W9-AEL-658

Eric Thornton

THE READER'S
ENCYCLOPEDIA

William Rose Benét

THE READER'S
ENCYCLOPEDIA

SECOND EDITION

THOMAS Y. CROWELL, PUBLISHERS
ESTABLISHED 1834
NEW YORK

81 82 83 15 14 13

Illustrations Editor: Robert H. Snyder, Jr.

Copyright © 1965 by Harper & Row, Publishers, Inc.
Previous editions copyright 1948, 1955 by Thomas Y. Crowell Company, Inc.

All rights reserved. Except for use in a review, the reproduction or utilization of this work in any form or by any electronic, mechanical, or other means, now known or hereafter invented, including photocopying and recording, and in any information storage and retrieval system is forbidden without the written permission of the publisher. Published in Canada by Fitzhenry & Whiteside Limited, Toronto.

Manufactured in the United States of America
Library of Congress Catalog Card No. 65–12510

ISBN 0–690–67128–8 (Plain)
0–690–67129–6 (Thumb-indexed)

Publisher's Preface

The Thomas Y. Crowell Company has been publishing reference books since 1886. During those seventy-nine years, many of these books have passed through several editions, each of which has represented a significant improvement over the previous edition. In general, these changes were part of that continuing process of gradual revision which makes good reference books better. The second edition of *The Reader's Encyclopedia,* however, is much more than a revision. It is a new book built on the foundations of the old.

The Reader's Encyclopedia was first published in 1948, under the editorship of the late William Rose Benét. In 1955 a 28-page supplement was added. Almost immediately thereafter work was begun on a complete revision of the book.

The new *Reader's Encyclopedia* contains 19 per cent more material than the old. This expansion has been achieved by increasing the dimensions of the page, while retaining the old type size. The additional material falls into three classes:

1. New entries. These cover literary developments of the last fifteen years, and also earlier writings in areas and periods of growing interest to modern readers, such as the Orient, the Soviet Union, Latin America, and the Near East.

2. Expansion of old entries. This process has aimed at a well-balanced coverage of world literature, with emphasis on areas of special interest today. For example, the article on Camus has been increased by 65 per cent, that on Li Po by 87 per cent, those on Dostoevski, Gabriela Mistral, and Aeschylus by 600, 700, and 800 per cent, respectively.

3. Addition of illustrations. The inclusion of 148 line cuts of title pages, old woodcuts, and cartoons on literary subjects enhances the usefulness, as well as the appearance, of the book.

Because a reference book is useful only in proportion to the accessibility of its information, special care has been taken with details of cross-referencing and the style of entry headings. Titles of non-English works, for example, are generally given both in English and in their original language, transliterated where necessary; Greek proper names appear in direct transliteration, as well as in their familiar latinized spellings. Basic data on authors and works are now included in the headings in uniform style.

The following persons contributed substantially to the present edition of *The Reader's Encyclopedia*:

JANE APTEKAR	PURSHOTAM LAL
DOLORES BAGLEY	THOMAS W. LOMBARDI
PATRICK A. BARRETT	MASON MARTENS
BENJAMIN K. BENNETT	JAMES MIROLLO
HARRIET A. BLUM	MARCIA NEWFIELD
SANDRA M-J BOSSY	ROBERT O'BRIEN
BETTY JO BROWN	GRAHAM PARRY
RICHARD J. CAREY	FREDERICK S. PLOTKIN
JOAN CENEDELLA	EDWARD QUINN
JON C. CHERUBINI	RICHARD C. ROBEY
CHRISTOPHER COLLINS	ARTHUR ROZEN
HELEN V. DELPAR	KENNETH SILVERMAN
KAREN S. EBBITT	ROBERT H. SNYDER, JR.
LEONORE FLEISCHER	DAVID STEPHENSON
JUAN FREUDENTHAL	EDWARD STEWART
ARTHUR G. HUDGINS	EDWARD TRIPP
PAUL R. JACKSON	DOROTHY J. TUCK
WALLACE B. KATZ	BETTE S. WEIDMAN
SUSAN KOTTA	PHILIP YAMPOLSKY

This book owes much to the work of Cyrena Jo Pondrom, Walter L. Hayward, and Charles F. Hollander, of the editorial and production staffs.

A Note on Using This Book

When a reader can find further information on a subject by consulting an additional entry, he is referred to it in one of two ways: by the use of SMALL CAPITALS (e.g.: He was associated with the GEORGIAN poets.) or by the word "see" (e.g.: **Golgotha.** See CALVARY). The first word printed in small capitals is the one under which the cross reference is alphabetized. In general, readers are referred from one entry to another only when the second entry provides significant information relevant to the first. Cross-references are plentiful, however, in the entries on mythology, where it is often helpful to be able to trace a complex tale through two or more entries.

Entries are alphabetized without reference to definite or indefinite articles. Titles beginning with frequently met phrases such as *The History of* . . . or *The Adventures of* . . . are found under the first significant word. (E.g. *Tom Sawyer, The Adventures of.*) Authors with pen names appear under the name by which they are best known: Marie Henri Beyle is found under his famous pseudonym, Stendhal, with a cross-reference under Beyle; Dickens appears under his own name, with a cross-reference under Boz. When the original title of a non-English work is commonly used by English speakers, its entry is found under that title, with a cross-reference under a well-known English title. (E.g.: **Would-be Gentleman, The.** See LE BOURGEOIS GENTILHOMME.) Works better known under English titles are found there, but with cross-references from their original titles, if these are frequently encountered. (E.g.: **A la Recherche du Temps Perdu.** See REMEMBRANCE OF THINGS PAST.)

The date of a play is that of its first production, when known, unless production was long delayed; otherwise the date is that of the first known printing.

Preface to the First Edition

At the end of the nineteenth century there died an English schoolmaster and clergyman whose life had spanned most of it. He was born in 1810. Two books in my father's library made me familiar, at an early age, with the Englishman's name. They were Brewer's *A Dictionary of Phrase and Fable* and Brewer's *The Reader's Handbook*. His full name was Ebenezer Cobham Brewer. Years later, when I was asked to edit a *Reader's Encyclopedia*, using *Crowell's Handbook for Readers and Writers* as nucleus, I discovered that, according to the preface of the first editor of that volume, it had originally owed much to the fascinating books of Dr. Brewer. (I always imagined him with a delightful beard—something like Edward Lear's—in which nested all the oddities of learning. Alas, I can boast no such receptaculum!) However, the *Handbook for Readers and Writers* had given his material extremely detailed revision, to say nothing of supplying a great deal that was new, relating to the Victorian era and to subsequent years, with especial attention to American literature and allusion. Since that time, of course, almost as many changes in taste, viewpoint, and interest have occurred as the handbook's editor found to have taken place between 1897 (when Dr. Brewer died) and 1925 (when the *Crowell Handbook* appeared). Twenty or more recent years have shown as many alterations as the previous thirty. And now, in the midst of the new Atomic Age, there are changes that even a modern editor could not have anticipated several years ago!

I wish immediately to acknowledge my indebtedness, not only to the editor of *Crowell's Handbook for Readers and Writers*, Miss Henrietta Gerwig, but also to an intermediate reviser, Miss Irene Hendry, whose knowledge of modern literature has proved indispensable to the present volume. Miss Gerwig's handbook was designed as "a dictionary of famous characters and plots in legend, fiction, drama, opera, and poetry, together with dates and principal works of important authors, literary and journalistic terms and familiar allusions." Miss Hendry's work, never before appearing in print, is incorporated here. But the original handbook is only one of several ancestors of the present work. Since the handbook's publication, so many people have contributed ideas and suggestions that the present volume has, in a sense, been composed for you by inquiring readers from all parts of the country. It is no mere revision, but veritably a new book.

Original entries on established authors of the past have been enlarged, with modern treatment. Full advantage has been taken of all the most modern reference books. More attention has been given to obscure works and figures in literature both of the distant and recent past. And, in line with the methodological advance in literary criticism of the past fifteen years or so, "whereby an author is interpreted not only in terms of the literal content of his works and the facts of his biography, but also in terms of the general intellectual forces of his time," entries have been chosen of significant figures, movements, and terms in aesthetics, science, philosophy, economics, and politics. Freud, Jung, Karl Marx, Lenin, The New Deal, the stream-of-consciousness tendency in fiction, and even futurism and surrealism have received due consideration. The fields of art and music are now extensively covered, incorporating important twentieth-century additions.

Such is the nature of an encyclopedia of this kind that one could go on almost indefinitely adding new information to that already accumulated. The limitations of such a volume are hard to establish. What is it that intelligent readers and writers do *not* wish to know? One simply has to set a term, and mark boundaries. Therefore, for this new book, much more grist has actually been gathered than has come through the mill. At that, it deserves to be called a one-volume literary encyclopedia.

I have endeavored carefully to check over what was already amassed, to expand, to fill up gaps, to carry on what was unfinished; to add biographical, historical, and other data that unfolding world events made obligatory; to comb for word, phrase, and allusion such reference works as had been searched either superficially or not at all; to discard the obsolete; to bring to light the overlooked; and to play, in general, the role of Argus-eyed modernizer. I am bound to have made errors both of omission and commission. But, with the able assistance of Dr. Alexander Gode and the invaluable final rechecking of that brilliant literary detective, Earle F. Walbridge, I believe that this encyclopedia will now prove one of the most complete and practicable in existence. It will be found to cover an unusual range of information, to provide a reference to most allusions occurring in your reading, to give all the important myths and legends and a great many of the most important themes and characters in fiction old and new, to include references that constantly crop up in the critical writing of yesterday and today, to furnish information as to literary schools, trends, and movements past and present and biographical data on most "people of importance." Likewise it will prove a real aid to the vocabulary and allusiveness of writers, as well as providing them with a genuine source book of ideas. As for cross-word puzzlers, they will, of course, discover it to be a necessity!

The curious mind inevitably stores up what it has sometimes characterized as "much useless information." Yet, in literature, it is often these peculiar bits of learning that serve most to adorn and give flavor to a style. I have, however, endeavored to rid the book of all that is merely archaic. I have tried to maintain balance and proportion between the modern world and the world of antiquity. People used to speak of "dead languages." Yet, in English derivations, the dead languages still live. In the same way, the mythology of the past constantly reappears in the poetry of the present; and the classics may furnish groundwork for the most modern fiction. (One has only to think of *Ulysses*.) All of this such a book as the one before you must comprehend. It must also show itself thoroughly familiar with modern literature and thought of all kinds, with modern invention and science, with new art media, with the continuity of history.

Either my memory is at fault or there is one essay that neither Charles Lamb, William Hazlitt, nor Christopher Morley ever wrote: one on Reference Books. The phrase for them, now cliché, has been "mines of information." But a mine, at best, is a rather dark and dreary excavation—not to say *dank*, at times. I prefer to think of the book before you as a cave like the famous one stumbled upon by Aladdin. I might go on from there to describe its revelation of treasure of so many varieties and kinds, yet each in its own particular bin. For the office of a reference book is, after all, to bring some sort of order out of chaos. But it is also to present to you a well-organized supplementary memory, in one volume. The delights of such a memory may be inexhaustible; the safaris of research it can initiate, endless; the urge to literary creation which it can supply, present on every page. And remember, that to enter this domain of learning and imagination you have not even to use that mysterious phrase, "Open Sesame!"

WILLIAM ROSE BENÉT

THE READER'S
ENCYCLOPEDIA

A

Aakjaer, Jeppe (1866–1930). Danish poet and novelist. As a novelist, Aakjaer was intensely concerned with social misery and the need for reform. *Vredens Børn* (*The Children of Wrath*, 1904) describes the oppressed existence led by servants on peasant farms. He is best known, however, for his lyric poetry, in which he celebrates the courage of the peasants and the beauties of his native Jutland. A merry simplicity characterizes the poetry of such collections as *Fri Felt* (1906), *Rugens Sange* (*Songs of the Rye,* 1906), and *Den Sommer og den Eng* (1910).

Aaron. In the Bible, the brother of Moses, the founder of the priesthood and the 1st high priest. He helped Moses in calling down the TEN PLAGUES and leading the Children of Israel out of Egypt (c. 1200 B.C.). Aaron directed the construction of the golden calf (made of gold earrings and other jewelry), which was idolatrously worshipped by the Israelites as the god of their deliverance, while Moses was receiving the Ten Commandments from Jehovah (Ex. 32). Aaron did not receive an inheritance in Canaan, as a punishment for doubting God's ability to bring water out of a rock.

Aaron's Rod. The name given to the rod of the tribe of Levi, used by Aaron during the 10 Plagues and the crossing of the Red Sea. When Aaron left his rod in front of the Ark, in the Tabernacle, it miraculously blossomed and bore almonds. This was interpreted as evidence of Jehovah's choice of Aaron as high priest (Num. 17:8).

Aaron. In Shakespeare's TITUS ANDRONICUS, the Moorish lover of the vengeful Tamora, with whom he plots the destruction of the Andronicus family. He flees Rome with the black child to whom Tamora gives birth, having substituted a white child and killed all witnesses, and is later condemned to death by Lucius.

Aaru. In Egyptian mythology, the fields of Aaru are the abode of the blessed dead and of the gods and goddesses.

Aasen, Ivar Andreas (1813–1896). Norwegian philologist. Aasen made from various dialects a Norwegian literary language called New Norwegian or *landsmaal,* in contrast to the Dano-Norwegian *rigsmaal.* In the poems of *Symra* (1863) he uses the *landsmaal* to describe peasant life and to voice his own subdued sadness.

Abaddon. The angel of the bottomless pit in *The Revelation of St. John the Divine.* Milton uses the name for the bottomless pit itself.

Abano, Pietro d'. Also **Petrus de Apono** (c. 1250–c. 1316). Italian philosopher, physician, astrologer. In his *Conciliator Differentiarum quae inter Philosophos et Medicos Versantur* ("reconciler of the differences among philosophers and doctors"), he advocated the systems of Averroes and other Arabic writers. He was so successful a scientist and physician that he was accused of black magic and heresy; brought twice before the Inquisition, he was acquitted once and died in prison before the second trial.

Abaris. A mythical Greek sage of the 6th century B.C. Surnamed "the Hyperborean," he is mentioned by Herodotus, Pindar, etc. Apollo gave him a magic arrow which rendered him invisible, cured diseases, gave oracles, and on which he could ride through the air. Abaris gave it to Pythagoras, who, in return, taught him philosophy.

Abbassids. The 2nd long dynasty (37 Caliphs, 750–1258) of the Muslim Empire. They claimed descent from Abbas (566–652), eldest uncle of Muhammad. Their reign was most firmly established and the court at Baghdad most splendid under HAROUN-AL-RASCHID, the Caliph described in the *Arabian Nights,* and his son Mamun (reigned 813–833).

Abbaye Group, the. A group of French writers and artists. They bought a house in Créteil near Paris, called it "L'Abbaye," and lived there communally for 14 months (1906–1907). After their separation they were influential in spreading the ideas of UNANIMISM, introduced to them by Jules Romains, a frequent visitor to the Abbaye. Among the group were René Arcos (1881–   ), Georges DUHAMEL, Luc Durtain (1881–1959), Pierre Jean JOUVE, Charles VILDRAC, and the cubist painter Albert Gleizes (1881–   ).

Abbé Constantin, L' (1882). A novel by Ludovic HALÉVY. This gentle tale, which owes its popularity to the simple, melodious grace of its author's style, tells of the effects of the sale of the largest chateau in the Abbé's parish. The ingredients of young love, charity, and fortune serve to placate the Abbé's fears for his parish and his godson.

Abbey Theatre. The famous Dublin home of the Irish National Theatre Society. It was established in 1901 for Irish actors in plays by Irish dramatists about Ireland; especially about her heroic past and peasantry. William Butler YEATS was influential in founding it. A. E. (q.v.), Lady GREGORY, and John Millington SYNGE wrote for it; and, in later years, so did Sean O'CASEY. See IRISH RENAISSANCE.

Abbot, The (1820). A novel by Sir Walter SCOTT centering on the escape from prison and flight to England of Mary, queen of Scots.

Abbot of Misrule or **Unreason.** See LORD OF MISRULE.

Abbotsford. The baronial mansion built by Sir Walter Scott on the Tweed near Melrose.

Abbott, George (1889–   ). American playwright and producer. He collaborated with James Gleason on *The Fall Guy* (1925), with Philip Dunning on *Broadway* (1926), with Ann Preston Bridgers on *Coquette* (1928), and with John Cecil Holm on *Three Men on a Horse* (1935). Thereafter, he turned to directing and producing. He is the author of a candid autobiography, *Mister Abbott* (1963).

Abbott, Lyman (1835–1922). American Congregational minister and editor. Abbott wrote a *Life of Henry Ward Beecher* (1903), but he is best known for his work as editor of the famous weekly THE OUTLOOK and of its immediate predecessor *The Christian Union* magazine. A liberal in theology and politics, Abbott exerted considerable influence on the American scene.

A B C Book or **Absey Book.** A primer or speller which used to be used as a child's first lesson book and contained merely the alphabet and a few rudimentary lessons often set in catechism form, as is evident from Shakespeare's lines:

> That is question now;
> And then comes answer like an Absey book.
> *King John*, i, 1

Abdera, Abderitan. Abdera was a maritime city of Thrace whose inhabitants were proverbial in ancient times for their stupidity. "Abderitan laughter" came to mean scoffing or incessant

The New England Primer (1727), an American A B C Book.

NEW YORK PUBLIC LIBRARY

A — In *Adam's* Fall We Sinned all.

B — Thy Life to Mend This *Book* Attend.

C — The *Cat* doth play And after slay.

D — A *Dog* will bite A Thief at night.

E — An *Eagles* flight Is out of sight.

F — The Idle *Fool* Is whipt at School.

laughter. It was so called because Abdera was the birthplace of Democritus, the laughing philosopher, who is regarded as the greatest among the Greek physical philosophers.

Abderite, the. See DEMOCRITUS.

Abdiel (*Heb.,* "servant of god"). In Milton's PARADISE LOST, the faithful seraph who opposes Satan when he urges the angels to revolt.

Abednego. See SHADRACH, MESHACH, AND ABEDNEGO.

Abel. See CAIN.

Abélard, Pierre (1079–1142). French scholastic philosopher and theologian. He studied under Roscellinus (b. 1050), exponent of extreme NOMINALISM, then under William of Champeaux (1070–1121), supporter of realism. In this controversy of medieval theology Abélard evolved a middle position called *conceptualism,* holding that both particular objects and universal concepts are real. However, he angered the clergy, who emphasized faith rather than dialectic argument and proof, with his rationalistic approach to Church dogma, especially the dogma of the Trinity. Thus Saint BERNARD OF CLAIRVAUX persecuted him as a heretic, and Abélard died on his way to Rome to appeal to the Pope against a condemnation on this charge. Nevertheless, Abélard had been extremely popular as a lecturer; when he had to leave Notre Dame, his students followed him to various monasteries. His influence and his writings, such as SIC ET NON, increased the popularity of Aristotelian logic over that of Platonic theory.

His popular fame, however, resulted from his tragic love affair with HÉLOÏSE. Moved by his *Historia Calamitatum* (c. 1134), Héloïse wrote to him, and they exchanged their famous letters of love and suffering, including Abélard's advice on how she should conduct the convent he had turned over to her in 1129.

Abe Lincoln in Illinois (1938). A play by Robert E. SHERWOOD. Awarded a Pulitzer Prize, it deals with the life of Lincoln up to his election to the presidency; the dialogue contains selections from a number of Lincoln's own speeches and writings.

Abell, Kjeld (1901–1961). Danish playwright. The work of Abell is a provocative mixture of light, witty comedy and bitter satire. In 1937, *The Melody that Got Lost* (*Melodien, der blev Voek;* 1935), a clever play about the office proletariat, was produced in London; it was followed by *Eva aftjener sin Barnepligt* (*Eva Serves Her Time as a Child,* 1936). *Anna Sophie Hedvig* (1939), whose school-teacher heroine murders her principal to save a child from persecution, is a violent protest against injustice.

Abencerrages (Sp. *Abencerrajes*). A family of Moors in Granada in the 15th century. They are famous in romance for their feud with the family of the Zegris (Sp. *Cegríes*). Chateaubriand wrote a novel called *The Last Abencerrage.*

abenteuerliche Simplicissimus, Der. See SIMPLICISSIMUS.

Abercrombie, Lascelles (1881–1938). English poet, critic, and writer of verse drama. He was associated with the GEORGIAN poets. His collections of poems include *Interludes and Poems* (1908) and *Twelve Idylls* (1928); *The Sale of St. Thomas* (1911) is a verse drama.

Abessa. See FAERIE QUEENE, THE.

Abhorrers. See PETITIONERS AND ABHORRERS.

Abie's Irish Rose (1922). A comedy by Anne Nichols. It had one of the longest records of performance (2,327) in the history of the theater. A Jewish boy and an Irish Catholic girl, fearing to tell their fathers that they are in love, are married by a Methodist minister. The play formed the basis for a novel (1927), a radio program (1942), and a movie (1946).

Abigail. In the Old Testament, the wife of Nabal and later of David (I Sam. 25:3). She referred to herself as the handmaid of David. In Elizabethan usage, the name came to signify a lady's maid. It is used in works by Marlowe, Beaumont and Fletcher, Swift, and Fielding. The name was further popularized by Abigail Hill (Mrs. Masham), the influential waiting-woman to Queen Anne.

Abnaki or **Abenaki.** An Algonquian Indian tribe. The English and French used the name to designate a loose confederacy of tribes occupying Maine and parts of New Brunswick and Quebec. The tribes fought as allies of the French until France lost its North American possessions.

abomination of desolation. An epithet, used in *Daniel* and in *Matthew,* referring to a pagan idol or statue set up in the temple at Jerusalem. The phrase is now used for anything very hateful or destructive.

Abou Ben Adhem. A short poem by Leigh HUNT. Because Abou begged to be written as "one who loves his fellowmen," his angel visitor

> . . . showed the names whom love of God had blest
> And lo! Ben Adhem's name led all the rest.

Abou Hassan. A young merchant of Baghdad, hero of the tale called "The Sleeper Awakened" in *The Arabian Nights.* While Abou Hassan is asleep, he is conveyed to the palace of HAROUN-AL-RASCHID where the attendants are ordered to do all they can to make him fancy himself the Caliph. He subsequently becomes the Caliph's favorite. See SLY, CHRISTOPHER.

Abra. A favorite concubine of Solomon. In his poem SOLOMON ON THE VANITY OF THE WORLD (1718), Matthew Prior describes her devotion in the celebrated lines:

> Abra was ready ere I called her name,
> And though I called another, Abra came.

Abrabanel or **Abarbanel, Judah León.** Known as **León Hebreo** (It., **Leone Ebreo**) or **Leo the Jew** (c. 1465–1535). A Jew expelled from Spain who came to Italy and practiced medicine while studying and writing philosophical material. His fame rests on the *Dialoghi d'Amore* (Dialogues of Love, 1535), a prose work that sets forth in a series of lively conversations Renaissance theories of love. The dialogues reveal the preoccupation in the Italy of the period with Neoplatonism and ancient learning in general.

abracadabra. A cabalistic charm, supposedly constructed from the initials of the Hebrew words Ab (Father), Ben (Son), and Ruach Acadasch (Holy Spirit), and once used as an antidote against various physical ills. From its role as charm it has come to be associated with any meaningless jargon

and is a term frequently used by magicians. The word was originally written on parchment and suspended from the neck by a linen thread, in the following form:

```
A B R A C A D A B R A
A B R A C A D A B R
A B R A C A D A B
A B R A C A D A
A B R A C A D
A B R A C A
A B R A C
A B R A
A B R
A B
A
```

Abraham. The founder of the Hebrew people and its first patriarch. With his wife Sarah and his nephew LOT, he migrated from UR of Chaldees into the land of Canaan, where he settled and prospered. To test his faith, Jehovah commanded him to sacrifice his son ISAAC as a burnt offering; however, a ram caught in a thicket was provided instead, just when Abraham was about to draw the knife. The story of Abraham is told in Gen. 11–25 and in various Muslim legends.

Abrahamic covenant. God made a covenant with Abraham (Gen. 17) that He would be God to him and all his children and that they should inherit and dwell in the land of Canaan.

Abraham ben Meïr ibn Ezra (1092–1167). Spanish Jewish scholar. He wrote scientific treatises, biblical commentaries, and outstanding poems. He is the Rabbi ben Ezra of Browning's poem.

Abraham Lincoln. A biography by Carl SANDBURG. The first part, entitled *Abraham Lincoln: The Prairie Years,* was published in two volumes in 1926, and the second part, *Abraham Lincoln: The War Years,* was published in four volumes in 1939. For Sandburg, Lincoln was the archetypal figure of American democracy; the preparation of the biography, the second part of which won a Pulitzer Prize, occupied many years of the poet's life.

Abraham-man or **Abram-man.** A begging impostor, a pretended lunatic. In Tudor and early Stuart times, inmates of Bedlam who were not dangerously mad were kept in the "Abraham Ward," and allowed out from time to time in distinctive clothes, to supplement their scanty rations by begging. Richard Head, a writer of the latter part of the 17th century, says that many healthy rogues, imitating these TOM o' BEDLAMS, "used to array themselves with party-coloured ribbons, tape in their hats, a fox-tail hanging down, a long stick with streamers, and beg alms; but for all their seeming madness, they had wit enough to steal as they went along."

Abraham Newland. A bank note, so called from the name of Abraham Newland (1730–1807), the chief cashier of the Bank of England from 1782 to 1807, without whose signature no Bank of England notes were genuine.

Abraham's bosom. The repose of the happy in death (Luke 16:22).

abraxas. A cabalistic word. It was used by the Gnostics to denote the Supreme Being, the source of 365 emanations, the sum of the numbers represented by the Greek letters of the word totaling 365. It was frequently engraved on gems (hence known as *abraxas stones*) that were used as amulets or talismans. By some authorities the name is given as that of one of the horses of Aurora, the dawn goddess.

Absalom. In the Old Testament, the handsome and rebellious 3rd son of David, king of Israel, who "stole the hearts of the men of Israel" and plotted to become king in his father's stead (II Sam. 15:6). Riding on a mule in the decisive battle at Ephraim, Absalom was caught by his hair in an oak tree; finding him so suspended, one of David's army killed him despite previous commands of the king. David's lament, "O my son Absalom, my son, my son Absalom! would God I had died for thee, O Absalom, my son, my son!" has become a classic expression of paternal grief.

Dryden gave the name Absalom to the duke of Monmouth, Charles II's natural son, in his satire *Absalom and Achitophel* (1681).

Absalom, Absalom! (1936). A novel by William FAULKNER. The story centers on Thomas Sutpen, the son of a West Virginia poor white, and his attempts to fulfill his "grand design," to be accepted as a Southern aristocrat and founder of a wealthy family. He establishes himself in Jefferson, Miss., and at the climax of his career he is elected colonel of Jefferson's regiment in the Civil War. Returning to his estate, Sutpen's Hundred, after the war, he finds the plantation in ruins. His daughter's half brother and part-Negro lover has been killed by Sutpen's son, who has disappeared, and she has become a confirmed spinster. Sutpen's attempt to have another son by a poor-white girl ends in his murder by her grandfather. When the Sutpen saga comes to an end in 1910, all that is left of his dream is an idiot Negro, Jim Bond, Sutpen's only living descendant, howling in the ashes of the burned house.

In place of the sustained interior monologue Faulkner used in *The Sound and the Fury,* the story is projected by means of three narrators; their personalities and concerns are revealed as each tells the story of Sutpen. Miss Rosa COLDFIELD, Sutpen's sister-in-law, first tells the story to Quentin Compson shortly before his departure for Harvard; her story is supplemented by that of Quentin's father; and Quentin, in turn, relates the whole story with his own interpretation to his Harvard roommate, Shreve McCannon. See SUTPEN.

Absalom and Achitophel (1681). A political satire in verse by John DRYDEN. Written in heroic couplets, the poem attacks Puritan attempts to exclude the duke of York, the legitimate heir, from the throne of England because of his Catholicism. Using Biblical terminology, Dryden describes the efforts of Achitophel (the earl of Shaftesbury) to incite Absalom (the duke of Monmouth, illegitimate son of Charles II) to rebellion against his father. A second part, written by Nahum TATE and revised by Dryden, who added 200 lines, appeared in 1682.

Absentee, The (1812). A novel by Maria EDGEWORTH. The "absentee," Lord Clonbrony, allows his foolish wife to persuade him to leave his estate in Ireland and try to force a way into fashionable London society.

Absey Book. See A B C BOOK.

Absolute, Captain Jack. The hero of Sheridan's comedy THE RIVALS. The clever and gallant son of Sir Anthony Absolute, he is a rival of Bob Acres for the hand of Lydia Languish, to whom he is known only as Ensign Beverley.

Absolute, Sir Anthony. A character in Sheridan's comedy THE RIVALS. He is a testy, but warm-hearted old gentleman who imagines that he possesses a most angelic temper and that, when he quarrels with others, it is they, not he, who are out of sorts.

absurd. Modern philosophical term. Used by Albert CAMUS to describe the meaninglessness of human existence in the modern world, it is presented especially in his essay THE MYTH OF SISYPHUS (1942) and his novel THE STRANGER (1942). Jean-Paul SARTRE describes the absurdity of the human condition, which he makes a precondition for the philosophy of EXISTENTIALISM, in his novel NAUSEA (1938). The "Literature of the Absurd," however, usually refers to those works which deliberately violate or distort the conventions of the novel or the theater, grimly making them ridiculous in an attempt to show the absurdity of the human lives they represent. They often use either a barren setting or an emphasis on things —inanimate material objects—to express the a-human sterility of modern values. The tone may range from the broadly comic aspect of the absurd to the unsettling, the grotesque, or even the terrible. Alfred JARRY's UBU ROI (1896) is often considered the first direct ancestor of the movement, and Franz KAFKA's novels the first examples. The absurd shocked its way to widespread recognition in France with the novels and plays of Samuel BECKETT and the plays of Jean GENET and Eugène IONESCO. In America it finds expression in the work of the avant-garde playwrights Edward ALBEE and Jack GELBER, in England in the plays of Harold PINTER. The Swiss dramatist, Friedrich DÜRRENMATT, also writes in the absurd tradition.

Absyrtus. See the ARGONAUTS.

Abzu. In Sumerian mythology, the river that is supposed to surround the earth. The Abzu seems almost identical with the Greek Oceanus, the "river of ocean." In Babylonian mythology it is personified as Apsu, the fresh water, who has existed from the beginning of time with his wife Tiamat, the salt water; he plays an important role in the WAR OF THE GODS. The Sumerian ENKI and the Babylonian EA, almost identical gods of water and of wisdom, live in a palace in the Abzu, which was probably the Persian Gulf, the shores of which in early days may have reached northward to the city of Eridu.

academe. A place of study or instruction. It is so called from Plato's ACADEMY.

Académie française. The French Academy. Originating in secret meetings of men of literary taste in Paris around the year 1630, the Academy was established by order of the king and at the behest of Cardinal Richelieu in the year 1635. Made up of 40 members, supposedly the most distinguished living men of French letters, the Academy took as its purpose the protection and perfection of the French language and to that end began compiling its dictionary in the year 1639; the task has not yet been completed. The Academy also undertook the composition of definitive treatises on grammar, poetry and rhetoric. Ordered by Richelieu to censure Corneille's *Le Cid,* the Academy early adopted a policy of advocating old rules and traditions at the expense of innovation and change. In the late 18th century the *philosophes* gained a majority in the Academy and briefly lent it an influential voice. Inactive during the revolution, the Academy was reestablished in 1803 by Napoleon as part of the Institut de France and two years later took up headquarters in the Palais Mazarin, which it still occupies. Inevitably the Academy is a conservative body, reflecting the tastes of its membership—men, by definition, of age and secure reputation. Including many of the most significant names in past and present French literature, criticism, and philosophy, the membership list nonetheless reveals several surprising omissions, most regrettably that of Molière. In this century the Academy may be said to have fairly represented the cultural life of France and, in general, to have exercised a beneficent effect upon the preservation of the language.

Académie Goncourt. See PRIX GONCOURT.

Academy, the (Akademe). The name of PLATO's school near Athens. It was named after a legendary hero, Hecademus or Academus. The school had a long history, continuing until Justinian suppressed the philosophic schools in 529 A.D.

Acadia. The old name for Nova Scotia, so called by the French from the river *Shubenacadie.* In 1621 Acadia was given to the Scot, Sir William Alexander, and its name changed; and in 1755 the old French settlers were driven into exile by George II. Many of them migrated to Louisiana, where their descendants are still known as "Cajuns" (Acadians). Longfellow has made this the subject of a poem in hexameter verse, EVANGELINE.

Acastus (Akastos). In Greek mythology, a son of PELIAS. He sailed with the ARGONAUTS and, after his father's death, became king of Iolcus. Believing the lie of his wife Cretheis that PELEUS had made advances to her, he tried to kill him. Later Peleus conquered Iolcus and killed Acastus.

Accademia Della Crusca (It., "Academy of the Chaff"). Florentine literary academy founded in 1583 to purify Tuscan, the literary language of the Italian Renaissance. It was opposed to Tasso in the debate over the merits of his GERUSALEMME LIBERATA. The first part of its official dictionary appeared in 1612 and the work is still in progress.

accent meter. (1) Accentual METER, that is, verse based on the alternation of accented and unaccented syllables. English prosody is based on accent meter as opposed to quantitative meter, or verse based on the alternation of long and short syllables, which is the basis of Greek and Latin prosody.

(2) Meter that depends only upon the number of accented syllables in the line and disregards the unaccented syllables. The feet that make up the line may be of any kind, including the monosyllabic foot. Accent verse has always been prevalent in popular ballads and songs, and it is often deliberately used in modern poetry. An example from *Sir Patrick Spens,* an early Scottish ballad of unknown authorship, is:

O LANG, / LANG, / may the LA/dies STAND
Wi thair GOLD / KEMS / in thair HAIR,
WAITING / FOR thair / AIN deir / LORDS,
For THEY'LL / se THAME / na MAIR.

Accolti, Bernardo (1458–1535). Italian poet and dramatist. Born in Arezzo, he is known as the Unique Aretine for his supposedly impromptu recitations of sonnets before the courts of Renaissance Italy. His *Virginia,* a play drawn from Boccaccio's *Decameron (Gillette of Narbonne,* III, 9), was first performed in 1494. He is a prominent interlocutor in Castiglione's *Cortegiano.*

Accoramboni, Vittoria (1557?–1585). Her husband was murdered so that she might marry the Duke of Bracciano. After Bracciano's death in 1585, she was herself murdered by assassins hired by one of his relatives. She is a principal figure in Webster's play THE WHITE DEVIL, OR VITTORIA COROMBONA.

Account of My Hut, An (Hōjō ki). Japanese miscellany, a brief account of the personal experiences of Kamo no Chōmei (1153–1216). It details the natural disasters that visited Kyoto during the late Heian period (794–1185) and describes the life led by the author at his hermitage. It is strongly Buddhist in tone.

Aceldama (Gr., "field of blood"). A field in the Hinnon Valley near Jerusalem which, in Matthew (27:6–8), was purchased by the priests with the 30 pieces of silver ("the blood money") thrown down by Judas Iscariot after his betrayal of Jesus. It was used as Jerusalem's "potter's field" (so called because potters used such fields to obtain clay) for the burial of strangers. According to The Acts (1:18), Judas bought the field, fell into it, and "burst asunder." The usual version (Matt. 27:5) of Judas' death is that he hanged himself.

Acestes. In Vergil's AENEID, the Trojan son of the river god Crimisus. During the funeral games held for Anchises in Sicily, where Acestes had established himself before the arrival of Aeneas, he discharges his arrow with such force that it takes fire from the friction of the air (Book V).

Acevedo Díaz, Eduardo (1851–1924). Uruguayan statesman and novelist. Trained as a lawyer, Acevedo Díaz was active in Uruguayan politics, spent part of his life in exile, and held several diplomatic posts. He described Uruguay's war for independence in an impassioned trilogy which he called "a hymn of blood": *Ismael* (1888), *Nativa* (1889–1890), and *Grito de gloria* (1894). His masterpiece is *Soledad* (1894), often considered the archetype of the gaucho novel. See GAUCHO LITERATURE.

Achard, Marcel (1899–   ). French dramatist. His characters are usually idealistic vagabonds and dreamers. His plays, such as *La Vie est belle* (1928), *Jean de la lune* (1929), *Domino* (1931), *Le Corsaire* (1938), and *Patate* (1957), are full of fantasy and the joy of life.

Achates. In Vergil's AENEID, the constant companion of Aeneas. Thus, a *fidus Achates* is synonymous with a faithful companion and bosom friend.

Achelous (Acheloos). In ancient Greece, the large river that separated Aetolia from Acarnania, and the god thereof. This bull-headed god wrestled Heracles as a rival for Deianira, and lost one of his horns as well as the prize. When ALCMAEON, pursued by the ERINYES for the murder of his mother Eriphyle, sought a land that had not existed at the time of the murder, he found it in the delta of the Achelous, which was formed by new silt. Achelous gave his daughter Callirrhoe in marriage to Alcmaeon but she proved to be his death.

Acheron. (Gr., the River of Sorrows.) The river of the infernal regions into which Phlegethon and Cocytus flow; also, the lower world (HADES) itself.

Several actual Greek rivers, in addition, were given that name. See STYX.

Achilles. In Greek mythology, the son of PELEUS and the Nereid THETIS, and king of the MYRMIDONS, a Thessalian tribe. He is the hero of Homer's ILIAD and became the prototype of the Greeks' conception of manly valor and beauty. He took part in the Trojan War on the side of the Greeks as their most illustrious warrior, and slew the Trojan hero Hector. Achilles had been dipped in the STYX by his mother, which rendered him invulnerable except in the heel by which she held him. He was fatally wounded there by an arrow shot by Paris, Hector's younger brother, or, according to another version of the story, by the god Apollo who had assumed Paris' shape. The phrase *Achilles' heel* is used to describe the vulnerable point in the character of a man or nation.

Achitophel. In the Old Testament, David's traitorous counselor. He deserted to ABSALOM, who was trying to supersede his father, but hanged himself when his advice was disregarded (II Sam. 17). In his satire, *Absalom and Achitophel* (1681), Dryden used this name for the earl of Shaftesbury.

Acis (Akis). In classical legend, a handsome Sicilian youth, son of Faunus and the naiad Symaethis. The lover of Galatea, he was killed by his rival, the Cyclops POLYPHEMUS. The blood flowing forth from Acis' body changed into water and formed the river Acis. The story is the subject of an opera by Handel, *Acis and Galatea* (1721).

Acmeism. A movement in Russian poetry, active from about 1910 to 1917. The Acmeists, who belonged to a group known as the Poets' Guild, got their name from the high poetic standards they professed. They advocated concision in poetry, clear and concrete imagery, and precise use of words. The movement was a reaction against the mysticism and stylistic vagueness of the symbolist school of poetry, which had held sway in Russian literature from about 1895. The leading Acmeists were Nikolai GUMILIOV, Anna AKHMATOVA, and Osip MANDELSHTAM.

Acquainted with the Night (1928). A sonnet by Robert FROST. Written in *terza rima* and one of Frost's few poems set in the city, it is a mystical poem of loneliness and despair; "the time was neither wrong nor right," it declares.

Acrasia. See FAERIE QUEENE, THE.

Acres, Bob. A character in Sheridan's comedy THE RIVALS. A country gentleman, he is the rival of Captain Jack Absolute for the hand of Lydia Languish. He tries to ape the man of fashion, affects elaborate oaths, and blusters mightily, but when his courage is put to the test he proves himself an abject coward.

Acrisius. In Greek mythology, king of Argos and the father of Danae. An oracle declared that Danae would give birth to a son who would kill him, so Acrisius kept his daughter shut up in a brazen tower. Here she became the mother of Perseus by Zeus who appeared in the form of a shower of gold. The king of Argos now ordered his daughter and her infant to be put into a chest, and cast adrift on the sea, but they were rescued by Dictys, a fisherman. When grown to manhood, Perseus accidentally struck the foot of Acrisius with a quoit, and the blow caused his death, thus fulfilling the oracle.

acropolis (akropolis; Gr., high city). The citadel of a Greek city, generally situated on a hill. The Acropolis at Athens, a rocky plateau about 200 feet high, was the site of the ancient town. It was surrounded by walls which were destroyed by the Persians in 480 B.C., and later rebuilt by Themistocles. The Acropolis was the center of religious activity; many temples and statues of Athene were located there. The ERECHTHEUM, the PARTHENON and the Propylaea are among the best known of its monuments. The acropolis of Thebes was the Cadmeia; that of Corinth, the Acrocorinth.

acrostic. A composition, often in verse, in which a set or sets of letters (such as the first, middle, or last of each line) spell out a word, a word group, or part of the alphabet. 12 Psalms of the Old Testament are written acrostically, the 119th being an ingenious alphabetic acrostic. The Latin poets wrote acrostic verse, and the early English poet CYNEWULF signed his name to his works in acrostic runes. The Elizabethan Sir John Davies wrote 26 *Hymns of Astraea,* in which the first letters of the lines spell *Elisabetha Regina* 26 times. Edgar Allan Poe demonstrated skill in devising acrostics on the names of his loved ones. Charles Lamb devised a well-known acrostic conundrum spelling his name (*Lamb*) and pseudonym (*Elia*). Abecedarian hymns, designed to aid the memorizing of the alphabet, may be counted acrostics, and perhaps for this reason men of letters have held the form in low esteem as being little more than a childish riddle. The word "acrostic" is also applied to any word square which reads the same horizontally as vertically.

Actaeon (Aktaion). In Greek mythology, the son of Aristaeus and Autonoë. Having accidentally observed Artemis in her bath, while hunting on Mount Cithaeron, he was changed by the goddess into a stag and torn to pieces by his own hounds.

acte gratuite. See André GIDE.

Actes and Monuments. See John FOXE.

Actian games. The games celebrated at ACTIUM and in Rome in honor of Apollo. They were founded by Octavius Caesar to celebrate his naval victory over Antony in 31 B.C. and were held every four years.

Action Française, L'. A political group whose organ was the newspaper *L'Action Française,* founded in 1899. An extreme right-wing movement, it advocated monarchist, anti-Semitic, and Roman Catholic principles, serving as a focal point for rightist sympathies. Leon DAUDET and Charles MAURRAS were the chief editors of *L'Action Française;* its last issue was published on August 24, 1944 and spoke out in favor of Marshal Pétain.

Actium. A promontory in northwestern Greece at the mouth of the Ambracian Gulf. In a famous naval battle (31 B.C.) near here, Octavius (see AUGUSTUS) defeated the combined forces of ANTONY and Cleopatra, making himself master of the Roman world. During the battle Cleopatra's ships fled and, when Antony himself followed, his land forces surrendered to Octavius. See ACTIAN GAMES.

Act of Settlement. An act passed during the reign of William III (1701) in England, limiting the crown, after Queen Anne's succession, to members of the House of Hanover, provided they were Protestant. As a result of this act, the reign of the House of Stuart ended and that of Hanover began.

Act of Union. Specifically, the Act of 1706 declaring that on and after May 1, 1707, England and Scotland should have a united parliament. The two countries had been united under one sovereign since 1603. The term is also applied to the Act of 1536 incorporating Wales with England, and to that of 1800, establishing a legislative union of Great Britain and Ireland on and after January 1, 1801.

Acts of the Apostles. A book of the New Testament. It is the earliest contemporary history of the Christian Church in existence, beginning with Jesus' Ascension and ending with St. Paul's imprisonment. The best passages are written in a vivid first-person style by a traveling companion of Paul. It is thought that the author of *Acts* is Luke the physician, author of the Gospel bearing his name. The protagonist is St. Paul, who released Christianity from the conservative restrictions of Judaism and preached it as a new, universal religion.

Adad. The principal Babylonian storm-god. He took over this role after ENLIL, the Sumerian god of air and storms, and MARDUK, the Baal of Babylon, became more generalized in their functions.

Adam. In Shakespeare's As You LIKE IT, a faithful old family retainer who accompanies Orlando into the forest and offers to give him his savings. The well-known phrase "a faithful Adam" is based on this character.

Adam, Juliette. Born Lamber. Pen names: Juliette Lamber; La Messine; and Comte Paul Vasili (1836–1936). French novelist and editor. She founded and edited the periodical *La Nouvelle Revue*.

Adam, Paul [Auguste Marie] (1862–1920). French novelist. Originally associated with the symbolists, he was later concerned with the analysis of group action, as in mobs, in his novel series *Le Temps et la vie* (16 v., 1899–1903).

Adam and Eve. The first man and woman, according to the Old Testament. The initial chapters of Genesis tell the story of their creation, their sin in eating the FORBIDDEN FRUIT from "the tree of knowledge of good and evil" (Gen. 3:9), and their expulsion from Paradise, or the Garden of Eden, to thereafter "till the ground." Milton retells the story of "man's first disobedience" in *Paradise Lost* (1667). See LILITH.

the old Adam; the offending Adam. Adam, as the head of unredeemed man, stands for "original sin," or "man without regenerating grace."

the second Adam; the new Adam. Jesus Christ is so called.

Adam's ale. Water, because the first man had nothing else to drink; in Scotland, it is sometimes called *Adam's wine.*

Adam's apple. The protuberance in the forepart of the throat, the anterior extremity of the thyroid cartilage of the larynx; so called from the superstition that a piece of the forbidden fruit stuck in Adam's throat.

Adam's Peak. A mountain in Ceylon where, according to Muslim legend, Adam bewailed his expulsion from Paradise, standing on one foot for 200 years to expiate his crime; Gabriel then took him to Mount Arafat, where he found Eve.

Adamastor. The spirit of the stormy Cape (Good Hope). It is described by Camões in the *Lusiad* as a hideous phantom that appears to Vasco da Gama and prophesies disaster to all seeking to make the voyage to India.

Adam Bede (1859). A novel by George ELIOT. The highly principled Adam Bede loves Hetty Sorrel, a pretty, superficial girl. Although Adam tries to save her, she fancies herself the wife of the young squire, Arthur Donnithorne, who seduces her and then leaves her. In her grief she consents to marry Adam, but before they are wed she discovers that she is pregnant. She tries in vain to find Arthur, but in the end is found guilty of the murder of her child and is transported for life. Adam finally marries Dinah Morris, a young Methodist preacher.

Adam de la Hale (or Halle) (c. 1230–c. 1286). French poet and composer, author of the first known opera or play with music, *Li Gieus de Robin et Marion* (*The Play of Robin and Marion*), performed before the French court at Naples in 1275 or 1285.

Adamic, Louis (1899–1951). Yugoslav-born American writer. Adamic came to this country when he was 15. His own life as an immigrant is described in *Laughing in the Jungle* (1932). *The Native's Return* (1934) gives his impressions of revisiting Yugoslavia, and *Grandsons* (1935) is the saga of a Slovenian family in America. Always concerned with America as a melting pot, Adamic felt increasingly that the process was too slow; *My America* (1938) reflects this belief.

Adamites. The name for various heretical sects. Their belief was that they might attain to primitive innocence by rejecting marriage and clothing. There was such a sect in North Africa in the 2nd century; the *Abelites* were similar. The heresy reappeared in Savoy in the 14th century, and spread over Bohemia and Moravia in the 15th and 16th centuries. One Picard, of Bohemia, was leader in 1400, and styled himself "Adam, son of God." The paintings of Hieronymus Bosch are thought to have been influenced by his adherence to an Adamite sect.

Adamov, Arthur (1908–1970). Russian-born French dramatist. His *Ping-Pong* (1955) and *Paolo Paoli* (1957) are bitterly disillusioned satires of modern commercial society. Other plays include *L'Invasion* (1949), *Taranne* (1951), and *Les Âmes mortes* (1959).

Adams, Abigail [Smith] (1744–1818). Wife of John ADAMS, noted as a letter writer. The daughter of a Congregational minister, she married Adams in 1764. Her lively, perceptive letters, first published in 1840 in a selected form by her grandson Charles Francis Adams, mirror the affection and respect that existed between the Adamses and give a valuable picture of social and political life in the infant republic; they are included in their entirety in *Family Papers* (2 vols., 1963), the second series of *The Adams Papers* published by Harvard University.

Adams, Charles Francis, Jr. (1835–1915). American lawyer, railroad expert, and historian. This grandson of John Quincy, brother of Henry Adams, was a successful businessman who in time became disgusted with the "low instinct" of money-getting, and turned to writing history. He was chiefly interested in the history of Massachusetts, and wrote *Three Episodes of Massachusetts History* (1892), and *Massachusetts: Its History and Historians* (1893). Earlier he had exposed corruption in railroads in *Chapters of Erie and Other Essays* (1871) and

Railroads: Their Origins and Problems (1878). He published lives of Richard Henry Dana (1891) and of his father (1900), as well as an *Autobiography* (1916).

Adams, Franklin P[ierce] (1881–1960). American columnist best known as **F.P.A.** He wrote a column, "The Conning Tower," which appeared in several New York newspapers from 1913 to 1941.

Adams, Hannah (1755–1831). American historian. The first professional woman writer in the United States, she wrote *Alphabetical Compendium of the Various Sects . . . from the Beginning of the Christian Era* (1784) and *A Summary History of New England* (1799).

Adams, Henry [Brooks] (1838–1918). American historian, scholar, and man of letters. A member of the famous Adams family of statesmen, Henry Adams was temperamentally fitted, not for political action, but for the equally arduous task of studying and writing history. Working for a time as a journalist, he became editor of the *North American Review;* at the same time, he held an assistant professor-

A page from Hannah Adams'
Alphabetical Compendium. . . .

NEW YORK PUBLIC LIBRARY

ENC   59

and made use of a book which they ſtiled, *The goſpel according to the Hebrews.*

Moſheim's Eccleſ Hiſt vol. 1. p. 173, 174.
Hearnes Dueſtor Hiſtoricus. vol. 2, p. 74.

EICETÆ, A ſect in the year 680, who affirmed, that in order to make prayer acceptable to God, it ſhould be performed dancing.

Dufreſnoy's Chronological Tables. vol 1. p. 213.

EFFRONTES, So called from their ſhaving their foreheads till they bleed, and then anointing them with oil, uſing no other baptiſm but this.

They ſay, the Holy Ghoſt is nothing but a bare motion inſpired by God in the mind ; and he is not to be adored.

R ſi's View of all Reigions, p. 233.

ELCESAITES, A ſect in the ſecond century ; ſo denominated from their prophet Elceſai. His fundamental doctrine was, that Jeſus Chriſt, who was born from the beginning of the world, had appeared from time to time under divers bodies.

Hiſtory of Religion, vol. 4.   [See Elceſaites]

ENCRATITES, or **CONTINENTS,** A name given to a ſect in the ſecond century, becauſe they condemned marriage, forbid the eating of fleſh, or drinking of wine, and rejected, with a ſort of horror, all the comforts and conveniencies of life.   Tatian, an Aſſyrian, was the leader of this denomination. He regarded Matter as the fountain of all evil ; and therefore recommended, in a peculiar manner, the mortification of the body. He diſtinguiſhed the creator of the world from the Supreme
I   Being ;

ship of history at Harvard, where he taught medieval, European, and American history. Adams' first important book was the nine-volume study, *The History of the United States of America During the Administrations of Thomas Jefferson and James Madison* (1889–1891). Men, Adams deterministically argued, cannot change the course of history.

In 1872, Adams married Marian Hooper; after her suicide in 1885, he traveled to the Orient, and renewed an interest in science. His most important books, MONT-SAINT-MICHEL AND CHARTRES and THE EDUCATION OF HENRY ADAMS, reflect his lifelong quest for order and unity in a world he considered to be in the process of disintegration.

Adams' two novels, DEMOCRACY and ESTHER, reflect two of his absorbing concerns: corruption in a capitalistic government, and loss of religious faith caused by new scientific discoveries. Adams' letters, edited and published during the last 15 years, often reveal him at his best.

Adams, James Truslow (1878–1949). American historian. He won a Pulitzer Prize for *The Founding of New England* (1921), but is perhaps best known as the author of *The Epic of America* (1931), which has been translated into nine languages. Among his other works are *Revolutionary New England* (1923), *The March of Democracy* (2 vols., 1932–1933), *Building the British Empire* (1938), and *The American* (1943), an analysis of the American character. Adams was also the editor of the *Dictionary of American History* (6 vols., 1940).

Adams, John (1735–1826). Second president of the U.S. (1797–1801). A graduate of Harvard, Adams was admitted to the bar in 1758 and was carrying on a successful law practice when the Stamp Act crisis of 1765 drew him into politics. In a series of articles, later collected as *A Dissertation on the Canon and Feudal Law* (1768), he argued that the Stamp Act was contrary to the "inherent rights of mankind." He was a delegate to the first and second Continental Congresses and was an ardent advocate of the Declaration of Independence when it was presented to the congress.

In 1785, after several years' service as minister to France, Britain, and Holland, he began to write his *Defense of the Constitutions of Government of the United States of America* (1787–1788), in which he discussed the history of republican government. Elected vice president under Washington, he became president in 1797. He quarreled with Hamilton over a treaty with France in 1800, and the resulting split in the Federalist Party contributed to his loss to JEFFERSON in 1800. After his retirement from the presidency, he returned to his home in Quincy, Mass., and renewed his old friendship with Jefferson. Both men died within a few hours of each other on July 4, 1826.

Adams' essentially conservative political philosophy placed him between the extreme federalism of Hamilton and the agrarianism of Jefferson. His concept of republicanism was based on a "balance" of power that would prevent the power-hungry from gaining control, and his awareness of the weaknesses and vices of mankind led him to put his faith in the "natural aristocracy" of a few men, who, like himself, would use the power vested in them for the good of the people rather than for their private ends. The *Diary and Autobiography of John Adams* (4 vols., 1961) and *Family Papers* (2 vols., 1963) have been published as the opening sections of *The Adams Papers* by Harvard University Press. See Abigail ADAMS.

Adams, John Quincy (1767–1848). Sixth president of the U.S. (1825–1829). Adams accompanied his father, John Adams, to France in 1778, studied in European schools, and was graduated from Harvard in 1787. In 1791 in a series of 11 articles signed Publicola, he replied to Thomas Paine's *Rights of Man,* defending the rights of the minority in opposition to Paine's contention that the majority must prevail. After holding several diplomatic posts, Adams became secretary of state in 1817; he secured Florida from Spain in 1819 and was largely responsible for the promulgation of the MONROE DOCTRINE in 1823. In 1824 Adams, Andrew Jackson, and Henry Clay were among the four candidates for the presidency. Since no candidate received a majority of the electoral votes, the election was given to the House of Representatives. Clay threw his support to Adams, who was elected, and when Adams named Clay secretary of state, Jackson's followers cried "corrupt bargain." This charge, though undoubtedly baseless, hounded Adams during his term of office and contributed to his defeat in 1828. In 1830 he was elected to the House of Representatives, where he served for nearly 17 years, opposing the annexation of Texas and defending free speech in the face of efforts to stifle debate on the slavery question. Adams' diary, covering more than 60 years, was edited by his son, Charles Francis Adams, and published in 12 volumes as *The Memoirs of John Quincy Adams* (1874–1877).

Adams, Léonie [Fuller] (1899–   ). American poet. Her poems are marked by a deeply mystical view of nature, by vigorous metrics, and by a sense of song that lends delicacy to the packed meaning of her lines. Her books include *Those Not Elect* (1925), *High Falcon* (1929), *This Measure* (1933), and *Poems: A Selection* (1954).

Adams, Nick. The central character in most of the stories of IN OUR TIME, a collection by Ernest Hemingway. He appears also in the famous short story THE KILLERS.

Adams, Parson Abraham. The quixotic, vain, staunch friend of the hero of JOSEPH ANDREWS (1742), a novel by Henry Fielding. He is a guileless clergyman, totally ignorant of the ways of the world, always seeking the good of others. The element of paradoxical discussion that he introduces into the novel gives the book its truly comic character. He was drawn from Fielding's friend, the Rev. William Young, who edited Robert Ainsworth's *Latin-English Dictionary* (1752).

Adams, Samuel (1722–1803). American patriot and pamphleteer. Active in arousing public opinion against England before the American Revolution, he was responsible for the creation of a committee of correspondence to communicate Boston's grievances to other towns in Massachusetts and "to the World," and prepared for the committee a radical declaration, *State of the Rights of the Colonies* (1772). He was the leading spirit behind the Boston Tea Party and served in the Continental Congress (1774–1781), where he advocated immediate independence.

Adams, Samuel Hopkins (1871–1958). American writer. An effective member of the staffs of *McClure's* and *Collier's* magazines during the muck-raking days, Adams was active in exposing frauds, especially in the field of medicine, and was instrumental in bringing about the Pure Food and Drug Act (1906). He later wrote a long series of books dealing with the American background in fictional terms. He attacked dishonest journalism in his novel *The Clarion* (1914) and the scandals of the Harding administration in *Revelry* (1926). The latter book was supplemented by *The Incredible Era: The Life and Times of Warren Harding* (1939). He also wrote biographies of Daniel Webster and Alexander Woollcott.

Adams, William T. Pen name **Oliver Optic** (1822–1897). The author of various series of books for boys. He edited the journal *Our Boys and Girls,* founded in 1867 as a weekly, subsequently a monthly.

Addams, Jane (1860–1935). American leader in social work and the peace and women's suffrage movements. She is famous for her pioneering work at Hull House, a Chicago settlement house that she founded in 1889. In 1931 she, together with Nicholas Murray Butler, was awarded the Nobel Peace Prize. She wrote a number of books and articles on social problems, among them two autobiographical works: *Twenty Years at Hull House* (1910) and *The Second Twenty Years at Hull House* (1931).

Adding Machine, The (1923). A play by Elmer RICE. The dramatist uses expressionistic techniques to satirize the morality of the machine age. Mr. Zero loses his position when his employer installs adding machines. In a fit of temporary insanity, he murders the employer and is executed. Along with a coworker, Daisy Diana Dorothea Devore, who has committed suicide to be with him, he finds himself in the Elysian Fields. Happily operating the celestial adding machine, Mr. Zero scorns the company of such men as Swift and Rabelais. He is finally reincarnated and returns to earth to continue evolving into the perfect soulless slave.

Addison, Joseph (1672–1719). English poet, essayist, and critic. In association with Richard STEELE, he perfected the essay as a literary form in his contributions to THE TATLER and THE SPECTATOR. His prose style was the model for pure and elegant English until the end of the 18th century; his comments on manners and morals were widely influential in forming the middle-class ideal of a dispassionate, tolerant, Christian world-citizen. *The Campaign* (1704), celebrating the victory at Blenheim, and his hymn *The Spacious Firmament on High* (1712) are his most famous poems. His musical play *Rosamond* (1705) was an attack on popular Italian operas, and his blank-verse tragedy *Cato* (1713) was enormously popular, combining an appeal to the party-spirit of the Whigs, and an avowed intention to purge the stage of immorality. Addison is bitterly attacked by Alexander Pope in EPISTLE TO DR. ARBUTHNOT (1735) in the character of Atticus. See Thomas TICKELL.

Address to the Deil (1786). A poem by Robert BURNS attacking the corrupt clergy of Scotland.

Ade, George (1866–1944). American humorist and playwright. Ade first achieved popularity in the columns of the Chicago *Record* with the creation of the brash but good-hearted Artie. Stories of a colored bootblack and a gentlemanly liar were added, the three becoming the titular heroes of *Artie* (1896), *Pink Marsh* (1897), and *Doc' Horne* (1899). In

1898 he began to write the stories that were collected as FABLES IN SLANG. He commenced his career as a playwright with a successful musical comedy, *The Sultan of Sulu* (1902), later writing *The County Chairman* (1903), a play directed against political corruption; THE COLLEGE WIDOW; and *Father and the Boys* (1908).

Adenauer, Konrad (1876–1967). First chancellor of the German Federal Republic (1949–1963), who led his country in its economic and political recovery after World War II. He was mayor of Cologne (1917–1933) but lost this position because of conflict with the Nazis. In 1945 he helped to found the Christian Democratic Union, his political party. He retired from public life in 1963.

Adler, Alfred (1870–1937). Austrian psychoanalyst. A disciple of Sigmund FREUD, he later rebelled against his master's teachings and held to a system of "individual psychology." In this he maintained that psychological differences among individuals—in behavior, attitude, and the like—were due to the differences in their means of attaining a feeling of superiority in their relations with society.

Adler, Felix (1851–1933). German-born American philosopher, teacher, and founder of the Ethical Culture movement. Adler came to America at the age of 16; he founded the New York Society of Ethical Culture while teaching at Cornell University in 1876. The society emphasized the need for a stronger morality, and advocated the moral education of children as well as various kinds of labor and social reforms. Adler established the first free kindergarten for the children of the poor in New York City; this later grew into a vocational school, the first to include manual training and ethical instruction in its curriculum. In 1884 Adler helped to establish the Tenement House Commission; he arranged for trained nurses to visit the poor, argued for parks and playgrounds in poor areas of the city, and opposed child labor. Ethical Culture societies have since sprung up in several cities of the United States and Europe. Among Adler's books are *The Moral Instruction of Children* (1892), *Marriage and Divorce* (1905), *What the Ethical Culture School Stands For* (1910), and *The Reconstruction of the Spiritual Ideal* (1923).

Admetus (Admetos). See ALCESTIS; ARGONAUTS.

Admirable Crichton, The (1902). A dramatic fantasy by J. M. BARRIE. The Earl of Loam, his family, and one or two friends are wrecked on a desert island, where the butler, the admirable Crichton, proves himself to be a man of infinite resource and power, far superior to the rest of the party. Barrie took the title from an epithet bestowed upon James Crichton (1560–1585?), Scottish traveler, scholar, and swordsman, by Sir Thomas Urquhart.

Admiral Hosier's Ghost (1739). A ballad by Richard GLOVER, based on the capture of Porto Bello by Admiral Edward Vernon in 1739. Admiral Francis Hosier (1673–1727) is sent with 20 ships to the Spanish West Indies to block up the galleons of that country. He arrives at the Bastimentos, near Porto Bello, but has strict orders not to attack and his men perish, not in battle, but from disease. Hosier dies of a broken heart. Upon Admiral Vernon's victory, Hosier and his 3,000 men rise from the dead and lament the cruel orders that forbade them to attack the foe, for "with 20 ships he surely could have achieved what Vernon did with only 6."

Adolphe (1815). A novel by Benjamin CONSTANT DE REBECQUE. Adolphe, the novel's young protagonist, has been influenced by his early relationship with a woman of strong intellectual convictions, and is unable to adopt the conventional masks of society. Having finished his studies, he sets out upon a period of travel in Germany and Poland. While visiting at a small German court, he establishes a liaison with Ellénore, mistress of Count P—. Adolphe, who began the affair out of pride rather than love, is deeply probed by the author who points out his inability to terminate the relationship as a result of his guilt, which leaves him desolate when Ellénore dies. The work, considered to be based in part on Constant's relationship with Mme. de STAEL, is a precursor of the modern psychological novel.

Adonai. See JEHOVAH.

Adonais (1821). A poem by Percy Bysshe SHELLEY. When Keats died in 1821, Shelley was moved to compose this elegy for his friend. He gave Keats the name of Adonais, probably in allusion to the mourning for Adonis. *Adonais* is considered one of the greatest elegies in the English language.

Adonis. In Greek mythology, a beautiful youth. Adonis was born of Myrrha (Smyrna) after she had been turned into a tree to escape her father, for whom she had an incestuous love. APHRODITE fell in love with Adonis when he was still a youth, but he was killed by a boar, which, according to some accounts, was Aphrodite's jealous lover Ares in disguise. From his blood sprang the anemone. According to another story, Aphrodite gave the infant Adonis in a chest to Persephone to take care of, but Persephone fell in love with him and would not return him. Zeus judged the case and ordered that Adonis should spend one third of the year with each goddess, the third where he chose. He chose to spend the extra third as well with Aphrodite.

This myth, the scene of which is laid in Asia, is one of the many in which a young god of vegetation dies and is resurrected. A part of the cult included the planting of "gardens of Adonis"—seeds in shallow soil which withered as quickly as they sprouted. The name of the god is derived from *adon* (lord), which appears in the Hebrew *adonai,* used as a substitute for the name of Yahweh (Jehovah). See TAMMUZ; VENUS AND ADONIS; ADONAIS.

Adramelech. One of the fallen angels. Milton has him overthrown by Uriel and Raphael in PARADISE LOST.

Adrasto (Adrastus). In the GERUSALEMME LIBERATA of Tasso, the commander of the Indian forces allied with other enemies of the crusaders. During the assault upon Jerusalem he is killed by Rinaldo at the final battle, which results in the fall of the city.

Adrastus (Adrastos). In Greek mythology, a king of Argos and leader of the expedition of the SEVEN AGAINST THEBES. He was the only member of the expedition to return alive.

Adrian or **Hadrian IV** (originally **Nicholas Breakspear**) (d. 1159). The only Englishman to be elected Pope (1154–1159). He crowned Emperor Frederick Barbarossa (1155), but soon entered a great conflict with him over the assertion of papal prerogatives. There is much historical controversy over his reputed gift of the feudal sovereignty of Ireland to Henry II of England.

Adriana. A character in Shakespeare's COMEDY OF ERRORS. She is the high-spirited and impatient wife of Antipholus of Ephesus and sister of Luciana.

Adullam. The cave in which David took refuge when he fled from King Saul. This stronghold attracted "every one that was in debt, and every one that was discontented" (I Sam. 22:1–2).

Advancement of Learning, The (1605). A treatise on philosophy by Francis BACON. Considered an excellent example of Renaissance thought, it extols the pursuit of learning and critically surveys the existing state of knowledge. Bacon later wrote a greatly expanded version, *De Dignitate et Augmentis Scientiarum* (1623), to form the first part of his projected INSTAURATIO MAGNA.

Advent (Lat. *adventus,* the coming to). The four weeks immediately preceding Christmas. It commemorates the first coming of Christ, and anticipates the second: the one to redeem, the other to judge the world. The season begins the Sunday on or nearest St. Andrew's Day (Nov. 30th). There is an old tradition of preaching on the "Four Last Things" on the Advent Sundays: Death, Judgment, Heaven, and Hell.

Adventists. Christian religious sects believing that the second coming of Christ and the end of the world are near at hand.

Adventures. For many titles beginning with the words *The Adventures of . . .* , see the following proper names. For example, *The Adventures of Tom Sawyer* will be found under *Tom Sawyer, The Adventures of.*

Adventures of Philip, The (1862). A novel by William Makepeace THACKERAY. The hero, Philip Firmin, revolts against the hypocrisy of his father, Dr. George Brandon Firmin, whose sham marriage to Caroline Gann forms the subject of an earlier novel. As a boy he is befriended by Caroline, now known as Mrs. Brandon, or "the little Sister," and throughout the book he champions her cause. He is brought up in luxury, but, owing to his father's scheming, loses his money and is forced to earn a living as an editor. He marries Charlotte Baynes, the daughter of his guardian, whom his father had tricked to secure his fortune. After numerous difficulties, Philip comes into a fortune from Lord Ringwood, a wealthy relative. The novel is a sequel to *A Shabby Genteel Story* (1840), which is usually printed as its prologue.

Advice to the Privileged Orders (1792). A prose tract by Joel BARLOW. Barlow argues that the state exists not to protect property but to assure the political rights of the individual. The piece aroused a great deal of discussion and unfavorable criticism in England and was the subject of debate in the House of Commons. The Pitt ministry ordered it burned and Barlow jailed.

Æ or **A.E.** Pen name of **George William Russell** (1867–1935). Irish poet, painter, mystic, patriot of Irish Nationalism, and one of the organizers of the Irish Agricultural Co-operative movement. In 1886 he was associated, as was William Butler Yeats, with the founding of the Dublin Lodge of the Theosophical Society, for occult and Hermetic study.

His mystical poetry is based on visions, magic, and Eastern religious ideas; he writes about these interests in *The Candle of Vision* (1918). Among his collections of poetry are *Homeward: Songs by the Way* (1894), *The Earth Breath* (1897), and *House of the Titans* (1934). He also wrote *Deirdre* (1902), one of the first verse plays performed at the ABBEY THEATRE, and *The Living Torch* (1937), a collection of essays.

Aeacus (Aiakos). Greek mythological character. A son of Zeus and Aegina, king of Pythia, noted for his piety. He was the father of Telamon and Peleus by Endeis and of Phocus by Psamathe. The elder sons killed Phocus from jealousy and were banished. When all Greece was ravaged by drought because of PELOPS' murder of Stymphalus, Aeacus' prayers brought rain. At his death he became either a warder or a judge in Hades.

aedile. In ancient Rome, one of 4 magistrates whose duty it was to maintain order in the city and to take charge of public games and buildings. An aedile corresponds roughly to a modern commissioner of public works. His supervision of public games gave him great opportunities for gaining favor with the populace. Although a small sum was appropriated from the public treasury for these games, an aedile generally expended much more from his own purse to make the show magnificent and thus win votes for the next office in the CURSUS HONORUM, that of praetor.

Aeëtes (Aietes). See MEDEA.

Aegeon. In Shakespeare's COMEDY OF ERRORS, a merchant of Syracuse, the father of the two Antipholi and the husband of Aemilia. He is detained in Ephesus, pending ransom, because of the law barring Syracusans from the city.

Aegeon. See BRIAREUS.

Aegeus (Aigeus). A legendary king of Athens, father of THESEUS. Aegeus threw himself into the sea, thinking mistakenly that Theseus' expedition to Crete had failed. The Aegean Sea, according to tradition, was so named as a result of this event.

Aegipan (Aigipan). The god PAN. His horns, ears, and legs were goatlike. The name literally means goat Pan.

Aegis (Aigis). The shield or cuirass of Zeus. Made by HEPHAESTOS, it was the symbol of divine protection. An aegis was also worn by Athene. The word indicates that it was originally merely a goatskin.

Aegisthus (Aigisthos). See House of ATREUS.

Aegyptus (Aigyptos). In classic myth the father of 50 sons. They were married to the 50 daughters of his twin brother Danaus and all except one of them were murdered by their brides on the wedding night. See DANAIDES.

Aelfric, called **Grammaticus,** or **"the Grammarian"** (c. 955–c. 1020). English clergyman and scholar, a prolific writer in both Latin and Old English. He wrote a series of 120 homilies and saints' lives (990–998), then a treatise on the Old and New Testaments and a *Heptateuch,* a vernacular translation of portions of the first seven books of the Bible. His prose is alliterative and rhythmical, the finest in Old English. Concerned with the revival of learning, he wrote a Latin grammar and Latin-English glossary.

Aemilia. The virtuous mother of the twins, Antipholus of Ephesus and Antipholus of Syracuse, and the wife of Aegeon in Shakespeare's COMEDY OF ERRORS. When her family is lost to her in a storm, she becomes an abbess.

Aeneas. The hero of Vergil's AENEID. He was the son of the mortal ANCHISES and the goddess Aphrodite. According to Homer, he fought against the Greeks in the Trojan War and after the sack of Troy reigned in the Troad. Vergil, however, used another legend, according to which Aeneas carried his father Anchises on his shoulders out of the burning city and with a band of followers set out to establish a new nation; after wandering for many years, he is said to have arrived in Italy, where he founded the colony from which the Romans traced their origin. The epithet often applied to him is *pious*, i.e., devoted to the service of the gods and deeply aware of his obligations to his family and his country. See ASCANIUS.

Aeneas Silvius. See PIUS II.

Aeneid. An epic poem by VERGIL, composed of 12 books, in which the legendary Trojan origin of the Roman people is glorified. Vergil traces the lineage of the Julii from Iulus or ASCANIUS, the son of the Trojan hero AENEAS, down to Octavius Caesar (later Augustus), whose newly established principate the poem endorses. The poem was written at the request of the emperor and, though it was left unfinished at the sudden death of the poet (19 B.C.), it was greeted with enthusiasm by all educated Romans because of its nationalistic purpose.

In Book I, Aeneas and his Trojan followers are driven by a storm to the shores of Carthage and are hospitably entertained by Queen DIDO. In Book II, Aeneas tells the tale of the wooden horse and of the destruction of Troy. He describes his escape from the burning city with his father ANCHISES, his son Ascanius, and several followers. His wife was lost and died during their flight. The narrative is continued in Book III, in which Aeneas recounts the perils he encountered on the westward voyage from Troy and the death of his father. Book IV tells of Dido's love for Aeneas, his departure from Carthage, and her suicide and cremation on a great funeral pyre. In Book V, Aeneas and his followers reach Sicily and hold funeral games in honor of Anchises. (See ACESTES.) Aeneas visits Anchises in the underworld in Book VI, sees the future generations of Romans, and is told of their exploits. Here appear the much quoted lines of Anchises to Aeneas concerning the task of the Romans: "Roman, remember that you shall rule the nations by your authority, for this is to be your skill, to make peace the custom, to spare the conquered, and to wage war until the haughty are brought low."

In Book VII, LATINUS, king of the Latini, entertains Aeneas and promises his daughter LAVINIA to him in marriage; but Prince TURNUS, who has already been betrothed to her by her mother, raises an army to resist Aeneas. Book VIII tells of the preparations for war on both sides and of Aeneas' visit to Latium, the future home of the Romans. In Book IX, Turnus, in the absence of Aeneas, fires the Trojan ships and assaults their camp. The episode of NISUS AND EURYALUS occurs here. The war between Turnus and Aeneas is depicted in Book X. Here MEZENTIUS and his son Lausas are slain by Aeneas. In Book XI, the battle continues. Book XII tells of the single combat between Aeneas and Turnus, and of the death of Turnus. See ACHATES; GYAS AND CLOANTHUS; HELENUS; PALINURUS.

Aeolus (Aiolos). In Greek mythology, the god of the winds, which he kept imprisoned in the Aeolian islands. He freed them at his own choice or the wish of other gods. In the *Odyssey*, Book X, he aided Odysseus in his homeward voyage by fastening the unfavorable winds in a leather bag and giving it into Odysseus' keeping, with a warning not to open it. While Odysseus slept, however, his seamen, thinking that he was secreting treasure from them, opened the bag and the ship was blown back to its starting point. Angrily Aeolus refused to cooperate further.

Aeolus (Aiolos). The grandson of Deucalion, the Greek Noah, and eponymous ancestor of the Aeolian Greeks.

Aerodrome, The (1941). A Kafkaesque social and political allegory by Rex WARNER. Its main character tries to impose his totalitarian system on a disorganized, easy-going village. The villagers successfully resist him.

Aeschylus (Aischylos) (525–456 B.C.). A Greek tragic dramatist. Aeschylus was born of an aristocratic family in Eleusis. In his youth, he fought against the Persians in the great battles of Marathon, Salamis, and Plataea. He seems to have been prouder of these feats than of his immense success as a playwright, which he did not even mention in the epitaph that, according to tradition, he wrote for himself. After 16 years of writing, he won his first prize for tragedy in 484 B.C.; he won his last with his masterpiece, the ORESTEIA, 25 years later. In 476 B.C. he had paid a successful visit to the court of Hiero I, Tyrant of Syracuse; three years before his death, he again went to Sicily, this time to Gela. According to a popular story, he was killed when an eagle dropped a tortoise on his bald head, mistaking it for a stone. The story is improved with the mention of an oracular prophecy that he would die of a blow from heaven.

Aeschylus wrote 90 plays, but only seven of them have survived: THE SUPPLIANT WOMEN, THE PERSIANS, the SEVEN AGAINST THEBES, PROMETHEUS BOUND, and the *Oresteia*, a trilogy. This last is the only extant example of the trilogies on related themes that were common in Aeschylus' day; it includes *Agamemnon*, The *Libation Bearers*, and the *Eumenides*. Aeschylus is noted for the grandeur of his language and of his subjects, which encompass not only the struggles between historical heroes (*The Persians*) and mythical (*Agamemnon*), but the grim conflict between the old laws and the new (*Eumenides*), and, in a sense, between man and gods (*Prometheus Bound*). Aeschylus' poetry is tense, closely packed, exciting, often somewhat rough, compared with the polished lines of Sophocles. His imagery is strong, startling, and sometimes forced, but always effective. The antithesis of Euripides' relatively colloquial speech, Aeschylus' dialogue is far from natural, but is well suited to the tragic immensity of his themes.

Aeschylus was a practical and imaginative man of the theater, as well as an inspired poet. He was the first to use a second actor in addition to the chorus;

this permitted for the first time dialogue between individuals. He also introduced elaborate costumes
and the high-soled *cothurnoi* that gave his actors
added stature. He seems to have enjoyed colorful
effects; *The Persians* is filled with pageantry, and old
Oceanus appears in *Prometheus Bound* riding on a
sort of four-legged bird, perhaps the original of
modern vaudeville's two-man horse. Tradition says
that some of his costumes were so splendid that the
hierophants at Eleusis copied them for their own
vestments. The story is also told that his presentation
in *Eumenides* of the chorus of Erinyes, hideous creatures with black skins and red tongues, so terrified
the audience that women had miscarriages and children convulsions.

Aesculapius. See ASCLEPIUS; FAERIE QUEENE,
THE.

Aesir. The collective name of the Norse gods
who lived in heavenly ASGARD. There were said to be
12 gods and some 24 to 30 goddesses, but the number
seems variable. The following may be mentioned:
(1) Odin, the chief of the gods; (2) Thor, Odin's
eldest son and god of thunder; (3) Tiu, another son,
the god of wisdom; (4) Balder, the Scandinavian
Apollo; (5) Bragi, god of poetry; (6) Vidar, god
of silence; (7) Hoder the blind, slayer of Balder;
(8) Hermoder, Odin's son and messenger; (9) Ho-
enir, a minor god; (10) Odnir, husband of Freya,
the Scandinavian Venus; (11) Loki, the god of
mischief; (12) Vali, Odin's youngest son.

Wives of the Aesir. Odin's wife was Frigga; Thor's
wife was Sif; Balder's wife was Nanna; Bragi's wife
was Iduna; Loki's wife was Siguna.

The important deities mentioned above are more
fully treated under their names. See ASYNJA; VANIR.

Aesop. Greek fabulist. According to tradition,
the author of *Aesop's Fables* was a Phrygian slave
who probably lived from 620 to 560 B.C. It is inferable
from Aristotle's mention of Aesop's acting as a public defender that he was freed from slavery, and
Plutarch's statement that the Athenians erected a
noble statue of him would tend to contradict the
tradition that Aesop was deformed. There is little
information on Aesop's life, and several scholars
have consequently been led to doubt that he ever
existed at all. The earliest extant collections of
Aesop's stories were made by various Greek versifiers and Latin translators, to whose compilations
were added tales from Oriental and ancient sources
to form what we now know as *Aesop's Fables.* The
majority of European fables, including those of LA
FONTAINE, are largely derived from these succinct
tales, in which talking animals illustrate human
vices, follies, and virtues. Since some of Aesop's
fables have been discovered on Egyptian papyri
dating from 800 or 1,000 years before his time, it
cannot be claimed that he was, by any means, the
author of all the fables.

aesthetics. The branch of philosophy dealing
with art and beauty. The term was first used by the
German philosopher Alexander Baumgarten (1714–
1762), though occidental preoccupation with problems of aesthetics goes back to the Greeks of the 4th
century B.C.

Aetna. See ETNA.

Affair, The (1959). A novel by C. P. SNOW.
It is a melodrama about an unpopular college teacher

with Communist sympathies. He is unjustly accused
of forgery, but eventually justice prevails. The novel
is part of the STRANGERS AND BROTHERS series.

Affliction (1633). A poem by George HERBERT.
The author rebels against the way God has "deceived" him into abandoning his worldly hopes for
His service, afflicted him with illness, loss of friends,
a sense of uselessness. The poem concludes with the
famous lines:

> Ah, my dear God! though I am clean forgot,
> Let me not love thee if I love thee not.

aficionado. See DILETTANTE.

Afinogenov, Alexander Nikolaevich (1904–
1941). Russian dramatist. His plays describe the
early struggles and problems of the Soviet regime.
They include *At the Breaking Point* (1926), *The
Crank* (1929), *Fear* (1931), *Distant Point* (1934),
Spain, Salute! (1936), *The Mother of Us All* (1940),
Mashenka (1941) and *On the Eve* (1941).

Afreet or **Afrit.** In Muslim mythology the
second most powerful of the five classes of JINN or
devils. They are of gigantic stature, very malicious,
and inspire dread. Legend holds that King Solomon
once tamed an Afreet, and made it submissive to his
will.

African Farm, The Story of an (1883). A semiautobiographical novel by Olive SCHREINER. She gives
a vivid account of life on a Boer farm like her childhood home and describes the religious doubts and intellectual and emotional development of an ardent
young feminist like herself.

African Queen, The (1935). A novel by C. S.
FORESTER. It is the comic-heroic story of a missionary's
sister and a timid Cockney engineer who try to blow
up a German gunboat from their asthmatic steam
launch, *The African Queen.*

After Many a Summer Dies the Swan (1939).
A novel by Aldous HUXLEY. Centered around Jo
Stoyte, a Californian oil magnate afraid of old age
and death, it is a satire of some aspects of American
life. Jeremy Pordage, working on some old English
manuscripts, discovers that an 18th-century earl
used the same rejuvenating system Stoyte is experimenting with. They go to England and find the
earl, over 200 years old, a filthy ape. Old Mr.
Propter is spokesman for Huxley's spiritual philosophy.

Afternoon of a Faun, The. See L'APRÈS-MIDI
D'UN FAUNE.

Agadir Crisis (1911). An international incident
precipitated by the arrival of a German gunboat at
Agadir in French-controlled Morocco. German demands for African territory were repulsed.

Against the Grain, or **Against Nature (A
Rebours;** 1884). A novel by Joris Karl HUYS-
MANS. Its subject is the quest of its DÉCADENT hero,
Des Esseintes, for the rare and perverse in sensation. Restless and discontent, Des Esseintes seeks release from the ennui of existence in perfumes, music, painting, the love of circus acrobats, or the study
of medieval Latin literature.

Agamedes. See TROPHONIUS.

Agamemnon. In Greek legend the king of
Mycenae, son of ATREUS and leader of the Greeks
at the siege of Troy. Homer makes him ruler over all
Argos. He was the brother of Menelaus, the theft of

whose wife Helen by Paris brought on the Trojan War. Before the expedition against Troy could sail, Agamemnon's daughter IPHIGENIA was sacrificed to Diana to appease that goddess for a sacred stag Agamemnon had killed. At Troy, Agamemnon's quarrel with Achilles cost the Greeks many lives and delayed the end of the war. (See ILIAD.) After the sack of Troy, Agamemnon returned home only to be murdered by his wife Clytemnestra, who was living as the paramour of Aegisthus.

Aganippe. Fountain of the MUSES, at the foot of Mount Helicon in Boeotia. Its waters were thought to inspire those who drank them.

agape. See LOVE FEAST; FAERIE QUEENE, THE.

Agapemone. A 19th-century English society. This communistic establishment of men and women was suspected of free-love practices.

Agassiz, Jean Louis Rodolphe (1807-1873). Swiss naturalist, teacher, and author. Agassiz came to the U.S. in 1846 as a lecturer with an established reputation; deciding to remain permanently, he became widely known as a professor at Harvard and curator of the Agassiz Museum at Cambridge. He was the founder of the Marine Biological Laboratory at Woods Hole, Mass. A fluent writer on geology and zoology, Agassiz showed an astonishing command of English. His major work is called *Contributions to the Natural History of the United States of America* (4 v., 1857-1862). An effective teacher of laymen and scientists, he epitomized his method in the directive: "Go to Nature; take the facts in your own hands; look, and see for yourself!" Opposed to the Darwinian theory of evolution, Agassiz did succeed in arousing interest in the natural sciences and establishing methods of study and classification. A member of the famous Saturday Club, he exchanged ideas with leading men of letters.

Agastya. In Hindu mythology, the legendary sage and pioneer in the epic age of the Aryanization of south India. Supposed to have been born in a jar, he is also known as Kumbhayoni, or "jarborn." Legend says that to his pupil Rama he presented the invincible bow and inexhaustible quiver of Vishnu. Another legend describes him as drinking the sea dry. As he was walking one day with Vishnu, the insolent ocean asked the god who the pigmy (the "jar-born" dwarf) was that strutted by his side. When Vishnu replied that it was the patriarch Agastya, who would restore earth to its true balance, the ocean contemptuously spat its spray in Agastya's face. Agastya, in revenge, drank it dry.

Agate, James Evershed (1877-1947). English dramatic critic. He wrote for the *Manchester Guardian*, the *Saturday Review*, and the *Sunday Times*.

Agathocles (361-289 B.C.). Tyrant of Sicily (316-304 B.C.). He was the son of a potter, and raised himself from the ranks to become general of the army. There is a story that he always kept an earthen pot at hand in memory of his origin. When he attacked the Carthaginians, he "carried the war into Africa" and "burned his ships behind him" that his soldiers might feel assured they must either conquer or die. Agathocles died of poison administered by his grandson. He is the hero of an English tragedy by Richard Perrington, a French tragedy

by Voltaire and a German novel by Caroline Pichler, all called by his name.

Agave (Agaue). In classic mythology, a daughter of Cadmus and mother of Pentheus, whom she tore to pieces in a mad fury under the illusion that he was a wild beast. This episode forms a part of Euripides' drama *Bacchae*. See BACCHANTS.

Agee, James (1909-1955). American novelist and film critic. Agee was raised in the Cumberland mountain area of Tennessee, the setting for his two novels. In 1936 he lived for a few weeks with several "typical" Alabama sharecropper families in order to write a magazine article on the plight of such people. Instead of a magazine article the result was the book *Let Us Now Praise Famous Men* (1941), with photographs by Walker Evans. During the 1940's Agee was a film reviewer. His work has been compiled as the first volume of *Agee on Film* (1958). After 1948 he worked almost exclusively for the motion pictures. The second volume of *Agee on Film* (1960) contains five of his screen plays. His first novel was *The Morning Watch* (1954). *A Death in the Family* was posthumously published in 1957 and was awarded a Pulitzer Prize. Dramatized by Tad Mosel as *All the Way Home* in 1960, the play too was a Pulitzer Prize winner. A collection of Agee's letters to Father Flye, an Episcopalian minister he had met as a youth, appeared in 1962.

Age of Anxiety, The (1947). A long poem by W. H. AUDEN. It concerns three men and a woman who meet by chance in a New York bar in wartime; all are suffering from the modern malaise, and feel guilty, isolated, and rootless. In a common dream they set out on a quest through a barren waste land. Hope in Christianity is presented as the solution to their problems. The title has frequently been used as a name to describe our age.

The Age of Anxiety is also the name of a ballet, danced to Leonard Bernstein's Second Symphony.

Age of Innocence, The (1920). A novel by Edith WHARTON. A satirical picture of social life in New York during the 1870's, it describes the marriage of Newland Archer to May Welland, who is bound by the tribal code of the elite. Although he is attracted to her unconventional cousin, Ellen Olenska, they are both too obedient to the code to seek happiness together.

Age of Reason, The (1794-1796). A controversial treatise by Thomas PAINE, expounding the deistic view of revealed religion. The work was widely denounced in America as immoral and atheistic.

Age of Reason, The. See ROADS TO FREEDOM, THE.

Agésilas (1666). A tragedy by Pierre CORNEILLE. Set in Ephesus in the time of Agesilaus, king of Sparta, it centers on the conflict between public opinion and the king's desire to marry a Persian. A compromise is effected, and he is finally able to marry the woman of his choice.

Aggravaine, Sir. In Arthurian legend, a son of MARGAWSE and a knight of the Round Table. In Malory's *Morte d'Arthur,* he is the brother of the knights Gawain, Gareth, Gaheris, and half brother of Mordred.

Agib. The third CALENDER in the *Arabian Nights*. He was wrecked on a loadstone mountain, lived for a year in the palace of the forty princesses, and lost an eye for his curiosity.

Agincourt, Battle of (1415). Battle in northern France. The English army defeated the more numerous, better armed French. It is the setting for Shakespeare's HENRY V and Michael Drayton's *The Ballad of Agincourt* (c. 1605).

Aglaia. (1) One of the three Charites (GRACES) of classic mythology.

(2) In Dostoevski's novel THE IDIOT, the fiancée of Prince Myshkin.

Aglaos. A poor Arcadian peasant. He was called by the Delphic oracle "happier than King Gyges of Lydia," because he was contented.

Agnès. In Molière's comedy L'ECOLE DES FEMMES, the girl on whom Arnolphe tries out his educational experiments, with the aim of turning her into a perfect wife for himself. She has been brought up in a country convent and kept totally in ignorance of the difference between the sexes, conventional proprieties, the mysteries of marriage, and so on. When removed from the convent, she treats men like schoolgirls, playing with them and kissing them. An *Agnès* is therefore any naïve and innocent young girl. The French have the expression, *Elle fait l'Agnès,* that is, she is pretending to be wholly unsophisticated and ingenuous.

Agnes Grey (1847). A novel by Anne BRONTË, published with her sister Emily's *Wuthering Heights*. It is a quiet account of the life of an ill-treated, lonely governess who eventually marries Mr. Weston, a curate.

Agni. The Hindu god of fire, sunlight, and lightning and lord of the gods of the earth. He is one of the more important deities described in the Vedas.

agnostic (Gr., *a*, not, *gignoskein*, to know). Thomas Huxley coined this term in 1869, alluding to the altar to "the Unknown God" mentioned in St. Paul's writings. Huxley meant to indicate the mental attitude of those who withhold their assent from whatever is incapable of proof, such as an unseen world, a First Cause, etc. Agnostics neither dogmatically accept nor reject such matters, but simply say *agnosco* (I do not know): they are not capable of proof.

Agramante (Agramant). The emperor of Africa who fights Charlemagne and the paladins in the Orlando poems of Boiardo and Ariosto. In the latter's poem he is killed by Oliviero (see ORLANDO FURIOSO).

Agrarians. A group of 20th-century American writers in the South. Among its members were Allen TATE, John Crowe RANSOM, and Robert Penn WARREN. Drawing their inspiration from the past, they favored agriculture as the economic base for the South; this would supposedly enable the South to return to its regional aristocratic heritage. These critics expressed their views in the symposium *I'll Take My Stand: The South and the Agrarian Tradition by Twelve Southerners* (1932). Many members of the original group have since abandoned their early position.

Agricane (Agrican). In Carolingian legend the King of Tartary who fights against the Christian forces of Charlemagne and his paladins. In the ORLANDO INNAMORATO of Boiardo, he besieges the

lovely princess Angelica at Albracca, but is killed in combat by Orlando. Before he dies, he asks for and is given baptism.

Agrippa I (d. A.D. 44). A son of Herod. He was one of the Roman rulers before whom St. Paul was tried. His tribute, "Almost thou persuadest me to be a Christian" (Acts 26:28), is often quoted.

Agrippina. (d. A.D. 59). Daughter of Agrippina and GERMANICUS CAESAR, sister of the emperor Caligula, and mother of the emperor Nero. She persuaded her husband the emperor CLAUDIUS, to name Nero, her son by a previous marriage, as his successor over his own son BRITANNICUS; subsequently she had Claudius poisoned. After he became emperor, Nero, after many elaborate and thwarted attempts, finally succeeded in having Agrippina murdered.

Agrippina's mother was the granddaughter of Augustus, wife of Germanicus Caesar and mother of Caligula. She was banished by Tiberius to the isle of Pandatarra where she died (A.D. 33).

Aguecheek, Sir Andrew. In Shakespeare's TWELFTH NIGHT, a silly old fop with "3,000 ducats a year." Very fond of the table but with a shrewd understanding that "beef had done harm to his wit," Sir Andrew thinks himself "old in nothing but in understanding," and boasts that he can "cut a caper, dance the coranto, walk a jig, and take delight in masques," like a young man.

Ahab. (1) In the Old Testament, a king of Israel whose name has become a byword for wickedness. He is remembered especially for his hostility to the prophet Elijah and countenance of profane cults. At the instigation of his wife Jezebel, he executed Naboth on false charges in order to obtain possession of a vineyard which Naboth owned and refused to sell. His story is told in I Kings 16–22.

(2) The monomaniacal captain of the *Pequod* in Melville's MOBY DICK (1851).

Ahasuerus. (1) In the Old Testament, king of the Medes and Persians, as related in the book of ESTHER.

(2) In medieval legend, one of the names given the WANDERING JEW.

Ahi. In Vedic myth, the sky dragon that releases the rain when Indra's thunderbolt is hurled.

Ahmed, Prince. A character in the *Arabian Nights,* noted for the tent given him by the fairy PARIBANOU, which would cover a whole army but might be carried in one's pocket; he is also associated with the apple of Samarkand, which would cure all diseases.

Aho, Juhani. Pen name of **Johannes Brofelt** (1861–1921). Finnish novelist and short-story writer. Influenced by the realist movement, Aho depicted in his earlier work the daily lives of common people. He was not, however, motivated by a passion for social reform, but sought instead to paint a true portrait and to record his often humorous insights. In both *Papin Tytar (The Parson's Daughter,* 1885) and *Papin Rouva (The Parson's Wife,* 1893), he portrays the inner struggles of a young woman who is married to a man she does not love. A new strain appeared in Aho's work with the publication of the novel *Panu* (1897): national romanticism now colored his realism. In the short stories of *Lastuja (Chips,* 1891–1921), he shows himself a fine poet.

Aholah and **Aholibah.** In the Old Testament, the names of 2 harlots who symbolize the religious idolatry and pursuit of false faiths in Samaria and Jerusalem (Ezek. 23:4).

Aholibamah. In the Old Testament, the name of one of Esau's wives (Gen. 36:2) and of a duke, or leader, of Edom (Gen. 36:41). In Byron's poem, *Heaven and Earth* (1824), she is a proud, ambitious, queenlike beauty, the daughter of Cain's son and loved by the seraph Samiasa.

Ahriman or **Ahrimanes.** In the dual system of ZOROASTER, the spiritual enemy of mankind, also called Angra Mainyu and Druj (deceit). He has existed since the beginning of the world and is said to be in eternal conflict with Ahura Mazda or ORMUZD.

Ah Sin. The Chinese card player in Bret Harte's PLAIN LANGUAGE FROM TRUTHFUL JAMES.

Ahura Mazda. See ORMUZD.

Aïda. A spectacular opera by Giuseppe VERDI. The libretto by Camille du Locle was translated into Italian by Ghislanzoni and considerably reworked by Verdi himself. The story was based on a sketch by the French Egyptologist Mariette, who had originally thought of it as appropriate for ceremonies opening the Suez Canal. Verdi, however, did not consent to begin writing the opera until 1870, the year after the opening of the canal, and the only connection it retained with Mariette's original purpose was that the khedive of Egypt, who commissioned the opera, required that it should open in Cairo.

Aïdes, also **Aïdoneus.** See HADES.

Aiglon, L'. A drama by Edmond ROSTAND. It is based on the tragic career of Napoleon's son and heir, whom Victor Hugo called l'Aiglon (the eaglet).

Aiken, Conrad [Potter] (1889–   ). American poet. A graduate of Harvard, Aiken was influenced by Freud, Havelock Ellis, and William James, as well as by Edgar Allan Poe. Of his novels, perhaps the best known are THE BLUE VOYAGE and the autobiographical USHANT. He won a Pulitzer Prize in 1930 for his *Selected Poems* (1929). Among his volumes of poetry are *The Jig of Forslin* (1916), *The House of Dust* (1920), *Priapus and the Pool* (1922), *Serlin* (1925), *Time in the Rock* (1936), and *And in the Human Heart* (1940). *Costumes by Eros* (1928) is a collection of short stories. See KID, THE. His collected novels appeared in 1964.

Ainsworth, William Harrison (1805–1882). English historical novelist. From 1840 on he was editor of *Bentley's Miscellany, Ainsworth's Magazine,* and the *New Monthly.* He wrote 39 novels, including *Rookwood* (1834), *Jack Sheppard* (1839), *Old St. Paul's* (1841), *Windsor Castle* (1843), and *The Flitch of Bacon* (1854).

Airavata. In Hindu myth the holy elephant, Indra being its rider. He is supposed to have been created by seven chants from the mouth of Brahma.

Ajax (Aias). The most famous hero of the Trojan War after Achilles. He was king of Salamis, a man of giant stature, daring and self-confident, son of Telamon. When the armor of Hector was awarded to Odysseus instead of to himself, he turned mad from vexation and stabbed himself. His deeds are narrated by Homer and later poets. Sophocles wrote a tragedy called *Ajax,* in which "the madman"

scourges a ram he mistakes for Achilles. His encounter with a flock of sheep, which he fancied in his madness to be the sons of Atreus, Agamemnon, and Menelaus, has been mentioned at greater or less length by several Greek and Roman poets. This Ajax is introduced by Shakespeare in his drama TROILUS AND CRESSIDA.

Ajax (Aias) the Less. In Greek legend, son of Oileus, king of Locris. The night Troy was taken, he offered violence to Cassandra, the prophetic daughter of Priam; in consequence, his ship was driven on a rock, and he perished at sea.

Akenside, Mark (1721–1770). English poet and physician to the queen (1761). He is the author of *The Pleasures of the Imagination* (1774), in blank verse, and of various minor poems.

Akhmatova, Anna. Pen name of **Anna Andreyevna Gorenko** (1888–1966). Russian poet. An outstanding member of the Acmeist school (see ACMEISM), she married the poet Nikolai GUMILIOV in 1910 and divorced him in 1918. Between 1912 and 1923 she published half a dozen volumes of poems, the best of which included *Evening (Vecher;* 1912) and *Anno Domini* (1922). Her poetry, principally intimate and personal love lyrics, is in the Acmeist tradition of clarity and sharpness of imagery. Akhmatova's abstinence from political themes led to an attack on her in 1946 by the Soviet cultural overseer, Andrei Zhdanov. She had published little since 1923 —being completely unpublished at all for one 17-year stretch—and after the attack issued only a few second-rate verses. In 1956, at the height of the Soviet thaw in the arts, two of her poems were reprinted in a Moscow literary journal.

Akins, Zoë (1886–1958). American dramatist. She won a Pulitzer Prize for her adaptation (1935) of Edith Wharton's THE OLD MAID. She also wrote such light romantic comedies as *A Royal Fandango* (1923) and *The Greeks Had a Word for It* (1930). In later years Miss Akins wrote screenplays, among them one for Edna Ferber's *Show Boat* (1926).

Aksakov, Sergei Timofeyevich (1791–1859). Russian writer. Born in Ufa, in the eastern steppes of Russia, Aksakov attended the University of Kazan and entered government service in Moscow. His early writing consisted mainly of essays and articles on the theatre. The novelist Gogol, who became a close friend of Aksakov's in the early 1830's, urged him to write the reminiscences of his early life in the steppe country. Aksakov produced three autobiographical works: *Semeinaya khronika (The Family Chronicle,* 1856), *Vospominaniya (Reminiscences,* 1856), and *Detskiye gody bagrova vnuka (Years of Childhood of Bagrov's Grandson,* 1858). In the *Chronicle* and *Years of Childhood,* Aksakov used fictitious names for his family. All three of these works, which are masterpieces of description and narration, have become classics in Russian literature. Aksakov's prose style is placed on a level with the best Russian prose writers, including Pushkin, Lermontov, and Turgenev. The love of the old patriarchal Russian way of life that is revealed in Aksakov's memoirs was passed on to his children. Two of his sons, Konstantin (1817–1860) and Ivan (1823–1886), became leading members of the SLAVOPHILES.

Akutagawa Ryūnosuke (1892–1927). Japanese short-story writer, noted for his novel subject matter, presented in a vivid and realistic style. Many of his stories have been translated into English. He committed suicide with an overdose of veronal.

Al Aaraaf (1829). A poem by Edgar Allan POE. It is the title poem of his second collection, called *Al Aaraaf, Tamerlane, and Other Poems.* In Arabian folklore, Al Aaraaf is the region between Heaven and Hell, presided over by Nesace, a beautiful maiden. Poe's Al Aaraaf is a wondrous star, surrounded by four suns. The youth, Angelo, is brought there with the hope of entering Heaven; an earthly love prevents him from hearing Nesace's call.

Aladdin. One of the most celebrated characters in the *Arabian Nights,* hero of the story *Aladdin or the Wonderful Lamp.* The son of Mustafa, a poor tailor of China, Aladdin is a lazy, obstinate and mischievous boy when the tale opens. One day an African magician accosts him, pretending to be his uncle, and sends him into a cave to bring up a "wonderful lamp," giving him a "ring of safety." Aladdin secures the lamp but will not hand it to the magician till he is out of the cave; whereupon the magician shuts him up and departs for Africa. Wringing his hands in despair, Aladdin accidentally rubs the lamp and learns of its magic power as two genii appear to do his bidding. He asks to be delivered from the cave and is returned to his home. By means of this lamp, he obtains untold wealth, builds a superb palace, and marries BADROULBOUDOUR, the sultan's daughter. After a time, the African magician, offering new lamps for old, obtains the lamp from Aladdin's wife and causes the palace to be transported into Africa. Ultimately, however, Aladdin poisons the magician, regains the lamp and has his palace restored to its original place in China.

Aladino (Alandine). In the GERUSALEMME LIBERATA of Tasso, the aged king of Jerusalem who opposes the armies of the First Crusade led by Goffredo (Godfrey). He is killed in the final battle that precedes the Christian conquest of the holy city.

Alain. Pen name of **Emile Chartier** (1868–1951). French philosopher, essayist, and teacher. He took his pseudonym from the 15th-century poet Alain Chartier. Believing that to be alive is to be awake, Alain imbued a generation of disciples with the will to resist conformity. His writings were most often in the form of propos, short aphoristic essays much like fables or parables, which taught a practical lesson through imagistic narrative. Some of the many thousands of these propos have been collected in books about politics, his militant pacifism, psychology, philosophy, and literary criticism, including *Les Cent et un Propos d'Alain* (5 v., 1908–1929) and *Mars, ou la Guerre jugée* (1921).

Alain-Fournier. Pen name of **Henri Fournier** (1886–1914). French novelist. Alain-Fournier grew up in the beautiful countryside of La Chapelle-d'Angillon, in the department of Cher. The son of two schoolteachers, he wandered from the merchant marine, to military service, to a career in journalism. In 1914, Alain-Fournier died in action, leaving one work which alone secured his reputation as a significant French novelist: LE GRAND MEAULNES.

Alamanni, Luigi (1495–1556). Florentine poet and playwright. A leading Renaissance imitator of classical forms in the vernacular, his most substantial works are the *Coltivazione* (On Cultivation, 1546),

a didactic poem in imitation of Virgil's *Georgics* similarly dealing with the care of fields and gardens; and two epics: *Gyrone il cortese* (1548), which relates the adventures of the courteous knight Gyrone; and the *Avarchide* (1570), on the siege of Bourges (Lat., Avaricum) by King Arthur.

Alamo. A fortified mission in San Antonio, Texas. In 1836, during the Texas rebellion against Mexico, a force of Texans under William B. Travis was besieged there by a much larger Mexican army led by General Santa Anna. When the Mexicans succeeded in gaining entrance after a 13-day bombardment, every remaining defender was killed in hand-to-hand combat. Among those killed were Davy Crockett and James Bowie. "Remember the Alamo!" became a battle slogan of the Mexican War.

Alan-a-Dale or **Alin-a-Dale.** See ALLAN-A-DALE.

Alarcón, Pedro Antonio de (1833–1891). Spanish novelist. Alarcón's fame rests on his shorter works, particularly his humorous tale based on popular ballad tradition, *El sombrero de tres picos* (*The Three Cornered Hat,* 1874). His humor again raised him to prominence with the publication of the novelette *El capitán Veneno* (*Captain Venom* or *Poison,* 1881). Also well known is his full-length work, *El escándalo* (1875), which points out the redeeming effects of an innocent girl's love upon a quarrelsome aristocrat, and the novel *El niño de la bola* (1880).

Alarcón y Mendoza, Juan Ruiz de (c. 1581–1639). Mexican-born Spanish dramatist. Alarcón, who spent most of his life in Spain, studied at Salamanca and was appointed to the Council of the Indies in 1626. His humped back and touchy temperament made him a target for the gibes of rival dramatists, such as Lope de Vega.

A restrained and painstaking artist who paid close attention to style and characterization, he wrote 24 plays, most of which were published in 1628 and 1634. The best known of these are the "comedies of ethics," in which the comic element enforces a moral lesson: *Las paredes oyen,* a study of slander; *Mudarse por mejorarse,* which assails inconstancy in love; *La prueba de las promesas,* an attack on ingratitude; and LA VERDAD SOSPECHOSA.

A la Recherche du Temps Perdu. See REMEMBRANCE OF THINGS PAST.

Alaric. (370?–410). Gothic king and conqueror. As king of the Visigoths, he invaded Greece (395–396) and plundered Rome (410).

Alas y Ureña, Leopoldo. Also known as **Clarín** (1852–1901). Spanish novelist and critic. Though he exerted some critical influence during his period, his chief claim to fame lies in his two-volume novel *La Regenta* (1884–1885), considered one of the major works of European fiction in the 19th century. It applies a mixture of naturalism, akin to that of French writers, and psychological interpretation to Spanish provincial life, concentrating upon the plight of a heroine crushed by the boredom and malice present in her native town.

Albanact. Son of BRUTE, in Geoffrey of Monmouth's *History of the Kings of Britain.* According to Geoffrey, Albanact gave his name to Albany (Scotland).

Albany, duke of. In Shakespeare's KING LEAR, the gentle, wise, and courageous husband of the ruthless Goneril, eldest daughter of Lear. He is horrified at Goneril's behavior toward her father. At the play's end, he and Edgar are left to rule England.

albatross. The largest web-footed bird. It is the subject of many superstitions, especially among sailors. Coleridge's RIME OF THE ANCIENT MARINER is based on the belief that it is fatal to shoot an albatross.

Albee, Edward [Franklin] (1928–   ). American playwright. His first play, written in three weeks in 1958, was the one-act *Zoo Story,* performed first in German (W. Berlin, 1959). This was followed by *The Death of Bessie Smith,* a one-act play on the effects of racial discrimination in the lives of whites; it was produced on Broadway in 1961, paired with Albee's *The American Dream.* He also wrote two 15-minute plays: *The Sandbox,* a prelude to *The American Dream,* and *Fam and Yam,* a dialogue between playwrights. Albee's first three-act play was *Who's Afraid of Virginia Woolf?* (1962), a virulent unveiling of the relationship between a history professor and his wife, the daughter of the president of the college. In 1963 he dramatized Carson McCullers' novel *The Ballad of the Sad Café.*

Alberich. In Scandinavian and German legend, the dwarf who guards the treasure of the Nibelungs, owners of a magic ring. He plays a prominent part in both the *Völsunga Saga* and the *Nibelungenlied.* In Wagner's musical drama, *Der* RING DES NIBELUNGEN (1876), Loki and Wotan steal the ring and treasure, and Alberich's curse follows the ring wherever it goes.

Albers, Joseph (1888–   ). German artist. He taught at the BAUHAUS and, emigrating to the U.S., headed the art department of Yale University until 1958. His teaching has considerably influenced industrial design.

Albert, Prince. Full name **Albert Francis Charles Augustus Emmanuel of Saxe-Coburg-Gotha** (1819–1861). German husband of Queen VICTORIA and prince-consort of England, son of the Duke of Saxe-Coburg-Gotha. Through his tact and abiding interest in the arts and science, he overcame the initial distrust of the English people. It was largely through his work that the great Exhibition of 1851 was successful. His death left the queen and the nation in deep mourning.

Albertanus of Brescia. See MELIBEE.

Alberti, Leone Battista (1404–1472). Florentine humanist. He wrote poetry, plays, moral and philosophical essays, dabbled in painting and sculpture, and practiced architecture, designing the Rucellai Palace and Loggia and the facade of Santa Maria Novella in Florence. In Rimini, he redesigned the church of San Francesco for the tyrant Sigismondo Malatesta in 1445; one of the earliest examples of Renaissance classical style, it was called the *Tempio Malatestiano* because of its resemblance to pagan temples. In Rome, he was one of the early contributors to the architectural plans for Saint Peter's. He is particularly known for his treatises, on painting, *De pictura* (1435), on sculpture, *De statua* (1464), and on architecture, *De re aedificatoria* (1452, pub. 1485) in which he popularized Filippo Brunelleschi's innovations concerning the scientific study of vision and the use of ancient monuments as sources; he also described a system based on human proportions which allows the correct placement of figures within pictorial space.

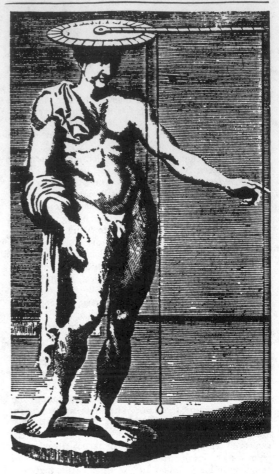

From Alberti's *De statua,* showing human proportions.

Among his literary works are a play written in such perfect imitation of the Latin poets that Aldo Manutius thought it an original; an autobiography (1460); and his masterpiece, the treatise *On the Family (Della famiglia),* which uses the dialogue form to discuss his social philosophy, and presents a valuable portrait of life in his day.

Alberti, Rafael (1902–   ). Spanish poet and playwright. His early volumes, *Marinero en tierra* (1925), *La amanta* (1926), *El alba del alhelí* (1927), and *Cal y Canto* (1927), reveal his initial interest in folklore as an art motif. Later, as in his best-known work, *Sobre los ángeles* (1928), he shifted his focus, concentrating upon surrealist poety. Alberti is also known for his popular plays *El hombre deshabitado* (1931), *El adefesio* (1944), and the tragedy *La Gallarda.*

Albertine disparue. See REMEMBRANCE OF THINGS PAST.

Albertine [Simonet]. The mistress of the narrator in Marcel Proust's REMEMBRANCE OF THINGS PAST. She refuses him when they meet at Balbec, but later comes to live with him in Paris, although secretly continuing to have affairs with other women. Tormented by his jealousy, she leaves him—only to be killed accidentally by being thrown from a horse.

Albert the Great. See ALBERTUS MAGNUS.

Albertus Magnus. (1206?–1280). German scholastic philosopher and churchman. His works include paraphrases of Aristotle's works, and he was very advanced for his day in his knowledge of experimental science. His teachings had great influence; Thomas AQUINAS was one of his students. He was canonized in 1932.

Albion. An ancient and poetical name for Great Britain. It is thought to have been so called from the white (Lat. *albus*) cliffs that face Gaul, but possibly from the Celtic *alp, ailp,* a rock, cliff, mountain. It was Napoleon who called England *Albion Perfide* (Perfidious Albion).

Albracca. In Boiardo's famous epic ORLANDO INNAMORATO, a fortress in Cathay to which ANGELICA retires in grief when Rinaldo fails to return her love. Here she is besieged by Agricane, king of Tartary, until Orlando kills him.

Albright, Ivan Le Lorraine (1897–   ). American painter. He spotlights, with microscopic realism, the pores, wrinkles, textures, and blemishes of humanity.

Alcaic verse or Alcaics. A Greek lyrical metre, so called from Alcaeus, a lyric poet. He is said to have invented it. Alcaic measure is little more than a curiosity in English poetry; probably the best example is Tennyson's:

O migh/ty-mouthed / in/ventor of / harmonies,
O skilled / to sing / of / Time or E/ternity.
God-gift/ed or/gan-voice / of Eng/land,
    Milton, a / name to re/sound for / ages.

Alcalde de Zalamea, El (The Mayor of Zalamea, c. 1640). A tragic drama by Pedro CALDERÓN DE LA BARCA. This play was originally written by Lope de Vega, but Calderón re-adapted it, giving to the realism of the former master a more profound and intellectual outlook. Among the characters created by Calderón is the hero, Pedro Crespo, a farmer who is elected *alcalde,* or mayor, of Zalamea.

Don Álvaro, an army captain quartered in Pedro's home, violates his host's daughter and refuses to marry her; he does not believe that he has to answer to commoners for his conduct. After Pedro has Don Álvaro jailed, Don Lope, the captain's superior officer, demands his freedom, and King Philip II, who has arrived in Zalamea, agrees that Pedro has exceeded his authority. However, when Pedro reveals that the captain has been strangled in prison, the king, forced to admit that justice has been done, makes Pedro perpetual mayor of the town. This play, like many of Lope's works, is a protest against the capricious and despotic feudal nobility and upholds the dignity of the middle class.

Alceste. The hero of Molière's comedy LE MISANTHROPE. Alceste is disgusted with society. Courtesy seems to him the vice of fops, and the customary forms of civilized life no better than hypocrisy. He is in love with Célimène, a coquette who produces caustic "portraits" of her friends behind their backs and who embodies all the qualities with which he is most impatient.

Alcestis (Alkestis). The first extant play (438 B.C.) by EURIPIDES. It tells the story of Alcestis, a daughter of Pelias and wife of Admetus, king of Pherae. In gratitude for past kindnesses, Apollo had promised that Admetus might escape death if someone would consent to die in his place. When the time came, Admetus' aged parents refused to do so, but Alcestis voluntarily descended to Hades, from which Heracles soon rescued her. The drunken, comic Heracles makes this a tragicomedy; it was originally presented in lieu of a SATYR PLAY. By implication, it called into question the Athenian attitude toward women. In Gluck's opera *Alceste* (1767), the heroine is saved by the intervention of Apollo.

Alchemist, The (1610). A comedy by Ben JONSON. Subtle, a clever quack, and his whorish colleague, Doll Common, set up shop in the house of Lovewit while the latter is away. With the help of Lovewit's servant, Jeremy or Face, the "alchemists" succeed in tricking a whole series of gullible scoundrels, such as Abel Drugger, who seeks charms and advice on how to set up his tobacco shop for maximum good fortune; Dapper, a gambler in need of a familiar spirit (whom he is forced to await while bound in a privy with a gingerbread gag in his mouth); two sanctimonious Puritan Brethren, Ananias and Tribulation Wholesome, who hope to extend their philanthropies and their power by means of alchemy; and, most important, Sir Epicure Mammon, a miser and lecher who dreams of inordinate sensual pleasure. These and others, including Kastril, a young country fellow who wishes to learn to quarrel like a gallant, are adroitly fleeced by Subtle and his colleagues, until the return of Lovewit, who cleverly routs the quacks and takes advantage of their various accumulated gains.

Alcibiades (Alkibiades; c. 450–404 B.C.). An Athenian general and politician. Arrogant and ambitious, Alcibiades called democracy "acknowledged folly." He was brilliant but dissolute and ostentatious, earning both the admiration and the disgust of his fellow citizens. Alcibiades' courage and ambition won him an appointment as general. When Segesta appealed to Athens for aid against Selinus, Alcibiades spoke in favor of the ill-omened expedition. Spurred on by his speech, the Athenians sent him at the head of a huge fleet (415 B.C.). Just before the sailing he was implicated in a sacrilegious mockery of the Eleusinian mysteries. After the fleet had sailed he was recalled for trial, but escaped to Sparta. There, in revenge for the Athenians' confiscation of his property and sentencing him to death, he traitorously informed the Spartans of Athens' weak defenses. Sparta successfully cut off Athens' control over the farmlands through Decelea. Finally, he was forced to flee Sparta because of the jealousy of their leaders. When the Athenian democracy was overthrown, he was welcomed back to his native city. There, on the eve of a battle with Sparta, he was distrusted again. He fled to Persia, where on Sparta's orders he was killed. Alcibiades' return to Athens is incidentally treated in Shakespeare's *Timon of Athens;* he also appears in Plato's dialogues the *Phaedo* and the *Symposium,* and is caricatured in Aristophanes' *The Clouds.*

Alcina. The sister of Morgana and a personification of sensual pleasure in the Orlando poems of Boiardo and Ariosto. In the latter's poem, ORLANDO FURIOSO, she reigns, like Circe, over an island of oblivion filled with luring enchantments. She turns her lovers into trees, stones and wild beasts after tiring of them. RUGGIERO, one of her victims, stays with her until rescued by Melissa, who also restores Astolfo to himself after Alcina had turned him into a myrtle tree.

Alcinous (Alkinoos). See PHAEACIANS.

Alcione or **Alcyone.** See HALCYONE AND CEYX.

Alciphron (Alkiphron). A Greek rhetorician of the 2d or 3d century. He was the author of fictitious letters giving details of domestic life and manners of his time.

Alciphron, or the Minute Philosopher (1732). The title of a series of dialogues by Bishop BERKELEY, so called from the name of the chief speaker, a free-thinker.

Alcmaeon (Alkmeon or **Alkmaion).** In Greek mythology, a son of Amphiaraus and ERIPHYLE. As children, he and his brother Amphilochus were enjoined by their father to avenge him on his wife for the treachery that drove him into the fatal war as one of the SEVEN AGAINST THEBES. When Alcmaeon was grown, Eriphyle, bribed by Thersander, repeated her treachery by sending Alcmaeon too into war with Thebes. He led the EPIGONI to victory and, on his return, killed his mother. Dying, she laid a curse on any land that would shelter him, and the ERINYES drove him mad.

Alcmaeon wandered through many lands. Phegeus, king of Psophis, married him to his daughter Arsinoe and Alcmaeon gave her HARMONIA'S NECKLACE, with which his mother had been bribed. Eriphyle's curse brought famine on the land and Alcmaeon left Psophis. He wandered to the river Achelous. On its delta, which had not existed when the curse was laid, he was at last free from madness. The river god Achelous gave Alcmaeon his daughter Callirrhoe.

She bore him two sons, Acarnan and Amphoteros, but soon demanded the necklace for herself. Alcmaeon returned to Psophis and tricked Phegeus into giving him the necklace. As he was leaving, the trick was discovered and Alcmaeon was killed by Phegeus' sons. Callirrhoe, meanwhile, had been lending her favors to the amorous Zeus. At her request, he caused her sons by Alcmaeon to grow to manhood overnight. They killed Phegeus' sons and finally dedicated the necklace to Apollo at Delphi, where it was still shown in classical times.

Alcman (Alkman). A celebrated Dorian lyric poet of Sparta. He flourished in the first half of the 7th century B.C.

Alcmena or **Alcmene (Alkmena, Alkmene).** In Greek mythology, the mother of HERACLES by Zeus. Her cuckolded husband was AMPHITRYON.

Alcofribas. The pseudonym assumed by François RABELAIS in Books I and II of his GARGANTUA AND PANTAGRUEL. Alcofribas Nasier is an anagram of François Rabelais. Books III, IV, and V were all signed "M. Fran. (or Francoys) Rabelais, Docteur en Médecine."

Alcoran, see KORAN.

Alcott, [Amos] Bronson (1799–1888). American philosopher, teacher, and poet. After a period as itinerant peddler, Alcott organized an unorthodox school whose advanced methods and racially mixed enrollment caused public indignation. For a time he ran a cooperative experimental farm called FRUITLANDS. He then served as superintendent of schools in Con-

cord, Mass., but it was not until his daughter Louisa May ALCOTT succeeded as a writer that any measure of financial security was assured his family. In Concord he set up a school of philosophy with William T. Harris; together, they disseminated Alcott's benevolent philosophy. He published little but kept extensive journals; his most important published work includes *Tablets* (1868), *Observations on the Principles and Methods of Infant Instruction* (1830), and his contributions of ORPHIC SAYINGS to *The Dial.*

Alcott, Louisa May (1832–1888). American novelist and poet. Determined to write, she had to work to help support the family. Her father, Bronson ALCOTT, to whom the family was very devoted, kept them poor with a succession of philanthropic and educational schemes. Miss Alcott wrote her first book, *Flower Fables,* when she was 16; her first success was *Hospital Sketches* (1863), a volume based on the letters she wrote for soldiers as an untrained nurse in Georgetown Hospital, during the Civil War. Louisa May Alcott became famous in 1869, with the publication of LITTLE WOMEN. She continued with a series of books read by children and adults: *An Old-Fashioned Girl* (1870), *Little Men* (1871), *Eight Cousins* (1875), *Rose in Bloom* (1876), and *Under the Lilacs* (1878).

Her fiction is semiautobiographical and is still widely read; eight of the books are still in print.

Alcuin of York (735–804). English scholar. Trained at the cathedral school of York, set up by one of the Venerable Bede's students, he was invited to France by Charlemagne to aid in the revival of learning and ecclesiastical reform (see CAROLINGIANS). He established a school at the royal court and another at Tours, thus helping to return to the Continent the Christian learning and culture that had been preserved mainly in the English monasteries.

Aldanov, Mark. Pen name of **Mark Aleksandrovich Landau** (1886–1957). Russian *émigré* novelist. He is best known for his novel *The Fifth Seal (Nachalo kontza;* 1939), set during the Spanish Civil War.

Alden, John. See COURTSHIP OF MILES STANDISH, THE.

Aldigieri of Chiaramonte. In the MORGANTE MAGGIORE of Pulci and the Orlando poems of Ariosto and Boiardo a knight of Charlemagne's company who holds the castle of Agrismonte. In Pulci's poem he is killed by the traitorous Gano of Maganza.

Aldine editions. Editions of the Greek and Roman classics printed and published at Venice and elsewhere by Aldo Manuzio or Aldus Manutius (1450–1515) and his family from 1490 to 1597. Their handy octavo size and scholarly accuracy made them popular throughout Europe and helped promote Renaissance Humanism's ideal of reviving the classics. Aldo invented the type called *italics,* once called *Aldine,* and first used in a 1501 edition of Virgil.

Aldington, Richard (1892–1962). English poet, novelist, biographer, and translator. At one time married to the American poet Hilda DOOLITTLE, he was a member of the group that introduced IMAGISM. He was among those who, after World War I, found England barren and sterile. His collection of poems *Images of War* (1919) expresses his disgust with the war itself; *Soft Answers* (1932) is a collection of savage satires. His chief novels are DEATH OF A HERO and *All Men Are Enemies* (1933). His best-known biographies are *D. H. Lawrence: Portrait of a Genius, But . . .* (1950), and *Lawrence of Arabia* (1955). *Life for Life's Sake* (1941) is an autobiography.

Aldrich, Bess Streeter (1881–1954). American novelist. She is noted for her studies of pioneer life, especially *A Lantern in Her Hand* (1928), the story of a pioneer mother in Nebraska, and *Song of Years* (1939), a novel of pioneer Iowa. *Miss Bishop* (1933) is the story of a Middle Western teacher who misses marriage and brings up other women's children.

Aldrich, Thomas Bailey (1836–1907). American poet, editor, novelist, and dramatist. After an early career as journalist and war correspondent, Aldrich became the editor of *The Atlantic Monthly* in 1881. He later retired to devote himself to writing.

Aldrich was a member of a brilliant literary circle in New York; although he was a man of great wit, his work is marred by excessive gentility and sentimentality. His most famous book is the novel, THE STORY OF A BAD BOY, based on his own childhood. His well-known short story, MARJORIE DAW, is included in the collection, *Marjorie Daw and Other People* (1873). Other popular works are *The Stillwater Tragedy* (1880), a collection of verse called *The Bells* (1855), and a series of plays.

Alecto (Allekto). In classic myth, one of the ERINYES (Furies).

Aleichem, Sholem or Shalom. Pen name of Solomon J. Rabinowitz (1859–1916). Russian-born Yiddish humorist. A noted author of tales in Yiddish, he was the son of Russian-Jewish storekeepers. For some years a rabbi, he escaped from the 1905 pogrom in Russia and, later, emigrated to the U.S. Sholem Aleichem's stories of Jewish life are noted for their combination of humor and pathos. Much of his large output has been translated into English, but the special quality of the Yiddish language, particularly in the uses of humor, loses a great deal in the translation, so that his reputation has failed to spread as far as it deserves.

Aleixandre [y Merlo], Vincente (1898–   ). Spanish poet. An emphasis upon the linking of strange metaphors, a favoring of free verse, and the presence of great technical skill are the main characteristics of his collected poems: *Ambito* (1928), *Espadas como labios* (1932), *Pasión de la tierra* (1935), *Sombra del paraíso* (1944), and *Mis poemas mejores* (1961). Aleixandre has had a profound influence upon younger, contemporary Spanish poets.

Alemán, Mateo (1547–after 1613). Spanish novelist. The son of a prison doctor, Alemán studied in Seville, Salamanca, and Alcalá and spent some 20 years as a government accountant. He was twice imprisoned for debt. In 1608 he went to Mexico in the company of Archbishop García Guerra, whose life he published in 1613.

Alemán is remembered chiefly as the author of GUZMÁN DE ALFARACHE, the second great picaresque novel after *Lazarillo de Tormes* (1554). The first part appeared in 1599 and, after Juan Jose Martí, a Valencian lawyer, produced a spurious sequel (1602), Alemán himself wrote a continuation (1604), in which he good-naturedly lampooned Martí. Alemán also wrote a biography of Saint Anthony of Padua (1604) and *Ortografía castellana* (1609), a treatise on spelling.

Alembert, Jean Le Rond d' (1717–1783). French mathematician and skeptical philosopher. He was the natural son of Mme. Claudine Guérin de TENCIN. As coeditor (1751–1759) with Diderot of the ENCYCLOPÉDIE, he wrote the *Discours préliminaire (Introduction)*, a veritable synthesis of human knowledge; numerous scientific, philosophical, and literary articles; and supervised all entries on mathematics. He was a member of the Academy of Science (1741), and the ACADÉMIE FRANÇAISE (1754), being secretary to the latter from 1772. He is best known for his *Traité de dynamique* (1743) and a history (1787) of the members of the French Academy who had died between 1700 and 1772.

Alencar, José Martiniano de (1829–1877). Brazilian novelist. Probably Brazil's finest romantic novelist, Alencar is known for his idealized portraits of Indians and for his deep feeling for the Brazilian landscape. His most popular novels are *O Guarani* (1857) and *Iracema* (1865), both of which deal with love between Indian and white.

Aleria. In the ORLANDO FURIOSO of Ariosto, an Amazon, one of ten married forcibly to GUIDONE SELVAGGIO (Guido the Savage) after he had killed the ten male champions of the Amazons who held him captive. Aleria, Guidone's favorite wife, helps him escape to join the armies of Charlemagne against the pagans.

Alete. In the GERUSALEMME LIBERATA of Tasso, an Egyptian ambassador who comes to the camp of Goffredo (Godfrey), the Christian commander, with Argante the infidel champion. He subtly tries to dissuade Goffredo from attacking Jerusalem, but when the attempt fails, he and Argante promptly declare war on the Crusaders.

Alexander (Aleksandros). The name given to Paris, son of Priam, by the shepherds who brought him up. Ironically, in view of its owner's character, the name means "protector of men."

Alexander VI, Pope. See BORGIA.

Alexander I (Aleksandr Pavlovich; 1777–1825). Czar of Russia (1801–1825). Alexander was given a liberal education by his grandmother Catherine the Great, and hopes were high in Russia that his reign would prove less despotic than that of his father, Paul I. However, Alexander showed little concern for reform. The invasion by Napoleon in 1812 and the subsequent years of war and political activity in Europe took up all of his attention. The renewed contact with Western political ideas, which the war brought about, once again stirred young Russians to thought and action. It was during this period that secret political groups were formed that finally made an unsuccessful attempt at a *coup d'état* in the DECEMBRIST REVOLT of 1825.

Alexander II (Aleksandr Nikolayevich; 1818–1881). Czar of Russia (1855–1881). Alexander II's reign was a period of major reform in Russia. In 1861 the long-awaited emancipation of the serfs took place. Three years later, elective assemblies (*zemstva*) were set up for local self-government. Judicial reforms, including public trial by jury, were also instituted. Despite these reforms, revolutionary activity increased. Several attempts were made on Alexander's life by the terrorist organization known as the People's Will (*Narodnaya volya*) before a successful attack on his life was made in March, 1881. Shortly before he was killed, Alexander had approved plans for an elective legislative assembly.

Alexander III (Aleksandr Aleksandrovich; 1845–1894). Czar of Russia (1881–1894). Alexander III was a conservative ruler, partially because of the influence of his former tutor and adviser, Konstantin POBEDONOSTZEV. Plans for constitutional government, which were begun by Alexander II, were dropped. Revolutionary agitation and terrorism continued, and the reign became a series of efforts by the regime to eradicate the revolutionaries and attempts by the latter on the life of the czar. A bomb plot in 1887 was squelched, and five of the conspirators were executed. Among these was Alexander Ulyanov, the older brother of Lenin, who reportedly swore vengeance for his brother's death.

Alexander, Sir William. Earl of Stirling (c. 1567–1640). Scottish poet. Alexander at one time held all of eastern Canada under royal grant, but died insolvent. A serious, plodding poet, he wrote sonnets, Senecan tragedies, and didactic poems. He is best known for *Doomsday* (1614), an epic poem in 12 books.

Alexander of Hales (c. 1175–1245). English theologian and scholastic philosopher, called "Doctor Irrefragabilis," a Franciscan after 1222. In his lectures at the University of Paris and in his Latin *Summa Universae Theologiae* he amalgamated the current Augustinianism of Christian doctrine with Aristotelian philosophy and the works of the Arabian commentators. His teaching greatly influenced St. Thomas Aquinas, St. Bonaventure, and others.

Alexander the Corrector. Self-assumed nickname of Alexander Cruden (1701–1770). A Scottish bookseller in London and compiler of the *Concordance to the Bible* (1737), he petitioned Parliament to constitute him "Corrector of the People." Confined on several occasions to an insane asylum, he developed a compulsion for carrying a sponge to wipe out licentious scrawls.

Alexander the Great (Alexander III of Macedon, 356–323 B.C.). The son of PHILIP OF MACEDON, and conqueror of the civilized world. He was appointed to his father's position as leader of the Greek confederation. He did away with his rivals to the throne, razing Thebes to the ground. He then began the invasion and conquest of Asia, and defeated Darius III, king of Persia. He marched through Syria, Egypt, Babylon, Susa, and Persepolis, founding the city of Alexandria in 331 B.C. Adopting the oriental customs of his captives, Alexander married a series of eastern princesses. On their way through India his exhausted troops rebelled, and Alexander was forced to begin the return to Macedon. He fell ill of a fever, and died after three days' illness at the age of 33. Alexander achieved the extension of Greek civilization into the East. His reign ushered in the Hellenistic Age. See BUCEPHALUS.

Admired for his courage and frequent generous and humane acts, Alexander figures in many English and French medieval romances. French heroic verse of six feet became known as the *Alexandrine*. Alexander's life is the subject of a tragedy by Racine (ALEXANDRE LE GRAND) and of Lyly's *Alexander and Campaspe* (1581).

Alexandre le Grand (Alexander the Great, 1665). A tragedy by Jean RACINE. Combining love and intrigue with historical details of Alexander's Indian campaign, the drama reaches its climax with Alexander's admiration for his betrayed enemy, the brave king Porus, and his consequent renunciation of the kingdom that he had conquered.

Alexandrian Library, the. The most famous library of antiquity. Located in Alexandria, it was, under the Ptolemies, the principal center of Hellenistic culture and contained hundreds of thousands of rolls. Among its earliest librarians were Callimachus and Apollonius of Rhodes. In his *Caesar and Cleopatra* G. B. Shaw treats humorously the burning of the library by Julius Caesar. It was burned and partly consumed in 391; and in 642, according to a dubious legend, the caliph Omar seized the city and used the library's books to "heat the baths of the city for six months." It is said that it contained 700,000 volumes, and the reason given by the Muslim destroyer for the destruction of the library was that the books were unnecessary in any case, for all knowledge that was necessary to man was contained in the Koran, and any knowledge contained in the library that was not in the Koran must be pernicious.

Alexandrian school. An academy of learning. It was founded about 310 B.C. by Ptolemy Soter, son of Lagus, and Demetrius of Phaleron; especially famous for its grammarians and mathematicians.

Alexandria Quartet, The. Four novels by Lawrence DURRELL: *Justine* (1957), *Balthazar* (1958), *Mountolive* (1958), and *Clea* (1960). The complex plot is made more complex by Durrell's attempt "to complete a four-decker novel whose form is based on the relativity proposition." Each novel presents a different point of view, and different truths about the same characters. Diaries and letters and novels-within-novels give still other views. *Justine* is about the love affair between the narrator, Darley, and the fascinating, enigmatic Justine. In *Balthazar* Darley learns, through Balthazar, a mutual friend, that Justine really loved his successful rival author, Pursewarden. Her apparently serene marriage to Nessim was really a cover for their illegal political activities—gun-running into British-held Palestine. *Mountolive* is a third-person novel (the "time" element in the relativity scheme) about a British diplomat in love with Nessim's mother but obliged to discover who is organizing the gun-running. *Clea,* narrated again by Darley, brings the threads of the story together and ends in an idyllic love between him and the serene painter, Clea.

Brilliant exotic and melodramatic episodes and a flamboyant poetical style enrich the works. Among the vivid characters are Melissa, a sad, lost night-club dancer; Narouz, a primitive, silent man who suddenly becomes a religious prophet; and Scobie, a comical old English homosexual. Durrell calls *The Quartet* "a big city poem." It is a wonderful evocation of Alexandria, an exotic and sordid city haunted by figures from its past, from the ancient alchemists to Antony and Cleopatra. *The Quartet* is also an investigation of modern love and a study of the growth of an artist.

Alexandrine. In prosody, a line of 6 iambic feet (iambic hexameter). The Alexandrine is the standard French heroic line, just as iambic pentameter is the standard line for English heroic verse. The name is thought to derive from *Li romans d'Alexandre,* a 12th-century French romance written in that measure relating the deeds of Alexander of Macedon. The Alexandrine was introduced in England by Michael Drayton and others in the 16th century, but never took root as a dominant measure in English poetry, perhaps because English, being an uninflected language, requires fewer syllables than French to express its meaning. However, the Alexandrine is used singly as the final line of the Spenserian stanza, where it affords a contrast to the predominant iambic pentameter.

Alexeyev, Konstantin Sergeyevich. See Konstantin STANISLAVSKI.

Alexis, Willibald. Pen name of **Wilhelm Häring** (1798–1871). German historical novelist. His early works *Walladmor* (1823) and *Schloss Avalon* (*Avalon Castle,* 1827) were strongly under the influence of Walter Scott and were even thought to be Scott's work in translation. Alexis' most famous later novel is *Ruhe ist die erste Bürgerpflicht* (*Quiet Is the First Civic Duty,* 1852), about the Napoleonic invasion of Germany.

Alexius Comnenus (1048–1118). Byzantine emperor (r. 1081–1118). He appealed to the West for military help against the Turks, giving impetus to the first of the CRUSADES. His daughter, **Anna Comnena** (1083–1148), wrote the *Alexiad* in Greek; although more a panegyric than a history of her father's career, it is an important source of information on this period.

Alfheim. In Scandinavian mythology, the region between heaven and earth inhabited by the elves.

Alfieri, Vittorio (1749–1803). Italian dramatist and poet. He wrote 19 tragedies (1775–1787) scrupulously observant of the classical unities and typified by a portrayal of the protagonist's struggle against moral and political tyranny. Among his dramas are *Cleopatra; Filippo,* whose protagonist is Philip II of Spain; *Antigone; Agamennone; Oreste; Virginia; Saul; Mirra;* and *Bruto Primo,* dedicated to George Washington, "the liberator of America," 1787. He also wrote sonnets and odes, five of which are grouped under the title *L'America Libera* (1781–1783) to celebrate the newly acquired independence of the U.S. In his lengthy and exciting *Vita* (*Autobiography*), he analyzed and exalted himself as a poet dedicated to the extirpation of all forms of political and intellectual bondage. His hatred of tyranny and love of freedom helped to revive the national spirit of Italy.

Alfonso X. Known as **El Sabio** ("The Sage" or "The Learned") (1221–1284). King of Castile and Leon (1252–1284), scholar, and poet. Alfonso is generally regarded as a political failure, his reign being marred by his futile attempts to capture the imperial crown and by a disastrous conflict with his second son, later Sancho IV. His true fame rests on his activities as a patron of art and learning. Scholars flocked to his court where, under his direction, they translated Arabic and Latin writings, copied manuscripts, and compiled historical, scientific, and legal works. Under his guidance, Castilian laws and customs were codified in *Las siete partidas,* begun about 1256, which presents a minute and accurate picture of 13th-century society. He was also responsible for

the compilation of the *Primera crónica general* or *Estoria de España,* a history of Spain from the deluge through the reign of Ferdinand III, Alfonso's father. Begun in 1270 and completed during the reign of Sancho IV, it is drawn from biblical, classical, and Arabic sources as well as from Spanish chronicles and epics, such as the *Poema de mio Cid.* Many scholarly and literary works are also ascribed to Alfonso's authorship, notably the charming *Cantigas de Santa María,* over 400 poems in Galician in honor of the Virgin.

Alfred, called **the Great** (c. 849–c. 900). King of Wessex in England (871–900). He began fighting against the Danes in 866 under his brother Aethelred, completing his first series of battles the year of his accession to the throne. He repulsed further attacks in 878 and between 893 and 897, when the Danes were defeated and retreated toward the north or into France.

Aside from his military successes, which made possible his successors' reconquest and unification of the rest of England, Alfred is known for the excellence of his domestic rule. He codified the laws and established a court school with scholars from abroad to promote the education of his people. He began a great translation project, determined to make available in Old English vernacular prose all the books he considered important, which then existed only in Latin. He himself translated Pope Gregory I's *Pastoral Care,* the world history by OROSIUS, and the *Consolation of Philosophy* by Boethius. His *Blostman* ("blossoms," i.e. "anthology") is largely culled from the *Soliloquies* of St. Augustine of Hippo. He had other scholars translate Gregory's *Dialogues* and Bede's *Ecclesiastical History of the English People,* and undertook the writing of the ANGLO-SAXON CHRONICLE. See also ASSER.

Algeciras Conference (1906). An international meeting at Algeciras, Spain. It was held largely at the urging of Kaiser Wilhelm II, who sought to curb French influence in Morocco. The conference members supported France.

Alger, Horatio, Jr. (1832–1899). American writer of books for boys. The oldest child of a Unitarian minister, Alger attended Harvard College and Harvard Divinity School, but fled to Paris as a rebellious bohemian. He was finally persuaded to return to the U.S. and became a minister. In 1866 he was made chaplain of a Newsboys' Lodging House, to which he devoted his time, money, and affection for the rest of his life.

Although Alger wished to write novels for adults, he actually turned out about 120 books for boys. Among the most popular were the *Ragged Dick Series* (1867), the *Luck and Pluck Series* (1869), and the *Tattered Tom Series* (1871). The heroes were bootblacks or newsboys whose virtue was invariably rewarded with riches and success. Alger also wrote juvenile biographies of famous men.

Algerine Captive, The (1797). An early American novel by Royall TYLER. It recounts the adventures of the hero, Updike Underhill, in his native New England backwoods, in Philadelphia where he meets Franklin, in London where he sees Tom Paine, and finally as a captive among the Algerines. The book is famed chiefly for its preface, which contained the first significant plea for native American fiction.

Algonquian or Algonkian. A linguistic family of widely distributed American Indian tribes whose territory stretched from Newfoundland to the Rocky Mountains. The tribes were mainly agricultural and sedentary.

Algren, Nelson (1909–   ). American novelist and short-story writer. Best known for his novel THE MAN WITH THE GOLDEN ARM, Algren is identified with the realistic school centered in Chicago; that city's west-side slums have been the principal inspiration of his work. His other works include *Somebody in Boots* (1935); *Never Come Morning* (1942); *The Neon Wilderness* (1947), a collection of short stories; *A Walk on the Wild Side* (1956); and *Who Lost an American?* (1963), a book of essays and travel pieces.

Alhambra. A citadel and palace at Granada, Spain, built by Moorish kings in the 13th century. Its name is derived from the Arabic *kal'-at al hamra* ("the red castle"). The buildings stand on a plateau some 35 acres in area and are surrounded by a reddish brick wall. Considered one of the finest examples of Moorish architecture in Spain, the palace consists largely of two rectangular courts:—the Court of the Pool or of the Myrtles and the Court of the Lions, —and their adjoining chambers. The latter court contains a famous central fountain, consisting of an alabaster basin supported by 12 lions of white marble. While he was an attaché at the American legation in Madrid, Washington Irving spent much time in the Alhambra and wrote a well-known volume of sketches and tales called *Legends of the Alhambra* (1832, 1852).

Ali Baba and the Forty Thieves. One of the most popular stories in the *Arabian Nights*. Hidden in a tree, the poor woodcutter Ali Baba sees a band of robbers enter a secret cave by saying the magic words, "Open Sesame." When they leave, he repeats the spell, gains access to the treasure, and becomes rich by carrying off gold from the stolen hoards. His brother, Cassim, also discovers the secret but forgets the word "Sesame" and cries "Open, Wheat! Open, Barley" to the door; he is killed by the thieves who find him trapped within the cave. Their captain tries several schemes to catch Ali Baba, but is always outwitted by the woodcutter's female slave, MORGIANA, who kills the whole band by pouring boiling oil into the jars where they have hidden themselves.

Alibert, François Paul (1873–   ). French poet. His works, primarily classical despite symbolist influence, include *L'Arbre qui saigne* (1907), *Odes* (1922), *Eglogues* (1923), and *Elégies romaines* (1923).

Alice Adams (1921). A novel by Booth TARKINGTON. It describes the disintegration of the middle-class Adams family in a small Midwestern town. The father, a minor employee in a drug company, has a nagging, ambitious wife and a shiftless son. Alice, his daughter, yearning for wealth and admiration and seeing herself always in a romantic role, almost deceives herself into believing that her fanciful explanations for the crudities of her family are valid. At the end of the book, her hopes doomed, she is seen bravely entering the stairway that leads to Frincke's Business College.

Alice's Adventures in Wonderland (1865). A whimsical story by Lewis CARROLL. The little girl Alice falls down a well into a strange country where everything happens with a fantastic illogicality. She finds that she can become a giantess or pygmy by nibbling alternate sides of a magic mushroom, and she has a series of remarkable adventures with the WHITE RABBIT, the CHESHIRE CAT, the MOCK TURTLE, the QUEEN OF HEARTS, the HATTER, the MARCH HARE, the DUCHESS, the DORMOUSE, and other strange characters. See THROUGH THE LOOKING-GLASS, and FATHER WILLIAM.

Alice W---n. The old love conjured up by Charles Lamb in his DREAM CHILDREN: A REVERIE as the mother of his imaginary children. She has been identified as the actress Frances Maria Kelly.

Alien and Sedition Acts (1798). 3 congressional acts that gave the president power to deport or imprison any alien considered dangerous to the nation, and to punish any person engaging in treasonable acts or issuing writings considered to be seditious. These measures were directed by the Federalists against propagandists for the French Revolution and the Democratic-Republican Party in the U.S.

Aljubarrota. A village in Portugal, some 40 miles north of Lisbon. It was the site of a battle (1385) between the forces of John I of Portugal and those of John I of Castile. The Portuguese routed the enemy, firmly establishing the independence that they had first won three centuries earlier.

Allah. The Arabic name of the Supreme Being, from *al,* the, and *illah,* god. *Allah il Allah,* the Muslim war cry, and also the first clause of the confession of faith, is a corruption of *la illah illa allah,* meaning "there is no God but the God."

The Garden of Allah. A novel by Robert Hichens (1904), the title of which refers to a region of the Sahara Desert.

Allan-a-Dale, Allin-a-Dale, or **Allen-a-Dale.** A minstrel in the Robin Hood ballads, who appears also in Scott's novel *Ivanhoe* (1820). He is assisted by Robin Hood in carrying off his bride when she is on the point of being married against her will to a rich old knight.

allegory. In literature, an extended METAPHOR in which characters, objects, incidents, and descriptions carry one or more sets of fully developed meanings in addition to the apparent and literal ones. John Bunyan's *Pilgrim's Progress,* for example, is apparently about a man named Christian who leaves his home and journeys to the Heavenly City. However, it is clear that Christian stands for any Christian man, and the incidents of his journey represent the temptations and trials that beset any Christian man throughout his life on earth.

Allegory has been a favorite form all over the world, and was particularly strong in Europe during the Middle Ages. Spenser's *Faerie Queene* (1590-1596), though late, is perhaps the best-known example.

In art, especially of the Middle Ages, allegory was also a favorite device; in particular it was used to depict good and evil engaged in symbolic action. See PERSONIFICATION.

Allegro, L' (1632). A poem by John MILTON, the title of which means literally the cheerful or merry one. It is a pastoral idyl, celebrating a mood of gaiety and contrasting with the author's Il Penseroso. The poem, like its companion piece, is written in Milton's early style, characterized by an Elizabethan freshness and vividness and a remarkable command of verbal music.

Allen, Ethan (1738–1789). American Revolutionary soldier and hero of early Vermont. He commanded the Green Mountain Boys, a regiment originally raised by some Vermont settlers to fight a claim on their land by Governor Tryon of New York. With 83 of the Green Mountain Boys and aided by Benedict Arnold, Allen seized Fort Ticonderoga in 1775. His own *Narrative of Captain Ethan Allen's Captivity* tells of his capture by the British after a rash attempt to take Montreal. He is the hero of Daniel Pierce Thompson's novel *Green Mountain Boys* (1839).

Allen, Frederick Lewis (1890–1954). American editor and writer. On the editorial staffs successively of the *Atlantic Monthly* and *Century Magazine,* he joined *Harper's Magazine* in 1921 and later became its editor in chief. He is also known for his lively social histories: *Only Yesterday* (1931), an account of the 1920's in the U.S.; *Since Yesterday* (1940), a similar treatment of the 1930's; and *The Big Change* (1952), an account of the transformation of the U.S. from 1900 to 1950.

Allen, [William] Hervey (1889–1949). American historical novelist. He is best known for his first novel, the long and phenomenally successful Anthony Adverse. Allen began his career with several volumes of verse and also wrote *Israfel* (1926), a biography of Edgar Allan Poe.

Allen, James Lane (1849–1925). American novelist and short-story writer. He is noted for the Kentucky setting of his books, among them A Kentucky Cardinal, *Aftermath* (1896), and *The Choir Invisible* (1897), an historical romance of pioneer Kentucky. *Flute and Violin* (1891) is a collection of Kentucky short stories. Allen also wrote the sketches of *The Blue-Grass Region of Kentucky* (1892).

Allen, Ralph (1694–1764). A noted English philanthropist, friend and benefactor of both Pope and Fielding. Fielding may have depicted him as Squire Allworthy in *Tom Jones,* and Pope wrote of him:

> Let humble Allen, with an awkward shame,
> Do good by stealth, and blush to find it fame.

All for Love, or The World Well Lost (1678). A tragedy in blank verse by John Dryden. In strict observance of the classical unities, Dryden describes the last day on earth of Antony and Cleopatra. Simpler in plot, though less stirring than Shakespeare's version of the famous story, Dryden's play focusses on the conflict between Cleopatra, on the one hand, and Antony's wife, Octavia, his general Ventidius, and his friend Dolabella on the other, as they vie for possession of Antony's soul.

All God's Chillun Got Wings (1924). A play by Eugene O'Neill. White Ella Downey marries Negro Jim Harris, who is struggling to become a lawyer. The tragic consequences of her mental inferiority are intensified by the latent racial prejudice she shows in a desperate effort to gain superiority before lapsing into insanity and a regression to childhood.

All Hallows' Day. See All Saints' Day.

All Hallows' Eve. See Hallowe'en.

Allingham, William (1824–1889). Irish poet, best known for light lyrics employing Irish folk lore and dialect. He was briefly editor of *Fraser's Magazine* (1874–1879) and much esteemed as a critic by Dante Gabriel Rossetti and Coventry Patmore. He published over a dozen volumes of poetry, perhaps the most famous of which is *The Fairies* (1883).

alliteration. In poetry and prose, the repetition of consonants, especially initial consonants, as in the sentence "Peter Piper picked a peck of pickled peppers." Like assonance and consonance, alliteration tends to unify the passage or poem in which it occurs, and in that function may be considered a form of rhyme.

Alliterative Morte Arthur, The. See Arthurian legends.

alliterative verse. Form of versification of Old English poetry such as *Beowulf,* similar to that of some early medieval Continental poetry. In Old English (or Anglo-Saxon) poetry, each line has four accented syllables and a varying number of unaccented syllables, divided into two halves of two strong stresses each. There must be alliteration between at least one stressed syllable in the first half and one in the second; preferably three, and sometimes all four, of the accented syllables in a line are alliterative. The use of this form declined under the influence of the strictly syllabic meters and rhyme schemes in French and Italian poetry; it was revived, however, during the 14th century in such works as *Piers Plowman* and *Sir Gawain and the Green Knight.* Poets of the late 19th and 20th centuries have adapted alliterative verse in the trend away from conventional toward accentual meters.

All Men Are Brothers. See Shui Hu Chuan.

All Quiet on the Western Front (Im Westen nichts Neues; 1929). A novel by Erich Maria Remarque. It is the best known of the antiwar literature written during the period 1920–1939, expressing the horror and futility of war.

All Saints' Day or **All Hallows.** A feast in honor of all Christian saints. Between 603 and 610 Pope Boniface IV changed the heathen temple called the Pantheon into a Christian church, and dedicated it to the honor of all the martyrs. The feast was first observed on May 1, but in 834 it was changed to November 1, and its use extended to the whole Christian Church. It is a major feast of the Church.

The medieval English name *All Hallows* is derived from *halig,* Old English for holy (man), hence, a saint. In France the day is called *Toussaint.* Much folk lore and superstition are associated with the eve of the day, called Hallowe'en.

All Souls' Day. The popular name for the Commemoration of All the Faithful Departed. It is observed by the Roman Catholic Church on November 2. It was instituted by Abbot Odilo of Cluny in 993 and soon spread to the rest of the Western Church. In many parts of Europe it is the custom to place lighted candles on graves of friends and family the previous evening.

All's Well that Ends Well (c. 1602). A comedy by William Shakespeare. After curing the king of France of a malady, Helena, the daughter of a famous physician, is rewarded by the king's giving her in marriage to BERTRAM, the young count of Rousillon, whom she has long loved. He, however, scorns her and departs for the Florentine war, stating that until Helena obtains the ring on his finger and produces his child, he will not return nor can she call him husband. Disguised as a pilgrim, Helena follows Bertram to Florence, where she discovers that he is enamored of a young Florentine girl. She arranges an assignation and takes the girl's place, obtaining the ring and conceiving the child. Hearing false reports of Helena's death, Bertram returns to France. When she suddenly appears, having fulfilled his terms, she at last wins his love.

The plot is taken from Boccaccio's *Decameron* and was a familiar folk legend reworked by Shakespeare. See countess of ROUSILLON; PAROLLES.

All the King's Men (1946). A novel by Robert Penn WARREN. Jack Burden, a young intellectual, narrates the story of the rise and fall of Willie Stark, a Southern demagogue obviously modeled on the Louisiana politician Huey Long. Burden is forced to confront the problem of good and evil in Stark's career and at the end of the book is led to a new self-understanding. The novel won a Pulitzer Prize.

Allworthy, Squire [Thomas]. In Henry Fielding's TOM JONES, a wealthy justice of the peace, foster father to the foundling Tom Jones. One of the best-known characters in English fiction, he is a man of sturdy rectitude, modesty, and benevolence, completely disinterested as regards money and fame. He is strongly contrasted with his neighbor Squire WESTERN. Fielding's friend Ralph ALLEN is believed to have been the model for Squire Allworthy.

Bridget Allworthy. The sister of Squire Allworthy, who, as it turns out, is the mother of Tom Jones.

Alma. See FAERIE QUEENE, THE.

Almagest (Arab. article *al*, Gr. *megiste*, greatest). An astronomical treatise by the 2d century Alexandrian scholar PTOLEMY. The work was extensively used during the Middle Ages in an Arabic translation.

Almanach de Gotha. A European social register. A German periodical publication begun in 1763, it gives data on all royal or titled European families.

Almanack, Poor Richard's. See POOR RICHARD'S ALMANACK.

Almaviva, Count and Countess. Leading characters in Beaumarchais' comedies THE BARBER OF SEVILLE and THE MARRIAGE OF FIGARO and in the operas based upon them.

Almayer's Folly (1895). A novel by Joseph CONRAD. Almayer, an English trader in the (then) Dutch East Indies, is moved by two passions: the desire to find gold and love for his half-caste daughter. "Almayer's Folly" is an absurdly fine house he moves into after his daughter has gone away with a Malay prince. See OUTCAST OF THE ISLANDS, AN.

Alnaschar. In the story the "Barber's Fifth Night" in the *Arabian Nights,* the visionary character who invests all his money in a basket of glassware, which he fancies will bring him wealth and the vizier's daughter. As he dreams of the grand life he will lead, he grows angry with his supposed wife, upsets his basket, and smashes all the wares that have started his visions of wealth. Hence, an *Alnaschar dream* is counting one's chickens before they are hatched.

Alonso. The king of Naples and father of the innocent Ferdinand in Shakespeare's THE TEMPEST. Alonso's greed and enmity toward Prospero caused him to accept the tributes of Antonio, Prospero's brother, and to endorse the usurpation of Prospero's dukedom.

Alonso, Dámaso (1898–   ). Spanish poet and scholar. A translator of Joyce and Eliot, Alonso is known for his poetry, particularly the volumes *Poemas puros; poemillas de la ciudad* (1921) and *Hijos de la ira* (1944), the latter being a treatment of religion in the modern poetic idiom. As a scholar and literary critic he is known for his studies of the Spanish baroque poet Góngora, particularly *La lengua poética de Góngora* (1935).

Alonzo the Brave. A ballad by Matthew Gregory LEWIS which first appeared in his novel, THE MONK. It is a variant of the widespread traditional theme of the specter lover, popularized in the ballad *Lenore* by Gottfried August Bürger. Imogen was betrothed to Alonzo, but, during his absence in the wars, became the bride of another. At the wedding feast Alonzo's ghost sat beside the bride, and, after rebuking her for her infidelity, carried her off to the grave.

alpha and omega. The first and last letters of the Greek alphabet; hence the beginning and the end. In the Bible, Jesus says, "I am Alpha and Omega, the beginning and the end, the first and the last" (Rev. 22:13).

Alroy, David. A half-mythical Jewish medieval prince, local governor of his people under Muslim rule, with the title, Prince of the Captivity. He is the hero of Benjamin Disraeli's prose romance, *The Wondrous Tale of Alroy* (1833).

Alsop, Joseph [Wright] (1910–   ) and **Stewart [Johonnot Oliver]** (1914–   ). American journalists. From 1945 to 1958 the two brothers wrote "Matter of Fact," a syndicated newspaper column on politics. After 1958, when Stewart became a contributing editor and later Washington editor for the *Saturday Evening Post,* Joseph continued the column alone.

Alsop, Richard (1761–1815). American satirical poet, a member of the group known as the HARTFORD WITS. Alsop frequently collaborated with Theodore Dwight, Lemuel Hopkins, and others in the two series of Federalist verse satire known as *The Echo* (1791–1805) and *The Political Greenhouse* (1798).

Also sprach Zarathustra. See THUS SPAKE ZARATHUSTRA.

Altamira. Site near Santander, Spain, of a cave decorated with paleolithic mural paintings. It was discovered in 1879.

Altamirano, Ignacio Manuel (1834–1893). Mexican novelist and poet. A full-blooded Indian, Altamirano was an adherent of Benito Juárez and fought against the French intervention in Mexico. In 1869, he founded *Renacimiento,* a review to encourage literary activity, almost moribund after 15 years of turbulence. He became the mentor of the younger generation, to whom he advocated the importance of creating a literature rooted in national life. His poetry consists of a single volume of *Rimas* (1880), written before 1867 and notable for its description of the Mexican landscape. Altamirano's preoccupation with purely Mexican scenes and customs is also evident in the prose works for which he is best known: *Clemencia* (1869), a love story set against the background of the French intervention; *La navidad en las montañas* (1870), a novelette; and *El Zarco* (1901), a novel dealing with bandits in the state of Morelos.

Altamoro (Altamore). A fierce Saracen warrior in the GERUSALEMME LIBERATA of Tasso. He leads the Persian and African forces against the Christian armies at Jerusalem and is also a champion of Armida, who has sworn to give herself to any infidel knight who kills Rinaldo of Este. It is he who surrenders the remnants of the pagan armies to the Christian general Goffredo, signalling the final victory of the Crusaders at the holy city.

Alton Locke, Tailor and Poet (1850). A novel by the Rev. Charles KINGSLEY. This novel won for the author the title of The Chartist Clergyman (see CHARTISM) because of its picture of Alton Locke and his radical Chartist friends who move through the depressed regions of the London sweatshops. It was one of the first English novels to present a study of industrial conditions.

Altruria. See A TRAVELLER FROM ALTRURIA.

Alvarez, A[lfred] (1929–   ). English poet and critic, a follower of William EMPSON. *The Shaping Spirit* (1958) and *The School of Donne* (1962) are books of criticism.

Alvarez Quintero, Serafín (1871–1938) and **Joaquín** (1873–1944). Spanish dramatists, brothers who collaborated in their work. The brothers Álvarez Quintero are known for their light and amusing comedies; the best known of the more than 100 written are *Los galeotos* (1900), *El patio* (1900), *El amor que pasa* (1904), and *Doña Clarinés* (1909).

Alvaro, Corrado (1895–1956). Italian novelist, poet, essaylst, and moralist. Alvaro was a world traveler who wrote several books of verse and travel, the latter noted for the author's keen perception and description of people, places, and customs. His numerous short stories have been collected in *Revolt in Aspromonte* (*Gente in Aspromonte;* 1930). For the most part these tales describe the hard, primitive life of Calabrian shepherds. His finest novels are *Man is Strong* (*L'Uomo E' Forte;* 1938) and *L'Età E' Breve* (1946), the first book of a three-novel cycle entitled *Memorie del Mondo Sommerso* describing Italian political and cultural life during the fascist period.

Alvaro, Don. (1) The husband of Mencia of Mosquera in Le Sage's GIL BLAS DE SANTILLANE.

(2) A character in Verdi's opera *La Forza del Destino.*

(3) A character in the romantic drama *Don Alvaro o La fuerza del sino* by Angel de Saavedra y Ramírez, duke of Rivas.

Alving, Oswald. The principal character in Ibsen's GHOSTS. A neurotic and dissipated young man, he becomes insane from congenital syphilis. His mother, embittered by her experiences, is in revolt against a society in which such conditions exist.

Amadís de Gaula (Amadis of Gaul). A 16th-century Spanish romance of chivalry. The first extant version (1508), consisting of four books, was compiled by Garci Ordóñez or Rodríguez Montalvo, a *regidor* of Medina del Campo, who stated that he was merely revising the original text; however, the fourth book is his own addition. The origin of the story is still obscure, though it was known in both Spain and Portugal at least as early as the 14th century.

The romance incorporates many details from the Breton cycle of the Round Table. Amadís, who exemplifies the chivalric ideals of valor, purity, and fidelity, is the illegitimate son of Perión, king of Gaul (Wales) and Elisena, princess of Brittany. Soon after birth he is abandoned by his mother, who puts his cradle in the sea; for this reason he is also known as *el Doncel del Mar,* or "Child of the Sea." He is rescued by the knight Gandalés and is educated in the court of the king of Scotland, where at the age of 12 he falls in love with Oriana, daughter of Lisuarte, king of England. Amadís then performs a series of incredible exploits, triumphing over sundry giants and monsters, but he always remains faithful to his lady-love. Other notable characters include Galaor, Amadís' brother; his cousin Agrajes; the Fairy Urganda, *la Desconocida,* or "the Unknown"; and Archeläus, a mischievous enchanter.

The work won enormous popularity throughout Europe and inspired numerous sequels and imitations, including Montalvo's *Las sergas de Esplandián* (1510) about the son of Amadís. The barber and priest in Cervantes' *Don Quixote* called it "the best of all the books of its kind," a verdict in which later generations have concurred.

Amado, Jorge (1912–   ). Brazilian novelist. In a series of novels beginning with *O País do Carnaval* (1931), Amado explores various aspects of life in his native state of Bahia. His works reflect his Marxist political views in their sympathy for the downtrodden and their keen awareness of social injustice. His best-known novels are probably *Terras do Sem Fim* (*The Violent Land,* 1942), about the cacao boom in the frontier districts of Bahia, and *Gabriela, Cravo e Canela* (*Gabriela, Clove and Cinnamon,* 1958), about social and political change in the

Illustration from a 1533 edition of *Amadis de Gaula.*

NEW YORK PUBLIC LIBRARY

city of Ilheus in 1925–1926. Among his other novels are *Suor* (1934), *Jubiabá* (1935), and *Mar Morto* (1936).

Amahl and the Night Visitors. A one-act opera by Gian Carlo MENOTTI. It was written (1951) for production on television. Amahl, a crippled boy, adds his crutch to the gifts of the Magi and is cured.

Amaimon. One of the chief devils in medieval demonology. He is king of the eastern portion of hell; Asmodeus is his chief officer. He can be restrained from doing harm from the third hour until noon and from the ninth hour until evening.

Amalia (1851–1855). A novel by José Mármol (1817–1871), Argentine poet and novelist. Written while Mármol was in exile in Uruguay, the book is an impassioned denunciation of the barbarism and terror of the dictatorship of Juan Manuel de ROSAS. Although the plot is melodramatic and the principal characters are one-dimensional, Mármol's descriptions of life in Buenos Aires and of actual personages, such as the dictator himself, are vivid and convincing.

Amalthea. In Roman legend, the sybil who sold the sibylline books to Tarquin.

Amaltheia. The goat that suckled the infant Zeus in the cave in the Cretan mountain Dicte. Her horn became the *cornucopia*, the horn of plenty that has been a symbol of the earth's bounty since very ancient times.

Amanda. See PEREGRINE PICKLE.

Amants magnifiques, Les (The Magnificent Lovers, 1670). A COMÉDIE-BALLET in prose by MOLIÈRE. Written for the king and based on a subject chosen by him, the play recounts amid songs and dances the courtship of a princess by two princes and her preference for a lowly soldier.

Amaryllis. A rustic sweetheart. The name is borrowed from a shepherdess in the pastorals of Theocritus and Vergil. In Spenser's *Colin Clout's Come Home Again,* Amaryllis is intended for Alice Spenser, countess of Derby.

Amasis, ring of. Herodotus relates that Polycrates, tyrant of Samos, was so fortunate in everything that Amasis, king of Egypt, fearing such unprecedented luck boded ill, advised him to part with something which he highly prized. Polycrates accordingly threw into the sea a ring of great value. A few days afterwards, a fish was presented to the tyrant, in which the ring was found. Amasis now renounced friendship with Polycrates, as a man doomed by the gods; and not long afterwards, a Persian satrap put the too fortunate despot to death by crucifixion.

Amavia. See FAERIE QUEENE, THE.

Amazons (Amazones). A mythical race of women warriors. Ancient accounts differ as to where they lived; Herodotus places them in Scythia, north of the Black Sea; Apollonius Rhodius' *Argonautica* has them inhabiting a portion of the south shore. According to the legend, they were a hardy lot, burning off their right breasts in order that they might draw the bow better. They either destroyed or sent away any male children they had as a result of encounters with neighboring tribes. There are among the Greek myths many legends of encounters with them. HERACLES fought them in order to acquire the

girdle worn by their queen, Hippolyta. He acquired it either by killing Hippolyta or by capturing her general, Melanippe, and holding her for ransom. Theseus also fought the Amazons and made one of them, either named HIPPOLYTA or Antiope, his wife. His son Hippolytus was their offspring. Hippolyta appears as the wife of Theseus, duke of Athens, in Shakespeare's *A Midsummer Night's Dream.*

Ambassadors, The (1903). A novel by Henry JAMES. The central character and first "ambassador," Lambert Strether, is sent to Paris by Mrs. Newsome, a wealthy widow whom he plans to marry, in order to persuade her son Chad to come home. Chad is deeply involved with a charming French woman, Madame de Vionnet, and the novel deals chiefly with Strether's gradual conversion to the idea that life may hold more real meaning for Chad in Paris than in Woollett, Mass. Strether comes to this conclusion in spite of his discovery that Chad and Mme de Vionnet are, in fact, more than just good friends. After the arrival of a second ambassador, Chad's sister Sarah, Strether decides to return to Woollett, urging Chad to remain in Paris. The essence of the novel is in Strether's remark, "Live all you can; it's a mistake not to."

ambiguous oath. A folklore motif, especially popular in medieval literature. An outstanding example may be found in the legend of TRISTAN AND ISEULT. Setting forth for the trial that is to determine whether she is guilty of a love affair with Tristan, Iseult sends word to Tristan to disguise himself as a poor pilgrim and meet her on the way. At her request, he then carries her across a stream so that she will not get wet. She is then able to swear at the trial that no one but King Mark (her husband) and "that poor pilgrim" who carried her across the stream has ever held her in his arms. She is subsequently absolved.

Ambler, Eric (1909–). English novelist and screenwriter. Ambler is best known for his realistic novels of espionage, usually dealing with ordinary Englishmen who find themselves enmeshed in a web of international intrigue. These include *Epitaph for a Spy* (1938), *The Mask of Dimitrios* (1939; U.S. title, *The Coffin of Dimitrios*), *Journey into Fear* (1940), *Judgment on Deltchev* (1951), and *Passage of Arms* (1959).

Ambrose. A tavern keeper. His name suggested the title for the celebrated NOCTES AMBROSIANAE, a series of imaginary conversations chiefly by Christopher North (John Wilson), published in *Blackwood's Magazine.* The blue parlor of Ambrose's Hotel in Edinburgh was in reality a rendezvous for Wilson and his friends, although the Ambrosian Nights were largely imaginary.

Ambrose, St. (c. 340–397). Bishop of Milan (374–397) and one of the Fathers of the Latin Church. A constant champion of the Church in its conflicts with paganism and the various early heresies, Ambrose was instrumental in driving the Arians out of Italy. He baptized Augustine of Hippo, who later became St. Augustine.

ambrosia (Gr. *a,* privative, *brotos,* mortal). The food of the gods. It is so called because it made them immortal. Anything delicious to the taste or fragrant in perfume is so called from the notion that whatever is used by the celestials must be excellent.

In actuality, ambrosia was probably the common and rather primitive cereal food of early Greece.

Ambrosio, or the Monk. See MONK, THE.

Amelia (1751). A novel by Henry FIELDING. Amelia, the idealized heroine, is the long-suffering, virtuous wife of Captain Booth, an impoverished army officer who has been unjustly thrown into prison. During his absence, his false friend Captain James makes overtures to Amelia, but her virtue prevails against him. In prison with Captain Booth is Miss Matthews, an adventuress who lures him into an affair, leaving him conscience-stricken. He is released from prison and Amelia forgives him, but soon after, he is thrown into debtor's prison for gambling. The situation is saved when Amelia receives an inheritance, and the two retire to the country to live a peaceful life.

Amélie. A character invented by Pierre Corneille in his tragedy CINNA. She encourages Cinna to lead a conspiracy against the emperor Augustus and is the cause of jealous friction between Cinna and his coconspirator MAXIME.

Amen, Ammon, Amun, or **Amen-Ra.** Among the ancient Egyptians, a deity usually represented as a man with a crown of two long plumes, and sometimes with a ram's head on a man's body. Originally a minor local deity of Thebes, he was brought into prominence about 2000 B.C. when his name was joined with that of RA, the sun god. As the composite figure Amen-Ra, he reigned as supreme King of the Gods; Amen appealed to the Theban patriot; Ra to the educated man. His oracle was in the Libyan oasis where Alexander the Great was told he was the son of Ammon. The Greeks identified Amen with Zeus.

America. Designation for both North and South America. Loose usage applies it chiefly to the U.S. Its origin is the name of Amerigo VESPUCCI, a Florentine merchant and traveler who claimed to have made a voyage in 1497 during which he discovered what is now the mainland of South America. His claim, although never proved, was perpetuated in the name given to the new continent in the West.

American, The (1877). A novel by Henry JAMES. Christopher Newman, a wealthy, self-made American in France, hopes to marry Claire de Cintré, a widowed daughter of the De Bellegardes, but that aristocratic old French family finally succeeds in circumventing him. Although Newman plans to retaliate by publishing proof that Claire's mother and brother were the virtual murderers of her father, he decides to give up his design because revenge is "really not his game." Both the contrast between the simple, innocent American and the sophisticated, corrupt European, and the necessity for renunciation later became common Jamesian themes.

American Academy of Arts and Letters. The inner circle of the National Institute of Arts and Letters. The latter, founded in 1898, created the smaller society to honor its more distinguished members. The first seven men elected to its membership were William Dean Howells, Augustus Saint-Gaudens, E. C. Stedman, John La Farge, Mark Twain, John Hay, and Edward MacDowell. The aim of the academy is to give "the stamp of its approval" to the best in literature and art that both the past and the present have to offer.

American Caravan, The (1927–1936). An annual publication of American poetry and fiction. Its aim was to exhibit the best of contemporary literature, and its first editor was Van Wyck Brooks. He was followed by Lewis Mumford, Alfred Kreymborg, and Paul Rosenfeld. A number of well-known writers, including Ernest Hemingway, were represented in its pages.

American Civil War (1861–1865). A war between the U.S. and 11 Southern states which seceded from the Union and formed the Confederate States of America. The war was the result of longstanding social and economic differences between North and South that gradually became apparent after the War of 1812. Sectional conflict over such issues as the tariff and the extension of slavery was temporarily abated by the activities of men such as Henry CLAY and Daniel WEBSTER, but in the 1850's the position of each side became progressively more rigid; whether the war could have been averted is still a subject for discussion among historians.

Upon receiving the news of Abraham LINCOLN's election in 1860, South Carolina seceded, followed by 10 other Southern states, which then organized the Confederate government and elected Jefferson DAVIS president early in 1861; with the Confederate attack on Fort SUMTER, the actual fighting began. To the North, the principal objective was the preservation of the Union, though emancipation of the slaves became a secondary aim after 1862.

Although Union hopes for a quick victory were dashed by the rout at BULL RUN, it gradually became evident that, despite the brilliant leadership of such Confederate generals as Robert E. LEE and Thomas ("Stonewall") JACKSON, the superior human and industrial resources of the North would ultimately prevail. This was especially true after the Union victory at GETTYSBURG and Gen. GRANT's successful siege of Vicksburg (1863) ended Confederate hopes of securing foreign recognition and aid. In 1864, Grant, now supreme commander of the Union forces, turned to the conquest of Richmond, the Confederate capital, while W. T. SHERMAN undertook his famous march to the sea. After a gallant defense, Lee was forced to evacuate Richmond (April 2, 1865) and surrendered to Grant at Appomattox Courthouse, Va., on April 9.

With the possible exception of the Napoleonic Wars, no other conflict has produced more books. Among the most famous of the novels inspired by the war are Stephen Crane's RED BADGE OF COURAGE, Winston Churchill's THE CRISIS, and Margaret Mitchell's GONE WITH THE WIND. Other novelists who wrote about the war include Thomas Nelson PAGE, Mary JOHNSTON, Ellen GLASGOW, and MacKinlay KANTOR. Verse dealing with the war was written by such poets as Henry TIMROD, Paul Hamilton HAYNE, John Greenleaf WHITTIER, Walt WHITMAN, and Stephen Vincent BENÉT. Edmund Wilson's *Patriotic Gore* (1962) consists of essays about 19th-century Civil War literature.

See John Brown; George B. McCLELLAN; SHILOH; ANTIETAM.

American Crisis, The. A series of 16 pamphlets written by Thomas PAINE between 1776 and

1783, widely distributed in the American colonies
and touching on all of the important issues of the
Revolution. The famous first *Crisis* paper, beginning,
"These are the times that try men's souls," was ordered by Washington to be read to his troops on the
eve of the battle of Trenton. In later *Crisis* papers,
Paine called for a strong federal union.

**American Democrat, The, or Hints on the
Social and Civic Relations of the United States
of America** (1838). A political essay by James
Fenimore COOPER, written on his return to New
York, after a seven-year stay in Europe. Although a
firm democrat, Cooper opposed a tyranny of the
majority. Socially conservative, he favored an aristocracy of landowners; this cultured class would
maintain stable values in American society. The
book is Cooper's fullest statement of his beliefs, and
is one of a series of volumes in which he criticizes
the politics and manners of his countrymen. The
other books are *A Letter to His Countrymen* (1834),
Homeward Bound (1838), *Home as Found* (1838),
and THE MONIKINS.

Cooper's outspoken criticism caused him to be denounced in the American press; acting as his own
lawyer, he fought and won many libel suits. Although he lost most of his fortune, he helped to
codify the libel laws of the U.S.

American Language, The (1919, 1921, 1923,
1936; *Supplement One,* 1945; *Supplement Two,*
1948). A treatise by H. L. MENCKEN. Believing at
first that the American language and English were
diverging, Mencken found that by 1923 American
had become the more powerful tongue and was leading English along with it. He set out to examine the
two streams of language and their differences in
vocabulary, spelling, and pronunciation. He treated
American slang, proper names, and non-English dialects in America. Ironically, his work won him a
place among the scholars he had attacked and
scorned.

American Mercury, The. An iconoclastic
magazine founded in 1924 and edited by H. L.
MENCKEN and George Jean NATHAN. For a decade,
previously, both men had worked together as editors
and part-owners of the *Smart Set.* Nathan retired as
coeditor of the *Mercury* after a year, but remained as
a departmental editor until 1930. Some departments
were continued from the *Smart Set,* for example, the
"Americana," a collection of absurdities in popular
culture and cults, arranged geographically by states.
But the magazine also contained articles on literary
figures and other positive aspects of American culture. Among its contributors were Lewis Mumford,
Sinclair Lewis, Carl Sandburg, and Vachel Lindsay.
After Mencken's retirement in 1933, it was published as a pocket-size miscellany of conservative
tendencies by Lawrence E. Spivak. It eventually became a rightist organ of limited circulation, owned
by millionaire J. Russell Maguire.

American Notes (1842). A volume of travel
sketches by Charles DICKENS. The book was well received in England, but gave great offense in the
U.S. Dickens, besides advocating the abolition of
slavery, made many harsh and somewhat patronizing
observations about the rawness and narrowness of
life and manners in America.

American Revolution (1775–1783). The war
for independence waged by the former British colonies in the present U.S. against the mother country.
The conflict stemmed from the political and economic
grievances of the colonists, especially after the FRENCH
AND INDIAN WAR, when the British decided to end
their former policy of "salutary neglect" toward the
colonies by enacting such revenue-raising measures as
the STAMP ACT and the Townshend Acts of 1767.
Fanned by the writings of Samuel ADAMS and others,
American resentment increased and erupted in such
incidents as the BOSTON MASSACRE and the BOSTON
TEA PARTY. The gathering of the first CONTINENTAL
CONGRESS in 1774 was followed by the clash of
British regulars and MINUTE MEN at LEXINGTON
and Concord; Congress named George WASHINGTON
commander-in-chief of its forces in 1775 and promulgated the DECLARATION OF INDEPENDENCE, largely
the work of Thomas JEFFERSON, the following year.
Important American leaders in the battles that followed were Ethan ALLEN, Benedict ARNOLD, Horatio
GATES, George Rogers CLARK, Anthony WAYNE,
Francis MARION, and John Paul JONES. The entry
of France into the war against England in 1778 was
a major factor in the final American victory; at the
siege of YORKTOWN, a French fleet blockaded the
harbor, while Washington was assisted by the forces
of the Comte de ROCHAMBEAU and the Marquis de
LAFAYETTE. The Treaty of Paris, signed after lengthy
negotiations by John ADAMS, Benjamin FRANKLIN,
and John JAY, ended the war.

The American struggle for freedom was accompanied by much literary activity, most of it political
in nature, as seen in the works of Thomas PAINE,
John TRUMBULL, and Francis HOPKINSON. Philip
FRENEAU is sometimes called "the poet of the American Revolution."

See battle of BUNKER HILL; Patrick HENRY; Paul
REVERE; John HANCOCK; Nathan HALE.

American Scene, The (1907). A travel book
by Henry JAMES. The volume is mainly an examination of life in Saratoga, Newport, and other important American social and cultural centers, remembered as they were in the 1870's and 1880's and
described as James saw them again in 1904, on a visit
to the U.S.

American Scholar, The (1837). A Phi Beta
Kappa address delivered by Ralph Waldo EMERSON
at Harvard. Emerson called for a reliance on direct
perception and native abilities, rather than a pale
imitation of European culture. For the scholar, or
Man Thinking, books must be secondary tools.
O. W. Holmes called the address our "intellectual
declaration of independence."

American Songbag, The (1927). A collection
of folk songs and ballads made by Carl SANDBURG.
In tours of the country, Sandburg himself sang
many of these songs, accompanying them on his
banjo or guitar. A number of them have been recorded by him, perhaps the best known being *The
Boll-Weevil.*

American Tragedy, An (1925). A novel by
Theodore DREISER. The author based his realistic
and vivid study on the actual case of Chester Gillette,
who in July, 1906, murdered Grace Brown at Big
Moose Lake in the Adirondacks. Dreiser, who gave
his protagonist the name Clyde Griffiths, at times

faithfully follows the original facts; at other moments he transcends them with his own interpretations. Clyde Griffiths' boyhood, for example, reproduces some of the details of Dreiser's own earlier years.

In revolt against the poverty and piety of his Midwestern family, Clyde becomes a bellboy in a luxurious hotel and, after being involved in an automobile accident for which he is legally responsible, is employed by a distant relative, owner of a collar factory in upper New York State. There Clyde seduces Roberta Alden, an employee at the factory, but falls in love with Sondra Finchley, a girl of the local aristocracy, who symbolizes the wealth and glamor that he has been seeking. Clyde's relationship with Sondra is menaced when Roberta, now pregnant, demands that he marry her, and he carefully devises a plan to murder her. He lacks the courage to carry out his scheme, when he takes Roberta rowing on an isolated lake, but the boat accidentally overturns, and he allows Roberta to drown while he swims away. Clyde is accused of murder, and the remainder of the book is a powerful depiction of his subsequent trial, conviction, and execution. Although Clyde is portrayed as a weakling, Dreiser squarely indicts America's industrial society for dazzling persons like Clyde with the dream of an unattainable and meretricious luxury.

America the Beautiful (1895; rev. 1904, 1911). A poem by Katharine Lee Bates (1859–1929), best known as a patriotic song to the tune of Samuel A. Ward's hymn, *Materna*.

Amerika (1927). An unfinished novel by Franz KAFKA that was published posthumously. Less radically abstruse than his other two novels, *The Trial* and *The Castle,* it deals with the adventures of a European boy in an unreal, expressionistically depicted America. Its first chapter was completed and published separately in 1913 as *The Stoker (Der Heizer).*

Amethyst Ring, The (L'Anneau d'améthyste; 1899). A novel by Anatole FRANCE. The tale centers about the actions of its protagonist M. BERGERET.

Amfortas. Guardian of the GRAIL in medieval legend, grandson of TITUREL. Because he has sinned, he has been wounded by the sacred lance which wounded Christ and can only be cured by a blameless fool. See PARSIFAL and PARZIVAL.

Amidism, or Pure Land Buddhism. A Chinese and Japanese Buddhist salvationism. Its aim is rebirth in the Western Paradise of Amida (Sans. *Amitabha;* Ch. *A-mi-t'o*) Buddha. Stemming from northern India and Central Asia, it spread rapidly in China, incorporating many elements from popular folk religions. In the Ming period (1368–1644) it merged with Ch'an (Zen) Buddhism. In Japan Amida pietism sprang up at the Tendai Buddhist center of Mt. Hiei. Its leading exponents were Genshin (942–1017), Hōnen (1133–1212), founder of the Jōdo Sect, and Shinran (1173–1262), the first patriarch of the Shin Sect. Amidism developed during the Heian (794–1185) period and marks a shift from a Buddhism for the elite toward one with an appeal for the common people. Emphasis is placed on the recitation, with faith, of the *nembutsu,* or invocation of the Buddha's name, as the single requirement for rebirth in Amida's Paradise. Its thought has had a lasting influence on both literature and the arts. The Shin was the first sect to allow its priests to marry. Shin and Jodo have the greatest number of adherents among Japanese Buddhist sects.

Amiel, Denys (1884–   ). French dramatist of the "school of silence" (see Jean-Jacques BERNARD). After *Le Voyageur* (1912, produced 1922), he collaborated with André Obey on *The Wife With the Smile (La Souriante Mme. Beudet;* 1921) and *La Carcasse* (1926). Other plays by Amiel include *Décalage* (1931), *Three and One* (1932), and *Café-Tabac* (1932).

Aminta. A famous Renaissance pastoral play by TASSO, written and first performed in 1573. The plot begins with the appearance of Venus' son Amor in the guise of a shepherd, determined to aim his arrows at the most obdurate nymph of Diana, Silvia, whose haughtiness has repulsed all lovers. Her friend Dafne (Daphne) tries to persuade her to fall in love with the shepherd Aminta, but she prefers the hunt; at the same time, Aminta spurns Amarilli, who loves him desperately. Aminta tells his friend Tirsi that there is no hope of gaining Silvia, as the wise Mopso has seen the future and confirmed the hopelessness of the pursuit. Now Satiro (the Satyr), also enamored of Silvia, decides to take her by force while she bathes. Aminta rescues her, but she flees from him. Later, believing Silvia dead, Aminta attempts suicide; but he survives to find Silvia convinced of his love and loving him in return. They wed and the play closes with the appearance of Venus, arrived to discover her unruly son and put an end to his mischief by taking him back to the Olympian court from which he had strayed.

Amis, Kingsley (1922–   ). English novelist and poet. His comic novels include the best-selling LUCKY JIM and *That Uncertain Feeling* (1955), *I Like It Here* (1958), and *Take a Girl Like You* (1960). *A Case of Samples* (1956) is a collection of intellectual, light-hearted poems. See ANGRY YOUNG MEN.

Amis and Amile. Also **Amys and Amylion** or **Amiloun.** French CHANSON DE GESTE based on an Oriental tale, made popular in 13th century French and English romance. The story celebrates an extraordinarily devoted friendship. Amis perjures himself to take Amile's place in a trial by combat, and is punished by leprosy. A vision reveals to Amile that only the blood of his children can cure his friend, so he kills them and effects the cure. But this generous sacrifice is miraculously rewarded: a visit to the children's dead bodies discovers them to be merely sleeping.

Amish. The Amish Mennonites, a strict sect of the 17th century, named from Jacob Ammann or Amen, a Swiss MENNONITE bishop.

Ammers-Küller, Johanna van (1884–   ). Dutch novelist. Her best-known novel is *The Rebel Generation* (1925), which was a best seller in Holland and widely translated.

Ammon. See AMEN.

Ammonius Saccas (c. 175–c. 242). An Alexandrian philosopher. The teacher of PLOTINUS, Ammonius made his students vow that they would not reveal his doctrines in writing. He was born a Christian but abandoned the faith.

Amores. See OVID.

Amoret. See FAERIE QUEENE, THE.

Amoretti (1595). Sonnet sequence by Edmund SPENSER.

Amorous History of the Gauls. See BUSSY-RAMBUTIN.

Amos. In the Old Testament, one of the Minor Prophets and the name of the oldest of the prophetic books in point of time. Amos had disquieting visions of the corruption of his city contemporaries. His pleas for personal and social righteousness are simply and movingly framed.

amour courtois. See COURTLY LOVE.

Amour médecin, L' (Love, the Doctor, 1665). A COMÉDIE-BALLET in prose by MOLIÈRE. By pretending to be a doctor, the hero Clitandre dupes the selfish Sganarelle into giving him the hand of his daughter and her dowry as well. See JOSSE; LUCINDE.

Ampère, André Marie (1775–1836). French physicist. Ampère made important discoveries in the fields of magnetism and electricity; these paved the way for the present-day study of electrodynamics. The *ampere*, the unit measure of intensity of an electric current, is named in his honor. Specific scientific orientation is less frequently found in his later work *Essai sur la philosophie des sciences* (1834–1844).

Amphiaraus. In mythology, the son of Oecles. It is not certain whether he was originally a man or god, although his name means "very sacred." Foreknowing the outcome of the expedition of the SEVEN AGAINST THEBES, Amphiaraus refused to take part in it until he was compelled to do so by his wife, ERIPHYLE. He attacked Thebes at the Homoloian Gate, but was driven off. While attempting to escape, he was swallowed up in a cleft in the ground made by Zeus's thunderbolt.

Amphion. A son of Zeus and Antiope. He became a famous musician and reigned, with his twin brother, in Thebes. Antiope, a daughter of Nycteus, the ruler of Thebes, lay with Zeus, but was driven from the city by her angry father. While fleeing to Sicyon, she gave birth to twins, Amphion and Zethus, on Mount Cithaeron. They were raised by shepherds and, on reaching manhood, learned of their mother's fate. Nycteus having died, his brother Lycus, now king, had brought Antiope back to Thebes, where he and his wife Dirce had long mistreated her. The twins went to Thebes, killed Lycus, and tied Dirce to the horns of a bull; she died at the Theban spring named for her.

Amphion and Zethus now shared the Theban throne and together built the city walls, though Amphion accomplished his part of the task by playing such ravishing music that the stones moved into place of their own accord. Amphion married NIOBE, but her arrogance led to the slaying by Apollo and Artemis of their many children and, according to some accounts, of Amphion himself. Zethus married Thebe, who gave her name to the city.

Amphitrite. In classic mythology, a goddess of the sea. She was the wife of Poseidon, daughter of Nereus and Doris, and mother of Triton.

Amphitryon. In Greek mythology, a king of Mycenae cuckolded by Zeus. The god assumed the likeness of Amphitryon for the purpose of visiting his wife, Alcmena, and gave a banquet at his house; but Amphitryon came home, and claimed the honor of being the master of the house. As far as the servants and guests were concerned, the dispute was soon decided: "he who gave the feast was to them the host." Alcmena became the mother of HERACLES. This legend is the subject of three famous comedies by Plautus, Molière, and Dryden, all called *Amphitryon*. In 1929 there appeared a play entitled *Amphitryon 38,* meaning that it was the 38th treatment of the famous theme, by the French dramatist Jean Giraudoux (1882–1944).

Amphitryon (1668). A comedy by MOLIÈRE. It is derived from Plautus' treatment of the Amphitryon legend. Jupiter, smitten with Alcmène, assumes the appearance of her husband Amphitryon, the better to effect her seduction, while his attendant Mercury takes on the appearance of Amphitryon's servant Sosie. The play recounts the mounting confusion caused by the arrival of the real Amphitryon and Sosie. Eventually, Jupiter clears up the matter by explaining the deception.

Heinrich von KLEIST's *Amphitryon* (pub. 1808) is an adaptation of Molière's version, but concentrates much more on the tragic implications of the situation, especially for Alcmène.

amrita or **amreeta** (*Sans.,* without death). In Hindu mythology, the elixir of immortality, corresponding to the AMBROSIA of classical mythology. To the early Aryans, it was probably the juice of the soma plant, from which a sweet ritual wine was prepared.

Amun. See AMEN.

Amundsen, Roald (1872–1928). Norwegian polar explorer. Amundsen located the exact geographical position of the north magnetic pole on a voyage through the Northwest Passage (1903–1906). On December 14, 1911, he reached the South Pole and is known as its official discoverer. He flew across the North Pole with Lincoln Ellsworth in the dirigible *Norge* (1926). Amundsen disappeared (June, 1928) while on a flight to rescue the Italian explorer Nobile, who was lost returning from the North Pole. With Ellsworth and others he published *North West Passage* (1908), *South Pole* (1912), *Our Polar Flight* (1925), and *First Crossing of the Polar Sea* (1927).

Amusements sérieux et comiques d'un Siamois. See Charles Rivière DUFRESNY.

Amyclaean silence. Named for Amyclae, a Laconian town south of Sparta. Amyclae was ruled by the mythical TYNDAREUS. The inhabitants had so often been alarmed by false rumors of the approach of invading Spartans that they made a decree forbidding mention of the subject. When the Spartans actually came no one dared give the warning, and the town was taken. Hence the phrase "more silent than Amyclae."

Amys and Amylion. See AMIS AND AMILE.

An. The Sumerian god of heaven. Born of Nammu, the primeval sea, An and his sister-wife Ki (Earth) were originally joined as one, but their offspring ENLIL, the god of the air, separated them. An's place as head of the Sumerian pantheon was taken by Enlil. An is the same as the Babylonian god ANU.

Anabaptists. A general name for many Protestant sects which appeared in Germany during the 16th and 17th centuries. Although the various groups were usually in conflict with one another, most of them believed that they were restoring the purity of the primitive Christian church. Most practiced adult baptism, as described in the Bible, and several were involved with social and economic agitation. See MÜNSTER ANABAPTISTS.

Anabase (1924). A poem by St.-John PERSE. It was translated into English by T. S. Eliot in 1930. In this long work, the "upward journey" of the human spirit is portrayed through the expeditions of a Conqueror making his way across inhabited lands and deserts in Asia. He is loath to leave the pleasures and people of each successive city; yet restlessly he dreams of new travels and conquests and sets forth again.

Anabasis. See XENOPHON.

Anacharsis. The protagonist in a once celebrated historical romance entitled *Le Voyage du jeune Anacharsis en Grèce dans le milieu du IVᵉ siècle avant l'ère vulgaire* (1788) by Jean Jacques BARTHÉLÉMY. The author, inspired by his archaeological research in Pompeii during a trip to Italy in 1755, seeks in this novel to bring alive classical antiquity in the time of Philip of Macedon and Demosthenes, and emphasizes particularly those aspects of science, art, and customs that history frequently neglects.

The real Anacharsis was a Scythian sage who, according to Herodotus, visited many countries in search of knowledge during the 6th century B.C.; Barthélémy's work, however, is completely original.

Anacreon (Anakreon). A Greek lyric poet. He wrote chiefly in praise of love and wine. He lived from about 563 to 478 B.C.

Anadyomene. An epithet of APHRODITE, alluding to her rising from the sea at birth.

anagoge. An elevation of the mind to things celestial. Specifically, the term is used to refer to exegesis that gives a mystical or spiritual meaning or application to the words of the Bible, as opposed to their literal, moral, or allegorical interpretation. See FOUR SENSES.

Anak. In the Old Testament, a giant of Palestine, whose descendants were terrible for their gigantic stature. The Hebrew spies said that they themselves were mere grasshoppers compared with the *Anakim*.

Analects (Lun-yü). One of the Chinese FOUR BOOKS. A brief, unsystematic collection of fragmentary writings attributed to Confucius and his school. Memorized until recently by every schoolboy, it is one of the most influential works in the history of Chinese thought. See Arthur Waley, *The Analects of Confucius* (1938).

Anand, Mulk Raj (1905–   ). Indian novelist writing in English. Educated in the Punjab and at Cambridge, he edited *Marg,* an art quarterly, and organized an Asian Writers' Conference in Delhi in 1956. His novels include *Coolie* (1936), *Two Leaves and a Bud* (1938), *Untouchable* (1947), and *Private Life of an Indian Prince* (1955).

Ananias. In the New Testament, an early Christian of Jerusalem. With his wife Sapphira, Ananias was struck dead for lying about the price of a piece of land they had sold in order to give the proceeds to their church (Acts 5). His name has since become a general term for one who lies.

anapest. In English prosody, a metrical foot consisting of three syllables, the first two unaccented and the third accented. The word "cig-a-RETTE" is an anapest. The METER made up of such units is called anapestic meter, and the following lines are a good example.

> i am MON/arch of ALL / i survey . . .
> i am LORD / of the FOWL / and the BRUTE.
>
> Cowper, *Alexander Selkirk*

Anarchiad, The (1786–1787). An American satirical epic poem, published anonymously in 12 installments of the New Haven *Gazette.* David Humphries, Lemuel Hopkins, Joel BARLOW, John TRUMBULL, and other HARTFORD WITS collaborated in its composition. It is chiefly an attack on French philosophy, paper money, Shays' Rebellion, and the condescending attitude of Europeans towards Americans.

Anat or **Anath.** Canaanite goddess, sister of Baal. A somewhat vengeful and violent deity, but loyal to her brother Baal, she has some characteristics in common with the Greek Artemis. She figures prominently in THE POEM OF BAAL and THE POEM OF AQHAT.

Anatol (1891). A play by Arthur SCHNITZLER. It presents several sentimental and erotic episodes from the life of a Casanovalike adventurer who constantly flits from one girl to another. Anatol's carefree and often shallow attitude toward life is contrasted with that of his more solid and sensible friend Max, but there is no real conflict, and the whole is pervaded with a light-hearted and sensuous humor. Hugo von Hofmannsthal wrote a preface in verse for the play.

Anatomy of Melancholy, The (1621). A prose work by Robert BURTON. Elaborately organized as a medical treatise, the *Anatomy* not only deals with various morbid mental states, their causes, symptoms, and cures, but is a compendium of notable utterances on the human condition in general, compiled from classical, scholastic, and contemporary sources. Melancholy, for Burton, embraced everything from raving lunacy to philosophical and occasional pessimism; as his quotations illustrate, it is "the character of mortality." The book is witty, pedantic, quaint, imaginative, inexhaustively rich, and, from Milton on, it has been pillaged by numerous authors.

Anaxagoras (500?–428 B.C.). A Greek philosopher, teacher of Pericles, Thucydides, Euripides, and possibly of Socrates. He believed in a dualistic universe, consisting of a chaotic mass of tiny particles or seeds that compose matter, and an ordering force that imparts motion. He called this force nous, or mind. Anaxagoras was also an astronomer, and correctly explained eclipses. He studied the size of the sun, the phases of the moon, and the behavior of meteors. Because his views conflicted with the state religion, Anaxagoras was charged with impiety and banished from the Athens he had made the center of philosophic argumentation. He is sometimes referred to as Anaxagoras of Clazomenae, after his birthplace in Asia Minor.

Anaximander (611?–547 B.C.). Greek philosopher of the MILESIAN SCHOOL, pupil of Thales. According to Anaximander, primary matter, which he called the *apeiron,* is eternal and indestructible. Motion and the separation of contradictory elements within this indefinite mass are the causes of plurality and variety in the universe. A practical scientist, Anaximander invented the sundial and was the first to prepare a map. He is known as the first Greek author to write in prose, although his philosophical treatise has perished.

Anaximenes (fl. 525 B.C.). Greek philosopher of the MILESIAN SCHOOL, associate of Anaximander. He believed that the condensation and rarefaction of air or *aether,* the primary substance, give rise to matter in all its forms.

Anaximenes of Lampsacus (c. 380–c. 320 B.C.). Greek rhetorician and historian, companion of Alexander the Great on his Persian expeditions. He wrote histories of Greece and biographies of Philip of Macedon and of Alexander. He is also thought to be the author of the only surviving work on rhetoric before Aristotle.

Anchises. In classic legend, a member of the royal house of Troy and the father of AENEAS by Aphrodite, who had fallen in love with him because of his beauty. According to Vergil, when Troy fell, Aeneas carried his aged father out of the burning city on his shoulders. Anchises died during Aeneas' wanderings and was buried in Sicily (AENEID, Book III).

Ancient Mariner, The Rime of the. See RIME OF THE ANCIENT MARINER, THE.

Ancient of Days. A scriptural title for the Deity (Dan. 7:9).

Ancients and moderns. See QUERELLE DES ANCIENS ET DES MODERNES.

Andersen, Hans Christian (1805–1875). Danish writer of fairy tales, poet, novelist, and dramatist. A skilled writer in all these genres, Hans Christian Andersen owes his worldwide fame to his fairy stories. Always popular with children, the 168 tales contain a mature wisdom together with gay whimsy. Andersen invested stories of folk and legendary origin with moral and symbolic significance. He could convey a fine perception of life's ironies while describing the fate of a tin soldier or a drab duckling. Among his best-known stories are *The Red Shoes, The Ugly Duckling, The Emperor's Clothes, The Tinder Box,* and *The Fir Tree.* The tales appeared from 1835 to 1872. Andersen's complete tales have been issued in several English editions.

Anderson, Marian (1902–   ). American contralto. She is the first Negro to have sung as a permanent member of the Metropolitan Opera Company in New York. She is greatly admired as a concert artist, especially in Europe, where she first established her reputation.

Anderson, Maxwell (1888–1959). American playwright. He is known for his experiments in verse drama, his insistence on the necessity of an inner moral struggle, and his success in the field of historical drama. After an early play, *White Desert* (1923), Anderson began collaborating with Laurence STALLINGS, the two producing WHAT PRICE GLORY?; *First Flight* (1925), about Andrew Jackson; and *The Buccaneer* (1925), a play about Sir Henry Morgan. In the late 1920's he wrote *Outside Looking In* (1925), based on Jim Tully's *Beggars of Life,* and *Saturday's Children* (1927), a domestic comedy. He then wrote with Harold Hickerson the first play to deal with the SACCO-VANZETTI case, *Gods of the Lightning* (1928). Anderson was to return later to this theme in his successful WINTERSET.

In the 1930's Anderson returned to historical drama, writing two plays dealing with 16th-century themes, *Elizabeth the Queen* (1930) and *Mary of Scotland* (1933). *Valley Forge* (1934), a reinterpretation of Washington, followed. During the 30's, Anderson wrote better than a play a year; some of these are NIGHT OVER TAOS; BOTH YOUR HOUSES; *High Tor* (1937), which mingles real people and ghosts, past and present; *Knickerbocker Holiday* (1938), a musical with Kurt Weill; and *Key Largo* (1939), about a man who struggles to redeem himself for an act of cowardice committed during the Spanish Civil War.

World War II was reflected in several Anderson plays of the early 40's: *Candle in the Wind* (1941), an anti-Nazi play set in Paris; *The Eve of St. Mark* (1942); and *Storm Operation* (1944). After the war Anderson returned again to historical drama with *Joan of Lorraine* (1946); *Anne of the Thousand Days* (1948), a favorable interpretation of Henry VIII; and *Barefoot in Athens* (1951), a play about Socrates. Also noteworthy among Anderson's late dramas were *Lost in the Stars* (1949), a dramatization of Alan Paton's *Cry the Beloved Country,* and *The Bad Seed* (1955), the story of a grotesquely evil little girl, based on a novel by William March.

Anderson, Robert W[oodruff] (1917–   ). American playwright. He is the author of the successful play *Tea and Sympathy* (1953), the story of a preparatory school student unjustly suspected of homosexuality. He later wrote *All Summer Long* (1959) and *Silent Night, Lonely Night* (1959).

Anderson, Sherwood (1876–1941). American short-story writer and novelist. Born in Ohio, largely self-educated, Anderson worked at various trades and for several years was a copywriter in Chicago. There he met Midwestern writers associated with the Chicago literary renaissance, notably Theodore Dreiser and Carl Sandburg, and began his own literary career. His third book, WINESBURG, OHIO, a collection of related short stories dealing with individuals in a typical Midwestern town, brought him recognition as a leader in the revolt against established literary traditions.

Though his style has been decried by a later generation of writers and critics as artless and sentimental, it was for Anderson's time a significant breakthrough to an individual and original expression; not realistic in the sense of being an accurate reproduction of Middle Western speech, it has yet a kind of stylized realism that evokes the flavor of the Midwestern town, the pathos of lives trapped by conventionality and commercialism, the adolescent yearning to know and despair at discovery. Anderson was repelled by the industrial and commercial society he saw growing up all around him, and he frequently contrasted the contemporary scene with an earlier one devoted to craftsmanship and personal concern. For Anderson, modern society and the worship of materialistic success resulted in the erection of walls between people, a sterile sexuality, and a loss of skill in handicraft and the arts. Such walls, he believed, could only be broken down by love, creative human relationships, and a return to a personal involvement in one's craft.

Anderson never again equalled his achievement in *Winesburg, Ohio,* though his novel DARK LAUGHTER became a best seller. He was most at home in the short story, some of his best stories being *I'm a Fool, Death in the Woods,* and *I Want to Know Why.*

His stories are collected in THE TRIUMPH OF THE EGG and *Horses and Men* (1923). His novels include *Windy McPherson's Son* (1916), *Marching Men* (1917), POOR WHITE (1920), and *Many Marriages* (1923). A STORY TELLER'S STORY and *Tar: A Midwest Childhood* (1926) are autobiographical. His *Memoirs* (1942) and *Letters* (1953) were published posthumously.

Andō Hiroshige (1787–1858). Japanese painter and wood-block artist. He is famous for his *Tōkaidō Gojūsan-tsugi* (fifty-three stations along the Tōkaidō Highway), and as the last great master of the woodblock (*ukiyoe*) print. His work is said to have influenced Western painters, notably Whistler.

And Quiet Flows the Don. See QUIET DON, THE.

André, John (1751–1780). English army major to whom Benedict Arnold delivered the plans for the betrayal of West Point during the American Revolution. He was caught and hanged as a spy. He is the hero of *André* (1798), a play by William Dunlap.

Andrea del Sarto (1855). A poem by Robert BROWNING. Written in the form of a dramatic monologue, del Sarto, known as "the Faultless Painter," reveals his own character as he tells of the consuming passion for his beautiful, unscrupulous wife, Lucrezia, which prevented him from reaching the artistic stature of Raphael and Michelangelo.

Andreas Capellanus or **André le Chapelain** (late 12th–early 13th century). French chaplain at the court of Philip II. He wrote a Latin *Liber de Arte Honeste Amandi* (*Book on the Art of Loving Honestly*), a treatise on the art of love in the tradition of Ovid's *Ars Amoris*. It became a handbook of the theory and practice of COURTLY LOVE.

Andrew, St. One of the twelve disciples of Jesus; the brother of St. Peter. He is depicted in Christian art as an old man with long white hair and beard, holding the Gospel in his right hand, and leaning on a cross like the letter X, termed St. Andrew's cross. His day is November 30. It is said that he suffered martyrdom in Patrae (A.D. 70).

André Walter, Les Cahiers d' (1891). A short novelistic work by André GIDE. It purports to be the notebooks of a sensitive youth who is suffering romantic anguish because his beloved has obeyed her mother and married another. Its melodrama reveals the conflict between spiritual love and fleshly desire as irreconcilable. Gide also called his first book of poems *Les Poésies d'André Walter* (1892).

Andrews, Joseph. See JOSEPH ANDREWS.

Andrews, Pamela. See PAMELA, OR VIRTUE REWARDED.

Andreyev, Leonid Nikolayevich (1871–1919). Russian writer. Born in the province of Oriol, Andreyev studied law at the universities of St. Petersburg and Moscow, during which time extreme mental depression led to several suicide attempts. He graduated in 1897 but turned to writing instead of law for a living, receiving aid and encouragement from Maksim Gorki. Among the best of Andreyev's earlier works were *In the Fog* (*V tumanye*; 1902) and *Thought* (*Mysl*; 1902), the first dealing with awakened sexuality in a young boy, the second with insanity and murder. Such sensational themes were at this time still treated in a realistic manner by Andreyev, but, from this period on, his work became increasingly complex, often strained in its search for sensational effect and symbolic import. This is especially apparent in a work such as *The Red Laugh* (*Krasnyi smekh;* 1904), a horrorific tale of the madness and terror of war. The same tendencies are evident in Andreyev's plays, which include HE WHO GETS SLAPPED, *The Black Maskers* (*Chiorniye maski;* 1908), *Anathema* (*Anafema;* 1909), and *The Life of Man* (*Zhizn cheloveka;* 1906).

Andrič, Ivo (1892–   ). Yugoslav novelist. Born in Bosnia of a family of artisans of very modest means, Andrič managed to secure an education in universities in several cities in what is now Yugoslavia, Poland, and Austria. He was active in the National Revolutionary Youth Organization before World War I, and after it served in the diplomatic service in Rome, Bucharest, Trieste, Graz, and Berlin. During the German occupation, he lived in retirement in Belgrade and wrote his major novels, all about Bosnia: *Miss; The Travnik Chronicle;* and THE BRIDGE ON THE DRINA. He was little known outside his own country until the last novel was translated into English. In 1961 he was awarded the Nobel prize for literature.

Androcles or **Androclus.** According to Aulus Gellius, Androcles was a Roman slave of the 1st century who removed a thorn from the paw of a lion. When Androcles was later thrown into the arena, the grateful beast began to caress him and they were both set free. George Bernard Shaw used this story as the basis of his play ANDROCLES AND THE LION.

Androcles and the Lion (1912). A play by George Bernard SHAW. Using the story of ANDROCLES as the basis of the plot, Shaw's play is about the early Christians' faith. The first act opens as a band of first-century Christians is being led to the arena in Rome to be martyred. Androcles, a meek tailor, whose fabled encounter with the lion has taken place in the prologue, is in the group. As they proceed toward Rome, they sing hymns and aver their faith. The two main characters are a Roman captain and Lavinia, a beautiful, young Christian. She enunciates the theme of the play: to make life worth living, one must have something to die for. In the arena one of the Christians fights so well that the emperor pardons them all, but one person must still be thrown to the lion to keep the crowd happy. Androcles volunteers and discovers that the lion is the same one that he had helped in the forest.

Andromache. In Homer's *Iliad,* the wife of Hector. She appears in Euripides' THE TROJAN WOMEN and is the heroine of his *Andromache* (430–424 B.C.). In the latter play, she has been carried off to Thessaly by Neoptolemus, Achilles' son; has borne him a child, and has been abandoned in favor of Hermione, the daughter of Menelaus and Helen. Her sufferings at their hands are the substance of the play, which, in portraying the Spartans as cruel and cowardly, served as an effective political indictment of the Athenians' enemies. Racine wrote a tragedy about Andromache entitled *Andromaque*.

Andromaque (1667). A tragedy by Jean RACINE. It is based on the Greek legend of ANDROMACHE but differs from it in several details of interrelation between the characters. The play is set in Epirus after the fall of Troy. Andromaque is loved by her captor

Pyrrhus whom she hates, but his action arouses the jealousy of his fiancée Hermione. Pyrrhus threatens to surrender Andromaque's son Astyanax to the Greeks if she will not yield to him. In exchange for his promise to protect her son, she agrees to marry Pyrrhus, but secretly intends to remain faithful to her dead husband Hector by killing herself after the wedding. The rejected Hermione persuades Orestes, the Greek ambassador, who has come to demand Andromaque's son, to murder Pyrrhus, and in exchange agrees to flee with him. But after the murder she reviles him and in her remorse commits suicide upon the funeral pyre of her adored Pyrrhus. Orestes goes mad. *Andromaque* is held by French critics to constitute the first representation in tragedy of the psychology of passion.

Andromeda. In Greek mythology, the daughter of Cepheus and Cassiopeia. Because her mother boasted that she was more beautiful than the Nereids, they induced Poseidon to send a sea-monster against Ethiopia, and an oracle declared that Andromeda must be sacrificed to it. Chained to a rock near Joppa, she was rescued by PERSEUS, who married her. He also killed Phineus, her former betrothed, and all his companions. She was placed among the stars upon her death.

Andromède (1650). A play by Pierre CORNEILLE. Based on the Andromeda legend, it exploited the most spectacular scenic effects of its day.

Andvari. King of the dwarfs in Scandinavian mythology, especially in the *Edda* and the *Völsunga Saga*, who gave up his treasure and magic ring to Loki in exchange for his liberty.

Anelida and Arcite (probably c. 1380 or 1381). An unfinished poem by Geoffrey CHAUCER, in 357 lines. Although Chaucer gives Statius as his authority, he apparently draws more on Boccaccio's *Teseida*. The story of how Arcite faithlessly leaves Queen Anelida for a new love is told in RHYME ROYAL. It introduces the better poetry of Anelida's song of complaint, written in stanzas of nine lines, except for two of sixteen.

angel (Gr., *angelos*, "messenger"). (1) In theology, a celestial being. In postcanonical and apocalyptic literature, angels are grouped in varying orders, and the hierarchy thus constructed was adapted to church uses by the early Christian Fathers. In his *De Hierarchia Celesti* the pseudo-Dionysius (early fifth century) gives the names of the nine orders; they are taken from the New Testament (Eph. 1:21 and Col. 1:16) and are as follows:

(i) SERAPHIM, Cherubim, and Thrones, in the first circle of the heavenly hierarchy.

(ii) Dominions, Virtues, and Powers, in the second circle.

(iii) Principalities, Archangels, and Angels, in the third circle.

The seven holy angels are Michael, Gabriel, Raphael, Uriel, Chamuel, Jophiel, and Zadkiel. Michael and Gabriel are mentioned in the Bible; the others appear in Apocryphal books.

Milton (*Paradise Lost*, Bk. 1, 392) gives a list of the fallen angels.

Muslims say that angels were created from pure, bright gems, the genii from fire, and man from clay.

(2) An obsolete English coin, current from the time of Edward IV to that of Charles I, bearing the figure of the archangel Michael slaying the dragon. Its value varied from 6s. 8d. in 1465 (when first coined) to 10s. under Edward VI. It was the coin presented to persons touched for the King's Evil.

Angelica. The bewitching heroine of the Orlando poems of Boiardo and Ariosto (see ORLANDO FURIOSO). A princess of Cathay, her arrival at the court of Charlemagne sows discord among the paladins, especially Rinaldo and Orlando. The latter goes mad for a time when he discovers that she has fallen in love with the simple Moorish youth Medoro and escaped to Cathay with him. By introducing her as the main plot impulse, Boiardo made the first important blending of the Carolingian legends with the amatory motifs of the Arthurian cycle.

Angelico, Fra [Giovanni]. Real name: **Guido di Pietro** (1387–1455). Italian painter. A Dominican friar of Fiesole, near Florence, he worked in Rome, Orvieto, and Florence. It was there that he completed the well-known series of frescoes for the monastery of San Marco, as a result of the patronage of Cosimo de Medici. In 1447, Fra Angelico was summoned to Rome by Pope Nicholas V for the purpose of painting several scenes from the life of Saint Lawrence, which were to be hung in the Vatican. A religious painter of grace and simplicity coupled with an admirable purity and delicacy of color, he did not share his contemporaries' enthusiasm for the new scientific naturalism of the day.

Angelo. (1) In Shakespeare's MEASURE FOR MEASURE, the puritanical lord deputy who governs Vienna in the absence of Duke Vincentio. Although he is widely known as "a man of stricture and firm abstinence," his austerity masks a violent inner nature.

(2) In Shakespeare's COMEDY OF ERRORS, a goldsmith who, having fashioned a gold chain for Antipholus of Ephesus, mistakenly gives it to Antipholus of Syracuse.

Angel Pavement (1930). A novel by J. B. PRIESTLEY. Set in London, it is the story of small businessmen and a grasping capitalist.

Angel Street (1942). A long-run mystery play (1295 performances) by the English playwright Patrick Hamilton (1909–1962).

Angelus. A Roman Catholic devotion in honor of the Incarnation. It is so called from the first words, *Angelus Domini* (The angel of the Lord). The prayer is recited three times a day at 6 A.M., noon, and 6 P.M., at the sound of a bell called the *Angelus*. Millet made a well-known painting with this title.

Angelus Silesius. Pen name of **Johann Scheffler** (1624–1677). German baroque poet. His most famous work, *Cherubinischer Wandersmann (The Cherubic Wanderer,* 1657) is a collection of religious epigrams of mystical character. Although he was a Catholic, Scheffler's thought is not unrelated to the earlier Protestant mysticism of Jakob Böhme and to the later movement of Pietism.

Anglo-Saxon Attitudes (1956). A satirical novel by Angus WILSON. The hero is an elderly medieval historian who decides to investigate a possible academic fraud with which he was once indirectly connected. In the process he discovers some truths about his family and himself.

Anglo-Saxon Chronicle, The [also called **Old English Annals**] (c. 891–924). An Old English history of England begun under the direction of

[facsimile of Anglo-Saxon Chronicle manuscript, Old English script]

BRITISH MUSEUM

The years 701–710 from *The Anglo-Saxon Chronicle.*

King ALFRED, still a major historical source. The early material is adapted from BEDE's work and from records kept by the monasteries. After the account of Alfred's wars against the Danes the *Chronicle* was officially kept up year by year until 924, after which the various extant manuscript copies of it show fragmentary continuations by different authors, one with entries as late as 1154.

Angry Young Men. A nickname coined by Fleet Street journalists for a group of English writers who came into prominence in the 1950's. The Angry Young Men, generally of working or middle-class origins, expressed the discontent and disillusion of a generation enfranchised and university-educated by British socialism but unable to effect an entrance into the restricted power circles of British politics, education, criticism, or literature. They expressed their suspicion and resentment of upper-class culture, manners, and snobbism and their disgust with Britain and with what they took to be British hypocrisy chiefly through the novel and the drama. They produced several works of undeniable power, won enormous press publicity and critical favor, and achieved an impressive commercial success which, in the opinion of several critics, has modified their fervor. The movement may be said to be in decline in the 60's. The leading Angry Young Men were John OSBORNE, notable for the fury and bitterness of his plays, and Kingsley AMIS, remarkable among the group for the coherence and humor of his novels.

Animal Farm (1945). A satirical fable by George ORWELL. Some farm animals get tired of their servitude to man and start a revolution to run the farm as they want. They are betrayed, however, by their leaders, the pigs, into a worse servitude. The pigs' slogan is, "All animals are equal, but some animals are more equal than others." The book is a satire on the development of the Russian revolution under Stalin.

Animal Kingdom, The (1932). A play by Philip BARRY. It is the story of Tom Collier, who finds years of happiness with his mistress, Daisy Sage. After returning to his wife, he abandons her again for Daisy.

animal magnetism. See MESMERISM.

animals in heaven. The 10 animals which, according to Muslim legend, have been allowed to enter paradise. They are (1) Jonah's *whale;* (2) Solomon's *ant;* (3) the *ram* caught by Abraham and sacrificed instead of Isaac; (4) the *lapwing* of Balkis; (5) the *camel* of the prophet Saleh; (6) Balaam's *ass;* (7) the *ox* of Moses; (8) the *dog* Kratim or Katmir of the Seven Sleepers; (9) Al Borak, Muhammad's *ass;* and (10) Noah's *dove.*

Anker Larson, Johannes (1874–1957). Danish novelist and playwright. His novel *The Philosopher's Stone* (*De Vises Sten,* 1923) won the coveted Gyldendal prize and brought fame to the little-known writer. Anker Larson's absorbing interest in mysticism finds expression in all his novels, among them *Martha and Mary* (*Martha og Marie;* 1925), *With the Door Open* (*For aaben Dør;* 1926), and *Stranger in Paradise* (*Sognet, som vokser ind i Himmelen;* 1928).

Ann, Mother. See Ann LEE.

Annabel Lee (1849). A poem by Edgar Allan POE. Its subject, Poe's favorite, is the death of a beautiful woman.

Anna Christie (1922). A drama by Eugene O'NEILL. Anna is the daughter of Chris Christopherson, a Swedish captain who has come to regard all evil and misfortune as the work of "dat old davil sea." He had sent her away to be brought up in Minnesota, but in the play she turns up in port and falls in love with both the sea and with a brawny Irish seaman named Mat Burke. When she confesses to a shameful past in St. Paul, both her father and lover repudiate her. In the end, however, she is forgiven by them both. The play won a Pulitzer Prize in 1922. It was made into the musical comedy *New Girl in Town* (1957) by George Abbott.

Anna Comnena (1083–?1148). A daughter of the Byzantine emperor ALEXIUS COMNENUS. She wrote a history of her father's career entitled the *Alexiad.*

Anna Karenina (1873–1876). A novel by Count Leo TOLSTOI. The author's second great major novel, it is the story of a tragic, adulterous love. Anna meets and falls in love with Aleksei Vronski, a handsome young officer. She abandons her child and husband in order to be with Vronski. When he tires of her and leaves her to go to war, she kills herself by leaping under a train. The idea for the story reputedly came to Tolstoi after he had viewed the body of a young woman who committed a similar suicide. A subplot concerns the contrasting happy marriage of Konstantin Levin and his young wife Kitty. Levin's search for meaning in his life and his love for a natural, simple existence on his estate are reflections of Tolstoi's own moods and thoughts of the time. While working on the novel, Tolstoi began to experience the doubts and torments which he describes in *A Confession*.

Annales Cambriae (c. 955). A Latin history of Wales, importantly connected with the origins of ARTHURIAN LEGEND. It notes that at the battle of Mount Badon, a historical Arthur (prototype of King Arthur) wore a cross on his shield, and that Arthur and Medraut (a historical MORDRED) fell at the battle of Camlan in the year 537.

Anna Livia Plurabelle. In James Joyce's novel FINNEGANS WAKE, the personification of the Irish river, the Liffey, representing H. C. Earwicker's wife Anna. The initials A. L. P. are interwoven throughout the novel to represent the universal feminine principle.

Anna of the Five Towns (1902). A novel by Arnold BENNETT. The first of Bennett's novels dealing with the Potteries region, it is a naturalistic account of an ordinary woman's dull life. It is also a study of the repressive effects of Wesleyan religion. Anna is the daughter of Ephraim Tellwright, a miser and former preacher, who looks after the fortune Anna has inherited from her mother and forces her to extort high rent from her tenants. Anna becomes engaged to marry Henry Mynors, a pillar of the Church and a successful businessman, who is interested in her money. When she finds that she really loves Willie Price, son of a tenant her father has forced her to ruin, she cannot break the habit of years of obedience and marries Henry. Old Mr. Price and Willie commit suicide.

Anne Boleyn (c. 1507–1536). Queen consort of HENRY VIII, mother of ELIZABETH I. A lady of honor to Henry's first queen, Catherine of Aragon, Anne soon attracted the attention of the king, to whom she was secretly married in January, 1533. Some months later Henry's first marriage was declared invalid, and Anne was crowned queen. After the disappointing birth of a daughter (the future Queen Elizabeth), a miscarriage, and a stillborn son, Anne lost favor with Henry. In 1536 she was made to stand trial for adultery, was condemned, along with five men accused of being her lovers, and executed.

Annenski, Innokenti Fiodorovich (1856–1909). Russian poet. A classical scholar and translator of Euripides and the French Parnassians, Annenski wrote lyric poems that were models of concision and exquisite finish. His small output of poetic work was published mainly in *Quiet Songs* (*Tikhiye pesni;* 1904) and *The Cypress Chest* (*Kiparisovskii laryetz;* 1910). Annenski was a potent influence on the poetry of the Acmeists and the early work of Boris Pasternak.

Anne of Austria (**Anne d'Autriche;** 1602–1666). Daughter of Philip III of Spain, consort of Louis XIII of France, and regent during the minority of her son Louis XIV.

Anne of Cleves (1515–1557). The fourth wife of HENRY VIII of England. Henry's marriage with Anne, a German, was arranged by Thomas Cromwell to create an alliance with the German Protestants.

Henry, however, disliked her, and after six months had the marriage declared null and void.

Anne of Geierstein, or The Maiden of the Mist (1829). A novel by Sir Walter SCOTT. Exiled Lancastrian supporters become involved with the defeat of Charles the Bold, duke of Burgundy, by the Swiss in the 15th century.

Anne of Green Gables. See L. M. MONTGOMERY.

Anniversaries, The. The general title of two long elegiac poems by John DONNE: *An Anatomy of the World* (1611) and *Of the Progresse of the Soule* (1612). Ostensibly written in memory of Elizabeth, young daughter of his patron, Sir Robert Drury, they are more concerned with the typical Donne themes of intellectual disorder and temporal decay.

anno Domini (*Lat.*). In the Year of our Lord; *i.e.,* in the year since the Nativity: generally abbreviated to A.D. It was Dionysius Exiguus who fixed the date of the Nativity; he lived in the early 6th century, and his computation is probably late by some three to six years. The custom of determining dates on this basis is said to be the result of the work of the Venerable Bede.

Annonce faite à Marie, L'. See TIDINGS BROUGHT TO MARY, THE.

Annual Register, The. A summary of the chief historic events of the year, first published by John and Robert Dodsley in 1758. It is still issued annually in England.

Annunciation, the Day of the. March 25, the day of the angel's (traditionally Gabriel's) announcement to the Virgin Mary of the forthcoming birth to her of the Messiah. It is also sometimes called Lady Day, which in medieval England was the first day of the legal year. The Annunciation was often represented in mystery plays, and is the subject of paintings by, among others, Fra Angelico, Andrea del Sarto, Titian, Tintoretto, and Murillo. The earliest authentic record of its celebration as a church festival is in 656.

Annus Mirabilis (*Lat.,* "year of wonders"; 1667). A poem by John DRYDEN. The poem describes the London fire and the Dutch war, the chief events of the year 1666. In a preface to the poem, Dryden discusses his conception of the poetic imagination.

Ann Veronica (1909). A novel by H. G. WELLS. It is the story of the heroine's struggle for independence, sexual freedom, and equality with men.

Anouilh, Jean (1910–). French dramatist and screen writer. *The Ermine* (1932) first presented his major recurrent theme, the "great thirst for purity." His plays, ANTIGONE (1942) and THE LARK (1953) for example, frequently oppose the freshness of youth to the staleness or even sordidness of age. Youth is embodied in the person of a young girl, poor but innocent and lovely; age is personified by a man who is usually wealthy and in a position of control. Allied to this contrast is the theme of the opposition between the poetry of fantasy or art and the sullying demands of practicality in the real world. The devices of play-within-a-play and disguised or pretended identity give symbolic expression to this conflict between artifice and actuality. Anouilh is never able to resolve these antitheses in an optimistic manner. The young and pure, however beautiful, is fragile and unreal, compelled to face the inevitable bitterness and ugliness of actual human existence. The increasing bitterness and pessimism of his later work is half hidden beneath a veil of facile but charming satiric wit.

Anouilh's serious plays are often adaptations of well-known legends; the settings of his popular comedies range from castles to bourgeois domesticity. His plays published as *Pièces roses* (rosy plays) include *Thieves' Carnival* (*Le Bal des voleurs,* 1932) and *Time Remembered* (*Léocadia,* 1939). *Restless Heart* (*La Sauvage,* 1934), *Eurydice* (1941; also translated as *Legend of the Lovers* and *Point of Departure*), *Romeo and Jeanette* (1945), and *Medea* (1946) were published as *Pièces noires* (dark plays). *Pièces brillantes* (sparkling plays) were *Ring Round the Moon* (*L'Invitation au Chateau,* 1947; translated by Christopher Fry), *Cecile* (1949), *The Rehearsal* (*La Répétition,* 1950) and *Colombe* (1951). *Pièces grinçantes* (grating plays) include *Ardèle* (1948) and *The Waltz of the Toreadors* (1952). Anouilh's later plays are *L'Hurluberlu* (1959) and *Becket* (1959).

Anshar. Babylonian sky-god. Born of Lahmu and Lahamu, he fathered by his sister, Kishar, ANU, the god of heaven.

Anstey, Christopher (1724–1805). English poet. He became famous as the author of *The New Bath Guide* (1766), a series of verse letters supposedly written by Simpkin Blunderhead and other members of his family, describing the resort town of Bath. Tobias Smollett later used the same device in *The Expedition of Humphrey Clinker.*

Anstey, F. Pen name of **Thomas Anstey Guthrie** (1856–1934). English humorist, novelist, and playwright. Among his works are VICE VERSA, OR A LESSON TO FATHERS (1882), a satiric novel, and *The Man from Blankley's* (1901), a play very popular in its day.

Antaeus (Antaios). In Greek mythology, a gigantic wrestler, a son of Earth and Sea, Ge and Poseidon. His strength was invincible as long as he touched the earth; and when he was lifted from it, his strength was renewed on touching it again. It was Heracles who succeeded in killing this charmed giant by lifting him from the earth and squeezing him to death.

Antenor. A Trojan in Homer's ILIAD. It was he who advised that Helen return to Menelaus. He appears also in Chaucer's *Troilus and Criseyde* and in Shakespeare's *Troilus and Cressida.*

Anteros. In late Greek mythology, a son of Aphrodite and brother of Eros, the avenger of unreturned love. Or, according to some authorities, the opponent of Eros.

Anthony, St. First Christian monastic. He lived in the third or fourth century and founded a fraternity of ascetics who lived in the deserts of Egypt. The story of his temptations by the devil is a well-known subject of literature and art. It is the basis of Flaubert's novel, *La Tentation de Saint Antoine.*

Anthony, Susan Brownell (1820–1906). American reformer and teacher. She organized the Woman's State Temperance Society of New York, and was president of the National American Woman Suffrage Association (1892–1900). A firm abolitionist, she was among the first, after the Civil War, to support Negro suffrage. She conducted many lecture tours,

and tested the suffrage law in the case of *United States vs. Susan B. Anthony.*

Anthony Adverse (1933). A historical novel by Hervey ALLEN. An enormous popular success, the book is set in the Napoleonic era and takes its hero all over the world in a series of rousing adventures. The enthusiastic response of readers to the book's great length surprised the publishing world and caused a trend, influencing numerous other works.

Anthony of Padua, St. (1195–1231). Franciscan friar, preacher, and theologian. He was born in Portugal, but spent his life teaching theology in France and Italy; he died in Padua, Italy. There is a legend that St. Anthony preached to a school of fishes that listened attentively until he was finished.

Antic Hay (1923). A satirical novel by Aldous HUXLEY. Comical and bitter, it is about a group of London intellectuals and their long, learned, futile conversations, in which everything seems valueless— God, love, art, learning, social reform, science. The central character is timid Theodore Gumbril, Junior, who gives up his job as a teacher to try to sell a new kind of trousers with built-in air cushion seats. He purchases a thick beard to help him act the part of a confident, aggressive man in business and in love. As in *Crome Yellow,* the general atmosphere of despair is deepened when the hero loses his girl.

Antichrist. Biblical term, occurring in the Epistles of John (I John 2:18), which refers to a "man of sin" (II Thess. 2:3) who denies the Father and Son and disowns the incarnation and messianic role of Jesus. Many legends are connected with the Antichrist, or deceiver, whose presence was supposed to precede the Second Coming of Christ and betoken the end of the world. Such stories are founded chiefly in II Thess. 2:1–12 and Rev. 8. The blasphemous beast with 7 heads and 10 horns, associated with the mystic numer 666, is identified with the Antichrist (Rev. 13–14). The early Christians associated the Antichrist with Caligula and Nero; Muhammad was also called Antichrist; and the name has since been applied figuratively to Hitler, Stalin, and other disturbers of world peace.

Antietam. A creek near Sharpsburg, Md., and the site of one of the bloodiest battles (Sept. 17, 1862) of the U.S. Civil War. Although the battle was a draw, the Union claimed victory because General Lee withdrew the Confederate troops to Virginia. General McClellan, the Union commander, was severely criticized for failing to pursue Lee and was soon replaced. See EMANCIPATION PROCLAMATION.

Antigone. In Greek mythology, the elder daughter of Oedipus. She is the heroine of Sophocles' tragedy ANTIGONE, and a principal character in his *Oedipus at Colonus* and Euripides' PHOENICIAN WOMEN. She appears briefly in the interpolated ending of Aeschylus' SEVEN AGAINST THEBES.

Antigone. One of the earliest extant tragedies of SOPHOCLES. After the defeat of the expedition of the SEVEN AGAINST THEBES, Creon, now king, decrees that the body of Polyneices shall lie unburied, in defiance of the rites due the dead. Antigone, OEDIPUS' daughter, gives her brother a token burial and, though she is affianced to his son Haemon, Creon condemns her to burial alive. Warned by TIRESIAS, he regrets his act too late; Antigone and Haemon kill themselves and Creon's wife Eurydice does the same on hearing the news.

Antigone (1942). A play by Jean ANOUILH first produced despite censorship as an allegory of France under the Vichy government.

Antigonus. A Sicilian lord and the beleaguered husband of the bold and strong-minded Paulina, in Shakespeare's WINTER'S TALE. When, at the command of King Leontes, he attempts to abandon the king's infant daughter in a deserted place, he is eaten by a bear.

Antilochus (Antilochos). In Greek legend, the son of Nestor and friend of Achilles. He was chosen to break to Achilles the news of Patroclus' death. Antilochus was killed by Memnon, the son of Aurora and Tithonus. The three friends, Antilochus, Achilles, and Patroclus were buried in the same mound. Odysseus saw them walking together in the underworld.

Antin, Mary. See PROMISED LAND, THE.

Antiochus. In Pierre Corneille's tragedy RODOGUNE, the stepson of the wicked queen Cleopatra and the betrothed of Rodogune.

Antiope. (1) See AMPHION.

Antiope. (2) A queen of the AMAZONS. See THESEUS.

Antipholus of Ephesus and **Antipholus of Syracuse.** In Shakespeare's COMEDY OF ERRORS, the lost twin sons of Aegeon and Aemilia. Antipholus of Ephesus is the husband of Adriana. Antipholus of Syracuse comes to Ephesus in search of his lost brother and becomes enamored of Adriana's sister, Luciana.

Antiphon (c. 479–410 B.C.) A Greek Sophist and rhetorician. Against PROTAGORAS and the early Sophists, who believed in the supremacy of conventional law, he argued that men were by nature seekers after life, comfort, and unlimited pleasure, and that all law and restraint were consequently opposed to nature, which was for him the standard of right. He advised men to evade the law whenever possible; to obey it when expedient. Other Sophists developed the doctrine that might makes right from his work.

antipope. See POPE.

Antiquary, The (1816). A novel by Sir Walter SCOTT, and his own favorite among his works. It deals with the love of William Lovel for the daughter of Sir Arthur Wardour in the time of George III. See Jonathan OLDBUCK and Edie OCHILTREE.

Antisthenes. See CYNICS.

Antoine, André (1858–1943). French actor and theater director. Antoine is known for his directorship of the *Théâtre Libre* (1887–1894). A passionate love for the theater accompanied his desire to see more freedom and more possibility for experimentation on the French stage. Avant-garde in its bold unconventionality, the *Théâtre Libre* produced principally the plays of the naturalists, although it also played the works of contemporary Scandinavian, Russian, and German dramatists. Financial failure did not discourage Antoine, who opened another theater, the *Théâtre Antoine,* in 1897. He had already done much to revolutionize French theater, to encourage naturalness and to dispense with artificial stage conventions.

Antoinette, Marie. See MARIE ANTOINETTE.

Antonello da Messina (c. 1430–1479). Italian painter. After his early years at Messina, Sicily, he went to Naples; there he encountered the Flemish style of painting, particularly the use of oils, in such works as those of Jan van Eyck. In the years following 1475, both in Venice and other Italian cities, he became the chief sponsor of the new technique. His works, which favor the miniature still life, are noted for their handling of light and mastery of perspective. Among those considered his masterpieces are *Saint Jerome in his study* and the *Virgin Annunciate*.

Antonio. (1) The title character of Shakespeare's MERCHANT OF VENICE.

(2) The treacherous brother of Prospero in Shakespeare's THE TEMPEST. With the help of Alonso, the king of Naples, he has usurped Prospero's dukedom and cast him and his infant daughter adrift on a rotting bark. He is never troubled by conscience, but is, at last, forced to restore his brother's rightful position to him.

Antony, Mark or Marc. In Latin, Marcus Antonius (c. 82–30 B.C.). Roman triumvir and general. He was one of the tribunes who, in 49 B.C., supported Caesar and joined him before crossing the RUBICON. He was appointed consul in 44 and, after Caesar's death, swung the populace against the assassins to his favor with his eloquent oratory. It was at this time that CICERO delivered his famous Philippics (orations) against Antony. In 43, the Second TRIUMVIRATE of Antony, Octavian (later Augustus), and Lepidus was formed. Caesar's assassins, Brutus and Cassius, were defeated at Philippi in 42. From the year 40 on, Antony lived chiefly at Alexandria with CLEOPATRA, queen of Egypt, abandoning his wife Octavia, sister of Octavian. Open hostilities between Octavian and Antony broke out, and, in 31, the combined forces of Antony and Cleopatra were defeated by Octavian at ACTIUM. Antony committed suicide in Egypt after hearing a false report of Cleopatra's death (circulated, some say, by Cleopatra herself in an attempt to win Octavian's favor by causing Antony's death).

In Shakespeare's JULIUS CAESAR, he is portrayed as a devoted friend of Caesar. Though he is fond of revelry and amusements, he is also a shrewd strategist and capable general. After Caesar's death, he skillfully turns public opinion against the assassins by means of his funeral oration, which begins with the famous lines:

> Friends, Romans, countrymen, lend me your ears;
> I come to bury Caesar, not to praise him.
> The evil that men do lives after them,
> The good is oft interred with their bones;
> So let it be with Caesar.

Antony is depicted in Shakespeare's ANTONY AND CLEOPATRA as a declining hero, torn between his love for Cleopatra and his political ambitions. After his death, Agrippa utters a fitting epitaph:

> A rarer spirit never
> Did steer humanity; but you, gods, will give us
> Some faults to make us men.

Antony and Cleopatra (c. 1607). A tragedy by William SHAKESPEARE. Having given himself over to a life of sensual pleasure with CLEOPATRA in Egypt, Marc ANTONY returns to Rome upon hearing of his wife's death and of an attack on Italy by the forces of Sextus Pompeius. In Rome the differences between Antony and the two other triumvirs, Octavius CAESAR and Lepidus, are patched up by Antony's marriage to OCTAVIA, the sister of Octavius. When Antony, succumbing to Cleopatra's enticements, returns to Egypt, Octavius seizes upon the insult to his sister as a pretext for attacking his erstwhile ally. Octavius wins the naval battle of Actium when Cleopatra's fleet deserts. Antony, after unsuccessfully seeking to make terms with the victor, hurls defiance at him. Defeated in a later land battle and believing Cleopatra dead, the despairing Antony falls on his sword. Hearing that she is still alive, he is taken to her and lives long enough to lay his last kiss upon her lips. When Cleopatra learns that Octavius, now sole master of the empire, plans to lead her in triumph through Rome, the proud and imperious queen applies an asp to her bosom and joins her lover in death.

Shakespeare's source for the play was Sir Thomas North's translation (1579) of Plutarch's *Lives*. Dryden's drama *All for Love* (1678) also describes the last days of Antony and Cleopatra, and for many years was more frequently performed than the Shakespearean version. See Domitius ENOBARBUS.

Anu. The Babylonian god of heaven. A development of the Sumerian god AN, he was descended from Tiamat, the sea; his own parents were Anshar and Kishar. He was deposed and emasculated by KUMARBI, but replaced on his throne by his son Ea, the god of water and wisdom, who became far more important in the Babylonian pantheon than Anu himself.

Anubis. In Egyptian mythology, a deity who presided over funeral rites and insured the accuracy of the scales weighing the souls of the dead. He was the son of Osiris, the judge of the infernal regions, and was represented as a man with a jackal's head.

Anunnaki. The Sumerian deities of the underworld. Originally followers of the god of heaven, ANU, they somehow became gods of the underworld where they were inferior to its queen, ERESHKIGAL. Their demotion may have been punishment for some crime, or merely the result of Anu's displacement as principal god of the pantheon by Enlil.

Anville, Evelina. See EVELINA, OR THE HISTORY OF A YOUNG LADY'S ENTRANCE INTO THE WORLD.

Anzengruber, Ludwig (1839–1889). Austrian dramatist. He is best known for his dialect plays depicting rustic life, such as *Der Meineidbauer* (*The Farmer Forsworn*, 1872) and *Der Doppelselbstmord* (*The Double Suicide*, 1876). Because of his use of dialect and his treatment, especially in *Das vierte Gebot* (*The Fourth Commandment*, 1877), of family problems, he was important in the genesis of dramatic NATURALISM.

Aonian. Pertaining to Aonia, the region of Mts. Helicon and Cithaeron, in Boeotia. The Muses were supposed to live there. The Aonian fount was the fountain of Aganippe at the foot of Mt. Helicon.

Apache. The name of a nomadic and predatory tribe of North American Indians of Athapascan linguistic stock. They occupied what is now the southwestern U.S. The name is often applied to the hooligans of Paris; an *apache* dance is a violently acrobatic exhibition supposedly danced by a Parisian apache and his partner.

Apemantus. The churlish, cynical philosopher in Shakespeare's TIMON OF ATHENS. He foresees Timon's ruin and chides him for his pride, as great in ruin as it was in wealth. His hatred of mankind is paralleled and later surpassed by Timon's misanthropy.

Apes of God, The (1930). A novel by Wyndham LEWIS. It is an epic satire on the rich Bohemian artistic coteries which in Lewis's eyes reflected the social decay of the period. Among writers satirized are the Sitwell family, Gertrude Stein, James Joyce, and Virginia Woolf and the Bloomsbury group.

Aphrodite. The Greek goddess of erotic love and marriage. Although Homer calls her a daughter of Zeus and Dione, it was the more common story that she was born from the foam that gathered about the severed parts of the emasculated Uranus. She is said to have first stepped ashore on the island of Cythera, just off the coast of Laconia, hence her epithet Cytherea. Her name was identified by the Greeks with the word *aphros,* seafoam. As an Olympian deity, she was the wife of Hephaestus, but the lover of Ares. A familiar story about her tells how Hephaestus trapped her in bed with Ares by throwing a delicate golden net over them, and displayed their embarrassment to the other gods. In late Greek myth, Aphrodite was called the mother of EROS.

It is generally agreed that Aphrodite was originally an Asiatic goddess similar to ISHTAR. An ancient center of her worship was the island of Cyprus for which she was often called Cypris. In Rome, she was identified with Venus. See ADONIS.

Apicius, Marcus Flavius (fl., A.D. 14–37). A Roman epicure in the time of Tiberius. He wrote a book on the ways of tempting an appetite. Having spent a fortune in supplying rare delicacies for his table, and having only 10 million sesterces (about $400,000) left, he hanged himself, not thinking it possible to exist on such a wretched pittance. *Apicia* has become a stock name for certain cakes and sauces, and his own name is still proverbial in all matters of gastronomy.

Apis. In Egyptian mythology, the bull of Memphis, sacred to Osiris, of whose soul it was supposed to be the image; others said it was the union of divine and animal souls. The sacred bull had to have natural spots forming a triangle on the forehead and a half-moon on the breast. It was allowed to live only 25 years, when it was sacrificed and buried with great pomp.

apocalyptic literature (Gr., *apokalupsis,* "uncovering"). A type of prophetic literature common in ancient Hebrew and early Christian writing. It is filled with veiled symbolism (see FOUR HORSEMEN OF THE APOCALYPSE) and inspired by visions of the future triumph of the Messianic kingdom. THE REVELATION OF ST. JOHN THE DIVINE is often called the *Apocalypse.*

Apocrypha (Gr., *apokrupto,* "hidden"). Certain Old Testament books of doubtful authority. These books are included in the Greek (Septuagint) and Latin (Vulgate) versions of the Old Testament, but are usually regarded as noncanonical or of secondary value by other Christians and Jews. They are seldom printed in Protestant Bibles, but in the Authorized Version of 1611 they are given immediately after the Old Testament. The New Testament also has a large number of apocryphal books associated with it, consisting of later gospels, epistles, apocalypses and such fragments as the *Logia*. ORIGEN was the first to apply the term to books used by the church, to designate writings of a questionable character; it has come to signify false and heretical literature.

Apollinaire, Guillaume [born **Wilhelm Apollinaris de Kostrowitski**] (1880–1918). French poet and critic. In 1898, he met Alfred JARRY in Paris and was attracted to *l'esprit nouveau*, the new spirit in esthetic theory. A friend of Picasso, Braque, and other avant-garde artists, he wrote *Antitradition futuriste* and *The Cubist Painters* in 1913. The latter work first established CUBISM as a school of painting. The poems in *Alcools* (1913) combined free and classical verse forms; those in *Calligrammes* (1918) used words to draw lines, the controversial typography carrying poetry to its extreme limits. He called *Les Mamelles de Tirésias* (1903, pub. 1917) a "drame surréaliste," apparently the source of the name of the surrealist movement. It was made into an opera (1947) by Francis Poulenc, Apollinaire's other works include fiction: *L'Hérésiarque et Cie* (1910) and *The Poet Assassinated* (1916); the verse play *Couleur du Temps* (1918); and the posthumously published *Ombre de mon amour* (1948), poems, and *Tendre comme le souvenir* (1952), letters.

Apollo (Apollon). A Greek god, son of Zeus and Leto. Originally, perhaps, a god of flocks, he also became a god of healing, music, and archery. As Phoebus Apollo, he came to be the god of light, but not properly of the sun. He was born, with his sister Artemis, on the island of Delos, where his mother had taken refuge from the jealous Hera. At an early age, he killed the Python, the sacred snake of the DELPHIC ORACLE, and took charge of that oracle, which had previously belonged to a succession of earth godesses. Though implacable in anger, as the fates of MARSYAS and NIOBE show, he was surprisingly unsuccessful in love, to judge from the number of nymphs and mortals, such as DAPHNE and MARPESSA, who rejected his advances. Nevertheless, he has been called "the most Greek of Greek gods," speaking more than once for modern concepts of justice and human relations as opposed to the more primitive traditions. The most notable example of this tendency is his defense of Orestes on the Areopagus, dramatized in Aeschylus' *Eumenides*.

Apollodorus (Apollodoros). A Greek mythographer. Nothing is known of him, but his one extant work (if it is his), *The Library* (*Bibliotheke*), is one of the most important sources of Greek mythology. Though it draws on the works of APOLLONIUS OF RHODES and the Athenian dramatists, it was largely based on a lost book by Pherecydes of Leros, dating from the early fifth century B.C.

Apollonian and Dionysiac. Terms used by Friedrich Nietzsche in THE BIRTH OF TRAGEDY to designate the two central principles in Greek culture. The Apollonian, which corresponds to Schopenhauer's *principium individuationis* ("principle of individuation"), is the basis of all analytic distinctions. Everything that is part of the unique individuality of a man or thing is Apollonian in character; all types of *form* or *structure* are Apollonian, since form serves to define or individualize that which is formed; thus, sculpture is the most Apollonian of the arts, since it relies entirely on form for its effect. Rational thought is also Apollonian since it is structured and makes distinctions.

The Dionysiac, which corresponds roughly to Schopenhauer's conception of "will," is directly opposed to the Apollonian. Drunkenness and madness are Dionysiac because they break down a man's individual character; all forms of enthusiasm and ecstasy are Dionysiac, for in such states a man gives up his individuality and submerges himself in a greater whole; music is the most Dionysiac of the arts, since it appeals directly to man's instinctive, chaotic emotions and not to his formally reasoning mind.

Nietzsche believed that both forces were present in Greek tragedy, and that true tragedy could only be produced by the tension between them. He used the names Apollonian and Dionysiac for the two forces because Apollo, as the sun-god, represents light, clarity, and form, whereas Dionysus, as the wine-god, represents drunkenness and ecstasy.

Apollonius of Rhodes (Apollonios Rhodios). An Alexandrian poet of the 3d-2d centuries B.C. According to tradition, he was a pupil of Callimachus, but quarreled with him and, when his youthful work the *Argonautica* proved unpopular, went to Rhodes. He later abridged this epic of the voyage of the ARGONAUTS; it won favor and he was appointed head of the Alexandrian Library.

Apollonius of Tyana or **Apollonios Tyanaios** (fl. A.D. 50). Greek Neo-Pythagorean philosopher. He studied in the temple of Asclepius at Aegae. An ascetic, he traveled through India, Babylonia, and Persia, absorbing mysticism. He had a school at Ephesus, and was credited with magical powers. Philostratus wrote a biography of Apollonius, recording his miraculous feats; the work is regarded as religious fiction.

Apologia pro vita sua, or a History of My Religious Opinions (1864). An autobiographical treatise by John Henry NEWMAN. In it the author outlines and defends the intellectual development that led to his conversion from the Anglican to the Roman Catholic Church. One of the most famous of English autobiographies, it is noted for its candor and intellectual passion, its subtle and musical prose style.

Apologie for Poetrie, An. An essay by Sir Philip SIDNEY, written during 1580–1583 in answer to an attack on poetry by the Puritan Stephen Gosson in THE SCHOOL OF ABUSE (1579). Sidney's essay defines as poetry all imaginative writing. In addition to defending its worth and replying to Puritan accusations against it, Sidney gives his own critical appraisal of the poetry and drama of the time. Two different editions of the essay, one titled *An Apologie for Poetrie*, the other *The Defense of Poesie*, were posthumously published in 1595.

Apology for Raymond Sebond (Apologie de Raimond Sebond). The longest of the ESSAYS of Michel de MONTAIGNE. It gives fullest expression to his skeptical philosophy. Montaigne's "defense" of the treatise of Sebond, a 15th-century Spaniard who attempted to demonstrate the existence of God by analogy with the hierarchy of nature in which man occupies the highest rung, was a pretense for demolishing the validity of reasoning altogether. Sebond's proof, asserted Montaigne, was no less credible than any other proof. Man vainly believes himself superior to the rest of creation by virtue of his reason, whereas in fact all his theorizing has not uncovered a single universal truth. Montaigne's skepticism was an affirmation of the relativity of knowledge and essentially a healthy reaction to the excessive faith in reason of the early Renaissance. It cleared his mind of preconceptions and prepared him for a search for wisdom based, not on intellectual speculation, but on his own experience.

Apology for the Life of Mrs. Shamela Andrews, An (1741). A novel by Henry FIELDING satirizing Samuel Richardson's PAMELA. Shamela is presented as a designing woman who deliberately tricks her master into marrying her.

Apolonio, Libro de. A Spanish heroic poem of the first half of the 13th century by an anonymous author, probably an Aragonese. Consisting of 2624 verses, it one of the oldest examples of CUADERNA VÍA. The story, based on a Greek legend, deals with Apollonius, prince of Tyre, who is separated from his wife, Luciana, and their daughter, Tarsia; after many adventures they are finally reunited. Other authors have utilized this theme, notably Shakespeare in *Pericles.*

Apophis. In Egyptian mythology, the power of darkness in the form of a serpent against whom the sun god Ra waged daily war.

aposiopesis. Deliberate failure to complete a sentence for rhetorical effect. As a figure of speech the form is often used to convey an impression of extreme exasperation or to imply a threat, as, for example, in "If you do that, why, I'll—" The rest of the sentence is understood.

apostles (Gr., *apostolos,* messenger, envoy). Jesus' 12 original disciples: PETER, ANDREW, JAMES THE LESS, JOHN, PHILIP, BARTHOLOMEW, THOMAS, MATTHEW, SIMON THE CANAANITE (also Simon Zelotes), JUDE (also Thaddaeus and Lebbaeus), JAMES THE GREATER, and JUDAS ISCARIOT. Jesus gave His message to these men personally and gave them the task of being his witness after His death. He shared with them the LAST SUPPER, which has become the fundamental sacrament of Christian worship.

To the apostles, Jesus entrusted the work of establishing the Church, with Peter to be the "rock" upon which it was built. Matthias was later chosen to take Judas Iscariot's place. All of the apostles met martyr's deaths except John and, of course, Judas Iscariot who committed suicide.

Beside Judas Iscariot, two other apostles have not been canonized: Philip and Simon the Canaanite. Paul, though not one of the original 12, is always classed as an apostle as is often Barnabas, Paul's companion in his first mission.

Apostolic Fathers. Christian authors born in the 1st century, when the apostles lived. John is supposed to have died about A.D. 99; Polycarp, the last of the Apostolic Fathers, born about 69, was his disciple. The *Five Apostolic Fathers* most referred to are Clement of Rome, Barnabas, Hermas, Ignatius, and Polycarp.

apostolic succession. A theological doctrine first enunciated by Irenaeus (fl. 190). It maintains that the bishops of the church are direct spiritual descendants of the apostles and of the bishops consecrated by them, and that authority over the church's faith and discipline resides in them.

Apostolius, Michael (1422–1480). Greek scholar in Italy during the Renaissance. He defended Plato against the Greek Aristotelians.

apostrophe. A figure of speech using the direct address of a person or thing, usually absent, for rhetorical effect. The thing addressed is often personified, as in "Hence, loathed Melancholy!" which begins Milton's *L'Allegro.* The object of the apostrophe is frequently a real person, living or dead, as in "Milton, thou shouldst be living at this hour," the beginning of Wordsworth's sonnet on Milton.

Appian Way (Lat., *Via Appia*). The oldest and best preserved of all the Roman roads, it leads from Rome to Brundisium (Brindisi) by way of Capua. This "queen of roads" was commenced by Appius Claudius, the censor, in 312 B.C.

Appius Claudius. Roman decemvir (451–450 B.C.). He was one of 10 decemvirs appointed to draw up a code of Roman law. According to tradition, his passion for the beautiful plebian VIRGINIA caused an uprising, led by her father, which overthrew the decemvirate and established a tribunate.

apple of discord. In Greek mythology, the initial cause of the Trojan War. All the gods and goddesses except Eris (Discord) were invited to the wedding of Thetis and Peleus. In revenge, Eris threw among the guests a golden apple inscribed "For the fairest." Hera, Athene, and Aphrodite claimed it and were referred to Paris, the handsomest man in the world, for judgment. See the JUDGMENT OF PARIS.

Appleseed, Johnny. Nickname of **John Chapman** (1774–1845). American orchardist and folk hero. Born in Massachusetts, Chapman wandered westward to Pennsylvania, Ohio, Illinois, and Indiana. For 50 years he led a nomadic existence, preaching and distributing apple seeds to all he met. It is said that the orchards of the four states above owe their origin to Chapman's seeds.

Johnny Appleseed has become a favorite American folk hero, celebrated in many stories and poems. The poet Vachel Lindsay, who frequently referred to him, wrote a long poem called *In Praise of Johnny Appleseed* (1923).

apples of perpetual youth. In Scandinavian mythology, magical golden apples. They were in the keeping of Idhunn, daughter of the dwarf Svald and wife of Bragi. It is by tasting them that the gods preserve their youth.

apples of Sodom. Fruit which, in classical tradition, grew beside the Dead Sea. They are lovely in appearance, but full of ashes within. Josephus, Strabo, Tacitus, and others speak of them, probably referring to the gall-nuts produced by the insect *Cynips insana.*

Après-midi d'un faune, L' (The Afternoon of a Faun, 1876). A poem by Stephane MALLARMÉ. It presents the wandering thoughts of a faun on a drowsy summer afternoon. The poem inspired Debussy's *Prélude à l'Après-midi d'un faune* (1894), which was choreographed and danced by Nijinsky for Diaghilev's Russian Ballet in 1912.

Apsu. See ABZU.

Apsyrtus (Apsyrtos). See the ARGONAUTS

Apuleius, Lucius (fl., c. A.D. 155). Latin writer. He is best known today for his prose romance *Metamorphoses,* or THE GOLDEN ASS, the only Latin novel that survives in its entirety. Apuleius was born in North Africa. After studying in Carthage and Athens, he spent a number of years traveling and delving into the magic lore of the Mediterranean countries. He incorporated his vast knowledge and experience into the 11-volume *The Golden Ass.* Here, in a prose style as odd and fanciful as the tale itself, he narrates the story of a man who, transformed into a donkey, wanders from land to land observing the preposterous and brutal foibles of mankind. In one of the episodes, Apuleius recounts the famous story of Cupid and PSYCHE.

Aqhat. Hero of the Canaanite THE POEM OF AQHAT. The young son of the chieftain Danel, he is given a divine bow belonging to Anat. She kills him and he is eaten by eagles, but avenged by his sister Paghat. It is probable that in the lost final section of the poem, Aqhat revived.

Aquilante. In the Orlando poems of Boiardo and Ariosto he is the son of Oliviero and brother of Grifone (see ORLANDO FURIOSO). He is called *il nero* (the black) and his brother *il bianco* (the white) because each is protected by an enchantress of that color. The black enchantress had saved him from an eagle (hence his name) which had stolen him from his mother Ghismonda.

Aquinas, St. **Thomas** (c. 1225–1274). Italian scholastic theologian and philosopher, often called the Angelic Doctor (Lat., *Doctor Angelicus*). He came from a noble family, who strongly objected when he joined the Dominican Order in 1243 and forcibly detained him for over a year. He finally reached Paris and began his studies under ALBERTUS MAGNUS, whom he followed to Cologne in 1248. He began teaching at Paris in 1252, and thereafter taught alternately in Paris and in Italy. In 1254 he began his commentaries on the *Sentences* of Peter LOMBARD, on Boethius, and on the Bible, revealing Albertus Magnus and St. AUGUSTINE of Hippo as the greatest influences on his thought.

The treatises that followed were later incorporated into his two great *Summae,* or summaries of human knowledge. The *Summa [de Veritate Catholicae Fidei] contra Gentiles* (1259–1264) defends "the truth of the Catholic faith against the pagans" by making clear the distinction between the realms of reason and of faith: reason seeks knowledge from experimental and logical evidence, while faith seeks understanding through revelation, but uses the knowledge provided by reason. Thus they can never be in conflict, and both come from and reveal God as the source of all truth. The SUMMA THEOLOGICA, his greatest work, continues on this basis to summarize all that is known about God and man from the sources of both reason and faith.

Aquinas' followers were called *Thomists* in later scholastic disputes, especially with the Scotists (see John DUNS SCOTUS). His synthesis of theology and philosophy, known as Thomism, has since been officially recognized as a cornerstone in the doctrines of the Roman Catholic Church.

Arabian Nights' Entertainments, The, or **A Thousand and One Nights.** A collection of ancient Persian-Indian-Arabian tales, originally in Arabic, arranged in its present form about 1450, probably in Cairo. Although the stories are discrete in plot, they are unified by SCHEHERAZADE, the supposed teller; she postpones her execution by telling her husband, SCHAHRIAH, a story night after night, without revealing the climax until the following session.

The first European translation, into French, was Antoine Galland's 12-volume (1704–1717) free rendering of the oldest known manuscript of 1548. In 1840, E. W. Lane published a new scholarly English translation (three vols.); John Payne's translation appeared in nine volumes, 1882–1884; and Sir Richard Burton's monumental (10-vol.) English version was issued only to subscribers by the Kamashastra Society of Benares in 1885–1886. Among the more recent editions is a four-volume edition by Powys Mathers, completed in 1937. See ABOU HASSAN; ALADDIN; ALI BABA AND THE FORTY THIEVES; CALENDER; CARPET, MAGIC; HAROUN-AL-RASCHID; SINBAD THE SAILOR; Sidi NOUMAN.

Arachne. In Greek mythology, Arachne was a Lydian maiden. She challenged Athena to compete with her in needle tapestry. Athena metamorphosed her into a spider out of jealousy. *Arachnida* is the scientific name for spiders, scorpions, and mites.

Araf or **Al Araf.** In the Koran, the Islamic equivalent of purgatory, between heaven and hell. It is a place both for those neither morally good nor bad, and for those who, because their good and evil deeds were about equally balanced, must await their ultimate admission to heaven.

Edgar Allan Poe has a poem called AL AARAAF.

Arafat, Mount. A hill southeast of Mecca where, according to Muslim tradition, Adam met Eve after a punitive separation of 200 years during which time he was a wanderer on the face of the earth. He was conducted to its summit by the angel Gabriel.

Aragon, house of. A noble family of Spanish origin. Its members ruled in Sicily and later in southern Italy from the 13th through the 15th century. At Naples, the outstanding King Alfonso of Aragon (1385–1458), surnamed the Great, who ruled from 1443, was a celebrated patron of Humanists and poets. Under his inspiration, the men of letters gathered at his court founded the Neapolitan Academy, which included such men as Pontano and Sannazaro.

Aragon, Louis (1897–   ). French novelist, poet, and essayist. After brief associations with Cubism and DADAISM, Aragon wrote the novel *Le Paysan de Paris* (1926) as a participant in SURREALISM. He criticized the ideal of "pure poetry" in *Traité du style* (1928), however, and became a Communist in 1930, thereafter to devote his art to the ideal of social revolution. He was prosecuted for his poem *The Red Front* (1931), but responded with more poetry: *Persécuteur persécuté* (1931) and *Hourra l'Oural* (1934), and with leftist magazines. Social novels depicting "the real world," as the series is collectively titled include: *The Bells of Basel* (*Cloches de Bâle,* 1936) and *Passengers of Destiny* (*Les Voyageurs de l'impériale,* 1941; also trans. *The Century Was Young*). *Aurelien* (1944) and *Les Communistes* (1949) are autobiographical. Aragon abandoned current politics, however, in *Holy Week* (*La Semaine Sainte,* 1958), a panoramic epic of the flight of Louis XVIII at the beginning of Napoleon's 100 days in 1815.

His books of poetry include *Le Crève-Coeur* (1941), *Les Yeux d'Elsa* (1942), *Brocéliande* (1943), and *Le Nouveau Crève-Coeur* (1948). Many of these describe his participation in the Resistance and his love for his Russian-born wife **Elsa Triolet** (1896–1970), author of the novels *The White Charger* (1943) and *Fine of 200 Francs* (1945), as well as novels dealing with postwar social problems.

Aramis. One of the famous trio in Dumas' THE THREE MUSKETEERS, and a prominent character in its sequels TWENTY YEARS AFTER and THE VISCOUNT of BRAGELONNE. Aramis, always soberly garbed in black, regularly swore that he would soon forego his adventures for a pious life in a monastery.

Aranha, José Pereira de Graça. See José Pereira de GRAÇA ARANHA.

Ararat, Mount. See NOAH.

Araucana, La (1569–1590). An epic poem by Alfonso de Ercilla y Zúñiga (1533–1594), Spanish soldier and poet who went to Chile after the conquest and fought against the indomitable Araucanian Indians. The stubborn resistance of the Araucanians against Spanish rule is the theme of the poem. Ercilla stresses the nobility and valor of the Indians and of their leaders Lautaro and Caupolicán, who are drawn in Homeric proportions.

Arbante. In a tale from Ariosto's ORLANDO FURIOSO he is the son of King Cimosco of Frisia, the spouse of Olimpia, and the victim of the latter's unwillingness to marry him. Olimpia has him killed before they wed.

Arbaud, Joseph d' (1874–   ). Provençal poet and novelist. Recorder of the old language and traditions of the Provence region, Arbaud presented in *The Laurel of Arles* (*Lou Lausié d'Arle;* 1913) his philosophy that a tree—or a culture—must have deep roots to grow high. His works include poems: *Songs of the Marshes* (*Li Cant palustre;* 1919), *The Brazen Boughs* (*Li Rampau d'aram;* 1920), and *Vision of the North* (*La Visioun de l'Uba;* 1921). Among his novels are *The Beast of the Vaccares* (*Lu Bèstiò dòu Vacarés;* 1924), *The Gypsy* (*La Caraco;* 1926). *Wild Animals* (*La Souvagino;* 1929) is a story collection.

Arber, Edward (1836–1912). English scholar. He was the editor of *Arber's English Reprints* (1868–1880) and other series of cheap, accurate editions of 15th-18th century works. He also edited *Transcript of the Registers of the Company of Stationers of London, 1554–1640* (1875–1894) and *Term Catalogues, 1668–1709* (1903–1906), basic sources for research in English literature and publishing.

Arbor of Amorous Devices, The. An anthology of Elizabethan lyric poetry. Published in 1597, it was one of many such published in England after the success of TOTTEL'S MISCELLANY. It was attributed by the printers to NICHOLAS BRETON, but it contains the work of other poets as well.

Arbuthnot, John (1667–1735). Scottish writer and court physician to Queen Anne. He was a close friend of Alexander Pope and Jonathan Swift and formed with them the SCRIBLERUS CLUB. His works include *The History of* JOHN BULL, which typified and fixed John Bull as the personification of England; *The Art of Political Lying* (1712), an essay; *Know Thyself* (1734), a philosophic poem; and *The Memoirs of* MARTINUS SCRIBLERUS (1741), an attack

THE ARBOR OF amorous Deuises.

VVherin, young Gentlemen

may reade many plesant fancies, and fine deuises: And thereon, meditate diuers sweete Conceites, to court the loue of faire Ladies and Gentlewomen
By N. B, Gent.

Imprinted at London by Richard Iohnes, dwelling at the Signe of the Rose and Crowne, neere Saint Andrewes Church in Holborne,
1597.

THE HUNTINGTON LIBRARY

Title page of *The Arbor of Amorous Devices* (1597).

on pedantry. He is the addressee of Pope's EPISTLE TO DR. ARBUTHNOT.

Arcades ambo (Lat., "both Arcadians"). Two people with similar skills and tastes, such as CORYDON and THYRSIS in Vergil's *Seventh Bucolic,* who were "both in the flower of youth, both Arcadians and peers of pastoral song." When used ironically, the term implies that both are simpletons or scoundrels.

Arcadia (Arkadia). A district of the Greek Peloponnesus. According to Vergil, it was the home of pastoral simplicity and happiness. This notion was an early example of an illusion that has beset sophisticated intellectuals ever since: namely, that a simple, rustic life is not only idyllic, but somehow nobler than a more complex urban existence. The Arcadians were, as a matter of fact, the most backward of the Greeks, retaining to a relatively late date primitive, even savage customs that had long since died out elsewhere in Greece. Hence, to less poetically minded authors, the term Arcadian came to have a derogatory meaning.

The name Arcadia was taken by Sir Philip Sidney as the title of his famous pastoral romance (1590) and was soon generally adopted into English with much the old Virgilian significance. A 17th-century painting by Guercino, and a more famous one by Poussin of a slightly later date, show a shepherd's tomb on which is the inscription *Et in Arcadia ego* (Even in Arcadia am I), signifying presumably that death is present even in the most ideal earthly life.

Arcadian Academy (Accademia dell' Arcadia). An Italian literary academy founded at Rome (c. 1690) at the suggestion of Queen Christina of Sweden and headed by Giovanni Maria Crescimbeni, an historian of Italian poetry.

The academy's members proposed to counteract the fashionable mannerism of MARINISM by a return to the simple, unsophisticated pastoral motifs of the classical poets (hence the name Arcadia). Their program included the use of an unpretentious language, a close imitation of the classical poets, and a preference for short verse forms: the ode, sonnet, and canzonetta. Among its members were Carlo Frugoni (1692–1768), generally considered the most typical exponent of Arcadian ideals ("Frugoneria" describes his sonorous style); Paolo Rolli (1687–1765), lyric poet, librettist for Handel, and tutor at the English court; and METASTASIO.

The academy came under the special protection of the royal house of Sweden and was never formally disestablished. It still maintains a formal existence although its role as arbiter of Italian literary taste came to an end with romanticism. See LEO XIII.

archangel. A chief angel. In Judeo-Christian Scriptures and legend there are four: Michael, the warrior; Raphael, the healer; Gabriel, the herald; and Uriel, bringer of light. In the Koran, the four are Michael, the champion of the faith; Gabriel, the angel of revelations; Azrael, the angel of death; and Israfel, who sounds the trumpet of the resurrection. In the medieval hierarchy (see ANGEL) the archangels comprise the second order of the third division.

Archbishop of Granada. In Lesage's novel GIL BLAS DE SANTILLANE, a very rich, proud, and inflexible church dignitary. Gil Blas becomes his secretary and favorite. When he dares to criticize the archbishop's oratorical excellence, he is dismissed.

Archer, Isabel. The heroine of Henry James' THE PORTRAIT OF A LADY. A girl of great vitality, Isabel has an insatiable thirst for experience which causes her to reject the proposal of Lord Warburton, a wealthy and cultivated Englishman, and to marry the shadowy and sinister Osmond. At all times treated sympathetically by James, she comes to realize the danger of her American expansiveness. Nevertheless, she asserts her inner freedom by refusing to leave the man she married.

Archilochian bitterness. Ill-natured satire. It is so named from Archilochus, the Greek satirist (714–676 B.C.).

Archiloro. A Negro giant in an episode from the ORLANDO INNAMORATO of Boiardo. He is killed at the battle of Albracca by Agricane, the king of Tartary, who hopes to win the hand of Angelica, princess of Cathay.

Archimago. The enchanter in Books I and II of Spenser's FAERIE QUEENE, typifying hypocrisy and false religion.

Archimedes (c. 287–212 B.C.). Syracusan mathematician, astronomer, and inventor. Several of his treatises, including that on the sphere and the cylinder, are still extant. Archimedes discovered the principle of the displacement of water, which, by means of specific gravity, he used to test the amount of base metal in the crown of Hieron, ruler of Syracuse. He is said to have exclaimed "EUREKA," or "I have found it," when the principle occurred to him as he stepped into his bath.

Archipenko, Alexander Porfirievich (1887–1964). Russian sculptor. Settling in the U.S. in 1923, he experimented with plastic materials and with the effects of transparency and reflection, tending toward abstraction in his sculpture.

Archpoet. See GOLIARDIC VERSE.

archy and mehitabel. The famous cockroach and cat created by Don MARQUIS in his newspaper column. Their stories were written at night in Marquis' deserted office by literary archy, who was obliged to write without capitalization because he could not operate the shift key on the typewriter. Archy often related the ribald adventures of the indomitable mehitabel, whose motto was "toujours gai." *The lives and times of archy and mehitabel* (1940) contains the original collection of the columns, *archy and mehitabel* (1927), and its sequels, *archy's life of mehitabel* (1933) and *archy does his part* (1935).

Arcita. See TESEIDA.

Arcite. (1) See ANELIDA AND ARCITE.

(2) See KNIGHT'S TALE.

Arcos, René. See ABBAYE GROUP, THE.

Arcturus. See GREAT BEAR.

Arendt, Hannah (1906–   ). German writer on political philosophy. Now resident in the U.S., she was educated at the universities of Marburg and Freiburg, and received her doctorate at the University of Heidelberg. In this country, she has taught at a number of universities, including those of California, Chicago, Princeton, and Wesleyan. Her best-known book, *Eichmann in Jerusalem: A Report on the Banality of Evil* (1963), is a study of the implications of the famous, emotionally charged trial of a high-placed Nazi official; it created a storm of controversy upon publication and was debated for months in literary journals. Her other books include *The Origins of Totalitarianism* (1951), *The Human Condition* (1958), *Between Past and Future: Six Exercises in Political Thought* (1961), and *On Revolution* (1963). She has also contributed to numerous publications, such as the *Partisan Review, Commentary, Review of Politics,* and *Journal of Politics.*

From 1944 to 1946, Miss Arendt was research director for the Conference on Jewish Relations, and 1949–1952 director of Jewish Cultural Reconstruction.

Areopagitica (1644). A famous pamphlet by John MILTON, written as an argument against restriction of freedom of the press. Probably Milton's best-known prose work because of the greatness of its cause and the eloquence of its rhetoric, it commands more interest than most of his other theological or political writings.

Areopagus (Areiopagos). The hill of Ares, located in Athens, west of the Acropolis. According to Greek myth, it was so named because it was there that Ares was tried for the murder of Halirrhothios, son of Poseidon. According to another story, the hill was named after an epithet of Athene, who had cast the deciding vote in the second trial of Orestes, supposedly held on this hill.

The name was also applied to a council of former *archons,* who assembled there. Under DRACO, the council had the duty of judging murderers, and exercised general administrative powers. Ephialtes and PERICLES reduced the scope of its function.

Ares. The Greek god of war, a son of Zeus and Hera. He was a lover of APHRODITE, by whom he had several children, but he also had various other mistresses. Probably Thracian in origin, Ares had no characteristics except belligerence, and, therefore, was rather disapproved of by the Greeks.

Aretino, Pietro (1492–1556). Italian Renaissance author. Aretino is famous throughout Europe for the volume and audacity of his writings. A self-styled Scourge of Princes, he aimed his satire at the powerful men of his day, but primarily at its social customs and literary pretensions. He was honored by princes and popes, and a friend of artists such as Titian, who painted Aretino's portrait. Among his many works— letters, dialogues, poems, comedies and tragedies— are both lascivious sonnets and a book on Christ. His best-known work is the comedy *La cortigiana* (*Life at Court*), written in 1525.

Arévalo Martínez, Rafael (1884–   ). Guatemalan novelist and poet. Though little is known of it, Arévalo's life has been apparently as bizarre as some of his writing; he was reported dead in 1920, only to turn up as director of Guatemala's National Library. He is best known as the creator of the "psychozoological" story. The most famous of these is *El Hombre que Parecía un Caballo* (1915), a Kafka-esque tale whose protagonist, modeled on a Colombian poet, resembles a splendid race horse, not only physically but, also, in his lack of moral sense. His other words include *Las Rosas de Engaddi* (1927), a collection of verse, and *El Mundo de los Maharachías* (1938), which deals with a shipwrecked traveller who finds himself in the land of the Maharachías, monkey-like beings superior to men.

Argalia. The brother of ANGELICA, the princess of Cathay who comes to sow discord in Charlemagne's court in the Orlando poems of Boiardo and Ariosto. In Boiardo's poem he is killed, but his horse Rabicane remains in the plot of Ariosto's version.

Argan. The hypochondriacal central character in Molière's comedy LE MALADE IMAGINAIRE. He attempts to marry his daughter Angélique to a doctor, in order to avoid the expense of apothecary's bills. At the conclusion of the play he is made a mock doctor in a burlesque ceremony of investiture, conducted in macaronic Latin.

Argante (Argantes). One of the two leading warriors among the infidels opposing the Crusaders in Tasso's GERUSALEMME LIBERATA. His death at the hands of Tancredi precipitates the conquest of the holy city by Goffredo (Godfrey), the commander of the Christian armies.

Argillano. In the Tasso epic GERUSALEMME LIBERATA an Italian Crusader among the Christian forces assaulting Jerusalem. When rumor reaches Argillano that the champion Rinaldo of Este is dead, he leads a revolt against the authority of Goffredo, the Christian commander who had caused Rinaldo to leave them in anger. Later, to amend for his rebellion, he plunges vigorously into battle and finds a noble death at the hands of Solimano, the Turkish king. Rinaldo eventually avenges Argillano's memory with the slaying of Solimano.

Argo. The galley, built by Argus, that carried Jason and the ARGONAUTS in search of the Golden Fleece. It was reputed to have been the first seagoing vessel.

Argonautica. See APOLLONIUS OF RHODES; ARGONAUTS.

Argonauts. A group of mythological heroes. They sailed to Colchis to recover the GOLDEN FLEECE. Jason had demanded the throne of Iolcos from Pelias, who had usurped it from his brother Aeson, Jason's father. Pelias agreed, if Jason would first return the Fleece to Greece. Those who joined Jason in this adventure included Heracles, Orpheus, Castor and Polydeuces, Peleus, Melampus, Mopsus, Meleager, Atalanta, Admetus, the winged sons of Aeolus, Calais and Zetes, the lynx-eyed Lynceus and his quarrelsome brother Idas, Telamon, Pelias' own son Acastus, and many others. Argus built their ship, the *Argo,* under Athene's direction, and Hera aided them throughout the voyage so as to punish Pelias for refusing to worship her.

Their first stop was Lemnos, where the women, lonely after having killed their husbands a year before, vainly entreated them to stay. They were hospitably received by the Doliones, but killed their king Cyzicus by mistake. In Mysia, when Heracles' beautiful young favorite Hylas was drowned in a spring by a love-struck naiad, Heracles would not give up the search for Hylas and had to be left behind. The Argonauts were challenged to box by Amycus, king of the Bebryces, who had killed many strangers in this manner. Polydeuces accepted the challenge and quickly killed Amycus. At Salmydessus they saw blind old King Phineus whose days were made miserable by the Harpies; they stole or befouled his food before he could eat—a punishment for his having revealed too much, as a seer, of the ways of Zeus. Zetes and Calais saved him by pursuing the Harpies until Iris promised that they would not return. In gratitude, Phineus gave the Argonauts much useful advice.

With the help of this advice and of Athene, they passed through the Clashing Rocks, which usually sprang together to crush ships between them. Later, shouts and the clashing of shields drove off the birds of Ares, which attacked them with a hail of sharp plumes. By a happy chance they saved the four sons of Phrixus from shipwreck and were led by them to their home, Colchis, where King Aeetes kept the Fleece. The cruel Aeetes promised to relinquish the Fleece if Jason could pass a test: he must plow a field with two fire-breathing bulls, sow dragon's teeth, and fight the armed men who would spring up (see also SPARTI). Jason succeeded with the secret aid of Aeetes' daughter MEDEA, who had fallen in love with him. Aeetes refused to honor his promise, but Medea lulled to sleep the dragon that guarded the Fleece and escaped with the Argonauts.

They were pursued, but escaped again when Jason and Medea treacherously slew her half-brother Apsyrtus and (according to some versions) flung pieces of his body from the ship. Zeus ordained that the Argonauts suffer many hardships for this outrage before reaching home. Making their way via the Danube, Rhine, and Rhone to the Mediterranean, they reached the island of Aea, where Circe, Aeetes' sister, purified Jason and Medea of murder. Thetis helped them past the Wandering Rocks; the singing of Orpheus got them safely past the SIRENS. While they were entertained by the Phaeacians, Queen Arete secretly arranged the marriage of Jason and

Medea and King Alcinous protected the Argonauts from pursuing Colchians.

Blown to the coast of Africa, they were marooned with their ship in the desert, but they were helped or encouraged by Libyan nymphs, by the Hesperides, and by the god Triton. As they neared Crete, the bronze giant Talus nearly crushed their ship with rocks, but was destroyed by Medea's sorcery. The Argonauts returned to Iolcos, where a trick of Medea's disposed of Pelias and, Aeson having died, Acastus became king. Jason returned the Fleece to the temple of Laphystian Zeus in Orchomenus.

Next to the Trojan War, the voyage of the *Argo* was the event most often celebrated in Greek epic. It is the subject in particular of the *Argonautica*, the masterpiece of Apollonius of Rhodes, which is notable for the psychological realism with which its characters are treated, its memorable picture of Medea, and its remarkably unheroic portrayal of its hero, Jason.

Arguedas, Alcides (1879–1946). Bolivian novelist, historian, and diplomat. Although Arguedas spent many years in Europe, especially in France where he was Bolivian consul, his best-known writings reflect his abiding concern with the problems of his homeland. He is remembered primarily for three works, each in a different field. *Pueblo enfermo* (1909) is a pessimistic and controversial analysis of Bolivian society. One of the most famous of the Indianist novels, *Raza de bronce* (1919) describes the exploitation of Bolivian Indians by inhuman landlords. Arguedas' most enduring work may be his five-volume *Historia de Bolivia* (1920–1929), which covers that country's history from 1809 to 1872.

Argus (Argos). A fabulous creature. According to Greek mythology, Argus had 100 eyes, for which he was called *Panoptes*. Hera set him to watch Io, of whom she was jealous. Hermes, however, acting under orders of Zeus, who had his eye on Io, charmed Argus to sleep and slew him. Hera changed Argus into a peacock, whose tail was full of eyes. "Argus-eyed," therefore, means jealously watchful.

Argus (Argos). The builder of the ship *Argo* for the ARGONAUTS. He was assisted by Athene.

Argus (Argos). Odysseus' faithful dog, who, in the *Odyssey*, recognized his old master on his return to Ithaca.

Argyropoulos, Johannes (1410–1490). Greek scholar in Italy during the revival of classical studies. He taught at Florence and Rome, was a member of the Medici circle, and engaged in the translation and the editing of texts.

Ariadne. In Greek mythology, daughter of Minos, king of Crete. She gave Theseus a clew of thread to guide him out of the Cretan LABYRINTH. Theseus married his deliverer, but when he arrived at Naxos forsook her. Later she became the wife of Dionysus. It is generally agreed that Ariadne was the name of a Cretan mother-goddess. Richard Strauss wrote an opera called ARIADNE AUF NAXOS (1912).

Ariadne auf Naxos (1912; rev. 1916). An opera by Richard STRAUSS, with a libretto by Hugo von HOFMANNSTHAL. It was originally intended as an interlude to be introduced into a performance of Molière's LE BOURGEOIS GENTILHOMME. In it a serious drama about Bacchus and ARIADNE is played simultaneously with the improvisations of a *commedia dell' arte* troupe. For the Vienna performance of 1916 Strauss wrote a long Prologue so that the opera could be performed independently of the play.

Arians. The followers of ARIUS, a presbyter of the church of Alexandria, in the 4th century. He maintained (1) that the Father and Son are distinct beings; (2) that the Son, though divine, is not equal to the Father; (3) that the Son had a state of existence previous to His appearance on earth, but not from eternity; and (4) that the Messiah was not real man, but a divine being in a case of flesh. The Arian tenets varied from time to time and also among their different sections. The heresy was formally anathematized at the COUNCIL OF NICAEA (325), but the sect was not, and never has been, wholly extinguished. See also ATHANASIUS.

Aridano. In the ORLANDO INNAMORATO of Boiardo a giant who guards the treasure of the witch Morgana at the bottom of a lake. Orlando kills him and seizes the treasure.

Ariel. A sprite in Shakespeare's THE TEMPEST. Ariel has been freed by Prospero from a pine rift in which he was imprisoned by the evil witch Sycorax. Invisible at will, all light and spirit, he seems to symbolize man's imagination. After serving Prospero faithfully, Ariel is at last freed when his master renounces his magic.

Ariel (1900). An essay by José Enrique RODÓ, which had a tremendous impact on Hispanic American intellectuals. Rodó appealed to the youth of Spanish America to aspire to the spirituality, idealism, and rationality symbolized by Shakespeare's Ariel and to reject the brutishness and sensuality represented by Caliban. Because Rodó censured U.S. materialism and utilitarianism in the essay, many readers erroneously assumed that he was pitting Anglo-Saxon crassness against Latin idealism. The essay is, however, a generalized guide for the future.

Arioch. In Milton's PARADISE LOST, one of the fallen angels. The word means "a fierce lion"; Milton took it from Dan. 2:14, where it is the name of a man.

Ariodante (Ariodantes). The beloved of GINEVRA in Ariosto's ORLANDO FURIOSO. The blame for his supposed suicide because of her infidelity is placed on her hands and she is doomed unless rescued by a champion. Rinaldo saves her and she is reunited with Ariodante, who is alive and arrives to defend her, when his identity is revealed.

Arion. A Greek poet and musician. He flourished about 700 B.C. According to legend, he was cast into the sea by mariners, but carried to Taenaros on the back of a dolphin.

Arion. A horse born of the union of Poseidon and Demeter. His magical swiftness saved his master ADRASTUS, the only one of the Seven Against Thebes to escape alive from the siege of Thebes.

Ariosto, Lodovico (1474–1533). Italian poet. He was born at Reggio, in Modena, and served the Este family of Ferrara for most of his life. His poems, satires, and learned plays were popular and respected in his day, but his masterpiece remains the ORLANDO FURIOSO (*Roland Mad*). A continuation of BOIARDO'S ORLANDO INNAMORATO (*Roland in Love*, 1495), it is a long narrative poem in octave stanzas dealing with the adventures of ROLAND and other knights of Charlemagne in wars against the Saracens.

Aristaeus (Aristaios). In classical mythology the son of Apollo and Cyrene. He was the god-hero protector of cattle and fruit trees. Aristaeus had offended the nymphs by pursuing Eurydice, the wife of Orpheus, who in her flight had been bitten by a serpent and died. In revenge the nymphs destroyed his bee hives, but, when he had propitiated them, new bees swarmed from a rotting carcass. He was the father of Actaeon by Autonoe.

Aristarchus (fl. 156 B.C.). Aristarchus of Samothrace, the greatest critic of antiquity and head of the Alexandrian library. His labors were chiefly directed to the *Iliad* and *Odyssey* of HOMER. He divided them into 24 books each, marked every doubtful line with an obelus, and every one he considered especially beautiful with an asterisk.

Aristides (Aristeides; 530–468 B.C.). An Athenian statesman and general. He is called "The Just" for his impartiality and honesty, which have become proverbial. According to tradition, an illiterate Athenian once came to Aristides, whom he did not recognize, and asked him to write the name of Aristides on a ballot demanding his ostracism from the state. The man explained that he had grown tired of hearing Aristides forever called "The Just." Without revealing his identity, Aristides wrote his own name.

Aristides of Miletus. See MILESIAN FABLES.

Aristippus (Aristippos; c. 435–c. 356 B.C.). Greek philosopher, pupil of Socrates. Aristippus founded the Cyrenaic School, named after his birthplace, Cyrene. This school, similar to the Epicurean, holds that pleasure is the goal of life, and that prudence should be exercised to avoid pain.

Aristophanes (445 B.C.–c. 380 B.C.). A Greek comic playright. Little is known of Aristophanes' life except that his first produced play won a second prize when he was only 18, and he continued to write fine comedies at a rate of about one a year for more than 20 years. His last two extant plays, *Ecclesiazusae* (392) and *Plutus* (388), were produced after the fall of Athens in 404 B.C. Perhaps because it was no longer possible for him to criticize the state freely, these comedies are considerably inferior to his earlier works.

Aristophanes was a brilliant if somewhat wide-swinging social satirist, who used the traditional freedom of OLD COMEDY to ridicule public figures, institutions, and even the gods. His favorite butts were the demagogue Cleon, whom he attacked in THE KNIGHTS and several other plays, and Euripides, who was lampooned in THE FROGS and THESMOPHORIAZUSAE. Socrates is the victim in THE CLOUDS, in which Aristophanes inaccurately and unfairly makes him a wily sophist who teaches men to cheat others through cunning argumentation. It is apparent that the playwright was conservative in his views, disapproving of Euripides' humanizing of the gods and heroes, of modern trends in music and philosophy, and of the war with Sparta, whose rigid traditionalism he may even have admired. As a practical writer of comedy, however, he also knew that it is easier to draw laughter by ridiculing newfangled fads than by pointing out absurdities in modes of behavior that are generally accepted.

Another indication of the license permitted Old Comedy is the open but never prurient obscenity of the plays, a custom that began with their origin in one aspect of the fertility rites of Dionysus. (Aristophanes' eleven plays are the only surviving examples of the genre.) It is all the more striking that Aristophanes does not hesitate to make Dionysus, the patron of the dramatic festivals, an absurd figure in *The Frogs,* or to give men the upper hand over the gods in THE BIRDS.

Aristophanes was the most imaginatively original of the Greek playwrights, in that, while they wrote of (supposedly) historical figures, he invented not only completely new characters and situations but even entire worlds out of whole cloth. He was also a fine poet who wrote delicate and charming lyrics in his choral songs. His masterpiece, *The Birds,* is a remarkable example of both these outstanding qualities. In it he creates a delightfully improbable kingdom of birds and men, Cloudcuckooland, and his characters, both feathered and otherwise, sing one lovely lyric after another all through the play. Unfortunately for modern audiences, some of the qualities that make Aristophanes' comedies successful are difficult or impossible to reproduce in modern English: his poetry, his topical satire, and his knack for puns and garbled literary allusions. In spite of this, his comic genius was so universal that a great deal of the humor of his plays still comes through.

Aristophanes of Byzantium (fl. 195 B.C.). A leading critic, head of the Alexandrian library. He is known for his editing of the works of Homer, and for devising, or at least standardizing, the accents since used in the Greek language. These accents were intended for the benefit of foreigners learning Greek, a language that all educated people were expected to know in the days of the Roman empire.

Aristotelian unities. See UNITIES.

Aristotle (Aristoteles; 384–322 B.C.). Greek philosopher, born at Stagira. Brought up in a family of moderate wealth and position, Aristotle went at the age of 18 to Athens to study in Plato's Academy, where he remained for 20 years, until the death of his teacher. He moved to Assos, then to Mytilene, then to Macedon, whence he was invited by King Philip to tutor the young Alexander. Aristotle remained in Macedonia for eight years, until Philip was assassinated (336 B.C.) and Alexander succeeded to the throne. During the time he spent in Assos, Mytilene, and Macedon, much of Aristotle's work in natural history was done. On his return to Athens, he taught at the LYCEUM. Finally, in 323 B.C., at Alexander's death, Aristotle left Athens, where there was an upsurge of anti-Macedonian feeling, and retired to Chalcis, where he died a year later.

The works for which he was most widely known among the ancients have been lost, but fragments indicate that they were dialogues written in a highly polished rhetorical style. These are referred to as his exoteric writings, or those designed for the general public outside his school. A second class of writings, the esoteric, or those designed for use by the students of the Lyceum, has survived. These are called the acroamatic writings, and are known to us as the treatises of Aristotle. A third class of writings, the hypomnematic, or memoranda, have also been lost.

The treatises include first the logical works (*Categories, Topics, De Interpretatione, Prior Analytics, Posterior Analytics, Sophistical Refutations*) known as the *Organon*, or instrument. For Aristotle, logic was preparation for scientific knowledge, not knowledge itself. He was the first to insist on rigorous scientific procedure, and his method of demonstration by the syllogism and by dialectic, or reasoning from the opinions of others, became standard philosophic method. Aristotle maintained that all human knowledge originates in sensible experiences, out of which the soul perceives the universal.

Aristotle's natural philosophy, contained in the eight books of the *Physics*, examines the physical universe. They include the important distinction between the substance (or essence) of a thing and its accidental properties. Other works in this group include *On the Heavens (De Caelo), On Coming into Being and Passing Away (De Generatione et Corruptione),* and *Meteorology (Meteorologic). Parva Naturalia* and *De Anima* are the titles of his works on psychology. He wrote an introduction to biology called *Historia Animalium,* in which he classified the animals, their methods of reproduction, and their evolution. In his treatises on metaphysics, known as *Metaphysica,* Aristotle discusses theology, or primary philosophy, which he considered the highest type of theoretical science. Unlike his teacher Plato he did not posit a separate world of perfect Forms or Ideas, but always finds form immanent in matter.

There are two Aristotelian ethical treatises, known as the *Nicomachean Ethics* and the *Eudemian Ethics.* According to the former, happiness is the goal of life. Pleasure, fame, and wealth, however, will not bring one of the highest happiness, which is achieved only through the contemplation of philosophic truth because it exercises man's peculiar virtue, the rational principle.

In Aristotle's *Politics* (eight books), the good of the individual is identified with the good of the city-state. The study of human good is thus a political inquiry, as it is in Plato. Aristotle discusses different types of government, finally preferring monarchy, an aristocracy of men of virtue, or constitutional government of the majority. Slavery is considered natural in Aristotle's politics, because some men are adapted by nature to be the physical instruments of others. Aristotle's *Rhetoric* treats methods of persuasion; the *Poetics* is his great contribution to literary criticism.

Called by Dante "the master of those who know," Aristotle mastered every field of learning known to the Greeks. His influence on St. Thomas Aquinas and the medieval world, through the translation of the Arabic scholar Averroes, was profound and enduring.

Arius (c. 256–336). Greek ecclesiastic. He lived and taught in Alexandria. His teachings on the nature of God constitute what is called the Arian heresy or Arianism. Arius felt that God is separate from the world, alone and unknowable. He taught that Jesus was a mortal, created being, not fully divine, and as such should be worshiped as secondary to God. At the church councils of Nicaea (325) and Constantinople (381), Arius and his followers were condemned as teachers of false doctrine. See ARIANS.

Arjuna (*Sans.,* the sinless). One of the five Pandava brothers and a hero of the great Hindu epic, the MAHABHARATA, especially prominent in the BHAGAVADGITA.

Ark of the Covenant. A wooden chest (possibly a model of a temple) overlaid with gold in which the presence of Jehovah was believed to dwell when communicating with Israel. The Ark was portable and was carried into battle. Its contents are thought to have been the stone tablets recording the law as given to Moses. It was installed in the Holy of Holies of Solomon's temple at Jerusalem. The fate of the original Ark is not known: it disappeared after the fall of Jerusalem in 586 B.C.

Arlen, Michael (1895–1956). Armenian-born English author. He is best known for a popular novel entitled THE GREEN HAT.

Arlequin. See HARLEQUIN.

Armada, Spanish. Also known as the **Invincible Armada.** The fleet assembled in 1588 by PHILIP II of Spain for the conquest of England. The armada, which consisted of some 130 ships and carried over 30,000 troops, set sail from Lisbon on May 29 under the command of the duke of Medina Sidonia. Its destination was the Netherlands, where the fleet was to pick up an army under Alexander Farnese, the duke of Parma, and transport it across the channel for an invasion of England.

After being forced by a storm to put in at Corunna for repairs, the armada was sighted by the English near Plymouth on July 29. Medina Sidonia, who was under orders to sail directly to the Netherlands, retired before the lighter and more maneuverable ships of the English fleet, suffering several losses, until he anchored at Calais on Aug. 6. Farnese's army, hemmed in by the Dutch fleet, was unable to stir. On Aug. 7, the English sent fire ships among the Spanish vessels, forcing them to flee. The following day the bitterest engagement of the campaign was fought off Gravelines, the Spaniards being bested by the gunnery of the combined English and Dutch fleets. A favorable change of wind enabled the armada to make for the North Sea and return to Spain by sailing around Scotland and Ireland, where severe storms caused further losses. The Spaniards lost over 63 ships and 9000 men in the campaign, and Spanish prestige suffered a severe blow.

Armado, Don Adriano de. A fantastical Spanish knight in Shakespeare's LOVE'S LABOUR'S LOST. A posturing, self-important fellow, given to absurd rhetoric, he is a satire on the popular Spanish knight of the Elizabethan era.

Armageddon. The name given in *The Revelation of St. John the Divine* (Rev. 16:16) to the site of the last great battle between good and evil before the Day of Judgment; hence, any great final struggle or conflict. Theodore Roosevelt popularized the term in connection with his break from the Republicans to form the Progressive Party in the presidential election of 1912. It has been frequently used in connection with the First World War.

arme Heinrich, Der. See HEINRICH, DER ARME.

Armida. In Tasso's GERUSALEMME LIBERATA, a beautiful sorceress, niece of the enchanter Idraote, sent by him to the Christian camp in hopes of sowing discord and confusion there. In the camp, she tells Goffredo, general of the Crusaders, a tearful story and requests ten of his knights to assist her in reclaiming her own lost kingdom. In the arguments that follow, Goffredo's leadership is severely tested, and more than ten of his most puissant knights fly after her. For a time she holds in her power the Christian champion Tancredi, who is rescued by Rinaldo of Este, himself soon a captive victim of her charms. When Rinaldo, whom she loves, is also rescued, Armida sets fire to her palace and flies in her chariot to the camp of the Egyptians, where she offers herself to any champion who will kill Rinaldo. In the final battle for Jerusalem she is put to flight by Rinaldo; she then tries to kill herself, but he persuades her to live and trust her future to him:

"Behold," she says, "thy handmaid; I obey:
  Thy lips my future life, thy will my fortune sway!"
                         (XX, 136)

Armida's Garden. The enchantress Armida, of Tasso's GERUSALEMME LIBERATA, lives in a castle that contains a garden of gorgeous sensual delights, from lush flowers and fruits to alluring nymphs bathing in fountains. It symbolizes the attractions of the senses and their power over human reason. As such, it links Armida with Circe and Alcina and is the inspiration of Spenser's Bower of Bliss.

Armida's Girdle. The enchantress Armida, of Tasso's GERUSALEMME LIBERATA, wears a magical girdle of incomparable beauty and worth. The source of many of her powers, it enables her to know and do whatever she wills.

Arminianism. A religious heresy, opposed to Calvinism. It began in Holland in the early 17th century and then spread to England and the colonies in America. It denied the leading Calvinistic tenets that only the elect were to benefit by the sacrifice of Christ's death, and that the human will was powerless to reject or to forfeit divine grace once it had been received; it also opposed the doctrine of absolute predestination. Jonathan Edwards violently attacked Arminianism in America.

Arminius, probably the Latin form of **Hermann** (18 B.C.–A.D. 21). Hero-chieftain of the Germanic Cherusci tribe. Although he served in the Roman army for a while, he came home to find his people suffering under Roman dominion, and in A.D. 9 won a crushing victory over the Roman governor Varus. He was finally defeated by GERMANICUS in A.D. 16. His exploits survive in popular legend and in plays such as F. G. Klopstock's *Hermanns Schlacht* (1769) and *Hermann und die Fürsten* (1784).

Armory Show. An exhibition of American and European modern art held in the 69th Regiment Armory, New York City in 1913. Among the organizers and contributors were Arthur Davies and John SLOAN. At this show Americans got their first look at the revolutionary work of such artists as Matisse, Kandinsky, Brancusi, Maillol, Picasso, and Braque. The painting that most attracted public attention was Marcel Duchamp's *Nude Descending a Staircase,* which one critic renamed "explosion in a shingle factory." In general, the conservative art critics were hostile to the show, especially to the foreign works that were much more extreme than those from the U.S. The public, however, flocked to the show: over 250,000 people paid to see the wild-looking European painting and sculpture. A few were conscious at once of what the Armory Show implied for art in America: modern art had arrived full-fledged from Europe, and it was in the U.S. to stay.

In the winter of 1963, the 50th anniversary of the Armory Show was celebrated in the same building. All of the works hung in the original show that could be traced were re-exhibited, most of those jeered at in 1913 being now considered masterpieces—or even outmoded.

Arms and the Man (1894). A play by George Bernard SHAW. Set in Bulgaria, it satirizes romantic attitudes about war. The title is taken from the first line of Vergil's *Aeneid: Arma virumque cano* (I sing of arms and the man). The libretto of the comic opera *The Chocolate Soldier* (1909) by Oskar Straus was unofficially based on the play.

Armstrong, John (1709–1779). Scottish poet and physician. He is noted for his didactic, blank-verse poem, *Art of Preserving Health* (1744).

Arnauld, Antoine (1612–1694). French writer and theologian. A Jansenist and a bitter opponent of all that he took to be false doctrine, Arnauld was a lifelong opponent of the Jesuits. A storm of controversy arose over his exposition of Jansenism in *La Fréquente Communion (The Frequent Communion,* 1643). *La Perpétuité de la foi de l'église catholique touchant l'Eucharistie (The Perpetuity of the Faith of the Catholic Church Regarding the Eucharist,* 1669–1676), written in collaboration with Pierre NICOLE, criticized the Calvinist conception of the Eucharist, and the *Traité des vraies et des fausses idées (Treatise on True and False Ideas,* 1683) demolished the pantheistic philosophy of Malebranche. *Lettre à un duc et pair (Letter to a Duke and Peer,* 1655), Arnauld's outspoken criticism of Jesuit practices in the confessional, brought about his condemnation by the Sorbonne, which in turn caused Pascal to write the *Lettres Provinciales.* Forced into hiding for almost 20 years of his life, Arnauld died in exile.

Arnauld-d'Andilly, Angélique. Known as **Mère Angélique de Saint Jean** (1624–1684). French nun and writer. Mistress of the novices at Port-Royal-de-Paris when the community was disbanded by order of the archbishop of Paris in 1664, she was moved to another convent and confined to a solitary cell without sacraments. She described her sufferings in the *Relation de Captivité (Account of Captivity,* 1760). From 1678 until her death she was abbess of Port-Royal-des-Champs.

Arndt, Ernst Moritz (1769–1860). German patriotic poet of great importance during Germany's wars of liberation from Napoleon (1813–1815). His most famous collection is *Lieder für Deutsche (Songs for Germans,* 1813), which includes the well-known song *Der Gott, der Eisen wachsen liess (The God Who Made Iron Grow).*

Arne, Thomas Augustine (1710–1778). English composer of operas, masques, and scores for plays. He wrote an English grand opera *Artaxerxes,* a score for Milton's COMUS, and songs for revivals of *As you like it* (1740) and *The Tempest* (1746). His patriotic song *Rule Britannia* is from the music for the masque *Alfred* (1740).

Arnim, Elisabeth ("Bettina") von, born **Brentano** (1785–1859). Wife of Achim von Arnim, sister of Clemens Brentano. In her youth she was a fervent admirer of Goethe, and her correspondence with the poet, *Goethes Briefwechsel mit einem Kinde* (*Goethe's Correspondence with a Child*, 1835) reveals the perfect emotional purity of her nature. Her *Dies Buch gehört dem König* (*This Book Belongs to the King*, 1843) is a naïve plea for royal assistance to alleviate poor economic and social conditions among the Silesian weavers.

Arnim, Ludwig Joachim ("Achim") von (1781–1831). German romantic poet. He was a close friend of Clemens Brentano, whose sister he married in 1811. With Brentano, he edited the folksong collection DES KNABEN WUNDERHORN. His unfinished novel *Die Kronenwächter* (*The Guardians of the Crown*, 1817), about 16th-century Germany, is important in the development of the German historical novel. See GERMAN ROMANTICISM.

Arnim, Gräfin von. See ELIZABETH, Countess Russell.

Arnold, Benedict (1741–1801). American army officer and traitor. Beginning his career as a patriot, Arnold led the attack with Ethan Allen on Fort Ticonderoga, N.Y. (1775), and he is now generally given credit for winning the important battle of Saratoga (1777). He was given command of the fort at West Point by Washington, but embittered by repeated slights from Congress and other Americans, he arranged for its surrender to the British, and was made a brigadier general in the British army. After the war he sailed to England, where he died. He appears in William Dunlap's play *André* (1798) and in Kenneth Roberts' novel *Arundel* (1930). See John ANDRÉ; Horatio GATES.

Arnold, Sir Edwin (1832–1904). English poet, journalist, translator, and traveler. A student of Indian languages, Persian, and Turkish, Arnold traveled widely in the Orient. His best-known work, *The Light of Asia* (1879), is an epic poem on the life of Buddha; many of his other poems also deal with Eastern themes. He was the author of a number of translations of Oriental literature, including *The Indian Song of Songs* (1875) and *Indian Idylls* (1893).

Arnold, Matthew (1822–1888). English critic and poet. The son of Thomas ARNOLD, the clergyman who became headmaster of Rugby and made it one of England's most renowned public schools, young Arnold began his literary career as a poet, publishing *The Strayed Reveler and Other Poems* (1849); *Empedocles on Etna and Other Poems* (1852); *Poems* (1853); *Poems, Second Series* (1855); *Merope*, a dramatic poem (1858); and *New Poems* (1867). His poetry tends to be elegiac and brooding, and at its best is among the finest expressions of the plight of the sensitive Victorian caught between "two worlds, one dead,/ The other powerless to be born." His most famous poems are THE SCHOLAR-GIPSY, based on a legend of an Oxford student who, in poverty, joined a band of gypsies; *Stanzas from the Grande Chartreuse* (1855), in which the narrator, visiting a Carthusian monastery, mourns the loss of faith in the modern world; *Thyrsis* (1866), an elegy written on the death of Arnold's friend Arthur Hugh Clough, which Swinburne adjudged, after Milton's *Lycidas* and Shelley's *Adonais*, the finest elegy in the English language; and DOVER BEACH (1867), perhaps his best-known poem, which uses the image of the sea as a metaphor for the Sea of Faith, ebbing away from the naked shores of the world.

In 1857, Arnold was elected to the professorship of poetry at Oxford, and during the 10 years that he held this position he delivered many of the lectures that were to become part of his essays on criticism. The best-known collections of these are *On Translating Homer* (1861); *Essays in Criticism* (1st series, 1865; 2nd series, 1888); CULTURE AND ANARCHY (1869); and *Literature and Dogma* (1873). Seeing literature as both shaper and sustainer of the highest elements of culture, he urged that the great mass of the public—the "Philistine" middle class—be educated to improve its response to literature (and culture). He argued for high standards of literary judgment, using the "lines and expressions of the great masters . . . as a touchstone to other poetry." He believed that the English were too immersed in the spirit of "Hebraism," or strictness of conscience and rightness of conduct, and not sufficiently touched by the symmetry and spontaneity of "Hellenism"; he saw religious fundamentalism as one expression of this Hebraism, and attempted to interpret the Bible as literature and show that, as in all great poetry, the poetry of the Bible contained the moral and spiritual truths that were the essence of religion. He saw the task of the critic as "a disinterested endeavor to learn and propagate the best that is known and thought in the world." He is of importance as a shaper of both English and American criticism, up to the time of T. S. Eliot. See Arminius von THUNDERTENTRONCKH.

Arnold, Thomas (1795–1842). English educator, historian, and headmaster of Rugby (1828–1842). The father of Matthew ARNOLD, he is often referred to as "Arnold of Rugby," being chiefly remembered for his tenure there as headmaster, where he exerted great personal influence and set the modern pattern for the entire English public-school system. His literary works include a collection of sermons (1829–1834), an edition of Thucydides (1830–1835), a history of Rome (3 vols., 1838–1843), and *Lectures on Modern History* (1842).

Arnold of Brescia (c. 1100–1155). Italian theologian and reformer. He was persecuted by St. Bernard of Clairvaux as being a follower of Pierre ABÉLARD's Aristotelian philosophy. A preacher of asceticism, he railed against the wealth and temporal power of the clergy, and in 1145 encouraged a revolution in Rome against the Pope's civil authority. In 1155 the rebellion was suppressed and Arnold was hanged, then burned.

Arnolphe. In Molière's comedy, L'ECOLE DES FEMMES, a man of wealth with stern ideas on the proper training of girls to make good wives. He applies his educational methods to Agnès whom, in time, he intends to make his wife.

Arnothy, Christine (1928–   ). Hungarian-born French novelist. She won notice with the autobiographical *I am Fifteen and I Don't Want to Die* (1956), about a Hungarian family escaping the Russian siege of Budapest. The sequel, *It is Not So Easy to Live* (1957), moves through refugee camp experiences to marriage in Paris. Her novels include

God Is Late (1955), *The Charlatan* (1959), and *The Serpent's Bite* (1961).

Arnoux, Mme Marie. One of the main characters in the novel L'Education Sentimentale by Gustave Flaubert. Frédéric Moreau suffers the passion of unrequited love for Mme Arnoux during the years of her marriage. In an ironic conclusion, when a middle-aged widow she comes to him, Frédéric rejects her offer of love.

Arouet, François Marie. See Voltaire.

Around the World in Eighty Days (Le Tour du monde en quatre-vingt jours; 1873). A romance by Jules Verne. The hero, Phileas Fogg, undertakes his hasty world tour as the result of a bet made at his London club. He and his French valet Passepartout meet with some fantastic adventures, but these are overcome by the loyal servant, and the endlessly inventive Fogg. The feat they perform is incredible for its day; Fogg wins his bet, having circled the world in only 80 days.

Arp, Hans. Also known as **Jean Arp** (1887–). German poet and sculptor. As a sculptor he is best known for his use of subtle, curved forms. With Hugo Ball and others he founded the Dada Cabaret Voltaire in Zürich (1916). A recent selection of his poetry is entitled *Wortträume und schwarze Sterne* (*Word-Dreams and Black Stars,* 1953).

Arrow of Gold, The (1919). A novel by Joseph Conrad. It is a story of romance and adventure during the Second Carlist War. Conrad himself, when he was about 20, had been involved at the fringe of these events.

Arrowsmith (1925). A novel by Sinclair Lewis. It follows the career of Dr. Martin Arrowsmith from his training under Max Gottlieb, through a small-town practice, the health department of a small city, an "institute" sponsored by a rich man and his wife, to an isolated West Indian island and an equally isolated Vermont farm. In his quest for pure science, Arrowsmith encounters meanness, corruption, and misunderstanding; he is often frustrated, and finally fails when he himself refuses to carry his principles to their logical extreme. Filled with medical lore, the details of which Lewis got from Paul de Kruif, the novel is frequently satiric and caused much controversy when it was first published.

'Arry and 'Arriet. Two characters from the pages of the English *Punch*. 'Arry, a good-natured but vulgar costermonger, and his wife 'Arriet were the creation of the *Punch* artist Edwin J. Milliken. 'Arry made his debut in *Punch's Almanac* of 1874 in *'Arry on 'orseback*.

Ars Amatoria, or Ars Amoris. See Ovid.

Arsenal at Springfield, The (1845). A poem by Henry Wadsworth Longfellow. A poem about peace, its theme was suggested by his wife.

Arsete (Arsetes). In the Gerusalemme Liberata of Tasso, a eunuch, custodian of the warrior maid Clorinda. He had been given the child by her mother, the Ethiopian queen, who feared that its white complexion would arouse the suspicions of King Senàpo (Senapus). Arsete neglects to baptize her, despite her Christian parentage, but he tells her the story of her birth before the battle that results in her death at the hands of her beloved Tancredi. The latter baptizes her and receives her forgiveness as she dies in his arms.

Arsinoé. (1) The false prude of Molière's comedy Le Misanthrope.

(2) The scheming stepmother in Pierre Corneille's tragedy Nicomède.

Ars Poetica (Lat., "the art of poetry"). A treatise by the Roman poet Horace, laying down rules for the writing of poetry. English critics of the Renaissance and post-Renaissance periods were greatly influenced by this work.

Artabano (Artabane). In the Gerusalemme Liberata of Tasso, a Saracen king who leads the African forces against the Crusaders during the battle for the holy city. His death at hands of the English baron Odoardo (Edward), takes place in the last canto of the poem.

Artagnan, Charles de Baatz d'. One of the famous guardsmen whose amazing adventures Alexandre Dumas narrates in The Three Musketeers, Twenty Years After, and The Viscount of Bragelonne. The works follow d'Artagnan through his various exploits to his death as Comte d'Artagnan, marshal of France. He is always the soldier—quick-witted, quick-tempered, and extraordinarily brave.

Artaud, Antonin (1895–1948). French dramatic theorist and producer. Artaud influenced many playwrights by urging that the theater should translate experience into universal and primitive images, as explained in *The Theater of Cruelty* (1935) and *The Theater and Its Double* (1938).

Artegal or **Arthgall.** See Elidure; Faerie Queene, The.

Artemidorus. In Shakespeare's Julius Caesar, a teacher of rhetoric who tries to warn Caesar of the plot against him. He passes Caesar a note naming the conspirators, but Caesar fails to read it.

Artemis. Greek goddess of hunting and childbirth, daughter of Leto and sister of Apollo. Perhaps originally a Cretan goddess of fertility, she came to be regarded as a virgin, who demanded chastity from her female attendants, and even her male devotees, such as Hippolytus. Her attendants (who were either local goddesses or local versions of Artemis herself) included Hecate, Callisto, Opis, Britomartis, and the mortal Iphigenia. She figures importantly in Euripides' plays Hippolytus and *Iphigenia in Aulis* (see Iphigenia).

Artemis of Ephesus, temple of. One of the Seven Wonders of the Ancient World. It contained a famous statue of the goddess—a cone surmounted by a bust covered with breasts—which was said to have fallen from Heaven. However, Minucius, in the second century A.D., described it as a wooden statue, and Pliny, a contemporary, claimed that it was made of ebony. As Diana of the Ephesians, this goddess, who bears a somewhat doubtful relationship to the Greek Artemis, appears in an episode in Acts 19:24–28.

art for art's sake. English equivalent of the French *l'art pour l'art,* which itself derives from Edgar Allan Poe in *The Poetic Principle:*

There neither exists nor can exist any work more thoroughly dignified . . . than the poem which is a poem and nothing more—the poem written solely for the poem's sake.

The doctrine which this represents, that the aim of art should be creation and the perfection of technical expression rather than the service of a moral, political, or didactic end, had been evolving ever since the romantic period. It was adumbrated by Coleridge and given early expression by Poe in the above treatise, flowered among the French symbolist poets and their English associate Walter Pater, and reached its culmination in surrealism and the aesthetic theory of I. A. Richards. It was the dominant theory of art and especially of poetry until the 1930's, when the proletarian and Marxist movements in literature threatened for a time to revive the 18th-century didactic theories. After the beginning of World War II in 1939, the latter movements began to lose much of their influence.

Artful Dodger, the. A young thief in Charles Dickens' OLIVER TWIST, pupil of Fagin. He became perfectly adept in villainy, and pickpocketing especially.

Arthur. The hero of a great cycle of medieval romance (see ARTHURIAN LEGEND). There was a historical Arthur, a Celtic chieftain who lived in Wales during the 6th century. Little is known of him except that he was mortally wounded (according to the ANNALES CAMBRIAE) in the battle of Camlan and was taken to GLASTONBURY where he died. However, while elements of the historical Arthur have been infused into the medieval romances, evidence indicates that there was an earlier, mythical Arthur, possibly a Celtic deity, whose origins are unknown. As they told and retold the story of Arthur, and in attempting to produce a coherent narrative out of diverse sources, the medieval romancers introduced Christian and other elements, not originally Arthurian, thus further confusing its origin. Despite the strong influence of Christianity in the later versions of Arthur, scholars detect the Celtic myth in which the GRAIL is a thinly disguised caldron of plenty and the opponents of Arthur and his knights the last echoes of earlier long-displaced deities.

By the time the Arthurian legends were given permanent shape in Malory's *Morte d'Arthur* (c. 1469), the figure of Arthur as a legendary hero had become fairly distinct. He was the natural son of UTHER

Arthur and his knights of the Round Table. Frontispiece from the *History of Prince Arthur* (1634).

PENDRAGON and IGRAINE (see MERLIN), and was raised by Sir Ector. By pulling the sword EXCALIBUR from a block of stone, he proved his right to the throne of England. He subdued 12 rebellious princes of whom LOT, king of Norway, was chief, and won 12 great battles against the Saxon invaders. About his ROUND TABLE he gathered a group of knights whose deeds of daring and chivalry won his court high renown. Arthur himself became known far and wide as a mighty warrior and a just and generous ruler. His wife was GUINEVERE, his most valiant knight LAUNCELOT. In the earlier romances the ruin that finally overtakes Arthur was due entirely to Guinevere and the traiterous MORDRED; the story of her illicit love for Launcelot and its demoralizing effect on the court was added later. In distinct contrast to Malory and the older romancers, who say that Arthur's sons were born out of wedlock, Tennyson in his IDYLLS OF THE KING makes Arthur a man of the highest morals, not only absolutely loyal to Guinevere but requiring that his knights "cleave to one maiden only." The treason that brought an end to Arthur's court was hatched while he was away on conquest. After his return and defeat in a final, terrible battle, the mortally wounded king was borne away to the island of AVALON, where some accounts say that he was buried while others say that he dwells with his sister MORGAN LE FAY "till he shall come again full twice as fair to rule over his people."

Arthur, Prince. See FAERIE QUEENE, THE.

Arthur, Timothy Shay. See TEN NIGHTS IN A BAR-ROOM.

Arthurian legend. A great body of literature that revolves around the partly mythical, partly historical figure of King ARTHUR. It seems to have neither traceable beginning nor foreseeable end, but the earliest extant written references to Arthur are found in Welsh literature of the 6th century. Sources of information include the writings of the historian GILDAS (c. 540); a poem entitled GODODIN (c. 600); the work of the historian NENNIUS (c. 800); the ANNALES CAMBRIAE (c. 955); THE SPOILS OF ANNWN (10th century); and the very important MABINOGION, a collection of tales which includes *Kulhwch and Olwen*, perhaps the earliest, full-fledged Arthurian romance.

In the 12th century the fame of Arthur spread to England where it was noted by William of Malmesbury in his GESTA REGUM ANGLORUM. In Geoffrey of Monmouth's Latin HISTORY OF THE KINGS OF BRITAIN, Arthur attained full stature, becoming a great national figure, the hero-king of marvelous deeds accompanied by such figures as MERLIN, Guinevere, Gawain, and Mordred. Uther Pendragon also made his appearance in context with the now traditional story of Arthur's conception, and there is what may be the first mention of Arthur's departure, mortally wounded, for Avalon.

The Norman poet, Wace, transformed the work of Geoffrey of Monmouth into an elegant verse chronicle, ROMAN DE BRUT. In this adaptation, the chivalric setting was expanded; the Round Table was introduced for the first time; the death of Arthur was further dramatized by the suggestion that he had gone to Avalon to be healed of his wounds, with the expectation of returning one day to Britain.

The innovations of the French poet CHRÉTIEN DE

TROYES involved, essentially, the unification of existing Arthurian materials into new narrative form. He wrote individual tales that highlighted the deeds of individual knights. The best known of these is *Lancelot,* a story that recounts the intensely enacted drama of Launcelot's adventures in the name of his great and undying love for Queen Guinevere, thus introducing into the stream of Arthurian legend that wondrous knight, Launcelot, and the important medieval theme of COURTLY LOVE.

The English priest Layamon (fl. 1198–1207) took the chronicle of Wace as his model and wrote THE BRUT—perhaps the first of the legends of Arthur to be composed in the English language. Layamon elaborated on the Round Table motif, effectively mixed native folk tradition with Norman elegance, and drew upon Celtic lore for a description of Arthur's journey to Avalon where Morgan le Fay waited to heal his wounds.

During the 13th century, the tales of Arthur enjoyed a period of popularity in Germany, which resulted in such works as those of GOTTFRIED VON STRASSBURG and WOLFRAM VON ESCHENBACH. In the 14th century, Arthurian legend saw an artistic revival that produced two especially important pieces of English literature: *The Alliterative Morte Arthur* (c. 1360) and SIR GAWAIN AND THE GREEN KNIGHT. In the first, an anonymous work, Gawain is the central figure, and it is his death, not Arthur's, that is the dramatic high point of the poem. Even his murderer, Mordred, weeps bitterly that it was his destiny to kill such a knight. The emphasis is on an early English kind of epic treatment, so that this version has an affinity more with *Beowulf* than with the customary form of Arthurian romance. Norman lightness and Celtic magic have no place in this work. When Arthur dies, he is carried to Glastonbury, not Avalon, for a Christian burial.

The second important poem of the 14th century English revival, *Sir Gawain and the Green Knight,* is one of the most important examples of Arthurian literature; its unknown author ranks with Chaucer as one of the greatest of the Middle English poets. Part of the brilliance of this particular poem is found in its unusual imagery and dramatic effects. An excellent example of the latter is the sudden appearance of the Green Knight at the court of King Arthur, during New Year festivities, and his shocking challenge; Gawain accepts the challenge, and the story is essentially a testing and development of his character.

In the 15th century, the legends of Arthur were gathered together and given ultimate shape in Sir Thomas Malory's great English prose classic, LE MORTE D'ARTHUR. This rendition is, above all else, the work of a master story-teller. Malory utilized traditions other than those of Arthurian romance, elaborating most effectively on the GRAIL theme, and making good use of material from the TRISTAN AND ISEULT stories. The life of Arthur is recounted, including the story of his miraculous conception and birth, events leading to his coronation, various military exploits, and his ultimate death at the hands of Mordred. In this work, the mysterious Lady of the Lake stretches her arm from the depths of the lake and provides Arthur with the marvelous sword, Excalibur. There is an enchanted forest through which disguised knights go galloping in search of odd beasts, the Holy Grail, perilous castles, ladies in distress, and behind almost any tree Morgan Le Fay may be waiting to capture passing knights of the Round Table. A villainous King Mark forever pursues the gallant Sir Tristram who is forever devoted to Queen Iseult. The exemplification of chivalry, Sir Launcelot, has many dramatic adventures in the name of love for Queen Guinevere or loyalty to King Arthur, while his son, the pure Galahad, is granted sight of the Holy Grail. *Le Morte d'Arthur* ends on the traditional, tragic note of Arthur's death and the dissolution of the Order of the Round Table.

Even in its own time, Malory's version of the Arthurian legend enjoyed considerable popularity. It was one of the works chosen for publication in 1485 by William Caxton, the first English printer, who gave it the title *Le Morte d'Arthur* and complained in a famous preface that Arthur was far better known and appreciated in other countries than his own. Caxton's complaint was subsequently more than answered as, one after the other, English poets dipped into Arthurian legend; the legend and the characters, however, changed, and the many versions reflect the changes in ideals, tastes, and preferences wrought by time. The Arthur in Spenser's *Faerie Queene* (1590, 1596, 1611), for example, is the ideal of manhood and bears little resemblance to earlier portraits of Arthur.

Perhaps the best-known modern retelling of the story of Arthur is Tennyson's IDYLLS OF THE KING (1859–1885). Like all the later romancers, Tennyson leaned heavily on Malory, but his approach is very different. The sin of Launcelot and Guinevere as the evil cause of the failure of the Round Table is strongly emphasized. Tennyson is often criticized for his shadowy, unreal, almost symbolic depiction of Arthur.

The story of Arthur has been told in the 19th and 20th centuries by such men as William Morris, Edwin Arlington Robinson, John Masefield, and Mark Twain, who burlesqued the romance of Arthur in *Connecticut Yankee in King Arthur's Court* (1889).

The popularity of the story of Arthur continues, being more recently retold, for example, by T. H. White in *The Once and Future King* (1958). This work has served to demonstrate once more the astonishing appeal of the legendary king, once a remote Celtic chieftain, whose name has already figured in literature for at least 1400 years.

Arthur Mervyn (Part I, 1799; Part II, 1800). A novel by Charles Brockden BROWN. The titular hero is a young man who becomes involved with a criminal, but later clears himself. The book is especially notable for its description of the yellow fever epidemic in Philadelphia in 1793.

Articles of Confederation and Perpetual Union. The constitution by which the United States was governed from 1781 until the ratification of the new CONSTITUTION in 1789. The central government created by the Articles lacked strength because each state remained sovereign and independent; there was no effective executive officer, and Congress lacked the power to levy taxes. To remedy these defects, a Constitutional Convention was called in 1787 and resulted in the writing of a new constitution.

Artzybashev, Mikhail Petrovich (1870–1927). Russian novelist and dramatist. His novel *Sanin* (1907) created a sensation because of its frank treatment and discussion of sex. His other works include *The Death of Lande* (1904) and *At the Brink* (1912).

Arundel (1930). A historical novel by Kenneth ROBERTS. The first of the author's stirring and authentic narratives, it deals with Benedict Arnold's expedition against Quebec. Arundel was the original name of Kennebunk, Me., Roberts' birthplace, and it had been his intention to give the history of Maine in a family chronicle, but he gave up the idea as he became more interested in the history of the country as a whole. Benedict Arnold's story is continued in RABBLE IN ARMS.

Arundhati. In Hindu legend, the wife of the great sage Vashishtha. Traditionally, she, along with Sita, represents the ideal Hindu wife.

Aruru. The Babylonian goddess who molded man, and later the hero Enkidu, out of clay. She appears in the *Epic of* GILGAMESH.

Arveragus. See FRANKLIN'S TALE.

Arviragus. (1) In Shakespeare's CYMBELINE, the valiant and noble younger son of Cymbeline, king of Britain. He is abducted by Belisarius as an infant and raised as his son under the name of Cadwal.

(2) In Chaucer's FRANKLIN'S TALE there is a character named Arviragus (or Arveragus). See GUIDERIUS.

Aryan language (from Sans. *arya,* noble). The Indo-European family of languages, from the name by which the Hindus and Iranians used to distinguish themselves from the nations they conquered. The place of origin of these languages is not definitely known, authorities differing so widely as between a locality enclosed by the river Oxus and the Hindu-Kush Mountains, and the shores of the Baltic Sea. The Aryan family of languages includes the Persian, Indic (Hindi, Sanskrit, etc.), Latin, Greek, and Celtic, with all the European except Basque, Turkish, Hungarian, and Finnic. It is sometimes called the Indo-European, sometimes the Indo-Germanic, and sometimes the Japhetic.

Aryan race. A term used by the German Nazis to designate, without any scientific basis, the original Indo-European race from which the German people were descended. They claimed that German superiority depended on the purity of the race, or in practical terms, on the extermination of the Jews. See Houston Stewart CHAMBERLAIN; Alfred ROSENBERG.

Ascalaphus (Askalaphos). In Greek mythology, an inhabitant of the underworld. When Hades gave Persephone permission to return to the upper world as she had eaten nothing, Ascalaphus said that she had partaken of a pomegranate. In revenge Persephone turned him into an owl by sprinkling him with the water of Phlegethon.

Ascalon, the Hermit of. In the GERUSALEMME LIBERATA of Tasso, a good wizard who helps Ubaldo and Guelfo break the power of Armida over the Christian champion Rinaldo of Este. With his help they are able to reach her castle on the Fortunate Isles and bring him to his senses. His return to the fray results in the final victory of the Crusaders.

Ascanius. Also known as **Iulus.** In classic legend, the son of AENEAS. He escaped with his father from Troy and later ruled over the kingdom in Italy which his father had secured. After Aeneas' death, Ascanius himself built its capital, Alba Longa. The gens Julia (or Iulia), to which Julius Caesar and Octavius Caesar belonged, supposedly derived its name from Ascanius' other name, Iulus, and accordingly sought to trace its lineage from the earliest ancestors of the Roman people. See AENEID; JULIAN EMPERORS.

Ascapart. A legendary giant conquered by Sir Bevis of Hamton. He was 30 feet high, and the space between his eyes was 12 inches. This mighty giant, whose effigy may be seen on the city gates of Southampton, could carry Sir Bevis and the latter's wife and horse under his arm with no difficulty.

Ascasubi, Hilario. See GAUCHO LITERATURE.

Ascent of F6, The (1936). A drama in verse and prose by W. H. AUDEN and Christopher ISHERWOOD. In a political crisis involving a border dispute in "British Sudoland," Sir James Ransom asks his brother Michael, a famous mountaineer, to lead a British expedition up F6, a mountain on the colony's frontier, which the Sudoland people believe to be haunted. Michael Ransom is reluctant to go, for he does not want to turn mountaineering into a political weapon, or to help his brother and his powerful, upper-class friends in their unscrupulous careers. But his mother urges him to go, to do a great deed; he agrees. The mountan is inhabited only by a strange order of monks, whose Abbot tells Ransom that the mountain is haunted in that each man meets his own demon there. The other climbers are killed one by one because of their particular obsessions or defects of character. At the top Ransom, delirious, goes through a nightmare trial scene with the other characters and finally sees *his* demon, his mother, and dies. As in Auden's other early work, the poet is concerned with both social and psychological diseases, and expresses himself through symbolism. Mr. and Mrs. A., ordinary English people, make up the chorus as they listen to the radio announcer's account of the expedition and comment on it. Benjamin Britten composed the music for the play.

Asch, Sholem (1880–1957). Polish-born American novelist. Asch, who wrote his books chiefly in Yiddish, is best known for his biblical novels: *The Nazarene* (1939), *The Apostle* (1943), and *Mary* (1949). These books reflect his conviction that Christianity should be considered the logical continuation of Judaism. *East River* (1946), a novel set in New York, illustrates the formation of the American character through the merging of diverse races and creeds. Asch's later works include *Moses* (1951), *A Passage in the Night* (1953), and *The Prophet* (1955).

Ascham, Roger (1515–1568). English prose writer and teacher, tutor to Elizabeth before her accession to the throne, later connected with her court as Greek preceptor. In his writings he urged the adoption of sports in an educational curriculum and defended English prose as a literary medium. His best known works are *Toxophilus* (1545), a treatise on archery, and *The* SCHOOLMASTER (1570), which expounds his pedagogical theories.

Aschenbach, Gustav von. See DEATH IN VENICE.

Asclepius (Asklepios). Greek god of healing, son of Apollo and Coronis. Apollo killed the mother for infidelity, but saved the unborn child, giving it into the care of CHIRON. Asclepius became extraordinarily proficient in medicine, but when he brought Hippolytus back to life, Zeus, thinking he had gone too far in interfering with divine prerogative, destroyed him with a thunderbolt. In revenge Apollo killed the Cyclopes. Asclepius was the father of Podalirus and Machaon, heroes at Troy, and of various daughters who were mere personifications of one form or another of healing.

Asem, An Eastern Tale, or A Vindication of the Wisdom of Providence in the Moral Government of the World (1759). A tale by Oliver GOLDSMITH concerning Asem, a hermit and misanthrope, who sees a vision of a world free from vice.

Asgard (from *as*, a god; *gard*[*h*], an enclosure, yard). The celestial dwelling place of the Scandinavian gods, equivalent to the Olympus of Greek mythology. It was said to be situated in the center of the universe and be accessible only by the rainbow bridge (*Bifrost*). Valhalla was the most famous great hall of its many regions and mansions, which also included Gladsheim, Vingolf, Valaskjalf, and Ydalir.

Ashcan School or **The Eight.** A term applied to a group of realistic American artists. They painted bars, prizefights, and street scenes rather than the pretty pictures fashionable at the turn of the 20th century. Their first exhibition in 1908 met with an uproar of disapproval that gave rise to the name of the group. Their members were Robert Henri (1865–1929), John SLOAN, Maurice Prendergast (1861–1924), Arthur B. Davies (1862–1928), George Luks (1867–1933), Everett Shinn (1873–1953), William Glackens (1870–1938), and Ernest Lawson (1873–1939).

Ashenden. The name W. Somerset MAUGHAM used for his own appearances in CAKES AND ALE and *The British Agent.*

Asherah or **Asherat.** The mother of the Canaanite gods, and consort of El. She lives in a palace in the north and exerts great influence over her husband. Even more than El himself, she seems hostile to the younger gods, such as Baal. Although her epithets refer to her as a sea-goddess, she fills a role in the Canaanite pantheon similar to that of Ge (Earth) in the Greek. See THE POEM OF BAAL.

Ashford, Daisy (1882–1972). English child author of the story THE YOUNG VISITERS. The book was published in 1919, wth a preface by J. M. Barrie claiming that the author, then a mature woman, was nine when she wrote it.

Ashkenazim. The middle and northern European Jews, as distinguished from the SEPHARDIM. It was originally the name of a people from Ashkenaz, near Ararat, mentioned in the Old Testament (Jer. 51:27). Ashkenaz is also the name of the eldest son of Gomer (Gen. 10:3).

Ashley, Lady Brett. The principal female character in Ernest Hemingway's novel THE SUN ALSO RISES. An Englishwoman, in Spain while she divorces her husband, she seeks to hide the emptiness of her life in friendship with the impotent Jake Barnes and an affair with the bullfighter Pedro Romero. She typifies the aimless pursuit of leisure of "the lost generation."

Ashnan. The Sumerian goddess of grain.

Ashtar. Canaanite god of artificial irrigation. During the period that the rain-god Baal spends in the underworld, he reigns on earth, but is not quite equal to the job. This role, clearly shown in THE POEM OF BAAL, is obviously an allegorical statement of the practical fact that irrigation cannot fertilize the earth as effectively as rain.

Ashton, Helen Rosaline (1891–1958). English novelist. She is the author of popular stories about doctors such as *Doctor Serocold* (1930), and fictional biographies such as *William and Dorothy* [Wordsworth] (1938) and *Parson Austen's Daughter* (1949).

Ashton, Lucy. See THE BRIDE OF LAMMERMOOR.

Ashton, Winifred. See Clemence DANE.

Ashtoreth. See ISHTAR.

Ashur. See ASSUR.

Ash Wednesday. The first day of Lent, so called from the ancient custom of sprinkling ashes on the heads of clergy and people. The ashes are prepared from the palms blessed on Palm Sunday the previous year.

Ash Wednesday (1930). A poem by T. S. ELIOT. The first of his poems to celebrate the peace found in orthodox Christianity, it is a poetic liturgy, meditation, and approach to mystical communion with God.

Asia. In classic mythology, one of the Oceanides, usually spoken of as wife of Iapetus and mother of Prometheus. In his PROMETHEUS UNBOUND, Shelley makes her play an important part as Prometheus' wife.

Asia. According to the Koran the wife of that Pharaoh who brought up Moses. Her husband tortured her for believing in Moses; but she was taken alive into paradise. Muhammad numbers her among the four perfect women.

As I Lay Dying (1930). A novel by William FAULKNER. It tells the story of the death of Addie Bundren and the ordeals her family undergo in carrying the body to Jefferson, Miss., for burial. Her husband, Anse; her four sons, Cash, Darl, Jewel, and Vardaman; her daughter, Dewey Dell; and several neighbors all reveal their relationships with Addie in the course of the story. A series of mishaps besets the family: in crossing a flooding river, the mules are drowned, Cash's leg is broken, and the coffin is upset and rescued by Jewel. Later, the family rests at a farmhouse, where Darl sets fire to the barn in an attempt to destroy the now-putrescent corpse; again the coffin is rescued by Jewel. The family finally reaches Jefferson, where Addie is buried; Darl is taken to the insane asylum, and Anse acquires a new wife.

In the course of the narrative it is revealed that Jewel was born of Addie's affair with Whitfield, a local preacher. Her relationship to Anse had been spiritually and emotionally barren, based on words alone. Significantly, Jewel is a silent man, active and passionate, while Darl is sensitive and perceptive, living in the world of his own mind.

The story unfolds in some 60 short sections, each labeled with the name of the character who narrates his thoughts and perceptions; as in *The Sound and the Fury*, Faulkner uses the stream-of-consciousness technique. A grim story of the ordeals of fire and water, the novel is often comic, ending with the new wife who is "duck-shaped" and popeyed.

Asimov, Isaac (1920–   ). Russian-born American author known primarily as a science-fiction writer, Asimov has published more than 40 books interpreting science to the general public. *Building Blocks of the Universe* (1957) and *The Living River* (1959) both received awards for their excellence. *The Intelligent Man's Guide to Science* (2 vols., 1960) is an encyclopedic work for the layman. His books of science fiction written for those in high school are published under the pseudonym Paul French.

Asín Palacios, Miguel (1871–1944).   Spanish philologist and professor of Arabic studies. Author of the famous *La escatología musulmana en la Divina Comedia* (*Islam in the Divine Comedy*, 1919), which deals with the influence of Arabian authors, notably Aben Arabí, upon Dante, Asín Palacios was responsible for many of the discoveries pointing to the interrelationship between the Islamic and early Christian cultures. Also among his best-known works is the volume *El Islam cristianizado* (1931).

Asir. See AESIR.

Ask or Askr. In Norse mythology, the first man, created out of an ash tree by Odin, Vili, and Ve. The first woman was EMBLA.

Asmodée. The devil-companion of Don CLÉOFAS, in Alain René LESAGE's picaresque novel *Le Diable Boiteux* (1707), sometimes entitled *Asmodeus* or *The Devil on Two Sticks* in English translations. He is an engaging little lame devil, with a great deal more gaiety than malice. He takes pleasure in showing his companion human ugliness and depravity by lifting the roofs off houses in Madrid.

Asmodeus. The "evil demon" who appears in the Apocryphal book of *Tobit*. His business was "to plot against the newly wedded and . . . sever them utterly by many calamities." According to Hebrew mythology, Asmodeus fell in love with Sara, daughter of Raguel, and slew her seven husbands in succession, each on his bridal night. He was exorcised and driven into Egypt by a charm made by TOBIAS (on the advice of the angel Raphael) from the heart and liver of a fish burnt on perfumed ashes (Tobit 6:14; 7:2). In the Talmud, Asmodeus is called "king of the devils."

Aspasia. A Milesian woman (fl. 440 B.C.) celebrated for her beauty and talents. She lived at Athens as mistress of PERICLES, and her house became the center of literary and philosophical society; hence a fascinating and cultured courtesan. Walter Savage Landor wrote a series of imaginary letters, *Pericles and Aspasia* (1836).

Aspasia. Titular heroine of Beaumont and Fletcher's drama, *The* MAID'S TRAGEDY (1610). She is betrothed to Amintor but the King, wishing to provide a husband for his mistress Evadne, commands Amintor to marry her instead. Aspasia is a pathetic figure, the very type of ill-fortune and wretchedness, but she bears her fate with patience even when she becomes a jest and byword. Her tragic death gives the drama its name.

Aspects of the Novel (1927). A literary study by E. M. FORSTER. Defining the novel as any work

of prose fiction, Forster discusses not only plot and character, but also "fantasy," "prophecy" (or symbolism), and "pattern and rhythm" (writing of the structure of a novel as though it is, or should be, like a symphony).

Aspern Papers, The (1888). A novelette by Henry JAMES. According to passages in his notebook, James based *The Aspern Papers* on a story he had heard concerning the mistress of Byron, then living, who was in possession of several unpublished papers and letters of both Byron and Shelley. The narrator of *The Aspern Papers* learns that the former mistress of the romantic poet Jeffrey Aspern is still living in Venice and has in her possession a collection of the poet's papers which she will not permit to be published. In hope of gaining access to the papers, the narrator rents a room from the old lady and her middle-aged niece, but his plans are frustrated when, at the old lady's death, the niece demands marriage as the price of the papers.

Assassins. A small Islamic sect. For two hundred years it terrified Europe with its secret murders. It was founded by Hassan-i-Sabbah near the end of the 11th century. From the nearly impregnable mountain stronghold of Alamut in Persia, and later from the Syrian stronghold of Masyad, the Assassins harried the Crusaders and their rival Islamic sects, remaining unbroken in power even by the great Saladin. They were finally destroyed in the 13th century by the Tatar prince Hulagu and, somewhat later, in Syria, by the Egyptian Sultan Baybars.

The name Assassins is derived from *hashish*, a drug made from hemp, with which, according to tradition, the victorious Assassins were rewarded upon their return from successful depradations. The secret of their long reign of terror was the absolute obedience that the young men of the sect were required to give to their leaders. The name of the sect soon came into the languages of Europe as a synonym for murderer.

Assembly. During the FRENCH REVOLUTION, a representative body which had three names: the National, Constituent, and Legislative. In 1789 the *tiers état* (THIRD ESTATE) declared itself to be the National Assembly and controlling body, and took the so-called OATH OF THE TENNIS COURT. Shortly thereafter, reinforced by a majority of clergy and a minority of nobles, it called itself the Constituent Assembly; in 1791 it framed and voted the first written constitution in French history. The Constituent Assembly was succeeded by the Legislative Assembly (1791), which voted the war against Austria and the imprisonment of Louis XVI, thus opposing the constitutional monarchy. In September, 1792 the Legislative Assembly was succeeded by the National Convention which immediately decreed the abolition of the monarchy. With this formality, the struggle among the various republican factions—GIRONDISTS, JACOBINS, CORDELIERS, adherents of ROBESPIERRE—began.

Asser (d. 909?). Welsh monk, later bishop of Sherborne (after c. 900). About 885 King ALFRED the Great invited him to his court as tutor and companion; he helped Alfred with his ambitious program of creating a center of popular learning. He wrote a biography of Alfred (c. 893), which includes a history of England from 849 to 887 and of Alfred's career until 887.

Assommoir, L' (The Dram Shop, 1877). One of the novels in the ROUGON-MACQUART series by Emile ZOLA. Written in the argot of the Paris streets, *L'Assommoir* is a study of the demoralizing effects of alcohol on the lives of working-class people. Although Zola had great compassion for these miserable people, his book was attacked as immoral because of the sordid nature of the subject.

assonance. In poetry and prose, the identity of vowel sounds, as in the words "scream" and "beech." Assonance is one of the many phonetic devices that serve to unify poetry and prose. In poetry it is frequently substituted for RHYME, and in this use is sometimes referred to as vowel rhyme. See CONSONANCE; ALLITERATION.

Assumption, Feast of the. August 15th, so called in honor of the Virgin Mary. In Catholic tradition, she was taken to heaven that day (A.D. 45) in her corporeal form, being at the time seventy-five years of age. There is a legend that the Virgin was raised soon after her death, and assumed to glory by a special privilege before the general resurrection.

Assumption of Hannele, The (Hanneles Himmelfahrt; 1893). A symbolic drama by Gerhart HAUPTMANN. It is the story of a maltreated girl who tries to drown herself and is taken to a wretched almshouse where she lapses into delirium. In her dreams she transforms the place and its dreary inhabitants into a fairy paradise of immense poetic beauty.

Assur or **Ashur.** The principal god of Assyria, which bears his name. The Baal of the Assyrian capital of Nineveh, he took over much of the dominant role that had been played by the Babylonian MARDUK.

Assur-bani-pal or **Ashurbanipal** (d. 626? B.C.). King of Assyria. The son of Esar-Haddon, he ruled Assyria, while his twin brother Samus-sum-yukin ruled Babylonia. Against great odds, Assur-bani-pal maintained his supremacy over Egypt and put down a Tyrian revolt. The most powerful of Assyria's rulers, he either subjugated or dominated the Manna, the Elamites, and the Cilicians. He also quelled a revolt by his brother in Babylonia, and harassed the northern Arabians. However, Assur-bani-pal had overreached himself and exhausted the resources of his own country to the extent that it collapsed completely not long after his death. He left behind him, however, a legacy of enormous importance for modern times: he had caused to be prepared for his royal library a large number of the most important literary works of the Near East; preserved on tablets, these were excavated in the middle of the 19th century in the ruins of Nineveh, his capital. Some characteristics of Assur-bani-pal are recognizable in the legendary SARDANAPALUS.

Astarotte. A fiend in Pulci's comic epic MORGANTE MAGGIORE. He takes Rinaldo from Egypt to the battle of Roncesvalles in a few hours by magic, discoursing on the way about theological questions. He has been regarded as Pulci's mouthpiece in the poem.

Astarte. See ISHTAR.

Astolfo. In medieval romance one of the twelve famous PALADINS of Charlemagne. An English duke, he joined the Emperor in his struggles against the Saracens. Known primarily for his great boasting, he was also generous, courteous, gay, and singularly handsome. In the *Morgante Maggiore* of Pulci and the Orlando poems of Boiardo and Ariosto he appears as Astolfo. In Ariosto, he rides a whale to the enchanted island of the witch Alcina and is detained by her until she tires of him. Transformed into a myrtle tree, he is rescued by MELISSA. Astolfo then journeys to the moon in search of Orlando's lost wits, which he brings back in a phial.

Astor, John Jacob (1763–1848). German-born American fur trader. Astor opened a fur store in New York City in 1786 and became the dominant figure in the fur trade of the Old Northwest. He later shifted his attention to the Far West, establishing Astoria, a trading post near the mouth of the Columbia River, in 1811. At his death he was the wealthiest man in the U.S. Washington Irving, on commission from the Astor family, wrote a laudatory account of ASTORIA.

Astoreth. See ISHTAR.

Astoria, or, Anecdotes of an Enterprise Beyond the Rocky Mountains (1836). A narrative arranged by Washington IRVING from material supplied by John Jacob Astor. Irving assumed the part of Astor's glorifier because he needed money, but parts of the work remain interesting as a record of life on the northwestern frontier. Astoria is a town established by Astor on the site of Fort Clatsop in Oregon, at the mouth of the Columbia River. Astor opened his fur-trading post there in 1811 and sold it to the British in 1812. It was subsequently returned to the U.S. by the treaty of Ghent (1814).

Astraea (Astraia). In classic mythology, the goddess of justice. She was generally said to be the daughter of Themis and Zeus. She was the last of the immortals to withdraw from the earth after the Golden Age. Afterward she became the constellation Virgo.

Astrate, Roi de Tyr (Astrate, King of Tyre, 1664). The most popularly successful tragedy of Philippe QUINAULT. The commoner Astrate loves Elise, queen of Tyre, but discovers that she has usurped the throne and that he is the lost son of the murdered king. The play aroused Boileau's harshest ridicule; the dilemmas of love, however improbable, are a recurring theme in Quinault's work.

Astrolabe, A Treatise on the (1391). An unfinished adaptation by Geoffrey CHAUCER of contemporary lore on astronomy and astrology. It is addressed to "little Lewis my son" (probably his own son, but possibly his godson Lewis Clifford), and explains the work of Messahala (eighth-century Arabian astronomer, known to Chaucer in Latin) in terms a child can understand. Of all Chaucer's prose works, it is the one that follows its model least closely, and therefore the best indication of Chaucer's own prose style.

Astrophel and Stella. A sonnet sequence by Sir Philip SIDNEY, written 1580-1584 and posthumously published in 1591. The "Stella" of the sonnets was Penelope Devereux. "Astrophel" (meaning starlover) is a Greek pun on Sidney's name. After Sidney's death in 1586 his friend Edmund Spenser wrote an elegy called *Astrophel*.

Astyanax. See TROJAN WOMEN, THE.

Asur. See Assur.

Asura. In Hindu mythology, a demon, an opposer of the gods.

Asushu-Namir. In Babylonian mythology, a hermaphroditic creature. It was created by the god Ea to rescue Ishtar from the underworld.

Asvins. In Hindu mythology, twin gods of light, the youngest of the gods. More than 50 hymns of the Rig Veda are addressed to them. See Vedas.

Asynja. The goddesses of Asgard; the feminine counterpart of the Aesir.

As You Like It (c. 1600). A pastoral comedy by William Shakespeare. Duke Frederick has banished the rightful duke, who is his brother and Rosalind's father, to the Forest of Arden. Rosalind first meets Orlando after a contest in which he has felled Duke Frederick's wrestler Charles. Shortly afterwards, Orlando is forced to flee to the forest to escape the plots of his jealous brother Oliver. When Rosalind incurs her uncle's wrath and must also flee, Frederick's daughter Celia and Touchstone the clown accompany her. In the forest of Arden, Rosalind, who has disguised herself as a youth by the name of Ganymede, meets Orlando and leads him through a series of episodes in which he unwittingly confides his love for her. Meanwhile, Oliver comes to the forest and, when Orlando saves him from death, the brothers are reconciled. In subsequent scenes, Touchstone woos the dull-witted Audrey, Oliver woos Celia, the shepherd Silvius woos Phebe, and Phebe woos the disguised Rosalind. At last, Rosalind reveals her identity, and the four pairs of lovers are united in the feast of Hymen before the banished duke and his followers. Rosalind's father is restored to his dukedom when Duke Frederick is converted by a monk and decides to enter a monastery. The story is based on Thomas Lodge's romance *Rosalynde: Epuphues' Golden Legacie* (1590). See Jaques.

Atahualpa (1500?–1533). Inca emperor of Peru. Becoming ruler of the northern part of the Inca empire upon the death of his father Huayna Capac in 1527, Atahualpa wrested the southern portion from his half-brother Huascar. The dissension produced by this fratricidal conflict facilitated the Spanish conquest led by Francisco Pizarro, who captured Atahualpa in 1532. Although Atahualpa was promised his freedom in exchange for a huge ransom of gold and silver, Pizarro accused him of conspiring against the Spaniards and had him executed.

Atala (1801). A novel by François René de Chateaubriand. A melancholy tale of violent passion, set in the primeval woods of North America, it is generally cited as signalizing the beginning of the romantic movement in French literature.

Atalanta (**Atalante**). In Greek legend, a daughter of Iasus (some authorities say Zeus) and Clymene. She took part in the Calydonian boar hunt and drew first blood. Being very swift of foot, she refused to marry unless the suitor should first defeat her in a race. Melanion overcame her at last by dropping, one after another, during the race, three golden apples that had been given him for the purpose by Venus. Atalanta was not proof against the temptation to pick them up, and so lost the race and became a wife. In the Boeotian form of the legend Hippomenes takes the place of Melanion. In some legends, Atalanta was also one of the Argonauts. William Morris made this legend the subject of one of the tales in his *Earthly Paradise* and Swinburne wrote a dramatic poem *Atalanta in Calydon* on the same theme.

Atalanta in Calydon (1865). A tragedy by Algernon Charles Swinburne. It is based on the Greek legend of Atalanta and the Calydonian boar. It is remembered today chiefly for its choruses, particularly the *Hymn to Artemis*.

Atalide. In Jean Racine's tragedy Bajazet, the princess beloved by the titular hero.

Ate. See Faerie Queene, The.

Atellanae, or **Atellan farces.** Low comedy interludes in the Roman theaters, introduced from Atella, in Campania. The characters of Macchus and Bucco are the forerunners of the modern Punch and Clown.

Athaliah. In the Old Testament (II Kings 11), the daughter of Ahab and Jezebel, and wife of Joram, king of Judah. After the death of her son Ahaziah, she gained the throne by murdering 42 princes of the house of David. She reigned six years, but in the seventh, Joash who had escaped the massacre was proclaimed the rightful king. Attracted by the shouts of the people at his coronation, Athaliah entered the temple where she was killed by the mob. Racine's last tragedy *Athalie* (1691) is based on this story.

Athalie (1691). A tragedy by Jean Racine. It is based on the Old Testament story of Athaliah and Joash. Because it was written for the schoolgirls of St-Cyr, the play includes songs sung by a chorus of Levite maidens. *Athalie* was Racine's last work for the stage, and is considered by many critics the most perfect example of French classical tragedy.

Athamas. A mythological Greek king of Boeotia, son of Aeolus and brother of Sisyphus and Salmoneus. He married the phantom Nephele at Hera's command and by her had a son, Phrixus, and a daughter, Helle. The sacrifice of these children was prevented by the arrival of a ram with Golden Fleece. Athamas also fathered Learchus and Melicertes by Ino.

Athanasius, St. Called Athanasius the Great (293?–373). A Greek father of the Church and lifelong opponent of the Arians. He is not the author of the Athanasian creed, which originated in the 5th or 6th century.

Atheist's Tragedy, The (1611). A tragedy by Cyril Tourneur. It presents the downfall of the self-seeking materialist D'Amville, whose early successes later turn to death and destruction.

Athene. The Greek goddess of war, handicraft, and wisdom. According to the most familiar story, she sprang fully armed from the head of Zeus when Hephaestus split it open with an axe. Zeus had previously swallowed his consort Metis, her mother, on learning that she would bear a child who would rule the gods. Another story, perhaps earlier, indicates that her birth was associated with some stream or lake; this may have been told of her as an ancient pre-Hellenic deity. In a dispute with Poseidon as to who should be patron of Athens, she won that distinction by bestowing on the Athenians the boon of the olive tree. The Parthenon was dedicated to her.

In most myths, Athene was a virgin, though originally she may have been a mother-goddess. She appears in innumerable myths, but none better displays her unique intellectual qualities than her role in the ODYSSEY as the constant friend and adviser of the clever and imaginative Odysseus.

Athens. The capital of modern Greece and one of the chief city-states of ancient Greece, situated in Attica. Its name was synonymous with outstanding cultural achievement for centuries after its political ascendancy had ceased to exist with its defeat in the PELOPONNESIAN WAR.

Atherton, Gertrude [Franklin] (1857–1948). American novelist. Among her numerous books, the most famous are *The Conqueror* (1902), a fictional biography of Alexander Hamilton, and *Black Oxen* (1923), a novel about the rejuvenation of an older woman. Much of her writing deals with California, as in *The Californians* (1898) and *California: An Intimate History* (1914).

Athos. One of the famous friends and adventurers in Dumas' THE THREE MUSKETEERS. Athos also appears in the sequels TWENTY YEARS AFTER and THE VISCOUNT OF BRAGELONNE. He is unfailingly the gallant gentleman, quiet and reserved.

Atlante (Atlantes). A magician and sage in the Orlando poem of Boiardo and Ariosto. Atlante is the teacher of RUGGIERO the Saracen warrior destined to be converted and marry Bradamante.

Atlantic Monthly, The. An American magazine founded in Boston in 1857. Named by Oliver Wendell Holmes, it has been edited by a series of distinguished men: James Russell Lowell, James T. Fields, William Dean Howells, Thomas Bailey Aldrich, Horace E. Scudder, Walter Hines Page, Bliss Perry, Ellery Sedgwick, and Edward A. Weeks. Among its contributors are numbered the most outstanding writers in America. Since 1938, the magazine has been noted for greater breadth, international outlook, and increased interest in current affairs. Several collections have been issued, including *Atlantic Harvest* (1947) and *Jubilee* (1957), a selection from the magazine's first hundred years.

Atlantis. A mythic island of great extent, anciently supposed to have once existed in the western sea. It is mentioned by Plato (in the *Timaeus* and *Critias*), and Solon was told of it by an Egyptian priest, who said that it had been overwhelmed by an earthquake and sunk beneath the sea 9,000 years before his time. See LEMURIA; LYONNESSE; NEW ATLANTIS, THE.

Atlas. In Greek mythology, one of the TITANS, son of Iapetus and Clymene. He was condemned by Zeus for his share in the war of the Titans to uphold the heavens on his shoulders. He was stationed on the Atlas mountains in Africa, and the tale is merely a poetical way of saying that they prop up the heavens, because they are so lofty. The PLEIADES were Atlas' daughters.

The figure of Atlas with the world on his back was employed by the Flemish geographer Mercator (1512–1594, real name Gerhard Kremer), on the title page of his collection of maps in the 16th century. The name has since been used to mean a book of maps.

atman (Sans., "breath, self, soul"). In Hinduism the internal essence of the single individual. *Atman* can also be used to refer to the universal Self, the source of all other selves.

atomists. See LEUCIPPUS.

atonality. In music, the absence of tonality. Atonality negates the primacy of a keynote or tonic; the notion of a scale built upon the tonic, to which certain of the 12 notes of the chromatic scale belong and to which others are foreign; the building of harmonic combinations exclusively in thirds; and the distinction between consonant and dissonant combinations, especially the need to resolve dissonances into consonances.

Arnold SCHOENBERG is generally considered to have been the first composer of atonal music and the prime systematizer of its methods. He eventually elaborated a 12-tone method of composition in which the notes of the chromatic scale were organized into an inviolable order, or "row," so that no note might be emphasized at the expense of any other. While the term *atonal* first implied an experimental rebellion against the single tonal center, it eventually came to designate the systematic negation of tonality through absolute equality of all tones. The organizational methods by which such music has sought to preserve its atonality have proved to be of greater value to contemporary music than the somewhat negative doctrine of atonality itself. Theoreticians, including Schoenberg, have questioned whether it is not a contradiction in terms to speak of "atonal music," and many hold that true atonality is, in practice, impossible.

Atreus, the house of. The royal line of Mycenae, whose terrible story was a favorite source for the Athenian tragic dramatists. Atreus and Thyestes, sons of Pelops, became rivals for the throne of Mycenae, left vacant by the death of their brother-in-law Sthenelus and his son Eurystheus. Thyestes suggested that it should go to the possessor of the golden lamb. Atreus, who had previously hidden one in a chest, agreed, not knowing that his wife Aerope had given it to Thyestes, who had seduced her. Thyestes won the throne, but lost it when Atreus, with the aid of Zeus, made the sun move backward, an omen that proved Thyestes a usurper. Learning of the seduction, Atreus invited Thyestes to a banquet, served him his sons in a stew, then banished him, but not before Thyestes had cursed the house of Atreus.

Thyestes learned from the Delphic oracle that only by begetting a son by his own daughter Pelopia could he avenge himself. He ravished her at night, unrecognized. Atreus, having killed Aerope, the mother of Agamemnon and Menelaus, now married Pelopia, thinking her the daughter of King Thesprotus of Sicyon. Bearing Thyestes' child, she exposed it out of shame, but it was rescued by shepherds and named Aegisthus. Atreus learned of the child and believed it to be his own. Later he sent Aegisthus to kill Thyestes, but Thyestes revealed himself as Aegisthus' father. Pelopia killed herself in shame, but Aegisthus killed Atreus. Thyestes, avenged, became ruler of Mycenae again. Later, however, Atreus' son Agamemnon drove out Thyestes and killed his son Tantalus, married the latter's wife Clytemnestra, and became king of Mycenae.

Clytemnestra bore a son, Orestes, and three daughters, IPHIGENIA, ELECTRA, and Chrysothemis. She never forgave her husband for the sacrifice of Iphigenia, but, taking Aegisthus as a lover, conspired with him to kill Agamemnon. When he returned from the Trojan War, they slew him in his bath. They also slew his captive, CASSANDRA. Electra, however, had smuggled away Orestes for his safety to the Phocian king Strophius, who brought him up with his own son Pylades. Grown to manhood, Orestes returned and, with Electra's help, avenged his father by killing both his mother and Aegisthus.

For this crime, which had been approved in advance by the Delphic oracle, he was driven mad by the ERINYES (Furies) of his mother. Later he was tried for his crime on the Areopagus, with Apollo pleading his case. He did not regain his sanity, however, until, on the advice of Apollo, he recovered an image from the temple of Taurian Artemis. There his life was saved by Iphigenia, who had been transported thither by Artemis at the time of the supposed sacrifice. Returning to Mycenae, he killed the new king Aletes, Aegisthus' son, and ultimately ruled Argos and Sparta, as well. His friend Pylades, who had accompanied him to Tauris, married Electra. With the return of Orestes' sanity, Thyestes' curse on the house of Atreus—or that of Myrtilus on the seed of Pelops—was finally lifted.

The events from the return of Agamemnon to the trial of Orestes are told in the only extant trilogy of Greek tragedies, the *Oresteia* (458 B.C.) of Aeschylus: the *Agamemnon* recounts his murder; *The Libation Bearers* (*Choephori*), the vengeance of Orestes; the *Eumenides* his trial. Various parts of the story are also told in Sophocles' ELECTRA, Euripides' ELECTRA, ORESTES, and his plays on Iphigenia, and in Seneca's *Thyestes* and *Agamemnon*. Eugene O'Neill retold much of the story in modern terms in his MOURNING BECOMES ELECTRA. Jean-Paul Sartre adapted the story for his play THE FLIES.

Atropos. In Greek mythology, that one of the three FATES whose office it was to cut the thread of life with a pair of scissors.

Atticus, Titus Pomponius (109–32 B.C.). Roman man of letters. He left Rome in 88 B.C. and took up residence in Athens (hence his added surname Atticus), where he remained for 23 years. He was famed for his ability to keep on good terms with men of conflicting personalities and political views, such as Brutus, Marcus Antonius, and Cicero. In his Athenian villa, he kept a staff of slaves whose work was to make copies of contemporary writings. It was Atticus' publishing house which preserved the letters of Cicero, the *Epistulae ad Familiares* and the *Epistulae ad Atticum,* invaluable sources of information about behind-the-scenes politics in the last years of the Roman republic.

Attila (d. 453). King of the Huns. He is notorious for his attacks and inroads upon Europe during the final stages of the Roman Empire. He overran the Balkans (447–450) causing great destruction. In 451 he invaded Gaul, but was forced to withdraw after a series of defeats. He and his soldiers were feared for their cruelty and vandalism; Attila himself was called "the scourge of God." Pierre Corneille made him the hero of a tragedy *Attila* (1667). He appears in the *Nibelungenlied* under the name Etzel and in the *Völsunga Saga* as Atli.

Attila (1667). A tragedy by Pierre CORNEILLE. One of Corneille's least successful works, it recounts the villainy and death of the murderous king of the Huns.

Attucks, Crispus. See BOSTON MASSACRE.

Atwill, Lionel (1885–1946). English-born stage and screen actor. Famous for his roles in Ibsen plays, he supported Katharine Cornell and Helen Hayes and played opposite Nazimova. In the movies most of his parts were in horror pictures.

Atys or **Attis.** The Phrygian counterpart of the Greek Adonis and Phoenician TAMMUZ. He was beloved by Cybele, the mother of the gods, but out of jealousy, she drove him mad. He castrated himself, died at a pine tree, and violets sprang from his blood. Catullus wrote a poem in Latin on the subject, which has been translated into English by Leigh Hunt.

Aub, Max (1903–). Spanish author and dramatist. Aub, a prolific writer, is known for his ironic humor, revealed in his novels *Campo de sangre* (1945) and *Las buenas intenciones* (1954). He is also the author of a tragedy, *Deseada* (1950).

Auber, Daniel François Esprit (1782–1871). French composer of opera, especially comic opera. His best known work is FRA DIAVOLO. He was director of the Paris Conservatoire, 1842–1871.

Aubignac, Abbé d'. François Hédelin (c. 1604– c. 1673). French writer. Although Aubignac was a mediocre playwright, his *Pratique du Théâtre* (*Theatrical Practice,* 1657), urging the observance of the classical unities in drama, offers useful information on the French theater of the 17th century.

Aubigné, [Théodore] Agrippa d' (1552–1630). French poet and historian. A fervent supporter of the Protestant cause during the religious wars, he fought in numerous campaigns and, for 20 years, was the friend and adviser of Henry IV. *Les Tragiques* (1616), his great epic poem of the religious wars, combines satire, allegory, and invective. Composed of seven books, it describes the horrors of the war, the vice and corruption of the Valois kings and the courts of justice, the sufferings of the Protestant martyrs and concludes with a vision of the final judgment in Heaven. The use of the Alexandrine in *Les Tragiques* was influential in establishing it as the vehicle of elevated French poetry. The third volume of his *Histoire Universelle* (1616–1619), an account of the Protestant struggle in Europe from 1553 to 1601, was ordered burned by the Parlement of Paris.

Aubrey, John (1626–1697). English antiquary. His best-known work is the anecdotal *Minutes of Lives,* now commonly known as *Brief Lives,* which first appeared as part of Anthony à Wood's *Athenae Oxonienses* (1690). First published separately in 1813, it is a valuable source of information on the lives of important 17th-century figures.

Auburn. The name of the village in Oliver Goldsmith's poem THE DESERTED VILLAGE. It is an imaginary English village, but some of its features support Goldsmith's wistful recollections of his own youth in the Irish village of Lissoy where his father was pastor.

Aucassin and Nicolette (early 13th century). French *chante-fable* in alternating prose and verse, one of the best medieval love romances. Aucassin, son of the Provençal Count of Beaucaire, falls in love with Nicolette, a slave captured from the Saracens. The Count separates them by imprisonment, but Nicolette escapes and Aucassin follows, and they spend three years together until they are captured by Saracens. Aucassin is shipwrecked near home and, his father having died, becomes Count. Nicolette is carried to Carthage, where she is recognized as the king's daughter; but she flees an unwelcome marriage and finds her way to Beaucaire disguised as a minstrel, so that the lovers are happily reunited.

Auchincloss, Louis [Stanton] (1917–   ). American novelist and short-story writer. A member of a prominent family and a successful practicing lawyer himself, Auchincloss is known for his stories dealing with the upper echelons of society. *The Injustice Collectors* (1950) and *The Romantic Egoists* (1954), both thematically unified collections of short stories, won critical acclaim. His first novel, *The Indifferent Children* (1947), was published under the pseudonym Andrew Lee. Other novels include *Sybil* (1952), *A Law for the Lion* (1953), *The Great World and Timothy Colt* (1956), *Pursuit of the Prodigal* (1959), *Portrait in Brownstone* (1962), and *The Rector of Justin* (1964). *Powers of Attorney* (1963) is a collection of short stories.

Auden, W[ystan] H[ugh] (1907–   ). English poet and dramatist. His most influential work was written during the 1930's. He was the best known of the group of British writers of Marxist sympathies who hoped that socialism might be the answer to the economic and political problems of the period. The group included the poets C. Day-Lewis and Stephen Spender, and the dramatist and novelist Christopher Isherwood. Auden served in the Spanish Civil War. In 1938 he married Erika Mann, daughter of the novelist Thomas Mann. In 1939 he emigrated to the U.S. and later became an American citizen.

During World War II, Christianity took the place of socialism as Auden's central preoccupation, and the influence of Marx and Freud gave way to the influence of Kierkegaard and the modern Protestant theologians. In his early work Auden expressed the idea that civilization could be cured of its economic and political diseases by socialism, and from its psychological diseases by psychoanalysis, the general cure being love. The same themes appear in his later work but with an added spiritual dimension. Auden's indebtedness to T. S. Eliot is particularly evident in the imagery of his earlier poems. The poem *New Year Letter* (1941; U.S. title *The Double Man*) is an analysis of the poet's intellectual development and changing views. He edited and rewrote subsequent reprints of his poetry in order to omit what no longer suited his poetic, political, or religious ideas. He also wrote much verse in the popular music-hall tradition.

Auden's chief early works are *Poems* (1930), THE ORATORS, *Look Stranger* (1936; U.S. title *On this Island*), and *Another Time* (1940). For the GROUP THEATRE he wrote the Marxist and experimental plays *The Dance of Death* (1933) and, in collaboration with Christopher Isherwood, THE DOG BENEATH THE SKIN, THE ASCENT OF F6, and *On the Frontier* (1938). He collaborated with Louis MacNeice on the verse and prose work *Letters from Iceland* (1937), and with Christopher Isherwood on *Journey to a War* (1939), about the war between Japan and China (it contains Auden's sonnet sequence *In Time of War*). The work of Auden's later period includes *The Quest* (1941), a sonnet sequence; FOR THE TIME BEING, a "Christmas Oratorio"; *The Sea and the Mirror* (1944), a "commentary" on *The Tempest;* and THE AGE OF ANXIETY. *Nones* (1951), *The Shield of Achilles* (1955), and *Homage to Clio* (1960) are collections of poetry. Auden collaborated on the libretto of Stravinsky's opera THE RAKE's PROGRESS. *The Enchafed Flood* (1950) and *The Dyer's Hand* (1963) are critical works. He edited the *Oxford Book of Light Verse* (1938) and selections from Kierkegaard (1952, 1955).

Audiberti, Jacques (1899–1965). French novelist, poet, and dramatist. All his writing is characterized by verbal extravagance and imaginative exaltation of modern man. His works include poetry: *Race des hommes* (1937) and *Toujours* (1944); novels: *Abraxas* (1938) and *Carnage* (1941); plays: *Quoat-Quoat* (1946), *Le Mal court* (1947), *Les Femmes du Boeuf* (1948), and *La Hobereaute* (1956).

Audrey. In Shakespeare's As You LIKE IT, an awkward country wench who jilts William for TOUCHSTONE.

Audubon, John James (1785–1851). Haitian-born American naturalist and artist. Educated in France, Audubon came to the U.S. in 1806. He traveled widely in the U.S. and Canada in search of material for his study of animals, which he depicted in firm, detailed drawings tinted in clear watercolor. His drawings reveal a good sense of design in the placement of animals and in the suggestion of their setting. *The Birds of America,* published in England from 1827 to 1838, is his most famous work.

Aue, Hartmann von. See HARTMANN VON AUE.

Auerbach, Berthold (1812–1882). German novelist of Jewish background, known especially for his collection of stories about rustic life, *Schwarzwälder Dorfgeschichten* (*Village Stories from the Black Forest,* 1843–1854). His deep awareness of problems faced by the Jews led him to write both the essay *Das Judentum und die neueste Literatur* (*Judaism and Recent Literature,* 1836) and a novel *Spinoza* (1835–1837).

Aufidius, Tullus. In Shakespeare's CORIOLANUS, the Volscian general whom Coriolanus defeats in battle. Coriolanus refers to him as "a lion that I am proud to hunt." Although Aufidius is responsible for the death of Coriolanus, he is immediately remorseful and vows to honor his memory.

Aufstieg und Fall der Stadt Mahagonny. See RISE AND FALL OF THE TOWN MAHAGONNY.

Aufzeichnungen des Malte Laurids Brigge, Die. See NOTEBOOKS OF MALTE LAURIDS BRIGGE, THE.

Augean stables. The stables of Augeas (Augeias), a mythological king of Elis, in Greece. These stables, in which he kept 3,000 oxen, had not been cleaned for thirty years. One of the labors of Heracles was to clean them, which he did by causing two rivers to run through them. Hence the phrase *to cleanse the Augean stables* means to clear away an accumulated mass of corruption.

Augie March, The Adventures of (1953). A novel by Saul BELLOW. This modern picaresque novel about a Chicago youth who grows up during the depression years brought its author national recognition. Because he will not accept any defining role in life, Augie finds himself being swept along in a current of alternately hilarious and tragic events. Unlike his brother Simon, who marries the daughter of a wealthy Chicago coaldealer in order to rise from his lower-class Jewish environment, Augie refuses every opportunity for a settled existence. He suffers some hard knocks, but, as he says, there is an *"animal ridens* in me, the laughing creature, forever rising up."

Augier, Emile (1820–1889). French dramatist. Reacting against the extravagances of the romantic drama, Augier wrote comedies that affirmed respectable bourgeois values. His *Gabrielle* (1849) satirizes exaggerated sentiment, while *Le Fils de Giboyer* (1862) levels a sharp attack on current attempts to disregard the differences between politics and religion. Among his other works are *Le Gendre de Monsieur Poirier* (1854), *Les Effrontés* (1861), and *Maître Guérin* (1865).

Augustan age. The golden age of Roman literature which covered the reign of AUGUSTUS Caesar (27 B.C.–A.D. 14). The Augustan age has, also, come to describe the apogee of any national literature, as, for example, the age of Swift and Pope in 18th-century England, which is often called the Augustan age of English prose.

The imperial period of Roman history begins with the establishment (27) of the principate (a thinly disguised monarchy) of Augustus after his decisive defeat of Mark Antony at ACTIUM (31 B.C.). Unlike republican Rome (see CICERONIAN AGE), the long, dictatorial peace of Augustus was not a time of free public debate. Oratory was useless, for there was no one to be swayed by skillful argument: the senate was a rubber-stamp parliament, and the people were voiceless. Augustus alone steered the ship of state. Historians had to be wary of adhering too closely to the facts of recent history. Only LIVY, with his lofty, patriotic aim of reminding his contemporaries of the glories of their republican past, could survive as a practicing historian.

Poetry, however, was not so inhibited. Under the patronage of the emperor and his wealthy supporter MAECENAS, the period was the crowning epoch of Latin poetry. VERGIL, perhaps the greatest of the Roman poets, began his first successful work, the *Bucolics,* in the year of Cicero's death (43 B.C.). He soon found encouragement and patronage in the retinue of the young Octavius (Augustus). His subsequent works, the *Georgics* (30 B.C.) and the *Aeneid* (19 B.C.), were intended, at least in part, to support the large-scale reforms in public morality and public thinking instituted by Augustus.

Another great poet of the period, the satirist and lyricist HORACE, was very different from Vergil in style and subject. His great achievement was to give new life to Roman satire and to naturalize in Rome the metrical forms of the older Greek odes. Other poets of this period include TIBULLUS and PROPERTIUS, both writers of love elegies.

Although the Augustan Age was an age of poetry, the one great poet who was born at its beginning and who was, in certain ways, its popular spokesman, died in exile three years after the emperor's death. This poet was OVID, who wrote love elegies, mock didactics, and the phantasmagorical epic, *The Metamorphoses.* This poet's last, pathetic years on the bleak shores of the Black Sea bring to a close the Augustan Age of Roman literature.

Augustine, St. Lat., **Aurelius Augustinus** (354–430). Early Christian church father and philosopher. Born in Roman North Africa of a Christian mother and a pagan father, he received his early training primarily in Latin literature and earned his living as a teacher of rhetoric in Carthage, Rome, and Milan from 374 to 387. He joined the MANICHAEANS for a number of years, but was disillusioned and after a period of skepticism was converted to Christianity by St. AMBROSE and baptized in 387. He returned to Africa and established a monastic community; in 391 he had ordained a priest at Hippo, becoming bishop there in 395. His CONFESSIONS vividly record his spiritual experiences and development during this period.

For the remainder of his life he preached and wrote prolifically, defining points of Christian doctrine and engaging in theological controversy with the Manichaeans, the Donatists, and the Pelagians. He maintained the importance of a single, unified Church, and developed a theory of sin, grace, and predestination that became basic to the doctrines of the Roman Catholic Church, but that later was also used as the justification for the tenets of Calvin, Luther, and the Jansenists.

St. Augustine (Strassburg, 1490).

Other important writings include *On the Trinity* (*De Trinitate;* 400–416), THE CITY OF GOD, *On Nature and Grace* (*De Natura et Gratia;* 415), and the *Retractions* (*Retractationes;* 426), in which he revised some of the more exaggerated statements he had made earlier.

Augustine of Canterbury, St. (d. 604?). First archbishop of Canterbury. He was responsible for the Christianization of England and called "Apostle of the English." A prior of the Benedictine monastery of St. Andrew in Rome, he was sent by Pope Gregory I (c. 595) to lead a missionary group of 40 monks to England. When he landed at Thanet in 597, King Ethelbert of Kent received him hospitably; Ethelbert's Frankish wife Bertha was already a Christian, and he soon accepted baptism. Augustine went to Arles in France to be consecrated as "bishop of the English," then returned and with Ethelbert's support of his mission baptized 10,000 converts the same year. He was made archbishop of Canterbury in 601, consecrated Christ Church there in 603, and tried in vain to reconcile the Celtic bishops in the rest of England with the Roman Church.

Augustus. Original name, **Caius Octavius** (63 B.C.-A.D. 14). First emperor of Rome. After his adoption by his great-uncle Julius Caesar (about 45 B.C.), he called himself Caius Julius Caesar Octavianus. It was thus, as Caesar's lawful heir, that the 19-year-old Octavius, upon Caesar's assassination (44 B.C.), skillfully lured Caesar's legions over to his side and formed, with Mark ANTONY and Lepidus, the Second TRIUMVIRATE. He pressed the war against Caesar's assassins, Brutus and Cassius, and after helping to crush the rebels at PHILIPPI (42 B.C.) he successfully maneuvered Antony into accepting as his share of empire the eastern Mediterranean provinces. Between the years 40 and 31 B.C., Octavius consolidated his control over the West, that is, Italy, Gaul, and Spain. His "cold war" with Antony finally broke out into open hostilities at ACTIUM (31 B.C.) off the northwestern coast of Greece. There the combined naval forces of Antony and of CLEOPATRA, the ambitious queen of Egypt, met Octavius' well-trained armada and were decisively defeated.

After this victory, Octavius celebrated a splendid triumph: Rome greeted him as her savior and showed herself willing to accept his sole sovereignty for 44 years. In 28 B.C. he was made *princeps senatus* (first senator); on January 17 of the next year he received the honorary title Augustus (by which he was thenceforth known); and in a series of senatorial bequests, he was made consul, tribune, and proconsul. Despite this gradual assumption of complete dictatorial power, his avowed aim was the restoration of the Roman Republic and the purification of its social and religious life. Whatever reforms he did accomplish, however, he did so on his own, by-passing the Senate and the Comitia. (See PRINCEPS.)

The accomplishments of Augustus include the construction of public buildings (libraries, temples, monuments—he boasted that he had found Rome in brick and left it in marble); the revival of ancient religious rites; the restoration of the calendar (the month August was named after him); the reorganization of the political structure of the Empire; and the fostering of a native Roman literature. (See AUGUSTAN AGE.) His greatest accomplishment, however—the one that made all these others possible—was the long periods of peace he was able to maintain through his mastery of the art of statesmanship.

Octavius Caesar appears briefly in Shakespeare's JULIUS CAESAR. In Shakespeare's ANTONY AND CLEOPATRA, he is presented as a cold and puritanical man of relentless purpose, the "man of the future" as contrasted with the declining Antony.

Auld Hornie. An epithet for the devil in Scotland. Pan, with his horns, crooked nose, goat's beard, pointed ears, and goat's feet, was transformed by the Scottish into Satan. In Scotland and northern England, Satan is also *Auld Clootie, Auld Hangie, Auld Nick,* and *Auld Ane.* The use of *Auld* seems to imply that he can appear only as an old man.

auld lang syne. In the olden time, in days gone by. *Lang syne* is Scotch for long since. *Auld Lang Syne,* the song (1788, pub. 1796), usually attributed to Robert BURNS, is really a new version by him of a very much older song; in Watson's Collection (1711), it is attributed to one Francis Sempill (d. 1682), but it is probably even earlier. Burns, in a letter to James Thomson, writes that "It is the old song of the olden times, which has never been in print. . . . I took it down from an old man's singing." See Robert AYTOUN.

aulos. See GREEK MUSIC.

Auric, Georges (1899–   ). See LES SIX.

Aurispa, Giovanni (1376–1459). Sicilian scholar and teacher in several northern Italian cities. He is noted for his trip to Constantinople to obtain manuscripts for Italian patrons of the new learning in the Renaissance.

Aurora Leigh (1856). A narrative poem by Elizabeth Barrett BROWNING. The heroine, a talented girl who is left an orphan without financial resources, learns to support herself by her pen. She falls in love with and eventually marries her cousin, Romney Leigh, a man whose passion for social reform has involved him in strange and varied experiences.

Aus dem Leben eines Taugenichts (**From the Life of a Ne'er-Do-Well,** 1826). A story by Joseph von EICHENDORFF, about a lazy young man who picks up his fiddle one day and goes off to see the world. His light-hearted adventures carry him through Germany, Austria, and Italy, but finally he settles down and marries the girl of his dreams. The basic attitude of the book is summed up in the last words: "And everything, everything was good."

Auslander, Joseph (1897–1965). American poet. In collaboration with Frank Ernest Hill, he wrote *The Winged Horse* (1927), a history of poetry for young people. His own poetry employs conventional forms with varied themes. His collections include *Sunrise Trumpets* (1924), *Cyclops' Eye* (1926), *Riders at the Gate* (1938), and *The Unconquerables* (1943).

Austen, Jane (1775–1817). English novelist, often regarded as the greatest of women novelists. The seventh child of a country parson, Jane Austen passed her days, like many an English lady of the time, almost entirely within her family circle. The only dramatic event of her life was an attachment to a clergyman who died before they could become engaged, but this was an obscure and doubtful episode, producing little outward change in her life. She never married; had no contact with London literary life; spent all her time, when not writing, on ordinary domestic duties, among her numerous nephews and nieces. Out of the materials of such a narrow world, precisely by sticking scrupulously to that narrow world, she made great literature. Her completed novels, SENSE AND SENSIBILITY, PRIDE AND PREJUDICE, MANSFIELD PARK, EMMA, NORTHANGER ABBEY, and PERSUASION, are distinguished by their satirical wit and brilliant comedy, complex and subtle view of human nature, exquisite moral discrimination, and unobtrusive perfection of style. These qualities elevate her little world of struggling clerical families, husband-hunting mothers and daughters, eligible clergymen and landowners, country fools and snobs, into an enduring microcosm of the great world.

Austerlitz, battle of. Also called the **battle of the three emperors** (December 2, 1805). A famous battle taking place in Moravia (now Czechoslovakia) where Napoleon Bonaparte inflicted a heavy defeat upon the armies of Russia and Austria. The emperors of all three states were on the field, being in personal command of their forces.

Austin, William. See PETER RUGG, THE MISSING MAN.

Autobiography of Alice B. Toklas, The (1933). An autobiography by Gertrude STEIN, written as though the author were her secretary, Miss Toklas. Although the book provoked an attack by other Parisian writers and artists in *Testimony Against Gertrude Stein* (1935), it remains a fascinating account of expatriate life in the Paris of the period.

Autobiography of Benjamin Franklin, The. One of the most popular works of Benjamin FRANKLIN, translated into virtually every language. Covering only the period of his life up to his prewar stay in London as representative of the Pennsylvania Assembly, it was written at intervals beginning in 1771; the final segment was completed shortly before the author's death. Parts of the autobiography were published in France between 1791 and 1798, but the complete work did not appear until 1868. Franklin's many interests—philosophy, politics, religion, literature, and practical affairs—and his energetic pursuit of them have made his autobiography an American classic.

Autocrat of the Breakfast-Table, The (1858). A series of essays by the elder Oliver Wendell HOLMES. A heterogeneous collection of boarders gather around the table, providing an audience for the wit and philosophy of the Autocrat. The essays take the form of conversations that generally develop into monologues. Cleverly and epigrammatically, the Autocrat discourses on social, theological, and scientific topics. The book, seemingly disconnected, is unified by the recurring themes and personalities. Holmes includes several of his poems.

auto-da-fé (*Port.* act of faith). The ceremony accompanying the pronouncement of judgment by the Inquisition. It was followed by the execution of sentence by the secular authorities. This ceremony usually took the form of a procession through the chief streets of the city or town to the church where a sermon was preached on the true faith.

Autolycus (Autolykos). A notorious thief of Greek mythology. A son of Hermes, he taught Heracles to wrestle, but later sold him mares stolen from Eurytus. Traveling with Heracles to Amazon country, he was stranded in Paphlagonia, but rescued by the Argonauts. When he stole Sisyphus' cattle, changing their color by magic, he was detected by the owner, who seduced his daughter Anticleia in revenge. Thus he became the grandfather of Odysseus.

Shakespeare uses his name for the merry balladmonger and peddler in THE WINTER'S TALE, who "having flown over many knavish professions, . . . settled only on rogue." His songs, such as "When daffodils begin to peer," are justly famous.

Automedon. According to Homer, the companion and the charioteer of Achilles, but according to Virgil the brother-in-arms of Achilles' son, Pyrrhus. Hence, a coachman.

Autonoë. In Greek mythology, a daughter of Cadmus. She married Aristaeus and bore him Actaeon. Having joined with Ino and Agave in denying that the lover of their dead sister SEMELE had been Zeus, she was punished by the son of this union, Dionysus. Driven into a Bacchic frenzy by the god, she helped to kill her nephew, the Theban king Pentheus. See BACCHANTS, THE.

auto sacramental. A one-act religious drama popular in Spain from the 13th to the 18th century. Performed at Corpus Christi, these dramas were allegorical in character, dealing with historical, biblical, and mythological subjects by which the tenets of Catholicism could be expounded. The genre was perfected by CALDERÓN, who wrote over 80 *autos*. In 1736 Charles III prohibited their performance.

Avalon. (1) In ARTHURIAN LEGEND, the island to which King ARTHUR is taken after he has been mortally wounded in the terrible, final battle. One of the earliest mentions of the island occurs in the 12th-century Latin *History of the Kings of Britain* by Geoffrey of Monmouth. A short time later, in his *Roman de Brut*, Wace mentions that King Arthur expects to return from Avalon as "the hope of Britain" after his wounds have been healed. Later versions of this dramatic incident elaborate on and expand the whole considerably. In Malory's *Morte d'Arthur* (c. 1469), for example, the barge that comes to take Arthur to Avalon is signaled to by throwing the sword EXCALIBUR into the lake, and the barge itself is filled with the three mysterious and beautiful, other-world queens. See GLASTONBURY.

(2) A Celtic word meaning "the island of apples," and applied in Celtic mythology to the Island of Blessed Souls, an earthly paradise set in the Western seas.

Avanti. Another name for Ujjain, the capital of Malwa, often mentioned in classical Sanskrit literature.

Avare, L' (The Miser, 1668). A comedy by MOLIÈRE. It is derived from Plautus' *Aulularia*. HARPAGON, a wealthy miser, wishes to marry his daughter Elise to an old man, Anselme, since Anselme does not require a dowry. The miser himself wants to marry his son Cléante's beloved, Mariane. Cléante arranges the theft of his father's money box, and in order to regain his treasure Harpagon permits Cléante to marry Mariane. Elise is allowed to marry her beloved, Calère, when her father discovers him to be the son and heir of Anselme. A happy ending balances the grim picture of inhuman greed.

avatar (Sans., *avatara,* descent; hence, the incarnation of a god). In Hindu mythology the advent to earth of a deity in a visible form. The 10 avatars of VISHNU are the most celebrated. The word is used metaphorically to denote a manifestation or embodiment of some idea or phase.

Ave atque vale! (Lat., "Hail and farewell!"). The words of Catullus at his brother's tomb.

Ave Maria, or **Hail Mary** or **Angelic(al) Salutation.** A prayer to the Virgin Mary. Its first phrases are based on the angel's address to Mary (the Annunciation, Luke 1:28) and the greeting of her cousin Elizabeth (Luke 1:42). The present form of the prayer was fixed by Pope Pius V in the 16th century. It has appeared in many musical settings, the most popular of which are by Schubert and Gounod. The smaller beads of a rosary are often called *Aves* or *Hail Marys,* the longer ones *paternosters* or *Our Fathers.*

Avernus. A lake in Campania in central Italy. Its sulphurous and mephitic vapors gave rise in ancient times to the belief that it was the entrance to the infernal regions. Hence, Avernus is used as a synonym for hell or the infernal regions.

Averroes or **Averrhoes.** Arabic name: **Ibn-Rushd** (1126–1198). Spanish Muslim philosopher and scholar. He is best known for his commentaries on Aristotle, which had an important influence on medieval Christian scholasticism. He also wrote treatises on astronomy, medicine, and jurisprudence. All his works were written in Arabic, but became widely known through Hebrew and Latin translations.

Avesta. The sacred book of the Zoroastrians and Parsees, dating in its present form from the third and fourth centuries A.D., collected from the ancient writings, sermons, and oral traditions of Zoroaster before 800 B.C. The books are sometimes called the *Zend-Avesta* from a misunderstanding of the term *Avesta-Zend* (*Avesta* means the text and *zend* its interpretation; hence the latter name has been given to the ancient Iranian language in which the Avistak-va-Zand is written).

It is only a fragment and consists of five parts: (1) the Yasna, the chief liturgical portion, including Gathas, or hymns; (2) the Vispered, another liturgical work; (3) the Vendidad, which, like the biblical Pentateuch, contains the laws; (4) the Yashts, dealing with stories of the different gods; (5) the Khordah, a book of private devotions.

Avicenna (Arab. **Abn-Ali al-Husayn ibn-Sina;** c. 980–c. 1037). Persian philosopher and physician. A Latin translation of his *Canon of Medicine* was used in Europe as the stàndard medical textbook until the 17th century. His *al-Shifa* (book of recovery), including sections on *Logic, Physics,* and *Metaphysics,* reveals his own adaptation of Aristotle's philosophy.

Avignon captivity, the (1309–1377). The period of the residence of seven popes at the palace of Avignon in Provence, under the control of French kings. During the papal schism two anti-popes resided there from 1378 to 1408. Clement VI bought the palace in 1348, and it remained a papal possession until 1791.

Avocat Pathelin, L'. See PATHELIN, LA FARCE DE MAISTRE PIERRE.

Avvakum, Archpriest (1621–1682). A leader of the OLD BELIEVER religious sect in Russia He is famous for his *Life* (*Zhitiye;* 1672–1675), written in a racy mixture of Church Slavonic, the old church language, and Russian vernacular.

Awake and Sing! (1935). A play by Clifford ODETS. It presents the various frustrations and tragedies of the Bergers, a lower-class Jewish family in the Bronx. The mother, with the best of intentions, browbeats her husband, forces her daughter to marry a man she doesn't love, and opposes her son's romance with a poor orphan. The results are disastrous but lead the one idealistic son to devote his life to the betterment of humanity.

Awkward Age, The (1899). A novel by Henry JAMES. It concerns the emergence of an English society girl from "the awkward age" into maturity and understanding. A rival of her mother in love for young Vanderbank, Nanda Brookenham is surrounded by older persons who are scheming and plotting. Vanderbank marries neither her nor her mother, and Nanda, disillusioned by her friends, goes to live in the country home of Mr. Longdon, an older man who had once been in love with her grandmother.

Axe-Helve, The (1917). A poem by Robert FROST. Written in blank verse, it tells of a conversation between Frost and a neighbor, and then describes the poet's visit to the neighbor's home. Ostensibly the story of a craftsman who hates the inferior products of the machine age, the poem is reinforced by religious references which give it a deeper meaning.

Axis powers. See ROME-BERLIN AXIS.

Ayer, A[lfred] J[ules] (1910–   ). English philosopher. Approaching truth and logic through a study of the nature of language, he is a leading exponent of LOGICAL POSITIVISM; his best-known book is *Language, Truth, and Logic* (1936).

Aymé, Marcel (1902–1967). French fiction writer. His novels are usually sophisticated satire, such as *The Green Mare* (*La Jument Verte;* 1933), *The Secret Stream* (*Le Moulin de la Sourdine;* 1936), *The Miraculous Barber* (*Travelingue;* 1941), *The Second Face* (*La Belle Image;* 1942), *The Transient Hour* (*Le Chemin des Ecoliers;* 1946), and *The Barkeep of Blémont* (*Uranus;* 1948). His short stories are known for the wittily realistic development of fantastic or burlesque situations. English collections are *Across Paris and Other Stories* (1958), including *The Walker Through Walls* (*Le Passe-Muraille;* 1943), and *The Proverb and Other Stories* (1961). His children's books include *Les Contes du chat perché* (1939), *The Wonderful Farm* (1951), *Magic Pictures* (1954). *Clérambard* (1958) is a play.

Aymon, Four Sons of (*Fr.* **Les Quatre Fils Aymon**). French CHANSON DE GESTE. Aymon is the father of Guiscard, Alard, Richard, and Renaud de Montauban, who escape from Charlemagne's court after Renaud kills the emperor's nephew. Charlemagne forces a long war on them until his paladins urge a settlement, whereupon Renaud goes to Palestine to fight the Saracens. For Renaud's exploits in the Italian romances see RINALDO.

Aymot, Jacques (1513–1593). French humanist and translator. Tutor and then chaplain to Charles IX and Henry II, he later became bishop of Auxerre, which he made a center of humanism. He is best remembered for his translation (1559) of Plutarch's *Lives*.

Aytoun or **Ayton, Sir Robert** (1570–1638). Scottish poet and courtier. A friend of Ben Jonson, he was one of the first Scots to use English as a literary language. He is believed by some to be the author of the original version of AULD LANG SYNE.

Aytoun, William Edmonston (1813–1865). Scottish poet and teacher. His best work consists of parodies of Tennyson, the Brownings, and other poets, and ballads in the vein of Scott. The former are collected in *Bon Gaultier's Ballads* (1845, with T. Martin); the latter in *Lays of the Scottish Cavaliers* (1848) and *Ballads of Sotland* (1858). He is also known as the originator of the name SPASMODIC SCHOOL for P. J. Bailey and his followers.

Azazel. A Hebrew name symbolizing an evil spirit living in the wilderness. It is mentioned in connection with services held on the Day of Atonement (Yom Kippur), in which lots were cast on two goats; one for the Lord and the other for Azazel (Lev. 16). The goat for Azazel was referred to as the SCAPEGOAT. Milton uses the name for the standard-bearer of the rebel angels in *Paradise Lost* (1667).

Azeglio, Marchese d'. See Marchese Massimo Taparrelli D'AZEGLIO.

Azevedo, Aluízio (1857–1913). Brazilian novelist. The first exponent of naturalism in Brazil, Azevedo was a shrewd critic of contemporary society. His best-known work, *O Mulato* (1881), deals with the status of the mixed-blood in Brazil. He also wrote *Casa de Pensão* (1884), about the residents of a boarding house in Rio de Janeiro, and *O Cortiço* (1890), translated as *A Brazilian Tenement*.

Aziz, Dr. See PASSAGE TO INDIA, A.

Azorín. See José MARTÍNEZ RUIZ.

Azrael. In Muslim theology, the angel of death who watches over the dying and takes the soul from the body. He is one of the four highest angels at the throne of Allah, whom he serves as messenger. He will be the last to die, but will do so at the second trump of the archangel.

the Wings of Azrael. The approach of death; the signs of death coming on the dying.

Aztecs. A Nahuatl-speaking tribe of Indians who dominated much of Mexico at the time of the Spanish conquest (1519–1521) under Hernán CORTEZ. In the 12th century, the Aztecs moved into the valley of Anahuac from the northwest and gradually subdued neighboring tribes, turning them into tribute-paying vassals. The "emperor" of the Aztecs was chosen by a supreme council which represented the 20 clans that comprised the Aztec tribe. See TENOCHTITLÁN; MONTEZUMA II; CUAUHTÉMOC.

Azuela, Mariano (1873–1952). Mexican novelist. After participating briefly in the Mexican Revolution, Azuela moved to Mexico City in 1916 and devoted the rest of his life to his two professions, medicine and writing. In his 41 novels, which touch on virtually every aspect of Mexican life during the 20th century, Azuela revealed an abiding concern for social justice and human dignity as well as angry dismay at the cynicism and corruption that he so often found in all levels of society. Among his best-known works are *Mala yerba* (1909), an indictment of the powerful land-owning class; Los DE ABAJO, probably his finest novel; *Los caciques* (*The Bosses,* 1917), an attack on the political bosses of a small Mexican city; *Las moscas* (*The Flies,* 1918), a trenchant examination of political opportunism; *La Malhora* (1923), the story of a woman who is dogged by misfortune; and *Nueva burguesía* (1940), a bitter satire on the lower middle classes of Mexico City.

B

B., Mr. In Samuel Richardson's novel PAMELA, a gentleman of station who attempts to seduce Pamela, but ends by marrying her. Henry Fielding satirically expanded the initial "B" into "Booby" in *Shamela* (1741), his parody of *Pamela,* and in JOSEPH ANDREWS; some of the later editions of *Pamela,* however, attempted to avoid the implication by giving Mr. B. the name of Boothby.

Baal. An epithet for any of a number of ancient Semitic gods. A Semitic word meaning lord or possessor, it was usually applied to a god as lord of a city or other place. The title thus became applied to a great many local gods; even the Hebrew Yahweh was so referred to in earlier days by the ancient Israelites. Originally a sort of fertility demon, Baal became individualized in various localities, notably as the Babylonian BEL and the Canaanite Baal. As the storm-god, he plays the principal role in the Canaanite POEM OF BAAL. Variations of the name also occur in the Greek Belus and in such Carthaginian compounds as Hannibal. In Tyre, the local Baal was known as MELKARTH. The worship of Baalim was firmly established in Canaan at the time of the Israelites' entry. The Israelites adopted many of the Canaanite rites in their own worship of Jehovah. Moses, ELIJAH, and other prophets denounced this form of Baalim worship as heathenism; hence Baal came to mean a false god. Baal was also a nature god symbolizing generation whose appearance, along with that of Ashtoreth (ISHTAR), was considered a necessary prelude to spring.

Babar. The little elephant in a series of French children's books. Written and illustrated by Jean de Brunhoff (1899–1937), and translated into English, they proved very popular in the U.S.

Babbitt (1922). A satirical novel by Sinclair LEWIS. It presents a portrait of George Follansbee Babbitt, a middle-aged realtor, booster, and joiner in Zenith, the Zip City. He is unimaginative, self-important, and hopelessly middle class. Withal, he is vaguely dissatisfied and tries to alter the pattern of his life by flirting with liberalism and by entering a liaison with an attractive widow, only to find that his dread of ostracism is greater than his desire for escape. He does, however, encourage the rebellion of his son, Ted, saying "Don't be scared of the family. No, nor all of Zenith. Nor of yourself, the way I've been." The name of the book identified an American type and gave a new word to the language.

Babbitt, Irving (1865–1933). American critic, essayist. One of the founders of the NEW HUMANISM movement of the second decade of the 20th century, Babbitt taught at Harvard for many years and in many ways epitomized the "professors" against whom H. L. Mencken and other "literary radicals" railed for their conservatism and traditionalism. A theorist about criticism rather than a critic per se, he saw in a return to the classical concept of man a possible solution to the excesses of romanticism and naturalism, and urged the necessity of moral and ethical standards for the evaluation of literature. His books include *The New Laokoön* (1910); *The Masters of Modern French Criticism* (1912); *Rousseau and Romanticism* (1919); *Democracy and Leadership* (1924), an extension in the political realm of his theories about literature; and *On Being Creative* (1932).

Babel, Isaak [Emmanuilovich] (1894–?1939). Russian short-story writer. Babel was born in Odessa of a middle-class Jewish family. He developed an early interest in literature, particularly the works of Flaubert and Maupassant. His first published stories appeared in a journal edited by Maksim Gorki. The older writer recognized Babel's talent, but advised him to see more of life before doing more writing. During the civil war following the revolution, Babel was attached to the cavalry detachment of General Budenny fighting in Poland. He recorded his experiences in the volume of stories entitled RED CAVALRY. The next year he published ODESSA TALES about his early life in the port city. A memorable character of the Odessa stories is Benya Krik, the Jewish gangster leader.

The success of Babel's work was immense. His vivid descriptions of the brutality rampant during the war in Poland were rendered in short, exquisitely polished stories. A unique feature of his work was his habit of treating his romantic material in a sharply honed classical style, reminiscent of Maupassant at his most concise. Babel's knowledge of the powerful effect of concision in literature is revealed in a line from one of his stories: "There is no iron that can enter the human heart with such stupefying effect as a period placed at just the right moment." The effort it took to achieve his remarkable effects is revealed by Babel's friend, the writer Konstantin Paustovski in his reminiscences. Babel showed Paustovski a 200-page manuscript, which turned out to be 22 versions of one of Babel's short stories.

Babel's popularity waned in the 1930's. The chief reasons for this seem to have been his neglect of political themes in his work and a growing resentment, under Stalin, of the way he depicted the warriors of Budenny's regiment. He disappeared about 1938, apparently a victim of the purges then going on. He is reputed to have been executed or to have died in a concentration camp, but no real facts about his fate have been divulged.

Babel, Tower of. A structure erected after the Flood by the descendants of Noah when they reached Babylonia. According to Gen. 11, the plan was to build a tower that would reach to heaven; but Jehovah, to prevent its completion, "confounded their language" so they could not understand one another. Thus, a tower of Babel has come to signify a visionary scheme, while the word babel itself has become associated with a confused uproar in which nothing can be heard but hubbub.

Babes in the Wood. Characters in an old English ballad and nursery tale.

Babeuf, François Noël. Pen name of **Gracchus Babeuf** (1760–1797). French journalist during the French Revolution. His ideas anticipated present-day communistic theories. Accused of conspiring to overthrow the Directory and re-establish the constitution of 1793, he was guillotined.

Babington's conspiracy. A plot against the life of Elizabeth I. Anthony Babington (1561–1586), formerly a page to MARY, QUEEN OF SCOTS, was induced by the priest John Ballard to organize a conspiracy in 1586 to assassinate Queen Elizabeth, lead a Catholic uprising, and release Mary from confinement. The plot was detected and Babington and a dozen others were executed. A few months later Mary was beheaded, largely on the grounds of evidence of her complicity in the plot supposedly contained in letters between her and Babington.

Baboon, Lewis. A character in John Arbuthnot's political satire *The History of* JOHN BULL. He is meant to represent King Louis XIV of France and, in a larger sense, the French nation. Baboon is a play upon the word Bourbon.

Bacbuc. See ORACLE OF THE HOLY BOTTLE.

Bacchanalia. Festivals held in ancient Rome in honor of BACCHUS, the name under which the Greek god Dionysus was better known in Rome. Like the Greek Dionysia, the feast was eventually characterized by drunkenness, debauchery, and licentiousness of all kinds, so that the word *bacchanalian* came to mean wild and drunken.

bacchants (bakchoi). Followers of the Greek god DIONYSUS or Bacchus. Also known as *maenads*, they engaged in wild ritual dancing on wooded mountains, during which they tore apart and ate fawns and perhaps human victims. They are probably an oriental addition (see CYBELE) to the cult of the Thracian god Dionysus. Their revels on Mount Cithaeron are detailed in Euripides' drama *The Bacchants*.

Bacchants, The (Bacchae; 408–406 B.C.). A tragedy by EURIPIDES. It deals with the tragic punishment of Pentheus, king of Thebes, who imprisons DIONYSUS and is torn to pieces by his own mother, Agave, during a bacchanalian orgy. Gilbert Murray pointed out that this of all plays most closely resembles in form the Dionysian mysteries from which Greek tragedy sprang. (See BACCHANTS.)

Bacchelli, Riccardo (1891–   ). Italian critic, novelist, dramatist, and poet. A writer of historical novels, he has been compared to Alessandro Manzoni because of the serenity of his outlook on life, his congenial humor, serious scholarship, and preoccupation with language and style.

Bacchelli was an artillery officer in World War I and the editor of *La Ronda* (1919–1923), an influential literary review published in Rome. The review proposed that contemporary Italian literature reaffirm its classical traditions by drawing inspiration from the Renaissance, Leopardi, and Manzoni.

Bacchelli's best-known work is the 2,000-page historical novel, *Il Mulino del Po* (1935–1940; pub. 1948–1950), translated as *The Mill on the Po* and *Nothing New Under the Sun*. The novel is a saga of Italian life from the Napoleonic Wars to World War I. The principals are several generations of the Scacerni family, Lombard millers whose gristmill stands for over a century on the banks of the River Po. The author draws from their story the conclusion that life itself is an unebbing flow of pain and sorrow, as regular and rhythmic in its course as the river that runs alongside the mill. Another historical novel, *Il Diavolo di Pontelungo* (1927), narrates the attempts of the Russian anarchist Michael Bakunin to foment a revolution in Italy and concludes with a description of an unsuccessful socialist revolt in Bologna (1864). *Mal d'Africa* (1934) recounts the African travels of the 19th-century Italian explorer Gaetano Casati.

Bacchus. In Roman mythology, the god of wine. He was, in fact, a Greek god (Bakchos was one of the names of the Greek DIONYSUS), the Roman god of wine having been LIBER. Bacchus was worshipped in the annual, riotous festival called the BACCHANALIA, similar to the Greek Dionysia. However, the fat and drunken Bacchus familiar from so many paintings of the Renaissance period was a later concept, completely out of keeping with the classic view of Bacchus as a handsome young man and a powerful god. In the *Lusiad* (1572) of Camoëns, Bacchus is the guardian power of Islam and an evil demon of Zeus.

Bach, Johann Sebastian (1685–1750). Outstanding German composer of the late Baroque. He came of a family that produced many musicians in the 17th and 18th centuries. His vast output includes all types of music current at the time, except opera; he was also a violinist and a renowned organist. By the end of his life his compositions were considered old fashioned, even by his gifted composer sons. Though Bach's music attracted some attention from Mozart and others in the period 1750–1829, its modern revival may be said to date from Mendelssohn's revival, in the latter year, of the *St. Matthew Passion* (1729). Other large choral works are *St. John Passion* (1723), *Mass in B minor* (1733–1738), and *Christmas Oratorio* (1734). Bach also wrote 198 cantatas for various occasions of the church year, 23 secular cantatas, orchestral music, chamber music, and outstanding works for organ, harpsichord, and clavichord. For the organ, he wrote sonatas, fantasias, preludes, fugues, toccatas, and 143 chorale preludes based on Lutheran hymn tunes; for harpsichord or organ, French suites, English suites, partitas, the Italian concerto (1735), Goldberg variations (1742), and *Das wohltemperirte Clavier* (*The Well-tempered Clavier*, 1722 and 1744). The last is two monumental sets of preludes and fugues in each of the 24 major and minor keys, written to exploit the advantages of equal temperament or tuning, which made it possible to play equally well in all keys; up till then this had not been possible.

Bachaumont, François de (1624–1702). French writer. He is coauthor with Claude-Emmanuel Chapelle of *Voyage en Provence et Languedoc (Journey to Provence and Languedoc,* 1656), a humorous compilation in prose and verse of outrageous scenic and gastronomic descriptions, laced with literary satires and burlesques.

Bachelier de Salamanque, Le (1736). The last novel of Alain René LESAGE. It is the story of the adventures of a young Spanish bachelor of arts, Don Chérubin de la Ronda, who meets a vast number of people in his profession of tutor. The novel is a vehicle for a cynical satire of the ruling classes: the nobility, the bourgeoisie, and the clergy. The picaresque plot, though Spanish in setting, is merely an excuse to penetrate the thousand and one turpitudes of French society, in which those who have succeeded in life have done so only by intrigue.

Bacheller, Irving [Addison] (1859–1950). American newspaperman and novelist. His most popular novel was *Eben Holden* (1900); the story of a young man in the middle years of the 19th century, it sold over 1,000,000 copies. *D'ri and I* (1901) was a novel set at the time of the War of 1812. *A Man for the Ages* (1919) dealt with Lincoln. His other novels include *Keeping Up with Lizzie* (1911) and *A Candle in the Wilderness* (1930).

Bachofen, Johann Jakob (1815–1887). Swiss jurist and classical scholar, known for his recognition of a matrilineal principle in ancient societies. In *Das Mutterrecht (Matriarchal Right,* 1861), which has since been refuted, he claimed that the matriarchal stage precedes the patriarchal in the social development of all peoples.

Back to Methuselah (1922). A 5-play cycle by George Bernard SHAW. Extremely long and not very dramatically theatrical, this collection of plays is a satirical fantasy on the prolongation of life and the perfectibility of the human race. The scenes are laid in the Garden of Eden, in England at the time of the play's composition, and in successive stages of the future, until the span of life has been increased and man has become almost wholly intellect. This progress is accomplished, not through science, but through the strength of the human will engaged in creative evolution.

Bacon, Francis (1561–1626). English philosopher, statesman, and essayist. Having served as solicitor general and attorney general, he was appointed lord chancellor in 1618; he was created Baron Verulam in the same year and Viscount St. Albans in 1621. With the intention of becoming a "second Aristotle," he carried on scientific and philosophic investigations and planned to reorganize on an experimental basis the systems of thought and the practical methods of obtaining power over nature that were current in his day. He was violently opposed to reasoning from authority and the syllogistic quibbling to which scholastic philosophy had declined in the early 17th century, and argued always for clarity of observation and the development of keen critical faculties of mind.

Most of his work on philosophy and science was written in Latin. Bacon's most important writings are THE ADVANCEMENT OF LEARNING and NOVUM ORGANUM, which formed the first two parts of his projected INSTAURATIO MAGNA; *Sylva Sylvarum* (1627); and NEW ATLANTIS. He is best known in the field of literature for his series of ESSAYS. See BACONIAN CONTROVERSY.

Bacon, Frank (1864–1922). American actor and playwright. He is best known for his role of the amusing liar Lightnin' Bill Jones in LIGHTNIN', a play he wrote in collaboration with Winchell SMITH.

Bacon, Leonard (1887–1954). American poet and critic. Known for his satiric verse, he won the Pulitzer Prize with his book of poems, *Sunderland Capture* (1940). Other volumes of verse are *Ulug Beg* (1923), *The Legend of Quincibald* (1928), and *Day of Fire* (1944). *Semi-Centennial* (1939) is his autobiography.

Bacon, Nathaniel. See BACON'S REBELLION.

Bacon, Roger (c. 1214–1294). English philosopher and scientist. He was called "Doctor Mirabilis" or "the Admirable Doctor." His encyclopedic *Opus Majus* (1267) urged that in order to make the Roman Catholic Church the leader in the civilization of mankind, Christian studies should be expanded to include all the sciences; he placed great emphasis on the importance of mathematics and experimental science, disciplines practically ignored in the learning of the time. His writings indicate his own interest in optics, chemistry, and astrology, and he is credited with having foreseen the practical possibilities of the telescope, lenses to correct vision, gunpowder, and mechanical navigation and flight. His *Opus Minus* is an alchemical treatise; the *Opus Tertium* stresses the utility of scientific knowledge, saying that without it philosophy becomes absurd. In 1278 the Franciscans, whom he joined about 1250, declared his

Title page of *The History of Frier Bacon* (c. 1660).

THE
Famous History
OF
FRIER BACON.
Containing the wonderful things that he did in his Life ; Also the manner of his Death, with the Lives and Deaths of the two Conjurers *Bungey,* and *Vandermast.*

Very pleasant and delightful to be read.

Blijdschap doet, het leven verlanghen.

London, Printed for W. Thackery, at the Angel in Duck-lane, and C. Bates next the Crown Tavern in West-smithfield.

works heretical, and he was imprisoned until 1292. He was working on a "compendium of theological studies" when he died.

Because of his advanced thinking on the need for experimental science and its practical possibilities, the popular imagination credited him with all sorts of magical achievements, supposedly the result of a league with the Devil. These legends began gathering at the beginning of the 14th century and appear in such works as Robert Greene's comedy *Friar Bacon and Friar Bungay* (1589).

Baconian controversy. An argument, first advanced in the mid-18th century, that William SHAKESPEARE did not write the plays attributed to him. The idea is based on the notion that Shakespeare, being a nobody from provincial Stratford, lacked the social background, education, and temperament to have written his masterpieces. The first claim for Sir Francis BACON as the true author was put forth by William Henry Smith in 1856; the following year Delia Bacon made an elaborate defense for Bacon's authorship in *The Philosophy of Shakespeare's Plays.* New "proof," in the form of a cryptogram of Bacon's signature in some of the plays, was offered by Ignatius Donnelly in *The Great Cryptogram* (1888) and by Mrs. E. W. Gallup in *The Bi-Lateral Cypher of Francis Bacon* (1900). Other writers, not satisfied that the evidence of authorship pointed to Bacon, attempted to prove the plays were really the work of Edward de Vere, earl of Oxford; or Roger Manners, earl of Rutland; or William Stanley, earl of Derby; or Henry Wriothesley, earl of Southampton; or Christopher Marlowe. There is no evidence that any of these men except Marlowe (who died in 1593 at the age of 29) ever wrote a line of blank verse. In orthodox Shakespearean scholarship, these controversies are ignored and it is assumed that Shakespeare wrote the plays.

Baconian philosophy. A philosophical system oriented toward experimental science and based on the principles laid down by the English philosopher Francis BACON in the second book of his NOVUM ORGANUM.

Bacon's Epitaph. 2 elegiac poems, first published in 1814, on the death (1676) of Nathaniel Bacon, the leader of Bacon's Rebellion, "made by his man." The poems are attributed to John and Ann Cotton of Queen's Creek, Va., and express opposed views of Bacon's character. Most critics consider them to be among the best early American poems. See BURWELL PAPERS.

Bacon's Rebellion (1676). An uprising of Virginia colonists, led by Nathaniel Bacon (1647–1676), a recent settler. Ostensibly the colonists wanted to quell Indian disturbances in the region, but they were actually protesting the tyranny (1642–1651, 1660–1676) of Governor William Berkeley (1606–1677). Although Bacon and his followers won some successes and burned Jamestown, his sudden death from fever resulted in the collapse of the rebellion.

Bactrian sage. A name given to ZOROASTER, or Zarathustra, the founder of the Perso-Iranian religion, which flourished in Bactria (the modern Balkh) before 800 B.C.

Badebec (*Fr.,* "open-mouthed"). In Rabelais' GARGANTUA AND PANTAGRUEL, the wife of Gargantua and mother of Pantagruel. The effort of giving birth to Pantagruel, as well as to a train of mules, dromedaries, and camels laden with salted and smoked foods, costs Badebec her life.

Badon or **Mount Badon, battle of** (c. A.D. 520). In Arthurian legend, the place of King Arthur's great victories over the pagan Saxon invaders. See ANNALES CAMBRIAE.

Badroulboudour. In the *Arabian Nights,* the daughter of the sultan of China who becomes the wife of ALADDIN. Twice she nearly causes his death: by exchanging "the wonderful lamp" for a new copper one, and by giving hospitality to the false FATIMA.

Baedeker, Karl (1801–1859). German printer who began the publication of a widely known series of guidebooks. His name has since become almost synonymous with guidebook.

Baena, Cancionero de. See CANCIONERO DE BAENA.

Bagehot, Walter (1826–1877). English economist and critic. He was editor of the *Economist* (1860–1877) and is known for his lucid, highly readable, idiosyncratic works on political economy, history, and literature. His *The English Constitution* (1867) is a classic in its field; other works of note are *Physics and Politics* (1872) and *Literary Studies* (1879).

Baglioni. A notorious Italian family. It dominated the affairs of the city of Perugia during the medieval period and the early Renaissance. When they were not slaughtering the rival Oddi family and other enemies, they were kept busy by internal feuds.

Bagnold, Enid. Maiden and pen name of Lady Roderick Jones (1889–). English novelist and playwright. She is the author of the successful novels *Serena Blandish* (1925) and NATIONAL VELVET. In later life she wrote such plays as *The Chalk Garden* (1956) and *The Chinese Prime Minister* (1961).

Bahaism. The doctrines of the Bahais, emphasizing the spiritual unity of mankind, advocating universal peace, and imbued with mild Oriental mysticism. The Bahais succeeded the Persian religious sect of Babism. Bahaism was founded (1863) by Mizra Husayn Ali.

Bahr, Hermann (1863–1934). Austrian critic and playwright. Like the writers of German naturalism, he wished to see the growth of a literary movement which would take account of the peculiarities of the modern age; but in his *Die Überwindung des Naturalismus* (*The Overcoming of Naturalism,* 1891) he made it clear that he favored a more sophisticated style than that of naturalism. His best-known play is *Das Konzert* (*The Concert,* 1909), an urbane and witty comedy.

Baiardo. Also known as **Bajardo** or **Bayard.** Rinaldo's horse, of a bright bay color, once the property of Amadis of Gaul. He was found by Malagigi, the wizard, in a cave guarded by a dragon, which the wizard slew. According to tradition he is still alive, but flees at the approach of man, so that no one can ever hope to catch him.

In Boiardo's ORLANDO INNAMORATO, the pagan king Gradasso comes to Paris to fight Charlemagne's paladins in hopes of winning the horse and Orlando's Durindana, a sword supposed to have belonged to Hector of Troy.

Baïf, Jean Antoine de (1532–1589). French poet and member of the PLÉIADE, who is remembered not so much for his poetry as for his inexhaustible interest in experimentation. Besides writing love poetry—*Amours de Méline* (1552) and *Amour de Francine* (1555)—he tried his hand at scientific poetry in *Le Premier des Météores* (1567), championed a reform in spelling, and introduced his own metric form, *le vers baïfin*. Perhaps his most promising project was the short-lived *Académie de Poésie et de Musique*, which he persuaded Charles IX to found in 1570 in the interest of uniting the two arts.

Bailey, Nathan or **Nathaniel** (d. 1742). English lexicographer. His *Universal Etymological English Dictionary* (1721) marks the beginning of modern English lexicography in the sense of objective registration of the complete body of words in the language. It served as the point of departure for the famous dictionary of Samuel Johnson.

Bailey, Philip James (1816–1902). English poet. He wrote *Festus,* a long and heavily moralized version of the legend of FAUST which won fleeting critical esteem and enduring popularity throughout the 19th century. The poem alternates ratiocinative writing with bursts of nebulous rhapsody; the portions in the latter manner were imitated by the SPASMODIC SCHOOL of poets. *Festus* kept reappearing in new and larger editions, incorporating other works of Bailey, until by 1889 it had quadrupled in size (40,000 lines).

Bailly, Harry. See CANTERBURY TALES.

Bairam. The name given to two great Muslim feasts. The *Lesser* begins on the new moon of the month Shawwal, at the termination of the fast of RAMADAN, and lasts three days. The *Greater* is celebrated on the 10th day of the 12th month, Dhul Hijja, lasts for four days, and forms the concluding ceremony of the pilgrimage to Mecca. It comes 70 days after the Lesser Bairam.

Baisecul. See Lord KISSBREECH.

Bajardo. See BAIARDO.

Bajazet (1672). A tragedy by Jean RACINE. The play is purportedly based on actual events that took place in Constantinople in 1638. It depicts the imprisoned Bajazet's pretense of love for the sultana Roxane, who plans to free him in order to marry him and place him on the throne, which is to be seized from her husband. Discovering Bajazet's love for the princess Atalide, Roxane allows him to be executed; discovering her infidelity, the sultan orders Roxane's execution; and, discovering her lover's death, Atalide commits suicide.

Baker, Ray Stannard. Pen name, **David Grayson** (1870–1946). American journalist and authorized biographer of Woodrow Wilson. Baker joined the staff of *McClure's Magazine* during the muckraking days and continued his contributions to that movement as an editor of the *American Magazine.* (See MUCKRAKERS.) Under his pen name, he wrote a series of essays which first appeared in the latter magazine and were later published in book form as *Adventures in Contentment* (1907) and similar volumes.

baker, the. A name applied to LOUIS XVI of France. He was called "the baker" (*le boulanger*), his queen MARIE ANTOINETTE, "the baker's wife" (*la boulangère*), and the dauphin "the shop boy" (*le petit mitron*) by the rabble who, after besieging Versailles on Oct. 6th, 1789, escorted them to Paris. When the king learned from them that there was a bread famine in Paris, he ordered supplies of flour sent there. During the return to Paris, chariots loaded with wheat and flour preceded the king's carriage, and National Guards carried loaves of bread, or sausages, on the end of their bayonets.

Bakunin, Mikhail Aleksandrovich (1814–1876). Russian revolutionary and anarchist leader. Born into a cultured noble family, Bakunin was educated at a military school in St. Petersburg, and served for a short time as an army officer. He resigned from the army and moved to Moscow, where he met the radical journalists Vissarion Belinski and Alexander Hertzen and plunged into the study of German philosophy, which was in vogue with the Russian intellectuals of the time. In 1840, Bakunin went to Berlin to continue his studies. He befriended the novelist Ivan Turgenev, who was also studying in Berlin. Turgenev is reputed to have used Bakunin as the model for the idealistic hero of his novel *Rudin.* While in Berlin, Bakunin published one of his most important early articles, *Reaktziya v germanii* (*Reaction in Germany,* 1842). In the article is the phrase that was later adopted as an anarchist slogan: "The passion for destruction is also a creative passion."

Bakunin took part in revolutionary agitation in Germany, Austria, and France during 1848. He was arrested and extradited to Russia the following year. After being in prison for almost 10 years he was exiled to Siberia, from which he escaped in 1861, making his way to Europe via Japan and the U.S. He remained in Europe for the rest of his life, mostly in Geneva and London. By the late 1860's, Bakunin's anarchist views were fully formed, and he expounded them in the periodical *Narodnoe Delo* (*The People's Cause*), which he published in Geneva.

Bakunin was a tireless, if not always effective, revolutionary schemer. An observer of his activities during the Paris revolt of 1848 said of him: "On the first day of a revolution he is a treasure; on the second he ought to be shot." This kind of revolutionary zeal led to Bakunin's expulsion from the First INTERNATIONAL in 1872 on charges of opposing the leadership, headed by Karl Marx, and of setting up a rival revolutionary organization.

Balaam. In the Old Testament (Num. 22–23), a prophet of Pethor whom Balak, king of Moab, had persuaded to prophesy against the Israelites invading his territory. On the way to utter the curse, Balaam was forced three times to beat the ass upon which he was riding when it stopped short, blocked by God's angel. "Then Jehovah opened the eyes of Balaam and he saw the angel of the Lord standing in the way" (Num. 22:31). Balaam refused to curse Israel, but pronounced his blessing instead.

Balan. The name of a strong and courageous giant in many medieval romances. He was the father of Sir Fierabras, a paladin in Charlemagne's court. In the Arthurian cycle, he is brother of Sir BALIN.

balance of power. A policy of preventing one nation from gaining so much power that it will be in a position to threaten the security of other nations. It was formulated by Prince Metternich at the Congress of Vienna in 1815, and became a leading principle of the continental policy of Great Britain with regard to France and Germany. In European history after Napoleon it played an important part in the wars and shifting diplomatic alliances of the nations on the continent.

Balaustion. An imaginary character of ancient Greece in Browning's *Balaustion's Adventure* (1871) and *Aristophanes' Apology, including a Transcript from Euripides, being the last Adventure of Balaustion* (1875). *Balaustion's Adventure* is for the most part a free version of Euripides' drama ALCESTIS.

Balbec. The French seaside resort visited by the narrator in Marcel PROUST's *Remembrance of Things Past*. It is based on resorts of the Normandy coast, such as Trouville and Cabourg.

Balboa, Vasco Núñez de (1475–1517). Spanish explorer. Sailing to America in 1500, Balboa became leader of the small colony of Darien on the isthmus of Panama. In 1513, after an arduous trek across the isthmus with 190 picked companions, Balboa discovered the Pacific Ocean, which he named the "South Sea," and took possession of it in the name of Spain. He later incurred the enmity of Pedro Arias de Avila (known as Pedrarias), governor of Panama, who had him beheaded on a trumped-up charge of treason.

Balbuena or **Valbuena, Bernardo de** (1568–1627). Spanish-born Mexican poet and bishop of Puerto Rico. Balbuena is remembered mainly for two long poems, both examples of the baroque style in literature: *La grandeza mexicana* (1604), a patriotic description of Mexico City, and *El Bernardo* (1624), a fantastic epic of chivalry.

Balchin, Nigel (1908–1970). English novelist. He is the author of *The Small Back Room* (1943), a story of wartime scientific researchers, or "back room boys"; *Mine Own Executioner* (1945), a psychological thriller; and *Seen Dimly Before Dawn* (1962), a novel about a 15-year-old English schoolboy.

Balcony, The (Le Balcon; 1956). A drama by Jean GENET. Men who come to Madame Irma's brothel to enact their secret ambitions begin to fulfill the roles of the images they have been playing. All, however, find that active responsibility is less satisfying than their dream projections. The Chief of Police discovers that he cannot *become* the modern hero until a customer comes to enact a heroic image of him.

Balder or **Baldur.** In Norse mythology, the god of light, summer, innocence, and purity, called "the good." The son of Odin and Frigga, he dwelt at Breidhablik, one of the mansions of Asgard. He is said to have been slain by his rival Hoder while fighting for possession of the beautiful Nanna after Holder had obtained Miming's sword, by which alone Balder could be wounded. Another legend tells that Frigga bound all things by oath not to harm him, but accidentally omitted the mistletoe. Loki learned this and armed his blind brother Hoder with a mistletoe twig, with which, after all else had been tried, Balder was slain. His huge ship was used for his funeral pyre, where he was joined by his faithful wife Nanna. His death brought general consternation to the gods, and formed the prelude to their final overthrow. See VALI.

Among modern poems written around the Balder legend are Matthew Arnold's *Balder Dead*, William Morris' *Funeral of Balder*, Robert Buchanan's *Balder the Beautiful*, and Longfellow's *Tegner's Drapa*.

Balderstone, Caleb. In Scott's BRIDE OF LAMMERMOOR, the intensely loyal but tedious old butler of the master of Ravenswood. His ingenuity in concealing the signs of poverty is equaled only by the faithfulness with which he serves the impoverished Ravenswoods without hope of reward.

Baldovino Di Buglione (Baldwin of Bouillon). The brother of Goffredo (Godfrey of Bouillon), commander of the Crusaders in Tasso's epic GERUSALEMME LIBERATA. Baldovino, one of the best fighters in the Christian camp, staunchly defends his brother when the Crusaders rebel against Goffredo's leadership.

Bald Soprano, The (La Cantatrice chauve; 1948). An antiplay by Eugène IONESCO. It burlesques the nonsensical stuffiness of a middle-class English home by stringing together the clichés of a foreign language phrase-book.

Baldwin, Faith [Cuthrell] (1893–). American novelist. Miss Baldwin, who has been called a "circulating-library" novelist, has written with great popular success a steady stream of lightly sentimental books for the feminine audience. Her many titles include *Those Difficult Years* (1925), *Three Women* (1926), *Woman on Her Way* (1946), *Blaze of Sunlight* (1959), and *Testament of Trust* (1960).

Baldwin, James (1924–). American novelist and essayist. His first novel, *Go Tell It on the Mountain* (1953), tells of the religious awakening of a 14-year-old Negro boy living in the Harlem section of New York City, where Baldwin himself was born. With this book Baldwin established his reputation as a writer of deep insight. His nonfiction, which includes *Notes of a Native Son* (1955), *Nobody Knows My Name: More Notes of a Native Son* (1961), and *The Fire Next Time* (1963), contains a passionate and clearly articulate statement on the suffering of the American Negro and an angry indictment of a society that permits such conditions to exist. Many feel that Baldwin is more distinguished as an essayist than as a novelist, although both of his later novels have received critical praise. *Giovanni's Room* (1956), a novel about a homosexual relationship, is set in Paris, where Baldwin exiled himself for a number of years. *Another Country* (1961) is a powerful though uneven novel of personal relationships among Negroes and whites.

Baldwin, Stanley. 1st Earl of Bewdley (1867–1947). English statesman. Baldwin, who became a Conservative member of Parliament in 1908, served as prime minister in 1923–1924, 1924–1929, and 1935–1937. The abdication of Edward VIII (later the duke of WINDSOR) occurred during Baldwin's third term.

Bale, John (1495–1563). English author and prelate. He was one of the most outspoken and vituperative critics of Roman Catholicism at the time of the English Reformation. A protegé of Thomas Cromwell and under Cromwell's patronage, Bale produced a number of morality plays and interludes attacking the Catholic clergy. The most important of these is his *Kynge Johan* (c. 1548), considered the first example of the CHRONICLE PLAY later developed by Shakespeare. Bale is also noted for his *Illustrium Majoris Britanniae Scriptorum*

(1548; revised edition, 1557–1559), a valuable, although often inaccurate, catalogue of British writers and their work.

Balfour, John, 3rd baron of **Burley** (d. 1688). A character in Scott's *Old Mortality* (1816). Scott, who depicted him as a bold and violent leader of the COVENANTERS, confused him with John Balfour of Kinloch.

Balfour Declaration (1917). An assurance by Great Britain of protection for the Jewish settlement of Palestine. After British forces had captured Palestine, the British Government declared its support for limited Jewish immigration into the area. Arthur James Balfour, the foreign secretary, drew up the statement of policy, which thus acquired his name. The Balfour Declaration formed the basis for British policy on the mandate of Palestine for the next 30 years.

Balin, Sir. One of the knights of the Round Table in Arthurian legend, brother of Sir Balan. In Malory's *Morte d'Arthur* (c. 1469), the two brothers unwittingly kill each other in single combat, neither recognizing the other until just before death. At their request they are buried in one grave by Merlin. Tennyson gives a much altered version of the story in *Idylls of the King* (1859–1872).

Balisand (1924). A novel by Joseph HERGESHEIMER. The story of a Federalist in tidewater Virginia in the days of the Revolution and afterward, *Balisand* pictures the conflict between the ideals of aristocracy and Jeffersonian democracy.

Balisarda. In the ORLANDO FURIOSO of Ariosto a famous sword made in the garden of Orgagna by the sorceress Falerina. It has the power to cut through even enchanted substances and was given to Ruggiero for the purpose of killing Orlando:

> He knew with Balisarda's lightest blows,
> Nor helm, nor shield, nor cuirass could avail,
> Nor strongly tempered plate, nor twisted mail.

Ball, Hugo (1886–1927). German writer and actor. He was one of the founders of the DADA movement in Zürich (1916). His *Hermann Hesse, Sein Leben und sein Werk* (*Hermann Hesse, His Life and Work*, 1927), a biography, stems from a personal acquaintance with the novelist.

ballad. A narrative song, originally chiefly of popular origin. Ballads fall into types according to subject and include the domestic tragedy, concerning a murder or family feud; the historical ballad, dealing with historical events; the outlaw ballad, celebrating a popular rebel against established law, such as Robin Hood or Jesse James; the Scottish coronach, or lament ballad; and the folkloric ballad. Among early ballads, coronach and historical ballads and those involving romance elements were usually composed by minstrels attached to noblemen's courts and were written with a sense of literary values and for a definite audience. The other types were popular products transmitted by oral tradition and had much charm but little artistic finish. In the U.S. many folk ballads are survivals or variants of the old English ballads. However, there are a number of indigenous types dealing with such subjects as occupational pursuits (*Casey Jones*), the Negroes and other national or ethnic groups (*John Henry*),

various sections of the country, famous battles, and actual or legendary heroes.

English and Scottish ballads dating from the 14th to the 16th century are found in Percy's RELIQUES OF ANCIENT ENGLISH POETRY and Child's *English and Scottish Popular Ballads*. Many literary ballads have been written by later poets; among them may be mentioned Campbell's *Lord Ullin's Daughter*, Scott's *Rosabelle*, Rossetti's *Sister Helen*, and Stephen Vincent Benét's *Ballad of William Sycamore*.

ballade. A traditional verse form first appearing in Provençal literature. The ballade was developed in France and reached its height during the 14th century, when it first came into English. François Villon (15th century) probably wrote the best-known ballades in literary history.

The ballade consists of three stanzas and an envoi, and its distinguishing feature is a refrain that appears as the last line of each stanza. The stanza may be of seven, eight, or ten lines. The ballade royal, written in RHYME ROYAL, has a fourth stanza instead of an envoi. Only three or four rhymes are used in all. The refrain adds to the meaning of the poem in every occurrence; the envoi is usually addressed to the poet's patron or to someone concerned with the subject of the poem. Chaucer's *Ballade of Good Counsel* and Swinburne's *Ballad of Dreamland* are good examples in English. See CHANT ROYAL.

Ballad of Dead Ladies, The (1869). An English translation by Dante Gabriel ROSSETTI of the famous *Ballade des dames du temps jadis* of the medieval French poet François Villon.

Ballad of Reading Gaol, The (1898). A poem by Oscar WILDE. It is the study of a man condemned to die and is drawn from the author's experiences in the prison of the title.

ballata. An Italian dance song popular among the folk as well as the learned during the Middle Ages and the Renaissance. Derived from the Italian word for dance (*ballo*), it was usually made up of a stanza of varying length and a two-line refrain intended for a soloist and a chorus of dancers. *Ballate* were written by Boccaccio, Poliziano, Lorenzo de' Médicis, and many others. Many were set to music by such famous composers as Francesco Landini.

ballet. An art form combining music, dance, and pantomime. Ballet originated in ancient Roman pantomimic performances, and was a popular entertainment at the courts of the Italian princes. In the 17th century Catherine de' Médicis imported ballet to France, where it acquired the *corps de ballet,* elaborate sets and costumes, and dramatic plots, often the work of leading poets and playwrights. After the French Revolution, ballet in western Europe became an adjunct to the opera, but survived in Russia in its classical form. The ballet of the 20th century, largely the creation of the Ballet Russe (Russian ballet) of Serge DIAGHILEV, is a synthesis of classical dance with modern dance of the sort pioneered by the American Isadora Duncan. Contemporary ballet can range from pure dance, without dramatic plot or incident, to danced drama, with fully developed plot and characterization, lacking only speech. Balletic elements have infiltrated and influenced opera, films, and stage plays.

balm. A curative. In the Bible, Jeremiah asks, "Is there no balm in Gilead?" meaning is there no medicine, or consolation (Jer. 8:22). "Balm" in this passage is the Geneva Bible's translation of the Hebrew *sori*, which probably means mastic, the resin yielded by the mastic tree, *Pistacia lentiscus*, which was formerly used in many medicines. In Wyclif's Bible the word is translated "gumme," and in Coverdale's "triacle." Balm of Gilead is also the name given to the black or balsam poplar.

Balmont, Konstantin Dmitriyevich (1867–1943). Russian poet. He was the first of the Russian SYMBOLISTS to become widely popular, primarily because of the musical quality of his poetry. His first work appeared in 1890, followed by other collections and translations, chiefly from English poetry. His favorite foreign poets were Shelley and Poe. Balmont emigrated after the revolution and lived in France until his death.

Balor. In the Gaelic mythological cycle, a FOMORIAN giant with an evil eye, which kills whomever it is turned on. In the tale BATTLE OF MOYTURA, he is slain by Lug who casts a stone from his sling into the eye of Balor, so that the eye comes "out through the back of his head."

Balsamo, Giuseppe. See Count Alessandro di CAGLIOSTRO.

Balthazar. (1) One of the three MAGI.

(2) In Shakespeare's COMEDY OF ERRORS, a merchant and friend of Antipholus of Syracuse.

(3) A servant to Don Pedro in Shakespeare's MUCH ADO ABOUT NOTHING.

(4) One of the four novels in Lawrence Durrell's ALEXANDRIA QUARTET.

Balue, Jean de la (1422–1491). French cardinal and politician. Accused of treason by Louis XI, he was imprisoned, it is said, in an iron cage. After 11 years he was freed as a result of papal intervention. Balue is a character in Scott's *Quentin Durward* (1823).

Baly or **Bali.** One of the great kings in the legends of India. He founded the city called by his name, redressed wrongs, upheld justice, was generous and charitable, so that at death he became one of the judges of hell. One day a dwarf asked the mighty monarch to allow him to measure three of his own paces for a hut to dwell in. Baly smiled and gave him permission. The first pace of the dwarf encompassed the earth, the second the heavens, and the third the infernal regions. Baly realized immediately that the dwarf was an incarnation of Vishnu and worshiped him. Vishnu made Baly king of hell and permitted him to revisit the earth once a year, on the first full moon of November.

Balzac, Honoré de (1799–1850). French novelist. Born at Tours, Balzac attended the Sorbonne where he acquired a passionate interest in literature. Unsuccessful experiments in the sensational novel and increasing debts marked his early years. At the age of 30, Balzac published his first successful novel, LES CHOUANS, and began the literary career that was to be as astoundingly prolific as it was important—he wrote more than 90 novels and tales. As in Stendhal and Flaubert, the romantic and the realistic coexist in both Balzac's character and his writings. Considered to be a founder of the realistic school, Balzac uses vast reams of meticulous detail

and faithfully depicts ordinary and undistinguished lives. Carefully documented, his novels are objective in their point of view and wide in their scope. Juxtaposed, however, with these realistic elements are the flagrantly romantic qualities of melodramatic plots, violent passions, and rhetorical passages. Balzac's characters are romantic in their extremism. Like the men and women of Dickens, they are painted in such bold strokes that they move away from human reality. Character traits, in such people as M. Grandet or Père Goriot, become heightened and exaggerated.

LA COMÉDIE HUMAINE is Balzac's tour de force, his masterpiece. The product of 20 years of creative labor, *La Comédie Humaine* is an attempt to present a complete social history of France in a thorough and scientific manner. The conception alone testifies to Balzac's almost superhuman energy and his unfailing vitality. Some of the finest novels in the series include EUGÉNIE GRANDET, LE PÈRE GORIOT, LA RECHERCHE DE L'ABSOLU, and CÉSAR BIROTTEAU. In style, Balzac's works are not graceful and polished. A strain of coarseness in the man and the work, a lack of concern with delicacy and subtlety, contributed to the clumsy strength of his prose. Balzac worked in breadth, not depth, and on his enormous canvas an unwieldly but intensely alive panoramic vision of France took shape.

Ban, King. In Arthurian legend (e.g., Malory's *Morte d'Arthur*), the king of Benwick and father of Sir Launcelot.

Bancroft, George (1800–1891). American diplomat and historian. A Democrat when most men of his background in Massachusetts were Whigs, Bancroft was named collector of the port of Boston as a reward for his party services in 1837. He later served as secretary of the navy and as minister to Great Britain and to Germany. He is best known, however, as the author of a 10-volume *History of the United States* (1834–1874), which he revised and cut to six volumes in 1876. A final revision (1883–1885) contained a volume on the *History of the Formulation of the Constitution*. Bancroft's historical work, which reflects his ardent faith in democracy and in the American people, has sometimes been compared to a Fourth-of-July oration. Although it is often considered outmoded, it is representative of 19th-century American nationalism.

Bandello, Matteo (1485–1561). Italian author. His *Novelliere* (1554), a collection of more than 200 short tales (see NOVELLA) which were translated into French and English, provided the basic plots for Shakespeare's *Romeo and Juliet, Much Ado About Nothing*, and *Twelfth Night*.

Banerjee, Tarashankar (1898–   ). Bengal's greatest living novelist. His writings are largely concerned with the decay of the landlord class and reveal his sympathetic attitude toward the oppressed peasants in Bengal's villages. *Rai Kamal* (1934) is considered his greatest work, but his enormously prolific output makes it difficult to assess the quality of his achievement.

Bang, Herman Joachim (1857–1912). Danish novelist and short-story writer. Acute sensitivity, loneliness, and compassion for those who suffer color all his work. After an abortive stage career, Bang turned to writing; his work is sometimes marked, however, by a certain preciousness and affectation that recalls the actor. *Tine* (1889) is a critical account of the weakness shown by the Danes in the defeat of 1864. In the novel *Det hvide Hus* (*The White House*, 1898), he paints a vivid reminiscence of his childhood and of his mother, who died when he was 14. *Ved Vejen* (*By the Wayside*, 1886) and *Ludvigsbakke* (*Ida Brandt*, 1896) are both tragic idylls, which depict with sympathy the drab, gray lives of unhappy women. Although his subjects are naturalistic, Bang never attempts detachment, but views the world from the perspective of his own misery and isolation. His impressionistic style is delicate and graceful.

Bangorian controversy. A theological war of words. It was stirred up by a sermon preached March 31, 1717, before George I, by Dr. Hoadly, bishop of Bangor, on the text, "My kingdom is not of this world," the argument being that Christ had not delegated His power or authority to either king or clergy. Arguing against High Church prerogative, Hoadly denied virtually all independent political power to the Established Church. Hoadly was strongly attacked on this point by William Law. The sermon, which was printed by royal command, led to such discord in Convocation that this body was prorogued, and from that time till 1852 was allowed to meet only as a matter of form.

Banks, John (c. 1650–1706). English dramatist. He wrote the tragedies *Virtue Betrayed, or Anna Bullen* (1682) and *The Island Queens, or The Death of Mary, Queen of Scotland* (pub. 1684).

Banks' horse. A horse called Marocco trained to do all manner of tricks. It belonged to one Banks about the end of the reign of Queen Elizabeth. One of Marocco's supposed exploits was the ascent of the steeple of old St. Paul's. He is frequently mentioned in contemporary literature.

Bankside. The southern bank of the Thames River. In Elizabethan times it was outside the city limits of London and therefore suitable for the production of plays. (Puritan opposition to the theaters outlawed the presentation of theatrical events within the city.) Shakespeare's Globe was located on the Bankside.

Banquo. In Shakespeare's MACBETH, the thane of Lochaber and a general in the king's army. He is slain by order of Macbeth because the witches had foretold that his descendants would reign over Scotland. His ghost later appears to Macbeth at a banquet, though it is invisible to the others present. Described as having a "royalty of nature," a "dauntless temper of mind," and a "wisdom that doth guide his valor," he serves as a foil to the ambition-driven Macbeth.

The name Banquo is given in many old genealogies of the Scottish kings, but Shakespeare's character is not drawn from history. See FLEANCE.

banshee. The domestic spirit of certain Irish or Highland Scottish families. Banshees were supposed to take an interest in the welfare of the family, and to wail at the death of one of its members. The word is the Old Irish *ben side,* a woman of the elves or fairies.

Banville, Théodore de (1823–1891). French poet, dramatist, and man of letters. Banville was a contributor to the *Parnasse Contemporain* (1866).

His best collections of poetry are *Les Stalactites* (1846), *Le Sang de la coupe* (1857), and *Les Exilés* (1867). See PARNASSIANS.

banzai (Jap. *ban,* ten thousand; *sai,* year). A Japanese cheer of enthusiasm or victory.

Baptes. Priests of the goddess Cotytto. She was the Thracian goddess of lewdness, whose midnight orgies were so obscene that they disgusted even the goddess herself. They received their name from the Greek verb *bapto,* to wash, because of the so-called ceremonies of purification connected with her rites. (Juvenal, ii, 91.)

baptism. The rite of Christian initiation. It is performed by pouring or sprinkling water on a person, or by immersing him briefly in water, accompanied usually with the formula "I baptize thee in the name of the Father, and of the Son, and of the Holy Ghost." The rite is held to wash away the stain of ORIGINAL SIN and to make the recipient a member of the Christian church. Much controversy has surrounded the mode of administration, and the age at which baptism should be administered. See ANABAPTISTS; SACRAMENT.

Baptista. In Shakespeare's TAMING OF THE SHREW, a rich gentleman of Padua, the father of Katharina and Bianca.

Barabbas. The robber and insurrectionary leader whom Pilate released from prison instead of Jesus, according to the custom that, at the feast of Passover, one prisoner, by popular demand, should be freed (Matt. 27).

Various baptismal practices ridiculed in Daniel Featly's *The Dippers Dipt* (1660).

NEW YORK PUBLIC LIBRARY

Barabbas (1950). A novel by Pär LAGERKVIST. The book tells the story of the fate of Barabbas, the criminal who was released instead of Christ, by Pilate. A reprobate, Barabbas is strangely affected by the Crucifixion and drawn, almost against his will, toward Christ's believers. Tortured by doubt, isolated from his fellow human beings, Barabbas seeks some certain meaning in existence. He dies with a cry of uncertainty still on his lips. Lagerkvist uses the biblical story to express his vision of man's anguish, his loneliness, and his desperate quest for meaning. He offers no simple, sure solution, but he does offer an intense compassion.

Barbara Allan (1724). A ballad by Allan RAMSAY, which appears in Percy's *Reliques*. Sir John Grehme is dying of love for Barbara Allan. Barbara goes to see him and, drawing aside the curtain, says, "Young man, I think ye're dyan'." She then leaves him, but she has not gone more than a mile away when she hears the death-bell toll and bitterly repents what she has said.

Barbara Frietchie (1863). A poem by John Greenleaf WHITTIER. The central incident in the poem is the fictional encounter between Barbara Frietchie and Stonewall Jackson. He forbade his Confederate troops to harm her, when she prominently displayed a Union flag. Ninety-six years old, she stood at her window in Frederick, Md.

> "Shoot, if you must, this old gray head,
> But spare your country's flag," she said.

Barbarossa (*It.,* "red-beard"). The surname attached to Frederick I (1123?–1190). King of Germany and Holy Roman emperor (1152–1190), he was a gifted ruler who helped unite Germany, but spent much of his time in the subjugation of Italy. He died on his way to the Third Crusade. There was a legend that he never died, but is still sleeping in the Kyffhäuser in Thuringia. There he sits at a stone table with his six knights, waiting the "fulness of time," when he will come from his cave to rescue Germany from bondage, and give her the foremost place of all the world. His beard has already grown through the table's slab, but must wind itself thrice round the table before his second advent. This legend originally grew up about Frederick's equally remarkable grandson, Frederick II.

Barbe-bleue. See BLUEBEARD.

Barberino, Andrea da (c. 1370–?1431). Tuscan *cantastorie* or minstrel and author of popular prose narratives of romantic material. *I Reali di Francia* (*The Nobility of France*) deals with the Carolingian heroes and feats; *Guerrino il Meschino* (*Guerrino the Wretched*) is his own creation of epic material, and is still popular today.

Barber of Seville, The (1775). The title of a comedy by BEAUMARCHAIS, and of two operas, one by Rossini (1816) and the other by Giovanni Paisiello (c. 1776), both based on the play. FIGARO, a rascal of a barber, aids his former master, Count Almaviva, to gain entrance to the house of Bartholo, so that the count can woo the latter's ward, Rosine, a beautiful young girl with whom Almaviva is in love. He succeeds with Figaro's help in marrying her in spite of old Bartholo's precautions.

barber's pole. A spirally painted pole, striped in red and white, displayed outside barber shops. A relic of the days when the callings of barber and surgeon were combined, it is symbolical of the winding of a bandage round the arm previous to blood-letting. The gilt knob at its end represents a brass basin, which is sometimes actually suspended on the pole.

Barbey d'Aurevilly, Jules (1808–1889). French novelist and critic. A minor romantic, Barbey d'Aurevilly is the author of two excellent novels, *L'Ensorcelée* (1854) and *Le Chevalier des Touches* (1864). Writing as literary or dramatic critic for such papers as the *Constitutionnel,* he produced reviews that were vigorous and perceptive, if somewhat prejudiced by his Royalist and Roman Catholic sympathies.

Barbizon school. The name given to a group of French landscape painters. Opposed to the classical teachings of the Academy, they withdrew and, from 1830 to 1870, made their center at Barbizon in the forest of Fontainebleau, seeking a new directness of observation from nature. Among them were Jean Baptiste Camille COROT, Jean François MILLET, Théodore Rousseau, and Charles Daubigny.

Barbour, John (1316?–1395). Scottish poet. He was archbishop of Aberdeen in 1375 and one of the auditors of the exchequer in 1372, 1382, and 1384. He is best known for his epic poem, THE BRUCE. Other poems, almost certainly his, include *Legend of Troy* and *Legends of the Saints,* both translations of works of Guido da Colonna.

Barbusse, Henri (1873–1935). French novelist and journalist. Barbusse is most famous for *Under Fire* (*Le Feu;* 1916), a brutally realistic picture of the absurdity of war. Other novels include *L'Enfer* (*The Inferno,* 1908), *Clarté* (*Light,* 1919), and *Les Enchaînements* (*Chains,* 1925).

Barchester Towers (1857). One of the best known of the novels of Anthony TROLLOPE in the BARSETSHIRE series. A sequel to *The Warden,* it is a novel of clerical intrigue showing the struggle between the trenchant Mrs. PROUDIE, the bishop's wife, and the insidious chaplain, Mr. Slope. Each wishes to become the dominant voice in the quiet cathedral town of Barchester. Mrs. Proudie eventually triumphs.

Barclay, Alexander (1475?–1552). English poet and divine. Barclay is famous for THE SHIP OF FOOLS (*The Shyp of Folys of the Worlde,* 1509), a satire on English life based on the German *Das Narrenschiff* by Sebastian Brant. He wrote a volume of *Eclogues* (1513?), which is considered to be one of the earliest examples of pastoral verse in English. He also translated some of the Latin poetry of Aeneas Silvius (1405–1464), who became Pope Pius II.

Barclay, Florence (1862–1921). English popular novelist. Her THE ROSARY was sensationally successful. Her ingredients were love, blood, tears, and purple religiosity.

Bard, The (1757). A Pindaric ode by Thomas GRAY, concerning a prophecy made by a Welsh bard to the invading King Edward I of England. It is based on Welsh legendary material and contains the famous line: "weave the warp and weave the woof." The central idea of the poem is that mankind from earliest times has been visited by the highest poetic inspiration.

Bardell, Mrs. In Charles Dickens' PICKWICK PAPERS, a widowed landlady of "apartments for single gentlemen" in Goswell Street. Long an admirer of Mr. Pickwick, she misinterprets some innocent remarks of his as a proposal of marriage and is induced by the unprincipled DODSON AND FOGG to sue for breach of promise. A verdict is obtained against Pickwick, but Mrs. Bardell is subsequently arrested for refusing to pay the costs of the trial and lodged in prison.

Bard of Avon. A popular epithet for William Shakespeare, who was born and buried at Stratford on Avon.

Bardolph. Sir John Falstaff's corporal in Shakespeare's HENRY IV: PART I and PART II and THE MERRY WIVES OF WINDSOR. In HENRY V he is promoted to lieutenant. He is a lowbred, drunken swaggerer whose red, pimply nose wins him the nickname "Knight of the Burning Lamp."

Barea, Arturo (1897–1957). Spanish novelist. Exiled as a result of the Spanish Civil War, he is best known for his autobiographical novel, *The Forging of a Rebel* (*La forja de un rebelde;* 1951), originally published in English in three parts: *The Forge* (*La forja*), *The Track* (*La ruta*), and *The Clash* (*La llama*). He also wrote the essay *Lorca, the Poet and his People* (*Lorca, el poeta y su pueblo;* 1944).

Barefoot Boy, The (1855). A poem by John Greenleaf WHITTIER. Its subject is the joy of a country childhood.

Baring, Maurice (1874–1945). English novelist, essayist, poet, and playwright. Until 1912 he worked as a journalist in Russia, and wrote several studies of Russian culture and literature. His interesting autobiography is entitled *The Puppet Show of Memory* (1922).

Barker, George (1913–   ). English poet. Like that of his contemporary, Dylan Thomas, his poetry is ecstatic, romantic, and violent, characterized by extravagant imagery and great technical dexterity in the use of puns, rhythms, and verbal devices. It is often also didactic, and concerned with moral and political issues. Collections of his poetry include *Poems* (1935); *Calamiterror* (1937), inspired by the Spanish Civil War; *Lament and Triumph* (1940); *Eros in Dogma* (1944); and *A Vision of Beasts and Gods* (1954).

Barker, Harley Granville-. See Harley GRANVILLE-BARKER.

Barker, James Nelson (1784–1858). American dramatist. In his plays, Barker, who held numerous public offices, expressed his ardent Americanism and his interest in politics. His best work is probably *Superstition* (1823), a blank-verse tragedy dealing with the English regicide Goffe and witchcraft trials in New England. He also wrote *The Indian Princess* (1808), in which Pocahontas figures prominently, and *Marmion* (1812), an adaptation of Scott's poem.

Barkis. In Charles Dickens' DAVID COPPERFIELD, the carrier who courts Clara PEGGOTTY by asking David to tell her "Barkis is willin'." Peggotty takes the hint and becomes Mrs. Barkis.

Barkley, Catherine. The heroine of Ernest Hemingway's novel A FAREWELL TO ARMS. An English nurse in an Italian hospital, she has a brief affair with the American lieutenant Frederic Henry but dies bearing his child.

Barlaam and Josaphat. An Eastern romance, probably written in the seventh century and popular in the Middle Ages, telling how Barlaam, an ascetic monk of the desert of Sinai, converted the Indian prince Josaphat to Christianity. It is believed to have been put in its final form by St. John of Damascus, a Syrian monk of the eighth century. Some authorities consider this a Christianized version of the story of Buddha. It includes the story of the three caskets which was used by Shakespeare in *The Merchant of Venice* (c. 1595).

A poetical version of the romance was written in the 13th century by the minnesinger Rudolf von Ems.

Barlach, Ernst (1870–1938). German dramatist and famous sculptor. His expressionistically tinged plays include *Der tote Tag* (*The Dead Day,* 1912) and *Die Sündflut* (*The Flood,* 1924).

Barleycorn, Sir John. An old song. As it was written down by Robert Burns, his neighbors vowed that Sir John should die, so they hired ruffians to "plough him with ploughs and bury him"; this they did, and afterward "combed him with harrows and thrust clods on his head," but did not kill him by these or by numerous other means which they attempted. Sir John bore no malice for this ill usage, but did his best to cheer the flagging spirits even of his worst persecutors. The song seems to recall fertility rites at corn-planting time.

Jack London wrote an autobiography called *John Barleycorn* (1913), which he described as his "alcoholic memories."

Barlow, Joel (1754–1812). American poet and diplomat, a leader of the anti-Federalist party, and one of the best-known of the HARTFORD WITS. In 1788 he left for Europe as a representative of some American business interests. He stayed abroad for 17 years and in 1795 was appointed American consul to Algiers. In Europe he shed his conservatism, became an ardent democrat, and befriended Thomas Paine.

Barlow's most popular poem was THE HASTY PUDDING; his most ambitious was *The Vision of Columbus*, first published in 1787, and later revised, lengthened, and reissued in epic form as THE COLUMBIAD. He was one of the authors of THE ANARCHIAD and also wrote ADVICE TO THE PRIVILEGED ORDERS, a controversial prose tract embodying his democratic ideals.

Barmecide feast. An imaginary feast where the dishes are empty; hence a reference to any appealing illusion. The allusion is to such a banquet given in jest for the poor Schacabac by a rich Barmecide prince in the *Arabian Nights'* story, "The Barber's Sixth Brother." The starving Schacabac pretends to eat and enjoy the empty dishes set before him, but when illusory wine is offered him, he feigns drunkenness and knocks the Barmecide down. The latter sees the humor of the situation, forgives Schacabac, and provides him with food to his heart's content.

Barnabas. In the New Testament, a companion of Paul and Mark. He accompanied them both on the first missionary journey. Barnabas was to go with Paul on his second journey and urged Paul to take

Mark, Barnabas' nephew, with them. Paul refused, however, since Mark had left them before the first journey was over. As a result, Paul took Silas with him and neither Mark nor Barnabas went. It is thought that Mark wrote his Gospel at the urging of Barnabas, perhaps under his direction.

Barnaby Rudge (1841). A novel by Charles DICKENS. The book revolves around the anti-Catholic GORDON RIOTS of 1780 in which the titular hero innocently participates for the pleasure of carrying a flag and wearing a blue bow. Barnaby is a half-wit, a fact mysteriously connected with the fact that his father murdered his employer and a fellow servant on the night of Barnaby's birth. Of conspicuous appearance, Barnaby is pale with long red hair; he dresses all in green and carries a large raven named Grip in a basket on his back. He is identified as a leading rioter and condemned to death, but is reprieved through the influence of Gabriel Varden. He spends the rest of his life with his mother in a cottage near Maypole, happily employed with his poultry and his garden.

Barnaby's father, Mr. Rudge, is mistakenly believed to have been murdered the same night as Mr. Haredale, his employer. After the murder, he is seen by many in the locality, but is thought to be a ghost. Years later he joins the Gordon rioters and is sent to Newgate. but makes his escape when it is burned down.

The plot of this book is one of Dickens' weakest, and the novel's chief interest lies in its depiction of the terrible riots. In exploring causes for the riots, Dickens finds the answer in a government that is heedless of the needs of its poor. A similar theme is dealt with in A TALE OF TWO CITIES.

Barnacle. The name given by Charles Dickens in LITTLE DORRIT to a "very high family and a very large family" active in governmental circles, nine of whom appear in the novel. They are bungling and incompetent. In all of them—particularly in Mr. Tite Barnacle, a permanent official in the CIRCUMLOCUTION OFFICE—Dickens satirizes governmental red tape.

Barnburners. The reform wing of the Democratic Party in New York during the 1840's. They were so called in allusion to the Dutch farmer who burned his barn in order to get rid of the rats. Led by Martin Van Buren, his son John, and Silas Wright, the Barnburners were opposed to the extension of slavery; in 1848 they bolted the Democratic Party and joined other antislavery elements to form the FREE-SOIL PARTY.

Barnes, Barnabe (1569?–1609). English poet. Barnes wrote *Parthenophil and Parthenophe, Sonnets, Madrigals, Elegies, and Odes* (1593) and *A Divine Century of Spiritual Sonnets* (1595).

Barnes, Djuna (1892–   ). American novelist and short-story writer. For many years a resident of Europe, Miss Barnes is the author of three experimental plays produced in 1919–1920 by the Provincetown Players: *Three from the Earth, An Irish Triangle,* and *Kurzy from the Sea. Ryder* (1928) and *Nightwood* (1936) are her best-known books. The latter, which has an introduction by T. S. Eliot, is a novel dealing with the Parisian artistic underground. *The Antiphon* (1958) is a surrealistic play in blank verse.

Barnes, Jake. The principal male character in Ernest Hemingway's novel THE SUN ALSO RISES. Made impotent by a war wound, he is hopelessly attracted to Lady Brett Ashley. Though in many ways his life is as aimless as the other "lost generation" characters, he lives by a code of behavior that gives him considerable stability.

Barnes, William (1801–1886). English poet and philologist. Of Dorsetshire yeoman stock, Barnes educated himself to such purpose that he became acquainted with some 60 languages, in addition to being a capable wood engraver, archaeologist, musician, and mathematician. He spent most of his life as a country schoolmaster and parson, publishing numerous philological works and composing the poems in Dorset dialect on which his fame rests. The poems are distinguished by simplicity and humor, fresh and vivid descriptions of nature, an unaffected and native pastoral quality. His works include *Poems of Rural Life in the Dorset Dialect* (1844, 1862), and *Poems of Rural Life in Common English* (1868).

Barnfield, Richard (1574–1627). English poet, author of *The Affectionate Shepherd* (1594), *Cynthia* (1595), and *The Encomium of Lady Pecunia* (1598). His fame, in large measure, rests on the fact that three of his lyrics, published (1599) in THE PASSIONATE PILGRIM, were long thought to be Shakespeare's.

Barnhelm, Minna von. See MINNA VON BARNHELM.

Barnum, Phineas T[aylor] (1810–1891). American circus man, impresario, and author. Barnum exhibited the midget, General Tom Thumb, in 1844, and brought Jenny Lind to America during 1850–1852. He entered into partnership with James A. Bailey, to present the famous Barnum & Bailey show; after Bailey's death in 1906, the show was absorbed by Ringling Brothers. Barnum's shows appealed to public curiosity, and the thirst for the sensational and the novel; the originator of this type of showmanship in America wrote *The Humbugs of the World* (1866) and possibly the *Life of P. T. Barnum, Written by Himself* (1855, frequently revised).

Baroja y Nessi, Pío (1872–1956). Spanish novelist. Known for his individualism and the cynical stoicism of his works, Baroja was a member of the GENERACIÓN DEL 98. His best-known work is the novel *El árbol de la ciencia* (*The Tree of Knowledge,* 1911). The tale is a study of Andrés Hurtado, a restless and selfless intellectual, who ends in suicide—thus reflecting the author's skepticism. Baroja is also the author of the trilogy *Tierra vasca* (1900–1909), *La sensualidad pervertida* (1920), and a novel dealing with Basque maritime life, *Las inquietudes de Shanti Andía* (*The Restlessness of Shanti Andía,* 1911).

baroque. A term applied to certain tendencies in European art in the latter 16th, the 17th, and the first half of the 18th centuries. Initially, and still primarily, the term referred to a free, exuberant style of architecture which supplanted the restrained and balanced style of the earlier Renaissance, but it was later applied to similar tendencies in painting, music, sculpture, and literature. The baroque style was dramatic, grandiose, ornate, full of motifs and forms expressive of conflict and energy. Originating in Italy and Spain, it spread throughout Europe, but is closely identified, especially in architecture, with Catholic Europe and was virtually the official style of the Counter Reformation. In literature the baroque spirit manifested itself in such movements as MARINISM in Italy, GONGORISM in Spain, and EUPHUISM in England. The word *baroque* has been used pejoratively, signifying a false, fantastic, overemphatic style, but such a sense would be justified, if at all, only when applied to late baroque style such as ROCOCO.

Barr, Amelia E[dith] (1831–1919). English-born American novelist. She is noted for her highly romantic and sentimental works. Especially popular were *Jan Vedder's Wife* (1885); *The Bow of Orange Ribbon* (1886), a novel of early New York; and *Remember the Alamo* (1888).

Barr, Robert (1850–1912). Scottish editor and popular novelist. He concluded Stephen Crane's unfinished novel, *The O'Ruddy* (1903).

Barrack-Room Ballads (1892). A volume of poems by Rudyard KIPLING, celebrating the British soldier and army life throughout the Empire, in ballad meters and, frequently, cockney diction. See TOMMY ATKINS; GUNGA DIN; FUZZY WUZZY; MANDALAY.

Barrault, Jean Louis (1910–). French producer and actor. In 1947, Barrault founded the *Compagnie Jean-Louis Barrault–Madeline Renaud* with his actress wife. On the stage of their theater, the *Théâtre Marigny,* could be seen experimental productions, some of which Barrault describes in his two published works: *Reflexions sur le théâtre* (1945) and *Nouvelles Reflexions sur le théâtre* (1961).

Barren Ground (1925). A novel by Ellen GLASGOW. It is a realistic work of ingenious incidents and rich characterization in which Miss Glasgow touches successfully on many themes. The antithesis of the conventional romance, it is the story of Dorinda Oakley, a poor white who has been disappointed in love and turns her father's barren acres into a prosperous farm, but is less successful in her relations with the opposite sex.

Barrès, [Augustin-] Maurice (1862–1923). French novelist, journalist, and politician. His first novel trilogy, *Le Culte du moi* (1888–1891), portrayed the inner life of an egoist who in trying to develop his individual self discovers his need for others. The trilogy *Le Roman de l'énergie nationale* (1897–1903) is a social and philosophical commentary based on his own public life. Most famous of the nationalistic trilogy *Les Bastions de l'Est* (1905–1921) is *Colette Baudoche; The Story of a Young Girl of Metz* (1918). Barrès wrote other novels, including *The Sacred Hill* (*La Colline inspirée;* 1913), and many articles about World War I, collected in *L'Ame Française et la guerre* (11 vols., 1917–1922) and *Chronique de la Grande Guerre* (14 vols., 1920–1924).

Barretts of Wimpole Street, The (1930). A successful play by Rudolf Besier (1878–1942). It was produced in London and New York and based on the romance of Robert and Elizabeth Barrett Browning.

Barrie, Sir J[ames] M[atthew] (1860–1937). Scottish dramatist and novelist, known for the whimsy and sentimental fantasy of his work. His best-known plays are QUALITY STREET, THE ADMIRABLE CRICHTON, PETER PAN, *Alice Sit-by-the-Fire* (1905), WHAT EVERY WOMAN KNOWS, and *Dear Brutus* (1917). His outstanding prose works include *A Window in Thrums* (1889); MARGARET OGILVY, a biography of his mother; THE LITTLE MINISTER, a novel dramatized in 1897; and SENTIMENTAL TOMMY, a novel. See KAILYARD; THRUMS.

barring out. The closing of a schoolroom against a schoolmaster, a prank once common in British schools. *The Barring Out: or, Party Spirit* is the title of a novel by Maria EDGEWORTH.

Barrington, E. See Mrs. Lily Adams BECK.

Barrios, Eduardo (1884–). Chilean novelist and short-story writer. After wandering throughout Latin America and working at a variety of jobs, Barrios settled in Santiago, where he served as minister of education and director of the national library in the 1920's. Regarded as a master of the psychological tale, he excels in the portrayal of the hypersensitive personality. Such is the 10-year-old protagonist of the novelette *El niño que enloqueció de amor* (1915), who suffers physical and mental torment when he falls in love with Angélica, a friend of his mother, and ultimately loses his reason. In *Un perdido* (1917), the hero is an overwrought weakling who, unable to cope with reality, finds refuge in alcohol. Barrios' best work is probably *El hermano asno* (1922), which deals with the inner conflicts of two Franciscan monks: Brother Lázaro, who fears that he may violate his monastic vows, and Brother Rufino, who is disturbed by his reputation for sanctity.

Barry, Philip (1896–1949). American playwright. His work consists of sophisticated comedies and dramas of life among the wealthier classes, although he experimented with fantasy and mysticism in such plays as HOTEL UNIVERSE and *Here Come the Clowns* (1938). Notable among his plays are *You and I* (1922), *Paris Bound* (1927), *Holiday* (1929), THE ANIMAL KINGDOM, and THE PHILADELPHIA STORY.

Barrymore. The name of an American family of actors. Maurice Barrymore, whose real name was Herbert Blythe (1847–1905), and his wife Georgiana Drew (1856–1893), the daughter of the famous actor John Drew (1827–1862), were the initial users of the name. Their children were Lionel (1878–1954), Ethel (1879–1959), and John (1882–1942). Among them they scored many great stage and motion-picture successes. *The Royal Family* (1927), a play by George S. Kaufman and Edna Ferber, is considered a satire on the family. Gene Fowler's *Good Night, Sweet Prince* (1943) is mainly about John, but tells much about the others also.

Barsetshire, Chronicles of. A series of novels by Anthony TROLLOPE. Known also as the Cathedral Stories, they comprise *The Warden* (1855), BARCHESTER TOWERS, *Doctor Thorne* (1858), *Framley Parsonage* (1861), *The Small House at Allington* (1864), and *The Last Chronicle of Barset* (1867). In them Trollope disturbs the placidity of the cathedral town of Barchester with a series of agitations that ripple the clerical pools. The same characters reappear in most of them; among the best-known characters are Bishop and Mrs. PROUDIE, Archdeacon

Grantly, Rev. Septimus Harding, Rev. Mr. Crawley, the Thornes, Mr. Slope, Lady Arabella Gresham, and Signora Madeleine Neroni. Descendents of these families appear in the novels of Angela Thirkell.

bar sinister. In heraldry, a bar drawn in the reverse of the usual way. It was popularly but erroneously supposed to indicate bastardy. See BATON.

Bart, Lily. See HOUSE OF MIRTH, THE.

Bartas, Guillaume du (1544–1590). French poet, recognized throughout Europe in his time as the master of grave religious themes. Of a retiring and studious nature, he spent some time in the service of Henry IV during the religious wars. Despite his Protestant sympathies, his poetry was impartially Christian and appealed to Protestants and Catholics alike. His works include *Judith* (1573); *La Semaine* (1578), an account of the Creation; and the uncompleted *Seconde Semaine* (1584), in which he proposed to follow man from the Garden of Eden to the Last Judgment. Though frequently achieving eloquence and grandeur, his religious epic poetry lacked taste and abounded in the extravagant metaphors in vogue at the time. Soon outdated, it had dropped into obscurity by the 17th century.

Barthélémy, Jean Jacques (1716–1795). French orientalistist, man of letters, numismatist, and author. It was his erudition and love for antiquity that brought him, during the years 1757–1788, to write the historical romance *Le Voyage du jeune Anacharsis en Grèce, dans le milieu du IVe siècle avant l'ère vulgaire* (see ANACHARSIS). The book enjoyed a huge success and opened the doors of the French ACADEMY to Barthélémy in 1789.

Bartholdi, Frédéric Auguste. See Statue of LIBERTY.

Bartholomew, St. One of the 12 disciples of Jesus. The symbol of this saint is a knife, in allusion to the knife with which he was flayed alive. He is commemorated on August 24.

Bartholomew Anglicus (13th century). English scholar and Franciscan friar. His comprehensive Latin encyclopedia, *De Proprietatibus Rerum* (c. 1230–1250), was translated into all the European languages—into English by John de TREVISA—and remained in widespread popular use through the 16th century.

Bartholomew Fair (1614). A comedy by Ben JONSON. The enormous vitality of the fair, and not the plot, is the focus of attention. In this noisy and colorful play, Puritans and prostitutes, bumpkins and pickpockets, salesmen, rogues, gallants, and do-gooders rub shoulders and occasionally clash. Among the many incidents: a "reforming" but bungling justice constantly gets into trouble with the authorities and is carted off to the stocks; a foolish young man loses his fiancée through his own stupidity; and a crusading Brother loses a debate with a puppet on the morals of the theater. The exuberance of the play places it among Jonson's finest dramatic works.

Bartleby the Scrivener (1853). A long short story by Herman MELVILLE. The narrator, who operates a law firm on Wall Street, employs a scrivener, Bartleby, whose job it is to copy and proofread legal documents. Eventually he rejects these chores, stares blankly at an empty wall, and answers all entreaties with, "I should prefer not to." Unable to persuade Bartleby to work or to leave, the narrator moves to a new office, and the scrivener is taken to prison. Refusing all the privileges his former employer's vague sense of responsibility has bought for him, he dies of starvation.

Bartlett, John (1820–1905). American bookseller, editor, and publisher. Self-taught, Bartlett impressed the customers in the University Book Store in Cambridge, Mass. with the breadth of his learning. He was employed by Little, Brown & Co., becoming in time a partner (1865) and a senior partner (1878). His most famous book was the collection of *Familiar Quotations* (1855), which ran through nine editions in his lifetime. It has subsequently been revised and issued three more times. Bartlett also published *A New Method of Chess Notation* (1857), *A Shakespeare Phrase Book* (1882), and *A New and Complete Concordance to Shakespeare* (1894).

Bartók, Béla (1881–1945). Hungarian composer, pianist, and collector of folk songs. The folk songs of his native land provided material for a number of musical arrangements and scholarly treatises, but they also partly inspired the style of his original compositions, such as *The Castle of Duke Bluebeard* (1911), an opera with libretto by Balázs (see BLUEBEARD); *Allegro barbaro* (1911), a popular piano piece; a dance suite for orchestra (1923); *Music for String Instruments, Percussion and Celesta* (1937); *Mikrokosmos* (6 vols., 1926–1937), a famous pedagogical work for piano; string quartets; and piano concertos.

Bartolommeo, Fra. Real name, **Bartolommeo di Pagolo del Fattorino.** Familiarly, **Baccio della Porta** (c. 1472–1517). Italian painter. He worked in his native Florence, and at Venice and Rome. His style, strongly influenced by that of Leonardo da Vinci, is characterized by the employment of noble types and gestures, and by a relieflike clarity of outline. Among his masterpieces are the *Last Judgment*, the *Virgin and Child with Saints,* and the posthumous portrait of Savonarola, of whom he was an ardent follower.

Barton, Bernard (1784–1849). English poet known as the Quaker Poet. Barton is chiefly remembered as a close friend of Charles Lamb. A collection of his work, *Poems and Letters of Bernard Barton,* was published by his daughter Lucy in 1849.

Barton, Clara. Full name **Clarissa Harlowe Barton** (1821–1912). American philanthropist and founder of the American Red Cross. During the Civil War, although she had no official connection with any organization, she gathered and distributed supplies for the sick and wounded and ministered personally to casualties at the front. In 1882, as a result of her efforts, the U.S. joined the International Red Cross, and she became the first president of the American branch. Hers was the innovation whereby the Red Cross alleviates distress in peacetime disasters as well as in war.

Bartram, William (1739–1823). American botanist, explorer, and writer. He is best known for his *Travels Through North and South Carolina* (1791). His descriptions of tropical plants and animals were used as source material by a number of writers, including Wordsworth and Coleridge.

Baruch, Bernard M[annes] (1870–1965). American businessman and statesman. A graduate of the City College of New York, whose school of business administration is named after him, Baruch held several government posts connected with the war effort during World War I. In 1943 he became adviser to James F. Byrnes, war mobilization director, and was named U.S. representative to the UN Atomic Energy Commission in 1946. He is the author of *American Industry in the War* (1941), *A Philosophy for Our Time* (1954), *Baruch: My Own Story* (1957), and *Baruch: The Public Years* (1960). Long known as America's "elder statesman," he served for many years as a valued, if unofficial, adviser to presidents, his office a park bench opposite the White House.

Barzun, Jacques [Martin] (1907–   ). French-born American critic and educator. Dr. Barzun is now provost of Columbia University. He brings a scholarly point of view to the study of contemporary problems. Among his books are *Race: A Study in Modern Superstition* (1937), *Romanticism and the Modern Ego* (1943), *Teacher in America* (1945), *Berlioz and the Romantic Century* (2 vols., 1950), *God's Country and Mine* (1954), *The House of Intellect* (1959), and *Science: The Glorious Entertainment* (1964).

Basel, Council of (1431–1443). The last of the great reform councils of the 15th century. Beginning at Basel and continuing at Ferrara, Florence, and Rome, it brought about a temporary reunion of the Greek and Roman churches and further stimulated the REVIVAL OF LEARNING.

Bashō. See MATSUO BASHŌ.

Basic English. A simplified system of learning English from a selected vocabulary of the 850 most essential words. It was set up by C. K. OGDEN and propagated, also as an international auxiliary language, by the Orthological Institute, Cambridge, England. I. A. RICHARDS was one of its strongest advocates. Supporters claim that the system, which has no emotive words, encourages logical thought and expression; opponents say it destroys stylistic modulation, and they point to such examples as the translation into Basic of a famous phrase coined by Sir Winston Churchill: "Blood and eye-water and face-water."

Basile, Giambattista (c. 1575–c. 1632). Italian writer. He was the author of a collection of 50 stories in the Neapolitan dialect, called *Lo cunto de li cunti* (*The Story of Stories*). Because its storytelling is divided into five days and its general structure resembles that of the *Decameron,* it is also called *Il Pentamerone* (*The Pentameron*). Published posthumously in 1634, it is one of the first European books of folk tales, including such favorites as *Cinderella, Puss in Boots,* and *Beauty and the Beast,* which were later popularized by Perrault's *Contes des Fées* (1697). The Neapolitan was translated into Italian by Benedetto Croce and into English by Sir Richard Burton.

basilisk (Gr., *basileos,* a king). The king of serpents, a fabulous reptile, also called a COCKATRICE. It was alleged to be hatched by a serpent from a cock's egg. It was supposed to have the power of "looking any one dead on whom it fixed its eyes."

Bassani, Giorgio (1916–   ). Italian novelist and writer of short stories. His most noted novel, *Il Giardino dei Finzi-Contini* (1962), narrates the plight of an aristocratic Jewish family of Ferrara during the Fascist racial persecutions. His short stories are collected in *Cinque Storie Ferraresi* (1956). Bassani's writing describes his native Ferrara, and his fictional characters are seen as they experience the tensions of certain periods in history.

Bassanio. The impecunious and quick-witted friend of Antonio in Shakespeare's MERCHANT OF VENICE. He borrows 3,000 ducats from Antonio in order to woo Portia, a wealthy heiress of Belmont. In accordance with her father's will, Portia can marry only that one of her suitors who successfully chooses from among three caskets the one that contains her portrait. With the help of a hint from Portia, Bassanio rejects the gold and silver caskets and, selecting the leaden one, opens it to find "fair Portia's counterfeit."

Basse, William (c. 1583–c. 1653). English poet. A member of the SPENSERIAN SCHOOL, he was the author of *Sword and Buckler* (1602), *Three Pastoral Elegies* (1602), and *Great Britain's Sunset* (1613), an elegy on the death of Prince Henry, the elder son of James I.

Basselin, Olivier. A French song writer of the 15th century. He is especially known for his drinking songs.

Bassett, John Spencer (1867–1928). American writer and educator. He was a bold commentator on the Negro question, and, from 1906 on, a teacher at Smith College. Among his writings are *Anti-Slavery Leaders of North Carolina* (1898), *The Life of Andrew Jackson* (1911), and *Expansion and Reform* (1926).

Basso, Hamilton (1904–1964). American novelist. Basso is best known for *Sun in Capricorn* (1942), which depicts a demagogue thought to be modeled on Huey Long, and for *The View from Pompey's Head* (1954), a novel of the South and New York. His other works include *Courthouse Square* (1936), *The Light Infantry Ball* (1959), *A Quota of Seaweed* (1960), and the biography *Beauregard: The Great Creole* (1933).

Bastille (O. Fr., *bastir,* now *bâtir,* to build). A famous state prison in Paris. It was commenced by Charles V as a royal chateau in 1370, and was first used as a prison by Louis XI. It was seized and sacked by the mob in the French Revolution, July 14, 1789, a date that has become Bastille Day, which is celebrated much as is the American Fourth of July. The final demolition of the prison was commenced and the Place de la Bastille laid out on its site. A Bastille has come to mean a state prison for political offenders.

Bataille, [Felix-] Henry (1872–1922). French dramatist and poet. Bataille usually portrayed the psychological drama of morbidly passionate women in such plays as *Maman Colibri* (1904), *Poliche* (1906), *La Femme nue* (1908), and *La Vierge Folle* (1910).

Bates, Charley. In Charles Dickens's OLIVER TWIST, one of Fagin's pickpockets-in-training. He is always laughing uproariously and is almost equal in artifice and adroitness to the Artful Dodger.

Bates, H[erbert] E[rnest] (1905–   ). English writer of novels, novellas, and short stories. Bates is the author of *Fair Stood the Wind for France* (1944), *The Jacaranda Tree* (1948), *The Nature of Love* (1954), *When the Green Woods Laugh* (1960), and *The Day of the Tortoise* (1961). Always fond of a country setting, he uses it notably in *The Darling Buds of May* (1958) and in other novels about the comic, Rabelaisian farming family of Pop and Ma Larkin.

Bates, Miss. A character in Jane Austen's EMMA. An old maid, garrulous and a dreadful bore, she is nevertheless "a happy woman and a woman no one named without good will. . . . She loved everybody, was interested in everybody's happiness."

Bates, Ralph (1899–   ). English proletarian novelist. He described life in Spain and the Spanish civil war (1936–1939) in *Lean Men* (1934), *The Olive Field* (1936), and *Sirocco and Other Stories* (1939).

Bathsheba. In the Old Testament, the beautiful wife of Uriah, the Hittite, sinfully loved by David who gave orders that Uriah, his captain, should be sent into the most dangerous part of the battle where he was slain. She was afterwards the wife of David and mother of Solomon (II Sam. 11:1–24).

baton. In heraldry, a bend or double line, from an upper corner of a shield to the opposite base point. When cut off at the ends, the baton indicated bastardy, as the bar or bend sinister was erroneously thought to have done.

Batrachomyomachia. See BATTLE OF THE FROGS AND MICE.

Battle Hymn of the Republic, The (1862). A patriotic song whose words were written by Julia Ward Howe. It was written in December, 1861, during the Civil War after a visit to a detachment of McClellan's army near Washington, D.C., when Dr. James Freeman Clark, a member of the party accompanying Mrs. Howe, urged her to write new words for the music of *John Brown's Body,* a song then popular with the Union soldiers. That night, towards dawn, Mrs. Howe awakened and found the words of a poem in her head, ready to march with the tune. She sprang out of bed, she relates, and without a light, in order not to awaken a baby who slept near her, wrote the *Battle Hymn*.

Battle of Britain. A term applied to bombing raids on Great Britain by German airplanes during World War II, especially during the summer of 1940.

Battle of Moytura, The. A 9th or 10th century Gaelic tale from the MYTHOLOGICAL CYCLE. It is a tale of battle between the TUATHA DÉ DANANN and the FOMORIANS. The principal figure of the Fomorians is BALOR whose evil eye is put out by LUG, thus turning the battle in favor of the Tuatha Dé Danann.

Battle of the Books, The (1704). A prose, mock-heroic satire by Jonathan SWIFT, written in 1697 and published with A TALE OF A TUB. It ridicules a literary squabble of the day as to the comparative merits of ancient and modern authors, touched off by Sir William TEMPLE's essay *Of Ancient and Modern Learning* and continued by Richard BENTLEY, among others. Swift showed his contempt for the entire controversy and, more broadly, for modern scholarship, criticism, and poetry by giving an account of a battle between modern and ancient books in St. James's Library, the outcome of which remains uncertain. The mock epic similes of the spider, signifying the moderns, and the bee, signifying the ancients, are among the most famous in all of literature.

Battle of the Frogs and Mice (Batrachomyomachia). A mock-heroic Greek poem of early date. War is caused by a frog's leaving his mouse friend to drown in the middle of a pond. When both sides are arrayed for battle, a band of gnats sounds the attack, and after a bloody battle the Frogs are defeated; but an army of land-crabs coming up saves the race from extermination, and the victorious Mice make their way home in terrible disorder. The name of the Mouse-king is Troxartes, probably a pun on *Tros,* a Trojan, and the poem is in many ways a burlesque of the *Iliad*. There is a 14th-century German skit on the same theme by G. Rollenhagen, a Meistersinger.

Battle of the Giants (1515). The battle of Marignano, in which Francis I of France won a complete victory over the duke of Milan and his Swiss allies. The battle is so called because the skill and obstinacy shown by the contenders on both sides.

Battle of the Herrings (Feb. 12, 1429). A battle during the seige of Orleans in the Hundred Years' War. The French attempted to intercept a supply of food being brought to the English by Sir John Fastolf, but the English repulsed them with barrels of herrings.

Battle of the Kegs, The (1778). A humorous ballad by Francis HOPKINSON. Composed to the tune of "Yankee Doodle," it tells of the alarm felt by the British over kegs, charged with gunpowder which were floated down the Delaware.

Battle of the Lake Regillus, The. A ballad by Thomas Babington Macaulay in his LAYS OF ANCIENT ROME. Lake Regillus was the name of a small lake near Rome, traditional site of a Roman victory over the Latins (496 B.C.).

Battle of the Moat. A battle between Muhammad and Abu Sofian, chief of the Koreishites, before Medina. The Prophet had a moat dug before the city to keep off the invaders, and in it much of the fighting took place.

Battle of the Spurs. (1) A battle (1302) near Courtrai, Belgium, between a Flemish army and the French under Philip IV. The battle is so called because the victorious Flemings gathered from the field more than 700 gilt spurs worn by French nobles slain in the fight.

(2) A battle (1513) near Guinegate, France, between the English under Henry VIII and the French under Louis XII. The name is said to derive from the flight of the French cavalry.

Battle-Pieces and Aspects of the War (1866). A collection of poems by Herman MELVILLE. The tone of these 72 poems is elegiac rather than vengeful. Melville does not celebrate martial spirit in the best of his work; he mourns the early death of young men and the ruin of the country.

Baty, Gaston (1892–1952). French theater director and producer. His company, *Les Compagnons de la Chimère,* formed in 1922, performed such expressionistic plays as *Le Simoun* by Henri Lenormand and *Martine* by Jean Bernard. Noted for his splendid and imaginative settings, costumes, and lighting effects, Baty created drama in his *Théâtre Montparnasse* that joined stage magic and reality.

Baubo. In myth, an Eleusinian slave woman. In the allegory of Goethe's *Faust,* Part II, she symbolizes sensuality.

Baucis and Philemon. See PHILEMON AND BAU-CIS.

Baudelaire, Charles Pierre (1821–1867). French poet, one of the most important figures among the French SYMBOLISTS. His typically DÉCADENT life was ultimately tragic; his debauched, violent, and eccentric existence brought him to an early and painful death at the age of 46. In Paris he first began to write as a critic and translator, introducing the works of Edgar Allan Poe to Europe through translations that have since become French classics. Baudelaire published only a single volume of poetry, LES FLEURS DU MAL. Stylistically, in its pure and carefully classical form, his verse in some ways resembles that of the Parnassians, but it is far more significant in that it foreshadows the development of modern poetry. Baudelaire's poems are filled with subtle nuances and with almost painfully delicate suggestiveness. The sensuous matter of a poem is conveyed in beautifully striking images. He is famous for his doctrine of correspondences, an exploration of the relationship of the various senses that lends a startling newness to his work. Not only Baudelaire's technique but his subject matter—the beauty of the perverse or the morbid, and the probing analysis of complex emotional states—has been reflected in 20th-century poetry.

Bauhaus (*Ger.,* "house of architecture"). A school of architecture and design, founded in Weimar, Germany, in 1919 by Walter GROPIUS. Its purpose was to unite the creative arts and the technology of modern mass production with 20th-century architecture. In addition to more strictly architectural studies, courses in painting, handicrafts, the theater, and typography were given by outstanding artists, including Lyonel Feininger, Vassily Kandinsky, and Paul Klee. Functionalism, or the international style, in architecture and a number of examples of industrial design, such as tubular lighting and steel furniture, were first developed at the Bauhaus. In 1925 the school moved to the buildings designed for it by Gropius in Dessau; three years later, Mies van der Rohe became its director. During the rise of Hitlerian Germany, the Bauhaus came increasingly under attack, and in 1933 it was forced to close; but in Europe and the U.S., through its masters and students, its great influence on modern architectural thought continued.

Baum, L[yman] Frank (1856–1919). American writer of children's books. He was the author of *The Wonderful Wizard of Oz* (1900) and a subsequent series of tales for young folk dealing with the mythical country of Oz. The later books did not match the excellence of the first.

Baviad, The (1794). A biting verse satire by William GIFFORD written to ridicule the DELLA-CRUSCANS and their poetry. It was republished the following year with a second part called *The Maeviad*. Bavius and Maevius were two minor poets pilloried by Virgil in his *Eclogues*, and their names are still used for inferior versifiers.

Bax, Clifford (1886–). English dramatist and poet. Among his plays are *The Poetasters of Ispahan* (1912), *The Rose without a Thorn* (1932), and *Circe* (1948). His books include *Ideas and People* (1936) and *Some I Knew Well* (1951).

Baxter, Richard (1615–1691). English divine. A member of the Parliamentarian faction during the English Civil War, he opposed the execution of Charles I. He supported the Restoration, but suffered imprisonment as a nonconformist under Charles II. His *Saint's Everlasting Rest* (1650), a fervent appeal for the Christian life, is a classic of English religious writing.

Bayard (bay-colored). (1) The horse of the four sons of Aymon. He grew larger or smaller as one or more of the four sons mounted him. According to tradition, one of his footprints may still be seen in the forest of Soignes, and another near Dinant.

(2) The French name for Rinaldo's horse BAIARDO.

Bayard, Seigneur de. Pierre du Terrail (1473?–1524). French knight and national hero, renowned for his valor. Known as *le chevalier sans peur et sans reproche,* he distinguished himself in the Italian campaigns of Charles VIII, Louis XII, and Francis I.

Bayle, Pierre (1647–1706). French philosopher. The son of a Calvinist minister, a convert to Catholicism and ultimately reconverted to Calvinism, he held that neither faith nor reason can lead to certainty. He condemned superstition and advocated religious tolerance in *Pensées sur la comète* (*Thoughts on the Comet,* 1682) and *Commentaire philosophique sur les paroles de Jésus-Christ* (*Philosophical Commentary on the Words of Jesus Christ,* 1686). The *Dictionnaire Historique et Critique* (*Historical and Critical Dictionary,* 1697–1706), his most important work, treats its biographical, theological, and philosophical subjects orthodoxly and reserves dissent for the voluminous footnotes. Its directness pleased the philosophes, and it influenced Diderot in the compiling of the *Encyclopédie.*

Bay Psalm Book (1640). A metrical translation of the Biblical psalms by Richard MATHER, Thomas Welde, John ELIOT, and 27 other ministers of the Massachusetts Bay Colony. The book—the first bound book printed in the English colonies—was published by Stephen DAY in Cambridge in an edition of 1,700 copies. Its full title is *The Whole Booke of Psalms Faithfully Translated into English Metre.* (See title page on page 86.)

Bayreuth Festival. The musical festival at Bayreuth, Germany, for the representation of Richard WAGNER's operas.

Bazarov, Evgeni Vasil'yev. The central character of Ivan Turgenev's novel, FATHERS AND CHILDREN. A representative of the young democratic generation rising in Russia about the middle of the 19th century, Bazarov is a hard-headed materialist with nothing but scorn for the old aristocratic order. He is regarded as one of Turgenev's most successful character portrayals.

Bazin, Hervé (1917–). French novelist, grandnephew of René Bazin. In *Viper in the Fist* (*Vipère au Poing;* 1947), he describes the psychological battle between a boy and his extraordinarily hateful mother. His later novels describe various kinds of love-hate relationships, usually in provincial settings: *Head Against the Wall* (*La Tête contre murs;* 1949); *Constance* (*Lève-toi et marche;* 1952); *In the Name of the Son* (*Au nom du Fils;* 1960).

Bazin, René (1853–1932). French novelist. His books concerned with the country life of rural Catholics are *This, My Son* (*Les Noellet;* 1890), *Those of His Own Household* (*Madame Corentine:*

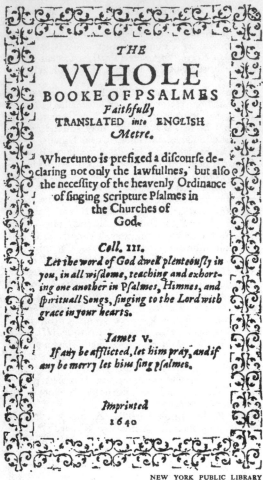

THE

VVHOLE

BOOKE OF PSALMES
Faithfully
TRANSLATED *into* ENGLISH
Metre.

Whereunto is prefixed a difcourfe declaring not only the lawfullnes, but alfo
the neceffity of the heavenly Ordinance
of finging Scripture Pfalmes in
the Churches of
God.

Coll. III.
Let the word of God dwell plenteoufly in
you, in all wifdome, teaching and exhort-
ing one another in Pfalmes, Himnes, and
fpirituall Songs, finging to the Lord with
grace in your hearts.

Iames V.
If any be afflicted, let him pray, and if
any be merry let him fing pfalmes.

Imprinted
1640

NEW YORK PUBLIC LIBRARY

Title page of the *Bay Psalm Book* (1640).

1893), and *Redemption* (*De toute son âme;* 1897). The problem of the desertion of the land for the cities is treated in *The Penitent* (*Donatienne;* 1903) and *The Coming Harvest* (*Le Blé qui lève;* 1907). Bazin discusses the political destiny of the disputed Alsace-Lorraine in *The Children of Alsace* (*Les Oberlé;* 1901).

BBC. See BRITISH BROADCASTING CORPORATION.

Beaconsfield, 1st earl of. See Benjamin DISRAELI.

Beacon Street. A famous street in Boston. It runs from Tremont Street along the Common and westward through the Back Bay district. Because of its residents, it became synonymous with wealth, social position, culture, and conservatism.

Bear, The. See Go DOWN, MOSES.

Beard, Charles A[ustin] (1874–1948). American historian. Having joined the faculty of Columbia University in 1904, Beard resigned in 1917 to protest the dismissal of two other professors for pacifism. Later he helped to organize the New School for Social Research.

Beard's best-known work is *An Economic Interpretation of the Constitution* (1913), in which he examined the backgrounds of the men who framed the U.S. Constitution and concluded that as property-owners they were interested chiefly in constructing a charter to protect their wealth. Beard, denied, however, that he was an economic determinist. He also wrote several books with his wife, Mary R[itter] Beard (1876–1958), notably *The Rise of American Civilization* (1927), *America in Midpassage* (1939), and *The American Spirit* (1942). In his later years, Beard became increasingly conservative and isolationist, expressing his views in such works as *American Foreign Policy in the Making* (1946) and *The Coming of the War* (1948). He also wrote *Economic Origins of Jeffersonian Democracy* (1915) and *The Economic Basis of Business* (1922).

Beardsley, Aubrey Vincent (1872–1898). English artist. Beardsley is known for his black-and-white drawings on fantastic and erotic subjects, chiefly as illustrations for books and periodicals representative of an English aesthetic movement during the 1890's.

Beatitudes. The sayings of Jesus in the opening verses of the SERMON ON THE MOUNT (Matt. 5:3–12), beginning "Blessed are the poor in spirit" and naming the virtues that make their possessor blessed.

beat movement. A part-social, part-literary phenomenon of the mid 1950's centered in Greenwich Village in New York, the North Beach district of San Francisco, and Venice West, a suburb of Los Angeles. Socially, the beat movement represented a rejection of middle-class values, of commercialism, and of conformity to a social norm; it advocated voluntary poverty, individualism, and release or "illumination" through jazz, sexual experience, and drugs. The term "beat" is meant to convey the usual connotations of worn-out and exhausted, but also to suggest beatitude or blessedness.

The chief spokesmen of the movement are Allen GINSBERG, Jack KEROUAC, Gregory Corso, William S. Burroughs, Lawrence Ferlinghetti, and Gary Snyder. Ginsberg was at least partially responsible for bringing the movement to national attention when his *Howl and Other Poems* (1956) was charged with obscenity and became something of a *cause célèbre*. Like Ginsberg, most of the beat writers are poets, and most work in loose structures and in the free-verse, incantatory tradition of Whitman. One of the more sensitive of the beat poets is Gary Snyder (1930–   ), whose poems of the Pacific Northwest, where he spent part of his childhood, are controlled and sometimes compelling. His books include *Riprap* (1959) and *Myths and Texts* (1960). Lawrence Ferlinghetti (1919–   ) is both poet and publisher (City Lights Books) and has published the work of many of the beat writers. His poetry includes *Pictures of the Gone World* (1955) and *A Coney Island of the Mind* (1958). Gregory Corso (1930–   ) tends to be provocative and impudent in his work, which is collected in *Gasoline* (1958) and *The Happy Birthday of Death* (1960).

Of the beat novelists the most widely known is Jack Kerouac, many of whose loosely constructed, picaresque works are set in beat environments. His books include *On the Road* (1957), *The Subterraneans* (1958), and *The Dharma Bums* (1960). William S. Burroughs (1914–   ), also a novelist, is known for *The Naked Lunch* (Paris, 1959; U.S.,

1962), a savage novel of the extremes of depravity experienced in dope addiction. Books on the beats include *The Beats* (1960), edited by Seymour Krim, and *A Casebook on the Beat* (1961), edited by Thomas Parkinson.

Beatrice. (1) The beloved of DANTE. He records the history of his love for her in LA VITA NUOVA, increasingly idealizing her until she becomes his spiritual inspiration. Thus, in the DIVINE COMEDY she is the symbol of divine revelation through faith, and guides him through Paradise. The original Beatrice was probably Beatrice Portinari (1266–1290), who married Simone de' Bardi.

(2) The high-spirited niece of Leonato in Shakespeare's MUCH ADO ABOUT NOTHING. Although she has sworn to have no man, she is attracted to Benedick, with whom she engages in a constant battle of wits. She is one of Shakespeare's most famous heroines.

Beattie, James (1735–1803)'. Scottish poet and philosopher. His opposition to the skeptical philosophy of Hume is set forth in his common-sense and orthodox reply, the *Essay on Truth* (1770). The essay contains what may be called an official doctrine of preromanticism. His best-known poem is THE MINSTREL; OR, THE PROGRESS OF GENIUS.

Beauchamp, Lucas. A character in William Faulkner's INTRUDER IN THE DUST and in his *Fire and the Hearth,* a short story in GO DOWN, MOSES. Lucas, the part-Negro grandson of Carothers McCaslin, is a dignified and independent man who lives on the borderline between the white and black worlds, thus causing a great deal of consternation among those white people who consider him arrogant and disrespectful.

Beauchamp, Mary Annette. See ELIZABETH, Countess Russell.

Beau Geste (1924). A best-selling novel by P. C. WREN about life in the French Foreign Legion. Beau Geste is the name the hero assumes.

Beauharnais, Joséphine de. Born **Marie Joséphine Rose Tascher de la Pagerie** (1763–1814). French empress. Born in Martinique, Josephine was first married to the vicomte Alexandre Beauharnais, who was executed as a counter-revolutionist in 1794. She had two children by this marriage, Eugène and Hortense, who became queen of Holland and mother of Napoleon III.

Josephine was a prominent figure in Parisian society when she met NAPOLEON BONAPARTE, then a comparatively obscure army officer whose reputation was on the rise. He fell passionately in love with her, as his letters testify, and they were married on March 9, 1796. At Napoleon's coronation she was crowned empress of France (Dec. 2, 1804). In 1809 Napoleon divorced his wife and empress as she had not provided him with an heir. She spent her last years in retirement at her lovely home in La Malmaison, occasionally receiving a visit from Napoleon.

Beaumarchais. Assumed name of **Pierre Augustin Caron** (1732–1799). French dramatist, courtier, and watchmaker to Louis XV. He is best known for his two comic masterpieces THE BARBER OF SEVILLE and *The Marriage of Figaro* (1784), both of which deal with the exploits of one of the world's cleverest servants, FIGARO. In addition to his

Mémoires (1774), he wrote three minor plays: *Eugénie* (1767), *Les Deux amis* (1770), and *La Mère coupable* (1792). He was also librettist of the opera *Tarare* (1787).

Beaumont and Fletcher. Beaumont, Francis (c. 1584–1616) and Fletcher, John (1579–1625), English dramatists. Their names are always linked together because of the plays on which they collaborated; these include such tragi-comedies as PHILASTER, *A King and No King* (1611), and THE MAID'S TRAGEDY. In these and other plays, Beaumont and Fletcher foreshadowed and influenced Restoration drama. Other fruits of the collaboration include *The Nice Valour* (1606?), *Wit at Several Weapons* (1606), *The Captain* (c. 1611), *Love's Pilgrimage* (1615?), and *The Scornful Lady* (c. 1614).

In addition, Fletcher wrote a number of plays both alone and in collaboration with other dramatists. He was at his best when he could bring his lyric talents and sophistication to bear on such comedies of manners as THE WILD GOOSE CHASE, *The Scornful Lady* (c. 1614), *Wit without Money* (1614), and *Rule a Wife and Have a Wife* (1624). He also excelled at tragi-comedy, a form he and Beaumont had made their own. His unaided plays in this genre include *A Wife for a Month* (1624) and *The Humorous Lieutenant* (1619). Fletcher is the author of the famous pastoral play THE FAITHFUL SHEPHERDESS. In collaboration with Philip Massinger, he wrote *The Bloody Brother* (1615?), *The Tragedy of Sir John Van Olden Barnavelt* (1619), *The False One* (1620), and *The Double Marriage* (1620). He is said to have collaborated with Shakespeare on HENRY VIII and THE TWO NOBLE KINSMEN.

Beaumont also wrote several plays alone, two of which are noteworthy: THE KNIGHT OF THE BURNING PESTLE and *The Woman Hater* (c. 1606), a comedy of humors.

Beautiful Litigant, The. See François de BOIS-ROBERT.

Beauty and the Beast. A well-known fairy tale. Beauty saves the life of her father by consenting to live with the Beast. The Beast, being freed from a spell by Beauty's love, becomes a handsome prince, and marries her.

Beauvoir, Simone de (1908–   ). French novelist and essayist. She abandoned the teaching of philosophy with the publication of her first novel, *She Came to Stay* (*L'Invitée,* 1943), which, like THE MANDARINS, is important as a barely fictionalized document about Jean-Paul Sartre, his circle of leftist intellectuals, and their interpretations of EXISTENTIALISM. *The Blood of the Others* (*Le Sang des autres;* 1944) and *All Men Are Mortal* (*Tous les hommes sont mortels;* 1947) are novels that preach existentialist doctrines about human possibility in a world without God.

The long esssay *The Second Sex* (*Le Deuxième Sexe;* 1949) analyzes the difficult position of woman in the modern world; *The Long March* (1957) is a sympathetic description of Communist China. *Memoirs of a Dutiful Daughter* (*Memoire d'une jeune fille rangée;* 1958) is her autobiography to the age of 21; *The Prime of Life* (*La Force de l'âge*) continues it through the Resistance and records her close personal attachment to Sartre. Her other works include the essays in *Pyrrhus et Cinéas* (1944), the play *Les*

Bouches inutiles (1945), and the travel diary *America Day by Day* (1948).

Beaux' Strategem, The (1707). A comedy by George FARQUHAR. Thomas Aimwell and his friend Archer, the two beaux, having run through all their money, set out fortune-hunting and come to Lichfield as "master and man." Aimwell pretends to be very unwell, and as Lady Bountiful's hobby is tending the sick, she orders him to be removed to her mansion. Here he and Dorinda, daughter of Lady Bountiful, fall in love and finally marry. Archer falls in love with Mrs. Sullen, wife of Lady Bountiful's son Squire Sullen.

Beaver Coat, The (Der Biberpelz; 1893). A comedy by Gerhart HAUPTMANN. It recounts the machinations of the thieving washerwoman, Mrs. Wolff, and her poacher husband. She steals a beaver coat and then manages to escape detection by the stupid and officious magistrate, Wehrhahn. In fact, in the end she convinces him that she is the most virtuous and upright woman in the village.

Bebel, August (1840–1913). German socialist and member of the Reichstag. He was a very popular and influential leader of the German Social Democratic Party, which he and Wilhelm Liebknecht had helped to found in 1869, and was opposed to Bismarck's war policies.

Beccadelli, Antonio. See PANORMITA, I.

Beccari, Agostino (d. 1590). Italian poet. A native of Ferrara, he wrote the first Renaissance pastoral drama, the *Sacrificio* (1554). It influenced Tasso's *Aminta*.

Beccaria, Cesare (1735–1794). Italian economist and penologist. In his influential and humanitarian *Tratto dei Delitti e delle Pene* (1764) he opposed capital punishment and torture. He also was a contributor to the review IL CAFFÈ.

Becher, Johann Joachim. See PHLOGISTON.

Beck, Beatrix (1914–   ). French novelist, formerly secretary to André Gide. In *The Passionate Heart* (*Léon Morin, prêtre;* 1952) the narrator is converted by a beloved Catholic priest during the Occupation.

Beck, Mrs. L[ily] Adams, born **Moresby** (d. 1931). English popular romantic novelist and mystical Orientalist, who wrote under the pen names E. Barrington and Louis Moresby as well as under L. Adams Beck. As E. Barrington she wrote best-selling historical novels, including *The Divine Lady* (1924), about Nelson and Lady Hamilton, and *Glorious Apollo* (1925), about Byron.

Becker, Carl [Lotus] (1873–1945). American historian. A disciple of Frederick Jackson Turner and professor of history for many years at Cornell University, Becker published a number of important books, including *The Declaration of Independence: A Study in the History of Political Ideas* (1922), *Our Great Experiment in Democracy* (1924), *The Heavenly City of the Eighteenth-Century Philosophers* (1932), *Progress and Power* (1936), and *Modern Democracy* (1942).

Becket (1959). A drama by Jean ANOUILH about St. THOMAS À BECKET.

Beckett, Samuel (1906–   ). Irish-born French novelist and dramatist. A close friend of James Joyce, he settled in Paris in 1937. The novels *Murphy* (1938) and *Watt* (1944, pub. 1953) were written in English; in 1945 Beckett began writing first in French, then translating most of his own works into English. From 1947 to 1949 he wrote the novel trilogy composed of MOLLOY, MALONE DIES, and THE UNNAMABLE, and the play WAITING FOR GODOT. Later plays are ENDGAME, KRAPP'S LAST TAPE, *Happy Days* (1961), and *Play* (1963). *Krapp's Last Tape* and *Happy Days* were written in English. In 1969 he received the Nobel Prize in literature.

Considered major works in the literature of the ABSURD, all Beckett's pieces present a comically pessimistic allegory of man's condition. Often the traditionally farcical gestures of the circus clown and the vaudeville actor are used to portray human weakness, frustration, and helplessness. Beckett's plays often parody past literary classics, or Cartesian rational thought. His characters typically advance through worsening stages of decrepitude or paralysis. Such human bonds as they form are the coupling of tyrant and victim, or at best of two pathetically groping dependencies. The only freedom they have exists within their own minds, where they invent characters whose existence becomes the proof of their own. Nevertheless, the freedom to invent is linked with the compulsive need to express, in the absence of anything to express or any meaningful language for expression. This need is the only life-sustaining force in a world of progressive disintegration.

Other works include the English radio plays *All That Fall* (1957, translated as *Tous Ceux Qui Tombent*) and *Embers* (1960; translated as *Cendres*), and the French novel *Comment C'est* (1960).

Beckford, William (1760–1844). English man of letters. He is best known for VATHEK, AN ARABIAN TALE; an Oriental romance, it was written in French and translated into English probably by Samuel Henley in 1786. The associated *Episodes of Vathek* was translated from the French by Sir F. T. Marzials in 1912. Beckford's eccentric literary career and his penchant for the extravagant Gothic form in art and architecture (particularly his estate at Fonthill Abbey) place him in the tradition of Horace Walpole.

Beckmesser. The town clerk, a leading character in Wagner's opera, DIE MEISTERSINGER. He is the savage caricature of a contemporary critic named Hanslick, who had criticized Wagner's poetic accomplishments. The composer was dissuaded by his friends from naming the character Hans Lick.

Becque, Henry (1837–1899). French dramatist. Becque wrote plays that were naturalistic both in subject matter and in technique. In such dramas as *Michel Pauper* (1870), *Les Honnêtes Femmes* (1880), *Les Corbeaux* (*The Vultures,* 1882), and *La Parisienne* (1885), he presented realistic portraits of life, handicapped by a dearth of action and colorless characterization.

Bécquer, Gustavo Adolfo (1836–1870). Spanish poet. With the exception of some individual poems his works first appeared posthumously as *Rimas* (1871). Approximately 80 poems are to be found in this work, but though few in number, their quality established Bécquer's reputation as one of the major poets of the romantic era. With apparent simplicity, he created a delicately lyrical and deeply spiritual tone which infuses such poems as *Volverán las oscuras golondrinas* or *Del salón en el* *ángulo obscuro* and reappears in his prose treatments of legend, as in *Los ojos verdes.*

Beddoes, Thomas Lovell (1803–1849). English poet and playwright. An eccentric, melancholy man with a taste for the macabre, he wrote in the tradition of the Elizabethan poetic drama. He was a great admirer of Shelley and was in some degree influenced by him. His chief work, *Death's Jest Book, or The Fool's Tragedy,* was printed posthumously in 1850.

Bede. Called **the Venerable** [also **Baeda** or **Beda**] (c. 673–735). English historian and scholar. A monk at the Northumbrian monastery at Jarrow, he wrote over 30 works of history, grammar, science, theological commentary, etc. His best-known work is the Latin *Ecclesiastical History of the English People* (*Historia Ecclesiastica Gentis Anglorum;* 731), from the Roman invasion of England to 731, now a major source of historical and legendary information. It was translated into Old English under King ALFRED, and also provided the material for the early part of the ANGLO-SAXON CHRONICLE.

Bede, Cuthbert. See Edward BRADLEY.

Bedivere, Sir. In Arthurian legend, a dignitary of King Arthur's court. In Malory's *Morte d'Arthur* (c. 1469), it is he who, at the request of the dying Arthur, throws the sword Excalibur into the lake, and then bears the king to the barge that waits to carry him to AVALON.

bedlam. A lunatic asylum or madhouse. The word is a contraction of *Bethlehem,* St. Mary of Bethlehem being the name of a religious house in London that was converted into a hospital for lunatics in 1402. See TOM o' BEDLAM.

Bednyi, Demyan. Pen name of **Efim Alekseyevich Pridvorov** (1883–1945). Russian poet. A peasant by origin, Bednyi became the most popular Soviet poet in the early years of the regime, churning out topical verse in profusion. His pen name, Bednyi, means "poor" in Russian. His crude propaganda poetry earned him a prominent place in Soviet letters until 1936 when his opera libretto, *Epic Heroes (Bogatyri),* displeased the authorities because of its spoofing of the Russian epic tradition of folk poetry and of the introduction of Christianity to Russia. The old Bolshevik failed to realize that, at that point in history, the party viewed the epic tradition as a national treasure and the spread of Christianity as a progressive occurrence. Bednyi was reprimanded, and never regained his popularity.

Beebe, Lucius [Morris] (1902–). American journalist. Known also as a chronicler of café society, in 1952 he revived and became editor of the *Territorial Enterprise,* a weekly in Virginia City, Nev., for which Mark Twain once wrote. The colorful history of the paper is recounted in *Comstock Commotion, The Story of The Territorial Enterprise* (1954). He is also known for his books on trains, the latest of which is *Mr. Pullman's Elegant Palace Car* (1961).

Beecham, Sir Thomas (1879–1961). English conductor. Noted for the performance of works of Handel, Mozart, and Delius, whose works he championed, he is also remembered for his acid wit and pungent comments. He wrote an autobiography, *A Mingled Chime* (1944).

Beecher, Henry Ward (1813–1887). American clergyman, editor, and writer. The son of Lyman Beecher and brother of Harriet Beecher Stowe, he attended a school conducted by his sister Catherine in which he was the only boy among some 40 girls. He was graduated from Amherst College in 1834 and from Lane Theological Seminary in Cincinnati in 1837. An intensely emotional man, Beecher won a huge following with his sermons, in which he extolled the love of God and man; he also attacked slavery and advocated woman's suffrage and free trade. From 1861 to 1864 he was editor of *The Independent,* and from 1870 to 1881, of *The Christian Union.* In 1874 he was sued for damages by Theodore Tilton, who accused him of adultery with Mrs. Tilton. Although the jury could not reach a verdict and a council of Congregational churches found him innocent, Beecher's reputation was permanently damaged.

His *Seven Lectures to Young Men* (1844), a series of addresses on such topics as "Industry and Idleness" and "Gamblers and Gambling," was widely read. He also wrote a book of essays, *Plain and Pleasant Talk about Fruits, Flowers, and Farming* (1859) and *Norwood* (1867), a novel.

Beecher, Lyman (1775–1863). American preacher and author. Beecher became one of the outstanding preachers of his day; he was the father of a large family of which four children became famous: Catherine, Edward, Henry Ward, and Harriet Beecher Stowe. Opposed to Catholicism and the use of liquor, Beecher supported traditional Calvinism, and instituted drastic domestic discipline in his home. Even he, however, was accused of heresy, although he was finally acquitted by the synod. In addition to several pastorates in New England and New York, Beecher was president of the Lane Theological Seminary in Cincinnati (1832–1852). His sermons and articles were collected in *Works* (1852), and his *Autobiography* appeared in 1864. The Beecher household probably provided the details for Harriet Beecher Stowe's *Oldtown Folks* (1869).

Beelzebub. One of the "false gods" worshiped by the Israelites. He was originally a local Philistine god (or Baal) of Ekron, whose name meant "Lord of Flies." In this capacity, Baalzebub, as his name was properly spelled, probably had the power to send or protect from sickness, which was known to be carried by flies. Another Lord of Flies was Zeus Apomyios to whom the Greeks annually sacrificed at Actium. The Romans also sacrificed to flies in the temple of Hercules Victor. In the New Testament (Matt. 12:24) the Jews accuse Christ of driving out devils by the power of Beelzebub, called the Prince of Devils. In *Paradise Lost,* Milton makes Beelzebub one of the chief lords of Hell, next to Satan in power and rank.

Beer, Thomas (1889–1940). American writer. The author of three novels, *The Fair Rewards* (1922), *Sandoval* (1924), and *The Road to Heaven* (1928), Beer is better known for his book on Stephen Crane (1923) and for THE MAUVE DECADE, a study of the 1890's. *Hanna* (1929) dealt with the same decade. *Mrs. Egg and Other Barbarians* (1933) is a collection of short stories.

Beerbohm, Sir Max (1872–1956). English essayist and caricaturist. The half-brother of Sir Herbert Beerbohm-Tree, he was a brilliant figure in the London of the decadents and the Gay Nineties, contributing to the *Yellow Book*, and writing irreverent parodies (as in *A Christmas Garland*, 1895) and drawing brilliant caricatures under the signature "Max." His later works included the novel ZULEIKA DOBSON, essays such as those collected in the volume *In Defense of Cosmetics* (1922), and *Around Theatres* (1930). He remained a legend for his wit, brilliance, and powers of satire even after he had retired to live quietly in Italy during his middle and old age.

Beer-Hall Putsch (1923). A revolt in Munich led by Adolf HITLER and General Erich LUDENDORFF, who sought to overthrow the Bavarian government. Hitler was arrested and spent several months in prison, where he wrote MEIN KAMPF.

Beer-Hofmann, Richard (1866–1945). Austrian poet and playwright with neoromantic leanings. Active in Vienna and a friend of Hugo von HOFMANNSTHAL, he often treated Jewish themes, as in his plays *Jaakobs Traum* (*Jacob's Dream*, 1918) and *Der junge David* (*Young David*, 1933).

Beethoven, Ludwig van (1770–1827). German composer. A student of Haydn, he added the new, emotional qualities of romanticism to the tradition of formal precision that he inherited from the 18th-century masters of music. His nine symphonies are the most widely known among his works, although he wrote in a number of other musical forms, including chamber music, sonatas, and concertos. The most famous symphonies are the Third, called the EROICA, the Fifth (1808), the Sixth, or *Pastoral* (1808), and especially the Ninth, or *Choral* (1823). See FIDELIO.

Beggar on Horseback (1924). A fantastic comedy by George S. KAUFMAN and Marc CONNELLY, with music by Deems Taylor. A satire on business in the form of a dream, it is the story of a poverty-stricken composer, Neil McRae, who is persuaded to propose to a rich girl, Gladys Cady. In a dream he learns the horrible consequences of such a marriage; he is set to work in the Cady factory, murders the Cady family, and is thrown in prison. Upon awakening he is released from the engagement.

Beggar's Opera, The (1728). A ballad opera by John GAY, first produced at Lincoln's Inn Fields in London, a theater managed by John RICH. Very little escapes satiric treatment in this work; barbs are aimed at the elaborate, current Italian operatic style, at the prime minister Walpole, at marriage, at ladies and gentlemen, at lawyers, and at trade. The songs, many of them set to popular English and Scottish tunes, were arranged and scored by John Christopher Pepusch, who composed the overture.

The story concerns Peachum, a receiver of stolen goods. His biggest business is done with Captain Macheath, a highwayman with whom Peachum's daughter Polly has fallen in love. They marry secretly, and Peachum, now unable to use Polly in his business, gets his revenge by informing on Macheath and collecting the reward money. Macheath is taken off to Newgate prison which is run by the corrupt Lockit, who is in league with Peachum. Lockit's daughter Lucy falls in love with Macheath and helps him to escape. He is captured but saved from hanging by the mock intervention of a beggar and a player, since it would never do to let the fine hero die. This happy ending satirizes the sentimental tragedy of the day. Bertold Brecht and Kurt Weill used *The Beggar's Opera* as the basis for their THREEPENNY OPERA.

Behan, Brendan (1923–1964). Irish playwright and wit. Born in Dublin at the time of civil strife in Ireland, Brendan Behan reflected in his life and works the zest, vitality, and macabre sense of humor of that tempestuous era. His early life was strongly influenced by the close association of his family with the Irish Republican Army, an association continued by Brendan who, at the age of 16, was arrested by English authorities for the possession of explosives with the intent of blowing up a battleship. He was found guilty and sentenced to three years in an English reform school, an experience he recounts with uninhibited gusto in the autobiographical *Borstal Boy* (1958). Behan subsequently served two more prison terms, the second of which resulted in his being deported to France. Having spent a good portion of his youth in jail, he utilized this experience as the basis of his two plays, *The Quare Fellow* (1956), a memorable exercise of "gallows humor," and *The Hostage* (1958). Despite his considerable reputation as a playwright, he was perhaps better known for his alcoholic exploits, accounts of which were featured prominently in the English and American press. For this reason he was dismissed by some critics as a buffoon, more interested in publicity than in playwrighting, and trading on a stereotyped conception of the wild young Irishman. For Behan, however, drinking was an essential expression of his approach to (and quarrel with) social reality. *Hold Your Hour and Have Another* (1964) is a collection of Behan's humorous pieces. A novel, *The Scarperer* (1964), was published posthumously.

Behemoth. The animal described in Job 40:15-24. If an actual animal were intended, it would seem to describe the hippopotamus; but modern scholarship tends to the opinion that the reference is purely mythological.

Behn, Mrs. Aphra (1640–1689). English novelist and dramatist. The first English female professional writer, she wrote a number of complicated comedies of intrigue, such as *The Rover, or The Banished Cavaliers: Parts I and II* (1677, 1680), *Sir Patient Fancy* (1678), and *The City Heiress, or Sir Timothy Treat-All* (1682). Her best-known novel is *Oroonoko, or the History of the Royal Slave* (c. 1678). She served Charles II as a spy in Antwerp.

Behrman, S[amuel] N[athaniel] (1893–). American playwright. He is especially known for his sophisticated comedies of ideas. *The Second Man* (1927) was his first play. Among his better-known later works are *Serena Blandish* (1928), a dramatization of a novel by the British novelist and playwright Enid Bagnold; *Biography* (1932), about a woman portrait painter and a journalist; *Rain from Heaven* (1934), one of the earliest anti-Nazi plays; END OF SUMMER; *Amphitryon 38* (1937), an adaptation from Jean Giraudoux; *Wine of Choice* (1938), on liberalism and its difficulties; NO TIME FOR COMEDY; and *I Know My Love* (1949). Behrman is the author of two biographies: *Duveen* (1952), a work on the famous art dealer, and *Portrait of Max* (1960), a profile of Max Beerbohm. He has also written several film scripts. In 1958 he dramatized his autobiographical *The Worcester Account* (1954) as *The Cold Wind and the Warm.*

Being and Nothingness (**L'Etre et le Néant;** 1943). A long philosophical treatise by Jean-Paul SARTRE. Subtitled "an essay on phenomenological ontology," it is Sartre's major attempt to systematize his theoretical analysis of man's condition and consciousness which underlies EXISTENTIALISM. Postulating that for man existence precedes essence, he concludes that the very "nothingness" of man's essence in a world without God or meaning allows each person infinite potentialities in the shaping of his life, limited by the facts of the external world, but not by any *a priori* conditions of the so-called human nature.

Beith, Sir John Hay. See Ian HAY.

Bekenntnisse des Hochstaplers Felix Krull. See CONFESSIONS OF FELIX KRULL: CONFIDENCE MAN.

Bel. The supreme Babylonian god of the earth and atmosphere, called the god of lords. He is said to have created man and the universe and symbolizes male generative power. Bel is the same word as BAAL in Phoenician and Hebrew.

In the story *Bel and the Dragon,* an Old Testament Apocryphal book appended to the book of *Daniel,* Daniel exposes the trickery of the priest of Bel in Babylon and convinces the king that Bel is only an image and not an actual living deity.

Belarius. In Shakespeare's CYMBELINE, a noble and worthy lord banished by Cymbeline, king of Britain. He kidnaps Cymbeline's two sons and, using the name Morgan, raises them in a rustic region of Wales as his own sons. He is a spokesman for the pastoral life far from the deceit and intrigues of the court.

Belasco, David (1859–1931). American actor, theatrical producer, and dramatist. Belasco produced nearly 400 plays, many of them by native dramatists, and greatly influenced the American theater in the direction of greater emotionalism and more realistic stage properties. He developed the talents of many performers, such as David Warfield and Minnie Maddern Fiske.

His best-known plays include *The Heart of Maryland* (1895), a Civil War story inspired by Rose Hartwick Thorpe's poem *Curfew Must Not Ring Tonight!* (1867); THE GIRL OF THE GOLDEN WEST; and *The Return of Peter Grimm* (1911), a fantasy to which Cecil B. DeMille also contributed. Belasco also collaborated with other writers, notably with James A. Herne on *Hearts of Oak* (1879) and with John Luther Long on *Madame Butterfly* (1898).

Belcari, Feo (1410–1484). Florentine writer of sacred plays and a celebrated life of Giovanni Colombini. His *sacra rappresentazione* (mystery or miracle play) entitled *Abramo ed Isac* is one of the best of the genre, as well as the earliest by a known author.

Belch, Sir Toby. In Shakespeare's TWELFTH NIGHT, Olivia's riotous, bibulous uncle. He extracts drinking money from the foolish Sir Andrew Aguecheek by pretending to advance the latter's suit for Olivia.

Belfagor. A famous novella by Niccolò MACHIAVELLI about the adventures on earth of the archdevil Belfagor. He has been sent here from Hell to determine whether matrimony has been the principal cause of the damnation of its residents, as they all claim. In Florence, he poses as a Spaniard, Roderigo of Castile, and marries Onesta Donati, but the more he loves her the haughtier she becomes, until he is forced to flee from her. Later, faced with the possibility of living with her again, he prefers to return to Hell.

Belford, John. The libertine friend and correspondent of LOVELACE in Samuel Richardson's epistolary novel CLARISSA HARLOWE. Horrified by the rape of Clarissa, he reforms; he becomes Clarissa's executor and the editor of her voluminous correspondence.

Belgard. See FAERIE QUEENE, THE.

Belge. See FAERIE QUEENE, THE.

Belinda. The heroine of Alexander Pope's mock-heroic poem THE RAPE OF THE LOCK, who is described as the fairest of mortals:

> If to her share some Female Errors fall,
> Look on her Face and you'll forget 'em all.

Belinski, Vissarion Grigoryevich (1811–1848). Russian literary critic and journalist. Belinski gained prominence in literary circles for his *Literaturnye mechtaniya* (*Literary Reveries,* 1834), dealing with the development of Russian literature since the 17th century. He became the literary critic on the influential journal *Otechestvennye Zapiski* (*Fatherland Notes*), and, from 1846 to his death, on the *Sovremennik* (*The Contemporary*). The critical articles he wrote during these years, such as his annual surveys of Russian literature, were to have an overwhelming influence on the future course of Russian literary criticism. Belinski's ideas formed the theoretical basis for the NATURAL SCHOOL in Russian literature, which insisted that literature treat its subjects—especially poverty and exploitation of the people—realistically, with the aim of social reform. Although later critics exaggerated the social aspect of Belinski's literary doctrine, he was not entirely unaware of artistic quality. This fact is particularly evident in parts of the series of articles that he wrote from 1843 to 1846 on the work of Pushkin. But Belinski's fervent interest in social issues did occasionally blind him in regard to literary facts; he hailed Gogol as a great realist, and this erroneous label stuck to Gogol until the 20th century. Whatever confusion he introduced into Russian critical theory and practice, Belinski did, at least, serve Russian literature by insisting on its importance. He also encouraged the early efforts of some of Russia's finest writers, such as Lermontov, Gogol, Turgenev, and Dostoevski. Belinski's social bias has made him one of the ever quoted oracles of Soviet literary criticism.

Belinus. One of the kings in Geoffrey of Monmouth's HISTORY OF THE KINGS OF BRITAIN. According to the writer, Belinus founded CAERLEON, and, when he died, his ashes were put into an urn and then placed on top of a tower.

Belisarius (505–565). Byzantine general, responsible for the military success of Justinian I. Accused of conspiring against the life of the emperor, he was imprisoned in 562 and released in 563. Much later, an exaggerated version of his punishment made him a blind beggar, and this account was popularized by Jean-François Marmontel's philosophical novel *Bélisaire* (1767).

Belkin, Tales of (Povesti Belkina; 1830). A cycle of 5 short stories by Aleksandr PUSHKIN, with an introduction dealing with the life of the fictitious compiler of the tales, Ivan Petrovich Belkin. The tales are *Vystrel* (*The Shot*), *Metel'* (*The Snowstorm*), *Grobovshchik* (*The Undertaker*), *Stantzionnyi smotritel'* (*The Stationmaster*), and *Baryshnya-Krest'yanka* (*The Lady-Rustic*). The best known of the tales is probably *The Stationmaster*, which contains one of the first carefully drawn portraits in Russian literature of a character who is not a member of the nobility. The fictitious compiler of the tales, Ivan Belkin, whose rather commonplace life is recounted in the introduction, became famous as a literary character in his own right. Pushkin later wrote a prose fragment, *Istoriya sela Goryukhina* (*History of the Village of Goryukhin,* 1830), which purports to be an autobiography of Belkin. The extraordinary description of such an ordinary figure as Belkin is credited with being one of the first steps toward the realism which predominated in later 19th-century Russian literature.

Bell, Acton, Ellis, and Currer. The pseudonyms adopted by Anne, Emily, and Charlotte BRONTË respectively. In 1846 they published a volume entitled *Poems by Currer, Ellis, and Acton Bell*.

Bell, [Arthur] Clive [Howard] (1881–1964). English critic of art and literature. A member of the Bloomsbury group, he married Vanessa Stephen, the sister of Virginia Woolf. His major works of criticism include *Art* (1914), *Since Cézanne* (1922), *Proust* (1929), and *Account of French Painting* (1931). His son Julian (1908–1937), author of *Work for the Winter* (1936), a collection of poems, was fatally wounded while driving an ambulance for the Loyalists during the civil war in Spain.

Bell, Gertrude (1868–1926). English travel writer and authority on Arabia. Her books include *The Desert and the Sown* (1907). Her interesting *Letters* were published in 1927.

Bell, Laura. The heroine of William Makepeace Thackeray's PENDENNIS. As Mrs. Arthur Pendennis, she also appears in *The Newcomes* (1853–1855) and *The Adventures of Philip* (1862).

Bell, The (1958). A comic, philosophic novel by Iris MURDOCH. The story is set in a lay religious community attached to a convent and is concerned with the complex needs and self-deceptions that bind each member to the group. The bell, which represents the ideals of the community, precipitates the final scandal that forces the group to disband. The members regain their freedom, but not all are able to deal with it.

Bellamy, Edward (1850–1898). American novelist and reformer. He is best known for his popular utopian novel LOOKING BACKWARD: 2000–1887. Bellamy earlier wrote several romances, including *The Duke of Stockbridge* (1879), dealing with Shays's Rebellion, and two psychological studies, *Dr. Heidenhoff's Process* (1880) and *Miss Ludington's Sister* (1884). His short stories were collected in *The Blind Man's World and Other Stories* (1898).

Bellamoure, Sir. See FAERIE QUEENE, THE.

Bellay, Joachim Du. See Joachim DU BELLAY.

Bell, Book and Candle (1950). A play by John VAN DRUTEN. It is about a beautiful present-day witch who falls in love with a man and loses her powers as a sorceress.

Belle au bois dormant, La (The Sleeping Beauty). A charming nursery tale that first appeared in the CONTES DE MA MÈRE L'OYE of Charles PERRAULT. A magic spell confines a beautiful princess to a castle where she must sleep for 100 years. Only the kiss of a young prince brave enough to penetrate the dark wood which springs up about the castle can, and eventually does, awaken her from the enchanted sleep.

Belle Dame sans Merci, La (1819). A ballad by John KEATS. Its title and general theme are taken from an early French poem by Alain Chartier that was translated into English by Sir Richard Ros, and not by Geoffrey Chaucer, to whom it is often mistakenly attributed. Keats retains much of the medieval imagery of the French original.

Belle Plaideuse, La. See François de BOISROBERT.

Bellerophon or Bellerophontes. A grandson of Sisyphus. While living at the Argive court of King Proetus, he incurred the enmity of the queen, Antaea, by rejecting her advances. She falsely accused him to her husband, who sent Bellerophon with a letter to Iobates, the king of Lycia, his wife's father, recounting the charge, and praying that the bearer might be put to death. Iobates, unwilling to slay him himself, gave him many hazardous tasks (including the killing of the CHIMAERA), but as he was successful in all of them, Iobates made him his heir and gave him his daughter for a wife. Later Bellerophon is fabled to have attempted to fly to heaven on the winged horse Pegasus, but Zeus sent a gadfly to sting the horse, and the rider was overthrown. The revenge of Antaea is a familiar theme in folktale, found also in the stories of PHAEDRA and of Joseph and Potiphar's wife.

Bellerus. A giant, the legendary guardian of Lands End, England, once known as Bellerium.

Bell for Adano, A (1944). A novel by John HERSEY. It details the attempt of a sympathetic American officer to secure a new bell for an Italian village church which has been partially destroyed in World War II. Hersey won a Pulitzer Prize for the novel, which was later dramatized.

Bellini, Giovanni (c. 1430–1516). Venetian painter. The son of the artist **Iacopo Bellini** (c. 1400–c. 1470), both he and his brother **Gentile Bellini** (c. 1427–1507) were strongly influenced by their father's work and also by their brother-in-law, the painter Andrea. MANTEGNA, during their early years at Padua. Within the context of the new medium of oil painting, however, Giovanni moved away from Mantegna's severity, towards a great richness and mellowness of color. His devoutly religious Madonnas and serene altarpieces also reveal a deep appreciation of landscape, and of the effect of light and color on atmosphere. His interest in light and color, when contrasted with the Florentine emphasis on line and modeling, was to become in the hands of Giorgione and Titian, his two greatest pupils, the glory of the Venetian school of painting. Among his masterpieces are *Christ Blessing*, the *Pietà*, and the *Agony in the Garden*.

His father Iacopo left few surviving works, but influenced his sons chiefly through his sketchbooks, which have entitled him to be called the initiator of the Venetian Renaissance in painting. His brother Gentile is noted for his ceremonial pageant pictures (especially the *Miracle of the Cross*) and for his portrait of Muhammad II, for whom he was court painter at Constantinople. Despite the Islamic prohibition of images, Gentile was cherished by the sultan because of his great artistry.

Bellini, Vincenzo (1801–1835). Italian opera composer. His works are characterized by elegance and lyrical charm. His principal operas are NORMA (his masterpiece), *I Puritani,* and *La Sonnambula.* Bellini was a close friend of Chopin, and his music is thought to have had some influence on the work of that composer.

Bellisant. The mother of the twins VALENTINE AND ORSON in French romance and the sister of the CAROLINGIAN king Pepin. Falsely accused of infidelity, she is banished to the forest for a while by her husband, Alexander of Constantinople.

Bello, Andrés (1781–1865). Venezuelan scholar and poet. As one of the most promising young men in Caracas, Bello studied classical literature, law, and philosophy; his interest in the natural sciences was stimulated by his meeting with Alexander von Humboldt, who greatly influenced him. In 1810, Bello was sent to England to seek support for the revolutionary junta of Caracas as part of a three-man delegation that also included Simón Bolívar. In England, where he remained for nearly 20 years, he began his famous edition of the *Poema del Cid,* based on the 12th-century text, and wrote his best-known poems: *Alocución a la Poesía* (1823), a declaration of literary independence in which he exhorts the Muse to abandon Europe for America, and *La agricultura de la zona tórrida* (1826), notable for its description of the plants of America in which realistic detail is combined with classical allusions. From 1829 until his death, Bello resided in Chile where he held important government posts, was a founder and first president of the University of Chile, and was the chief architect of the Chilean civil code. During this period, he published *La oración por todos* (1843), an adaptation of Hugo's *La prière pour tous* (1830) which is sometimes considered better than the original. His most enduring achievement, however, is probably his *Gramática de la lengua castellana* (1847), still the outstanding authority on Spanish grammar. See Domingo Faustino SARMIENTO.

Belloc, Hilaire. Pen name of **Joseph Hilaire Pierre Belloc** (1870–1953). English writer. Born in France, Belloc was a prolific author of light verse, essays, travel books, history, biography, works of Roman Catholic and conservative polemic, and fiction. Like G. K. Chesterton, with whom he had many attitudes in common, he engaged in a great deal of influential controversy attacking the ideas of H. G. Wells and Bernard Shaw; Shaw called the pair "the Chesterbelloc." He is now best remembered for his light, witty writing and for his verse for children. His humorous, mock-moral books for children include *The Bad Child's Book of Beasts* (1896), CAUTIONARY TALES, and *Cautionary Verses* (1941). His elegant, witty essays appeared in such volumes as *On Nothing* (1908) and *On Everything* (1909). *The Path to Rome* (1902) is a travel book strongly flavored with humor and Catholic feeling; *Places* (1942) is a collection of short travel essays. He also wrote *History of England* (1925–1927) and biographies of Robespierre (1901), Wolsey (1930), and others. A collection of his letters was published in 1959.

Belloc Lowndes, Marie Adelaide. See Mrs. Belloc LOWNDES.

Bellona. In Roman mythology, the goddess of war and either wife or sister of Mars.

Bellow, Saul (1915–   ). American novelist. Best known for his picaresque ADVENTURES OF AUGIE MARCH, Bellow has a style that is rich, complex, and often comic. His first novel, *Dangling Man* (1944), is the story of a young man who is waiting to be inducted into the army. His second novel, *The Victim* (1947), deals with relations between Jew and Gentile. *Seize the Day* (1956) contains the excellent long story that entitles the volume, a play, and a shorter story, *Looking for Mr. Green.* The hero of *Henderson the Rain King* (1959) is a giant of a man with aspirations that match his bulk; the book departs from a realistically described American setting to a fantasy world where Henderson finds his destiny in a series of comic adventures that culminate in his becoming the rainmaker for a savage tribe. *Herzog* (1964), a novel about a college teacher, is highly autobiographical.

Bellows, George Wesley (1882–1925). American painter and lithographer. He is best known for his scenes of prizefights.

Bells and Pomegranates (1841–1846). A series of pamphlets containing poems by Robert BROWNING. They were issued by his publishers in an effort to popularize his work.

beloved disciple. John the evangelist, one of the 12 apostles.

beloved physician. Luke the evangelist. The beloved physician mentioned by St. Paul in *Colossians* (4:14) is presumed to be this Luke.

Beloved Returns, The (Lotte in Weimar; 1939). A novel by Thomas MANN. It is based on an imaginary incident in the life of Goethe: Charlotte ("Lotte") Buff, who was Goethe's sweetheart when he was young and who is thought to have been the model for the character Lotte in Goethe's THE SORROWS OF YOUNG WERTHER, comes to Weimar many years later and re-encounters the now old and established Goethe. Although in real life this incident never occurred, Mann has used it to make many intriguing explorations into Goethe's work and personality.

Beloved Vagabond, The (1906). A best-selling novel by William J. LOCKE. The vagabond is Paragot, a Bohemian philosopher and violinist, who wanders about Europe with a stray small boy (Anticot, who tells the story) and a homeless country girl.

Belphoebe. See FAERIE QUEENE, THE.

Belshazzar. The son of Nebuchadnezzar and the last of the Chaldaean dynasty, whose name means "may Bel protect the king." When his father fled the city of Babylonia after being defeated by Cyrus, Belshazzar assumed the throne in 539 B.C.; he was killed the next year in the sack of the city by Cyrus. According to scriptural narrative, he was warned of his coming doom by Daniel who interpreted the HANDWRITING ON THE WALL (Dan. 5:5–27).

Beltine (Cétshamain). May 1, one of the 4 great feast days of the ancient Celtic year. SAMAIN and Cétshamain (Beltine) are the feast days that divide the year into two halves, the hot and the cold seasons. See IMBOLC; LUGNASAD.

Belvidera. See VENICE PRESERVED.

Bely, Andrei. Pen name of **Boris Nikolayevich Bugayev** (1880–1934). Russian poet and novelist. One of the SYMBOLISTS, Bely, like Blok, was early in his career under the influence of the mystical ideas of the philosopher Vladimir SOLOVIOV. A student of philosophy and mathematics at the University of Moscow, Bely published his first poetry in 1901. He greeted the revolution enthusiastically with a long poem, *Christ Is Risen* (*Khristos voskrese;* 1918). Bely's best work is his prose, which includes the novels *The Silver Dove* (*Serebryanyi golub';* 1910), *Petersburg* (*Peterburg;* 1913), and *Kotik Letayev* (1918). Bely's prose style is rich, ornamental, and complex, often reminiscent of that of James Joyce in English. His later ideas had their source mainly in the anthroposophy of Rudolf Steiner, of whom Bely became a disciple. Bely left Russia in 1921, but returned in 1923, when he tried unsuccessfully to acclimate himself to the new society. His last years were spent writing his three volumes of memoirs which were published between 1929 and 1933: *On the Border of Two Centuries* (*Na rubezhe dvukh stoletii*), *The Beginning of a Century* (*Nachalo veka*) and *Between Two Revolutions* (*Mezhdu dvukh revolyutsii*). In his memoirs he included his reminiscences of Aleksandr Blok, his friend and fellow poet.

Bembo, Cardinal **Pietro** (1470–1547). Italian prelate and man of letters. Famed as a reformer and legislator of language and literature, he imposed classicist norms on the Tuscan tongue through his writings and inspired writers such as Petrarch to raise themselves to the level of classical models. Made a cardinal in 1539, he was a candidate for the papacy at the time of his death. His most famous works are the *Asolani* (1505), a group of dialogues on the nature of love which take their title from Asolo, the setting of the work, and the *Prose della volgar lingua* (*Essays on the Vernacular Tongue,* 1525).

Bemelmans, Ludwig (1898–1962). Austrian-born American writer and painter. Bemelmans' experiences in the hotel and restaurant business furnished material for his many entertaining stories and novels; he is also known for the charm of his books for children, especially *Madeleine* (1939). His work, written in a seemingly naïve though highly sophisticated style, was often illustrated by his own water colors and drawings. Among his many books are *Hansi* (1934), *My War with the United States* (1937), *Hotel Splendide* (1940), *Now I Lay Me Down to Sleep* (1944), *The One I Love Best* (1954), *The World of Bemelmans* (1955), *My Life in Art* (1958), and *Are You Hungry Are You Cold* (1960).

Benares or **Varanasi.** A holy city on the Ganges River in central India, famous as a place of pilgrimage.

Benassis, Dr. See COUNTRY DOCTOR, THE.

Benavente [y Martínez], Jacinto (1866–1954). Spanish playwright. Benavente was one of the leaders of Spanish drama during his day. He was a prolific writer whose works stress social satire or rural life. *Los intereses creados* (1907) is considered Benavente's masterpiece and is reminiscent of the Italian *commedia dell' arte.* His other well-known plays include *La mal querida* (*The Passion Flower,* 1913) and *Señora ama* (1908). In 1922 he was awarded the Nobel Prize for literature.

Ben Bolt. A popular song by Thomas Dunn English. It was first published in *The New Mirror* (1843). The heroine of George du Maurier's novel, *Trilby,* sings the song while hypnotized by Svengali. Several tunes have been used for English's lyrics, which begin "Oh, don't you remember sweet Alice, Ben Bolt?"

Benchley, Robert [Charles] (1889–1945). American drama critic, essayist, humorist, actor, and screenwriter. Highly successful in movies and on the radio, Benchley was admired for his short film *How to Sleep* (1935) and his famous sketch, *The Treasurer's Report* (1930). In his essays, Benchley portrayed his life as a series of frustrations and humiliations; his humor is based on the situation of the average American man, faced with the complexities of 20th-century life. Among his works are *20,000 Leagues under the Sea, or, David Copperfield* (1928), *From Bed to Worse* (1934), *My Ten Years in a Quandary* (1936), *Benchley Beside Himself* (1943), and the posthumous *Chips Off the Old Benchley* (1949). His son, Nathaniel, wrote a biography of him in 1955.

Benda, Julien (1867–1956). French philosopher and essayist. A violent defender of strict rationalism, he wrote a controversial attack on Bergsonism in 1912 and condemned the esthetics of contemporary literature for sensational emotionalism in *Belphégor* (1918). Benda is best known, however, for his attack on THE TREASON OF THE INTELLECTUALS. *The Yoke of Pity* (*L'Ordination;* 1912) is a novel.

bend sinister. In heraldry, two parallel lines from the upper right hand corner of a shield to the opposite base point. It was erroneously supposed to indicate bastardy. See BATON.

Benedick. In Shakespeare's MUCH ADO ABOUT NOTHING, a self-assured, cynical, and witty young nobleman of Padua. Although he has forsworn women, he constantly engages in repartee with the sharp-tongued Beatrice, with whom he is at last united through the conspiracy of their friends.

Benediktsson, Einar (1864–1940). Icelandic poet. Benediktsson was the leader of a nationalist movement that reacted against the bleakness and pessimism of the naturalist school. Active in political affairs, he published the newspaper *Dagskrá* for several years. In his verse, too, he expressed both optimism and patriotism, as well as his mystic beliefs. His volumes of poetry include *Sögur og Kvoeoi* (1897), *Hrannir* (1913), *Hvammar* (1930), and *Ljóomoeli* (3 vols., 1945).

Benelli, Sem (1877–1949). Italian dramatist. His best-known play is *La Cena delle Beffe* (1909), a melodrama set in Renaissance Florence, which was produced (1919) in New York as *The Jest* with John and Lionel Barrymore. He also wrote *La Maschera di Bruto* (1909) and *L'Amore dei Tre Re* (1910), which was the source of Italo Montemezzi's opera (1913) of the same name.

Beneš, Eduard (1884–1948). Czechoslovak statesman. Named foreign minister of Czechoslovakia when the republic was created in 1918, Beneš served for 17 years and was elected president in 1935. He held the post again after World War II, but resigned after the Communist coup d'etat of 1948.

Benét, Laura (1884?–   ). American poet and biographer. The sister of William Rose and Stephen Vincent Benét, she has published several books of verse, including *Fairy Bread* (1921) and *Is Morning Sure?* (1947), as well as a series of biographies for young people. Among her later books are *Coleridge, Poet of Wild Enchantment* (1952) and *Famous American Humorists* (1959).

Benét, Stephen Vincent (1898–1943). American poet and short-story writer. Known for his interest in fantasy and American themes, Benét also used his literary gifts as a novelist and writer for radio. His early collections of verse include *Five Men and Pompey* (1915), *Young Adventure* (1918), *Heavens and Earth* (1920), *The Ballad of William Sycamore* (1923), and *Tiger Joy* (1925). *King David* (1923) is a narrative poem about the biblical ruler. Benét's most famous poem, John Brown's Body, won a Pulitzer Prize. In *Litany for Dictatorships* (1935), he attacked totalitarian states. *Western Star* (1943), the first part of an American epic left incomplete at his death, was awarded a posthumous Pulitzer Prize.

Benét's first collection of short stories was *Thirteen O'Clock* (1937), which includes The Devil and Daniel Webster and *Sobbin' Women*. Other stories were collected in *Tales Before Midnight* (1939) and *The Last Circle* (1946). His novels include *Spanish Bayonet* (1926) and *James Shore's Daughter* (1934). Interested in the dramatic possibilities of radio, he wrote *They Burned the Books* (1942) and *A Child Is Born* (1942), a retelling of the birth of Jesus.

Benét, William Rose (1886–1950). American poet, critic, and editor. The elder brother of Stephen Vincent Benét, he wrote much poetry, collected in such volumes as *Merchants from Cathay,* (1913), *Starry Harness* (1933), *The Stairway of Surprise* (1947), and *The Spirit of the Scene* (1951). *Rip Tide* (1932) is a novel in verse. His verse autobiography, *The Dust Which Is God* (1941), won a Pulitzer Prize. One of the founders of the *Saturday Review of Literature,* he served on its editorial board and conducted the column of literary miscellany called "The Phœnix Nest" for many years. He was the original editor of *The Reader's Encyclopedia.*

Bengal Lancer. See Francis Yeats-Brown.

Bengodi. (*It.,* "enjoy well.") The name of a "land of Cockaigne" in Boccaccio's Decameron (VIII, 3). This is the land where "they tie the vines with sausages, where you may buy a fat goose for a penny and have a gosling in the bargain; where there is also a mountain of grated Parmesan cheese, and people do nothing but make cheesecakes and macaroons." It occurs in the tale of *Calandrino and the Heliotrope,* and is described to Calandrino by his friends, who are trying to persuade him that he will find precious stones there. But since it is "farther away even than the Abruzzi," he decides not to go.

Bengtsson, Frans Gunnar (1894–1954). Swedish poet, historian, novelist, and essayist. *Legenden om Babel* (1925) is a collection of poems that express in polished verse a love of the heroic. His most famous work, the novel *Röde Orm* (*Red Orm,* 1943; *The Long Ships,* 1954) also deals with the heroic: it is a lusty and amusing account of Viking exploits.

Ben-Hur: A Tale of the Christ (1880). A novel by Lew Wallace. The book grew out of a railroad car discussion that the author had with Robert Ingersoll, the free thinker. They discussed the divinity of Christ, and Wallace decided to study the life and times of Jesus. The book centers around Judah Ben Hur, a young aristocratic Jew, who is falsely accused of seeking to murder the Roman governor of Palestine. Sent to the galleys, he escapes, becomes a Roman officer, engages in a climactic chariot race with his betrayer, the false friend Messala, and is finally converted to Christianity. The book, highly popular, has been staged and twice made into a motion picture.

Benito Cereno (1856). A short story by Herman Melville, collected in his volume Piazza Tales. Benito Cereno, the captain of a slave ship, appears to be in command; in reality, he is the prisoner of the slaves, who are led by Babo, a Senegalese posing as Cereno's valet. The story is narrated by Captain Amasa Delano, an innocent who can only suspect the presence of evil. Finally, the conspirators are undone, Cereno dies, and Babo is executed.

Benivieni, Girolamo (1453–1542). Florentine poet, member of the Medici circle. Benivieni is the author of a famous Renaissance poem, the *Canzone dell'-Amor Divino* (*Song of Divine Love*), which summarizes the Platonic love theory of Ficino. The poem was the subject of an extensive commentary by Pico Della Mirandola, and influenced such writers as Bembo, Castiglione, and Spenser.

Benjamin. In the Old Testament, the youngest and favorite son of Jacob and Rachel, whose name means "son of the right hand." When, during the famine, Jacob sent his sons forth from Canaan to buy bread, he refused to let Benjamin go "lest peradventure mischief befall him" (Gen. 42:4). Jacob's son Joseph who was in charge of the granaries in Egypt told his brothers, without revealing his own identity, that they must bring Benjamin with them if they returned for more corn. When they did so, Joseph feasted them and gave them grain, but sent word after them that his silver cup was missing; when search was made it was found in Benjamin's sack, where it had been placed by Joseph's orders. Joseph then disclosed his identity and arranged for his father's migration to Egypt.

Benjamin's descendants formed the tribe of Benjamin; they were stalwart warriors and defenders of freedom. Israel's first king, Saul, came from this tribe as did the Apostle Paul.

Benn, Gottfried (1886–1956). German poet, short-story writer, and essayist. He was strongly influenced by Nietzsche. His early collections of expressionistic verse, *Morgue* (1912), *Fleisch* (*Flesh,* 1916), and *Schutt* (*Rubble,* 1919), are the best known.

Bennet, Elizabeth. See Pride and Prejudice.

Bennett, [Enoch] Arnold (1867–1931). English novelist, playwright, and journalist. His finest novels are THE OLD WIVES' TALE and CLAYHANGER. Both are set in the industrial district in the English midlands where he was born, known as Five Towns in his novels. A humble clerk with literary ambitions, Bennett went to London at 21 (his autobiographical *A Man from the North* [1898] describes this period). He became a successful journalist, editing a woman's magazine, writing "Pocket Philosophies" such as *How to Live, on 24 Hours a Day* (1908), and doing influential reviewing. In 1903 he went to live in Paris for some years and married a Frenchwoman. Influenced by the writings of Emile Zola, Bennett wrote naturalistic novels, studies of how his characters are the creatures of their environment. Among these are his two best novels, and ANNA OF THE FIVE TOWNS, *Whom God Hath Joined* (1906), *Hilda Lessways* (1911), *These Twain* (1915), *Riceyman Steps* (1923), *Lord Raingo* (1926), and *Imperial Palace* (1930). Among his collections of short stories are *Tales of the Five Towns* (1905) and *The Matador of the Five Towns* (1912). His successful comic novels are *A Great Man* (1904), BURIED ALIVE, THE CARD (*Denry the Audacious* in the U.S.), and *Mr. Prohack* (1922). He wrote, with Edward Knoblock, *Milestones* (1912), a successful drama about the rise of an industrial family. Bennett also wrote deliberate commercial fiction, such as *Sacred and Profane Love* (1905), for he wanted—and achieved—success, a famous-actress mistress, and a yacht.

Like the naturalistic novelists who were his contemporaries, his friend H. G. Wells and John Galsworthy, Bennett was attacked by the modernist Virginia Woolf, and is now somewhat neglected. His best work is distinguished by his rendering of the passage of time, his accurate descriptions of ordinary, apparently quite dull and unromantic lives, and his sympathetic portrayals of women.

Bennett, James Gordon (1795–1872). Scottish-born American newspaper editor. Bennett came to America in 1819 and settled finally in New York City, serving on the staff of *The Enquirer* and *The Courier*. On May 6, 1835, he founded the *New York Herald* and remained its editor until his retirement in 1867. It was an aggressive, widely read paper, notable for its extensive news coverage and lively editorials. According to Gerald W. Johnson, Bennett "filled his paper with vulgarity, vituperation, and scandal, but he got the news." His son, James Gordon Bennett (1841–1918), succeeded him as editor in 1867. The younger Bennett sent Stanley to Africa to find Livingstone and supported other expeditions to Africa and the Arctic. He was the founder of the Paris edition of the *Herald* (1887).

Benoît de Sainte-Maure or **Sainte-More** (12th century). Medieval French poet, attached to the court of Henry II of England from 1154 to 1189. He is said to be the author of the *Roman de Troie* (*Romance of Troy,* c. 1160), which gives the history of the Trojan War the atmosphere of medieval feudalism and the chivalric code; this seems to be the first appearance of the story of TROILUS and Cressida (here called Briseida). Benoît is also considered the author of the *Chronicle of the Dukes of Normandy* to 1135.

Benserade, Isaac de (1613–1691). French poet. A member of the Académie Française, Benserade specialized in writing masques and ballets, the popular court entertainments of his day. His sonnet on Job was so admired that a dispute arose whether this or Voiture's sonnet *Uranie* was better. Corneille had to call for an end to the quarrel, which had divided the literary world into *Jobelins* and *Uraniens.*

Benson, A[rthur] C[hristopher] (1862–1925). English scholar, best known as the author of volumes of essays, including *From a College Window* (1906). He wrote the words of the song *Land of Hope and Glory.* His father was archbishop of Canterbury; his brother, E[dward] F[rederic] Benson (1867–1940), wrote light novels, including *Dodo* (1893), which was supposed to be based on the character of the future Lady Oxford and created a sensation; a third brother, R[obert] H[ugh] Benson (1871–1914), became a Roman Catholic and wrote historical and contemporary novels with a strongly religious tone.

Benson, Sally (1900–   ). American short-story writer. She is the author of *Junior Miss* (1941), a best seller which was later made into a highly successful play, a movie, and a radio series. Among her other books are *People Are Fascinating* (1936), *Meet Me in St. Louis* (1942), and *Women and Children First* (1944).

Benson, Stella (1892–1933). English novelist and adventurous traveler. Her novels include *Tobit Transplanted* (1931), a retelling of the apocryphal story in a Korean setting.

Bentham, Jeremy (1748–1832). English philosopher of the utilitarian school. His social and philosophical ideas are to be found in his *Fragment on Government* (1776) and *Introduction to Principles of Morals and Legislation* (1789). His watchword was "the greatest good for the greatest number," and he tried to work out scientifically on a quantitative scale the values of pleasure and pain in moral motivation. See UTILITARIANISM.

Bentleman, Lawrence (1942–   ). Indian poet writing in English. He has worked for a commercial firm, a newspaper in Calcutta, and is currently a columnist for a New Delhi weekly. *Graffiti* (1962) is a collection of poems.

Bentley, E[dmund] C[lerihew] (1875–1956). English writer of detective stories and originator of a form of humorous biographical verse called CLERIHEWS. TRENT'S LAST CASE is a classic of detective fiction.

Bentley, Phyllis (1894–   ). English regional and historical novelist. Her Yorkshire novels include *The Inheritance* (1932) and *The House of Moreys* (1953). *O Dreams, O Destinations* (1962) is an autobiography.

Bentley, Richard (1662–1742). English classical scholar. His *Dissertation on the Letters of Phalaris* (1699) is one of the first studies to use philology as a test of authenticity. It sprang from a controversy (1695–1699) with Charles Boyle which Jonathan Swift continued in the BATTLE OF THE BOOKS. Swift, like other literary men of the day, saw nothing but modern pedantry in Bentley's painstaking scholarship. Bentley's Homeric studies are fragmentary, but historically important for showing that early Greek had a sound, later lost, which was represented by the letter *Digamma* and pronounced like the English *w*.

Benton, Thomas Hart (1782–1858). American statesman. From 1821 to 1851, Benton represented Missouri in the U.S. Senate, where he strongly favored Western interests. A vigorous supporter of Andrew Jackson, he fought the U.S. Bank, and was finally defeated for re-election because he championed the Union against the South. He wrote a well-known autobiography, *Thirty Years View* (2 vols., 1854, 1856). His daughter Jessie married John C. Frémont.

Benton, Thomas Hart (1889–   ). American painter and muralist. Born in Missouri, he became a leading advocate of regionalism, depicting in his work a contemporary view of life in the Middle West. He inveighed against all the European movements and is the author of *An Artist in America* (1937), which he also illustrated.

Benu. The Egyptian prototype of the Greek phoenix. It was a heronlike bird, the embodiment of Ra, worshiped under the composite form of Osiris with the head of a bird.

Benvolio. In Shakespeare's ROMEO AND JULIET, a nephew of Montague and Romeo's friend. Hoping that Romeo will be cured of his infatuation for the fair Rosaline, Benvolio persuades him to attend the Capulets' ball, so that he can compare her with the other beauties present. On several occasions he tries unsuccessfully to avert strife between the feuding Montagues and Capulets.

Beolco, Angelo (1502–1542). Italian dramatist. He is also known as *Ruzzante* (the Howler), after the chief peasant character in his dramas. They were performed by one of the first acting companies organized in Italy. The best of his seven comedies are the *Moschetta* (*Little Mosquito,* 1520) and the *Fiorina* (*Florin,* 1521).

Beowulf (early 8th century?). An Old English (Anglo-Saxon) epic of almost 3200 lines in ALLITERATIVE VERSE. It is the earliest extant written composition of such length in English, and indeed in all Teutonic literature. Its content was based on Norse legends merged with historical events of the early sixth century in Denmark; this oral tradition was carried to England by Danish invaders of the mid-sixth century, fused with the Christianity they absorbed there, and finally written down by a single but unknown poet shortly before or after 700.

Hrothgar, king of the Danes on the island of Zealand, has built the mead hall Heorot for feasting his warriors, but they abandon it because of the murderous ravages of the monster GRENDEL. Beowulf, nephew of King Hygelac of the Geats (on the coast of southern Sweden facing the Danes), comes with 14 warriors to challenge the monster, and is received by Hrothgar at a great feast. The Geats spend the night in the mead hall; Grendel comes, and in a mighty fight Beowulf with his bare hands wrenches the monster's arm from his shoulder, and mounts it as a trophy. The next day Hrothgar gives a triumphant feast in Heorot; but as they sleep that night, Grendel's mother comes to avenge her son, slaying a Dane and stealing the severed arm. Beowulf plunges into the demon-infested pond where the monsters live and wrestles with Grendel's mother. His own sword Hrunting proves of no use, but he

A page from a manuscript of *Beowulf.*

finds a sword crafted by the giants and beheads her. Then he severs the head of Grendel, who has died there of his wound, to bring back as a trophy. He and his Geats receive many gifts from Hrothgar when they leave, and from Hygelac when they reach home. Hygelac and his son both die in wars with the Swedes, so that Beowulf eventually becomes king of the Geats, ruling well for 50 years. Then a fire-breathing dragon, angered because a man has stolen a goblet from his hoarded treasure, begins to ravage the land. Beowulf goes out to slay it, but all his warriors fearfully desert him, except young Wiglaf. Although together they kill the dragon, Beowulf receives his own death-wound. Wiglaf berates his companions for cowardice, and Beowulf is given a stately burial.

The story is not told chronologically, however; events are often anticipated in prophecy or interpolated later in retrospect. Long speeches of celebration or lamentation, long descriptions of the feasts, and digressions into genealogy and history all give a colorful picture of life at that time. Memorable episodes not actually a part of the main action include Unferth's insult to Beowulf at the first feast and Beowulf's answering description of his swimming contest with Breca, and the tale of Finn and Hildeburh, sung by a minstrel at the second feast (see FINNSBURG).

Beppo (1818). A satirical poem by Lord BYRON. Beppo is the husband of Laura, a Venetian lady. He is taken captive at Troy, becomes a Turk, joins a band of pirates, grows rich, and, after several years' absence, returns to his native land, where he discovers his wife at a carnival ball with her *cavaliero servente*. He makes himself known to her, and they live together again as man and wife.

Béranger, Pierre Jean de (1780–1857). French folk poet. His songs, variously sentimental or witty, ribald or light-heartedly gay, assured him of fame during his lifetime. In such songs as *Le Roi d'Yvetot* (1813) he gave expression to popular feeling after the Napoleonic Wars when the French people, weary of the quest for glory, longed instead for comfort and for peace. His song *Le Marquis de Carabas* (1816) satirized the vain pretensions of nobles during the Bourbon restoration. Although *Chansons inédites* (1828), his collection of political verse celebrating Napoleon Bonaparte, won him a prison term, it earned him staunch popular approval.

Berceo, Gonzalo de (c. 1180–c. 1246). Earliest Spanish poet known by name. A secular priest at the Benedictine monastery of San Millán de la Cogolla, Berceo was a prolific writer of pious religious verse in the vernacular. His best-known poems are works dedicated to the Virgin, notably *Milagros de Nuestra Señora,* and lives of saints, such as *Vida de Domingo de Silos*. See MESTER DE CLERECÍA.

Berchtesgaden. A district in Bavaria, site of Hitler's country house. It was razed by Allied bombings in 1945.

Bercilak. See SIR GAWAIN AND THE GREEN KNIGHT.

Berdyayev, Nikolai Aleksandrovich (1874–1948). Russian religious philosopher. A Marxist in his youth, Berdyayev turned to religious views and played a large part in the renaissance of religious and philosophical thought in Russian intellectual life early in the 20th century. His writings, mainly aphoristic in form, often deal with the problem of freedom and man's relationship to the world in the light of this problem. His works include *The Spiritual Crisis of the Intelligentsia* (*Dukhovnyi krisis intelligentziya;* 1910), *The Philosophy of Freedom* (*Filosofiya svobody;* 1911), *The Meaning of Creativity* (*Smysl tvorchestva;* 1916), and studies of Dostoevski and of Russian religious and philosophical thinkers.

In 1922, with a number of other Russian intellectuals, Berdyayev was expelled from the Soviet Union. He went to Berlin and then to Paris in 1925 where he continued to write, edited a journal (*The Way;* Russian *Put'*), and worked for the Y.M.C.A. Press, a publisher of religious and philosophical works.

Bérénice (1670). A tragedy by Jean RACINE. The emperor Titus, newly acceded to the throne, learns that the Romans object to his marrying the foreigner Bérénice, queen of Palestine. Despite his love for her, he obeys the mandate of his people, and the lovers separate forever. Literary tradition holds that the duchesse d'Orléans arranged for Racine and Corneille to write plays on this subject, each in ignorance that the other was doing the same. In the resulting contest, Racine's play was judged the better. See TITE ET BÉRÉNICE.

Berenice (1835). A tale by Edgar Allan POE. Egaeus is in love with his epileptic cousin, Berenice.

Fascinated by her teeth, he draws them when she is presumed dead, after a fit. Berenice returns to life in a comic-horror climax.

Berenson, Bernard (1865–1959). Lithuanian-born American art connoisseur. A longtime resident of Italy, he was recognized by his generation as the greatest authority on Italian art from the 13th to the 17th century. Collectors and specialists alike have relied on his judgment. His *Italian Painters of the Renaissance* and other books and monographs remain classics in their field. *I Tatti,* his villa near Florence, with its magnificent library and superb art collection, has become, since his death, a European outpost of Harvard University. Excerpts from the diaries he kept from 1947 to 1956 were published as *The Passionate Sightseer* (1960).

Beresford, John Davys (1873–1949). English novelist. He was the author of *Jacob Stahl* (1911), a once popular story about a young man growing up.

Berezina. A river in western Russia. It flows into the Dnieper, and was the scene of battles in both 1812 when Napoleon's army retreated westward and in 1941 when the German army invaded the Soviet Union.

Bergamín, José (1894–). Spanish critic and dramatist. Bergamín directed (1933–1936) the critical review *Cruz y Raya* whose literary influence favored Spanish neo-Catholicism. He is also known for his dramas, which include *La hija de Dios* (1945), *Una mujer con tres almas* (1950), and for his collection of essays, *El cohete y la estrella* (1922).

Bergengruen, Werner (1892–). German novelist, known for his interest in historical subjects and for the humor of his style. Among his novels are *Der Grosstyrann und das Gericht* (*The Tyrant and the Court,* 1935), *Am Himmel wie auf Erden* (*In Heaven as on Earth,* 1940), and *Das Feuerzeichen* (*The Fiery Sign,* 1949).

Bergeret, M. The central figure in the four satiric novels that comprise Anatole FRANCE's *Histoire Contemporaine*. In the first volumes M. Bergeret holds an official position in a French provincial university. In the last two books, he is divorced from his wife and lives in Paris. These last books in the series deal extensively with the Dreyfus case, Bergeret serving as a vehicle for many of France's own feelings and convictions on the subject.

Bergman, Hjalmar Frederik (1883–1931). Swedish dramatist, novelist, and short-story writer. The son of a wealthy banker, Bergman did not develop his own unique literary qualities until his father's financial failure forced him to write for a living. Lively humor and ironic tenderness characterize Bergman's work; in both his novels and his plays the people are amusingly grotesque clowns. Among his novels and stories are *Hans nåds testamente* (1910), *Markurells i Wadköping* (*God's Orchid,* 1919) and *Chefen fru Ingeborg* (*The Head of the Firm,* 1924). His plays include *Marionettspel* (1917), *Swedenhielms* (1925), and *Patrasek* (1928).

Bergman, Ingmar (1918–). Swedish motion-picture director, writer, and producer. The son of a clergyman, Bergman has throughout his career been associated with A. B. Svensk Filmindustri; he first came to public attention with the script he wrote for *Torment* (1944). His own productions, made with a small company of devoted actors, are often concerned with questions of faith and belief; they include *Smiles of a Summer Night* (1955), *The Seventh Seal* (1956), *Wild Strawberries* (1957), *The Magician* (1958), *The Virgin Spring* (1959), *Through a Glass Darkly* (1960), *Winter Light* (1962), and *The Silence* (1963).

Bergotte. A famous author in Marcel Proust's REMEMBRANCE OF THINGS PAST. His work greatly influences the narrator, who admires the delicate, exquisite style of his writing.

Bergson, Henri (1859–1941). French philosopher. During his lifetime Bergson enjoyed wide popularity as a professor at the *Collège de France;* his lectures were always crowded and his books were eagerly read. His influence upon modern literature and thought has been of profound significance. Bergson's philosophy is complex, but the basic premise of his intellectual system is a faith in direct intuition as a means of attaining knowledge. To the experimental and rationalistic methods of science he opposed an antirational and mystical approach to understanding. Change or movement, Bergson believed, was the basis of all reality. Time should not be measured scientifically or mechanically, since for the human being time operates as a continuous flow in which past and present are inseparable to the consciousness and the memory. This theory of time in relation to the human self figures prominently in the long work of Marcel Proust, REMEMBRANCE OF THINGS PAST.

Bergson's interest in biological evolution led to the formulation of his theory of *élan vital,* a spirit of energy and life that moves all living things, and to the publication of his famous work *L'Evolution créatrice* (1907). His chief philosophical works are *Essai sur les données immédiates de la conscience* (1888; translated as *Time and Free Will*), *Matière et mémoire* (1896), *L'Energie spirituelle* (1919; translated as *Mind-Energy*), *Durée et simultanéité* (1922), *Les Deux Sources de la morale et de la religion* (1932), and *La Pensée et le mouvant* (1934). Of Jewish parentage, Bergson renounced the honors and posts awarded him by the French government in 1940, as a protest against hostile legislation passed by the Vichy government against the Jews.

Berkeley, George (1685–1753). Irish-born English bishop and philosopher. He was one of the earliest and most influential thinkers of the philosophic school of idealism. The exponent of a theory of philosophical immaterialism based on the proposition that to be is to be perceived, he maintained that material objects are ideas in our minds, with no independent existence, and that, therefore, the whole of reality consists of ideas in the mind of God. His chief works are ESSAY TOWARDS A NEW THEORY OF VISION; *Treatise concerning the Principles of Human Knowledge* (1710); *Three Dialogues between Hylas and Philonus* (1713); ALCIPHRON, OR THE MINUTE PHILOSOPHER, a collection of popular pseudo-Platonic dialogues; *Theory of Vision* (1733); and SIRIS: A CHAIN OF PHILOSOPHICAL REFLECTIONS AND INQUIRIES CONCERNING THE VIRTUES OF TAR-WATER. He was active in attacking the opinions of freethinkers, and was associated with a number of prominent 18th-century literary figures including Addison, Pope, and Swift. From 1728 to 1732, he lived in America, in the colony of Rhode Island, where he wrote *Alciphron* and founded the Literary and Philosophical Society and a college for the education of colonists and Indians.

Berkeley, Sir William. See BACON'S REBELLION.

Berlichingen, Götz von. See GÖTZ VON BERLICHINGEN.

Berlin, Irving. Real name, **Israel Baline** (1888–). Russian-born American composer. He is known for his popular songs and lyrics, especially of a sentimental or patriotic nature, such as *Blue Skies* (1927), *God Bless America* (1939), and *White Christmas* (1942). He also wrote the scores for many musical comedies, including *As Thousands Cheer* (1933), *Annie Get Your Gun* (1946), and *Call Me Madam* (1954).

Berlioz, [Louis] Hector (1803–1869). French composer and conductor. His *Treatise on Modern Instrumentation and Orchestration* (1844) established a new concept of the symphony orchestra, and is still a basic text. His literary works give excellent descriptions of his musical environment, and have been collected in 10 volumes. His musical works are conceived almost entirely as musical embodiments of literary ideas. The *Symphonie Fantastique* (1830), subtitled *episode in the life of an artist,* is the first piece of sustained narrative music, the forerunner of the tone poems of Franz Liszt and Richard Strauss. Berlioz also invented the *idée fixe,* a basic theme that occurs in various forms in all movements of a work. *Harold en Italie* (1834) and *Roméo et Juliette* (1839) are two other programmatic symphonies. Other important works are the *Grande Messe des Morts (Requiem Mass)*, the oratorio *L'Enfance du Christ (The Childhood of Christ)*, and the gigantic opera *Les Troyens (The Trojans,* 1865–1869), which is based on the tragic love of Dido and Aeneas.

Berma. A great actress in Marcel Proust's RE-MEMBRANCE OF THINGS PAST. Partially modeled on Sarah Bernhardt, she is particularly famous for her roles in Racine's plays.

Bermoothes. An old name for Bermuda and the name of the island in Shakespeare's THE TEMPEST. The adventures of Sir George Somers, who was shipwrecked there with a group of colonists in 1609, may have furnished some of Shakespeare's material for the play.

Bernabò of Genoa. A tale from Boccaccio's DECAMERON (II, 9). Bernabò makes a wager with a fellow merchant, Ambrogiuolo, that his wife Ginevra will not succumb to any man in his absence. Ambrogiuolo, stealing into Ginevra's room while she is asleep, removes some of her garments and observes that she has a mole under her breast. He then confronts Bernabò with the items he stole and his knowledge of the mole as proof of his having slept with Ginevra. Convinced he has truly lost his wager, and deeply grieved by his wife's supposed infidelity, he orders her death. But Ginevra persuades her executioner to show Bernabò her blood-stained garments and let her flee into exile. Disguising herself as a youth, Sicurano da Finale, Ginevra goes to sea with a Catalan merchant and reaches Alexandria, where the sultan takes her into his service. One day, she encounters Ambrogiuolo, who has come to sell his goods, including the garments taken from her room in Genoa that fateful night. Recognizing them, she asks to buy them and persuades him to tell how he got them. Knowing the truth at last, she sends for Bernabò and calls upon the sultan to judge Ambrogiuolo. She then startles all three of them by revealing herself as Ginevra. The sultan condemns Ambrogiuolo to death and sends Ginevra and Bernabò home, reconciled and joyous, to Genoa. The plot is that of Shakespeare's *Cymbeline*.

Bernadette of Lourdes, St. Real name, **Bernadette Soubirous** (1844–1879). French peasant girl canonized as a saint on Dec. 8, 1933. Bernadette was tending her sheep in February, 1858, when the Virgin Mary appeared to her several times in a vision and revealed the miraculous healing properties of the waters springing from the grotto in which she was standing. Lourdes, a town of the Gave de Pan in the department of Hautes-Pyrénées, is the site of the famous grotto which has become one of the principal Roman Catholic shrines and where many miraculous cures have been reported. Emile Zola drew inspiration from this story for his novel *Lourdes* (1894). THE SONG OF BERNADETTE is a similarly inspired historical novel by Franz Werfel.

Bernanos, Georges (1888–1948). French novelist and political writer. His novels reflect his fervent Catholicism and his intense concern with moral and spiritual problems. *Sous le Soleil de Satan* (*Under the Sun of Satan*, also translated as *The Star of Satan*, 1926), and DIARY OF A COUNTRY PRIEST both stress the heroism of sanctity in the struggles of rural clerics. His other novels include MONSIEUR OUINE and *Un mauvais rêve* (1951). In his political essays, Bernanos opposed parliamentary democracy because it did not provide enough protection from the greedy and the power mad, and urged a return to monarchy to institute a new moral order. *Les Grands Cimetières sous la lune* (*A Diary of My Times*, 1938) was inspired by his fury against Franco in the Spanish Civil War. His anti-Vichy writings of World War II are collected in *Lettre aux Anglais* (*Plea for Liberty*, 1942), *La France contre les robots* (1947), and *Le Chemin de la Croix des Ames* (1948). *Dialogues des Carmélites* (1949), a play, is the basis of Poulenc's opera of the same name.

Bernard. A leading character in Virginia Woolf's novel THE WAVES. He speaks the memorable final soliloquy.

Bernard, Jean Jacques (1888–   ). French dramatist, son of Tristan Bernard. A major exponent of the school of silence, he maintained that the theater is the art of "expressing what is unspoken," using delicate dialogue about trivia to capitalize on what is not said. Among his plays are *The Sulky Fire* (*Le Feu qui reprend mal;* 1921), *Martine* (1922), and *The Unquiet Spirit* (*L'Ame en Peine;* 1926).

Bernard, Tristan. Pen name of **Paul Bernard** (1866–1947). French dramatist and novelist. Bernard is best known for his popular traditional comedies, such as the two he wrote with A. Godferneaux: *Triplepatte* (1905), adapted by Clyde Fitch as *Toddles* (1908), and *Monsieur Codomat* (1907). His own comedies include *Le Petit Café* (1911), *Jules, Juliette, et Julien* (1929), and *Le Sauvage* (1931).

Bernard de Ventadour. See TROUBADOURS.

Bernardin de Saint-Pierre, Jacques Henri (1737–1814). French author and one-time civil engineer. He travelled extensively from 1761 to 1766 in western Europe, with the intention of promoting

a scheme to regenerate society. A malcontent like ROUSSEAU, he returned to Paris in 1770, where he became the former's disciple and intimate friend, sharing his love of nature and horror of civilization. In 1784 he published his *Etudes de la Nature,* a remarkable series of exotic descriptions of nature. Their object is to show the perfection of Nature, the work of a good God solicitous of man's welfare. The precision, charm, and mastery of the language, new to French literature, are marred at times by the infantilism of the author's reasoning and by his sentimentality; his "philosophy" is at times a caricature of Rousseau's. The fourth part of these *Etudes* comprises his most famous work, the short novel PAUL ET VIRGINIE. Stylistically, Bernardin de Saint-Pierre is a precursor of Chateaubriand in his vivid use of pictorial description.

Bernardino da Siena (1380–1444). Italian Franciscan friar. Famous for his sermons, he was a frequent subject for the artists of the time.

Bernardo. See MARCELLUS.

Bernard of Clairvaux, St. (1090–1153). French ecclesiastic. In 1113 he entered the Cistercian abbey of Citeaux; two years later he became the founder and abbot of a new Cistercian monastery at Clairvaux, a post he held until his death. His fame as a preacher soon spread, bringing crowds of pilgrims to Clairvaux, but Bernard refused all offers of ecclesiastical preferment. Nevertheless, his importance and prestige grew rapidly: through his work, the Cistercians became the greatest order in western Christendom, and he himself the greatest influence, at first in France and later throughout western Europe. He was instrumental in the success of Pope Innocent II's cause over the claims of the antipope, Cardinal Peter of Leon. In 1141 he secured an official condemnation of Pierre Abelard's works at the Council of Sens. In 1146 he summoned the people to join in a crusade, in the name of Pope Eugenius II, and Louis VII of France with many others was moved to organize the Second Crusade. He was canonized in 1173.

Bernard of Cluny or **Morlaix** (c. 1100–c. 1156). French Benedictine monk. He wrote a Latin poem *De Contemptu mundi,* famous through the English translation of John Mason Neale.

Berners, Lord. See John BOURCHIER.

Bernesque satire or **poetry.** See Francesco BERNI.

Berni, Francesco (c. 1498–1536). Florentine author of popular satires on contemporary social and literary conventions. His favorite forms were the extended or tailed sonnet, and the long poem in *terza rima* called *capitolo*. One of the latter, his *Capitolo al Fracastoro,* is widely admired for its vividly humorous description of a night's lodging in a vicarage, cast in the form of a letter to his friend Fracastoro. Bernesque satire, or the Bernesque style, refers to his treatment in a seriocomic way of such trivial subjects as eels, melons, peaches, or jelly. He is also noted for his rewriting of Boiardo's *Orlando Innamorato* in a pure Tuscan style.

Bernini, [Giovanni] Lorenzo (1598–1680). Italian sculptor and architect. The dominant influence on European sculpture for over a century, he was a typically baroque artist and did not shy away from whirling movement and illusionistic representation in stone. He is known for his consummate portrait busts and his fountains, particularly the fountain of Trevi, and, in Rome, the fountain of the Four Rivers. His religious works include the skillfully carved Saint Theresa group in Rome's Santa Maria della Vittoria, theatrically lit by a hidden overhead window, and the exuberant setting for the chair of Saint Peter. His best-known architectural achievement is the double colonnade of the Piazza of Saint Peter (1656–1668).

Bernstein, Eduard (1850–1932). German socialist. His *Die Voraussetzungen des Sozialismus und die Aufgaben der Sozialdemokratie* (*The Premises of Socialism and the Tasks of Social Democracy, 1899*) modified Marxist theory. He denied the necessity for a proletarian revolution, and urged the workers to improve their position through democratic activity.

Bernstein, Leonard (1918–   ). American conductor and composer. He is widely known for his television lectures on music, some of which were published as *The Joy of Music* (1959). He has written classical pieces, such as the Symphony No. 2 (1949), subtitled *The Age of Anxiety,* after W. H. Auden's poem, and musical comedies, such as *Candide* (1956) and *West Side Story* (1957). He succeeded Dimitri Mitropoulos as musical director of the N.Y. Philharmonic Orchestra in 1958.

Béroul (12th century). Medieval French poet. He wrote one of the early versions of the TRISTAN legend.

Berowne. See BIRON.

Berryman, John (1914–1972). American poet and short-story writer. Berryman's *Poems* appeared in 1942, and was followed by *The Dispossessed* in 1948. *Homage to Mistress Bradstreet* (1956) is a long poem dealing with the 17th-century American poet Anne Bradstreet. Berryman has also written short stories and a biography of Stephen Crane (1950).

berserker. In Scandinavian mythology, a wild, ferocious, warlike being who was sometimes possessed of supernatural strength and fury. One account says the name originated from the grandson of the eight-handed Starkader, called *boer-serce* (bare of mail) because he went into battle unharnessed. Another holds that the name means simply men who have assumed the form of bears. The word is used in English both as an adjective denoting excessive fury, and a noun denoting one possessed of such.

Berthe aux grands pieds (*Fr.,* "Bertha with the large feet"). The title of a popular *chanson de geste* by the 13th-century minstrel Adenet le Roi. Historically, Berthe was the wife of Pepin the Short. She was influential at court in guiding the policies of her son Charlemagne (see CAROLINGIANS) until her death in 783.

Bertram. In Shakespeare's ALL'S WELL THAT ENDS WELL, the arrogant young count of Rousillon, who initially spurns the lovely Helena because she is a commoner.

Bertram, Edmund. See MANSFIELD PARK.

Bertram, Harry. See GUY MANNERING.

Bertran[d] de Born (c. 1140–c. 1215). Provençal warrior and TROUBADOUR. He is denounced in Dante's *Inferno* for having stirred up hostility between Henry II of England and his sons.

Berzelius, Baron **Jöns Jakob** (1779–1848). Swedish chemist. Founder of the present system of writing chemical symbols, Berzelius discovered selenium and thorium, and experimented in the field of electrolysis. A passage in his writings dealing with elective affinities in chemistry became the nucleus of Goethe's famous novel, *Die Wahlverwandtschaften. Larebok i Kemien* (1808–1828) is a handbook on chemistry.

Bes. The Egyptian god of pleasure.

Besant, Annie, born **Wood** (1847–1933). English author, theosophist, and political radical. A clergyman's wife, Mrs. Besant separated from her husband and became associated with Charles BRADLAUGH in the free thought movement. An advocate of socialism and social reform, she was a member of the FABIAN SOCIETY, an organizer of labor unions, a worker among impoverished and delinquent children. Later, after meeting Mme. Blavatsky, she became a leading theosophist in England. Interest in occult theology took her to India (1889) where she founded the Central Hindu College at Benares. Both in India and later back in England, she agitated for home rule in India. Among her best-known religious works are *Karma* (1895), *Four Great Religions* (1897), and *Wisdom of the Upanishads* (1906). Her other works include *Autobiography* (1893), *How India Wrought for Freedom* (1915), and *India, Bond or Free* (1926). See THEOSOPHY.

Besant, Sir **Walter** (1836–1901). English novelist, historian, and critic. A prolific writer, Besant is best known for his novels dealing with social evils in East London, such as *All Sorts and Conditions of Men* (1882) and *Children of Gibeon* (1886). His interest in social reform led to his participation in the founding of The People's Palace in London (1887), an institution for the recreation and education of workingmen that ultimately developed into part of London University. He was also actively engaged in the improvement of copyright laws, and the betterment of the financial position of authors. His other works include historical novels and books on French literature and on the history of London, fields in which he was a noted authority. His *Autobiography* appeared in 1902.

Besier, Rudolf. See BARRETTS OF WIMPOLE STREET, THE.

Bess, Good Queen. ELIZABETH I of England.

Bessarion (1403–1472). Greek churchman and scholar. He came to Italy for the unity council of 1438–1439 and stayed to become a Roman Catholic cardinal. His scholarly activities influenced the revival of classical learning and Italian Renaissance Humanism generally. His collection of books became the nucleus of the Venetian Library of St. Mark's.

Bessie Bell and Mary Gray. A ballad by Allan RAMSAY. Two young ladies of Perth, to avoid the plague of 1666, retire to a rural retreat called the Burnbraes, the residence of Mary Gray near Lynedock. A young man in love with both carries provisions to them. They all die of the plague and are buried at Dornock Hough.

bestiaries. Allegorical poems or books giving descriptions of various animals, or stories concerning them, with a Christian application or moral appended to each. Although the characteristics and habits assigned to each animal were largely legendary, the bestiaries were often treated during the

Cocodrillus (crocodile). From a 13th-century bestiary.

Middle Ages as treatises on natural history as well as moral instruction, and were highly popular.

The beast-fable, popular from Aesop to the medieval *Reynard the Fox,* was usually satirical and pragmatic in its moral; a fourth-century work in Greek was probably the first to turn animal descriptions into specifically Christian allegory, and its translations into Latin *Physiologi* were the basis of most English and Continental bestiaries. The best known are the Latin *Physiologus* (11th century) by the abbot Theobaldus, the *Bestiary* by the Anglo-Norman poet Phillippe de Thaün, and an anonymous Middle English *Bestiary* (c. 1250).

Besuch der alten Dame, Der. See VISIT OF THE OLD LADY, THE.

Bethany. A town of Palestine on the Mount of Olives. It was the home of Lazarus, brother of Mary and Martha, who was raised from the dead by Christ.

Bethgelert or **The Grave of the Greyhound** (1811). A ballad by William Robert Spencer (1769–1834) retelling a story common in Oriental and then in medieval European literature. In this version Gelert is a hound given by King John to Llewelyn the Great, who returns from the hunt one day to find his dog covered with blood and his infant son missing from an overturned cradle. Believing that Gelert has eaten the child, Llewelyn stabs him; but the hound's dying scream awakens the infant, who cries out from where he is hidden under a pile of coverings, and under the bed is found a huge wolf killed by Gelert.

Bethlehem. The ancient town in Judea, Palestine, where Jesus was born. Also the scene of Ra-chel's death, the home of Ruth and Naomi, and the city of David, it is mentioned frequently in both the Old and the New Testament.

Bethmann-Hollweg, Theobald von (1856–1921). Chancellor of the German Empire (1909–1917). He defended the German violation of Belgian neutrality (1914) at the beginning of WW II.

Betjeman, John (1906–   ). English poet and architectural authority. In satirical light verse, his poems celebrate the English countryside and ordinary provincial and suburban life. They nostalgically evoke the Victorian era and a past or passing English culture. Among collections of his poems are *Continual Dew* (1937), *New Bats in Old Belfries* (1945), *A Few Late Chrysanthemums* (1955), and *Summoned By Bells* (1960), a verse autobiography. He was named poet laureate in 1972.

Betterton, Thomas (1635?–1710). English actor. The son of an under-cook in the service of Charles I, he joined Davenant's company at Lincoln's Inn Fields Theatre in 1661 and became its manager upon Davenant's death. The greatest actor on the Restoration stage, he excelled in Shakespearean roles, being equally adept in tragedy and comedy. His wife, Mary Saunderson, was a leading actress of the times.

Bettina. The name taken by Elisabeth Brentano, Countess von ARNIM (1785–1859), in her publication *Goethe's Correspondence With a Child* (1835) which purported to be her correspondence with Goethe.

Between the Acts (1941). A novel by Virginia WOOLF. It describes a pageant on English history, written and directed by Miss La Trobe, and its effects on the people who watch it. Most of the audience misunderstand it in various ways; a clergyman reduces its vision to a sermon. But, for a moment, Virginia Woolf implies, the pageant, or art, has imposed order on the chaos of human life.

Beulah, land of. In Bunyan's PILGRIM'S PROGRESS, that land of heavenly joy where the pilgrims tarry until they are summoned to enter the Celestial City; the paradise before the resurrection. The name occurs in the Bible (Isa. 62:4).

Beveridge, Albert [Jeremiah] (1862–1927). American historian and statesman. Elected to the U.S. Senate in 1899, Beveridge was defeated in 1911 when Old Guard Republicans refused to support him. He joined Theodore Roosevelt's Progressive Party and later turned to writing biographies. His *Life of John Marshall* (2 vols., 1916, 1919) won a Pulitzer Prize. At his death he was working on a biography of Lincoln, two volumes of which were published in 1928.

Beverley, Ensign. See CAPTAIN JACK ABSOLUTE.

Beverly, Robert (c. 1673–1722). American historian of the Virginia colony. His chief work is *The History and Present State of Virginia,* issued in London in 1705. It is one of the earliest self-consciously American works. "I am an Indian," Beverly wrote, "and don't pretend to be exact in my language."

Bevis of Hamton or **Southhampton, Sir.** A medieval chivalric romance. It has a slight connection with the Charlemagne cycle. In the English version, found in Michael Drayton's *Polyoblion,* (1622), the mother of Bevis slays his father and sells Bevis as a slave to Eastern merchants when he tries to avenge the murder. After many adventures, Bevis converts Josian, the daughter of the Soldan, to

Christianity and carries her off to England, where he finally revenges the death of his father. See ASCAPART.

Beyle, Marie Henri. See STENDHAL.

Beyond Good and Evil (Jenseits von Gut und Böse; 1886). A philosophical work by Friedrich NIETZSCHE in the form of a collection of aphorisms. In it, Nietzsche expresses his desire for a "transvaluation of all values." He contends that no human values are absolute; that all value distinctions (such as that between "good" and "evil") are artificial, the result of mere traditional prejudices; and that man should discard his old, outmoded values (such as "good" and "evil") in favor of ones more suited to contemporary cultural reality.

Beyond the Horizon (1920). A play by Eugene O'NEILL. The Mayo brothers love the same girl; Robert, who had wanted to seek adventure "beyond the horizon," stays home to marry the girl, and the prosaic Andrew goes to sea and later to the Argentine. In the end Robert dies embittered but happy "with the right of release—beyond the horizon." The play was awarded a Pulitzer Prize.

Bezukhov, Pierre. A central character in Count Leo Tolstoi's novel WAR AND PEACE. Like Prince Andrei Bolkonski, Pierre has a poor first marriage, but later falls in love with Natasha Rostova. After an attempt to assassinate Napoleon, Pierre is captured by the French and must take part in their disastrous retreat from Moscow. Released during a Cossack raid, Pierre learns of the death of his wife and of his great friend, Prince Andrei. Nearly overwhelmed by life, Pierre at last learns of the sheer joy of being alive. His eventual marriage to Natasha is a happy one for them both. Pierre represents to Tolstoi the triumph of a humanistic way of life.

Bhagavadgita (*Sans.*, the song of God). An 18-part discussion between Krishna and Arjuna on the nature and meaning of life. It forms part of the MAHABHARATA. The dialogue takes place on the battlefield of Kurukshetra, the scene of the epic battle between the Kauravas and the Pandavas described in the *Mahabharata*. Arjuna, dejected and confused, refuses to fight his kinsmen, and Krishna counsels him on the "selfless act" performed within the context of duty, on the three ways to *moksha* or liberation (work, knowledge, and devotion) and on the three *gunas*, or qualities that constitute nature, human or otherwise. The *Gita* has profoundly influenced philosophers and creative writers in the West. It is paraphrased in Edwin Arnold's *Song Celestial* (1885). A readable contemporary version, *The Song of God* (1954), is by Christopher Isherwood and Swami Prabhavananda.

Bhagirath. In Hindu legend, the bringer of the Ganges River from heaven to earth after a 1,000-year penance. He wanted to cleanse the honor of his ancestors, who were cursed by the sage Kapila and burnt into cinders. The Ganges is sometimes known as the Bhagirathi.

Bharata. (1) In Hindu legend, the son of Dasharatha by Kaikeyi (in the epic, the RAMAYANA).
(2) The author of the NATYA-SHASTRA, a first-century treatise on drama.
(3) The name of the son of Dushyanta and Shakuntala in Kalidasa's play *Shakuntala*.
(4) The eldest son of the ancient sage Rishab-

hadeva. India, therefore, is sometimes called Bharatavarsha, or land of Bharata.

Bhasa (3rd century?). Sanskrit dramatist. His works show great skill in narration, exquisite poetry, and excellent stagecraft. *Svapna-Vasavadatta* (*The Dream of Vasavadatta*) is the most popular of the 13 Bhasa plays unearthed in 1912 in Trivandrum, South India, by Pandit Ganapati Sastri.

Bhattacharya, Bhabani (1906–). Indian novelist writing in English. Educated in India and at the University of London, he was for a time press attaché at the Indian embassy in Washington. He has published *So Many Hungers* (1948), *Music for Mohini* (1952), *He Who Rides a Tiger* (1954), and *A Goddess Named Gold* (1961).

Bhavabhuti (8th century). Sanskrit playwright. He is praised for subtle handling of poignant scenes. Two of his plays, *Mahavira Charita* (*Portrait of a Hero*) and *Uttara-rama-charita* (*The Later Story of Rama*), retell the *Ramayana* story in a highly dramatic and sometimes sentimentalized form; a third, *Malati and Madhava*, deals with a legendary tale.

Biadice. See GOLDEN FLEECE.

Bianca. (1) In Shakespeare's TAMING OF THE SHREW, the younger daughter of Baptista of Padua. She is as gentle and meek as her sister Katharina is violent and irritable.
(2) In Shakespeare's OTHELLO, the mistress of Cassio. She unwittingly aids Iago in his plot against Othello.

Bianchi and Neri (Whites and Blacks). Rival factions within the Guelph party in Tuscany about 1300 (see GUELPHS AND GHIBELLINES). The Bianchi wanted to maintain Florence as a democratic constitutionally independent of both emperor and pope; the Neri were willing to compromise with the pope to gain power against the emperor. See DANTE.

Bianchon, Horace. A tolerant and charitable Parisian physician who appears in many of the novels of Balzac's COMÉDIE HUMAINE. Bianchon is a member of Balzac's fictional CÉNACLE.

Biberius, Caldius Mero. The punning nickname of Tiberius Claudius Nero, the Roman emperor Tiberius who reigned from A.D. 14 to 37. Biberius means drink-loving; Caldius Mero, by metathesis is *calidus mero*, which means hot with wine.

Biberpelz, Der. See BEAVER COAT, THE.

Bible. The Christian sacred book. Actually a collection of books, the Holy Bible, as it is often called, is divided into two parts: the OLD TESTAMENT and the NEW TESTAMENT. The former contains 39 books according to the Protestants, with a supplement of 14 books known as the APOCRYPHA; other churches include either part or all of the Apocrypha in the Old Testament. The New Testament contains 27 books.

The word *bible* is from the Greek word *biblos*, which means book, and is derived from *byblos*, "papyrus."

The Old Testament was compiled from the 13th to the first century B.C. No original manuscripts have survived and present versions are based on two primary sources: the SEPTUAGINT, a Greek translation made from the Hebrew in Alexandria about 250 B.C., and the Massoretic Text, the work of a group of trained Jewish scholars, beginning in the

sixth century after Christ, whose purpose was to
correct and preserve the Hebrew versions then available. The Massoretic Text was completed by the
end of the 10th century. The Septuagint became the
accepted Christian version of the Old Testament,
while the Massoretic Text has remained the Hebrew
canon. Other important versions of the Old Testament are the Samarian Pentateuch, a fourth-century
B.C. text preserved by the Samaritan community, and
the VULGATE, a Latin translation by St. Jerome begun
in A.D. 382. The Vulgate is still the authorized Roman
Catholic version.

The New Testament was written, probably in
Greek, during the first century; however, the earliest manuscripts date from the third and fourth centuries. There is no doubt that, in the years between
the date of its original composition and those of
extant manuscripts, numerous textual changes were
made through poor copying and interpretive additions or subtractions. There are five general types
of text identifiable in early manuscripts. When the
New Testament canon was defined in 367, an attempt was made to standardize the texts. Of the
150,000 variants of New Testament text only 50 are
significant, and no essential doctrine is affected by
any of them.

The greatest number of New Testament texts are
in Greek, but there are early Latin texts, parts of
which were incorporated into the Vulgate. The New
Testament is by far the best preserved document
from the ancient world; there are about 175 papyri
from the second to the fourth centuries and close to
3,000 manuscripts that date from before the invention of printing.

Bible, English versions. The principal versions
of the English Bible are:

American Revised Version. A separate version
published in 1901, the work of the American Committee on the Revised Version. It differs in a few
particulars from the Revised Version (see below).

Authorized or *King James Version.* The version
in general use in England. It was made by a body of
scholars working at the command of King James I
(hence sometimes known as the King James Bible)
from 1604 to 1611, and was published in 1611. The
modern Authorized Version is, however, by no
means an exact reprint of that originally authorized
by King James; a large number of typographical
errors which occurred in the first edition have been
corrected, the orthography and punctuation have
been modernized, and the use of italics, capital
letters, etc. altered. The Bishops' Bible (see below)
was used as the basis of the text, but Tyndale's,
Matthew's, Coverdale's, and the Geneva translations
were also followed when they agreed better with
the original. The King James Version became the
Bible of almost all English-speaking Protestant sects,
and its influence can be detected in nearly every
subsequent version. It is still much in use and remains, in its simplicity and eloquence, the most
beautifully written of all Bibles in the language. Its
literary influence is inestimable; besides its direct
effect on many important writers, it has been regarded as a major force in keeping English relatively unchanged since the 17th century. See HAMP-
TON COURT CONFERENCE.

Bishops' Bible. A version made at the instigation of

Archbishop Parker (hence also called "Matthew
Parker's Bible"), to which most of the Anglican
bishops were contributors. It was a revision of the
Great Bible (see below); it first appeared in 1568
and by 1602 had reached its 18th edition. It is this
edition that forms the basis of the Authorized Version. See Treacle Bible (below).

Coverdale's Bible. The first complete English Bible
to be printed. It was published in 1535 by Miles
Coverdale. As Coverdale knew neither Hebrew nor
Greek, his translation is from Latin and German
sources, notably the Vulgate, another Latin version
by Sanctes Pegninus (1527–1528), Luther's German
version (1534), and the Swiss-German version of
Zwingli and Juda (Zurich, 1527–1529). He used Tyndale's translations of the New Testament and the
Pentateuch. The first edition was printed in Antwerp,
but the second (Southwark, 1537) was the first Bible
printed in England. Matthew's Bible (see below) is
largely based on Coverdale's. See Bug Bible (below).

Cranmer's Bible. A name given to the Great Bible
(see below) of 1540. It, and later issues of it, contained a prologue by Archbishop Cranmer, and on
the title page a woodcut by Holbein shows Henry
VIII seated while Cranmer and Thomas Cromwell
distribute copies to the people.

Douay Version. A translation of the Vulgate made
by English Catholic scholars in France. The New
Testament was published in Rheims in 1582 and the
Old Testament in Douay in 1609. It is sometimes
called the Rheims-Douay Version. See Rosin Bible
(below).

Geneva Bible. A revision of Tyndale and the Great
Bible, undertaken by English exiles in Geneva during the Marian persecutions and first published in
1560. It was the work of William Whittingham (a
brother-in-law of Calvin), assisted by Anthony Gilby
and Thomas Sampson. Whittingham had previously
published a translation of the New Testament (1557).
The Genevan version, one of the most important in
the history of the English Bible, was the first to be
printed in roman type instead of black letter, the
first in which the chapters are divided into verses
(taken from Robert Stephan's Greek-Latin Testament of 1537), and the first in which italics are used
for explanatory and connective words and phrases
(taken from Theodore Beza's New Testament of
1556). It was immensely popular; from 1560 to 1616
no year passed without a new edition, and at least
200 are known. It was the Bible used by Shakespeare.
In every edition the word "breeches" is used in
Gen. 3:7; as a result this is popularly called the
Breeches Bible (see below). See Goose Bible; Place-
makers' Bible (below).

Great Bible. Coverdale's 1539 revision of his own
1535 edition collated with Tyndale and Matthew.
It was made at the request of Thomas Cromwell.
Its name comes from its large size (10 by 15 in.).
The printing was begun by Regnault in Paris, halted
by the Inquisition, and completed by Richard Graf-
ten and Edward Whitchurch in London. A second
revision in 1540 is often called Cranmer's Bible (see
above).

King James Bible. See Authorized Version
(above).

Matthew Parker's Bible. The Bishops' Bible
(above).

Matthew's Bible. A pronouncedly Protestant version published in 1537 as having been "truly and purely translated in English by Thomas Matthew," which was a pseudonym, adopted for purposes of safety, of John Rogers, an assistant of Tyndale. It was probably printed in Antwerp. The text is made up of the Pentateuch from Tyndale's version together with his hitherto unprinted translation of Joshua to II Chronicles inclusive and his revised edition of the New Testament, with Coverdale's version of the rest of the Old Testament and the Apocrypha. It was quickly superseded by the Great Bible (see above), but it is of importance as it formed the starting-point for the revisions which culminated in the Authorized Version. See Bug Bible (below).

Revised Standard Version. The newest American version which appeared in 1952; the New Testament was published in 1946. It employs a modern American idiom and has been widely accepted by Protestant churchmen.

Revised Version. A revision of the Authorized Version begun in 1870 by a body of 25 English scholars (assisted and advised by an American Committee). The New Testament was published in 1881, the complete Bible in 1885, and the Apocrypha in 1895.

Rheims-Douay Version. See Douay Version (above).

Taverner's Bible. An independent translation by a Greek scholar, Richard Taverner, printed in 1539 (the same year as the Great Bible) by T. Petit for T. Berthelet. It had no influence on the Authorized Version, but is remarkable for its vigorous, idiomatic English, and for being the first English Bible to include a third book of Maccabees in the Apocrypha.

Tyndale's Bible. The first printed English New Testament, translated by William Tyndale (Cologne, Worms, 1525). He followed it with the Pentateuch (Marburg, Hesse, 1530 or 1531), Jonah, Old Testament lessons appointed to be read in place of the Epistles, and a manuscript translation of the Old Testament to the end of Chronicles that was afterwards used in Matthew's Bible (see above). His revisions of the New Testament were issued in 1534 and 1535. Tyndale's principal authority was Erasmus' edition of the Greek Testament, but he also used Erasmus' Latin translation of the same, the Vulgate, and Luther's German version. Tyndale's version fixed the style and tone of the English Bible: about 90 per cent of his translation is retained in the Authorized Version. In 1535 he was arrested and put to death as a heretic the following year.

Wyclif's Bible. The name given to two translations of the Vulgate, one completed in 1380 and the other a few years later. Wyclif was neither the translator nor concerned with the translation of either of these. Nicholas of Hereford made the first version as far as Baruch 3:20; who was responsible for the remainder is not known. The second version has been ascribed to John Purvey, a follower of Wyclif. The Bible of 1380 was the first complete version in English, being a word-for-word translation of the Vulgate into a Midland dialect. The complete Bible remained unprinted until 1850, when the monumental edition of both versions was published by Forshall and Madden. Printings of the New Testament had appeared in the previous century.

Bible, specially named editions. The following Bibles are named either from typographical errors or archaic words that they contain, or from some special circumstance connected with them:

Adulterous Bible. The "Wicked Bible" (see below).

Bamberg Bible. The "Thirty-six Line Bible" (see below).

Bear Bible. The Spanish Protestant version printed at Basle in 1569; so called because the woodcut device on the title-page is a bear.

Bedell's Bible. A translation of the Authorized Version into Irish carried out under the direction of Bedell (d. 1642), bishop of Kilmore and Ardagh.

Breeches Bible. A name given to the Geneva Bible because Gen. 3:7 is translated, "The eyes of them bothe were opened . . . and they sowed figge-tree leaves together and made themselves breeches." This reading occurs in every edition of the Geneva Bible, but not in any other version though it is given in the then unprinted Wyclif manuscript ("ya sewiden ye levis of a fige tre and madin brechis"), and also in the translation of the Pentateuch given in Caxton's edition of Voragine's *Golden Legend* (1483).

Brother's Bible. The "Kralitz Bible" (see below).

Bug Bible. A name given to Coverdale's Bible (see above) of 1535 because Ps. 91:5 is translated, "Thou shalt not nede to be afrayed for eny bugges by night." The same reading occurs in Matthew's Bible and its reprints; the Authorized and Revised Versions both read "terror."

Complutensian Polyglot. The great edition, in six folio volumes, containing the Hebrew and Greek texts, the Septuagint, the Vulgate, and the Chaldee paraphrase of the Pentateuch with a Latin translation. It also includes Greek and Hebrew grammars and a Hebrew dictionary; it was prepared and printed at the expense of Cardinal Ximenes, and printed at Alcala (the ancient Complutum) near Madrid, 1513–1517.

Discharge Bible. An edition printed in 1806 containing *discharge* for *charge* in I Tim. 5:21, "I discharge thee before God, . . . that thou observe these things. . . ."

Ears to Ear Bible. An edition of 1810, in which Matt. 13:43 reads, "Who hath ears to *ear,* let him hear."

Ferrara Bible. The first Spanish edition of the Old Testament, translated from the Hebrew in 1553 for the use of the Spanish Jews. A second edition was published in the same year for Christians.

Forty-two Line Bible. The "Mazarin Bible" (see below).

Goose Bible. The editions of the Geneva Bible printed in Dort (or Dordrecht), Holland; the Dort press had a goose as its device.

Gutenberg Bible. The "Mazarin Bible" (see below).

He and She Bible. The two earliest editions of the Authorized Version (both 1611). In the first (now known as the "He Bible"), Ruth 3:15 reads, "and he went into the city"; the other (now known as the "She Bible") has the variant "*she.*" "He" is the correct translation of the Hebrew, but nearly all modern versions—with the exception of the Revised Version—perpetuate the confusion and print "she."

Idle Bible. An edition of 1809 in which "the idole shepherd" (Zech. 11:17) is printed "the idle shepherd." In the Revised Version the translation is "the worthless shepherd."

Kralitz Bible. The Bible printed by the United Brethren of Moravia (hence, known as the Brother's Bible) at Kralitz (1579–1593).

Leda Bible. The third edition (second folio) of the Bishop's Bible published in 1572, and so called because the decoration to the initial in the Epistle to the Hebrews is a startling and incongruous woodcut of Jupiter visiting Leda in the guise of a swan. This, and several other decorations in the New Testament of this edition, were from an edition of Ovid's *Metamorphoses;* they created such a storm of protest that they were never afterwards used.

Leopolita Bible. A Polish translation of the Vulgate by John of Lemberg (ancient Leopolis) published in 1561 at Cracow.

Mazarin Bible. The first Bible to be printed (an edition of the Vulgate), and the first large book to be printed from movable metal type. It contains no date, but was probably printed in 1455, and was certainly on sale by the middle of 1456. It was printed at Mainz, but there is some question about who the printer was; it is now thought to have been either Johannes GUTENBERG or Fust and Schöffer. It is frequently called the *Gutenberg Bible.* By bibliographers it is usually known as the *Forty-two Line Bible* (having 42 lines to the page), to differentiate it from the Bamberg Bible of 36 lines. Its popular name is due to the fact that the copy found in the Mazarin Library, Paris, in 1760, was the first to be known and described.

Murderers' Bible. An edition of 1801 in which the misprint *murderers* for *murmurers* makes Jude 16 read, "These are murderers, complainers, walking after their own lusts . . . "

Old Cracow Bible. The "Leopolita Bible" (see above).

Ostrog Bible. The first complete Slavonic edition, printed at Ostrog, Volhynia, Russia, in 1581.

Pfister's Bible. The "Thirty-six Line Bible" (see below).

Place-makers' Bible. The second edition of the Geneva Bible, 1562; so called from the printer's error in Matt. 5:9, "Blessed are the placemakers [peacemakers], for they shall be called the children of God." It has also been called the "Whig Bible."

Printers' Bible. An edition of about 1702 which makes David pathetically complain that "printers [princes] have persecuted me without a cause" (Ps. 119:161).

Proof Bible (Probe-Bible). The revised version of the first impression of Luther's German Bible. A final revised edition appeared in 1892.

Rebecca's Camels Bible. An edition printed in 1823 in which Gen. 24:61 reads, "Rebecca arose, and her camels," instead of "her damsels."

Rosin Bible. A name sometimes given to the Douay Version, of 1609, so called because it has in Jer. 8:22, "Is there noe rosin in Galaad." The Authorized Version translates the word by "balm," but gives "rosin" in the margin as an alternative. See Treacle Bible (below).

Sacy's Bible. A French translation, so called from Louis Isaac le Maistre de Sacy, director of Port Royal, 1650–1679.

Schelhorn's Bible. A name sometimes given to the "Thirty-six Line Bible" (see below).

September Bible. Luther's German translation of the New Testament, published anonymously at Wittenberg in September, 1522.

She Bible. See He Bible (above).

Standing Fishes Bible. An edition of 1806 in which Ezek. 47:10 reads, "And it shall come to pass that the fishes [fishers] shall stand on it, . . ."

Thirty-six Line Bible. A Latin Bible of 36 lines to the column, probably printed by A. Pfister at Bamberg in 1460. It is also known as the Bamberg and Pfister's Bible, and sometimes as Schelhorn's, as it was first described by the German bibliographer J. G. Schelhorn in 1760.

Thumb Bible. An edition printed at Aberdeen in 1670; it measures one inch square by a half inch thick.

To-remain Bible. A Bible printed at Cambridge in 1805, in which Gal. 4:29 reads, "he that was born after the flesh persecuted him that was born after the spirit to remain, even so it is now." The words "to remain" were added in error by the compositor, the editor having answered a proofreader's query as to the comma after "spirit" with the penciled reply "to remain" in the margin. The mistake was repeated in the first 8vo edition published by the Bible Society (1805) and in their 12mo edition (1819).

Treacle Bible. A popular name for the Bishops' Bible (1568) because in it Jer. 8:22 reads, "Is there no tryacle in Gilead, is there no phisition there?" In the same Bible "tryacle" is also given for "balm" in Jer. 46:11, and Ezek. 27:17. Coverdale's Bible (1535) also uses the word "triacle." See Rosin Bible (above).

Unrighteous Bible. An edition printed at Cambridge in 1653, containing the printer's error, "Know ye not that the unrighteous shall inherit the Kingdom of God?" (I Cor. 6:9). It should read "shall *not* inherit." The same edition gave Rom. 6:13 as, "Neither yield ye your members as instruments of righteousness unto sin," in place of "*un*righteousness." This edition is sometimes known as the "Wicked Bible."

Vinegar Bible. An edition printed at the Clarendon Press, Oxford, in 1717 with the heading to Luke 20, "Parable of the Vinegar" instead of "Parable of the Vineyard."

Wicked Bible. An edition in which the word *not* is omitted in the seventh commandment, making it, "Thou shalt commit adultery." It was printed in 1632 in London by Barker and Lucas who were fined £300 for their unfortunate error. See Unrighteous Bible (above).

Wife-hater Bible. An edition of 1810 in which the word "life" in Luke 14:26 is printed "wife." It reads, "If any man come to me, and hate not his father . . . yea, and his own wife also. . . ."

Wuyck's Bible. The Polish Bible authorized by the Roman Catholics and printed at Cracow in 1599. The translation was made by the Jesuit Jacob Wuyck.

Zurich Bible. A German version (1530) composed of Luther's translation of the New Testament and portions of the Old, with the remainder and the Apocrypha by other translators.

Bible in Spain, The (1843). A travel book by George Borrow, considered one of the best in the English language. Supposedly based on the author's experiences in Spain as a colporteur for the Bible Society, it probably contains much material of his own invention. However, the book is thought to give a valid picture of Spanish life during the Carlist troubles.

Biblia Pauperum (*Lat.*, "the poor man's Bible"). A picture-book, widely used by the illiterate in the Middle Ages in place of the Bible. It was designed to illustrate the leading events in the salvation of man; later manuscripts as a rule had a Latin inscription to each picture. These *Biblia* were probably the earliest books to be printed, first from blocks and later with movable type.

Bibliotheke. See Apollodorus.

Bickerstaff, Isaac. A fictitious astrologer invented by Jonathan Swift to silence John Partridge, an almanac maker who had achieved a reputation as something of a prophet. In his almanac *Predictions for the ensuing year by Isaac Bickerstaff* (1708), Swift predicted Partridge's death on March 29. On March 30, he published a convincing account of the prophecy's fulfillment in *An Elegy of Mr. Partridge* (1708). The hoax was successful despite Partridge's protests that he was still very much alive. The joke was popular, and Richard Steele capitalized on Bickerstaff's fame by making him the supposed editor of the Tatler.

A page from a German *Biblia Pauperum* (1471).

Bickerstaffe-Drew, Monsignor Count **Francis Browning Drew** (1858–1928). English Roman Catholic clergyman and author. Under the pen name John Ayscough he wrote several novels, including *Dromina* (1909), *Mezzogiorno* (1910), and *Faustula* (1912).

Biddle, Nicholas (1786–1844). American financier. Named president of the bank of the United States (1822), he opposed Andrew Jackson's contention that the bank charter was unconstitutional. His attempt to renew the national charter was defeated, and in 1836 the bank was renamed the Bank of the United States of Pennsylvania (1836); Biddle resigned in 1839.

Bidpai (also **Bidpay, Pilpay**), **Fables of.** Also known as **Kalilah and Dimnah** (c. 750). An Arabic version of a collection of Indian fables common to Buddhism and Brahminism. They were collected in the Sanskrit *Panchatantra* and translated into Persian about A.D. 55. *Bidpai* means court scholar, and the allegorical animal stories are told as a wise man's advice to a young Indian prince.

Biedermeier. In German literature, a tendency found most strongly in the period 1815–1848, during which most parts of Germany were governed by oppressive conservative regimes such as those of Prussia and Austria. It is often thought of as the antithesis of the *Jung Deutschland* (Young Germany) movement. Whereas the Young Germans stressed social criticism in thought, vigorous realism in style, and heroism in their characters, *Biedermeier* authors favored social conservatism in thought, didacticism in style, and a capacity for quiet resignation in their characters. The *Biedermeier* tendency is distinguished from romanticism by its emphasis on a sober, resigned attitude toward the world, as opposed to the romantics' highflown, fundamentally optimistic striving for the ideal. The late Swabian phase of German romanticism, however, nearly coincides with the *Biedermeier*. No major authors are purely and simply *Biedermeier*, but the three most important figures in whom the tendency is clearly marked are Grillparzer, Mörike, and Stifter.

Bienville, Sieur de. **Jean Baptiste Lemoyne** (1680–1768). French explorer of the lower Mississippi and Red River (1699). He was a lieutenant of the French king in Louisiana (1700) and governor of the colony (1701–1712; 1718–1725; 1733–1743). In 1718 he founded New Orleans.

Bierce, Ambrose [Gwinett] (1842–?1914). American journalist, short-story writer, and poet. Bierce had little education and was frankly ashamed of his sternly religious Ohio family; he fought bravely in the Civil War and left the federal army with the brevet title of major. Later coming to doubt the cause for which he had fought, he refused a large sum in back army pay, saying bitterly, "When I hired out as an assassin for my country, that wasn't part of the contract."

Bierce settled in San Francisco after the war, holding a variety of jobs. He published in local newspapers, *The Overland Monthly,* and his own newsletter; soon he became the literary dictator of the West Coast, his gibes determining the fate of books and authors. Bierce began to publish his stories, and with his friends, Joaquin Miller, Bret Harte, and Mark Twain, formed an important literary circle.

He married the daughter of a wealthy Nevada miner, whose wedding gift of $10,000 enabled the young couple to live abroad for four years. When Bierce returned from England, he had become witty and polished. Back in San Francisco, he wrote his famous column, "The Prattler," a mixture of literary gossip, epigrams, and short stories. Employed by the young William Randolph Hearst in Washington, he also wrote for *The Cosmopolitan* and prepared a collected edition of his works (12 vols., 1909–1912). Divorced from his wife in 1904, he broke off connections with his whole family. In 1913, tired of existence, he disappeared into Mexico. According to one story, he was killed in the war between Villa and Carranza.

Bierce's wit is cruel and brilliant; he was a clever epigrammatist and a forerunner of such American realists as Stephen Crane. His fame rests on three volumes in his collected works: IN THE MIDST OF LIFE, a collection of short stories; *Can Such Things Be?* (1893), a group of weird stories; and *The Devil's Dictionary* (1906). Bierce has been called a difficult genius who never attained full stature.

Bifrost (Icel., *bifa*, tremble; *rost*, path). In Scandinavian mythology, the rainbow bridge between Asgard, heaven, and Midgard, earth. The various colors of the rainbow were said to be reflections of its precious stones. Heimdall was keeper of the bridge, which was expected to collapse at Ragnarok under the weight of the onrushing sons of Muspelheim.

Big Ben. London's famous bell. It is attached to "the Westminster clock," standing in the Parliament tower, or St. Stephen's Tower. Big Ben weighs 13½ tons; it is named after Sir Benjamin Hall, chief commissioner of works in 1856, when the bell was cast.

Big Bertha. See KRUPP.

Big Brother. A tyrannical political leader who assumes the role of protective elder brother. The term was invented by George Orwell. See 1984.

Bigelow, John (1817–1911). American writer and diplomat. Bigelow served as American consul-general at Paris and later as minister to France. He worked with William Cullen Bryant on the New York *Evening Post* and was secretary of state to the New York governor, Samuel J. Tilden. Out of these experiences he wrote two biographies, *William Cullen Bryant* (1893) and *Samuel J. Tilden* (1895). Bigelow's autobiography is called *Retrospections of an Active Life* (5 vols., 1909–1913). He is also the author of several historical works.

Big-Endians. In Jonathan Swift's GULLIVER'S TRAVELS, a religious faction in the kingdom of LILLIPUT, who make it a matter of conscience to break their eggs at the big end. They are looked on as heretics by the orthodox party, who break theirs at the little end. The Big-Endians typify the Catholics, and the Little-Endians the Protestants.

Biggers, Earl Derr. See Charlie CHAN.

Biglow Papers, The (1848). A series of poems and prose sketches by James Russell LOWELL. A second series was issued during the Civil War and collected in 1867.

This work marks Lowell's first appearance as poet, abolitionist, and defender of American democracy. The first series is concerned with the Mexican War, while the second treats the Civil War; the poems are written in dialect, while the accompanying prose remains in standard English. There are three central characters: Hosea Biglow, a forthright commentator on current affairs; his friend, Birdofredom Sawin, a scoundrel; and the Reverend Homer Wilbur, used by Lowell as a foil for the first two characters. The series satirizes politicians and their doctrines, the cowardice of editors, and the follies of the wealthy, North and South. More significant than his satire is Lowell's use of language. His treatment of Yankee dialect is an important contribution to the literature of the American language. See COURTIN', THE.

Big Money, The (1936). A novel by John Dos Passos, the last book in the trilogy U.S.A. (q.v.). It portrays the extravagance and corruption of the 1920's, culminating in the stock-market crash of 1929 and in the personal tragedy or moral defeat of several of the leading characters. There are short interspersed biographies of such men as Henry Ford, Frank Lloyd Wright, William Randolph Hearst, and Rudolph Valentino.

Bildungsroman (*Ger.*, "novel of Education"). Also called **Entwicklungsroman** ("novel of development"). A type of novel common in German literature, which treats the personal development of a single individual, usually in youth. The definitive example of the form is *Wilhelm Meisters Lehrjahre* (*Wilhelm Meister's Apprenticeship*, 1795–1796; see WILHELM MEISTER) by Goethe, which exercised an extremely strong influence on subsequent German novels. The *Bildungsroman* represents the culmination of a long tradition, but strictly speaking, the term may not be applied to any work earlier than *Wilhelm Meister*. Both Wolfram's *Parzival* (early 13th century) and Grimmelshausen's *Simplizius Simplizissimus* (1668 ff.), though treating individual development, are *primarily* concerned with depicting a Christian world order; and Wieland's *Agathon* (1766) concentrates more on philosophical ideas than on personal development as such. Among the greatest 19th-century *Bildungsromane*, all of which were influenced by *Wilhelm Meister*, are Novalis' *Heinrich von Ofterdingen* (1802), Eichendorff's *Ahnung und Gegenwart* (*Presentiment and the Present*, 1815), Stifter's *Der Nachsommer* (*Indian Summer*, 1857), and Keller's GREEN HENRY. A 20th-century example is Mann's *The Magic Mountain* (1924), and among English novels Dickens' *David Copperfield* (1850) shows the general characteristics of the form. See KÜNSTLERROMAN.

Billings, Josh. Pen name of **Henry Wheeler Shaw** (1818–1885). American auctioneer, real-estate agent, and humorist. After taking up many occupations, Shaw turned to writing humorous essays; when he studied the techniques of Artemus WARD and adopted cacography he became famous. He published volumes of *Sayings* (1865, 1866) and a series of *Allminax* (1869–1879). Among his other writings are *Josh Billings on Ice and Other Things* (1868), *Josh Billings' Struggling with Things* (1881), and *Josh Billings, His Works Complete* (4 vols., 1888). The Yankee humorist has been both highly praised and ignored; Charles H. Smith called him "Aesop and Ben Franklin, condensed and abridged."

Billingsgate. The site of an old passage through that part of the city wall that protected London on the river side. It was so called from the Billings, who were the royal race of the Varini, an ancient tribe mentioned by Tacitus. Billingsgate has been the site of a fishmarket for many centuries, and its porters and other workers were famous at least 300 years ago. Hence billingsgate became a synonym for vulgar and profane language.

Bill of Divorcement, A. A play by Clemence DANE.

Bill of Rights. The first 10 amendments to the CONSTITUTION OF THE UNITED STATES, guaranteeing civil liberties against infringement by the federal government. Among these rights are freedom of speech, of press, of religion, and trial by jury. The Bill of Rights became part of the Constitution on Dec. 15, 1791.

Billy Budd, Foretopman (post. 1924). A novella by Herman MELVILLE. Billy, innocently good, is cruelly antagonized by Claggart, the evil master-at-arms. Unjustly accused before the captain by Claggart, Billy, speechless with rage, strikes the schemer and kills him. Captain Vere, who loves Billy as his son, decides that he must hang the boy and uphold law. Vere's first obligation is the preservation of social welfare; justice, rather than mercy, must be administered to maintain order. Billy, understanding, mounts the yardarm willingly, crying "God bless Captain Vere."

Bimini. An island of the Bahama group. The FOUNTAIN OF YOUTH on Bimini, according to the legend, conferred eternal youth on all who drank its waters. Many journeys were made in search of it. See PONCE DE LEÓN.

Bing, Rudolf (1902-   ). Viennese-born American opera impresario. After important posts with various opera companies in Europe, he became general manager of the Metropolitan Opera House in New York in 1950.

Bingham, George Caleb (1811–1879). American painter. He is best known for scenes of life on the Mississippi and Missouri rivers. Their clear and strong composition is imbued with the poetry of subtle colors intensified by bright accents. The creator of political genre paintings, he became increasingly involved in politics, to the detriment of his painting.

Binyon, Laurence (1869–1943). English poet, dramatist, and art historian. His best-known work is his translation of Dante's *Divine Comedy* into English *terza rima*. His volumes of poetry include *The Burning of the Leaves* (1944), and his poetic dramas include *Attila* (1907).

Biographia Literaria (2 vols., 1817). A prose work by Samuel Taylor COLERIDGE. It contains essays on literary criticism and develops the author's distinction between FANCY and IMAGINATION. The book also contains a discussion of the distinction between reason and understanding, a trenchant critical analysis of Wordsworth's poetry, and detailed discussions of portions of the philosophies of Kant, Schelling, and Fichte.

Bion (2d century B.C.). Greek pastoral poet of Smyrna. A contemporary of Theocritus, he was best known for *Lament for Adonis*.

Biondello. In Shakespeare's TAMING OF THE SHREW, one of the servants of Lucentio, the future husband of Bianca.

Biondo, Flavio (1392–1463). Italian historian. He was the author of *Historiarum ab Inclinatione Romanorum Decades,* the first attempt at treating the "decline and fall" of the Roman empire.

Birch, Harvey. The hero of Cooper's THE SPY.

Birches (1916). A poem by Robert FROST. One of Frost's best-known poems, *Birches* describes the trees bent to the ground by ice storms; the poet imagines that they had been bent by a boy swinging on them, and wishes, when he himself is "weary of considerations," to climb toward heaven in a birch tree "till the tree could bear no more,/ But dipped its top and set me down again."

Bird, Robert Montgomery (1806–1854). American physician, dramatist, and novelist. Bird reputedly gave up his medical practice because of an unwillingness to collect fees. He sold several of his plays to an unscrupulous friend, actor Edwin Forrest, who allowed him only a tiny fraction of the profits, while refusing to let him publish his own work. The plays include *The Gladiator* (1831), *Oralloosa* (1832), and *The Broker of Bogota* (1834). Dr. Bird turned to novel writing, publishing NICK OF THE WOODS, his best book; *Calavar* (1834); *The Infidel* (1835); *The Hawks of Hawk Hollow* (1835); and others. Most of Bird's plays were included in *Life and Dramatic Works of Robert Montgomery Bird* (1919).

Birds, The (Ornithes; 414 B.C.). A famous comedy by ARISTOPHANES. Euelpides and Pithetaerus, fugitives from Athenian taxation and litigation, persuade the birds to found a city in the clouds, Nephelococcygia (Cloud-cuckooland). There they will be strategically placed to prevent the delightful smoke from the sacrifices of mortals from reaching the gods, unless the gods comply with the birds' demands. The plan is successful, the gods capitulate, and the birds and their two Athenian friends presumably live happily ever after. The comedy, filled with delightful fancies and lovely lyrics, is Aristophanes' masterpiece.

Bireno. In Ariosto's ORLANDO FURIOSO, the duke of Selandia. He is loved by Olimpia, whom he deserts after falling in love with the daughter of King Cimosco of Frisia.

Birkin, Rupert. The hero of D. H. Lawrence's novel WOMEN IN LOVE, in which he is Lawrence's spokesman.

Birmingham, George A. Pen name of James Owen Hannay (1865–1950). Irish clergyman and author. He wrote farcical novels of Irish life, the best of which was *Spanish Gold* (1908).

Biron or Berowne. One of the three lords of Navarre who take a three-year vow of celibacy and devotion to learning with King Ferdinand in Shakespeare's LOVE'S LABOUR'S LOST. Biron differs from the others in that, being a sensualist and a realist, he takes the oath only because he does not intend to be outdone by them.

Birrell, Augustine (1850–1933). English essayist and statesman. A lawyer, professor of law, parliamentarian, and one-time chief secretary of Ireland (1907–1916), Birrell is known for his essays on English authors and literature, OBITER DICTA, *Res Judicatae* (1892), *Collected Essays and Addresses* (1922), and *More Obiter Dicta* (1924). These are usually acute, judicious, and trenchantly witty. He also wrote the biographies, *Charlotte Brontë* (1885), *Hazlitt* (1902), and *Marvell* (1905).

Birth (1918). A novel by Zona GALE. Family and associates look upon Marshall Pitt as a tiresome nonentity. His wife leaves him, he fails in all his ventures, and finally dies trying to rescue a pet dog. His son recognizes his goodness and courage too late. *Mr. Pitt,* a dramatization of the novel by the author, appeared in 1924.

Birthmark, The (1846). A story by Nathaniel HAWTHORNE. Aylmer, a scientist, insists on removing a small birthmark from the cheek of his otherwise perfect wife, Georgiana. He succeeds, but Georgiana, no longer human, must die. In his attempt to master nature, Aylmer has "rejected the best the earth could offer."

Birth of Tragedy from the Spirit of Music, The (*Die Geburt der Tragödie aus dem Geiste der Musik;* 1872). A long philosophical essay by Friedrich NIETZSCHE. As a work of classical scholarship, it marks the final overthrow of WINCKELMANN's naïve conception of Greek culture as being perfectly static and blissful. Nietzsche sees in ancient Greece the tension and interaction of two opposed forces: the Apollonian, on one hand, which corresponds to Winckelmann's ideas, and the dark, mysterious Dionysiac, on the other. (See APOLLONIAN AND DIONYSIAC.) In particular, he attempts to trace the development of Greek tragedy from the original Dionysiac chorus and to show its decline as a result of Euripides' and Socrates' excessive Apollonian rationalism. The book ends with the hope that modern German music, specifically that of Richard Wagner, might give birth to a new tragic age. Nietzsche's early idolization of Wagner is still strong here, but in 1876 he broke with the composer and later polemicized frequently against him.

Bishop, Elizabeth (1911–   ). American poet. Winner of the Pulitzer Prize for poetry in 1956 for *Poems* (1955), Elizabeth Bishop writes mainly descriptive poems in the modern idiom with great stylistic subtlety. A regular contributor to periodicals, she brought out her first book of poems, *North and South,* in 1946. She was born in Worcester, Mass., and now lives in Petropolis, Brazil. She has held several fellowships, was a consultant at the Library of Congress 1949–1950, and was appointed honorary consultant in American letters in 1958.

Bishop, John Peale (1892–1944). American poet and essayist. Educated at Princeton, he was for a time managing editor of *Vanity Fair* and one of the American expatriates in Paris in the 1920's. Bishop is the author of several volumes of distinguished poetry, including *Green Fruit* (1917); *The Undertaker's Garland* (1922), with Edmund Wilson; *Now with His Love* (1933); *Minute Particulars* (1936); and *Selected Poems* (1941). After his return to the U.S., he wrote less poetry and produced some of his best work of criticism. *Many Thousands Gone* (1931) is a collection of short stories; *Act of Darkness* (1935) is a novel. His contributions both as poet and critic may be seen in the two volumes published after his death: *Collected Poems* (1948), edited with a memoir and preface by Allen Tate, and *Collected Essays* (1948), edited with an introduction by Edmund Wilson.

Bishop Blougram's Apology (1855). A poem in the form of a dramatic monologue by Robert BROWNING, originally published in his collection *Men and Women.* The speaker, Sylvester Blougram, confesses to intellectual skepticism yet continues to stand before the world as an exponent of doctrines he no longer holds. He justifies his position to Gigadibs, a young poet.

Bismarck, Prince Otto von (1815–1898). German statesman. As chancellor of Prussia (1862–1890) and the German Reich (1871–1890), he pursued a practical, opportunistic course that led to the formation of the German Reich in 1871. (See BLOOD AND IRON; EMS TELEGRAM; Count MOLTKE.) In the later years of his office he was respected for his conservative, responsible statesmanship. See DROPPING THE PILOT; KULTURKAMPF.

Bitter Sweet. (1) A long metrical narrative (1858), by Josiah Gilbert HOLLAND, at one time widely read.

(2) A popular operetta (1929), by Noel COWARD.

Bitzius, Albert. See Jeremias GOTTHELF.

Bizet, Alexandre César Léopold, called **Georges** (1838–1875). French composer. He is best known for his suite of incidental music to Alphonse Daudet's play *L'Arlésienne* (1872) and for his opera CARMEN. The latter was Nietzsche's favorite opera after he had turned his back on Wagner's music.

Björnson, Björnstjerne (1832–1910). Norwegian poet, novelist, and playwright. Björnson is known for his interest in his people and their history, first reflected in his "peasant novels" *Synnöve Solbakken* (*Trust and Trial,* 1857), *Arne* (1858), *A Happy Boy* (1860), and *The Fisher Maiden* (1868). For two years the manager-director of the National Theater at Bergen, he carried his interest in Norwegian history and legend over into his early plays, notably the trilogy of *Sigurd Slembe* (*Sigurd the Bastard,* 1862). A friend and rival of Henrik IBSEN, he also wrote plays of social realism which, though inferior to Ibsen's work, had greater popular success; the best of these are *The Editor* (1874), *A Bankruptcy* (1875), *The Gauntlet* (1883), and *Beyond Our Strength* (1883). Björnson published two volumes of poetry, *Poems and Songs* (1870) and *Arnljot Gelline* (1870), an epic. Interesting among his later novels are *Flags Are Flying in Town and Port* (1884) and *In God's Way* (1889), both of which are concerned with the problems of heredity and education. He was awarded the Nobel Prize in 1903.

Black and Tan. A member of the irregular force enlisted in England for service in Ireland as auxiliaries to the Royal Irish Constabulary during the disturbances of 1919–1922. The name arose because the original uniform of the force was the army khaki with the black leather accouterments of the R.I.C.

Black Beauty, The Autobiography of a Horse (1877). An imaginary autobiography of the horse, Black Beauty, by Anna SEWELL. In describing the ill treatment the horse receives from a series of owners, the author pleads for humane treatment of animals.

Black Book, The (1938). A novel by Lawrence DURRELL. Strongly influenced by Henry Miller's *Tropic of Cancer* (1934), the novel is a bizarre, erotic, surrealistic attack on "the English Death." The story is narrated by "Lawrence Lucifer." T. S. Eliot admired the book—understandably, since "the English Death" is Durrell's version of a sexually oriented waste land.

Blackburn, Thomas (1916–   ). English poet. Among his collections of mystical and visionary verse is *A Smell of Burning* (1961).

Black Dwarf, The (1816). A novel by Sir Walter SCOTT. It is the tale of an apparently malignant dwarf dwelling in seclusion in 18th-century Scotland, who proves ultimately to be of kind disposition. He finally reveals himself as Sir Edward MAULEY in order to prevent a forced marriage between Sir Frederick Langley and Isabella Vere.

black flag. The banner of a pirate ship. It usually was decorated with the skull and crossbones, and was known as the Jolly Roger.

Blackfriars. The name of 2 successive London theaters, both housed in the same building of an old Black Friars' monastery between Ludgate Hill and the Thames. The building was first leased as a theater (1576) by Sir William More to the Master of The Children of Windsor Chapel for the public performance of their plays before production at Court, and was used by them until 1584.

The second Blackfriars Theatre was housed in the same building after James Burbage's purchase (1596) of the property from More. After Burbage's death (1597) the property became his son Richard's, who leased it (1600) to Henry Evans and Nathaniel Giles for performances by the Children of the Chapel. Evans gave up his lease in 1608, and Burbage formed a company of owners consisting of himself, his brother Cuthbert, four of the King's Men (Shakespeare, Heminge, Condell, and Sly), and Thomas Evans. In 1609 the King's Men moved into their new theater, which became the center of the WAR OF THE THEATRES. Beaumont and Fletcher's plays and Shakespeare's last plays date from this time.

Blackfriars remained in operation as a theater until 1642, when all the theaters were closed. The building was dismantled in 1655. The site is now occupied by the offices of the London *Times*.

Black Hole of Calcutta. The punitive cell, measuring 14 ft. 10 in. by 18 ft., of the barracks at Fort William, Calcutta. In 1756, by order of Suraja Dowlah, 146 Europeans were thrown into it for a whole night; 23 survived to the next morning. Hence, a black hole is any lockup in military barracks.

Black Mass. See SATANISM.

Black Mischief (1932). A novel by Evelyn WAUGH. It is a farcical satire on various attempts to "civilize" a primitive country. The emperor himself introduces boots and contraceptives, which his subjects eat. The English and French try to take over the country; in the course of their efforts the hero, at a native banquet, is given some of his girl-friend to eat.

Blackmore, Richard Doddridge (1825–1900). English novelist. He wrote a number of novels of romance and adventure, of which LORNA DOONE is best known. His books are particularly notable for their secondary characters and for descriptions of England's West country, in which many of them are set. Among his other works are *Craddock Nowell* (1866), *Clara Vaughan* (1864), and *Christowell* (1882).

Blackmur, R[ichard] P[almer] (1904–1965). American critic and poet. In *The Double Agent* (1935) he analyzed modern poetry, arguing that form and content *together* comprise the poem's meaning. In the title essay of *Language As Gesture* (1952), Blackmur described linguistic gesture as "the outward and dramatic play of inward and imaged meaning." Among his other books are *The Expense of Greatness* (1940), *The Lion and the Honeycomb* (1955), and *Form and Value in Modern Poetry* (1957).

Black Prince. An epithet for Edward, prince of Wales (1330–1376), eldest son of King Edward III of England. Froissart says he was "styled black by terror of his arms." The appellation is sometimes thought to refer to the color of his armor, but usually to his martial deeds.

Black Riders and Other Lines, The (1895). A book of poems by Stephen CRANE. Partly inspired by the work of Emily Dickinson, the "other lines" of this collection are often epigrammatic parables written in free verse. The title poem comes from a boyhood experience in which Crane, after watching the waves beat against the shore, dreamed of black riders on black horses riding up, out of the water.

Black Shirt. One of the Italian Fascisti under Mussolini. The black shirt was the distinctive part of their uniforms. See S.S.

Blackstone, Sir William (1723–1780). English jurist. The famous *Commentaries* bearing his name for more than a century were fundamental in any study of English law. Hence Blackstone is synonymous with the law.

Black Tulip, The (La Tulipe Noire; 1895). An historical romance by Alexandre DUMAS. Set in Holland in the 17th century, the tale revolves about the struggle between two political factions.

Blackwood, Algernon (1869–1951). English writer of adventure stories and tales of the supernatural. *John Silence* is a series of stories about a psychical detective.

Blackwood's Magazine. A Scottish literary magazine, founded in 1817. It was strongly Tory in its political sympathies and violently opposed in its literary outlook to the so-called COCKNEY SCHOOL of poets. John Gibson Lockhart and James Hogg were well-known and influential members of *Blackwood's* staff.

Blagden, Isabella (1816–1873). English friend of the Robert Brownings. *Dearest Isa* (1951) is a collection of 154 letters written to her by Browning after his wife's death.

Blaine, James G[illespie] (1830–1893). American statesman. After serving in Congress (1862–1876), Blaine was a leading contender for the Republican presidential nomination in 1876 and was nominated in a famous speech by Robert G. Ingersoll, who referred to him as the "plumed knight," a designation with which he was henceforth associated. Blaine lost the nomination because of charges that he had used his political office for personal gain, but he became the candidate in 1884 against Grover Cleveland. Blaine's defeat is often ascribed to a remark by an overzealous supporter who described the Democratic Party as the party of "Rum, Romanism, and Rebellion," alienating Irish-American voters in the key state of New York. As secretary of state (1889–1892), he convened the first Pan-American Conference. The character of Sen. Ratcliffe in Henry Adams' DEMOCRACY is supposedly modeled on Blaine.

Blair, Eric. See George ORWELL.

Blake, Nicholas. The pen name under which C. DAY-LEWIS has written detective stories.

Blake, William (1757–1827). English poet, engraver, painter, and mystic. Apprenticed in 1771 to an engraver, he later illustrated his own work with copperplate engravings and water colors. He also illustrated Young's *Night Thoughts,* Gray's *Poems,* the Book of Job, and Dante's *Divine Comedy.* As a poet, he is known for his mysticism and complex, sometimes obscure symbolism. His visionary world is extremely important to his work. An antinomian, he bypasses the Church and experiences God directly; from boyhood on he had his visions, and from them created his personal mythology, of which URIZEN is a part. As his devoted wife remarked, "I have very little of Mr. Blake's company; he is always in Paradise." His works, in some of which both text and illustrations were engraved, include *Poetical Sketches* (1783); SONGS OF INNOCENCE and SONGS OF EXPERIENCE; and the so-called prophetic books including THE BOOK OF THEL, THE MARRIAGE OF HEAVEN AND HELL, *The Gates of Paradise* (1793), *The Visions of the Daughters of Albion* ([1793] see title page, below); *The Song of Los* and *The Book of Los* (1795). He also wrote JERUSALEM, *The Emanation of the Giant Albion* (1804), and MILTON.

Blanc, [Jean Joseph Charles] Louis (1811–1882). French socialist. Regarded as the father of state socialism, he founded (1839) the journal *Revue du Progrès* to promulgate his doctrines. One of the most prominent leaders of the abortive revolution of 1848, Blanc was forced to flee France that same year. His 12-volume *Histoire de la révolution française* (1847–1862) was written in England, where he lived until he returned to France in 1871.

A Blake title page designed and printed by the author.

The Eye sees more than the Heart knows.
Printed by Will.ᵐ Blake : 1793.

Blanchefleur or **Blancheflor.** See FLORES AND BLANCHEFLEUR.

Blanco Fombona, Rufino (1874–1944). Venezuelan novelist, short-story writer, poet, and essayist. Blanco Fombona was an exile during the long dictatorship of Juan Vicente Gómez, returning to Venezuela after the latter's death in 1935. His writing reflects his angry dismay at the stupidity, iniquity, and sordidness that he seemed to find everywhere. Accordingly his novels are weakened by bits of heavy-handed social satire and political propaganda. They include *El hombre de hierro* (1907), which depicts the triumph of evil over virtue; *El hombre de oro* (*The Man of Gold,* 1916), which exposes the venality and incompetence of Venezuelan politicians; and *La mitra en la mano* (1927), the story of an ambitious priest, who has been called a Venezuelan Elmer Gantry. *Cuentos americanos* (1904) and *Dramas mínimos* (1920) are his best-known collections of short stories. His poetry, which includes the collections *Pequeña ópera lírica* (1904) and *Cantos de la prisión y del destierro* (1911), shows the influence of MODERNISM. Among his other works are *Letras y letrados de Hispano-América* (1908) and *Grandes escritores de América* (1917), literary criticism; *La lámpara de Aladino* (1915), autobiographical sketches; and *El conquistador español en el siglo XVI* (1922), a study of the Spanish conquerors. He also edited the letters of Simón Bolívar, and edited and published several series of great American books.

Blandamour. See FAERIE QUEENE, THE.

Blanketeers. The name given to a body of Manchester workers who assembled in St. Peter's Field, Manchester, on March 10, 1817, with the purpose of marching to London to petition against what they considered unfair practices on the part of their employers. Each man was outfitted with provisions and a blanket. The leaders and some of the followers were arrested and imprisoned; the rest never got to London.

blank verse. In prosody, unrhymed verse. In English, the term usually means unrhymed iambic pentameter. In classical prosody, rhyme was not used at all; with the introduction of rhyme in the Middle Ages blank verse disappeared. It was reintroduced in the 16th century, and in England became the standard medium of dramatic poetry and frequently of epic poetry; Shakespeare's plays, for example, are written in blank verse.

Blanqui, Louis Auguste (1805–1881). French socialist. A fiery revolutionist who advocated the dictatorship of the proletariat, Blanqui served 46 years in prison for his efforts to bring about the overthrow of Louis Philippe.

Blarney Stone. A triangular stone in the wall of the castle at Blarney, Ireland, about 20 feet from the top and difficult of access. It contains the inscription "*Cormac McCarthy fortis me fieri fecit, A.D. 1446.*" Tradition says that whoever can kiss this wins the power of being able to obtain all his desires by cajolery. As it is almost impossible to reach, a substitute has been provided by the custodians of the castle, and it is said that this is in every way as efficacious as the original.

Blas, Gil. See GIL BLAS DE SANTILLANE, HISTOIRE DE.

Blasco Ibañez, Vicente (1867–1928). Spanish novelist. His early, naturalistic novels, dealing with life in his native Valencia, are generally considered his best; these include *La barraca* (*The Cabin*, 1898) and *Cañas y barro* (*Reeds and Mud*, 1902). Later he wrote the novels that won him great popularity and financial rewards, perhaps at the expense of his literary reputation. Among these are *Los cuatro jinetes del Apocalipsis* (*The Four Horsemen of the Apocalypse*, 1916), a World War I story, and *Sangre y arena* (*Blood and Sand*, 1909).

Blast. A "little" magazine edited by Wyndham Lewis in association with Ezra Pound. In unconventional typography it advocated VORTICISM in art and literature.

Blatant Beast. See FAERIE QUEENE, THE.

blaue Blume. See BLUE FLOWER.

Blaue Reiter, Der (The Blue Rider). A group of artists established in 1911 in Munich around Wassily Kandinsky and Franz Marc. Interested in an expressionistic use of color to convey emotion, the group organized exhibitions of the works of such painters as Henri Rousseau, Georges Braque, Pablo Picasso, Casimir Malevitch, and Paul Klee. Their 1912 yearbook contained articles on cubism and other artistic movements in France, Germany, and Russia, as well as an article dealing with the music of Arnold Schoenberg. The group dispersed in 1914, with the outbreak of the First World War. See BRÜCKE, DIE.

Blavatsky, Helena Petrovna, called **Mme. Blavatsky** (1831–1891). Russian-born spiritualist medium, magician, and occultist. She founded the Theosophical Society (see THEOSOPHY). She wrote *Isis Unveiled* (1877) and *The Secret Doctrine* (1888), influential books of occult lore. She toured India, Europe, and the U.S., developing and preaching her doctrines. The poet William Butler Yeats was profoundly influenced by her work.

Bleak House (1852). A novel by Charles DICKENS. The heroine is Esther Summerson, or rather Esther Hawdon, illegitimate daughter of Lady Dedlock and Captain Hawdon; Esther herself does not know her origins, and Lady Dedlock believes Esther to be dead. A ward of Mr. Jarndyce, Esther lives with him at Bleak House. Lord Dedlock's lawyer, Mr. Tulkinghorn, begins to suspect Lady Dedlock's secret past and unravels it; when Tulkinghorn is found dead, Lady Dedlock is suspected; she disappears and is later found dead. Tulkinghorn was actually killed by Lady Dedlock's maid. Esther ultimately marries Dr. Woodcourt.

In the background of the novel is the interminable suit of *Jarndyce* vs. *Jarndyce*. Beginning as a dispute as to how the trusts under a Jarndyce will were to be administered, the suit drags on from year to year, from generation to generation. Two of the heirs are Richard Carstone and Ada Clare, his pretty cousin, who marry and live at Bleak House with John Jarndyce and Esther. When the case is finally settled, it is in Carstone's favor, but all the funds have been dissipated by the litigation. Carstone dies and Ada lives on at Bleak House with their son.

In this novel, Dickens attacks the delays and archaic absurdities of the courts, which he knew about firsthand from his frustrating and unprofitable experience of trying to sue the pirate publishers of *A Christmas Carol*. See Mr. BUCKET; The Rev. Mr. CHADBAND; Miss FLITE; Mrs. JELLYBY; Jo; KROOK; Harold SKIMPOLE.

Blefescu. In Jonathan Swift's GULLIVER'S TRAVELS, an island, northeast of LILLIPUT, inhabited by pygmies. It is supposed to represent France.

Bleibtreu, Karl (1859–1928). German author in the movement of NATURALISM. In his critical work, *Revolution der Literatur* (*Revolution of Literature*, 1886) he advocates what he calls "true romanticism," a genuine, heartfelt striving for human ideals. Among his creative works, *Dies Irae* (1882), the fictional diary of a French officer in the Franco-Prussian War, was most influential.

Blenheim, battle of (1704). During the War of the Spanish Succession, the battle in which John Churchill, duke of MARLBOROUGH, defeated Marshal Tallard at Blenheim on the upper Danube. It was the most resounding and decisive victory enjoyed by the British on the Continent since Agincourt. Louis XIV's schemes for pushing his frontiers up to the Rhine were thus thwarted and French prestige was badly shaken. The poem *The Battle of Blenheim* (1798) was written by Robert Southey.

Blenheim Steps. The site of an anatomical school on Bond Street in London, over which Sir Astley Cooper presided. Here "resurrectionists" were sure to find a ready mart for their gruesome wares, for which they received sums of money varying from £3 to £10, and sometimes more. Hence, *going to Blenheim Steps* means going to be dissected, or unearthed from one's grave.

Blessed Damozel, The (1850). A poem by Dante Gabriel ROSSETTI giving expression to the longing of the "blessed damozel" in heaven for her lover on earth.

Blessington, countess of. Marguerite Power (1789–1849). Irish writer. Her *Conversations with Lord Byron* (1834) are still interesting, but she is better known for her dramatic life. Sold by her father into marriage at 14, she fled from a brutal husband into a liaison with an English officer, who later gave her up (for £10,000) to the earl of Blessington. Her remarkable beauty, cleverness, and charm established her as a leading hostess of the day. After Blessington's death (1829), she became the companion, if not mistress, of Alfred, count d'Orsay, 12 years her junior, celebrated for his looks and accomplishments. To provide for "the last of the dandies" and her own luxurious tastes, she took to writing, but her novels and travel books failed to avert bankruptcy in 1849. She died a few months later, after following d'Orsay to France.

Blest Gana, Alberto (1830–1920). Chilean novelist. One of the outstanding realists of Latin-American fiction, Blest Gana, who spent many years in France, sought to be the Balzac of Chile. His best-known novel is *Martín Rivas* (1862). Dealing with the experiences of an impoverished provincial youth who falls in love with a girl of the aristocracy, the work gives an incisive, satirical view of Chilean society in the 1850's. Other works by Blest Gana include *Durante la Reconquista* (1897), an epic of Chile's struggle for independence, and *Los trasplantados* (1904), which depicts decadent Chilean émigrés in Paris.

Blifil, William. See TOM JONES.

Bligh, William (1754–1817). English admiral and master of the H.M.S. *Bounty*. Having sailed with Captain Cook on his second expedition when the breadfruit tree was discovered, Bligh was sent in 1787 on the *Bounty* to acquire specimens of the tropical tree for transplantation in the West Indies. His extreme severity led to mutiny, and Bligh, with 18 others, was set adrift. He succeeded in navigating nearly 4,000 miles of open sea and lived to carry out his original mission. His adventure is known from Byron's poem *The Island* and from a trilogy of novels by Charles Nordhoff and James Norman Hall, beginning with MUTINY ON THE BOUNTY.

Blind Bard or **Poet.** An epithet frequently applied to Homer. The tradition of Homer's blindness may possibly be related to that of DEMODOCUS, the blind rhapsode at the court of Alcinous in the *Odyssey*.

Blind Harry. See HENRY THE MINSTREL.

Bliss (1920). A short story by Katherine MANSFIELD. It describes a blissful afternoon and evening in the life of Bertha Young, who loves her husband, her baby and her home. In Mansfield's typically ironic ending, Bertha discovers that her husband is being unfaithful to her.

Blithedale Romance, The (1852). A novel by Nathaniel HAWTHORNE. Blithedale, a Utopian community, is modeled on BROOK FARM, the Transcendentalist experiment at West Roxbury, Mass., in which Hawthorne had participated 10 years before he wrote the novel. Miles Coverdale, the narrator, is a coldly inquisitive observer; in revealing his knowledge of the other members of the community, he reveals himself. Zenobia, a dark, queenly woman, is in love with Hollingsworth, an egoistic reformer who plans to convert Blithedale into an experiment in prison reform.

Priscilla, a pale innocent girl, fallen under the evil influence of the mesmerist Westervelt, has performed as the Veiled Lady. Taking refuge at Blithedale, she is revealed to be the half-sister of Zenobia. When Hollingsworth admits his love for Priscilla, Zenobia drowns herself. Hollingsworth, shocked by the experience, abandons his schemes, depending on Priscilla for strength. Coverdale, in the final chapter, admits that he, too, had always loved Priscilla. See Margaret FULLER.

Blitzkrieg (*Ger.*, "lightning warfare"). A form of large-scale surprise attack involving motorized forces with air support, developed by Germany in World War II.

Blitzstein, Marc (1905–1964). American composer and playwright. He is known for his experimentation with formal technique and his use of proletarian themes. *The Cradle Will Rock* (1937), an experimental play with music on the capital-labor theme, is his best-known work. He also wrote *I've Got the Tune* (1937), a radio song-play, *No for an Answer* (1941), and the libretto for the American adaptation of Bertolt Brecht and Kurt Weill's *Threepenny Opera*.

Blixen, Baroness **Karen.** See Isak DINESEN.

Bloch, Ernest (1880–1959). Swiss-born composer. Many of his works have a Hebraic flavor derived from traditional Jewish melodies and modes, such as his cello rhapsody, *Schelomo* (1916). His *Concerto Grosso No. 1* (1925) is a typical example of the return to old forms engendered by neoclassicism.

Bloch-Michel, Jean (1912–   ). French novelist. Active in the Resistance movement, Bloch-Michel worked on the journal *Combat* during the Liberation years. His novels are similar in spirit to the work of Albert Camus: sober, stoical, and grimly honest about the human condition. *Les Grandes Circonstances* (1949), *Journal du désordre* (1955), and *Un Homme estimable* (1956) are among his works.

Blok, Aleksandr Aleksandrovich (1880–1921). Russian poet. The greatest of the Russian SYMBOLISTS, he is generally ranked as one of the half-dozen major poets in Russian literature. Blok's early poems *Songs of the Beautiful Lady* (*Stikhi o prekrasnoi damye*; 1904) are hymns to a mystical vision of Sophia, a tendency originating with the philosopher Vladimir SOLOVIOV that played a large role in Russian symbolist poetry. Blok's loss of faith in his mystical experience of the eternal feminine was reflected in later poetry and plays, which grew increasingly bitter, gloomy, and ironic. In his lyrical drama, *The Puppet Show* (*Balaganchik*; 1905) he ridiculed his former beliefs. Another play, *The Stranger* (*Neznakomka*; 1906), depicts the former Beautiful Lady as a common prostitute. A poem of this title, written at the same time, expresses Blok's wish to escape the pain of his disappointment in drink. He also attempted to find solace in love affairs although toward the end of his life he claimed that he had had only two loves in his life: his wife Lyubov (a daughter of the scientist Mendeleyev) "and all the others."

Blok's masterpiece is his long poem THE TWELVE, an impressionistic picture of St. Petersberg during the early days of the revolution. Another well-known work is *The Scythians* (*Skify;* 1918), an address of both challenge and proffered friendship to the West from the new revolutionary Russia. Blok worked on a long autobiographical poem, *Retribution* (*Vozmezdiye*), from 1910 until his death, completing one chapter and parts of two others.

Blok's standing as one of the greatest Russian poets is based on a large body of lyrics, several excellent verse dramas, and his long poem *The Twelve*. His importance as an innovator in Russian prosody is also great. He created the new accentual verse in Russian known as *dolniki*, which is based only on the number of stresses per line, allowing any number of unstressed syllables between the stresses. This break with the classic prosody of syllabic-accentual verse, which took into account both stressed and unstressed syllables, introduced a new freedom into modern Russian poetry, which was used to good account by later poets such as Mayakovski, Esenin, and Anna Akhmatova.

Blood and Iron (*Ger.*, "Blut und Eisen"). A phrase used by BISMARCK at a meeting with members of the Reichstag (1862), to describe his political policies. He said, "The great questions of the day will not be settled by resolutions and majority votes, . . . but by blood and iron."

Blood Wedding. See Federico GARCÍA LORCA.

Bloody Assizes. The popular name for the trials conducted in England in 1685 by Lord Chief Justice George JEFFREYS after the collapse of Monmouth's Rebellion. Hundreds of both actual and presumed supporters of the duke of MONMOUTH were executed or sold into West-Indian slavery. The trials, which were brief, brutal, and flagrantly unjust, became a byword for relentless cruelty.

Bloody Mary. See MARY I.

Bloom, Hyman (1913–   ). Latvian-born American painter. He is known for his hypnotic, horrifying pictures.

Bloom, Leopold. The central character in James Joyce's novel ULYSSES. Bloom is an advertising canvasser of Jewish origin, living in Dublin. He is an unheroic but affirmative character, whose wanderings about Dublin are ironically contrasted with the epic voyage of Ulysses. Humane and generous, self-conscious and guilt-ridden, throughout the book his quest for love is frustrated and his best instincts are stifled. Only through his daydreams does Bloom find fulfillment as a social, political, and ethical human being. His rejection by Ireland may thus be seen as Joyce's indictment of a culture that is only artificially civilized. Symbolically, he is linked to a variety of literary and historical figures, among them, Elijah, Moses, and Christ.

Bloom, Molly. One of the three chief characters in James Joyce's novel ULYSSES. She is the wife of Leopold Bloom, to whom she is unfaithful. A sardonic counterpart of Penelope in the *Odyssey*, she is a sensual, intuitive woman, for Joyce a symbol of the universal feminine principle. The final section of the novel consists of her famous stream-of-consciousness monologue: a single, uninterrupted sentence ending in an affirmative of life, "Yes."

Bloomsbury group. The name given to a group of English writers, artists, and philosophers who began to meet about 1906. They include the writers Virginia and Leonard WOOLF, E. M. FORSTER, and Lytton STRACHEY; the artists and art critics Roger FRY and Vanessa and Clive Bell; the economist John Maynard KEYNES; and the philosopher Bertrand RUSSELL. Bloomsbury was then an artistic, Bohemian section of London.

Blot in the 'Scutcheon, A (1843). A poetic drama by Robert BROWNING. Thorold, Earl Tresham, boasts that no blot has ever stained his noble family's escutcheon. Henry, Earl Mertoun, who is Thorold's neighbor, asks permission to marry Thorold's young sister Mildred. Thorold, unaware that Mertoun has already seduced Mildred, consents; but when he learns the truth he is beside himself with fury and shame. He kills Mertoun and poisons himself; Mildred dies soon after.

Bloudy Tenent, The (1644). A tract pleading for religious toleration, written by Roger WILLIAMS during a controversy with John COTTON. Its full title is *The Bloudy Tenent of Persecution, for Cause of Conscience, Discussed in a Conference between Truth and Peace*. It urges freedom of belief for Catholics, Jews, and pagans, as well as for Protestants. An advocate of democracy in government, Williams also declared that the "foundation of civill power lies in the people." Cotton wrote a reply entitled *The Bloudy Tenent, Washed, and Made White in the Bloud of the Lamb* (1647). Williams rejoined with *The Bloudy Tenent Yet More Bloudy by Mr. Cotton's Endeavour to Wash it White in the Bloud of the Lamb* (1652), in which he reaffirmed that each man must believe what his conscience tells him. Both writings are considered to be among the

most forceful and eloquent prose written in the American colonies in the 17th century.

Bloy, Léon [Marie] (1846–1917). French novelist and essayist. Bloy was a Catholic author who attacked contemporary society and prophesied an impending transformation in *Le Salut par les Juifs* (1892), *La Femme Pauvre* (1897), *Le Pélerin de l'absolu* (*Pilgrim of the Absolute*, 1914).

Bluebeard. The villain of the tale *Barbe-bleue* (1697) by Charles PERRAULT in his CONTES DE MA MÈRE L'OYE. Bluebeard entrusts the keys of his castle to each of his new brides in turn with the warning not to open a door behind which, unknown to them, are strewn the bodies of his previous wives. None can restrain her curiosity, and Bluebeard murders six wives for their disobedience before the seventh bride has the good fortune to escape him. Based on the crimes of the murderer Gilles de RETZ, the Bluebeard story has been the basis for numerous burlesques and dramatizations. Maurice Maeterlinck made it the subject of his *Ariane et Barbe-bleue* (1901).

Béla BARTÓK's opera *Duke Bluebeard's Castle* (1911) was composed to a libretto by Béla Balász in which the horrific elements of the tale were minimized and Bluebeard became a discontented, searching philosopher. Jacques OFFENBACH's operetta *Barbe-Bleue* (1866) was a rollicking burlesque, based only loosely on the Bluebeard theme.

blue flower (Ger., *blaue Blume*). A symbol in Novalis' novel HEINRICH VON OFTERDINGEN. It was later taken by a number of authors, including Heine in his *Die romantische Schule* (*The Romantic School*, 1833), as the representative symbol of all German romanticism. At the beginning of Novalis' novel young Heinrich is filled with a longing whose actual object he does not yet know, and the blue flower appears to him in a dream as the fulfillment of this longing. Thus, basically, it symbolizes the yearning for an ideal so distant that one does not yet know what it is, the romantic yearning for infinity. Novalis might have been thinking of the blue haze of distance when he chose the color of the flower.

Blue Hotel, The (1899). A short story by Stephen CRANE. First published in the volume *The Monster and Other Stories*, it is one of Crane's finest works. In the story, a Swede comes to a Nebraska hotel with his mind filled with the romantic violence of Western dime novels. Expecting the same violence, he finally causes a fight, leaves the hotel, and is killed in another argument in a bar. The story dramatizes the question of who was responsible for the Swede's death. Although one of the characters remarks, "Every sin is the result of a collaboration," the actual point of the story is not the moral complicity of the characters but rather the inexplicable mystery of a universe which, like the blizzard that rages throughout the story, cares nothing for the trials of mankind.

blue laws. The name given to all statutory regulations of personal conduct in matters of conscience. While the term has no technical legal meaning, it is also used to describe the severe laws passed at various times and places in colonial America, whose object was to stamp out "heresy," enforce a strict observance of the Sabbath, and even regulate kissing between husbands and wives. "Blue laws" may also refer to Puritan legislation in England. Connecticut, because of an especially rigid group of laws passed at New Haven in 1732, is sometimes called the *Blue Law State*.

blues. Negro folk songs, distinguished by certain expressive out-of-tune notes, called "blue notes," by their prevailing melancholy (though often ironically humorous), and by their unique poetic and musical form. The latter is as simple as it is effective: within each three-line stanza the first two lines are approximately the same; the third line resolves the tension caused by this repetition. Each line is followed by a brief musical interlude. Some poets have consciously imitated this form, notably Langston Hughes.

Blues and Grays. In the American Civil War, the Union and Confederate forces respectively, from the color of their uniforms. *The Blue and the Gray* (1867), a sentimental poem by Francis Miles Finch which was often recited at Memorial Day ceremonies, was inspired by women in Columbus, Miss., who strewed flowers over the graves of both Union and Confederate dead.

bluestocking. A female pedant, a woman of pretentious intellectual and literary interests. The term was originally applied (c. 1750) to meetings which took place at the home of Elizabeth MONTAGU, where literary discussions replaced cards and gossip. Among the guests was Benjamin Stillingfleet who always wore blue stockings (instead of the customary white for formal wear). It is in reference to him that the group—and later any group like it—came to be called derisively "the Bluestocking Club."

Blue Voyage, The (1927). A novel by Conrad AIKEN. It describes the people and incidents of a transatlantic voyage, largely in the stream-of-consciousness technique.

Blum, Léon (1872-1950). French statesman and political leader. Leader of the Socialist party (from 1919) and editor of its newspaper *Le Populaire,* Blum first served as premier in a Popular Front government (June 4, 1936–June 21, 1937). He carried through radical reforms in banking, labor, and agriculture. For brief periods in 1938 and 1946–1947, Blum again occupied the office of premier. Arrested by the Vichy government, he was imprisoned in a German concentration camp but released in 1945 by the Allies.

Blunden, Edmund (1896-   ). English poet and critic. Associated with the GEORGIAN poets, he served in World War I, receiving the Military Cross; *Undertones of War* (1928) is a major book of wartime reminiscence. His volumes of poems include *The Shepherd* (1922), *Shells by a Stream* (1944), and *A Hong Kong House* (1962).

Blunderhead, Simpkin. See Christopher ANSTEY.

Blunt, Wilfrid Scawen (1840-1922). English poet, author, diplomat, and explorer. Blunt traveled in a diplomatic and private capacity throughout Europe, the Near East, and India. He was bitterly opposed to 19th-century British policies of imperialism and exploitation, and once served a prison term for an inflammatory speech in Ireland. His best poems, a few lyrics from *Love Sonnets of Proteus* (1880) and *A New Pilgrimage* (1889), survive through their genuine force, pathos, and subtlety.

Blunt also wrote long political poems, such as *The Wind and the Whirlwind* (1883) and *Satan Absolved* (1899). Of his numerous prose works—mostly dealing with injustices of the British Empire—the most interesting are the famous *My Diaries, 1888–1914* (1920–1921), which were withdrawn by their publisher because of their revelations of British secret diplomacy. *The Poetical Works* (two volumes). appeared in 1914.

Blut und Eisen. See BLOOD AND IRON.

Bly, Nelly. See Elizabeth Cochrane SEAMAN.

Boadicea (d. A.D. 62). Celtic queen of the Iceni, Britons of Norfolk and Suffolk. Also known as the Warrior Queen, she rebelled against Roman rule, taking poison after being defeated in battle when the revolt was quelled.

Boanerges (Gr., "sons of thunder"). Christ's name (Mark 3:17) for his disciples James and John, because they wanted to call "fire to come down from heaven" to consume the Samaritans for not "receiving" Jesus (Luke 9:54).

Boar's Head Tavern. A London tavern. It was made immortal by Shakespeare in HENRY IV, as the favorite haunt of Prince Hal and Sir John Falstaff. The tavern was located in Eastcheap, on the site of the present statue of William IV, and was in existence until 1831.

Boaz. See RUTH.

Bobadil, Captain. A character in Ben Jonson's comedy EVERY MAN IN HIS HUMOUR. A military braggart, he is an ignorant, clever bully, completely cowardly, but thought by his dupes to be an amazing hero.

bobby. A London policeman. This slang word is probably derived from Sir Robert PEEL who was home secretary when the new Metropolitan Police Act was passed in 1828. Bobbies were also known as "peelers," a name originally applied to the Irish constabulary established by Peel.

Boccaccio, Giovanni (1313-1375). Italian prose writer and poet. He was born at Certaldo (or possibly, as he hinted in one of his works, at Paris) and spent part of his youth at Naples (1327-1341). He enjoyed fashionable Neapolitan society, but not his father's merchant trade and the study of the law. From 1341 to his death he was mainly at Florence, where he pursued his chosen career as a man of letters. His prolific output, including many works of prose and poetry that were the first of their kind in Italian or European literature, entitle him to a place beside Petrarch as a founder of the Italian Renaissance. His scholarly works in Latin were written mainly towards the end of his life, when a spiritual crisis persuaded him to reject all vernacular writing as sinful. While not enjoying the popularity of his earlier efforts, these Latin works, with their interest in classical antiquity, were seminal in the growth of Humanism. Of the same order are his attempts to have Homer translated and made more accessible at a time when few knew Greek. On the recommendation of his close friend Petrarch, he supported an incompetent Greek scholar in his own home until a bad translation was completed. Still loyal to the vernacular tradition, he also lectured on Dante and wrote a eulogy of him during that final period.

His works and their chronological order are as

follows: *Caccia di Diana* (*Diana's Hunt*), the first Italian hunting poem in terza rima, written 1334–1336; the prose romance FILOCOLO, including the THIRTEEN QUESTIONS OF LOVE; the FILOSTRATO, a romance in ottava rima and the first of its kind written by a man of letters; the TESEIDA, in octaves, the first Tuscan epic; the *Ameto* (1341–1342), a prose romance with pastoral setting and characters; the *Amoroso Visione* (1342–1343), an allegorical poem in *terzine;* FIAMMETTA, a psychological romance whose heroine may be a real woman (see MARIA D'AQUINO) or the poetic equivalent of Beatrice and Laura; the *Ninfale Fiesolano* (1346), the first Italian idyll, done in octaves; the DECAMERON, his most famous work. His last Italian works (1355–1375) were the *Corbaccio* (1366), a satire against women; the eulogy of Dante; and a commentary on the *Divine Comedy.* The Latin works of the final period were *De Casibus Virorum Illustrium* (*The Fate of Illustrious Men*); *De Claris Mulieribus* (*On Famous Women*); and *De Genealogiis Deorum Gentilium* (*Genealogies of the Pagan Gods*), whose 13th book contains a defense of poetry.

Boccalini, Traiano (1556–1613). Italian satirist. His *Ragguagli di Parnaso* (*Dispatches from Parnassus,* 1612–1614), literary and political satires, were popular and widely influential in 17th-century Europe because of their literary topicality and their anti-Spanish, prorepublican sentiments.

Bocksgesang. See GOAT SONG.

Bodenheim, Maxwell (1893–1954). American poet and novelist. One of the most notorious of the Bohemians who came to Greenwich Village during the 1920's, Bodenheim in his early work was influenced by the romanticists and imagists, but later, for example in his novel *Lights in the Valley* (1942), he espoused various proletarian causes. Among his volumes of poetry are *Introducing Irony* (1922), *Bringing Jazz* (1930), and *Selected Poems, 1914–1944* (1946). *Crazy Man* (1924), *Sixty Seconds* (1929), and *Naked on Roller Skates* (1929) are novels. Bodenheim carried on several feuds with his literary contemporaries, the most famous one being with Ben HECHT. In 1954 he and his third wife were found murdered in a dingy, heatless room.

bodhisattva (*Sans.,* "being of wisdom"). In Buddhism one who has attained the status of a Buddha but who postpones his entry to Buddhahood in order to assist others in their quest for the Truth.

Bodin, Jean (1530–1596). French lawyer and political philosopher. He is noted for his *Six Books of a Republic* (1576) and his *Method for the Easy Comprehension of History* (1566). Almost alone among 16th-century thinkers, Bodin attempted to devise a comprehensive theory of political society. He strove to discover some principle of order and unity that would reconcile liberty and subjection, yet satisfy conscience and reason, without regard to divine or supernatural sanction. Two principles are evident in his political philosophy. In the attempt to find a principle of order, he defined political sovereignty in terms of power, that is, he defined the state in terms of a relation between political inferiors and a political superior, and law as a command from the latter to the former. And in the hope of resting this structure on grounds consonant with conscience, he affirmed the principle of natural law as an ethical and authoritative foundation for political power: both the Sovereign, or political superior, and the subject, or political inferior, were bound by natural law; the Sovereign to command in accordance with justice, the subject to obey in accordance with justice. These two tendencies in his thought were, however, not adequately drawn together, and consequently, each strain was given separate and definitive formulation later. Bodin's theory of sovereignty was systematically developed by HOBBES; his conception of natural law as an ethical foundation for the state, by GROTIUS and LOCKE.

Bodkin, Maud (1875–   ). English scholar. She applied Jung's psychoanalysis to literary criticism in her influential study, *Archetypal Patterns in Poetry* (1934).

Bodleian library. A celebrated library at Oxford University in England. Projected by Sir Thomas Bodly in 1598, it was opened in 1602. It is famous for its collection of rare books and valuable manuscripts.

Bodmer, Johann Jakob (1698–1783). Swiss scholar and critic. He was a translator of Milton and a patron of Klopstock and Wieland. A strong opponent of GOTTSCHED, he is most famous for his editions of medieval German literature, such as *Parcival* (the *Parzival* of Wolfram von Eschenbach, 1753) and *Fabeln aus dem Zeitpunkte der Minnesinger* (*Stories from the Time of the Minnesingers,* 1757), including the *Nibelungenlied.*

Body of Liberties, The (1641). A code of laws for the government of the Massachusetts colony, combining the common law of England with the Mosaic law. Prepared by a committee led by Nathaniel WARD, it is ranked by some critics with the Magna Charta and the Bill of Rights in its recognition of fundamental human rights. In 1648 an enlarged code was published under the title of *The Laws and Liberties of Massachusetts.*

body snatcher. See RESURRECTION MAN.

Boece (probably 1381 or 1382). A prose translation by Geoffrey CHAUCER of the CONSOLATION OF PHILOSOPHY by Boethius.

Boehme, Jakob. See Jakob BÖHME.

Boeotian. A rude, unlettered person; a dull blockhead. The ancient Boeotians loved agricultural and pastoral pursuits, so the Athenians used to say they were as dull and thick as their own atmosphere. On the other hand, Hesiod, Pindar, Corinna, Pelopidas, Epaminondas, and Plutarch were all Boeotians.

Boer War (1899–1902). The usual name for the war between Great Britain and the joint forces of the Transvaal Republic and the Orange Free State. The war was the culmination of a long-standing conflict between the British and the Boers (South Africans of Dutch descent), both of whom had interests in South Africa. The immediate cause of the war was Great Britain's refusal to withdraw troops stationed in Transvaal. The Boers had considerable success in the beginning of the war, but soon gave way to Britain's superior force. The war ended with the fall of Pretoria (1900) and organized Boer resistance disappeared. Peace was not formally arrived at until 1902.

Boethius, [Anicius Manlius Severinus] (c. 480–c. 524). Roman philosopher. Appointed in 510, he served as consul under Theodoric the Great, until he was accused of treason and executed. Boethius is best known for his famous work, THE CONSOLATION OF PHILOSOPHY, written while he was imprisoned, awaiting final sentence. He also translated works by Aristotle and the neo-Platonist Porphyry, and wrote a number of philosophical treatises, especially on logic, which became textbooks for the Schoolmen of the Middle Ages and their major source of knowledge about the thinkers of antiquity.

Boffin, Nicodemus. In Charles Dickens' OUR MUTUAL FRIEND, the kindly "olden dustman," residuary legatee of John Harmon. He pretends that his inheritance has made him miserly and hardhearted, but actually he is keeping the fortune for young John Harmon, the rightful heir.

Bogan, Louise (1897–1970). American poet and critic. Miss Bogan's poetry, subtle and intellectual, shows the influence of the English metaphysical poets. Her work has appeared in *Body of This Death* (1923), *Dark Summer* (1929), *Sleeping Fury* (1937), and *Collected Poems* (a co-winner of the Bollingen Prize, 1954). A poetry reviewer for *The New Yorker*, Miss Bogan has also written the well-received *Achievement in American Poetry, 1900–1950* (1951) and *Selected Criticism: Poetry and Prose* (1955).

Bohème, La (1896). An opera by Giacomo PUCCINI. It is based upon Henri Murger's *Vie de Bohème* (1848). The story deals with the love affair of Rodolfo, a poet, and Mimi, a Paris seamstress, as well as with Rodolfo's penniless friends and the ups and downs of artist life in the Latin Quarter. Mimi is ill and finally dies.

Bohemian. A term applied to literary men and artists of loose and unconventional habits living on what they can pick up on their wits. Originally the name was applied to the gypsies, from the belief that before they appeared in Western Europe they had lived in Bohemia, or because the first who arrived in France came by way of Bohemia (1427). When they presented themselves before the gates of Paris they were not allowed to enter the city, but were lodged at La Chapelle, St. Denis.

Böhl de Faber, Cecilia. See Fernán CABALLERO.

Böhme or **Boehme, Jakob** (1575–1624). German mystic. His thought is often termed nature mysticism because of his belief in the unity of nature as a vehicle for immediate contemplation of the divinity and because of his concept of natural language (*lingua adamica*) as the language of the Holy Ghost. Böhme, who was a shoemaker by trade, thought of his ideas as a development of Protestantism, but found himself under attack by the Protestant as well as the Catholic clergy. His most famous works are *Aurora oder die Morgenröte im Aufgang* (*Aurora, or the Rising Dawn,* 1612), *Beschreibung der drei Prinzipien gottlichen Wesens* (*Description of the Three Principles of Divine Essence,* 1619), and *Mysterium Magnum* (1623). He was of great influence on subsequent German thought, especially in the movement of romanticism.

Bohn, Henry George (1796–1884). English publisher. His Bohn's Libraries of standard works at cheap prices became famous.

Boiardo or **Bojardo, Matteo Maria.** Count of **Scandiano** (1441–1494). Italian poet at the ducal court of Ferrara. While serving the Este family as their regent for Modena and Reggio, he composed love poems and his famous romantic epic, ORLANDO INNAMORATO (*Roland Enamoured*). It was left unfinished at his death, then taken up and continued by ARIOSTO in his ORLANDO FURIOSO (*Roland Mad*).

Boileau[-Despréaux], Nicholas (1636–1711). French poet and critic. He was one of the earliest and most characteristic of the neoclassicists, who urged prudence, moderation, common sense, and obedience to authority in the writing of literature. In his *Satires* (1666) he imitated Horace and Juvenal and attacked the social and literary foibles of his day, while his LE LUTRIN is a mock epic in the manner of Pope's *Rape of the Lock*. His chief work is *Art Poétique* (1674), in which he formulated in verse the literary principles that were dominant throughout the 18th century. Known as *le législateur du Parnasse* ("the legislator of Parnassus"), Boileau greatly influenced his friends and literary associates, who included Racine, Molière, and La Fontaine.

Bois de Boulogne. A large park west of Paris, France. It contains the famous race tracks of Longchamp and Auteuil. Parisians call it simply *le Bois*.

Bois-Guilbert, Sir Brian de. In Scott's IVANHOE, the violent preceptor of the Knights Templars, who first insults Rebecca, then rescues her from a burning castle. When Rebecca is charged with sorcery, she demands a trial by combat, and Sir Brian is appointed to sustain the charge against her, while Ivanhoe is her champion. Sir Brian is found mysteriously dead in the lists, and Rebecca is declared innocent.

Boisrobert, François de (1592–1662). French playwright. With the exception of *La Belle Plaideuse* (*The Beautiful Litigant,* 1654), a depiction of the Parisian life of the time, his comedies and tragicomedies are today largely forgotten. One of the original members of the Académie Française and one of Richelieu's *cinq auteurs*, he generously employed his influence with the cardinal to the advantage of other writers.

Boito, Arrigo (1842–1918). Italian poet, librettist, and composer. Strongly influenced by the romantic cult of the Middle Ages, he wrote verse which linked an antiquarian's interest in medieval lore with a moralist's preoccupation with the Faust-like struggle of good and evil in the individual. A member of the SCAPIGLIATURA group of writers, he published his collected verse in *Il Libro dei Versi* (1877). A legend in verse, *Re Orso*, was published the same year.

Boito wrote the music and libretti for *Mefistofele* (1868) and *Nerone,* first presented at La Scala in 1924. An admirer of Shakespeare, he wrote excellent libretti for Verdi's *Otello* (1885) and *Falstaff* (1893). He based his libretto for Ponchielli's *La Gioconda* (1879) on Hugo's *Angelo,* but used a pen name, apparently embarrassed over its old-fashioned melodrama.

Bojer, Johan (1872–1959). Norwegian novelist. A popular writer outside his own country, Bojer enjoyed a prolific literary career. His best known work in English translation is *The Great Hunger* (*Den store hunger;* 1916). More valuable for their artistic merit are his sensitive and powerful novels of peasant life: *Den siste viking* (1921) and *Folk ved sjøen* (*Folks by the Sea*, 1929).

Bok, Edward W[illiam] (1863–1930). Dutch-born American editor. Under his 30-year stewardship (1889–1919), the *Ladies' Home Journal* exerted great influence on the American home, and Bok made it the vehicle for his campaigns on behalf of world peace and against billboards and the common drinking cup. His autobiography, *The Americanization of Edward Bok* (1920), won a Pulitzer Prize.

Boldrewood, Rolf. See Thomas Alexander Browne.

Bolerium. In ancient geography, Land's End.

Boleyn, Anne. See Anne Boleyn.

Bolingbroke, Viscount. See Henry St. John.

Bolívar, Simón. Known as **El Libertador** (1783–1830). Venezuelan revolutionary leader and statesman. The scion of a wealthy Creole family, Bolívar was educated largely in Europe, where he absorbed the ideas of the Enlightenment and fell under the spell of Napoleon's reputation. During a visit to Rome, it is said, he vowed on the Aventine hill to free America from Spanish domination. Upon his return to Venezuela in 1810, he plunged into the separatist movement and emerged as its leader by 1813. Undismayed by numerous setbacks, he declared a war to extinction and won the independence of Colombia at the battle of Boyacá and that of Venezuela at the battle of Carabobo. The two regions, together with Ecuador, were incorporated in the republic of Gran Colombia with Bolívar as president.

After his famous meeting with San Martín at Guayaquil, Bolívar proceeded to Peru, most of which was still controlled by Spain. Bolívar's victory at Junín and that of his chief lieutenant, Antonio José de Sucre, at Ayacucho virtually ended Spanish resistance to the independence movement. He approved the creation of an independent republic, which was named Bolivia in his honor, in the region of Upper Peru and wrote a constitution for it embodying his republican, though authoritarian, principles. One of the first advocates of hemispheric solidarity, Bolívar sponsored a congress of American states in Panama (1826). Although unsuccessful, the congress is regarded as the forerunner of the contemporary Pan-American movement. Bolívar's last years were embittered by disputes with his former associates and by the disintegration of Gran Colombia; in 1828 he barely escaped assassination in Bogotá.

Because of the vigor and lucidity of his prose, Bolívar is considered an important figure in Latin-American literature. One of his best-known works is his letter from Jamaica (1815), an analysis of conditions in South America and a political program for the future. Another is his address to the congress of Angostura (now Ciudad Bolívar, Venezuela; 1818), in which he outlined a constitution for Gran Colombia that would provide order with freedom.

Bolkonski, Prince Andrei. One of the central characters of Count Leo Tolstoi's novel War and Peace. In his unhappy first marriage, Prince Andrei was arrogant and cynical. The loss of Natasha, whom he loves, causes him to take on a new fierceness in the war with Napoleon. He and Natasha fall in love again after she nurses his wounds received at Borodino, but he dies as a result of these wounds.

Böll, Heinrich (1917–   ). German novelist and short-story writer. Most of his writing was done after World War II. The religious and moral principles on which his critical attitude toward modern society is based are set forth in his *Brief an einen jungen Katholiken* (*Letter to a Young Catholic*, 1958). His best known novels are *Und sagte kein einziges Wort* (*And Did Not Say a Single Word*, 1953) and *Billard um halbzehn* (*Billiards at Nine-Thirty*, 1959). In 1972 he won the Nobel Prize in literature.

Bollingen Prize. An annual award in poetry. First given in 1949 under the auspices of the Library of Congress, the award was supported by the Bollingen Foundation, a philanthropic trust created by Paul Mellon. A distinguished board of writers gave the first award to Ezra Pound for his Pisan Cantos, causing a lengthy and bitter controversy. The debate centered on whether the political and social views of a poet should affect an appraisal of his work, and thereafter the Bollingen Foundation canceled further prizes. In 1950, however, it was announced that the Bollingen Prize in poetry would be awarded by Yale University Library. Since then, distinguished living poets have been given the prize annually. Among the recipients are Wallace Stevens, Marianne Moore, E. E. Cummings, and Yvor Winters.

Bolshevik or **Bolshevist.** A member of the Russian revolutionary party headed by Lenin that seized power in October, 1917. The origin of the term was the congress of the Russian Social Democratic Party in London in 1903, when Lenin's radical wing of the party prevailed in a dispute, and the name *Bolshevik* was adopted by the group. The word comes from the Russian word *bolshe*, meaning "larger," while the name *Menshevik* adopted by the contending faction comes from *menshe*, "smaller."

Bona Dea (*Lat.*, "good goddess"). A Roman goddess of fertility and chastity, worshipped exclusively by women. She was the female counterpart of Faunus and was sometimes called Fauna. It was the rites of the Bona Dea that Clodius Pulcher profaned.

Bonaparte, Napoleon. See Napoleon.

Bonarelli, Guidobaldo (1553–1608). Italian dramatist. He wrote a famous pastoral play, *Filli di Sciro* (1607), which was translated into English as *Phyllis of Scyros*.

Bonario. A young soldier disinherited by his avaricious father, Corbaccio, in Jonson's comedy Volpone, or the Fox. His own blustering honesty proves to be his greatest disadvantage when he fights for his rights against such subtle rogues as Volpone and his own father.

Bonaventura. The pseudonym of the author of the German romantic novel *Die Nachtwachen des Bonaventura* (*The Night-Watches of Bonaventura*, 1805). The book is a witty and ironic account of the experiences of an ex-poet who has taken work as a town's night watchman in order to observe men without their deceptive, daytime façades. The author was probably Friedrich Gottlieb Wetzel (1779–1819), an otherwise insignificant poet.

Bonaventure or **Bonaventura, St.** Originally **Giovanni di Fidanza** (c. 1221–1274). Italian theologian, mystic, and scholastic philosopher, called the

"Seraphic Doctor." A Franciscan, he placed more emphasis on faith and less on reason than St. Thomas Aquinas, and is best known for his *The Journey of the Mind to God (Itinerarium Mentis ad Deum)*. This, like his other works, explains that the direct contemplation of God is the goal of all the arts and sciences; philosophy's task is to discern intimations of God first in the external world, then in the soul itself, which is the image of God, and thus to prepare the mind for its ultimate mystic union with God. Bonaventure furthered the cult of the Virgin Mary, and wrote lives of Christ and St. Francis of Assisi, as well as the treatises *Breviloquium, Soliloquium,* and *De Reductione Artium ad Theologiam*.

Bond, James. The tough hero of popular novels of espionage by Ian FLEMING.

Bonhomme Richard. The French form of Benjamin Franklin's pseudonym, Richard SAUNDERS. It is also the name of John Paul JONES's famous man-of-war, a refitted French vessel, which was rechristened in Franklin's honor.

Bonjour Tristesse (1954). A short novel by Françoise SAGAN about teenage Cécile's jealous and tragic plot to prevent her father's remarriage by scheming with his mistress and her own lover.

Bonnard, Sylvestre. See CRIME OF SYLVESTRE BONNARD, THE.

Bonnefoy, Yves (1923–   ). French poet and critic. Bonnefoy is concerned with the mystic role of words in trying to immobilize experience in art. His poetry, imagistic and hermetic, includes *Du Mouvement et de l'immobilité de Douve* (1953), *Hier régnant désert* (1958), and *Pierre écrite* (1959).

bonnet rouge. The red cap of liberty worn in 1789 by the most fanatical French revolutionaries. It was officially adopted by the Commune in 1792, and is the emblem of red republicanism. The cap seems to have been derived from the Phrygian cap (see LIBERTY CAP) given to the freed slaves of Greece and Rome, and from the *bonnet rouge* worn by convicts. See CARMAGNOLE.

Bonnie Prince Charlie. See PRETENDER.

Bonnivard, François de (1495–1570). Genevan prelate and politician. He appears in idealized form as the hero of Lord Byron's THE PRISONER OF CHILLON.

bonsai. Japanese dwarf trees. Potted, they are stunted and trained, and attain great age.

bonseki. Japanese tray landscapes.

Bonus Army. A so-called army of unemployed U.S. World War I veterans. They came to Washington in 1932 to try to persuade Congress to vote immediate payment of the bonus due them in 1945 through the World War Adjusted Compensation Act of 1925. The men camped near the Capitol, picketed the Congressional buildings, and were finally dispersed with tear gas. The bonus was finally given in 1936.

bonze. The European name for the Buddhist clergy of the Far East, particularly Japan.

Booby, Lady. In Henry Fielding's novel JOSEPH ANDREWS, a vulgar upstart who tries to seduce her footman, Joseph Andrews. She is a foil to Parson ADAMS as well as a caricature of Samuel Richardson's PAMELA.

Book of Changes (I-ching). One of the Chinese FIVE CLASSICS. A divination manual adopted into the Confucian canon, it contains mystical speculations and is the subject of numerous commentaries. See Richard Wilhelm, *The I-ching or Book of Changes* (1950).

Book of Documents (Shu-ching). One of the Chinese FIVE CLASSICS. The first Chinese work of history, it contains speeches, pronouncements, and treatises dating to the Chou dynasty (1027–256 B.C.). The language is obscure and much of the text is of doubtful authenticity. See Bernhard Karlgren, *The Book of Documents* (1950).

Book of Marriage, The (1926). A symposium on the subject of marriage with Count Hermann Alexander KEYSERLING as editor and chief contributor. George Bernard Shaw declined to participate because he felt that no man can tell the truth about marriage while his wife is alive.

Book of Martyrs, The. The popular title given to John FOXE's *Actes and Monuments* (1563).

Book of Odes (Shih-ching). One of the Chinese FIVE CLASSICS. The first collection of poetry, it contains some 305 songs and was compiled around 600 B.C. See Arthur Waley, *The Book of Songs* (2d ed., 1954).

Book of Rites (Li-chi). One of the Chinese FIVE CLASSICS. A compilation of the first century B.C., it is composed of various older texts dealing with music, ritual practice, education, and other subjects. It is traditionally but inaccurately attributed to the disciples of Confucius.

Book of the Dead. A collection of magic incantations, prayers, and exorcisms, used in the religion of ancient Egypt as a guidebook for the dead on their journey through the underworld. Though not exactly such, it has been described by some as the Egyptian Bible.

Book of the Duchess, The (1369). A poem by Geoffrey CHAUCER, of 1335 lines in octosyllabic couplets. Based largely on French sources, particularly the *Roman de la Rose* and several works of Guillaume de Machaut, it was almost certainly written as an elegy on the occasion of the death of Blanche of Lancaster, first wife of Chaucer's patron, John of Gaunt. The poet reads the story of HALCYON AND CEYX until he falls asleep. Then he dreams of

A vignette from a *Book of the Dead*. The god Anubis weighs the dead man's tongue against his soul.

joining a hunt and meeting a knight in black, who laments the way Fortune has beaten him at the game of life by introducing him to a most perfect lady, letting him marry her and live with her in bliss, then snatching her away in death.

Book of Thel, The (1789). The first of William BLAKE's mystical writings known collectively as his prophetic books. Its theme is death, redemption, and eternity. It is written in free verse.

Boone, Daniel (1734–1820). American frontiersman. He is known for his exploration and settlement of Kentucky and has been celebrated by a number of American and English writers, including Cooper and Byron in *Don Juan* (1823). His adventures were popularized in the supposedly autobiographical account included in *Discovery, Settlement and Present State of Kentucky* (1784), written by John Filson, and have passed into American folklore.

Boötes (*Gr.,* "the ploughman"). The name of the constellation which contains the bright star, Arcturus. According to ancient mythology, Boötes invented the plough, to which he yoked two oxen, and at death, being taken to heaven with his plough and oxen, was made a constellation. Homer calls it the wagoner.

Booth, Amelia. See AMELIA.

Booth, Edwin [Thomas] (1833–1893). American actor, son of Junius Brutus BOOTH. One of the most noted of Shakespearean actors, Booth was the founder and first president of the Players Club. His letters were edited by Otis Skinner in a volume called *The Last Tragedian* (1939).

Booth, John Wilkes (1838–1865). American actor and assassin. The son of Junius Brutus Booth and brother of Edwin Booth, he was known for playing Shakespearean roles. During a performance of *Our American Cousin* at Ford's Theater in Washington on April 14, 1865, he shot President Lincoln and escaped, shouting *"Sic semper tyrannis!* The South is avenged!" Two weeks later he was trapped in a barn near Bowling Green, Va.; the barn was fired after he refused to surrender, and he probably shot himself.

Booth, Junius Brutus (1796–1852). English-born American actor. Coming to the U.S. in 1821, Booth toured the country playing in romantic dramas of violence and bloodshed. Junius Booth was the father of Edwin BOOTH, who also became famous as a tragedian, and of John Wilkes BOOTH.

Booth, William (1829–1912). English preacher, founder of the SALVATION ARMY (1865). He is noted for his work among the urban poor. He is the subject of a poem by Vachel Lindsay, GENERAL WILLIAM BOOTH ENTERS INTO HEAVEN.

Borachio. In Shakespeare's MUCH ADO ABOUT NOTHING, a villainous follower of Don John of Arragon.

Borah, William E[dgar] (1865–1940). American statesman. As U.S. senator from Idaho (1907–1940), he strongly opposed the World Court and American entry into the League of Nations. He was chairman of the powerful Senate Foreign Relations Committee from 1924 until his death, and was a leading isolationist in the period before World War II.

Borak, al. Muhammad's horse. It conveyed Muhammad from earth to the seventh heaven. It was milk-white, had the wings of an eagle and a human face, with horse's cheeks. Every pace it took was equal to the farthest range of human sight. The name is Arabic for "the lightning."

Bordeaux, Henry (1870–1963). French novelist and historical biographer. A Catholic writer of the Savoy region, Bordeaux is best known for the novels *The Will to Live* (*Les Roquevillard;* 1906), *Footprints Beneath the Snow* (*La Neige sur les pas;* 1912), and *The Gardens of Omar* (*Yamilé sous les cèdres;* 1923).

Borden, Lizzie (1860–1927). American woman indicted in a celebrated murder case. She was charged with having murdered (Aug. 4, 1892) her father and stepmother with an axe in their home in Fall River, Mass., and her trial was followed with eager interest all over the country. She was acquitted, but the murder became the theme of several ballads and poems that failed to accept the verdict, and of an anonymous but widely quoted quatrain: "Lizzie Borden took an ax/ And gave her mother forty whacks;/ When she saw what she had done,/ She gave her father forty-one." The crime has never been solved. Edmund Pearson, who wrote *The Trial of Lizzie Borden* (1937), was convinced of Lizzie's guilt, but she was ardently defended by Edward Radin in *Lizzie Borden: The Untold Story* (1961).

The case has been the subject of numerous literary works, notably the dramas *Nine Pine Street* (1933) by John Colton and *The Legend of Lizzie* (1959) by Reginald Lawrence; a one-act play, *Goodbye, Miss Lizzie Borden* (1947), by Lillian de la Torre; and a novel, *The Long Arm* (1895) by Mary E. Wilkins Freeman. *Fall River Legend* (1948) is a ballet by Agnes de Mille.

border-thief school. A term coined by Thomas Carlyle in his *Sartor Resartus.* He applied it to Sir Walter Scott and others who celebrated the achievements of freebooters and bandits like Rob Roy.

Boreas. In Greek mythology, the god of the north wind, and the north wind itself. He was the son of Astraeus, a Titan, and Eos, the morning, and lived in a cave of Mount Haemus in Thrace. He loved the nymph Orithyia and tried to be gentle with her. Since he could not speak soothingly or sing softly, he carried her off, true to his real character. He was by her the father of Zetes and Calais who both took part in the Argonauts' expedition.

Bores, The. See FÂCHEUX, LES.

Borges, Jorge Luis (1899–). Argentine short-story writer, essayist, and poet. Until about 1930, Borges devoted himself mainly to verse. His poems, such as those in *Fervor de Buenos Aires* (1923), *Luna de enfrente* (1925), and *Cuaderno de San Martín* (1929), are nostalgic and nationalistic treatments of Argentine themes. He also wrote concise and lucid essays on metaphysics, literature, and language. Later, however, as his failing eyesight and poor health made him a semi-invalid, he turned to the creation of the short fictional narratives for which he is best known today. Similar in some respects to the work of Kafka, Poe, and Valéry, these stories are fantastic and esoteric, reflecting the author's irony and skepticism. Among his work of fiction are *Historia universal de la infamia* (1935), *Ficciones* (1945, 1956), and *El Aleph* (1949). His collections of essays include *Inquisiciones* (1925),

El tamaño de mı esperanza (1926), El idioma de los argentinos (1928), and Otras inquisiciones (1952). In 1962 an English translation of some of his stories and essays appeared under the title Labyrinths.

Borgese, Giuseppe Antonio (1882–1952). Italian novelist, critic, poet, professor, and advocate of world unity. An outspoken opponent of fascism, he emigrated to the U.S. in 1931, where he became a citizen (1938) and taught at the University of Chicago. He wrote in excellent English his Goliath (1937), which describes the rise and consolidation of fascism and presents an intelligent analysis of authoritarian rule. He returned to Italy in 1948.

His best-known novel, Rubé (1921), is a fictionalized study of an idealistic generation's disillusionment and embitterment at the outbreak of World War I. Borgese also wrote the novel I Vivi e I Morti (1923). Collections of his short stories include La Città Sconosciuta (1924), Le Belle (1927), and Il Sole Non E' Tramontato (1929). Collections of verse include La Canzone Paziente (1910) and Poesie (1922). Noteworthy among his works written for the theater are L'Arciduca (1924) and Lazzaro (1925).

Borgia or **de Borja.** A Spanish family that rose to prominence in Italy during the Renaissance. It has since become a symbol of unbridled power, lust, and greed because of the legends it spawned. Its chief figures are

Alonso Borgia (1385–1458), who became Pope Calixtus III in 1455 and laid the foundation of his family's power and influence in Italy.

Rodrigo Borgia (1431–1503), who reigned as Pope Alexander VI from 1492. A nephew of Calixtus III and father of Cesare and Lucrezia, he exerted tremendous efforts in order to secure wealth and high station for his children.

Lucrezia Borgia (1480–1519), daughter of Rodrigo Borgia and sister of Cesare Borgia, one of the most famous (and infamous) women of history. A pawn in the designs of her father and brother, she was married three times. The first marriage was annulled; the second ended when her husband was murdered; the third, to Alfonso I of Este, duke of Ferrara, was a purely political match forced down the reluctant throats of the Estensi. Despite Lucrezia's exemplary life at Ferrara, gossip, scandal, rumors, and legends swirled about her and her family, so that she came down to posterity burdened with imputations of poisonings, incestuous relations with brother and father, illegitimate children, and generally whorish behavior. Thus Victor Hugo's play Lucrèce Borgia (1833), and Donizetti's opera Lucrezia Borgia (1833) tell the story of her natural son Gennaro, who turned against his mother before a final recognition and reconciliation, but there is no basis for the tale in fact. Modern scholars discount much, but not all, of her evil reputation on the grounds that as a Borgia and a Spaniard, as well as an illegitimate daughter of a pope, she became the target for the hatred stirred by her family's power and political activity in Italy. The praise heaped upon her by the poets Bembo and Ariosto is now regarded as more than mere flattery.

Cesare Borgia (1476–1507), son of Rodrigo, brother of Lucrezia and, for many, the very embodiment of Renaissance individualism in its sinister form.

The favorite of his father, he was made archbishop of Valencia in 1492 and a cardinal the following year. In 1498, released from ecclesiastical duties, he traveled to France as papal legate and was made duc de Valentinois by a grateful Louis XII (thereafter he was known as Valentino, or il duca Valentino). After a marriage to the sister of the king of Navarre, Cesare returned to Italy and became standard bearer of the Church as well as its captain general. Using his military skill and cunning, he proceeded to consolidate the states of the church and to carve out a principality for himself among the conquered territories, incidentally winning the admiration of Machiavelli, who found his swift cruelty and treachery appropriate to the goal envisioned. The death of his father and the accession to the throne of Peter by the hostile Julius II brought his brief but meteoric career to a halt, for he was unable to rally his forces in the midst of a serious illness and soon found himself compelled to leave Italy under guard. In Spain, where he managed to free himself from prison, he finally met his end in a skirmish at the age of 31. Like the other Borgias, he left behind a legend filled with murders, including that of his own brothers, incest with his sister, insatiable greed, and unbridled cruelty. Modern scholars doubt the incest and many of the murders, but cannot find evidence that the other ingredients of his reputation are mere fiction.

Borglum, [John] Gutzon [de la Mothe] (1871–1941). American sculptor. His most famous undertaking was the carving of the faces of Washington, Jefferson, Lincoln, and Theodore Roosevelt in gigantic scale on Mount Rushmore, South Dakota.

Boris Godunov (1825). An historical drama by Aleksandr Pushkin. It is based on the career of Boris Feodorovich Godunov when he was czar of Russia (1598–1605). In the play Boris is haunted by his guilt over the murder of the czarevich Dmitri. A false pretender to the throne who claims to be Dmitri but is actually an ambitious young monk invades Russia. Boris tightens his rule and prepares to defend his throne, but falls ill and dies, tortured by visions of the prince he murdered. The composer Mussorgski used this play as the basis of his opera (1869–1874) of the same name.

Börne, Ludwig (1786–1837). German journalist. He was an outspoken liberal and advocate of social and intellectual equality for the Jews. Like Heine, he entered voluntary exile in Paris (1830 on), but though many of his views were shared by Heine, the two constantly quarreled in print. His Briefe aus Paris (Letters from Paris, 1832–1834) were filled with criticism of Prussia and were prohibited by the government.

Borodin, Alexander Porphyrievich (1833–1887). Russian composer, one of "The Five," also a chemist. He made use of Russian folk themes in much of his music and is considered to have influenced Debussy, Ravel, Stravinsky, and Sibelius. He wrote operas, symphonies, chamber music, and numerous songs. His best-known works are In the Steppes of Central Asia (1880), a tone poem, and the Polovtsian Dances from Prince Igor, an unfinished opera later completed by Rimski-Korsakov and Alexander Glazunov.

Borodino. The site of a decisive battle between Napoleon's forces and the Russian armies in September, 1812. The battle, which opened the way for Napoleon's entry into Moscow, has been dealt with in Russian literature. The most famous description is by Tolstoi in WAR AND PEACE.

Borrow, George (1803–1881). English traveler, philologist, and writer, noted for his works on gypsies. He wrote several volumes about his experiences as an agent of the Bible Society in Spain and Russia, including *The Zincali; or Account of the Gypsies in Spain* (1841), THE BIBLE IN SPAIN, LAVENGRO, and *The Romany Rye* (1857). Part autobiography and part fantasy, these works are exuberant, racy, and vivid in their description of scenes and incidents of vagabond life. As a philologist, Borrow is best known for his *Romano Lavo-Lil* (1874), a work on Romany, the gypsy language.

Bors, Sir. In Arthurian legend, one of the knights of the Round Table and uncle of Launcelot. In Malory's *Morte d'Arthur* (c. 1469), he is one of the three knights to be granted sight of the Holy Grail, the others being Percival and Galahad, who wins the quest.

Boru, Brian. See BRIAN BORU.

Bos, Charles Du. See Charles DU BOS.

Boscán Almogáver, Juan (c. 1498–1542). Spanish poet. A native of Barcelona, Boscán served as a soldier in Italy and a tutor to the duke of Alba. In 1526 he met Andrea Navagiero, the Venetian ambassador, who persuaded him to write Castilian poetry employing Italian forms and meters. Because of his efforts, he is remembered for having popularized Italianate verse in Spain. In 1543, the year after his death, his widow published his collected poetry. Included in this work are 92 sonnets and 11 *Canciones;* a long *Historia de Leandro y Hero* in unrhymed hendecasyllables; two *Epístolas,* one of which is addressed to Diego Hurtado de Mendoza; and *Octava Rima,* an allegory based on Bembo's *Stanze.* He also wrote an excellent prose translation (1534) of Castiglione's *Il Cortegiano* (1528). See GARCILASO DE LA VEGA.

Bosch, Hieronymus or **Jerome.** Real name, **Hieronymus van Aken** (1450?–1516). Flemish painter. Bosch, who was so named from his birthplace Hertogenbosch, Netherlands, painted religious pictures, scenes of heaven and hell, and allegories in which exquisite panoramas serve as background to the action of fantastic creatures and demons. His personal symbolism of sin and evil, dependent on contemporary literature, astrology, and popular beliefs, has led to contradictory interpretations, but the extreme delicacy, the refinement, and the richness of imagination displayed by his work is incontrovertible. After Bosch's death, a large portion of his work, including the famous *Gardens of Delight,* was brought to Spain by Philip II.

Bosco, Henri (1888–   ). French novelist of the Provence region. His stories, characterized by poetic fantasy, are filled with both sensual human warmth and a mystic Catholicism. Best known for *Le Mas Théotime* (*The Farm Théotime,* 1946, also translated as *Farm in Provence*), he has also written *L'Ane culotte* (1937), *Le Jardin Hyacinthe* (1940), *Monsieur Carré-Benoît in the Country* (1947), *Dark Bough* (*Un Rameau de la Nuit;* 1950), and *Barboche* (1958).

Bose, Buddhadeva (1908–   ). Indian poet and novelist in Bengali. Head of the comparative literature department of Jadavpur University, and visiting professor at New York University in 1959–1960, he has published over 100 volumes, one of the latest being a book of verse, *Je Andhar Alor Adhik.* He founded and edits *Kavita,* a poetry quarterly in Bengali.

Bosinney, Philip. In John Galsworthy's A FORSYTE SAGA, an architect, lover of Soames Forsyte's wife, Irene.

Boss, The (1911). A play by Edward SHELDON. The hero, Michael Regan, a corrupt contractor and politician, is based on James (Fingy) Connors of Buffalo, N.Y. He ultimately falls in love with a wealthy girl who marries him to save her father.

Bossuet, Jacques Bénigne (1627–1704). French prelate. A Roman Catholic bishop, educated by the Jesuits, Bossuet tutored the dauphin 10 fruitless years; it was for this apathetic pupil that he wrote his most important work, the *Discours sur l'histoire universelle* (*Discourse on Universal History,* 1681), a treatise on history from the Christian viewpoint. Turning to ecclesiastical duties, Bossuet preached sermons in which he united exposition of pure dogma with a simple, moving style. In his funeral orations for such personages as Anne of Austria and Marie Thérèse, wife of Louis XIV, he eloquently drew from the lives of the illustrious the "great and terrible lessons" which God teaches kings and men. Bossuet tirelessly defended the Catholic faith against Protestants and heretics; his *Relation sur le Quiétisme* (*Statement on Quietism,* 1698) is a criticism of the quietist movement.

Boston (1928). A novel by Upton SINCLAIR. Its central character is a lady of the Boston Brahmins who suffers pangs of social conscience and goes to work in a factory, where she meets Sacco and Vanzetti. She observes at close range the events following their arrest, appeal, and execution. Seething with indignation, the book partly follows the transcript of the trial.

Boston Hymn (1863). A poem by Ralph Waldo EMERSON. The poet celebrates freedom, denouncing kings and aristocrats. *Boston Hymn* is one of Emerson's most fervent expressions.

Bostonians, The (1886). A novel by Henry JAMES. James satirically portrays a strong-minded Boston feminist, Olive Chancellor, representing a new generation of "do-gooders," who thinks she has found a kindred soul in a beautiful and impressionable girl, Verena Tarrant. The plot turns on the domination of one woman by another and on the struggle between Olive and Basil Ransom for Verena. The theme was suggested by Alphonse Daudet's *Evangeliste* (1883), but James intended it to be at the same time "a tale very characteristic of our social conditions." Bostonians attacked the novel angrily as a false portrayal of their city, and many American critics censured James for his lack of local feeling. It was one of the first American novels to deal more or less explicitly with Lesbianism.

Boston Massacre (March 5, 1770). A clash between the townspeople of Boston and British troops. Sent to Boston to protect the customs commissioners, the soldiers fired on a mob of men and boys, killing five civilians. Further violence was averted by the withdrawal of the troops to some islands in the harbor. The slain leader of the mob was the Negro hero, Crispus Attucks (1723?–1770).

Boston News-Letter. The first newspaper published in the American colonies to have a permanent life. John Campbell, postmaster at Boston, published the first issue on April 24, 1704. The paper ran until 1776.

Boston Public Occurrences. The first newspaper to be published in the American colonies, appearing in 1690. It lasted only one day because its publisher failed to get a government license.

Boston Tea Party (Dec. 16, 1773). The destruction in Boston Harbor of 342 chests of tea by citizens disguised as Indians and led by Samuel Adams. The colonists were protesting an act of Parliament designed to save the East India Co. from bankruptcy at the expense of the colonists.

Boswell, James (1740–1795). Scottish man of letters and biographer. He is best known as a diarist and as the biographer of Dr. Samuel JOHNSON. He was called to the Scottish bar in 1766 and practiced law for 20 years. He met Dr. Johnson in 1763 and visited him yearly on vacations to London until he moved there. In 1786 he settled permanently in London, entered the English bar, but met with little success there. His literary fame and success began with *An Account of Corsica* (1768), a defense of Corsica's abortive struggle for freedom against the republic of Genoa. In 1773 he accompanied Dr. Johnson on a journey to Scotland; his account of the trip, *The Journal of a Tour to the Hebrides with Samuel Johnson, LL.D.*, appeared in 1785, by which time he was already working on THE LIFE OF SAMUEL JOHNSON, LL.D. Boswell was a man of great wit and charm; his personality was marked with fascinating turns of hypochondria and gaiety. He noted with amusement the fact that while he defended Corsican liberty abroad, he was opposed to further extensions of liberty at home. His papers are full of detailed plans for reform and admonitory addresses to himself such as, "Desperate. This day, *Easter* rouse. Be Johnson. You've done no harm. Be *retenu* [restrained], &c. *What* am I?" Occasionally he even took his own advice. See BOSWELL PAPERS.

Boswell Papers. The papers of James BOSWELL. Long believed to have been lost or destroyed, they constitute one of the most important literary finds of the 20th century. The discoveries include letters and manuscripts of Dr. Samuel JOHNSON and Sir Joshua REYNOLDS, as well as the manuscripts of THE LIFE OF SAMUEL JOHNSON, LL.D, *The Journal of a Tour to the Hebrides with Samuel Johnson, LL.D,* and Boswell's private journals. The bulk of the material was acquired by Yale University in 1949 and is in the process of being published in two series. The annotated "research edition" will run to at least 30 volumes A shorter "trade edition" is being published under the editorship of Frederick A. Pottle and others: *Boswell's London Journal, 1762–1763* (1950), *Boswell in Holland, 1763–1764* (1952), *Boswell on the Grand Tour: Germany and Switzerland, 1764* (1953), *Boswell on the Grand Tour: Italy, Corsica, and France, 1765–1766* (1955), *Boswell in Search of a Wife, 1766–1769* (1956), *Boswell for the Defense, 1769–1774* (1959), and *Boswell's Journal of a Tour*

to the Hebrides with Samuel Johnson, 1773 (1962), which was originally published in 1785. The Reynolds manuscript, *Portraits by Sir Joshua Reynolds,* was published by Yale in 1952.

Bosworth, battle of (Aug. 22, 1485). The concluding battle of the WARS OF THE ROSES. In the struggle, RICHARD III, the last Yorkist king, was slain, and the victor, Henry Tudor, became HENRY VII of England.

Botero, Giovanni (1540–1617). Italian political theorist. He defended church and monarchy in the *Ragion di Stato (Reason of State,* 1589), an anti-Machiavellian treatise which summed up the political thought of the Counter Reformation. Its title became a popular phrase in future political discussion.

Both Your Houses (1933). A play by Maxwell ANDERSON. A young congressman compiles evidence to prove political corruption, but finds that the father of the woman he loves is among those involved. It was awarded a Pulitzer Prize.

bo tree. The pipal tree or *Ficus religiosa* of India, related to the banyan tree. It was under one of these trees that Gautama attained enlightenment or perfect knowledge (Sans., *bodhi*) and so became the Buddha.

Botticelli, Sandro. Real name, **Alessandro di Mariano dei Filipepi** (1444–1510). Florentine painter. A pupil of Fra Lippo LIPPI, he depicted both religious and mythological subjects in a style dependent on the decorative patterns of flowing draperies and exquisite detail, on the graceful elongation of idealized figures, and on the swaying beauty of linear design. The *Primavera* (c. 1477) and *The Birth of Venus* (c. 1485), painted for the Medici and now in the Uffizi Gallery in Florence, are his masterpieces in this style. He also painted portraits of the Medici family and did some illustrations of Dante's *Divine Comedy*. At Rome he was commissioned to plan and execute with other artists the frescoes for the walls of the Sistine Chapel. His own contribution was the *Punishment of Korah, Dathan, and Abiram*. He became a follower of the religious reformer Savonarola during the last years of the 15th century and turned towards the illustration of allegories in a harsher, barer style.

Bottom. A weaver and the leader of the bumbling tradesmen-players who perform the tragedy of Pyramus and Thisbe for Duke Theseus in Shakespeare's MIDSUMMER NIGHT'S DREAM. He is a blustering, pompous, but lovable character who constantly misuses words and wants to enact every part in the play.

Bottom is finally persuaded to settle for the part of Pyramus in one of Shakespeare's funniest burlesques. Flute the bellows mender is chosen to play the heroine Thisbe, though he has "a beard coming." Snug the joiner, who is "slow of study," has the sole task of roaring like a lion. Snout the tinker, who is also given to bombast, takes the part of a most garrulous "Wall." Robin Starveling plays the Moon but "wanes" early, and Peter Quince, in bewildered fashion, essays the direction of the whole affair and speaks the prologue. Their combined efforts provide one of Shakespeare's greatest low comedy scenes.

Bottome, Phyllis. Pen name of **Mrs. Ernan Forbes-Dennis** (1884–1963). English novelist. A prolific writer, she is best known for two novels. *Private Worlds* (1934) is heavily influenced by the author's study with Alfred Adler, a prominent psychologist. In 1937 she published *The Mortal Storm,* an anti-Nazi novel written to warn the West. Phyllis Bottome also made several lecture tours in the U.S. before World War II. *Search for a Soul* (1948) is the first volume of an autobiography; the second, *Challenge* (1952), covers the years from adolescence to the early thirties. *Walls of Glass* (1958) is a book of short stories.

Bottomley, Gordon (1874–1948). English poet and poetic dramatist. Associated with the GEORGIANS, he dedicated himself to the revival of English verse drama; his works in this genre include *The Crier by Night* (1902), *King Lear's Wife* (1915), and *Gruach* (1921). Among his poems are *Chambers of Imagery* (1907 and 1912).

Boucher, François (1703–1770). French painter. His works include scenes, pastorals, portraits, and tapestry cartoons in the rococo style. He was very successful as a decorative artist in spite of a tendency toward the florid and sensual. His fashionable elegance made him a favorite of Madame de Pompadour and won him the title of court painter in 1765.

Boucicault, Dion. Original name, **Dionysius Lardner Boursiquot** (1820–1890). Anglo-Irish playwright, theatrical manager, and actor. Born in Ireland, he was educated in London and achieved success there, while still a minor, with the production of his play *London Assurance* (1841). In 1853, his reputation already established, he journeyed to New York City and became a leading figure on the U.S. stage. Boucicault dramatized Mayne Reid's novel *The Quadroon* (1856), which he rechristened THE OCTOROON, and he collaborated with Joseph Jefferson on the famous stage version of RIP VAN WINKLE, which began its long run in London in 1865. In his later years, he specialized more and more on plays with an Irish setting, among them *Arrah-na-Pogue* (1865) and *The Shaughraun* (1874). He has been described as "a director-playwright with a genius for theatrical effect."

Bouhours, Dominique. Known as **le père Bouhours** (1628–1702). French Jesuit and grammarian. In *Doutes sur la langue française* (*Doubts concerning the French Language,* 1674), Bouhours supported the reforms proposed by the Académie Française and aimed at raising the standard of the language. After the death of Claude Vaugelas, Bouhours became the leading grammarian of France.

Boulanger, Georges Ernest Jean Marie (1837–1891). French general. Boulanger, who enjoyed tremendous popular support, advocated militarism and revenge upon Germany after the Franco-Prussian War; the political movement Boulangism adopted his name and his aims. Elected deputy of the department of the Seine in 1889, Boulanger might have seized dictatorial powers; accused of conspiracy, he fled the country without awaiting trial. His popular cognomen, Man on Horseback, resulted from his habit of appearing mounted before Paris crowds.

Boulanger, Nadia (1887–   ). French conductor and composer. Herself once a pupil of Gabriel Fauré, she is famous as a teacher of composers, especially two generations of Americans, including Virgil Thomson, Aaron Copland, Roy Harris, Walter Piston, and Elliott Carter. She has also revived much old music, including works of Monteverdi.

Boulez, Pierre (1925–   ). French composer of extremely complex, pointillistic music. He is best known for *Le Marteau sans Maître* (1955), with a text by Réné Char.

Boulle, Pierre (1912–   ). French novelist. Like *The Bridge Over the River Kwai* (1952), most of his books are set amid the difficulties of war, international intrigue, or wilderness outposts. The novels satirize either the British code of conduct or the often ignoble origins of so-called heroism: *Not the Glory* (1950), *Face of a Hero* (1953), *The Test* (*L'Epreuve des hommes;* 1955), S.O.P.H.I.A. (1959), and *A Noble Profession* (*Un métier de seigneur;* 1960).

Bounderby, Josiah. In Charles Dickens' HARD TIMES, a vulgar banker and mill owner described as a "bully of humility." He is always boasting of his old ignorance and poverty, of an infancy passed in an "egg-box" under the care of his drunken grandmother. Actually, his parents doted on him, educated him at considerable sacrifice, and he now pays them a monthly stipend to keep out of sight. Bounderby marries Louisa Gradgrind, but later she separates from him.

bounds, beating the. An old custom, still kept up in many English parishes, of going round the parish boundaries on Holy Thursday, or Ascension Day. The schoolchildren, accompanied by the clergymen and parish officers, walked through their parish from end to end; the boys were switched with willow wands all along the lines of boundary, the idea being to teach them to know the bounds of their parish. Beating the bounds was called in Scotland *riding the marches* (bounds), and in England the day is sometimes called *gang-day.*

Bourbon. A French royal family whose line also formed ruling dynasties in Spain and Naples. The Bourbon kings of France were Henry IV, Louis XIII, XIV, XV, and XVI (1589–1793). It was said that the family "learned nothing and forgot nothing." Hence a Bourbon is anyone who fails to learn by experience. In the U.S., the name was given to the Democratic Party by its opponents.

Bourchier, John. 2nd Baron **Berners** (1467–1533). English translator, a high court official under Henry VIII. At the king's request he translated Froissart's *Chronicles* (2 vols., 1523, 1525), a classic of Tudor English prose, and the French romance *Huon de Bordeaux. The Golden Boke of Marcus Aurelius* and *The Castell of Love* were translated from French versions of Spanish works by Antonio de Guevara and Diego de San Pedro, and printed after his death.

Bourdaloue, Louis (1632–1704). French Jesuit priest and preacher. He delivered his first sermons in Paris in 1669, and till his death he was considered the greatest preacher of his era. Dealing chiefly with moral and practical questions, his sermons were as calm and rational as Bossuet's were emotional and stirring. Bourdaloue was a formidable opponent of the Jansenists.

bourgeois drama (**drame bourgeois**). A type of French play, developed from the COMÉDIE LARMO-

YANTE, which deals seriously with middle-class family relationships, problems, and duties. Representative plays of this type were often sentimental, morally edifying, melodramatic, mediocre, and humorless. The most famous of these plays are DIDEROT's *Le fils naturel* (1771) and *Le Père de famille* (1761); SEDAINE's *Le Philosophe sans le savoir* (1765); and Beaumarchais' *La Mère coupable* (1792). Diderot's theories about this type of drama were to have an influence on the social theater of Emile Augier and Dumas *fils*.

Bourgeois Gentilhomme, Le (The Would-be Gentleman, 1670). A COMÉDIE-BALLET by MOLIÈRE. M. JOURDAIN, a bourgeois and a boor, is determined to make a gentleman of himself and to that end studies dancing, fencing, and philosophy, allows himself to be fleeced by the unscrupulous nobleman DORANTE, and forbids his daughter's marriage to her beloved CLÉONTE or to any other commoner. The resourceful Cléonte disguises himself as the son of the Grand Turk and, babbling pseudo-Turkish, dupes M. Jourdain into granting him the girl's hand. A delightful comedy in its own right, the play has survived in the repertory for almost three centuries and has often served as a pretext for lavish ballets and *divertissements*.

Bourget, Paul Charles Joseph (1852–1935). French novelist and critic. Bourget's work occupies an important place in the development of the psychological novel, probing with new care and accuracy the state of the inner man. Among his finest novels are *Cruelle Enigme* (1885), *Le Disciple* (1889), *Cosmopolis* (1893), and *L'Etape* (1903). His critical works, such as *Etudes de Portraits* (1888) and *Pages de Doctrine et de Critique* (1912), use a similar analytical method. The tone of the later work, however, changed, becoming increasingly moralistic and didactic in such novels as *L'Emigré* (1907) and *Le Démon de midi* (1914).

Bourgh, Lady Catherine de. An overbearing "great lady" in Jane Austen's PRIDE AND PREJUDICE. An inveterate snob, she tries to prevent the marriage of Elizabeth and Darcy.

Bourjaily, Vance [Nye] (1922–). American writer. His first novel, *The End of My Life* (1947), was the story of a young man's mental and moral disintegration during World War II. Bourjaily was also an editor of *discovery*, a paperback periodical of the 1950's devoted to new authors. He has written several other novels and *The Unnatural Enemy* (1963), a book about the ethics of hunting.

Bourke-White, Margaret (1906–1971). American photographer. Known for her photographic studies of industry, social and economic conditions, and news personalities, she has worked in 34 countries, including the Soviet Union and the Arctic. She was a United Nations' war correspondent in Korea for *Life* magazine (1952) and was also associated with *Fortune* and *PM* as editor and photographer. She described her successful struggle against Parkinson's disease in her autobiography, *Portrait of Myself* (1963). See Erskine CALDWELL.

Bourne, Randolph [Silliman] (1886–1918). American literary critic and essayist. An early accident made Bourne a helpless cripple; he succeeded, however, in studying at Columbia University and abroad. He held radical views on education and politics and was an outspoken pacifist during World

War I. He wrote for several publications, including *The Dial*, *The New Republic*, and *The Masses*. Among his books are *Youth and Life* (1913), *The Gary Schools* (1916), *Education and Living* (1917), and *Untimely Papers* (1919). After Bourne's death, Van Wyck Brooks edited *The History of a Literary Radical* (1920; reprinted 1956).

Bourrienne, Louis Antoine Fauvelet de (1769–1834). French diplomat, friend and secretary (1797–1802) to Napoleon. He wrote *Mémoires sur Napoléon* (10 vols., 1829), a vivid but untrustworthy work.

Boutelleau, Jacques. See Jacques CHARDONNE.

Bovary, Emma. The heroine of Gustave Flaubert's novel MADAME BOVARY.

bowdlerize. To expurgate a book. In 1818 an English physician, Thomas Bowdler (1754–1825), gave to the world a 10-volume edition of Shakespeare's works "in which nothing is added to the original text; but those words and expressions are omitted which cannot with propriety be read aloud in a family." Bowdler later treated Gibbon's *Decline and Fall* in the same way. Hence, we have the words *bowdlerist, bowdlerizer, bowdlerism, bowdlerization*, etc.

Bowen, Catherine [Shober] Drinker (1897–). American biographer. An accomplished musician who first wrote about music, Mrs. Bowen later turned to biography. Two early biographies were of musicians: Tchaikovsky (*Beloved Friend*, 1937) and Anton and Nicholas Rubinstein (*Free Artist*, 1939). These were followed by *Yankee from Olympus: Justice Holmes and His Family* (1944), *John Adams and the American Revolution* (1950), *The Lion and the Throne: The Life and Times of Sir Edward Coke* (1957), *The Adventures of a Biographer* (1959), and *Francis Bacon: The Temper of a Man* (1963).

Bowen, Elizabeth [Dorothea Cole] (1899–1973). Anglo-Irish novelist and short-story writer. She knew members of the Bloomsbury group and wrote in the tradition of sensibility, following Henry James and E. M. Forster. With satire, irony, and occasional melodrama she explores the relationships, emotional crises, and failures of feeling of her upper-middle-class characters. Her best-known novels are THE HOTEL, THE HOUSE IN PARIS, THE DEATH OF THE HEART, and THE HEAT OF THE DAY. Among her other books are *The Last September* (1929), *A World of Love* (1955), *A Time in Rome* (1960), and *The Little Girls* (1964). *Bowen's Court* (1942) studies the history of the Bowen family house in Ireland and 10 generations of the family. *Seven Winters & Afterthoughts* (1962) consists of two sections. The first, an autobiographical fragment, was first published in 1943; the second is a collection of critical essays. Among her collections of short stories are *The Cat Jumps* (1934), *Look at All Those Roses* (1941), and *The Demon Lover* (1945).

Bowen, John (1924–). English novelist. Among his satirical novels are *The Truth Will Not Help Us* (1956) and *After the Rain* (1958).

Bowen, Marjorie. See G. M. V. LONG.

Bower of Bliss. See FAERIE QUEENE, THE.

Bowers, Claude [Gernade] (1878–1958). American historian and diplomat. His historical works include *Jefferson and Hamilton* (1925) and *The Tragic Era: The Revolution after Lincoln*

(1929). In *My Mission to Spain* (1954), and *My Life* (1963), he described his experiences in politics and as ambassador to Spain and Chile.

Bowery. A district of New York City, now known as the last refuge for derelicts of all types. Bowery or *bouwerij* is the old Dutch word for farm; and Bowery Lane received its name because it led to the farm of Peter Stuyvesant, one of the Dutch governors of colonial days. It was for a long time the height of fashion to live on Bowery Lane, but with the growth of the city the character of the district underwent a radical change, becoming the site of dance halls and gambling resorts. *The Bowery*, a popular song by Charles H. Hoyt, gives an indication of the reputation of the district at the close of the 19th century.

Bowling, Lieutenant Tom. In Tobias Smollett's novel RODERICK RANDOM, the generous uncle of the hero. A man too frankly the product of the sea to be anything but ill at ease on land, he is careless of the niceties of life ashore.

Bowra, Sir [Cecil] Maurice (1898–1971). English classical scholar and author of criticism on ancient and modern European literature. Among his books are *Greek Lyric Poetry* (1936), *Heroic Poetry* (1952), and *Primitive Song* (1962).

Bow Street. A street near Covent Garden in London which contains the principal police court. The early police were called "Bow Street runners."

Box and Cox (1847). A farce by John Maddison Morton (1811–1891). It has been called "the best farce for three characters in the English language." The principal characters are Box and Cox; the third is the thrifty landlady who rents the same rooms to Box and Cox (one of whom is employed by night, the other by day) in the vain hope that her two tenants will remain ignorant of each other's existence. Hence, there developed the term a *Box and Cox arrangement.*

Boxer. A member of a secret society in China. This society took a prominent part in the rising against foreigners in 1900, which was suppressed by joint European action. The Chinese name was *gee ho chuan,* signifying "righteousness, harmony and fists," and implying training as in athletics for the purpose of developing righteousness and harmony.

Boy Bishop. St. Nicholas of Bari. He was so called because from his cradle he manifested marvelous indications of piety. The custom of choosing a boy from the cathedral choir on his day (December 6th), as a mock bishop, is very ancient. The boy possessed episcopal honor for three weeks, and the rest of the choir were his prebendaries. If he died during his time of office he was buried *in pontificalibus.* Probably the reference is to Jesus Christ sitting in the temple among the doctors while he was a boy. The custom was abolished in the reign of Henry VIII.

boycott. To refuse to have commerce of any sort with a person, group, or country for punitive or retaliatory reasons. The term is derived from the experience of Charles Cunningham Boycott (1832–1897). In his capacity of agent for a large landowner in County Mayo, Ireland, Captain Boycott was thus ostracized (even his servants left him) by the Irish agrarian insurgents of 1880.

Boyd, Nancy. A pen name of Edna St. Vincent MILLAY. It was used on the title page of a series of sketches, *Distressing Dialogues* (1924).

Boyle, Kay (1903–   ). American short-story writer and novelist. Miss Boyle was an expatriate for many years, living in France. As early contributor to "the little magazines," she is known for the stylish polish of her prose and psychological interest in character. Her books include *Wedding Day* (1931), *The White Horses of Vienna and Other Stories* (1936), *The Crazy Hunter* (1940), *American Citizen* (a poem, 1944), *1939* (1948), *His Human Majesty* (1949), *The Seagull on the Step* (1955), and *Generation without Farewell* (1959).

Boyle, Robert (1627–1691). Irish-born English physicist and chemist. Boyle's Law states that, if the temperature remains constant, the volume of a gas varies inversely with the pressure.

Boz. The pen name of Charles DICKENS. His *Sketches by Boz* (two series) appeared in 1836. "Boz, my signature in the Morning Chronicle," he tells us, "was the nickname of a pet child, a younger brother, whom I had dubbed Moses, in honor of [Goldsmith's] *The Vicar of Wakefield,* which, being pronounced Bozes, got shortened into Boz."

Brabançonne. The national anthem of Belgium, composed by Van Campenhout in the revolution of 1830. It is named from Brabant, of which Brussels is the chief city.

Brabantio. In Shakespeare's OTHELLO, a Venetian senator and father of Desdemona. When he learns of Desdemona's secret marriage to Othello, he accuses the Moor of having won his daughter by witchcraft. Since Desdemona insists on remaining with her husband, he is forced to accept the situation, but warns Othello:

> Look to her, Moor, if thou hast eyes to see:
> She has deceiv'd her father, and may thee."

Bracciolini, Poggio (1380–1459). Italian Humanist. He served as chancellor of Florence and papal secretary during a varied career that saw him spend four years in England and many others in search of lost manuscripts of classical writers in continental monasteries. Among the early Italian Renaissance humanists, he wrote the best Latin letters and dialogues and was especially known for his *De varietate fortunae (On the Vagaries of Fortune)*; a history of Florence; and a collection of jests and anecdotes, the *Liber facetiarum.*

Bracebridge Hall, or The Humorists (1822). A collection of tales and sketches by Washington IRVING. The book is a less successful sequel to *The Sketch Book of Geoffrey Crayon, Gent.*

Bracegirdle, Anne (1663?–1748). English actress. A protegée of Thomas Betterton, she was the intimate friend of Congreve and made her greatest successes as the heroines of his comedies, particularly as Millamant in *The Way of the World.* She retired in 1707, probably out of fear of being eclipsed by Mrs. Oldfield, a younger rival.

Brackenridge, Hugh Henry (1748–1816). American novelist and poet. One of the first writers to consider the native American scene valid material for literature, he collaborated with Philip Freneau on *The Rising Glory of America* (1772), a commencement ode at Princeton, and also wrote *The*

Battle of Bunker Hill (1776) and *The Death of General Montgomery* (1777), blank-verse dramas in the 18th-century style. His most important work is MODERN CHIVALRY, OR THE ADVENTURES OF CAPTAIN JOHN FARRAGO AND TEAGUE O'REGAN HIS SERVANT.

Bradamante or **Bradamant.** The warrior maiden of Carolingian legend, prominent in the Orlando poems of Boiardo and Ariosto (see ORLANDO FURIOSO) as the sister of Rinaldo and the beloved of Ruggiero. Known as the Virgin Knight, she wears white armor and a white plume; her spear magically unhorses any knight it touches. Her marriage to the Moor Ruggiero after his conversion, and the subsequent defeat of Rodomonte in single combat, form the subject of the last book of Ariosto's poem. The marriage of Bradamante and Ruggiero also enables Ariosto to flatter his noble patrons, the Este family, since it is said to be the forerunner of the future house of Este. She is also the title character of a play by Robert Garnier.

Bradamante (1582). A play by Robert GARNIER. It is derived from the Carolingian legend of BRADAMANTE and from Ariosto's *Orlando Furioso*. Centering on a combat between the knight Roger and the warrior-maiden Bradamante, with emphasis upon Roger's dilemma in choosing between the claims of love and duty, the play was the first of the French tragicomedies—an enormously popular genre in which romance and adventure led to a happy ending, the classical unities being freely disregarded.

Bradbury, Ray [Douglas] (1920–   ). American writer of science fiction. Bradbury is noted for his unearthly, fantastic tales, many of which have appeared in short-story anthologies. Among his books are *Dark Carnival* (1947), *The Martian Chronicles* (1950), *The Golden Apples of the Sun* (1953), *Dandelion Wine* (1957), and *A Medicine for Melancholy* (1959).

Bradby, Anne. See Anne RIDLER.

Braddock, Edward (1695–1755). English general. He led an ill-fated expedition against Fort Duquesne during the French and Indian War. Washington was one of his junior officers.

Braddon, Mary Elizabeth. Pen name, **Babington White** (1837–1915). English novelist. She is best known for her first (and one of her weakest) books, the melodramatic *Lady Audley's Secret* (1862). She was the author of some 80 other novels of a high-flown, romantic character, which, though ephemeral, were not devoid of quality.

Bradford, Andrew (1686–1742). American printer and publisher. On Dec. 22, 1719, he brought out the first number of the *American Weekly Mercury*, the earliest newspaper in Pennsylvania. It continued for more than 26 years. From 1713 to 1723 Bradford was the only printer in Pennsylvania.

Bradford, Gamaliel (1863–1932). American biographer. He is best known for his "psychographs," interpretative portraits concerned with depicting the subjective life of literary and historical figures. Perhaps the best of these are contained in *American Portraits* (1922), discussing Mark Twain, Henry Adams, Henry James, and others, and *Bare Souls* (1924), portraying Keats, Lamb, Voltaire, and other writers. *Damaged Souls* (1923), analyzing P. T. Barnum, Aaron Burr, and others, was perhaps his

most popular volume. His other books include *Types of American Character* (1895), *Confederate Portraits* (1914), *Portraits of Women* (1916), and *Elizabethan Women* (1936).

Bradford, Roark (1896–1948). American short-story writer and playwright. He is best known for the stories of OL' MAN ADAM AN' HIS CHILLUN. *John Henry* (1931), dealing with the legendary Negro, was dramatized in 1940. Other books by Bradford include *Ol' King David an' the Philistine Boys* (1930), *Let the Band Play Dixie* (1934), a collection of short stories; and *The Three-Headed Angel* (1937).

Bradford, William (1590?–1657). English-born American statesman. A leader in the founding of Plymouth, he was governor of the colony from 1621 to his death, except for five years during which he refused election. He was one of the authors of an account of the settlement of Plymouth known as MOURT'S RELATION, and is best known for his *History of Plimouth Plantation,* a chronicle of events in the colony from 1620 to 1646, which was not discovered and published until 1856.

Bradlaugh, Charles (1833–1891). English social and political reformer. Like Mrs. Annie BESANT, with whom he was associated, he was a free thinker. Although he was elected to Parliament for six years, he was not seated because as a free thinker he wished to affirm instead of swear on the Bible. Ultimately he won his point, and in 1886 was seated.

Bradley, Edward. Pen name, **Cuthbert Bede** (1827–1889). English clergyman and humorist. He wrote and illustrated *Adventures of Mr. Verdant Green, an Oxford Freshman* (1853–1856), *Tales of College Life* (1856), and other amusing, Dickensian accounts of Oxford life.

Bradstreet, Anne (1612?–1672). English-born poet of the Massachusetts Bay Colony. By birth an aristocrat, she was the daughter of one governor of the colony and wife of another. Although her verse in general alternates between scenes of domestic affection and conventional professions of piety, it shows a sensitivity to beauty not usually associated with the Puritans. THE TENTH MUSE LATELY SPRUNG UP IN AMERICA is the only edition of her poems published in her lifetime and the first volume of original verse to be written in America. She also wrote *Religious Experiences,* an autobiographical sketch, and *Meditations, Divine and Moral,* a collection of aphorisms for the instruction of her son. John Berryman wrote a remarkable poem, *Homage to Mistress Bradstreet* (1956), in which the sexual tenderness of Anne Bradstreet is set against the sternly chaste background of Puritan New England.

Brady, Cyrus Townsend (1861–1920). American clergyman and author. He wrote many books for boys and historical stories, biographies of Paul Jones, Andrew Jackson, and others.

Brady, Mathew B. (1823?–1896). American photographer. The first significant representative of his profession in the U.S., he is best known for his photographic record of the Civil War and for portraits of Abraham Lincoln and other outstanding personalities of the time.

Braes of Yarrow. See YARROW.

braggadocio. A braggart; one valiant with his tongue but a great coward at heart. The character is from Spenser's FAERIE QUEENE, in which Braggadochio appears as a kind of "Intemperance of the Tongue."

Bragi. In Scandinavian mythology, the son of Odin and Frigga, husband of Iduna, and god of poetry, eloquence, and song. He was represented as an old man with a long white beard. With Hermod, he received and welcomed to Valhalla all heroes who fell in battle.

Bragi's apples. An instant cure for weariness, decay of power, ill temper, and failing health. The supply was inexhaustible; after one was eaten another took its place immediately.

Bragi's cup. A cup which each new king had to drain and pledge by before he ascended the high seat of his fathers.

Bragi's story. A lengthy but interesting tale.

Bragmardo, Janotus de. In Rabelais' GARGANTUA AND PANTAGRUEL, a professor of theology sent by the Sorbonne to recover the bells of Notre Dame from Gargantua, who had taken them to hang around his mare's neck. Although he has already decided to return the bells, Gargantua listens to the sophist's harangue and is so amused by it that he sends him away amply rewarded.

Brahe, Tycho (1546–1601). Danish astronomer. He attempted to establish a system of astronomy midway between that of Copernicus and that of Ptolemy. The earth, he maintained, was motionless, and the five planets revolved around the sun, which circled the earth once every year. On Nov. 11, 1572, he discovered the celebrated "new star" in Cassiopeia, the first in a universe previously considered fixed for eternity, and his account of it, *De Nova Stella,* was published in 1573. He wrote a number of treatises on astronomy in Latin, the most important being *Astronomiae Instauratae Progymnasmata* (1602–1603), edited by Kepler, which dealt with the motions of the sun and the moon.

Brahma. In Hinduism, the Absolute, or God conceived as entirely personal. The theological abstraction was endowed with personality, and became the creator of the universe, the first in the divine TRIMURTI, or triad, of which the other partners were Vishnu the Preserver and Siva the Destroyer. The Brahmins claim Brahma as the founder of their religious system.

Brahma (1857). A poem by Ralph Waldo EMERSON. In terms of Hindu philosophy, the poet expresses the pantheistic belief that God is everywhere and is found in the act of seeking.

Brahmin. A member of one of the four castes of Hinduism, representing the priestly and meditative order. See CASTE; BRAHMA.

Brahmo Samaj (*Bengali,* "the union of God"). A monotheistic offshoot of Hinduism. It was established in 1830 in Calcutta by Ram Mohun Roy (1774–1833), a wealthy and extraordinarily erudite Brahmin who wished to reform the ritualistic excesses of institutionalized Hinduism by founding an order free from idolatry and superstition. In 1844 the "church" was reorganized by Debendro Nath Tagore, and its reforming zeal and intellectual influence impressed sensitive Hindus everywhere, but especially in Bengal. The Samaj provided a spearhead of morally excellent people whose example succeeded in convincing even orthodox Hindus of the necessity of reform; it also supplied an alert élite of educated Indians who did much for national autonomy, social reforms, and political independence. After 1947 its influence has gradually declined, partly because most of its ideas have been accepted and incorporated into the progressive sections of Hinduism.

Brahms, Johannes (1833–1897). German romantic composer. His works include four symphonies, concertos, chamber music, songs, and choral works, including the popular *Ein deutsches Requiem* (*A German Requiem,* 1867). He was the most successful of the romantic composers in reconciling the conflicting claims of lyricism and classical form, partly because of his study and editing of 16th-, 17th-, and 18th-century music.

Braille, Louis (1809–1852). French teacher of the blind. In 1829, Braille, who was himself blind from the age of three, developed an alphabetic system of raised points that enabled the blind to read.

Braine, John (1922–). English novelist. One of the ANGRY YOUNG MEN, he is author of the best-selling novel ROOM AT THE TOP. A sequel, *Life at the Top,* was published in 1962.

Brainworm. In Ben Jonson's comedy EVERY MAN IN HIS HUMOUR, the servant of Kno'well. A veritable Proteus in his metamorphoses, he appears first as Brainworm, then as Fitz-Sword, then as a reformed soldier whom Kno'well takes into his service, then as Justice Clement's man, and lastly as valet to the courts of law. By his various transformations he is able to play upon the same group of characters, and his rascalities serve as the catalyst to the comedy.

Braithwaite, William Stanley Beaumont (1878–1962). American poet and anthologist. He originated and edited for 17 years the *Anthology of Magazine Verse and Year Book of American Poetry.* Much of his own poetry appears in *Selected Poems* (1948).

Bramah, Ernest. See Ernest Bramah SMITH.

Bramante. Real name, **Donato d'Agnola** (c. 1444–1514). Italian architect and painter. Born in Urbino, he worked mainly at Milan, serving Lodovico Sforza, and then at Rome for the papacy, where he was consulted on all important architectural undertakings. One of his paintings, *Christ at the Column,* is considered a masterpiece, but his great fame rests on his achievements as an architect. One of the finest examples of his work is the *Tempietto,* the severely classical, small-scale, and perfect circular temple erected at Rome in 1502 on the spot where Peter allegedly was crucified. In 1506, he began to execute his design for the new basilica that eventually became the modern St. Peter's. Supposedly a rival of Michelangelo, he is thought to have secured for the latter the torturous and unwelcome task of decorating the ceiling of the Sistine Chapel.

Bramble, Matthew. The chief character in Tobias Smollett's novel HUMPHREY CLINKER. An irascible, eccentric, somewhat valetudinarian bachelor, he initiates the family expedition partly because of ill health and partly to distract the mind of his young niece Lydia Melford, who has fallen in love with a supposedly itinerant actor.

Tabitha Bramble. In the same book, the sister of Matthew Bramble, noted for her bad spelling. She is vain, prim, uncharitable, and in violent search for a husband. She contrives to marry Captain LISMA-HAGO, who is content to take her for the sake of her £4,000.

Bramine's Journal, The. A journal kept by Laurence STERNE and addressed to Mrs. Eliza Draper, whom he met in London. It is dated from April, 1767, to August, 1767, after her departure for India. See ELIZA.

Brancati, Vitaliano (1907–1954). Italian novelist and essayist. He is noted for his satire of contemporary social manners and his ironic appraisals of fascist culture. His works include *Don Giovanni in Sicilia* (1942), a light-hearted spoofing of anachronistic Sicilian customs; *Il Vecchio con gli Stivali* (1945), a humorous treatment of the Italian bourgeoisie's belief in fascist dreams of national glory; and *Il Bell'Antonio* and *Paolo Il Caldo*, both political satires. Brancati was essentially a realist of the school of De Roberto. He freely employed dialect in his fiction and, as a rule, used his native Catania as the setting of his novels.

Branch, Anna Hempstead (1875–1937). American poet. Noted for her lyricism, she wrote *Nimrod*, a narrative poem based on the biblical story. *The Monk in the Kitchen* (1905) is perhaps her best-known poem. Among her works are *The Heart of the Road, and Other Poems* (1901), *The Shoes that Danced* (1905), and *Sonnets from a Lock Box and Other Poems* (1929).

Brancusi, Constantin (1876–1957). Romanian sculptor, settled in France in 1904. He is known for his simplified abstracted forms, executed in wood, steel, stone, and bronze, and finished to a great smoothness or polish. His best-known work in the U.S. is *Bird in Space* (1919), a vertical swelling shaft of highly polished metal.

Brand (1866). A verse drama by Henrik IBSEN. The first of Ibsen's major plays, *Brand* deals with a passionate and uncompromising idealist, a minister who sacrifices the health and finally the life of his child and his wife rather than violate his stern sense of duty to his parish. Finally, Brand tries to lead his parishioners to the greater Church of Life in the mountains, but the people fall behind and abandon him. In the symbolic closing scene on the mountain Ice Church, Brand, about to be crushed by an avalanche, calls out to God. He is answered by a voice saying "God is Love."

Brand, Max. Pen name of **Frederick Faust** (1892–1944). American writer. Although he published two books of verse under his own name, he is best known for his Max Brand books, which are old-style Westerns done with great storytelling power. *The Untamed* (1918) is the first of this lengthy series, while *Destry Rides Again* (1930) is perhaps the most famous. He also wrote the books and motion pictures about Dr. Kildare.

Brandan or **Brendan**, St. A semilegendary Irish saint. He is said to have been buried at Clonfert (at the age of about 94), in 577, where he was abbot over 3,000 monks. He is best known because of the very popular medieval story of his voyage in search of the EARTHLY PARADISE, which was supposed to be situated on an island in mid-Atlantic. The voyage lasted for seven years, and the story is crowded with marvelous incidents, the very birds and beasts they encountered being Christians and observing the fasts and festivals of the Church. As late as 1755 St. Brandon's Island, or the Island of San Borandan, was set down in geographical charts as west of the Canary group.

Brandeis, Louis D[embitz] (1856–1941). American jurist. Born in Louisville, Ky., Brandeis practiced law in Boston, becoming known as the "people's attorney" because of his opposition to vested interests and monopolies in every form. He was appointed to the U.S. Supreme Court by President Wilson in 1916, his nomination being confirmed only after a bitter struggle. Often joining Holmes and later Cardozo in their dissents, Brandeis served on the court until his retirement in 1939. He wrote several books, including *Business, A Profession* (1914) and *The Curse of Bigness* (1934). Brandeis University, founded in 1948 in Waltham, Mass., is named after him.

Brandes, Georg Morris Cohen (1842–1927). Danish literary critic and scholar. Brandes exercised great influence upon Scandinavian thought and literature, serving as leader of *Det moderne gennembruch* ("the modern breaking-through"). In 1871 he began to formulate the principles of a new realism and naturalism, condemning abstract idealism and fantasy in literature. Brandes was the author of several critical biographies, including a study of Henrik Ibsen, who shared his literary goals, in his volume of *Critical Studies* (1899). His other studies include *Søren Kierkegaard* (1877), *Esaias Tegnér* (1878), *Wolfgang Goethe* (1914–1915), and *François de Voltaire* (1916–1917). After spending several years in Germany, Brandes came under the influence of Nietzsche's philosophy and disavowed democracy for an aristocratic radicalism.

Brandimarte. In the Orlando poems (see ORLANDO FURIOSO) of Boiardo and Ariosto, the son of king Monodante, brother of Origille, and the trusted companion of Orlando, who had baptized him. He is followed about continually by his faithful wife Fiordiligi until Gradasso kills him.

Brandt, Margaret. In Charles Reade's historical novel THE CLOISTER AND THE HEARTH, the heroine and mother of Erasmus. Peter Brandt, her father, is also a prominent character.

Brangwen, Ursula. The heroine of 2 novels by D. H. Lawrence. In THE RAINBOW, her experience as a teacher and rebel from her environment reflects Lawrence's own; in the sequel, WOMEN IN LOVE, she is based more on Lawrence's wife, Frieda LAWRENCE.

Brant, Joseph. Indian name, **Thayendanegea** (1742–1807). Mohawk Indian chief. During the American Revolution, he commanded the Indian forces cooperating with the British and ravaged the Mohawk Valley of New York. An earnest Christian, he also translated the Book of Common Prayer into the Mohawk tongue.

Brant, Sebastian (1458–1521). German didactic poet and satirist. Most famous for THE SHIP OF FOOLS, Brant was a highly conservative, even hidebound thinker. Although he is often classified as a humanist, he was very much afraid of change in any form, and cannot properly be so called.

Brantôme, Seigneur de. Pierre de Bourdeilles (1540?–1614). French soldier, adventurer, and memorialist. His two chronicles, *Vies des hommes il-*

Das Narren Schyff.

Gen Narragonien.

Hi sunt qui descendunt mare in nauibus
faciétes opationem in aquis multis.
Ascendūt vsqȝ ad cęlos/ & descēdunt vsqȝ
ad abyssos: aia eorū in malis tabescebat.
Turbati sunt & moti sunt sicut ebrius: &
omnis sapientia eorū deuorata est.
.Psalmo .Cvi.

Title page of Sebastian Brant's *Ship of Fools* (1494).

lustres et grands capitaines français and *Vies des dames galantes* (1665–1666), reveal him as credulous and uncritical, impressed by spectacle and fascinated by trivialities and gossip, but they survive as an interesting portrait of French-Renaissance manners.

Braque, Georges (1882–1963). French painter, associated with Pablo Picasso in the development of CUBISM. His subjects were chiefly still lifes. In 1952 he began a series of designs of birds which bring to a culmination of simplicity his elegance of line and precision of color.

Brass, Sampson. In Charles Dickens' OLD CURIOSITY SHOP, a knavish, servile attorney, affecting great sympathy with his clients but in reality fleecing them without mercy.

Sally Brass. Sampson's sister, and an exaggerated edition of her brother.

Brave New World (1932). A satirical novel by Aldous HUXLEY. Set in the year 632 AF (After Ford), it is a grim picture of the world which Huxley thinks our scientific and social developments have already begun to create. Human embryos are developed in bottles and conditioned to collectivism and passivity. A "savage" is found in New Mexico and imported as an experiment. He has educated himself by reading Shakespeare and believes in spirituality and moral choice; in the new world he soon goes berserk and kills himself. The title, which is highly ironic, is from Shakespeare's *The Tempest*.

brazen head. A theme of many legends. The legend of the wonderful head of brass that could speak is common in early romances, and is of Eastern origin. In *Valentine and Orson,* a gigantic head kept in the castle of the giant Ferragus of Portugal tells those who consult it whatever they require to know, past, present, or to come. The most famous brazen head in English legend is that fabled to have been made by Roger Bacon. It was said if Bacon heard it speak he would succeed in his projects; if not, he would fail. His familiar, Miles, was set to watch, and while Bacon slept the head spoke thrice. "Time is"; half an hour later it said, "Time was." In another half-hour it said, "Time past," fell down, and was broken to atoms. References to Bacon's brazen head are frequent in literature.

Bread and Wine (Pane e Vino; 1937; revised, 1962). A novel by Ignazio SILONE. The hero, Pietro Spina, returns to his native Abruzzi after 15 years of exile to continue his antifascist agitation. As he travels through the country, disguised as a priest, he sees the inroads made upon the Italian character by Mussolini's rule. Finding that the underground movement is in chaos and doubting the validity of his old revolutionary slogans, he eventually flees to avoid certain arrest. Other important characters include the devout Cristina and Don Benedetto, a priest who is an uncompromising opponent of the regime and who is poisoned by the sacramental wine he drinks as he celebrates mass. In the 1962 version of the novel, the Italian title was changed to *Vino e Pane.*

Break, Break, Break (1842). A poem by Alfred TENNYSON, one of those inspired by the death of his friend Arthur HALLAM.

Break of Noon (Partage de Midi; 1906). A poetic drama, revised in 1948, by Paul CLAUDEL. Mesa, struggling with his devotion to God, suddenly falls in love with Yse, mysterious and fecund wife of his friend De Ciz, and acknowledges her as the necessary complement of his own being. However, when she senses that Mesa still secretly feels their human love is a barrier to spiritual love, Yse abandons him and her De Ciz children and takes Mesa's child to rejoin her former lover Amalric. When Mesa comes to woo her back, their child is dead, and they recognize the necessary impossibility of their earthly happiness.

Breasted, James Henry (1865–1935). American historian and archaeologist. He is noted for his many books on ancient Egyptian history. His *Ancient Times: A History of the Early World* (1916) was reissued as *The Conquest of Civilization* (1926).

Brecht, Bertolt (1898–1956). German dramatist. Despite his explicit commitment to Marxist dogma, his plays have been immensely popular in the West. His early plays, such as *Trommeln in der Nacht (Drums in the Night,* 1922), *Im Dickicht der Städte (In the Jungle of Cities,* 1924), and *Mann ist Mann (Man Is Man,* 1927), are closely related in technique to the movement of EXPRESSIONISM, and though they are permeated by the cynical and critical irony toward modern society that appears in all his works, they do not yet systematically advocate any political doctrine. Brecht's decisive turn to Marxism, however, came shortly afterward in THE THREEPENNY OPERA and RISE AND FALL OF THE TOWN MAHAGONNY. It is also in these plays that his mature technique is first fully exemplified, the technique of the EPIC THEATER that was to dominate his subsequent production. In 1933, Brecht was driven from Germany by the rise of Nazism, and began a 14-year exile in Denmark, Sweden, Finland and, from 1941 to 1947, in the U.S. The plays written during this exile include direct attacks on Nazism, such as THE PRIVATE LIFE OF THE MASTER RACE and *Schweyk im Zweiten Weltkrieg* (*Schweyk in the Second World War*, written 1944–1945); plays with historical settings such as LIFE OF GALILEO and MOTHER COURAGE AND HER CHILDREN; and two Chinese parables, THE GOOD WOMAN OF SEZUAN and THE CAUCASIAN CHALK CIRCLE. In 1947, Brecht returned to Zürich and went from there to East Berlin in 1948 where he founded his own company; his works of the last period consist almost entirely of adaptations.

Breck, Alan. In Robert Louis Stevenson's novel KIDNAPPED, a high-spirited, courageous, and slightly unscrupulous supporter of the Stuart claimant to the throne. After being shipwrecked, he and David Balfour, the young hero of the book, travel through Scotland. His full name is Alan Breck Stewart (or Stuart) and he is very proud to bear the name of a king. He appears in Stevenson's *Catriona* (1893) also.

Bregendahl, Marie (1867–1940). Danish novelist. A regionalist writer, she described peasant life in her native Jutland with quiet skill and sober sympathy. Her most important works are *En Dødsnat* (*A Night of Death*, 1912) and *Sødalsfolkene* (7 vols., 1914–1923).

Breitmann, Hans. The hero of a series of ballads written in German-American dialect; also, the pen name of his creator, Charles Godfrey Leland (1824–1903). The first and most famous of the ballads is *Hans Breitmann'· Party*, published in *Graham's Magazine* (May, 1857), of which Leland was then editor. Leland's published collections about Breitmann, a jovial Pennsylvania Dutchman, include *The Breitmann Ballads* (1871), *Hans Breitmann in Tyrol* (1894), and *Hans Breitmann's Ballads* (1914).

Bremond, Henri (1865–1933). French literary critic and historian. Bremond left the Jesuit order for a literary career, but his principal work, *Histoire littéraire du sentiment religieux en France* (1916–1933), is an 11-volume study of religious elements in French literature.

Brennius. One of the kings in Geoffrey of Monmouth's HISTORY OF THE KINGS OF BRITAIN. He struggled with Belinus for the kingdom, but ultimately made a treaty with him.

Brentano, Clemens Maria (1778–1842). German romantic poet. He was the brother of Bettina von Arnim. In his lyrics, he had a genius for capturing the folk spirit, and it was he who invented the so-called folk legend of the LORELEI, in a poem that appeared in his novel *Godwi* (1800–1801). But he was also capable of highly sophisticated poems, especially on religious subjects, as in his unfinished *Romanzen vom Rosenkranz* (*Romances of the Rosary*, written 1810 ff.). With his friend (and later brother-in-law) Achim von Arnim, he edited DES KNABEN WUNDERHORN, a collection of folk songs; and his private collection of folk books (see VOLKSBUCH) provided the material for Görres' treatise on the subject. Brentano's short narrative works include the novella *Geschichte vom braven Kasperl*

und dem schönen Annerl (*Story of Upright Casper and Lovely Annie*, written 1816, pub. 1838), and numerous MÄRCHEN. See GERMAN ROMANTICISM.

Brest-Litovsk, Treaty of (1918). A treaty between Germany and the Russian Bolshevik government, signed in the Polish city of the same name. Russia withdrew from World War I and ceded vast territories in eastern Europe.

Brethren of the Common Life. A group of mystics in Germany and the Low Countries during the 14th and 15th centuries. It was founded by Gerard Groote (1340–1389), a Dutchman. The Brethren lived together communally and through their schools assisted greatly in establishing reforms in education and religion. Erasmus and Martin Luther were at one time their pupils, and the *Imitation of Christ* was one of the products of the influence of the sect's brand of mysticism.

Breton, André (1896–1966). French poet, novelist, and essayist. He was greatly influenced by his reading of Arthur Rimbaud's poetry, his studies of Freudian theory, and his own work in psychiatry. His friendship (1916–1919) with Jacques Vaché (1895–1919), who committed suicide as a deliberate mark of his contempt for modern society, also made a deep impression. In 1919 Breton met Tristan Tzara and led a group of friends into the DADA movement. By 1921, however, he had rejected Tzara's nihilistic use of the irrational as a mockery of reason in favor of a serious research into the subconscious as the autonomous source of truth and beauty. The results of his experiments in automatic writing were published as *Les Champs magnétiques* (1921), written with Philippe Soupault.

In 1924 he founded SURREALISM; his three manifestoes (1924, 1930, 1942) are the most important theoretical statements of the movement. Other critical essays in its defense include *Les Pas perdus* (1924), *Légitime Défense* (1926), *Le Surréalisme et la peinture* (1928), and *What Is Surrealism?* (1934).

A growing interest in the study of dreams and psychic states led to the novel NADJA and *Les Vases communicants* (1932), a study of dreams. Breton joined the Communist Party in 1927, but left it in 1935 after trying unsuccessfully to identify surrealism as the artistic representative of social revolution.

His poems exalting love include those in *Le Revolver à Cheveux Blancs* (1932), *L'Amour Fou* (1937), *Fata Morgana* (1941), and *Arcane 17* (1945).

Breton, Nicholas (1545?–1626). English poet, author of numerous prose pamphlets, moral, religious, and lyric verse. He is known primarily as a pastoral poet, and the best examples of his verse can be found in *England's Helicon* (1600). He is represented in *Breton's Bower of Delights* (1591) and *The Arbor of Amorous Devices* (1597); though both of these books were assigned to him by the printers, the work of other poets is also included.

Bréton de los Herreros, Manuel (1796–1873). Spanish playwright. The clarity of the work of this prominent social satirist makes up for the lack of bitter irony in his comedies of middle-class life. His classic, *Marcela o ¿cuál de los tres?* (*Marcela*, 1831), deals with the problems of a widow beset by three suitors: one arrogant, another loud, and the third melancholy. Among his best-known dramas are *La* *escuela del matrimonio, A Madrid me vuelvo,* and *Muérete y verás.*

Breton lais or **lays.** Rhymed stories popular in England in the 14th century. They usually deal with Celtic themes and often use Arthurian material. The origin of this literary form is unknown, but it was perfected in the 12th century by MARIE DE FRANCE who wrote, among others, the lai *Sir Launfal.* The Franklin in Chaucer's *The Canterbury Tales* (1388) speaks of the old Bretons who rhymed their tales and sang them to the accompaniment of a musical instrument. *Sir Orfeo* is one of the best-known English Breton lais.

Breton's Bower of Delights. See Nicholas BRETON.

Brett, Dorothy (1891–). English painter and friend of D. H. Lawrence. She is the author of *Lawrence and Brett* (1933), a book of reminiscences.

Brian Boru, Boroimhe or **Borumha** (926–1014). Irish king (after 1002) and national hero. His victory over the Danes at Clontarf (1014) put a permanent end to their sovereignty over Ireland, but he was murdered in his tent after the battle.

Briareus (Briareos). In classic legend, a huge monster with 100 arms and 50 heads. With his brothers, Cottus and Gyges, he conquered the Titans by hurling at them 300 rocks at once. Thetis called him to the aid of Zeus when Hera, Athene, and Poseidon rebelled against him. He was also called Aegeon (Aigaion).

Bricklayer, the. A nickname for Ben JONSON, from his stepfather's trade.

Bricks Without Straw (1880). A novel by Albion W. TOURGÉE. This book, a sequel to the earlier A FOOL's ERRAND, is one of the earliest to deal with racial problems in the postwar South. The novel has as its hero a New England schoolteacher in the South who sympathizes with the Negroes.

Bride Comes to Yellow Sky, The (1898). A short story by Stephen CRANE. Published in the collection *The Open Boat and Other Tales of Adventure,* it deals with the conflict between Sheriff Jack Potter and Scratchy Wilson, one of the old frontier gunfighters. Potter brings his new wife to Yellow Sky and encounters Scratchy, who is looking for a fight. When Scratchy realizes that Potter has no gun, he realizes that the old days are gone forever.

Bridehead, Sue. See JUDE THE OBSCURE.

Bride of Abydos, The (1813). A poem by Lord BYRON. The heroine is Zuleika, daughter of Giaffer, pasha of Abydos. She is the plighted bride of Selim; but Giaffer shoots him, and Zuleika dies of a broken heart.

Bride of Lammermoor, The (1819). A historical novel by Sir Walter SCOTT, set in the reign of William III. The titular heroine is Lucy Ashton, daughter of Sir William Ashton, an unscrupulous man who has made great gains in fortune and position by bringing the estate of Lord Ravenswood to ruin through legal trickery. Though he has sworn vengeance, Ravenwood's son Edgar falls in love with Lucy; the lovers plight their troth at the Mermaid's Fountain, but while Edgar is away, Lucy is forced by her parents to marry the unpleasant, dissolute Frank Hayston, laird of Bucklaw. Deranged with grief, Lucy stabs and critically wounds her bridegroom; she dies in convulsions the following day. Edgar, hearing of the marriage and taking it as Lucy's rejection of him, is on his way to a duel with her brother when he is lost in the quicksand of Kelpies Flow, fulfilling an ancient prophecy. The novel is based on historical incident.

In Donizetti's opera *Lucia di Lammermoor* (1835), which is based on the novel, Bucklaw dies of the wound inflicted by his bride and Edgar, heartbroken at Lucy's death, stabs himself. See Caleb BALDERSTONE.

Bride of the Sea. Venice. The city was so called from the ancient ceremony of the wedding of the sea by the doge, who threw a ring into the Adriatic, saying, "We wed thee, O sea, in token of perpetual domination." This took place each year on Ascension Day, and was enjoined upon the Venetians in 1177 by Pope Alexander III, who gave the doge a gold ring from his own finger in token of the victory achieved by the Venetian fleet at Istria over Frederick Barbarossa, in defense of the pope's quarrel. See BUCENTAUR.

Brideshead Revisited (1945). A novel by Evelyn WAUGH, subtitled *The Sacred and Profane Memories of Captain Charles Ryder.* As an undergraduate Ryder met Sebastian Marchmain and later visited him and his family at Brideshead, their home. Billeted there during World War II, Ryder recalls the members of this family and their individual responses to their Catholic faith.

Bridewell. An ancient London prison in Bridge Street, Blackfriars. It was built as a hospital on the site of a former royal palace over a holy well of medicinal water, called St. Bride's (Bridget's) Well.

Bridge, The (1930). A long poem by Hart CRANE. In this, his most important work, Crane attempted to synthesize a picture of modern America by the use of symbols from its past and present, centered about Brooklyn Bridge as a chief symbol of man's aspiration and achievement. Written in several sections, the poem makes use of such figures from the American past as Columbus, Whitman, Poe, and Emily Dickinson; they themselves function as bridges, connecting and fusing the disparate elements of American life into an organic whole. Not only past and present, but time and eternity are fused, the latter bridge being furnished by the Mississippi River.

Bridge of San Luis Rey, The (1927). A novel by Thornton WILDER. The winner of a Pulitzer Prize, it tells of the collapse of a bridge in Peru in 1714. Five travelers on the bridge are killed, and the accident is witnessed by Brother Juniper, a Franciscan friar. The priest wonders whether it really was an accident or a deliberate plan of the Almighty, and it is his subsequent investigation into the lives of the five people that forms the core of the book.

Bridge of Sighs. An enclosed bridge in Venice, connecting the Doge's Palace with the state prisons. According to popular tradition, prisoners were conveyed across this bridge from the judgment hall to the place of execution.

Bridge on the Drina, The (Na Drini Cúprija; 1945). A chronicle by Ivo ANDRIĆ. This long narrative, which its author appropriately called a chronicle, relates in a series of episodes the history of a bridge near the Bosnian town of Višegrad. That history covers three and a half centuries, through much of which the Bosnians lived under Turkish overlords. This is probably the most important of Andrić's several novels about his native Bosnia.

Bridge Over the River Kwai, The. See Pierre BOULLE.

Bridge Perilous. See FAERIE QUEENE, THE.

Bridges, Robert (1844–1930). English poet, appointed British poet laureate in 1913. His poetry is classical in spirit and in diction (he advocated a return to the diction of the 18th century and was a co-founder of the SOCIETY FOR PURE ENGLISH). His prosody is mildly experimental. He did important work in metrics, including a study of *Milton's Prosody* (1893). *His Poetical Works* was published in 1912, and THE TESTAMENT OF BEAUTY in 1929. *A Passer-by* is his finest lyric. He also wrote plays, chiefly on classical subjects, and critical essays. Bridges was a friend of Gerard Manley Hopkins, and published his poetry in 1918.

Bridie, James. Pen name of **Osborne Henry Mavor** (1888–1951). Scottish playwright. His plays are famous for their wit and fancy. *The Anatomist* (1930) and *The Sleeping Clergyman* (1933) are dramatizations of well-known criminal cases. *Storm in a Teacup* (1936) is set in Scotland. *One Way of Living* (1939) is autobiographical.

Bridlegoose, Judge. An anglicism for Juge Bridoie, the judge in Rabelais' GARGANTUA AND PANTAGRUEL who decides the cases brought before him by a throw of dice. He explains to Pantagruel that he had never made a mistake until his eyesight began to fail. The dice-throwing and Bridlegoose's insistence that volumes of documents are necessary to allow a case to mature properly are a lively satire on legal procedures.

Beaumarchais in the *Marriage of Figaro* (1784) named his judge "Bridoison," but his magistrate, a slave to legal procedure, bears little resemblance to Rabelais' character.

Bridoie, Juge. See Judge BRIDLEGOOSE.

Bridoison. See Judge BRIDLEGOOSE.

Brieux, Eugène (1858–1932). French dramatist. Brieux's early works—*Ménages d'Artistes* (1890) and *Blanchette* (1892)—were first produced at Antoine's Théâtre Libre. In *Les Trois Filles de M. Dupont* (1899), Brieux, at heart a moral and social reformer, leveled violent criticism at parents who seek to manipulate the lives of their children. *La Robe Rouge* (1900) demands that criminal law be reformed; *La Femme Seule* (1913) staunchly defends women's rights. Although Brieux did not possess the depth necessary for excellent drama of ideas, he did possess a large fund of sympathy and a vigorous sense of protest.

Briffault, Robert Stephen (1876–1948). English anthropologist. He was the author of the once widely read study *The Mothers* (1927).

Brigge, Malte Laurids. See NOTEBOOKS OF MALTE LAURIDS BRIGGE, THE.

Bright, John (1811–1889). English statesman and orator. A liberal, he was strongly opposed to the CORN LAWS and the Crimean War and favored the North in the U.S. Civil War. He is the author of *Speeches on Parliamentary Reform* (1867), *Speeches*

on Questions of Public Policy (1869), and *Speeches on Public Affairs* (1869).

Brighton Rock (1938). A novel by Graham GREENE. Set in an English seaside resort, it is the story of Pinkie, a teen-age criminal gang leader and murderer. The novel has elements of a detective story, psychiatric case history, and essay on moral theology.

Brigliadoro (Golden Bridle). Orlando's horse in the poems of Boiardo and Ariosto (see ORLANDO FURIOSO).

Brihat-kathasaritsagara. See KATHASARITSAGARA.

Brillat-Savarin, Anthelme (1755–1826). French politician and gourmet. His *Physiologie du goût* (1825) is a famous work on gastronomy.

Brimming Cup, The (1921). A novel by Dorothy Canfield FISHER. In this story set in Vermont, Mrs. Fisher tells how a man of the world, mature and selfish, seeks to win Marise Crittendon from her husband, Neale. The latter is too honorable to seek to hold her, but events convince her that she needs his integrity more than Vincent Marsh's passion. *Rough-Hewn* (1922) tells of Neale and Marise earlier in their lives.

Brinnin, John Malcolm (1916–   ). American poet and editor. He was the editor of various avant-garde periodicals and later published several volumes of poetry, including *The Garden Is Political* (1942), *The Lincoln Lyrics* (1942), and *The Sorrows of Cold Stone* (1951). After inviting Dylan Thomas to give readings in the U.S., he wrote *Dylan Thomas in America* (1955) and edited *A Casebook on Dylan Thomas* (1960).

Brinton, [Clarence] Crane (1898–1968). American historian, biographer, and educator. A teacher at Harvard since 1923, Brinton has written numerous books, among them *The Political Ideas of the English Romantics* (1926), *The Jacobins* (1930), *Nietzsche* (1941), and *The Shaping of the Modern Mind* (1953).

Brinvilliers, Marquise de. Born **Marie Madeleine d'Aubray** (1630–1676). Notorious French poisoner and a favorite subject for writers. Mme. de Sévigné describes Brinvilliers' execution in her letters.

Briscoe, Lily. A painter, a leading character in Virginia Woolf's novel TO THE LIGHTHOUSE.

Briseida. The beloved of TROILUS in the *Roman de Troie* of BENOÎT DE SAINTE-MAURE. In later versions of the story she is known as Criseida or Cressida.

Briseis. The daughter of Briseus. She was the subject of the quarrel in the ILIAD between Agamemnon and Achilles; when the former robbed Achilles of her, Achilles refused any longer to go to battle, and the Greeks lost ground daily.

Brissot [de Warville], Jacques Pierre (1754–1793). French revolutionist and journalist. His antimonarchical pamphlets, inspired by the ideas of Rousseau, caused him to be exiled. He traveled in the Netherlands, Switzerland, England, and the U.S. Returning to France in 1789, he became editor of the newspaper *Le Patriote français* until his death; he was a leader of the GIRONDISTS, and the paper became their organ. Brissot's humanitarian interests led him to advocate penal reform in France, and later to found the society of the "Amis des noirs" in 1788, dedicated to the abolition of slavery. An admirer of the U.S., he founded the Gallo-American Society; he wrote *Considerations on the Relative Situation of France and the United States* (1788, in English) and *The Commerce of America with Europe* (1794, in English). When the JACOBINS overthrew the Girondists, Brissot was guillotined.

Bristol Boy, the. An epithet for the poet Thomas CHATTERTON. He is so called because his chief poetic works deal with the imagined 15th century antiquities of the port city of Bristol.

Britannia. A personification of the British Empire. The first known representation of Britannia as a female figure sitting on a globe, leaning with one arm on a shield, and grasping a spear in the other hand, is on a Roman coin of Antoninus Pius, who died A.D. 161. The figure reappeared on the English copper coin in the reign of Charles II, 1665.

Britannicus. Original name, **Claudius Tiberius Germanicus** (c. A.D. 41–55). Son of Messalina and the emperor Claudius, heir apparent to the throne. Through the scheming of his stepmother, AGRIPPINA, he was denied succession to the throne. It is believed that Nero, his half brother, poisoned Britannicus at a banquet. The name Britannicus was given to him by the senate because the conquest of Britain took place at about the time of his birth. He is the subject of a tragedy (1669) by Racine.

Britannicus (1669). A tragedy by Jean RACINE. The material of the play is derived from Tacitus. Smitten with Junia, the beloved of his half brother Britannicus, the emperor Nero attempts to win her; unsuccessful, he causes Britannicus to be arrested and poisons him. Junia escapes from the palace and becomes a vestal virgin. The play abounds in political subplot and marks Racine's first challenge of Corneille on the older playwright's homeground: political drama.

British Broadcasting Corporation. Called the BBC. The publicly owned radio and television broadcasting body in Great Britain. The home radio networks are called the Light Programme, the Home Service, and the Third Programme. It is the last that is famous for its extremely erudite programming. The BBC was established in 1922.

Britomart. In Spenser's FAERIE QUEENE (Books III and IX), a lady knight, the personification of chastity.

Britomartis. A Cretan goddess, later an attendant of Artemis. Loved by King Minos, she hid from him for nine months and finally flung herself into the sea to escape him. She was saved by being caught in, or hiding under, fishermen's nets.

Brittain, Vera. Pen name of **Mrs. George Edward Gordon Catlin** (1896–1970). English essayist and novelist. She wrote *Testament of Youth* (1933), an autobiography, and *Testament of Friendship* (1940), a memorial to her friend Winifred Holtby. *Testament of Experience* (1957) is a companion piece to her earlier autobiography and covers the years from 1925 to 1950.

broadside ballads. Popular songs and poems, written in doggerel. They were printed in black letter on a single sheet of paper, decorated with woodcuts, with the name of the tune to which the ballads in question were to be sung, and sold for a penny or two on the street corners of England in the late 16th and early 17th centuries. Their subject

The Revvard of Murther,
In the Execution of *Richard Smith*, for murthering *Mary Davis* widow, to whom hee made a promise of Marriage after he had gotten her with Childe: she was found drownd in a Pond neare More Fields, the 27. of *November* last, and the said *Richard Smith*, executed this present Saterday, being the 12. of *December*, 1640. for the same fact.

To the tune of, *Ned Smith.*

An English broadside ballad (1640).

matter was taken from political events, battles or wars, murders, strange happenings, executions, freakish births, domestic quarrels, and the like, and also included moral exhortations and religious propaganda.

Broadway. The main street of New York City, extending from near the lower tip of Manhattan northward through the length of Manhattan and the Bronx to beyond the city line. Though famous in its own right, the street is mainly known today for its association with the theater: since nearly all commercial drama originates in New York City, the term Broadway is practically synonymous with the American theater. Most of the major theaters in the city are not more than a block or two from Broadway. In a more general sense, Broadway denotes the gay night life of the American metropolis in a quasi-legendary conception.

In the 1950's, the term Off Broadway became prominent in referring to the growing number of small theaters in other parts of Manhattan which offered theater fare considered commercially unprofitable for Broadway. These theaters were often tiny, grubby, and impoverished, but some of them gave fine performances of experimental plays or classical revivals that could not otherwise have been seen. In time, the Off-Broadway theater became highly popular, and, with rising costs, was beset by many of the financial ills of Broadway. However, it also attracted first-class actors and even some outstanding playwrights, such as Tennessee Williams, who consented to have new works performed off Broadway.

Brobdingnag. The country of giants 12 times the size of man in Jonathan Swift's satire GULLIVER's TRAVELS. Told by Gulliver of European customs and institutions, the king observes, "I cannot but conclude the bulk of your natives to be the most pernicious race of little vermin that nature ever suffered to crawl upon the earth." The inhuman nobility of this view contrasts with the meanness and pettiness of the people of LILLIPUT. See GLUMDALCLITCH.

Broch, Hermann (1886–1951). Austrian novelist. He is best known for his *Der Tod des Vergil* (*The Death of Vergil*, 1945) in which mythical and penetrating psychological elements are blended in an original and powerful manner that has excited comparisons with such writers as James Joyce and Thomas Mann. His most famous earlier work, more directly concerned with social and historical problems, is *Die Schlafwandler* (*The Sleepwalkers*, 1931–1932), a trilogy of novels. Broch, whose widely varied background influenced his writing, studied philosophy and mathematics, was active in the textile industry, wrote numerous sociological and literary essays in addition to his novels, and died while engaged in research on mass psychology at Yale University. He had left his homeland after being imprisoned by the Nazis.

Brocken. The highest peak of the Harz range in Saxony. On the eve of May Day, i.e., the feast of Walburga (Walpurgis) or Walpurgis Night, the Brocken was the scene of a famous witches' Sabbath. It is also known for the specter of the Brocken, an optical illusion, first observed on the Brocken, in which shadows of the spectators, greatly magnified, are projected on the mists about the summit of the mountain opposite. In one of De Quincey's opium dreams there is a powerful description of the Brocken specter.

Brod, Max (1884–1968). Austrian writer. He is best known for his edition of the works of his friend Franz Kafka, who bequeathed him all his unfinished manuscripts. He also wrote a fine biography entitled *Franz Kafka* (1937) and several critical works on the same author. He now lives in Tel Aviv, and his own lyric and narrative writing deals largely with Jewish themes.

Brofelt, Johannes. See Juhani Aho.

Broken Heart, The (c. 1629). A tragedy by John Ford. The feud between the Spartan families of Crotolon and Thrasus was to have been ended by the marriage of the former's son Orgilus to the latter's daughter Penthea. However, Thrasus dies, and his son Ithocles gives Penthea to the jealous old merchant Bassanes. Meanwhile, Ithocles' friend Prophilus has fallen in love with Orgilus' sister Euphranea. He marries her, and the breach between the two families seems to have been healed. Orgilus even intercedes as an arbiter in Ithocles' suit for the hand of Calantha, the king's daughter. Soon her loveless marriage is too much for Penthea. She loses her mind and, shortly thereafter, dies. On a visit to her bier, Orgilus avenges himself by stabbing Ithocles to death. Apprehended, Orgilus is allowed to open a vein and bleed to death. Calantha dies of a broken heart.

Broken Jug, The (Der zerbrochene Krug; written 1803, pub. 1811). A one-act comedy by Heinrich von Kleist. The plot revolves around the figure of a Dutch village judge named Adam who, on the very day that his court is being observed by a government inspector, finds that he must hear a case in which he himself is the guilty party. By his swift inventiveness, he manages to keep the truth hidden for a while, but is finally discovered.

Brome, Alexander (1620–1666). English attorney and royalist poet. Noted for his drinking songs and satirical verse, he was the author of *The Cun-*

ning Lovers (1654), a comedy, and *Songs and Poems* (1661).

Brome, Richard (d. 1652). English dramatist known for his realistic and satirical comedies of life in London. His best plays are A Jovial Crew *The City Wit, or The Woman Wears the Breeches* (c. 1628), *The Weeding of Covent Garden* (1632), and *The Sparagus Garden* (1635). He was the last of the comic dramatists of the Tudor-Stuart period.

Bromfield, Louis (1896–1956). American writer. Bromfield established his reputation with his early novels, the four books of a tetralogy called *Escape:* The Green Bay Tree, *Possession* (1925), *Early Autumn* (1926), and *A Good Woman* (1927). He also received praise for his factual and descriptive accounts of the 1,000-acre Ohio farm he purchased and turned into a productive showcase: *Pleasant Valley* (1945), *Malabar Farm* (1948), *Out of the Earth* (1950), and *From My Experience* (1955). One of his numerous other novels, *The Rains Came* (1937), is set in Malabar, the coastal region of India after which his farm was named.

bromide and sulphite. Words coined by Gelett Burgess in his humorous essay *Are You a Bromide, or The Sulphitic Theory* (1907). In it he explains the terms bromide and sulphite as applied to psychological rather than chemical analysis. The bromide, according to Burgess, "does his thinking by syndicate. He follows the main-traveled roads, he goes with the crowd." The sulphite, on the other hand, is unconventional, original, everything that the bromide is not.

Bronnen, Arnolt (1895–1959). German dramatist in the movement of expressionism. His violently emotional works include *Vatermord* (*Parricide*, written 1915, performed 1922), and *Katalaunische Schlacht* (*Catalaunian Battle*, 1924). Bronnen was a socialist and friend of Brecht until the two parted company when Bronnen turned to Nazism.

Bronstein, Lev Davidovich. See Leon Trotsky.

Brontë family. An English family, originally of Irish descent, that produced three 19th-century novelists: Charlotte, Emily, and Anne. On the death of his wife in 1821, the Reverend Patrick Brontë, a curate, sent for his sister-in-law to help him bring up his six children. A few years later all the girls except Anne were sent to board at the Clergy Daughters' School at Cowan Bridge; conditions at the school were dreadful, and worsened by the administration's belief that physical discomfort was spiritually edifying. The two eldest girls died at the school in 1825, and Charlotte and Emily were returned home. Lowood School in Jane Eyre was based on Charlotte's unhappy memories of Cowan Bridge. During much of their childhood, the four remaining Brontë children were free to roam and play in the Yorkshire moors, giving free reign to their imaginations. Charlotte, with the help of her brother Branwell, created Angria, a vast African empire, and wrote of the lives and adventures of its inhabitants. At the same time Emily kept a journal, the *Gondal Chronicle*, on the wars and intrigues of the Royalists and Republicans in a mysterious North country.

In 1831, *Charlotte* (1816–1855) was sent to Roe Head School, where she returned to teach from 1835–1838. She worked for a time as a governess and then, in 1842, went with Emily to Brussels to study at the school of Constantine Héger, where she taught the following year. Many of the scenes of VILLETTE are based on Charlotte's experiences at the school and on her deep but frustrated emotional attachment to Héger. In 1845, Charlotte made the accidental discovery that Emily and Anne had been writing verse. She herself had composed many poems, and she collected them all into a volume (1846) of poetry signed by Currer (Charlotte), Ellis (Emily), and Acton (Anne) Bell, pseudonyms that they retained throughout their later work. The book, published at their expense, was unsuccessful, selling only two copies. Charlotte soon submitted her first novel, *The Professor,* to a number of publishers, and it was rejected so many times that she finally withdrew it. She nevertheless set to work to complete *Jane Eyre,* which was published and achieved spectacular success.

On the strength of her one novel, WUTHERING HEIGHTS, and the best of her poems, *Emily* (1818–1848) is generally considered to be of greater genius than her sisters. Her mysticism is reflected in her work, especially in her extraordinary novel and in such poems as *The Prisoner, Remembrance, The Old Stoic,* and *The Visionary.* Some skeptics have maintained that *Wuthering Heights* was actually the work of her dissipated brother, **Patrick Branwell** (1817–1848), on the grounds that no woman, let alone one who led such a circumscribed life, could have written such a turbulent and passionate book. But Branwell, who was tubercular and addicted to alcohol and possibly to opium, had no literary talent. He died in 1848, and Emily, who caught cold at his funeral, died a few months later.

Anne (1820–1849), the least talented of the sisters, wrote two novels, AGNES GREY and THE TENANT OF WILDFELL HALL. It is possible that neither of these books would be remembered today if she were not the sister of Charlotte and Emily.

After her sisters' death Charlotte devoted herself to the care of her father, who was going blind. She completed SHIRLEY, which was well received, as was *Villette,* her last novel. These were years of social lionization, and in London and elsewhere she met Thackeray, Matthew Arnold, Mrs. Gaskell, Harriet Martineau, and others. She married Arthur Bell Nichols, her father's curate, in 1854 and died the following year. *The Professor* was published posthumously in 1857, and *Emma,* a fragment, appeared in 1860.

Bronze Horseman, The (Mednyi Vsadnik; 1833). A long poem by Aleksandr PUSHKIN. Its theme is the conflict between the desires of an ordinary individual, represented by the poor clerk Evgeni, and the demands of a powerful state, represented by Peter the Great. A flood inundates St. Petersburg, the capital city built on the Neva River at Peter's orders, and drowns Evgeni's fiancée. Demented by his grief, Evgeni stands before the imposing statue of the emperor and curses Peter's inhuman willfulness, which he blames for his fiancée's death. In a hallucination, he imagines that Peter is chasing him through the streets of the city. After this, Evgeni is cured of his rebelliousness. Whenever he passes the statue of the emperor, his manner once again shows respect and fear.

The poem displays one aspect of Pushkin's attitude toward Peter the Great. Pushkin also recognized that, however much Peter's sometimes cruel power was to be deplored, the emperor had done Russia great service. In the long poem, *Poltava* (1828–1829), Pushkin extolled Peter for his service to the country.

Bronzino, Il. Real name, **Agnolo di Cosimo Allori** (1503–1572). Florentine portraitist. A pupil of the mannerist Pontormo, he was strongly influenced by Michelangelo's religious paintings. His best-known works include the *Portrait of Ugolino Mantelli* and the *Portrait of Eleonora of Toledo with her Son.*

Brooke, Dorothea. The idealistic heroine of George Eliot's MIDDLEMARCH. Her sister Celia and their uncle, Squire Brooke, with whom they live, are also prominent characters.

Brooke, Frances [Moore] (1724–1789). English-born Canadian novelist. The wife of a clergyman, Mrs. Brooke followed her husband to Canada, where he was chaplain to the garrison at Quebec. Her four-volume *History of Emily Montague* (1769) had a Canadian setting and is often considered the first Canadian novel. However, Mrs. Brooke's work was based on English models and had no perceptible effect on Canadian literature, though it does give a vivid picture of social life in 18th-century Quebec.

Brooke, Henry (1703–1783). Irish poet and novelist. His best known works are *Universal Beauty* (1735–1736), a philosophical poem dealing with physical and theological concepts; *Gustavus Vasa* (1739), a play; and THE FOOL OF QUALITY, a novel.

Brooke, Rupert (1887–1915). English poet. He was widely known and admired for his war poetry, especially the series of sonnets called *1914;* it expressed the patriotic idealism of the early years of World War I. He died in service during the war, of septicaemia. He was a traditional, GEORGIAN poet; *Grantchester* and *The Great Lover* are well-known examples of his early work. Later he was influenced, like T. S. Eliot, by his study of 17th-century poetry (he published a study of John Webster in 1916), and began to write such witty, original poems as *Heaven* and *Dust.* St. John Ervine is said to have drawn the hero of his novel *Changing Winds* from Rupert Brooke.

Brook Farm. A utopian community established in 1841 at West Roxbury, Mass. The members of the Brook Farm Institute of Agriculture and Education, led by George RIPLEY, shared equally in work, benefits, and remuneration; among those associated with the community were Theodore Parker, William Henry Channing, Nathaniel Hawthorne, Margaret Fuller, Charles A. Dana, G. W. Curtis, and Albert Brisbane. The group, later influenced by FOURIERISM, changed its name to the Brook Farm Phalanx; in 1846, when the "Central Phalanstery" burned down, it disbanded. Emerson viewed this experiment made by his fellow Transcendentalists with skepticism; he called Brook Farm "the Age of Reason in a patty-pan." Hawthorne, who came to West Roxbury in the hope of finding an economical way to live and write, soon found communal living unattractive. He modeled the community in THE BLITHEDALE ROMANCE on Brook Farm.

Brook Kerith, The (1916). A novel by George MOORE. A presentation of the life of Jesus, the author follows the customary account as far as the Crucifixion, but later Joseph of Arimathea finds Jesus still alive. For 30 years afterward He lives as a shepherd by the Brook Kerith. He has rejected his early belief in himself, which he considers blasphemy, and when he finally meets Paul the Apostle and hears his version of the story, he is horrified and plans to go to Jerusalem and reveal the truth. Paul, however, forces him to realize that his story would not be believed.

The ravens fed Elijah by this brook of Palestine, called Cherith in the Bible.

Brooks, Cleanth (1906–   ). American literary critic and educator. Brooks became associated with the NEW CRITICISM when he coedited (1935–1942) THE SOUTHERN REVIEW with Robert Penn WARREN. He wrote two college textbooks: *Understanding Fiction* (1943), in collaboration with Warren, and *Understanding Drama* (1945), with Robert Heilman. In these texts, and in his own volumes, *Modern Poetry and the Tradition* (1939) and *The Well-Wrought Urn* (1947), he influenced contemporary methods of teaching literature. Brooks's approach to literature emphasizes close reading and structural analysis; he tends to look for and favor in poetry the central qualities of wit, irony, paradox, symbolism, and dramatic structure. Since 1947, he has taught at Yale University; with Warren he has written *Modern Rhetoric* (1949), and with W. K. Wimsatt, Jr., *Literary Criticism: A Short History* (1957). *William Faulkner: The Yoknapatawpha Country*, the first of a proposed two-volume study, appeared in 1963.

Brooks, Van Wyck (1886–1963). American critic and biographer. His early writings, such as *The Wine of the Puritans* (1908), were critical of the narrowness and insularity of the Puritan heritage and urged a broader, more unified cultural ideal for the nation. In the five volumes of the "Makers and Finders" series, Brooks created the first composite picture of American cultural and literary development. The best-known volumes of the series are *The Flowering of New England, 1815–1865* (1936), which was awarded a Pulitzer Prize, and *New England: Indian Summer, 1865–1915* (1940). Brooks also wrote *America's Coming of Age* (1915), *The Ordeal of Mark Twain* (1920), *The Pilgrimage of Henry James* (1925), and *The Life of Emerson* (1932).

Broteas. In Greek mythology, an extremely ugly son of Tantalus and brother of Pelops who flung himself onto a pyre because of his ugliness or blindness. He was said to have carved a still existing statue of Rhea on the side of Mount Sipylus.

Brother Jonathan. The generic name for a New Englander, hence for Americans and America. One account of its origin tells how, when Washington was in want of ammunition, he called a council of officers, but no practical suggestion could be offered. "We must consult Brother Jonathan," said the general, meaning His Excellency Jonathan Trumbull, governor of the state of Connecticut. This was done, and the difficulty was remedied. "To consult Brother Jonathan" then became a set phrase, and Brother Jonathan became a name for the typical shrewd Yankee. He appears as a character in *The Contrast* (1787), a play by Royall Tyler.

Brothers Karamazov, The (Brat'ya Karamazovy; 1879–1880). A novel by Feodor DOSTOEVSKI. Considered his best work, it is one of the outstanding novels in literature. The main plot involves Feodor Pavlovich Karamazov and his four sons: Dmitri, Ivan, Alyosha, and the bastard Smerdyakov (see KARAMAZOV). Feodor Pavlovich, a depraved buffoon, is Dmitri's rival for the affections of the local siren, GRUSHENKA. Violent quarrels over her and over Dmitri's disputed inheritance ensue until Feodor Pavlovich is murdered. Dmitri is arrested and brought to trial for the crime. This basic line of action is complicated throughout the novel by a host of other factors masterfully linked to the main plot. The second son, Ivan, a tortured intellectual, gradually realizes that he has secretly wished for his father's death and may have transmitted this wish to Smerdyakov, a grotesque caricature of the brilliant Ivan. Dmitri's relations with his ex-fiancée, KATERINA IVANOVNA, also prove to have a bearing on his involvement in the crime and his unwillingness to defend himself against the charges. The youngest son, Alyosha, plays no direct part in the crime, but acts throughout the book as a religious foil to the depraved Feodor Pavlovich, the passionate Dmitri, and the rationalistic Ivan. By means of Alyosha, the elder ZOSIMA, who expresses the author's religious views, is introduced into the novel.

Balancing, or perhaps outweighing, Zosima's religious message is the expression of unbelief enunciated by Ivan. His attitude is forcefully conveyed in the famous "Legend of the GRAND INQUISITOR," a parable of his own invention which he relates to Alyosha. Essentially a pessimistic look at man's religious possibilities, the Legend has been regarded by some critics as evidence of Dostoevski's own religious doubts.

Besides being a story of crime and a novel of religious and ethical ideas, the book is, in part, a social document. The intellectual and political ideas current in 19th-century Russia are introduced by Ivan and the careerist Rakitin, while the Legend may be read as a critique of the socialist utopia as well as of religious orthodoxy. The judicial reforms of the later 19th century and the effects they had are revealed during the trial of Dmitri.

The literal, religious, social, and ethical levels of the novel are buttressed by the psychological probings for which Dostoevski is well known. The book abounds in instances of the author's mastery in this area, from the portrayal of the corrupt yet shameful Feodor Pavlovich, to the mental disintegration of the brilliant Ivan, to the painful adolescence of Kolya Krasotkin.

Broun, Heywood [Campbell] (1888–1939). American journalist and novelist. Known for his liberal sympathies and opposition to social injustice, Broun wrote for several New York newspapers and magazines. He was equally well known and loved as a kindly, unpunctual fellow whose huge bulk and untidy appearance led him to be called a "one-man slum." The Newspaper Guild, which Broun helped found, has established an annual award for reporting done "in the spirit of Heywood Broun." A *Collected Edition* of his writings appeared in 1941.

Brown, Charles Brockden (1771–1810). American novelist and editor. Regarded as the first American professional author, he introduced the Indian into U.S. fiction and was among the first Americans to win a hearing abroad. Brown anticipated the later deep interest in psychotic characters, foreshadowing Poe's interest in the horrifying. His fame rests on six Gothic romances: WIELAND, *Ormond* (1799), ARTHUR MERVYN, EDGAR HUNTLY, *Clara Howard* (1801), and *Jane Talbot* (1801).

Brown, Ford Madox (1821–1893). English painter. He represented historical or social and moralizing subjects with accurate draftsmanship characterized by repeated areas of color. He was never a member of the PRE-RAPHAELITE BROTHERHOOD, but there was a reciprocal influence between that group and himself.

Brown, John (1800–1859). American abolitionist. In the 1850's Brown, an abolitionist since his youth, became obsessed with the idea of freeing the slaves by force. In 1855 he and five sons went to Kansas, then a battleground between pro- and anti-slavery forces. The following year, with his approval, a small band, including four of his sons, murdered five settlers near Potawatomi Creek during an anti-slavery raid. Later he and 40 men resisted an attack on Osawatomie by proslavery men.

Now nationally known as "Old Brown of Osawatomie," he made plans to foment a slave insurrection in the South. On Oct. 16, 1859, he attacked Harper's Ferry, Va. (now West Va.) with 21 men and seized the U.S. arsenal and armory there. A detachment of marines under Col. Robert E. Lee defeated and captured Brown. During his trial for treason, he conducted himself with dignity, maintaining that he had been an instrument in the hands of God. He was convicted and hanged on Dec. 2, a martyr in the eyes of abolitionists.

His career inspired the Civil War marching song *John Brown's Body Lies A-Mouldering in the Grave* and numerous literary works, notably Stephen Vincent Benét's narrative poem, *John Brown's Body* (1928).

Brown, John (1810–1882). Scottish physician and author. He is famous for his dog story RAB AND HIS FRIENDS and his essay on *Marjorie Fleming* (1863), the 10-year-old prodigy and pet of Sir Walter Scott.

Brown, Thomas. See John FELL.

Brown, Tom. See TOM BROWN'S SCHOOL DAYS.

Brown, William Hill (1765–1793). American novelist, poet and dramatist, probably the author of THE POWER OF SYMPATHY. Born in Boston, Brown also wrote a series of verse fables, a tragedy, a comedy, and another short novel of incest and seduction, *Ira and Isabella* (1807).

Browne, Charles Farrar. See Artemus WARD.

Browne, Hablot Knight. See PHIZ.

Browne, Sir Thomas (1605–1682). English writer and scholar. Browne was a successful physician who, except for his years of schooling at Oxford and in Europe, spent his life in the town of Norwich. He was knighted in 1671 by Charles II as a steadfast Royalist famous for his antiquarian scholarship. As Browne himself knew, he had a curiously mixed nature: by temperament melancholy, mystical, and credulous, he was by training a scientist and philo-sophical skeptic. He was also a lover of language and classical learning, and his sonorous, stirringly cadenced prose style, rich in exotic coinages and striking images, is one of the most remarkable accomplishments in English literature. He is most brilliant when he treats themes that allow the full display of his personality, such as religion in RELIGIO MEDICI and morality and oblivion in HYDRIOTAPHIA OR URN BURIAL. His other works are *Pseudodoxia Epidemica,* also called VULGAR ERRORS; *The Garden of Cyrus* (1658); and *Christian Morals,* edited in 1756 by Samuel Johnson.

Browne, Thomas Alexander. Pen name, **Rolf Boldrewood** (1826–1915). Australian novelist who wrote some 30 novels of adventure. His best-known book is *Robbery Under Arms* (1888), which depicts life in the Australian gold fields.

Browne, William (c. 1591–?1643). English poet. The most influential member of the early 17th-century SPENSERIAN SCHOOL of pastoral poets, he was the author of *Two Elegies* (1613) on the death of Prince Henry, the elder son of James I, and of *Britannia's Pastorals* (1613, 1616). His poems were also published in *The Shepherd's Pipe* (1614), a book of eclogues in which George Wither and Sir John Davies, prominent Spenserians, were also represented. *Britannia's Pastorals* is said to have influenced Milton and Keats.

brownie. The house spirit in Scottish superstition. At night he is supposed to busy himself in doing little jobs for the family over which he presides. Farms are his favorite abode. Brownies are brown or tawny spirits, in opposition to fairies, which are fair ones. In the U.S. the adventures of the brownies were popularized by a series of *Brownie Books* by Palmer Cox.

Browning, Elizabeth Barrett (1806–1861). English poet, wife of Robert BROWNING. In childhood she suffered a spinal injury and, until her meeting with Browning, seemed to be doomed to invalidism and seclusion from the world. The Brownings' courtship under the eyes of Elizabeth's jealous, tyrannical father, their elopement, and subsequent happy married life in Italy form one of the most celebrated of literary romances. Hawthorne described Mrs. Browning as "a pale, small person scarcely embodied at all," and this ethereality of her physical appearance is reflected by the palpitating fervor, the unworldly tenderness and purity of her work. Often, however, these qualities decline into stridency, diffuseness, and confusion. Her themes were dictated by her broad humanitarian interests; a deep if unorthodox religious feeling; her affection for her adopted country, Italy; and, of course, her love for Browning. Her greatest work, SONNETS FROM THE PORTUGUESE, a sequence of love sonnets addressed to her husband, remains an extraordinary and living achievement. Her other works include *Essay on Mind, With Other Poems* (1826), a translation of Aeschylus' *Prometheus Bound* (1833), *The Seraphim And Other Poems* (1838), *Poems* (1844), CASA GUIDI WINDOWS, AURORA LEIGH, *Poems Before Congress* (1860), and *Last Poems* (1862). See CRY OF THE CHILDREN, THE; LADY GERALDINE'S COURTSHIP.

Browning, Robert (1812–1889). English poet. The son of a bank clerk, Browning was long unsuccessful as a poet and financially dependent upon his family until he was well into adulthood. When in his teens, he discovered Shelley and adopted Shelleyian liberalism in opinion and confessionalism in poetry. Accordingly, his first poems—*Pauline* (1833), PARACELSUS, SORDELLO,—were long, personal, and self-consciously poetic, though the latter two supposedly had as their subject actual historic personages. All three works were considered failures, and, from 1837 to 1846, Browning attempted to write verse drama for the stage, again unsuccessfully. In 1845 he met Elizabeth Barrett, then considered one of the outstanding poets of the day, and married her the following year. Partially because of her ill health and partially because of her father's opposition to the marriage, Browning took his wife to Italy, and remained there until her death in 1861. The story of their love has been dramatized by Rudolf Besier in THE BARRETTS OF WIMPOLE STREET.

PIPPA PASSES, a dramatic poem included in the collection BELLS AND POMEGRANATES, was among Browning's first significant works; Pippa, a little Italian girl, passes by singing, and unwittingly influences the lives of four groups of people. During the next 25 years Browning published many volumes of poetry, all of which sold badly: *Dramatic Lyrics* (1842), which contained *Porphyria's Lover,* MY LAST DUCHESS, *Soliloquy in a Spanish Cloister,* and *The Pied Piper of Hamelin; Dramatic Romances and Lyrics* (1845), which included How THEY BROUGHT THE GOOD NEWS FROM GHENT TO AIX and *The Bishop Orders His Tomb at St. Praxed's Church; Christmas Eve and Easter Day* (1850), a long poem; and *Men and Women* (1855), which contained many of his best-known poems: FRA LIPPO LIPPI, ANDREA DEL SARTO, BISHOP BLOUGRAM'S Apology, *Two in the Campagna,* and *A Grammarian's Funeral.* In the collection *Dramatis Personae* (1864) were RABBI BEN EZRA and PROSPICE.

After 40 years of poetic obscurity, Browning abruptly came into his own with the publication of the massive THE RING AND THE BOOK. The story, which Browning found in an old manuscript, deals with a 17th-century murder case; in the poem, each of 12 characters presents his view of the action in a long dramatic monologue.

Though his philosophy is now considered less profound than it was at the height of his success, Browning is notable for his psychological insight into character and motivations, his sometimes abrupt but forceful colloquial English, his perfection of the form of the dramatic monologue in which a speaker tells something of himself and reveals more than he intends or realizes, his learning, and his predilection for Italian Renaissance subjects. See Elizabeth Barrett BROWNING; BLOT ON THE 'SCUTCHEON, A; LURIA; RETURN OF THE DRUSES.

Browning Version, The (1948). A one-act play by Terence RATTIGAN. It is set in an English boys' school. An old teacher, universally disliked by the students, has his hard exterior cracked by a sympathetic and understanding boy. *The Browning Version* was made into a motion picture with a fine performance by Michael Redgrave as the teacher.

Brownism. The teachings of Robert Browne (1550?–1633), an English divine. He first formulated the principles of Congregationalism.

Brownshirts. See S.A.

Brownson, Orestes Augustus (1803–1876). American writer on theology and philosophy. Brownson was a New Englander so thoroughly individualistic that he could not agree long with anybody—even with himself. Raised as a strict Puritan, he became successively a Presbyterian, a Universalist, and a Unitarian; in 1844 he was converted to Roman Catholicism but was severely criticized when he tried to promulgate his own American form of Catholicism. His political views were similarly varied; at first, he was a Utopian socialist, an admirer of Robert Owen; later, he helped to organize a Workingmen's Party. He then became active in Democratic Party politics, until he lost faith in the intelligence and integrity of the common people.

To spread his beliefs, Brownson established the *Boston Quarterly Review* (January, 1838), which in 1842 was merged with the *United States Democratic Review;* in 1844 it became *Brownson's Quarterly Review,* continued until 1865, was revived in 1872, and terminated in 1875. His writings include *New Views of Christianity, Society, and the Church* (1836); a semiautobiographical novel, *Charles Elwood, or The Infidel Converted* (1840); and *The Convert* (1857), an autobiography.

Bruce, Robert. Called the Bruce (1274–1329). Scottish national hero, king of Scotland from 1306. Though at first he swore fealty to Edward I of England as king of Scotland (1296), Robert Bruce soon followed the popular leader Sir William WALLACE and raised arms against Edward in a struggle to gain Scottish independence. In July, 1297, however, he signed the capitulation of Irvine whereby Scottish lords were pardoned in return for their allegiance. Bruce took no part in Wallace's continued struggle and final downfall, but remained, to all outward appearances, loyal to the English. He was appointed co-regent of Scotland together with William Lamberton and John Comyn; he entered into a secret agreement with Lamberton binding him to uphold the patriotic cause.

After the execution of Wallace, Bruce murdered (1306) Comyn, an enemy of long standing, and was thenceforth openly committed to the Scottish cause. He was crowned Robert I of Scotland at Scone in 1306; he then set about to win his kingdom. He suffered defeat at Methven, took refuge on the coast of Ireland, was outlawed, and was excommunicated by the pope. After the death of Edward I and Edward II's accession to the throne, Bruce faced an easier opponent. He returned to Scotland and in a series of engagements, wrested most of Scotland from the English; his crusade finally culminated in the treaty (1327) by which Edward III recognized Scotland as independent and Bruce as her sovereign. Bruce died in 1329 of leprosy, barely enjoying the fruits of his own achievement. See BRUCE, THE; BRUCE AND THE SPIDER.

Bruce, The (c. 1375). An epic poem by John BARBOUR. The poem, a mixture of anecdote and accurate history, concerns the deeds of Robert BRUCE, James DOUGLAS, and the struggle for Scottish independence.

Bruce and the spider. It is said that when Robert BRUCE was forced by the English to retreat to Ireland, he took heart from a spider: one day he watched the spider try six times to fix its web on a beam in the ceiling. "Now shall this spider," said Bruce, "teach me what I am to do, for I also have failed six times." The spider's seventh effort was successful, whereupon Bruce left Ireland, collected 300 followers, landed at Carrick, and at midnight, surprised the English garrison at Turnberry Castle. In *Tales of a Grandfather,* Sir Walter Scott tells us that in remembrance of this incident, it has always been deemed a foul crime in Scotland for any of the name of Bruce to harm a spider.

Brücke, die (The bridge). A group of German painters, formed in 1905 in Dresden. In rebellion against impressionism, they aimed to found a truly expressive school of German painting. Ernst Ludwig Kirchner and Eric Heckel were among the leaders of the group, whose members were influenced by the art of Africa and the South Seas and by primitive German religious art. Using color in an expressionistic manner, these artists painted dramatic landscapes and nudes, mystical and visionary compositions, and depicted the anguish and loneliness of the street, the circus, and the *café dansant.* *Die Brücke* was incorporated into the BLAUE REITER movement in 1912.

Bruckner, Anton (1824–1896). Austrian organist and composer of church and symphonic music. A friend of Richard Wagner, he taught theory and organ at the Vienna Conservatorium from 1868 to 1891. His style is a mixture of homely simplicity and Catholic mysticism. His works include nine symphonies, three masses, and numerous shorter works for the church.

Bruegel or **Brueghel** or **Breughel, Pieter** (1525?–1569). Flemish painter. He painted scenes from peasant life, fantastic recreations of biblical subjects such as the tower of Babel, and landscapes composed of closely observed details combined to form an immense panorama in which small figures enact religious dramas and perform common tasks. His splendidly composed and brightly colored, realistic paintings are noted for their keen and often humorous observation of nature and mankind. Bruegel had two sons, Pieter the Younger (1564?–1637?), who often copied his father, and Jan (1568–1625), called "Velvet Bruegel," who painted landscapes, allegorical pictures, and still lifes.

Brueys, L'Abbé David-Augustin de. See BATHELIN, LA FARCE DE MAISTRE PIERRE.

Bruin, Sir. See REYNARD THE FOX.

Bruller, Jean. See VERCORS.

Brumaire. The 2nd month in the French REVOLUTIONARY CALENDAR. It began Oct. 22, 23, or 24, depending on the year, and ended Nov. 21, 22, or 23. The name comes from *brume* (Fr., "fog"), and was used because this season was often marked by foggy weather. The celebrated 18th Brumaire (Nov. 9, 1799) was the day on which the Directory was overthrown and Napoleon established his supremacy.

Brunanburh, battle of (10th century). An Old English poem of 73 lines in ALLITERATIVE VERSE, included in the *Anglo-Saxon Chronicle.* It celebrates the victory (937) of the English under King Aethelstan over the invading Vikings and Scots.

Brunelleschi, Filippo (1377–1446). Florentine architect and goldsmith. He used his knowledge of Gothic and Romanesque architecture in spanning the immense space covered by his dome for the cathedral of Florence, while in such buildings as the Pazzi Chapel, the Church of San Lorenzo, the Pitti Palace (1446), the Hospital of the Innocenti (1419), and the Church of the Santo Spirito (1435), he introduced the classical elements—columns, arches, ornamental details—that form such an integral part of Renaissance architecture. His classicism was spurred by a trip made to Rome in 1433 with his friend DONATELLO for the purpose of studying the Roman ruins. Along with Donatello and other Florentine artists, he shared the patronage of Cosimo de' Medici. He also invented linear perspective: the mathematical device for the construction of a rational space, with depth and interval, as seen from a single point of view.

Brunello. In the Orlando poems of Boiardo and Ariosto, a cunning dwarf and expert thief who steals Angelica's magic ring and then loses it to Bradamante, who needs it to free her beloved RUGGIERO from the enchanter Atlante.

Brunetière, Vincent de Paul Marie Ferdinand (1849–1906). French literary critic. Conservative and neoclassical in his tastes, Brunetière opposed the naturalistic school because he deplored its lack of moral purpose. Dogmatic in his beliefs, he applied the principles of Darwinian evolution to the development of literature. Among his most important works are *Le Roman Naturaliste* (1883), *Etudes critiques sur la littérature française* (1880–1907), *Evolution des genres* (1890–1894), and *Histoire de la littérature française classique* (1904–1907), which was begun in 1904 and left unfinished at the time of the author's death.

Brunetto Latini. See Brunetto LATINI.

Brunhild. See VÖLSUNGA SAGA; NIBELUNGENLIED; Wagner's RING DES NIBELUNGEN.

Bruni, Leonardo (1374–1444). Italian humanist and historian. Also known as Leonardo Aretino, from his birthplace at Arezzo, he was a chancellor of Florence, his adopted city and a papal secretary. One of the outstanding early Italian Renaissance Humanists, he wrote in Latin, Greek, and Italian, and did translations and other scholarly works. His *History of Florence (Historiarum Florentinarum libri xii;* 1610) is sometimes described as the first modern history because of its break with medieval methods of narrating past events.

Bruno, Giordano (1548–1600). Italian philosopher. Bruno is sometimes referred to as the Nolan from his birthplace at Nola, near Naples. After studying at the university of Naples and entering the Dominican order, he fled from his vows and his native land in 1576 in order to begin his career as an itinerant teacher of controversial philosophical subjects. In 1582, at Paris, he wrote his first literary work, the comedy *Il Candelaio.* While in England during the next few years, he met Sir Philip Sidney and Fulke-Greville, debated at Oxford, and produced several philosophical dialogues in Italian. *La cena de le ceneri (Ash Wednesday Supper,* 1584) defended the Copernican system and Bruno's notion of the infinite universe, while *De la causa, principio e uno (On Cause, Principle, and Unity,* 1584) and *De l'infinito universo e mondi (On the Infinite Universe and Its Worlds,* 1584) offered an anti-Aristotelian metaphysics grounded largely in mystical Neoplatonism and Pantheism. The *Spaccio della bestia trionfante* (*Banishment of the Triumphant Beast*, 1584), dedicated to Sidney, deals largely with ethics; the *Cabala del cavallo pegaseo* (*Cabala of the Pegasean Steed*), also written during this period, is a satire against pretentious ignorance and obscurantism, in the form of an ironic praise of asininity that recalls a similar "praise of folly" by Erasmus. *De gli heroici furori* (1585), also dedicated to Sidney, deals with heroic enthusiasms, such as the aspirations of the intellectual mind and the inspirations of poetry. The discussion revolves about a group of poems by Bruno himself and by Luigi Tansillo, who is an interlocutor in the dialogue.

Between 1585 and 1591, Bruno wandered through France, Switzerland, and Germany, everywhere encountering opposition to his unorthodox ideas and irascible personality. In 1591, at Frankfurt, he published a group of Latin works in which he continued to expound his philosophy. In scope these works range from mnemonics and monism to the atom and the monad, from the pre-Socratic philosophers to Nicholas of Cusa and Copernicus. The most important of the works is *De immenso et innumerabilis seu de universo et mundis* (*On Immensity and Innumerability, or on the Universe and Its Worlds*), consisting of verse, prose commentary, and diagrams. In 1592, he was betrayed to the Inquisition at Venice; a year later he was in a Roman prison, where he languished for seven years. His refusal to recant earned him condemnation as a heretic and execution at the stake on February 17, 1600.

Despite the difficulty of his style and the obscurity of his thought, Bruno influenced contemporaries such as Spenser. Among modern authors, his influence is present in Joyce's *Finnegans Wake*. In philosophy he anticipated Leibniz and other subsequent thinkers.

Brush, Katharine [Ingham] (1902–1952). American novelist, short-story writer, and columnist. She is known for her successful works of fiction appearing in *Cosmopolitan* and other magazines. An annalist of "the jazz age," she is the author of a number of novels, including *Glitter* (1926), *Young Man of Manhattan* (1930), and *Red-Headed Woman* (1931). Collections of her short stories are *Night Club* (1929) and *Other Women* (1932).

Brut, The (c. 1205). A Middle English verse rendition by the English priest Layamon (fl. 1189–1207) of Wace's Norman French ROMAN DE BRUT. A mixture of alliteration and rhyme, it is the first long poem in Middle English with any claim to literary quality, and marks the first appearance of the story of King Arthur in English. It relates the mythical history of Britain from its founding by BRUTE, a descendant of Aeneas, to the year 689. It contains versions of the stories of King LEIR (Lear), CYMBELINE, and other legendary kings of Britain. See ARTHURIAN LEGEND.

Brute (**Brutus**). In Geoffrey of Monmouth's HISTORY OF THE KINGS OF BRITAIN, a mythical ancestor of the British. According to Geoffrey, he is the great-grandson of the Trojan Aeneas. After an adventurous life, he lands in England, which—says the writer—he calls Britain after his own name. His three sons are ALBANACT, CAMBER, and LOCRINE.

Brutus, Decius. In Shakespeare's JULIUS CAESAR, a conspirator against Caesar. By flattering Caesar's pride, he persuades him to attend the Senate despite Calpurnia's pleas.

Brutus, Lucius Junius. Roman CONSUL (509 B.C.). One of the first two consuls in Rome's history, he is known as "the founder of the Roman Republic." According to legend, he feigned idiocy in order to escape the fate of his father and brother who were killed by his uncle Tarquinius Superbus, king of Rome. When Sextus, son of Tarquinius Superbus, ravished LUCRETIA, Brutus, casting off his feigned simple-mindedness, swore vengeance; he led an insurrection which expelled the Tarquins from Rome and changed the magistracy of kings to that of consuls. Brutus and Tarquinius Collatinus, husband of Lucretia, were chosen consuls.

Brutus, Marcus Junius (c. 85–42 B.C.). Roman politician and general. He was known for his devotion to the ideals of the republic, and, in the civil struggle between CAESAR and Pompey, he supported the latter, who had legality on his side. After the battle at Pharsalus (48 B.C.), which ended in the defeat of Pompey, Caesar pardoned Brutus and made him one of his companions. Caesar appointed him governor of Cisalpine Gaul (46) and praetor (44). His love for Caesar notwithstanding, Brutus was persuaded by CASSIUS to murder Caesar; he was deluded into thinking that this act would recall the ideals of the republic which had disintegrated under Caesar's dictatorship. Accordingly, Caesar was murdered on the IDES of March in 44 by a group of conspirators under Brutus and Cassius. Mark ANTONY turned public opinion against the conspirators in his oration at Caesar's public funeral, and Brutus and Cassius fled Rome. Both raised armies, and Antony and Octavius, Caesar's lawful heir (later Augustus), temporarily suspended their struggle for power and marched against them. In the first engagement at Philippi (42) Brutus was victorious over Octavius while Cassius, overwhelmed by Antony's forces, committed suicide. In the second engagement, Brutus' forces were surrounded by those of Octavius, and Brutus committed suicide. According to Plutarch, when Antony found Brutus' body, he wrapped it up in his own robe for burial and had the ashes sent to Servilia, Brutus' mother. Another story, however, says that Antony had Brutus' head cut off and flung it at the feet of a statue of Caesar. See ET TU, BRUTE.

In Shakespeare's JULIUS CAESAR, Brutus is depicted as an idealist, "high in all the people's hearts," who joins the conspiracy out of love of country. Antony's eulogy is famous:

> This was the noblest Roman of them all;
> All the conspirators save only he
> Did that they did in envy of great Caesar;
> He only, in a general honest thought,
> And common good to all, made one of them.

Bryan, William Jennings. Known as the **Great Commoner** and the **Boy Orator of the Platte** (1860–1925). American political leader and orator. Having been twice elected to Congress (1890, 1892), Bryan became editor of the Omaha *World-Herald* after an unsuccessful Senate bid in 1894. In 1896 he won the Democratic presidential nomination when, as an advocate of the free coinage of silver, he electrified the convention with the famous "Cross of Gold" speech that ended, "You shall not press down upon the brow of labor this crown of thorns, you shall not crucify mankind upon a cross of gold." After a strenuous campaign, in which he won the support of Southern and Western agrarians, he lost to William McKinley by fewer than 600,000 votes. In 1901 he founded a weekly newspaper, the *Commoner*, which he edited until 1913. Again an unsuccessful presidential candidate in 1900 and 1908, he was named secretary of state by President Wilson, but he resigned in 1915 when he felt that the president's policies might involve the U.S. in World War I. After the war his fundamentalist religious beliefs led him to take part in a movement to prevent the teaching of evolution in American schools; in 1925 he served as prosecutor in the celebrated SCOPES TRIAL.

Bryan was one of the most popular lecturers on the Chautauqua circuit; best loved of all his talks was one on *The Prince of Peace*, which he repeated innumerable times until 1924. Vachel Lindsay paid tribute to Bryan in his poem *Bryan, Bryan, Bryan: The Campaign of 1896, as Viewed at the Time by a 16-Year-Old* (1919), but he was pilloried in H. L. Mencken's *In Memoriam: W. J. B.* (*Prejudices*, 5th Series, 1926).

Bryant, William Cullen (1794–1878). American poet, critic, and editor. Bryant's early beliefs were Calvinist; his politics were Federalist and his tastes, classical. During his life, he moved from these attitudes to almost opposite ones, finally achieving a balanced view.

After beginning at the law, he achieved early fame when his poems were published in 1817. In 1825, he went to New York from his native Massachusetts to work on the New York *Evening Post*. Later he became its editor, and a leading democrat; he supported Lincoln, encouraged liberal causes, and espoused a less severe religion. Throughout his life he continued to write poetry, but rarely achieved the quality of his earliest work, THANATOPSIS, TO A WATERFOWL, and INSCRIPTION FOR THE ENTRANCE TO WOOD. Bryant's important works include early political satire in *The Embargo* (1808), collected *Poems* (1832), *The Fountain* (1842), and *The Flood of Years* (1876). He translated the *Iliad* (1870) and the *Odyssey* (1871).

Bryce, James. Viscount **Bryce of Dechmont** (1838–1922). English statesman and historian. Ambassador to the U.S. from 1907 to 1913, he was one of the founders of the League of Nations. His best-known writings are *The Holy Roman Empire* (1862) and *The American Commonwealth* (1888), both highly regarded studies in history and political science. He wrote a number of other books on travel, biography, jurisprudence, and political science.

Bryher. Pen name of **Winifred Bryher** (1894–   ), English historical novelist. She authentically and poetically recreates Greece and Rome in *Gate to the Sea* (1958) and *Roman Wall* (1954). English historical scenes are portrayed in *Ruan* (1960), the Celts; *The Fourteenth of October* (1952), the battle of Hastings; and *The Player's Boy* (1953), early seventeenth century. *Heart to Artemis* was published in 1962 and *Coin of Carthage* in 1963.

Brynhild. See VÖLSUNGA SAGA; NIBELUNGENLIED; Wagner's RING DES NIBELUNGEN.

Bryusov, Valeri Yakovlevich (1873–1924). Russian poet. One of the founders of the symbolist movement, Bryusov established in 1904 a journal *The Scales* (*Vesy*), which became an important showcase for the symbolist work of the next five years. Bryusov was heavily influenced by the French SYMBOLISTS and transmitted this influence into the Russian movement. His major collections of verse are *Urbi et Orbi* (1903) and *Stephanos* (1905). Bryusov accepted the Bolshevik regime, and as a consequence his work, while not as politically oriented as the Soviets would like, is at least accepted and reprinted in the Soviet Union.

Bubastis. The Greek name of Bast, or Pasht, the Artemis of Egyptian mythology. She was the daughter of Isis and sister of Horus, and her sacred animal was the cat.

Buber, Martin (1878–1965). Jewish theologian, philosopher, and writer. He has contributed to the modern development of HASIDISM and has devoted much of his life to winning recognition of the cultural value of Judaism. His writings include *Moses*, *The Revelation and the Covenant* (1946), *The Prophetic Faith* (1949), *Two Types of Faith* (1951), *Eclipse of God* (1952), and *Tales of the Hassidim* (1961).

bucentaur (Gr., *bous*, "ox"; *centaurous*, "centaur"). A gaily ornamented ship or barge, from the name of the Venetian state galley employed by the doge on Ascension Day when he went to wed the Adriatic (see BRIDE OF THE SEA). It was probably so called from the galley's figurehead, a man's head with an ox's body.

Bucephalus (Gr., *boukephalos*, "bull-headed"). The favorite horse of Alexander the Great. Philip II had determined to destroy the high-spirited horse no one could mount, but allowed his son to try his skill first. Observing that the horse was terrified by its own shadow, Alexander turned its eyes into the sun, and was able to mount. By taming him Alexander fulfilled an oracle concerning the succession to the throne of Macedon.

Buchan, Sir John. 1st Baron **Tweedsmuir** (1875–1940). Scottish writer and governor general of Canada. He wrote many romantic adventure stories with idyllic natural settings. His first successful book was *Prester John* (1910), a romance of South Africa. THE THIRTY-NINE STEPS, *Greenmantle* (1916), and *The Three Hostages* (1924) are adventure and spy novels whose hero is Richard HANNAY. Other stories, such as *Huntingtower* (1922), are about a group of Scottish slum boys called the Gorbals Die-Hards. *John Macnab* (1925) is about poaching, hunting, and fishing in Scotland. Buchan's biographies include a life of *Cromwell* (1934) and a life of Cromwell's Scottish contemporary, *Montrose* (1928). *Memory-Hold-the-Door* (1940) is an autobiography.

Buchanan, Robert Williams (1841–1901). Scottish poet, dramatist, critic, and novelist. He is remembered for his cruel literary attack, entitled THE FLESHLY SCHOOL OF POETRY, which began a literary and personal quarrel that lasted several years. He was a prolific and successful dramatist, and his

Poetical Works (1901) contains a number of poems of interest.

Büchner, Georg (1813-1837). German dramatist. He is known especially for the brilliant imagination and theatrical skill with which he treats social, human, and metaphysical problems in the plays DANTONS TOD and WOYZECK. Inspired in his student days by the ideals of the French Revolution of 1789, he became a political radical and, in 1834, publicized a militant socialist program in his *Der hessische Landbote* (*The Hessian Messenger*), a tract which violently attacked the oppressive archduchy of Hesse. As a dramatist, he reinforced his socialist sympathies with a brutally stark, realistic style that caused him to be regarded as a forerunner of naturalism. But he was also a master of metaphysical symbolism, and his works contain passages of the highest poetic beauty. Other products of his short career are the comedy *Leonce und Lena* (written 1836) and the fragmentary novella *Lenz* (1879) about the life of the poet Reinhold Lenz.

Buck, Pearl [Sydenstricker] (1892-1973). American novelist. The daughter of American missionaries, Mrs. Buck was raised in China and is best known for her books about Chinese life. Part of her purpose has been to make the East known to the West. She was awarded a Pulitzer Prize in 1932 for THE GOOD EARTH, the first novel in a trilogy called *The House Of Earth*, finished in 1935. She received the Nobel Prize for Literature in 1938.

Mrs. Buck is the author of many other novels about the Far East, including *Dragon Seed* (1942), *Pavilion of Women* (1946), and *The Living Reed* (1963), and of two autobiographical works, *My Several Worlds* (1954) and *A Bridge for Passing* (1962). She also translated a Chinese classic under the title *All Men Are Brothers* (1933) and wrote several novels with an American setting under the pseudonym John Sedges.

Bucket, Mr. A shrewd detective in Charles Dickens' BLEAK HOUSE. He discovers that Hortense, the French maid of Lady Dedlock, murdered Mr. Tulkinghorn. Speaking of the detectives of fiction, Swinburne calls Bucket "that matchless master of them all."

Buckingham, 1st duke of. George Villiers (1592-1628). English nobleman, whose erratic political and military policies caused continual friction with Parliament and foreign powers. The profligate favorite of James I, he was known for his good looks, and his face at death was described as "the face of an angel." He was assassinated by John FELTON. He was used as a character by Scott in *The Fortunes of Nigel* (1822) and by Dumas in *The Three Musketeers* (1844).

Buckingham, 2nd duke of. Henry Stafford (1454-1483). English nobleman, a staunch supporter of Richard III in the early part of his reign. He later rebelled against Richard and was captured and executed. In Shakespeare's RICHARD III, he is depicted as the crafty "second self" of the king, but he balks at Richard's demand that he kill the two sons of Edward IV.

Buckingham, 2nd duke of. George Villiers (1628-1687). English nobleman and writer. The son of the 1st duke of Buckingham and a favorite of Charles II, he was a member of the court clique known as the CABAL, his name furnishing the third letter of the famous acronym. With Samuel Butler, Thomas Sprat, and others, he wrote *The Rehearsal* (1671), a burlesque tragedy satirizing Dryden. He is a character in Scott's *Peveril of the Peak* (1822) and *Woodstock* (1826) and in Dryden's *Absalom and Achitophel* (1681).

Buckle, Henry Thomas (1821-1862). English historian. He is known chiefly for the first volume of his *History of Civilization in England* (1857), which caused a sensation in England and the U.S. because of its bold thinking. Buckle's special theory was that climate, soil, food, and other aspects of nature play a large role in the intellectual progress of mankind. A second volume of his *History* appeared in 1861, but was generally considered inferior to the first.

Bucolics (Bucolica). Also known as **Eclogues (Eclogae).** Ten pastoral poems by VERGIL, written in the years 43-37 B.C. Though based on the idyls of Theocritus, the *Bucolics* are sophisticated tours de force and subtle allegories of contemporary events and persons. As Vergil's first notable achievement, they mark the beginning of his writing career and his entry into the literary circle of Augustus and Maecenas.

The first bucolic portrays the anguish of a shepherd forced to leave his ancestral lands. This is a reference to the threatened confiscation of Vergil's lands by Mark Antony in 43. The second is the love song of CORYDON for the boy Alexis. An amoebaean contest, i.e., a singing contest in which one shepherd sings an impromptu couplet to which the other must reply with a variation of tone and subject matter, composes the third poem. Interwoven into this rustic game of wits are references to Vergil's

Woodcut of Vergil's first *Bucolic* (Strassburg, 1502).

patrons and to the farm which, through their influence, was restored to the poet.

The fourth poem is perhaps the most famous bucolic of all. In it, Vergil predicts a new age of peace for the world which will be ushered in by the birth of a child. Often called the *Messianic Eclogue,* this poem has been variously interpreted as a natal poem for an expected child (either that of Mark Antony and Octavia or of Octavius Caesar and Scribonia) and as an inspired prophecy of the birth of Christ. It was because of this poem that medieval Christians revered Vergil as a pagan prophet whom God had chosen to prepare the world for the coming of the Prince of Peace.

The fifth poem is an elegant exchange of songs by two shepherds; its subject is elegaic—the death of a young shepherd, Damon—but it actually refers to the death of Julius Caesar. The sixth is the "Song of Silenus," a capsule cosmogony which seems to show Vergil's acquaintance with Lucretius' *De Rerum Natura.* The seventh poem is another amoebaean singing contest.

The eighth bucolic contains two love elegies, in both of which the singers use magical refrains. The poem is sometimes called *Pharmaceutria* (sorcery). The ninth is a gracious exchange of songs between a young man and an old man in which there are many oblique references to the death of Caesar, the Roman civil wars, and the confiscations.

The final bucolic is dedicated to Gallus, a leading patrician and writer of elegies who was an early protector of Vergil. This poem is in the form of a consolation sent to Gallus, who is brokenhearted over the infidelity of his mistress. Many authorities now claim that this artificial piece is a clever pastiche of Gallus' own love lyrics.

Vergil's *Bucolics* were the principal influence on pastoral tradition after the Renaissance, and it was their calm elegance that became the dominant tone of pastoral verse. The refrain "Sweete Themmes, runne softly, till I end my song" in Spenser's *Prothalamion* is an echo of the recurrent refrain in the eighth *Bucolic: Incipe Maenalios mecum, mea tibia, versus;* and the opening of Milton's *Lycidas,* "Yet once more, O ye laurels, and once more, / Ye myrtles brown . . . / I come to pluck" is an adaption of *Et vos, o lauri, carpam te, proxima myrte.* (*Bucolic* II).

Budd, Lanny. See Upton SINCLAIR.

Buddenbrooks (1901). A novel by Thomas MANN. It treats the decline of a prosperous North German commercial family. Both Johann Buddenbrook, Sr., the patriarch when the novel opens, and his son Johann, Jr. (Consul Buddenbrook) are exemplary bearers of the family's solid and rational tradition. But symptoms of decadence appear in the consul's children: Toni, the daughter, is an aimless personality; Christian is an outright ne'er-do-well; and Thomas, who takes over the family business, has a repressed potential for decadence, which shows itself in his occasional attraction to art and philosophy and in his inability to keep the family fortune from declining. In Thomas' son Hanno, finally, the symbolic connection between art and decadence and the symbolic antithesis between art and life culminate. Hanno is frail and sickly, fond of music and filled with creative longings; he dies as a boy, bringing the family line to an end.

Buddha (*Sans.,* "the enlightened"). Real name, Siddhārtha GAUTAMA. Also known as **Shākyamuni.** The founder of BUDDHISM. He is traditionally said to have died in 544 B.C.

Buddhism. The system of religion inaugurated by the Buddha in India in the 6th century B.C. The four sublime verities of Buddhism, the "Four Aryan or Noble Truths," are as follows:

(1) Pain exists.

(2) The cause of pain is "birth sin." The Buddhist supposes that man has passed through many previous existences, and all the sins accumulated in these previous states constitute man's "birth sin."

(3) Pain is ended only by NIRVANA.

(4) The way that leads to nirvana is the "Eightfold Path": right faith, right judgment, right language, right purpose, right practice, right obedience, right memory, and right meditation.

The abstract nature of the religion, together with the overgrowth of its monastic system and the superior vitality and energy of Brahminism, caused it to decline in India itself; but it spread rapidly to the surrounding countries and took so permanent a hold that it has millions of adherents in India, Ceylon, Tibet, China, and Japan.

Early Indian Buddhism (Theravāda or Hīnayāna) emphasized personal salvation; later Mahāyāna Buddhism developed, promising salvation for all. Mahāyāna Buddhism spread to Central Asia, China, and Japan and is the principal Buddhism in these countries. Hīnayāna is still practiced in Ceylon. Numerous sects and variant teachings exist, ranging from highly academic and abstruse doctrines to simple salvationism.

Budé, Guillaume (1468-1540). French scholar and humanist. Secretary and librarian to Francis I, he translated Greek texts into Latin and published them with critical analyses of the works themselves, rather than of previous commentaries on the works as had been done previously. In correspondence with humanists like Erasmus, More, and Rabelais, he zealously advocated classical studies, not only to gain erudition, but to cultivate the mind and regain classical wisdom. Along with others close to Francis I, he was instrumental in the founding of the COLLÈGE DE FRANCE (1530), where for the first time Greek and Hebrew were taught in addition to Latin.

Buffalo Bill. See William F. CODY.

Buffon, Comte **Georges Louis Leclerc de** (1707-1788). French naturalist, curator of the Jardin du Roi from 1739. He is best known for his *Histoire naturelle* (36 vols., 1749-1788), continued in eight volumes by his assistants and published in 1804; his *Epoques de la nature* (1779); and *Théorie de la Terre* (1749). His works deal with the earth, minerals, animals, and man. He helped lay the foundations for 19th-century work in natural science, especially in zoology and comparative anatomy, and was the first to write a history of the earth in terms of a series of successive geologic stages. His theories (*e.g.,* his development of geographic zoology) anticipated those of Lamarck and Darwin. The *Discours sur le style,* his inaugural address to the French ACADEMY in 1753, reflects his concern with literary style: "Style is the man himself" is a famous quotation from it. His writing is vivid, eloquent, and majestic.

Building of the Ship, The (1849). A poem by Henry Wadsworth LONGFELLOW. Often considered his best ode, the poem describes the building of a ship, interweaving the details with those of the approaching marriage of the builder's daughter and the owner's son. The ship is used as a symbol for life itself, and at the end, for the Union.

Bukharin, Nikolai Ivanovich (1888–1939). Russian Communist leader and editor. He joined the Bolsheviks in 1906 and was a leader in the movement by 1912 when, with Lenin, he co-edited the party organ, *Pravda*. In 1916 he was the editor of the revolutionary paper *Novy Mir* (*The New World*) in New York. The head of the Third International (1926–1929), he was expelled from the party only to be reinstated. Suspected of being a supporter of Trotsky, he was arrested and executed in the purges of 1938.

Bulba, Taras. See TARAS BULBA.

Bulfinch, Thomas (1796–1867). American teacher and writer. Bulfinch held a business post throughout his life, devoting his leisure to writing. His *Age of Fable* (1855) is still used in American schools as an introduction to Greek, Roman, Scandinavian, and Celtic mythology. *The Age of Chivalry* (1858), another straightforward, expurgated popularization of mythology, has pleased many young readers.

Bulgakov, Mikhail Afanasevich (1891–1940). Russian dramatist. He is best known for his DAYS OF THE TURBINS and for his dramatizations of Gogol's *Dead Souls* (1932) and Cervantes' *Don Quixote* (1940).

Bull, Olaf Jacob Martin Luther (1883–1933). Norwegian poet, short-story writer, and playwright. Love for the bare beauty of sea and mountain and pine forest, characteristically Norwegian, finds expression in Bull's poetry. In 1918 he spoke out violently against the destructive impact of German militarism on all fineness and beauty in life. A painstaking craftsman, Bull wrote intellectual, highly introspective verse. His collections include *Digte* (1909), *Digte og Noveller* (1916), *Stjernerne* (1924), *De hundrede aar* (1928) and *Oinos og Eros* (1930).

Bull, The Sacred. See APIS.

Bulldog Drummond. The hero of stories by Sapper (pen name of H. C. McNEILE). Drummond is a patriotic Englishman and a modern Robin Hood.

Bullitt, William C[hristian] (1891–   ). American diplomat. He was ambassador to Russia (1933–1936), to France (1936–1941), and ambassador-at-large (1941–1942). He wrote one novel, *It's Not Done* (1926), in addition to such nonfiction as *Report to the American People* (1940) and *The Great Globe Itself* (1946).

Bull Run. A brook in Virginia and the site of two battles during the U.S. Civil War. In the first battle of Bull Run (July 21, 1861), Union forces, confident of an easy victory that would enable them to push on to Richmond, were initially successful. But the stand of the Confederate brigade led by Thomas Jackson, which won him the nickname "Stonewall," and the arrival of reinforcements turned the apparent Union victory into rout. The second battle of Bull Run (Aug. 30, 1862) also ended in defeat for the Union. These battles are sometimes

known as the battles of Manassas from nearby Manassas Junction.

Bulwer-Lytton, Edward George Earle Lytton. 1st Baron **Lytton** (1803–1873). English novelist and dramatist. A member of Parliament for 15 years, Bulwer-Lytton served as colonial secretary from 1858 to 1859 and was created a peer in 1866. Among his notable historical novels are EUGENE ARAM, THE LAST DAYS OF POMPEII, *Rienzi* (1835), *Leila* (1838), THE LAST OF THE BARONS, and *Harold* (1848). Scholarly in their historical detail and often heavy, but just as often thrilling in their narrative, these books held the interest of several generations of readers. In addition, Bulwer-Lytton wrote the supernatural tales ZANONI and *A Strange Story* (1862), the long poem *King Arthur* (1849), and numerous dramas, including *Richelieu* (1839) and *Money* (1840)—the latter reflecting his occasional attraction to social themes. See CAXTONS, THE.

Bumble, Mr. In Charles Dickens' OLIVER TWIST, a minor official in the workhouse where Oliver is brought up. He is a cruel, fussy man with mighty ideas of his own importance. He has given to the language the word "bumbledom," for the officious arrogance and conceit of the petty dignitary. After marriage to Mrs. Corney, the high and mighty Bumble is sadly henpecked.

Bumppo, Natty. The central figure in THE LEATHERSTOCKING TALES, a series of novels by James Fenimore COOPER. Called by many names in the novels, among them Leatherstocking, Hawkeye, Deerslayer, Pathfinder, and *La Longue Carabine*, Natty remains the uncorrupted natural man. Companioned by Chingachgook, a Mohican chief, Natty prefers the moral code of the Indian to the selfish exploitation of nature by white settlers. Superior to the Indians in woodcraft, he is loyal and courageous, a voluntary outcast who follows the wilderness westward.

Bunch, Mother. A noted London alewife of the late Elizabethan period, nominal source of many jests and anecdotes, and often mentioned in Elizabethan drama. The "Epistle to the Merrie Reader" in *Pasquil's Jests, mixed with Mother Bunches Merriments* (1604) gives the following description of her:

She spent most of her time in telling tales, and when she laughed, she was heard from Aldgate to the Monuments at Westminster, and all Southwarke stood in Amazement. . . . She dwelt in Cornhill, neere the Exchange, and sold strong Ale . . . and lived an hundreth, seventy and five years, two days and a quarter, and halfe a minute.

Other books were named after her, such as *Mother Bunch's Closet newly Broke Open* (1609), "containing rare secrets of art and nature, tried and experienced by learned philosophers, and recommended to all ingenious young men and maids, teaching them how to get good wives and husbands."

Bundren, Addie. The principal character in William Faulkner's novel AS I LAY DYING. Although she dies near the beginning of the story, much of the action of the characters is determined by their relationships with the dead woman.

Bungay or Bongay, Friar. A famous necromancer of the 13th century. His story is much overlaid with legend. It is said that he "raised mists and vapors which befriended Edward IV at the battle of Barnet." In the old prose romance, *The Famous History of Friar Bacon,* and in Greene's *Honourable History of Friar Bacon and Friar Bungay* (1591), he appears as the assistant to Roger Bacon (d. 1294) in his diabolical scientific experiments; he also appears in Bulwer-Lytton's novel *Last of the Barons* (1843).

Bunin, Ivan Alekseyevich (1870–1953). Russian novelist, short-story writer, and poet. He was the first Russian to win the Nobel Prize for literature (1933). Bunin emigrated from Russia in 1918 and lived in France until his death. He is famous chiefly for his prose works, which had a closer kinship with the prose of the 19th-century masters than with the modernist experiments of his own period. His novels, *Derevnya* (*The Village,* 1910) and *Sukhodol* (*Dry Valley,* 1912), written in the restrained "classical" style of Turgenev, Goncharov, or Chekhov, depict the stagnation of life in provincial Russia. His short story, *Gospodin iz San-Frantzisko* (*The Gentleman from San Francisco,* 1916), is world famous. Bunin's poetry is less highly esteemed than his prose, but he did a number of successful translations in Russian, notably of the works of Longfellow and Byron.

Bunker Hill, battle of (June 17, 1775). The first great battle of the American Revolution. To control the high ground overlooking Boston, American troops built a redoubt on nearby Breed's Hill. Under General Howe, 2,400 British troops assaulted the hill but were repulsed twice with heavy losses. After the third assault, the Americans, their powder exhausted, retreated to Bunker Hill, where nearly a fourth of them were slain or wounded.

Bunner, H[enry] C[uyler] (1855–1896). American short-story writer, poet, novelist, and editor of *Puck,* a weekly humor magazine. Bunner wrote such novels as *The Midge* (1886), a story about a bachelor and his orphan ward, but he is best remembered for his short short stories, especially *Short Sixes: Stories to Be Read While the Candle Burns* (1891). He also published *Made in France: French Tales with a United States Twist* (1893) and other books. The best of his *vers de société* appeared in *Airs from Arcady and Elsewhere* (1884).

Bunsen, Robert Wilhelm [Eberhard von] (1811–1899). German chemist. His many contributions to experimental science include the method of spectrum analysis, developed with Gustav Kirchhoff, and the bunsen burner, a heating apparatus.

Buntline, Ned. See E. Z. C. JUDSON.

Bunyan, John (1628–1688). English writer and preacher. The son of a Bedfordshire tinker, Bunyan adopted his father's trade and served in the Parliamentary army from 1644 to 1646. In 1648 or 1649 he married a woman whose dowry included two devotional books which, he later said, first turned his thoughts to religion. After a period of intense spiritual struggle, he joined the Baptist church at Bedford and later became a lay preacher. His refusal to bow to royal edicts banning nonconformist preaching led to his imprisonment from 1660 to 1672. During these 12 years he devoted himself to study of the Bible and Foxe's *Book of Martyrs* and wrote many of his books, including his autobiography,

GRACE ABOUNDING TO THE CHIEF OF SINNERS. Upon his release he became minister of the nonconformist church at Bedford, a position which he held for the rest of his life. In 1675 he was again imprisoned for a few months, during which time he wrote his most celebrated work, PILGRIM'S PROGRESS.

His other writings, all religious in character, most of them allegorical, include *The Holy City, or the New Jerusalem* (1665), *A Confession of My Faith, and a Reason of My Practice* (1672), THE LIFE AND DEATH OF MR. BADMAN, and THE HOLY WAR. An outstanding narrative genius, he wrote in a style that has been highly praised for its simplicity, vigor, and concreteness.

Bunyan, Paul. A legendary lumberjack of the American northwestern forests. A comic folk hero, he is frequently the subject of "tall tales," in which each storyteller strives to surpass the others. It is said that the dragging of Bunyan's pick cut out the Grand Canyon. When he builds a hotel, he has the "last seven stories put on hinges so's they could be swung back for to let the moon go by."

The legend of Paul Bunyan may have first appeared in Quebec, or northern Ontario; James Stevens traced him to a French-Canadian logger named Paul Bunyon, who won a reputation as a prodigious fighter in the Papineau Rebellion against England in 1837, and later became famous as the boss of a logging camp. Paul Bunyan's first appearance in print seems to be in an advertising pamphlet, *Paul Bunyan and His Big Blue Ox* (1914), published by the Red River Lumber Company. Written and illustrated by W. B. Laughead, it immediately became popular and was reissued many times. Among those who have retold the Bunyan stories are Virginia Tunvey, Esther Shepard, James Stevens, Glen Rounds, Dell J. McCormick, and Acel Garland. Daniel Hoffman studied the legend in his book, *Paul Bunyan: Last of the Frontier Demigods* (1952).

Burbage, Cuthbert. See Richard BURBAGE.

Burbage, James (d. 1597). English actor and theater-builder. In 1576 Burbage leased land in Shoreditch and built on it the first theater in England specifically intended for stage performances. It was known simply as "The Theater." In 1596 he acquired a house in Blackfriars which, being roofed over, was used for plays during the winter months. After Burbage's death his sons tore down The Theater and re-erected it in Bankside, where it became the GLOBE Theater. See Richard BURBAGE.

Burbage, Richard (1567?–1619). English actor, son of James Burbage. Richard and his brother Cuthbert Burbage inherited a share in their father's two playhouses, The THEATER and the BLACKFRIARS. Because of difficulties about the lease of the site of The Theater, they transported the building to a location in Bankside, where it was reassembled as the GLOBE Theater. Richard, one of the chief actors of his day, acted every major part in the plays of Shakespeare, as well as in those of Ben Jonson and Beaumont and Fletcher, and was particularly celebrated for his roles in tragedy. He was also a painter of some note, and the Felton portrait of Shakespeare is sometimes ascribed to him.

Burbank, Luther (1849–1926). American plant breeder. Born in Massachusetts, Burbank took up the profession of market gardening at the age of 21.

There he produced his first new creation, the Burbank potato. Moving to California, he settled down in Santa Rosa in a nursery garden and greenhouse. His aim, the cultivation of "better fruits and fairer flowers," did not include theoretic formulation; in 1905, the Carnegie Institute persuaded him to accept a salary and allow them to gather the data his experimenting accumulated. The arrangement was unsuccessful, and soon ended. By importation of foreign plants, hybridization to eliminate undesirable characteristics, and selection, Burbank was able to create new varieties of plums, berries, lilies, roses, apples, peaches, quinces, nectarines, potatoes, tomatoes, corn, asparagus, and innumerable others. His acknowledged master and the source of his earliest inspiration, Burbank wrote, was Charles Darwin.

Burchiello. Real name **Domenico di Giovanni** (1404–1448). Florentine barber, author of humorous sonnets. He influenced Berni and other Renaissance satirical writers. One of the verses in his *Sonetti* (1757) is a debate between Poetry and his Razor, concerning the amount of time that the barber spends on each. He was called *il Burchiello* (*It.*, "canal barge or wherry"), possibly because of a sign in his shop.

Burckhardt, Jakob Christoph (1818–1897). Swiss historian of art and culture. His best-known work is *The Civilization of the Renaissance in Italy* (*Die Kultur der Renaissance in Italien;* 1860), for many years the classic analysis of the Renaissance. According to Burckhardt, Italy's unique political organization, based on the city-state rather than feudalism, had fostered the individualism upon which the Renaissance spirit rested. Thus, Italy was the cradle of the Renaissance and of modern man.

Burd, Ellen. In Scotch legend, a sister of CHILDE ROWLAND. She is rescued by him from the fairies who had shut her up in a castle in Elfland.

Bürger, Gottfried August (1747–1794). German poet of the STURM UND DRANG, close to the GÖTTINGER HAIN group. Under Herder's influence, he wrote ballads in folk style, the most famous of which is LENORE.

Burgess, [Frank] Gelett (1866–1951). American humorist and illustrator. He was the author of *Goops and How to Be Them* (1900), *Are You a Bromide* (1907), *Look Eleven Years Younger* (1937). He also wrote the famous nonsense quatrain beginning "I never saw a purple cow." See BROMIDE AND SULFITE.

Burgess, Thornton Waldo (1874–1965). American author of *Bedtime Stories,* a syndicated series of animal stories for children. Beginning in 1912, they appeared daily in numerous newspapers throughout the U.S. He also published a large number of his stories in book form.

Burghley or **Burleigh**, Baron. **William Cecil** (1520–1598). English statesman, the chief adviser to Elizabeth I.

Burgoyne, John (1722–1792). English army officer and dramatist. While commander-in-chief of the northern army, he was forced to surrender to the Americans at Saratoga in 1777. He later took part in the impeachment of Warren Hastings. Garrick produced his *Maid of the Oaks* (1775); his *The Heiress* (1786) enjoyed enormous popularity. He figures prominently in George Bernard Shaw's *The Devil's Disciple* (1897) and in Kenneth Roberts' *A Rabble in Arms* (1933).

Buried Alive (1908). A humorous novel by Arnold BENNETT. Priam Farll, a famous but shy painter, allows his rascally valet, Henry Leek, to be buried in Westminster Abbey under his name. Farll attends his own funeral, posthumously marries the splendid, comfortable Alice Chalice, and is accused of forging his own paintings. The book contains much satire of the London art world.

Burke, Edmund (1729–1797). Irish-born English statesman and author, known for his orations in the House of Commons. He was sympathetic toward the American colonies and the Irish Catholics, and was a strong enemy of the French Revolution. Among his most famous speeches are ON AMERICAN TAXATION, ON CONCILIATION WITH THE COLONIES, and *On the Nabob of Arcot's Private Debts* (1785), in which Burke discusses the great prosecution of Warren HASTINGS and tries to make him the scapegoat for all the abuses connected with the regime of the East India Company. His published works include *A Vindication of Natural Society* (1756), an ironic attack on deism; *A Philosophical Inquiry into the Origin of Our Ideas of the Sublime and Beautiful* (1756), a pioneer study in the psychological basis of aesthetic enjoyment; *Observations on the Present State of the Nation* (1769); *Thoughts on the Cause of the Present Discontents* (1770), in which Burke declares that politics deals with men and nations in actuality, never in bloodless abstractions; *Letter to the Sheriffs of Bristol* (1777); REFLECTIONS ON THE FRENCH REVOLUTION; and *Letters on the Proposals for Peace with the Regicide Directory of France* (1796–1797). He was associated with Samuel Johnson and Sir Joshua Reynolds in 1764 in forming the LITERARY CLUB. His influence on early 19th century German national economists is particularly pronounced.

Burke, Kenneth [Duva] (1897–   ). American literary critic, philosopher, and translator. Burke's translations of the German authors Thomas Mann, Emil Ludwig, Oswald Spengler, and Hugo von Hofmannsthal contributed greatly to making them known in the U.S. Among Burke's own writings are *Philosophy of Literary Form—Studies in Symbolic Action* (1941), *A Grammar of Motives* (1945), and *Rhetoric of Motives* (1950).

Burke, Thomas (1886–1945). English novelist and essayist. He wrote romantic, melodramatic stories about the Limehouse slum district in London. They include *Limehouse Nights* (1916) and *Abduction* (1939).

Burlador de Sevilla y el convidado de piedra, El (The Libertine of Seville and the Stone Guest, pub. 1630). A play by TIRSO DE MOLINA. It gave to world literature one of its most enduring character types, Don Juan. Based on a 14th-century Sevillan chronicle, Tirso's play relates how Don Juan Tenorio, a dissolute young rake, kills Don Gonzalo Ulloa, father of one of his lady loves, in a duel. Later Don Juan pulls the beard of a stone effigy of Don Gonzalo and invites the figure to dinner. The statue accepts and returns the hospitality by inviting Don Juan to an entertainment at his tomb, where he is strangled by the stone figure and his soul is carried off to hell.

Tirso's Don Juan, the first in a long line of successors, ignores the conventions of honor; he seeks only to secure his pleasure. At the same time he is profoundly religious and noble, exemplifying the conflict between the morality inherited from the Middle Ages and the libertinism fostered by the Renaissance. Among the most notable of later works in which Tirso's character appears are Byron's DON JUAN, Mozart's DON GIOVANNI, Zorrilla's DON JUAN TENORIO, and Shaw's MAN AND SUPERMAN.

Burlingame, [William] Roger (1889–1967). American writer. After being associated with Charles Scribner's Sons from 1914 to 1926, he turned to writing as a full-time occupation. In addition to several novels, including *You Too* (1924), a satire on advertising, Burlingame wrote a number of books showing his knowledge and interest in the history of technology in the U.S.

Burnand, Sir Francis Cowley (1836–1917). English playwright and editor of the periodical *Punch* (1880–1906). He wrote many burlesques including *Cox and Box* (1867), with music by Sir Arthur Sullivan. *Happy Thoughts* (1866), originally a series for *Punch*, has been widely read. He also wrote *The Incompleat Angler* (1887).

Burne-Jones, Sir Edward Coley (1833–1898). English painter. A member of the PRE-RAPHAELITE BROTHERHOOD, he was accorded wide public adulation. He painted classical, religious, medieval, literary, and symbolic scenes, marked by mysticism, emotion, and exotic decoration.

Burnet, Gilbert (1643–1715). English historian and churchman, bishop of Salisbury. Deeply involved in the religious and political controversy of the times, a confidential adviser to William and Mary, Burnet found time to write two important histories: *A History of the Reformation of the Church of England* (1679–1714) and the *History of His Own Time* (1724–1734). These books, based on original documents or personal experience, are early models of scientific historical research.

Burnet, Thomas (1635?–1715). English clergyman and author. He is known for his chief work *Telluris Theoria Sacra* (1681), translated as *The Sacred Theory of the Earth*, a prose exploration into the origin and development of the cosmos.

Burnett, Frances Eliza Hodgson (1849–1924). English-born American author of popular romances and books for children. Her works include LITTLE LORD FAUNTLEROY, *Sara Crewe* (1888), and *The Secret Garden* (1911).

Burnett, W[illiam] R[iley] (1899–   ). American writer. A leading exponent of HARD-BOILED FICTION, Burnett made his fortune with *Little Caesar* (1929), a story of gangsters in the prohibition era. Turned into a movie, it made Edward G. Robinson a star. Among his later books are *Iron Man* (1930), *Dark Hazard* (1933), *Nobody Lives Forever* (1944), *The Asphalt Jungle* (1949), *Pale Moon* (1956), and *Underdog* (1957).

Burney, Fanny [Madame d'Arblay] (1752–1840). English author. The daughter of a prominent musician and keeper of robes in the queen's household, she is chiefly known for her *Diaries and Letters, 1778–1840* (1842–1848), *Early Diary, 1768–1778* (1889), and her novels EVELINA, OR THE HISTORY OF A YOUNG LADY'S ENTRANCE INTO THE WORLD; CECILIA, OR MEMOIRS OF AN HEIRESS; *Camilla;* and *The Wanderer, or, Female Difficulties* (1814). She was one of the first novelists to deal with the experiences of a young girl coming in contact with the social world, and may be regarded as a link between Samuel Richardson and Jane Austen in the history of the novel.

Burning Babe, The (written c. 1593, pub. 1595). A mystical religious poem by Robert SOUTHWELL in which the poet has a vision of the suffering infant Christ on Christmas day.

burning bush. In the Old Testament, a bush burning with fire and not consumed (Ex. 3:2). It was out of this bush that the voice of God spoke to Moses on Mount Horeb, telling him that the Children of Israel were to be delivered from the oppression of the Egyptians and brought, under the leadership of Moses, into the land of Canaan. Because of its scriptural connotation and in commemoration of its early history of persecution, the burning bush became an emblem of the Presbyterian Church.

Burning Bush, The. See Sigrid UNDSET.

burning ghat. A Hindu cremation place. One of the best known is at Kalighat in Calcutta.

Burns, John Horne (1916–1953). American novelist. Burns is best known for his first book, *The Gallery* (1947), a series of connected sketches about American and British soldiers in Naples during World War II. He also wrote *Lucifer with a Book* (1949) and *A Cry of Children* (1952).

Burns, Robert (1756–1796). Scottish poet, generally considered the greatest of his nation. Self-educated, the son of a humble cotter and a farm laborer himself, Burns became a social as well as a literary sensation with the publication of his early poems in 1786. He is best known for his lyrics, written in the Scottish vernacular, on nature, love, patriotism, and peasant life. Among the most famous of these last are those addressed to a clergyman with whose theology he disagreed and against whom he had a personal grudge: THE HOLY FAIR, *Holy Willie's Prayer, Address to the Unco Guid,* and ADDRESS TO THE DEIL. He also wrote *To a Mouse, To a Mountain Daisy, Sweet Afton, Ye Flowery Banks, A Red, Red Rose,* SCOTS, WHA HAE, *John Anderson My Jo,* AULD LANG SYNE, and *A Man's a Man for a' That,* which expresses Burns's democratic opinions. His longer poems include THE COTTER'S SATURDAY NIGHT, TAM O'SHANTER, and THE JOLLY BEGGARS.

Like Chaucer and Byron, Burns was a master of the technique of using conversational rhythms in poetry. He almost always wrote to an old tune for which he sought appropriate words: "These old Scottish airs are so nobly sentimental that when one would compose for them, to *south* the tune, as our Scotch phrase is, over and over, is the readiest way to catch the inspiration, and raise the bard into that glorious enthusiasm so strongly characteristic of our old Scotch poetry." See SYLVANDER; HIGHLAND MARY; MARY CAMPBELL.

Burnt Njal. The hero of one of the best known of the early Icelandic sagas, *The Story of Burnt Njal.* The plot concerns the grim blood feud between the families of two well-to-do landowners, Njal and Gunnar, who are personal friends. Hallgerda, the spiteful and selfish wife of Gunnar, is the instigator of the feud, which progresses with a regular alternation of murders between the two sides until it culminates in the burning of Njal's home and his death within.

Burnt Norton. See FOUR QUARTETS.

Burnt-Out Case, A (1960). A novel by Graham GREENE. Set in a leper colony in the Congo, it is the story of a famous architect who is a spiritual leper and "burnt-out case."

Burr, Aaron (1756–1836). American politician. After distinguishing himself in the American Revolution, Burr served in the U.S. Senate (1791–1797) and organized a strong Democratic machine in New York through the previously nonpolitical Tammany Society. He was vice president (1801–1805) under Jefferson, whom he had tied in electoral votes in the election of 1800. Burr's long-standing enmity with Alexander Hamilton culminated in a duel (1804), in which Hamilton was killed and which ruined Burr personally and politically. In 1806 he became involved in a conspiracy in the Old Southwest, the nature of which has never been fully clarified, and was tried and acquitted of treason. Burr appears as a character in several novels, including H. B. Stowe's *The Minister Wooing* (1859), Gertrude Atherton's *The Conqueror* (1902), and Kenneth Roberts' *Arundel* (1930).

Burroughs, Edgar Rice. See TARZAN.

Burroughs, John (1837–1921). American naturalist, essayist, and poet. A farm boy who deeply loved nature, Burroughs was for a time a treasury clerk in Washington, D.C., where he met Walt Whitman. They became close friends, and Burroughs made the first biographical study of Whitman, *Notes on Walt Whitman as Poet and Person* (1867), a considerable portion of which was written by Whitman himself. Later the book was expanded into *Walt Whitman: A Study* (1896).

After working as a bank examiner (1873–1884), Burroughs settled at Riverby on the Hudson River, and the fame he acquired by his numerous essays on nature and his natural history collections attracted many visitors. He became a national figure, with his snowy white beard and his broad forehead and benign expression. He became a close friend of Theodore Roosevelt.

Reading Burroughs is for many people almost like actually seeing what he describes, so vivid, concrete, and pleasant is his writing. As he expressed it in *The Summit of the Years* (1913), "I go to books and nature as a bee goes to a flower, for a nectar that I can make into my own honey." His best-known collections include *Wake-Robin* (1871), *Riverby* (1894), *Ways of Nature* (1905), and *Leaf and Tendril* (1908).

Burroughs, William S. See BEAT MOVEMENT.

Burt, [Maxwell] Struthers (1882–1954). American novelist and short-story writer. Burt combined his personal knowledge of Philadelphia society and Wyoming ranches in his novel *The Delectable Mountains* (1927). He also wrote *John O'May and Other Stories* (1918), *The Interpreter's House* (1924), and several other volumes, including some poetry.

Burton, Sir Richard Francis (1821–1890). English explorer and writer of travel books. His *First Footsteps in Eastern Africa* (1856) is an account of his travels with John Speke (1827–1864). In 1858 the two went to East Africa again where Burton discovered Lake Tanganyika and Speke discovered Lake Victoria. As British consul, Burton traveled in West Africa, Brazil, Damascus, and Trieste. He published more than 30 narratives on his travels. He also made a literal translation of the *Arabian Nights*.

Burton, Robert (1577–1640). English churchman and prose writer. Burton entered Oxford as a student in 1593, later becoming vicar of St. Thomas, Oxford, and keeper of his college library. Thereafter he never left the little university town. He was a passionate scholar with a consuming curiosity about every phase of learning: medicine, history, literature, science, and theology. He possessed, moreover, an extraordinary memory, a great power of systematizing facts, and the gifts of eloquence, sympathy, and dry wit. Except for a few minor Latin pieces, he left only one work, THE ANATOMY OF MELANCHOLY, into which he poured a lifetime's hoard of classical and curious learning.

Burwell Papers. An account of Bacon's Rebellion, written around 1676 near Williamsburg, Va., by a planter named John Cotton. It was first printed in 1814 from an 18th-century copy owned by the Burwell family of Virginia. The lost original was the source for a verse history of the rebellion by Ebenezer Cook. The two epitaphs on Bacon contained in the Burwell Papers have been called the finest poems written in colonial America. See BACON'S EPITAPH. The account is also known as *The History of Bacon's and Ingram's Rebellion,* the title of the 1866 edition.

Bury the Dead (1936). A one-act play by Irwin SHAW. A pacifist fantasy, it deals with six men, killed in World War I, who refuse to be buried and at last persuade their living fellow soldiers to join them in a revolt against war.

busby. A tall headdress of fur worn in the British Army by hussars, artillerymen, and engineers. A bag of the same color as the facings of the regiment hangs from the top on the right.

Busch, Niven (1903–). American writer. A successful writer of popular fiction, Busch uses backgrounds that range from the Old West to 20th-century Europe. *Duel in the Sun* (1944), a novel of the Southwest in the 1880's, is perhaps his best-known work. He is also the author of *The Carrington Incident* (1941), *Day of the Conquerors* (1946), *The Furies* (1948), *The Hate Merchant* (1953), *The Actor* (1955), and *California Street* (1959).

Busch, Wilhelm (1832–1908). German humorous poet and illustrator. His well known book of verses, *Max und Moritz* (1865), illustrated by himself, is a veiled but sometimes bitter satire of average bourgeois complacency. "Max und Moritz" is still a common phrase in German, used in reference to mischievous children in general.

Buscón, Vida del (1626). A PICARESQUE novel by Francisco de QUEVEDO. Probably written about 1607, it is witty, cruel, and cynical, devoid of any feeling for humanity. Its full title is *Historia de la vida del Buscón, llamado Don Pablos, ejemplo de vagamundos y espejo de tacaños.* It relates the career of Pablos, the son of a Segovian barber and a woman of loose morals, who enters the service of a young gentleman, Don Diego Coronel. They both lodge at a boarding house in Salamanca, whose keeper, the avaricious Licenciado Cabra, was probably the prototype of Dickens' Squeers. After numerous unsavory adventures, Pablos emigrates to America, where he hopes to improve his fortunes.

bushidō (*Japanese,* "way of the warrior"). The code of ethics formerly adopted by the military leaders and feudal clan rulers of Japan. Not a written code, its provisions varied with the times, but the general emphasis was on loyalty and duty. Also involved was a certain aesthetic sensitivity and an attachment to ZEN discipline.

Busirane. See FAERIE QUEENE, THE.

Busiris. A mythical king of Egypt, who, in order to avert a famine used to sacrifice to the gods all strangers who set foot on his shores. Hercules was seized by him; and would have fallen a victim, but he broke his chain, and slew the inhospitable king. He is the titular hero of a blood-and-thunder tragedy (1719) by Edward Young.

Buson. See TANIGUCHI BUSON.

Bussy D'Ambois (c. 1604). A tragedy by George CHAPMAN. Bussy, a poor countryman who has gained the patronage of Monsieur, the king's brother, finds favor at the court of Henri III, despite the enmity of the duke of Guise, whose wife Bussy has been courting. Soon, however, his attentions turn to Tamyra, countess of Montsurry, and he becomes Monsieur's rival for the lady's affections. Where Monsieur fails, Bussy succeeds and becomes Tamyra's lover. Eventually, Count Montsurry forces Tamyra, his wife, to write a letter to Bussy imploring him to come to her. Bussy falls into the trap and is killed by Montsurry.

Bussy-Rambutin, Comte de Bussy. Roger de Rambutin (1618–1693). French soldier and writer. His *Histoire amoureuse des Gaules* (*Amorous History of the Gauls,* 1665), a collection of anecdotes libeling ladies of the court and presenting a disagreeable portrait of his cousin Mme. de Sévigné, earned him 17 years' exile and brought his military career and royal favor to a dismal end. Not surprisingly, the book enjoyed a wild popularity. Bussy-Rambutin was elected a member of the Académie française.

Butler, Joseph (1692–1752). English bishop and philosopher. He is known for his defense of revelation, *The Analogy of Religion* (1736). Unlike the optimistic deists, who found sufficient evidence of God's perfection and of His moral government in nature and in the heart of man, Butler stressed the imperfection of nature and of man. Accordingly, he argued that if nature, even with all its defects, furnished proof of Divine Creation, then the revealed religion of Scripture, with *analogous* defects, might also be considered the work of God.

Butler, Rhett. The rugged and free-living hero of Margaret Mitchell's historical novel, GONE WITH THE WIND.

Butler, Samuel (1612–1680). English poet, most famous for HUDIBRAS, a mock-epic satirizing the Puritans. Butler's work is distinguished by its relentless exposure of cant, hypocrisy, and human absurdity, its arresting figures of speech, odd rhymes, and witty parade of learning. His *Genuine Remains in Verse and Prose* (1759) contains a set of *Characters* in the manner of THEOPHRASTUS and THE ELEPHANT IN THE MOON, a verse satire on the Royal Society.

Butler, Samuel (1835–1902). English satirist, novelist, Homeric scholar, and translator. Son of a clergyman and grandson of Bishop Samuel Butler, whose biography (1902) he wrote, Butler too was destined for the church; upon graduation from Cambridge, however, religious doubts caused him to abandon it and he emigrated to New Zealand (1859–1864) where he accumulated a small fortune in sheep farming.

A brilliant amateur biologist, Butler was immediately attracted to Darwin's theory of evolution, but, believing Darwin had excluded mind from the life process, he subsequently took exception to certain aspects of it in a series of criticisms which he elaborated throughout his life. His essay *The Deadlock in Darwinism* and his books on evolution—*Life and Habit* (1877), *Evolution, Old and New* (1879), *Unconscious Memory* (1880), and *Luck or Cunning?* (1887)—are still very readable.

His satiric masterpiece, EREWHON, attacked contemporary attitudes in social morals, religion, and science. *The Fair Heaven* (1873) is a subtle, ironic attack on revealed religion presented in the guise of a convincing defense of the gospels, yet in fact undermining them. *Erewhon Revisited* is a continuation of his attack on revealed religions.

Butler also wrote *The Authoress of the Odyssey* (1897), in which he seriously defends his conviction that the *Odyssey* was written by a woman; *Shakespeare's Sonnets Reconsidered* (1899); and THE WAY OF ALL FLESH, a novel, and perhaps his best-known work. He was an extremely versatile, original, and brilliant writer, one of the most searching critics of his age.

Butor, Michel (1926–   ). French novelist and essayist of the NEW WAVE. *A Change of Heart* (*La Modification,* 1957; also translated as *Second Thoughts*) and *Passing Time* (*L'Emploi du Temps;* 1956) are experimental novels showing the effect of the passage of time on human relationships. His other novels, too, deal symbolically with psychological rather than objective time and memory: *Passage de Milan* (1954) and *Degrees* (1960). He explained his literary theories in *Le Génie du Lieu* (1958) and the autobiographical *Repertoire* (1960).

Buzfuz, Serjeant. In Charles Dickens' PICKWICK PAPERS, the pleader retained by DODSON AND FOGG for the plaintiff in the celebrated case of *Bardell* v. *Pickwick.* Serjeant Buzfuz is an able orator, who proves that Mr. Pickwick's innocent note about "chops and tomato sauce" is a declaration of love, and that his reminder "not to forget the warming-pan" is only a flimsy cover to express the ardor of his affection.

Byles, Mather (1707–1788). American clergyman and poet. The son of a Boston saddler, and nephew of Cotton Mather, Byles graduated from Harvard in 1725. His two chief collections were *Poems on Several Occasions* (1744) and *The Conflagration* (1755), verse greatly influenced by Alexander Pope with whom Byles corresponded. A sort of official greeter for New England, Byles was the most noted wit of 18th century America.

byliny. The epic poems of the Russian peasantry in song form. A number of specific heroes reappear throughout these songs. Their feats are fantastic and are often engagingly ingenuous. Many of the *byliny* are divided into cycles, such as the cycle of Kiev, the cycle of Novgorod, the cycle of Ivan the Terrible, and others. They range in time from the earliest mythological periods to the 18th century.

Bynner, [Harold] Witter (1881–1968). American poet. Bynner early wrote *An Ode to Harvard* (1907) and later did editorial work for *McClure's Magazine*. In 1916 he was involved with Arthur Davison Ficke in the Spectra hoax. In 1922 he published *A Book of Plays*. Interested in the art of China and India, he published *The Jade Mountain* (1929), a translation of Chinese poetry; *Indian Earth* (1929), a volume of verse; and *The Way of Life According to Laotzu* (1944). Among his other books are *Journey with Genius* (1951), an account of time spent with D. H. Lawrence, and *New Poems* (1960).

Byrd, Richard E[velyn] (1888–1957). American polar explorer. A descendant of the Virginia planter William Byrd, he flew by airplane over the North Pole (1926) and the South Pole (1929), and took part in three expeditions to Antarctica (1928–1930, 1933–1935, 1939). He described his adventures in *Skyward* (1928), *Little America* (1930), and other books.

Byrd, William (1543?–1623). English composer. Known in 16th-century Europe as the "Father of Music," he wrote much church music, chamber and instrumental music, and a number of songs and madrigals on texts by Sir Philip Sidney, Ovid, Ariosto, and other famous poets. He is considered to have originated the solo song with string accompaniment. Although he wrote music for the Anglican Church, Byrd remained a devout Catholic.

Byrd, William (1674–1744). American historian of the Virginia colony, scholar, explorer, and member of the Royal Society of London, one of the most cultivated men in colonial America. His best-known works are *The History of the Dividing Line*, concerning the dispute over the boundary between Virginia and North Carolina; *A Journey to the Land of Eden;* and *A Progress to the Mines.* They are included in a collection of his papers, known as *The Westover Manuscripts*, first published in 1841. Diaries which Byrd kept in shorthand as a hobby for several years were discovered nearly 200 years after his death and published as *The Secret Diary of William Byrd of Westover* (1941) and *Another Secret Diary* (1942).

Byrne, Donn. Original name, **Brian Oswald Donn-Byrne** (1889–1928). Irish-American novelist and short-story writer. Best known for his novel Messer Marco Polo, Donn Byrne always tried to hide the fact that he had been born in Brooklyn. A romantic imagination, the use of fantasy, and a graceful style mark his writing. *Blind Raftery* (1924) is a novel about the Gaelic poet Anthony Raftery (1745?–1835). His many stories were collected in *The Changeling* (1923), *Rivers of Damascus* (1931), and *The Woman of the Shee* (1932).

Byron, George Gordon [Noel]. 6th baron **Byron of Rochdale.** Called **Lord Byron** (1788–1824). English poet. In both his works and his life he created the "Byronic hero"—a defiant, melancholy young man, brooding on some mysterious, unforgivable sin in his past. Whatever Byron's sin was, he never told, but neither did he deny the legends of wildness, evil, and debauchery that grew up about his name. The heroes of Byron's poems are generally swashbuckling brigands who perform heroic feats. Byron himself, however, was short, somewhat stout, and limped from a club foot.

His profligate father died when Byron was three years old, and he was raised in Scotland by his mother. He was educated at Harrow and at Trinity College, Cambridge, receiving an M.A. from the latter in 1808. In 1809 he took his seat in the House of Lords, having come into the family title and estates through the death of his great-uncle in 1798. His first published work, Hours of Idleness, a collection of poems, was given a devastating, although accurate, review by the *Edinburgh Review*. This review was answered by Byron in the virulent satire, English Bards and Scotch Reviewers. After a very short time in Parliament, Byron and his friend J. C. Hobhouse left England for a tour of the Mediterranean that took them from Spain to the Near East. The trip fired Byron's romantic nature with tantalizing views of the Orient and supplied material for many of his later works.

Following his return to England (1811), Byron published the first two cantos of Childe Harold's Pilgrimage, a fictionalized account of his trip. *Childe Harold* was an immediate success; as Byron put it, he woke up one morning to find himself famous. In the next two years he published *The Giaour* (1813), The Bride of Abydos, The Corsair, and *Lara* (1814).

Byron was much admired by women and had been involved in several intrigues before he married Anne Isabella Milbanke in 1815. However, his promiscuous behavior after the marriage completely destroyed his reputation. Shortly after the birth of their daughter (1815), Lady Byron separated from her husband. Byron later spoke bitterly of the marriage, referring to their honeymoon as a "treaclemoon," and once a deed of separation had been signed he left England, never to return.

He traveled to Switzerland, where he lived with the Shelleys at Lake Geneva. Byron began a liaison with Clara Clairmont, but moved restlessly on, arriving in Venice in November, 1816, in the company of his friend Hobhouse. He spent the next six years in Italy, always championing and often taking part in the Italian nationalist movement. In 1819, Byron met and fell in love with the 17-year-old countess Theresa Guiccioli, and critics have attributed much of the poet's enthusiasm for Italy to her influence. With Leigh Hunt, Byron edited *The Liberal* (1822), but after the collapse of the *Carbonari* movement they were left without a cause. The next year, following the death of Shelley, Byron outfitted a ship and sailed to Greece to take part in the battle for Greek independence. He died, fever-stricken, at Missolonghi in January, 1824. After being given full military honors in Greece, his body was shipped back to England for burial at Newstead Abbey, his baronial seat.

Byron's poetic output was never slowed down by his political and personal adventures. While in Italy he finished *Childe Harold* (1816, 1817) and wrote The Siege of Corinth, Parisina, and The Prisoner of Chillon, all poetic narratives. In 1817 he wrote his first poetic drama, Manfred, which was followed by Marino Faliero, *Cain, a Mystery* (1821), *Heaven and Earth* (1822), Werner, and The Deformed Transformed. Among Byron's most accomplished works are his satires, such as Beppo, The Vision of

JUDGEMENT, in which he answers the attack on him by the poet Robert Southey; *The Age of Bronze* (1823); and his masterpiece, DON JUAN. *Don Juan,* begun in 1819, was still unfinished when Byron died. This 16,000 line poem in 16 cantos was continually added to by the poet, and as such it can be read as a contemporaneous account of the author's moods and feelings. Byron used *Don Juan* as a platform to express many of his sardonic opinions of people and events. The protagonist is, of course, Byron himself, only thinly disguised as the famous Spanish rake.

As a poet and especially as one of the English romantics, Byron has found less favor than Keats or Shelley; he is looked on as the embodiment of romanticism rather than its spokesman. The bizarre aspects of Byron's life have somewhat overshadowed his technical virtuosity as a poet: the man has been more closely examined than his work. However, at its best Byron's poetry shows an extraordinary rhyming ability combined with a free-flowing, dynamic style. His work rarely has the profundity found in that of Shelley or Keats, but his opus as a whole is a forceful expression of the majesty and desolation of history, the vanity of pomp, and the fleeting quality of fame. His work has always been more popular in Europe, especially Germany, than in England and the U.S. See DESTRUCTION OF SENNACHERIB, THE.

Byron, Harriet. See SIR CHARLES GRANDISON.

Byrsa. The citadel of Carthage. It was built, according to legend, by DIDO, who was told by the local ruler that she might purchase as much land as could be enclosed within a bull's hide. By cutting the hide into narrow strips, she obtained a sizable piece of land. The hide (Gr., *byrsa*) supposedly gave the place its name; historically, the name comes from a Phoenician word meaning *citadel.*

Byzantine Empire. The eastern or Greek division of the Roman Empire, sometimes called the Later or Eastern Roman Empire. For the purposes of administration, DIOCLETIAN (r. 284–305) divided the rule of the empire among four emperors, an experiment that led to 20 years of civil strife after his abdication. The empire was reunited in 324 when CONSTANTINE THE GREAT, defeating all his rivals, became sole ruler of the whole empire.

The Byzantine Empire may be dated from Constantine's creation of a second capital, modeled on Rome, at BYZANTIUM which he renamed Constantinople (now Istanbul). From the establishment of this city as a second Rome the division of east from west was formalized, and the east soon emerged as the dominant half. More important, unlike Rome with its pagan history, Constantinople was, from the very first Christian, and it was Greek, thus dividing east from west still further. As Rome declined and finally fell (476), the Byzantine Empire flourished: it was a major, if not the major, power in Europe up to the mid-11th century. Politically, it played the highly significant role of protecting Europe, through the Middle Ages, against invasions from western Asia. The absolute monarchy, with the monarch elected by God, instituted by Constantine the Great remained largely unchanged throughout the long life of the empire, which fell at the hands of the Turks in 1453. See JUSTINIAN.

The iconography of the Byzantine Empire developed out of Christian symbolism. Its chief features are the circle, dome, and round arch; its chief symbols are the lily, cross, vesica, and nimbus. Saint Sophia at Constantinople and Saint Mark's at Venice are fine exemplars of Byzantine architecture and decoration.

Byzantium. A city on the European shore at the mouth of the Thracian Bosporus. It was first established by Megarian colonists (c. 657 B.C.). In the sixth century B.C. it came under Persian rule and then alternately under Spartan and Athenian rule in the fifth and fourth centuries. After its revolt from the second Athenian League (357), it was independent and became an ally of Rome at the time of the Third Macedonian War. It subsequently came under Roman rule and was chosen by Constantine the Great for his new capital; he renamed it CONSTANTINOPLE, and it is now called Istanbul, a major city in Turkey.

Byzantium appears as a central symbol in the poetry of William Butler YEATS. It occurs in *Sailing to Byzantium* and *Byzantium,* where it represents the richness of an artistic civilization and the triumph of art over time and death.

C

Caaba or **al Caaba.** See KAABA.

Cabal. In English history, an influential clique of ministers at the court of Charles II from 1667 to 1674. The group derived its name from the initials of its members (Clifford, Ashley, Buckingham, Arlington, and Lauderdale), who were notorious for their intrigues and corruption. The word *cabal,* which is now used to signify a body of political intriguers, was probably popularized by the activities of the English Cabal, but it had long been associated with secrecy and magic. See CABALA.

cabala or **kabbalah.** The oral traditions of the Jews, said to have been delivered by Moses to the rabbis and handed down through the centuries by word of mouth. The word comes from *qabbalah,* the Hebrew word for "tradition," and in the Middle Ages was a popular term for the Jewish theosophy describing the World of Souls. The rabbis, or cabalists, who were the guardians of the cabala were feared as possessing secrets of magical powers.

Caballero, Fernán. Pen name of **Cecilia Böhl de Faber** (1796–1877). Spanish novelist. Of Spanish descent, Fernán Caballero was born in Switzerland but emigrated to Spain in 1813. The appearance of her first novel, *La Gaviota* (*The Seagull,* 1849) marked the beginning of the regional school in Spanish literature. The tale relates the progress of a low-born singer who marries a German surgeon, becomes a well-known opera star, has an affair with a bull-fighter, and after marrying again, returns to her native province. Set in Andalus` , the novel is noted for its colorful descriptions of life in that province. She also wrote *Clemencia* (1852) and *La familia de Alvareda* (1856).

Cabbages and Kings (1904). A volume of 19 connected stories by O. HENRY. The stories are set in a fictional country called Coralio in Central America. The title, from the ballad of the Walrus and the Carpenter in Lewis Carroll's *Alice in Wonderland,* announces the intention "to talk of many things." The picture of life presented is one of mingled romance and realism.

Cabell, James Branch (1879–1958). American novelist and essayist. Cabell belonged to an old Virginian family, and some of his most laborious writings are concerned with the genealogies of his own and other families. His first book, *The Eagle's Shadow,* appeared in 1904. While writing his second book, *Gallantry* (1907), Cabell became irritated by having to describe a scene he had never visited. As a result, he created his own mythical country, the medieval French province of Poictesme, the name of which is probably a compound of Poitiers and Angoulême. In a long series of symbolic and satirical novels, he traced the history of the imaginary province from 1234 to 1750, describing in great detail its laws, easy sexual morality, courtly manners, legends, and habits. (See Dom MANUEL).

It was not until the publication of JURGEN in 1919 that Cabell received any popular success, and his acceptance was due largely to the attempt to suppress the book on the grounds of immorality. In the 18-volume *Storisende Edition* (1927–1930), Cabell arranged the Poictesme novels in sequence of action rather than in the order in which they were published. Among the books in the series are *Beyond Life* (1919), *The Soul of Melicent* (1913; revised as *Domnei,* 1920), *Chivalry* (1909), *Jurgen, Gallantry* (1907), THE CREAM OF THE JEST, *The Silver Stallion* (1926), and *Something about Eve* (1927). Cabell also wrote numerous books of poetry and nonfiction.

When asked how to pronounce his name, Cabell rhymed, "Tell the rabble my name is Cabell."

Cabeza de Vaca, Alvar Núñez (c. 1490–c. 1557). Spanish explorer and governor. Cabeza de Vaca saw military action in Italy and Spain before joining an ill-fated expedition (1528) to Florida under Pánfilo da Narváez, during which he and a few companions were marooned on Galveston Island near Texas. After spending six years as a merchant among Indian tribes in the area, Cabeza de Vaca began his long journey back to civilization. During a period of captivity among the natives, he met two other Spaniards and a Negro slave, also survivors of the Narváez expedition; the four of them managed to escape and headed for Mexico, winning the favor of Indians along the way by healing the sick. They reached Culiacán on the Pacific coast of Mexico in 1536. Cabeza de Vaca himself described his adventures in *Naufragios* (1542).

In 1540 he was appointed governor of the province of La Plata in South America. After an unsuccessful attempt to reach the legendary city of Manoa, he was deposed by a revolt in Asunción, supposedly because he was usurping royal authority, but probably because he insisted on decent treatment for the Indians.

Cable, George Washington (1844–1925). American short-story writer and novelist. He is known for his tales dealing with the Creoles of New Orleans; Cable was part of the local color movement of the late 19th century, and a master of the various dialects of his native city. His first literary success was OLD CREOLE DAYS, a collection of stories to which *Madame Delphine* (1881) was added in later editions. THE GRANDISSIMES, a complex novel of social forces and his most widely read work today, showed Cable to be an important writer whose treatment of race relations and violence was to foreshadow such later Southern writers as William Faulkner and Robert Penn Warren. *Dr. Sevier* (1884) attacked the corruption of New Orleans in the period before the Civil War.

An enemy of slavery and a reformer, Cable published *The Silent South* in 1885. This argument for better treatment of Negroes and for prison reform increased the animosity of the Creoles toward Cable, forcing him to move to Massachusetts, where he continued to write on social problems in *The Negro Question* (1888) and *The Southern Struggle for Pure Government* (1890). Cable's later fiction is thought to be inferior to his earlier work. It includes *Strong Hearts* (1899), *"Posson Jone'"* and *Père Raphaël* (1909), and *Gideon's Band* (1914).

Cabot, John (1450–1498) and **Sebastian** (c. 1476–1557). Outstanding Italian navigators and explorers. The senior Cabot traveled to the Orient in 1480 in hope of improving the spice trade. While there he became impressed with the need for a northwest passage to Cathay: this was to become the ruling passion of his career and that of his son. Cabot traveled to England, settling in Bristol, where he received a patent of discovery from Henry VII and set sail in 1497 accompanied by his son on a voyage of discovery. He reached Baffin Land and cruised along the Newfoundland coast, which he thought to be Asia; a second voyage in 1498 carried him to the Delaware Capes and Hatteras. He is generally credited with the discovery of the North American continent.

His son Sebastian, an expert cartographer as well as explorer, made an unsuccessful attempt to locate the Northwest Passage in 1509. He was then commissioned by the Spanish to explore the possibility of a southwest passage to the Pacific and from 1526 to 1529, he was in South America, following the River Plate. In 1533 he became the governor of a joint stock Company of Merchant Adventurers whose aim was to find a northeast passage to China; their expedition reached Russia and opened trade possibilities instead. Sebastian died wealthy and famous, but he never realized his elusive goal.

caccia. A poem in free verse, employing mainly short lines. Popular during the Italian Renaissance, *caccia* are generally used to portray hunting scenes or any outdoor experience, serving to provide the necessary shouts, exclamations, and conversational examples that form the body of the poem. The literal meaning of the word *caccia* is the hunt or chase. Many poems cast in this form appeared, usually anonymously, between 1350 and 1450; these were set to music but few have survived.

Caccini, Giulio (1546–1618). Italian musician and composer. Caccini was a member of the Florentine *Camerata*, a group of theorists and composers, including V. Galilei, Peri, Rinuccini, and Monteverdi, who created the first operas. He wrote the music, not extant, for Chiabrera's *Rapimento di Cefalo*, performed in 1600.

Cacus. In Roman mythology, a famous robber son of Vulcan. He is represented as three-headed, and vomiting flames; he lived in Italy, and was strangled by Hercules. It is thought that, with his sister Caca, Cacus was actually a primitive god of the hearthfire.

Cadalso y Vázquez, José (1741–1782). Spanish poet, essayist, and soldier. Once described as a man who wrote classicism and lived romanticism, Cadalso is best known for such satirical works as *Los eruditos a la violeta* (1772), directed against superficial learning, and *Cartas marruecas* (1793), essays notable for their acute analysis of Spanish decadence. *Noches lúgubres* (1792) are prose dialogues in which he described an attempt to disinter the body of his dead mistress. His best poetry appears in *Ocios de mi juventud* (1773).

Cade, Jack [originally **John**] (d. 1450). Irish-born English rebel who assumed the name of Mortimer and claimed York kinship. He led an insurrection, usually called "Cade's Rebellion," of about 30,000 heavily armed Kentishmen protesting oppressive taxation and unjust administration of the government under King Henry VI. They defeated a royal army and occupied London (July, 1450) for two days, executing two of the king's ministers. On the third day, however, their plundering turned the citizenry against them. Cade tried to make a stand, but a promise of pardon dispersed most of his army, and he was pursued into Sussex and slain. He appears in Shakespeare's HENRY VI: PART II, and in R. T. Conrad's tragedy *Jack Cade* (1835), rewritten as *Aylmere* (1852) and very popular in 19th-century America.

Cadenus. One of Swift's many pseudonyms, an anagram of *decanus* (Lat., "dean"). It appears in *Cadenus and Vanessa* (1713, pub. 1726), one of Swift's best poems, which gives an account of his relationship with Esther Vanhomrigh and was written to dispel her passion for him. The poem also reflects Swift's zeal for improving the minds of young ladies, which had begun with his tutorship of Esther JOHNSON. At the request of Esther Vanhomrigh, *Cadenus and Vanessa* was published after her death.

Cade's Rebellion. See Jack CADE.

Cadignan, Diane de. The Duchess of Maufrigneuse, afterwards Princess of Cadignan. One of Balzac's most heartless and brilliant women, the Princess is the mistress of many of the men who appear in the novels of LA COMÉDIE HUMAINE. She is the heroine of LES SECRETS DE LA PRINCESSE DE CADIGNAN.

Cadmus (Kadmos). In Greek mythology, a son of Agenor and Telephassa. Sent from their Phoenician home to seek their sister Europe, he and his brothers were told not to return without her. The Delphic oracle advised him to give up the search and to found a city where a cow with a moon-shaped mark lay down to rest. This he did at Thebes in Boeotia. Killing a dragon sacred to Ares, he sowed its teeth and armed men sprang up from the ground (see also SPARTI). When he flung a stone among them, they killed each other, except for five who became his allies.

At a wedding attended by the gods Cadmus married Harmonia, daughter of Ares and Aphrodite; she bore him a son, Polydorus, and four daughters, Autonoë, Ino, Agave, and SEMELE. He fortified the Theban acropolis, the Cadmeia. In his old age he resigned the throne to his grandson Pentheus, after whose early death Cadmus and Harmonia migrated to Illyria and ultimately became serpents. Through Polydorus, Cadmus fathered the ill-fated dynasty that ended with Oedipus' grandsons. He appears in Euripides' tragedy *The Bacchae* as a follower of Semele's son Dionysus. (See BACCHANTS, THE.)

Cadou, René Guy (1920–1951). French poet. The best of his deceptively simple and sentimental poetry is collected in *Poèmes Choisies* (1950) and *Hélène; ou, le règne végétal* (1952).

Caduceus. An ancient Greek herald's wand (*kerykeion*) entwined with snakes or ribbons. Perhaps originally associated in Greek religion with fertility *daimones* (see DAEMON) it became especially identified with Hermes, the herald of the gods, and ASCLEPIUS (Aesculapius), the demigod of healing. Through the latter, it became a symbol of the physician's profession, as it is today.

Caedmon (d. 680?). Old English religious poet. According to Bede he was an illiterate herdsman who received divine inspiration in a dream to write religious poetry. He entered a monastery and made narrative poetry in ALLITERATIVE VERSE of the scriptural histories told to him. Actually, there is only one hymn which he certainly composed; the rest of the "Caedmonian manuscript" is the work of several different authors. The first "book" has adaptations of Genesis, Exodus, and Daniel. The second, called *Christ and Satan,* is of much later date, perhaps even ninth century (see CYNEWULF).

Caeneus (**Kaineus**). See LAPITHS.

A page from a manuscript of *Caedmon's Hymn.*

BODLEIAN LIBRARY, OXFORD

Caerlon (Welsh, "city of legions"). A place name prominent in Arthurian legend as the seat of King Arthur's court. The most noted early references to Caerlon in connection with Arthurian literature occur in the writings of the Welsh historians. From Geoffrey of Monmouth (12th century), for example, we learn that Caerlon was situated on the river Usk, that it was founded by Belinus, and that it became the archbishopric for Cambria (Wales). See CAMELOT; CARDUEL.

Caesar, [Caius] Julius (100–44 B.C.). Roman general and statesman. After a brilliant early career in politics, where he distinguished himself in oratory, and in generalship which he displayed in Spain (61–60 B.C.), Caesar was elected consul in 59. In the year 60 B.C. he joined with Pompey and Crassus in the First TRIUMVIRATE. After his consulate, as was customary, he was allotted the governorship of a province: his choice was GAUL. For nine years (58–49) he pushed back the boundaries of Roman Gaul until he had conquered all of central Europe from the Rhine to the Pyrenees. In 49, Pompey and the leaders of the Senate, fearing the prestige of Caesar and the strength of his fanatically loyal legions, ordered him to resign his command and return to Rome without his army. This he refused to do; "The die is cast," he is reported to have said as he led his army across the RUBICON into Italy. Pompey fled together with many members of the senatorial party, including Cicero and Cato the Younger. Following his opponents to Thessaly in northern Greece, Caesar defeated them in the battle of Pharsalus (48). In subsequent campaigns, he secured his firm hold on the empire in several ways: he placed CLEOPATRA on the throne of Egypt (48); he defeated the king of Pontus at the Battle of Zela (47); he crushed the remainder of the senatorial army at Thapsus in North Africa (46). His return to Rome in the spring of 46 was marked by lavish public festivals. He was hailed as a demigod; the name of the fifth month (*Quintilis*) in the Roman calendar was changed to *Julius* (July) in his honor. During the year that followed, Caesar made many reforms in the senatorial system and in the general management of the empire. His most durable reform, however, was his revision of the calendar. With the help of an Alexandrian astronomer, he established the Julian calendar which, with minor changes, is the one we use today. It went into effect on January 1, 45 B.C.

Opposition to Caesar on the part of the aristocratic party was still seething beneath the surface of Roman politics. On March 15, 44 (the IDES of March), a group led by CASSIUS Longinus and Marcus Junius BRUTUS assassinated Caesar, thus bringing to a sudden end uncompleted plans for the reorganization of Rome and the empire.

Caesar was one of the foremost orators of his age; only Cicero was esteemed the more persuasive of the two speakers. He also found time to record some of the history that he himself helped to make. His COMMENTARIES ON THE GALLIC WAR (51) and his *Commentaries on the Civil War* (45), which was unfinished, show him as a clear and vigorous prose stylist.

Even in his lifetime, the name *Caesar* represented the Roman *Imperium*. By the time of Christ—75 years later—it was used to connote civil government.

When Diocletian, at the end of the third century, split the empire into East and West, he appointed two Caesars as vice-regents. Through the Middle Ages to the present day, Caesar's name has survived as Kaiser and Czar. (See JULIAN EMPERORS.)

Caesar appears in many historical dramas, notably in Shakespeare's JULIUS CAESAR and George Bernard Shaw's CAESAR AND CLEOPATRA. In *Julius Caesar,* Brutus is actually the main interest of the play while Caesar is drawn as a weakling and a braggart. This characterization has often been criticized as untrue to history.

Caesar's famous dispatch *"Veni, vidi, vici"* (I came, I saw, I conquered) was written to the senate to announce his overthrow of Parnaces, king of Pontus. *Caesar's wife must be above suspicion.* When Pompeia's name became linked with Clodius', Caesar divorced her, not because he believed her to be guilty, but because the wife of Caesar must not even be suspected of crime. See CALPURNIA.

Caesar and Cleopatra (1899). A play by George Bernard SHAW. A wise, unsentimental Caesar is the center of a loose plot about political intrigue in ancient Egypt. Shaw gives unfamiliar personalities to both Caesar and Cleopatra. Not Shakespeare's "serpent of the old Nile," this Cleopatra is a giddy teenager, convinced the Romans are monsters. Under Caesar's tutelage she loses her charm and becomes a precocious adult. Caesar, balding and practical, is amused by Cleopatra, history, and himself. Shaw's plot is taken directly from Plutarch's *Parallel Lives.*

caesura. In prosody, a break or pause in the flow of a line of poetry for rhetorical effect. The caesura is as related to meaning as to verse technique, since it must be occasioned by a sense pause such as the end of one sentence and the beginning of another. Formerly subject to the strict rules of classical prosody, the caesura is now used freely and naturally to vary the music of the line and thus of the entire poem.

Caffè, Il (*Ital.,* "The Coffeehouse"). An Italian literary gazette (1764–1766). Although carrying some articles of a purely literary nature, it was mainly concerned with promoting economic, social, and political reform on the basis of ideas formulated by the luminaries of the French Enlightenment. The review's founders and chief contributors were the economist Pietro Verri (1728–1797), his brother Alessandro, and the penologist Cesare Beccaria. Voltaire and d'Alembert praised its efforts to familiarize the Italian public with French rationalist thought.

Cagliostro, Count Alessandro di. Real name: **Giuseppe Balsamo** (1743–1795). Italian charlatan. He traveled throughout Europe with his wife, posing as a man of rank and duping the credulous with his feats of magic and alchemy. Later the couple founded a secret masonic sect which gained many adherents. Implicated in the DIAMOND NECKLACE AFFAIR in 1785, he was imprisoned in the Bastille. In Rome he was condemned to death by the Inquisition for heresy, but the sentence was commuted to life imprisonment.

Cahan, Abraham (1860–1951). Russian-born American novelist and editor. Cahan came to America in 1882, joined the staff of Yiddish journals in New York City, and became a founder and editor-in-chief of the *Jewish Daily Forward.* His best-known

novel is THE RISE OF DAVID LEVINSKY, dealing with the archetypal immigrant experience. Other works include *Yekl, a Tale of the New York Ghetto* (1896) and *The Imported Bridegroom and Other Stories of the New York Ghetto* (1898).

Cahiers de la quinzaine. See Charles PÉGUY.

Caiaphas. In the New Testament, a high priest before whom Jesus was brought to trial. He was a member of the SANHEDRIN.

Cain. In the Old Testament, the son of Adam and Eve and murderer of his brother Abel. Cain killed his brother out of jealousy when Abel's sacrifice of the firstlings of his flock proved more acceptable to Jehovah than his own sacrifice of the fruit of the ground. Then Jehovah, to signify his disapproval cast his curse upon him and made Cain "a fugitive and a vagabond in the earth." The rivalry of a shepherd for the approval of a deity is as old as Sumerian literature (see DUMUZI).

According to Muslim tradition, Cain refused to follow his father's desire that he marry Abel's twin sister, Jumella, and instead married his own twin sister Aclima. God rejected Cain's sacrifice to signify his disapproval of this marriage.

Byron wrote a dramatic poem *Cain, a Mystery* (1821) based on the Bible narrative. Coleridge's prose poem *The Wanderings of Cain* (1798) is on the same subject.

Cain, James M[allahan] (1892–   ). American novelist. Cain established a reputation as a writer of hard-boiled fiction with his first novel, *The Postman Always Rings Twice* (1934). It is the story of a young hobo who has a love affair with the wife of the owner of a roadside stand and plots with her to murder her husband and collect his insurance. Later novels include *Serenade* (1937), *Mildred Pierce* (1941), *Past All Dishonor* (1946), and *Mignon* (1955).

Caine, [Sir Thomas Henry] Hall (1853–1931). English novelist. His books were phenomenally successful and earned him a fortune. Among the best known are *The Manxman* (1894), *The Eternal City* (1901), and *The Prodigal Son* (1904). As a young man he served as secretary to D. G. Rossetti, and published his *Recollections* of the poet in 1882.

Caine Mutiny, The (1951). A novel by Herman WOUK. It takes place aboard the *Caine,* a World War II mine sweeper, whose officers rebel against the cowardly and inefficient Captain Queeg. A book of sustained and gripping narrative power, it had a tremendous impact on the American reading public. A section of it was later equally effectively dramatized by the author as *The Caine Mutiny Court Martial* (1953).

Ça Ira (Fr. "it will go"). Name and refrain of a popular patriotic song (1790) of the French Revolution. The rallying cry was borrowed from Benjamin Franklin, who used to say in reference to the American revolution, *"Ah! ça ira!"* ("we'll succeed!")

Caius, Dr. An irascible French physician in Shakespeare's MERRY WIVES OF WINDSOR. His courtship of Anne Page has the backing of her mother, Mrs. Page.

Cakes and Ale (1930). A novel by W. Somerset MAUGHAM. It is a satire of English literary life in which ASHENDEN and Kear (a popular novelist based on Hugh Walpole) re-examine the life of the great

Victorian writer Driffield. Driffield was said to be based on Thomas Hardy, but Maugham vigorously denied it. The central character is Rosie, Driffield's first wife, an exuberant, promiscuous barmaid.

Calais (Kalais). See ARGONAUTS.

Calamity Jane. The nickname of **Martha Jane Burke** (1852?–1903). Born in a Montana mining community, she was a well-known frontier character, pony-express rider, and scout. She became the heroine of *Deadwood Dick on Deck, or Calamity Jane the Heroine of Whoop Up,* one of a series of dime novels by Edward L. Wheeler that began in 1884. The name has come to be a synonym for one who is always predicting misfortune, one who puts the worst possible interpretation on any turn of events.

Calamus (1860). A group of poems in Walt Whitman's LEAVES OF GRASS. Intended as a complementary section to *Children of Adam,* the poems celebrate "the manly love of comrades." Calamus is a hardy and aromatic kind of grass or rush, often called sweet flag.

Calandrino and the Heliotrope. A tale from Giovanni Boccaccio's THE DECAMERON. It tells of the simpleton Calandrino and his belief that there is a stone called the heliotrope that can make him invisible. Imagining he has found it, he eludes his friends Bruno and Buffalmacco and returns home. When his wife scolds him for bringing home so many stones, he beats her, convinced that she has destroyed the virtues of his find. Only when his friends confess the jest, is he persuaded not to beat her again. Calandrino appears in several of the *Decameron* stories.

Calder, Alexander (1898–   ). American artist. He is known for his graceful mobiles.

Calderón de la Barca [y Henao], Pedro (1600–1681). Spanish dramatist, one of his country's great literary figures. Born in Madrid of a prosperous family of the lower aristocracy, Calderón was educated at the Jesuit college there and attended the university at Salamanca. Beginning his literary career about 1620, he was a soldier as well as a successful playwright. In 1651 he became a priest. After his ordination he wrote only AUTOS SACRAMENTALES and command plays for the court theater.

Calderón brought to the theater a fine power of reasoning, an intellectual outlook, a keen dramatic instinct, and a delicate imagination. He was a typical writer of the Baroque period, frequently given to metaphors and artificially imposed symbols. His philosophy was influenced by such stoics as Epictetus and Seneca and by St. Augustine and St. Thomas Aquinas. His pessimism can be traced to a biblical origin in the Book of Job and Ecclesiastes. Most of the *comedias* and *autos* written at the end of his life proclaim the vanity of life and the emptiness of human existence.

Calderón wrote more than 120 plays and some 70 *autos;* there are, in addition, about 20 short pieces, such as *entremeses* and *zarzuelas.* Among the best-known works of Calderón's early period, in which he gave vent to his rebellious and restless personality, are EL ALCALDE DE ZALAMEA, considered one of his finest plays; *La devoción de la cruz* (*Devotion to the Cross*), which shows how devotion to the cross can negate even the most heinous crimes; *El cisma de*

Inglaterra, dealing with Henry VIII and Anne Boleyn; *La niña de Gómez Arias;* and *Luis Pérez el Gallego.*

Like other dramatists of Spain's Golden Age, Calderón wrote several dramas based on *pundonor,* or the point of honor, a theme with which he is often associated. The concept in this case is limited to conjugal honor. According to the code, apparently condoned by Calderón, the barest rumor of a wife's infidelity gave her husband the right to take her life. Plays in this vein include EL MÉDICO DE SU HONRA, *A secreto agravio, secreta venganza,* and *El pintor de su deshonra.*

Calderón also wrote intricate, ingenious *comedias de capa y espada,* or cloak-and-sword comedies, filled with duels, secret hiding places, and veiled women. Among the best of these are *Hombre pobre todo es trazas, El astrólogo fingido,* and *La dama duende.* In the more philosophical epoch of Calderón's career, the following plays are noteworthy: LA VIDA ES SUEÑO, often considered his masterpiece; EL MÁGICO PRODIGIOSO; *En esta vida todo es verdad y todo es mentira;* and *Saber del bien y del mal.*

Calderón is regarded as the outstanding writer of *autos sacramentales,* a genre which he perfected. His *autos* include EL GRAN TEATRO DEL MUNDO, LA CENA DE BALTAZAR, and *El divino Orfeo.*

Caldwell, Erskine [Preston] (1903–   ). Amerian novelist and short-story writer. A native of the Deep South, Caldwell is noted for his vivid studies, earthy or starkly tragic, of life among Southern sharecroppers and Negroes in Georgia's back country. In spite of its implied plea for social justice, Caldwell's work has often been attacked on the grounds of immorality. TOBACCO ROAD is his best-known novel, though GOD'S LITTLE ACRE has also been tremendously popular.

Caldwell began his career with some powerful short stories, notably *Country Full of Swedes* (1933). He collaborated with Margaret Bourke-White, his former wife, on three picture-and-comment documentaries, including *You Have Seen Their Faces* (1937). During World War II, they were in Russia as war correspondents, an experience which produced his *All Out on the Road to Smolensk* (1942) and other works. *Call It Experience* (1951) is a literary autobiography. Other works of fiction include *Trouble in July* (1940); two volumes of short stories, *Jackpot* (1940) and *The Sure Hand of God* (1947); *A Place Called Estherville* (1949); another volume of stories, *The Courting of Susie Brown* (1952); and *Claudelle Inglish* (1959).

Caldwell, [Janet Miriam] Taylor (1900–   ). English-born American novelist. Miss Caldwell's career, during which she produced a long succession of best sellers, began with *Dynasty of Death* (1938), a story of two families who control a huge munitions trust. This story was continued in *The Eagles Gather* (1940) and *The Final Hour* (1944). *The Earth Is the Lord's* (1941) is a romance about Genghis Khan, and *The Turnbulls* (1943) describes the life of an English cotton industrialist. She again dealt with families of wealth and power in *This Side of Innocence* (1946). Other books include *Dear and Glorious Physician* (1959) and *Your Sins and Mine* (1961). Miss Caldwell has occasionally used the pseudonym Max Reiner.

Caleb. In the Old Testament, a Hebrew leader at the time of the conquest of Canaan. He was one of the 12 spies sent by the Israelites to appraise the strength of Canaan and to judge whether the Israelites were strong enough to invade it. Because he and Joshua were the only ones who reported favorably, they were the only ones of their generation permitted to enter the Promised Land.

Caleb Williams, The Adventures of, or Things as They Are (1794). A novel by William GODWIN. Highly suspenseful, it anticipates, in some respects, detective fiction, and is a social commentary on the relative positions of the privileged and lower classes. Caleb Williams is a young man in the service of Falkland, an aristocrat who values his good name above everything else. Quite accidentally, Caleb discovers that Falkland has committed a murder for which an innocent person has been executed. Although Caleb would never reveal his master's crime, Falkland has him imprisoned on false charges. Caleb then escapes from prison, but is relentlessly tracked down by the suspicious Falkland. As a last resort, Caleb tells the truth and Falkland is forced to confess. Caleb suffers terrible self-reproach at having caused his master's ruin. This novel was dramatized by George Colman, the younger, under the title of *The Iron Chest*.

Caledonia. Scotland; the ancient Roman name, now used only in poetry and in a few special connections.

calender (from Persian *galandar*). A member of a begging order of dervishes, founded in the 13th century by Qalandar Yusuf al-Andalusi, a native of Spain, who obliged its members to be perpetual wanderers. This feature has made the calenders prominent in Eastern romance. The story of the Three Calenders in the *Arabian Nights* is well known; they are three royal princes, disguised as begging dervishes, each of whom has lost his right eye.

Tale of the First Calender. No names are given. This calender was the son of a king, and nephew of another king. While on a visit to his uncle, his father died and the vizier usurped the throne. When the prince returned, he was seized and his right eye pulled out. The uncle died and the usurping vizier made himself master of this kingdom also. The hapless young prince assumed the garb of a calender, wandered to Baghdad, and being received into the house of "the three sisters," tells his tale in the hearing of the Caliph HAROUN-AL-RASCHID.

Tale of the Second Calender. No names given. This calender, like the first, was the son of a king. On his way to India he was attacked by robbers, and though he contrived to escape, lost all his possessions. In his flight, he came to a large city where he encountered a tailor who gave him food and lodging. In order to earn a living, he became a woodsman and accidentally discovered an underground palace in which a beautiful lady was kept confined by an evil genius. Intent on liberating her, he kicked down the talisman; the genius killed the lady and turned the prince into an ape. As an ape he was taken on board ship and transported to a large commercial city where he was made vizier to the sultan. The sultan's daughter undertook to disenchant him, but to accomplish this she had to fight with the malignant genius. She succeeded in killing

the genius and restoring the enchanted prince, but received such severe injuries in the struggle that she died, and a spark of fire that flew into the right eye of the prince destroyed it. The sultan was so heartbroken at the death of his only child that he insisted on the prince's quitting the kingdom without delay. He assumed the garb of a calender and being received into the hospitable house of the three sisters, tells his tale before Caliph Haroun-al-Raschid.

Tale of the Third Calender. This calender, King Agib, was wrecked on the loadstone mountain which drew all the nails and iron bolts from his ship; but he overthrew the bronze statue on the mountaintop, the cause of the mischief. Agib then visited ten young men, each of whom had lost his right eye, and was carried by a roc to the palace of 40 princesses, with whom he stayed a year. The princesses were then obliged to leave for 40 days, but entrusted him with the keys of the palace, with free permission to enter every room but one. On the 40th day, curiosity finally induced him to open this room, where he saw a horse which carried him through the air to Baghdad. The horse then deposited him, and knocked out his right eye with a whisk of its tail, as it had done to the 10 young men whom it had previously met.

calends. The first day of the Roman month. See IDES; NONES.

Calhoun, John C[aldwell] (1782–1850). American statesman. A native of South Carolina, Calhoun was elected to Congress in 1810 and became one of the "war hawks" who advocated war with Great Britain. He was secretary of war (1817–1825) and vice president under J. Q. Adams and Andrew JACKSON. After the passage of the protectionist "Tariff of Abominations," Calhoun wrote his *South Carolina Exposition* (1828), defending state sovereignty and the right of NULLIFICATION, a doctrine he elaborated in a letter (1832) to Governor Hamilton of South Carolina. Breaking with Jackson over nullification and other issues, Calhoun resigned the vice presidency in 1832 and was elected to the U.S. Senate the same year. Except for a brief term as secretary of state, he sat in the Senate until his death, the leading spokesman for the minority interests of the South.

A political theorist of considerable originality, some of whose ideas anticipated those of Karl Marx, he was austerely intellectual; it is said that on one occasion he tried to write a poem, produced the single word "Whereas," and never repeated the attempt.

Caliban. In Shakespeare's THE TEMPEST, the deformed, half-human slave of Prospero. The son of the witch Sycorax and a devil, Caliban symbolizes mankind's primitive urges.

Robert Browning's poem, *Caliban upon Setebos, or Natural Theology in the Island*, is an attempt to express for such a creature as Caliban his crude philosophy of God and the universe. Percy MacKaye wrote a poetic drama, *Caliban* (1916), showing the regeneration of Caliban through love for Miranda.

Caliban by the Yellow Sands (1916). A masque by Percy MACKAYE. In this poetic drama, drawn in part from Shakespeare's *Tempest*, Caliban is seen as "that passionate child-curious part of us all," who is regenerated through Prospero's wisdom and his own love for Miranda.

Calidore, Sir. See FAERIE QUEENE, THE.

Caligorante. In the ORLANDO FURIOSO of Ariosto, a huge sea monster defeated by Astolfo with his magic horn, given to him by the good witch Logistilla. Astolfo ties the monster in its own net and goes from city to city, dragging the monster behind him in order to display the great victory he has achieved.

Caligula. Original name, **Caius Caesar** (A.D. 12–41). Roman emperor (37–41). Son of Agrippina and GERMANICUS CAESAR, he was brought up among the legions in Germany where the soldiers gave him his nickname, Caligula, because he wore the soldier's boot (*caliga*). He was held high in the emperor Tiberius' favor, and on Tiberius' death, which was either caused or helped along by Caligula, he succeeded to the throne. Caligula was at first revered by the people as the son of Germanicus, but after a serious illness, he appeared very much changed and behaved like a madman. His wild extravagance led him to extortion and plunder. He was finally murdered and was succeeded by his uncle Claudius. He is the main character in the play CALIGULA by Albert Camus.

Caligula (1944). A play by Albert CAMUS. The author makes the Roman emperor a sensitive man horrified by what Camus calls elsewhere the absurd condition of human life. Caligula adds to the senselessness by arbitrary acts of violence, obeying the mistaken logic that he can escape the condition of man by severing all his ties with humanity and thus by asserting his own freedom achieve the impossible. His seemingly mad complicity in his own assassination symbolizes his failure.

Calisto y Melibea, La tragicomedia de. See CELESTINA, LA.

Callaghan, Morley [Edward] (1903–). Canadian novelist and short-story writer. After meeting Ernest Hemingway in Toronto in the 1920's, Callaghan went to Paris, where he became acquainted with the American expatriates there and contributed to *This Quarter, transition,* and similar periodicals. His novels, which are noted for their "hard-boiled" realism, include *Strange Fugitive* (1928), *The Loved and the Lost* (1951), *The Many Colored Coat* (1960), and *A Passion in Rome* (1962). *Now That April's Here* (1936) and *Stories* (1959) are collections of short stories. His years in Paris are recounted in *That Summer in Paris* (1963).

Callimachus (**Kallimachos;** born c. 310 B.C.). Greek poet, born in Cyrene. According to tradition he was head of the ALEXANDRIAN LIBRARY, and was highly regarded in his own time, and thereafter, for his short poems. He is said to have engaged in a literary feud with APOLLONIUS OF RHODES.

Calliope (**Kalliopeia**). The Muse of epic poetry, and chief of the MUSES. She was the mother of Orpheus by Apollo or King Oeagrus.

Callirrhoe (**Kallirrhoe**). See ALCMAEON.

Callirrhoe (**Kallirrhoe**). The lady-love of Chaereas in Chariton's Greek romance, the *Loves of Chaereas and Callirrhoe.* It was probably written in the 6th century A.D.

Callisto and **Arcas** (**Kallisto, Arkas**). Callisto was an Arcadian nymph metamorphosed into a she-bear by ARTEMIS for not remaining a virgin like her other attendants. Her son Arcas, having met her in the chase, would have killed her, but Zeus converted him into a he-bear, and placed them both in the heavens, where they are recognized as the Great and Little Bear. Arcas was the eponymous ancestor of the Arcadians.

Call of the Wild, The (1903). A novel by Jack LONDON. This famous story tells how the dog Buck is stolen from his comfortable home and pressed into service as a sledge dog in the Klondike. At first he is abused by both men and doge, but he learns to fight ruthlessly and finally finds in John Thornton a master whom he can respect and love. When Thornton is murdered, Buck breaks away to the wilds and becomes the leader of a pack of wolves. See WHITE FANG.

Calpe. See PILLARS OF HERCULES.

Calpurnia. Third wife of Julius CAESAR. They were married in 59 B.C. On the night before he was assassinated she dreamed that a templelike gable, dedicated in his honor, smashed to the ground and that Caesar lay dying in her arms. She is a character in Shakespeare's JULIUS CAESAR; she begs Caesar not to attend the Senate. Caesar's first two wives were Cornelia and Pompeia.

Calvary or **Golgotha** (Lat., *calvaria,* Aram., *gŭlgŭtha,* "skull"). The place outside the wall of Jerusalem where Jesus was crucified. Its exact location is unknown; tradition ascribes it to the present site of the Church of the Holy Sepulcher.

Calverley, Charles Stuart (1831–1884). English poet and parodist. He wrote light verse, parodies, and translations, including *Verses and Translations* (1862); *Theocritus Translated into English Verse* (1869); and *Fly Leaves* (1872).

Calvin, John. Adapted form of **Jean Cauvin** (1509–1564). French Protestant reformer. His theological doctrines had tremendous influence, particularly in the Puritan religion of England, Scotland, and later America.

Calvin had an early background of humanism, being a student of Latin and Greek and familar with the writings of Plato, Seneca, and St. Augustine. Because of the radical Protestant views expressed in a public speech he wrote in 1533 to be delivered at an inaugural ceremony at the University of Paris, Calvin was forced to flee the capital and soon France as well. He establshed himself in Geneva, where eventually he became an absolute dictator, strictly enforcing his theological doctrines and rules of conduct. His greatest work is INSTITUTES OF THE CHRISTIAN RELIGION.

Calvinism as a religious system recognized only the Bible as a source of knowledge and authority in questions of belief. Its chief principles were (1) the total depravity of man as a result of Adam's fall; (2) the absolute power of the will of God; (3) the superiority of faith to good works, since man has no will of his own; (4) salvation by grace from God rather than by any act of the will of man; and (5) the divine predestination of those to be saved, or the Elect, although, since no one can tell whether he is a member of the Elect, all must lead holy and pious lives, acknowledging God's supreme power and obeying His commands.

Calydonian boar. A creature of Greek legend.

Oeneus, king of Calydon, in Aetolia, having neglected to sacrifice to Artemis, was punished by the goddess' sending a ferocious boar to ravage his lands. A band of heroes collected to hunt the boar, which was eventually slain by MELEAGER after he had been first wounded by Atalanta. A dispute over the boar's head led to a war between the neighboring tribe of Curetes and the Calydonians. This was one of the most famous sagas of Greece, but is not recorded in any outstanding single work.

Calypso (Kalypso). In Homer's ODYSSEY, the nymph of the island of Ogygia. She detains the shipwrecked Odysseus there seven years. Loyal to Penelope, he refuses her offer of immortality if he stays, and at last, at Zeus's command, she helps him to continue on his way toward Ithaca.

Cama. See KAMA.

Cambel. See FAERIE QUEENE, THE.

Camber. In Geoffrey of Monmouth's HISTORY OF THE KINGS OF BRITAIN, a son of BRUTE, and the person after whom Wales (Cambria) was said to be named.

Cambina. See FAERIE QUEENE, THE.

Cambrai, League of. A league formed in 1508 by the Papacy, France, Spain, and the Holy Roman Empire against Venice. The War of the League of Cambrai (1508–1510) resulted in the defeat of the Venetians.

Cambridge, Richard Owen (1717–1802). English man of letters who wrote the famous mock-epic *Scribleriad* (1751). He was an intimate of Samuel Johnson.

Cambridge critics. A group of influential 20th-century English critics. They were centered at the University of Cambridge. They rejected the traditional method of studying literature in the light of its historical period, the author's biography, and other external influences. They preferred to make a detailed, quasi-scientific analysis of the work itself. This method had its best results when applied to complex poetry, and these critics praised symbolistic, metaphysical, witty, and modern poetry at the expense of more traditional verse. I. A. RICHARDS and William EMPSON were pioneers in the study of exact meanings in poetry. See LOGICAL POSITIVISM; F. R. LEAVIS; SCRUTINY; NEW CRITICISM.

Cambridge Platonists. A group of English liberal philosophic-religious thinkers of the latter half of the 17th century, whose general aim was to effect a reconciliation between reason and mystical religiosity. Their mode of thought and terminology were taken chiefly from Plato and the Neoplatonists. They were vehemently opposed to Hobbes's materialism, their most important doctrine being the absolute existence of right and wrong. The outstanding members of the group were Ralph Cudworth (1617–1688), Nathaniel Culverwel (1618–1651), Joseph GLANVILL, Henry MORE, Benjamin Whichcote (1609–1683), and John Smith (1616–1652). Their thought may be summarized in Smith's words: "To follow reason is to follow God."

Cambuscan or **Cambyuskan.** See SQUIRE'S TALE.

Cambyses II (d. 522 B.C.). A Persian ruler. He succeeded his father Cyrus the Great, reigning from 529 to 522 B.C. Reputed to be tyrannical, he conquered Egypt and made that country part of the Persian Empire. His throne was assumed by an impostor, and he died while returning to Persia to defend it.

Camelot. A place name prominent in Arthurian literature, one of the spots where King Arthur held court. In many of the legends, we find both Camelot and CAERLEON as court capitals, each being appropriate, apparently, to certain times of the year. For example, Caerleon is sometimes found to be the place where King Arthur and his court celebrated Pentecost and Camelot the place where the court went for the celebration of Christmas. See CARDUEL.

Camilla. In Vergil's Aeneid, a warrior maiden who fought fearlessly against the Trojans in their war with TURNUS, and was killed in battle. She was so speedy, says Vergil, that she could run across a field of corn without bending a single blade or cross the sea without even wetting her feet.

Camille. See DAME AUX CAMÉLIAS, LA.

Camille. In Pierre Corneille's tragedy HORACE, the sister of Horace and the fiancée of Curiace, Horace's opponent in combat. When Horace kills Curiace, Camille curses Rome, and her infuriated brother slays her.

Camillo. An honorable and faithful counsellor to Leontes, king of Sicilia, in Shakespeare's WINTER'S TALE. Commanded by Leontes to poison Polixenes, he leaves his beloved country rather than commit the crime. When he at last returns, he marries the bold and courageous PAULINA.

Camino Galicia, León Felipe. See LEÓN FELIPE.

Camisards. The Calvinists of Cevennes who in 1703 rebelled against Louis XIV after his revocation of the Edict of Nantes. Their leader, Jean Cavalier (1680–1740), escaped to England and became governor of Jersey. The word *camisard* refers to the insurgents' white shirts.

Camlan, Battle of. See ANNALES CAMBRIAE.

Camões or **Camoëns, Luis Vaz de** (1524?–1580). Portuguese poet. After being banished from court because of his romance with Caterina de Ataíde (the "Natercia" of his poems), a lady-in-waiting to the queen, Camões served in North Africa, where he lost his right eye in an engagement with the Moors. In 1552 he was imprisoned for wounding a court official in a street brawl. Sailing to India in 1553 as a common soldier, he was later named official trustee for the property of the dead and absent in Macao and was briefly imprisoned for allegedly embezzling government funds. After numerous hardships, he managed to return to Lisbon in 1570.

Camões' best-known work is his epic poem, Os LUSIADAS, notable for its synthesis of national, religious, and humanistic themes. He is also regarded as one of Portugal's greatest lyric poets, largely because of his sonnets and *canções*. His other works include three plays: *Os anfitriões*, which was inspired by Plautus' *Amphitruo; El-Rei Seleuco*, based on an episode in Plutarch; and *Philodemo*.

Campagna di Roma. Territory of Old Latium surrounding Rome, about 30 by 100 miles in extent. It is usually simply called the Campagna and is not to be confused with ancient Campania, the territory directly south of Latium.

Campanella, Tommaso (1568–1639). Italian philosopher. Born in Calabria, he spent most of his life in the prisons of Naples, Padua, and Rome because of his interest in astrology, naturalistic philosophy, and radical political schemes. After his final imprisonment in Rome, he fled to France in 1634, where he died. A prolific writer, he produced many Italian lyrics, a critical treatise on poetry, and his masterpiece, *La città del sole (Civitas Solis* or *City of the Sun,* 1623). Written in 1602 during his imprisonment, and based on Plato and Thomas More, it describes his utopia, a society organized communistically and ruled by a priest-philosopher. His Latin works, dealing largely with metaphysics and theology, also include a treatise on the Spanish monarchy and an apology for Galileo.

Campaspe. Also called **Pancaste.** A beautiful woman, the favorite concubine of Alexander the Great. Apelles, it is said, modeled his Aphrodite Anadyomene from her. According to Pliny, Alexander gave her up to Apelles, who had fallen in love with her while painting her likeness. John LYLY produced, in 1583, a drama, *Alexander and Campaspe.*

Campbell, Joseph (1879–1944). Irish poet. He published some of his work under his Gaelic name, Seosamh MacCathmhaoil. His works include *Rushlight* (1906), and *Irishry* (1913).

Campbell, Mary. One of the women loved by Robert BURNS. She died of fever in 1788, and the poem *To Mary in Heaven* (1789) was written on the first anniversary of her death. See HIGHLAND MARY.

Campbell, Mrs. Patrick, born **Beatrice Stella Tanner** (1865–1940). English actress who played important roles beginning with the title role in Pinero's *The Second Mrs. Tanqueray.* She originated the part of Eliza Doolittle in Shaw's *Pygmalion,* written expressly for her.

Campbell, Roy (1902–1957). South African poet. A neofascist and disciple of Wyndham Lewis, he wrote satires and poems of colorful nature description. He was converted to Catholicism in about 1935. He fought on the fascist side on the Spanish Civil War; *Flowering Rifle* (1939) is a long satiric poem celebrating Franco's victory. Among his collections of poems are *The Flaming Terrapin* (1924), *Adamastor* (1930), and *Talking Bronco* (1946). He has done translations of the poems of St. John of the Cross, and written two autobiographies: *Broken Record* (1934) and *Light on a Dark Horse* (1952).

Campbell, Thomas (1777–1844). Scottish poet, best known for his literary ballad LORD ULLIN'S DAUGHTER. He also produced some notable martial lyrics, including *Ye Mariners of England* (1800); *Hohenlinden* (1802); and *The Battle of the Baltic* (1809). Of his longer narrative works only GERTRUDE OF WYOMING retains interest. Campbell was an editor *(The New Monthly Magazine)* and anthologist of some influence in his day. See LOCHIEL.

Campbell, Walter Stanley. Pen name, **Stanley Vestal** (1887–1957). American writer. An authority on the Old West, under his own name he has edited documents and books relating to Indians and explorations. Under his pen name he has written such books as *Fandango, Ballads of the Old West* (1927), *Kit Carson* (1928), *Mountain Men* (1937), *Queen of Cowtowns: Dodge City* (1952), and *Joe Meek* (1952).

Campbell, [William] Wilfred (1861–1918). Canadian poet and novelist. After studying at the Episcopal Divinity School in Cambridge, Mass., Campbell was ordained in 1885 and was given a parish in West Claremont, Mass. In 1891 he resigned from his church offices, feeling that their formality and dogmas restricted him. His books of poetry include *Snowflakes and Sunbeams* (1888), *Lake Lyrics* (1889), and *Beyond the Hills of Dream* (1899). He also wrote historical novels, notably *Ian of the Orcades* (1906) and *A Beautiful Rebel* (1909).

Campbell, William Edward March. See William MARCH.

Campbells Are Coming, The. A famous song composed in 1715. The earl of Mar raised the standard for the Stuarts against George I. John Campbell was commander-in-chief of His Majesty's forces and the rebellion was quashed.

Campion, Thomas (1567–1620). English poet and musician. He is famous for his songs written to music of his own composition, collected in such volumes as *A Book of Airs* (1601), *Two Books of Airs* (c. 1613), and *The Third and Fourth Books of Airs* (c. 1617). His lyrics possess rare charm and freshness, as well as a melodiousness and metrical variety that reflect their musical origin. He was also the author of *Observation in the Art of English Poesy* (1602), an argument for the use of classical, quantitative meters in English verse, which prompted Samuel Daniel's *Defence of Ryme* (1602).

Campistron, Jean Galbert de (1656–1723). French soldier and playwright. An admirer and imitator of Racine, he wrote several tragedies characterized by their melancholy treatment of classical subjects, among them *Arminius* (1684) and *Andronic* (1685). His greatest successes were the tragedy *Tiridate* (1691), which depicted the denobling power of passion, and the comedy *Le Jaloux désabusé (The Jealous Man Undeceived,* 1709).

Campo, Estanislao del. See GAUCHO LITERATURE.

Campoamor, Ramón de (1817–1901). Spanish poet. His best-known work may be sampled in the volumes *Doloras* (1846), *Humoradas* (1872), and *Pequeños Poemas* (1872–1874). These are filled with poems in the style favored by Campoamor: philosophical epigrams expressing a humorous point of view.

Campus Esquilinus. The burial place for the lowest classes, just outside the Servian Wall of Rome.

Campus Martius. The field of Mars. A grassy plain along the east bank of the Tiber in ancient Rome, used for elections, martial exercises, public games, and the like.

Camus, Albert (1913–1960). Algerian-born French philosopher, novelist, dramatist, journalist. After studying philosophy at Algiers, Camus organized (1935) the Théâtre de l'Equipe, a young avant-garde dramatic group, and worked with it until 1938. Then, until the beginning of World War II, he worked both in North Africa and in Paris as a journalist. It was between 1937 and 1941 that he wrote the works that made him famous upon their publication during the war: the novel THE STRANGER, the essay THE MYTH OF SISYPHUS, and the play CALIGULA. He also sketched THE MISUNDERSTANDING, which he finished in 1943. All four present the feeling of the ABSURD, the plight of man's need for clarity and rationality in confrontation with the unreasonable silence of the universe, and various tragedies of man's failure to assume proper consciousness of his condition, or, if he does, to find the human values by which he can shape his life.

After the occupation of France by the Germans in 1941, Camus became one of the intellectual leaders of the Resistance movement. He helped found the underground newspaper *Combat* in 1943, was its chief editor during the war, and continued to write for it until 1946, when it began open publication after the liberation of France. Camus was a close associate of Jean-Paul SARTRE and his circle; although they cooperated in Resistance activities, however, the differences between their philosophical positions became more and more apparent. Camus has sometimes been classified among the existentialists, but he himself refuted their position in many of his writings (see EXISTENTIALISM).

His refusal to take solace in a concept of divine or cosmic meaning for human life did not conflict with Camus' humanistic attitude that man is capable of a certain degree of dignity in honestly facing his solitary condition and trying to find and assert the human values, such as the maximum possible individual freedom, intercommunication, and even love, within the limitations of that condition. His commitment to this humanistic attitude, and consequently to humanitarian causes, is reflected in the novel THE PLAGUE, about men doing the futile best they can in the face of disaster. The short novel THE FALL more bitterly comments on the difficulty of finding a mode of active life compatible with total consciousness both of the absurd and of one's inescapable solidarity with other human beings.

During the late 1950's, Camus renewed his active interest in the theater, writing and directing stage adaptations of William Faulkner's *Requiem for a Nun* and Dostoevski's *The Possessed*. He was awarded the Nobel Prize for literature in 1957.

THE REBEL gives a book-length statement of his philosophical attitudes. In *Actuelles I-III* (1950, 1953, 1958) are essays on political, social, and literary questions collected from *Combat* and elsewhere; *Resistance, Rebellion, and Death* (1961) is an English selection from these. Other works include the early essays *L'Envers et l'endroit* (1937) and *Noces* (1939), mostly sympathetic sketches of North Africa; *Letters to a German Friend* (*Lettres à un ami allemand;* 1945), written during the war; the plays *State of Siege* (*Etat de Siège;* 1948) and *The Just Assassins* (*Les Justes;* 1950); and the six short stories in *The Exile and the Kingdom* (*L'Exil et le Royaume;* 1957).

Canaan. An ancient region of vague boundaries. It lay roughly between the Jordan River and the Mediterranean Sea. This "Promised Land" of the Israelites was actually rather infertile. A mixture of Semites and Indo-Europeans lived there until the Israelites conquered much of the area. The Semites, worshippers of *baalim* (see BAAL), had a fairly rich culture, many evidences of which have been uncovered in the 20th century at UGARIT and elsewhere. Most of them were under the domination of Egypt or, for a time, of the Hittites. The civilization of Phoenicia was to a considerable extent a continuation of that of Canaan.

The rabbinical tradition that Canaan, a son of

Ham, was the first of the seven sinners who made idols for the heathens, reflects the regrettable history of Israelitish backsliding into the baal-worship of their Canaanite neighbors. For Canaanite literature see the POEM OF BAAL and the POEM OF AQHAT.

Canace. See FAERIE QUEENE, THE.

Canacee. See SQUIRE'S TALE.

Canaletto or **Canale, Antonio** (1697–1768). Venetian painter, known for his broad views of Venice. He rendered architectural detail with great precision and flawless perspective, and bathed his scenes in a clear light of sharp contrasts. Bernardo Bellotto (1724–1780), his nephew and pupil, is also sometimes called Canaletto.

Canby, Henry Seidel (1878–1961). American literary critic, biographer, editor, and teacher. Canby served as literary editor of the New York *Post,* helped to found and edit the *Saturday Review of Literature* (1924), and acted as chairman of the Book-of-the-Month Club (1926–1954). He taught at Yale University for more than 20 years. Among his many volumes are *The Short Story* (1902), *Thoreau: A Biography* (1939), *Walt Whitman: An American* (1943), and *Turn West, Turn East: Mark Twain and Henry James* (1951). *American Memoir* (1947) is an autobiography.

Cancer. One of the twelve signs of the zodiac (the Crab, June 21st to July 23rd). It appears when the sun has reached its highest northern limit, and begins to go backward toward the south; but, like a crab, the return is sideways.

According to fable, Hera sent Cancer against HERACLES when he combated the HYDRA of Lerna. It bit the hero's foot, but Heracles killed the creature, and Hera set it in the sky.

Cancionero de Baena. An anthology of 576 poems compiled in 1445 by Juan Alfonso de Baena (1406–1454) for John II of Castile. The poems, lyrics of the courtly, aristocratic school, show the development of Spanish poetry in the 14th and 15th centuries. The works of over 50 authors are included, notably Alfonso Alvarez de Villasandino, a representative of the Galician-Portuguese school, and Micer Francisco Imperial, who was influenced by Dante.

Candida (1903). A play by George Bernard SHAW. This is one of Shaw's most theatrically successful works; its subject is marriage. Candida Morell's husband is a hearty, popular Christian Socialist clergyman. Eugene Marchbanks is an 18-year-old rhapsodic, visionary poet who is in love with Candida. Forced to choose between them she remains with her husband when she realizes that he needs her, being the weaker of the two men. The plot of *Candida* shows the influence of Ibsen's *A Doll's House.* Shaw, however, has reversed the roles of puppet and master: Morell's seeming strength wholly rests on Candida's dignity and character.

Candide, ou L'Optimisme (1759). VOLTAIRE's most popular philosophical novel. It satirizes the optimistic creed of LEIBNIZ: "All is for the best in this best of all possible worlds." Dr. PANGLOSS, tutor to the hero, Candide, is the embodiment of this theory, maintaining it through thick and thin, despite the most blatant evidence to the contrary. Misadventures begin when young Candide is kicked out of the castle of Thunder-ten-tronckh for making love to the baron's daughter, Cunégonde. Thereafter, he, Cunégonde, and Pangloss embark—sometimes singly, sometimes together—on a long series of disastrous adventures. After being impressed into the Bulgarian army, Candide is beaten nearly to death; he deserts and flees to Holland where he learns that Cunégonde and her family have been massacred. He and Pangloss go to Lisbon, arriving in time for the historic earthquake (1755); there they are condemned by the Inquisition, and Pangloss is hanged. But Cunégonde —alive, after all—saves Candide, who later finds it necessary to kill a Jew and an Inquisitor to discourage them from pursuing Cunégonde. Still hunted by the Inquisition, Candide leaves Cunégonde and, with his valet Cacambo, flees to safety among the Jesuits, who are warring on Spain and Portugal. Candide kills their general, a Jesuit who is none other than Cunégonde's brother. He flees to El Dorado, but because he misses Cunégonde, leaves, loaded with riches. He returns to France, where he is threatened with imprisonment and cheated out of his fortune by swindlers. He travels to Portsmouth and then to Venice, where he learns that Cunégonde has been captured by pirates and is washing towels in Constantinople. On the ship to Turkey, Candide discovers that two of the galley slaves are none other than Cunégonde's brother, whom he did not kill, and Pangloss, who had not been properly hanged. He finally finds Cunégonde, now very ugly, and marries her against his will. All of them finally settle down on a little farm. Pangloss insists that all these calamities happened for the best. Candide replies, *"Il faut cultiver notre jardin"* (Fr., "We must cultivate our garden"). All the disasters in the novel have historical precedents, and we may conclude from Candide's last remark either that work is far more profitable than vain speculation, or that work is the antidote to man's unhappy lot.

Candlemas Day. The popular name for the Feast of the Purification of the Virgin Mary, February 2. On this day Christ was presented by her in the Temple. The feast is so called from the custom of blessing on this day all the candles which will be used in a church throughout the year. They symbolize Christ as "the light of the world" and "a light to lighten the Gentiles," phrases spoken of Jesus at the time of his Presentation by the aged Simeon. There is also a weather legend associated with the day. See GROUNDHOG DAY.

Canfield, Dorothy. See Dorothy Canfield FISHER.

Canidia. A Neapolitan, beloved by the poet HORACE. When she deserted him, he held her up to contempt in certain of his epodes and satires as an old sorceress who could by magic spell unsphere the moon.

Canidius. In Shakespeare's ANTONY AND CLEOPATRA, the lieutenant general of Antony's land forces. Canidius vainly advises Antony against engaging Octavius Caesar in naval battle and later defects to the enemy.

Cannae. The battlefield in southeast Italy where HANNIBAL defeated the Romans under Varro and L. Aemilius Paulus with great slaughter in 216 B.C. Any fatal battle that is the turning point of a great general's prosperity may be called his Cannae. Thus, Moscow was the Cannae of Napoleon.

Cannery Row (1945). A novel by John STEINBECK. In this episodic work, Steinbeck returns to the style of *Tortilla Flat* to produce a rambling account of the adventures and misadventures of workers in a California cannery and their friends. One character, Doc, was reportedly modeled on the marine biologist Edward F. Ricketts (1896–1948), with whom Steinbeck collaborated on *The Sea of Cortez* (1941).

Canonization, The (1633). A poem by John DONNE in which he claims that the reciprocal love between him and his mistress is so deep and unworldly as to make them saints of love. It is a fine example of the vehemently colloquial and ingeniously conceited style typical of Donne.

Canon's Yeoman's Tale, The. One of the CANTERBURY TALES of Geoffrey CHAUCER. In the *Prologue* a Canon and his Yeoman overtake the pilgrims. The Host asks if the Canon can tell a story, and the Yeoman begins to reveal his master's craftiness as a fraudulent alchemist. The Canon bids him be silent, but he has decided to leave the alchemist's service, so he continues his vituperative report, and the Canon rides off to avoid shame. The Yeoman bitterly describes the apparatus and processes of the "cursed craft" of alchemy, and all the money and labor lost in searching for the elixir to turn base metals into gold. Then he tells a tale about a canon, not his ex-master, who pretends to take a priest into his confidence and let him help in the conversion of quicksilver and copper to silver. The canon effects the exchange by sleight of hand, but the duped priest believes in the actual transmutation of the metal and asks to buy the formula. The canon accepts forty pounds, making him think it a bargain price, and can never be found by the priest again.

Canossa, Count Ludovico of (1476–1532). Italian courtier and prelate. He is noted for his diplomatic missions and his participation in the dialogues of THE COURTIER by his kinsman Castiglione.

cantari. See CANTASTORIE.

cantastorie. Tuscan minstrels, or singers of tales, of the 14th century who composed and performed, usually in the public places of Italian towns and villages, *cantari,* long narrative poems in *ottava rima.* Although the preferred subject was the Carolingian legends, especially the loves and battles of Orlando (Roland), Christian and classical material also helped to form the repertoire of the *cantastorie.* Though many of their works died with the anonymous singers, some survived to influence the later Renaissance *romanzo* (romantic epic) of Pulci, Ariosto, and Boiardo.

Cantatrice Chauve, La. See BALD SOPRANO, THE.

Canterbury Tales, The (c. 1387–1400). Poetic work by Geoffrey CHAUCER. Although unfinished, it is his longest and his finest work, written in decasyllabic couplets except as noted in the entries for individual tales. The *General Prologue* establishes the framework for the stories: the poet has joined with 30 others (although the *Prologue* says 29) to make the usual April pilgrimage to Becket's shrine at Canterbury; he describes each of his companions, who are of widely varying classes and occupations. Their host at the Tabard Inn, Harry Bailly, proposes to come with them and serve as judge in a story-telling contest to occupy the long hours of the journey;

¶ The tale of the chanons yeman

¶ And begynneth the tale

With this chanon I dwellyd vij yere,
And of his scienc am I neuer the nere.
Al that I had I haue lost ther by,
And god wot so haue mo than I.
Ther as I was wont to be right fressh & gay
Of clothynge and of other good aray,
Now may I were an hose vp on myn hed;
And where my colour was both fressh & red,
Now it is wan and of a leden hewe.
Who so it vseth sore shal he rewe.
And of my swynk y slent is myn eye.
Lo suche auauntage it is to multeplye.
That slydyng scienc hath made me so bare
That I haue no good wher that euer I fare.
And yet I am endetted so sore therby,
Of gold that I borowed trewly.

From Caxton's 2nd edition of the
Canterbury Tales (1483).

each pilgrim is to tell two stories on the way to Canterbury, two on the way back, and the teller of the best tale will get a free dinner at the Tabard upon their return. Chaucer only wrote 24 tales, however: 21 are told by characters described in the *Prologue,* one is told by the Canon's Yeoman, who joins the group after they have already started, and Chaucer himself begins one tale, and when interrupted tells a second. In addition to the characters who do narrate tales (see below) Chaucer describes the Knight's Yeoman, two Priests accompanying the Prioress, a Haberdasher, a Carpenter, a Weaver, a Dyer, a Tapicer (weaver of tapestry), and a Plowman.

Although such "frame stories" were common in Chaucer's day, Chaucer was an innovator in his choice of such a diverse assembly of narrators, in the concomitant diversity of style of their tales (from chivalric romance to bawdy *fabliau,* from folk tale to sermon), and in the way he develops the drama of the interaction of his characters' personalities. With a few exceptions, where Chaucer obviously had not thoroughly worked out his scheme, the tales and the manner of their telling (except for the convention of being in verse) are completely suited to the nature of their tellers. And between the actual narratives are interludes in which the characters talk—often argue— with each other and with the host, revealing much about themselves. These episodes usually occur in the "prologues" to the tales, and each is described in connection with the tale it accompanies. See:

CANON'S YEOMAN'S TALE (the fraudulent alchemist)
CLERK'S TALE (patient Griselda)
COOK'S TALE (Perkin)
FRANKLIN'S TALE (Dorigen, Arveragus, and Aurelius)
FRIAR'S TALE (the summoner and the Devil)
KNIGHT'S TALE (Palamon and Arcite)
MANCIPLE'S TALE (the tell-tale crow)
MAN OF LAW'S TALE (Constance)
MELIBEE (told by Chaucer)
MERCHANT'S TALE (January and May)
MILLER'S TALE (Nicholas, Alison, and Absolon)
MONK'S TALE (the falls of illustrious men)
NUN'S PRIEST'S TALE (Chauntecleer and Pertelote)
PARDONER'S TALE (the revellers who seek Death)
PARSON'S TALE (sermon on Penitence)
PHYSICIAN'S TALE (Virginia)
PRIORESS'S TALE (the murdered boy who sings)
REEVE'S TALE (the miller's family and the students)
SECOND NUN'S TALE (Life of St. Cecilia)
SHIPMAN'S TALE (the miserly merchant, his wife, and the monk)
SQUIRE'S TALE (Cambuscan and Canacee)
SUMMONER'S TALE (Thomas and the friar)
THOPAS, SIR (told by Chaucer)
WIFE OF BATH'S TALE (the knight and the hag)

Canth, Minna (1844–1897). Finnish playwright and novelist. In Finland she was the pioneer of the new naturalism, depicting drab lives and indicting the upper classes with passionate fervor for their neglect of such misery. In the plays *Työmiehen Vaimo* (*The Laborer's Wife,* 1885) and *Papin Perhe* (*The Parson's Family,* 1891) she speaks against restriction and limitation of the human being, whether by unjust social laws or by the narrow prejudices of the older generation.

Cantos. An incomplete epic poem by EZRA POUND. It was published in separate sections: *Cantos I-XVI* (1925), *A Draft of XXX Cantos* (1930), *Eleven New Cantos XXXI-XLI* (1934), *Fifth Decad of Cantos* (1937), *Cantos LII-LXXI* (1940), *Cantos* (1948), PISAN CANTOS, SECTION: ROCK DRILL 85–95 DE LOS CANTARES, *Thrones: 96–109 de los Cantares* (1959). The earliest of the *Cantos* were published in magazine form as early as 1917. One of the most important 20th-century works of poetry, the *Cantos* have a loose musical structure and were once described by Pound himself as a ragbag. Central to their conception is the use of Odysseus as a man in search of a culture and of Ovid's *Metamorphoses* as a touchstone of individual and cultural transformation. Pound quotes widely from the literary and historical documents of the ancient Greeks, the medieval Provençal poets, writers of the Italian Renaissance, and American statesmen of the Jeffersonian period. His economic beliefs, especially regarding usury, play an important part throughout the work; they appear particularly in large sections devoted to American politics and to the Chinese.

Canty, Tom. The beggar boy in Mark Twain's PRINCE AND THE PAUPER. He changes places with Prince Edward VI.

Canute or **Knut** (994–1035). Danish king who finally became King of England (after 1016) as well, taking an English wife and maintaining peace and security. A 12th-century legend describes how he rebuked his flatterers by commanding the waves to stand still—in vain, of course—to show the limits of his power. *The Song of Canute* is an early 12th-century lyric in Middle English, supposedly composed by Canute while rowing past the abbey of Ely and hearing the music of the services.

canzone. Italian lyric form of verse, popular during the Middle Ages and the Renaissance. Derived from the Provençal *canso*, it normally consisted of from five to seven stanzas, each echoing the first in number of lines and in rhyme scheme. A final short stanza (the *congedo*, or *commiato*) follows the pattern of the Provençal *tornada* or the French *envoi* in addressing the poem itself or in directing it on a mission to some personage. The subject matter is usually amatory, but might also be political, satiric, or humorous. *Canzoni* were written at the Sicilian court of Emperor Frederick II in the 13th-century and later by Dante, Petrarch, Boccaccio, and the leading poets of the Renaissance. In English, an example of the canzone form is Spenser's marriage hymn, the *Epithalamion*.

Capaneus (Kapaneus). In Greek mythology, one of the SEVEN AGAINST THEBES. He was struck dead by a thunderbolt for declaring that not Zeus himself should prevent his scaling the city walls. Evadne, his wife, threw herself into the flames while his body was burning.

Čapek, Karel (1890–1938).   Czech dramatist, novelist, and essayist. Čapek's early scientific training enabled him to devise convincing backgrounds for his plays and novels dealing with the scientific and fantastic. An ardent defender of and worker for the short-lived Czech republic, he was simultaneously founder and director of the Vinohradsky Art Theater, an editor on a Prague newspaper, and a creative writer. In his essays he reveals himself politically an idealist and optimist, while in his fiction and stage works he emerges a highly imaginative moralist and ironist. His best known play is R.U.R. (q.v.); other plays include *The Life of the Insects* (1922); *The Makroupolos Secret* (1925), dealing with the scientific prolongation of life; *Power and Glory* (1938); and *The Mother* (1939). *Money and Other Stories* (1929) is a collection of short stories; *War with the Newts* (1937) and *The Cheat* (1941) are novels. His essays include *President Masaryk Tells His Story* (1934) and *The First Rescue Party* (1939).

Capetians. The third dynasty of the kings of France (reigned 987–1328). Their feudal domain was Ile de France; its central location facilitated their consolidation of power and administration. The succeeding Valois and Bourbon dynasties were branches of the Capet family.

Capital (*Das Kapital*; 1867–1894). A systematic critical study of capitalist economy by Karl MARX, based on the ideas which he formulated, with Friedrich ENGELS, in *The Communist Manifesto*. Volume one appeared in 1867; volumes two and three were completed by Engels from Marx's notes (1885–1894).

Capitoline geese. Sacred geese kept on the Capitoline Hill of Rome. According to tradition, when the Gauls invaded Rome, a detachment in single file clambered up the hill of the capitol so silently that the foremost man reached the top without being challenged. When he was striding over the rampart, some geese, disturbed by the noise, began to cackle, and awoke the garrison. Marcus Man-

lius rushed to the wall and hurled the fellow over the precipice. To commemorate this event (390 B.C.) the Romans carried a golden goose to the capitol every year.

Capitoline Hill. Of the seven hills on which ancient Rome was built, the one which held the capitol.

capitolo. The Italian word means, literally, chapter, but its literary usage refers to any lengthy poem in TERZA RIMA. During the Renaissance, it was predominantly the vehicle for satirical verse of the kind written by Francesco Berni, although *capitoli* were also composed on sacred subjects and sometimes used as the form for verse epistles.

cap of liberty.   See LIBERTY CAP.

Caporetto. A town in Yugoslavia, formerly belonging to Italy. It was the scene of a disastrous defeat (1917) sustained by Italian forces under General Cadorna during World War I. The subsequent Italian retreat is vividly described in Hemingway's FAREWELL TO ARMS.

Capote, Truman (1924–   ). American novelist and short-story writer. Although he was born in New Orleans, Capote does not consider himself primarily a Southern writer. His concern with the Gothic romance, however, does provide a link with the Southern literary tradition. His special mark is the exploration of the dividing-line between dream and reality.

Capote's first novel was OTHER VOICES, OTHER ROOMS. *The Grass Harp* (1951) deals with a young orphan who goes to live with two aunts, Dolly and Verena Talbo, who respectively represent an imaginative view of life and a grasping sense of reality. *Breakfast at Tiffany's* (1958) is the story of Holly Golightly's search for identity in New York. Capote's other works include *Local Color* (1950), a book of essays and travel sketches, and *A Tree of Night* (1956), a collection of short stories.

Capri. An island off the coast of Italy not far from Naples. During the last years of Tiberius' reign, the emperor spent most of his time there. It is now a popular tourist resort, known especially for its Blue Grotto, with phosphorescent waters.

Captain Bonneville, The Adventures of (1837). A narrative prepared by Washington IRVING from the documents of Captain Benjamin L. E. de Bonneville (1796–1878). Bonneville explored the Northwest during his career in the army, and met Irving while the latter was at work on *Astoria*. Irving agreed to do Bonneville's story as a sequel. Irving, sympathetic to the Indians, condemns the treatment they received at the hands of the white trappers.

Captain Brassbound's Conversion (1900). A play by George Bernard SHAW. Lady Cecily Waynflete talks Brassbound out of his plan for revenge on his uncle. Set in Morocco, using the U.S. Navy as a *deus ex machina,* and written in a variety of dialects, this is one of Shaw's less dramatically successful plays. It was written for the actress Ellen Terry, who said it was "more fitted for the closet than the stage."

Captain Craig (1902).   The title poem of a book of verse by Edwin Arlington ROBINSON. One of the author's long and characteristic narratives, it describes a picturesque and talkative old vagabond, Captain

Craig, who preaches the doctrine that "God's humor is the music of the spheres" and that one must "laugh with God."

Captain of Köpenick, The (Der Hauptmann von Köpenick; 1931). A satirical comedy by Carl ZUCKMAYER. It caricatures the narrowness of Prussian militarism and bureaucracy. Wilhelm Voigt, a penniless cobbler who, because he is an ex-convict, can obtain neither a work permit nor a passport to leave the country, gets possession of an army captain's uniform. By taking advantage of people's slavish respect for the military, he arrests the mayor of Köpenick and robs the town hall. What he really wants is a passport, but all he finds is money. In the end, when he gives himself up, the authorities refuse to believe that as silly-looking a character as he could have been the impostor.

Captain's Doll, The (1923). A short story by D. H. LAWRENCE. In it he puts forward some of his ideas about marriage. A German countess makes and sells a puppet of her lover, who is a captain in a Scottish regiment. He says that romantic love always makes a doll of its object, and that their marriage must be based instead on her vows to "honor and obey" him.

Captain Singleton (1720). The hero and shortened title of *The Life, Adventures and Piracies of the famous Captain Singleton,* a first-person narrative of piracy and buccaneer raids on the African coast written by Daniel DEFOE.

Captive, The. See REMEMBRANCE OF THINGS PAST.

Capuana, Luigi (1839–1915). Italian novelist and critic. The champion of Zolaesque realism in Italy, he began his literary career as drama critic for the noted Florentine newspaper *La Nazione.* A member of the SCAPIGLIATURA group of writers, Capuana was a fervent admirer of the psychological novels then popular in France, England, and Russia. They influenced his later novels and short stories in which a detailed investigation into the psychological behavior of exceptional, pathological individuals is joined by a scrupulous regard for realistic descriptions and a precise, unadorned style. Capuana's theorization of Zolaesque realism laid the foundation for *verismo,* its Italian counterpart.

Capuana's first novel, *Giacinta* (1879), is perhaps the best example of his "pseudo-scientific" technique. The plot is in itself unimportant for it only serves to give an insight into the protagonist's peculiar behavior. Giacinta takes a lover on the day of her marriage to a man whom she despises yet whom she wanted as her husband. The lover's eventual feeling of repugnance for her causes her to commit suicide. The author explains her behavior in terms that reflect a psychoanalysis of her personality and suggest Freudianism *avant la lettre:* Giacinta inherited a sexually promiscuous appetite from her mother and was traumatically affected by being raped at the age of 14.

Il Marchese di Roccaverdina (1901) traces the life of the marquis of Roccaverdina from the time he murders his mistress' husband to his own suicide, brought about by feelings of guilt although he is never suspected by his mistress or by the police.

The novel *Profumo* (1890) describes the unreasoning hysteria of a woman whose nervous condition causes her body to emanate an odor of orange blossoms.

Among Capuana's many works are collections of short stories, depicting the customs and landscape of Sicily, and critical essays: *Le Novelle Appassionate* (1893), *Le Novelle Paesane* (1894), *Fausto Bragia* (1897), *Lo Sfinge* (1897), *Il Decameroncino* (1901), *Coscienze* (1905), and *La Voluttà di Creare* (1906).

Capulet and Montague. The English names of the Capelletti and the Montecchi, two noble families of legends of 14th-century Verona. The feud between the two houses has been immortalized by Shakespeare's ROMEO AND JULIET.

Old Capulet, Juliet's father, is an irascible, unimaginative man who loves his daughter but is incensed when she refuses to marry Paris, the husband he has chosen for her. Upon hearing of the death of the two lovers, he is reconciled with Lord Montague, Romeo's father, who vows to erect a golden statue to the "true and faithful Juliet."

Caracalla. Full Latin name, **Marcus Aurelius Antonius** (A.D. 188–217). Roman emperor (211–217). He was nicknamed Caracalla after the long, hooded tunic worn by the Gauls, which he wore after he became emperor. He and his brother Geta succeeded to the throne after their father's death, but Caracalla had his brother assassinated, along with several of the most distinguished statesmen in the country. His reign was marked by cruelty and treachery. He was murdered by the praetorian prefect.

Caractacus or Caradoc. A legendary king of the Silures in Britain. He withstood the Roman armies for nine years; but he was finally betrayed by Carthismandu, queen of the Brigantes, and led captive to Rome in A.D. 51. He is a prominent figure in the Welsh *Triads* and in Michael Drayton's *Polyolbion* (1622).

Caractères de Théophraste traduits du grec, avec les caractères ou les Moeurs de ce siècle. See Jean de LA BRUYERE.

Caravaggio, Michelangelo Merisi da (1569–1609). Italian painter. Reacting against MANNERISM and idealism, he introduced a powerful realism into his paintings of biblical scenes by employing crude peasant types and dramatizing them by means of harsh light and violent contrasts. His naturalistic method earned him much opposition in his day, but his influence was important for such later painters as George de la Tour, Velázquez, and Rubens. Typical of his best work is the masterpiece *Christ at Emmaus.*

Carbonari (*Ital.,* "charcoal burners"). The name given to a secret political association that flourished in Italy and France early in the 19th century. The group first came into being during the reign (1808–1815) of Joachim Murat in Naples. The movement originally sought to free Italy from foreign domination, but democratic and republican sentiments later arose as well. After the failure of several uprisings, the Carbonari were absorbed by MAZZINI's Young Italy society. The movement gained prominence in France after 1820.

Carco, Francis. Pen name of **François Marie Alexandre Carcopino-Tusoli** (1886–1958). French poet, novelist, and critic. He is a recorder of the charms of Montmartre in such poetry as *La Bohème* *et mon coeur* (1912) and *Poèmes en prose* (1948). Carco's argot-filled novels of bohemian life and morals include *Perversité* (1925, translated by Ford Madox Ford), *Rue Pigalle* (1927), and *The Hounded Man* (*L'Homme traqué;* 1921, also translated as *The Noose of Sin*). He is also known for his memoirs *The Last Bohemia* (*De Montmartre au Quartier Latin;* 1927), and for his biographies of Villon (1927) and Verlaine (1939).

Card, The (1911). A humorous novel by Arnold BENNETT. The card is a good-humored, comic, smart young man called Denry. He earns a living by playing ruthless, remunerative tricks on Five Towns citizens.

Cardano, Girolamo (1501–1576). Italian philosopher. Skilled in medicine and mathematics, Cardano was familiar with many of the intellectual centers of the Italian Renaissance. His *Ars magna* (*Great Art,* 1545) was an important and influential mathematical treatise embodying many of his achievements.

Cardinal, The (1641). A tragedy by James SHIRLEY. Duchess Rosaura, a rich young widow, is betrothed to the heroic Don Columbo, nephew of the mighty cardinal, despite her preference for the Count d'Alvarez. While Columbo is away at war, she breaks the engagement and prepares to marry Alvarez. Columbo, after winning a great victory, returns and kills Alvarez. Rosaura then promises to marry Colonel Hernando, an officer who hates Columbo, if he will avenge her. When Columbo is killed, suspicion falls on Hernando, and the cardinal cleverly arranges to become Rosaura's guardian. He plans to rape and poison her, but Hernando, returning just in time, stabs first the cardinal and then himself. The cardinal confesses his crimes, pretends to have poisoned Rosaura, and offers her an antidote, which is actually poison. Thus, the dying cardinal has his revenge.

Cardozo, Benjamin Nathan (1870–1938). American jurist and associate justice of the U.S. Supreme Court (1932–1938). A liberal who believed that law should reflect social change, Cardozo wrote five important books: *The Nature of the Judicial Process* (1921), *The Growth of the Law* (1924), *The Paradoxes of Legal Science* (1928), *The Law and Literature* (1931), and *Law Is Justice* (1938). For both style and content his legal opinions are regarded as classics.

Carducci, Giosuè (1835–1907). Italian poet and literary critic. Self-proclaimed antiromantic classicist, patriot, liberal, and freemason, he was professor of Italian literature at the University of Bologna from 1860 to 1904. The aims and struggles of the *Risorgimento* are reflected in such works as *Juvenilia* (1860), *Levia Gravia* (1868), *Giambi ed Epodi* (1879), and *Rime Nuove* (1887), while *Odi Barbare* (1877–89) and *Rime e Ritmi* (1898) reveal his predilection for classical motifs and meters and archaic language; throughout, there is a positive endorsement of liberal ideology. *The Hymn to Satan* (*L'Inno a Satana,* 1863; pub. 1870) is a vigorous manifesto of rebellion in which the obscurantism and asceticism of traditional religion are denounced while human achievement in material progress is praised. Awarded the Nobel Prize for literature (1906), he is considered the national poet of modern Italy.

Carduel. In the Breton lai *Sir Launfal* by MARIE DE FRANCE, the place in which King Arthur holds his court at Pentecost. See CAMELOT; CAERLEON.

Carêmeprenant. See KING LENT.

Carew, Thomas (c. 1595–c. 1639). English poet. One of the SONS OF BEN, he was the first and probably best of the CAVALIER POETS. A courtier of Charles I, Carew was a sensualist and libertine who, it is said, repented on his deathbed. His work shows the influence of Donne as well as of Jonson: not only are there phrases, cadences, and themes reminiscent of Donne, but Carew's poetry has a richness of conceit and a play of intellect rare in Cavalier verse. In their essential spirit, however—their melody, grace, and polish—his poems reflect the art of Jonson. Carew wrote numerous songs and light love lyrics, such as the song *Ask Me No More Where Jove Bestows* and *Mediocrity in Love Rejected,* and a number of more serious pieces distinguished by their perspicacity, tact, and feeling, such as the lovely epitaph on Maria Wentworth. His collected poetry appeared in the posthumous volume *Poems* (1640), and he was also the author of a masque *Coelum Britannicum* (1633).

Carey, Henry (1687?–1743). English poet and composer. He wrote farces, burlesques, songs, and often accompanying music for the stage. His best-known ballad is SALLY IN OUR ALLEY (1729). His other works include *Namby Pamby* (1725), a poem, the title of which he also gave as a nickname to Ambrose PHILIPS; CHRONONHOTONTHOLOGOS (1734), a burlesque tragedy; *The Dragon of Wantley* (1737), a burlesque opera relating the tale of the slaying of a dragon; and *The Honest Yorkshire Man* (1735), a ballad-farce. There was a rumor that Carey was also the author of *God Save the King.*

Carey, Mathew (1760–1839). Irish-born American editor and author. He founded the *American Museum* (1787–1792), one of the first successful American literary periodicals, which printed works by Francis Hopkinson, Benjamin Franklin and the Hartford Wits. For a time Carey also edited the COLUMBIAN MAGAZINE. As a writer he is best known for *The Porcupiniad* (1796), an attack on William Cobbett for the latter's criticism of America, and *The Olive Branch* (1814), a plea for Anglo-American reconciliation after the War of 1812.

Cariteo or **Chariteo. Benedicto Gareth** (c. 1450–1514). Italian poet. Born in Barcelona, Cariteo spent most of his life at Naples in the service of the house of Aragon and as a member of the Neapolitan literary academy. His fellow academicians, noting the resemblance between his Catalan name Gareth and the Greek *Charites* (the Graces), addressed him with the Latinized form, *Chariteus;* the Italian equivalent, Cariteo, or Chariteo, then became standard. His lyrics, to which he gave the title *Endimione* (Endymion) because in them the object of his love is called Luna (the Moon), were published in 1506. These are essentially Petrarchan in style, but more exuberant and daring in the choice of metaphors (see CONCEIT), and were influential in establishing a style that contrasted with the purer Petrarchism championed by Bembo. His imitators were and are sometimes called Chariteans.

Carker, James. In Charles Dickens' DOMBEY AND SON, the business manager of the firm of Dombey. He not only brings the firm to bankruptcy, but he elopes with Dombey's second wife Edith. Edith leaves him at Dijon, and Carker, returning to England, is accidentally killed by a railway train.

Carlo Magno. The Italian form of Charlemagne and the name used to designate him in the three great Italian poems on the Carolingian material: the *Morgante* of Pulci and the Orlando poems of Boiardo and Ariosto.

Carlos, Don (1545–1568). Spanish prince. The son of Philip II by his first wife, Mary of Portugal, Don Carlos was mentally and physically unsound and was subject to fits of maniacal rage. He was betrothed to Elizabeth of Valois, but Philip married her himself. Later he conceived a bitter hatred for his father, hindering his policies whenever possible. When he laid plans to leave Spain secretly, he was imprisoned at Philip's orders and died a few months later. Although he probably died of natural causes, it was widely rumored that he had been murdered at his father's instigation. The unlucky prince was the subject of Schiller's tragedy DON CARLOS and of dramas by Thomas Otway and Vittorio Alfieri. Verdi based one of his finest operas, *Don Carlo* or *Don Carlos* (1867) on Schiller's play.

Carlota or **Charlotte** (1840–1927). Belgian-born empress of Mexico. The daughter of King Leopold I of Belgium, she was the wife of the ill-fated MAXIMILIAN, whom she urged to accept the Mexican crown offered by Napoleon III of France. In 1866, when Maximilian's empire seemed on the verge of collapse, she went to France in a futile attempt to persuade Napoleon not to withdraw his troops from Mexico. During a visit to the Vatican, she lost her mind and never fully regained her sanity.

Carlovingians. See CAROLINGIANS.

Carlyle, Thomas (1795–1881). Scottish-born English prose writer. He is remembered for his explosive attacks on sham, hypocrisy, and excessive materialism; his distrust of democracy and the mob; and his highly romantic belief in the power of the individual, especially the strong, heroic leader. During much of his own life he struggled courageously, though hardly quietly, with poverty and "dyspepsia" (probably painful gastric ulcers). He was influenced in his early career by German literature, which he helped to popularize in England, being a particular admirer of Schiller and Goethe.

Carlyle's best-known book is the THE FRENCH REVOLUTION. Of his public lectures, the famous *On Heroes, Hero-worship, and the Heroic in History* (1841) best expresses his cult of the leader. His hatred of *laissez faire* policies, fears of the destruction of personality by the machines of industrialism, and his distrust of social legislators are to be found in the essays *Chartism* (1839), *Past and Present* (1843), and *Latter Day Pamphlets* (1850). Among his biographies are *Life of Schiller* (1823–1824), *Cromwell* (1845), *The Life of Sterling* (1851), and *History of Frederick II of Prussia, Called Frederick the Great* (1858–1865). SARTOR RESARTUS, called a spiritual biography, is one of his most characteristic works and aroused violent protest when published. Carlyle's style is savage and apocalyptic; it is marked by unusual words and figures of speech, agitated and mounting rhythms, and expressions influenced by the German language. See Jane WELSH; CRAIGENPUTTOCK.

Carmagnola, Count of. Francesco Busone (1390–1432). The famous Italian CONDOTTIERE who fought for the Visconti of Milan and the republic of Venice until the latter, fearing his successes, had him killed.

carmagnole. (1) Costume of French Revolutionists: wide-collared jacket, wide, black pantaloons, red cap (see BONNET ROUGE), and scarlet or tricolored waistcoat. The jacket was adopted from that worn in the south of France by the Piedmontese workmen of Carmagnola.

(2) A Red Republican song and dance of the time of the French Revolution, with the refrain:

> *Dansons la Carmagnole,—Vive le son, vive le son—*
> *Dansons la Carmagnole,—Vive le son du canon!*

Carman, [William] Bliss (1861–1929). Canadian poet, essayist, and lecturer. He is best known for his collaboration with Richard HOVEY on *Songs from Vagabondia* (1894) and its sequels. In 1928, Carman was made Poet Laureate of Canada. Among his other volumes are *Low Tide on Grand Pré* (1893), *Behind the Arras* (1895), and *The Rough Riders and Other Poems* (1909).

Carmelites. An order of mendicant friars. It was founded at Mt. Carmel by the Crusader Berthold in the 12th century. Expelled from the Holy Land by the Saracens in the 13th century, they came to Europe. The order of Carmelite nuns dates from 15th century, the greatest being the Spanish mystic Saint Teresa of Avila, who organized the austere branch of the discalced (shoeless) Carmelites in contrast to the traditional Carmelites of the mitigated rule.

Carmen (1875). An opera by Georges BIZET based on Mérimée's novel of the same name. Carmen, a gypsy, flirts with the young Spanish officer Don José, and he lets her escape arrest for stabbing another girl. She persuades him to desert and cast in his lot with a band of gypsy smugglers. Soon, however, she forgets José in her interest in the torero Escamillo. When she refuses to return to him, José stabs her.

Carmer, Carl [Lamson] (1893–). American writer. While teaching at the University of Alabama, Carmer composed the popular *Stars Fell on Alabama* (1934), a volume of Alabama folklore. He has also written a similar volume in the folklore of New York, his native state, *Listen for a Lonesome Drum* (1936). His other books include *The Hudson* (1939); *Genesee Fever* (1941), a novel; *Windfall Fiddle* (1950), a distinguished juvenile; and *The Susquehanna* (1955).

Carmilhan. A legendary phantom ship of the Baltic. The captain of this ship swore he would double the Cape, whether God willed it or not. For this impious vow he was doomed to abide for ever and ever captain in the same vessel, which always appears near the Cape, but never doubles it. The kobold of the phantom ship, named Klaboterman, helps sailors at their work, but beats those who are idle. When a vessel is doomed, the kobold appears smoking a short pipe, dressed in yellow, and wearing a nightcap. See also FLYING DUTCHMAN.

Carmina Burana. See GOLIARDIC VERSE.

Carné, Marcel (1906–). French film director and producer. Representative of the early portion of Marcel Carné's career are *Quai des Brumes* (1938) and *Le Jour se Lève* (1939), realistic studies of tragic lives with an emphasis on character and milieu. His later work is characteristic of the French cinema during the five years of German occupation. Like Cocteau, he took refuge in the romantic allegory touched with fantasy and mysticism. His most renowned works of this period, produced in collaboration with Jacques PRÉVERT, are *Les Visiteurs du Soir* (1942) and *Les Enfants de Paradis* (1945).

Carnegie, Andrew (1835–1919). Scottish-born American industrialist and philanthropist. Starting as a bobbin boy in Pennsylvania at $1.20 a week, Carnegie achieved a commanding position in the steel industry through his organizing ability and acumen as a judge of men. After selling his steel interests to the U.S. Steel Corp. for $250 million in 1901, he devoted himself to philanthropy, providing funds for numerous public libraries and for such institutions as the Carnegie Endowment for International Peace. His philanthropy was inspired by his conviction that men who amassed great wealth were morally obligated to use it for the public good. He first expressed this doctrine, known as "the gospel of wealth," in an article, *Wealth,* in 1889. His other writings include *Triumphant Democracy* (1886), *The Gospel of Wealth and Other Timely Essays* (1889), and an *Autobiography* (1920).

Caro, Annibale (1507–1566). Italian diplomat and humanist. He wrote Petrarchan verse, comedies, and letters. His most famous work was his verse translation (1563–1566) of Vergil's *Aeneid* and his prose version of Longus' *Daphnis and Chloe.*

Carolingians or **Carlovingians.** Second dynasty of Frankish kings. They held the office of "mayor of the palace" under the weak later Merovingian kings, but they were the virtual rulers, particularly CHARLES MARTEL and his son Pepin the Short (c. 714–768), who finally deposed the nominal ruler in 751 and was anointed king of the Franks by the Pope in 754. His two sons jointly inherited the crown, but when Carloman (751–771) died, CHARLEMAGNE became sole king. His battles greatly enlarged his territory to include most of France, Germany, and northern Italy, and in 800 Pope Leo III crowned Charlemagne Emperor of the West, thus identifying his temporal power with the interests of Christianity. He was an effective administrator, especially known for his attempt to revive learning and culture, sometimes known as the *Carolingian Renaissance.* To re-educate the clergy, he established schools and imported scholars from abroad, including ALCUIN of York. After his death, however, internal divisions weakened the empire, and the reign of his successors ended in Germany in 911 and in France in 987.

The *Carolingian legends* are the romances of medieval and Renaissance Europe dealing with the supposed adventures of Charlemagne's PALADINS. See especially those associated with ROLAND.

Caron, Pierre Augustin. See BEAUMARCHAIS.

Carpaccio, Vittore (c. 1450–c. 1526). Venetian painter. A student of the Bellini brothers, he is noted for his ceremonial and narrative pictures, which abound in colorful detail. His masterpiece is the series of canvases that relate the *Story of St. Ursula.* His most important student and disciple was Veronese.

Carpenter, Edward (1844–1929). English poet and writer. Originally a clergyman, Carpenter's socialist views caused him to leave the church and earn his living as lecturer, farmer, and sandal-maker. A disciple of Walt Whitman, whose poetry his own verse closely resembles, he was also a partisan of democracy and apologist for homosexual love. His best-known prose works are *England's Ideal* (1887), *Civilization: Its Cause and Cure* (1889), and *Love's Coming of Age* (1896). Collections of his poetry include *Narcissus* (1873), *Toward Democracy* (1883–1905), and *Sketches from Life in Town and Country* (1908).

carpet, magic. In Eastern wonder tales and romances, a stock device for transporting a character to any place he wished to go. It is sometimes termed *Prince Housain's carpet* because of the role it plays in the well-known story of Prince Ahmed in the *Arabian Nights.* The most popular magic carpet, however, was that of King Solomon which, according to the Islamic legend related in the Koran, was of green silk. When he traveled, his throne was placed on it, and it was large enough for all his forces to stand upon; in order to screen his party from the sun, the birds formed a canopy over them with their wings.

carpetbagger. In U.S. history, a derisive epithet applied to Northerners who went south to take part in Reconstruction governments. To disgruntled Southerners, the carpetbags these men carried were indicative of their transience and lack of property interests in the South.

Carr, John Dickson. Pen names, **Carter Dickson, Carr Dickson** (1906–   ). American writer of detective and mystery stories. Many of Carr's books are set in England, where he lived for many years, and feature the astute sleuthing of the corpulent Dr. Gideon Fell. Carr emphasizes the puzzle element in the solutions of his mysteries, occasionally adding a touch of the macabre, and often using authentic historical backgrounds. Among his many books are *The Bride of Newgate* (1950), *Behind the Crimson Blind* (1952), *Cut-Throat* (1955), *The Dead Man's Knock* (1958), and *The Men Who Explained Miracles* (1963).

Carracci, Annibale (1560–1609). Italian painter. With his brother **Agostino** (1557–1602) and his cousin **Lodovico** (1555–1619), he founded an academy in Bologna, in 1582, where artists followed a course of study that served as a model for later academies. Based on the principle of eclecticism, it combined elements from the art of the Venetian school and that of Correggio, Raphael, and Michelangelo in an effort to achieve classical beauty. Annibale Carracci's religious pictures and large decorative schemes, notably his frescoes in the Farnese Gallery in Rome, reveal that he was the most talented member of this artistic family. His leading disciples were Domenichino and Guido Reni.

Carranza, Venustiano (1859–1920). Mexican political leader. An associate of Francisco Madero in the revolutionary movement of 1910, Carranza became provisional president in 1915 and was elected president in 1917. His administration saw the promulgation of the nationalistic Constitution of 1917, still in force today, but he ignored its provisions for social and economic reform. Despite U.S. recognition of the Carranza government in 1915, the border raids of Pancho VILLA and American agitation against "godless and socialistic Mexico" brought the two countries to the verge of war. When it became apparent that Carranza planned to name his own successor, revolt broke out; attempting to flee with a trainload of loot, Carranza was murdered at the hands of his own men.

Carrillo y Sotomayor, Luis (1583?–1610). Spanish poet and soldier. Considered a forerunner of Góngora, he wrote difficult, latinate verse, such as *Fábula de Acis y Galatea*. In his *Libro de la erudición poética*, he argued that Spanish should be latinized and that poetry should be cultivated only by the learned. His works were first published in 1611.

Carroll, Lewis. Pen name of **Charles Lutwidge Dodgson** (1832–1898). English author, mathematician, and photographer. A lecturer in mathematics at Christ Church, Oxford, Carroll was shy and stammering, reputedly a boring lecturer, whose mathematical writings include *An Elementary Treatise on Determinants* (1867), *Euclid and His Modern Rivals* (1879), *Curiosa Mathematica* (1888), and *Symbolic Logic* (1896). He was ordained as a deacon but never preached, and was a talented portrait photographer. His principal enthusiasm, however, was for little girls, for whom he created many amusing games and puzzles and for one of whom, Alice Liddell, he wrote his famous ALICE'S ADVENTURES IN WONDERLAND and THROUGH THE LOOKING GLASS. These became highly popular among adult readers; theorists of surrealism in the 20th century seriously interpreted Carroll's works as early embodiments of their own principles; and Freudians have made much of the symbolism of the Alice books. Carroll's other works of fantasy and nonsense include *The Hunting of the Snark, An Agony in Eight Fits* (verses, 1876), *Sylvie and Bruno* (1889), and *Sylvie and Bruno concluded* (1893). Through these works run veins of satire, parody, masterfully inverted logic, and extremely suggestive symbolism. See Sir John TENNIEL.

Carryl, Charles Edward (1842–1920). A New York financier and writer of children's books of a type reminiscent of those of Lewis Carroll, as *Davy and the Goblin* (1886); *The Admiral's Caravan* (1892). They contain some brilliant nonsense verse.

Carson, Christopher. Known as **Kit Carson** (1809–1868). American trapper and guide. Carson crossed the Mohave Desert in 1830 and served as a guide for Frémont's first western expedition (1842). He took an important part in the conquest of California during the Mexican War and fought in New Mexico during the Civil War, rising to the rank of brigadier general. Joaquin Miller's poem *Kit Carson's Ride* (1871) tells how Carson rescued his Indian bride from a prairie fire on their wedding day. Carson also appears in numerous dime novels and folk legends.

Carson, Rachel L[ouise] (1907–1964). American writer and scientist. Miss Carson's *The Sea Around Us* (1951) and *The Edge of the Sea* (1956) are known as works of literary as well as scientific merit. She maintained her impeccable style and aroused far more discussion and controversy with *The Silent Spring* (1962), in which she contended that the indiscriminate use of weed killers and insecticides constitutes a hazard to wildlife and to human beings.

Carstone, Richard. See BLEAK HOUSE.

Carswell, Mrs. Catherine (1879–1946). Scottish novelist and critic. Her biography of D. H. Lawrence, a close friend, was suppressed as libelous.

Cartaphilus or **Kartaphilos.** The doorkeeper of the Judgment Hall under Pontius Pilate in the variant of the WANDERING JEW legend told by the historians of St. Albans, Roger of Wendover (d. 1236) and Matthew PARIS. They reported that an Armenian archbishop, visiting St. Albans in 1228, said that he had recently dined with a man named Joseph who as Cartaphilus had been rude to Christ and had consequently become the Wandering Jew. The Flemish chronicler Philip Mousket (13th century) wrote a similar version about 1243.

Carte de tendre. See CLÉLIE, HISTOIRE ROMAINE.

Carter, Nick. A fictional American detective who has appeared in over 1,000 stories. He was apparently invented by John R. Coryell (1848–1924), who worked in a writing team with Thomas Chalmers Harbaugh (1849–1924) and Frederick Van Rensselaer Dey (1861?–1922); Nick made his first appearance in *The Old Detective's Pupil* (1886). The Nick Carter dime novels were extremely popular, and other writers continued the series in stories, movies, and radio plays.

Carteret, Philip (1639–1682). English colonial governor of New Jersey (1664–1676) and, after division of the colony, of East New Jersey (1676–1682). He came into conflict with Sir Edmund Andros, governor of New York, who challenged his right to collect duties on goods entering Jersey ports.

Carthage. Ancient city and state in North Africa. Founded in the ninth century B.C. by Phoenicians from the kingdom of Tyre, it was located on a peninsula near the site of modern Tunis. According to Roman legend, it was founded by DIDO. It became dominant among Phoenician cities in North Africa, founded several colonies in Africa, and held sway over the native agricultural population of a large region. Carthage carried on considerable trading activities along the coasts of the Mediterranean and founded colonies in Spain, Sardinia, and Sicily. There existed between Rome and Carthage a number of treaties restricting Rome from interfering with Carthaginian trade. These treaties governed the relations between Rome and Carthage until the PUNIC WARS. Carthage was ultimately burned to the ground by the Romans in the Third Punic War (149–146 B.C.).

Carthago delenda est. (Lat., "Carthage must be destroyed.") This is the phrase with which CATO THE ELDER ended all his speeches in the senate.

Carthusians (from *Chartreuse,* near Grenoble in France). An order of monks. It was founded in 1084 by St. Bruno. They were sworn to perpetual silence, continuous wearing of hair shirts, and eating of only one meal a day.

Cartier, Jacques (1491–1557). French navigator. During the second of his three voyages to America, he sailed up the St. Lawrence River, which he discovered, to an Indian village called Hochelaga, the site of modern Montreal, and named it Mount Royal.

Carton, Sydney. The hero of Charles Dickens' A TALE OF TWO CITIES. He is a dissipated young man whose temperament is contrasted with that of Charles Darnay; the great physical resemblance of the two is an important factor in the plot. Carton loves Lucie Manette, but, knowing of her attachment to Darnay, never attempts to win her. His love for her, however, brings out his nobler qualities, and ultimately brings him to die on the guillotine in place of Darnay. His last thoughts are the famous lines, "It is a far, far better thing that I do, than I have ever done; it is a far, far better rest, that I go to, than I have ever known." See Bully STRYVER.

Cartwright, William (1611–1643). English preacher, dramatist, and poet. Highly regarded by his contemporaries, Cartwright was one of the sons of Ben, or poets influenced by Ben Jonson. His best-known plays are *The Ordinary* (1634) and *The Royal Slave* (1636), which were first presented at Oxford University.

Caruso, Enrico (1873–1921). Italian dramatic tenor of worldwide popularity. The tremendous power and brilliance of his voice combined with an impassioned delivery and dynamic personality earned him many admirers, but also partially caused his death from overwork and strain. He was especially famous in the lead roles in *Pagliacci*, *Aïda*, *La Bohème*, and *Tosca*.

Carvajal, Micael or **Miguel de** (c. 1480–c. 1560). Spanish dramatist. He is best known for his *Tragedia Josefina* (c. 1535), a tragedy in four acts about Joseph and his brethren.

Carver, John (c. 1576–1621). 1st governor of the Plymouth Colony. He also hired and outfitted the *Mayflower*, and helped obtain financial backing for the voyage.

Cary, Joyce (1888–1957). Anglo-Irish novelist. He is the author of two trilogies, the first consisting of *Herself Surprised* (1941), *To Be a Pilgrim* (1942), and THE HORSE'S MOUTH, and the second of PRISONER OF GRACE, *Except the Lord* (1953), and *Not Honour More* (1955). The semiautobiographical *A House of Children* (1941) gives an impression of his Irish childhood. Trained as an artist, he brought his knowledge of a painter's problems to his best-known novel, *The Horse's Mouth*. From 1913 to 1920 Cary worked for the Nigerian political service. All his first novels are set in Africa and are about Africans, interracial problems, and the duties of government and law. His African novels are *Aissa Saved* (1932), *An American Visitor* (1933), *The African Witch* (1936), and MISTER JOHNSON. Cary's later books are Dickensian in their humor and wealth of characters, and are concerned with English social history. In this group are *Charley Is My Darling* (1940), *The Moonlight* (1946), *A Fearful Joy* (1949), *The Captive and the Free* (1959), and the trilogies. A celebrant of the power of the creative imagination, Cary presents it in many forms—in an African clerk (*Mister Johnson*), an artist (*The Horse's Mouth*), and a politician (the *Prisoner of Grace* series).

Casabianca. A poem by Felicia HEMANS celebrating the heroic death of Giacomo Jocante Casabianca, the little son of a French naval captain. The boy was set by his father on watch. The ship caught fire, and his father was burnt to death. As the flames spread, the boy called to his father, but stood by his post until the ship blew up.

Casa de Bernarda Alba, La. See Federico GARCÍA LORCA.

Casa Guidi Windows (1851). A long poem by Elizabeth Barrett BROWNING, written on behalf of the national aspirations of the Florentines.

Casals, Pablo or **Pau** (1876–   ). Spanish cellist and conductor. His mastery of interpretation and technique on the cello is now legendary; he has extended his profound musical insight to his teaching and conducting. Since the defeat of the Spanish Loyalists in 1939, Casals has chosen voluntary exile: first in Prades, France, where he established an annual music festival, later in Puerto Rico, where the festivals continued. *Conversations with Casals* (1956), by J. M. Corredor, surveys Casals' life and thought.

Casanova [de Seingalt], Giovanni Jacopo (1725–1798). Italian adventurer. After his expulsion from a Venetian seminary for scandalous misconduct, Casanova commenced a lively career as charlatan, gambler, and lover that took him to all the capitals of Europe. His fortunes fluctuated widely: in 1755, for example, he was imprisoned in Venice for impiety and magic, but after making a daring escape, he turned up in Paris, where he enjoyed temporary affluence as director of the state lottery and came in contact with such luminaries as Louis XV and Mme. de Pompadour. In 1785 he was made librarian at Count Waldstein's castle of Dux in Bohemia, where he remained until his death. His famous *Mémoires* (12 vols., 1826–1838) are no doubt unreliable as to his own career but are of great interest historically.

Casaubon, Rev. Mr. See MIDDLEMARCH.

Casca. In Shakespeare's JULIUS CAESAR, a conspirator against Caesar. He is known for his blunt, unadorned language.

Casey Jones. American ballad about a train wreck. It is probably based on the wreck in 1900 of the "Cannonball Express," whose driver, John Luther Jones (1864–1900), was born in Cayce, Kentucky, hence the nickname "Casey." Two railroad men, T. Lawrence Seibert and Eddie Newton, published the song in 1909 and may have been the authors.

casket letters, the. Eight letters and a series of poems supposedly written by MARY, QUEEN OF SCOTS to James, Earl of Bothwell. At least one of these was held to prove her complicity with Bothwell in the murder of her husband, Henry, Lord Darnley. The letters were found in a casket that fell into the hands of the Earl of Morton in 1567, four months after Darnley's death and a few days after Mary's surrender to the rebelling Scottish lords. The following year the letters were used as evidence in the investigation of the charges brought against Mary by the rebels. All trace of the original letters disappeared after 1584, and their authenticity is still a matter of dispute.

Casona, Alejandro. Pen name of **Alejandro Rodríguez Alvarez** (1903–   ). Spanish playwright. Spanish audiences received his *La Sirena Varada* (1934) and *Nuestra Natacha* (1936) with great acclaim. Since 1939, Casona has resided in Argentina where his *La Dama del Alba* (1944) and *Los Arboles Mueren de Pie* (1949) have been similarly well received.

Casperl. See GASPAR.

Cassandra (Kassandra). In Greek mythology, a daughter of Priam and Hecuba. She was gifted by Apollo with the power of prophecy. However, when she refused the god's advances he ordained that no one would believe her predictions, although they were invariably correct. She was carried off to Argos by Agamemnon and was killed with him by Clytemnestra and Aegisthus. She appears prominently in Euripides' *The Trojan Women* and Aeschylus' *Agamemnon*, as well as in Shakespeare's *Troilus and Cressida*. Her name has become synonymous with all prophets of doom.

Cassatt, Mary (1845–1926). American painter and print maker. She resided most of her life in France, where she was associated with Edgar Degas and the impressionists. She treated the theme of maternity with objectivity and an interest in simple everyday gestures, but she derived her style of clear lines, flat colors, and unusual composition from Japanese art.

Cassim Baba. See ALI BABA AND THE FORTY THIEVES.

Cassio, Michael. In Shakespeare's OTHELLO, the handsome young Florentine whom Othello appoints as his lieutenant. Iago, jealous of the preference shown to Cassio, encourages his weakness for drink and involves him in a brawl, causing his dismissal. Iago then convinces Othello that Cassio is Desdemona's lover. When Iago's plot is uncovered, Othello reinstates Cassio and asks his pardon before committing suicide.

Cassiopeia (Kassiopeia). In Greek mythology, the wife of Cepheus, king of Ethiopia, and mother of ANDROMEDA. In consequence of her boasting of the beauty of her daughter, she was sent to the heavens as the constellation Cassiopeia, the chief stars of which form the outline of a lady seated in a chair and holding up both arms in supplication.

Cassius. Full Latin name, **Caius Cassius Longinus** (d. 42 B.C.). Roman general and politician. During the civil war between CAESAR and Pompey, Cassius allied himself with Pompey. After Pompey's defeat at Pharsalus (48 B.C.), Caesar pardoned Cassius and made him praetor (44). Unlike BRUTUS, however, Cassius never ceased to be Caesar's enemy, in spite of the favor shown him. It was Cassius who conceived the plot against the dictator's life, and he who persuaded Brutus to join the conspiracy. After Caesar's murder, public opinion turned against the conspirators, and they fled from Rome. Cassius and Brutus met the forces of Octavius and Antony at Philippi (42), and during the first engagement Cassius, overwhelmed by Antony's forces, precipitately committed suicide, not knowing that Brutus had driven Octavius from the field. Brutus' forces were defeated some days later.

In Shakespeare's JULIUS CAESAR, Cassius is depicted as the instigator of the plot to assassinate Caesar. Grasping and ambitious, he urges the reluctant Brutus to join the conspiracy, pointing out, in a famous speech, that each man controls his own destiny:

> The fault, dear Brutus, is not in our stars,
> But in ourselves, that we are underlings.

Caesar says of him:

> Yon Cassius has a lean and hungry look;
> He thinks too much: such men are dangerous.

At Philippi, rashly assuming that Brutus has been defeated, Cassius commits suicide and thus helps turn Brutus' initial victory into overwhelming defeat.

Cassola, Carlo (1917–   ). Italian novelist. Inspired by Italy's fascist experience, his novels include *Fausto and Anna* (*Fausto e Anna;* 1952), *I Vecchi Compagni* (1953), *La Casa di Via Valadier* (1956), *Un Matrimonio del Dopoguerra* (1958), *Bebo's Girl* (*La Ragazza di Bubé;* 1960), and *Un Cuore Arido* (1961), which depicts the love life of a Tuscan seamstress in prewar Italy.

Interested in sociopolitical problems of postwar Italy, Cassola has written a notable polemical study about the conditions of Tuscan miners, *I Minatori della Maremma* (1956).

Castalia. A fountain of Parnassus sacred to the Muses. Its waters had the power of inspiring with the gift of poetry those who drank of them.

Castaway, The (1803). A tragic poem, his last, by William COWPER. It was based on an incident described in *A Voyage Round the World* (1748), by Admiral George Anson (1697–1762), a celebrated seaman of the eighteenth century. It tells of a lonely death at sea and compares this with the poet's own in a mood of despairing prophecy.

caste (Port. *casta*, race). One of the hereditary classes of society in India. The four great Hindu castes are the *Brahmin* (the priestly and meditative order), the *Shatriya* or *Kshatriya* (soldiers and rulers), *Vaishya* (husbandmen and merchants), and *Sudra* (peasants and laborers). The untouchables or outcastes form a fifth group, to whom the religious books are sealed; they are held cursed in this world, and without hope. Mahatma Gandhi and the present Indian government have done much to improve the position of this last group.

Castelar, Emilio (1832–1899). Spanish statesman and orator. A professor of history at Madrid university, he became president of the first Spanish republic in 1873. His speeches, which may be studied in his *Discursos* (1871), raised him to the position of Spain's greatest orator and exerted an influence upon European affairs. He is also the author of *Fra Filippo Lippi* (1877) and an account of his travels in Italy, *Recuerdos de Italia* (1872).

Castelo Branco, Camilo (1825–1890). Portuguese novelist. Castelo Branco was a prolific writer whose works reflect his own turbulent existence. Born out of wedlock, he had numerous love affairs, briefly contemplated entering the priesthood, and in 1861 was imprisoned for adultery. During his incarceration he wrote his best-known novel, *Amor de Perdição* (1862), a semiautobiographical tale of thwarted passion. Considered an outstanding prose stylist, he later turned toward realism, particularly in *Novelas do Minho* (1875), studies of rural life, and *A Brasileira de Prazins* (1882). He also wrote *Onde Está a Felicidade?* (1856), *Um Homem de Brios* (1857), and *Eusébio Macário* (1879), a parody of Zolaesque realism.

Castelvetro, Lodovico (1505–1571). Italian Renaissance literary critic. He is noted for his commentary (1570) on Aristotle's *Poetics;* its influence was felt in Europe through the 18th century.

Castiglione, Baldassare (1478–1529). Italian diplomat, writer, and courtier. One of the most important and influential authors in Europe during the Renaissance, he was born at Mantua, where he served the Gonzaga family, then moved to Urbino and the service of its duke, Guidobaldo da Montefeltro. In 1506, he was in England to receive the Order of the Garter for his master from Henry VII. In 1524, he went to Spain as papal envoy and died there in 1529, universally mourned. Although he wrote poetry in various genres, his chief work is *Il Libro del Cortegiano* (*The Book of the Courtier*), known simply as *Il Cortegiano* (THE COURTIER). Finished in 1518, the book sets forth in a series of dialogues the author's conception of the ideal courtier and the norms of courtesy in a cultured society. Castiglione's portrait, done by his friend Raphael, is one of the masterpieces of the Louvre museum.

Castillejo, Cristóbal de (1490?–1550). Spanish poet. A Cistercian monk, he spent most of his life in the service of Archduke Ferdinand, later king of the Romans. His poems, which were published in 1573, include *Sermón de Amores; Diálogo de la Vida de Corte,* a satire on court life; and *Contra los que Dejan los Metros Castellanos,* a diatribe on poets who adopted Italian meters.

Castillo y Solórzano, Alonso de (1584–c. 1648). Spanish novelist and dramatist. He is best known for his numerous picaresque novels, notably *Las Harpías en Madrid* (1631), *Aventuras del Bachiller Trapaza* (1637), and *La Garduña de Sevilla* (1642).

Castle, Egerton (1858–1920). English novelist. In collaboration with his wife Agnes (d. 1922), he wrote a series of popular romantic novels including *The Pride of Jennico* (1898), *The Bath Comedy* (1900), and *The Secret Orchard* (1901). Several of his books were dramatized.

Castle, Joyous. See FAERIE QUEENE, THE.

Castle, The (Das Schloss; 1926). An unfinished novel by Franz KAFKA, published posthumously. In its bare essentials, it is the story of a man against a bureaucracy and in this is similar to THE TRIAL. The hero, a land surveyor known only as K., is constantly frustrated in his efforts to gain entrance into a mysterious castle, which is administered by an extraordinarily complicated and inaccessible bureaucratic hierarchy. The book invites allegorical interpretation; K.'s striving has been seen as the human quest for comprehension of the ways of an incomprehensible God and his frustration has been seen as symbolic of the actual human condition. But apart from any exact interpretation, the novel clearly reflects Kafka's convictions about the problematic nature of human existence, as well as his stylistic mastery and frequent ironic humor.

Castle Dangerous (1832). A novel by Sir Walter SCOTT. Castle Dangerous or the PERILOUS CASTLE of James DOUGLAS was so called because it was taken from the English three times between 1306 and 1307. In the novel Black Douglas promises to release his prisoner, Lady Augusta, if the castle is surrendered to him. Sir John de Walton consents, gives up the castle, and marries the lady.

Castle Garden. A large circular building at the Battery, New York City. It was built as a fort in 1807. It became a concert hall where Jenny Lind gave a famous concert. Later an immigrant station, than an aquarium, it has been restored to its original form and is a federal monument.

Castle of Indolence (1748). A poem in Spenserian stanzas by James THOMSON. The castle of the poem is situated in the land of Drowsiness, where every sense is steeped in enervating delights. The owner is an enchanter who deprives all who enter his domains of their energy and free will. In Canto II, Selvaggio, the Knight of Arts and Industry, breaks the spell cast by the wizard Indolence. It is considered Thomson's best work by many critics.

Castle of Otranto, The (1764). A GOTHIC NOVEL, the first of that genre in English, by Horace WALPOLE. The villain, Manfred, prince of Otranto, inhabits the castle of Otranto and rules the realm unlawfully; his grandfather had poisoned Alfonso, the rightful ruler, and it had been cryptically prophesied that the usurpers would prevail so long as the castle was big enough to hold the rightful ruler. Manfred plans to marry his son Conrad to Isabella, daughter of the marquis of Vicenza, but in one of many supernatural events, Conrad is crushed to death by a gigantic helmet in the courtyard. Manfred then determines to marry Isabella himself in the hope that she will present him with another heir, whom he needs in order to maintain control of the realm. Isabella, terrified of Manfred, is aided by the handsome young peasant Theodore in her escape. In fulfillment of the prophesy, Alfonso's ghost, grown too large for the castle, tears it down and rises from the ruin, proclaiming Theodore, future husband of Isabella, the true heir to Otranto.

Castle Rackrent (1800). A novel by Maria EDGEWORTH depicting the dissolute life of Irish landlords of the 18th century. A succession of irresponsible members of the Rackrent family, watched by their ineffectual tenantry, dissipate their fortunes until they reach the verge of destitution.

Castor (**Kastor**) **and Polydeuces** (**Polydeukes, Pollux**). In Greek mythology, sons of Leda and Tyndareus or Zeus, called the **Dioscuri.** Beginning with their births, their lives and adventures are told in many versions. Both may have been the mortal sons of Tyndareus, or both immortal sons of Zeus; but the commonest tale makes Castor mortal. They sailed with the Argonauts, and it was Polydeuces, a great boxer, who killed Amycus, the brutal Bebrycian king, in a boxing match. Later, they quarreled with another pair of twins, Lynceus and Idas, and in the ensuing fight, all but Polydeuces were killed. Polydeuces begged his father Zeus to let him share his immortality with his brother. This wish being granted, they either spend one day together in heaven, the next in Hades, or they alternate in spending a day in each.

Castor and Polydeuces became patron gods of mariners, appearing in St. Elmo's fire. In late myth they were identified as the constellation Gemini. Their cult became highly popular in Rome, where Polydeuces was known as Pollux.

Castorp, Hans. The central figure in Thomas Mann's novel THE MAGIC MOUNTAIN. He is a young marine engineer of middling talents, the son of a Hamburg merchant family. He is described early in the book as an "unwritten sheet of paper," by which Mann means that his personality has yet to take shape. He is essentially passive and reflects the characters and events about him, more than he acts upon them.

Castro, Inés de (c. 1310–1355). Spanish noblewoman. She was the mistress of Dom Pedro, eldest son and heir of King Alfonso IV of Portugal. Pedro married her after the death of his first wife, and Alfonso, fearful that she and her powerful family constituted a threat to the dynasty, had her put to death. Upon his accession to the throne in 1357, Pedro had her body exhumed and placed upon a throne, forcing his courtiers to render her the homage denied her in life. Her remains were later taken to Alcobaça, where a magnificent mausoleum was built. Many writers have retold her tragic story, notably Camões in Os LUSIADAS and Luis Vélez de Guevara in *Reinar Después de Morir.*

Castro Alves, Antônio de (1847–1871). Brazilian poet. The chief representative of the *condoreira* school of poets, so called because their poetic flights resembled those of the Andean condor, Castro Alves was strongly influenced by Victor Hugo, whom he acclaimed as "master of the world." A handsome, dashing youth, he was "discovered" by José de Alencar and Machado de Assis, who were impressed by his *Gonzaga* (1867), a prose drama about an abortive revolution in 18th-century Minas Gerais. After a shooting accident resulted in the loss of a foot, Castro Alves was stricken by tuberculosis, which caused his death at the age of 24. He spent his last months in the preparation of *Espumas Fluctuantes* (1870), his best-known collection. Effectively combining the ideals of romanticism with social criticism, his poetry is characterized by great verbal opulence and emotional force, though critics point out that it is often overwrought and bombastic. He is affectionately remembered by his countrymen as "the poet of the slaves," because of the ardent abolitionist sentiments he expressed in such poems as *Vozes d'Africa* and *O Navio Negreiro,* both included in the 1921 edition of *Os Escravos,* the first to follow the author's plan.

Castro y Bellvís, Guillén de (1569–1631). Spanish dramatist. A soldier turned writer, Castro was a disciple of Lope de Vega. His fame rests largely on *Mocedades del Cid* and its sequel, *Hazañas del Cid,* which were derived almost entirely from popular ballads about the medieval hero. These plays were the direct source of Corneille's *Le Cid* (1636).

Casuarina Tree, The (1926). A collection of short stories by W. Somerset MAUGHAM. Maugham successfully dramatized the title story as *The Letter* in 1927; it is the story of a white woman in Malaya who shoots her lover when he confesses that he is now in love with a Chinese woman.

cat. A domesticated feline to which many curious beliefs have adhered. It was called a "familiar," from the medieval superstition that Satan's favorite form was a black cat. Hence witches were said to have cats as their familiars.

In ancient Rome the cat was a symbol of liberty. The goddess of Liberty was represented as holding a cup in one hand, a broken scepter in the other, with a cat lying at her feet. No animal is more an enemy to all constraint than a cat.

In Egypt the cat was sacred to Isis, or the moon. It was held in great veneration and was worshiped with great ceremony as a symbol of the moon not only because it is more active after sunset but from the dilation and contraction of its pupils, symbolical of waxing and waning. The goddess Bast (Bubastis), representative of the life-giving solar heat, was portrayed as having the head of a cat, probably because that animal likes to bask in the sun. Diodorus tells us that whoever killed a cat, even by accident, was by the Egyptians punished by death, and according to Egyptian tradition, Artemis assumed the form of a cat, and thus excited the fury of the giants.

catachresis. (1) The wrong use of one word for another, as in "his action was most affective" instead of "effective."

(2) The use of an especially far-fetched figure of speech such as one involving literal impossibility or paradox, as in a mixed metaphor.

Catcher in the Rye, The (1951). A novel by J. D. SALINGER. It deals with two days in the life of Holden Caulfield, who has run away from his prep school just before the start of the Christmas vacation; unwilling to go home, he drifts about in New York, getting himself into a series of wryly humorous adventures. The sophistication and amazing but credible articulateness of this slightly unbalanced adolescent uniquely convey contemporary youth's dissatisfaction with adult society.

Catchpoles. An anglicism for the Chicanous in Rabelais' GARGANTUA AND PANTAGRUEL, who live on the Isle of Procuration. They make their living by offering to be beaten for a fee. Through these strange creatures Rabelais satirized the legal officers whose unpleasant task it was to deliver court summonses.

Câteau-Cambrésis, Treaty of. See DISASTROUS PEACE.

categorical imperative. See CRITIQUE OF PRACTICAL REASON.

Cather, Willa [Sibert] (1876–1947). American novelist. As a child, Willa Cather, who was born in Virginia, was taken to Nebraska, which later provided her with the setting for much of her finest work. After working as a newspaperwoman in Pittsburgh and as a teacher in Allegheny, Pa., she joined the staff of *McClure's Magazine* in New York City.

Miss Cather's first novel was *Alexander's Bridge* (1912), the story of an engineer, Bartley Alexander, torn between love for his wife and an actress he had known in his youth. She then wrote three excellent novels dealing with the life of the immigrant settlers in the Middle West: O PIONEERS!, THE SONG OF THE LARK, and MY ÁNTONIA. Two later novels, ONE OF OURS and A LOST LADY, are concerned with the Midwest and their characters' relation to its pioneer past. With THE PROFESSOR'S HOUSE and DEATH COMES FOR THE ARCHBISHOP, Miss Cather turned to the Southwest. Her interest in Roman Catholicism shown in the latter book was continued in SHADOWS ON THE ROCK, a novel about 18th-century Quebec. Other novels by Miss Cather are *My Mortal Enemy* (1926), *Lucy Gayheart* (1935), and *Sapphira and the Slave Girl* (1940). Her short stories and novelettes were collected in *The Troll Garden* (1905), YOUTH AND THE BRIGHT MEDUSA, *Obscure Destinies* (1932), and *The Old Beauty and Others* (1948).

In time Miss Cather's high regard for the courage and industry of the pioneers seemed to become a deep hatred for the modern world. She was, according to Maxwell Geismar, "an aristocrat in an equalitarian order, an agrarian writer in an industrial order, a defender of the spiritual graces in the midst of an increasingly materialistic culture."

Catherick, Anne. See THE WOMAN IN WHITE.

Catherine de Médicis (1519–1589). Italian-born queen of France. The great-granddaughter of Lorenzo the Magnificent, she married the future Henry II of France in 1533, and was the mother of Francis II, Charles IX, and Henry III. As regent during the minority of Charles, she intrigued with both the Huguenots and the Roman Catholic party and in 1572 persuaded him to order the MASSACRE OF ST. BARTHOLOMEW.

Catherine Parr (1512–1548). The sixth and last wife of HENRY VIII of England. Catherine took Henry as her third husband in 1543. An accomplished scholar and a woman characterized by piety and kindness, she was undoubtedly a wholesome influence on the king. She brought Mary and Elizabeth, who had been regarded as illegitimate for many years, back to court and treated them as princesses. She also tried to lessen the religious persecutions of the time. Shortly after Henry's death she married Sir Thomas Seymour, a former suitor and the uncle of the new king, Edward VI. She died after the birth of her first child in 1548.

Catherine the Great or **Catherine II (Ekaterina Alekseyevna; 1729–1796).** Empress of Russia (1762–1796). Her reign was marked by increased contact with the West. At that time, French culture was predominant in Europe and the empress herself took part in the intellectual life of the continent, corresponding regularly with Voltaire, Baron von Grimm, and Diderot. The beginning of Catherine's reign promised a liberalization of the regime in Russia. She intended to reform the legal code of the country, for this purpose composing a *Nakaz* (*Instruction*) on which the reforms were to be based. Much of the material in the *Nakaz* came from such liberal thinkers as Montesquieu and Beccaria. Catherine's liberal attitude changed as a result of the peasant uprising (1773–1774) led by Emelyan PUGACHEV and the French Revolution in 1789. The change in attitude led to the banning of satirical journals in Russia, which the empress had encouraged for a time. The primary target of the ban was Nikolai Ivanovich Novikov, whose criticism of Russian society was becoming too sharp for Catherine's taste. Novikov was imprisoned in 1791 and was freed after her death. Another victim of the empress's conservatism was Aleksandr Nikolayevich RADISHCHEV, who published his now famous *Puteshestviye iz peterburga v moskvu* (*A Journey from Petersburg to Moscow*) in 1790. Radishchev's criticisms of Russian life incensed Catherine and the author was exiled to Siberia.

Catherine's chief political achievements were the acquisition of land in the Ukraine that had been long held by Poland and the establishment of Russia's frontier on the coast of the Black Sea. Her dream of conquering Constantinople from the Turks was unfulfilled and was later taken up by other nationalist political thinkers.

Cathleen Ni Houlihan (1904). A one-act play by William Butler YEATS. It concerns a young Irish peasant who leaves his home and fiancée in order to follow a poor old woman. She is Cathleen Ni Houlihan, symbol of Ireland, who promises fame to those who help her recover her land from the strangers (the English) who have taken it. The part was written for Maud GONNE.

Cathos. One of the 2 ridiculous snobs in Molière's comedy LES PRÉCIEUSES RIDICULES.

Catiline. Full Latin name, **Lucius Sergius Catilina** (d. 62 B.C.). Roman conspirator. An able but unscrupulous patrician, Catiline organized a conspiracy of similarly desperate men to overthrow the Roman government by force. The plot was discovered by CICERO, who exposed it in his four eloquent orations: *In Catilinam*. Driven from Rome by Cicero's first speech, Catiline later fell in battle against the Roman army. He is the subject of a tragedy (1611) by Ben Jonson.

Catlin, George (1796–1872). American artist. He lived with Indians in the Middle West and in Central and South America, taking notes, gathering material, and picturing their life. His collection was placed in the National Museum in Washington and proved of great documentary value. He is the author of several books, including *Life Amongst the Indians* (1861).

Cato, Marcus Porcius. Known as **Cato the Elder** (234–149 B.C.). Roman statesman. His long public career was a constant struggle against enemies of the state abroad and moral laxity at home. As censor, Cato became the stern arbiter of Roman manners and did his utmost to suppress all innovations in thought and behavior. All that did not fit his severe code of moral rectitude he labeled "un-Roman." Despite the decisive defeat of Carthage in 202 B.C., he still regarded it as Rome's persistent enemy, and he would end each of his speeches in the Senate with the phrase *Carthago delenda est* ("Carthage must be destroyed"). In 146, three years after the death of Cato, Carthage was at last evacuated and burnt, and its rubble was leveled with ploughs and oxen.

Except for his treatise *De Re Rustica* (also known as *De Agri Cultura*), Cato's writings, including his great work on Roman history *Origines,* are now lost. His prose style was admired for its vigor and terseness.

Cato, Marcus Porcius. Known as **Cato the Younger** (95–46 B.C.). Roman statesman. The great-grandson of Cato the Elder, he is often considered the last of the Romans of the old school. Unwilling to win an election by bribing the populace, he lost it but gained the admiration of the Roman nobility. In Caesar's conflict with Pompey, Cato backed the latter and, after Pompey's defeat at Pharsalus, went with him into exile. When Caesar's legions defeated the army of the nobility in North Africa, Cato—then at Utica—took his own life. The conservative Senatorial Party went on to revere him as a saint and renamed him *Cato Uticensis* ("Cato of Utica") for his last stoic act of defiance. Of him, Lucan wrote: *Victrix causa diis placuit, sed victa Catoni!* ("The gods were pleased with the cause that won—Cato with the cause that lost!"). His death is described in Addison's tragedy *Cato* (1713).

Cat on a Hot Tin Roof (1955). A play by Tennessee WILLIAMS. It deals with the neurotic Pollitt family living in the Mississippi Delta. "Big Daddy" Pollitt is dying of cancer; Gooper, the oldest son, and his wife plot to gain the father's property. Brick, the younger son, an alcoholic ex-football star, and his wife, Maggie ("the cat"), are driven apart when Brick accuses Maggie of being responsible for his friend's death. In a confrontation with his father, Brick admits his failings and Maggie untruthfully announces that she is pregnant in an attempt to help her husband gain his inheritance. At the end of the play, the audience is left with a hope of reconciliation between Brick and Maggie. The play was awarded a Pulitzer Prize.

Cattle-Raid of Cooley, The. In Gaelic literature, an 8th-century epic tale from the ULSTER CYCLE. It is perhaps the most important of the early Irish sagas. Queen MEDB brings war against the Ulstermen, and CÚ CHULAINN alone defends the territory against her army for a long period. The most poignant moment in the tale is the combat between Cú Chulainn and his own foster brother, Ferdiad, whom he ultimately kills. This tale had considerable influence on the writers involved in the 19th-century Irish Renaissance.

Catton, Bruce (1899–). American historian and journalist. After working for various newspapers in Cleveland, Boston, and Washington, Catton entered government service in 1942 and later served as director of information for the War Production Board. From this experience came *The War Lords of Washington* (1948). He became deeply interested in the American Civil War, but it was not until 1952 that he began devoting his full time to writing Civil War history. His works in this field include *Mr. Lincoln's Army* (1951), dealing with the early years of the war; *Glory Road* (1952), relating the campaigns of 1862–1863; *A Stillness at Appomattox* (1953), which won a Pulitzer Prize; and *Grant Moves South* (1959). *The Coming Fury* (1961) and *Terrible Swift Sword* (1963), the first two volumes of his centennial history of the war, cover events from the Democratic convention at Charleston in April, 1860, to the fall of 1862.

Catullus, Gaius Valerius (87–?54 B.C.). Roman lyric poet. Born in Verona, he went to Rome as a young man. Through his charm and precocious brilliance he gained easy admittance to the refined and prodigal society of the day; through his ardent susceptibility he fell disastrously in love with a young Roman matron who became the "Lesbia" of his poems. She was the beautiful, gifted, and unscrupulous Clodia, sister of the notorious Clodius Pulcher (see CICERO). She became the dark muse of his poetry, and her life and personality are closely intertwined with the life and lyrics of Catullus.

At 30, Catullus found himself bankrupt, emotionally as well as financially, and in 57 B.C., after his final break with Clodia, he traveled to Asia with his friend Gaius Memmius, who was taking the post of propraetor of Bithynia. On his way back to Rome, a year later, he passed his brother's grave near Troy. Here he probably wrote the famous ode which ends *Frater, ave atque vale* (Brother, hail and farewell). He died himself not long afterwards, at the age of 30, or 33 at the most.

Of his poems, 116 composed in a number of lyric meters are extant. Among them are such celebrated love lyrics as *Vivamus, mea Lesbia, atque amemus* and *Odi et amo;* the mock threnody on the death of Lesbia's parrot; the *Lament of Atthis;* the miniature epic on the marriage of Peleus and Thetis; and a host of stinging epigrammatic attacks on his personal enemies.

Catullus brought many Greek rhythms into Latin literature, and was the first Roman poet to exploit fully the classical lyric meters. He exerted wide influence on subsequent poets, such as Tibullus, Propertius, Ovid, and Horace and Martial. In English literature his influence can be traced in the Elizabethan wedding odes and in the Caroline lyrics.

Caucasian Chalk Circle, The (Der kaukasische Kreidekreis; 1944–1945). A play by Bertolt BRECHT. Based on a Chinese fable (see THE CIRCLE OF CHALK), it concerns the conflict between a rich, powerful woman who has abandoned her baby son and a peasant girl who has brought him up. Both women claim the child, and the judge before whom the case is brought instructs each of them to take one of the child's hands and attempt to pull him out of a circle chalked on the floor, to show the strength of their love. The rich woman yanks with all her might and succeeds, because the peasant girl, afraid of hurting the boy, lets go. The judge, however, awards the child to the peasant girl, for he recognizes that she has shown the greater love.

Caudine Forks. A narrow pass in the mountains near Capua, now called the valley of Arpaia. It was here that the Roman army, under the consuls T. Veturius Calvinus and Sp. Postumius, fell into the hands of the Samnites (321 B.C.) and was made to pass under a yoke made up of three spears, two stuck into the ground parallel to each other and the third placed above them. The army was then allowed to depart in ignominy.

Caudwell, Christopher. Pen name of **Christopher St. John Sprigg** (1907–1937). English literary critic and writer of detective stories. His Marxist literary criticism was influential during the leftist 1930's: *Illusion and Reality* (1937). He was killed fighting with the International Brigade in the Spanish Civil War.

Cautionary Tales (1907). Verses for children by Hilaire BELLOC. They are mock-moral anecdotes about the fearful fates of children who Chew String, Tell Lies, or Bang Doors.

Cauvin, Jean. See John CALVIN.

Cavafy, Constantine P. Pen name of **C. P. Kavafis** (1863–1933). Greek poet. Though Greek culture and the Greek past is the subject of much of his finest verse, Cavafy lived most of his life in Alexandria, where he was born. During his lifetime he published only one small book of poems, which he later revised. Most of his poems were distributed only among his personal friends. They were scarcely known to readers of English until some of them were translated in 1952. Esteemed by critics as one of the finest modern Greek poets, Cavafy's work was brought to wider notice by their admiration.

There are two main classes of Cavafy's poems: narrative poems of events in the Greek past, and personal lyrics often concerned with homosexual love. In both the author's remarkable capacity for objectivity shows itself. The first, far from being heroic, are ironic in tone; the second are straightforward and unsentimental. The style and tone of Cavafy's work, expressed in simple, almost dry language, is peculiarly his own. *The Complete Poems of Cavafy*, translations by Rae Dalven, was published in 1961.

Cavalcade. See Noel COWARD.

Cavalcanti, Guido (1250–1300). Italian poet. He was one of the STILNOVISTI group and a close friend of Dante. Most of his "love songs," the *Canzone d'amore,* were addressed to a French lady named Mandetta. They were translated by Dante Gabriel Rossetti (1861) and by Ezra Pound (1911).

Cavalier, Jean. See CAMISARDS.

Cavalier of the Rose, The. See ROSENKAVALIER, DER.

Cavalier poets. English lyric poets associated with the court of Charles I, chief of whom were Robert HERRICK, Thomas CAREW, John SUCKLING, and Richard LOVELACE. They are best known as writers of frank, high-spirited, gracefully fanciful love poems and songs. See SONS OF BEN.

Cavalleria Rusticana (Rustic Chivalry). An opera by Pietro MASCAGNI (1890) based on a novella by Giovanni VERGA.

Cavender's House (1929). A narrative poem by Edwin Arlington ROBINSON. It tells how Cavender, who pushed his wife off a cliff because he suspected her of infidelity, is still uncertain of her guilt 12 years later.

Cavendish, Margaret. Duchess of Newcastle (1624?–1674). English noblewoman, one of the outstanding writers of her sex in the 17th century, known for her eccentricity of dress and behavior. She wrote prolifically, producing 13 printed books. Her best-known work is her *Sociable Letters* (1664), presenting a vivid picture of her times. She also wrote *The Life of William Cavendish* (1667), a biography of her husband, the duke of Newcastle, who had been a devoted follower of both Charles I and Charles II.

Caves du Vatican, Les. See LAFCADIO's ADVENTURES.

Cavour, Conte **Camillo Benso di** (1810–1861). Italian statesman. Named prime minister of Sardinia in 1852, he devoted himself to the cause of Italian unification. His efforts saw fruition in 1861 when Victor Emmanuel II of Sardinia became king of all Italy excepting Rome and Venetia.

Cawdor, and Other Poems (1928). A collection of poems by Robinson JEFFERS. *Cawdor,* the title poem, is based on the story of Phaedra and Hippolytus; it deals with the desire of Fera Cawdor for her stepson, Hood, who rejects her advances. Cawdor, suspecting the boy has seduced Fera, kills him. Later Cawdor learns that Hood was innocent, and suffers from his inability to expiate his guilt.

Cawein, Madison [Julius] (1865–1914). American poet. He is best known for his *Kentucky Poems* (1902), a selection published in England with a laudatory introduction by Edmund Gosse. He wrote more than 30 books, including *Blooms of the Berry* (1887) and *The Cup of Comus* (1915).

Caxton, William (c. 1422–1491). The first English printer, also an important translator. He moved to Bruges, where he established himself as a dealer in textiles, remaining active in commerce until about 1470, even serving as governor (1465–1469) of the English Association of Merchant Adventurers in the Low Countries. Between 1469 and 1471 he translated a French romance about the Trojan War, then, to meet the great demand for the book, set about learning the new art of printing, probably with Colard Mansion at a press in Bruges. In 1474 or 1475 his *Recuyell of the Historyes of Troye* became the first book ever printed in English. The second was *The Game and Playe of the Chesse* (1475), which he had also translated from the French.

Caxton established a printing press in Westminster when he moved to England in 1476, and thereafter printed nearly 80 books, including the *Mirrour of the World* (1481), *The Golden Legend* (1483), Malory's *Morte d'Arthur* (1485), and the works of Boethius, Geoffrey Chaucer, and John Gower. Many of the books were his own translations from the French, including a great many of the Carolingian and Arthurian romances. What Caxton chose to print naturally became the staple reading matter for the English reading public of his time. His assistant Wynkyn de Worde became his successor after his death, reprinting many of Caxton's most popular titles.

Caxtons, The (1849). A novel by Edward BULWER-LYTTON. Along with its sequels, *My Novel* (1853) and *What Will He Do with It* (1858), it narrates the history of an upper middle-class English family. The story is supposed to be written by

Caxton's advertisement, which he printed in 1477. It is thought to be the earliest English broadside.

Pisistratus Caxton. His father, Austin Caxton, is an impractical philosopher and scholar, lost in vague dreams and plans for his proposed masterpiece on *The History of Human Error*. The launching of this magnum opus is finally made possible by the money that Pisistratus brings back from Australia. Others of the Caxton family are the gay, irresponsible Uncle Jack, who is an inveterate and not too lucky promoter; the fine old soldier, Captain Roland, also an uncle of Pisistratus; and Roland's son Herbert, a wild young man with gypsy blood in his veins, who dies a heroic death in India.

Cayrol, Jean (1911–   ). French poet and novelist. The novel trilogy *Je vivrai l'amour des autres* (1947–1950) depicts a Lazarus figure, a wandering beggar who assumes the miseries of the world. This theme is continued in the essay *Lazare parmi nous* (1950) and in many of his poems, such as *Pour tous les temps* (1955). Other works include *Poèmes de la Nuit et du Brouillard* (1945) and *Passetemps de l'homme et des oiseaux* (1947).

Cecchi, Giovanni Maria or **Giammaria** (1518–1587). Florentine notary and wool merchant who was also one of the first professional Italian playwrights. He wrote some 50 comedies, farces, and religious plays, his best being the comedy *L'Assiuolo* (*The Horned Owl*).

Čech, Svatopluk (1846–1908). A Czech epic poet and satirist. He celebrated Slavic traits and democratic ideals in his epic poems, though his novels were mildly satirical. Perhaps his best work, however, was in his lyrics.

Cecil, Lord [Edward Christian] David [Gascoyne] (1902–   ). English literary critic and biographer. Among his urbane studies are *Early Victorian Novelists* (1934); *The Young Melbourne* (1939); *Lord M.* (1954), the second part of his biography of Melbourne; and *The Fine Art of Reading* (1957).

Cecil, William. See William Cecil BURGHLEY.

Cecilia, St. A Roman lady who underwent martyrdom in the 3d century. She is the patron saint of the blind, being herself blind; also patroness of musicians, and inventor of the organ. According to tradition an angel fell in love with her for her musical skill, and used nightly to visit her. Her husband saw the heavenly visitant, who thereupon gave to both a crown of martyrdom, which he brought from Paradise. Dryden and Pope have written odes in her honor, and both speak of her charming an angel by her musical powers. See SECOND NUN'S TALE.

Cecilia, or Memoirs of an Heiress (1782). A novel by Fanny BURNEY. In order to keep her fortune, Cecilia Beverly, an heiress of somewhat inferior birth, must marry a man who will adopt her name. Mortimer Delvile loves her, but his family is proud of its antiquity and only he can perpetuate its name. Their love is thwarted by this and other obstacles, particularly the schemes and prejudices of those who wish to make use of Cecilia for their own ends. The two finally marry secretly, but further misunderstanding separates them until Delvile locates her by placing an advertisement in the "agony column" of the daily newspaper.

Cecrops (**Kekrops**). The traditional founder of Athens and first king of Attica. Supposed to have sprung from the ground, he was represented as half man, half serpent.

Cela, Camilo José (1916–   ). Spanish novelist. *La familia de Pascual Duarte* (1942), his first novel, was a huge success both in Spain and abroad. The tale, an example of the TREMENDISMO technique, presents the self-narrated account of the life of a murderer awaiting execution. Cela is also known for his social satire *La colmena* (*The Hive*, 1951) and is considered one of the most able of contemporary Spanish writers.

Celebrated Jumping Frog of Calaveras County, The (1865). A story by Mark TWAIN. It is based on an actual event reported in the California newspapers. Jim Smiley, a miner, bets that his frog, Dan'l Webster, can outjump any other. A stranger accepts the dare; while Jim is distracted, he pours quail shot into Dan'l. The story, reprinted many times, appeared in Clemens' first book, a collection of tales called *The Celebrated Jumping Frog* (1867).

Celestial City. See PILGRIM'S PROGRESS.

Celestina, La (1499). The popular title of *La tragicomedia de Calisto y Melibea,* a Spanish novel in dialogue by an anonymous author. The oldest known edition, dating from 1499, contains 16 acts which were increased to 21 in a 1502 edition. There is some doubt as to the author of the first act and of the 1502 additions, but it is generally agreed that Acts 2–16 were written by Fernando de Rojas, a lawyer and converted Jew from Toledo who served as *alcalde mayor,* or chief magistrate, of Talavera.

The plot deals with the noble young Calisto and his love for Melibea. When she proves cold to his advances, he enlists the aid of Celestina, an unscrupulous, self-seeking crone, who persuades Melibea to relent. Just when the romance is progressing smoothly, Calisto is killed by a fall from a ladder. In despair, Melibea flings herself from a tower to her death.

Most of the interest in the novel centers about the demonic figure of the go-between Celestina. Although the young lovers move in a world of idealized passion, Celestina and the servants, prostitutes, and other low-life characters who surround her give a coarse but vivid picture of the common people of 15th-century Spain.

Unsuitable for the stage because of its length, the *Celestina* strongly influenced Spanish writers, notably Lope de Vega. It was widely translated, the English version (1631) by James Mabbe being especially well known. See Juan RUIZ.

Celeus (**Keleos**). In Greek legend, a king of Eleusis, husband of Metanira. He sheltered DEMETER when she was wandering in search of her daughter. In return, Demeter wished to give his son Demophon immortality. When Metanira objected to her placing the infant in the fire to immortalize him, Demeter angrily revealed herself as a goddess. She instituted the famous ELEUSINIAN MYSTERIES and bestowed on Celeus' other son TRIPTOLEMUS the honor of being mankind's teacher in the use of the plough.

Celia. The very virtuous, naïve young wife of Corvino in Jonson's comedy VOLPONE, OR THE FOX. Inexperienced in the ways of the world, she is victimized by the lecherous Volpone, by the jealous Lady Politick Would-Be, and above all by her own greedy husband.

Celia. Rosalind's cousin, daughter of Duke Frederick, in Shakespeare's As You Like It. She is a merry young lady who cheerfully follows her cousin into banishment for the sake of their friendship and eventually weds Oliver.

Célimène. In Molière's comedy Le Misanthrope, a coquette courted by Alceste, the misanthropist. Hence, the name has become a synonym for any flagrant coquette.

Céline, Louis-Ferdinand. Pen name of the doctor **Louis-Ferdinand Destouches** (1894–1961). French novelist. Celine is known for the misanthropic invective of Journey to the End of the Night (1932) and Death on the Installment Plan (Mort à crédit; 1936), which expose almost everything as either evil or insane. He looked to communism, but after a trip to Russia renounced it in Mea Culpa (1937). He turned to fascism with the violently anti-Semitic diatribe Bagatelles pour un massacre (1937) and the attack on the "degenerate" French in Ecole des cadavres (1938). When he returned from his exile in Germany, he wrote D'un château l'autre (1957) and Nord (1960).

Cellini, Benvenuto (1500–1571). Florentine goldsmith, sculptor, and author of one of the world's great autobiographies. First published in 1730, the work was actually begun in 1558, when Cellini started dictating his memoirs to an apprentice. It tells of his adventures in Italy and France, his relations with popes and kings and with fellow artists, his production of works like the Perseus statue. A fairly complete picture of the times emerges from the work, though exaggerated by the author's distortion of his own role in events. Its realism, vivid descriptions, racy style, and, above all, its portrait of a genuine personality have exerted a strong influence on historians of the Renaissance, as Burkhardt, who see it as confirming the view that the key to the period is the emergence of modern individualism. Goethe's translation and Berlioz' musical interpretation are examples of its continuing impact on other artists.

Cement (Tzement; 1925). A novel by Feodor Vasilyevich Gladkov. The book was one of the first to deal with the problems of reconstruction and industrialization in Russia after the civil war. It is now ranked as one of the early Soviet classics.

Cénacle. In 19th-century France, the name of a literary and political group meeting in the salon of Charles Nodier and, later, the name of a similar group led by Victor Hugo. Honoré de Balzac made use of this designation in some of the novels of his La Comédie Humaine; among the most active members of this fictional cénacle were Daniel d' Arthez, Henri de Marsay, and Horace Bianchon.

Cena de Baltazar, La (Belshazzar's Feast). An auto sacramental by Pedro Calderón de la Barca. Heedless of the prophet Daniel's call to repentance, Belshazzar, king of Babylon, revels with his wives Vanity and Idolatry and his jester, Thought. He is finally struck down by Death.

Cenci, Beatrice (1577–1599). A historical personage. She is known as the Beautiful Parricide, from a famous portrait in Rome's Barberini palace attributed to Guido Reni. She was the daughter of Francesco Cenci (1549–1598), a choleric, cruel, and vice-laden Roman nobleman. With her mother and two brothers, Beatrice successfully plotted the death of her father at the hands of hired bravos. It is possible, however, that the immediate provocation of the murder was Francesco's discovery of his daughter's intimacy with one of the family's stewards.

The plot was revealed by one of the bravos, and the conspirators were brought to trial. Great sympathy was aroused by the plight of the young, beautiful Beatrice, and her attorney attempted to play upon this by falsely claiming that Francesco had tried to commit incest with her. However, Pope Clement VIII refused the sought-for pardon and on September 11, 1599 Beatrice was beheaded. Her story has been a favorite theme of poetry and art, the most famous use being Shelley's tragedy The Cenci (1819), in which she is treated sympathetically.

Cendrars, Blaise (1887–1961). French poet and novelist. An innovator in his verse forms, he was lyrical even in his prose, especially in the autobiographical L'Homme foudroyé (1945). His novels of adventure include Le Panama ou les Aventures de mes sept oncles (Panama, or, The Adventures of my Seven Uncles, 1919), L'Or (Sutter's Gold, 1925), Moravagine (1926), Rhum (1930), and Bourlinguer (1948).

censor. In ancient Rome, a magistrate of high rank. His duty was to take the census, see that Senate vacancies were filled, take inventory on government finances, allot government contracts for public works, and investigate and, if necessary, correct the state of public morality. Originally, two censors were elected for a five-year period, called a lustrum; in 433 B.C., the term of office was shortened to 18 months. As a distinct office, the censorship disappeared in the reign of Domitian (84 A.D.).

Centaurs (Kentauroi). In classic mythology, beings who were half horse and half man. They fought with the Lapiths at the marriage feast of Pirithous, were expelled from their country, and took refuge on Mount Pindus. Chiron was the most famous of the centaurs. Both Lapiths and Centaurs are thought to have been actual Thessalian tribes.

Centlivre, Mrs. Susannah (1667–1723). English dramatist and actress. She wrote a number of comedies of intrigues such as The Busy Body (1709), The Wonder, a Woman Keeps a Secret (1714), and A Bold Stroke for a Wife (1718).

Cent nouvelles nouvelles, Les (1462). A collection of prose tales by an unknown member of the court of Philip of Burgundy. Modeled on Boccaccio's Decameron (1353) and Poggio's Facetiae (early 15th century), the stories are comic, often licentious, anecdotes purportedly told by the members of the court.

cento (Lat., a patchwork). A literary composition, especially a poem, of lines or parts from the writings of established authors, and with a meaning and message different from the original. Centos were freely produced during the decadent period of Greece and Rome; Ausonius (c. 310–395), who put together the scandalous Cento Nuptialis with lines taken from Vergil, enunciated rules concerning their composition. Among well-known examples are the Homerocentones, taken by Byzantine compilers from Homer, the Cento Vergilianus by Proba Falconia (4th century), which used Vergil to relate Biblical history, and the Christian hymns devised by the monk

Metellus (12th century) from the works of Vergil and Horace.

Central Powers. In World War I, Germany and her allies: Austria-Hungary, Bulgaria, Turkey.

Century of Louis the Great, The. See Charles PERRAULT.

Cephalus (Kephalos) and Procris. In classic legend, Cephalus was Procris' husband. She deserted him, out of jealousy. Searching for her, he rested a while under a tree. Procris, knowing of his whereabouts, crept through some bushes to ascertain if a rival was with him; and he, hearing the noise and thinking it to be made by some wild beast, hurled his javelin into the bushes and slew her. When the unhappy man discovered what he had done, he slew himself in anguish of spirit with the same javelin.

Cerberus (Kerberos). In Greek mythology, the three-headed dog, keeper of the entrance of the infernal regions. Heracles dragged the monster to earth to show him to Eurystheus, and then took him back. The Sibyl who conducted Aeneas through the lower world threw the dog into a profound sleep with a cake seasoned with poppies and honey (*Aeneid* vi, 417–425). The phrase *give a sop to Cerberus* therefore means to give a bribe, to quiet a troublesome person.

Ceres. An Italian goddess of fertility, later identified with the Greek DEMETER.

Cerf, Bennett [Alfred] (1898–1971), American publisher and editor. In 1925, with Donald S. Klopfer, Cerf bought the Modern Library series of inexpensive reprints of the classics from Boni and Liveright. He made the series a tremendous success and added many new titles over the years. In 1927 he and Klopfer founded Random House, which merged with Harrison Smith and Robert Haas in 1936 and has published many noted writers. Cerf has compiled and edited a number of books, many of them anthologies of humor.

Cernuda, Luis (1904–   ). Spanish poet. His early works include *Perfil del aire* (1927), and *La invitación a la poesía* (1933). These have been described as romantic, but possess a strain of hardy intellectualism. Cernuda left Spain during the revolution, traveling to the continent and later to England. In 1947 he was a member of the faculty of Mount Holyoke College. His recent work includes the prose poem *Ocnos* (1943) and *Tres narraciones* (1948).

Cervantes [Saavedra], Miguel de (1547–1616). Spanish novelist, dramatist, and poet. Born in Alcalá de Henares, Cervantes came from a good though impecunious family. Little is known of his education except that in 1568 he was a student of the Madrid humanist Juan López de Hoyos, who edited an elegaic volume on the death of Queen Isabel de Valois to which Cervantes contributed some verses. In 1569 he went to Italy, became a soldier, and fought in the battle of Lepanto (1571), in which he acquitted himself with distinction and lost the use of his left hand; he was extremely proud of his role in the famous victory and of the nickname he had earned, *el manco de Lepanto*. As Cervantes was returning to Spain with his brother on the galley *El Sol* in 1575, the ship was captured by Barbary pirates, and the two brothers were taken to Algiers as slaves. Miguel remained in captivity for five years, during which he made several romantic if futile efforts to escape. His ransom of 500 ducats was finally paid by the Trinitarian friars.

Having returned to Spain, Cervantes married Catalina de Salazar y Palacios in 1584, fathered an illegitimate daughter, and in 1587 secured employment as a purchasing agent for the navy. In this capacity he traveled throughout the country, often becoming involved in disputes with communities reluctant to part with their crops; on one occasion he was excommunicated for seizing grain that belonged to the church. Twice he was imprisoned for debt.

In 1605 Cervantes and his family, who were then living in Valladolid, were accused of complicity in the death of a young nobleman. They were later absolved, but the records of the case give evidence of the poverty and wretchedness of Cervantes' mode of existence at the time. His position improved considerably, however, after the publication of the first part of DON QUIXOTE in the same year. Although Cervantes' previous literary efforts had met with little success, *Don Quixote* immediately caught the fancy of the reading public. Moving to Madrid, he devoted his last years to writing.

Cervantes' reputation as one of the greatest writers in history rests almost entirely on *Don Quixote* and on the 12 short stories known as the NOVELAS EJEMPLARES. His literary production, however, was considerable. *La Galatea* (1585), a pastoral romance, was his first long work; similar in form and content to other novels of this type, it received little contemporary notice and is remembered largely because of its authorship. Cervantes repeatedly promised to write a continuation, but it never appeared.

He next turned his attention to the stage and wrote between 20 and 30 plays in the years immediately following 1585. Two extant dramas of this period are *El trato de Argel* and *La Numancia,* both of which were first printed in 1784. The former, dealing with the life of Christian slaves in Algiers, is of interest only because of its autobiographical details. The latter, which recounts the siege and capture of Numantia by the Romans under Scipio Africanus, has won wider approbation, partly because of some powerful scenes and partly because of its expressions of patriotism. In 1615 Cervantes published his *Ocho comedias, y ocho entremeses nuevos.* Only one of the full-length plays, *Pedro de Urdemalas,* has met with critical favor, but the *entremeses,* or interludes, are highly regarded for their sprightly and realistic pictures of Bohemian life.

Cervantes himself realized that he was deficient in poetic gifts, a judgment confirmed by later generations. Aside from his plays, his most ambitious work in verse is the *Viaje del Parnaso* (1614), an allegory which consists largely of a rather tedious though good-natured review of contemporary poets. *Los trabajos de Persiles y Sigismunda* (1617) is a verse romance in the manner of Heliodorus, which Cervantes thought would be either the worst or the best book in the Spanish language. Though some critics have boggled at the fantastic geography of its early scenes and the incredible adventures of its characters, others have praised its polished style.

Regardless of its merits, the *Persiles* will be remembered, if only for its dedication and prologue. Addressed to the conde de Lemos, the dedication was signed on April 19, 1616, just four days before Cervantes' death. Quoting an old ballad, *Puesto ya el pié en el estribo* ("One foot already in the stirrup"), Cervantes takes leave of his patron and of the world with the same gallantry and grace that characterized both his life and his work.

César Birotteau, Histoire de la grandeur et de la décadence de (1837). A novel by Honoré de BALZAC. The title character is a perfume dealer who is admitted to the Legion of Honor. Dazzled by the honor, he gives a lavish ball to celebrate the event. This necessitates the complete remodeling of his home, and as a result of all this expense and of several unwise investments, he is completely ruined. Within three years he is able to pay his debts, but, ironically, he dies soon afterward. The novel, which forms part of LA COMÉDIE HUMAINE, is said to reflect Balzac's own unhappy experiences in business.

Cesbron, Gilbert (1913–   ). French novelist, essayist, and dramatist. His novels usually have moral and social themes. *Saints in Hell* (*Les Saints vont en enfer;* 1952) concerns the struggles of worker-priests in Paris, and *Lost Children of Paris* (*Chiens perdus sans collier;* 1954) is about juvenile delinquency. Other works include the novels *The Innocents of Paris* (1944), *La Tradition Fontquernie* (1947), *Avoir Eté* (1960), and the play *No Plaster Saint* (*Briser la statue;* 1952).

Céspedes, Alba de (1911–   ). Italian writer. Her novels sympathetically explore the position of the modern Italian woman. Her best-known novel, *Il Quaderno Proibito* (*The Secret,* 1954), concerns the gradual deterioration of a marriage; it is written in the form of a diary kept secretly by the wife.

cestus (kestos). (1) The girdle of Aphrodite, made by her husband Hephaestus. It was reputed to possess magical power to move to ardent love. By a poetical fiction, all women of irresistible attraction are supposed to be wearers of Aphrodite's girdle, or the *cestus.* It is introduced by Spenser in *The Faerie Queene* as the girdle of Florimel. It gave to those who could wear it "the virtue of chaste love and wifehood true," but if any woman not chaste and faithful put it on, it "loosed or tore asunder." (2) The *cestus* in Roman games was a covering for the hands of boxers, made of leather bands and often loaded with lead or iron.

Cézanne, Paul (1839–1906). French painter. The great master of postimpressionism and perhaps the greatest figure in modern French painting, Cézanne was born in Aix-au-Provence, the son of a banker. His early works were low in key and heavy in medium, but after 1870 he began to paint out of doors and allied himself with the impressionists. By 1876 he had already begun to accentuate mass, rather than light, in an effort to achieve a better illusion of volume. Cézanne's statement that "Nature must be treated through the cylinder, the sphere, the cone," summarizes his desire "to make of impressionism something as solid and durable as the painting in the museums." This search led him to displace visual planes, to raise the horizon, to construct his paintings in such a way that each departure from nature would increase the impression of form and depth. He retained the pure colors of impressionism, but used them to build up volume through the contrast of tones. He spent much of his life as a recluse in Provence, painting the famous still lifes, landscapes,

and portraits, that were then unknown except to a few of his contemporaries. It was not until the last decade of the century that his reputation began to grow. Cézanne is said to have been in the mind of Emile Zola, his former schoolmate and friend, during the composition of *L'Œuvre* (1886); Zola represents his hero as a restless painter and failure.

Chaadayev, Piotr Yakovlevich (1794–1856). Russian philosophical thinker. He is famous for his *Philosophical Letters* which unfavorably compared Russia's past and present condition to that of the Western nations. The publication of the first letter in 1836 brought down a storm of abuse and police persecution on Chaadayev, who was officially declared insane and put under house arrest for a time.

Chadband, Rev. Mr. In Charles Dickens' BLEAK HOUSE, a typical, canting hypocrite "in the ministry."

Chagall, Marc (1889–   ). Russian-born French painter. From his earliest paintings, scenes of Russian village life, he developed an individualistic style of great poetry, fantasy, and brightness, typified by his pair of lovers floating over, or nesting in, large bouquets of flowers. With World War II, he introduced social and religious elements in his art, painting numerous crucifixions. He designed theatrical scenery and stained-glass windows, and illustrated Nikolai Gogol's *Dead Souls* (1948) and the *Fables* of La Fontaine (1952).

Chairs, The (*Les Chaises;* 1951). A tragic farce by Eugène IONESCO. It presents a Kafka-like image of modern man. An old lighthouse keeper, preparing to die, invites a group of guests to a gathering where his final words of wisdom will be delivered. In a scene that is both a dramatic and a symbolic *tour de force,* he and his wife rush desperately about to seat an enormous crowd of imaginary guests. The bare, empty stage juxtaposed with the frenzied human effort offer an absurd image of modern man, isolated, frustrated, and unable to order the chaos of life. A final irony, ludicrous and bitter, is the audience's discovery that the orator can neither read nor write.

Chakravakas. Sanskrit for red geese or sheldrake, favorite symbols with classical Indian writers. In legend, these birds were supposed to be ideally happy during the daytime, but at night a curse separated them and they bewailed each other's absence from the opposite banks of a river.

Chalciope (Chalkiope). See GOLDEN FLEECE, THE.

Chalcondyles, Demetrius (d. 1511). Greek editor of classical texts. He prepared early and influential editions of Homer (1488) and Euripides (1493). Also a scholar and teacher at Padova, Florence, and Milan, he numbered among his students Castiglione, Reuchlin, Trissino, and the future Pope Leo X.

Chaliapin, Feodor Ivanovitch (1873–1938). Russian basso, famed for his acting as well as his singing, especially in the title role of *Boris Godunov.* He wrote two volumes of memoirs: *Pages from My Life* (1926) and *Man and Mask* (1932).

Challenger, Professor. An adventurous, iconoclastic, rather opinionated scientist of imposing girth who appears in Conan DOYLE'S *The Lost World* (1912). Doyle regarded him as his most amusing character.

Chambered Nautilus, The (1858). A poem by Oliver Wendell HOLMES. The sea creature that enlarges its shell as it grows is an example to the human being:

Build thee more stately mansions, O my soul,
. . . .
Leaving thine outgrown shell by life's unresting sea!

Chamberlain, Houston Stewart (1855–1927). British-born political philosopher who became a German citizen in 1916. His *Foundations of the Nineteenth Century* (*Die Grundlagen des neunzehnten Jahrhunderts;* 1899), a historical defense of the superiority of the Germanic race, contains anti-Semitic theories that were later developed by the NAZIS. See ARYAN RACE.

Chamberlain, Neville (1869–1940). Conservative prime minister of England from 1937 to 1940. He is remembered chiefly for his role in the Munich meeting with Hitler in September, 1938, in which he pursued a policy of appeasement. For a time, his name became synonymous with betrayal in the writing of Marxists and liberals, who considered that he had delivered Czechoslovakia into the hands of the Nazis. He was succeeded in office by Winston Churchill.

Chamber Music (1907). A volume of poems, mainly love lyrics, by James JOYCE. They show the influence of the Elizabethan poets and of the early William Butler Yeats and his circle.

Chambers, Charles Haddon (1860–1921). Australian playwright. His best comedy, *The Tyranny of Tears* (1902), was produced by Charles Wyndham.

Chambers, Sir E[dmund] K[erchever] (1866–1954). English literary scholar. His books on *The Medieval Stage* (1903), *The Elizabethan Stage* (1923), and *William Shakespeare* (1930) are among the standard works on the subjects.

Chamisso, Adalbert von (1781–1838). German poet and botanist. He is famous for his ballads and the story, PETER SCHLEMIHLS WUNDERSAME GESCHICHTE. He was one of the first poets to turn away from the unswerving idealism of earlier GERMAN ROMANTICISM, and to write with a genuine love for the common people; for example, he wrote poems about beggars and washerwomen. He was appointed botanist to a Russian ship and published a diary of his expedition around the world. He was custodian of the botanical gardens in Berlin.

Champion, or British Mercury, The (1739–1741). A tri-weekly periodical edited by Henry FIELDING under the pseudonym of Captain Hercules Vinegar. Modeled on Richard Steele's *Tatler,* it was predominantly a vehicle of opposition to the government of Sir Robert Walpole.

Champlain, Samuel de (1567–1635). French explorer. He discovered and explored Lake Champlain and in 1608 founded the colony of Quebec.

Champollion, Jean François (1790–1832). Famous French Egyptologist. As a result of his study of the Rosetta Stone, he obtained a clue for deciphering Egyptian hieroglyphics.

Chamson, André (1900–   ). French novelist and essayist. At first a regional writer of the Protestant Cévennes area—he has written poems in Provençal—he became famous for his novels *Roux le Bandit* (1925), *Les Hommes de la route* (1927),

and *Le Crime des Justes* (1928), all translated by Van Wyck Brooks. As a result of his widening interest in ethical and political problems he wrote *La Galère* (1939); *Le Puits des miracles* (1945), an account of life during the German Occupation; *L'Homme qui marchait devant moi* (1948); *La Neige et la fleur* (1951); and *Le Chiffre de nos jours* (1954).

Chan, Charlie. A shrewd Chinese detective living in Hawaii who appears in several stories by Earl Derr Biggers (1884–1933). Given to wise, philosophical reflections, Chan acts on the assumption that if he can understand a man's character, he can predict his actions in any given circumstance. He first appeared in *The House Without a Key* (1925). Later Chan stories include: *The Chinese Parrot* (1926); *Behind That Curtain* (1929); *Charlie Chan Carries On* (1930); *Keeper of the Keys* (1932).

Chanakya (3rd century B.C.). Author of the Sanskrit *Chanakya-niti* or *The Laws of Chanakya* and the well-known *Artha-shastra,* an elaborate explanation of the science of national economics and statecraft. He was the minister of Emperor Chandragupta Maurya and is sometimes called Vishnugupta or Kautilya.

Ch'an Buddhism. Japanese ZEN. The Meditation School in China. Meditation was widely used in all forms of BUDDHISM in India and China, but Ch'an was the first to put almost exclusive emphasis on it. Traditionally Bodhidharma (fifth century) is given as the founder in China, and the sixth patriarch, Hui-neng (d. 713), is honored as the developer of the sect as a religion. The actual history is unclear, but by the T'ang Dynasty (618–906) Ch'an had gained great popularity and there were numerous teachers throughout China. Ch'an advocates "direct seeing into one's own mind" and realizing Buddhahood in oneself. It emphasizes the teacher-disciple relationship and transmission from mind to mind rather than through written words. After the persecutions of Buddhists (845) it became the dominant school in China. By the Sung period (960–1279) it had split into various sects and an organized church had been developed. It was the Ch'an of this time that was transmitted to Japan, together with the elaborate KOAN system. The two principal branches are Lin-chi (Japanese *Rinzai*) and Ts'ao-tung (Japanese *Sōtō*), both of which flourish in Japan today. By the Ming period (1368–1644) Ch'an had lost its vitality and became mixed with the Pure Land School, or Amidism.

Chance (1913). A novel by Joseph CONRAD. Flora de Barral marries Captain Roderick Anthony, and she and her father put to sea with him on the *Ferndale.* Flora fears that her husband has married her only out of pity, because her father is a broken man, a financier just out of prison for fraud. She is a tortured soul, suffering from an obsessional relationship with her father. Finally De Barral's attempt to poison Anthony, discovered and thwarted by mere "chance," clarifies the situation. Most of the story is told by MARLOW.

Chance Acquaintance, A (1873). A novel by William Dean HOWELLS. Kitty Ellison falls in love with Miles Arbuton, a young Bostonian, while they travel on the St. Lawrence River. They become engaged, but Miles, meeting some fashionable and snobbish friends, ignores Kitty. She breaks the engagement, knowing she cannot be happy with a Boston Brahmin.

Chancellor, Olive. See BOSTONIANS, THE.

Chancellorsville, battle of (May 2–4, 1863). In U.S. history, a Civil War battle near Fredericksburg, Va., in which the Union army under Gen. Joseph Hooker was defeated by Confederate forces under Gen. Robert E. Lee. Thomas ("Stonewall") Jackson, the Confederate general, was accidentally shot by his own men during the battle and died of pneumonia on May 10. This battle is said to have furnished the background for Stephen Crane's *Red Badge of Courage* (1895).

Chand, Prem. Pen name of Nawab Rai (1880–1936). Greatest short-story writer and novelist in Hindi. His early work was written in the Urdu language, but lack of a sufficiently large audience made him write his best novels in Hindi. *Seva-Sadan* (1907) describes the predicament of an innocent wife forced into prostitution. *Premashran* (1922) depicts the conflicting interests of tenant and landlord. *Nirmala* (1923) deplores the evils of the dowry system. *Ranga-bhumi* (1924) attacks the depredations of capitalists. *Karma-buhmi* (1925) is a strong indictment of British colonial rule in India. Prem Chand's work, loaded with social content, finds its best expression in his last novel, *Godan (The Cow-Gift;* 1936), a harrowing tale of the difficulties of the life of the Indian peasant. To critics who complained of the propagandistic "realism" in his writings, he explained that he wrote with "a touch of humanity, a poetic nuance. These make a story. All else fails."

Chandala (*Sans.,* outcaste). In India the child of a Sudra father and a Brahmin mother. See CASTE.

Chandler, Raymond (1888–1959). American detective-story writer. A master of the hard-boiled, though literate, crime story, Chandler was the creator of the private detective Philip Marlowe. His best-known novels include *The Big Sleep* (1939), *Farewell, My Lovely* (1940), and *The Long Goodbye* (1954). *The Simple Art of Murder* (1950), a collection of short stories and novelettes, contains an excellent and well-known essay on the writing of crime fiction.

Changeling, The (c. 1623). A tragedy by Thomas MIDDLETON and William ROWLEY. Beatrice Joanna, a young noblewoman betrothed to Alonzo De Piracquo, falls in love with Alsemero, a Venetian gentleman. After postponing the wedding she calls in Deflores, the ugly servant of her father whom she has always despised, and enlists his aid in killing Alonzo. After Deflores, who adores Beatrice Joanna, has dispatched Alonzo, he claims her person as his reward. Horrified, she refuses, but Deflores, a desperate man, swears to tell all unless she becomes his mistress. Trapped, she agrees. She marries Alsemero but, fearful of exposure, substitutes her virginal servant Diaphanta in the bridal bed. When Diaphanta lingers too long, Deflores sets fire to the house and kills the girl in her burning chamber. But by this time, Beatrice Joanna and Deflores have been found out. Confronted by Alsemero, they confess, and Deflores kills both Beatrice and himself.

Channing, Edward Tyrell (1790–1856). American editor and teacher. One of the famous Channings of New England, Edward Tyrell Channing practiced law and helped to found and edit the *North American Review* (1815), one of the most important American review magazines. As Boylston Professor of Rhetoric at Harvard, he had great influence on literature; among those he guided were Emerson, Thoreau, Holmes, Lowell, Edward Everett Hale, and R. H. Dana, Jr. Dana edited Channing's *Lectures* (1856). These reveal that he taught his students to dispense with ornament in style.

Channing, William Ellery (1780–1842). American clergyman. An ordained Congregational minister, he came to reject Calvinism, especially its emphasis on the depravity of mankind. At the ordination of Jared Sparks in 1819, he delivered a sermon that led to the formal emergence of Unitarianism, and he became the apostle of the movement. An advocate of abolition and other social reforms, he was one of the leading propagandists of the era. His ideas are believed to have contributed to the development of Transcendentalism.

cha-no-yu. Japanese tea ceremony. It arose during the Muromachi period (1333–1600) and was brought to its highest refinement by Sen no Rikyū (1521–1591), a Zen priest. There are many schools of tea ceremony, and during the Tokugawa period (1600–1868) it was greatly refined and elaborated. It consists of the drinking of thick green tea served in tea bowls, often of great artistic merit, under an elaborate ceremonial etiquette supervised by a tea master. Simplicity, harmony, and quietude form its basic spirit.

Chanson de Roland. See ROLAND.

chansons de geste (*Fr.* songs of deeds). The medieval French metrical romances celebrating the heroic deeds of historical and legendary knights. The epics of the 11th and early 12th centuries were divided into lays (Fr., *laiss*) or stanzas of irregular length, usually with 10-syllable lines united by assonance or a single rhyme. They glorified the code of chivalric honor in battle and gave little place to women. By the 13th and 14th centuries the role of women and romantic love became more important, regular rhyme schemes were introduced, and the alexandrine (12-syllable line), which later became the standard for French classical verse, became popular.

Most of the *chansons de geste* were written by TROUVÈRES about the PALADINS of Charlemagne or the knights who were his enemies, and arranged in cycles according to the ancestor of each group of heroes. They were sung by JONGLEURS and court minstrels.

One of the earliest and best was the *Chanson de* ROLAND. Other groups center on Charlemagne's childhood, his wars in Spain, his pilgrimage to Jerusalem. There is an important cycle about *Garin de Monglane* and his descendants, including the chanson *Girard de Viane,* which describes Roland's meeting with OLIVIER. Another is the *Geste de* DOON DE MAYANCE, grouping the traitors and the families at war with Charlemagne.

Chanticleer. See under NUN'S PRIEST'S TALE.

chanties. See SHANTIES.

chant royal. An elaboration of the BALLADE form. The chant royal was developed in medieval France and used for serious and stately themes. It was not introduced in England until the latter part of the 19th century during the revival of interest in French forms. It is a 60-line poem having 5 stanzas of 11 lines and an envoi of 5 lines, each ending with the refrain, as in the ballade.

Chaos. In Greek mythology, the original void. Out of Chaos, according to Hesiod, came Earth, Tartarus, Eros (Love), Erebus (Darkness), and Nyx (Night). The Orphics (see ORPHISM) claimed that Chaos, Night, and Darkness coexisted, and Love came from an egg laid by Night; Eros parthenogenetically produced the first generation of gods.

Chapayev. See Dmitri FURMANOV.

chapbook. Originally one of the books carried about for sale by *chapmen* (tradesmen, *chap* meaning purchase or bargain). Hence, any book of a similar nature, a tract, small collection of ballads, or the like.

Chapelain, Jean (1595–1674). French critic and man of letters. For 20 years he labored at an epic poem, *La Pucelle* (the first part was published in 1656), generally reckoned to be a failure. He was a regular visitor at the Hôtel de Rambouillet, where his advocacy of classical forms in literature and especially of the three unities in drama had considerable influence. Conservative and a founding member of the Académie française, he conceived the plan of the Académie's dictionary, and at Richelieu's request he drafted that institution's censure of Corneille: *Sentiments de l'Académie sur Le Cid* (1638).

Chapelle, Claude Emmanuel Luillier (1626–1686). French poet. An intimate of Boileau, Molière and Racine, Chapelle was coauthor with François de BACHAUMONT of the entertaining *Voyage en Provence et Languedoc* (1656) and an enthusiastic admirer and exponent of the philosophy of Pierre GASSENDI.

Chaplin, Charlie. Real name, **Charles Spencer Chaplin** (1889–   ). English-born motion-picture actor, director, writer, producer, and composer. He is internationally famous as the creator of the inimitable tramp character Charlie. The tramp wears baggy pants, oversized shoes, and a derby hat; he carries a bamboo cane and has an awkward walk. His naïve approach invariably involves him in dangerous situations from which he extricates himself effortlessly by sheer good will. The tramp has enormous trust and affection for all men, and the ludicrous predicaments into which these lead him are resolved as if by divine grace. Chaplin made his screen debut with Mack Sennett's Keystone Company in 1914. In the next few years he appeared in *Tillie's Punctured Romance, The Count, Easy Street,* and *The Cure.* In 1918 he became an independent producer with his own company, First National Films, and in 1923 he was one of the founders of United Artists. Among his most notable films are *The Kid* (1919), *The Gold Rush* (1926), *City Lights* (1931), *Modern Times* (1936), *The Great Dictator* (1940), *Monsieur Verdoux* (1947), and *Limelight* (1952). He has published *My Autobiography* (1964).

Chapman, George (1559?–1634). English poet, scholar, and playwright. Chapman is best remembered today for his translation of the works of Homer, which began with his *Seven Books of the Iliad* in 1598. In 1611 he published the entire *Iliad*, in 1615 the *Odyssey*, and in 1616 *The Whole Works of Homer.* The translation, in rhymed couplets, often departs from and expands upon the original, but it is a notable poetic achievement in its own right. It was praised by Lamb and Coleridge, and most

memorably by Keats in his sonnet *On First Looking into Chapman's Homer.* Among Chapman's poems are *The Shadow of Night* (1594) and *Ovid's Banquet of Sense* (1595). He completed Christopher Marlowe's unfinished *Hero and Leander* (1598), and wrote a number of plays, of which the best known are the tragedies BUSSY D'AMBOIS (c. 1604) and its sequel, *The Revenge of Bussy D'Ambois* (c. 1610). However, some scholars feel his best plays were his romantic comedies, such as *All Fools* (c. 1599) and *May Day* (c. 1602). His other plays include *The Blind Beggar of Alexandria* (1596); *An Humorous Day's Mirth* (1597); *The Gentleman Usher* (c. 1602); *Monsieur D'Olive* (1604); and *Charles, Duke of Byron,* I & II (1607–1608).

Chapman, John. See Johnny APPLESEED.

Chaque Homme dans sa nuit (Each in His Darkness, 1960). A novel by Julian GREEN. The hero Wilfred Ingram, a Catholic, moves in a sordid, carnal world. He is not able to deny his faith, however, but suffers in his knowledge of his own sin. When he is dying, Ingram's face is transformed by an expression of joy and peace: his faith, in spite of sin, has transcended death. Characteristically, Green's vision remains hopeful, although he probes the depths of human evil and misery.

Char, René (1907–   ). French poet of the Midi region. The poems he wrote while associated with the surrealistic movement are collected in *Le Marteau sans maître* (1934). Like his poetry of the Resistance, *Seuls Demeurent* (1945) and *Feuillets d'Hypnos* (1946), included in the English *Hypnos Waking: Poetry and Prose* (1956), Char's later poetry tends to be brief and hermetic. It reveals a close communion with nature and seeks a humanistic exaltation of man.

character writers. A school of English prose writers in the first half of the 17th century. They wrote sketches of men and women—either as individuals or types—in descriptive, analytical, or satirical form as observed in the life of their time. Many of them were influenced by the work of Theophrastus, the Athenian Peripatetic philosopher, who wrote studies of 30 types of personality, such as the Flatterer and the Grumbler, under the title of *Characters.* The best-known English character writers are Joseph HALL, Owen FELLTHAM, Sir Thomas OVERBURY, and John EARLE.

Chardin, Jean (1643–1713). French writer and traveler. He is the author of *Voyage en Perse et aux Indes Orientales (Journey to Persia and to the East Indies,* 1711).

Chardin, Jean Baptiste Siméon (1699–1779). French painter. He is known for his calm still lifes, domestic scenes, and portraits. His paintings of kitchen utensils, game, and fruit are painted with great subtlety and richness of color, animated by bright flashes of light, and unified by reflections of tone. Chardin's sure sense of form and harmonious composition has made his work become a source of study for later artists, notably Edouard MANET and Georges BRAQUE.

Chardonne, Jacques. Pen name of **Jacques Boutelleau** (1884–   ). French novelist. Chardonne, who writes in the classical tradition about the spiritual problems of married life, is best known for his trilogy *Les Destinées sentimentales* (1934–1936).

Other novels include *L'Epithalame* (1921), *Eva* (1930), and *Chimériques* (1948).

Charge of the Light Brigade, The. A poem by Alfred TENNYSON celebrating the famous "death charge of the 600" at Balaclava in the Crimea, Oct. 25, 1854. A British brigade, knowing the folly of their orders, charged the Russian line and was decimated:

> Theirs not to make reply,
> Theirs not to reason why,
> Theirs but to do and die.
> Into the valley of Death
> Rode the six hundred.

Chariclea (Charicleia). The lady-love of Theagenes. She appears in the exquisite erotic Greek romance called ETHIOPICA, the story of Theagenes and Chariclea, by Heliodoros.

Charis. According to Homer, one of the Graces and wife of HEPHAESTUS. In later times the name was applied to any of the three Graces (Charites).

Charites, the. See GRACES, THE.

Charlemagne or **Charles the Great** (742–814). Frankish king, crowned Emperor of the West in 800. See his history under CAROLINGIANS. He and the knights said to be his paladins became the center of a number of *chansons de geste,* or medieval epic romances, most having very little basis in fact except for the defeat of the rear guard at RONCESVALLES. Famous versions of these legends include the French *Chanson de* ROLAND and in Italian Pulci's MORGANTE MAGGIORE, Boiardo's ORLANDO INNAMORATO, and Ariosto's ORLANDO FURIOSO.

Charles. In Shakespeare's As You LIKE IT, a wrestler in Duke Frederick's court, whom Orlando challenges and defeats.

Charles I (1600–1649). Stuart king of England (1625–1649) and 2nd son of James I. The first years of his reign were marked by disputes with Parliament over matters of finance, religion, and foreign policy. In 1629 he dissolved Parliament and ruled alone for 11 years, but in 1640 he was compelled to recall Parliament to deal with the problems of the Scottish rebellion and a growing lack of money. From this point on, the conflict between King and Commons became more intense; the former's stubbornness and duplicity and the latter's insistence on its rights and its generally anti-Anglican (Puritan) character led to the CIVIL WAR and Charles's beheading in 1649. In his private personality, Charles was a virtuous, deeply pious, and courageous man, as his deportment at his trial and execution revealed; but his public character was marred by double-dealing, obstinacy, ingratitude to friends, and a lack of political intelligence. Charles is a prominent character in Dumas' *Twenty Years After* (*Vingt Ans Après,* 1845). See EIKON BASILIKÉ; PETITION OF RIGHT.

Charles II (1630–1685). Stuart king of England (1660–1685). He was proclaimed king in Scotland after the death of his father Charles I, but it was only after 11 years of exile, struggle, and disappointment that he assumed the throne of England. This restoration was brought about by compromise and Parliament's invitation, not by force of arms, and throughout Charles's reign, he was obliged to intrigue and maneuver for parliamentary support. A brother of the openly Catholic James, he was anxious to obtain a wider measure of religious tolerance in England and also to strengthen the monarchy and ensure the succession of James. He failed in his first goal and attained only a very partial and transient success with the latter. His reign was disturbed by shifting alliances, several wars, numerous actual and fictitious conspiracies, the Great Plague (1665), and the Fire of London (1666), but was productive of much in literature, science, and architecture. Charles II was an easygoing, intelligent, pleasure-loving, witty man, notorious for the number of his amours and illegitimate offspring. He is an important character in Scott's *Peveril of the Peak* (1823) and *Woodstock* (1826). See Nell GWYNN.

Charles VII (of France). See DAUPHIN.

Charles, Duc d'Orléans (1391–1465). French poet, son of Louis d'Orléans (brother of King Charles VI) and father of King Louis XII. In 1415 he was taken captive to England, where he wrote most of his graceful *ballades* and *rondeaux.* After his ransom in 1460 he established a miniature court at Blois as a patron of the arts, entertaining François Villon and others.

Charles V. Also known as **Charles I** of Spain (1500–1558). Holy Roman Emperor. The son of Philip the Fair of Flanders and Joanna the Mad of Spain, Charles inherited Burgundy and Flanders upon his father's death (1506) and, because of his mother's insanity, acceded to the throne of Spain after the demise of his grandfather, Ferdinand II, in 1516. Spanish resentment against the Flemish-born youth was heightened when he secured election as Holy Roman Emperor in 1519 at great expense and without consulting the *cortes,* or parliaments, of Spain. During Charles's absence in Germany, this resentment erupted in the revolt of the *comuneros,* or townsmen, in which nobles and commoners were at first arrayed against the monarchy but later turned into a class struggle. Other rebellions broke out in Valencia and among the *Moriscos,* or converted Moors, of Spain.

After the suppression of these revolts, Spain enjoyed internal peace and prosperity while Charles devoted himself to foreign affairs. There were several wars with France, whose ruler, FRANCIS I, feared Hapsburg domination of Europe. (See PAVIA.) Challenging Turkish designs in the Mediterranean and in central Europe, Charles captured Tunis in 1535 but failed to take Algiers in 1541. He also attempted to suppress Lutheranism in Germany.

Disillusioned by the frustration of his hopes for religious and political peace in Europe and burdened by debt, Charles decided to give up his many crowns, assigning the imperial title to his brother Ferdinand and his hereditary possessions to his son Philip. In 1556 he retired to the Hieronymite convent of Yuste in Estremadura, where he lived in seclusion until his death.

Charles, Nick. A detective created by Dashiell HAMMETT. He first appeared in *The Thin Man* (1932). A witty and debonair man, he was a striking contrast to Hammett's other famous detective, Sam Spade.

Charles Martel or **Charles the Hammer** (689?–741). Frankish ruler, grandfather of Charlemagne. See CAROLINGIANS. He is famous for his victory over the Moors near Tours in 732.

Charles's Wain, Charles' Wain. An old popular name for the Great Bear. The constellation forms the rough outline of a wheelbarrow or rustic wagon, and the "Charles" stands for Charlemagne. One possible etymology suggests that King Arthur (Lat., *Arturus*) became identified with *Arcturus*, a bright star in Boötes, the constellation which seems to be directing the wagon. Confusion between the legendary cycles of romance connected with Arthur and Charlemagne established the name Charles's Wain in the popular mind.

Charles the Great. See CHARLEMAGNE.

Charleston School. A group of American men of letters. They supported the Southern position in the years before the Civil War. The group, including Paul Hamilton HAYNE, William Gilmore SIMMS, and Henry TIMROD, had its headquarters in Charleston, South Carolina.

Charlot, André Eugène Maurice (1882–1956). British theatrical manager and producer. He was born in Paris and was well known for *Charlot's Revue*.

Charlotte Temple (pub. in England, 1791; U.S., 1794). An early American novel by Susannah Haswell ROWSON. Originally entitled *Charlotte, a Tale of Truth*, it has run through more than 100 editions and is still occasionally read. The heroine is lured from her English home and deserted in New York by a British officer named Montraville, who later repents. Mrs. Rowson wrote a sequel *Charlotte's Daughter*, better known as *Lucy Temple*, published posthumously in 1828.

Charlus, Baron Palamède [Mémé] de. An important aristocrat in Marcel Proust's REMEMBRANCE OF THINGS PAST. One of the GUERMANTES, he cultivates his reputation as a virile woman-chaser, but is secretly a homosexual.

Charmian. In Shakespeare's ANTONY AND CLEOPATRA and Dryden's ALL FOR LOVE, a gay, kind-hearted attendant on Cleopatra. After the queen's death, she kills herself by applying one of the asps to her own arm.

Charnwood. 1st baron **Godfrey Rathbone Benson** (1864–1945). English biographer. He is best known for his *Abraham Lincoln* (1916).

Charon. In classic myth, the ferryman of the STYX. Charon's toll was a coin, about equal to a penny, placed in the mouth or hand of the dead by the ancient Greeks to pay Charon for ferrying the spirit across the river Styx to ELYSIUM.

Charpentier, Gustave (1860–1956). French composer. He is mainly known for his opera *Louise* (1900), which had a striking success at the time of its premiere. Its realistic libretto deals with the lives and loves of working-class Parisians.

Charpentier, Marc Antoine (1634–1704). Most important French-born composer of the 17th century. Charpentier is known principally for his church music and his oratorios. He was unable to write for the Opéra until after Lully's death, for that composer enjoyed a monopoly of the musical stage, but his one opera, *Medée*, was finally produced in 1693. Because of Lully's quarrel with Molière, Charpentier wrote the elaborate musical score for Molière's last play, *Le Malade Imaginaire*.

Charrière, Isabelle de. See ZÉLIDE.

Charterhouse of Parma, The (La Chartreuse de Parme; 1839). An historical novel by STENDHAL. In essence the tale is a chronicle of the adventures of its young hero, Fabrizio del Dongo. Set in the post-Napoleonic era, this remarkable analysis of ROMANTICISM leads us through the battle of Waterloo, life and intrigue in a small Italian court, romantic love, imprisonment, the priesthood, and finally terminates in a Carthusian monastery.

Charteris, Leslie (1907–   ). English novelist. The son of a Chinese surgeon and an Englishwoman, he was originally named Leslie Charles Bowyer Lin. A naturalized American citizen, Charteris is known for his very popular stories about a gentleman burglar nicknamed THE SAINT.

Chartier, Alain (c. 1390–c. 1435). French poet, prose writer, and diplomat under Charles VII. In his first poem, the *Livre des quatre dames*. (1415), four ladies lament the death of their lovers in the French defeat by Henry V at Agincourt. He described the confused condition of France in the years that followed in his best-known prose work, the *Quadrilogue Invectif* (1422). His prose style, modeled on that of the Latin orators, marked the revival of classicism in French literary style. The title and theme of his popular poem *La Belle Dame sans merci* (1424) were used by John KEATS. Other works include the poem *Bréviaire des nobles* (c. 1424) and the prose *Traité de l'espérance* (c. 1428).

Chartier, Emile. See ALAIN.

Chartism (1838–1849). The political movement and program of the group of English reformers known as Chartists. Their main target of criticism was the Reform Bill of 1832, which had failed to extend the vote to the workingman. Their principal demands, published in "the People's Charter," were for universal manhood suffrage and for the annual election of parliament, abolition of property qualifications and payment to its members, vote by ballot, and equal representation in electoral districts. Members of the group were mostly industrial workers led by radical intellectuals. Chartism disappeared from the political scene after 1849, but all the Chartists' aims, with the exception of annual parliaments, were ultimately realized.

The Chartist Clergyman. Charles KINGSLEY, so called because of his sympathy with the Chartists and other working-class movements.

Charybdis. See SCYLLA AND CHARYBDIS.

Chase, James Hadley. Pen name of **René Raymond** (1906–   ). English author of crime and adventure fiction. His most widely read novel was *No Orchids for Miss Blandish* (1939).

Chase, Mary C[oyle] (1907–   ). American playwright. She is best known for her Pulitzer Prize-winning play HARVEY. Her earlier plays had achieved little success, but two later plays were well received: *Mrs. McThing* (1952) and *Bernardine* (1952). *Midgie Purvis* was produced on Broadway in 1961.

Chase, Mary Ellen (1887–   ). American novelist and teacher. Miss Chase is noted for her regional novels dealing with the Maine seacoast, her native setting. Of these, *Mary Peters* (1934) and *Silas Crockett* (1935) are perhaps her best. The latter, chronicling the fortunes of a Yankee family through four generations, has as its theme the hardships inflicted on the old clipper sailors by the introduction of steamships. Other novels are *The Plum Tree* (1949) and *The Edge of Darkness* (1957). For many years professor of English literature at Smith College, Miss Chase has also written stories for young people, including *Mary Christmas* (1926) and *Gay Highway* (1933), and several volumes of nonfiction, most notably *The Golden Asse; and Other Essays* (1929), *This England* (1936), and *Psalms for the Common Reader* (1962). Her autobiography, *A Goodly Heritage* (1932), and its sequel, *A Goodly Fellowship* (1939), deal with her experiences as a teacher.

Chase, Stuart (1888–   ). American economist and semanticist. Under the influence of Henry George, Chase became interested in social problems, especially those relating to conservation, consumer education, semantics, and labor. Among his books are *The Tragedy of Waste* (1925), *Your Money's Worth* (in collaboration with F. L. Schlink, 1927), *A New Deal* (1932), *The Tyranny of Words* (1938), and *Live and Let Live* (1960).

Chastelard (1865). A tragedy by Algernon Charles SWINBURNE, the first of a trilogy on Mary Queen of Scots. It is based on the life of Pierre de Boscosel de Chastelard, a French poet who was executed for his love for Mary. The other dramas in the trilogy are *Bothwell* and *Mary Stuart*.

Chastellain, Georges. See RHÉTORIQUEURS, LES GRANDS.

Chateaubriand, Vicomte **François René de** (1768–1848). French writer, forerunner of the romantic movement. The work of Chateaubriand is characterized by egotistical melancholy, impassioned emotion, and a love of untamed nature. His interest in Roman Catholicism and the Middle Ages, in exotic countries and primitive tribes, foreshadows typically romantic concerns (see ROMANTICISM). Chateaubriand is famous for his fictional portrayal of America. His novels ATALA, RENÉ, and LES NATCHEZ all deal with North America and the North American Indians. *Les Martyrs* (1809) and *L'Itinéraire de Paris à Jérusalem et de Jérusalem à Paris* (1811) are concerned with Greece, the Holy Land, and the Near East. Other works include LE GÉNIE DU CHRISTIANISME and MÉMOIRES D'OUTRE-TOMBE. Chateaubriand's political career was a stormy one. He favored the Bourbon monarchy and served it as ambassador to England, Italy, and Germany, and as minister of foreign affairs.

Châtelet, Marquise **du. Gabrielle Emilie Le Tonnelier de Breteuil** (1706–1749). French mathematician and   physicist. Mistress of VOLTAIRE, she lived with him at Montjeu and at her château at Cirey (in Lorraine). The liaison lasted 14 years until her death. The marquise had an intense interest in the theories of Leibniz and Newton and propagated the latter's ideas in France. She wrote *Traité sur le bonheur* (1749) and *Traduction des principes de Newton* (1756). See EMILIE.

Chats-Fourrés. See FURRY LAWCATS.

Chatterley, Lady. See LADY CHATTERLEY'S LOVER.

Chatterton, Thomas (1752–1770). English poet. His literary fabrications are distinguished by their poetic genius. While still a mere boy, living in Bristol, he wrote a number of poems couched in elaborately archaic spelling that he declared to be the work of one Thomas Rowley, a nonexistent monk, poet, and

antiquarian of the 15th century. In this way, Chatterton evolved a romance of Bristol centering around William Canynges, a merchant who became lord mayor. Notable poems in this series are: *Bristowe Tragedie: or, the Dethe of Syr Charles Bawdin* (1772) and *An Excelente Balade of Charitie* (1777). His deception was successful for awhile, although it was exposed in 1777–1778 by Thomas Tyrwhitt and Thomas Warton. Chatterton also wrote *Apostate Will* (1764), a satire, and *The Revenge* (1770), a successful burlesque opera. In despair at his poverty, after moving to London, he killed himself at the age of 17 by taking poison. A volume of his collected works was published in 1803. Chatterton was a favorite figure of the English Romantic poets, becoming for them the prototype of the neglected genius. See MARVELLOUS BOY; BRISTOL BOY, THE.

Chaucer, Geoffrey (c. 1343–1400). English poet and public servant, by far the most important writer of Middle English and considered one of the finest poets in literature. His family had been in the royal service, and in 1357 Chaucer is known to have been already in the service of the wife of Prince Lionel, and to have met John of Gaunt, another of the King's sons, who became one of his most important patrons. He joined the English army's invasion of France in 1359, was captured, and was ransomed by King Edward III in 1360. His activities for the next six years remain unknown: he may have been with Lionel in Ireland, he may have attended law school, he may already have entered the King's service. About 1366 he married Philippa, one of the Queen's

A page from William Morris'
Kelmscott Chaucer (1896).

attendants and the sister of Katherine Swynford, later John of Gaunt's mistress, then wife, Philippa apparently gave him two sons, "little Lewis" (see *Treatise on the* ASTROLABE) and Thomas, highly successful in public service in the 15th century. There may have been one daughter, or perhaps two, but the evidence is uncertain.

In 1367 Chaucer was given a life pension by the King, and apparently remained in the royal service thereafter, going abroad on a number of more or less secret diplomatic missions between 1368 and 1378, mostly to France. The two trips into Italy (1372–1373) and 1378) proved extremely important in his literary development because of his discovery of the works of Dante, Boccaccio, and Petrarch, which greatly influenced his own; it is probable that he read all their major works except Boccaccio's *Decameron,* and he knew many of those tales through Petrarch and French translations.

In 1374 he was given a house of his own and made Controller of Customs on wools, skins, and hides; in 1382 he was also given control of Petty Custom on wines and other goods. About 1385 he established his residence in Kent, where he was elected justice of the peace and briefly (1386) a member of Parliament. After his wife died in 1387, his financial fortunes worsened, possibly through political retaliation for his opposition to the Gloucester cause in the years of Richard II's minority following Edward's death in 1377. At any rate, soon after Richard came of age, he appointed Chaucer Clerk of the King's Works (1389), in charge of the maintenance and repair of public buildings, parks, bridges, etc. Chaucer resigned this position in 1391, and was appointed deputy forester of a royal forest in Somerset. He retained his residence at Kent and his activities in London, however. In 1394 Richard awarded him another life pension, Chaucer having resigned the first one in 1388. He seems to have been in attendance (1395–1396) on Henry Bolingbroke, John of Gaunt's son, who deposed Richard in 1399, and as Henry IV increased Chaucer's annuity.

Chaucer's early work is heavily influenced by the French tradition of the poetry of love. It includes the BOOK OF THE DUCHESS and the *Romaunt of the Rose* (probably c. 1370; a translation, of which only the beginning is now extant, of the French ROMANCE OF THE ROSE), both in octosyllabic couplets. *Saint Cecilia,* later used as the SECOND NUN'S TALE, was probably written about 1373, most of the tragedies incorporated into the MONK'S TALE about 1374.

The HOUSE OF FAME and ANELIDA AND ARCITE, written about six years later, are considered transitional works, for they begin to show the influence of Italian literature, although still essentially in the French tradition. Soon afterward Chaucer translated as *Boece* the CONSOLATION OF PHILOSOPHY by Boethius. About the same period he wrote the PARLIAMENT OF FOWLS and within a few years *Palamon and Arcite,* later adapted as the KNIGHT'S TALE, as well as TROILUS AND CRISEYDE and the LEGEND OF GOOD WOMEN. This is called his period of Italian influence.

His period of maturity is considered to begin in 1387 with the writing of the *General Prologue* to the unfinished CANTERBURY TALES. He certainly worked on them through 1394, and probably until his death. In addition, he revised some of his earlier work and

wrote the *Treatise on the Astrolabe.* There are also 16 short poems, written at various periods in his career in different stanzaic forms, and 5 poems of doubtful authorship.

In the early 1370's Chaucer began to abandon the octosyllabic couplets of his early works—although he used the form once more in the *House of Fame*— largely in favor of RHYME ROYAL, although he also tried eight- and nine-line stanza forms. In the mid-1380's he first began to use the decasyllabic couplet, probably in *Palamon and Arcite* (although it was possibly first written in stanzaic form and then adapted for the *Knight's Tale*) and certainly in the *Legend of Good Women.* This is the first known English use of the decasyllabic couplet, which Chaucer then used for most of the *Canterbury Tales,* and which evolved into the heroic couplet.

Chaucerian roundel. A variation of the French RONDEL form, first written by Chaucer. The Chaucerian roundel is characterized by the repetition of the first as a refrain at the end of the second and third stanzas. It has 10 lines and its rhyme scheme is: A-b-b, a-b-A, a-b-b-A (A being the refrain).

Chauchat, Clavdia. In Thomas Mann's novel THE MAGIC MOUNTAIN, a Russian tubercular patient with whom Hans CASTORP falls in love and whose presence is a major cause of his remaining at Haus Berghof. Her fingernail-biting, careless dress, and door-slamming reflect the lax and decadent way of life she represents.

Chauncey, Charles (1705–1787). American clergyman. He is best known for his opposition to the revivals and conversions of the "GREAT AWAKENING," which he attacked in such works as *Seasonable Thoughts on the State of Religion* (1743), a reply to Jonathan Edwards' *Some Thoughts Concerning the Present Revival of Religion* (1742). Chauncey's *Salvation of All Men,* published anonymously in 1782, marked the beginning of Universalism in New England. An ardent patriot before and during the Revolution, he also wrote a number of political tracts.

Chauntecleer. See under NUN'S PRIEST'S TALE.

chauvinism. Blind and pugnacious patriotism of an exaggerated kind; unreasoning jingoism. Nicholas Chauvin, a soldier of the French Republic and Empire, was madly devoted to Napoleon and his cause. He was introduced as a type of exaggerated bellicose patriotism into a number of plays, including Scribe's *Le Soldat laboureur,* Cogniard's *La Cocarde tricolore,* Bayard and Dumanoir's *Les Aides de camps,* and Charet's *Conscrit Chauvin.* The term *chauvinism* spread quickly into a great number of languages.

Chávez, Carlos (1899–   ). Outstanding Mexican composer and conductor of the century. He was director of the National Conservatory in Mexico City, and conductor of the Orquesta Sinfónica de México from 1928 to 1952. His music, principally orchestral, makes considerable use of elements from Mexican Indian folk music.

Cheapside. A London street running east from St. Paul's Churchyard. Formerly it was noted for its shops. Before the Great Fire of 1666, it was an open square, called The Cheaps, where markets and fairs were held.

Cheeryble brothers. In Charles Dickens' novel NICHOLAS NICKLEBY, two brothers, Ned and Charles.

Wealthy, self-made London merchants, they are ever ready to help those struggling against the buffets of fortune.

Cheever, John (1912–   ). American short-story writer and novelist. Subtle, ironic attacks on suburbia characterize most of Cheever's writing. His stories, many of which originally appeared in *The New Yorker*, have been collected in such books as *The Enormous Radio and Other Stories* (1953), *The Housebreaker of Shady Hill and Other Stories* (1958), and *Some People, Places and Things That Will Not Appear in My Next Novel* (1961). *The Wapshot Chronicle* (1957) was a best-selling novel. Its sequel *The Wapshot Scandal* appeared in 1964.

Cheka. In early Soviet Russian history, the secret police body established in 1917 to guard against counterrevolutionary activity. The name is an abbreviation for "Extraordinary Commission for the Combat of Counterrevolution, Sabotage and Breach of Duty by Officials." In 1922 it was replaced by the GPU, or Gay-Pay-Oo (State Political Administration), which shortly thereafter became the OGPU (United State Political Administration). In 1934 secret policy duties were taken over by the NKVD (People's Commissariat of Internal Affairs). In 1946 this body was changed to the MVD (Ministry of Internal Affairs). After 1946, the Soviet security service was placed in the hands of the KGB (Committee of State Security), which employed less terror than its predecessors.

Chekhov, Anton Pavlovich (1860–1904). Russian short-story writer and playwright. Noted for his masterful short stories and lyrical dramas, Chekhov was born in Taganrog in the south of Russia, the third of six children. He was the son of a merchant and the grandson of an ex-serf who had purchased his freedom. Chekhov attended secondary school in Taganrog, and in 1879 enrolled in the School of Medicine at the University of Moscow. He graduated in 1884. While at the university, Chekhov had to earn money to help support the large family. Following the example of his older brother, Aleksandr, he began contributing short sketches, stories, and jokes to humorous journals and papers. Many of these early stories were published under such pen names as Antosha Chekhonte, Anton Ch., and The Doctor Without Patients. *Skazki Mel'pomeny* (*Tales of Melpomene*, 1884), was the first volume of Chekhov's stories published. Other early collections of tales were *Piostrye rasskazy* (*Motley Tales*, 1886) and *V sumerkakh* (*In the Twilight*, 1887).

Chekhov's work attracted the attention of the writer Dmitri Grigorovich, who encouraged the young author to continue writing and introduced him to Alexei Suvorin, publisher of *Novoye Vremya*, a leading St. Petersburg daily. The more secure financial position offered by this connection enabled Chekhov to pay more attention to improving the quality of his stories. The number of stories written each year fell steadily, but the artistic quality of the work improved, and Chekhov's reputation grew.

In 1890, Chekhov made a trip to the prison island of Sakhalin in the Far East. His observations and experiences were related in *Ostrovo sakhalina* (*Sakhalin Island*, 1893). The trip was made despite Chekhov's weakened condition from the tuberculosis that had appeared while he was still a student at the university. The whole of Chekhov's short life was a constant struggle against the steady advance of the disease. After his return to Russia, Chekhov took part in relief work during the 1892 famine. He then bought a small estate at Melikhovo, not far from Moscow, and moved there with his family. While living at Melikhovo, Chekhov created some of his best-known works, including the tales WARD No. 6, *Uchitel' slovestnosti* (*The Teacher of Literature*, 1894), MY LIFE, and PEASANTS. During this period he also produced two of his major plays, THE SEA GULL and UNCLE VANYA. *The Sea Gull* was first performed in St. Petersburg in 1896. It was so badly received that Chekhov vowed to give up playwriting. Two years later, however, the drama was put on with great success by the newly formed Moscow Art Theatre. Chekhov's play was so important in establishing the reputation of the new repertory theater that the directors made a gull the company's emblem.

His failing health forced Chekhov to move in 1898 to the milder southern climate of Yalta in the Crimea. Here he often met with the writers Maksim Gorki and Count Leo Tolstoi. From this time until the end of his life, Chekhov's creative activity was concerned mainly with drama. The few major stories of these later years were *Dama s sobachkoi* (*The Lady with the Dog*, 1898), IN THE RAVINE, *Arkhiyerei* (*The Bishop*, 1902), and *Nevesta* (*Betrothed*, 1903).

In 1901, Chekhov married Olga Knipper, a Moscow Art Theatre actress. The couple lived apart much of the time, because Chekhov's ill health forced him to remain in the warmer climate at Yalta. During this period Chekhov wrote for the Art Theatre his two famous plays, THE CHERRY ORCHARD and THE THREE SISTERS.

Chekhov's failing health induced his doctors to send him to the health resort at Badenweiler, Germany, in 1904. He died there in July.

The main theme of Chekhov's prose fiction is life's pathos, caused by the inability of human beings to respond to or even to communicate with one another and the pervading mood of sadness and hopelessness arising from this situation. This characteristic theme is clearly seen in A DREARY STORY, which is usually regarded as the first work of Chekhov's mature period, that is, after his comic and satirical stories. Chekhov was equally adept at creating a lyrical atmosphere, engendered by man's response to nature and untouched by the pain of relations as they exist between people. His most successful story of this type is *Step'* (*The Steppe*, 1888), describing a long trip across the plains as experienced by a young boy on his way to school in a distant town.

Chekhov is famed as a master of the short story. Even though some of his best prose pieces are almost novel-length, these stories, as well as his better-known short works, achieve their effect with the minimum of artistic means. All of his best work is an illustration of Chekhov's dictum: "Conciseness is the sister of talent."

Chekhov's plays deal with the passing of the vitality of the Russian landed gentry. His characters, helpless before the changes taking place in 19th-century Russia, take refuge in elaborate, improbable dreams of renewed prosperity. His plots are simple, mere outlines for the creation of atmosphere and delineation of character at which he excels. The result is a group of plays, combining comedy, pathos, anti-climax, and digression in a wholly natural effect that seems to belie the careful workmanship of the dramatist. *Ivanov* (1887) and the four major plays already mentioned are among the finest in the modern repertory. His shorter plays include *Medved'* (*The Bear,* 1888), *Tragik ponevole* (*A Tragedian in Spite of Himself,* 1889), *Svadba* (*The Wedding,* 1889), *Na bolshoi doroge* (*On the High Road,* 1884), *Yubilei* (*The Jubilee,* 1891), *Predlozheniye* (*The Proposal,* 1888), and *Lebedinaya pesnya* (1887).

Chemins de la liberté, Les. See ROADS TO FREEDOM, THE.

Chénier, André Marie de (1762–1794). French poet, often considered the greatest of 18th-century France. His *Bucoliques* and, to a lesser extent, his *Elégies* reflect his early love and remarkable understanding of Greek antiquity. At first sympathetic with the French Revolution, he was later horrified at the excesses of the Jacobins and wrote denunciatory pamphlets. He was arrested by order of Robespierre, whom he had attacked. During his imprisonment and before he was guillotined, he wrote, on bits of smuggled paper, his satiric and bitter *Iambes* against his persecutors, and his last, most famous ode *La Jeune captive,* inspired by a fellow victim. His philosophical poetry (e.g., *L'Invention*) gives poetic expression to the scientific ideas of his age. Most of his works were published posthumously in 1819. His life inspired Giordano's opera *Andrea Chénier* (1896).

Chernyshevski, Nikolai Gavrilovich (1828–1889). Russian critic and editor. For three years after graduation from the university at St. Petersburg, Chernyshevski was a schoolteacher in his native Saratov. In 1853 he returned to St. Petersburg and began his journalistic career on the *Sovremennik* (*The Contemporary*), which he turned into the period's leading radical publication. Chernyshevski became the chief spokesman for the radical wing in literature; he and his younger colleague Dobrolyubov in their critical writings gave further emphasis to the social aspect of literature, which the renowned critic BELINSKI had brought to light. Chernyshevski supplied an example of the literature he praised in his didactic novel, *Chto Delat'?* (*What Is To Be Done?;* 1863). In the novel, he expounded his ideas of how the true revolutionary should think and behave. Though the work is more of an ideological tract than a novel, it suited the mood of the times and attained wide popularity. It is now regarded in the Soviet Union as a revolutionary classic. Chernyshevski was arrested in 1862 for revolutionary activities; he was sentenced to 7 years at hard labor with 20 years of exile in Siberia. In 1883, he was permitted to leave Siberia because of his health; he returned to Russia and lived out his life in Saratov.

Cherry Orchard, The (**Vishnovyi sad;** 1904). A play by Anton CHEKHOV. Its four acts portray the declining fortunes of the Ranevskis, a landowning family, who are about to lose their estate and beloved cherry orchard. Poor management, neglect, and impracticality have brought the family to the point of bankruptcy, but no one is able to act as head off the disaster. The suggestion of the practical businessman Lopakhin that the family chop down the orchard and build houses on the land is met with horror. For the Ranevskis, the orchard represents the pleasant past,

before the mysterious forces of the changing times threatened their idyllic existence. The estate is finally sold from under the hapless family. Lopakhin buys the land and proceeds to carry out his plan to destroy the orchard and erect houses. As the family sadly prepares to depart, the sound of an ax chopping down a cherry tree is heard off stage.

The play, regarded as one of Chekhov's finest dramatic works, is both a penetrating study of the changing way of life in Russia at the end of the 19th century and a vivid depiction of what the change means to the people involved. The stage portraits of the Ranevskis, with their inability to do anything to save themselves, and of Lopakhin, the representative of a new rising class in society, are masterpieces of dramatic creation.

Cherubim, Don. See BACHELIER DE SALAMANQUE, LE.

Cherubini, [Mario] Luigi [Carlo Zenobio Salvatore] (1760–1842). Italian composer. He settled in Paris in 1788. His principal works are his operas, of which he wrote 24. *Medée* (1787) has recently been revived with great success. He was the favorite composer of Napoleon, and was much admired by Beethoven.

Cheshire cat. In Lewis Carroll's ALICE'S ADVENTURES IN WONDERLAND, a creature that has the ability to vanish at will, its grin being the last thing to go.

Chesnutt, Charles W[addell] (1858–1932). American novelist. Chesnutt, who is sometimes called the first Negro novelist, was a teacher, newspaperman, and lawyer. His first story, *The Goophered Grapevine,* appeared in the *Atlantic* in 1887. His first book, *The Conjure Woman* (1899), centered about Uncle Julius McAdoo, a character not unlike Uncle Remus. His later books dealt with race prejudice: *The Wife of His Youth and Other Stories of the Color Line* (1899), *The House Behind the Cedars* (1900), *The Colonel's Dream* (1905). In 1928, Chesnutt received the Spingarn gold medal for his pioneer work in depicting the struggles of the American Negro.

Chester, George Randolph. See GET-RICH-QUICK WALLINGFORD.

Chester Cycle. A series of 24 medieval English MYSTERY PLAYS performed by the guilds of Chester at Whitsuntide (13th to 16th centuries).

Chesterfield, 4th earl of. Philip Dormer Stanhope (1694–1773). Statesman and man of letters. A friend of Alexander Pope and an important patron of letters, Lord Chesterfield was unsuccessful in his belated attempt to patronize Samuel Johnson's DICTIONARY OF THE ENGLISH LANGUAGE after it had been completed. Johnson's rebuke is famous:

Is not a patron, My Lord, one who looks with unconcern on a Man struggling in the water and when he has reached ground encumbers him with help?

Johnson's comment on Chesterfield's *Letters* to his natural son Philip Stanhope is equally well known: "They teach the morals of a whore, and the manners of a dancing master." The judgment is too severe. Written between 1737 and 1768, Lord Chesterfield's *Letters to his Son* (1774) form one of the classic portraits of an ideal 18th-century gentleman.

Chesterton, G[ilbert] K[eith] (1874–1936). English journalist, essayist, novelist, and poet; author of biography, history, literary criticism, and polemical works. Like his friend, Hilaire BELLOC, he was a propagandist of his Catholicism and his conservative political views (the two were referred to as Chesterbelloc). Chesterton became a Catholic in 1922, but had always been a traditionalist, admiring the Victorians, romanticizing the Middle Ages, and attacking H. G. Wells and Bernard Shaw. He is best remembered for his essays, such as *On running after one's hat* (1908), which are gay and witty, and for such poems as *Lepanto* (1911), which are full of gusto. Sometimes he conveyed his serious ideas in fantastic novels, as in THE NAPOLEON OF NOTTING HILL, THE MAN WHO WAS THURSDAY, and a series of detective novels, beginning with *The Innocence of Father Brown* (1911), in which the priest Father Brown is sleuth. Chesterton wrote a good history of *The Victorian Age in Literature* (1913). Among his polemical works are *Heretics* (1905), *Orthodoxy* (1908), *What's Wrong with the World?* (1910), and *The Everlasting Man* (1925), an outline of history.

Chettle, Henry (c. 1560–?1607). English dramatist. The only extant play solely his work is *The Tragedy of Hoffman* (1602). He also collaborated with John Day, Thomas Dekker, and Anthony Munday.

Chevalier à la mode, Le (1687). A comedy of manners by Florent DANCOURT. It recounts the exploits of an impudent and imprudent chevalier who almost succeeds in his simultaneous courtship of two rich widows and the niece of one of them. The play gives a lighthearted but not inaccurate picture of the French society of Dancourt's day.

Chevallier, Gabriel (1895–   ). French novelist whose *Clochemerle* (1934) is a grotesquely comic caricature of village life. His other novels include *Sainte-Colline* (1937) and *The Euffe Inheritance* (1945).

Chevy Chase. One of the oldest ballads in English. There is some evidence that it may have grown out of the Battle of Otterborne, and a Scottish version exists earlier than 1549. It is included in Percy's *Reliques* (1765).

Cheyney, Peter (1896–1951). English writer of tough, adventurous crime fiction. He wrote *Dames Don't Care* (1937) and numerous other novels.

Chiabrera, Gabriello (1552–1638). Italian lyric poet and satirist. He is noted for his numerous *canzonette;* 30 satirical *Sermoni;* the pastoral poem *Alcippo* (1604); and odes in imitation of Horace, Pindar, and Anacreon. Wordsworth admired him greatly and translated several of his epitaphs.

Chiang Kai-shek (1886–   ). Chinese statesman and general. An early follower of SUN YAT-SEN, he studied in Russia and on Sun's death in 1925 became leader of the Nationalist movement. In 1927 he broke with the Russian communists in China. After several years of civil war between the communists and the Nationalists, a truce was reached in 1936 so that a united China led by Chiang might face the threat of Japanese aggression. Upon the outbreak of war with Japan in 1937, Chiang became commander of China's forces and was named provisional president in 1943. Elected president in 1948, he was forced to abandon the mainland of China in the face of communist military successes and in 1949 settled on the island of Taiwan (Formosa), which

he maintained, with extensive American aid, as the last stronghold of the republic of China. He was reelected president in 1954 and in 1960.

Chiang Mei-ling (1898–   ). American-educated, Christian Chinese wife of CHIANG KAI-SHEK. She became known throughout the world for her activities in the administration of the national affairs of her country, for her influence on the policies of her husband, and for her importation of Western ideas and methods into China. *China Fights for Her Life* (1938), *China in Peace and War* (1940), and *This Is Our China* (1940) are books by Mme. Chiang written in English.

Chicago Group or **Chicago Renaissance.** A group of American writers. From about 1912 to about 1925, Chicago seemed well on its way to becoming the literary capital of the U.S. Although many of the writers dealt with Middle Western subjects, the literary activity also had a cosmopolitan scope, especially through such literary magazines as Harriet Monroe's POETRY: A MAGAZINE OF VERSE and Margaret Anderson's *Little Review.* The term is variously used to include such writers as H. B. FULLER, Theodore DREISER, Ben HECHT, Sherwood ANDERSON, Edgar Lee MASTERS, and Carl SANDBURG.

Chicanous. See CATCHPOLES.

Chichen-Itza. An ancient city of Yucatán, Mexico, with well-preserved ruins of the Mayan civilization.

Chichikov, Pavel Ivanovich. The central character of Nikolai Gogol's DEAD SOULS. Plump and prosperous-looking, appearing as respectable as he claims to be, Chichikov is actually an unctuous swindler. A totally mediocre man, whose only abilities are a knowledge of social form and a talent for flattery, he almost succeeds in his dishonest scheme because he allows the people he is swindling to believe they are swindling him.

Ch'ien-lung. Name of Chinese era (1736–1795). A period of great literary and academic ferment.

Chikamatsu Monzaemon (1653–1725). Japanese dramatist. Composer of puppet plays (*joruri*) and *kabuki* drama. He is famous for both his historical spectacles (*jidaimono*) and domestic plays (*sewamono*) many of which are still performed today. Cf. *Major plays of Chikamatsu* (1961) by Donald Keene.

Child, Francis James (1825–1896). American philologist. Professor of Middle English at Harvard, he was an authority on Chaucer and his contemporaries. For many years Child occupied himself with the collection in eight volumes of *English and Scottish Popular Ballads* (1857–1858). It was revised from 1883 to 1898, and issued in 10 volumes. This most authoritative work in its field printed 305 distinct English and Scottish ballads, as many as possible from manuscript sources, with varying versions and exhaustive critical comment and notes.

Childe. A medieval title of honor. In times of chivalry, noble youths who were on probation as candidates for knighthood were called *infants, valets, damoysels, bacheliers,* and *childe.*

Childe Harold's Pilgrimage (Cantos I & II published 1812; Canto III, 1816; Canto IV, 1818). A long narrative poem in Spenserian stanzas by Lord BYRON. The romantically melancholy hero, Childe Harold, disillusioned with a life devoted to the pursuit of pleasure, embarks on a solitary pilgrimage through Portugal, Spain, the Ionian Islands, Albania, Greece, Belgium, the Rhine valley, the Alps, and the Jura. The poet evokes the events and people associated with each place: Rousseau and Julie, Napoleon, the battles of Waterloo and Spain, the bondage of Greece. In the fourth canto Byron drops the device of the hero to speak directly to the reader, describing the great men and historical associations of the Italian cities. The poem satisfied the popular craving for descriptive travel literature of Byron's day and did much to establish the poet's fame.

Childermass, The. See HUMAN AGE, THE.

Childe Rowland (sometimes spelled **Roland**). Younger brother of "the fair Burd Ellen" in the old Scottish ballad. Guided by the enchanter Merlin, he undertakes to bring back his sister from Elfland, whither the fairies have carried her, and succeeds in his perilous exploit. See BURD ELLEN.

Childers, Erskine (1870–1922). Anglo-Irish writer, soldier, and politician. He is best known for his novel *The Riddle of the Sands* (1900), which describes an imaginary German plot to invade Britain. He devoted himself to Irish republicanism and was captured and executed in its cause.

Childhood (Detstvo; 1913–1914). 1 volume of an autobiographical trilogy by Maksim GORKI. The other two volumes are *In the World* (*V lyudakh;* 1916) and *My Universities* (*Moi universitety;* 1923). Of the three volumes, *Childhood* is the richest in insight and incident, chiefly because of the memorable portrait in it of Gorki's grandmother, Akulina Ivanovna Kashirina.

Childhood, Boyhood, Youth (Detstvo, Otrochestvo, Yunost'; 1852, 1854, 1857). An autobiographical trilogy by Count Leo TOLSTOI. *Childhood* was the first of Tolstoi's works to receive wide attention. The descriptions of life on a provincial estate are among the best depictions of nature in Russian literature.

Children of Adam (1860–1867). A group of poems in Walt Whitman's LEAVES OF GRASS. The poems praise physical love and procreation; Whitman claims that Adam's children have lost the Garden of Eden through the degradation of their senses. Body and soul are not separate, but one. "Lusty, phallic," Whitman is the unashamed "chanter of Adamic songs."

Children of Heracles, The (Heracleidae; 427? B.C.) A tragedy by EURIPIDES. Eurystheus, the cruel king of Argos who had forced HERACLES to perform the 12 labors, has continued to persecute the hero's children after his death. Led by old Iolaus, Heracles' trusted friend, they win the protection of Demophon, king of Athens. Iolaus, made young again for one day, fights with the Athenians against the Argives. Eurystheus is captured and put to death.

Written at the height of the Peloponnesian War, the play praises Athens as a champion of freedom and points out that Sparta, now her enemy, should be grateful to the city that had defended the children of Heracles, from whom the Spartans claimed descent.

Children of the Ghetto (1892). A novel by Israel ZANGWILL. It consists of a number of episodes in the lives of the poor, striving people in London's Jewish community. Zangwill paints vivid portraits of his characters.

Children of the Soil (1894). A novel by H. SIENKIEWICZ. It gives a vivid and comprehensive picture of Polish life.

Children's Hour, The (1860). A poem by Henry Wadsworth LONGFELLOW. It is devoted to his three daughters, whose mother was Mary Potter, the poet's first wife.

Childs, Marquis W[illiam] (1903–   ). American journalist and writer. Childs writes a syndicated political column and is the author of a number of books of nonfiction, including *Sweden: The Middle Way* (1936) and *Eisenhower, Captive Hero* (1958). *The Cabin* (1944) and *The Peacemakers* (1962) are novels.

Child's Garden of Verses, A (1885). A small collection of verses by Robert Louis STEVENSON. Written expressly for children and from a child's point of view, they have nevertheless delighted adults as much as children since they were written. Among the favorite titles are *My Shadow* and *The Lamplighter.*

Chillingsworth, William (1602–1644). English writer. Although he was at one time a Roman Catholic, he is best known for his *Religion of the Protestants a Safe Way to Salvation* (1638).

Chillingworth, Roger. The vengeful husband of Hester Prynne in Hawthorne's THE SCARLET LETTER.

Chillon. See PRISONER OF CHILLON, THE.

Chimaera (Chimaira). One of the monstrous offspring of TYPHON and ECHIDNA. It is generally represented as having the head of a lion, the body of a goat, and the tail of a serpent. It was killed by BELLEROPHON, mounted (in most versions) on the winged horse Pegasus.

Ch'in. The first Chinese empire (221–207 B.C.). It saw the country unified for the first time. A canal system and the Great Wall were constructed, and the various writing styles reduced to one. The thought of the LEGALIST SCHOOL prevailed during this brief but important dynasty.

Chinatown. The Chinese quarter of a city, especially of New York or San Francisco in the U.S. Until recently, the Chinatowns in these two cities were famous for their gambling dens, vice, and opium trade. These illegal activities were under the control of the TONGS, and were the cause of murderous tong wars and feuds. Once the power of the tongs was broken, Chinatowns began a new prosperity in the tourist trade. As a result of the trade embargo on Communist Chinese goods, most souvenirs now for sale in Chinatowns are of Japanese origin. The Chinese quarter of London is called Limehouse.

Chinese literature. Two varying literary streams may be found in the first historical records (11th-3d centuries B.C.) left by the Chinese: the shamanistic, represented by the divination inscriptions on oracle bones used in scapularmancy, and the official, found in the inscriptions on bronzes, which generally contain information concerning the king's relationships with his ministers. Both of these types of inscriptions are written in an archaic form of writing, whose stylization attests to a long period of development. Among ancient texts, the BOOK OF DOCUMENTS, which represents the official tradition, contains speeches and proclamations of a historical nature, and the ELEGIES OF CH'U, although of dubious authenticity, contains material relating to shamanism, as does the first poetry collection, the BOOK OF ODES. After the eighth century B.C. a period of incessant warfare among rival feudal principalities disrupted the nation and there arose from the sixth century on a variety of philosophical systems that sought to propound solutions to the political and ethical problems of the times. Confucius, an unsuccessful would-be advisor to the government of his state, spread his moral and political teachings; they were later elaborated upon by his disciples and further developed by Mencius and other philosophers. The passive, yielding doctrines of Taoism found much favor, and came into conflict with Confucianism. For a brief period during the Ch'in Dynasty (221–207 B.C.) the Legalist School of ruthless and practical expediency gained the upper hand, and a vast number of books were destroyed by governmental order. By the second century B.C., however, the scattered texts had been reassembled (although not without many accretions and much tampering with the originals) and Confucianism had established itself as a political and ethical system which was to endure, with modifications, until the 20th century. The Han Dynasty (202 B.C.-A.D. 220) found the writing of history established as a major literary form. SSU-MA CH'IEN's *Shih chi,* covering the whole span of Chinese history, set the pattern for the later DYNASTIC HISTORIES, 24 in number, which detailed the events of each dynasty as viewed by the regime that replaced it. As governmental compilations they reflect the official Confucian doctrine. The third to sixth centuries A.D. saw the introduction of Buddhism from India and Central Asia. Missionaries and later Chinese priests undertook the translation of Buddhist texts, frequently using Taoist terminology to approximate the meaning of newly introduced philosophical concepts. All forms of Indian Buddhism were imported indiscriminately, and a number of highly complex philosophical systems developed, each based on Indian texts or interpretations of them. There was a gradual sinicization of this new religion with many purely Chinese works being added to the canon; although Confucianism continued its hold, many emperors and high officials became zealous converts to Buddhism. During the T'ang Dynasty (618–906) Ch'an (Zen) Buddhism gained wide acceptance; the vast temple complexes and land holdings of the other sects placed a severe economic burden on the nation, leading to the persecution of 845, from which Ch'an emerged as the dominant Buddhist sect. The revival of Confucianism in the 12th century and the gradual introduction of Amidist beliefs into Ch'an accounted for the decline in importance of this type of Buddhism from the 14th century on. The T'ang Dynasty was noted for a great revival of poetry as a popular literary form. Poetry, philosophical works and their commentaries, essays, and histories had always been the principal forms of Chinese literary expression: with the writings of Po CHÜ-I, LI PO, WANG WEI, TU FU and others, poetry gained heights hitherto unattained. The origins of Chinese fiction can be traced to the Han Dynasty, but official disapproval of such literature worked against its preservation. Some early works of fiction from the T'ang Dynasty have been found among the documents unearthed at TUN-HUANG. Written in colloquial language, they are tales of the supernatural, Buddhist stories, and prose romances, many deriving from the oral tradition. HSI YU CHI, stemming from this tradition, reached its final form in the 16th century and details the fantastic adventures of the priest Hsüan-tsang and his companions. The SHUI HU CHUAN and the CHIN P'ING MEI are major novels whose popularity continues unabated. The HUNG LOU MENG, characterized by a sensitivity and depth of character development not found in other works, has been described as the greatest Chinese novel. Novels have frequently been the subject of suppression and censorship, particularly during the Ch'ing Dynasty (1644–1912), when officials found them too critical of existing conditions. The Ch'ing period saw great literary activity, with enormous collectanea, encyclopedias, and works in all fields of scholastic and scientific endeavor being compiled. In the 20th century much fiction, notably short stories, has been produced, the writings of LU HSUN being of particular importance. See CIRCLE OF CHALK.

Ch'ing or **Manchu** Chinese dynasty (1644–1912). An alien dynasty. It replaced the Ming, and became gradually sinicized. Ineffectual in the face of the Western nations, the Ch'ing dynasty was eventually destroyed by the Chinese themselves with the establishment of the Republic in 1912.

Ching-t'u Buddhism. See AMIDISM.

Chin P'ing Mei. Chinese novel of the Ming Dynasty (1368–1644). It details the history of Hsi Men and his six wives. Highly satirical, it is set in the declining years of the dynasty and has been frequently banned and censored for its sexual detail. See *Chin P'ing Mei, The Golden Lotus* (1940). Introduction by Arthur Waley.

Chios. One of the seven cities claiming to be the birthplace of HOMER. Two different lists of these cities exist in Greek epigram: *Smyrna, Chios, Colophon, Salamis, Rhodos, Argos, Athenae;* or, *Smyrna, Chios, Colophon, Ithaca, Pylos, Argos, Athenae.*

Chirico, Giorgio di (1888–   ). Italian painter. His important work, from 1911 to 1920, greatly influenced surrealism. He is known for enigmatic landscapes in which solitary figures and elements of classical architecture create a feeling of premonition by means of exaggerated perspective, lengthened shadows, and lonely sense of space. During the 1920's, when he was associated with surrealism, he painted faceless figures suggestive of dummies, but later reverted to academism.

Chiron (Cheiron). A learned centaur. He taught music, medicine, and hunting to Achilles, Hercules, Asklepios, Jason, and many other heroes. A son of Cronos and Philyra, he is often spoken of as a king or leader of the Thessalian centaurs. Accidentally wounded by one of Heracles' poisoned arrows, Chiron gave up his immortality to Prometheus in order to find relief from the unbearable pain in death.

chivalry. The system of customs and conventions connected with knighthood in the Middle Ages. Derived from the French word *chevalier,* meaning horseman or knight, it was originally associated with the business of recruiting knights for the purpose of making war. It came to include the curriculum of training the young knight to fight, to hunt, to serve his lord, to govern his own vassals, and ultimately it evolved into that courtly ideal in which the true knight was not only courageous and skillful in war but also generous, pious, and courteous. When the championing of the weak began to be emphasized as part of the ideal, chivalry became as important in peace as in war, and, among other things, the tournament flourished. Another component of the chivalric code was the ideal of COURTLY LOVE, an element that further refined the knight by requiring that he be poet and musician and that he be dedicated to some lady of his choice.

Chivers, Thomas Holley (1809–1858). American poet and physician. The son of a wealthy landowner, Chivers preferred writing verse and joining the cults of his day to practicing medicine systematically. He published several volumes of verse, including *The Lost Pleiad and Other Poems* (1845), *Eonchs of Ruby, A Gift of Love* (1851), *Memoralia* (1853), and *Virginalia* (1853). Sometimes his extraordinary combinations of words resulted in exquisite melody; at other times, they became sheer nonsense. A friendly rival of Edgar Allan Poe, Chivers offered his less fortunate friend a permanent haven on his estate. After Poe's death, he charged that Poe had plagiarized from him. Chivers' influence has also been traced in the work of Rossetti and Swinburne.

Chloe. The shepherdess beloved by Daphnis in the pastoral romance of Longus, entitled DAPHNIS AND CHLOE. Hence Chloe has become a generic name among romance writers and pastoral poets for a rustic maiden, not always of the artless variety.

Chloe. See STREPHON.

Chocano, José Santos (1875–1934). Peruvian poet. Considered the outstanding exponent of MODERNISM in Peru, Chocano led a colorful life as revolutionary and political agitator; he was murdered while riding a streetcar in Chile. He early revealed his concern with American themes in *La epopeya del morro* (1899), written when he was 20, which describes the suicide of a group of Peruvian soldiers who threw themselves into the sea rather than surrender during the so-called War of the Pacific (1879–1883). His subsequent poetry glorified the Indian, the tropical landscape, and the legacy of Spain. In *La epopeya del Pacífico,* which appears in his best-known collection, *Alma América* (1906), he expressed his misgivings about the power of the U.S. Although he could be simple and spontaneous, his style tended to be florid and, at times, grandiloquent.

Chopin, Frédéric [François] (1810–1849). Composer and pianist. Born near Warsaw of a French father and Polish mother, he was resident in France for most of his career. He was the outstanding pianist and composer for the piano in the Romantic era. Nearly all his compositions are for piano: preludes, scherzos, sonatas, waltzes, ballades, études, polonaises, mazurkas, nocturnes, etc. Chopin was a close friend of the painter Delacroix and was admired by the composer Schumann. For several years he was associated with George SAND, the novelist, in an unhappy affair which ended in a quarrel and estrangement. Chopin died of tuberculosis of the larynx, a disease that had caused him much weakness and suffering.

Chopin, Kate [O'Flaherty] (1851–1904). American short-story writer and novelist. She is known for her portrayal of Creole life in Louisiana. Her best works were included in two collections of short stories: *Bayou Folk* (1894) and *A Night in Acadie* (1897). Her novel, *The Awakening* (1899), a tale of extramarital love and miscegenation, created a storm of criticism when it was first published.

Choquette, Robert (1905–   ). U.S.-born Canadian poet. Although Choquette wrote a long radio series, *Métropole,* and some rural novels, his greatest achievement is his poetry. In his first book of poems, *A Travers les Vents* (1925), he showed a passionate feeling for the north country, more lyrical and less morbid than much Canadian writing about that region. The poems in his second book, *Metropolitan Museum* (1931), contrast the serene art in the museum with the frantic life of the city around it. His other works include *Poésies Nouvelles* (1933) and *Suite Marine* (1953).

choragos. An earlier term in Greek classical drama, for the leader of the chorus. See CORYPHAEUS.

Chou. The second Chinese dynasty (c. 1027–256 B.C.). The classic age of Chinese civilization, which saw the development of a feudal state and society. The *Book of Odes* is a product of this age, as well as the thought of Confucius, the Taoist religious system, and other important philosophical concepts. The Chou kings held actual power only briefly, and the period was marked by almost incessant warfare among rival principalities.

Chouans, Les (1829). A historical novel by Honoré de BALZAC. His first literary success, it now forms part of LA COMÉDIE HUMAINE. The heroine is the beautiful spy Marie de Verneuil, and the hero is the marquis de Montauran, a Royalist leader. The Chouans themselves were French peasant insurgents, supporters of the royalist cause at the time of the Revolution. Jean Cottereau, their first leader, was nicknamed *Chouan*—a corruption of the French *chatuant* (a screech owl)—because of his secret call in times of danger.

Chou En-lai (1898–   ). Premier of Communist China. Educated in Japan and France, he was one of the founders of the Communist party in China. Joined Sun Yat-sen (1924); became active in the Red Army (1931); founded Chinese Soviet Republic (1931); began all-out military operations against Chiang Kai-shek (1947). Premier of Communist China (1949–   ).

Chou Shu-jen. See LU HSUN.

Chrétien de Troyes (fl., 1160–1190). French poet at the court of Marie de Champagne and Philip of Flanders. He wrote some of the earliest Arthurian romances including EREC ET ENIDE, *Cligés,* and YVAIN, OU LE CHEVALIER AU LION. Two of his most important works are *Lancelot, ou le chevalier de la charrette* (*Launcelot, or the Knight of the Cart*) and *Perceval, ou le conte du Graal* (*Perceval, or the Story of the Grail*), which were left incomplete at his death. *Lancelot* deals with the adventures of the Arthurian LAUNCELOT, and *Perceval* (see PERCIVAL) is the earliest literary version of the Grail legend. *Guillaume d'Angleterre,* a version of the life of St. Eustace, has been attributed to him by some scholars.

Christabel (1816). A fragmentary poem by Samuel Taylor COLERIDGE. It is known for its interesting

metrical form and its distinctive effects of the supernatural, which are often compared with THE RIME
OF THE ANCIENT MARINER. Christabel's purity and
innocence are threatened by the wicked enchantress,
Lady Geraldine.

Christian. (1) A follower of Christ. The first
use of the word occurred at Antioch (Acts 11:26).

(2) The pilgrim hero of Bunyan's PILGRIM'S PROG-
RESS. His journey from the City of Destruction to the
Celestial City forms the substance of Part I.

Christian, Fletcher. The leader of the mutinous
sailors in the novel MUTINY ON THE BOUNTY by
Charles Nordhoff and James Norman Hall.

Christian Hero, The (1701). A pamphlet by
Richard STEELE, written when the author was in the
British army, and perhaps occasioned by a duel in
which Steele was wounded. It is an attack on dueling and the code of honor.

Christian Science. A religious movement whose
teaching is that healing is done by spiritual means
rather than by surgery or medicine. It preaches spiritual confidence in the face of disaster, and by an understanding of God as the impersonal, infinite Mind.
Christian Science, founded by Mary Baker EDDY in
1866, has spread throughout the U.S., the British
Empire, Germany, and the rest of Europe. The First
Church of Christ, Scientist, in Boston, Mass., has
more than 3,000 branches. Mrs. Eddy's book, *Science
and Health with Key to the Scriptures* (1875) contains the teachings of the religion. Mark Twain wrote
a savage attack on the cult in *Christian Science*
(1907).

Christian Socialism. A religious political movement founded in England in the 1840's under the
leadership of Frederick Denison MAURICE. Its aim
was to remedy the condition of the laboring class by
a program of education and legislative reform, and
by encouraging the propertied class to practice Christian ethics in their dealings with the poor. The movement opposed the heartless individualism and com-
petitiveness of 19th-century capitalism. Aside from
Maurice, one of the chief adherents of the movement
was Charles KINGSLEY. The movement was influenced
by the work of William Godwin and Thomas Carlyle.

Christie, Agatha (1891–   ). English detective-
story writer and playwright. She is the prolific author
of consistent best sellers. Her detective hero is usually
Hercule Poirot, a Belgian. *The Murder of Roger
Ackroyd* (1926) is generally considered to be her
most ingenious book. In addition to her many mystery stories, she has written "straight" novels under
the pen name of Mary Westmacott. Among her numerous books are *The Pale Horse* (1962), a mystery
story with a supernatural theme, and *Double Sin
and Other Stories* (1961), a collection of short pieces.
Her mystery play, *Witness for the Prosecution*
(1953), was successful in both London and New
York.

Christie Johnstone (1855). A novel by Charles
READE. It is primarily the story of the titular character, a Scottish fishergirl, and her artist lover, Charles
Gatty. Gatty's mother opposes the match, but when
Christie saves Charles' life Mrs. Gatty relents. The
subplot concerns the Viscount Ipsden, whose health
has been impaired by his cousin Barbara Sinclair's
refusal to marry him. He meets Christie while fol-

lowing his doctor's prescription to mingle with
humble folk and "relieve one fellow creature a day."
Eventually Barbara marries the viscount.

Christina (1626–1689). A queen of Sweden,
daughter of Gustavus Adolphus (1594–1632). She
was given the education of a man and made her
court a center of intellectual activity to which she invited distinguished foreign scholars, artists, and philosophers. The French philosopher Descartes died
while in Christina's employ as tutor. Before she
came of age, the affairs of state, troubled by the
Thirty Years' War, were conducted by Axel Oxen-
stierna. She herself reigned for ten years (1644–1654)
and abdicated in favor of her cousin Charles X. She
embraced Roman Catholicism (1655) and died in
poverty in Rome.

Christina de Pisan (c. 1364–c. 1430). Italian-born
French poet and scholar. She turned to writing at 25
when she was left a widow with three children,
and was probably the first woman since antiquity to
earn her livelihood as an author. Her poetry includes
love lyrics, a patriotic glorification of Joan of Arc,
and three longer philosophical poems. Her prose
works include *La Cité des dames* (*The City of
Ladies*), largely adapted from Boccaccio's *De Claris
Mulieribus*, treatises on education and history; and
two defenses of women (1399, 1400) against the
satirical accusations in Jean de Meung's *Roman de la
Rose* (see ROMANCE OF THE ROSE).

Christmas, Joe. The protagonist of William
Faulkner's LIGHT IN AUGUST. The illegitimate child
of Milly Hines and a man supposedly Mexican, Joe
is placed in an orphanage by his fanatically religious
grandfather, who believes him to be part-Negro. He
is adopted by a strict Calvinist couple, who know
nothing of his origins. After wandering over the
Southwest for several years, Joe arrives in Jefferson,
Miss., where he has an affair with a white woman,
kills her, and becomes the object of a manhunt. At
home in neither the world of the whites nor that of
the Negroes, Joe continually alienates himself from
both worlds and rushes to castration and death at
the hands of a mob.

Christmas Carol, A (1843). A Christmas story
by Charles DICKENS. The subject is the conversion of
Scrooge, "a grasping old sinner," by a series of visions of Christmases past, present, and to come.
Scrooge has glimpses of his life as a schoolboy, apprentice, and young lover; of the joyous home of Bob
CRATCHIT, his underpaid clerk; of what his lot would
be if he were to die now, heartless and despised.
These visions wholly change his nature, and he
becomes benevolent and cheerful, loving all and by
all beloved. Although Dickens wrote the story
partly for the income it would bring, he said afterwards that he laughed and cried over it as he did
over no other story.

Christmas Day. The popular English name for
the Feast of the Nativity of Jesus Christ, December
25. This date was first set in 336, by the Roman
Church, the Eastern Churches having earlier settled
on the date of January 6 as the Feast of the EPIPHANY.
December 25 was observed in pagan Rome as the
festival *Natalis Invicti Solis* (Birth of the Unconquered Sun), sacred to the sun god Mithras. Christmas became a great popular festival in the Middle
Ages, which led to objections by some of the Re-

formers. The observance was forbidden in England under the Commonwealth (1644–1660), and in Calvinist New England.

Christophe, Henri (1767–1820). Negro king of Haiti. Christophe served as lieutenant to Toussaint L'Ouverture in the revolution against the French (1791). He succeeded DESSALINES as head of the government under the title Henri I. In 1820 a rebellion of his subjects caused him to commit suicide, with a legendary silver bullet.

Christopher, St. A saint of the Greek and Latin churches. Legend relates that St. Christopher was a giant who one day carried a child over a brook, and said, "Child, thou hast put me in great peril. I can bear no greater burden." To this the child answered, "Marvel thou nothing, for thou hast borne all the world upon thee, and its sins likewise." As Christopher sank beneath his load, the child told the giant He was Christ, and Christopher resolved to serve Christ and Him only. He died three days afterward and was canonized. The Greek and Latin churches look on him as the protecting saint against floods, fire, and earthquake.

Christopher Robin. The son of A. A. MILNE, for whom he wrote the POOH books. Christopher Robin is the only human character in a world of small animals.

Christ Stopped at Eboli (Cristo Si E Fermato a Eboli; 1945). An autobiographical work by Carlo LEVI. It is an eloquent and moving description of the life the author shared for a year with the peasants of a remote area of Italy, where he was exiled for his political views during the fascist regime.

Christy Minstrels. A troupe of Negro minstrels organized in New York (c. 1842) by Edwin P. Christy (1815–1862). Some of Stephen C. FOSTER's music was written for them.

Chronicle, The Anglo-Saxon. See ANGLO-SAXON CHRONICLE.

Chronicle of the Kings of England. See GESTA REGUM ANGLORUM.

Chronicle play. A play employing—sometimes very loosely—historical events as the basis of its action. The earliest example in English is John Bale's *Kynge Johan* (c. 1548). The finest examples are Shakespeare's Richard II and Henry IV plays (1594–1598) and Christopher Marlowe's *Edward II* (1592).

Chronicles, I and II. Two Old Testament canonical books, originally one book in Hebrew, which follow II Kings. The author, known only as "the chronicler," parallels the epochs described in II Samuel and II Kings. He stresses certain aspects to present a colorful picture of the traditions and attitudes of the time.

Chronicles of England, Scotland, and Ireland (1577). A history by Raphael HOLINSHED. The *Chronicles* was the source of much of the material used in Shakespeare's *Macbeth, King Lear,* and *Cymbeline.* The section concerning the history of Scotland is said to be chiefly a translation of *Scotorum Historiae* (1527) by Hector Boece. In 1587 a second and expanded edition was published, but parts of it did not please Queen Elizabeth, and she tried to have it suppressed.

Chrononhotonthologos (1734). A burlesque of contemporary drama by Henry CAREY, subtitled "the

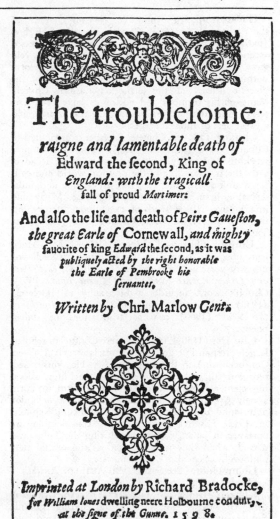

The troublesome raigne and lamentable death of Edward the second, King of England: with the tragicall fall of proud *Mortimer*:

And also the life and death of *Peirs Gaueston,* the great Earle of Cornewall, and mighty fauorite of king *Edward* the second, as it was publiquely acted by the right honorable the Earle of Pembrooke his seruantes.

Written by Chri. Marlow *Gent:*

Imprinted at London by Richard Bradocke, *for William Iones dwelling neere* Holbourne conduit, *at the signe of the* Gunne. 1 5 9 8.

Title page of Marlowe's chronicle play
Edward II (1598).

Most Tragical Tragedy that was ever Tragedized by any company of Tragedians." The title is the name of the King of Queerumania, the pompous main character, and is used for any bombastic person who delivers inflated address. The play is noted for its frank criticism of the theater of its day.

Chryseis. In Homer's ILIAD, daughter of Chryses, a priest of Apollo. She was famed for her beauty. During the Trojan War, Chryseis was taken captive and allotted to Agamemnon, king of Argos. When he refused to accept ransom, Chryses evoked a plague and Agamemnon was forced to let her go.

Chrysippus (Chrysippos). See PELOPS.

Chrysoloras, Manuel (d. 1415). Greek scholar. He was invited to Florence to teach in 1396, the first of many who came to Italy to foster the revival of classical studies during the Renaissance. His teaching and scholarly activities did not prevent him from traveling widely in Italy and throughout Europe, as well as his native Constantinople.

Chrysostom, St. John (c. 345–407). One of the Fathers of the Greek Church, elected archbishop (patriarch) of Constantinople in 398. He stressed asceticism and knowledge of the Scriptures in religion, as well as charity, social justice, and reform within the Church; he established the basis of the present liturgy of the Orthodox Eastern Church. Many of his sermons and addresses have been preserved, including *On Priesthood, On the Statues,* and a great deal of Biblical exegesis.

Chuang Tzu. A Chinese Taoist text attributed to Chuang Chou (369?–286? B.C.). The first Chinese work to deal solely with spiritual subjects, it advocates the transcending of the physical world and calls for a union with the Tao, the mysterious and indescribable first principle of the universe. Witty and imaginative, it is a work of exceptional literary distinction. See H. A. Giles, *Chuang Tzu* (1926). See TAOISM.

Chubb, Thomas Caldecot (1899–1972). American poet and biographer. In addition to such volumes of verse as *Ships and Lovers* (1933), *Cliff Pace and Other Poems* (1936), and *Cornucopia* (1953), Chubb's work includes a biography of Boccaccio (1930) and one of Aretino (1940). *The Months of the Year* (1960) contains translations of Italian poems.

Chu Hsi (1130–1200). Chinese Confucian scholar, largely responsible for the Confucian revival (Neo-Confucianism) in the Sung Dynasty. He synthesized, reorganized, and reinterpreted the teachings, adopting elements from Buddhism and Taoism, to form a new Confucian system that became the orthodox philosophy until the establishment of the Republic in 1912. His teachings were of considerable importance in Japan, particularly during the Tokugawa period, when they were adopted as the official state philosophy. See also CONFUCIANISM.

Ch'un-ch'iu. See SPRING AND AUTUMN ANNALS.

Chung-yung. See MEAN, THE.

Church, Benjamin (1639–1718). American soldier known as one of the outstanding guerilla fighters in the wars between the New England colonists and the Indians. From his notes his son Thomas Church (1673–1748) wrote *Entertaining Passages Relating to Philip's War* (1716), an account of the elder Church's experiences.

Church, Richard [Thomas] (1893–1972). English poet, novelist, and literary critic. His books of poetry include *Collected Poems* (1948), *The Inheritors* (1957), and *North of Rome* (1960). Among his prose works are *Over the Bridge* (1955) and *Calm October* (1961).

Church, Thomas. See Benjamin CHURCH.

Churchill, Charles (1731–1764). English poet and clergyman, known for his biting satiric verse. His major works are *The Rosciad* (1761), an attack on London actors and acting which is often ranked with Pope's *Dunciad; The Ghost* (1762), an account of the notorious COCK LANE GHOST episode ridiculing Samuel Johnson for his interest in it; THE PROPHECY OF FAMINE, A SCOTS PASTORAL, a verse satire voicing English distrust of Scotland; *The Duellist* (1764), a poem defending the political position of John Wilkes and attacking all his detractors, particularly Smollett; *Gotham* (1764), a verse epistle setting forth the "idea of a patriot king" (see Henry ST. JOHN); and *The Candidate* (1764), a poetic attack on the conservative political policies of Cambridge University.

Churchill, John. See 1st duke of MARLBOROUGH.

Churchill, Sarah (1914–   ). English actress. The daughter of Sir Winston Churchill, she married Vic Oliver (Viktor Samek) in 1936 (divorced 1945) and Anthony Beauchamp in 1949. She has appeared on the American stage in *Gramercy Ghost* (1951) and on television.

Churchill, Winston (1871–1947). American novelist. He is noted for his enormously successful historical romances. Although his first novel, *The Celebrity* (1898), supposedly a satire on Richard Harding Davis, was moderately popular, it was with his second, RICHARD CARVEL, that he established his literary reputation. THE CRISIS, THE CROSSING, CONISTON, and *Mr. Crewe's Career* (1908), a story about the control of state politics by railroad interests, followed. Churchill was interested in social questions and religion, and his later books reflect these preoccupations. *The Inside of the Cup* (1913) deals with the relations of religion and modern society. Other books are *A Far Country* (1915), a story of a modern prodigal son; *The Dwelling Place of Light* (1917), an account of a New England factory strike; and *The Uncharted Way: The Psychology of the Gospel Doctrine* (1940).

Churchill, Sir Winston [Leonard Spencer] (1874–1965). English statesman and author. A political Conservative, he held many important governmental offices between 1911 and 1955. He is best remembered, however, as Prime Minister during World War II. He became popular both in England and in the U.S. because of his personality and his confidence in the capacity of Britain to survive against odds. He was noted for the eloquence of his speeches and his capacity for making memorable phrases. He has written many books, including a history of World War II, in six volumes, and *A History of the English-Speaking Peoples,* in four volumes. He was awarded the Nobel Prize for Literature (1953).

Churchyard, Thomas (1520?–1604). English poet and soldier. Churchyard is best remembered for the verse accounts of Cardinal Wolsey and Jane Shore in *The Mirror for Magistrates. Shore's Wife* is considered his best work. Some of his poems and ballads appeared in broadsheets or in popular Elizabethan miscellanies. His works, primarily autobiographical, appeared as *Churchyard's Chips* (1575), *Churchyard's Choice* (1579), *Churchyard's Charge* (1580); *Churchyard's Challenge* (1593); etc.

Chūshingura. Japanese *joruri* and *kabuki* play by Takeda Izumo (1691–1756). Known in English as the *League of the Loyal Ronin,* it concerns the revenge taken by 47 loyal retainers whose master was forced to take his life. After attaining their objective, all 47 likewise commit *harakiri.* It is based on a historical incident.

Chute, La. See FALL, THE.

Ch'u Tz'u. See ELEGIES OF CH'U.

Ciappelletto, Ser. The hero of a tale from Giovanni Boccaccio's THE DECAMERON. He makes a false confession about his wicked life before his death and soon becomes a legendary paragon of virtue, St. Ciappelletto.

Ciardi, John (1916–   ). American poet, teacher, and critic. Ciardi's essays on the art of reading and enjoying poetry are notable for their lively wit, perception, and common-sense attitudes. Among his collections of critical writings are *How Does a Poem Mean?* (1959) and *Dialogue with an Audience* (1963). His poetry tends to be ironic but is not without muted depths and power. His earliest collection, *Homeward to America* (1940), was followed by *Other Skies* (1947), *As If* (1955), *I Marry You* (1958), *39 Poems* (1959), *In the Stoneworks* (1961), and *In Fact* (1962). He translated Dante's *Inferno* (1954) in *terza rima* and in idiomatic English to recall Dante's use of the vernacular. His translation of the *Purgatorio* appeared in 1961.

Cibber, Colley (1671–1757). English dramatist, poet, and actor. He is best known for the sentimental comedy *The Careless Husband* (1704), and such others as *Love's Last Shift* (1696), *She Would and She Would Not* (1702) and *The Provoked Husband* (1728), an adaptation of Molière's *Tartuffe*. He also wrote a famous description of the Restoration and early 18th-century theater, *Apology for the Life of Mr. Colley Cibber, Comedian* (1740). Cibber was poet laureate for 27 years from 1730, was generally considered one of the worst poets to hold the office, and even admitted that he was granted the post for being a good Whig.

Cicero, Marcus Tullius (106–43 B.C.). Roman orator, statesman, and man of letters. After carefully preparing himself for a career in law, Cicero made his oratorical debut under the dictatorship of Sulla, his first public success occurring in 80 B.C. The next two years he spent in Greece and Rhodes, where he continued his study of philosophy and rhetoric. After his return to Rome, he was elected quaestor (76) and aedile (70). In the year of his aedileship he was asked by the Sicilians to be their attorney against their former governor Verres. Even though his opponent was Hortensius, the most famous orator of the day, Cicero was able to amass such a convincing array of evidence of the dishonesty and cruelty of Verres that the defendant took the first chance to slip into voluntary exile. In 67 Cicero was overwhelmingly elected praetor, and as such came out in favor of the Manilian Law, the proposal that would confer on Pompey complete command in his war with Mithradates. Thus, in his first purely political oration, Cicero registered himself on the side of Pompey and the aristocratic party.

Cicero himself, however, was of equestrian rank; he was a parvenu, or *novus homo*, whose family had never been distinguished by holding public office. Although he was a member of the aristocratic party, he was looked down upon by many members of his own faction. Nevertheless, in 64 he succeeded in being elected consul of Rome. It was this year of his consulate (63) that marked his greatest success: the almost singlehanded foiling of the conspiracy of CATILINE. His four brilliant orations against Catiline (*In Catilinam*) show that Cicero was not only a master of the Roman art of pleading but also a master of the equally Roman art of politics; he emerges as a beleaguered patriot protecting himself from paid assassins, a shrewd chief of state gathering the means to overcome a civil criminal, and a clever propagandist presenting himself to the people as one greater than Romulus, for Romulus merely founded Rome while Cicero was its savior. Catiline and his army were defeated, and the principal conspirators were summarily executed.

Soon afterward, however, Cicero's influence waned. His enemies became more outspoken. Finally, in 58, CLODIUS PULCHER had a bill passed which declared that anyone who had executed a Roman citizen without trial should be declared an outlaw. In the face of growing popular indignation, Cicero voluntarily retired to Greece. The sentence of banishment was pronounced *in absentia*, his properties destroyed or confiscated, and his wife and daughter harassed.

Through the influence of his friends, he was, within a year and a half, recalled from exile and entirely restored to his former rank within the commonwealth, but he found himself obliged to spend the next six years defending these same friends from their political enemies. His orations in defense of Sestius, Plancius, and Milo date from this period. In the 50's he also found time for study and for writing. He returned to the two great enthusiasms of his youth: philosophy and the art of rhetoric. Between the years 54–51 he wrote *De Re Publica*, a six-book work on political philosophy of which about one third is extant. In 55 he wrote his great treatise on oratory, *De Oratore*. Written in the form of a dialogue, this treatise deals with the proper training for an orator, the style and treatment appropriate to particular themes, and the manner of delivery most apt to sway an audience.

But there was no longer a place for oratory in the Roman world. The senate was dwarfed by the figures of Julius Caesar and Pompey, and these two giants called for war. In 49, after long hesitation, Cicero left Italy and pledged his life and fortune to the cause of Pompey. In the next year, when Caesar crushed Pompey in the battle of Pharsalus, Cicero realized that the cherished traditions of republican Rome were crumbling. Even though the victorious Caesar pardoned him and welcomed him back to Rome, Cicero, shaken and disillusioned, remained aloof from politics. He retired to his villa in the mountains of Tuscany and sought out what he called *otium cum dignitate* (leisure with dignity). Between the years 47 and 44, he wrote the five books of the *Tusculanae Disputationes*, on the subject of happiness; his works on theology and augury, *De Natura Deorum* and *De Divinatione;* his two dialogues on old age and friendship, DE SENECTUTE and DE AMICITIA; and his handbook on Stoic morality, *De Officiis*.

In 44, with the death of Caesar, Cicero, then in his 63rd year, saw his chance to re-enter politics and to save Rome from demagoguery and chaos. He hoped to play the role of the elder statesman and to serve as guardian to the young Octavius. Accordingly, he attacked Mark Antony in 14 orations known as Philippics. But Octavius turned against his would-be ally and, joining Antony and Lepidus in the Second TRIUMVIRATE, declared Cicero an outlaw. He tried to escape to Greece but was overtaken by a mob of bounty hunters; his head and right hand were presented to his enemy Antony, who had them placed on the rostrum in the Forum, where the orator had first won his glory.

Cicero was not only Rome's greatest orator; he was

perhaps its most articulate philosopher. Through his philosophical treatises, he helped to make Latin a strong, yet surprisingly flexible, vehicle for logical speculation. Through his mastery of Latin prose, he transformed Latin from a blunt utilitarian language —one most fit for merchants, generals, and lawyers —to a rich chromatic language that rivaled Greek in its capacity to convey at the same time the gamut of feelings and the fine distinction of ideas.

Cicero's prose style is rhetorical, in the best sense of the word; it is intended to persuade. It has always been contrasted with the style of Tacitus and Sallust, who both preferred a tight, tersely emphatic prose to the symphonic sonorities of Cicero. These two stylistic schools continued in conflict into the 16th and 17th centuries when in England the Tacitean style of Francis Bacon was contrasted with the Ciceronian style of Jeremy Taylor. See ATTICUS; CICERONIAN AGE.

Ciceronian age. In its intellectual aspects, the last years of republican Rome are often referred to as the Ciceronian age, or the age of CICERO, dating from the emergence of Cicero (80 B.C.) to the empire under Augustus (27 B.C.). The prose—as well as the politics—of the late republic was dominated by Marcus Tullius Cicero. Like Cato the Elder, Cicero was a versatile writer-statesman, but where Cato was representative of the sharp, straightforward, vernacular Latin style, Cicero was the creator and pre-eminent representative of the smooth and rhetorically powerful Hellenized style. A master of oratory, Cicero was also a thoughtful and thorough student of literary criticism, a foremost authority on Stoic philosophy, and a brilliant letter writer. Other prose writers of the period include the historians Julius CAESAR and SALLUST, both of whom set a high standard of excellence for all subsequent Roman historians, and Terentius VARRO, reputedly the most learned and productive scholar of his time.

Although the Ciceronian age is conspicuously an age of prose, it also embraces LUCRETIUS and CATULLUS, two of the most significant poets in Latin literature. Lucretius wielded the dactylic hexameter of Ennius in his long and passionate poem on Epicurean science, De Rerum Natura. Catullus was the first truly successful writer of Latin lyric poems. These he modeled on the literary forms of the Alexandrine school of Hellenistic Greek literature.

With the murder of Cicero (43), the last great voice of Roman republicanism was stilled. The transition to the imperial period had begun and its dominant figure was to be the young Octavius Caesar, later Augustus. In his struggle with Mark Antony, from the death of Julius Caesar (44) to its culmination at ACTIUM (31), Rome leaves behind her old republican ideals to become an empire, and the Ciceronian age gives way to the AUGUSTAN AGE.

Cid, Le (The Cid, 1637). A tragedy by Pierre CORNEILLE. One of Corneille's most powerful tragedies, Le Cid is considered by many critics to mark the beginning of modern French drama. The playwright borrowed from Guillén de Castro's treatment of the subject, but compressed the material into a swiftly moving play.

Cid, Poema del or Cantar de mio. An epic poem in Spanish, written about 1140 by an unknown Castilian bard. The poem has survived only in a single manuscript copy from which several pages are missing, made in 1307 by one Per Abbat. It was first published in 1779 by Tomás Antonio Sánchez.

The poem is based on the exploits of Rodrigo or Ruy Díaz de Bivar (c. 1043–1099), who was known as el Cid (from Arabic Sidi, "lord"). Born near Burgos, he was named chief marshal, or alférez, of the royal army by Sancho II of Castile and later served under Sancho's brother and successor, Alfonso VI, who banished him because of personal differences. The Cid fought both for and against the Moorish rulers who at that time controlled much of the Iberian peninsula. A highlight of his career was his conquest of Valencia (1094), which halted Almoravid expansion in Spain. In 1074 he married Doña Jimena Díaz, a niece of Alfonso. He was also known as el Campeador ("the Champion").

Consisting of 3735 lines, the poem is divided into three parts, or cantares. The first deals with the Cid's exile and concludes with his defeat of the count of Barcelona. A famous episode describes his entry into Burgos, where no one will speak to him until a little girl explains that King Alfonso has warned the people to refuse him lodging. In the second part, the Cid captures Valencia, is reconciled with the king, and marries his two daughters, Doña Elvira and Doña Sol, to two nobles, the infantes, or heirs, of Carrión. The third part recounts the outrageous conduct of Rodrigo's sons-in-law, who beat and abandon their wives. The Cid avenges himself by defeating them in a trial by combat and then arranges the marriage of his daughters to the princes of Navarre and Aragon.

Similar in form to the Chanson de Roland, the poem is notable for its simplicity and directness and for its exact, picturesque detail. Despite the inclusion of much legendary material, the figure of the Cid, who is depicted as the model Castilian warrior, is not idealized to an extravagant degree.

The Cid appeared in many other medieval poems, among them the epic Cantar de Rodrigo, which was written about 1400 and is based almost entirely on legend. Later authors also made use of this theme, notably Juan de la Cueva, Lope de Vega, Guillén de Castro, and Juan Eugenio Hartzenbusch. Castro's Mocedades del Cid was the direct source of Corneille's LE CID. Present knowledge about the historical character and the Poema de mio Cid is derived largely from the exhaustive investigations of Ramón Menéndez Pidal, who published a three-volume critical edition (1908–1911).

Cimabue, Giovanni. Real name, **Cenni di Pepo** (c. 1240–c. 1302). Florentine painter. Tradition celebrates him as "the father of Italian painting" and the teacher of GIOTTO. He was himself taught by Byzantine artists, so that several iconlike Madonnas and Crucifixions have been attributed to him, but there are no extant works that can be positively established as his. His renown among his contemporaries is attested to by Dante, who describes him in the Purgatorio, as having "held the field" until surpassed by Giotto.

Cimber, Metellus. In Shakespeare's JULIUS CAESAR, a conspirator against Caesar. After he unsuccessfully appeals to Caesar to revoke a decree banishing his brother from Rome, he and the other conspirators fall on Caesar and stab him to death.

Cimetière marin, Le (The Graveyard by the Sea, 1920). A poem by Paul VALÉRY. Written in decasyllabic six-line stanzas, it describes the dazzling noon of the Mediterranean coast, where Valéry spent his boyhood. The narrator ironically contrasts the attractive clarity of timeless intellectuality with the inevitable decay of all that lives in reality. He concludes, however, that for a mortal being "It is necessary to try to live."

Cimmerians (Kimmerioi). A legendary tribe. Homer placed them beyond Oceanus, in a land of never-ending gloom. Immediately beyond was Hades. Pliny placed Cimmeria near the Lake Avernus, in Italy, where "the sun never penetrates." The phrase "Cimmerian darkness" signifies intense darkness.

Historically, the name Cimmerians is given to a nomad tribe from the Crimean region who, under pressure from the Sarmatians and Scythians, overran Asia Minor in 635 B.C.

Cimosco. In the ORLANDO FURIOSO of Ariosto, the King of the Frisians. His son Arbante is supposed to wed the unwilling Olimpia. When the latter causes the death of Arbante, Cimosco plans to take revenge on her lover, Bireno. But while in captivity, Bireno falls in love with Cimosco's daughter and deserts Olimpia for her.

Cincinnatus, Lucius Quinctius. An early Roman hero. According to tradition, he was appointed DICTATOR in 458 B.C. and sent to rescue a Roman army besieged by the Aequians on Mount Algidus. Cincinnatus routed the Aequians and, after a dictatorship of 16 days, renounced public life and returned to his farm.

Cinderella. The heroine of an ancient fairy tale. Her name (Fr., *Cendrillon*; Ger., *Aschenbrötel*) means literally the little cinder girl. The story, probably of Eastern origin, was mentioned in 16th-century German literature and was popularized in Perrault's *Contes de ma mère l'oye* (1697). Cinderella is the drudge of a household while her elder sisters go to balls. At length, a fairy godmother enables Cinderella to go to the Prince's ball. The Prince, of course, falls in love with her, and she is later rediscovered by him by means of a glass slipper that she has dropped, and that will fit no foot but her own. The details of the complete story, not found in most children's books, are somewhat gruesome. Rossini's delightful opera *La Cenerentola* (1817) is based on a considerably modified version of the story.

Cinna. In Shakespeare's JULIUS CAESAR, a young poet. After Caesar's murder, he is mistaken for Cinna the conspirator by the irate Roman citizens.

Cinna (1640). A tragedy by Pierre CORNEILLE. It is based on an episode in Roman history recounted in Seneca's *De Clementia*. Though trusted by the emperor Augustus, Cinna leads a conspiracy to overthrow him, encouraged by his beloved Amélie who desires to avenge the death of her father. Maxime, a fellow conspirator also in love with Amélie, betrays the plot, hoping to cause Cinna's arrest. The last act focuses on Augustus' struggle to choose between mercy and revenge. Ultimately, he pardons the lovers as well as the treacherous Maxime. The play reflects Corneille's interest in political subjects.

cinq auteurs (Fr., "five authors"). The French playwrights BOISROBERT, COLLETET, CORNEILLE, L'Estoile, and ROTROU, who were hired by Cardinal RICHELIEU to write plays under his supervision conforming to his strong views on the drama. A man with literary ambitions of his own, Richelieu occasionally chose the subject matter with which his authors were to deal, but more frequently merely dictated the treatment. Few of the plays he commissioned are remembered, though several were performed for the king.

cinquain. In prosody, a quintet or five-line stanza. The term is also used to designate the five-line poem of two, four, six, eight, and two syllables respectively; this form was invented by Adelaide Crapsey who was greatly influenced by the Japanese HAIKU and TANKA.

> Just now,
> Out of the strange
> Still dusk—as strange, as still—
> A white moth flew. Why am I grown
> So cold?
> Adelaide Crapsey, *The Warning*

cinquecento (*It.*, the five hundreds). Italian designation of the 16th century. This is the age of the high RENAISSANCE—of Ariosto and Castiglione, Machiavelli and Aretino. In art history, the age of Raphael, Leonardo da Vinci and Michaelangelo, and of the advent of Mannerism and the proto-Baroque.

Cipolla, Brother. A friar in one of the tales from Giovanni Boccaccio's THE DECAMERON. He specializes in duping villagers with fake relics. Planning to display a feather from the wings of the archangel Gabriel, he discovers that some coals have been substituted for it; quickly, he recovers his poise and announces that they are from the brazier on which Saint Lawrence met his death.

Circe (Kirke). A sorceress of Greek mythology. She lived in the island of Aeaea. When Odysseus landed there, Circe turned his companions into swine, but he resisted this metamorphasis by virtue of a herb called *moly*, given him by Hermes.

Circe was Aetes' sister and the aunt of Medea. She purified Jason and Medea for the murder of Absyrtus and gave them advice on their homeward journey.

Circle of Chalk, The. A Chinese classical play of the Yuan dynasty (1259–1368), sometimes attributed to Li Hsing-Tao. The lovely Chang-hi-tang is sold to a teahouse by her destitute family and is bought by Mr. Ma, the tax collector, to whom she bears a son. Jealous for her position as head wife and heir, Mrs. Ma poisons her husband's tea and bribes witnesses to prove that Chang-hi-tang has murdered him and that the concubine's child is really her own. The new emperor, who has ordered all cases involving the death penalty retried before him, listens to the evidence; he then places the child in a chalk circle and directs Mrs. Ma and Chang-hi-tang each to take hold of one of the baby's arms and, thus, gain the child by pulling him out of the circle. When Mrs. Ma wins this contest, for Chang-hi-tang is unwilling to hurt the child by pulling at all, the emperor decides that the concubine is the rightful mother and Mrs. Ma the murderess, and he leaves it to Chang-hi-tang to pronounce justice. She orders Mrs. Ma to make herself a cup of tea and to let her conscience decide what sort of tea it ought to be. In later adaptations additional symbolic chalk circles and a love affair between the emperor and Chang-hi-tang were added. Bertolt Brecht used the play as the basis of his *Caucasian Chalk Circle,* in which the stagecraft is purportedly modeled on the classical Chinese convention and moralistic and socio-economic didacticisms replace the subtlety and beautifully lyric verse that distinguish the original.

A very similar story is told in the Bible of a wise judgment of SOLOMON.

circumlocution (literally, talking around). A deliberately roundabout and wordy way of saying something. Frequently it represents an evasion of a plain but perhaps unpalatable truth.

Circumlocution Office. A term applied in ridicule by Charles Dickens in LITTLE DORRIT to public offices in England, because each person tries to shuffle off every task onto someone else. Hence, routine formality and the red tape of bureaucracy.

Ciriaco [Pizzicolli] D'Ancona (1391-1455). Italian archeologist and scholar. One of the genuine enthusiasts for antiquity in the Italian Renaissance, he roamed widely in search of inscriptions, monuments, and ruins. He is reported to have said of his journeys, "I go to awake the dead!"

Cithaeron (Kithairon). A mountain range between Attica and Boeotia. Near to both Thebes and Athens, it was the scene of many events of Greek mythology. Perhaps most notable of these were the death of Pentheus at the hands of his mother Agave and her BACCHANTES, and the exposing of both the infant Oedipus and the twins Amphion and Zethus.

Cities of the Plain. See REMEMBRANCE OF THINGS PAST.

Citizen of the World, The (1762). An epistolary novel by Oliver GOLDSMITH. In almost colloquial prose, it is supposedly written by a Chinese philosopher, LIEN CHI ALTANGI, who visits England and reports on it to his friends in the East. The letters were published with the subtitle *Letters from a Chinese Philosopher Residing in London to his Friends in the East.* In these "Chinese Letters," Goldsmith is typical of his day in his praise of simplicity. Here the main catchword is Nature's "simple plan." The philosopher's observations are supplemented by those of his friend, the MAN IN BLACK, by Beau TIBBS, and by Lady Betty TEMPEST. The letters are linked by a subplot, in which the philosopher's son rescues the Man in Black's daughter from captivity in Persia, brings her to England, and marries her. The novel first appeared as a series of essays in Newbury's *Public Ledger* (1760-1761) under the title, *The Chinese Letters.* This device of the Oriental traveler was perfected in Montesquieu's *Lettres Persanes* (1721).

City, The (La Ville; 1890). A poetic drama, revised in 1897, by Paul CLAUDEL. It presents in allegorical form the building, the destruction, and the salvation of the City of Men.

City in the Sea, The (1831). A poem by Edgar Allan POE. The poet evokes a grim landscape in melodic lines. His description of the shrine includes the well-known lines:

> Whose wreathèd friezes intertwine
> The viol, the violet and the vine.

City of Destruction. In Bunyan's PILGRIM'S PROGRESS, the world of the unconverted. Bunyan makes Christian flee from it and journey to the Celestial City, thereby showing the "walk of a Christian" from conversion to death.

City of Dreadful Night, The (1874). A long poem by the Victorian poet James THOMSON, published in *The City of Dreadful Night, And Other Poems.* It describes an imaginary city of misery and horror created out of the author's own sense of despair as, afflicted with insomnia, he walked at night through the streets of London.

City of God, The (De Civitate Dei; 22 vols., 413-426). A long treatise by St. AUGUSTINE. It is an apology for Christianity against the accusation that the Church was responsible for the decline of the Roman Empire. It interprets human history as a conflict between the City of God (*Civitas Dei*), which includes the body of Christians belonging to the Church, and the Earthly City (*Civitas Terrena*), composed of pagans and heretical Christians. Augustine foresees that through the will of God the people of the City of God will eventually win immortality, those in the Earthly City destruction.

city of refuge. A sacred area. Moses, at the command of God, set apart three cities on the east of Jordan, and Joshua added three others on the west, whither any person might flee for refuge who had killed a human creature inadvertently. The three on the east of Jordan were Bezer, Ramoth, and Golan; the three on the west were Hebron, Shechem, and Kedesh (Deut. 4:43; Josh. 20: 1-8).

Medina, in Arabia, where Muhammad took refuge when driven by conspirators from Mecca, is known as the *city of refuge.* He received a warm welcome when he entered Medina in A.D. 622.

Civil Disobedience (1849). An essay by Henry David THOREAU. Its major premise is "that government is best which governs least." Thoreau asserts that a man's first loyalty is to his own nature; true to himself, he may then be true to a government. The essay influenced Gandhi's doctrine of passive resistance.

Civil War, American. See AMERICAN CIVIL WAR.

Civil War, English, or **Great Rebellion.** A civil war brought on by conflict between CHARLES I and the LONG PARLIAMENT over economic, political, and religious issues. The war had two phases. The first (1642-1646) was fought between the Royalist party, which included most of the nobles and gentry and adherents of the Church of England, and the Parliamentary party, which was supported by Presbyterians and other dissenters and the middle classes in general. In 1643 the Scottish COVENANTERS joined the Parliamentary cause. After initial Royalist successes, this phase ended with Parliamentary victories at MARSTON MOOR and NASEBY.

The second phase, which lasted from about 1648 to 1652, followed the acquisition of power by the Parliamentary army and more radical dissenters, or INDEPENDENTS, led by Oliver CROMWELL. The struggle was now between this group and the king, who was executed in 1649, conservative members of Parliament, Irish Royalists, and the Scots, now allied with Charles II. In the Preston campaign (1648), the Irish War (1649-1650), and the battles of Dunbar (1650) and Worcester (1651), Cromwell emerged victorious. See GRAND REMONSTRANCE; John HAMPDEN; NEW MODEL ARMY; PRIDE'S PURGE; and John PYM.

Clair, René (1898–   ). French film director and producer. From his first effort in 1923, *Paris qui dort*, René Clair revealed a unique sense of the absurd, especially as embodied in the French bourgeois. His talent culminated during the silent era in the *Italian Straw Hat* (1927), a witty film version of Eugène Labiche's famous 19th-century farce of the same name. With the introduction of sound, Clair began new experimentation. His famous trilogy, *Sous les toits de Paris* (1929), *Le Million* (1931), and *A nous la liberté* (1931), is characterized by an ingenious mingling of music and dialogue with silent film techniques. In 1934 he went to work for the British and American film industry, later returning to France.

Clairmont, Clara Mary Jane. Known as **Claire** (1798–1879). Stepdaughter of William Godwin and mother of Lord BYRON's daughter Allegra. She was a friend of the Shelleys.

Clan-na-Gael. An Irish secret organization. It was founded in Philadelphia in 1881, and was successor to the Fenian brotherhood (1856). Its avowed object was to secure "the complete and absolute independence of Ireland from Great Britain, and the complete severance of all political connection between the two countries, to be effected by unceasing preparation for armed insurrection in Ireland." See FENIANS.

Clare, Ada. See BLEAK HOUSE.

Clare, Angel. See TESS OF THE D'URBERVILLES.

Clare, John (1793–1864). English poet. Clare was born into a barely literate, impoverished Northamptonshire peasant family, had little formal education, and long supported himself as a farm laborer. After the appearance of his first book (*Poems Descriptive of Rural Life and Scenery*, 1820), he became famous as a peasant poet, the curiosity of one London season. Thereafter, however, he was plagued by ill-health, neglect, poverty, and finally, madness. In 1837 he was committed to a mental asylum and died in confinement. Much of Clare's voluminous verse lacks distinction, but his best poems possess a startling originality and directness of vision, ranking high among English nature poetry. Aside from his first volume, his works include *The Village Minstrel* (1821); *The Shepherd's Calendar* (1827); and *The Rural Muse* (1835). The recent edition of *Selected Poems of John Clare* (1950) by Geoffrey Grigson includes many poems written in madness.

Clarel: A Poem and a Pilgrimage in the Holy Land (1876). A long poem by Herman MELVILLE. Clarel, a young theological student, oscillates between faith and doubt. In love with Ruth, a Jewish girl, he leaves her to join a group of pilgrims traveling from Jerusalem to Gethsemane, the Dead Sea, and Bethlehem. The pilgrims, conversing with Clarel, represent almost every persuasion. They are: Nehemiah, a saintly old man who knows the time of the Second Coming; Vine, a seclusive aesthete resembling Melville's friend, Nathaniel Hawthorne; Derwent, an Emersonian optimist; Mortmain and Ungar, cynical pessimists; Margoth, a materialist; a Dominican friar, and many others. When Clarel returns, he finds that Ruth has died; he is left alone to face reality, the possessor of new wisdom. Melville asks if civilization can survive, after science has caused a loss of faith. His poem, though technically weak, has considerable intellectual strength.

Clarence, 3rd duke of. **George** (1449–1478). English noble, son of Richard Plantagenet, duke of York. He originally took up arms against his brothers Edward (IV) and Richard (III), but was later reconciled with them. Convinced that Clarence was plotting against him, Edward had him imprisoned, and it is said that he was drowned in a butt of malmsey wine. In Shakespeare's RICHARD III, he is depicted as the victim of Richard's machinations and is arrested when Richard revives an old prophecy that "G of Edward's heirs the murderer shall be." He also appears in Shakespeare's *Henry VI: Part III*.

Clarendon, 1st earl of. **Edward Hyde** (1609–1674). English historian and statesman. An influential adviser to Charles I and lord chancellor under Charles II, he was falsely accused of treason and banished in 1667. In France he wrote his *Life* (1759) and completed his chief work, *The History of the Rebellion and Civil Wars in England* (1702–1704). The *History* is best known for Clarendon's perceptive and tolerant character sketches of the leading personages of the time. His daughter Anne married the duke of York, later James II, and bore two daughters who became Queen Mary and Queen Anne.

Clarendon Press. A printing establishment connected with Oxford University, England. It was founded partly with the profits from the 1st earl of Clarendon, Edward Hyde's *History of the Rebellion*.

Clares, Poor. See POOR CLARES.

Claretie, Jules (1840–1913). French journalist and writer. Claretie served as director of the COMÉDIE FRANÇAISE in 1885. His 20-volume work *La Vie à Paris* (1881–1911) is a piece of facile, clever writing.

Claribell. See FAERIE QUEENE, THE.

Clarín. See Leopoldo ALAS Y UREÑA.

Clarissa Harlowe (1747–1748). An epistolary novel by Samuel RICHARDSON, generally considered to be his masterpiece. Its original title is *Clarissa, or, The History of a Young Lady*. It is the longest novel in the English language, totaling about one million words. It is noted for its subtle and penetrating psychological treatment of character. Clarissa has been coldly commanded by her tyrannical family to marry Mr. Solmes, a man she despises. She refuses, even though it pains her to defy her parents. Locked in her room, isolated from family and friends, Clarissa corresponds secretly with Robert LOVELACE, a suitor disapproved of by her family; she finally throws herself upon his protection and flees with him. It soon becomes clear to her, however, that Lovelace's sole aim is to seduce her. Her virtue is so great that Lovelace becomes obsessively absorbed in breaking it down; convinced finally that she will never yield to him, he becomes desperate, drugs and rapes her. He then proposes marriage, but Clarissa refuses, retires to a solitary dwelling, and dies of grief and shame. Lovelace, whose heart the reader never really knows, is killed in a duel with Colonel Morden, Clarissa's cousin. Rousseau was greatly influenced by *Clarissa Harlowe* in his novel, JULIE, OU LA NOUVELLE HÉLOÏSE. See John BELFORD; Anna HOWE.

Clarisse. See Anne LENCLOS.

Clark, George Rogers (1752–1818). American Revolutionary frontier leader. His victories over the

British at Kaskaskia and Vincennes (1778–1779) assured American control of the Old Northwest.

Clark, Walter van Tilburg (1909–1971). American novelist and short-story writer. Although he was born in Maine, Clark lived most of his life in the Far West, and it is with this region that his talents are almost entirely identified. He is best known for *The Ox-Bow Incident* (1940), his forceful first novel that tells of the lynching of three supposed cattle rustlers just as word arrives that they are innocent. He is also the author of two other novels: *City of Trembling Leaves* (1945) and *The Track of the Cat* (1949). *The Watchful Gods* (1950) is a collection of short stories.

Clarke, Austin (1896–   ). Irish poet and writer of verse plays and novels. His work is inspired by the Irish countryside, legends, and history. His *Collected Poems* appeared in 1936, and *Collected Later Poems*, in 1961. *The Singing Men at Cashel* (1936) and *The Sun Dances at Easter* (1952) are novels. *Collected Plays* appeared in 1963.

classical. (1) Usually, a term referring to the classics, or to the period of greatest power among the Greeks and Romans, especially their culture.

(2) In literature and art in general, a term used to express, with reference to a single work as well as to an entire age, dominance of form over content: technical precision over emotional expressiveness; clarity, restraint, and rationality over ambiguity, extravagance, and free play of the imagination. It is opposed to ROMANTICISM. See NEOCLASSICISM.

(3) In music, the term is applied to work that accepts certain basic conventions of form and structure as the natural framework for the expression of ideas, as distinguished from music that is more concerned with the expression of individual emotions than with the achievement of formal unity. The term is usually restricted to music from 1750 to 1830, the period marked by the rise of the symphony and the composers HAYDN and MOZART. BEETHOVEN stands as a transitional figure to the Romantic era. The term is also used commonly to denote all serious or art music, as distinguished from all popular and folk music.

classics. The Romans were divided by Servius into five classes. Any citizen who belonged to the highest class was called *classicus;* the rest were said to be *infra classem,* that is, beneath the class. Accordingly, authors of the best or first class were termed *classici auctores* (classic authors). The term has come to describe any work or body of works of the first or highest order; thus we have English classics, French classics, and so on.

Claudel, Paul [Louis Charles Marie] (1868–1955). French dramatist, poet, and diplomat. After spending his boyhood in a small village, Claudel came with his family to Paris. He believed he had lost the conventional Catholic faith of his parents, but at 18 he rediscovered in the prose poems of Arthur Rimbaud's *Les Illuminations* and *Une Saison en Enfer* the revelation of the supernatural; that Christmas Eve during a service at Notre Dame Cathedral he suddenly felt himself permanently converted to fervent faith. He spent four years discovering the literature which was to influence him most, including the Bible, Aeschylus, Vergil, and Dante, and attending Mallarmé's salons.

In 1890 he published TÊTE D'OR and wrote THE CITY, both showing much symoblist influence. In 1893 he began his career as a foreign diplomat and came as a consul to Boston and New York; he wrote *The Exchange* (*L'Echange;* 1893), a play set on the east coast of the United States, and translated the *Agamemnon* of Aeschylus into French. In 1895 he went to China, which he describes in the prose poems of *The East I Know* (*Connaissance de l'Est;* 1900). Thereafter he traveled widely, serving in the Far East, Germany, Italy, Brazil, and again in the U.S. until 1935, after which he lived in retirement, primarily at a country home in France. *L'Arbre* (1901), a collection of all his plays to that date, includes *La Jeune fille Violaine,* which Claudel later adapted as the well-known THE TIDINGS BROUGHT TO MARY. He published BREAK OF NOON IN 1906, and THE HOSTAGE in 1909, soon followed by the last two plays of the Coûfontaine trilogy. In 1916 he completed the translation of the last two plays of Aeschylus' *Oresteia* trilogy. Between 1919 and 1924 he wrote the long play THE SATIN SLIPPER, greatly influenced by the Nō theater of Japan (he went to Tokyo as ambassador in 1921). Among his later works the best known are the dramatic oratorios *The Book of Christopher Columbus* (*Le Livre de Christophe Colomb;* 1927), with music by Darius Milhaud, and *Jeanne d'Arc au Bûcher,* with music by Arthur Honegger.

Claudel's plays, as well as his lyric poems, are written in poetic "versets" of irregular length, often of several lines, without rhyme or conventional meter; the dynamic, vigorous rhythm often resembles that of biblical verse. His inspiration is primarily religious, but he writes as passionately and eloquently of the physical world as of the spiritual; for him all things are manifestations of God, fulfilling His designs and redounding to His glory. The plays describe the conflict in men between their earthly desires and needs—to plow and reap, to explore and conquer, to delight in sensual pleasures, to love one another—and their eventual spiritual destination. The harmony of the physical cosmos, which he presents with sweeping magnificence, represents for Claudel the grandeur of God; similarly, the energy men bring to their human passions becomes the medium through which they can come to an intimation of divine love; and the greater the capacity of a character's soul for intense passion of any kind, the greater the value and the joy of its final mystic surrender to God.

Shorter lyrical poems include *Cinq Grandes Odes* (1910), *Corona benignitatis anni Dei* (1914), and *Ode jubilaire* (1921), about Dante. His prose includes discussions of his own poetic form and of poetry in general, religious meditations as in *A Poet Before the Cross* (*Un Poète regarde la Croix;* 1932), and much biblical commentary.

Claudine. Heroine of four semiautobiographical novels by COLETTE: *Claudine at School* (*Claudine à l'école;* 1900), *Claudine in Paris* (*Claudine à Paris;* 1901), *Claudine Married* (*Claudine en ménage;* 1902), and *The Innocent Wife* (*Claudine s'en va;* 1903).

Claudio. The brother of the virtuous Isabella in Shakespeare's MEASURE FOR MEASURE. He is the pivotal character in the play, embodying humanity's weakness and standing between the strict purity of Isabella and the cruel austerity of Angelo.

Claudio. In Shakespeare's MUCH ADO ABOUT NOTHING, a handsome young Florentine lord, who has served with distinction in the army of Don Pedro. He falls in love at first sight with Hero.

Claudius I. Full Latin name, **Tiberius Claudius Drusus Nero Germanicus** (10 B.C.-A.D. 54). Roman emperor (A.D. 41–54). He was excluded from public affairs by Caligula, his predecessor and nephew. When Caligula was murdered in A.D. 41, Claudius was proclaimed emperor by the praetorian guard. He was persuaded by AGRIPPINA, his second wife, to set aside his own son BRITANNICUS and adopt her son by a former marriage, Lucius Domitius (later NERO), as his successor. When Claudius, too late, repented this move, he was poisoned by Agrippina. Claudius was noted for his writing, but none of his work is extant. He is the principal character in two historical novels, *I, Claudius* (1934) and *Claudius the God* (1934), by Robert Graves.

Claudius. In Shakespeare's HAMLET, the uncle of Hamlet. He has poisoned his brother, the king of Denmark, married his widow, and ascended the throne before the play opens. Shakespeare depicts him as a sensual though able ruler whose lust for power fails to be tempered by the gnawing of his conscience.

Claudius, Matthias (1740–1815). German poet, known for his simple, sincere Christianity and his love for the common people and nature. His works include *Tändeleien und Erzählungen* (*Triflings and Stories*, 1763) and a periodical that he edited, *Der Wandsbecker Bothe* (*The Wandsbeck Messenger*, 1771–1775).

Claudius the God (1934). A novel by Robert GRAVES. A sequel to *I, Claudius*, it is an unusual historical and psychological novel, written in the form of the autobiography of the Emperor Claudius. It does not present the traditional view of Claudius as a despicable weakling.

Claus, Peter. See KLAUS, PETER.

Claus, Santa. See SANTA CLAUS.

Claussen, Sophus (1865–1931). Danish poet and essayist. Influenced by the French symbolist movement, and particularly by the work of Baudelaire, Claussen was Denmark's leading symbolist poet. His poetry, woven of esoteric imagery and intricate paradox, expresses a sensuous joy in life. In a romantic manner he worshiped the creative vitality of nature, likening it to the vigorous creativity of the poet figure. Among his collections are *Naturbørn* (1887), *Frøken Regnvejr* (1894), *Pileføjter* (1899), *Danske vers* (1912), *Heroica* (1925), and *Hvededynger* (1930).

Claveret, Jean (1590–1666). French playwright and author. In *Traité du poème dramatique*, Claveret challenged the classical rule restricting the action of a drama to a 24-hour period. His play *L'Esprit fort* (1630), which ridicules a man who pretends to be of strong character and independent judgment but who is actually a moral coward, is notable as the first French comedy of manners.

Clavers, Mrs. Mary. See Caroline KIRKLAND.

Clavileño. In Cervantes' DON QUIXOTE, the wooden horse on which the knight and his squire make a fantastic journey through the air. It is governed by a wooden pin in its forehead. The horse is a well-known figure in European and Near Eastern folklore.

Clay. A short story in James Joyce's DUBLINERS (1914). It is about a very ordinary, ineffectual, pitiful spinster called Maria who goes to the family party of a man to whom she was nurse when he was a child. The story, which has little action, is largely a character study of Maria. During a blindfold party game the children play a trick on her, making her put her fingers in a dish of wet clay. The clay is a symbol of her character; she herself is a symbol of Ireland.

Clay, Henry (1777–1852). American statesman, often called "The Great Pacificator." As a member of Congress from Kentucky, he was Speaker of the House (1811–1820, 1823–1825) and a leader of the "war hawks" who urged war with Great Britain before 1812. After running unsuccessfully for the presidency in 1824, he was named secretary of state by John Quincy ADAMS. He later served in the U.S. Senate (1831–1842, 1849–1852), where he espoused an "American System" of internal improvements and protective tariffs to strengthen the national economy. In 1832 and 1844 he was the unsuccessful Whig candidate for president; he is credited with saying, "I would rather be right than be President." Devoted to the preservation of the Union, he was largely responsible for the enactment of the COMPROMISE OF 1850. See John RANDOLPH.

Clayhanger (1910). The 1st novel in a series by Arnold BENNETT. Under the domination of his unimaginative puritanical father, Edwin Clayhanger is forced to give up his ambition to become an architect and enters the family printing business. He falls in love with Hilda Lessways, but his father will not give him enough money to marry, and he learns that Hilda is already married. Hilda's husband, George Cannon, is found to be a bigamist, old Clayhanger dies, and Edwin and Hilda are married. The novel has notable descriptions of Five Towns life, the conflict between father and son, and the son's own inner conflicts. In *Hilda Lessways* (1911) the same events are narrated from Hilda's point of view; *These Twain* (1916) is a study of the couple in married life; and *The Roll Call* (1918) is about Hilda's son, George.

Clea. See ALEXANDRIA QUARTET, THE.

Cléante. The name given by Molière to 3 of his characters. (1) In LE MALADE IMAGINAIRE, the lover of Angélique, the daughter of Argan.

(2) In L'AVARE, the son of Harpagon.

(3) In LE TARTUFFE, the brother-in-law of Orgon.

Cleisthenes (**Kleisthenes**; fl. 507 B.C.). Athenian statesman, considered the second founder of the democracy. Cleisthenes saw that the divisiveness of the clans would forever keep SOLON's government from working well. Cleisthenes' organization aimed to do away with local political influence. Taking the natural divisions of the *demes* as the basis for the Athenian state, he divided the country into three regions: the city, the coast, and the inland area. Each of the regions was divided into ten *trittyes*, a total of 30. From the 30 *trittyes*, Cleisthenes formed ten groups of three, so that none of the ten groups had two *trittyes* from the same region. Each group, though it was based on artificial geography, was known as a tribe. Local political action was ended, and all citizens worked for the general good. Cleisthenes replaced Solon's Council of 400 (based on the four clans) with a Council of 500, fifty from each tribe. The operation of the Council shows that the Athenians understood representative government. Cleisthenes is also supposed to have initiated the practice of ostracism.

Clelia. See CLOELIA.

Clélie, Histoire Romaine (1654–1660). A novel in 10 volumes by Madeleine de SCUDÉRY. Derived and enormously elaborated from the Roman legend of Cloelia, the novel recounts the tribulations endured by Clélie as hostage of Sextus Tarquinus and climaxes with her swimming of the Tiber and her long-sought reunion with her lover Aronce. Rich in digressions, the novel includes the *carte de tendre,* an imaginative map of the amorous sentiments, drawn up by Madeleine de Scudéry with the aid of her salon.

Clemenceau, Georges (1841–1929). French statesman. During the Civil War Clemenceau served as a correspondent with Grant's army. He was an ardent supporter of Dreyfus and agitated for a new verdict in the case. Serving first as a senator (1902–1920), then as Minister of the Interior (1906), Clemenceau became premier of the Third Republic (1906–1909). Premier again in 1917, he led France to victory in World War I and headed the French delegation to the Peace Conference at Versailles.

Clemens, Samuel Langhorne. See MARK TWAIN.

Clement VII, Pope. See MEDICI.

Clementina della Porretta, The Lady. In Samuel Richardson's novel SIR CHARLES GRANDISON, a devout young Catholic deeply in love with Sir Charles.

Cléofas Pérez Zambullo, Don. The high-spirited hero of two picaresque novels: *Le Diable boiteux* (1707) by Alain René LESAGE; the other (on which Lesage modelled his novel), *El Diablo cojuelo* (1641) by Luis Vélez de Guevara. In both books Don Cléofas uncorks the little devil ASMODEUS from a bottle, and as a reward, the latter shows him the vices of Madrid.

Cleon or **Kleon** (d. 422). Athenian demagogue and leader of the war party during the Peloponnesian War. He is chiefly remembered today as one of the favorite butts of Aristophanes, particularly in his comedy THE KNIGHTS.

Cléonte. In Molière's LE BOURGEOIS GENTILHOMME, the suitor for the hand of M. Jourdain's daughter. Since he is a commoner and M. Jourdain will have none but a nobleman for son-in-law, Cléonte is forced to disguise himself as the son of the Grand Turk in order to win her hand.

Cleopatra. In the chronology of Egyptian queens, Cleopatra VII (69–30 B.C.). Last Macedonian queen of Egypt. From 51 to 49 B.C. she was joint ruler with and wife of her brother Ptolemy XIII, in accordance with Egyptian tradition. She was driven from the throne by her brother, but reinstated by Julius CAESAR in 48; this gave rise to a war between Caesar and Ptolemy XIII in which the latter was killed, and his younger brother Ptolemy XIV ascended the throne and married Cleopatra. Cleopatra lived with Caesar in Rome from 46 to 44 and had by him a son, Ptolemy XV, who was later put to death

The *carte de tendre* from an English edition of *Clélie.* In the form of a map, it outlines the course of love.

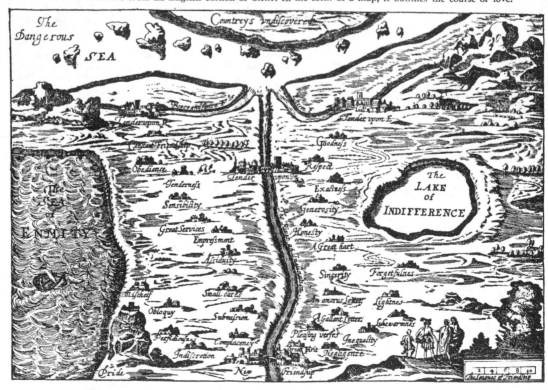

by Augustus. Returning to Egypt after Caesar's assassination, Cleopatra gave her support to the Second Triumvirate of ANTONY, Octavius (later Augustus), and Lepidus against the republicans Brutus and Cassius. Mark Antony, who had been appointed to rule over Asia and the East, succumbed completely to her charms and abandoned his wife Octavia to live with Cleopatra. They had three children. After the defeat of Antony and Cleopatra at ACTIUM, Antony killed himself on hearing a false report of her death; some say she spread the report herself to gain favor with Octavius by causing Antony's death. When she heard that Octavius planned to exhibit her triumphantly in Rome, she committed suicide by applying a poison asp to her bosom. Famed for her extraordinary charm and beauty, she was also highly cultivated.

The capricious and imperious queen is one of the most complex and fully developed of Shakespeare's female characters. In his ANTONY AND CLEOPATRA, she is a wildly erratic, jealous, and avaricious woman, but withal sincerely in love with Antony. The famous speech of Enobarbus aptly describes her:

> Age cannot wither her, nor custom stale
> Her infinite variety; other women cloy
> The appetites they feed, but she makes hungry
> Where most she satisfies; for vilest things
> Become themselves in her, that the holy priests
> Bless her when she is riggish.

She also appears in Dryden's ALL FOR LOVE OR THE WORLD WELL LOST and Shaw's CAESAR AND CLEOPATRA.

Cleopatra's Needle. Either of two obelisks, one in Central Park in New York City, the other on the Thames Embankment in London. They were erected by Thothmes III, a pharaoh of the 18th dynasty, in Heliopolis. Augustus had them removed to Alexandria about 9 B.C. They antedated Cleopatra by many centuries.

clerihew. A form of verse invented by Edmund Clerihew BENTLEY. It consists of two couplets that humorously characterize a person whose name is one of the rhymes.

Clerk's Tale, The. One of the CANTERBURY TALES of Geoffrey CHAUCER, written in RHYME ROYAL and based on a Latin adaptation by Petrarch of the 100th tale in Boccaccio's *Decameron* (see GRISELDA). The people of Saluzzo urge their Marquis Walter to marry and provide a successor. He chooses Griselda, the virtuous, lovely, and hard-working daughter of the poorest man in town. She promises that she will always willingly obey him, proves well gifted for helping him rule, and is much beloved by the people, but he insists on trying her steadfast devotion to the extreme. He takes both of their children away from her shortly after birth, telling her that he must kill them because the people feel that his heirs must not share her lowly ancestry. Finally he divorces her, sending her home, then recalling her to supervise the preparation of the palace and the reception of a new bride. She does everything willingly, until finally Walter reveals that the supposed bride and her brother are Griselda's own children, secretly raised by Walter's sister, and all live in affectionate happiness thereafter. Chaucer implies humorously that the story cannot literally mean that Griselda's behavior, any more than Walter's, is worthy of emulation, but

rather is an allegory of the constancy all men should show in unavoidable adversity.

Cleveland, [Stephen] Grover (1837–1908). 22d and 24th president of the U.S. (1884–1888, 1892–1896). Having served as mayor of Buffalo, N.Y., and as governor of New York, Cleveland was elected to the presidency on the Democratic ticket in 1884, defeating James G. BLAINE. In 1886 he married Frances Folsom in the first presidential wedding held in the White House. He ran for a second term in 1888 and was defeated by Benjamin Harrison, whom he in turn defeated in 1892. During the Panic of 1893 he secured the repeal of the Sherman Silver Purchase Act to end a drain in U.S. gold reserves. In 1894 he alienated labor by sending troops to Illinois to prevent interference with the mails during the Pullman Strike. He also invoked the Monroe Doctrine to help settle a boundary dispute between Venezuela and British Guiana. The hero of Paul Leicester Ford's THE HONORABLE PETER STIRLING is supposedly modeled on Cleveland.

Cleveland or **Clieveland, John** (1613–1658). English METAPHYSICAL POET. A reader in rhetoric at Cambridge and a Royalist during the English Civil War, he wrote satire in both verse and prose against the Puritans. In his poetry the metaphysical CONCEIT was carried to its point of greatest extravagance, degenerating often to a kind of witty ornamentation. He was very popular in his day and was imitated by numerous lesser poets. The most complete and authentic volume of his work was *Clievelandi Vindiciae, or Clieveland's Genuine Remains* (1677).

Cliff Dwellers, The (1893). A novel by Henry B. FULLER. Fuller, a pioneer in the depiction of city life, perhaps originated the term "cliff dwellers" to describe the denizens of huge apartment houses and skyscrapers. A Chicago skyscraper is the central locale of the book, which explores the subject of wealth and its effects on a large number of characters.

Clifford, Mrs. Lucy, born **Lane** (?–1929). English novelist and playwright, best known for her literary associations—with Leslie Stephen, George Eliot, James Russell Lowell, and Henry James. Her most successful novel was *Mrs. Keith's Crime* (1885), the story of parents who are tried for ending the misery of their hopelessly ill and suffering child.

Cligés. See CHRÉTIEN DE TROYES.

Clinker, Humphrey. See HUMPHREY CLINKER.

Clinton, Sir Henry (1738?–1795). English general in the American Revolution. Named commander-in-chief of all British forces in America, he captured Charleston, S.C. (1780). His delay in sending reinforcements to Cornwallis contributed to the British surrender at Yorktown.

Clio. In classic mythology, one of the nine MUSES, the inventor of historical and heroic poetry. Addison adopted the name as a pseudonym, perhaps because many of his papers in the *Spectator* are signed by one of the four letters in this word, probably the initial letters of Chelsea, London, Islington, Office.

Clitandre. The impostor-hero of Molière's *comédie-ballet* L'AMOUR MÉDECIN. Also, a tragicomedy by Pierre CORNEILLE (1632).

Clitus. In Shakespeare's JULIUS CAESAR, a servant of Brutus. When Brutus asks Clitus to kill him, he refuses, saying that he would rather kill himself.

Clive, Robert. Baron **Clive of Plassey** (1725–1774). Founder of the empire of British India and governor of Bengal (1764), who obtained for the East India Company sovereignty over the whole province. On his return to England in 1767, he met a storm of obloquy and inquiries into his actions, and although he was acquitted, he later committed suicide.

Clodius Pulcher, Publius (d. 52 B.C.). Roman patrician and tribune. He was known as a profligate and as a bitter enemy of CICERO. Cicero had disproved Clodius' alibi when the latter was accused of profaning the rites of the BONA DEA by attending them in disguise, and, though through bribery Clodius was acquitted, he hated Cicero and harassed him from then on. It was Clodius who passed a bill exiling anyone who put a Roman to death without right of appeal—a measure directed against Cicero who had members of the Cataline conspiracy executed—and thus sent Cicero into exile (58). Clodius was the brother of the notorious Clodia, the "Lesbia" of Catullus' poetry.

Cloelia or **Clelia.** In the legendary history of Rome, a Roman maiden, one of the hostages given to Lars Porsena. She made her escape from the Etruscan camp by swimming across the Tiber. She was sent back by the honorable Romans; Porsena, however, not only set her at liberty in recognition of her courage but also released her fellow hostages. Mlle. de Scudéry took this story as the framework for her celebrated romance *Clélie,* published in 10 volumes (1654–1660).

Cloete, [Edward Fairly] Stuart [Graham] (1897–   ). South African novelist. His novels, such as *Turning Wheels* (1937), are often set in South Africa and are usually historical, about the early Boer settlers. *West with the Sun* (1962) is a travel book.

Cloister and the Hearth, The (1861). A historical novel by Charles READE. The action takes place on the Continent in the latter years of the 15th century. Among the historical characters of note whom Reade introduces into the narrative are Froissart, Gringoire, Deschamps, Luther, Villon, and—as a child—Erasmus. The story centers around the tragically thwarted love of Erasmus' parents: Gerard, a talented calligrapher, and the red-haired Margaret, daughter of Peter Brandt. A forged letter convinces Gerard of Margaret's death; and, after a period of despair and wild living, he becomes a monk of the Dominican order, unaware that Margaret has given birth to Erasmus, his son. When after many adventures and misadventures the pair meet again, Gerard is unable, because of his vows, to live with his family. He manages, however, to settle nearby. Margaret soon dies of the plague, and the heartbroken Gerard dies shortly thereafter.

Clootie, Auld. See AULD HORNIE.

Cloridano. In the ORLANDO FURIOSO of Ariosto, a Moorish soldier, companion of Medoro, who goes with the latter to retrieve from the battlefield the body of their king Dardinello, after he had been killed by Rinaldo at the siege of Paris. Surprised by Zerbino, he leaves the body to Medoro and flees, but later dies defending his friend.

Clorinda. In the GERUSALEMME LIBERATA of Tasso, a pagan warrior maid from Persia. She is the daughter of King **Senapo** (Senapus) of Ethiopia, but when she was **born,** her mother the queen, fearful that the child's white complexion would arouse the suspicions of the king, substitutes a Negro child for her and gives her up to the care of the eunuch Arsete. At one point, Arsete loses her and she is suckled by a tiger. Later, he finds her again and takes her to the East, where she grows up skilled in arms. At the battle of Antioch, to which she comes to fight the knights of the First Crusade, she meets briefly and falls deeply in love with TANCREDI (Tancred), one of the leading Crusaders. When she offers her arms to the king of Jerusalem, Aladino, in exchange for the lives of Sofronia and Olindo, she finds herself once again in combat with her beloved. Unwittingly, Tancred wounds her in a night attack. Before she dies in his arms, she seeks baptism, having learned from Arsete of her Christian parentage. Tancred, in desperate grief, grants her wish and receives her forgiveness. Later, he has a vision of her in heaven.

Closterman, Pierre (1921–   ). French novelist. The work of Closterman, a World War II aviator, has risen to popularity in France with the work of other explorers and adventurers, among them Maurice Herzog who writes of mountain climbing, and Alain Bombard who writes of the sea. Testaments to man's courage and to his powers of endurance, Closterman's works include *Le Grand Cirque* (*The Big Show,* 1948) and *Feux du ciel* (*Flames in the Sky,* 1951).

Cloten. In Shakespeare's CYMBELINE, the son of the second wife of Cymbeline by a former husband. He is an arrogant, vindictive lout who does, however, display some good sense. Cloten is the rejected lover of Imogen.

Clotho. See the FATES.

Cloud, The (1820). A poem by Percy Bysshe SHELLEY. A lyrical description by a cloud of its cyclical journey from the sky to the earth and back once more to the sky, it expresses the poet's pantheism and his idea of nature's eternal alteration, rebirth, and recurrence.

Cloud-cuckoo-land (Gr., **Nephelococcygia**). A Utopian city built in the sky by the birds in Aristophanes' comedy *The Birds.* It has come to refer to visionary schemes in general.

Clouds, The (**Nephelai**). A comedy by Aristophanes (423 B.C.). This clever satire unfairly equates Socrates with the Sophists, noted for their capacity to use argument cunningly to prove whatever point they wished to make, whereas the actual Socrates seriously criticized them, believing that argument was useful only if it arrived at truth. A dishonest farmer, Strepsiades encourages his son Phidippides to enroll in Socrates' school, the Thinkery, where he can learn to evade his numerous creditors through shrewd argument. Strepsiades is delighted with his son's immense success until the young man turns his new talent against his father. At this point the old man regrets turning away from the old virtues and ends by setting fire to the Thinkery.

Clouet, François (c. 1510–c. 1572). French painter. Appointed court painter by Francis I, he is known for his soberly accurate portrait drawings and paintings. His father, Jean (c. 1486–1541), who served in a similar capacity, was a noted miniaturist.

Clovis I. *Ger.* **Chlodwig**, equivalent to later *Fr.* **Louis** (c. 466–511). King of the Salian Franks (after 481) who reunited the kingdom of his grandfather Merovée and firmly established the MEROVINGIAN dynasty. He married a Christian princess and had himself and all his people baptized, thus securing the political backing of the Roman Catholic Church.

cluricaune. In Irish folklore, an elf, particularly one guarding secret treasure.

Clutton-Brock, Arthur (1868–1924). English critic and essayist. He is highly regarded for his style. He wrote studies of Shelley (1909) and William Morris (1914). He was a Fabian socialist.

Clymene (Klymene). In Greek mythology, the daughter of Oceanus and Thetis, wife of Iapetus, and mother of Atlas, Prometheus, and Epimetheus. Clymene is, also, the name of many other heroines in Greek mythology and legend, especially that of the mother of Phaethon.

Clytemnestra (Klytaimnestra or **Klytaimestra).** In Greek legend, the daughter of Tyndareus and Leda. She became the wife of Agamemnon, whom she and her paramour Aegisthus murdered after his return from Troy. She was slain by her son Orestes. See the House of ATREUS.

Clytie (Klytie). In classical mythology, an ocean nymph, in love with the Sun-God. Her love passed unnoticed, and she was changed into the heliotrope, or sunflower, which, traditionally, still turns to the sun, following him through his daily course.

Coates, Robert M[yron] 1897–1973). American writer and art critic. During the 1920's Coates was an expatriate in Europe, where he wrote his first novel, *The Eater of Darkness* (1929). He later became art critic for *The New Yorker.* He is also the author of *The Outlaw Years* (1930), a history of the Natchez Trace pirates, and *Wisteria Cottage* (1948) and *The Farther Shore* (1957), two fictional studies of criminal psychology.

Cobb, Humphrey (1889–1944). American novelist. He is best known for *Paths of Glory* (1935), his powerful World War I novel belonging to the school of Remarque. It was made into a successful play by Sidney Howard and into an excellent movie.

Cobb, Irvin S[hrewsbury] (1876–1944). American writer, humorist, and newspaperman. Noted especially for his Judge PRIEST stories, Cobb earlier was a newspaperman for the New York *Sun* and the *World.* He later wrote for *The Saturday Evening Post* and, from 1922 to 1932, for *Cosmopolitan.* Cobb was in the main stream of American humor and was a direct follower of Artemus Ward and Mark Twain. The number of books and stories he wrote was immense. His first book was *Back Home* (1912). In addition to the Judge Priest books, Cobb wrote humorous skits, travel books, such as *Europe Revised* (1914), and an autobiography, *Exit Laughing* (1941).

Cobbett, William (1762–1835). English writer and journalist. He is best known for his pro-British pamphlets written in the U.S. under the pseudonym Peter Porcupine, and for his newspaper *Cobbett's Political Register,* published in England beginning in 1802. He became a member of Parliament in 1832. *Rural Rides* (1830), descriptions of life and agricultural conditions in the English countryside, remains his most interesting work today.

Cobden, Richard (1804–1865). English statesman and publicist. He is especially known as an advocate of free trade and peace. He was a member of Parliament most of the time from 1841 to his death, but refused party affiliation and opportunities to become a cabinet minister. He was a leader, with John Bright, of the Anti-Corn Law League (see CORN LAWS) and earned some unpopularity for his opposition to the Crimean War. He was an adherent of the North in the U.S. Civil War. His *Political Writings* were published in 1867 and his *Speeches on Questions of Public Policy* in 1870.

Cobweb. See PEASE-BLOSSOM.

Coccioli, Carlo (1920–   ). Italian-born writer who now publishes in French. In 1946 Coccioli published his first novel, *Il Migliore et l'Ultimo. Le Ciel et la Terre* (1952, translated from the Italian) is the story of the struggles of a parish priest, Don Ardito Piccardi. In its concern with spiritual problems it reveals a marked kinship with the work of Georges Bernanos. *La Ville et le Sang* (1955), *Manuel le Mexicain* (1956), and *La Table Ronde* (1957) were written in French.

cockatrice. A fabulous and heraldic monster with the wings of a fowl, tail of a dragon, and head of a cock. It was so called because it was said to be produced from a cock's egg hatched by a serpent. According to legend, the very look of this monster would cause instant death. In consequence of the crest with which the head is crowned, the creature is called a basilisk. Isaiah (King James version) says, "The weaned child shall put his hand on the cockatrice' den" (xi, 8), to signify that the most obnoxious animal should not hurt the most feeble of God's creatures.

Cock Lane Ghost. The ghost of one Mrs. Kent; she appeared as a "luminous lady" and was supposedly responsible for mysterious noises. This fraud, perpetrated in Cock Lane, Smithfield, London by a man and his 11-year-old daughter, was exposed in 1762. Samuel Johnson took an interest in the ghost and was satirized for believing in it by Charles CHURCHILL in his poem *The Ghost;* Johnson's interest, of course, did not stem from credulity, but from a determination to expose the fraud.

Cockney School. An epithet applied by John Gibson LOCKHART to the group of writers that included Leigh Hunt, Hazlitt, Shelley, and Keats. The group was largely composed of Londoners, and Lockhart, who was a devoted partisan of the LAKE POETS and a fierce enemy of writers whose aims or principles varied from his own, sneeringly referred to Hunt as "the Cockney Homer" and to Hazlitt as "the Cockney Aristotle."

Cocktail Party, The (1949). A poetic drama by T. S. ELIOT. On one level the play is a contemporary drawing-room comedy; on another it is a profound religious work concerned with universal themes. The cocktail party is a trivial affair at which ordinary Edward tries to hide from his friends the fact that his wife, Lavinia, has just left him. Edward and Celia are lovers, and Celia urges Edward to take the opportunity, divorce his wife, and marry her. However, Edward suddenly feels he needs his wife most. An unidentified stranger at the party warns Edward that his decision has set in motion events that he may not be able to control. When Lavinia returns the couple go together to a psychiatrist, Sir Henry Harcourt-Reilly, who turns out to be the stranger who was at the party. He reconciles the couple, telling them there are two kinds of good life, the acceptance of ordinary day-to-day duties, such as they have chosen, and the way of self-dedication and self-sacrifice, which Celia has finally chosen; Celia's choice is the best. Two years later, at another cocktail party, the guests learn that Celia has been martyred on a tropical island. The psychiatrist and Julia, a meddling old woman, are god and guardian-angel figures, and put forward Eliot's Christian point of view. The verse, characterized by passages of incantation and repetition, is written in the rhythms of conversation.

Cocteau, Jean (1889-1963). French poet, novelist, dramatist, essayist, film writer, and director. In the vanguard of almost every experimental artistic movement of the century, especially cubism and surrealism, Cocteau did much to promote the work of such innovators as Picasso, Chirico, Stravinsky, and the Groupe des six. Through all his works runs the theme of the poet-angel, defier of Destiny and guardian of the divine in man. The poet can be glimpsed in children and legendary heroes, but he risks being lost in the disorder of the modern world.

The most famous of his modernistic ballets are *Parade* (1916), music by Erik Satie, scenery by Picasso; *Le Boeuf sur le toit* (1920), music by Darius Milhaud; and *Les Mariés de la tour Eiffel* (1921), music by the Groupe des six.

His poetic novels are *Thomas the Impostor* (1923), set in World War I, *The Grand Ecart* (1923), and LES ENFANTS TERRIBLES (1930).

For the theater Cocteau adapted a number of myths and legends: *Antigone* (1922), *Romeo et Juliette* (1924), *Orphée* (1926), *Oedipus Rex* (1928; a libretto for an opera by Stravinsky), THE INFERNAL MACHINE (1934; also on the Oedipus myth), *Les Chevaliers de la Table Ronde* (1937), and *Bacchus* (1951). Original plots include those of *The Human Voice* (1930; made into an opera by Francis Poulenc), *Intimate Relations* (*Les Parents terribles;* 1938), *The Typewriter* (*La Machine à écrire;* 1941), and *The Eagle Has Two Heads* (*L'Aigle a Deux Têtes;* 1946).

His most famous films include the surrealistic *The Blood of a Poet* (*Le Sang d'un Poète;* 1932), *The Eternal Return* (1944), *Beauty and the Beast* (*La Belle et la Bête;* 1945), *Les Parents terribles* (1948) and *Les Enfants terribles* (1950).

In addition to a number of volumes of poetry his works include the cartoons, verse, and prose of *Le Potomak* (1913, pub. 1919); the critical essays of *A Call to Order* (1926); the personal account *Opium: A Diary of a Cure* (1930); and the autobiography *Portraits-Souvenir* (1935).

Cocu imaginaire, le. See SGANARELLE.

Cocytus (Kokytas). One of the five rivers of hell in Greek mythology. The word means the river of lamentation. The unburied were doomed to wander about its banks for 100 years. It flows into the river Acheron. See STYX.

Code of Justinian. See JUSTINIAN I.

Cody, William F[rederick]. Known as **Buffalo Bill** (1846-1917). American scout, showman, and folk hero. An expert horseman and marksman, Cody was a rider for the pony express, a frontier scout,

and a hunter of buffalo. After 1883 he toured the U.S. and Europe in his "Wild West Show." Cody's career was popularized by the dime novels of E. Z. C. JUDSON (Ned Buntline), who claimed that he had given Cody his sobriquet.

Coffin, Robert P[eter] Tristram (1892-1955). American poet. Coffin is noted for his writings dealing with his native state of Maine. A Pulitzer Prize winner in poetry for *Strange Holiness* (1935), he wrote many volumes of verse, including *Golden Falcon* (1929), *Maine Ballads* (1938), and *People Are Like Ballads* (1946). He also wrote several prose works about Maine and the volume called *The Kennebec* (1937) for the Rivers of America series. Positive and optimistic (America, he said, "is promises—promises kept"), both his prose and poetry are marked by a frank colloquialism.

Coghill, Nevill (1899-   ). English literary scholar. He is best known for his translation of Chaucer's *The Canterbury Tales* into modern English (1951).

cogito ergo sum. The axiom of DESCARTES. It was formulated as the starting place of his system of philosophy. It means "I think, therefore I exist." Descartes, at the beginning, provisionally doubted everything, but he could not doubt the existence of the *ego,* for the mere fact that *I* doubt presupposes the existence of the *I:* in other words, the doubt could not exist without the *I.*

Cohan, George M[ichael] (1878-1942). American actor, song writer, playwright, and producer. As a child Cohan acted in vaudeville in a family theatrical group, "The Four Cohans." The first play that he wrote, produced, and acted in was *The Governor's Son* (1901). He followed this with *Little Johnny Jones* (1904), in which he played a role always thereafter associated with him, "the Yankee Doodle Boy." Among his musicals and dramas were *Forty-Five Minutes from Broadway* (1906); GET-RICH-QUICK WALLINGFORD; *Broadway Jones* (1912), a play and musical about a young spendthrift; and *Seven Keys to Baldpate* (1913), based on a novel by Earl Derr Biggers. In the course of his career, Cohan wrote many songs which have remained American favorites: *Over There, I'm a Yankee Doodle Dandy, Grand Old Flag, Give My Regards to Broadway,* and *Mary Is a Grand Old Name.*

Cohen, Octavus Roy (1891-1959). American writer of short stories and detective fiction. Best known for his stories about stereotyped Negro characters, he was the creator of Florian Slappey and Epic Peters. They appeared in such books as *Florian Slappey Goes Abroad* (1928), *Epic Peters, Pullman Porter* (1930), and *Florian Slappey* (1938).

Coignard, Jérôme. A character created by Anatole France. Coignard is an irreverent, licentious abbé who also manages to be a wise and witty philosopher. The chief personage in AT THE SIGN OF THE REINE PÉDAUQUE and *Les Opinions de Jérôme Coignard* (1893), Coignard is one of France's most popular characters. Many of the author's own beliefs and opinions are voiced by him.

Colbert, Jean Baptiste (1619-1683). French statesman. After hastening the downfall of Fouquet, Colbert was made controller general of finance by Louis XIV in 1665. Although Colbert initiated many wise reforms, the costs of the king's wars and courtly extravagances defeated his plans to increase national prosperity. Colbert founded several academies and was a patron of men of letters.

Colchis (Kolchis). In Greek mythology, a city at the eastern end of the Black Sea on the River Phasis. It was ruled by Aeetes, from whom the Argonauts stole the GOLDEN FLEECE.

Cold Comfort Farm (1932). A novel by Stella GIBBONS. A brilliant parody of the novel of rustic pessimism, such as those written by Mary WEBB and other writers in the Hardy tradition, it virtually put an end to a widely popular genre.

Coldfield, Rosa. A narrator and important character in William Faulkner's novel ABSALOM, ABSALOM! Her empty life centers in her hatred of Thomas Sutpen, her brother-in-law, whom she sees as a monster, though he has long been dead.

Cole, King. Legendary English king best known as the "Old King Cole" of the nursery rhyme. He is sometimes identified with the Coel who according to Geoffrey of Monmouth made himself king of the Britons in the third century, was the father of St. Helena, and thus the grandfather of the Emperor Constantine the Great. He appears often in literature, as in John Masefield's poem *King Cole* (1921).

Cole, Thomas. See HUDSON RIVER SCHOOL.

Coleridge, Samuel Taylor (1772–1834). English poet, essayist, and critic. The son of a Devonshire clergyman, Coleridge was a precocious, dreamy boy; he attended Christ's Hospital school where he met Charles Lamb and formed a friendship that was to last a lifetime. He attended Cambridge (1791–1793, 1794), but did not receive a degree. In 1794 he

Program of Coleridge's lectures on
Shakespeare (1808).

LONDON PHILOSOPHICAL SOCIETY,

SCOT'S CORPORATION HALL,

CRANE COURT, FLEET STREET,

(ENTRANCE FROM FETTER LANE.)

MR. COLERIDGE

WILL COMMENCE

ON MONDAY, NOV. 18th,

A COURSE OF LECTURES ON SHAKESPEAR AND MILTON;

IN ILLUSTRATION OF

THE PRINCIPLES OF POETRY,

AND THEIR

Application as Grounds of Criticism to the most popular Works of later English Poets, those of the Living included.

After an Introductory Lecture on False Criticism, (especially in Poetry,) and on its Causes: two thirds of the remaining course, will be assigned, 1st, to a philosophic Analysis and Explanation of all the principal *Characters* of our great Dramatist, as OTHELLO, FALSTAFF, RICHARD 3d, IAGO, HAMLET, &c.: and 2nd, to a critical *Comparison* of SHAKESPEAR, in respect of Diction, Imagery, management of the Passions, Judgment in the construction of his Dramas, in short, of all that belongs to him as a Poet, and as a dramatic Poet, with his contemporaries, or immediate successors, JONSON, BEAUMONT and FLETCHER, FORD, MASSINGER, &c. in the endeavour to determine what of SHAKESPEAR'S Merits and Defects are common to him with other Writers of the same age, and what remain peculiar to his own Genius.

The Course will extend to fifteen Lectures, which will be given on Monday and Thursday evenings successively. The Lectures to commence at ½ past 7 o'clock.

Single Tickets for the whole Course, 2 Guineas; or 3 Guineas with the privilege of introducing a Lady: may be procured at J. Hatchard's, 190, Piccadilly; J. Murray's, Fleet Street; J. and A. Arch's, Booksellers and Stationers, Cornhill; Godwin's Juvenile Library, Skinner Street; W. Pople's, 67, Chancery Lane; or by Letter (post paid) to Mr. S. T. Coleridge, J. J. Morgan's, Esq. No. 7, Portland Place, Hammersmith.

met Robert Southey at Oxford, and the two developed their plan, called PANTISOCRACY, to establish a small, ideal community in the U. S. Unable to finance their project, they had to abandon it. In the meantime, because marriage was an essential factor in the pantisocratic scheme, Coleridge became engaged to Sarah Fricker, sister of Southey's fiancée, only to discover, too late, that his love for Mary Evans was reciprocated. His unfortunate marriage (1795) to Miss Fricker ended in separation some seven years later.

In 1796, Coleridge published his first volume of poetry and in the same year began the publication of *The Watchman,* a liberal political periodical, which lasted only 10 issues. He was by now in great financial difficulty and was considering entering the Unitarian ministry when the brothers Josiah and Thomas Wedgwood granted him an annuity of 150 pounds, thus enabling him to pursue his literary career.

In 1797, Coleridge formed a friendship with Wordsworth, a friendship that stimulated Coleridge's finest achievements in poetry, including THE RIME OF THE ANCIENT MARINER, KUBLA KHAN, and the first part of CHRISTABEL. Wordsworth and Coleridge together published LYRICAL BALLADS, and subsequently traveled to Germany where Coleridge studied philosophy at Göttingen University and mastered the German language. On their return to England (1799), Coleridge translated Schiller's *Wallenstein.* Afflicted by the damp climate of the Lake District, where he had settled in order to be near Wordsworth, Coleridge took up opium as a remedy and swiftly became addicted. After writing the second part of *Christabel* and *Dejection: An Ode,* Coleridge wrote very little poetry from then on. Hoping to improve his health, he sailed to Malta in 1804 but returned to England in 1806 without improvement. From 1808 to 1819 he gave seven series of lectures on Shakespeare and other literary subjects, which were brilliant if disorganized. During the years 1809 and 1810 he published a politico-philosophical review, *The Friend,* and a revised version of his tragedy *Osorio* (written 1797) was successfully produced in 1813. Three years later Coleridge took up residence with a doctor, in order to control his opium addiction. In 1817 he republished his earlier poems and BIOGRAPHIA LITERARIA, which contains a good deal of information on Wordsworth as well as much of Coleridge's finest literary criticism. Although his poetic achievement was small in quantity, Coleridge was without a doubt the most perceptive English critic of his time and virtual intellectual spokesman for the English romantic movement.

Colette. Pen name of **Sidonie Gabrielle Colette** (1873–1954). French novelist. The CLAUDINE books, written with her husband, were published under his pseudonym Willy. After their collaboration ended in 1904 and until 1916, she used the name Colette Willy, then Colette. She became a music-hall dancer and mime, and wrote *La Vagabonde* (1910), *L'Envers du music-hall* (1913), and *Mitsou* (1919). Remarried twice, she continued to write wry, penetrating novels of the demimonde and the feminine heart: often the older one, as in *Chéri* (1920) and *La Fin de Chéri* (1926). Her best-known works include *Gigi* (1945); her childhood reminiscences in *La Maison* *de Claudine* (1922) and *Sido* (1929); her description of German Occupation in *Paris de ma fenêtre* (1944); and her late memoirs published in *L'Etoile Vesper* (1946) and *Le Fanal Bleu* (1949).

Colette Baudoche. See Maurice BARRÈS.

Coligny, Gaspard de (1519–1572). French admiral. During the reign of Charles IX he was leader of the Huguenots and made several attempts to establish colonies for French Protestants in America. He was a victim of the MASSACRE OF ST. BARTHOLOMEW.

Colin and Lucy. A tragic love ballad by Thomas TICKELL (1720). It was called by Oliver Goldsmith "the best ballad in our language." Colin was betrothed to Lucy but forsook her for a bride "thrice as rich as she." Lucy was sad, but was present at the wedding; when Colin saw her, "the damps of death bedewed his brow, and he died." Both were buried in one tomb, and many betrothed maidens came there "to deck it with garlands and true-love knots."

Colin Clouts Come Home Againe (1595). A long allegorical pastoral poem by Edmund SPENSER. The shepherd Colin Clout describes to his fellow-shepherds his journey with the Shepherd of the Ocean (Sir Walter Raleigh) to the land of the beautiful shepherdess Cynthia (Queen Elizabeth). Colin Clout also appears in THE SHEPHEARDES CALENDER.

Collar, The (1633). A poem by George HERBERT, in which the author, after rebelling against his profitless service of God, is abruptly and totally reconciled. The poem makes use of irregular line-lengths and rhymes to achieve a remarkable dramatic effect. The collar is the clerical collar, emblem of servitude to God.

Collean, May. The heroine of a Scottish ballad. "Fause Sir John" carried her to a rock in order to throw her down into the sea; but May outwitted him and subjected him to the fate he had designed for her.

Collection, The (1962). A one-act play by Harold PINTER. It is about a homosexual who is accused of making love to another man's wife. The husband enters into a strange, aggressive relationship with the homosexual, perhaps in an attempt to enrage the homosexual's partner as he himself feels outrage and injury.

The Collection was first produced on BBC television (1961).

Collège de France. An institution of higher learning in Paris. Founded by Francis I in 1530 at the instigation of Guillaume BUDÉ, it represented an attempt to place humanistic studies on an equal footing with the theological studies provided at the Sorbonne. Hebrew and Greek were taught for the first time, thus earning it the plaudits of enthusiastic humanists such as Rabelais and Ronsard. First known as the Collège des Lecteurs royaux, it has been called the Collège de France since the Revolution.

College Widow, The (1904). A comedy of college life by George ADE. In the play, the daughter of the college president is asked to use her charms on a certain halfback to induce him to play for the right team. Extremely popular in its day, it has continued to be produced.

Colleoni, Bartolommeo (1400–1475). A famous Italian CONDOTTIERE. Following a brilliant military career highlighted by his tactical genius with artil-

lery, Colleoni lived in pleasant retirement as lord of Bergamo; most of his fellow *condottieri* met violent ends. The statue made of him by the sculptor Verrocchio, still to be seen in Venice, is the major prop of his present-day fame.

Colletet, Guillaume (1598–1659). French poet and playwright. One of the original members of the Académie and one of Richelieu's CINQ AUTEURS, Colletet is less remembered for his plays than for his poems, which include *Divertissements* (1631–1633), *Banquet des Poètes* (1646), and *Epigrammes* (1653).

Collier, Constance. Stage name of **Laura Constance Hardie** (1880–1955). English actress. Once an Edwardes Gaiety Girl, she appeared in *Peter Ibbetson* (1917), *Our Betters* (1923), which had 548 performances, and many other plays. *Harlequinade* (1929) is her autobiography.

Collier, Jeremy (1650–1726). English clergyman, known for his *Short View of the Immorality and Profaneness of the English Stage* (1698), an attack on the licentiousness of the Restoration theater. His work drew an angry reply from CONGREVE, whom he had signaled out for censure, along with Dryden, D'Urfey, and Vanbrugh.

Collier, John (1901–   ). English-born American short-story writer and novelist. Collier's first novel, *His Monkey Wife: Or Married to a Chimp* (1930), was written in the sardonic and fantastic vein that characterized his later work. His other novels include *Epistle to a Friend* (1931), *Full Circle* (1933), and *Defy the Foul Fiend* (1934). Best known for his numerous short stories, which are witty, satiric, grotesque, often macabre, and graced with a delicate and impeccable style, he is often compared to Saki. Among his short-story collections are *No Traveller Returns* (1931), *Green Thoughts* (1932), *The Devil and All* (1934), *Variations on a Theme* (1935), *A Touch of Nutmeg* (1935), and *Presenting Moonshine* (1941). Many of the stories in these collections, as well as previously unpublished works, were reprinted in *Fancies and Goodnights* (1951).

Collin, Jacques. The consummate villain of Honoré de Balzac's LA COMÉDIE HUMAINE. Collin plays a part in many of the novels. In LE PÈRE GORIOT, under the name and disguise of Vautrin, he makes love to the landlady and eats her cheap scanty food until the spiteful Mlle Michonneau gives him up to the police. Collin also appears in *Les Splendeurs et misères des courtisanes* (1843) and *La Dernière incarnation de Vautrin* (1847) as a Spanish priest and philosopher.

Collingwood, R[obin] G[eorge] (1889–1943). English philosopher. He wrote on art, history, religion, and science; among his best-known books are *Principles of Art* (1937), *The Idea of History* (1945), and *The Idea of Nature* (1946). He also published an *Autobiography* (1939).

Collins, Mr. In Jane Austen's PRIDE AND PREJUDICE, a self-important clergyman, very much the toady and prig. Elizabeth Bennet refuses his proposal of marriage, and he marries Charlotte Lucas instead.

Collins, [William] Wilkie (1824–1889). English novelist, best known as the author of THE WOMAN IN WHITE and THE MOONSTONE. He is considered by some to have been the first English author of *bona fide* detective and mystery novels. Collins was a good friend of Charles Dickens, a contributor to Dickens' magazines and occasional collaborator. The two men reciprocally admired and influenced one another, and though their talents are in other respects unequal, Collins occasionally rivaled Dickens in the creation of character and mood, excelled him in handling plot. Among Collins' other books are *The New Magdalen* (1873), *The Haunted Hotel* (1879), and *Heart and Science* (1883).

Collins, William (1721–1759). English poet. One of the preromantics of the eighteenth century, Collins wrote only a small quantity of poetry, consisting chiefly of odes on nature subjects in a quiet, melancholy vein, distinguished by their smoothness and their skillful use of sound-effects. Such work, centering about a personified abstraction, came to be called the "descriptive" or "allegorical" ode. His best-known poems, many of which were published in *Odes on Several Descriptive and Allegorical Subjects* (1746), are *Ode to Evening* (1746); *How Sleep the Brave* (1746); *Dirge in Cymbeline* (1744); and *Ode Occasioned by the death of Mr. Thomson* (1749), commemorating his significant literary relationship with the poet James Thomson. Collins' view of poetry, as set forth in his *Ode on the Poetical Character*, is that it is essentially imaginative, divine in origin, and wild and impassioned in method and insight. All his life Collins suffered from poverty and illness, and he was insane before his death.

Collodi. See PINOCCHIO, THE ADVENTURES OF.

Colman, George. Known as **Colman the elder** (1732–1794). English dramatist. He is best remembered for such comedies as *The Clandestine Marriage* (1766), written with David Garrick, and *The Jealous Wife* (1761).

Colman, George. Known as **Colman the younger** (1762–1836). English playwright known for *The Heir at Law* (1797) and *John Bull* (1803), both comedies. See DELLA-CRUSCANS.

Coloma, Luis (1851–1915). Spanish priest and author. He is best known for the satiric novel *Pequeñeces* (*Currita, Countess of Albornoz*, 1891). This vigorous and realistic work was widely enjoyed during the period at the expense of the real personages so easily identifiable with its characters.

Colonel Jack (1722). The hero and shortened title of *The History of the Most Remarkable Life and Extraordinary Adventures of the truly Hon. Colonel, Jacque, vulgarly called Colonel Jack*, written in the form of an autobiographical novel of a convicted pickpocket, by Daniel DEFOE. The colonel (born a gentleman and bred a pickpocket) goes to Virginia, and passes through all the stages of colonial life, from "slave" to slave owner and landowner, while his haunting sense of guilt and wrong-doing gradually vanishes.

Colonna, Francesco (1432?–?1527). Italian author and Dominican monk. He created one of the most beautiful and mystifying books of the Italian Renaissance, the *Hypnerotomachia Poliphili* (*The Strife of Love in a Dream with the Lover of Polia*); written in 1467, it was published by Aldus in 1499 with nearly 20 woodcuts. In two books and in a Latinized Italian prose, the author tells of the dream-journey of Poliphilus and of his love for Polia. Beneath the surface of its allegorical and romantic plot are various esoteric meanings and devices, such as the fact that the initial letters of its chapters spell out the author's name and address. An anonymous Elizabethan translation spread its influence then; but its appeal extended to modern times, as in Charles Reade's *Cloister and the Hearth*.

Colonna, Vittoria (1492–1547). Italian poet. She was a friend of Michelangelo, who addressed several of his poems to her. Her own poems include sonnets on her dead husband, Ferrante d'Avalos, and upon religious themes. They were published in her *Canzoniere* (*Song Book,* 1538).

Coloquio de los perros, El. One of the stories in Cervantes' NOVELAS EJEMPLARES. In this PICARESQUE tale, the dog Berganza is given the power of speech for one night and describes to another dog his experiences under various masters, satirizing human behavior in the process.

Colossians, The Epistle of Paul the Apostle to the. A book of the New Testament. It is a letter written by Paul, while he was in prison, to the early Christians of Colossae, the ancient city of Phrygia in Asia Minor. He urges them to ignore the syncretic ideas then common in the Near East.

Colossus of Rhodes. A gigantic statue of HELIOS on the island of Rhodes. Completed about 280 B.C., this famous statue commemorated the successful defense of Rhodes against Demetrius Poliorcetes in 304 B.C. One of the Seven Wonders of the World, it stood 105 feet high, and is said to have been made from the warlike engines abandoned by Demetrius. It was designed and built by the sculptor Chares, a pupil of Lycippus. The story that it destroyed the harbor arose only in the 16th century.

Colum, Mary (1886?–1957). Irish-American literary critic; wife of Padraic Colum. *From These Roots* (1937) is a book of criticism and *Life and the Dream* (1947) is an autobiography that throws light on the literary life of Ireland in the early 20th century.

Colum, Padraic (1881–1972). Irish poet and dramatist; later resident in the U.S. and president of the Poetry Society of America. He was associated with the IRISH RENAISSANCE and the Irish National Theater, in company with William Butler Yeats, A. E., Lady Gregory, and John Millington Synge. *The Fiddler's House* (1907) and *Thomas Muskerry* (1910) are earthy, Ibsenish plays. *Wild Earth* (1907) is a collection of poems about Irish country life. Many of his lyrics have been set to music and are familiar as near-folk songs. He also wrote books on travel and folklore. *The Poet's Circuits* appeared in 1960.

Columba, St. (Ir., *Colum*; 521–597). An Irish saint. After establishing several churches and monasteries in Ireland, the nobly born Columba converted the Picts in northern Scotland, where he founded more monasteries.

Columban, St. (543–615). An Irish saint. Most of his life was devoted to the founding of monasteries in France, Switzerland, and Italy. Several of his erudite writings are extant.

Columbiad, The (1807). An epic poem by Joel BARLOW, first published in briefer form as *The Vision of Columbus* (1787). Columbus is taken by Hesper, the spirit of the Western World, to the Mount of Visiton and there foresees the future of the North American continent.

Columbian Magazine. An early American literary magazine, founded in Philadephia in 1786.

Among its editors were Mathew Carey and Francis Hopkinson. It ran until 1792 and featured an unusual amount of American fiction.

Columbine. A stock character in old Italian comedy. She first appeared about 1560 and was shortly thereafter transplanted to English pantomime. She is the daughter of PANTALOON and the sweetheart of HARLEQUIN. Like Harlequin, she is supposed to be invisible to mortal eyes. See PIERROT.

Columbus, Christopher (*Sp.* Cristóbal Colón; *It.* Cristoforo Colombo; 1451–1506). Discoverer of America. The son of a Genoese wool weaver, Columbus went to sea as a youth, becoming a skilled navigator. He conceived a plan to reach Asia by sailing westward, but was rebuffed at the English, French, and Portuguese courts; in 1492 Ferdinand and Isabella of Spain finally agreed to sponsor the voyage, naming him Admiral of the Ocean Sea, Viceroy, and governor of the lands he might discover.

Columbus set sail from Palos, Spain, on Aug. 3, 1492, with a fleet of three ships: the *Niña*, the *Pinta*, and the flagship *Santa María*—and some 90 officers and men. On October 12 he made his first landfall at an island in the Bahamas, probably Guanahuani, which he called San Salvador. Ignorant of the fact that he had discovered a new world, Columbus then reached Cuba and Hispaniola (Santo Domingo), where he established a settlement called Navidad, and sailed for Spain.

During his second voyage (1493–1496), Columbus discovered Puerto Rico and Jamaica. However, he began to have difficulties with the Spaniards on Hispaniola, who chafed at his iron discipline. Returning to America in 1498, he touched Trinidad and sailed along the coast of Venezuela. Meanwhile, the trouble on Hispaniola continued, and Francisco Bobadilla, who had been sent as royal commissioner to investigate complaints against Columbus, ordered him back to Spain in chains. Though none of his political powers were restored, Columbus was permitted to undertake a fourth voyage (1502–1504), during which he explored the coast of Central America. After being marooned on Jamaica for over a year, he returned to Spain, where he died in poverty and neglect. Both Seville and Santo Domingo claim to possess his remains.

The best known of Columbus' writings is the journal of his first voyage. Washington Irving wrote a biography, *History of the Life and Voyages of Columbus* (1828), based on material he gathered while serving as an attaché at the American legation in Madrid. Poems about the great discoverer include James Russell Lowell's *Columbus* (1847), Walt Whitman's *The Prayer of Columbus* (1874), and Joaquin Miller's *Columbus* (1896). Paul Claudel wrote a dramatic oratorio, *The Book of Christopher Columbus* (1927), with music by Darius Milhaud.

Columbus, History of the Life and Voyages of (1828). A multivolume biography by Washington IRVING. He gathered the material while serving in the U.S. embassy at Madrid. The book includes some of the documents made available by the duke of Veraguas, a descendant of Columbus. Although Irving idealized the explorer, the book remains readable. He later added a volume called *The Companions of Columbus* (1831).

Combat. See Albert CAMUS.

Combray. A French village in Marcel PROUST's *Remembrance of Things Past*. The narrator's family visit relatives there, and it is the scene of many of his childhood memories, including the walks along the Méséglise Way and the Guermantes Way. Based on the village of Illiers, southwest of Chartres on the Loire River, it includes some details from Proust's birthplace in the Parisian suburb Auteuil.

comedia de capa y espada (Sp., "cloak-and-sword play"). A form of Spanish drama, dealing with the upper middle classes and deriving its name from the typical street costume of these groups. Stressing incident rather than characterization, these plays have complex and romantic plots that employ such devices as mistaken identities, disguises, and mutual misunderstandings. Lope de VEGA and CALDERÓN wrote excellent examples of this type of play.

comédie-ballet. A theatrical form, originally devised by MOLIÈRE for the entertainment of Louis XIV, consisting of comedy with ballet inserted between the acts. The *comédie-ballet* was one of the most popular entertainments of 17th-century France.

Comédie-Française. French national theater, now known as the *Théâtre-Français* and housed in a Paris theater of that name. A troupe of MOLIÈRE's actors, established at the *Théâtre de Petit-Bourbon* in 1658, became the core of a new theater formed in 1681 by the union of several theatrical companies and titled officially the *Comédie-Française*. The company was often called *La Maison de Molière*. After the Revolution, the *Comédie-Française* was renamed the *Théâtre-Français* (1791) and given the theater where its performances are still held today.

Comédie Humaine, La (The Human Comedy). The title given by Honoré de BALZAC in 1841 to the whole body of his work, including both completed and projected novels. The vast canvas of the work is France itself, seen from a variety of perspectives and peopled by more than 2,000 characters. Individuals of all social classes are depicted with accuracy and massive detail. A forerunner of such naturalistic works as those of Zola and the Goncourt brothers, *La Comédie Humaine* is divided into three main areas of study: manners, philosophy, and marriage. The first group is subdivided into scenes of private life, provincial life, Parisian life, country life, political life, and military life. Among the best known of these novels are LES CHOUANS, EUGÉNIE GRANDET, LE PÈRE GORIOT, LA RECHERCHE DE L'ABSOLU, CÉSAR BIROTTEAU, *Le Curé de village* (1839), LA COUSINE BETTE, THE COUNTRY DOCTOR, and COUSIN PONS.

comédie larmoyante (Fr., "*tearful comedy*"). A popular French 18th-century type of sentimental comedy in which the exaggeratedly pathetic situations of the characters made the audience weep. Concern with the triumph of virtue afforded playwrights the opportunity of moralizing to excess. Examples of this type of play are to be found in LA CHAUSSÉE's *La Fausse antipathie* (1733), *Le Préjugé à la mode* (1735), and *Mélanide* (1741); in Voltaire's *L'Enfant prodigue* (1736) and *Nanine* (1749); and in DESTOUCHES' *Le Glorieux* (1732). The comédie larmoyante was to develop into the BOURGEOIS DRAMA.

Comedy of Errors, The (c. 1594). A comedy by William SHAKESPEARE. AEMILIA, wife of AEGEON, has twin sons, both named ANTIPHOLUS, who shipwrecked in infancy have been carried, one to Syracuse, the other to Ephesus. The play represents Antipholus of Syracuse going in search of his brother; and to make the confusion of identities more absurd, the brothers each have a slave named DROMIO, and the Dromios are also indistinguishable twins. ADRIANA, the wife of the Ephesian, mistakes the Syracusan for her husband and later has her real husband arrested as a madman. Great confusion results, but ultimately the matter is brought into court. Not only do the brothers recognize each other at last, but their mother Aemilia, now an abbess in whose priory the Syracusan had taken refuge during the excitement, and their father Aegeon, who had come to Ephesus to search for his son, appear in court, and the entire family is reunited. The sources of the plot are the *Menaechmi* and the *Amphitruo* of Plautus, both written in the second century B.C.

Come Hither (1923). An anthology of verse and prose compiled by Walter DE LA MARE. It has become a classic book for children.

Come into the Garden, Maud. Well-known first line of Alfred Tennyson's MAUD.

Comendador de Ocaña, El. See PERIBÁÑEZ O EL COMENDADOR DE OCAÑA.

Comical History of the States and Empires of the Moon and **Comical History of the States and Empires of the Sun.** See CYRANO DE BERGERAC.

comic relief. The relaxation of the audience's tension by means of an interpolated comic episode in a serious play. Its function is to permit a stronger renewal of the emotional surge. A good example is the grave-diggers' scene in *Hamlet.* Some critics hold that the function of such scenes is not relief but increased tension through senseless and ironical juxtaposition of opposites.

Comines (also **Commines** or **Commynes**), **Philippe de** (c. 1446–1511). Flemish-born French chronicler and diplomat, in the service of Charles the Bold, then Louis XI, then Charles VIII. The largest part of his *Memoirs* (written 1489–1490) describes the reign of Louis XI; the last part (written 1497–1498) concerns the Italian expedition of Charles VIII. The *Memoirs* are more serious and impartial than any European history written up until that time; and they were the basis for Scott's novel QUENTIN DURWARD.

Coming Struggle for Power, The (1932). The chief work of John STRACHEY. It predicts a close and final conflict between capitalism and Communism, and the doom of capitalism.

Cominius. In Shakespeare's CORIOLANUS, the Roman general under whom Coriolanus serves in the battle against the Volscians. He has a judiciousness and humility which Coriolanus lacks.

Comintern. See INTERNATIONAL.

comitia. In ancient Rome, an assembly of the people that had the authority to act on certain matters submitted to them through official channels. They met at the foot of the Capitol at a place called *Comitium.*

Commager, Henry Steele (1902–   ). American historian. A native of Pittsburgh, Pa., Commager was educated at the University of Chicago. From 1939 to 1956 he was professor of history at Columbia University; in the latter year he joined the faculty of Amherst College. His writings are popular among both scholars and the general public.

His works include *The Growth of the American Republic* (1930), written with S. E. Morison and subsequently revised and expanded; *Theodore Parker* (1936); *The Heritage of America* (1939), with Allan Nevins; and *The American Mind* (1950). He also edited *Documents of American History* (1934).

Commander of the Faithful. A title of the Caliphs, first assumed by Omar I (581, 634–644).

commedia dell'arte (*It.,* comedy of the profession or of skill). Italian dramatic genre dating from the mid-16th century, when professional theatrical companies, especially the famous *Gelosi* (*The Jealous Ones*) began to include in their repertoire a new form of comedy characterized by improvisation upon a bare outline of plot (*scenario*), and the use of stock characters, some wearing masks, that combined features of the learned as well as the popular drama. It is this testing of the actor's virtuosity and skill that gave the genre its name, not an association with a professional craft or guild. Among the famous and enduring stock characters were "the beautiful young lady," an ingenue with a name such as Julia or Lucinda; her "lover," handsome but impecunious, sometimes called Octavio; Pantalone, a Venetian merchant as foolish as he is wealthy; the Doctor, sometimes called Graziano, who is a hopeless pedant; a braggart captain, later called SCARAMUCCIA; and a collection of servants who provide anything from sparkling wit to acrobatics as they move in and out of the story, sometimes helping, at other times hindering the affairs of their masters and mistresses. The oldest of the wily or blundering manservants is Zanni (a dialect version of Gianni or Giovanni); later the word was used to designate a whole troupe of comedians. Following variations of the type included Arlecchino or Harlequin, famous for his particolored costume (derived from the original patched garments he wore); he is sometimes called Truffaldino or Mezzetino; Tartaglia, noted for his eyeglasses and his comic stuttering; Brighella, the usual companion of Arlecchino; and Pulcinella, who speaks in Neapolitan dialect, has a tremendous nose, and is always hungry—he survives in the PUNCH AND JUDY shows of the puppet theater. The *commedia dell'arte* was popular in Italy and throughout Europe (thanks to traveling companies) for several hundred years; it strongly influenced the development of European comedy and of individual writers such as Molière, Goldoni, and Gozzi.

Commemoration Ode (1865). A poem by James Russell LOWELL, more accurately entitled *Ode Recited at the Harvard Commemoration.* It was written on request in honor of the Harvard students who had died in the Civil War. In its published form, Lowell added 66 lines, beginning with the famous "Such was he, our Martyr-Chief."

Commentaries on the Gallic War (c. 58–44 B.C.). An historical work in 7 books by Julius CAESAR. Written in a brisk, straightforward third person, each book covering one year, it narrates the campaigns, starting in 58 B.C., by which Caesar made Gaul a permanent part of the empire. Though not intended as polished literature, the work is valued as a masterpiece of clear, concise Latin and historical accuracy. Caesar, who had never lost a campaign or left the field before the enemy, had no reason to exaggerate or misrepresent; perhaps the only subjective note in the *Commentaries* is introduced in his justification of the war.

Commines or **Commynes, Philippe de.** See COMINES.

Committee of Public Safety (*Comité de salut public*). Formed on April 6, 1793, it assumed direction of the government during the French Revolution from 1793 to 1795. Although theoretically subordinate to the Constitutional Convention, this committee soon concentrated all power in its hands and instituted the REIGN OF TERROR. Its most famous members were ROBESPIERRE, Antoine Saint-Just, Georges Couthon, Lazare Carnot, and Bertrand Barrère.

Commodus, Lucius Aelius Aurelius (A.D. 161–192). Roman emperor (180–192). He succeeded to the throne on the death of his father Marcus Aurelius. His reign was marked by his prodigality, self-indulgence, and violence. He prided himself on his gladiatorial skill and was strangled by an athlete in a conspiracy.

Common, Doll. The mistress and assistant in charlatanry of Subtle in Jonson's THE ALCHEMIST.

Common Sense (1776). A political treatise by Thomas PAINE, urging immediate separation from England. In a few months more than 100,000 copies were published in America. The work was influential in bringing about the Declaration of Independence.

Commune of Paris. The revolutionary government established in Paris during 1792 by the representatives of the communes, the smallest administrative districts of France. It led to the period known as the Reign of Terror. More commonly, the term is applied to the insurrectionary government that took possession of Paris (March 18–May 28, 1871), after the withdrawal of the Prussian troops.

Communist Manifesto, The (*Das Kommunistische Manifest;* 1848). A pamphlet by Karl MARX and Friedrich ENGELS, the classic document of communist theory. It analyzes history in terms of class conflict, predicts the imminent overthrow of the ruling bourgeoisie by the oppressed proletariat, and envisions a resulting classless society in which personal property would be abolished. The *Manifesto* calls upon the proletariat of the world to unite and strengthen itself for this final revolution.

Company of Jesus. See JESUITS.

Compensation (1841). An essay by Ralph Waldo EMERSON. The writer claims that evil is balanced by good, that "every sweet hath its sour; every evil its good." The doctrine of compensation, precluding the necessity for an afterlife, caused Emerson to be criticized by the religiously orthodox, as well as the liberals who considered his view too naïve.

Compleat Angler, The, or the Contemplative Man's Recreation (1653). A treatise on fishing by Izaak WALTON. It takes the form of a dialogue in which Piscator (an angler) tries to convince Venator (a hunter) that fishing is the superior sport. Their friend Auceps, a fowler, is silenced early in the work. Charles COTTON wrote a continuation which appeared in the fifth edition (1676).

Compromise of 1850. In U.S. history, a collective name for five acts of Congress which attempted to settle the controversy over the extension of slavery into the territory recently acquired from Mexico. In the Senate, Henry Clay and Daniel WEBSTER supported compromise measures, while John C. Calhoun pleaded for equal rights for the South, and William Seward argued that "a higher law" forbade constitutional safeguards for slavery. The compromise bills provided for the admission of California as a free state and for the establishment of territorial governments in New Mexico and Utah without restrictions regarding slavery; in addition, the Fugitive Slave Law was strengthened, and the slave trade was abolished in the District of Columbia.

Compson. A family in THE SOUND AND THE FURY and other works by William FAULKNER. One of the old, aristocratic families of YOKNAPATAWPHA County, the Compsons trace their American ancestry back to the early 18th century, but by the early 20th century the family is decaying. In the 1930's the family property is sold and the last male Compson is a childless bachelor. The family includes Benjamin, the idiot of *The Sound and the Fury;* Candace (Caddy), a girl whose checkered career includes a seduction, a marriage to a banker and another to a motion-picture executive, and who is last seen in Paris during the German occupation; Jason Lycurgus Compson I, the first of the family to settle in Mississippi; Jason II, a brigadier general in the Civil War to whom Thomas Sutpen of ABSALOM, ABSALOM! tells part of his story; Jason III, an intelligent but ineffectual lawyer who first sells some of the family property; Jason IV, a shrewd and selfish storekeeper who sells the remaining property; Quentin Compson, the illegitimate daughter of Caddy; Quentin MacLachan Compson, an introspective young man who commits suicide at Harvard in 1910.

In addition to *The Sound and the Fury,* the Compson family appears in the short story *That Evening Sun,* and Quentin MacLachan Compson is one of the three narrators in *Absalom, Absalom!*

Compton-Burnett, Ivy (1892–1969). English novelist. A pitiless observer of human cruelty and lust for power, she writes witty and terrifying social comedies of family life—all in dialogue. Her wit, irony, and malice are like a fiercer Jane Austen's. All her novels follow the same form. They are set in large country houses, between 1885 and 1901, and consist almost entirely of polite, mannered, aphoristic dialogue between the members of the ingrown household. The background story concerns a struggle for power between a tyrant and his victim (often servants or precocious children), and a murder or some other melodramatic event. Some of her titles are *Pastors and Masters* (1925), *Brothers and Sisters* (1929), *A House and Its Head* (1935), *Elders and Betters* (1944), *Manservant and Maidservant* (1947, U.S. title, *Bullivant and the Lambs*), *Two Worlds and Their Ways* (1949), *Mother and Son* (1955), and *The Mighty and Their Fall* (1962).

Comte, [Isidore] Auguste [Marie François] (1798–1857). French philosopher. Known as the founder of positivism, Comte sought to apply the methods of observation and experimentation used in the sciences to philosophy, social science, and even religion. He hoped that through the use of such methods, rather than through idealistic appeal to absolute principles, social reform might be achieved. The philosophy of positivism only admits knowledge gained by the scientific method as real or positive.

Cours de philosophie positive (6 vols., 1830–1842) is Comte's basic formulation of the doctrine. Comte had a significant influence on the thought of his time. Both Taine and John Stuart Mill show the effect of his ideas in their own philosophical writings.

Comus (1634). A MASQUE by John MILTON. In late Roman mythology, Comus was the god of sensual pleasure, son of Bacchus and Circe. The name is from the Greek *komos* meaning "revel." In the masque, a young lady is left in the woods by her two brothers who have gone to find food for her. She falls into the hands of Comus, who tries to persuade her to become his consort, queen of his band of riotous monsters. She resists, is almost rescued by her brothers aided by an attendant spirit, but a spell has been cast upon her, which is broken by the power of Sabrina, nymph of the river Severn.

The masque was first performed in the Ludlow castle of the earl of Bridgewater, whose three children played the parts of the brothers and sister. Its theme is the struggle between chaste temperance and sensual pleasure; both causes are eloquently represented, and its richness of language and fancy make it one of the greatest works of its kind.

Conan Doyle. See Sir Arthur Conan DOYLE.

conceit. A whimsical, ingenious, extended METAPHOR. In a conceit an object, scene, person, situation, or emotion is presented in terms of a simpler analogue, usually chosen from nature or a context familiar to author and reader alike. First developed by Petrarch, the conceit became a standard stylistic device in poetry and spread to England in the 16th century.

The METAPHYSICAL POETS, by extending the range of poetic analogy into the realms of science, religion, learning, and practical life, produced a distinct and arresting kind of conceit. Their aim was to startle the reader by showing a very exact correspondence between a thought or emotion and some particular aspect of a seemingly alien and inappropriate object. A famous example is found in these lines from Donne's *A Valediction: Forbidding Mourning* in which, parting from his mistress, he uses the figure of a drawing compass to describe the bond between their souls:

> If they be two, they are two so
> As stiffe twin compasses are two,
> Thy soule the fixt foot, makes no show
> To move, but doth, if th'other doe.
>
> And though it in the center sit,
> Yet when the other far doth rome,
> It leanes, and hearkens after it,
> And growes erect, as that comes home.

Here the conceit is adapted as the best means of expressing a complicated thought; its exactitude and naturalness give it force. With the later metaphysical poets, like John Cleveland and Abraham Cowley, the conceit becomes more fanciful, less exact, at best a kind of witty ornament, at worst absurdity, as when Cleveland speaks of his mistress' hand:

> So soft, 'tis air but once removed,
> Tender as 'twere a jelly gloved.
> Cleveland, *Fuscara*

conceptism or **conceptismo** (from Sp., *concepto,* "a conceit"). A 17th-century Spanish stylistic form which sought to express clever and penetrating ideas by means of verbal devices such as puns, antitheses, and epigrams. Often, however, originality and wit were achieved at the expense of thought and common sense. Conceptism is best exemplified in the works of Baltasar GRACIÁN, whose *Agudeza y arte de ingenio* (1648) exhaustively describes every type of literary conceit. See GONGORISM.

Conciliatore, Il. An Italian semiweekly published in Milan (1818–19). Edited by Silvio PELLICO, it adopted a liberal, progressive position on political, social, and literary questions and, accordingly, favored the romantic movement just then emerging in Italy. It was suppressed by the Austrian police because of its politically liberal point of view.

Concord, Battle of. See LEXINGTON.

Concord Hymn (1836). A poem by Ralph Waldo EMERSON. Written at the completion of the Concord Monument, the poem includes the famous lines:

> Here once the embattled farmers stood
> And fired the shot heard round the world.

Condenado por desconfiado, El (pub. 1635). A religious drama by TIRSO DE MOLINA, dealing with the problem of free will and predestination. Paulo is persuaded by the devil to leave his hermitage and seek Enrico, whose fate, he is told, will be the same as his. Discovering that Enrico is a cheat and a bully, Paulo becomes a bandit in despair. An angel disguised as a shepherd asks him to repent and trust in God, but Paulo refuses. Enrico, however, repents before he dies and is saved. Unwilling to believe in Enrico's salvation, Paulo refuses to confess his sins and is damned for his pride and lack of faith.

Condensed Novels and Other Papers (1867). A series of parodies by Bret HARTE. The book imitates such writers as Dickens, Cooper, Simms, Hawthorne, and Irving. Not all travesties, some of the sketches reflect Harte's admiration and respect for writers who influenced him.

Condillac, Etienne Bonnot, Abbé (1715–1780). French philosopher. He contributed articles on philosophy to the ENCYCLOPÉDIE. In his *Essai sur l'origine des connaissances humaines* (1746) and *Traité des sensations* (1754), he shows, as a disciple of Locke, that thought is not innate, but is derived from sensations and experience. He exerted considerable influence on the IDÉOLOGUES.

Condition humaine, La. See MAN'S FATE.

Condorcet, Marquis de. Marie Jean Antoine Nicolas Caritat (1743–1794). French philosopher and mathematician. He advocated the theory of the "infinite perfectibility of man" in his *Esquisse d'un tableau historique des progrès de l'esprit humain* (1794). In this work, Condorcet traces human development through 9 epochs, and predicts that man will become perfect in the 10th. Arrested as a member of the GIRONDIST faction, he died in prison.

condottiere (It.). A professional soldier of fortune who leads or conducts a band of mercenaries. During the Italian Renaissance, these captains were commissioned to fight wars in support of the city states and petty duchies. Some of them, such as the Sforza, eventually became nobles themselves; others (the Gonzaga and Montefeltro families) sold their armed services even though they were already nobles in possession of states and petty principalities. Foreigners, such as the famous Sir John Hawkwood, an English captain, numbered among their ranks. Their legendary cruelty is captured by Verrocchio in his statue of Bartolommeo Colleoni, which still frightens tourists in Venice.

Confessio Amantis (1386/1390). Poem in Middle English by John GOWER, of over 30,000 lines in octosyllabic couplets. The narrator is an unhappy lover who appeals to Venus and is sent to confess to her priest Genius, who instructs him concerning the seven deadly sins against Love; each lesson is embellished with one or more stories from Biblical or classical legend. Chaucer had certainly read this work when he wrote the *Man of Law's Tale* and the *Wife of Bath's Tale,* although Gower was not his only source for the stories. The tale of Apollonius of Tyre also was a source for Shakespeare's *Pericles, Prince of Tyre.*

Confession, A (Ispoved'; 1879–1881). An account by Count Leo TOLSTOI of the spiritual crisis leading to the formation of the religious and philosophical ideas he preached in his later years. The work records Tolstoi's growing discontent with life as he experienced it in civilized society, and his gradual conclusion that a life close to nature was requisite for the ideal life. *A Confession* is regarded as one of Tolstoi's most powerful nonfiction works because of its effective depiction of the intense spiritual struggles of one of the world's great geniuses.

confessions. A form of autobiography or simulated autobiography. Intimate and possibly guilty matters not usually disclosed are "confessed," presumably to serve some sort of didactic purpose. Confessions constitute a literary genre which began with the *Confessions of St. Augustine.* They reached the height of their development in the era of romanticism, when they already began to show symptoms of narcissistic decadence. Among the most famous confessions in literature are Rousseau's *Confessions* and De Quincey's *Confessions of an English Opium Eater.*

Confessions. An autobiography by Jean Jacques ROUSSEAU. Written between 1766–1770, it was published posthumously (Books I–VI in 1781, Books VII–XII in 1788). In this work, Rousseau "frankly and sincerely" reveals the details of his erratic and rebellious life. Scholars find, however, that his unconscious motivation was to justify himself in the eyes of his supposedly numerous persecutors. The autobiographical account given in *Confessions* is supplemented by the three dialogues written in 1775–1776: *Rousseau juge de Jean-Jacques, Rêveries du promeneur solitaire,* and *Correspondance.* They inaugurated a fashion in literature for confessions, but Rousseau's successors, such as Chateaubriand, Lamartine, George Sand, and Renan lack his openness.

Confessions of an English Opium Eater (1822). A largely autobiographical work by Thomas DE QUINCEY. It gives an account of the poet's early life and describes the growth and effects of his habit of taking opium.

Confessions of a Thug. See Philip Meadows TAYLOR.

Confessions of Felix Krull: Confidence Man (Bekenntnisse des Hochstaplers Felix Krull; 1954). A novel by Thomas MANN. In its adventurous and episodic quality, it is his closest approach to the picaresque novel. Krull, like many of Mann's characters, represents the artist, and his profession indicates the symbolic connection in Mann's mind between the artist and the actor or charlatan.

Confessions of Harry Lorrequer, The (1839). A novel by Charles LEVER. It relates the scrapes and adventures of the high-spirited young Irish hero, Harry Lorrequer. The first part of the book is concerned with his part in Wellington's campaigns.

Confessions of Saint Augustine, The (397–401). A spiritual autobiography by St. AUGUSTINE. He describes his devoutly Christian mother, Monica, his life with the concubine who gave him his son Adeodatus (371–389), his exploration of Manichaeanism and neo-Platonism, and his conversion to Christianity. Designed to show the details of the soul's progress, from enjoyment of the beauties outside itself to a study of its own nature and finally to joy in the knowledge of God, the work was the first in literature to be concerned entirely with an introspective analysis of the author's own spiritual and emotional experiences.

Confidence-Man, The: His Masquerade (1857). A novel by Herman MELVILLE. The scene is a Mississippi River boat, ironically named the *Fidele.* A plotless satire taking place on April Fool's Day, the book is filled with characters difficult to distinguish from one another; most of them are different manifestations of the confidence man. A sign hanging on the door of the *Fidele's* barbershop expresses the theme: "No Trust." The confidence man, king of a world without principle, succeeds in gulling men by capitalizing on false hopes and offering false pity. At the end of the book, the flickering light hanging above the table where an old man reads the Bible goes out completely.

Confucianism. Chinese political and moral philosophy based on the teachings of CONFUCIUS. Originally one of the several rival teachings during the Chou Dynasty (1027–256 B.C.), it found little favor at first, but by the second century B.C. had become the official creed of China. Essentially a guide for statecraft and a moral teaching, it was enlarged upon and developed by MENCIUS, often regarded after Confucius as the second Chinese sage. In the third century B.C. the HSÜN TZU further elaborated and organized the teachings, and by the Han Dynasty (202 B.C.–A.D. 220) it was the orthodox teaching, dominating Chinese political and ethical thought until the early 20th century. During the Han Dynasty many extraneous elements, such as the YIN AND YANG theory, were introduced, attempts were made to deify Confucius, and to use Confucian doctrines as justification for the absolute right of the emperors. Throughout its history Confucianism came into frequent conflict with Buddhism and Taoism, but it retained its position as the official state philosophy, largely because of the Imperial University and the examination system for government employees that perpetuated its power. The Sung Dynasty (960–1279) witnessed a great Confucian revival under the leadership of CHU HSI and his school. Known as Neo-Confucianism, the teachings were reorganized; a minute examination of the precepts of the Confucian sages as well as of all external phenomena was called for, and the FOUR BOOKS became the basis for all education. Neo-Confucianism had great influence in Japan, where it became the basis on which the Tokugawa government was organized.

Confucius (551?–479 B.C.). Chinese political and ethical philosopher and would-be reformer. Failing to achieve personal ambitions and success, he taught a large number of disciples who carried on, developed, and greatly altered his teachings, so that by the second century B.C. they formed the dominant philosophy in China. Confucius advocated a this-worldly, rational philosophy, which emphasizes humanity (*jen*), reverence for the ancient sages, and government by personal virtue.

Congo, The: A Study of the Negro Race (1914). A poem by Vachel LINDSAY. He attempted to represent Negro ragtime rhythms in verse by means of various verbal effects. It falls into three sections: "Their Basic Savagery," "Their Irrepressible High Spirits," and "The Hope of Their Religion."

Congregationalist. A member of the Congregational Church. Its doctrines, known as evangelical or orthodox, include autonomy tempered by co-operation and fellowship of the individual congregations.

Congreve, William (1670–1729). English dramatist, usually considered the greatest master of the Restoration comedy of manners. The son of an English army officer stationed in Ireland, Congreve was educated at the Kilkenny School, where Swift was a schoolmate, and at Trinity College, Dublin. His

Confucius in court costume.

first play, *The Old Bachelor* (1693), which was produced under Dryden's auspices, was widely acclaimed. It was followed by three other comedies: *The Double Dealer* (1693), LOVE FOR LOVE, and his masterpiece, THE WAY OF THE WORLD. In these plays Congreve revealed a genius for urbane, scintillating wit that rivalled Molière's. He also wrote a tragedy, *The Mourning Bride* (1697), remembered chiefly as the source of such oft-quoted phrases as "Music hath charms to soothe a savage breast." The same year he engaged in controversy with the Reverend Jeremy COLLIER, who attacked the lewdness of the English stage, and was apparently bested in the exchange. After 1700, Congreve gave up writing for the theater and spent the rest of his life in the company of such friends as Swift, Steele, and Pope, who dedicated his translation of the *Iliad* to him; the visiting Voltaire, however, regretted that the "writer" had turned into a "gentleman." See Anne BRACEGIRDLE.

Coningsby, or the New Generation (1844). A novel by Benjamin DISRAELI. It contains many of his political opinions on the social issues of his day. There appear in the book several prominent contemporary figures, thinly disguised, and much of the book's popularity may be credited to the interest in identifying them. Gladstone is said to be depicted as Millbank, the Marquis of Hertford as the Marquis of Monmouth, and Coningsby may represent either Lord Littleton or Lord Lincoln. A notable character is the Jew, Sidonia, said to be drawn partly from Baron Alfred de Rothschild, partly from the author himself.

Coniston (1906). A historical novel by Winston CHURCHILL. Churchill became interested in the politics of New Hampshire, where he lived for many years, and to some extent embodied his observations and conclusions in this story, laid in the years between the administrations of President Jackson and President Grant. His chief character is Jethro Bass, an able but corrupt Vermont politician whose quest for power leads him to break with the woman he loves. Bass was modeled on Ruel Durkee, a New Hampshire political boss.

Conjectures on Original Composition, in a Letter to the Author of Sir Charles Grandison (1759). An essay by Edward YOUNG which undertakes to defend originality against slavish imitation. Young restates many of the arguments in the old controversy between the Ancients and Moderns (see BATTLE OF THE BOOKS), and concludes that, in the long run, it is in the nature of man and the universe that the future shall surpass the past and that the progress of art is basically the result of the efforts of the original genius.

Connecticut Wits. See HARTFORD WITS.

Connecticut Yankee in King Arthur's Court, A (1889). A novel by Mark TWAIN. A blow on the head conveys the superintendent of a Hartford arms factory back to the days of King Arthur. When the Yankee's ingenuity and know-how encounter the world of medieval superstition, Mark Twain takes the opportunity to satirize the Old World, chivalry, kings, and the church. Many of the Arthurian knights are seen through the unimpressed eyes of the Yankee. He marries and has a child, but another blow restores him to his own time.

Connell, Norreys. See Conal O'RIORDAN.

Connelly, Marc[us Cook] (1890–). American playwright. Connelly collaborated with George S. Kaufman on several plays: Dulcy; *To the Ladies* (1922), a study in illusions; *Merton of the Movies* (1922), a dramatization of Harry Leon Wilson's satiric novel about Hollywood; and Beggar on Horseback. By himself he wrote *The Wisdom Tooth* (1926), a clerk's futile but pleasant dream of how he defies his employer; The Green Pastures; *The Farmer Takes a Wife* (1934), with characters taken from Walter D. Edmonds' *Rome Haul* (1929); and *A Story for Strangers* (1948), a parable about a talking horse.

Connolly, Cyril (1903–). English essayist, critic, and novelist. He ran the magazine *Horizon* (1940–1949). His best-known book is *The Unquiet Grave* (1945), a collection of melancholy pensées, aphorisms, and quotations. It was published under the pen name **Palinurus** (Connolly thinks Palinurus fell into the sea through a typically modern will to failure). His other works are his partly autobiographical *Enemies of Promise* (1938); *The Condemned Playground* (1946), a collection of essays and literary criticism; the novel *The Rock Pool* (1936); and *The Missing Diplomats* (1953).

Conquest of Canaan, The. (1) A 9,000-line epic poem (1785) by Timothy Dwight, based on the Old Testament Book of Joshua and called by its author "the first American epic." Joshua, who in the poem represents George Washington, was the leader under whom the Jews entered the Promised Land of Canaan and defeated the inhabitants. In the poem, one critic has remarked, 18th-century Americans with Hebrew names talk like Milton's angels and fight like prehistoric Greeks.

(2) A novel (1905) by Booth Tarkington. Canaan is a town in Indiana where intolerance and narrow-mindedness hold sway. Joe London, making his way against great obstacles, wins out against the townspeople, marries a beautiful heiress, Ariel Tabor, and becomes the town's mayor.

Conquistador (1932). A narrative poem by Archibald MacLeish. Awarded the 1933 Pulitzer Prize in poetry, it is based on an eye-witness account of the Spanish expedition led by Hernando Cortez to Mexico in the 16th century written by Bernal Díaz del Castillo. Heroic and realistic, it emphasizes the love of individual men for adventure, rather than official plans for expansion, as the real motive for the expedition.

Conrad. The hero of Lord Byron's poem The Corsair. He is said to have been partly modeled on Jean Lafitte, the famous pirate who assisted Andrew Jackson at the Battle of New Orleans.

Conrad, Joseph (1857–1924). Polish-born English novelist, whose original name was Teodor Jósef Konrad Korzeniowski. Best known in his own time as a writer of sea stories, he is now more admired as a novelist of moral exploration and a master of narrative technique. He was influenced by the technique of Henry James. (See Marlow.) Nostromo, Heart of Darkness, and Lord Jim are regarded as his greatest works. His earliest novels, including Almayer's Folly and An Outcast of the Islands, are full of romantic description, with a mysterious, mystical atmosphere and much analysis and brooding. Youth, Typhoon, and The Shadow-Line—and, indeed, in some respect, most of his tales—describe men's characters being tested in conditions of extreme danger and difficulty. Almost all his mature novels are concerned with moral dilemmas, isolation, and the psychology of men's inner urges. Among these are The Nigger of the Narcissus, The Secret Agent, Under Western Eyes, Chance, Victory, The Arrow of Gold, and The Rescue. The Secret Sharer is a remarkable short story. Conrad collaborated with Ford Madox Ford on the novels *The Inheritors* (1901) and *Romance* (1903). He also wrote *The Mirror of the Sea* (1906), *Some Reminiscences* (1912, U.S. title, *A Personal Record*), and *Notes on Life and Letters* (1921).

The son of a Polish nobleman, writer, and militant nationalist, Conrad had an adventurous youth. (See *Arrow of Gold* and, for an account of his smuggling days, *Mirror of the Sea*.) From 1878 to 1894 he worked at sea on British merchant ships, rising to the rank of captain. As a boy he had educated himself by reading widely in Polish and French, but he began to learn English only when he became a seaman. He was a naturalized British citizen. In 1895 he published his first novel, *Almayer's Folly*, left the sea, married, and settled down near London to write. Conrad is regarded as a major 20th-century novelist and a distinguished stylist in the English language.

Conradi, Hermann (1862–1890). German author and radical exponent of naturalism. In the preface to the anthology *Moderne Dichtercharaktere* (*Modern Figures in Poetry*, 1884) edited by him, he expresses the desire for a "modern" poetic movement, meaning timeliness and sincerity, as opposed to formal polish and artificiality. Among his own works are a collection of prose sketches, *Brutalitäten* (*Brutalities*, 1886), and a novel *Adam Mensch* (*Adam Man*, 1889).

Conrart, Valentin (1603–1675). French grammarian and man of letters. An original member of the Académie française, he was appointed perpetual secretary of that organization and enormously influenced its policies on grammar and style. Not a prolific author, he is remembered chiefly for the extant fragments of his *Mémoires* (1824), which include an account of the Fronde.

Conscience, Hendrik (1812–1883). Flemish novelist. *In't Wonderjaer 1566* (*In the Year of Marvels, 1566*), published in 1837, was his first novel and the first book to be published in modern Flemish. *De Leeuw van Vlaanderen* (*The Lion of Flanders*) of 1838 is one of his more than 100 books that is likely to continue to be read.

conscience clause. A clause in an act of Parliament. It relieves persons with conscientious scruples from certain requirements in the act in which it appears. It generally has reference to religious matters, but came into wider prominence with the English Compulsory Vaccination Act of 1898, and with the introduction of conscription in the First World War.

conscript fathers. (Lat., *Patres conscripti*.) The senators of ancient Rome. Romulus instituted a senate consisting of 100 elders, called *Patres*. After the Sabines joined the state, another hundred were added. Tarquinius Priscus, the fifth king of Rome, added a third hundred. When Tarquinius Superbus, the seventh and last king of Rome, was driven out by Junius Brutus, several of the senate followed him. Brutus appointed new men to the vacancies. The new members were enrolled in the senatorial registry and called *Conscripti;* the entire body was then addressed as *Patres et Conscripti,* or *Patres conscripti.*

conservation of energy. See Julius Robert Mayer.

Consolation of Philosophy, The (De Consolatione Philosophiae; c. 524). A philosophical work by Boethius. Written while Boethius was in prison awaiting execution, it consists of a dialogue in alternating prose and verse between the author, lamenting his own sorrows, and a majestic woman who is the incarnation of his guardian Philosophy. She develops a modified form of Neoplatonism and Stoicism, demonstrating the unreality of earthly fortunes, then proving that the highest good and the highest happiness are in God, and reconciling the apparent contradictions concerning the existence of evil, if God is all-good and all-powerful, and the existence of man's free will, if God has foreknowledge of everything. The work became very popular; it inspired many translations, including English ones by King Alfred, Chaucer, and Queen Elizabeth.

consonance. In poetry and prose, the identity of consonants, as in the words "leaves" and "lives." Like assonance and alliteration, consonance may be considered a form of rhyme since it involves degrees of identity of sound and serves to unify a poem.

Constable, Henry (1562–1613). English poet. A convert to Catholicism, Constable lived much of his life on the Continent. He wrote sonnets and pastoral poems, which are represented in *England's Helicon* (1600) and other anthologies. His sonnet sequence *Diana* was published in 1592 and expanded in 1594. A series of religious sonnets, *Spiritual Sonnets to the Honor of God and His Saints* (published 1815) is attributed to him.

Constable, John (1776–1837). English landscape painter. Mostly self-taught, he repeatedly sketched the same scenes, notably Salisbury cathedral, under varying conditions. In order to impart to his naturalistic landscapes the impression of moving clouds and changing light, he used looser, less blended brushstrokes than were usual at his time. He painted more finished exhibition pieces, yet gained little recognition in England. In France, however, Eugène Delacroix learned much from his brighter colors, the Barbizon school was influenced by the directness of his observation, and later, the Impressionists admired his temporary effects of light.

Constance. See under Man of Law's Tale.

Constance, Council of (1414–1418). The church council that brought about the end of the Great Schism, which had seen rival French and Roman popes reigning at the same time, each claiming supreme authority.

Constant de Rebecque, Henri Benjamin. Known as **Benjamin Constant** (1767–1830). Swiss-born French politician, journalist, novelist, best remembered for his short novel Adolphe. His famous liaison with Mme. de Staël began in 1794 and lasted for 17 years. From 1816 he devoted himself to his brilliant political career, writing political and religious treatises, including a pamphlet attacking Napoleon. His journals are of great interest.

Constantine I. Called **the Great** (A.D. 272–337).

Roman emperor (306–337). On the death of his father, Constantine laid claim to part of the empire and was acknowledged as master of the countries beyond the Alps. He defeated Maxentius, who had possession of Italy, in the battle of the Milvian Bridge (312), where, according to legend, a cross appeared to him in the sky bearing the words *in hoc signo vinces* ("by this sign you will conquer"). He was converted to Christianity in 313. He defeated Licinius (323), who had gained possession of the East, and thus became sole emperor of the whole empire. He called the great Council of Nicaea (325) where the Nicene Creed was adopted. Constantine chose Byzantium as his capital and renamed it Constantinople after himself. See Byzantine Empire.

Constantinople. The Christian capital of the Roman empire founded by Constantine the Great and dedicated in A.D. 330 on the site of ancient Byzantium. It remained the center of the Byzantine Empire, the successor to the Eastern Roman Empire, until 1453 when it fell to the Turks. Constantinople is now the Turkish city of Istanbul.

Constant Nymph, The (1924). A consistently popular novel by Margaret Kennedy. It concerns the family and friends of Albert Sanger, an eccentric musician who is the father of numerous children. His children, both legitimate and illegitimate and all talented, are known collectively as Sanger's circus. The nymph is 15-year-old Teresa Sanger, who has to deal with adult problems of love and fidelity.

Constitution. A 44-gun frigate, U.S. Navy, launched in 1797. The *Constitution* took part in the Tripolitan War against the Barbary corsairs of North Africa. Later, in the War of 1812, under the command of Isaac Hull (1773–1843), she forced the surrender of the British frigate *Guerrière* off Cape Race, Newfoundland (Aug. 19, 1812), and was victorious in seven other encounters. When the *Constitution* was ordered dismantled, Oliver Wendell Holmes wrote the poem *Old Ironsides* (1830), which prompted her rebuilding. She is now permanently moored at Boston and houses a museum.

Constitution of the United States of America. The fundamental law framed in 1787 and in effect since March, 1789, supplanting the Articles of Confederation signed in 1781. The Constitution established a republican form of government for the U.S., with separate executive, legislative, and judicial branches. Twenty-four amendments to the original instrument have been adopted. The 24th amendment, ratified in 1964, forbids the collection of poll taxes as a requirement for voting in presidential and congressional elections. See Bill of Rights.

Consuelo (1842). A novel by George Sand. The title character, a gypsy girl raised in the streets of Venice, is discovered by the maestro Porporo and becomes a successful opera singer. She eventually marries a Bohemian count and travels with Joseph Haydn to Vienna. Her adventures end in Berlin, where she is feted and admired by Frederick the Great. *La Comtesse de Rudolstadt* (1843–1845) is a sequel.

consul. One of the two chief magistrates of the ancient Roman republic chosen annually in the Campus Martius. In the early ages of Rome they were chosen by noble families, but in 367 B.C. the people were extended the privilege of electing one from among themselves. The consuls were the highest civil authority; they commanded the army and presided over the senate. At the expiration of one year of office, the consul was sent to govern a province and was then called a proconsul. The office continued under the empire and, although almost entirely stripped of its power, was a coveted position until A.D. 534. The original consulate was established in 509 B.C. when the people chose Tarquinius Collatinus and Lucius Junius BRUTUS as consuls, after Brutus had driven Tarquinius Superbus, seventh and last of the Roman kings, out of Rome.

Consul, The (1950). A three-act tragic opera by Gian Carlo MENOTTI about a woman who desperately needs to leave her country and is frustrated by bureaucratic red tape.

Contes de ma mère l'Oye (Mother Goose Tales, 1697). A book of fairy tales by Charles PERRAULT. Drawing upon popular folk stories, Perrault collected the tales into a single volume and gave them the simple and graceful form in which they are known today. The *Contes* included LA BELLE AU BOIS DORMANT (*The Sleeping Beauty*), *Le Petit Chaperon Rouge* (LITTLE RED RIDING-HOOD), *La Barbe-Bleue* (BLUEBEARD), *Le Maître-chat ou le chat botté* (*Puss-in-Boots*), *Les Fées* (*The Fairies*), *Cendrillon ou la petite pantoufle de verre* (*Cinderella, or The Little Glass Slipper*), *Riquet à la houppe,* and *Le Petit Poucet* (*Tom Thumb*).

Contes Drôlatiques (Droll Stories, 1832–1837). A collection of tales by Honoré de BALZAC. Written in the style of the medieval *fabliaux,* these frequently gross tales are related with verve and gusto.

Contes et nouvelles en vers (1664–1674). A collection of tales derived from Ariosto, Boccaccio, Machiavelli, Petronius, and others by Jean de LA FONTAINE. Though set in graceful verse and popular in their day, the tales have often been criticized for their ribaldry, and upon his religious conversion, in 1692, La Fontaine publicly disavowed them.

Continental Congress. The congress of representatives from the British colonies of North America, first convened in Philadelphia in 1774 to consider grievances against the mother country. The Second Continental Congress adopted the Declaration of Independence, organized the Revolutionary Army, and conducted diplomatic negotiations with foreign nations. After the ratification of the Articles of Confederation (1781), it functioned as the central governing body of the new republic under the title, "The United States in Congress Assembled."

Contrast, The (1787). A play by Royall TYLER. Opening at the John Street Theater in New York City on April 16, 1787, it marked the true beginning of American drama. The plot involves the romantic affairs of Billy Dimple, a wealthy Anglophile, whose engagement to the clever Maria does not prevent him from flirting with other women. He eventually loses Maria to the staid but attractive Captain Manly, a Revolutionary officer. The most notable character, however, is Manly's servant Jonathan, first of the innumerable stage Yankees of American drama, whose plain practicality and wisdom make him a symbol of rural virtue.

Conversation at Midnight (1937). A long poem by Edna St. Vincent MILLAY. Eight men, assembled after dinner in a Washington Square house, discuss controversial social, political, and aesthetic issues of the time.

Conversations with Goethe. See Johann Peter ECKERMANN.

Convidado de piedra, El. See BURLADOR DE SEVILLA, EL.

Conway, Thomas. See CONWAY CABAL.

Conway Cabal (1777). A faction that tried unsuccessfully to remove Washington and make General Gates commander-in-chief of the American forces. Doubt still exists as to the nature and extent of the plot, but General Thomas Conway (1735–c. 1800), the man for whom it is named, probably did not play the leading role.

Cook or **Cooke, Ebenezer** (c. 1672–1732). American colonial poet, self-styled "Poet-laureate of Maryland." What little is known of Cook's life derives from his long satiric poem, *The Sot-Weed Factor* (1708), a diatribe against the crudities of life in the New World by one forced to live there because of "Friends unkind, and empty Purse." A revised edition of the poem appeared in 1731, with changes presenting a less harsh picture of colonial life. In the same volume, Cook published a verse history of Bacon's Rebellion based upon the *Burwell Papers.* Published by William Parks, the volume is entitled *The Maryland Muse* and is the first volume of American poetry published in the South. In 1960, John Barth published *The Sot-Weed Factor,* a satirical novel based on Cook's life.

Cook, George Cram (1873–1924). American novelist and playwright. Although Cook wrote *Roderick Taliaferro* (1903), a story of Montezuma's empire, and *The Chasm* (1911), a socialist novel, he is best known for his association with the American little theater movement. Cook and his wife, Susan GLASPELL, organized the PROVINCETOWN PLAYERS in 1915 in Provincetown, Mass. There, under Cook's direction, the early plays of Eugene O'Neill were first produced. Re-established in New York in 1916, the group continued to produce O'Neill's plays. *Suppressed Desires* (1915) was a one-act comedy on a Freudian theme by Cook and his wife. His play *The Spring* was produced in New York in 1921. After the success with the Provincetown Players, Cook, who had no interest in competing with commercial theater, gave up the project and sailed in 1921 for Greece, where he lived until his death.

Cook, James. Known as **Captain Cook** (1728–1779). English navigator and explorer who discovered New Caledonia and the Sandwich (Hawaiian) Islands. He was murdered by the natives in revenge for a flogging administered to one of them for stealing a boat.

cook one's goose. To ruin one's prospects. According to legend, Eric, king of Sweden, came to a certain town with very few soldiers. The enemy, in mockery, hung out a goose for him to shoot at. Finding, however, that the king meant business, and that it would be no laughing matter for them, they sent heralds to ask him what he wanted. "To cook your goose for you," he replied.

Cook's Tale, The. An unfinished fragment in the CANTERBURY TALES of Geoffrey CHAUCER. Roger the Cook laughs at the *Reeve's Tale* and offers to tell a similarly bawdy jest. He begins a story about the apprentice Perkin, a reveller too fond of dice and women for his master's taste. A metrical romance sometimes called *The Cook's Tale of Gamelyn* has been erroneously attributed to Chaucer, who probably at one time intended to adapt it. See GAMELYN.

Coolidge, [John] Calvin (1872–1933). 30th president of the U.S. (1923–1929). Coolidge first won national attention when, as governor of Massachusetts, he broke the Boston police strike of 1919, declaring that there was "no right to strike against the public safety by anybody, anywhere, any time." In 1920 he became the Republican vice-presidential nominee and, succeeding to the presidency on the death of Warren G. Harding, was elected in his own right in 1924. In 1927 he announced that he did not "choose to run" for the presidency again. An uncompromising Republican, noted for his taciturnity and frugality, Coolidge wrote an *Autobiography* (1929). He was the subject of a well-known biography by William Allen White, *A Puritan in Babylon* (1938).

Cooper, Anthony Ashley. See 1st earl of SHAFTESBURY.

Cooper, James Fenimore (1789–1851). American novelist. James Fenimore Cooper, a son of the wealthy landowner Judge William Cooper, who founded Cooperstown, N.Y., was born in Burlington, N.J. After his expulsion from Yale, he became a sailor; in 1811, he married Susan DeLancey, and occupied himself as a gentleman farmer. At the age of 31 he wrote his first novel. Although *Precaution* (1820) was a failure, Cooper continued to write. In 1823, he wrote THE PIONEERS and THE PILOT, both works of signal importance in American literature. *The Pilot* is the first American novel of the sea, and *The Pioneers* introduces the character of Natty BUMPPO, the natural man uncorrupted by civilization. Natty has taken on mythic significance in the history of the American imagination. Cooper's audience demanded that he be revived in THE LAST OF THE MOHICANS, THE PRAIRIE, THE PATHFINDER, and THE DEERSLAYER.

From 1826 to 1833 the Coopers lived abroad. Turning out novels at a prolific rate, Cooper returned to Jacksonian America dismayed to discover that the democracy he had defended abroad had turned to mobocracy. He was outspoken in his criticism, and was denounced in the American press. In the 1840's, while involved in numerous lawsuits, he wrote an Antirent trilogy, THE LITTLEPAGE MANUSCRIPTS, in which he defended the existence of a landed gentry as a stabilizing force in democracy. SATÁNSTOE, with its lively portraits of contrasting Yankee, Middle Colony, and Dutch manners in colonial New York, is one of Cooper's most successful books.

Although Cooper's literary craftsmanship can rarely be admired, his 50-odd volumes, in their use of the American landscape and their unique creation of Leatherstocking, constitute the foundation of American literature. See LEATHERSTOCKING TALES, THE; SPY, THE; MONIKINS, THE; AMERICAN DEMOCRAT, THE.

Cooper, Peter (1791–1883). American industrialist and philanthropist. The owner of a Baltimore iron works, Cooper designed and built the first American steam locomotive, popularly known as "Tom Thumb," in 1830. In 1857 he founded Cooper Union, an educational institution in New York City dedicated to the "advancement of science and art." He ran for the presidency in 1876 as the candidate of the Greenback Party.

Cooper, Samuel (1725–1783). American clergyman, known for his revolutionary writings against British rule in the colonies. He was the author of sermons, pamphlets, and articles for the *Boston Gazette*. His most famous work is *The Crisis* (1754), a pamphlet attacking the currently proposed bill for excise taxes in America. Cooper also worked prominently in support of the alliance with France (1778) made by Benjamin Franklin.

Copeau, Jacques (1879–1949). Theatrical producer and critic. From 1904 to 1910, Copeau wrote as a drama critic; his essays are collected in *Critiques d'un autre temps* (1923). With Gide and Rivière, he helped to found the *Nouvelle Revue Française* in 1909, and later became its editor in chief (1912–1914). Best known for his theatrical career, Copeau opposed the realism of Antoine and Lugné-Poë. With Charles Dullin and Louis Jouvet, he directed the *Théâtre du Vieux-Colombier,* an experimental playhouse that sought to bring poetry and subtle evocation back to the theater. Dullin and Jouvet eventually left to begin their own theaters; Copeau spent some years training young actors and from 1936 to 1941 served as a producer of the *Comédie Française.*

Copernicus, Nicolaus. Latinized form of **Niklas Koppernigk** (1473–1543). Polish astronomer. It was Copernicus who laid the foundations for modern astronomy by upsetting the Ptolemaic system of astronomy, which had prevailed since the second century. PTOLEMY placed the earth at the center of the universe; Copernicus advanced the theory that the earth and all the other planets revolved around the sun in individual orbits while spinning on their axes. He finished his treatise on this subject, *De Revolutionibus Orbium Coelestium* (*On the Revolutions of Heavenly Bodies*), in 1530, but it was not published until 1543, when its author lay dying. Opposition to his theories was theological as well as scientific: not only had Copernicus ignored the wisdom of the ancients, he had displaced man from the center of the universe.

Cophetua. A mythical king of Africa. Of great wealth, he fell in love with a beggar girl, Penelophon (Zenelophon in Shakespeare's *Love's Labour's Lost,* IV, i.), and married her. He is the hero of a ballad in Percy's *Reliques,* and Tennyson versified the tale in *The Beggar-Maid.*

Copland, Aaron (1900–　). American composer. He is probably the best known representative of American nationalism in music. His most popular works employ American subjects and styles, often modeled on jazz or folk music, for example, in *Music for the Theatre* (1925), *El Salón México* (1937), and *Appalachian Spring* (1944, a ballet). Since the 1930s he has been concerned with improving general understanding of modern music by organizing concerts and writing such books as *What to Listen for in Music* (1939), *Our New Music* (1941), and *Music and the Imagination* (1952).

Copley, John Singleton (1738–1815). American painter. He began his career as a portrait painter in Boston; in 1775, he settled in England, where he turned to historical painting. He is best known for his early portraits, sharply observed and executed in a severe and uncompromising manner.

Coppard, A[lfred] E[dgar] (1878–1957). English short-story writer and poet. *Adam and Eve and Pinch Me* (1921) was his first collection of short stories. Ranging from realism to fantasy, his stories are marked by pathos and gentle irony, and possess the direct narrative interest of the folk tale. His *Collected Tales* were published in 1951 and *Lucy in Her Pink Jacket* in 1954; his *Collected Poems* appeared in 1928.

Coppée, François Edouard Joachim (1842–1908). French poet and playwright. Coppée was a contributor to the *Parnasse Contemporain* (1866). His poetic works include *Le Reliquaire* (1866), *Intimités* (1868), *Les Humbles* (1872), *Le Cahier Rouge* (1874), and *Les Récits et les Elégies* (1878).

Copperheads. In U.S. history, Northerners, mainly Democrats, who during the Civil War favored the Confederate cause and advocated a negotiated peace.

Copts. Christian Egyptians who hold that St. Mark founded their church at Alexandria. They belong to the Jacobite branch of the Eastern Orthodox Church and, since the Council of Chalcedon in 451, have possessed the patriarchal chair of Alexandria. The word is probably derived from Coptos, the metropolis of the Thebaid. The Copts conduct their worship in a dead language called "Coptic," derived from ancient Egyptian but written in Greek capital letters. St. Anthony (c. 250–350), the founder of Christian monachism, was a Copt.

copyright. The exclusive right to reproduce, publish, and sell works of literature, music, or art. The first copyright act in England was that of 1709, subsequently subject to various modifications and additions. In 1842 a new act was passed granting copyright for 42 years after publication or until 7 years after the author's death, whichever should be the longer period. This act was superseded by the Copyright Act of 1911, under which the period of protection was extended to 50 years after the death of the author, irrespective of date of publication. This act also deals with copyright in photographs, engravings, architectural designs, musical compositions, and phonograph records.

The first copyright act in the U.S. was enacted by the states of Connecticut and Massachusetts in 1783, following vigorous agitation by Noah Webster. The first national statute, passed in 1790, was modelled upon the then existing British law. Additional acts were passed in 1846, 1856, 1859, and 1865. At present, U.S. copyrights may be secured under the Act of March 4, 1909 (as amended), for a period of 28 years; a 28 year renewal period is allowed, bringing the maximum period of copyright to 56 years.

Influenced by lobbyists for book manufacturers reluctant to extend U.S. copyright to books manufactured abroad, the U.S. did not sign the Berne International Copyright Convention (1886), and thus, until the formulating of the Universal Copyright Convention under the auspices of UNESCO, a certain confusion existed in the field of U.S.-international copyright. Though the U.S. and most of the members of the Berne convention have signed the Universal Copyright Convention, a worldwide international copyright does not at the moment exist, the Soviet Union preferring in general to remain outside copyright conventions.

A common-law copyright, secured to the author by the act of creation and requiring no formality, is recognized in the U.S. and in England.

Coq d'or, Le (The Golden Cockerel, 1909). A satirical opera by RIMSKY-KORSAKOV, flaying the foibles of royalty.

Coquette, The (1797). An American novel by Hannah Webster FOSTER. It is a *roman à clef* in epistolary form, in which the heroine is seduced by an army officer and is later deserted by a minister who had once wooed her. Inconclusive attempts have been made to identify her as the daughter of a prominent Yale trustee, and her seducer as Aaron Burr or as the son of Jonathan Edwards.

Corbaccio (Carrion Crow). A miserly Venetian in Jonson's comedy VOLPONE, OR THE FOX. He disinherits his own son in a vain attempt to inherit the wealth of Volpone. His desperate attempts to acquire more wealth than he has already are the more ironic in that Corbaccio himself is so old and decrepit that he will be unable to enjoy it.

Corbacho, El. See Alfonso MARTÍNEZ DE TOLEDO.

Corbet, Richard (1582–1635). English churchman and poet, known for his joviality. Although he served as bishop of Oxford and of Norwich, he was too convivial and tolerant to be an efficient prelate; his success was mainly due to his reputation as an anti-Puritan and his assiduous courtship of the powerful. A friend of Ben Jonson, he was popular at the Mermaid Tavern because of his skill at extemporizing poetry. Of his written works the best known is *The Fairies' Farewell* (1647), a humorous lament for the departure of England's merrier fairies, which Corbet blames on Puritanism.

Corbière, Edouard Joachim. Known as Tristan Corbière (1845–1875). French poet. Associated with the symbolist school, in his *Gens de mers* (published in *Les Amours jaunes,* 1873), Corbière treats the world of those who live upon the sea in a realistic and forceful manner. See SYMBOLISTS.

Corbin, Alice. See Alice Corbin HENDERSON.

Corceca. See FAERIE QUEENE, THE.

Corday, Charlotte (1768–1793). French patriot who stabbed Jean Paul MARAT to death in his bath. She was an adherent of the Revolution and sympathized with the GIRONDISTS, but was repelled by the excesses of the REIGN OF TERROR. She was guillotined on July 17, 1793.

Cordelia. In Shakespeare's KING LEAR, the youngest daughter of Lear. She is disinherited by Lear because she lacks the "glib and oily art" of flattery. Her simplicity and sincerity move the king of France to marry her despite her disinheritance. It is of her that Lear speaks the famous lines: "Her voice was ever soft, gentle and low, an excellent thing in woman."

Cordelier (*i.e.* cord-wearer). A Franciscan friar of the strict rule. In the Middle Ages they distinguished themselves in philosophy and theology. DUNS SCOTUS was one of their most distinguished members. The traditional origin of the name is that in the reign of St. Louis they repulsed an army of infidels, and the king asked who those *gens de cordelics* (corded people) were.

Cordeliers, the. French Revolutionary club of 1790 known officially as *La Société des Amis des Droits de l'Homme et du Citoyen.* MARAT, DANTON, and ROBESPIERRE were among the speakers at its meetings. The club played an active part in overthrowing both the monarchy and the GIRONDISTS. It ceased to function in 1794 when its leading members were guillotined. The name "Cordeliers" comes from the old (Franciscan) Cordelier monastery, where the club held its meetings.

Corelli, Archangelo (1653–1713). Italian violinist and composer. He had a wide European reputation, and was the first to establish a characteristic style of writing for the violin. His best-known work is a set of variations on the Spanish dance *La Folia.*

Corelli, Marie. Pen name of **Mary Mackay** (1855–1924). English romantic novelist. She was sensationally popular at the end of the 19th century. At first ambitious to be a musician, she turned to literature after a "psychical experience." Her first novel, *A Romance of Two Worlds* (1886), like most of her later books, was about "spirit power and universal love." She also wrote *Vendetta* (1886), *Barabbas* (1893), *The Sorrows of Satan* (1895), *The Master Christian* (1900), and many other novels.

Corin. In Shakespeare's As You LIKE IT, a philosophical old shepherd who assuages Silvius' romantic grief and befriends Rosalind.

Corinna's Going A-Maying (1648). A poem by Robert HERRICK, in which the poet implores his late-sleeping mistress to rise and join the May Day festivities. Against a background of spring freshness and picturesque country rite, he sings of life's shortness, urging love and "the harmless folly of the time."

Corinne, or Italy (1807). A romantic novel by Mme. de STAËL. Oswald Nevil, an English lord, recuperating in Rome, meets the famous poetess Corinne, who, half-English and half-Italian, has exiled herself from her native England; they fall in love. Nevil wishes to marry Corinne, but she hesitates, fearing the rigidity of the English life she once knew; her present unconventional life is too dear to her. Oswald, forced to return to England, later gives in to the pressures of his social milieu and marries the wholly English Lucile, half sister of Corinne. When she learns of the marriage, Corinne dies of grief. Idealistic and passionate, *Corinne* is a psychological study of two tormented souls, and a celebrated description of Italian civilization and mores.

Corinthians, The First Epistle and **The Second Epistle of Paul the Apostle to the.** Two books of the New Testament. They are letters written by Paul to the troubled Christian church in the cosmopolitan Greek city of Corinth. The two canonical letters incorporate parts of two other letters. The Christians in Corinth were exposed to the very worldly, licentious atmosphere of this city. Paul tells them to ignore these influences; he also deals with a crisis over internal dissension and local authority. These two books are of particular historical interest because of the insight they offer into first-century Christians' problems with the pagan world. The 13th chapter of I Corinthians contains Paul's beautiful discourse on Christian love, one of the most noteworthy chapters in the Bible.

Coriolanus, The Tragedy of (c. 1608). A tragedy by William SHAKESPEARE. Caius Martius, an honorable but haughty patrician, defeats the Volscians under Tullus AUFIDIUS at Corioli and is given the name of Coriolanus. He is then persuaded to seek election to the consulship, though the thought of currying favor with the masses repels him. When Brutus and Sicinius, two unscrupulous tribunes, incite the populace against him, Coriolanus angrily denounces the plebeians for their fickleness and ingratitude and is driven from the city. Enraged by the treatment he has received, he joins the forces of Aufidius, who is preparing another attack on Rome. As the Volscian army menaces Rome, MENENIUS and COMINIUS, two old friends, unsuccessfully plead with Coriolanus to spare the city, but he remains obdurate until VOLUMNIA, his mother, and Virgilia, his wife, add their appeals to the others. Coriolanus raises the siege and tries to explain his conduct to the Volscians. Aufidius, envious of the Roman's prestige, accuses him of treachery, and as the Volscians hurl abuse at him, Coriolanus is murdered by agents of Aufidius.

The direct source of the play is Thomas North's translation (1579) of Plutarch's *Lives,* which records the career of the legendary patrician.

Cornaro, Luigi (1467–1566). Italian author. He wrote four *Discorsi della vita sobria (Discourses on the Life of Moderation).* His work was translated by George Herbert and admired by many subsequent authors, including Addison.

Corneille, Pierre (1606–1684). French dramatist. Son of a lawyer, he abandoned a career at the bar in order to write for the theater, initially under the patronage of Richelieu as one of the cardinal's CINQ AUTEURS. *Mélite* (1629), his first play and a comedy of manners, was successfully produced in Paris. There followed the tragicomedy *Clitandre* (1632), seven comedies of only moderate interest, and his first tragedy, MÉDÉE (1635). Although LE CID (1637) won an enormous popular success, Richelieu persuaded the Académie française to censure the play's violation of the dramatic unities as well as its emotional style. Madame de Rambouillet's salon also expressed doubt concerning the play's merit. For three years, chastened and disturbed, Corneille wrote nothing for the theater. He finally broke his silence with the tragedies HORACE, CINNA, POLYEUCTE, RODOGUNE, HÉRACLIUS, LA MORT DE POMPÉE, NICOMÈDE, ANDROMÈDE, and a comedy, LE MENTEUR. With *Le Cid,* these tragedies marked Corneille's brief leadership of the French stage. After the failure of *Pertharite* (1651), Corneille withdrew to Rouen. In 1659 he returned to the theater with OEDIPE, only to find that during his absence the public had come to prefer the directness and simplicity of Racine to the complexity of his own late style. The plays of Corneille's decline include the tragedies *La Toison d'or (The Golden Fleece,* 1660), *Sertorius* (1662), *Sophonisbe* (1663), *Othon* (1664), AGÉSILAS, ATTILA, *Suréna* (1674), and the comedies TITE ET BÉRÉNICE (1670) and *Pulchérie* (1672). Corneille eventually retired from the theater and translated *The Imitation of Christ* into French verse.

Corneille can be considered the prime shaper of the French classic theater. While earlier writers had attempted a tragedy of actions, Corneille sought tragedy in the depiction of the human soul, thus substituting an interior drama for the exterior drama of his predecessors. Borrowing the greater part of his subjects from classical mythology and history, Corneille excelled in the creation of tragic protagonists: men and women of heroic dimension caught in the conflict of reason, will, or duty with an all-powerful love or hatred. Propelled by the highest sentiments and gifted with an enormous will to triumph over the obstacles of destiny, his characters are drawn in large, bold strokes and sometimes, in the magnificence of their deeds and language, exceed the bounds of humanity and rise to the superhuman.

Corneille, Thomas (1625–1709). French playwright and brother of Pierre Corneille. A skilled technician and an accomplished imitator, he kept the French theater stocked with workmanlike though not highly original plays during the interval between Pierre Corneille's great tragedies and those of Racine. Notable among his works are the romantic tragedy *Timocrate* (1656), based on an episode in La Calprenède's *Cléopâtre,* and the heroic tragedy *Ariane* (1672), based on the Ariadne legend.

Cornelia. See GRACCHI.

Cornelius. See VOLTIMAND.

Cornford, Frances Crofts (1886–1960). English poet. The granddaughter of Charles Darwin and wife of Francis Macdonald Cornford, she usually wrote restrained poems about nature; her best-known poem is the ironic *To a Fat Lady Seen from the Train.* Her *Collected Poems* appeared in 1954.

Cornford, Francis Macdonald (1874–1943). English scholar. He wrote *From Religion to Philosophy* (1912), an anthropological study, and *The Origin of Attic Comedy* (1914), in which he traces comedy back to the Dionysian fertility rites.

Cornhuskers (1918). A collection of poems by Carl SANDBURG. It includes such well-known poems as *Cool Tombs, Prairie, Caboose Thoughts, Wilderness, Chicago Poet, Testament,* and *Haunts.*

corn laws. Laws passed at various times in English history, from 1436 to 1842, regulating the domestic and foreign grain trade of England. The most controversial corn laws were those of the 19th century, which levied a high duty on imports and raised domestic prices, causing great hardship among the poor of England, especially in the manufacturing districts. Feeling against the laws ran high and when the Corn Law of 1815 was passed in order to counteract the post-Napoleonic depression, there were riots. In 1839, an Anti-Corn Law League was formed to bring about repeal of the laws. Richard COBDEN and John BRIGHT were the leading orators associated with the Anti-Corn Law League. The grain tariff was reduced in 1849 and entirely abolished in 1862.

Cornucopia. The horn of plenty, an ancient symbol of the bounty of growing things. Often identified with the horn of Amaltheia, the goat that had suckled the infant Zeus, it was frequently shown in art as an attribute of various forms of a fertility DAEMON.

Cornwall, duke of. In Shakespeare's KING LEAR, the grasping, ruthless husband of Lear's daughter Regan. When Gloucester shelters Lear, Cornwall plucks Gloucester's eyes out in revenge. A servant, horrified at the cruel deed, kills Cornwall and is in turn killed by Regan.

Cornwallis, Charles, 1st marquis (1738–1805). English major general in the American Revolution. He defeated General Greene at Guilford Courthouse, N.C., but was forced to surrender at Yorktown shortly thereafter. He later served as viceroy of Ireland and governor-general of India.

Coronado, Francisco Vásquez de (1510–1554). Spanish explorer. In 1540 Coronado left Mexico as commander of an expedition to conquer the Seven Cities of Cibola in present New Mexico, which earlier explorers had described in glowing terms. After undergoing extreme hardships and traversing Arizona, New Mexico, Texas, Oklahoma, and Kansas, Coronado returned to Mexico empty-handed and disillusioned. One of his men, García López de Calderón, discovered the Grand Canyon on a side expedition.

Corot, Jean Baptiste Camille (1796–1875). French landscape painter. The least realistic of the BARBIZON SCHOOL, his style evolved from the influence of contemporary classicism to the poetic rendition of landscapes in which a silver-grey haze envelops and harmonizes perfectly balanced figures and trees. Corot's work also includes historical subjects and figure paintings, the latter being only less prized than his landscapes today.

Corpus Juris Civilis. See under JUSTINIAN I.

Correggio, Antonio Allegri da (c. 1489–1534). Italian painter. He is known for his use of chiaroscuro and blurred outlines in mythological paintings. These have a sensuous, almost seductive, sweetness and reveal his use of light and trompe l'oeil to create the illusion of church ceilings opening up into the heavens. His mythological paintings—*Antiope, Jupiter and Io, Ganymede*—strongly influenced French painting during the 18th century. His frescos on the octagonal cupola of the cathedral at Parma was a leading source of later baroque ceiling decoration in Italy and throughout Europe.

Corsair, The (1814). A narrative poem by Lord BYRON. The pirate chief CONRAD disguises himself as a dervish, in order to enter the palace of Sultan Seyd. He is discovered and imprisoned, but Gulnare, queen of the harem, releases him, and he returns to the pirates' isle, only to find that Medora, his true love, has died in his absence. He, therefore, returns to his native Greece, where he heads a rebellion and is shot. Upon his death, his page Kaled is discovered to be Gulnare in disguise. *Lara* (1814), another narrative poem, deals with Conrad's last adventures in Spain, where he has returned as Lara. He lives a strange and secluded life until he is recognized and killed. Conrad and Lara are prototypes of the Byronic hero, extravagant, romantic, and mysterious. See Sir EZZELIN.

Corso, Gregory. See BEAT MOVEMENT.

Cortez or **Cortés, Hernando** or **Hernán** (1485–1547). Spanish conqueror of Mexico. Cortez arrived in the New World in 1504 and was mayor of Santiago, Cuba, when he was ordered by Governor Velázquez to lead an expedition to Mexico. Velázquez later tried to halt the voyage, but Cortez had already set sail (1519). Reaching the mainland, he was fortunate in acquiring the services of two interpreters, one of whom was the famed Malinche or Doña Marina, daughter of an Aztec chieftain, whom the Maya had enslaved; she became Cortez' mistress as well as his confidante.

After founding the city of Vera Cruz, Cortez moved against the Aztec capital at Tenochtitlán, forming alliances with other Indian tribes, such as the Tlaxcalans, who hated the Aztecs. When some of the more faint-hearted Spaniards spoke of returning to Cuba, Cortez ordered their ships to be destroyed.

Although MONTEZUMA, the Aztec chief at Tenochtitlán, was outwardly friendly, Cortez captured him and held him as a hostage. Upon hearing that Velázquez, in an attempt to reassert his authority over Mexico, had dispatched another expedition under Pánfilo de Narváez, Cortez returned to the seacoast and persuaded Narváez' men to desert their commander and join him. Back in Tenochtitlán, he found that the actions of Pedro de Alvarado, his deputy, had incited the Indians to revolt and that Montezuma had been killed. During the disastrous *noche triste,* or "sad night" (June 30, 1520), the Spaniards were forced to flee with the loss of many men. Cortez immediately began to plan another campaign against Tenochtitlán, which was captured the following year. Though he was granted many honors and was created marquis of the Valley of Oaxaca, Cortez gradually lost his political power in Mexico and was supplanted in 1535 by the first viceroy, Antonio de Mendoza.

Cortez himself gave a vivid description of the conquest of Mexico in five letters he wrote to Charles V of Spain. The best-known account, however, is the history of Bernal Díaz DEL CASTILLO, which Archibald MacLeish used as the basis of his poem *Conquistador* (1932). Novels laid in this period include Lew Wallace's *The Fair God* (1873) and Samuel Shellabarger's *Captain from Castile* (1945). See CUAUHTÉMOC.

Corvino (It., "Raven"). A greedy merchant in Jonson's comedy VOLPONE, OR THE FOX. Though very jealous of his innocent young wife, Celia, he willingly offers her to the lecherous Volpone in the hope of inheriting some of his money.

Corvo, Baron. See Frederick ROLFE.

Cory, William Johnson (1823–1892). English poet, classicist. Cory published a single volume of verse, *Ionica* (1858), in which is found the famous translation from Callimachus, *Heraclitus,* beginning "They told me, Heraclitus, they told me you were dead."

Coryate or **Coryat, Thomas** (1577?–1617). English traveler and buffoon at court. *Coryate's Crudities* (1611) is a curious account of his travels on foot through France, Savoy, Italy, and other countries.

corybantes (**korybantes**). See CYBELE.

Corydon. A conventional name for a rustic or shepherd; a brainless, love-sick youth derived from the shepherd in Vergil's *Bucolic* II. See ARCADES AMBO.

Corydon (1924). An essay in dialogue form by André GIDE. Written during the years 1911–1920, it maintains that the homosexual is not unnatural, nor harmful either to himself or to society. It provoked violent criticism, directed less toward the book than toward Gide himself.

Coryell, John R. See Nick CARTER.

coryphaeus (**koryphaios**). The leader of the chorus in Greek classical drama. An earlier term for the same office was *choragos.* Both words have been used figuratively to apply to the leader of any group, or, more especially, its most active member.

Cosette. In Victor Hugo's novel LES MISÉRABLES, the daughter of Fantine and the adopted daughter of Jean Valjean.

Cosimo, Piero di (1462–1521). Florentine painter. He is noted for the lyric quality of his paintings and his penchant for the fantastic and the strange. In his religious works or in his mythological scenes, harshness alternates with tender melancholy. VASARI says he boiled his eggs with the varnishes, 50 at a time, in order to devote every minute to his work. His best-known works include the *Death of Procris,* the *Passage of the Red Sea* (one of the Sistine Chapel frescoes), and the *Memorial Portrait of Simonetta Vespucci,* the celebrated Florentine beauty used by Botticelli as a model for his *Primavera* and *Birth of Venus.*

Cossacks, The (*Kazaki;* 1863). A novel by Count Leo TOLSTOI. The central character, Olenin, tired of life in civilized society, attempts to find happiness among the wild, free-living Cossacks of the Caucasus. The portraits of the old Cossack Eroshka and the native girl Maryana are especially successful. Critics generally cite this short work as the finest book written by Tolstoi before *War and Peace.*

Costain, Thomas B[ertram] (1885–1965). Canadian-born American writer. Costain came to the U.S. in 1920 and became fiction editor of *The Saturday Evening Post.* He is best known for his historical novels, notably *The Black Rose* (1945), which is set in medieval England and China, and *The Silver Chalice* (1953), a biblical tale woven around the chalice of Antioch. Costain also wrote *Joshua* (1943), a biography of the biblical hero, and several volumes of popular history, including *The Three Edwards* (1958) and *The Last Plantagenets* (1962). *Son of a Hundred Kings* (1950) is a semiautobiographical novel about a Canadian boy.

Costard. In Shakespeare's LOVE'S LABOUR'S LOST, an unlettered clown who tries to imitate the learned court wits of Elizabethan times. He uses the word "honorificabilitudinitatibus" and speaks of the "contempts" of a letter.

Coster, Charles de (1827–1879). A Belgian writer. His best-known work, *La Légende de Thyl Ulenspiegel et de Lamme Goedzak* (1868), succeeds in making of Tyll Eulenspiegel a delightful incarnation of the Flemish folk spirit.

Côté de chez Swann, Du. See REMEMBRANCE OF THINGS PAST.

Côté de Guermantes, Le. See REMEMBRANCE OF THINGS PAST.

Cotter's Saturday Night, The (1786). A sentimental poem in Spenserian stanzas by Robert BURNS, famous for its description of Scottish peasant life and for the story of Jenny.

Cotton, Charles (1630–1687). English poet and translator. Cotton is best known for his translation 1685) of Montaigne's *Essays,* a clear, faithful, and vigorous version which is often preferred to the earlier Florio translation. An intimate friend of Izaak Walton, he wrote a treatise on fly-fishing which was included in the fifth edition (1676) of THE COMPLEAT ANGLER. Cotton was also the author of several other translations from the French, some rather scurrilous burlesques of Vergil and Lucian, and a number of poems on fishing, country life, and related subjects, which have a certain homely charm and fidelity to the rural scene. These last, collected in *Poems on Several Occasions* (1689), were admired by Wordsworth, Coleridge, and Lamb.

Cotton, John (1584–1652). English-born Puritan clergyman and writer. Dissatisfied with conditions in England, Cotton, who was already a famous clergyman, emigrated to Boston in 1633 and became one of the colony's most influential leaders. Known for his tireless scholarship and aristocratic political views, he wrote numerous works including *The Keys of the Kingdom of Heaven* (1644); *Milk for Babes* (1646), a children's catechism; and *The Bloudy Tenent Washed* (1647), part of a celebrated controversy with Roger Williams (see BLOUDY TENENT, THE). Cotton Mather was his grandson.

Cotton, Sir Robert Bruce (1571–1631). English antiquary, collector of books, manuscripts, coins, medals, etc. He was the founder of the famous Cottonian Library, now in the British Museum, which contained many otherwise unobtainable manuscripts saved from destroyed monasteries, including those of *Beowulf*, *The Pearl*, and *Gawain and the Green Knight*. The identifying titles of the manuscripts were derived from the busts of Roman emperors which adorned the bookcases holding these collections; thus, the *Beowulf* manuscript is called "Cotton Vitellius A XV" from the Emperor Vitellius, and the manuscript of *The Pearl* is known as "Cotton Nero A X" from the Emperor Nero.

Cotton allowed the free use of his library to leading scholars of his time and presented manuscripts from his collection to the Bodleian Library when it was founded. His library was bequeathed to the English nation on the death of his grandson in 1701.

Cotytto. The Thracian goddess of fertility, worshiped at Athens with licentious rites. See BAPTES.

Council of Nicaea (325). The first ecumenical council of the Christian Church. Called by CONSTANTINE THE GREAT, it was held in Nicaea, a small town in Bithynia, Asia Minor. The major undertaking of the council was a discussion of the views of ARIUS, who held that Jesus was the most exalted human of all time, but had not been created out of nothing nor was he eternally existent, and that he was capable of right and wrong in his own free will. The council's decision was against Arius, ascribing a purely divine nature to Jesus (see TRINITY).

The council published a confession of faith called the Nicene Creed (from the Latin *credo*, "I believe"). It was based on an older creed that had been used in Caesarea, but carefully defined the orthodox doctrine of the Trinity. The Nicene Creed is used (with minor changes) in the liturgies of the Roman, Greek, and Anglican churches, and its doctrinal teachings have been accepted by most Protestants.

Counterfeiters, The (Les Faux-Monnayeurs; 1926). A novel by André GIDE. The novelist Edouard keeps a journal of events in order to write a novel about the nature of reality. The intrigues of a gang of counterfeiters symbolize the "counterfeit" personalities with which people disguise themselves to conform hypocritically to convention or to deceive themselves. The adolescent boys Bernard Profitendieu and Olivier Molinier, having left home in order to be free to find and develop their true selves, encounter many varieties of hypocrisy and self-deception in human relationships and barely escape falling into such poses themselves. Both begin by seeking a close emotional tie with Edouard. Each, however, comes to recognize that Edouard is inadequate as an ideal for emulation, particularly when the novelist cannot recognize the psychological reality of the schoolboy Boris' useless suicide, which is an indirect result of the counterfeiters' machinations.

Counter Reformation. A term used to describe the Roman Catholic reaction to the Protestant Reformation of the 16th century. Beginning with the Council of Trent, and later through the efforts of the INQUISITION and the JESUITS, the Roman church sought to consolidate its position and win back its former adherents. Literature and the other arts became involved as vehicles for the renewal of faith and the propagandizing of Roman Catholic dogma. Artists were bound by conscience and external pressure to help or at least not hinder the cause. The so-called Counter-Reformation style in literature, sometimes identified with or considered a part of the baroque style, flourished during the latter half of the 16th century and the first half of the 17th century. It was characterized by the use of rhetoric, a straining after the ironic, the paradoxical, and the witty, attempts to render reality as well as the world of the spirit in concrete and highly sensuous imagery, especially in religious verse. Though its leading practitioners in Italy, Spain, France, and England, poets such as Tasso, Marino, Ceppède, Góngora, Lope de Vega, Southwell, and Crashaw were Catholics, the style left its mark on such Protestant poets as D'Aubigné and Donne in their use of the metaphysical conceit.

Countess Cathleen, The (1891). A poetic drama by William Butler YEATS. It describes how the countess Cathleen sells her soul to the devil in exchange for the souls of the starving Irish peasants. In her wanderings through Ireland the Countess Cathleen is accompanied by Oona, an old nurse, and Aleel, a poet who loves her in vain. The part of the countess was written for Maud GONNE. The play was one of the first produced by the company that was later to become the ABBEY THEATRE company. At its first production it provoked a riot by Catholics offended at what they considered Yeats's theological irregularity in having God save the heroine's soul at the end.

Count of Monte Cristo, The (Le Comte de Monte Cristo; 1844). A romance by Alexandre DUMAS. The hero, Edmond Dantès, is about to begin a blissful existence as captain of his vessel and husband of his sweetheart, when a false political charge condemns him to life imprisonment. He escapes, in a highly dramatic manner, and flees to the island of Monte Cristo. With the aid of a treasure he unearths, Dantès becomes a powerful and darkly mysterious figure. Eventually, all who wronged him suffer his revenge.

Country Doctor, The (Le Médecin de campagne; 1833). A novel, part of LA COMÉDIE HUMAINE, by Honoré de BALZAC. The title character is Dr. Benassis, whose kindly spirit and indefatigable efforts on behalf of the people of his village make him universally beloved.

Country House, The (1907). A novel by John GALSWORTHY. It is a naturalistic social study of the traditions and attitudes of the English landed aristocracy. These traditions are threatened in the Pendyce family when the dashing young son, George Pendyce, becomes involved in a divorce scandal. Eventually, through the coercion of his father and the sentimental persuasions of his mother, George is extricated. Thus

Galsworthy ends by supporting the values of country house life and reassuring his conservative readers that they need not take his satire and criticism too seriously.

Country of the Pointed Firs, The (1896). A book of tales and sketches by Sarah Orne JEWETT. Thinly bound together by a faint thread of plot, the entire series describes a Maine seaport town from the point of view of a summer resident. The portraits of the townspeople are sympathetically drawn. Willa Cather thought so well of the book that she placed it beside *Huckleberry Finn* and *The Scarlet Letter.*

Country Wife, The (1675). A comedy by William WYCHERLY. Pinchwife, an overly jealous husband, brings his simple country wife, Margery, to London for the marriage of his sister Alithea to the credulous Sparkish. Despite Pinchwife's efforts, Margery soon becomes familiar with the fashionable ways of the city and ends by cuckolding him with the libertine Horner, who has spread the rumor that he is a eunuch to facilitate his access to willing wives. Thus, Pinchwife's jealousy leads his wife to infidelity while Sparkish eventually loses Alitha because of excessive confidence in her loyalty.

In 1766 Garrick rewrote the play as *The Country Girl,* modifying some of its bawdiness.

Couperus, Louis Marie Anne (1863–1923). Dutch novelist. He is known as the outstanding writer of the Dutch realist school of fiction. His most important works chronicle the lives of insignificant people with great insight and attention to detail. THE SMALL SOULS, the first of a tetralogy, is the best example of this preoccupation, though *Old People and the Things That Pass* is probably his outstanding single novel. He wrote more than 30 novels.

couplet. In prosody, a pair of lines forming a unit. This is usually because they are either set off as a separate stanza or because they rhyme. The best known couplet is the so-called HEROIC COUPLET.

Courbet, Gustave (1819–1877). French painter. Spokesman of realism, he painted straightforward and unembellished, oversized scenes of everyday life and autobiographical events. Although he was decried by his conservative contemporaries, he rejected harmonious composition and color in his desire to express truth, and achieved a forceful expression, especially in his landscapes.

Cours de Philosophie Positive. See Auguste COMTE.

Courtier, The (Il Cortegiano; 1528). A Renaissance courtesy book by Baldassare CASTIGLIONE. Written in 1518, its four books of dialogues describe the conversations held at the court of Urbino on four successive evenings in 1507. The main interlocutors are Federico Fregoso, Lodovico Di Canossa, Bernardo Bibbiena, Giuliano de' Medici, Pietro Bembo, Ottaviano Fregoso, and Emilia Pia, who along with the hostess, Elisabetta Gonzaga, acts as moderator. In the first book, the ideal courtier is said to require noble birth, skill in arms, courage, a handsome appearance, and dexterity in swimming, hunting, dancing, and the arts. He must be able to write and speak well, but above all without affectation. The manner of doing these things must be nonchalant and natural (*sprezzatura*).

The second book is devoted to language, the kind and the occasion of speech as well as the manner of

Title page of Hoby's translation of
The Courtier (1577).

addressing oneself to princes and friends. Bibbiena dominates the discussion with a long treatment of jests and witticisms. The third book features Giuliano de' Medici's discourse on the *donna di palazzo,* the court lady, who is required to maintain her femininity while displaying a knowledge of letters, the arts, and how to entertain the court. She must be morally superior, an injunction that produces a lengthy debate on the chastity of women and the problems of amatory relationships at court.

The fourth book deals with the final and true role of the ideal courtier: to guide his prince in matters of government and state. After further discussion of the education of the prince and the best forms of political organization, Bembo concludes the book with a rhapsodic explanation of Platonic Love, the union of beauty and goodness in the ascent to God.

Not long after its publication, the book was translated into French, German, Spanish, and Russian. The English version of Sir Thomas Hoby (1561) insured its popularity in England, where it influenced the writings of Spenser and Sidney, the plays of Shakespeare, and the educational and social theory and practice of the English Renaissance. With the courtesy books of Guazzo and Della Casa, it formed a trio of crucial landmarks in the development of English attitudes towards the requirements of being a gentleman.

Courtin', The (1867). A poem by James Russell LOWELL. Written in Yankee dialect, it was originally published in the second series of THE BIGLOW PAPERS. This tale of rural courtship was introduced as a diversion from the discussions of politics with which the rest of the *Biglow Papers* are concerned. The poem is still valued as a fine example of native American humor and sentiment.

courtly love or (*Fr.*) **amour courtois.** A medieval code of attitudes toward love and of the highly conventionalized conduct considered suitable for noble lords and ladies. It postulates the adoration and respect of a gallant and courageous knight or courtier for a beautiful, intelligent, lofty-minded noblewoman who usually remains chaste and unattainable. He performs noble deeds for her sake, but suffers terribly because she remains indifferent or, even if she favors his devotion, because her purity and his respect for it prevent the consummation of their love. Often he must keep secret the name of his beloved, although he carries her scarf or glove into battle or celebrates her beauty in song, for the lady is usually married to someone else; a basic tenet of the code is the incompatibility of love with marriage. Nevertheless, the lover welcomes the suffering of his passion, for it ennobles him and inspires him to great achievements.

The tradition of courtly love seems to have first been popularized by the Provençal TROUBADOURS of southern France in the 11th century. Through ELEANOR OF AQUITAINE's patronage of the troubadours, the convention spread to the royal courts of northern France, of England, and then of Germany (see MINNESINGERS). Eleanor's daughter Marie de Champagne urged her chaplain Andreas Capellanus to write a treatise on the art of love; and the "court of love," in which a group of court gentlefolk gather to debate specific theoretical problems of conduct in the interpretation of the code, became popular as a social pastime and a literary convention. The principles of courtly love were embodied in the first part of the allegorical ROMANCE OF THE ROSE, and in medieval romances such as the cycles concerning King Arthur, Tristan and Iseult, and Troilus and Cressida, most notably in the version of the Launcelot legend by Chrétien de Troyes.

In Italy the STILNOVISTI of the late 13th century adapted the tradition in a "sweet new style," which further idealized the role of woman in the spiritual elevation of the man who adores her. This worship of the beloved thus became fused with the cult of the Virgin Mary, and with the concept of the ideal in Platonism. By the 16th century courtly love had become only one aspect of the code governing the entire bearing and conduct of the courtier and his lady. The most famous handbook of courtly behavior was Castiglione's THE COURTIER, translated into English by Sir Thomas Hoby in 1561. This and the Stilnovistic works of Dante and Petrarch, all identifying physical beauty and social decorum with moral and ultimately with spiritual worth and the approach to a Platonic ideal, greatly influenced much Elizabethan writing, such as that of Sir Philip Sidney and Edmund Spenser. The exaltation of a worthy woman because of the elevating aspect of courtly love is especially prominent in Spenser's *Four Hymns.*

Courtship of Miles Standish, The (1858). A long narrative poem by Henry Wadsworth LONGFELLOW. The captain of the Plymouth settlement, Miles STANDISH, sends his friend John Alden to woo Priscilla Mullins for him. Despite his honest pleas for the older man, Priscilla prefers John as a husband.

When Miles is reported killed, the lovers plan their marriage. On the eve of the wedding Standish returns to give his blessings to the young couple.

Cousin, Victor (1792–1867). French philosopher and teacher. A professor of philosophy at the Sorbonne, Cousin delivered brilliant lectures, helping to increase the reputation of the university. A student of German philosophy, he met both Hegel and Schelling. Not a philosophical creator, but a synthesizer who drew upon former systems, Cousin is considered the founder of the Eclectic school. Among his published works are *Cours d'histoire de la philosophie moderne* (1841–46) and *Fragments pour servir à l'histoire de la philosophie* (1865).

Cousine Bette, La (1846). A novel, part of LA COMÉDIE HUMAINE, by Honoré de BALZAC. The title character, Lisbeth Fischer, is a harsh old spinster who masks frustration and bitterness behind a facade of good will. Driven by fierce jealousy, she deliberately destroys a romance between her young niece and a Polish sculptor.

Cousin Pons, Le (1847). A novel, part of LA COMÉDIE HUMAINE, by Honoré de BALZAC. The hero, Silvain Pons, is a musical composer who squanders most of his income on works of art. Ugly and lonely, he becomes a glutton and social parasite as he grows older.

Cousins, Norman (1912–). American journalist and editor. Cousins became editor of the SATURDAY REVIEW in 1942. A decade later he dropped the words "of Literature" from the title and broadened the magazine's scope to reflect his interest in world affairs and arts of communication other than literature. Cousins has also written books on world federalism and foreign policy, including *Modern Man Is Obsolete* (1945) and *In Place of Folly* (1961).

Cousteau, Jacques-Yves (1910–). French underwater explorer and writer. Inventor of the Aqua-Lung and other devices for submarine investigation, he records many of his experiments and discoveries in *The Silent World* (1953) and *The Living Sea* (1963).

Covenanters. A term applied, during the 16th and 17th centuries, to the Scottish Presbyterians who banded together in a series of agreements, or covenants, to defend their religion against royal encroachments. In 1643 the English Parliament and the Scots drew up a Solemn League and Covenant that provided for changes in the English church in conformity with Presbyterian principles; in return, the Covenanters agreed to join the Parliamentary struggle against Charles I.

Coventry Cycle. A cycle of MIRACLE PLAYS. Supposedly they were performed at Coventry, England. They are among the best of the surviving plays of this genre.

Coverdale, Miles (1) (1488–1568). An English priest, converted to Lutheranism and translator of the first complete Bible in English (1535). See BIBLE, ENGLISH VERSIONS.

(2) The narrator of Hawthorne's BLITHEDALE ROMANCE and a leading character in the story.

Coverley, Sir Roger de. The simple, good, and altogether delightful country squire created by Richard STEELE as a chief character in the imaginary club that supposedly wrote THE SPECTATOR. He was further developed by Joseph ADDISON, and it is to

Addison that we are indebted for this portrait of a perfect English gentleman in the reign of Queen Anne. Roger de Coverley is the name of a country-dance similar to the Virginia Reel and it was Addison's fiction that Sir Roger's great-grandfather invented the dance.

Covetous Knight, The. See LITTLE TRAGEDIES.

Coxey's Army. A group of about 400 unemployed who marched on Washington, D.C., in 1894 during a period of economic distress. Led by Jacob S. Coxey (1854–1951), they demanded federal legislation to create jobs and increase the amount of money in circulation. The army disbanded after Coxey and two other leaders were arrested for trespassing on the grounds of the Capitol. Coxey led another army in 1914.

Coward, Noel [Pierce] (1899–   ). English actor, composer, and playwright. He is best known for his witty, brittle, and sophisticated comedies of the British "leisure class." His works for the theater, in addition to musical revues, include *The Vortex* (1925), a serious drama; *Bitter Sweet* (1929), an operetta; *Private Lives* (1930), his most successful comedy; *Cavalcade* (1931), a patriotic play on the British Victorian tradition in the history of a single family; and *Blithe Spirit* (1941). *Present Indicative* (1937) is an autobiography; *Pomp and Circumstance* (1960) is a novel. He wrote, directed, and acted in a war movie *In Which We Serve* (1942). The second volume of his autobiography *Future Indefinite* was published in 1954; it describes his experiences as an entertainer in the second World War. His costume piece *Quadrille* (1952), starring the Lunts, had long runs in both London and New York. He has appeared on television and in night clubs.

cowboy. A Western cattle herder. The name was originally applied to Tory raiders during the American Revolution who plundered neutral land. The Western version is a breed that learned much of its way of life from the Mexican *vaquero*. Dime novels did much to make the cowboy a popular folk figure in the U.S., and the tradition has been carried on with apparently untiring success by the motion pictures and, later, by television.

Cowley, Abraham (1618–1667). English META-PHYSICAL POET and essayist. His conceits were fantastic and extreme, popular in his own day, but regarded with disfavor by the time of Dryden. He was also famous as the originator of the English Pindaric ode. Cowley published his first volume, *Poetical Blossoms* (1633), at the age of 15; later works include DAVIDEIS, his best-known poem.

Cowley, Mrs. Hannah (1743–1809). English dramatist. One of the earliest English female playwrights, she wrote a number of comedies of manners touched with sentimentality. Among the best are *The Belle's Stratagem* (1780) and *A Bold Stroke for a Husband* (1783).

Cowley, Malcolm (1898–   ). American critic and poet. A member of the American colony in France during the 1920's, Cowley discussed expatriate psychology in *Exile's Return: A Narrative of Ideas* (1934; rev., 1951). His other works include two volumes of poetry, *Blue Juniata* (1929) and *The Dry Season* (1942), and *The Literary Situation* (1954), an analysis of the writer's place in American society. He wrote an influential study of William Faulkner's

works as the introduction to the *Viking Portable Faulkner* (1946), which he edited.

Cowper, William (1731–1800). English pre-romantic poet. From the time he was 24, Cowper suffered from a religious mania and was subject to fits of despair—he was convinced that he was excluded from salvation—and intermittent attacks of insanity. After his first breakdown, he went to Huntingdon to board with Morley Unwin until Unwin's death (1767). He then moved, with the widowed Mary Unwin, to OLNEY and continued to live with her until her death (1796). His poetic career began late in life, with the production of hymns, didactic verse, nature lyrics, and religious poetry. His best-known poem is THE TASK. Others, also well known, include *Truth, The Progress of Error, Expostulation, Hope, Charity, Conversation,* and *Retirement,* all published in 1782, *The Diverting History of* JOHN GILPIN, a humorous ballad published with *The Task,* and the *Olney Hymns* (1779). He also translated Homer (1791) and on his death left many letters and introspective autobiographical writings. Cowper was interested in freeing English verse from the facility of the followers of Pope. "Give me a manly rough line," writes Cowper, "with a deal of meaning in it, rather than a whole poem full of musical periods, that have nothing but their oily smoothness to recommend them." See THE CASTAWAY; STRICKEN DEER.

Cowperwood, Frank Algernon. The central character in a trilogy of novels by Theodore DREISER. Patterned after the life of Charles T. Yerkes, Cowperwood is a man with an overweening desire for power, which drives him on to ruthless pursuit of financial dominance but fails to bring him happiness. The three novels are THE FINANCIER, THE TITAN, and *The Stoic.*

Coyle, Kathleen (1886–1952). Irish novelist. *A Flock of Birds* (1930) is a sensitive novel about the Irish revolution. In *Immortal Ease* (1939), the character Victoria Rising is supposed to be based on Elinor Wylie.

Cozzens, James Gould (1903–   ). American novelist. His *S.S. San Pedro* (1931), a novel based on the sinking of the *Vestris* in 1928, was the first of his works to attract wide attention. *Guard of Honor* (1948), which received a Pulitzer Prize, deals with soldiers and civilians at a Florida air force base during World War II. *By Love Possessed* (1957) became a best seller and was highly praised by many critics. Perhaps because it was so highly praised, a critical reaction set in, and Cozzens' work was attacked, most notably by Dwight Macdonald in *Commentary* in an article called "By Cozzens Possessed." Other novels by Cozzens include *The Last Adam* (1933), *Men and Brethren* (1936), and *The Just and the Unjust* (1942).

Crabbe, George (1754–1832). English poet. He escaped extreme poverty through the financial assistance of Edmund Burke. Considered a transitional figure between neoclassicism and romanticism, Crabbe wrote in the heroic couplet; his sympathies were humanitarian but opposed to sentimentality. His best-known poem is THE VILLAGE, a realistic answer to Oliver Goldsmith's *The Deserted Village*. Other poems by Crabbe, similar in theme to *The Village,* include *The Newspaper* (1785), *The Parish Register* (1807), and *The Borough* (1810). *Peter Grimes,* one of the most powerful tales in *The Borough,* is the subject of a tragic opera, first produced in 1945, by Benjamin Britten.

Crabbed Age and Youth. An anonymous Elizabethan lyric (1599), presenting a series of antitheses between youth and age.

Crabtree, Cadwallader. In Tobias Smollett's novel PEREGRINE PICKLE, an embittered and misanthropic old Welshman, who assists the hero in his satiric exposés of society's folly.

Craddock, Charles Egbert. See Mary Noailles MURFREE.

Craig, [Edward] Gordon (1872-   ). English actor, stage designer, producer, and writer on subjects related to the theater. He organized and published a journal, *The Mask* (1908), and founded a theatrical school at the Arena Goldoni in Florence, Italy. He is the son of Ellen Terry and Edward Goodwin.

Craigenputtock. A lonely farm near Dumfries, Scotland, owned by Jane WELSH, the wife of Thomas CARLYLE. The couple lived there from 1828 to 1834, and it was there that Carlyle wrote much of his best work. Ralph Waldo Emerson visited the Carlyles at Craigenputtock in 1833.

Craigie, Pearle Mary Teresa. Pen name **John Oliver Hobbes** (1867-1906). American-born English novelist and dramatist. Her best-known work— such as her play *The Ambassadors* (1898) and the novels *Some Emotions and a Moral* (1891) and *The Herb-Moon* (1896)—is marked by sophistication and satirical wit. Though a devout, even mystical Catholic, Mrs. Craigie was very much a woman of the world, active in the fashionable life of London.

Craig's Wife (1925). A play by George KELLY. It is a study of a selfish, narrow woman, more interested in her house than in her husband; by the end of the play everyone has left her and she is alone with the house. It was awarded a Pulitzer Prize.

Craik, Dinah Maria Mulock (1826-1887). English novelist, author of over 40 volumes including novels, tales for children, books of travel, and poetry. Her only novel of note is JOHN HALIFAX, GENTLEMAN. Most of her work is characterized by a note of rather tedious piety and sentimentality.

Cranach or **Kranach, Lucas** (1472-1553). German painter and engraver. He owes his fame to his altarpieces and to his portraits of Martin Luther and other German reformers. As court painter to the elector of Saxony, he also painted a number of biblical and mythological scenes.

Crane, [Harold] Hart (1899-1932). American poet. One of the first to attempt to express the spirit of a mechanized 20th century in valid and appropriate poetic terms, Crane is known for his unique, imaginative, and powerful creative talent. Strongly influenced by such poets as Arthur Rimbaud and T. S. Eliot, he nevertheless created his own distinctive style of dramatic rhetoric and extremely complex, compact imagery. In constant revolt from a father who had little appreciation for his poetic gifts, Crane often used elements from his own life for the stuff of his poetry. As a young man he came to New York from Ohio, worked at various jobs, and wrote poetry which was finally published in *Poetry,* the *Little Review,* and other little magazines. In 1926 he published his first collection of verse, *White Buildings,* contain-

ing an inscription from Rimbaud, whose influence is clear.

Crane reacted strongly to the poetry of T. S. Eliot, recognizing the power of the verse at the same time that he rejected the negative view of modern culture found especially in *The Waste Land.* THE BRIDGE was, in part, an answer to Eliot, an attempt to evoke the "myth of America," to write a poem that would fuse American culture, past, present, and future, into one ecstatic whole. (This rejection of cultural pessimism was not new to Crane; it infused several of the poems in *White Buildings,* notably *For the Marriage of Faustus and Helen.*) The poem remains one of the major achievements of 20th-century poetry.

Always torn by personal difficulties, in the throes of despair over what he considered his failing literary powers, Crane committed suicide by jumping overboard from the ship bringing him back from Mexico, where he had gone on a Guggenheim fellowship to write a poem on the Spanish Conquest.

After his death, a volume of poems collected for publication, *Key West: An Island Sheaf,* was found. This group, together with other unpublished poems, was included in *Collected Verse* (1933). See Samuel GREENBERG.

Crane, Ichabod. A character in Washington Irving's tale, THE LEGEND OF SLEEPY HOLLOW. Crane is a gawky schoolmaster, described as resembling "some scarecrow eloped from a field."

Crane, Stephen [Townley] (1871-1900). American novelist, short-story writer, poet, and war correspondent. In his short life, Crane managed to produce work that assured him a permanent place in American literature. Best known for his novel THE RED BADGE OF COURAGE, he has been variously described as an impressionist, a realist, and a symbolist. Ignored by critics in the years immediately after his death, he has since been the subject of much critical controversy, but his importance as a writer is indisputable.

Crane was born in Newark, N.J., the son of a Methodist minister and writer of religious tracts. His mother was also a writer, for a time editor of the *Christian Advocate.* After one semester each at Lafayette College and Syracuse University, he gave up formal schooling and devoted himself to journalism and literature.

His first novel was MAGGIE: A GIRL OF THE STREETS. Although published by Crane at his own expense and ignored by reviewers, this realistic study brought him the respect of Hamlin Garland and William Dean Howells. In 1895, Crane published both *The Red Badge of Courage,* which brought him immense prestige, especially in England, and his first volume of poems, THE BLACK RIDERS. GEORGE'S MOTHER appeared the following year.

Sent to cover a filibustering expedition to Cuba, Crane was on board the *Commodore* when it sank on New Year's Day, 1897. From this experience came THE OPEN BOAT, the short story that has been called one of the finest in the English language. Meanwhile, Crane had fallen in love with Cora Taylor, whom he had met in Florida, and together they went to Greece as war correspondents, an experience responsible for the novel *Active Service* (1899). At the close of the war, they established themselves in England.

During the Spanish-American War, Crane went to

Cuba as a reporter for the New York *World* and the New York *Journal*. Plagued by ill health and financial difficulties, he returned for the last year of his life to England, where among his close friends was Joseph Conrad, who greatly admired his writing. Of the work of his last years, the stories THE BRIDE COMES TO YELLOW SKY and THE BLUE HOTEL may be singled out for special praise, the latter being included in the collection *The Monster and Other Stories* (1899). Other works include *The Little Regiment and Other Episodes of the American Civil War* (1896), *The Third Violet* (1897), WAR IS KIND, WHILOMVILLE STORIES, *Wounds in the Rain* (1900), *Great Battles of the World* (1901), *Last Words* (1902), *The O'Ruddy* (1903), and *Sullivan County Sketches*, compiled by Melvin Schoberlin in 1949.

Cranford (1853). A story by Mrs. GASKELL dealing with the life of the peaceful little English village of Cranford, inhabited chiefly by old ladies who practice elegant economy and a quaint social decorum under the leadership of the Honorable Mrs. Jamieson. The chief characters are the two Miss Jenkyns: Miss Deborah and Miss Mattie.

Cranmer, Thomas (1489–1556). Archbishop of Canterbury. Cranmer first came to the attention of HENRY VIII through his suggestions regarding Henry's divorce from Catherine of Aragon. He was made Archbishop in 1533, and contributed substantially to the progress of the English Reformation by encouraging the circulation of the Bible in English, in the preparation of the First and Second Prayer Books of Edward VI, and in the formulation of the 42 (now 39) Articles of Religion. In 1553 he was persuaded to sign the dying request of Edward VI to give the crown to Lady Jane GREY. After Lady Jane's brief reign and the accession of the Catholic Mary, Cranmer was sent to the Tower. He was burned at the stake for heresy in 1556.

Crapsey, Adelaide (1878–1914). American poet. A teacher at girls' schools and at Smith College, Miss Crapsey wrote her poetry in the last year of her life, developing her own form, the CINQUAIN, derived from Japanese poetry. Her work resembles that of the imagists in its firmness and concentration. Her poetry was posthumously published in *Verse* (1915). See Jean WEBSTER.

Crashaw, Richard (1612–1649). English METAPHYSICAL POET. Although Crashaw's father was a Puritan preacher, the poet became a convert to Catholicism in his early 30's. From the beginning of the English Civil War until his death, he lived in exile on the continent, first in Paris and later attached to the household of Cardinal Palotto and to the shrine of Loreto in Italy.

Crashaw is best known for his religious verse, though he wrote a good deal of secular verse and much Latin poetry. Even before his conversion, his religious poems reflected a straining, passionate mysticism and a love of lush, sensuous imagery and ornate conceits in the manner of the Marinist Italian poetry of the 16th and early 17th centuries. Although he was partly inspired to write religious verse by his reading of George Herbert's *The Temple* (1633), Crashaw's work is distinguished by a luxuriance and high-keyed emotiveness alien to Herbert. His style is highly individual and uneven: he is capable of an ardor and brilliance hardly surpassed in literature, but he can also be overwrought and tasteless.

In 1646 Crashaw published *Steps to the Temple,* a collection which contains his well-known secular poems MUSICS DUEL and WISHES TO HIS SUPPOSED MISTRESS, and his religious poems to Sts. Theresa and Mary Magdalene. *The Flaming Heart,* a hymn to St. Theresa, which deals with her precocious piety and mystic transports, shows Crashaw at his strongest; but *St. Mary Magdalene, or The Weeper,* in which he describes her penitential tears in a series of extended and extravagant images, contains overelaborate conceits and bathetic passages. Other works by Crashaw are *Epigrammatum Sacrorum Liber* (1634) and *Carmen Deo Nostro* (1652).

Crassus, Marcus Licinius. Surnamed **Dives,** i.e., "the Rich" (115?–53 B.C.). Roman financier and politician. Shortly after the civil war of Marius and Sulla, Crassus came into political prominence by defeating the slave army of SPARTACUS in 71. After this military victory, he turned his talents to business and by shrewd speculation was able, within 10 years, to amass a vast fortune. In 60 he joined Caesar and Pompey in the First TRIUMVIRATE and was allotted the command of Asia Minor. He was killed fighting the Parthians at Carrhae.

Cratchit, Bob. In Charles Dickens' A CHRISTMAS CAROL, the clerk of Ebenezer Scrooge. Though Cratchit has to maintain nine dependents on meager wages, his home, unlike his employer's, is filled with happiness and love.

Tiny Tim Cratchit. The little lame son of Bob Cratchit, a winsome and beloved child. In the ordinary course of events he was doomed to an early death, but Scrooge, after his change of character, makes Tiny Tim his special care.

Crawford, F[rancis] Marion (1854–1909). American novelist. He is best known for popular romances with historical backgrounds and glamorous depictions of life in cosmopolitan society. His first novel, MR. ISAACS, achieved enormous popularity. Novels with a contemporary setting include those of the SARACINESCA series, *Dr. Claudius* (1883), and *The White Sister* (1909). His historical novels include *Via Crucis* (1898) and *In the Palace of the King* (1900).

Crawford, Mary and Henry. See MANSFIELD PARK.

Crawley, Captain Rawdon. The husband of Becky Sharp in Thackeray's VANITY FAIR. Separated from his wife, he ends his days as governor of Coventry Island.

Sir Pitt Crawley. Rawdon's father. A rich, vulgar baronet, he is "a philosopher with a taste for low life." On the death of his second wife, Sir Pitt proposes to Becky Sharp, but she has already married his son.

Mr. Pitt Crawley. Sir Pitt's eldest son. He inherits fortunes from his father and from the aunt who disowned Crawley for his marriage to Becky.

Mr. and Mrs. Bute Crawley. A "tall, stately, jolly, shovel-hatted rector," brother of Sir Pitt, and his politic little wife.

Crayon, Geoffrey. A pen name of Washington IRVING. He published THE SKETCH BOOK and *The Crayon Miscellany* (1835) under this pseudonym.

Crazy Jane. A beggar, the spokesman and heroine of a series of poems by William Butler YEATS.

Advocating the natural joys of life, she flouts conventional morality, especially in *Crazy Jane and the Bishop.*

Creakle. In Charles Dickens' DAVID COPPERFIELD, a hard, vulgar schoolmaster to whose charge David is entrusted and in whose school he first makes the acquaintance of STEERFORTH. The portrait of Creakle is Dickens' protest against the harsh treatment meted out to children by schoolmasters.

Cream of the Jest, The (1917). A novel by James Branch CABELL. This "comedy of evasions" is the story of an author, Felix Kennaston, who by means of a hieroglyphic disk escapes into a dream world where he pursues a changing yet always similar image of his beloved. She turns out to be his wife.

Creasey, John (1908–). English writer of crime fiction. One of the ablest and most prolific practitioners of his craft, Creasey is perhaps best known for his documentary novels about George Gideon of Scotland Yard, which he writes under the pseudonym of J. J. Marric. These include *Gideon's Day* (1955), *Gideon's Week* (1956), *Gideon's Staff* (1959), and *Gideon's Risk* (1961). Creasey also uses other pen names, including Michael Halliday, Gordon Ashe, and Jeremy York.

Creasy, Sir **Edward Shepherd.** See FIFTEEN DECISIVE BATTLES OF THE WORLD.

creation myths. The earliest known myth of the creation is from Sumer of the third millennium B.C. First was the goddess Nammu, the primeval sea; she gave birth to An, the sky-god, and Ki, the earth-god —earth and sky, both solid elements, being joined together. Their offspring Enlil, the god of air, separated them. He lighted his realm by begetting Nanna, the moon-god, who in turn fathered Utu, the sun-god. Enlil next impregnated Ki, who gave birth to Enki, the god of water and of wisdom. Enki ordered the universe, but was unable to create man—a task that the goddess Nintu accomplished by molding him of clay.

In the Babylonian creation myth of the WAR OF THE GODS (*Enuma elish*), Marduk forms man out of the blood and bones of Kingu, a henchman of the defeated Tiamat. An Egyptian belief was that the original sun-god, Atum, standing on a mound in the midst of the slowly receding primeval waters, gave birth parthenogenetically to the other gods and to those parts of the universe which they embodied. According to the familiar biblical story in the first chapter of Genesis, the universe and man were created by Yahweh in seven days, beginning with light and ending with man and woman. In the second chapter appears a variation on the creation of man, which is older and closer to folk tale; woman is created of a rib detached from Adam while he sleeps. Christian theology added that the Son and the Holy Ghost existed with Yahweh from before the creation. The Eastern branch of the Church, however, denied that Jesus had existed from the beginning and the resulting "*filioque* controversy" was the ostensible cause of the split between Eastern and Western churches in 1054.

The first Greek description of creation, in the *Theogony,* attributed to Hesiod, seems to have been a theological elaboration of genuine myth. First to exist was Chaos, from which came Earth, Tartarus, Love, Darkness, and Night. Night and Darkness gave birth to Day and the upper air (Aether). Earth parthenogenetically produced Heaven, Mountains, and Sea. After this prelude, the Hesiodic version proceeds with nearly universal mythic elements that are probably far older. Uniting with Heaven (Uranus), Earth (Ge) gave birth to Oceanus and the Titans. The last of these was Cronus, who overthrew and emasculated his father, only to be supplanted in turn by his son Zeus (see KUMARBI). A highly artificial myth current in the doctrines of Orphism claimed that Chaos, Night, and Darkness existed at the beginning; Love (Eros) sprang from an egg laid by Night and himself gave birth to the other gods. The creation of man seems not to have interested the Greeks very deeply; of various versions, the most prominent made Prometheus their creator—he having molded them of clay.

In Vedic mythology, creation began with Aditi, celestial space. Sky and Earth were sometimes regarded as the first goddesses, sometimes as the original male and female elements, which are known to so many other mythologies; later the sky was personified as Varuna. The first man was Manu; his daughter-mate Ida was born of the food that he offered as a sacrifice to Vishnu in gratitude for being saved from the flood.

Crébillon, Claude Prosper Jolyot de (1707–1777). French author and son of Prosper Jolyot de CRÉBILLON. His novels, tales, and dialogues reflect the moral laxity of his day. *Le Sopha* (1745), for example, tells the experiences of a man transformed by metempsychosis into a sofa, and the scandalous adventures which take place on it. His other works include *L'Ecumoire* (1733) and *La Nuit et le moment* (1755). He was, like his father, one of the dramatic censors of the French government.

Crébillon, Prosper Jolyot de (1674–1762). French dramatist. His tragedies rely more on violence and horror than on grandeur. Nicolas Boileau called him a "drunken Racine." His best play, *Rhadamiste et Zénobie* (1711), whose subject was taken from a novel of Jean Segrais, enjoyed considerable popularity; his other plays did not. He was elected to the French ACADEMY in 1731, and became one of the official dramatic censors of the time. Though he considered himself a literary descendant of Racine, he is merely a precursor of the romantic melodrama.

credo (*Lat.,* "I believe"). A creed or confession of faith. The most important historical Christian creeds are the *Apostles'* and the *Nicene* (both 4th century), and the *Athanasian* (5th century). Later credal statements of importance are found in the *Decrees of the Council of Trent* (1563), the *Augsburg Confession* (1530), and the *Westminster Confession of Faith* (1647).

Creevey, Thomas (1768–1838). English diarist of the Georgian era. His journals and correspondence covering a period of 36 years were published in 1903 as the *Creevey Papers.*

Cremona. A fine violin made in Cremona, in Lombardy. There, in the 17th and early 18th centuries, lived violin makers of worldwide renown, such as Andrea Amati (c. 1520–c. 1610), Nicolò Amati (1596–1684), Antonio Stradivari (1644–1737), and numerous members of the Guarneri family, especially Giuseppe (1687–1744).

Creon (Kreon). (1) In Greek mythology, a king of Thebes. The brother of Jocasta, he served as regent after the death of her husband Laius, and became king after the death of Eteocles in the War of the SEVEN AGAINST THEBES. He condemned Oedipus' daughter ANTIGONE to death and, repenting too late, lost his own son Haemon as a consequence.

(2) A king of Corinth, whose daughter Glauce married Jason and met her horrible fate through the jealousy of MEDEA. He appears in Euripides' tragedy *Medea*.

Crepuscolari, I (*Ital.,* "the twilight poets," a name coined by the critic G. A. Borgese). A group of Italian poets of the early 20th century whose work is notable for its use of musical and mood-conveying language and its general tone of despondency. Their attitude represents a reaction to the content-poetry and rhetorical style of CARDUCCI and D'ANNUNZIO, favoring instead the unadorned language and homely themes typical of PASCOLI. An affinity existed with the French SYMBOLISTS (Valéry, Rimbaud, and Mallarmé). Guido GOZZANO was the most competent exponent of the movement.

Cressida. See CRISEYDE.

Cretheis. See ACASTUS.

Crétin, Roger Auguste. See Roger VERCEL.

Creusa (Kreousa). (1) See ION.

(2) In the *Aeneid,* the daughter of Priam and Hecuba and wife of AENEAS.

Crèvecœur, Michel Guillaume Jean de. Pen name **J. Hector St. John** (1735–1813). French author, agronomist, traveler and settler in America from 1754 to 1780. After having traveled through Canada, the Great Lakes region, and Pennsylvania, he settled on a farm in the colony of New York. Here, between 1770 and 1781, he wrote LETTERS FROM AN AMERICAN FARMER, an extremely popular series of essay-letters. On his return to the U.S. to serve as French consul in 1783, he did much to improve Franco-American relations. More letters, found in 1922 and published as *Sketches of Eighteenth Century America* (1925), give informative and accurate descriptions of colonial American rural life. He also wrote *Voyage dans la haute Pennsylvanie et dans l'état de New York, par un membre adoptif de la nation Onéida* (1801), an account of his early travels and of the American Indians, which he pretended to have translated from an original manuscript. Selections from *Voyage* were translated and published under the title *Crèvecœur's Eighteenth-Century Travels in Pennsylvania and New York* (1961) by Percy G. Adams.

Cricket on the Hearth (1845). A Christmas tale by Charles DICKENS. In the happy home of John Peerybingle and his wife Dot, the cricket on the hearth chirps when all is well and is silent when unhappiness pervades. They take in an elderly boarder whom John soon discovers is a young man in disguise. His suspicions are aroused when he sees this man with his arm around Dot. The cricket takes things in hand, counseling John not to find fault. Soon, the young man, who turns out to be Edward Plummer, bursts in with his young bride May Fielding. He explains all: after his long absence he came back disguised so that he could ascertain whether May truly loved Tackleton, the man she was to marry. Happiness returns to the house and Edward

is reunited with his father Caleb and his blind sister Bertha.

Crillon, Louis des Balbis de Berton de (1541–1615). French general, known as *L'Homme sans peur* (*Fr.,* "the man without fear"). He fought against the Huguenots in the French religious wars and took part in the battle of Lepanto. He later entered the service of Henry IV, who called him "bravest of the brave," and fought at the battle of Ivry.

Crime and Punishment (Prestupleniye i nakazaniye; 1866). A novel by Feodor DOSTOEVSKI. The poor student Raskolnikov, after a long period of brooding over his poverty and the helpless position of his mother and young sister, plans and carries out the murder of an old woman pawnbroker. Surprised in the act, he has to kill the old woman's sister, also. His motives for the murder are then re-examined. Raskolnikov, whose name is derived from the Russian word for *schismatic,* has claimed that he needed the money to help his family, that with the money he could raise himself and become a benefactor to mankind, and finally that by transgressing the law he showed a boldness that put him in the same category as a Napoleon. One by one Raskolnikov's motives are proven false, as his conscience works on him. He instinctively feels disgust for his act, and is unable to bring himself to use the money he has stolen. The torments of conscience he endures prove to him that he lacks the qualities of an amoral superman. He turns for sympathy to SONYA Marmeladova, a young girl forced into prostitution to support her drunken father, his wife, and three small children. Sonya urges him to confess his crime. The police inspector Porfiri Petrovich, an astute psychologist, already strongly suspects Raskolnikov and simply waits for the confession he is sure will come. Raskolnikov finally does break down, although he stubbornly refuses to admit sorrow for having killed the old pawnbroker. He is sentenced to Siberia, where Sonya devotedly follows him, and there he gradually begins to achieve the peace and humility necessary for his sincere repentance.

The novel, the first of Dostoevski's five large works, reveals the mastery of psychological observation and analysis for which the author is hailed. Beside the depiction of Raskolnikov's anguished mind before, during, and after his crime, there are vivid studies of the profligate SVIDRIGAILOV, the saintly Sonya, and her drunken father, MARMELADOV.

Crimean War (1854–1856). A war between Turkey with its allies (England, France, and Sardinia) and Russia. It succeeded for the time being in shattering Russia's ambitions of leadership in southeastern Europe. The chief battles were at Alma, Balaklava, Inkerman, and the famous siege of Sevastopol. The result was the Treaty and Declaration of Paris (1856), in which the integrity of Turkey was guaranteed, the Black Sea neutralized, and Danubian navigation declared free. An event in this war was celebrated by Tennyson in his poem *The Charge of the Light Brigade*. It was also the scene of Florence Nightingale's heroic activities as a nurse.

Crime of Sylvestre Bonnard, The (Le Crime de Sylvestre Bonnard; 1881). A novel by Anatole FRANCE. Sylvestre Bonnard is a kind-hearted, absent-minded old archeologist. The aged scholar's crime is the kidnapping of Jeanne Alexandre, the orphaned daughter of his former love, from a school in which she is abused and unhappy. Threatening complications result, but when it is discovered that Jeanne's guardian is an embezzler, she is made the legal ward of M. Bonnard.

Criseida. The heroine of Giovanni Boccaccio's romance FILOSTRATO and the prototype of Chaucer's heroine in his *Troilus and Criseyde.*

Criseyde. Beloved of Troilus in Geoffrey Chaucer's TROILUS AND CRISEYDE. She is more complicated than her prototype in Boccaccio's *Il Filostrato;* although a practical opportunist, she is genuinely affectionate, not the heartlessly fickle girl she becomes in Shakespeare's *Troilus and Cressida.*

Crishna. See KRISHNA.

Crisis, The (1901). A historical novel by Winston CHURCHILL. The action centers in St. Louis during the controversy over slavery. The hero, Stephen Brice, is a Yankee; the heroine, Virginia Carvel, a Southerner. The novel shows the inevitability of the Civil War, yet stresses the fact that neither side wanted it. The book includes a notable portrait of Lincoln.

Criterion, The (1922–1939). A quarterly literary review. It was edited in London by T. S. ELIOT and reflected his opinions.

Critical Fable, A (1922). Amy LOWELL's imitation of her kinsman James Russell Lowell's FABLE FOR CRITICS. For a time the poem was thought to have been written by Leonard Bacon, an attribution encouraged by Miss Lowell. The poem consists of a dialogue with the earlier Lowell, during the course of which many poets of the 1920's are discussed.

critical philosophy. See Immanuel KANT.

Criticón, El (1651, 1653, 1657). A philosophical novel by Baltasar GRACIÁN. Divided into three seasons (the spring of childhood, the autumn of manhood, and the winter of old age), it describes the encounter on a desert island of the wise and noble Critilo with the savage Andrenio. Critilo brings Andrenio in contact with civilization, acting as his guide to human society. The pessimistic conclusions of both men probably explain at least part of the admiration that Schopenhauer felt for the book.

Critique of Judgment (Kritik der Urteilskraft; 1790). A philosophical work by Immanuel KANT. It contains Kant's aesthetic philosophy. He believed that the representation of a thing in art constitutes a partial understanding of the thing in itself (*Ding an sich*).

Critique of Practical Reason (Kritik der praktischen Vernunft; 1788). A philosophical work by Immanuel KANT. Kant constructed a philosophy of ethics based on practical reason, or the free will of man. Since the moral law itself is unconditional and universal, it is called the categorical imperative; its basic formulation is "Act only on that maxim whereby you can at the same time will that it should become a universal law." Our knowledge of God is obtained through our moral feelings, not through pure reason.

Critique of Pure Reason (Kritik der reinen Vernunft; 1781). A philosophical work by Immanuel KANT, in which he maintained that all sense experience must be inherently rational, and therefore, that rational knowledge about experience is

possible. But although reason can understand a thing considered as an object of experience, reason cannot understand the thing-in-itself (*Ding an sich*).

Crito (Kriton; fl. 400 B.C.). An Athenian friend and follower of Socrates. Plato wrote a dialogue called *Crito* in which his friend attempts to persuade Socrates to escape from prison. Socrates refuses to break the law of Athens. His well-known last words were, "Crito, I owe a cock to Aesculapius."

Croce, Benedetto (1866–1952). Italian philosopher, literary critic, and historian. A prolific writer of encyclopedic range, Croce set forth his philosophical system, in which the influence of German idealism is discernible, in the four volumes of his *Filosofia dello Spirito: Estetica Come Scienza dell'Espressione e Linguistica Generale* (1902), *Logica Come Scienza del Concetto Puro* (1905), *Filosofia della Pratica, Economica, ed Etica* (1908), and *Teoria e Storia della Storiografia* (1916). He was perhaps most influential as an aesthetician, emphasizing the intuitive nature of art.

He also wrote numerous works of literary criticism, including *La Poesia di Dante* (1920) and the six-volume *Letteratura della Nuova Italia* (1914–1940). Among his other works are *Materialismo Storico ed Economia Marxista* (1900), *Breviario di Estetica* (1913), and *Storia d'Italia dal 1871 al 1915* (1927). For 27 years he edited *La Critica,* a bimonthly magazine.

A staunch liberal during the fascist regime, he was a member of the post-World War II Committee of Liberation, a delegate to the constitution-making Italian Parliament (1945–1947), and president of the Italian Liberal Party until 1947.

Crockett, David or **Davy** (1786–1836). American frontiersman, public official, and folk hero. After serving as a scout under Andrew Jackson in the Creek War of 1813–1814, Crockett became a justice of the peace in Tennessee; he later boasted that none of his decisions, which were based on "natural-born sense instead of law learning," was ever reversed. He was also a prodigious hunter of bears and claimed to have killed over 100 in eight or nine months. A humorous suggestion that he run for Congress led him to undertake the race, and he was elected for three terms (1827–1831, 1833–1835), becoming known as the "coonskin Congressman." His opposition to the policies of President Jackson endeared him to the Whigs but cost him his seat, and he decided to go to Texas, where he died fighting heroically at the ALAMO. He was speedily made into an American folk hero who could talk the language of animals, ride the lightning, lie with extravagant grandeur, and whip his weight in wildcats.

Several books have been attributed to Crockett, notably *A Narrative of the Life of David Crockett* (1834). He may also have had a hand in some of the *Crockett Almanacs,* which appeared from 1835 to 1856. They contained the usual meteorological and astronomical data, as well as tall tales involving such figures as Crockett, Daniel Boone, and Kit Carson.

Crockett, Samuel Rutherford (1860–1914). Scottish novelist. Abandoning the ministry for a literary career, he participated in the romantic revival. A member of the KAILYARD school of writers, he wrote *The Stickit Minister* (1893) and many fine and exciting historical novels.

crocodile. A symbol of deity among the ancient Egyptians. According to Plutarch, it is the only aquatic animal that has its eyes covered with a thin transparent membrane, by reason of which it sees and is not seen, as God sees all, Himself not being seen. To this, he adds: "The Egyptians worship God symbolically in the crocodile, that being the only animal without a tongue, like the Divine Logos, which standeth not in need of speech" (*De Iside et Osiride*). Achilles Tatius says, "The number of its teeth equals the number of days in a year." Another tradition is that during the seven days held sacred to Apis, the crocodile will harm no one. See TROCHILUS.

crocodile tears. Hypocritical tears. The tale is that crocodiles moan and sigh like a person in deep distress to allure travelers to the spot, and even shed tears over their prey while in the act of devouring it. Shakespeare refers to this in the second part of *Henry VI* (1592).

Crocus. In classic legend, a young man enamored of the nymph Smilax. She did not return his love. The gods changed him into the crocus flower, to signify unrequited love.

Croesus (Kroisos; fl. 550 B.C.). King of Lydia famous for his wealth. According to a story recounted by Herodotus, Croesus was once visited by SOLON, who, instead of calling Croesus the happiest of mortals, as the vain ruler had expected, said, "Account no man happy before his death." Croesus indignantly dismissed Solon, but the Greek proved to be right. Later, misinterpreting an oracle from Delphi that war with Persia would cause the fall of a great empire, Croesus attacked Cyrus, king of Persia, in 546 B.C. The kingdom to fall turned out to be his own. Sentenced to death by fire, Croesus called the name of Solon, recalling too late his wisdom. Cyrus, upon inquiry, learned the story of the interview, and countermanded the death sentence. Instead he made Croesus one of his trusted advisers.

Unfortunately for the story, it is chronologically impossible, since the dates of Croesus and Solon did not coincide. The remark attributed to Solon was a popular proverb; it appears as the final lines of Sophocles' *Oedipus Tyrannos,* among other places.

Crofts, Freeman Wills (1879–1957). Anglo-Irish writer of detective stories and creator of Inspector French. *The Cask* (1920) is one of his cleverest novels.

Crome Yellow (1921). A satirical novel by Aldous HUXLEY. It is concerned with the odd, learned conversations and comic adventures of a group of people gathered at a country house party: Mrs. Wimbush, who believes in spiritualism; Mr. Wimbush, who reads aloud portions of his absurd history of his house, Crome; Mr. Scogan, who is planning a "Rational State" much like the one Huxley describes in *Brave New World;* and other eccentrics. The central character is Denis Stone, an ineffectual young poet whose banal verse is included in the novel. His one decisive action takes him away from the girl he shyly and secretly loves.

Crommelynck, Fernand (1885–). Belgian dramatist. *Le Cocu magnifique* (1920) is the best known of his poetic, sardonic farces. Among his other plays are *Le Sculpteur de masques* (1908), *Tripes*

d'or (1925), and *Chaud et Froid ou L'Idée de monsieur Dom* (1934).

Crommyonian sow. In Greek mythology, a dangerous wild pig. This animal roamed the land of Crommyon on the Isthmus of Corinth. Theseus killed it.

Cromwell, Oliver (1599–1658). English Puritan leader and Lord Protector of the Realm (1653–1658). As commander of the famous cavalry regiment called Ironsides, he contributed to the Parliamentary victories at Edgehill and Marston Moor and, as joint commander of the NEW MODEL ARMY, defeated the Royalists at Naseby. After the execution of Charles I, he led an army against the rebellious Roman Catholics of Ireland, whom he persecuted so relentlessly that his name is still regarded there with odium. Although he refused the title of king, his powers as lord protector were such that he was able to rule as virtual dictator. An efficient administrator, he permitted religious toleration and pursued a vigorous foreign policy. His son, Richard, trained to be his successor, alienated both the army and Parliament and was dismissed in 1659.

Cromwell, Thomas, Earl of Essex (1485?–1540). English statesman. In 1524 Cromwell was employed by Cardinal Wolsey to survey some of the smaller monasteries with a view to their suppression. He was attached to Wolsey until the latter's fall from royal favor in 1529, after which time Cromwell himself rose steadily in power. According to Cardinal Pole, Cromwell urged HENRY VIII to proclaim himself head of the church and thereby make unnecessary a papal dispensation for his divorce from Catherine of Aragon. When in 1534 the Act of Supremacy established the king as head of the Church, Cromwell's policy was made law, and he became Henry's chief adviser in ecclesiastical matters. He became Lord Chamberlain in 1539, but the following year incurred Henry's disfavor over the king's marriage to Anne of Cleves, which Cromwell had fostered in the hope of gaining the support of German Protestants. He was accused of treason by his enemies, and executed in 1540.

Cronin, A[rchibald] J[oseph] (1896–). Scottish novelist and physician. Many of his bestselling novels are about the medical profession. Among his best-known books are *Hatter's Castle* (1931), *Three Loves* (1932), *The Citadel* (1937), *The Stars Look Down* (1935), *The Keys of the Kingdom* (1941), *The Spanish Gardener* (1950), and *The Judas Tree* (1961).

Cronos (Kronos). One of the TITANS of Greek mythology, and father of Zeus. Born of Uranus (sky) and Ge (earth), he married his sister-titan Rhea. Learning from Ge that his son would dethrone him, he swallowed their children, Hestia, Demeter, Hera, Hades, and Poseidon, but Rhea and his sons rescued Zeus. This son did indeed dethrone Cronos, as had been predicted.

Cronos is believed to have been an ancient pre-Hellenic god of fertility. The sickle with which he is depicted in art probably was his attribute as a god of crops, though the Greeks explained that this was the sickle with which he had castrated his father Uranus. The Romans identified Cronos with their equally vague deity SATURN.

cross. An ancient symbol of many uses. Long before the birth of Christ, it was used in Carthage for ornamental purposes. Runic crosses were set up by the Scandinavians as boundary marks, and were erected over the graves of kings and heroes. According to Cicero, the staff with which the Roman augur marked out the heavens was in the shape of a cross. The Egyptians employed it as a sacred symbol, and two buns marked with crosses were discovered at Herculaneum. It was a sacred symbol among the Aztecs long before the landing of Cortez. It was worshiped in Cozumel and Palenque; in Tabasco, it symbolized the god of rain. It was also the emblem of Quetzalcoatl as lord of the four cardinal points and their respective winds.

There are many legends about the cross of the crucifixion. It is said to have been made of four kinds of wood: palm, cedar, olive, and cypress, signifying the four quarters of the globe. Another legend says that Solomon cut down a cedar and buried it on the spot where the pool of Bethesda later stood. Shortly before the crucifixion, the cedar floated to the surface of the pool, and was used as the upright of the cross. During the Middle Ages, enough fragments of the "true cross" were sold as relics to account for an entire forest of crosses. According to legend, the Emperor Constantine, on his march to Rome, saw a luminous cross in the sky, with the motto *"In hoc signo vinces"* (by this sign conquer). The night before the battle of Saxarubra (312) a vision appeared to the emperor in his sleep instructing him to inscribe the cross and the motto on the shields of his soldiers. He obeyed the voice and the vision, and won the battle. A very similar legend has been applied to various other conquerors, however. The cross generally associated with the crucifixion in art is a Latin cross, or *crux immissa*. St. Andrew's cross, the *crux decussata*, is shaped like an X; the *tau* cross, or *crux commissa*, is a very ancient symbol of a T shape, thought to have been originally a phallic emblem.

The *tau* cross with a circle at the top, the *crux ansata*, was common to various Egyptian deities, including Isis and Osiris. The circle signifies the eternal preserver of the world. The *tau* is the monogram of Thoth, the Egyptian Hermes, the god of wisdom.

Crossing, The (1904). A historical novel by Winston CHURCHILL. It deals mainly with the settlement of Kentucky and with the conquest of the Northwest Territory by George Rogers Clark during the American Revolution. The hero, a youth named David Ritchie, takes part in Clark's campaign.

Crossing Brooklyn Ferry (1856). A poem by Walt WHITMAN. The poet is one with all those who cross from shore to shore. Regardless of time and space, he shares the experience of life itself.

Crossing the Bar (1889). A famous poem by Alfred TENNYSON, which uses, as a metaphor for death, a description of putting out to sea on a calm evening. Before his death the author instructed his publishers to insert it at the end of each section of his works.

Crossman, R[ichard] H[oward] S[tafford] (1907–   ). English writer on politics, economics, and philosophy; journalist and leftist politician. He is best known as editor of THE GOD THAT FAILED, a collection of essays by ex-Communists.

Cross Purposes. See MISUNDERSTANDING, THE.

Crotchet Castle (1831). A novel by Thomas Love PEACOCK. A delightful satire on romantic themes, being a humorously erudite discussion of various curious topics. The central one is an argument to determine the most desirable period of history, with the Rev. Folliott contending for Athenian Greece, Mr. MacQuedy for contemporary Scotland, and Mr. Chainmail for the Middle Ages.

Crothers, Rachel (1878–1958). American playwright. She is interested in the place of women in the modern world. *Susan and God* (1937) is a play about a woman who masks her selfishness under a new-found religious zeal. Among her plays: *Nice People* (1921), *Let Us Be Gay* (1929), and *When Ladies Meet* (1932).

Crouse, Russel (1893–1966). American journalist, playwright, and theatrical producer. Crouse early wrote the libretto for the musical *The Gang's All Here* (1931) and published two books on 19th-century American life: *Mr. Currier and Mr. Ives* (1930) and *It Seems Like Yesterday* (1931). With Howard LINDSAY he dramatized LIFE WITH FATHER and *Life with Mother* (1948), based on the books by Clarence Day; *State of the Union* (1945), a Pulitzer Prize-winning satire on American politics; *Call Me Madam* (1950), a musical comedy; and *Tall Story* (1959). Also with Lindsay he produced Joseph Kesselring's comedy *Arsenic and Old Lace* (1940), the story of two old ladies who poison people for their own good. Crouse wrote the book on which *The Sound of Music* (1960) was based.

Crowdero. In Butler's HUDIBRAS, one of the rabble leaders encountered by Hudibras at a bearbaiting. The original was one Jackson or Jephson, a milliner.

Crowe, Captain. In Tobias Smollett's novel *The Adventures of Sir LAUNCELOT GREAVES*, the attendant of Sir Launcelot in his peregrinations to reform society. Sir Launcelot is a Georgian Don Quixote; Captain Crowe is his Sancho Panza.

Crowley, [Edward] Aleister (1875–1947). English poet and author of books on magic and occult lore. He was a legendary figure, notorious for his celebrations of Black Magic rites. He wrote such books as *Songs of the Spirit* (1898) and *The Diary of a Drug Fiend* (1922). He is the subject of Somerset Maugham's novel *The Magician*.

Crowne, John (c. 1640–c. 1703). English dramatist, best known for his lively comedy *Sir Courtly Nice, or It Cannot Be* (1685). His other plays include the heroic drama *The Destruction of Jerusalem by Titus Vespasian* (1677), *The Country Wit* (1675), *The English Friar* (1689), *The Married Beau* (1694), and a string of meretricious tragedies.

Crowninshield, Frank [Francis Welch] (1872–1947). American editor. Associated with various magazines, including *The Bookman*, he is best known as the editor of *Vanity Fair* (1914–1935). A witty after-dinner speaker, he was one of the founders of the Museum of Modern Art and wrote such books as *Manners for the Metropolis* (1908) and *The Bridge Fiend* (1909).

Crucible, The (1953). A play about the Salem, Mass., witchcraft trials of 1692 by Arthur MILLER. Raising the question of freedom of conscience, it provided a parallel to McCarthyism in America during the early 1950's.

Cruden, Alexander. See ALEXANDER THE CORRECTOR.

Cruikshank, George (1792–1878). English illustrator and caricaturist. He is famous as the illustrator of Dickens (*Sketches by Boz* and *Oliver Twist*) and Scott, and as a social and political satirist.

Crummles, Mr. Vincent. See NICHOLAS NICKLEBY.

Cruncher, Jerry. A minor character in Charles Dickens' A TALE OF TWO CITIES. He works in a bank by day and is a RESURRECTION MAN by night. His wife is continually saying her prayers, which Jerry terms "flopping."

Crusades. Wars undertaken in late medieval times by Christians against the Turks and Saracens for the recovery of the Holy Land and, nominally at least, for the honor of the cross. The word is derived from *Lat.* crux, "cross."

Crusoe. A self-reliant solitary man who adjusts himself to the primitive conditions he finds, from the tale ROBINSON CRUSOE by Daniel Defoe.

Crusts. See HOSTAGE, THE.

Cruz, Sor Juana Inés de la. See JUANA INÉS DE LA CRUZ, SOR.

Cruz Cano y Olmedilla, Ramón de la (1731–1794). Spanish dramatist. His humorous one-act plays, or *sainetes*, form the body of his work. These may be described as classical only insofar as their satiric mirroring of 18th-century Spanish life remains didactic in nature. The most famous of his portrayals of middle-class mores are *La pradera de San Isidoro, El rastro por la mañana, Le Plaza Mayor por Navidad,* and *El fandango del candil.*

Cry of the Children, The (1843). A poem by Elizabeth Barrett BROWNING, expressing intense sympathy for the victims of child labor in the English mines and factories of her day and indicting those who were responsible for their exploitation.

Cry, The Beloved Country (1948). A widely read and influential novel by Alan PATON. It is the moving story of a Zulu country parson who comes to Johannesburg to find that the environment has forced his sister to become a prostitute and his son a murderer. The language is Biblical and poetic. The novel was made into a musical play entitled *Lost in the Stars* (1949), with words by Maxwell Anderson and music by Kurt Weill.

cuaderna vía. A form of medieval Spanish versification. The stanza consists of four 14-syllable lines with a single rhyme, and each line is divided into two equal hemistichs. *Cuaderna vía* was always used for poetry written in the style known as MESTER DE CLERECÍA.

Cuauhtémoc (1495?–1525). Last Aztec emperor of Mexico. The nephew and son-in-law of Montezuma, Cuauhtémoc became emperor after the latter's death and led the Indian resistance to the Spaniards after they had been driven out of Tenochtitlán. He was seized by Cortez after the capital had been taken and was put to torture when he refused to reveal the location of a supposedly fabulous Aztec treasure. Forced to accompany Cortez on an expedition to Honduras, he was accused of inciting the Indians to revolt and was executed.

cubism. An artistic movement begun in 1907 in Paris. It was influenced by the structural simplifications of African sculpture and by CÉZANNE's concepts of geometry in the visual representation of objects. Cubism is characterized by a reduction of objects, figures, and occasionally of landscapes to their basic geometric forms. This effect is achieved by flattening and superimposing planes without the use of perspective or light. Analytical cubism (1910–1912) increased the breakdown of forms and simultaneously represented various aspects of the same object. Monochromatic and austere, this phase led to the inclusion on the canvas of such materials as sand, glass, newspaper, and cloth. With synthetic cubism (1913–1914) the planes grew larger and more varied, form and color reappeared, and reality was represented in its most general terms. Pablo PICASSO and Georges BRAQUE were the founders of cubism in the visual arts, and its most outstanding representatives.

In literature, the poets Guillaume APOLLINAIRE, Max JACOB, Pierre REVERDY, and André SALMON helped to form cubist doctrines and collaborated on the cubist bulletins, although they preferred the term *l'esprit nouveau* (new spirit) to cubism. They experimented with cubistic poetry, arranging apparently imagistic lines in clear-cut blocks. The results were the immediate precursors of surrealistic poetry: Apollinaire's *Alcools* (1913) and *Calligrammes* (1918); Jean Cocteau's *Ode à Picasso* (1917); Jacob's *Le Laboratoire central* (1921); Reverdy's *Les Ardoises du toit* (1918) and *Cravates de chanvre* (1922); and Salmon's *Prikaz* (1919).

Cú Chulainn. Also known as **Cuculain, Cuchullin, Cuchulain,** and **Cu Cullin;** original name **Setanta.** In Gaelic literature, chiefly the ULSTER CYCLE, an Irish warrior of pagan times, a great hero of legendary feats. He is sometimes described as "the Achilles of the Gael." Ostensibly of mortal parentage, Cú Chulainn is represented to be in fact the son of the sun god Lugh. When, as a mere child, he is attacked by a ferocious hound, he kills it; when he sees the grief of its owner, Culain, he takes on the role of watchdog until a hound can be found to replace the one he killed. He is thereafter known as "the hound of Culain," or Cú Chulainn. As a young man he receives training at arms from the woman warrior Scathach on the isle of Scathach, now Skye. When Scathach is attacked by Aoife, another female warrior, Cú Chulainn subdues Aoife and makes love to her; when leaving the island, he instructs her to send their son Conlaoch to Ireland when he comes of age, under a vow to let no man stop him or force him to reveal his name. Conlaoch arrives in Ireland years later and kills so many warriors that he becomes embattled with Cú Chulainn who kills him, learning his identity too late. In one version, they kill each other; in another, Cú Chulainn, in his grief, does battle with the sea and finally sinks, exhausted, into it.

In the most widely known version of the Cú Chulainn story, Cú Chulainn singlehandedly deters the invading army of Queen Maeve until the Red Branch warriors of Ulster awaken from an enchantment. In this version Cú Chulainn duels with his foster brother, Ferdiad. (See CATTLE-RAID OF COOLEY.) Some years later, MEDB gathers an army for the express purpose of killing Cú Chulainn and succeeds by creating, with the help of magic, an imaginary host with whom he fights to exhaustion. Fatally wounded, Cú Chulainn binds himself to a pillar and dies standing and facing the enemy. Emer, his widow to whom he had returned after being seduced by Fand, the wife of the sea god Mananaan, throws herself into his grave and dies. During the Irish Renaissance, Cú Chulainn became a favorite subject for poets, notably William Butler Yeats, who describes his central exploit in *On Baile's Strand*.

cuckold. The husband of an adulterous wife. The name derives from *cuckoo,* the chief characteristic of this bird being to deposit its eggs in other birds' nests. Dr. Johnson explained that "it was usual to alarm a husband at the approach of an adulterer by calling out Cuckoo, which by mistake was applied in time to the person warned." The cuckold was traditionally supposed to wear horns as the attribute of his condition. The usage is ancient; the Romans used to call an adulterer a cuckoo.

Cudworth, Ralph. See CAMBRIDGE PLATONISTS.

Cueva de Garoza, Juan de la (1550?–?1610). Spanish dramatist and poet. Cueva was one of the first playwrights to compose dramas dealing with events in Spanish history, such as *Los siete infantes de Lara* and *Cerco de Zamora.* For, as he maintained in his *Exemplar poético* (1606), he believed that dramatists should use native themes and meters instead of blindly imitating Greek and Latin models. The principal character of his comedy *El infamador* is considered a forerunner of Tirso's Don Juan. Cueva's poems include *Coro febeo de romances historiales* (1587), a collection of old ballads, and *La conquista de la Bética* (1603), an epic about the conquest of Andalusia.

Cuff, Sergeant. See MOONSTONE, THE.

Cullen, Countee (1903–1946). American poet. Known for his poetry on Negro themes, Cullen established his reputation with his first book, *Color* (1925). In addition to a novel, *One Way to Heaven* (1931), he published several other collections of verse including *The Ballad of the Brown Girl* (1928), *Copper Sun* (1927), *The Black Christ and Other Poems* (1929), and *The Medea and Some Poems* (1935). *The Lost Zoo* (1940) and *My Lives and How I Lost Them* (1942) are children's books.

Culloden, or **Drummossie Moor.** A heath in Scotland where the duke of Cumberland defeated Prince Charles Edward Stuart (the Young PRETENDER) on April 27, 1746. The old Scottish ballad of Culloden begins "Drummossie Moor, Drummossie Day!" See Flora MACDONALD.

Culprit Fay, The. See Joseph Rodman DRAKE.

Culture and Anarchy (1869). A collection of essays on political and social conditions by Matthew ARNOLD. In these are found some of his most famous arguments for the role of literary culture in the spiritual life of England. The collection includes the famous essay HEBRAISM AND HELLENISM.

Culverwel, Nathaniel. See CAMBRIDGE PLATONISTS.

Cumberland, Richard (1732–1811). English dramatist. He is the author of a number of sentimental domestic comedies such as *The West Indian* (1771), *The Jew* (1794), *The Fashionable Lover* (1772) and *The Brothers* (1769).

Cumberland Road. The first main road to the American West, begun in 1811 and built for the most part with Federal money. It ran from Cumberland, Md., over the mountains to Wheeling and Zanesville on the Ohio and finally to Vandalia, Illinois. When completed it was about 600 miles long, 60 feet wide, and had a paved strip 20 feet wide in the middle. Over this National Pike ran the Western mails.

Cummings, E[dward] E[stlin] (1894–1962). American poet. One of the most gifted and independent poets of his era, Cummings was born in Cambridge, Mass., and was educated at Harvard. He is known for the eccentricity of his typography and punctuation, which he employed to indicate the rhythmic pattern and interwoven meaning of his poems. Until the 1930's he preferred the lower case e. e. cummings.

His work includes lyrical love poems, humorous character sketches, and bitter satires on the foibles and institutions of his time. Tough characters of the sort well publicized in the U.S. in the 1920's frequently appear in his poems, along with contemporary slang and dialect and the rhythms of jazz. Cummings' first published work was THE ENORMOUS ROOM, a novel based on his experiences in a French prison in World War I. This was followed by the first of his many volumes of poetry, *Tulips and Chimneys* (1923). His other volumes of verse include *XLI Poems* (1925), *&* (1925), *Is 5* (1926), *ViVa* (1931), *No Thanks* (1935), *50 poems* (1940), *1 × 1* (1944), *Poems 1923–1954* (1954), and *Ninety-five poems* (1958). He also published two plays, HIM and *Santa Claus* (1946), a book of drawings and paintings called *CIOPW* (1931); a travel book, EIMI; a satirical ballet, *Tom* (1935); and *i, six nonlectures* (1953).

Cummins, Maria Susanna. See LAMPLIGHTER, THE.

Cunctator (*Lat.,* "the delayer"). Epithet for Quintus Fabius Maximus (d. 203 B.C.). He was the Roman general who harassed Hannibal by avoiding direct engagements, and wore him out by marches, countermarches, and skirmishes from a distance. The English FABIAN SOCIETY was so named in honor of his policy.

Cunégonde. See CANDIDE.

Cunha, Euclides da. See SERTÕES, Os.

Cunningham, Allan (1784–1842). Scottish poet, essayist, and biographer. Many of his poems are in Scottish dialect or are adaptations of traditional lyrics. His *Songs of Scotland* (1825) includes the well-known *A Wet Sheet and a Flowing Sea.* Other verse collections by Cunningham are *Songs* (1813) and *Songs and Poems* (1847). He is also known for his *Lives of the Most Eminent British Painters, Sculptors, and Architects* (1829–1833) and for his *Memoirs of Burns* (1834).

Cunninghame-Graham, Robert Bontine (1852–1936). Scottish-Spanish travel and story writer and historian. At different times he was an adventurer in South America, a Labour member of Parliament, and a friend of W. H. Hudson, Joseph Conrad, and Bernard Shaw. He wrote *Mogreb-el-Acksa, or Journey in Morocco* (1898); *Scottish Stories* (1914) and other collections of short stories; and many biographical and historical works on South America, including *The Conquest of New Granada* (1922).

Cunstance. See MAN OF LAW'S TALE.

Cupid. In Roman mythology, the god of love, son of Venus and Mercury, and counterpart of the Greek Eros. He is usually represented as an exquisite boy with wings, bearing a bow and quiver of arrows, and is often described as blind or blindfolded. The bow is used to shoot the arrows, which are invisible and which cause the one shot to fall irrevocably in love. Originally depicted as a young man, as in the myth of Cupid and Psyche, Cupid later developed into the familiar cherubic but mischievous little boy.

Curate of Meudon. See François Rabelais.

Curel, François de (1854–1928). French dramatist. Curel's career began in 1892, when Antoine, director of the *Théâtre Libre,* accepted some of his plays, among them *Les Fossiles* and *L'Envers d'une sainte.* A landed aristocrat who did not depend on the theater for his living, Curel wrote erratically. His work may be seen, however, in terms of a gradual dramatic evolution. The early plays, *Sauvé des eaux* (1889, later produced as *L'Amour brode* [1893]), and *La Danse devant le miroir* (1913), *L'Invitée* (1893), and *L'Envers d'une sainte* (1892), are dramas of passion that portray a conflict between some desired ideal and a brutal reality. The next group of plays, *La Nouvelle Idole* (1895), *Le Repas du lion* (1897), *La Fille Sauvage* (1902), are rather weighty dramas of ideas, although the emphasis still falls on inner turmoil. His last plays, among them *L'Ame en folie* (1919), *Ivresse du sage* (1922), and *Orage mystique* (1927), are characterized by a biting gaiety and contain more autobiographical elements than the earlier work.

Curetes (Kouretes). In Greek mythology, sons of Rhea. They protected the infant Zeus from Cronos by covering his cries with the clashing of their shields as he grew up in a cave on Mount Dicte in Crete. They were regularly associated with the rites of Zeus' mother Rhea, and were identified by the Greeks with the Corybantes, who performed a similar function in the rites of Cybele. Jane Harrison, in her *Themis,* suggests that both were minor divinities who had originally been the young men (*kouroi*) who took children from their mothers at puberty and initiated them in noisy rites into manhood and full membership in the tribe. (The Curetes were also a tribe who were neighbors of the Calydonians.)

Curiace. In Pierre Corneille's tragedy Horace, the opponent of Horace in the combat between the cities of Rome and Alba. Although Curiace is the fiancé of Horace's sister Camille, Horace must kill him for the honor and safety of his native city, Rome.

Curiatii, the. In legendary Roman history, the three brothers who engaged in combat against the three Horatii.

Curie, Marie Sklodowska (1867–1934). Polish scientist. She is best known for her discovery, with her husband, Pierre Curie, of radium. With A. H. Becquerel, they were awarded the Nobel Prize for physics (1903) for this discovery. She again won the Nobel Prize for chemistry in 1911. *Madame Curie* (1937) is a biography written by her daughter Eve Curie. Another daughter, Irène Curie-Joliot (with her husband Frédéric Joliot) won the Nobel Prize for chemistry (1935).

Curran, John Philpot (1750–1817). Irish orator and magistrate. He is noted for his defense of the leaders of the Irish insurrection of 1798, for his defense of parliamentary reform, and for his support of Catholic emancipation.

Currier and Ives. Nathaniel Currier (1813–1888) and **James Merritt Ives** (1824–1895), American lithographers. In 1835 Currier began to sell lithographs of notable current events and later (1857) he formed a partnership with Ives, his former bookkeeper. The firm published lithographic prints illustrating scenes of farm life, sports, famous disasters on land and sea, and all the mechanical and technical innovations of the age. Drawn in great detail by a number of artists, these prints were soon supplanted by photography, but they are a valuable record of the middle and latter part of the 19th century.

Curry, John Steuart (1897–1946). American painter. He is known for his portrayals of rural life in his native Kansas.

Curse of Kehama, The (1810). An epic poem by Robert Southey. Kehama is the mighty raja of the world. To save his daughter Kailyal from the advances of Kehama's son, Ladurlad kills him. In retaliation Kehama curses Ladurlad, charming his life so that, while he cannot be harmed by disease, weapons, or age, neither can he eat or drink. The curse turns out to be a blessing, for Ladurlad is able, through his immunity, to save his daughter from countless dangers. Eventually, Kehama tries to take over hell and, drinking a potion of immortality, finds he has drunk of immortal death and is forever condemned to hell as a supporter of the lord of hell. Kailyal also drinks the potion and is brought to immortality in the Bower of Bliss, while Ladurlad dies and awakes in heaven. The background of the poem is Hindu folklore and mythology.

Cursor Mundi (c. 1300). Anonymous religious poem in a northern dialect of Middle English, of about 24,000 lines largely in rhyming couplets. Very popular in its day, it describes the "course of the world" in seven ages from the creation to doomsday; its history is based on the Old and New Testaments, interspersed with numerous legends and saints' lives from medieval lore, and told in a style resembling that of the chivalric romances.

cursus honorum (*Lat.,* "course of honors"). In ancient Rome, the steps up the ladder of political success. In order of influence, the magistrates whose offices were generally included in the *cursus honorum* were the tribune, the quaestor, the aedile, the praetor, and the consul. By the time he reached the consulate, the Roman politician had usually made his fortune and was ready to be assigned the comfortable governorship of a conquered province.

Curtain Theatre. Famous Elizabethan playhouse. It was located in Shoreditch and used as an "easer" (an annex to accommodate overflow crowds) to the neighboring Theatre. Shakespeare's company, the Lord Chamberlain's Men, occupied the Curtain between the closing of the Theatre in 1597 and the opening of the Globe in 1599. Some scholars believe it to be the "wooden O" referred to in Shakespeare's *Henry V.*

Curtis, George William. See Potiphar Papers.

Curtis, Jean-Louis (1917–). French novelist. *The Forests of the Night* (1947) analyzes young participants in the Resistance; *The Side of the Angels*

(*Les Justes Causes;* 1954) does the same for members of postwar intellectual movements. Acute insights into the ideals and habits of his generation shape other works such as *Chers Corbeaux* (1951), *L'Echelle de soie* (1956), and *La Parade* (1960).

Curtius, Marcus. Legendary Roman hero of 4th century B.C. He is said to have leaped in full armor on horseback into a chasm that had been opened in the Forum at Rome by an earthquake; in so doing he fulfilled a soothsayer's proclamation that the sacrifice of Rome's chief treasure, which Curtius interpreted to mean a brave man, would close the fissure.

Cusa, Nicholas of (Nicholas Krebs or Krypffs). Also known as **Nicolaus Cusanus** (1401–1464). Born at Cusa (Kues) near Trier in Germany, he became a cardinal, an ecclesiastical statesman, and a theologian, but was also an outstanding humanist, philosopher, and mathematician. Known mainly as an early forerunner of the Copernican theory, he was more famous in his day as a brilliant student at Padua, a papal legate at the age of 25, and an influential figure at the Council of Basel (1433). His trip to Constantinople a few years later brought about the Council of Ferrara (1438), which led to the temporary union of the Eastern and Western churches and brought many Greek scholars to Italy (See REVIVAL OF LEARNING and HUMANISM). As deputy to his friend Pope Pius II, he was able to write philosophical works in peace and deal in them with esoteric and subtle ideas. He intuited notions later explored by Copernicus and BRUNO (the infinity of the universe, the cosmological relevance of mathematics, the coincidence of opposites). His most famous work, *De docta ignorantia* (*On Learned Ignorance*), insists on the simplicity of truth against the Aristotelian weaving of abstractions and verbal webs.

Custer, George Armstrong (1839–1876). American general. Custer is best known for his "last stand" (1876) at the Little Big Horn River in Dakota Territory when he and his troops were overwhelmed and annihilated by Sioux warriors under Crazy Horse. Custer's wife, Elizabeth Bacon Custer (1843–1933), described their life together in *Boots and Saddles* (1885). See SITTING BULL.

Custom of the Country, The (1913). A novel by Edith WHARTON. The heroine is Undine Spragg, a ruthless social climber who, through several marriages and divorces, samples the pleasures of money and aristocratic titles before finding her own level and marrying the youth from her home town who has become a millionaire.

Cutty Sark. A witch in Robert BURNS' poem TAM O'SHANTER. The term means "short shirt" (*cutty* being the Scottish word for short, *sark* being Scottish for shirt), and Burns uses it jocularly to describe the witch that catches Tam's eye. *Cutty* is also used to describe a short, plump woman and, by extension, is used playfully to describe a hussy.

Cuvier, Baron **Georges Léopold Chrétien Frédéric Dagobert** (1769–1832). French zoologist and paleontologist. Cuvier was instrumental in founding the sciences of comparative anatomy and paleontology. He published a series of lectures on his findings, *Leçons d'anatomie comparée* (1800–1805), and a work entitled *Recherches sur les ossements fossiles* (1821–1824).

Cuzco, El. A city in Peru, once the capital of the Inca empire. According to one Inca legend, it was founded about 1100 by the first emperor, Manco Capac, who was given a golden staff by the sun god and told to establish a city on the spot where the staff sank into the ground.

Cybele (Kybele or Kybebe). An ancient Asian goddess identified by the Greeks with RHEA. Originally a bisexual earth goddess, she was made a female by the gods. Jealously in love with the beautiful youth Attis, who was preparing to marry a nymph, she drove him to madness, in which he castrated himself and died. She mourned for him thereafter. Cybele was celebrated in orgiastic rites by eunuch priests.

In her rites she was always associated with the corybantes, a group of young men who dance and play musical instruments. Because these rites were similar to those of Rhea and her attendant CURETES, which were also widely practiced in Phrygia, the two became identified. Cybele, one of whose names was the Great Mother, became an important goddess in Rome, where she was known as *Magna Deum Mater.*

Cyclic poets. Epic poets. For some centuries after Homer, the Cyclics continued to write narratives filling out the story of the Trojan War and a cycle of poems about Thebes. In spite of various traditions, little is known about either the poems or their authors. Undoubtedly, however, they supplied later mythographers with a great deal of their material.

cyclopean masonry. The gigantic old Pelasgic ruins of Greece, Asia Minor, and Italy, such as the Gallery of Tiryns, the Gate of Lions at Mycenae, the Treasury of Athens, and the Tombs of Phoroneus and Danaos. They are composed of huge blocks fitted together without mortar, with marvelous nicety, and are fabled to be the work of the CYCLOPS. The term is also applied to similar structures in many parts of the world.

Cyclops (Gr., *kyklops,* circular eye). Any of a group of giants, offspring of Ge and Uranus. Hesiod listed three of them, named Brontes, Steropes, and Arges, who forged Zeus's thunderbolts. Each had only one eye, which was set in the middle of his forehead.

The most famous of the Cyclopes, however, was Polyphemus, whose cannibal welcome to Odysseus and his sailors is related both in the *Odyssey* and in Euripides' satyr play *Cyclops.*

Cygne, Le (The Swan). A poem by Stéphane MALLARMÉ. The swan serves as a symbol representing the cold and sterile solitude of the poet, who lives in a world set apart from that of ordinary men. Images of whiteness, ice, and snow are used to create the poem's atmosphere.

Cymbeline. One of the kings in the 12th-century HISTORY OF THE KINGS OF BRITAIN written by Geoffrey of Monmouth. When Caesar invaded the British island, he forced the Britons to pay tribute and took Cymbeline with him as a hostage. Cymbeline was brought up in Rome as a Roman. When he became king of Britain, he lived peacefully with the Romans. After his death, his sons Guiderius and Arviragus refused to pay tribute, and a new Roman invasion ensued. Some five centuries later, he became the central, titular figure of Shakespeare's play *Cymbeline*.

Cymbeline (c. 1610). A play by William SHAKE-SPEARE. Upon hearing of the secret marriage between his daughter IMOGEN and POSTHUMUS LEONATUS, a gentleman of his court, Cymbeline, king of Britain, banishes Posthumus, who goes to Rome. There he meets the cynical IACHIMO, who makes a wager that, going to Britain, he will cause Imogen to be unfaithful. When Imogen scorns his advances, Iachimo resorts to subterfuge. He gains access to her bedroom in the dead of night, steals her bracelet, and convinces Posthumus that he has won the wager. The outraged husband orders his servant PISANIO to murder Imogen, but the kindly fellow allows her to escape dressed as a boy. In the wilds of Wales she comes upon the banished lord BELARIUS, who is living with Cymbeline's two sons, GUIDERIUS and ARVIRAGUS, whom he had abducted as infants. Eventually Iachimo's villainy is exposed, Imogen and Posthumus are reconciled, and Cymbeline is reunited with his sons.

The historical source of the play is Holinshed's *Chronicles* (1577), but the theme of the wager is taken from Boccaccio's *Decameron*. Although the highly complicated plot often seems to be a parody of the extravagance of Elizabethan drama, the play itself contains much beautiful and moving poetry, "Hark! hark! the lark" and "Fear no more the heat o' the sun" being famous examples.

Cymocles. See FAERIE QUEENE, THE.

Cymodoce. A sea nymph and companion of Venus, in Vergil's *Georgics* and *Aeneid*. See FAERIE QUEENE, THE.

Cynara. The lady to whom the best-known poem of Ernest DOWSON is addressed. Each stanza closes, "I have been faithful to thee, Cynara, in my fashion." The poem has a Latin title: *Non sum qualis eram bonae sub regno Cynarae.*

Cynewulf or **Cynwulf** (early 9th century). Old English religious poet. His identity is known because he wove RUNES spelling his name into the ends of four poems in ALLITERATIVE VERSE: *The Fates of the Apostles,* the *Ascension, Juliana,* and *Elene,* the story of St. Helena and her son Constantine. In the EXETER BOOK the *Ascension* is preceded by the *Incarnation* and followed by the *Last Judgement,* also attributed to Cynewulf, the three poems being commonly known as *Christ.* The more than 80 "riddles" in the *Exeter Book* were long attributed to Cynewulf, but he probably wrote very few of them. His work probably influenced the unknown authors of *Christ and Satan* (see under CAEDMON), *Andreas,* and the remaining "riddles," which are short poems of descrip-

tion, some simple, some very obscure. See VERCELLI BOOK.

Cynics. A Greek school of philosophy. It was founded at Athens by Antisthenes (c. 455–c. 360 B.C.), a pupil of Socrates. Antisthenes held that happiness is only to be attained by freedom from desires. The principles of the Cynics were illustrated in the life of DIOGENES. The school may have been named after Antisthenes' school in the gymnasium at Cynosarges, or it may have been derived from *kyon* (dog), Diogenes' nickname. The views of the Cynics were later adopted and modified by the Stoics under Zeno.

Cynthia. The moon; a surname of ARTEMIS or Diana. The Roman Diana, who personified the moon, was so called from Mount Cynthus in Delos, where she was born.

Cyprian, St. Full name **Thascius Caecilius Cyprianus** (c. 200–258). The first Christian bishop to suffer martyrdom. The son of a wealthy patrician family, he was converted to Christianity (246), made bishop of Carthage (248), and there beheaded as a martyr (258). His *Letters* are an important source of information about the early Christian church.

Cyrano de Bergerac, Savinien (1619–1655). French author and playwright. In his fantasies *Histoire comique des états et empires de la lune* (*Comical History of the States and Empires of the Moon,* 1656) and *Histoire comique des états et empires du soleil* (*Comical History of the States and Empires of the Sun,* 1661) Cyrano recounts his imaginary visits to the moon and sun; his descriptions of their people and institutions are broadly satirical of the society and politics of his own day. He also composed the comedy *Le Pédant joué* (*The Pedant Tricked,* 1654) and the tragedy *La Mort d'Agrippine* (*The Death of Agrippina,* 1653), both still recognized as poetic and remarkable works. A freethinker and a soldier, famed for his skill in duels as well as for his inordinately long nose, Cyrano served as inspiration for the central character in Edmond ROSTAND's play *Cyrano de Bergerac* (1897).

Cyrenaic School. See ARISTIPPUS.

Cyrus the Great (d. 529 B.C.). The founder of the Persian Empire. Cyrus dethroned his grandfather Astyages, and conquered Lydia and Babylonia. He permitted the exiled Jews to rebuild Jerusalem, as recorded in the Old Testament and treated generously the conquered Lydian king CROESUS. Legends surrounding his birth are related by Herodotus.

Cytherea (Kytherea). An epithet of APHRODITE. It resulted from her first setting foot on the island of Cythera after her birth from seafoam.

D

Dabit, Eugène (1898–1936). French novelist of the working class. Like *Hôtel du Nord* (1929), his other novels treat sympathetically the life of the laborer: *Villa Oasis* (1932), *Faubourgs de Paris* (1933), and *Le Mal de Vivre* (1939).

dactyl. In English prosody, a metrical foot consisting of three syllables, the first accented and the second and third unaccented. The word "WON-der-ful" is a dactyl. The METER made up of such units is called dactylic meter. The six-foot dactylic line was the epic verse of Latin and Greek poetry and was used by Homer and Vergil. An example in English is: "THIS is the/ FOREST pri/MEVAL, the MURMuring/ PINES and the /HEMlocks . . ." from Longfellow's *Evangeline*.

Dactyls (Daktyloi). Sacred smiths vaguely connected with the worship of RHEA in Crete and sometimes identified with the CURETES and the Corybantes (see CYBELE). The idea that they were possessed of magical powers is related to the ancient notion that all smiths were magicians.

Dada or Dadaism. A literary and artistic movement founded in 1916 and devoted to the negation of all traditional values in philosophy and the arts. Its form was a protest against what its leaders felt to be the insane destruction of civilized life and thought during World War I. Organized in Zurich by Tristan TZARA, with Hans ARP, the German poet Hugo Ball, and medical student Richard Huelsenbeck, the movement produced the *Dada* review. This review proclaimed its intention to replace logical reason in thought with deliberate madness, and to substitute intentionally discordant chaos for established notions of beauty or harmony in the arts. Dada meetings turned into riots; art exhibits were mocking hoaxes. The former cubist painter Francis Picabia, who had been leading a similar movement in New York with Marcel DUCHAMP, joined Tzara's group in 1918. The next year they joined in Paris with André BRETON, who with Louis ARAGON, Paul ELUARD, and Philippe SOUPAULT founded the ironically named review *Littérature*. While Tzara continued his sensational efforts at pure negation, the Germans adapted the revolt to the service of Communism. Breton and his group became interested in the subconscious, breaking with Tzara in 1921 and officially founding SURREALISM in 1924. Dadaism revived in the 1930's in England and America, as a revolt against traditional artistic values.

Daedalus (Daidalos). In Greek mythology, a fabulously cunning artisan. An Athenian, the son of Metion and descendant of Hephaestus, he was exiled from Athens for murdering his apprentice Talus or Perdix. Fleeing to Crete, he earned a questionable distinction by constructing the wooden cow in which Minos' queen PASIPHAË was able to satisfy her passion for a bull. He was then faced with the necessity of providing a place to keep their offspring, the Minotaur; for this purpose he built the famous LABYRINTH.

Having made himself so useful to Minos, he was imprisoned in his own Labyrinth so that he could not leave the king's service. Making wings of wax and feathers for himself and his son Icarus, he flew away to Sicily. Icarus, however, disobeying his father's instructions, flew too close to the sun; the wings melted and he fell to his death in the sea.

daemon (daimon). A minor divinity in ancient Greece. Originally beneficent spirits of the dead who insured fertility and often had animal as well as human forms, certain daemones became more individualized in function and ultimately developed into heroes or gods. Dionysus retained most clearly the character of a fertility daemon.

daemonic (Ger., das Dämonische). In a special sense, a quality of certain characters in Goethe's works, such as the heroes of GÖTZ VON BERLICHINGEN and EGMONT. The daemonic figure is endowed with a powerful, uncannily attractive individual force that sweeps other people along in its violent destiny. In FAUST, it is Mephistopheles rather than Faust himself who exemplifies this quality. In his famous poem *Urworte, Orphisch (Primal Orphic Words*, 1817), Goethe defines the basic elements in human destiny as Daemon, Chance, Love, Necessity, and Hope, Daemon referring to each man's unique, inborn, developmental force, the unalterable law of his own individual growth.

Daffodils, The (1807). A famous nature poem by William WORDSWORTH. The poem is characteristic of English romanticism in its appreciation of an object of nature for its own sake.

Dagon. A god of the Philistines. He was supposed (from very uncertain etymological and mythological indications) to have been symbolized as half man and half fish. He is mentioned by Milton in *Paradise Lost* and *Samson Agonistes*.

Dahl, Roald (1916–   ). Welsh-born American short-story writer. Dahl popularized the mythical gremlins in his book *The Gremlins* (1944). In 1946 he published *Over to You,* 10 stories of flying and fliers. Moving to the U.S., he began publishing stories in *The New Yorker* and soon became known for his mastery of the macabre. His books include *Some Time Never* (1948), *Someone Like You* (1953), *Kiss, Kiss* (1960), and *James and the Giant Peach* (1961), a juvenile book.

Dahn, Felix (1834–1912). German author, best known for his "professorial novels," so called because of the antiquarian and scholarly exactness that destroys their artistic value. The most famous is *Ein Kampf um Rom* (*A Struggle for Rome*, 1876).

Daiches, David (1912–   ). Scottish literary critic. He wrote *The Novel and the Modern World* (1939), *Virginia Woolf* (1942), *Robert Burns* (1951), *Willa Cather* (1951), and *A Critical History of English Literature* (1960). *Two Worlds: An Edinburgh Jewish Childhood* (1956) is an autobiography.

daimyō (*Jap.*, "great name"). Feudal lord. It was used chiefly in reference to the clan heads and owners of large fiefs during the Tokugawa period (1600–1868).

Daisy Miller (1878). A novelette by Henry JAMES. It deals with an unsophisticated, "strikingly, admirably pretty" girl from Schenectady who runs athwart the conventions of a group of Europeanized Americans who enforce the rules with unthinking severity.

Daladier, Edouard (1884–1970). Premier of France three times: in 1933, 1934, 1938–1940. With the English prime minister Neville Chamberlain, Daladier was responsible for signing the Munich pact with Hitler in 1938. In 1939 Daladier signed the declaration of war against Germany; he resigned as premier just before the German invasion and the surrender of France. Daladier was arrested, first by the Vichy regime, and was later imprisoned in Germany. After the war he was elected to a seat in the National Assembly.

Dalai Lama. See LAMA.

Dalcroze. See JAQUES-DALCROZE.

Dali, Salvador (1904–   ). Spanish painter and etcher. He is best known for his paintings of irrational subjects done in a meticulously realistic style. Long a disciple of SURREALISM, he has also experimented with pointillism, scientific cubism, futurism, constructivism, and bulletism. The last-named involves shooting a 16th-century blunderbuss filled with graphite at a blank etching plate and printing the resulting pattern. Many critics and a great deal of the public dismiss Dali as merely an artistic prankster; however, his work has been purchased and displayed by the Museum of Modern Art (New York) and the Metropolitan Museum of Art (New York). Perhaps his most famous painting is *Persistence of Memory* (1931), a desolate landscape with limp, melting watches sagging over cliffs and leafless trees.

Dalinda. The servant of the calumnied Ginevra in an episode of the ORLANDO FURIOSO of Ariosto. Her revelations to Rinaldo expose the villain Polinesso, the slanderer of her mistress, and he is then denounced and killed in a duel.

Dalloway, Mrs. See MRS. DALLOWAY.

Daly, Arnold (1875–1927). American actor and producer. In 1903 he produced Shaw's *Candida* and thereafter appeared exclusively in Shaw's dramas. His arrest, trial, and acquittal after the first performance of MRS. WARREN'S PROFESSION (1905) is a famous case. The play caused a sensation because Mrs. Warren's profession is prostitution.

Daly, T[homas] A[ugustine] (1871–1948). American newspaperman and poet. He is best known for his poems in Italian and Irish dialect, especially *Mia Carlotta*. Among his books are *Canzoni* (1906), *Carmina* (1909), *Madrigali* (1912), and *McAroni Ballads* (1919).

Damascus. A city in Syria on the edge of the desert. Famous for its silks and steel, it is generally considered the oldest city to have continuing existence in the world. It is frequently referred to in the Old Testament (Gen. 14:15; 15:2). Its role in the history of Paul's conversion is told in the New Testament, Acts 9.

Damayanti. See NALA.

Dame aux Camélias, La (Camille, 1852). A play by Alexandre DUMAS, *fils*. The work, which was first published as a novel (1848), met with great success, both at home and abroad. The heroine Marguerite Gauthier, known in America as Camille, is a beautiful courtesan who has become part of the fashionable world of Paris. Scorning the wealthy Count de Varville who has offered to relieve her debts should she once more become his mistress, she escapes to the country with her penniless lover Armand Duval. Here Camille makes her great sacrifice. Giving Armand whom she truly loves the impression that she has tired of their life together, but actually at the request of his family, she returns to Paris and her life of frivolity. The tale concludes with the ultimate tragic reunion of Armand and the dying Camille. This sentimental story, dealing with a real moral and social problem, is also the basis of Verdi's opera *La Traviata*.

Damien de Veuster, Joseph. Known as **Father Damien** (1840–1889). A Belgian Roman Catholic missionary. He is noted for his work with the lepers in a government hospital on Molokai Island in the Hawaiian group, where he contracted leprosy and died. Robert Louis Stevenson wrote a famous essay, *Father Damien: An Open Letter to the Rev. Dr. Hyde* (1890).

Damkina. In Babylonian mythology, the wife of MARDUK.

Damnation of Theron Ware, The (1896). A novel by Harold FREDERIC. The main character, an earnest young clergyman, suffers emotional conflict when he realizes the deficiencies of the church. The book, suggesting the disintegration of religious orthodoxy, was sensational at the time of its publication.

Damocles' sword. A symbol of anxiety. Damocles, a sycophant of Dionysius the Elder, of Syracuse, was invited by the tyrant to try the felicity he so much envied. Accepting, he was set down to a sumptuous banquet, but overhead was a sword suspended by a hair. Damocles was afraid to stir, and the banquet was a tantalizing torment to him.

Damoetas. A herdsman. Theocritus and Vergil use the name in their pastorals.

Damon and Pythias. Two inseparable friends of Greek legend. They were Syracusans of the first half of the fourth century B.C. Pythias, condemned to death by Dionysius the tyrant, obtained leave to go home to arrange his affairs on condition that Damon agree to take his place and be executed should Pythias not return. Pythias was delayed, Damon was led to execution, but his friend arrived just in time to save him. Dionysius was so struck with this honorable friendship that he pardoned both of them.

Dämonische, das. See DAEMONIC.

Dampier, William (1652–1715). English navigator and buccaneer. Perhaps the first Englishman to see Australia, he discovered and named New Britain Island in the Pacific, and Dampier Archipelago, off the coast of Australia, is named after him. During a voyage around the world, he marooned Alexander Selkirk, the prototype of Robinson Crusoe, on the Juan Fernandez Islands near Chile, and subsequently was the pilot of the privateering company that rescued Selkirk in 1709. He wrote several accounts of his experiences, the best known of which is *A New Voyage Round the World* (1697).

Damrosch, Walter [Johannes] (1862–1950). German-born conductor and composer. He championed the cause of Wagner in the U.S., and was the originator of educational radio concerts. *My Musical Life* (1923) is his autobiography. His father, Leopold Damrosch (1832–1885) and his brother, Frank [Heino] Damrosch (1859–1937), were also conductors.

Dana, Charles Anderson (1819–1897). American journalist. Reformer and editor, Dana became assistant secretary of war under Stanton. After the Civil War he bought the New York *Sun,* which soon became one of the leading newspapers in the U.S. Although he competed with Godkin's *Post* in sensationalism, Dana surrounded himself with the best newspaper writers of the day. H. L. Mencken said that he "produced the first newspaper on earth that was decently written." Dana discussed his craft in *The Art of Newspaper Making* (1895).

Dana, Richard Henry, Jr. (1815–1882). American lawyer and writer. During his student days, Dana had serious difficulty with his eyes; he shipped out as a common sailor to improve his health. Dana might have traveled as a passenger, but chose the more strenuous course of working on the *Pilgrim* on a voyage around Cape Horn in 1834. He returned home in 1836, his health much improved. From the journal he had kept, he wrote the American sea classic, TWO YEARS BEFORE THE MAST. The same year, he finished law school and was admitted to the bar; his experiences at sea led him to become a sailor's lawyer. He wrote a manual for sailors, *The Seaman's Friend* (1841), which became an authority on naval law. His sympathy for the downtrodden did not allow him to amass wealth as a lawyer, nor did it leave him much time for writing. He did collect the lectures of a famous teacher, Edward Tyrell CHANNING (1856).

Dana, Richard Henry, Sr. (1787–1879). American poet, editor, and lecturer. A founder of the *North American Review,* he also published his own journal, called *The Idle Man* (1821–1822). In 1833, his work was collected in the two-volume *Poems and Prose Writings* (enlarged, 1850).

Danaë. The daughter of King Acrisius of Argos. Because the Delphic oracle predicted that his death would come at the hands of his daughter's son, Acrisius built a tower of brass and shut Danaë in it. But Zeus visited her as a shower of gold and made her the mother of PERSEUS. Acrisius then set mother and son adrift in a chest, but they were saved by Zeus.

Danaides. The 50 daughters of Danaos. They were punished in Hades for having murdered their husbands on their wedding night by having to draw water everlastingly in sieves from a deep well. The reason for their gory deed was told in a trilogy of plays by Aeschylus, of which only THE SUPPLIANT WOMEN remains.

dance of death. An allegorical representation of the triumph of Death over people of every age and class, reminding men of their mortality. Originating in the Middle Ages as a MORALITY PLAY, it became even more popular as a subject for pictures, such as the woodcuts by Hans Holbein. Closely related is the *danse macabre,* in which the dead themselves lead the dance, rather than an abstract personification of Death.

Goethe used "dance of death" for the title of his ballad *Todtentanz;* W. H. Auden's *The Dance of Death* (1933) is a dramatic poem satirizing the decline of the English middle class.

Dance of Death, The (1901). A double play by August STRINDBERG. One of Strindberg's most powerful plays, *The Dance of Death* is characterized by intense psychological realism in its presentation of a love-hate relationship between husband and wife. Alice has been virtually imprisoned by Edgar, her tyrannical husband, for 25 years; now he is gravely ill, and the conflict focuses on his attempts to maintain his domination of his wife and her attempts at retaliatory torture.

Dance to the Music of Time, A. A sequence of novels by Anthony POWELL. It includes *A Question of Upbringing* (1951), *A Buyer's Market* (1952), *The Acceptance World* (1955), *At Lady Molly's* (1957), *Casanova's Chinese Restaurant* (1960), and *The Kindly Ones* (1962). The novels describe the narrator's schooldays, youth, and maturity, and the lives of his various friends. Though primarily satiric in tone, they are indebted to Marcel Proust for the underlying sadness they express about life and time.

Dancourt, Florent Carton. Known as Sieur d'Ancourt (1661–1725). French comic playwright. Jesuit-educated and intended for the law, Dancourt married an actress and devoted himself to acting and playwriting instead. His prose comedies are informal in style and often reveal their hasty composition, but rollicking satire and topical subject matter redeem such works as LE CHEVALIER À LA MODE, *La Loterie* (*The Lottery,* 1697), *Le Notaire obligeant* (*The Obliging Notary,* 1685), *Les Bourgeoises à la mode* (1692), *Le Mari retrouvé* (*The Rediscovered Husband,* 1698), *Les Bourgeoises de Qualité* (1700), and *Les Agioteurs* (*The Stock-Speculators,* 1710), in which Dancourt lampooned decadent aristocracy, social climbers, financial fraud, speculation, judicial inefficiency, and other vices and foibles of his day.

Dandaka. In Hindu legend, a king of the solar dynasty (Raghu), who raped the daughter of his *guru.* He was punished by having his kingdom turned into the forest known as Dandakaranya, often mentioned in classical Indian writing (Sans. *aranya,* forest).

Dandin. The mad magistrate and central figure of Jean Racine's comedy LES PLAIDEURS. Locked up in the house by his son and prevented from judging in court, he hears farcical cases involving neighbors, household servants, and pets.

Dandin. See Perrin DENDIN.

Dane, Clemence. Pen name, taken from the church of St. Clements Dane in London, of Winifred Ashton (1888–1965). English novelist, dramatist, and poet. Her best-known play *A Bill of Divorcement* (1921) made the reputation of Katharine Cornell; she adapted it for the stage from her novel *Legend* (1919). Her other well-known novels are *Regiment of Women* (1917) and *Broome Stages* (1931), about a theatrical family whose history parallels that of the Plantagenet family. Her other plays include *Will Shakespeare* (1921); *Naboth's Vineyard* (1925), a play about Jezebel; *Come of Age* (1934), a poetic play about Thomas CHATTERTON; and *Till Time Shall End* (1961).

Danel or **Daniel.** Father of the young hero in the Canaanite THE POEM OF AQHAT. Danel is a powerful but pious chieftain, who is granted a son by El only to lose him at the hands of Anat.

Dangeau, Marquis de. Philippe de Courcillon (1638–1720). French courtier and favorite of Louis XIV. His ill-written but scrupulously detailed *Mémoires*, a record of court affairs from 1684 to 1720, are an invaluable historical source and aided SAINT-SIMON in the composition of his own *Mémoires*.

Dangerfield, Thomas. See MEAL-TUB PLOT.

Dangerous Corner (1932). A play by J. B. PRIESTLEY. A chance remark at a party is the "dangerous corner" which leads to embarrassing revelations about those present. At the end of the play the opening conversation is renegotiated, this time successfully.

Daniel. A biblical hero whose deeds and prophecies are recorded in the Old Testament book of his name. For continuing to pray to his own God while a captive in Babylon, he was cast into a den of lions, but divinely delivered. Especially gifted with "understanding in all visions and dreams" (Dan. 2:17), he successfully exercised this gift by interpreting Nebuchadnezzar's disquieting dreams, as well as the mysterious handwriting on the wall which disturbed the revelry of Belshazzar (Dan. 5:5).

Nothing is known of Daniel except what appears in his book. The first half of the book tells the story of the Hebrew prophet living in Babylon during the exile; the second half is his prophetic vision. It is now thought that *Daniel* was written c. 164 B.C. instead of in the sixth century B.C., that Daniel's "predictions" were history by the time of writing.

Daniel, Arnau[l]t (12th century). Provençal TROUBADOUR, for a while attached to the court of Richard the Lion-hearted. He invented the SESTINA, and was greatly praised by Dante and Petrarch for the technical virtuosity of his versification.

Daniel, Samuel (c. 1562–1619). English poet and dramatist. Daniel is known for the purity of his diction, the smoothness and grace of his verse: he was called "well-languaged Daniel" by contemporaries. His works include the famous sonnet sequence, *Delia* (1592, with numerous later "augmented" editions); *The Complaint of Rosamund* (1592), a first-person narrative of the sort found in the MIRROR FOR MAGISTRATES; *The Civil Wars* (1595–1609), a verse history of the Wars of the Roses; *A Defense of Rime* (1603), an essay answering Thomas CAMPION's attack on English rhymed and accentual verse; and *The Vision of the Twelve Goddesses* (1604), the first masque to be written for the new court of James I. He wrote two tragedies in the style of Seneca, *Cleopatra* (c. 1593) and *Philotas* (1604).

Daniel Deronda (1874–1876). The last novel of George ELIOT. The heroine, Gwendolyn Harleth, marries Henleigh Grandcourt in order to avoid impending destitution of herself and her mother; this she does in spite of a previous promise not to, made to the mother of his illegitimate children. Grandcourt turns out to be a tyrannical, selfish man, bent on breaking Gwendolyn's high-spiritedness. When Grandcourt drowns in a moment of delay before Gwendolyn throws him a rope, she blames herself. In her distress she turns to Daniel Deronda, a man of fine character whom she has long admired. His sympathetic advice and her suffering, caused by the realization that he will never marry her, serve to develop her finer qualities. Deronda, a man of the highest ideals, has been brought up by his rich guardian as a Christian, but learns that he is a Jew. He marries Mirah Cohen whom he had saved from suicide. In Mordecai, who turns out to be Mirah's lost brother, he finds a friend who inspires him with the cause of Jewish nationalism. After Mordecai's death he and Mirah go to Palestine to live.

Daniello, Bernardino (d. 1565). Italian critic from Lucca. He wrote the first Italian Renaissance treatise on the art of poetry, *La poetica* (1536).

Daniels, Jonathan [Worth] (1902–). American journalist and writer. The son of Josephus Daniels, he succeeded his father as editor of the Raleigh, N. C., *News and Observer*. From 1943 to 1945 he was an administrative assistant to President Roosevelt. *Frontier on the Potomac* (1946) describes the Washington scene during those years. He also wrote *A Southerner Discovers the South* (1938), *Tar Heels: A Portrait of North Carolina* (1941), and *The End of Innocence* (1954).

Daniels, Josephus (1862–1948). American journalist and statesman. Born in Washington, N. C., Daniels was editor of the Raleigh *Times and Observer* from 1884 until his death. He served as secretary of the navy (1913–1921) and as ambassador to Mexico (1933–1941). His autobiographical volumes are of great historical interest: *Editor: In Politics* (1940), *The Wilson Era* (2 vols., 1944, 1945), and *Shirt Sleeve Diplomat* (1947).

Daniel the Stylite. See STYLITES.

Daninos, Pierre (1913–). French novelist. His experience as liaison officer with the British army inspired the character of Marmaduke Thompson. Thompson first appeared in a newspaper in 1943, then in the ironically humorous novels *The Notebooks of Major Thompson* (1954) and *The Secret of Major Thompson* (1956). *Un Certain Monsieur Blot* (1960) shows Daninos as the amused philosophical observer of his time. Other novels include *Les Carnets du Bon Dieu* (1947), *L'Eternel Second* (1949), and *Sonia, les autres, et moi* (1952).

Dannay, Frederic. See Ellery QUEEN.

D'Annunzio, Gabriele (1863–1938). Italian poet, novelist, dramatist, and soldier. He was an exceptionally prolific writer whose principal artistic aim seems to have been the detailed and verbally precise analysis of passion. His position as a decadent results from the absence of any real concern for morality, conscience, and thought in his work, so that the well-exercised pleasures of the senses alone give meaning to life. His heroes are unfettered by the bourgeois ethic; their refined ability to enjoy sensual pleasure and to experience "perfect passion" make them a law to themselves, suggestive of Nietzsche's superman.

The D'Annunzian hero first appeared in the novel *Il Piacere* (*The Child of Pleasure,* 1889) in the person of the amoral sybarite Andrea Sperelli. His other novels include *Giovanni Episcopo* (*Episcopo & Company,* 1892), *L'Innocente* (*The Intruder,* 1892), *Il Trionfo della Morte* (*The Triumph of Death,* 1894), and THE FLAME OF LIFE, based on his celebrated liaison with Eleonora Duse. Among his best-known dramas are *La Città Morta* (*The Dead City,* 1898), LA GIOCONDA, *Francesca da Rimini* (see PAOLO AND FRANCESCA), and *La Figlia di Jorio* (*The Daughter of Jorio,* 1904). His finest lyric poems are probably included in *Le Laudi* (1903–1912), particularly in the third book, *Alcione.* He also wrote short stories describing peasant life in his native Abruzzi: *Terra Vergine* (1882), *Libro delle Vergini* (1884), and *San Pantaleone* (1886).

An ardent nationalist, he led an expedition into the city of Fiume in 1919 and held it for 15 months in defiance of Italy's obligations under the Treaty of Versailles. He later supported the chauvinistic Fascist Party.

danse macabre. See DANCE OF DEATH.

Dante. Full name, **Dante (or Durante) Alighieri** (1265–1321). Italian poet. The first important author to write in Italian and one of the greatest poets in all literature, he was born in Florence, where he became thoroughly educated in both classical and Christian literature. As a young man, Dante joined actively in both the politics and the actual fighting in the wars between the GUELPHS

Dante entering the woods (*Inferno* Canto I). Frontispiece from a 1506 edition of *The Divine Comedy.*

AND GHIBELLINES. He belonged to the BIANCHI, one of the rival factions within the Guelph party, and when the Neri finally achieved power late in 1301, Dante and many others were sentenced (1302) to perpetual banishment, condemned to death by burning should they be caught again in Florence. The Bianchi soon made an alliance with the Ghibelline party and attempted several unsuccessful attacks on Florence. Their hopes ended with the death (1313) of the emperor Henry VII, who they had hoped would reunite Germany and Italy. Thereafter, Dante spent most of his time writing his *Commedia* (see THE DIVINE COMEDY) under the patronage of Ghibelline leaders, one in Verona, then one in Ravenna. The exact period of the composition of the *Commedia* is unknown. Dante may have begun it as early as 1300, more probably 1307, but the major part of the writing was almost certainly done after 1315, and the last section completed shortly before his death.

Dante had first met BEATRICE in 1274 when he was nine; their second meeting was nine years later. After her death in 1290 he wrote LA VITA NUOVA, which reveals the significance of his idealized love for her as the inspiration for most of his works. He finally married Gemma Donati (1292?), by whom he had two sons and one or two daughters; she did not, however, accompany him into exile in 1302.

Dante's early works include a number of amatory lyrics in the form of the CANZONE and the sonnet, many of which appear in *La Vita Nuova* and in the unfinished *Il Convivio* or *Convito* (*The Banquet,* 1304–1307), which consists of three long commentaries, encyclopedic in scope, each on one of his own *canzoni* (see STILNOVISTI).

De vulgari eloquentia (1304–1306) is a Latin treatise "on the vernacular tongue." In opposition to the general assumption of his day that Latin must be used for all important writing, Dante urges that the courtly Italian used for amatory lyrics be enriched with the best from every spoken dialect and established as a serious literary language, thus unifying the separated Italian territories by the creation of a national culture. He also analyzes several Italian dialects, anticipating the much later science of linguistics, and considers various problems of literary style and specific poetic forms, especially the *canzone.* In fact, Dante used his native Tuscan for the *Commedia* and *La Vita Nuova,* and thereby established that dialect as the ancestor of modern Italian.

In the Latin treatise *De Monarchia* (*On Monarchy,* usually translated as *On World Government,* c. 1313) Dante presents the political perspective that also becomes a major theme in the *Commedia.* He believes that a unified temporal authority, the Holy Roman Empire, is necessary, but deplores the rivalry for supreme political power currently raging between the emperors and the papacy. He prophesies that peace will only be achieved when the universal monarchy of the empire is established and recognized as being dependent only on God, although reverent toward the spiritual authority of the Church. Then Church and State will be allies with separate responsibilities in guiding mankind to peaceful happiness on earth and bliss in heaven.

Other works include two *Eclogues* (c. 1319) in Latin verse; the *Quaestio de aqua et terra* (1320), a scholastic treatise on physics; and 13 Latin *Epistles,* including both personal and political letters.

Dantès, Edmond. See COUNT OF MONTE CRISTO.

Danton, Georges Jacques (1759–1794). French lawyer, orator, and leader of the FRENCH REVOLUTION. He became a leader of the CORDELIERS early in the Revolution, a member of the Legislative ASSEMBLY in 1792, and was a major figure in the storming of the Tuilleries. In the new republic he was the minister of justice. He instituted the Revolutionary Tribunal (Mar. 10, 1793). Now a partisan of peace, he came into increasing conflict with ROBESPIERRE, who later charged him and his followers with a conspiracy to overthrow the government. His trial was a mockery and he was guillotined. His death is the subject of a dramatic poem, *Dantons Tod* (Ger., *Danton's Death,* 1835) by Georg Büchner. In a speech (Sept. 2, 1792) inspired by the dangers of the European alliance against revolutionary France, Danton uttered the famous words: *"Il nous faut de l'audace, encore de l'audace, et toujours de l'audace, et la France est sauvée."* (Fr., "We must dare and dare, and dare again—and France is saved.").

Dantons Tod (Danton's Death, 1835). A drama by Georg BÜCHNER, depicting with convincing psychological perception and frequent ironic humor the steps leading up to the execution of George Jacques DANTON. The play is starkly realistic; Danton first appears in it as a tired, apathetic, somewhat licentious, and rather unrevolutionary character. But this, by contrast, only increases the effectiveness of his idealistic commitment when he finally defies Robespierre.

Daphne. In Greek mythology, the daughter of a river-god, loved by Apollo. She fled from the amorous god, and escaped by being changed into a laurel, thenceforth the favorite tree of Apollo.

Daphnis. In Greek mythology, the Sicilian shepherd who invented pastoral poetry. Though the son of Hermes and a nymph, and a half-brother of Pan, he was unfortunate in love, being blinded by a nymph for a not very clear reason. He made up sad but lovely songs on the subject, and was eventually taken up to heaven by Hermes. On the other hand, Theocritos, the human inventor of the pastoral, claims in his first idyl that Daphnis died of unrequited love, a punishment from Aphrodite for having refused the love of women.

Daphnis and Chloë. A Greek pastoral poem, generally ascribed to the sophist Longus (fourth or fifth century A.D.). It tells the story of the tender love of Daphnis and Chloë, the children of a goatherd and a shepherd. It owes its fame in modern times to the French version by Amyot (1559). Major works in its later tradition are Tasso's *Aminta,* Montemayor's *Diana,* and Saint-Pierre's *Paul et Virginie.* Maurice Ravel made two highly popular orchestral suites from his ballet music for *Daphnis and Chloe* (1912).

Da Ponte, Lorenzo (1749–1838). Italian librettist and poet. Appointed poet to the Italian Theater in Vienna, he was commissioned by Mozart to write the librettos for *Le Nozze di Figaro* (1786; see FIGARO), DON GIOVANNI, and *Così Fan Tutte* (1790). In 1805 he emigrated to the U.S., where he was appointed professor of Italian literature at Columbia

University. His colorful memoirs, *Memorie,* first appeared in 1823.

Da Porto, Luigi (1486–1529). Italian soldier and courtier. Da Porto took a story by Masuccio and turned it into *Giulietta e Romeo* (see ROMEO AND JULIET), first published in 1530. Although it reached Shakespeare through such intermediary sources as Bandello and English translators, it was Da Porto who first gave it its definitive plot and characters.

Dapper. A character in Ben Jonson's comedy THE ALCHEMIST (1610). A lawyer's clerk, he goes to Subtle, the "alchemist," to be supplied with a familiar to make him win in horse-racing, cards, and all games of chance.

Darby and Joan. A designation for a loving, old-fashioned, virtuous married couple. The names appear in a ballad called *The Happy Old Couple,* probably written by Henry Woodfall, and the original characters are said to have been John Darby of Bartholomew Close, who died in 1730, and his wife. Woodfall served his apprenticeship as a printer to John Darby. Some authorities attribute the ballad to Matthew Prior. It was originally distributed as a broadside ballad in 1748.

Darcy. See PRIDE AND PREJUDICE.

Dardanelles. The ancient HELLESPONT, a strait between Europe and Asiatic Turkey. During World War I the Allies attacked the Turks here, and suffered defeat. In 1941 it was the gateway to Russia from the Mediterranean but Turkey, as neutral, refused passage of it. Its fortifications were so strong that no attempt on it was made by sea.

Dardinello. In the ORLANDO FURIOSO of Ariosto, the King of Zumara in Africa, son of Almonte, and one of the leading pagan warriors besieging the forces of Charlemagne at Paris. He is killed by Rinaldo.

Dare, Virginia (1587–?). The first child of English parents born in America. She and her parents were among the settlers who disappeared from the "lost colony" at Roanoke Island.

Dares Phrygius. In Homer's *Iliad,* the priest of Hephaestus in Troy. He allegedly wrote a poem on the siege of Troy. A Latin poem of the fifth century after Christ, *De Excidio Troiae Historia,* allegedly a translation of Dares Phrygius' work. The translation is attributed to Cornelius Nepos because it is prefaced by a forged letter from him to Sallust claiming to have found the old manuscript written in Phrygian characters. Although now known to be a literary forgery, the decidedly inferior poem was one of the versions by which the story of Troy was known to the Middle Ages. See DICTYS CRETENSIS.

Darío, Rubén. Pen name of **Félix Rubén García** (1867–1916). Nicaraguan poet and essayist, famed as the founder and high priest of MODERNISM. Raised by relatives, Darío wrote verse as a child and was known in Central America as "the boy poet." In 1886, he went to Chile, where he published his first major work, *Azul* (1888), a collection of verse and prose sketches that bore the imprint of French PARNASSIANISM and revealed the fondness for lush, exotic imagery that was to characterize his work. In 1890, he returned to Central America, where he embarked on the first of his two unhappy marriages, and, after a short visit to Spain in 1892, moved to Buenos Aires. The appearance of *Prosas profanas* (1896), in which the influence of French SYMBOLISM is fused with that of the Parnassians, marked the highpoint of the modernist movement. In 1898, Darío went to Spain as a correspondent for *La Nación*, a Buenos Aires newspaper with which he was long associated. He was acclaimed by the intellectuals of Spain's "generation of '98," who, like Darío, were profoundly affected by the outcome of the Spanish-American War. *Cantos de vida y esperanza,* generally regarded as his best work, appeared in 1905. Not only does it show the technical excellence and lyric beauty of his earlier poetry, but there is greater freedom and a new feeling for native themes, which he had previously rejected. Darío's concern for "our America" is also evident in "A Roosevelt," a poetic diatribe against the U.S. motivated by the seizure of Panama in 1903, and in *Canto a la Argentina* (1910). Darío's later work also reveals a deepening disillusionment and despair. Although he was named Nicaraguan minister to Spain in 1908, Darío's last years were marred by financial difficulties and poor health due in part to his heavy drinking. In 1915, after an unsuccessful lecture tour of the U.S., he was stricken by pneumonia in New York and died soon after his return to Nicaragua. Darío's influence on Spanish poetry can be measured by the statement of Pedro Henríquez Ureña that "of any poem written in Spanish it can be told with certainty whether it was written before or after him."

Darius I. Known as **Darius the Great** (c. 550–486 B.C.). King of Persia. A member of a younger branch of the royal family, Darius assumed the throne in 521 after quelling a rebellion led by the magician Gautama, who claimed to be Bardiya, brother of the dead king Cambyses. Darius was an excellent administrator, extended the boundaries of the Persian Empire, and built an imposing capital at Persepolis. His exploits are recorded on the famous monument at Behistun in Iran.

According to legend, Darius was one of seven Persian princes who agreed that he should be king whose horse neighed first; his was the first to do so when he tethered a mare near it.

Darius III. Surnamed **Codomannus** (c. 380–330 B.C.). Last king of Persia. Defeated by Alexander the Great at the Granicus river, at Issus, and at Arbela, he was killed by one of his own satraps.

Legend relates that when Alexander succeeded to the Macedonian throne, Darius sent to him for the traditional tribute of golden eggs, but Alexander answered, "The bird which laid them is flown to the other world, where Darius must seek them." The Persian king then sent him a bat and ball, in ridicule of his youth; but Alexander told the messengers that with the bat he would beat the ball of power from their master's hand. Lastly, Darius sent him a bitter melon as emblem of the grief in store for him; but the Macedonian declared that he would make the shah eat his own fruit.

Dark Ages. The earlier centuries of the MIDDLE AGES. Roughly, it encompasses the era between the death of Constantine and the close of the Carolingian dynasty. It was so termed because of the intellectual darkness supposedly characteristic of the period, but nowadays few writers dare to use the term without the qualification "so-called."

Dark Laughter (1925). A novel by Sherwood ANDERSON. It deals with the escape of John Stockton, a Chicago newspaperman, from a life he regards as sterile and oppressive, ruled by the machine. In conscious imitation of Mark Twain's Huckleberry Finn, Stockton travels by boat down the Mississippi River. Eventually, he takes a job as a laborer, under the name of Bruce Dudley, in a factory in his former hometown in Indiana, and there he and Aline Grey, the wife of his employer and a woman similarly dissatisfied with a mechanical life, fall in love and elope. The "dark laughter" of the title is that of the American Negro, who, uncorrupted by white civilization and white morality, is alone still capable of a simple, uninhibited joy.

Darkness at Noon (1941). A novel by Arthur KOESTLER. Analyzing various kinds of Communist psychology, it is an account of the moral struggles of an idealistic revolutionary who is persuaded by his superiors to confess to crimes against the state which he did not commit.

Darley, George (1795–1846). Irish-born English poet, mathematician. In his use of symbols to express abstract ideas, he anticipates the symbolist school of poetry. He first earned a living writing mathematical textbooks and, but for a severe speech impediment, might have been an eminent professor of that subject. Later he wrote astute, if harsh, criticism of drama and art. His work includes the verse drama *Sylvia* (1827), and the collections *Errors of Ecstacie* (1822) and *Nepenthe,* published posthumously in 1876.

Darling, Wendy, Michael, and John. See PETER PAN.

Darnay, Charles. In Charles Dickens' A TALE OF TWO CITIES, a teacher of languages who loves Lucie Manette and marries her. He is a French aristocrat, nephew of the Marquis de St. Evrémonde, and has changed his name, emigrating to England in rebellion against his family, who have committed grave injustices against peasants. Because of his family, he is considered an enemy of the revolution and when he returns to Paris to help an old servant unjustly imprisoned, he himself is arrested and sentenced to the guillotine; he is saved by the self-sacrificing intervention of Sydney Carton.

Darnel, Aurelia. See LAUNCELOT GREAVES.

Darnley, Henry Stuart, Lord (1545–1567). Great-grandson of Henry VII, and the second husband of MARY, QUEEN OF SCOTS. Displeased at not receiving the crown matrimonial from Mary, Darnley became jealous of David Rizzio, one of her favorite counselors, and was an accomplice in his murder. Shortly thereafter Darnley himself was murdered—possibly with Mary's knowledge—at Kirk o' Field, a solitary house near Edinburgh; the house was blown up with gunpowder, and Darnley's body, apparently strangled, found nearby.

Darrow, Clarence [Seward] (1857–1938). American lawyer, lecturer, and writer. A well-paid railroad lawyer, Darrow viewed the cases he defended unsympathetically. In the famous Eugene DEBS case, Darrow resigned his position with the railroads and won a national reputation for his defense of Debs. Later he defended Nathan Leopold and Richard Loeb, who murdered a young boy (1924), and saved them from execution. He was the chief counsel for J. T. Scopes, who was accused of violating Tennessee law by teaching evolution in a public school. (See SCOPES TRIAL.) Although Darrow lost the case, he destroyed the reputation of the prosecuting attorney, William Jennings Bryan.

Darrow wrote two novels, *Farmington* (1904) and *An Eye for an Eye* (1905). Among his other volumes are *Crime: Its Cause and Its Treatment* (1922); *Infidels and Heretics* (with Wallace Rice, 1929), an anthology; and *The Story of My Life* (1932). He appears as a character in *Inherit the Wind* (1955), a play based on the Scopes trial, by Robert E. Lee and Jerome Lawrence, and in Meyer Levin's book *Compulsion* (1956), based on the Loeb-Leopold case.

D'Artagnan. See Charles de Baatz d'ARTAGNAN.

Darwin, Charles Robert (1809–1882). English naturalist, grandson of Erasmus DARWIN. An original expounder of the theory of evolution by natural selection, since known as Darwinism, he was to have a profound influence on human concepts of life and the universe. Although he studied medicine at Edinburgh and prepared for the ministry at Cambridge, his abiding interest was natural history, and it was as naturalist that he sailed on the *Beagle* (1831–1836) on an expedition to southern islands, South American coasts, and Australia. On his return to England he published *Zoology of the Voyage of the Beagle* (1840). As secretary of the Geological Society (1838–1841), he came into contact with the noted geologist Sir Charles Lyell (1797–1875), who urged him to write on his experiments in inbreeding and his theory of evolution by natural selection. He received (1858) from Alfred Russel Wallace (1823–1913) an abstract outlining an identical theory of natural selection, independently arrived at. He published Wallace's essay along with his own, written in 1844, in 1858. In 1859 he published his ORIGIN OF SPECIES; it is said that the first edition sold out in one day, and immediately a raging controversy arose. Within one year, the book's importance, still felt today, as the leading work in natural philosophy in the history of mankind, was recognized. Darwin's later important works include *The Movements and Habits of Climbing Plants* (1865), *The Variation of Animals and Plants under Domestication* (1868), *The Descent of Man* (1871), and *Selection in Relation to Sex* (1871). See SCOPES TRIAL.

Darwin, Erasmus (1731–1802). English physician, botanist, and poet. He is the author of *The Botanic Garden* (1789, 1791), a didactic poem in heroic couplets discoursing on plants and flowers according to the theories of Linnaeus. Darwin's *Zoönomia* (1794–1796) is a treatise on evolutionary development, not, however, in the sense that his grandson Charles Robert DARWIN was to assign to that term.

Das, Deb Kumar (1936–   ). Indian poet writing in English; also a research scientist. He published *The Night Before Us* (1960).

Dasharatha. In Hindu legend, a king of the solar dynasty; in the Ramayana, father of Rama. He had three chief queens, and when the sage Rishyasringa performed a special sacrifice for him, Rama was born to Kaushalya, Lakshmana and Shatrughna to Sumitra, and Bharata to Kaikeyi. His daughter was Shanta. After he ordered Rama into fourteen years' exile in order to keep a promise he had made to the evil-minded Kaikeyi, he died of a broken heart.

Dashwood, Elinor and **Marianne.** See SENSE AND SENSIBILITY.

Dashwood, Elizabeth Monica. See E. M. DELAFIELD.

Datta, Sudhindranath (1901–1960). Indian poet and critic in Bengali. He was a leader of the modernist movement in Bengali and translated European poetry. His best-known work is *Orchestra.*

Daudet, Alphonse (1840–1897). French novelist of the naturalist school. Daudet is noted for his keen observation, his sympathetic portrayal of character, and his vivid presentation of incident. His novels deal with life in Provence, his birthplace, and with the various social classes of Paris. The Provençal stories (see TARTARIN), vigorous and good-humored, include LETTRES DE MON MOULIN, *Tartarin de Tarascon* (1872); *Tartarin sur les Alpes* (1885), and *Port-Tarascon* (1890). Daudet's novels of Parisian manners include *Le Nabob* (1877), NUMA ROUMESTAN, *Les Rois en exil* (1879), and *Sapho* (1884).

Daudet, Léon (1868–1942). French journalist and writer. The son of Alphonse Daudet, he gave up medicine to devote himself to political journalism. His intemperate, antidemocratic articles, polemical essays, and diatribes at first appeared in *Le Gaulois, Le Figaro,* and the fanatically anti-Semitic *La Libre Parole;* then, in 1908, Daudet became coeditor with Charles Maurras of the ultraroyalist Catholic journal L'ACTION FRANÇAISE. For 20 years the force of his invective was feared, and he wielded a political influence that enabled him to be elected to the Chamber of Deputies, where he served from 1919 to 1924. His influence was, however, insufficient to sustain a murder charge which he had brought against the chauffeur in whose cab his son had committed suicide. The chauffeur prosecuted him, and, following a noisy trial, he was sentenced to prison for defamation. With royalist help he escaped and fled to Belgium in 1927. Daudet wrote the novels *L'Astre noir* (*The Black Heavenly Body,* 1893), *Les Morticoles* (1894), and *Sylla et son destin* (1922). His nonfiction books include *L'Avant-guerre* (1913). *Souvenirs* (1914), *L'Hérédo* (1916), *Le Monde des images* (1919), and *Le Stupide XIXe siècle* (*The Stupid XIXth Century,* 1922).

Daumier, Honoré (1808–1879). French painter and caricaturist. On the staff of *La Caricature* and *Charivari,* he produced an enormous number of powerful lithographs commenting with bitter humor, scathing satire, or tragic seriousness upon the faults of the bourgeoisie, the corruption of the law, and the injustices of his age. His direct, economically stated paintings with their superb handling of light and shade remained unappreciated until after his death.

Dauphin. The heir to the French crown under the Valois and Bourbon dynasties. Guy VIII, count of Vienne, was the first so styled, apparently because he wore as his emblem a dolphin. The title descended in the family until 1349, when Humbert III ceded his *seigneurie,* the Dauphiné, to Philippe VI (du Valois), one condition being that the heir of France assume the title of *le Dauphin.* The first French prince so called was Jean, who succeeded Philippe; the last was a Duc d'Angoulême, son of Charles X, who renounced the title in 1830. The

Dauphin remembered in connection with JOAN OF ARC was Charles VII (1403–1461), the son of the feeble-minded Charles VI. The early part of his reign was wasted in internal dissensions within the court which the weak Dauphin was unable to put down. Thanks to the efforts of Joan, he was crowned in 1429, but it was not till some years later that a group of more vigorous councillors than he had previously had were able to make the new king take a firm policy. Eventually, partly due to the influence of his remarkable mistress Agnes Sorel, Charles became a fairly strong monarch. Apparently embarrassed over his lack of support for Joan during her lifetime, he arranged for her rehabilitation about 25 years later.

The so-called Lost Dauphin was Charles, son of Louis XVI and Marie Antoinette, called after his father's death Louis XVII by French loyalists. According to official accounts he died in prison two years later, but the secrecy surrounding his death inevitably led sympathizers to believe that he had actually escaped. In later years, innumerable pretenders appeared who claimed to be the Lost Dauphin.

Davenant or **D'Avenant**, Sir **William** (1606–1668). English dramatist and poet, thought by some to be an illegitimate son of Shakespeare. His SIEGE OF RHODES, a heroic tragedy with "musical recitative," is considered the first English opera. Though his writing was very popular in his time, his only outstanding work is *Gondibert* (1651), a heroic poem formed on the aesthetic theories of Hobbes and anticipating Dryden's style.

Davenport, **Marcia** (1903–   ). American novelist. Mrs. Davenport is the daughter of the famous singer Alma Gluck, and her first book was a life of Mozart (1932; rev. 1956). She followed this with several highly popular novels, including *Of Lena Geyer* (1936), *The Valley of Decision* (1942), *East Side, West Side* (1947), *My Brother's Keeper* (1954), and *Constant Image* (1960).

David. The shepherd-king of the Old Testament and the reputed author of many of the Psalms. The youngest son of Jesse, he was secretly anointed king by the prophet Samuel while Saul was still on the throne. Stories of his early life are concerned with his immortal friendship for Saul's son Jonathan, and with Saul's growing jealousy. Though he charmed away the black moods of Saul with his harp (I Sam. 16:23), he was, for many years, forced to flee from Saul's anger. When no one else would venture to respond to the giant's challenge, he killed Goliath, the huge champion of the Philistines, with only his slingshot and some stones (I Sam. 17).

After the death of Saul and Jonathan, David became the second king of Israel (c. 1000–c. 960 B.C.). His latter years were concerned with his guilty love for BATHSHEBA, and his grief over the revolt of his son ABSALOM.

David, St. (*fl.* 6th century A.D.). The patron saint of Wales. Legend relates that he was son of Xantus, Prince of Cereticu, now called Cardiganshire; was brought up a priest, became an ascetic in the Isle of Wight, preached to the Britons, confuted Pelagius, and was preferred to the see of Caerleon or Menevia (i.e., *main aw*, narrow water or firth). Here the saint had received his early education, and when Dyvrig, the archbishop, resigned his see to him, St. David removed the archiepiscopal residence to Menevia, which was henceforth called St. David's. The waters of Bath "owe their warmth and salutary qualities to the benediction of this saint." The leek

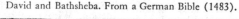

David and Bathsheba. From a German Bible (1483).

worn by Welshmen on *St. David's Day* is in memory of a complete victory obtained by them over the Saxons (March I, 640). This victory is ascribed to the prayers of St. David, and his judicious adoption of a leek in the cap, that the Britons might readily recognize each other. The Saxons, having no badge, not unfrequently turned their swords against their own supporters.

David, [Jacques] Louis (1748–1825). French painter. An accomplished realist, he lent the precision of his drawing to the formulation of a measured and heroic art inspired by the antiquity of republican Rome, and became the indubitable leader of French classicism. During the French Revolution, he supported Robespierre and produced one of his masterpieces, *The Death of Marat* (1793); he then became court painter on the accession of Napoleon. The figures of his historical paintings are sharply lit and sculptural in quality, but often harshly colored and theatrically posed. His exactitude was more suited to the art of portraiture, of which he has given us some admirable examples.

David Copperfield (1849–1850). A novel by Charles DICKENS, admittedly autobiographical. As a mere boy, after his mother's death, David is sent by his cruel stepfather Mr. Murdstone to London to make his living; here he pastes labels on bottles in a warehouse by day and is the single lodger of the poverty-stricken though optimistic Mr. MICAWBER and his family. David finally runs away to his great-aunt Betsey TROTWOOD, who becomes his guardian. After a period of school life in CREAKLE's school, he settles down to work with Mr. WICKFIELD, a lawyer, and finds a warm friend in Wickfield's daughter Agnes. Unaware of Agnes's deep devotion to him, David marries Dora SPENLOW, a rattlebrained childlike woman, who dies soon after. Neither his literary success nor his marriage has brought him the peace and happiness he yearns for, and David turns to Agnes with the realization that he has always loved her. She is involved in extricating her father from the deceits of the unctuous Uriah HEEP, who has gained a financial hold over them. With the help of Mr. Micawber, Uriah Heep is foiled; David marries Agnes and together they find happiness.

David Copperfield is a devastating exposé of the inhuman treatment of children in 19th-century England. Among the well-known secondary characters in the book are BARKIS, the PEGGOTTY family, STEERFORTH, and Tommie TRADDLES.

Davideis (1656). An epic poem in four books by Abraham COWLEY, describing the troubles of King David of the Hebrews. The poem is incomplete.

Davidson, Jo (1883–1952). American sculptor. He was a portraitist of eminent personalities, such as Franklin D. Roosevelt and Georges Clemenceau.

Davidson, John (1857–1909). Scottish poet, playwright, and author. Known in his day as the poet of Anarchy from the gloomy, pessimistic philosophy expressed in his long poetic *Testaments* (1901, 1902, 1908), Davidson survives through a few lyrics such as *The Ballad of Hell* (1894) and *A Runnable Stag* (1906). Collections of his verse include *Fleet Street Eclogues* (1893, 1896) and several volumes of *Ballads* (1894, 1897, 1899). He also wrote successful plays, several novels, translations, and criticism.

Davidson, Lawrence H. The pen name under which D. H. LAWRENCE published *Movements in European History* (1921).

Davie, Donald (1922–   ). English poet and critic. A witty, antiromantic poet like other followers of William Empson, he published *New and Selected Poems* in 1961.

Davies, Sir John (1569–1626). English poet of the SPENSERIAN SCHOOL. The author of epigrammatic and ingenious poetry and treatises in verse, he is known for the vigor and intelligence of his writing. Among his works are *Orchestra* (1596), a treatment in poetry of the dance; *Hymns to Astraea* (1599), a collection of acrostic hymns praising Queen Elizabeth; and *Nosce Teipsum* (1599), a philosophical poem on the immortality of the soul.

Davies, W[illiam] H[enry] (1871–1940). Welsh-born English poet. He wrote simple, Wordsworthian poems on nature, and was associated with the GEORGIANS. Until he was over 30, he was a hobo and peddler by choice. His best-known book is his prose *Autobiography of a Super-tramp* (1908).

Daviot, Gordon. See Elizabeth MACKINTOSH.

Davis, Clyde Brion (1894–1962). American newspaperman and novelist. Davis worked on many newspapers from coast to coast, but he is best known for his novel *"The Great American Novel"* (1938), the story of a newspaperman whose roving life is spent in dreaming about the great American novel he expects to write. *The Anointed* (1937) is the story of a sailor who thinks he is divinely inspired. Davis also wrote *The Arkansas* (1940) for the Rivers of America series, and over 15 other novels with American settings.

Davis, Elmer [Holmes] (1890–1958). American journalist and radio commentator. Born in Indiana, Davis worked for the New York *Times* and wrote a history of the newspaper (1921). Having joined the staff of CBS in 1939, he interrupted his work there to head the Office of War Information (1942–1945), then returned to radio work. Known for his fearless interpretation of the news, he attacked Senator McCarthy in a collection of essays called *But We Were Born Free* (1954). Davis also wrote several works of fiction, notably *Giant-Killer* (1928), a novel telling the story of King David from a rationalist viewpoint.

Davis, H[arold] L[enoir] (1896–1960). American novelist. He became well known for his realistic historical novel *Honey in the Horn* (1935), a story of frontier life in Oregon. He is also the author of *Harp of a Thousand Strings* (1947), a narrative dealing with the French Revolution; *Beulah Land* (1949) and *Winds of Morning* (1951), both frontier novels; *Team Bells Woke Me* (1953), a collection of short stories; and *Distant Music* (1957), a family chronicle set in southeastern Oregon.

Davis, Jefferson (1808–1889). American statesman. A graduate of West Point, Davis was wounded at the battle of Buena Vista in the Mexican War. In 1847 he became U.S. Senator from Mississippi and later served as secretary of war under Franklin Pierce. Again elected to the Senate in 1857, he resigned when Mississippi seceded and was chosen president of the Confederacy in 1861. His policies, however, aroused much controversy within Confederate ranks. After the Civil War, he was captured and imprisoned; in 1866 he was indicted for treason, but was never tried.

Davis, Owen (1874–1956). American playwright. He is the author of numerous popular melodramas, the most celebrated of which are *Nellie, the Beautiful Cloak Model* (1906) and *The Nervous Wreck* (1923). He won a Pulitzer Prize for *Icebound* (1923), the story of a family who greedily wait for the mother to die. Davis successfully dramatized *Ethan Frome* (1936) and a number of other novels.

Davis, Rebecca [Blaine] Harding (1831–1910). American author and mother of Richard Harding DAVIS. She was one of the earliest American realists, known for her attempts to deal in fiction with the life of industrial workers, the problem of the Negro, and political corruption. Her early success was the "muckraking" *Life in the Iron Mills,* published in *The Atlantic Monthly* in April, 1861. This was followed by *Margaret Howth* (1862), a novel set in an Indiana milltown. *Waiting for the Verdict* (1868) was a story about racial bias; *John Andross* (1874) was a tale of political corruption.

Davis, Richard Harding (1864–1916). American journalist and novelist. The son of novelist Rebecca Harding Davis, he covered wars all over the world, and his vivid, dramatic dispatches made him the leading reporter of his day. Aided by his good looks and sartorial elegance, he became equally famous as a personality, the embodiment of "the mauve decade" of the 1890's. Although his fiction is considered somewhat slick and superficial, he was a skillful storyteller and created several memorable characters, notably Gallegher, the enterprising office boy, and Cortland Van Bibber, the Robin Hood of the social set. Davis' works of fiction include *Gallegher and Other Stories* (1891), *Van Bibber and Others* (1892), *Soldiers of Fortune* (1897), *Captain Macklin* (1902), and *The Bar Sinister* (1903). He also wrote more than 20 plays, including *The Dictator* (1904).

Davis, Stuart (1894–1964). American painter. He evolved a meticulous language of abstract symbols and intense color.

Davis, Thomas Osborne (1814–1845). Irish poet. Davis founded, with John Blake Dillon and Charles Gavan Duffy, *The Nation* (1842), in its day the most influential organ of Irish nationalism. He is best known for his ballads, collected in *Poems* (1846).

Davy Jones. A sailor's name for the evil spirit of the sea. The term seems to be a corruption of *Duffy* or *Duppy Jonah,* the word *duffy* or *duppy* standing, among the Negroes of the West Indies, for "a haunting spirit or ghost." Jones is a corruption of Jonah, the prophet who was thrown into the sea. "He's gone to Davy Jones' locker" is the nautical way of saying that a messmate is dead and has been buried at sea.

Day, Clarence [Shepard], Jr. (1874–1935). American writer. He was best known as the author of two unique collections of humorous sketches based on recollections of his parents: LIFE WITH FATHER, and *Life with Mother* (1936). Day also wrote *This Simian World* (1920), *God and My Father* (1932), and *Scenes from the Mesozoic* (1935).

Day, John (1522–1584). English printer. He printed the first church music book in English (1560) and the first English edition of John Foxe's *Actes And Monuments* (1563).

Day, John (c. 1574–c. 1640). English dramatist. He is best known for *The Parliament of Bees* (1608) and part one of *The Blind Beggar of Bethnal Green, or Thomas Strowd* (1600), written with Henry Chettle. His other plays include *The Isle of Gulls* (1606) and *The Travels of Three English Brothers* (1607). He also collaborated with Thomas Dekker.

Day or Daye, Stephen (1594?–1668). The first printer in New England. He brought out the *Bay Psalm Book* (1640), the first book printed in the English colonies. The town of Cambridge, Mass., granted him 300 acres of land for "being the first that sett upon printing."

Day Lewis, C[ecil] (1904–1972). Irish-born English poet and author of detective stories under the pen name Nicholas Blake. Associated during the 1930's with the Marxist poets W. H. Auden and Stephen Spender, he, like them, wrote much didactic verse, and used the imagery of industrial society. His later poetry is more personal and reflective. Among his collections of poetry are *From Feathers to Iron* (1931), *The Magnetic Mountain* (1933), *A Time to Dance* (1935), and *An Italian Visit* (1953). *A Hope for Poetry* (1934) and *Revolution in Writing* (1935) are critical essays on the aims of the Marxist poets. He has made good verse translations of Vergil's *Georgics* (1941) and *Aeneid* (1952), and has also written children's books. Among his detective novels is *The Worm of Death* (1961). He was named poet laureate in 1968.

Day of Atonement or **Yom Kippur.** The most solemn Jewish fast. It culminates the 10 days of penitence at the beginning of the Jewish New Year, falling on the 10th day of the 7th month (*Tishri*). In ancient times, a priest made atonement for the whole community; a bullock was sacrificed; its blood sprinkled on the Ark of the Covenant; and a SCAPEGOAT selected to carry the poeple's sins "into a solitary land." It involved abstinence from all labor, food or drink and the recitation of penitential prayers.

Day of Doom, The (1662). A celebrated poem by Michael WIGGLESWORTH. It describes the Day of Judgment and the sentencing to punishment in Hell of sinners and of infants who died before baptism. So popular was the poem that no first or second edition of it exists; the copies were apparently thumbed to shreds. It is estimated that one out of every 20 persons in the Bay colony bought a copy, making it the first American best seller.

Day of the Locust, The (1939). A novel by Nathanael WEST. Set in Hollywood, the book deals with the failure of the American dream. The central character is Homer Simpson, who arrives in California only to find monotony and boredom. The book culminates in a surrealistic riot at a movie premiere.

Day of the Rabblement, The (1901). An attack by James JOYCE on the parochial nationalism of the Irish Literary Theatre (see ABBEY THEATRE). He accused this theater movement of neglecting true art in trying to appease the people, or Irish rabblement.

Days (1852). One of the best poems by Ralph Waldo EMERSON. It expresses this thought from his essay, *Works and Days:* "He only is rich who owns the day."

Days of the Turbins (Dni Turbinikh; 1926). A drama by Mikhail BULGAKOV. It gives a well-balanced account of the conflict during the Russian Revolution between the Czarist White Guard and the forces of the Red Army.

Dazai Osamu. Pen name of **Tsushima Shuji** (1909–1948). Japanese novelist, author of pessimistic works, widely read in the postwar period. He died with a woman in a suicide pact. Several of his works have appeared in translation: *Shayō* (*The Setting Sun,* 1947) and *Ningen Shikaku* (*No Longer Human,* 1948), both translated by Donald Keene.

D'Azeglio, Marchese. **Massimo Taparrelli** (1798–1866). Italian patriot and writer of historical novels which were inspired by the Italian struggle for national independence (the RISORGIMENTO). Most noted are *Ettore Fieramosca* (1833) and *Niccolò de' Lapi* (1841). He is also known for his polemical writings and for his memoirs, *I Miei Ricordi* (1867).

Deacon's Masterpiece, The, or, The Wonderful "One-Hoss Shay" (1858). A poem by Oliver Wendell HOLMES. The deacon built his shay so sturdily that it would never break down; based on logic, it lasted a hundred years. The shay never did break down; it simply fell apart all at once: "Just as bubbles do when they burst." Clearly Holmes was satirizing Calvinist dogma, or any inflexible though highly logical system designed for permanence.

Dead, The. The last and most famous of the short stories in James Joyce's DUBLINERS (1914). It concerns Gabriel Conway, an Irish college teacher. Gabriel and his wife Gretta spend the evening at his elderly aunts' Christmas dance, a rather moribund affair; one incident after another makes Gabriel feel more and more a social failure. Seeing his wife look radiant after hearing an old song, he takes her home in a romantic mood. She tells him the song reminded her of a boy called Michael Furey, who was once in love with her, but who died when he was 17. In a famous last paragraph Joyce describes Gabriel looking at the snow and thinking of his aunts who will soon be dead, of himself who is spiritually almost dead, and of his wife's dead lover.

Dead End (1935). A play by Sidney KINGSLEY. It depicts life in New York's slums by means of typical scenes taking place in a dead-end street.

Dead Sea Scrolls (also called **Qumram manuscripts**). The fragmentary remains of a large library of the ancient Jewish sect of Essenes. They were discovered in 1947 in a cave around the Qumram Valley of the Dead Sea. Thousands of fragments of manuscripts comprise the archaelogical discovery; over 100 scrolls of Old Testament books—all except the book of Esther—have appeared. The oldest texts date from 200 B.C., 1,000 years older than any previously existing documents.

Dead Souls (Myortvye Dushi; 1842). A novel by Nikolai GOGOL. It relates the adventures of an archswindler, Pavel I. CHICHIKOV. The hero, who has already been in trouble for shady deals when he appears on the scene, has conceived a weird scheme for making his fortune anew. He intends to buy from landowners all of their serfs who have died since the last census was taken. These serfs are still alive according to government records, and the landowner has to pay taxes on them until the next census strikes them off the list. Chichikov's plan is to pay the owner a small sum, assume the burden of the taxes on these "dead souls" himself, and become the rightful owner of them. Then he intends to mortgage them and to acquire a real estate of his own in eastern Russia. The novel follows Chichikov as he makes friends with the right people in town and visits the local landowners, to each of whom he gently puts his strange proposition. He neglects to tell them, however, what he plans to do with the dead souls once he has them. The description of the landowners he visits, their reactions to his proposal, and Chichikov's reactions to their reactions make up some of the finest scenes in the novel. Eventually rumors spread through the town about Chichikov's deals with the landowners MANILOV, SOBAKEVICH, KOROBOCHKA, and PLYUSHKIN. The obnoxious NOZDRYOV adds lies of his own invention to the rumors, and Chichikov finally wings away from the town in his troika.

Gogol was working on a second part to the novel in which Chichikov was to be reformed and become a genuinely respectable citizen. The author destroyed most of the manuscript shortly before his death and only fragments of it have survived.

Dead Souls has been unanimously acclaimed as one of the greatest novels in the Russian language, for its characterizations, humor, and style. The perpetual question of whether Gogol was a realist or a fantasist has created differences of opinion, however, about just what kind of novel Gogol wrote. The influential critic Vissarion Belinski accepted Gogol's fiction as being truthful to Russian life. This view, retained by later radical critics, is the official Soviet doctrine on Gogol. Other critics have stressed the many fantastic elements in Gogol's work: the grotesque caricatures of real people that compose his characters, the extravagance of his imagery, and use of hyperbolic language.

De Amicis, Edmondo (1846–1908). Italian educator, moralist, and essayist. De Amicis is noted for the sentimental and moral tenor of his writings. An admirer of Manzoni and politically a moderate socialist, he was chiefly interested in the pedagogical and social problems of post-Risorgimento Italian society. His fiction—*Le Novelle,* a collection of short stories (1872); *Gli Amici* (1884); and *Il Cuore* (1886)—is candidly didactic. *La Vita Militare* (1869) recounts his experiences as an infantry officer in the Italian army during the Austro-Prussian War (1866). *Romanzo di Un Maestro* (1890) and *Idioma Gentile* (1905) are interesting essays in practical pedagogy: the former discusses state-run public schools; the latter treats informally the correct spoken and written usage of the Italian language.

A world traveler, De Amicis was one of the first men of letters to write carefully detailed accounts of the places he visited: *Londra* (1874), *Spagna* (1873), *Olanda* (1874), *Marocco* (1876), *Constantinopoli* (1878), and *Parigi* (1879). In his later years he devoted himself to improving the lot of the impoverished Italian proletariat. His *Sull'Oceano* (1889) vividly narrates the plight of Italian emigrants to the Americas.

De Amicitia (44 B.C.). A dialogue on the subject of friendship by CICERO. The chief interlocutor is Gaius Laelius Sapiens. Hence the essay is also known as the *Laelius.*

Dear Judas, and Other Poems (1929). A collection by Robinson JEFFERS. The title poem is an attempt to rehabilitate the reputation of Judas. He is presented as a man who loves Jesus but finds him grown too fond of power. Judas therefore betrays him in the belief that he will be jailed for a few days and then released, escaping later execution as a rebel.

Death and the Fool. See TOR UND DER TOD, DER.

Death Comes for the Archbishop (1927). A novel by Willa CATHER. It describes the missionary efforts of the French bishop Jean Latour and his vicar, Father Joseph Vaillant, to establish a diocese in the territory of New Mexico. The novel is based on the lives of the two eminent French clerics, Bishop Jean Baptiste Lamy (1814–1888) and Father Joseph Machebeuf. They prevail over all adversities to build a cathedral in the wilderness.

Death in Venice (Der Tod in Venedig; 1913). A novella by Thomas MANN. Gustav von Aschenbach, the hero, is a successful author, proud of the self-discipline with which he has ordered his life and work. On a trip to Venice, however, he becomes aware of mysterious decadent potentialities in himself, and he finally succumbs to a consuming love for a frail but beautiful Polish boy named Tadzio. Though he learns that there is danger of a cholera epidemic in Venice, he finds he cannot leave the city, and eventually he dies of the disease. The story is permeated by a rich and varied symbolism with frequent overtones from Greek literature and mythology.

Death of a Hero (1929). A novel by Richard ALDINGTON. It expresses the author's disillusionment with the idealistic patriotism of World War I. The "hero" is so disgusted by a corrupt and wasteful English society, neurotic parents, and the complications in his love life, that he invites his own death.

Death of a Salesman (1949). A play by Arthur MILLER. A bitter indictment of American values, it is the story of Willy Loman, a traveling salesman, who experiences a profound sense of failure as he discovers signs of aging in himself and takes stock of his accomplishments. The play ends in his suicide.

Death of Ivan Ilyich, The (Smert' Ivana Ilyicha; 1886). A story by Count Leo TOLSTOI. It concerns the thoughts on life and death of a dying man. An ordinary man who had never particularly bothered himself about large questions, Ivan is forced into his contemplation by the discovery that he will soon die of cancer. The problems he ponders are similar to those that acutely occupied Tolstoi himself when he went through the spiritual crisis described in *A Confession*. Ivan's acceptance of death as part of the natural order of things recalls a similar conclusion reached by Prince Andrei Bolkonski in *War and Peace*.

Death of Pompey, The. See MORT DE POMPÉE, LA.

Death of Seneca, The. See François L'HERMITE.

Death of the Heart, The (1938). A novel by Elizabeth BOWEN. It is the story of Portia, an illegitimate 16-year-old girl who comes to live with her half brother when her mother dies. To escape from the arid, artificial, unfeeling social world of her London relatives she falls in love with ordinary, insensitive Eddie—who is soon found holding hands with someone else. Innocence and idealism die in Portia's heart, but she also grows up into an acceptance of the world as it is.

Death of the Hired Man, The (1914). A poem by Robert FROST. It narrates the argument between a farmer and his wife over whether or not to keep a defeated old hired hand, who, in his last hours, has returned to them. When the farmer seeks out the man he finds him dead. The poem contains the kind of folk wisdom that made Frost popular, but also has an almost mystical undercurrent giving layers of meaning beyond the obvious debate.

Débâcle, La (The Downfall, 1892). A novel in the ROUGON-MACQUART series by Emile ZOLA. The characters in *La Débâcle* are dwarfed by Zola's realistic and thoroughly detailed account of the Franco-Prussian War.

de Barral, Flora. The heroine of Joseph Conrad's novel CHANCE. She is torn between her husband and her father.

De bello Gallico. See COMMENTARIES ON THE GALLIC WAR.

Deborah. In the Old Testament, a Hebrew prophetess and judge of Israel (Judg. 4:4). She summoned Barak to fight against the tyranny of Jabin, prophesied success, and accompanied him in battle against Sisera, captain of Jabin's army. After their victory over the Canaanites, she sang a famous song of triumph (Judg. 5), considered by scholars to be one of the oldest pieces of writing in the Old Testament.

Debrett, John (1752–1822). English publisher and original compiler of the *Peerage of England, Scotland, and Ireland* (1802) and the *Baronetage of England* (1808).

Debs, Eugene V[ictor] (1855–1926). American socialist leader. Founder of the Social Democratic Party and its leader during the period of its greatest influence (1897–1916), Debs was a candidate for the presidency five times, and was renowned for his campaign oratory. He came to prominence as a leader of the famous Pullman strike in Chicago (1894) and was imprisoned for his participation. (See Clarence DARROW.) A powerful figure in American politics, he always insisted on the primacy of democratic procedures. His *Writings and Speeches* were collected in 1948 by Arthur M. Schlesinger, Jr.

Debussy, Claude [Achille] (1862–1918). French composer. He is identified with musical impressionism, although he preferred to call himself simply *musicien français*. Certain revolutionary characteristics of his work, such as unresolved discords, exotic scales, and free forms, prepared the way for many developments of modern music. His best-known pieces include *Suite Bergamasque*, a piano suite containing the famous *Clair de Lune; Prélude à l'après-midi d'un faune* (1894), a tone poem inspired by Mallarmé's eclogue *L'Après-midi d'un faune (Afternoon of a Faun,* 1876); *Pelléas et Mélisande* (1902), his only opera, composed to Maeterlinck's play; *La Mer* ("The Sea," 1905), a tone poem; *Children's Corner Suite* (1908), a piano suite; and *Jeux* ("Games," 1913), a ballet.

décadents. A term applied narrowly to the group of French poets whose leaders were Rimbaud, Verlaine, and Mallarmé (see SYMBOLISTS). Broadly and more popularly the term *décadents* is applied to the poets and prose writers, chiefly French, of the postromantic period. Morbid and perverse tastes, unconventional and often sensational social behavior, and hyperaesthetic temperaments characterize the *décadents*. In their writings, they placed emphasis upon creative self-expression, advancing the ideal of pure art. In his novel AGAINST THE GRAIN (*A Rebours*), J. K. Huysmans creates a hero who is the epitome of the *décadent*. Oscar Wilde is the leading figure in the English counterpart of this French phenomenon.

Decalogue. See TEN COMMANDMENTS.

Decameron, The. A collection of tales by Giovanni BOCCACCIO, written 1351–1353. The title (from Gr., *deca*, ten, and *hēmera*, day) refers to the frame story: in the year of the black death, 1348, seven young ladies and three young gallants meet in a Florentine church and decide to escape from the city to the hills of Fiesole. There they spend the time in telling stories on 10 days. The 100 novelle, ranging from anecdotes and fabliaux to folk tales and fairy tales of ancient lineage, include many that became famous and influential in European literature: *Ser Ciappelletto*, BERNABÒ OF GENOA, GILLETTE OF NARBONNE, THE REVENGE OF TANCRED, ISABELLA, OR THE POT OF BASIL, THE EATEN HEART, BROTHER CIPOLLA, A GARDEN IN JANUARY, CALANDRINO AND THE HELIOTROPE, TITUS AND GISIPPUS, THE PATIENT GRISELDA. It is unlikely that Chaucer knew the book, though he used similar stories; but the tales have appeared in the works of other English and European writers in a steady stream up to modern times. They have also been used for plays, operas, and paintings.

De Casseres, Benjamin (1873–1945). American newspaperman, poet, and biographer. An innovator and radical individualist, he wrote flamboyant essays for the New York papers. His books include *The Shadow-Eater* (1915), *Black Suns* (1936), and *Don Marquis* (1938).

Decatur, Stephen (1779–1820). American naval officer. He commanded the squadron that sailed to Algeria in 1815 to impose upon the British a peace on American terms. On his return, he uttered his famous toast at a banquet: "Our country! In her intercourse with foreign nations may she always be in the right; but our country, right or wrong!"

Decembrist revolt. A short-lived, unsuccessful uprising in Russia in December, 1825. Led by young nobles of some of Russia's oldest families, the Decembrists wanted to institute a constitutional form of government and deny the throne to Nicholas I following his accession on the death of Alexander I. The insurgents were arrested; 5 were executed, and over 100 exiled to Siberia. The revolt was the first such uprising led by members of the aristocracy. The event has been a constant point of reference for Russian revolutionaries and writers as an example of a courageous bid for freedom. The Decembrists included many friends of the poet Pushkin, but he was never proved to have been involved in the affair.

De Civitate Dei. See CITY OF GOD, THE.

Declaration of Independence. The public act by which the Second Continental Congress, on July 4, 1776, declared the 13 North American colonies to be free and independent of Great Britain. New York alone did not ratify the act until July 9. It was signed on Aug. 2, 1776, by the representatives of all 13 colonies. The document was nominally the work of a drafting committee, but actually Thomas Jefferson wrote it practically in its entirety.

Declaration of the Rights of Man (La Declaration des droits de l'homme et du citoyen). In French history, a document setting forth the principles of the FRENCH REVOLUTION. Consisting of a preamble and 17 articles, it was modeled on the American Declaration of Independence and was voted by the Constituent ASSEMBLY on August 27, 1789.

Decline and Fall (1928). A bitter, farcical, satiric novel by Evelyn WAUGH. Paul Pennyfeather, the unfortunate hero, is unjustly expelled from Oxford and turns to teaching at an appalling boys' school. He falls in love with the mother of one of his pupils, and is arrested and imprisoned for unknowingly working in her white slave trade business. Finally he returns to Oxford to study theology.

Decline and Fall of the Roman Empire, The History of the (1776–1788). A history by Edward GIBBON. Although later scholarship has superseded much of the information in this work, it has taken its place among the classical works of historical literature in the English language. The work is divided into three periods and covers a total of 13 centuries: from the rule of Trajan and the Antonines to the decay of the Western Empire; from the era of Justinian in the Eastern Empire to the founding of the Holy Roman Empire in the west under Charlemagne; and from the restoration of the Western Empire to the capture, in 1453, of Constantinople by the Turks. Gibbon's point of view is best expressed in his observation that history is a record of "little more than the crimes, follies, and misfortunes of mankind."

decorum. The ideal of propriety, or appropriateness. Stemming from classical authors, it was defined and put into practice as a literary principle by the neoclassicists of the latter part of the 17th and the 18th centuries. In accordance with this principle, literature, especially poetry, was required to be polished, dignified, clear, rational, moderate, conventional, and "elevated"; in order to achieve elegance, Latinized diction and generality and abstraction in figurative language were preferred elements of style. Wide use of the epithet was one result of the latter tendency. Leading exponents of the principle of decorum were Boileau, Pope, and Samuel Johnson. See NEOCLASSICISM.

Woodcut from a 1518 edition of *The Decameron.*

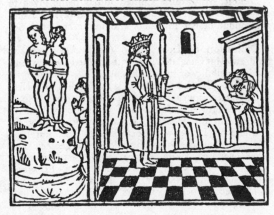

Decoud, Martin. A character in Joseph Conrad's novel NOSTROMO. A cynic with no inner resources, he kills himself when he is stranded on an isolated island.

decretals. The name of ecclesiastical historians for the second part of the canon law. It contains the decrees and decisions of the early popes on disputed points.

The false or forged decretals were designed to support the claim of the popes to temporal as well as spiritual authority, and purport to be the decisions of some thirty popes of the first three centuries.

The ninth century forgery known as the *Donation of Constantine* is among the false decretals. This purports to relate how Constantine the Great, when retired to the Bosporus in 330, conferred all his rights, honors, and property as Emperor of the West on the Pope of Rome and his successors. It is said, also, to have been confirmed by Charlemagne.

Dedalus, Stephen. The hero of James Joyce's novel A PORTRAIT OF THE ARTIST AS A YOUNG MAN and one of the three chief characters in his novel ULYSSES. Stephen's character, background, and life history are closely modeled on Joyce's own. His name is clearly symbolic of the creative artist (see DAEDALUS).

Portrait concerns Stephen's struggle to gain his identity as an artist by freeing himself from his family ties, the narrowness of his Catholic upbringing, and the cultural aridity and frenzied nationalism of Ireland. The book ends on an affirmative note as Stephen is about to leave Dublin for Paris. In *Ulysses*, however, Stephen has returned to Ireland, defeated and undeceived. Still emotionally involved with the cultural and religious values his intellect rejects, Stephen is paralyzed as an artist. In the earlier book Stephen is portrayed fairly straightforwardly; his adolescent sense of superiority and colossal pride are presented with no trace of irony. But Joyce's detached portrayal of Stephen in *Ulysses* stands in ironic contrast to his earlier vision.

Dedlock, Lady. See BLEAK HOUSE.

Dee, John (1527–1608). English mathematician and astrologer. A magician who had practiced at various European courts, Dee was imprisoned in England soon after the accession of Mary Tudor on the charge of having practised sorcery against her life. He was released in 1555, and later enjoyed the favor of Elizabeth, whom he instructed in astrology. He wrote numerous works on astrology and mathematics.

Deeping, [George] Warwick (1877–1950). English novelist. He is the author of SORRELL AND SON and other popular novels.

Deerslayer, The (1841). A novel by James Fenimore COOPER. Although it was the last of THE LEATHERSTOCKING TALES to be written, *The Deerslayer* is the novel of Natty BUMPPO's youth. The scene is Lake Otsego, N. Y., called Glimmerglass in the story. Young hunters, Natty and his friend Hurry Harry March live with the Delaware Indians. They fight the Hurons with the aid of the British. Part of the story deals with the fruitless attempts of Judith Hutter to interest Natty romantically. Chingachgook, the Delaware chief who becomes Natty's companion in other volumes, enters the hero's life in this book.

Defarge, M. In Charles Dickens' A TALE OF TWO CITIES, a revolutionist, keeper of a wine shop in the Faubourg St. Antoine, in Paris. He is a rough, bull-necked, implacable-looking man.

Mme Defarge. M. Defarge's wife, a harsh, remorseless woman and a revolutionary fanatic. It is her sister whom St. Evrémonde attacks and in her revenge she is instrumental in having Charles Darnay sentenced to the guillotine because he is related to the marquis. She has compiled a list of aristocrats and enemies of the Revolution, encoded in the stitches of her knitting. Knitting incessantly while watching the daily executions at the guillotine, she is a perfect example of the TRICOTEUSES.

Defender of the Faith (Fidei Defensor). Henry VIII of England. A title given to him by Pope Leo X in 1521, for a Latin treatise *On the Seven Sacraments*.

Défense et Illustration de la Langue française (1549). A treatise on poetry by Joachim DU BELLAY which served as the doctrine of the French poets of the PLÉIADE. It contained two main propositions: (1) that the French language be "defended" as a mode of poetic expression against those who were trying to rival the classic poets by writing in Latin; (2) that in order to attain its full potential of expression, French must be "illustrated" or embellished by borrowing from Greek and Latin and by the use of archaic, dialectal, and technical words. "Illustration" also included the imitation of literary formulas discovered by the ancients and the adoption of poetic forms such as the classical ode and the Italian sonnet. None of these ideas was new with Du Bellay, who sought to raise poetry to the eminence it had enjoyed in ancient times, but by fitting them into a coherent system, he gave form to the revolutionary aims of the Renaissance poets.

Defense of Poesie, The. Alternate title of AN APOLOGIE FOR POETRIE by Sir Philip Sidney.

Deffand, Marquise du. Marie de Vichy-Chamrond (1697–1780). Witty and cynical French noblewoman, leader in Parisian social life and literary and philosophical circles. Her salon was frequented by Turgot, d'Alembert, Marivaux, Baron de Grimm, and others. When she lost her sight in 1754, she engaged Julie LESPINASSE as a companion; a violent quarrel between the two broke up the salon. Her correspondence with Voltaire, Montesquieu, Horace Walpole, and others documents 18th-century society.

Déficit, Madame. Contemptuous name given to MARIE ANTOINETTE because she was always demanding money of her ministers and never had any. See BAKER.

Definition of Love, The (1681). A poem by Andrew MARVELL, dealing with exalted passion and the impossibility of its fulfillment.

Defoe, Daniel (1660–1731). English novelist, pamphleteer, journalist, and political agent. He is celebrated for his frank and dramatic realism in fiction, and the accuracy, vigor, and lucidity of his journalism. Defoe was born Daniel Foe, son of a London tallow-chandler (he added the genteel "De" when over forty years of age). He is best known for his novels ROBINSON CRUSOE and MOLL FLANDERS, and for his JOURNAL OF THE PLAGUE YEAR, a historical reconstruction. Others of his works include *The True-Born Englishman* (1701), a rugged, satirical poem on English hatred of foreigners when, in fact, there is no true-born Englishman; *The Shortest Way with the Dissenters* (1702), satirizing ecclesiastical intolerance in the extreme right of the Church of England by ironically proposing that all Non-Conformist preachers be hanged—and for which he was imprisoned and pilloried; *A Tour Thro' the Whole Island of Great Britain* (1724–1727), in three volumes, an important source for early English economic life; and several novels other than his most famous, including *Memoirs of a Cavalier* (1720), a romance concerning the Cavalier's service under Gustavus Adolphus, King of Sweden; CAPTAIN SINGLETON; COLONEL JACK; and *Roxana, or, the Fortunate Mistress* (1724), which purports to be a true account of a strumpet flourishing among the aristocracy. Defoe edited, from 1704 to 1713, *The Review*, a newspaper which anticipated the *Tatler* and the *Spectator*, though it laid much greater stress on discussions of commerce and the news than did the others. He supported King William III and was later a secret agent in the pay of the moderate Tories under Robert Harley (1705). Defoe was also the first author of ghost-stories in modern English literature, an example of which is *A True Relation of the Apparition of One Mrs. Veal*. See Mrs. VEAL.

De Forest, John William (1826–1906). American novelist and memoirist. At the outbreak of the Civil War, De Forest joined the Union army; after Lee's surrender he served as the head of the Freedman's Bureau in South Carolina. His best-known novel, MISS RAVENEL'S CONVERSION FROM SECESSION TO LOYALTY, includes a realistic treatment of war; also based on his Southern experience is *Kate Beaumont* (1872). Among De Forest's other books are the novels *Witching Times* (1856), *Seacliff* (1859), *Overland* (1871), and *Honest John Vane* (1875). His posthumously published memoirs are included in *A Volunteer's Adventures* (1946) and *A Union Officer in the Reconstruction* (1948). An early American realist, De Forest was admired by William Dean Howells, and is considered a forerunner of Stephen Crane.

Deformed Transformed, The (1824). An unfinished poetic drama by Lord BYRON. The hero Arnold hates life because he is horribly deformed, but when he is by magic transformed into the shape of his own choosing, he goes forth a young Achilles, bent on adventure. He joins the besieging Bourbon army at Rome and attempts to rescue the beautiful but disdainful Olimpia; here the drama breaks off.

Degas, [Hilaire Germain] Edgar (1834–1917). French painter. Associated with the impressionists, although he was not interested in landscape, Degas is noted for his mastery of motion, his superb line and color, and the veracity of his observation. He painted, drew, made lithographs, etchings, and modeled clay figures, but his favorite medium was pastels. He portrayed ballet dancers at work or in the glare of spotlights, milliners, laundresses, and women at their toilet, with scientific attention to the strained, even ungraceful, momentary positions of unobserved movement and transfigured his subjects. It was from the Japanese, whose prints became known in France about 1860, that Degas derived much of the intimacy of presentation, originality of composition, and heightened decorative quality that marks his painting.

de Gaulle, Charles [André Joseph Marie] (1890–1970). French general and statesman. After the surrender of France to German forces in 1940, de Gaulle rallied his countrymen to the cause of a Free France, refusing to accept the terms of the armistice with Germany. Court-martialed in absentia and condemned to death (August, 1940), he appointed himself leader of the Free French and established his headquarters in England. At the Casablanca Conference with Winston Churchill and Franklin D. Roosevelt he represented France. After the war de Gaulle served as head of a provisional government, from November, 1944 to January, 1946. During twelve years of retirement from political life he wrote and published his three-volume memoirs, *Mémoires de guerre* (1954–1959). In English the books are titled *The Call to Honour* (1940–1942), *Unity* (1942–1944), and *Salvation* (1944–1946). In June 1958, at the height of the Algerian crisis, de Gaulle became the last premier of the Fourth Republic. A new constitution, providing for a much strengthened executive branch, was drafted and de Gaulle was elected the first President of the French Fifth Republic in December, 1958.

Degée, Olivier. See Jean TOUSSEUL.

Dehmel, Richard (1863–1920). German lyric poet influenced by Nietzsche. His early work, like that of his friend Liliencron, shows characteristics of naturalism, but he quickly developed an ecstatic subjective style similar to that of expressionism. His best-known volumes include *Erlösungen* (*Salvations*, 1891), *Weib und Welt* (*Woman and the World*, 1896), and *Schöne wilde Welt* (*Beautiful Wild World*, 1913).

Deimos. See PHOBOS.

Deiphobus (Deiphobos). In classic legend, one of the sons of Priam. Next to Hector, he was considered the bravest and boldest of all the Trojans. On the death of his brother Paris, he married Helen; but Helen betrayed him to her first husband, Menelaus, who slew him. He appears in the *Iliad* and *Aeneid*, and also in Shakespeare's *Troilus and Cressida*.

Dei plenus. Full of the god. Inspired, or possessed by frenzy as the Maenads in Greco-Roman mythology, who celebrated the orgiastic rites of DIONYSUS or the CORYBANTES dancing to Cybele.

Deirdre. The heroine of the greatest love story in Irish legend, found in the ULSTER CYCLE. Like the elopement tale PURSUIT OF DIARMAID AND GRÁINNE, the story of Deirdre is an early parallel to episodes in the Tristan and Iseult legend. The story has many versions, but, in general, Deirdre is the daughter of Felim, storyteller to Conchobar, king of Ulster. When she is born it is prophesied that she will be the most beautiful woman of Ireland and that she will bring bloodshed and death. To avert the prophecy, Conchobar determines to marry her when she comes of age. She is raised by the nurse Lavarcham in a secluded house in the woods where she sees no one but a few servants. Lavarcham's stories about Noisi, nephew of Conchobar and son of Usnech, fire her young imagination, and her constant pleas finally persuade Lavarcham to bring him to the house. Deirdre falls in love with him, and the two with Noisi's two brothers flee to Alba, or Scotland, to avoid the wrath of Conchobar. Ultimately they are persuaded to return and, betrayed, the sons of Usnech are killed. In some versions Deirdre kills herself at the grave of Noisi; in others, finding herself a captive of Conchobar, she dashes her brains against a rock. Synge's play *Deirdre of the Sorrows* (1910) is based on this legend, as is Yeats's *Deirdre* (1907).

deism. A belief in the existence of a personal God who is manifested neither supernaturally in history nor immanently in nature. Deism has been called "natural religion"; it is based on reason as opposed to revelation. It sprang up with the spread of scientific knowledge during the Renaissance and reached its height in the 18th century. Notable adherents of deism included Lord Herbert of Cherbury, the 3d earl of Shaftsbury, and Henry St. John in England, and Voltaire and the Encyclopedists in France. Their views affected literature—for example, Pope's ESSAY ON MAN—and the views of nature entertained by Wordsworth, Coleridge, and others.

De Jong, David Cornel (1905–1967). Dutchborn American writer. *Belly Fulla Straw* (1934) tells the story of a Dutch immigrant family. *Domination of June* (1944) is a volume of poetry. *Snowon-the-Mountain* (1946) contains some of his short stories. *With a Dutch Accent* (1944) describes his own experiences. *The Desperate Children* (1949) and *Two Sofas in the Parlor* (1952) are both novels.

Dekker, Thomas (1572?–?1632). English dramatist. He was one of the Henslowe group who worked long and hard to produce the quantities of plays needed by that company. Consequently, his plays are often hastily constructed but brightened by charming verse and Dekker's warm, easy feeling for people. Among his best are THE SHOEMAKER'S HOLIDAY, THE HONEST WHORE: PARTS I AND II, and the allegorical OLD FORTUNATUS. Most of his plays, however, were written in collaboration: THE ROARING GIRL, with Thomas Middleton; *The Virgin Martyr* (c. 1620), with Philip Massinger; *The Witch of Edmonton* (1621), with John Ford and William Rowley; and *The Sun's Darling* (1624), with Ford.

De Kooning, Willem (1904–   ). Dutch-born American artist. He began in 1948 a series of large paintings entitled *Woman*, whose unrestrained color and violent emotional brushwork immediately impressed many younger painters.

De Koven, Reginald (1857–1920). American composer of light operas (*The Begum*, 1887; *Robin Hood*, 1890; *Student King*, 1906) and the grand opera *Canterbury Pilgrims* (1917), with a libretto by Percy MacKaye. He is also known for his musical setting for Kipling's *Recessional*.

de Kruif, Paul (1890–1971). American bacteriologist and popular writer on science and medicine. De Kruif (whose name rhymes with *knife*) collaborated with Sinclair Lewis on much of the medical background for *Arrowsmith*. His own books on great figures and events in medical history are written in a lively style and have been very popular. Among them are *Microbe Hunters* (1926); *The Hunger Fighters* (1928); *Men Against Death* (1932); *Yellow Jack* (1934), a play written in collaboration with Sidney Howard; *The Fight for Life* (1938); *Man Against Insanity* (1957). His autobiography, *The Sweeping Wind*, appeared in 1962.

Delacroix, [Ferdinand Victor] Eugène (1799–1863). French painter. Leader of the romantic movement, he opposed the fire of his vision to the clarity of Ingres. He often used for his compositions past historical subjects, but he was also involved in contemporary struggles as evidenced by two of his most famous paintings: *The Massacre of Chios* (1824) and *Liberty Leading the People* (1831). A visit to North Africa, in 1832, furnished him with further subjects, notably hunting scenes, which he continued to paint throughout his life. Delacroix stressed movement and color for emotive and dramatic purposes. His vibrant palette, heightened by the juxtaposition of complementary colors, and his observation that shadows have color anticipated the discoveries of the impressionists. His famous *Journals* (1893–1895) are a distinguished contribution to literary and artistic criticism.

Delafield, E. M. Pen name of **Elizabeth Monica Dashwood** (1890–1943). English novelist. She wrote ironic comedies of manners, among them DIARY OF A PROVINCIAL LADY and *The Provincial Lady in America* (1934).

De la Mare, Walter (1873–1956). English poet, novelist, and anthologist. He was a romantic writer whose work expressed his interest in childhood, nature, dreams, and the uncanny. Much of his writing is nominally for children. Among his collections of poetry are *The Listeners* (1912), the title poem of which is his most famous and successful lyric; *Peacock Pie* (1913); and *Collected Poems* (1942). His prose writings include the novels *Henry Brocken* (1904), THE RETURN, and MEMOIRS OF A MIDGET; *Crossings, a Fairy Play* (1921), *Early One Morning* (1935), a book about children; and short stories. Among De la Mare's fine anthologies are COME HITHER and *Behold, This Dreamer!* (1939).

Deland, Margaret [ta Wade Campbell] (1857–1945). American novelist and short-story writer. Often associated with the local colorists, she was the creator of the Pennsylvania town of Old Chester, home of Dr. Lavendar, a kindly rector who appears in many of her stories. The town is the setting for *Old Chester Tales* (1898); *The Awakening of Helena Richie* (1906), a novel about a woman who must choose between her lover and her adopted son; and its sequel, *The Iron Woman* (1911). Other novels by Mrs. Deland include *John Ward, Preacher* (1888), about an orthodox minister married to a woman of liberal religious views, and *Philip and His Wife* (1894), about the conflict of an artist and his wife over the rearing of their only child.

Delaney, Shelagh (1936–   ). English playwright. She writes with wit and bawdy humor about the English lower class into which she was born. Her first play, *A Taste of Honey* (1958), was written when she was 18. The heroine is pregnant with the illegitimate child of a Negro sailor. She is helped by the companionship of her friend, a homosexual artist. Delaney's second play, *The Lion in Love* (1960), is the story of an impecunious street peddler and his extravagant wife. As with her first play, this work is filled with an extraordinary collection of vivid, unique characters.

de la Roche, Mazo (1879–1961). Canadian novelist. Miss de la Roche's novels of the Whiteoak family of Jalna, an estate in southern Ontario, have sold over two million copies. Among the many titles in the series are *Jalna* (1927), *Whiteoaks of Jalna*

(1933), *Young Renny* (1935), *Whiteoak Harvest* (1936), *Whiteoak Heritage* (1940), *Return to Jalna* (1946), *The Whiteoak Brothers* (1953), *Centenary at Jalna* (1958), *Morning at Jalna* (1960). *Ringing the Changes* (1957) is an autobiography.

Delectable Mountains. See PILGRIM'S PROGRESS.

Deledda, Grazia (1875–1936). Italian novelist. She is noted for her many novels and short stories depicting the peasantry of her native Sardinia. An incidental rather than deliberate realist, she was concerned chiefly with the inner experiences of her characters. Among her best known works are *Racconti Sardi* (1894), *Anime Oneste* (1895), *Elias Portolu* (1903), *Cenere* (1904), *L'Edera* (1908), and *La Madre* (*The Mother,* 1920), which was made into a motion picture with Eleonora Duse. She was awarded the Nobel Prize for literature in 1926.

Delia. The name of many ladies addressed in poetry. She was a shepherdess in Vergil's *Eclogues,* the lady love of Tibullus, and the lady to whom Samuel Daniel addressed his sonnets. The Delia of Pope's satires is the second Lady Delorraine of Ledwell Park.

Delias. The Delian ship (i.e. the ship of Delos) that according to legend, Theseus made; it carried him to Crete when he slew the Minotaur. In memory of this it was sent every fourth year with a solemn deputation to the Delian Apollo. During the festival, which lasted 30 days, no Athenian could be put to death, and as Socrates was condemned during this period his death was deferred till the return of the sacred vessel. The ship had been so often repaired that not a stick of the original vessel remained at that time.

Delibes, Léo (1836–1891). French composer. While he is most famous for his ballets, Delibes is also the composer of LAKMÉ, a staple of the French repertory of opera. His ballets include *La source* (1866), *Coppélia* (1870), *Jean de Nivelle* (1880), and *Kassya,* which was finished by Massenet after the composer's death.

Delight in Disorder (1648). A poem by Robert HERRICK. He pleads for "a sweet disorder in the dress" on the grounds that the little imperfections in a lady's dress are particularly beguiling.

Delilah. A Philistine woman in the Old Testament who was mistress of SAMSON and betrayed him. When she discovered that Samson's strength lay in his hair, she cut it off so that he was able to be captured by the Philistines (Judg. 16). Her name has come to be associated with any fascinating and deceitful woman.

Dell, Ethel M. Maiden name and pen name of **Ethel Mary Savage** (1881–1939). English novelist. She was the author of such novels as *The Way of an Eagle* (1912) and *Sown Among Thorns* (1939).

Dell, Floyd (1887–1969). American novelist, playwright, and editor. Early associated with the CHICAGO GROUP of writers, Dell moved to New York in 1914 and became an associate editor of the leftist periodicals *The Masses* and the *Liberator.* He later became known for a number of novels dealing with postwar disillusion, youth in the jazz age, and the Bohemian life current at the time in Greenwich Village. His most popular novel is MOON-CALF. *The Briary-Bush* (1921) is a sequel. *Janet March* (1923) and *Runaway* (1925) are other novels similar in theme and treatment. His most successful play was the comedy *Little Accident* (1928), based on his novel *The Unmarried Father* (1927). In 1927 he edited with Paul Jordan Smith an excellent edition of Burton's *Anatomy of Melancholy. Love in the Machine Age* (1930) is a reasoned statement of his attitudes toward sex. *Homecoming* (1933) is an autobiography.

Della Casa, Giovanni (1503–1556). Florentine cleric and author of the popular courtesy book, *Il Galateo,* written 1551–1555. Unlike *The Courtier* of Castiglione, it is realistically concerned with minor problems of good manners in polite, rather than courtly, society. It was translated by Peterson in 1576, in time to influence Elizabethan concepts of courtesy. To this day, *sapere il galateo* ("to know the *Galateo*") is a popular Italian phrase signifying that one is polite.

Della-Cruscans. A clique of English poets who met originally in Florence in the latter part of the 18th century. Their sentimental, affected work, which appeared in the periodical magazines the *World* and the *Oracle,* created for a time quite a furore, but was

Title page of Della Casa's *Il Galateo* in Robert Peterson's translation (1576).

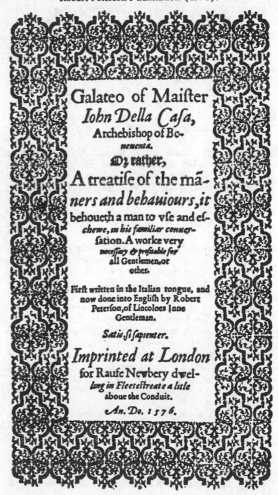

Galateo of Maifter *Iohn Della Cafa,* Archebishop of Beneuenta.

Or rather,

A treatife of the māners and behauiours, it behoueth a man to vfe and efchewe, in his familiar conuerfation. A worke very neceffary & profitable for all Gentlemen, or other.

Firft written in the Italian tongue, and now done into Englifh by Robert Peterfon, of Lincolnes Inne Gentleman.

Satis, fi fapienter.

Imprinted at London for Raufe Newbery dwelling in Fleeteftreate a litle aboue the Conduit.

An. Do. 1576.

mercilessly gibbeted in THE BAVIAD and *The Maeviad* of William Gifford. The clique took its name from the famous Academia della Crusca (literally, "Academy of Chaff") which was founded in Florence in 1582 with the object of purifying the Italian language —sifting away its "chaff"—and which published an important dictionary in 1611. Members of the clique included Robert Merry, who signed himself "Della Crusca," Mrs. Hannah Cowley, who signed herself Anna Matilda, James Cobb, a writer of farces, James Boswell, Thomas Morton, George Colman, and Mrs. Elizabeth Robinson.

Della Porta, Giambattista (1535-1615). Neapolitan author and amateur scientist. Della Porta wrote some 30 comedies as well as books on various scientific subjects. His plays were known in England by such dramatists as Middleton, and his *Magia naturalis* (1589) gained popular attention in its translation as *Natural Magic*.

Della Rovere. Italian family prominent during the Renaissance.

Francesco della Rovere (1414-1484) became Pope Sixtus IV in 1471. The famous Sistine Chapel of the Vatican bears his name.

Giuliano della Rovere, nephew of Francesco, became Pope Julius II in 1503, at the age of 60; still he led the papal forces in the field. Before his death in 1513, he had founded the Vatican Museum, begun the construction of St. Peter's, and employed Raphael, Bramante, and Michelangelo in various projects. In 1506, the Della Rovere became dukes of Urbino when Guidobaldo of Montefeltro died leaving no heir.

Deloney, Thomas (1543?-?1600). English prose writer, a silk-weaver and author of numerous BROADSIDE BALLADS. He is best known for his vivid tales of life among the craftsmen and laborers of London. The most famous of these is THE GENTLE CRAFT (1597).

Delos. A small island in the Cyclades where Apollo and Artemis were born. Having been the only place to accept Leto when she was ready to give birth to these gods, it was honored by becoming sacred to Apollo. This story is told in the *Homeric Hymn to Delian Apollo.* Delos was said to have been a floating island, which Poseidon finally made fast to the bottom of the sea.

Delphic oracle. An ancient oracle at Delphi, on the southern slope of Mount Parnassus. It was of extremely ancient origin, having originally belonged to a chthonic deity. Aeschylus' claim in the *Eumenides* that it belonged successively to Ge, Themis, and Phoebe—two of whom, at least, were earth goddesses —may not be far from wrong. In later times, the oracle was taken over by Apollo, who, according to the *Homeric Hymn to Pythian Apollo,* killed the python, a sacred snake associated with the oracle. The oracular utterances were made by the Pythia, a priestess who sat on a tripod over a cleft in the rock. Her incomprehensible mouthings were interpreted by a priest.

Although there were many oracles in the Greek world, the Delphic oracle was regarded as a final authority in religious matters. A great many of the most famous Greek myths involve the working out of oracles that issued from Delphi.

Associated with the shrine was the *omphalos,* a sacred stone that was regarded as the navel of the world, though various other centers made the same claim. Some authorities believe that the *omphalos* was the phallic cap of a tomb, possibly that of the python, since many oracles were associated with the tombs of heroes. In the first part of the *Eumenides,* Orestes clings to the *omphalos* in seeking sanctuary from the Erinyes or Furies.

Delphine (1802). Epistolary romantic novel by Mme de STAËL. It is the story of unfulfilled love between Delphine and Léonice (a character inspired by Benjamin CONSTANT DE REBECQUE). In the end he is shot as a traitor and she poisons herself. The book is one of the first feminine autobiographies in French literature. See Mme de VERNON.

Deluge, The. The second in a trilogy of historical novels by Henryk SIENKIEWICZ. See WITH FIRE AND SWORD.

De Marchi, Emilio (1851-1901). Italian novelist. Like Manzoni, he believed that the novel could be used legitimately as a guide to moral living. He was also influenced by the SCAPIGLIATURA and by the prose style of Verga and Capuana. His three best-known novels—*Demetrio Pianelli* (1889), *Arabella* (1892), and *Giacomo L'Idealista* (1897)—reflect his interest in contemporary social and moral problems. His protagonists are defeated by evil forces operating in society, yet their defeat awakens in them an attitude of resignation and purposeful self-sacrifice that seem to the writer the final victory of the human spirit. Demetrio Pianelli, for example, is an unassuming government clerk who realizes a capacity for love and self-sacrifice through a succession of tragic events.

An interesting example of De Marchi's narrative skill is *Il Cappello del Prete* (1888), which describes the hallucinating experiences of a priest's murderer. The scene is Naples, and the action centers on the Neapolitans' proverbial passion for the national lottery, a theme exploited by Matilda Serao in *Il Paese della Cuccagna* (1891).

Demeter. The Greek goddess of corn. Her principal myth concerned the abduction of her daughter Persephone by Hades, which took place in Sicily. When the young goddess, called also simply Kore (daughter), plucked a certain flower, the earth opened and Hades snatched her away to the underworld in his chariot. Demeter, bearing torches, sought her all over the world until Helios told her what had happened. She left Olympus in anger that the gods had permitted the abduction, and the earth grew desolate. Appearing as an old woman in the village of Eleusis, she was hospitably received by King Celeus and his wife Metaneira. She tended their son Demophoon, and would have immortalized him in the fire had not Metaneira seen her doing so and screamed. The goddess thereupon revealed her true identity and commanded that her rites should be celebrated at Eleusis.

Disturbed at the blight on the earth, Zeus approached Hades to bring about a reconciliation. Because Persephone had eaten pomegranate seeds in the underworld, she was not allowed to leave permanently, but it was arranged that she should spend two thirds of every year with her mother. In gratitude for Eleusinian hospitality, Demeter gave a bag of seeds to Celeus' son Triptolemus and sent him in a chariot by winged dragons throughout the world to plant corn and teach its culture. Demeter was very widely worshiped, but her most important cult center remained Eleusis, her major festival the ELEUSINIAN MYSTERIES. For other legends of Demeter see PELOPS and IASION.

Demetrius. In Shakespeare's MIDSUMMER NIGHT'S DREAM, a young man betrothed to Hermia by her father's decree. When she escapes to the forest with her lover Lysander, he pursues them and is pursued in turn by Helena, his jilted sweetheart.

De Mille, Cecil B[lount] (1881–1959). American motion-picture producer and director. De Mille began his long association with Hollywood when he went there in 1913 with Jesse L. Lasky and Samuel Goldwyn and directed *The Squaw Man,* one of the first full-length movies ever made. In 1921 he became president of Cecil B. De Mille Productions and began to produce the monumental motion-picture extravaganzas so identified with his name. Among the best-known of these are *The Ten Commandments* (1923; remake, 1956), *The King of Kings* (1927), *The Sign of the Cross* (1932), *The Plainsman* (1936), *Union Pacific* (1939), and *The Greatest Show on Earth* (1952).

Demiurge (Demiourgos). Any power or personality creating a world, real or imaginary. From the Greek for "worker of the people." The modern meaning goes back to Plato's use of the word for the inferior god who created the world.

Democracy (1880). A novel by Henry ADAMS, first published anonymously. A social and political satire based on the corruption of the second Grant administration, the book includes characters modeled on President Hayes and James G. Blaine. A charming and intelligent young widow, Madeleine Lee, moves to Washington "to touch with her own hands the massive machinery of society." She finally rejects an offer of marriage from a senator who has compromised his moral integrity for political advantage.

Democratic Vistas (1871). An essay by Walt WHITMAN. The poet, alarmed by the "hollowness of heart" in post-Civil War America, sees a decline in vigor and moral consciousness. Although the U.S. has enjoyed "unprecedented materialistic advancement," it has become increasingly superficial in social, moral, and intellectual spheres. "We live," says Whitman, "in an atmosphere of hypocrisy throughout."

Turning to the future, he envisions, in an America disburdened of foreign imitation, the rise of a group of artists. These men and women are needed, for "the work of the New World is not ended, but only fairly begun."

Democritus (Demokritos; c. 460–c. 370 B.C.). A philosopher, also called the Abderite and the Laughing Philosopher. He was born in ABDERA and traveled widely. He adopted the atomistic theory of LEUCIPPUS, holding that the universe is composed of atoms that move about in space and form themselves into bodies. Atoms are eternal, while bodies perish; the soul is a form of fire, which animates the human body. Democritus also held that pleasure, along with self-control, was the goal of life. His cheerful disposition won him the epithet of the Laughing Philosopher. He is supposed to have put out his eyes in order that he might think without outside disturbances.

Demodocus (Demodokos). A minstrel. According to Homer (ODYSSEY viii), he sang the amours of Ares and Aphrodite in the court of Alcinous while Odysseus was a guest there.

Demogorgon. A terrible deity, whose very name was capable of producing the most horrible effects. He is first mentioned by the 4th-century Christian writer, Lactantius, who, in so doing, is believed to have broken the spell of a mystery, for *Demogorgon* is supposed to be identical with the infernal Power of the ancients, the very mention of whose name brought death and disaster, to whom reference is made by Lucan and others. Hence Milton speaks of "the dreaded name of Demogorgon" in *Paradise Lost.* According to Ariosto, Demogorgon was a king of the elves and fays who lived on the Himalayas, and once in five years summoned all his subjects before him to give an account of their stewardship. Spenser, in *The Faerie Queene,* says that he dwells in the deep abyss with the three fatal sisters. Shelley so calls eternity in *Prometheus Unbound.*

De Morgan, William (1839–1917). English novelist. A retired manufacturer, De Morgan achieved immediate success at the age of 67 with his somewhat old-fashioned, Dickensian first novel, *Joseph Vance* (1906). *Alice-for-Short* (1907) and other successful novels followed.

Demosthenes (383–322 B.C.). The most famous of Greek orators. Opposed to the encroachment of Philip II of Macedon, Demosthenes delivered the first *Philippic* in 351 B.C. Five years later he was sent as an ambassador, with nine others, to conclude a peace with Philip. Dissatisfied with the agreement, Demosthenes refused to honor its terms. When Philip broke the treaty shortly afterward, the Greek patriotic party chose Demosthenes as its leader. After Philip's assassination in 336 B.C., Demosthenes was one of the leaders of the anti-Macedon uprising. Alexander demanded his arrest, but he was spared. When Harpalus, the Macedonian treasurer, fled to Athens, the 700 talents he had stolen from Alexander were placed in a vault to be returned; later, Demosthenes was accused of having accepted part of the money as a bribe. He was forced into exile, though the patriotic party recalled him at the death of Alexander. In 322 B.C. the joint rulers of Macedon, Antipater, and Craterus captured Athens, and Demosthenes took poison to escape arrest. His major orations are the three *Philippics* (351, 344, 341 B.C.), three *Olynthiacs* (349, 349 B.C.), *On the Peace* (346 B.C.), *On the Embassy* (344 B.C.), *On the Affairs of the Chersonese* (341 B.C.), and *On the Crown* (330 B.C.).

Demosthenes is traditionally supposed to have overcome speech defects by speaking over the roar of the sea with pebbles in his mouth. He rigorously applied himself to the development of a fine style, combining great rhetorical skill with simplicity and directness of language. His arguments were designed to appeal to a popular audience. Sixty-one speeches have come down to us under his name, although some are not considered genuine. He influenced, among others, Cicero, Quintilian, Burke, Fox, and Pitt.

demotic writing. An Egyptian hieroglyphic script, developed in the 5th century B.C. A simplified form of *hieratic* writing, running from left to right in horizontal lines, it was first used mainly for social and business purposes, but later for religious and literary purposes as well; it continued to be employed by the priests of Isis as late as A D. 452.

Dendin or **Dandin, Perrin** (*Fr.*, "Ninny"). In Rabelais' GARGANTUA AND PANTAGRUEL, an old man whom Judge BRIDLEGOOSE cites for the extraordinary number of disputes he settles, though he is not a judge by profession. When his son, Tenot Dendin, attempts to carry on his practice, he fails to settle a single quarrel because, as his father explains, he always intervenes at the very beginning of the dispute when the litigants are still averse to compromise. Perrin's secret is to wait until both parties are so tired of their dispute that they will welcome any judgment that will bring an end to their wrangling.

Racine gave the name "Dandin" to a character with a mania for judging in his comedy *Les Plaideurs* (1668). In La Fontaine's *Fables* (1678–1679), "Perrin Dandin" settles the dispute between two pilgrims over an oyster by eating it himself.

Denham, Sir John (1615–1669). Irish-born English poet. He was an architect by profession and was for a time surveyor general of works, with the young Christopher Wren as his assistant. Denham was famous in his own day for *The Sophy* (1642), a melodramatic tragedy, and *Cooper's Hill* (1642), a didactic poem. The latter was praised by Dryden, and imitated by Pope in *Windsor Forest* (1713). See George WITHER.

Denikin, Anton Ivanovich (1872–1947). Russian general. In 1917, he supported Kornilov's attempt to overthrow the Bolshevik regime. After Kornilov's death, during the civil war, he succeeded him as supreme commander of the White armies, and led the anti-Bolshevik forces in southern Russia until General Wrangel took over the command in 1920. Denikin then fled to Constantinople and, in 1926, went to live in France.

Dennis, Nigel (1912–   ). English novelist. He is the author of *Cards of Identity* (1955), a fantastic, nightmarish satire about modern man's loss of his sense of identity.

dénouement (*Fr.*, "the untying"). In drama and fiction, the final unwinding of the tangled elements of the plot which ends the suspense; it follows the climax. The word is also applied to the final solution of complicated sets of actions in life.

Denry the Audacious. See CARD, THE.

Deor's Lament or **The Complaint of Deor** (9th century?). Old English poem of 42 lines in ALLITERATIVE VERSE. The poet describes the misfortunes of Germanic heroes, which overshadow his own sad luck in being ousted by his lord in favor of another minstrel; there are seven unequal stanzas with the recurring refrain that as "that has passed, this will too."

de profundis (*Lat.* "out of the deep;" hence, an extremely bitter cry of wretchedness). Ps. 130 is so called from the first two words in the Latin version. It forms part of the Roman Catholic burial service. Oscar Wilde's letter to Lord Alfred Douglas, a personal essay of confession and reminiscence written in prison bore the title *De Profundis* (1905).

De Quincey, Thomas (1785–1859). English essayist and critic. He is famous for CONFESSIONS OF AN ENGLISH OPIUM-EATER, a fascinating memoir distinguished by great imaginative power and prose that is splendid and elaborate without stiffness. These qualities are also present in his personal and fugitive essays such as *Suspiria de Profundis* (1845), *The English Mail Coach* (1849), and *Murder Considered as One of the Fine Arts* (1827, 1839). One of the major critics of the romantic movement, he had clear, judicious taste and remarkable insight, and was learned and original though sometimes prolix and vague. He was closely associated with Wordsworth and Coleridge, residing for a time in the Lake Country, and was also acquainted with Lamb, Hazlitt, Hood, and other literary figures. Much of his work appeared in such journals as *Blackwood's Magazine* and was collected by himself in the 24-volume *Writings* (1851–1859).

Derain, André (1880–1954). French painter. He was an original member of the FAUVES and was closely associated with Matisse and Vlaminck. He exhibited at the first Fauve show in 1905 at Paris. By 1913 he began to evolve a more distinctive style in his work, influenced by primitive sculpture, cubism, and the works of van Gogh, Gauguin, and Seurat.

De Rerum Natura. See LUCRETIUS.

Derleth, August [William] (1909–1971). American novelist. He is best known for his *Sac Prairie Saga,* a group of regional novels depicting life in a Wisconsin community (modeled on Sauk City) from 1830 to the present; included in the series are *Still Is the Summer Night* (1937), *Wind Over Wisconsin* (1938), and *Restless Is the River* (1939). His *Wisconsin Saga* includes *Bright Journey* (1940) and *The Hills Stand Watch* (1960). He is also the author of *Still Small Voice* (1940), a biography of Zona Gale; *Selected Poems* (1944); *Sac Prairie People* (1948) and *Wisconsin Earth* (1948), collections of short stories; and several volumes of detective and science fiction.

De Roberto, Federico (1866–1927). Italian novelist. He is known as a leading exponent of the precisely realistic fiction produced by the *verismo* literary movement (see Luigi CAPUANA). A member of the Milanese circle of naturalistic writers among whom were G. VERGA and G. ROVETTA, De Roberto gave an objective, scholarly description of contemporary Italian society in his two major historical novels: *The Viceroys* (*I Vicerè;* 1894) and *L'imperio* (1929). *The Viceroys* is a lengthy account of the political fortunes of an aristocratic Sicilian family, the Uzedas of Francalanza, in the period between the collapse of the Bourbon dynasty and the proclamation of Italian unity (1859–1861). De Roberto's interest centers on a detailed study of character types, and his purpose is to show the determining influence of inherited family traits in the Uzedas' reaction to a critical moment in history.

L'imperio continues the study of the Uzeda family describing the fortunes of the youngest member, Count Consalvo, when he becomes a deputy to the new Italian parliament.

De Roberto began his writing career as a literary and art critic for the Milanese newspaper *Corriere della Sera.* A devoted friend of Verga at a time when the author of *The Malavoglias* was unfavorably received by the critics, De Roberto wrote his biography (which was never completed).

His minor novels are *Ermanno Raeli* (1889), *L'Illusione* (1891), *La Sorte* (1891), and *Spasimo* (1897).

Derzhavin, Gavril Romanovich (1743–1816). Russian poet. Though his verse is less polished than that of such poets as Pushkin and Tyutchev, Derzhavin's work can bear comparison with any Russian poetry for power and vividness. His best-known works are *Bog* (*Ode to God*, 1784), *Na smert' knyazya Meshcherskogo* (*On the Death of Prince Meshcherski*, 1779), and *Felitza* (*Felitsa*, 1782). This last is an ode to Catherine the Great, whom Derzhavin served as court poet and administrator.

Desai, Anita (1937–   ). Indian novelist writing in English. Born of Indian-German parentage, she was educated in Delhi. Her novel, *Cry the Peacock* (1963), reveals fine craftsmanship and subtle, delicate feeling.

De Sanctis, Francesco (1817–1883). Italian literary critic. Minister of education in the first Italian cabinet (1861) and professor of comparative literature at the University of Naples (1871–1877), he is noted as the founder of modern literary criticism in Italy. Influenced by Hegel, he formulated an aesthetic theory which maintains that an artist's formal expression is intrinsically linked to his idea-content; this theory, in turn, influenced Benedetto Croce. De Sanctis wrote critical essays such as *Saggi Critici* (1865) and *Nuovi Saggi Critici* (1872), and a celebrated *Storia della Letteratura Italiana* (1870–1871).

Descartes, René (1596–1650). French mathematician and philosopher. Father of the modern scientific method, he is also known as the originator of analytic geometry and progenitor of modern physiological psychology. Seeking absolute certainty in the application of "methodical doubt" to all received opinions, Descartes challenged the metaphysical view of the universe in his principal works, *Discours de la Méthode* (*Discourse on Method*, 1639) and *Principia philosophiae* (*Principles of Philosophy*, 1644), in which he divided the universe into mutually exclusive but interacting spirit and matter, the spirit subject to reason and the matter subject to mechanical laws. The resulting philosophy is called *Cartesianism* after its creator. Descartes formulated the principle Cogito, ergo sum (I think, therefore I am) and held it to be a model of certainty. See Nicolas Malebranche.

descent to the underworld. The motif of numerous stories in the mythology and folk lore of all peoples. The descent is usually made to rescue someone either abducted or rightfully dead, to find the answer to a question or discover a secret from the ruler of the underworld, or to seize some treasure. To partake of the food of the dead (or of fairyland in later folk lore) prevents the visitor from ever returning. Among the most famous descent stories are the Greek myths of Orpheus and Eurydice, Demeter and Persephone, and Heracles' bringing of Cerberus up from Hades and his rescue of Alcestis. Also well known are the Babylonian story of Ishtar's descent to rescue Tammuz, the Norse myth of Hermod's journey to Hel to bring back Balder. There are similar tales in Hindu, Chinese, and Japanese writings, and among the Ainus, Melanesians, North American Indians, and Eskimos. Descents to Hell are common also in early Christian literature.

Deschamps, Eustache (c. 1346–c. 1406). French poet and diplomat. He wrote a great number of bitterly satirical *ballades* and *rondeaux* about the political situation in France and the wars with England, and the first known critical treatise on the writing of poetry in French. His long, unfinished poem *Miroir de mariage* is a satire against women, including the prototype of the mother-in-law of French farce.

Desdemona. The innocent, artless, and lovely heroine of Shakespeare's Othello. She is the daughter of Brabantio.

De Senectute (44 b.c.). An essay on old age by Cicero, written in the form of a dialogue. Its main speaker, Cato the Elder, discourses to his younger friends on the advantages of a serene old age. From his name, it is often called the *Cato Major*.

Deserted Village, The (1770). A poem by Oliver Goldsmith, portraying the rural depopulation of the latter half of the eighteenth century. He attributes it to the increase in luxury, foreign trade, the enclosure of open pastures by absentee landowners, and the cancerous growth of London. The poem is dedicated to Sir Joshua Reynolds. See Auburn.

De Sica, Vittorio (1902–   ). Italian motion-picture director and actor. He made his screen debut in *What Rascals Men Are* (1932); he directed his first motion-picture, *Red Roses,* in 1939. He is best known for his highly distinguished films: *Shoe Shine* (1946) and *The Bicycle Thief* (1949).

Desire Under the Elms (1924). A tragedy by Eugene O'Neill. Set in New England, it deals with Ephraim Cabot and his new young wife, Abbie. Abbie seduces Eben, the youngest son of Ephraim, hoping to bear a son she can claim is Ephraim's. When it appears to Eben that Abbie has used him only for her own ends, he threatens to expose her infidelity; to prove her love for him she smothers the child. The play exemplifies O'Neill's interest in Freudian psychology and in the conflict between a repressive Calvinism and Dionysian surrender.

Desmarets de Saint-Sorlin, Jean (1596–1676). French poet, novelist, and playwright. An original member of the Académie française and holder of an administrative post by virtue of his intimacy with Richelieu, Desmarets opposed the Jansenists of Port-Royal in religious controversies and vehemently objected to Boileau's condemnation of national and Christian themes as subjects for epics, deriving his own epics *Clovis ou la France Chrestienne* (*Clovis, or Christian France,* 1657) and Esther (1673) from French history and the Bible respectively. His novel *Ariane* (1632) evokes the Rome of Nero, and his comedy *Les Visionnaires* (*The Visionaries,* 1637) ridicules the extravagances of certain fashionable ladies of his day, with cutting reference to Madame de Rambouillet. The play served Molière as model for *Les Femmes Savantes.*

Desmoulins, Camille (1760–1794). French journalist, pamphleteer, and collaborator with Mirabeau during the French Revolution. He was called *Procureur de la lanterne* (Fr., "agent of the lantern") for his anti-aristocratic pamphlet *Le Discours de la lanterne aux Parisiens.* As deputy to the Convention (1792), he had a small rôle to play, and two years later he was executed with Danton by Robespierre.

Desnos, Robert (1900–1945). French poet. At first associated with surrealism, he later turned to simple lyrics, like the love song *Poème à la mystérieuse* (1926) and other poems of love and liberty in *Corps et Biens* (1930) and *Fortunes* (1942). His

30 Chante-fables pour les enfants sages (1944) are animal fantasies in a singsong rhythm.

de Soto, Hernando or **Fernando** (1500?–1542). Spanish explorer. Having served with Pizarro in Peru, de Soto won permission from Charles V to conquer Florida, where he landed in 1539 with some 600 men. For the next three years he wandered through present Georgia, the Carolinas, Alabama, Mississippi, Arkansas, and Louisiana; though he found no gold, he is credited with discovering the Mississippi River in 1541. He died on the banks of the Mississippi, and his body was sunk in the river by his men.

Despair. See FAERIE QUEENE, THE.

Desportes, Philippe (1546–1606). Foremost French poet at the court of Henry III and successor to the Pléiade poets. Solely concerned with pleasing his protectors, he confined himself to writing love poetry so impersonal as to be applicable to any occasion (*Premières Oeuvres* [1573] and *Dernières Amours* [1583]) and to translating the *Psalms* (1591) to flatter the piety of Henry III. He cultivated the modish Petrarchan theme of idealized love and imitated the elaborate metaphors dear to the Italian poets. Clarity, suppleness, and harmony still lend charm to his poetry, otherwise lacking in substance.

Dessalines, Jean Jacques (1758–1806). Negro revolutionary leader and emperor of Haiti. As leader of the insurgent slaves, Dessalines fought alongside of Toussaint L'Ouverture and aided by the English, he succeeded in driving out the French in 1803. In 1804, Dessalines established the republic of Haiti, and the following year, under the title Jacques I, he became the country's emperor (1805–1806). His cruel reign led rapidly to his assassination by Henri CHRISTOPHE and Pétion.

Destouches, Louis Ferdinand. See Louis Ferdinand CÉLINE.

Destouches, Philippe. Pen name of **Philippe Néricault** (1680–1754). French dramatist. Famous for *Le Philosophe marié* (1727), *Le Glorieux* (1732) and other sentimental comedies, Destouches sought to make comedy morally edifying. His plays are early forerunners of the COMÉDIE LARMOYANTE.

Destruction of Sennacherib, The (1815). A well-known poem by Lord BYRON. It vividly portrays the annihilating plague that struck down the invading army of the Assyrian king Sennacherib in Palestine during the seventh century B.C.

Deucalion's Flood. The Deluge of Greek legend. Deucalion (Deukalion) was son of Prometheus and Clymene, and was king of Phthia, in Thessaly. When Zeus sent the deluge, Deucalion built a ship, and he and his wife, Pyrrha, were the only mortals saved. The ship at last rested on Mount Parnassus, and Deucalion was told by the oracle of Themis that to restore the human race he must cast the bones of his mother behind him. The two cast the stones of their mother Earth as directed. Those thrown by Deucalion became men, those thrown by his wife became women.

Bayard Taylor has a lyrical drama entitled *Prince Deukalion* (1878), in which he takes Deukalion and Pyrrha over all the earth and through all ages of history.

deus ex machina. A theatrical device used in Greek tragedy. In several plays of Euripides, a god appears at the last moment to provide the solution to the tangled problems of the main characters. The god is let down from the sky on a sort of crane. The phrase has come to refer to a playwright's use of external means to solve the problems of his characters—a practice generally frowned upon.

Deuteronomy. A book of the Old Testament, the last book of the Pentateuch. It reiterates the Mosaic law and, ending with the death of Moses, contains the final episodes in his life. It was probably written during the reign of Manasseh (c. 698–643 B.C.). Either suppressed or forgotten for a generation, the book was discovered in 621 B.C. hidden in the temple. It has been expanded by later writers. The original parts (most of chaps. 5–26 and 28) are thought to be the first book ever canonized as divine law.

Deutsch, Babette (1895–   ). American poet and critic. Her poems, which often have social implications, have been collected in many volumes, from *Banners* (1919) and *Honey out of the Rock* (1925) to *Animal, Vegetable, Mineral* (1954) and *Coming of Age: New and Selected Poems* (1959). *Potable Gold* (1929) and *This Modern Poetry* (1935), enlarged as *Poetry in Our Time* (1952, 1956, 1962), are critical works. Among her other books is one on Whitman (1941) and *Poetry Handbook* (1957; rev., 1961). Miss Deutsch is also a translator of German and Russian verse, usually in collaboration with her husband, Avrahm Yarmolinsky.

Deval, Jacques (1894–1972). French playwright of popular comedies. Best known for *Tovaritch* (1934), about a group of Czarist emigrés in France, Deval also wrote the play *Mademoiselle* (1932).

de Valera, Eamon (1882–   ). Irish statesman. De Valera was born in New York City of a Spanish father and an Irish mother. President of the Irish home rule party Sinn Fein from 1917 to 1926, he became the leading statesman of the Irish Free State, as prime minister and later as president.

de Vere, Aubrey Thomas (1814–1902). Anglo-Irish poet, essayist. A friend of Cardinal Newman, de Vere was a convert to Catholicism; his poetry found its inspiration in religion and in the myths and legends of Ireland, a country that he also defended in such prose works as *English Misrule and Irish Misdeeds* (1848). Three-volume editions of his poetry (*Poetical Works*) and criticism (*Critical Essays*) were published between 1884 and 1889. His *Recollections* (1897)—he was a friend of Tennyson, Browning, Carlyle—are interesting.

devil. In Jewish and Christian theology, an apostate spirit. The name is also given to the chief of devils, known as *the Devil,* who is the supreme spirit of evil, the adversary of God, the enemy and tempter of man, and the ruler of Hell. In the Bible and Apocrypha the Devil or devils are variously referred to as SATAN, ASMODEUS, BEELZEBUB, SAMAEL, and, according to the Church Fathers, as LUCIFER. Devils' names in literature and popular usage include MEPHISTOPHELES, Auld Nick, AULD HORNIE, Auld Ane, Clootie, and Hangie.

The Devil and devils are frequently represented with a cloven foot, since rabbinical writers refer to them as *seirizzim* (goats). As the goat is the prototype of uncleanliness, the prince of unclean spirits is aptly represented under this emblem.

Devil and Daniel Webster, The (1937). A short story by Stephen Vincent BENÉT. First published in the *Saturday Evening Post,* it was adapted as an opera (1938) with music by Douglas Moore, and later was made into a play. In it, a New England farmer, Jabez Stone, sells his soul to the Devil for material prosperity, but is saved from paying his debt by the oratorical eloquence of Daniel Webster before a demonic jury.

Devil and Tom Walker, The (1824). A story by Washington IRVING. It first appeared in his collection, TALES OF A TRAVELLER. The story concerns the devil's attempt to hold Tom tc his bargain. Despite Tom's wiles, the devil succeeds.

Devils, The. See POSSESSED, THE.

Devil's Advocate. The *advocatus diaboli,* a man appointed to attest the claims of a candidate for canonization before a papal court. He advances all arguments he can against the candidate, who is defended by the *advocatus dei* (God's advocate), who says all he can in support of the proposed canonization. By extension, the term is used of a destructive critic, or one who deliberately searches for flaws in order to bring out the whole truth.

Devil's Disciple, The (1897). A play by George Bernard SHAW. It is set in America during the Revolution. Dick Dudgeon, a reprobate, allows himself, to his own surprise, to be arrested by the English and sentenced to death in place of Parson Anderson. The parson, too, finds a new side to his personality, when he leads an armed band to fight the British and rescue Dick. Shaw's thesis is that convention and circumstance fix a person's life, but under crisis people make startling discoveries about themselves. An exciting and brilliant play, *The Devil's Disciple* makes particular fun of the military.

Devil's General, The (Des Teufels General; 1946). A play by Carl ZUCKMAYER. It depicts the inner struggle of a Nazi *Luftwaffe* general who, though in principle opposed to Nazism, manages to rationalize his position as a servant of the regime. But when he is confronted by a saboteur, a man true to his principles, who is doing his best to hamper the German war effort, the general recognizes the untenability of his own compromise and deliberately flies off to his death in a sabotaged plane.

De Vinne, Theodore Low (1828–1914). American master printer and historian. He founded and managed Theo. L. De Vinne & Co., later the De Vinne Press, and became widely known for the excellence of his printing and engravings. He was the founder and sixth president of the Grolier Club (1884), a society of bibliophiles in New York City. Among his books are *The Invention of Printing* (1876), and *The Practice of Typography* (4 v., 1900–1904).

Devoción de la cruz, La. See Pedro CALDERÓN DE LA BARCA.

Devotions upon Emergent Occasions (1624). A series of meditations on the "Variable, and therefore miserable condition of Man" by John DONNE. The work was ostensibly written during a long, grave illness. Its style is highly metaphorical and complex. It contains the famous passage from which Ernest Hemingway drew the title of *For Whom the Bell Tolls* (1940):

No man is an Iland, intire of it selfe; every man is a peece of the Continent, a part of the maine; if a Clod bee washed away by the Sea, Europe is the lesse, as well as if a Promontorie were . . ; any mans death diminishes me, because I am involved in Mankinde; And therefore never send to know for whom the bell tolls; It tolls for thee.

De Voto, Bernard [Augustine] (1897–1955) American historian and critic. De Voto first gained public attention with his *Mark Twain in America* (1932), a rebuttal to Van Wyck Brooks's *Ordeal of Mark Twain* (1920). He also taught at Harvard, filled "The Easy Chair" of *Harper's* from 1935 to 1955, and wrote several novels, including *The Crooked Mile* (1924) and *Mountain Time* (1947). The work that he himself rightly regarded as his most important was his historical writing, principally *The Year of Decision: 1846* (1943); *Across the Wide Missouri* (1947), which won a Pulitzer Prize; and *The Course of Empire* (1952).

Devushkin, Makar Alekseyevich. The hero of Feodor Dostoevski's short novel, POOR FOLK. Devushkin is a timid clerk, desperately in love with Varvara Alekseyevna Dobroselova, and acutely conscious of the impossibility of his love because of his greater age and extreme poverty. His condition is sharply brought home to him when he reads Nikolai Gogol's short story, *The Overcoat,* which portrays a downtrodden clerk too much like Devushkin himself. He complains about writers dealing with such subjects in one of his letters to Varvara.

Dewey, George (1837–1917). American naval officer. As commander of the Asiatic Squadron during the Spanish-American War, Dewey moved his fleet into Manila Bay and in a seven-hour battle destroyed the Spanish naval force in the Far East. He then blockaded Manila Bay, enabling General Wesley Merritt to land his troops and effect the conquest of the Philippines.

Dewey, John (1859–1952). American teacher, philosopher and educational reformer. A believer in William James's PRAGMATISM, Dewey employed the principles of that philosophy in his progressive movement in education. He advocated "learning by doing," rejecting traditional methods of teaching by rote. Although his principles have been adopted by many, not all of Dewey's disciples are restrained by his common sense. Among his many books are *The School and Society* (1900; rev. 1908, 1932), *Interest and Effort in Education* (1913), *Democracy and Education* (1916), *The Quest for Certainty* (1929), *Art as Experience* (1934), and *The Problems of Man* (1946).

Dewey, Melvil (1851–1931). American librarian. Dewey invented his decimal system of library classification while still a student librarian at Amherst College (1874–1876). Referred to as the DEWEY DECIMAL SYSTEM, it is widely used in the U.S. Dewey later became the librarian of Columbia University, and there founded the first school of library science (1887). He was director of the New York State Library from 1889 to 1906.

Dewey decimal system. A system of book classification for library cataloguing. It was devised by Melvil DEWEY in 1876. The system divides books into 10 main groups, represented by figures, as in the following example:

800–899 Literature (novels, plays, poetry, criticism).

Each of the main classes is then further subdivided. When the distinctions between books become fine, decimals are used; this gave the system its name. Unusually large libraries have abandoned the Dewey system for that used by the Library of Congress, but approximately 85% retain it.

Dexter, Timothy (1747–1806). American merchant and eccentric. Becoming enormously wealthy as the result of a series of transactions that should logically have proved disastrous, he named himself "Lord Timothy Dexter" and built a great mansion in Newburyport, Mass. He wrote an admiring and amusing account of his own exploits in *A Pickle for the Knowing Ones, or Plain Truths in a Homespun Dress* (1802). The book had no punctuation, but Dexter satisfied his critics by including a page full of various punctuation marks in a second edition, inviting his readers to "peper and solt it as they plese." John P. Marquand wrote a biography, *Lord Timothy Dexter,* in 1925, which he revised in 1960 as *Timothy Dexter Revisited.*

Dey, Frederick Van Rensselaer. See Nick CARTER.

dharma (*Sans.,* "that which binds"). An ethical code, way of life, social conscience, truth, the natural order. To a Hindu, *sva-dharma* (*sva,* self) would mean one's right to perform the duties dictated by one's nature and conscience. In Buddhism *dharma* is the law of the Buddha.

Dhôtel, André (1900–   ). French novelist. In such tales as *Faraway* (*Le Pays où l'on n'arrive jamais,* 1955), Dhôtel creates a poetic atmosphere of magic and suspense.

Diablo cojuelo, El. See Luis VÉLEZ DE GUEVARA.

Diafoirus. The name of 2 quack doctors, father and son, in Molière's comedy LE MALADE IMAGINAIRE. As their name suggests, they are obsessed with the liver.

Diaghilev, Sergei Pavlovitch (1872–1919). Art critic, impresario, and founder (1909) and director of the Russian Ballet in Paris. He encouraged new ideas and techniques, first as an art critic, later in his ballets, which provided an audience for experiments in the various arts of music, painting, costume design, and dance. As a result, he attracted the talents of such composers as Claude Debussy, Maurice Ravel, Igor Stravinsky, and the members of Les SIX; such artists as Pablo Picasso, Leon Bakst,

The punctuation from Dexter's *A Pickle,* etc.

[Note to Dexter's Second Edition.]

fouder mister printer the Nowing ones complane of my book the fust edition had no stops I put in A Nuf here and thay may peper and solt it as they plese

,,
,,
,,
::
.............!!!!!!!!!!!!!!!!!!!!
...............!!!!!!!!!!!!!
................!!!!!!!
.................!
,,
,,,.............. ?????????????????????? ....,

Henri Matisse, and Georges Braque; such dancers and choreographers as M. M. Fokine, Anna Pavlova, Vaslav Nijinsky, and Léonide Massine. Many studies of Diaghilev and his ballet have been written.

Dial, The. A magazine founded in New England in 1840. The organ of the Transcendentalist movement, its founders were Theodore PARKER, Bronson ALCOTT, Orestes BROWNSON, Margaret FULLER, and Ralph Waldo EMERSON. Miss Fuller served as editor from 1840 to 1842, and Emerson, with Thoreau's help, took over until 1844, when the magazine ceased publication. During its short history, it wielded a great deal of influence in literary, philosophic, and religious thought. In addition to publishing the work of its founders, *The Dial* published the poetry of Jones Very and William Ellery Channing.

Since 1844, three other magazines have taken the same name. Moncure Conway founded the second *Dial* in 1860, in Cincinnati. In 1880, a conservative group founded the third *Dial* in Chicago. When it moved to New York in 1918, it became the outstanding literary review of its time. Until 1920, with the aid of Conrad AIKEN, Randolph BOURNE, and Van Wyck BROOKS, it published articles by leading radical thinkers including John Dewey and Thorstein Veblen. After 1920, it was devoted to the encouragement of *avant-garde* authors. Marianne MOORE became editor in 1926. The magazine ceased publication three years later.

The present *Dial,* a literary quarterly, was founded in 1959. It is edited by James Silberman.

Dialogues des morts. See Bernard le Bovier de FONTENELLE.

Dialogues of the Dead. See Bernard le Bovier de FONTENELLE.

Diamond. See FAERIE QUEENE, THE.

diamond jousts. Jousts instituted by King Arthur, "who by that name had named them, since a diamond was the prize." The story, as embroidered by Tennyson in his *Launcelot and Elaine* from Malory, is that Arthur found nine diamonds from the crown of a slain knight and offered them as the prize of nine jousts in successive years. Launcelot had won them all, but when he laid them before the queen, Guinevere, in a fit of jealousy—the result of believing false rumors about Launcelot and Elaine—flung them into the river a moment before the corpse of Elaine passed in the barge.

Diamond Necklace Affair. A famous scandal in French history (1783–1785). The jewelers Böhmer and Bassenge had originally made the necklace, containing 500 diamonds, for Mme Du Barry; but, after the death of Louis XV, they were unable to dispose of it. To recoup their investment, they repeatedly but unsuccessfully pressed MARIE ANTOINETTE to buy it. The scheming, so-called Comtesse, Jeanne de La Motte, a high-class courtesan, knowing that Cardinal de Rohan, a rich, profligate churchman, wished to ingratiate himself with the queen—partly because he fatuously believed he could become her lover, and partly to regain royal favor—fraudulently persuaded him that Marie Antoinette secretly wished to buy the necklace, convincing him that the queen had chosen him to negotiate with the jewelers on her behalf. He agreed to act as intermediary and to deliver the necklace to Mme de La Motte who, in turn, would deliver it to Marie Antoinette. To lend credibility to her ruse, Mme de La Motte arranged for a young modiste and woman of the streets to impersonate the queen at a short garden meeting with Rohan; she also forged several letters which fanned the cardinal's infatuation and confirmed his role as go-between. He made a down payment on the necklace and delivered it to Mme de La Motte who, with her young accomplice and lover Rétaux de Villette, took it apart, sold the individual diamonds in England and Paris, and kept the money herself. Böhmer tried to collect the balance from the Queen, insisting that she had authorized Rohan to purchase it. The Queen, indignant at being accused of dishonesty, reported the affair to her husband, Louis XVI, who caused a sensation by having the cardinal arrested publicly. At the ensuing trial, Rohan was exonerated, but exiled to the country by the king, who still believed him guilty; Marie Antoinette was cleared of any duplicity; Mme de La Motte was publicly branded, whipped, and sentenced to life imprisonment. She later escaped to England where she wrote her memoirs, accusing the queen.

Diana. An ancient Italian and Roman divinity, later identified with the Olympian goddess ARTEMIS.

Diane de Poitiers (1499–1566). Mistress of Henry II of France. She wielded immense power over Henry, who was 10 years her junior, until his death in 1559. She spent her last years at her château at Anet, which had been designed for her by Philibert Delorme, a celebrated architect.

Dianora. See GARDEN IN JANUARY, A.

Diary of a Country Priest, The (*Journal d'un curé de campagne*; 1936). A novel by Georges BERNANOS. It describes the struggles of a young priest with his diseased body and his ineffective parish projects. He is uncertain about whether his intervention in the affairs of the Count's family is true service to God.

Diary of Anne Frank. See Anne FRANK.

Diary of a Provincial Lady (1930). A novel, in diary form, by E. M. DELAFIELD. A phlegmatic husband, disconcerting children, temperamental servants, and dreadful neighbors are the problems of ordinary upper-middle-class domestic life of the period.

Diary of a Scoundrel, The (*Na vsyakogo mudretza dovolno prostoty*; 1868). A comedy by Aleksandr OSTROVSKI. A clever rogue, Glumov takes advantage of the foibles of society to advance himself. He is discredited by the discovery of his diary, in which he ridicules the pretensions and stupidity of his associates, but he brazenly confronts the discoverers and triumphs.

Diary of a Writer, A (*Dnevnik pisatelya*; 1873, 1876–1877, 1880–1881). A series of collected articles and short sketches published in the form of a journal by Feodor DOSTOEVSKI. He began the project as a section in *Grazhdanin* (*The Citizen*), a weekly newspaper he edited in 1873–1874. The so-called diary was concerned mostly with political and social questions, although Dostoevski did publish in it a few of his short stories, including *Krotkaya* (*The Meek One*, 1876), and *Son smeshnogo cheloveka* (*The Dream of a Ridiculous Man*, 1877). In 1880, the *Diary* contained Dostoevski's famous speech at the Pushkin celebration in Moscow.

Díaz, Porfirio (1830–1915). Mexican dictator. An erstwhile supporter of Juárez, Díaz seized power in 1876 and ruled Mexico for 35 years. Although his regime brought political and fiscal stability, only a handful of politicians, landowners, and foreign capitalists prospered, while the rural masses lived in virtual servitude. Díaz was ousted in 1911 and died in exile in Paris.

Díaz de Bivar, Rodrigo or **Ruy.** See CID, POEMA or CANTAR DE MIO.

Díaz del Castillo, Bernal (1496–1584). Spanish soldier and historian. Díaz was one of the 400 soldiers who took part in the Spanish conquest of Mexico; he later settled down on an estate in Guatemala. Piqued by an official history of the conquest which he felt unduly glorified the achievements of Cortez, Díaz, then an octogenarian, attempted to tell what really happened in his *Historia verdadera de la conquista de la Nueva España* (*True History of the Conquest of New Spain*, 1632), perhaps the best popular history in the Spanish language. With a plethora of minute yet vivid detail, Díaz celebrates the exploits of the common soldiers who accompanied Cortez in a style remarkable for its homely vigor. An intensely personal document in which Díaz does not minimize his own achievements and depicts Cortez as a very fallible human being, the work gives an excellent picture of the individuality and tenacity that characterized the 16th-century conquistadors.

Dichtung und Wahrheit (**Poetry and Truth,** 1811–1833). An autobiography by Johann Wolfgang von GOETHE. It is not so much a simple recounting of the events of his life as an attempt to explain the major strains of his inner development and set forth the essential principles on which his poetic activity was based.

Dickens, Charles (1812–1870). English novelist, the most popular and considered by many the greatest of his country. Like that of the children in many of his novels, Dickens' childhood was a difficult and unhappy one; his father, a navy clerk, was constantly in debt and was thrown into debtors' prison, and Dickens was sent to work in a blacking factory at the age of 12. Most bitter for him was his parents' failure to educate him. He reacted to this indifference by working hard, a lifelong characteristic. He became an office boy in a law firm, then a county reporter, and finally a reporter of debates in Parliament for the *Morning Chronicle* in 1835. His *Sketches by Boz*, satires on daily life, were serialized in the *Old Monthly Magazine* (1833–1835). Immediately asked to do another series, he wrote *The Posthumous Papers of the Pickwick Club*, better known simply as PICKWICK PAPERS; these were illustrated by Phiz (H. K. Browne) and made Dickens successful at 24. With OLIVER TWIST, Dickens began his indictment of the society of his place and time, a society that grossly mistreated and abused the poor, especially children, driving them to crime. While working on *Twist*, his wife Catherine's sister died; his deep grief and lifelong utterances of love for this sister-in-law underline his less profound relationship with his wife, from whom he was separated in 1858. They had 10 children.

NICHOLAS NICKLEBY, like *Oliver Twist*, was serialized in *Bentley's Miscellany*. The next two, BARNABY RUDGE and THE OLD CURIOSITY SHOP, were serialized in Dickens' own, new weekly periodical, *Master Humphrey's Clock*; they were his least successful novels. In 1842, Dickens made a trip to the U.S. where he trod on native sensibilities by urging the abolition of slavery and the establishment of an international copyright. Back in England, he published his insulting AMERICAN NOTES and MARTIN CHUZZLEWIT, a powerfully satiric novel of selfishness, hypocrisy, and financial speculation as it bloomed in insular England and the open spaces but narrow minds of the U.S. Dickens met with sensational success with the publication of A CHRISTMAS CAROL and he followed it in consecutive years with other Christmas books including A CRICKET ON THE HEARTH. His next novel, DOMBEY AND SON, was written in Switzerland.

In 1850 Dickens founded the weekly *Household Words*, and in 1859 another weekly, *All the Year Round*, both of which he kept until his death; most of his later works were published in these periodicals.

With DAVID COPPERFIELD, his more mature works begin. Autobiographical, it was Dickens' own favorite. In BLEAK HOUSE, an exposé of political corruption and court delay, Dickens displays a gloomy lack of faith in the ability of governmental institutions, held together with red tape and filled with archaic practices, to benefit the people. HARD TIMES is a protest against utilitarian lack of feeling and imagination and is perhaps Dickens' most single-minded social novel. Further disillusionment came in LITTLE DORRIT, which included memories of Dickens' father in debtors' prison. Next came his dramatic novel A TALE OF TWO CITIES. This was soon followed by GREAT EXPECTATIONS, considered by many as his finest work. OUR MUTUAL FRIEND is highly regarded by some critics; but others find it humorless, diffuse, and contrived. In 1858, Dickens began to give public readings, which he continued on his second visit to the U.S. in 1867–1868. He died in England while working on his novel *The Mystery of* EDWIN DROOD. He was buried in Westminster Abbey.

No other English writer has created a world of characters so distinctively cruel or suffering, comic or repugnant as Dickens has; no other writer has written so convincingly of the wrongs inflicted on children by adults in the 19th century. Attacks on Dickens' sentimentality and tendency to caricature have detracted little from his stature as a great humorist and creator of characters; these he brought to life with a wealth of meaningful detail, a myriad of odd gestures, expressions, speech patterns, and physiognomies. As a social critic he focused sharply on the iniquities and inequities of his environment. See BOZ.

Dickens, Monica (1915–   ). English novelist, great-granddaughter of Charles Dickens. Her popular early books were entertaining accounts of her experiences in new jobs—as a cook in *One Pair of Hands* (1939) and nurse in *One Pair of Feet* (1942). Other books include *Man Overboard* (1958), *The Heart of London* (1961), and *Cobbler's Dream* (1963).

Dickinson, Emily (1830–1886). American poet. One of the three children of Edward Dickinson, lawyer and treasurer of Amherst College, she shared a cultivated family life. After attending Amherst Institute and Mount Holyoke Female Seminary, she retired to her home; later, dressing only in white, she rarely came down from her room to meet her guests. Her father, a stern Calvinist who served a term in Congress, dominated his daughter's life. Among the other men who influenced her were the Reverend Charles Wadsworth, whose trip to California is cryptically referred to in the poetry; Samuel Bowles, editor of the *Springfield Daily Republican*, where one of her poems appeared; Benjamin F. Newton, a short-lived scholar and lawyer, who introduced her to the works of Emerson; T. W. HIGGINSON, soldier and critic; and Judge Otis P. Lord, a family friend.

Throughout her adult life Emily Dickinson wrote poetry; only two of the almost 2,000 poems she wrote were published in her lifetime. Uniformly short, consisting usually of four-line stanzas, the poems are written in a terse, aphoristic style. Although she personally rejected Calvinist theology, Emily Dickinson was influenced by the philosophy of Jonathan Edwards; like Emerson, she found that spirit manifested in nature. Physically isolated, she belongs in the tradition of American poetry that includes Whitman and Robert Frost.

Dickinson, Goldsworthy Lowes (1862–1932). English philosopher, essayist, and worker for international peace. *The Greek View of Life* (1896) is among his books.

Dickson, Carter or **Carr**. See John Dickson CARR.

Di Costanzo, Angelo (1507–1591). Italian Renaissance sonneteer and historian of his native city, Naples. He was important in the development of Petrarchism and Marinism because of his attempts at bringing to the sonnet the witty effects of epigrams. He was especially popular in the 18th century, among the Arcadians. His *Rime* (*Verses*) were not published until 1709.

dictator. In ancient Rome, the temporary supreme commander. In times of great national danger, the senate would call upon the consuls to appoint a dictator who would hold office for no longer than six months. See CINCINNATUS.

Dictator of Letters. Epithet for VOLTAIRE (François Marie Arouet), who was also called "the Great Pan."

Dicte (Dikte). A Cretan mountain where, in a cave, the infant Zeus was tended by nymphs and the CURETES and suckled by the goat Amaltheia. An actual cave on this mountain has proved through excavation to have been a center of an important Minoan cult centering about a young child.

diction. Word choice in verbal expression with all that such choice implies in questions of correctness, clarity, and style. The *mot juste*, or exactly right word, is the ideal of good diction. Popularly, it is often confused with enunciation.

Dictionary of the English Language (1755). A monumental work by Samuel JOHNSON, which made his reputation and was the standard dictionary until Noah Webster's. In 1747, Johnson applied to Lord CHESTERFIELD for patronage and was refused; upon completion of the work, Chesterfield made a belated offer, which Johnson then refused in a famous letter. In his preface to the *Dictionary,* addressing critics, Johnson wrote, ". . . and it may repress the triumph of malignant criticism to observe, that if our language is not here fully displayed, I have only failed in an attempt which no human powers have hitherto completed."

Dictys Cretensis. Reputed author of an alleged, eye-witness account in Latin of the siege of Troy, which was one of the versions of the Troilus legend known to the Middle Ages. Both Dictys Cretensis and DARES PHRYGIUS are names mentioned by Homer.

didactic poetry. Poetry to teach factual information or moral lessons. Didactic verse has since time immemorial combined the mnemonic virtues of rhyme and rhythm with information to be memorized, as in the nursery rhyme "Thirty days hath September." In the view of some philosophers, the underlying aim of all literature is at least in part didactic; but aside from such an underlying aim, purely didactic poetry is no longer written. Some examples of didactic poetry in literary history are: Lucretius's *De Rerum Natura*, Vergil's *Georgics*, Erasmus Darwin's *Botanic Garden*, and Pope's *Essay on Man*.

Diderot, Denis. Nicknamed **Pantophile Diderot** (1713–1784). French encyclopedist, materialistic philosopher, novelist, satirist, dramatist, and art critic. Until recently, he was famous mainly for having compiled and edited, with d'ALEMBERT and others, the ENCYCLOPÉDIE OU DICTIONNAIRE RAISONNÉ DES SCIENCES, DES ARTS ET DES MÉTIERS (28 vols., 5 suppls., 2 index vols.). Among his philosophic works are *Pensées philosophiques* (1746), which is deistic in thought and a defense of human passions; *Lettre sur les aveugles . . .* (1749), a study of how the blind learn, containing his view on materialism (he was imprisoned for three months because of this work); *Lettre sur les sourds et les muets* (1749), one of the first studies on the deaf and dumb, as well as an inquiry into aesthetics; *Pensées sur l'interprétation de la nature* (1753), containing ideas which foreshadow discoveries in biology, the theory of transformism, and natural selection. Diderot's audacity and profundity in scientific thought are strikingly illustrated in his *Le Rêve de d'Alembert* (1769, pub. 1830), one of his three dramatic dialogues in which he presents surprising insights into the physical, moral, and social universe; in it is found the first modern conception of the cellular structure of matter. His novels include *Les Bijoux indiscrets* (1748); *La Religieuse* (written 1760, pub. 1796), an attack on life in convents; LE NEVEU DE RAMEAU, a dialectical satire on contemporary society and conventional morality; and the satirico-philosophical JACQUES LE FATALISTE, in which Diderot poses the problem of freedom versus predeterminism, and at the same time experiments with the form of the novel. Among Diderot's plays, the most famous are *Le Père de famille* (1758) and *Le Fils naturel* (1757). Moral in tone, and rather mediocre, they illustrate his theories on the drama and became prototypes for the BOURGEOIS DRAMA. Diderot's theories on the drama, which he developed in several essays, e.g., *Paradoxe sur le comédien* (1773–1778, pub. 1830), were put into practice by Emile Augier and Dumas fils, in their moralistic, social-minded plays. In the *Salons*, written for Baron de Grimm's *Correspondance littéraire, philosophique et critique*, Diderot inaugurated art criticism as a literary genre. His *Lettres à Sophie Volland* attest to his genius as a letter-writer.

Dido. Also known as **Elissa.** The name given by Vergil in his AENEID to the founder and queen of Carthage. According to Roman legend, she fled from Phoenicia to North Africa after her brother Pygmalion, king of Tyre, had murdered her husband, Sychaeus, for his wealth. (See BYRSA.) The name Dido was also an epithet of the Phoenician goddess Astarte.

In Vergil's poem, she hospitably receives Aeneas and the Trojans when they are shipwrecked on her shores. Through the plotting of the goddess Venus, she falls in love with Aeneas and tries to persuade him to settle in North Africa and share Carthage with her. But when the will of the gods is announced to him by their messenger Mercury, Aeneas yields, half against his will: he must abandon Dido and found his own nation in Italy. After his departure, Dido, in grief, takes her life by the sword, and is cremated on a great funeral pyre which Aeneas, now far out to sea, beholds burning on the shore.

Ovid's *Heroides* contains a letter, supposedly written by Dido to Aeneas, in which she reminds him of all she has done for him and begs him to remain. Other works dealing with the unfortunate queen include Nash and Marlowe's tragedy *Dido, Queen of Carthage* (c. 1593), Purcell's opera *Dido and Aeneas* (1689), and Piccinni's opera *Didon* (1783).

Diego [Cendoya], Gerardo (1895–). Spanish poet and scholar. His well-known earlier collections, *Imagen* (1922), *Manual de espumas* (1924), and *Versos humanos* (1925), reveal a style which relates the growth of a poem to that of a living organism. His recent work includes the volume *Romancero de la novia* (1944).

Diego, San. A modification of Santiago (*Span.*, St. JAMES, patron saint of Spain).

Dies Irae (*Lat.*, Day of Wrath). A famous medieval hymn on the last judgment, probably composed by Thomas of Celano, a native of Abruzzi, who died in 1255. It is derived from the Vulgate version of Joel 2:31, and used in the Mass for the Dead and on All Souls' Day.

Dietrich of Bern. See THEODORIC THE GREAT.

Digby, Sir Kenelm (1603–1665). English naval commander, diplomat, writer, and council member of the Royal Society. He discovered the necessity of oxygen for plant life. Among his works are *A Treatise of the Nature of Bodies* (1644), *A Treatise Declaring the Operations and Nature of Man's Soul* (1644), and his allegorical *Memoirs* (1827).

dilettante (from Italian; literally, one who takes delight in a thing). Like *amateur*, which means literally, one who likes a thing, the term *dilettante* is especially applied with reference to the fine arts. Since mere fondness of an art guarantees neither knowledge nor ability, *amateur* as well as *dilettante* have come to mean one who dabbles in a given subject. The Spanish word *aficionado*, popularized in English with the flurry of interest in bullfighting, carries the sense of the knowledgeable enthusiast that the other two words have nearly lost.

Dill Pickle, A (1920). A short story by Katherine MANSFIELD. A pair of lovers meet by chance in a restaurant after they have been separated for six years. In the half hour they spend together she rediscovers his charm and regrets ever leaving him, then rediscovers his faults and leaves him sitting in the restaurant. A sour dill pickle in an anecdote he tells functions as a symbol for the whole experience.

Dillon, George (1906–1968). American poet, translator, and editor. Editor of POETRY from 1937 to 1950, Dillon earlier published his own poetry in *Boy in the Wind* (1927) and *The Flowering Stone* (1931). The latter won a Pulitzer Prize. In collaboration with Edna St. Vincent Millay, he published a translation of Baudelaire's *Les Fleurs du Mal* (1935).

dimeter. In prosody, a line of verse containing two metrical feet. It may be in any meter, usually identified together with the name of the meter, as iambic dimeter, trochaic dimeter, etc.

Dimmesdale, Arthur. The guilty minister in Hawthorne's THE SCARLET LETTER.

Dinarzade. Sister of SCHEHERAZADE in *The Arabian Nights*.

Dindenault. See DINGDONG.

Dindymus. In ancient geography, a mountain range between Phrygia and Galatia, sacred to Cybele, the Great Mother of the Gods, often also called Dindymene.

Dîners Magny. A restaurant in Paris, the scene of informal meetings held by an inner circle of French novelists between 1862 and 1875. Among the men who gathered there, for dinner and discussion, were Edmond and Jules de Goncourt, Théophile Gautier, Alphonse Daudet, Ernest Renan, Gustave Flaubert, and Charles Sainte-Beuve.

Dinesen, Isak. Pen name of Baroness **Karen Blixen**, born **Dinesen** (1883–1962). Danish short-story writer. Married to her cousin Baron Blixen, Isak Dinesen lived from 1914 to 1931 on a coffee plantation in British East Africa, now Kenya. *Out of Africa* (1937), published simultaneously in English and Danish, is a sensitive account of her experiences. Her first book, *Seven Gothic Tales* (1934), was published in English and received immediate critical acclaim; *Winter's Tales* (1942) is another well-known collection. During the German occupation of Denmark, Isak Dinesen published a symbolic critique of the conquerors, *Gengoeldelsens Veje* (*The Angelic Avengers*, 1947) under the name of Pierre Andrézel. A delicate subtlety of both mood and expression characterizes her acutely perceptive, often mysterious stories.

Ding an sich. See CRITIQUE OF PURE REASON; CRITIQUE OF JUDGMENT.

Dingdong. An anglicism for Dindenault, the sea-going sheep trader in Rabelais' GARGANTUA AND PANTAGRUEL who sells PANURGE a ram for an exorbitant price. Panurge punishes Dingdong by heaving the ram overboard, thus causing the whole herd to stampede into the sea, dragging the trader with them. Panurge declares that such good sport was well worth the price he had paid for the ram.

Dinggedicht (*Ger.,* "thing poem"). A lyric poem about an objective entity which, though it is most often a material thing, may also be a person or situation. The poet seeks not so much to describe from his own point of view as to recreate the intrinsic essence of the object in question, to get inside the object, as it were. Ideally, the reader should react to the poem as though he were reacting, on a deeper and more perceptive level than usual, to the thing itself. In many poems of this type, those by Eduard Mörike and Conrad Ferdinand MEYER for example, the subject is a work of art; but Rainer Maria RILKE, with whom the term *Dinggedicht* is most often associated, expanded the technique to include such subjects as living animals, human situations, and common household objects. The *Dinggedicht* is recognized in German literary criticism as a distinct poetic form.

Dinmont, Dandie. An eccentric and humorous farmer in Scott's GUY MANNERING. He owns two terriers, Mustard and Pepper, reputedly the progenitors of the Dandie Dinmont breed.

Diocletian [Gaius Aurelius Valerius] (A.D. 245–313). Roman emperor (284–305). He inaugurated the period of the Partnership of Emperors. He ruled with Maximian from 285, and divided the empire again (293) to include Constantius Chlorus and Galerius as rulers. Diocletian governed the eastern portion. At the instigation of his colleague Galerius, he began a terrible 10-year persecution of the Christians in 303. Diocletian abdicated (305) and retired to his native Dalmatia, where he spent the last years of his life.

Diogenes (c. 412–323 B.C.). The Greek CYNIC philosopher, pupil of Antisthenes. According to Seneca, he lived in a tub. The ascetic Diogenes is said to have searched in daylight with a lantern for an honest man. He exposed the vanity and selfishness of men. Diogenes' contempt for worldly goods is indicated by his reply to Alexander the Great, when the latter asked if he could do the philosopher any favor. Diogenes answered, "Yes, move out of my sunshine." Diogenes' nickname was *kyon,* or dog, a comment on his mode of living.

Diogenes Laertius (c. 200–250). A Greek author. Nothing is known of this writer's life. He wrote *Lives and Opinions of Eminent Philosophers,* of unknown date. He included the biographies of 82 Greek thinkers from Thales to Epicurus, which he compiled from the works of earlier writers. Diogenes chiefly records anecdotes to illustrate the viewpoint or character of his subject. The greatest value of the book is its preservation of three epistles and the maxims of Epicurus.

Diomedean swap. An exchange in which all the benefit is on one side. The expression is based on an incident related by Homer in the *Iliad.* During the proscribed exchange of credentials before a fight to the death, the Greek hero Diomedes and the Trojan hero Glaucus discover that their families had been allied. Forgetting their quarrel, they exchange armor, but Glaucus' armor is pure gold, while Diomedes' is only brass. Homer remarks that Zeus must have addled Glaucus' wits.

Diomedes. In Shakespeare's ANTONY AND CLEOPATRA, an attendant of Cleopatra. He brings word to Antony that Cleopatra, whom he has been told is falsely dead, is actually still alive.

Diomedes or **Diomed.** In Greek mythology, a king of Argos. He is described as one of the bravest warriors at the siege of Troy. He survived the siege, but on his return home, found his wife living in adultery, and saved his life by living in exile in Italy. See also DIOMEDEAN SWAP.

Dione. A titaness and consort of Zeus to whom, according to one Greek myth, she bore Aphrodite. Her name was later occasionally applied to Aphrodite.

Dionysiac. See APOLLONIAN AND DIONYSIAC.

Dionysus (Dionysos). Also known as **Bacchus** in Roman mythology. The Greek god of wine and fertile crops, the son of Zeus and Semele. Saved from his dead mother, the unborn child was sewed into Zeus's thigh. After his birth, he was torn to pieces by the Titans at the jealous Hera's instigation. Revived by Rhea, he was transformed into a kid and raised by nymphs. As a young man, he invented wine and introduced the vine to many lands, accompanied everywhere by a troop of maenads and suitors. Those who opposed his orgiastic rites were driven mad or otherwise destroyed. He married Ariadne, whom Theseus had deserted in the island of Naxos. Later he took the place of Hestia as one of the twelve Olympians and raised his mother from Hades under the name of Thyone.

The important festivals, among them the Eleusinian Mysteries and the Athenian Antestheria, celebrated the cult of Dionysus as the DAEMON of reviving vegetation in the spring. An influential development of this cult was Orphism, which in turn influenced the philosophies of Pythagoras and Plato. Euripides' play THE BACCHANTS (408–406 B.C.) tells the story of Dionysus' gory triumph over Pentheus, king of Thebes. It is generally acknowledged that drama, especially tragedy, developed out of the traditional ceremonies performed at Dionysian festivals to celebrate the death and resurrection of the god.

Dioscuri (Gr. *Dios kouroi,* sons of Zeus). See CASTOR AND POLYDEUCES.

Diotima. An Arcadian prophetess, the teacher of Socrates. She is quoted by him in Plato's *Symposium.*

Dircaean Swan. PINDAR; so called from Dirce (see AMPHION), a fountain in the neighborhood of Thebes, the poet's birthplace.

Dirce (Dirke). See AMPHION.

Directory, the. The name of the executive body of government in France created by the Constitution of 1795 during the FRENCH REVOLUTION; it lasted from October, 1795 to November, 1799. The Directory consisted of five men elected by the Council of 500 and the Council of the Elders (or *Anciens*). Ineffective because of internal dissensions, corruption, and bankruptcy, it was overthrown by Napoleon.

Dirty Hands (Les Mains sales; 1948). A drama by Jean-Paul SARTRE. The play, translated into English, was produced on Broadway under the title *Red Gloves.* Louis' faction of the Proletarian Party consider Hoederer's policies inexpedient. To kill him, the young intellectual Hugo is sent to Hoederer's house as a secretary, accompanied by his wife Jessica. Hugo delays his murder, however, increasingly impressed by Hoederer. He finally shoots him when he finds Hoederer kissing Jessica, but he does it with no definable motive, neither jealousy nor political conviction. The Party eventually switches to Hoederer's policies, and, after his prison term Hugo is examined to see if he is "salvageable" for further Party work; if not, he will be shot. In despair because Hoederer's death now has no public meaning, as the act of killing had no private meaning for him, Hugo tries to claim the significance of both by refusing to be "salvageable." The play dramatizes the dilemma that, in order to accomplish anything, a man must

Dionysus riding in a chariot drawn by a satyr, who carries a wine storage jar. Dionysus is crowned with grape leaves.

be willing to have "dirty hands"—that is, apparently, to accept the argument that the end justifies the means. Hoederer, who does so, seems most "real" as a person to Hugo and Jessica; idealistic Hugo suffers when he discovers that he cannot.

Dis. A name for HADES and hence the lower world.

Disastrous Peace, the (La Paix malheureuse). A name given to the Treaty of Câteau-Cambrésis (1559). It followed the battle of Gravelines. It was signed by France, Spain, and England, and by it France ceded the Low Countries to Spain, and Savoy, Corsica, and 200 forts to Italy.

Discours de la méthode. See René DESCARTES.

Discours sur l'histoire universelle. See Jacques Bénigne BOSSUET.

Disenchanted, The (1950). A novel by Budd SCHULBERG. The central character is Manley Halliday, a famous alcoholic novelist of the 1920's, based on F. Scott Fitzgerald. Schulberg had known the senior writer, and the book—a fictional re-creation of his personal experiences—is a melodrama approximating the tragedy of Fitzgerald's own life in Hollywood. The book was dramatized in 1958.

disestablishment. The act of withdrawing from a church its established position or privileges in relation to the state. The Irish Church was disestablished by an act of Parliament in 1869. The Church of England was disestablished in Wales by several acts in 1920.

Dismas or Dysmas. The usual name in the apocryphal gospels for the penitent thief. He was crucified with Jesus. He became the patron saint of thieves. The impenitent thief is commonly known as *Gesmas* or *Gestas.* Longfellow, in his *Golden Legend,* calls the penitent Titus and his fellow thief Dumachus.

Disney, Walt[er Elias] (1901–1966). American pioneer in animated cartoons and motion-picture producer. Disney studied at the Chicago Academy of Fine Arts and later became a commercial artist. In 1923 he went to Hollywood and began to create the first of his famous animated cartoons. His series of films featuring Oswald the Rabbit won wide favor, after which came those featuring Mickey Mouse and Donald Duck, his almost universally known creations. Disney made *The Three Little Pigs* in 1933 and, thereafter, turned his attention to making full-length pictures in this technique; *Snow White and the Seven Dwarfs* (1938), *Fantasia* (1940), and *Dumbo* (1942) are among the best known of these. *The Living Desert* (1953) was the first of a number of documentary films on wild life and nature that Disney subsequently produced.

Disraeli, Benjamin. 1st earl of Beaconsfield (1804–1881). English statesman and novelist. A member of Parliament, leader of the opposition in Commons, thrice chancellor of the exchequer, and twice prime minister, Disraeli was created a peer in 1876. It was by his initiative that Britain acquired the Suez canal in 1875, and he was responsible for having Queen Victoria proclaimed "Empress of India" and for negotiating "peace with honor" at the Congress of Berlin. As a young man, Disraeli had hesitated in deciding between a political and a literary career; his best novels, written at this time, are marked by acute wit, sharp realism, and a totally individual and often fantastic style. They include VIVIAN GREY, *The Young Duke* (1831), his two earliest works; *Contarini Fleming,* a psychological romance (1832), and *The Wondrous Tale of Alroy,* a historical novel (1832), both of which reveal the pride which Disraeli, a baptized Anglican, felt in his Jewish ancestry, a pride which he was to retain throughout his life; *Henrietta Temple,* a love story (1836); *Venetia* (1837), which presented in fictionalized form episodes from the lives of Byron and Shelley; CONINGSBY, OR THE NEW GENERATION, first in a projected political trilogy; SYBIL, OR THE TWO NATIONS, the second in the series, a depiction of the Chartist movement with such a frank portrayal of labor conditions that it was instrumental in provoking factory reform; TANCRED, OR THE NEW CRUSADE, the last novel in the trilogy, an implicit proposal that English politics and church seek a revitalizing inspiration from Semitic sources; and two political novels dating from late in his political career, LOTHAIR (1870) and *Endymion* (1880). Disraeli's nonfictional works are now chiefly of historical interest, but like his novels they exemplify his conservative convictions, his disdain for the theories of abstract rights and the a priori systems of the utilitarians, his trust in democratic Toryism, his acceptance of the duty of social reform, and his pride in empire and crown.

D'Israeli, Isaac (1766–1848). Father of Benjamin DISRAELI. Isaac's father, Benjamin D'Israeli, was a Jewish merchant descended from a family of Spanish refugees who came to England in 1748. Isaac had several works published anonymously, including *Curiosities of Literature* (6 vols., 1791–1834) and *Amenities of Literature* (3 vols., 1841).

Dissertation on Roast Pig, A. One of the most famous of Charles LAMB's *Essays of Elia,* it is a humorous account of the "accidental discovery" of the process of cooking pork.

Dissertation upon Parties (1735). A well-known political pamphlet by Henry ST. JOHN, Viscount Bolingbroke, which rejects the notion of divine right of kings and sets forth the idea of a king, free from the restrictions of party factionalism, who would assume leadership and preserve both a balanced government and traditional civil liberties.

dissociation of sensibility. A phrase coined by T. S. Eliot in *The Metaphysical Poets* (1921). According to Eliot, the 17th-century poets could "feel their thought as immediately as the odour of a rose," but after them a "dissociation of sensibility" set in and poets became either intellectual or emotional, but not both. Like the French symbolists, Eliot was trying to recapture that lost fusion of thought and feeling.

distich. The classical designation of a unit of two lines in a strophic poem for choral recitation. The term is used in English only in relation to or in translations of poetry from other languages. The elegaic distich of classical times consists of a hexameter followed by a pentameter, a form also used by the German poets Goethe and Schiller in poetic aphorisms. An example by Schiller, which is a characterization of the distich, reads, in Coleridge's translation:

In the hexameter rises the fountain's silvery column,
In the pentameter aye falling in melody back.

dithyramb (Gr., *dithyrambos*, a choric hymn). Originally a wild, impetuous kind of Dorian lyric in honor of Dionysus. It was traditionally ascribed to Arion of Lesbos (about 620 B.C.), who was thereafter called *the father of dithyrambic poetry*. It was said to be the origin of drama.

Ditzen, Rudolf. See Hans FALLADA.

Dive Bouteille, Oracle de la. See ORACLE OF THE HOLY BOTTLE.

Diverting History of John Bull and Brother Jonathan (1812). A satire by James Kirke PAULDING, under the pseudonym of Hector Bullus. The book relates the settling of Jonathan's farms (the U.S.) and their revolt from Bullock Island (England). Violently anti-British in tone, the story was continued in a sequel, *The History of Uncle Sam and His Boys* (1835).

Diverting History of John Gilpin, The. See JOHN GILPIN.

Divine Comedy, The (Commedia, completed 1321; called **Divina Commedia** after the 16th century). An epic poem by DANTE, his major work. It has 100 cantos in TERZA RIMA, divided equally (after an introductory canto in the first section) into three sections of 33 cantos each. The poet finds himself lost in the wood of Error on Good Friday, 1300. He is met by the spirit of Vergil, the great classical poet whom Dante considers the incarnation of the highest knowledge attainable by the human mind. Vergil conducts him through Hell to free him of the temptation to sin; then on Easter morning they begin the ascent of the mountain of Purgatory to purify Dante's soul of even the capacity for error. Vergil must leave Dante at the top of the mountain, for man alone, without grace, can go no further; but in the Earthly Paradise there Dante meets BEATRICE, who represents divine revelation, and she conducts him through Paradise to God. For details of each section see INFERNO; PURGATORIO; PARADISO.

The cosmology, angelology, and theology of the work are based firmly on the system of St. Thomas AQUINAS, but Dante considered the Church of his time a "harlot" no longer serving God—he meets seven popes in the Inferno, for instance—and was therefore frequently considered a heretic. The characters whom Dante meets on his journey are drawn largely from ancient Roman history and from recent and contemporary Italian history, including Dante's personal friends and enemies; their vivid portraiture and the constant allusions to human affairs make the work, although in structure a description of the Beyond, actually a realistic picture and intensely involved analysis of every aspect of earthly human life. Dante's literal journey is also an allegory of the progress of the individual soul toward God, and the progress of political and social mankind toward peace on earth; it is a compassionate, although moral, evaluation of human nature and a mystic vision of the Absolute toward which it strives. Thus the universality of the drama and the lyric vigor of the poetry are far more important than the specific doctrinal content.

Divine Pagan. See HYPATIA.

Divinity School Address, The (1838). An address by Ralph Waldo EMERSON. Delivered before the graduates of the Harvard Divinity School, the address shocked Boston's conservative clergymen. Emerson stressed the divinity of man and the humanity of Christ. He denied miracles and did not quote scripture. Evil was represented as possessing a negative character; instead of a positive force, it became a vacuum into which good would easily flow. Further, he upheld intuition, rather than ritual, as a means of knowing God.

Dix, Dorothy. Pen name of **Elizabeth Meriwether Gilmer** (1870–1951). American newspaper writer. She is known as the author of a widely syndicated column of advice on domestic problems, which was first published in 1896 in the New Orleans *Picayune*.

Dixie. A nostalgically regarded American paradise in the South. It is also the popular name of a song, originally entitled *I Wish I Was in Dixie's Land*, composed by Daniel Decatur Emmett in 1859. A great favorite in the South, it was taken up by the soldiers in the Confederate army. Fanny Crosby wrote a Union version of the text in 1861, known as *Dixie for the Union*.

The origin of the word Dixie is obscure. It has been suggested that it is related to the Mason and Dixon line; others believe that a Louisiana bank, printing its pre-Civil War bills in French with a big Dix (ten) in the middle of the 10-dollar notes, made the South the land of "dixies." A further, and ironic derivation is from the name of a slaveholder on Manhattan Island in the late 18th century; so benevolent was he that when his slaves were moved down south, they pined for "Dixie's land" up north.

Dixon, Jim. In Kingsley Amis's novel LUCKY JIM, a young university teacher beset by comic misfortunes.

Djinnestan. See JINNISTAN.

Dobell, Sydney (1824–1874). English poet and critic. Probably the most estimable member of the SPASMODIC SCHOOL, Dobell wrote such long poems as *The Roman* (1850) and *Balder* (1854) and many ballads and sonnets. While there are numerous fine passages and striking lines in the former, Dobell was an uneven writer and his reputation rests largely on shorter works, such as the ballad *Keith of Ravelston* (1857).

Dobie, J[ames] Frank (1888–1964). American teacher, historian, and folklorist. Dobie, who is especially identified with the University of Texas, has taught in a number of universities. He was a visiting professor at Cambridge University and from this experience came a book of observations, *A Texan in England* (1945). Among the books of this cultural historian of the Southwest are *Coronado's Children* (1931), *Tales of the Mustangs* (1936), *Apache Gold and Yaqui Silver* (1939), *Guide to Life and Literature in the Southwest* (1943; revised and enlarged, 1952), *The Mustangs* (1952), and *I'll Tell You a Tale* (1960).

Döblin, Alfred (1878–1957). German novelist and essayist, known as a leading representative of EXPRESSIONISM. His major novel, however, *Berlin Alexanderplatz* (1929), is less expressionistically tendentious, more scenic and realistic than his earlier works, and shows the influence of John Dos Passos and James Joyce. Döblin, a physician, emigrated from Germany in 1933 and became a French citizen.

Dobrée, Bonamy (1891–   ). English authority on Restoration drama. Dobrée is the author of

Restoration Comedy (1924) and *Restoration Tragedy* (1929).

Dobrolyubov, Nikolai Aleksandrovich (1836–1861). Russian journalist and literary critic. After graduation from the St. Petersburg Pedagogical Institute in 1857, Dobrolyubov began his brief career on the journal *Sovremennik* (*The Contemporary*). Like his colleague CHERNYSHEVSKI, Dobrolyubov emphasized the social usefulness of literature. The best-known of his critical essays are *Tiomnoye Tzarstvo* (*The Kingdom of Darkness,* 1859), a study of Ostrovski's drama *The Storm; Chto takoye oblomovshchina?* (*What is Oblomovshchina?* 1859), on Goncharov's novel *Oblomov;* and *Kogda zhe prediot nastoyashchi den'?* (*When Will the Real Day Come?* 1860), on Turgenev's novel *On the Eve.* Belinski, Chernyshevski and Dobrolyubov formed the triumvirate of 19th-century critics most often cited in Soviet literary criticism.

doctor. A scholastic or honorary title conferred by a university. Today the word is commonly synonymous with physician, from the degree M.D., Doctor of Medicine. In the medieval universities doctors were advanced students who were usually also teachers. The Schoolmen, or theologians who lectured in the cloisters and cathedral schools, were also called doctors.

Doctor. For titles beginning with *Doctor*, see also under Dr.

Doctors of the Church. Certain early Christian Fathers, especially four in the Greek (or Eastern) Church and four in the Latin (or Western) Church.

Eastern Church. St. Athanasius of Alexandria (d. 373), who defended the divinity of Christ against the Arians; St. Basil the Great of Caesarea (d.? 379) and his co-worker St. Gregory of Nazianzus (d.? 389); and the eloquent St. John Chrysostom (d. 407), Archbishop of Constantinople.

Western Church. St. Jerome (d. 420), translator of the Vulgate, St. Ambrose (d. 397), bishop of Milan; St. Augustine (d. 430), bishop of Hippo; and St. Gregory the Great (d. 604), the pope who sent St. Augustine, the Apostle of the Anglo-Saxons, to England.

Doctor Zhivago (Doktor Zhivago; 1957). A novel by Boris PASTERNAK. This famous book centers around the experiences of a member of the intelligentsia during the Russian Revolution. The story's hero, Yuri Zhivago, is a young doctor with a mild interest in the coming revolution and a great interest in literature. He composes poems, mostly with religious overtones; 25 of his verses form the last part of the novel. Zhivago's discussions with his uncle Kolya and his friends contain most of the explicit anti-Marxist passages that offended Soviet censors. The novel was refused publication in the Soviet Union, but was published abroad, bringing down the wrath of Soviet officialdom on Pasternak's head. Soviet authorities were as much bothered by the religious spirit pervading the novel as they were by the outspoken opposition to Marxism. Pasternak's opposition is implied throughout the book in the frequent contrast between the revolution's attempt to order men's lives rationally and the free, living spirit Zhivago finds in nature and in such characters as his mistress, Lara. Zhivago's, and the author's, sympathies are always obviously with life as opposed to the ideas about life held by the Marxists. The poetic spirit of the book is enhanced by the language in which it is written. In the original Russian, the lines often fall into the cadences of verse and almost always strike the reader with the intense force usually expected from well-written poetry.

Doctrine and Discipline of Divorce (1644). A famous prose argument by John MILTON on the religious justifications and legality of divorce. It may have been prompted, in part, by his own marital difficulties with his first wife, Mary Powell.

Dodd, William E[dward] (1869–1940). American historian and diplomat. Dodd was ambassador to Germany from 1933 to 1937, when he resigned to lecture against Nazism. His *Ambassador Dodd's Diary* (1941) contains his reactions to Nazism. Earlier he had written several books on American history, including *Statesmen of the Old South* (1911), *Lincoln or Lee* (1928), and *The Old South* (1937).

Doderer, Heimito von (1896–   ). Austrian novelist. Influenced by Robert Musil, he was known for his critical attitude toward what he regarded as the militaristic orientation of the 20th century. His best known novel is *Die Strudelhofstiege* (1951), which takes its title from the name of a stone stairway in Vienna.

Dodge, Mary Mapes (1831–1905). American writer and editor of *St. Nicholas Magazine* (1873–1905). Her books for children, *Hans Brinker, or the Silver Skates* (1865) and *Donald and Dorothy* (1883), are classics.

Dodgson, Charles Lutwidge. See Lewis CARROLL.

Dodona. A famous oracle in the village of Dodona in Epirus, and the most ancient of Greece. It was dedicated to Aeus, and the oracles were delivered from the tops of oak and other trees, the rustling of the wind in the branches being interpreted by the priests. Also, brazen vessels and plates were suspended from the branches, and these, being struck together when the wind blew, gave various sounds from which responses were concocted. Hence the Greek phrase Kalkos Dodones (brass of Dodona), meaning a babbler, or one who talks an infinite deal of nothing.

According to tradition, two black pigeons took their flight from Thebes, in Egypt; one flew to Libya, and the other to Dodona. On the spot where the former alighted, the temple of Zeus Ammon was erected; in the place where the other settled, the oracle of Zeus was established, and there the responses were made by the black pigeons that inhabited the surrounding groves. This fable is probably based on a pun upon the word *peleiai*, which usually meant "old women," but in the dialect of the Epirots signified pigeons or doves.

Dodsley, Robert (1703–1764). English poet, playwright, and the most important publisher and bookseller of the eighteenth century. With the aid of Alexander Pope, he opened his bookshop at the sign of Tully's Head in Pall Mall, London, and was soon publishing the works of Pope, Samuel Johnson, Edward Young, William Collins, and many others. His publication of poetry culminated in *A Collection of Poems by several hands* in 6 volumes (1748–1758); his chief connection with English fiction was the London edition of *Tristram Shandy.* Dodsley was also the editor of a collection of *Old Plays* (12 vols., 1744), beginning with a morality play, which went through several revised and enlarged editions.

Dodson and Fogg, Messrs. In Charles Dickens' Pickwick Papers, two unprincipled lawyers who undertake on speculation to bring an action against Mr. Pickwick for breach of promise, and file accordingly the famous suit of *Bardell* v. *Pickwick*. The names Dodson and Fogg are frequently used as synonymous with unscrupulous or dishonest solicitors.

Dodsworth (1929). A novel by Sinclair Lewis. Samuel Dodsworth, a rich automobile manufacturer in the Midwestern city of Zenith, retires and goes to Europe with his frivolous wife, Fran. Fran becomes involved in several love affairs with European adventurers, and Dodsworth, lonely and unhappy, meets Edith Cortwright, an American widow who teaches him to appreciate the traditions of Europe. He eventually leaves his wife for the more mature companionship of Edith. The novel was dramatized in 1934 by Sidney Howard.

dog. An animal that in medieval art symbolizes fidelity. A dog is represented as lying at the feet of St. Bernard, St. Benignus, and St. Wendelin; as licking the wounds of St. Roch; as carrying a lighted torch in representations of St. Dominic. In monuments the dog is placed at the feet of women to symbolize affection and fidelity, as a lion is placed at the feet of men to signify courage and magnanimity. Many of the Crusaders are represented with their feet on a dog, to show that they followed the standard of the Lord as faithfully as a dog follows the footsteps of his master.

Dog Beneath the Skin, The (1935). A satiric drama in prose and verse by W. H. Auden and Christopher Isherwood. Parodying traditional fairy-tale themes and the technique of the popular 20th-century musical comedy, it concerns the quest for Sir Francis Crewe, a missing English heir.

Dogberry. A pompous but comical constable in Shakespeare's Much Ado About Nothing. He has a habit of confusing his words, sagely remarking, for example, that "comparisons are odorous." He and his crony Verges take Borachio into custody as a suspicious character and ask Leonato to question him. Leonato fails to comprehend their garbled story, however, and Don John's plot against Hero and Claudio nearly succeeds.

doggerel. Originally, loose and irregular verse, often comic or burlesque. It gave the impression of having been quickly and casually composed, as in *Hudibras,* Butler's satirical epic. A pejorative meaning has now become attached to the word, connoting triviality of subject matter and inexpertness of technique, as in "mere doggerel."

Dog Star. Sirius, the brightest star in the firmament. Its influence was supposed in ancient times to cause great heat, pestilence, etc. It was called Dog Star (Caniculus) because it belongs to the constellation *Canis Major* (larger dog).

Doktor Faustus (1947). A novel by Thomas Mann. In it the intense and tragic career of the hero Adrian Leverkühn, a composer, is made to parallel the collapse of Germany in World War II. To achieve this end, Mann employs the device of having another character, Serenus Zeitblom, narrate Leverkühn's story from memory, while the war is going on, and interperse his narrative with remarks about the present situation. In this way, it is implied that it is the same demonic and always potentially destructive energy inherent in Leverkühn's music that is also, on a larger scale, behind the outburst of Nazism. Mann thus suggests that the violent Faustian drive, when it is not diverted into art, or when there is no single artistic genius to harness it into creative process, will be perverted and result in grossly subhuman degradation. Thus, Mann is concerned here with his favorite theme, the artist's isolation in the world; but whereas earlier treatments such as Tonio Kröger had shown the artist attempting to get along with the world's values, here the world is seen attempting to cope with a force that is proper only to art.

Dolce, Lodovico (1508–1566). Italian dramatist. He wrote Senecan tragedies in the modern manner of Giraldi, which influenced the Elizabethan drama. His best-known work is the *Marianna* (1565).

dolce stil nuovo. See Stilnovisti.

Dolet, Etienne (1509–1546). French scholar and printer. From his printing press at Lyons he issued works by Rabelais, Clément Marot, and others, as well as his own *Commentarii linguae Latinae* (1536–1568), a philosophical study. Convicted of heresy and blasphemy, he was hanged and then burned in Paris.

Dolgoruki, Arkadi Makarovich. The hero of Feodor Dostoevski's novel, A Raw Youth. Arkadi is the illegitimate son of Versilov.

Makar Ivanovich Dolgoruki. The nominal father of Arkadi, Makar is an old former serf who has become a religious pilgrim. He preaches humility and love and a striving for seemliness in relations among men. He has often been compared to a similar peasant philosopher, Platon Karatayev in Tolstoi's *War and Peace.*

Dolittle, Dr. The animal-loving doctor hero of children's stories by Hugh Lofting.

Dollfuss, Engelbert (1892–1934). Chancellor of Austria (1932–1934). He was assassinated in a Nazi *Putsch.*

Dolliver Romance, The (1876). An unfinished novel by Nathaniel Hawthorne. It was supposed to have been published serially in *The Atlantic Monthly,* but the author died before his plans were realized.

Dr. Dolliver attempts to prepare an elixir of life so that he might live to care for his granddaughter, Pansie. In contrast to the selfless Dolliver, Colonel Dabney demands the elixir for purely selfish reasons. Dabney finally dies, ironically, of an overdose of the elixir.

Doll's House, A (1879). A play by Henrik Ibsen. Sheltered, petted, and expected to behave like an amiable nitwit by first her father and then her husband, Nora Helmer has committed forgery in order to get money to save her husband's life. Though she has repaid the money, her husband finally finds out about her act. His behavior makes Nora realize that in their eight years of marriage he has never looked on her as a human being, but only as a doll, and she leaves him in order to learn to become a person in her own right.

Dolopathos. See The Seven Wise Masters.

Dombey and Son (1848). A novel by Charles Dickens. The proud, unfeeling Mr. Dombey has but one ambition in life: to have a son that his firm might be called Dombey and Son. When his son Paul is born he promises to fulfill this ambition, which overrides even grief at the death of Mrs. Dombey. Young Paul, a delicate, sensitive boy, is quite unequal to the great things expected of him; he is sent to Mr. Blimber's school and gives way under the strain of the discipline. In his short life he wins the love of all who know him. Mr. Dombey is embittered by Paul's death. Florence, his daughter, lives on with him trying desperately to win his love, but she has succeeded only in incurring his hatred because she lives while her brother died. Dombey marries again, but his second wife, Edith Granger, runs off with Mr. CARKER, his business manager. Florence marries the kind young Walter Gay. Dombey's firm fails, and alone and miserable, he finds himself longing for the sweet and kind daughter whom he treated so coldly. The two are reconciled, and Dombey tries to expiate his past through his grandchildren.

The novel is noted for its complex structure. The symbolism of death as the sea and life as the flow of the river into the sea, used often in his later novels, is first used here.

Dom Casmurro (1900). A novel by Joachim Maria MACHADO DE ASSIS. The narrator, a middle-aged lawyer nicknamed Dom Casmurro (roughly, "Mr. Peevish") because of his difficult disposition, reflects on his adolescence and on his youthful romance with Capitú, whom he later married. An aura of uncertainty and ambiguity hovers over the book —not even the question of Capitú's adulterous relationship with Escobar, her husband's best friend, is fully settled. Written in a limpid, wryly humorous style, the novel is largely plotless and is frequently interrupted by the narrator's asides.

Domdaniel (Lat. *domus,* house or home; *Danielis,* of Daniel). A fabled abode of evil spirits, gnomes, and enchanters, "under the roots of the ocean" off Tunis, or elsewhere. It first appears in Chaves and Cazotte's *Continuation of the Arabian Nights* (1788–1793), was introduced by Southey into his *Thalaba,* and used by Carlyle as synonymous with a den of iniquity.

Domenichino, il. Real name, **Domenico Zampieri** (1581–1641). Italian painter. A product of the eclectic academy of the CARRACCI at Bologna, he is noted for his religious and mythological works, including the *Last Communion of St. Jerome* (1614) and several fresco and easel treatments of the life of St. Cecilia, patroness of music.

Domesday or **Doomsday Book** (1086). Latin record of a census and survey of most of England. It was compiled at the order of William the Conqueror. All property is described and evaluated in detail, along with a census of its inhabitants and its domestic animals, as of (1) the time of Edward the Confessor, (2) the time of William's bestowal of the estates on their new owners, and (3) the time of the survey and future potential. *Domesday* means "day of judgment," and the records were probably so named because they were the final authority for property litigation; they served as the basis for tax assessments until 1522. Other similar records were often called the *Domesday Book* of a given locality; E. L. Masters used the title for a collection of verse (1920).

Dominic, St. (1170–1221). Spanish-born Roman Catholic priest and founder of the Dominican order.

An important church official in his native Spain, he went to Languedoc in 1205 to preach orthodox doctrine to the Albigenses, but, contrary to the tradition, he was not an "inquisitor," nor did he take a personal part in the bloody massacre of the Albigenses, who held to the Manichaean heresy. In 1215, he organized his band of followers into the Dominican order, or Preaching Friars, devoted to missionary work.

Dominicans. The popular name for the Order of Preachers founded by St. Dominic in 1215. The most famous member of the Order was a theologian, St. Thomas AQUINAS. The Dominicans early acquired the punning sobriquet *Domini canes* (*Lat.,* "dogs of the Lord") because of their swift and vigorous penetration into the life of the Church over all of Europe. In England they were formerly called Black Friars from their black dress, and in France Jacobins, because their mother establishment in Paris was in the rue St. Jacques.

Dom Juan ou le Festin de Pierre (Don Juan or the Stone Guest, 1665). A prose comedy by MOLIÈRE. It is derived from the play EL BURLADOR DE SEVILLA Y EL CONVIDADO DE PIEDRA of Tirso de Molina. The rake DON JUAN abducts Elvire, marries her, and abandons her—not the first time he has so mistreated a woman. He then ironically invites the statue of a man he has murdered to dinner; the statue accepts and returns the invitation, and as it takes Don Juan by the hand a fiery chasm opens and swallows him. Molière added the character Elvire as well as many characteristic touches to this grim tale. There are scenes of sparkling comedy; the valet Sganarelle is timidity incarnate, and Don Juan assumes the traits common to the libertine nobility of Molière's day. Perhaps for this reason the play, though enormously popular, was suppressed. It was later put into verse by Thomas Corneille.

Domus Aurea (*Lat.,* "golden house"). A palace of the emperor Nero, at or near the site of the Colosseum. It was the scene of many banqueting orgies.

Doña Bárbara (1929). A novel by Rómulo GALLEGOS. The central character Doña Bárbara, as her name implies, symbolizes barbarism. Believing herself possessed of supernatural powers, she rules a vast domain on the Venezuelan *llanos* and bends men to her will through bribery, intimidation, and murder. Some saw in Doña Bárbara's rapacity and ruthlessness a resemblance to the practices of Juan Vicente Gómez, Venezuelan dictator when the book was published.

Donalbain. In Shakespeare's MACBETH, the younger son of Duncan, the murdered king, and the brother of Malcolm. He flees to Ireland after his father's death.

Don Alvaro o la fuerza del sino (1835). A romantic tragedy in prose and verse by Ángel Saavedra, duque de RIVAS. Don Alvaro, in love with Doña Leonor, accidentally kills the girl's father, then slays her two brothers in a duel. Before he dies, the younger brother kills Doña Leonor in the mistaken belief that she is the paramour of his father's murderer. Stricken with grief, Don Alvaro leaps to his death. This play was the basis of Verdi's opera *La Forza del Destino* (1862).

Donatello. Real name, **Donato di Niccolò dei Bardi** (1386–1466). Florentine sculptor. An associate of Filippo Brunelleschi and Lorenzo Ghiberti, he studied antique sculpture but rejected the serenity of its idealized beauty in favor of a more vigorous style. In stone and bronze, in reliefs and in free-standing statues admirably integrated with their architectural setting, he stressed power of expression and dramatic action. His masterpieces include *The Boy David,* the first large bronze free-standing nude since classical times, and the bronze equestrian statue of GATTAMELATA, also the first of its kind since antiquity.

Donation of Constantine. See DECRETALS.

Donatus. In full, **Donatus de octibus partibus orationis.** The most famous Latin grammar. It was named after its author Aelius Donatus, Roman grammarian of the fourth century, who was one of the instructors of St. Jerome.

Don Carlos (1787). A play by Friedrich SCHILLER, based on the life of the son of the Spanish king Philip II. Don CARLOS' libertarian idealism is shared by the older and more experienced Marquis Posa, and the two plot against the tyrannical king. The prince, however, is suspected, and in order to save him, Posa contrives to draw all suspicion upon himself and is murdered by the king. Carlos is then offered his freedom, but in a last, unconsidered burst of idealism, he defies the king, and is turned over to the Inquisition for execution. The play is the basis of Verdi's opera *Don Carlos* (1867).

Don Flows Home to The Sea, The. See QUIET DON, THE.

Don Giovanni (1787). An opera by Wolfgang Amadeus MOZART, with a libretto by Lorenzo DA PONTE. It deals with the adventures of the Spanish libertine DON JUAN. After he and his servant Leporello have committed one piece of villainy after another, the statue of a nobleman Don Giovanni has murdered appears and takes him off to the infernal regions. It is regarded as one of the supreme works of art.

Doni, Anton Francesco (1513–1574). Florentine author and unfrocked priest. He is noted for his dialogues *I Marmi* (*The Marble Steps*) and *I Mondi* (*The Worlds*). The latter was influenced by the *Utopia* of Thomas More, the first example of an English Renaissance work stirring Italian imitation. Doni's work was, in turn, utilized by Campanella in his utopia, *The City of the Sun.*

Donizetti, Gaetano (1797–1848). Prolific Italian composer of operas. The best known are *Don Pasquale* (1845), *Lucrezia Borgia* (1833), LUCIA DI LAMMERMOOR, and *La Favorita* (1840).

Don Juan. A legendary profligate. The origin of the central theme of his widespread legend—that of a statue of a dead man who accepts a libertine's invitation to dinner—is not known. Its first appearance in any literary form was in Tirso de Molina's EL BURLADOR DE SEVILLA (1630), which gave the hero the identity that he has retained ever since: Don Juan, a young nobleman of Seville. It also suggested the internal complications of his nature that have endlessly fascinated writers and composers. The name of Tirso's hero quickly became a synonym for an obsessive and unscrupulous pursuer of women.

The basic plot of this play soon reached France, by way of Italy, and was used in several plays, most notably Molière's DOM JUAN OU LE FESTIN DE PIERRE,

which introduced the figure of Elvire, Don Juan's wife. The attempts of English writers to treat Don Juan, such as Shadwell's *The Libertine* (1676), were unimpressive until G. B. Shaw included his "Don Juan in Hell" scene in MAN AND SUPERMAN. The only significant one of several Spanish versions of the legend after *El Burlador de Sevilla* was DON JUAN TENORIO (1844), by José Zorrilla y Moral. Among the French versions after Molière's day were stories and plays by Prosper Merimée, Dumas père, Alfred de Musset, Balzac, and Flaubert. Pushkin wrote a short verse drama that closely followed the Don Juan legend, *The Stone Guest* (see LITTLE TRAGEDIES).

The most famous of all forms of the story is undoubtedly Mozart's great opera DON GIOVANNI, written to a libretto by Lorenzo da Ponte, although there were several slightly earlier operatic versions. Another outstanding musical work inspired by the Don Juan legend is Richard Strauss's tone poem *Don Juan.*

Don Juan (1819–1824). An unfinished epic satire by Lord BYRON. Byron's DON JUAN only slightly resembles the legendary Spanish rake. He begins his adventures in Spain, but is sent abroad at the age of 16 by his mother, Donna INEZ. His ship is wrecked and he is cast up on a Greek island, where he is nursed back to health by the beautiful HAIDÉE. Lambro, the girl's father, discovers the lovers together, captures Juan, and sells him as a slave to GULBEYAS, the sultana of Constantinople. However, Juan then falls in love with DUDU, a beautiful girl in the harem, and so arouses the jealousy of Gulbeyas that he barely escapes with his life. His next adventure takes him to Russia, where as a soldier he attracts the favor of the Empress Catherine. She sends Juan to England as a courier. The poem breaks off with Juan in England.

Don Juan is sprinkled with long digressions in which Byron, through his hero, gives his views on wealth, power, society, chastity, poets, diplomats, and England. It is written in *ottava rima* and even in its incomplete state contains 16,000 lines in its 16 cantos.

Don Juan in Hell. See MAN AND SUPERMAN.

Don Juan Tenorio (1844). A drama in verse by José ZORRILLA Y MORAL. In Zorrilla's version of the DON JUAN legend, the hero falls in love with the virtuous Doña Inés, repents of his sins, and is saved by her prayers on his behalf. Though Zorrilla himself deprecated his work, it is one of Spain's most popular plays and is regularly performed during the first week in November.

Donnay, Maurice (1859–1945). French playwright. Donnay began his dramatic career with humorous short pieces which he wrote for the Montmartre cabaret Le Chat Noir. A gay, quick wit characterizes his comedies, the best of which also contain psychological insight: *Amants* (1895), *La Douloureuse* (1897), *L'Autre Danger* (1902), and *Paraître* (1906). His problem plays, marked by a perceptive wit, include *La Clairière* (1900) and *Les Eclaireuses* (1913), a study of feminism.

Donn-Byrne, Brian Oswald. See Donn BYRNE.

Donne, John (1572?–1631). English poet, first and greatest of the METAPHYSICAL POETS. Donne was of good family, bred as a Roman Catholic, well educated in theology and law, and in his youth a lover of company and elegant women. In 1614, after a long period of hardship following his secret marriage to Anne More, and as his hopes of secular preferment waned, he was converted to Anglicanism. Ordained in 1615, he became dean of St. Paul's Cathedral six years later and possibly the most influential preacher in England.

Donne's best-known poetry falls into two classes, the early ironic and erotic verse and the later religious poems. In his verse satires and in such lyrics as Go And Catch a Falling Star (often entitled *Song*) and *Woman's Constancy,* Donne makes a witty display of worldliness, skepticism, and fickleness. Other poems, such as *The Extasie,* The Anniversaries, The Canonization, and Twicknam Garden, are moving expressions of passion or grief. Donne's love poetry is remarkable for its close analysis of the nature and psychology of love; in its emotional sophistication and highly personal tone, it differs markedly from the conventional courtly love poetry of Donne's day. The later religious poems powerfully express the yearning for union with God of a man obsessed with death, oppressed by his sense of human limitation and sin, by an almost invincible doubt of salvation. Among the most famous of these poems are the sonnets, *Death Be Not Proud* and *Batter My Heart; Three Person'd God;* and the *Hymne to God the Father.*

Donne also wrote numerous elegies, epigrams, and verse letters, many sermons, and the Devotions, an extraordinary series of meditations on the theme of sickness and mortality. This last prose work, together with *The Anniversaries,* reveals his preoccupation with the themes of mutability and death, the paradoxical human union of spirit and matter, themes which are crucial even in the love poems.

Donne's poetry is marked by intellectual power, deep learning, and intense emotion. His imagery, to which the adjective "metaphysical" was chiefly applied, is powerful and striking; it was drawn from Scholastic philosophy, the science of the day, trades and professions, and the simple, commonplace things of everyday life. His meter is irregular and dramatic, preserving the cadence and immediacy of ordinary speech.

Donne's poems were published in 1633 and were very popular and widely imitated during the next generation. He was almost unknown, however, during the 18th century and was disapproved of by Samuel Johnson. A few of the Romantics liked him, but it was only in the 20th century that interest in him was revived to any considerable extent. See conceit.

Donnithorne, Arthur. See Adam Bede.

Donnybrook Fair. A fair held near Dublin in August from the time of King John till 1855. It is noted for its bacchanalian orgies and light-hearted rioting. The name has become proverbial for a disorderly gathering.

Don Pasquale (1845). The title of a comic opera by Gaetano Donizetti.

Don Quixote (de la Mancha, El ingenioso hidalgo) (1605, 1615). A novel by Miguel de Cervantes Saavedra. Alonso Quijano is a gaunt country gentleman, kindly and dignified, who lives in the province of La Mancha. His mind is so crazed by reading romances of chivalry that he believes himself called upon to redress the wrongs of the whole world. Changing his name to Don Quixote de la Mancha, he is knighted by an innkeeper whose miserable hostelry he mistakes for a castle. As his lady love he chooses a peasant girl named Aldonza Lorenzo whom he transforms into Dulcinea del Toboso. Don Quixote now sallies forth into the world but after several mishaps, including a beating administered by some merchants whom he challenges to a passage at arms, he returns to his home. Undaunted, he asks Sancho Panza, an ignorant rustic, to be his squire and promises to reward him with the governorship of the first lands they conquer. Riding Rocinante, a nag as bony as himself, Don Quixote sets out a second time, accompanied by Sancho on his ass Dapple.

During his travels Don Quixote's overexcited imagination invariably blinds him to reality: he thinks windmills to be giants, flocks of sheep to be armies, and galley-slaves to be oppressed gentlemen. Toward the end of the novel, Sancho is named governor of the isle of Barataria, a mock title given to him by some noblemen whose only aim is to make sport of the squire and his master. After being bested in a duel with the Knight of the White Moon, in reality a student of his acquaintance in disguise, Don Quixote, tired and disillusioned, returns to La Mancha, and shortly before his death, renounces books of knight-errantry.

The first part of *Don Quixote,* which may have

Title page of the first edition of *Don Quixote* (1605).

EL INGENIOSO
HIDALGO DON QVI-
xote de la Mancha.

Compuesto por Miguel de Ceruantes Saauedra.

DIRIGIDO AL DVQVE DE
Bejar, Marques de Gibraleon, Conde de Benalcaçar, y
Bañares, Vizconde dela Puebla de Alcozer, Señor
de las villas de Capilla, Curiel,
y Burguillos.

Impresso con licencia, en Valencia, en casa de
Pedro Patricio Mey, 1605.

A costa de Iusepe Ferrer mercader de libros,
delante la Diputacion.

been conceived while Cervantes was in prison, was first printed in 1605 in Madrid by Juan de la Cuesta. In 1614 a second part was published by an unknown author who used the pseudonym Alonso Fernández de Avellaneda. This bit of plagiarism, though not an unusual practice at the time, spurred Cervantes to complete his own sequel, which appeared the following year and is usually considered superior to the first part.

Although it is generally agreed that Cervantes meant his novel to be a satire on the exaggerated chivalric romances of his time, some critics have interpreted it as an ironic story of an idealist frustrated and mocked in a materialistic world. Others have seen it as a veiled attack on the Catholic church or on contemporary Spanish politics. To many, the contrasting figures of Don Quixote and Sancho Panza, the visionary idealist and the practical realist, symbolize the duality of the Spanish character. With its variegated assortment of minor characters, shepherds, innkeepers, students, priests, and nobles, the novel also gives a panoramic view of 17th-century Spanish society. At the same time its essential humanity has made it a universal favorite. See CLAVILEÑO.

Don Ramón. In D. H. Lawrence's THE PLUMED SERPENT, a scholarly Mexican, the political, religious, and sexual hero of the novel.

Don Segundo Sombra (1926). A novel by Ricardo Güiraldes (1886–1927), Argentine novelist and short-story writer. Güiraldes was a wealthy cosmopolite who travelled widely, but *Don Segundo Sombra* reveals his native roots and draws on his childhood experiences at *La Porteña*, his family's ranch in Buenos Aires province. The narrator of the novel is a boy who runs away from the aunts who have raised him and attaches himself to Don Segundo Sombra, an itinerant ranch worker. During their five-year odyssey, Don Segundo not only teaches him to be an expert cowboy and horseman, but also shows him how to live with courage and honor, according to the gaucho code. After discovering that he is the illegitimate son of a wealthy rancher who has left him his estate, the narrator, by now a young man, acquires a measure of formal culture. Don Segundo, feeling that there is no longer need for his tutelage, goes on his lonely way. In this novel, considered the outstanding fictional example of GAUCHO LITERATURE, Güiraldes captured the essence of the gaucho myth in his scenes of life on the pampas and, above all, in the idealized figure of Don Segundo.

Dooley, Mr. See Finley Peter DUNNE.

Doolittle, Hilda. Pen name, **H.D.** (1886–1961). American poet. Miss Doolittle went to Europe in 1911 where she became acquainted with poets practicing IMAGISM, the movement with which her own name and work are primarily identified. She married the English poet Richard Aldington and thereafter lived abroad. Her work shows the influence of the Greek classics and is distinguished for its simple, clear, and precise visualizations of scenes, images, and objects. *Sea Garden* (1916), her first book of poetry, was followed by *Hymen* (1921); *Heliodora and Other Poems* (1924); *Collected Poems* (1925 and 1940); *Hippolytus Temporizes* (1927), a verse tragedy; and *The Flowering of the Rod* (1946). *Helen in Egypt* (1961), a book-length poem, was published

posthumously. She also wrote fiction, usually dealing with historical themes, as in *Palimpsest* (1926) and *Hedylus* (1928).

Doomsday Book. See DOMESDAY BOOK.

Doon. A river in Ayrshire, Scotland, celebrated in the poems of Robert BURNS.

Doon de Mayence. A medieval cycle of CHANSONS DE GESTE about the heroes opposed, at least part of the time, to Charlemagne. They include the histories of GANELON, OGIER THE DANE, and the *Four Sons of* AYMON.

Doppelgänger (Ger., *doppel*, double; *gänger*, walker). The ghostly or spiritual double of a living being, the appearance of which supposedly presages that person's imminent death. The *Doppelgänger* theme is a favorite with German romantic authors and has been treated by E. T. A. Hoffmann and Heinrich Heine; the latter's poem, *Der Doppelgänger*, was set to music by Franz Schubert.

Dora. See Dora SPENLOW.

Doralice. In the Orlando poems of BOIARDO and Ariosto, the daughter of King Stordilano of Granata and the betrothed of Rodomonte, whom she deserts for Mandricardo, thus causing a fatal discord in the camp of the pagan warriors opposed to Charlemagne and his paladins.

Dorante. The unscrupulous nobleman in Molière's LE BOURGEOIS GENTILHOMME. He fleeces the social-climbing M. Jourdain of a great deal of his wealth under the pretext of offering him social advancement.

Doré, [Paul] Gustave (1833–1883). French illustrator and painter. He is famous for masterly and imaginative illustrations of such classics as the works of Rabelais, Balzac, Dante, Cervantes, and the Bible.

Doria, Andrea (c. 1468–1560). Genoese admiral; called "Father of Peace" and "Liberator of Genoa." In 1951 his name was given to a luxury liner of the Italian Line, that sank (July 25, 1956) during a transatlantic crossing after having been rammed by the S.S. *Stockholm.* The name is also that given to one of the main characters in Schiller's *Fiesko.*

Dorian or **Doric.** Pertaining to the Dorians, traditionally the last of the groups of tribes who invaded Greece in pre-Classical times. The so-called Dorian invasion, probably from the North, early in the 12th century B.C., put an end to the Mycenaean era and was long thought to have caused a protracted Dark Age, although the process is now considered to have been much less clear-cut and complete than was formerly supposed.

In Classical times, Doric attitudes were identified with solidity and simplicity, as in the "Doric order" of architecture characterized by plain, chaste forms. The "Dorian mode" in music, a scale that may be reproduced by playing all the white notes from one D to the next on a piano, was regarded by Plato as being conducive to sobriety and other virtues needed by the citizen of an ideal state. See GREEK MUSIC.

Dorigen. See FRANKLIN'S TALE.

Dormouse, the. The mouse in ALICE'S ADVENTURES IN WONDERLAND. He is thrust into a teapot by the Hatter and the March Hare. The word dormouse probably means "sleeping mouse" (from Fr., *dormir*, "to sleep").

Dorotea, La (1632). A prose romance in dialogue by Lope de VEGA. He called it "the most beloved of my works." The novel is partly autobiographical, and the Dorotea of the title is the actress Elena Osorio, with whom Lope had an affair and whom he called Filis in other works. He wrote the book at an early age but revised it years later, including details of his liaison with Marta de Nevares. *La Dorotea* was influenced by LA CELESTINA, whose main character is reincarnated in Lope's work by Gerarda.

Dorothea, St. A martyr under Diocletian about 303. She is represented with a rose branch in her hand, a wreath of roses on her head, and roses with fruit by her side; sometimes with also an angel carrying a basket with three apples and three roses. The legend is that Theophilus, the judge's secretary, scoffingly said to her, as she was going to execution, "Send me some fruit and roses, Dorothea, when you get to Paradise." Immediately after her execution, while Theophilus was at dinner with a party of companions, a young angel brought to him a basket of apples and roses, saying, "From Dorothea in Paradise," and vanished. Theophilus, of course, was a convert from that moment. The story forms the basis of Massinger's tragedy, *The Virgin Martyr* (1622).

Dorr Rebellion (1842). A rising in Rhode Island led by Thomas Wilson Dorr (1805–1854) to revise the state constitution, which severely restricted suffrage. In 1842 Dorr was elected governor by the reformers, while Samuel King was chosen at the regular elections; thus the state had two separate governments, Dorr basing his authority on the power of the people. The movement collapsed after Dorr's attempt to seize the state arsenal was frustrated by King, who had declared martial law. A constitution providing for nearly universal suffrage was adopted in 1843.

Dorset, Thomas Sackville, earl of. See Thomas SACKVILLE.

Dory, John. See JOHN DORY.

Dos Passos, John (1896–1970). American novelist. Best known for his trilogy *U.S.A.* (q.v.), Dos Passos was one of the group of Harvard writers who graduated shortly before World War I. With E. E. Cummings, who had also gone to Harvard, and Ernest Hemingway, who had not, Dos Passos joined the Norton-Harjes Ambulance Service during the war. From this experience came his first important novel, THREE SOLDIERS.

After the war he was a newspaperman and freelance writer. His next novel, MANHATTAN TRANSFER, was a major step toward the technical perfection of his later trilogy. The work also reveals the conflict between Dos Passos' concern for individual liberty and his social conscience which was to remain characteristic of his work as a writer. In the late 1920's, he turned to the theater with three plays noted for their "movie" technique: *The Moon Is a Gong* (1926), *Airways, Inc.* (1928), and *Fortune Heights* (1933).

In 1930, Dos Passos published THE 42ND PARALLEL, the first novel of his trilogy. *1919* (q.v.) and THE BIG MONEY completed the series, which was published as *U.S.A.* in 1938. A massive achievement, the trilogy is noted for its technical brilliance and mastery of language. Combining such special devices as the "news-reel" and the "camera eye" with many short, well-written biographies and the narrative proper, *U.S.A.* is a vast panorama of American life; indeed, the country itself is its subject and protagonist.

Dos Passos began a new trilogy, which was later published under the single title *District of Columbia* (1952), with ADVENTURES OF A YOUNG MAN. This saga of the Spottswood family also includes *Number One* (1943) and *The Grand Design* (1949). This trilogy and THE GROUND WE STAND ON mark a change in Dos Passos' social and political attitudes; always concerned with the freedom of the individual, he became much more conservative during this period. His books of nonfiction include *State of the Nation* (1944), *Tour of Duty* (1946), *The Prospect Before Us* (1950), *Chosen Country* (1951), *The Theme Is Freedom* (1956), *The Great Days* (1958), *Prospects of a Golden Age* (1959), and *Midcentury* (1961).

Dostoevski, Feodor Mikhailovich (1821–1881). Russian novelist. One of the most outstanding and influential writers of modern literature, Dostoevski was born in Moscow, the son of a doctor and the second of eight children. When he was 16 years old, Dostoevski's mother died. A year later, he was enrolled in the Military Engineering School in St. Petersburg. His elder brother Mikhail had also applied, but was turned down by the medical examiners. Young Dostoevski was left alone, in an atmosphere uncongenial to his nature, without Mikhail, his closest friend, and with what he considered an insufficient allowance. His letters to his father begin to sound a note that is to be heard often in his later correspondence: his desperate need for more money. Another problem was his work at the school; drawing plans for military fortifications interested him far less than reading literature. Before his graduation (1843), Dostoevski had already decided that his career would not be that of a military engineer. He remained in the army's service just a little over a year after graduation; he then resigned and took up his lifelong occupation as a writer.

Dostoevski's first publication (1844) was a translation of Balzac's novel *Eugénie Grandet*. Meanwhile, he was working on a novel of his own, a work in epistolary form entitled POOR FOLK. The manuscript reached the leading critic of the day, Vissarion BELINSKI, probably by way of Dostoevski's friend Dmitri Grigorovich and the poet Nikolai Nekrasov. Belinski read the work and launched into ecstatic praise of it. *Poor Folk* perfectly fulfilled his idea of what literature should be; it showed compassion for the poor and downtrodden and succeeded in stirring the reader's humanitarian feelings. Belinski's approval was enough to insure Dostoevski's reputation as a talented new writer. The novel was published (1846) in the *Petersburg Miscellany* (*Petersburgski sbornik*), edited by Nekrasov. A few weeks later Dostoevski's second work, THE DOUBLE, appeared. This short novel, a study of a poor clerk's mental disintegration, was less pleasing to both critics and public. In 1846, Dostoevski also published a short story, *Gospodin Prokharchin* (*Mr. Prokharchin*). The critical acclaim at first given Dostoevski's work was now absent: *The Double, Mr. Prokharchin,* and *Khozayka* (*The Landlady,* 1847) were all failures in Belinski's estimation. The adverse criticism strained Dostoevski's relations with Belinski and the circle of young writers surrounding him, including Nekrasov and Ivan TURGENEV—the feud with Turgenev becoming a lifetime preoccupation of Dostoevski.

A more serious problem than bad reviews or literary feuds began at about this time for the young author: the onset of the epileptic attacks that were to plague him throughout his life. Some writers, including Sigmund Freud, have speculated that these attacks actually began earlier, about the time Dostoevski's father was murdered by his serfs (1839). This theory holds that the attacks were a form of self-punishment for Dostoevski's suppressed wish for his father's death and that his later gambling mania was similarly caused. The preoccupation with the theme of parricide in Dostoevski's last novel, THE BROTHERS KARAMAZOV, is also evidence of Dostoevski's feeling of guilt, according to this view.

In 1848, Dostoevski published three short stories: *Slaboye serdtze* (*A Faint Heart*), *Chestnyi vor* (*The Honest Thief*), and *Belye nochi* (*White Nights*). In the last of these stories, the emphasis on the unreal, miragelike quality of St. Petersburg foreshadows a theme that was developed further in some of his later works. At this time, Dostoevski was also working on a novel, *Netochka Nezvanova*, but he never completed it. It was during this year that he became involved with a group of young intellectuals headed by Mikhail Vasilyevich Petrashevski (1819–1867). The Petrashevski circle, as the group was known, met to read and discuss the works of the French Utopian socialists and other political and social topics forbidden open discussion by the Czarist regime. In 1849 the members of the group were arrested. They were charged, among other things, with having read the banned Belinski letter to Nikolai Gogol and of having conspired to set up a secret printing press. After eight months in prison, during which time he wrote another short story, *Malenkyi geroi* (*The Little Hero*), Dostoevski was taken with his alleged fellow conspirators to the site of their execution. At the very last moment, they were informed that their sentence was actually to be exile and imprisonment in Siberia. The shattering experience of the near execution never left Dostoevski. He used the episode in his novel THE IDIOT, and mentioned it in his journalistic writings.

Dostoevski was sentenced to four years in the labor camp at Omsk, after which he was obliged to enlist for a four-year term in the army, most of which time he served at Semipalatinsk. These years have been described by Dostoevski as vitally important ones for his development as a writer. His enforced contact with the convicts at Omsk gave him a knowledge of the Russian lower classes, possessed by no other Russian author. During his prison term the only book allowed him was the New Testament, which he read constantly and which directed his thought toward the religious view of life so prominent in his novels. The fruits of his observations and thought in the Omsk prison were contained in his THE HOUSE OF THE DEAD.

While serving his army term, Dostoevski met and, after a hectic courtship, married (1857) the widow Marya Dmitrieyevna Isayeva. In 1859 he was allowed to resign from the army and to return to European Russia, settling first in Tver and then returning to St. Petersburg. While still in Siberia, he had begun writing again, and he arrived in St. Petersburg with two short novels: *Dyadushkin son* (*Uncle's Dream*) and A FRIEND OF THE FAMILY, both published in 1859. In 1861 his brother Mikhail began to publish the journal *Vremya* (*Time*). In this periodical Dostoevski published the novel THE INSULTED AND INJURED in which one of his major ideas, the beneficial effects of suffering, was first enunciated. He also serialized his *House of the Dead* in the journal.

In the summer of 1862, Dostoevski made his first trip to Europe, visiting Paris, London, and Geneva. His impressions of what he saw were contained in *Zimnye zametki o letnikh vpechatleniyakh* (*Winter Notes on Summer Impressions,* 1863).

The journal *Vremya* was suppressed by the government in 1863, because of an unfortunate article on the Polish rebellion of that year. Dostoevski, who had been editing the publication, made his second trip abroad at this time. This time, however, he had a companion, Apollinariya (Polina) Suslova, a young woman who had contributed a short piece to *Vremya* in 1861. Dostoevski's relations with his wife had been strained for some time. Whether Polina was a cause or a result of this situation is unclear. It is certain, however, that Polina was a torment to him. She was reputedly Dostoevski's model for "the infernal woman" whom he depicted in his later novels. On the trip through Europe, Dostoevski visited the gambling houses at Wiesbaden, Germany, where he gave in to the mania that, for some years, was to continue to trouble him.

Returning to Russia (1864), Dostoevski became editor of the new journal published by his brother. In this periodical, *Epokha* (*Epoch*), appeared NOTES FROM UNDERGROUND, the work that is generally cited, because of its artistic excellence and psychological acuteness, as the first of Dostoevski's mature writings. Dostoevski wrote the work while tending his dying wife, who was, at last, succumbing from consumption which had long afflicted her. Shortly after her death, Dostoevski had another blow: the death of his brother Mikhail. Left with the care of Mikhail's family as well as with that of his own stepson, he labored desperately to make *Epokha* a successful publication. The conservative political slant he gave the journal lessened its popularity, however, and in 1865 the venture had to be abandoned. Dostoevski made another trip to Europe where he again met Polina, did some gambling, and worked on a novel he hoped would pull him out of his financial predicament. This work, CRIME AND PUNISHMENT, was published in 1866. In the same year Dostoevski published a short novel, THE GAMBLER. The deadline for this work was fast approaching, and the novelist had to hire a stenographer to take down the work in shorthand and transcribe it. The girl hired for this job, Anna Grigoryevna Snitkina, became Dostoevski's second wife in 1867. The couple went abroad to escape creditors the following year. They lived in Dresden, Baden-Baden, and Geneva, always in financial straits made worse by Dostoevski's intermittent gambling sprees. On the trip to Geneva, they stopped off in Basle where Dostoevski saw Holbein's painting *Dead Christ* in the museum. The strong impression of the work prompted Dostoevski to include a discussion of it in the novel he was then writing. This work, published in serial form in 1868, was *The Idiot*. The effort involved in attempting to portray the saintly Myshkin in the novel was made more agonizing by the death of his infant daughter Sonya, who died at the age of three months.

During 1869, Dostoevski and Anna moved restlessly about Europe, from Switzerland, to Italy, to Austria, and finally to Dresden again. There a second daughter, Lyubov, was born. Dostoevski was at work during this period on one of his best short novels, THE ETERNAL HUSBAND. At the same time he was making preliminary notes for a massive work, to be contained in several novels, that would deal with the religious problems which had been the center of his thought for some years. The work was to be "the life of a great sinner," tracing his early growth, his falling away from faith, and his ultimate redemption. The broad scope of ideas contained in the plan was to include all of Dostoevski's late novels. STAVROGIN, the sinister hero of THE POSSESSED, could be taken as a depiction of the great sinner who had lost his faith, as could IVAN KARAMAZOV. Arkadi, the young hero of A RAW YOUTH, in some respects resembles the nascent sinner, who has not yet set out on the journey through the "furnace of doubt" that leads to religious faith. The idea of the movement into the world and back to faith is also present in *The Brothers Karamazov*.

After his return to Russia (1871), Dostoevski again entered journalistic work, editing the weekly *Grazhdanin* (*The Citizen*), in 1873–1874. In 1876 he published the first part of his DIARY OF A WRITER. This publication, which was also issued in 1877 and in 1880–1881, contained articles on political, social, and literary topics, as well as some original short stories, including *Krotkaya* (*A Gentle Spirit*, 1876) and *Son smeshnogo cheloveka* (*The Dream of a Ridiculous Man*, 1877). These last years of Dostoevski's life were financially the easiest ones he had known. Professionally, he was also at his peak, especially after the publication of *The Brothers Karamazov*. The climax of his long career came with his speech at the Pushkin celebration in Moscow in 1880, in which he cited the poet as a model of his own ideas about the unique, all-embracing universality of the Russian character. In January, 1881, Dostoevski died in St. Petersburg.

Since his death Dostoevski's reputation has steadily grown as one the greatest writers in literary history. The acuteness of his psychological perceptions and analyses have amazed later experts in psychology, including Freud. Dostoevski's philosophical profundity has provided a rich field of investigation and imitation for writers and philosophers. His range of philosophical ideas and approaches has led to his being claimed as a forerunner by such diverse groups as Russian Orthodox thinkers and atheistic existentialist writers. With TOLSTOI Dostoevski ranks as a supreme master of the realistic novel which is Russia's major contribution to literature. Dostoevski's artistic methods have until recently received less attention than his psychological and philosophical ideas. That he was above all a master artist has been attested by readers the world over and, perhaps more convincingly, by other great novelists who have an intimate knowledge of the craft of fiction.

In his own country, Dostoevski has less public recognition than he has in other countries. His well-known animus toward socialism, his emphasis on religion and on the irrationalism in the psychological processes of the individual mind have made him unattractive to the rulers of Soviet literary opinion, particularly during the most rigid periods of intellectual censorship under Stalin. As better ways are found to explain away embarrassing aspects of Dostoevski's work, Soviet publishers will undoubtedly tend to reprint his novels more often.

Dotheboys Hall. See NICHOLAS NICKLEBY.

Double, The (Dvoinik; 1846). A short novel by Feodor DOSTOEVSKI. *The Double* is a fantastic tale, similar in style and manner to some of Gogol's work, particularly to *Diary of a Madman,* which also depicts the mental disintegration of the hero. Yakov Petrovich GOLYADKIN, the hero of *The Double,* is a lowly civil servant who awkwardly and unsuccessfully pursues the daughter of his employer. After some cruel rebuffs, a strangeness enters Golyadkin's world and another Golyadkin, his absolute double, appears on the scene. Where the old Golyadkin had fumbled, the young Golyadkin is adroit. He is soon a favorite in exactly the way the first Golyadkin yearned to be. The nightmare ends when Golyadkin is taken away from his phantoms to the madhouse.

At the time of its publication, *The Double* aroused no enthusiasm in the critics. They were more interested in work which made some kind of social comment, such as Dostoevski's *Poor Folk,* than they were in depictions of the processes of psychological breakdown. The influential critic Belinski was especially displeased with the work and began to rue his earlier high praise of the author.

Doubting Castle. See PILGRIM'S PROGRESS.

Doughty, Charles Montagu (1843–1926). English traveler and writer. He is best known for his *Travels in Arabia Deserta* (1888), an account of two years of tribulation and wandering in Arabia notable for its vivid picture of Bedouin life and its curious, intriguing style, which combines English words and phrases with many Arabic expressions. Doughty also wrote a number of poems—which share some of the peculiarities of his prose—of which the best known is the lengthy *The Dawn in Britain* (1906).

Douglas. A family in Scottish history, legend, and romance. There were two branches: the *Black Douglases,* or senior branch, and the *Red Douglases,* who came to the fore later. They are prominent in Sir Walter Scott's novels, notably the following:

(1) *Sir James,* the first of the Black Douglases. See James DOUGLAS.

(2) *Archibald the Grim,* natural son of "the Good Sir James." He is prominent in *The Fair Maid of Perth.*

(3) *James Douglas,* earl of Morton, one of the Red Douglases. He figures prominently in THE MONASTERY and THE ABBOT.

(4) *Ellen Douglas.* Heroine of Scott's narrative poem, *The Lady of the Lake.*

Douglas, Lord Alfred (1870–1945). English poet, noted as a sonnet writer. His relationship with Oscar Wilde provoked his father, Lord Queensberry, to action that led to Wilde's conviction for homosexual practices. See DE PROFUNDIS.

Douglas, Gawain or **Gavin** (1474?–1522). Scottish poet, bishop of Dunkeld. He was the author of *The Palace of Honor* (printed c. 1553) and *King*

Hart (first printed in 1786), two allegorical poems, and a translation of the *Aeneid* (completed 1513), which is called the earliest translation of a Latin classic into English. Douglas was a member of the group called the Scottish Chaucerians.

Douglas, James. Called **Black Douglas** (1286–1330). In the days of Robert Bruce and Edward II, Douglas invaded England and plundered many towns and villages in the North. In his *History of Scotland*, Scott writes: "It was said that the name of this indefatigable and successful chief had become so formidable that women in the northern countries, used to still their froward children by threatening them with the Black Douglas." He destroyed an English garrison three times, and it is on one of these incidents that Scott based his novel CASTLE DANGEROUS.

Douglas, Lloyd C[assel] (1877–1951). American novelist. A clergyman, Douglas was over 50 when he published his first book, *Magnificent Obsession* (1929), and thereafter he published several best-selling novels of a piously didactic, inspirational character. Perhaps the best known of these is *The Robe* (1942), the story of what happened to Christ's robe after the Crucifixion. Other novels are *Precious Jeopardy* (1933), *Green Light* (1935), *White Banners* (1936), *Disputed Passage* (1939) and *The Big Fisherman* (1948).

Douglas, [George] Norman (1868–1952). English novelist and travel writer. Best known for the novel SOUTH WIND, Douglas lived for many years on the island of Capri and in Italy and other Mediterranean countries, and made these the settings for his books. An art lover and a scholar (biologist, geologist, archaeologist, and classicist), he was also a hedonist and a skeptic. His interests are uniquely blended in his books. In *Siren Land* (1911), his first book, he established his style. It is a traveler's lively description of Sorrento and Capri, interspersed with learned, fantastic, and lightly satirical essays. *Fountains in the Sand* (1912) is about Tunisia, and *Old Calabria* (1915), considered his best travel book, is about southern Italy. The novels *They Went* (1920) and *In the Beginning* (1927) are fantasies about mankind's early history. Among Douglas's other books are *London Street Games* (1916); *Birds and Beasts of the Greek Anthology* (1927); *Some Limericks* (1928); *How About Europe?* (1929), a claim that Christianity is causing the decay of our society, and *Looking Back* (1933), a fragmentary autobiography.

Douglas, Stephen A[rnold] (1813–1861). American statesman, known as the "Little Giant." After holding several state offices in Illinois, Douglas was elected to Congress in 1843 and to the U.S. Senate in 1847. He introduced the KANSAS-NEBRASKA ACT, which incorporated the principle of popular sovereignty, but lost the support of Southern Democrats when he opposed the proslavery Lecompton constitution for Kansas, which he claimed violated popular sovereignty. During his famous debates (1858) with Abraham Lincoln when both were candidates for the Senate, Douglas formulated his "Freeport doctrine," maintaining that the people of a territory might admit or exclude slavery because slavery could not exist unless it was supported by local police regulations. Although Douglas won the Senate seat, the Freeport doctrine further alienated Southerners and probably cost him their backing for the 1860 Democratic nomi-

nation. In 1860 Douglas was the presidential candidate of Northern Democrats and lost to Lincoln.

Douglas, William O[rville] (1898–   ). American jurist and author. Beginning as a high-school teacher in Yakima, Wash., Douglas then studied law, practiced in New York City, and taught at Columbia and Yale universities. He entered government service in 1929 and was appointed to the U.S. Supreme Court by President Roosevelt 10 years later.

Several of his books, based on trips abroad, give expert reports on political conditions and vivid depictions of foreign scenes; these include *Strange Lands and Friendly People* (1951), *Beyond the High Mountains* (1952), and *North from Himalaya* (1953). Douglas, an outdoor man and a lover of nature, also wrote *My Wilderness: The Pacific West* (1960). Among his other works are *An Almanac of Liberty* (1954), *America Challenged* (1960), *A Living Bill of Rights* (1961), and *Mr. Lincoln and the Negroes* (1963).

Douglass, Frederick (1817?–1895). American abolitionist, orator, and journalist. The son of a Negro slave and a white father, Douglass escaped to the North in 1838. A speech he delivered at an antislavery convention in Nantucket in 1841 made such an impression that he was soon in great demand as a speaker. Mobbed and beaten because of his views, he described his experiences in an outspoken *Narrative of the Life of Frederick Douglass* (1845). After a two-year stay in Great Britain, where he earned enough money to buy his freedom, he founded *The North Star*, a newspaper which he published for 17 years, advocating the use of Negro troops during the Civil War and civil rights for freedmen. He held various public offices after the war.

Doukhobors. See DUKHOBORS.

Dove Cottage. The house where Dorothy and William WORDSWORTH made their home, from 1799 to 1807, at Grasmere in the English Lake District. See LAKE POETS.

Dover Beach (1867). A poem by Matthew ARNOLD expressing his pessimism with regard to the future of the modern world and advocating personal fidelity and love as the rather desperate substitute for the ebbing "sea of faith":

> Ah, love, let us be true
> To one another! for the world, which seems
> To lie before us like a land of dreams,
> So various, so beautiful, so new,
> Hath really neither joy, nor love, nor light. . . .

Dowden, Edward (1843–1913). Anglo-Irish essayist, poet, and critic. He is known chiefly for his numerous books on Shakespeare such as *Shakespeare, His Mind and Art* (1875), *A Shakespeare Primer* (1877), and *Introduction to Shakespeare* (1893). He was also the author of a notable *Life of Shelley* (1866).

Dowland, John (1563–1626). Composer and lutenist. Dowland was born in Ireland and died in London, but spent much of his life in France, Germany, and Denmark. He ended his days as lutenist to the King of England. A man of melancholy temperament, Dowland is accounted the greatest lutenist the world has ever known, and his compositions for lute, and for voice and lute, are the finest of their type.

Downing Street. Figuratively, the British government in power (because the Prime Minister lives at No. 10, and his cabinet usually meets there) or the foreign office (which is also located there). It is in Westminster.

Dowsabell. A common name for a sweetheart, especially an unsophisticated country girl, in poems of Elizabethan times. It is from the French *douce et belle*, sweet and beautiful. Michael Drayton wrote a poem called *The Ballad of Dowsabell* (1606).

Dowson, Ernest [Christopher] (1867–1900). English poet. Dowson is best known for his poem CYNARA, properly entitled *Nom Sum Qualis Eram Bonae Sub Regno Cynarae*.

Doyle, Sir **Arthur Conan** (1859–1930). English novelist, known chiefly for his series of tales concerning Sherlock HOLMES. Also noteworthy are his historical novels, *Micah Clarke* (1888) and THE WHITE COMPANY, and his imaginative fantasy *The Lost World* (1912). The Holmes stories, conceived to augment Doyle's income from an unsuccessful medical practice, quickly made their author famous. At one point, tiring of the detective, Doyle attempted to exterminate him in *The Memoirs of Sherlock Holmes* (1894), but the clamor of his admirers forced him to resurrect Holmes for several further volumes, and his popularity has waned little since. Doyle was much interested in the occult, and wrote a *History of Spiritualism* (1926). Among his finer characters are Professor CHALLENGER and Brigadier GERARD.

Drachenfels (*Ger.* dragon-rock). The home of the dragon slain by Siegfried in the NIBELUNGENLIED.

Drachman, Holger (1846–1908). Danish poet. At first, Drachman joined the "Modern Awakening" movement led by Georg Brandes and wrote poems of passionate sympathy for suffering laborers. Among his early collections are *Doempede Melodier* (1875), *Ungdom i Digt og Sang* (1879), *Ranker og Roser* (1879), and *Princessen og det halve kongerige* (1878). In the 1880's, however, he turned his lyric gifts to new ends and produced the romantic, patriotic verse of such collections as *Dybe Strenge* (1884), *Sangenes Bog* (1889), and *Unge Viser* (1892).

Draco; (Drakon; fl. 650 B.C.). An Athenian legislator. In 621 B.C. he was given extraordinary power to codify the laws of Athens for the first time. His work was designed to replace individual revenge with public justice. His code was known for its severity, and was said to have been written in blood, rather than ink. The death penalty was prescribed for several crimes, and cases of murder were to be tried by the AREOPAGUS. Under Draco's Code, debtors could be claimed as slaves. SOLON abolished the Code except for the law relating to murder.

dragon. A mythical beast. Found in the mythology and folklore of innumerable peoples, it was commonly conceived of as a kind of large serpent of hostile disposition. In its earliest forms, it was a monster sea serpent, perhaps suggested to the primitive mind by the undulating surface and unruly habits of rivers and seas. The first known example is the Sumerian KUR, though its precise appearance is not clear from the three extant myths in which he or she appears. Kur, like all dragons, seems to have existed mainly to be killed by a hero; the Sumerian champions who accomplished this feat were ENKI, NINURTA, and the goddess Inanna.

The basic theme of the sea dragons slain by a hero was developed further by the Babylonian conquerors of Sumeria in the story of the WAR OF THE GODS, in which the primeval sea, TIAMAT, the mother of the gods, is regarded as a dragon; she is killed by the hero Marduk. Among the Canaanites it is Baal, the storm god, who subdues YAM, the dragon of the sea. The Hebrew Yahweh is similarly credited with the destruction of the leviathan, of Rahab, and of simply "the dragon." Several Greek heroes slay dragons that are also associated with water and with the Near East. PERSEUS rescued Andromeda from a sea monster in Canaan; the Canaanite CADMUS killed a dragon that guarded a spring at Thebes. The HYDRA, as the name implies, was also a water creature, and Heracles had many Near Eastern connections. Even the famous feat attributed to St. GEORGE is an echo of the Perseus myth, for George killed his dragon at Lydda very near to Joppa, where Perseus' dragon ravaged the land.

Another common class of dragons guarded sacred places. This notion may have sprung from the widespread belief that the dead returned as serpents (Cadmus, himself, became one) and were often venerated as such. Sacred snakes were associated with many oracles, including that at Delphi, and for such religious festivals as the Thesmophoria at Athens. Dragons (Gr. *drakon*, snake) guarded the apples of the HESPERIDES and the GOLDEN FLEECE. The less benevolent dragons of northern Europe guarded hoards of treasure, which were wrested from them by such heroes as BEOWULF and Sigurd (SIEGFRIED).

The dragons of the Chinese and Japanese mythology are totally different from the hostile varieties. Powerful spirits of air, sea, and earth, they are generally benevolent and are responsible to a considerable degree for the orderly functioning of natural phenomena.

Among the many Christian saints who are usually pictured with dragons may be mentioned St. Michael; St. Margaret; St. Sylvester, the pope; St. Samson, archbishop of Dol; St. Donatus; St. Clement of Metz; St. Romain of Rouen, who destroyed the huge dragon, La Gargouille, which ravaged the Seine; St. Philip the Apostle, who killed another at Hierapolis, in Phrygia; St. Martha, who slew the terrible dragon, Tarasque, at Aix-la-Chapelle; St. Florent, who killed a dragon that haunted the Loire; St. Cado, St. Maudet, and St. Pol, who did similar feats in Brittany; and St. Keyne of Cornwall.

Among the ancient Britons and Welsh the dragon was the national symbol on the war standard; hence the term, PENDRAGON for the *dux bellorum*, or leader in war (*pen* = head or chief). See FAFNER; GRENDEL.

Dragontina. In the ORLANDO INNAMORATO of Boiardo, an enchantress who rules the Island of Forgetfulness. At one point in the story, Orlando is her prisoner until rescued by Angelica, who needs him to defend her fortress at Albracca.

Drake, Sir **Francis** (1540?–1596). First English circumnavigator of the globe. After sailing as a privateer against Spanish vessels in the West Indies, Drake in December, 1577, set off on his round-the-world voyage. He passed through the Straits of Magellan, up the coast of South America, and as far as 48° north latitude along the North American coast, which he named New Albion and claimed in the name of Elizabeth. He then sailed to Celebes, around the Cape of Good Hope, and back to England, returning in October of 1580. He fought against the Spanish Armada in 1588, and died in the course of an expedition to the West Indies.

Drake, Joseph Rodman (1795–1820). American poet and satirist. Drake studied medicine but after obtaining his degree opened a pharmacy in New York City. His early death from tuberculosis prevented his full development as a poet. With Fitz-Greene HALLECK, Drake composed the witty *Croaker Papers;* he is best known for the posthumously published tale in verse called *The Culprit Fay* (1835). A nature fantasy, the poem tells the story of a fay who loved a mortal maiden. Another well-known poem is the eulogy, *The American Flag* (1819). Drake is buried in the New York City park that was named in his honor.

Drake, Temple. A character in William Faulkner's SANCTUARY and REQUIEM FOR A NUN. A 17-year-old college student in *Sanctuary,* Temple is a provocative and irresponsible girl who invites by her actions the rape she half fears and half desires. Playing the part of the victim, she subsequently allows herself to be kept at a brothel by POPEYE and perjures herself at the murder trial of an innocent man, less out of malice toward the accused than out of indifference. In *Requiem for a Nun,* she persists in her former attitudes by refusing, until the very end, to see herself as anything but a respectable woman wronged by circumstance.

dramatic irony. A theatrical device, consisting in the conscious production by the author of an ironical situation, i.e., a marked incongruity between a character's words and the action; as for instance in Schiller's *Wallenstein* when the hero (not aware of the plot on his life of which the audience has been informed) says before going to bed: "I intend to take a long rest." The understanding of the unintentional play on words imparts to the audience for a moment the role of "an omniscient god of the drama."

dramatic unities. See UNITIES.

Drapier's Letters (1724–1725). A series of pamphlets by Jonathan SWIFT, purporting to be from the pen of a linen draper, "M. B. Drapier." They attack a patent for coining halfpence granted to William Wood by King George I and Sir Robert Walpole without the consent of the Irish Parliament, and advise the Irish not to accept the coinage. Although Wood's halfpence were certified a sound coinage, the scheme was defeated after severe riots by the Dublin mob.

Draupadi. In Hindu legend, daughter of king Drupada and wife of the five Pandava brothers (in the MAHABHARATA). In the epic, she is a strongwilled, proud character, whose outrage at being disrobed in the palace hall by Duryodhana is one of the major factors in leading up to the battle of Kurukshetra, when the Pandavas take revenge on Duryodhana.

Draupnir. In Scandinavian mythology, a magic ring, the symbol of fertility, made for Odin by the dwarfs. Every ninth night it dropped eight rings equal in size and beauty to itself.

Drayman Henschel (Fuhrmann Henschel; 1898). A drama by Gerhart HAUPTMANN. A man

has promised his late wife to be faithful to her memory. However, he is trapped into marriage by the machinations of his ambitious housekeeper. Oppressed and bullied by her, he finally commits suicide.

Drayton, Michael (1563–1631). English poet. Born in the same county (Warwickshire) as Shakespeare, he matched the master in the range, if not the quality, of his poetic achievement. Always experimenting and continually revising, Drayton wrote sonnets, dramas, odes, mythological poems, satires, pastorals, and historical verse narratives. His works include *Idea, the Shepherd's Garland* (1593); *Idea's Mirror* (1594), a sonnet sequence; *England's Heroical Epistles* (1597); POLYOLBION, a poetical survey of the topography of England; NIMPHIDIA, a charming minor epic set in a fairy atmosphere; *Idea,* a completely revised version of his earlier sonnet sequence; and *The Muses Elyzium* (1630). Drayton also wrote a number of plays that have not survived. According to one tradition, it was as a result of a "merry meeting" with Drayton and Ben Jonson that Shakespeare contracted the illness that resulted in his death.

Dream Children: A Reverie (1822). One of the best-known essays of Charles LAMB, prompted by the death of the author's brother James. In it, Lamb describes an imaginary conversation held with the children he has never had. See ALICE W—N.

Dream of Gerontius, A. A poem by John Henry NEWMAN in which Gerontius makes his last journey

Title page of Drayton's satire *The Owle* (1604).

to God, carried by his guardian angel through a world of good and evil spirits. *A Dream of Gerontius* has been set to music in the form of an oratorio by Sir Edward Elgar (1900).

Dream of the Red Chamber. See HUNG LOU MENG.

Dream of the Rood, The. Old English religious poem, one of the finest, of 156 lines in ALLITERATIVE VERSE. A fragment of it is inscribed (early eighth century) on a stone cross in Scotland, and the VERCELLI BOOK has a complete version (late ninth century). The poet lyrically describes dreaming that the Rood, or True Cross, speaks to him about its own history and urges him to promote its cult. Then he tells how the dream has changed his life, alluding to Christ's life in his own prayer for heavenly reward.

dreams, the gates of. Two gates in Hades, one of ivory and one of horn. Dreams that delude pass through the ivory gate, those that come true pass through the gate of horn. This fancy depends upon two puns: ivory in Greek is *elephas,* and the verb *eliphairo* means to cheat with empty hopes; the Greek for horn is *keras,* and the verb *karanoo* means to accomplish. Anchises dismissed Aeneas through the ivory gate, on quitting the infernal regions, to indicate the unreality of his vision.

Dreary Story, A (Skuchnaya istoriya; 1889). A story by Anton CHEKHOV subtitled *From the Notebook of an Old Man.* The story is usually regarded as the starting point of Chekhov's mature writings. In it he introduces the theme of the difficulty of real communication between people, which he was to take up in so many of his later works. The old man of the tale, Professor Nikolai Stepanovich, realizes as his life draws to a close that he has lived his years without a unifying ideal to make a whole of his personal, professional, and social relationships. As he reviews it, his life seems fragmented, aimless, and worthless. The same kind of despair is experienced by his young ward Katya. Because neither can really communicate with the other, both the professor and Katya are left to endure their agonies singly.

Dred Scott decision (1857). A U.S. Supreme Court decision in the case of Dred Scott (1795?–1858), a Negro slave who had been taken by his master from Missouri to Illinois and Wisconsin, where slavery was prohibited. After his return to Missouri, Scott sued for his liberty on the basis of his residence in free territory. Deciding against Scott, the court held that he was not a citizen of the U.S. and therefore could not bring suit in a federal court, and that the MISSOURI COMPROMISE, which forbade slavery in Wisconsin, was unconstitutional because it deprived persons of their property (i.e., their slaves) without due process of law. The decision was bitterly attacked by Northern abolitionists because it declared in effect that slavery could not be barred from the territories.

Dreigroschenoper, Die. See THREEPENNY OPERA, THE.

Dreiser, Theodore [Herman Albert] (1871–1945). American novelist. Dreiser is known as one of the principal exponents of American NATURALISM; though many critics have inveighed against the clumsiness and crudeness of his style, the power and importance of his work cannot be denied.

The son of a highly religious father and a sensitive and loving mother, Dreiser knew poverty from an early age and was later to react strongly against organized religion. After a year at the University of Indiana and a career as a newspaperman in Chicago, St. Louis, Pittsburgh, and New York, he submitted his first novel, SISTER CARRIE, to Doubleday, Page & Co. Read by Frank Norris, who was very enthusiastic, the novel was accepted for publication, only to be withdrawn later after only 1,000 copies had been printed (but not distributed) when Doubleday himself objected to the book's frankness and its lack of conventional moral viewpoint.

Despondent about *Sister Carrie,* Dreiser contemplated suicide, but was guided by his brother Paul into a very lucrative position with the Butterick publications; in a few years he had become head of the firm. After a 10-year interval, Dreiser published JENNIE GERHARDT. Like *Sister Carrie,* it is an absorbing study of a fallen woman. THE FINANCIER began "the trilogy of desire," the story of a captain of high finance, Frank Cowperwood. Influenced by the evolutionary theories of Herbert Spencer and by Nietzsche's concept of the superman, Dreiser still managed to combine with these ideas a poetic sense of the mystery and beauty of the universe. While these ideas are subordinate in *The Financier* and THE TITAN, in the final work of the trilogy, *The Stoic* (1947), they assume great importance.

THE "GENIUS," the most autobiographical of all Dreiser's novels, is generally considered one of his least successful works. During this period Dreiser also published three autobiographical books: *A Traveler at Forty* (1913), *A Hoosier Holiday* (1916), and *A Book About Myself* (1922; later republished as *Newspaper Days*). *Hey-Rub-a-Dub-Dub: A Book of the Mystery and Terror and Wonder of Life* was published in 1919.

In 1925 came AN AMERICAN TRAGEDY, a book based on the famous case of Chester Gillette's murder of Grace Brown. In 1927, Dreiser visited Russia, publishing after his return the two books that marked his acceptance of socialism and the rejection of his former despairing emphasis on fate and determinism: *Dreiser Looks at Russia* (1928) and *Tragic America* (1931). From this point on Dreiser concerned himself more and more with socialism and left-wing politics.

The Bulwark, which was begun as early as 1910, was published posthumously in 1946, and *The Stoic,* the last of the Cowperwood trilogy, in 1947. Both show the influence of the mystic strain which, although present in Dreiser's character from the beginning, became pronounced in his last years. Other works include *Plays of the Natural and Supernatural* (1916), *Free and Other Stories* (1918), *The Hand of the Potter* (1919), *Twelve Men* (1919), *The Color of a Great City* (1923), *Moods* (1926), *A Gallery of Women* (1929), *Fine Furniture* (1930), and *Epitaph* (1930).

Drepane. See PHAEACIANS.

Dressler, Marie (1873–1934). The stage name of Leila Koerber, a Canadian-born American comedienne. She had great success on the stage and in motion pictures, mainly in broad comic roles that were lifted out of mediocrity through the honesty and warmth of her personality. She made famous a song, *Heaven Will Protect the Working Girl.*

Dreyfus, Alfred (1859-1935). Central figure in the famous Dreyfus case which divided France for almost four years. An officer in the French artillery of Jewish descent, Captain Dreyfus was accused and convicted of having betrayed military secrets. In 1894 he was sent to Devil's Island to serve a life imprisonment sentence. Evidence attesting to the innocence of Dreyfus and to the guilt of a Major Esterhazy was uncovered but suppressed by the military. Dreyfus was finally pardoned in 1906 by the *Cour de Cassation.* He transcended, however, his individual significance, becoming a symbol of injustice for liberal intellectuals who vigorously opposed right-wing reactionary forces such as the military and the church. Emile Zola wrote the letter J'ACCUSE, and many other men of letters were ardent Dreyfus supporters. In *A la recherche du temps perdu,* Marcel Proust gives an excellent picture of the alignment of French opinion on the controversial case.

Dr. Faustus, The Tragical History of (first performed in 1588; first published in 1604). A play by Christopher MARLOWE. The yearning for the infinite that characterizes Marlowe's heroes is embodied in Dr. Faustus, the seeker after power through knowledge. The legend of the scholar who sells his soul to the Devil becomes a powerful portrait of a man torn by conflicting desires. In a scene that borrows from earlier morality drama, a good and bad angel, external representations of inner conflict, battle over the soul of Faustus. Despite the moral at the end, which advises the wise to heed the awful fate of Faustus, Marlowe's attitude throughout is one of sympathy and understanding for the boundless longings of his hero. See FAUST.

Drinkwater, John (1882-1937). English poet, dramatist, and biographer. His poetry belongs to the GEORGIAN school. He wrote historical and biographical plays, such as *Abraham Lincoln* (1918) and *Mary Stuart* (1921). *Inheritance* (1931) and *Discovery* (1932) are autobiographical volumes.

driver of Europe (Fr., *cocher de l'Europe*). The designation the empress of Russia used for the duc de Choiseul (1719-1785), minister of Louis XV, because he had spies all over Europe, and thus ruled its political cabals.

Dr. Jekyll and Mr. Hyde. See STRANGE CASE OF DR. JEKYLL AND MR. HYDE, THE.

Dromio of Ephesus and Dromio of Syracuse. In Shakespeare's COMEDY OF ERRORS, the merry identical twins who are the servants of the identical twins Antipholus of Ephesus and Antipholus of Syracuse. The twin Dromios are roundly beaten and sent hither and yon in the confusion which results when they and their masters, unbeknownst to each other, end up in the same city.

Dropping the Pilot. The title of a political cartoon in the English magazine *Punch* by Sir John Tenniel. It dramatized the resignation of Bismarck after his disagreement with Kaiser Wilhelm II in 1890. Bismarck, as the old pilot, solemnly leaves his ship while the youthful emperor, now in sole command, watches.

Droste-Hülshoff, Annette von (1797-1848). German poetess. She is remembered especially for ballads in which she combines vivid renderings of natural scenes from her Westphalian homeland with a swift, subtle narrative gift and a compact use of language. Another side of her nature, deeply religious, is seen in the collection *Das geistliche Jahr* (*The Spiritual Year,* 1851). Her famous novella, *Die Judenbuche* (*The Jews' Beech Tree,* 1842), though set in a simple rustic atmosphere, is psychologically deep and succeeds in evoking a powerful sense of mystery about the workings of fate.

Drugger, Abel. A character in Ben Jonson's comedy THE ALCHEMIST (1610). A seller of tobacco, he is artless and gullible in the extreme. He is building a new house, and comes to Subtle the "alchemist" to know on which side to set the shop-door, how to dispose the shelves so as to ensure most luck, on what days he may trust his customers, and when it will be unlucky for him to do so.

Druid. A member of the ancient Gaulish and British order of priests, teachers of religion, magicians, or sorcerers. The word is the Lat. *druidae,* or *druides* (always plural), which was borrowed from the Old Irish *drui* and Gaelic *draoi.* Practically our only literary sources of knowledge of the druidic cult are Pliny and the *Commentaries* of Caesar, which say that the rites of the Druids were conducted in oak groves and that they regarded the oak and the mistletoe with peculiar veneration; that they studied the stars and nature generally; that they believed in the transmigration of souls, and dealt in "magic." Their distinguishing badge was a serpent's egg (see DRUID'S EGG), to which powerful properties were credited. The order seems to have been highly organized, and, according to Strabo, every chief had his druid, and every chief druid was allowed a guard of thirty men.

In Samuel Butler's *Hudibras* there is an allusion to the

> Money by the Druids borrowed,
> In t'other world to be restored.

This refers to a legend recorded by one Patricius (St. Patrick?) to the effect that the Druids were wont to borrow money to be repaid in the life to come.

Druid's egg. A fabled egg hatched by the joint labor of several serpents, and buoyed into the air by their hissing. The person who caught it had to ride off at full speed, to avoid being stung to death; but was sure to prevail in every contest, and to be courted by those in power. Pliny says he had seen one of them, and that it was about as large as a moderate-sized apple.

Drummond, William Henry (1854-1907). Irish-born Canadian poet and physician. Drummond is best known for his verse in French-Canadian dialect about rural life in Quebec. These poems are a mingling of humor and sentiment, at times slightly satirical. Collections of his work include *The Habitant and Other French-Canadian Poems* (1897) and *Johnnie Courteau and Other Poems* (1901).

Drummond of Hawthornden, William (1585-1649). Scottish poet. Owner of an extensive library and ardently Royalist in politics, he translated French and Italian lyric poetry, especially the works of Ronsard, Passerat, and Desportes. His own verse, which includes *Flowers of Zion* (1623), is known for its grace and smoothness. He also left interesting notes on Ben Jonson's conversation during the latter's visit to Hawthornden in 1618.

Drums Along the Mohawk (1936). A historical novel by Walter D. EDMONDS. The bitter struggle in the Mohawk Valley between the supporters of the American Revolution and their British foes is vividly portrayed. Stress is laid on the destructiveness of the Tories and their Indian allies. The novel is based on the kind of careful research that Edmonds describes in *How You Begin a Novel* (*Atlantic Monthly,* Aug., 1936).

Druon, Maurice. Pen name of **Maurice Kessel** (1918–). French novelist. *The Curtain Falls* (*La Fin des hommes*) is a detailed chronicle of the moral and commercial corruption of two bourgeois families between the world wars. The work includes *The Magnates* (*Les Grandes Familles;* 1948; first translated as *The Rise of Simon Lachaume*), *Feet of Clay* (*La Chute des corps;* 1950), and *Rendezvous in Hell* (1951). *The Accursed Kings* (6 vols., 1956–1961) is a series of historical novels about the French monarchy of the 14th century. *The Glass Coffin* (1963) is a collection of short stories.

Drury Lane. A street in London named after Drury House, which was built by Sir William Drury in the time of Henry VIII. The street has been the site of several theaters of the same name, the first of which was built by Thomas Killigrew in 1663 as the Theatre Royal and was described by Samuel Pepys. After it was destroyed by fire in 1672, a new theater, designed by Christopher Wren, was erected on the site of the present Drury Lane Theatre and was opened in 1674.

Druses. A people and sect of Syria living south of Damascus near the mountains of Lebanon and Anti-Libanus. Their unitarian faith combines Moslem, Christian, Jewish, and Sufist ideas. They offer devotions both in mosques and churches, worship the images of saints, and observe the fast of RAMADAN. Their name is probably derived from that of their first apostle, Ismail Darazi or Durzi (11th century A.D.).

Browning wrote a tragedy, *Return of the Druses* (1841).

dryad. In Greek mythology, a tree nymph. Originally, the dryads were specifically oak-nymphs (*drys,* oak), but the name came to be applied to all tree nymphs. Nature spirits who died with the trees they inhabited, they were also called *hamadryads.* The most famous of them, perhaps, was Eurydice, the wife of Orpheus.

Dryden, John (1631–1700). English poet, dramatist, and critic. He was the outstanding figure in letters during the Restoration and literary dictator of his age.

Dryden came from a good, but impecunious, country family with a Parliamentarian and Church of England background. In his middle 20's he went to London, where his gifts were quickly recognized in intellectual circles, though he had to struggle for years to earn a respectable living by means of his plays and translations. Dryden made several radical shifts in his religion and politics: in 1659 he eulogized Cromwell in the *Heroick Stanzas;* a year later he celebrated Charles II in *Astraea Redux;* in 1682 he published RELIGIO LAICI, a defense of Anglicanism; five years later THE HIND AND THE PANTHER revealed him as an ardent partisan of Catholicism and Catholic James II. In 1688, however, he refused to take an oath of allegiance to William and Mary, remaining loyal to James II at the cost of important offices, including the laureateship of England.

Dryden's earliest work, such as his elegy *Upon the Death of Lord Hastings* (1650), is in the extravagant late metaphysical vein of Cowley. Soon he developed a more restrained and natural style, close to normal cultivated speech and employing the heroic couplet to emphasize its finish and point. This was to be the dominant poetic style for a century, though perhaps never again more forceful and various than it was in Dryden's hands. It was a vehicle particularly well-adapted to satirical and didactic works, such as ABSALOM AND ACHITOPHEL, THE MEDAL, MACFLECKNOE, *Religio Laici,* and *The Hind and the Panther.* Dryden also used it in his translations of Virgil and other Latin poets and in a number of his plays, although his greatest play, ALL FOR LOVE, is written in blank verse. His prose writings are also of great importance: the orderly, lucid, and masculine style which distinguishes his prefaces and critical essays, such as the ESSAY OF DRAMATIC POESY, became one of the chief models for modern prose. These works reveal Dryden as an acute and extraordinarily sensible critic.

In addition to those referred to above, the following poems by Dryden also deserve mention: the lyrics *To Mrs. Killegrew* (1686), *A Song for St. Cecilia's Day* (1687), and *Alexander's Feast* (1697); a number of longer poems, such as ANNUS MIRABILIS; and his paraphrases and translations of Chaucer, Boccaccio, Ovid, Juvenal, Lucretius, and Homer. Other memorable plays by Dryden are *The Indian Emperor* (1665), *Almanzor and Almahide, or The Conquest of Granada* (1670), *Aurengzebe* (1675), and *Don Sebastian* (1690). See John SHEFFIELD.

Dryope. In Greek legend sister of Iole and wife of Andraemon. For having plucked inadvertently the lotus into which the nymph Lotis had been changed, Dryope herself was changed into a lotus.

Dry Salvages, The. See FOUR QUARTETS.

Duat. In Egyptian mythology, one of the abodes of the dead in the underworld through which the sun passed by night.

Du Barry, Comtesse. **Mari Jeanne Bécu** (1743–1793). Adventuress and mistress of Louis XV from 1768 to his death (1774). She ruled both king and court, and was famous for her prodigality as a patron of artists and men of letters. She was guillotined on Dec. 7, 1793.

Du Bellay, Joachim (1522–1560). French poet. A companion of Ronsard at the Collège de Coqueret in Paris, Du Bellay was one of the founders of the PLÉIADE and author of its poetic program: DÉFENSE ET ILLUSTRATION DE LA LANGUE FRANÇAISE. His melancholy nature easily lent itself to the Petrarchan type of idealized love then in vogue, a tendency reflected in his first work, *L'Olive* (1549), the first French collection of sonnets. Yet the following year he produced *A une Dame,* a biting satire of this very convention. In 1553, ailing and downcast at his failure to win royal favor, he accompanied his cousin Cardinal Du Bellay to Rome as his secretary. He approached Rome with the reverence of a confirmed Latinist and left it four years later greatly disillusioned. Upon his return to France in 1558, he published four volumes: the *Poemata,* written in Latin in the style of the Italian humanists; *Les Antiquités de Rome,* in which he exalted ancient Rome; *Les Regrets,* in which he bitterly satirized the mediocrity of contemporary Rome and expressed his regrets over his self-imposed exile; and the *Divers jeux rustiques,* in which he freed himself from his cares and relaxed into pastoral pieces and sensual love poems. The *Poète courtisan* (1559) was a last embittered satire on the court poets.

Second only to Ronsard in the eyes of his contemporaries and posterity, Du Bellay could not reconcile himself to this position and harbored a jealousy which he did not always attempt to hide.

Dubliners (1914). A collection of short stories by James JOYCE. By dealing successively with incidents in the childhood, adolescence, maturity, and public life of Dubliners, Joyce provides a picture of the paralyzing world from which he fled. Most of the characters and scenes are mean and petty, sometimes tragic; they are drawn from ordinary Catholic middle-class life. The style is simple and moving, more in the manner of Anton Chekhov than in that of the author's more famous works. In all the stories, Joyce uses a device he named the EPIPHANY, having a sudden remark, symbol, or moment that epitomizes and clarifies the meaning of a complex experience. Among the best known of the stories are THE SISTERS, *Counterparts,* CLAY, IVY DAY IN THE COMMITTEE ROOM, and THE DEAD. Several of the characters introduced in *Dubliners* reappear in *Ulysses.*

Joyce had difficulty in finding a publisher for his book, and it did not appear until many years after it had been written. It was severely attacked because the names of actual persons and places in Dublin are mentioned in it.

Du Bois, William E[dward] B[urghardt] (1868–1963). American writer, editor, and teacher. The descendant of a French Huguenot and an African slave, Du Bois was trained as a sociologist and did much to promote greater understanding of Negroes. *The Souls of Black Folk* (1903), a collection of essays, is his best-known work. He wrote many other works, among them *The Negro* (1915), *Black Folk: Then and Now* (1930), *Color and Democracy* (1945), *In Battle for Peace* (1952), and *The Black Flame, A Trilogy,* which consists of *The Ordeal of Mansart* (1957), *Mansart Builds a School* (1959), and *Worlds of Color* (1961).

Du Bos, Charles (1882–1939). French critic. Du Bos combined Catholicism with the influence of Walter Pater to become a leading commentator on the literary production of his time. Much of his thought is collected in *Approximations* (7 vols., 1922–1937) and his *Journal Intime* (8 vols., 1946–   ).

Duccio di Buoninsegna (c. 1260–1319). Italian painter. He was the founder of the Sienese school of painting and is noted for the refinement and delicacy of his style. His masterpiece is the *Virgin in Majesty,* (1311), a panel in the cathedral of Siena; equally celebrated scenes from the life of Christ are to be found on its reverse side.

Duchamp, Marcel (1887–1968). French painter of the DADA movement. His *Nude Descending a Staircase* (1912) caused a sensation at the ARMORY SHOW. His brother, Raymond Duchamp-Villon (1876–1918), was a cubist sculptor.

Duchess, the. A character in Lewis Carroll's ALICE'S ADVENTURES IN WONDERLAND. The duchess wallops her baby till it howls and sings this lullaby to it:

> Speak roughly to your little boy,
>   And beat him when he sneezes;
> He only does it to annoy,
>   Because he knows it teases.

Duchess of Malfi, The (c. 1613). A tragedy by John WEBSTER. The last of the great Elizabethan dramas, it deals movingly with the disastrous marriage of a noblewoman and a commoner. The duchess, the widowed sister of Ferdinand, duke of Calabria, and of the cardinal, offends them by marrying her steward, Antonio. The lovers are forced to separate: Antonio flees, and the duchess is kept prisoner in her house, where she is subjected to mental torture. Bosola, the cardinal's henchman, strangles the duchess and her children and later murders Antonio. The play is based on William Painter's *The Palace of Pleasure* (1566–1567).

Duclos, Charles Pinot (1704–1772). French historian, moralist, and man of letters. On succeeding Voltaire as historiographer of France in 1750, he wrote *Mémoires pour servir à l'histoire des moeurs du XVIII° siècle* (1751). He also wrote novels and short stories, including *Histoire de la baronne de Luz* (1741), and *Les Confessions du comte de . . .* (1741). As secretary of the French ACADEMY, he supervised the 1762 edition of its famous dictionary.

Du côté de chez Swann. See REMEMBRANCE OF THINGS PAST.

Dudintzev, Vladimir (1918–   ). Russian novelist. His novel, NOT BY BREAD ALONE, created a sensation with its criticism of the Soviet bureaucracy. Dudintzev was attacked by Soviet critics in violent terms until Khrushchev, in May, 1959, finally put an end to the prolonged controversy by declaring that Dudintzev was not an enemy of the regime, but had merely erred in his efforts to criticize some aspects of Soviet society. Since that time Dudintzev has issued only a short work entitled *A New Year's Tale* (*Novogodnaya skazka*), which Western critics have hopefully interpreted as another anti-Soviet jibe. The work, however, is obscure, and Dudintzev's intention cannot easily be discerned.

Dudley, John, duke of **Northumberland** (1502?–1553). Protector of Edward VI. In an attempt to transfer the crown from the Tudor dynasty to his own family Northumberland persuaded the dying Edward VI to will the succession to Lady Jane GREY, Northumberland's daughter-in-law. After the attempt to place Queen Jane on the throne failed, he was executed.

Dudley, Robert, earl of **Leicester** (1531–1558). Favorite of Elizabeth I. The brother of Guildford Dudley (the husband of Lady Jane GREY), Robert Dudley was condemned to death after the attempt to place Lady Jane on the throne had failed. He was pardoned by ELIZABETH I and became Master of Ordnance and one of her chief favorites at court. She made him a Knight of the Garter, created him earl of Leicester, and gave him a castle at Kenilworth. His wife, Amy Robsart, died under somewhat suspicious circumstances, but there is no proof that her death—which freed Leicester to marry Elizabeth if she would have him—was anything but accidental. He is a main character in Sir Walter Scott's novel *Kenilworth.*

Dudone. One of the paladins of Charlemagne in the Carolingian stories centered about Orlando. He also appears in the MORGANTE MAGGIORE of Pulci and the poems of Orlando of Boiardo and Ariosto. In the latter's ORLANDO FURIOSO he is given the command of a complete navy magically created by Astolfo. Dudone's new fleet then routs the pagan army sailing with Agramante their leader to fight the Christians. In the GERUSALEMME LIBERATA of Tasso, he is Dudone of Consa (Contz), one of the adventurers among the crusading knights. When he is killed by the pagan warrior Argente, the Crusaders withdraw from battle to honor his corpse.

Dudu. In Lord Byron's narrative poem DON JUAN, one of the beauties of the harem into which Juan has been admitted in female attire. Next day, the sultana, out of jealousy, orders that both Juan and Dudu be stitched in a sack and cast into the sea; but, by the connivance of Baba, the chief eunuch, they effect their escape.

Duessa. An evil enchantress in Spenser's FAERIE QUEENE (Books I, II, and V), representing variously the Roman Catholic Church, Mary Tudor, and Mary, Queen of Scots.

Dufay, Guillaume (c. 1400–1474). Flemish (Belgian) composer. He lived and worked in Italy, Savoy, Burgundy, and Flanders. At the end of his life, Dufay was the most highly regarded composer in Europe. His finest music was written for the church. It was he who first established the practice of having polyphonic music sung by a chorus; hitherto each part had been performed by a single voice or instrument.

Dufresny, Charles Rivière (1648–1724). French playwright and novelist. His *Amusements sérieux et comiques d'un Siamois* (*Serious and Comic Amusements of a Siamese,* 1699), which criticized French institutions by the then novel device of recounting the reactions to Paris of a visiting Siamese, did much to set the fashion and establish the pattern for similar works, notably Montesquieu's *Lettres Persanes.* Among his plays, *Le Chevalier Joueur* (*The Gambling Knight,* 1697), which dealt realistically with the gambling mania, and the comedies *L'Esprit de Contradiction* (*The Spirit of Contradiction,* 1700) and *Le Double Veuvage* (*The Double Widowing,* 1702) were the most successful.

Dufy, Raoul (1877–1952). French artist, painted still lifes, harvest, street, and racetrack scenes. He developed a distinct style of briefly drawn details and fresh colors.

Duhamel, Georges. Pen name **Denis Thévenin** (1884–1966). French dramatist, novelist, critic, and poet. A leading member of the ABBAYE GROUP, Duhamel then turned to the theater and wrote *The Light* (1911), *In the Shadow of Statues* (1912), and *Combat* (1913). He also published *The New Book of Martyrs* (1917) and *Civilisation,* stories of World War I. Duhamel's works also include two long novel series, the cycle of SALAVIN (5 vols., 1920–1932) and the PASQUIER CHRONICLES (10 vols., 1933–1945). His essay *The Heart's Domain* (*La Possession du monde;* 1919) urges, as do his novels, the cultivation of the inner life on which is based the fraternity of mankind. He won the Prix Goncourt in 1918 for *Civilisation.*

Duino Elegies (**Duineser Elegien;** 1923). A series of poems by Rainer Maria RILKE. They are elegiac in mood, though not, strictly speaking, in form and meter. In them, Rilke develops his own, highly personal solution to some of the human problems posed by Existentialism, without, however, committing himself as a follower of that school of philosophy and poetry. "Duino" is the name of a castle near Trieste where Rilke, in 1911–1912, was a guest of the Princess Marie von Thurn und Taxis, to whom he presented the poems.

Dujardin, Edouard (1861–1949). French writer. A poet and a distinguished editor, he allied himself with the symbolists. He is known for his influential novel LES LAURIERS SONT COUPÉS, the first example of interior monologue.

Dukhobors or **Doukhobors** (Russ. *Dukhobortsi,* "spirit wrestlers"). A religious sect that arose among Kharkov peasants in the mid-18th century. Guided by "inner light," they rejected the authority of Church and State, and led communal lives under "inspired" leaders. Their beliefs have been compared to those of Quakers. Internal dissensions and resistance to military service subjected them to a series of forced migrations and dispersals.

Thousands removed to western Canada in 1898, where they founded prosperous if turbulent settlements as the "Christian Community of Universal Brotherhood." Their sporadic protests against taxes and compulsory education (especially those led by the violent "Sons of Freedom") have taken the form of fires, bombings, and marches in the nude, which abated in the late 1950's after a new threat of expulsion.

Dulce et Decorum Est (1920). A poem by Wilfred OWEN, bitterly denouncing war. The title is ironic, being a quotation from Horace: *Dulce et decorum est pro patria mori* (It is sweet and fitting to die for one's country).

Dulcinea del Toboso. The lady love of DON QUIXOTE in Cervantes' novel. Her real name is Aldonza Lorenzo, but the knight dubs her Dulcinea del Toboso. "Her flowing hair," says the knight, "is of gold, her forehead the Elysian fields, her eyebrows two celestial arches, her eyes a pair of glorious suns, her cheeks two beds of roses, her lips two coral portals that guard her teeth of Oriental pearl, her neck is alabaster, her hands are polished ivory, and her bosom whiter than the new-fallen snow." According to Sancho Panza, she is "a stout-built sturdy wench, who could pitch the bar as well as any young fellow in the parish."

Dulcy (1921). A comedy by George S. KAUFMAN and Marc CONNELLY. It is based on a character created by the columnist Franklin P. Adams. In the course of her well-meaning, self-appointed task of helping her husband put through an important business deal, Dulcy makes one blunder after another, but her efforts unexpectedly turn out all right.

Dull, Anthony. A dull-witted constable in Shakespeare's LOVE'S LABOUR'S LOST. He becomes the butt of the pedantic wit of Holofernes and Sir Nathaniel and understands absolutely nothing of what they say.

Dullin, Charles (1885–1949). French actor, director, and producer. Associated with Jacques COPEAU in the *Théâtre de Vieux-Colombier,* Dullin founded his own company at the *Théâtre de l'Atelier* in 1921. He stressed poetry and fancy on the stage, rather than a naturalistic portrayal of reality. Dullin produced plays by a wide variety of playwrights, among them Marcel Archard, Stève Passeur, Armand Salacrou, Jules Romains, and Pirandello.

Duma. Russian parliamentary body created in 1905. Its function was to advise Czar Nicolas II in matters of legislation. It was overthrown by the Russian Revolution (1917).

Dumachus. See DISMAS.

Dumain. In Shakespeare's LOVE'S LABOUR'S LOST, one of the three young lords who join the king of Navarre in an oath of celibacy and study. He becomes enamored of Katherine.

Dumas, Alexandre. Known as **Dumas fils,** or the younger (1824–1895). French dramatist. The natural son of Alexandre Dumas the novelist, the younger Dumas became an extremely popular playwright during the Second Empire. In technique his plays were realistic; for subjects he chose moral and social problems, depicting the adulterous intrigues and financial scandals of the upper social classes. Among Dumas's most successful works were: LA DAME AUX CAMÉLIAS, *Le Demi-Monde* (1855), *La Question d'argent* (1857), *Un Père Prodigue* (1859), *L'Ami des Femmes* (1864), *Les Idées de Mme Aubray* (1867). Heavy-handed didacticism characterized his later dramas.

Dumas, Alexandre. Known as **Dumas père** (1802–1870). French novelist and dramatist. Alexandre Dumas has become almost legendary for his prolific literary output (almost 300 volumes), and the rollicking gusto with which he lived and wrote. Dumas maintained a corps of collaborators—whom he termed his factory—who were engaged in searching through earlier memoir writers for suitably exciting plots. Accused of altering historical fact to suit his fictional purposes and of pilfering unscrupulously from other writers, Dumas remained supremely indifferent to such charges. His historical romances, all of the swashbuckling variety, include such favorites as THE COUNT OF MONTE CRISTO, THE THREE MUSKETEERS, THE BLACK TULIP, THE VISCOUNT OF BRAGELONNE, and TWENTY YEARS AFTER. Critics point quickly, and rightly, to his lack of psychological perception, and to his careless style, but the color and drama of his novels continue to insure their popularity. In France Dumas is noted for his plays: *Henri III et sa cour* (1829), *Napoléon Bonaparte* (1831), *Antony* (1831), and *La Tour de Nesle* (1832).

du Maurier, Daphne (1907–   ). English novelist and short-story writer. Her popular novels, compounded of melodrama, romance, the scenery of Cornwall, and some history, include *Jamaica Inn* (1936), *Rebecca* (1938), *Frenchman's Creek* (1942), *Hungry Hill* (1943), *The King's General* (1946), *My Cousin Rachel* (1951), and *The Glass-Blowers* (1963). She is a granddaughter of George du Maurier and daughter of the actor Sir Gerald du Maurier (1873–1934). Her *Gerald, A Portrait* (1934) is a biography of her father.

du Maurier, George [Louis Palmella Busson] (1834–1896). English novelist and illustrator. He illustrated the work of Thackeray, Hardy, James, and Meredith, and was famous for his caricatures in *Punch.* His novels, PETER IBBETSON, the highly successful TRILBY, and *The Martian* (1896), are tinged

with social satire and colored with the memories of the author's days as an art student in Paris. He also wrote light verse in English and French, which was popular in its day.

Dumbwaiter, The (1960). A one-act play by Harold PINTER. The two characters are assassins waiting in a hotel room for their victim to arrive. When an order for a Chinese meal is sent to them on the dumbwaiter they assume that their room was once a restaurant. They fill the order as best they can with candy and biscuit. They are deluged with orders for food from an unknown person who they feel is testing them. As the time approaches for the killing one of the assassins, a questioning, childish person, starts to feel remorse for their other victims. He leaves the room; when he returns, his partner kills him.

Dumuzi. A Sumerian shepherd-god, known elsewhere as TAMMUZ. He was loved by INANNA (Ishtar). Although he does not appear in the extant Sumerian myth of her descent into the underworld, the close parallel with Ishtar's search for Tammuz makes it highly likely that that was the purpose of Inanna's descent.

Dumuzi also is a central figure in a myth in which he, a shepherd, disputes with the farmer god Enkimdu for the favor of Inanna. Although Dumuzi is elsewhere her lover, she here prefers the farmer. This is one of several Sumerian myths with an obvious parallel to the story of CAIN and Abel.

Dunbar, Paul Laurence (1872–1906). American poet. Dunbar is noted for his highly skilled use of Negro themes and dialect. Writing at a time when literary regionalism was in vogue, he was undoubtedly influenced by Thomas Nelson Page. Although he was the son of a slave, his poetry is sentimental and lacks the bitterness of the work of later Negro writers. *Lyrics of Lowly Life* (1896) is his most famous collection. It was followed by *Lyrics of the Hearthside* (1899), *Lyrics of Love and Laughter* (1903), and *Lyrics of Sunshine and Shadow* (1905). He also wrote novels, including *The Uncalled* (1898) and *The Sport of the Gods* (1902).

Dunbar, William (1465?–?1530). Scottish poet. For a time he was a Franciscan friar and later a diplomatic agent for James IV of Scotland. His works include *The Thrissel and the Rois* (*The Thistle and the Rose,* 1503), a political allegory; *The Dance of the Sevin Deidly Sinnis* (1503–1508), a religious dream vision; *The Goldyn Targe* (c. 1508), an allegory in the tradition of *The Romance of the Rose; Lament of the Makaris* (i.e., poets; c. 1508), an elegy on the death of great poets of the past that has been compared to the poetry of François Villon; and *The Two Marryit Women and the Wedo* (c. 1508), a satire on women. Dunbar is considered one of the greatest of the SCOTTISH CHAUCERIANS.

Duncan. In Shakespeare's MACBETH, the generous and gracious king of Scotland whom Macbeth murders to attain the crown. When prodded by his wife to do the deed, even Macbeth protests against it, extolling Duncan's virtues:

> Besides, this Duncan
> Hath borne his faculties so meek, hath been
> So clear in his great office, that his virtues
> Will plead like angels trumpet-tongued against
> The deep damnation of his taking-off.

Duncan, Isadora (1878–1927). American dancer. She was acclaimed in London, Paris, and on the Continent, and established a German school of dancing near Berlin in 1904 and later one in Moscow. In 1926–1927, she wrote her autobiography, entitled *My Life*. She choreographed compositions by Tchaikovsky and Chopin. She was strangled in an automobile accident when her scarf was caught in a wheel.

Duncan, Robert [Edward] (1919–   ). American poet. At one time an editor of the *Experimental Review* and of *Phoenix,* Duncan has been influential among the younger poets both as an artist and a theorist. His work is highly distinctive and is characterized by lyricism, irony, and intensity. Collections of his poetry include *Selected Poems* (1959) and *The Opening of the Field* (1960).

Dunciad, The (1728; final version, 1743). The "dunce-epic," a satire in heroic couplets by Alexander POPE. The first version, in three books, was written under the influence of Swift; it attacked all critics of Pope's works, poetasters, publishers, and pedants. In 1729 this version, with changes, was republished as *The Dunciad Variorum.* A fourth book, *The New Dunciad,* appeared in 1742 and the final version, *The Dunciad in Four Books,* was published a year later. In the first book, the leading role was initially given to Lewis THEOBALD, but in the final version it is Colley CIBBER who is named king of the Dunces, his rule extending over the empires of Emptiness and Dullness. The second book, a burlesque of the account of funeral games for Anchises in Vergil's *Aeneid,* depicts Cibber's coronation; it is celebrated with games and contests, and as everyone drowses off to sleep, poetry-reading. In the third book, Cibber falls asleep and sees, in his dreams, the past, present, and future; in all three, Dullness prevails. In the fourth book, Dullness reigns supreme over scholarship, art, and science. The goddess of Dullness, thus firmly entrenched, gives directions to her several agents to encourage foolish and trifling pursuits and to discourage thought, and night and chaos are finally restored. *The Dunciad* is considered by many to be among Pope's crowning achievements, and, in spite of its topicality, its satire is still fresh and biting.

Dunne, Finley Peter (1867–1936). American journalist and humorist. Dunne worked for several newspapers in his native Chicago, writing his first "Mr. Dooley" essays for the *Evening Post.* Later he became part owner of the *American Magazine,* to which he contributed a pungent department entitled "In the Interpreter's House," and was editor of *Collier's* (1918–1919).

Dunne's fame rests entirely and solidly on his creation of Martin Dooley, an imaginary Irishman who presided over a small saloon on Chicago's West Side. Dooley was modeled, Dunne said, on a saloon-keeper named James McGarry. In his earlier pieces Dunne called his philosophic barkeeper Col. McNeery, but when McGarry objected to the too-ready identification, Dunne changed the name to Dooley.

From the days of the Spanish-American War to World War I, Mr. Dooley reviewed public men and affairs with a wit and wisdom that made him a national institution. He made his remarks to his faithful friend and customer, Malachi Hennessey. Possibly Mr. Dooley's most famous utterance was, "Whether th' Constitution follows th' flag or not, th' Supreme Court follows th' illiction retarns." "There's only one thing," said Dooley elsewhere, "that would make me allow mesilf to be a hero to the American people, and that is it don't last long."

Dunne wrote more than 700 essays about Mr. Dooley, some of which were collected in *Mr. Dooley in Peace and War* (1898), *Mr. Dooley in the Hearts of his Countrymen* (1899), and other books. *Mr. Dooley Remembers: The Informal Memoirs of Finley Peter Dunne* (1963) was edited by his son Philip Dunne.

Dunne, John William (1875–1949). English author of *An Experiment with Time* (1927) and *The New Immortality* (1938). These books of popular philosophy purported to demonstrate, through mathematics, the immortality of the soul and the principle of serialism (that the individual passes through a single sequence of time as he lives, but all other times and places exist simultaneously always). His books influenced J. B. PRIESTLEY and others.

Dunsany, Lord. Edward John Moreton Drax Plunkett (1878–1957). Irish dramatist and poet. A member of the Anglo-Irish gentry, he was educated at Eton. After service in the Boer War (1899–1902), he became active in the newly founded ABBEY THEATRE. In 1909 his play *The Glittering Gates* was produced at the Abbey by William Butler Yeats and won quick acclaim. This was followed by a number of other successes, many of them one-act plays, the best known of which are *A Night at an Inn* (1916), his finest play; *The Laughter of the Gods* (1916); and *If* (1922). Superficially his work appears to be merely the naive expression of Celtic whimsy with the usual assortment of fairies and other supernatural creatures. Dunsany, however, employed this background to satirize human behavior with a disarmingly simple, seemingly unconscious, wit.

Duns Scotus, John (c. 1265–c. 1308). Scottish scholastic theologian, known as the "Doctor Subtilis." He joined the Franciscans and was a teacher at Oxford, Paris, and Cologne, becoming famous for his defense of the dogma of the Immaculate Conception, and his description of man's free will as a horse capable of throwing off grace, its rider. Declaring that the existence of God or the immortality of the human soul cannot be proved by human reason, he thus challenged the harmony of faith and reason, of theology and philosophy, so important in the system of St. Thomas Aquinas. For centuries his followers, called *Scotists,* disputed with the Thomists over this and other doctrinal questions. Eventually Scotism was modified until it resembled Thomism on most issues.

Duns Scotus' theories are formulated in his metaphysical treatises *De Rerum Principio, Quaestiones, Opus Oxoniense,* and the commentaries on the *Sentences* of Peter Lombard. Although he had tried to urge philosophy's greater dependence on divine revelation by showing the limitations of human reason, the controversy had the opposite effect of lessening philosophy's concern with theology. His opposition to classical studies led in the Renaissance to the use of his name (Duns, Dunse, or Dunce) for a pedantic sophist incapable of real learning, and thence to the current meaning of *dunce* as a stupid, dull-witted person.

Dunstable, John (c. 1370–1453). The most important English composer of the 15th century; also a mathematician and astronomer. He infused beauty and grace into the rigid and angular English music of the 14th century, and had an influence on French music.

Duomo. See GIOTTO'S TOWER.

Dupes, Day of (*Journée des Dupes*). November 11, 1630, when Marie de Médicis and Gaston, Duc d'Orléans extracted from Louis XIII the promise that he would dismiss his minister Cardinal Richelieu. The cardinal went immediately to Versailles, the king repented, and Richelieu became more powerful than ever. Marie de Médicis and Gaston, the dupes, paid dearly for their short triumph.

Dupin, Aurore Amantine Lucille. See George SAND.

Dupin, C. Auguste. An amateur detective created by Edgar Allan POE. Appearing in the three stories Poe called his ratiocinative tales, Dupin works solely by deductive method. His unofficial status, bewildered friend, and cold logic have become familiar characteristics of the literary detectives modeled on him. See MURDERS IN THE RUE MORGUE, THE; PURLOINED LETTER, THE.

Du Pont, Eleuthère Irénée (1771–1834). American gunpowder manufacturer, son of Pierre Samuel DU PONT DE NEMOURS. He came to the United States in 1799 and founded, in Wilmington, Del., the gunpowder and textile firm of E. I. Du Pont de Nemours & Co. (1802–1804). In 1822, he was appointed director of the Bank of the United States.

Du Pont de Nemours, Pierre Samuel (1739–1817). French economist, friend and disciple of FRANÇOIS QUESNAY, the PHYSIOCRAT. He was imprisoned during the French Revolution and emigrated to the United States in 1799. At Jefferson's request he prepared a scheme for national education which, although never adopted in the U.S., influenced the French educational code. He returned to France (1802–1815), but again emigrated to the U.S. two years before his death.

Durandal, Durendal, Durandana, or Durindana. The magic sword of ROLAND (Orlando). Once used by Hector, it was given to Roland by Charlemagne in some stories, by MALAGIGI the magician in others.

Durant, Asher. See HUDSON RIVER SCHOOL.

Durant, Will[iam] [James] (1885–   ). American teacher, philosopher, and historian. Durant, perhaps the greatest popularizer of philosophic ideas in American publishing history, originally wrote *The Story of Philosophy* (1926) as a lecture series; the book was so popular that it was translated into a dozen languages and soon sold over a million copies. Durant then began a series on *The Story of Civilization: Our Oriental Heritage* (1935), *The Life of Greece* (1939), *Caesar and Christ* (1944), *The Age of Faith* (1950), *The Renaissance* (1953), *The Reformation* (1957), and *The Age of Reason Begins* (1961) and *The Age of Louis XIV* (1963), both written with his wife, Ariel Durant.

Duras, Marguerite (1914–   ). French novelist who usually presents events in terms of their psychological significance, most often to a woman, as in *Sea Wall* (*Un Barrage contre le Pacifique;* 1950), *Le Marin de Gibraltar* (1952), and *The Square* (1955). Other works include the film scenario *Hiroshima mon amour* (1959) and the novels *La Vie tran-*

quille (1944) and *Moderato Cantabile* (1958). She adapted *Moderato Cantabile* for the screen.

Durbeyfield, Tess. See TESS OF THE D'URBERVILLES.

Dürer, Albrecht (1471–1528). German painter and engraver. Travels in Italy in 1494 and 1505 familiarized him with Italy's search for clarity in art. At first he followed the German Gothic tradition of linear unrest and vehemence, but this style gradually gave way to greater breadth and simplicity, until he achieved a classical art of great expressiveness. Acutely aware of his own importance as an artist and increasingly interested in the teachings of Martin Luther, he sought to reconcile the strictness of the Reformation with the humanistic aspects of the Renaissance and its classical conern with ideal beauty. In the process he created the greatest expression of German Renaissance art. He painted a number of famous religious works and self-portraits, but he is particularly renowned for his numerous woodcuts and engravings depicting Apocalyptic visions, allegories, the Passion of Christ, and the life of the Virgin. The delicacy and strength of his hand is also demonstrated by portrait and landscape drawings and by minute studies of animals and details of nature. During his last years he wrote theoretical works on geometry and perspective, and on anatomy and human proportion.

D'Urfey, Thomas or Tom (1653–1723). English dramatist and song writer. He is known for such comedies as *Love for Money* (1691), *The Marriage-*

A Dürer woodcut for Brant's *Ship of Fools* (1494).

Hater Matched (1692), and *The Comical History of Don Quixote: Parts I, II, and III* (1694–1696). There is also a six-volume collection of his songs: *Wit and Mirth* (1719–1720).

Durga. The wife of Shiva. She is also known as Uma, Parvati, and KALI. The *Durga Puja* is Bengal's greatest religious festival, usually taking place in September or October.

Durrell, Gerald [Malcolm] (1925–   ). English zoologist and writer about animals. The brother of Lawrence Durrell, he is the author of *My Family and Other Animals* (1956). Other books include *A Zoo in My Luggage* (1960) and *The Whispering Land* (1961).

Durrell, Lawrence [George] (1912–   ). Anglo-Irish novelist, poet, and playwright. He is best-known for THE ALEXANDRIA QUARTET, a series of novels set in Egypt. Most of Durrell's other works are set on Mediterranean islands or in Europe, where he has spent most of his life. Henry Miller helped him to publish his first prose work, THE BLACK BOOK, in France in 1938. Employed by the British Council and the British Foreign Office in Egypt, Argentina, Belgrade, and Cyprus, Durrell wrote boys' adventure stories, humorous sketches of diplomatic life, and novels and travel books about Mediterranean islands. His Aegean books are *Prospero's Cell* (1945), *The Dark Labyrinth* (1947), *Reflections on a Marine Venus* (1953), and *Bitter Lemons* (1957), about life in Cyprus during the Turkish-Greek-British struggles. Like Norman Douglas, Durrell compares Anglo-Saxons unfavorably with Southern Europeans, who have, he thinks, a better sense of history and art, and more sexual freedom.

Durrell's poems have been appearing consistently since 1938. Usually on Mediterranean and classical subjects, they are romantic, taut, and sometimes humorous. *The Death of General Unkebunke* (1938) is an ironic biography. Durrell's *Collected Poems* appeared in 1956. His poetic dramas are *Sappho* (1950) and *Acte* (1961).

Dürrenmatt, Friedrich (1921–   ). Swiss playwright. Dürrenmatt, who writes in German, is especially known for his mastery of the bizarre and for the penetrating irony with which he comments on both the contemporary world and the helplessness of the human situation in general. His two most significant works are both tragicomedies: *Die Ehe des Herrn Mississippi* (*The Marriage of Mr. Mississippi,* 1952), a grotesque depiction of what has happened to moral and social values in our day, and the famous THE VISIT OF THE OLD LADY, which is an ironic modern counterpart to classical tragedy, treating the theme of the death of one man for the sake of the community. His other well-known plays include *Romulus der Grosse* (*Romulus the Great,* 1949) and *Ein Engel kommt nach Babylon* (*An Angel Comes to Babylon,* 1954). In his stage technique Dürrenmatt, like his countryman Max Frisch, follows Brecht's lead by frequently disrupting the stage-illusion in order to make the audience think in a more direct way about the ideas being presented. Besides his plays he has also written several detective stories with overtones of deeper meaning, including *Der Verdacht* (*Suspicion,* 1953), and a well-known essay entitled *Theaterprobleme* (*Problems of the Theater,* 1955), treating the subject of modern drama.

Durtain, Luc. See ABBAYE GROUP, THE.

Durvasas. In Hindu legend, one of the 7 great sages. In Kalidasa's play SHAKUNTALA, he is an ancient ascetic who curses Shakuntala because she neglects to serve him when he visits Kashyapa's *ashram* (hermitage).

Du Ryer, Pierre (c. 1600–1658). French playwright. Du Ryer's output was of wide range and included the pastoral *Les Vendages de Suresne* (*The Grape Harvests of Suresne,* 1635), unorthodox in the realism of its setting, the Seine of his own day; the romantic tragedy *Alcionée* (1640); the biblical tragedies *Saul* (1642) and *Esther* (1644); and historical tragedies, which are considered his best work. Of these, *Scévole* (1647), based on the legend of Mucius Scaevola, is generally reckoned his masterpiece.

Duse, Eleonora (1859–1924). Italian actress. Descended from a theatrical family, she scored her first great success when, aged 14, she played Juliet in Verona. Later she was acclaimed for her Camille and her interpretations of Ibsen's heroines. In 1895, she and Sarah Bernhardt, both appearing in London in Sudermann's *Magda,* invited the critics to choose between them; George Bernard Shaw was among those who preferred Duse. When she was in her late 30's, she entered into an artistic and romantic liaison with Gabriele D'ANNUNZIO, playing the title roles in his *La Gioconda* and *Francesca da Rimini.* An actress of great emotional power, she was noted for her great simplicity and lack of theatrical artifice.

Dutch Courtezan, The (1603). A drama by John MARSTON. Freevil, in love with the gentle Beatrice, wishes to break off his old relationship with Franceschina, the Dutch courtesan. To twit his upright friend Malheureux, he takes him to Franceschina's house where the young man falls under the courtesan's spell. Discovering the facts about Freevil's forthcoming marriage, Franceschina turns to Malheureux and promises to give herself to him when he brings her Freevil's ring as a token that the latter is dead. Malheureux informs Freevil of her offer, and the two stage a mock quarrel. Malheureux hurries to Franceschina with the ring and then finds that she has betrayed him to the authorities. As Malheureux is about to be executed, Freevil appears and reveals the subterfuge.

Dutchman's Fireside, The (1831). A novel by James Kirke PAULDING. A faithful depiction of Dutch life in 18th-century America, the book follows the adventures of Sybrandt Nestbrook in the French and Indian Wars. The hero, reported dead, returns in time to win the hand of Catalina Vancour.

Dutch Wars. Three wars fought between England and the United Provinces (Holland) in 1652–1654, 1664–1667, and 1672–1674. The first two were inspired by commercial rivalry and consisted largely of naval engagements and raids upon shipping and colonies. Among these was the British raid on New Amsterdam in 1664 which brought about the cession of that colony. The third war, very unpopular in England, was brought about by the desire of Charles II's ally, Louis XIV of France, to seize the Spanish Netherlands, and French land campaigns were important. Overall the wars were to England's advantage, but the Dutch were able to preserve the integrity of their home territory and government.

Dutourd, Jean (1920–   ). French novelist and essayist. Dutourd is the satirical humorist of such works as *A Dog's Head* (*Une tête de chien;* 1950), *The Best Butter* (*Au Bon Beurre;* 1952, also translated as *The Milky Way*), and *Five A. M.* (*Doucin;* 1955). *The Taxis of the Marne* (1956) is an autobiographical and political essay.

Duun, Olav (1876–1939). Norwegian novelist. In both subject and style Duun is a regionalist writer. *Juvikfolke* (*The People of Juvik,* 6 vols., 1918–1923), a novel series and his finest work, is set in his native Namdalen. He writes in *landsmaal,* the spoken language of Norway, and not in the traditional literary Dano-Norwegian *riksmaal.*

Duval, Claude. A highwayman, famed in legend and ballad. He was hanged at Tyburn in 1670 and provided with an epitaph beginning: "Here lies Du Vall: Reader, if male thou art look to thy purse, if female, to thy heart."

Duveneck, Frank (1848–1919). American portrait painter and etcher. The Ashcan School was influenced by his direct presentation and by the vigorous brushwork, learned in Munich, Germany, with which he defined the planes of a face on the canvas.

Du Vergier de Hauranne, Jean. Abbé de Saint-Cyran (1581–1643). French theologian. A man of austere and unshakable religious conviction, Du Vergier defended the rights of bishops against the Jesuits in his pamphlets *Petrus Aurelius* (1632–1633). Appointed director of Port-Royal in 1635, he introduced into the convent the moral and theological convictions of JANSENISM, which he had acquired from his teacher and friend Cornelius Jansen. In 1638, Richelieu became uneasy at Du Vergier's enormous religious influence and ordered him sent to prison where he remained till the year of his death.

Dvořák, Antonin (1841–1904). Czech composer. He was director of the National Conservatory of Music in New York City (1892–1895), and head of the Conservatory in Prague (1901). He wrote many operas and symphonies (among these the *New World Symphony*), symphonic poems, overtures, rhapsodies, nocturnes, scherzos, concertos, and choral works.

dwarf. A tiny, often misshapen person. Dwarfs have figured in the legends and mythology of nearly every race, and Pliny gives particulars of whole races of them, possibly following travelers' reports of African Pygmies. Among the Teutonic and Scandinavian peoples, dwarfs held an important place in mythology. They generally dwelt in rocks, caves, and recesses of the earth, were the guardians of its mineral wealth and precious stones, and were very skilful in the working of these. They had their own king, as a rule were not inimical to man, but could, on occasion, be intensely vindictive and mischievous. They play an important role in Wagner's RING DES NIBELUNGEN.

Dwight, Theodore (1764–1846). American lawyer and writer. Like his brother Timothy, he was one of the HARTFORD WITS and wrote satirical verse in collaboration with Richard ALSOP. He also wrote a pro-Federalist *History of the Hartford Convention* (1833).

Dwight, Timothy (1752–1817). American poet and educator, a grandson of Jonathan Edwards, and leader of the Hartford Wits. A Calvinist in religion and Federalist in politics, Dwight was president of Yale (1795–1817), whose staff and curricula he brilliantly developed. His most popular poems were THE CONQUEST OF CANAAN, *The Triumph of Infidelity* (1788), and *Greenfield Hill* (1794). A clergyman as well, Dwight served as a chaplain in the Revolutionary army and wrote many sermons, 173 of which were collected as *Theology, Explained and Defended* (1818–1819).

Dyer, Sir Edward (1540?–1607). English poet of the Elizabethan period. A friend of Sir Philip Sidney, Fulke Greville, and Edmund Spenser. He was best known for his lyric beginning "My mind to me a kingdom is."

Dyer, John (1699–1757). English poet and painter. He was a member of a literary coterie which included James Thomson and Richard Savage, and studied painting with Jonathan Richardson. His first major poem GRONGAR HILL is in Pindaric form and deals with the tradition of evening contemplation which was popularized by Milton's *Il Penseroso.* Other important poems are *The Ruins of Rome* (1740) and *The Fleece* (1757), a didactic account of sheep-raising and the wool trade in supposed imitation of the pastorals of Vergil and Alexander Pope.

dynastic histories. Chinese historical works detailing the history of the various ruling houses. They begin with the Han Dynasty (202 B.C.–A.D. 220) and continue until the Ch'ing or Manchu (1644–1912). There are altogether 24 such histories, each composed by writers of the dynasty following one which had fallen.

Dynasts, The. See Thomas HARDY.

Dysmas. See DISMAS.

Dzhugashvili, Iosef Visarionovich. See Joseph STALIN.

E

Ea. The Babylonian god of water and of wisdom. Developed from the Sumerian ENKI, he was one of the most important gods in the pantheon. It was he who, to a considerable extent, established the orderly functions of earth, sky, and sea, especially as they affect man, though specific functions such as irrigation or the growth of grain were in the hands of lesser gods. It was he whose wisdom or cunning often saved the universe and the other gods from disaster. He disposed of the stone monster of KUMARBI when it threatened heaven; he alone of the gods found the means to save ISHTAR from the underworld; and he saved mankind from the flood by warning Utnapishtim to build his ark, as explained in the *Epic of* GILGAMESH.

Each and All (1839). A poem by Ralph Waldo EMERSON. Written on the occasion of a seashore walk, it is an expression of faith in the oneness of the universe. The poet praises the "perfect whole" in which all parts are interdependent. *Each and All* was later collected in Emerson's *Poems* (1847).

eagle. A large, powerful predatory bird. It is used in many lands and ages as an emblem symbolizing strength and swiftness. The Romans used it from the time of Marius as the ensign of a legion. The French under the Empire assumed the same device. The golden eagle and the spread eagle, devices of the emperors of the East, adapted from the ensigns of the ancient kings of Babylon and Persia, of the Ptolemies and the Seleucides, came to commemorate the Crusades. In Christian art, the eagle is emblematic of St. John the Evangelist, because, like that bird, he looked on "the sun of glory." St. Augustine, St. Gregory the Great, and St. Prisca are also often shown with an eagle.

When Charlemagne was made leader of the Holy Roman Empire, he joined the German eagle, which faces right, to the Roman eagle, which faces left. The resulting double-headed eagle thus became the emblem of the Holy Roman Empire and of the Austrian Empire which regarded itself as its successor. In Russia, the same emblem symbolizes the Eastern or Byzantine Empire and the Western or Roman Empire, supposedly combined under the Russian Ivan Vasilyevich when, in 1472, he married Sophia, the niece of Constantine XIV, the last emperor of Byzantium. The phrase in Psalm 103, "Thy youth is renewed like the eagle's," refers to an ancient superstition that every ten years the eagle soars into the fiery region and plunges thence into the sea, where, molting its feathers, it acquires new life. See PHOENIX.

Eakins, Thomas (1844–1916). American painter. He studied anatomy in Philadelphia, where he settled, making dissections and taking casts. A realistic painter, he made full use of this knowledge in scenes of sports, especially rowing. Experimenting in various directions, he painted genre scenes, did some sculpture, and is known for penetrating, uncompromisingly objective portraits such as *The Clinic of Dr. Gross.*

Earhart, Amelia (1898–1937). American aviator. She was the first woman pilot to cross the Atlantic Ocean in an airplane (June 17, 1928). She was married to George Palmer Putnam, the publisher, and was herself the author of several books, notably *Last Flight* (1938), edited by her husband. In July, 1937, she was lost in an attempt to fly across the Pacific.

Earle, John (1601?–1665). English prose writer and prelate. His *Microcosmography* (1628) is considered one of the best works by the 17th-century CHARACTER WRITERS; it is a miniature human comedy, both witty and contemplative.

Earnshaw, Catherine. See WUTHERING HEIGHTS.

Earthly Paradise, the. A place of perfect beauty, peace, and immortality, widely believed in the Middle Ages to exist on earth in some as yet undiscovered land or island. It was sometimes identified with the Biblical Garden of Eden and located in the Near East; sometimes it was situated in the Far East, as in a legendary letter from PRESTER JOHN, which locates it within three days' journey of his kingdom, or in *The Travels of Sir John* MANDEVILLE; other maps and reports place it variously in the Atlantic, Pacific, and Indian Oceans. See ST. BRANDAN.

William MORRIS' *The Earthly Paradise* (4 vols., 1868–1870) is a long collection of narrative poems modeled on Chaucer's. The prologue tells how a band of Norse sailors flee the Black Death and go in search of the Earthly Paradise. They finally come to rest in "a nameless city in a distant sea." Then follows a series of banquets at which 24 tales are told; each month one of the Norsemen tells a medieval saga or romance, and one of the hosts relates a classical myth. In between are lyric interludes describing the changing landscape, a poem for each month.

Earwicker, Humphrey Chimpden. The protagonist of James Joyce's novel FINNEGANS WAKE. Literally a middle-aged Irish tavern keeper with a guilty conscience, he represents all sinful mankind. His initials, HCE, are interwoven throughout the book.

East Coker. See FOUR QUARTETS.

Easter. The Christian Paschal festival. The name was adopted from A.S. *eastre*, a heathen festival held at the vernal equinox in honor of the Teutonic goddess of dawn, called by Bede *Eostre* (cognate with L. *aurora* and Sanskrit *ushas,* dawn). On the introduction of Christianity it was natural for the name of the heathen festival to be transferred to the Christian, since the two fell at about the same time.

Easter Day is the first Sunday after the 14th day of the Paschal moon. The Paschal moon is the first moon whose 14th day comes on or after the vernal equinox (March 21). Consequently, Easter Sunday cannot be earlier than March 22, or later than April 25. This was fixed by the council of Nicaea, A.D. 325. It was formerly a common belief that the sun danced on Easter Day.

Easter Rebellion (1916). An abortive revolution staged on Easter Monday, 1916 in Dublin by the revolutionary Fenian organization attempting to secure Irish independence from England. Frustrated by the English delay in granting home rule, the FENIANS —under the leadership of Patrick Pearse (1879–1916) and James Connolly (1870–1916)—seized the general post office and a number of other locations in Dublin, proclaiming an Irish republic. The rebels, about 2000 in number, held their positions for six days before succumbing to the overwhelming superiority of the English forces. The ruthless behavior of the British soldiers, coupled with the execution of all the rebel leaders, led to a wave of violent anti-English sentiment, and the rebellion became a rallying point for all Irishmen. The events were celebrated in a number of literary efforts, notably in Yeats's *Easter Sunday* and, with considerable irony, in O'Casey's play *The Plough and the Stars*.

Easter Wings (1633). A poem by George HERBERT. The two stanzas of the poem are composed of lines that become progressively shorter, then longer, creating a shape resembling a pair of wings. The sense of the poem, which deals with the Fall and man's participation in Christ's Resurrection, fits perfectly in this form.

Eastlake, Sir **Charles Lock** (1793-1865). English painter and art critic. He made sketches of Napoleon as a prisoner aboard H.M.S. *Bellerophon,* from which he developed two large portraits. He served as keeper of the National Gallery (1843–1847) and became its director in 1855. He is known for his pictures of Italian banditti and for several paintings of episodes in the life of Christ.

East Lynne (1861). A novel by Mrs. Henry WOOD which was immensely popular, particularly in a dramatic version. Its heroine, Lady Isabel Vane, after running off with another man, returns to her remarried husband disguised as a nurse to care for her own children. After keeping up this pretense for a considerable time, she is at last reconciled to her husband.

Eastman, Max [Forrester] (1883–1969). American critic, poet and essayist. Eastman began his career as a teacher of philosophy and psychology at Columbia University. During this period he was occupied with aesthetics and wrote *The Enjoyment of Poetry* (1913). When the First World War broke out, Eastman turned to political and social controversy. He became a Marxist, but opposed the Stalinist development of Soviet Russia. Eastman helped to found two important magazines, THE MASSES and *The Liberator* (1917); he was tried for sedition when *The Masses* was suppressed for antiwar writings in 1917. Some of Eastman's other books are *Marxism: Is It Science?* (1940); *Heroes I Have Known* (1942); *Lot's Wife* (1942), a narrative poem; *Enjoyment of Living*

(1948); *Poems of Five Decades* (1954); *Reflections on the Failure of Socialism* (1955); and *Great Companions—Critical Memoirs of Some Famous Friends* (1959).

East of Eden (1952). A novel by John STEINBECK. Based on the biblical story of Cain and Abel, the book centers on the lives of Adam Trask and his two sons, Cal and Aron. Adam settles in the Salinas Valley in California with his wife, Cathy, who bears the two boys, leaves her husband, and becomes a prostitute. Adam, who favors Aron, is at first unable to forgive Cal when he drives Aron to his death by telling him that their mother is a prostitute.

Eaten Heart, The. A tale from THE DECAMERON of Giovanni Boccaccio. In this story, William of Roussillon gives to his wife the heart of her lover. When she discovers that she has eaten the heart, she kills herself and is buried with her lover.

Eaton, Margaret or **Peggy O'Neale** (1796–1879). Wife of John H. Eaton, U.S. secretary of war (1829–1831). The daughter of a Washington tavern-keeper, Peggy was the wife of John B. Timberlake, a navy purser, when Andrew JACKSON and his friend Eaton lodged at her father's inn in 1823. After Timberlake's death, Eaton married the pretty widow in 1829 amid rumors that he had been overly familiar with her while her husband was alive. When Jackson named Eaton secretary of war in 1829, the wife of Vice President Calhoun and the wives of other Cabinet members refused to call on her. The president, however, remained loyal to his friends, perhaps remembering the social abuse to which the recently deceased Mrs. Jackson had been subjected. The feud eventually turned into a political issue, resulting in the resignations of Eaton, Secretary of State Van Buren, and other Cabinet members, and widened the growing rift between Jackson and Calhoun.

Eberhart, Richard (1904–   ). American poet and teacher. Eberhart's first collection was *A Bravery of Earth* (1930). Among his later works are *Song and Idea* (1942), *Burr Oaks* (1947), *Undercliff: Poems, 1946–1953* (1953), *Great Praises* (1957), and *Collected Poems, 1930–1960* (1960). His poetry is characterized by short lines, few rhymes, and the use of simple, homely things from which the poet draws a parallel to some metaphysical truth. He was a founder of the Poets' Theater at Cambridge, Mass.; his verse play *The Apparition* was first produced there (1951). His *Collected Verse Plays* appeared in 1962.

Ebers, Georg (1837-1898). German novelist and Egyptologist. He is known for his pedantic "professorial novels," such as *Eine ägyptische Königstochter* (*An Egyptian Princess,* 1874) and *Kleopatra* (1894).

Ebert, Friedrich (1870-1925). German statesman. He was the first president of the Weimar Republic (1919–1925) and leader of the Social Democrats.

Eblis. In Muslim legend, the Devil, called Azazel before the fall, who rules over the evil genii or JINN. When Adam was created, Allah commanded all the angels to worship him, but Azazel replied, "Me thou hast created of smokeless fire, and shall I reverence a creature made of dust?" Allah was angry at this insolent answer, and turned the disobedient angel into a Sheytan (devil) and he became the father of devils. Another Muslim tradition has it that before life was breathed into Adam, all the angels came to look at the shape of clay, among them Azazel, who, knowing that Allah intended man to be his superior, vowed never to acknowledge him as such and kicked the figure until it rang.

Eblis had five sons: *Tir,* author of fatal accidents; *Awar,* the demon of lubricity; *Dasim,* author of discord; *Sut,* father of lies; *Zalambur,* author of mercantile dishonesty.

Ebuda. In the ORLANDO FURIOSO of Ariosto an island of the Hebrides, west of Scotland. Here Angelica and later Olimpia are exposed to the cruel sea monster called the Orc. Ruggiero rescues Angelica and Orlando rescues Olimpia from the beast.

Eça de Queiroz, José Maria (1845–1900). Portuguese novelist and short-story writer. Considered Portugal's greatest novelist, he is best known for *O Crime Do Padre Amaro* (*The Sin of Father Amaro,* 1876), a naturalistic satire directed against clerical corruption which was based on his observations as a municipal official in the province of Leiria. His gift for ironic social criticism was further revealed in *O Primo Basilio* (*Cousin Basilio,* 1878), a study of a middle-class Lisbon family, and *Os Maias* (1880), about upper-class life. He also wrote a fanciful short novel, *O Mandarim* (1880); the novel *A Reliquia* (*The Relic,* 1887); *A Cidade e as Serras* (*The City and the Mountains,* 1901), short stories; *Prosas Bárbaras* (1905), a collection of articles and stories; and *Cartas de Inglaterra* (1945), letters about Victorian England, where he lived from 1874 to 1888.

Ecbasis Captivi. Full title **Ecbasis cuiusdam Captivi, per Tropologiam (The Escape of a Certain Captive, with Allegorical Significance,** usually called **The Escape of the Calf,** c. 940). A Latin tale about a calf running away from his stable, only to be threatened by a wolf until rescued by a fox. It probably represents a monk running from his vows and his monastery, and in danger of great sin until rescued by discipline. Its importance, however, is in the development of the beast-epic, for some of the animals and events reappear in the clerical satire *Ysengrimus* (1148), direct ancestor of REYNARD THE Fox.

Ecclesiastes. A book of the Old Testament. It was formerly ascribed to Solomon because of its opening verse, "The words of the Preacher, the son of David, king in Jerusalem," but it is now generally assigned to an unnamed author of the third century B.C. The book's refrain is "vanity of vanities; all is vanity." (Eccl. 1:2).

Ecclesiastical History of the English People. See BEDE.

Ecclesiazusae (Ekklesiazousai). See ARISTOPHANES.

Echegaray [y Eizaguirre], José (1832–1916). Spanish dramatist. His works, which enlarge upon the romantic theme of melancholic passion, are noted for their high degree of technical skill. The best known of his fustian compositions are *O locura o santidad* (1877), in which a Quixotic hero is accused of folly for attempting to pass along his fortune to its rightful owners, and EL GRAN GALEOTO. This last mentioned work relates the transformation of the three virtuous and honorable members of a triangle situation, society being blamed for their corruption. In 1904 Echegaray received the Nobel Prize.

Echeverría, Esteban (1805–1851). Argentine poet. During a five-year stay in Paris, Echeverría absorbed the tenets of French romanticism which permeate his works of poetry, especially *Elvira, o la novia del Plata* (1832), *Consuelos* (1834), and *La cautiva* (1837), notable for its depiction of the Argentine pampa and its inhabitants. Echeverría's opposition to dictator Juan Manuel de ROSAS led him and other idealistic youths to form the *Asociación de Mayo,* a secret revolutionary group dedicated to liberal, democratic principles. His hatred for Rosas also inspired him to write EL MATADERO, the work for which he is probably best known today.

Echidna. A monster of classical mythology, half woman, half serpent. By Typhon she was mother of the CHIMAERA, the many-headed dog Orthos, the hundred-headed dragon of the Hesperides, the Colchian dragon, the Sphinx, Cerberus, Scylla, the Gorgons, the Lernaean hydra, the vulture that gnawed away the liver of Prometheus, and the Nemean lion.

Spenser makes her the mother of the Blatant Beast in the *Faerie Queene* (1596).

Echo. A nymph of Greek mythology. There are several stories of why she seemed to be merely a disembodied voice. Perhaps the commonest is that she pined away from unrequited love for NARCISSUS until only her voice remained. According to another story, Hera, annoyed at Echo's babbling while she was trying to spy on Zeus, took away the nymph's speech, allowing her only to echo others. Yet a third version explains that Pan, furious that she could not love him, maddened some shepherds until they tore her into such tiny pieces that nothing was left but her voice.

Eckermann, Johann Peter (1792–1854). A friend and literary assistant to Goethe. He helped Goethe prepare the *Ausgabe letzter Hand* (final edition) of his works. His *Gespräche mit Goethe* (English edition, *Conversations with Goethe,* in 3 vols., 1836–1848) are daily records of Goethe's personal talks with Eckermann and constitute in their remarkable authenticity a monument to the ideal amanuensis.

eclectic (from *Gr.* "ek-legein," to choose, select). Selectiveness as a way of living. The name given to those who do not attach themselves to any special school (especially philosophers and painters), but pick and choose from various systems, selecting and harmonizing those doctrines and methods that suit them.

eclogue. Specifically, a pastoral dialogue in verse. The speakers, usually two shepherds or a shepherd and his mistress, discuss topics ranging from the state of their hearts to that of the nation, from the management of sheep to that of verse. Loosely, any short poem with pastoral elements may be called an eclogue. See BUCOLICS.

Ecole des femmes, L' (The School for Wives, 1662). A verse comedy by MOLIÈRE. ARNOLPHE has arranged for his beloved AGNÈS to be raised in total innocence, in order that she may never prove unfaithful when he marries her. Because of her unsophistication, Horace is able to win her affections and persuades her to run away with him. Unaware of Arnolphe's relation to the girl, Horace asks him to hide her. Arnolphe is about to spirit her away to a convent when it is revealed that Agnès' father, the rich Enrique, has arranged with Horace's father for their children to be married. The play was criticized for supposed moral as well as literary flaws, and Molière replied to his critics in two works: *La Critique de l'Ecole des Femmes* (1663) and *L'Impromptu de Versailles* (1663).

Ecole des femmes, L'. A novel trilogy by André GIDE about the position of women in the modern world. It includes *The School for Wives* (1929), *Robert* (1929), and *Geneviève* (1936).

Ecole des maris, L'. See SGANARELLE (2).

Ector, Sir. In Malory's *Morte d'Arthur* (c. 1469), the foster father of King Arthur and father of Sir KAY.

Edda. The name given to two Icelandic collections of early Scandinavian mythology. The manuscripts comprising the *Elder* or *Poetic Edda* (written 9th to 12th century) were discovered about 1643 by the Icelandic Bishop Brynjolf Sveinsson (1605-1675), who erroneously attributed them to Saemund Sigfusson (1056-1133) and called the work *The Edda of Saemund.* The 34 lays, or poems, tell the mythological stories of the Old Norse gods and heroes.

The *Younger* or *Prose Edda,* also called the *Snorra Edda* (early 13th century), was written by SNORRI STURLUSON. In five parts, it includes a prefatory account of the creation of the world and of pagan poetry; the stories of early Scandinavian mythology; further legends of the gods, given as the "sayings of Bragi," god of poetry; the *Skalda,* a detailed account of the rules of ancient prosody; and the *Hattatal,* a technical analysis of meters. Other linguistic treatises and a list of poets were added after Sturluson's death.

Eddy, Mary Baker (1821-1910). American religious leader, editor, and author. The founder of CHRISTIAN SCIENCE, Mrs. Eddy published *Science and Health* (1875) as an exposition of her ideas and as the official statement of the organization she headed. In this book and others of her *Miscellaneous Writings* (1896) she taught that pain, disease, old age, and death were "errors." She founded the Church of Christ, Scientist, in Boston (1879), and the newspaper, *The Christian Science Monitor* (1908). Mrs. Eddy was influenced by Transcendentalism, and particularly, by the work of Ralph Waldo Emerson. Toward the end of her career, she was attacked by the New York *World, McClure's Magazine,* and Mark Twain, who wrote a book on *Christian Science* (1907) ridiculing her beliefs. The doctrines of Christian Science are summarized in the first sentence of Mrs. Eddy's *Science and Health:* "The Prayer that reforms the sinner and heals the sick is an absolute faith that all things are possible to God."

Edel, Leon (1907-). American critic and biographer. A professor of English at New York University, Edel has edited much of the work of Henry James. *Henry James: The Untried Years, 1843-1870* (1953) is the first volume of a proposed four-volume biography. For *Henry James: The Conquest of London, 1870-1881* and *Henry James: The Middle Years, 1882-1895* (both published in 1962), Edel was awarded the Pulitzer Prize and the National Book Award. His other books include *James Joyce: The Last Journey* (1947); *Willa Cather, A Critical Biography* (1953), written with E. K. Brown; and *The Psychological Novel, 1900-1950* (1955).

Eden. Paradise, the country and garden in which ADAM AND EVE were placed by God (Gen. 2:5). The word means delight, pleasure; it has often been used

metaphorically to describe a place of charming scenery.

Edgar. In Shakespeare's KING LEAR, the legitimate son of the earl of Gloucester. He is disinherited because of his bastard brother Edmund's lies. After Gloucester has been blinded and ousted from his castle by Regan and Cornwall, Edgar finds him and saves him from suicide. He then kills the treacherous Edmund.

Edgar Huntly; or, Memoirs of a Sleep-Walker (1799). A novel by Charles Brockden BROWN. Really a detective story, the plot involves a supposed murder, an attempted murder, and a real murder. The Indians, who turn out to have committed the crime, are not idealized; the novel had a great influence on James Fenimore Cooper.

Edgeworth, Maria (1767-1849). An Irish novelist, best known for her novel CASTLE RACKRENT. Many of her other works have their setting in Irish life, among them *Belinda* (1801), THE ABSENTEE, *Vivian* (1812), and *Ormond* (1817). She wrote in the tradition of the novel of manners in which Jane Austen excelled, but was also very sensitive to local atmosphere, and portrayed national character with great sympathy. In this respect she exercised a fair influence on her friend Sir Walter Scott. Her letters as well as her novels are still highly readable.

Edict of Nantes. See NANTES, EDICT OF.

Edison, Thomas A[lva] (1847-1931). American inventor. Born in Ohio, Edison was educated at home by his mother and at the age of 12 was a newsboy on the railroad; later he became a telegraph operator. Edison patented over 1000 inventions, including the incandescent electric lamp, the microphone, the phonograph, and the Edison accumulator. In 1913 he produced talking motion-pictures. He is credited with the definition of *genius* as 2% inspiration and 98% perspiration.

Editions de Minuit, Les. See VERCORS.

edle Einfalt und stille Grösse. See Johann Joachim WINCKELMANN.

Edmonds, Walter D[umaux] (1903-). American historical novelist. Edmonds made his native region of northern New York as much his own literary property as it is possible for an author to do. The Black River, the Black River Canal, and the Erie Canal dominated his imagination. His books are authentic in research and setting, vivid in their style and narrative. They include *Rome Haul* (1929), *Erie Water* (1933), DRUMS ALONG THE MOHAWK, *Chad Hanna* (1940), *In the Hands of the Senecas* (1947), and *The Wedding Journey* (1947). He has also written *The First Hundred Years* (1948), *They Fought With What They Had* (1951), *Uncle Ben's Whale* (1955), and a number of juveniles.

Edmund. In Shakespeare's KING LEAR, the bastard son of the earl of Gloucester. He instigates the disinheritance of his half-brother Edgar, betrays his father, and schemes with Lear's daughter Goneril to poison her husband, Albany. Mortally wounded by Edgar, the repentant Edmund tries unsuccessfully to save Cordelia, Lear's youngest daughter, from execution.

Edo. See TOKYO.

Edo period. See TOKUGAWA.

Education of Henry Adams, The (privately printed, 1907; posthumously published, 1918). An autobiographical work by Henry ADAMS. Subtitled *A Study in 20th-Century Multiplicity,* it complements MONT-SAINT-MICHEL AND CHARTRES. Adams' book, written in the third person, might have been an account of the experience of any sensitive man; he uses himself as a model of modern man, searching for coherence in a fragmented universe. Adams considers his education a failure, for it had not prepared him for the conflicts to be faced.

The book is not a complete autobiography; it omits any mention of the 13 years of Adams' marriage, and the seven years following his wife's suicide. It does, however, present a vivid picture of places and people the author knew. In the chapter, "The Virgin and the Dynamo," Adams compares two eras; the dynamo, symbol of mechanistic force, acts on passive man in the 20th-century "multiverse," while the Virgin, symbol of unity, correspondingly stands for the 13th-century concept of an ordered universe.

Education sentimentale, L' (Sentimental Education, 1869). A novel by Gustave FLAUBERT. Flaubert presents a picture of life among French dilettantes, intellectuals, and revolutionaries at the time of the decline and fall of Louis Philippe's monarchy and the Revolution of 1848. The events of the Revolution and the establishment of the Second Empire, carefully documented, provide a further background for the main action. The novel's protagonist, Frédéric Moreau, is an egotistical and ambitious young man who comes to Paris from the provinces determined to pattern his life upon literature's romantic hero. He undergoes the romantic passion of unrequited love for MME ARNOUX, but does not forego involvement in several less ideal and ultimately disillusioning affairs. Like the desires of Emma Bovary (see MADAME BOVARY), his dreams are pathetic and sometimes contemptible. Like Emma, too, Moreau is a wholly real person, whom Flaubert draws with truly objective detachment and complete artistic mastery.

Edward. A medieval English ballad which has many versions. In most of these, a young man named Edward explains to his mother that he has killed his father. In some variations, there is the suggestion that the mother encouraged the murder. A modern version of this "domestic tragedy" ballad may be found in a poem by Robinson Jeffers: *Such Counsels You Gave To Me* (1937).

Edward II (1284–1327). King of England (after 1307). He is the subject of a play by Christopher MARLOWE.

Edward VI. Edward Tudor (1537–1553), King of England (1547–1553). The son of Henry VIII and his third wife, Jane Seymour, Edward became king when he was only nine years old. He was under the Protectorate first of his uncle, Edward Seymour, lord Somerset, and then of John Dudley, duke of Northumberland. Largely through Northumberland's machinations, Edward signed a deposition willing the crown to his second cousin, Lady Jane GREY, who was also Northumberland's daughter-in-law.

Edward VIII. See duke of WINDSOR.

Edwardian. Pertaining to English life and letters in the early years of the 20th century, a period corresponding roughly to the reign (1901–1910) of Edward VII. In general, the era witnessed a relaxation of Victorian conservatism and complacency, together with a questioning and criticism of authority and accepted social values. G. B. Shaw, Arnold Bennett, and H. G. Wells were among the writers who reflected these tendencies. The term is also used to refer to the opulence and elegance of the period. Victoria Sackville-West described the era in her novel *The Edwardians* (1930).

Edwards, Harry Stillwell (1855–1938). American lawyer, editor, public official, and writer. Edwards won the Chicago *Record* $10,000 prize (1896) for his novel, *Sons and Fathers.* When he was 64 years old, he wrote the book for which he is well known: *Eneas Africanus* (1919). It is the story of a Negro slave who becomes separated from his master in 1865; for eight years he wanders through the South in a humorous pilgrimage in the wilderness until he and his master are reunited. Edwards also wrote *Eneas Africanus, Defendant* (1921).

Edwards, Jonathan (1703–1758). American theologian and philosopher. In his early youth Edwards was a precociously brilliant scholar, showing a keen interest in scientific observation. His early philosophical thought tended toward Idealism under the influence of Locke, and many of his ideas resembled those of George Berkeley, whose work at that time he did not know.

Edwards' theology was more basically Calvinistic than that of earlier Puritan divines, who emphasized the covenantal relation between God and man, rather than the absolute supremacy of a God bound by no contract. He believed "that the essence of all religion lies in holy love" and that sin was a "property of the species," which both justified God's punishment of man and made possible mercy and redemption. His sermon on *Sinners in the Hands of an Angry God* (1741), so horrifying to later readers, was in fact an exhortation on the necessity of salvation, as well as a reminder of the torments that awaited the unregenerate. His beliefs on the place of the emotions in religious experience led him to champion the "GREAT AWAKENING," in which he saw dramatic conversions as evidence of the "peculiar and immediate" manifestation of God. Among his works are *A Faithful Narrative of the Surprising Work of God in the Conversion of Many Hundred Souls* (1737) and *A Careful and Strict Enquiry into Freedom of the Will* (1754).

Edwards, Richard (1523?–1566). English dramatist and poet. Edwards' only extant play is *Damon and Pythias* (published 1571). Some of his poems appeared in THE PARADISE OF DAINTY DEVICES (1576).

Edwin Drood, The Mystery of (1870). An unfinished novel by Charles DICKENS. The orphans Edwin Drood and Rosa Bud have been betrothed by their fathers, and are to marry when Edwin is 21, though the obligatory nature of the agreement has in fact made love between them impossible. Rosa arouses the admiration of two men: Edwin's ostensibly devoted Uncle Jasper, a disagreeable hypocrite who loves her passionately, and Neville Landless, a youth who detests Edwin for his mistreatment of the young girl. At their last meeting before they are to be wed, Edwin and Rosa acknowledge that they can never be happy together and break their engagement. The same night Edwin mysteriously disappears, and Jasper, who has done all he can to aggravate the enmity between Edwin and Neville, accuses the latter of murdering his nephew. Rosa's guardian notices

Jasper's displeasure on learning that the engagement had been broken before the disappearance. Neville is arrested, but, since no body can be found, he is released untried. Jasper, however, continues to connive against Neville and to pursue the terrified Rosa, while a mysterious Mr. Datchery appears on the scene to frustrate Jasper's intrigues. At this point the novel breaks off. In the absence of any solution left by Dickens, it has been a favorite puzzle of literary detectives to attempt to solve the mystery. The most convincing proposed solutions generally hinge on two questions: whether or not Edwin is actually dead, and what Mr. Datchery's true identity is. Some have held that Datchery is actually Edwin.

Egeria. In Roman legend, the nymph who instructed NUMA POMPILIUS, 2nd king of Rome, in his wise legislation. Hence, a woman counselor, especially a woman who advises and influences a statesman.

Egeus. In Shakespeare's MIDSUMMER NIGHT'S DREAM, the stern father of Hermia. He forces her betrothal to Demetrius despite her love for Lysander, who is just as desirable a suitor.

Eggleston, Edward (1837–1902). American novelist and clergyman. He is known for regional fiction dealing with Indiana, and especially for THE HOOSIER SCHOOLMASTER. An ardent reformer, Eggleston wrote several other novels of importance, including *The Circuit Rider* (1874), a book describing the impact of Methodism on the frontier; *Roxy* (1878), the story of the trials of a young woman in frontier Indiana; and *The Graysons* (1888), a novel introducing Lincoln as a young lawyer.

Egil. The brother of Wieland or Volund, the Vulcan of Norse mythology. Egil was a famous archer; in the Saga of Thidrik there is a tale about him which is the counterpart of the famous story of WILLIAM TELL and the apple.

Eglamour, Sir. In Shakespeare's Two GENTLEMEN OF VERONA, a chivalrous old knight who helps Silvia escape from Milan to find her beloved Valentine.

Egmont (publ. 1788). A tragedy by Johann Wolfgang von GOETHE. It is based on the downfall of a historical Count Egmont (1522–1568) who was executed in connection with the Netherlandic revolt against Spain. Like Goethe's earlier GÖTZ VON BERLICHINGEN, Egmont is upright and straightforward in his striving for freedom, but unable to survive in an atmosphere of subtle political machinations. Though Goethe was already working on the play in 1776, in his STURM UND DRANG period, he did not finish it until his second year in Italy, when his ideas had already taken a strong turn toward the classical. This change is reflected in the play's relative polish of form and language as compared with *Götz*. Beethoven wrote his famous *Egmont* music for Goethe's play. See DAEMONIC.

Egoist, The (1879). A novel by George MEREDITH. The "egoist" is Sir Willoughby Patterne of Patterne Hall, possessed of good looks, wealth, and all the virtues except humility and a sense of humor. He invites his fiancée, Clara Middleton, and her father, a clergyman who loves good food and wine, to spend a month at the Hall, where he is the idol of his two old aunts. Clara—"a rogue in porcelain" as Mrs.

Mountstuart Jenkinson, the clever widow who regulates the social life of the countryside, pronounces her —is soon longing to extricate herself from the attentions of her self-centered lover. She is thankful for the diversion of Patterne's gay Irish guest, De Craye, who makes violent love to her, but gives her confidence to Vernon Whitford, Patterne's cousin and secretary. Patterne, who has had a sad experience previously, is in mortal dread of being jilted by Clara, and to preserve his dignity he proposes to his former worshiper Laetitia Dale, whom he had made use of for this same purpose before. Many complications arise, but Vernon and Clara finally confess their love, and Patterne is forced to plead with the now thoroughly disillusioned Laetitia to become the mistress of Patterne Hall.

Egoist, The. An English little magazine. Originally founded as a feminist periodical in 1911, it became the chief organ of imagist poetry (see IMAGISM). Ezra POUND, T. S. ELIOT, Hilda DOOLITTLE, Richard ALDINGTON, Rebecca WEST, and Harriet Weaver were associated with its publication.

Egyptian, The. See Mika Toimi WALTARI.

Ehrenburg, Ilya Grigoryevich (1891–1967). Russian novelist, poet, and journalist. Much of his early life was lived in Paris where he published his first book of poems (1911). He covered the Spanish Civil War for Soviet papers in 1936–1937 and during World War II spent some years in Paris. His first important novel, *The Extraordinary Adventures of Julio Jurenito* (*Neobyknovennoye priklyucheniya Julio Jurenito;* 1922), is a satire on modern European civilization. His other novels include *The Fall of Paris* (*Fadeniye Parizha;* 1941), dealing with the war in Western Europe before Russia's involvement; *The Storm* (*Burya;* 1948), a war novel; and *The Thaw* (*Ottepel';* 1954, 1956), an outspoken work about shortcomings under Stalin's regime which gave its name to the period of greater relaxation after Stalin's death.

In installments during 1961–1963, Ehrenburg published his memoirs, entitled *People, Years, and Life* (*Lyudi, gody, zhizn*), which contain interesting revelations about the maneuverings of Soviet intellectual life. Ehrenburg himself has often been accused of being an opportunist who knew too well how to avoid purges in the literary world. He was, however, a fairly persistent advocate of greater intellectual freedom in Soviet letters and served as a rallying point for Soviet admirers of Western culture.

Eichendorff, Joseph Freiherr von (1798–1857). German romantic poet. He is most famous for his many poems that treat idyllically the unspoiled woods of his Silesian homeland, and for the long story AUS DEM LEBEN EINES TAUGENICHTS. His novel *Ahnung und Gegenwart* (*Presentiment and the Present,* 1815), a BILDUNGSROMAN, reflects Eichendorff's Catholicism in that the hero ends by renouncing this world and entering a monastery. During his career, Eichendorff was a friend of many of the German romantics (see GERMAN ROMANTICISM), including F. Schlegel, Arnim, and Brentano, and later in life he wrote a number of works on literary history, for example, *Über die ethische und religiöse Bedeutung der neueren romantischen Poesie in Deutschland* (*On the Ethical and Religious Importance of Recent Romantic Poetry in Germany,* 1847).

Eichmann, Adolf (1906–1962). German Nazi, in charge of the execution of Jews (1942–1945). He escaped capture after the war, but in 1960 was apprehended by Israeli security forces in Argentina. Worldwide controversy was aroused during his trial (1961) by an Israeli court, which condemned him to death for crimes against humanity.

Eiffel Tower. An iron tower 984.25 feet high. It was built for the Paris Exposition of 1885 on the Champ de Mars. It was named for the engineer Alexandre Gustave Eiffel (1832–1923) who also built the framework for the Statue of Liberty and designed the locks for the Panama Canal. Its sections were prefabricated and assembled on the spot.

Eikon Basiliké (*Gr.*, "royal image"; 1649). A book purporting to be the spiritual autobiography of CHARLES I. Published at the time of Charles's execution, it contains his meditations and prayers during his political troubles as well as his advice to his son. Its authorship is often attributed to John Gauden (1605–1662), an Anglican clergyman who became bishop of Worcester. The book was so popular that Parliament authorized Milton to write an official reply, his *Eikonoclastes* (*Gr.*, "image-breaker"; 1649).

Eimi (1933). A narrative of travel in Russia by E. E. CUMMINGS. Written in a stream-of-consciousness style, including puns, parodies, and typographical innovations, the book is an impressionistic study of what Cummings himself had seen, heard, and felt. The title (pronounced to rhyme with Mamie) is Greek and means *I am*.

Ein' feste Burg (*Ger.* A mighty fortress). The first words of Martin LUTHER's metrical version of Psalm 46. It is used in the opera *Les Huguenots* by MEYERBEER.

Einstein, Albert (1879–1955). German-Swiss-American physicist. Einstein is best known for his theory of relativity, first enunciated in 1905, which made possible the modern concept of the atom. In 1921 he won a Nobel Prize. Einstein left Germany after the rise of the Nazis and settled in the U.S., where he worked at the institute for Advanced Study in Princeton, N.J., until 1945.

Eisenhower, Dwight D[avid] (1890–1969). American general and 34th president of the U.S. (1953–1961). Born in Denison, Texas, Eisenhower graduated in 1915 from the U.S. Military Academy at West Point. In 1942 he was made commander of the Allied forces landing in North Africa. He became a full general in February 1943, was appointed Supreme Commander of the Allied Expeditionary Forces in Europe, led the Normandy invasion, and directed the overthrow of the Nazis (1944–1945). He later became chief of staff in Washington and told his own story of the European war in *Crusade in Europe* (1948). He was president of Columbia University from 1948 to 1952, taking a leave of absence to serve as Supreme Allied Commander in Europe and to set up the forces of the North Atlantic Treaty Organization.

Eisenhower was eyed by both Republicans and Democrats for the presidential nomination in 1952. He accepted the Republican bid and defeated Adlai E. Stevenson in the election. As president he generally took a middle road in his policies, continuing foreign aid and advocating a balanced budget while he opposed government control in private enterprise.

He was reelected in 1956, again defeating Stevenson. *Mandate for Change, 1953–1956,* the first volume of Eisenhower's account of his administrations, *The White House Years,* appeared in 1963.

Eisenstein, Sergei M[ikhailovich] (1898–1948). Russian motion-picture director. Acclaimed as one of the greatest of all film directors, whose methods of cutting and mounting film to gain the effects of montage and dynamic progression have been widely imitated, Eisenstein was trained as a civil engineer and as an architect, then served in the Bolshevik army as a volunteer (1918–1920). His first film, *Strike* (1924), was notable for its skillful handling of crowd movement. Several remarkable scenes in *Potemkin* (1926) were even more significant as milestones in the development of cinematic technique. Among his other famous films are *Ten Days That Shook the World* (1928), the never-completed epic *Que Viva Mexico* (1931–1932), *Alexander Nevsky* (1928), and *Ivan the Terrible* (*Part I*, 1941; *Part II*, 1946), which was originally planned as a trilogy.

Eisteddfod. The Welsh national congress of bards. It had its origin in an extremely old Welsh assembly called the Gorsedd; in its present form it probably began in the twelfth century. Eisteddfod means literally "a session." Minstrelsy has been an important part of Welsh culture from the earliest days, and the present purpose of the Eisteddfod is to maintain an interest in the ancient traditions.

El. The supreme god of many ancient Semitic races in the Near East. He was represented in the form of a bull. The golden calf of the Old Testament probably was sacred to one of his offspring. See THE POEM OF BAAL and THE POEM OF AQHAT.

Elaine. In Arthurian romance, the name given to two ladies, both of whom love LAUNCELOT. In Malory's *Morte d'Arthur* (c. 1469), the first Elaine is the daughter of King Pelles. Falling in love with Sir Launcelot, she takes on for a night the likeness of Queen Guinevere, in order to deceive him. As a result, a son is born to them, and he is given the name of GALAHAD.

The second Elaine, known as the "lily maid of Astolat" is the Elaine of Tennyson's *Lancelot and Elaine* in his *Idylls of the King,* in which he recasts Malory's version of the story. This Elaine loved Launcelot "with that love which was her doom." Her love is so great that she dies of it. According to her request, her dead body is then placed on a barge, a lily in her right hand and a letter, avowing her love and showing the innocence of Launcelot, in her left. The barge, steered by an old servitor, moves down the river, and, when it stops at the palace entrance, Arthur orders the body borne in. The letter is read, and Arthur directs that the maiden shall be buried like a queen, with her sad story blazoned on her tomb. Tennyson has also told her story in his *The Lady of Shalott.*

Elba. An island in the Mediterranean to which Napoleon Bonaparte was banished when he abdicated power in 1814. After 10 months, he escaped from Elba and returned to France for the Hundred Days that ended at WATERLOO.

El Dorado (*Sp.*, the gilded). A legendary king. El Dorado was the supposed King of Manoa, a fabulous city of immense wealth localized by early explorers on the Amazon. He was said to be covered with oil and then powdered with gold dust. This operation had been performed so many times that he was permanently, and literally, gilded. Many expeditions, from both Spain and England (two of which were led by Sir Walter Raleigh), tried to discover El Dorado, and the name was later transferred to his supposed territory. Hence, the term refers to any place or realm of fabulous richness.

Eleanor of Aquitaine (c. 1122–1204). Queen of Louis VII of France (1137–1151), then of Henry II of England (1152–1204), mother of Richard I and King John. Because she was heiress of Aquitaine, about half of southern France, England claimed possession of the region, thus precipitating about 400 years of wars between France and England. She backed the rebellion of her sons against Henry II (1173), for which she was imprisoned (1174–1189). Richard released her after his accession to the throne, and when he went on his crusade, she protected his interests against John. Later she reconciled the brothers and continued to be politically important during John's reign. An ardent patron of the Provençal TROUBADORS, she was influential in bringing them and their works to her courts.

Elective Affinities, The. See WAHLVERWANDT-SCHAFTEN, DIE.

Electra (Elektra). (1) In Greek mythology, a daughter of Agamemnon and Clytemnestra, and sister of Orestes. Her tragic story (see House of ATREUS) was told by each of the three great Athenian dramatists, Aeschylus in his *Oresteia* trilogy, Sophocles and Euripides in their plays called *Electra*. Richard Strauss wrote an opera of a version of Sophocles' play by Hugo von Hofmannsthal (1903). *Mourning Becomes Electra* (1931), a trilogy of plays by Eugene O'Neill, is a retelling of the *Oresteia* story set in 19th century New England. Jean Giraudoux also adapted the story for his play *Electre* (1937).

(2) One of the PLEIADES, daughter of Atlas, mother of Dardanus. She is known as "the lost Pleiad," for it is said that she disappeared a little before the Trojan war, that she might be saved the mortification of seeing the ruin of her beloved city. She showed herself occasionally to mortals, but always in the guise of a comet.

Electra (Elektra; 414? B.C.). A tragedy by SOPHOCLES (414? B.C.). It deals with the return of Orestes to Argos and the murder of Clytemnestra. Electra is the heroine; as in the *Philoctetes* and the *Oedipus at Colonus,* Sophocles isolates his tragic hero in order to emphasize the qualities of heroism and tragic endurance. As a consequence, the murder of Clytemnestra and Aegisthus is left to the very end; the climax of the play is the long recognition scene between Orestes and Electra. Also, in order to develop the character of Electra to the fullest extent, Sophocles leaves Orestes almost blank; he is the avenger, a paragon of virtue, and nothing more. Thus the recognition scene is the fitting climax, since Electra's trials are now over. Clytemnestra is the real enemy, and Aegisthus is no threat. Euripides reverses this emphasis in order to make Clytemnestra's death more unnecessary and more horrible; Sophocles' determination to represent the murder as an example of "natural recoil" necessitates a strong character for the queen.

Electra (Elektra; 413 B.C.). A drama by EURIP-IDES (413 B.C.). Aegisthus has forced Electra to marry a kindly old farmer so that she cannot enter into a dangerous marriage with some great prince. Electra has no power to avenge her father as the wife of a peasant; her only hope is Orestes. The play opens in the peasant's small hut in the mountains. The peasant speaks the prologue, after which Orestes and Pylades enter furtively. Various devices lead gradually to the recognition of brother and sister, which comes about through the summoning of the old servant of Agamemnon who rescued Orestes as a baby. In this play the murder of Aegisthus precedes that of Clytemnestra. Aegisthus is portrayed as the real force behind the usurpation; Clytemnestra is represented as being to some degree the victim of circumstances. In this way the play leads up to the murder of Clytemnestra, who is summoned to the peasant's hut on the pretext that Electra has just had a child. Clytemnestra goes inside, to be met by Orestes and Electra. Euripides' presentation is designed to inspire the utmost horror at the act and great pity for the victim. The play ends with the beginning of the madness of Orestes, brought on by the Erinyes.

Elegies of Ch'u (Ch'u Tz'u). Chinese poetry anthology attributed to Ch'ü Yüan of the Chou Dynasty (1027–256 B.C.). It contains 17 poem cycles, dealing with the virtues, largely unrecognized, and the misfortunes of the poet. Also included are nine poems of shamanistic import. The text is corrupt and contains many Han Dynasty accretions. See Arthur Waley, *The Nine Songs: a Study of Shamanism in Ancient China* (1956); David Hawkes, *Ch'u Tz'u: The Songs of the South* (1959).

elegy. In classical prosody a poem in elegiac distichs, in modern prosody a lyrical poem of plaintive content and mood, especially a poem of lament for someone or something departed. Thought to be among the greatest elegies in English are Milton's *Lycidas,* Shelley's *Adonais,* Tennyson's *In Memoriam,* and Matthew Arnold's *Thyrsis,* all poems of mourning, and Gray's *Elegy Written in a Country Churchyard* in a more general plaintive vein.

Elegy Written in a Country Churchyard. A poem by Thomas GRAY (1742?–1750, pub. 1751), probably the most popular—and often considered the greatest—poem written in the eighteenth century. Its familiar theme deals with rural life combined with the tragic dignity inherent in man. This pastoral idealization and meditation on death is made even more subjective at the end by the introduction of "The Epitaph."

Elephant in the Moon, The. A satire on the Royal Society by Samuel BUTLER. In it, an elephant discovered on the face of the moon is revealed to be only a mouse imprisoned in the telescope. The work was first published in a posthumous collection of Butler's *Genuine Remains in Verse and Prose* (1759).

Eleusinian Mysteries. Ancient Greek religious rites. They were performed in honor of DEMETER and her daughter Persephone (Kore) at Eleusis in Attica. Begun probably in late Mycenaean times, with the introduction of the worship of Demeter to Eleusis, these rites became the most famous mysteries in the Greek or Roman world, and continued to be celebrated well into the Christian era. The secret of the rites was so successfully guarded that, in spite of their tremendous importance, no one can say precisely what they were. It is known, however, that they centered about the abduction of Persephone by HADES, her return, and the subsequent reconciliation of Demeter and Hades. In short, they celebrated the revival of corn in the springtime. Also connected with the rite in some way was a youthful godling Iacchus, about whom almost nothing is known, except that he was later identified with Dionysus.

Elgar, Sir Edward (1857–1934). English composer. His most notable compositions include the oratorios *Dream of Gerontius* (1900), *The Apostles* (1903), and *The Kingdom* (1906); *Pomp and Circumstance,* a march (1902); *Enigma Variations* (1899). He also wrote symphonies, songs, and sonatas.

Elgin marbles. A collection of Greek sculptures, mainly of the Phidian school (see PHIDIAS). It includes the bulk of the surviving sculptural decoration of the Parthenon. The works were removed from Athens (1803–1812) by Lord Elgin and were purchased by the British government in 1816. The collection now resides in the British Museum in London.

Elia. See Charles LAMB.

Elidure. Legendary king of England. According to Geoffrey of Monmouth he became king after his elder brother Artegal (or Arthgall) was presumed dead. When Artegal returned after a long exile, Elidure nobly resigned the throne to him. The story appears in John Milton's *History of Britain* and William Wordsworth's poem *Artegal and Elidure.*

Elihu. A name given to several Old Testament characters, the most notable being found in the book of Job. Here, Elihu attempts to reason with Job about his troubles, after the three false comforters have spoken (Job 32).

Elijah. In the Old Testament, a Hebrew prophet who lived during the ninth century B.C. in the reign of Ahab. During the great drought which he foretold, he was fed miraculously by ravens near the stream Cherith, and by Zarephath's widow whose dead son he restored to life. He opposed the prophets of Baal and challenged them to a dramatic contest on Mount Carmel where two altars were built, one to Baal and one to Jehovah. Baal was deaf to the repeated cries of his prophets, but Jehovah answered Elijah by sending fire from heaven. The story of Elijah's discouragement under the juniper tree is well known (see I Kings 19:4). He did not die but was carried up to heaven in a whirlwind (II Kings 2:11). He cast his mantle on Elisha whom he had anointed prophet in his stead; hence, the phrase *Elijah's mantle* signifies succession to any office.

Eliot, Charles William (1834–1926). American teacher and chemist. President of Harvard from 1869 to 1909, he helped to make that school one of the best known in the world. In 1894, Eliot helped to establish Radcliffe College for women. Introducing the elective system, he influenced college education everywhere in the U.S. He improved the graduate and professional schools at Harvard, attracting great scholars to the faculty. Believing that "All the books needed for a real education could be set on a shelf five feet long," he was persuaded to edit the famous Harvard Classics, a 50-volume set.

Eliot, George. Pen name of **Mary Ann or Marian Evans** (1819–1880). English novelist. Of the first rank among Victorian novelists, George Eliot was the daughter of a Warwickshire land agent, a man of strong Evangelical Protestant feeling. Her severance from her father's religion was a great source of conflict for her and distress for him. Early in the 1840's she became acquainted with the new and "advanced" biblical and theological scholarship of Germany and translated D. F. Strauss's *Leben Jesu* (*Life of Jesus,* 1846). After her father's death, she began to associate with a group of rationalists in London; one of them, John Chapman, took her on as assistant editor for the *Westminster Review,* a post she held from 1851 to 1854. She became a friend of Herbert Spencer and through him met George Henry LEWES. Although Lewes was separated from his wife, he could not obtain a divorce, and, in 1854, George Eliot entered into an irregular union with him that lasted until his death (1878); they lived as man and wife and were accepted as such by their friends.

George Eliot was on the verge of midde age before she wrote her first fiction. In 1857 (when she assumed her pen name) her first works of fiction—three short stories—appeared in *Blackwood's* and were published later that same year as the volume *Scenes of Clerical Life.* ADAM BEDE, her first full-length novel, followed soon after, and in 1860 came two more novels: THE MILL ON THE FLOSS and SILAS MARNER. Inspired by a trip to Florence, she did a great deal of painstaking research in the Italian Renaissance and produced her only historical novel, ROMOLA in 1863. Turning again to the contemporary scene in England she wrote FELIX HOLT, THE RADICAL and MIDDLEMARCH, generally considered her finest work. Her last novel, DANIEL DERONDA, is peopled with characters who illustrate her moral philosophy. In 1880, two years after Lewes's death, she married J. W. Cross, a clergyman; she died later that same year.

George Eliot's fiction is a vehicle for the serious discussion of social and moral problems of her time; her purpose is primarily didactic. She presents, on a vast scale and crowded with detail, a beautifully observed world of peasants and townsfolk. Her greatest preoccupation is with moral problems, and, more particularly, with the moral development of her characters, many of whom strive with the difficulty of arriving at an individual and mature view of life. See SPANISH GYPSY, THE.

Eliot, John (1604–1690). English-born American teacher, missionary, and linguist. Emigrating to Massachusetts in 1631, Eliot devoted himself to converting the Indians to Christianity; he established 14 colonies of "Praying Indians" and translated the Bible into the dialect of the Naticks, an Algonquian tribe, in 1663. Most of his work was destroyed during King Philip's War. Eliot also wrote *The Christian Commonwealth* (1659), in which he advocated a society based entirely on obedience to the Scriptures. The book was suppressed by Massachusetts authorities for fear of angering the restored monarchy in England. See BAY PSALM BOOK.

Eliot, Lewis. The hero and narrator of the STRANGERS AND BROTHERS novels by C. P. Snow.

Eliot, Sir Thomas. See Sir Thomas ELYOT.

Eliot, T[homas] S[tearns] (1888–1965). American-born English poet, critic, and dramatist. He lived in England from 1914 and became a British subject in 1927. Universally recognized as one of the major

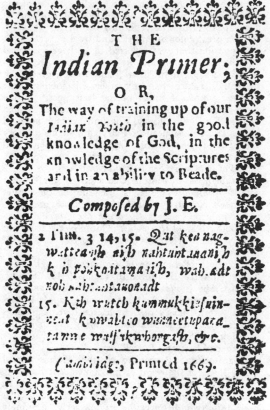

EDINBURGH UNIVERSITY LIBRARY

Title page of John Eliot's *Indian Primer* (1669).

poets of the 20th century, Eliot's reputation grew to almost mythic proportions during his own lifetime. Because of its radical innovations in poetic technique and subject matter, his poetry revolutionized the literary conventions bequeathed by the Romantics and Victorians and gave expression to the spirit of the post-World War I world.

Eliot was born in St. Louis, Missouri. He was educated at Harvard, where his flair for eclectic scholarship and his keen sensitivity to the social-psychological currents of the day were already marked characteristics, according to the reminiscences of his fellow students. Realizing that the poetry of his own day could be of little use to him as literary models, he turned to the poetry of other nations and epochs. The English Jacobeans and the French Symbolists were a revelation to him; his indebtedness to Laforgue and Baudelaire is already apparent in his undergraduate poems. After doing graduate work at Harvard, the Sorbonne, and Oxford, Eliot settled in London in 1915. There he came under the influence of Ezra Pound, who recognized Eliot's genius at once, and criticized and encouraged his work. Pound was also largely responsible for getting the early poems into print; he saw to the publication of THE LOVE SONG OF J. ALFRED PRUFROCK in *Poetry* in 1915 and introduced Eliot to Harriet Weaver, who published his first volume of verse, *Prufrock and Other Observations,* in 1917. With his early work in print, Eliot's reputation

quickly grew. By the time THE WASTE LAND appeared in 1922, his position was firmly established among the avant garde, and he had become the recognized leader of younger poets.

In technique, as in subject matter, Eliot's poetry broke with the literary conventions of his day, conventions that he felt were inadequate to express the experience of the modern world. In order to capture the spirit of a new age he believed it was necessary to create new poetic forms and a new poetic language, which, in turn, might break up current modes of perception and change contemporary attitudes. Perhaps his most important technical innovations were twofold: instead of "poetic diction" Eliot used the idiom and natural rhythms of speech, and instead of relying on abstractions he expressed himself solely through sense impressions (see OBJECTIVE CORRELATIVE and DISSOCIATION OF SENSIBILITY). The subject matter of his early poems also reflected the world about him. For material, he drew upon his own social background as well as the surrounding squalor of an industrial age. In such poems as *Prufrock,* PORTRAIT OF A LADY, GERONTION, the SWEENEY poems, *The Waste Land,* and THE HOLLOW MEN, he depicts the emotional impoverishment, boredom, and spiritual emptiness common to both the dying genteel world of devitalized social rituals and the new urban materialistic world. Eliot's later poetry reflects his conversion to the Anglican Church in the late 1920's. In poems such as ASH WEDNESDAY, *The Journey of the Magi,* and *Marina,* he portrays alternating stages of despair, skepticism, hope, and joy in the soul's struggle for renewal. FOUR QUARTETS is generally acknowledged to be the major work of this latter period. It is a series of four long meditative poems in which Eliot weaves together his complex thoughts on the irreconcilable tension between man's position in the space-time world and his desire to escape its dimensions. He has also written poems in a lighter vein, such as THE HIPPOPOTAMUS and OLD POSSUM's *Book of Practical Cats* (1939).

In an early essay, TRADITION AND THE INDIVIDUAL TALENT, Eliot propounded the doctrine that poetry should be impersonal, transmuting private feelings into general truths. This view is closely connected with his belief in the indebtedness of the poet to the tradition of the past and the necessity for incorporating the experience of the past into the poetry of the present. His early critical essays were collected in *The Sacred Wood* (1920), a volume that established his reputation as a critic and had an enormous impact on contemporary literary taste. By exalting the Elizabethan dramatists, metaphysical poets, Dante, and the French poets of the 19th century, and attacking Milton and the Victorian and Romantic poets, he effected a general change in literary values. Among his critical works are *The Use of Poetry and the Use of Criticism* (1933) and *The Classics and the Man of Letters* (1942). After joining the church, Eliot devoted much of his prose writing to cultural problems, particularly the place of religion in society. *After Strange Gods: A Primer of Modern Heresy* (1934), *The Idea of a Christian Society* (1939), and *Notes Towards a Definition of Culture* (1948), are books of social criticism. In *For Lancelot Andrewes,* a collection of essays published in 1929, Eliot declared himself "an Anglo-Catholic in religion, a classicist in literature, and a royalist in politics," and the labels stuck, despite his changing opinions. For from his earlier exploratory essays in literary values to his later essays, in which he frequently reversed or modified his previous positions, Eliot's judgments have often been taken to be dogmatic, though in fact he has always viewed them as tentative.

In *Poetry and Drama* (1951) Eliot discusses the problems he faced in attempting to revive poetic drama for the modern stage. His first play, MURDER IN THE CATHEDRAL, is generally considered to be his best. It was followed by THE FAMILY REUNION, THE COCKTAIL PARTY, *The Confidential Clerk* (1954), and *The Elder Statesman* (1958).

Eliot was long associated with Faber & Faber, Ltd., British publishers, and was a director of the firm at his death. He received the Nobel Prize in 1948.

Elise. The illicit queen of Tyre in Quinault's tragedy ASTRATE, ROI DE TYR. Elise is also the name of the miser's daughter in Molière's comedy L'AVARE.

Elisha. In the Old Testament, a Hebrew prophet. He was selected by ELIJAH to be his successor. In contrast to his predecessor, Elisha was urbane and sophisticated. His ministry lasted for 50 years during which time he was counselor to four kings of Israel (c. 850–790 B.C.). His work (which included many civic projects) and his prophecies are recorded in II Kings.

Elissa. See DIDO; FAERIE QUEENE, THE.

elixir of life. The potion of the alchemists to prolong life indefinitely. It was imagined sometimes as a dry drug, sometimes as a fluid. *Elixir* (*Arabic,* a powder for sprinkling on wounds) also meant among alchemists the philosopher's stone, the tincture for transmuting metals, and the name is now given to any sovereign remedy for disease, especially one of a quack character.

Eliza. A character in Harriet Beecher Stowe's UNCLE TOM'S CABIN.

Eliza. Eliza Draper, wife of an official of the East India Company, to whom Laurence Sterne addressed THE BRAMINE'S JOURNAL and the *Letters of Yorick to Eliza* (1775). The letters are a sentimental account of their passionate but Platonic love affair in 1766. *The Letters of Eliza to Yorick* (1775) and *Letters supposed to have been written by Yorick and Eliza* (1779) are forgeries.

Elizabeth I. Elizabeth Tudor (1533–1603). Queen of England (1558–1603), daughter of HENRY VIII and ANNE BOLEYN. Elizabeth was proclaimed queen by Parliament on the death of her elder half-sister, Mary Tudor. She re-established Protestantism and the supremacy of the English ruler over the Pope, ended foreign religious and political domination, and helped, with her claim of being "mere English" and her refusal to take a foreign consort, to strengthen England's growing sense of nationality and unity. Among the major political events of her reign was the execution of Mary, Queen of Scots, for complicity in a Catholic plot against the life of Elizabeth. The death of the Catholic queen may have been the final stroke that moved Philip of Spain to action; the following year, in 1588, he sent the "invincible Armada" against England, and was soundly defeated.

Elizabeth's long reign was marked by domestic peace and prosperity, by the growth of England as a naval power, by the beginnings of what was to become a great colonial empire, and by a general spirit of expansion that was reflected in both geographical and literary exploration; it was an age that produced perhaps more "firsts" and more "greats" in English literature than any other. Elizabeth's Court was the source of much of the lyric poetry of the time, and she numbered among her courtiers such men as Sir Philip Sidney. Edmund Spenser honored her as Gloriana, Queen of Fairyland, in his allegory *The Faerie Queene.* She was fond of plays and pageants, and many of Shakespeare's plays were presented at her Court. See ELIZABETHAN.

Elizabeth is a central character in Sir Walter Scott's *Kenilworth.* She is the subject of Lytton Strachey's biography *Elizabeth and Essex,* and Maxwell Anderson's drama *Elizabeth the Queen.*

Elizabeth II (1926–   ). Queen of Great Britain and Northern Ireland (1952–   ). She is married to Philip, duke of Edinburgh.

Elizabeth. Pen name of Countess **Russell,** born **Mary Annette Beauchamp** (1866–1941). English novelist. She is best known for *Elizabeth and Her German Garden* (1898), a semiautobiographical novel in diary form; it is a meditative, sensitive, sometimes satirical account of the author's trying life in Prussia as wife of Count von Arnim. Her second husband was a brother of Bertrand Russell.

Elizabethan. Pertaining to the 45-year period (1558–1603) of the reign of ELIZABETH I of England, sometimes considered the English renaissance. In both literary and political history her reign divides itself into two distinct phases: an early, seemingly undistinguished period in which Elizabeth's tenuous hold on royal authority and the Elizabethan writer's experimental probing of his language (which had hitherto been regarded as an inferior, even barbaric tongue) were gradually becoming consolidated; and a later, dazzlingly brilliant and enormously successful era. This began, in the political realm, with the execution of Mary Stuart (MARY QUEEN OF SCOTS) in 1587, and in literature with the publication of Edmund Spenser's THE SHEPHEARDES CALENDAR (1579). It is this latter quarter of a century that is generally identified as Elizabethan. (In drama the term is often used to embrace all activity relative to the stage until the closing of the theatres in 1642.) Nevertheless, it was in the early period that the groundwork was laid for the later, great achievements.

The first two years of Elizabeth's reign were marked by two events in literature, insignificant in themselves but representative of interests, attitudes, and linguistic developments that were to bear fruit near the close of the century. These were the publication of the first full translation of Vergil's *Aeneid* into English and of the first extant edition of A MIRROR FOR MAGISTRATES. These two works, both of which were extremely popular throughout the reign, reflected the two chief sources of the Elizabethan inheritance: classical humanism, with its grand and noble conception of the dignity of man, and in the case of *A Mirror for Magistrates,* the medieval tragic sense of life, with its intense concentration on the fact of death. From these diverse sources, the later Elizabethans managed to fuse a picture of man and the universe that was sweeping and heroic, and at the same time circumscribed by the overwhelming sense of human mortality. One of the most comprehensive portrayals of this conception is Christopher Marlowe's Dr. FAUSTUS. Surely the finest expression of this vision is Hamlet's apostrophe on man:

What a piece of work is a man! how noble in reason! how infinite in faculty! in form and moving how express and admirable! in action how like an angel! in apprehension how like a god! the beauty of the world! the paragon of animals! And yet, to me, what is this quintessence of dust?

Although the greatest literary achievement of the Elizabethans lies in drama, their accomplishments in the other genres are only slightly less substantial. To the development of English the Elizabethans contributed, on one level, the ornate, rhetorical, expansive prose derived from Cicero and culminating in the massive dignity of Richard Hooker's *Laws of Ecclesiastical Polity*. On another level, the Elizabethans enriched the language through the racy colloquialism that characterizes the prose pamphlets of the period, written by such men as Robert GREENE, Thomas NASHE, and the pseudonymous "Martin Marprelate." (See MARPRELATE CONTROVERSY.) Probably the finest prose achievement in this latter category is John Florio's magnificent translation of the *Essays of Montaigne*.

In poetry the great monument of the Elizabethan era (as well as being in tone and style a very representative poem) is Edmund Spenser's THE FAERIE QUEENE. In the six elaborately constructed, enormously detailed allegorical books comprising the poem, he attempted to write a great moral epic that would glorify Elizabeth and England as Vergil had glorified Augustus Caesar and Rome. Spenser also contributed to another significant Elizabethan poetic development: the sonnet sequence. But here both Spenser, in his AMORETTI, and Sir Philip Sidney, in his pioneering sequence ASTROPHEL AND STELLA, were overshadowed by the mysterious, unorthodox, untitled collection we know as the SONNETS OF SHAKESPEARE. Other well-known sequences were Samuel DANIEL's *Delia* and Michael DRAYTON's *Idea*.

It is in the drama of the period, however, that the vitality, splendor, and diversity we identify as Elizabethan is exuberantly displayed. Emerging from the primitive morality plays and INTERLUDES of the earlier part of the century, Elizabethan drama, possibly as a result of the new upsurge of national identity and patriotic fervor that followed the victory over the Spanish ARMADA, began to attract a new school of playwrights. Chief of these was the titanic figure of Christopher MARLOWE, defying all moral and metrical conventions as he attempted to capture the spirit of the age in his portraits of the "overreachers" in such plays as TAMBURLAINE, THE JEW OF MALTA, and *Dr. Faustus*. The instrument of Marlowe's expression was blank verse, a new and staid meter that he transformed into a thundering drum roll, later characterized by Ben Jonson as "Marlowe's mighty line." At the same time the drama was developing in lesser keys. George PEELE and John LYLY experimented to combine light fantasy and romantic comedy in such plays as *The Arraignment of Paris* and *Endymion* to the delight of the Court, the agency which stood as

a buffer between the acting companies and the growing militance of the Puritan opposition to the stage. This opposition forced the players to set up their theaters outside London proper in a suburb on the south side of the Thames. Playgoing became increasingly popular among the non-Puritan population. Plays such as Thomas Kyd's THE SPANISH TRAGEDY enjoyed an unparalleled success and the Theatre (the first public theater, built in 1576 by James BURBAGE) became so popular that by 1585 a second playhouse, the CURTAIN, was being used to accommodate the overflow.

Into this heady atmosphere stepped the man whom many regard as the supreme literary artist of all time. In 1588 William SHAKESPEARE was 24 and, like the nation itself, newly conscious of his powers and of the capacity of the English language as a fit vehicle to serve those powers. He capitalized on the revolutionary treatment that Marlowe had given blank verse, achieving a greater range and flexibility than his predecessors had been capable of, and he responded to the newly developing national mood with a series of chronicle plays (the Histories). These plays helped to articulate a sense of national self-identity best epitomized by John of Gaunt's speech in RICHARD II:

> This royal throne of kings, this sceptred isle,
> This earth of majesty, this seat of Mars,
> This other Eden, demi-paradise,
> This fortress built by Nature for herself
> Against infection and the hand of war,
> This happy breed of men, this little world,
> This precious stone set in the silver sea,

This glorification of the nation proved, however, to be the least of his contributions. He managed to run the gamut of comic potential, ranging from the slapstick farce of THE MERRY WIVES OF WINDSOR through the romantic fantasy of A MIDSUMMER NIGHT'S DREAM to the dark satire of MEASURE FOR MEASURE. Finally he produced in his tragedies those explorations of the human condition that are familiar to everyone.

By 1600, three years before the death of Elizabeth, the Elizabethan vision had begun to fade, and the literature that mirrored the life of its time underwent a change (see JACOBEAN). The literature of the 1590's, a literature rich in harmony, profuse and expansive in detail, and essentially affirmative in its vision of life, had lost its vitality and splendor and had already begun to be parodied. The old queen, now almost 70, and childless, had not designated an heir. The earl of Essex, whose brilliance and daring epitomized the era, had suffered a humiliating defeat in the Irish campaign, and insurrection was in the air. The Renaissance in England was over and the "counter-Renaissance" had begun.

Elizabeth of Hungary, St. Patron saint of queens, being herself a queen. She died in 1231 at the age of 24, and her day is November 19. She gave so bountifully to the poor that she starved her own household. One day her husband met her going out with her apron filled with something heavy, and demanded of her what she was carrying. "Only flowers, my lord," said Elizabeth, and to save the lie God converted the loaves of bread into flowers. She is the heroine of Kingsley's dramatic poem *The Saint's Tragedy* (1846).

Elle et Lui (He and She, 1859). A novel by George SAND. The author describes in retrospect her version of the love affair with Alfred de Musset. Musset had died two years earlier, but his brother Paul published *Lui et Elle* as a protest against Miss Sand's interpretation of the affair and its complexities.

Elliott, Anne. See PERSUASION.

Elliott, Ebenezer (1781–1849). English poet called the Corn-Law Rhymer because much of his verse consisted of invective against the CORN LAWS, so ruinous to England's laboring classes. These poems were forceful and cogent enough to play a significant part in the repeal of the laws. He wrote *The Village Patriarch* (1829); *Corn Law Rhymes* (1831); *The Splendid Village* (1833–1835); and many miscellaneous poems.

Ellis, [Henry] Havelock (1859–1939). English psychologist, essayist, and art critic. He is best known for his pioneering and at that time scandalous studies in sexual psychology, including *Man and Woman* (1894), *Studies in the Psychology of Sex* (6 vols., 1897–1910), and *The Erotic Rights of Women* (1918). *The Dance of Life* (1923), in which the dance is made to symbolize the vital rhythm of the universe, was his most popular book. He also wrote essays on art and literature, *Little Essays of Love and Virtue* (1922, 1931), and *My Life* (1939), a revealing autobiography. He was a close friend of the novelist Olive Schreiner.

Ellison, Ralph [Waldo] (1914–   ). American writer. Ellison, who studied at Tuskegee Institute, has lectured at a number of colleges and published work in various periodicals in both the essay and short-story form. His impressive first novel, INVISIBLE MAN, which won a National Book Award, was hailed as an outstanding work on the Negro in America.

Ellwood, Thomas (1639–1714). English Quaker and writer. Milton's friend and Latin reader, he is said to have suggested the writing of *Paradise Regained* (1671). His books include a *Sacred History of the Old and New Testaments* (1705–1709) and an *Autobiography* (1714).

Elmer Gantry (1927). A novel by Sinclair LEWIS. It deals with a brazen ex-football player who enters the ministry and, through his half-plagiarized sermons, his physical attractiveness, and his unerring instinct for promotion, becomes a successful evangelist and later the leader of a large Middle Western church. Carefully researched, the novel was realistic enough to shock both the faithful and unfaithful.

Elmire. In Molière's comedy LE TARTUFFE, the wily wife of Orgon. By a clever ruse she unmasks the hypocrite Tartuffe and finally convinces her husband of his duplicity.

Elm Tree on the Mall, The (L'Orme du Mall; 1897). A novel by Anatole FRANCE. The tale centers about the actions of its protagonist M. BERGERET.

Elohim. See JEHOVAH.

Elohistic and Jehovistic Scriptures. Elohim and Jehovah (Yahwe) are the most common of the many names given by the ancient Hebrews to the Deity. The fact that they are both used with interchangeable senses in the Pentateuch gave rise to the widely held theory that this group of five books was written in two different periods. The Elohistic paragraphs, being more simple, more primitive, more narrative, and more pastoral, are held to be the older. The later Jehovistic paragraphs, which indicate a knowledge of geography and history, seem to exalt the priestly office, and are of a more elaborate character, were subsequently woven into the Elohistic narrative.

This theory was originally stated by Jean Astruc, the French scholar, in his *Conjectures sur les mémoires originaux, dont il paroit que Moyse s'est servi pour composer le livre de la Genèse* (1753), a book that formed the starting point for all modern criticism of the Pentateuch.

Elpenor. In Homer's *Odyssey*, a member of Odysseus' crew. He falls from a roof during their stay with Circe and is killed. He is the first man Odysseus meets when visiting Hades, and he asks that his body be buried.

Elsie Dinsmore. Title of one of the 26 Elsie Books by Martha Finley (pen name, Martha Farquharson, 1828–1909). The books deal with the trials and adventures of Elsie Dinsmore. Elsie is a pious little prig who remains a paragon of all the virtues, although she is persecuted by associates, relatives, and even her father. Her story proved so popular with 19th-century girl readers that the series was continued until long after Elsie had become a grandmother.

Elsie Venner: A Romance of Destiny (1861). A novel by Oliver Wendell HOLMES. Elsie, whose mother was bitten by a snake while carrying her, has distinctly serpentine qualities. Isolated from other human beings, she never removes the heavy gold necklace that presumably hides an unsightly and revealing mark. Although she falls in love with Bernard Langdon, the young schoolteacher, her strange and repellent nature forbids the return of affection. Only her Negro mammy understands Elsie's mystery. In the attempt to humanize herself, the girl dies. Through Elsie Venner, Holmes opposes the Calvinist belief that a human being may be held morally responsible for an inherited flaw. He considered the doctrine of Original Sin a barbarism. For Holmes, the physician or psychologist, not the preacher, should treat the morally diseased.

Elsinore. The English name of Helsingör, a city in Denmark on the island of Zealand, It is the site of Kronberg Castle, the traditional scene of Shakespeare's HAMLET.

Elstir. A great painter in Marcel Proust's REMEMBRANCE OF THINGS PAST. His work is an idealized composite of that of a number of French impressionist painters, particularly of Claude Monet's.

Eluard, Paul. Pen name of **Eugène Grindel** (1895–1952). French poet. After his interest in DADAISM Eluard became, with André Breton, one of the founders of SURREALISM. *Les Nécessités d'une vie et les conséquences des rêves* (1921) gave flashes of the "living reality" of dreams; *Mourir de ne pas mourir* (1924) built a bridge of pure and passionate poetry between dream and reality. Then Eluard became the poet of the couple, of loving communion with the other as well as with the universe of nature: *Capitale de la douleur* (1926), *L'Amour, la poésie* (1929), *La Rose Publique* (1934), and *Les Yeux fertiles* (1936). Deeply moved by the Spanish Civil War and World War II, Eluard extended this communion to the fraternity of mankind in *Livre ouvert*

(1940, 1941), *Poésie et Vérité* (1942), *Au Rendez-vous allemand* (1944), *Poèmes politiques* (1948), and *Le Dur Désir de Durer* (translated by Stephen Spender, 1950).

Elvire. In Molière's DOM JUAN OU LE FESTIN DE PIERRE, the woman whom Juan abducts and marries, only to abandon.

Elyot or **Eliot, Sir Thomas** (1499?–1546). English humanist, diplomat, and prose writer. Elyot is best known for *The Book Named the Governor* (1531). The first treatise on education published in English, it is regarded as one of the important 16th-century contributions to the development of English prose. He also wrote *Of the Knowledge Which Maketh a Wise Man* (1533); *The Castel of Helth* (1534), a popular treatise on medicine; and the first complete Latin-English dictionary (1538). His many translations from Latin and Greek helped to spread the reading of the classics throughout the educated classes of England. Elyot is said to be an ancestor of the 20th-century American-born poet T. S. ELIOT, in whose poem *East Coker* (1940) are quotations from the work of Sir Thomas.

Elysium (Elysion). The abode of the blessed in Greek mythology. Hence the Elysian Fields, the Paradise or Happy Land of the Greek poets. Elysian means happy, delightful.

Elzevir. A family of Dutch publishers and printers flourishing in the 17th century. A style of type was named *Elzevir* after this family. Books of their printing are of special value. The best are editions of classical and French authors. The Elzevir imprint is found in 1213 books: 968 Latin, 44 Greek, 126 French, 32 Flemish, 22 Oriental, 11 German, 10 Italian.

Emancipation Proclamation (Jan. 1, 1863). A proclamation issued by President Abraham Lincoln declaring that all slaves in areas still in rebellion against the U.S. were henceforth to be free. The proclamation did not affect slaves in the border states nor in territory under U.S. military occupation. A preliminary proclamation had been issued on Sept. 22, 1862 after the Union success at Antietam had bolstered the likelihood of ultimate victory over the Confederacy. Slavery was not completely abolished until the adoption of the 13th amendment to the Constitution in 1865.

Embla. The first woman, in Norse mythology, created out of an elm by the gods Odin, Vili, and Ve. The first man was Ask.

emblem books. Originally a symbolic picture illustrating a moral idea, but during the Renaissance and baroque periods, when emblems were immensely popular, the picture was always accompanied by a motto or pungent phrase and a short poem (epigram, sonnet, etc.) expanding upon the moral significance of the scene depicted (see IMPRESA). The illustration is commonly called the *cor* (heart), and the accompanying poetry the *anima* (soul) of the emblem. An example would be a depiction of Hercules standing between a bearded sage representing wisdom and a satanic figure representing vice. The motto above says, "When Vice and Vertue Youth shall wooe,/ Tis hard to say, which way 'twill go." Below the picture is a stanza in which the idea is treated at greater length (from George WITHER's *A Collection of Emblemes,* 1635). A famous European collection, or

Fruſtra quis ſtabilem figat in Orbe Gradum.

This changing World no lasting Joys can give,
The slipp'ry Ground your Footsteps will deceive.

An 18th-century reprint of an emblem
by Francis Quarles.

emblem book, was that of the Italian Andrea Alciati; in England, Francis QUARLES' *Emblems, Divine and Moral* (1635) was immensely popular. Emblems and emblem books, the latter's appeal boosted by the development of engraving, influenced many poets in their choice and treatment of subject matter and descriptive detail.

Emerald Isle. Ireland. This term was first used by Dr. William Drennan (1754–1820), in the poem *Erin.* It refers to the bright verdure of the island.

Emerson, Ralph Waldo (1803–1882). American poet, essayist, and philosopher. After a studious but undistinguished career at Harvard, and a brief period of teaching, Emerson entered the ministry. He was appointed to the Old Second Church in Boston, his native city, but soon became an unwilling preacher. Unable in conscience to administer the sacrament of the Lord's Supper, he resigned his pastorate at the death of his young wife, Ellen Tucker. The following year, 1832, he sailed for Europe. Visiting Landor, CARLYLE, and Coleridge, he began to formulate his own philosophy. Emerson's friendship with Carlyle was both lasting and significant. The insights of the British thinker helped him to reconcile some of his own confusions. Two other trips to England followed, in 1847 and 1872, but neither was as vital as the first.

On his return to New England, Emerson became known for the challenges to traditional thought in his essays and lectures. His first book, NATURE, summarized his major ideas. In 1835, he married Lydia Jackson and settled in Concord, Mass. The center of a literary circle, "the sage of Concord" became the chief spokesman for TRANSCENDENTALISM. Other members of his group included Margaret Fuller, Bronson Alcott, Henry Thoreau, and W. E. Channing.

Among Emerson's best work are ESSAYS, FIRST AND SECOND SERIES, *Poems* (1847), REPRESENTATIVE MEN, ENGLISH TRAITS, and THE CONDUCT OF LIFE (1860). His best-known addresses are THE AMERICAN SCHOLAR and THE DIVINITY SCHOOL ADDRESS. For two years, 1842–1844, Emerson edited the Transcendentalist journal, THE DIAL.

Emerson's philosophy is characterized by its reliance on intuition as the only way to comprehend reality. His conception of life as "spiritual vision" owes much to the work of Plotinus. He was influenced, too, by Swedenborg and Boehme. Like Thoreau and Whitman, he was attracted to mystical Indian literature and philosophy.

Emerson's unit of thought is the epigrammatic sentence. His prose style is not clearly organized or easy to follow, but has moments of great brilliance. Emerson wrote a poetic prose; intuitive rather than logical in form, the essays are ordered by recurring themes and images. His poetry, on the other hand, is often called harsh and didactic; he knew himself to be a "husky singer."

A believer in the "divine sufficiency of the individual," Emerson was a steady optimist. His refusal to grant the positive existence of evil caused Melville, Hawthorne, and Henry James, Sr., among others, to doubt his judgment. In spite of skepticism, Emerson's beliefs—that each man shares in the Over-Soul, or God; that Nature is a manifestation of Spirit; and that man possesses, within himself, the means to all knowledge—expressed in his memorable sentences, are of central importance in the history of American culture. See BOSTON HYMN; BRAHMA; CONCORD HYMN; DAYS; EACH AND ALL; MERLIN; THRENODY; Jones VERY.

Emesh and **Enten.** The brothers in Sumerian mythology who were created by the god of the air, Enlil. Each was assigned special duties connected with fertility; they quarreled, however, over which was the more important, and Enlil decided in favor of Enten, who thereafter was designated the god of farmers. This tale may have been a forerunner of the story of Cain and Abel.

Emilia. (1) In Shakespeare's OTHELLO, Iago's sharp-tongued wife and faithful waiting-woman to Desdemona. When she publicly denounces Iago's villainy, he stabs her, and she dies at her mistress' feet.

(2) Heroine of Boccaccio's TESEIDA.

Emilia Galotti (1772). A tragedy by Gotthold Ephraim LESSING in which Emilia, a middle-class girl, unwittingly arouses the passion of a prince, who has her bridegroom murdered and hopes to make her his mistress. In the end, to preserve her honor, her father stabs her to death.

Emile, ou l'Education (1762). An educational romance by Jean Jacques ROUSSEAU. It describes, in loose, story form, the bringing up of the boy Emile according to what Rousseau calls the principles of nature. He emphasizes character formation, learning by experience and observation, physical exercise, the mastery of useful trades, judgment, and hard work. One of the dominant principles of Rousseau's theory is that the child is not an adult and should not be treated as such until he is ready. Hitherto education was usually inconsiderate of the various psychic stages of a child's development; Rousseau deserves credit for showing that the object and the methods of education should change with these stages. In Book IV, Emile's moral and religious education is summarized in the *Profession de foi du vicaire* SAVOYARD. The natural religion that Rousseau advocates in this section led to his persecution by the church authorities. Book V deals with the education of Sophie, a girl intended for Emile's wife. Her unique purpose is to please men, and to be charming, modest, virtuous, and submissive. (Curiously enough, in his sequel *Emile et Sophie,* Rousseau relates the infidelity of Sophie and the breakup of their marriage.) The work had a notable influence on pedagogical theory in France, Germany, and England. It was immediately translated into English. The thinking of educators of the 19th century, Friedrich Wilhelm August Froebel, Johann Heinrich Pestalozzi, and Johann Friedrich Herbart, is derived directly from Rousseau.

Emilie. The "divine Emilie," to whom VOLTAIRE wrote verses, was Marquise du CHÂTELET, with whom he lived at Cirey from 1734 to her death in 1749.

Emireno (**Emirene**). In the GERUSALEMME LIBERATA of Tasso, a Christian convert to the Islamic faith and the chief of the allied forces of the infidels against the Crusaders. He is killed by Goffredo, the Christian commander, during the final battle for the holy city.

Emma (1816). A novel by Jane AUSTEN. Charming, wilful Emma Woodhouse has no responsibilities other than the care of an indulgent father. To amuse herself she plays with other people's affairs, planning their lives the way she sees fit. Her first project is pretty, vapid Harriet Smith, a parlor-boarder at a nearby school and the natural daughter of an unknown person. Encouraging her to aspire to the hand of Mr. Elton, a young clergyman, Emma prevents Harriet's accepting the offer of the far more appropriate Robert Martin, a young farmer. Emma's plans go awry: the snobbish, ambitious Elton first aspires to Emma's hand, and, haughtily rejected, chooses instead the crass, pretentious daughter of a wealthy family for his bride. Other moves, notably Emma's interference in the courtship of Jane Fairfax and Frank Churchill, are not any more successful. When Harriet shows signs of attachment to Knightly, a somewhat dictatorial but frank and generous gentleman, Emma appreciates the folly and thoughtlessness of her meddling; she discovers that her long friendship with Knightly has grown into love. Propriety and common sense prevail: Emma marries Knightly, Harriet her first love, Robert Martin. The book is much concerned with the themes of self-delusion and notions of class and decorum fundamental to English society. See Miss BATES.

Emmanuel, Pierre. Pen name of Noël Mathieu (1916–   ). French poet and essayist. Both the style and the symbolism of much of his poetry were inspired by the Bible and Greek mythology: *Tombeau d'Orphée* (1942), *Sodome* (1946), and *Babel* (1951). The volumes *Jours de Colère* (1942) and *La Liberté guide nos pas* (1945) are poetry of the Resistance. *Cantos* (1944), *Chansons du dé à coudre* (1947), and *Versant de l'age* (1958) represent elaborate attempts to express the mystery of existence. *Poésie raison ardente* (1947), *Qui est cet homme?* (1947), and *L'Ouvrier de la onzième heure* (1954) are prose essays.

Emmet, Robert (1778–1803). Irish patriot. The son of a liberal-minded, well-to-do physician, Robert became involved, while still in college, in the cause of the UNITED IRISHMEN; the latter fought, sometimes with violence, for the rights of Irish Catholics who had been deprived of their land under Cromwell. In 1803, Emmet was part of an insurrection that was put down by the British. Although he could have escaped, he remained in Dublin to protect his followers and the girl he loved, Sarah Curran. He was tried for treason, and executed at the age of 25 by hanging and decapitation.

Empedocles (Empedokles; fl. 444 B.C.). A Greek philosopher, interested in biology, medicine, and physics. In his work called *On Nature,* an epic poem in hexameters, Empedocles identifies four immutable elements in the universe: earth, air, fire, and water. The things of this world are produced by the association and dissociation of these elements. Empedocles called the two opposing forces love and strife. In another poem, called *Purifications,* Empedocles approves of the doctrine of transmigration. According to Greek tradition, Empedocles threw himself into the crater of Mt. Etna. In his poem *Empedocles on Etna,* Matthew Arnold found the philosopher a figure expressive of his own pessimism.

Emperor Jones, The (1920). A play by Eugene O'NEILL. Set on an island in the West Indies, the play deals with a former Pullman porter, Brutus Jones, who has set himself up as emperor. When the play begins the natives are beginning to revolt, and Jones is forced to flee. As he rushes through the jungle the tom-toms beat steadily, and he becomes more and more the victim of his own terror. Jones retrogresses on the evolutionary ladder, becoming a participant in a slave auction and finally the victim of his—and mankind's—aboriginal fears. In the end he is killed by the natives who use the silver bullets Jones had said were necessary. A sensation as a play, *Emperor Jones* was also successful as an opera (1933) by Louis Gruenberg, with a libretto by Kathleen de Jaffa.

empirics. An ancient Greek school of medicine founded by Serapion of Alexandria (2nd century B.C.). He contended that it is not necessary to obtain a knowledge of the nature and functions of the body in order to treat diseases, but that experience is the surest and best guide (Gr. *empeiros,* experienced, from *peira,* trial). The empirics were opposed to the dogmatic school founded by HIPPOCRATES, which made certain dogmas or theoretical principles the basis of practice. Now, any quack or pretender to medical skill is called an *empiric.*

empyrean. In Ptolemaic philosophy, the last of the 5 heavens. It was made of pure elemental fire and was the seat of the deity. Called the empyrean from the Gr. *empyros,* fiery, it was employed in Christian angelology—for instance, by Dante in his *Divine Comedy*—as the abode of God and the angels.

Empson, William (1906–   ). English poet and critic. A mathematician before he became a poet, Empson wrote verse characterized by scientific references and by wit, ingenuity, and obscurity. The poet's complicated notes on his verse add to the crossword-puzzle effect. His poems are restrained in technique, often being written in such traditional forms as the VILLANELLE and TERZA RIMA. They are sometimes humorous. *Poems* appeared in 1935 and *The Gathering Storm,* in 1940. Although he has published little poetry, his work had a great effect on the young English poets of the 1950's such as Kingsley Amis, A. Alvarez, Donald Davie, Thom Gunn, and John Wain.

Empson's criticism has also been influential. A leading CAMBRIDGE CRITIC, he has been influenced by the ideas of I. A. Richards. His critical works include *Seven Types of Ambiguity* (1930), *Some Versions of Pastoral* (1935), *The Structure of Complex Words* (1951), and *Milton's God* (1962), a controversial attack on Christianity, denouncing it as a cruel religion.

Ems telegram (1870). The report of an interview between King Wilhelm of Prussia and the French ambassador at the resort of Ems, originally sent to Bismarck. Bismarck condensed the text so that it appeared to report a diplomatic insult, and then released it to the press. The resulting international furor incited declaration of the Franco-Prussian War, just as Bismarck had planned.

Encina or **Enzina, Juan del** (1468?–?1529). Spanish dramatist and poet. Encina took minor orders as a youth, was in the service of the duke of Alba, and later lived in Rome. In 1519 he visited the Holy Land, where he was ordained and said his first mass. Often called "the father of Spanish drama," he is best known for his dramatic pieces, usually called *églogas* or "eclogues," which were published in various editions of his *Cancionero* (1496). Most of these plays have religious themes and were performed before aristocratic audiences; the characters, however, are usually Spanish peasants, realistically and humorously portrayed, who speak a rustic dialect, *sayagués,* that became a stock theatrical device. Among his most famous works in this genre are the two eclogues in which Pascuala, Mingo, and the squire Gil appear; the Carnival *Egloga de Antruejo,* and the farcical *Auto del repelón,* dealing with a brawl between peasants and Salamanca students. After his stay in Rome, Encina wrote three plays which reveal the influence of Italian pastoral poetry and represent an attempt to elevate the drama; these are *Egloga de Plácida y Victoriano, Egloga de tres pastores,* and *Egloga de Cristino y Febea.* He also wrote numerous *villancicos,* or Christmas carols, which were used at the end of most of his plays.

Encyclopédie, ou Dictionnaire raisonné des sciences, des arts et des métiers (Methodical Dictionary of the Sciences, Arts, and Trades, 1751–1780). A French encyclopedia. Based originally on an idea to translate the English *Cyclopaedia* of Ephraim Chambers, the work's whole scope was greatly expanded by DIDEROT, and his coeditors d'ALEMBERT and Louis de Jaucourt. The contributions of such famous *encyclopédistes* (also called *philosophes*) as CONDILLAC, HELVÉTIUS, MONTESQUIEU, ROUSSEAU, QUESNAY, TURGOT, and Diderot himself helped make it the great literary monument of the 18th century, even though many of the articles were written by hack writers under the direction of Jaucourt. The work mirrors that French brand of 18th-century philosophical skepticism and scientific determinism which was derived from Bacon, Locke, and Descartes among others. Its spirit of inquiry led it to combat superstition; the supernatural; religious authority, intolerance, and persecution; unequal distribution of wealth; fiscal privileges; and abuses of justice. Attention was paid to the latest scientific discoveries, particularly in the natural sciences. Reforms in government, education, and commerce were prudently advocated, also. One new feature of the encyclopedia was the inclusion of articles and plates on the mechanical trades (weaving, paper-making, printing, etc.). An ingenious system of cross references often led the reader to another article that ridiculed the contradictions accepted in the theological discussion of the first article; hence, the Jesuits opposed it, causing the encyclopedia to be temporarily suppressed in 1752 and 1759 by the government, and condemned by the pope in 1759. Though the history of the suppression of this work is generally recounted as one of energetic and efficacious persecution by the government and the church, in fact this is not so. The relatively few attempts at suppression were half-hearted on the part of the government and had little or no effect on its final publication. Mme. de POMPA-DOUR along with several government officials, among whom was Chrétien-Guillaume de MALESHERBES, an enlightened administrator and director of *la librairie* (the governmental censoring body), did everything in their power to encourage its publication for the public good. Diderot, with the help of Jaucourt, worked tirelessly to bring out the "clandestine" edition in Paris, which appeared in 17 volumes (plus 11 volumes of plates) between 1751 and 1772. Diderot had no hand in the five-volume supplement (1776–1777), or in the two analytical index volumes (1780). Other editions followed. In spite of its imbalance (for example, six lines devoted to *Alpes* and one column to artichoke recipes), errors, and unacknowledged plagiarism, it was a highly successful business venture. At one point there were 4,000 subscribers, and the profit is said to have been 300 per cent.

Endgame (Fin de partie; 1957). A play by Samuel BECKETT. The blind chair-bound autocrat Hamm, whose parents Nagg and Nell are confined to ashcans, learns from his servant Clov of the disappearance of objects and the deaths of people in a disintegrating world.

Endicott or **Endecott, John** (1589?–1665). English-born governor of the Massachusetts Bay Colony. He served as the first governor of the colony (1628–1630) until the arrival of John Winthrop. A zealous Puritan, he persecuted Quakers and the followers of Thomas Morton. He is the title character of *Endicott and the Red Cross* (1837), a short story by Nathaniel Hawthorne, and of one of Longfellow's *New England Tragedies* (1868).

End of Summer (1936). A play by S. N. BEHRMAN. Set in a summer home in Maine, it includes a brilliant portrait of a psychiatrist.

Endor, witch of. See WITCH.

Endymion. In Greek mythology, a beautiful youth, sometimes a shepherd. As he slept on Mount Latmus he so moved the cold heart of Selene, the moon goddess, that she came down and kissed him and lay at his side. He woke to find her gone, but the dreams that she gave him were so strong and enthralling that he begged Zeus to give him immortality and allow him to sleep perpetually on Mount Latmus. Other accounts say that Selene herself bound him by en enchantment so that she might come and kiss him whenever she liked. There are, in fact, innumerable explanations in myth of Endymion's sleep. Keats used the story as the framework of his long allegory, *Endymion* (1817), and it forms the basis of Lyly's comedy, *Endimion, the Man in the Moone* (1585).

Enfants Terribles, Les (1929; also translated as **The Holy Terrors**). A novel by Jean COCTEAU about the fantasy-world rituals and fierce amoral passions of a group of children.

Engels, Friedrich (1820–1895). German socialist and collaborator of Karl MARX, whom he met in Paris in 1844. Together they wrote THE COMMUNIST MANIFESTO, although Engels gave Marx the credit for its theoretical formulation. Engels completed CAPITAL after Marx's death.

England, rulers of. Egbert, originally king of the West Saxons, conquered the other English realms, making himself master of all England.

SAXONS	
Egbert	829– 839
Ethelwulf	839– 858
Ethelbald	858– 860
Ethelbert	860– 866
Ethelred I	866– 871
Alfred the Great	871– 899
Edward the Elder	899– 924
Athelstan	924– 940
Edmund I	940– 946
Edred	946– 955
Edwy	955– 959
Edgar	959– 975
Edward the Martyr	975– 978
Ethelred II	978–1016
Edmund II	1016

DANES	
Canute	1016–1035
Harold I	1035–1040
Hardecanute	1040–1042

SAXONS	
Edward the Confessor	1042–1066
Harold II	1066

HOUSE OF NORMANDY	
William I	1066–1087
William II	1087–1100
Henry I	1100–1135
Stephen	1135–1154

HOUSE OF PLANTAGENET	
Henry II	1154–1189
Richard I	1189–1199
John	1199–1216
Henry III	1216–1272
Edward I	1272–1307
Edward II	1307–1327
Edward III	1327–1377
Richard II	1377–1399

HOUSE OF LANCASTER	
Henry IV	1399–1413
Henry V	1413–1422
Henry VI	1422–1461

HOUSE OF YORK	
Edward IV	1461–1470

HOUSE OF LANCASTER	
Henry VI	1470–1471

HOUSE OF YORK	
Edward IV	1471–1483
Edward V	1483
Richard III	1483–1485

HOUSE OF TUDOR	
Henry VII	1485–1509
Henry VIII	1509–1547
Edward VI	1547–1553
Lady Jane Grey	1553
Mary I	1553–1558
Elizabeth I	1558–1603

HOUSE OF STUART	
James I	1603–1625
Charles I	1625–1649

COMMONWEALTH	
Council of State	1649–1653
Oliver Cromwell (Lord Protector)	1653–1658
Richard Cromwell (Lord Protector)	1658–1659

HOUSE OF STUART	
Charles II	1660–1685
James II	1685–1688
William III and Mary II (d. 1694)	1689–1702
Anne	1702–1714

HOUSE OF HANOVER	
George I	1714–1727
George II	1727–1760
George III	1760–1820
George IV	1820–1830
William IV	1830–1837
Victoria	1837–1901

HOUSE OF SAXE-COBURG	
Edward VII	1901–1910

HOUSE OF WINDSOR	
George V	1910–1936
Edward VIII	1936
George VI	1936–1952
Elizabeth II	1952–

England's Helicon (1600). One of the miscellanies (see TOTTEL'S MISCELLANY), or collections of poetry, published in the Elizabethan period. It is distinguished by the good taste shown in the selection of its contents, and unique in that the editors deliberately limited the book to pastoral poetry. It contains work by Shakespeare, Sidney, Spenser, Drayton, Lodge, among others.

English Bards and Scotch Reviewers (1809). A long verse satire by Lord BYRON. Neoclassical in flavor and written in heroic couplets, it was occasioned by the harsh reception given to Byron's first book of poems, *Hours of Idleness* (1807), by the *Edinburgh Review*. In the poem, Byron not only attacks his critics but the older generation of English romantic poets as well, including Wordsworth, Coleridge, Scott, and Southey.

English Traits (1856). An analysis of the English people by Ralph Waldo EMERSON. The book grew out of a series of lectures delivered by Emerson after two visits to England. He discusses some of his English contemporaries, Wordsworth, Carlyle, and Coleridge. Amused by English pomp, the American is impressed by the practical sense of the English and by their writers.

English Woman's Love Letters, An. See Laurence HOUSMAN.

Engstrom, Albert (1869–1940). Swedish author and artist. Engstrom's fame rests upon his perceptive cartoons and on the illustrated stories that depict life in Småland and on the Stockholm archipelago. Among his collections of tales are *Samlade berättelser* (1915–1934), and *Nationalupplaga* (*Twelve Tales*, 1934). As editor of the comic journal *Strix* from 1924 to 1940, he revealed a keen but kindly satirical wit.

Enki. The Sumerian god of water and of wisdom. He lived near the ancient city of ERIDU in his watery palace in the ABZU—probably the Persian Gulf. This god, like his later Babylonian counterpart EA, was principally responsible for ordering the functions of the elements that affect life on earth. Cleverest of the gods, he provided the land with sweet water, fathered Uttu, the goddess of plants, found a way to rescue Inanna from the underworld, and saved mankind from extermination in the great flood. He was not, however, infallible. While in his cups, he let the seductive goddess slip away with his "divine decrees," which would give supremacy to her favored city of Erech instead of to Eridu. His attempt to create man was a pathetic failure, and it was left to the goddess NINTU to mold of clay a satisfactory human being.

Enkidu. A friend of Gilgamesh in the *Epic of* GILGAMESH. Molded of clay, and at first a wild man who lives with the beasts, he becomes a hero who first defeats Gilgamesh in wrestling, then becomes his fast friend. They share various adventures together, but Enkidu is condemned to death by the gods for his part in slaying the storm bull of heaven. Gilgamesh's search for the secret of eternal life is the result of his grief over Enkidu's death. He appears also in Sumerian mythology.

Enkimdu. A Sumerian farmer god. He disputed with the shepherd god DUMUZI for the favor of Inanna and won it.

Enlightenment, the. The 18th century. This period is variously called the Age of Reason and, in France, *Le Siècle des Lumières* because its writers as a whole applied reason to religion, politics, morality, and social life. Aside from purely historical events, the 18th century does not lend itself to a chronological view; its unity lay not in a coherent development or progression of ideas, but rather in the intellectual energy and enthusiasm which characterized its writers. Intensely aware of their heritage and dependency upon the ancients, these men clarified, sifted, and developed this heritage.

The rule of Louis XIV had been an oppressive one, and the somber religious tone which it took before the Sun King's death caused the reaction to it to be all the greater. The government, continued by the monarchies of Louis XV (1715–1774) and Louis XVI (1774–1793), fell ever deeper into discredit. The failure of John Law's MISSISSIPPI BUBBLE (June, 1720), the increasing national debt due to royal prodigality, and the repeated hiring and dismissal of incapable finance ministers—and even of capable ones like Cardinal Fleury, Turgot, and Necker—all contributed to the economic instability of France. The necessity for reform became clear. The century culminated in the FRENCH REVOLUTION, a crisis that reflected these economic and social ills; the application of reason to the human situation, so typical of the 18th century, perhaps made it clear to the middle class that the old order did not have to prevail. In most aspects of French culture, the influence of the increasingly economically independent bourgeoisie was to replace that of the aristocracy.

The Enlightenment began by breaking down the older forms of metaphysical and philosophical knowledge; Cartesianism, with its spirit of systems (*esprit de système*), was replaced by a systematic spirit (*esprit systèmatique*)—the a priori by the a posteriori. In contrast to the 17th century, in which reason represented tradition, authority, stability, the 18th century saw reason as a tool, a means to authority. Questions were no longer envisaged under the aspect of pure thought, but were examined from a social and practical point of view. This preoccupation with the useful caused men to turn to the physical world; writers like VOLTAIRE, DIDEROT, d'ALEMBERT, and MONTESQUIEU made literature out of the natural sciences, astronomy, law, travel, philosophy, politics, and education. The investigation into natural and social phenomena, what we would today broadly designate as science, was called philosophy in the 18th century. The *philosophe* represented an ideal, as did the *honnête homme* in the 17th century, or as the universal man characterized the Renaissance. The philosophers of this age were in search of a concrete anthropology, a knowledge of man in general. This common goal by no means implied a homogeneous point of view: one has only to compare the differences between Voltaire and ROUSSEAU, BUFFON and CONDILLAC, Diderot and HELVÉTIUS.

It is perhaps CONDORCET who, in his *Sketch for a historical picture of the progress of the human mind* (written in 1793–1794) best summarizes the optimism and faith in human reason so characteristic of the age. In tracing man from the dawn of history, Condorcet first emphasized the liberation of mankind from ignorance, tyranny, and superstition by means of his science and his reason; he then sketched a hopeful future in which mankind would be free, equal in wealth, in education, and with sexual equality; he finally envisaged the moral, intellectual, and physical improvement, indeed perfection, of humanity that would arise through better instruction, laws, and institutions.

Enlil. The Sumerian storm-god of the air. He was born of the union of An (heaven) and Ki (earth), who were regarded as joined together. Enlil separated them—the element air may have been thought to separate the vault of heaven from earth by its own expansion. Enlil married Ninlil, who bore him three gods of the underworld (Nergal, Ninazu, and an unknown god) and Nanna the moon, who in turn became the father of Utu, the sun. Next Enlil impregnated his mother Ki and produced NINTU, another earth goddess. Enlil became more important in the pantheon than his father An, and in turn he was himself to a degree supplanted from his place as principal god by ENKI. Enlil was the chief god of the Sumerian city of Nippur. In the Baby-

lonian period, MARDUK took on many of his attributes, and Adad became the storm-god.

ennead (from Gr. *ennea*, nine). A group of 9 units, as, for example, the 9 gods found in the pantheon of the ancient Egyptians.

The title *The Enneads* was given to the works of the neo-Platonist Plotinus because each of the six books contains nine chapters.

Ennius, Quintus (239–?169 B.C.). Latin poet. The earliest of the great epic poets of Rome, he is regarded as one of the founders of Latin literature. His successful use of Greek meters in his dramas and epic poetry ushered in a new era in the development of literary Latin. As an epic poet, employing the Greek dactylic hexameter in Latin, he is a precursor of Vergil, Rome's greatest poet.

Enobarbus, Domitius. In Shakespeare's AN-TONY AND CLEOPATRA, a trusted officer of Antony. He deserts Antony after Actium, but when the latter magnanimously sends him his treasure, he is so remorseful that he commits suicide. His astute and witty observations on the behavior of Antony and Cleopatra make him one of Shakespeare's most engaging secondary characters.

Enoch Arden (1864). A narrative poem by Alfred TENNYSON. Arden is a seaman who has been wrecked on a desert island, and returning home after a long absence finds his wife married to another. Seeing her happy and prosperous, he resolves not to make himself known, so he leaves the place and dies of a broken heart. Hence, any story that involves a long-lost mate returning to discover his spouse remarried is often described as having an Enoch Arden plot.

Enormous Room, The (1922). An autobiographical novel by E. E. CUMMINGS. It describes a period of imprisonment in a French military concentration camp near Paris (1917–1918), where the author was incarcerated on a false charge of treason. Cummings' own experiences and the personalities of the various other prisoners are presented with their individual psychological reactions to the injustices of their treatment. Ironically structured on John Bunyan's *Pilgrim's Progress,* the book is highly vivid, often even lyrical, in its bitter attack on man's inhumanity to man.

Enquiry Concerning Political Justice, An (1793). A political and philosophical treatise by William GODWIN with the subtitle "its influence on General Virtue and Happiness." The author examines the systems of government, law, and religion of his day, and concludes that monarchy is corrupt and all government, in fact, an obstacle to the development of mankind. It urges the abolition of all social and political institutions created by man, including government, law, wealth, and marriage, and places total confidence in the fundamental perfectibility of man. This treatise was regarded with horror by the conservative elements of the day, and had a great influence on the English Romantic poets, particularly Shelley.

Enten. See EMESH.

entente; *entente cordiale* (Fr.). A cordial understanding between nations; not quite amounting to an alliance, but something more than a *rapprochement.* The term is not new, but is now usually applied to the *entente* between England and France that was arranged largely by the personal endeavors of Edward VII in 1906.

Triple Entente. A friendly alliance between Great Britain, France, and Russia before World War I. During the war Great Britain, France, and Italy were referred to as the *Entente*.

Little Entente. An alliance between Czechoslovakia, Yugoslavia, and Romania entered into after the signing of the Treaty of the Trianon (1920), with the avowed purpose of defeating any Hungarian plan for a restoration of the Hapsburgs.

Entwicklungsroman. See BILDUNGSROMAN.

Enuma elish. See WAR OF THE GODS.

Envy (Zavist'; 1927). A novel by Yuri OLIOSHA. A notable work of fiction, it portrays the struggle of the individual against the encroachments of the growing collectivist society in Soviet Russia. This hackneyed theme is rendered fresh by Oliosha's imaginative use of images and language and by his creation of the memorable characters Ivan Babichev and Nikolai Kavalerov. Both are disaffected with the society, though for different reasons: Babichev because he sees the danger of human feelings being destroyed, and Kavalerov because he yearns for personal glory and envies the less talented people who can adjust and make their way in the new system. Babichev's brother, Andrei, is a representative of the adjusted man. He is a director of a Soviet food combine, briskly going about his business, which consists of planning new, cheap cafeterias to feed the masses. Whether Andrei actually does triumph over his good-for-nothing brother Ivan is, at the book's end, a moot point. This fact apparently began to worry Soviet critics who praised the novel at first and then began to criticize it severely.

Eos. In Greek mythology the goddess of the dawn. She is the daughter of Hyperion and Thea and drives across the sky in a chariot drawn by two horses. It was Eos who asked Zeus to give TITHONUS immortality; however, she forgot to have Tithonus made eternally youthful.

Eothen, or Traces of Travel Brought Home from the East. See Alexander William KINGLAKE.

Epée, Charles Michel de l' (1712–1789). French abbé. He was a pioneer in the development of a system of manual communication for the deaf and dumb.

Epeios. Builder of the TROJAN HORSE. He was the principal craftsman with the Greek forces at Troy.

Ephesian letters. Characters assumed to be of a mystic nature by the Ephesians, a people greatly addicted to magic. Magic characters were marked on the crown, cincture, and feet of Diana. At the preaching of Paul in Ephesus, many converts who had used "curious," or magical, books burned them (Acts 19:19).

Ephesians, The Epistle of Paul the Apostle to the. A New Testament book. Traditionally ascribed to Paul, this letter was probably written by some one who used his name and borrowed freely from his epistle to the COLOSSIANS for its content. Consisting of two parts, it first explains God's plan to unite all humanity in Christ and then shows the role of the Church in the working of this plan.

Ephialtes. See OTUS.

Ephyre. A prehistoric Greek city. It was iden-

tified in Classical times with Corinth. Founded by Sisyphus, it was later ruled by Jason. Indeed, since no significant Mycenaean remains have been found at Corinth, it is likely that most myths involving Corinth should be referred to Ephyre, which was probably one of the many Mycenaean towns unearthed on the Isthmus near the present Corinth.

epic. A very long narrative poem presenting adventures on a grand, heroic scale organically united through a central figure of heroic proportions. The adventures are made up of episodes which contribute to the formation of a race or nation. The earliest epics were formed from various works of unknown poets. Among the best-known of these folk epics are the *Iliad* and *Odyssey* (attributed to Homer), the Anglo-Saxon *Beowulf*, the East Indian *Mahabharata*, the Spanish *Cid*, the Finnish *Kalevala*, the French *Song of Roland*, and the German *Nibelungenlied*.

The so-called classical or art epic is distinctly the work of a single author. Influenced largely by Vergil, it developed certain almost universal characteristics. These include beginning *in medias res,* the invocation of the muse, and the statement of the epic purpose. Other conventions, usually observed by writers of epic, are descriptions of warfare and the use of the supernatural. Familiar classical epics include Vergil's *Aeneid,* Dante's *Divine Comedy,* Tasso's *Jerusalem Delivered,* Spenser's *Faerie Queene,* and Milton's *Paradise Lost.*

Epicasta (Epikaste). The name given to Jocasta in the *Iliad* and some other Greek works. See OEDIPUS.

Epic Cycle. The name given a series of very early (c. 800–500) epic poems by authors other than Homer or Hesiod, all of which are lost, but which are recounted in later synopses. They deal with events connected with the Trojan War not included in the *Iliad* or the *Odyssey.* Poems of the Epic Cycle include the *Theogonia* and *Titanomachia,* on the creation and early history of the world; *Cypria,* on the theft of Helen; *Aethiopis, Ilias Parva, Iliu Persis,* and *Nostoi,* continuations of the *Iliad;* and *Telegonia,* on the death of Odysseus. There are other cyclic poems, such as those on Thebes and on heroes such as Heracles, Theseus, and the Argonauts; strictly speaking, however, the term "Epic Cycle" refers to the Trojan stories alone.

Epicene, or The Silent Woman (1609). A comedy by Ben JONSON. A gentleman named Morose has resolved to disinherit his nephew, Sir Dauphine, by marrying and producing an heir. A man who can bear no noise, he has discovered a perfect mate, a woman who "spends but six words a day." But just after the wedding, Epicene, the silent woman, turns into a shrill harpy who belabors her husband mercilessly. Alarmed, Morose tries mightily to break the match, even going so far as to offer Sir Dauphine a generous allowance and his inheritance if he will take the lady off his hands. Sir Dauphine complies immediately by plucking off Epicene's wig, revealing that "she" is a boy whom Dauphine has carefully trained and employed.

Epic of Creation, Babylonian. See WAR OF THE GODS.

Epictetus (Epiktetos; fl. A.D. 100). A Greek Stoic philosopher. An emancipated slave, Epictetus taught in Rome until A.D. 94, when Emperor Domitian banished all philosophers from the city. He moved to Nicopolis, where he established a school. No written works survive, but his pupil Arrian preserved his essential doctrines in a manual. Epictetus counseled men to wish for nothing that is not under their control. He advocated a serene life, free from unfulfilled desires, and calm in the face of death. He said that a man should behave in life as he would at a banquet, taking only a polite portion of what is offered. See STOICISM.

Epic Theater. A term used by Bertolt BRECHT to designate his own style of playwriting as opposed to the style of conventional drama. In conventional drama, suspense is created by means of a tightly woven plot, which constantly develops and welds the play together into a unity; in the Epic Theater, suspense is deliberately avoided, and the play consists of a loose sequence of virtually independent scenes (just as the individual scenes of an epic poem are usually less dependent on one another than those of a conventional drama). Conventional drama attempts to capture the audience's emotions, to create a powerful and continuous illusion in which the audience will become emotionally involved; the Epic Theater, on the other hand, deliberately avoids playing on the audience's emotions, seeks rather to make the audience emotionally detached, and attempts to convey its meaning entirely on an intellectual plane. One specific technique often used by Brecht for achieving the effect of the Epic Theater consists in having a character step to the front of the stage and directly address the audience, thereby breaking the illusion and inviting the audience to regard the play intellectually.

Epicurus (Epikouros, c. 340–c. 270 B.C.). Greek philosopher, founder of the Epicurean School. The school is often referred to as the Garden, after the place in which Epicurus taught in Athens. Only fragments remain of his work, but his biographer DIOGENES LAERTIUS gives the texts of three epistles and forty maxims, which indicate that Epicurus advocated reliance on the senses. In order to reduce man's anxiety, he posited a materialistic physics, in which the universe consisted of Democritean atoms and void. He tried to eliminate superstition and the dread of death. Pleasure, by which Epicurus meant freedom from pain, is the highest good. Serenity, the harmony of mind and body, is best achieved, he said, through virtue and simple living. The current usage of the term *epicure* to describe one devoted to sensual pleasures, reflects a misunderstanding of the philosophy of Epicurus.

epicycles. See PTOLEMY.

Epigoni (Epigonoi). In Greek mythology, the sons of the SEVEN AGAINST THEBES. They were led by ALCMAEON, a son of Amphiaraus, who had demanded that his sons avenge his death at Thebes. Alcmaeon might have forgotten this vow, but Thersander, the son of Polynices, bribed his mother, Eriphyle, to urge him on, as she had earlier urged Amphiaraus. TIRESIAS had warned the Thebans that the city would fall when the last of the Seven died. The only one to survive the earlier siege had been Adrastus, king of Argos. On learning that his son, Aegialeus, one of the Epigoni, had been killed in the new siege, Adrastus died of grief.

Tiresias then advised the Thebans to flee the city at once, which they did, under cover of night. Tiresias, who had lived through seven generations of Theban rulers, at last died. The escaping Thebans continued as far as Hestiaea, where they founded the city. The Epigoni razed Thebes.

epigram. A brief, pithy, pointed, and witty piece of poetry or prose. The epigram was especially popular as a literary form in classic Latin literature and in European and English literature of the Renaissance and neoclassical periods. Coleridge wrote of it:

> What is an epigram? A dwarfish whole,
> Its body brevity, and wit its soul.

epilogue. (1) The final part of a work of literature (except a play), completing and rounding it off; the opposite of preface. (2) After a play, the speech (frequently in verse) addressed by an actor or group of actors to the audience; the opposite of prologue. (3) In rhetoric, the last of the five divisions of a model oration. (4) In music, the final section of a composition, the coda. A free use of the term occurs in Goethe's *Epilogue to Schiller's Bell (Epilog zu Schillers Glocke)*, written in commemoration of the younger poet's death.

Epimenides (7th century B.C.). A Cretan poet and philosopher. According to Pliny (*Natural History*) he fell asleep in a cave when a boy, and did not wake up for 57 years, when he found himself endowed with miraculous wisdom.

Epimetheus. In classic myth, the brother of Prometheus and husband of PANDORA. The name signifies afterthought, in contrast to Prometheus, forethought.

Epinay, Louise Florence Pétronille de la Live d' (1726–1783). French author. She is well known on account of her friendship with Diderot, d'Alembert, Baron d' Holbach, Baron de Grimm, and others. For Rousseau she built a cottage in the garden of her château near Montmorency. About her *Mémoires et correspondance* (1818), Sainte-Beuve has written: "The memoirs of Mme d'Epinay are not a work, they are an epoch."

Epinicia (Epinikia). Odes of victory in national games, as the Olympic, Pythian, Delphic, Nemean, and Isthmian games. There are among PINDAR's extant works 44 Epinicia.

Epiphany (Gr. *epiphaneia*, appearance or manifestation). The feast on January 6, commemorating the showing of Christ to the nations, at the time of the visit of the MAGI. One of the oldest of Christian festivals, it originally was the feast of the birth of Christ, as it still is in the Eastern Churches. In England it was called Twelfth Day, from which comes TWELFTH NIGHT.

epiphany. A term coined by James JOYCE for the sudden revelation of the essential nature of a thing, person, or situation. It is the moment in which "the soul of the commonest object . . . seems to us radiant," and may be manifested through any chance word or gesture. Among Joyce's earliest works were little sketches or prose poems, which attempted to record such moments; he called them epiphanies. Some are incorporated in his novel *Stephen Hero;* in this novel he also gives the clearest explanation of what he means by epiphany.

Epipsychidion (1821). A poem by Percy Bysshe SHELLEY. The title, a word coined by Shelley from Greek, means "this soul out of my soul." Of over 700 lines, the poem is addressed to Emilia VIVIANI, whom Shelley regarded as an embodiment of the ideal love and beauty that he constantly sought. Along with an allegorical history of the poet's soul, the poem includes rapturous praise of Emilia Viviani, a famous justification of free love, and a glowing vision of an Edenic isle in the Aegean.

Epistle to Dr. Arbuthnot (1735). A satiric poem by Alexander POPE in the form of a dialogue between the poet and Dr. John ARBUTHNOT, a physician and man of letters who was a friend of Pope. The poem gives Pope's judgment on his own work and pitilessly attacks his contemporaries, especially Joseph ADDISON, who is characterized as "the jealous Atticus," and Lord John HERVEY who is satirized as the effeminate "Sporus."

Epistolae Obscurorum Virorum (Letters of Unknown Men, 1515, 1517). A satire on scholasticism. It is directed specifically at the reactionary University of Cologne, in the form of letters supposedly written by various church figures to a Cardinal Ortwinus. The book parodies a collection of letters that Ortwinus himself had published under the title of *Epistolae Clarorum Virorum (Letters of Famous Men)*. The *Epistolae Obscurorum Virorum* are a central document of German humanism, and implicitly support Johann REUCHLIN in his struggles with the renegade Jew Pfefferkorn. The authors are not known, but it is quite likely that Ulrich von HUTTEN wrote part of the book.

Epithalamion (1595). Lyric poem by Edmund SPENSER. It was written to celebrate his marriage. It has been called his highest poetic achievement.

E Pluribus Unum (*Lat.,* One From Many). A motto of the seal of the U.S. First proposed on Aug. 10, 1776, by a committee composed of Franklin, John Adams, and Jefferson, it appeared officially for the first time on a coin in New Jersey in 1706.

Epstein, Sir Jacob (1880–1959). American-born British sculptor. Epstein settled in London after studying in Paris under Rodin. He made no attempt at realism in his figures; as a result his work has been criticized as unpleasantly grotesque. Among Epstein's best known figures are *Mother and Child, Rima, Day, Night, Adam, Genesis, Ecce Homo, Venus*. He has also done portrait busts of prominent statesmen and artists, including Churchill, Bernard Shaw, Joseph Conrad, and Lady Gregory. He wrote an autobiography called *Let There Be Sculpture* (1940).

Equicola, Mario (1470?–1525). Italian man of letters and courtier who served the Este family at Ferrara. He wrote a history of Mantua, but was noted in his time for an influential book, *De natura de Amore (On the Nature of Love,* 1525). It was one of several philosophical treatises on love that spread Neoplatonic doctrine among such Renaissance writers as Ficino, Benvieni, and Castiglione.

Erasmus, Desiderius (1466–1536). Dutch scholar and philosopher, noted for his satire, *The Praise of Folly*. Erasmus called his religious outlook "the philosophy of Christ," yet his thought was influenced by varied tendencies, some Christian, some secular. He was affected by the German religious tradition, which stressed personal piety in religion, as well as by the work of Italian humanists such as Pico della Mirandola. He adhered to the view of German pietism that religion was less a matter of ceremony and doctrine than of morality and rational piety, and his classical education and the influence of Pico and other humanists tended to stimulate in him a skeptical, critical attitude toward superstition, clericalism, and excessive religious zeal. He tried to combine the critical, rational, and secular attitude of classical antiquity and Italian humanism with the religious piety of the German Middle Ages. Aware of ecclesiastical corruption, and hostile to the intolerant dogmatism of the Church of his time, he was at first sympathetic to the Reformation and the attempts of Luther to reform the Church. Yet, humane and moderate at a time when the Reformation was fanning religious conflict, war, and hatred, he was forced finally to oppose the extremism of Luther and become an enemy of the Reformation.

Erato. In Greek mythology, the muse of love poetry. She is usually represented holding or playing a lyre.

Ercilla y Zúñiga, Alonso de. See ARAUCANA, LA.

Erda. In Wagner's RING DES NIBELUNGEN, the earth goddess NERTHUS.

Erebus (Erebos). In Greek mythology, the son of CHAOS and brother of Night; hence darkness personified. His name was given to the gloomy cavern underground through which the Shades had to walk in the course of their passage to Hades.

Erec et Enide. The earliest Arthurian romance in French, written in the 12th century by CHRÉTIEN DE TROYES. It tells of Erec, a knight at the court of King Arthur, who goes out in search of adventure and stays overnight at a run-down castle; here he meets Enide, the beautiful daughter of the baron who is master of the castle. Erec asks for her hand, marries her, and then retires from the active life of a knight in order to enjoy the pleasures of domestic life. His reputation soon begins to suffer from this, however, and one day he overhears his wife bemoaning the situation. The knight thereupon blames her for the state of affairs in which they find themselves, and sets out once more in search of adventure, forcing Enide to accompany him. They have amazing adventures in which Erec proves himself to be of prodigious strength and valor, although he is harsh in his treatment of his wife. Eventually she is kidnaped by a robber baron while the knight lies in an apparent state of death. He revives in time to rescue her, and at length they are reconciled.

Erech or **Uruk.** An ancient Sumerian city. It is best known as the capital of the hero GILGAMESH. It was also the favored city of INANNA, who tricked the god Enki into giving it preference over his own city of Eridu.

Erechtheum (Erechtheion). A temple of the tutelary deities of Athens in the ACROPOLIS of Athens. It derived its name from King Erechtheus.

Ereshkigal. The Sumerian queen of the underworld. She is said to have been carried off by KUR into the underworld; the god Enki then went out to do battle with Kur, but the outcome is unknown. Later, however, Ereshkigal reigns in the underworld and appears as a baleful figure in the myth of

INANNA's descent. Her role bears a striking resemblance to that of the Greek Persephone, who was carried off by Hades and thereafter reigned—at least, part of the year—in the underworld. The further parallel of the rivalry of Persephone and Aphrodite for the love of ADONIS suggests that Inanna may have descended to the underworld in search of her lover TAMMUZ; the closely related myth of ISHTAR and Tammuz supports this conclusion.

Erewhon (1872). A satirical novel by Samuel BUTLER about a UTOPIA. In the institutions of Erewhon (an anagram of "Nowhere") Butler satirizes contemporary English attitudes towards religion, science, crime, etc. *Erewhon* is probably the most brilliant specimen of 19th century Utopian novels. A sequel, *Erewhon Revisited,* was published in 1901.

Ericson (also **Ericsson, Erikson, Eriksson**), **Leif** (fl. 1000). Norse explorer, son of Eric the Red. According to legend he was returning from Norway to Greenland (c. 1000) when a storm drove his ship to a shore he called *Vinland* (also *Vineland, Wineland),* variously said to have been Labrador, Newfoundland, or New England. Thus it is asserted that he, not Columbus, was the first European to discover North America.

Eric the Red (c. 950–c. 1000). Norwegian explorer, father of Leif Ericson. He fled Norway, then Iceland, to escape murder charges. He named Greenland, which had been discovered 100 years before, and founded its first colony about 985.

Eridu. An ancient Sumerian city. In ancient times it was probably on the shores of the Persian Gulf, which no longer extends so far northward. It was the cult center of the god Enki and of his Babylonian counterpart, Ea.

Erifilla. A giantess in the ORLANDO FURIOSO of Ariosto, who guards the entrance to Alcina's enchanted castle. She is defeated by Ruggiero, who then falls prey to Alcina's subtle enchantments for a time.

Erigena, Johannes Scotus. See Johannes SCOTUS ERIGENA.

Erinyes. The Furies of Greek mythology. Snaky-haired and hideous women who sprang from the blood of Uranus when he was castrated by his son Cronos, they lived in the underworld, from which they issued to pursue and drive mad those who had committed such heinous crimes as patricide. They appeared prominently in Aeschylus' *Eumenides,* where, after relentlessly harassing Orestes for murder of his mother (see the House of ATREUS), they give up vengeful insistence on the ancient law of blood for blood and are thenceforward worshiped in Athens as the Eumenides (Kindly Ones). In some accounts there were three, named Tisiphone, Alecto, and Megaera.

Eriphile. The slave girl in Jean Racine's tragedy IPHIGÉNIE EN AULIDE who, infatuated with Achilles, betrays the plot to save Iphigénie from being sacrificed to the gods. Far from winning Achilles or achieving her rival's death, her treachery seals her own doom, for the priests demand her sacrifice instead.

Eriphyle. In Greek mythology, the sister of Adrastus and wife of Amphiaraus. In a quarrel, the two men agreed henceforth to let Eriphyle decide their differences. Later, POLYNICES persuaded Adrastus to help him attack Thebes, but Amphiaraus, a seer, opposed the expedition of the SEVEN AGAINST THEBES, foreseeing that only Adrastus would survive it. Polynices won the support of the vain and greedy Eriphyle by bribing her with HARMONIA'S NECKLACE. Amphiaraus, bowing to his wife's will because of his vow, joined the expedition, but enjoined his young sons, ALCMAEON and Amphilochus, to avenge his death on his mother and on the Thebans.

On growing to manhood, Alcmaeon might have forgotten his mother's crime had she not repeated it at his own expense. Bribed by Thersander, Polynices' son, she urged Alcmaeon to lead the EPIGONI against Thebes. Alcmaeon returned from the war victorious and, learning of his mother's double treachery, killed her. Like Orestes, he was pursued by the ERINYES through many tragic events.

Eris. The goddess of discord, sister of Ares. He flung the APPLE OF DISCORD. See JUDGMENT OF PARIS.

Erlking or *Ger.* **Erlkönig,** king of the alders (a mis-translation of the Danish *eller-konge,* king of the elves). A malevolent goblin of the Black Forest who lures people, especially children, to destruction. Never actually a part of medieval German folk tradition, he was first popularized by Goethe in his famous ballad *Der Erlkönig.* One of Franz Schubert's most famous songs is a setting of Goethe's poem.

Erminia. In the GERUSALEMME LIBERATA of Tasso, a Syrian maiden whose life was spared by the Crusader Tancredi (Tancred) at the battle of Antioch. Though she loves him, he is enamored of Clorinda, the warrior maid from Persia. At one point Erminia, learning that Tancredi lies wounded, goes to him in Clorinda's armor; but both he and the other Christian knights pursue her in the belief that she is Clorinda. Taking pleasant refuge in a beautiful wood, she is cared for by an old shepherd, who extolls the virtues of the pastoral life. Later, in the camp of the Egyptian armies, she informs Vafrino, the shield-bearer of Tancredi sent as a spy, of a plan to disguise a group of infidel warriors in Crusaders' dress so that they can close with and kill Goffredo, the Christian general. On the way to Jerusalem with Vafrino she encounters the wounded Tancredi and nurses him tenderly back to health. After she takes him back to the camp outside the holy city, she disappears from the plot and Ariosto says nothing further of her fate.

Ermonide. In the ORLANDO FURIOSO of Ariosto, a Dutch knight who is killed by the Scottish warrior Zerbino when he attempts to slay the old hag Gabrina, an ancient enemy of his family.

Ernst, Max (1891–). German painter. A member of the surrealists and the earlier Dadaists, Ernst originally studied philosophy while at the universities of Cologne and Bonn. He was drawn into art with no formal training through his friendship with André Breton and Louis Aragon. He has written for the surrealist publication *Literature and the Surrealist Revolution.* His paintings include *The Chaste Joseph* and *Max Ernst showing a Girl his Father's Head.*

Eroica. BEETHOVEN's Symphony No. 3. Its first title was *Sinfonia grande Napoleon Bonaparte.* When he learned about Napoleon's accession to the imperial throne of France (May 18, 1804), Beethoven changed it in a fit of rage to *Sinfonia eroica com-*

posta per festiggiare il sovvenire d'un grand'uomo (*Heroic symphony composed to celebrate the memory of a great man*).

Eros. The Greek god of love. According to the accounts in Hesiod, Eros was one of the earliest gods, born of Chaos at the same time as Mother Earth. He came to be the patron god of beautiful young men. Only in late myth did he become a child, the naughty son of Aphrodite, as he appears in the *Argonautica* and elsewhere. It was in this form that he was identified with the Latin CUPID.

Eros. In Shakespeare's ANTONY AND CLEOPATRA, a faithful soldier of Antony. Commanded by Antony to kill him, he commits suicide rather than take his master's life.

Erostratus or **Herostratus.** The Ephesian who set fire to the temple of Artemis on the day that Alexander the Great happened to be born (356 B.C.). This he did to make his name immortal; and, in order to defeat his object, the Ephesians forbade his name ever to be mentioned.

Erra-Pater. The assumed name of the author of an almanac published about 1535 as *The Pronostycacion for ever of Erra Pater: A Jewe born in Jewery, a Doctour in Astronomye and Physycke.* It is a collection of astrological tables, rules of health, and the like, and is arranged for use in any year. It is occasionally referred to in contemporary literature.

Title page of Erra-Pater's almanac (c. 1535).

THE BRITISH MUSEUM

[He] had got him a suit of durance, that would last longer than one of Erra Pater's almanacks, or a cunstable's browne bill.—Thomas Nashe, *Lenten Stuffe* (1599)

The almanacs were frequently reprinted, and nearly a hundred years later Samuel Butler says of William Lilly, the almanac maker and astrologer:

> In mathematics he was greater
> Than Tycho Brahe or Erra Pater.
> *Hudibras*, i, 1 (1663)

Error. See FAERIE QUEENE, THE.

Erymanthian boar. In Greek mythology, a devastating boar. It had its haunt on the mountain range of Erymanthus between Arcadia and Achaia. It was finally captured by HERACLES.

Erysichthon. In classic myth, an impious person. He profaned a grove sacred to Demeter by cutting down a great oak. He was punished by terrible, incessant hunger.

Erythraean main. Literally, the Red Sea. In ancient geography, the Erythraean Sea was the Indian Ocean including the Red Sea and the Persian Gulf.

Esau. In the Old Testament, the eldest son of Isaac and Rebekah. The name itself means in Hebrew "rough" or "covered with hair." In return for a mess of pottage, it was Esau who sold his birthright to his twin brother JACOB (Gen. 25:33–34). In another story, Jacob put on a hairy animal skin and secured the blessing that his blind father had intended for Esau (Gen. 27).

Escalus. In Shakespeare's ROMEO AND JULIET, the prince of Verona. He orders the feuding Montagues and Capulets to end their public brawls on pain of death and later banishes Romeo from Verona for killing Tybalt.

Escamillo. The toreador in Bizet's opera CARMEN.

Escorial or **Escurial, El.** A royal palace some 25 miles northwest of Madrid, built (1563–1584) by PHILIP II. Dedicated to St. Lawrence, on whose feast day the battle of St. Quentin was fought in 1557, the building is in the shape of a gridiron, in commemoration of the gridiron on which St. Lawrence was martyred, and is famed for its artistic and bibliographic treasures. It also contains a monastery with a celebrated art collection and library, a church, and a mausoleum where the kings of Spain lie buried.

Escosura [y Morrogh], Patricio de la (1807–1878). Spanish novelist and dramatist. Escosura is best known as the author of romantic historical novels, patterned on the Waverley novels of Sir Walter Scott. The most famous of these is *Ni Rey ni roque* (1835), whose value lies in its portrayal of the native Spanish landscape.

Escragnolle, Alfredo d'. See Viscount TAUNAY.

Esenin, Sergei Aleksandrovich (1895–1925). Russian poet. Born of peasant parents, Esenin used the theme of the passing of rural Russia in his poetry. One of the finest lyric poets of the early Soviet period, he was for a time connected with a literary group called the Imaginists, founded in 1919, which, like the English and American Imagists, stressed the importance of the image in poetry. His growing popularity went hand in hand with an increasingly wild life. For a chaotic year (1922–1923), he was married to the dancer Isadora Duncan. His drinking bouts grew in length, and he died, having slashed his wrist in a hotel room in Leningrad and written a farewell poem with his blood, by hanging himself. His suicide was attributed by the Soviet regime to his mental instability, and Esenin's works have not been suppressed as have those of other disaffected literary figures. His four volumes of lyrics, with their glowing pictures of the Russian countryside, are still popular in Russia.

Esmeralda. A beautiful gypsy girl, the heroine of Victor Hugo's novel THE HUNCHBACK OF NOTRE DAME.

Esmond, Henry or **Harry.** The hero of Thackeray's novel HENRY ESMOND.

Francis Esmond. The supposed heir to the Castlewood estate. He brings up Henry with his own children but allows him to believe he is an illegitimate son of the dead viscount to whom the estate belonged.

Rachel Esmond (Lady Castlewood). The wife of Francis. After his death she marries Henry Esmond.

Frank Esmond. The son of Francis and Rachel. Like Henry, he is an ardent supporter of the Pretender.

Beatrix Esmond. The daughter of Francis and Rachel; a beautiful coquette. After numerous affairs, notably one with James Edward Stuart, the Pretender, which destroys his chances for the throne, she marries Tusher, her brother's tutor, and succeeds in having him made bishop. "She was imperious," says the author, "she was light-minded, she was flighty, she was false. She had no reverence for character and she was very, very beautiful."

esoteric (Gr.). Those within, as opposed to *exoteric,* those without. The term originated with Pythagoras, who stood behind a curtain when he gave his lectures. Those who were allowed to attend the lectures, but not to see his face, he called his exoteric disciples; but those who were allowed to enter the veil, his esoterics.

Aristotle adopted the same terms; those who attended his evening lectures, which were of a popular character, he called his exoterics; and those who attended his more abstruse morning lectures, his esoterics.

Espina [de la Serna], Concha (1880–1955). Spanish novelist. Her works include *La esfinge maragata* (1913), a regional novel, and *El metal de los muertos* (1920), which deals with the plight of Spanish mine workers. She is known for her feminine sensitivity and the thoroughness of her narration.

Esprit des lois, De l'. See SPIRIT OF LAWS, THE.

Esprit Fou, L'. See Jean CLAVERET.

Espronceda y Delgado, José (1808–1842). Spanish poet. Espronceda was a romantic in word and in deed. An early conspiracy left him with no choice but to flee Spain; later he was an ardent supporter of liberalism in Holland, while in 1830 he joined the revolutionary cause in Paris. His work stresses patriotic and Byronic themes. His most famous short poems, which appeared in his *Poesías* (1840), include *A Jarifa en una orgía, El verdugo, El mendigo,* and *A la patria.* However, his reputation rests upon two longer works: *El estudiante de Salamanca* (1839), which deals with the adventures of Félix de Montemar, a typical romantic hero who witnesses his own funeral, and the long dramatic

poem *El diablo mundo* (1840–1841), considered his masterpiece, which resembles Byron's *Don Juan* and contains a famous *Canto a Teresa,* dealing with the poet's lost love.

Esquemeling, Alexander Olivier (1645?–1707). A Dutch buccaneer. His book, *De Americaensche Zeerovers* (*The Buccaneers of America,* 1678), has become an important source for the history of piracy.

Essay Concerning Human Understanding, An (1690). A treatise by John LOCKE dealing with the origin and scope of human knowledge. Its basic premise is the empirical origin of ideas, which can be described as the raw material with which the mind works. The mind of man at birth, Locke claimed, is like a blank sheet of paper and possesses no "innate ideas." Man acquires knowledge through experience, which is made up of sensation, impressions of the external world derived through the senses, and reflection, the internal operation of the mind. Knowledge stems from the perception of relationships among ideas. Locke's essay contributed greatly to the growth of 18th-century rationalism and, through its impact on the work of Hume, Kant, and others, influenced modern theories of knowledge.

Essay for the Recording of Illustrious Providences, An (1684). A pseudoscientific treatise by Increase MATHER. The work is a collection of reports involving supernatural incidents in New England, which Mather examines in an attempt to prove and illustrate the intervention of God in human affairs. The book was republished twice in the 19th century as *Remarkable Providences.*

Essay of Dramatic Poesy (1668). A famous critical essay by John DRYDEN. It is in the form of a conversation among four Englishmen who have ventured out on the Thames in a barge in hope of witnessing an engagement between the Dutch and English fleets. They discuss Greek, French, and English drama, the merits of several dramatists, and the use of blank and rhymed verse in plays.

Essay on Criticism, An (1711). A didactic poem in heroic couplets by Alexander POPE, written when he was 21 or younger. It is a discussion, based on neoclassical doctrines, of literary taste and style, principles of verse structure and of criticism, and gives a brief history of criticism. Standards of taste are to be derived from the order found in nature:

> Those rules of old discovered, not devised,
> Are nature still, but nature methodized.

The poem is sprinkled with well-known couplets:

> A little learning is a dangerous thing;
> Drink deep, or taste not the Pierian spring.

> True wit is nature to advantage dressed,
> What oft was thought, but ne'er so well expressed.

> Good nature and good sense must ever join;
> To err is human, to forgive divine.

Essay on Man, An (1733–1734). The best-known poem of Alexander POPE. Written in heroic couplets, it is divided into four Epistles dealing respectively with man's relation to the universe, to himself, to society, and to happiness. The poem is addressed to, and was inspired by, Henry St. John, Lord Bolingbroke; it expresses a deistic philosophy (see DEISM) loosely derived from Leibniz, being intended to set forth a coherent scheme of the universe, to "vindicate the ways of God to man" and to declare that "whatever is, is right." It is optimistic and shows the characteristic neoclassical faith in reason and respect for tradition and authority.

Essays (Essais; 1580, 1588). The masterpiece of the French moralist Michel de MONTAIGNE, creator of the personal discursive essay. Loosely constructed, they ramble at will over any number of subjects like a spirited conversation. The order in which the chapters appear and the division into three books had no logical significance. However, the order in which Montaigne actually wrote has been established and reveals a certain progression in his thought from a classic stoic attitude to one of skepticism (see APOLOGY FOR RAYMOND SEBOND) to a final affirmation of the possibilities in human nature. He found that the knowledge he sought resided in man alone, of which he was a representative. To extract knowledge, therefore, he must learn to know himself, as his great model Socrates had taught. In the *Essays*, he delved into his own experience, gleaned the lessons it held for him, and gradually filled out his "self-portrait." The ideas he expressed on such topics as death, friendship, virtue, suffering, education, politics, freedom, nature, and man are peculiarly his own. At the same time they are universal, since the truth Montaigne found is rooted in human nature itself. Montaigne was highly original in turning attention from academic learning and intellectual theorizing to man himself. Freed from the prejudices of his time, he cleared the way for the consideration of morality, politics, and justice as separate disciplines, independent of religious dogma, whose successful practice was closely related to an understanding of human nature. He has endured because every reader has found not only the portrait of Montaigne in the *Essays*, but glimpses of his own image.

Essays or Counsels, Civil and Moral, The. A collection of brief essays by Francis BACON, published in three editions during his lifetime: a first edition of 10 essays (1597); a second of 38 (1612); and a third of 58 (1625). Generally, they deal with questions of personal or public conduct and philosophical or religious matters. They are written in a witty, pithy, widely metaphorical, and highly original style.

Essays, First and Second Series (1841; 1844). Two collections of essays by Ralph Waldo EMERSON. The *First Series* includes the essays called *History*, SELF-RELIANCE, COMPENSATION, *Spiritual Laws, Love, Friendship, Prudence, Heroism*, THE OVER-SOUL, *Circles, Intellect*, and *Art*. The *Second Series* includes *The Poet, Experience, Character, Manners, Gifts, Nature, Politics*, and *Nominalist and Realist*.

Essays in Idleness (Tsurezure gusa). Japanese miscellany of the Muromachi Period (1333–1600) by Yoshida Kenkō (1283–1350), a court official and Buddhist monk. The 243 passages, of varying length, are mainly sketches, comments, and anecdotes, which reflect both a cynical worldliness and a rather shallow Buddhistic outlook.

Essay towards a New Theory of Vision (1709). A philosophical treatise dealing with the doctrine of immaterialism by George BERKELEY.

Establishment. Popular name for those who, wielding power in Britain, are sometimes humorously and sometimes resentfully considered to form an ex-

clusive society that runs the country. The Establishment is conceived of as an arm of the British upper class, dedicated to preserving the values, rights, and powers of that class, generally at the expense of the rest of the population. Its membership includes virtually all royalty, nobility, money, power, and influence in British life, from debutante to prime minister, from playwright to press baron. The Establishment periodically assimilates to its bosom all competition or opposition that can be ingratiated or bought off and squashes the rest. It is, consequently, self-preserving, self-perpetuating, and unbeatable.

Este. Italian noble family, lords of the province of Ferrara from the 13th through the 16th century, who took their name from the city of Este (hence also *Estensi*). Their influence on literature and the other arts was especially great during the Renaissance, when their court was a center of activity in the drama and devoted to the romanzo, or romantic epic. The most famous recipients of their patronage were the poets Boiardo, Ariosto, and Tasso. Among the outstanding Estensi were:

Leonello d'Este (1407–1450). Marquis of Ferrara, man of letters, patron of such artists as Alberti, and himself a minor poet of some ability.

Ercole 1 d'Este (1431–1505). Duke of Ferrara (1471–1505). Patron of Boiardo, father of two celebrated Renaissance women: Beatrice d'Este (1475–1497), wife of Lodovico Sforza of Milan; and Isabella d'Este (1474–1539), wife of Francesco Gonzaga of Mantua and one of the most learned and cultivated women of her time.

Alfonso II d'Este. Duke of Ferrara (1559–1597). Patron of Tasso, who was forced to confine the poet in an asylum after a mental breakdown. Alfonso's sister Eleonora d'Este (1537–1581) was once thought to have been the object of Tasso's love, and the reason for his confinement, but this is now considered a fiction.

Ippolito d'Este. Cardinal (1479–1520). Friend of Leonardo da Vinci and patron of the poet Ariosto.

Luigi d'Este (1538–1586). A cardinal and patron of the poet Tasso until 1572, when the latter entered the service of Duke Alfonso.

Estébanez Calderón, Serafín (1799–1867). Spanish statesman and author. His most famous work is the colorful *Escenas andaluzas* (1847), which deals with the picturesque life, customs, and dress of the inhabitants of the province of Andulasia.

Estensi. See ESTE.

Esterhazy, Marie Charles Ferdinand Walsin (1847–1923). French army officer. Esterhazy confessed in 1899 that he had forged the documents that led to the conviction of Alfred DREYFUS. He spent the remainder of his life in exile in England.

Esther. The name of an Old Testament heroine (in Hebrew, *Hadassah*) whose story is told in the book bearing her name. In place of Queen Vashti, King Ahasuerus chose the beautiful Jewish maiden Esther as his queen. She kept her religion secret, on the advice of her uncle and guardian Mordecai, until the evil Haman conceived a plot to destroy all Jews in the kingdom. As queen, she made a courageous plea for her people to Ahasuerus, and Haman was hung on the gallows he intended for Mordecai. Orthodox Jews still celebrate the feast of Purim to commemorate this deliverance.

Esther (1673). An epic by Jean DESMARETS DE SAINT-SORLIN, based on the Old Testament Book of Esther.

Esther (1689). A tragedy in 3 acts by Jean RACINE. Based on the Book of Esther and relating the story of Esther and Ahasuerus, the play was written for the schoolgirls of St.-Cyr at the request of Mme. de Maintenon; the nature of the commission explains the unorthodox interpolation of songs by a chorus of Israelite maidens.

Esther (1884). A novel by Henry ADAMS. Esther Dudley, a free-thinking young painter, falls in love with the clergyman Stephen Hazard, but, hostile to his church and alienated by his orthodox views, she breaks their engagement. The character of Esther is thought to be modeled after that of Adams' wife Marian. The artist Wharton, a character in a romantic subplot, may have been drawn from the sculptor Augustus St. Gaudens, who created the impressive memorial to Mrs. Adams in the Rock Creek Cemetery in Washington.

Esther Waters (1894). A novel by George MOORE. It is the story of an English servant and her long struggle to bring up her illegitimate son. The boy's father, William Latch, who had been footman in the household where Esther had her first position, finally turns up as a bookmaker and innkeeper and marries her, but her happy married life is only an interlude in a distressed and melancholy existence.

Estienne, Henri (1531–1598). French humanist, printer, and philologist. The son and grandson of illustrious printers, he lived in Geneva, but he also spent much time among the humanists of Paris. His publication of the works of Anacreon (1554) and of other Greek authors exercised a great influence on the Pléiade poets. An admirer of Greek, which he considered the only worthy predecessor to French, he published a *Thesaurus graecae linguae* (1572) and five works on the French language. His most important work in French, *Apologie pour Hérodote* (1566), is a satire on his age; *Dialogues du nouveau françois italianisé* (1578), a satire, laments the corruption of the French language by Italian influences.

Estrées, Gabrielle d' (1573–1599). Mistress of Henry IV of France. The daughter of the marquis of Cœuvres, she won the affection of Henry when he visited the castle of Cœuvres and became his mistress in 1592, bearing him several children, who were legitimized. Henry's plans to marry Gabrielle after his divorce from Margaret of Valois were cut short by her death.

Estrildis. See LOCRINE.

Etaples, Jacques Lefèvre d' (1453–1536). French theologian. He was one of the first French theologians to reject medieval scholasticism in favor of the humanism of the Renaissance. Rather than teach from commentaries on the classics, as had been done previously, he taught from his own editions of the texts, such as Aristotle's *Physics* (1492–1494), *Ethics* (1494), and *Politics* (1506). Under the influence of Erasmus, he wrote his Latin commentaries (1522) on the New Testament, which led him to reject the body of Church dogma and to consider Scripture as the only sound basis of Christianity. He thus became one of the forerunners of the Protestant reform movement.

Eteocles (**Eteokles**). In Greek legend, a son of OEDIPUS and Jocasta. See SEVEN AGAINST THEBES.

Eteoclus (**Eteoklos**). See SEVEN AGAINST THEBES.

Eternal City, the. Rome. The epithet occurs in Ovid, Tibullus, and other writers, and in many official documents of the Empire. In Vergil's *Aeneid*, Jupiter tells Venus that he would give to the Romans *imperium sine fine* (an eternal empire).

eternal feminine. A phrase from the last lines of Goethe's FAUST, "Das Ewig-Weibliche/Zieht uns hinan" ("The eternal feminine/Draws us onward"). Goethe symbolizes this idea in the Virgin Mary at the end of *Faust*, and both GRETCHEN and HELEN are manifestations of it, but its full meaning is more general. Whereas Mephistopheles represents nihilism, the complete lack of upward striving, the eternal feminine is the goal of all upward striving, of all man's attempts, however futile or misguided, to improve himself or his world.

Eternal Husband, The (**Vechnyi muzh**; 1870). A short novel by Feodor DOSTOEVSKI. It is a brilliant psychological study of the relations between a cuckolded husband and his wife's ex-lover. The husband, Pavel Pavlovich Trusotzki, torments himself as well as the lover, Aleksei Ivanovich Vel'chaninov. He hints to Vel'chaninov that the daughter his wife bore before she died was actually Vel'chaninov's. Trusotzki horribly mistreats the little girl who loves him, nevertheless, and who falls ill and dies when she is separated from him. Vel'chaninov hopes he has seen the last of Trusotzki, but the half-mad little man turns up again, urging Vel'chaninov to come and meet his prospective second wife, as if inviting cuckoldry all over again.

Ethan Brand (1851). A short story by Nathaniel HAWTHORNE. Brand, setting out to discover the Unpardonable Sin, finally finds it in his own heart. For this "sin of an intellect that triumphed over the sense of brotherhood with man and reverence for God," he destroys himself.

Ethan Frome (1911). A short novel by Edith WHARTON. In a typical New England village, the title character barely makes a living out of his stony farm and exists at odds with his wife Zeena, a whining hypochondriac. When Mattie, Zeena's cousin, comes to live with them, love develops between her and Ethan. They try to end their hapless romance by steering a bobsled into a tree; but both end up cripples, tied to a long life of despair with Zeena. Zeena, however, is transformed into a devoted nurse while Mattie becomes the nagging invalid.

Etherege, Sir George (1634–1691). English dramatist. He is noted for such brilliant, if licentious, comedies as *The Comical Revenge, or Love in a Tub* (1664), *She Would If She Could* (1668), and THE MAN OF MODE.

Ethiopians (*Gr.* burnt-faces). A legendary race of people in Greek mythology. The country of the Ethiopians lay south of Egypt, close to the stream of Ocean. Cepheus, husband of Cassiopeia and father of Andromeda, was one of their kings. Memnon, the son of Aurora and Tithonus who fell in the Trojan War, was another. In Greek drama mention is often made of various gods being off in Ethiopia, meaning they were a great distance removed from the action of the play.

Ethiopica. The story of the loves between Theagenes and Chariclea, by Heliodoros (Heliodorus), Greek romance writer and later bishop of Tricca, in Thessaly, in the 4th century. The book, considered the earliest of extant Greek romances, was formed by 10 volumes, largely borrowed from by subsequent novelists, and especially by Madeleine de Scudéry, Tasso, Guarnini, and D'Urfé.

Etna or **Aetna.** The famous Sicilian volcano. In the Aeneid, Vergil ascribes its eruption to the restlessness of Enceladus, a giant who lies buried under the mountain, where the Greek and Latin poets also placed the forges of Vulcan and the smithy of the Cyclopes.

Etourdi, L' (The Scatterbrain, 1665). Molière's 1st comedy. In the play, which is set in Messina, Lélie has fallen in love with Clélie but has not the money to buy her. His servant Mascarille contrives a series of maneuvers for obtaining the girl, but the hare-brained Lélie fumbles them all. Nonetheless, he finally obtains Clélie.

Etranger, L'. See Stranger, The.

Etre et le Néant, L'. See Being and Nothingness.

Etruria. See Etruscans.

Etruscans. An ancient non-Italic race which established itself in northern Italy some time before the 7th century B.C. Modern Tuscany is roughly the center of what was their kingdom, Etruria. The Tusci, as they were called by the Romans, gained great power in Italy and the western Mediterranean, and held sway over Rome until 509 B.C. when the last Etruscan king was expelled from that city. The Romans feared and hated them for many years thereafter, although they were finally absorbed both politically and culturally into the Roman state. Their art shows influences from Greece, Egypt, Syria, Cyprus, and Mesopotamia, and it, in turn, influenced Roman art. Their language remains undeciphered and their origin a mystery, although the Greek historian Herodotus asserts that they came from Lydia in Asia Minor.

Ettrick Shepherd, the. See James Hogg.

Et tu, Brute. According to Suetonius in his *Lives of the Caesars*, Julius Caesar on being stabbed by Marcus Junius Brutus, whom he had counted among his trusted friends, exclaimed: *Et tu, Brute fili* ("You also, O Brutus, my son"). Shakespeare, in his play Julius Caesar, immeasurably heightened the effect of the passage by adding to it an expression of utter despair at such betrayal: "Et tu, Brute! Then fall, Caesar!" The phrase is currently used as an expression of amazement at a sudden revelation of treachery or ingratitude.

Etzel. The name given Attila of the Huns in German legends such as the Nibelungenlied. He is known as Atli in the Völsunga Saga.

Eucharist (from Gr. *eucharistein,* to give thanks). The sacrament of the Lord's Supper (see Last Supper).

Euclid (Eukleides; fl. 300 b.c.). A Greek mathematician. He lived and taught at Alexandria. His *Elements* (of geometry) in 13 books became the basis of future geometry. He is celebrated in Edna St. Vincent Millay's well-known line, "Euclid alone has looked on beauty bare."

Eugene Aram (1832). A novel by Edward Bulwer-Lytton, founded on a famous murder case. The real Eugene Aram (1704–1759) was a Knaresborough schoolmaster convicted of murdering a shoemaker, Daniel Clarke, to whom he owed money. Bulwer-Lytton makes the youthful Aram commit murder to secure money to further his own idealistic purposes. He goes free for a time, falls in love, all unknowingly, with a relative of the murdered man, and is in his wedding clothes when he is accused of the crime.

Eugene of Savoy, Prince (1663–1736). French aristocrat who served the Austrian Hapsburgs as military commander and administrator. He drove the invading Turks out of Hungary in 1697.

Eugene Onegin (Evgeni Onegin; 1831). A novel in verse by Aleksandr Pushkin. For the influence it had on later Russian literature and in its own right, *Eugene Onegin* is probably Pushkin's most important work. The novel relates the experiences of its Byronic hero, Eugene. Bored with the social life in St. Petersburg, he visits his country estate and meets Tatyana, a young girl who falls in love with him and naïvely offers herself to him. The bored Eugene is not interested and rather bluntly tells Tatyana this. For lack of any other amusement, he then provokes a duel with Lenski, a young romantic poet who has become his friend. Lenski is killed, and Onegin goes back to the world of society. After his departure, Tatyana visits Eugene's country manor, browses through his library, and begins to realize how hollow and artificial he is.

A few years later when Eugene meets Tatyana, who is now the wife of a prince and a prominent member of St. Petersburg society, her beauty and charm, and perhaps her eminence in society, turn his head. He announces his love to her in a letter, as Tatyana had to him in years before. Tatyana admits she still loves him, but refuses him because of her duty to her husband.

Pushkin's novel has been a rich source of character types for Russian writers. His use of an ironic narrator to tell the story has perhaps been equally influential. This narrative device was especially well developed by Dostoevski. The libretto for Tchaikovsky's opera *Eugene Onegin* (1879) was faithfully adapted from Pushkin's tale by the composer's brother Modeste.

Eugénie, Empress. Full name, **Eugénie Marie de Montijo de Guzmán.** Comtesse de Téba (1826–1920). Wife of Napoleon III, and empress of the French (1853–1871). A leader of fashion, her feminine charm added brilliance to the French court. Her influence upon her husband reveals her lack of interest in liberal and democratic ideas. After the downfall of the empire, she fled to England, where she was befriended by Queen Victoria.

Eugénie Grandet (1833). A novel, part of La Comédie Humaine, by Honoré de Balzac. Félix Grandet, the embodiment of greed and domestic tyranny, destroys the romance of his daughter Eugénie with her cousin Charles, condemning her to a futile, joyless existence.

Eulenspiegel or **Ulenspiegel, Till** or **Tyll.** Called in English **Tyll Howleglas** or **Owlglass.** A German peasant popular in legend as a player of pranks. Tradition makes him a native of Brunswick who died in 1350. The stories associated with his name tell of the often brutal tricks and practical jokes he

LA VIE
Joyeuse et recréative
DE
THIEL-ULESPIÉGLE,

*De fes faits merveilleux & fortunes qu'il a eu;
lequel par aucune rufe ne fe laiffa pas tromper.*

A TROYES,
Chez A P F. André. Imp Lib. & Fabricant de
Papier, Grand rue, v s à vis la Belle-Croix.

A 16th-century French edition of *Till Eulenspiegel.*

played, mostly on innkeepers and other tradespeople, but sometimes on priests or noblemen. The first written account was probably a Low German one of about 1483, the next a High German text of 1515. The satire of these seems to emphasize the tricks as the revenge of the peasant upon the townsmen who scorn him as inferior. The rogue's adventures, highly popular and adapted in translations all over Europe, had been printed in England by 1560. Charles de Coster wrote a modernized version in 1867, and Richard Strauss used the theme musically in his tone poem *Till Eulenspiegel's Merry Pranks* (1894).

eulogy. A formal piece of writing or an oration in praise of a person or thing; by extension, it has come to mean any general expression of praise.

Eumaeus (Eumaios). The faithful slave and swineherd of Odysseus in the ODYSSEY.

Eumenides. See ERINYES.

Euphorion (*Gr.*, well-bearing). In late classical tradition, the son of the shades of Achilles and Helen of Troy.

In Part II of FAUST, Goethe makes him the son of Faust and Helen and uses him as an allegory for Lord Byron's career. Euphorion lives only for the joy of the moment and, like Icarus, finally flings himself too high, only to fall and die. Helen follows him to the underworld, leaving Faust behind.

Euphrasia. The heroine of Arthur MURPHY's tragedy *The Grecian Daughter* (1772). She nurses her starving father Evander, King of Syracuse, with milk from her own breast when he is imprisoned by Dionysius the younger. The incident is not historical, but is related of other heroines of legend.

Euphrosyne (*Gr.* Joy). In classic mythology, one of the three Charites, or GRACES.

Euphues. The chief character of John LYLY's *Euphues, The Anatomy of Wit* (1579) and *Euphues and his England* (1580). Euphues is a witty, pleasure-loving young Athenian who, sojourning in Naples, attempts to win Lucilla, fiancée of his friend Philautus. This procedure estranges him from Philautus, but when Lucilla chooses a third lover, the unworthy Curio, the two friends are united in disillusionment. There is little plot in either romance; the interest lies chiefly in long philosophic discussions and in the elaborate and affected style that gave rise to the terms EUPHUISM and *euphuist.* This style, marked by ingenious antitheses, alliteration, exempla, complicated figures, and skillfully balanced sentences, was for a while in great vogue. It was frequently parodied, however, and by 1590 a reaction in favor of a more masculine, pithy style had set in.

euphuism. An artificial style of English speech and writing popular in the late Elizabethan and Jacobean periods. It derived its name from *Euphues: The Anatomy of Wit* (1579) by John LYLY, who either invented the style or derived it from translations of certain works of a Spanish writer, Antonio de GUEVARA. It was characterized by exaggerated Baroque refinement and artificiality of style, with plentiful references to mythical birds and beasts, constant alliteration, and the frequent use of unduly neat antitheses. The intent of this elaborate elegance was to woo feminine readers by seeming to edify them, while avoiding scholarly solemnity. The attempt was so successful that even Queen Elizabeth began to affect the euphuistic style. The fashion lasted for half a century, and Lyly had many imitators, notably Robert GREENE and Thomas LODGE. (See EUPHUES.)

eureka (*Gr.*, more correctly *heureka,* I have found it). An exclamation of delight at having made a discovery. Originally that of ARCHIMEDES, the Syracusan philosopher, when he discovered how to test the purity of Hiero's crown. The tale is that Hiero, a famous tyrant of Syracuse, delivered a certain weight of gold to a smith to be made into a votive crown, but, suspecting that the gold had been alloyed with an inferior metal, asked Archimedes to test it. The philosopher did not know how to proceed, but in stepping into his bath, which was quite full, observed that some of the water ran over. It immediately struck him that a body must remove its own bulk of water when it is immersed; silver is lighter than gold, therefore a pound weight of silver will be more bulky than a pound weight of gold, and would consequently remove more water. In this way he found that the crown was deficient in gold. Vitruvius says: "When the idea flashed across his mind, the philosopher jumped out of the bath exclaiming, '*Heureka! heureka!*' and, without waiting to dress himself, ran home to try the experiment."

Eureka (1848). An essay on the material and spiritual universe by Edgar Allan POE. Under the influence of Laplace and Newton, Poe presented his view of the universe as a mystic and material unity. An interesting contribution to scientific and philosophic thought, the piece indicates that Poe saw the possibility of non-Euclidean geometry. Many of his notions are surprisingly in agreement with the latest theories of cosmic origin.

Euripides (480?–405 B.C.). A Greek tragic playwright. A slightly younger contemporary of Aeschylus and Sophocles, and less honored in his time, Euripides is now admired for his remarkably modern attitudes and his profound insights into psychology. In spite of Aristophanes' taunt that his mother had sold vegetables, he was actually high born and well educated. He was twice married, both times unhappily. Although he wrote between 80 and 90 plays, Euripides won prizes only four times. In 409 B.C., he left Athens and died at the court of King Archelaus of Macedonia.

According to tradition, Euripides was withdrawn and bookish, and his plays reveal a sharply inquiring mind that must have made him many enemies in Athens. He was cruelly lampooned by Aristophanes in two comedies, THE CLOUDS and the THESMOPHORIAZUSAE. The slanders against him and the relative unpopularity of his plays may account for his leaving Athens when he was still at the height of his powers; yet Sophocles dressed his chorus in mourning when news of Euripides' death reached Athens.

Seventeen tragedies by Euripides remain, beginning with the ALCESTIS in 438 B.C., and ending with THE BACCHANTS in about 405 B.C. He also wrote the fragmentary SATYR PLAY CYCLOPS about 424–423 B.C., and may have written another existing tragedy, *Rhesus*, of which the date is unknown. Although called a tragedy, the *Alcestis* has a strong comic element that relates it more closely to the satyr plays.

Three qualities in Euripides' plays have especially attracted modern readers: his biting social criticism, his subtle psychological analyses of his characters, and their humanity, as compared to the larger-than-life remoteness of the heroes and heroines of Aeschylus and Sophocles. Euripides attacked, at least by implication, many attitudes accepted by the Athenians: the subordinate position of women (*Alcestis*), and foreign women in particular (MEDEA); the unjust treatment of illegitimate children (*Hippolytus*); above all, the glory of war (THE TROJAN WOMEN). His own attitude toward his home city of Athens seems to have changed strikingly in the decade between his ANDROMACHE and *The Trojan Women*. The earlier play bitterly attacks the Spartans as cruel and cowardly, and seems to imply that the Athenians would never behave in such a manner. In *The Trojan Women*, however, they behave in much the same way to the defeated Trojans, killing the child Astyanax out of fear that the line of Hector will be perpetuated. This play reflected Euripides' disillusionment and outrage over the massacre by Athenians of the inhabitants of Melos, because they had remained neutral in the PELOPONNESIAN WAR. This disgust with war is evident also in the IPHIGENIA IN AULIS, one of his last plays. Even as early as the *Andromache*, however, it was clear that Euripides found no glory in war, but only needless suffering and inhumanity.

Some of the irony of the *Alcestis*, in which Admetus gallantly allows his wife to die for him, may have been lost on the Athenians, who considered men's lives more valuable than those of women. But in the *Medea* the sharp-tongued heroine makes his criticism of the treatment of women abundantly clear. Medea, like Electra and Phaedra (in the *Hippolytus*), is drawn with extraordinarily acute insights into her emotions. They are queens, yet they are extremely human women, rather than heroic personages of tragedy. It was in this reduction of tragic figures to human proportions that Euripides laid the groundwork for the New Comedy that was to come. Euripides' characters speak a much more colloquial language than that of the other tragedians, but it is still poetry of a high order, especially in the choral odes.

Euripides' other plays include ION, IPHIGENIA in TAURIS, HELEN, ELECTRA, ORESTES, HECUBA, and THE SUPPLIANT WOMEN.

euroclydon. A tempestuous northeast wind of the Mediterranean. Also called *gregale*, i.e., the wind from Greece. The first part of Euroclydon is the word *eurus*, the east wind of classical antiquity; the second *clydon*, a wave. The word occurs in the New Testament (Acts 27:14) and may be a popular adaptation of the manuscript variant (now preferred) *Euraquilo*, in which the second part is *Aquilo*, the north wind.

Europa (Europe). In classic myth, a daughter of Agenor, or, according to the *Iliad*, daughter of Phoenix. She was famed for her beauty. Zeus in the form of a white bull carried her off and swam with her to the island of Crete. She was the mother of Minos, Rhadamanthus, and Evandros or Sarpedon, and, according to some forms of the legend, of the Minotaur.

Europeans, The (1878). A novel by Henry JAMES. The plot centers about the visit of "the Europeans," Felix Young, an artist, and his sister Eugenia, the morganatically married Baroness Muenster whose husband is about to repudiate their marriage, to the farm of their New England relatives, the Wentworths. The Europeans hope to gain much from their American cousins; the baroness futilely tries to make a wealthy marriage, and Felix paints portraits of the Bostonians he meets, eventually marrying a kinswoman who is eager to escape from her bleak environment. James tends to treat his themes here comically, and although he portrays the Wentworths' moral solidity with respect, he nevertheless calls attention to their provincialism and timidity.

Euryanassa. See TANTALUS.

Eurydice. See ORPHEUS.

Eurylochus (Eurylochos). In classic myth, the only companion of Odysseus whom CIRCE was unable to change into a hog.

Eurystheus. In Greek mythology, a king of Mycenae, and cousin of HERACLES. On the urging of Hera, or for some other reason, he imposed upon that hero his twelve famous labors.

Eurytion. (1) A centaur. In Greek legend, at the marriage feast of Pirithous, King of the LAPITHS, with Hippodamia, he became intoxicated and offered violence to the bride, thus causing the celebrated battle of the Lapiths and Centaurs.

(2) Eurytion was also the name of the giant guarding Geryon's castle slain by HERACLES.

Eusebius of Caesarea (260?–?340). A theologian, called the "father of ecclesiastical history." He wrote a Christian Church history in 10 books and also a universal history.

Eustace and Hilda. A trilogy by L. P. HARTLEY, consisting of *The Shrimp and the Anemone* (1944, U.S. title *The West Window*), *The Sixth Heaven* (1946), and *Eustace and Hilda* (1947). In the first book Eustace, as a little boy, tries ineffectually to rebel against his emotionally dominating elder sister. In *The Sixth Heaven,* as a student at Oxford, he tries to rid himself of Hilda by encouraging a romance between her and one of his schoolfellows. In the last book, after Hilda has been seduced, deserted, and has had a mental breakdown, Eustace restores her to health at the cost of his own life. Their relationship is emphasized by symbolic imagery. As a child Eustace is shown watching a sea anemone (Hilda) devouring a shrimp (himself); the shrimp struggles free, carrying the anemone's entrails with him.

Eustace Diamonds, The (1873). A novel by Anthony TROLLOPE. It is the story of the beautiful, mendacious Lady Elizabeth Eustace who tries to keep a valuable diamond necklace she had from her husband before he died. Since it is a family heirloom, the Eustace family tries to retrieve it. Lady Elizabeth fails in her attempt to keep it, is humiliated, and marries the dubious Mr. Emilius, an apparent bigamist.

Eustazio (Eustache of Bouillon). In Tasso's epic poem GERUSALEMME LIBERATA, the younger brother of Goffredo (Godfrey), the Christian commander He opposes his brother, urging the Crusaders to help the enchantress Armida regain her kingdom. Later he becomes her slave until released by Rinaldo of Este.

Euterpe. One of the 9 Muses, the inventor of the double flute. She was the muse of Dionysiac music, patroness of joy and pleasure, and of flute-players.

Evadne. (1) In Greek legend, wife of CAPANEUS. She threw herself on the funeral pile of her husband, and was consumed with him.

(2) Name of one of the principal characters of Beaumont and Fletcher's drama, *The Maid's Tragedy* (1610). The sister of Melantius, Amintor was compelled by the King to marry her, although he was betrothed to Aspasia, the "maid" whose death forms the tragic event of the drama.

Evangeline, A Tale of Acadie (1847). A narrative poem by Henry Wadsworth LONGFELLOW. The lovers, Gabriel Lajeunesse and Evangeline Bellefontaine, are separated when the British expel the Acadians from Nova Scotia. He is carried to Louisiana, and she to New England. The two spend years searching for one another. Nursing the sick in an epidemic in Philadelphia, she recognizes him as the dying man in her care. Now an old woman, Evangeline also dies, and the two are buried together.

Evan Harrington (1860). A novel by George MEREDITH. The hero, Evan Harrington, is the son of Melchisedec Harrington, the tailor, "the great Mel." Mel, who is ambitious, has succeeded in marrying his three daughters into good society, and with their assistance proposes to make a gentleman of Evan. Through the scheming manipulations of his sister the Countess de Saldar, "the most consummate liar in literature," Evan is introduced under false pretenses among the guests at a house party at the home of the high-born Rose Jocelyn. Evan and Rose fall in love; she half suspects the truth; he tries to confess it. Meantime "the great Mel" has died, leaving huge debts, and the sensible and forthright Mrs. Mel makes every effort to persuade her son to assume the business. The truth comes out at last, but the romance survives the shock.

Evans, Caradoc (1883–1945). Welsh novelist, playwright, and journalist. He wrote scathing satires on Welsh life: *My Neighbors* (1919), *Nothing to Pay* (1930), *Wasps* (1933) and *This Way to Heaven* (1934).

Evans, Mary Ann. See George ELIOT.

Evans, Maurice (1901–). English-born American actor. He scored a great success in performances of Shakespeare's plays directed by Margaret Webster, and in Shaw's *Man and Superman*. Though usually at his best in roles calling for great vitality, he was particularly moving as Richard II.

Evans, Nathaniel (1742–1767). Colonial American poet. Born in Philadelphia, where he attended a Moravian boarding school, Evans later went to England, where he was ordained a minister in the Society for the Propagation of the Gospel. Settling in Haddonfield, N.J., he wrote gifted Spenserian and Miltonic verse, collected after his death and published in 1772 as *Poems on Several Occasions*. He was a protégé of William Smith and a close friend of Thomas Godfrey, to whom he dedicated some poems.

Evans, Sir Hugh. In Shakespeare's MERRY WIVES OF WINDSOR, a pedantic Welsh parson and schoolmaster of extraordinary simplicity and native shrewdness.

Evans, William (d. 1632). An English giant, nearly 8 feet tall. A porter of Charles I, he carried Sir Jeffrey Hudson, the queen's dwarf, in his pocket. Sir Walter Scott wrote of him in *Peveril of the Peak* (1823).

Eve (from Heb., *hawwāh*, life). The 1st woman, the wife of Adam, and "the mother of all living" (Gen. 3:20). Because Eve persuaded Adam to eat the forbidden fruit in the Garden of Eden, her name is often used as a synonym for a temptress. See ADAM AND EVE.

Evelina, or The History of a Young Lady's Entrance into the World (1778). A novel by Fanny BURNEY. After having been brought up in the country by Reverend Arthur Villars, a friend of her grandfather, Evelina Anville is sent to live in London with Villars' friend Lady Howard. Here Evelina is introduced to the ways of society. Though courted by Sir Clement Willoughby, whom she recognizes for the rake that he is, she prefers the gentlemanly Lord Orville. However, they are kept apart by numerous misunderstandings and by the mystery and stigma surrounding Evelina's birth; she turns out to be the daughter of Sir John Belmont and all ends happily.

Evelyn, John (1620–1706). English diarist and miscellaneous writer. A man whose interests ranged from gardening to numismatics, Evelyn held a number of offices under Charles II and was a prominent member of the Royal Society. His varied background and participation in the political events of his day lend interest and importance to his *Diary* (1818) which covers the years from 1640 to 1706.

Eve of St. Agnes, The (1819). A poem by John Keats. It is based on the legend that on the Eve of St. Agnes, young maidens are allowed a glimpse of their future husbands. Porphyro thus comes to Madeline on St. Agnes' Eve and soon they depart into the timeless world of love. Some of Keats's most striking sensuous imagery is found in this poem.

Eve of St. John, The (1800). A ghostly romantic ballad by Sir Walter Scott.

Everdene, Bathsheba. See Far from the Madding Crowd.

Everlasting Mercy, The (1911). A narrative poem by John Masefield. It describes the redemption of a drunken villager. It was a popular success and influenced other poets. The Georgian poets were influenced by its rural setting, and younger, experimental poets admired its sometimes harsh and colloquial language and its occasional use of oaths.

Ever Victorious Army, the. See Charles George Gordon.

Everyman (c. 1500). Most famous of the morality plays, probably translated into English from the Dutch *Elckerlijk* (1495). When Everyman receives a summons from Death, he tries vainly to persuade his friends Fellowship, Kindred, Worldly Goods, Beauty, and others to journey with him; but only Good Deeds remains faithful, although so weak because of Everyman's neglect that Knowledge and

First page of the morality play *Everyman* (c. 1500).

Confession must renew his strength so that he can accompany Everyman to the grave. The subtitle reads "A Treatise how the hye Fader of Heven sendeth Dethe to somon every creature to come and gyve a counte of theyr lyves in this Worlde."

Hugo von Hofmannsthal's *Jedermann* (1911) is a reworking of the play into German verse.

Every Man in His Humour (1598). A comedy by Ben Jonson. A familiar classic plot is used as a vehicle for the study of a series of characters, each of whom is possessed by a particular humour or dominating characteristic. The plot, which is rife with incident and misunderstanding, concerns the efforts of Young Kno'well and Wellbred to escape or contain the displeasure of their father and brother-in-law respectively. The characters to whom the title applies are: Captain Bobadil, whose humour is bragging of his brave deeds and military courage, and who is thrashed as a coward by Downright; Kitely, whose humour is jealousy of his wife and who is befooled and cured by a trick played on him by Brainworm; Stephen, whose humour is verdant stupidity and who is played on by everyone; Kno'well, whose humour is suspicion of his son; Dame Kitely, whose humour is jealousy of her husband, but she, like him, is cured by a trick devised by Brainworm.

The play exists in two versions, the first of which uses Italian names and places. A sequel, *Every Man Out of His Humour* (1599), has even less coherency of plot but presents a rich collection of the foibles of the time.

Everyman's Library. A series of books, popularly priced, including, among its hundreds of titles, most of the best works of the greatest authors of the past. The idea of the library was conceived by Ernest Rhys, and the first fifty titles appeared in 1905.

Evil May Day. The name given to the 1st of May, 1517, when the young apprentices in London rioted against the French residents of the city. A serious riot, it was put down only with difficulty. Sir Thomas More, and the earls of Shrewsbury and Surrey were among those helping to quell the riot. Of the thousands of apprentices involved, 278 were arrested, and 15 were hanged, drawn, and quartered. The incident forms the basis of an anonymous Elizabethan play, *Sir Thomas More*.

Ewald or **Evald, Johannes** (1743–1781). A Danish national lyric poet and dramatist. He was the author of the first original Danish tragedy *Rolf Krage* (1770) and the national festival drama, *The Fishers* (1779), containing the song, *King Christian Stood by the Lofty Mast,* which has become a Danish national song.

Ewig-Weibliche, Das. See Eternal feminine.

Excalibur (OFr., *Escalibor*). The sword of King Arthur in Arthurian romance. It is called *Caliburn* by Geoffrey of Monmouth, and *Caledvwlch* in the *Mabinogion.* There is in Irish legend a famous sword called *Caladbolg,* a name that is thought to mean "hard belly," i.e., capable of consuming anything; this and the name Excalibur are probably connected.

The way that Arthur gains the sword is variously told in Arthurian legend. In some versions, Excalibur is the sword, magically fixed in a stone, that can be withdrawn only by one who is the rightful king of England, and Arthur proves to be the only knight that can pull the sword from the stone. In Malory's

Morte d'Arthur (c. 1469), Excalibur is a gift to Arthur from the Lady of the Lake. After the last battle, when Arthur lies mortally wounded, he commands Sir Bedivere to return Excalibur to the lake. Sir Bedivere throws it into the water, and an arm, clothed in white samite, appears to receive it.

Excursion, The. A long didactic poem by William Wordsworth, forming part of *The Recluse* (1814). It includes discussions of virtue, religious faith, the industrial revolution and its social effects, and the education of children.

Exemplary Novels. See Novelas ejemplares.

Exeter Book (Codex Exoniensis; c. 975). Collection of manuscripts of Old English poetry, presented to Exeter Cathedral (c. 1070) by Leofric, its first bishop. It includes Widsith, The Seafarer, The Wanderer, Deor's Lament, and a number of poems attributed to Cynewulf, including *Christ, Juliana,* and the "riddles."

Exiles (1918). A play by James Joyce. The central character is Richard Rowan, who, like Joyce himself, is an Irish writer who has spent much of his life abroad and feels estranged from Irish society on his return to Dublin. The action concerns various love entanglements between Richard, his common law wife, Bertha, and his friends. It is a naturalistic play, indebted to the work of Ibsen, whom Joyce greatly admired. Only moderately successful on the stage, *Exiles* is chiefly important for the light it throws on the development of Joyce's ideas about the artist's alienation from society.

existentialism. A contemporary movement in philosophy. Although it grew out of the development of the philosophical tradition all over Europe, it was highly popularized in France in the 1940's and is usually associated with the theories expressed by Jean-Paul Sartre. The beginnings of existentialism are found in the writings of the Danish Søren Kierkegaard, the German Friedrich Nietzsche, and the Russian Feodor Dostoevski, although none of them formulated a logical system. The works of the Germans Martin Heidegger and Karl Jaspers were the most immediate influence on Sartre's thinking, along with the method of approach of the phenomenologist Edmund Husserl.

All existentialists are concerned with ontology, the study of being. The point of departure is human consciousness and mental processes. In contrast to most previous philosophical systems, which maintain that an *a priori* essence precedes or transcends the individual existence of people or of objects, the existentialists conclude that existence precedes essence. The significance of this for human beings is that the concept that a man has an essential self is shown to be an illusion. A man's self is nothing except what he has become; at any given moment, it is the sum of the life he has shaped until then. The "nothing" he begins with is thus the source of man's freedom, for at each moment it is man's will that can choose how to act or not to act. However, each such decision affects the future doubly: a man is or should be responsible for the consequences of his actions; and each action necessarily excludes the other potential actions for that moment, and their consequences, and thus at least partially limits the potentialities for future actions.

By what standards, then, should man make his decisions? Man's mind cannot discern any meaning for this existence in the universe; when he abandons his illusions, he finds himself horrified by the absurdity of the human condition. The question of the existence of God (or some cosmic purpose) is irrelevant, according to Sartre and the atheistic existentialists, because even if He does exist (which they usually deny), He does not reveal to men the meaning of their life. Thus man must create a human morality in the absence of any known predetermined absolute values. Honesty with oneself is perhaps the major value common to existentialist thinking; all their writings describe the emotional anguish of trying to achieve it. Sartre calls the "man of good faith" one who understands the human condition described above and fully accepts the responsibility of the freedom it entails. The "man of bad faith" accepts illusion, is deliberately hypocritical, or tries to use the excuse of "good intentions" to escape responsibility for the consequences of his actions, the ramifications of which always involve other people. The man of good faith judges a potential action by estimating the result if everyone, not just himself, were to perform it. Yet despite the difficulty of choice, he does not withdraw from life, but is *engagé*, actively engaged in the business of living with himself and with other men.

The Christian existentialists agree that man can never know God's purpose, but they affirm that it exists and that through a "leap of faith" man can establish his values in accordance with it. However, they too describe the anguish and the responsibility of honest action, for a man can never be certain that his decision is actually based on an intuition of the divine and not on the disguised temptation of evil.

Other writers in the existentialist tradition are Gabriel Marcel, leader of Christian existentialism in France, the Spaniards Miguel de Unamuno and José Ortega y Gasset, and the Jewish mystic Martin Buber.

Albert Camus is often classified with the movement, but he considers many of Sartre's postulates as much an unjustifiable "leap of faith" as that of the religious existentialists. His "man of the Absurd" resembles Sartre's "man of good faith" in that both acknowledge man's lonely condition in the face of the silence of the universe; both reject despair and commit themselves to the anguish and responsibility of living as best one can; and both consider the exercise of one's own freedom inseparable from the opportunity for all men to exercise theirs, which is contingent on their freedom from poverty, political oppression, and other avoidable external limitations. However, Camus' writings do not attempt to constitute an organized philosophical system of ontology, as do Sartre's.

exodos. In classical Greek drama, the last choral passage in a tragedy or comedy, recited or sung as the chorus left the orchestra. See parodos.

Exodus (*Gr.,* a going out). The escape by the Jews from their bondage in Egypt (c. 1200 b.c.). Led by Moses, they crossed the Red Sea and wandered for 40 years in the Sinai wilderness, finally reaching Canaan. During this time God revealed His name, His laws, and the destiny of Israel. The covenant between God and Israel promised Israel a "land flowing with milk and honey" in return for homage and reverence.

The book of Exodus is the second volume of the Pentateuch. It gives the account of Moses' birth, the Israelites' departure from Egypt, and the beginning of their long journey to Palestine. The 20th chapter of Exodus contains the Ten Commandments.

Exodus is the title of a novel by Leon Uris (1958) about the establishment of the modern state of Israel.

ex pede Herculem. From this sample we may judge of the whole. Literally (*Lat.*), Hercules [may be drawn] from his foot. Plutarch says that Pythagoras calculated the height of Heracles (*Gr.* for the *Lat.* Hercules) by comparing the lengths of various stadia in Greece. A stadium was 600 feet in length, but Heracles' stadium at Olympia was much longer; therefore, said the philosopher, the foot of Heracles was proportionately longer than an ordinary foot; and as the foot bears a certain ratio to the height, so the height of Heracles can be easily ascertained. *Ex ungue leonem* (a lion [may be drawn] from its claw) is a similar phrase.

expressionism. In European art, a movement beginning about 1900, in which strong expression of the artist's subjective feelings becomes all important. The expressionist artists sought to portray, not what they perceived from without, as the impressionists did, but only what they felt from within themselves. Moreover, they rejected harmony and beauty as criteria of art, and used violent distortion, instead, in order to represent intense emotions, especially terror, pathos, or agony. The movement flourished mainly in Germany, where it was developed by such groups as *Der* BLAUE REITER (The Blue Rider) and *Die* BRÜCKE (The Bridge). Major expressionist artists include the Norwegian painter Edvard Munch (1863–1944); the German sculptor Ernst Barlach (1870–1938); and the Austrian painter Oskar Kokoschka (1886–   ). The roots of expressionist style may be found in earlier European art, for example, the turbulent lines and violent colors used by van Gogh, the fantastic caricatures in Goya's graphic work, and the contorted forms of Grünewald's religious art.

In reference to literature, expressionism denotes a movement, from about 1910 to 1925, closely akin to the corresponding movement in art. Basically, the expressionists tended to stress the individual's *will* and the *expression* of purely internal visionary experience, as opposed to the emphasis in impressionism and symbolism upon the individual's more or less passive *reception* of experience, and the emphasis in naturalism upon thorough objectivity.

Expressionism made its first major breakthrough in the field of lyric poetry with such figures as Georg Trakl, Georg Heym, Franz Werfel and Ernst Stadler, whose verses are fired with an ecstatic, hymnlike quality and written in a language that seeks to compress as much concentrated meaning in as small a space as possible. Expressionist drama, likewise, takes compression as one of its principal goals: everything not immediately necessary for expressing the play's central idea is omitted; the external world is merely sketched in; the dramatis personae are not characters but types, without fully developed personalities and often without names; the successive scenes are often connected only by ideas, not by any continuity of action; and the dialogue is often compressed into a "telegram-style." Major playwrights include Georg Kaiser, Reinhard Sorge, Walter Hasenclever, Ernst Toller, Fritz Unruh, Ernst Barlach, and Bertolt Brecht in his earlier work. Narrative prose, finally, did not come into its own as an expressionist medium until after the movement had passed its peak. Major figures are Leonhard Frank, Alfred Döblin, and again, Franz Werfel. In terms of history and politics, expressionism may be seen as a continuation of the satirical rejection of complacent bourgeois values begun by such writers as Sternheim and Frank Wedekind; then, with the coming of World War I, most of the expressionists took a strong pacifistic stand. After the war, several of the most powerful figures, including Kaiser, Toller, and Brecht, came out for social revolution; but by the mid-20's, revolutionary fervor had, for the most part, given way to a resigned skepticism or even outright cynicism, and expressionism was past.

Expurgatory Index. See INDEX, THE.

Eyck, Hubert van (1366?–1420) and **Jan van** (1390?–1441). The founders of the Flemish school of painting. The brothers van Eyck are reputed to have originated the modern process of oil painting. The only known authentic work by Hubert's hand is the celebrated altarpiece, the *Adoration of the Lamb* at Ghent, which was completed by Jan. A polyptich containing over 20 panels, it is generally considered one of the great masterpieces of Western art, in its magnificence of color, skillful handling of light and atmosphere, and deeply religious tone. Both men were artists of keen observation, rendering with vigorous realism and infinite detail the world they saw around them, whether the beauty of flowers, trees, and common objects or the richness of materials and jewels. Through the artistic genius of their religious paintings and portraits and their technical innovations, the brothers van Eyck exerted an enormous influence, revolutionizing painting in northern Europe by breaking with the Gothic tradition and instituting a new realistic vigor.

Eyeless in Gaza (1936). A novel by Aldous HUXLEY. It is about Anthony Beavis, a weak-minded man who spends most of his life behaving badly in a meaningless, valueless world. In middle age he is converted to Huxley's own mystical doctrines. Sunbathing with his mistress on the roof of his house, he is bespattered with blood when a dog falls from a passing plane. Beavis goes to Mexico and meets a mystical anthropologist who converts him to pacificism, vegetarianism, and Eastern mysticism, thereby reshaping his character. The title is from John Milton's *Samson Agonistes,* who was

Eyeless in Gaza, at the mill, with slaves.

Eyre, Simon (d. 1459). English shoemaker. According to tradition he enjoyed a fast-rising political career and became Lord Mayor of London in 1445. He appears in Thomas Deloney's *The Gentle Craft* and in Thomas Dekker's THE SHOEMAKER'S HOLIDAY.

Ezekiel (6th century B.C.). A Hebrew prophet during the Babylonian Exile. His sermons to Israel are found in the Old Testament book bearing his name. He stresses the moral responsibility of the Jews for their captivity and calls for a return to godliness and faith.

Ezekiel, Nissim (1926–   ). Indian poet writing in English. Editor of *Quest,* an influential "little magazine" (1954–1960), he became associate editor of *Imprint,* a Bombay literary monthly. His books of poetry include *A Time to Change* (1951), *Sixty Poems* (1953), *The Third* (1959), and *The Unfinished Man* (1960).

Ezra. In the Old Testament, a Jewish priest who led a band of 1,500 Jews back to Jerusalem from their captivity in Babylon (c. 390 B.C.). The Old Testament book of Ezra, grouped with Nehemiah in early Hebrew canon, tells about the journey and Ezra's attempts to re-establish the temple and morally purify the Jewish community.

Ezzelin, Sir. In Lord Byron's *Lara* (1814), a gentleman who recognizes Lara as the corsair Conrad. A duel ensues, resulting in the death of Ezzelin. See CORSAIR, THE.

F

Fabian. In Shakespeare's TWELFTH NIGHT, a sharp-witted servant of Olivia and a participant in the merry pranks on Malvolio.

Fabian Society. An association of socialists founded in 1883 by a small group of middle-class intellectuals, including George Bernard Shaw and Sidney Webb. The name is derived from Quintus Fabius (275–203 B.C.), a Roman general who won his way against Hannibal by wariness and caution rather than violence and defiance. See CUNCTATOR.

fable. A short tale, usually epigrammatic, with animals, men, gods, and even inanimate objects as characters. The action of a fable illustrates a moral which is usually (but not always) explicitly stated at the end. This moral often attains the force of a proverb. The fable form appears early in man's cultural development, being a common part of the oral folk literature of primitive tribes. It appeared in ancient Egyptian papyri of c. 1500 B.C., and in Greece a recognizable fable was included in the works of Hesiod in the 8th century B.C.; by far the most famous fables are those attributed to AESOP, a Greek slave who lived about 600 B.C. In India the fable also appeared early, the great Indian collection, the *Panchatantra*, having been composed in the 3rd century. Modern fables have been in the main dominated by the genius and style of LA FONTAINE, the great French fabulist of the 17th century, who wrote fables in polished and witty poetry that have been almost universally translated and imitated. Among the best-known modern fabulists are Gay (England, 17th century); Lessing (Germany, 18th century); and James Thurber (U.S., 20th century).

Fable, A (1954). A novel by William FAULKNER. Set in France during World War I, *A Fable* is both an allegory of the passion of Christ and a study of a world that has renounced individualism and chosen submission to authority and the secular values of power and chauvinism. The novel centers on a young corporal, born in a cow-shed, who enlists in the French army, incites a mutiny, and is eventually executed for cowardice. When the gravesite is struck by an enemy shell, his body disappears. The characters of the novel tend to be either personifications of abstractions or modern versions of biblical figures.

Fable for Critics, A (1848). A long verse satire by James Russell LOWELL. The fable of Apollo and his dealings with an American critic is of little interest; the poem's value is in the witty profiles in verse of leading writers. Among the writers satirized in pungent and accurate sketches are Emerson, Longfellow, Hawthorne, Poe, Cooper, Whittier, Holmes, and Lowell himself. The poet makes the important assertion that American literature has come of age.

Fables choisies, mises en vers (Selected fables, set in verse, 1668, 1678–1679, 1694). A collection of verse fables by Jean de LA FONTAINE. Though freely derived from ancient and modern sources, the fables are stamped with La Fontaine's own gently ironic view of life and society. In colorful and ingenious free verse, by means of animal symbols and spirited dialogues, the author propounds a philosophy of sense and moderation, drawing practical lessons from the tribulations of crows, mice, ants, and the like and holding his fellow men up to affectionate ridicule. The fables, however, are not primarily moralistic in intent, but graceful and worldly stories told for the pleasure of telling.

Fables in Slang (1899). A collection of sketches by George ADE that first appeared in the Chicago *Record*. Humorous tales illustrating the common sense of ordinary people, the *Fables* won attention for their rendering of contemporary American speech. Ade's "slang," however, is not slang, but a picturesque prose with numerous racy colloquialisms and many luxuriant figures of speech.

fabliaux (12th–14th centuries). Short humorous tales, often ribald or scurrilous. Highly popular in the Middle Ages, they are situation comedies burlesquing the weaknesses of human nature; women, priests, and gullible fools are often the butts of the buffoonery, which sometimes becomes savagely bitter. The material derives from the oral folk tradition of bawdy anecdotes, practical jokes, and clever tricks of revenge, but the term *fabliau* was first specifically applied to a medieval French literary form, a narrative of 300–400 lines in octosyllabic couplets. About 150 of these are still extant. Similar prose tales became popular all over Europe, as in Boccaccio's *Decameron*. Apparently only a few narratives in the style of the *fabliau* were written in England; the most notable are the ones Chaucer included in his *Canterbury Tales*, such as the tales told by the Miller, the Reeve, the Friar, the Summoner, and the Shipman.

Fabre, Jean Henri (1823–1915). French naturalist. Fabre is the author of *Souvenirs entomologiques* (1879–1907), a 10-volume work on insect life. After his death, his laboratory became a national museum.

Fabriano, Gentile da (c. ´1370–1428). Italian painter. His is a delicate and richly patterned style, Gothic in its attention to detail and incident, but Renaissance in its assimilation of contemporary themes and techniques. His best-known works include *The Flight into Egypt* and the *Adoration of the Magi*.

Fabricius, Gaius (d. c. 270 B.C.). Roman hero, famed for his honesty and incorruptibility. In Rome's struggle with King Pyrrhus of Epirus, he was sent as envoy to the enemy camp for the exchange of prisoners. There he was offered casks of gold and jewels if he would divulge state secrets. When bribery failed, the king ordered a flap of his tent opened, revealing a gigantic elephant only inches from the Roman envoy. Through both trials, Fabricius stood undismayed. When he departed, he left Pyrrhus with a striking example of Roman honor and bravery.

Fâcheux, Les (The Bores, 1661). The first COMÉDIE-BALLET by MOLIÈRE. Written in haste for a royal fete, it is based on satires of Horace and Régnier. The play depicts the maddening interruptions of the hero's courtship by an endless variety of bores, most of them drawn from the author's own observation. The production was enormously successful and started the fashion for *comédie-ballet*.

factotum (Lat., *facere totum,* to do everything). One doing for his employer all sorts of services. Sometimes called a *Johannes Factotum.* Formerly the term meant a busybody, or much the same as our Jack-of-all-trades, and it is in this sense that Robert GREENE used it in his famous reference to Shakespeare:

There is an upstart Crow beautified with our feathers, that with his *Tygers hart wrapt in a Players hyde,* supposes he is as well able to bumbast out a blanke verse as the best of you: but being an absolute *Johannes fac totum,* is in his owne conceit the onely Shake-scene in a countrie. (*Groatsworth of Wit,* 1592)

Facundo (1845). The popular title of a book by Domingo Faustino SARMIENTO. Its full title is *Civilización y barbarie, Vida de Juan Facundo Quiroga.* One of the classics of Hispanic-American literature, the book is partly an attack on the dictatorship of Juan Manuel de ROSAS, partly a somewhat fanciful biography of Facundo, an Argentine political boss, and partly a sociological analysis of Argentine society. Argentina's troubles, Sarmiento believed, stemmed from the conflict between the civilization of the Europeanized urban classes and the barbarism of the ignorant, untamed gauchos, as exemplified by Rosas and Facundo. Written in a vigorous, spontaneous style, the work is also famous for its description of the Argentine pampas and of gaucho types, such as the outlaw and the tracker. *Facundo* was first translated into English by Mary Tyler Mann, wife of Horace Mann, who was a good friend of Sarmiento.

Fadeyev, Aleksandr Aleksandrovich (1901–1956). Russian novelist. His early novel, *The Rout* (*Razgrom;* 1927), also translated as *The Nineteen,* reintroduced the psychological realism of the 19th-century novel into Soviet literature. Fadeyev's novel came after a number of so-called proletarian works, which often were little more than tedious documentation of socialist construction without human characters or concerns. His story of a band of Red partisans fighting in the Far East contains both excitement and psychological portraits of the characters that make them vivid to the reader. Fadeyev's next work, *The Last of the Udegs* (*Poslednyi iz Udege;* 1928–1936), also set during the Civil war in the Far East sector of the fighting front, was not as successful. His third work, *The Young Guard* (*Molodaya gvardiya;* 1945), depicted underground resistance

of young Communists living under the German occupation. The book was criticized for not stressing the leading role of the Communist Party in the resistance; and Fadeyev dutifully revised the work. From 1939 to 1953, he was secretary of the Union of Soviet Writers, a post from which he was moved after Stalin's death. Fadeyev committed suicide in 1956.

Faerie Queene, The (Books I–III, 1590; IV–VI, 1596). An allegorical epic poem by Edmund SPENSER. *The Faerie Queene* was conceived as a work of 12 books, each of which was to have portrayed, in the person of its leading knight, one of the 12 private moral virtues; the work as a whole was to be unified by the figure of Prince Arthur, the "image of a brave knight," in whom all these virtues were perfected. In the prefatory letter to Sir Walter Raleigh, Spenser indicated that, if the first 12 books were well received, he would go on to "frame the other part of politic virtues" in Arthur after he became king. However, only 6 books of 12 cantos each and 2 additional cantos on Mutability (publ. 1609) were published, the other books, if they existed, possibly having been burned in the fire that destroyed Spenser's castle at Kilcoman in 1598.

Gloriana, the Faerie Queene, signifies both the abstract concept of Glory and Queen Elizabeth in particular. Drawing heavily from the chivalric romances, Spenser has Prince Arthur see her in a vision and

The Red Cross Knight (*The Faerie Queene,* 1598 ed.).

determine to "seek her out in Faeryland." Gloriana is holding her annual 12-day feast, on each day of which one of the 12 adventures which were to form the 12 proposed books was to begin. Following the traditional epic form, *The Faerie Queene* begins not with the scene of the feast and the begging of the first knight for a boon, but *in medias res,* with the knight already setting out on his adventure.

As a religio-political allegory of the times, *The Faerie Queene* presents aspects of Roman Catholicism in the evil figures of the false Duessa and the wicked enchanter Archimago (Bks. I and II), and attacks the Catholic emperor Philip of Spain, England's greatest enemy, as the tyrant Grantorto (Bk. V); Duessa, executed by Queen Mercilla (Elizabeth) in Book V, here figures as the Catholic Mary, Queen of Scots. The moral allegory is explored in the trials and temptations undergone by the knights representing the virtues. The spiritual allegory of man's quest for salvation is carried on throughout by the structure of the chivalric quest-motif. In each book, the leading knight is associated with a particular virtue.

Book I: The Legend of the Red Cross Knight, or of Holiness. The RED CROSS KNIGHT (Holiness), having put on the Christian armor mentioned by St. Paul, is sent by Gloriana to rescue the parents of the virgin UNA (Truth), who have been imprisoned and their kingdom laid waste by a Dragon. With Una the Knight comes to the den of Error, a monster half woman and half serpent; after a dreadful battle Error is vanquished. They then meet with ARCHIMAGO (Hypocrisy), a seemingly pious, aged man, and spend the night in his hut. There the Red Cross Knight is subjected to dreams that make him believe Una false, and he abandons her. He comes upon the Saracen knight Sansfoy, accompanied by his lady Fidessa (DUESSA, Falsehood). The Red Cross Knight slays the Saracen and is beguiled by the lies of Fidessa. Thinking to make a garland for her head he plucks a branch from a tree, which bleeds, and which reveals itself to be Fradubio (the Doubter), who had been transformed into a tree by Duessa. Meanwhile Una, following her Knight, meets a Lion, who afterward attends her. She spends the night in the hut of Abessa (Superstition), daughter of Corceca (Blind devotion). Kirkrapine (Churchrobber) comes to bring his plunder to his mistress Abessa, but is slain by the Lion. Una travels on, followed by Archimago in disguise as the Red Cross Knight. He overtakes her and they meet Sansloy, who attacks the disguised Archimago and exposes him, and takes Una off to a wild forest. The real Red Cross Knight, by this time, has come with Duessa to the House of Pride, magnificent in appearance but built on a foundation of sand, and ruled by Queen Lucifera (Pride, and chief of the Seven Deadly Sins). Sansjoy arrives and does battle with the Red Cross Knight, who would have killed him but for the magic intervention of Duessa, who causes Sansjoy to disappear and carries him in the car of Night to the Infernal regions, where he is healed of his wounds by Aesculapius. Meanwhile Una, being attacked by Sansloy, is rescued by a troop of fauns and satyrs. Sir Satyrane (Natural Chivalry) finds her and accompanies her on her journey. They meet Archimago disguised as a pilgrim, who tells them that the Red Cross Knight is dead.

Duessa, having returned from her journey to the Underworld, persuades the Red Cross Knight to drink from an enchanted pool, which robs him of his strength. He is taken captive by the giant Orgoglio (Arrogant pride), who also makes Duessa his mistress. Una learns of her hero's plight, and meeting by chance Prince Arthur, persuades him to go to the Knight's rescue. Arthur slays the giant, strips Duessa of her rich robes and reveals her as a loathsome hag. The Red Cross Knight and Una travel on and soon meet Despair, who tempts the Knight to end his life. He is rescued by Una, who brings him to the house of Holiness to be healed. After this he and Una journey to Eden, the land of her captive parents, and after a three-day battle the Knight slays the Dragon. He and Una are betrothed, but before the marriage can take place Archimago, disguised as a messenger, brings a letter from Duessa, who claims that the Knight is betrothed to her. Their falseness is revealed, Archimago is captured and bound in prison, and Una and her Knight are married.

Book II: The Legend of Sir Guyon, or of Temperance. Archimago, having escaped from his confinement, meets Sir Guyon (Temperance) and a Palmer (Sobriety or Prudence), and tells them that the Red Cross Knight has shamefully attacked a virgin; to insure the desired effect, he has disguised Duessa as a weeping virgin and placed her beside the road, and she complains of her dreadful treatment at the hands of the Knight. They travel on and soon they meet the Red Cross Knight, with whom Sir Guyon almost comes to blows before each recognizes the Christian emblem on the other's shield.

Sir Guyon and the Palmer discover the dying Amavia, who tells them how her dead husband, Sir Mordant, had succumbed to the wiles of the enchantress Acrasia (Intemperance), who lives in the Bower of Bliss on the Wandering Island. Amavia dies, and Guyon swears vengeance. They come to a castle in which live three half-sisters, Medina (Golden Mean), Perissa (Excess), and Elissa (Deficiency). Sir Guyon entrusts to Medina Amavia's infant, which he has named Ruddymane because its hands are stained with its mother's blood. He then meets raging Furor and his mother, the hag Occasion; he silences Occasion, whose constant ranting spurs Furor to anger, by putting a lock on her tongue, and binds Furor with a hundred iron chains. Phaon (or Phedon), the young squire whom Furor had been tormenting, tells how through jealousy and rage he had slain his innocent sweetheart, Claribell, and poisoned Philemon, the friend who deceived him. Pyrocles (Fiery anger) arrives, and he and Sir Guyon fight. Brought to his knees, Pyrocles begs for mercy, and is spared. He unbinds Occasion and Furor, but soon falls a victim to them himself.

Cymocles (Loose living), hearing that his brother Pyrocles is dead, leaves the Bower of Bliss and his mistress Acrasia and travels to find Sir Guyon. He is ferried into the Idle Lake by Phaedria (Wantonness), whose dalliance with him soon makes him forget about revenge. Taking him to the Floating Island, she lulls him to sleep, and returns to the strand where she encounters Sir Guyon seeking a ferry. They meet the awakened and enraged Cymocles, who attacks Guyon, but Phaedria stops their battle. Meanwhile Pyrocles, inflamed by Furor, tries to end his torments by drowning himself in the Idle Lake, but is saved and healed of his fiery wounds by Archimago.

Sir Guyon comes to the den of Mammon, who takes him to the House of Riches, which adjoins Hell. He tries to tempt Guyon to covet his treasure, but the knight refuses all temptations, and asks to be taken back to earth. He is found in a trance by the Palmer just before Pyrocles and Cymocles arrive, bent on vengeance. Thinking him dead, they are about to strip him of his armor when Prince Arthur appears. After a dreadful battle in which both Pyrocles and Cymocles are killed, Guyon revives from his trance and he and Arthur travel to the castle of Alma (the Soul), besieged by the enemies of Temperance. The leader of this rabble is Maleger, the incarnation of evil passions; his twelve troops typify the seven deadly sins and the lusts of the five senses. Arthur gives him terrific battle, but each time Maleger is cast to the ground he rises up even more powerful. Finally Arthur remembers that Earth is Maleger's mother, and restores him each time he falls; so Arthur squeezes the life out of him and throws him in a lake.

After a perilous sea journey Sir Guyon and the Palmer arrive at the Bower of Bliss, where they capture Acrasia in a net, destroy the Bower, and restore to their normal shape the lovers whom Acrasia had transformed into beasts.

Book III: The Legend of Britomart, or of Chastity. Sir Guyon sends the captive Acrasia to the Faery Court, and he and Arthur travel on in search of adventure. Meeting an unknown knight, Guyon charges, but is unhorsed, for the strange knight is the lady Britomart (Chastity), who wields an enchanted lance. When Arthur and Guyon go off to rescue the fair Florimell, pursued by a lustful forester, Britomart remains behind, and soon comes to the Castle Joyous, where she finds six knights attacking one. She learns that the lady of the castle demands the love of every knight who comes that way, and if he loves another he is forced to do battle with the six knights. She subdues them and enters the castle, where Queen Malecasta (Lust), thinking her a man, tries to seduce her.

Meanwhile Arthur's squire, Timias, separated from his master, is ambushed by the lustful forester and his brothers, whom he kills in a bloody battle. Badly injured himself, he is discovered by the virgin huntress Belphoebe. She cures his wounds with herbs, but he pines away from love of her. Florimell, fleeing the forester, comes to the cottage of a wicked witch, whose churlish son lusts after the fair virgin. Again she flees, pursued by a monster sent by the witch, and reaching the sea escapes in a boat in which a fisherman is sleeping. The witch, however, then creates a counterfeit Florimell, who is borne away one day by Braggadocchio, only to have her taken from him by another knight. The true Florimell, out on the sea, resists the advances of the lustful fisherman; her cries bring the help of Proteus, who takes her to his bower at the bottom of the sea.

Meanwhile Sir Satyrane meets the libertine Sir Paridell, and they come to the castle of Malbecco (Jealousy), an aged miser, and his beautiful young wife Hellenore. A cunning seducer, Paridell soon persuades Hellenore to run away with him, but before leaving her husband she steals part of his money and sets fire to the rest. Malbecco, torn between pursuing his wife and rescuing his burning money, knows not what to do. Finally he sets off in search of Hellenore, whom Paridell has by now abandoned and who has gone to live with the satyrs. After watching the satyrs with Hellenore Malbecco is consumed with jealousy, and tries to persuade her to return to him, but she refuses. He returns to his buried treasure, only to find that it has been stolen by the servant of Braggadocchio. Mad with jealousy and fury, he casts himself from a cliff—but he is so consumed by wrath that there is nothing left of him but an airy sprite. He crawls into a cave, where he dwells forever in misery.

Britomart comes upon Scudamore (Shield of Love), who is prostrated with grief that his beloved Amoret is a captive of the enchanter Busirane, who torments her because she will not renounce her love for Scudamore. Britomart promises to rescue Amoret, and she and Scudamore ride to Busirane's enchanted castle, which is guarded by a fire through which only Britomart is able to pass. Having found in the empty but lavishly decorated castle an iron door that will not open, she waits; and at midnight the door flies open and a strange Masque of Cupid passes through it. When the door opens at midnight the next night, she rushes in, finding the room empty save for Amoret, bound to a pillar, and Busirane. The enchanter and Britomart fight, and Busirane is subdued. He is forced to undo his enchantments and restore Amoret to health, and is himself bound in chains.

Book IV: The Legend of Cambel and Triamond, or of Friendship. Amoret and Britomart, in search of Scudamore, meet the knights Blandamour and Paridell, accompanied by Duessa and Ate (Dissension), a foul old hag. Later, Blandamour and Paridell come upon Scudamore, and Paridell attacks him but is badly beaten. Ate lyingly tells Scudamore that she has seen Amoret false to him with Britomart. At this point arrives Sir Ferraugh with the false Florimell he had taken from Braggadocchio. Blandamour, desiring the lovely false Florimell, rides against her knight and captures her. Paridell, egged on by envy and the querulous counsel of Ate, demands that Blandamour share Florimell with him, and the two erstwhile friends come to blows. Later, they come upon the knights Cambel and Triamond and their ladies Cambina and Canace. Canace, a fair and modest lady loved by many, had refused to love any of her suitors; in order to end the strife among her would-be lovers, her brother Cambel agreed to do battle with the stoutest three, the victor to have his sister. The three bravest and boldest were the triplets Priamond, Diamond, and Triamond, sons of Agape. Cambel, protected by a magic ring, was able to slay both Priamond and Diamond; however, their fairy mother had been granted by the Fates that the spirits of the first of her two sons to die would enter the body of the third, so that when Cambel gave the death-stroke to Triamond it failed to kill him. Neither knight could kill the other, and finally their battle was ended by the appearance of the triplets' sister Cambina, who brought peace. Canace was married to Triamond, and Cambina to Cambel.

Together, all agree to go on to the Tournament held by Sir Satyrane in honor of the lost Florimell, whose golden girdle he had found and now offers as a prize to the lady judged the loveliest. The false Florimell is acclaimed the fairest, but the magic cestus, which will girdle only the waists of the virtuous, will not stay fastened.

Meanwhile Scudamore meets Artegal disguised, and both swear vengeance on Britomart, whom they believe has wronged them. They meet her but are both quickly unhorsed. Artegal, fighting her on foot, strikes off her helmet, and seeing her face falls into a rapture of love. Britomart recognizes Artegal's face as the image of her true love she had seen in her magic mirror, and they become betrothed.

The true Florimell, imprisoned in a dungeon by Proteus, still rejects his advances and is true to her beloved Marinell—who has no use for women, and is still suffering from a wound given him by Britomart. Finally his wound is cured by Tryphon, and he and his mother Cymodoce go to the house of Proteus for a great banquet. Marinell chances to overhear Florimell's complaint of her love of him from her dungeon, suddenly falls in love with her, and ultimately has her released.

Book V: The Legend of Artegal, or of Justice. Irena (Ireland) goes to the court of the Faerie Queene to complain of the tyrant Grantorto (Great wrong), who withholds her inheritance. Gloriana sends Artegal (Justice) and with him her own groom Talus (Iron Man). On their journey Artegal kills Pollente, a Saracen who stations himself on the Bridge Perilous and kills and robs travelers, bestowing the spoils on his daughter Munera. Talus then forces his way into the castle stronghold, casts Munera over the wall and into the river, burns the spoils, and destroys the castle utterly. On their way to the wedding of Florimell and Marinell, Artegal and his groom meet Braggadocchio and the false Florimell. Artegal changes armor with Braggadocchio and wins the tournament thus clad. Later, wearing his own armor as victor of the tournament, Braggadocchio presents the false Florimell; Artegal then proclaims Braggadocchio a fraud and confronts the false Florimell with her true image. The false Florimell promptly melts away and vanishes.

Artegal and Talus rescue Terpine from a band of Amazons about to hang him, and besiege the Amazon city. Radigund, the Queen, offers to meet Artegal in single combat, the winner to become the servant of the loser. Artegal, struck with pity at the sight of Radigund's beautiful face, surrenders to her, and is made her thrall. Talus, however, escapes and brings news of Artegal's plight to Britomart, who kills Radigund and frees Artegal. Traveling on, Artegal meets Prince Arthur rescuing Samient, handmaiden to Queen Mercilla (Mercy). On their way to the Queen they encounter the robber Malengin (Guile), who tries to escape by turning himself into various animals, but is captured and killed by Talus. Arriving at the palace, the knights find Queen Mercilla about to dispense justice; Duessa is brought to the bar and charged with having tried to usurp Mercilla's crown, judged guilty, and executed. At this time appear at the palace two sons of Belge, whose land is held by the tyrant Geryoneo, asking Mercilla for aid. Prince Arthur goes off to rescue Belge, slays the

monster, and restores her to her rightful kingdom. Artegal completes his original quest, and frees Irena and conquers Grantorto.

Book VI: The Legend of Calidore, or of Courtesy. Sir Calidore (Courtesy) in pursuit of the Blatant Beast (Slander), finds the fair Pastorella, the fosterdaughter of a shepherd, and falls in love with her. Finally he rescues her from brigands and takes her to castle Belgard, ruled by Sir Bellamoure and his wife the fair Claribell. Calidore leaves Pastorella there and continues on his quest for the Beast. Through a distinctive birthmark Pastorella is revealed to be the long-lost daughter of Bellamoure and Claribell. Calidore conquers the Blatant Beast and binds it in chains.

Fafner. In Wagner's DER RING DES NIBELUNGEN, one of the giants who built Valhalla for Wotan. He and his brother Fasolt accept Alberich's golden ring in place of Freya, the price originally agreed on. Fafner kills Fasolt and changes himself into a dragon to guard the hoard which is now his. He is killed by Siegfried. In the Norse sources, Fafnir (not Fafner) has no brother and is guarding Andvari's gold as a venom-breathing dragon from the start.

Fagin. In Charles Dickens' OLIVER TWIST, a villainous old Jew who leads a gang of thieves, mostly boys. These he trains to pick pockets and pilfer. Fagin assumes a suave and fawning manner but is grasping and full of cruelty. He is ultimately arrested, tried, and condemned to death. Fagin is one of Dickens' most famous characters.

Faguet, Emile (1847–1916). French literary critic and professor of literature at the Sorbonne. Faguet published several volumes of French literary history and such critical studies as *Les Grands Maîtres du XVII siècle* (1885).

Fahrenheit, Gabriel Daniel (1686–1736). German physicist who devised the thermometer scale that bears his name. On the Fahrenheit thermometer, the freezing and boiling points of water are designated as 32° and 212° above the zero of its scale.

Fairfax, Edward (d. 1635). English poet and translator. Fairfax is remembered as the author of the first complete translation of Tasso's *Jerusalem Delivered.* Published in 1600, it was called *Godfrey of Bulloigne, or the Recoverie of Jerusalem,* and was written in heroic couplets and characterized by rich and imagistic language. Fairfax also wrote eclogues, most of which have never been published.

Fairfax, Thomas. 3rd Baron **Fairfax of Cameron** (1612–1671). English military leader and statesman. As commander-in-chief of the Parliamentary forces, he organized the New Model Army and defeated Charles I at Naseby. Less able in civilian affairs, he became an instrument in the hands of stronger men and reluctantly acquiesced to the execution of the king. He later participated in negotiations for the Restoration and headed the commission dispatched to Charles II at The Hague.

Fair God, The (1873). A historical novel by Lew WALLACE. The book is set in Mexico during the conquest by Cortez, when Montezuma futilely tried to resist the Spaniards. The fair god is Quetzalcoatl, Aztec god of the air. The result of 30 years of research and writing, the book went through 20 editions in 10 years.

Fair Maid of Perth, The (1828). A novel by Sir Walter SCOTT set in the 14th century. The Fair Maid is Catherine Glover, daughter of a glovemaker of Perth, who kisses Henry Smith, the armorer, in his sleep on St. Valentine's Day. Smith proposes marriage, and although Catherine refuses at first, she becomes his wife at the end of the novel. The concurrent plot is the romance of Prince James, son of Robert III of Scotland, and LOUISE, THE GLEEMAIDEN.

Fair Maid of the West, The: Parts I and II (c. 1631). A romantic drama by Thomas HEYWOOD. It deals with the love of Bess Bridges, a gallant and virtuous barkeep, for Spencer, an adventurer about to embark for the Azores. Hearing that he is dead, she outfits a ship and sails off to bring his body home. She captures a Spanish vessel on which Spencer is being held prisoner, and the two sail for Morocco where the dark King Mullisheg is much taken with the white girl. However, Bess manages to gain the king's consent to her marriage with Spencer.

In Part II, the king tries to seduce Bess but she and Spencer escape, are recaptured, are released, then shipwrecked and separated. Penniless, Bess is rescued by the duke of Florence who tries to make love to her. Eventually though, Spencer turns up and the lovers are reunited.

Faithful Shepherdess, The (1609). A pastoral play by John FLETCHER. (See BEAUMONT AND FLETCHER.) Clorin, the faithful shepherdess, tends the grave of her dead lover and gathers medicinal herbs to benefit mankind. To her is drawn Thenot, who adores her for her loyalty and pines for her so long as she remains indifferent to his pleas. At the opposite pole of behavior are the lusty Amarillis and Cloe, for whom no lover is too forward, and the conniving lechery of the Sullen Shepherd. After many complications in which all the shepherds' and shepherdesses' reactions are tested in various situations, virtue and chastity triumph;—lust and lechery are repudiated.

fakir. In Arabic-speaking Muslim lands, a religious beggar or mendicant. Many are wanderers who attract attention and alms by performing such acts of austerity as lying on beds of nails; others perform menial offices connected, for example, with burials and the cleaning of mosques.

Falerina. In the ORLANDO INNAMORATO of Boiardo, a witch who presides over the enchanted garden of Orgagna. Here Orlando finds a book that teaches him how to break Falerina's enchantments, and as a result she is forced to do his bidding for a time.

Falerno. An Italian sweet wine. It was grown in what the ancients called *Falernus Ager*, a fertile district some 20 miles north of Naples. It was celebrated by Horace.

Faliero, Marino. See MARINO FALIERO.

Falkberget, Johan Petter (1879–   ). Norwegian novelist. The novel cycle *Christianus Sextus* (6 vols., 1927–1935), his most important work, is set in the mining town of Röros. Although his own early experiences in the mines gave Falkberget an understanding of hardship and suffering, his work is marked by Christian faith and a firm optimism.

Falkenhayn, Erich von (1861–1922). Chief of the German General Staff (1914–1916). The suc-

cessor to Helmuth von Moltke, he was dismissed after the unsuccessful attack at Verdun and replaced by Paul von Hindenburg.

Falkner, John Meade (1858–1932). English novelist and antiquarian. *The Lost Stradivarius* (1895) is a story of demoniacal possession in a musical setting. *Moonfleet* (1898) is a boys' adventure tale about smugglers. *The Nebuly Coat* (1903) is a romance in which all Falkner's interests—music, architecture, church history and heraldry—are skillfully combined.

Fall, The (La Chute; 1956). A short novel by Albert CAMUS. A former Parisian lawyer explains to a stranger in an Amsterdam bar his current profession of judge-penitent. His bitter honesty prevented him first from winning his own self-esteem through good deeds, then from exhausting his own self-condemnation through debauchery. Knowing that no man is ever innocent, he is still trying to forestall personal judgment by confession, by judging others, and by avoiding any situation demanding action.

Falla [y Matheu], Manuel [Maria] de (1876–1946). Spanish composer. Spain's first major composer of instrumental music since the 17th century, Falla studied in Paris, was influenced by the impressionist technique of Debussy, and developed a brilliant and individual style of orchestration. Aside from *Noches en los Jardines de España* (*Nights in the Gardens of Spain*, 1915) and the *Concerto for Harpsichord* (1926), his best known music, all of it Andalusian in coloring, was written for the stage. His operas include *La Vida Breve* (*Life is Short*, 1905) and EL RETABLO DE MAESE PEDRO (*Master Peter's Puppet Show*, 1923); his ballets include *El Amor Brujo* (*Love, the Magician*, 1915) and *El Sombrero de Tres Picos* (*The Three-Cornered Hat*), the latter based on a comedy of Alarcón. Falla's dramatic cantata *Atlántida* was posthumously completed and performed in 1963.

Fallada, Hans. Pen name of **Rudolf Ditzen** (1893–1947). German novelist. Inclined toward EXPRESSIONISM in his youth, he later became known as a sympathetic depictor of the lower classes. He wrote the best-selling *Kleiner Mann—was nun?* (*Little Man, What Now?*, 1932), a novel about Germany during the depression of the 1920's and 1930's.

Fallersleben, Hoffmann von. See August Heinrich HOFFMANN.

Fall of the House of Usher, The (1839). A tale by Edgar Allan POE. A friend visits Roderick Usher in his old family mansion. The two read together, the friend attempting to dispel Roderick's gloom. Usher plays strange music of his own composition and shows his friend one of his paintings. Although his twin sister, Madeline, has been placed in the family vault dead, Usher is convinced she lives. When she suddenly appears in her blood-stained shroud, brother and sister fall dead together. The visitor, hurriedly departing, turns to see the house split asunder and sink into the tarn.

Falls of Princes. A very long poem by John LYDGATE, written in rhyme royal between 1430 and 1438, and first printed in 1494. Based on Boccaccio's *De Casibus Virorum Illustrium*, the poem deals with great men from the time of Richard II (1377–1399) and their rise to and decline from fame and power, subject to the fluctuations of fortune. The ghost of each appears before the poet and relates his sufferings.

Falstaff, Sir John. The most famous comic character created by Shakespeare. He appears in HENRY IV: PARTS I and II, and THE MERRY WIVES OF WINDSOR, and his death is given some attention in *Henry V.* Falstaff is a monumentally self-indulgent braggart, the culmination of a line that can be traced back to Plautus' *Miles Gloriosus* and the *capitano* of the *commedia dell'arte.* Falstaff is totally unapologetic: he revels in his lechery and chicanery, lies without scruple and, when caught in a lie, unabashedly seeks to turn everything to his own advantage. But his knavery is so engaging and his lust for life so keen that he has become one of the favorite characters of dramatic literature. He holds forth at the Boar's Head Tavern with a rascally crew that includes Bardolph, Nym, Peto, Pistol, and Prince Hal's companion Poins. Later, commissioned by the king to recruit for the army, he assembles the following company: Ralph Mouldy, Simon Shadow, Thomas Wart, Francis Feeble, and Peter Bull-calf.

familiar. A spirit bound to its master's service by a supernatural tie. It is usually represented in the form of a small animal such as a cat, mouse, or poodle.

Family Reunion, The (1939). A drama in verse by T. S. ELIOT. Combining elements of social comedy and Greek tragedy, it deals with the return of Harry, Lord Monchensey, to his English family home for the birthday of his old mother, Amy. The family think Harry is behaving oddly. Only his wise aunt, Agatha, understands that he has murdered his wife and is seeing the Eumenides, or avenging furies. She tells him that when he was born his father wanted to kill his mother, and would have done so if Agatha had not dissuaded him. Harry is bound to suffer from the family curse, especially in the decaying old family house. Agatha presides over Harry's flight; over the disintegration of the rest of the family; and over Amy's death. Like Sir Henry Harcourt-Reilly and Julia in *The Cocktail Party*, she serves as Eliot's mouthpiece.

fancy. In English romantic aesthetic theory, the clever, playful faculty of mind that combines sensations, observations, impressions—the various materials of art—and brings them to bear in a work of art. It is distinguished from IMAGINATION, notably by S. T. Coleridge in his BIOGRAPHIA LITERARIA, in that fancy does not transcend its material to produce truly inspired literature.

Faneuil Hall. A market house containing an assembly hall in Boston, Mass., given in 1742 to his fellow citizens by the merchant and slave trader Peter Faneuil (1700–1743). After the fire of 1761, it was rebuilt by the city and became the meeting place of American patriots during the Revolution. It is now remembered as "the cradle of liberty."

Fangen, Ronald August (1895–1946). Norwegian novelist, playwright, and critic. In all his work Fangen speaks eloquently and soberly of a Christian solution to the world's problems; he rejects belief in the communist and materialist doctrines popular between the wars. Among his plays are *Synde fald* (1920), *Den forjoettede dag* (1926), and *Som det kunde ha gått* (1925). His novels include *Nogen*

unge mennesker (1929), *Duel* (1932), *Pà bar bunn* (1936), and *En lysets engel* (*Both are My Cousins*, 1945).

Fanshawe (1828). A novel by Nathaniel HAWTHORNE, published anonymously. Fanshawe, a pale, serious student, falls in love with Ellen Langdon, the ward of Dr. Melmoth, president of Harley College. Rescuing her from an attempted seduction, Fanshawe gives Ellen up to the man he knows she loves, and soon dies. The college and its environs are modeled on Hawthorne's *alma mater*, Bowdoin College, in Maine. Influenced by Scott and the Gothic novel, *Fanshawe* illustrates Hawthorne's developing technique.

Fantine. One of the principal characters in Victor Hugo's novel LES MISÉRABLES. She is the mother of Cosette.

Faraday, Michael (1791–1867). English chemist and physicist. As a journeyman bookbinder he heard a lecture by Sir Humphry Davy who impressed him so deeply that he resolved to turn all his attention to the natural sciences. He became one of the greatest chemists of his time and a pioneer in the young science of electricity. His publications are numerous. His monograph on candles deserves to rank as a classic in popular scientific literature.

Farange, Maisie. See WHAT MAISIE KNEW.

farce. An exaggerated type of comedy, full of ludicrous incidents and expressions. The word is the OFr. *farce*, stuffing (from Lat. *farcire*, to stuff); originally meaning a passage in the vernacular inserted in a Latin text or liturgy, the farce in medieval France came to resemble the earlier FABLIAUX, but specifically for dramatic representation. Like *La Farce de maistre Pierre* PATHELIN, the most famous, most farces were written in octosyllabic couplets, and burlesqued the foibles and vices of ordinary life, setting the pattern for future French comedy.

Farewell Address (Sept. 17, 1796). The address prepared by George WASHINGTON just before his retirement from the presidency. Probably written with the aid of Hamilton and Madison, it was never delivered publicly. In it Washington explained his reasons for refusing to run for a third term and warned against the dangers of the party system. He advised the U.S. to avoid permanent alliances with foreign nations and to trust to "temporary alliances for extraordinary emergencies." It did not contain the phrase "entangling alliances," with which it is often associated and which appeared in Jefferson's first inaugural address.

Farewell to Arms, A (1929). A novel by Ernest HEMINGWAY. It deals with the romance of Frederic HENRY, an American lieutenant in the Italian ambulance service during World War I, and Catherine Barkley, an English nurse. She becomes pregnant, and after the disastrous Italian retreat from Caporetto (superbly described by Hemingway), Henry deserts, joins Catherine, and escapes with her to Switzerland, where she dies in childbirth. This is one of the best-known novels depicting the tragedy and destruction of World War I.

Far from the Madding Crowd (1874). A novel by Thomas HARDY. Bathsheba Everdene is loved by Gabriel Oak, a young farmer who becomes bailiff of the farm she inherits; by William Boldwood, who owns a neighboring farm; and by Sergeant Troy, a handsome, inconsiderate young adventurer. She marries Troy, who mistreats her and squanders her money. When he leaves her and is presumed drowned at sea, Bathsheba becomes engaged to Boldwood. Troy however reappears, and is murdered by Boldwood, who goes mad as a result of his action and is sent to an institution instead of being sentenced. Bathsheba then marries Gabriel, the steadiest and most faithful of her three suitors.

Fargue, Léon-Paul (1876–1947). French poet. His early works reflect the influence of Mallarmé's symbolist salons. Fargue moves through a surrealist concern with the reality of the dream world to an eerily melancholy expression of the poetry of modern city life. His style varies from regular verse to poetically rich prose in such works as *Tancrède* (1911), *Espaces* (1921), *D'après Paris* (1931), and *La Piéton de Paris* (1939).

Farigoule, Louis. See Jules ROMAINS.

Farinelli (real name **Carlo Broschi**; 1705–1782). Italian castrato soprano, the most famous singer of the 18th century.

Farmer George. King George III of England (1738–1820), who reigned from 1760 to his death; so called from his farmerlike manners, taste, dress, and amusements.

A better farmer ne'er brushed dew from lawn.
—Byron, *Vision of Judgment*

Farnol, [John] Jeffery (1878–1952). English writer of popular historical romances, such as *The Broad Highway* (1910) and *The Amateur Gentleman* (1913).

Farquhar, George (1678–1707). English comic dramatist of the early 18th century. His plays reveal the growing taste for sentiment, which was beginning to replace the brilliance and wit of the Restoration. His best-known plays are THE BEAUX' STRATAGEM, *The Recruiting Officer* (1706) and *The Constant Couple* (1699).

Farrago, Captain. See MODERN CHIVALRY.

Farrar, Geraldine (1882–). American dramatic soprano. She knew many roles but was most famous as Carmen and Madama Butterfly. She acted in several silent films. *Such Sweet Compulsion* (1938) is her autobiography.

Farrell, James T[homas] (1904–). American novelist. Known for his lengthy studies of lower-middle-class Irish-Catholic life, Farrell was born in the South Side section of Chicago, which forms the background for his own works. His stories dealing with STUDS LONIGAN began to appear in 1932; they aroused heated controversy, for Farrell practiced a frankly naturalistic mode of writing that did not hesitate to unveil the crudities of life among the people of his novels. The characters of the novels, which sometimes use a stream-of-consciousness technique, are presented with what is often a sociologist's objectivity. The emphasis is on poverty, religious bigotry, economic inequality, individual frustration, vice, and the destructive influence of environment. Some critics assert that the very dreariness and turgidity of Farrell's style has defeated the author's aim, but others praise the powerful, cumulative effect of personal tragedy that distinguishes Farrell's most famous work; the Studs Lonigan trilogy, which is comprised of *Young Lonigan, The Young Manhood of Studs Lonigan,* and *Judgment Day.* Five other novels concern Danny O'NEILL. Farrell's *Note on Literary Criticism* (1936) is one of the most important literary statements of the "proletarian" point of view of the 1930's. *The Silence of History* (1963) also deals with an Irish-American youth in Chicago in the 1920's.

fasces. In ancient Rome, a symbol of authority. They were bundles of birch or elm rods fastened together by a red strap with the blade of an ax projecting from the bundle. The *fasces* were carried by the left hand, on the left shoulder by the LICTORS who accompanied magistrates. The rods and the ax represented the king's authority to punish or execute criminals. Within the city of Rome, the ax was removed in recognition of the accused's right to appeal to the people in the matter of life and death.

Benito Mussolini's Fascist Party, which controlled Italy from 1922 to 1944, used the *fasces* as its emblem. Fasces have appeared on U.S. coins and adorn many government buildings.

fascism. An authoritarian and totalitarian political system characterized by aggressive nationalism and the absolute sovereignty of the state over individual rights and interests. Its principles were put into practice by Benito MUSSOLINI and his Fascist Party in Italy. See Vilfredo PARETO; NAZI.

Fasolt. See FAFNER.

Fast, Howard (1914–). American novelist and short-story writer. Born in New York City, he is known for his vivid historical novels, many of which espouse radical political causes. *Citizen Tom Paine* (1943) and *Freedom Road* (1944) avowedly grew out of his association with the Communist Party. Fast later broke with communism, describing his disillusionment in *The Naked God* (1957). Among his better-known novels are *The American* (1946), a sympathetic treatment of Governor John Peter Altgeld of Illinois, and *Spartacus* (1958), a portrayal of the Roman revolutionary leader.

Fastnachtsspiel (*Ger.,* Shrovetide-play). A form of simple, often slapstick, comedy with a clear moral message, current in Germany in the 15th and 16th centuries. The earliest example, however, comes from the 13th century, and the origins of the form are thought to go back to spring fertility rites among the Germanic tribes. Hans SACHS is considered to have perfected the form.

fata (*It.,* a fairy). A female supernatural being introduced in Italian medieval romance, usually under the sway of DEMOGORGON. In ORLANDO INNAMORATO we meet with the "Fata Morgana" (see MORGAN LE FAY); in Boiardo, with the "Fata Silvanella," and others.

Also called *Fata Morgana* is a sort of mirage in which objects are reflected in the sea, and sometimes on a kind of aerial screen high above it. It is occasionally seen in the neighborhood of the Straits of Messina, and named from Morgan le Fay, who was fabled by the Norman settlers in England to dwell in Calabria.

fatal raven. The emblem on the Danish standard, *Landeyda,* which was consecrated to the war god Odin. It was said to have been woven and embroidered in one noontide by the daughters of Regner Lodbrok, son of Sigurd. If the Danish arms were destined to defeat, the raven hung his wings; if victory was to attend them, he stood erect and soaring, as if inviting the warriors to follow.

Fates, the (*Gr.*, moirai; *Lat.*, parcae or fata). In Greek mythology, 3 daughters of Nyx (Night). They controlled the destinies of men. Originally birth-goddesses, the Fates came to be represented as three old women who spun the thread of life. They were identified by Hesiod as Clotho (or Kloto), who spun the thread; Lachesis, who measured it out; and Atropos, who cut it. Generally, even Zeus himself is subject to their decisions.

Father, The (1887). A play by August STRINDBERG. Dealing with the psychological antagonism between men and women, *The Father* centers on the Captain and his inability to prevent the female members of his family from subjugating him. His wife, Laura, torments him by leading him to suspect that Bertha is not his daughter, spreads rumors that he is insane, and finally succeeds in driving him mad and to his death.

Father Brown. A Catholic priest and detective, hero of a series of stories by G. K. CHESTERTON.

Fathers and Children or **Fathers and Sons** (*Ottzy i deti;* 1862). A novel by Ivan TURGENEV. it portrays the conflicts between the older aristocratic generation and the new democratic intelligentsia in Russia during the 1860's. The chief character is the nihilist BAZAROV, who espouses a strictly materialistic attitude toward life. His chief adversary is Pavel Petrovich KIRSANOV, an uncle of Bazarov's friend Arkadi, who upholds the aristocratic traditions in the face of Bazarov's ridicule. The novel, which is considered one of Turgenev's finest works, originally aroused widespread controversy in Russia, with both radicals and conservatives denying the accuracy of the portrayal of Bazarov. One side considered it slandered the younger generation; the other accused Turgenev of presenting too favorable a picture of the nihilist. Only Dmitri Pisarev among the radicals accepted the portrayal of Bazarov as accurate.

Father William. A humorous ballad by Lewis CARROLL appearing in ALICE'S ADVENTURES IN WONDERLAND; it is a parody of *The Old Man's Comforts* (1799), a poem by Robert Southey.

Fatima. (1) According to the Koran, the daughter of Muhammad, and one of the 4 perfect women. The other three are Khadijah, the prophet's first wife; Mary, daughter of Imran; and Asia, wife of the Pharaoh drowned in the Red Sea.

(2) The name usually given to the last wife of BLUEBEARD.

(3) A female hermit in the *Arabian Nights* (1548) who was murdered by the African magician as a part of his schemes against Aladdin.

Faulconbridge, Philip. In Shakespeare's KING JOHN, the natural son of Richard I (Coeur de Lion). Leader of John's forces, he is a blunt, fiercely patriotic Englishman who sums up his philosophy in his final speech:

> This England never did, nor never shall.
> Lie at the proud foot of a conqueror,
> But when it first did help to wound itself.
> . . . Nought shall make us rue,
> If England to itself do rest but true.

Faulkner, William (1897–1962). American novelist and short-story writer. Faulkner, who was awarded the Nobel Prize in 1949, is generally recognized as a great American novelist. In his novels, many of them set in the imaginary YOKNAPATAWPHA COUNTY, he created a complex social structure within which he explored the burden of the Southern past, the inability of the Southern aristocracy to meet the demands of modern life, the relations between Negro and white, and the alienation and loneliness that so beset 20th-century man. But more than this he drew an immense gallery of characters, vivid and unforgettable.

Faulkner came from an old Mississippi family, and elements of the family past appear in his books. His great-grandfather Col. William C. Faulkner (who later spelled his name Falkner) wrote a popular romance, *The White Rose of Memphis* (1880). His violent death in 1889 furnished his great-grandson with material for SARTORIS and THE UNVANQUISHED, in which Colonel John SARTORIS is modeled on Colonel Falkner. In 1918, William Faulkner enlisted in the Canadian Air Force but did not see active service. After the war he briefly attended the University of Mississippi and worked at many odd jobs. He published a book of verse, *The Marble Faun*, in 1924 and, with the help of Sherwood Anderson, secured the publication of his first novel, *Soldier's Pay*, the following year. Neither this book nor his second novel, *Mosquitoes* (1927), are considered among Faulkner's best.

In *Sartoris* (1929), Faulkner created Yoknapatawpha County, which was to be the setting for most of his subsequent works. In the same year appeared THE SOUND AND THE FURY, usually considered among Faulkner's masterpieces. Although the styles of the two books are radically different—*The Sound and the Fury* owes much to James Joyce and the stream-of-consciousness technique—both deal with the breakup of old aristocratic Southern families. In As I LAY DYING, Faulkner relates a terrifyingly comic story of a ritualized burial journey. But it was not until SANCTUARY that Faulkner created a sensation and achieved anything like popular success. Faulkner himself did much to mislead the reaction to this novel by suggesting that it was hurriedly written as a mere potboiler. It is true that *Sanctuary* is often grotesquely shocking, but it is, nevertheless, a book of great craft, allegorical in intent.

It was followed by LIGHT IN AUGUST, which relates the agonizing story of Joe Christmas, and the equally brilliant ABSALOM, ABSALOM!, considered by Cleanth Brooks to be Faulkner's best book.

For many critics, *Absalom, Absalom!* marks a high point in Faulkner's development. While *The Unvanquished* has occasionally been highly praised, it is generally considered one of Faulkner's weaker books. THE HAMLET is the first part of the trilogy that now includes *The Town* (1957) and *The Mansion* (1959).

The collection Go DOWN, MOSES AND OTHER STORIES contains the justly famous story *The Bear*. INTRUDER IN THE DUST and REQUIEM FOR A NUN, in some ways a sequel to *Sanctuary,* are generally not thought to be Faulkner at his best. The same judgment has been made of A FABLE, in which Faulkner left Yoknapatawpha County for the French army in World War I. Other works are THESE THIRTEEN, *A Green Bough* (verse, 1933), *Doctor Martino and Other*

Stories (1934), *Pylon* (1935), THE WILD PALMS, KNIGHT'S GAMBIT, and *Big Woods* (stories, 1955).

In the 1930's, many critics saw only the melodramatic violence in Faulkner's writing. It was not until Malcolm Cowley's introduction to *The Portable Faulkner* in 1946 that the continuity and consistency in Faulkner's work, as well as his concern with "the tragic fable of Southern history," were really seen and understood.

Faunus. In Roman mythology, a rural deity, grandson of Saturn and father of Lavinia's father Latinus. He, as well as Silvanus, came to be more and more identified with the Greek PAN, with whom he had many traits in common. His priests were the Luperci, his main festival the LUPERCALIA. When not viewed as an individual, he appeared in the multiformity of the fauns, possibly under the influence of the Greek pans, satyrs, and sileni in their relation with Pan. The fauns were satyrlike beings with tails, horns, goats' legs and feet, and furry, pointed ears. Two festivals called *Faunalia* were held on February 13 and December 5.

Hawthorne wrote a novel, *The Marble Faun* (1860), in which it is hinted that the hero is a faun. It was suggested by the statue of a youthful faun by Praxiteles, now in the Capitoline Museum in Rome. The same title is used by William Faulkner for a collection of verse (1924).

One of the best-known poems of Stéphane Mallarmé is his *L'Après-midi d'un faune* (*Afternoon of a Faun*). Debussy's orchestral tone poem *Prélude à l'après-midi d'un faune* (*Prelude to Afternoon of a Faun*, 1892) became the firm foundation of its composer's fame.

Fauré, Gabriel [Urbain] (1845–1924). French composer, organist, and teacher. He became choir director at the Madeleine in Paris in 1877, and organist in 1896, taught composition at the Paris Conservatoire from 1896, and was its director from 1905 to 1920. His best-known works are the *Requiem Mass* (1887), and many songs, which include settings of poems by Verlaine, Rimbaud, Baudelaire, and Sully Prudhomme. Maurice Ravel was a pupil of his.

Faust. A legendary figure, the subject of many literary works. The historical personage behind all the various Faust legends seems to have been a German necromancer named Georg Faust (1480?–?1538). Bits of his life are known from contemporary testimony, including that of Philipp Melanchthon, but it is impossible to make a complete biography of him. His career was not without success, for he sometimes gained influence in powerful ecclesiastical and worldly courts. The power he enjoyed, combined with the boasting for which he was famous, captured the imagination of many after his death, and various altered and exaggerated versions of his exploits soon began to appear in print (see FAUSTBUCH). The name Johann, given him in the folk books and by Marlowe in DR. FAUSTUS, probably results from confusion with a different magician.

Johann Wolfgang von GOETHE was first attracted to the Faust legend by the *Faustbuch* and a Faust puppet-show he saw in his youth. But it was not until 1808 that the completed play, *Faust, Der Tragödie erster Teil* (*Faust, The First Part of the Tragedy*) first appeared. It is in this Part I that Goethe develops the character of Faust as the old scholar who yearns to comprehend not so much all knowledge as all experience, but finds that in order to do so he must promise his immortal soul to the destructive tempting spirit, MEPHISTOPHELES. The latter helps rejuvenate Faust, who then falls in love with and seduces a young girl named GRETCHEN. She bears him a child, but panics and drowns it, and the last scene of Part I is set in the dungeon where, awaiting execution for her crime, she refuses to flee with Faust and puts her trust in God.

In Part I, Mephistopheles promises to show Faust both "the small world" of personal feeling and experience, and "the great world" of history, politics, and culture. This distinction neatly parallels the difference between the two parts. In Part II (1832), which is much longer and more allegorical than Part I, Goethe took the opportunity to develop many of his ideas on mythology, cultural development, art, statesmanship, war, courtly life, economics, natural science, and religion, to the extent that the plot is sometimes lost from view. Toward the end, Faust attempts to justify his existence by reclaiming land from the sea in order to found an ideal society, but the plan fails. Faust's soul is finally rescued by a choir of angels who speak the motto *Wer immer strebend sich bemüht, / Den können wir erlösen* ("He who exerts himself in constant striving, / Him we can save"). See URFAUST; WAGNER; WALPURGISNACHT; MOTHERS, THE; HOMUNCULUS; HELEN; EUPHORION; ETERNAL FEMININE.

Thomas Mann, in his DOKTOR FAUSTUS, does not directly treat the Faust legend, but uses it as a parallel to the fall of his own hero, Adrian Leverkühn.

The Faust legend has inspired several operas, including Boïto's *Mefistofele* (1866), Berlioz' *La damnation de Faust* (1893), and Busoni's *Doktor Faust* (1925). The most famous of these is Charles Gounod's *Faust* (1859), which is based on Goethe's play.

Faust, Frederick. See MAX BRAND.

Faustbuch, Das (Ger., "Faust-book"). A term referring to any of the several German folk books (VOLKSBUCH) which relate the career of Dr. Johann Faust. The first such book was printed by Johann Spies in 1587, and many variations appeared shortly afterwards. Goethe's main sources, however, seem to have been a much later version by Nikolaus Pfitzer (1674) and an abridgment of Pfitzer's book which appeared in 1725.

Faustian. Of or pertaining to either the historical FAUST or any of his fictional counterparts. From this basic meaning the term has broadened until, in modern usage, it is often used when characterizing any unswerving and unquenchable will to possess all of human knowledge or experience.

Faustina [Annia Galeria]. The name of 2 Roman empresses. Faustina the Elder was married to the emperor Antoninus Pius, and died in A.D. 141. Faustina the Younger, her daughter, was married to the emperor Marcus Aurelius, the adopted son and successor of Antoninus, and died in 175. Both were notorious for their evil lives, though Marcus Aurelius professed to believe his wife the best of women. Swinburne's poem *Faustine* was written with these empresses in mind.

Fauves, les. A group of French artists (ROUAULT, DERAIN, DUFY, VLAMINCK, etc.) who grouped around Matisse and exhibited together from 1905 to 1907. The movement is characterized by the use of violent

THE HISTORIE
OF
THE DAMNABLE
LIFE, AND DESERVED
DEATH OF DOCTOR
IOHN FAVSTVS.

Newly printed, and in conuenient places, imperfect
matter amended : according to the true Copie printed
at *Frankfort* ; and translated into English,
By P. R. Gent.

Printed at London for *Iohn Wright*, and are to be sold at the Sign of the
Bible in' Giltspur-Street without Newgate. 1636.

An English translation of a German *Faustbuch* (1636).

color and the rejection of modeling. The outraged
contemporary reaction gave their name to *les Fauves,*
the wild beasts.

Faux-Monnayeurs, Les. See COUNTERFEITERS,
THE.

Favonius. In Roman mythology, a personification
of the west wind. He is a promoter of vegetation,
identical with the Greek Zephyrus.

Favorite, The (Les Personnages; 1961). A
novel by Françoise MALLET-JORIS showing that even
Cardinal Richelieu was only an instrument in the
hands of Destiny rather than a maker of history.

Fawkes, Guy. See GUNPOWDER PLOT.

Fawley, Jude. See JUDE THE OBSCURE.

Fearing, Kenneth [Flexner] (1902–1961).
American poet and novelist. He is noted for his
satiric attacks upon the mechanized society of America, often using such elements as the comic strip and
advertising as symbols of that society. Fearing published several volumes of poetry, including *Poems*
(1935), *Dead Reckoning* (1938), *The Afternoon of
a Pawnbroker and Other Poems* (1943), and *New
and Selected Poems* (1956). *The Hospital* (1939) is
a serious novel. He also wrote mystery novels, the
best known being *The Big Clock* (1946), the story
of a manhunt in which the quarry must track himself down. *The Crozart Story* appeared in 1960.

Feast During the Plague, The. See LITTLE
TRAGEDIES.

Feast of Fools. A kind of Saturnalia, popular
in the Middle Ages. Its chief object was to honor the
ass on which Jesus made his triumphant entry into
Jerusalem. This blasphemous mummery was held on
the Feast of the Circumcision (Jan. 1). The office of
the day was chanted in travesty, then a procession
was formed and all sorts of foolery was indulged in.
An ass was an essential feature, and from time to
time the whole procession imitated braying, especially in the place of "Amen."

Feast of Lanterns. A popular Chinese festival.
It is celebrated at the first full moon of each year.
Tradition says that the daughter of a famous mandarin fell into a lake one evening. The father and
his neighbors went with lanterns to look for her, and
happily she was rescued. In commemoration thereof,
a festival was ordained, and it grew in time to be the
celebrated Feast of Lanterns.

Federalist, The (1787–1788). A series of 85
papers or essays written to urge New York voters to
approve the U.S. Constitution. About 50 of the series
are said to have been written by Alexander HAMIL-
TON, the others by James MADISON and John JAY. The
essays were intended to show how the proposed constitution would create an effective national government in conformity with republican principles. They
are now considered outstanding studies in the practical application of political theory.

Fedin, Konstantin Aleksandrovich (1892–).
Russian novelist. After serving in the Red Army
during the civil war, Fedin became connected with
the SERAPION BROTHERS and published his first story,
The Orchard (*Sad*) in 1920. The theme of the story,
which recurs in several of his later works, is the
conflict between the old and new in changing Soviet
society. His first novel, *Cities and Years* (*Goroda i
gody;* 1924), also uses this theme, contrasting the
vacillating Andrei Startzov, a type of SUPERFLUOUS
MAN, with the devoted Communist, Kurt Wahn,
who eventually kills Startzov as a traitor to the
cause. The novel constituted a departure from the
style then prevalent in Russian fiction. Instead of
the wildly romantic treatment of its subject, rendered
in vivid and exotic language, found in the work of
Pilnyak, Vsevolod Ivanov, and other young writers,
Fedin used the calm, objective description and sober
psychological probing typical of the 19th-century Russian novel. He departed from it, however, in his complicated handling of the chronological sequence of the
narrative, beginning with the novel's denouement,
and flashing back and forth in time to tell his story.

Fedin's second novel, *The Brothers* (*Bratya;* 1928),
treated the same theme of an individual's acclimation
to the revolution in a manner even closer to the classical Russian novel's realism. His next large work,
The Rape of Europe (*Pokhishcheniye evropy;* 1934–
1935), concerned relations between the West and
the new Soviet society.

After the war Fedin published two more novels,
which are considered his best works: *First Joys*
(*Pervye radosti;* 1945–1946) and *Unusual Summer*
(*Neobyknovennoye leto;* 1948). Both portray life in
the Volga region of Saratov shortly before World
War I and during the revolution.

Feininger, Lyonel [Charles Adrian] (1871–
1956). American artist. Of German descent, and
associated with the BAUHAUS throughout its existence,

he became a leader of the nonrepresentational movement in painting. In his landscapes of sea or city he divides forms and space into segmented planes, limited by straight lines. His son Andreas Feininger (1906–), a talented photographer, has published *The World As I See It* (1963).

Feisi or **Feiyasi, Abul Feis ibn Mubarak** (1547–1595). Indo-Persian poet and scholar, crowned king of poesy (c. 1572) by the Mogul Emperor Akbar the Great. He translated parts of the *Mahabharata* into Persian.

Félibrige. An association of Provençal poets. It was founded near Avignon (1854) for the cultivation of Provençal as a literary language. The school's first leader was Joseph Roumanille, and its membership included Frédéric MISTRAL, Rémy Marcellin (1832–1908), Jean Brunet (1823–1894), Paul Giéra (1816–1861), Anselme Mathieu (1828–1925), Alphonse Tavan (1833–1905) and Théodore Aubanel (1829–1886).

Felipe, León. Pen name of **León Felipe Camino Galicia** (1884–). Spanish poet. He is best known in Spain for his early work, *Versos y oraciones del camino* (1920), and abroad for the larger volume *Antología rota, 1920-1947* (1947). His poetry, simple and direct, reveals the influence of Walt Whitman whom Felipe has translated.

Felix Holt the Radical (1866). A novel by George ELIOT. Felix Holt is an ardent young man of strong social convictions who attempts, by living as a watchmaker among the lower classes in his area, to encourage them to better themselves. Against him is set Harold Transome, who is running for Parliament as a radical, yet possesses none of the social sense of Felix. Felix finds himself in love with Esther, imagined to be the daughter of the local curate, Rufus Lyon. Eventually, Esther has to choose between Felix and Transome. As a complication, Felix, in his efforts to prevent the workers from rioting on Election Day, has accidentally killed a man and is on trial. His trouble brings Esther to the realization that she loves him, and when he is pardoned she becomes his wife. Running through the novel are the legal problems concerning the inheritance of the Transome property, and the attending mystery surrounding Esther's birth.

Felix Krull. See CONFESSIONS OF FELIX KRULL: CONFIDENCE MAN.

Fell, Dr. See John FELL.

Fell, John (1625–1686). English scholar and prelate, subject of the well-known quatrain by Thomas Brown (1663–1704):

> I do not love thee, Dr. Fell,
> The reason why I cannot tell;
> But this I know, and know full well,
> I do not love thee, Dr. Fell.

Brown is said to have composed these lines when Fell, who was dean of Christ Church, Oxford, promised to remit a sentence of expulsion if the youth could make an impromptu translation of Martial's 33rd epigram:

> Non amo te, Sabidi, nec possum dicere quare;
> Hoc tantum possum dicere non amo te.

Fellini, Federico (1920–). Italian motion-picture director and writer. He appeared as an actor for a short time before 1940, when he began his career as a script writer and director. Among the films for which he has received international acclaim are *La Strada* (1956), *La Notta di Cabiria* (1957), *La Dolce Vita* (1960), and *8½* (1963).

Felltham or **Feltham, Owen** (1602?–1668). English essayist, poet, and CHARACTER WRITER. His two major works are *Resolves, Divine, Moral, and Political* (1628) and *A Brief Character of the Low Countries* (1652). An ardent Royalist, he once referred to Charles I as "Christ the Second."

Felton, John (1595?–1628). English soldier and assassin. In 1628 he assassinated the Duke of Buckingham, who had refused him the command of a company, and was hanged at Tyburn. He appears in Dumas' *The Three Musketeers* (1844).

Femmes savantes, Les (The Learned Ladies, 1672). A comedy by MOLIÈRE. It satirizes women who devote themselves to women's rights, science, and philosophy to the neglect of domestic duties and wifely amenities. Philaminte, who is capable of discharging a servant for employing bad grammar, wants to marry Henriette, her daughter, to Trissotin, a man whose tastes and opinions match her own. Her daughter Armande advocates Platonic love and science, and her sister Bélise is a self-styled philosopher who imagines that everyone is in love with her. Henriette, who has no sympathy with the lofty flights of her female relatives, is in love with Clitandre, but is prevented from marrying him until her father loses his property through the "savant" proclivities of his wife and Trissotin withdraws his suit of the girl. Clitandre and Henriette are thereupon united, Clitandre declaring his beloved the "perfect" or thorough woman—in distinction, Molière implies, to the rest of her family.

Fénelon, François de Salignac de la Mothe- (1651–1715). French prelate and writer. Fénelon's success in tutoring the duc de Bourgogne, grandson of Louis XIV, won him an appointment to the Académie française, the title of archbishop, and a favored position at court. He lost favor embracing the unorthodox doctrines of Quietism, and upon publication of his epic TÉLÉMAQUE, which in offering political advice to the dauphin indirectly reproved the policies of the king, Fénelon was exiled to his diocese. Liberal in his political and educational theories, Fénelon expressed his convictions in *De l'Education des filles (Concerning the Education of Girls,* 1687) and *Table de Chaulnes* (1711).

Fenian cycle. In GAELIC LITERATURE, a group of tales revolving around the deeds of FIONN MAC CUMHAIL and his son Oisín, or OSSIAN. The term *Fenian* comes from "fian," a band of warriors. The chief Fenian text is the *Colloquy of Old Men,* a discussion between St. Patrick and Ossian; also important is THE PURSUIT OF DIARMUID AND GRÁINNE. Paganism is somewhat modified in the Fenian cycle, Christianity reaching Ireland in the old age of Ossian.

Fenians or **Fenian Brotherhood.** An anti-British, secret association of disaffected Irishmen founded in New York in 1857 with a view to securing the independence of Ireland. The movement spread over the U.S. and through Ireland (where it absorbed the pre-existing Phoenix Society); several attempts at insurrection in Ireland were made as well as an invasion of Canada from the U.S. Eleven "national congresses" were held by the Fenian Brotherhood in the U.S. between 1863 and 1872, after which it continued as a secret society. It was a forerunner to the Irish Republican Brotherhood. The name Fenian is derived from Fionn mac Cumhail, the name of the great, semimythological hero of Ireland. See CLANNA-GAEL; SINN FEIN; YOUNG IRELAND; EASTER REBELLION.

Fenollosa, Ernest Francisco (1853–1908). American poet, art critic, and Orientalist. After living in Japan and teaching for 12 years at the University of Tokyo, Fenollosa returned to the U.S.; he became curator of the Boston Museum of Fine Arts and was a widely received lecturer. He later returned to Japan, and finally moved to England, where he died. His collected poems appeared as *East and West* (1893). *Epochs of Chinese and Japanese Art* (2 v., 1912), his greatest art book, was published posthumously. During the Westernization of Japan, Fenollosa saved many ancient art treasures from mishandling and destruction. His private collection formed the nucleus of the Fenollosa-Weld Collection in the Boston Museum. After his death, Fenollosa's wife turned his notes and papers over to the poet Ezra Pound. From Fenollosa's work, Pound made the celebrated translations from Li Po that appear in his *Cathay* (1915), as well as the versions of classical Japanese drama found in *Certain Noble Plays of Japan* (1916).

Fenrir or **Fenris-wolf.** In Scandinavian mythology, the wolf of Loki and brother of Hel, typifying the goading of a guilty conscience. It was said that when he gaped, one jaw touched earth and the other heaven. Odin sought vainly to chain him but the wolf was expected to swallow Odin at the day of doom. Percy MacKaye wrote a dramatic poem entitled *Fenris the Wolf* (1905).

Fenton. In Shakespeare's MERRY WIVES OF WINDSOR, a young gentleman who woos and finally wins "sweet Anne Page." He had formerly been a companion of Prince Hal.

Ferber, Edna (1887–1968). American novelist and short-story writer. Edna Ferber started her long career as a highly successful writer of fiction with several collections of short stories. Her best-selling novels include *The Girls* (1921); *So Big* (1924), which was awarded a Pulitzer Prize and which deals with the struggles of the widowed Selina DeJong to support herself and her son Dirk; SHOW BOAT; and *Cimarron* (1930), a story of the spectacular land rush of 1889 in Oklahoma. In collaboration with George S. Kaufman, Miss Ferber wrote several popular plays: *Minick* (1924), based on one of her best short stories; *The Royal Family* (1927), which exhibited the Barrymores in a humorous vein; *Dinner at Eight* (1932), about a fashionable dinner party; and *Stage Door* (1936). Among her many later novels are *Giant* (1952) and *Ice Palace* (1958).

Ferdinand. (1) The young king of Navarre who takes an oath with three friends to make his court "a little Academe, still and contemplative in living art" in Shakespeare's LOVE'S LABOUR'S LOST.

(2) The son of Alonso, king of Naples, in Shakespeare's THE TEMPEST. Untouched by worldly corruption, he falls in love at first sight with Prospero's daughter Miranda and willingly undergoes the labors Prospero imposes to test his love for her.

Ferdinand II of Aragon or **Ferdinand V** of Castile (1452–1516). King of Spain. In 1469 Ferdinand married Isabella of Castile and, upon her accession to the throne in 1474, the two great kingdoms of Spain were permanently united. During their reign Ferdinand and Isabella sought to consolidate royal power and to assure the racial and religious purity of Spain. The first aim they accomplished by destroying the privileges of the unruly Castilian nobility and by limiting the once-considerable independence of the towns. The second aim was achieved by the establishment of the Spanish INQUISITION (1478) and by the conquest (1492) of Granada, the last Moorish kingdom in Spain. In the same year the Jews of Spain were ordered to become Christians or face expulsion; the same alternatives were offered to the Moors of Castile in 1502. Perhaps the most important event of their reign was the discovery of America in 1492 by Christopher Columbus, whose voyage was made possible by Isabella. Ferdinand expanded Spanish power in Europe as well, acquiring Naples in 1503 and the kingdom of Navarre in 1512. Upon the death of Isabella in 1504, he ruled Castile as regent for their demented daughter, Joanna the Mad. In 1506 he took a second wife, Germaine de Foix.

Ferdinand Count Fathom, The Adventures of (1753). A novel by Tobias SMOLLETT. The titular hero, son of a harridan mother, is an amoral Machiavellian rogue who nearly succeeds in destroying Monimia, the fiancée of his master and friend, Count de Melvil. Reduced to ignominy and disgrace when his schemes miscarry, he is finally rehabilitated by the benevolent Melvil, and reforms under an assumed name. The novel professes to terrify the iniquitous into virtue through an appeal to the "impulses of fear." Fathom, completely reformed and prosperous, reappears as a character in *The Expedition of* HUMPHREY CLINKER.

Fergus. A famous warrior in the ULSTER CYCLE of Gaelic literature. Fergus also appears in James Joyce's *Ulysses* (1922).

Ferlinghetti, Lawrence. See BEAT MOVEMENT.

Fernández de Avellaneda, Alonso. See DON QUIXOTE.

Fernández de Lizardi, José Joaquín (1776–1827). Mexican novelist and journalist. Fernández de Lizardi is often called *El Pensador Mexicano* (*Sp.*, the Mexican Thinker), the name of a newspaper he established in 1812 as a vehicle for his ideas on morality and patriotism. It is, however, as a novelist that he is best known, notably for EL PERIQUILLO SARNIENTO, often considered the first Hispanic-American novel, and for *La quijotita y su prima* (1818–1819), which was inspired by Rousseau's theories of education.

Fernández de Moratín, Leandro. See Leandro Fernández de MORATÍN.

Fernández Flórez, Wenceslao (1886–   ). Spanish writer. The journalistic style of his early newspaper career reappears in the ironic humor of his novels, including *Valvoreta* (1917), *Las siete columnas* (*The Seven Pillars,* 1926), and *Los que no fuimos a la guerra* (1930).

Fernández y González, Manuel (1821–1888). Spanish novelist and dramatist. He is known for his prolific output of historical novels patterned on the works of the English romanticists. His best-known novels are *Los siete infantes de Lara* (1853), *El cocinero de Su Majestad* (1857), and *Historia de un murciélago* (1857). He also wrote the drama *Cid Rodrigo de Vivar* (1858).

Ferney, the patriarch or philosopher of. Epithet for VOLTAIRE (François Marie Arouet). Ferney is the name of the estate that Voltaire bought near Geneva in 1758 and where he spent the last 20 years of his life. He is known as the patriarch of Ferney because of his fatherly interest in the management of the estate and in his staff of servants. For them and for the local inhabitants, Voltaire built a pottery factory and a church. His grand manner of entertaining his numerous famous visitors also explains this epithet. Secure from political and religious interference at Ferney, because of its geographical location, Voltaire poured forth innumerable vitriolic pamphlets attacking just about everyone who disagreed with him.

Ferragù, Ferrau, Ferracute, or Ferragus. In Ariosto's ORLANDO FURIOSO, a Saracen knight, son of Lanfusa. Having lost his helmet in a river, he vowed to wear none other than Orlando's. In the ORLANDO INNAMORATO of Boiardo, he was supposed to wed Angelica, as her brother Argaglia wished; but she fled from him. In the Ariosto continuation, he is finally killed by Orlando when wounded in the navel, his only vulnerable part.

Ferrar, Nicholas (1592–1637). English theologian. With several members of his family he established a religious colony at LITTLE GIDDING in Huntingdonshire that was renowned for its piety. Ferrar translated religious works, wrote the *Story Books of Little Gidding*, first published in 1899, and was responsible for publishing the work of George Herbert, his friend. The last of T. S. Eliot's *Four Quartets* (1943) is entitled *Little Gidding*, the poet using Ferrar's community as an example of achieved spiritual life.

Ferrars, Edward. See SENSE AND SENSIBILITY.

Ferraugh, Sir. See FAERIE QUEENE, THE.

Ferrex and Porrex. Sons of King Gorbodug in the HISTORY OF THE KINGS OF BRITAIN by Geoffrey of Monmouth. The king divided his kingdom between them, but Porrex drove his brother from Britain. When Ferrex returned with an army he was slain, but Porrex was shortly after put to death by his mother, whose favorite was Ferrex. The story forms the basis of the Tudor drama GORBODUC (1592), the first English tragedy by Norton and Sackville.

Ferumbras. See FIERABRAS.

Feste. Olivia's clown in Shakespeare's TWELFTH NIGHT. He takes part in the pranks against Malvolio, and he also sings the well-known song, "O mistress mine!"

Festin de pierre, Le. See DOM JUAN OU LE FESTIN DE PIERRE.

Festus. See Philip J. BAILEY.

Fet, Afanasi Afanasyevich (1820–1892). Russian lyric poet. Fet was the illegitimate son of Afanasi Shenshin, a landowner, and a German woman named Foeth (Fet in Russian). He retained the name Fet throughout his literary career. His first volume of poems (1840) received little notice. With the publication of two more books of verse in 1850 and 1856, however, Fet's reputation was established as a lyric poet whose work was unexcelled in its melodic quality, his chief themes being love and nature. The quality and the concerns of Fet's work were not palatable to the utilitarian critics of the 1860's. They cited his poetry as an example of the sterility of "art for art's sake." One of their favorite targets for ridicule was a short poem by Fet, *Shopot, robkoe dykhan'e* (*Whispering, timid breathing*). An impressionistic description of the break of dawn, the poem contains no verbs. The unfriendly critical reception of his work induced Fet to stop publishing poetry for more than 20 years. He lived quietly on his estate near the home of his friend, Leo Tolstoi. In the 1880's, several more volumes of Fet's poems were published.

Feuchtwanger, Lion (1884–1958). German novelist. He was noted for his treatment of historical and political themes, and for his application of psychoanalytic ideas to the development of character. Among his novels are *Die hässliche Herzogin Margarete Maultasch* (*The Ugly Duchess*, 1923), *Jud Süss* (1925, translated as *Power*), *Der jüdische Krieg* (1932, translated as *Josephus*), and *Der Wartesaal* (*The Waiting Room*), a trilogy including *Erfolg* (*Success*, 1930), *Die Geschwister Oppenheim* (1933, translated as *The Oppermanns*), and *Exil* (1939, translated as *Paris Gazette*). Feuchtwanger was active as a pacifist and a socialist, and was forced into exile by the rise of Nazism. He was a friend of Bertolt Brecht and collaborated with him on several plays including *Leben Eduards II von England* (*Life of Edward II of England*, 1923), and adaptation of *Edward II* by Marlowe. See Arnold ZWEIG.

feudalism or feudal system. The system of distribution of land and political allegiance prevalent throughout Europe during the Middle Ages. According to its purest form, the king owns all the land over which he rules, but gives portions of it as inheritable fiefs to his vassals, in exchange for loyalty and a specified amount of military service. These feudal lords similarly divide their land among their followers, and the subdivision continues, forming a pyramidal hierarchy in which each nobleman has an obligation to the lord above him and authority over those below him. At the base of the pyramid are the serfs, the farmers who belong to the land they work, owing most of its produce to its lord and changing masters when the land changes hands through gift or marriage alliances or wars.

The feudal system was dominant from the 9th to the 14th century, when the rise of the merchant class and the growing importance of the towns began to change the social structure. Some feudal elements, however, such as the hierarchy of the propertied class of nobles, continued through the 19th century.

Feuerbach, Ludwig (1804–1872). German philosopher. He analyzed religion from a psychological and anthropological viewpoint in *Das Wesen des Christentums* (*The Essence of Christianity*, 1841) and *Das Wesen der Religion* (*The Essence of Religion*, 1845). Denying the traditional antithesis of the divine and the human, he maintained that divinity is man's projection of his own human nature. Love and morality, the basis of human relations, are the essence of religion. This tendency toward secularization of religion in the mid-19th century is also found in the work of David Friedrich Strauss and Ernest Renan.

Feuillants, Le Club des. A French political club born of a schism between members of the JACOBIN Club in July, 1791. They were more moderate than the Jacobins in their wholehearted support of the constitutional monarchy provided for by the Constitution of 1791, and in their distrust of the political influence of the Parisian mob. The Feuillants came to power early in 1792, but were soon replaced by the GIRONDISTS over the question of war with Austria. Their political power rapidly waned and they were suppressed by the Jacobins after the fall of the monarchy in September, 1792. The club's members met in the old convent of the Feuillants, a branch of the Cistercian Order, hence their name.

Feuillet, Octave (1821–1890). French author and playwright. One of the most appreciated, popular writers of his period, Feuillet is the author of the sentimental novel *Roman d'un jeune homme pauvre* (1858). The young hero of this tale refuses to marry his wealthy beloved and later destroys the proof which would enable him to take possession of her family fortune. His honor does not go unrewarded, however, for he soon inherits an even larger fortune and is at last united with his love. Feuillet's dramas, which received the same approval as his novels, include *La Belle au bois dormant* (1867) and *La Partie de dames* (1883).

feuilleton. The section of a French newspaper devoted to tales, serials, light literature, and criticism. The title of this early 19th-century phenomenon is derived from the French *feuille* (a leaf) as the first feuilletons were printed on the detachable, lower portion of the page. The word is now applied to pamphlets, generally of a political nature, that are distributed on the street.

Few Figs from Thistles, A (1920). A collection of poems by Edna St. Vincent MILLAY. The second of her collections, this volume differs from the earlier *Renascence and Other Poems* (1917) in its greater tone of sophisticated flippancy. Seeming to epitomize youthful Bohemianism, the poems were widely quoted in Greenwich Village, among the best known of them being *First Fig, Recuerdo,* and *The Philosopher.*

Fiammetta. The lady celebrated by Giovanni Boccaccio in his verse and prose works. The literal meaning of her name, flickering or darting fire, suggests his passion for her. *Fiammetta* is also the title of a psychological romance written by Boccaccio in 1344–1346, in which she is the heroine describing her abandonment by Panfilo and her subsequent grief. Since she is also called Maria, it was once assumed that Fiammetta was really MARIA D'AQUINO. Modern scholars now hold that she was purely fictional, a Boccaccian equivalent of LAURA and other ladies of the lyric tradition.

Fichte, Johann Gottlieb (1762–1814). German philosopher and political thinker. An important force in the development of GERMAN ROMANTICISM, in his *Grundlage der gesammten Wissenschaftslehre (Foundation of the Complete Theory of Knowledge,* 1794), he developed the distinction made earlier by Kant between phenomenal reality and the thing-in-itself (see CRITIQUE OF PURE REASON). He maintained that the essence of the universe is ego—mind, that is, or spirit—and that the ego itself posits the material world by a process called productive imagination.

Man's ideas do not come from experience of the material world, for his mind is part of the universal creative ego and finds fulfillment in self-conscious unity with it. Fichte's main political work is *Reden an die deutsche Nation (Addresses to the German Nation,* 1808), in which his earlier enthusiasm for the French Revolution is replaced by a stern condemnation of Napoleon. Fichte, who believed in the nobility of the German spirit, hoped that Germany would unite and free Europe from French rule.

Ficino, Marsilio (1433–1499). Italian philosopher and scholar. The first and most influential Platonist of the Renaissance, as a child he was taken into the Florentine household of Cosimo de' Medici for the express purpose of learning the philosophy of Plato and his followers, the Neoplatonists. He soon became the center of a group of intellectuals, including Angelo Poliziano and Pico della Mirandola, loosely called the Florentine Academy. He translated Greek works into Latin, wrote such commentaries as the famous one on Plato's *Symposium* (in Latin and Italian), and composed original treatises. His main impulse seems to have been the desire to reconcile Platonism (actually Neoplatonism) with the tradition of Christian thought, as in his *Theologia platonica de immortalitate animorum (The Platonic Theology of the Immortality of Souls).* Among the many European and English writers influenced by his writings are Benvieni, Pico della Mirandola, Bembo, Castiglione, Spenser, and Chapman. Among the poets who read and used him, it was frequently the Platonic theory of spiritual or philosophic love that appealed rather than theological or cosmological theory.

Ficke, Arthur Davison (1883–1945). American poet and critic. Ficke's interests were divided between art—especially Japanese art—and poetry. In the former field he published *Twelve Japanese Painters* (1913) and *Chats on Japanese Prints* (1915). As a poet he was noted for his sonnets; his two interests combined in *Sonnets of a Portrait Painter* (1914). He was involved with Witter BYNNER in the SPECTRA hoax.

Fiddler's Green. The Elysium of sailors; a land flowing with rum and lime juice; a land of perpetual music, mirth, dancing, drinking, and tobacco; a sort of Dixie Land or land of the leal.

Fidei Defensor. See DEFENDER OF THE FAITH.

Fidelio (1805). An opera by Ludwig von Beethoven, based on Bouilly's *Lenore.* The hero is Don Fernando Florestan, a state prisoner in Spain, and the heroine his faithful wife Leonora, who disguises herself as a man and under the name Fidelio becomes the jailer's servant in order to protect her husband and bring about his release. It is the only opera Beethoven wrote. Beethoven composed four overtures for *Fidelio* that are often performed in concert.

Fidessa. See FAERIE QUEENE, THE.

Field, Arthur William (1888–   ). Australian novelist. Born in Gosport, England, Field was sent as a boy to Australia where his early literary influences were Charles Dickens, Sir Arthur Conan Doyle, and Alexandre Dumas. He led an adventurous life as a sheepherder, cowhand, gold miner, fur trapper, and soldier. Many of his actual experiences are vividly related in his books: *House of Cain* (1929), *Murder Down Under* (1937), *The Devil's*

Steps (1940), *The New Shoe* (1951), *Death of a Love* (1954), *The Sinister Stones* (1954).

Field, Eugene (1850–1895). American poet and journalist. Expelled from three colleges because of his pranks, Field turned to journalism. He settled in Chicago, where he wrote a column, "Sharps and Flats," for the *Daily News*. Collecting his newspaper verses into several books, he published *The Tribune Primer* (1882), *A Little Book of Western Verse* (1889), *Love Affairs of a Bibliomaniac* (1896), and several other volumes. He wrote many popular and sentimental poems for children, including *Little Boy Blue* (1889).

Field, Michael. Joint pen name of **Katharine Harris Bradley** (1846–1914) and **Edith Emma Cooper** (1862–1913). English authors, they collaborated (from 1884) on lyric poetry and poetic closet dramas. Their lyrics—their best work—are represented by *A Selection From the Poems of Michael Field* (1923).

Field, Nat[han] or **"Nid"** (1587–?). English actor and dramatist. He became one of the Children of the Chapel Royal in 1600, remaining with that company until 1613, when he was absorbed into the Lady Elizabeth's Players. Two years later he joined the King's Men. He was apparently an excellent actor, generally playing the part of young lovers. His name comes 17th on the list of 26 actors in the 1623 Shakespeare folio. He was the author of two come-

Title page of Field's *Amends for Ladies* (1639 ed.).

AMENDS FOR LADIES.

With the merry prankes of Moll Cut-Purfe: Or, the humour of roaring:

A Comedy full of honeſt mirth and wit.

As it was Acted at the *Blacke-Fryers,* both by the P R I N C E S Servants, and the Lady E L I Z A B E T H S.

By *Nath. Field.*

LONDON,
Printed by *Io. Okes,* for *Nath. Walbaneke,* and are to be fold at his Shop, at *Grayes-Inne* Gate 1639.

dies, *A Woman Is a Weathercock* (1609?) and *Amends for Ladies* (pub. 1618), and is believed to have collaborated with Philip Massinger, John Fletcher, and Francis Beaumont.

Fielding, Henry (1707–1754). English novelist and playwright, an important figure in the development of the English novel. His career as a dramatist has been eclipsed by his career as a novelist, and all that is remembered today of his plays is TOM THUMB, a brilliant farce, and *Pasquin* (1736) and *The Historical Register for 1736* (1737), two social and political satires. Robert Walpole's Licensing Act of 1737 ended the use of the stage for political satire, and so terminated this phase of Fielding's career. Turning to the study of law, he was admitted to the bar; in 1749 he became London's first police magistrate and, with the organization of the Bow STREET Runners, a pioneer in the detection of crime.

In the meantime his literary career continued. From 1739 to 1741 he edited the periodical CHAMPION. When Richardson's PAMELA was published, Fielding was moved to parody it, first in APOLOGY FOR THE LIFE OF MRS. SHAMELA ANDREWS, and once again, more brilliantly, in JOSEPH ANDREWS. In 1743 he published three volumes of *Miscellanies*, which included his ironic satire JONATHAN WILD. TOM JONES, his greatest novel, and AMELIA, an early example of social realism, appeared soon after. In 1754, in an attempt to restore his failing health, he made a trip to Portugal and wrote an account of it in A JOURNAL OF A VOYAGE TO LISBON. He died at Lisbon.

Field of the Cloth of Gold. A plain near Guisnes, France. There Henry VIII (of England) had his interview with Francis I (of France) in 1520; so called from the splendor and magnificence displayed there on that occasion.

Fierabras or **Ferumbras.** One of Charlemagne's PALADINS in medieval French and English romances. A Saracen giant, son of King Balant of Babylon, he has conquered Rome and taken the holy relics. But Olivier defeats him in a duel, and he becomes a Christian knight. His sister Floripas is also baptized and marries Guy of Burgundy.

Fiesole. A village near Florence, Italy, chiefly famous for a Dominican monastery decorated by Fra Angelico.

Fiesole, Mino da (1431–1484). Tuscan sculptor. His tombs, particularly that of Pope Paul II (1473), portrait busts, and reliefs, are known for their finish, delicacy of detail, and strongly devotional aspects.

fifteen, the. The JACOBITE rebellion of 1715, when James Edward Stuart, "the Old PRETENDER," with the Earl of Mar, made a half-hearted and unsuccessful attempt to gain the throne of England. The reference is to the year of the attempt, to distinguish it from the forty-five (1745) revolt of "the Young Pretender," Charles Edward Stuart.

Fifteen Decisive Battles of the World (1851). A historical work by Sir Edward Creasy (1812–1878). The author discusses those battles which in his opinion have effected some great and permanent political changes in Western history. The battles under discussion are Marathon; Syracuse; Arbela; Metaurus; Teutoberg Forest; Chalons; Tours; Hastings; Orléans; the defeat of the Spanish Armada; Blenheim; Poltava; Saratoga; Valmy; Waterloo.

fifth column. Enemy sympathizers engaged in sabotage. The term was first used during the Spanish Civil War (1936–1939) by General Mola, who stated in a broadcast that he had four columns of soldiers advancing on Madrid and a fifth column of sympathizers within the city who would arise to attack the defenders from the rear. It was made the title of a play (1938) by Ernest Hemingway; the term came into wide use during the German invasion of Holland, Belgium, Luxembourg, and France in 1940, when fifth columnists were active. During World War II, the term applied to a systematic organization of spies penetrating the civilian life of the enemy country to acquire information, obstruct military preparations, alarm, confuse, and divide the populace, and assist or join the invading army. It was also applied to citizens who were enemy sympathizers. The fifth column, in fact and in rhetoric, is the modern equivalent of the Trojan Horse.

Fifth Monarchy Men. A fanatical sect of millenarians in England at the time of the Commonwealth, who maintained that the fifth monarchy, when Christ should reign on earth 1,000 years, was near at hand and that they must establish it by force. They listed Assyria, Persia, Greece, and Rome as the preceding four monarchies. Their uprisings (1657 and 1661) came to nothing.

Figaro. The rascally hero of two comedies by BEAUMARCHAIS: THE BARBER OF SEVILLE and its sequel *Le Mariage de Figaro, ou La folle journée* (1784). The complicated plot of the latter play concerns Count Almaviva, who is tired of his wife Rosine and tries to find solace elsewhere. Figaro, now the count's doorkeeper, loves Suzanne, Rosine's maid. Almaviva, himself taken with Suzanne, is in favor of the marriage between Figaro and Suzanne, provided he can exercise his feudal rights over Suzanne. His attempts to achieve his ends are constantly thwarted by various conspiracies, rendering him constantly ridiculous. His infidelity to Rosine is exposed, and Figaro, having outwitted his master, finally marries Suzanne. Beaumarchais' bitter criticisms of the ruling classes caused the play to be suppressed for three years; he was even imprisoned five days for his audacity; but the public demanded its performance, and its success was possibly the greatest any play has ever had in the history of French theater. In Figaro's famous, daring monologue (Act V, scene 3), he says: "What have you [the nobility] done to deserve such wealth? You took the trouble to be born, and nothing else." Mozart composed an opera based on this play: *Le Nozze di Figaro* (*The Marriage of Figaro*, 1786), in which the political implications are absent.

Filarete, Il. Real name, **Antonio Averlino** (c. 1400–1470). Florentine sculptor and architect. He worked for the Sforza family in Milan, where he built the Ospedale Maggiore (1457) and the Medici bank. In Rome, he carved the bronze doors for the old St. Peter's, which were retained for the present structure. His treatise on architecture, *Trattato dell' architettura* (1464), was described by VASARI as "perhaps the most stupid book ever written;" it contains plans for what he called *Sforzinda*, an ideal, wholly symmetrical city.

Filelfo, Francesco (1398–1481). Venetian diplomat and scholar. Like other Humanists of the Italian Renaissance, he wrote Latin verse and translated from Greek, which he had studied at Constantinople (see HUMANISM). His activities as teacher and scholar centered in the university at Florence and the court of Milan.

Filicaia, Vincenzo da (1642–1707). Italian lyric poet. A member of the ARCADIAN ACADEMY, he is known for his odes and sonnets on religious and patriotic themes. His most famous sonnet, *Italia*, was translated by Byron in *Childe Harold's Pilgrimage* (Canto III, 1. 110).

Filioque controversy. An argument that long disturbed the Eastern and Western branches of the Christian Church. The difference of opinion still forms one of the principal barriers to their fusion. The point was: Did the Holy Spirit proceed from the Father *and* the Son (*filio-que*), or from the Father only? The Western Church maintains the former position and the Eastern the latter.

Filippovna, Natasha. In Feodor Dostoevski's novel THE IDIOT, the beautiful, tormented woman whose proud nature is continually exacerbated by the memory of a shameful seduction in her youth. Prince Myshkin tries to help her, but is able only to offer her his pity. She finally runs away with the passionately jealous ROGOZHIN, who kills her.

Filocolo, Il. A lengthy prose romance by Giovanni Boccaccio. Its title, a Greek coinage meaning *Love's Labor*, refers to the travails of its leading characters, Florio and Biancofiore. Derived from the French tale FLORES AND BLANCHEFLEUR, it was filled with many episodes and digressions by Boccaccio which later were used by European and English writers. The most famous of these digressions is the THIRTEEN QUESTIONS OF LOVE.

Filostrato, Il. A romance in octaves by Giovanni Boccaccio, whose title means "a man overwhelmed by love." The man is Trojan Troiolo (Troilus), who loves and wins Criseida with the help of her cousin and his friend Pandaro (Pandarus). But when she leaves the Trojan camp to return to her father on the Greek side, she quickly betrays Troiolo's trust, leaving him stunned by grief. Boccaccio drew the plot from the *Roman de Troie* of Benoît de Sainte-More, then supplied Chaucer with the story of his *Troilus and Criseyde*. See GUIDO DELLE COLONNE.

Filumena, St. (Philomena). A saint unknown till 1802. A grave was discovered in that year in the catacomb of St. Priscilla on the Salarian Way (leading from Rome to Ancona), with this inscription on tiles: *"lumena paxte cymfi,"* which, being rearranged, makes *Pax tecum Filumena*. Filumena was at once popularly accepted as a saint, though never canonized, and so many wonders were worked by her that she has been called *La Thaumaturge du Dixneuvième Siècle*. In 1961, the Vatican officially prohibited her further veneration.

Financier, The (1912). A novel by Theodore DREISER. It is the first volume in the trilogy that includes THE TITAN and *The Stoic* (1947). All three deal with a typical industrial and financial magnate of the late 19th century. Dreiser admitted that he based his central character, Frank Algernon Cowperwood, on the figure of Charles T. Yerkes (1837–1905), who gained control of the Chicago street-railway system. The book begins with a famous scene in which Cowperwood as a young boy in Philadelphia watches a lobster devour a squid, this act becoming for him a symbol of what life really is. Working his way upward, the hero is caught in a stock-market crash and receives a prison sentence for illegal dealings. At the end of the book, when he is released, he marries and goes to Chicago to begin his climb again.

Fin de partie. See ENDGAME.

Fingal, An Ancient Epic (1761). An epic poem by James MACPHERSON. Purportedly a translation from Gaelic, the poem was attributed by him to OSSIAN, son of Fingal, and told of the adventures of the legendary hero Fingal or FIONN MAC CUMHAIL.

Finnabair. In Gaelic literature, the Irish GUINEVERE, daughter of MEDB and Ailill. One of the figures in the Ulster cycle, she appears in such tales as the *Cattle-Raid of Cooley* and *Fled Bricrenn*.

Finnegans Wake (1939). The last and most revolutionary experimental novel by James JOYCE. It is almost inaccessible to readers who have not done some special study; a great many volumes of explication have been published since the novel's first, controversial appearance. The main difficulty is in the language. Joyce uses an elaborate language of his own devising, made up of puns, portmanteau words, and words from foreign languages, with endless philological variations. He incorporates literary, historical, and philosophical allusions; names of people and places in Dublin; Irish references; slang; phrases from newspapers, popular songs, art, and the world of sport; and words and syllables from every other imaginable source. By means of this complex language and its rich connotations, Joyce is able to relate his slight, rather obscure central story to the whole historic, psychological, religious, and artistic experience of mankind. Critics relate Joyce's difficult linguistic method to the scholasticism he encountered during his strict Catholic education, and his presentation of different levels of meaning simultaneously to the influence of medieval allegory.

Most literally, the novel presents the dreams and nightmares of H. C. Earwicker and his family as they lie asleep at night. Their anxieties, secret thoughts, unexpressed desires, and the events of the past day recur in their minds. Humphrey Chimpden Earwicker, a Protestant Irishman of Scandinavian descent (and thus, like Bloom of *Ulysses,* an outsider) is the middle-aged keeper of a tavern in Dublin. He has a wife, Anna, and three children: Isobel, a daughter now in her teens, and twin sons, Kevin and Jerry. At some time in the past Earwicker has accosted someone in Phoenix Park, but it is never made clear whether this was a young girl or a man; he still feels guilty and fears investigation by the authorities. In his dream Earwicker's personal guilt is related to various religious taboos and legends, and he is associated with Lucifer, Adam, Humpty Dumpty, and other figures. Another sexual taboo and guilt complex in Earwicker's dream concerns his daughter Isobel, whom he substitutes as a love object for his wife; however, to avoid incest he transforms her into Iseult the Fair and himself into Tristram. He also imagines himself as Jonathan Swift, the Irish writer who loved two women. Because of the similarity in names, Earwicker is also associated with earwigs (see Persse O'REILLY). Earwicker represents Everyman and general maleness. His initials, HCE, are interwoven throughout the book, particu-

larly in the recurrent phrases Here Comes Everybody and Haveth Childer Everywhere. Anna, his wife, like Molly Bloom of *Ulysses,* resents the universal feminine principle, and becomes identified with the River Liffey, personified in the novel as Anna Livia Plurabelle. The Anna Livia Plurabelle sections are among the most remarkable in the novel, being triumphs of Joyce's poetic prose. Eventually all the women in the novel merge into this figure as the river merges into the sea. Earwicker's two sons are complementary opposites. Jerry, who appears as Shem the Penman, is a rebellious, introverted artist of the type of Stephen Dedalus, and Kevin, or Shaun the Postman, is a man of action and an average, extroverted citizen.

In structure the novel is entirely circular, ending in an unfinished sentence which is completed by a half sentence at the beginning. The history of mankind and the river-to-sea progression of time and individual life are also seen as circular. In Christian thought the fall of man is followed by the resurrection; Earwicker's mysterious misdeed took place in Phoenix park, and the title of the novel refers both to the Irish hero Finn MacCool, who was supposed to return to life some day to be the savior of Ireland, and to Tim Finnegan, the hero of a music hall ballad about a man who jumped up indignantly in the middle of his own wake. Joyce used the ideas of cyclical repetition of Giambattista Vico; Freud's dream psychology; Jung's theory of a collective unconscious; and Giordano Bruno's theory of the complementary but conflicting nature of opposites (Shem and Shaun).

Joyce began writing *Finnegans Wake* in 1922. During the 17 years of its composition the novel was known as *Work in Progress,* and several parts of it were published separately as they were completed; the whole work was revised before publication.

Finn MacCool. See FIONN MAC CUMHAIL.

Finnsburg (or **Finnesburh**), **The Fight at** (8th century?). Old English (Anglo-Saxon) poem, of which only a 50-line fragment is extant. In the version of the story incorporated in BEOWULF, King Finn of the Frisians has married Hildeburh of the Danes, but treacherously attacks her brother Hnaef and his followers while they are his guests. The following spring the Danes under Hengest kill Finn and carry Hildeburh back to Denmark.

Fionn mac Cumhail. Also known as **Finn mac Cumhail, Finn MacCool.** Legendary Irish hero, hero of the FENIAN CYCLE, and leader of the Fenians, a band of warriors. He is now believed to have an historical basis, dating back to the third century B.C. The Fenians and Fionn himself were famous for their remarkable strength and stature, their fearlessness, and their extraordinary feats. As a child, Fionn was educated in the forest by a poet. His profound wisdom came from his having tasted the salmon of knowledge which fed on the hazelnuts of wisdom. His life is one of countless adventures with giants and hags; in the service of the high king at Tara, he performs many deeds, and it is for the king that he organizes the Fenians, or Fianna. His life knows two great loves: his first wife, Sedb, mother of his son Oísin, or OSSIAN, and his second wife, Gráinne, who betrays him with his kinsman Diarmuid. THE PURSUIT OF DIARMUID AND GRÁINNE is the best known of the stories of Fionn. Fionn is the hero of James Macpherson's poem FINGAL, AN ANCIENT EPIC, a spurious translation from the Gaelic.

Fiordiligi or **Fiordelisa**. In the Orlando poems of Boiardo and Ariosto, the daughter of King Dilistone. As a child she was stolen from her parents and brought up with BRANDIMARTE, a knight whom she loves and follows everywhere on his adventures. Eventually, the revelation of her royal birth enables them to marry, but Brandimarte is killed soon after. She builds a tomb for him and encloses herself within it to await her own death.

Fiorentino, Ser **Giovanni**. The Italian author of a collection of 50 *novelle* in imitation of the *Decameron* of Boccaccio, entitled by later readers *Il Pecorone* (*The Numbskull*). The author, about whom nothing is known, says he finished the tales in 1385. One of the stories, "Giannetto and the Lady of Belmont," provided Shakespeare with the pound of flesh and other details of *The Merchant of Venice*.

Firbank, Ronald (1886–1926). English novelist. Heir of the decadents of the 1890's, and a Catholic, Firbank was an escapist who created fantastic, elegant wish-fulfilment myths, and a wit who was master of brilliant dialogue. Gaily vicious, his characters are society ladies, ecclesiastics, lesbians, kings, nuns, and Negroes. The mid-century is seeing a revival of interest in his work, with a successful musical-comedy adaptation of VALMOUTH. *The Flower Beneath the Foot* (1923) is a romance and a saint's life. *Prancing Nigger* (1924) is a sympathetic account of a Negro family in Haiti who leave their village to educate their daughters—disastrously—in the big city. *Concerning the Eccentricities of Cardinal Pirelli* (1926) describes that dignitary's death in pursuit of a pretty choirboy through the cathedral.

Fir Bolg. In Gaelic literature, the 3rd race to invade and inhabit Ireland. They were defeated by the fourth race of invaders, the TUATHA DÉ DANANN.

Firdousī or **Firdusī** or **Firdausī**. (Born **Abul Qāsim Mansur** or **Hasan**; ?941–1020). Persian epic poet. His major work is the epic SHAH-NAMA. It was written at the request of the Sultan Mahmud ibn Sabuktagin who wanted a history of Persia. Its completion required 35 years. When it was finished in 1010, the sultan did not send the promised reward of a thousand gold pieces for every thousand couplets (60,000 in all), but substituted silver instead. In anger Firdousī gave the silver away, wrote a bitterly scurrilous satire that he sent to the sultan, and fled to exile. In Baghdad he wrote a long poem, *Yusuf and Zuleikha*, on the Koranic version of the loves of Joseph and Potiphar's wife, a popular theme in Persian literature. After nine years he returned to his birthplace of Tūs, Persia, where he died shortly thereafter.

Firenzuola, Angelo (1493–c. 1548). Florentine author. His best-known work is the dialogue *Della bellezza delle donne* (1541) concerning the beauty of women. This work is a study of the Renaissance conception of the ideal female type familiar in the paintings of the period.

Fire of London, Great. A fire that broke out in a baker's shop in Pudding Lane in 1666 and burned for three days and three nights. Much of the city was destroyed, including the old Gothic cathedral of St. Paul's. In his *Diary*, Samuel Pepys described how the fire spread "in corners and upon steeples, and between churches and houses as far as we could see . . . in a most horrid malicious bloody flame."

First-Born. See GIANTS.

First Folio. The first collection of the plays of William SHAKESPEARE. It was compiled by his fellow actors John Heminges and Henry Condell, and published in 1623, seven years after his death. It contained 36 plays (omitting *Pericles*, but otherwise including all the plays now considered to be authentic) arranged under the headings of comedies, histories, and tragedies. It was dedicated to two literary patrons, the earl of Pembroke and the earl of Montgomery, and for many years was considered to be a more authoritative text than the earlier quarto editions of individual plays. Several editions appeared, the third of which (second issue, 1664) included seven additional plays of which only one, the sometimes-disputed *Pericles*, is considered to be the work of Shakespeare. A facsimile edition of the First Folio was published by the Oxford University Press in 1902, and by Yale University Press in 1954.

Fischer, Lisbeth. See COUSINE BETTE, LA.

Fischer, Louis (1896–1970). American writer and journalist. Fischer is especially known for his keen interest in modern political developments in Russia and India. His books include *The Soviets in World Affairs* (1931), *Men and Politics, An Autobiography* (1941), *Gandhi and Stalin* (1947), *The Life and Death of Stalin* (1952), *Russia Revisited* (1957), and *Russia, America and the World* (1961). He also edited *Mahatma Gandhi* (1950), the autobiography of the great Indian leader whose personal disciple Fischer became.

fish. As a symbol for Christ it was used by the early Christians. The letters of the Greek word for fish, ICHTHYS, formed an acrostic of the words Jesus Christ, Son of God, Saviour.

Fisher, Dorothy Canfield [formerly **Dorothy Canfield**] (1879–1958). American novelist and short-story writer. Mrs. Fisher was a kindly but discriminating interpreter of American life, especially in New England, from the beginning of her career. Among her most widely read novels are THE SQUIRREL-CAGE, *The Bent Twig* (1915), THE BRIMMING CUP, *Rough Hewn* (1922), *Her Son's Wife* (1926), and *The Deepening Stream* (1930). In *Four-Square* (1949) 17 of her short stories were collected. The best of her nonfiction work is *Vermont Tradition; The Biography of an Outlook on Life* (1953).

Fisher, [Alvero] Vardis (1895–1968). American novelist. Fisher first became known with his tetralogy of novels dealing with the life of Vridar Hunter, an autobiographical hero who is carried through childhood, adolescence, and maturity in a quest for the meaning of life: *In Tragic Life* (1932), *Passions Spin the Plot* (1934), *We are Betrayed* (1935), and *No Villain Need Be* (1936). His novel about the early Mormons, *Children of God* (1939), won the Harper Prize Novel award. With *Darkness and the Deep* (1943) he began a series of stories portraying the development of primitive man, which he called *Testament of Man*. *Peace Like a River* (1958), *My Holy Satan* (1959), and *Orphans in Gethsemane* (1960) are part of this series. Two later books are *Love and Death* (1960) and *Suicide or Murder: The Strange Death of Meriwether Lewis* (1962).

Fisherman's ring. The Pope's signet ring for attesting papal briefs. It bears his name encircling a figure of Peter, a fisherman and first bishop of the Roman Church. A new ring is made for each Pope and is destroyed at his death, to avoid forged documents.

Fitz Boodle Papers, The (1842–1843). A series of sketches and tales by William Makepeace THACK-ERAY. The principal character is a lazy young nobleman, George Savage Fitz Boodle, with a flair for Bohemian life.

FitzGerald, Edward (1809–1883). English translator, man of letters. During his lifetime, FitzGerald was known only (and by few) for his wit and personal sweetness; he was "dear old Fitz" to such as Thackeray and Tennyson. His *Six Dramas of Calderon* (1853) was poorly received when published, though later acclaimed as great translation. His famous translation of the RUBÁIYÁT OF OMAR KHAY-YÁM was ignored until discovered by Dante Gabriel Rossetti and others after FitzGerald's death. His reputation is largely founded on this poem, so free in rendition as to be virtually an original work, and masterful in its concentration, music, and command of tone. FitzGerald's *Letters and Literary Remains* (ed. W. A. Wright, 1899) are also of much interest.

Fitzgerald, F[rancis] Scott [Key] (1896–1940). American novelist and short story writer. One of the most gifted writers of his generation, Fitzgerald became known for his novels and stories of the 1920's; he called it the "Jazz Age" and described it as "a new generation grown up to find all Gods dead, all wars fought, all faiths in man shaken." As a spokesman for the Jazz Age, Fitzgerald created glittering characters, cynical and irresponsible, trying to turn life into an endless, gay party; as the moralist he felt himself essentially to be, he infused his novels and stories with the sense that something was desperately wrong.

Fitzgerald was born in St. Paul, Minnesota, where his mother's well-to-do middle class family had its roots; he was named after the author of *The Star-Spangled Banner,* an ancestor of his father. He attended Princeton, but did not receive his degree; here it was that he began his lifelong friendship with Edmund Wilson. He served in the army, but never saw action, and in fact spent most of his time working on his first novel THIS SIDE OF PARADISE. Published in 1920, it was a spectacular success both financially and critically. In the same year he married the beautiful Zelda Sayre and together they embarked on a life that reads like one of his novels, commuting between the plush hotels and better speakeasies of the U.S. and the fashionable resorts of Europe, where they mingled with other wealthy, sophisticated expatriates. They made homes on the Riviera, and in Paris, New York, Long Island, and Washington. It was a glamorous life that was to end tragically with Zelda's incurable mental illness and Fitzgerald's break-down.

Fitzgerald followed his first success with a collection of short stories *Flappers and Philosophers* (1920), and a second novel *The Beautiful and Damned* (1921), in which he describes the pervading goal of his day as "the final polish of the shoe, the ultimate dab of the clothes brush, and a sort of intellectual There!" *Tales of the Jazz Age* (1922) and *The Vegetable* (a play; 1923) were followed by THE GREAT GATSBY, often considered his finest work. As was his custom, he immediately followed the novel with another collection of short stories, *All the Sad Young Men* (1926).

From this point on in his career, Fitzgerald had an increasingly difficult time in keeping abreast of the enormous financial and emotional demands besetting him. His next novel, TENDER IS THE NIGHT, was not published until 1934, its progress having been constantly interrupted with attempts to meet his expenses by writing stories for magazines. The strain of Zelda's severe mental illness and of trying desperately to bring her back to health contributed to his own personal crisis which he described in *The Crack-Up* (1936). His determined, and to some extent, successful efforts to put the pieces of his life back together and to devote himself to writing ended with his early death. His last novel, *The Last Tycoon* (1941), incomplete at his death, is considered by many critics to be his best.

Fitzgerald was also a master of the short story form; among his finest are *The Rich Boy, The Diamond as Big as the Ritz,* and *Babylon Revisited.*

Fitzgerald has been the subject of a great number of biographical and critical works; the central character of Budd Schulberg's novel *The Disenchanted* (1950) is modeled closely on Fitzgerald in his declining years. His *Letters,* edited by Andrew Turnbull, appeared in 1963.

Fitzgerald, Robert David (1902–   ). Australian poet. His work is noted for its vitality and metaphysical content. His *Essay on Memory* won the Australia-wide competition that took place during the 150th anniversary celebration. His writings include *The Greater Apollo: Seven Metaphysical Songs* (1927), *To Meet the Sun* (1929), *Moonlight Acre* (1938), *This Night's Orbit* (1953), *Between Two Tides* (1952), and *The Wind at Your Door* (1959).

Fitzmaurice-Kelly, James (1857–1923). English authority on Spanish literature. He wrote authoritative works in his field and was editor of *The Oxford Book of Spanish Verse* (1913).

Five, The. A group of late 19th-century Russian composers who, fervent nationalists, hoped to develop an indigenous school of music. It consisted of Mily Balakirev (1837–1910), who was leader, César Cui (1835–1918), MUSSORGSKY, BORODIN, and RIMSKY-KORSAKOV.

Five Classics. Works in the Confucian canon. They are: BOOK OF ODES, BOOK OF CHANGES, BOOK OF RITES, BOOK OF DOCUMENTS, and the SPRING AND AUTUMN ANNALS. Together with the *Four Books,* they served as the basis of Chinese education until recent times.

Five-Foot Shelf. A popular name for the HARVARD CLASSICS.

Five Nations. (1) A confederation of five related tribes of the Huron-Iroquois linguistic stock: the Mohawks, Oneidas, Onondagas, Cayugas, and Senecas. See IROQUOIS LEAGUE.

(2) The Five Civilized Nations or Tribes were the Cherokee, Chickasaw, Choctaw, Creek, and Seminole, so called because they had gone far in absorbing the civilization of the white settlers.

Five-Year Plan. A period of industrial construction and consolidation in the Soviet Union. The first plan lasted from 1928 to 1932. At the instigation of the literary group RAPP, many novels, stories, and plays were produced depicting the time. Among the best were works by Valentin Katayev (*Time, Forward!*) and by Leonid Leonov.

Flaccus, Quintus Horatius. See HORACE.

Flag Day. June 14, celebrated in the U.S. as the anniversary of the formal adoption of the Stars and Stripes in 1777, though not a legal holiday.

Flagellants. Members of religious associations who hold that the wrath of God can be appeased only by self-flagellation. The first wave of this movement spread over Europe, starting from Italy, about the year 1260. Scenes of public processions with the exhibition of bloody self-castigation were repeated on a larger scale at the time of the plague called the black death (about 1348). For a modern group with similar tenets see PENITENTES.

Flagstad, Kirsten (1895–1962). Norwegian dramatic soprano. She was famous for her Wagnerian interpretations, especially in the role of Isolde. Her autobiography, *The Flagstad Manuscripts* (1952), was narrated to the music critic, Louis Biancolli.

Flaherty, Robert Joseph (1884–1951). Canadian explorer, writer, and pioneer documentary motion-picture director. From 1910 to 1916, he led a number of expeditions into the subarctic regions of eastern Canada. Among his classic documentary films are *Nanook of the North* (1922), *Moana of the South Seas* (1925), *Tabu* (1931), *Man of Aran* (1934), *Elephant Boy* (1935), and *Louisiana Story* (1948). He wrote the autobiographical *A Film-Maker's Odyssey* (1939) and the novels *The Captain's Chair* (1938) and *White Master* (1939).

Flame of Life, The (Il Fuoco, 1900). A novel by Gabriele D'ANNUNZIO. It deals with the love affair of La Foscarina, a great tragic actress in her prime, and Stelio, a young poet. Inspired by the author's liaison with Eleonora DUSE, the novel caused a scandal upon publication.

Flaminio, Marcantonio (1498–1550). Venetian lyricist. He is noted for his prolific output of secular and religious verse in Latin during the Renaissance. Especially noteworthy is the *Lusus Pastorales* (*Pastoral Fancies*, 1552), eight books of bucolic verse.

Flanders, Moll. See MOLL FLANDERS.

Flaubert, Gustave (1821–1880). French novelist. Born at Rouen in Normandy, Flaubert is one of the great literary artists of the 19th century. Although his name is associated with the naturalist movement, his artistic beliefs and ideals may not be so neatly summarized. Victor Hugo, Chateaubriand, and Gautier were the writers whom Flaubert most admired. A deep strain of romanticism in his own nature, which found expression in lyricism and vivid imaginings, was resolutely curbed in the service of his theories of art. Like Gautier, Flaubert believed in perfection of form and in the absolute value of art: *l'art pour l'art* ("art for art's sake"). In technique, his work is marked by exactness and accuracy of observation, extreme impersonality and objectivity, and extraordinary balance and precision of style. But his precise, careful portrayal of object and event, although naturalistic in method, was not naturalistic in aim. Flaubert's concern was to create reality through the art of exact selection and the chiseled perfection of his style. Beset by ill health and by personal misfortune, he led a solitary life of rigid discipline. His obsession with the writer's craft is legendary. Hour after hour, he would labor over the rhythm or the music of a particular sentence, seeking *le mot juste*. He wrote MADAME BOVARY, SALAMMBÔ, L'EDUCATION SENTIMENTALE, *Tentation de Saint-Antoine* (*The Temptation of Saint Anthony*, 1874), and the unfinished *Bouvard et Pécuchet* (1881). The short stories *Un Coeur Simple* (A SIMPLE HEART), *La Légende de Saint-Julien-l'Hospitalier*, and *Hérodias* appeared in the single volume *Trois Contes* (1877); these masterful tales revealed Flaubert's great command of this genre.

Flavius. In Shakespeare's TIMON OF ATHENS, the "true and honest" servant of Timon. His loyalty to Timon never wavers, even when his master is reduced to ruin. Flavius shares his savings with Timon's other servants and offers to give Timon the remainder.

Flavius and Marullus. In Shakespeare's JULIUS CAESAR, two tribunes, supporters of the defeated Pompey. They bitterly reproach the Roman masses for their fickleness, reminding them that they had once paid Pompey the same homage that they now give to Caesar.

Fleance. In Shakespeare's MACBETH, the son of Banquo. After the assassination of his father, he escapes to Wales. From him, according to legend, proceeded in a direct line the Stuart line of Scotland, thus fulfilling the witches' prophecy that Banquo's descendants would be kings.

Flecker, James Elroy (1884–1915). English poet and dramatist. He is known for his iconoclastic manner, his interest in Greece and the Orient, and the pictorial richness of his writing. His poetic works include *The Bridge of Fire* (1908), *The Golden Journey to Samarkand* (1913), *The Burial in England* (1915), and *Collected Poems* (1916). His plays are *Don Juan*, produced in 1925, and *Hassan*, which was widely celebrated in the 1923 production. He wrote one novel, *King of Alsander* (1914). Flecker was called "the last of the Parnassians."

Flecknoe, Richard. See MACFLECKNOE.

Fleet marriages. Clandestine marriages that were performed without banns or license by needy chaplains, in Fleet Prison, London. As many as thirty marriages a day were sometimes celebrated in this manner. This practice was suppressed and declared null and void in 1774.

Fleet Street. A street in London now synonymous with English journalism and newspaperdom. It was a famous thoroughfare centuries before the first newspaper was published there at the close of the 18th century. The name derives from the old stream, the Fleet, now subterranean, which flowed nearby.

Fleming, Henry. The hero of Stephen Crane's novel THE RED BADGE OF COURAGE and of his short stories *Lynx-Hunting* and *The Veteran* (see WHILOMVILLE STORIES). In the novel, Fleming learns the meaning of fear and later, almost accidentally, of courage.

Fleming, Ian (1908–1964). English author of crime and adventure fiction. The hero of most of his novels is James Bond, a secret agent for British Intelligence. Among Fleming's works are *From Russia With Love* (1951), *Casino Royal* (1954), *Dr. No* (1959), *Goldfinger* (1959), and *Thunderball* (1961).

Fleming, Paul (1609–1640). German baroque poet. Although a close follower and admirer of Martin Opitz, he shows more depth of personal feeling in his verse. A complete edition of his works, *Teutsche Poemata* (*German Poems*, 1642), appeared posthumously.

Fleming, Peter (1907–1971). English travel writer and novelist. Among his books are *Brazilian Adventure* (1933); *News from Tartary* (1936); *Operation Sea Lion* (1957), dealing with a projected invasion of England during World War II; *Siege at Peking* (1959), about the Boxer Rebellion; and *Bayonets to Lhasa* (1961), an account of a British invasion of Tibet in 1904.

Fleshly School of Poetry, The (1871). An article in the *Contemporary Review* by Robert Buchanan. It is a vitriolic diatribe against the poetry of the Pre-Raphaelite Brotherhood, particularly that of Dante Gabriel Rossetti. These writers were accused of morbidity, nastiness, perverted sensuality, and indifference to larger and more exalted concerns of poetry. Buchanan, who wrote the piece over the signature Robert Maitland, at first denied authorship, but was later obliged to admit it. Swinburne became involved in the celebrated quarrel that followed, and his trenchant reply is to be found in *Under the Microscope* (1872). *The Fleshly School of Poetry* was reprinted in the volume *Notorious Literary Attacks* (1926), edited by Albert Mordell. See Stealthy School of Criticism.

Fletcher, Giles, the younger (1588?–1623). English poet. He is best known for Christ's *Victorie and Triumph in Heaven and Earth* (1610), a religious poem modeled on the work of DuBartas and Spenser, which is thought to have had a great influence on Milton's *Paradise Regained* (1671). He was the son of Giles Fletcher, the elder (1549?–1611), who wrote *Licia* (1593), an early book of sonnet sequences.

Fletcher, John. See Beaumont and Fletcher.

Fletcher, John Gould (1886–1950). American poet and critic. First associated with Imagism and later with the Agrarians, he felt that modern poetry needed new patterns and new subject matter. His *Selected Poems* (1938) won a Pulitzer Prize. *Irradiations: Sands and Spray* (1915), his first volume of poetry, was followed by such other collections as *Goblins and Pagodas* (1916), *Breakers and Granite* (1921), *The Black Rock* (1928), and *XXIV Elegies* (1935). His prose works include a book on Gauguin (1921), *John Smith—Also Pocahontas* (1928), *The Two Frontiers: A Study in Historical Psychology* (1930), and the autobiography *Life Is My Song* (1937).

Fletcher, Phineas (1582–1650). English poet. The brother of Giles Fletcher the younger, he was a follower and imitator of Spenser. He is best known for *The Purple Island* (1633), an allegorical poem on man in terms of the topography and settlement of an island. Among his other works are *Locustae* (1627), an anti-Jesuit poem in Latin, its paraphrased English title being *The Apollyonists*; *Britain's Ida* (1627), a mythological poem in the manner of Spenser and first published as the work of Spenser; *Piscatory Eclogues and Other Poetical Miscellanies* (1633). Milton's Satan is believed to have been suggested by the Lucifer of *The Apollyonists*.

fleur-de-lis. See Lily of France.

Fleurs du mal, Les (The Flowers of Evil, 1857). A volume of poetry by Charles Baudelaire. Faced with the conflict of good and evil, Baudelaire discards the conventional distinctions and seeks beauty or good in the perverse, the grotesque, and the morbid. His sensibility, painfully alive to all emotions and sensations, lends unity to the various poems.

Flies, The (Les Mouches; 1943). A play by Jean-Paul Sartre. The plot is an adaptation of Aeschylus' story of Orestes. Zeus shares with Aegistheus "the bitterness of knowing men are free," although the townsfolk are content to let their king shoulder their decision-making along with their responsibility for guilt. Orestes is the dangerous man who knows that he is free, and that "human life begins on the far side of despair." To teach his people to be free and responsible, Orestes kills Aegistheus and takes with him the crowd of repulsive flies, the Furies of the Greek drama, who symbolize conscious acceptance of the consequences of one's acts. When it was first produced during the Occupation, the play had overtones of a call to resistance to the Vichy government's collaboration with the Nazis.

Flint, F[rank] S[tuart] (1885–1960). English imagist poet (see Imagism) and translator. His collections of poetry are *In the Net of the Stars* (1909), *Cadences* (1915), and *Otherworld* (1915).

Flirtatious Mother, The. See Philippe Quinault.

Flite, Miss. In Charles Dickens' Bleak House, a pathetic old woman, demented because of the delay of her suit in chancery.

Floating Island. See Faerie Queene, The.

Flodden or **Flodden Field, Battle of.** A battle in Northumberland on Sept. 9, 1513. James IV of Scotland was defeated and killed by the forces of the earl of Surrey, who was in charge of the action in the absence of Henry VIII. The battle, in which there were up to 10,000 Scottish dead, among them all Scotland's leaders, was made the subject of poems by John Skelton, Thomas Deloney, and others. The battle is described in the 6th canto of Sir Walter Scott's *Marmion, A Tale of Flodden Field*.

flood myths. A very widespread theme in mythology is the destruction of the world by a flood and the survival of one human being, often with his family, thanks to the good will of a god. The most famous flood narrative, that of Noah, is based closely on the far older Babylonian story of Utnapishtim, told in the *Epic of* Gilgamesh. This in turn was based on the Sumerian legend of Ziusudra. In Hindu mythology, Vishnu appears to Manu, the first man, as a fish and warns him of the coming flood; the god himself leads Manu's ship to a safe mooring in the mountains of the North. In the Greek myth, Deucalion (see Deucalion's Flood), the son of Prometheus, is the hero who, with his wife Pyrrha, is saved and repopulates the earth. The Hittite Noah was Ullush. Stories of a great flood are also found in many parts of Asia, in Australia, and in North and South America, though they are uncommon in Europe. It has been suggested that these myths arose either from traditions of local floods or from attempts to explain striking configurations of the landscape.

Flora. In Roman mythology, goddess of flowers. Hence, in natural history all the flowers and vegetable productions of a country or locality are called its *flora.*

Flora. See TURN OF THE SCREW, THE.

Flores (or Floris) and Blanchefleur (*Fr.* **Floire et Blancheflor**). A medieval metrical romance in French and English. Flores and Blanchefleur are a Christian prince and princess who are brought up together and fall in love. Before Blanchefleur is carried off as a slave by the Saracens, she gives Flores a ring that will tarnish when she is in danger. It warns him, and he pursues her through many adventures to an Oriental Emir's harem, which he enters concealed in a basket of roses. When he is discovered, the lovers are sentenced to death, but are pardoned by the Emir because of the beauty of their love for each other. Boccaccio adapts this tale in his IL FILO-COLO.

Florian, Jean Pierre Claris de (1755–1794). French dramatist, novelist, and fabulist, admitted to the French ACADEMY in 1788. His comedies, such as *Les Deux billets* (1799) and *Le Bon ménage* (1782), depict bourgeois life in which Arlequin appears as a sentimental character. Marie Antoinette called Florian's novels "milk soup," such was their insipidity; among these are *Galatée* (1783, adapted from Cervantes) and *Numa Pompilius* (1786, a feeble imitation of Fénelon's *Télémaque*). His fame rests on his agreeable, limpid *Fables,* which are similar to those of La Fontaine, though much less pessimistic.

Florimell. See FAERIE QUEENE, THE.

Florio, John (1553–1625). English lexicographer and translator. The son of an Italian Protestant refugee, Florio compiled an Italian-English dictionary, *A Worlde of Words* (1598), revised as *Queen Anne's New World of Words* (1611); he is best known, however, for his famous and enduring translation of Montaigne's *Essays* (1603).

Floris. See FLORES AND BLANCHEFLEUR.

Florismart. One of Charlemagne's PALADINS in medieval romances, a close friend of Roland.

Florizel. The son of Polixenes, king of Bohemia, in Shakespeare's WINTER'S TALE. During a hunting expedition, he sees Perdita, supposedly the daughter of a shepherd, falls in love with her, and courts her under the assumed name of Doricles. When Polixenes objects to the match, Florizel flees with her to Sicilia, where it is revealed that she is the long-lost daughter of that country's king, Leontes.

Flower and the Leaf, The (15th century). Anonymous allegorical poem of about 600 lines in rhyme royal, for a long time erroneously attributed to Geoffrey Chaucer. The knights and ladies of the Flower, fond of frivolous sports and amusements, are given shelter from a shower by the more serious company of the Leaf.

flower arrangement, Japanese. See IKEBANA.

Flowering Judas (1930). A collection of short stories by Katherine Anne PORTER. Originally printed in a limited edition, it was later reprinted with four stories added. It was the first major work to establish its author's reputation.

Flower of Chivalry. An epithet. It was often applied to Sir Philip Sidney, statesman, poet, and soldier (1554–1586) and to the Chevalier de Bayard, *le Chevalier sans Peur et sans Reproche* (1476–1524).

Fluellen. A pedantic Welsh captain in Shakespeare's HENRY V. He attempts to draw a comparison between Henry and Alexander the Great, but after he points out that one was born at Monmouth and the other at Macedon, both of which begin with the same letter, and that there is a river in both cities, he finds that he has exhausted his parallelisms.

Flute. See BOTTOM.

Flutter, Sir Fopling. See MAN OF MODE, THE.

Flying Dutchman. A legendary spectral ship. Supposedly, it can be seen in stormy weather off the Cape of Good Hope; it is considered an omen of ill luck. Sir Walter Scott, in his note to *Rokeby,* says that the ship was originally a vessel laden with precious metal, on which a horrible murder was committed; then plague broke out among the crew, and no port would allow the vessel to enter. The ill-fated ship still wanders about like a ghost, doomed to be sea-tossed, never more to enjoy rest. Captain Marryat's novel *The Phantom Ship* (1839) tells of Philip Vanderdecken's successful but disastrous search for his father, the captain of the *Flying Dutchman.* WAGNER's opera *The Flying Dutchman* (*Der Fliegende Holländer;* 1843) embodies the legend in a different form. An old Dutch captain, in the midst of a struggle with the elements, has sworn an impious oath to round the Cape even if it takes an eternity to do it. The curse, which is laid on him for centuries, will only be lifted if he finds a wife willing to sacrifice everything for his sake. The opera deals with the lifting of the curse by the Norwegian maiden Senta.

Foch, Ferdinand (1851–1929). Marshal of France, made supreme commander of the Allied forces in 1918, the last year of World War I.

Fogazzaro, Antonio (1842–1911). Italian novelist and poet. A representative of liberal Catholicism, he attempted to reconcile traditional dogma with modern science. His finest novel, *Piccolo Mondo Antico* (*The Patriot,* 1896), dramatizes the antithetical attitudes toward religion held by Franco Maironi, a rigid Catholic, and his wife Luisa, a rationalist. Only a shared tragedy succeeds in reconciling their mutual antagonisms in favor of a trusting Christian faith. Other major novels include *Malombra* (1881), *The Politician* (*Daniele Cortis;* 1885), *Piccolo Mondo Moderno* (1901), *Il Santo* (1906), and *Leila* (1911). They describe a curious symbiosis of exalted mysticism and impassioned sensuality, suggestive of symbolist influence. *Il Santo* was judged heretical by church authorities. See Piero MAIRONI.

Fogg, Phileas. Hero of AROUND THE WORLD IN EIGHTY DAYS by Jules Verne.

Földes, Jolán, Anglicized as **Yolanda** (1903–   ). A Hungarian novelist, permanently established in London. Her novel *The Street of The Fishing Cat* was awarded the All-Nations Novel prize in 1936.

Folengo, Teofilo or **Girolamo** (1496–1544). Italian satiric poet and Benedictine monk. He is famous for his mock epic poem, *Baldus.* Published in two parts totaling 25 books, the poem was written in Macaronic Latin, a mixture of the classical tongue with Italian. In its satire it was influenced by earlier writers like Erasmus, Pulci, and Boiardo; its chief impact was on Rabelais, who used several of its characters and incidents. It has sometimes borne the title *Macaronicae,* and Folengo, also, has been known by the pseudonym he affixed to the poem, Merlin Cocai.

Folk book. See VOLKSBUCH.

Folle de Chaillot, La. See MADWOMAN OF CHAILLOT, THE.

Fomorians. In Gaelic literature, a race of giants who periodically came from the sea to raid prehistoric Ireland and inevitably tangled with whoever happened to be inhabiting the island at the time. See BATTLE OF MOYTURA, THE.

Fontaine, Jean de la. See Jean de LA FONTAINE.

Fontainebleau. A town 37 miles southeast of Paris. Its palace was from the Middle Ages a favorite residence of the royal families of France. Several treaties were signed there. The forest of Fontainebleau is considered the most beautiful in France. It was the resort of the Barbizon school of painters, also known as the Fontainebleau or Fontainebleau-Barbizon school.

Fontane, Theodor (1819–1898). German novelist, perhaps his country's greatest master of the social novel. In his youth, he was primarily a ballad writer but is not highly regarded as such; and it was not until the 1870's that he turned to novel writing. His style is realistic and witty, and he uses a great deal of dialogue to recreate the atmosphere of the society he depicts. Without being excessively gloomy, he is constantly skeptical of men's ability to rise above the foolishness they have inherited from the past. Most of his novels treat the decline of the Prussian nobility and the rise of the bourgeois, and most of his plots concern either persons who are living in the past or those who unsuccessfully try to transcend traditional values. His best-known novels are *Irrungen, Wirrungen* (*Mistakes, Confusions,* 1888), about a nobleman who finally chooses a socially acceptable bride over the girl he loves; *Frau Jenny Treibel* (1892), about *nouveau riche* families who jockey for social position by marrying their children to the right persons; and *Effi Briest* (1895), his greatest work, about a middle-class girl who is obliged by her family to marry the old baron who had once been her mother's sweetheart. As a critic, Fontane was one of the first to appreciate the young authors of naturalism, particularly Gerhart Hauptmann.

Fontanne, Lynn (1887?–   ). British-American actress. She is married to the actor Alfred LUNT, with whom she has starred in many stage productions, mainly light comedies. One of her finest performances was as the old lady in Dürrenmatt's *The Visit of the Old Lady*.

Fontenelle, Bernard le Bovier de (1657–1757). French man of letters. *Entretiens sur la pluralité des mondes* (*Conversations on the Plurality of Worlds,* 1686), the best known of his writings, discusses the solar system in terms easily grasped by the general reader. In *Dialogues des morts* (*Dialogues of the Dead,* 1683), historical figures conduct imaginary and witty dialogues on a variety of philosophical subjects. Ostensibly opposing the pagan belief in oracles and upholding the scientific method, the *Histoire des oracles* (*History of Oracles,* 1686) levels a subtle attack at religious orthodoxy and blind obedience to authority. In *Digressions sur les anciens et les modernes* (*Digressions upon the Ancients and the Moderns,* 1688) Fontenelle sides with the moderns, predicting unlimited progress in the arts and sciences.

Fonvizin, Denis Ivanovich (1745–1792). Russian satirical dramatist. He is best known for two classic comedies: *The Brigadier* (*Brigadir;* 1769) and *The Minor* (*Nedorosl';* 1782). The second play, considered his masterpiece, satirizes the barbaric habits of the semieducated gentry of the time.

Fool, Lear's. In Shakespeare's KING LEAR, the strangely wise companion in motley who travels in the storm with Lear, commenting on the behavior of mankind and peppering his words with song. The character is enigmatic in intent, "a pestilent gall" to Lear because of his bitter, mocking wit. He disappears at that point in the play at which Cordelia returns to help Lear, and he is believed in some way to represent truth, a trait also reflected in Cordelia, sometimes referred to by Lear as his "fool."

Fool of Quality, The (1765–1770). A long novel by Henry BROOKE, describing the education of young Harry Moreland, destined to become earl of Moreland and to marry a princess of Morocco. It presents, as Charles Kingsley remarked, "the education of an ideal nobleman by an ideal merchant prince"; and it teaches that "all virtues, even justice itself, are merely different forms of benevolence."

fools. Attendants at court. From medieval times until the 17th century licensed fools or jesters were commonly kept at court, and frequently in the retinue

Will Sommers, the court jester of Henry VIII.

of wealthy nobles. Thus we are told that the regent Morton had a fool, Patrick Bonny; Holbein painted Sir Thomas More's jester, Patison, in his picture of the chancellor; and as late as 1728 Swift wrote an epitaph on Dickie Pearce, the fool of the earl of Suffolk, who died at the age of 63 and is buried in Berkeley Churchyard, Gloucestershire. Dagonet, the fool of King Arthur, is also remembered.

Among the most celebrated court fools are: Rayère, of Henry I; Scogan, of Edward IV; Thomas Killigrew, called "King Charles jester" (1611–1682); Archie Armstrong (d. 1672), and Thomas Derrie, jesters in the court of James I; James Geddes, to Mary Queen of Scots; his predecessor was Jenny Colquhoun; Patch, the court fool of Elizabeth, wife of Henry VII, Will Sommers (d. 1560), Henry VIII's jester, and Patche, presented to that monarch by Cardinal Wolsey; and Robert Grene, jester in the court of Queen Elizabeth I.

The fools of Charles V of France were Mitton and Thévenin de St. Léger; Haincelin Coq belonged to Charles VI, and Guillaume Louel to Charles VII. Triboulet was the jester of Louis XII and Francis I (1487–1536); Brusquet, of whom Brantôme says "he never had his equal in repartee," of Henri II; Sibilot and Chicot, of Henri III and IV; and l'Angély, of Louis XIII.

The guild fools of medieval times played an important part in the spread of literature and education. They formed a branch of the Troubadour organization, a force that permeated Europe.

Fool's Errand, A (1879). A novel by Albion W. Tourgée. This book, published anonymously by "one of the fools," was admired by the public and the critics. The fool's errand was the attempt to rebuild the South, after the Civil War, in the image of the North. The novel concludes that Reconstruction is a failure. Tourgée discusses such groups as the new Ku Klux Klan in the passages of social history interwoven with the story. The story of a Union colonel from Michigan who moves to a Southern plantation after the war, the novel is semiautobiographical.

foot. See METER.

Foote, Samuel (1720–1777). English playwright and actor known for his sensational and libelous plays. In *The Minor* (1760), Foote satirizes METHODISM and George Whitefield; in *The Maid of Bath* (1761), he derides the suitors of the famous singer Elizabeth Linley, then wife-to-be of Richard SHERIDAN. His "scandal-chronicle" comedies gave Foote an opportunity to display his remarkable mimicry and to caricature mercilessly his enemies. Foote's other popular "noonday-skits" include *The Diversions of the Morning* (1747), *An Auction of Pictures* (1748), and *Taste* (1752). His biting wit earned him the epithet "the English Aristophanes."

Forbes, Esther (1894?–1967). American historical novelist. Miss Forbes's favorite setting was New England. Among her books are *O Genteel Lady!* (1926); *A Mirror for Witches* (1928), a powerful novel of a 17th-century girl accused of witchcraft; *The General's Lady* (1938); *Johnny Tremaine* (1943); *The Running of the Tide* (1948); and *Rainbow on the Road* (1954). *Paul Revere and the World He Lived In* (1942) was awarded a Pulitzer Prize.

Forbes, Kathryn. Pen name of **Kathryn Anderson McLean** (1909–1966). American writer. Miss Forbes's short stories about her maternal grandmother, a Norwegian immigrant, were collected as *Mama's Bank Account* (1943). I REMEMBER MAMA, a dramatization of the book by John Van Druten, appeared the following year. Miss Forbes is also the author of *Transfer Point* (1947), the story of a 10-year-old girl and a San Francisco trolley car, and *Dog Who Spoke to Santa Claus* (1956), a collection of Christmas stories.

Forbidden City. The city of LHASA in Tibet. It was so called because of the hostility of the lamas to visitors other than pilgrims. Also the section of Peking with the Imperial palace, which was formerly closed to the general public.

forbidden fruit. Figuratively, unlawful indulgence, from the fruit of the tree of the knowledge of good and evil eaten by ADAM AND EVE in disobedience of God's command. According to Muslim tradition, the forbidden fruit was the banana or Indian fig, because fig leaves were employed to cover the disobedient pair when they felt shame as the result of sin.

Forced Marriage, The. See SGANARELLE (3).

Ford, Ford Madox. Original name, **Ford Madox Hueffer** (1873–1939). English novelist and editor. His mother was the daughter of Ford Madox Brown, the Pre-Raphaelite painter, and sister-in-law of William ROSSETTI. Violet HUNT was Ford's mistress for some time. His best novels, THE GOOD SOLDIER and the tetralogy PARADE'S END, are studies of the emotional relationships in marriage and adultery. The early novels *The Inheritors* (1901) and *Romance* (1903) were written in collaboration with Joseph Conrad, whose oblique narrative method Ford admired and imitated. He wrote critical studies of Conrad (1924) and of Henry James (1913). An important literary editor, Ford founded the *English Review* in 1908 and edited the *Transatlantic Review*, from Paris, from about 1924. He "discovered" D. H. Lawrence (see MIRIAM) and was a friend of James Joyce and Ezra Pound. Among his volumes of autobiography and memoirs are *No Enemy* (1929), *Return to Yesterday* (1931), and *It Was the Nightingale* (1933). During the 1950's, Ford began to be increasingly recognized as a major 20th-century writer.

Ford, Henry (1863–1947). American industrialist. Founder of the Ford Motor Co. (1903), he is famous for introducing the principles of mass production to the manufacture of inexpensive automobiles. The Ford Foundation, established in 1936, has done much toward furthering peace, improving college salaries, and protecting freedom of speech, even though Ford himself was often extremely conservative in his social outlook. With Samuel Crowther he wrote several books, among them *My Life and Work* (1923).

Ford, John (1586–c. 1640). English dramatist. He is known for his portrayal of passion and for his concentration on incest and other sexual abnormalities, as revealed in such works as 'TIS PITY SHE'S A WHORE and THE BROKEN HEART. These characteristics are less apparent in PERKIN WARBECK. His other plays include *The Lovers' Melancholy* (1628), *The Lady's Trial* (1638), *The Fancies, Chaste and Noble* (c. 1635), *Love's Sacrifice* (1630), *The Sun's Darling* (1624), and *The Witch of Edmonton* (c. 1623), written with William Rowley and Thomas Dekker.

Ford, Paul Leicester (1865–1902). American novelist and historian. His fame rests principally on two novels: THE HONORABLE PETER STIRLING and JANICE MEREDITH. With his brother, Worthington Ford, he issued some important bibliographies, *Winnowings in American History* (15 v., 1890–1891). Among his various historical and biographical works are *The True George Washington* (1896) and *The Many-Sided Franklin* (1899).

Forester, C[ecil] S[cott] (1899–1966). English novelist, creator of Horatio HORNBLOWER. He is best known for his Hornblower books, but he also wrote the successful *Payment Deferred* (1926), a crime novel; *The Gun* (1933), and THE AFRICAN QUEEN. His recent works include *The Naval War of 1812* (1957) and *Hunting the Bismarck* (1959).

Forest Lovers, The (1898). A popular historical romance by Maurice HEWLITT. Set in the Middle Ages, it is the story of the colorful adventures of Prosper le Gai. Out of pity he marries a waif who turns out to be the Coutess Isoult of Morgraunt.

Forever Amber. See Kathleen WINSOR.

formalism. A movement in Russian literary theory and criticism during the 1920's. It was characterized by its members' interest in aesthetic as opposed to social aspects of art. Although they lost the dominant place in Soviet literature to the advocates of proletarian and socialist art, the movement did inject a healthy interest into Russian literary criticism in the nature of literature and the problems of literary craft. Such interests had been generally subordinate to social concerns since the 19th-century critic Vissarion Belinski set the tone and direction of Russian criticism with his socially-oriented analyses and evaluations. The leading formalist theorists and critics were Victor Shklovski, Boris Eikenbaum, Yuri Tynyanov, Victor Zhirmunski, Boris Tomashevski, and Victor Vinogradov.

Forman, Harry Buxton (1842–1917). English critic and editor. He was responsible for painstaking editions of the works of Keats (1890) and Shelley (1876) and was a supporter of Rossetti, Morris, Meredith, and other contemporary poets.

Fornovo, battle of. In 1495, the French troops of King Charles VIII fought an army of Italian and mercenary troops and safely extricated themselves from defeat. However, a year later, at Atella, they were defeated; for the Italians, it was a major victory against the foreigner; and the basis of the fame of their leader, Francesco Gonzaga.

Fors Clavigera. See John RUSKIN.

Forster, E[dward] M[organ] (1879–1970). English novelist, short-story writer, and essayist. He is known for his liberal humanism, notably exemplified in his greatest novel, A PASSAGE TO INDIA, which is a study of the prejudices and injustices of the English rule over colonial India. With quiet irony, in all his novels he reveals the moral and emotional deficiencies of English middle-class life. HowARDS END is based on his well-known motto "Only connect." Forster believes that people of different races and classes should "connect" with one another, and that within themselves individuals should "connect the prose with the passion"—be imaginative, mystical, and sensitive to nature as well as practical. Like Norman Douglas and D. H. Lawrence, Forster believes that middle-class English people tend to lack the capacity for passion and intuition, and must learn it from other countries, especially Southern Europe, and perhaps from the lower-class English. The novels WHERE ANGELS FEAR TO TREAD and A ROOM WITH A VIEW, both set in Italy, revolve about this theme. Forster's novels are technically enriched by the symbolic and structural devices discussed in his critical work ASPECTS OF THE NOVEL.

Brought up in the country in the house he later celebrated as Howards End, Forster was educated at King's College, Cambridge and continued to live there and in the village of Abinger. His novel THE LONGEST JOURNEY gives a picture of Cambridge life. Abinger is celebrated in *Abinger Harvest* (1936). In Cambridge and London Forster was associated with the BLOOMSBURY GROUP. He traveled to Europe and India, and lived in Alexandria for a while, writing about it in *Pharos and Pharillon* (1923), a collection of essays. He also wrote a number of short stories, chiefly of an allegorical kind, which he published in *The Celestial Omnibus* (1911) and *The Eternal Moment* (1928).

After an early burst of creative activity, Forster wrote no more novels. After 1924 he published only collections of literary and sociological essays such as *Abinger Harvest* and *Two Cheers for Democracy* (1951), biographies, and books of literary criticism. One of the great English novelists of our time, Forster has sometimes been underestimated because all his work belongs to the first quarter of the century.

Förster-Nietzsche, Elisabeth (1846–1935). Sister of Friedrich Nietzsche. In her additions to the works he left unfinished when he went insane, especially *Der Wille zur Macht* (*The Will to Power*, 1901), she distorted his views to make him appear a racist.

Forsyte Saga, The. A series of novels by John GALSWORTHY. Galsworthy continued to write novels about the Forsyte family throughout his life, but strictly the *Saga* consists of *The Man of Property* (1906), *In Chancery* (1920), and *To Let* (1921). The whole work was published with two additional "interludes," *Indian Summer of a Forsyte* and *Awakening*, in 1922. The Forsytes are a large upper-middle-class London family of conventional, materialistic businessmen. When the *Saga* opens, 10 members of the oldest generation are still alive. Most of the novels are concerned with two members of the second generation, Soames Forsyte and Young Jolyon, and their children.

The "man of property" of the first and best-known novel is Soames Forsyte, a typical member of the Forsyte family. His wife Irene, whom he regards as just another piece of property, falls in love with Philip Bosinney, a young architect. Soames devotes all his money and power to punishing them, and Philip is killed in an accident. *In Chancery* tells of the Forsytes' divorce. Irene marries Young Jolyon, the only sensitive member of the Forsyte family, and Soames marries a French girl, Annette. In *To Let*, Soames' daughter Fleur falls in love with Jon, the son of Young Jolyon and Irene; when the young couple learn the truth about their parents Jon draws back in order to remain loyal to his mother.

A Modern Comedy (1929) is a second series of novels about the Forsytes; it consists of *The White*

Monkey, The Silver Spoon, Swan Song, and two "interludes." This series carries the story up to Galsworthy's own day and is full of descriptions of the contemporary scene—toward which the aging author was unsympathetic. Most of the novels are about Fleur, her husband Michael Mont, and their friends. *End of the Chapter* (1933) is a little-read trilogy which is also concerned with Fleur and her friends. The Forsytes recur in many of Galsworthy's short stories and even in novels centered about other families.

In *The Forsyte Saga* itself Galsworthy satirizes Soames Forsyte and his materialistic values and champions the artist, the rebel, and the underdog. But in later novels he praises Soames' solid traditionalism, preferring him to the members of the modern young generation.

Fort, Paul (1872–1960). French poet and dramatist. In 1890 he reacted against the naturalist *Théâtre Libre* of ANTOINE by founding the *Théâtre d'art,* which became the influential *Théâtre de l'Oeuvre* under the director LUGNÉ-POË. Fort wrote a number of symbolic plays with historical subjects for the new theater, among them *La Petite Bête* (1890), *Ysabeau* (1924), and *Les Compères du Roi Louis* (1927). A native of central France, he celebrated her history and culture in forty volumes of *Ballades françaises* and *Chroniques de France* (1897–1951), versified poetry usually printed as prose paragraphs.

For the Time Being (1944). A Christmas oratorio in verse and prose by W. H. AUDEN. It retells the Nativity story in contemporary idiom, with modern allusions, and with some comic, music-hall ballads as well as lyrical choruses. Auden equates the bad political and spiritual condition of the world just before the birth of Christ with the contemporary situation.

Fortinbras. In Shakespeare's HAMLET, the prince of Norway. A man of action unlike the introspective Hamlet, he has planned to invade Denmark but, deterred by his uncle and Claudio, marches on Poland instead. When Hamlet dies, Fortinbras arrives to claim the Danish throne and to restore order to the kingdom.

Fortuna. In Roman mythology, the goddess of fortune or chance. She was identified with the Greek Tyche, and she was often depicted with a rudder, as the pilot of destiny, with wings, or with a wheel. The wheel of fortune was a widely used symbol in medieval art and literature, forming the concept on which Lydgate's *Falls of Princes* (1494) and Chaucer's *Monk's Tale* from the *Canterbury Tales* (1387–1400?) were based.

Fortunate Islands. Also called **Islands of the Blessed** or the **Happy Islands.** Imaginary islands in the ocean. Here the souls of the good lived in eternal bliss. The name was later applied to Canary and Madeira Islands.

Fortunatus. A hero of medieval European legend. A native of Cyprus, he meets the goddess of Fortune, who offers him any one of her gifts: wisdom, long life, riches, and the like. He chooses riches, and she gives him a purse that refills itself whenever he draws from it. On his travels he steals a magic wishing cap from the sultan of Cairo. These apparent treasures, however, eventually prove the ruin of him and his two sons, pointing the moral that worldly goods do not bring happiness. The story first appears in print in a German collection of 1509. It was dramatized by Hans Sachs in 1553, Thomas DEKKER in 1660, and J. L. TIECK (*Phantasus,* 1812–1816). See SCHLEMIHL, PETER.

Fortunes of Nigel, The (1822). A novel by Sir Walter SCOTT set in the period of James I, in which James himself is a character. It relates the attempts of Lord Nigel Olifaunt to secure his properties and a wife.

forty. A number of frequent occurrence in Scripture. Hence it was formerly treated as, in a manner, sacrosanct. Moses was 40 days in the mount; Elijah was 40 days fed by ravens; the rain of the flood fell 40 days, and another 40 days expired before Noah opened the window of the ark; 40 days was the period of embalming; Nineveh had 40 days to repent; Jesus fasted 40 days; He was seen 40 days after His resurrection.

St. Swithin betokens 40 days' rain or dry weather; a quarantine extends to 40 days; 40 days, in the Old English law, was the limit for the payment of the fine for manslaughter; the privilege of sanctuary was for 40 days; the widow was allowed to remain in her husband's house for 40 days after his decease; a knight enjoined 40 days' service of his tenant; a stranger, at the expiration of 40 days, was compelled to be enrolled in some tithing; Members of Parliament were protected from arrest 40 days after the prorogation of the House, and 40 days before the House was convened; a new-made burgess had to forfeit 40 pence unless he built a house within 40 days.

The ancient physicians ascribe many strange changes to the period of 40; the alchemists looked on 40 days as the charmed period when the philosopher's stone and elixir of life were to appear.

forty-five, the, sometimes '**45**. The second rebellion of the JACOBITES which occurred in 1745 and failed. Prince Charles, "the Young PRETENDER," had to escape to France with the aid of Flora MACDONALD. See FIFTEEN, THE.

42nd Parallel, The (1930). A novel by John Dos Passos, 1st book in the trilogy later called *U.S.A.* (q.v.). Set in the period immediately before World War I, the novel interweaves episodes from the lives of several characters with the "newsreel" and "camera eye" devices and with biographies of Eugene Debs, Luther Burbank, William Jennings Bryan, Andrew Carnegie, Edison, and others.

The characters, some of whom appear in other parts of the trilogy, include Fainy McCreary ("Mac"), who eventually joins the Mexican Revolution; the ruthless J. Ward Moorehouse; Eleanor Stoddard, with whom he has an affair; and Charley Anderson, who later becomes a war hero and airplane manufacturer. These various interlocking strands are designed to show the U.S. on the eve of the First World War, rather than the development of particular individuals. Although the book is sometimes confusing, it is, nevertheless, a powerful presentation of a vast canvas of human nature and history.

forty stripes save one. A punishment. The Jews were forbidden by the Mosaic law to inflict more than 40 stripes on an offender, and for fear of breaking the law they stopped short of the number. If the scourge contained three lashes, 13 strokes would equal forty save one.

Forty Thieves. See ALI BABA AND THE FORTY THIEVES.

For Whom the Bell Tolls (1940). A novel by Ernest HEMINGWAY. Set against the background of the Spanish Civil War (1936–1939), it tells the story of Robert Jordan, an idealistic American college professor, who has come to Spain to fight with the Republican army. He has been assigned to a band of guerrillas led by Pablo and his wife, Pilar, a powerful peasant woman. Jordan's task is to blow up a bridge of strategic importance. He falls in love with Maria, a young Spanish girl who has been raped by the Fascists, and, during the three days they are together, they try to forget the impending event in their passion for each other. There is jealousy and distrust among the peasant members of the guerrilla company, several are killed, and the inefficiency and jealousies of the Communist leaders are revealed, but Jordan carries out his mission. He blows up the bridge successfully, but is wounded and left on the hillside to die. The title of the novel is taken from one of the best-known passages in the DEVOTIONS of John Donne.

Foscari, Francesco (1373–1457). Famous *doge* (leader) of the Venetian republic. His long service to his city ended tragically with his expulsion from office. The story of how his enemies used the weaknesses of his son to humiliate him attracted the interest of Lord Byron, who immortalized the affair in his *Two Foscari.*

Foscolo, Ugo (1778–1827). Italian novelist, poet, and patriot. He was the author of *Le Ultime Lettere di Jacopo Ortis* (1802), the first Italian novel in the modern sense of the word. Influenced by Goethe's *Werther,* and told in the form of exchanged letters, it relates the story of the futile love of the young student Ortis for a married woman; Ortis' sufferings, compounded of fruitless passion and frustrated patriotism, eventually drive him to suicide. Foscolo's best-known poem, *I Sepolcri* (1807), reveals his dual poetic personality in its romantic spirit and neoclassical style.

A zealot for the cause of Italian national unity, he fought with Napoleon's Italian army and went into voluntary exile when Austria regained possession of Venetia and Lombardy. While in England (1816–1827), he wrote critical essays on literary, historical, linguistic, and political topics relating to Italy.

Foster, Hannah Webster (1759–1840). American novelist, author of THE COQUETTE. She wrote one other book, *The Boarding School* (1798), a series of didactic lectures on "female deportment."

Foster, Stephen Collins (1826–1864). American song writer and popular composer. Among his best-known songs are MY OLD KENTUCKY HOME, OLD FOLKS AT HOME, *Old Black Joe,* and *Jeanie with the Light Brown Hair.* His OH! SUSANNA appeared in 1848 and, becoming extremely popular with the goldrush "forty-niners," established his success. Many of his songs were used by the Negro minstrel troupes popular at the time and have become genuine American folk songs. Foster died, almost destitute, in the charity ward of Bellevue Hospital in New York.

Fouché, Joseph. Duke of **Otranto** (1763–1820). French minister of police. A master of political intrigue, Fouché was renowned for his espionage system. He served in turn as minister of police, senator, minister of the interior, and again as minister of police. In 1816, Fouché was exiled from France. Stefan Zweig has written a biographical study entitled *Joseph Fouché.*

Fountainhead, The (1943). A novel by Ayn RAND. The hero of this widely sold book, who is supposedly modeled on Frank Lloyd Wright, is an architect of enormous conceit who nevertheless succeeds in justifying his faith in the permanent values of honest design.

Fountain of Youth. In popular folk tales, a fountain supposed to possess the power of restoring youth. Expeditions were fitted out in search of it, and at one time it was supposed to be in BIMINI. See PONCE DE LEÓN.

Fouqué, Friedrich von. Baron de la Motte (1777–1843). German author of fantastic tales and sentimental romances. He was prominent in the movement of GERMAN ROMANTICISM. His most famous work is the tale UNDINE.

Fouquet, Jean (c. 1420–c. 1480). French painter. The leading representative of French 15th-century painting, he was deeply influenced by both the work of the early Florentine school and the Flemish tradition of the Van Eycks. The court painter of Louis XI, he is known equally as a miniaturist and portrait painter.

Fouquet or **Foucquet, Nicolas** (1615–1680). French superintendent of finance under Cardinal Mazarin. At best a haphazard financier, Fouquet bestowed generous favors upon men of letters and incurred the disfavor of King Louis XIV. Arrested by royal order in 1661, he was tried for speculation and sentenced to life imprisonment. He died after 19 years in prison.

Fouquier-Tinville, Antoine Quentin (1746–1795). French revolutionist. He was a public accuser of unexampled ferocity before the Revolutionary Tribunal (March 1793–July 1794). He wrote articles of accusation against Marie Antoinette and ROBESPIERRE, who was once his benefactor.

Fourberies de Scapin, Les. See SCAPIN.

Four Books. The four principal works in the Confucian canon. They are: The ANALECTS, the GREAT LEARNING, The MEAN, and the MENCIUS. Except for the *Analects,* these were relatively unimportant works until raised to an exalted status by Chu Hsi during the Sung Dynasty (960–1279). From this time they were used as the primary textbooks in the Chinese educational system and served as the basis for civil service examinations until 1905. See the FIVE CLASSICS.

Four Horsemen of the Apocalypse. The personifications of the evils of war who appear in the Revelation of St. John the Divine (Rev. 6). They are Conquest, Slaughter, Famine, and Death, and are seen on white, red, black, and pale horses, respectively. The Spanish novelist Vicente Blasco-Ibáñez entitled his widely read novel of World War I *The Four Horsemen of the Apocalypse (Los cuatro jinetes del apocalipsis;* 1916); it has twice been produced as a motion picture.

four hundred, the. The inner circle of New York society, the élite. The term originated in 1892 when only 400 guests were invited to a ball given by

Mrs. William Astor since her ballroom had space for only that number. See FOUR MILLION, THE.

Four Hymns to Love and Beauty (1596). A set of poems by Edmund SPENSER. The first two, *A Hymn in Honor of Love* and *A Hymn in Honor of Beauty,* were written in Spenser's youth. According to his introductory note, he desired to "amend" his youthful praise of natural love and beauty, and so wrote the second two hymns to heavenly love and beauty. All four poems, however, partake strongly of the Platonist and neo-Platonist ideas that mark much of his work, and there is little ideological conflict between the two sets of hymns.

Fourierism. The social system advanced by François Marie Charles Fourier (1772–1837), French reformer and economist. In order that men might live in the harmony to which they were naturally predisposed and which could be developed under proper conditions, Fourier envisioned a society in which economic activities would be carried on by phalanxes, groups consisting of some 1600 persons, who would live in common buildings called phalansteries. Products would be divided among the members of each phalanx, with labor receiving the largest share; private property, however, would not be abolished. A republican form of government, with elective officials, would be established. Fourier outlined his ideas in several works, including *Théorie des quatre mouvements* (1808), *Traité de l'association domestique agricole* (1822), and *Le Nouveau Monde industriel* (1829–1830). A number of Fourieristic communities and periodicals were founded in France, and several novels by George Sand show the influence of his ideas. Introduced into the U.S. in 1842 by Albert Brisbane, Fourierism was adopted by the members of BROOK FARM.

Four Million, The (1906). A collection of 25 short stories by O. HENRY. The title, referring to the actual population of New York City at the time, was selected as a rebuttal to Ward McAllister's famous remark that "there are only about 400 people in New York society." The book contains O. Henry's famous story, THE GIFT OF THE MAGI, although perhaps its best piece is *An Unfinished Story.* O. Henry's favorite characters—shop girls, tramps, the humble and lowly in general—people these tales and give utterance to the author's unique brand of gently ironic sentimentality.

Fournier, Henri. Real name of ALAIN-FOURNIER.
Fournier, Pierre. See Pierre GASCAR.
Four P's, The (performed c. 1520; published 1544). An INTERLUDE by John Heywood. It is a debate among a Palmer, a Pardoner, and a Potecary, with a Pedlar acting as judge, as to who can tell the biggest lie. The Palmer, who asserts that he never saw a woman out of temper, wins the prize.

Four Quartets (1936–42). A long poem by T. S. ELIOT. Considered by many critics to be Eliot's major poetic achievement, it is an elaborate, allusive meditation on time and eternity, consisting of four poems named for four different places. The first (published in 1936), is set in *Burnt Norton,* a house with a rose garden in which children are playing. The second is *East Coker* (1940), the village in England from which Eliot's 17th-century ancestor set out for the New World. *The Dry Salvages* (1941) is a group of rocks off the coast of Massachusetts, where Eliot lived

as a boy; the poem also has descriptions of the Mississippi, St. Louis having been his childhood home. The last poem (1942) is inspired by LITTLE GIDDING and its chapel. It is a wartime poem; there are references to the bombing in London alongside references to the English Civil War. The whole work is as elaborately constructed as a piece of music, with its recurrent imagery, series of symbols (the separate poems are concerned, respectively, with air, earth, water, and fire), and literary, historical, and Christian references. Each poem ends with some words about the poet's craft and the problems of creating a work of art.

Four Saints in Three Acts (1927). An opera by VIRGIL THOMSON to a libretto by GERTRUDE STEIN, first produced in 1934 with an all Negro cast. The text exemplifies Miss Stein's unique style: repetitive, sonorous, contradictory, and obscure. The opera is actually divided into four acts, with about a dozen saints, some historical and others fictitious. One famous line is "Pigeons on the grass alas."

four senses. The 4 varieties of Scriptural interpretation: 1. historical or literal, 2. allegorical, 3. moral, 4. anagogical. "Jerusalem is *literally* a city in Palestine, *allegorically* the Church, *morally* the believing soul, *anagogically* the heavenly Jerusalem."

fourteener. (1) In English prosody, a line containing 14 syllables, usually 7 iambic feet. It was widely used in English verse about the middle of the 16th century. See POULTER'S MEASURE.

(2) A poem of 14 lines, a sonnet or any other variation of this length, is now sometimes referred to as a fourteener.

Fourteen Points. A statement of American peace aims during World War I. It was made by President Woodrow WILSON in an address to Congress on Jan. 8, 1918. Briefly abridged, the Fourteen Points are as follows:

(1) Open covenants of peace, openly arrived at.

(2) Freedom of navigation upon the seas, except by international action.

(3) Removal of economic barriers and establishment of equality of trade conditions.

(4) Adequate guarantees of reduction of national armaments to the lowest point consistent with domestic safety.

(5) An impartial adjustment of all colonial claims with fair consideration for the interests of populations and governments concerned.

(6) Full cooperation in obtaining for Russia an unhampered opportunity for the independent determination of her own political development.

(7) The evacuation of Belgium.

(8) The restoration of Alsace-Lorraine to France.

(9) The readjustment of Italian frontiers on clearly recognized lines of nationality.

(10) Autonomous development for the peoples of Austria-Hungary.

(11) The relations of the Balkan states to be determined along historically established lines of allegiance and nationality.

(12) Autonomous development for other nationalities under Turkish rule; freedom of the Dardanelles.

(13) The establishment of an independent Polish state.

(14) The establishment of a general association of nations for the purpose of affording mutual guaran-

tees of political and territorial integrity to great and small alike.

In Nov., 1918, the other Allies reluctantly accepted the Fourteen Points, with reservations, as the basis for an armistice. The treaty of VERSAILLES, which ended the war, incorporated several of Wilson's points, including the covenant of the League of Nations.

fourth estate. The daily press. It is reputed to be the most powerful of all, the others being the Lords Spiritual, the Lords Temporal, and the Commons. Edmund Burke, referring to the Reporters' Gallery, is credited with having said, "Yonder sits the fourth estate, more important than them all," but it does not appear in his published works.

Fourth of July. An American national holiday in celebration of the Declaration of Independence, July 4, 1776, which declared the 13 colonies free and independent and absolved of all allegiance to Great Britain. It is also called *Independence Day.*

Fowler, Gene. Real name, **Eugene Devlan Fowler** (1890–1960). American writer. Born in Denver, Colo., Fowler had a successful career both as a newspaperman and script-writer. He is best known, however, for his lively biographies of picturesque contemporaries whom he knew personally. The first of these, *The Great Mouthpiece* (1931), was about a New York lawyer. It was followed by *Timberline* (1933), an account of two Denver editors. His best book is *Good Night, Sweet Prince* (1943), a biography of John Barrymore. Other books include *Beau James* (1949), the story of Jimmy Walker; *A Solo in Tom-Toms* (1946); and *Schnozzola: The Story of Jimmy Durante* (1951).

Fowler, Henry Watson (1858–1933). English lexicographer. With his brother F. G. Fowler (1870–1918), he wrote *The King's English* (1906). Fowler compiled a number of dictionaries based on the great *Oxford English Dictionary.* His most famous work is *A Dictionary of Modern English Usage* (1926), a remarkable compilation of learning, wit, humor, and good taste.

Fox, Charles James (1749–1806). Celebrated English statesman and orator. He was a Tory member of Parliament at the age of 20, and two years later became lord of the admiralty under Lord North. Removed from his post at the insistence of King George III, who disliked him both for his personal independence and for the dissoluteness of his life, Fox led the opposition to North's coercive measures against the American colonies. He was foreign secretary (1782–1783), first under Rockingham and then in Portland's coalition ministry, the latter being turned out of office by the king's intervention against Fox's India reform bill. He was kept out of office by the king until 1806 when William Pitt the younger died and he again held the portfolio of foreign secretary in the so-called All-The-Talents ministry during the last year before his own death. Fox once gave a toast: "Our Sovereign, the people." He urged abolition of slavery, favored the French Revolution, and objected to English participation in continental wars. He loved literature and made one venture into authorship with *History of the Early Part of the Reign of James II* which, unfinished, was published two years after his death.

Fox, George (1624–1691). The founder of the Society of Friends, or QUAKERS. The son of a weaver, and an apprentice to a cobbler, he became an itinerant lay preacher. He was an unusual combination of mystic and highly practical man, a fact that led him to denounce social evils in forthright terms that nine times landed him in prison. Nevertheless, he was very widely respected and loved for his remarkable personal qualities. He traveled as a missionary to the West Indies and America, and to Holland and Germany. Beginning about 1650, many persons had been so attracted to his teachings that they were organized in the Society of Friends, who were nicknamed Quakers. Because of his limited education, his writings were inelegantly though often effectively expressed.

Fox, John [William], Jr. (1863–1919). American writer of fiction. He achieved enormous popularity with his two best-selling novels, THE LITTLE SHEPHERD OF KINGDOM COME and THE TRAIL OF THE LONESOME PINE. An earlier novel, *The Kentuckians* (1898), contrasts the prosperous inhabitants of Kentucky's bluegrass region with its impoverished mountaineers. Fox's short stories and sketches were collected in *A Cumberland Vendetta* (1895), *Hell for Sartain* (1897), *Blue Grass and Rhododendron* (1901), and *Christmas Eve on Lonesome, and Other Stories* (1904).

Foxe, John (1517–1587). English martyrologist. Educated at Oxford, Foxe was made a Deacon in 1550. He was exiled between 1554 and 1559, the years of the reign of the Catholic Mary I, during which time he wrote a first Latin draft of his great work on martyrs. A revised and longer version was published in English in 1563 as *Actes and Monuments of These Latter Perilous Days* (commonly known as *The Book of Martyrs*). Two volumes, enlarged further, appeared in 1570. The *Actes and Monuments* was tremendously influential, being used practically as a companion-volume to the Bible in English churches and households for many years. The work is of interest historically for its many accounts of the deaths of contemporary Protestant martyrs.

F.P.A. See Franklin Pierce ADAMS.

Fracastoro, Girolamo (1483–1553). Veronese physician and poet. He is noted for his Latin verse,

Burning Anne Askew (1546). From Foxe's
Actes and Monuments.

especially the *Syphilis sive de morbo gallico* (*Syphilis or the Gallic Disease*), a combined mythological and scientific treatment of the subject. He is also the author of an important critical treatise, the *Navigerius,* which uses the dialogue form to discuss Renaissance literary problems and theories.

Fra Diavolo (1830). A highly popular comic opera by D. F. E. Auber. It is founded on the exploits of Michele Pezza (1771?–1806), a celebrated brigand and renegade monk, who evaded pursuit for many years amidst the mountains of Calabria. The libretto is by Scribe.

Fradubio. See Faerie Queene, The.

Fragonard, Jean Honoré (1732–1806). French painter. A versatile imitator of Antoine Watteau and Giambattista Tiepolo, he painted and drew landscapes, mythological love-scenes, and fashionable outdoor gatherings. With verve and charm, he extended the popularity of rococo up to the time of the French Revolution.

Fra Lippo Lippi (1855). A poem in the form of a dramatic monologue by Robert Browning. The painter, speaking to street guards of Florence who have come upon him in the midst of a night adventure, gives his biography and his views on life and art. See Fra Lippo Lippi.

Framley Parsonage, The. See Barsetshire, Chronicles of.

France, Anatole. Pen name of **Jacques Anatole François Thibault** (1844–1924). French novelist, poet, and critic. An eminently civilized man of letters, Anatole France occupied the chief position in the French literary world for many years. In 1872, he published *Les Poèmes dorés,* a volume of poetry in the manner of the Parnassians—pure in form and classical in spirit. A poetic drama *Les Noces corinthiennes* was published in 1876. France's career as a critic began in 1888, when he was appointed literary editor of *Le Temps,* a popular daily. His criticism is avowedly impressionistic and subjective, the imaginative play of a finely developed mind and cultivated sensibility responding to and revealing his world and age. Elected to the French Academy in 1896, he reached the peak of his fame during the turn of the century. By the time of his election he had published his famous novels The Crime of Sylvester Bonnard; Thaïs, made into an opera by Massenet (1894); At the Sign of the Reine Pédauque; The Red Lily; and a volume of short stories, *L'Etui de Nacre* (*The Mother-of-Pearl Box,* 1892). Highly allusive in nature, France's subtle and ironic work displays an urbane cynicism and tolerant mockery. His style, like the tone of his writing, is sophisticated, delicate, and graceful. His later novels include Penguin Island, The Gods are Athirst, and the Revolt of the Angels. *Histoire Contemporaine* (1896–1901) is a collection of four satirical novels: The Elm Tree on the Mall, The Wickerwork Woman, The Amethyst Ring, and *M. Bergeret à Paris.* France's autobiographical works include *Le Livre de mon ami* (*My Friend's Book,* 1885), *Pierre Nozière* (1899), *Le Petit Pierre* (*Little Pierre,* 1918) and *La Vie en Fleur* (*The Bloom of Life,* 1922). The relaxed detachment of many of France's writings may be juxtaposed with his passionate interest in the Dreyfus case. France's character, like his career, is interesting for its many

facets. He was awarded the Nobel Prize for literature in 1921.

France, king of. In Shakespeare's King Lear, the husband of Cordelia, Lear's youngest daughter. Recognizing her virtues, he marries her although she has been disowned by her father.

France, rulers of. Like earlier members of his house, Pepin the Short ruled the domain of the Franks as mayor of the palace on behalf of the ineffectual Merovingians; the Carolingian dynasty began when Pepin set aside the last of the "do-nothing kings" and had himself crowned in 751.

THE CAROLINGIANS

Pepin the Short	751 – 768
Charlemagne	768 – 814
Louis I	814 – 840
Charles I	840 – 877
Louis II	877 – 879
Louis III	879 – 882
Carloman	882 – 884
Charles II	884 – 888
Eudes (Odo)	888 – 898
Charles III	898 – 922
Robert I	922 – 923
Rudolf	923 – 936
Louis IV	936 – 954
Lothair	954 – 986
Louis V	986 – 987

THE CAPETS

Hugh Capet	987– 996
Robert II	996–1031
Henry I	1031–1060
Philip I	1060–1108
Louis VI	1108–1137
Louis VII	1137–1180
Philip II	1180–1223
Louis VIII	1223–1226
Louis IX	1226–1270
Philip III	1270–1285
Philip IV	1285–1314
Louis X	1314–1316
John I	1316
Philip V	1316–1322
Charles IV	1322–1328

HOUSE OF VALOIS

Philip VI	1328–1350
John II	1350–1364
Charles V	1364–1380
Charles VI	1380–1422
Charles VII	1422–1461
Louis XI	1461–1483
Charles VIII	1483–1498
Louis XII	1498–1515
Francis I	1515–1547
Henry II	1547–1559
Francis II	1559–1560
Charles IX	1560–1574
Henry III	1574–1589

HOUSE OF BOURBON

Henry IV	1589–1610
Louis XIII	1610–1643
Louis XIV	1643–1715
Louis XV	1715–1774
Louis XVI	1774–1792

FIRST REPUBLIC

National Convention	1792–1795
Directory	1795–1799
Napoleon (Consul)	1799–1804

FIRST EMPIRE	
Napoleon I	1804–1814

HOUSE OF BOURBON	
Louis XVIII	1814–1824
Charles X	1824–1830

HOUSE OF ORLÉANS	
Louis Philippe	1830–1848

SECOND REPUBLIC	
Louis Napoleon	1848–1852

SECOND EMPIRE	
Napoleon III	1852–1870

THIRD REPUBLIC—PRESIDENTS	
Thiers, Louis Adolphe	1871–1873
MacMahon, Marshal	1873–1879
Grévy, Jules	1879–1887
Carnot, Sadi	1887–1894
Casimir-Périer, Jean Paul	1894–1895
Faure, François Félix	1895–1899
Loubet, Emile	1899–1906
Fallières, Armand	1906–1913
Poincaré, Raymond	1913–1920
Deschanel, Paul	1920
Millerand, Alexandre	1920–1924
Doumergue, Gaston	1924–1931
Doumer, Paul	1931–1932
Lebrun, Albert	1932–1940

VICHY GOVERNMENT	
Pétain, Henri Philippe	1940–1944
Laval, Pierre	1942–1944

PROVISIONAL GOVERNMENT—PRESIDENTS	
de Gaulle, Charles	1944–1946
Gouin, Félix	1946
Bidault, Georges	1946
Blum, Léon	1946–1947

FOURTH REPUBLIC—PRESIDENTS	
Auriol, Vincent	1947–1954
Coty, René	1954–1959

FIFTH REPUBLIC—PRESIDENT	
de Gaulle, Charles	1959–

Francesca, Piero della. Real name: **Piero dei Franceschi** (1420?–1492). Italian painter and mathematician. Born in Umbria, he came in contact with the monumental tradition of Masaccio and the scientific studies of Brunelleschi and Alberti during a stay in Florence. His own work, in which an almost abstract simplification of forms is fused with a sensitive observation of light effects, creates a world of great solidity, simplicity, and calm. He wrote two mathematical treatises on perspective and on the five regular solids, and was the first to treat optics and perspective with a purely scientific method. Among his masterpieces are *The Legend of the Holy Cross,* a series of frescoes in the sanctuary of the church of St. Francis at Arezzo; the *Portrait of Federigo da Montefeltro; The Resurrection;* and the *Brera Madonna,* his last work. His leading pupils were Melozzo da Forlì and Luca Signorelli.

Francesca da Rimini. See PAOLO AND FRANCESCA.

Francis I (1494–1547). King of France (1515–1547). After conquering Milan by his victory at Marignano (1515), Francis tried unsuccessfully to be elected Holy Roman Emperor and waged four wars against his victorious rival Charles V, who advanced claims to the French duchy of Burgundy and also to Milan. The first war (1521–1525) came to an end when Francis was defeated and taken prisoner at Pavia. In the second war (1527–1529) he lost his hold on Italy by the treaty of peace signed at Cambrai for him by his mother Louise of Savoy and known as the *Paix des Dames.* The third war (1536–1538) led to a truce. The fourth war (1542–1544) was terminated with the peace of Crespy which left Francis in possession of Burgundy while Charles retained Milan. Francis' reign is marked by the Renaissance in France. He himself was a patron of the arts. His sister was the celebrated Margaret of Navarre.

Franciscans. Also called **Friars Minor, Minorites,** and **Grey Friars.** A Catholic religious order. It was founded by Saint FRANCIS OF ASSISI (1209) simply as a confraternity and approved informally by Pope Innocent III (1210). The members made the usual vows of obedience, chastity, and a strict poverty permitting no possessions and dependent solely on the offerings of the faithful. Honorius III confirmed (1223) a new set of rules (including the requirement of a novitiate, etc.) for the now numerous order; but administrative struggles over the conviction of some that the order should be permitted to own the buildings it used and other necessaries eventually split the order (1415) into the Conventuals, following the modified rules, and the more traditional Observants. About 1528 even stricter reforms were instituted by a third branch, the Capuchins. About 1214 Francis had instituted a second order for nuns, called Poor Clares from their leader St. Clara; and about 1221 he organized the Brothers and Sisters of Penance as a third order of laymen, hence called Tertiaries. This important innovation was soon imitated by other religious orders.

Francis Ferdinand (1863–1914). Archduke of Austria, nephew of Francis Joseph and heir to the imperial throne of Austria. His assassination at Saravejo, Bosnia, by Gavrilo Princip, a member of a Serbian secret society, precipitated the outbreak of World War I.

Francis Joseph I or **Franz Josef** (1830–1916). Emperor of Austria (1848–1916). He succeeded to the throne upon the abdication of his uncle, Ferdinand I, during the revolution of 1848 in Vienna. Throughout his reign he opposed the forces of liberalism and maintained a traditional imperial court. There was much tragedy in his personal life: he was the brother of the ill-fated MAXIMILIAN of Mexico; his wife Elizabeth was assassinated in 1898; his only son Rudolf committed suicide; and the assassination of his nephew and heir, Archduke Francis Ferdinand, precipitated World War I.

Francis of Assisi, St. Originally **Giovanni Francesco Bernardone** (1181 or 1182–1226). Italian monk, founder of the Order of FRANCISCANS. The son of a prosperous merchant, he turned at about 26 to a life of asceticism and mysticism, devoting himself to the care of the poor, the sick, and the leprous, as well as to prayer. Feeling a divine call to imitate Christ's life and to preach, he gathered about him a small group of followers and drew up (1209) the rules of life for the monastic order called the Friars Minor, later known as the Franciscans. They journeyed to Rome in 1210 and received verbal confirmation from the Pope. Francis joined a pilgrimage to Palestine (1219–1220), then resigned his leadership of the now numerous Friars Minor because of internal disputes about administration.

Francis' approach to religion was characterized by its joyousness and its love of nature; he called both animate and inanimate creations his brothers and sisters, and his preaching to the birds has become a popular subject for artists, as has the episode when two years before his death he is said to have received on his body the *stigmata* resembling Christ's wounds after 40 days of fasting on Mount Alverno. He was canonized as a saint in 1228, two years after his death; and about a century later the legends and anecdotes about his life, along with his sermons and sayings, were collected as the *Little Flowers of St. Francis Fioretti di S. Francesco d'Assisi*).

Franck, César Auguste (1822–1890). Belgian-French organist and composer. Among his works are the *Symphony in D minor* and the *Mass for Three Voices*, from which comes the familiar *Panis Angelicus*. His style is romantic and expansive, full of chromatic harmony and restless modulation. Among his pupils were Alexandre Guilmant, Vincent d'Indy, and Charles Bordes. These three founded a school, the *Schola Cantorum* (1894) to perpetuate their master's influence and methods.

Franco, Francisco (1892–   ). Spanish political leader. Chief of staff of the Spanish army at the beginning of the Civil War (1936–1939), Franco became leader of the insurgents after the death of generals José Sanjurjo and Goded. With the help of Germany and Italy, favored by British and American "nonintervention," he consolidated his position and assumed dictatorial powers shortly after the fall of Madrid (March 28, 1939). He is sometimes known as *el Caudillo* ("the leader").

Franco, Matteo (1447–1494). Florentine poet and priest. A partisan of the Medici, he wrote verse concerning the behavior of his parishioners, and exchanged sonnets with Pulci in a bitter literary feud. The *Sonetti* were first published in 1759.

Franco, Niccolò (1515–1570). Italian poet. Born in Benevento, he was the author of a group of dialogues and verses entitled *La Filena* (1537–1542). He was at first a friend and partisan, then a bitter enemy of Aretino.

Franco-Prussian War. Also known as the **Franco-German War** (1870–1871). A war between France, then ruled by Napoleon III, and Prussia, whose prime minister at the time was Otto von Bismarck. Relations between the two powers deteriorated when Bismarck supported the candidacy of Prince Leopold Hohenzollern-Sigmaringen, a relative of King William of Prussia, to the vacant throne of Spain. Prince Leopold eventually withdrew, but Bismarck, who wanted war, edited the famous Ems TELEGRAM describing an interview between William and the French ambassador in such a way as to make it seem that the king had insulted France, which retaliated by declaring war on July 19, 1870. The French were overwhelmed by the well-trained, well-organized Prussian forces, and a large part of the French army and Napoleon himself were forced to surrender at Sedan. A republic was then proclaimed in Paris, which was besieged by the Prussians and capitulated on Jan. 28, 1871. By the treaty of Frankfort, France lost the provinces of Alsace and Lorraine and agreed to pay an indemnity of five billion francs; an army of occupation would remain in France until the indemnity was paid. Bismarck used the victory to complete German unification, and after the states of Bavaria, Baden, and Württemberg had joined the German Confederation, King William was proclaimed German emperor on Jan. 18, 1871 in the Hall of Mirrors at Versailles.

Frank, Anne (1929–1944). German-Jewish girl who hid from the Nazis with her parents and several friends in an Amsterdam warehouse from 1942 to 1944. Her diary, covering the years of hiding, was found by friends and published as *Het Achterhus* (*Du.,* "the annex"; 1947); it was later published in English as *The Diary of a Young Girl* (1952). Against the background of the mass-murder of European Jewry, the book presents a vivid picture of a group of hunted people forced to live and survive together in almost intolerable proximity. Written with humor as well as insight, it offers an extraordinary picture of a girl growing up and conveys all the preoccupations of adolescence and first love. The diary ends three days before the Franks and their friends were discovered by the Nazis. Anne died in the extermination camp at Bergen-Belsen in 1944. The book was dramatized as *The Diary of Anne Frank* and performed the world over.

Frank, Bruno (1887–1945). German novelist and playwright. He was influenced by Thomas Mann and noted for his historical and psychological realism. His best-known works are *Zwölftausend* (*Twelve Thousand,* 1927), a play, and *Cervantes* (1934), a story.

Frank, Leonhard (1882–1961). German playwright and novelist with socialist leanings. He is best known for his short novel *Karl und Anna* (1926, dramatized 1929).

Frank, Waldo [David] (1889–1967). American writer. Waldo Frank was noted for his criticism of contemporary civilization, often from the point of view of political liberalism. Novels of his that attracted attention were *The Dark Mother* (1920), *Rahab* (1922), *Holiday* (1923), *The Death and Birth of David Markand* (1934), *The Bridegroom Cometh* (1938), *Summer Never Ends* (1941), *The Invaders* (1948), and *Not Heaven* (1953). His works of nonfiction include *Virgin Spain* (1926), *Dawn in Russia* (1932), *Chart for Rough Water* (1940), *Bridgehead: The Drama of Israel* (1957), *The Rediscovery of Man* (1958), and *Cuba: Prophetic Island* (1961).

Frankau, Gilbert (1884–1952). English popular novelist, author of *World Without End* (1943).

Frankau, Pamela (1908–1967). English novelist, daughter of Gilbert Frankau. Among her novels is *A Wreath for the Enemy* (1954), the story of a girl growing up.

Franken, Rose (1895–   ). American novelist and playwright. She is best known for the Claudia series of novels, dealing with the happy domestic life of a girlish heroine. A stage version of *Claudia* (1929), the first novel in the series, was produced in 1941. Her other plays include *Mr. Dooley, Jr.* (1932) and *Another Language* (1934).

Frankenstein, or the Modern Prometheus (1818). A romance by Mary Wollstonecraft SHEL-

LEY. Frankenstein, a young student, animates a soulless monster made out of corpses from churchyards and dissecting rooms by means of galvanism. Longing for sympathy and shunned by everyone, the creature ultimately turns to evil and brings dreadful retribution on the student for usurping the Creator's prerogative, finally destroying him. Several movies have been based on the novel. Mrs. Shelley gave no name to the monster, but he is commonly called Frankenstein after his creator, the student. This, of course, is an error.

Frankfurter, Felix (1882–1965). Austrian-born American jurist and teacher. After a brief career practicing law, Frankfurter taught at Harvard Law School (1914–1939) and engaged in various governmental pursuits until his appointment to the U.S. Supreme Court (1939–1962). He wrote many legal textbooks as well as *The Case of Sacco and Vanzetti* (1927), *The Public and Its Government* (1930), *Mr. Justice Holmes and the Supreme Court* (1939), and *Law and Men* (1956). *Felix Frankfurter Reminisces,* edited by Harlan B. Phillips, appeared in 1960.

Frankie and Johnny. One of the most famous of American folk ballads. It relates Frankie's pursuit and murder of her unfaithful sweetheart, Johnnie. The refrain is: "He was her man, but he done her wrong." It inspired a series of paintings by Thomas Hart Benton, another by John Held, Jr., and several dramas.

Franklin, Benjamin (1706–1790). American statesman, author, inventor, printer, and scientist, sometimes called "the wisest American." The son of a Boston tallow chandler, Franklin was apprenticed at 12 to his brother James, a local printer, to whose newspaper he contributed a series of Addisonian essays, the *Dogood Papers* (1722). In 1723 he ran away to Philadelphia, where he set up his own newspaper, published POOR RICHARD'S ALMANACK, and with intense energy established a subscription library, a philosophical society, a fire company, a hospital, a militia, became postmaster of Philadelphia, proposed the University of Pennsylvania, devised bifocal spectacles, a stove, and a water-harmonica. He later performed electrical experiments leading in 1752 to his invention of the lightning rod, which earned him election to the Royal Society in London, the compliments of Louis XV of France, and several honorary degrees. Active for the colonies throughout the Revolution, he helped draft and was a signer of the Declaration of Independence. He concluded an alliance with France (1778) and was one of the diplomats to negotiate the treaty of peace with Great Britain (1783). In 1787 he attended the Federal Constitutional Convention. His AUTOBIOGRAPHY is considered one of the classics of the genre. Herman Melville introduced him into *Israel Potter* (1855), and he also appears in Irving Bacheller's *In the Days of Poor Richard* (1922).

Franklin Evans, or The Inebriate (1842). A novel by Walt WHITMAN. In this conventional temperance tract, a country boy suffers degradation and torment when he falls under the influence of alcohol in New York City. Finally reforming, he lives an honorable life.

Franklin's Tale, The. One of the CANTERBURY TALES of Geoffrey CHAUCER. Apparently it is based on a tale in Boccaccio's *Il Filocolo* and similar to his tale of a GARDEN IN JANUARY in the *Decameron,* although Chaucer attributes it to a Breton *lay.* The Franklin opposes the views in the WIFE OF BATH's TALE, saying that love flies when constrained by sovereignty. In his tale, Dorigen accepts her husband Arveragus (or Arviragus) as her servant in love but her lord in marriage. When Arveragus goes off to war, she refuses the advances of the squire Aurelius, playfully promising that she will be his when he removes all the rocks from the coast of Brittany. Arveragus returns, and Aurelius pines until a magician succeeds in making it appear that the rocks have disappeared. Aurelius reminds Dorigen of her promise. She decides she should rather kill herself than dishonor her marriage; but when Arveragus learns the story, he says she must keep her promise, and sends her to meet Aurelius. The squire meets this display of nobility by releasing her from her promise, and the magician, not to be outdone, releases the squire from his 1000-pound debt, since the magic did not achieve its purpose.

Fraser, G[eorge] S[utherland] (1915–   ). Scottish poet and critic. Associated with the NEW APOCALYPSE movement, he wrote *Vision and Rhetoric* (1960) and works on Dylan Thomas and Ezra Pound.

Fraunhofer lines. The dark lines in the solar spectrum, caused by the passage of light through certain gases in the atmosphere. They were named after the Bavarian physicist Joseph von Fraunhofer (1787–1826), who was the first to classify them. See Gustav Robert KIRCHHOFF.

fravashi. In Persian religion, a spiritual protector or guardian angel of each individual, especially of the believer. It is the pre-existing archetype of every man in the presence of ORMUZD and corresponds to the Roman GENIUS.

Frazer, Sir James George (1854–1941). Scottish scholar and anthropologist. He is best known for his famous work THE GOLDEN BOUGH, which is noted for its important contributions to the study of early religion and anthropology. Other works include *Totemism* (1887); *Folk-lore in the Old Testament* (1918); and numerous translations of such classical writers as Ovid, Pausanias, and Apollodorus.

Fréchette, Louis [Honoré] (1839–1908). Canadian poet and journalist. He is best known for *La légende d'un peuple* (1887), a series of epic poems inspired by the leading events and personages in French-Canadian history. In 1880 the French Academy honored two other poetic works by Fréchette, *Les fleurs boréales* (1879) and *Les oiseaux de neige* (1880), and he became Canada's first poet laureate.

Frederic, Harold (1856–1898). American novelist and journalist. He is known for realistic portrayals of small-town and rural life. His most popular novel, THE DAMNATION OF THERON WARE, was a pioneering work in the development of psychological realism. Frederic is credited with helping to prepare the way for the works of Stephen Crane and Theodore Dreiser. *Seth's Brother's Wife* (1887) is a story of a triangular love affair. *In the Valley* (1890) is a historical novel dealing with the battle at Oriskany in 1777.

Frederick II, known as **Frederick the Great** (1712–1786). King of Prussia (1740–1786). He was an enlightened despot who built up the Prussian state through vast territorial acquisitions and domestic reforms. An enthusiastic amateur of music he composed and played chamber music. He was a patron of the arts, friend of Voltaire. He wrote voluminously, almost always in French. He built the palace of Sans Souci (1747) near Potsdam. During his later years he was known as *der Alte Fritz* (Old Fritz).

Frederick, Duke. The uncle of Rosalind and father of Celia in Shakespeare's As You Like It. "Of rough and envious disposition," he has usurped his older brother's dukedom, but he is finally converted by a monk and enters a monastery.

Frederick the First. See Barbarossa.

Frederick the Great. See Frederick II.

Free Kirk. The church organized by those who, in 1843, left the national Church of Scotland (thereafter often referred to as the Auld Kirk), in order to be free from state control in spiritual matters. In 1929 the United Free Church of Scotland was reunited with the established Church of Scotland, thus bringing together the large majority of all Scottish Presbyterians.

Freeman, Douglas Southall (1886–1953). American historian. An editor of the Richmond *News Leader,* Freeman won a Pulitzer Prize for his exhaustive *Robert E. Lee* (4 vols., 1934). He continued his studies with *Lee's Lieutenants* (3 vols., 1942–1944) and then went further back in American history with a seven-volume life of *George Washington* (1948–1957), the last volume of which was completed by his assistants, J. A. Carroll and M. W. Ashworth.

Freeman, Mary E[leanor] Wilkins (1852–1930). American novelist and short-story writer of the local-color school. She is known for her use of dialect and her character studies of the frustrated and decadent New Englanders left after the Western expansion. Among the collections of her short stories, the genre in which she did her best work, are *A Humble Romance and Other Stories* (1887), A New England Nun and Other Stories, and *The Wind in the Rose Bush* (1903). Her novels include *The Revolt of Mother* (1890), *Jane Field* (1893), and *The Portion of Labor* (1901).

Freeman, Richard Austin (1862–1943). English scientific detective-story writer. His detective hero is the physician Dr. John Thorndyke.

Freemasons. A fraternal organization claiming, without basis, to trace its origins to Hiram of Tyre and the Temple of Solomon. The modern secret fraternity had its origin in England in the 18th century, and its connection with masons, the workers in stone, arises from the fact that the founders adopted many of the practices of the old masonic guilds as being most suitable to their purpose. These medieval guilds consisted of workmen who, by the nature of their calling, had to move from place to place, and their secret passwords and other rituals were adopted so that when on their travels they could prove without difficulty that they were actually Free and Accepted Masons, and so secure the comradeship of their brother masons as well as get employment. In each district where cathedrals and churches were being built, lodges were created, much as a branch of a trade union would be today, and these had their masters, wardens, and other officials.

Free-Soil party. An American political party opposed to the extension of slavery. It was formed in 1848 by antislavery Democrats and Whigs and by members of the Liberty party. In 1848 Martin Van Buren, their presidential candidate, failed to carry a single state and, by splitting the Democratic vote in New York, helped win the election for Zachary Taylor, the Whig nominee. In 1854 the Free-Soilers were part of the coalition that formed the Republican party. See Barnburners.

free verse or **vers libre.** In prosody, verse free of the rules of versification. Free verse is composed in lines cadenced according to meaningful stress rather than the mechanical alternation of accent and nonaccent; the starts, stops, and pauses of line division play an important part in its rhythm.

The term *vers libre* was coined by the French poets of the Symbolist movement (see Symbolism), notably Jules Laforgue and Gustave Kahn, to describe their verse technique. Whitman, of course, had written such verse before them, as had the ancient Hebrew poets of the Psalms and other parts of the Bible.

Free verse became the prevailing poetic form for a brief time in the 1920's, and subsequently in the 20th century has continued as one of the main prosodic streams alongside traditional and modernist traditional forms. Poets who have worked substantially in free verse in English include: H. D. (Hilda Doolittle), Robinson Jeffers, D. H. Lawrence, Amy Lowell, Edgar Lee Masters, Ezra Pound, Carl Sandburg, Wallace Stevens, and William Carlos Williams.

Fregoso, Federico (1480–1541) and **Ottaviano** (d. 1524). Genoese noblemen. The nephews of Guidobaldo of Montefeltro, they appear as interlocutors in The Courtier of Castiglione. Federico was later made archbishop of Salerno by Pope Julius II; Ottaviano became doge of Genoa in 1513, and later served as governor when it fell to Francis I.

Freiligrath, Ferdinand (1810–1876). German liberal political poet, a revolutionary during the 1840's and later a strong admirer of Bismarck. His most famous volume is the *Glaubensbekenntnis* (*Declaration of Faith,* 1842) that led to his break with the Prussian government.

Freischutz (*Ger.* "free-shooter"). Legendary marksman popular in German folk lore of the 14th to 16th century. The Devil gives him seven bullets, six of which will infallibly hit what the marksman aims at, but the last will be directed by the Devil. The account in Apel's *Gespensterbuch* (book of ghosts, 1810–1815) suggested Weber's opera *Der Freischutz* (1821), libretto by Friedrich Kind (1768–1843). The woodsman Max must win a sharpshooting contest to win the hand of Agathe. Because his marksmanship is not perfect, he allows his colleague Caspar, already a servant of the Devil, to arrange for him to make a pact with the Black Huntsman for the magic bullets. The seventh shot, aimed at a dove, would have killed Agathe, but her bridal wreath deflects it, and Caspar dies instead.

Frémont, John C[harles] (1813–1890). American explorer, soldier, and politician. Frémont, an officer in the U.S. Topographical Corps, made three important expeditions to the Far West, and his *Report of the Exploring Expedition to the Rocky Mountains* (1843), which he wrote with the help of his wife, Jessie, daughter of Thomas Hart Benton, was widely read. During the Mexican War, he played a controversial role in the conquest of California; he was later found guilty of mutiny and disobedience by a court-martial and although President Polk remitted his sentence, he resigned from the army. In 1856 he ran for the presidency on the anti-slavery platform of the newly formed Republican Party. After the outbreak of the Civil War, Frémont was given a command in the Department of the West, but was removed because of his radical antislavery policies. From 1878 to 1883 he was territorial governor of Arizona. Irving Stone's *Immortal Wife* (1944) is a biographical novel about the Frémonts.

Fremstad, Olive (1871–1951). Swedish-born American dramatic soprano. Although she began singing as a contralto, she soon proved herself a foremost interpreter of soprano roles in both German and Italian opera. Thea Kronborg, the heroine of Willa Cather's novel, *The Song of the Lark* (1915), was modeled after her.

French, Alice. Real name of **Octave Thanet** (1850–1934). American novelist and short-story writer. Miss French's stories, laid mostly in the villages of rural Arkansas, are part of the LOCAL-COLOR school. Her special interest was the labor problem; she advocated cooperatives rather than labor unions. Among her books are *The Man of the Hour* (1905), *Knitters in the Sun* (1887), and *The Heart of Toil* (1893).

French Academy. See ACADÉMIE FRANÇAISE.

French and Indian War (1754–1763). The last, most decisive conflict in the 150 years' struggle between France and England for possession of the North American continent. It was the American phase of the SEVEN YEARS WAR and ended with the cession of Canada to Great Britain in the Treaty of Paris (1763).

French Renaissance. The French Renaissance roughly encompasses the 16th century.

Fervor for the Italian Renaissance took hold of the French court following the military campaigns of Charles VIII, Louis XII, and FRANCIS I in Italy. As traffic between Italy and France increased, French art, architecture, and most particularly literature felt the effects. Clément MAROT introduced the Italian sonnet into French poetry. Queen MARGARET OF NAVARRE wrote the first collection of French tales modeled on the *Decameron* of Boccaccio. However, the Italian influence in this period was more intellectual than artistic. French writers developed a new critical spirit and moral sense from reading Greek and Latin literature, which had been rediscovered in Italy. They were humanists, interested in the full development and enjoyment of man's capacities, and they cultivated a taste for the refinements of Italian Renaissance society.

The influence from the north affected particularly the scholars. It was characterized by a philosophical questioning of the long-entrenched dogmas of the Church. French scholars became avid for knowledge as the old taboos fell and the flood of printed matter opened up formerly neglected fields of learning. Francis I engaged Guillaume BUDÉ as his librarian and, at Budé's instigation, founded the COLLÈGE DE FRANCE, where Greek and Hebrew were taught for the first time. The Collège soon became a rallying point for the "Evangelists," those who sought the basis for faith in the Scriptures themselves, rather than in papal bulls and church decrees.

The two currents of new ideas from the north and from the south merged in the short-lived marriage between humanism and Evangelism which marks the first flowering of the French Renaissance around 1530. The writers of this period shared in differing degrees the general excitement, and all participated in the burst of intense optimism, feverish activity, and exaltation. François RABELAIS emerges as the most important literary figure of the period. While his GARGANTUA AND PANTAGRUEL is largely a continuation of the medieval fabliaux in form, it fairly breathes the new spirit in its rich multilingual vocabulary and its sheer amassing of detail in every field of knowledge.

The second half of the century saw a distinct change in the tenor of the French Renaissance. The glorious reign of Francis I was followed by the rule of four ineffective kings (Henry II, Francis II, Charles IX, and Henry III), the last three more or less subservient to their mother, CATHERINE de Médicis. After the publication of John CALVIN's *Institutes* in French in 1541, the happy alliance between humanism and Evangelism had been irrevocably ruptured. The early Evangelists were succeeded by militant Protestant reformers who not only challenged Roman Catholicism, but menaced the very basis of French royal authority as well, thereby losing its protection. Henceforth, the Protestant Reformation and humanism went their separate ways. The universal exuberance of the first humanism gave way to a notion of a distinctly French art nourished by Italian and classical example but proudly asserting French genius in the French language. Joachim DU BELLAY gave the clarion call of this new artistic consciousness with his DÉFENSE ET ILLUSTRATION DE LA LANGUE FRANÇAISE in 1549. The *Défense* signaled the formation of the PLÉIADE, a group of poets led by Pierre de RONSARD, whose mission was to raise French poetry to the eminence of Italian and ancient poetry. A parallel group of poets at Lyons, headed by Maurice SCÈVE and Louise LABÉ, had no declared mission, but its poetry was so personal in tone that it too contributed to the liberation of the French literary idiom.

Meanwhile, the rise of Protestantism led to civil war. The country became a bloody battleground of the contending Protestant and Catholic ideologies. Eventually these wars produced their own poets, notably the impassioned Agrippa d'AUBIGNÉ. His narrative poem, *Les Tragiques* (1616), recounting the horrors suffered by the Protestant martyrs and the divine retribution to come, introduced into French literature the visions of a soul possessed.

The end of the century saw the birth of a new spirit which was to develop into the classicism of the 17th century. Primitive attempts at a new drama distinct from the popular mystery plays and passion plays of the Middle Ages produced the tragi-comedies of Robert GARNIER, from which Corneille would later draw inspiration. The political chaos resulting from the religious wars brought the realization that national stability depended upon a strong central government free from religious ideology. King HENRY IV established absolute rule which Louis XIV was later to consolidate. The great literary figure of the period was Michel de Montaigne, friend and unofficial counselor to Henry IV. In his Essays, a genre which he invented, Montaigne reflected the general disillusionment over the first period of humanistic optimism and over the ensuing bloody conflicts of the religious wars. He called for a rejection of ideologies in the interest of the first priority, man himself. His greatest concern was the requirements imposed by human nature for its proper development. To learn these requirements nothing less was needed than a rigorous search for the lessons of individual experience. In turning inward to study human psychology as the source of knowledge, Montaigne gave a new and modern meaning to the term "humanism," which extended beyond France to affect all of Europe. He was the great precursor of the ideal *honnête homme* of the 17th century.

French Revolution. The world-famous revolution in France of the third estate against the clergy and nobility, which formally began in May, 1789, and ended in December, 1799, with Napoleon's dictatorship. Until this time, France had been ruled as a monarchy with two privileged classes: the nobility and the clergy. Under this old order there was no place for either the new class of economically independent bourgeois or the new class of industrial workers. They, as well as the peasants, bore the brunt of excessive spending on the part of the nobility. Heavy taxes, *corvées* (obligatory services to the king), military service, backward agricultural methods, and internal tariff barriers—all medieval feudal institutions still existing in 18th-century France—were also contributory causes to the revolution; they had been systematically attacked by the major writers of this Age of Reason, particularly by the physiocrats. The badly needed economic reform which these latter advocated failed because of the unwillingness of the ruling classes to relinquish any of their privileges. France's national debt was also increased by her participation (which she could ill afford) in the American Revolution. On May 5, 1789, the States-General (the assembly of the three Estates of the Realm) was convoked by Louis XVI and Necker in an effort to obtain a general fiscal reform. The third estate, constituting a majority against the

ruling classes, defiantly proclaimed itself the National Assembly on June 17, and later, when Louis XVI closed their meeting place, adjourned to an indoor tennis court and took the Oath of the Tennis Court. The king, on June 27, yielded and legalized this assembly, but at the same time dismissed Necker, at Marie Antoinette's insistence, and surrounded Versailles with his troops. On July 14, a Paris mob led by Desmoulins, stormed the Bastille. Louis then recalled Necker and recognized the legal existence of the Constituent Assembly (as the new National Assembly was called). The Assembly adopted the Declaration of the Rights of Man, proclaiming the fundamental principles of the revolution, and drafted a new constitution creating a limited monarchy. In addition, church lands were nationalized and religious orders suppressed. Meanwhile, radical political clubs, especially the Jacobins, were gaining power in Paris.

Louis XVI finally accepted the constitution and on October 1, 1791, a new Legislative Assembly was convened. In the same year Louis tried to flee France, as many nobles had already done, but was brought back a prisoner to Paris. The Legislative Assembly consisted of members of various political clubs, more or less radical, like the Feuillants, and the Cordeliers. During this era some of the leaders of the revolution wore the bonnet rouge, and "Liberty, Equality, and Fraternity," was their motto. At first, foreign governments were sympathetic to the revolution, but because both the king and French émigrés were inciting European monarchs to intervene on behalf of French royalty, they began to be frightened by the progress of the lower classes. Austria and Prussia issued threats, and on April 20, 1792, war was declared on Austria, and three months later Prussia declared war on France. This war began the succession of foreign wars which in turn led to the Napoleonic Wars. The repeated defeats of the Revolutionary armies were attributed to Royalist treason and on September 2 and 3, 1792, the people invaded the prisons and massacred 1,200 prisoners (the September Massacres). In Paris, the National Convention, headed by Marat and Danton, succeeded the Legislative Assembly, and its first act was to abolish the monarchy; the king was tried for treason and beheaded on Jan. 21, 1793. The Convention tried to continue the war, which by now included England, Spain, and most of the other European countries, but it was torn by internal dissention among the Girondists, the Montagnards, and the Cordeliers. The Convention established the Committee of Public Safety which ruled France. Robespierre, now in control of the Jacobins, joined the Committee at the insistence of Saint-Just, and, as its leader, established a virtual dictatorship. The period following is known as the Reign of Terror, which, because of its excesses, was eliminated by the Convention's coup of 9 Thermidor. Once Robespierre was executed, a period of reaction set in, and a new constitution (1795) set up the Directory. The incompetence, corruption, and intrigues of the Directory, and the military reverses of the army brought France to the brink of disaster. Napoleon Bonaparte, hero of the Italian Campaign, returned from Egypt, and with the help of the army and his supporters, overthrew the Directory on 18 Brumaire, and established the Consulate. He was the

Contemporary woodcut of Parisians celebrating the fall of the Bastille (July 14, 1789).

VUE DE LA PLACE DE GREVE LE JOUR DE LA PRISE DE LA BASTILLE • NOUS CEDONS A L'AMOUR DE LA LIBERTÉ

ruler of France until 1814 when the Bourbon kings were restored to power.

French Revolution, The (1837). A history in 3 parts by Thomas CARLYLE. Critics have preferred to call it a drama or a prose epic rather than a history. The central motif is the nemesis that follows upon the oppression of the poor. The work established Carlyle's reputation as a historian and remains widely read to this day.

Freneau, Philip [Morin] (1752–1832). American poet. One of the first American poets to achieve renown for his verse in the U.S., he is best known for his political poems, most of them written at the time of the American Revolution: *A Poem on the Rising Glory of America* (1772), written in collaboration with Hugh Henry Brackenridge on their graduation from Princeton; *American Liberty* (1775); *General Gage's Confession* (1775); and *The British Prison-Ship* (1781), an account of his experiences as a prisoner of war after capture at sea near the West Indies. His poems on nature and on the Indian, considered precursors of the romantic movement in America, include: *The Wild Honey Suckle* (1786), *The Indian Burying Ground* (1788), *On a Honey-Bee Drinking from a Glass of Wine* (1809).

Freneau was anti-Federalist in his politics and a deist in religion. Admired by Jefferson, he edited the *National Gazette* from 1791 to 1793, in which he attacked Alexander Hamilton.

Fréquente Communion, La. See Antoine ARNAULD.

Frere, John Hookham. Pen name **William and Robert Whistlecraft** (1796–1846). English diplomat, satirist, translator. After holding several important offices Frere became ambassador to Spain at the outbreak of the Spanish insurrection against Napoleon. Dissatisfaction with his part in early English defeats in the Peninsular War forced his replacement and retirement from diplomacy. His articles for the *Anti-Jacobin* (1797), an antiradical weekly, are good examples of his satirical writing. His famous translations of Aristophanes (1839) and other writing is collected in his *Works* (1872).

Freud, Sigmund (1856–1939). Austrian psychologist, the originator of PSYCHOANALYSIS. Freud was trained as a medical doctor at the University of Vienna. He graduated in 1881, but never practiced internal medicine. He soon became interested in neuropathology and studied hypnotism and cerebral anatomy.

He became dissatisfied with hypnotism as a treatment for hysterical patients. However, he had noticed that some patients had fallen into reveries in which they had talked about their problems and afterwards had felt better. From these observations he began to formulate his theory of "free association" which is the kernel of psychoanalysis. In Freudian practice, patients under the guidance of an analyst attempt to recall emotional episodes that aggravated conflicts, and thus recognize and release frustrated emotions. Freud used dream interpretation as one of his basic tools in analysis. The patient's dreams were analyzed for their symbolic content and were used as a guide to the patient's internal life. Freud viewed dreams as a person's means of expressing repressed emotions, and repression was seen as the source of neurotic behavior.

Freud postulated the existence of three internal forces that govern a person's psychic life: (1) the *id*, the instinctual force of life—unconscious, uncontrollable and isolated; (2) the *ego*, the executive force that has contact with the real world; (3) the *superego*, the governing force, or moral conscience, that seeks to control and direct the ego into socially acceptable patterns of behavior.

As his theories began to take concrete form, Freud started to publish his findings. *The Interpretation of Dreams* (1900) was one of the first reports on his independent studies of the subconscious. By this time his work had begun to attract attention outside his native Vienna, and others took up his cause. In 1908 the first International Congress of Psychoanalysis met in Vienna. Many young doctors, some of them now famous in their own right, attended this meeting; among them were Alfred ADLER, A. A. Brill, Ernest Jones, and Carl JUNG.

From the beginning the very nature of his work made Freud the center of controversy. His theories about sex have been, in general, misunderstood by the public and in varying degrees rejected by many of his followers. Freud maintained that the primary motivating factor in human psychology and human behavior is sexual, but he did not limit this to its purely erotic connotations. The sexual instinct, as Freud saw it, has many of the aspects ordinarily referred to as "social." He found elements of strong sexuality among children and ascribed most neuroses to the repressive influence of social and individual inhibitions on sex.

While many of Freud's ideas have been superseded he is still considered the great innovator in the field of psychiatry, and is almost worshiped in some circles. The work of only one other man in this century, Albert Einstein, has had as great an impact on man's way of thinking and acting. Freud's influence has been especially strong on artistic expression, both the fine arts and literature. Such authors as Thomas Mann and James Joyce have embodied much of his thought in their works.

Among Freud's important works are *Three Contributions to the Theory of Sex* (1910), *Wit and Its Relation to the Unconscious* (1916), *Leonardo da Vinci: A Psychosexual Study of an Infantile Reminiscence* (1916), *Totem and Taboo* (1918), *The Ego and the Id* (1927), and *Moses and Monotheism* (1939).

Freud, a Jew, was forced to flee from the Nazis in 1938. He and his family moved to England where he died, an honored and respected man.

Frey or Freyr. The Scandinavian god of peace and fertility, the dispenser of rain, and the patron god of Sweden and Iceland. The son of Niörd and husband of Gerda, he was originally one of the Vanir but was received among the Aesir after the war between the two. Among his treasures was a magic ship, *Skithbathnir*, which could be folded up like a tent, a golden helmet with the crest of a wild boar, *Gullinbursti*, and his horse *Blodighofi* (Bloody hoof).

Freya. The Norse goddess of love, fecundity, and death. She was the wife of Odin, but he deserted her for Frigga because she loved finery better than her husband. One account says that she flies through the air with the wings of a falcon, another that she rides in a chariot drawn by two cats. The chief legends concerning Freya relate the efforts of the giants to carry her off. In one instance Thor, dressed as a veiled bride, impersonates Freya in order to recover his hammer from the giant Thrym.

She is also known as *Frea, Frija, Frigg, Frige,* and the like, and it is from her that our Friday is named. In Teutonic mythology, Freya and Frigga are the same.

Freyre, Gilberto [de Mello] (1900–   ). Brazilian sociologist, anthropologist, and social historian. Freyre is best known for *The Masters and the Slaves* (*Casa-Grande e Senzala;* 1933) and *The Mansions and the Shanties* (*Sobrados e Mucambos;* 1936), brilliant studies of Brazilian patriarchal society from the 16th to the 19th centuries. In these and later books, notably *Brazil: An Interpretation* (1945), revised and expanded as *New World in the Tropics* (1959), he has maintained that the fusion of diverse ethnic and cultural elements—Portuguese, Amerindian, and African—has resulted in a distinctively Brazilian civilization. The Portuguese settlers in Brazil, he claims, were particularly suited for creating this new tropical culture because of their racial tolerance and previous colonial experiences in India and Africa.

Freytag, Gustav (1816–1895). German novelist and playwright, known for his detailed realism in both style and choice of subject matter. He was a political liberal and was strongly interested in the problems of his day, as is seen in his comedy *Die Journalisten* (*The Journalists,* 1854), which deals with international politics, and his novel *Soll und Haben* (*Should and Have,* 1855) about commercialism. But he always attempted to see his own time in the light of the past, as in *Die Ahnen* (*The Ancestors,* 1873–1880), a series of six novels covering most of German history, and *Bilder aus deutscher Vergangenheit* (*Scenes from the German Past,* 1859 ff.), a historical study.

friar (Lat., *frater,* brother). A monk, especially one belonging to one of the four great mendicant orders: FRANCISCANS, DOMINICANS, Augustinians, and CARMELITES.

Friar John. An anglicism for Frère Jean des Entommeures (Fr., *entamer,* to carve the first slice, hence Friar John of the Hearty Eaters or Trenchermen), a major character in Rabelais' GARGANTUA AND PANTAGRUEL. As Gargantua's comrade in arms in Book I, he is the hero of the war against PICROCHOLE. At the end of the war Gargantua gives him the abbey of THÉLÈME as a reward for his bravery. Friar John has all the faults of monks but none of their vices. Ignorant, unclean, and gluttonous, he is also frank, lusty, and courageous. Rabelais clearly had great affection for Friar John and created in him one of his most picturesque characters.

Friar Laurence. See Friar LAURENCE.

Friar Rush or **Bruder Rausch** (*Ger.* "intoxication"). In late medieval German legend, a demon disguised as a friar. He leads monks and friars into wickedness by all sorts of devious and generally amusing devices. He appears in the English prose *History of Friar Rush* (1568) and several minor tales and plays.

Friars Major (Lat. *fratres majores*). The Dominicans.

Friars Minor (Lat. *fratres minores*). The Franciscans.

Friar's Tale, The. One of the CANTERBURY TALES of Geoffrey CHAUCER. The Friar and the Summoner reveal their enmity, and the Summoner promises to retaliate after the Friar tells his tale. The Friar describes an extremely lewd and dishonest summoner who meets the Devil disguised as a bailiff. The two swear friendship and gossip about their respective techniques of extortion. They pass a carter cursing his horse and cart and hay for being stuck in the mud, his words consigning them to the Devil. But the Devil explains to the Summoner that he cannot take them because the carter does not really mean the curse. Then the Summoner decides to extort money from an innocent woman by threatening her with a summons to the archdeacon for adultery. He ignores her words that send him to the Devil, but the Devil ascertains that she really means them, and gleefully carries the Summoner off to Hell.

Friar Tuck. A fat, jovial vagabond friar in the ROBIN HOOD ballads and a character in the May-day plays. His costume consists of a russet habit of the Franciscan order, a red corded girdle with gold tassel, red stockings, and a wallet. He appears in Sir Walter Scott's novel *Ivanhoe* (1820) as the "holy clerk of Copmanhurst."

Fricka. In Wagner's RING DES NIBELUNGEN, the goddess of marriage and wife of WOTAN. See FRIGGA.

Fricker, Sara. See Samuel Taylor COLERIDGE.

Friday. The sixth day of the week. It is named for the goddess FREYA. In the Romance languages it is named for the corresponding Roman goddess Venus. Friday is traditionally the day when Adam was created, when he was expelled from Paradise, when he repented, when he died, when Christ was crucified, when the dead will rise for the last judgment. In many Christian churches Friday is a fast day. To spill salt on Friday is a bad omen. It used to be the day for the execution of capital punishment and is often called hangman's day.

Frieda. See Frieda von Richthofen LAWRENCE.

Friend of the Family, The, or **The Village of Stepanchikovo** (*Selo Stepanchikovo;* 1859). A short novel by Feodor DOSTOEVSKI. It portrays the horrible spectacle of a petty and talentless ex-toady, Foma Fomich Opiskin, ruling a household by playing on the guilt feeling he induces in the master of the house. Foma, with his immense aptitude for hypocritical self-righteousness, is a sort of Russian Tartuffe.

Frigga or **Frigg.** The supreme Norse goddess of Asgard, and wife of Odin. She presided over marriages and may be identified with the Roman Juno. In Teutonic mythology, she is identified with Freya.

Frisch, Max (1911–   ). Swiss playwright and novelist, writing in German. He is noted for his ironic and original treatments of the problems of man in the age of technology. Among his plays, which show the influence of Bertolt Brecht, are *Als der Krieg zu Ende war* (*When the War Was Over,* 1949), and *Don Juan oder Die Liebe zur Geometrie* (*Don Juan or The Love of Geometry,* 1953). His two best-known novels, both of which treat the problem of human identity in the modern world, are *Stiller* (1954) and *Homo Faber* (1957).

Frison-Roche, Roger (1906–). French novelist. He has produced adventure stories such as *First on the Rope* (*Premier de cordée*, 1943), *Grand Crevasse* (1948), and *The Lost Trail of the Saharas* (1950).

Frobisher, Sir Martin (1535?–1594). English navigator. Frobisher led three expeditions in search of the Northwest Passage between 1576 and 1578, and discovered Frobisher Bay. He commanded the *Triumph* against the Spanish Armada, was vice-admiral under Sir Francis Drake in his expedition to the West Indies (1586), and vice-admiral in Sir John Hawkins' expedition to the Portuguese coast in 1590.

Fröding, Gustaf (1860–1911). Swedish poet. A writer of lyric and religious verse, Fröding's first collection of poems, *Guitarr och dragharmonika* (1891), revealed his unique poetic gifts; he achieves a blend of irony, melancholy, and humor. Other early collections were *Nya dikter* (1894), and *Stank och flikar* (1896). The poem "En Morgondröm" in the latter volume was branded pornography and led to a court case. Acquitted, but shaken and deeply disturbed, Fröding suffered a mental breakdown and was confined to an asylum in 1898. Although he left the asylum, the remaining years of his life were marked by ill health. *Gralstänk* (1898) contains a series of religious poems expressing a faith in the divinity of all things in the world.

Frog, Nicholas. A character in John Arbuthnot's *The History of* JOHN BULL who represents the Dutch people.

Frogs, The (Batrachoi, 405 B.C.). A comedy by ARISTOPHANES. In it, Dionysus, the patron of the drama, having grown weary of the lack of inspiring dramatists in Athens, decides to go down to Hades to bring back Euripides. Knowing that Heracles has already been there, he borrows his famous lion skin as a disguise, and sets off with his slave Xanthias. When he arrives in Hades, he discovers that Heracles, who had once stolen the guardian dog Cerberus, is not popular there, and hastily changes costume with Xanthias. After further confusion over which of the two is actually Dionysus, the god finds Euripides. However, having listened to an argument between him and his rival playwright Aeschylus, he decides to return to earth with Aeschylus instead, because he is the weightier playwright. Besides being a charming comedy, the play is a striking example of the freedom of speech allowed the writer of Old Comedy. Dionysus is made an absurd figure, though he was the patron of the festivals at which the comedy was performed.

Froissart, Jean (1337?–?1410). French poet and historian. He enjoyed the patronage of Queen Philippa of England from 1361 until her death in 1369, and then the protection of two French noblemen. He traveled widely throughout western Europe seeking firsthand accounts of the events of the Hundred Years' War. His *Chronicles* (1369–c. 1400) give a vivid picture of Europe from 1325 to 1400, although dates and geography are often inaccurate, and the history is often distorted by perspective, the first volume sympathizing with the English, the last three espousing the French cause. The description of events until 1356 is largely a revision of the chronicle by Jean le Bel (c. 1290–c. 1370).

Froissart also wrote a number of graceful lyrics and a long verse romance, *Méliador*.

Frollo, Claude. The villain of Victor Hugo's novel THE HUNCHBACK OF NOTRE DAME. Frollo is an archdeacon whose reputation for sanctity is seriously undermined by his base passion for Esmeralda.

From Here to Eternity (1951). A novel by James JONES. It is a story of life in the regular army before the Japanese attack on Pearl Harbor in 1941. A sprawling (861 pages), powerful, occasionally vulgar book, it caused a sensation at its publication. Jones's writing is vigorous, vivid, and fluent. The title is taken from the well-known phrase "damned from here to eternity," a quotation from *Gentlemen Rankers*, Kipling's poem of British army life.

Fromm, Erich (1900–). German-born American psychoanalyst and philosopher. Fromm came to the U.S. in 1934 and has worked for the National Institute for Social Research in New York City and taught at various universities. His books have done much to elucidate and popularize many current philosophical and psychological ideas. His works include *Escape from Freedom* (1941); *Man for Himself: An Inquiry into the Psychology of Ethics* (1947), its sequel; *Psychoanalysis and Religion* (1950); *The Forgotten Language: An Introduction to the Understanding of Dreams, Fairy Tales, and Myths* (1951); *The Art of Loving* (1956); *May Man Prevail? An Inquiry into the Facts and Fictions of Foreign Policy* (1961); *Beyond the Chains of Illusion: My Encounter with Marx and Freud* (1962); and *The Dogma of Christ, and Other Essays on Religion, Psychology, and Culture* (1963).

From Morn Till Midnight (Von Morgens bis Mitternachts; 1916). A play by Georg KAISER. The hero, a bank teller, attempts to break out of his pitifully circumscribed existence by embezzling a large sum of money. He embarks on a wild spree, spending money by the fistful in a frantic pursuit of pleasure that is to give meaning to his life, but is finally disillusioned and commits suicide.

Fronde. An insurrectionary French political party during the minority of Louis XIV and the ministry of Cardinal Mazarin. The Fronde revolted against the crown (1648–1652), but, though successful in temporarily holding the capital, were unable to achieve their aim of curbing royal power. Members were called *frondeurs* by the Court Party, who likened them to boys slinging stones in the streets and scampering away at the approach of authority.

Frondeurs. See FRONDE.

Front de Boeuf, Sir Reginald. A vicious opponent of IVANHOE, in Scott's novel. He dies at the siege of his castle at Torquilstone.

Frontino. A fiery steed in the ORLANDO FURIOSO of Ariosto. Formerly belonging to Sacripante, it was stolen by the dwarf Brunello and given to the warrior Ruggiero.

Frost, Robert (1874–1963). American poet. Although he was born in San Francisco, he is best known for his verse dealing with New England life and character. Frost moved east in 1885, attended Dartmouth and Harvard for brief intervals, and held various odd jobs. From 1900 to 1905 he farmed in New Hampshire. But poetry was his real vocation, and in 1912, after his failure to be published in the U.S., he went to England, where for three years he wrote poetry, talked with poets, and published two collections, *A Boy's Will* (1913) and *North of Boston* (1914). The latter book contains several of Frost's best-known poems, including MENDING WALL, THE DEATH OF THE HIRED MAN, *Home Burial,* and *A Servant to Servants.*

Back in America in 1915, Frost began to gather a reputation, following the American publication of *North of Boston.* Maintaining his own creative independence, aloof from the poetic movements of the day, he next published *Mountain Interval* (1916), a volume containing THE ROAD NOT TAKEN, *An Old Man's Winter Night,* and BIRCHES. With *New Hampshire* (1923), there is the first indication of Frost's awareness of himself as poet; as he says in the title poem, he is "a creature of literature." There is also present a tone of irony that had earlier been muted. THE AXE-HELVE, STOPPING BY WOODS ON A SNOWY EVENING, and *Two Witches* appear in this volume.

A FURTHER RANGE saw the introduction of contemporary concerns in Frost's poetry and the beginning of his later tendency toward abstract philosophizing, which was to result in the two verse dramas *A Masque of Reason* (1945) and *A Masque of Mercy* (1947). Frost's other collections include WEST-RUNNING BROOK, *A Witness Tree* (1943), *Steeple Bush* (1947), *Complete Poems* (1949), and *In the Clearing* (1962).

Frost is often seen as opposed to the main tendencies of modern poetry. He is the clear, simple, moral poet who sings of rural, democratic joys and who is, above all, the lover of nature. But although Frost is perhaps most closely akin to Emerson and Emily Dickinson, he clearly learned much from modern poetic movements. If he is the positive poet of rural America, he is also the chronicler of the dark night of the human soul, the sophisticated poet, full of irony and ambiguity. He wrote in traditional verse forms, but within the poems he created a tension of thought and feeling, reinforced by tension between colloquial speech and traditional metrics, that is unmatched in American poetry. The poem, as he said in *The Figure a Poem Makes,* is "a momentary stay against confusion."

Frost was awarded the Pulitzer Prize in 1924, 1931, 1937 and 1943 for *New Hampshire, Collected Poems, A Further Range,* and *A Witness Tree.*

Froth, Master. In Shakespeare's MEASURE FOR MEASURE, a foolish gentleman, too shallow for great crime and too light for virtue. See Mistress OVERDONE.

frottola. An Italian verse form popular among both folk and learned poets during the early Renaissance. It is characterized by a long discursive style, chiefly in short lines, that comments on topical as well as literary subjects. Its nearest English analogue is the so-called Skeltonic verse practiced by John SKELTON.

Froude, James Anthony (1818–1894). English historian. He wrote a *History of England from the Fall of Wolsey to the Defeat of the Spanish Armada* (1856–1870). As executor of Thomas Carlyle he wrote *Reminiscences of Carlyle* (1881) and a *Life of Thomas Carlyle* (1884). With his brother, Richard Hurrell Froude (1803–1836), who contributed to TRACTS FOR THE TIMES, Froude was associated for a time with the Oxford Movement.

Fruitlands. An experimental cooperative community (1842–1843) founded by Bronson ALCOTT at Harvard, Mass. Its plan included vegetarianism, farming, and teaching. Alcott's daughter, Louisa May Alcott, described the colonists with gentle humor in *Transcendental Wild Oats* (1876), a fictional sketch.

Fruits of the Earth, The (Les Nourritures terrestres; 1897). A poetic work by André GIDE. It is a hymn in prose and poetry to the beauty of all experience, exhorting youth to prepare itself for receiving all the joy of life by casting off all that is artificial or merely conventional. In the 1920's a generation of restless youth welcomed the work as a popular handbook of self-liberation.

Fry, Christopher (1907–   ). English dramatist. He was born Christopher Harris, but took his mother's name. His plays are most often in verse forms; they are witty and full of poetic conceits. The heroine of *The Lady's Not for Burning* (1949) is a young witch. Among his other plays are *A Phoenix Too Frequent* (1949); *A Sleep of Prisoners* (1951), designed to be produced in churches; *Venus Observed* (1950); *Ring around the Moon* (1950), a translation of *L'Invitation au Château* by Jean Anouilh; *The Dark is Light Enough* (1954); and *Curtmantle* (1961).

Fry, Elizabeth (1780–1845). English Quaker philanthropist, noted as promoter of wide-ranging prison reforms, particularly in the treatment of female prisoners. Her *Memoirs* were published in 1847.

Fry, Roger (1866–1934). English art critic and painter. A member of the BLOOMSBURY GROUP, he was a pioneer in introducing the work of Cézanne and other POST-IMPRESSIONIST painters. He was at one time curator of paintings at the New York Metropolitan Museum. Among his books are *Vision and Design* (1920), *Transformations* (1926), *Cézanne: A Study of his Development* (1927), and *Reflections on British Painting* (1934). He also edited *Sir Joshua Reynolds' Discourses* (1905). Virginia Woolf wrote his biography (1940).

Fudge Family. A family whose adventures are related in Thomas MOORE's satire *The Fudge Family in Paris* (1818). Each member of the family writes letters to friends back home in England; they are meant to satirize the *parvenu* English abroad.

Fuenteovejuna (The Sheep Well, c. 1619). A drama by Lope de VEGA. Based on actual historical records, the story takes place during the reign of Ferdinand and Isabella. Commander Fernán Gómez, the lascivious lord of Fuenteovejuna, violates Laurencia, a peasant girl of the community. She tells her misfortune to the townspeople who, enraged by her words, storm the commander's castle and put him to death. The king sends a judge to discover the identity of the murderer, but all the villagers, even under torture, will say only that Fuenteovejuna killed him. Impressed by the heroic behavior of the people, the king pardons them and puts the village under the crown's protection.

Führer, der (*Ger.,* "Leader"). A title assumed by Adolf HITLER, who claimed to be the true representative of the German people. It was also used by leaders of subdivisions within the Nazi Party.

Fuhrmann Henschel. See DRAYMAN HENSCHEL.

Fujiwara. See HEIAN.

Fujiyama. More correctly **Fuji-no-Yama,** but commonly called **Fujisan.** The sacred mountain of Japan. The mountain, Japan's highest (12,394 feet), is in the province of Suruga, 60 miles southwest of Tokyo. It is a snow-capped volcano, inactive since 1708, a resort of pilgrims and prominent in Japanese art.

Fuller, Henry B[lake] (1857–1929). American novelist. Fuller won success with his first novel, *The Chevalier of Pensieri-Vani* (1890), written under the pseudonym Stanton Page, but his best-known book is THE CLIFF DWELLERS, the first successful novel about an American city. Working as a book critic for Chicago newspapers, he was active in Chicago's literary circles, especially those engaged in making POETRY the most important magazine of its kind in the country. Fuller himself issued two collections of verse: *The New Flag* (1899) and *Lines Long and Short* (1917).

Fuller, [Sarah] Margaret. Marchesa **Ossoli** (1810–1850). American editor, essayist, poet, and teacher. A brilliant and well-educated woman, Miss Fuller edited *The Dial* for two years. She had a gift for languages, and translated Goethe, spreading enthusiasm for his work. She held Saturday "conversations" regularly, and wrote critical articles for the New York *Tribune.* Unfavorably criticizing Longfellow and Lowell, she alienated the Boston Brahmins from the Transcendentalists. In 1846, Miss Fuller went abroad; visiting Italy, she mingled with leading authors, and became involved in Italy's struggle for freedom. She met Giovanni Angelo, Marquis Ossoli, who was 10 years younger than she, and became his mistress. They had a son, and were later married. Miss Fuller became very active in the hospitals when fighting began in Italy; she started to write a book on Giuseppe Mazzini and the war of liberation. In May, 1850, the family set sail for New York; their vessel was shipwrecked off Fire Island. The body of the infant son washed ashore, but the others were never recovered.

Margaret Fuller published a number of books, among them *Summer on the Lakes* (1844), *Woman in the Nineteenth Century* (1845), and *Papers on Literature and Art* (1846). She was attacked in James Russell Lowell's A FABLE FOR CRITICS, and Hawthorne is said to have modeled his character, Zenobia, in THE BLITHEDALE ROMANCE, on the dynamic and paradoxical figure of Margaret Fuller.

Fuller, Roy (1912–   ). English poet. His early poems were sociological, in the manner of W. H. Auden, and his later poems more romantic and mythological. His collections include *Poems* (1939) and *The Ruined Boys* (1959).

Fuller, Thomas (1608–1661). English clergyman and writer. One of the most popular preachers and authors of his day, Fuller was appointed chaplain to Charles II after the Restoration. His writing is remarkable for its wit, tolerance, and common sense. Among his works are *The History of the Holy War* (1639), an account of Palestine during the Crusades; *The Holy State and the Profane State* (1642), a series of character sketches; *Good Thoughts in Bad Times* (1645), brief essays on contemporary religious conflicts; and *The History of the Worthies of England* (1662), a collection of biographical sketches.

Fulton, Robert (1765–1815). American inventor. After working as an artist and draftsman, Fulton went to Europe in 1786 where he remained for 20 years, devoting himself to science and mechanics. Although he made several important inventions, he is best known for his applications of steam to navigation. He designed the first commercially successful steamboat, the *Clermont,* which traveled from New York to Albany and back (Aug. 17–22, 1807) in 62 hours of operating time.

Fulvia (d. 40 B.C.). A Roman matron married successively to the demagogue Clodius Pulcher, Curio, and Mark Antony. It is said that when Cicero was murdered by Antony's orders, his head was brought to Fulvia who drove a needle through his tongue in revenge for the things he had said against her husband in his famous Philippics.

Funeral Oration. See PERICLES.

Furcht und Elend des Dritten Reiches. See PRIVATE LIFE OF THE MASTER RACE.

Furies. See ERINYES.

Furmanov, Dmitri Andreyevich (1891–1926). Russian novelist. He is the author of the much-praised Soviet classic *Chapayev* (1923). A story of the civil war, it contrasts the characters of an emotional, haphazard guerilla leader, General Chapayev, and a cool, detached, and efficient Bolshevik commissar, who was Furmanov himself.

Furness, Horace Howard (1833–1912). American Shakespearian scholar. In 1871 he began to edit the *New Variorum* edition of Shakespeare's works. It was carried to completion by his son, **Horace Howard Furness** (1865–1930). The elder Furness' treatment of the text of Shakespeare's plays is considered conservative; his edition includes abstracts of previous criticism as well as variant readings. His son's work reveals less scholarship and judgment. On the latter's death, he bequeathed his great Shakespearian library to the University of Pennsylvania.

Furnivall, Frederick James (1825–1910). An English philologist. He was the founder of innumerable English literary societies, including the Early English Text Society (1864), the Chaucer Society and the Ballad Society (1868), the New Shakespeare Society (1873), the Browning Society (1881), the Wyclif Society (1882), and the Shelley Society (1885). He edited the *Six-Text Print of Chaucer's Canterbury Tales* (1868–1875) and began a dictionary for the Philological Society that developed into the *Oxford English Dictionary.*

Furor. See FAERIE QUEENE, THE.

Furphy, Joseph. Pen name, **Tom Collins** (1843–1912). Australian novelist. A perfect example of late literary blooming, Furphy was 60 when his novel *Such is Life* (1903) was published. And though, as a youth, he showed great promise with a prize-winning poem on the death of Abraham Lincoln, he published only some verses and sketches in the next 20 years, during which period his brilliant style developed. *Such is Life* caught the notice of only a small group upon its publication. Later, however, the book proved to be a starting point for the longer form of Australian novel. Furphy, a self-educated man, flouted all the rules, and in this way wrote a novel of complete originality. *Such is Life* has recently been recognized as one of the best frontier novels in English.

Furry Lawcats. An anglicism for the Chats-Fourrés, who inhabit the Wicket, where Pantagruel and his friends are arrested in Rabelais' GARGANTUA AND PANTAGRUEL. The Furry Lawcats, so called in allusion to the ermine-bordered robes worn by judges, are a rapacious breed who use their incomprehensible subtleties to devour everything. Among them, vice is deemed virtue, and evil passes for good; though they plunder the universe, their authority is unquestioned. Pantagruel and his companions are released only when Panurge, after answering a riddle posed by Graspall, or Grippeminaud, archduke of the Furry Lawcats, tosses them a bag full of gold coins. This episode was Rabelais' most violent satire on the courts of justice.

Furtado, R. de L. (1922–   ). Indian poet writing in English, currently Professor of English in Delhi University. *The Centre,* poems, appeared in 1955; *Shelley,* literary criticism, in 1958; *The Oleanders and Other Poems* in 1960.

Further Range, A (1936). A collection of poems by Robert FROST. It contains several humorous and satirical pieces and a group of epigrams called *Ten Mills.* The longest poem in the book, *Build Soil,* reflects the poet's concern with contemporary political developments. Also included in the collection are *Desert Places, Neither out Far Nor in Deep, Design,* and *Provide, Provide.*

futurism. A radical movement in literature and art initiated in 1909 by the Italian poet and novelist Filippo Tommaso Marinetti (1876–1944). His *Manifeste du Futurisme* (1909) called for a revolutionary attitude toward life and art in general, exalting such aspects of contemporary life as speed, machinery, and war. The special manifesto on literature (1912) insisted on courage, audacity, and rebellion as the essential elements of poetry; it advocated freedom for the word (*parole in libertà*), the abolition of syntax, and similar anarchic, "liberating" tendencies. In the field of art, futurism produced its most interesting works before World War. In their effort to portray dynamic movement and force, futurist painters often presented a moving object in successive stages of motion. Among the representatives of futurist art were the painters Giacomo Bella and Gino Severini and the sculptor Umberto Boccioni. The movement won for a time the endorsement of the Italian fascists.

Futurism influenced modern European literature and art and was also a forerunner of cubism, dadaism, expressionism, and surrealism. Its most immediate effect was felt in Russia where futurists attempted to do away with what they regarded as stale and hackneyed in Russian poetry, especially the kind of work written by the symbolist poets. The chief members of the Russian futurists were Velemir Khlebnikov and Vladimir Mayakovski. The Fauvist attitude of the futurists was revealed in their manifesto, *A Slap in the Face of Public Taste* (*Poshchiochina obshchestvennomu vkusu;* 1912), which voiced their demand: "Throw Pushkin, Dostoevski, Tolstoi . . . overboard from the steamship of modernity." The search for new poetic techniques led Khlebnikov to experiment with "trans-sense language" (Russ., *zaumnayi yazik* or *zaum*), in which words are shorn of their meanings and used only for their sound values. One of Khlebnikov's experiments consisted of a poem, written in 1910, made up of neologisms derived from the word *smekh* ("laughter"). Mayakovski, the greatest poet of the group, was more successful in developing a new kind of poetry. Its chief features were a rhetorical style, original rhymes, powerful rhythms, and an emphasis on the individual word, rather than the line, as the basis of poetic organization.

Although revolutionary in temper and tone, the work of the futurists was too literary for the Soviet cultural overseers. To propagate their views, the futurists formed the organization known as LEF (Left Front of the Arts) in 1923 and published a journal under that name. The journal failed in 1925, and was revived briefly in 1927–1928 as *Novyi LEF* (*New LEF*), but eventually the project died. By this time the proletarian trend in literature, advocated by RAPP (q.v.), was dominant.

Fuzzy Wuzzy (1892). Title of one of Rudyard Kipling's BARRACK-ROOM BALLADS celebrating the bushy-haired warriors of the Sudan who fought Gordon and Kitchener.

> So 'ere's to you, Fuzzy Wuzzy, at your 'ome in
>   the Soudan;
> You're a pore benighted 'eathen but a first-class
>   fightin' man.

G

Gaboriau, Emile (1835–1873). A literary pioneer who popularized the detective story in France. Gaboriau created the memorable hero Monsieur LECOQ.

Gabriel. One of the archangels who appears in the Jewish, Christian, and Muslim systems of belief. in Hebrew mythology, he is sometimes regarded as the angel of death, the prince of fire and thunder, but more frequently as one of the Deity's chief messengers and the only angel who can speak Syrian and Chaldee. In the Talmud, he appears as the destroyer of Sennacherib's armies, as the man who showed Joseph the way, and as one of the angels who buried Moses.

Christians hold that Gabriel was the angel of the Annunciation who appeared to the Virgin Mary; he also announced to Zacharias the future birth of John the Baptist. It is he who is to blow the trumpet on Judgment Day.

The Muslims call Gabriel the chief of the four favored angels and the spirit of truth. He was the angel who, according to the Koran, revealed the sacred laws to Muhammad.

Milton, in his *Paradise Lost* (1667), makes Gabriel chief of the angelic guards placed over Paradise.

Gabriel Conroy (1876). A novel by Bret HARTE. The longest of his fictional writings, it gives a vivid picture of mining conditions during the early days of the California gold rush. Among the best-drawn characters is the professional gambler, Jack Hamlin.

Gabrieli, Giovanni (1555–1612). Venetian composer, pupil of his uncle, Andrea Gabrieli (c. 1515–1586), also a composer of note. From 1576 to 1580 he was in Munich with Orlando de Lassus. He was a teacher of Michael Praetorius and Heinrich Schütz. Long associated with the Cathedral of St. Mark's in Venice, Gabrieli brought to its peak the Venetian style of polychoral writing (pieces for two or more groups of instruments or voices in different parts of the building). He is also important as a bridge between the Renaissance and Baroque styles in music.

Gabrina. In the ORLANDO FURIOSO of Ariosto an old hag whose ugliness evokes laughter in anyone who looks at her, but prompts quarrels among the knights who defend her. When the warrior maiden Marfisa, her protectress, defeats the Scottish knight Zerbino, the latter is compelled to keep Gabrina's company and follow her. He saves her from her enemy Ermonide, but she ungraciously charges him with the death of Pinabello. Zerbino, rescued by Orlando, later punishes the false knight Oderico by compelling him to keep Gabrina's company. Eventually, Oderico hangs her.

gadfly. A fly that bites or annoys cattle. In Greek mythology, Hera sent a gadfly to torment the white-horned cow in whose shape Zeus tried to protect his beloved Io from his wife's jealousy. A gadfly also bit Pegasus and caused him to send BELLEROPHON plunging to the earth.

Gaelic League. An organization founded in Dublin in 1863. Its purpose is to preserve and extend the vernacular use of the Gaelic language, the native tongue of Ireland.

Gaelic literature. The literature of Gaelic-speaking Ireland and Scotland. Irish literature is usually divided as follows: Old Irish (up to 900); Middle Irish (up to 1350); Late Middle, or Early Modern, Irish (up to 1650); and Modern Irish (from 1650). Up until the 12th century, Gaelic literature was entirely oral; it was committed to memory by bards and transmitted orally from generation to generation. In the middle period, a few monks began to set it down lest it be entirely forgotten.

Old Irish literature survives in medieval manuscripts, which are copies of older manuscripts; among the most important of these are *Lebor na Huidre* (*The Book of the Dun Cow*), *The Book of Leinster, The Yellow Book of Lecan, The Book of Ballymote,* and *The Speckled Book.* The romances and sagas contained in these books have been grouped according to characters and subject matter. The major groupings of these hero sagas are three: the MYTHOLOGICAL CYCLE, the ULSTER CYCLE, and the FENIAN CYCLE. The mythological cycle relates various traditions about the early settlement and conquest of Ireland. The Ulster cycle deals with Irish heroes, the greatest of whom is Cú Chulainn. The Fenian cycle deals with a much later period and extends into the Christian era which comes in the extreme old age of Oisin or Ossian, poet of the Fenians. The cycles are prose narratives interspersed with poetic dialogue.

The later Middle Irish literature written in Gaelic is generally less significant than that of the older periods; unlike the earlier literature, the bulk of which is anonymous, the later medieval literature was written by known poets, several of whom are worthy of mention. The chief bards of the 13th through 15th century are Gilbride Albanach McNamee (13th century), the religious poet Donough Mor O'Daly (13th century), and Teig Og O'Higgins (15th century). To this late medieval period also belongs the celebrated Gaelic narrative collection *The Three Sorrows of Story Telling.* The 16th and 17th centuries saw a great poetic revival and the rise of Modern Irish prose. As England conquered Ireland and as Protestantism became firmly established in England, Gaelic literature evinced fiercer patriotism and affirmed Catholicism. The decline of bardic poetry, however, was already under way before Cromwell's arrival (1649) in Ireland. The prose of the 16th and 17th century is transitional; the religious writings and monumental history of Ireland of Geoffrey Keating (1570–c. 1650) is the very foundation of Modern Irish literature. The number of Gaelic-speaking Irish declined somewhat after the arrival of Cromwell and the settling of English in Ireland; however, the potato famine of 1847 dealt the most severe blow, for, in the consequent depopulation of the country, the Gaelic west was hardest hit and the proportion of Gaelic speakers in Ireland dropped in three short years from three fourths to one quarter.

In the later 19th century, through the efforts of Irish scholars, there came the great Gaelic literary revival that continued into the 20th. See GAELIC LEAGUE; IRISH RENAISSANCE.

Gaheris, Sir. See MARGAWSE, QUEEN.

Gainsborough, Thomas (1727–1788). English painter. He rivaled Sir Joshua REYNOLDS as a fashionable portraitist, but his work shows greater simplicity and a lighter, rapid, and vibrant touch. One of the first painters to depict English scenery, he painted landscapes for his own pleasure and liked to portray his sitters in the open, but he allowed his art to be limited by the fashion of the day, which rejected landscape as a minor genre. Among his delightful portraits is the well-known *Blue Boy*.

Galafrone. In the ORLANDO INNAMORATO of Boiardo, the king of Cathay. He sends his daughter Angelica and his son Argalia to Paris to fight against Charlemagne and his paladins, the one using her beauty, the other his enchanted arms.

Galahad, Sir. In the later legends of King Arthur, the purest and noblest knight of the Round Table. Best known from Malory's *Morte d'Arthur* (c. 1469), he is the illegitimate son of Sir Launcelot and the princess ELAINE and the last descendant of Joseph of Arimathea. He alone is qualified to fill the SIEGE PERILOUS at the Round Table, and he alone achieves the quest for the Holy GRAIL. His career ends in Sarras, after he has completed the quest. Later writers, particularly of the romantic period, wrote newer versions of Sir Galahad into the Arthurian legend. Among these are Tennyson and Mark Twain. The name of Sir Galahad has become, in fact, synonymous with the chivalrous, the perfect knight.

Galápagos Islands. An archipelago of volcanic islands on the equator, west of Ecuador. It is noted for its large tortoises (Sp. *galápago,* tortoise), elephant seals, and other species that exist nowhere else. It was investigated by Darwin during his voyage in the *Beagle,* later by William Beebe. It is the setting of Melville's short story *The Encantadas.*

Galatea (Galateia). (1) A Nereid; see ACIS. (2) See PYGMALION.

Galatians, The Epistle of Paul the Apostle to the. A New Testament book. It is a letter from Paul to the various Christian churches in Galatia. Paul argues for the universality of the Christian faith, and tries to save it from becoming merely a Judaistic sect.

Galba (5 B.C.?–A.D. 69). Roman emperor (A.D. 68–69). He was made emperor after Nero's death by the Praetorian guard, but was killed after a few months because he was unwilling to fulfill the expectations of his followers.

Gale, Zona (1874–1938). American novelist and short-story writer. Born in Wisconsin, Miss Gale is best known for her work dealing with small-town life in the Middle West. She joined the staff of the New York *World* in 1901, but soon left to devote her time to writing. Her first novel, *Romance Island,* was published in 1906. The sentimentality that characterized Miss Gale's early writing was evident in her popular series of stories about the mythical Friendship Village. But despite their one-sided view, the author's talent for accurate observation gave them an aura of reality.

During World War I Miss Gale was again living in Wisconsin. Her pacifist views brought her the enmity of her neighbors, and her views of village life were greatly altered. This change of attitude is reflected in BIRTH and in her short novel MISS LULU BETT, which was an immediate success. In the same realistic vein were *Faint Perfume* (1923), which pitted the sensitivity of her heroine against the crassness of middle-class life, and two collections of short stories, *Yellow Gentians and Blue* (1927) and *Bridal Pond* (1930). A strain of mysticism, hinted at in earlier work, was apparent in *Preface to a Life* (1926) and in much of her later writing.

Galen (Klaudios Galenos, 2d century). A famous Greek physician and philosopher. For centuries he was the supreme authority in medicine; hence, any physician.

Galeoto or **Galeotto.** The Italian name of Gallehault, one of the forms of GALAHAD, which has attached to itself a quite divergent meaning. Its modern connotations come from a passage in Dante's *Inferno* telling how PAOLO AND FRANCESCA read of a guilty kiss between Launcelot and Guinevere and yielded to the suggestion. Gallehault was the knight who had brought Launcelot and the queen together, and he performed the same office for Paolo and Francesca, for "Galeoto was the book and he who wrote it. That day we read no more." Hence, though far from the character of Galahad, Galeoto has become a term for a panderer in Italy and Spain. In José Echegaray's tragedy EL GRAN GALEOTO, gossip is the "Galeoto."

Galiana. A Moorish princess, whose father, King Gadalfe of Toledo, reputedly built a palace for her on the Tagus River. It was so splendid that the phrase, a palace of Galiana, became proverbial in Spain.

Galilei, Galileo. Known as **Galileo** (1564–1642). Italian astronomer, physicist, and philosopher. Galileo's achievements led to a new physical and mathematical concept of nature. He discovered the isochronism of the pendulum (1583), hydrostatic balance (1586), Jupiter's satellites (1610), sun spots (1610), the moon's libration (1637), among other accomplishments. A staunch advocate of COPERNICUS, he found himself in difficulties with the Church, but was not unduly harassed until the publication of his *Dialogo dei due massimi sistemi* (*Dialogue on the Great World Systems,* 1632). The following year he was tried before the INQUISITION on charges of proclaiming and defending the Copernican system, which had been denounced as heretical. Unwilling to sacrifice his remaining years and his work to a fruitless heroism, he recanted his views. Legend has it that after doing so, he muttered *"Eppur si muove!"*

(And yet it moves!), in quiet insistence on the earth's motion. During his remaining years he was under close watch, in virtual house arrest, but he was widely acclaimed and revered. The *Dialogue* was the first scientific treatise written in Italian, the layman's language, rather than in the customary Latin. He is the subject of Brecht's play THE LIFE OF GALILEO.

gall. Bile; the very bitter fluid secreted by the liver. The word is used figuratively as a symbol of anything of extreme bitterness. The phrase "gall and wormwood" compounds the bitterness.

The gall of bitterness means the bitterest grief; extreme affliction. The ancients taught that grief and joy were subject to the gall as affection was to the heart, knowledge to the kidneys, and the gall of bitterness means the bitter center of bitterness, as the heart of hearts means the innermost recesses of the heart or affections. In the Acts it is used to signify the sinfulness of sin, which leads to the bitterest grief. According to tradition, pigeons have no gall, because the dove sent from the ark by Noah burst its gall out of grief, and none of the pigeon family has had a gall ever since.

Gall, Franz Joseph (1758–1828). German physician and phrenologist. His major scientific treatise is *Anatomie et physiologie du système nerveux en général* (*Anatomy and Physiology of the Nervous System in General,* 1810–1819). See PHRENOLOGY.

Gallegos [Freire], Rómulo (1884–1969). Venezuelan novelist, educator, and political leader. When lack of funds forced Gallegos to abandon his legal studies, he turned to teaching and, from 1912 to 1930, was director of various educational institutions. The publication of DOÑA BÁRBARA, Gallegos' best-known novel, aroused the hostility of Juan Vicente Gómez, Venezuela's dictator, who tried to silence the author by offering him a seat in the senate. Gallegos chose voluntary exile instead, living in the U.S. and Spain, where he was an employee of the National Cash Register Co. Returning to Venezuela, after the death of Gómez in 1935, he served briefly as minister of education, directed motion-picture versions of several of his novels, and was an unsuccessful presidential candidate in 1942. In 1945 a coup engineered by Acción Democrática, a liberal political party of which Gallegos had been a founder, overthrew the government, and he was elected president of Venezuela for the term 1948–1952. Late in 1948, however, Gallegos was deposed by a military junta and remained in exile until the overthrow of Marcos Pérez Jiménez in 1958.

As a novelist, Gallegos is famed for his interpretation of the people and customs of the Venezuelan *llanos,* or tropical prairies. Besides *Doña Bárbara,* his best-known novels are *La trepadora* (1925), a psychological study of an illegitimate son who seeks his family's acceptance; *Cantaclaro* (1934), which relates the adventures of a wandering minstrel on the *llanos; Canaima* (1935), a story laid in the tropical forest where the evil spirit "canaima" dwells; and *Pobre negro* (1937), which describes slavery and mulatto life in 19th-century Venezuela.

Gallehault. The name for GALAHAD in the old French romance *Lancelot du Lac.* See GALEOTO.

Gallic Wars. See COMMENTARIES ON THE GALLIC WAR.

Gallup, George H[orace] (1901–   ). Amer-

ican public-opinion statistician. Having founded the Institute of Public Opinion (1935) and spent some time measuring public reactions by means of polls, Gallup began to forecast the results of such reactions, particularly in the realm of political elections. He is the author of *The Pulse of Democracy: A New Technique for Measuring Reader Interest* (1940) and numerous articles on public opinion.

Galotti, Emilia. See EMILIA GALOTTI.

Galsworthy, John (1867–1933). English novelist and playwright, known for his portrayals of the British upper classes and for his social satire. His most famous work is his novel series beginning with THE FORSYTE SAGA (1906–1922); Galsworthy continued to write novels about the Forsyte family throughout his life. His plays are remarkable realistic and satirical studies based on various different social problems. Like Bernard Shaw and other contemporary writers of dramas of ideas, Galsworthy was influenced by the drama of Henrik Ibsen.

Born into an upper-middle-class family like the ones he usually wrote about, Galsworthy was trained as a lawyer and his legal knowledge colors many of his novels and plays. He turned to literature after he had met Joseph Conrad on a voyage. A passionate romance with Ada Galsworthy, his cousin's wife, who encouraged his writing, led to their marriage some 10 years later, in 1905. Galsworthy's earliest works, written under the pseudonym of John Sinjohn, were volumes of short stories and two novels influenced by Turgenev: *Jocelyn* (1898) and *Villa Rubein* (1900). He came to artistic maturity in 1906, with the publication of his novel *The Man of Property* (the first installment of *The Forsyte Saga*) and the production of his play *The Silver Box.* In the work of this early period Galsworthy attacked the smug conventionality and self-righteous hypocrisy of the middle classes, and championed the artist, the rebel, and the underdog (see his play JUSTICE). He became less satirical and more sentimental and traditional in his subsequent novels, such as THE COUNTRY HOUSE and THE PATRICIAN, and the plays *The Skin Game* (1920) and *Loyalties* (1922). He refused knighthood in 1918 but accepted the Order of Merit in 1929 and the Nobel Prize in 1932.

Galuppi, Baldassare (1706–1785). Italian composer, principally of opera. The work that inspired Browning's poem *A Toccata of Galuppi's* is thought to have been the *Toccata in A major* by the Italian composer Pietro Domenico Paradies or Paradisi (1707–1791).

Gálvez, Manuel (1882–   ). Argentine novelist. Gálvez is best known for his naturalistic novels in which he mercilessly exposed Argentina's social evils, revealing a Dickensian sympathy for the downtrodden. *La maestra normal* (1914), often considered his best work, is a tale of seduction notable for the author's depiction of the pettiness and monotony of life in the provincial city of La Rioja. Córdoba is the setting for *La sombra del convento* (1917), which describes the conflict between conservative clericalism and liberalism. Gálvez' most popular novel was *Nacha Regules* (1919); although its plot is melodramatic, dealing with the redemption of a fallen woman through true love, the novel gives a chilling portrait of conditions in a Buenos Aires brothel and among the poor in general.

Gama, Vasco da (c. 1460–1524). Portuguese explorer. The first European to discover a sea route to the East, he rounded the Cape of Good Hope on Nov. 22, 1497, sailed along the coast of Africa, and crossed the Indian Ocean to reach Calicut on May 20, 1498. He made a second trip to the East in 1502–1503 and was named viceroy of India in 1524. He is the hero of Camões' LUSIADAS, and Meyerbeer's opera *L'Africaine.*

Gambara, Veronica (1485–1550). Italian poet. She wrote sonnets on Petrarchan love themes and on the political events of her day. Her *Rime* (*Verses*) and *Lettere* were published in 1759.

Gambetta, Léon (1838–1882). French lawyer and statesman. Violently opposed to Napoleon III, he served as a member of the new government of National Defence (September, 1870). In a futile attempt to organize national resistance, Gametta made a spectacular balloon escape during the Prussian siege of Paris. He served as president of the Chamber of Deputies (1879–1881) and as premier of France (1881–1882), during the Third Republic.

Gambler, The (Igrok; 1866). A short novel by Feodor DOSTOEVSKI. The gambling mania of the tale's hero, Aleksei Ivanovich, is a reflection of the author's own tendency. The heroine of the story, Polina, is based on Polina Suslova, Dostoevski's lover in 1862–1863.

Gamelin, Evariste. Chief character in the novel THE GODS ARE ATHIRST by Anatole France. A young artist, Gamelin becomes an avid member of the revolutionary tribunal. Ironically, he himself is put to death by the guillotine.

Gamelyn, The Tale of. A metrical romance in Middle English. Often called **The Cook's Tale of Gamelyn,** it has been erroneously attributed to Chaucer (see COOK'S TALE). Gamelyn is the youngest of three brothers. The eldest robs him of his share of their father's property, and after a series of successes and reverses in reclaiming it, Gamelyn takes to the forest and eventually becomes chief of a band of outlaws. The second brother tries to help him and winds up in chains, but Gamelyn returns to overthrow their wicked brother, now sheriff, as well as the dishonest judge and jury. Thomas Lodge adapted the story in his romance *Rosalynde* (1590), a major source for Shakespeare's As You LIKE IT.

Gamesmanship. A term popularized by Stephen POTTER through his humorous book *Theory and Practice of Gamesmanship, or the Art of Winning Games without Actually Cheating* (1947).

Gammer Gurton's Needle (1566). The second oldest English comedy. It was first performed at Cambridge in 1566, and published in 1575. It was formerly ascribed to John Still (1543?–1607), Bishop of Bath and Winchester, but the claim of William Stevenson (d. 1575?) is now generally favored. A coarse and vigorous comedy, it deals with the housewife Gammer Gurton's loss of her needle as she is mending her servant Hodge's breeches; it closes with the painful but farcical discovery of the missing needle in the seat of Hodge's pants.

Gamp, Sarah, usually called **Sairey.** A disreputable nurse in Charles Dickens' MARTIN CHUZZLEWIT, famous for her bulky umbrella and perpetual reference to Mrs. Harris, a purely imaginary person

Title page of *Gammer Gurton's Needle* (1575).

whose opinions always confirm her own. She is fond of strong tea and more potent stimulants.

Hence, a regular Gamp came to signify a low-class, drink-sodden, uncertificated maternity nurse, and an umbrella, especially a large, badly rolled cotton one, came to be called a gamp.

gandharva (*Sans.*, celestial musician). In the Hindu tradition, marriage by the mere exchange of garlands, a love union, recognized by Manu, the Hindu law codifier, as one of the eight acceptable types of marriage.

Gandhi, Mohandas Karamchand, called **Mahatma** (great-souled) **Gandhi** (1869–1948). Hindu nationalist leader. He is considered the architect of Indian independence and self-rule. He studied law in England and practiced in India. In 1893 he went to South Africa to help in the struggle of Indian settlers to gain political rights; it was here that Gandhi first used the technique of passive resistance that later became his chief weapon against the British in India. After returning to India in 1914, he supported the British in World War I, but in 1919 he formed the Satyagraha, a politico-religious movement of non-cooperation with the British, which caused him to be imprisoned for "civil disobedience." In 1924 he became president of the Indian National Congress, a position he held until 1934. He urged the boycott of all English goods in 1932, the same year that he began his "fast unto death" in protest to the official treatment of the untouchables. He won his point after six days. During World War II he was again arrested by the British. He was shot and killed in 1948 by a Hindu Nationalist. His tremendous popularity in India was due to his devotion to Hindu ideals, his asceticism, his efforts to overcome the social and economic distress of the Indian peasants, and his campaign to eliminate untouchability from Hindu society. His simple costume of white worn by the wrinkled old man in the plain steel glasses appealed to the Western imagination as did the form of his protest that proved effective against the might of the British Empire. His works include *Indian Home Rule* (1922), *Young India* (1924) and *Autobiography* (1949).

Ganelon. Also **Gan of Mayence, Gano of Maganza.** The traitor among Charlemagne's paladins. In the *Chanson de* ROLAND his betrayal is responsible for the defeat at RONCESVALLES, and he figures prominently as the instigator of discord among the knights in Pulci's *Morgante Maggiore*, Boiardo's *Orlando Innamorato,* and Ariosto's *Orlando Furioso.* He is cited as one of history's notorious traitors in Dante's *Inferno* and Chaucer's *Nun's Priest's Tale.*

Ganesh or **Ganesa.** The god of wisdom or prudence in Hindu mythology. He is the son of Shiva and Parvati, and is always represented with an elephant's head. He is propitiated at the commencement of important work and at the beginning of sacred writings because he is the legendary scribe of the Hindu epic, the *Mahabharata,* which was dictated to him nonstop by the sage Vyasa. His worship is confined largely to west India, but he is one of the most popular Hindu deities.

Ganges or **Ganga.** The most sacred river of India. It rises in the Himalayas, flows about 1500 miles, and empties into the Bay of Bengal by many mouths. It is also known as the Bhagirathi. Its source, in Hindu legend, lies at the feet of Brahma, and its descent to the earth was through the matted locks of Shiva, the king of *yogis* or ascetics; hence the ritual necessity for orthodox Hindus to bathe in the holy river on certain days in order to be rid of their imperfections. See BHAGIRATH.

Ganivet, Angel (1865–1898). Spanish philosopher and critic. His most famous work is the philosophical inquiry into the Spanish national character entitled *Idearium español* (1898), which points the way toward the *Generación del 98* in its analysis of abulia, a lack of will in the Spanish people. Ganivet is also the author of two novels, considered semiautobiographical in nature, *La conquista del reino de Maya* (1897) and *Los trabajos del infatigable creador Pio Cid* (1898).

Ganor, Ganora, Geneura, Ginevra, Genievre, Guinevere, Guenever. Various ways of spelling the name of King Arthur's wife. She is called Guanhumara or Guanhumar by Geoffrey of Monmouth, but Tennyson made GUINEVERE the popular English form.

Gant, Eugene. The central character in Thomas Wolfe's autobiographical novels LOOK HOMEWARD, ANGEL and OF TIME AND THE RIVER. Gant is a young man of robust energies and intense emotion; he feels "different" from others, and has vast, romantic yearnings toward love, adventure, personal achieve-

ment, and a semimystical, unknown goal which carries him on a virtual pilgrimage through the U.S. and Europe. Other characters with the same family name are likewise drawn from life: Oliver Gant, Eugene's father; Eliza Gant, his mother; and Ben Gant, his older brother.

Ganymede (Ganymedes). In Greek mythology, the cup-bearer of Zeus, successor to Hebe, and a type of youthful male beauty. The son of Tros, an early king of Troy, he was carried off by Zeus on the back of an eagle because of his unusual beauty.

García de la Huerta, Vicente (1734–1787). Spanish playwright. His work is thought to have anticipated romanticism while preserving neoclassical principles. His most successful work is the verse drama *Raquel* (1778), dealing with the love between Alfonso VIII and a Jewish girl from Toledo, a theme previously treated by Lope de Vega and by Mira de Amescua.

García del Castañar. See Francisco de ROJAS ZORRILLA.

García Gutiérrez, Antonio (1813–1884). Spanish dramatist. The most popular of his many plays is *El trovador* (1836), a romantic historical tragedy that was the basis of Verdi's opera IL TROVATORE. He also wrote *Venganza catalana* (1864) and *Juan Lorenzo* (1865), sometimes considered his masterpiece.

García Lorca, Federico (1898–1936). Spanish poet and playwright. He is considered the most deeply appreciated Spanish poet, both at home and abroad. Born in Madrid, he began his career with the study of law; however, he abandoned this for verse and travel. After a period of great initial creativity revealing an even greater promise, García Lorca was brutally murdered by Falangists during the Civil War. His tragic death created a vacuum in Spanish literature, which present-day poets are still seeking to fill.

García Lorca's first poetic venture, *Libro de poemas* (1921), met with little success, but revealed his poetic bent. His next work, *Romancero gitano* (1928), breathing new life into the old tradition of the Spanish ballad, skyrocketed Lorca to fame. The work is a collection of Andalusian ballads, each containing the intense strains of the native gypsy songs (*cante-jondo*) of the area. One of the best-known of the ballads is *Muerte de Antonito el Camborio.* The poet's preoccupation with death is apparent in the title of his most famous poem, *Llanto por Ignacio Sánchez Mejías* (*The Death of a Bullfighter,* 1935). This work is considered to be the greatest elegy in modern Spanish poetry. García Lorca's well-known collections also include *Poeta en Nueva York* (*The Poet in New York,* 1940), which contains the poem *El rey de Harlem,* and *El diván del Tamarit* (1936).

García Lorca has an equally merited reputation as a dramatist. His plays, which have been translated into several languages, are among the most popular in Spanish literature. The most famous of his tragedies are *Bodas de sangre* (*Blood Wedding,* 1933), which relates the story of a young bride who runs off with a previous lover—he is subsequently murdered by her husband; *Yerma* (1934); and *La casa de Bernarda Alba* (*The House of Bernarda Alba,* 1936), the story of a brutal woman bent on a course of action which results in anguish and suicide for her daughters.

García Lorca was also an accomplished musician and amateur painter.

Garcilaso de la Vega (1501?–1536). Spanish poet and soldier. Garcilaso spent much of his brief life in Italy, where he lived, as he himself wrote, "Now using the sword, now the pen" (*Tomando, ora la espada, ora la pluma*). Often called "the Spanish Petrarch" because of his successful imitation of Italian poetry, he was a close friend of Juan Boscán, whose widow published his works with those of her husband in 1543. Garcilaso wrote 38 sonnets, five *canciones*, five odes, two elegies, and one *epístola* or "epistle," which are notable for their technical excellence and delicacy of sentiment. His first eclogue, dealing with the unhappy loves of the shepherds Salicio and Nemoroso, is generally considered his masterpiece.

Garcilaso de la Vega. Known as **El Inca** (1539–1616). Peruvian historian. The son of a Spanish knight and an Inca princess, Garcilaso is often regarded as the first spokesman for the South American mestizo. After fighting in European wars for 30 years, he settled in Spain, was ordained a priest, and devoted himself to history. His masterpiece is the *Comentarios reales* (*Royal Commentaries*, 1609), in which he described the Inca Empire and its conquest by Spain. Although some critics have claimed that it gives too fanciful and idealized a picture of Inca civilization, it is still considered a major source of information about pre-Columbian America. Garcilaso also wrote *Florida del Inca* (1605), an account of De Soto's explorations in what is now the southern U.S.

Garden, Mary (1877–   ). Scottish-born operatic soprano. Noted for the dramatic qualities of her singing, she was chosen over Maeterlinck's mistress to sing the first Mélisande in Debussy's opera, which estranged the poet from the composer. She wrote *Mary Garden's Own Story* (1951) with Louis Biancolli's help.

Garden, The (1681). A poem by Andrew Marvell. It was written while he was a tutor at the country estate of the Cromwellian general Thomas Fairfax. The poet dwells on the contrast between the innocence, peace, and beauty of the garden and the stress and trouble of the outside world. At the height of his contemplation of the garden, his mind performs a typically Marvellian transformation:

> Annihilating all that's made
> To a green thought in a green shade.

Garden in January, A. A tale from Giovanni Boccaccio's The Decameron. Dianora tells Ansaldo, an unwelcome suitor, that he can have her if he can make her garden as gay with flowers in January as it is in May. With the help of a magician, to whom he promises a generous reward, Ansaldo succeeds. Dianora's husband, learning of her plight, agrees to the fulfillment of the pact, whereupon Ansaldo matches his generosity by releasing Dianora from the pledge. The magician, too, joins in the general display of courtesy by refusing his reward. This is essentially the *Franklin's Tale* of Chaucer.

Garden Party, The (1922). A short story by Katherine Mansfield. While a wealthy woman and her daughters are preparing for their garden party, a poor laborer is killed in an accident. Young Laura is sent to take the widow and orphans the cakes left over from the party; the experience makes her see her own life in a new light for a moment. The reality of the outer world has intruded suddenly and violently upon the delicate artifice she has known as life.

Gardner, Erle Stanley (1889–1970), American writer of detective stories. One of the most successful writers of crime detection in the history of American publishing, Gardner, who has written over 100 books, usually employs two sleuths: the lawyer Perry Mason, hero of a long series that began with *The Case of the Velvet Claws* (1933), and Douglas Selby, who appears in *The D.A. Calls It Murder* (1944). Using the pseudonym A. A. Fair, Gardner has also created the engaging Donald Lam and Bertha Cool, who are featured in *Pass the Gravy* (1959) and other works.

Gareth, Sir. In Arthurian legend, one of the knights of the Round Table. In Malory's *Morte d'Arthur* (c. 1469) he is the youngest son of King Lot and Margawse. His mother, to deter him from entering Arthur's court, says jestingly that she will consent to his doing so only if he conceals his name and goes as a scullion for 12 months. He agrees to this, and Sir Kay, the king's steward, nicknames him "Beaumains," because his hands are unusually fine and large. At the end of the year he is knighted, and obtains his first quest when Linet begs the aid of some knight to liberate her sister Liones held prisoner by Sir Ironside in Castle Perilous. Linet treats Sir Gareth with great contempt, calling him a washer of dishes and a kitchen knave, but he overthrows five knights and frees Liones, whom he marries. Tennyson retells the story in *Gareth and Lynette* in his *Idylls of the King* (1859–1872).

While rescuing Queen Guinevere from death at the stake, Sir Launcelot unwittingly kills Sir Gareth, who is standing guard, and thus evokes the vow of revenge from Gareth's brothers that ultimately effects the downfall of King Arthur's court and the end of the Round Table. See Sir Gawain.

Gargamelle. In Rabelais' Gargantua and Pantagruel, the daughter of the king of the Parpaillos (*Fr.*, "butterflies"), wife of Grandgousier and mother of Gargantua. In the eleventh month of her pregnancy she goes into labor as a result of eating too much tripe and, after taking an astringent, gives birth to Gargantua through her left ear.

Gargantua (*Sp.*, "gullet"). The name of a giant-hero in medieval folk literature, whom Rabelais made the father of Pantagruel in his satire Gargantua and Pantagruel. He figures in four of the five books, but as a major character only in *La Vie inestimable du grant Gargantua, père de Pantagruel* (1534), which is now known as Book I.

Son of Grandgousier and Gargamelle, Gargantua miraculously enters the world through Gargamelle's left ear, shouting "Drink, drink, drink!" The narrative continues in a similar vein, recounting his extraordinary childhood and adolescence; his trip to Paris on his famous mare, whose tail switches so violently that she fells the entire forest of Orléans; his lawsuit over stealing the bells of Notre Dame Cathedral to hang around his mare's neck; his encyclopedic course of studies in Paris; his defense of his father's lands against the assaults of PICROCHOLE; and his founding of the abbey of THÉLÈME at the war's end. Apart from the buffoonery, the work also provides a biting and realistic satire on various aspects of contemporary society—monasticism, scholastic education, the legalistic pedantry of the theologians at the Sorbonne—and on the causes and effects of tyrannical power. It vividly describes student life in the Latin Quarter of Paris, and provincial life and manners in Rabelais' native Chinon. It contrasts antiquated educational programs with the humanistic studies that were just coming into prominence; despotism with intelligent, humane government; and oppressive monasticism with healthy living.

Gargantua and Pantagruel (1532–1564). The English title for a 5-part satirical work by François RABELAIS. Derived in part from the medieval fabliaux, it was published as follows:

Les Horribles et espovantables faictz et prouesses du tres renommé Pantagruel, Roy des Dipsodes, fils du grant géant Gargantua (1532), later known as Book II, recounts the life of PANTAGRUEL up to the war against the Dipsodes in UTOPIA.

La Vie inestimable du grant Gargantua, père de Pantagruel (1534), which is now known as Book I, describes the life of GARGANTUA through the founding of the abbey of THÉLÈME.

Le Tiers Livre des faictz et dictz heroiques du noble Pantagruel (Book III, 1546) presents a discussion of the problem faced by Pantagruel's companion PANURGE, who cannot decide whether or not to marry. Pantagruel accompanies Panurge as the latter consults a sibyl, a mute, a poet, an astrologer, a theologian, a physician, a philosopher, and a madman, none of whom can provide a solution. Panurge then persuades Pantagruel and his friends to embark on a voyage to the ORACLE OF THE HOLY BOTTLE for the answer. The book is rich in humanistic learning in the fields of divination, botany, and moral philosophy; at the same time it satirizes poets, judges, fortune-tellers, etc.

Le Quart Livre (Book IV, 1552), which relates the departure for the Holy Bottle in Cathay, reflects the keen interests of the period in the great voyages of discovery. Although in Book II, Pantagruel had reached Utopia by sailing around the Cape of Good Hope, this time the voyagers follow the North Atlantic route taken by the French explorer Jacques Cartier. Pantagruel and his companions visit several islands, where they meet the PAPIMANIACS, the POPE-FIGS, and other peoples who serve as targets for Rabelais' satirical thrusts against contemporary society. Like its predecessors, this book was condemned by the Sorbonne for its attacks on the Church.

The posthumous *Cinquième et dernier livre* (Book V, 1564), which includes L'ISLE SONANTE, is probably not entirely of Rabelais' authorship. Most modern scholars believe it was published by an imitator who developed sketches and drafts left by Rabelais. As the voyage to Cathay continues, Rabelais launches into a violent satire on religious and legal institutions. (See FURRY LAWCATS.) At last Pantagruel and his friends arrive at the temple of the Holy Bottle, where the oracle answers Panurge's question by a single word, "Drink!" This reply has been taken to mean that each man must eventually solve his own problems and that life's aim is a never-ending quest for knowledge, from which comes wisdom.

Rabelais was a man of his time who delighted in satirizing the religious, political, legal, and social institutions and practices of 16th-century France. He displayed a characteristically Renaissance thirst for erudition, but he also exalted the development of all human faculties, in accordance with his basic belief that human nature is fundamentally good. His universal genius reached far beyond his own century and has influenced numerous later writers, including La Fontaine, Molière, Voltaire, Swift, Balzac, Hugo, and Gautier.

Garibaldi, Giuseppe (1807–1882). Italian patriot. An ardent republican and associate of Mazzini, he was forced to flee from Italy because of his political activities and lived in South America (1834–1848). On his return he served in the army of the short-lived Roman Republic and upon its defeat made a dramatic retreat through central Italy. He escaped to the U.S. (1850–1854), where he became a naturalized citizen and worked for a while as a candlemaker on Staten Island. Returning to his native land, in order to secure the unification of Italy, he swore allegiance to King Victor Emmanuel of Sardinia. After taking part in the war against Austria, he invaded the so-called Kingdom of the Two Sicilies with his famous band of 1,000 men known as the Red Shirts. After the conquest of Sicily, he crossed to the mainland and drove Francis II from Naples. When the Sicilian king capitulated and Victor Emmanuel was proclaimed king of Italy (1861), Garibaldi withdrew to his farm in Caprera. He later led two unsuccessful expeditions of liberation against Rome and fought on behalf of the French republic in the Franco-Prussian War. On his statue on the Janiculum overlooking Rome is engraved his famous cry, *Roma o Morte* ("Rome or Death").

Garigliano, battle of (1503). The meeting at which the Spanish forces defeated the French armies in a struggle over possession of the kingdom of Naples, to which both laid claims.

Garland, [Hannibal] Hamlin (1860–1940). American short-story writer and novelist. Garland is best known for his realistic studies of the hardships and frustrations of farm life in the Middle West. Born in Wisconsin, Garland went to Boston and became a friend of William Dean Howells and others in the Boston literary circle. In 1887 he returned to the Midwest, where the barren and difficult lives of the farmers impressed him as being the stuff of fiction. Influenced by the realism of Howells and the single-tax ideas of Henry George, he began to write the stories and sketches published in MAIN-TRAVELLED ROADS. Other stories were collected in *Prairie Folk* (1892) and *Wayside Courtships* (1897), later published under the single title, *Other Main-Travelled Roads* (1910). Always interested in social reform, Garland's novels of the period center around political corruption: *Jason Edwards* (1892), *A Member of the Third House* (1892), and *A Spoil of Office* (1892).

In 1894 Garland issued his literary manifesto, *Crumbling Idols,* a group of essays calling for the repudiation of any imitation of past masters. Garland called his brand of realism "veritism," a concern for truth which emphasized local color, impressionism, and an art which is basically "sociologic." Although he was seldom able to live up to his own precepts, Garland influenced other writers, notably Stephen Crane.

A Little Norsk (1892) and *Rose of Dutcher's Coolly* (1895) both dealt with the drudgery of farm life. Garland then turned to writing novels about the Indians and the Far West. *The Captain of the Gray-Horse* (1902), which contains an appeal for justice to the Indians, is the most famous of these. *Cavanaugh, Forest Ranger* (1910) was also very popular. Garland also wrote four autobiographical narratives, the first two of which were A SON OF THE MIDDLE BORDER and the Pulitzer Prize-winning *A Daughter of the Middle Border* (1921).

Garneau, François Xavier (1809–1866). Canadian historian and poet. Garneau is best known for his four-volume *Histoire du Canada* (1845–1852), the first major literary achievement by a French-Canadian author.

Garnett, Constance. See Edward GARNETT.

Garnett, David (1892–   ). English novelist, son of Edward and Constance Garnett. He wrote fantasies, including LADY INTO FOX and *A Man at the Zoo* (1924), and the delicate, odd love story, *Aspects of Love* (1955). Garnett also published autobiographies which include accounts of his father's Bloomsbury life, beginning with *The Golden Echo* (1953). He also edited *The Letters of T. E. Lawrence* (1938) and *The Essential T. E. Lawrence* (1951). Other recent works include *A Shot in the Dark* (1958), *A Net for Venus* (1959), and *The Familiar Faces* (1962).

Garnett, Edward (1868–1937). English critic, biographer, and essayist. He was the son of Richard GARNETT. The best-esteemed publisher's reader in London, he encouraged and helped to publicize such writers as Joseph Conrad, John Galsworthy, and D. H. Lawrence. His wife, Constance Garnett (1862–1946), was renowned for her translations of Dostoevski and other Russian authors, much of whose work she made available to English readers for the first time.

Garnett, Richard (1835–1906). English librarian, literary historian, poet, critic, biographer, chief keeper of printed books at the British Museum (1890–1899). Garnett edited *Relics of Shelley* (1862) and contributed to the *Encyclopædia Britannica* and the *Dictionary of National Biography*. He also wrote poetry, numerous biographies, translations, essays, and an excellent collection of original fables, *The Twilight of the Gods* (1888). He was the father of Edward GARNETT.

Garnier, Robert (1544–1590). French dramatist. A fervent Catholic, he was concerned with restoring morality and faith during the religious wars. His own conviction expressed itself in the most lyrical and successful tragic verse dramas written in France before the great period of 17th-century French tragedy. His tragi-comedy BRADAMANTE and tragedy *Les Juives* (1583) are the high points of French Renaissance theater.

Garratt, the mayor of. Garratt is in England, near Earlsfield, Wimbledon; the first "mayor" was elected in 1778. He was really the chairman of an association of villagers formed to put a stop to encroachments on the public common, and as his election coincided with a general election, the society made it a law that a new "mayor" should be chosen at every general election. These elections gave rise to several satirical *Addresses by the Mayors of Garratt,* and Samuel Foote wrote a farce on the subject entitled *The Mayor of Garratt.*

Garrick, David (1717–1779). English actor and theater manager. He was educated in Lichfield and went to London with Samuel Johnson, his teacher and friend. He and his brother started a wine business, but were unsuccessful. Garrick turned to acting and his quick success enabled him to buy part of the patent for Drury Lane; his career as manager began in 1747. He did much to revive Shakespeare's popularity and wrote many theater pieces himself—largely farces and light comedies.

Garrison, William Lloyd (1805–1879). American abolitionist. In 1831 Garrison founded *The Liberator,* a weekly newspaper in which he denounced slavery and slaveholders with such vehemence that he was nearly killed by a Boston mob in 1835. He sought complete and immediate freedom for the slaves and demanded that the North repudiate its ties with the South, condemning the Constitution as "a convenant with death and an agreement with hell." *The Liberator* ceased publication in 1865 after the passage of the 13th amendment to the Constitution, which abolished slavery.

Garter, the Most Noble Order of the. The highest order of knighthood in Great Britain, instituted by Edward III on April 23, 1349. St. George is considered its special patron, and it is sometimes called the Order of St. George. Originally limited to 25 knights in addition to the king, it was reorganized and expanded in 1831 to include the Prince of Wales and to provide for the admittance of other members of the royal family, as well as of foreign royalty. The emblem of the order is a blue garter bearing the words *Honi soit qui mal y pense.*

The story is that Joan, countess of Salisbury, while dancing with the King, let fall her garter, and the gallant Edward, perceiving a smile on the faces of the courtiers, picked it up, bound it round his knee, and exclaimed, *"Honi soit qui mal y pense."* ("Evil to him who evil thinks.") The blue garter and the motto of the order are thus accounted for.

Garth, Sir Samuel (1661–1719). English physician and poet. His best-known work is *The Dispensary* (1699), a mock-heroic poem satirizing apothecaries. He was also a member of the KIT-CAT CLUB.

Garuda. In Hindu mythology, a supernatural being, half man and half bird, with golden body and red wings. Vishnu rides on Garuda.

Gary, Romain (1914–   ). Russian-born French novelist and diplomat. Gary is best known for *A European Education* (1945), about the Polish resistance in World War II, and THE ROOTS OF HEAVEN. Almost all of his novels satirize men's weaknesses and condemn many specific modern types, yet point hopefully to the potential dignity of man. His works include *The Company of Men* (*Le Grand Vestiare;* 1949), *The Colors of the Day* (1952); *Lady L.* (1958). *Promise at Dawn* (*La Promesse de l'aube;* 1960) is an autobiographical account of his youth.

Gas. The general name given to a loose trilogy of plays by Georg KAISER: *Die Koralle* (*The Coral,* 1917), *Gas I* (1918) and *Gas II* (1920). Taken together, they constitute a monumental indictment of the overmechanization in modern society.

The hero of *The Coral*, who is called the Billionaire, has risen to the highest possible position in industry, but is nonetheless constantly tormented by memories of his unhappy childhood. In an attempt to escape himself, he murders the Secretary, who is his double, and acquires the little piece of coral that symbolizes the latter's identity. Though he is executed for the crime, he still feels a kind of exhilaration at having broken clear of his rut. In *Gas I*, the Billionaire's son has taken over the plant which is now producing the gas that drives all other industry. The machinery fails, however, and there is a huge explosion that brings the son to his senses and prompts him to offer the workers land instead of a new gas plant, to offer them mastery over themselves rather than new enslavement to the machine. But the Engineer persuades the workers to rebuild the plant, and the Billionaire's son is killed in an ensuing riot. In *Gas II*, the final drama, the state has taken over the gas plant and is using it to fight a war. The workers attempt to make peace with the enemy, but fail; and the Great Engineer then persuades them to produce and use his new superweapon, a gas bomb. The device is detonated, and the play ends in a vision of total annihilation.

Gascar, Pierre. Pen name of **Pierre Fournier** (1916–   ). French fiction writer, journalist. His prisoner-of-war experiences inspired the cruel realism of his short novel *The Season of the Dead*. The novel was published with the six brutal allegories of *The Animals* (both 1953) in *Beasts and Men*. His travels as a journalist, which produced the reports *Chine ouverte* (1955) and *Voyage chez les vivants* (1958), also inspired the novel *The Coral Barrier* (1958), set against the racism and colonialism of Italian Somaliland. *The Seed* (1955) recalls his own boyhood in a provincial factory town.

Gascoigne, George (1525?–1577). English poet, playwright, and prose writer. Gascoigne was educated at Cambridge, studied law, and was elected a member of Parliament (1557/59). In 1566 he produced at Gray's Inn *The Supposes*, a prose adaptation of Ariosto's comedy *Gli Suppositi*, and the first prose comedy in English. This was followed by the blank-verse tragedy *Jocasta*, written in collaboration with Francis Kinwelmersh and adapted from a play by Euripides. Military adventures took Gascoigne away from England for three years, during which time a collection of his verse and other writings appeared. Called *A Hundred Sundry Flowers* (1572) and published without his permission, it caused a mild sensation, and Gascoigne himself published an enlarged edition in 1575. The same year appeared his "tragical comedy" *A Glass of Government*. In July of 1575 he accompanied the party of Queen Elizabeth visiting Kenilworth Castle, where he was commissioned by Leicester to write verses and masques for entertainment. *The Princely Pleasures at the Court of Kenilworth* (1576) contains some of his writings for that occasion. His blank verse satire *The Steel Glass* (1576) is one of the first satires in English; it was prefixed by a commendatory sonnet by Sir Walter Raleigh—the first of his poems to appear in print. In 1577 Gascoigne dedicated to Elizabeth a collection of moral elegies called *The Grief*

of Joy. He was the stepfather of Nicholas Breton, and is considered one of the leading men of letters during the period before Spenser and after Wyatt and Surrey.

Gaskell, Elizabeth Cleghorn, born **Stevenson** (1810–1865). English novelist. She is known for her depictions of English country life and for her pioneering studies of conflicts between capital and labor in Victorian industrialism. In the former class are the novels CRANFORD and *Wives and Daughters* (1864–1866), which show a fine degree of observation and characterization. Her social novels, chiefly MARY BARTON and *North and South* (1855), are notable for their sympathetic portrayal of the oppressed laboring classes in mid-19th-century England. She herself lived mainly in Manchester, a center of the depressed regions. Mrs. Gaskell was the friend of many literary figures in England, including Charlotte Brontë, whose biography she wrote in 1857, and George Eliot, whose work she influenced. Among her other books *Ruth* (1853) and *Sylvia's Lovers* (1863) are worthy of notice.

Gaspar or **Caspar** (the white one). One of the three MAGI. His offering to the infant Jesus was *frankincense*, in token of divinity. At some point in medieval dramatic presentations of the nativity, he became a comic figure. He soon degenerated in Germany into Casperl, a popular comic servant who appeared in puppet shows, notably the Faust play, in which he is Faust's servant.

Gaspé, Philippe Aubert de (1786–1871). Canadian novelist. Gaspé was high sheriff of the district of Quebec for many years until forced to withdraw from public life because of business difficulties and debts. At the age of 76 he published *Les anciens canadiens* (*The Canadians of Old*, 1863), a historical romance considered a classic of French-Canadian literature. His *Mémoires* (1866) is a collection of notes and hints for historians.

Gassendi, Pierre (1596–1655). French philosopher and mathematician. An opponent of the mechanistic world view of Descartes and an advocate of the atomistic theory of Epicurus, Gassendi wrote works on mathematics and philosophy, as well as lives of the astronomers Copernicus, Regiomontanus, and Tycho Brahe. Appointed professor of mathematics at the Collège de France in 1645, he achieved influence in learned and literary circles, and is said to have numbered Molière and Chapelle among his disciples.

Gaster. See MESSER GASTER.

gate of horn and ivory gate. In Greek mythology, the two gates of the abode of Sleep. Through them dreams come forth. Those passing through the gate of horn are true.

Gates, Horatio (1728?–1806). American general. At the time he was given credit for repulsing Burgoyne's army at Saratoga (1777), though modern historians maintain that the victory was due at least as much to Benedict Arnold. After suffering a serious defeat at Camden, S.C. (1780), Gates was relieved of his command. See CONWAY CABAL.

Gatomaquia (The Battle of the Cats, 1634). A mock-heroic poem by Lope de VEGA. Notable for its biting irony and wit, this burlesque of the Italian epic deals with the romantic affairs of the cat

Zapaquilda and her two suitors, Marramaquiz and Micifuf.

Gattamelata (It., *Honeyed Cat*). The popular cognomen of a notorious Italian CONDOTTIERE, Erasmo da Narni, who fought mainly for the Venetian republic and died in 1443. His equestrian statue, the work of Donatello, still stands before the church of Saint Anthony in Padua.

gaucho literature. A term used to describe literary works dealing with the gaucho, or outlaw cattle hunter, of the Rio de la Plata region of South America. In many works of this type he is treated realistically, and some writers, notably Sarmiento in his FACUNDO, decried his influence on the national life of Argentina and Uruguay. Elsewhere, however, he emerges as a romantic symbol of a pure and uncomplicated past.

The literary manifestations of gaucho folklore sprang from the extemporaneous songs of the gaucho minstrels known as *payadores*. One of the first writers to compose a literary work on the gaucho theme was Hilario Ascasubi (1807–1875), author of *Santos Vega* (1851; 1872), a poem narrated by the *payador* Santos Vega, a familiar figure in gaucho legend. The work is notable for the author's careful description of rural life and setting and for his use of authentic gaucho terminology. *Fausto* (1866) by Estanislao del Campo (1834–1880) is a mock-epic in which a gaucho who has witnessed a performance of *Faust* describes the action in his own crude language. The outstanding example of gaucho poetry is probably MARTÍN FIERRO, whose title character is drawn in heroic proportions.

Among the first prose writers to concentrate on the gaucho was Eduardo Gutiérrez (1853–1890) whose "thrillers," especially *Juan Moreira* (1880), demonstrated the vitality of the genre. Gutiérrez' dramatization (1884) of his work was extremely successful, and the gaucho soon became a familiar theatrical character, notably in the plays of Florencio SÁNCHEZ.

Soledad (1894) by Eduardo ACEVEDO DÍAZ is generally considered the prototype of later gaucho novels. Other novelists concerned with the subject were the Uruguayans Javier de Viana (1872–1926), author of the naturalistic *Gaucha* (1899), and Justino Zavala Muniz (1897–   ) and the Argentine Benito LYNCH, whose *Romance de un gaucho* (1930) is written entirely in gaucho idiom. Güiraldes' DON SEGUNDO SOMBRA, an able synthesis of American material and European technique, is widely regarded as the finest gaucho novel.

Gaudeamus igitur (Lat. "Therefore let us rejoice"). The first words of a Latin student song of German origin. The words date from 1267, the tune is 18th century. It is quoted by Brahms in the *Academic Festival Overture*.

Gauden, John. See EIKON BASILIKÉ.

Gauguin, [Eugène Henri] Paul (1848–1903). French painter. One of the most remarkable figures in modern painting, in 1883 he abandoned his job as a brokerage clerk, and the support of his family, in order to devote himself to painting. Poor and restless, he traveled, visiting Vincent Van Gogh in Arles and finally setting out for Tahiti in 1891. He returned to France only once and spent the rest of his life in the South Pacific, living among the natives. Gauguin developed a very decorative, highly original, personal style consisting of simplified forms and generally flat planes limited by a sinuous line and the use of brilliant, pure, unmixed color exaggerated to the point at which a reddish tinge in the foliage becomes pure vermillion, sand pink, and tree trunks blue. Gauguin's painting, especially his color, had great influence on later artists, notably on Henri MATISSE and the expressionists. He himself left an autobiographical account of his life on Tahiti, *Noa Noa* (1897), while W. Somerset Maugham's novel *The Moon and Sixpence* (1919) is a reconstruction in fictional terms of the whole of Gauguin's life.

Gaul (Lat., *Gallia;* hence, the English adjective *Gallic*). In classical geography the territory that comprises modern France and Belgium and part of northern Italy. *Cisalpine Gaul,* that is, Gaul on *this* (the Italian) side of the Alps, extended almost as far south as Florence. *Transalpine Gaul,* that is, Gaul beyond the Alps, included all the Gallic, German, and Celtic tribes from the Rhine to the Pyrenees. Gaul has been used as a literary name for modern France.

gauntlet, to run the. To be attacked on all sides, to be severely criticized. The word came into English at the time of the Thirty Years' War as *gantlope*, meaning the passage between two files of soldiers, and is the Swedish *gata*, a way, passage and *lopp* (connected with our *leap*), a course. The reference is to a punishment formerly common among soldiers and sailors; the company or crew, provided with rope ends, were drawn up in two rows facing each other, and the delinquent had to run between them, while every man dealt him as severe a chastisement as he could.

"To throw down the gauntlet" means to challenge. The custom in the Middle Ages, when one knight challenged another, was for the challenger to throw his gauntlet on the ground, and if the challenge was accepted the person to whom it was thrown picked it up.

Gautama. The personal name of Buddha. His family name was Siddhartha, his father's name Suddhodana, and his mother's Maya. *Buddha* means the enlightened, the one who knows. He assumed this title at about the age of 36, when, after seven years of seclusion and spiritual struggle, he believed himself to have attained the perfect Truth.

Gauthier, Marguerite. See DAME AUX CAMÉLIAS, LA.

Gautier, Théophile (1811–1872). French poet and novelist. The early poems and prose tales of Gautier move in the realm of the fantastic and the macabre. In his later poetry, however, Gautier stresses perfection of form and achieves a carefully polished beauty. His emphasis on form and his doctrine of *l'art pour l'art* (art for art's sake) make him a forerunner of the Parnassian school. Gautier's poetry includes *Poésies* (1830); *Albertus* (1832), a fantastic narrative poem; *La Comédie de la Mort* (1833), another long poem dealing with the sensual and the ideal; and *Emaux et Camées* (1852), considered the best example of his pure, minutely chiseled style (see PARNASSIANS). Among Gautier's novels and tales are *Les Jeune-France* (1833), *Mlle. de Maupin* (1835), *La Jettatura* (1856), and *Le Captaine Fracasse* (1861–1863).

Gawain, Sir. In ARTHURIAN LEGEND, one of the knights of the Round Table, nephew (in some versions, cousin) of King Arthur, and probably the original hero of the GRAIL quest. One of the earliest figures in the legends of Arthur, he appears in the Welsh *Triads* and the *Mabinogion* as Gwalchmei. He is the central figure in two major 14th-century English works: *The Alliterative Morte d'Arthur* and SIR GAWAIN AND THE GREEN KNIGHT. He is known as "the Courteous" and is first represented as the flower of chivalrous knighthood, but later writers (including Malory) downgraded him. In Malory's *Morte d'Arthur* (c. 1469) he is the son of King Lot and Queen MARGAWSE. He is King Arthur's favorite cousin and one of the most outstanding of the Round Table knights. He avenges the death of his father by killing King Pellinore, kills Sir LAMEROK, who is the lover of his mother, and kills his cousin Sir Uwayne, who is the son of Morgan Le Fay. Then, when Sir Launcelot unwittingly kills his youngest brother, Sir GARETH, Sir Gawain swears revenge. Twice he challenges Sir Launcelot to single combat at the siege of Benwick, and the second time is fatally wounded by that great knight who so unwillingly fought him. Returning to Britain, Sir Gawain dies, but not before repenting and writing a letter of reconciliation to Sir Launcelot.

Gay, John (1685-1732). English poet and playwright. A friend of Alexander Pope, he is known for his pungent satire and contemporary realism. THE BEGGAR'S OPERA, a satire of Sir Robert Walpole and the court of George II, won him enduring fame. Among his other works are *Rural Sports* (1713), a poem dedicated to Pope; *The Shepherd's Week* (1714), six pastorals written partly to parody the pastorals of Ambrose Philips; *Trivia, or the Art of Walking the Streets of London* (1716), a humorous but realistic depiction of the grotesque aspects of 18th-century London; POLLY, a sequel to *The Beggar's Opera*, which was suppressed until 1777 because of the virulence of its political satire; and *Fables* (1727-1738) a collection of 66 tales, the last 16 of which were published posthumously. In the 18th century, these last rivalled *The Beggar's Opera* in popularity. See John RICH.

Gay-Lussac, Joseph Louis (1778-1850). French chemist and physicist. Gay-Lussac made the first balloon ascent for purposes of scientific investigation. He discovered hydrosulphuric and oxychloride acids, and his name is associated with the law of volumes, or Gay-Lussac's law, concerning the proportions in which gases combine.

Gay Science. A translation of *gai saber,* the old Provençal name for the art of poetry. A guild called the *Gai Saber* was formed at Toulouse in 1323 with the object of keeping in existence the dying Provençal language and culture. Its full title was "The Very Gay Company of the Seven Troubadors of Toulouse."

Gaza, Theodore (d. 1475). Greek scholar. Born in Salonika, he was one of the first Greek scholars to arrive in Italy to help stimulate the revival of classical studies during the RENAISSANCE. He taught at Ferrara and in Rome, under the patronage of Pope Nicholas V.

Ge or **Gaea.** In Greek mythology the personification of the Earth. She is the offspring of Chaos, or at least comes into being after it. Uranus is both her child and husband. Their children, besides such things as seas and mountains are the Titans and Cyclopes. After her separation from Uranus she bore the Erinyes and Giants, being fertilized by the blood from his castration. Later she gave birth to Typhon, whose father was Tartarus.

Geb. In Egyptian religion, the god of earth, represented in human form, with beard and staff and a goose on his head. He was the husband of his sister Nut, the sky goddess, with whom he fathered Isis and Osiris.

Geber or **Jabir** (*Arab.*, **Jabir ibn Hayyan**; *fl.* 721-776). An Arabian alchemist, born at Thous, in Persia. He wrote in the usual mystical jargon of the period several treatises on the art of making gold, which led to the creation of the word gibberish in imitation of his name.

Geburt der Tragödie aus dem Geiste der Musik, Die. See BIRTH OF TRAGEDY FROM THE SPIRIT OF MUSIC, THE.

Geddes, Norman Bel (1893-1958). American stage and industrial designer. He made his reputation with his first production, *Nju,* in 1916. Thereafter he designed well over 200 theatrical productions; his settings for Max Reinhardt's *The Miracle* (1923) attracted particular attention. He also produced designs for ships, offices, and furniture, and devised a scheme for automobile highways described in his book *Magic Motorways* (1940).

geese, Capitoline. See CAPITOLINE GEESE.

Gehenna. The New Testament name for the Valley of Hinnom surrounding Jerusalem. It is the place of eternal torment, the "valley of slaughter" (Jer. 19:6) where sacrifices to Baal and Moloch were offered. See TOPHET.

Geibel, Emanuel (1815-1884). German poet, capable of classicistic elegance in style, but not known as a creator or innovator. Besides lyrics, he produced several dramas, including a tragedy *Brunhild* (1858).

Geijerstam, Gustaf af (1858-1909). Swedish novelist and playwright. Such early novels as *Grakallt* (1882), *Fattigt folk* (1884), and *Erik Grane* (1885) were gloomy naturalistic studies that delved into abnormal psychology. In his later works, however—*Minapojkar* (*My Boys,* 1896) and *Boken om lille-bror* (*The Book About Little Brother,* 1900), for example—Geijerstam waxed sentimental and domestic. His popular folk plays include *Svärfar* (1888), *Aldrig i lifvet* (1891), and *Per Olsson och hans käring* (1894).

Geisel, Theodor Seuss. Pen name, **Dr. Seuss** (1904-   ). American comic draughtsman and writer and illustrator of immensely popular humorous children's books.

geisha. A Japanese professional singing and dancing girl. Hence, especially in Western misconception, a licensed prostitute.

Gelber, Jack (1932-   ). American playwright. His first play, *The Connection* (1959), with its minutely realistic depiction of drug addiction, its stretches of obscenity and junkie argot, and its improvised jazz assault upon the audience, came to be regarded as an important expression of the generation who grew up in the 1950's. Gelber's second play, *The Apple* (1961), carried the attack on conventional dramaturgy and on the spectator even further and was received with mingled admiration and distaste. As in *The Connection,* the actors mingled with the audience between the acts, a device pioneered by Eugene O'Neill in *Marco Millions.*

Gelée, Jacquemart. See under REYNARD THE FOX.

Gelli, Giambattista (1498–1563). Florentine shoemaker and amateur moral philosopher. Gelli's aim in writing his treatises was to popularize learning for his fellow artisans. His *Circe* (1549), in 10 dialogues, had already been translated into English by 1570. He also wrote 20 short lives of Florentine artists and gave lectures on Dante and Petrarch at the Florentine Academy.

Gemara (Aram., "complement"). The 2nd part of the TALMUD. It consists of annotations, discussions, and amplifications of the MISHNAH, which is the first part. The Mishnah is the interpretation of the written law, the Gemara is the interpretation of the Mishnah. There is a Babylonian Gemara and a Palestinian Gemara. The former, which is the more complete, is by the academies of Babylon, and was finished by the sixth century; the latter, compiled in Palestine, was completed at the close of the fourth century.

Generación del 98. A group of Spanish writers of the early 20th century. Profoundly affected by the outcome of the Spanish American War (1898), they probed deeply into Spanish life and institutions in order to find the reasons for their country's disastrous defeat. Members of the group included José MARTÍNEZ RUIZ, Eduardo MARQUINA, Antonio MACHADO, Ramón PÉREZ DE AYALA, Juan Ramón JIMÉNEZ, Jacinto BENAVENTE, the brothers ALVAREZ QUINTERO, Ramón del VALLE-INCLÁN, Pío BAROJA, and Miguel de UNAMUNO. Their goal was betterment of Spanish life through education and opposition to bossism and to clericalism. In literature the movement advocated simplicity of style, the discarding of exaggeration, international rather than purely Spanish inspiration, the exalting of the countryside, and a contempt for patterns—it was felt that the pattern of life itself should be sought by playwrights and novelists.

General William Booth Enters into Heaven (1913). A poem by Vachel LINDSAY. Written after the death of the leader of the Salvation Army, it was first published in *Poetry.* It is written in the rhythmic drumbeats of a Salvation Army band, and is intended to be sung to the music of *Washed in the Blood of the Lamb.*

Genesis (Gr., "origin"). The 1st book of the Old Testament. In Hebrew, it is called *Bereshith,* "In the beginning," from the initial words of the text.

The first 11 chapters deal with the early days of the creation of the world; the remaining (12–50) are an account of the patriarchs of Israel: Abraham, Isaac, Jacob, and Joseph.

Genêt, Edmond Charles Edouard (1763–1834). French diplomat in the U.S. As minister of the First Republic, "Citizen" Genêt hoped to draw the U.S. into France's war against England and Spain. Attacking the government for its policy of neutrality, he sought to create a change of presidential attitude through popular agitation. He also commissioned privateers in American ports to prey upon English ocean commerce. He was recalled on the insistence of Washington, but meanwhile the Girondists—his faction of moderate republicans ruling the First Assembly—had fallen from power, and he lived for the rest of his life on Long Island.

Genet, Jean (1910–   ). French dramatist and essayist. A professional thief who had served a number of jail sentences, he was freed by the intervention of Jean-Paul Sartre and Jean Cocteau. His plays reveal a concern with the illusory nature of reality, particularly with the ambiguous definitions of good and evil in a society characterized by repression and hypocrisy. Of all the dramatists of the ABSURD, Genet probes most deeply into the inner self: its dreams, illusions, deceptions, and bitterly frustrated longings. Among his stylized, lurid, and nightmarishly disillusioning plays are: THE MAIDS, *Deathwatch* (*Haute Surveillance;* 1949), THE BALCONY, and *The Blacks* (*Les Nègres;* 1958). His other works include the prose *Our Lady of the Flowers* (*Notre-Dame des Fleurs;* 1949), *The Thief's Journal* (*Journal de voleur;* 1949, with a preface by Sartre), and *Poèmes* (1948).

Geneva. The capital of the Swiss canton of Geneva. Situated on the Lake of Geneva, or Lac Leman, it was a center of the Reformation under Calvin (1536–1564). It was also the birthplace of Jean-Jacques Rousseau. It served as the seat of the League of Nations after World War I.

Geneva Bible. See BIBLE, ENGLISH VERSIONS.

Geneva convention. An agreement made by the European powers at Geneva (1864; supplemented 1868). It established humane regulations for the treatment of disabled soldiers in war. It was revised and brought into accord with modern methods of warfare in 1906 and has since been ratified by almost every country.

Genevieve (earlier **Genovefa**) **of Brabant.** Heroine of an old German folk tale, wife of Count Palatine Siegfried of Trèves. Their majordomo Golo falsely accuses her of infidelity during the absence of Siegfried, who orders her killed. But the executioner allows her to escape into the forest, where she lives with her infant son, nourished by a doe. Siegfried learns of his error, and six years later, when he discovers the hiding place by chance while pursuing the doe, they are reunited.

Genghis (**Jenghiz**) **Khan** (1162–1227). A Mongol emperor. Named **Temujin,** by his father, who died when the boy was 13 years old, he took the title by which he is commonly remembered, and which means "perfect warrior." Genghis, with the aid of his mother, quickly regained the supremacy of the allied tribes who had defected after his father's death, and then proceeded to extensive conquests. He took vast territories in north China, then moved westward through Iran and Iraq, subduing nations wherever he passed. He pillaged considerable sections of India as well. Genghis' generals ravaged considerable parts of Russia before returning to their homeland.

Barbarously cruel, Genghis was one of the most brilliant generals of history. His successors, however, could not hold his vast empire together, and it lasted only a fairly short period. (See TAMERLANE.) His conquests, nevertheless, had far-reaching effects on history, for they set in motion a chain of events that led to the westward invasions of the Turks and helped to establish the Ottoman Empire. See KUBLAI KHAN; GOLDEN HORDE.

Génie du Christianisme, Le (**The Genius of Christianity**, 1802). A treatise on Christianity by François René de CHATEAUBRIAND. The author extols Christianity, describing it as the great force that develops the soul of man, and citing it as the chief source of progress in the modern world. This work, not only won great popular approval for Chateaubriand, but also earned him the good will of Napoleon.

genii or **ginn.** See JINN.

Genius (pl. *Genii*). In Roman mythology, the spirit that presides over the birth of every man and attends him throughout his life. (Women had no individual Genii, but were under the general protection of Juno.) The Genius, as the individual life-principle, was especially honored on a man's birthday; considered as one's higher self, it was also called to witness a man's oath. There were also corporate Genii: Genii of the family, the tribe, and the nation. Under the empire, the Genius of the emperor was worshiped throughout the Roman World. Moral philosophers, seeking to explain moral conflict within human nature, posited an opposing, evil Genius. In Christian times these two Genii became the guardian angel and his diabolical counterpart.

"Genius," The (1915). A novel by Theodore DREISER. The hero of this semiautobiographical work is Eugene Witla, a Middle Western artist, who becomes the art director of a large magazine corporation, has numerous love affairs, attains financial and social success, and marries Angela, who dies in childbirth. Witla himself suffers a breakdown but recovers his health and devotes himself thereafter to painting and to the care of his daughter. According to Helen Dreiser, in her book *My Life with Dreiser* (1951), Witla is a composite of three real persons: the artist Everett Shinn, an art editor whom Dreiser knew, and Dreiser himself.

Genji, The Tale of. See TALE OF GENJI, THE.

Genovefa. See GENEVIEVE OF BRABANT.

Genroku. The name of a Japanese era (1688–1703). The greatest flowering of Japanese literature and culture during the Tokugawa period (1600–1868) occurred during this era. See CHIKAMATSU MONZAEMON, MATSUO BASHŌ, and IHARA SAIKAKU.

genteel tradition. A term first used by George SANTAYANA. In *The Genteel Tradition at Bay* (1931), he applied it to those American writers at the close of the 19th century who upheld traditional social, moral, and literary standards, emphasizing correctness and conventionality. Among these writers were Richard Henry STODDARD, Bayard TAYLOR, Edmund Clarence STEDMAN, and Thomas Bailey ALDRICH. Santayana associated the term with New England, and attacked the later flowering of the genteel attitude in Paul Elmer MORE, Irving BABBITT, and the NEW HUMANISM.

Gentle Craft, The. A tale by Thomas DELONEY (1597), celebrating shoemakers and their craft. Part I deals with St. Hugh, the patron saint of cobblers, and St. Winifred. Part II tells of St. Crispin and St. Crispinian, also patron saints of cobblers. Part III, the best-known section of the story, gives an account of Simon EYRE, the shoemaker Lord Mayor of London.

Gentleman from Indiana, The (1899). A novel by Booth TARKINGTON. The hero is John Harkless, the young editor of a country newspaper in Indiana, who fights courageously against political corruption and is eventually elected to Congress.

Gentleman's Magazine, The. An English periodical, founded in 1731 by Edward Cave, a printer at St. John's Gate, Clerkenwell. It was the first periodical to call itself a "magazine." The publication was at first a miscellany of essays extracted from weekly journals, together with a systematic chronicle of current news. Samuel JOHNSON was a regular contributor and an editor in the early 1740's, and, under his direction, the extracts were largely replaced by original matter. The magazine was issued until 1914.

Gentlemen Prefer Blondes (1925). A humorous novel by Anita Loos. Subtitled "The Illuminating Diary of a Professional Lady," it tells the story of Lorelei Lee, a good-looking but not very intelligent girl, who manages to do very well for herself with Mr. Gus Eisman, the Button King. A satire on "the gold-diggers" of Hollywood, the book had an enormous vogue, though rumor has it that some fraction of its popularity may be ascribed to the fact that it was taken seriously by girls who thought it a useful handbook on how to get rich.

Geoffrey of Monmouth (c. 1100–c. 1155). Medieval English historian. A canon at Oxford, he wrote the important Latin prose HISTORY OF THE KINGS OF BRITAIN (*Historia Regum Britanniae*), one of the sources of the ARTHURIAN LEGEND and of considerable literary influence. He is considered to be the creator of the heroic image of King Arthur.

George, St. The patron saint of England since about the time of the institution of the Order of the Garter (c. 1348). He was "adopted" by Edward III. He is commemorated on April 23. St. George had been popular in England from the time of the early Crusades, for he was said to have come to the assistance of the Crusaders at Antioch (1098), and many of the Normans (under Robert, son of William the Conqueror) then took him as their patron.

That St. George is a historical character is beyond all reasonable doubt. He is now believed to have been

St. George. Woodcut from a broadside ballad.

a Cappadocian official in Diocletian's army, martyred April 23, A.D. 303. There are various versions of his *Acta,* one saying that he was a tribune and that he was asked to come and subdue a dragon that infested a pond at Silene, Libya, and fed on the dwellers in the neighborhood. St. George came, rescued a princess (Sabra) whom the dragon was about to make its prey, and slew the monster after he had wounded it and the princess had led it home in triumph by her girdle.

The legend of St. George and the dragon is in part a universal folk theme (see ANDROMEDA), in part an allegorical expression of the triumph of the Christian hero over evil, which St. John the Divine beheld under the image of a dragon. Similarly, St. Michael, St. Margaret, St. Sylvester, and St. Martha are all depicted as slaying dragons; the Saviour and the Virgin as treading them under their feet. A snake or a dragon biting its tail was sometimes an attribute of Father Time in Renaissance art.

The legend forms the subject of an old ballad given in Percy's *Reliques.* Spenser introduces St. George into his *Faerie Queene* as the Red Cross Knight. See KALYB.

George, Henry (1839–1897). American economist and reformer, known for his study of the problems of poverty. His most famous theory is that of the single tax, or a tax on land, which was the most important form of wealth in his day, set forth most persuasively in PROGRESS AND POVERTY. Other works are *The Irish Land Question* (1881), *Social Problems* (1884), *Protection and Free Trade* (1886), and *Science of Political Economy* (1897). The Fabian Society in England and later movements for economic reform in the U.S. were influenced by George's theories. He died while campaigning for the office of mayor of New York (for the second time) as an independent Democratic candidate.

George, Stefan (1868–1933). German poet. Strongly influenced by Nietzsche in his youth, he adopted an aristocratic doctrine of the poet as a chosen being, from which he never entirely departed; but later in his career, under the impact of World War I, he became more concerned with political reality and developed a conception of the poet as priest, with a duty not only to himself and his art, but also to his people. The poet, he believed, must preserve traditional spiritual values and prevent his people from succumbing to the excitement of wartime brutality and regarding war as an end in itself. Despite his development toward an idealistic patriotism, George's cultural interests were always international in scope. He was a prolific translator (e.g., Baudelaire, Dante, Shakespeare, the English Pre-Raphaelites) and came into personal contact with the French symbolist poets Verlaine and Mallarmé, by whom he was strongly influenced. Of his own works, the following collections of poems are most famous: *Das Jahr der Seele* (*The Year of the Soul,* 1897), *Der Stern des Bundes* (*The Star of the League,* 1914), and *Das neue Reich* (*The New Kingdom,* 1928). His style abounds in esoteric mythical allusions and archaic linguistic forms, and his works are rendered still less accessible by innovations in punctuation and typography. The "George-circle," a small group of literary apostles whom he collected about himself, is credited with a major role in the critical "rediscovery"

of such important German writers as Friedrich Hölderlin and Jean Paul Richter, whose works had fallen into neglect around the turn of the century. See Hugo von HOFMANNSTHAL; Friedrich GUNDOLF; Karl WOLFSKEHL.

George's Mother (1896). A novelette by Stephen CRANE. This is the story of the mother of George Kelsey, who battles unsuccessfully against the lures of the city for her son's allegiance. A religious woman, she dies still believing in her idealized view of George, not knowing that she has really lost. The story was early hailed for its social realism and its artful manipulation of common people and everyday events.

Georgians. A group of English poets, whose style dominated the early years of the 20th century, and who wrote poetry of nature and rustic life in the traditional manner of Wordsworth. The trend was inaugurated by John Masefield's THE EVERLASTING MERCY and A. E. HOUSMAN's Shropshire ballads; it was turned into a movement by Edward Marsh, who published the biennial anthology *Georgian Poetry* (1912–1922). The name reflects the accession of King George V in 1910. The chief Georgian poets were Lascelles ABERCROMBIE, Edmund BLUNDEN, Gordon BOTTOMLEY, Rupert BROOKE, W. H. DAVIES, John DRINKWATER, W. W. GIBSON, Ralph HODGSON, Harold MONRO, T. Sturge MOORE, Robert NICHOLS, J. C. SQUIRE, Edward THOMAS, and Francis Brett YOUNG.

Georgia Scenes, Characters and Incidents, &c., in the First Half Century of the Republic (1835). A collection of 18 humorous sketches by Augustus Baldwin LONGSTREET. In this popular book, Longstreet alternates Addisonian essays with excellent tales of the folkways of Georgia. A pioneer regionalist, he faithfully reproduced Georgia's language.

Georgics (*Georgica*). A didactic poem in 4 books on the subject of agriculture, composed in 37–30 B.C. by VERGIL. As Vergil's *Bucolics* were based on Theocritus' *Idyls,* so his *Georgics,* also, had a classical Greek precedent: Hesiod's *Works and Days.* Although the work was conceived and executed within the classical genre of the simple didactic, it is more than an agricultural handbook: it is the subtle and profound work of a philosopher-poet. Like the *De Rerum Natura* of Lucretius, to which it is in many ways a reply, Vergil's *Georgics* is built upon a solid didactic foundation from which it rises naturally to peaks of impassioned eloquence.

Book I contains advice on farming in general. After giving an account of the ills that followed the assassination of Julius Caesar, the poet prays that the Roman blood spilled at PHARSALUS and PHILIPPI may be sufficient to expiate the nation's ancestral guilt and that the young Octavius Caesar will save the world from civil war.

In Book II, Vergil concerns himself with grape vines and fruit trees, though he again rises above mere instruction. This book also contains a famous paean to the crops and heroes of Italy.

At the beginning of Book III, the poet rededicates himself to his work. He takes up the care and propagation of livestock, and at the end of the book describes the effect of a plague which killed all living things.

Unlike Lucretius, who ends his poem with a similar scene of a plague in Athens, Vergil passes directly into the sunny Book IV of his *Georgics* and tells a tale of miraculous regeneration. The book is formally concerned with the raising of honey bees, but its most important sections deal with two myths of death and resurrection, one within the other. The bees of Aristaeus, god of beekeeping, have suddenly died. His mother, the sea divinity Cyrene, advises him to consult Proteus, who tells Aristaeus that his bees have been killed by the dryads. The nymphs were avenging the death of Eurydice who, while being pursued by Aristaeus, stepped on a snake and died of its bite. Proteus then relates the pathetic tale of Orpheus and Eurydice. At his mother's suggestion, Aristaeus sacrifices four bulls and four heifers to the shades of Orpheus and Eurydice. After he has let their carcasses rot for nine days, he beholds a swarm of living bees issuing forth from the decaying bellies of the cattle.

Geraint, Son of Erbin. A medieval Welsh tale from the MABINOGION in which King Arthur figures. This story has a parallel in the tale EREC ET ENIDE of Chrétien de Troyes. Tennyson drew his characters Geraint and Enid in his *Idylls of the King* (1859–1872) from the same source.

Gerard, Brigadier. An egotistical, swashbuckling, braggart Napoleonic soldier, hero of a series of tales by Sir Arthur Conan DOYLE.

Gerhardi, William Alexander (1895–   ). English novelist. A disillusioned satirist, he wrote *Futility* (1922), *The Polyglots* (1925), and *Resurrection* (1934). His other works include the novels *Of Mortal Love* (1936) and *My Wife's the Least of It* (1938), the plays *I Was a King in Babylon* (1948) and *Rasputin* (1960), *The Romanoffs: An Historical Biography* (1940), and *The Life and Times of Lord Beaverbrook* (1963).

Géricault [Jean Louis André] Théodore (1791–1824). French painter. The exhibition in 1819 of his masterpiece *The Raft of Medusa*, a realistic and dramatic indictment of death and suffering, caused a storm of protest, and marked the beginning of the struggle between the classical and romantic schools of painting. A powerful draftsman and superb colorist, Géricault is equally known for his paintings of animal life and vivid historical scenes.

Germ, The. This "little magazine" was published from January to April, 1850, by the PRE-RAPHAELITE BROTHERHOOD. In its pages the Pre-Raphaelites printed poems, reproductions of their paintings, and expositions of their artistic ideas.

Germanicus Caesar (15 B.C.–A.D. 19). Roman general. He was adopted by his uncle, the emperor Tiberius and received command of the legions in Germany. He scored a huge success in his campaign against the Germans (A.D. 11–16), but just when he was about to conquer the whole country between the Rhine and the Elbe, Tiberius, alarmed at his strength, recalled him to Rome. It was believed by many that Germanicus was poisoned, possibly at Tiberius' bidding. Germanicus had nine children by Agrippina, among whom were the notorious Caligula and AGRIPPINA, mother of Nero.

German romanticism. Romanticism in Germany was not one movement but a series of separate ones. The first of these, called Jena romanticism after the small university town where most of the writers met, flourished around 1798–1802 and centered about the brothers F. and A. W. SCHLEGEL. The Schlegels, however, did not regard themselves as the founders of a romantic movement for, in their definition, romantic meant simply modern (from the Middle Ages on), as opposed to classical (Greek and Latin). As romantic authors, they wished to go beyond the classics, but *not* to deny them; in fact, they were very much a part of the philhellenic tradition that also produced WEIMAR CLASSICISM.

But they did set out in new directions. F. Schlegel urged writers to strive for a progressive universal poetry, by which he meant that romantic poetry must constantly develop, that it must not cease to be progressive, and that its ultimate goal must be universal, a synthesized comprehension of the entire world; these ideals of dynamism and universality were opposed to the Weimar classical ideals of balance and limitation. NOVALIS and Wackenroder strove for a new synthesis of art and religion. And Tieck and Novalis made new advances in the characteristically romantic form of the MÄRCHEN, which was later developed by BRENTANO and E. T. A. Hoffmann.

The second of Germany's romantic movements, which flourished in Heidelberg around 1804–1808, was less urbane than Jena romanticism and tended more to stress the beauties of unspoiled nature. It was also in Heidelberg romanticism that the romantic interest in German history and folklore, which had begun with Wackenroder and Tieck, first really took root. Major figures in this phase were Achim von Arnim, Brentano, Görres, Eichendorff, and the brothers Grimm.

But in the atmosphere of growing nationalism that culminated in the wars of liberation against Napoleon (1813–1815), German literature took a turn toward realism, and it is mainly this which characterizes the work of the Berlin group of about 1808–1813, although in their idealism and their frequent use of the *Märchen*-form they are still recognizably romantic. Major figures were E. T. A. Hoffmann, Fouqué, Chamisso, Heinrich von Kleist, and again, Arnim and Brentano.

Finally, after the wars of liberation, under the conservative Prussian and Austrian regimes of 1815–1848, German romanticism again followed the tenor of the times. The Swabian School, which Heine attacked vigorously in his *Die romantische Schule* (*The Romantic School*, 1833) and which included Uhland, Kerner, Lenau, Hauff and Schwab, was a primarily conservative group, interested in the preservation of tradition, and was already very like the postromantic BIEDERMEIER movement.

Disparate though it was, there is a unifying principle inherent in German romanticism. In the 18th century, some voices had already been heard against the prevailing rationalism of the age: Hamann, Herder, Jacobi, Klopstock, the poets of the STURM UND DRANG and of Weimar classicism. In very general terms, German romanticism may be seen as the culmination of all these movements, the final overthrow of the enlightenment, and the definitive redirection of 19th-century literature into nonrationalistic areas of experience. The philosophers most closely associated with German romanticism were Fichte and Schelling. See romantic IRONY.

Germinal (1885). A novel by Emile ZOLA, one of the ROUGON-MACQUART novels. *Germinal* is a study of the bitter sufferings of workers in the French mines. Zola's intense sympathy for the lower classes and his pleas for social reform find powerful expression in this careful portrait of life in the mines.

Germinie Lacerteux (1869). A novel by the GONCOURT brothers. Based on the sordid life of one of the Goncourts' own servants, and composed with attention to realistic detail, this work is naturalistic in both its form and subject matter.

Gernando of Norway. In the GERUSALEMME LIBERATA of Tasso, a Christian knight who is the rival of Rinaldo of Este for the command vacated as a result of the death of Dudone. When the quarrel results in his death, Rinaldo is charged with the crime by Goffredo, the Christian general. Like Achilles, Rinaldo stalks off in anger and leaves the Crusaders without one of their leading warriors.

Geronimo. Indian name: **Goyathlay** (1829–1909). American Apache chieftain. In 1885–1886 he led an attack on white settlers; he was captured by General George Crook (1829–1890), escaped, and later surrendered to General Nelson A. Miles (1839–1925). He finally settled down with members of his tribe on farmland and ranches at Fort Sill, Okla. There he joined the Dutch Reformed Church in 1903, and dictated an account of his life to Stephen M. Barrett; it was published as *Geronimo's Story of His Life* (1906). A town in Arizona is named for the Indian chief. During World War II, American parachutists would often begin their jump by yelling "Geronimo." The reason for their adoption of the Indian name is unknown.

Géronte. The name of the old man who is a stock figure in early French comedy. By Molière's time the character had taken on the unpleasant traits exemplified by the Géronte of LE MÉDECIN MALGRÉ LUI.

Gerontion (1920). A poem by T. S. ELIOT. Spoken by "an old man in a dry month," it is a despairing poem about old age, aridity, the spiritual decay of the world, and the need and unlikelihood of salvation.

Gerontius, The Dream of. See DREAM OF GERONTIUS, THE.

Gershwin, George (1897–1937). American composer. He began his career by composing popular songs, soon combined them into musical comedies, such as *George White's Scandals* (1920–1924), *Funny Face* (1927), and *Of Thee I Sing* (1931; the first musical to win a Pulitzer Prize). However, his chief importance resulted from his ability to bring jazz and popular styles into the realm of classical music, especially with the internationally famous works, *Rhapsody in Blue* (1924) and *Porgy and Bess* (1935; see PORGY). His songs have been collected in *George Gershwin's Song Book* (1932). His brother Ira Gershwin (1896–   ) was a popular Broadway lyricist who wrote lyrics for many of George's shows.

Gerson, Jean Charlier de (1363–1429). French theologian. Court preacher to Charles VI, he was famous for his sermons in both Latin and French. Gerson was a prominent scholar, the chancellor of the University of Paris, and a delegate to the councils of Pisa and Constance where he strove for church unity and ecclesiastical reforms. He was one of the leading opponents of the *Romance of the Rose,* which he condemned to be burned (1399) as a threat to morality. The authorship of the *Imitation of Christ* is sometimes attributed to Gerson, instead of to Thomas à Kempis.

Gertrude. In Shakespeare's HAMLET, the queen and mother of Hamlet. A weak-willed woman, who has married her husband's brother and murderer, she draws from Hamlet the cry: "Frailty, thy name is woman!"

Gertrude of Wyoming (1809). A poem by Thomas CAMPBELL. The setting is in the wilds of the Wyoming Valley in Pennsylvania. The heroine, Gertrude, is the daughter of the patriarch Albert; the hero is Henry Waldegrave, who as a boy spends three years in the patriarch's home and later returns to marry Gertrude. The settlement is attacked by a mixed army of Indians and British and both Albert and Gertrude are shot. Henry then joins the army of Washington.

Gerusalemme liberata (Jerusalem Delivered). The celebrated romantic epic by Torquato TASSO. Written during the Italian Renaissance, some time between 1559 and 1575, it was published in a definitive version of twenty cantos in 1581. The whole work had been translated into English by 1600, the accomplishment of Edward Fairfax. Unlike other Renaissance romances, it was based on the historic events of the First Crusade (1096–1099) and utilized several historical characters. The plot begins with the fictional war in its sixth year and the election of Goffredo (Godfrey) as the chief of the Christian armies encamped on the plains of Tortosa. As they prepare to attack Jerusalem, its king Aladino learns from the enchanter Ismeno that the city will not fall if a statue of the Virgin is removed from a Christian church and placed in a mosque. Finding the statue stolen, Aladino plans revenge on the Christian community of the city, but a young Christian maiden, Sofronia, offers to take the blame, as does her beloved, Olindo, who hopes thereby to save her. Aladino promptly orders both put to death, and they are saved only by the timely appearance of the warrior maiden Clorinda, who offers her sword in return for their lives. Now the pagan warrior Argante (Argantes), having failed to dissuade Goffredo from the attack, declares war upon the Crusaders. When the Christians attack the holy city, Argante kills their champion Dudone and the Christians withdraw to do him honors. Heeding the infernal decree of Plutone (Pluto), the enchanter Idraote sends his beautiful niece Armida to confound the Christian camp. She tells Goffredo of her need for ten knights to retake the city of Damascus; he is unwilling, but many more than ten Crusaders follow her away, among them the most puissant in the Christian army. Rinaldo also departs in anger because Goffredo has denounced him for the murder of Gernando, his rival for the command vacated because of the death of Dudone. Argante now challenges the Christian knights and kills Ottone, but his ferocious duel with Tancredi (Tancred) is interrupted when Erminia, who loves the latter, lures him away by disguising herself as his beloved Clorinda. Goffredo's depleted forces now face the challenge of Solimano (the Soldan, or Solyman), leader of the Arabs, but the archangel Gabriel intervenes to save them. Solimano soon joins forces with Aladino. In the renewed assault by the Crusaders, Tancredi unknowingly wounds Clorinda, who forgives him and is baptized before dying. Goffredo, learning from a vision that only Rinaldo can break the enchantments of Ismeno and free the armies to continue their assault upon the city, sends Guelfo and Ubaldo to bring him back. Dallying with Armida, Rinaldo is finally disenchanted and persuaded to return. With his return, the Crusaders are soon victorious. The unyielding Argante is killed by Tancredi, but the Egyptian forces, spurred by Armida, try to renew the battle. Rinaldo administers the final defeat to the infidels by killing Solimano and subduing Armida. With Aladino dead and the Egyptian king killed by Goffredo, the Crusaders can enter the great city at will. There, at dawn, led by Goffredo, they worship at the sepulcher of Christ.

Gervaise. One of the principal characters in the novels of Emile Zola's ROUGON-MACQUART series. She first appears in L'ASSOMMOIR.

Geryon. In Greek mythology, a monster with three bodies and three heads. His oxen ate human flesh and were guarded by Orthrus, a two-headed dog. HERACLES slew both Geryon and the dog.

Geryoneo. See FAERIE QUEENE, THE.

Geschichten Jaakobs, Die. See JOSEPH AND HIS BROTHERS.

Gesmas. The impenitent thief. He was crucified with Jesus. In the apocryphal *Gospel of Nicodemus*, he is called Gestas. The penitent thief was DISMAS.

Gespräche mit Goethe. See Johann Peter ECKERMANN.

Gestapo. The abbreviated name of the Nazi *Geheime Staatspolizei* (Secret Political Police), taken from the initial syllables of the words. Formed by Goering (1933), it became under HIMMLER the state's arm of terror.

Gesta Regum Anglorum (Chronicle of the Kings of England, c. 1120–1128). Latin history by WILLIAM OF MALMESBURY. It covers the history of England from 449 to 1128, including an account of Arthur, which indicates that the legends surrounding the hero were already prevalent in England.

Gesta Romanorum ("Deeds of the Romans"). Latin collection of tales, many of them of Oriental origin, very popular in the Middle Ages. It may have been compiled in England in the late 13th century; it was printed in 1473 and frequently thereafter, different versions including about 100 to 200 tales. The episodes are usually arbitrarily assigned to the reign of a Roman emperor, but there is little real history; similarly, a "moral" or "application" follows each tale, purportedly for the use of preachers, but it is not a religious work. Chaucer, Shakespeare, and later English writers have drawn frequently on the tales for plot material.

Gestas. See GESMAS.

Gesualdo, Carlo (c. 1560–1613). Italian composer and Prince of Venosa, near Naples. One of the most curious composers in musical history, Gesualdo was responsible for the brutal murder of his first wife (his first cousin) and her lover. His often experimental madrigals and other compositions are harmonically daring, filled with constant chromatic modulation, and nervously restless. He was a close friend of the poet Torquato Tasso, whose poems he set. Tasso's name has been linked with that of Leonora d'Este, Gesualdo's second wife.

Gethsemane. An olive grove or garden on the western slope of the Mount of Olives. It was here that Jesus went to pray after the Last Supper, and that Judas Iscariot betrayed him to the Roman soldiers (Mark 14:32–43; Matt. 26:36–49). Centuries-old olive trees growing on the site are today tended by monks of the Greek, Armenian, Russian, and Roman Churches.

Get-Rich-Quick Wallingford (1908). A group of related stories by George Randolph Chester (1869–1924). Wallingford, whose name has become part of American folklore, is a company promoter. With his satellite Blackie Daw, he engages in many dubious enterprises, but always manages to escape the hand of the law. Chester continued his adventures in several other books: *Young Wallingford* (1910), *Wallingford and Blackie Daw* (1913), *Wallingford in His Prime* (1913). George M. Cohan made a successful dramatization of the stories in 1910.

Gettysburg. A town in southern Pennsylvania and the site of a major battle (July 1–3, 1863), often considered the turning point of the American Civil War. The Confederates under Gen. Lee were defeated by numerically superior Union troops under Gen. George Meade. Casualties are estimated at about 23,000 for the Union Army, about 28,000 for the Confederates. Though Lee's retreat into Virginia was temporarily blocked by the flooding of the Potomac, Meade's failure to attack permitted the Confederates to escape on July 13 after the river fell.

Gettysburg Address (Nov. 19, 1863). An address prepared and delivered by President Abraham Lincoln at the dedication of the national cemetery at Gettysburg battlefield. Lincoln's brief address, which followed a two-hour oration by Edward Everett, the principal speaker of the day, is perhaps the most moving and eloquent statement of the American creed. Mary Raymond Shipman Andrews wrote "a sentimental footnote to history" in *The Perfect Tribute* (1906), a fictional account of the delivery and effects of the address.

Ghebers or **Guebres.** PARSEES, or followers of the ancient Persian religion, Zoroastrianism. The name, bestowed upon them by their Arabian conquerors, is now applied generally to fire worshipers.

Ghelderode, Michel de (1898–1962). Belgian dramatist. In the 1920's he wrote plays for marionettes, and his later works often use a similar stylization. Sometimes the human actors are masked to resemble puppets, for his characters are often the grotesque caricatures of farce and fantasy. Ghelderode was inspired by the flamboyance of Shakespeare and the Golden Age of Spain, the satiric realism of the Flemish painters, and the allegories of traditional folklore. His plays, mingling the burlesque and the mystical, did not begin to be widely known until 1946. They include *Christopher Columbus* (1927), *Escurial* (1928), *Barabbas* (1928), *The Women at the Tomb* (1928), *Chronicles of Hell* (*Fastes d'enfer*, 1929), *Pantagleize* (1930), *Sire Halewyn* (1934), *Hop, Signor!* (1935), and *School for Buffoons* (*L'Ecole des bouffons;* 1937).

Ghéon, Henri. Pen name of **Henri Vangeon** (1875–1944). French dramatist, essayist, and critic.

Ghéon was associated with the *Nouvelle Revue française* and published in it a series of critical articles: *Nos Directions: réalisme et poésie* (1911). He is best known for the religious plays that he wrote after his conversion to Catholicism, especially *Le Pauvre sous l'Escalier* (1920).

Ghibellines. See GUELPHS.

Ghiberti, Il. Real name, **Lorenzo di Cione di Ser Buonaccorso** (1378–1455). Florentine sculptor. His style combines tradition and innovation: the grace of medieval sculpture and a vivid pictorial quality, unparalleled elsewhere, caused by the use of perspective and the manipulation of planes in relief. He executed the famous north and east doors of the baptistry of Florence (1402–1422 and 1427–1452, respectively), which are elaborately decorated with panels in gilt bronze relief. Toward the end of his life he wrote three *Commentaries* (*I Commentarii*) on art, which survive in very imperfect form and include his autobiography and the first account of the lives of the artists of the 14th century.

Ghirlandaio, Il. Real name, **Domenico di Tommaso Bigordi** (1449–1495). Florentine painter. He was noted for his religious easel pictures and his narrative frescoes. Influenced by Fra Lippo Lippi, he in turn influenced the young Michelangelo, who worked in his studio. Among his best-known works are the frescoes behind the high altar of Santa Maria Novella in Florence, especially *The Birth of the Virgin;* portraits of Florentine humanists of the Medici circle; the touching *Portrait of an Old Man and a Boy;* the *Adoration of the Shepherds in the Uffizi;* and the wall frescoes of the Sistine Chapel, done with Botticelli.

Ghismonda. See TANCRED, THE REVENGE OF.

Ghosts (1881). A play by Henrik IBSEN. Ten years after her husband's death, Mrs. Alving is about to open an orphanage dedicated to his memory. Her son, Oswald, has just come home from abroad. She reveals to the moralistic Pastor Manders, who many years before had advised her against leaving her husband, that the late Captain Alving had lived and died drunken and profligate, and that Regina, the serving-girl, is actually his daughter. Oswald is beginning to go insane from hereditary syphilis, a legacy from his father; and Mrs. Alving realizes that, in basing her actions on duty rather than love, she has been indirectly responsible both for her husband's dissoluteness and her son's incipient insanity. The "ghosts" of the title are the dead conventions and beliefs that prevented Mrs. Alving from living for "the joy of life."

Giacometti, Alberto (1901–1966). Swiss painter and sculptor. His fleshless, elongated, gloomy figures display his interest in surrealism. He lived and worked in Paris.

Giacosa, Giuseppe (1847–1906). Italian dramatist, poet, librettist, and short-story writer. Giacosa is considered the leading Italian playwright of the late 19th century. The themes of his dramas undergo an observable change paralleling the changing literary tastes of the public for whom he wrote. Initially (c. 1870–1890) he composed graceful, charming verse plays reflecting the romantic cult of the Middle Ages and naturalistic interest in scientifically precise descriptions of character and setting. To this period belong *La Partita a Scacchi* (1873), *Il Trionfo d'Amore*

(1875), *La Signora di Challant,* written for Sarah Bernhardt (1891). Subsequently he wrote serious social dramas influenced by the problem plays of Henrik Ibsen and the popularity of French, Russian, and English psychological novels. Among his plays of social criticism are *Tristi Amori* (1888), *I Diritti dell'Anima* (1900), *Come Le Foglie* (1900), and *Il Più Forte* (1905). In collaboration with Luigi Illica, he wrote the libretti for Puccini's *La Bohème* (1896), *La Tosca* (1900), and *Madama Butterfly* (1904).

Giacosa's nondramatic writings include *Novelle e Paesi Valdostani* (1886), short stories set against the background of his native Val d'Aosta (Piedmont), and a collection of travel essays on America.

Giafar, or **Jaffar the Barmecide.** Vizier of the Caliph Haroun-al-Raschid and companion of his adventures. He appears frequently in the *Arabian Nights.*

Giall. In Scandinavian mythology, the river on the frontiers of Niflheim or hell, equivalent to the Greco-Roman Styx. Over it pass the doomed on a golden bridge.

Giambullari, Pier Francesco (1495–1555). Florentine historian. His history of Europe, *Istoria d'Europa,* covering the years 887–947, was published posthumously (1566) in its unfinished state. It was one of the first Humanist (see HUMANISM) histories to look at the past from the wider viewpoint of the Empire, rather than from the narrower interest of one city or state.

Gian ben Gian. In Arabic legend, a king of the JINN and founder of the Pyramids. He was overthrown by Eblis, the Muslim Lucifer.

Giant Despair. See PILGRIM'S PROGRESS.

Giants (Gigantes) or **Earth-Born (Gegeneis).** In Greek mythology, offspring of Ge (earth), impregnated by blood from the castrated URANUS (sky). They were in most accounts of human form, but with serpents' tails instead of feet. They warred on the gods, hurling whole trees and giant rocks. They were finally defeated only with the aid of HERACLES. Immortal, they were buried alive under mountains—generally volcanoes. Possibly oriental in origin, they are thought to have been personifications of the violent forces in nature. They should not be confused with the HUNDRED-HANDED or OTUS AND EPHIALTES.

Giants in the Earth: A Saga of the Prairie (1924–1925 in Norwegian; 1927 in English). A novel by Ole E. RÖLVAAG. The first volume of a trilogy that includes *Peder Victorious* (1929) and *Their Father's God* (1931), it is a stark and realistic work describing the hardships, both mental and physical, of a small group of Norwegian farmers who set out from Minnesota with their families in 1873 to settle in the then unopened Dakota Territory. The novel centers on Per Hansa, his devotion to the land, the growing religious fanaticism of his wife, Beret, and his final disappearance in a blizzard.

The hero of the two succeeding novels is Peder Victorious Holm, Per Hansa's youngest son, who marries a devout Irish Catholic, Susie Doheny, and later quarrels with her over the raising of their son, Petie.

Giants in the Earth was successfully dramatized (1928) by Thomas Job and made into an opera (1951) by Douglas Moore.

giaour. Among the Muslims, a term used contemptuously for one, especially a Christian, who does not adhere to their faith.

Byron wrote a poem, *The Giaour* (1813). In it, Leilah, the beautiful concubine of the Caliph Hassan, flees with a Giaour to her destruction; the Giaour later becomes a monk and tells his story while on his deathbed.

Gibbon, Edward (1737-1794). English historian, noted for his masterpiece *The History of the* DECLINE AND FALL OF THE ROMAN EMPIRE. He formed the plan for this great work during a tour of Italy (1764) while "musing amidst the ruins of the Capitol." He entered Parliament in 1774 and was made commissioner of trade and plantations. The first volume of his "History," which appeared in 1776, was very well received, though his chapters on Christianity provoked severe criticism from some quarters. Succeeding volumes were not as warmly received as the first. Gibbon's *Memoirs,* put together by Lord Sheffield, were published in 1796.

Gibbon, Lewis Grassic. See James Leslie MITCHELL.

Gibbons, Stella (1902–). English novelist and poet. Her best-known book is COLD COMFORT FARM, a brilliant parody of the novel of rustic pessimism.

Gibbs, A[rthur] Hamilton (1888-1964). English-born American novelist. The youngest of three writing brothers, he wrote best-selling novels, including *Soundings* (1925), *Chances* (1930), *The Need We Have* (1936), and *Obedience to the Moon* (1956).

Gibbs, Cosmo Hamilton. See Cosmo HAMILTON.

Gibbs, Sir Philip [Hamilton] (1877-1962). English journalist and novelist. The second of three writing brothers, he was knighted for his work as a frontline correspondent during World War I. His books of essays and social commentary include *Realities of War* (1920), *Now It Can Be Told* (1920), and *The New Elizabethans* (1953).

Gibraltar. A famous rock fortress at the western entrance to the Mediterranean Sea.

Gibson, Charles Dana (1867-1944). American illustrator. The creator of "the Gibson Girl," he modeled his drawings on his wife, the beautiful, dignified, and fashionable Irene Langhorne. Nearly every woman during the gay 90's imitated her clothes, looks, and manners. Gibson also illustrated many books, most notably the stories of Richard Harding Davis.

Gibson, W[ilfred] W[ilson] (1878-1962). English poet, associated with the GEORGIAN group. His most successful poems are about the grim, industrial lives of working people, as in *Daily Bread* (1910) and *Thoroughfares* (1914).

Gide, André (1869-1951). French writer and editor. Brought up in an austere Protestant household, Gide reacted passionately against the prohibitions of revealed religion. Yet his search for self—the underlying theme of his more than 80 published works—remained essentially a religious search, and Gide is as well known for his influence as a moralist and a thinker as for his contributions to literature.

At 18 he met Pierre Louÿs and other aspiring writers and artists, and attended the literary salons of José-María de Hérédia and Stéphane Mallarmé. In 1891 he published *Les Cahiers d'*ANDRÉ WALTER, reflecting his spiritual love for his cousin Madeleine and his conviction that physical desire must be suppressed. He published his first poems the next year, but by 1900 he had practically abandoned this form of writing. Gide shared Paul Valéry's fascination with the myth of Narcissus as a symbol of man's hopeless and misdirected yearning for perfection. His friends read the essay *Le Traité du Narcisse* (1891) as a definition of symbolism, but its theories were actually quite differently intended, and Gide soon separated from the group.

With his first trip to North Africa in 1893, Gide broke with his entire past. He rejected mortification of the flesh, believing that harmony of body and soul was possible only if both were satisfied, and deliberately sought sensual experience. His discovery of his homosexual leanings troubled him, but the tolerance of the North Africans and the open encouragement of Oscar Wilde in 1895 freed him of embarrassment. THE FRUITS OF THE EARTH is a hymn to the joy of the search for experience.

Gide considered himself a disturber of youth, ever urging individual self-cultivation, while paradoxically warning against a narcissistic concern with self. His fiction is autobiographical only to the extent that each major figure is an exaggerated personification of one aspect of his own character. Thus, THE IMMORALIST and STRAIT IS THE GATE were conceived as companion pieces to show the unhappy consequences of amoral hedonism in the first and of equally selfish self-abnegation and asceticism in the second.

Always concerned with motivation and the function of man's will, Gide was influenced by Dostoevski (his translations and analyses did much to make the Russian novelist popular in France) and agreed that there are both good and evil impulses, not traceable to common motives such as love, hate, or self-interest. He was fascinated by examples of the apparently disinterested *acte gratuit,* or gratuitous act, and concluded that it is motivated solely by a personal need to assert one's individuality and thus the only human act that reveals one's essential character; LAFCADIO'S ADVENTURES presents a murder as such an act.

Gide was twice tempted to find self-development in commitment to something outside himself. His correspondence with his friends Francis Jammes (pub. 1948) and Paul Claudel (pub. 1949) reveal their unsuccessful attempt to convert him to Catholicism. Then on a trip to French Equatorial Africa in 1925 he was horrified by the French treatment of the natives. He expressed his views on the subject in *Travels in the Congo* (*Voyage au Congo;* 1927, and *Le Retour du Tchad;* 1928), and began to advocate the reform of social institutions, becoming an admirer of the ideal of Communism and its practical experiment in the Soviet Union. But he could not accept the party's orthodox dogma without the right to question, and in 1936 was disillusioned by a visit to the Soviet Union, described in *Return from the USSR* (*Retour de l'URSS;* 1936) and *Afterthoughts on the USSR* (*Retouches à mon retour de l'URSS;* 1937).

The novel THE COUNTERFEITERS exposes the hypocrisy and self-deception with which people try to avoid sincerity. Gide's own obsessive concern with personal and public honesty often led him to face public scandal—especially with his insistence that the bounds of the natural include homosexuality. When CORYDON drew violent criticism, Gide answered with IF IT DIE. . . . He pursued this ideal of perfect frankness in his comprehensive private, literary, and philosophical *Journals* (1939–1950), omitting only the details of his marriage with his cousin Madeleine. After her death (1938) he wrote the painful account of their mutual love and unhappiness, published posthumously as *Et nunc manet in te* (1951), translated as *Madeleine* (1952).

Gide was one of the most influential editors of LA NOUVELLE REVUE FRANÇAISE. In 1947 he was awarded the Nobel Prize for his varied contributions to literature.

Other important works by Gide, available in English, include the satires *Paludes* (1895) and *Le Prométhée mal enchaîné* (1899), collected as *Marshlands and Prometheus Misbound* (1953); the plays *Philoctète* (1899), *Le Roi Candaule* (1901), *Saül* (1903), *Bethsabé* (1912), and *Perséphone* (1934), collected as *My Theater* (1951); the play *Oedipe* (1931) and the tale *Thésée* (1946), collected as *Two Legends: Theseus and Oedipus* (1950); and the tales *Isabelle* (1911) and THE PASTORAL SYMPHONY, included in *Two Symphonies* (1931). See ECOLE DES FEMMES.

Gideon. In the Old Testament, a Hebrew liberator, reformer, and one of the judges of Israel for 40 years. With a company of 300 men, he delivered his people from the Midianites. The army was purposely reduced to 300 by eliminating all who were afraid and all who drank from a stream instead of lapping the water from their hands. To give the impression of being a huge army, they made a great noise by breaking pitchers and blowing trumpets (Judg. 7:16–20).

Gielgud, Sir [Arthur] John (1904–   ). English actor. He has appeared in plays by Wilde, Shakespeare, and Sheridan as well as contemporary works. He has been seen on the movie and television screen in both England and America.

Gifford, William (1756–1826). English literary critic and poet, first editor (1809–1824) of the *Quarterly Review*. He edited Elizabethan plays and wrote the verse satires THE BAVIAD and *The Maeviad* (1795).

Gift of the Magi, The (1906). A short story by O. HENRY. Containing perhaps the most famous of O. Henry's trick endings, this Yuletide narrative tells how a nearly penniless young husband and wife are each determined to buy the other a suitable Christmas present. He sells his watch to buy her a set of combs; she has her beautiful hair cut off and sells the tresses to buy him a watch fob. The tale was included in THE FOUR MILLION.

Gilbert, Sir **Humphrey** (1539?–1583). English navigator. The half-brother of Sir Walter Raleigh, Gilbert made a voyage with him in 1578. He wrote a *Discourse of a Discoverie for a new passage to Cataia* (published 1576, written and circulated earlier), in which he urged exploration for the discovery of a northwest passage (see NORTHEAST PASSAGE). His arguments probably influenced Sir Martin Frobisher's voyages in search of such a passage in 1576–1578. He established the first British colony in North America

at St. John's, Newfoundland (August 5, 1583), but went down with his ship on the return voyage to England.

Gilbert, Sir **William** S[chwenck] (1836–1911). English dramatist and writer of humorous verse. He is best remembered as librettist of the GILBERT AND SULLIVAN comic operas. Among his other dramatic pieces are *The Palace of Truth* (1870), *Pygmalion and Galatea* (1871), and *Engaged* (1877). Several of the Gilbert and Sullivan operas owe their origin to Gilbert's collection of humorous ballads, *Bab Ballads* (1866–71), which show his great facility in versifying. He had a penchant for whimsicality, nonsense, and topical satire.

Gilbert and Sullivan operas, also called **the Savoy Operas.** A series of comic operas, text by William Schwenck GILBERT and music by Arthur Seymour SULLIVAN, originally produced (1881 et seq.) at the Savoy Theatre in London by Richard D'Oyly Carte. An outstanding achievement in music collaboration, the titles are *Thespis or The Gods Grown Old* (1871), *Trial by Jury* (1875), *The Sorcerer* (1877), H. M. S. PINAFORE (1878), THE PIRATES OF PENZANCE OR THE SLAVE OF DUTY (1879), PATIENCE OR BUNTHORNE'S BRIDE (1881), IOLANTHE OR THE PEER AND THE PERI (1882), *Princess Ida or Castle Adamant* (1884), THE MIKADO OR THE TOWN OF TITIPU (1885), *Ruddigore* (1887), THE YEOMEN OF THE GUARD (1888), *The Gondoliers* (1889), *Utopia, Limited* (1893), and *The Grand Duke* (1896). The first of these operas, and the last two, written after a serious quarrel between Gilbert and Sullivan, are almost never performed. Highly satiric, the operas poke fun at contemporary Victorian life. The Gilbert and Sullivan following, called Savoyards after the name of the theater, is still considerable.

Gilberte. The first girl beloved by the narrator in Marcel Proust's REMEMBRANCE OF THINGS PAST. Daughter of Charles SWANN and ODETTE DE CRÉCY, she repudiates her Jewish background when her mother remarries, and eventually marries Robert de SAINT-LOUP.

Gil Blas de Santillane, Histoire de (1715, 1724, 1735). A PICARESQUE novel in four volumes by Alain René LESAGE. The extraordinary number of episodes in this novel render any coherent plot summary impossible. The setting is Spanish, but the society depicted is really French. The hero, Gil Blas, leaves home at 17 to try his fortune at Salamanca; in his journeys he meets a large number of people—adventurers, thieves, valets, actors, authors, doctors, clergymen, and noblemen. Lesage has very little good to say about any of them. Gil Blas himself, though full of good intentions, is a singularly weak character. One critic (Lester G. Crocker) says that Gil Blas goes through the three stages of innocence, corruption, and the triumph of virtue. Among the more famous portraits in the novel are the ARCHBISHOP OF GRANADA, DON ALVARO, and DR. SANGRADO. (See also THE SOUL OF PEDRO GARCIAS.) From the literary historical view, Lesage continues the traditions of the realistic novels written in the 17th century by Charles Sorel, Antoine Furetière, and Paul Scarron. This novel also affords a good example of the evolution of the French language between the 17th and 18th centuries, in that an increase in the concision of narrative style is apparent.

Gildas (c. 500). An early Welsh historian who wrote about the battle of Mount Badon. This battle was later hailed as the greatest triumph of an historical Arthur who may be the prototype of the literary King Arthur. There is no mention of the name in Gildas' work, however. See ARTHURIAN LEGEND.

Gilded Age, The (1873). A novel by Mark TWAIN and Charles Dudley WARNER. Colonel Beriah Sellers, a schemer who always fails, persuades his friend, Squire Hawkins, to join him in an ill-fated land speculation scheme in Missouri. Hawkins' adopted daughter is seduced by Colonel Selby, whom she later murders. All the characters are modeled on real people; among them are William Weed and his political gang, based on the Tweed Ring in New York. The phrase "gilded age" has been adopted as a description of the hectic post-Civil War period.

Gilder, Richard Watson (1844–1909). American newspaper and magazine editor and poet. He edited *Scribner's Monthly* (1870–1881) and *The Century Magazine* (1881–1909). Among his volumes of poetry are *The New Day* (1876) and *Five Books of Songs* (1900). Gilder's refusal to receive Robert Louis Stevenson, because rumors had led him to doubt the latter's respectability, has gained him a degree of notoriety.

Gilderoy. Real name: **Patrick Macgregor** (d. 1636). Scottish cattle-stealer and highwayman. According to an old ballad, he robbed Cardinal Richelieu in the presence of the king, picked Oliver Cromwell's pocket, and hanged a judge. He was hanged in Edinburgh.

Gildippe. In Tasso's GERUSALEMME LIBERATA, the wife of Odoardo (Edward). Having accompanied her husband on the crusade, this capable fighter deals the infidels many stout blows before being killed by Solimano, their leader.

Giles, St. Patron saint of cripples. The tradition is that Childeric, king of France, accidentally wounded a hermit in the knee when hunting; and the hermit, that he might better mortify the flesh, refused to be cured, remaining a cripple for life. His day is September 1, and his symbol a hind, in allusion to the "heaven directed hind" which went daily to his cave near the mouth of the Rhone to give him milk. He is sometimes represented as an old man with an arrow in his knee and a hind by his side. Churches dedicated to St. Giles were usually situated in the outskirts of a city, and originally without the walls because some cripples and beggars were not permitted to pass the city gates.

Gilgamesh. A mythical hero of Sumer and Babylonia. Though he is best known from the famous Babylonian EPIC OF GILGAMESH, he was originally a Sumerian hero, the king of the ancient city of Erech. In a Sumerian myth, he comes to the aid of the goddess INANNA who is distressed because she is unable to cut down the *Huluppu* tree in the garden, in order to have furniture made of it: a snake, a dangerous bird, and Lilith have all taken up residence in it. When Gilgamesh chases them away and chops down the tree, Inanna gives him (untranslatable) gifts, but he accidentally drops them into the underworld. His companion Enkidu undertakes to go after them, but fails to observe the precautions essential in such ventures and cannot return. His ghost, however, is permitted to come back long

UNIVERSITY MUSEUM, PHILADELPHIA

Sumerian shell inlay of Gilgamesh taming two monsters.

enough to carry on a lengthy conversation with Gilgamesh. The ending of the myth is unknown from the fragmentary tablets on which it was found.

Gilgamesh, Epic of. A Babylonian poem (c. 2000 B.C.). One of the oldest and most important major epics in literature, it was first discovered on clay tablets in the library of ASSUR-BANI-PAL (668–626 B.C.). Like the ILIAD and the ODYSSEY, it is composed of far earlier elements of myth and folklore that have been joined into a single poem through a process of gradual accretion. Also, like Homer's epics, it enjoyed immense popularity for centuries; passages from it were frequently quoted in later literature. The epic includes stories, originally separate, of GILGAMESH, a legendary king of Sumerian origin; ENKIDU, a sort of primeval man; Utnapishtim, the Babylonian Noah; and several other tales.

Gilgamesh was a mighty, part-immortal king of Erech whose subjects eventually prayed for relief from his tyranny. Taking pity on them, the lord of heaven ordered the goddess Aruru to mold out of clay a hairy wild man named Enkidu. This monstrous creature lived with and ate like the beasts, whom he saved from the snares of hunters. Learning of his existence, Gilgamesh sent a young woman to seduce him, after which the animals would have no more to do with him. The woman told him of Gilgamesh's tyranny, and Enkidu resolved to challenge his power. This he did at the New Year's festival, but when he had defeated Gilgamesh in wrestling, the two became fast friends.

The first exploit that they undertook together was to cut down a cedar in the sacred wood guarded by the monster Humbaba, who breathed fire and plague and had one eye that could turn men to stone. They felled the cedar and Humbaba came roaring to the attack, but the sun-god (at the plea of the goddess Ninsun, Gilgamesh's mother) saved them by blinding the monster with hot winds. After the friends defeated and beheaded Humbaba, the goddess ISHTAR endeavored to seduce Gilgamesh, but he reminded her bluntly how she had treated TAMMUZ and other lovers, turning many of them into beasts. Furious, she belabored the lord of heaven with threats until he sent the storm bull of heaven against them, but the two youths promptly killed it and offered its heart to the sun-god. Enkidu now had a series of dreams which revealed to him that the gods, outraged at this act, had decreed his death. Lying on his bed, he gradually grew weaker until he died.

Grief-stricken, Gilgamesh determined to learn the secret of eternal life by seeking out the sage Utnapishtim, the only mortal ever to have escaped death. In spite of many trials and warnings, Gilgamesh reached the ocean of death and was rowed across it by the ferryman Urshanabi into the presence of Utnapishtim. The old man told him of how, in the early days of the earth, a great flood had destroyed his fellow men. He, warned by EA, the god of wisdom, had saved himself and his family by building an ark in which they had floated for seven days and nights until the ark grounded on a mountain. Utnapishtim had then sent out a dove, a swallow, and a raven; and, when the last of these having found dry land did not return, he and his family had offered thanks to the gods for their safety. Utnapishtim and his wife, thereafter, had been sent to the island at the end of the earth where they now lived, and where they had become immortal.

Gilgamesh now understood that this immortality was a special gift of the gods, and that neither Utnapishtim nor any other mortal would ever learn the secret of eternal life. The sage told him, however, of a herb growing at the bottom of the sea that would restore his youth. Taking leave of the old man, Gilgamesh tied stones to his feet, dived into the sea, and found the plant. After he had gone a long way on his journey home to Erech, he stopped to rest and bathe in a spring, laying the plant on the ground. A snake quickly appeared and made off with it; tasting the plant, it cast off its old skin and was made young again. Gilgamesh wept. Now he understood that no human being can escape old age and death. Resigned to the fate that he shared with all men, he returned to his homeland, where he died.

Gillette of Narbonne. The heroine of a tale from Giovanni Boccaccio's THE DECAMERON. As a reward for curing the king of France, she obtains the right to marry Bertrand of Roussillon. The reluctant bridegroom flees angrily to Florence, where he loves a young woman, until discovering that he has slept with his own wife thinking she was his mistress, and that she has borne him two sons, he is finally reconciled. This is essentially the story of Shakespeare's play *All's Well That Ends Well.*

Gil y Zárate, Antonio (1793–1861). Spanish playwright. He is well known for his abandonment of neoclassic principles; this is apparent in his *Carlos II, el hechizado* (1844), a moderate romantic drama which attacks reactionary political views. He is also the author of *Guzmán el Bueno* (1847).

Giménez Caballero, Ernesto (1899–). Spanish writer and academician. Giménez is the founder of the avant-garde publication *La Gaceta Literaria* (1927). His best-known writings include *Notas marruecas de un soldado* (1923); *Yo, inspector de alcantarillas* (1928), a surrealistic novel; and

Genio de España (1931), which is considered his best work.

Ginevra. In Ariosto's ORLANDO FURIOSO, a Scottish princess unjustly accused by LURCANIO of causing the death of his brother and her beloved, Ariodante (Ariodantes). Doomed to die unless a champion appears to fight Lurcanio, she tells her story to Rinaldo, who, having learned from her maid Dalinda that Ginevra was betrayed by Polinesso, denounces the latter before the king and then kills him in a duel. Ariodante, who is actually alive and present to defend Ginevra, reveals himself and wins her hand.

Ginsberg, Allen (1926–). American poet. A leading poet of the BEAT MOVEMENT, Ginsberg writes an incantatory, loosely structured line reminiscent of Whitman. *Howl and Other Poems* (1956) is a violent lament for what society has done to his generation; it became something of a *succès de scandale* when it was charged with, and subsequently cleared of, obscenity. Ginsberg has also written *Kaddish and Other Poems* (1961) and *Empty Mirror: Early Poems* (1961).

ginseng. A Chinese herb valued as a medicine. Its root, often forked, explains why it corresponds in Chinese folk lore to the Western MANDRAKE.

Ginza. Street in Tokyo, running from Shimbashi to Kyobashi. It is the center of a high-class shopping and entertainment district.

Gioconda, La. A portrait by LEONARDO da Vinci. One of the most famous of paintings, it is better known as the Mona Lisa. Its subject was a Neapolitan noblewoman, Madonna (Mona) Lisa del Giocondo. The portrait, which hangs in the Louvre, is especially noted for the lady's smile, which inspired *The Gioconda Smile,* one of Aldous Huxley's best-known short stories. It has been pointed out, however, that similar enigmatic smiles were a popular feature of portraits for this period.

Gioconda, La (1876). An opera by Amilcare Ponchielli based on Victor Hugo's *Angelo the Tyrant of Padua.* The libretto was written by Arrigo Boïto under the pseudonym Tobia Goria—presumably through embarrassment over its melodramatic plot.

Gioconda, La (1898). A drama by Gabriele D'Annunzio. The title character is a model for a brilliant young sculptor, Lucio Settala. Out of loyalty to his devoted wife Silvia, he tries to resist the fascination that Gioconda exercises over him. Eventually, however, he leaves Silvia for Gioconda, who he feels is the real inspiration of his art. Eleonora Duse, to whom the play is dedicated, scored a great success in the title role.

Giocondo. Hero of an episode in the ORLANDO FURIOSO of Ariosto, his name is better known in its French paraphrase Joconde.

Giono, Jean (1895–). French novelist of the Provence region. This countryside is presented with sensuous realism in such early works as *Hill of Destiny (Colline;* 1928), *Lovers Are Never Losers (Un de Baumugnes;* 1929), *Harvest (Regain;* 1930), and the semiautobiographical *Blue Boy (Jean le bleu;* 1932). Preferring a Hellenistic pantheism and the earthy life of the peasant to Christianity and modern civilization, he expressed his love of life in *The Song of the World (Le Chant du monde;* 1934) and *Joy of Man's Desiring (Que ma joie demeure;* 1935). Al-

though he fought in the First World War, he went
to prison rather than serve in the Second, upholding
the principles of his pacifist essay *Refus d'obéissance*
(1937). His other works include the short story *La
Femme du boulanger* (1935, filmed as *The Baker's
Wife,* 1939) and the plays *Lanceurs de graines* (1937)
and *Le Bout de la Route* (1941). Among his novels
are *Le Grand Troupeau* (1931), *Les Grands Chemins*
(1951), and *The Malediction* (*Le Moulin de Pologne;*
1952).

Giorgione, Il. Real name, **Giorgio da Castelfranco** (c. 1478–1510). Little is known of his life
and scarcely a half dozen paintings can be safely
ascribed to him, yet this young and influential student
of Giovanni Bellini is known as the chief master of
the Venetian school of his day. He is celebrated for
the sensuous and poetic grace of his work and for his
introduction of a new range of subject matter:—
idyllic scenes of pastoral love that depend for their
effect on the golden color harmony which unifies the
whole. Among his authenticated works are the
enigmatic *Tempest* (1506), the *Fête Champêtre,* the
Castelfranco Madonna, and *Sleeping Venus.*

Giotto [di Bondone] (1266?–1337). Florentine
painter. The greatest Italian painter of the pre-
Renaissance, he was, according to tradition, a pupil
of CIMABUE and a friend of Dante. VASARI acclaimed
him for breaking with the rigid Byzantine tradition of
his time by introducing the direct observation of nature, and recounted that, when asked by the pope
for a sample of his work, the artist sent only a perfect circle painted with a free movement of his arm
from the elbow. His monumental work brought a new
strength and force to art. He created architectural and
landscape backgrounds for his massive, sensitively
drawn figures, while his subdued colors and masterly
compositions contribute to the expressive power of
each scene. The quality of his genius is best seen in
the series of 38 frescoes in the Scrovegni (Arena)
Chapel in Padua, depicting the life of Christ and
other Biblical subjects (1304–1306); the extent of
his actual contribution to the earlier frescoes in the
Church of St. Francis at Assisi is debatable. He also
frescoed the Bardi and Peruzzi chapels of the Church
of Santa Croce in Florence and is said to have done
frescoes and mosaics for the old St. Peter's in Rome.
In 1334, Giotto became the official architect of
Florence. He is generally considered to have begun
the construction of the separate *campanile,* or bell
tower, of the Florence cathedral; it is likely that he
also carved some of its reliefs with Andrea Pisano.

Giotto's tower. The campanile of the Duomo
(the church of Santa Maria del Fiore) in Florence.
It was designed by GIOTTO, and the construction
begun in 1334. However, much of the final form of
the building may be due to Giotto's successor Andrea
Pisano. The Duomo, begun in 1298, was not completely finished until 1888.

Giovannitti, Arturo (1884–1959). Italian-born
American poet. A crusader for social and economic
change, he was jailed during the Lawrence, Mass.,
textile strikes, an experience which caused him to
write *The Walker* and several other prose poems.
In 1917, he wrote *When the Cock Crows,* a poem inspired by the lynching of the labor leader Frank
Little. His principal collection of verse is *Arrows
in the Gale* (1914).

Giovio, Paolo (1483–1552). Italian Renaissance
historian. He wrote a history of his own times; a
group of lives of famous men; the *Elogia virorum
illustrium,* a series of prose and verse inscriptions for
the portraits collected in his private museum; and a
treatise on IMPRESE, or devices, which was translated
by Samuel Daniel in 1585.

Gipsy. See GYPSY.

Giraldi, Giambattista Cinzio or **Cinthio** (1504–
1573). Ferrarese scholar, teacher, and author of
novelle, plays, and literary criticism. His collection
of 100 *novelle,* called *Gli Ecatomiti,* was a plot source
of Shakespeare's *Othello* and *Measure for Measure.*
In his tragedies, Giraldi followed the style of Seneca
and was influential in popularizing tragedies filled
with horror and bloodshed. He also used happy endings for some of his plays, thus becoming a pioneer
of the tragi-comedy. His critical discourses were
also important in Renaissance discussion of literary
types, and imitation of the ancient writers.

Giraudoux, [Hippolyte] Jean (1882–1944).
French dramatist, novelist, essayist, and diplomat.
All Giraudoux's works are characterized by a verbal
extravagance, an elegance and virtuosity of imagery
and style that verges on poetic fantasy; even in a
serious play like TIGER AT THE GATES, it masks the
horror of the apparent inevitability of tragedy.

The novel *My Friend from Limousin* (*Siegfried et
le Limousin;* 1922) was transformed into the play
Siegfried (1928), portraying the Franco-German conflict. The plot of the novel *Bella* (1926) centers in
an antithesis within French politics, that of *Eglantine*
(1927) in the social antithesis of a simple-minded
country gentleman and a rich Jewish banker. These
two and especially the earlier novels *Suzanne and
the Pacific* (1921) and *Juliette Visits the Land of
Man* (*Juliette au pays des hommes;* 1924) show
Giraudoux's predilection for charming young girl
characters who represent the candid innocence of
divinity, of nature, of ideal Truth. To grow up or to
fall in love is to enter the "terrible convent of human
beings" with its heartache, disillusion, and even
tragedy; his treatment of the UNDINE tale in the play
Ondine (1939) has the same theme. Giraudoux has
a humanistic and compassionate view of the adult
world; nevertheless, he delights in escaping from it
in extravagant comedies like THE MADWOMAN OF
CHAILLOT.

Many of his plays are based on Greek myth or the
Bible, but make very free with the legends; for
instance, his *Judith* (1931) falls in love with Holo-
fernes before she kills him. Among his other adapta-
tions—besides the above-mentioned *Siegfried* and
Tiger at the Gates—are *Amphitryon 38* (1929),
Electre (1937), *The Apollo of Bellac* (1942), and
Sodome et Gomorrhe (1943).

Other works include *Amica America* (1918), about
his stay in the United States; *Adorable Clio* (1920),
vignettes from World War I; the plays *The Enchanted* (*Intermezzo;* 1933) and *The Virtuous Island*
(*Supplément au voyage de Cook;* 1935); the novels
The School for Indifference (*L'Ecole des indifférents,*
1911), *Simon the Pathetic* (1918), *The Adventures of
Jérôme Bardini* (1930), and *The Chosen One* (*Choix
des élues;* 1938).

Girl of the Golden West, The (1905). A play
by David BELASCO. The heroine is a courageous

saloonkeeper in a Western mining camp who falls in love with an outlaw. The play was the basis of Puccini's *La Fanciulla del West* (1910), the first grand opera written on an American theme.

Girondists, or **the Gironde,** or **the Girondins.** A middle class political party during the FRENCH REVOLUTION (1791–1793). They were so named because many of their members were from the department of the Gironde. Their point of view was republican: they advocated overthrow of the monarchy, an agressive foreign policy, and were anticlerical. Although the most powerful party for a time, they were overthrown in June, 1793, because of their attempt to soften the ever-rising spirit of fanaticism among the more extreme revolutionists. Among their ranks were Jacques Pierre BRISSOT (their leader, and after whom they were sometimes called *Brissotins*), CONDORCET, and the adherents of Madame ROLAND.

Gironella, José María (1917–   ). Spanish novelist. His works, which have been very popular in translation, include *Un hombre* (*The Soil was Shallow*, 1946), his initial success; the well-known *Los cipreses creen en Dios* (*The Cypresses Believe in God*, 1951), a tale of events leading up to the Spanish Civil War; and its sequel, *Un millón de muertos* (1961).

Girty, Simon (1741–1818). American soldier, known as "the Great Renegade." He deserted from the Revolutionary Army (1778) and later led British and Indian raiding expeditions. Although he is said to have saved the life of Simon Kenton, Girty was widely known for his brutality. He is the title character of Elinor Wylie's poem, *Simon Girty* and also appears in Stephen Vincent Benét's *The Devil and Daniel Webster* (1937).

Gish, Lillian (?1896–   ). American stage and screen actress. After her first success in *Birth of a Nation*, she played in many other films, including *The Scarlet Letter, Broken Blossoms, Orphans of the Storm*, etc. She appeared on stage in *Camille, Uncle Vanya, The Star Wagon*, and others. Her sister Dorothy is also well-known as an actress.

Gissing, George [**Robert**] (1857–1903). English novelist, critic, and essayist. Gissing's brilliant academic career was cut short when, attempting to reform and support a young prostitute, he was caught stealing money from classmates. He was expelled and imprisoned; soon after he spent a year of privation and wandering in the U.S., then returned to England. He married the prostitute, entering a life of misery and poverty, and when she died, he remarried, again unhappily.

Gissing's love of the classics, the hardships of his life, and his mixed idealism and pessimism, are reflected in his best-known novels *The Nether World* (1881) and NEW GRUB STREET. These books are characterized by their realism and psychological acuteness, and by the subtlety, grace, and subdued passion of their style. Other aspects of his temperament and talent are exhibited in THE PRIVATE PAPERS OF HENRY RYECROFT and his fine *Charles Dickens: A Critical Study* (1898). Other novels include *Demos* (1886), *Thyrza* (1887), *A Life's Morning* (1888), *Born in Exile* (1892), *The Odd Women* (1893), and *In the Year of Jubilee* (1894).

Giusti, Giuseppe (1809–1850). Italian satiric poet. His clever satires held up to ridicule the so-called "humaneness" of the guillotine (*La Guigliottina a Vapore*, 1833), foreign domination of Italy (*Lo Stivale*, 1836), and many other aspects, both important and trivial, of 19th-century society.

Giustinian, Leonardo (1388–1446). Venetian scholar and poet. Giustinian wrote and composed the music for popular songs in Venetian dialect. He excelled in *strambotto, canzonetta*, and *laude*, so much so that variations and adaptations of such of his poems as *Se li arbori sapessen favellare* (If the trees could speak) are still heard in the Italy of today.

Gjellerup, Karl (1859–1919). Danish writer long resident in Germany. His interest in German art and music found expression in *Richard Wagner i hans Hovedwaerk* (*Richard Wagner in his Chief Work, the Ring of Nibelung*, 1890). His novels include *En Idealist* (1878), *Germanernes Laerling* (1882), and *Der Pilger Kamanoto* (*The Pilgrim Kamanoto*, 1906), a novel set in India and the only novel by Gjellerup to be translated into English. In 1917 he shared the Nobel prize for literature with another Danish writer, Henrik Pontoppidan.

Gladkov, Feodor Vasilyevich (1883–1958). Russian novelist. He is famous as the author of CEMENT, one of the first proletarian novels of Soviet literature, which had an immense success with Soviet critics. In 1932–1938, Gladkov published *Energy* (*Energiya*), describing the building of Dneprostroi dam during the Five-Year Plan. One of his best works is his autobiography, *Story of My Childhood* (*Povest' o detstve*; 1949), reminiscent of Gorki's autobiography in style and quality.

Gladstone, William Ewart. Called the **Grand Old Man** (1809–1898). English statesman, financier, and orator. His high abilities were early recognized by his party (Whig), and during the short-lived administration of Sir Robert Peel (December 1834–April 1835), he was made first junior lord of the treasury and then undersecretary for the colonies. During his brilliant career he was chancellor of the exchequer (1852–1855), leader of the Liberal Party (1867), and Prime Minister four times (1868–1874; 1880–1885; 1886; 1892–1894). Milestones in his career are the disestablishment of the Irish Church, two Home Rule bills for Ireland (1886, 1893), both defeated, and the denunciation of Turkish atrocities in Bulgaria. The most prominent man in politics of his time, he was rivaled only by his Tory opponent, Benjamin Disraeli. In spite of his full career, he found time for considerable writing. His works include *The State in its Relations to the Church* (1838), *Letters on the State Persecutions of the Neapolitan Government* (1851), *Studies on Homer and the Homeric Age* (1858), *Juventus Mundi* (1869), and pamphlets on *Bulgarian Horrors* (1876, 1877), *Homeric Synchronism* (1876), and *Gleanings of Past Years* (1879).

Glanvill, Joseph (1636–1680). English clergyman and philosopher, one of the CAMBRIDGE PLATONISTS. Although he was a scientist and a skeptic who supported the Royal Society in his *Plus Ultra, or the Progress and Advancement of Knowledge since the time of Aristotle* (1668), in other works he defended the pre-existence of souls and belief in witchcraft. His best-known book *The Vanity of Dogmatizing* (1661) contains the theme of Matthew Arnold's poem *The Scholar Gypsy* (1853).

Glasgow, Ellen [Anderson Gholson] (1874–1945). American novelist. One of her country's greatest regional writers, Ellen Glasgow confined her work to the study of the South as typified in Virginia, her native state. In all, she wrote 19 novels, and Henry Seidel Canby has said, "she was a major historian of our times, who, almost singlehandedly, rescued Southern fiction from the glamorous sentimentality of the Lost Cause."

Although her early books, such as *The Battle-Ground* (1902), were in the tradition of the Southern romance, she was already in revolt against what she called the "sanctified fallacies" of the South, and the growth of her art may be measured by contrasting these with VIRGINIA, a characteristic study of a woman in a particular time and place. The years following World War I saw the appearance of what was probably her most distinguished work, the novels BARREN GROUND, THE ROMANTIC COMEDIANS, *They Stooped to Folly* (1929), and *The Sheltered Life* (1932). As she grew older, she became more conservative, rejecting the work of such Southerners as William Faulkner and regretting the loss of manners that the modern world had brought.

Her later works include *Vein of Iron* (1935) and *In This Our Time* (1941), which was awarded a Pulitzer Prize. *A Certain Measure: An Interpretation of Prose Fiction* (1943) is a valuable statement on her art as well as a helpful account of the grand design of her novels. *The Woman Within* (1954), her autobiography, and *Letters of Ellen Glasgow* (1958) were published after her death.

Glaspell, Susan (1882–1948). American novelist and dramatist. Miss Glaspell early wrote short stories and, in 1909, a novel, *The Glory of the Conquered*. With her husband, George Cram COOK, she organized the PROVINCETOWN PLAYERS, an experimental theater designed to combat the commercialism of Broadway. For its opening, she and her husband wrote the satiric one-act play, *Suppressed Desires* (1915). Miss Glaspell wrote several other novels: *Fidelity* (1915), *Brooks Evans* (1928), and *Judd Rankin's Daughter* (1945). Among her plays are *The People* (1917), *Bernice* (1919), *The Verge* (1921), and *Alison's House* (1930), which was based on the life of Emily Dickinson and awarded a Pulitzer Prize. *The Road to the Temple* (1926) is a biography of her husband.

Glasperlenspiel, Das. See MAGISTER LUDI.

Glass, Montague [Marsden] (1877–1934). English-born American writer of fiction. He is best known as the creator of the titular heroes of POTASH AND PERLMUTTER (1910).

Glass Menagerie, The (1944). A play by Tennessee WILLIAMS. With Tom Wingfield narrating both the introduction and the conclusion, the play is set in memory. It takes place shortly before Tom left home for the merchant marines and focuses on his mother, who constantly imagines scenes of the "gentlemen callers" of her girlhood, and on his sister Laura, a partial cripple who has withdrawn from the real world into the private universe of her glass animals. The mother insists that Tom bring home a gentleman caller for Laura, and when he does the friend breaks the horn on Laura's glass unicorn, making the animal less of a freak and allowing her momentarily to break out of the world of her menagerie. However, after kissing Laura, the friend admits that he is already engaged; Laura's emergence from her fragile world is left in doubt.

Glastonbury. An ancient town in Somerset, England, dating from Roman times. It is traditionally associated with Arthurian legend and with the Holy Grail. It is at Glastonbury that JOSEPH OF ARIMATHEA is said to have established the first Christian Church in England and, earlier, to have planted his staff, which took root and became the Glastonbury thorn that burst into blossom every Christmas eve. Local legend has it that Arthur and Guinevere are buried there, and it has been recorded of the historical Arthur that he was buried there. Most of the Arthurian romances, however, place Arthur in AVALON after his death.

Glaucus (Glaukos). Once a fisherman of Boeotia. He became a sea-god endowed with the gift of prophecy and instructed Apollo in the art of soothsaying.

Glaucus (Glaukos). In ancient Greek myth, a son of Sisyphus and father of Bellerophon. Because he would not allow his horses to breed, Aphrodite maddened them until they killed him.

Glaucus (Glaukos). A mythical leader of Lycian troops in the Trojan War. For the story of his meeting with Diomedes, see DIOMEDEAN SWAP.

Glaucus (Glaukos). In ancient Greek myth, a son of Minos. He drowned in a vat of honey. Minos ordered the seer Polyidos, once he had found the child, to revive him. The CURETES told Polyidos to find the most pat simile for a cow of three colors. When Polyidos mentioned the fruit of the dog rose, he saw a snake and killed it. The snake's mate restored the first snake with a herb, which Polyidos promptly used on Glaucus with success. Later, however, Polyidos was angry with Minos for confining him to the palace. He had taught the art of divination to Glaucus, but on finally leaving Crete, he made Glaucus spit into his mouth and the boy forget everything he had learned.

Gleizes, Albert. See ABBAYE GROUP, THE.

Glencoe or **Glen Coe.** The valley of the river Coe in western Scotland. It was the scene of the massacre of Glencoe (1692), in which governmental troops led by a member of the clan of Campbell treacherously murdered 38 members of the Macdonald clan because of their Jacobite sympathies.

Glinka, Mikhail Ivanovich (1804–1857). The first important Russian composer. He wrote *Ivan Susanin*, or *A Life for the Czar*, the first Russian national opera, in 1836; *Russlan and Ludmilla*, after a poem by Pushkin, in 1842; and overtures, symphonies, and orchestral suites.

Globe, The. Elizabethan playhouse built in 1599 by Richard and Cuthbert Burbage on the Bankside south of the Thames. It became the permanent home of the Lord Chamberlain's (later King's) Men, Shakespeare's company, and it was here that his greatest plays, including *Hamlet, Macbeth, King Lear,* and *Othello,* were first presented. The Globe was unquestionably the most popular theater in London and its design—about which there is considerable controversy among scholars—became the model for the numerous theaters that sprang up in the early years of the 17th century. In June, 1613, the Globe was consumed by fire during a presentation of Shakespeare's *Henry VIII*. The theater was rebuilt in 1614 and remained standing until 1644, when it was pulled down to make room for residences.

Gloriana. The Queen of Faeryland in Spenser's FAERIE QUEENE.

Glorious Revolution. The name given by English Whigs to the movement (1688–1689), in which JAMES II was driven from the throne and the crown was offered to William of Orange and his wife Mary, eldest daughter of James. Carried out by those who opposed James's attempts to impose Catholicism on the country and to restore absolute monarchy, the revolution established the supremacy of Parliament. Although there was little opposition to the revolution in England, James had many supporters in Scotland and Ireland. James's Scottish adherents won the battle of Killiecrankie (1689), but James himself was defeated at the battle of the Boyne in Ireland (1690). See RIGHT, DECLARATION OF.

gloss. (1) An explanation or interpretation, the rendering of an obscure expression. The term is especially used to denote a marginal or interlinear note, of the kind abounding in medieval literature where Latin, Greek, or Hebrew words had to be rendered in the vernacular Teutonic, Romanic, and Celtic tongues. These special glosses are philologically very important and represent the oldest rudiments of bilingual dictionaries.

(2) A running commentary amplifying and explaining a difficult text.

(3) In prosody, a poetic composition which is a variation on a theme. A "texte" is chosen from some poetic work, and succeeding stanzas use a line or a couplet of the texte as the last line or lines until it has all appeared in the composition.

Gloucester, earl of. In Shakespeare's KING LEAR, the faithful old lord who shelters Lear from the storm. His aid to Lear is betrayed by his bastard son, Edmund, and his eyes are plucked out by Lear's daughter Regan and her husband, Cornwall. Evicted from his castle and bent on suicide, Gloucester is saved by his loyal son, Edgar, whom he had previously disinherited.

Glover, Richard (1712–1785). English poet, author of the ballad ADMIRAL HOSIER'S GHOST, which was published in Percy's RELIQUES OF ANCIENT ENGLISH POETRY. His chief work *Leonidas* (1737; enlarged in 1770 to 12 books), probably the most discussed blank-verse epic poem of the half-century, was translated into French and German and owed its success in part to the use Robert Walpole's opponents could make of it, for it was chiefly written in support of the Opposition Party.

Glubdubdrib. The island of sorcerers and magicians off the coast of Balnibarbi in Jonathan Swift's GULLIVER'S TRAVELS, where Gulliver is shown Homer, Aristotle, Vergil, and other famous men of antiquity.

Gluck, Christoph Willibald [von] (1714–1787). Austrian opera composer. In *Orfeo* (1762; see ORPHEUS) he created a new style of Italian opera. Conventional virtuosity was abandoned in favor of dramatic truth and a moving simplicity of expression, and the use of chorus and ballet was adopted from French opera. His adoption of this style was largely due to his librettist, Raniero de' Calzabigi. Later "reform" operas were *Alceste* (1767), *Paride e Elena*

(1770), *Iphigénie en Aulide* (1774), *Armide* (1777) and *Iphigénie en Tauride* (1779).

Gluckists. The supporters of GLUCK in a foolish rivalry in Paris (1774–1780) between the admirers of that composer, an Austrian, and those of PICCINI, an Italian. Marie Antoinette was a Gluckist, and consequently Young France favored the rival claimant. In the streets, coffee-houses, private houses, and even schools, the merits of Gluck and Piccini were canvassed, and all Paris was ranged on one side or the other.

Glumdalclitch. In Jonathan Swift's GULLIVER'S TRAVELS, a girl, nine years old, 40 feet high, who is Gulliver's nurse in BROBDINGNAG.

Glyn, Elinor (1864–1943). English novelist. Replete with tiger skins and violent passion, her best-selling romantic novels were once considered daring and slightly scandalous. *Three Weeks* (1907), *It* (1927), and *Romantic Adventure: The Autobiography of Elinor Glyn* (1936) are among her best known works.

gnome. According to the Rosicrucian system, a misshapen elemental spirit. It dwells in the bowels of the earth and guards the mines and quarries. The word seems to have been first used (perhaps invented) by Paracelsus, and to be derived from Gr. *ge-nomos*, earth-dweller.

Gnomic poets. Greek poets, such as Theognis of Megara and Solon, the lawgiver, whose writings are gnomic or aphoristic, containing maxims.

Gnostics (Gr. *gnosticos*). *Knowers*, as opposed to *believers;* various sects in the first six centuries of the Christian era. They tried to accommodate Christianity to the speculations of Pythagoras, Plato, and other Greek and Oriental philosophers. They taught that knowledge, rather than mere faith, is the true key of salvation. In the Gnostic creed Christ is esteemed merely as an eon or divine attribute personified, like Mind, Truth, Logos, Church, etc., the whole of which eons made up this divine pleroma or fullness. St. Paul, in several of his epistles, speaks of this "fullness [pleroma] of God."

Go and Catch a Falling Star (1633). The first line of a famous lyric by John DONNE, often entitled *Song*. A series of impossible feats are declared to be less difficult than the task of finding a woman "true and faire."

goat. An animal associated from very early times with the idea of sin (see SCAPEGOAT) and with devil lore. It is an old superstition in England and Scotland that a goat is never seen during the whole of a twenty-four-hour period, for once a day it pays a visit to the devil to have its beard combed. Formerly the devil himself was frequently depicted as a goat; and the animal also typifies lust and lechery.

Goat Song (Bocksgesang; 1921). A play by Franz WERFEL. It deals with the elemental frenzy of a group of peasants in revolt who worship a monster, half man and half ram, that has appeared out of the woods. The revolt is suppressed, and the monster killed; but one of the peasant girls bears its child, which symbolizes the continued existence of a chaotic potential in man.

Gobbo, Old. In Shakespeare's MERCHANT OF VENICE, the "sand-blind, high-gravel blind" father of Launcelot Gobbo. He encounters his son after an absence in an amusing scene of reconciliation.

Launcelot Gobbo. A clownish servant, the son of Old Gobbo. He leaves Shylock's service for shorter hours, more pay, and more sleep in the service of Bassanio.

Go-Between, The (1953). A novel by L. P. HARTLEY. A tragic love triangle is observed by an uncomprehending 13-year-old schoolboy, who carries messages between the adult characters.

Gobineau, Comte **Joseph Arthur de** (1816–1882). French diplomat, writer, and Orientalist. His best-known work, the sociological treatise *Essai sur l'inégalité des races humaines* (1853–5), advanced an early form of the theory of Aryan, or Teutonic, racial superiority. His skillful Oriental tales, such as *Akrivie Phrangopaulo* (1872), *Mademoiselle Irnois* (1847), or *Adélaïde* (1913), represent Gobineau's best writing. He also published works concerning the Italian Renaissance, and Oriental religions and philosophies.

goblin. A familiar demon. It lived, according to popular belief, in private houses and chinks of trees; in many parts miners attribute those strange noises heard in mines to them. The word is the Fr. *gobelin*, probably a diminutive of the surname *Gobel*, but perhaps connected with Gr. *kobalos*, an impudent rogue, a mischievous sprite, or with the Ger. KOBOLD. As a specimen of forced etymology, it may be mentioned that Johnson, in his *Dictionary*, records that

this word some derive from the *Gibellines,* a faction in Italy; so that *elfe* and *goblin* is *Guelph* and *Gibelline* because the children of either party were terrified by their nurses with the name of the other.

Godden, Rumer. Pen name and maiden name of Mrs. **Rumer Haynes Dixon** (1907–   ). English novelist. Her novels *Black Narcissus* (1939) and *The River* (1946) are both set in India. *Take Three Tenses* (1945) is an experiment in the handling of time. Other successes are *Kingfishers Catch Fire* (1953), *An Episode of Sparrows* (1955), *The Greengage Summer* (1958), and *The Battle of the Villa Fiorita* (1963). She also wrote books for children, including *Miss Happiness and Miss Flower* (1961).

Godey, Louis Antoine. See GODEY'S LADY'S BOOK.

Godey's Lady's Book. An American magazine of the mid-19th century. Famous for its hand-colored fashion plates and its art reproductions, *Godey's Lady's Book* found its way into 40,000 homes. Louis A. Godey (1804–1878) founded the magazine in 1830, and was its sole editor for six years; he then bought Sarah Josepha Hale's *Ladies' Magazine* and shared his editorship with her. Mrs. Hale (1788–1879), the author of *Mary Had a Little Lamb* (1830), was an advocate of women's rights and leader of the movement for a national Thanksgiving Day. Mrs. Hale retired in 1877, Godey died the following year, and the magazine continued publication only until 1898.

Godferneaux, A. See Tristan BERNARD.

Godfrey, Thomas (1736–1763). American poet and dramatist. The son of a Philadelphia glazier, Godfrey was apprenticed to a local watchmaker at 13. Wholly self-educated, he wrote songs and Chaucerian adaptations which attracted the attention of William Smith and the young poets at the College of Philadelphia. He died while on military duty in North Carolina. Two years later his friend Nathaniel Evans collected and published his poems as *Juvenile Poems*

on Various Subjects. The volume included Godfrey's PRINCE OF PARTHIA, often called the first American play.

Godfrey de Bouillon. See GOFFREDO.

Godiva, Lady (11th century). English benefactress, wife of Earl Leofric of Mercia. According to tradition, she asked her husband to relieve Coventry of certain burdensome taxes (c. 1040), but he jested that he would do so only if she would ride naked through the marketplace at midday. She did, covered only by her long hair, and Leofric kept his promise. In some versions, she had previously requested all the townspeople to stay indoors at the appointed hour, and not to look at her; one tailor, since known as "Peeping Tom of Coventry," looked through his window, for which a miracle struck him blind. The legend appears as one of Walter Savage Landor's *Imaginary Conversations* (1829), Alfred Tennyson's poem *Godiva, A Tale of Coventry* (1842), and a number of other literary works.

Godkin, Edwin Lawrence (1831–1902). Irish-born American journalist, editor, and author. In 1865 Godkin helped to found *The Nation* and became its first editor. When the magazine became the weekly edition of the New York *Post* (1881), Godkin became associate editor of that newspaper, and later, editor-in-chief (1883–1900). Among his achievements was the establishment of higher standards for book reviewing. His published works include *Reflections and Comments, 1865–95* (1895), and *The History of Hungary and the Magyars* (1853).

Gododin (c. 600). A poem by the Welsh bard Canu Aneurin (fl., c. 600). It is important in connection with ARTHURIAN LEGEND because it contains the first known reference to an Arthur. The poem is about the battle of Cattraeth (603) in which the tribe of the Gododin was defeated by the Saxons.

Go Down, Moses (1942). A collection of short stories by William FAULKNER. Set in Faulkner's mythical YOKNAPATAWPHA COUNTY, the stories are unified by a common theme, the ritual of the hunt—whether it be a hunt for Old Ben in *The Bear*, for the lovesick Negro in *Was*, for buried gold in *The Fire and the Hearth*, or for the Negro killer in *Pantaloon in Black*. All but the last deal with the members, black and white, of the complicated McCASLIN family, beginning with the second generation in *Was* and ending with the sixth in *Delta Autumn*. There is, in addition, an underlying theme of initiation into manhood and the responsibility of carrying out the social traditions.

The Bear, the most famous of the stories and possibly Faulkner's best, deals mainly with the hunt for Big Ben, an enormous and elusive bear. A shorter but equally important section tells how Isaac McCaslin, through the discovery of his grandfather's Negro offspring, rejects his claim to the McCaslin plantation and the guilt of slavery with which it is stained.

Godoy Alcayaga, Lucila. See Gabriela MISTRAL.

Gods Are Athirst, The (Les Dieux ont soif; 1912). An historical novel by Anatole FRANCE. It deals with the French Revolution. See Evariste GAMELIN.

God's Determinations Touching His Elect. A long poem on the Puritan theory of Grace by Edward

TAYLOR, begun around 1685 but unpublished until 1939. It combines elements of the cycle of lyric poems and of the medieval morality play. The imagery is alternately regal and homely, using 11 different verse forms. While not a play, the poem is cast as a drama. The first act traces man's predicament since the Fall; the second shows Christ and Satan battling for man's soul; the third describes the difficulties of the Christian life and the soul's fear of unworthiness; the last shows the soul entering the royal coach of Grace and flying to the feast of love in heaven.

God's Little Acre (1933). A novel by Erskine CALDWELL, dealing with shiftless and amoral Georgia mountaineers. The protagonist has set aside one acre of his land the income of which is to go to the church, but he constantly shifts the acre's location according to his own momentary plans and needs.

gods of classical mythology. The deities of the Greeks and Romans. The Romans identified many of their own deities with those of the Greeks. Since Greek mythology was far richer and more imaginative, the characteristics of the Greek gods tended to dominate those of the Roman deities. However, in later ages, knowledge of Greek mythology was generally gained through Roman sources, and the Roman names of the gods—and even the Latinized spelling of the Greek names—were more widely known. Those Greek and Roman deities who, in later times, were regarded as equivalent are as follows:

GREEK	ROMAN
Zeus	Jupiter
Apollon	Apollo
Ares	Mars
Hermes	Mercury
Poseidon	Neptune
Hephaestus	Vulcan
Hera	Juno
Demeter	Ceres
Artemis	Diana
Athena	Minerva
Aphrodite	Venus
Hestia	Vesta

These were the 12 chief gods, the Olympians of Greek mythology. Other well-known gods were:

Dionysus (Bakchos)	Bacchus
Eros	Cupid
Hades (Plouton)	Pluto
Kronus	Saturn
Persephone	Proserpina

A Greek hero equally popular with the Romans was Heracles, whose Latin name is Hercules.

For the chief deities of Scandinavian mythology, see AESIR and VANIR.

God that Failed, The (1950). A collection of essays edited by R. H. S. CROSSMAN. Written by persons who were attracted to Communism in the 1930's and were later disillusioned, it is an important document on a phase of modern history and thought. The contributors are Arthur Koestler, Ignazio Silone, Richard Wright, André Gide, Louis Fischer, and Stephen Spender.

Godunov, Boris Feodorovich (1552–1605). Russian czar (1598–1605). After the death of Ivan IV (Ivan the Terrible) in 1584, Godunov became regent for the imbecile Feodor I. He was elected to the throne on the death of Feodor. The mysterious death of the czarevich Dmitri (1591) is presumed to have been caused by Boris to clear his path to the throne. As regent he brought new vitality to the Russian nation, regaining land in Sweden and colonizing Siberia. After he became czar he lost the support of the nobility; his prestige was weakened by the appearance of a pretender claiming to be the murdered Dmitri. Boris died shortly after the false Dmitri invaded from Poland, but before the two men had confronted each other.

The poet Pushkin wrote a play called BORIS GODUNOV, which was the basis of Mussorgski's opera of the same name.

Godwin, William (1756–1836). English novelist and political theorist. A leading radical of the 18th century, he believed that it is impossible to be rationally persuaded and not act accordingly, and that therefore, man could live in harmony without law and institutions; he believed in the perfectibility of man. He was influenced by the ideas of ROUSSEAU and the French Encyclopedists, and in turn had a great influence on the English Romantics, particularly Wordsworth, Coleridge, Shelley, and Byron; Shelley's *Preface* to his *Revolt of Islam* is an excellent exposition of Godwin's ideas. Among Godwin's works are AN ENQUIRY CONCERNING THE PRINCIPLES OF POLITICAL JUSTICE, AND ITS INFLUENCE ON GENERAL VIRTUE AND HAPPINESS; *The Adventures of* CALEB WILLIAMS, OR THINGS AS THEY ARE, a novel; *St. Leon* (1799) a supernatural tale; and a *History of the Commonwealth* (1824–1828). Godwin's wife was the feminist Mary WOLLSTONECRAFT, and his daughter, Mary Wollstonecraft SHELLEY, was Shelley's second wife.

Goebbels, Paul Joseph (1897–1945). Minister of propaganda in Nazi Germany. After the collapse of Germany in World War II he poisoned himself and his family.

Goering, Hermann Wilhelm (1893–1946). Minister of aviation in Nazi Germany. Captured by the Allies (1945), he committed suicide before his scheduled execution.

Goes, Hugo van der (1440–1482). Flemish painter. Belonging to the school of the van Eycks, his religious scenes are known for their vigorous personalization of figures, strength of color, and tension in attitudes and spatial conception.

Goethe, Johann Wolfgang von (1749–1832). German poet, playwright, and novelist. Besides writing, he held an important cabinet post at the ducal court in Weimar, directed the theater in that city, and carried on extensive research in science, especially plant biology, on which he wrote *Die Metamorphose der Pflanzen* (*The Metamorphosis of Plants*, 1790), and optics, the subject of his *Zur Farbenlehre* (*On the Theory of Colors*, 1810). In his scientific studies, he always attempted to see the individual phenomenon as part of an organic, developing whole, in opposition to the categorizing science of his time. His poetic works, too, are characterized by this interest in the natural, organic development of things, rather than in any idealistic schemes.

In his early career (1769–1776), Goethe was recognized as a leading figure in the STURM UND DRANG. His well-known poem *Prometheus* (written 1774?), with its insistence that man must believe not in gods but in himself alone, might be seen as a motto for the whole movement. HERDER's strong influence upon his thinking during these years is reflected, for example, in his essay *Von deutscher Baukunst* (*On German Architecture,* 1773). The plays GÖTZ VON BERLICHINGEN, *Clavigo* (1774), *Stella* (1774), and EGMONT belong to this initial phase of his development, as do the earliest Faust sketches and the short novel THE SORROWS OF YOUNG WERTHER.

Goethe's youth was emotionally hectic to the point that he sometimes feared for his reason, but in 1775, after a relaxing trip to Switzerland, he made a decisive break with his past and left his native Frankfurt am Main for the small city of Weimar. It was there that he first assumed serious governmental responsibility; and it was there that he met the woman he was to worship for a decade, Charlotte von STEIN. These years, until 1786, were not very productive for Goethe the writer, but they did contribute much to the characteristic personal balance that appears in his later work.

Goethe spent the years 1786–1788 in Italy, a trip that he later described in his *Italienische Reise* (*Italian Trip,* 1816) and which significantly influenced his growing commitment to a classical view of art. In Italy, he completed his play IPHIGENIA IN TAURIS, which, along with his *Römische Elegien* (*Roman Elegies,* 1788–1790, pub. 1795) and the play TORQUATO TASSO, is customarily taken as the beginning of WEIMAR CLASSICISM.

From this point on, Goethe's life was relatively settled and though he traveled much, his base was always Weimar where he was, in effect, the court's cultural director. But his poetic development was by no means finished. In 1794 began his close and fruitful friendship with SCHILLER, and the ensuing years saw his work expand into new directions, as in the epic poems REINEKE FUCHS and HERMANN UND DOROTHEA, and the novel WILHELM MEISTER. He was also in contact with the founding figures of GERMAN ROMANTICISM, especially the brothers Schlegel, but marked romantic tendencies do not begin to appear in his work until later: for example, in the novel DIE WAHLVERWANDTSCHAFTEN or in *Der West-ostliche Divan* (*The West-Eastern Divan,* 1819), a lyric cycle that shares the romantics' interest in the Orient; and in Part II of FAUST.

In a sense, Goethe's development came full circle. At the beginning of his so-called classical period (1788–1805) he had repudiated the emotionalism of his own *Werther;* but as time went on, he tended back toward his earlier attitudes. In his lyric *Trilogie der Leidenschaft* (*Trilogy of Passion,* 1824), one poem, addressed to the character Werther, shows the extent of his regained understanding and sympathy for his own youthful works.

At times, Goethe was grossly insensitive to the merits of such great authors as Hölderlin, Kleist, and Heine, but with himself he was never less than honest; despite the extraordinary length of time spanned by his career, he never stagnated, but was always learning and expanding, seeking to grasp more of what he regarded as the poet's proper domain, the entire world.

Valuable material about his life and personality may be found in his autobiographical DICHTUNG UND WAHRHEIT and in Johann ECKERMANN's *Gespräche mit Goethe* (*Conversations with Goethe,* 1836). See also DAEMONIC; MÄRCHEN; Johann LAVATER.

Goffe, William (1605?–?1679). English regicide. One of the judges at the trial of Charles I, he fled to America in 1660 with his father-in-law, Edward Whalley (1616?–?1675). Their mysterious wanderings in New England, where they lived for many years, turned them into semilegendary figures. Goffe appears in numerous literary works, notably Scott's *Peveril of the Peak* (1823), Cooper's *The Wept of Wish-Ton-Wish* (1829), and J. K. Paulding's *The Puritan and His Daughter* (1849).

Goffredo (Godfrey de Bouillon). The principal character of Tasso's romantic epic GERUSALEMME LIBERATA. When the poem was first translated by Thomas Carew in 1594, and completed by Edward Fairfax in 1600, its English title was *Godfrey of Bullogne.* Godfrey, duke of Lorraine, was the chosen commander of the allied Crusaders who assaulted Jerusalem in the year 1099. He was also for a time king of Jerusalem. In Tasso's poem, though divinely appointed, he must contend with infidel forces, enchantments, infernal spirits, and division in his ranks; but he finally leads the triumphant Christian army into the city. In worship at the sepulcher of Christ, he hangs his arms in fulfillment of his vow to recover the holy city.

Gog. In the Bible (Ezek. 38:39), the king of Magog, a northern land whose fierce hordes were to invade Israel. Scholars sometimes identify Gog with Gyges, a ruler of Lydia in Asia Minor. In Revelation 20:7, Gog and Magog symbolize the enemies of the kingdom of God, in this case Gog being associated with Magog, a son of Japheth (Gen. 10:2). Elsewhere (I Chron. 5:4), Gog is a descendant of Reuben, eldest of the 12 sons of Jacob.

In British legend, Gog and Magog are the sole survivors of a monstrous brood, the offspring of the 33 infamous daughters of the Emperor Diocletian, who murdered their husbands and, being set adrift in a ship, reached Albion, where they fell in with a number of demons. Their descendants, a race of giants were extirpated by Brute and his companions, with the exception of Gog and Magog, who were brought in chains to London and were made to do duty as porters at the royal palace, on the site of the London Guildhall, where their effigies have been at least since the reign of Henry V. The old giants were destroyed in the Great Fire of 1666, and the present ones, 14 feet high, were carved in 1708 by Richard Saunders.

Gogarty, Oliver St. John (1878–1957). Irish physician and writer of memoirs, essays, and poetry. He was said to be the original of Malachi (Buck) Mulligan in James Joyce's *Ulysses.* His exuberant memoirs are full of reminiscences of his friends, including Joyce, William Butler Yeats, and other Irish writers. Among his books of memoirs are *As I Was Going Down Sackville Street* (1937) and *I Follow St. Patrick* (1938).

Gogol, Nikolai Vasilyevich (1809–1852). Russian novelist, dramatist, and short-story writer. Gogol was born in the Ukraine in the province of Poltava. His father, a member of the petty nobility, had a small estate and was an amateur playwright. Gogol used some lines from his father's plays as epigraphs for his early stories in the collection *Vechera na* *khutore bliz Dikan'ki (Evenings on a Farm Near Dikanka;* 1831–1832). After attending school in the Ukraine, Gogol went to St. Petersburg where he worked as a government clerk and as a teacher, for a short while lecturing in history at St. Petersburg University. His first attempt at literary work, a short poem called *Italia* (1829) was mildly successful. This encouraged Gogol to try a long narrative poem, *Hanz Keuchelgarten* (1829), which turned out to be a disaster. In 1831, Gogol met Pushkin and established a friendship that lasted until the great poet's death. Pushkin was impressed with Gogol's Dikanka tales, which were largely based on Ukrainian folklore with an admixture of Gogol's own fantasy. Even these early tales reveal some features characteristic of Gogol's mature style: a rich mixture of vulgarisms and high-flown rhythmical rhetoric with often sharp juxtapositions between the two levels.

Gogol's next published work was *Arabeski (Arabesques,* 1835), containing a collection of essays and three of his St. Petersburg stories: *Nevski prospekt (Nevski Prospect), Portret (The Portrait),* and *Zapiski cumashedshego (Diary of a Madman).* The last story is a remarkable depiction of the mind of the lunatic Poprishchin, a civil servant who comes to believe that he is the king of Spain. In the same year Gogol published a collection of Ukrainian stories entitled *Mirgorod,* including *Starosvetskiye pomeshchiki (Old-world Landowners),* TARAS BULBA, *Vii,* and *Povest' o tom, kak possorilsya Ivan Ivanovich s Ivanom Nikiforovichem (The Story of How Ivan Ivanovich Quarreled with Ivan Nikiforovich).* Two more stories, *Kolyaska (The Carriage)* and *Nos (The Nose),* appeared in 1836. *The Nose* is another example of Gogol's predilection for fantasy, a story about a man whose nose abruptly leaves him and gads about town, wearing clothes and riding in a fine carriage. In April, 1836, the first performance of Gogol's satiric comedy THE INSPECTOR GENERAL was given. The mixed reaction to the play upset the author, who was always extremely sensitive about the public's attitude to his work. He left Russia for Europe, traveled in Italy, Germany, Switzerland, and France, and finally settled down in Rome. Except for short visits to Russia in 1839–1840 and 1841–1842, he was abroad for 12 years. Gogol had taken with him from Russia a few chapters of his novel, DEAD SOULS, which was completed in Rome and published in 1842 in a four-volume edition of his works. Also in the edition was his famous story THE OVERCOAT and all his previously published work.

After the publication of the first part of *Dead Souls,* which was well received in Russia, Gogol began writing to friends and publishing requests for material to use in the planned second part of the work. Whether he felt his creative power failing or whether he really believed that accounts of daily life from amateur correspondents would be useful is obscure. In ill health and increasingly obsessed with a religious mania, Gogol aimlessly traveled about Europe, took a pilgrimage to Palestine, and eventually returned to Russia in 1848. His reception in his homeland was cool, at least among the radical intelligentsia. Two years before his return, Gogol had published a didactic work entitled *Vybrannye mesta iz perepiski c druz'yami (Selected Passages from Correspondence with Friends,* 1846) in which he upheld the autocratic

Czarist regime and the patriarchal Russian way of life and advised landowners to allow their peasants to read only the Bible lest they pick up dangerous ideas. The book stirred up a storm of protest among the radicals and elicited a violent letter from the critic Vissarion Belinski, which became at least as well known in Russia, though it was banned from print, as the book that caused it to be written. What Belinski and the other radicals failed to notice was that Gogol himself had never explicitly criticized the social system in Russia. His critics merely assumed that previously such was the implication of his writings.

From 1848 until his death (1852), Gogol fell more and more into melancholia, aggravated by his fears of spiritual damnation. Shortly after burning some of his manuscripts, including the second part of *Dead Souls,* he took to his bed and died.

Gogol is recognized as one of the greatest writers in Russian literature from the point of view of the imaginativeness and stylistic richness of his work. No Russian author has handled the wealth of the Russian language so well. Gogol's choice of everyday life as the basis of much of his work had a profound effect on future Russian literature, although the degree and the purposes of his realism as interpreted by Belinski and later radical critics are doubtful. Whether he intended it or not, Gogol's work was held up as a model for later Russian writers, who turned their attention to a sympathetic observation and realistic description of the lower levels of Russian society.

Despite his later evidences of conservatism and religiosity, Gogol is viewed by Soviet critics, as he was early in his career by Belinski, as a realist who used his work to point out social evils with the aim of bringing about reform. His development in the last years of his life, including the *Selected Passages,* is regarded officially as the result of mental aberration.

Gokak, V. K, (1909–   ). Indian poet, playwright, essayist, and critic writing in Kannada. Currently professor of English at the Karnatak University, he was president of the Karnatak Poets' Conference (1934). His publications include *The Poetic Approach to Language* (1948) in English; *Pavana,* poems, and *Sahityaaalli Pragati,* criticism, in Kannada.

Gold, Michael. Pen name of **Irving Granich** (1894–1967). American writer. One of the major figures in American "proletarian literature," Gold was the first to define the term clearly in his article *Towards Proletarian Art* published in *Liberator* magazine (Feb. 1921), while his later novel *Jews Without Money* (1930) became a model for aspiring proletarian novelists.

Goldberg, Isaac (1887–1938). American writer. He is known for his interest in language, which resulted in *The Wonder of Words* (1938), and for his books introducing Latin-American literature to the American public: *Studies in Spanish-American Literature* (1920) and *Brazilian Literature* (1922). Other works include a book on William S. Gilbert and the Gilbert and Sullivan operettas (1913), *Tin Pan Alley* (1930), and biographies of H. L. Mencken (1925) and Havelock Ellis (1926).

Gold Bug, The (1843). A story by Edgar Allan POE. William Le Grand accidentally discovers a cipher giving the location of buried treasure. Unraveling its instructions, he drops the beetle, or gold bug, through one eye of a skull, and unearths a fortune. The story takes place on Sullivan's Island off South Carolina.

Golden Apple. See APPLE OF DISCORD; ATALANTA.

Golden Ass, The (2nd century). The common, alternative title of the *Metamorphoses,* a satirical romance, by Lucius APULEIUS. It is narrated in the first person by Lucius, a licentious young man with insatiable curiosity about people and things. While visiting a sorceress in Thessaly, he induces a maid to steal a magic potion which will turn him into an owl. He takes the wrong potion and turns into an ass instead. In this disappointing form he wanders throughout Greece, passing through the hands of a series of owners who mistreat him. Interspersed throughout the narrative are lively stories of intrigue, witchcraft, and love, most famous of which is Cupid and PSYCHE. Lucius is finally restored to his human form with the help of the goddess Isis.

Ever since its first appearance, *The Golden Ass* has enjoyed an unusually sustained popularity. The book's influence has been considerable and can best be seen in such writers as Boccaccio, Cervantes, and Rabelais. Apuleius borrowed his stories and plots from Greek predecessors; he may have based his book on the same work by Lucius of Patrae that inspired LUCIAN's novel *Lucius, or the Ass.*

Golden Bough, The (1890–1915). A comprehensive work on comparative religion and mythology by Sir James George FRAZER. The general title of the 12 volumes refers to the branch broken from a sacred tree by Aeneas before his descent into the underworld. Although many of his conclusions have been discredited, Frazer's book was a seminal work in its field, and most subsequent scholarship recognizes a great debt to it. In its single-volume condensation, it has become a popular classic. *The Golden Bough* had a significant influence on the literary world, and played an important part in the conception of *Finnegans Wake* by James Joyce and of *The Waste Land* by T. S. Eliot. See KING OF THE WOOD.

Golden Bowl, The (1904). A novel by Henry JAMES. The heroine, Maggie Verver, the daughter of an American millionaire, marries the impoverished Prince Amerigo. Her old school friend, Charlotte Stant, who has had an affair with the prince, later marries Adam Verver, Maggie's father, and continues her relationship with her lover. The second part of the novel deals with Maggie's discovery of the liaison and with her reaction to it. This is generally considered to be James's most difficult work.

golden calf. An image of worship made of gold earrings and other jewelry by the Hebrews under the direction of Aaron, while Moses was receiving the Ten Commandments (Ex. 20) on Mount Sinai. When Moses returned with the two stone tablets on which were written the laws and found his people adoring the image (a form of BAAL-worship), he destroyed the tablets and threw the powdered dust of the calf into the spring of Marah. After he had led his people in repentance, he returned to the mount and received two new tablets.

Golden Dog, The (unauthorized, 1877; auth. ed., 1896). A novel by William Kirby (1817–1906), English-born Canadian novelist and editor. This was the first Canadian novel to achieve widespread popularity. The story, set in old French Quebec, served as a model for numerous Canadian historical romances in the 19th century and later.

Golden Fleece, the. In Greek mythology, the fleece of pure gold, taken from a miraculous winged ram. Athamas, a son of Aeolus and ruler of Boeotia, married the phantom Nephele (see IXION), who bore him a son Phrixus and a daughter Helle. He also became the father of Learchus and Melicertes by Cadmus' daughter INO. Jealous of Nephele, Ino persuaded the Boeotian women secretly to parch the seed wheat, then caused a false oracle to be brought from Delphi: only the sacrifice of Phrixus and Helle would save the crops. At the last moment, a winged, golden ram was sent by Hermes, and Phrixus and Helle escaped on its back. As it flew, Helle fell and was drowned in the Hellespont, the straits thereafter named in her honor. Phrixus reached Colchis at the eastern end of the Black Sea; he gave the ram to King Aeetes, who nailed its fleece to an oak in the grove of Ares, and married Aeetes' daughter Chalciope, who bore him four sons. The fleece was later seized by the ARGONAUTS and returned to Iolcus.

Golden Horde. A body of Mongol Tartars of the 13th century. They overran eastern Europe, and were so called from the magnificent tent of Batu Khan, grandson of Genghis Khan. The kingdom of the Golden Horde at its height reached from the Dniester to central Asia. It was overthrown by Ivan III of Russia (1480), and broke up into a number of smaller khanates with that of Astrakhan representing the Golden Horde.

Golden Legend, The (1483). A compilation of lives of the saints and other ecclesiastical commentaries, one of the most popular books published by William Caxton. It drew on the material in the Latin *Legenda Aurea* of Jacobus de Voragine (1230–1298), but was based mostly on French and English versions.

Golden Legend, The (1872). A poem by Henry Wadsworth LONGFELLOW. It is the second part of a trilogy called *Christus: A Mystery.* The theme is a variant of the Faust legend, reflecting the attitudes of the Middle Ages toward Christian truths.

Golden Rose, the. The annual custom whereby the Pope bestowed upon a worthy individual or place an exquisite rose made of gold. In 1494, Pope Alexander VI presented the rose to King Charles VIII of France in hope of dissuading him from invading Italy—to no avail.

Golden Treasury of the Best Songs and Lyrical Poems in the English Language, The (1861; second series 1897). An anthology of poetry from the 16th to mid-19th century by F. T. PALGRAVE. A monument to late romantic taste (particularly in its predilection for the short lyric), it was one of the most influential of English anthologies.

Golding, Louis (1895–1958). English novelist. Among his novels of Jewish life in a large industrial town are *Magnolia Street* (1932) and *Five Silver Daughters* (1934).

Golding, William (1911–   ). English novelist. He is the author of *The Inheritors* (1955), LORD OF THE FLIES, PINCHER MARTIN (U.S. title *The Two Deaths of Christopher Martin*), *Free Fall* (1959), *The Inheritors* (1962), and *The Spire* (1964). Golding calls his books fables and uses them to express his rather grim view of the world—the view that most men are basically evil and life is a tooth-and-claw

Hoe begynneth the hystorye of Noe the first sonday in ❧ Sexagesimé //

NEW YORK PUBLIC LIBRARY

Noah in the ark. From Caxton's
Golden Legend (1484).

affair. His World War II experiences in the navy and his years spent teaching small boys have helped to shape his philosophical attitudes. Master of strange situations and ironic surprise twists, Golding also enriches his books with symbols and literary, mythological, and Christian allusions.

Goldoni, Carlo (1707–1793). Italian dramatist. Born in Venice, he wrote some 150 comedies through which he became the creator of the modern Italian comedy in the style of Molière, superseding the traditional COMMEDIA DELL'ARTE, then vigorously defended by Carlo Gozzi. His comedies, written in Italian and in the Venetian dialect, depict the foibles of the middle and lower classes of Venice and offer a true-to-life portrayal of character and action absent in the older *commedia* technique of improvisation carried out by stock characters. His finest comedies appeared in the years 1748–1760. Among them are *La Bottega del Caffè, La Locandiera, La Vedova Scaltra, La Famiglia dell'Antiquario,* and the dialect plays *I Rusteghi* and *Le Baruje Chiozote.* In his *Mémoires* (trans., 1877), which like his last plays were written in French, he described his verbal warfare with the traditionalists of the theater and stated: "The secret of the art of a writer of comedies is to cling to nature and never to leave her." A writer for the Italian theater in Paris and pensioned by Louis XIV, he was impoverished as a result of the French Revolution.

Goldsmith, Oliver (1731–1774). Irish-born English poet, playwright, and novelist. Educated in Ireland, he left for Edinburgh in 1752, and never returned. He studied medicine for a while at Leyden in 1754, then made the Grand Tour of the Continent, returning to England in 1756, where he became engaged in literary hackwork, and, for a time, was employed by Samuel Richardson, the printer and novelist. His literary fame began with THE TRAVELLER, a didactic poem surveying national modes of happiness, which was praised by Samuel Johnson and other members of the LITERARY CLUB. His major works include *An Enquiry into the Present State of Polite Learning in Europe* (1759), a prose essay attributing the decline of polite learning to the inferiority of poets; *The Bee* (1759), a periodical containing perhaps his most famous tales—REVERIE AT THE BOAR'S HEAD TAVERN and ASEM, AN EASTERN TALE; THE CITIZEN OF THE WORLD, a satiric epistolary novel in imitation of Montesquieu's *Lettres Persanes* (1721); THE VICAR OF WAKEFIELD, a novel; THE DESERTED VILLAGE, a poem; and THE GOOD NATUR'D MAN and SHE STOOPS TO CONQUER, comedies. A beloved member of Dr. Johnson's circle, he was noted for his comic verbal *faux-pas,* though it seems that Goldsmith buffooned purposely on occasion without his friends ever suspecting it. At the end of his life he retorted to their raillery in a series of brilliant caricatures, *The Retaliation* (1774). See GOLDY; GOODY TWO-SHOES; HERMIT, THE.

Goldy. The pet name given to Oliver GOLDSMITH by Dr. Samuel Johnson. David Garrick said of Goldsmith, "He wrote like an angel and talked like poor Poll."

Golgotha. See CALVARY.

Goliardic verse. The light Latin verse of 12th- and 13th-century Germany, France, and England by university students and wandering clerics, minstrels, and *jongleurs.* This poetry was of two types: scurrilous satire defying all kinds of civil and ecclesiastical authority, including the Pope; and gay, nonchalant, ribald celebrations of nature, women, and wine, including some drinking songs still popular. The Goliards, as the authors were called, often referred to a mythical Golias as their leader and patron, ironically dignifying him with the titles of "Bishop" (*episcopus*) and "Archpoet" (*archipoeta*). He is sometimes identified with Primus, a 12th-century scholar from Orleans. The *Confession of Golias,* as well as much other Goliardic verse, was once attributed to Walter MAP. A large collection of this poetry was published in Germany as *Carmina Burana* (1847), some of which J. A. Symonds translated in his *Wine, Women, and Song* (1884). Carl Orff set *Carmina Burana* to music in 1935.

Goliath. See DAVID.

Golovlyov Family, The (Gospoda Golovlyovy; 1872–1876). A novel, written under the pen name N. Shchedrin by Mikhail SALTYKOV. It depicts the dissolution of a Russian provincial landowning family. Arina Petrovna, the rapacious mother of the family, dominates her husband and alienates her four children, caring only for adding to her estates. The land eventually passes to her son Porfiri, who is nicknamed IUDUSHKA (Little Judas). He proves to be just as grasping and unloving as his mother had been, driving away his own children. The gloomy chronicle comes to an end with the unctuous Iudushka sinking into ruin and death through drink. The novel is one of the classics of 19th-century Russian realism.

Golyadkin, Yakov Petrovich. The hallucination-ridden hero of Feodor Dostoevski's short novel, THE DOUBLE.

Gomberville, Marin le Roy, Sieur de (1600–1674). French novelist. An original member of the ACADÉMIE FRANÇAISE, Gomberville wrote novels of heroic adventure, usually set in exotic lands and historical periods with which the author had little familiarity. *La Caritie* (1621), *Polexandre* (1629–1637), and *La Cythérée* (1640) lushly evoked an imagined Central America and North Africa. *Polexandre,* the author's most important work, was the five-volume tale of a beautiful island queen and the travels of her knight Polexandre around the world; it included the first description of seascape and tempest to be found in French literature. Upon his conversion to Jansenism in 1651, Gomberville published *La Jeune Alcidiane,* a Christian sequel to *Polexandre,* with the intention of counteracting what he supposed to be the nefarious effect of the earlier book.

Gómez de la Serna, Ramón (1888–). Spanish writer. A prolific author, he is known for his biographies, which range in scope from Goya to *Oscar Wilde* (1929) and include *Lope de Vega* (1945), El Greco, Azorín, and Valle-Inclán. His major achievement, however, is his invention and subsequent use of *greguería,* a strange literary form which joins humor with the metaphoric conceit in a startling manner: "the pillows resting on the window sill are *pulcinellas* tired of the night's performance," or "Bottle, wine's coffin." This style forms the basis of such works as *El torero Caracho* (1926), *La malicia de las acacias* (1927), and *La Nardo* (1934).

Gomorrah. See SODOM AND GOMORRAH.

Gompers, Samuel (1850–1924). English-born American labor leader. Arriving in the U.S. in 1863, Gompers joined the Cigarmakers' Union and became its president in 1877. He played an important role in the organization of the American Federation of Labor, which he headed from 1886 until his death (except for the year 1895). Devoted to practical ends, such as improvements in wages and hours, he believed that unions should avoid political alliances.

Gonçalves Dias, Antônio (1823–1864). Brazilian poet and ethnologist. Perhaps Brazil's first truly national poet, Gonçalves Dias was a fervent patriot who wrote verse glorifying the Indian and the tropical landscape. His best-known poem is *Canção do Exilio* (*Song of Exile,* 1846), whose first lines—"There are palm trees in my homeland, where the sabiá sings"—are familiar to every literate Brazilian.

Goncharov, Ivan Aleksandrovich (1812–1891). Russian novelist. Born in Simbirsk (now Ulyanovsk), Goncharov spent his childhood on the family estate. The richness and comfort of the old patriarchal way of life he experienced there was later immortalized in his major novel, OBLOMOV. Goncharov's idyll in the country ended in 1822, when he was sent to Moscow to complete his education. He was miserable in the city and consoled himself by reading extensively, forming an interest in literature that led him to enroll in Moscow University's faculty of letters. He graduated in 1834 and entered the civil service. Goncharov's first important novel, *Obyknovennaya istoriya* (*A Common Story,* 1844), dealt with the loss of idealistic dreams when a young provincial encounters life in the city. The theme was later to be touched on in *Oblomov.* The critic Vissarion Belinski called *Obyknovennaya istoriya* "a terrible blow to romanticism, dreaminess, sentimentality, and provincialism."

In 1849, Goncharov had already completed the first chapters of his masterpiece. He published one of the chapters, "Oblomov's Dream," in that year. Work on the novel was interrupted by a world cruise he took as secretary for a Russian expedition on the ship *Pallada* from 1852 to 1855. He published a description of the journey in *The Frigate 'Pallada'* in 1858. The following year, *Oblomov* appeared.

Goncharov retired from government service in 1867 and completed his third novel, *Obryv* (*The Precipice,* 1869), on which he had been working for almost 20 years. The novel contrasted the materialist views of the socialists with those of the old Russian patriarchal world. Goncharov's unmistakable preference for the conservative way of life scandalized the radicals. During the remaining years of his life, Goncharov lived a secluded life in his St. Petersburg apartment, occasionally pulling himself free from his mental depression and illnesses to take a trip abroad. His writings during this period consisted mainly of sketches, articles, and reminiscences. The best known of these works is *Mil'on terzani* (*A Million Torments,* 1872), an essay on *Woe from Wit,* the classic Russian comedy by Aleksandr S. Griboyedov.

Goncourt, Edmond (1822–1896) and **Jules de** (1830–1870). French writers known as the **Brothers Goncourt,** who collaborated in their work. Early leaders in the movement of NATURALISM, the Goncourt brothers are forerunners of Emile Zola. Such novels as GERMINIE LACERTEUX and *Madame Gervaisais* (1869) are studies of pathological or degenerate subjects. *La Fille Elisa* (1877), written by Edmond alone, is a realistic description of prostitution. The Brothers Goncourt went to great lengths in order to depict a subject with precision and accuracy. To write *Sœur Philomène* (1861), for example, they went into hospitals, studying the exact conditions. Their work is episodic in form and impersonal in tone. In addition to their naturalistic novels, the Goncourts wrote several studies of 18th-century costumes, art, and furniture. They were also avid collectors of objets d'art and are thought to have been the first to introduce Japanese art into France. See PRIX GONCOURT.

Goneril. In Shakespeare's KING LEAR, the eldest daughter of Lear. The instigator of the cruelties perpetrated on Lear, she refuses to house her father's large entourage. Later she plots with Edmund to kill her husband, the duke of Albany, poisons her sister Regan, who also loves Edmund, and finally stabs herself when the plot is discovered.

Gone with the Wind (1936). A historical novel by Margaret MITCHELL, an American. At the time of the author's death, it had won a Pulitzer Prize and had sold more than 8,000,000 copies; a motion picture version (1939) was equally successful. The heroine of this, her only book, is Scarlett O'Hara, a fiery Southern belle, whose love for Ashley Wilkes is frustrated when he marries gentle Melanie Hamilton; after being widowed twice, Scarlett weds Rhett Butler, who proves more than a match for her. The novel also depicts, from a Southern viewpoint, the tumult and suffering caused by the Civil War and Reconstruction.

Góngora y Argote, Luis de (1561–1627). Spanish poet. A native of Córdoba, Góngora studied at Salamanca and though he probably had little vocation for the priesthood, he took minor orders, becoming prebendary of Córdoba's cathedral. In 1617 he was ordained and was named chaplain to King Philip III. After suffering an apoplectic stroke in 1626, he retired to Córdoba, where he died.

Góngora's literary career had two distinct phases. Initially, as a disciple of Fernando de Herrera, he wrote verse that was relatively simple and remarkable for its exuberance, charm, and wit. These early poems include Italianate sonnets; *romances* or ballads (*Amarrado al duro banco, Servía en Orán al rey, Angélica y Medoro*); and *letrillas* or songs (*Aprended, flores de mí*).

After 1600, however, Góngora deliberately cultivated the abstruse style to which he gave his name, GONGORISM, and for which his enemies dubbed him *Príncipe de las Tinieblas* ("Prince of Darkness"). Written for the intellectual elite, his poems in this manner, particularly the *Fábula de Polifemo y Galatea* and the *Soledades,* caused a sensation. Though many, including Cervantes, hailed Góngora's innovations, others, notably Lope de Vega and Quevedo, bitterly attacked him.

Góngora's works were first collected by Juan López de Vicuña in 1627. A more complete collection, including the play *Las firmezas de Isabela* and fragments of two other dramas, was issued in 1633 by Gonzalo de Hozes y Córdoua.

Gongorism (Gongorismo). A Spanish literary style, sometimes called *cultismo* or *culteranismo,* used by Luis de GÓNGORA and other 17th-century poets. Designed to appeal to the cultivated (*los cultos*), it is characterized by an emphasis on Latin terms and syntax, by frequent allusions to classical mythology, and lavish use of tropes, metaphors, hyperbole, and antitheses. Gongorism can also be considered as a purely stylistic variant of the contemporaneous literary trend known as CONCEPTISM, which appeared mainly in prose. It had counterparts in the Marinism of Italy and the Euphuism of England. Although Góngora used the style to enhance the sonority and richness of his verse, in the hands of lesser poets it became mere affectation, and Gongorism later became synonymous with bad writing.

Gonne, Maud (1866–1953). Irish patriot and philanthropist. In 1903 she married Major MacBride, an Irish patriot who was executed (1916) by the British after the Easter Rebellion. She was the first diplomatic emissary (1921) of the Irish Free State to Paris. Famous for her beauty and known as an actress, painter, and linguist, she is the heroine of several poems and plays by William Butler Yeats. *A Servant of the Queen,* her autobiography, was published in 1940.

Gonzaga. Italian noble family of Mantua. It was famed during the Renaissance for its cultural patronage. Outstanding were:

Lodovico Gonzaga (1414–1478), the marquis who employed the painter Mantegna, the architect Alberti, the scholars Pico della Mirandola and Poliziano, and the educator Vittorino da Feltre.

Federico Gonzaga (1440–1484) continued his father's patronage, was skilled in diplomacy, and excelled as a CONDOTTIERE.

Francesco Gonzaga, son of Federico (1466–1519), married the famous Isabella d'Este and was a military commander during the period.

Elisabetta Gonzaga, his sister (1471–1526), married Duke Guidobaldo of Urbino (see MONTEFELTRO) and became the duchess of Castiglione's *Cortegiano* (*The Courtier*).

Federigo Gonzaga, (1500–1540), Francesco's son continued the family tradition by employing Giulio Romano and Pietro Aretino. He was the first duke of Mantua, having received the title from Emperor Charles V.

González Prada, Manuel (1848–1918). Peruvian essayist and poet, famed as a polemicist. A member of a distinguished Peruvian family, González Prada fought in the so-called War of the Pacific (1879–1883), in which Peru suffered a humiliating defeat at the hands of Chile. In a famous speech (1886), he uttered the phrase "old men to the tomb, young men to work," which became the battle cry of those who sought changes in the established order. Uncompromising and incorruptible, he devoted his life to exposing his country's ills in scathing but highly polished prose, hurling his most impassioned invective at the politicians and at the Roman Catholic Church. He became the intellectual mentor of several generations of Peruvian reformers and revolutionaries. Some of his best-known articles and speeches are collected in *Páginas libres* (1894) and *Horas de lucha* (1908). He also wrote several volumes of poetry, the best of which is probably *Baladas peruanas* (1935), which gives a realistic portrayal of Indian life.

Gonzalo. In Shakespeare's THE TEMPEST, the kindly old counsellor who peppers his words with wisdom and is mocked for his garrulity by Alonso and Antonio. His ministrations helped save Prospero's life.

Goodbye, Mr. Chips (1934). A best-selling short novel by James HILTON. It deals sentimentally with the life of an English schoolmaster.

Good Companions, The (1929). A novel by J. B. PRIESTLEY. Good humored, and filled with comic characters and varied scenes from English life, it is the story of a group of oddly assorted people who run a touring music-hall company called The Good Companions.

Good Earth, The (1931). A novel by Pearl BUCK. It describes the rise of Wang Lung, a Chinese peasant, from poverty to the position of a rich landowner, helped by his patient wife, O-lan. Their vigor, fortitude, persistence, and enduring love of the soil are emphasized throughout. Generally regarded as Pearl Buck's masterpiece, the book won universal acclaim for its sympathetically authentic picture of Chinese life.

Good Friday. The Friday preceding Easter Day, the anniversary of Jesus' Crucifixion. "Good" here means *holy;* Christmas, as well as Shrove Tuesday, used to be called "the good tide." According to old superstition, those born on Christmas Day or Good Friday have the power of seeing and commanding spirits.

Good Natur'd Man, The (1768). A comedy by Oliver GOLDSMITH. The story concerns Honeywood, a likeable young man prone to extravagance. His uncle, in order to demonstrate that his friends will abandon him if he has no money, has Honeywood arrested for debt. Honeywood is in love with the beautiful, wealthy Miss Richland. When he is released from prison he assumes that a friend of his in the government is responsible for his freedom, though actually it is Miss Richland who is responsible. In the end Honeywood's uncle arranges a match with Miss Richland.

Good Queen Bess. ELIZABETH I of England.

Goodrich, Samuel Griswold (1793–1860). American publisher, editor, author of children's books, and memoirist. Adopting the pseudonym of Peter Parley, Goodrich published a series for children beginning with *The Tales of Peter Parley About America* (1827). For about 30 years he wrote volumes of history, geography, science, and travel for children, with the help of several collaborators, including Hawthorne. His best book is considered *Recollections of a Lifetime* (1856).

The patron of many American authors, he introduced Nathaniel Hawthorne to the public in his magazine *The Token* (1828–1842); some of the best of the *Twice-Told Tales* first appeared there. Goodrich's *Parley's Magazine* (1833–1844) also had some distinguished contributors.

Good Samaritan. See SAMARITAN, GOOD.

Good Soldier, The (1915). A novel by Ford Madox FORD. The narrator discovers that for the past nine years his wife has been the mistress of his best friend, Captain Ashburnham, the apparently honorable "Good Soldier" of the title. Conventional appearances and bitter truth are ironically juxtaposed.

Good Soldier Schweik, The (Osudy Dobrého Vojáka Švejka za Světové Války, 1920–23; Eng. translation, 1930). A novel by Jaroslav HAŠEK. The author originally planned this gargantuan satire on the military bureaucracy of Austria and on war in general as a six volume work, but lived to complete only four volumes. The novel chronicles the laughable misadventures of the kindhearted Schweik, which by their very absurdity point up the stupidity of war. The book has been variously hailed as a brilliant lampoon, as an epic defense of pacifism, and as a Czech *Don Quixote*.

Good Women, The Legend of. See LEGEND OF GOOD WOMEN.

Good Woman of Sezuan, The (Der gute Mensch von Sezuan; 1938–1940). A play by Bertolt BRECHT. Three gods come to earth to find a "good man," and the only person in the town of Sezuan who will give them shelter is the prostitute Shente. With the money they give her, she opens a tobacco shop, but her own natural charity soon brings her to bankruptcy. She disguises herself as a "male cousin," Shui Ta, and by ruthless business policies gains back the money she had benevolently given away. Basically, the play criticizes the social order in which a good person must pretend to be bad in order to survive.

Goody Blake and Harry Gill (1798). A poem by William WORDSWORTH. Gill is a farmer who forbids old Goody Blake to carry home a few sticks of firewood which she has picked up from his land. She curses him for his meanness, saying that he will never from that moment cease from shivering with cold, and from that hour, a-bed or up, summer or winter, at home or abroad, his teeth "chatter, chatter, chatter still."

Goody Two-shoes (1765). A nursery tale written for the publisher John Newbery by Oliver GOLDSMITH. Goody Two-shoes is a very poor child, whose delight at having a pair of shoes is so unbounded that she cannot forbear telling everyone she meets that she has "two shoes"; whence her name. In time, she acquires knowledge and becomes wealthy.

Googe, Barnabe (1540–1594). English poet and translator, best known for his volume of *Eclogues, Epitaphs and Sonnets* (1563), regarded as containing some of the earliest examples of pastoral poetry in English. His work is considered representative of English poetry between the period of WYATT and SURREY and that of SPENSER. It is particularly marked by alliteration and the use of the FOURTEENER, an iambic line of seven feet.

Gookin, Daniel (1612?–1687). English-born American author and colonial administrator. Known for his humanitarian interest in the Indians, in 1656 he was appointed superintendent of all the Indians who acknowledged the government of Massachusetts. He wrote *Historical Collections of the Indians in New England* (1792) and *An Historical Account of the Doings and Sufferings of the Christian Indians in New England* (1836).

Goose, Mother. A mythical character famous as giving the name to *Mother Goose's Nursery Rhymes*. This name seems to have been first used in English in *Songs for the Nursery, Or Mother Goose's Melodies for Children*, published by T. Fleet in Boston, Mass., in 1719. PERRAULT's *Contes de ma mère l'oye* (*Tales of my Mother Goose*) had appeared in 1697.

Goose Bible. See BIBLE, SPECIALLY NAMED EDITIONS.

goose step. A step formerly used in the Prussian army on ceremonial occasions. At each pace the thigh had to be brought to a right angle with the erect body. It was supposed to look extremely dignified when carried out by a well-drilled body of men, but it was unmercifully ridiculed by the Allies during World War I.

Gorboduc, or Ferrex and Porrex (produced 1561, published 1565). A play by Thomas Sackville and Thomas Norton, the first Senecan tragedy in English, the first English play to be written in blank verse, and one of the first to use English historical material. The story is based on the legendary history of England of Geoffrey of Monmouth. Gorboduc, a British king, has two sons, Ferrex and Porrex. He divides his kingdom between them, but they quarrel, and Porrex kills his brother. Soon afterward, Porrex himself is murdered in his bed by his mother, who loved Ferrex better. The people, horrified, rebel and kill both the old king and queen. The nobility then kill many of the rebels. Soon, since there are no heirs to the throne, the country falls into civil war and is laid waste.

Gorbodug. One of the kings in Geoffrey of Monmouth's HISTORY OF THE KINGS OF BRITAIN. He reappears in the pre-Shakespearean tragedy GORBODUC by Sackville and Norton.

Gordian knot. An intricate problem. Gordias, a peasant, was chosen king of Phrygia, and dedicated his wagon to Zeus. The wagon yoke was fastened to a pole so cleverly that it was said that whoever undid the knot would reign over the empire of Asia. Alexander cut the knot with a single stroke of his sword. "Cutting the Gordian knot" became proverbial for the decisive and bold completion of a complicated action.

Gordon, Caroline (1895–   ). American novelist and short-story writer. Miss Gordon received both critical and popular acclaim for her first novel, *Penhally* (1931), the story of three generations on a Kentucky plantation. Her other books include *Aleck Maury* (1934); *The Garden of Adonis* (1936); *None Shall Look Back* (1937), a fictional study of the Confederate general Nathan Bedford Forrest; *Green Centuries* (1941); *The Forest of the South* (1945), a collection of 17 skillfully written short stories; *The Women on the Porch* (1946); *The House of Fiction* (1950), a textbook written with Allen Tate; *The Malefactors* (1956); and *Old Red and Other Stories* (1963).

Gordon, Charles George. Known as **Chinese Gordon** and **Gordon Pasha** (1833–1885). English soldier. In 1860 he was attached to a British force operating with the French against China, and commanded a Chinese force, called the Ever Victorious Army, against the Taiping rebels (1863–1864). He quelled the rebellions after 33 engagements and resigning his command, was presented by the emperor with the yellow jacket and peacock's feather of a mandarin of the first class. He was governor (1874–1876) of the equatorial provinces of central Africa in the service of the khedive of Egypt and in 1877 was created pasha by the khedive. As governor-general (1877–1879) of the Sudan, Darfur, the equatorial provinces, and the Red Sea littoral, he suppressed slave trade. Sent by the British government in 1884 to the Sudan to assist the khedive in withdrawing the garrisons of the country, which could no longer hold out against the Mahdi, he was besieged by the Mahdi at Khartoum and killed in the storming of the city. There is a fine biographical sketch of Gordon in Lytton Strachey's *Eminent Victorians* (1918).

Gordon Riots. The riots that occurred in London in 1780, fomented by Lord George Gordon, to compel the House of Commons to repeal the bill passed in 1778 for the relief of Roman Catholics. Charles Dickens has given a very vivid description of these riots in BARNABY RUDGE.

Gorgias (c. 483–375 B.C.). A Greek philosopher, SOPHIST, and teacher of rhetoric. He exercised a great influence on the development of classical Greek style: Plato's dialogue on rhetoric is called *Gorgias*. His lost work, *On Nature or the Non-existent,* is believed to be a refutation of Presocratic argument for a fundamental principle of unity in the universe which underlies all appearances.

Gorgons (**Gorgones**). Monsters of classical myth. With golden wings and claws of brass, their hair was a mass of live serpents and their aspect was so terrible that all who looked at them were turned to stone. There were three: Stheno, Euryale, and Medusa, daughters of Keto and the aged sea-god Phorcys and sisters of the Graiae, who guarded them. MEDUSA, their chief, and the only mortal one, was slain by Perseus. The Gorgon's head was a favorite subject in ancient Greek art; because they believed that its power would terrify the enemy, the Greeks

carved it on shields and armor and even on city walls. It was also used as an amulet to protect against enchantment.

Goriot, Père. See PÈRE GORIOT, LE.

Gorki, Maksim. Pen name of **Aleksei Maksimovich Peshkov** (1868–1936). Russian writer. Gorki was the first great Russian writer to emerge from the ranks of the proletariat. Born in Nizhni Novgorod (now named Gorki), he was orphaned at an early age and lived for a brief time with his grandparents. Financial difficulties soon forced the boy at the age of nine to go into the world to make his own way. He was a dishwasher on a Volga steamer, bakery-shop worker, fisherman, railroadman, and clerk, as well as a down-and-outer, before he began to write. His hard life drove him to a suicide attempt in 1887. His pen name, Gorki, is the Russian equivalent of "the bitter one." His first published story, *Makar Chudra* (1892), appeared in a Tiflis newspaper. His stories, sketches, and articles were published in local newspapers in provincial towns, until they finally attracted the notice of the writer and journalist Vladimir Korolenko, who helped him get his first stories placed in journals in St. Petersburg. The first story to appear was *Chelkash* (1895). This was followed by a stream of stories, and in 1898 two volumes of Gorki's stories and sketches were issued. By then the one-time tramp was famous all over the country. Gorki's work of this period drew heavily on the kind of life he had himself experienced, which of necessity meant that most of his characters and themes were taken from the lowest level of Russian society. Gorki both depicted the wretched lives of this class of "creatures that once were men" and infused his stories with a heavy dose of protest against the society that allowed such wretchedness to exist. His most successful story of this period was TWENTY-SIX MEN AND A GIRL.

Gorki's popularity and financial success allowed him to embark on a longer work: his first novel, *Foma Gordeyev* (1899), a study of a declining bourgeois merchant family in a Volga town. In the meantime, he had moved to St. Petersburg and founded a publishing house, *Znaniye* (*Knowledge*), that was later to publish such well-known writers as Andreyev, Kuprin, and Bunin. He also joined the Social-Democratic Party and contributed much of his literary earnings to furthering the Marxist revolutionary movement. This activity displeased the government, and, when he was elected an honorary member of the Russian Academy of Sciences in 1902, the government vetoed the choice. The authors Anton Chekhov and Vladimir Korolenko promptly resigned their memberships in protest.

Gorki's formerly romantically tinged realistic pictures of lower-class life became increasingly grim and angry. The most forceful expression of his attitude is the drama THE LOWER DEPTHS, his second play, regarded as his dramatic masterpiece. Gorki's first play was *The Petit-Bourgeois* (*Méshchanye;* 1901), an indictment of the philistinism of that class.

For his Bolshevik activities in the revolution of 1905, Gorki was arrested. Public indignation forced his release and he went abroad, visiting Europe and the U.S. and settling on Capri. In 1907, he issued his didactic novel about the revolutionary movement, MOTHER. Although artistically weak, the book's mes sage has made it a favorite with Soviet literary hucksters. *Tales of Italy* (*Skazki ob Itali;* 1911–1912) depicted the lives of the Italian working classes. The next years saw the production of one of Gorki's best works, his autobiographical trilogy. The first part, CHILDHOOD, appeared in 1913–1914. The second part, *In the World* (*V lyudakh*), came out in 1916, and the third volume, *My Universities* (*Moi universitety*), in 1923.

Gorki had been allowed to return to Russia in 1913. His former sympathy with the Bolsheviks had abated somewhat. He saw unbridled violence as a threat to the existence of what had been worthwhile in the cultural life of the past. When the advocates of proletarian Marxism attempted to sweep away the cultural past, Gorki did what he could to save it. He organized the publishing venture, *Vsemirnaya literatura* (*World Literature*), which helped many writers earn enough bread to stay alive during the chaotic months following the revolution. He also helped establish a "House of Arts" (*Dom iskusstv*) and a "House of Scholars" (*Dom uchonykh*), which offered writers a place to stay and, more important, a place to work. This aspect of Gorki's activity has caused him to be called a bridge between the old classical culture of Russia and the new Soviet culture.

The influence Gorki had with the Bolshevik leaders was often used to good advantage to help writers who were down and out or in trouble with the new regime. He, also, was active in discovering and encouraging new writers, such as Vsevolod Ivanov and Konstantin Fedin. Thus, he helped both to preserve the old culture and foster the new.

In 1921, Gorki, weakened by his strenuous work load, went abroad for a rest. He remained in Italy until 1928. During this period, beside the third volume of his autobiography, he wrote two novels—*The Artamonov Business* (*Delo Artamonovykh;* 1925) and *The Life of Klim Samgin* (*Zhizn Klima Samgina;* 1927–1936)—and two plays produced after his return to Russia—*Yegor Bulychov and Others* (*Yegor Bulychov i drugiye;* 1931) and *Dostigayev and Others* (*Dostigayev i drugiye;* 1932). The plays and *The Artamonov Business* all deal with the same theme, the decay of merchant families. *The Life of Klim Samgin,* a huge work of which four volumes were finished, also treats the decline of a particular class, the intelligentsia.

After his return to the Soviet Union, Gorki helped develop the literary doctrine of SOCIALIST REALISM, which was formed in 1932. His own ideas about what he meant by socialist realism differed somewhat from official doctrine as it was later interpreted.

Gorki died in 1936, while undergoing medical treatment. In the 1937–1938 purge trials, the ex-secret police chief Yagoda confessed that Gorki's death was ordered by him as part of a so-called Trotskyite plot. The real truth of the matter is still unknown.

Gorki's fictional work generally suffers from lack of a controlled style and a tendency to overindulge in philosophical discourse. His place in Russian literature is secure, however, for his autobiographical trilogy and for his *Reminiscences* (*Vospominaniya;* 1919) of Tolstoi, Chekhov, and Andreyev, which are full of sharp insights and interesting anecdotes.

Gorky, Arshile (1904–1948). Armenian-born American painter. A native of Turkish Armenia, Gorky came to the U.S. in 1920. A precise draftsman, he combined rich color and nongeometric forms derived from nature to create increasingly surrealistic works of art.

Görres, Joseph von (1776–1848). German scholar and political writer. He was a friend of BRENTANO and Arnim. His best-known scholarly work is *Die deutschen Volksbücher* (*The German Folk-books,* 1807), in which the word VOLKSBUCH was first used in its present sense. Politically, he was violently anti-Napoleonic during the French domination of Germany and expressed his views in the newspaper *Rheinischer Merkur* (*Rhenish Mercury*) which he founded in 1814. After Napoleon's defeat, however, he came into conflict with the Prussian government and was forced into exile in 1816.

Gospels. See MATTHEW, THE GOSPEL ACCORDING TO ST.; MARK, THE GOSPEL ACCORDING TO ST.; LUKE, THE GOSPEL ACCORDING TO ST.; JOHN, THE GOSPEL ACCORDING TO ST.

Gösta Berlings saga (1891). A novel of Swedish life by Selma LAGERLÖF. It relates the adventures of the impulsive and temperamental young hero, whose magnetic personality inevitably draws people to him. His turbulent passions just as inevitably involve him, and those attracted to him, in misfortune. Eventually he marries the Countess Elizabeth, whose husband has divorced her. Through Elizabeth's influence and his own efforts, he is able to begin a life that more nearly approximates his ideals.

Gotham, wise men of. Fools, wiseacres. The legend is that King John, on his way to Lynn Regis, intended to pass through Gotham, in Nottinghamshire, with his army, and sent heralds to prepare his way. The men of Gotham were resolved, if possible, to prevent this expense and depredation, so they resolved to play the fool. Some raked the moon out of the pond; some made a ring to hedge in a bird; others did equally foolish things. The king then abandoned his intention, and "the wise men" of the village cunningly remarked, "We ween there are more fools pass through Gotham than remain in it."

A collection of popular tales of stupidity was published in the reign of Henry VIII as *Merie Tales of the Mad Men of Gotham, gathered together by A.B. of Phisike, Doctour.* Since that date many other tales have been attached to the inhabitants of Gotham. The old nursery rhyme is well known:

> Three wise men of Gotham
> Went to sea in a bowl;
> If the bowl had been stronger
> My story had been longer.

The name *Gotham* was given to New York City by Washington Irving in his satirical *Salmagundi Papers* (1807) and has remained in current use.

Gothic novel. A type of novel characterized by horror, violence, supernatural effects, and a taste for the medieval, usually set against a background of Gothic architecture, especially a gloomy and isolated castle. The genre originated in England with Horace Walpole's CASTLE OF OTRANTO. In its early forms, and even as late as THE MYSTERIES OF UDOLPHO by Mrs. Ann Radcliffe, the supernatural is given a naturalistic explanation, the aim being to produce a "correct," i.e. probable, medieval romance. Even so, its excesses produced a satirical reaction as in Jane Austen's NORTHANGER ABBEY, while conversely, in William Beckford's VATHEK, where Gothic terrors merge with the terrors of an Oriental despotism, the very monstrosities themselves seem to verge on parody. Matthew Lewis' THE MONK marks a new departure: its horrors are frankly supernatural, but psychologically symbolic. This development culminates in MELMOTH THE WANDERER by Charles Robert Maturin, and, in America, in novels by Charles Brockden BROWN, Nathaniel HAWTHORNE, and Edgar Allan POE. A similar development took place on the Continent, especially in Germany. In the 20th century, the movement of SURREALISM claimed the Gothic novel as one of its forerunners.

Götterdämmerung. See RAGNAROK.

Gottfried von Strassburg (early 13th century). German minnesinger or court poet. His handling of the Tristan and Iseult legend (c. 1210) was one of the best court epics in Germany; it was the major source for Wagner's opera *Tristan und Isolde* (1865).

Gotthelf, Jeremias. Pen name of **Albert Bitzius** (1797–1854). Swiss novelist, writing in German, known especially for his conservative, didactic piety which is, however, sometimes lightened by humor. He was a well-established Protestant pastor for more than a decade before beginning to write his many novels about peasant life, such as *Der Bauernspiegel* (*The Peasants' Mirror*, 1837), *Wie Uli, der Knecht, glücklich wird* (*How Uli, the Servant, Becomes Happy*, 1841), and *Elsi, die seltsame Magd* (*Elsie, the Strange Maid*, 1850). His novella *Die schwarze Spinne* (*The Black Spider*, 1842) is a masterful treatment of the occult.

Göttinger Hain (Göttingen Grove). An association of German poets formed in 1772, most of whose members were students at the University of Göttingen. The name Hain (grove) was drawn from a poem by Klopstock, whom the young poets took as their model. Some members were Voss, Hölty, and the brothers Stolberg. Bürger was close to the group, but not a member. The tendencies of the group, which dispersed in 1774, were related to those of the STURM UND DRANG movement.

Gottlieb, Max. In Sinclair Lewis' ARROWSMITH, an old, disillusioned, but dedicated scientist who helps to train Arrowsmith in research methods. Gottlieb may have been modeled on Jacques Loeb (1859–1924), the great biophysiologist on the staff of the Rockefeller Institute for Medical Research (1910–1924).

Gottsched, Johann Christoph (1700–1766). German aesthetician and dramatist of the enlightenment, under the influence of French neo-classicism. He was strongly opposed by such figures as Bodmer and Lessing, who advocated artistic directions less dependent upon foreign models. His most famous play is *Der sterbende Cato* (*The Dying Cato*, 1732).

Götz von Berlichingen (1773). A play by Johann Wolfgang von GOETHE, freely adapted from the life of Götz von Berlichingen (1480–1562), a German knight. In Goethe's treatment, Götz becomes a typical STURM UND DRANG hero, a powerful individual personality, unwaveringly committed to his own straightforward conception of justice, but in the end not able to escape the subtle maneuverings of his political adversaries. Formally, Goethe wished to emulate Shakespeare, in opposition to the prevailing style of neoclassicism, and the play is written in a powerful, rough-and-ready prose, with short pithy scenes and constant changes of setting between them. See DAEMONIC.

Goudge, Elizabeth (1900–   ). English novelist. Her popular novels sensitively evoke the English countryside, English history, and the world of children. Among them are *A City of Bells* (1936), *Towers in the Mist* (1938), *Green Dolphin Street* (1944), *Gentian Hill* (1950), *The Rosemary Tree* (1956), and *The Scent of Water* (1963). *The Little White Horse* (1947) is a book for children.

Gould, Charles. A central character in Joseph Conrad's novel NOSTROMO, the owner of a silver mine in South America. Doña Emilia is his gentle wife.

Gounod, Charles François (1818–1893). French composer. His best-known operas are *Faust* (1859) and *Roméo et Juliette* (1867). He at first wrote sacred music; among his songs is the famous *Ave Maria* based on Bach's first prelude of the *Well Tempered Clavier.*

Gourmont, Rémy de (1858–1915). French literary critic and novelist. In his early years as a critic, Gourmont wrote perceptive, sympathetic articles on the symbolist poets, published in *Le Livre des masques* (1896) and *Promenades littéraires* (1904–1913). His novels, rather chilly in tone, emphasize the biological origins of all human behavior. They include *Les Chevaux de Diomède* (1897), *Le Songe d'une Femme* (1899), *Une Nuit au Luxembourg* (1906), and *Un Cœur Virginal* (1907). Among his essays are *L'Esthétique de la Langue Française* (1899), *Le Problème du Style* (1902), and *Physique de l'Amour* (1903). These are marked by irony, an interest in the sensual, and a quick, probing intelligence. Disfigured by a skin disease, Gourmont spent much of his life in seclusion.

Gower, John (1325?–1408). English poet, a friend of Chaucer, well known at the courts of Richard II and Henry IV. He wrote serious poetry of the allegorical and didactic type common in his day, urging moral and social reforms. His principal works are the French SPECULUM MEDITANTIS, the Latin VOX CLAMANTIS, and the English CONFESSIO AMANTIS, as well as some lighter short poems in all three languages.

Goya y Lucientes, Francisco José de (1746–1828). Spanish painter and etcher. He worked for the Royal Workshop as a designer of cartoons and became Royal Painter in 1786. After the death of Charles III he went on to serve his son, Charles IV, portraying the king, his family, and the nobility in brilliant, often cruelly truthful paintings which rank among the most discerning in the world of art. A severe disease left him deaf at 47, yet the following years mark the peak of his fame. The injustice and inhumanity of the period of the Spanish War of Independence against Napoleon's occupation (1808–1814) and of Ferdinand VII's reign (1814–1820) elicited a tortured reaction from him. He painted scenes of disasters, madness, and satanism, and executed the series of etchings entitled *The Disasters of War,* in which he indicted violence and murder with bitter realism and censured the moral dishonesty of those who would not rebel against human misery. In 1823, Goya left for Bordeaux, in France, where he continued to paint with unshaken confidence and originality. He left an extensive production: portraits, religious paintings, scenes of the Inquisition, of crime, of the people's everyday work, engravings of war and the bullfight. The paintings were little known outside Spain until 1896, and *The Disasters of War* were not published till 1863, yet Goya exerted a profound influence on modern art. Eugène Delacroix, Honoré Daumier, and Edouard Manet were among the first to be influenced by his visionary representation of the world and by his approach to art, from which he banished all academic conceptions of composition and draftsmanship in order to give color the double role of unifying loosely constructed paintings and of defining the forms.

Gozzano, Guido (1883–1916). Italian poet. Afflicted by poor health throughout his short life, Gozzano is best known for his lyric poetry, collected in *I Primi e gli Ultimi Colloqui* (1927). Although he was originally influenced by D'Annunzio, his work reveals a melancholy, passive attitude toward life that aligns him with the CREPUSCOLARI poets.

Gozzi, Count Carlo (1720–1806). Italian playwright. A member of the Granelleschi Society, whose purpose it was to preserve Tuscan literature from foreign influences, Gozzi ignored theatrical innovation and produced charming and witty plays, many of them dramatized versions of fairy tales. Goethe and Mme. de Staël, among others, were admirers of his work. His play *Re Turandot* (*King Turandot*, 1762) was translated into German by Schiller, and became the basis for operas by Weber, Busoni, and Puccini. *Fiaba dell' amore delle tre melarancie* (*Fable of the Love of Three Oranges*, 1761), which was derived from Basile's *Cunto delli Cunti* and presented the two rival dramatists Goldoni and Chiari under the satirical guises of a fairy and a magician, revived the stock characters of the Italian comedy of masks and enjoyed a huge popular success. Almost a century and a half later, it was used by Prokofiev as the basis for his opera *The Love of Three Oranges*. A portion of Gozzi's output was modeled on Spanish plays, and his later works include tragedies in which he experimentally introduced comic elements.

Gozzoli, Benozzo, or **Benozzo di Lese** (1420–1497). Italian painter. One of the leading figures of the early Florentine Renaissance, he was a pupil of Fra Angelico and strongly influenced by Gentile da Fabriano. His forte was the large-scale narrative fresco, in which he combined Italian realism and Gothic fantasy in a delightful way. For his patrons, the Medici, he decorated the chapel of their palace in Florence and included portraits of the family in his masterpiece, *The Journey of the Magi*. He is also known for his Old Testament scenes painted at the *campo santo* of Pisa, especially the *Story of Noah*.

Grabbe, Christian Dietrich (1801–1836). German playwright, known especially for the ironic, often pessimistically cynical and disillusioned attitude that permeates his works. His style is an early example of the 19th-century turn toward realism, away from the idealism of such dramatists as Schiller. Among his works are *Scherz, Satire, Ironie und tiefere Bedeutung* (*Joke, Satire, Irony and Deeper Significance,* pub. 1827) and *Don Juan und Faust* (1829).

Graça Aranha, José Pereira de (1868–1931). Brazilian diplomat, novelist, and man of letters. A champion of nationalism in literature, Graça Aranha is best known for *Canaan* (*Chanaan;* 1902). A novel of ideas, it consists largely of a conversation between two Germans, newcomers to Brazil, who discuss the development of the Brazilian nation.

Gracchi. A prominent family of republican Rome. Its most famous members were **Tiberius Sempronius Gracchus** (163?–133 B.C.) and his brother **Gaius Sempronius Gracchus** (d. 123 B.C.). As tribune (133), Tiberius secured the enactment, despite much opposition, of an agrarian reform law that would grant public lands to the impoverished Italian peasantry. When, in defiance of custom, he sought a second term as tribune, he and 300 of his followers were killed in an election riot.

His work was carried on by Gaius who, as tribune in 123 and 122, sought to regulate the price of grain in Rome and proposed extension of the franchise. Like his brother, he was killed at the instigation of the senate.

The mother of the Gracchi brothers was the famous Cornelia, daughter of SCIPIO AFRICANUS, who was considered the ideal Roman matron. According to tradition, she was once visited by a wealthy woman who displayed her jewels and asked to see Cornelia's. Pointing to her sons, Cornelia replied, "These are my jewels."

Grace Abounding to the Chief of Sinners (1666). An autobiography by John BUNYAN. Written while he was in prison, it describes his spiritual struggles and the development of his religious convictions.

Graces, the. In Roman mythology, the Gratiae, goddesses who embodied beauty and charm. Called by the Greeks the Charites, they were, by some accounts, named Aglaia (Brilliance), Thalia (the Flowering), and Euphrosyne (Joy), though their names and even their number varied. Although they were probably very early spirits of vegetation, they did not in classical times have any cult of importance. They are best known from their many appearances in art.

Gracián, Baltasar (1601–1658). Spanish prose writer and Jesuit priest. The outstanding exponent of CONCEPTISM, Gracián has been variously regarded as a moral philosopher of considerable depth and as an unoriginal intellectual poseur. His best-known works are EL CRITICÓN, an allegorical novel, and *Agudeza y arte de ingenio* (1642, 1648), a manual of conceptism, in which he defined the numerous varieties of literary *agudeza* ("fine distinction, ingenuity"). In *El Héroe* (1637), he drew a portrait of the ideal Christian hero. *El Discreto* (1646) discusses the 25 *realces,* or "adornments," which make up the well-bred gentleman, while the *Oráculo manual o arte de prudencia* (1647) is a collection of 300 maxims that offer a distillation of worldly wisdom.

gracioso. A comic servant in Spanish drama. Although the character appeared under the name of *simple* or *bobo* in the works of earlier dramatists, such as Torres Naharro and Lope de Rueda, Lope de Vega is often regarded as its creator.

Gracq, Julien. Pen name of **Louis Poirier** (1910–). French novelist and playwright. His works share a haunting mood partly Gothic, partly surrealistic, and an impressionistic, symbolic style. His novels include *The Castle of Argol* (1945), *A Dark Stranger* (*Un beau ténébreux;* 1945), and *Balcony in the Forest* (1958).

Gradasso. Oriental monarch who besieges Charlemagne at Paris in Boiardo's ORLANDO INNAMORATO; in Ariosto's ORLANDO FURIOSO, he is killed by Orlando and the other paladins in a battle to which he had challenged them.

Graeae (Graiai). Literally, the gray-haired women. In Greek myth, the sisters and guardians of the GORGONS. They owned only one eye and one tooth among them, which they shared in turn. PERSEUS, robbing them of these, forced them to show him the way to the Gorgons, and to give him their winged sandals, magic wallet, and cap of invisibility. Hesiod mentions only two Graeae, Enyo and Pephredo; later legends add a third, Deino.

Graham, Stephen (1884–   ). English travelwriter. He traveled mostly in Russia, writing about his experiences and the history and literature of the country in such books as *Undiscovered Russia* (1913) and *Summing Up on Russia* (1951). He tramped the American West with Vachel Lindsay and wrote *Tramping with a Poet in the Rockies* (1922).

Grahame, Kenneth (1859–1932). English author of children's books and essays. He wrote THE WIND IN THE WILLOWS, *The Golden Age* (1895), and *Dream Days* (1898).

Graham of Claverhouse, John. 1st Viscount **Dundee.** Known as **Bloody Claverse** and **Bonny Dundee** (1649?–1689). Scottish soldier. He was dubbed "Bloody Claverse" by the Scottish COVENANTERS, whom he persecuted with great severity for 20 years. In 1689 he raised an army of Highlanders to fight for James II and won the battle of Killiecrankie, but was mortally wounded. To Jacobites he became known as "Bonny Dundee," a semilegendary hero. He is a character in Scott's novel *Old Mortality* (1816).

Grail, Holy Grail, or **Sangreal (Sangraal).** A famous talisman (variously represented as a chalice, dish, stone, and cup into which a lance drips blood), the center around which a huge corpus of medieval legend, romance, and allegory revolve. The precise origin and nature of the Grail is unknown and has been the subject of countless scholarly researches; these have attempted to sort out the features of ancient fertility cults, Celtic myth, and Christianity in the Grail romances. The Grail is best known as the object of a quest on the part of the knights of the ROUND TABLE in Arthurian legend. It brings healing and food to those who touch it and can be found only by one absolutely pure.

The best-known accounts of the Grail are those that give it a Christian origin and generally run along the following lines: It is the vessel from which Christ drank at the Last Supper and that afterwards came into the possession of JOSEPH OF ARIMATHEA who caught in it some of the blood that flowed from the wounds of the crucified Saviour. He carried it with him to England, and it provided him with food, drink, and spiritual sustenance for the rest of his life. It was handed down to his successor and thence from generation to generation, GALAHAD, in Malory's *Morte d'Arthur* (c. 1469), being Joseph's last descendant. In some accounts it disappears after Joseph brings it to England. In still others, it is the

dish out of which Christ and his disciples ate the paschal lamb at the Last Supper. The theory of a Christian origin of the Grail, however, has been abandoned. Many now hold that the Grail was originally a female sex symbol used with the bleeding lance mentioned in Chrétien de Troyes' early account in ancient fertility rites. Jessie L. Weston's discussion of this theory in *From Ritual to Romance* (1920) was the source used by T. S. Eliot for his poem *The Waste Land* (1922), where the Grail theme occurs in this symbolic form.

The mass of literature concerning the Grail cycle, both ancient and modern, is enormous. The chief sources of the principal groups of legend are the *Peredur* in the *Mabinogion,* which is one of the most archaic forms of the story; the unfinished *Perceval, ou le conte du Graal* by Chrétien de Troyes, in which the Grail is a hollow dish, accompanied by a bleeding lance (see PERCIVAL); Wolfram von Eschenbach's PARSIFAL (c. 1210), the best example of the story as transformed by ecclesiastical influence; a chivalric version by Gottfried von Strassburg; the 13th-century French *Percival le Gallois* (founded on earlier English and Celtic legends that had no connection with the Grail), showing Percival in his later role as an ascetic hero, translated by Dr. Sebastian Evans (1893) as *The High History of the Holy Grail;* and the *Quête du St. Graal,* which, in its English dress, is found in Malory's *Morte d'Arthur.* It was the French poet Robert de Boron (fl., c. 1215), who, in his *Joseph d'Arimathie ou Le Saint Graal,* first definitely attached the history of the Grail to the Arthurian cycle and first mentioned the Grail as a chalice containing Christ's blood. The framework of Tennyson's *Holy Grail* in his *Idylls of the King* (1859–1885), is taken from Malory.

Gráinne. See PURSUIT OF DIARMUID AND GRÁINNE, THE.

Grand Canal. The chief water thoroughfare of Venice, Italy.

Grande Demoiselle, La. See Duchesse de MONTPENSIER.

Grandet, Eugénie. See EUGÉNIE GRANDET.

Grandgousier (*Fr.,* "great gullet"). In Rabelais GARGANTUA AND PANTAGRUEL, the king of Utopia, husband of Gargamelle, and father of Gargantua. Grandgousier, a just and peace-loving patriarch who lives at the Devinière, the house where Rabelais was born, has been identified with the latter's own father.

Grand Inquisitor, The Legend of the. In Feodor Dostoevski's THE BROTHERS KARAMAZOV, the parable related by Ivan to Alyosha, expressing the former's religious doubts. The tale relates how Christ returns to earth in Seville during the Inquisition, how He is recognized by the people, and immediately arrested by the Inquisition leaders. The Grand Inquisitor, a menacing old churchman, visits Christ's cell and upbraids Him for returning, saying that the Church no longer needs Him, that He has misapprehended man's nature and has burdened man with too much freedom. The Church, says the Inquisitor, understands that man does not want the burden of free choice but wants to be led. The Church's allegiance has been shifted to the Other, to the Devil, the Inquisitor claims, and Christ is now only an unwanted distraction. Henceforth, he says, man will be cared for by the few leaders of the Church who are strong enough to take on themselves the burden of freedom and to guide the weak masses. At the end of his tirade, the Inquisitor throws open the cell door and orders Christ to leave and never return. Christ, who has been silent throughout the interview, answers the old man with a kiss on the cheek before leaving, presumably an expression of His love even for the unbeliever.

The Grand Inquisitor is the most famous single section of the novel and is often excerpted as an independent piece for anthologies, although its thematic connections with the novel as a whole are strong. The ideas it expresses have been considered formulations of Dostoevski's own religious doubts.

Grandison, Charlotte. In Samuel Richardson's last novel, SIR CHARLES GRANDISON, the witty and inconsiderate sister of the hero, and major correspondent of Harriet Byron. Her flippant treatment of her husband Lord G., at once amusing and shocking, is in studied contrast to Harriet's serious affection for Sir Charles.

Grandison, Sir Charles. See SIR CHARLES GRANDISON.

Grandissimes, The: A Story of Creole Life (1880). A novel by George W. CABLE. It is set in New Orleans in the period of the Louisiana Purchase. An outside observer, Frowenfeld, learns of the family feuds, especially those between the De Grapions and the Grandissimes, the race feuds, and the struggle between the new order and the old. The book is filled with vivid characters, notably the Creole mother and daughter Nancanou, and the African king Bras Coupé, who allows himself to be tortured to death rather than be a slave.

Grand Meaulnes, Le (1913; translated as **The Wanderer** and **The Lost Domain**). The novel that won ALAIN-FOURNIER his reputation. Le Grand Meaulnes, the young hero, has a curious adventure at Christmastime. In the middle of the woods he discovers a gay party and a beautiful girl both hidden in an old house. His love for the girl, Yvonne, and his friendship with her brother, Franz, shape his life, bringing him intense joy and intense sorrow. The uniqueness of the novel lies in its delicate combination of fantasy and realism. Actuality and the dream world mingle indistinguishably in the experience of a young boy coming to manhood.

Grandonio of Volterra. In the ORLANDO FURIoso of Ariosto, a pagan knight from Spain, noted for his rude and discourteous manner. He is defeated by the warrior maiden Bradamante.

Grand Remonstrance. In English history, the protest passed by the House of Commons on Nov. 22, 1641. It listed the unconstitutional acts of Charles I and demanded reform.

Gran Galeoto, El (The Great Galeoto, 1881). A tragedy by José ECHEGARAY, in which spiteful gossip is the "GALEOTO" of the title. The heroine is suspected by the spying public and finally by her husband, Julian, of improper relations with his young secretary, Ernest. They are innocent, but are powerless to convince Julian, who dies from a wound received in a duel for his wife's honor.

Grani (gray-colored). Siegfried's horse, of marvelous swiftness.

Granich, Irving. See Michael GOLD.

Grant, Ulysses S[impson] (1882–1885). Ameri-can soldier and 18th president of the U.S. (1869–1877). A graduate of West Point and a veteran of the Mexican War, Grant later engaged unsuccessfully in farming and business. He entered the Union army in 1861 and after capturing Forts Henry and Donelson in Tennessee (1862), was promoted to major-general; he led the Union forces at SHILOH and captured Vicksburg (1863), splitting the Confederacy in half. Appointed commander-in-chief of the Union army in 1864, he moved against Richmond, the Confederate capital, in a slow and costly but ultimately successful campaign and accepted the surrender of General Lee at Appomattox Courthouse. His two presidential terms were marred by extensive graft and corruption that involved such highly placed officials as Secretary of War W. W. Belknap and O. E. Babcock, Grant's private secretary. After his retirement, Grant was left penniless through the failure of a brokerage firm, but his *Personal Memoirs* (1885), which he completed while dying of throat cancer, brought his family nearly $500,000.

Gran teatro del mundo, El (The Great Theater of the World). An AUTO SACRAMENTAL by Pedro CALDERÓN DE LA BARCA. It deals with the world in terms of a theatrical allegory. The Author (God) presents a performance in which a beggar, a rich man, and other figures, including personifications of vices and virtues, play out their roles. The play demonstrates that the things of this world pass away and only God is eternal.

Grantly, Archdeacon. See BARSETSHIRE, CHRONICLES OF.

Grantorto. See FAERIE QUEENE, THE.

Granville-Barker, Harley (1877–1946). English critic, dramatist, director, and actor. Before World War I, Granville-Barker was noted both as an actor, specializing in Shavian roles, and as the author of such plays as THE VOYSEY INHERITANCE and THE MADRAS HOUSE. In 1911–1913 his staging of *The Winter's Tale, A Midsummer Night's Dream,* and *Twelfth Night* effected a radical change in Shakespeare production. Today Granville-Barker is best known for his critical works, such as his *Prefaces to Shakespeare* (1923–1947), which analyze the plays from a director's point of view, and *A Companion to Shakespeare Studies* (1934), which he edited with G. B. Harrison.

Grapes of Wrath, The (1939). A novel by John STEINBECK. Awarded the Pulitzer Prize in 1940, this moving and highly successful proletarian novel tells of the hardships of the Joad family. "Okie" farmers forced out of their home in the Oklahoma dust-bowl region by economic desperation, they drive to California in search of work as migrant fruitpickers. The grandparents die on the way; on their arrival the others are harassed by the police and participate in strike violence, during which Tom, the Joad son, kills a man. At the conclusion of the novel, throughout which descriptive and philosophical passages alternate with narrative portions, the family is defeated but still resolute.

Graspall. See FURRY LAWCATS.

Gratiae. See GRACES, THE.

Gratiano. (1) In Shakespeare's MERCHANT OF VENICE, a friend of Antonio and Bassanio. He "speaks an infinite deal of nothing, more than any man in all Venice." Gratiano marries Nerissa, the waiting-gentlewoman of Portia.

(2) In Shakespeare's OTHELLO, the brother of Brabantio and uncle of Desdemona.

Grattan, Henry (1746–1820). Irish orator and statesman. He was a persistent advocate of Irish independence and Catholic emancipation. In 1782, when the legislative independence of Ireland was gained by Grattan and the "Protestant Volunteers," the British Parliament gave up the right to pass laws binding upon Ireland.

gratuitous act. See André GIDE.

Grau [Delgado], Jacinto (1877–1958). Spanish playwright. His output, though small, is appreciated both at home and abroad, and includes *El conde Alarcos* (1917), *El hijo pródigo* (1918), *Don Juan de Carillana* (1919), and *El señor de Pigmalión* (1930).

Grau, Shirley Ann (1929–). American short-story writer and novelist. Born in New Orleans and raised in Alabama, Miss Grau writes subtly and realistically of Southerners, black and white, in *The Black Prince and Other Stories* (1955). *The Hard Blue Sky* (1958) and *The House on Coliseum Street* (1961) are novels.

Graustark (1901). A romantic novel by George Barr McCUTCHEON. Subtitled *The Story of a Love Behind the Throne,* this enormously popular melodrama tells how an American named Grenfall falls in love with the Princess Yetive in the highly colorful kingdom of Graustark. McCutcheon's first novel, it was sold outright for $500 to a publisher who subsequently reaped a fortune from it. It was followed, however, by the sequels *Beverly of Graustark* (1904) and *The Prince of Graustark* (1914), which were equally and more equitably profitable.

Graves, Alfred Perceval (1846–1931). Irish man of letters and poet. The father of Robert GRAVES, he was a leader in the Irish literary renaissance. Among his works are *Songs of Killarney* (1872) and *Irish Songs and Ballads* (1879).

Graves, Morris (1910–). American artist. Deeply influenced by the spirituality of the Far East, he is known chiefly for his somber expressionistic paintings of birds.

Graves, Robert (1895–). English poet, novelist, and critic. His individualistic poems are polished and dryly humorous; often they make cosmic statements through quaint personal myths. Among his many collections of poetry are *Fairies and Fusiliers* (1917), *Collected Poems* (1959), *More Poems* (1961), and *New Poems* (1962). *Goodbye to All That* (1929) is a striking autobiography covering his experiences fighting in World War I.

Graves's historical novels are scholarly and mischievous; he often interprets his characters in psychologically convincing ways that are quite different from the conventional, traditional view. *I, Claudius* (1934), CLAUDIUS THE GOD, *Wife to Mr. Milton* (1943), *The Golden Fleece* (1944), *King Jesus* (1946), and *Homer's Daughter* (1955) are novels of this kind. Among his books of literary criticism are *A Survey of Modernist Poetry* (1927), with Laura Riding as co-author; THE WHITE GODDESS; and *Oxford Addresses on Poetry* (1962). *The Long Week-End* (1940) is a social history of the interwar years in England. *The Nazarene Gospel Restored* (1953), with Joshua

Podro as co-author, is a bold, scholarly reinterpretation of the origins of Christianity. He translated and commented on *The Greek Myths* (1955). Graves was a friend of T. E. Lawrence and Laura Riding, and encouraged the young English writer Alan Sillitoe. After having lived in Majorca for many years, he returned to England in 1961 to become professor of poetry at Oxford University.

Graveyard by the Sea, The. See CIMETIÈRE MARIN, LE.

graveyard school. A preromantic movement in English poetry of the 18th century, composed chiefly of followers and imitators of Edward YOUNG and Robert BLAIR. It is so named because of the meditative, melancholy tone of the characteristic verse of the school, the scene of which was often laid in graveyards and cemeteries, and because of the moral and religious reflections inspired by their thoughts of impending death.

Gray, Asa (1810–1888). American botanist and teacher. A professor at Harvard, he published a series of scientific studies of American flora and several textbooks. Among these are *Elements of Botany* (1836), *Manual of Botany of the Northern U.S.* (1848), and *How Plants Grow* (1858). Highly regarded by scholars, Gray made Harvard a center of botanical research in America.

Gray, Thomas (1716–1771). English poet and noted letter-writer. He was one of the forerunners of the romantic movement in England. His most important correspondence was with Horace Walpole, Thomas Wharton, and William Mason. His works, largely meditative lyrics and Pindaric odes are marked by love of nature and melancholy reflection. His poetry includes *Ode to Spring, Hymn to Adversity,* and *Ode on a Distant Prospect of Eton College* (1742); *Sonnet on the Death of Richard West* (1775), which contains the well-known lines ". . . where ignorance is bliss, 'Tis folly to be wise"; *Ode on the Death of a Favorite Cat, Drowned in A Tub of Gold Fishes* (1748), light verse in the neoclassic manner; ELEGY WRITTEN IN A COUNTRY CHURCHYARD, his most famous work; *The Progress of Poesy,* on the power of music; THE BARD; *The Fatal Sisters* and *The Descent of Odin* (1761), both in imitation of early Welsh and Norse verse. The biography published by his friend and correspondent William Mason, in 1775, contains many of his famous letters.

Gray expressed his poetic ideal thus: "Extreme conciseness of expression, yet pure, perspicuous, and musical, is one of the grand beauties of lyric poetry. This I have always aimed at, and never could attain." See STOKE POGES.

Grazzini, Anton Francesco (1503–1584). Florentine apothecary and author of stories and plays. He was also a founder of the Academy of the *Umidi,* in which his academic name was *Il Lasca* (the Roach). One of his plays, *La Spiritata (The Possessed),* has been translated into English under the title of *The Bugbears.*

Great Awakening. A religious revivalist movement (1740–1750) which swept through the American colonies and was marked by violent and sensational public repentance and conversion. It began in Massachusetts under the influence of the preaching of Jonathan EDWARDS and of the English evangelist George Whitefield. The movement was opposed by

S I N N E R S
In the Hands of an
Angry G O D.
A SERMON

Preached at *Enfield,* *July* 8th 1 7 4 1.

At a Time of great Awakenings ; and attended with remarkable Impreffions on many of the Hearers.

By *Jonathan Edwards,* A.M.
Paftor of the Church of CHRIST in *Northampton.*

Amos ix 2, 3. *Though they dig into Hell, thence fhall mine Hand take them ; though they climb up to Heaven, thence will I bring them down. And though they hide themfelves in the Top of Carmel, I will fearch and take them out thence ; and though they be hid from my Sight in the Bottom of the Sea, thence I will command the Serpent, and he fhall bite them.*

The Second Edition.

? T O N : Printed and Sold by S. KNEELAND ". GREEN in Queen-Street over againft the 1 7 4 2.

A popular sermon published during the Great Awakening.

a liberal group led by Charles CHAUNCEY whose ideas led in time to the doctrine of Unitarianism.

Great Bear and **Little Bear (Ursa Major** and **Ursa Minor).** Constellations. In Greek legend, Callisto, a nymph of Artemis, had a son by Zeus. His wife Hera (or Zeus himself) changed Callisto into a bear. When she was about to be shot by her son Arcas, Zeus converted mother and son into constellations. The name given to the two constellations considered as a single group, is Arctos.

The Greek word *arktos,* a bear, is still kept in the names Arcturus (the bear-ward, from *ouros,* guardian), and Arctic. The Sanskrit name for the Great Bear is from the verb *rakh,* to be bright, and it has been suggested that the Greeks named it *arktos* as a result of confusion between the two words. Arcturus was once the name given to the Pole Star.

Encompassed within Great and Little Bear are star formations popularly known as the Big Dipper and the Little Dipper; the latter contains the North Star, which is also known as the Pole Star, Polaris.

Great Bible. See BIBLE, ENGLISH VERSIONS.

Great Cham of Literature. A sobriquet for Dr. Samuel JOHNSON first used by Smollett in a letter to Wilkes. *Cham* is an obsolete word, synonomous with *Khan,* applicable to the ruler of the Tartars, the Mongols, and the emperor of China.

Great Divide, The (1906). A drama by William Vaughn MOODY. Originally entitled *The Sabine Woman,* the play has as its theme the conflict between Puritan New England and the American West. Ruth Jordan, from Massachusetts, is attacked by three men while alone in her brother's cabin in Arizona; she saves herself by agreeing to marry one of them and, eventually, after many trials, comes to love him and his Western independence.

Great Expectations (1860–1861). A novel by Charles DICKENS. The novel traces the growth of Philip Pirrip, called Pip, from a boy of shallow dreams to a man of depth and character. Pip is reared by his sister and her husband Joe Gargery, a blacksmith. In his youth he is influenced by the eccentric Miss HAVISHAM, who was jilted on her wedding night and who has brought up her adopted niece Estella to hate men. As a young man, Pip is informed that an unknown benefactor has provided money for his education and expects to make him his heir. Forsaking his humbler friends—particularly the faithful Joe—he sets off to London with the firm intention of becoming a gentleman and realizing his "great expectations." He soon learns that his patron is Abel MAGWITCH, a transported convict, whom Pip had helped years earlier; Magwitch also turns out to be Estella's father. With this knowledge Pip's dreams fade; he returns home after Joe saves him from imprisonment for debt, and sets himself to honest work. He marries Estella after her husband, Bentley Drummle, dies. Among the gallery of characters in the book are Biddy, who becomes Joe's second wife; the Pocket family; Uncle PUMBLECHOOK; Dolge Orlick, the murderer of Pip's sister; and Mr. JAGGERS.

The novel is regarded by many as Dickens' greatest achievement, although the happy ending, which according to Dickens' biographer John Forster was written on the advice of Bulwer-Lytton, detracts from the work somewhat.

Great Gatsby, The (1925). A novel by F. Scott FITZGERALD. The mysterious Jay Gatsby lives in a luxurious mansion on the wealthy Long Island shore, entertaining hundreds of guests at lavish parties that have become a legend on the island. Nick Carraway, the narrator, lives next-door to Gatsby, and Nick's cousin Daisy and her crude but wealthy husband Tom Buchanan live in the house directly across the harbor from Gatsby's. Gatsby reveals to Nick that he and Daisy had a brief affair before the war and her marriage to Tom; born Jay Gatz of a poor midwestern family, he has accumulated enormous wealth through shady transactions solely to make himself the kind of man he thinks Daisy admires: his one dream, and the reason he bought his house and gives his parties, is to win her back. He persuades Nick to bring him and Daisy together again, but ultimately he is unable to win her from her husband. Daisy, driving Gatsby's car, runs over and kills Tom's mistress Myrtle, unaware of the woman's identity. Myrtle's husband traces the car and shoots Gatsby, who has remained silent in order to protect Daisy. Gatsby's friends and business associates all desert him, and only Nick, Gatsby's father, and one habitué of the parties attend the funeral. The novel's power derives not from its violent plot, but from its sharp and antagonistic portrayal of wealthy society in America and from the exposure of the "Jazz Age," Fitzgerald's favorite subject, in all its false glamour, cultural barrenness, moral emptiness, and desperate boredom. Yet the novel transcends its own bitter view and is probably Fitzgerald's most humane work. It has enjoyed continuous popularity since its first publication, and, written in a fully-developed and easy style, it is now considered one of the chief texts of American literature of the post-World War I period.

Great God Brown, The (1926). A play by Eugene O'NEILL. Masks are used to symbolize the varying personalities of the characters as they are and as they appear to other people. The "great god Brown" is a successful businessman, devoid of inner resources; he eventually takes the mask of Dion Anthony (as his name suggests, a Dionysian character), a frustrated artist who dies. With Dion's mask, Brown is accepted by Dion's wife as the real Dion, for she has known and loved only her husband's mask, not his true self.

Great Learning, The. One of the Chinese FOUR BOOKS. Originally one chapter from the BOOK OF RITES, it was elevated to importance in the Confucian educational and philosophical system during the Sung Dynasty (960–1279). It emphasizes self-cultivation.

Great Mother, the. A nature goddess of ancient Anatolia. Her names and appellations include CYBELE, the mountain mother, the Idaean mother, and still others. In Greek mythology, Cybele is generally associated with Rhea.

Great Theater of the World, The. See GRAN TEATRO DEL MUNDO, EL.

Greaves, Sir Launcelot. See LAUNCELOT GREAVES.

Greco, El. Sobriquet of **Kyriakos Theotocopoulos** (c. 1541–1614). Greek-born Spanish painter. Having mastered the technique of icon painting in Crete, he went to Italy where he studied the work of Titian and Tintoretto. In 1577 he settled in Toledo, Spain, where, isolated from artistic influences, he developed a highly personal style which retains the movement of baroque drawing while suppressing the very spatial depth which baroque art sought to create. He painted intense portraits, mystic saints, and deeply expressive religious scenes. His use of such effects as discordantly contrasted cool colors, elongated distortions of the human frame, bright illumination, and flashing accents was misunderstood by contemporaries, and the significance of his art was not recognized until the 19th century. His best-known works include *Assumption of the Virgin* (1577), *Burial of the Count of Orgaz* (c. 1584), *Pentecost* (1604–1614), and *View of Toledo* (1600–1610).

Greek Anthology, The. A collection of several thousand poems, songs, gravestone inscriptions, epigrams, epitaphs, and the like, by numerous Greek writers, known and anonymous, from the 5th century B.C. to the 6th century A.D. Its original form was a collection called the *Garland of Meleager* (c. 60 B.C.), to which continuous additions were made. A number of the poems in *The Greek Anthology* have become famous. The Elizabethan poetic miscellany (see TOTTEL'S MISCELLANY) was a spiritual descendant of *The Greek Anthology*.

Greek epic poetry. Greek epic, a development from oral tradition. The earliest extant examples are the ILIAD and the ODYSSEY of HOMER. The functions of the Mycenaean rhapsode (*rhapsodos*) or minstrel are clearly shown in the character of Demodocus, the blind bard who entertained Odysseus and other guests at the court of the Phaeacian king Alcinous in the *Odyssey*. It was his duty to sing of the great heroes of past and present in order to entertain and please the kings and lords who could afford such a luxury. Unlike Demodocus, most bards probably traveled from court to court. Wherever they stopped, they would find it expedient to recite events that were especially gratifying to the local lord; his own exploits or those of heroes he claimed as forebears, much as Vergil later made the myths of Aeneas a paean to the glory of Rome and of his personal patron, Augustus. To this end the bard would often fabricate a connection between his patron of the moment and some great event or hero, such as the sack of Troy or the deeds of Heracles. This custom accounts in part for the apparent ubiquity of Heracles and Theseus and, more important, for the process of gradual accretion which, over a period of centuries, culminated in such epics as the *Odyssey,* in which a great mass of originally unrelated myths and folk tales adhered to the story of one hero.

An itinerant bard had to be able not only to recall an enormous number of tales, but to recite them in the dactylic hexameters which, by the time of Homer, had already been the traditional language of epic for centuries. Since writing, if it was used at all for literary purposes, must have been only a kind of shorthand, a bard was called upon to perform prodigious feats of memory. At the same time, in adjusting his tales to the requirements of the immediate situation, he had to be able to improvise at length.

The structure of the great Greek epics, even in the relatively literary form in which they have been preserved, show clearly their oral origins. One of their most striking characteristics is the great number of repeated phrases (for example, epithets such as "wine-dark sea" or "shepherd of the people") which are applied more or less indiscriminately to a variety of places or people. Every bard memorized a vast repertory of these formulae, which he could then apply on the spur of the moment in an appropriate spot in a poem according to the demands of the meter. It was probably this patchwork approach to poetry that earned him the name of rhapsode: "stitcher."

The repetition of stock phrases inevitably tends to monotony, especially when those phrases must, for practical reasons, be kept general enough in tone to be largely interchangeable. It is a measure of the genius of Homer, whoever he may have been, that he was able, within these traditional limitations, to achieve considerable individuality in his characters and to overcome monotony with sheer dramatic and poetic power.

Greek music. The music of ancient Greece. Music was extensively cultivated and studied in ancient Greece, and was considered important to the state, because of its supposed control of human passions and morals. Only fragments of the actual music have survived, but many important theoretical treatises still exist, and have had an important influence on music ever since. The principal modes (or scales) in which Greek music was written are: Phrygian, brisk and spirited; Dorian, bold and grave; Lydian, full of soft pathos; Mixolydian, dirgelike.

The principal instruments used in Greek music were the *aulos* and the *kithara*. *Auloi* is a generic name for wind instruments of the flute and oboe type; the *kithara*, and its close relative the *lyra* or lyre, was a plucked string instrument with 3 to 15 strings.

Greek Passion, The (Ho Christós Xanastauronetai; 1951). A novel by Nikos KAZANTZAKIS. Set in modern Anatolia, it is a story of the persecution of the Greek inhabitants of an impoverished village by their Turkish overlords and, worse, by each other. At the beginning, several of the villagers are chosen for roles they are to play eight months later in a local passion play. By the time Passion Week comes, the play has been forgotten in a succession of violent events—and the villagers have played out their assigned roles in real life. A powerful modern morality play, the novel reveals the darker passions in men's lives that deeply concerned Kazantzakis.

Greeley, Horace (1811–1872). American journalist and political leader. As a newspaper printer and editor in New York, Greeley advocated many reform movements including abolition. He served in Congress (1848–1849) and supported the candidacy of Lincoln for president. Averse to the Republican policy of revenge on the South following the Civil War, he ran unsuccessfully against Grant in 1872. Greeley supported the agrarian movement and worked for a liberal policy for settlers; one of his favorite sayings was "Go West, young man." In sympathy with the laboring classes in New York City, he also favored "magnanimity in triumph," a policy of universal amnesty and universal suffrage after the Civil War. His willingness to put up bail for Jefferson Davis brought him much abuse, but he never allowed his subscribers' threats to modify his editorial views.

Green, Anna Katharine (1846–1935). American novelist and short-story writer. She is especially remembered for *The Leavenworth Case* (1878), said to be the first detective fiction written by a woman. Other works include *The Hand and the Ring* (1883) and *The Filigree Ball* (1903).

Green, Anne (1899–   ). American novelist. Shortly after her birth, her family moved to Paris where her father was in business, and Miss Green, whose brother is Julian GREEN, has described the household in her volume of reminiscences: *With Much Love* (1948). Her novels include *The Selbys* (1930), *A Marriage of Convenience* (1933), *Fools Rush In* (1934), *The Silent Duchess* (1939), *Just Before Dawn* (1943), and *The Old Lady* (1947).

Green, Frederick Lawrence (1902–1953). Irish novelist, best known for his *Odd Man Out* (1945), a novel about a young Irish revolutionary.

Green, Henry. Pen name of **Henry Yorke (1905–   ).** English novelist and manufacturer. All his novels have extremely brief titles, such as *Blindness* (1926); *Living* (1929), a compassionate proletarian novel; *Party Going* (1939); LOVING, his best-known novel; *Back* (1946), an account of a man's return from the war; *Concluding* (1948), a satire on a future bureaucratic state; *Nothing* (1950); and *Doting* (1952). His novels, written almost entirely in realistic dialogue, are elegant and witty but ambiguous comedies of manners. Often two forces are brought into conflict, such as the old and the young,

the past and the present, the employer and the servant. Though the novels are apparently simple, even naïve, they have mysterious symbolical overtones (see *Loving*). *Pack My Bag* (1939) is a collection of reminiscences.

Green, Julian or Julien (1900–   ). French novelist of American parentage. He is the brother of Anne GREEN. Green is as much influenced by his Puritan heritage as by the Catholicism to which he was converted. His novels, originally written in French, reflect his obsessive sense of sin, his terrible consciousness of the violence and sadism of which men are capable, his fascination and fear of madness and death. Depicting a varied yet constant battle between good and evil, Green's works include *Avarice House (Mont-Cinère; 1926), The Closed Garden (Adrienne Mesurat; 1927), The Dark Journey (Leviathan; 1929), The Dreamer (Le Visionnaire; 1934), Then Shall the Dust Return (Varouna; 1940)*, MOÏRA, and CHAQUE HOMME DANS SA NUIT. *Sud* (1953), *L'Ennemi* (1954), and *L'Ombre* (1956) are plays; *Personal Record 1928–1939* (1939) and *Memories of Happy Days* (1942) are autobiographical volumes.

Green, Paul E[liot] (1894–   ). American playwright and teacher. He is best known for dramas portraying life in the South, often set in his native state of North Carolina. His most important plays are *In Abraham's Bosom* (1927), a Pulitzer Prizewinning drama about a mulatto who tries to establish a school for Negroes in a North Carolina town; *The Field God* (1927), concerning poor whites; *The House of Connelly* (1931), dealing with the contrast between aristocratic Southern landowners and the tenant farmers; and a dramatization (1940) of Richard Wright's *Native Son*. Green wrote scripts in Hollywood during the 30's, eventually returning to teach at the University of North Carolina. His later plays deal with folk customs and beliefs; among them are *The Lost Colony* (1937), a historical pageant dealing with the first settlement on Roanoke Island; *The Common Glory* (1947), set at the time of the Revolution; *Wilderness Road* (1955); and *The Stephen Foster Story* (1959).

Green, Thomas Hill (1836–1882). A British philosopher, noted for his *Prolegomena to Ethics* (1883) and *Principles of Political Obligation* (1895). Against Social Darwinists such as Spencer, who argued that man was determined by natural forces such as evolution, Green followed Hegel in asserting that man was a free and rational being who acted in relation to rational moral ideals; that the highest moral ideal revealed by reason was the ideal of the perfect state, that man's most important duties were therefore political. Freedom was not the ability to do as one liked, but the power to identify one's self with the highest rational good, i.e., the ideal of the perfect state, and the responsibility to criticize and reform the existing social order in accordance with this ideal.

Green Bay Tree, The (1924). A novel by Louis BROMFIELD. It tells the story of Lily Shane who begins life in a Middle Western industrial town and goes to Paris to bear an illegitimate child. Bromfield's first novel, it is also the first novel in the tetralogy entitled *Escape*.

Greenberg, Samuel (1893–1917). Austrian-born American poet. Greenberg, who came to the U.S. as a child, began writing poetry in a hospital for the tubercular. None of his poems was published during his lifetime, but, after his early death, Hart CRANE found his manuscripts. Crane was deeply impressed by the strange imagery and flights of intense imagination, and some of Greenberg's phrases are recognizable in Crane's own poems. *Poems: A Selection from the Manuscripts* was published in 1947, with a preface by Allen Tate.

Green Carnation, The (1894). A novel by Robert S. Hichens (1864–1950). It satirizes the decadence of the period at the end of the 19th century; in particular, it is intended as a lampoon on Oscar Wilde. The "green carnation" of the title is "the arsenic flower of an exquisite life." The hero, Lord Reginald Hastings, "too modern to be reticent," is put in his place by a heroine who, when he complains that she is almost ordinary, replies that she is glad of it and flatly refuses to marry him.

Greene, Graham (1904–   ). English novelist, short-story writer, and playwright. He is an ardent convert to Catholicism, and all his writings reflect his religious views. Greene's novels are unusual combinations of psychological studies, adventure thrillers, and essays on moral and theological dilemmas. Among the best known of his works are BRIGHTON ROCK, THE POWER AND THE GLORY (first published in the U.S. as *The Labyrinthine Ways*), THE HEART OF THE MATTER, and A BURNT-OUT CASE. He also wrote a number of lighter novels in which the thriller element predominates, but which are still about problems of good and evil. Some of these "entertainments," such as THE THIRD MAN, have made excellent movies.

Greene's settings are varied: Sweden in *England Made Me* (1935), wartime London in *The Ministry of Fear* (1943) and *The End of the Affair* (1951), Mexico, Africa, or an English seaside town. The place, however, is always in a state of seedy decay and the people in a state of spiritual and psychological chaos. Greene has a journalist's sense of topicality. Many of his novels were set in unusual places just before they became international crisis spots: *The Quiet American* (1955), about a fumbling idealist in cold-war Viet Nam; *Our Man in Havana* (1958), a Cuba spy-story "entertainment"; and *A Burnt-Out Case* (1960), set in the Congo. Greene has also written *Twenty-One Stories* (1954), a collection of short stories, meditative travel books such as *Journey without Maps* (1936), and plays such as *The Living Room* (1953), *The Potting Shed* (1956), and *The Complaisant Lover* (1959).

Greene, Robert (1560?–1592). English prose writer and dramatist. Greene traveled in Europe, took his M.A. degree from both Oxford and Cambridge, and then appeared in London, where he became known as a University Wit and a writer of rogue literature. During his brief life he was a remarkably prolific writer, having 38 publications—prose romances, pamphlets, dramas—to his credit at the time of his death. His early prose works, showing the influence of John LYLY and the Euphuistic style (see EUPHUISM), include *Mamilla* (1583); *The Myrrour of Modesty* (the story of Susanna, 1584); *Alcida, Greene's Metamorphosis* (1588). *Euphues, His Censure of Philautus* (1587), is a continuation of Lyly's work. *Pandosto, the Triumph of Time* (1588)

is a prose romance which provided Shakespeare with the plot for *A Winter's Tale. Menaphon* (1589, reprinted as *Greene's Arcadia*) is a pastoral romance modeled after Sir Philip Sidney's *Arcadia*.

All Greene's plays were performed posthumously. They include *The Comical History of Alphonsus, King of Arragon* (c. 1587); *Friar Bacon and Friar Bungay* (c. 1589, acted 1594), a comedy that may have been inspired by Marlowe's *Dr. Faustus*, dealing with the legendary alchemical pursuits of Roger Bacon and Thomas Bungay; *Orlando Furioso* (acted 1592), a free adaptation of Ariosto; *The Scottish History of James IV* (c. 1591); and, with Thomas Lodge, *A Looking Glass for London and England* (c. 1590, acted 1592). It is possible that Greene was in part responsible for the original plays dealing with HENRY VI, which Shakespeare allegedly revised and rewrote. In his last pamphlet, A GROATSWORTH OF WIT, Greene gives the first contemporary mention of Shakespeare in a warning to his fellow-playwrights to beware the upstart actor who, with his "tiger's heart wrapped in a player's hide," is encroaching on their territory and writing plays himself.

As one of the writers hired to reply to the Puritan pamphlets in the Martin MARPRELATE CONTROVERSY, Greene was attacked by Richard Harvey in *Plaine Percevall and the Peace-maker of England* (1590). Greene answered with *A Quip for an Upstart Courtier* (1592), directed against Harvey and his two brothers. By the time Gabriel HARVEY retaliated in *Foure Letters and Certaine Sonnets*, Greene was dead "of a surfeit of pickled herring and Rhenish wine," and his defense was taken up by Thomas NASHE. Gabriel Harvey wrote of Greene's last days.

Greene's repentance pamphlets, while in part autobiographical, should probably not be taken entirely as documents of personal repentance and confession. They include *Greene's Mourning Garment* (1590); *Never Too Late* (1590); *Farewell to Folly* (1591); and *A Groatsworth of Wit Bought with a Million of Repentance* (1592), which contains the allusion to Shakespeare. His "cony-catching" pamphlets (1591–92) are realistic descriptions of London low-life and underworld activity; they include *A Defense of Cony-Catching; Disputation between a He-Cony-Catcher and a She-Cony-Catcher; The Black Book's Messenger;* and *A Notable Discovery of Cozenage.*

Green-eyed monster. Iago's term for jealousy in Shakespeare's *Othello*. A greenish complexion was formerly held to be indicative of jealousy; and as cats, lions, tigers, and all the green-eyed tribe "mock the meat they feed on," so jealousy mocks its victim by loving and loathing it at the same time.

Green Hat, The (1924). A best-selling novel by Michael ARLEN. Its popularity was largely due to the way in which it captured the licentious, disillusioned spirit of the time. With a self-sacrificing heroine and a husband who kills himself on his wedding night because he has syphilis, the novel is a sentimental account of sexual license among the wealthy.

Green Henry (Der grüne Heinrich; first version, 1854; second, 1879–1880). A largely autobiographical novel by Gottfried KELLER in the tradition of the BILDUNGSROMAN. Heinrich Lee, the hero (called green because all of his boyish clothes were made from his dead father's green uniforms), wishes to become a great painter and expends a great deal of time and energy at this pursuit before he finally discovers that he can never achieve more than moderate competence. In the course of his adventures, however, he neglects his widowed mother, and it is in this aspect of the story that the novel's two versions diverge. In the early version, Heinrich assumes all the blame for his mother's eventual death; his attacks of conscience break both his spirit and body, and he dies. In the later version, however, Heinrich's guilt is not stressed, and he successfully adjusts himself to a life of civic service as a government official.

Green Knight. See Sir Gawain and the Green Knight.

Green Mansions (1904). A romance of the South American tropics by William Henry Hudson. The hero, Mr. Abel, tells the tragic story of his love for the bird girl, Rima, an ethereal maiden whose jungle upbringing has brought her close to the powers and beauty of nature. Abel has just succeeded in awakening the human emotion of love in the half-wild girl when she is killed by a band of savages.

Green Mountain Boys, The (1839). A novel by Daniel Pierce Thompson (1795–1868), American lawyer, novelist, and historian. The book's central character is the hero Ethan Allen. Immensely popular, the novel was the most successful of Thompson's attempts to preserve romantic episodes in early Vermont history and gives a vivid picture of Revolutionary times in Vermont.

Green Pastures, The (1930). A play by Marc Connelly, based on the sketches in Roark Bradford's Ol' Man Adam an' His Chillun. This famous play, which was awarded a Pulitzer Prize, presents reverent though humorous versions of Old Testament stories as they are told by an old Southern Negro preacher in terms of the lives of his congregation.

Greenwich Village or **The Village.** A section of New York City west of Washington Square. It was noted during the early 20th century and the years immediately preceding and following World War I as the haunt of Bohemian artists, writers, and radicals, who originally chose it as a place to live because of its cheapness. In former days it had been a quaint, small village reached from the city in lower Manhattan by stage coach.

By the time of the 1930's, Greenwich Village was chiefly a residential district for young business and professional couples, who could pay higher rents than their predecessors the Bohemians, and the artists and writers had moved to Brooklyn or to the Connecticut suburbs. Among the well-known personalities who have lived and worked in Greenwich Village at one time or another are: Floyd Dell, Gelett Burgess, Max Eastman, Emma Goldman, William Vaughn Moody, Eugene O'Neill, Edna St. Vincent Millay, William Rose Benét, Katherine Anne Porter, E. E. Cummings, Carson McCullers, and James Baldwin; among the little magazines published there were *The Little Review, The Masses,* and *The Seven Arts.* Several novels of Floyd Dell deal with the life in Greenwich Village in its heyday.

Greg, Sir W[alter] W[ilson] (1875–1959). English bibliographer and literary scholar. A pioneer in the use of scientific bibliography in literary criticism, he wrote *Pastoral Poetry and Pastoral Drama* (1906) and *A Bibliography of the English Printed Drama to the Restoration* (2 vols., 1939, 1951).

Gregorian chant. The ritual plain song, or *cantus firmus,* a kind of unison music in the eight church modes. A collection of these, edited by Pope Gregory I, has come down to us. It is still used in the services of the Roman Catholic Church and Greek Catholic Church.

Gregorian year. The civil year, according to the correction introduced by Pope Gregory XIII in 1582. The equinox, which occurred on March 25 in the time of Julius Caesar, fell on March 11 in the year 1582. This was because the Julian calculation of 365¼ days to a year was 11 min. 10 sec. too much. Gregory suppressed ten days, so as to make the equinox fall on March 21, as it did at the Council of Nice, and, by some simple arrangements prevented the recurrence in future of a similar error.

The New Style, as it was called, was adopted in England in 1752, when Wednesday, September 2, was followed by Thursday, September 14.

This gave rise to a double computation: Lady Day, March 25, Old Lady Day, April 6; Midsummer Day, June 24, Old Midsummer Day, July 6; Michaelmas Day, September 29, Old Michaelmas Day, October 11; Christmas Day, December 25, Old Christmas Day, January 6.

Gregory I. Called **Gregory the Great,** St. (c. 540–604). Benedictine monk elected Pope (590–604). He established the temporal power of the papacy, reformed monastic discipline, and sent Augustine with 40 monks to England. According to tradition it was he who established the liturgical music known as Gregorian chant.

Gregory VII, St. Original name, **Hildebrand** (c. 1020–1085). Italian pope (1073–1083). As pope he pursued a policy of establishing the papacy as the supreme office in the Church and of protecting the Church from the civil states in Europe. He issued a decree (1075) that prohibited lay investiture of the clergy, that is, clergy could no longer be appointed to office by civil authorities. He called Henry IV of Germany to Rome to answer charges of oppression of the Church and sacrilege. Henry was outraged at Gregory's play for authority and tried to depose him. Gregory responded by excommunicating Henry. Henry did penance in the snow before Gregory's palace at Canossa and gained conditional absolution (1077). In 1078, Gregory renewed the excommunication, and Henry declared war. He appointed Clement III as antipope (1080) and captured Rome in 1084. Gregory was rescued from the castle Sant' Angelo, and died in exile at Salerno the next year.

Gregory, Horace [Victor] (1898–   ). American poet, critic, and translator. Much of his poetry criticizes middle-class life and presents dramatic monologues or character studies of petty racketeers and gangsters and people of the city slums. Among his books are *Chelsea Rooming House* (1930), *No Retreat* (1933), *Chorus for Survival* (1935), *Poems: 1930–1940* (1941), *The Shield of Achilles: Essays on Poetry and Beliefs* (1944), *Selected Poems* (1951), and *Medusa in Gramercy Park and Other Poems* (1961). In 1931 he translated the poems of Catullus; in 1958 Ovid's *Metamorphoses.* He also wrote *Pilgrim of the Apocalypse* (1933), a study of D. H. Lawrence; *A History of American Poetry, 1900–1940* (1946), with his wife, Marya Zaturenska; and critical biographies of Amy Lowell (1958) and James Mc-Neill Whistler (1959).

Gregory, Lady **Isabella Augusta** (1852–1932). Irish dramatist. The first 40 years of Lady Gregory's life were from a literary viewpoint extremely uneventful, with little if any thought given to the subject. With the death of her husband, Sir William Gregory, in 1892, however, she developed a strong interest in Irish literature and history, and in 1898, when she met William Butler Yeats, she was ready to lend her talent, wealth, and position to the slowly developing sense of national consciousness that was to burgeon into the Irish literary renaissance. The major focus of her energy was directed to the Irish National Theatre, which later evolved into the Abbey Theatre and which she served as a director. In 1914 she wrote a history of the movement, *Our Irish Theatre.*

Her own literary efforts were primarily designed to reawaken the Irish national consciousness through translations and collections of ancient Celtic legend and folklore. She is best known, however, for her one-act plays, which were originally designed as "fillers" for the Abbey program. Among these the best known are *Spreading the News* (1904) and *The Rising of the Moon* (1907).

Her beautiful estate at Coole in western Ireland is celebrated in Yeats's lovely poem, *The Wild Swans at Coole*. See IRISH RENAISSANCE.

gregueria. See Ramón GÓMEZ DE LA SERNA.

Greif, Andreas. See Andreas GRYPHIUS.

Gremio. In Shakespeare's TAMING OF THE SHREW, a rich old gentleman, suitor to Bianca. He considers himself an ideal mate because of his advanced years.

Grendel. The monster in BEOWULF. He is described as a giant in human shape, a descendant of Cain who lives in a murky pond with his mother among other strange and vicious sea-beasts. For 12 years mother and son come to land occasionally and devour human victims, until Beowulf comes to kill them.

Grenfell, Sir **Wilfred** (1865–1940). English medical missionary and writer, widely known as Grenfell of Labrador. He wrote adventure tales and books of a religious nature, including *A Labrador Doctor* (1919) and others.

Grenville, Sir **Richard** (1541?–1591). English naval commander. The cousin of Sir Walter RALEIGH, Grenville commanded a fleet of seven of Raleigh's ships carrying colonists who were attempting to settle on Roanoke Island, off the coast of North Carolina (1585). When in 1591 his ship, the *Revenge*, was isolated by a fleet of fifteen Spanish ships off Flores, Grenville fought off the Spaniards for fifteen hours. His heroic battle is celebrated in Tennyson's ballad *The Revenge.*

Gresset, Jean **Baptiste Louis** (1709–1777). French poet and dramatist. He is noted for his poem *Vert-Vert* (1734), relating the adventures of a parrot, and a successful comedy *Le Méchant* (1745), which satirizes contemporary salon society.

Gretchen (German diminutive for Margarete). In Part I of Goethe's FAUST, the young and simple, lower-class girl whom Faust seduces with the aid of Mephistopheles' magic. She reappears as a penitent spirit at the end of Part II and greets Faust's salvation with joyful song. See ETERNAL FEMININE.

Grettir the Strong. A hero of *The Grettisaga*, a 14th-century Icelandic tale. Concerned with a historical hero of the late 10th and early 11th century, the story is of unusual interest because of resemblances to parts of the 8th-century Old English epic *Beowulf*. There is a translation of it by William Morris.

Grettisaga, The. See GRETTIR THE STRONG.

Greuze, Jean **Baptiste** (1725–1805). French painter. He was greatly admired by his contemporaries for his narrative genre scenes of morality, such as *The Paralytic tended by his Children* and *A Father's Curse: the Ungrateful Son*. Today these overdramatic, insincere, and sentimental paintings are found inferior to his portraits.

Greville, Sir **Fulke.** 1st Baron **Brooke** (1554–1628). English courtier and diplomat. Greville's epitaph reads: "Servant to Queen Elizabeth—Councillor to King James—and Friend to Sir Philip SIDNEY." It is in this last capacity that he is best remembered, and for his *Life* (1652) of Sidney. Greville had a distinguished career in government, becoming chancellor of the exchequer under James I. He was a patron of the arts and learning, and a fair poet in his own right.

Grey, Lady **Jane** (c. 1537–1554). The great-granddaughter of Henry VII and for nine days queen of England. At 16 she was married to Lord Guildford Dudley, whose father, the earl of Northumberland, was Protector of Edward VI. As part of a plan to change the succession of the crown from the Tudors to the Dudleys, Northumberland persuaded the dying Edward to settle the crown on Lady Jane and bypass the claims of Mary and Elizabeth. Lady Jane was proclaimed Queen on July 10, 1553, but by the 19th Mary had gathered powerful supporters, defeated the forces of Northumberland, and was proclaimed Queen by the Lord Mayor. Lady Jane and her husband were imprisoned and finally executed.

Grey, Zane (1875–1939). American writer of Westerns and articles on outdoor life. In 1904, Grey made up his mind that writing rather than dentistry was to be his career. A first-rate storyteller, he won enormous popular success with *Riders of the Purple Sage* (1912) and a long succession of later novels. Possibly his best books are *The Last of the Plainsmen* (1908) and the nonfiction collection *Tales of Fishing* (1925).

Grey Friars. Franciscans. Black Friars are Dominicans, and White Friars, Carmelites.

Griboyedov, **Aleksandr** **Sergeyevich** (1795–1829). Russian dramatist. His satirical masterpiece, WOE FROM WIT, is one of the classics of Russian drama. For most of his career, Griboyedov was a civil servant. His death was spectacular: serving as Russian minister to Persia, he was cut to pieces by a raging mob that sacked the Russian embassy in Tehran. Griboyedov was the subject of an interesting fictionalized biography entitled *The Death of Vazir-Mukhtar* (*Smert' Vazir-Mukhtara*; 1929) by the Soviet writer Yuri Nikolayevich Tynyanov (1894–1944).

Grieg, Edvard [**Hagerup**] (1843–1907). Norwegian composer. The rhythmic and melodic patterns of his work capture the spirit of his homeland. Grieg wrote operas, choral works, dances, songs, and concertos for various instruments; his PEER GYNT suite, written as incidental music to accompany Ibsen's play, is well known. His songs and chamber music employ subtle and delicate harmonies.

Grieg, [Johan] Nordahl [Brun] (1902–1943). Norwegian poet, novelist, and playwright. The vigor and the adventurous spirit that marked Grieg's life and his writings manifested itself first during his student days. A voyage as a seaman on a Norwegian freighter produced the realistic account *Skibet går videre* (*The Ship Sails On*, 1924); he also traveled through Europe living with tramps. Although he wrote plays during the 1920's, it was not until Grieg's trip to Russia (1933–1935) that his work acquired real force and dramatic vitality. Study of the Russian theater strengthened his sympathy for the working classes and led him to write his plays about controversial social issues. *Vår oere og vår makt* (*Our Honor and Our Might*, 1935) treats the greed of Norwegian ship owners during World War I; *Men imorgen* (*But Tomorrow—*, 1936) presents a conflict between labor and Nazism. In Spain during the civil war as a journalist with republican sympathies, Grieg published a novel, *Men ung må verden ennu voere* (*But Young the World Must Be*, 1938) based on his experiences in Russia, Spain, and Norway. He went to England with the Norwegian government in exile at the time of the German invasion, and flew missions over Germany in American bombers. Before his death, he wrote several war lyrics that express a deepened love for his country and an undaunted courage. *Flagget* (1945), *Friheten* (1945), and *Habet* (1946) are his posthumous collections of poetry.

Grierson, Francis. See Benjamin Henry Jesse Francis SHEPARD.

Grierson, Sir Herbert J[ohn] C[lifford] (1866–1960). Scottish scholar, critic, and editor who, in such books as *The First Half of the 17th Century* (1906), *Poems of John Donne* (1912), and *Metaphysical Poets from Donne to Butler* (1921), helped to bring about the current revival of interest in the Metaphysical poets.

Grieux, le Chevalier des. See MANON LESCAUT.

Grieve, Christopher Murray. See Hugh MacDIARMID.

griffin. A mythical monster. Also called *griffon*, *gryphon*, and similar names. It is fabled to be the offspring of the lion and eagle. Its legs and all from the shoulder to the head are like an eagle; the rest of the body is that of a lion. This creature was sacred to the sun, and kept guard over hidden treasures. The griffins were in perpetual strife with the Arimaspians, a people of Scythia, who rifled the gold mines for the adornment of their hair. The belief apparently grew out of the stylized animal commonly represented in Scythian art, originally perhaps a chicken.

Griffith, D[avid Lewelyn] W[ark] (1875–1948). American motion-picture director and producer. One of the pioneers in the early days of the film, he is especially known for his mobile and imaginative use of the camera and for having developed such techniques as the closeup, the long shot, the flashback, and the fadeout. After a period as actor and script writer, he became a director for the Biograph Company. Later he began to produce motion pictures independently, and in 1923 he was one of the founders of United Artists. Among his famous films are *The Birth of a Nation* (1915), *Hearts of the World* (1917), *Broken Blossoms* (1919), *Way Down East* (1920), and *Orphans of the Storm* (1921).

Grifone (Gryphon). In the Orlando poems of Boiardo and Ariosto, the son of Oliviero and brother of AQUILANTE. He is called *il bianco* (the white) and his brother *il nero* (the black), because each of them is protected by an enchantress of that color. The white enchantress rescued him from a griffin (hence his name), which had stolen him from his mother, Ghismonda.

Grigorovich, Dmitri Vasilyevich (1822–1899). Russian novelist and short-story writer. Grigorovich's father died when he was a child, and he was raised by his French mother and governess. Not until he attended school in Moscow did he learn to read and write Russian. In 1836 he entered the military engineering school in St. Petersburg. One of his fellow students was the future novelist Feodor Dostoevski. During his four years at the school, Grigorovich developed a strong interest in literature. He made the acquaintance of such leading figures as the critic Vissarion Belinski, the poet Nikolai Nekrasov, and the novelist Ivan Turgenev. About this time the NATURAL SCHOOL in Russian literature, originating from Belinski's literary doctrines, was in the ascendancy. Grigorovich became one of the leading members of this movement. His first contribution was *Peterburgskiye sharmanshchiki* (*Petersburg Organ-grinders*, 1844), a sketch realistically depicting the lives of organ-grinders in the capital. The piece appeared in *Fiziologiya Peterburga* (*Physiology of Petersburg*, 1845), an anthology devoted to an examination of life in St. Petersburg.

Grigorovich's best works were published in the following two years. *Derevnya* (*The Village*, 1846) was one of the first literary works to deal extensively with peasant life. It was followed by another study of the peasantry: *Anton-Goremyka* (1847). Although they were criticized as presenting a somewhat idealized picture, both these stories did much to make peasant life acceptable material for literature.

Grigoryev, Apollon Aleksandrovich (1822–1864). Russian poet and literary critic. Grigoryev grew up in the conservative middle-class section of Moscow, ZAMOSKVARECHYE, which Ostrovski often used as the setting for his dramas. After graduating from Moscow University, Grigoryev began a wandering career as literary critic for a series of journals. One of his most important associations was with the *Moskvityanin* (*The Muscovite*), where his contacts with Ostrovski and other supporters of an independent Russian culture had a great effect on his own literary theories. In 1856, Grigoryev went abroad for two years. On his return he wrote for the journal *Vremya* (*Time*), published by the novelist Feodor Dostoevski and his brother Mikhail Dostoevski. These men, together with the philosopher Nikolai Nikolayevich Strakhov (1828–1896), shared Grigoryev's views that Russian culture must be an organic growth rooted in Russian life, rather than an imitation of Western culture. Russian literature and art, they maintained, must grow from Russian soil (*pochva*). The ideas of the *pochvenniki*, as the group was known, were set forth by Grigoryev in his article *Paradoxy organicheskiye kritisizma* (*Paradoxes of Organic Criticism*). At about the same time, he wrote the autobiographical work, *Moi literaturniye i nravst-*

venniye skitalchestva (*My Literary and Moral Wan-derings*), in which he describes his intellectual development and, also, gives vivid sketches of life in Zamoskvarechye.

Grigoryev's poetry has received less attention than his critical writings. Taking Lermontov and Byron as his poetic masters, Grigoryev wrote mainly romantic lyrics describing his unfortunate love affairs. His narrative poem *Vverkh po Volge* (*Up the Volga*, 1857) describes his unsuccessful attempt to rehabilitate a prostitute. A cycle of poems also published in 1857, *Bor'ba* (*The Struggle*), contains some of his best lyrics, reputedly inspired by gypsy songs. Aleksandr Blok, who edited a collection of Grigoryev's verse in 1915, acknowledged the influence of some of these lyrics on his own work.

Grigson, Geoffrey (1905–   ). English poet, essayist, and critic. His volumes of poetry include *Several Observations* (1939) and his prose works include *Essays from the Air* (1951). He edited the periodical anthology *New Verse* (1933–1939).

Grillparzer, Franz (1791–1872). Austrian dramatist whose work is modeled on the dramas of Shakespeare and Calderón. Though his plays often show a deep, sentimental melancholy about the impossibility of reconciling reality with the ideal, his thought never degenerates into mere romantic lamentation and, like the writers of the BIEDERMEIER movement, he believes that a rewarding life is still possible for the man who recognizes and remains within the salutary limits of his nature. His early plays, which are more emotionally extravagant than his later ones, include *Die Ahnfrau* (*The Ancestress*, 1817), a fate-tragedy not unlike those of Zacharias Werner, and a tragedy (1818) about the Greek poetess Sappho. But with the trilogy *Das goldene Vliess* (*The Golden Fleece*, 1822), on the story of Jason and Medea, and with the historical tragedy *König Ottokars Glück und Ende* (*King Ottocar's Success and Downfall*, 1825), he hit his dramatic stride, and these plays are among his greatest. His works were not generally well-received, however, and after the dismal failure of *Weh dem, der lügt* (*Woe to Him Who Lies*, 1838) he became completely discouraged and never published another play. Still, he continued writing, and among the dramas he left behind at his death are two of his most famous: *Die Jüdin von Toledo* (*The Jewess of Toledo*, completed 1855) and *Ein Bruderzwist in Habsburg* (*A Fraternal Struggle in the House of Hapsburg*, written c. 1855). His well-known novella *Der arme Spielmann* (*The Poor Minstrel*, written 1831) is a sentimental but carefully constructed masterpiece.

Grimald, Nicholas (1519–1562). English poet, scholar, and clergyman. Grimald is best known for his 40 poems, most of them translations from Latin, which appeared in the first edition of TOTTEL'S MISCELLANY (1557). He also wrote two Latin plays and translated Cicero's *De Officiis* (1553).

Grimm, Jacob Ludwig Carl (1785–1863) and his brother **Wilhelm Carl** (1786–1859). German scholars, considered the founders of Germanic philology as a systematic study. Among the works on which they collaborated are *Deutsche Sagen* (*German Legends*, 1816) and the famous collection of *Kinder-und Hausmärchen* (lit., "Children's and Household Tales," 1812 ff.) known as *Grimm's Fairy-Tales* (see

MÄRCHEN). For the latter, they got most of their material not from written documents but from peasants whom they interviewed; Wilhelm, who tended more toward literary criticism and appreciation than his brother, did most of the transcription. Jacob, more the scholar, wrote a *Deutsche Grammatik* (*German Grammar*, 1819 ff.) in which he formulated "Grimm's Law," the first attempt to explain the consonantal differences between Greek and Latin words and their cognates in the Germanic languages. It was also Jacob who did most of the work on the definitive *Deutsches Wörterbuch* (*German Dictionary*, 1852 ff.), begun by the brothers and still in progress.

Grimmelshausen, Hans Jakob Christoffel von (1610?–1676). German novelist, strongly influenced by the tradition of the picaresque novel in France and Spain. Although contemporary with baroque poets such as Andreas Gryphius, Grimmelshausen used a less ornamented style, which was more accessible to the people. His most famous work is the novel SIMPLICISSIMUS.

Grindel, Eugène. See Paul ELUARD.

Grippeminaud. See FURRY LAWCATS.

Griselda or **Grisilda** (**The Patient**). The heroine of the final tale of Giovanni Boccaccio's THE DE-CAMERON. Her husband, the marquis of Saluzzo, chooses her from among the peasantry, then decides to test her fidelity. First, he pretends their two children are dead by his hand; then he feigns boredom and pretends he has married again, using his own daughter as the supposed new love. Turned out of the house, she endures her sufferings nobly and remains constant until Saluzzo relents; she is then restored to her home and children, having won the love and admiration of her husband and his people.

Basically the Job story in modern dress, the tale was known to Boccaccio from a French source; it was in turn translated into Latin by Petrarch. From this Latin version rather than from the Italian source Chaucer drew the CLERK'S TALE, to which he supplied his own ironic comment on the credibility of the tale:

> Grisilde is dead, and eek her pacience,
> And both at once buried in Italie.

Groatsworth of Wit Bought with a Million of Repentance, A (1592). A pamphlet written by Robert GREENE, supposedly while he was dying. It is in part a repentance tract and a warning to his fellow-playwrights to eschew evil and thus avoid his own bitter end. It contains the famous reference to SHAKESPEARE as "an upstart crow, beautified with our feathers, that . . . supposes he is as well able to bombast out a blank verse as the best of you; and being an absolute *Johannes fac totum*, is in his own conceit the only Shake-scene in a country." See illustration on page 426.

Grongar Hill (1726). A poem by John DYER imitative of the early poems of Milton. It presents a picturesque, contemplative, and melancholy landscape, in sharp contrast to its lively companion poem *The Country Walk*.

Groote, Gerard (1340–1384). A Dutch reformer and founder of the society of BRETHREN OF THE COMMON LIFE.

Gropius, Walter [Adolf] (1883–   ). German architect. The organizer and head of the BAUHAUS

GREENES, GROATS-VVORTH
of witte, bought with a
million of Repentance.

Deſcribing the follie of youth, the falſhood of make-
ſhifte flatterers, the miſerie of the negligent,
and miſchiefes of deceiuing
Courtezans.

Written before his death and publiſhed at his
dyeing requeſt.

Fælicem fuiſſe infauſtum.

LONDON
Imprinted for William Wright.
1 5 9 2.

NEW YORK PUBLIC LIBRARY

Title page of Greene's *A Groatsworth of Wit* (1592).

until 1928, he has been established in the U.S. since 1937. His influence in the field of education continued on this continent when he became chairman of the department of architecture at Harvard (1938–1953). His conception of architectural teamwork led to the formation of The Architects' Collaborative (TAC), designers of Harvard's Graduate Center. It has attracted commissions on the scale of a civic center for Tallahassee, Fla., and the new U.S. Embassy in Athens.

Grosseteste, Robert (c. 1175–1253). English prelate and scholar, bishop of Lincoln (after 1235). He is known for his determined struggle to protect the English clergy against both King Henry III and Pope Innocent IV, particularly as to the right of making ecclesiastical appointments. Also important to medieval intellectual life were his voluminous writings on everything from philosophy and theology to husbandry, largely in Latin, but also including *Le Château d'Amour* (*The Castle of Love*), a French poem of religious allegory.

Grossi, Tommaso (1790–1853). Italian poet and novelist. A member of the romantic school, he is the author of a novella in octaves entitled *Ildegonda* (1820), and a 15-canto epic poem *I Lombardi alla Prima Crociata* (1826). His novel *Marco Visconti* (1834), which follows Manzoni's model for the historical novel, is noted for its illustration of the theme of Italian independence. Verdi based the libretto for his opera *I Lombardi alla Prima Crociata* (1843) on the epic poem.

Grosz, George (1893–1961). German artist. He is known for his venomous satirical drawings which he used to attack militarism, the bourgeoisie, and capitalists. Greatly effected by the first World War, he participated in the Dada movement. When he was exiled to the U.S. after Hitler came to power, his satire became less aggressive.

Grote, George (1794–1871). English historian, educator. Active in the liberal and humanitarian movements of his day, Grote was, with John Stuart Mill and Henry Brougham, a founder of the University College, London. He was an advocate of parliamentary reform and higher education for women. He is best known for his *History of Greece* (1845–1856), for many years the definitive English work in its field, though now superseded by later scholarship. He was also the author of *Plato and the Other Companions of Socrates* (1865) and *Aristotle* (1872).

Grotius, Hugo. Latinized form of **Huig de Groot** (1583–1645). A Dutch jurist and statesman. His *De Jure Belli et Pacis* (1625), written after his escape to France as leader of the Remonstrants, is regarded as the real beginning of the science of international law. His voluminous writings include a number of tragedies.

Groto, Luigi (1541–1585). Italian dramatist and poet. Known as *Il Cieco d'Adria* (the Blind Poet of Adria) after his infirmity and his birthplace near Venice, he was the author of lyrics, comedies, and tragedies. One of the latter, *La Hadriana,* retells the story of *Romeo and Juliet,* but far more popular and influential were his epigrams and madrigals, mainly imitations of the *Greek Anthology.* He was also a diplomat and, at times, an actor, as when he performed the role of Tiresias in Sophocles' *Oedipus Rex* at the famous theatre of Vicenza built by Palladio.

ground-hog day. February 2. On that day, according to popular legend, the ground hog, or woodchuck, emerges from the hole in which he spent the winter, but if he sees his shadow he goes back to hibernate for six weeks more, and winter lasts that much longer. See CANDLEMAS DAY.

Ground We Stand On, The (1941). A collection of biographical sketches by John DOS PASSOS. Dos Passos in his novels had been passionately critical of contemporary American life. In these sketches he turned to the past to affirm the American Dream as it appeared exemplified in the philosophy of men who had made or influenced our earlier era, such as Roger Williams, Sam Adams, Tom Paine, Jefferson, Joel Barlow, and Hugh Henry Brackenridge.

Group Theatre, The. A London theater and acting company. It flourished during the 1930's, performing Marxist, labor-sympathizing, and experimental plays. W. H. AUDEN and Christopher ISHERWOOD wrote plays for this theater.

Groussard, Serge (1920–　). French novelist and journalist. His novels are a kind of fictionalized reporting of the contemporary scene: *Pogrom* (1948), about the Jews in Tripolitania, *Woman With No Past* (*La femme sans passé;* 1954), and *German Officer* (*Un officier de tradition;* 1954).

Grove, Sir George (1820–1900). English engineer and writer on music. He built the first iron lighthouse at Jamaica (1841). He is remembered chiefly as the editor of the standard *Dictionary of Music and Musicians* (1879–1886). He served as director of the Royal College of Music at Kensington from 1882 to 1894.

Grove, Lena. A character in William Faulkner's LIGHT IN AUGUST. Although not central to the main action of the story, Lena Grove offers an important and implicit contrast to the violence and death present in the plot. Her confinement symbolically reenacts the confinement of Joe CHRISTMAS' mother, and her placidity and animal unconcern make her a minor kind of Earth Mother, carrying out her natural function of reproduction in a context that seems, but for her, hostile to life and growth.

Growth of the Soil, The (*Markens Grøde;* 1917). Nobel prize-winning novel by Knut HAMSUN. Hamsun describes an elemental existence in the rough open country of Norway. Isak and Inger, the hero and heroine of the novel, are individuals, yet they possess a simple, hardy vitality that makes them personifications of pioneer life.

Grub Street. The former name of a London street (now Milton Street). Dr. Johnson says that it was "Much inhabited by writers of small histories, dictionaries, and temporary poems; whence any mean production is called *grubstreet.*" The word is used allusively for needy authors, literary hacks, and their work. George Gissing wrote a novel entitled NEW GRUB STREET.

Grumio. The clownish, punning servant of Petruchio in Shakespeare's TAMING OF THE SHREW. With his good-humored playfulness, he is a perfect foil for the lusty and vigorous Petruchio.

Grundtvig, Nicolai Frederik Severin (1783–1872). Danish poet, historian, and linguist. Until the death of his father, a clergyman, in 1813, Grundtvig served as a country curate. His prolific writing career began in Copenhagen where he published poems and articles; he also made several translations into Danish, including *Beowulf* (1820). After a term as vicar (1821–1826) that terminated in violent theological controversy, Grundtvig spent two years in England studying Anglo-Saxon manuscripts. He returned to Copenhagen where he became a bishop in 1861. As a historian, he practiced a romantic approach, treating Scandinavian mythology in *Nordens Mythologi* (1808). A religious reformer and educationalist as well, Grundtvig was a figure of great influence in Denmark.

Grundy, Mrs. *What will Mrs. Grundy say?* What will our very proper and strait-laced neighbors say? A phrase from Tom Morton's English comedy *Speed the Plough* (1800). In the first scene Mrs. Ashfield shows herself very jealous of neighbor Grundy, and farmer Ashfield says to her: "Be quiet, wull ye? Always ding, dinging Dame Grundy into my ears. What will Mrs. Grundy say? What will Mrs. Grundy think? . . ."

grüne Heinrich, Der. See GREEN HENRY.

Grünewald, Matthias (1480?–1528). German painter. He is generally regarded as the last and greatest representative of the German Gothic school. His work has great power and originality, its distortion in drawing, heavy chiaroscuro, and rich color adding to its emotional intensity. The complex, many-winged altarpiece—now in the Colmar Museum—is his masterpiece.

Grushenka. In Feodor Dostoevski's THE BROTHERS KARAMAZOV, the beautiful young woman loved by Dmitri and pursued by his father, Feodor Pavlovich. Although her past is checkered and her reputation not the best, Grushenka is as large-hearted in her way as Dmitri himself. Often referred to in the novel as a kitten and a cat, she shows both sets of qualities, being playful and soft at times and crafty and malicious at others. Her love for Dmitri grows, regenerates her, and at the end of the novel she prepares to follow him to his Siberian imprisonment.

Gryll Grange (1860). A novel by Thomas Love PEACOCK. The action, such as it is, takes place during a house party in an English country mansion. There is a great deal of witty and erudite conversation, while most of the events are of a cheerfully preposterous character, such as the simultaneous marriage of nine couples that ends the book.

Gryphius, Andreas. Pen name of Andreas Greif (1616–1664). German baroque poet and dramatist. Gryphius, like Grimmelshausen, was deeply affected by the Thirty Years' War. His works frequently deal with the theme of the vanity of human life and of petty human ambitions, and it is characteristic that in his two most famous historical tragedies, *Katharina von Georgien* (*Catherine of Georgia,* 1657) and *Carolus Stuardus* (*Charles Stuart,* 1657), the hero dies a martyr's death. Gryphius' tragic style was strongly influenced by Seneca and by the Dutch drama of his time, but his own originality is felt in such works as *Cardenio und Celinde* (1657), which has been called the first "bourgeois tragedy" in German, and in his comedies, the most famous of which is *Absurda Comica oder Herr Peter Squentz* (1663). In his lyrics he often combines religious subject matter and classical forms.

gryphon. See GRIFFIN.

Guanhumara. See GUINEVERE.

Guard, Theodore de la. See Nathaniel WARD.

Guardi, Francesco (1712–1793). Venetian painter, pupil of Antonio Canaletto. Using muted tones animated by dabs of bright color and a sketchy touch to suggest details and highlights, he painted intimate, poetic scenes of Venice, its courtyards, canals, and piazzas.

Guardian Angel, The (1867). A novel by Oliver Wendell HOLMES. Myrtle Hazard, an orphan brought from the tropics to live in an austere New England home, is descended from a line of ancestors of widely differing natures. Excitable and uncontrolled, she runs away; when she is returned to New England, she becomes ill and hysterical. Under the intelligent guardianship of Professor Gridley, she is restored to health and falls in love with the young sculptor, Clement Lindsay. During the Civil War, she goes with him to the front, and nurses the wounded. Proper treatment and environment overcoming heredity, her mental balance is restored.

Guarini, Giambattista (1538–1612). Ferrarese poet. He wrote one of the most popular and influential of Renaissance dramas, IL PASTOR FIDO. A pastoral tragicomedy in imitation of TASSO's AMINTA, it was translated into English by Sir Richard Fanshawe in 1647. In John Fletcher's *The Faithful Shepherdess* (1610), Guarini's faithful shepherd has changed sex, and the plot has been altered, but the English play is based upon the Italian. As a critic, Guarini defended his mixture of tragedy and comedy, and generally argued for greater freedom from classical rules in literary genres.

Guarino of Verona (1374-1460). Italian educator. Teaching mainly at the Ferrara court school, he used methods, based on Greek ideals, intended to educate the pupil completely. Both he and VITTORINO OF FELTRE exercised great influence on their pupils and on future educational theory.

Guarneri. See CREMONA.

Guazzo, Stefano (1530-1593). Italian diplomat and man of letters. His *La civile conversazione* (1574), is a courtesy book composed of four books of dialogues which offer a model for the would-be gentleman to follow in polite discourse. In England, the translation (1581-1586) by George Pettie and Bartholomew Young placed it beside THE COURTIER and the *Galateo* of Della Casa as indispensable reading.

Gudrun. (1) A German epic poem written about 1210 by an unknown Austrian, apparently in imitation of the *Nibelungenlied*. Its many sea settings are unusual among German tales. Of its three sections, the first concerns Hagen, king of Ireland, and the second describes Hetel's courtship of Hagen's daughter Hilde. In the third part, their daughter Gudrun is engaged to Herwig of Seeland, but is abducted by Hartmut of Normandy. She refuses to marry her captor, so for 13 years she is forced to do menial servant's work. At last Herwig, accompanied by Gudrun's brother, comes to her rescue; and the lovers are happily married.

(2) Sigurd's wife in the VÖLSUNGA SAGA, better known as Kriemhild in the NIBELUNGENLIED and Gutrune in Wagner's tetralogy of operas, DER RING DES NIBELUNGEN.

(3) The heroine of the Icelandic LAXDALE SAGA, and daughter of Queen Grimhild. She was a selfish, independent, forceful woman, married successively to Thorwald, Thord, and Bolli, and in love with Kjartan, whose death she caused.

(4) One of the two leading women characters in D. H. Lawrence's novel WOMEN IN LOVE. She is believed to have been based on Katherine Mansfield.

Guebres. See GHEBERS.

Guedalla, Philip (1889-1944). English historian and biographer who wrote in the manner of Lytton Strachey. Among his biographies are *Palmerston* (1926) and *The Duke* (1931), which is about Wellington.

Guelfo (**Guelph**) or **Carlo** (**Charles**) of Denmark. In the GERUSALEMME LIBERATA of Tasso, the Christian knight who narrates the death of Sveno in a massacre which he alone survived. He is also one of the two knights (the other, Ubaldo) sent by Goffredo the Christian general to bring back Rinaldo of Este. He and Ubaldo complete their mission with the aid of the Hermit of Ascalon, who shows them where to find Rinaldo and how to extricate him from the enchantments of Armida.

Guelphs (or **Guelfs**) and **Ghibellines.** Names of the rival political parties in 12th-century Germany, adopted by 13th- and 14th-century Italian parties. The Ghibellines were the supporters of the Holy Roman Emperor, at that time a German; the Guelphs were his opponents, usually supported by the papacy. At the time of DANTE the Guelphs of Tuscany were bitterly divided into two factions: see BIANCHI AND NERI.

Guérin, Georges Maurice de (1810-1839). French poet. His prose poem *Le Centaure* was published posthumously by George Sand in *Revue des Deux Mondes* (1840). His sister Eugénie Guérin (1805-1848) is famous for her *Journal,* a posthumously published diary.

Guermantes, de. A large family of the French aristocracy, in Marcel Proust's REMEMBRANCE OF THINGS PAST. Duc Basin, called the Prince de Laume before his father's death, is the elder brother of Baron de CHARLUS and of Mme de Marsantes, the mother of Robert de SAINT-LOUP. Basin's wife, Oriane, the Duchesse de Guermantes is even more of an aristocrat in her own right, being a descendant of the eighth-century Geneviève de Brabant and a cousin of many of the members of European royalty. She is represented as the most important hostess in French society, and the narrator in his youth goes through a period of worshiping her extravagantly. There are also the Prince and Princesse de Guermantes, and various other relatives by blood and marriage.

Guermantes Way, The. See REMEMBRANCE OF THINGS PAST.

Guerrazzi, Francesco Domenico (1804-1873). Italian novelist. He was a prolific author of historical novels with patriotic themes in keeping with the struggle for Italian independence. His best-known work is *L'Assedio di Firenze* (1836).

Guerre de Troie n'aura pas lieu, La. See TIGER AT THE GATES.

Guest, Lady Charlotte Elizabeth (1812-1895). Welsh writer. Her MABINOGION (1838-1849, 1877), a collection of tales translated from the Welsh, is a classic of Celtic folklore.

Guest, Edgar A[lbert] (1881-1959). English-born American writer of verse. At the age of 20, Guest began to conduct a daily column of verse in the Detroit *Free Press.* His sentimental, folksy, moralistic doggerel was widely syndicated, extremely popular, and known throughout the U.S. Among his collections are *A Heap o' Livin'* (1916), *Just Folks* (1917), and *Life's Highway* (1933).

Guevara, Antonio de (c. 1480-1545). Spanish historian and Franciscan monk. He wrote *The Dial of Princes* (*Libro Llamado Relox de Principes, en el Qual Va Encorporado el Muy Famoso Libro de Marco Aurelio;* 1529), a didactic novel giving an imaginary life of Marcus Aurelius, and a series of *Epístolas Familiares* (1539-1545), often called the *Golden Letters* because of their supposed worth. These works, translated into English by Thomas North and Edward Hellowes, may have been the inspiration for Lyly's *Euphues.* See EUPHUISM.

Guggenheim fellowships. Annual awards provided by the John Simon Guggenheim Memorial Foundation. Each year, 40 or 50 fellowships are given to Americans in the fields of literature, stagecraft, art, music, history, philosophy, and science. Among the writers who have received the award are John Dos

Passos, W. H. Auden, Jacques Barzun, Theodore Roethke, and Lewis Mumford.

Guicciardini, Francesco (1483–1540). Florentine historian and diplomat. Guicciardini's public career was spent in the service of the Medici and the papacy. Though critical of his contemporary, Machiavelli, he shares with him a realistic approach and a modern historical sense in his *Storia d'Italia* (*History of Italy*) and other writings. Passages of the *Storia*, translated into English by Geoffrey Fenton from a French version, appeared in the *Chronicles* of Holinshed, thus, exerting an important influence on English writers like Raleigh and Bacon.

Guiccioli, Countess **Teresa** (1801?–1873). Italian noblewoman, known for her long-lasting liaison with Lord BYRON. She was still a very young girl, married to a much older man, when in 1819 their relationship began; a year later she left her husband and became Byron's openly acknowledged mistress. The attachment, which lasted the rest of Byron's life, is considered to have had a steadying influence on the poet and to have contributed to his increasing literary skill and facility during his years in Italy. She wrote *My Recollections of Lord Byron* (1868).

Guiderius. In Shakespeare's CYMBELINE, the elder son of Cymbeline, king of Britain. He is abducted by Belarius as an infant and raised as his son under the name of Polydore. He and his brother Arviragus are "as gentle as zephyrs blowing below the violet . . . and yet as rough, their royal blood enchaf'd, as the rud'st wind."

Guidiccioni, Giovanni (1500–1541). Italian papal official. He is noted for his sonnets on Italian affairs during the crucial years 1526–1530, when the Spanish were gaining domination over Italy and the Papacy. His *Rime* (*Verses*) were published in 1557.

Guido delle Colonne (13th century). Sicilian poet. He is known for his *Historia Troiana* (c. 1285), a Latin work in which he embodies the Troilus story adapted from the *Roman de Troie* of Benoît de Sainte-Maure. Guido is considered to have been the source of Boccaccio's *Il Filostrato*. He visited England in the retinue of Edward I when the latter returned from the Crusades.

Guidone Selvaggio (**Guido the Savage**). In the ORLANDO FURIOSO of Ariosto, a younger brother of Rinaldo and kinsman of Astolfo. Having been shipwrecked on the coast of the Amazons, he is doomed to fight their ten male champions. He slays them all, but must then marry ten of the Amazons. With the help of his favorite wife, Aleria, and Astolfo, who uses his magic horn to scatter the Amazons, he escapes and joins the forces of Charlemagne against the pagan armies.

Guildenstern. See ROSENCRANTZ AND GUILDENSTERN.

Guillaume de Lorris (early 13th century). French poet famous for having written the first part of the ROMANCE OF THE ROSE.

Guillaume Tell. See William TELL.

Guillén, Jorge (1893–   ). Spanish poet and academician. Born in Valladolid, Guillén began a teaching career that took him from Seville to Wellesley and then to Harvard University. His cold, intellectual poetry reveals the influence of Paul Valéry; it appears in the volume *Cántico* (1928), which is enlarged with every new edition. Other recent volumes include *Maremágnum* (*Clamor*, 1957) and *Viviendo y otros poemas* (1958).

guillotine. A decapitating machine much used during the French Revolution. A similar device was already in use in the 16th century in the south of France and in Italy, where it was called *mannaia* and was used exclusively for beheading nobility. Joseph Ignace Guillotin (1738–1814), member of the Constitutional Assembly, proposed in 1789 that a uniform method of capital punishment be established and that a machine, surer and swifter than the headsman's hand, be devised to carry it out. Dr. Antoine Louis, then secretary of the French College of Surgeons, was the actual designer of the guillotine, and it was at first called *louison* or *louisette*. It was first used on April 25, 1792. It is still the legal method of execution in France.

Guinevere. In Arthurian legend, the wife of King ARTHUR. In the many versions in which she appears, her name is spelled a variety of ways. (See GANOR.) She is, for example, the Guanhumara of Geoffrey of Monmouth, the early Irish Finnabair, the Welsh Gwenhwyvar. In many of the romances, she is said to be the daughter of King Leodegrance who, when Arthur and Guinevere are married, gives to Arthur the famous ROUND TABLE.

Like her classical counterparts, Helen of Troy and Persephone, Guinevere is one of those legendary heroines who is always being abducted and whose beauty brings betrayal, war, disaster. In Geoffrey of Monmouth's *History of the Kings of Britain* (1137), she is seduced by Arthur's nephew (or son), MORDRED, thus ultimately bringing about the death of Arthur and an end to many others. In most versions, however, it is Sir LAUNCELOT with whom Guinevere is illicitly involved. In *Lancelot* (c. 1180) by Chrétien de Troyes, it is that ideal knight who must go to the rescue of Guinevere when she is kidnapped by an unknown knight.

In Malory's *Morte d'Arthur* (c. 1469), Sir Launcelot is not only often the rescuer of Guinevere, but also her abductor. Here also, however, it is Mordred who, in the absence of Arthur, has usurped the kingdom and wishes to seduce and marry Guinevere. Thus begins the closing tragedy that culminates in the death of Arthur and the end of the order of the Round Table. Arthur hastens back from his expedition against Leo, king of the Romans; Guinevere flees, and a desperate battle is fought in which Mordred is slain and Arthur mortally wounded. Guinevere renounces Launcelot after the death of Arthur and takes the veil at Almesbury, where later she dies. But even at the end, Launcelot must go to carry her away once more. In a vision one night, he is told that Queen Guinevere is dead. Sadly, he goes for her, carries her body to Glastonbury, and places it beside the body of King Arthur.

Tennyson, in his *Idylls of the King* (1859–1885) makes Guinevere guilty only in her passion for Launcelot, and not a party to Mordred's treachery.

Guinicelli or **Guinizelli, Guido** (c. 1240–c. 1276). Italian poet, founder of the STILNOVISTI school of poetry. Only a few of his sonnets and lyrics have survived; the most famous is the *canzone* called *Al Cor Gentil*, translated as *The Gentle Heart* (1861) by Dante Gabriel Rossetti.

Guinness, Sir Alec (1914–   ). English stage and screen actor. He was a member of the Old Vic (1936–1939), afterward touring Europe. He appeared on the stage in New York in Eliot's *The Cocktail Party* (1950). He is best known in America as a film actor for his outstanding, subtle comic roles in *Man in the White Suit, Kind Hearts and Coronets, The Lavender Hill Mob,* and *The Horse's Mouth* (for which he wrote the screen play). As a dramatic actor his depiction of Fagin in *Oliver Twist* so aroused the ire of pressure groups that the film was banned in the U.S. for several years.

Güiraldes, Ricardo. See DON SEGUNDO SOMBRA.

Guise. A French ducal house, a branch of the house of Lorraine. The Guise family acquired great political influence upon the accession (1559) of Francis II, who had married Mary, Queen of Scots, granddaughter of Claude, first duke of Guise. Henry, third duke of Guise (1550–1588), was known, like his father, as *le Balafré* (*Fr.,* "the scarred") because of a battle scar on his face. He became the leader of the Roman Catholic party in French politics and organized the HOLY LEAGUE. The idol of the Parisian mob, Henry probably aspired to the French throne and was murdered at the instigation of Henry III. The league, subsequently under the leadership of the duke of Mayenne, brother of the third duke, was crushed before the end of the 16th century. The direct line of the house of Guise became extinct in 1675. See also HENRY IV (of France).

Guiterman, Arthur (1871–1943). American poet. A deft light versifier, Guiterman, who was born in Vienna of American parents, first attracted attention with his *Rhymed Reviews* in *Life* magazine. He made an adaptation of Molière's *L'Ecole des Maris* in rhymed verse for the Theatre Guild (1933), and wrote the libretto and lyrics for Walter Damrosch's opera, *The Man Without a Country* (1937). *Betel Nuts* (1907), *The Laughing Muse* (1915), *Ballads of Old New York* (1920), and *Lyric Laughter* (1939) are among the collections of his verse.

Guitry, Sacha [**Alexandre Pierre Georges**] (1885–1957). French actor and dramatist, son of the actor Lucien Guitry (1860–1925). Extremely popular between the world wars for his light sparkling comedies, he wrote over 130 plays, such as *Le Page* (1902), *Sleeping Partners* (1916), *Mariette* (1928), and *Where There's a Will* (1934). Some, such as *Deburau* (1918), *Pasteur* (1919), and *Mozart* (1926), were historical biographies.

Guizot, François Pierre Guillaume (1787–1874). French historian and statesman. A professor of history at the Sorbonne during the earlier years of his career, Guizot published historical works that comprise a voluminous body of writing. He became involved in politics during the July Monarchy (see JULY REVOLUTION) and served in various ministerial capacities under LOUIS PHILIPPE (1830–1848).

Gulbeyas. The sultana in Lord Byron's DON JUAN. Having purchased Juan at the slave market and introduced him into the harem in female attire, she is outraged to find that he prefers Dudu, one of the attendant beauties, to herself. She attempts to have them drowned in the Bosphorus, but they escape.

Gulistan (Pers., **Rose Garden,** 1258). A collection of lyrics by the Persian poet SA'DI. Polished and accomplished, full of moral reflections, both witty and sweet, it contains sections on kings, dervishes, contentment, love, youth, old age, and social duties, together with many stories and philosophical sayings.

Gulliver's Travels (1726). Best-known title of *Travels into Several Remote Nations of the World, by Lemuel Gulliver,* a satiric masterpiece written in the form of a journal by Jonathan SWIFT. Lemuel Gulliver, a ship's physician, makes four voyages: to LILLIPUT, whose inhabitants are six inches tall; to BROBDINGNAG, a land of giants; to the flying island of LAPUTA, an empire of "wise men"; and to HOUYHNHNMLAND, inhabited by Houyhnhnms and Yahoos. Swift's bitterest work, *Gulliver's Travels* satirizes man's abuse of human reason as reflected in his political, social, and academic institutions; at best, man is foolish; at worst, he is nothing more than an ape. A multifarious book, it is various in its appeal: it is enchantingly playful and fantastic, and is often read by children; it is a witty, allegorical depiction of the political life and values of Swift's time; it is a bitter denunciation of mankind; finally it is Swift's reflections on man's corruption of his highest attribute, reason.

Gull's Hornbook, The (1609). A prose satire by Thomas DEKKER. In the form of a mock hornbook, or primer, it attacked the manners of emptyheaded dandies (gulls) through ironic instructions in the kind of behavior that would attract attention at the theater, the tavern, the gambling house, and other public places.

Gumiliov, Nikolai Stepanovich (1886–1921). Russian poet. Gumiliov was one of the founders of the Acmeist movement. His early travels in Africa were reflected in the exoticism of his poetry. Between 1910 and 1918, he was married to the poet Anna AKHMATOVA, also a member of the Acmeist group. After the revolution, Gumiliov openly expressed his opposition to the Bolsheviks, and was executed for conspiracy in 1921. See ACMEISM.

Gundolf, Friedrich. Pen name of **Friedrich Gundelfinger** (1880–1931). German literary historian, critic, and biographer. In his youth he was a member of the circle about Stefan GEORGE. His works include *Shakespeare und der deutsche Geist* (*Shakespeare and the German Spirit,* 1911); *Shakespeare in deutscher Sprache* (*Shakespeare in German,* 1908), a 10-volume translation done in collaboration with George; and works on the German romantics.

Gunga Din (1892). One of Rudyard Kipling's BARRACK-ROOM BALLADS, in praise of a Hindu water-carrier for a British Indian regiment.

> An' for all 'is dirty 'ide
> 'E was white, clear white, inside....
> . . . You're a better man than I am, Gunga Din.

Gunn, Thom[**son William**] (1929–   ). English poet. His verse, stylistically influenced by William Empson, often deals with violent, contemporary subject matter. Among his publications is *My Sad Captains* (1961).

Gunnar. See GUNTHER.

Gunnarsson, Gunnar (1889–   ). Icelandic novelist, poet, and playwright. Born into a farming family and largely self-educated, Gunnarsson celebrated in his work the courage and dignity of humble people in his native land. During his extended stay in Denmark (1910–1939), he published a nostalgic novel series, *Borgsloegtens Historie* (4 vols., 1912–1914). A longer novel series, planned as a narration of Iceland's history, includes *Edbrødre* (*The Sown Brothers*, 1918) and *Salige er de Enfoldige* (*Seven Days' Darkness*, 1920).

Gunpowder Plot. In English history, a conspiracy of a few Roman Catholics led by Robert Catesby to murder James I and the members of both houses of Parliament. The date selected for the attempt was Nov. 5, 1605, when James was to appear in person at the opening of Parliament. The plot was foiled when Guy Fawkes (1570–1606), who had undertaken to fire the gunpowder for the explosion, was arrested in the cellar under the House of Lords on November 4. The failure of the plot is still celebrated in England on November 5 as Guy Fawkes Day.

Gunther. Burgundian king who courts Brunhild in the NIBELUNGENLIED and Wagner's RING DES NIBELUNGEN, known as Gunnar in the VÖLSUNGA SAGA. He is probably partially based on Gundahar, a historical ruler overthrown by the Huns in 436.

Günther, Johann Christian (1695–1723). German poet admired by Geothe. His style is halfway between the mannerism of the late Baroque and the more personal lyric that developed in the 18th century. His works include a tragedy, *Die Eifersucht* (*Jealousy*, 1715).

Gunther, John (1901–1970). American journalist and writer. With *Inside Europe* (1936) Gunther established his reputation as a careful researcher and colorful writer. *Inside Asia* (1939), *Inside Latin America* (1939), *Inside U.S.A.* (1947), *Inside Africa* (1955), and *Inside Russia Today* (1958) followed, and a quarter century later, he came full circle with *Inside Europe Today* (1961). He is also the author of *Death Be Not Proud* (1949), a moving memorial on the death of his son, and *Roosevelt in Retrospect* (1950). Gunther described how and why he wrote the "Inside" books in *A Fragment of Autobiography* (1962).

guru. (Sans., "venerable"). In Hinduism one's personal spiritual teacher and religious guide. *Guru* was the title taken by the succession of SIKH spiritual and temporal leaders from 1469 to 1708.

Gustavus II, known as **Gustavus Adolphus** (1594–1632). A king of Sweden, the Lion of the North, or the Snow King. Supporting the Protestant cause in the Thirty Years' War (1630–1632), he won the battle of Lützen against Wallenstein, but was mortally wounded. One of the greatest generals of all times, he saved Protestantism in Germany. His death left Sweden under a regency with his six-year-old daughter CHRISTINA as nominal queen.

gute Mensch von Sezuan, Der. See GOOD WOMAN OF SEZUAN, THE.

Gutenberg, Johannes (c. 1400–c. 1468). German printer, usually considered the inventor of movable metal type. Documents dating from 1439 indicate that he was involved in various secret operations employing a press and a device presumed to be a type mold. In 1455 at Mainz he entered into a partnership with Johann Fust, a moneylender. The partnership was dissolved five years later when Gutenberg defaulted on the loan and Fust seized Gutenberg's equipment and stock and continued the opera-

tion himself with the help of Peter Schöffer. It is generally accepted that the so-called *Gutenberg Bible* —more properly called the *Mazarin Bible* from its discovery in 1760 in the library of Cardinal Mazarin in Paris (see BIBLE, SPECIALLY NAMED EDITIONS)— was issued from the press that Gutenberg established and Fust took over. Whether Gutenberg alone was responsible for this edition is uncertain. None of the work ascribed to him bears his name.

After he lost his press to Fust, Gutenberg came under the patronage of Conrad Humery, a counselor of Mainz, and continued to print books. The *Catholicon* of 1460 is a fine example of his later work.

Gutiérrez, Eduardo. See GAUCHO LITERATURE.

Gutiérrez Nájera, Manuel (1859–1895). Mexican poet and journalist. Generally considered a precursor of MODERNISM, Gutiérrez Nájera was strongly influenced by the French Parnassians and symbolists. His verse is graceful, subjective, and elegiac, distinguished by elegance of style and perfection of form. His best-known poems, such as *Tristissima Nox, Serenata de Schubert,* and *Non omnis moriar,* were written after 1880; his poetry remained scattered until 1896 when a collection of his *Poesías* appeared with a preface by Justo Sierra. Gutiérrez Nájera is also remembered as the founder of the *Revista Azul,* Mexico's first modernist review.

Gutrune. See KRIEMHILD.

Gutzkow, Karl (1811–1878). German novelist and dramatist in the movement of JUNG DEUTSCHLAND (Young Germany). His early novel *Wally, die Zweiflerin* (*Wally, a Doubting Girl,* 1835) aroused a storm of protest because of its extensive treatment of such generally avoided subjects as atheism and free love, and he was jailed for three months as a result. His later social novel, *Die Ritter vom Geiste* (*The Knights of the Spirit,* 1850–1851), though not as sensational as *Wally,* is more competent as a work of art. Among his dramas, the best known is *Uriel Acosta* (1846), which depicts the struggle of a Jew for intellectual freedom.

Guy Mannering (1815). A novel by Sir Walter SCOTT, set in Scotland at the time of George III. Guy Mannering, a young Englishman traveling in Scotland, stops overnight at the home of the laird of Ellangowan. A son is born to the laird that night and Mannering, a student of astrology, predicts two crises in the boy's life in his fifth and 21st years. He then goes on his way. Some time later, the son, Harry Bertram, disappears at the age of five. His mother dies of shock and the laird lives on only for a few years, leaving his daughter Lucy in the care of Dominie SAMPSON, a friend and schoolteacher, on his death. Mannering, returned from India after years of living there, invites Lucy and Dominie to live with him and his daughter, Julia. He is followed from India by a Captain Brown whom he erroneously suspects of loving his wife and with whom he has dueled. Brown is actually in love with Julia. In the climax of the book, Brown is recognized by a gypsy; he is Harry Bertram, although he did not know it, and was spirited off by the unscrupulous lawyer Glossin who got Harry's father's estate for himself since the heir had disappeared. All is restored to Harry and he wins the friendship of Mannering and the hand of Julia. The book is noted not so much for its plot, which brims with coincidences, as for

the creation of such notable characters as Meg MER-
RILIES and Dandie DINMONT.

Guy of Warwick (c. 1300). The title of a Middle English romance and the name of its hero. The
exploits and adventures of Guy of Warwick are typical of the heroes of non-Arthurian romance, such
as Bevis of Hampton, Havelock, and King Horn.
To obtain Phelis (Felice) as his wife, Guy of Warwick undertook many knightly deeds. He rescued the
daughter of the emperor of Germany, and went to
fight against the Saracens, slaying the doughty Col-
dran, Elmaye King of Tyre, and the soldan himself.
Then he returned and wedded Phelis, but in 40 days
went back to the Holy Land, where he slew the
giant Amarant, and many others. Having achieved
all this he became a hermit near Warwick. Daily he
went in disguise to his own castle and begged bread
of his wife Phelis; but on his death bed he sent her
a ring, by which she recognized him, and went to
close his dying eyes.

Guyon, Sir. See FAERIE QUEENE, THE.

Guzmán, Martín Luis (1887–   ). Mexican essayist and novelist. During the Mexican Revolution,
Guzmán was an adherent first of Venustiano Carranza, then of Pancho Villa. From 1923 to 1936 he
lived in Spain, where he wrote the books that
brought him immediate renown. Guzmán's best-
known work is *El águila y la serpiente* (*The Eagle*

Guy of Warwick killing the giant.
From the 1560 edition.

and the Serpent, 1928), an autobiographical collection of sketches describing scenes and personages of
the revolution. *La sombra del caudillo* (1929) is a
roman à clef exposing the cynicism and intrigue that
characterized Mexican politics in the 1920's. In the
four-volume *Memorias de Pancho Villa* (1938–1940),
Guzmán gives an account of the deeds and sayings
of the revolutionary hero.

Guzmán de Alfarache, Vida del Pícaro (1599,
1604). A PICARESQUE novel by Mateo ALEMÁN. The
book is supposedly the autobiography of a Sevillian
rogue who composes it while in forced retirement in
the galleys, where he has been sent for defrauding
a rich widow. After relating each of his adventures,
the narrator adds a long moral; these passages are
outstanding for their superb prose and good sense.
The book also contains numerous subsidiary tales,
such as the famous story of Ozmin and Daraja. Alemán's original title for the work was *Atalaya de la
vida* (*Watch-tower of Life*), but his contemporaries
insisted on calling it *El Pícaro*.

Gwendolen or **Guendolene.** See LOCRINE.

Gwenhwyvar. See GUINEVERE.

Gwyn or **Gwynne, Eleanor.** Known as **Nell
Gwyn** (1650–1687). English actress and mistress of
Charles II. She is said to have begun her career as
an orange-vendor in a London theater. As an actress,
she was noted for her skill in comedy roles, and her
gaiety and good nature made her a great favorite
with the public. She became Charles's mistress in
1668 and bore him two sons, one of whom was later
made Duke of St. Alban's. According to tradition,
the King's dying request to his brother was "Let not
poor Nelly starve."

Gyas and Cloanthus. In Vergil's AENEID, two
companions of Aeneas, generally mentioned together
as "fortis Gyas fortisque Cloanthus." The phrase has
become proverbial for two very similar characters.

gypsy. A member of a dark-skinned nomadic
race. Gypsies first appeared in England about the
beginning of the 16th century, and, as they were
thought to have come from Egypt, were named
Egyptians, which soon became corrupted to *Gypcians,*
and so to its present form. They call themselves
Romany (from Gypsy *rom,* a man, husband), which
is also the name of their language: a debased Hindu
dialect with large additions of words from Persian, Armenian, and many European languages. It is thought
that early gypsies migrated from Northern India.

The name of the largest group of European gypsies
is *Atzigan;* this, in Turkey and Greece, became
Tshingian, in the Balkans and Romania *Tsigan,* in
Hungary *Czigany,* in Germany *Zigeuner,* in Italy
Zingari, in Portugal *Cigano,* and in Spain *Gitano.*
The original name is said to mean dark man. See
BOHEMIAN.

There is a legend that the gypsies are waifs and
strays on the earth because they refused to shelter
the Virgin and her child in their flight to Egypt.

H

Habakkuk. An Old Testament book bearing the name of its author. It is a short, cogitative book written just before the fall of Jerusalem in 586 B.C. The author questions the actions of a god who uses a wicked enemy to punish his sinful people. Habakkuk resolves his problems by foreseeing a final triumph over evil by the forces of righteousness and faith.

Habington, William (1605–1654). English poet. He was the author of the lyrical collection *Castara* (1634), a series of elegant poems praising the chastity of his mistress and muse.

Hachette, Louis Christophe François (1800–1864). French publisher, founder of the Paris firm of Hachette et Cie (1826). The firm is noted for its carefully annotated, classical texts, its educational books, and dictionaries.

Hacker, Louis M[orton] (1899–   ). American historian and teacher. Interested in the impact of economics on American politics, public policy, and social and individual behavior, Hacker wrote *A Short History of the New Deal* (1934), *The Triumph of American Capitalism* (1949), *American Capitalism* (1957), and other books. He joined the faculty of Columbia University in 1934 and later became dean of the university's School of General Studies.

Hades (Haides, Aïdoneus). The place of the dead. In Homer, the name of the god, also called Plouton (Pluto), who reigns over the dead. In later mythology, the name was also applied to the abode of the departed spirits, a place of gloom, but not necessarily, like the Christian Hell, a place of punishment and torture. As the state or abode of the dead it corresponds to the Hebrew *Sheol,* a word which the translators of the Authorized Version frequently replaced with the misleading *Hell.* Hence Hades is often used as a euphemism for Hell.

Hadith (Arabic, "a saying or tradition"). The traditions about the prophet Muhammad's sayings and doings. This compilation, made in the 10th century by the Muslim jurists Moshin and Bokhari, forms a supplement to the Koran as the Talmud does to the Jewish Scriptures. The *Hadith* was originally not allowed to be committed to writing, but the danger of the traditions being perverted or forgotten led to their being placed on record.

hadji. A pilgrim; specifically, a Muslim who has completed the required pilgrimage or *hadj* to Mecca. The word is often prefixed to a name as an epithet of honor. See ISLAM.

Hadrian. Full Latin names **Publius Aelius Hadrianus** (A.D. 76–138). Roman emperor (117–138). As part of his policy of consolidation and of renouncing conquest, he established the Euphrates as the Eastern boundary of the Roman Empire. He effected the construction in Britain of Hadrian's Wall (120–123) from Solway Firth to the south of Tyne as a protection against the Picts and Scots. He profoundly admired Greek culture and did much to beautify Athens with new buildings. His tomb at Rome and his villa at Tibur are remarkable structures. Hadrian was a learned man, an amateur architect, and a writer of genuine gifts. His reign was one of the finest ages in Roman history, and it continued for many years longer through his foresight in choosing as his successors Antoninus Pius and Marcus Aurelius. Marguerite Yourcenar wrote a thoughtful fictional biography of Hadrian, which she called a "meditation on history," in *Mémoires d'Hadrien* (*Memoirs of Hadrian;* 1951).

Hadzhi Murad (1911). A novel by Count Leo TOLSTOI. A short book, written in 1904, it is set during a Cossack uprising in the Caucasus. Replaced as a leader by a rival, Hadzhi deserts to the Russians. He later changes his mind and, pining for his own people, decides to go back to them, even though he knows they will kill him for his desertion. The novel is generally considered one of the most artistic works of Tolstoi's later period.

Haeckel, Ernst (1834–1919). German zoologist and philosopher who popularized the ideas of Darwin. In *The Riddle of the Universe* (*Die Welträtsel;* 1899) he applied the doctrine of evolution to philosophy and religion.

Haemon (Haimon). See ANTIGONE.

Hāfiz. Pen name of **Shams-ud-din Muhammad** (c. 1300–1388). Persian poet. A student of both poetry and theology, Hāfiz became a dervish, a member of the Sūfi, an Islamic sect, and a professor of Koranic studies; his pen name, Hāfiz, "one who remembers," was the Persian term applied to a scholar who knew the Koran by heart. The *Dīvān of Hāfiz* is a large collection of odes (*ghazals*) written in 5 to 15 couplets (*distichs*) each. The second lines of the couplets rhyme throughout and the last couplet always introduces the poet's name. An example of a final couplet is: "The laughing wine, the sweet girl's tumbled tresses,/ Were more than even Hāfiz could deny!" The odes are arranged alphabetically in the book according to their rhymes. The subjects of the odes include love, wine, birds, flowers, the instability of all things human, and Allah and the prophets. Beside their apparent content, the odes have religious meaning in the mystical terms of the Sūfi.

Best known for his odes, Hāfiz also wrote in other forms, especially the *rubáiyát* (rhymed quatrains).

Hagar. In the Old Testament, the Egyptian servant of Abraham's wife Sarah. When she bore Abraham a son ISHMAEL, she grew haughty towards her mistress, who remained childless; but after the birth of Sarah's son Isaac, Hagar and Ishmael were cast out into the wilderness. On one occasion, when they were perishing of thirst, an angel of the Lord pointed out a spring of water in the desert, thereby saving the lives of Hagar and Ishmael (Gen. 21).

Hagen or **Hagan.** Murderer of Siegfried in German legend. A retainer of the Burgundian kings in the NIBELUNGENLIED, he is their half-brother (son of ALBERICH) in Richard Wagner's four-part opera RING DES NIBELUNGEN.

Haggadah. The portion of the MIDRASH that contains rabbinical interpretations of the historical and legendary, ethical, parabolic, and speculative parts of the Hebrew scriptures. The portion devoted to law, practice, and doctrine is called the *Halachah*. They were begun in the 2nd century and completed by the 11th.

Haggai. A book of the Old Testament named for its author. The prophet Haggai's main concern was with the correct and speedy rebuilding of the temple in Jerusalem after the return from exile in Babylon (c. 530 B.C.). He also expresses the Messianic hope.

Haggard, Sir [Henry] Rider (1856–1925). English novelist, whose tense, mysterious stories usually occur in some exotic African setting. His most effective novels are *King Solomon's Mines* (1885), *Allan Quartermain* (1887), SHE (1887), and its sequel *Ayesha* (1905). Many of his books, notably *She* and *King Solomon's Mines,* have been dramatized and made into motion pictures.

Hagia Sophia. See SANTA SOPHIA.

Hague Tribunal. An international court of arbitration meeting at The Hague. It arose out of the Hague Congress on disarmament in 1899 and has been superseded by the Permanent Court of International Justice.

Hahn, Otto (1879–1968). German chemist. He did important basic research in radiology and atomic fission. In 1938, with Lise Meitner and Fritz Strassman, he split the uranium atom. He won the Nobel Prize for chemistry in 1944.

Haidée. In Lord Byron's DON JUAN, the beautiful Greek girl who finds Juan when he is cast ashore on one of the Cyclades. She hides him in a cave, and the two soon fall in love. When her father, Lambro, a rich Greek pirate, returns from an expedition, the romance is discovered. Juan is exiled, and Haidée goes mad and dies after a lingering illness. There is also a Haidée who figures in Dumas' *Count of Monte Cristo.*

haikai. See HAIKU.

haiku. A form of Japanese poetry, composed of seventeen syllables (in 5, 7, 5 pattern), giving a complete impression or mood. Its greatest practitioner was MATSUO BASHŌ, who established the rules for the content of the poems and the allusions permitted. It developed from *haikai,* a form of linked verse (composed by various poets) popular in the 16th and 17th centuries. *Hokku* is the opening verse in a series of linked verse; *haiku* is a separate poem of the *haikai* school. The three terms are frequently confused. An example of *haiku* by Matsuo Bashō:

> This road:
> no one walks along it.
> Dusk in autumn.

See TANKA.

Haile Selassie (1891–   ). Name assumed upon coronation by Ras **Tafari,** emperor of Ethiopia (1930). Called the Lion of Judah, he was driven from Ethiopia by Italian conquest in 1936–1941, but restored to his throne in 1941.

Hairy Ape, The (1922). A play by Eugene O'NEILL. An expressionistic drama, it tells of a crude stoker on a transatlantic liner. Yank, who feels that he "belongs" in the depths of the ship, becomes disillusioned with his life when he and the men are inspected by a society girl. His attempt to climb the evolutionary ladder fails in New York City, where he finally goes to the zoo; realizing that the ape is his nearest kin in spirit, he releases the animal from its cage and is crushed to death by the beast.

Hajar-al-Aswad. In the Muslim faith, a famous black stone, irregularly oval, about seven inches in breadth and surrounded with a circle of gold, which is found in the northeast corner of the KAABA. According to legend, when Abraham wished to build the Kaaba, the stones came to him of their own accord and he commanded all the faithful to kiss this one. The stone was supposed to have been whiter than milk when it first came from Paradise, but became black through the sins of the millions that had kissed it. On the Day of the Resurrection, it is believed, the stone will have two eyes by which it will recognize all those who have kissed it, and a tongue with which it will bear witness to Allah.

The stone is probably an aerolite, and it was worshiped long before Muhammad's day. In the second century A.D. Maximus Tyrius spoke of the Arabians paying homage to it, and Persian legend states that it was an emblem of Saturn.

Hajji Baba of Ispahan, The Adventures of (1824). A PICARESQUE romance by James MORIER, dealing with life in Persia. The hero is a sort of Persian Gil Blas whose roguery takes him into all spheres of Persian society. In a satiric sequel, *Hajji Baba in England* (1828), he visits England as a government official, seeing familiar customs with a foreign eye.

Hajji Khalfah. Original name **Mustafa ibn-Abdallah** (1600?–1658). A Turkish historian and bibliographer. He compiled a bibliographical lexicon, with memoirs of the authors, of more than 25,000 books in Arabic, Turkish, and Persian.

Hakluyt, Richard (1553–1616). English scholar and clergyman. As a boy Hakluyt became interested in maps and explorations, and devoted his life to compiling and editing accounts of English voyages of discovery. In 1582 he published his first compilation, *Divers Voyages touching the Discovery of America.* This was followed in 1589 by *Principal Navigations, Traffics, Voyages, and Discoveries of the English Nation,* which was greatly enlarged to three volumes in 1598–1600. Called "the prose epic of the modern English nation," it contains accounts of the voyages of Raleigh, of the Cabots, of Drake's circumnavigation, of Martin Frobisher's search for the Northwest Passage, and the like. His work, which reflects the great exploring spirit of the Elizabethan age, gave additional impetus to English exploration, conquest, and colonization.

Halachah. The division of the MIDRASH that deals with the interpretation of the law, points of doctrine, etc. See HAGGADAH.

Halbe, Max (1875–1944). German dramatist in the movement of NATURALISM. He is best known for his early works, which include *Ein Emporkömmling* (*An Upstart,* 1889), a village tragedy; and *Die Jugend* (*Youth,* 1893), a lovers' tragedy of the Romeo and Juliet type, which also treats the conflict between modern personal values and traditional religious ones.

halcyon days. A time of happiness and prosperity. Halcyon is the Greek for a kingfisher, compounded of *hals,* the sea, and *kyo,* to brood on. The ancient Sicilians believed that the kingfisher laid its eggs and incubated them for 14 days before the winter solstice on the surface of the sea. During this time the waves of the sea were always unruffled.

Halcyone and Ceyx. A story told by Ovid and his medieval adapters, and used by Chaucer (spelled Alcione and Seys) as an introduction to his BOOK OF THE DUCHESS. Halcyone is often the daughter of Aeolus. She learns in a dream of the death of Ceyx, her husband, who has been drowned in a shipwreck. Next morning she finds his body cast up by the sea, and three days later she dies, usually by casting herself into the sea in grief.

Hale, Edward Everett (1822–1909). American clergyman and author. He is best known for his realistic story THE MAN WITHOUT A COUNTRY. He also wrote whimsical tales, historical romances, and scholarly works, and was the founder of *Old and New* (1870–1875), a magazine later absorbed by *Scribner's. A New England Boyhood* (1893, enlarged, 1900) and *Memories of a Hundred Years* (2 v., 1902) are autobiographical.

Hale, Nancy (1908–   ). American novelist and short-story writer. Born in Boston, the granddaughter of Edward Everett Hale, she is the author of a number of novels, among them *The Young Die Good* (1932), *Never Any More* (1934), *The Prodigal Women* (1942), and *The Sign of Jonah* (1950). Her perceptive short stories are collected in *The Earliest Dreams* (1936), *Between the Dark and the Daylight* (1943), and *The Empress' Ring* (1955). *A New England Girlhood* (1958) is her autobiography embroidered by fancy. She also wrote *The Pattern of Perfection* (1960) and *The Realities of Fiction: A Book About Writing* (1962).

Hale, Nathan (1755–1776). American hero in the Revolutionary War. He was sentenced by the British to be hanged as a spy and went to his death with the words, "I only regret that I have but one life to lose for my country." He is the hero of a drama by Clyde Fitch entitled *Nathan Hale* (1898).

Hale, Sarah Josepha. See GODEY'S LADY'S BOOK.

Halévy, Elie (1870–1937). French historian. A student of English social and political history of the 19th century, Halévy published a comprehensive study: *Histoire du peuple anglais au XIXᵉ siècle* (1912–1923, 1926–1932). His other works include *L'Angleterre en 1815* (1912), *Du Lendemain de Waterloo à la veille du Reform Bill* (*1815–1830*)

(1923), *De la crise du Reform Bill à l'avènement de Sir Robert Peel* (*1830–1841*) (1923).

Halévy, Ludovic (1834–1908). French dramatist and novelist. With Henri Meilhac (1832–1897), Halévy wrote gay, spirited librettos for the light operas of Offenbach, including *La Belle Hélène* (1865), *La Vie parisienne* (1867), and *La Grande Duchesse de Gérolstein* (1867). The partners also produced the libretto for Bizet's CARMEN and the two light, witty comedies *Froufou* (1869) and *La Petite marquise* (1874). Writing alone, Halévy enjoyed success as a novelist, his best-known work being the charming L'ABBÉ CONSTANTIN.

Half Moon. See Henry HUDSON.

Haliburton, Thomas Chandler (1796–1865). Canadian humorist. In 1856, Haliburton, a lawyer and judge, retired and went to England, was welcomed into literary and political circles, and was elected to the House of Commons. A fanatic conservative, he was critical of the U.S., frequently expressed contempt for what he called "the lower orders," and became an avowed enemy of democracy.

In 1835 Haliburton began writing in the newspaper *The Novascotian* humorous sketches about Sam SLICK, an itinerant Yankee clockmaker. This lampoon on Americans was apparently primarily intended to make Nova Scotians appreciate their own country and British institutions, but also to contrast Nova Scotian indolence with Yankee industry and shrewdness. The first sketches, with others added, were collected in *The Clockmaker, or, The Sayings and Doings of Samuel Slick of Slickville* (1837). This series was followed by several others, including *Sam Slick's Saws and Modern Instances* (1853). The books became very popular, first in Canada, then in the U.S. and England. Sam Slick became the best-known character in the field of Yankee humor and had many imitators. A shrewd, ruthless trader, ready to trick his customers at every opportunity, Sam is full of wise saws and has an unfailing supply of humorous stories. Some of his sayings gained wide currency, such as: "Politics makes a man as crooked as a pack does a peddler; not that they are so awful heavy either, but it teaches a man to stoop in the long run."

Halifax Law. A severe penalty peculiar to this English town. By this law, whoever committed theft in the precinct of Halifax was to be executed on the Halifax gibbet, a kind of guillotine. Hence the expression *go to Halifax.*

Hall, Donald (1928–   ). American poet and editor. At one time the poetry editor of the *Paris Review,* Hall has done much to make the younger contemporary poets more widely known by collecting their work in several anthologies. *The New Poets of England and America* (1957), compiled with Robert Pack and Louis Simpson, was an excellent representative collection of poets born between 1917 and 1935; it was followed by *The New Poets of England and America #2* (1962), with Robert Pack; *The Poetry Sampler* (1962); and *Contemporary American Verse* (1962). Hall's collections of his own poetry include *Exiles and Marriages* (1955) and *The Dark Houses* (1958).

Hall, James Norman (1887–1951). American novelist and short-story writer. Hall was coauthor with Charles Bernard NORDHOFF of the remarkably successful trilogy: MUTINY ON THE BOUNTY, *Men Against the Sea* (1933), and *Pitcairn's Island* (1934). During the First World War, Hall flew with the Lafayette Escadrille, an experience which provided him with material for subsequent books written both independently and with Nordhoff. Among the books on which they collaborated were *Lafayette Flying Corps* (1920), *Falcons of France* (1929), *The Hurricane* (1936), and *Botany Bay* (1941).

Hall, Joseph (1574–1656). English clergyman, satirist, poet, and CHARACTER WRITER. Named successively bishop of Exeter and of Norwich, he is known for his satires, such as *Virgidemiarum* (1597), in which he attacked contemporary institutions and individuals, and *Mundus Alter* (1605), directed against Roman Catholics. His *Characters of Virtues and Vices* (1608) is in the direct tradition of Theophrastus, except that its emphasis is on moral, rather than social, virtues and evils.

Hall, Radclyffe (1886–1943). English novelist and short-story writer. Her novel *The Well of Loneliness* (1928) caused a sensation because it treated with sympathy sexual perversion among women. It was banned in England and suspended in the U.S.

Hallam, Arthur Henry (1811–1833). English poet and essayist whose early death caused Tennyson to write IN MEMORIAM. Hallam, who was a close friend of Tennyson's and the fiancé of his sister Emily, was touring the Continent when he suddenly died in Vienna. His death was a profound shock to Tennyson and the cause of deep conflict between doubt and faith in the poet's life.

Halleck, Fitz-Greene (1790–1867). American poet, banker, and secretary to John Jacob Astor. Literature was Halleck's avocation. With his friend, Joseph Rodman DRAKE, he wrote the lively *Croaker Papers* (1819) for New York newspapers. Halleck's *Poetical Works* appeared in 1847. He is best known for his elegy (1820) written at Drake's death, beginning "Green be the turf above thee," and for his popular poem, *Marco Bozzaris* (1825).

Hallelujah (Heb., *halelu-Jah*, praise ye Jehovah). An exclamation used in songs of praise and thanksgiving.

Hallelujah lass. A name given, with a humorously contemptuous import, to female members of the Salvation Army in its early days.

Haller, Harry. The hero of Hesse's STEPPENWOLF. Part of the novel's vitality stems from the fact that Haller's experiences, like his initials, are patterned on Hesse's own.

Halley, Edmund (1656–1742). English astronomer. A friend of Newton, whose *Principia* (1687) he published at his own expense, Halley is best known for his study of comets. He concluded that the comets of 1531, 1607, and 1682 were in reality a single body and accurately predicted its return in 1758. The comet has since been known as Halley's Comet.

Hallowe'en. October 31, in the old Celtic calendar the last day of the year. Its night was the time when all the witches and warlocks were abroad and held their wicked revels. At the introduction of Christianity it was taken over as the eve of ALL SAINTS. It is still devoted to all sorts of games in which the old superstitions can be traced. See SAMAIN.

Halper, Albert (1904–   ). American novelist and short-story writer. He is chiefly known for his graphic studies of workingmen in large U.S. industries and of slum life, especially in his native Chicago. His style is naturalistic, and he is considered a writer of the proletarian school of the 1930's. *Union Square* (1933), though his first published work, was his fourth novel. His other works include *Sons of the Fathers* (1940), *The Little People* (1942), *The Golden Watch* (1953), and *Atlantic Avenue* (1956).

Hals, Frans (1580?–1666). Dutch portrait and genre painter. His sitters represent every class of society, from officers, burgomasters, and merchants to fishwives and itinerant entertainers. He represented them in animated and momentary attitudes, capturing a casual glimpse with quick and broad brushstrokes. His work is known for its vitality and, during his later period, for its gray and black tonal harmonies.

Ham. In the Old Testament, one of the three sons of NOAH, his brothers being Shem and Japheth. According to legend, Ham was the ancestor of the Hamitic races which populated Africa; their black skins were the result of Ham's iniquity in viewing his father drunk and naked, while his brothers walked backwards, with averted eyes, to cover Noah (Gen. 19: 22–23). One of his sons was Canaan.

Haman. See ESTHER.

Hamann, Johann Georg (1730–1788). German philosopher and aesthetician. In his *Des Ritters von Rosencreuz letzte Willensmeinung über den göttlichen und menschlichen Ursprung der Sprache* (*The Knight of Rosencreuz's Last Will, on the Divine and Human Origin of Language,* 1772), he contended that language is basically irrational, and thus he opposed the rationalism of enlightenment thought. He was influenced by pietism and was a teacher of Herder. See STURM UND DRANG.

Hamelin, Pied Piper of. See PIED PIPER OF HAMELIN.

Hamilcar Barca (270?–228 B.C.). Carthaginian general, father of HANNIBAL. He was appointed to the command of the Carthaginian forces in Sicily, in the 18th year of the First PUNIC WAR, in 247 B.C. After the defeat of the Carthaginians in 241, Hamilcar crossed over into Spain and, within nine years, obtained possession of a considerable portion of Spain for Carthage. He was drowned during a campaign.

Hamilton, Alexander (1757–1804). American statesman and chief author of THE FEDERALIST essays. He served as the first secretary of the treasury (1789–1795) and recommended fiscal measures, such as the creation of a national bank, that reflected his belief in a strong, centralized government. Distrusting the capacity of the common man, he advocated government by the elite. He was killed in a duel by Aaron Burr, whose political ambitions he had thwarted. He is the subject of Gertrude Atherton's "dramatized biography" *The Conqueror* (1902).

Hamilton, Anthony (1646–1720). Irish-born French writer. His brilliant style and humor are at their best in his short novel *Les Mémoires du Chevalier de Grammont* (1713), which recounts the adventures and amorous exploits of his brother-in-law and depicts scandals at the court of Charles II of England. He also wrote some short stories in imitation of *The Arabian Nights,* and some mordant poems.

Hamilton, Cosmo. Pen name of Cosmo Hamilton Gibbs (1872–1942). English popular novelist, dramatist, and short-story writer, eldest of the Gibbs brothers. *Mrs. Skeffington* (1910), a drawing-room comedy, is his best-known work.

Hamilton, Edith (1867–1963). American classical scholar. She is distinguished for her books translating for modern readers the meaning of Greek and Roman life. Her most famous works include *The Greek Way* (1930), *The Roman Way* (1932), *The Prophets of Israel* (1936), and *The Echo of Greece* (1957).

Hamilton, Lady Emma, born **Lyon** (1761?–1815). Wife of Sir William Hamilton, mistress of Horatio NELSON. Of humble birth but of great beauty, she became the mistress of Hamilton's nephew, Charles Greville, who sold her to the elderly diplomat in exchange for payment of his debts. She attained great popularity and influence at the court of Naples, where Hamilton was envoy, and there met Nelson, becoming his mistress in 1798. The lovers were extremely open about their relationship, and the birth of Nelson's daughter, Horatia (1801), gave further cause for scandal. After Nelson's death, her extravagance caused her to be imprisoned for debt (1813); she was released a year later and died in poverty in France.

Hamilton, Patrick. See ANGEL STREET.

Hamlet, The (1940). A novel by William FAULKNER, the 1st book of a trilogy that also includes *The Town* (1957) and *The Mansion* (1959). Spanning almost 50 years in time, the trilogy is centered on the innumerable and vicious members of the SNOPES family, the first of whom invades YOKNAPATAWPHA COUNTY early in the 20th century. In the hamlet of Frenchman's Bend, Flem Snopes begins as a clerk in Will Varner's store; through usury, connivance, and thrift, he becomes part-owner of the store and husband of Eula VARNER, Will's daughter. In Jefferson, Flem works his way into Colonel Sartoris' bank, finally becoming vice-president. In order to enrich himself still further, he drives the bank president, Manfred De Spain, from town. In *The Mansion,* Flem moves into the now-vacant De Spain mansion, one of the largest and oldest houses in Jefferson. Flem has no human feelings of any kind, caring only for money and for the outward appearance of respectability. He imports a number of cousins—Mink, I.O., Lump, Ike, Eck—whom he installs in various positions in the community, until the local citizens feel that they are overrun with Snopeses.

The novels are loosely episodic, humorous, and ironic. *The Hamlet* is made up of material dealing alternately with horse-trading and love—economic life vis-à-vis emotional life. *The Town* continues this contrast on a more sophisticated level, centering on the hopeless and almost comic love of Gavin STEVENS, first for Eula Varner Snopes and then for her daughter Linda, and on the machinations used by Flem to acquire more money. *The Mansion* departs from this scheme, dealing primarily with the attempts of Mink Snopes to return to Jefferson and murder Flem, and with the relationship between Gavin and Linda. Each of the novels is made up of sections narrated mainly by characters who observe the action rather than take part in it, such as V. K. RATLIFF, the ubiquitous sewing-machine salesman, and Chick MALLISON, the young nephew of Gavin Stevens.

Hamlet of A. MacLeish, The (1928). A poem by Archibald MacLEISH. In this dramatic monologue, the poet contrasts Hamlet's situation with that of modern man, symbolized by the poet himself. He attempts to show that the sensitive man today has no knowledge of the evil he tries to fight.

Hamlet, Prince of Denmark (c. 1601). A tragedy by William SHAKESPEARE. It is his most famous play and one of the most fascinating in world literature.

Hamlet, prince of Denmark, falls into melancholia after the death of his father, the king. CLAUDIUS, his father's brother, has assumed the throne and married Hamlet's mother, GERTRUDE, within two months of the king's death. His father's ghost appears to Hamlet, accuses Claudius of murdering him, and demands revenge. Hamlet then resolves to feign madness in order to disguise his intentions. His rejection by OPHELIA, to whom he has shown attention, leads her father, POLONIUS, to the conclusion that love has driven the prince mad. Unable to bring himself to action and beset by doubts as to the truth of the ghost's words, Hamlet persuades some traveling players to re-enact the death of his father. Claudius' violent reaction to the play convinces Hamlet of his uncle's guilt. Later, in his mother's chamber, the prince kills the eavesdropping Polonius, mistaking him for Claudius. Using this murder as a pretext for disposing of the prince, Claudius sends Hamlet to England with ROSENCRANZ AND GUILDENSTERN, who

Title page of the first quarto of *Hamlet* (1603).

THE HUNTINGTON LIBRARY

THE

Tragicall Hiſtorie of

HAMLET

Prince of Denmarke

By William Shake-ſpeare.

As it hath beene diuerſe times acted by his Highneſſe ſeruants in the Cittie of London : as alſo in the two Vniuerſities of Cambridge and Oxford, and elſe-where

At London printed for N.L. and Iohn Trundell.
1603.

bear secret letters to the king of England, advising him to put the prince to death. But Hamlet discovers the plot and manages to return to Denmark. Ophelia, driven mad by Hamlet's rejection and the death of her father, commits suicide. Her brother, LAERTES, who has been studying in Paris, returns for her funeral, intent upon revenging himself for the deaths of his father and sister. Inciting him further, Claudius arranges for a duel between Laertes and Hamlet, in which Laertes will be provided with a poisoned sword. To insure Hamlet's death, Claudius also prepares a cup of poisoned wine. During the duel, Laertes nicks Hamlet with the poisoned sword, while the queen accidentally drinks the poisoned wine and dies. Having unwittingly seized the poisoned rapier in the scuffle, the dying Hamlet kills both Laertes and Claudius. See FORTINBRAS.

Although *Hamlet* is a play of revenge, its greatness lies in the unique and thoughtful nature of the prince, whose temper is philosophical rather than active. He does not so much pursue his revenge as he is swept to it through the events of the play. His preoccupation with the nature and consequences of man's actions has led critics to call him "the first modern man." The complexity and richness of the play have furnished critics and performers with material for hundreds of interpretations.

The earliest source of the play is a story which first appeared in *Historia Danica* (1514) by the Danish chronicler Saxo Grammaticus, and was later translated in *Histoires Tragiques* (1570) by Pierre de Belleforest. An earlier version of the play (c. 1589), now lost, is referred to as "Ur-Hamlet," or source Hamlet.

Hammarskjöld, Dag (1905–1961). Swedish statesman. Hammarskjöld worked first in the field of public finance, serving as undersecretary of state in the Swedish department of finance from 1936 to 1946, and subsequently as financial advisor to the Swedish government. In 1953 he was chosen secretary-general of the United Nations; the diligence, imagination, and courage with which he performed his job earned him worldwide respect and admiration. Greatly concerned with the emerging African nations, Hammarskjöld was on his way to attempt some peaceful solution for the problems of the troubled Congo when he lost his life in a plane crash over Northern Rhodesia. In 1961 the Nobel Prize for peace was awarded to him posthumously. *Markings* (1964) is a collection of poems and entries from his personal journal which he called "a sort of white-book concerning my negotiations with myself and God."

Hammerstein, Oscar (1895–1960). American musical comedy librettist and producer. A talented and prolific theatrical craftsman, Hammerstein wrote, in collaboration or singly, the book and lyrics for 18 musicals, including *Rose Marie* (1924), *The Desert Song* (1926), *Show Boat* (1927), *New Moon* (1928), *Sweet Adeline* (1929), *Music in the Air* (1932), *May Wine* (1935), *Oklahoma* (1943), *Carmen Jones* (1943), *Carousel* (1945), *South Pacific* (1949), *The King and I* (1951), *Me and Juliet* (1953), *Flower Drum Song* (1958), and *The Sound of Music* (1959). He also wrote six screen plays, and with Rodgers produced five Broadway hit shows. Hammerstein collaborated with the best light composers of his day, including Romberg, Kern, and Rodgers.

Hammett, [Samuel] Dashiell (1894–1961). American writer of detective stories and movie scripts. An excellent craftsman, Hammett was the founder of the so-called hard-boiled school of detective fiction (see HARD-BOILED FICTION). In THE MALTESE FALCON he first presented his famous "private eye," Sam Spade. Of his many detective books, Hammett's favorite was *The Glass Key* (1931). *The Thin Man* (1932) offered another sleuth, Nick CHARLES, who was to become as well known as Sam Spade. Hammett's work was highly regarded by some European critics, notably André Gide.

Hammurabi. King of Babylon, 2067–2025 B.C. One of the greatest rulers of antiquity, he is chiefly remembered for his remarkable code of laws, which no doubt accounted in part for the success with which he governed much of Mesopotamia.

Hampden, John (1594–1643). English statesman. He became a popular symbol of resistance to royal tyranny when he fought the attempts of Charles I to collect ship-money from the inland counties without the consent of Parliament. At the outbreak of the Civil War he raised a regiment for the Parliamentary army and was mortally wounded at Chalgrove Field.

Hampden [Dougherty], Walter (1879–1955). American actor. One of the most distinguished on the American stage, he appeared in a number of Shakespearean roles and in *Cyrano de Bergerac, An Enemy of the People, Our Town,* and many other plays, as well as many motion pictures.

Hampton Court Conference (1604). A conference held under James I at Hampton Court, a royal palace on the Thames, to settle the differences between the Puritans and the High Church party of the Church of England. Although the Puritans failed to win their objectives, it was here that the first suggestion was made for the revision of the Bible that resulted in the King James or Authorized Version of 1611.

Hamsun, Knut Pederson (1859–1952). Norwegian novelist and playwright. Born of a farming family, Hamsun spent the years of his young manhood in poverty, wandering from one incongruous job to another. Two steamer voyages to the U.S. yielded positions as street-car conductor, dairyman, and finally as fisherman off the Grand Banks of Newfoundland. In 1890 his novel *Sult* (*Hunger,* 1899) appeared, establishing Hamsun's reputation as a significant author. He focused on the inner turmoil of his young hero, abandoning the current literary concern with social problems. In style, too, the work was original and provocative: the author experimented with the possibilities of the Norwegian rıksmaal. In his writings, Hamsun both affirms and attacks. Such novels as *Pan* (1894), *Victoria* (1898), and *En Vandrer spiller med Sordin* (*With Muted Strings,* 1909) express a mystical feeling for nature. Other novels— *Segelfoss By* (1915) and *Konerne ved Vandposten* (*The Women at the Pump,* 1920), for example—contain angry criticism of modern life. In 1920 he received the Nobel prize for *Markens Grøde* (THE GROWTH OF THE SOIL). An influential figure in the modern literary world, Hamsun lived during the latter part of his life in isolation from society, at Nøerholmen near the sea which he loved.

Han. Chinese dynasty (202 B.C.–A.D. 220). The Chinese imperial age, which witnessed great developments in science, literature, and the arts. Confucian thought was systematized and established as the dominant ethical and political philosophy. The *Shih chi*, the first historical annal, was composed during this period.

Hancock, John (1737–1793) American statesman. He served as president of the Continental Congress (1775–1777) and was the first signer of the Declaration of Independence. From the bold legibility with which he signed that document, there developed the expression a "John Hancock," meaning an autographed signature.

Handel, George Frideric (1685–1759). German-born composer, with Bach the greatest figure of the late Baroque in music. After study in Germany and Italy (1706–1709), he settled permanently in England in 1712, and became a naturalized British subject in 1726. Handel's works are nearly all in two genres, Italian opera and English oratorio and odes. Notable among his 39 operas are: *Giulio Cesare* (1724), *Rodelinda* (1725), *Sosarme* (1732), *Orlando* (1733), *Alcina* (1735), and *Atalanta* (1736). Full of beautiful music, these works for various reasons have been little performed since the 18th century, but in the last generation there have been many revivals, which still continue. His oratorios and odes, usually on Biblical subjects, are the outstanding large choral works in the English language. Most were written after 1738, when Handel faced financial ruin because of the failure of his operatic ventures. The best of the oratorios are: *Saul* (1739), *Israel in Egypt* (1739), *Messiah* (1742), *Belshazzar* (1744), *Hercules* (1744), *Solomon* (1748), and *Jephtha* (1751). The other secular choral works are: *Acis and Galatea* (1720), *Alexander's Feast* (1736; text by Dryden), *Ode for St. Cecilia's Day* (1739; text by Dryden), and *L'Allegro, il Penseroso ed il Moderato* (1740; text of the first two acts by Milton). He also wrote church music, chamber music, and harpsichord suites, but the best known of his other works are 12 *concerti grossi* for orchestra (1739), 12 organ concertos (1738–1740), the *Water Music* (1715–1717), and the *Fireworks Music* (1749), the last two being suites for orchestra.

Handful of Dust, A (1937). A novel by Evelyn WAUGH. Satirical in its treatment of upper-class English society, it is a comic novel about Tony Last, owner of a Gothic mansion which he loves. His old-fashioned values, however, cannot support him in the changing modern world. Deserted by his wife, he becomes an explorer in Brazil and is captured and enslaved by a mad old man who forces him to read Dickens aloud every afternoon.

Handlyng Synne ("handbook of sins," c. 1303). Religious poem by Robert MANNYNG, of 12,630 lines in octosyllabic couplets. It is a Middle English adaptation of the *Manuel des Pechiez,* written in Anglo-French by William of Wadington (late 13th century), a treatise on the ten commandments, the seven deadly sins, and the seven sacraments. However, Mannyng illustrates his homilies with legendary tales and contemporary anecdotes that give a lively and vivid picture of the customs of his time.

handwriting on the wall. An announcement of some coming calamity, or the imminent fulfilment of some doom. The allusion is to the handwriting on Belshazzar's palace wall announcing the loss of his kingdom. See DANIEL.

Handy Andy (1842). A novel by Samuel LOVER. The book's Irish hero, Andy Rooney, "had the most singularly ingenious knack of doing everything the wrong way." Despite his blunders Handy Andy finally wins his cousin, Oonah, and is declared heir to Lord Scatterbrain's title and wealth.

Han Fei Tzu. Chinese politico-philosophical work of the LEGALIST SCHOOL. The author, Han Fei Tzu (d. 233 B.C.) was a scholar and political adviser. Harsh, practical, and cynical, it propounded an anti-Confucian philosophy of government. Its teachings were put into practice during the short-lived CH'IN Dynasty (221–207 B.C.). See W. K. Liao, The *Complete Works of Han Fei Tzu* (1939, 1960).

Hanging Gardens of Babylon. One of the SEVEN WONDERS OF THE ANCIENT WORLD. According to Diodorus Siculus, the garden was 400 ft. square, rising in a series of terraces from the river in the northern part of Babylon. It was provided with earth to a sufficient depth to accommodate trees of a great size. According to tradition, it was built by Nebuchadnezzar to gratify his wife Amytis, who was weary of the flat plains of Babylon and longed for reminders of her native Median hills.

Hanley, James (1901–   ). English novelist. A merchant seaman at one time, Hanley writes most of his realistic novels about ships, sailors, and the sea. Among his works are *The Furys* (1934), *The Closed Harbour* (1952), *The Welsh Sonata* (1954), and *Levine* (1955). *At Bay* (1943), *Crilley* (1945), and *A Walk in the Wilderness* (1950) are collections of short stories.

Hannah. In the Old Testament, the wife of Elkenah and mother of the prophet SAMUEL. She made and kept a vow that if the Lord gave her a child, she would give him to the service of the temple (1 Sam. 1:2).

Hannay, James Owen. See George A. BIRMINGHAM.

Hannay, Richard. In John Buchan's THE THIRTY-NINE STEPS and its sequels, a South African mining engineer who becomes a British general and an energetic spy-catcher.

Hanneles Himmelfahrt. See ASSUMPTION OF HANNELE, THE.

Hannibal (247–183 B.C.). Carthaginian general, son of HAMILCAR BARCA. As a child he was taken to Spain by his father and made to swear eternal enmity to Rome, an oath he never forgot. His whole life was a struggle against the Romans. At the onset of the Second PUNIC WAR, he invaded Italy from Spain, crossing the Alps with elephants by way of the Little St. Bernard, and plunged Rome into immediate danger through his victory at CANNAE (216). He was ultimately defeated by SCIPIO AFRICANUS and recalled to Africa. Years later, he escaped extradition to Rome by committing suicide.

Hanno. Carthaginian navigator who led a colonizing expedition down the west coast of Africa (5th century B.C.).

Hanno the Great. Carthaginian politican of 3rd century B.C. He favored peaceful relations with Rome, in opposition to Hamilcar Barca and Hannibal.

Han of Iceland (Han d'Islande; 1823). A romance by Victor HUGO. Rich in elements of the macabre and the grotesque, it is a tale of 17th-century Norway. The title character is a bloodthirsty individual who boasts descent from the monster Ingulph the Exterminator. His career is a long succession of crimes and horrors.

Hansards. Official reports of Parliamentary proceedings in England, named after Luke Hansard (1752–1828), the printer of the House of Commons journals (from 1774). Hansard was also the printer for Robert Dodsley, the prominent publisher and bookseller. Thomas Curson Hansard, his eldest son, published *Typographia* in 1825.

Hans Brinker or The Silver Skates (1865). A well-known story for children by Mary Mapes DODGE. The hero is a Dutch boy, and the book gives an interesting picture of life in Holland.

Hanseatic League. A confederacy begun in the 13th century among towns of northern Germany for mutual defense, particularly of their trade routes. During the 14th century it expanded to include most German and Dutch cities, and reached the height of its political and commercial power, making trade agreements with other countries as a unit. The need for the League declined in the 16th century, and the last meeting was held in 1669.

Hänsel and Gretel. An opera for children by Engelbert HUMPERDINCK (1893) based on the well-known fairy tale by the brothers Jacob and Wilhelm GRIMM. It portrays the adventures of Hänsel and Gretel, the broom-maker's children, with the Sand Man, the Dew Man, and the terrible Crunch Witch.

Hanuman. In the RAMAYANA, the monkey helpful to Rama in constructing a bridge from India to Ceylon. With his followers, he enabled Rama to rescue his wife Sita from the stronghold of Ravana, the demon-king of Ceylon. In some parts of India he is worshiped as a deity.

Hapsburg. A royal Central European family. Germanic in origin, the family derived its name from the ancient castle of Hapsburg (hawk's castle) in what is now Switzerland. Counts of Hapsburg were known as early as the 11th century, and it is their descendants who occupied the thrones of Germany, Austria, Hungary, Bohemia, Spain, etc., and for nearly 400 years were the rulers of the Holy Roman Empire. The still current phrase, "a Hapsburg lip," refers to the familial characteristic of a protruding lower lip observable in 18 generations of Hapsburgs.

Hara. Another name for SHIVA, the destroying aspect of the Hindu *Trimurti*.

harakiri (Japanese *hara* abdomen, *kiri* cutting). More commonly called *seppuku* in Japan, the Sinico-Japanese reading of the same characters in reverse order. Harakiri is a method of suicide by disembowelment, which began to be used in the Kamakura period (1185–1333). Frequently a form of protest, it was also a type of death penalty imposed during the Tokugawa period (1600–1868) on criminals of high rank.

Harbaugh, Thomas Chalmers. See Nick CARTER.

Harbor, The (1915). A novel by Ernest POOLE. The changes of New York harbor over the years become symbolic of the changes in the hero's mind. An artist, he is divided between the vewpoint of his father-in-law, who helps to build the harbor into a great commercial center, and that of a col-

lege friend, who presents the side of the workers. In time he chooses the latter standpoint.

Harcourt-Reilly, Sir Henry. A gin-drinking psychiatrist and god-figure in T. S. Eliot's verse-drama THE COCKTAIL PARTY.

hard-boiled fiction. A type of detective or crime story current in 20th-century American literature. A sense of realism is generated by laconic and often vulgar dialogue, through the depiction of cruelty and bloodshed at close range, and the use of sordid environments. The genre was closely associated with the magazine *Black Mask* (founded 1919) and with its editor Joseph T. Shaw, who compiled *The Hard-Boiled Omnibus: Early Stories from Black Mask* (1946). Among the writers of hard-boiled fiction are Dashiell HAMMETT, Raymond CHANDLER, George Harmon Coxe, and W. R. BURNETT. At first, such fiction was a serious attempt not dissimilar in aim to the work of such major writers as Ernest HEMINGWAY and John Dos PASSOS; later, it tended to degenerate into the sensationalism and undisguised sadism of writers like Mickey SPILLANE.

Hard Cash. See LOVE ME LITTLE, LOVE ME LONG.

Hardenberg, Friedrich Leopold Freiherr von. See NOVALIS.

Harding, Warren G[amaliel] (1865–1923). 29th president of the U.S. (1921–1923). Originally the editor and publisher of a newspaper in Marion, Ohio, Harding served as lieutenant governor of the state and was elected to the U.S. Senate in 1915. In 1920 he became the Republican candidate for president after his nomination had been decided upon by a handful of party leaders "in a smoke-filled room." Harding waged a front-porch campaign, promising a "return to normalcy" that appealed to war-weary Americans and won him 404 electoral votes while his Democratic opponent, James M. Cox, received only 127. His administration, one of the least distinguished in American history, is remembered largely for the corruption that flourished as Harding's cronies, especially the notorious "Ohio gang," helped themselves at the federal till. (See TEAPOT DOME.) While returning from a trip to Alaska, Harding became fatally ill in San Francisco. Embolism was listed as the cause of death. *Revelry* (1926), a novel by Samuel Hopkins Adams, and *The Gang's All Here* (1959), a play by Jerome Lawrence and Robert E. Lee, are based on Harding's administration.

Hard Lot, A (Gorkaya sud'bina; 1859). A drama by Alexei PISEMSKI. Dealing with the tragic conflicts caused by a love affair between an estate owner and the wife of one of his serfs, the play is regarded as one of the most powerful realistic tragedies in Russian drama.

Hardouin, Jean (1646–1729). French Jesuit priest and scholar. Librarian to Louis XIV, Hardouin was so skeptical that he questioned the truth of all received history and denied the authenticity of the *Aeneid* of Vergil and the *Odes* of Horace. He thus came to epitomize the doubting philosopher.

Hard Times (1845). A novel by Charles DICKENS. Thomas Gradgrind, a fanatic of the demonstrable fact, has raised his children Tom and Louisa in an atmosphere of grimmest practicality. Louisa marries the banker Josiah BOUNDERBY partly to protect her brother who is in Bounderby's employ, partly because her education has resulted in an emotional atrophy that makes her indifferent to her fate. Tom, shallow and unscrupulous, robs Bounderby's bank and contrives to frame Stephen Blackpool, an honest and long-suffering mill hand. Meanwhile, Louisa's dormant emotions begin to awaken, stimulated by disgust for the vulgar Bounderby and the attentions of the charming, amoral James Harthouse. When she runs away to her father and when Tom's guilt is discovered, Gradgrind realizes how his principles have blighted his children's lives. Ultimately Louisa secures a separation from Bounderby and Tom flees the country. The novel is Dickens' harshest indictment of practices and philosophical justifications of mid-19th-century industrialism in England.

Hardwick, Nan. See TRAGEDY OF NAN, THE.

Hardy, Alexandre (c. 1569–1632). French playwright. A prolific author, Hardy wrote literally hundreds of plays and published 34 of them, including the biblical tragedy *Marianne,* in the years 1623–1628. An innovator with a sure theatrical flair, Hardy enlivened dramatic movement by omitting the chorus, pruning soliloquies and monologues, introducing confrontations between main characters, and permitting violence on stage. Though poetically and rhetorically inferior to much of his predecessors' work, Hardy's plays achieved an enormous popularity in their time and performed the invaluable service of bridging the gap between the French drama of the Middle Ages and Renaissance and that of the 17th century.

Hardy, René (1911–   ). French novelist. Known for his studies of men in war, Hardy wrote such novels as *The Sword of God* (*Le fer de Dieu;* 1953), set in Indo-China, and *Bitter Victory* (*Amère Victoire;* 1955).

Hardy, Thomas (1840–1928). English novelist and poet. Hardy was born in Dorsetshire, the region that he later called Wessex in his novels. He trained as an architect and began to practice in 1867, though he soon became disillusioned and sought another medium for expression. He had been writing poems for several years, but he could find no publisher for his verse; he attempted a novel, but his first book, *The Poor Man and the Lady,* was rejected. *Desperate Remedies* (1871) was published anonymously, as was *Under the Greenwood Tree* (1872). In 1873 he published A PAIR OF BLUE EYES under his own name; the book was successful, and he began a full-time literary career. In the next 24 years, he produced 11 novels: FAR FROM THE MADDING CROWD, *The Hand of Ethelberta* (1876), THE RETURN OF THE NATIVE, *The Trumpet-Major* (1879), *A Laodicean* (1881), TWO ON A TOWER, THE MAYOR OF CASTERBRIDGE, *The Woodlanders* (1887), TESS OF THE D'URBERVILLES, JUDE THE OBSCURE, and *The Well-Beloved* (1897). Hardy's view of life, particularly as shown in his major novels, was one shaped by the prevalent materialistic and deterministic theories of 19th-century science, which saw man as subject to forces he could neither understand nor control; a naturalist, Hardy wrote forceful studies of life in which his characters are continually defeated in their struggle against their physical and social environment, against their own impulses, and against

the malevolent caprices of chance. Though his style is often awkward, it has a harsh power that contributes to the almost tragic intensity of his best work.

Hardy's first volume of verses, *Wessex Poems,* appeared in 1898, though it contained poetry he had written since the 1860's. Abandoning the novel, probably because of the shocked public reaction to *Jude the Obscure,* he continued to write poetry, publishing six more volumes of lyrical verse, which were gathered together in the *Collected Poems* of 1931, and one later volume, *Winter Words in Various Moods and Meters* (1928). Sometimes colloquial, uneven, and ragged, Hardy's verse is highly original, and has a wide variety of metrical styles and stanza forms, and a wide scope of tone and attitude, as is apparent from the ironically humorous ballad on *The Ruined Maid,* the pensive *Darkling Thrush* or the simple but moving *She Hears the Storm.* Hardy's most ambitious poetic work, *The Dynasts* (1903, 1906, 1908), is an epic drama on the Napoleonic wars.

hare. According to tradition, it is unlucky for a hare to cross one's path, because witches transform themselves into hares. In medieval science, the hare was a most melancholy beast, and ate wild succory in the hope of curing itself. Its flesh was supposed to generate melancholy in any who partook of it.

Another superstition was that hares are sexless, or that they change their sex every year. Among the Hindus the hare is sacred to the moon because, as they affirm, the outline of a hare is distinctly visible in the full disk. The idea that a March hare is mad derives from the fact that hares are unusually shy and wild in March, their rutting season. Erasmus, however, says "Mad as a marsh hare," and adds, "hares are wilder in marshes from the absence of hedges and cover."

Hari. Another name for VISHNU, the preserving aspect of the Hindu *Trimurti.*

Häring, Willibald. See Willibald ALEXIS.

Harington or **Harrington, John** (1561–1612). English satirist and miscellaneous writer. A godson of Queen Elizabeth, he translated Ariosto's *Orlando Furioso* into English (1591) at her command. He was banished from court because of some of his ribald satires, such as *The Metamorphosis of Ajax* (1596), a history of water closets. He also wrote many pamphlets and epigrams.

Harleian Library. The celebrated library of rare books, papers, and documents collected by Robert HARLEY and his son Edward (1689–1741). The Harleian manuscripts were acquired by the British government for the British Museum. A selection of Harleian pamphlets was published as *The Harleian Miscellany* (1744–1746).

Harlem. A section of New York City. It is inhabited largely by Negroes and Latin Americans. It was popular among intellectuals and society people of the 1920's because of its cabarets and SPEAKEASIES and its jazz. During the latter 1930's it also became a center of attraction for devotees of swing and boogie-woogie music. Harlem is the scene of *Naked on Roller Skates,* by Maxwell Bodenheim; *All God's Chillun Got Wings,* by Eugene O'Neill; *Nigger Heaven,* by Carl Van Vechten, and *The Cool World,* by Warren Miller. The character of its residents is depicted in the works of such Negro writers as Countee Cullen, Langston Hughes, W. E. Du Bois,

Ann Petry (author of *The Street* [1946]) and James Baldwin.

Harlequin or **Arlequin.** Originally *Arlecchino,* a stock character of Italian comedy (possibly from the name of a medieval demon or goblin), Harlequin became the buffoon of French and then of English pantomime. He has a shaven head, wears a mask and particolored tights, and carries a wooden sword. Often invisible to all but COLUMBINE, he is a rival of PIERROT or some other Clown for her love. His character is adapted to the *opéra-comique* and the *comédie bourgeoise* by such writers as Jean-Pierre de FLORIAN, Pierre de MARIVAUX, and Alexis PIRON.

Harleth, Gwendolyn. See DANIEL DERONDA.

Harley, Robert. 1st earl of **Oxford** (1661–1724). English Tory statesman and politician who was chancellor of the exchequer and leader of the Tory ministry (1710). See HARLEIAN LIBRARY.

Harley Street. A street in London known for its many specialist physicians' and surgeons' offices.

Harlowe, Clarissa. See CLARISSA HARLOWE.

Harmon, John, alias **John Rokesmith.** See OUR MUTUAL FRIEND.

Harmonia's Necklace. An unlucky possession; something that brings evil to all who possess it. In classic mythology, Harmonia was the daughter of Ares and Aphrodite. On her marriage with Cadmus, she received a necklace that proved disastrous to all who possessed it after her. See ERIPHYLE; ALCMAEON.

Haroot and Maroot. Angels in medieval angelology. In consequence of their want of compassion to man, they were susceptible to human passions, and were sent upon earth to be tempted. They were kings of Babel, and teachers of magic and the black arts.

Haroun-al-Raschid or **Harun-Al Rashid.** *Aaron the Upright.* Fifth caliph of Arabia (785–809). He entertained friendly relations with Charlemagne, whom he resembled in his patronage of the arts and learning. He was idealized as the splendid caliph of the ARABIAN NIGHTS' ENTERTAINMENTS, where everything curious, romantic, and wonderful is associated with his name and reign. See ABOU HASSAN; CALENDER; GIAFAR.

Harpagon. The central character in Molière's comedy L'AVARE. Nothing in life, not even his children, is more important to him than his hoard of money. Both Harpagon and his son Cléante desire to marry Mariane; but when the former, having lost a casket of money, is asked which he prefers—the money or Mariane—he says that he prefers the money, and Cléante marries the lady. Harpagon imagines that everyone is out to rob him, and when his casket is stolen he seizes his own arm in a frenzy. He proposes to give his daughter Elise in marriage to an old man named Anselme, because no dowry will be required. When Elise's lover Valère cites reason after reason against the unnatural alliance, the miser makes but one reply: "sans dot" (without dowry). On another occasion, Harpagon solicits Jacques to tell him what people say about him; when told that he is called a miser and a skinflint, he becomes helplessly enraged and beats poor Jacques in his terrible passion.

Harpagus (Harpagos, 6th century B.C.). A Median general. According to legend, the Median king Astyages chose him to expose the infant CYRUS. He gave the task to a herdsman, who kept the infant alive. Astyages punished Harpagus by serving to him at a banquet the flesh of his own son. Harpagus afterward became Cyrus' most trusted general.

Harpers Ferry. A town in West Virginia. The arsenal of Harpers Ferry was raided on Oct. 16, 1859, by the abolitionist, John BROWN. Lee took it from a large Union force on Sept. 15, 1862.

Harper's Magazine. An American magazine founded in 1850 as *Harper's New Monthly Magazine.* It was called *Harper's Monthly Magazine* after 1900, and after 1925, simply *Harper's Magazine.* During the 19th century it was devoted to literature, and frequently published serials of English authors, including Dickens, Bulwer-Lytton, Trollope, Thackeray, and George Eliot. The department of comment called "The Easy Chair" was conducted by a series of distinguished editors, among them W. D. Howells and G. W. Curtis. Howells also published articles on the new realistic fiction in a department called the "Editor's Study," which he began in 1885. Later contributors were Mark Twain, Booth Tarkington, Frank R. Stockton, and Woodrow Wilson. After World War I, economic, social, and political problems received more emphasis in the magazine.

harpies (**harpyai**). In Greek mythology, predaceous birds with women's faces. They were

Cover of the first issue of *Harper's Magazine* (1850).

daughters of the titaness Electra and sisters of Iris. They are most familiar from the story that they regularly snatched away the food from the blind king PHINEUS until they were pursued and frightened away by the ARGONAUTS CALAIS and Zetes, winged sons of Boreas. They seem to have combined the primitive concepts of wind spirits and predatory ghosts with actual characteristics of carrion birds.

Homer mentions only one harpy. Hesiod gives two, and later writers three. Their names were Ocypeta (rapid), Celeno (blackness), and Aello (storm).

Harpocrates (Harpokrates). The Greek form of the Egyptian Heru-P-Khart (Horus the Child). He is represented as a youth. As he has one finger pointing to his mouth, he was adopted by the Greeks as the god of silence.

Harp-Weaver and Other Poems, The (1923). A collection of poems by Edna St. Vincent MILLAY. This volume, which was awarded a Pulitzer Prize in poetry, was especially praised for the excellence of the 39 sonnets included, especially for the one beginning "Euclid alone has looked on Beauty bare."

Harraden, Beatrice (1864–1936). English novelist. Her greatest success was the novel *Ships That Pass in the Night* (1893) which sold over a million copies. Miss Harraden's other books include *In Varying Moods* (1894); *Interplay* (1908), and *Rachel* (1926). She was a leader in the woman's suffrage movement in England.

Harrington (1811). A novel by Maria EDGEWORTH. The titular hero is a Jew, and the novel was one of the first deliberate attempts to portray a Jew in fiction in a favorable light. As such it is worthy of note, but the character of Harrington is generally dismissed as wooden and oversentimentalized.

Harrington or Harington, James (1611–1677). English political theorist. A republican, though a good friend of Charles I, he is best known for his controversial political romance, *The Commonwealth of Oceana* (1656). Harrington's analysis of politics was distinguished by its emphasis on the idea that the form of government possible for a country depends on the distribution of property, especially land.

Harris, Joel Chandler (1848–1908). American journalist and author. He is famous for his humorous adaptations of native Negro folk legends in the Uncle Remus stories. His tales, marked by simple humor and authentic Negro dialect, are undoubtedly the greatest in the school of Negro folk literature. He wrote many of his stories first for the Atlanta *Constitution* and later collected them into such works as UNCLE REMUS: HIS SONGS AND HIS SAYINGS, *Nights with Uncle Remus* (1883), and several other collections. They dealt chiefly with animals such as Brer Rabbit, and illustrated such maxims as the ability of intelligence to win out over brute force. Harris also wrote local-color stories of Southern life; these include *Mingo and Other Sketches in Black and White* (1884), which contrasts the aristocracy and the middle class, and the novel *Gabriel Tolliver* (1902), set in the Reconstruction period. *On the Plantation* (1892) is largely autobiographical. See TAR BABY.

Harris, John Beynon. See John WYNDHAM.

Harris, Roy [really Leroy] (1898–). American composer. Many of his works have been inspired by American folk music, for example, the Symphony No. 4 (*Folksong Symphony;* 1940) and *American Ballads* (piano piece; 1942).

Harrison, William Henry. See TIPPECANOE AND TYLER TOO; Martin VAN BUREN.

Hart, Heinrich (1855–1906) and his brother **Julius** (1859–1930). German poets who were the leading theoreticians of early NATURALISM. In their periodically published *Kritische Waffengänge* (*Critical Passages-at-Arms;* 1882–1884), they stated that they wanted a naturalism in literature like the "naturalness of Goethe's poems," as opposed to any classicistic artificiality. Heinrich's best-known volume of verse is *Weltpfingsten* (*Whitsuntide of the World;* 1872); Julius' is *Homo sum* (*I Am a Man;* 1889).

Hart, Moss (1904–1961). American playwright and librettist. Hart began his career with *The Hold-Up Man* (1925), but his first real success came with *Once in a Lifetime* (1930), the first of a long series of plays written in collaboration with George S. KAUFMAN. Together they wrote *Merrily We Roll Along* (1934), the Pulitzer Prize-winning YOU CAN'T TAKE IT WITH YOU, *I'd Rather Be Right* (1937), *The American Way* (1939), THE MAN WHO CAME TO DINNER, and *George Washington Slept Here* (1940). Hart wrote the libretto for Irving Berlin's *Face the Music* (1933) and for Kurt Weill's *Lady in the Dark* (1941). He also wrote *Winged Victory* (1943), *Light Up the Sky* (1948), and *The Climate of Eden* (1952). Hart won the Antoinette Perry Award for his direction of the musical *My Fair Lady.* His autobiography, *Act One* (1959), became a best seller.

Harte, [Francis] Bret[t] (1836–1902). American short-story writer, novelist, editor, and poet. Harte left school early and went to San Francisco, where he mined, taught school, and finally became a journalist. He began his literary career with humorous sketches, attracted some attention with his verses, and achieved great fame through his short stories.

Editing the OVERLAND MONTHLY during the late 60's, he published a collection of his poetry, *The Lost Galleon and Other Tales* (1867), and his satirical CONDENSED NOVELS.

It was during this period that he wrote his best-remembered stories: THE LUCK OF ROARING CAMP and OUTCASTS OF POKER FLAT. His PLAIN LANGUAGE FROM TRUTHFUL JAMES, a comic verse narrative, was written in 1870.

During the 1870's, Harte was unable to continue writing at this level; he lost popularity and a contract to write for the *Atlantic Monthly.* Neither the novel GABRIEL CONROY nor the play *Ah Sin* (1877), written with Mark Twain, helped to restore his finances. Later he became a consul in Germany and Scotland, and was a favorite in European literary circles. His last work was a second series of *Condensed Novels* (1902).

Harte's work is marked by sentimentality, humor, and a penchant for showing thieves, vagabonds, and miners as more admirable than conventional and law-abiding folk. He is remembered for his pioneering work in Western local color writing. See M'LISS.

Hartford Convention (1814). A secret meeting of New England Federalists who were opposed to the War of 1812 to discuss revision of the Constitution. The delegates adopted several resolutions designed to preserve the influence of New England in the federal government. The news of the peace treaty with Great Britain and of Andrew Jackson's victory at New Orleans made the delegates a target for public ridicule, and they were accused, without evidence, of sedition and treason.

Hartford Wits. The name given to a group of 18th-century American poets, including Timothy DWIGHT, John TRUMBULL, and Joel BARLOW. The group was also known as the Connecticut Wits and the Yale Poets. Other members of the group, not all of them Yale men, were Lemuel Hopkins (1750–1801), David Humphries (1752–1818), Theodore DWIGHT, and Richard ALSOP. Except for Barlow, the Wits were Federalist in politics and Calvinist in religion. See ANARCHIAD, THE.

Hartley, David (1705–1757). English philosopher. He is best known for his study of human psychology, the *Observations on Man* (1749). Inspired by Newton's principle of gravitation, which had bound all physical bodies in a harmonious unity, Hartley endeavored to find some principle which would similarly unite moral phenomena. Following Locke, he developed the principle of association of ideas, by which simple ideas "run into complex ones by means of Association." According to Hartley, the moral sense was not innate, but acquired through the association of pleasurable sensations with ever loftier and wider objects: the child began by loving the tree; the man, through association, learned to love its Creator. With the proper education, Hartley contended, every man might learn to associate pleasure with the right objects, and thus the perfectibility of man was conceivable.

Hartley, L[eslie] P[oles] (1895–1972). English novelist and short-story writer. He wrote the trilogy EUSTACE AND HILDA, *The Boat* (1949), *My Fellow Devils* (1951), THE GO-BETWEEN, *A Perfect Woman* (1955), and *Facial Justice* (1961). Hartley was a perceptive and ironic observer of the social scene, who gave his novels depth through his skillful use of symbolism.

Hartmann von Aue (c. 1170–c. 1215). German court poet. His epic romances *Erec* and *Iwein*, free adaptations of the work of Chrétien de Troyes, introduced the Arthurian legends into Germany. However, his most popular work was the much shorter *Der arme Heinrich*, the only one based on German legend. See HEINRICH, DER ARME.

Hartzenbusch, Juan Eugenio (1806–1880). Spanish dramatist. His best-known work, *Los amantes de Teruel* (*The lovers of Teruel*, 1837), is considered one of the major Spanish romantic dramas because of its successful fusion of intense passion, melancholy, and medieval romance. The play deals with the amatory relationship between Diego Marsilla and Isabel Segura and culminates in the tragic death of both lovers. Hartzenbusch also wrote *La jura de Santa Gadea* (1845), dealing with the Cid, and two plays of magic, *La redoma encantada* (1839) and *Los polvos de la madre Celestina* (1841).

Harvard, John (1607–1638). An English clergyman, the son of a butcher, for whom Harvard University is named. He settled at Charlestown, Mass., and became the first benefactor of the college at New Towne, bequeathing to it his library of 300 volumes and half his estate, valued at £800. The college was renamed Harvard College in his honor in the year of his death, the third year of its existence.

Harvard Classics (1909–1910). A 50-volume set of books, containing selections from the literature of the world. It was edited by Charles W. Eliot, president emeritus of Harvard University, and published by P. F. Collier & Son. The original idea for the set can be traced to a chance remark of Eliot: "All the books needed for a real education could be set on a shelf five feet long!" From this remark and its physical make-up, the set is also known as "the Five-Foot Shelf."

Harvey (1944). A play by Mary C. CHASE. Harvey is a six-foot rabbit who appears only to the amiable drunkard who is the play's protagonist. The comedy turns on the futile attempts of eminent psychiatrists to dispel Harvey forever. The play had a long success on Broadway and was awarded a Pulitzer Prize.

Harvey, Gabriel (1545?–1630). English poet and satirist. A friend and possibly the tutor of Edmund Spenser, Harvey is thought to be the "Hobbinol" of Spenser's *Shepheardes Calender* (1579). Some of the correspondence between the two men appears in *The Letter-Book of Gabriel Harvey, A.D. 1573–80* (published 1884). Harvey, a literary conservative and something of a pedant, tried to introduce classical meters into English poetry and considered himself to be the "father of English hexameter." He is best known, however, for his acrimonious pamphlet-battle with Robert GREENE and Thomas NASHE. In connection with the Martin MARPRELATE CONTROVERSY, Harvey's brother Richard attacked Greene and, as a side issue, Nashe. Greene replied, and a literary feud began which ultimately narrowed down to a duel of words between Harvey and Nashe. Harvey's contributions to this dispute include *Foure Letters, and Certaine Sonnets, especially touching R. Greene* (1592); *A New Letter of Notable Contents* (1593); and *The Trimming of T. Nashe* (1597). Finally, in 1599, the Archbishop of Canterbury put an end to the quarrel by ordering the Harvey-Nashe tracts burned and forbidding them to be reprinted.

Harvey, William (1578–1657). English physician, physiologist, and anatomist. The discoverer of the theory of the circulation of the blood, Harvey announced his theory to the College of Physicians in 1616, but did not publish his treatise on it until 1628 (*Exercitatio Anatomica de Motu Cordis et Sanguinis in Animalibus*). He also studied the reproductive functions of animals, and in his *Exercitationes de generatione animalium* (1651) theorized that both parents, not only the male, contribute to the form of the offspring.

Hašek, Jaroslav (1883–1923). A Czech novelist and short-story writer. His major work, THE GOOD SOLDIER SCHWEIK (English translation, 1930), is a satire in four volumes (planned as six), which has been compared with the creations of Rabelais and Cervantes.

Hasidism. The tenets of the Hasidim, a Jewish sect founded about 300 B.C. in protest against Hellenistic innovation. Its members, unlike many of their brethren, strictly observed the ritual of purification and separation, as commanded by Jewish law. In the middle of the 18th century, in reaction against growing Jewish secularism and intellectualism, the Polish rabbi Israel Ben Eliezer founded a Hasidic sect devoted to mysticism, a revival of the earlier Hasidim. Modern Hasidism is characterized by a wariness of secularism in religion and of intellectualism and rationalism pursued for their own sake. Its members continue the strict observation of ritual law of their predecessors and do not recognize the state of Israel, holding that Israel can be returned to the Jews only by the Messiah himself. A world-famous Yeshiva, or school for Talmudic study, has been established by the Hasidim in the Williamsburg section of Brooklyn, N.Y.

Hassan (1923). A romantic play by James Elroy FLECKER. Hassan is a poetic confectioner of Baghdad. He becomes the caliph's favorite but has to leave the court when he denounces the caliph's execution of young lovers. The play was spectacularly produced with ballets by Fokine and music by Delius.

Hassgesang. See HYMN OF HATE.

Hastinapur. The ancient site of Delhi, often referred to in classical Indian writing. It was situated on the Ganges, about 30 miles east of modern Delhi.

Hastings, Battle of (1066). Battle near Senlac in Sussex, England, where Harold II died defending his claim to the English throne against the Norman WILLIAM THE CONQUEROR. William was crowned shortly afterward, thus effecting the "Norman Conquest," which greatly influenced English history, language, and literature.

Hastings, Warren (1732–1818). English statesman and administrator of India. He went to Calcutta in the East India Company's service in 1750, becoming successively a member of the Calcutta council, governor of Bengal, and governor-general of India. He was impeached in 1788 for corruption and cruelty, chiefly because of his conduct in regard to the zamindar of Benares whom he deposed and the begum of Oudh whose treasures he had allegedly confiscated. Although he was prosecuted by Edmund Burke, among others, his famous trial resulted in acquittal in 1795. Hastings is the subject of a famous essay by Thomas Babington Macaulay.

Hasty Pudding, The (1796). A mock-heroic poem by Joel BARLOW, describing the making and eating of the celebrated New England mush. It was one of the most popular of Barlow's works.

Hasty Pudding Club. A Harvard undergraduate organization that gave the first of its annual dramatic productions in 1844. The plays produced are burlesques. Some of the university's most eminent graduates have taken part in these performances, from George Santayana to Robert Benchley. At early meetings hasty pudding, made of corn meal, was served.

Hatchway, Lieutenant Jack. In Tobias Smolletts' novel PEREGRINE PICKLE, a retired naval officer on half pay, the friend and companion of Commodore Hawser TRUNNION, and an abettor of the hero's mischief.

Hathaway, Anne. The wife of William SHAKESPEARE.

Hathor. The Egyptian sky goddess, worshiped under several forms, in whom the sun was supposed to rise and set. As the personification of the sky, she was the female counterpart of Osiris and was represented as a cow with a disc and two plumes. Like Isis, she was a goddess of love, mirth, and joy,

corresponding to the Greek Aphrodite. Her temple at Denderah still exists.

Hatter, The. A character in Lewis Carroll's ALICE'S ADVENTURES IN WONDERLAND. During the course of a mad tea party he puts a riddle to Alice, "Why is a raven like a writing desk?" to which there is no answer. He has a watch that tells the day but not the time, and his eccentric behavior includes pouring hot tea on the Dormouse in order to wake him. The character is a burlesque of the rather illogical expression, "MAD AS A HATTER."

Hauff, Wilhelm (1802–1827). German romantic poet. He is well known for ballads and for narratives in MÄRCHEN style, such as the famous *Phantasien im Bremer Ratskeller (Fantasies in the City Hall Tavern of Bremen,* 1826). His novel *Lichtenstein* (1827), which was influenced by Walter Scott, is a closely documented work about 16th-century Germany and, along with the works of Willibald Alexis, is important in the genesis of the German historical novel. See GERMAN ROMANTICISM.

Hauptmann, Gerhart (1862–1946). German dramatist. Though he wanted at first to be a sculptor, he turned early to writing and produced a romantic epic entitled *Promethidenlos (The Lot of the Promethides,* 1885). But in accordance with the literary tenor of the times, he soon turned to realism in the story *Bahnwärter Thiel (Trackwalker Thiel,* 1887), and then, in his first play, *Vor Sonnenaufgang (Before Sunrise,* 1889), he developed a naturalistic style. This play, dedicated to "the consistent realist Bjarne P. Holmsen" (see Arno HOLZ) and influenced by Ibsen, treats the dangers of alcoholism in a starkly down-to-earth manner; it aroused a storm of critical controversy at its first performance, and marked the establishment of German NATURALISM as a recognized literary movement. Hauptmann himself wrote several more plays in a similar style, such as *Das Friedensfest (The Celebration of Peace,* 1890) and THE WEAVERS; but in *Hanneles Himmelfahrt (Hannele's Ascension,* 1893) it became clear that his development was taking him away from naturalism. Though there are many naturalistic elements in this play, a large portion of it is taken up by an ecstatic, mystical vision of the heaven into which a dying girl is about to enter. Other plays, such as *Fuhrmann Henschel (Coachman Henschel,* 1898), *Rose Bernd* (1903), and *Und Pippa tanzt (And Pippa Dances,* 1906), also show this mixture of basically naturalistic style and subject matter with deeply symbolic overtones or insertions. And finally, in such plays as THE SUNKEN BELL and *Der Arme Heinrich (Poor Henry,* 1902), he does away with naturalistic elements altogether.

After becoming established, Hauptmann was long regarded as the patriarch of modern German literature, but none of his later works had the same immediate appeal or aroused the same stormy controversy as his earlier ones. And yet his later period was by no means barren, and among its notable products are *Der Narr in Christo Emanuel Quint (The Fool in Christ, Emanuel Quint,* 1910) and *Im Wirbel der Berufung (In the Confusion of Vocation,* 1936), both novels; *Der Ketzer von Soana (The Heretic of Soana,* 1918), a story; and an epic *Till Eulenspiegel* (1928). Among his late plays are *Vor Sonnenuntergang (Before Sunset,* 1932) and a monumental treatment of the story of the house of Atreus in his *Atriden-Tetralogie* (*Atrides Tetralogy*), which includes *Iphigenie in Delphi* (1941), *Iphigenie in Aulis* (1944), *Agamemnons Tod* (*Agamemnon's Death,* 1948) and *Elektra* (1948). He was awarded the Nobel Prize for literature in 1912. See Till EULENSPIEGEL.

Hauptmann von Köpenick, Der. See CAPTAIN OF KÖPENICK, THE.

Hauser, Kaspar (1812?–1833). German foundling who appeared as a youth of about 16 in Nuremberg. He showed no signs of ever having been in contact with other humans but displayed normal intelligence. He is the subject of the novel *Caspar Hauser* (1908) by Jakob WASSERMANN.

Haushofer, Karl (1869–1946). German geographer. He used geopolitical theories to justify German expansion in Europe, and his claim that Germany needed *Lebensraum* ("living space") had a strong influence on Nazi ideology.

Havelok the Dane. A hero of medieval romance. The orphan son of the Danish king Birkabegn, he is exposed at sea through the treachery of his guardians. When the raft drifts to the coast of Lincolnshire, a fisherman, Grim, finds the young prince and brings him up as his own son. Believed to be a peasant, he is united with a princess who is to be degraded because she stands in the way of certain ambitious nobles. But Havelok, having learned the story of his birth, obtains the aid of an army of Danes to recover his wife's possessions, and in time becomes the king of Denmark.

Havisham, Miss. In Charles Dickens' GREAT EXPECTATIONS, a rich, eccentric, old recluse who lives in a decaying mansion. Years before she was jilted on the eve of her wedding and has since worn a wedding dress, complete with veil, white satin shoes, and bridal flowers in her hair. She has adopted Estella with the design of using her as an instrument of vengeance on the male sex; this she does by educating Estella to hate and torture men. She repents of her schemes just before her death caused by shock and burns when her ancient gown catches fire.

Estella Havisham. Miss Havisham's ward, later revealed to be the daughter of Abel MAGWITCH. She is a beautiful, self-possessed girl, convinced of her own heartlessness. Pip loves her, but she marries Bentley Drummle, knowing that they will torture each other. After Drummle's death and the misery of her marriage, she is at last ready for Pip's love.

Hawes, Stephen (d. 1523?). English poet. Hawes became a member of the household of Henry VII, to whom he dedicated *The Pastime of Pleasure* in 1506. Printed by Wynken de Worde in 1509, it is a long and elaborate allegorical poem, influenced by the poetry of LYDGATE and anticipating in some of its aspects Edmund Spenser's FAERIE QUEENE. Hawes wrote several other pieces, among them *A Joyful Meditation,* written for the coronation of Henry VIII in 1509, and the allegorical poem *The Example of Virtue* (printed 1512).

Hawk, Sir Mulberry. See NICHOLAS NICKLEBY.

Hawkes, Jacquetta (1910–). English archeologist and writer, wife of J. B. PRIESTLEY. *A Land* (1951) is a poetic account of the physical and human evolution of Britain.

Hawkins, Sir Anthony Hope. Pen name Anthony Hope (1863–1933). English novelist, author

First page of Hawes's *A Joyful Meditation* (1509).

of THE PRISONER OF ZENDA (1894), its sequel, *Rupert of Hentzau* (1898), and *The Dolly Dialogues* (1894).

Hawkins, Jim. See TREASURE ISLAND.

Hawkins, Sir John (1532–1595). English navigator and naval commander. With the expeditions of his nephew Sir Francis Drake, Hawkins' privateering voyages to the Spanish-American coast helped bring about the break between England and Spain. As Rear Admiral, Hawkins helped defeat the Spanish Armada in 1588. He died at sea as second in command under Drake on an expedition to the West Indies.

Hawkwood, Sir John (1320–1394). A celebrated captain of mercenaries. He was knighted by Edward III for his services against the French. He organized a band of professional soldiers, called the White Company, and went to Italy. Known to the Italians as Giovanni Acuto (thus Machiavelli refers to him), he enjoyed great success as a CONDOTTIERE.

Hawthorne, Nathaniel (1804–1864). American novelist and short-story writer. Born into an old New England family, Hawthorne was very much aware of his ancestors. The Hathornes (as they spelled it) participated in the Salem witch trials in the 17th century, and later in the Quaker persecutions. The writer, reflecting on the past, always felt a sense of guilt and made this a theme in his work.

The son of a sea captain, Hawthorne was educated at Bowdoin College, where he knew Franklin Pierce and Henry Wadsworth Longfellow. For 12 years, after his graduation in 1825, he lived in his mother's house in Salem; in virtual retirement, he wrote sketches and stories for annuals and newspapers. In 1828, he anonymously published a novel, FANSHAWE, based on his college life. Suddenly ashamed of his work, he withdrew most of the copies and burned them. Devoting his energies to short fiction, he explored the nature of sin. Hawthorne's first important book was a collection of short tales and sketches called TWICE-TOLD TALES.

In Boston as surveyor of the Customs House, Hawthorne renewed his acquaintance with Longfellow and the literary world. He invested his savings in the Transcendentalist experiment at BROOK FARM in 1841, and married Sophia Peabody the following year. Having found communal living unattractive, Hawthorne brought his bride to the Old Manse in Concord, Mass. The Manse, owned by the Ripleys, had been the home of Ralph Waldo Emerson. Here the author enjoyed three and a half happy years, during which his first daughter, Una, was born. He published his second collection of stories, MOSSES FROM AN OLD MANSE; this volume was brilliantly reviewed by Herman Melville, establishing an important friendship between the two men.

Later the Hawthornes moved to Salem, where the writer served again as surveyor in a Customs House. Removed from duty in 1849 as a result of political maneuvering (see Charles Wentworth UPHAM), Hawthorne began to write his masterpiece, THE SCARLET LETTER. The book brought him fame and some degree of financial independence. Although collections of early short pieces appeared after 1850, the year marked the end of Hawthorne's dedication to short fiction. He turned to the composition of novels and a few books for children. Living in Lenox, Mass., near Melville, Hawthorne wrote THE HOUSE OF THE SEVEN GABLES and THE BLITHEDALE ROMANCE. He collected the tales and sketches of THE SNOW IMAGE AND OTHER TWICE-TOLD TALES and wrote a campaign biography for his friend Franklin Pierce. When Pierce was elected president, he appointed Hawthorne consul at Liverpool and Manchester (1853–1857). After 1857, Hawthorne traveled through Europe for three years, completing his last published novel, THE MARBLE FAUN, in England.

On his return, Hawthorne collected a series of sketches about England called OUR OLD HOME. During the last decade of his life he wrote only sporadically. At his death, four unfinished novels were found among his notes. Among these were SEPTIMUS FELTON and THE DOLLIVER ROMANCE.

Turning to the historical past, Hawthorne found Puritan New England a congenial setting for his work. Claiming the privileges of the romancer, he deplored the lack of material for the artist in contemporary America, a land of shadowless daylight. His precise, almost classic prose style and his use of symbol and allegory made a great impression on his contemporary, Herman Melville, and on the later American writers, Henry James and William Faulkner. See TANGLEWOOD TALES.

Hay, Ian. Pen name of Sir **John Hay Beith** (1876–1952), English novelist, dramatist, and soldier. His light, humorous novels are often about the life and ethos of English boys' boarding schools. The best known is *A Safety Match* (1911). Hay dramatized stories by his friend P. G. Wodehouse, and collaborated on a number of plays including *Admirals All* (1934) and *Housemaster* (1936). *The First Hundred Thousand* (1915) was a popular account of Kitchener's army.

Hay, John [Milton] (1838–1905). American statesman and man of letters. Hay was assistant to John G. Nicolay, President Lincoln's private secretary, and they later collaborated on the 10-volume *Abraham Lincoln: A History* (1890). After the Civil War, Hay held several diplomatic posts and wrote for the New York *Tribune*. In 1898 he became President McKinley's secretary of state, a position he continued to hold under Theodore Roosevelt, helping to effect the Open Door policy in China and the negotiations for the Panama Canal.

As a writer, Hay is best known for his *Pike County Ballads* (1871) in western dialect; included in the collection was *Jim Bludso of the Prairie Belle,* a poem about a steamboat engineer who sacrifices himself to save his passengers when his boat catches fire. *Castilian Days* (1871) is a travel book of observations on Spanish civilization. Hay also wrote an anonymous novel, *The Breadwinners* (1884), in which he defended the propertied classes against the "dangerous" demands of labor.

Hayakawa, S[amuel] I[chiye] (1906–   ). Canadian-born American semanticist and teacher. Hayakawa taught at various universities before becoming a professor of language arts at San Francisco State College. A follower of Alfred Korzybski, he adapted and popularized Korzybski's principles of general semantics in *Language in Action* (1941). The book was extensively revised as *Language in Thought and Action* in 1949. In 1943 he became one of the founders and editors of the magazine *ETC., A Review of General Semantics*. He has edited *Language, Meaning and Maturity* (1954) and *Our Language and our World* (1950), both collections of articles that originally appeared in *ETC.*

Haydn, Franz Joseph (1732–1809). Austrian composer. He was kapellmeister of the Esterhazy family at Esterhaz (Eisenstadt) in Hungary (1760–1790), where he wrote some of his greatest music. In England (1791–1792; 1794–1795) he wrote and conducted twelve symphonies. In Vienna (from 1795), he wrote his last six masses, his finest chamber music, and the two great oratorios, *The Creation* and *The Seasons*. His total output includes 104 symphonies, concertos, about 20 operas, 12 masses, other church music, 84 string quartets, much other chamber music, 52 piano sonatas, and songs. Haydn's music shows much development during his long creative life. In the beginning he was under the influence of a rather superficial group of Viennese composers, but in the long years in the country in Hungary, as Haydn himself says: "There was no one about me to confuse and torment me, and I was compelled to become original." In later years, important influences were the young Mozart and the choral works of Handel, which he heard in England; these inspired the writing of the oratorios and left their mark on the late masses.

Haydon, Benjamin Robert (1786–1846). English painter. He is noted for his works on historical subjects. His writings include *Lectures on Painting and Design* (1844–1846). Wordsworth and Keats addressed sonnets to him.

Hayes, Alfred (1911–). English-born American novelist and poet. Hayes grew up in New York City, and *The Big Time* (1944), his first book of poems, extensively uses the city background in its imagery. During World War II, he served in the army in Italy, an experience which provided material for his two novels *All Thy Conquests* (1946) and *The Girl on the Via Flaminia* (1949). His later work includes the novels *Shadow of Heaven* (1947) and *In Love* (1953). *Welcome to the Castle* (1950) is a book of poems.

Hayes, Helen (1900–). American actress. A native of Washington, D.C., Miss Hayes gave her first public performance at the age of six. Later she scored great successes in such plays as *Mary of Scotland* and *Victoria Regina,* and in 1932 won an Academy Award for her acting in the motion picture *The Sin of Madelon Claudet.* In 1928 she married playwright Charles MacARTHUR. A Broadway theater is named in her honor.

Haymarket. The name of a street in London. It is between Pall Mall and Piccadilly Circus and is the center of London's theater district. The Haymarket Theatre is the second oldest London playhouse still in use. The original building was erected in 1720, the current one dates from 1820.

Haymarket Square riot (May 4, 1886). A riot that occurred in Chicago's Haymarket Square when the police tried to disperse a labor protest meeting, organized by anarchists, and a bomb was thrown, killing 7 policemen and wounding 70 others. The trial of eight anarchist leaders followed; seven were sentenced to death, one to 15 years in prison. When petitions protesting the verdict were circulated by William Dean Howells and other prominent persons, the sentences of two of the prisoners were commuted to life imprisonment, but four others were executed in 1887. In 1893, Governor John Peter Altgeld freed the three men still in jail. The incident was a temporary setback to the labor movement in general.

Hayne, Paul Hamilton (1830–1886). American poet. Hayne contributed to the *Southern Literary Messenger* and collected his *Poems* in 1855. Two years later, he founded *Russell's Magazine,* named after the bookstore in Charleston where Hayne and his friend Henry TIMROD often met. Ardently patriotic, he wrote fervent poems on the Civil War; one of these is *The Battle of Charleston Harbor.* During Sherman's march to the sea, Hayne's mansion was destroyed. He moved to Georgia, where he supported his family entirely from his writings. Among these are *Legends and Lyrics* (1872), *The Mountain of the Lovers* (1875), and *The Broken Battalions* (1885). His work is chiefly distinguished for its landscapes of the South, as in *Aspects of the Pines* and *The Cottage on the Hill.* Hayne edited the poems of his friend Timrod in 1873.

Hayston, Frank. See BRIDE OF LAMMERMOOR, THE.

Hazard of New Fortunes, A (1890). A novel by William Dean HOWELLS. Dryfoos, a Pennsylvania German who has recently risen to great wealth, brings his family to New York. Hoping to dissuade his son, Conrad, from joining the ministry, he purchases a magazine, *Every Other Week,* making Conrad the publisher. Dryfoos is also the father of two girls who, with their newly acquired fortune, are striving to enter high society. Basil March, editor of the magazine, is faced with a moral problem when Dryfoos demands the dismissal of Lindau, an old German socialist, from the magazine's staff. Lindau resigns, and later, participating in a strike of streetcar drivers and conductors, he is beaten to death. Conrad, also present at the strike, attempts to defend the old man and is killed by a stray bullet. Dryfoos sells the magazine to March, and takes his daughters to Europe, so they may continue their social climbing.

Hazlitt, William (1778–1830). English essayist and literary critic. At first dedicated to a career as a painter, he realized his talent was insufficient and turned to writing. Hazlitt became known for his studies and lectures on contemporary authors and the Elizabethan playwrights. His firm political liberalism estranged him from his friends Wordsworth, Coleridge, and Southey because he felt they had betrayed the liberalism of their youth. He went to London in 1808 and became a contributor to newspapers and periodicals, notably the *Edinburgh Review* and the *Examiner.*

After Coleridge, Hazlitt is probably the most penetrating and erudite of the early romantic critics, and is still eminently readable. Among his important works are: *The Characters of Shakespeare's Plays* (1817); *The Round Table* (1817, with Leigh Hunt); *A View of the English Stage* (1818); *Lectures on the English Poets* (1818); *Lectures on the English Comic Writers* (1819); *Lectures on the Dramatic Literature of the Age of Elizabeth* (1820); *Table Talk* (1821–1822); *Liber Amoris* (1823), an account of an unhappy love affair; and *The Spirit of the Age* (1825). He is considered one of the greatest masters of English prose.

H.D. See Hilda DOOLITTLE.

Headlong Hall (1816). A novel by Thomas Love PEACOCK. A brilliantly witty piece, it presents the mildly philosophic opinions on life exchanged by Mrs. Foster, the optimist, Mr. Escot, the pessimist, and Mr. Jenkinson, the status-quo-ite. It is a satire on the idealistic aspirations of romanticism.

Heard, [Henry Fitz] Gerald (1889–1971). English writer, resident in the U.S. since 1937. He has written about mystical religion and science and was a commentator on popular science for the British Broadcasting Corporation. Many of his books prove through anthropology and psychoanalysis man's need for religion, and describe his own mystical, oriental-style faith. Among his books are *The Ascent of Humanity* (1929), *Code of Christ* (1941), *Gabriel and the Creatures* (1952), and *Human Venture* (1955). His ideas greatly influenced Aldous Huxley; Christopher Isherwood and Huxley have been associated with him in California in the study of Eastern religion. He has written detective novels under the name of H. F. Heard.

Hearn, [Patricio] Lafcadio [Tessima Carlos] (1850–1904). American journalist and author. Of Greek and English-Irish parentage, he was born in the Ionian Islands. He is noted for the poetic prose style of his exotic and fantastic tales; he dedicated himself to "the worship of the Old, the Queer, the Strange, the Exotic, the Monstrous." After some early publication, including translations of stories by Théophile Gautier (in *One of Cleopatra's Nights,* 1882),

Hearn achieved success in works set in Louisiana and the Caribbean. *Chita* (1887) is anovel about a young girl who survives a tidal wave on a small island; YOUMA is concerned with a slave insurrection.

Hearn's search for the exotic led him to Japan in 1890, where he spent the rest of his life teaching and writing about the Japanese scene. He married and became a Japanese citizen under the name of Koizumi Yakumo. He published several books on Japan, including *Kokoro* (1896), *In Ghostly Japan* (1899), and *Japan: An Attempt at Interpretation* (1904). But his best work was his first, *Glimpses of Unfamiliar Japan* (1894).

Hearst, William Randolph (1863–1951). American newspaper publisher. Beginning his career on the San Francisco *Daily Examiner* in 1887, Hearst acquired a vast newspaper and magazine empire, which he ruled from his estate, San Simeon, in California. His name early became synonymous with "yellow journalism," and his skill in the methods of mass communications helped magnify a Cuban insurrection into the Spanish-American War. A staunch isolationist, Hearst served in Congress (1903–1907) and later made an unsuccessful bid for the governorship of New York.

Heartbreak House (1920). A play by George Bernard SHAW. A complex, allegorical work in which Shaw indicts apathy, confusion, and lack of purpose as the causes of the world's problems. The characters —all larger than life and with symbolic names—are gathered at the home of an eccentric sea captain; they each represent an evil in the modern world. Into their midst comes young Ellie Dunn, whose search for a husband Shaw treats as a new generation searching for a way of life. While the play is essentially a pessimistic one, it ends on a note of optimism: The first bombs of a war caused by the old order kill Boss Mangan, the avaricious capitalist, and Ellie selects as her spiritual husband the eccentric old owner of Heartbreak House, who represents common sense.

Heart of Darkness (1902). A long short story by Joseph CONRAD. MARLOW tells his friends of an experience in the (then) Belgian Congo, where he once ran a river steamer for a trading company. He describes the cruel colonial exploitation there. Fascinated by reports about the powerful white trader Kurtz, Marlow went into the jungle in search of him, expecting to find in his character a clue to the evil around him. He found Kurtz living with the natives and brought him away, dying; Kurtz's last words were "The horror! The horror!" The "heart of darkness" is the jungle, and the primitive, subconscious heart of man.

Heart of Midlothian, The (1818). A novel by Sir Walter SCOTT. The title alludes to the old jail at the center of Edinburgh, where the novel opens with scenes of the Porteous riots in 1736, when the commander of the Civic Guard, Captain Porteous, was lynched by a mob of incensed citizens after he had fired on a crowd. The plot concerns Effie Deans, a farmer's daughter, who is seduced by George Staunton, and who is tried and sentenced to death for murdering their child. Her loyal half-sister Jeanie determines to walk to London to seek a pardon from George II, and in spite of all obstacles, actually accomplishes her task. Effie marries Staunton, but shortly afterward he is shot by a gypsy boy, in reality his illegitimate son, who had not died after all. Jeanie marries Reuben Butler, a Presbyterian minister. The novel has a factual basis.

Heart of the Matter, The (1948). A novel by Graham GREENE. Set in West Africa, its hero is Scobie, an English Roman Catholic who is torn between his adulterous love for a young girl and his duty to his wife and his religion.

Heathcliff. The central character of Emily Brontë's novel WUTHERING HEIGHTS. Spurned by his childhood love, Catherine, he is obsessed with a desire for revenge that not only poisons her life and his but very nearly taints their children. Heathcliff is a romantic, almost demonic figure drawn on a heroic scale.

Heathen Chinee, The. See PLAIN LANGUAGE FROM TRUTHFUL JAMES.

Heat of the Day, The (1949). A novel by Elizabeth BOWEN. Set in wartime London, it is a melodramatic but sensitive story of espionage, counterespionage, and suicide, and of the emotions of the people involved.

heaven (AS, *heofon*). The word properly denotes the abode of the Deity and his angels; also the upper air.

In the Ptolemaic system the heavens were the successive spheres of space enclosing the central earth at different distances and revolving around it at different speeds. The first seven were those of the so-called planets, the Moon, Mercury, Venus, the Sun, Mars, Jupiter, and Saturn; the eighth was the firmament containing all the fixed stars; the ninth was the crystalline sphere, invented by Hipparchus (second century B.C.), to account for the precession of the equinoxes. These were known as *The Nine Heavens;* the 10th—added much later—was the *primum mobile.*

According to the Muslims, there are seven heavens. *The first heaven* is of pure silver, and here the stars, each with its angel warder, are hung out like lamps on golden chains; it is the abode of Adam and Eve. *The second heaven* is of pure gold, and is the domain of John the Baptist and Jesus. *The third heaven* is of pearl, and is allotted to Joseph. Here Azrael, the angel of death, is stationed, and is forever writing in a large book the names of those just born and blotting out those of the newly dead. *The fourth heaven* is of white gold, and is Enoch's. Here dwells the Angel of Tears, whose height is "500 days' journey," and he sheds ceaseless tears for the sins of man. *The fifth heaven* is of silver, and is Aaron's. Here dwells the Avenging Angel, who presides over elemental fire. *The sixth heaven* is composed of ruby and garnet, and is presided over by Moses. Here dwells the Guardian Angel of heaven and earth, half snow and half fire. *The seventh heaven* is formed of divine light beyond the power of tongue to describe, and is ruled by Abraham. Each inhabitant is bigger than the whole earth and has 70,000 heads, each head 70,000 mouths, each mouth 70,000 tongues, and each tongue speaks 70,000 languages, all forever employed in chanting of the Most High.

To be in the seventh heaven is to be supremely happy. The cabalists maintained that there were seven heavens, each rising in happiness above the other, the seventh being the abode of God and the highest class of angels. See PARADISE.

Heaven and Hell (1956). An essay by Aldous HUXLEY. It describes the effects the drug mescalin has on the mind, and compares the ecstatic and depressed states it produces with mystics' accounts of heaven and hell. Huxley had described his own experiments with mescalin in *The Doors of Perception* (1954).

Hebbel, [Christian] Friedrich (1813–1863). German dramatist, known especially for the philosophical and historical theories which, though they sometimes enhance his works, often mar the dramatic effect. Almost all his plays take place at historical turning points, in accordance with ideas that he formulates in *Mein Wort über das Drama* (*My Word on the Drama*, 1843) and in the preface to his tragedy MARIA MAGDALENA. Among his plays are also a tragedy (1841) about the Biblical heroine JUDITH; *Herodes and Mariamne* (1850), which treats the Herod in whose reign Christ was born (see MARIAMNE); *Agnes Bernauer* (1855), a tragedy of love between a prince and a commoner; *Gyges und sein Ring* (*Gyges and His Ring*, 1856), based on the story of Candaules; and *Die Nibelungen* (1862), a trilogy based on the story of the Nibelungenlied. In style, Hebbel's plays are considered realistic, as opposed to the idealism of the classical and romantic authors of the earlier 19th century.

Hebe. In Greek mythology, goddess of youth. She was the cupbearer of the immortals before GANYMEDE superseded her. She was the wife of Heracles and had the power of making the aged young again.

Hebraism and Hellenism (1869). A well-known essay by Matthew ARNOLD. It appeared in the collection *Culture and Anarchy*. It analyzes and contrasts the Hebrew and the Greek cultures, the two strongest influences on British culture. Arnold maintains that the "uppermost idea" of Hellenism is "to see things as they really are," while that of Hebraism is "conduct and obedience."

Hebreo or **Ebreo, León.** See Judah León ABRABANEL.

Hebrews, The Epistle of Paul the Apostle to the. A New Testament book. Scholars place its date of writing around A.D. 100, but have been unable to identify its author; it is generally agreed that Hebrews is not an actual Pauline epistle. One of the most eloquent books in the New Testament, it stresses the powerful role of Jesus as the highest priest of God whose personal sacrifice was made for all men.

Hecate (Hekate). One of the TITANS of Greek mythology. The only one who retained her power under the rule of Zeus, she was the daughter of Perses and Asteria, and became a deity of the lower world after taking part in the search for Persephone. She taught witchcraft and sorcery, and was a goddess of the dead. As she combined the attributes of, and became identified with, Selene, Artemis, and Persephone, she was represented as a triple goddess and was sometimes described as having three heads: one of a horse, one of a dog, and one of a lion. Her offerings consisted of dogs, honey, and black lambs, which were sacrificed to her at crossroads.

In Shakespeare's MACBETH, she appears as the queen of witches. After berating the three "weird sisters" for having made prophecies to Macbeth without her knowledge, she joins them in completing his destruction.

Hecht, Ben (1893–1964). American journalist, playwright, and novelist. Born in New York City, Hecht began his career in Chicago, where he worked as a reporter and took part in that city's "literary renaissance." His first novel, *Erik Dorn* (1921), the story of an intellectual who throws over both wife and mistress for the excitement of European revolution, was based on his experiences as Berlin reporter for the Chicago *News*. *Count Bruga* (1926) and *A Jew in Love* (1930) are lampoons of Maxwell BODENHEIM, who had drawn an unflattering portrait of Hecht in *Ninth Avenue* (1926). Hecht's play *Winkelberg* (1958) is also about Bodenheim. A prolific writer, Hecht wrote numerous short stories during his Chicago days, many of them being included in *The Collected Stories of Ben Hecht* (1945).

Hecht collaborated with Charles MacArthur on two plays: *The Front Page* (1928), a fast-paced portrayal of newspaper life, and *Twentieth Century* (1932). He also wrote the scenarios for several films. Hecht attacked anti-Semitism in *Guide for the Living* (1944) and advocated an extreme form of Zionism at the time Israel was being formed. *Perfidy* (1961) is a polemical attack on some of the leaders of the Israeli government. *A Child of the Century* (1954) is his frank, entertaining, and unconventional autobiography.

Hector (Hektor). Eldest son of Priam, the noblest and most magnanimous of all the Trojan chieftains in Homer's ILIAD. After holding out for ten years, he was slain by Achilles, who lashed him to his chariot, and dragged the dead body in triumph thrice round the walls of Troy. The *Iliad* concludes with the funeral obsequies of Hector and Patroclus.

In modern times his name has somewhat deteriorated, for it is used today for a swaggering bully, and "to hector" means to browbeat, bully, bluster.

Hecuba (Hekabe). In Homer's *Iliad*, the wife of Priam and mother of Hector. She is a tragic figure in Euripides' THE TROJAN WOMEN. In his HECUBA, her grief has made her a kind of Fury. In revenge for the murder of her son Polydorus, she blinds the Thracian king Polymestor, after killing his children. According to myth (perhaps through confusion with Hecate), she was transformed into a fiery-eyed hellhound. In Shakespeare's *Hamlet,* the Player King is deeply moved by his own speech about her, and Hamlet marvels, "What's Hecuba to him, or he to Hecuba?"

Hecuba (?425 B.C.). A tragedy by EURIPIDES. Hecuba, queen of Troy, has seen all of her 50 children die except her daughter Polyxena and POLYDORUS, her youngest son, whom she sent to King Polymestor in Thrace at the beginning of the war. As the play begins, she lies exhausted in front of her tent in Chalcidice, where the Greek expedition has taken her. A messenger comes to announce the decision of the Greeks in council: Polyxena must die to assuage the shade of Achilles. Polyxena goes to her death with dignity; soon after, the body of Polydorus is brought onto the stage. When Hecuba learns which of her children this is, she yearns for revenge. She lures Polymestor to her tent, blinds him, and kills his sons. Polymestor is reduced to an animal state as he crawls and gropes his way out of the tent. The closing scene shows Polymestor and Hecuba arguing their cases before Agamemnon. When Agamemnon decides for Hecuba, Polymestor breaks into prophecy and foresees the murder of Agamemnon and the horrible death of Hecuba, who will bark like a dog.

Many critics, approaching the *Hecuba* as a drama of character, have found contradictions in the plot, which is divided into two parts: the death of Polyxena and the blinding of Polymestor. Hecuba is involved in both of them, and her character changes through the play, but Euripides' tragic conception concerns more than Hecuba. The theme of the play is the brutality of suffering. Though Hecuba is the principal actor, the climactic speech is the prophecy of Polymestor, which displays Polymestor and Hecuba at the same bestial level. The key to Euripides' purpose is his use of myth; the old tales of Agamemnon's murder and Hecuba's animal metamorphosis become the climax to the long series of brutalities in the play.

Hedda Gabler (1890). A play by Henrik IBSEN. Hedda, a ruthless, neurotic woman, is bored with her dull, scholarly husband, repelled by the idea of her possible pregnancy, and concerned that she may have to forgo certain luxuries if her husband fails to be appointed a professor at the university. She learns that meek Thea Elvsted has helped reform the brilliant but dissipated Eilert Lövberg, who had once been in love with Hedda, and that the success of Lövberg's new book has made him her husband's rival for the professorship. Determined to show her power over Lövberg and thwart Thea's good influence, she lures him back into dissipation. She finds the missing manuscript of a second book, far more important to Lövberg than the first, but lets him believe that it is lost beyond recall. When, in despair, he threatens to end his life, she gives him a pistol and urges him to "die beautifully." He dies quite horribly, and Hedda finds herself in the power of Judge Brack, who knows that Hedda gave Lövberg the pistol and intends to use his knowledge to make her his mistress. Hedda finds this situation unbearable and "dies beautifully" by putting a bullet through her head.

Hedin, Sven Anders von (1865–1952). Swedish geographer and explorer in Central Asia, China, and India. Accounts of his journeys include *Through Asia* (1898), *Central Asia and Tibet* (1904), *Overland to India* (1910), and *The Silk Road* (1936).

Heep, Uriah. In Charles Dickens' DAVID COPPERFIELD, a clerk of Mr. WICKFIELD. One of the most famous characters in fiction, he is a detestable sneak, who is everlastingly forcing on one's attention that he is "'umble." Actually, Uriah is designing and malignant and he becomes a blackmailing tyrant over Mr. Wickfield. His infamy is brought to light by Mr. Micawber.

Hegel, Georg Friedrich Wilhelm (1770–1831). German philosopher. He greatly influenced the study of history and metaphysics in that he saw reality as a dynamic process, rather than as a reflection of static ideals. The process of reality, he maintained, is governed by the dialectical law: every thesis implies its own contradiction, or antithesis, and their conflict ends in a synthesis which again brings forth its antithesis. History, understood in terms of the dialectic, is produced by the conflicting impulses and interests of men, but at the same time shows the progressive self-realization of human reason and freedom. Great men are those whose personal aims coincide with the aim of the historical process; and in the later years of his life, Hegel used this concept of history to justify support of the Prussian state. His concept of the dialectic was developed by many subsequent philosophers, notably Marx and Engels; but the latter discarded Hegelian idealism and applied the dialectic to a materialistic view of history. Hegel's works include *The Phenomenology of the Spirit* (*Die Phänomenologie des Geistes;* 1807) and *The Philosophy of Right* (*Grundlinien der Philosophie des Rechts;* 1821). He was a close friend of both Hölderlin and Friedrich Schelling, with whom he held many ideas in common.

Heggen, Thomas [Orlo] (1919–1949). American novelist. Heggen, who was a member of the staff of the *Reader's Digest,* used his wartime experiences in the navy to write MISTER ROBERTS, an extremely successful novel, later adapted for the stage by Joshua Logan.

hegira or **hijira** (Arabic, "the departure"). The flight of MUHAMMAD from Mecca to MEDINA when he was expelled by the magistrates, July 16, 622. In 639, the Caliph Omar decreed that the Muslim calendar would date from this event.

Heian. The second Japanese historical period (794–1185). It saw the development of an exquisitely refined culture under the Imperial Court at Kyoto (Heian). Literature and the arts were marked by an extreme elegance, strongly influenced by Buddhist and Chinese thought. The *Tale of Genji* and the *Pillow-book of Sei Shōnagon* are products of this age. It was dominated by the Fujiwara family and is also known as the Fujiwara period.

Heiberg, Gunnar Edvard Rode (1857–1929). Norwegian playwright and essayist. A clever satirist, Heiberg mocked the absurd pettiness of Norwegian political life and treated other current concerns in such plays as *Kong Midas* (1890), *Gerts have* (1894), and *Det store lod* (1895). In *Balkonen* (*The Balcony,* 1894) and *Kjoerlighedens tragedie* (*The Tragedy of Love,* 1904), he turns his lyric powers to an analysis of the primitive force of sexual passion.

Heidegger, Martin (1889–   ). German philosopher, influenced by Kierkegaard, whose ideas form the basis of the existentialist movement. In *Sein und Zeit* (*Being and Time,* 1927), he distinguishes between two types of being: human existence (*Dasein*) and nonhuman presence (*Vorhandensein*), such as that of physical objects. Human existence is characterized by personal consciousness and accompanied by feelings of insecurity and dread (*Angst*). *Angst* is not fear of anything specific, but a general dread of nothingness.

Heidenstam [Carl Gustaf] Verner von (1859–1940). Swedish poet and novelist. An aspiring painter, Heidenstam turned to another art form with the publication of his first collection of poetry, *Vallfart och vandringsår* (1888). The vigorous modern rhythms and exuberant mood of the poems had a significant effect on young writers who were rebelling against naturalism. *Dikter* (1895) and *Nya Dikter* (1915) revealed Heidenstam's lyrical gifts. After 1890 he became chiefly a prose writer; in 1916 he received the Nobel Prize for literature.

Heidi. A children's story of life in the Swiss Alps by Johanna Spyri (1827–1901).

Heifetz, Jascha (1901–   ). Russian-born American violin virtuoso. He was a child prodigy;

his technique and artistry continued to amaze people as he matured. He settled in the U.S. after the Russian Revolution and became one of the most popular violinists of the century.

Heike monogatari, see TALES OF THE HEIKE, THE.

Heimat, Die. See MAGDA.

Heimdall. One of the gods of Scandinavian mythology, son of the nine virgin daughters of Aegir and called the White God with the Golden Teeth. As watchman of Asgard, he dwelt on the edge of heaven, guarded the rainbow bridge Bifrost, and possessed a mighty horn whose blast could be heard throughout the universe. It was said that he could see for 100 miles by day or night, that he slept less than a bird, and could hear the grass grow. When Ragnarok, the twilight of the gods, comes, he will sound his Gjallarhorn to assemble the gods and heroes. See LOKI.

Heimskringla. The most important prose collection in Old Norse literature, containing 16 sagas of Norwegian history through 1177, sketched through the medium of biography, with a compendium of ancient Scandinavian mythology and poetry. Its name comes from its opening words, *Kringla heimsins,* the circle of the world. The authorship is attributed to SNORRI STURLUSON.

Heine, Heinrich. Name at birth: **Chaim Harry Heine** (1797–1856). German poet, satirist, and journalist of Jewish origin. His ambiguous attitude toward Germany, combining a sincere sentimental love for the land and the people with biting irony about many German institutions, customs, and literary trends, appears in the early *Reisebilder* (*Travel-Sketches,* 1826 ff.), one of which is *Die Harzreise* (*Trip in the Harz Mountains,* 1826), his first major literary success. Gradually, however, he began to realize that the conflict between his liberal political views and the oppressive conservative regime in Prussia would make it impossible for him to remain in Germany. His attention was specifically drawn to Paris, where both the political ferment of the July Revolution (1830) and the growth of Saint-Simonianism attracted him; in 1831 he went there and remained for the rest of his life. In Paris, he was primarily active as a journalist and critic, writing in both German and French, and much of his work was intended to promote better understanding between his native and adopted lands: for example, *Französische Zustände* (*The Situation in France,* 1833); *Zur Geschichte der Religion und Philosophie in Deutschland* (*On the History of Religion and Philosophy in Germany,* 1834), which was also published in French; and *Die romantische Schule* (*The Romantic School,* 1833). In 1835, a Prussian edict prohibited his writings in Germany, naming him as a leader in the JUNG DEUTSCHLAND (Young Germany) movement with which he had, however, been only peripherally associated.

In his early poems, notably the *Buch der Lieder* (*Book of Songs,* 1827 ff.), which includes his famous ballad on the LORELEI-theme, Heine stands close to GERMAN ROMANTICISM. But though romantic elements remain in his later verse, especially the collection *Romanzero* (1851), there is also a strong tendency toward irony about romanticism, as in the narrative poems *Atta Troll* (1843) about the death of a trained bear, and *Deutschland, ein Wintermärchen* (*Ger-*

many, a Winter Tale, 1844) a political and literary satire. See PLATEN, BÖRNE.

Heinrich, Der arme (**Poor Heinrich**) (early 13th century). A narrative poem by HARTMANN VON AUE, based on German legend. The nobleman Heinrich is told he will not be cured of his leprosy until a virgin is willing to die for him. As he cannot wish such a sacrifice, he gives away most of his possessions and goes to live with one of his tenant farmers. This man's daughter learns how the cure must be effected and offers herself as the victim. This is enough to cause an instant cure, and Heinrich marries her. Heinrich becomes Prince Henry of Hoheneck in H. W. Longfellow's *The Golden Legend* (1851), and the tale is retold in Gerhart Hauptmann's drama *Der arme Heinrich* (1902).

Heinrich von Ofterdingen. Legendary German minnesinger, or medieval court poet. See under WARTBURG. NOVALIS uses his name for the title and hero of an unfinished symbolic novel (pub. 1801) in which the BLUE FLOWER represents the union of the dream world and the real world for the poet. The novel treats the imaginary development of Heinrich from a completely naïve young man into an accomplished poet. Wagner makes him one of the competing minstrels in TANNHÄUSER.

Heinse, Johann Jakob Wilhelm (1749–1803). German novelist. His justification of immoralism on aesthetic grounds is related to the tendencies of the STURM UND DRANG. His critical works on art, especially Italian painting, are significant, and his interest in this field may also be seen in the novel *Ardinghello oder Die glückseligen Inseln* (*Ardinghello or The Isles of the Blessed,* 1787), which is important in the growth of the BILDUNGSROMAN (novel of education).

Hekatoncheires. See the HUNDRED-HANDED.

Hel or **Hela.** The daughter of LOKI in Scandinavian mythology, who was queen of the dead and goddess of the lower regions. Here she was cast by Odin to dwell beneath the roots of the sacred ash, Yggdrasil. The region of Hel was also the home of the spirits of those who had died in their beds, as distinguished from Valhalla, the abode of heroes slain in battle.

Heldenbuch, Das (book of heroes). Name given to several collections of medieval German epics. The

Woodcut from a German *Heldenbuch* (c. 1500).

earliest extant manuscript is from 1472, the first printed version about 1477, although the poems were probably composed in the 13th century. The episodes are grouped in two cycles, one concerning Dietrich of Bern (see THEODORIC THE GREAT), the other about the brothers ORTNIT and Wolfdietrich.

Helen (Helene). In Greek mythology, the daughter of Zeus and Leda and wife of Menelaus. Her abduction by Paris led to the Trojan War. In the ILIAD of Homer and The TROJAN WOMEN of Euripides, she appears as a shallow and self-centered woman, unconcerned with the havoc her infidelity has wrought. Throughout literature from Greek times to the present, she has been a symbol of womanly beauty and sexual attraction. As such she has appeared in many dramas, including Marlowe's *Doctor Faustus,* Goethe's *Faust,* and Jean Giraudoux' *Tiger at the Gates.* Euripides' HELEN, however, tells another version of the story. The Helen at Troy was a phantom created by Hera to cause war. Menelaus' faithful wife, kidnapped by Hermes, remained in Egypt throughout the war, but they were finally reunited, despite the attempt of the Egyptian king Theoclymenus to marry her by force. This story of the false Helen was attributed to the poet STESICHORUS, who was said by Plato to have been blinded by Helen (who was also a goddess) for maligning her in verse. He redeemed her reputation, and his own sight, by writing the story of the phantom. Gluck wrote an opera on the traditional Helen, *Paride ed Elena* (1770). At the imperial court in Part II of Goethe's *Faust,* Faust makes Helen and Paris appear in a magical vision but, forgetting that it is an illusion, falls violently in love with Helen and causes an explosion by his rash attempt to take her from Paris. In the classical WALPURGIS NIGHT, however, he finds the real Helen, and the two of them enjoy a brief idyll that symbolizes the romantic ideal (see the brothers SCHLEGEL) of a synthesis between Nordic and classical cultures. See EUPHORION; ETERNAL FEMININE.

Helen (Helene; 412 b.c.). A play by EURIPIDES. Following Stesichorus' version of the story of HELEN of Troy, the play opens in Egypt. Hermes has brought her there after Paris has abducted from Troy not Helen but a phantom created in her likeness by Hera. She has been kindly treated by King Proteus, but he has died and his son Theoclymenus, who hates the Greeks, wants to marry her. Teucer arrives and tells of the destruction of Troy seven years before. Thousands have died because of the woman they all believe is Helen; her own mother and brothers have killed themselves in shame at her conduct; Menelaus and his ships are lost.

Menelaus arrives, however, and, recognizing his wife—the phantom having vanished—bitterly realizes that the TROJAN WAR has been fought for nothing. Pretending that Menelaus is dead, Helen borrows a ship to hold obsequies for him at sea. Together they escape from Theoclymenus and sail for home.

Helena. (1) In Shakespeare's MIDSUMMER NIGHT'S DREAM, a young Athenian lady in love with Demetrius. She pursues him despite his love for Hermia and is at last rewarded when Puck anoints him with a love potion.

(2) The persistent and loving heroine of Shakespeare's ALL'S WELL THAT ENDS WELL. She loves the haughty Bertram despite his scorn for her.

Helen of Kirconnell. A famous Scottish ballad. Helen is the lover of Adam Flemming. One day, while they are standing on the banks of a river, a rival suitor points his gun at Adam. Helen throws herself in front of him and is shot. The two rivals then fight, and the murderer is slain. Wordsworth embodies the same story in his poem *Ellen Irwin.*

Helenus. In Vergil's AENEID, a Trojan prince and prophet, the only son of Priam to survive the fall of Troy. He falls to the share of Pyrrhus (Neoptolemus) when the captives are awarded, and eventually marries Andromache, his brother Hector's widow. In some versions of the legend he is said to have deserted to the Greeks, and in others he is said to have been captured by Odysseus.

Helicon (Helikon). A Boeotian mountain. It was known by the Greeks as the home of the Muses. It contained the fountains of Aganippe and Hippocrene, connected by "Helicon's harmonious stream." The name is used allusively of poetic inspiration.

Heliogabalus. Full Latin name, **Varius Avitus Bassianus** (204–222). Roman emperor (218–222). He began as a priest in the temple of the sun god Elagabalus (hence his name as emperor). He was put forward as the son of CARACALLA and proclaimed emperor by the soldiery. Giving himself up to infamous debauchery, he left affairs of state to his mother. He was killed by the Praetorian Guard.

Helios. The Greek sun god. He rode to his palace in Colchis every night in a golden boat furnished with wings. He appears principally in the myth of PHAËTON, though his cattle are important in the ODYSSEY. His cult was important on the island of Rhodes; the famous COLOSSUS OF RHODES was a statue of Helios. See HERACLES.

heliotrope (Gr., "turn-to-sun"). The sun god loved Clytie, but forsook her for her sister Leucothoe. On discovering this, Clytie pined away; and the god changed her at death to a flower, which, always turning toward the sun, is called heliotrope.

The bloodstone, a greenish quartz with veins and spots of red, used to be called heliotrope, the story being that if thrown into a bucket of water it turned the rays of the sun to blood color. This stone also had the power of rendering its bearer invisible.

Helle. See GOLDEN FLEECE, THE.

Hellen. In Greek legend, a king of Phthia, eponym of the Hellenic race.

Hellenore. See FAERIE QUEENE, THE.

Hellespont. The ancient name of the Dardanelles, named for Athamas' daughter Helle (see THE GOLDEN FLEECE). In the classical romance, Leander used to swim the Hellespont to visit Hero, a priestess of Sestos. Lord Byron prided himself upon duplicating this feat.

Hell-fire Club. See MEDMENHAM ABBEY.

Hellman, Lillian (1905-   ). American dramatist. She is noted for her plays of psychological conflict. *The Children's Hour* (1934) dealt with a young girl who starts the rumor that the two heads of her school are Lesbians. THE LITTLE FOXES and THE WATCH ON THE RHINE are two of Lillian Hellman's most successful dramas. Others include *The Searching Wind* (1944) and *Toys in the Attic* (1960).

Hellström, Gustaf (1882–1953). Swedish writer. A career as foreign correspondent gave a foreign flavor to his novels, which are set in such world capitals as New York, London, and Paris. Among his works are *Ungkarlar* (1904), *Kuskar* (1910), *Bengt Blancks sentimentala resa* (1917), *Snormakare Lekholm far en idé* (*Lacemaker Lekholm has an idea,* 1927), and the autobiographical series *En man utan humor* (1921–1944).

Helmholtz, Hermann Ludwig Ferdinand von (1821–1894). German physicist who developed the theory of the conservation of energy, first formulated by Julius Robert MAYER.

Héloïse (1101–1164). Niece of the Canon Fulbert of Notre Dame Cathedral, famous as the beloved of Pierre Abélard. He was her tutor when he fell in love and seduced her (1118). They were secretly married after the birth of their son Astrolabe, although Héloïse tried to dissuade him, fearing the marriage would ruin his career. And in fact, when the marriage became known, Fulbert had Abélard emasculated; Héloïse became a nun and Abélard a monk. Their famous exchange of letters (see under ABÉLARD) made their story popular as a romantic tragedy, and in 1817 their bodies were reburied in one grave.

helot. A serf of ancient SPARTA. Possibly members of the earlier population of the area enslaved by their Dorian conquerors, they constituted the lowest class in the city-state. According to tradition, Spartan fathers used to ply their helot slaves with liquor on occasion so that their sons might learn by their disgusting example to detest drunkenness.

Helper, Hinton Rowan (1829–1909). American writer. Helper, who was born in North Carolina and was raised on a plantation, is best known for *The Impending Crisis of the South: How to Meet It* (1857), in which he argued that the South was economically and culturally far behind the North because of its slave labor. He held that slavery should be taxed out of existence and that all Negroes should be sent back to Africa. The book was an immediate success in the North, but it became illegal in most parts of the South even to own a copy.

Helvétius, Claude Adrien (1715–1771). French materialistic philosopher and encyclopedist. In his most famous work, *De l'Esprit* (1758), he asserts that human minds at birth are uniformly blank and that general progress and well-being therefore depend upon education, institutions, and laws. Utilitarian in his thinking, he states that religion has failed in becoming the framework for morality and that the only real basis for morality and for law is the public interest, i.e., that which is good for the greatest number. For this heretical doctrine the Sorbonne, the Pope, and the *Parlement* had the work condemned and burned. Jeremy Bentham and James Mill acknowledge his influence.

Hemans, Felicia Dorothea, born **Browne** (1793–1835). English poet, best known for her lyrics, *The Landing of the Pilgrim Fathers* and CASABIANCA. Mrs. Heman's work was much admired in its day for what was deemed nobility and pathos. She was also famous for her beauty and learning. Her *Poetical Works* were edited by W. M. Rossetti in 1873.

Hemingway, Ernest [Miller] (1899–1961). American novelist and short-story writer. Starting his writing career as a newspaperman and foreign correspondent, Hemingway was a meticulous literary craftsman whose terse, economic style, dramatic understatement, and superb dialogue have been extremely influential on modern prose writers. Sometimes erroneously dismissed as being sentimentally obsessed with violence, Hemingway clearly portrays in his work the sensitivity of a man hurt by the violence which he sees as a characteristic of our time.

Hemingway's first published volume was *Three Stories and Ten Poems* (1923); it contained the stories *Up in Michigan, Out of Season, My Old Man,* and six poems which had been previously published in *Poetry* (January, 1923). The author's first major work, IN OUR TIME, was a collection of 15 stories, many of them dealing with the early biography of Nick Adams, whose boyhood was to be a prototype for those of later Hemingway heroes. His first novel, *The Torrents of Spring* (1926), with its burlesque of Sherwood Anderson, is significant only as a declaration of his literary independence. It was with the appearance of THE SUN ALSO RISES that Hemingway's reputation became widely established. Often considered his best work in this form, it depicts "the lost generation" and the disillusionment that followed World War I.

MEN WITHOUT WOMEN, a collection that includes the famous stories THE KILLERS and *Fifty Grand,* continued Hemingway's early success. For those critics who consider Hemingway at his best in the short-story form, this volume and the later *Winner Take Nothing* (1933) rank high indeed. Hemingway next wrote A FAREWELL TO ARMS, a romantic, vivid, and impeccably written novel whose genesis was derived from material published in the earlier volume *In Our Time.* Two works of nonfiction followed: *Death in the Afternoon* (1932), with its eulogy of ritualized bullfight, and *Green Hills of Africa* (1935).

In 1937, Hemingway's early dissociation from political questions gave way to a position of greater involvement. To HAVE AND HAVE NOT, with its dying hero gasping, "One man alone ain't got . . . no chance," was the first to mark this change. That same year, deeply sympathetic with the Loyalist cause, he went to Spain as a war correspondent during the Civil war. *The Fifth Column* (1938), a play presenting "the nobility and dignity of the cause of the Spanish people," continued this concern as did his novel FOR WHOM THE BELL TOLLS.

During the next decade, Hemingway was almost silent. Taking part in World War II as a correspondent and waging his own irregular war at the head of a make-shift corps of his own, he did not publish another novel until 1950 when *Across the River and into the Trees* appeared. This novel, in which an aging hero revisits the scene of his World War I wounding, was almost unanimously rated as inferior work. But in 1952 came THE OLD MAN AND THE SEA, a novelette that was widely acclaimed and awarded the Pulitzer Prize. In 1954, Hemingway was given the Nobel Prize in literature. He published nothing more of significance before his self-inflicted death in 1961.

The author's short stories were collected in *The*

Short Stories of Ernest Hemingway (1938). *A Moveable Feast* (1964), published posthumously, is a reminiscence of the author's early years in Paris. See SHORT HAPPY LIFE OF FRANCIS MACOMBER, THE; SNOWS OF KILIMANJARO, THE.

Hemlock and After (1952). A novel by Angus WILSON. The hero is a middle-aged writer who is trying to reconcile his high-minded ideals with his failures and homosexual impulses. Wilson's attitude toward his many characters is both satirical and diagnostic.

Hémon, Louis (1880–1913). French novelist. Although Hémon spent only a short time in Canada, he is best known for *Maria Chapdelaine* (1916), a novel of farm life in Quebec, which became very popular after its posthumous publication.

Henchard, Michael. See MAYOR OF CASTERBRIDGE, THE.

Henderson, Alice Corbin (1881–1949). American poet and editor. With Harriet MONROE, she founded the magazine POETRY, and served as its associate editor (1912–1916). Her own poetry was collected in *The Spinning Woman of the Sky* (1912), *Red Earth* (1920), and *The Sun Turns West* (1933). She also compiled with Miss Monroe, *The New Poetry: An Anthology* (1917).

Hengist and **Horsa.** Two brothers in Geoffrey of Monmouth's *History of the Kings of Britain.* They were Jute invaders of England (c. 449), whose aid in war against the Picts was enlisted by the ancient British king VORTIGERN. Horsa is said to have been killed in battle in 455, Hengist to have ruled the kingdom of Kent, which they founded, until 488.

Henley, William Ernest (1849–1903). English poet, dramatist, and editor. As editor of the *National Observer* (1889–1894) and the *New Review* (1898–1903), Henley was a revolutionary force in English literature, publishing and defending early works of such writers as Barrie, Hardy, Kipling, Wells, Shaw, and Conrad. In his own work he was a pioneer in the use of free verse (*In Hospital*, 1888) and wrote a number of poems of merit and technical accomplishment. Unfortunately, aggressive jingoism mars much of such volumes as *The Song of the Sword* (1893) and *For England's Sake* (1900) and Henley has had the ill-luck to be known, generally, as the author of a single poem, the meretricious INVICTUS. His collected *Poems* appeared in 1912. He also collaborated with his friend R. L. Stevenson on three plays, and was the author of numerous critical essays (*Works*, 1908).

Hennepin, Father Louis (1640–?1701). Belgian-born Franciscan friar and explorer. He accompanied La Salle through the Great Lakes (1679) and joined a party that explored the Upper Mississippi Valley. While a captive of the Sioux, he discovered the Falls of St. Anthony, near present-day Minneapolis. In France he published *Description de la Louisiane* (1683) and other, somewhat exaggerated, accounts of his experiences. His claim that he descended to the mouth of the Mississippi has since been shown to be false.

Henriade, La (1723, republished in 1728 with revisions). An epic poem in 10 cantos by VOLTAIRE. It recounts the struggle of Henry of Navarre (later HENRY IV of France) to obtain the throne. Voltaire depicts the assassination of Henry III and the religious wars with the HOLY LEAGUE, and by implication condemns civil strife and religious fanaticism.

Henrietta Maria (1609–1669). Queen consort (1625–1649) of Charles I of England and mother of Charles II and James II. The daughter of Henry IV of France, she was a Roman Catholic. Forced to flee to France (1644), she returned to England after the Restoration.

Henriques, Robert (1905–   ). English soldier and novelist. Among his works are *No Arms, No Armour* (1939), *Home Fires Burning* (1945), *Through the Valley* (1950), and *A Stranger Here* (1953).

Henry IV. Also known as **Henry Bolingbroke** and **Henry of Lancaster** (1367–1413). King of England (1399–1413), the 1st monarch of the house of Lancaster. The son of John of Gaunt and the grandson of Edward III, he was banished by RICHARD II in 1398. The following year he invaded England, overthrew Richard, and assumed the crown himself. He is a central character in Shakespeare's HENRY IV: PART I and PART II, and also appears in RICHARD II. The surname Bolingbroke refers to the castle in which he was born.

Henry V (1387–1422). King of England (1413–1422). The son of Henry IV, he invaded France in an attempt to reconquer England's former possessions there, winning an important victory at Agincourt (1415). Subsequent military successes and astute diplomacy resulted in the treaty of Troyes (1420), by which Henry was to marry Catherine of Valois, daughter of Charles VI, king of France, and inherit the French crown upon Charles's death. See HENRY V, THE LIFE OF KING.

Henry VII. Also known as **Henry Tudor** (1457–1509). King of England (1485–1509), the 1st monarch of the Tudor dynasty. As earl of Richmond and the principal representative of the Lancastrian claim to the throne of England, he defeated Richard III at Bosworth Field in 1485. His subsequent marriage to Elizabeth, daughter of Edward IV, marked the end of the WARS OF THE ROSES. Later he successfully suppressed a rebellion by the Yorkist pretender PERKIN WARBECK. He was succeeded by his son Henry VIII.

Henry VIII. Henry Tudor (1491–1547). Second of the Tudor kings, king of England (1509–1547). At the beginning of his reign Henry married Catherine of Aragon, his brother's widow; because of some ecclesiastical protest about the validity of such a union, he was forced to acquire a Papal dispensation. When, nearly twenty years later, Catherine had not borne him a son, personal and political reasons moved him to consider divorce. The Pope was unwilling, doubly so since Rome was in the hands of the Emperor Charles V, Catherine's nephew. Various delays occurred, and finally Henry chose the expedient of overthrowing papal jurisdiction, thus at one fell swoop making possible his divorce, channeling the revenues from monasteries and Church lands away from Rome to the Crown and, almost incidentally, and for political far more than religious reasons, initiating the English Reformation. Early in 1533, before any kind of divorce had been granted, he secretly married ANNE BOLEYN, and a few months later had his first marriage declared void and his second declared valid. This was followed by an Act of Succession, giving the right of succession to the throne to offspring of Anne and denying it to Mary (later MARY I), Catherine's daughter, on the grounds of her illegitimacy. To both this and the Act of Supremacy, by which Henry was made head of the Church, subjects were required to give an oath of acceptance, a thing that no devout Catholic could do, and in default of which Sir Thomas More, formerly Lord Chancellor, was executed for high treason.

Anne, like Catherine before her, bore only one child that lived, and that a daughter, the future ELIZABETH I. In 1536 Anne was dispatched on a charge of adultery, and Henry married Jane Seymour, who died bearing him the much-desired son, destined to become the boy-king Edward VI. In 1540 Henry married the German princess Anne of Cleves, but disliked her and divorced her almost immediately. Catherine Howard, the next of his wives, was soon charged with adultery and beheaded. His last wife was Catherine Parr, a patroness of the arts, who survived him. Before his death Henry fixed the succession in his will, giving it to Edward, Mary, and Elizabeth (though both of his daughters had previously been declared illegitimate), who succeeded him in that order.

Henry IV. Also known as **Henry of Navarre** and **Henry the Great** (1553–1610). King of France (1589–1610), the first of the Bourbon dynasty. Raised as a Calvinist, Henry became leader of the French Huguenot party in 1569 after the death of the first prince of Condé. He succeeded to the throne of Navarre as Henry III and married MARGARET OF VALOIS, sister of Charles IX of France, in 1572. When the death of the brother of Henry III, the reigning king of France, made Henry of Navarre heir presumptive, the refusal of the HOLY LEAGUE to recognize his title led to the conflict known as the War of the Three Henrys (Henry III of France, Henry of Navarre, and Henry, duke of GUISE). After the assassination of the king of France, Henry's victory over the league at Ivry and his conversion to Catholicism enabled him to secure the crown. One of France's ablest monarchs, Henry initiated a program to hasten recovery from the religious wars. He issued the Edict of NANTES and, in foreign affairs, followed a policy of opposition to the Hapsburgs. He was assassinated by François Ravillac, a Roman Catholic fanatic. See Gabrielle d'ESTRÉES; duc de SULLY; and HENRIADE, THE.

Henry IV (1050–1106). Holy Roman emperor. On the death of his father, Henry III, in 1056, he succeeded to the kingdoms of Germany, Italy, and Burgundy. In 1065 Henry was declared of age and assumed the throne. His reign was marked by the great struggle between empire and papacy over the question of lay investiture. Hitherto the emperors had filled the ecclesiastical positions within their dominions at their pleasure. But Pope GREGORY VII decided to claim this power for the papacy, and in 1075 he issued a decree forbidding lay investiture. Almost immediately, Henry responded by filling several sees in Italy with bishops of his own choosing. When Gregory threatened excommunication, Henry called together the German bishops and answered: "I, Henry, king by the grace of God, together with all our bishops, say unto thee, come down, come

down from thy throne and be accursed through all the ages." Gregory forthwith deposed the bishops, excommunicated Henry, and declared the thrones of Italy and Germany vacant. Henry was then faced with a revolt in his territories, as his vassals gave him notice that a new emperor would be chosen within the year if he did not relent. Accordingly, the emperor went in 1077 to meet the pope at Canossa. There, outside the castle, Henry garbed as a penitent waited for three days in the snow before Gregory would receive him and grant conditional absolution. When Henry returned to Germany, he found that the princes had elected a new emperor in spite of his penance. Gregory remained neutral for a time, then renewed the excommunication. After Henry had defeated and killed his rival Rudolf, duke of Swabia, he marched on Rome. An attempt at compromise through the convocation of a synod failed, and in 1083 Henry deposed Gregory and installed Clement III, who promptly crowned Henry emperor. Meanwhile, the German princes had chosen a new king, Hermann of Luxemburg, and Henry was compelled to renew the struggle. By 1088 he had restored his authority throughout Germany. He survived conspiracies by his second wife and his eldest son Conrad, only to be defeated by his second son Henry, later Henry V, who declared he owed no allegiance to an excommunicated father. In 1105 a diet in Mainz forced Henry IV to abdicate. After escaping to Cologne, he began negotiations with England, France, and Denmark. He was engaged in organizing an army when he died in 1106.

Henry IV: Part I (c. 1597–1598). A historical play by William SHAKESPEARE, depicting early years of the reign of England's HENRY IV. After defeating rebellious Scottish barons, Henry PERCY, the famous Hotspur, eldest son of the powerful earl of Northumberland, refuses to yield his prisoners to the king unless his kinsman Edmund Mortimer, captured by the rebellious Welshman Owen Glendower, is ransomed. Since Mortimer is pretender to the throne, Henry refuses his ransom. Angered, the Percy family joins the rebels. Meanwhile, the king's son and heir, Prince Hal, continues to annoy his father by keeping company with the band of revelers led by Sir John FALSTAFF. But, hearing of the uprising, Hal takes command of a part of his father's forces, helping to defeat the rebels at the battle of Shrewsbury (1403). Hal saves his father's life and kills Hotspur.

Henry IV: Part II (c. 1597–1598). A historical play by William SHAKESPEARE, completing the description of the reign of HENRY IV. Despite the death of Hotspur, the rebellion continues, under the leadership of the earl of Northumberland. Meanwhile, Hal has returned to the riotous company of FALSTAFF. Upon Northumberland's desertion, the rebels negotiate with the king's second son, John of Lancaster, who promises to redress their grievances if they will disband. They accept and are promptly killed by the treacherous prince. News of his enemies' defeat reaches the king on his deathbed. Hal is named king (Henry V) and promptly repudiates his misspent youth by banishing Falstaff from his presence. Shakespeare's source for both plays about Henry IV is Holinshed's *Chronicles* (1577).

Henry V, The Life of King (c. 1598–1599). A historical play by William SHAKESPEARE. Shortly after his coronation, HENRY V decides to press his claims to the French throne and leads an army into France. He defeats a vastly larger French army at Agincourt (1415), wins the hand of the French princess, Catherine of Valois, and is recognized as heir to the French throne. Against this background, Shakespeare reveals Henry's rapport with the doughty English soldiers. The death of FALSTAFF is also reported in the play.

In HENRY IV: PART I and PART II and in *Henry V,* Shakespeare chronicles Henry's life from his days as a profligate youth under the influence of Sir John Falstaff to his victory at Agincourt as king of England. His character is used by Shakespeare as a study in statesmanship. Although Henry steeps himself in the revels and schemes of Falstaff, part of him always remains aloof. For, as he explains:

> I know you all, and will awhile uphold
> The unyok'd humour of your idleness:
> Yet herein will I imitate the sun,
> Who doth permit the base contagious clouds
> To smother up his beauty from the world,
> That when he please again to be himself,
> Being wanted, he may be more wonder'd at.

Henry VI: Part I (c. 1590–1592). The 1st play of a historical trilogy by William SHAKESPEARE, depicting the early years of Henry's reign up to his marriage with MARGARET OF ANJOU. After the death of Henry V, the realm of the child king, Henry VI, falls under the control of his uncles, the regents John, duke of Bedford, and HUMPHREY, duke of Gloucester. War has broken out anew in France; under JOAN LA PUCELLE, the French begin to drive the English out. Meanwhile, Richard Plantagenet, having successfully pressed his claims to the title of the duke of York, quarrels with the powerful Beaufort family of the house of Lancaster, setting the stage for the Wars of the Roses. After a temporary reconciliation of Yorkists and Lancastrians, a marriage is arranged between Henry and the daughter of the French earl of Armagnac in order to seal a truce between England and France. However, at the urging of the earl of Suffolk, Henry chooses Margaret of Anjou to be his queen.

Henry VI: Part II (c. 1590–1592). The 2nd play of a historical trilogy by William SHAKESPEARE, covering the early years of the Wars of the Roses. After his marriage to Margaret, Henry is dominated by the queen and the duke of Suffolk, who plot the overthrow of the lord protector, Humphrey, the duke of Gloucester, by convicting Humphrey's wife, the duchess of Gloucester, of sorcery, and thus forcing his shameful retirement. Meanwhile, Richard Plantagenet, having convinced the earl of Salisbury and Richard Neville, earl of Warwick, of his right to the throne, waits for the opportunity to seize it. Before leaving to suppress a revolt in Ireland, he encourages Jack CADE to launch a rebellion in his absence. Subsequently, Richard returns to England and meets and defeats the king's forces at St. Albans (1455).

Henry VI: Part III (c. 1590–1592). The 3rd play of a historical trilogy by William SHAKESPEARE, covering the downfall of Henry and the victory of the house of York in the person of Edward IV. After the defeat of his forces at St. Albans, Henry begs Richard Plantagenet to allow him to reign during his lifetime. Richard agrees, but Margaret, Henry's queen, is set on destroying Richard. At Wakefield,

she defeats him and puts him to death. But Richard's sons, Edward (IV) and Richard (III), triumph over Margaret at Towton, and Edward becomes king. Henry, who has fled, returns to England and is imprisoned in the Tower of London. Edward sends Warwick to France to arrange a marriage with Bona, sister of Louis XI. In his absence, Edward marries Lady Elizabeth Grey, and Warwick, annoyed, goes over to Margaret. After several reverses, Edward defeats Margaret at Tewkesbury (1471) where Henry's son, Edward, prince of Wales, is killed. Shortly thereafter, Richard (III) murders Henry in the Tower. The principal sources for the trilogy about Henry VI were Holinshed's *Chronicles* (1577) and Edward Hall's *Union of The Noble and Illustrious Families of Lancaster and York* (1547).

Henry VIII, The Famous History of the Life of King (1613). A historical play by William SHAKESPEARE. John Fletcher (see BEAUMONT AND FLETCHER) may have written parts of the play.

The drama begins with the return of HENRY VIII from the Field of the Cloth of Gold. Edward Stafford, duke of Buckingham, is about to warn the king of the growing power of Cardinal Wolsey when he is falsely accused of treason and executed. Meanwhile, Henry who has met Anne Bullen becomes concerned with the legal aspects of his marriage to Katharine of Aragon. Through Wolsey, he negotiates with the pope for a divorce. But when Wolsey discovers that the king plans to marry Anne, he tries to stop the divorce, is found out, and, while under arrest for treason, dies. Henry's marriage is annulled by Thomas Cranmer, archbishop of Canterbury, and the king marries Anne. Katharine dies, commending her daughter, Mary, to Henry's protection. The nobles, jealous of Cranmer's growing influence, try to discredit him but Henry protects the archbishop and makes him godfather of the infant Elizabeth. The principal source of the play is Holinshed's *Chronicles* (1577); the portions dealing with Cranmer are derived from Foxe's *Book of Martyrs* (1563).

Henry, Frederic. A principal character in Ernest Hemingway's novel A FAREWELL TO ARMS. An American lieutenant in the Italian ambulance service during World War I, he falls in love with an English nurse, Catherine Barkley. He deserts to be with her, but she dies in childbirth.

Henry, John. A legendary Negro hero of American ballads and folk tales. Born supposedly in the "Black River country," he was employed in the building of railroads or as a roustabout on river steamboats. John Henry is a man of prodigious strength; in one well-known tale he dies from overexertion, after winning a contest against a steam drill. The tales are apparently based on the exploits of a giant Negro who worked on the Chesapeake & Ohio Big Bend Tunnel in the early 1870's. In 1931, Guy B. Johnson made a collection of varying ballads in *John Henry: Tracking Down a Negro Legend.* In the same year Roark Bradford based a novel, *John Henry,* on several tales. Bradford's novel was later dramatized with music by Jacques Wolfe (1931).

Henry, O. Pen name of **William Sydney** [earlier spelled **Sidney**] **Porter** (1862–1910). American short-story writer. An extremely popular and prolific writer during his lifetime, O. Henry is noted for his sentimental, semirealistic stories dealing with the lives of modest people and his mastery of the surprise ending, which came to be known as the "O. Henry ending" and has been widely imitated in commercial fiction. Born in North Carolina, he later went to Texas, where he became the editor and publisher of a humorous magazine THE ROLLING STONE. Charged with embezzling funds from a bank, he fled to Central America, subsequently the scene of CABBAGES AND KINGS. He later returned and, although there has been much debate over his actual guilt in the matter, served over three years in the federal penitentiary at Columbus, Ohio. While in prison, he published the first of his stories signed O. Henry—*Whistling Dick's Christmas Stocking* (1899)—in *McClure's Magazine*. The pen name is presumed to be the abbreviation for the name of a French pharmacist, Etienne-Ossian Henry, found in the *U.S. Dispensatory,* a reference work Porter used when he worked as prison pharmacist.

In prison O. Henry heard many stories that were the germs of his later narratives, among them the tale of Jimmy Connors, the thief who became the hero of A RETRIEVED REFORMATION. But his work is most identified with New York City, where he subsequently lived and to which he gave the name "Bagdad-on-the-Subway." In his own lifetime numerous collections of O. Henry's stories were published, including THE FOUR MILLION, and others appeared after his death. *Works of O. Henry* (2 vols., 1953) includes all of his stories and some of his poems. In 1918, the O. Henry Memorial Awards were established. These are given to the best stories published each year in American magazines, the prize stories and the leading contenders then being published together in an annual collection. See GIFT OF THE MAGI, THE; LAST LEAF, THE.

Henry, Patrick (1736–1799). American statesman and orator. As a member of the Virginia House of Burgesses, he offered a series of resolutions against the Stamp Act (1765). He later served in the Continental Congress and as governor of Virginia. Famous passages from his speeches include:

> Caesar had his Brutus; Charles the First, his Cromwell; and George the Third—*may profit by their example.* If *this* be treason, make the most of it. (Virginia House of Burgesses, 1765)

> Is life so dear, or peace so sweet, as to be purchased at the price of chains and slavery? Forbid it, Almighty God! I know not what course others may take; but as for me, give me liberty, or give me death! (Virginia Convention, 1775)

Henry Esmond, Esquire, The History of (1852). A historical novel by William Makepeace THACKERAY. It is written in the first person, supposedly by Henry ESMOND. He is brought up by Francis Esmond, heir to the Castlewood estate with Francis' own children, Beatrix and Frank, and grows up in the belief that he is the illegitimate son of Thomas Esmond, the deceased viscount of Castlewood. On his deathbed, Francis confesses to Henry that he is the lawful heir, but Henry keeps the information secret. He and Frank Esmond are ardent supporters of James Edward, the (Old) Pretender, who falls in love with Beatrix and ruins his chances for the throne. When Beatrix joins the prince abroad, Henry, who has been in love with her, renounces the Pretender;

he marries her mother, Rachel, Lady Castlewood, instead and takes her to America. The story of their descendants is related in Thackeray's THE VIRGINIANS.

Henryson, Robert (1430?–1506). Scottish poet, one of the group of SCOTTISH CHAUCERIANS. His works include *Tale of Orpheus* (printed 1508); *Testament of Cressid* (printed 1593), a treatment of the TROILUS legend, attributed to Chaucer until the 18th century; and *Moral Fables of Aesop the Phrygian* (printed 1621).

Henry the Minstrel, also known as **Blind Harry** (fl. 1470–1492). Scottish bard. His epic poem *Wallace* (c. 1482) celebrates the Scottish hero Sir William Wallace. The poem, which was widely popular, shows the influence of Chaucer.

Henry the Navigator (1394–1460). Portuguese prince. The younger son of John I, he planned and directed a campaign of exploration and discovery that subsequently led to Portugal's extensive conquests in the Orient and the New World. From his residence at Sagres, which became the foremost center of navigation in Europe, he dispatched several vessels each year into the uncharted seas to the south and west, meeting only failure until 1434 when Cape Bojador was rounded. On later voyages Madeira and the Azores were discovered.

Henschke, Alfred. See KLABUND.

Hephaestus (Hephaistos). In Greek mythology, the god of fire and metal-working. Later he was identified with the Roman VULCAN. Hephaestus was either the son of Zeus and Hera, or produced by Hera alone. Homer related that Hera threw her lame son out of heaven, ashamed of his deformity. In revenge, Hephaestus wrought a golden throne from which Hera could not arise. In another story, Hephaestus took the part of Hera against Zeus, who then hurled him from heaven. He fell for nine days and was finally picked up, lamed for life, on the island of Lemnos.

Married to the unfaithful APHRODITE, he became known as the special patron of cuckolds. Hephaestus (or Prometheus) delivered ATHENE from the head of Zeus with the stroke of an ax.

Heptaméron (1559). An unfinished collection of 72 tales by MARGARET OF NAVARRE. Modeled on the *Decameron* (1353) of Boccaccio, the work is otherwise original. All but one of the tales were probably based on her own experiences. Though weak in literary style, the work is distinguished for its psychological perception and its didactic quality.

heptameter. In prosody, a line of verse containing seven metrical feet in any METER. It is usually identified together with the name of the meter: for example, iambic heptameter.

Hera. A Greek goddess, daughter of Cronos and Rhea, and both sister and wife of Zeus. She appears most often in myth as a jealous wife who persecutes her husband's many mistresses (Semele, Io, Leto, and others) or their children (Dionysus, Heracles). Her worship, however, antedated that of Zeus in Greece, where she had important shrines at Argos and elsewhere. The Heraean Games for women were celebrated at Olympia long before the famous Olympic Games for men. She was the patroness of the ARGONAUTS.

Heracles (Herakles) (Lat. *Hercules*). A mythical Greek hero of fabulous strength. Heracles was the son of Zeus and Alcmena, who had caught Zeus' notice when her husband AMPHITRYON was away from Thebes. Amphitryon, however, returned the same night that Zeus had visited her, and in good time she gave birth to twins, Heracles and Iphicles, who was merely the son of Amphitryon. HERA, who had done everything possible to prevent the birth, did not give up. She sent two snakes to attack the twins, but Heracles strangled them in his crib. Heracles married the Theban king's daughter Megara, but, driven mad by Hera, he killed Megara and all their children. When he returned to his senses, he went into exile and bound himself to serve his cousin Eurystheus, the king of Mycenae, for 12 years. At the end of this time he would become immortal. Although he traveled far and wide for many of the famous Labors, Heracles' own home seems to have been at Tiryns. His Labors were as follows:

1. Killing the NEMEAN lion. This frightful beast, sent by Hera to ravage the Nemean plain and to annoy Heracles, he killed by clubbing and strangling it, although it was supposedly invulnerable. Henceforward he wore its skin.

2. Killing the HYDRA. This tremendous snake, one of the many delightful monsters spawned by Echidna, inhabited the Lernaean swamps. As soon as one of its numerous heads was lopped off, others grew in its place. Heracles persuaded his friend Iolaus to burn the stumps before the heads could grow and thus they disposed of the beast, as well as a crab sent by Hera to help it out. This crab became the constellation of Cancer.

3. Capturing the ERYMANTHIAN BOAR. Heracles brought this redoubtable beast back to Eurystheus and nearly scared him out of his wits.

4. Capturing the Hind of ARTEMIS. Heracles succeeded in capturing this sacred animal after a year's search and Artemis permitted him to carry it off to Argos if he promised to let it go, which he did.

5. Killing the man-eating Stymphalian birds. Heracles chased them from their hiding in the woods by banging a bronze rattle, then shot them down one by one.

6. Cleansing the AUGEAN STABLES. These stables, belonging to King Augeas of Elis, had never been cleaned. Heracles accomplished the task in a day by redirecting a river through them.

7. Capturing the Cretan Bull. This bull, which may have been the father of the Minotaur, was taken alive and shown to Eurystheus, like the Hind, then released.

8. Capturing the horses of Diomedes, son of Cyrene and Ares. These horses were fed on human flesh by their owner, the king of the Bistonians. They suddenly became tame when Heracles fed their master to them. He then took them back to Eurystheus and dedicated them to Hera.

9. Capturing the girdle of Hippolyta. Either alone or with an army, Heracles defeated the AMAZONS and either killed Hippolyta or secured the girdle by holding one of her generals, Melanippe, for ransom.

10. Killing the monster Geryon. Heracles threatened Helios with his bow until the god gave him his golden cup, in which Heracles sailed the river Oceanus to the far west. There, after disposing of the herdsman Eurytion and the ferocious dog Orthrus, he killed Geryon himself, stole his cattle, and returned with them, either in the cup or by a long and arduous route through Spain, France, and Italy.

11. Capturing Cerberus. Heracles made his way down to HADES, dragged up Cerberus, the three-headed dog that watches the gates, showed him to Eurystheus, and duly returned him to his proper place. According to one story Heracles actually fought with and wounded Hades himself.

12. Stealing the apples of the HESPERIDES. These apples grew on a tree guarded by a terrible dragon and belonging to the Hesperides, daughters of Night, who lived near the Atlas Mountains. There are various tales as to how Heracles plucked the apples: He either killed the snake or put it to sleep and took the apples himself, or he sent Atlas for them, holding the sky on his shoulders meanwhile.

Heracles had innumerable other adventures, either separately or incidentally to his main labors. He eventually died after donning the poisoned shirt dipped in the blood of the centaur NESSUS, which his wife Deianira had given him. He built himself a funeral pyre on Mount Oeta and persuaded Poeas with the gift of his bow and arrows to set it afire. After this he ascended to Olympus and married Hebe.

The last three labors of Heracles seem to indicate that he achieved immortality by his feats. A very considerable number of his adventures were added to his saga to explain the many places in which his cult flourished. Some authorities believe that the root of the Heracles saga is the adventures of an actual Mycenaean king of Tiryns who performed mighty feats at the bidding of his overlord, the high king of Mycenae. His feats were a favorite subject of art among the Greeks and in the Renaissance.

Heracles appears in two tragedies by Sophocles, *The Trachinian Women (Trachiniai)* and *Philoctetes,* in two by Euripides, *Alcestis* and *The Madness of Heracles (Herakles Mainomenos)*; and in Seneca's *Hercules Furens.* Euripides' *The Children of Heracles (Herakleidai)* tells of the final defeat of Eurystheus, who had continued to persecute Heracles' family after his death.

Heracles Mainomenos. See HERACLES.

Heraclitus (Herakleitos; fl. 500 B.C.). A Greek philosopher, belonging to one of the ruling families of Ephesus. Over a hundred fragments of his work have survived. The style is oracular, striving to indicate a truth rather than explicate it. Referred to as the dark philosopher, Heraclitus' best-known statement is "all things change." He considered the basic stuff of the universe to be fire.

Héraclius (1647). A tragedy by Pierre CORNEILLE. It is derived from the annals of Baronius. Héraclius, son of the murdered emperor of the East, has been raised by a loyal nurse as the son of the usurper Phocas; this masquerade, which has saved Héraclius' life, has been accomplished at the sacrifice of the nurse's own son. For political reasons, Phocas wishes Pulchérie, daughter of the former emperor, to marry Héraclius, supposedly his own son, who in reality are brother and sister. When Phocas learns the truth he almost kills Héraclius, but a conspiracy ends his life, and Héraclius becomes emperor. The play is further complicated by additional characters, disguises, and misunderstandings.

Herakleidai. See HERACLES.

Herbert, Sir A[lan] P[atrick] (1890–1971). English humorist, poet, and member of Parliament. He is known for his work in securing a modification of the English divorce laws; divorce is the subject of his novel *Holy Deadlock* (1934). He also campaigned for the improvement of English canals and waterways, which provide the setting for his novel *The Water Gipsies* (1930). His volumes of witty and humorous essays include *Light Articles Only* (1921), and his collections of light verse include *Less Nonsense* (1944).

Herbert, Edward. 1st Baron Herbert of Cherbury (1583–1648). English soldier, diplomat, and philosopher, brother of George Herbert. His attempts, in such works as *De Veritate* (1624) and *De Religione Gentilium* (1663), to discover a rational and universally self-evident basis for religion make him the first of the English deists. He also wrote an interesting *Autobiography*, which was discovered and published by Horace Walpole in 1764, and poetry in the metaphysical vein.

Herbert, George (1593–1633). English poet of the METAPHYSICAL SCHOOL. Herbert, who was a brother of Lord Herbert of Cherbury, came from a Welsh family famous for its soldiers and statesmen. For a long time he aspired to a government career, but a growing sense of religious vocation and the death of James I and other patrons led him to become an Anglican priest. In 1630 he was given the rural living of Bemerton, where he died a few years later, esteemed almost as a saint.

All of Herbert's poetry is religious, even that written during his period of secular ambition. In fact, a major theme of his work, revealed in poems like THE COLLAR and AFFLICTION (I), is the conflict between his calling and his ambition, his pride in his descent and his attainments. Other poems, such as THE SACRIFICE, deal with every facet of religious life: the vicissitudes of a believer's hopes and fears; the nature of God, with emphasis on His love and suffering for man; the festivals, institutions, and doctrines of the Church. Herbert often expresses deep religious anxiety, but his characteristic mood is one of sweetness and equilibrium, a trusting, intimate friendliness with God. Technically, his work is marked by simple diction, striking colloquial rhythms, and the use of symbols and images from ecclesiastical ritual, farming, the trades, science, and everyday household pursuits. He is also known for his extraordinary metrical inventiveness and his occasional "pattern poems": poems whose lines are arranged to form a given shape like an altar or wings or a cross, such as the well-known EASTER WINGS.

Herbert wrote one volume of poems, THE TEMPLE; a treatise on the life and duties of a country parson, *A Priest to the Temple* (1652); and several collections of proverbs. His work was highly popular in its day, but attacked in the later 17th century as overelaborate in conceit and perversely ingenious. He had some admirers in the 19th century, but it was not until the 20th century, with the general revival of interest in metaphysical poetry, that his work was once more appreciated.

Herbert, Victor (1859–1924). Irish-American conductor and composer. He was the conductor of the Pittsburgh Symphony, 1898–1904. He wrote some 30 operettas, including *Babes in Toyland* (1903);

Mlle. Modiste (1905); *The Red Mill* (1906); *Naughty Marietta* (1910). He also wrote a cello concerto, other orchestral music, and two grand operas.

Herbst, Josephine [Frey] (1897–1969). American novelist. Associated with the so-called proletarian novelists, she was born in Iowa and early became an advocate of radical political and social change. Three of her novels—*Pity Is Not Enough* (1933), *The Executioner* (1934), and *Rope of Gold* (1939)—were designed as a trilogy to portray the decay of capitalistic society. Her more recent books include *Somewhere the Tempest Fell* (1947), *New Green World* (1954), and *The Watcher with the Horn* (1955).

Hercules. See HERACLES.

Hercules Furens. See HERACLES.

Herder, Johann Gottfried (1744–1803). German philosopher, historian, and critic. He is known as the most prominent representative of 18th-century irrationalism. His interest in the folk spirit (see VOLKSGEIST) was not confined to Germany, and his collection of *Volkslieder* (*Folk Songs*, 1778–1779), which was prompted by Percy's *Reliques of Ancient English Poetry*, included Nordic, English, and Romance songs, as well as German. His ideas about the value of intuition in both creation and criticism were taken up and developed by Goethe, with whom he was closely associated, and by German romanticism. His other works include *Von deutscher Art und Kunst* (*On German Character and Art*, 1773), *Auch eine Philosophie der Geschichte zur Bildung der Menschheit* (*Another Philosophy of History for the Education of Mankind*, 1774), and *Briefe zur Beförderung der Humanität* (*Letters for the Furtherance of Humanity*, 1793–1797). See HAMANN; STURM UND DRANG.

Heredia, José María de (1803–1839). Cuban poet. Exiled at 20 for revolutionary activity against the Spanish regime in Cuba, Heredia imbued his poetry with the disillusion and frustration that was the lot of many Cuban intellectuals of his generation. After spending two unhappy years in the U.S., he settled in Mexico, where, except for a brief trip to Cuba in 1836, he remained for the rest of his life. Although Heredia's poetry is classical in form, he has been called the first romantic poet of Hispanic America because of the subjectivity and intensity that characterize his verse. The two poems generally considered his best are *En el teocalli de Cholula* (1820), in which Heredia reflects on the impermanence of all earthly endeavor, and *Niagara* (1824), in which the poet describes the scene in a style as torrential as the falls itself, and then laments his solitude, so far from home.

Hérédia, José Maria de (1842–1905). Cuban-born French poet. A pupil of Leconte de Lisle, Hérédia was one of the first PARNASSIANS. His finest poetry is contained in the 118 sonnets of *Les Trophées* (1893), which are remarkable for the richness of their imagery, the sonorousness and cadence of their language, and the evocative character of their historical impressions.

Hereward the Wake (1865). A historical novel by Charles KINGSLEY. The titular hero is a reckless young Saxon who for a time successfully opposes the Norman conquest. He plunders and burns the abbey of Peterborough, establishes his camp in the Isle of Ely where he is joined by Earl Morcar, is blockaded for three months by William I, but makes his escape with some of his followers.

Hergesheimer, Joseph (1880–1954). American novelist and short-story writer. A skillful popular writer, Hergesheimer won considerable acclaim with his novels *The Three Black Pennys* (1917), JAVA HEAD, and BALISAND. He is also known as the author of *Tol'able David,* a short story about a Virginia mountain boy who triumphs over great odds, which was first published in his collection of short stories, *The Happy End* (1919). His other works include the novels *Linda Condon* (1919), *Cytherea* (1922), *The Bright Shawl* (1922), and *The Party Dress* (1930).

Hermann. See ARMINIUS.

Hermann und Dorothea (1797). An idyllic epic in hexameters by Johann Wolfgang von GOETHE, set during the French invasions of Germany that followed the French Revolution. Goethe explicitly avoids the heroic and concentrates on the bourgeois honesty and simplicity of the love between his two main characters, which he sees as a balance to the unrest of the times.

hermaphrodite. A plant or animal containing both male and female organs of reproduction. The word is derived from the Greek myth of Hermaphroditus, son of Hermes and Aphrodite as told in Ovid's *Metamorphoses.* The nymph Salmacis became enamored of him, and prayed that she might be so closely united that "the twain might become one flesh." Her prayer was answered, and the nymph and boy became one body.

Hermes. Divine herald of Greek mythology. This ancient Arcadian deity was also a god of flocks, of roads, of trading, and of thieves, the inventor of the lyre, and the guide of souls on the way to Hades. The son of Zeus and Maia, he grew miraculously in both size and cunning, on the first day inventing the lyre and stealing Apollo's flocks. He was widely worshiped in the form of the herm, a phallic pillar. The amusing story of his exploits on the day of his birth was told in the fourth Homeric hymn and in Sophocles' satyr play, *Ichneutai.* The Romans identified him with Mercury (Mercurius), their god of tradesmen.

Hermes Trismegistus (*Gr.,* the thrice-great Hermes). A name applied by the Neoplatonists to the Egyptian god Thoth. He was almost identical to the Greek god Hermes.

The name was also applied, from about the third century, to the supposed author of a body of alchemic, occult, and mystical writings. Until the 17th century he was thought to have been a contemporary of Moses, and his writings were considered Christian and almost as sacred as the Bible. Actually the Hermetic books were composed by a group of teachers who lived in Alexandria in the first two centuries B.C. or A.D.; they were a composite of Egyptian magical writings, Jewish mysticism, and Platonism. The 20th century is seeing a revival of interest in the Hermetic writings, notably in the work of the French symbolists and the occult system of William Butler Yeats.

hermeticism. A name applied to a 20th-century school of Italian poets. It was first used by the noted Italian critic Francesco Flora to characterize the difficult, "occult-meaning" verse of a group of Italian poets headed by Salvatore QUASIMODO, Giuseppe UNGARETTI, and Eugenio MONTALE.

The verse of these poets originated in the French symbolist school of "pure poetry" as practiced by Mallarmé and Valéry. Decadent poetry entered Italy through the CREPUSCOLARI poets, and it is from them that "the hermetics" have evolved.

Typical of hermetic poetry is a deliberate rarefaction of poetic language; this is the result of the poet's attempt to verbalize a personal impression that seems to transcend common experience in a language that conveys it with the maximum fidelity and immediacy. The hermetics reject rhetoric and the stylistic mechanics of formal traditional poetry. They adopt instead a vocabulary that is extremely personal, idiosyncratic, and, to the uninitiated, abstruse and often meaningless.

Hermetic writings. See HERMES TRISMEGISTUS.

Hermia. In Shakespeare's MIDSUMMER NIGHT'S DREAM, the daughter of Egeus of Athens, who escapes to the woods with Lysander rather than marry her father's choice, Demetrius.

Hermione. (1) In Greek legend, the only daughter of Menelaus and Helen. She became the wife of Neoptolemus, son of Achilles, but Orestes assassinated him and married Hermione, who had already been betrothed to him. She appears in Euripides' ANDROMACHE as the cruel persecutor of the heroine.

(2) The virtuous and uncomplaining wife of Leontes, king of Sicilia, in Shakespeare's WINTER'S TALE.

Hermit, The (1721). See Thomas PARNELL.

Hermit, The (1765). A ballad by Oliver GOLDSMITH. The hero and heroine are Edwin and Angelina. Angelina is the daughter of a wealthy lord "beside the Tyne"; her hand is sought in marriage by many suitors, among whom is Edwin, "who had neither wealth nor power, but he had both wisdom and worth." Angelina loves him, but "trifles with him"; and Edwin, in despair, leaves her and retires from the world. One day, Angelina, in boy's clothes, seeks refuge at a hermit's cell; it is not long before she discovers that the hermit is Edwin, and from that hour they never part again. Goldsmith has been accused of borrowing his story from the ballad *The Friar of Orders Gray.*

Hermod or **Hermodr.** In Scandinavian mythology, the son of Odin and messenger of the gods. It was he who journeyed unsuccessfully to Hel to bring back Balder, killed by his blind brother Hoder. With Bragi, Hermod received and welcomed to Valhalla all heroes who fell in battle.

Hernández, José. See MARTÍN FIERRO.

Herndon, William Henry (1818–1892). American lawyer. The son of an Illinois tavern keeper, Herndon studied law with Abraham LINCOLN and became his law partner in 1844. Idealistic and well read, he is said to have influenced Lincoln's views on slavery. In the biography he wrote with Jesse Weik, *Herndon's Lincoln: The True Story of a Great Life* (1889), Herndon stated that Ann Rutledge had been the only woman Lincoln had ever loved; Mrs. Lincoln retaliated by labeling Herndon a drunkard and a ne'er-do-well. Regardless of the accuracy of these particular charges, the work contributed much valuable information about Lincoln's early life.

Herne, James A. Original name **James Ahearn** (1839–1901). American actor and dramatist. A capable actor whose daughters Julie and Crystal also attained prominence on the stage, Herne developed as a writer into an impressive realist. His best-known works include *Hearts of Oak*, written with David Belasco (1879), an adaptation of an English melodrama that was later revised as *Sag Harbor* (1899); *Margaret Fleming* (1890), a frank treatment of adultery that shocked contemporary audiences; *Shore Acres* (1892), a realistic study of Maine life; and *The Reverend Griffith Davenport* (1899), about a Southern Methodist circuit rider during the Civil War.

Herne's Egg, The (1938). A poetic drama by William Butler YEATS. Full of the symbolism and philosophy of Yeats's own occult system, it is the story of two warring Irish kings, their theft of the eggs of the sacred Great Herne and raping of the priestess of the Great Herne, and their death under a curse.

Hero. In Shakespeare's MUCH ADO ABOUT NOTHING, the greatly maligned daughter of Leonato, governor of Messina. She is of a quiet, serious disposition, and thus forms a contrast to the gay and witty Beatrice, her cousin.

Hero and Leander. Hero and heroine of a romantic Greek legend. Leander, who lived in Abydos, swam across the HELLESPONT every night to court Hero in *Sestos*. When he was drowned in a storm, she flung herself into the sea. They are well known from Marlowe's *Hero and Leander* (pub. 1598) and Byron's *The Bride of Abydos* (1813).

Herod Antipas. Son of HEROD THE GREAT, tetrarch of Galilee and Peraea (4 B.C.–A.D. 39). He married his niece Herodias, who had been the wife of his half brother Herod Philip. This incestuous marriage was loudly denounced by JOHN THE BAPTIST and brought about John's beheading at the request of Herodias' daughter SALOME. It was before this Herod that Pontius Pilate sent Christ; Herod "set him at nought, and mocked him, and arrayed him in a gorgeous robe, and sent him again to Pilate" (Luke 23:7–15). Herod was ultimately banished to Gaul in A.D. 39; Herodias voluntarily accompanied him.

Hérodiade (1869). A dramatic poem by Stéphane Mallarmé. The heroine soliloquizes upon the isolation of her existence. As is LE CYGNE she is a symbol of the chill sterility that characterizes the aesthetic life.

Herodias. See SALOME.

Herodotus (Herodotos; c. 480–c. 425 B.C.). A Greek historian, often called the Father of History. He was born at Halicarnassus, in Asia Minor, and traveled widely, living first at Samos and later at Athens. Herodotus was the first to carry on research into the events of the past and to treat them in a rational rather than a mythical manner. Although he lacked the political sense of Thucydides, his relation of incidents and anecdotes is extremely readable. His history of the Persian invasion of Greece until 479 B.C. is divided into nine books, named after the nine Muses. He is criticized for credulity, but admired for the charm of his narrative. The relation of the battles of Thermopylae, Salamis, and Plataea in Books VII, VIII, and IX is vivid, and his object, to perpetuate the memory of "great and wonderful deeds," is fully realized.

Herod the Great (73?–4 B.C.). King of Judea

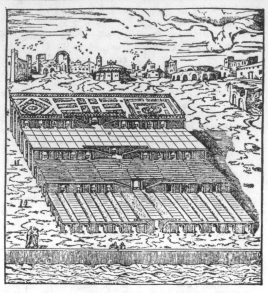

Herodotus: a woodcut of the Gardens of Babylon reconstructed from his description. From the *Histories* (1592).

under the Roman regime (37–4 B.C.). The birth of Jesus Christ took place in the last year of his reign (an error in chronology first assigned it to A.D. 1), and it was he who ordered the Massacre of the INNOCENTS.

Herod had his wife Mariamne (and later their two sons) put to death because he suspected her of adultery, a suspicion which was without foundation. The story of Herod and Mariamne has been the subject of several tragedies including Voltaire's *Mariamne* (1724) and Friedrich Hebbel's *Herodes und Mariamne* (1850). The expression "to out-herod Herod" means to surpass the worst of tyrants in violence and wickedness and refers to Herod the Great's tyrannical nature. He was the father of HEROD ANTIPAS.

On Heroes, Hero Worship, and the Heroic in History. See Thomas CARLYLE.

heroic couplet. In English prosody, a rhymed couplet written in iambic pentameters, the English heroic (or epic) line. The neoclassical rules of the 17th and 18th centuries in England required that the heroic couplet express a complete thought and allowed no enjambment between the lines; it was a "closed" couplet. These requirements, however, were a phenomenon of that period, and both before it, as in Chaucer's and Shakespeare's work, and after, from the romantics on, the construction of sentences has been allowed to carry over from line to line and couplet to couplet; such couplets are called "open" or "run-on" couplets.

Hero of Our Time, A (Geroi nashego vremeni; 1840). A novel by Mikhail LERMONTOV. It portrays a young aristocrat during the reign of Czar Nicholas I in the 1830's. The hero, Grigori Aleksandrovich Pechorin, faces the dilemma of all the young men of his time: to serve the state or to remain inactive. All other outlets for the talents and energies of the Russian aristocracy were closed. The willful and morbid

Pechorin reacts to this situation by assuming the pose of a world-weary Byronic wanderer. His sinister air, however, is no pose. His aimless willfulness is a real threat to all who come near him. Serving as an army officer in the Caucasus, he has a love affair with a native girl which indirectly leads to her death, briefly becomes involved with a band of smugglers which almost leads to his death, and kills another young officer in a duel. Exciting as the adventures are, the most notable thing about the novel is the revelation and analysis of Pechorin's personality as rendered by his old army companion Maksim Maksimych, by a fictional narrator who meets Pechorin, and by the hero himself in his journal, which make up the last three sections of the book. The portrayal is one of the best studies of the character of the SUPERFLUOUS MAN in 19th-century Russian literature. Lermontov's novel is ranked beside the works of the later great Russian novelists, whose narrative techniques and acute psychological analysis he anticipated.

Herrera, Fernando de (1534?–1597). Spanish poet. Herrera spent his uneventful life in his native Seville, disturbed only by his platonic passion for Doña Leonor, countess of Gelves, to whom he addressed elegant Petrachan sonnets. Known to his admiring contemporaries as *el Divino,* he sought to enrich and elevate Spanish lyric verse by the use of loftier themes and by verbal innovations. He unfolded his esthetic doctrines in his controversial *Anotaciones a las obras de Garcilaso de la Vega* (1580). His finest poems were inspired by patriotic sentiment. Among these are the song celebrating the Christian victory over the Turks at Lepanto; the ode to Don Juan of Austria, on the occasion of a Moorish revolt in the Alpujarras (1571); and the elegy on the death of King Sebastian of Portugal, killed at Alcázar Kebir in 1578. His other extant works include an account of the Cyprus war and the victory at Lepanto (1572) and a eulogy on the life and death of Thomas More (1592).

Herrera y Reissig, Julio (1875–1910). Uruguayan poet. A representative of the "baroque" or extravagant wing of MODERNISM, Herrera y Reissig was the leader of a Bohemian literary group that met in the attic of his father's home in Montevideo. His poetry, designed to appeal to the few, is characterized by experimentation in vocabulary and by unusual imagery, though his themes were often drawn from everyday life. His poems, which were not collected until after his death, include *Desolación absurda* and *Julio.*

Herrick, Robert (1591–1674). English poet, known for his pastoral and love lyrics. Herrick, though a clergyman, was a lover of London's society of poets and wits and, at first, regarded his appointment to a rural Devonshire living as bitter exile. However, his interest in country life produced contentment and much of his best poetry. A Royalist, Herrick lost his parish during the English Civil War. He lived happily in London until the Restoration when he regained his old living and there spent the rest of his days.

Herrick was a CAVALIER POET, one of the sons of Ben, or poets who followed the tradition of Ben Jonson. Like his master, he was strongly influenced by the Latin poets, but his classicism is devoid of pedantry, rooted in a natural spiritual affinity to the Latin lyricists. At its best, Herrick's poetry has an unaffected simplicity, a gracefulness compatible with robustness and humor, vivid pictorial fancy, and unfailing command of form and feeling. Many of his short poems make ideal song lyrics: his famous To THE VIRGINS, To MAKE MUCH OF TIME became one of the most popular songs of the 17th century. Herrick writes of rustic rites and superstitions, flowers, fairies, country content, wine, the making of verse, and a number of imaginary mistresses and their clothing, as in DELIGHT IN DISORDER. He also wrote some excellent religious verse in the *Noble Numbers* section of his collection HESPERIDES.

Herrick is essentially a happy poet. While such poems as *To the Virgins,* CORINNA'S GOING A-MAYING, and *To Daffodils* deal with the inevitability of age and death, the theme is treated with a gentle Epicurean melancholy which invites one to enjoy life's fleeting beauty. His love poems do not suggest passion's tragic possibilities, and his religious verse does not repudiate his secular poems in any absolute way. Poems dealing with aspects of religious anxiety, such as To His ANGRY GOD, are honest and touching, but not cries from the depths. More characteristically, he expresses gratitude or simple piety.

Herrick published only one volume of verse, *Hesperides,* which—in spite of the popularity of some of his songs—was quickly forgotten. Only near the end of the 18th century was his work rediscovered and appreciated.

Herrick, Robert (1868–1938). American teacher and novelist. While teaching at the University of Chicago, Herrick sought to describe and analyze the problems of modern industrial society, especially the corruption of the middle-class soul by commercialism. He himself drew a distinction between those of his novels that were realistic and a limited group that were, as he said, idealistic, manifesting a kind of broadminded Puritanism. His most widely read book was *The Master of the Inn* (1908), the story of a physician who cures mental illness. *The Common Lot* (1904) depicts the fashion in which a young Chicago architect succumbs to commercialism. Other novels by Herrick include *One Woman's Life* (1913), about a selfish socialite, and *Chimes* (1926), which gives an unfavorable picture of a large university, presumably the University of Chicago.

Herries Chronicle, The. A series of novels by Hugh WALPOLE. Set chiefly in the English Lake District, *Rogue Herries* (1930), *Judith Paris* (1931), *The Fortress* (1932), and *Vanessa* (1933) comprise the series. They form a romantic historical family saga, from the 18th century to the present day.

Herrings, Battle of the. See BATTLE OF THE HERRINGS.

Herriot, Edouard (1872–1957). French statesman. Leader of the Radical Socialist party, Herriot served twice as premier in 1924–1925 and in 1932. He held numerous public offices: among them, Senator, Minister of State (1934–1935), President of the Chamber of Deputies (1925–1926; 1936–1940, under the Popular Front), and President of the National Assembly (1947).

Herrnhuter. See MORAVIAN BRETHREN.

Herschel, Sir William. Originally **Friedrich Wilhelm Herschel** (1738–1822). English astronomer who discovered a new planet (1781) which he called

Georgium Sidus in honor of King George III. It is now known as Uranus. He also discovered moons of Saturn and Uranus and was a pioneer in sidereal science. His studies were continued by his son Sir John Frederick William Herschel (1792–1871).

Hersey, John [Richard] (1914–   ). American novelist and journalist. Hersey's early books of non-fiction, *Men on Bataan* (1942) and *Into the Valley* (1943), are direct reflections of his experiences as a war correspondent. His novel A BELL FOR ADANO, which won a Pulitzer Prize, was based on Hersey's careful observation of the American occupation of Italy. In 1946, Hersey visited Hiroshima and wrote an objective and horrifying account of the impact of the atomic bomb blast on six survivors. Appearing in *The New Yorker* magazine in 1946, it was re-printed in book form as *Hiroshima* (1946). Man's inhumanity and courage are also the themes of Hersey's most ambitious novel, THE WALL, the story of the extinction of the Warsaw ghetto by the Germans. Later novels include *A Single Pebble* (1956), *The War Lover* (1959), and *The Child Buyer* (1960). *Here to Stay* (1963) is a collection of biographical sketches illustrating human courage and tenacity.

Hertha. See NERTHUS.

Hertz, Heinrich Rudolf (1857–1894). German physicist, known for his experiments with electro-magnetic waves. His identification of radio waves (sometimes called "hertzian waves") led to the development of wireless telegraphy.

Hertzen or **Herzen, Aleksandr Ivanovich** (1812–1870). Russian journalist and political thinker. The illegitimate son of a nobleman, Hertzen very early interested himself in social and political problems. At Moscow University he became the leader of a group of students also interested in politics. Such activity led in 1834 to his arrest and exile to the provinces. He was allowed to return to the capital in 1836, but was again exiled in 1840. Finally, in 1847, he obtained permission to emigrate from Russia and never returned. He witnessed the 1848 revolutions in western Europe with some disappointment and finally settled in London in 1852.

In 1857, Hertzen began to publish his famous revolutionary periodical, *Kolokol* (*The Bell*), which had a large readership in Russia even though it had to be smuggled into the country. Czar Alexander II himself was reputed to be a regular reader of the publication. In the journal Hertzen carried on a spirited criticism of the social order in Russia and a constant advocacy of the necessity for Russia to adopt Western socialism.

Hertzen's major works are *S togo berega* (*From the Other Shore*, 1850), a series of articles on socialism and revolution, and *Byloe i Dumy* (*My Past and My Thoughts*, 1852–1855), an autobiography that describes the intellectual atmosphere of the 1850's.

Hervey, John. Baron **Hervey of Ickworth** (1696–1743). English politician and lord privy seal (1740–1742). He is the author of *Memoirs of the Court of George II*. Hervey was attacked by Alexander Pope, because of his well-known effeminacy, as "Sporus" in the EPISTLE TO DR. ARBUTHNOT: "that thing of silk, Sporus, that mere white curd of ass's milk."

Herwegh, Georg (1817–1875). German political poet. He is most famous for his *Gedichte eines Le-*

bendigen (*Poems of a Living Man*, 1841 ff.), which were directed against the reactionary regimes in Prussia and Austria and were part of the growing revolutionary sentiment that led to the upheavals of 1848. Later in life, he polemicized against Bismarck.

Herzog, Emile. See André MAUROIS.

Hesiod (**Hesiodos,** 8th century B.C.). A Greek poet known as the Father of Greek didactic poetry. The most important works ascribed to him are *Works and Days* and *Theogony*. The first consists of moral maxims and precepts on farming. It is a rich source of information on primitive beliefs concerned with everyday life. The *Theogony* is an account of the origin of the world and of the gods.

If the statements made in the *Works and Days* are authentic, Hesiod lived most of his life as a farmer in Boeotia. His father was an impoverished farmer who had taken to the sea to make ends meet. The *Works and Days* was addressed to Hesiod's brother, supposedly a wastrel who had cheated Hesiod of much of his share of the family property.

Hesione. In Greek legend, a daughter of Laomedon, king of Troy, and sister to PRIAM. Her father exposed her to a sea-monster in order to appease the wrath of Apollo and Poseidon, but she was rescued by Heracles who made the stipulation that he should receive a certain reward. Laomedon did not keep his promise, so Heracles slew him, took Troy, and gave Hesione to Telamon, by whom she became the mother of TEUCER. The refusal of the Greeks to give her up to Priam is given as one of the causes of the Trojan War.

Hesperia. From Greek *hesperos,* evening. Italy was so called by the Greeks, because it was to them the land of the setting sun and the evening star. The Romans, for a similar reason, transferred the name to Spain.

Hesperides. Three sisters who guarded the golden apples that Hera received as a marriage gift. They were assisted by the dragon Ladon. HERACLES, as the last of his twelve labors, slew the dragon and carried some of the apples to Eurystheus. Many poets call the place where these golden apples grew the garden of the Hesperides. The apples are thought to have been a symbol of immortality.

Hesperides is the title of Robert HERRICK's collected poetry (1648), in allusion to the idyllic, pastoral character of most of his poems.

Hess, Rudolf (1894–   ). German Nazi and close friend of Hitler, whom he met in 1920. (See MEIN KAMPF.) In 1941 Hess flew to Scotland, presumably for private negotiations, but was held as a prisoner of war. At the Nuremberg Trials he was sentenced to life imprisonment.

Hesse, Hermann (1877–1962). German novelist. He was known especially for his burgeoning imagination, as well as for the accuracy of his psychological and cultural observations. As the title of his verse collection *Romantische Lieder* (1899) reveals, in his early career he was strongly influenced by GERMAN ROMANTICISM, especially by the writings of Novalis, and several Romantic traits remained with him throughout his life: his intense interest in music, for example, and his tendency to combine the ideas of widely varying times and cultures into a single whole. But the mature Hesse was by no means dependent upon any school of writing; his later works are characterized by a highly individualized style and a strikingly original view of man and culture which combines, among other things, ideas from psychoanalysis and Asian religion. His most famous novels are *Demian, Die Geschichte einer Jugend* (*Demian, A Story of Youth*, 1919), STEPPENWOLF, *Die Morgenlandfahrt* (*Trip to the Orient*, 1932) and *Das Glasperlenspiel* (literally, *The Glass-Bead Game*, 1943), translated as MAGISTER LUDI. Hesse's style is lively and engaging, rich in human sympathy, imagination, and ironic humor. He was a Swiss citizen from 1921 to his death, and was awarded the Nobel Prize in 1946. His essays include *Zarathustras Wiederkehr* (1920) and *Blick ins Chaos* (*In Sight of Chaos*, 1920). His poetry was collected in *Gesammelte Dichtungen* (1952).

Hessian. One whose services in politics or war can be easily bought; so called from the German mercenaries, primarily from Hesse-Cassel and Hesse-Darmstadt, who fought for England in the American Revolution.

Hestia. A Greek goddess, later identified with Vesta, the Roman goddess of the hearth. Originally one of the twelve Olympians, she resigned her place to Dionysus.

Hesychasts (Gr., *hesychos*, still, calm). A sect of mystics or quietists in the Eastern Church, who lived on Mount Athos in the 14th century. By contemplating their navels, they aimed to attain perfect serenity and supernatural insight, which would enable them to feel, diffused through them, the uncreated but communicable divine light that shone on Mount Tabor at the transfiguration of Christ.

hetaera (**hetaira**). Literally, a female companion or comrade. In ancient Greece, a courtesan of the better class. Some hetaeras were freed women or even women of free birth. LAIS and PHRYNE are the most famous ones.

He Who Gets Slapped (**To, kto poluchayet poshchiochini;** 1914). A drama by Leonid ANDREYEV. The play's central character is a disenchanted intellectual who seeks refuge as a clown in a circus. The clown, famed for the number of slaps he can endure, apparently symbolizes intellect being buffeted for the amusement of the coarse, uncomprehending mob.

Hewlett, Maurice (1861–1923). English historical novelist. His very popular books were THE FOREST LOVERS, a romance set in the Middle Ages; *Richard Yea-and-Nay* (1900), about Richard Coeur de Lion (King Richard I); and *The Queen's Quair* (1904), a romance founded on the life of Mary Queen of Scots (see KINGIS QUAIR).

Hexam, Lizzie. In Charles Dickens' OUR MUTUAL FRIEND, heroine of the subplot. She is the daughter of a Thames waterman, and finally marries Eugene Wrayburn, whose life she has saved.

hexameron. Six days taken as one continuous period; especially the six days of the Creation.

hexameter. In prosody, a six-foot line. The word usually refers to the dactylic hexameter line which was the epic verse of classical poetry, whereas the French epic line of iambic hexameter is usually called the ALEXANDRINE. The hexameters of the ancients have been imitated in English in Longfellow's *Evangeline,* Clough's *Bothie,* and Kingsley's *Andromeda.* The Authorized Version of the Bible furnishes a number of examples of "accidental" hexameters; the following are well known:

How art thou fallen from Heaven, O Lucifer son of the Morning.
Why do the heathen rage and the people imagine a vain thing?
God is gone up with a shout, the Lord with the sound of the trumpet.

Hexapla (Gr., "sixfold"). The collection of Old Testament texts collated by ORIGEN. It contains in parallel columns the Hebrew text in Hebrew and in Greek characters, the SEPTUAGINT (with emendations), and the versions of Aquila, Theodotion, and Symmachus.

Hexateuch. The first 6 books of the Old Testament. It contains the PENTATEUCH plus Joshua, which relates the final settlement of the Jews in the Promised Land.

Heyer, Georgette (1902–   ). English popular novelist, author of romantic swashbuckling historical novels and detective stories. *The Grand Sophie* (1950), *The Reluctant Widow* (1947), and *Friday's Child* (1946) are among her works.

Heym, Georg (1887–1912). German poet. Very influential in early EXPRESSIONISM, he himself was under the influence of Baudelaire, Rimbaud, and Stefan George. His works include *Der Athener Ausfahrt* (*The Athenians' Sally,* 1907), a tragedy, and *Der ewige Tag* (*The Eternal Day,* 1911), a collection of poems.

Heyse, Paul (1830–1914). German novelist, immensely popular in his time but not highly regarded today. His technical mastery of the novella form, however, is undisputed; the most effective among his numerous novellas is *L'Arrabbiata* (*The Angry Girl,* 1855), a love story set in Italy. He also outlined a theory of the novella in the preface to the collection *Deutscher Novellenschatz* (*Treasury of German Novellas,* 1871 ff.), which he edited. Among his novels, *Kinder der Welt* (*Children of the World,* 1873) is respected; but his plays and lyric poetry are of little value. He received the Nobel Prize in 1910.

Heyst, Axel. A misanthropic but generous man, hero of Joseph Conrad's novel VICTORY.

Heyward, DuBose (1885–1940). American novelist, poet, and dramatist. He is best known for PORGY, his first novel, which became a successful play and served as the basis for George Gershwin's opera *Porgy and Bess. Mamba's Daughter* (1929) was another novel of Charleston Negro life, and it was also successfully dramatized (1939). Heyward's other novels include *Peter Ashley* (1932), a story set in the Civil War, and *Star-Spangled Virgin* (1939), about the Virgin Islands and the New Deal. Heyward began his career as a poet, publishing *Carolina Chansons* (1922) with Hervey Allen. He later published two more volumes of verse.

Heywood, John (1497?–1580?). English poet, a friend of Sir Thomas MORE, and a court musician and entertainer under Henry VIII, Edward VI, and Queen Mary. He made popular the court INTERLUDES that later became an important part of entertainment for royalty and the nobility in Elizabethan and Jacobean times. THE FOUR P's is his most famous work of this type. He also wrote epigrams and proverbs included in his *Works* (1562) and a satirical allegory on religion, *The Spider and the Fly* (1556).

Heywood, Thomas (c. 1570–1641). English dramatist. One of the Henslowe group, he wrote plays remarkable for their pictures of English domestic life. Among the best are A WOMAN KILLED WITH KINDNESS, THE FAIR MAID OF THE WEST: PARTS I AND II, *The Wise Woman of Hogsden* (c. 1604), *The Captives* (1624), and the masque *Love's Mistress* (1634). His other plays include *A Maidenhead Well Lost* (c. 1633), *A Challenge for Beauty* (c. 1635), *King Edward IV* (c. 1599), *The Royal King and the Loyal Subject* (c. 1602), *The English Traveller* (c. 1624), and a series of dramatizations of classical myths: *The Golden Age* (c. 1610), *The Silver Age* (c. 1610), *The Brazen Age* (c. 1610), and *The Iron Age*: *Parts I and II* (1610).

Hezekiah. In the Old Testament, a king of Judah for 29 years. He was noted for his efforts to abolish idolatry, which had flourished under his father Ahaz, and to restore the worship of Jehovah. The famous destruction of the Assyrian army under Sennacherib occurred during his reign (II Kings 18).

Hiawatha (1855). A long narrative poem by Henry Wadsworth LONGFELLOW. Hiawatha, an Ojibway Indian, is reared by his grandmother, Nokomis, daughter of the Moon. After detailing the hero's accumulation of wisdom, the poet recounts the deeds of Hiawatha in revenging his mother, Wenonah, against his father, the West Wind. Hiawatha eventually becomes the leader of his people, teaching peace with the white man. When his wife, Minnehaha, becomes ill, he goes with her to the land of the Northwest Wind. The poem has been endlessly parodied. See Henry Rowe SCHOOLCRAFT.

Hichens, Robert Smythe (1864–1950). English novelist. *The Green Carnation* (1894) is a novel satirizing Oscar Wilde. Among his popular successes were *The Garden of Allah* (1904) and *Bella Donna* (1909), both set in North Africa.

Hickok, Wild Bill [James Butler] (1837–1876). American soldier, scout, and U.S. Marshal. Hickok fought in many Civil War, frontier, and Indian battles. As marshal at Hays City and later in Abilene, Kan., he faced some of the toughest men on the frontier, killing only in self-defense or in the line of duty. In 1872, he toured the east with Buffalo Bill (William Cody). Four years later, he was murdered by the notorious Jack McCall, and was buried in Deadwood, S.D. He became a legend during his lifetime, and after his death, a folk hero. Hickok's friend, the poet scout Captain Jack Crawford, dedicated a ballad to him, called *The Burial of Wild Bill*. See PONY EXPRESS.

Hicks, Edward (1780–1849). American folk artist. A coach and sign painter, he was also a Quaker minister in Newton, Pa. He painted landscapes and allegorical scenes, notably *The Peaceable Kingdom* in which the lion and the calf, the wolf, the tiger, and the lamb rest together in toylike simplicity. The background opens up to reveal a historical antecedent of this hoped-for peace—William Penn signing his peace treaty with the Indians.

Hicks, Granville (1901–   ). American author and literary critic. He was known during the 1930's for his Marxist interpretations of literature; works from this period are *The Great Tradition* (1933), *John Reed* (1936), *I Like America* (1938), and *Fig-*

ures of Transition (1939). In 1939, after the non-aggression pact between the U.S.S.R. and Nazi Germany, Hicks resigned from the Communist Party. He edited *The Letters of Lincoln Steffens* (with Ella Winter, 1938) and *Proletarian Literature in the U.S.* (1935). His three novels are *Only One Storm* (1942), *Behold Trouble* (1944), and *There Was a Man in Our Town* (1952). Hicks conducts a column of fiction criticism in the *Saturday Review*.

Hidalgo y Costilla, Miguel (1753–1811). Mexican priest and revolutionary leader. Banished to the village of Dolores for his unorthodox views and irregular personal life, Hidalgo became the representative of the lower classes in Mexico's struggle for independence from Spain. On Sept. 16, 1810, in the parish church, he uttered the *grito de Dolores*—"Long live Our Lady of Guadalupe, death to bad government, death to the Spaniards!"—which became the battle cry of the insurgents. At the head of an ill-kempt army of Indians and mestizos, Hidalgo won victories at Guanajuato and Guadalajara but, perhaps because of a lack of ammunition, failed to attack Mexico City. In March, 1811, he was captured by the Spaniards and shot. Mexicans now celebrate Sept. 16 as their Independence Day.

hieratic (*Gr.*, "holy"). Consecrated to sacred uses. The Greeks applied the term to an Egyptian cursive form of hieroglyphic writing which, though originally used for all literature, came to be reserved for religious texts when DEMOTIC writing was adopted for secular use.

Hieronimo. The central character in Thomas Kyd's SPANISH TRAGEDY.

Higden, Ranulf (c. 1299–c. 1364). English chronicler, a Benedictine monk. His *Polychronicon*, a Latin history of the world from its creation to 1327, was continued by others through 1357 and popularized in English by John de TREVISA.

Higgins, F[rederick] R[obert] (1896–1941). Irish poet, editor, and director of the ABBEY THEATRE from 1935. His work includes *Salt Air* (1924) and *The Gap of Brightness* (1940).

Higginson, Thomas Wentworth (1823–1911). American Unitarian clergyman, soldier, editor, and writer. A New England abolitionist, Higginson led the first Negro regiment in the Civil War (1862–1864). He related his experience in *Army Life in a Black Regiment* (1870). A friend of many prominent writers, he told of them in *Cheerful Yesterdays* (1898). Emily Dickinson sent him several of her poems, and carried on a correspondence; after her death, Higginson and Mabel Loomis Todd edited her *Poems* (1890). A believer in women's rights, Higginson wrote a book called *Common Sense About Women* (1881). He published biographies of Margaret Fuller (1884), his ancestor Francis Higginson (1891), Longfellow (1902), and Whittier (1902). He also wrote essays, literary histories, a novel and some verse; his *Writings* were collected in seven volumes in 1900, and his *Letters and Journals* were published in 1921.

High Church. An unofficial division of the Church of England and the Episcopal Church in America. It is distinguished by the importance it places upon the priesthood, the sacraments, and, in general, the outward forms and ceremonies of liturgical ritual.

higher criticism. The name applied to modern textual criticism of the Bible, treating such problems as authorship, authenticity, dates of composition. By those who accept the doctrine of the literal inspiration of the Bible, the term is used in a pejorative sense. The phrase was first used in 1787 in Eichhorn's *Einleitung in das Alte Testament.*

Higher Pantheism, The. A poem by Alfred TENNYSON, written in 1869, in which the poet urges a belief that God not only is found in the world (pantheism) but also that He transcends it. Swinburne wrote a parody of this in *The Higher Pantheism in a Nutshell.*

Highland Mary. The most shadowy of Robert BURNS'S sweethearts, but the one to whom he addressed some of his finest poetry, including *My Highland Lassie, O, Highland Mary, Thou Ling'ring Star* and—perhaps—*Will ye go to the Indies, my Mary?* She is believed to have been Mary CAMPBELL.

high tea. A meal served by the British at the usual teatime. Besides tea, it includes fish, cold meats, pastry, and many other delicacies.

High Wind in Jamaica, A (1929, first published in U.S. as *The Innocent Voyage*). A novel by Richard HUGHES. A family of children living in Jamaica in the 19th century are sent to England after a hurricane has partly destroyed their home. Amiable pirates capture them by mistake, and the children bring about the pirates' ruin; one girl becomes a murderess. The irrationality and impenetrability of a child's amoral world and the horror of the whole situation are brilliantly conveyed.

Hiketides. See THE SUPPLIANT WOMEN (1) and (2).

Hilda Lessways. A novel by Arnold Bennett. See CLAYHANGER.

Hildebrand. (1) Hero of German legend, a follower of Theodoric the Great. In the *Hildebrandslied* (c. 800), a short poetic fragment, he is challenged to single combat by a young warrior. He discovers that the young man is his son Hadubrand, whom he has not seen for 30 years, and tries to stop the fight. Hadubrand, unbelieving, accuses him of a coward's evasive lie and insists on the battle, only to be slain by the older and better warrior. See the *Nibelungenlied* for Hildebrand's role there.

(2) The original name of Pope GREGORY VII.

Hillary, Richard (1919–1943). English fighter-pilot, who wrote a moving account of his experiences in *The Last Enemy* (1942, U.S. title *Falling Through Space*).

Hillyer, Robert [Silliman] (1895–1961). American poet and teacher. The winner of a Pulitzer Prize for his *Collected Verse* (1933), Hillyer also wrote critical essays, several novels, and made a rendering of the Egyptian *Book of the Dead* called *The Coming Forth by Day* (1923). His volumes of poetry include *Hills Give Promise* (1923), *Pattern of a Day* (1940), *The Death of Captain Nemo* (1949), *The Relic and Other Poems* (1957), and *Collected Poems* (1961).

Hilton, James (1900–1954). English novelist. His two best-selling books were GOODBYE, MR. CHIPS, and *Lost Horizon* (1933), a novel about the mythical land of SHANGRI-LA. He also wrote *Random Harvest* (1941), about a man suffering from amnesia.

him (1927). A play by E. E. CUMMINGS. Taking hints from the German expressionists, James Joyce,

and other literary pioneers, Cummings produced an extraordinary conglomeration of techniques and effects in this "phantasmagoria." It was produced by the Provincetown Players in 1928.

Himmler, Heinrich (1900–1945). High-ranking official in Nazi Germany. One of the founders of the party, he organized the S.S. (q.v.) (1929) and GESTAPO (1933) and became supreme police commissioner (1936). He poisoned himself after his capture by the Allies.

Hīnayāna. See BUDDHISM.

Hind and the Panther, The (1687). A poem by John DRYDEN in defense of the Catholic religion. The hind is the Church of Rome, and the panther is the Church of England. James II is the lion which protects the hind from the bear (Independents), the wolf (Presbyterians), the hare (Quakers), the ape (Freethinkers), the boar (Anabaptists), and the fox (Arians). One of Dryden's most celebrated works, the poem is notable for its wit, the brilliance of its argument, and its passages of rare eloquence and power.

Hindemith, Paul (1895–1963). German-born composer and violinist. One of the most prolific and versatile composers of his day, with an individual style that is generally dissonant and contrapuntal. *Mathis der Maler* (1938; text by Hindemith) is probably his best known opera; other works include *Das Marienleben* (1923, song cycle to poems by Rilke), *Ludus Tonalis* (piano pieces, 1943), and diverse chamber music. He also wrote several theory texts.

Hindenburg, Paul von (1847–1934). German general and statesman. He succeeded Falkenhayn as chief of the High Command during World War I and served as president of the Weimar Republic (1925–1934). In 1933 he was forced to make Hitler chancellor. See Eric LUDENDORFF.

Hind Horn. See HORN, KING.

Hindle Wakes. See William Stanley HOUGHTON.

Hindu calendar. This year is divided into 12 months. An intercalary month occurs after every month in which there are two new moons, which is once in every three years. This inserted month takes the name of the month preceding it. The months, the first of which begins about April 11, are Baisakh, Jeth, Asarh, Sawan, Bhadon, Asin (Kuar), Katik, Aghan, Pus, Magh, Phagun (Phalgun), and Chait.

Hinduism. The religious and social system of India, organically interrelated by DHARMA. Hinduism is based on birth and conduct, and because it has no founder or creed, tends to be nondogmatic. *Dharma* involves belief in *karma* or the principle of cause as affecting a future existence. Past *karma* can be "burnt away" and future *karma* annihilated by the performance of the "pure act" (selfless, detached, dedicated action), which leads to its by-product *moksha* or liberation (in Buddhism called NIRVANA), a state of release from the painful dualities, polarities, and ambivalences of the phenomenal world. Many techniques are prescribed for the attainment for *moksha*: worship, pilgrimage, *yoga,* many ascetic practices, and respect for a spiritual teacher or *guru.* If any of these are performed for the satisfaction of one's ego, the act becomes "impure" or tainted by *karma,* and falls under the category of the good or bad deed, leading to good or bad rebirth. The ultimate goal is serenity, not ecstasy or agony. The numerous sects of Hinduism implicitly recognize these principles, and their monistic or pantheistic philosophy is derived from the Vedas or the Upanishads, which were organized into a metaphysical framework known as Vedanta by the seventh century philosopher Shankaracharya, sometimes called the "Aquinas of India."

Hindus, Maurice [Gershon] (1891-   ). Russian-born American writer. Coming to the U.S. in 1905, Hindus has been principally concerned in his work with the land of his birth, which he has revisited many times. His numerous books on the subject include *Russian Peasant and Revolution* (1920), *Broken Earth* (1926), *Humanity Uprooted* (1929), *Red Bread* (1931), *Mother Russia* (1943), *The Cossacks* (1945), and *Crisis in the Kremlin* (1953). He is also the author of *To Sing with the Angels* (1941), a novel about the Nazi occupation of a small Czechoslovakian community, and *Green Worlds* (1938), an account of his youth.

Hinkson, Mrs. Katherine. See Katherine TYNAN.

Hinnom, the Valley of. See GEHENNA; TOPHET.

Hippalca, or Ippalca. In the ORLANDO FURIOSO of Ariosto, the maidservant of the warrior maiden Bradamante and a messenger between her mistress and the knight Ruggiero, Bradamante's beloved.

Hippius, Zinaida Nikolayevna (1867-1945). Russian poet. One of the Russian SYMBOLISTS, she was the wife of the author and critic Dmitri MEREZHKOVSKI. Her poetry, lyrical and introspective exercises, holds less interest than her reminiscences of the greater poets, such as Blok, Bryusov, and Sologub, whom she received in her St. Petersburg salon. In 1919 she and her husband emigrated to France.

hippocampus. In Greek mythology, a fabulous sea horse; head and forequarters of a horse and tail of a dolphin. It was represented as attached to chariots of Poseidon and the tritons. Paintings of hippocampi were found in Pompeii.

Hippocrates (Hippokrates; 460?-?377 B.C.). A Greek physician born on the island of Cos; known as Father of medicine. According to tradition, he devised a code of medical ethics that imposed on his disciples the oath still administered to men about to enter medical practice and known as the Hippocratic Oath. Eighty-seven treatises are attributed to him.

Hippocratic oath. An oath of allegiance to ethical professional standards. It is administered to M.D. candidates at each commencement at Columbia, Cornell, and other universities. Its original version is attributed to HIPPOCRATES. The form now commonly used is:

I do solemnly swear by that which I hold most sacred: That I will be loyal to the profession of medicine and just and generous to its members; That I will lead my life and practice my art in uprightness and honor; That into whatsoever house I shall enter, it shall be for the good of the sick to the utmost of my power, I holding myself aloof from wrong, from corruption, and from the temptation of others to vice; That I will exercise my art solely for the cure of my patients, and will give no drug, perform no operation for a criminal purpose, even if solicited, far less suggest it. That whatsoever I shall see or hear of the lives of men which is not fitting to be spoken, I will keep inviolably secret. These things I do promise, and in proportion as I am faithful to this my oath may happiness and good repute be ever mine—the opposite if I shall be forsworn.

Hippocrene (*Gr.* "hippos," horse; "krene," fountain). The fountain of the Muses on Mount HELICON, produced by a stroke of the hoof of PEGASUS; hence, poetic inspiration.

Hippodamia (Hippodameia). (1) The bride of Pirithous (see LAPITHS).

(2) The wife of PELOPS.

hippogriff (Gr. *hippos,* a horse, and *gryphos,* a griffin, thus a winged horse). The flying steed whose father was a griffin and mother a filly. In Ariosto's ORLANDO FURIOSO, it carries Ruggiero away from his beloved Bradamante to the island of the enchantress Alcina. It also takes Astolfo to Ethiopia, from whence he ascends to the moon to retrieve Orlando's lost wits. Further mention is made of the hippogriff in Milton's *Paradise Regained.*

Hippolyta (Hippolyte). An Amazon queen. When Eurystheus demanded her girdle, Heracles went to fetch it. He succeeded either by killing her, or by holding her general Melanippe for ransom. This queen, or another of the same name, attacked Attica and was defeated with her Amazons by Theseus. He married her and she bore him Hippolytus. Some, however, call her Antiope.

In Shakespeare's MIDSUMMER NIGHT'S DREAM, she is the proud and sophisticated woman who is betrothed to Theseus, duke of Athens. The play of the artisans is presented as a part of the celebration of the wedding.

Hippolyte. In Jean Racine's tragedy PHÈDRE, the stepson of Phèdre and the object of her guilty passion. He rebuffs her advances, but his father, King Theseus, is convinced of his guilt and brings about his death by invoking Neptune against him.

Hippolytus (Hippolytos, 428 B.C.). A tragedy by EURIPIDES. Aphrodite, angry at Hippolytus, the illegitimate son of Theseus by the Amazon Hippolyta, because he scorns the love of women, avenges herself on him by causing Theseus' wife Phaedra to fall in love with him. Though wasting away of her passion, Phaedra will not tell Hippolytus, but, during Theseus' absence, her nurse gives the story away. Hippolytus is horrified, but will say nothing to Theseus. Humiliated, Phaedra hangs herself, leaving a message for Theseus claiming that Hippolytus has tried to violate her. Theseus returns and, refusing to listen to Hippolytus' denials, lays on him one of three unfailing curses given him by his father Poseidon. Hippolytus is soon killed when a bull rising from the sea frightens his horses. Artemis, whose faithful servant Hippolytus has been, now reveals the truth to Theseus, who is grief-stricken over Hippolytus' death and his own guilt, although Hippolytus frees him of this guilt with his dying words.

This story was also told in Racine's masterpiece PHÈDRE, and in such lesser works as Seneca's *Phaedra,* Robinson Jeffers' dramatic poem *The Cretan Woman* (1954), and Mary Renault's novel *The Bull from the Sea* (1962).

Hippomedon. See SEVEN AGAINST THEBES.

Hippopotamus, The (1920). A rhyming, comic poem by T. S. ELIOT. It is about the "True Church."

Hiraoka Kimitake. See MISHIMA YUKIO.

Hirohito (1901-   ). Emperor of Japan (1926-   ). The name of his reign is Shōwa.

Hiroshige. See ANDŌ HIROSHIGE.

Hiroshima. The Japanese city which was the target of the first atomic bomb used in warfare (August, 1945). The bomb was dropped by the U.S. at the close of World War II. Hiroshima was largely destroyed by that attack, and afterward rebuilt. *Hiroshima,* by John Hersey (1946), gave a factual and devastating account of the event. Since then, Hiroshima has become a symbol of the tragic division and possible reconciliation between people.

Hirschfeld, Georg (1873–1935). German playwright. As a writer, Hirschfeld is identified with the movement of NATURALISM. His two best-known plays, both of which deal with women under extraordinary conditions of social pressure, are *Die Mütter* (*The Mothers,* 1896) and *Agnes Jordan* (1898).

His Family (1917). A novel by Ernest POOLE. A study of the results of immigration, depicting the contrasting ideals of two generations in New York City, this is the story of a father and his three daughters. One daughter is devoted to the welfare of her five children; another, a principal of a high school, sacrifices herself to the interests of young people; the third is a devotee of pleasure. The novel was awarded a Pulitzer Prize.

Histoire amoureuse des Gaules. See BUSSY-RAMBUTIN.

Histoire comique des états et empires de la lune and **Histoire comique des états et empires du soleil.** See Savinien CYRANO DE BERGERAC.

Histoire des oracles. See Bernard le Bovier de FONTENELLE.

Historia Ecclesiastica Gentis Anglorum. See BEDE.

History. For many titles beginning with the words *History of . . . ,* see the following proper names. For example, *The History of Tom Jones, a Foundling* will be found under *Tom Jones, a Foundling, The History of.*

History of New York from the Beginning of the World to the end of the Dutch Dynasty, A (1809). A satire by Washington IRVING. The book is presented as the work of a fictional character called Diedrich Knickerbocker. Beginning with a chapter on the creation of the world, the format of the volume mocks the pretensions of early historians. The burlesque became more pointed as Irving included many facts about the colony. The book contains lively descriptions of Dutch manners and morals. It was frequently reprinted after Irving expurgated racier passages, which offended descendants of the Dutch.

History of the Kings of Britain, The (Historia Regum Brittanniae; 1137). A Latin prose chronicle in 12 books by GEOFFREY OF MONMOUTH. The work is of special importance in relation to the development of ARTHURIAN LEGEND, and also as a source book (partly by way of Holinshed's *Chronicles*) for Elizabethan dramatists. It purports to be a true account of events involved in the founding of the English nation, but is a mixture of fact and fantasy. It begins with the arrival in England of the mythical BRUTE, or Brutus, great-grandson of the Trojan Aeneas. In subsequent pages, there are accounts of such ancients as HENGIST AND HORSA, VORTIGERN, King LEAR, FERREX AND PORREX, CYMBELINE, GORBODUG, many of whom turn up again in later literature, notably in the plays of Shakespeare.

The strongest influence of Geoffrey's work on other writers has been in the area of Arthurian legend. With the introduction of Merlin the magician, Uther Pendragon, and the building of Arthur into a towering national figure who conquers large chunks of Europe, the legends of Arthur achieved new impetus. Translations and adaptations of the *History of the Kings of Britain* soon appeared in other countries, the most notable of these being the French *Roman de Brut* (1155) of Wace.

Though Wace cautiously expressed doubts about the truth of Geoffrey's "history," the work was not seriously questioned by Englishmen for several centuries. Indeed, in the 16th century one claim to the throne was considerably strengthened by the popular belief that the claimant was directly descended from King Arthur. See BELINUS; BRENNIUS; LUD.

Histriomastix. An anonymous play satirizing the stage, probably written in part by John MARSTON in about 1599. It was answered by Ben Jonson in EVERY MAN OUT OF HIS HUMOUR (1599). See WAR OF THE THEATERS.

Hita, arcipreste of. See Juan RUIZ.

Hitler, Adolf (1889–1945). German NAZI and FÜHRER of the THIRD REICH (1933–1945), whose talents as popular orator and political tactician were the foundation of his demogogic power. Appointed chancellor (1933) by President HINDENBURG and granted temporary dictatorial powers by the legislature, he was given complete executive power by a plebiscite following Hindenburg's death (1934). Hitler promised to avenge the shame suffered by Germany after World War I and to reestablish the grandeur of the ARYAN RACE. His annexation of Austria and the Sudetenland (1938) and invasion of Poland (1939) brought on World War II. Although Hitler was an absolute dictator, much of his strength was based on the efficient administration of subordinates such as Goebbels, Goering, Himmler, Ribbentrop, and Schacht. It is thought that Hitler committed suicide after the collapse of Germany in 1945. See BEER-HALL PUTSCH; MEIN KAMPF.

H. M. Pulham, Esq. (1941). A novel by John P. MARQUAND. Unlike the title character in Marquand's *The Late George Apley,* Pulham partially escapes from his New England background by way of World War I and falls in love with a girl in New York; but like Apley he weds the girl his family selects for him. The book goes on to explore the price of conformity for both Pulham and his wife.

Hobbema, Meindert (1638–1709). Dutch painter. After Ruisdael, with whom he studied, Hobbema is considered the finest landscapist of the Dutch school. His works are distinguished by subdued colors, careful details, and the invariable presence of a water mill.

Hobbes, John Oliver. See Pearle Mary Teresa CRAIGIE.

Hobbes, Thomas (1588–1679). English philosopher. Hobbes spent most of his long life as tutor and companion to the Cavendish family (the earls of Devonshire), though he once tutored Charles II in mathematics. He also spent a number of years in Europe, where he became acquainted with such thinkers as Galileo and Descartes. In England, his friends included Harvey, Ben Jonson, Cowley, and

John Selden. An ardent Royalist, Hobbes defended secular monarchy in his best-known work, LEVIATHAN, OR THE MATTER, FORM, AND POWER OF A COMMONWEALTH, but its anticlericalism made his position difficult in Restoration England.

Hobbes has been called the father of materialism: his system reduces all events, even those of thought and memory, to some species of physical motion. He was a pioneer of modern political science, a forerunner of associational psychology, and a leader of modern rationalism, insisting on the complete separation of philosophy and theology. He was, in addition, the master of an unusually forceful and lucid prose style. His other works include *Elements of Law* (1651, 1655) and *Philosophical Rudiments* (1651), treatises on human nature and government.

Hobbit. A gnomelike creature, invented by the novelist J. R. R. TOLKIEN.

hobgoblin. An impish, ugly, and mischievous sprite, particularly Puck or Robin Goodfellow. The word is a variant of *Rob-Goblin,* i.e., the goblin Robin, just as Hodge is the nickname of Roger.

Hobson, Laura Z[ametkin] (1900–). American novelist. She is best known for her novel, *Gentleman's Agreement* (1947), which deals with anti-Semitism in the U.S. Mrs. Hobson worked for various magazines and newspapers until 1935, when she began to write short stories. Her first novel, *The Trespassers* (1943), dealt with the problems of refugees denied entrance to the United States because of the immigrant quota system. She has also written *The Celebrity* (1951) and *First Papers* (1964).

Hoby, Sir Thomas (1530–1566). English diplomat and translator, famous for his translation of *Il Cortegiano* (THE COURTIER) by Baldassare Castiglione. The book became a manual for English courtiers, and influenced the writings of Wyatt, Surrey, Sidney, and Spenser.

Hoccleve, Thomas. See Thomas OCCLEVE.

Hoder, Hodur, or **Höthur.** The Scandinavian god of darkness, called the blind old god, as opposed to his brother BALDER, the god of light. According to fable, Loki urged Hoder to kill Balder with an arrow made of mistletoe. Hoder was in turn slain by Vali, the guardian of justice.

Hodgson, Ralph (1871–1962). English GEORGIAN poet. His best-known poems, such as *The Bells of Heaven* and *The Bull,* are passionate protests against cruelty to animals.

Hoffmann, August Heinrich (1798–1874). Pen name: **Hoffmann von Fallersleben.** German political poet of libertarian sympathies. He wrote *Deutschland, Deutschland über alles* (*Germany, Germany, Over All,* 1841), a song that later (1919) became Germany's national anthem. Since the Nazi era in Germany, it has become popular belief that the poet wanted Germany to conquer all other nations; but in fact, Hoffmann was simply pleading for a single unified Germany to take precedence over all the numerous states into which the land was divided at the time.

Hoffmann, E[rnst] T[heodor] A[madeus] (1776–1822). German author, known especially for his fantastic and often humorous tales, two collections of which are the *Fantasiestücke* (*Fantasy-pieces,* 1814–1815) and the *Nachtstücke* (*Night-pieces,* 1817). His MÄRCHEN style represents a new departure in roman-

tic writing, for he weaves the fantastic world closely into the real world—as opposed, for example, to Novalis, whose idealistic *Märchen* have nothing of the real world in them. Thus, Hoffmann may be said to stand between romanticism and the realism of the later 19th century. The same mixture of fantasy and realism characterizes his two novels, *Die Elixiere des Teufels* (*The Devil's Elixirs,* 1816) and the unfinished *Kater Murr* (*Tom-Cat Murr,* 1820). The latter, which is the fictional autobiography of a cat, also includes the story of Hoffmann's most famous character, a composer named Johannes Kreisler who is a typical example of ZERRISSENHEIT. Hoffmann himself was a composer as well as an author, and wrote the music for the opera UNDINE based on a story by his friend Fouqué. See TALES OF HOFFMANN.

Hofmann, Hans (1880–). German abstract painter. Settling in the U.S. in 1932, he has exerted great influence through the schools he founded in New York and in Provincetown, Mass.

Hofmannsthal, Hugo von (1874–1929). Austrian playwright, poet, and essayist. His early writings (pre-1901) are typical of the movement of IMPRESSIONISM. Most of his lyric poetry, for example, was written during this period, and, like that of his friend Stefan George, it combines mysticism and exoticism in content with delicate balance in form and a style full of innuendoes that suggest more than they state. Among his most famous poems are *Manche freilich . . .* (*Many, it is true . . .*), about the mystical unity of all human destinies, and *Vorfrühling* (*Pre-Spring*), which suggests the feeling of the wind on a night just before spring. The short plays that he wrote during this period, including *Der Tod des Tizian* (*Titian's Death,* 1892), *Das kleine Welttheater* (*The Small World-Theater,* 1897), and DER TOR UND DER TOD, are very much like his lyrics; in them, the emphasis is not on action but on the poetic expression of a mystical mood, which permeates the situation.

The essay *Brief des Lord Chandos* (*Letter of Lord Chandos,* 1901), however, marks a clear turning point in Hofmannsthal's career. In it, he states that he no longer finds language adequate as a means of expression; even the word *apple,* he says, has so many different connotations for different people that one is never certain of exactly communicating one's meaning with it. He had become discouraged with the lyric as an expressive medium, and, in many of his post-1901 dramas, he attempts to compensate for the inadequacies of language by turning to traditional and mythical subject matter, that is, he attempts to communicate more directly with his audience by treating material that is part of everyone's cultural heritage. Examples of this tendency in his works are *Elektra* (1903), an adaptation of Sophocles' tragedy; *Ödipus und die Sphinx* (1906), on the story of Oedipus; *Jedermann* (EVERYMAN, 1911), an adaptation of the medieval morality play; *Das Salzburger grosse Welttheater* (*The Great World-Theater of Salzburg,* 1923), based on Calderón's *El gran teatro del mundo;* and *Der Turm* (THE TOWER, 1925), a free adaptation of Calderon's *Life Is a Dream.* Also, in these later plays, he makes more extensive use of dramatic action and stage arrangements for expressive purposes, rather than relying on language alone. Finally, his search for better means of communication led him to combine his art with music in the opera librettos he wrote for Richard Strauss, which include *Der* ROSENKAVALIER and *Die Frau ohne Schatten* (*The Woman with No Shadow,* 1919).

In his later period, Hofmannsthal became deeply interested in the structure and problems of culture, both in Austria and in Europe in general. Besides his dramatic works, he produced several essays on cultural questions, including the well known *Das Schrifttum als geistiger Raum der Nation* (*Letters as the Spiritual Environment of the Nation,* 1927).

Hofmann von Hofmannswaldau, Christian (1617–1679). German poet. His style is characterized as "late baroque" or "manneristic," because of the self-conscious richness, sometimes highly overloaded, of his imagery and language. His writing does not have the stoic, ascetic quality that is found in Gryphius' works, but he was nonetheless a religious man, and the influence of German mysticism is felt in his verse. A characteristic poem is his sonnet *Auf den Einfall der Kirchen zu St. Elisabeth* (On the Collapse of the Church in St. Elizabeth), in which a rich, detailed picture of the ruined building is given, followed by a moral comparing it to the religion of the time.

Hofstadter, Richard (1916–1970). American historian. A member of the faculty of Columbia University, Hofstadter won a Pulitzer Prize for *The Age of Reform: From Bryan to F.D.R.* (1955), an unsentimental analysis of populism and progressivism, which he viewed as the precursors of modern conservatism rather than of the New Deal. His other works include *Social Darwinism in American Thought* (1944); *The American Political Tradition* (1948), essays emphasizing the continuity in American politics; *The Development of Academic Freedom in the United States* (1955), in collaboration with Walter P. Metzger; and a study of the causes and manifestations of *Anti-Intellectualism in the United States* (1963).

Hogarth, William (1697–1764). English painter and engraver. Generally regarded as the greatest pictorial satirist of England, his reputation was established through the plates for Samuel Butler's *Hudibras* (1726). He then did a series of satirical paintings, *The Harlot's Progress* (1731), engravings of which he distributed the following year by subscription. They achieved a tremendous success and Hogarth went on to do other series of narrative paintings which he afterwards engraved. *The Rake's Progress* was distributed in 1735, *Marriage à la Mode* in 1745. Hogarth's fame rests on these satirical series, in which he expressed the hard morality of his age with sharpness and humor; however, his admirable portraits, with their strong sense of color and direct, free handling of paint, also make a claim to artistic greatness. His engravings are said to have furnished Henry Fielding with prototypes for his characters, and inspired the libretto of W. H. Auden and Chester Kallman for Stravinsky's opera *The Rake's Progress* (1951).

Hogg, James. Known as **the Ettrick Shepherd** (1770–1835). Scottish poet. He was so called because he was born in Ettrick and inherited the occupation of shepherd from his family. Largely self-educated, he is known for his verse celebrating Scottish rural scenes and pursuits and for his treatments of the Celtic folklore tradition. He was encouraged by Sir

Fencing master's advertisement engraved by Hogarth.

Walter Scott and in his later life was associated with *Blackwood's Magazine.*

Hogg, Thomas [Jefferson] (1792–1862). English lawyer, intimate friend and biographer of Shelley. At the request of Shelley's widow and family, Hogg undertook Shelley's biography, the first two volumes of which appeared in 1858. Dissatisfied with the results, Shelley's family denied him further access to the materials necessary to complete the work. Although what he did write was often more about Hogg than Shelley, the two volumes remain an accurate, valuable, and loyal account of the poet's early years.

Hōjō ki. See ACCOUNT OF MY HUT, AN.

hokku. See HAIKU.

Hokusai. See KATSUSHIKA HOKUSAI.

Holbein, Hans, the younger (1497–1543). German painter. His father (c. 1460–1524), after whom the son was named, was also a distinguished painter, noted for his altar-pieces. The younger Holbein studied and worked in Basel and was led by the artistic depression ensuing from the Reformation to undertake a trip to England (1526–1528), and finally to settle there in 1530. He executed smoothly finished, carefully detailed, precisely drawn, and richly colored portraits and religious paintings. His formal portraits preserve the features of Erasmus, Sir Thomas More and his family, Thomas Cromwell, and Henry VIII, in whose services he spent his last years.

Holcroft, Thomas (1744–1809). English dramatist. His *Tale of Mystery* (1802) has been called "the first English melodrama." His other plays include the sentimental drama *The Road to Ruin* (1792), the comedy *Love's Frailties* (1794) and translations of Beaumarchais' *Le mariage de Figaro* and Destouches' *Le glorieux*. He was a member of the DELLA-CRUSCANS.

Holda. See HULDA.

Hölderlin, Friedrich (1770–1843). German poet. In his predominant use of classical verse forms and syntax he was a follower of Klopstock, but his language is more compressed and powerful than the older poet's. He was not directly affilated with either of the two major literary movements of his time, Weimar classicism or romanticism, but his thought has elements in common with both. He shares the classicists' love of balance and repose, but couples it with a romantic yearning for complete oneness with nature and for a religion that could combine pantheism, Greek religion, and Christianity. Schelling and Hegel, friends of his since their school days, expressed similar ideas at times.

Hölderlin's life was never settled or happy. He lacked both money and recognition, and these strains, combined with that of his entirely platonic but socially suspect love affair with a married woman (Susette Gontard, whom he calls "Diotima" in his poems), drove him insane in 1803, so that his actual career lasted only about a decade. Neither Schiller nor Goethe recognized Hölderlin's greatness, but his lyric poetry and his novel HYPERION ODER EREMIT IN GRIECHENLAND are now counted among the greatest literary achievements in the language. Some of his finest lyrics (written 1800–1803) are *Brod und Wein* (*Bread and Wine*), an elegy celebrating both Christ and Dionysus; *Der Archipelagus,* an ode in which it is hoped that modern Germany will tend toward the character of ancient Greece; *Heidelberg* and *Der Rhein,* odes on the city and the river, respectively; and the patriotic ode *Germanien.*

Holger Danske. National folk hero of Denmark, usually identified with OGIER THE DANE. He supposedly still sleeps under Elsinore, waiting to arise when Denmark needs him.

Holgrave. The young daguerreotypist in Hawthorne's THE HOUSE OF THE SEVEN GABLES.

Holinshed or Hollingshead, Raphael (d. c. 1580). English historian. Holinshed is famous as the author of the CHRONICLES OF ENGLAND, SCOTLAND, AND IRELAND (1577). A massive history of the world had been begun by Reginald Wolfe; when Wolfe died in 1573 Holinshed took over the project and, with the assistance of Richard Stanihurst and William Harrison, completed it on a somewhat smaller scale as a history of England. The work is memorable primarily as a source of plots for Elizabethan dramatists, particularly Shakespeare.

Holland, Josiah Gilbert (1819–1881). American editor and writer. His early writings appeared under the pseudonym of Timothy Titcomb. He was popular in his period for his sentimental didacticism. Among his novels are *Arthur Bonnicastle* (1873), a partly autobiographical book, and *Sevenoaks* (1875), the story of an unscrupulous New England millionaire. Holland also wrote poetry and was especially well known for BITTER SWEET. In 1870 he became co-founder and co-editor of *Scribner's Monthly.*

Holley, Marietta. Pen name, **Josiah Allen's Wife** (1836–1926). American writer of humorous stories. While relating the adventures of Josiah Allen and his wife Samantha, the author—an ardent advocate of temperance and women's suffrage—often propagandized her own beliefs in her stories. *Samantha at the Centennial* (1877) and *Samantha in Europe* (1895) were two of her most popular books.

Hollow Men, The (1925). A poem by T. S. ELIOT. Mixing nursery rhyme and liturgy, it presents his view of the spiritual emptiness and doom of the 20th century through the symbol of a scarecrow (the guy of Guy Fawkes night; see GUNPOWDER PLOT). Its epigraph is from Joseph Conrad's *Heart of Darkness.*

Holm Saxe. See Helen Hunt JACKSON.

Holmes, Oliver Wendell, Sr. (1809–1894). American physician, professor, man of letters. By his own definition, he was a New England Brahmin, a man of cultivated family and sufficient fortune. Holmes earned local recognition as a youth with the poem OLD IRONSIDES.

A member of the Harvard Class of '29, Holmes frequently celebrated his classmates in topical verse. After graduation he spent two years in Paris (1833–1835) studying medicine. In 1836, a year typical of his active life, Holmes, at the age of 25, took a medical degree at Harvard, began his practice, became a member of the Massachusetts Medical Society, wrote a *Dissertation on Intermittent Fever in New England,* won the Boylston Prize, wrote the Phi Beta Kappa poem, and published his first volume of verse. The book contained two of his best-loved poems, "The Last Leaf," and "The Moral Bully." In 1847, the doctor accepted a Harvard professorship of anatomy and physiology and turned out another volume of verse. He was a witty and popular teacher, until his resignation in 1882 at the age of 73.

When THE ATLANTIC MONTHLY began publishing under James Russell Lowell, Holmes gave it its name, and contributed THE AUTOCRAT OF THE BREAKFAST-TABLE, a series that combined fiction, essay, conversation, drama, and verse. The *Autocrat,* modeled on the work of Addison and Steele, made Holmes famous for wit and originality. THE CHAMBERED NAUTILUS, his most frequently anthologized poem, appeared there. He continued the essays in two further series: *The Professor at . . .* (1859), and *The Poet at . . .* (1872).

A conversationalist in the tradition of Dr. Johnson, Holmes was in great demand as a guest and speaker. He was a familiar figure at the dinners of the Saturday Club, of which Emerson, Longfellow, Whittier, Lowell, Agassiz, and Motley were members.

Holmes always rebelled against his Calvinist upbringing. As an enlightened scientist, he urged that criminals be educated rather than punished. His poem THE DEACON'S MASTERPIECE is a satire on tightly constructed dogmas. Holmes's "medicated" novels, ELSIE VENNER, THE GUARDIAN ANGEL, and A MORTAL ANTIPATHY continue his attack on Calvinist theology.

Holmes was not only ahead of his time in social thought, but his essay on *The Contagiousness of Puerperal Fever* anticipated Semmelweis. In 1884, Holmes produced a biography of Emerson, and in 1888, wrote the series *Over the Teacups,* for the *Atlantic.* He was honored at Cambridge, Edinburgh, and Oxford during his 1886 trip to Europe. He was the father of the great jurist Oliver Wendell Holmes, Jr.

Holmes, Oliver Wendell, Jr. (1841–1935). American jurist. Son of the celebrated physician and author of the same name, Holmes graduated from Harvard University and served in the Union army for three years during the Civil War; he was wounded three times, twice severely. He was lost to sight for a while, and the elder Holmes reported his adventures in search of him in *My Hunt After "The Captain"* (*Atlantic Monthly,* November, 1862).

Holmes began to practice law in Boston in 1867, on his return from the first of many trips to England, and began to teach at the Harvard Law School in 1870. His lectures on *The Common Law* (1881) became classics. In 1882 he was appointed to the Supreme Judicial Court of Massachusetts and became chief justice in 1899. In 1902 he was appointed to the Supreme Court by President Theodore Roosevelt, and after a notable series of opinions and dissents was regarded as the leading exponent of law in Anglo-Saxon countries. He retired in 1932.

Known as "the great dissenter," he had certain fixed ideas, the chief of which was that the law was made for society, not society for the law. He held that the life of the law was not logic but experience, that law was not an absolute "but what the courts will enforce," and that "the first call of a theory of law is that it should fit the facts." It was an axiom of his that "certainty generally is an illusion, and repose is not the destiny of man." He said, "The best test of truth is the power of thought to get itself accepted in the market." His dissents often had great influence, and in time many of his views were accepted as good law, such as his pronouncements, always based on the Constitution, on the plenary power of Congress over commerce, on the taxing power of Congress, on the meaning of "police power," and on the provisions of the Bill of Rights, especially the first amendment.

In addition to *The Common Law,* Holmes published in his own lifetime *Speeches* (1891; rev. 1913) and *Collected Legal Papers* (1920). His correspondence with Sir Frederick Pollock and with Harold J. Laski has also been published.

Holmes, Sherlock. The most famous detective of fiction, a creation of Sir Arthur Conan DOYLE, who introduced him in his *Study in Scarlet* (1887). His adventures are continued in *The Sign of the Four* (1889); *The Adventures of Sherlock Holmes* (1891); *The Memoirs of Sherlock Holmes* (1894); *The Hound of the Baskervilles* (1902); *The Return of Sherlock Holmes* (1904); *The Valley of Fear* (1915); *His Last Bow* (1917); and *The Case Book of Sherlock Holmes* (1927). Holmes has such brilliant analytical faculties and indefatigable interest in any detective problem that he regularly puts Scotland Yard to shame. He is abrupt in manner, master of the violin and a dozen obscure sciences, and a victim of the cocaine habit. His admiring friend, Dr. Watson, usually records his triumphs. Holmes's inveterate enemy is the malevolent Moriarty.

Holmsen, Bjarne P. See Arno HOLZ.

Holofernes. A tedious, pedantic schoolmaster in Shakespeare's LOVE'S LABOUR'S LOST. Holofernes and Sir Nathaniel are described as "arts-men" who "have been at a great feast of languages and stolen the scraps."

Holofernes. See JUDITH.

Holt, Felix. See FELIX HOLT, THE RADICAL.

Holtby, Winifred (1898–1935). English novelist. Her best book was her last, *South Riding* (1936), a novel about Yorkshire life. See Vera BRITTAIN.

Hölty, Ludwig Heinrich Christoph (1748–1776). German poet, member of the GÖTTINGER HAIN group. Along with Bürger, he contributed much to the 18th-century revival of the German ballad. His *Gedichte* (*Poems,* 1783) were edited posthumously by Friedrich Stolberg and Johann Heinrich Voss.

Holy Alliance. A league formed by Russia, Austria, and Prussia in 1815. It was designed to regulate the affairs of Europe after the fall of Napoleon "by the principles of Christian charity." This meant that every endeavor would be made to stabilize the existing dynasties and to resist all change. It lasted until 1830, and was joined by all the European sovereigns except those of England and Turkey, and the Pope.

Holy Bible. See BIBLE.

Holy City. That city considered by the followers of a given faith to be sanctified by its connections with that faith. Allahabad is the Holy City of the Indian Muslims; Benares, that of the Hindus; Cuzco, of the ancient Incas; Fez, of the Western Arabs; Jerusalem, of the Jews and Christians; Kairwan, near Tunis, containing the Okbar Mosque in which is the tomb of the prophet's barber, that of North African Muslims; Mecca and Medina, of all Muslims; Moscow and Kiev, of the Russians, the latter city having been the cradle of Christianity in Russia.

Holy Cross or **Holy Rood Day.** September 14, the day of the Feast of the Exaltation of the Cross. Called by the Anglo-Saxons "Roodmass-day," it is kept in honor of the exposition of a portion of the true Cross in the basilica erected at Jerusalem by the Empress Helen (c. 326). Another event connected with it is the recovery of the piece of the Cross which had been stolen from Jerusalem in 614 by Chosroes, king of Persia, and by Heraclius in 629.

Holy Fair, The (1786). A poem by Robert BURNS ridiculing the Holy Fair at Mauchline. Three "sisters"—Fun, Superstition, and Hypocrisy—visit the Fair and view scenes of immorality.

Holy Family. The infant Jesus, Mary and Joseph. Anne, the mother of Mary, Elizabeth, and the infant John the Baptist are often also present in pictures of the Holy Family.

Holy Grail. See GRAIL.

Holy Land. Any land held to be holy by the devotees of a particular faith. The Christians call Israel the Holy Land, because it was the site of Christ's ministry. To Muslims, Mecca, the birthplace of Muhammad, is the Holy Land. The Chinese Buddhists regard India as holy because it was the native land of the Buddha. The Greeks considered Elis holy because it was the site of the temple of Olympian Zeus, near which the Olympic Games were held every four years.

Holy League, the. (1) Designation for an agreement arranged by Pope Julius II among the Italian and European powers. It was directed against France. The War of the Holy League (1511–1513) put an end to French plans for the domination of Italy. Another league, called the Second Holy League, was an agreement among the Papacy, France, and the Italian powers directed against Spain. The War of the Second Holy League (1526–1529), won by Spain, insured her control of Italy and the Papacy thereafter.

(2) An association formed in 1576 under the auspices of Henry, duke of GUISE, to defend the Roman Catholics against French Protestants and to win the French throne for the Guises. The league, which was subsidized by Philip II of Spain, was defeated by Henry IV of France at Arques and Ivry and lost its influence after his conversion to Catholicism.

Holy Living and Dying. A religious work by Jeremy TAYLOR. It was originally published in two parts: *The Rule and Exercise of Holy Living* (1650) and *The Rule and Exercise of Holy Dying* (1651).

Holy of Holies. The innermost quarter of the Jewish temple. In it the Ark of the Covenant was kept. Into this place only the high priest was allowed to enter, and that but once a year, on the Day of Atonement. The term, or its Latin equivalent, *sanctum sanctorum*, has been applied to any haven kept sacred from the world in general.

Holy Roman Empire. A loose confederation of German states ruled by various royal German houses who claimed the imperial authority of ancient Rome. The butt of generations of joking students ("it was neither Holy, Roman, nor an Empire"), the Holy Roman Empire lasted in name for over 1,000 years (800–1806). It began when Charlemagne was crowned emperor by Pope Leo III and ended when Francis II (Francis I of Austria) abdicated. While the power of the emperor and the cohesion of the empire always existed more in theory than in practice, the Holy Roman Empire did give a certain unity to the many German states.

The first German emperor was Henry the Fowler who was crowned in 919. Since the title was not hereditary, the emperor being elected by seven electors, the crown was held at various times by nearly all the royal German houses. The uninterrupted line of Hapsburg emperors began in 1438. The power and prestige of the Austrian Hapsburgs reflected on the empire as well. Under Maximilian I and Charles V the empire had its greatest strength. After Charles relinquished the crown in 1556, there began the steady decline that ended in 1806 with the empire's extinction.

Holy Sepulcher. The rock-hewn tomb in a garden outside the walls of Jerusalem, traditionally the burial place of the body of Christ after the Crucifixion. Although the site of the tomb has never been precisely identified, rumor has fixed it in a cave under the edifice known as the Church of the Holy Sepulcher in Jerusalem, which was begun by Constantine the Great in the fourth century, destroyed and rebuilt—once during the Crusades—and reconsecrated in 1810 after extensive repairs.

Holy Trinity. See TRINITY.

Holy War. A war in which religion plays or purports to play a considerable part. The Crusades, the Thirty Years' War, the wars against the Albigenses, and many others have been so called. A holy war launched by Muslims against Christians was known as a *jehad*.

Holy War, The (1682). An allegory by John BUNYAN, depicting the salvation of the soul of man. The city of Mansoul is captured by Diabolus, but is later liberated by the forces of Emmanuel, son of the builder of the city. Although the city falls into evil and is again assaulted by Diabolus, Emmanuel is ultimately victorious. It is thought that Bunyan's experiences in the English Civil War may have contributed to the military and political allegory in this work.

Holz, Arno (1863–1929). German author. A few of his poems appeared in Hermann Conradi's anthology *Moderne Dichtercharaktere* (*Modern Figures in Poetry*, 1884); in these, as well as in his own volume *Das Buch der Zeit, Lieder eines Modernen* (*The Book of the Time, Songs of a Modern Man*, 1886), he showed himself an exponent of the early, idealistic phase of German NATURALISM. But during 1888–1890, when he became a friend of Johannes SCHLAF, he turned strongly toward what he called consistent realism, and attempted to reproduce everyday reality in his writing. At the same time, he turned away from lyric poetry to narrative and drama, and with Schlaf, co-authored the two starkly realistic works: *Papa Hamlet* (1889), a collection of prose sketches which appeared under the pseudonym Bjarne P. Holmsen, advertised as a translation from the Danish, and the play *Die Familie Selicke* (*The Selicke Family*, 1890) about the troubles of a poor Berlin family. Shortly afterward, he wrote a theoretical work, *Die Kunst, ihr Wesen und ihre Gesetze* (*Art, Its Essence and Its Laws*, 1891), in which he strongly disputed the claim that art is a metaphysical absolute. The difference, he said, between a child's crude drawing and a true work of art is entirely relative; the artist simply has more skill in reproducing his perception of nature. Holz himself, however, turned away from naturalism and back to lyric poetry in his *Phantasus* (1898 ff.), and in a theoretical work *Revolution der Lyrik* (*Revolution of Lyric Poetry*, 1899) he defended the use of completely free verse.

Home, Daniel Dunglas (1833–1886). A Scottish spiritualist medium who was the subject of Robert Browning's poem, *Sludge the Medium* (1864). He conducted séances at courts and in public in the U.S., England, France, and Prussia and was the author of *Incidents of my Life* (1863).

Home, John (1722–1808). English playwright, known for his drama *Douglas* (1756) and for his friendship with David Hume and William Collins.

Homer. Ionian poet. To him the ILIAD and the ODYSSEY are traditionally attributed. As early as the Hellenistic period, a few scholars insisted that the epics were the work of different authors. Orthodox opinion, however, claimed that Homer had composed both works, and numerous biographies were written of him. Eight of these are extant, but their dates and authors are unknown and they are regarded as largely invention. There was a further firm tradition that Homer was blind. A measure of the reliable information about Homer known to the ancients is the fact that seven cities claimed to have been his birthplace: Chios, Colophon, Smyrna, Rhodes, Argos, Athens, and Salamis. The fact is that nothing whatever is known about Homer the man, including the crucial point of whether he existed.

Nevertheless, modern scholars have learned a great deal about the works that the Greeks attributed to Homer. These were not only the *Iliad* and the *Odys-*

sey, but also the BATTLE OF THE FROGS AND THE MICE and the HOMERIC HYMNS, and certain epics from the EPIC CYCLE, known today only in brief fragments. It has long been accepted as certain that of these only the first two can be considered as genuinely "Homeric," although the Homeric hymns were clearly written in imitation of Homer's style. Today even most "unitarians," who believe the *Iliad* and the *Odyssey* each to be the work of a single author, do not consider them the work of the same author. The diction and language of the *Odyssey* show it to be a somewhat later work.

All scholars are aware that GREEK EPIC POETRY of the Homeric age was the end product of a long period of gradual accretion during which historical events, legends, and folk tales were stitched together by many generations of rhapsodes or bards. In the case of the *Iliad* and the *Odyssey,* this process probably covered four centuries, from shortly after the series of events known as the TROJAN WAR in the early 13th century B.C. to the mid-ninth century, which seems the most likely date for Homer. The "analytic school" of Homeric scholars believe that this process continued up to the sixth century B.C., when PISISTRATUS had the epics arranged for regular recitation at the Panathenaic festivals. This would mean that the epics were compiled and edited from bits and pieces rather than composed to a significant extent by a single individual.

Although analytic theories tended to dominate Homeric studies after the pioneer work of F. A. Wolf in 1795, there has been in recent years a strong resurgence of the unitarians. The most widely held position today is that, although both the *Iliad* and the *Odyssey* are made up of traditional materials, each bears the unmistakable imprint of a single artistic intelligence. This belief is supported by the remarkable structural, dramatic, and stylistic unity achieved in both epics, in spite of numerous and obvious anachronisms and other discrepancies. The *Odyssey*, in spite of—or perhaps in part because of—its broader scope and greater variety, evidences more clearly than the *Iliad* the work of a single poet. It is remarkable for its extraordinarily modern structure, which employs the techniques of the "flash-back" and parallel lines of action common in the novel.

The *Iliad* and the *Odyssey* as they are known today are based on the texts edited in the sixth century B.C. for use in Athens. A considerable amount of tampering with the *Iliad* was done by the Athenians in order to increase their role in its events and the texts were further edited in the second century B.C. by two distinguished scholars in Alexandria: Aristarchus of Samothrace and Aristophanes of Byzantium. The extant texts are substantially those of Aristarchus.

Homer, Winslow (1836–1910). American painter. Beginning as an illustrator, he was special correspondent during the Civil War for *Harper's Weekly*. About 1880 he gave up illustration for painting. A realist, he presented the shooting of rapids or scenes from hunting and fishing with great directness. He settled on the Maine coast about 1884. His themes became the everyday life of fishermen, and the power of sea and wind. Maine and the West Indies, which he subsequently visited, inspired him to do superb watercolors, striking for their breadth of handling and economical suggestion of moving sea and air.

Homeric hymns. Poems in the epic style composed by poets known as Homeridae or sons of Homer. Modelled after the works of Homer, these hymns or Preludes were presented by the Homeridae before their recitation of Homer at public festivals. Thirty-three poems are extant, among them hymns to Demeter, Pan, Apollo, and others.

Home, Sweet Home. A popular song with lyrics by John Howard PAYNE. It was written to a tune by Sir Henry Rowley Bishop (1786–1855) and first sung in his opera, *Clari, or, the Maid of Milan* (1823).

Homme Révolté, L'. See REBEL, THE.

Homunculus (*Lat.,* "little man"). In Part II of Goethe's FAUST, a miniature man in a vial who is artificially created by WAGNER in an attempt to raise man above his dependency on sex for reproduction. Homunculus leads Faust and Mephistopheles to the classical WALPURGIS NIGHT.

Honegger, Arthur [Oscar] (1892–1955). French composer, member of LES SIX. His best-known works include *Pacific 231* (1924; an orchestral imitation of a steam locomotive) and two cantatas: *Le Roi David (King David;* 1921; text by René Morax) and *Jeanne d'Arc au Bûcher (Joan of Arc at the Stake;* 1938; text by Paul Claudet).

Honest Whore, The: Parts I and II (1604, 1605). A comedy by Thomas DEKKER. Hippolito, in love with Infelice, the daughter of the duke, believes that she is dead, and is inconsolable. Actually, she has been sent to a convent to separate her from Hippolito. Meanwhile, the constant Hippolito has been taken to the home of the courtesan Bellafont, whose advances he resists. She, however, falls madly in love with him and embarks on a life of chastity. Soon, Hippolito discovers that Infelice is alive and rushes to the convent to marry her. The duke arrives too late to prevent the match and becomes reconciled to the union. Bellafont, by order of the duke, is married to her first lover, Matheo. The subplot revolves around Candido, a linen draper, whom nothing perturbs. He is so mild and serene that his wife, in desperation, has him committed to an asylum. At the end, he is released, his brow gently furrowed with concern for his wife's sanity.

In Part II, the honest Bellafont's worthless husband Matheo is in prison, and she seeks help from Hippolito, who is struck by her beauty. When Matheo is released from prison, her sorrows only increase. Her husband stoops at nothing, even suggesting that she return to her old profession to provide money; Hippolito presses her with his unwanted attentions. Meanwhile, Orlando Friscobaldo, Bellafont's father, has disguised himself and become Matheo's servant, in order to watch over his daughter. Soon, Bellafont is falsely arrested for prostitution, and Matheo accuses her of infidelity with Hippolito. However, her father revealing himself, establishes her innocence, and Matheo is sternly warned to repent. Again the patient Candido appears, this time in the process of taming his second shrewish wife.

Honorable Peter Stirling, The (1894). A novel by Paul Leicester FORD. Its hero, an honest and fearless politician in New York City, is said to represent the young Grover Cleveland; this was denied by the author. The book is valued as an accurate picture of ward politics in the urban America of the 1890's.

Hood, Robin. See ROBIN HOOD.

Hood, Thomas (1799–1845). English poet and humorist. Hood suggested as his epitaph "Here lies one who spat more blood and made more puns than any man living." His actual epitaph reads "He sang the Song of the Shirt." Together they suggest something of the contradictory nature of his life and art: the long struggle with illness and poverty maintained with courage and gaiety, his unique standing as a poet both humorous and serious. He earned a livelihood through his light verse, which ranges from the penetrating but good natured satire of Miss KILMANSEGG to such pun-filled buffoonery as *Faithless Nelly Grey* (1834):

> O Nelly Grey! O Nelly Grey!
> Is this your love so warm?
> The love that loves a scarlet coat,
> Should be more uniform.

Among his serious works, his poems of social protest, such as *The Song of The Shirt* (1843), are most famous, but he wrote a wide variety of lyrics and ballads. Some of his collections are *Odes and Addresses to Great People* (1825), *The Midsummer Fairies* (1827), *Whims and Oddities* (1826, 1827).

Hooker, [William] Brian (1880–1946). American librettist and poet. He wrote the librettos for two operas composed by Horatio Parker: *Mona* (1911) and *Fairyland* (1915). With W. H. Post, he wrote the libretto for *The Vagabond King* (1925), an operetta based on Justin H. McCarthy's *If I Were King* (1901), with music by Rudolph Friml. Hooker's greatest success, however, is his translation (1923) of Edmond Rostand's *Cyrano de Bergerac,* which was first produced on Broadway with Walter Hampden in the title role. He also published a collection of *Poems* (1915)

Hooker, Richard (1554?–1600). English theologian. Hooker took holy orders in 1581. As a result of a controversy with a strict Calvinist, he attempted to clarify the position of the Church of England and wrote his great work, *The Laws of Ecclesiastical Polity* (1593–1597). The treatise treats church government from a philosophical and logical point of view, and anticipates the "common consent" grounds for government of Locke and Rousseau.

Hooper, J. J. See Captain Simon SUGGS.

Hoosier Schoolmaster, The (1871). A novel by Edward EGGLESTON. A widely read, realistic story of frontier life in the Middle West, it deals with the life of a schoolmaster in the days before the Civil War. It was followed by *The Hoosier Schoolboy* (1883).

Hoover, Herbert [Clark] (1874–1964). 31st president of the U.S. (1929–1933). After a successful career as a mining engineer and businessman, Hoover won an international reputation during World War I when he served as chairman of the American Relief Committee, as chairman of the Commission for Relief in Belgium, and as U.S. Food Administrator. As secretary of commerce (1921–1928), he organized his department in order to make it serve business interests more efficiently. In the 1928 presidential election he defeated Al Smith, the Democratic candidate, becoming the first Republican to crack the "Solid South." Faced by the great depression of 1929 soon after he entered the White House, Hoover, an advocate of self-help, was reluctant to use the power of the federal government to revive the economy, though he supported the Reconstruction Finance Corporation (1932) to extend loans to banks and other business enterprises. In 1932 he sought reelection but was defeated by Franklin D. Roosevelt. From 1947 to 1949 he headed a bipartisan commission to study ways of simplifying and improving the structure of the executive branch of the federal government. Hoover's books include *American Individualism* (1922), *The Challenge to Liberty* (1934), *Memoirs* (3 vols., 1951–1952), and *The Ordeal of Woodrow Wilson* (1958).

Hope, Anthony. See Sir Anthony Hope HAWKINS.

Hopkins, Arthur [Melancthon] (1878–1950). American producer and playwright. His producing career started with *The Poor Little Rich Girl* (1913) and closed with *The Magnificent Yankee* (1946). He put on plays by Shakespeare, Ibsen, and O'Neill, and was the author of several plays and books.

Hopkins, Gerard Manley (1844–1889). English poet and Jesuit priest. He is known for his small number of brilliant poems on religion and nature, and for his revolutionary innovations in poetic technique. His poetry is distinguished by an intricate type of rhythm, which he called SPRUNG RHYTHM; by puns, internal rhymes, and intricate patterns of wordplay; and by an extremely individual technique of elliptical phrasing and compound metaphor capable of great concentration of meaning. His work is thought to be indebted to Old English alliterative verse, to the METAPHYSICAL poets, especially George Herbert, and to traditional Welsh poetry.

Hopkins was a member of a large, artistically gifted family, and was himself talented in drawing and music as well as in poetry. He loved sensuous beauty; his earliest poems are lush and Keatsian, and for many years he kept diaries describing the beauties of nature. At Oxford University he was a student of Walter Pater and wrote a Platonic dialogue *On the Origin of Beauty*. He also came under the influence of Benjamin Jowett and Cardinal Newman. Converted to Roman Catholicism in 1866, he was inducted into the Jesuit order in 1868. He received his theological training in North Wales. Hopkins tried to compensate for his sensuous nature by entering on an extremely ascetic course of life. It was not till 1875 that, at the wish of his Rector, he broke a seven years' poetic silence and wrote THE WRECK OF THE DEUTSCHLAND, his first great poem. Subsequent poems celebrated the beauty and INSCAPE of God-made nature, and reflected his personal experience as a priest and his concern about social conditions and industrial materialism. He became a professor of Greek in Dublin University in 1884. His last poems include his "terrible" sonnets, which express his sense of alienation from God—a state commonly experienced by mystics.

Hopkins' poems were very much in advance of his time and none were published during his lifetime. He sent them, with long letters, to the poet Robert Bridges, his friend from Oxford days; Bridges published them in 1918. Because of the originality of his poetry and the date of its publication Hopkins tends to be regarded as a leading modern poet rather than as a Victorian. His techniques influenced a number of 20th-century British and American poets, notably W. H. Auden and Dylan Thomas. Hopkins' letters, notebooks, and papers were published in four volumes from 1935 to 1938. These contain details of his metrical and aesthetic theories, accounts of his spiritual progress, and many descriptions of nature. Among Hopkins' best-known individual poems are *The Windhover, Pied Beauty, The Caged Skylark, Felix Randall, Spring and Fall,* and *The Leaden Echo and the Golden Echo.*

Hopkins, Lemuei. See HARTFORD WITS.

Hopkinson, Francis (1737–1791). American politician, writer, and musician. Devoted to the cause of the American colonies, he wrote *A Pretty Story* (1774), an allegorical satire describing the quarrel between America and England, and THE BATTLE OF THE KEGS, his best-known work. He was also a signer of the Declaration of Independence. His *Seven Songs* (1788) was the first book of music published by an American composer. See also COLUMBIAN MAGAZINE.

hop-o'-my-thumb. A pigmy or midget. The name has been given to several dwarfs, as well as being commonly used as a generic term.

Hopper, Edward (1882–1967). American painter. His stark scenes of austere New England architecture are relieved by a crystalline light.

Horace. Full Latin name, **Quintus Horatius Flaccus** (65–8 B.C.). Roman lyric poet and satirist. The son of a freed slave, Horace was born at Venusia in southern Italy. His father, a tax collector, spared no effort or expense to provide his son with the best possible education; he took Horace to Rome to study under the best Roman grammarian. To complete his education, Horace, then a young man of 20, enrolled at the University of Athens (45 B.C.). While he was there, word came that Caesar had been assassinated. Like many Roman intellectuals, Horace rallied to the cause of revolution and liberty, and, when Brutus appeared at Athens, he followed him, entering the senatorial army as a military tribune. After the defeat of Brutus at Philippi (42), Horace returned penniless to Rome and managed to get a job with the Roman civil service as a clerk.

Here he began writing his first successful poetry: a group of clever satires and a mélange of iambic poems after the manner of Greek lyrics. These poems won him the admiration of Vergil who, in 38, introduced Horace to the influential patron MAECENAS. Thus began a lifelong friendship between the patron and the young poet, and, in 33, Maecenas gave Horace a small estate in the Sabine Hills. There he polished his satires (*The Sermones*) and his iambic poems (*The Epodes*); he published them in 30.

His great poetic work was his four-book collection of odes (*The Carmina*), the first three books of which appeared in 23. In them he displayed what Petronius termed a "painstaking felicity" of expression. Horace was the finished master of stanzaic meters, just as Vergil was the incomparable master of the larger and more sonorous dactylic hexameter. Horace's hexameters, as he used them in his satires and in his epistles (*The Epistulae,* composed 22–8), were deliberately unmajestic; they employed everyday diction, interspersed with occasional slang, and

were written in a conversational tone in which whole passages, nevertheless, have the feeling of elegant, musical prose. Throughout his poetry, his personality, though seldom obtrusive, is always evident. His poetry is, indeed, his own most vivid biography. Here we sense the presence of a sly but never ungenerous man, a sometimes aloof lover of independence who was also the devoted friend of the emperor Augustus, of Maecenas, and of Vergil; an epicurean in good times and a stoic in adversity; an artist and a country gentleman who had learned the advantages of cultivating his own garden in poetry as well as in politics.

Among Horace's other works are the *Carmen Saeculare,* a liturgical hymn composed for the secular games held at Rome in 17, and the ARS POETICA (*Art of Poetry*) which was adapted as a handbook on style by the neoclassicists of the 16th and 17th centuries. Horace died in 8, only a few months after the death of his friend and supporter Maecenas, beside whose grave he was buried. See CANIDIA.

Horace (1640). A tragedy by Pierre CORNEILLE. The material of the play is derived from Livy. Horace and his two brothers are chosen to represent Rome, Curiace and his two brothers to represent Alba, in a combat that will decide the war between the two cities. When his brothers are killed, Horace pretends to flee and thus contrives to kill each adversary separately. His sister Camille, the betrothed of Curiace, curses Rome. Infuriated, Horace kills her and is summoned before the king. Curiace's sister Sabine begs to be executed in Horace's place. His father pleads for him, and in view of his brave deed the king pardons Horace.

Horace. The young lover of Agnès in Molière's comedy L'ECOLE DES FEMMES.

Horatian Ode upon Cromwell's Return from Ireland, An (1650). A poem by Andrew MARVELL. It celebrates Cromwell as a kind of fated and elemental force, but with elements of pity for Charles I and strong suggestions of uneasiness about a future with Cromwell in supreme power.

Horatii, the three. In Roman legend, three brothers of the Horatia gens, or clan. They are celebrated for their combat with the three Curiatii, brothers from Alba Longa, to determine whether Rome or Alba was supreme. Two of the Horatii fell, while the Curiatii, though each was severely wounded, stood their ground. The surviving Horatius, unhurt, feigned flight. The Curiatii pursued him at unequal distances because of their wounds, and Horatius turned and killed them severally. He returned home in triumph bearing the bodies of the three Curiatii. His sister Horatia, recognizing one of the bodies as her betrothed, began to weep. Angered by her tears in his moment of triumph, Horatius plunged his sword into her breast, exclaiming: "So perish every Roman woman who bewails a foe." Horatius was condemned to death for this murder, but was acquitted with a token punishment: a beam symbolizing a yoke was erected across the street and Horatius passed under it with covered head, thus showing submission to Roman law. The beam came to be known as "sister's gibbet."

Horatio. In Shakespeare's HAMLET, the loyal friend and confidant whom the dying Hamlet adjures:

If thou didst ever hold me in thy heart,
Absent thee from felicity awhile,
And in this harsh world draw thy breath in pain,
To tell my story.

Horatius Cocles. Legendary hero of ancient Rome. When Lars Porsena attacked Rome in the 6th century B.C., Horatius and two companions defended a bridge across the Tiber against the entire Etruscan army while the bridge behind them was destroyed by the Romans. Horatius then swam the river safely. In his honor a statue was erected and he was given as much land as he could plow in a day. Another version has Horatius fighting alone and drowning in the Tiber.

Horatius' exploits are the subject of the poem *Horatius* in Macaulay's book of poems, *The Lays of Ancient Rome* (1842).

Horn, King. Hero of a 12th-century French metrical romance and a 13th-century English one. Son of the king of Sudenne, he is set adrift by the Saracen pirates who kill his parents. He comes to Westernesse, where he is brought up by the king and becomes the lover of the princess Rymenhild (or Rimel). A companion betrays the affair, and Horn is banished. As a disguised adventurer he defeats a Saracen invasion in Ireland, but declines the reward of marriage to the princess and returns to Westernesse to free Rymenhild from the threat of an unwelcome marriage, proving his identity by a magic ring she had given him. He leaves to recapture Sudenne from the Saracens, returns to release Rymenhild from a second unwelcome marriage, and finally takes her home to rule happily as king and queen of Sudenne. *Horn Childe* is a 14th-century English imitation with some variations. *Hind Horn* is a ballad describing Horn's return to Rymenhild disguised as a palmer.

Hornblower, Horatio. The courageous but sensitive hero of a series of popular novels by C. S. Forester. The novels, notable for their authentic historical background, follow Hornblower's naval career from midshipman to admiral in the wars against Napoleon. The character appeared in *The Happy Return* (1937), *Lord Hornblower* (1946), *Mr. Midshipman Hornblower* (1950), and other books.

Horn Childe. See Horn, King.

Hornie, Auld. See Auld Hornie.

Horn of Fidelity. A horn sent by Morgan le Fay to King Arthur. No lady could drink out of it who was not "to her husband true"; all others were sure to spill the contents. The horn was carried to King Mark, and "his queene with a hundred ladies more" tried the experiment. Only four ladies present managed to "drinke cleane." Ariosto's enchanted cup possessed a similar spell. See Mantle of Fidelity.

Horn of Plenty. See Cornucopia.

Horns of Cuckoldry. See cuckold.

Hornung, Ernest William (1866–1921). English novelist and short-story writer. He created Raffles, hero of *The Amateur Cracksman* (1899) and other books, and wrote novels about Australia. Hornung was the brother-in-law of Sir Arthur Conan Doyle.

Horsa. See Hengist.

Horse Sacrifice. In Hindu history, the *Ashvamedha.* This ritual was performed in ancient times by the absolute ruler of India in order to show his complete control over the land.

Horse's Mouth, The (1944). A novel by Joyce Cary, the third in his first trilogy. It is the story of Gulley Jimson, passionate artist and exuberant, rascally, comic old man, whose hero is William Blake. *Herself Surprised* (1941) is about one of Gulley's mistresses, the fascinating, down-to-earth Sara Monday. She is successively cook, fine lady, housekeeper, thief, and respectable middle-class wife. *To Be a Pilgrim* (1942) is the story of Sara's other lover, the religious, near senile lawyer, Mr. Wilcher. The central character of each book tells his own story in his own distinctive idiom.

Hortensio. A friend to Petruchio and unsuccessful suitor to Bianca in Shakespeare's Taming of the Shrew. It is at Hortensio's suggestion that Petruchio sets out to win the shrewish Katharina. Hortensio, rejected by Bianca, marries a rich but unmanageable widow.

Horus. A major god of the ancient Egyptians, the son of Osiris and Isis, sometimes referred to as the god of silence. The Greeks called him Harpocrates and portrayed "Horus the Child" as a boy with a finger in his mouth. As one of the solar deities, he was represented by a hawk, or as a hawk-headed man; his emblem was the winged sun disk.

Hosea. An Old Testament book named for its author, an 8th-century (B.C.) prophet. The book is in two distinct parts. The first, a personal history of the prophet's home life with an errant wife, can be read as an allegory of God's trials with a sinful Israel. The second part is a catalogue of Israel's wickedness.

Host (Lat. *hostia,* an animal offered as a sacrificial victim). Bread consecrated in the Eucharist. It is so called in the Latin Church because it is considered a real victim of flesh, blood, and spirit, offered up in re-creation of Christ's sacrifice. At the service of Benediction, or when carried in procession, it is exposed in a vessel called a *monstrance. The elevation of the Host* refers to that moment when the celebrant of the Mass lifts up the Host immediately after its consecration, so that it may be seen by the people.

Hostage, The (L'Otage; 1909). A poetic drama by Paul Claudel. It is the first of the plays, which with *Crusts* and *The Humiliation of the Father* form a trilogy, about the aristocratic Coufontaine family during the 19th century. Sygne de Coufontaine saves the pope by marrying her former servant Toussaint Turelure, an opportunist now become the most powerful man in France. However, she cannot complete her sacrifice by ceasing to hate her husband and their new-born son; consequently, when the cousin she loves tries to shoot Turelure, she intercepts the bullet and dies. In *Crusts* (Le Pain Dur; 1914) the son Louis causes his father's death and marries a Jewish woman, Sichel. *The Humiliation of the Father* (Le Père humilié; 1916) describes the love between their blind daughter Pensée and the brothers Orian and Orso de Homodarmes.

Hostos, Eugenio María de (1839–1903). Puerto Rican educator and man of letters. Hostos was educated in Spain where he wrote *La peregrinación de Bayoán* (1863), a political novel, and fought for the short-lived republic of 1868. His hopes that Puerto Rico might be granted autonomy with Santo Domingo and Cuba in a confederation of the Antilles were dashed by the imperialist attitude of the Spanish republicans. Hostos continued, however, to work for this goal in Santo Domingo, where he lived until

1889, establishing its first normal school. After a 10-year stay in Chile, he returned to Santo Domingo in 1900, bitterly disappointed at the results of the Spanish-American War, which finally doomed his dream of Antillean federation.

Hostos is remembered, not only as a patriot, but also as an enlightened teacher, dedicated to progress and truth. His best-known work, *Moral social* (1888), is a guide to ethical social conduct which was designed as a school text. He also wrote a famous essay (1872) on *Hamlet*.

Hotel, The (1927). A novel by Elizabeth BOWEN. She satirizes the empty social round of idle middle-class English people in a Riviera hotel. The heroine, Sydney Warren, passes through a period of devotion to a sophisticated older woman, a brief engagement to a clergyman, and then emerges from the hotel to freedom.

Hotel Universe (1930). A play by Philip BARRY. Stephen Field's experience of life and the depth of his philosophy enable the old man to act as a sort of mystic psychiatrist for a number of guests in his home in southern France.

Hotson, Leslie (1897–   ). American scholar. One of the most indefatigable of 20th-century Shakespearean scholars, Hotson has established a reputation as a literary detective, largely as a result of his exhaustive research among unpublished records. His discoveries include the details of Christopher Marlowe's murder (*The Death of Christopher Marlowe*, 1925); the uncovering of new records related to Shakespeare's life (*I, William Shakespeare*, 1937; *Shakespeare versus Shallow*, 1931); an extraordinarily well-documented account of the first performance of *Twelfth Night* (*The First Night of "Twelfth Night"*, 1954) and a highly controversial theory that Shakespeare's Globe was actually a theatre in the round (*Shakespeare's Wooden O*, 1959).

Houdon, Jean Antoine (1741–1828). French sculptor. He is famous for his animated, vigorously conceived yet delicately executed busts. He portrayed, among others, Voltaire, Diderot, Mirabeau, Jean Jacques Rousseau, George Washington, and Benjamin Franklin.

Hough, Emerson (1857–1923). American novelist. He is known especially for *The Mississippi Bubble* (1902), about the 18th-century French speculation in Louisiana. His other novels include *The Covered Wagon* (1922), about a train of 200 wagons moving westward in 1848, and *North of Thirty-Six* (1923), a story of herding on the Chisholm Trail.

Houghton, William Stanley (1881–1913). English dramatist. He became famous and made a fortune from one work, *Hindle Wakes* (1912). Within a year of the first performance in London, the play had been acted 2,000 times in London, Manchester, New York, and Chicago. It deals with the cotton mills districts of Lancashire. Houghton had begun his career in the business of his father, who was a cotton merchant.

Hougron, Jean (1923–   ). French novelist. His first six novels, including *Reap the Whirlwind* (*Tu récolteras la tempête;* 1950) and *Blaze of the Sun* (*Soleil au ventre;* 1952), describe aspects of the hatred caused by the war in Indo-China. Later books are psychological suspense stories, such as *Question of Character* (*Je reviendrai à Kandara;* 1955).

Hound of Heaven, The (1893). The best-known poem of Francis THOMPSON. In startling cosmic imagery, arresting cadences, it presents the "autobiography" of a fugitive from God's redemptive love.

houris. Black-eyed damsels said to be the reward of the faithful in the Muslim Paradise. Possessed of perpetual youth and beauty, they can renew their virginity at pleasure and are always equal in age with their husbands. According to the Koran, every believer will have 72 of these *houris* in Paradise and, depending on his wish, his intercourse may be fruitful or otherwise; if an offspring is desired, it will grow to full estate in an hour.

Hours, The (Horai). Greek goddesses of the seasons. In Greek, the word implied seasons, rather than hours, and these goddesses varied in number according to various concepts of the number of seasons in the year. Hesiod named them Eunomia, Dike, and Irene (Eirene).

Hours of Idleness (1807). The 1st book of poems published by Lord BYRON. He was only 19 at the time, and some of the poems were written years earlier. The severe criticism in the *Edinburgh Review* brought forth the satire ENGLISH BARDS AND SCOTCH REVIEWERS, Byron's first mature work.

House in Paris, The (1935). A novel by Elizabeth BOWEN. A story of complex love affairs, infidelities, and tragedy is revealed largely through two children who meet by chance at a house in Paris for a day. The boy Leopold, the illegitimate issue of his mother's early love affair, is finally taken home to his mother and her new husband.

House of Fame, The (probably 1379 or 1380). An unfinished poem by Geoffrey CHAUCER, of 2158 lines in octosyllabic couplets. It begins as a love-vision of the French type, but draws more on the works of Ovid, Vergil, and Dante. In the first "book" the poet introduces his dream and describes finding himself in the Temple of Venus. Here he finds engraved Vergil's story of Dido and Aeneas. In the second book he conducts a lively conversation with a great shining eagle who carries him to the House of Fame, presumably to learn more about love. But the third section shows lady Fame in her house distributing fame and slander among some of her applicants and denying any renown to others, all with arbitrary capriciousness. Then the poet is taken to the House of Rumor, inhabited by shipmen, pilgrims, couriers, and other gossips, who increase the falsity of their tidings with each retelling.

House of Life, The. A sonnet sequence by Dante Gabriel ROSSETTI, written during the period between 1848 and 1881. Chiefly autobiographical, it was inspired by Elizabeth SIDDAL, the author's wife. The title refers to the house of human life in astrology.

House of Mirth, The (1905). A novel by Edith WHARTON. Lily Bart, an orphan, tries to secure a wealthy husband, rejecting Lawrence Seldon, whom she loves but who lacks a fortune. Lily becomes involved with another man who tries to blackmail her, and is falsely accused of an intrigue with another woman's husband. Her fortunes become progressively worse until she becomes a milliner and eventually takes an overdose of sleeping pills. The intention of the novel was to satirize and reveal the weaknesses of New York society.

House of Pride. See FAERIE QUEENE, THE.

House of Riches. See FAERIE QUEENE, THE.

House of the Dead, The (Zapiski iz my-ortvogo doma; 1861–1862). An account of life in a Siberian prison by Feodor DOSTOEVSKI. The work is based on Dostoevski's own experiences in the Omsk prison (1850–1854), to which he was sentenced for having belonged to the Petrashevski circle, a study group interested in French Utopian socialism.

House of the Seven Gables, The (1851). A novel by Nathaniel HAWTHORNE. Iron-willed, grasping Colonel Pyncheon obtained the desirable land on which he built the pretentious House of the Seven Gables by accusing its humble owner, one Matthew Maule, of witchcraft. Old Maule, hanged for his crime, cursed the Colonel, saying "God will give him blood to drink." That curse, reverberating down the generations, affects the whole family.

At the time of the story, the withered old spinster, Hepzibah Pyncheon, and her brother Clifford live in the house. Desperately poor, Hepzibah must open a cent-shop in order to refuse aid from Judge Jaffrey Pyncheon, the intellectual and moral heir of the old colonel. Clifford has just returned from an extended imprisonment for the murder of an uncle. The murder, in reality committed by Jaffrey, enabled the latter to gain control of the Pyncheon fortune. Clifford, a weak-willed aesthete, has been destroyed by the 30-year sentence.

Phoebe, a visiting Pyncheon country cousin, and Holgrave, the young daguerreotypist boarding in the house, fall in love. Holgrave, a descendent of Matthew Maule, breaks the family curse, refusing to betray Phoebe by exercising his mesmeric powers. Hawthorne, in treating the weight of past guilt, once again reveals an unpardonable sin: the violation of another's soul.

Housman, A[lfred] E[dward] (1859–1936). English poet and Latin scholar. He is best known for his collection of poems called *A Shropshire Lad* (1896). These lyrics, set against a background of the English countryside and showing the influence of traditional English ballads and classical verse, are marked by their spirit of irony, and by their melancholy sense of youthful disillusionment, the transitoriness of youth and love, and the sadness of life. Their tone is ascribed to the author's disappointment at his mediocre performance at his final examinations at Oxford and to his passionate love for a college friend, Moses Jackson. Jackson is referred to in the poems by the classical name of Terence. In later years Housman became a professor of Latin, edited Manilius' *Astronomica*, and published *Last Poems* (1922). These poems, and those collected posthumously by his brother, Laurence Housman, in *More Poems* (1936), were mostly written during the same period as *A Shropshire Lad*. Shropshire is an English county. Two of Housman's best-known poems are *Loveliest of trees, the cherry now . . .* and *Terence, This* [poetry] *is Stupid Stuff. . . .*

Housman, Laurence (1865–1959). English novelist, dramatist, and illustrator. He was the brother of A. E. Housman. His first—almost his only—popular success came by accident. He published anonymously *An Englishwoman's Love Letters* (1900). They were accepted by the public as genuine. With 32 of his plays censored in one way or another, he has been called "England's most censored playwright,"

but his *Victoria Regina* (1934), with Helen Hayes, was an enormous success in America. His work is brilliantly versatile: he was a beautiful draughtsman, a fine poet, and a delightful writer of fantastic stories.

Houssain. The brother of Prince Ahmed in one of the *Arabian Nights* stories. He possesses a piece of carpet or tapestry of such wonderful power that anyone has only to sit upon it and be transported in a moment to any place he desires. See CARPET, MAGIC.

Houston, Sam[uel] (1793–1863). American soldier and statesman. Settling in Texas in 1833, Houston became a champion of Texan independence from Mexico. As commander-in-chief of the Texan army, he decisively defeated General Santa Anna at San Jacinto (1836) and served as president of the new republic (1836–1838, 1841–1844). After Texas was admitted to the Union in 1845, he became one of the first two senators from the state. He was elected governor in 1859 but was deposed when he refused to approve the entrance of Texas into the Confederacy.

Houyhnhnmland (pronounced whinnimland). The country of Gulliver's fourth voyage in Jonathan Swift's GULLIVER'S TRAVELS, inhabited by Houyhnhnms, a race of horses. The Houyhnhnms, an embodiment of all that is good in mankind, are endowed with virtue and reason and live an idyllic existence. They hold in subjection the YAHOO, an inferior race whom Gulliver closely resembles. The Houyhnhnms consider Gulliver inferior, but he learns from them—so much so that, when he returns finally to his own country, he finds his fellow man so repellent that he becomes a confirmed misanthrope.

Hovey, Richard (1864–1900). American poet and dramatist. Hovey studied painting, became a candidate for priest's orders (never completed), and finally turned to newspaper work. Known for his exaggerated behavior, he adopted the costume of Oscar Wilde. He was impressed by Mallarmé and Maeterlinck, translating several of the latter's plays into English. In 1892, he and his friend Bliss Carman went to Nova Scotia and New Brunswick; the two then published *Songs from Vagabondia* (1894). Hovey's best-known poems include *Men of Dartmouth, Eleazar Wheelock,* and *Stein Song.*

Howard, Leslie (1893–1943). English actor. He was popular in the U.S. as both a stage and screen performer, appearing in *Berkeley Square, Hamlet* and *The Petrified Forest.* He died in an airplane accident in World War II (his plane was probably shot down).

Howard, Sidney [Coe] (1891–1939). American dramatist. Howard early did adaptations from foreign plays and collaborated with Edward Sheldon on *Bewitched* (1924). His first original play to attract attention was the Pulitzer Prize-winning THEY KNEW WHAT THEY WANTED. Best known of his later plays are THE SILVER CORD and *Yellow Jack* (1934), a documentary dealing with the conquest of yellow fever, written with Paul de Kruif. Howard also wrote *Lucky Sam McCarver* (1925); *Ned McCobb's Daughter* (1926); *Salvation* (1928), with Charles MACARTHUR; *Lute Song* (1930), with Will Irwin; and *Dodsworth* (1934), with Sinclair Lewis.

Howards End (1910). A novel by E. M. FORSTER. It deals with an English country house called Howards End and its influence on the lives of the materialistic Wilcoxes, the cultured and idealistic Schlegel sisters, and the poor bank clerk Leonard Bast. The Schlegels try to befriend Bast. Mr. Wilcox, whom Margaret Schlegel later marries, gives him financial advice which ruins him. Helen Schlegel becomes his mistress for a short time and bears his son; thereupon Charles Wilcox thrashes and accidentally kills him. The house passes from intuitive, half-mystical Mrs. Wilcox to her husband's second wife, Margaret Schlegel, to Margaret's nephew, Leonard Bast's son. Illustrating Forster's motto "Only connect," the house brings together three important elements in English society: money and successful business in the Wilcoxes, culture in the Schlegels, and the lower classes in Leonard Bast.

Howe, Anna. In Samuel Richardson's novel CLARISSA HARLOWE, the friend and correspondent of Clarissa. She treats Clarissa with loyalty and affection, but more in the spirit of worldly prudence than with understanding. She is unable to save Clarissa, despite her sound and practical common sense.

Howe, E[dgar] W[atson] (1853–1937). American editor and novelist. He is known for his first novel, *The Story of a Country Town* (1883), one of the early examples of realism in American fiction. Howe wrote other novels of less importance and several collections of editorials and aphorisms, including *Lay Sermons* (1911), *Ventures in Common Sense* (1919), and *The Indignations of E. W. Howe* (1933).

Howe, Julia Ward (1819–1910). American poet and reformer. In 1843 she married Samuel Gridley Howe, the noted humanitarian and teacher of the blind, and soon came to know many of New England's distinguished men and women. After her husband's death she continued his work and lectured on woman suffrage, prison reform, and international peace. Although she is remembered chiefly for THE BATTLE HYMN OF THE REPUBLIC, she wrote several collections of verse, including *Passion Flowers* (1854) and *Later Lyrics* (1866), and is the author of *Sex and Education* (1874), *Modern Society* (1881), and *Reminiscences* (1899).

Howe, M[ark] A[ntony] DeWolfe (1864–1960). American biographer and editor. Howe was associated with several magazines, especially the *Atlantic Monthly*. Although his books have a wide range, he was preeminent in the field of biography. He wrote biographies of Phillips Brooks (1899), Charles Eliot Norton (1913), Barrett Wendell (1924), for which he was awarded a Pulitzer Prize, John Jay Chapman (1937), and several others. He also edited the series *Beacon Biographies* (31 vols., 1899–1910) and wrote several volumes of verse. *A Venture in Remembrance* (1941) is his autobiography.

Howe, Samuel Gridley (1801–1876). American physician, teacher, and humanitarian. After receiving a medical degree from Harvard in 1824, he sailed to Greece, where he spent six years aiding the Greeks in their struggle for independence from Turkey. In 1831 he was named director of the school for the blind in Boston that later became the Perkins Institute; his best-known patient was the blind deaf-mute Laura Bridgman (1829–1889), whom he trained by means of a raised type that he had devised and by other methods that later proved successful with Helen Keller. He was also interested in helping other handicapped persons. Active in the antislavery clause, he founded, with his wife, Julia Ward HOWE, an abolitionist newspaper, *The Commonwealth*. He subsequently returned to Europe to help the Cretans in their revolt against the Turks. His best-known work is *Historical Sketches of the Greek Revolution* (1828). Mrs. Howe wrote a *Memoir* (1876) of her husband's life.

Howell, James (1594?–1666). Welsh-born English author. He is best known for his *Epistolae Hoelianae: Familiar Letters* (1645–1655), most of which were written while he was imprisoned as a Royalist sympathizer during the Civil War. He also compiled a *Lexicon Tetraglotton* (1660), a polyglot dictionary of English, French, Italian, and Spanish.

Howells, William Dean (1837–1920). American novelist, editor, critic, and poet. Born and raised in Ohio, he had little schooling, but regularly contributed poems and tales to newspapers. Howells wrote of his boyhood and youth in the autobiographical *A Boy's Town* (1890) and *Years of my Youth* (1916). By the time he was 23, he had published a book of poems, *Poems of Two Friends* (1860), and a campaign life of Abraham Lincoln. In 1860, he made a literary pilgrimage to Boston, where he was received by Lowell, Holmes, and Fields.

The reward for his campaign biography was the consulship in Venice, where Howells spent the war years. On his return, he published *Venetian Life* (1866), a series of travel letters and impressions. He worked for several magazines, finally becoming the editor of THE ATLANTIC MONTHLY in 1871. A firm friend of Mark Twain, he also encouraged another admirer, the young Henry James.

Howells' most important contribution to literary criticism is his theory of realistic fiction. He shared with George Eliot a literary interest in the commonplace, and defined realism as "nothing more or less than the truthful treatment of material." Howells' bias is revealed, however, when he chooses Jane Austen as the most truthful of writers. Among his own books, THEIR WEDDING JOURNEY, A MODERN INSTANCE, and THE RISE OF SILAS LAPHAM illustrate his theory best.

Leaving the *Atlantic*, Howells wrote a column for *Harper's*; influenced by Tolstoy and the American socialist Laurence Gronlund, he supplemented his realism with liberal views. A HAZARD OF NEW FORTUNES and A TRAVELLER FROM ALTRURIA are studies of American social institutions. Later in life, his militant liberalism subsiding, Howells continued to write realistic novels. Among them, *The Landlord at Lion's Head* (1897) and *The Kentons* (1902) approach his best earlier work in quality. He issued a number of reviews and articles collected from magazines, the most important of which is *My Mark Twain* (1910).

Howells' reputation continued to grow; known as the dean of American letters, he was president of the American Academy of Arts and Letters. Although he praised the posthumously published poems of Emily Dickinson, and encouraged Stephen Crane and Frank Norris, he was regarded as a genteel sentimentalist by Sinclair Lewis, H. L. Mencken, and Theodore Dreiser. Modern evaluation, restoring his reputation, grants him unquestioned historical importance in the development of American literature. See A CHANCE ACQUAINTANCE; THE LADY OF THE AROOSTOOK; INDIAN SUMMER.

How Green Was My Valley (1940). A popular novel by Richard LLEWELLYN. Written in a lyrical style, it tells the story of a Welsh mining family.

Howleglas or **Owlglass, Tyll.** See EULENSPIEGEL.

How They Brought the Good News from Ghent to Aix (1845). A ballad by Robert BROWNING. Noted for its onomatopoetic effects, it describes a purely imaginary incident.

How to Write Short Stories (1924). A collection of 10 stories by Ring LARDNER. The sardonic preface discloses that the purpose of the volume is to discuss the art of short-story writing, the stories that follow being "samples." Among them are such classic Lardner tales as *Alibi Ike* and *Champion*.

Hrosvitha or **Hrotsvitha.** See ROSWITHA.

Hrothgar. See BEOWULF.

Hsi Yü Chi (Journey to the West). Chinese novel of the Ming Dynasty (1368–1644) by Wu Ch'eng-en (c. 1500–1580). Describes the adventures of the priest Hsüan-tsang during his pilgrimage to India in search of the scriptures, accompanied by Monkey and other creatures. Humorous, satirical, and absurd, it has enjoyed continued popularity. Partially translated by Arthur Waley, *Monkey* (1943).

Hsün Tzu. Chinese Confucian work attributed to Hsün Ch'ing (c. 300 B.C.). It exerted considerable influence during the Han period (202 B.C.–A.D. 220). The first Confucian text in expository form, it contradicts the *Mencius* by saying that man is by nature evil, and attacks superstition, extolling rationalism in its stead. It places great emphasis on the need for education.

Huang Ti. A legendary emperor of China (c. 2600 B.C.). He is credited with the invention of bricks, musical instruments, etc. His name means yellow emperor.

Hubbard, Elbert (1856–1915). American businessman, printer, and writer. At the age of 36, Hubbard stopped selling soap and toured Europe. Highly impressed by the Kelmscott Press of William Morris, he returned to East Aurora, New York, and founded the Roycroft Press. He issued many "arty" books and magazines, and produced such household objects as pottery, metal and leather work, and furniture. He wrote a series of 170 *Little Journeys* to the homes of notable men and women, and published two magazines, *The Philistine* (1895–1915) and *The Fra* (1908–1917), largely filled with his own writings. Himself a self-conscious aesthete, Hubbard was known as "Fra Elbertus" or "the Fra." His most successful publication was A MESSAGE TO GARCIA, an exhortation to fidelity and enterprise that became enormously popular among businessmen; they distributed copies to their employees to provide "inspiration." Hubbard appeared on the vaudeville stage, and attracted many people to East Aurora. He died when the *S. S. Lusitania* was sunk in the Irish Sea by a German submarine.

Huch, Ricarda (1864–1947). German novelist, poet, and essayist. She was especially noted for her historical sense as expressed, for example, in the novels of her Garibaldi cycle: *Die Verteidigung Roms* (*The Defense of Rome,* 1906), *Der Kampf um Rome* (*The Struggle for Rome,* 1907) and *Das Leben des Grafen Frederigo Confalonieri* (*Life of Count Frederigo Confalonieri,* 1910). Her essays on German romanticism are also well known.

Huckleberry Finn, The Adventures of (1884). A novel by Mark TWAIN. Huck escapes from the lonely cabin in which his drunken, brutal father had imprisoned him; on Jackson's Island he meets Jim, a runaway slave. Together they float down the Mississippi River on a raft, occasionally stopping at the banks. In these brief episodes Huck participates in the lives of others, witnessing corruption, moral decay, and intellectual impoverishment. He learns from Jim of the dignity and worth of a human being. Life on the river comes to an end when Jim is captured; Huck, reunited with TOM SAWYER, helps him to escape, subordinating society's morality to his own sense of justice and honor. When Tom's Aunt Sally says she wants to adopt Huck, he decides to head westward to avoid being "sivilized."

Hudibras (1663, 1664, 1678). A long satirical poem in three parts by Samuel BUTLER, directed against the hypocrisy and intolerance of the Puritans. Its hero Hudibras, modeled after various Presbyterian worthies of the Commonwealth, is a country justice who sets out with his squire Ralpho, an Independent, to reform abuses and enforce the laws for the suppression of popular amusements. Like Don Quixote, Hudibras is of comical appearance, humpbacked and potbellied, with an untidy yellow-red beard. He, too, rides a broken-down nag and receives much punishment in the performance of his exploits. The poem, written in jingling, doggerel couplets, gave rise to the adjective *hudibrastic,* meaning mock-heroic or in the style of *Hudibras.*

Hudson, Henry (died after 1611). English navigator and explorer. Engaged by the Dutch East India Co. to find a northern passage to the Orient, he sailed to America on the *Half Moon* and explored the river that now bears his name, reaching as far as Albany (1609). On a later voyage he was set adrift by his own men.

Hudson, Sir Jeffrey (1619–1682). English dwarf, at one time page to Queen Henrietta Maria. When he was 30 years old, he was under two feet high, but later reached a height of about three feet nine inches. He was a cavalry captain in the Royalist army during the Civil War. Afterwards he was captured by pirates and sold as a slave in Barbary, but managed to escape. He is a character in Scott's *Peveril of the Peak* (1823). See William EVANS.

Hudson, Stephen. Pen name, **Sidney Schiff** (1869–1944). English novelist and translator. Most of his novels are about a single group of persons and include *Tony* (1924), *Richard, Myrtle, and I* (1926), and *A True Story* (1930). Hudson completed Scott Moncrieff's translation of Proust's *Remembrance of Things Past.*

Hudson, William Henry (1841–1922). English naturalist and novelist, born in Argentina of American parentage. He became a naturalized British subject in 1900. He is best known for his writings on nature subjects, especially those with an Argentine background. His books include *The Purple Land* (1885), *Argentine Ornithology* (1888–1889), *Nature in Downland* (1900), *El Ombú* (1902), *Little Boy Lost* (1905), and *A Shepherd's Life* (1910). He is best remembered for GREEN MANSIONS and his autobiographical *Far Away and Long Ago* (1918).

"Hudibras Catechized." An engraving by Hogarth for Samuel Butler's *Hudibras*. (1726).

Hudson River School. The name given to a group of 19th century U.S. artists who painted rural scenes, especially in the Catskills, after 1830. Realistic, poetic, or fantastic interpretations were given to these landscapes, which were popularized by Thomas Cole (1801–1848) and Asher B. Durant (1796–1886). Cole, the leader of the movement, painted both visionary and more factual views, while Durant represented large scenes with patiently accurate draftsmanship.

Hudson's Bay Company. A joint stock company chartered in 1670 by Charles II for the purpose of purchasing furs from the Indians. Its territory, the Hudson's Bay Territory or Rupert's Land, included all the streams flowing into Hudson Bay. It was sold to the British government (1869) and incorporated with the Dominion of Canada (1870).

Hueffer, Ford Madox. See Ford Madox FORD.

Huerta, Vicente García de la. See Vicente GARCÍA DE LA HUERTA.

Hughes, Charles Evans (1862–1948). American jurist and public official. Hughes's distinguished legal career led to his being elected governor of New York in 1906 and 1908. In 1910 he was appointed to the Supreme Court by President Taft, but resigned to run against Woodrow Wilson for the presidency in 1916. Defeated by a narrow margin, he returned to law practice, but served as secretary of state from 1921 to 1926 when he became a member of the courts of international arbitration and justice at the Hague. In 1930 President Hoover appointed him chief justice of the Supreme Court; he served until 1941. Mod-

erately conservative in his views, he supported many of the measures proposed by President Roosevelt, although he fought the president's court reorganization plan and opposed government agencies that usurped the functions of courts.

Hughes, Hatcher (1881–1945). American dramatist and teacher at Columbia University. He is best known for the Pulitzer Prize-winning *Hell-Bent for Heaven* (1923), a play about a religious fanatic among the North Carolina mountaineers. With Elmer Rice he wrote *Wake Up, Jonathan* (1921), and alone he wrote several other successful plays.

Hughes, [James] Langston (1902–1967). American poet. Marked by the use of the rhythms of the blues and the ballad, often documentary in tone, his poems deal with the trials and joys of the American Negro. His collections of verse range from *Weary Blues* (1926) and *The Dream Keeper* (1932) to *Ask Your Mama* (1961). From his own poem, *Cross,* he made the play *Mulatto* (1935); this in turn was produced in a musical version called *The Barrier* (1950). He is also known for his humorous sketches, written originally for a Negro newspaper, which are collected in *Simple Speaks His Mind* (1950) and *The Best of Simple* (1961). His other works include the novel *Not Without Laughter* (1930) and *The Ways of White Folks* (1934), a short-story collection.

Hughes, Richard (1900–   ). English novelist and dramatist. The novel A HIGH WIND IN JAMAICA is generally considered to be his greatest achievement.

Hazard (1938) is a sea story. *The Fox in the Attic* (1961) is the first part of a long historical novel to be entitled *The Human Predicament*. Described by its author as a study of his own times, the novel opens in 1923 and is to close with the Second World War.

Hughes, Thomas (1822–1896). English jurist, reformer, and author. He wrote TOM BROWN'S SCHOOL DAYS and its sequel, *Tom Brown at Oxford* (1861). He was associated with Christian Socialism, and worked ardently to improve the conditions of the poor.

Hugh of Lincoln, St. (c. 1246–1255). English boy said to have been tortured and murdered by the Jews of Lincoln, a number of whom were hanged in consequence. Legends of miracles gathered around his name, such as the story that he spoke to his mother, though dead, and identified his murderer. His tragedy appears in Chaucer's PRIORESS'S TALE, *Alphonsus of Lincoln* (1459), Marlowe's *The Jew of Malta* (1589), and a number of ballads such as *Sir Hugh, Hugh of Lincoln, The Jew's Daughter*.

Hugh Selwyn Mauberley (1920). A poem in several sections by Ezra POUND. Although there has been much discussion on the exact relationship between Pound and his persona Mauberley, the poem represents Pound's farewell to London and is a vehement denunciation of a civilization marked by war, the commercialization of the arts, and a general and sexual sterility. The artist either prostitutes his art as did Arnold Bennett ("Mr. Nixon") or he manages to barely exist in a solitary and destitute state as did Ford Madox Ford (the "stylist"). Mauberley himself is finally capable of only a refined and delicate art in such a corrupt civilization. It has been suggested that Mauberley represents the poet Pound would have become had he remained the simple imagist, unconcerned by the cultural and economic problems that from this point on were to occupy him.

Hugin and Munin. In Scandinavian mythology, the two ravens, typifying Thought and Memory, which sat on Odin's shoulders and brought him news from earth.

Hugo, Victor [Marie] (1802–1885). French poet, novelist, dramatist, and leader of the romantic movement in France. Like Chateaubriand, the literary figure he so admired, Hugo played an active part in political life. Serving first as a peer under the monarchy of Louis Philippe, he transferred his loyalties to the republicans in 1848 and was elected to the popular assembly. Deeply disturbed by the restoration of the Second Empire, in 1851 Hugo fled France, living in exile for 18 years in the Channel Islands. His last public office was held under the Third Republic, in which he served as a senator. His love of liberty and his hopes for mankind were regarded, however, as a poet's dream, and Hugo had little real political influence during this period. If he lacked political influence, Hugo's influence upon French literature of the 19th century was unrivaled. In each genre he revealed himself as a romantic par excellence (see ROMANTICISM). The voice of his poetry is always musical, often highly personal, reflective, and sometimes characterized by gentle melancholy. Often considered France's greatest lyric poet, Hugo experimented with language and with rhythm, displaying a fine sensitivity to the sound and color of

words. *Les Feuilles d'Automne* (1831) and *Contemplations* (1856), both describe the moods and emotions of the poet in richly sonorous verse. In other volumes, however, such as *Les Châtiments* (1853) which attacked Napoleon III or *Les Chants du Crépuscule* (1835), Hugo conceived of the poet's role as public and prophetic. The poet should lead and guide the people, rather than express his own responses to nature's beauty or personal sorrow. This same strain appears again in Hugo's long novels which reveal a humanitarian interest in the problems and suffering of the common man. Stylistically the novels are marked by violent melodrama, panoramic sweep, and the colorful use of language. These novels, best known of Hugo's work to the English audience, include HAN OF ICELAND, THE HUNCHBACK OF NOTRE DAME, LES MISÉRABLES, TOILERS OF THE SEA, THE MAN WHO LAUGHS, and NINETY-THREE. In the drama his preface to *Cromwell* (1827) became a manifesto adopted by the romantic dramatists. Hugo asserted the playwright's independence from the rigid rules of classicism. He suggested such innovations as a mixture of the comic and the tragic, colloquial dialogue, new freedom in meter and from the traditional unities of time and place. His own plays, historical melodramas filled with rather wooden typically romantic personages, include *Hernani* (1830), *Ruy Blas* (1838) and *Les Burgraves* (1843). Some of these are better known today as sources for operatic librettos, notably *Hernani* and *Le Roi S'amuse* (1832; *Rigoletto*), both set to music by Verdi, and *Angelo* (1835), which became Ponchielli's *La Gioconda*.

Huguenots. A term applied to French Protestants during the religious wars of the 16th and 17th centuries. The name was first applied to citizens of medieval Geneva who resisted the claims of the dukes of Savoy over the city; it is probably an adaptation of *Eidgenossen* (*Ger.*, "confederates"). See NANTES, EDICT OF.

Huis Clos. See NO EXIT.

Hulda. Old German goddess of marriage and fecundity who sent bridegrooms to maidens and children to the married. The name means "the Benignant," and is an euphemistic appellation.

Hull, Edith Maude. See SHEIK, THE.

Hull, Isaac. See CONSTITUTION.

Hull, Hell, and Halifax. An old beggars' and vagabonds' "prayer." As quoted by Taylor, the Water Poet (early 17th century), it was:

> From Hull, Hell, and Halifax,
> Good Lord, deliver us.

Hell was probably the least feared as being farthest from them; Hull was to be avoided because it was so well governed that beggars had little chance of getting anything without doing hard labor for it; and Halifax, because anyone caught stealing in that town was beheaded without intermediate proceedings.

Hulme, Thomas Ernest (1883–1917). English critic and philosopher. He is noted for *Speculations* (1924) and *Notes on Language and Style* (1929). He was killed in World War I, but his ideas were later widely popularized by T. S. Eliot and Ezra Pound. Hulme distinguished classicism, which he considered true and "realistic," from humanism and romanticism, both of which he judged false and "unrealistic." Humanism, he claimed, erroneously described man as "naturally" good and capable of perfection; classicism, on the contrary, truthfully depicted man as "intrinsically bad or limited, but disciplined by order and tradition to *something fairly decent.*" Humanistic (and romantic) art, further, was undisciplined and imprecise, he concluded, while classic art was "clean, clearcut, and mechanical." See IMAGISM.

huma. A fabulous Oriental bird always on the wing. It is said that every head over which its shadow passes will wear a crown.

Human Age, The. A satirical prose epic by Wyndham LEWIS. It consists of *The Childermass* (1928), and *Monstre Gai* and *Malign Fiesta* (1955). The subject is a surrealistic journey to a nightmare heaven. The description is macabre and imaginative; the language is obscure—full of allusion, word-play, and parody.

Human Comedy, The. See COMÉDIE HUMAINE, LA.

Humanism. An attitude of the mind that accompanied the flowering of the RENAISSANCE. The term refers to several varied literary and scholarly activities inspired by the study of antiquity but differing in aim and scope. Humanism in the Renaissance took its name from the *studia humanitatis,* those studies (grammar, rhetoric, poetry, history, and moral philosophy) that were thought to possess human value: the ability to make man a fully realized human creature, elevated and distinct from the lower animals. The ancient writers of Greece and Rome were particularly revered, as it was felt that they had excelled in such studies and would thus be of value in teaching the modern Christian how to attain the perfections of life. This aspect of Humanism, sometimes called the REVIVAL OF ANTIQUITY, includes the study of the classics; editorial and philological work on ancient texts; the search of enthusiasts for unknown but extant manuscripts, statues, medals, and coins; the writing of modern works in classical Latin; and the teaching of the classics in universities and to the children of the nobility.

Our English term *humanists,* used to designate the participants in the above-mentioned activities, is derived from the Italian word *umanista,* which was first used in the late 16th century to describe a university teacher of the humanities. Renaissance humanists include scholars and poets such as Petrarch, often called the first humanist; instigators of "the revival" such as the Greek scholar Chrysoloras; the philologists Valla and Erasmus; archaeologists and antiquarians such as Poggio and Ciriaco; the educators Vittorino of Feltre and Guarino of Verona; philosophers, historians, and men of letters such as Pius II and Leonardo Bruni; and a host of secretaries, chancellors, legates, and other royal advisors who, having imbibed the spirit of the period, used their mastery of eloquence in practical labors. Outstanding English humanists during the Renaissance were More, Colet, Elyot, and Ascham.

The origins of Humanism have been found to lie in the introduction of Greek studies into Italy by refugee and other visiting scholars from the Byzantine world; and in the economic flowering of the Italian city-states, which provided the necessary wealth and leisure for cultural activities. From Italy, Humanism spread north to France, England, the Netherlands, and Germany as well as Spain. By the time of its arrival in the northern countries, however, the purely cultural aims gave way to the needs of the Reformation; theological disputation and educational theory assumed greater importance than the study and imitation of pagan authors and text. In succeeding centuries, the influence of Humanism persisted mainly in the school curricula.

Modern Humanism (see NEW HUMANISM) only vaguely resembles the Renaissance brand, and is primarily a secular philosophy devoted to the propagation of a self-sufficient system of human values.

Humbaba. A one-eyed monster in the *Epic of* GILGAMESH. This gorgon-faced giant, whose eye can strike men dead, who breathes fire and plague, and who speaks in a whirlwind, is the guardian of the forest of the gods. He is killed by Gilgamesh and Enkidu, with the help of the sun-god, who blinds him with searing winds.

Humboldt, Baron **Alexander von** (1769–1859). German naturalist. With Aimé Bonpland, a French botanist, he traveled throughout Latin America (1799–1804), studying physical geography and meteorology; in the Andes, he determined the relationship between altitude and temperature, and he also discovered the cool Peruvian current that now bears his name. The volumes in his *Voyage aux régions équinoxiales du Nouveau Continent* (1807 ff.) greatly influenced later explorers and give an excellent picture of political and economic conditions in Latin America on the eve of independence. His main work is *Kosmos* (1845–1862), a description of the physical universe. He was the brother of Wilhelm von Humboldt.

Humboldt, Wilhelm von (1767–1835). German philologist, statesman, and educator. The brother of Alexander von Humboldt, he was a friend of both Goethe and Schiller. His most important work is *Über die Kawisprache auf der Insel Jawa* (*On the Kawi Language of the Island of Java,* 1836–1840). See WEIMAR CLASSICISM.

Hume, David (1711–1776). Scottish philosopher and historian. His empirical outlook is clearly seen in his *Natural History of Religion* (1757), *Dialogues concerning Natural Religion* (1779), in which anthropomorphism is assailed, and in his essay *On Miracles* where he asserts that "no testimony for any kind of miracle has ever amounted to a probability, much less a proof." His philosophical skepticism, often referred to as Humism, restricts human knowledge to the experience of ideas and impressions, and has been of extraordinary importance in the history of modern metaphysical thinking. Hume was the author of many treatises and essays, and of a history of England during the reigns of James I and Charles I. His best-known work is *Philosophical Essays Concerning Human Understanding* (1748), later issued as *An Enquiry Concerning Human Understanding.*

Humevesne. See Lord SUCKFIST.

Humiliation of the Father, The. See HOSTAGE, THE.

humor. An obsolete medical term for the supposed four principal humors or liquids of the body. In medieval times, these were supposed to be blood, phlegm, yellow bile, and black bile. They were thought to correspond to the four principal temperaments: the sanguine, the phlegmatic, the choleric, the melancholic. This idea was still popular in Elizabethan days. Ben Jonson's comedy, *Every Man in His Humour,* makes his characters stereotyped with one ruling temperament for each. Albrecht Dürer is said to have thought of the four temperaments and humors in connection with his paintings of the four evangelists.

Humperdinck, Engelbert (1854–1921). German composer. A friend of Richard Wagner, he is best known for his fairy-tale opera HÄNSEL UND GRETEL (1893). He also composed incidental music for Shakespeare and for Maeterlinck's play *The Blue Bird.*

Humphrey. Duke of **Gloucester** and earl of **Pembroke** (1391–1447). English noble. The youngest son of Henry IV, he was known as a patron of learning and donated his library to Balliol College, Oxford. Upon the death of his brother Henry V, he served as protector for the young Henry VI. His first marriage having been annulled in 1428, he married his mistress, Eleanor Cobham, whose dabblings in sorcery contributed to his downfall in 1447. He appears in Shakespeare's HENRY IV: PART II, HENRY V, and HENRY VI: PART I and PART II.

Humphrey Clinker, The Expedition of (1771). An epistolary novel by Tobias SMOLLETT. The letters are written by Matthew BRAMBLE, his sister Tabitha, their niece, their nephew, and their maid Winifred JENKINS. Each correspondent has a highly individual style and caricatures himself unwittingly. The titular hero of this comic masterpiece, who plays a lesser role than the Brambles, is a workhouse lad who enters into their service by chance and who later becomes a Methodist preacher. He falls in love with Winifred, and is eventually found to be the natural son of Mr. Bramble. The "expedition" of the title is a family tour through England and Scotland, during which the correspondents express surprisingly varied reactions to the same events. Of particular note is the picture of Hot Wells (a sobriquet for the city of Bath), a fashionable watering place. See Captain LISMAHAGO.

Humphries, David. See HARTFORD WITS.

Hunchback of Notre Dame, The (**Notre Dame de Paris**) (1831). A romance of medieval times by Victor HUGO centering about the life of the great Parisian cathedral. The principal characters are Esmeralda, the gypsy dancer in love with Captain Phoebus, Claude Frollo, the hypocritical archdeacon, whose evil passion for Esmeralda causes him to denounce her as a witch, and Quasimodo, the "Hunchback of Notre Dame," a deformed bellringer, whose devotion saves Esmeralda for a time when she seeks protection from the mob in the belfry of the Cathedral. Esmeralda is finally executed, and Quasimodo throws Frollo from the heights of Notre Dame.

Hundred Days. The days between March 20 and June 28, 1815. On March 20, Napoleon reached the Tuileries after his escape from Elba; June 28 was the date of the second restoration of Louis XVIII. Napoleon left Elba February 26; landed near Cannes, March 1; entered Paris, March 20; and signed his abdication June 22, four days after the fateful battle at WATERLOO.

Hundred-Handed, The (**Hekatoncheires**). In Greek mythology, three hundred-armed giants, offspring of Ouranus and Ge. They assisted Zeus in his war against the Titans. Their names were Cottus (Kottos), Briareus (also called Aegaeon), and Gyes.

Hundred Years' War (1337–1453). The long series of wars between France and England, beginning in the reign of Edward III and ending in that of Henry VI.

The first battle was a naval action off Sluys, and the last the fight at Castillon. The war originated in English claims to the French crown, and resulted in the English being expelled from the whole of France, except Calais.

Huneker, James Gibbons (1860–1921). American critic and man of letters. Although Huneker's greatest area of concentration was music, he is known for his impressionistic criticism in all fields of art. *Iconoclasts* (1905) called attention to many European playwrights up to that time little known in the U.S. Other collections of critical and biographical pieces were *Mezzotints in Modern Music* (1899), *Chopin* (1900), *Overtones* (1904), *Egoists* (1909), and *New Cosmopolis* (1915). He also published two collections of short stories, *Melomaniacs* (1902) and *Visionaries* (1905), and one novel, PAINTED VEILS. *Steeplejack* (2 vols., 1919), his autobiography, contains many of his views on art.

Hungerford, Margaret Wolfe. Born **Hamilton** (1855?–1897). Irish novelist. She wrote more than 30 novels, of which the best-known is *Molly Bawn* (1878). Most of her books were signed "The Duchess."

hunger strike. The refusal of a prisoner or a prominent person to take any food until he has been released or secures some desired concession. The practice seems to have originated in Russia, but was widely employed by suffragette prisoners in England during the early years of the 20th century and later by Irish political prisoners. The hunger strike was used to particular effect by Mohandas K. GANDHI, the Indian nationalist, in his struggle with the British.

Hung Lou Meng. Chinese novel by Tso Hsueh-chin of the Ch'ing Dynasty (1644–1912). Autobiographical in nature, it details the decline in fortune of the Chia family, giving a vivid picture of the social life of the times. Written in the colloquial, it has had an enduring popularity. See Chi-chen Wang, *Dream of the Red Chamber* (1958).

Hunt, Henry. Called **Orator Hunt** (1773–1835). A persuasive orator who presided over the meeting in St. Peter's Field, Manchester, at the time of the PETERLOO MASSACRE (1819). Yeomen and soldiers charged upon the reform meeting, and the news of this outrage so aroused the poet Shelley in Italy that he wrote *The Masque of Anarchy.* Orator Hunt was sentenced to two years' imprisonment. Later he became a member of Parliament (1830–1833), and published his memoirs in 1820.

Hunt, [William] Holman (1827–1910). English painter. With John Everett Millais and Dante Gabriel Rossetti, Holman Hunt founded the PRE-RAPHAELITE BROTHERHOOD. In 1905 he published his two-volume *Pre-Raphaelitism and the Pre-Raphaelite Brotherhood;* in the same year he was awarded the Order of Merit.

Hunt, [James Henry] Leigh (1784–1859). English journalist, essayist, poet, and political radical. For years, in the face of poverty, vilification, and official persecution, Hunt edited a series of one-man journals.

From 1813 to 1815 he was imprisoned for attacking the future George IV in his *Examiner,* becoming a hero of the radicals. He is most important as an essayist and critic, early champion of Shelley and Keats. Byron was briefly Hunt's patron, but the two were unable to get along; Hunt's *Lord Byron and Some of His Contemporaries* (1828) reflects some bitterness. Though much of his prose is perspicacious and graceful, his poetry tends to be slight and sentimental. A few shorter poems, such as ABOU BEN ADHEM (1834) and *Jenny Kissed Me* (1844), and parts of *The Story of Rimini* (1816), are still of interest. Among his other works are: *Critical Essays* (1807); *The Round Table* (1817, with William HAZLITT); *The Months* (1821); *Men, Women and Books* (1847); *Autobiography* (1850).

Hunt, Violet (1866–1942). English biographer and novelist. She was daughter of the Pre-Raphaelite painter Alfred William Hunt and for some years mistress of Ford Madox FORD. Her autobiography *I Have This to Say* (1926) and her biography *The Wife of Rossetti* (1932) are valuable because she knew so many of the literary people of her day. Miss Hunt wrote garish novels, such as *White Rose of Weary Leaf* (1908), and macabre stories, such as *Tales of the Uneasy* (1910).

Hunter, Evan (1926–   ). American novelist. His first novel, *Blackboard Jungle* (1954), which grew out of his own experiences as a teacher, is a sensational exposé of the brutal underworld of a big-city high school. In *Strangers When We Meet* (1958), Hunter investigated marital infidelity in suburbia. He is also the author of *Matter of Conviction* (1959), and *Mothers and Daughters* (1961).

Hunter, Mr. and Mrs. Leo. In Charles Dickens' PICKWICK PAPERS, a celebrity-hungry couple who invite Pickwick and his friends to their house. Mrs. Hunter is the author of "Ode to an Expiring Frog," generally considered a masterpiece.

Huon de Bordeaux (early 13th century). French CHANSON DE GESTE, popularized through a prose version (1454) and the English translation by Lord Berners, *Huon of Burdeuxe* (c. 1540). Huon kills Charlot in self-defense, ignorant that his attacker is Charlemagne's son. His death sentence is suspended on condition that he go to the court of the Emir of Babylon, kill his most important knight, and kiss his daughter Esclairmonde three times. OBERON, king of the fairies, meets and befriends Huon, helping him to succeed in all his adventures and marry Esclairmonde. The tale was used by Christoph Martin Wieland in his epic poem *Oberon* (1780), and from there adapted by Weber for his opera *Oberon* (1826).

Hurd, Richard (1720–1808). English bishop, and author. His *Letters on Chivalry and Romance* (1762) set forth a historical approach to the study of the medieval romance in which the Gothic is contrasted with the classical art of Greece. Hurd's enthusiasm for the medieval and Gothic forms added greatly to the vogue of medievalism demonstrated in the poetry of James Macpherson, Thomas Chatterton, Thomas Percy, and others. Other works include an edition of the works of Horace (1749) and *Moral and Political Dialogues* (1759), which represents Joseph Addison and John Arbuthnot discussing feudalism amidst the ruins of Kenilworth.

Hurst, Fannie (1889–   ). American novelist and playwright. She began her long and successful career with such works as *Humoresque* (1919), a collection of stories about Jewish life in New York City. The title story tells of a poor boy who became a great violinist. *Lummox* (1923), the story of a servant girl whose greatness of soul shines amid her sordid surroundings, is one of her best-known novels. Her other books include *Star-Dust* (1921), *Back Street* (1931), *Imitation of Life* (1933), and *God Must be Sad* (1961). *Anatomy of Me* (1958) is her autobiography.

Hurstwood, George. A leading character in Dreiser's novel SISTER CARRIE. A wealthy man at the beginning of the novel, he helps Carrie in her rise to success but is himself destroyed in the process.

Hurtado de Mendoza, Diego (1503–1575). Spanish historian and poet. A member of one of Spain's noblest families, Hurtado was a humanist who read Greek, Hebrew, and Arabic as well as a distinguished diplomat who represented the king in Venice, Rome, and at the Council of Trent. A quarrel with another noble in 1568 led to his exile from Madrid. He retired to Granada, where he wrote his masterpiece, the *Guerra de Granada* (1627), a vivid history of the Morisco uprising of 1568–1571 which was modeled on the works of Tacitus and Sallust. His poetry is of two types: his sonnets and the *Fábula de Adonis, Hipómenes y Atalanta* reveal the influence of classical and Italian verse, but he was more successful with Spanish forms, as is shown by his witty, sometimes cynical, *redondillas*. The authorship of LAZARILLO DE TORMES has also been attributed to him. At his death he left all his books and manuscripts to the library of the Escorial.

Hu Shih (1891–1962). Ambassador to U.S. (1938–1942). President of Academia Sinica. One of modern China's greatest scholars, he wrote widely on philosophy, literature, and history. Author of *China's Place in the Present World Struggle* (1942).

Huss, John or **Jan Hus** (1369–1415). A Bohemian religious reformer. Rector of the University of Prague, he was condemned and burned at the stake for propagating a reform doctrine influenced by Wycliffe. His followers, the Hussites, organized a religious and political party and waged a fierce civil war (1419–1434). Their radical wing, the Taborites, became merged with the Bohemian Brethren. The conservatives or Calixtines later turned Lutheran or Roman Catholic.

Husserl, Edmund (1859–1938). German philosopher. He was a leader in the development of PHENOMENOLOGY as the basis for a new philosophical method. His work has had much influence on the existentialists, especially Jean-Paul Sartre, who studied under him from 1933 to 1934. His works include *Logical Inquiries* (*Logische Untersuchungen;* 1900–1901) and *Thoughts toward a Pure Phenomenology and Phenomenological Philosophy* (*Ideen zu einer reinen Phänomenologie und phänomenologischen Philosophie;* 1922).

Hussonet. A character in Gustave Flaubert's novel L'EDUCATION SENTIMENTALE. A friend of the hero Frédéric Moreau, Hussonet is an opportunistic journalist and editor. He voices firm support of the principles of 1848, but after Louis Napoleon's successful coup d'état he rapidly became an ardent supporter of the empire.

Hutchinson, Anne (1591–1643). English-born American religious teacher. Her assertion that salvation could come only through personal intuition of God's grace, and not through good works, conflicted with the beliefs of many clergymen in the Massachusetts Bay Colony and produced a bitter controversy that divided the entire settlement. In 1637 she was tried and banished from the colony "for traducing the ministers and their ministry." She and her family moved to Rhode Island, then to New York, where they were killed by Indians.

Hutchinson, A[rthur] S[tuart-]M[enteth] (1879–1971). Popular English novelist. He is author of IF WINTER COMES. Later works include *The Uncertain Trumpet* (1929), *He Looked for a City* (1940), and *Bring Back the Days* (1958).

Hutchinson, John. See Lucy HUTCHINSON.

Hutchinson, Lucy (1620–1675). English prose writer. She is known for her biography of her husband, Colonel John Hutchinson (1615–1664), an outstanding Puritan leader and soldier during the English Civil War. The work, entitled *Memoirs of the Life of Colonel Hutchinson*, was written after 1664 and published in 1806. It is considered noteworthy because of its character analysis of its subject, its defense of the Puritan character in general, and its picture of a 17th-century English Puritan household.

Hutchinson, R[ay] C[oryton] (1907–). English novelist. He has written many serious, sensitive books, including *The Answering Glory* (1932), *Recollection of a Journey* (1952), and *The Stepmother* (1955).

Hutten, Ulrich von (1488–1523). German humanist writer. Luther's most vigorous defender among the nobility, he was a progressive in religion and politics and wished to see Germany freed from the yoke of Rome, as is clearly expressed in his Lucianlike dialogue *Inspicientes* (*The Onlookers*, c. 1521). In matters of social change, however, he was conservative and opposed the rise of the cities. He has been suspected of writing the second half of the EPISTOLAE OBSCURORUM VIRORUM, but this is not certain.

Huxley, Aldous (1894–1963). English novelist, essayist, and satirist. He was the grandson of Thomas Huxley, great-nephew of Matthew Arnold, brother of Julian Huxley, and half-brother of Andrew Huxley (winner of the 1963 Nobel prize for physiology). Huxley's early work differs sharply from that of his later years, the break reflecting his conversion to mysticism. His early novels are witty, despairing evocations of society in the 1920's, satirizing the intellectual pretensions and poses of the era. Among the novels of this period are CROME YELLOW, *Antic Hay* (1923), *Those Barren Leaves* (1925), and POINT COUNTER POINT. Huxley's early short stories were collected in *Mortal Coils* (1922). In the 1930's Huxley's work began to reflect his growing preoccupation with occult studies. Among his later novels are EYELESS IN GAZA, AFTER MANY A SUMMER DIES THE SWAN, *Time Must Have a Stop* (1944), and *Island* (1962). Huxley is noted for his interest in science; his forty-fifth and last book, *Literature and Science* (1963) is an essay on both. BRAVE NEW WORLD, one

of his best-known books, expresses his concern over the dangers of scientific progress; *Ape and Essence* (1948) is a satire about the world after an atomic war. His most important essays are *Music at Night* (1931), *Beyond the Mexique Bay* (1934), *The Perennial Philosophy* (1946), *The Doors of Perception* (1954), HEAVEN AND HELL, and *Brave New World Revisited* (1958).

Huxley studied medicine, but was prevented from practicing by a disease of the eyes that temporarily blinded him. He was associated with J. Middleton Murry and Katherine Mansfield in editing the *Athenaeum*. A friend and admirer of D. H. Lawrence, Huxley edited his letters in 1932; it was Lawrence who encouraged him to begin to search for spiritual values when he was in despair. In 1947 he settled in California, where he became associated with the Ramakrishna Mission in Hollywood and pursued various occult studies.

Huxley, Julian [Sorell] (1887–). English biologist and writer, brother of Aldous Huxley. He is the author of *Essays of a Biologist* (1923), *The Science of Life* (with H. G. and G. P. Wells, 1929), *What Dare I Think?* (1931), *The Captive Shrew and Other Poems* (1932), *Evolution: the Modern Synthesis* (1942), *New Bottles for New Wine* (1957), *The Humanist Frame, 1961*.

Huxley, Thomas Henry (1825–1895). English biologist and teacher. He is known for his defense of the theory of evolution held by Darwin, and for his lectures and writings popularizing science. His books include *Man's Place in Nature* (1863), *The Physical Basis of Life* (1868), *Lay Sermons, Addresses, and Reviews* (1870), *Science and Morals* (1886), *Essays upon Some Controverted Questions* (1892), and *Ethics and Evolution* (1893). Huxley was called "Darwin's Bulldog" and engaged in a controversy with the English statesman Gladstone on the question of scientific evolutionary theories as opposed to Biblical lore. He was the grandfather of Aldous and Julian HUXLEY.

Huysmans, Joris Karl (1848–1907). French novelist. Of Dutch ancestry, Huysmans was born, lived, and died in Paris, where after a prolonged spiritual struggle, he became a convert to Roman Catholicism. His neurasthenia and perverse tastes mark Huysmans as a typical DÉCADENT. Stylistically, his work is characterized by vivid and concrete figures, fantastic description, and a gift for portraying the grotesque. Among his novels are *Marthe, Histoire d'une Fille* (1876), a naturalistic account of a young prostitute's life; AGAINST THE GRAIN; *Là-Bas* (1891), part of a spiritual autobiography; and *La Cathédrale* (1898).

Hyacinth (Hyakinthos). In Greek mythology, a beautiful youth loved by Apollo. Zephyr, the jealous west wind, spoiled Apollo's aim when he was throwing the discus; it struck Hyacinth and he died. From his blood sprang the hyacinth (not the modern flower), bearing on its petals the cry of grief, AI. Hyakinthos was, in fact, a pre-Hellenic local deity in Amyclae, antedating Apollo's appearance in Greece.

Hyde, Douglas (1860–1949). Irish poet, scholar, and statesman. The first president of Eire (1938–1945), he wrote much of his work in Gaelic and devoted himself to the restoration of Irish culture. He was one of the founders of the ABBEY THEATRE and wrote many books on Irish history, literature, and folk lore. His *Love Songs of Connaught* (1894) is a classic compilation. His other works include *Answer to Communism* (1949), and *I Believed* (1950), an autobiographical account of how he came to join the Communist party, grew disillusioned with it, and became a convert to Catholicism.

Hyde, Edward. See earl of CLARENDON.

Hyde, Mr. See STRANGE CASE OF DR. JEKYLL AND MR. HYDE, THE.

Hyde Park (1). A large park in west-central London. It has become a symbol of freedom of speech, for the many speakers who hold impromptu meetings there are traditionally allowed to say anything they please, however critical it may be of the government.

(2) A village in New York State, overlooking the Hudson and famous as the residence of Franklin D. Roosevelt and his family. It now contains a museum devoted to mementoes of Roosevelt's presidency.

Hydra. A monstrous serpent of Greek mythology. It was born of TYPHON and ECHIDNA. Living in the swamps of the river Lerna, it had many heads; when one was cut off, another grew in its place. HERACLES finally killed it by having his friend Iolaus burn the stumps with torches as soon as the heads were removed. Heracles poisoned his arrows with its blood. See CANCER.

Hydriotaphia, or Urn Burial (1658). An essay by Sir Thomas BROWNE. In part a scientific report on some Roman burial urns that had recently been unearthed in Norfolk, the essay becomes a moving meditation on mortality and oblivion. The famous last chapter on death is considered an example of nearly flawless English prose.

Hyksos (fr. Egyptian *hikan Khasut*, "rulers of foreign lands"; erroneously, "shepherd kings"). An ancient, semi-nomadic Semitic race whose dominion, centered in Palestine, extended from the Euphrates to the Nile. Between 1720 and 1710 B.C. they defeated the Pharaohs of the Middle Kingdom and ruled Egypt until about 1570 B.C. (XV–XVIII dynasties). The Hyksos introduced the horse-drawn chariot and the composite bow into Egypt, as well as the Canaanite deities. In Egyptian art they are depicted as barbarians who misruled the country and debased its culture.

Hymettus. A mountain E. and SE. of Athens, famous for its honey and for a marble used in building ancient Athens.

Hymir. In Scandinavian mythology, a giant with a frosty beard who personified the inhospitable sea. He owned the kettle in which the gods brewed their ale, and it was he who took Thor in his boat and robbed him of his prey when the latter god sought to kill the Midgard serpent.

Hymn of Hate (Hassgesang). A German poem popular during World War I by Ernst Lissauer (1882–1937). Its refrain "Gott strafe England" ("God punish England") was the source of the English verb "to strafe."

Hypatia (c. 370–415). Member of the Neoplatonic School of philosophy at Alexandria, in the 5th century A.D. A daughter of Theon, the mathematician, Hypatia was murdered by the Alexandrine mob. Her story is told in the historical novel HYPATIA (1853), by Charles Kingsley. She is also known as the *Divine Pagan*.

Hypatia (1853). A historical novel by Charles KINGSLEY, a romance of 5th-century Alexandria. The hero, a young monk named Philammon, leaves his monastery for a more active struggle with the brilliant pagan life of the great city. He is strongly drawn to Hypatia, a lecturer on Greek philosophy and a woman of rare spiritual charm, and is much moved by her discussions. But the fanatical Christians of the city cannot tolerate her teachings, and she is torn to pieces by an angry mob. Philammon then recedes into the desert to meditate upon tolerance.

hyperbole. In rhetoric, a figure of speech consisting of exaggeration or extravagance of statement. It is used deliberately for effect and not meant to be taken literally, as in "the waves were mountains high," or "I was fainting from hunger."

Hyperboreans. A happy people of early Greek legend. They were supposed to dwell on the other side of the spot where the North Wind had its birth, and therefore to enjoy perpetual warmth and sunshine. They were said to be the oldest of the human race, the most virtuous, and the most happy, dwelling for some thousand years under a cloudless sky, in fields yielding double harvests, and in the enjoyment of perpetual spring.

Later fable held that they had not an atmosphere like our own, but one consisting wholly of feathers. Both Herodotus and Pliny mention this fiction, which they say was suggested by the quality of snow observed to fall in those regions.

Hyperion. In Greek mythology, one of the TITANS, son of Uranus and Ge, and father of Helios, Selene, and Eos (the Sun, Moon, and Dawn). The name is sometimes given by poets to the sun itself. One of the best-known works of John KEATS is his "poetical fragment" of this name (1820).

Hyperion (1839). A romance by Henry Wadsworth LONGFELLOW. Paul Flemming travels in Europe, falling in love with Mary Ashburton. She scorns him, and he continues his search for the mythical blue rose of German legend, the symbol of the unattainable. Often called Longfellow's *Wilhelm Meister*, the book is studded with old legends.

Hyperion oder Der Eremit in Griechenland (Hyperion or the Hermit in Greece, 1797–1799). An epistolary novel by Friedrich HÖLDERLIN. It is set in modern Greece, but expresses an elegiac longing for the human and artistic perfection of ancient Greece.

Hypermnestra. In Greek legend, the wife of Lynceus and the only one of the fifty daughters of Danaus who did not murder her husband on their bridal night. See DANAIDES.

Hypnos. In Greek mythology, the god of sleep.

Hypocrite, The. See TARTUFFE, LE.

Hypsipyle. In Greek legend, a queen of Lemnos. When the women of her island killed their husbands to a man for infidelity, she saved her father Thoas, who escaped in a boat. When the ARGONAUTS arrived on their way to find the Golden Fleece, she and her women were so hospitable that they repopulated the island. Later, however, Hypsipyle was sold into slavery for having saved Thoas, and was the nursemaid who permitted the child OPHELTES to be fatally bitten by a snake.

I

Iacchus (Iakchos). An obscure Greek deity. A young man associated with the worship of Demeter and Persephone in the ELEUSINIAN MYSTERIES, he was later identified with DIONYSUS.

Iachimo. In Shakespeare's CYMBELINE, a Roman courtier who wagers with Posthumus Leonatus that he can seduce the latter's wife Imogen. A worldly and affected libertine, he has no redeeming qualities.

Iago. In Shakespeare's OTHELLO, the "ancient," or ensign, who is driven by bitterness against his master for having chosen Cassio as his lieutenant. Though outwardly the epitome of "honesty and trust," he causes the downfall and near-death of Cassio and weaves the Machiavellian plot that plants in Othello's mind the false suspicion of his wife's infidelity with Cassio.

Ironically, one of Shakespeare's most famous speeches on honor is delivered by Iago:

Good name in man and woman, dear my lord,
Is the immediate jewel of their souls:
Who steals my purse steals trash; 'tis something, nothing;
But he that filches from me my good name
Robs me of that which not enriches him
And makes me poor indeed.

His also is the famous phrase:

O, beware, my lord, of jealousy;
It is the green-eyed monster, which doth mock
The meat it feeds on.

iamb (or iambus). In English prosody, a metrical foot consisting of two syllables, the first unaccented, the second accented. The word "beTRAY" is an iamb. The METER made up of such units is called iambic meter, and the following lines are a good example:

As NIGHT/ drew ON,/ and, FROM/ the CREST
Of WOOD/ed KNOLLS/ that RIDGED/ the WEST,
The SUN,/ a SNOW/-blown TRAV/eller, SANK
From SIGHT/ beNEATH/ the SMOTH/ering BANK.
                    Whittier, *Snow-Bound*

Iambic meter is the most common English measure; insofar as one can generalize, it is the prevailing meter of natural English speech.

Ianthe. A poetic name much in use in the 19th century. The Ianthe to whom Byron dedicated his *Childe Harold* was Lady Charlotte Harley, only 11 years old at the time. He borrowed it from Walter Savage Landor, who had thus etherealized the middle name of his early sweetheart, Sophia Jane Swift. Landor wrote many poems in her praise. Shelley gave the name to the maiden to whom the fairy queen appears in *Queen Mab*.

Iapetus. In classical mythology, a TITAN son of Uranus and Ge, father of Atlas, Prometheus, Epimetheus, and Menoetius, and ancestor of the human race.

Iasion. According to a Greek myth, a mortal who was united with Demeter and made her the mother of Plutus. He was killed for his presumption by Zeus' lightning. The myth probably symbolizes the fertilization of the fields.

Ibarbourou, Juana de (1895–   ). Uruguayan poet, often known as "Juana de América." Married at 18, she led a quiet life as a wife and mother. She is best known for the poems in *Las lenguas de diamante* (1918) and *Raíz salvaje* (1922); simple, sensuous, and earthy, they are characterized by a subjectivity that has been described as narcissistic.

Iberia. Spain; the country of the Iberus, the ancient name of the river Ebro.

Iberville, Sieur d'. Pierre le Moyne (1661–1706). French-Canadian commander and explorer. Born in Montreal, Iberville served in the French navy and took part in successful engagements with the English in the Hudson Bay area. In 1699 he organized and led an expedition which located the mouth of the Mississippi. In 1702 he established colonies at Biloxi and Mobile.

ibis. A sacred bird of the ancient Egyptians. It was especially associated with the god Thoth who, in the guise of an ibis, escaped the pursuit of Typhon. Its white plumage symbolized the light of the sun, its black neck the shadow of the moon, its body a heart, and its legs a triangle. It was said to drink only the purest of water and to be so fond of Egypt that it would pine to death if transported elsewhere. The ibis was encouraged to make its nest in temples and was often mummified.

Ibraham. The Abraham of the Koran.

Ibsen, Henrik [Johan] (1828–1906). Norwegian poet and playwright. The son of a middle-class family that suffered severe financial reverses when he was a boy, Ibsen was apprenticed to a druggist in his teens, began to study medicine, but soon found his way into the theater. In 1851 he was appointed manager and official playwright of the new National Theater at Bergen, for which he wrote four plays based on Norwegian folklore and history, notably *Lady Inger of Östråt* (1855), dealing with the liberation of medieval Norway. He left the Bergen theater for the post of manager of the Norwegian Theater at Christiania (now Oslo), remaining there until the theater failed in 1864. To this period belong *The Vikings of Helgoland* (1858) and *The Pretenders* (1864), historical dramas; and *Love's Comedy* (1862), a satire. With the aid of a traveling scholarship,

Ibsen began a period of self-imposed exile from his homeland, living until 1891 in various cities on the Continent, primarily Rome, Munich, and Dresden. In 1891 he settled in Christiania, where he lived until his death in 1906.

Ibsen's first two major plays, both in verse, were the symbolic tragedy BRAND and the mock-heroic fantasy PEER GYNT. *The League of Youth* (1869), a political satire, was his first modern prose drama. It was followed by *Emperor and Galilean* (1873), a historical play in two parts on Julian the Apostate. *Pillars of Society* (1877) deals with the shady acts of a wealthy and hypocritical businessman. A DOLL'S HOUSE, a social drama on marriage, was alternately vilified and praised for its sympathy with woman's rights and the questions raised when Nora Helmer slammed the door on her doll's house and her duties and went out in the world to learn how to be a human being. GHOSTS touched on the forbidden subject of "social disease" and attacked social conventions and duty as destroyers of life and happiness. In *An Enemy of the People* (1882), Ibsen contrasted the enlightened and persecuted minority with the ignorant, powerful majority; Dr. Stockman is voted an "enemy of the people" because he insists that the town's famous and prosperous baths are dangerously polluted and must be shut down for expensive repairs. The play was followed by the poetic and symbolic drama THE WILD DUCK; ROSMERSHOLM, another play on the problems of idealism; *The Lady from the Sea* (1888), a play with supernatural overtones and a happy ending. HEDDA GABLER, one of Ibsen's greatest plays, is a striking study of a modern neurotic woman. THE MASTER BUILDER deals symbolically with the plight of the artist. *Little Eyolf* (1894) concerns parental responsibility. Ibsen's last two works, the realistic JOHN GABRIEL BORKMAN and the highly symbolic WHEN WE DEAD AWAKEN, both deal with men who are dead spiritually because they have sacrificed love.

Called the father of modern drama, Ibsen discarded the Scribean formula for the well-made play that had ruled the 19th-century theater. He brought the problems and the ideas of the day onto his stage, emphasized character rather than ingenious plots, and created realistic plays of psychological conflict. Throughout all his works, the social dramas as well as the symbolic plays, run the twin themes that the individual, not the group, is of paramount importance, and that the denial of love is the one unforgivable sin, tantamount to a denial of life.

Ibycus (Ibykos, 6th century B.C.). A Greek lyric poet. According to legend, he was murdered with only a passing flock of cranes as witnesses. In the presence of a large crowd one of the murderers betrayed himself, when he saw a flock of cranes pass overhead, by exclaiming: "The cranes of Ibycus!" This phrase signifies hence "unsuspected witnesses to a crime."

Icarius (Ikarios). In Greek legend an Athenian who was taught the cultivation of the vine by Dionysus. He was slain by some peasants who had become intoxicated with wine he had given them, and who thought they had been poisoned. They buried the body under a tree; his daughter Erigone, searching for her father, was directed to the spot by the howling of his dog Maera, and when she discovered the

Icarus and Daedalus (Freiburg, 1493).

body she hanged herself for grief. Icarius became the constellation *Boötes*, Erigone the constellation *Virgo*, and Maera the star *Procyon*, which rises in July, a little before the dog star.

Icarus (Ikarus). In Greek mythology, son of DAEDALUS. He flew with his father from Crete; but the sun melted the wax with which his wings were fastened on, and he fell into the sea, hence called the Icarian.

Iceland Fisherman, An. See PÊCHEUR D'ISLANDE.

I-ching. See BOOK OF CHANGES.

ichthys (*Gr.*, "fish"). An early symbol of Christ. The word is an anagram of the phrase *I*esous *CH*ristos, *TH*eou Yios, Soter, "Jesus Christ, Son of God, Saviour." This word, and the ichthys symbol, two facing curved lines which overlap at one end, are found on many early Christian seals, rings, urns, and tombs.

icon. In the Eastern Church, an image or representation of Christ, a saint, or an angel. Icons are sacred and honored with relative worship (kissing, incense, light) but not with supreme worship, which is due to God alone. They range from elaborate works of art in the church buildings to humble enamel and niello objects carried by the peasantry

iconoclasts (*Gr.*, "image breakers"). Reformers who rose in the Eastern Church in the seventh and eighth centuries, beginning under Emperor Leo III, the Isaurian. They destroyed sacred images or ICONS in the churches because they feared such visual representation would lead to pagan idol worship. The iconoclasts' crusade continued for 120 years under Constantine Copronymus, Leo the Armenian, Theophilus, and other Byzantine emperors, known as the *Iconoclast emperors*. Eventually, images were used in the Western Church, but in the Eastern Church sculptures are still excluded, though pictures are allowed.

A person who criticizes or seriously questions ideas and attitudes previously accepted as correct, just, and valuable by convention and tradition, rather than by independent examination and judgment, is also called an *iconoclast*.

Milton attacked the royal image of Charles II in his prose pamphlet *Eikonoclastes* (1649).

Idaean Mother. CYBELE, who had a temple on Mount Ida, in Asia Minor.

Idalian. Pertaining to Idalium, an ancient town in Cyprus, or to Aphrodite, to whom the place was consecrated.

Idas. In Greek legend, the son of Arene by Poseidon and brother of LYNCEUS. See ARGONAUTS.

Idea of a Patriot King (1749). A pamphlet by Henry ST. JOHN. It expressed the doctrine that the ideal government is without party and thus anticipated the actual political program of George III and strongly influenced the 19th-century Tory political ideology.

idéologues. A group of materialistic and pragmatic philosophers and psychologists of the late 18th century. They included disciples of CONDILLAC, CONDORCET, Pierre Jean Georges Cabanis, and Antoine Louis Claude Destutt de Tracy. Liberal and antireligious, they believed that ideas originate in physical sensation and that morality is therefore physical in origin; they proclaimed the self-sufficiency of man. Their literary influence is found in the works of Benjamin Constant and Stendhal, and in the literary criticism of Taine and Renan.

ides. In the Roman calendar, the 15th of March, May, July, and October, and the 13th of all the other months. The ides always fell eight days after the NONES.

According to Plutarch, Julius Caesar ignored a soothsayer's warning to beware the ides of March, the day on which he was slain.

Idiot, The (1868). A novel by Feodor DOSTOEVSKI. It is concerned with the effect of the saintly Prince Myshkin on worldly society in St. Petersburg. Myshkin's gentle, childlike nature and his refusal to take offense at anything have earned him the nickname of "the idiot." He himself admits to having been virtually an idiot for several years while under medical care in Switzerland. On the death of his benefactor, he returns to Russia to find himself heir to a large fortune. Almost immediately the trustful Myshkin is entangled in the affairs of the corrupt world of society. On the trip back to Russia he has already met the violently passionate ROGOZHIN who is obsessed by the beautiful Natasha FILIPPOVNA, the victim in her youth of an older man who brought her up as his mistress. The shame Natasha feels has driven the proud girl to degrade herself even more. Only when she meets Myshkin does she feel she has encountered a sympathetic being. This feeling eventually drives her to greater self-torment, when she realizes that Myshkin's apparent love is, in fact, pity.

Myshkin becomes involved with another woman, young Aglaya Epanchin, to whom he also cannot give the normal passionate love she wants, although he does ask her to marry him. His pity for Natasha, however, overcomes whatever love it is he feels for Aglaya, and he goes off to try again to redeem her. His vacillations manage only to hurt both women and, finally, to enrage the jealous Rogozhin to the point of murder. The latter tries unsuccessfully to kill Myshkin and, at the end of the novel he murders Natasha. Confronted with the scene, Myshkin relapses into idiocy.

Dostoevski's announced intention with the character of Myshkin was to portray a truly good man. The attempt has been viewed by critics as only partially successful, not only because Myshkin wreaks havoc with most of the characters he influences, but also because of the abstract, bloodless quality of the characterization itself. A more successful effort of this type is ALEXEI KARAMAZOV, in whose portrayal Dostoevski managed to blend harmoniously both human and Christlike attributes.

Dostoevski acknowledged that *The Idiot* was not completely successful, but insisted that the book was nevertheless his personal favorite among his works. Besides the figure of Myshkin, the author included in the novel many of his ideas on the superiority of Orthodoxy to Western religion and on the connections between Roman Catholicism and socialism.

Idiot's Delight (1936). A play by Robert E. SHERWOOD. Several travelers are detained at an Alpine resort hotel just before the outbreak of a second world war. They include a honeymooning English couple, a German scientist, a French munitions manufacturer, and a troupe of American actors. Harry Van, promoter of the troupe, recognizes Irene, the Russian mistress of the munitions manufacturer, as a woman he once knew slightly in Omaha. The outbreak of the war is announced, and "the little people" in and around the hotel become patriotic and join the army; they all leave but Irene, who has renounced her arms manufacturer and consequently lost her passport. Harry decides to remain with her; they are trapped in the hotel during an air raid. The play was awarded a Pulitzer Prize.

Idle Lake. See FAERIE QUEENE, THE.

Idler, The (1758–1760). A series of essays by Samuel JOHNSON. Published in the *Universal Chronical, or Weekly Gazette,* they are lighter in tone than the RAMBLER and incline to the satiric portrait and Oriental tale.

Idomeneus. King of ancient Crete, an ally of the Greeks at Troy. Part of his tale is told in the ILIAD. After the city was burned he made a vow to sacrifice whatever he first encountered, if the gods granted him a safe return to his kingdom. It was his own son that he first met. He offered him up to fulfill his vow, but a plague followed, and the king was banished from Crete as a murderer. See also JEPHTHAH; ISAAC.

Idraote (Idraotes). In the GERUSALEMME LIBERATA of Tasso, a wizard commissioned by Satan to prevent the Christian capture of Jerusalem. He sends his niece, Armida, to the Christian camp to use her seductive charms in sowing confusion there; she succeeds admirably.

Iduna, Idun, or **Ithunn.** In Scandinavian mythology, the goddess who kept in Asgard the golden apples eaten by the gods to preserve their eternal youth. The daughter of the dwarf Svald and wife of Bragi, she personified the year between March and September, when the sun was north of the equator. When the sun descended below the equator, Loki was said to carry her off to Giant-Land and steal her apples. When the sun rose again above the equator in March, Iduna made her escape in the form of a sparrow.

idyll. (1) A pastoral poem, usually brief, describing the picturesque in country life and conveying a mood of peace and contentment. The most celebrated idylls of antiquity are those of Theocritus and Vergil. Idylls may also be narrative poems, sometimes of epic stature, as in Tennyson's *Idylls of the King.*

(2) Any bucolic, peaceful, romantic episode or period in life or literature which might be a suitable subject for an idyll.

(3) In music, a romantic pastoral composition.

Idylls of the King (1859–1885). A series of poems in 10 books by Alfred TENNYSON. Based on ARTHURIAN LEGEND, they comprise *The Coming of Arthur, Gareth and Lynette, Geraint and Enid, Merlin and Vivien, Lancelot and Elaine, The Holy Grail, Pelleas and Etarre, The Last Tournament, Guinevere,* and *The Passing of Arthur*. In interpreting the Arthurian legend, Tennyson focuses on the introduction of evil into the hitherto unblemished Camelot through Lancelot's sin of adulterous love for Guinevere. Because of this approach, some commentators have found Tennyson's conception of Arthur lacking in substance.

If It Die . . . (Si le grain ne meurt; 1926). An autobiographical work by André GIDE. Written in 1920, it records Gide's experiences during his trips to North Africa in 1893 and 1894–1895. In part a confession of homosexuality, the book was intended to force public discussion of an issue then normally avoided.

If Winter Comes (1920). A once popular novel by A. S. M. HUTCHINSON. Bearing a thematic resemblance to the work of Warwick Deeping, it tells the story of Mark Sabre, unhappily married, who befriends a pregnant girl and is suspected of being the father of her illegitimate child. Sabre discovers that the real culprit is the idolized son of his business associate. When the boy's death at the front is reported, he knows that he will never be able to clear himself of the charges. Despite such misfortunes, the novel ends happily with Sabre's divorce and his remarriage to a woman he has always loved. The title is taken from the last line of Shelley's *Ode to the West Wind*: "If Winter comes, can Spring be far behind?"

Ignatius of Loyola, St. See St. Ignatius of LOYOLA.

Igraine, Igerne, or **Ygerne, Queen.** In Arthurian literature the mother of King ARTHUR. In many versions, she is the virtuous wife of Gorlois, duke of Tintagel, and she is innocently seduced by King UTHER PENDRAGON when the magic of Merlin gives him the appearance of her husband. In other versions, Uther and Gorlois fight, and the latter is slain. Uther then besieges Tintagel Castle, takes it, and compels Igraine to become his wife. Nine months afterwards, Uther dies, and on the same day Arthur is born.

Ihara Saikaku (1642–1693). Japanese novelist. He wrote erotic stories and tales of merchant class life. His writings reflect the new bourgeois culture centering in Osaka. His works enjoyed immense popularity and are still widely read. See *The Life of an Amorous Woman* (1962) by Ivan Morris.

I.H.S. The first three letters of the Greek form of Jesus, and a widely used Christian symbol. In time, the long "e" (H) was mistaken by people of Latin culture for a capital H, and various phrases arose that used these letters as initials, such as *Jesus Hominum Salvator* (Jesus, Savior of men) and *In hac salus* (safety in this, i.e., the Cross).

ikebana. Japanese flower arrangement. It was developed as an art during the Muromachi period (1333–1600), where it was used in conjunction with the tea ceremony. In the Tokugawa period (1600–1868) it became highly formalized, and a large number of schools arose, each with its own specialized techniques, most of which are still extant.

Ikeda Hayato (1899–1965). Japanese politician. In 1960 he became head of the Liberal Party and Prime Minister.

Ikshvaku. In Hindu legend, the first king of the solar dynasty. He is known as Raghu.

Ilf and Petrov. Pen names of the Soviet humorists **Ilya Arnoldovich Ilf** (1897–1937) and **Yevgeni Petrovich Katayev** (1902–1942). Their two comic novels, TWELVE CHAIRS and *The Little Golden Calf* (*Zolotoi telionok*, 1931), recount the hilarious machinations of the master con-man, Ostap Bender. The two writers also collaborated on a satirical account of their visit to the U.S., *One-Storied America* (*Odnoetazhnaya Amerika;* 1936). Ilf died of tuberculosis in 1937; Petrov was killed during the war in 1942.

Iliad. Greek epic poem (8th century B.C.?) attributed to HOMER. In 24 books of dactylic hexameter verse, it details the events of the few days near the end of the TROJAN WAR, focusing on the withdrawal of Achilles from the contest and the disastrous effects of this act on the Greek campaign. The plot is as follows:

Book I. AGAMEMNON, commander-in-chief of the Greek forces, refuses to return his captive Chryseis to her father Chryses, a priest of Apollo. An ensuing pestilence is divined to be the result of this unseemly act, and the Greeks insist that Agamemnon relinquish Chryseis. He grudgingly does so, but takes ACHILLES' captive Briseis in her place. Furious, Achilles refuses to fight with the Greeks. His mother, THETIS, persuades Zeus to turn the tide of battle so that the Greeks will see how much they need Achilles.

Book II. A false dream sent by Zeus leads Agamemnon to plan a battle. He tests his men by suggesting that they return home. To his dismay, they start to rush for the ships, and are only restrained when ODYSSEUS beats their leader Thersites. The "Catalogue of Ships" lists the combatants and their forces.

Book III. PARIS, whose abduction of HELEN from Sparta was the cause of the war, now engages in single combat with her husband, MENELAUS. About to be killed, Paris is spirited away by APHRODITE.

Book IV. ATHENA, who favors the Greeks, causes the Trojan PANDARUS to break the truce by treacherously shooting Menelaus, and the battle is joined.

Book V. DIOMEDES is the hero of the day, killing Pandarus and many others and even wounding Aphrodite and (with Athena's help) Ares, who are helping the Trojans.

Book VI. HECTOR, the Trojan leader, returns to Troy, bids the women pray to Athena, and bids farewell to Andromache, his wife, and his infant son in a touching scene. On the battlefield, Diomedes and GLAUCUS, finding that their godfathers were friends, refrain from fighting and exchange armor, Glaucus accepting bronze for gold.

Book VII. After an indecisive battle between the Trojan leader Hector and Great AJAX, there is a pause. Under pressure from the Trojans, Paris, though refusing to give up Helen, promises to make handsome restitution. The Greeks refuse his offer and build a wall to protect their ships.

Book VIII. Zeus orders the other gods not to interfere in the war. HERA and Athena at first defy him, but are chastened. The war turns in the Trojans' favor.

Book IX. Desperate, Agamemnon offers to return Briseis to Achilles and make further restitution. Odysseus, Ajax, and Phoenix, Achilles' old tutor, bear the offer to Achilles, but he indignantly refuses it and vows to start for home the next day.

Book X. Odysseus and Diomedes spy on the Trojans, and kill Dolon and the Thracian king, Rhesus.

Book XI. Agamemnon worries the Greeks, but he, Odysseus, Diomedes, and others are wounded. Achilles sends Patroclus to inquire about the course of the fighting. Nestor urges him to beg Achilles to fight or to send Patroclus with Achilles' MYRMIDONS.

Book XII. The Trojans under Hector break through a gate in the Greek walls.

Book XIII. In spite of Zeus's commands POSEIDON rallies the Greeks under Idomeneus and the Ajaxes.

Book XIV. Hera amorously deceives Zeus and puts him to sleep, while Poseidon helps the Greeks. The Trojans are driven back and Hector is wounded.

Book XV. When Zeus awakes, Poseidon is forced to cease aiding the Greeks and APOLLO rouses Hector to lead the Trojans as far as the Greek ships, where he tries to burn them. Patroclus meanwhile begs Achilles to fight.

Book XVI. Achilles gives Patroclus his armor and tells him to repel the Trojan advance, but no more. Patroclus drives the Trojans to the walls of Troy, killing SARPEDON and Hector's charioteer; but there Hector kills him, with the aid of Apollo.

Book XVII. Hector takes Achilles' armor, but, in a violent fight, Menelaus and the Greeks recover Patroclus' body.

Book XVIII. In spite of Thetis' warnings that he is fated to die, Achilles determines to avenge Patroclus in battle. Hephaestus makes him a new shield, richly engraved with many scenes.

Book XIX. Achilles announces that he will fight. Agamemnon makes amends. Achilles' immortal horses, Xanthus and Balius, warn him that this is the last time they will bear him safely from the field. Knowing that he is soon to die, Achilles goes into battle.

Book XX. Since Zeus's promise to Thetis now is fulfilled, the other gods are free to join in the war. Aligned with the Greeks are Athena, Hera, Poseidon, Hephaestus, and Hermes; with the Trojans, Apollo, Ares, Artemis, Aphrodite, and Leto. Aeneas fights with Achilles, but is rescued by Poseidon; similarly Hector is saved by Apollo.

Book XXI. Achilles routs the Trojans, killing many in the river Xanthus, which fights against him. Only Apollo saves the Trojans from destruction.

Book XXII. Hector waits alone outside the walls of Troy to meet Achilles. At first he flees from him three times about the city but then turns to fight. Abandoned by Apollo he is tricked by Athena and killed by Achilles, who drags his body behind his chariot to the ships, while his family and all Troy lament on the city walls.

Book XXIII. Achilles holds a great funeral for

Patroclus, burning 12 Trojan youths with his body. Games are held in his honor.

Book XXIV. For days Achilles continues to heap indignities on the corpse of Hector, until Zeus warns him through Thetis that the gods will be angered. The Trojan king, PRIAM, begs the body from Achilles, who recognizes in him a fellow-sufferer, and consents. A funeral is held for Hector.

The Trojan war is now known, thanks to the discoveries of SCHLIEMANN and his successors, to have been a historical event of the 13th century B.C., though hardly the glorious contest described in the *Iliad*. About that event there grew up a vast number of legends, which, during the succeeding centuries, were told and retold by the bards in accordance with the traditions of GREEK EPIC POETRY until a certain amount of order was imposed on the many variant strands. It was probably about four centuries after the war that a particular group of these myths were modeled into the dramatic and stylistic unit that became known as the *Iliad*. This work was attributed to an Ionian poet called Homer.

Controversy still rages on whether Homer was a single poet or many, but there is little question of the essential unity of concept that makes the *Iliad* a great poem. In spite of the monotonous similarity between one hand-to-hand combat and the next and in spite of the epithets and other bardic formulas that can apply as well to one hero as to another, the *Iliad* is far more than a vast, highly formalized panorama of battle. Many of the principal figures are considerably individualized; Achilles, Agamemnon, Nestor, Paris, Hector, Thersites, Dolon. There are amusing touches: the ignominious flight of the Greeks when Agamemnon tests their loyalty, Glaucus giving his gold armor in an access of hospitality; there are moving scenes: Hector's infant son frightened by the plume on his father's helmet, Achilles going into battle in spite of his horse's warning, Priam and Achilles weeping together over their mutual loss. All these scenes give the story a human significance that deeply involves the reader in its events. One of the most impressive qualities of the poem is the dramatic impact that the poet achieved by concentrating his attention not on the siege of Troy, but on the tragic results of one man's anger. In spite of Achilles' implacable and (to modern readers) childish resentment of a slight on his honor, he is a genuinely noble figure who knowingly embraces certain death rather than live a long life without glory.

The *Iliad* is written in the poetic line regularly associated with Greek epic, the dactylic hexameter. The dialect of the poem is primarily Ionic, with a strong subsoil of Aeolic, which had been the language of the earlier inhabitants of the part of Ionia from which Homer traditionally came. However, the language of the *Iliad*, or of epic in general, was more a traditional poetic diction than an actual speech.

The world of the Trojan War was very imperfectly remembered in the Homeric poem, written centuries later. Some of the traditional material, inherited and faithfully passed on by Homer, must have been incomprehensible to him: for example, the use of the Mycenaean full-length rectangular shield, which had long been obsolete. As a result, the soldiers in the *Iliad* are sometimes described as bearing the round bronze shield of the poet's day, whereas elsewhere they carry the ancient long shield. Such discrepancies as these have aided scholars in sorting out old and new material in the work. Other anachronisms are the result of deliberate tampering, in order to increase the role of Athens in the war and to diminish that of her enemies. This process may well have taken place in the days of PISISTRATUS, when the recitation of Homer became a regular part of the Panathenaic festival. The fact that certain barbarous customs, such as human sacrifice, torture, and mutilation, scarcely appear in the *Iliad* is probably also due to later expurgation.

I'll Take My Stand: The South and the Agrarian Tradition by Twelve Southerners. See AGRARIANS.

illuminism. A pseudoscientific movement of mystics and visionaries in the 18th century which influenced literature in the 19th century. A wave of mysticism, whose origins date from the Middle Ages, came from Germany, Switzerland, and Sweden, and reached France, forming a freemasonry of illuminists or mystics. At first inspired by Christian doctrines, they sought to live according to the Gospel and to regenerate their souls by direct contact with the divine. They also, however, believed in spiritism, magnetism, alchemy, and magic and professed to invoke the invisible and the arcane. Among the more famous illuminists were Swedenborg, who conversed with the dead; Lavater, a believer in black magic, who thought to contact God by magnetism; Claude de Saint-Martin ("the unknown philosopher"), who sought to hasten the coming of Christ by meditation and prayer; Mesmer; the Comte de Saint-Germain, who pretended to be several hundred years old and to possess the elixir of eternal life; Gall; and the famous Cagliostro, who evoked spirits. An almost instinctive reaction against 18th-century rational philosophies, illuminism under many names (e.g., millenarism, syncretism, neopaganism, pythagorism, theosophy, etc.) influenced some writers of the romantic period. It revived a sense of religious exaltation and mystery and created, or re-created, a need for the infinite, a belief in man's inner nature and a feeling for the mysteries of nature and of love. Among the writers who were influenced in the 19th century were Joseph de Maistre, in his *Soirées de St. Petersbourg;* Charles Fourier; the Christian philosopher Pierre-Simon Ballanche; Charles Nodier, in his fantastic tales; Balzac; and Gérard Nerval.

Illusionists, The (Le Rempart des béguines; 1950). A novel by Françoise MALLET-JORIS about a girl of fifteen who becomes the Lesbian lover of her father's mistress.

Ilmarinen. A smith in the KALEVALA, inventor of the SAMPO. He created one of his wives out of gold and silver and brought her to life, but she was so cold that whatever came near her would probably freeze.

Ilsan the Monk. A boisterous friar in the 13th-century German epic the *Rosengarten* (*The Rose Garden at Worms*). He brings home 52 garlands from an expedition against the garden, and presses their thorns into the flesh of his fellow friars until they consent to pray for the forgiveness of his sins.

Imaginary Cuckold, The. See SGANARELLE.

Imaginary Invalid, The. See MALADE IMAGINAIRE, LE.

imagination. In romantic aesthetic theory, the creative function of the intellect by which separate elements of experience are synthesized in a new whole differing from and transcending any of its original parts. S. T. Coleridge set forth the distinction between it and fancy in his BIOGRAPHIA LITERARIA. He said that imagination was the "shaping and modifying" power while FANCY was the "aggregative and associative" power; imagination "struggles to idealize and unify" while fancy is merely "a mode of Memory emancipated from the order of time and space."

imagism. A theory of poetry adopted about 1910 by a number of English and American poets who followed the leadership of T. E. HULME and Ezra POUND. The movement confessed to several predecessors—e.g., medieval philosophy, the aesthetics of Henri Bergson, and Japanese poetry—but it was primarily a reaction against the stultified form and diction of Georgian verse. It demanded absolute precision in the presentation of the individual image; in metrics it proposed the cadence of "the musical phrase," by which was meant a controlled free verse. Generally speaking, imagist poems were short, pointed observations, often no more than four or five lines in length and usually balanced on a single radically original metaphor.

Pound and Hulme were joined by a number of other poets, notably Hilda DOOLITTLE, Richard ALDINGTON, William Carlos WILLIAMS, and later, Amy LOWELL. They called themselves *Imagistes.* In 1912 Pound edited the first imagist anthology, *Some Imagiste Poets.* Meanwhile, he and the others propagandized vigorously for their beliefs, and Pound, who had become foreign editor of Harriet Monroe's POETRY magazine, published therein a number of manifestoes as well as his own and his friends' poems. Pound later abandoned the movement and with Wyndham Lewis went on to vorticism; though Amy Lowell carried on for a few years, by 1917 or 1918 the movement, as an institutional device, had expired. It had, however, exerted an enormous influence on the development of modern poetry and had provided the break with the immediate past which was necessary before a new literature could appear. Some of imagism's most enduring monuments have been translations such as those made by the English poet Arthur Waley from Chinese poetry and by Francis Densmore from American Indian poetry.

Imbolc. February 1, one of the 4 great feast days of the ancient Celtic year. See SAMAIN; BELTINE; LUGNASAD.

Imhotep. In the mythology of ancient Egypt, the god of learning in general, and a physician later deified as god of medicine. He corresponds to the Greek Asclepius.

Imitation of Christ (De Imitatione Christi; 1426). A religious treatise commonly ascribed to THOMAS A KEMPIS. It has been said that this book has had more influence on Christianity than any other book except the Bible. It is mystical in tone as it explores the inner life and the value of contemplation, yet remarkably clear in its simplicity. Other candidates for the authorship of this work are the brilliant chancellor of the University of Paris, Jean Gerson, and a Jean Gersen, who is only identified as the abbot of Vercelli.

Imlac. In Samuel Johnson's novel RASSELAS the son of a rich merchant of Goiama, a city near the mouth of the Nile. Imlac is a great traveler, philosopher and poet, who accompanies Rasselas on his journey and returns with him to the Happy Valley. Imlac, the moralistic spokesman for Johnson himself, teaches that man should make the most of what order and reason he can find, but that it is folly to stake one's hopes on a facile discovery of divine order in the world.

Immaculate Conception. The belief that the Virgin Mary, from the moment of her conception, was free from the stain of ORIGINAL SIN. The belief has been widespread among Christians as a pious opinion, but has also had many opponents, especially St. Thomas Aquinas in the 12th century. In 1854, in the bull *Ineffabilis Deus,* Pope Pius IX proclaimed it a dogma, making the belief binding for Roman Catholics. The feast is observed on December 8.

Immermann, Karl Lebrecht (1796–1840). German novelist and playwright. His *Die Epigonen* (*The Late-Comers,* 1836) is one of the earliest German social novels. It is set in the Germany of the 1830's when, partly because of the stultifying political conservatism of Austria and Prussia, there was a widespread feeling of having been born too late for the great and exciting ages of humanity. His later novel *Münchhausen* (1838–1839) is quite a daring experiment in form. It consists of two main stories developed in alternating episodes; though connected, they are independent enough to be separated, and one, entitled *Der Oberhof* (*The Upper Manor*), is often printed alone. *Der Oberhof* is a rustic village story reflecting the BIEDERMEIER tendency, whereas the remainder of the novel, a variation on the adventures of Baron Munchhausen, is an urbane document of social criticism. Immermann's best-known drama *Merlin* (1832) is more romantic than either of the novels.

Immoralist, The (L'Immoraliste; 1902). A tale by André GIDE. Michel takes his bride Marceline to North Africa, where he develops tuberculosis and becomes hyperconscious of physical sensations, particularly of his attraction to young Arab boys. Back on his French estate after being cured, he is encouraged by his friend Ménalque to rise above conventional good and evil and give free rein to all his passions. When Marceline falls ill with the tuberculosis she caught while nursing him, he takes her south. He neglects her demands on him more and more, however, in order to keep himself free, since his new doctrine demands that the weak be suppressed if necessary for the preservation of the strong. She dies, and he, guilt-ridden and debilitated by his excesses, tries to justify his conduct to a group of friends.

Imogen. In Shakespeare's CYMBELINE, the daughter of Cymbeline and the tender, faithful wife of Posthumus Leonatus. Attempting to find her husband, who erroneously believes that she has betrayed him, she disguises herself as a page and assumes the name of Fidele.

Impending Crisis of the South, The. See Hinton Rowan HELPER.

Importance of Being Earnest, The (1895). A comedy by Oscar WILDE. It is noted for its witty lines, its clever situations, and its satire on the British nobility and clergy. It deals with the aspirations of Jack Worthing to the hand of Gwendolen Fairfax, daughter of Lady Bracknell. Lady Bracknell objects to the marriage because of the obscurity of Worthing's background; he was found in a handbag in Victoria Station and has no information as to who his parents were. Eventually matters are straightened out by the revelation that Worthing is actually the son of Lady Bracknell's sister and was left in the handbag as an infant through the absentmindedness of a governess. His name is actually Ernest John Moncrieff and he is the brother of his friend Algernon Moncrieff. Worthing is particularly happy that his name turns out to be Ernest since he has created an imaginary younger brother of that name for the benefit of his ward Cecily Cardew (who eventually marries Algernon); this "Ernest," a purportedly rakish fellow whom Worthing had constantly to get out of scrapes, was Worthing's excuse for absenting himself from his country estate, where Cecily lived under the tutelage of Miss Prism, to go to London to see Gwendolen.

impresa. The Italian word for heraldic device or personal motto. Its literal meaning of enterprise suggests its key idea: an expression of the soul of an individual, his goal or chief characteristic. *Imprese,* very popular during the Renaissance and baroque eras in Europe, could be a single pungent phrase or a few lines, accompanied by illustration or used alone. The fact that many were collected and commented upon relates them to the popular EMBLEM BOOKS, which are, however, a somewhat different device. In English literature, an example is Spenser's *Shepheardes Calender,* in which each of the eclogues is prefaced by a motto appropriate to the character involved, as in Colin's *"Anchóra speme"* (Still I hope), inaccurately termed an emblem by Spenser.

impressionism. A term applied originally to the work of a group of 19th-century French painters in Paris. Associated with naturalism, rebelling equally against the academic and romantic schools, the impressionists attempted to convey in painting the impression gained from the direct observation of nature. Concerned principally with the study of light and its refractions, they used only the colors of the spectrum, and did much of their work out of doors, thus continuing the tradition of their forerunners, the BARBIZON SCHOOL. Claude Monet, Renoir, and Alfred Sisley are the most typical representatives of impressionism in its purest form, other important members of the group being Manet, Degas, Pissarro, and Cézanne. In 1874, when the work of several of these artists was rejected by the Salon, they organized their own separate exhibition, but for an entire generation their work was generally ignored or derided. Gradually the group began to disintegrate, each artist developing in his own manner, yet a vast spiritual unity continued to mark their work.

Impressionism had an enormous effect on the subsequent history and development of painting both in and outside of France. Among American-born painters its influence can be seen in the works of James McNeill Whistler, John Singer Sargent, Mary Cassatt, and Maurice Prendergast.

In German literature of the late 19th and early 20th centuries, impressionism denotes the style of writing characterized by extreme precision in language and emphasis on accurately rendering, in all their vagueness and complexity, subjective impressions of unique, individual experiences. Impressionism is therefore most commonly found in lyric poetry, especially that of Liliencron, Dehmel, the early George, Hofmannsthal, and the early Rilke; but it is also clearly an element in Thomas Mann's early prose style, especially in *Buddenbrooks,* and in the dramatic writing of Arthur Schnitzler. The subjectivity of impressionism constitutes a reaction against both the materialism of mid-19th-century philosophy and the programmatic objectivity of naturalism; but naturalism and impressionism still had much in common, particularly the wish to make words more precise and the tendency to concentrate on specific human situations, so that several major writers, including Hauptmann, Holz and Schlaf, were active in both movements. See EXPRESSIONISM.

In music, impressionism stresses sonorous effects for their own sake, i.e., the use of harmonies and instrumental timbres as musical "colors" that blend and change without clear direction or purpose other than the evocation of a general mood. Most impressionistic pieces have literary or pictorial titles; the programmatic implications are generally more important than form or structure. Claude Debussy, Maurice Ravel, Ottorino Respighi (1879–1936), and Charles Tomlinson Griffes (1884–1920) are among those composers associated with impressionism.

Im Westen nichts Neues. See ALL QUIET ON THE WESTERN FRONT.

Inanna or Ininni. A Sumerian goddess of erotic love and of war. She was a prototype of the goddess ISHTAR who, under various names but with remarkably consistent nature, was the chief female goddess of the Near East for 3,000 years. Many of her attributes caused her to be later identified with Artemis, Aphrodite, and other Greek goddesses. The most important of the many myths in which she figures is that of her descent into the underworld, whose queen is her dire sister Ereshkigal. Parallel myths of Ishtar make it likely that this dangerous journey was undertaken to rescue her lover DUMUZI or TAMMUZ. Inanna first orders her herald Ninshubur, if she does not return in three days, to notify the assembled gods. She then goes down into the underworld. As she approaches the queen's palace, her robes and ornaments are removed one by one until she is finally led naked before Ereshkigal. As Inanna had expected, she is killed by glances of death from the queen and the Anunnaki, judges of the underworld, and her body is hung from a stake.

On his mistress's instructions, Ninshubur begs the gods for aid, but only ENKI is willing to help. He sends two creatures to the underworld bearing the food and water of life, which they sprinkle on Inanna's body. Reviving, she returns to earth; but the dead swarm up out of the underworld and accompany her wherever she goes. The remainder of the myth has not been discovered.

In Camera. See NO EXIT.

Incas. A Quechua-speaking people who dominated pre-Columbian Peru. The name *Inca* was also given to their kings, absolute monarchs who were worshiped as descendants of the sun. From their capital at CUZCO, they gradually conquered neighboring regions, especially after 1438 when Pachacuti and his son, Topa Inca, extended Inca rule as far

north as Quito and as far south as northern Chile. See ATAHUALPA; Francisco PIZARRO; GARCILASO DE LA VEGA.

incunabula (Lat., "a cradle"). Works of art or industry of the infant stages in the development of a given field. In the history of bookmaking, books printed before 1500. They are sometimes called cradle books or fifteeners. In this sense the singular "incunabulum" can be used.

Independents. In the English CIVIL WAR, the radical wing of the Parliamentary party. It consisted of Puritans and other independent dissenters who were opposed to the Presbyterian faction. They came to power with the RUMP PARLIAMENT and were the dominant party during the rule of Oliver Cromwell.

Index, The. Official list of books that Roman Catholics are not allowed to read. The Roman Index includes both the *Index Librorum Prohibitorum* and the *Index Expurgatorius.* The former contains a list of such books as are absolutely forbidden to be read by faithful Catholics. The latter contains such books as are forbidden till certain parts are omitted or amended. The lists are made out by a board of cardinals called the *Congregation of the Index.*

Indiana (1832). A novel by George SAND. In this violently romantic work, which served as a springboard to establish George Sand's literary reputation, the events bear a provocative resemblance to those in the author's own life. Its heroine, a Creole named Indiana, abandons her old husband for a fascinating young lover.

Indian Summer (1886). A novel by William Dean HOWELLS. Theodore Colville, a journalist of 40, meets a childhood acquaintance, the widow Mrs. Lina Bowen, in Florence. He becomes engaged to her young ward, Imogene Graham. When Imogene

Incunabula: printing in the 15th century.

admits that she is in love with a younger man, Colville finally recognizes the more mature love he feels for Mrs. Bowen.

Indra. Also called **Mahendra** (from Sans., *maha, great*). The chief god in the Hindu pantheon of lower deities. In Hindu myth, he is also the god of heaven and ruler over thunder, lightning, and storm. He molested Ahalya and was cursed by her husband, the sage Gautama. See AHI; AIRAVATA; MATALI.

In Dubious Battle (1936). A novel by John STEINBECK. It deals with the problem of labor organization among the migrant fruit-pickers in California. Mac, the leading character, is a veteran organizer for the Communist Party who allows nothing to interfere with his service to the cause, not even the murder of his friend Jim Nolan. Another important character is Doc Burton, an uncommitted sympathizer who helps the striking workers.

Industrial Workers of the World. Called the **IWW.** A federation of industrial unions established at Chicago in 1905. Dedicated to the overthrow of capitalism by direct means, it called general strikes and resorted to sabotage. Many "wobblies," as members were called, refused to fight in World War I, claiming that it was a struggle between capitalists. The IWW became increasingly unpopular during the war, when ultrapatriotic feeling swept the U.S. In 1918 the U.S. government arrested, tried, and convicted its leaders, and by 1925 its influence had ended.

Inez, Donna. In Byron's poem DON JUAN, the mother of Juan. After worrying her husband, Don José, to death by her prudery and want of sympathy, Donna Inez endeavors to raise Juan by the strictest rules of propriety and make him a model of all the virtues. Unfortunately, he is seduced by her best friend, the equally proper and intellectual Donna Julia.

infantes de Lara, Cantar de los siete. See LARA, CANTAR DE LOS SIETE INFANTES DE.

Infant Phenomenon, The. The stage name of the allegedly 10-year-old Ninetta Crummles in Charles Dickens' NICHOLAS NICKLEBY. Actually, she is at least 15 and her low stature results from being kept up late every night and "an unlimited allowance of gin and water."

Infernal Machine, The (La Machine infernale; 1934). A tragedy by Jean COCTEAU. It uses the story of Oedipus as an example of a cosmic joke, "one of the most perfect machines constructed by the infernal gods for the mathematical annihilation of a mortal." Oedipus, who possesses the intuitive, imaginative qualities of Cocteau's ideal poet figure, is brutally crushed by a hostile external world.

Inferno (Hell). Part I of the DIVINE COMEDY by DANTE. Vergil conducts Dante through the region of damnation, where the souls suffer eternal punishments appropriate to their sins. In the anteroom are those who did nothing in life, neither good nor evil. Then follow nine levels of Hell, descending conically into the earth. The first is Limbo, where are the blameless but unbaptized spirits, including the great men of pagan antiquity. The circles of the sins of incontinence, least terribly punished, include the carnal sinners (see PAOLO AND FRANCESCA), the gluttons, the misers and the spendthrifts, the wrathful and the sullen. With the sixth circle, that of the

heretics, begin the horrible torments of the City of Dis, generally fiery. The seventh circle contains the violent against others (murderers), against self (suicides), and against God and Nature (blasphemers, perverts, and the like). The eighth level includes 10 categories of the fraudulent (seducers, sorcerers, thieves, hypocrites, and various kinds of liars and evil counselors). The most odious of the fraudulent, the traitors, are frozen in the ice of the ninth circle: the betrayers of their own relatives or country (see UGOLINO) and, at the very center of the earth, Lucifer with three heads gnawing on Brutus and Cassius, the betrayers of Julius Caesar, and Judas Iscariot, the betrayer of Jesus Christ. Turning around at Lucifer's waist, Dante and Vergil emerge through a tunnel into the opposite hemisphere, which is covered with water, to approach the island of the mountain of Purgatory.

Informer, The (1925). A novel by Liam O'FLAHERTY. It is a psychological melodrama describing the last day of Gypo Nolan, a destitute Irish revolutionary who turned a comrade in to the police for 20 pounds.

Inge, William (1913–   ). American playwright. He is known for his dramas dealing with average people of the Midwest. His first play, *Farther Off from Heaven* (1947), was produced by Margo Jones in her Dallas theater. *Come Back Little Sheba* (1950) won the George Jean Nathan and the Theatre Time awards; *Picnic* (1953) won the Pulitzer Prize and was later made into a movie. *Bus Stop* (1955) was a successful play and was also later made into a movie, as was *The Dark at the Top of the Stairs* (1957). *A Loss of Roses* was produced in 1960. Inge is also the author of a successful screenplay, *Splendor in the Grass* (1961).

Ingemann, Bernard Severin (1789–1862). Danish poet and novelist. Ingemann was the author of a series of popular historical novels set in the Danish middle ages. A schoolteacher in the old town of Sorø, he acquired a lively sense of the past and a love for the ancient chivalric values. Among his novels are *Valdemar Seier (Waldemar, surnamed Seir, or the Victorious,* 1826), *Erik Menveds Barndom (The Childhood of King Eric Menved,* 1828) and *Kong Erik og de Fredløse (King Eric and the Outlaws,* 1833). *Morgensange for Børn* (1837) and *Morgen og Aften sange* (1839) are collections of simple delicate lyrics that express a naïve vision of the world.

Ingénu, L' (1767). A satiric romance by VOLTAIRE. The hero, l'Ingénu, returns to France after having been brought up by the primitive Huron Indians in Canada. His simple, frank, and naturally good qualities are violently contrasted by Voltaire with the conventional mores and religious convictions of the civilized world. The story is a criticism of highly placed officials during Louis XV's time, a protest of the abuse of power, and a satire of the absurdities of society's conventions. See NOBLE SAVAGE.

Ingersoll, Robert G[reen] (1833–1899). American lawyer, public official, and orator. He was known as "the Great Agnostic" for his defense of free-thinking in religious matters. An active Republican, he became a sought-after orator when he eloquently nominated James G. BLAINE for the presidency (1876). Influenced by Voltaire and Paine, Ingersoll is known for such aphorisms as these: "Many people think they have religion when they are merely troubled with dyspepsia"; "With soap, baptism is a good thing"; and "An honest God is the noblest work of man." Among Ingersoll's books are *The Gods* (1872), *Some Mistakes of Moses* (1879), and *Why I Am an Agnostic* (1896). After his death appeared *The Works of Robert G. Ingersoll* (12 v., 1900). See BEN-HUR.

Ingmars, the. A Swedish family whose struggles and adventures are narrated in the short stories that comprise Selma Lagerlöf's JERUSALEM.

Ingres, Jean Auguste Dominique (1780–1867). French painter. The acknowledged leader of the classical school, he painted many religious, historical, and mythological subjects. These are less appreciated today than his portraits, but he is noted for the strong, refined purity of his drawing and the abstract grace of his form and line.

Iniquity, the. See VICE, THE.

In Memoriam (Lat., "in memory of"). A long poem written between the years 1833 and 1850 by Alfred TENNYSON, in memory of his friend Arthur HALLAM, who died in 1833. It is considered one of the great English elegies and, on the whole, the poet's most impressive longer work. The poem not only deals with Hallam's death and Tennyson's enduring sense of loss, but also attempts to grapple with many of the intellectual and religious problems of the mid-19th century: the decline of faith, the rise of skepticism and scientific materialism.

inner light. Spiritual illumination. Specifically, in QUAKER doctrine, the term designates a divine presence in the soul of every man, the light of Christ that gives moral guidance and religious and spiritual assurance to all who are willing to receive it.

Inner Temple and Middle Temple. See INNS OF COURT.

Innes, Hammond. Pen name of **Ralph Hammond-Innes** (1913–   ). English novelist, writer of thrillers with backgrounds marked by unusual accuracy of detail. Among his works are *The White South* (1949), *Naked Land* (1954), *Land God Gave to Cain* (1958), *Doomed Oasis* (1960), and *Harvest of Journeys* (1960), an autobiography.

Innes, Michael. The pen name under which J. I. M. STEWART writes his detective stories.

Inness, George (1825–1894). American landscape painter. The English landscapists and the BARBIZON SCHOOL influenced his portrayal of familiar landscapes in their varying moods. In his last years he allowed an increasing poetic vagueness to blur the delicately toned landscapes he created from memory.

Innocents, Massacre of the. The slaughter of the male children of Bethlehem "from two years old and under," when Jesus was born (Matt. 2:16). This was done at the command of Herod the Great in order to cut off "the babe" who was destined to become "King of the Jews." The Feast of the Holy Innocents commemorating this event is December 28.

In British parliamentary phraseology, the phrase denotes the withdrawal of the bills which there has not been time to consider and pass before the close of the session.

Innocents Abroad, The, or, The New Pilgrim's Progress (1869). A travel book by Mark TWAIN. It is based on a series of letters he wrote from Europe as a roving correspondent. The book burlesques the sentimental travel book popular in the mid-19th century. Admiring the leisure of Europeans, Clemens criticized some American manners.

Innocent Voyage, The. See HIGH WIND IN JAMAICA.

Innommable, L'. See UNNAMABLE, THE.

Inns of Court. The four legal societies that have the exclusive right of calling candidates to the English bar, and maintain instruction and examination for that purpose. They are all in London, and are the Inner Temple, the Middle Temple, Lincoln's Inn, and Gray's Inn. Each consists of a legal faculty governed by a board of "benchers."

Ino. In Greek mythology, a daughter of Cadmus and consort of ATHAMAS, by whom she had two sons, Learchus and Melicertes. Ino's jealousy drove the children of Athamas' first wife Nephele to the sacrificial altar, but they were saved by the GOLDEN FLEECE. Because Ino and Athamas helped Zeus to save the infant Dionysus from Hera's wrath, Hera revenged herself by driving them mad. Athamas killed Learchus, mistaking him for a stag; Ino escaped with Melicertes and flung herself into the sea, but Zeus, grateful because she had protected Dionysus, transformed her into the sea goddess Leucothea. He transformed Melicertes into the sea god Palaemon, and, under those names, both watch over storm-tossed sailors.

In Our Time (1924). A collection of short stories by Ernest HEMINGWAY. First published in France and the following year in the U.S., many of the stories deal with the development of young Nick Adams, who bears some resemblance to the author himself. In *Indian Camp*, Nick is introduced to the violence of life when he accompanies his doctor father; *Big Two-Hearted River* shows his mental state after he has been wounded in World War I. The stories alternate with imagistic "chapters" that give glimpses of the war and of bullfighting. See KILLERS, THE.

In Parenthesis (1937). A book by David JONES. It is a modernistic, poetic account of infantry life in the First World War. Realistic description is mixed with Celtic mythology, Arthurian legend, and Christian allusion.

In Praise of Johnny Appleseed (1921). A poem by Vachel LINDSAY. It follows the career of John Chapman over the Appalachians, his wanderings among the Indians and in the wilderness, and his vigorous old age.

Inquisition. A court commonly called the Holy Office. It was instituted to inquire into offenses against the Roman Catholic religion, and fully established by Gregory IX in 1235. Torture, as a means of extracting recantations or evidence, was first authorized by Pope Innocent IV in 1252, and those found guilty were handed over to the secular arm to be dealt with according to the secular laws of the land. This was followed by the founding of the *Congregation of the Inquisition* in Rome, 1542. The Inquisition was only once introduced into England (viz., at the trials of the Templars, who were suppressed in 1308); it was most active in southern Europe, and flourished sporadically in Spain until the 19th century. In the Provençal region of France, where the Inquisition fostered the rise of militant monastic orders designed to stamp out mass heretic movements, the Dominican order played a crucial role in the Albigensian Crusade; the Inquisition was suppressed in France in 1772.

Inquisition, Spanish. A tribunal for suppressing heresy in Spain, established by Pope Sixtus IV in 1478 at the request of Ferdinand and Isabella. The first Inquisitor-General was Tomás de Torquemada (c. 1420–1498), a Dominican monk whose name has become a byword for cruelty and severity.

Though nominally under papal control, the Inquisition was actually an agency of the crown, which often used it for political purposes. The principal victims of the Inquisition in Spain were the converted Muslims and Jews, known respectively as *Moriscos* and *Marranos*. It also investigated crimes against morality, such as polygamy and rape. Its procedures were secret, and suspects were not told the identity of their accusers; torture was sometimes used. Penalties, which were announced at solemn public gatherings called *autos de fé*, ranged from reprimand and warning to "relaxation," i.e., being delivered to the secular authorities to be burned at the stake. The Inquisition was suppressed in 1808 and its successor, the Tribunal of the Faith, was abolished in 1834.

Insarov. The hero of Ivan Turgenev's novel, ON THE EVE. A Bulgarian revolutionary who lives only to free his country from Turkish oppression, the dedicated Insarov inspires love in the young Russian Elena STAKHOVA.

inscape. A term coined by the poet Gerard Manley HOPKINS. Usually applied to an object or scene in nature, it means essential, intrinsic quality and oneness that is composed of a number of separate characteristics. *Instress* is the force that creates and maintains *inscape*.

Inscription for the Entrance to a Wood (1817). A poem by William Cullen BRYANT. The poet finds solace in the woods for the guilt and misery of the world.

Inspector General, The (Revizor; 1836). A comic drama by Nikolai GOGOL. It is regarded as one of the best plays in Russian dramaturgy. The action revolves about a case of mistaken identity. The central character Khlestakov, a run-of-the-mill civil servant from St. Petersburg, is stranded in a small provincial town. The corrupt officials of the town, hearing that a government inspector is on the way there, convince themselves that Khlestakov is the man. Khlestakov quickly catches on and goes along with the error, bragging of his high connections in the capital, taking bribes, and wooing the mayor's daughter and wife. He is unmasked when a gloating letter he has written to a friend in St. Petersburg is read by the inquisitive postmaster, but before he is found out, Khlestakov has prudently left town. While the town officials are fuming about the ruse, the real inspector general arrives.

The play was taken as a social satire at the time of its production and that view has remained the standard one in Russian criticism. There are, however, many fantastic aspects to the comedy, particularly in Khlestakov's inane chattering.

Instauratio Magna (*Lat.,* "great renewal"). A projected work by Francis BACON, designed to be a comprehensive survey of the principles, methods, and accomplishments of the "new philosophy," or experimental science. Only two of six parts were

completed: THE ADVANCEMENT OF LEARNING and NOVUM ORGANUM.

Institute of France (Institut de France). A national French society, established in 1795 by the Republican Convention "to advance the sciences and arts of research . . . and to prosecute those scientific and literary labors which shall have for their end general utility and the glory of the republic." The organization includes five academies: L'ACADÉMIE FRANÇAISE, *L'Académie des Inscriptions et Belles-Lettres, L'Académie des Sciences, L'Académie des Beaux Arts,* and *L'Académie des Sciences Morales et Politiques.*

Institutes of the Christian Religion (Institution de la religion chrétienne; 1536). The principal work of John CALVIN. It first appeared in Latin in 1536, and a French translation, made by Calvin himself, was published in 1541. Designed as a reply to attacks on Protestantism and as a guide to Scripture, the work states, with passionate conviction, the essential doctrines of the new religion.

Insulted and Injured, The (Unizhennye i oskorblyonnye; 1861). A novel by Feodor DosTOEVSKI. The first of his full-length novels, it is also the first of his works clearly to express Dostoevski's characteristic ideas about the purifying function of suffering. The book has a conventional, melodramatic plot, with Ivan Petrovich (Vanya), who is in love with Natasha Ikhmeneva, trying to aid her in her wooing of Alyosha Valkovski. Ivan, a young writer who bears some resemblance to the young Dostoevski, engages in philosophical duels with the cynical Prince Valkovski, Alyosha's father, an early sketch of the "predatory type" more fully developed in SVIDRIGAILOV in *Crime and Punishment* and STAVROGIN in *The Possessed.*

The sentimental atmosphere of the novel is heightened by the presence of a young girl, Nelly. Taken obviously from Dickens, she undergoes harrowing experiences at the hands of the prince before she is rescued.

interior monologue. See STREAM OF CONSCIOUSNESS.

interlude. A form of dramatic entertainment, originating during the reign of Henry VIII of England and popular at the Tudor court. The exact nature of the interlude is not known, but it is believed to have originated as a brief skit between the courses of a banquet. Court interludes, of which John HEYWOOD was the outstanding author, were usually lively and realistic and devoted chiefly to entertainment. Heywood's THE FOUR P's is a typical example. There were also educational interludes, didactically teaching an edifying moral; these were usually written in Latin, using type characters and situations, and were performed at public schools, such as Eton. The interlude is considered a transitional form between the miracle plays and MORALITY PLAYS of the Middle Ages and fully developed Elizabethan drama.

International. The name of 3 successive international associations, or congresses, designed to unite the working classes of all nations and promote Marxist socialism.

First International. The International Working Men's Association was founded in London in 1864 under the leadership of Karl MARX and Friedrich Engels. It had some success for the next five years, lending its support to aggrieved workers in England and in Europe, but, when the Russian anarchist Bakunin joined in 1869, a rift opened up between his followers and the less radical Marxists. Bakunin's group was expelled in 1872, but the organization lost the support of the nationalistic trade unions being formed at this time, and the last congress was held in Philadelphia in 1876.

Second International. Formed in 1889, the Second International followed the same Marxist theories as the First. After repeated attempts to avoid war, the movement lost most of its force when the First World War broke out and most of the members supported the war as national subjects, instead of opposing it as internationalists.

Third International. Also called the *Communist International* or *Comintern.* Established in Russia in 1919 as a result of the revolution, this International was formed to help spread Communist revolution throughout the world. The hostility of the Communists to the more moderate Socialists in the rest of Europe led to a revival of the Second International in the 1930's to provide a united Socialist front. The Third International was dissolved in 1943 by Stalin.

A so-called Second-and-a-half International was formed in Vienna in 1919; its attempt to reconcile the Socialists and Communists ended in total failure in 1922. Trotsky formed a Fourth, or Anti-Comintern, International in 1937 from his exile in Mexico, but it had little influence.

In the American Grain (1925). A volume of essays by William Carlos WILLIAMS. Attempting to discover the essential qualities of the American character, it includes sketches of such figures as Columbus, Poe, and Franklin, but it stresses minor figures of a less heroic nature. The book shares Van Wyck Brooks's search for a "usable past," and was used by Hart Crane in his attempt to create the myth of America in THE BRIDGE.

In the Midst of Life (1891). A collection of 26 stories by Ambrose BIERCE. In these tales of horror, Bierce implies that life is subject to accident and coincidence. The stories have twist endings rarely surpassed in literature. Ten of the tales deal with soldiers, and in every case, the young men die. Bierce's characters are generally abstractions, interesting not for their individuality but for their tragic fate. The mood of horror, established by realistic detail, is further exaggerated by the author's sardonic humor. Among the most famous of the stories are *An Occurrence at Owl Creek Bridge, A Horseman in the Sky, The Man and the Snake,* and *The Eyes of the Panther.*

In the Ravine (V ovrage; 1900). A long story by Anton CHEKHOV. A study of the brutal lives of the peasantry in a small provincial town, this work has long been considered one of Chekhov's best prose pieces. On its publication, it was unanimously acclaimed one of the outstanding works of Russian literature. The story's central characters are the shopkeeper Tzybukin, his two sons, and their wives, Aksinya and Lipa. Aksinya is a rapacious creature who eventually takes over the household and shop, drives out the old man, and causes the death of Lipa's small son.

Intruder in the Dust (1948). A novel by William FAULKNER. Lucas BEAUCHAMP, an aging Negro who has long nettled the townsfolk of Jefferson by his refusal to adopt the Negro's traditionally servile attitude, is wrongfully accused of murdering a white man and is threatened with violent death at the hands of a mob. Through the efforts of 16-year-old Chick MALLISON, Aleck Sander, Chick's Negro friend, and 70-year-old Miss Eunice Habersham, Lucas' innocence is proved and the real murderer captured. Because of his relationship with Lucas, Chick comes into manhood able to recognize other human beings as individuals, regardless of their color.

Invictus (*Lat.,* unconquered). The title of a well-known poem (usually deplored by critics) written in a tuberculosis hospital, by William Ernest HENLEY. Its last lines read:

> It matters not how strait the gate
> How charged with punishment the scroll,
> I am the master of my fate,
> I am the captain of my soul.

Invincibles, the Irish. An Irish secret society. It was founded in Dublin in 1881 with the object of doing away with the English tyranny. Members of this society were responsible for the Phoenix Park murders in 1882.

Invisible Man (1952). A novel by Ralph ELLISON. This unusual first novel is the record of a Negro boy's progression from youthful affirmation to a sense of total rejection; his final invisibility—that is, his loss of social identity—gives him a point of view often compared with that of the hero of Dostoevski's *Notes from the Underground.* Ellison's unnamed protagonist at first has a rather unrealistic trust in the motives of others. He is dismissed from a Negro college for showing one of the founders how Negroes actually live in the South. In New York City he plays a political role for the Communists, until he realizes that they are merely using him as a symbol of the Negro; as a person he is as invisible to them as to everyone else. During a surrealistic Harlem riot, he comes to the realization that to affirm his identity he would have to contend with both white people and the leaders of his own race.

Io. In Greek mythology, a priestess of Hera. Zeus seduced her, then transformed her into a cow to save her from Hera's wrath. Hera, however, sent a gadfly which drove Io over Greece and much of Asia. In Egypt she finally regained human form and gave birth to twins, Belus and Agenor, who fathered many dynasties of Greece, Crete, and Asia Minor. She appears in Aeschylus' PROMETHEUS BOUND.

Iolanthe; or, The Peer and the Peri (1882). An opera by GILBERT AND SULLIVAN. Iolanthe is a fairy banished because she married a mortal. Her son, Strephon, is a fairy down to the waist, but his legs are mortal. This leads to complications when he wishes to marry Phyllis, a shepherdess. The opera satirizes the House of Lords and the Courts of Chancery.

Iolcus or Iolcos (Iolkos). A city in Thessaly, the modern Volo, point of embarkation of the ARGONAUTS.

Ion (418 B.C.). A drama by Euripides. It treats the legend of Ion, son of Creusa and Apollo. He ultimately became king of Athens and ancestor of the Ionian race. It is one of Euripides' most dramatic plays. It has been interpreted by some as a skeptical drama that questioned the sanctity of Apollo and the honesty of his Delphic oracle.

Ionesco, Eugène (1912–   ). Romanian-born French dramatist of the ABSURD school. His earlier works are characterized by deliberate *non sequiturs,* the logic of nightmares, and strange metamorphoses. The stage is cluttered with inanimate or rotting things that proliferate until any remnant of the human is pathetically stifled. Nevertheless, these grimly grotesque farces remain essentially comic, because Ionesco is essentially sympathetic to the human attempt, however pitifully inadequate, at communication and love. THE BALD SOPRANO, *The Lesson* (1950), *Jack, or the Submission* (1950), THE CHAIRS, *Victims of Duty* (1952), and *Amedée* (1953) are all tragicomic in tone. Although the compassionate satire and the atmosphere of the fantastic remain, with *The Killer* (*Tueur sans gages;* 1958), Ionesco's plays begin to employ a more explicit symbolic technique and a more straightforward plot line. THE RHINOCEROS is almost a conventional allegory.

Iphiclus (Iphiklos). See MELAMPUS.

Iphigenia (Iphigeneia). In Greek mythology, the eldest child of Agamemnon and Clytemnestra. She was sacrificed by her father in order to gain favorable winds for the Greek fleet on its way to Troy (see IPHIGENIA IN AULIS). Her mother used this act as an excuse for murdering Agamemnon on his return. Their son Orestes, driven mad after killing Clytemnestra, went to the savage land of Tauris and there found his sister, whom Artemis had spirited away from her funeral pyre. Iphigenia saved Orestes and his friend, Pylades, and sailed away with them (see IPHIGENIA IN TAURIS).

Iphigenia in Aulis (Iphigeneia he en Aulidi; c. 405 B.C.). A tragedy by EURIPIDES. The seer Calchas has predicted that only the sacrifice of Iphigenia will save the Greeks from remaining trapped in the harbor at Aulis by unfavorable winds. Agamemnon has already sent for his daughter, pretending that she is to marry Achilles. He regrets his decision, but is dissuaded from altering it by the scorn of Menelaus. When Iphigenia arrives, with her mother Clytemnestra and her brother Orestes, even Menelaus relents, but Agamemnon orders the sacrifice, sure that Odysseus will force his hand in any case. Clytemnestra begs her husband to free his daughter, and Achilles, who has known nothing of the plot, offers to save her, but Iphigenia agrees to sacrifice herself for the Greeks.

The play was finished by Euripides' son after the playwright's death. An ending in which Iphigenia is saved when Artemis carries her off and substitutes a deer on the altar is thought to be a later interpolation. An altered version of this story was made into an opera by Gluck, *Iphigénie en Aulide* (1772).

Iphigenia in Tauris (Iphigeneia he en Taurois; c. 414–412 B.C.). A tragedy by EURIPIDES. After murdering his mother Clytemnestra (see ORESTEIA), ORESTES has been pursued by the Furies and Apollo has said he will be cured of madness only if he rescues the statue of Artemis from the savage inhabitants of Tauris (the Crimea), who kill all Greeks they find in their country. With his faithful friend Pylades, Orestes arrives in Tauris. The two are promptly

captured and are brought to the high priestess to be ritually prepared for their sacrifice. The priestess is Iphigenia, who had been transported to Tauris by Artemis (see IPHIGENIA IN AULIS). In a moving scene, she and Orestes recognize each other. After each of the friends has offered to die for the other, she manages by a ruse to save both and escape with them in a boat. They are driven back by the wind, but saved when Athena appears and orders Thoas, the Taurian king, to let them leave. A version of this story was made into an opera by Gluck, *Iphigénie en Tauride* (1779).

Iphigenia in Tauris (Iphigenie auf Tauris; prose version, 1779; final version in verse, 1787). A play by Johann Wolfgang von GOETHE after Euripides' play of the same title. Iphigenia, whom her father Agamemnon had wished to sacrifice in order to get good weather for the Greeks' voyage to Troy, has been snatched away by Artemis and left in Tauris as a priestess. Her brother Orestes, tormented by the Furies, then comes unwittingly to Tauris, is joyfully reunited with his sister, and both sail home. Goethe, however, does away with Euripides' *deus ex machina* and makes the play's resolution arise from what he later called pure humanity, the inner core of emotional sympathy that unites men, transcends all boundaries of nationality or religion, and ultimately assuages all guilt. See WEIMAR CLASSICISM; Charlotte von STEIN.

Iphigénie en Aulide (1679). A tragedy by Jean RACINE. Its material is freely drawn from the play by Euripides. An oracle declares that only the sacrifice of Iphigénie can release the Greek fleet from Aulis, where unfavorable winds have stranded it. Priests force Agamemnon to send his daughter word that Achilles, her betrothed, desires her at Aulis for an immediate marriage. Achilles is incensed to learn of the ruse, but Iphigénie obediently awaits her fate. Remorseful, Agamemnon arranges for his daughter to escape, but the slave-girl ERIPHILE (a character invented by Racine), who loves Achilles, reveals the plan. The priest Calchas declares Eriphile the victim the gods require, for her name at birth was Iphigénie. Eriphile kills herself on the altar, and Iphigénie is spared.

I.R.A. See IRISH REPUBLICAN ARMY.

Iras. In Shakespeare's ANTONY AND CLEOPATRA, the second lady-in-waiting to Cleopatra. She dies shortly before her mistress.

Ireland, William Henry (1777–1835). English forger of Shakespearean manuscripts and documents. His own blank verse play, *Vortigern and Rowena,* which he attributed to Shakespeare, was a complete failure on the stage (1796) and led to the exposure of the forgeries, and shortly thereafter Ireland wrote *An Authentic Account of the Shaksperian MSS.* He also published several ballads, poems, novels, memoirs, and translations.

I Remember Mama (1944). A play by John VAN DRUTEN. A dramatization of Kathryn Forbes' *Mamma's Bank Account* (1943), it is the amusing and tender story of a Norwegian mother and father raising their children in America in the early days of the 20th century. The situation later became the basis of a successful television serial starring Peggy Wood.

Irena. See FAERIE QUEENE, THE.

Irene. In John Galsworthy's FORSYTE SAGA, the sensitive, passionate heroine. Wife of Soames Forsyte, she falls in love with Philip Bosinney, is divorced, and marries Young Jolyon Forsyte.

Ireton, Henry (1611–1651). English general and statesman. The husband of Oliver Cromwell's daughter Bridget, he was a cavalry commander at the battle of Naseby. He became a member of Parliament in 1645 and was one of the judges at the trial of King Charles I.

Iriarte, Tomás de (1750–1791). Spanish fabulist and poet. His best-known work is the collection of fables, 76 in all, entitled *Fábulas literarias* (1782), which satirizes contemporary literature in a series of apologues including *El burro flautista* and *El oso y el mono.* Iriarte also completed a verse translation of Horace.

Iris. The Greek goddess of the rainbow, or the rainbow itself. In classic mythology, she is called the messenger of the gods when they intended discord, and the rainbow is the bridge or road let down from heaven for her accommodation. When the gods meant peace they sent Hermes.

Irish Renaissance. A term used to describe the outburst of creative activity at the turn of the last century, which grew out of the attempt to awaken the Irish people to the wealth and value of their native culture. The movement, which had been developing very slowly in the latter half of the 19th century, achieved its major impetus from the political martyrdom of the Irish leader Charles Stewart Parnell, an event which caused many thoughtful Irishmen to abandon the attempt to achieve a national identity within an English framework. The Gaelic culture with which the movement identified itself had been, prior to the English invasion in the 12th century, among the richest and most advanced in Europe, particularly distinguished by the enormous prestige with which it invested the tribal bard or storyteller.

The movement itself had two major developments: the activities of the Gaelic League, an organization founded in 1893 by Douglas Hyde to restore Gaelic as the official language of Ireland; and the formation of the Irish National Theatre Society in 1901, out of which grew the famous Abbey Theatre Company. The leading figures of this latter movement were William Butler Yeats, Edward Martyn (1859–1927), George Moore, Lady Gregory, and the actors William (1872–1947) and Frank (1870–1931) Fay. The Abbey Theatre soon became (and remained for the next 30 years) a storm center, the result of the brilliant but, at the time, controversial plays of Yeats, John M. Synge and Sean O'Casey. Riots and vigorous protestations greeted the productions of Synge's *Playboy of the Western World,* Yeats's *Countess Cathleen* and O'Casey's *The Plough and the Stars* (1926) and *Juno and the Paycock.* Despite the protests at home, the Abbey soon developed an international reputation, and the players, featuring such performers as Sara Allgood (1883–1950) and Barry Fitzgerald (1888–1961) enjoyed their greatest success, ironically enough, on tour in England. Other significant Abbey dramatists were Padraic Colum, Lennox Robinson, and Paul Vincent Carroll. Although the Abbey's greatest days are now past, its impact on the modern theatre is still felt and its legacy may be seen in the work of two recent Irish

dramatists of note, Brendan Behan and Samuel Beckett.

In nondramatic literature, the revival was sparked by the poetry of Yeats and A.E., the fanciful and charming re-creations of Irish legends in the novels and poems of James Stephens, the more realistic treatment of contemporary life in the novels and short stories of Liam O'Flaherty, Sean O'Faolain and Frank O'Connor. The irony that marks so much of the Irish Renaissance—its great achievement lies, not in the restoration of Irish culture, but in the immeasurable enrichment of English literature—is nowhere so pronounced as in one of its greatest products: James Joyce, who so steadfastly refused to be associated with the revival and yet whose work is saturated with Irish life.

Irish Republican Army (I.R.A.). A secret organization founded to work for Irish independence from England. It continued to exist even after the Republic of Ireland was established in 1937.

Iroldo. A character in Boiardo's ORLANDO INNAMORATO whose friend Prasildo falls in love with his wife Tisbina. He generously gives her up and leaves, but later Prasildo rescues him and they fight together.

Iron, Ralph. See Olive SCHREINER.

iron crown of Lombardy. The crown of the ancient Longobardic kings. It was used at the coronation of Agilulph, king of Lombardy, in 591, and among others who have since been crowned with it are Charlemagne, as king of Italy (774); Henry of Luxemburg (the emperor Henry VII), as king of Lombardy (1311); Frederick IV (1452); and Charles V (1530). In 1805, Napoleon put it on his head by his own hand.

In 1866, at the conclusion of peace, the iron crown was given up by Austria to Italy and was replaced in the cathedral at Monza, where Charlemagne had been crowned, and whence it had been taken in 1859. It is so called from the fact that there is within it a narrow band of iron, said to have been beaten out of one of the nails used at the Crucifixion. According to tradition, the nail was given to Constantine by his mother, St. Helena, who discovered the true cross. The outer circlet is of beaten gold, and set with precious stones.

Iron Heel, The (1907). A novel by Jack LONDON. Prophetically, it describes events from 1912 to 1918 when a fascistic organization, the Iron Heel, seizes power in the U.S. The hero is Ernest Everhard, a socialist who fights the Iron Heel.

Iron in the Soul. See ROADS TO FREEDOM, THE.

Iron Mask, Man in the. See MAN IN THE IRON MASK.

Ironsides. A name given to the cavalry troops that fought under Oliver Cromwell in the English Civil War, especially after the battle of Marston Moor (1644). Earlier, the name was applied only to a famous cavalry regiment led by Cromwell.

irony. In rhetoric, a deliberate dissembling for effect or to intensify meaning. An example is subtle sarcasm or language meant to be understood only by the initiated. Irony often takes the form of pretended ignorance as a device to lead on and eventually to confound an opponent, as in Socratic irony. Dramatic irony is the theatrical device of making a speaker utter words which have a hidden meaning intelligible to the audience but of which he himself is unconscious, as when Oedipus, in Sophocles' *Oedipus Tyrannus,* calls down curses upon the slayer of Laius, not knowing that they will fall upon his own head. In life, an occurrence or series of occurrences are said to be ironical that are quite the reverse of what might have been expected, as if fate had intended to be ironical in the rhetorical sense; "the irony of fate" expresses this meaning more explicitly.

irony, romantic. A literary technique first specifically defined by Friedrich SCHLEGEL. Romantic irony is basically the introduction of paradox into a literary work, as, for example, when the hero of a novel suddenly announces that the author of the novel has died and that he, the hero, will carry on the work, a situation that occurs in Brentano's *Godwi* (1800–1801). Another common ironic technique is for statements *about* a literary work to be included *within* the work. Examples of this are Tieck's play *Puss in Boots* (*Der gestiefelte Kater,* pub. 1797), in which a fictitious audience is put on the stage to criticize the play, and Schlegel's own novel *Lucinde* (1799), which embodies a theory of the novel.

Iroquois League. A confederacy of Iroquoian-speaking Indian tribes organized about 1570 in what is now western New York. The members of the league, who called themselves "People of the Long House" because they dwelt together in harmony, were the Mohawks, Oneidas, Onondagas, Cayugas, Senecas (and later the Tuscaroras). During the 17th century they warred against the French and other Indian tribes. Most of the Iroquois supported England in the American Revolution, and many settled in Canada after peace was concluded. Hiawatha, the Mohawk chief whose name was immortalized in Longfellow's *Song Of Hiawatha* (1855), played an important part in creating the League.

Irus (Iros). In Greek legend, the beggar of Ithaca. He ran errands for Penelope's suitors. When Odysseus returned home dressed as a beggar, Irus challenged him, and Odysseus broke his jaw with a blow. (See ODYSSEY.)

Irving, Sir Henry (1838–1905). English actor. He played successfully various roles and in 1874, with his performance of Hamlet, won real distinction. He took over the management of the Lyceum Theatre in 1878 and made many tours to the U.S. with his company, which included Ellen TERRY. He was the first actor to be knighted (1895), and was buried in Westminster Abbey.

Irving, Washington (1783–1859). American essayist, biographer, and historian. Although he prepared to be a lawyer, Irving was physically delicate, and his indulgent family allowed him to lead the life of a man of letters. His first published writing was a series of newspaper sketches appearing under the pseudonym of Jonathan Oldstyle, Gent. In 1807, in collaboration with his brother William, and James Kirk Paulding, Irving wrote the SALMAGUNDI papers; these humorous and satirical pieces modeled on Addison brought him local renown in New York. His first book, A HISTORY OF NEW YORK FROM THE BEGINNING OF THE WORLD TO THE END OF THE DUTCH DYNASTY, supposedly by Diedrich Knickerbocker, created the character of the phlegmatic Dutchman. A quaint and humorous figure, Knickerbocker is a familiar byword, particularly in New York.

After the death of his fiancée, Irving sailed for Europe, where he remained for 17 years. His best-known book, THE SKETCH BOOK OF GEOFFREY CRAYON, GENT., was published there in 1820, followed by BRACEBRIDGE HALL and TALES OF A TRAVELLER. For financial reasons, Irving accepted a position in the U.S. embassy in Madrid. Fascinated by Spain, he enthusiastically wrote four works: HISTORY OF THE LIFE AND VOYAGES OF COLUMBUS, *The Conquest of Granada* (1829), *Companions of Columbus* (1831), and THE LEGENDS OF THE ALHAMBRA. He returned home, and journeyed across the prairies, recording his trip three years later in A TOUR ON THE PRAIRIES. He contracted with John Jacob Astor to write the history of ASTORIA and produced a sequel, *The Adventures of* CAPTAIN BONNEVILLE. From 1842 to 1846 Irving served as U.S. minister to Spain. He then retired to Sunnyside, his home in Tarrytown, N.Y. As an old man, he wrote biographies of Goldsmith and Mahomet, and completed a five-volume biography of George Washington (1855–1859) shortly before his death.

Irving took as his models Scott, Addison, and Goldsmith, never attempting to develop an original idiom. Though he rarely manifests moral or intellectual awareness, the charm, delicacy, and pictorial quality of his writing give it lasting value. Irving proved to skeptics at home and abroad that the world would read an American book. Further, among the delightful tales and sketches are a few that have become part of American folklore. See WOLFERT'S ROOST.

Irwin, Wallace [Admah] (1875–1959). American newspaperman, writer of humorous verse and fiction. Irwin won national fame with *The Love Sonnets of a Hoodlum* (1902), a remarkable collection of Petrarchan verses in the American vernacular. He is also known for creating the character of Hashimura Togo, a Japanese schoolboy, under whose name he wrote epistolary stories for at least 20 years. The first collection of these was *Letters of a Japanese Schoolboy* (1909). He also wrote *Mr. Togo, Maid of All Work* (1913); *The Rubaiyat of Omar Khayyam Jr.* (1902); *Seed of the Sun* (1921), a serious novel about the problems of the Japanese living in California; and *Yankee Doctor in Paradise* (1941), in collaboration with Dr. Sylvester Lambert.

Is. See Ys.

Isaac. In the Old Testament, the only son of ABRAHAM and Sarah, the husband of Rebekah, and the father of JACOB and ESAU. He was nearly offered as a sacrifice to prove his father's faith, but at the last moment God intervened and told Abraham to slay a ram instead (Gen. 24–28).

Isaacs, Jorge. See MARÍA.

Isabella. In the ORLANDO FURIOSO of Ariosto, the Saracen princess, daughter of the king of Galicia and beloved of the Christian knight Zerbino. After the latter is killed by Mandricardo, she lets herself be slain by Rodomonte, who in grief builds a shrine to commemorate the unfortunate lovers.

Isabella. The beautiful and intensely virtuous religious novice who is the heroine of Shakespeare's MEASURE FOR MEASURE. She is finally united with the introverted, philosophical Vincentio, duke of Vienna.

Isabella I. Known as la Católica ("the Catholic") (1451–1504). Queen of Castile. The daughter of John II of Castile, she married FERDINAND II of Aragon in 1469. Her accession to the throne of Castile upon the death of her brother Henry IV in 1474 led to the permanent union of the two great kingdoms of Spain.

Isabella, or The Pot of Basil (1820). A poem by John KEATS, adapted from a tale by Boccaccio. Set in Florence, it tells of Isabella's love for Lorenzo. Her brothers, discovering this love, revenge themselves by murdering Lorenzo in a forest. The ghost of Lorenzo appears to Isabella and tells her of the crime; she goes to the forest, digs up his head, and plants it in a pot of basil, keeping it by her and watering it with her tears. Her brothers discover her grotesque secret and steal the pot, leaving Isabella to die of grief.

Isaiah. A prophetical book of the Old Testament. In its present form it is the work of at least three distinct authors in three successive stages of Jewish history from c. 750 to c. 450 B.C. The first part is strongly political, the author having been a counselor of the Judaean kings. Urging peace with Israel's enemies, he can still foresee the coming tragedy of the Babylonian Exile. The middle chapters of Isaiah (40–55) were written after 586, when Jerusalem fell. They call on Israel not to lose faith in its god and prophesy the return of his loving care. The last part reflects the period of Nehemiah's return to Jerusalem and the rebuilding of the city and temple (c. 450). It is nationalistic and stresses the ritualistic side of Judaism.

All three parts of Isaiah are filled with Messianic hope. The life of the Messiah is told in Isaiah.

Ischia, battle of (1464). The Neapolitan fleet of the Aragonese monarchs defeated the French navies in this battle, thus ending the efforts of the Angevins to regain the throne of Naples, lost to Alfonso of Aragon in 1442.

Isenbras or **Isumbras, Sir** (14th century). Hero of a Middle English verse romance. Strong and prosperous but arrogant, he is offered the choice of suffering either in youth or in old age. Choosing the former, he is beset by great misfortunes, which humble him. After performing many deeds of generosity and bravery for 21 years, he is restored in happiness to all he had lost.

Isengrim. See REYNARD THE FOX.

Iseult. The name of the heroine in the medieval cycle TRISTAN AND ISEULT. There are many other versions and parallels of this cycle, beginning with early Irish tales (see THE PURSUIT OF DIARMUID AND GRAINNE) and appearing in the modern world in such forms as the music drama of Richard Wagner; Iseult's name appears in various forms: Isolde, Isolt, Ysolt, etc. In general, Iseult the Fair is an Irish princess, wooed and won by TRISTAN for his uncle, King MARK of Cornwall. But in the process of journeying to the court of King Mark, both Iseult and Tristan drink a magic potion that causes them to fall in love with one another, a love which is completely binding, even in the face of death. The major part of this cycle is concerned with the adventures of the pair, after the marriage of Iseult to King Mark, in the name of their great love. Ultimately Tristan is banished and goes to Brittany where he marries another, Iseult of the White Hands. When he is about to die, he sends for his love, Iseult the Fair, but she arrives too late. Lying beside the body of Tristan, she too dies. When the two lovers are buried next to one another, a briar grows up from the grave of Tristan and curves over to take root on the grave of Iseult.

Three times it is cut down and three times it grows again, until King Mark commands that it be left alone. Iseult is depicted as very beautiful, gifted (among other things, she has great skill in healing wounds), shrewd, and something of a sorceress. In James Joyce's *Finnegans Wake* (1939), the wife and daughter of Earwicker represent the two Iseults of Tristan.

Isherwood, Christopher [William Bradshaw] (1904–   ). English novelist, short-story writer, and playwright. He was a member of the talented group of left-wing young writers of the 1930's that included W. H. Auden, C. Day-Lewis, and Stephen Spender. Living in Germany during Hitler's rise to power, Isherwood brilliantly described the social corruption and disintegration in his *Berlin Stories*: MR. NORRIS CHANGES TRAINS, *Sally Bowles* (1937), and *Goodbye to Berlin* (1939). He collaborated with W. H. Auden on the verse plays THE DOG BENEATH THE SKIN, THE ASCENT OF F6, and *On the Frontier* (1938), a political melodrama. He traveled to China with Auden and collaborated on *Journey to a War* (1939), about the war between Japan and China. At the outbreak of the European war he, like Auden, emigrated to the U.S. Auden abandoned Marxism for earnest Christianity; Isherwood abandoned it to become a disciple of Aldous Huxley in the study of Eastern religions and yoga. Among Isherwood's other publications are the novels *All the Conspirators* (1928), *The Memorial* (1932), *Prater Violet* (1945), *The World in the Evening* (1954), *Down There on a Visit* (1962), and *A Single Man* (1964). He has also translated Baudelaire's *Intimate Journals*.

Ishmael. In the Old Testament, the son of Abraham and HAGAR. In general, the name refers to any outcast from society because of the prophecy: "And he will be a wild man; his hand will be against every man, and every man's hand against him" (Gen. 16:12). After the birth of Isaac, Ishmael was cast out of Abraham's household, married, and settled at Paran; the Arab people were descended from his 12 sons.

Herman Melville gave the name Ishmael to the narrator of MOBY DICK.

Ishtar. The Babylonian goddess of love and war. Known to the Canaanites as Astarte, to the Israelites as Ashtoreth, to the Arabs as the god Athtar, she developed from the Sumerian goddess INANNA, and was the most widely worshiped of all the deities of the Near and Middle East. According to one version of the myth, she was the daughter of Sin (the moon) and sister of Shamash (the sun); according to another, the daughter of Anu, the lord of heaven; in both, she was identified with the planet Venus. Though the goddess of erotic love, she was often warlike and, at best, had a remarkably irritable disposition. Her worship involved ritual prostitution, which was severely condemned by the Hebrew prophets. She may have been "the queen of heaven" mentioned by Jeremiah; Solomon built a temple to her.

Of the many myths in which she figured, the most famous tells of her love for Tammuz, a young fertility god. In some unexplained way, her love caused his death. She mourned him extravagantly—her lamentations were ritually commemorated yearly when the summer sun dried up the vegetation—and finally descended into the underworld to bring back her lover. At each of the seven gates through which she passed, she was divested of one of her ornaments or pieces of clothing, until she stood naked before her terrible sister ERESHKIGAL, goddess of the underworld. She was imprisoned there, and the gods were powerless to help her, until EA fashioned a hermaphroditic creature called Asushu-Namir and sent it armed with magic spells against Ereshkigal. These were successful, and, after Asushu-Namir had poured over her "the water of life," Ishtar returned to earth, taking Tammuz with her. Ishtar's love for Tammuz and her struggle for him with the goddess of the underworld obviously influenced the myth of Aphrodite's rivalry with Persephone over ADONIS.

As Tammuz discovered, the love of Ishtar was a mixed blessing. In the *Epic of* GILGAMESH, the hero resists her advances and, employing many unflattering epithets, reminds her that her other lovers have regretted their good fortune, many being turned (literally or figuratively) into beasts. In her fury at this rude treatment, Ishtar induces her father Anu to send the bull of heaven against Gilgamesh, but he and Enkidu kill it. It is for this crime that Enkidu dies.

Isis. The principal goddess of ancient Egypt, forming with her husband-brother Osiris and son Horus the major triad of deities. As the patron saint of mariners in Alexandria, she was often identified with the moon; the cow was sacred to her, its horns representing the crescent moon which, in Egypt, appears lying on its back. Her chief temples were at Amydos, Busiris, and Philae. She is represented as a queen, her head being surmounted by horns and the solar disk or by the double crown.

The later Greeks and Romans also identified her with the goddess of nature and Apuleius, in the *Golden Ass* (second century A.D.), describes her as "the universal mother nature." Representations of Isis suckling Horus were possible prototypes of the Madonna and Child.

Milton, in *Paradise Lost* (1667) places Isis among the fallen angels. In the *Faerie Queene* (1596), Spenser used the legend of Isis and Osiris to symbolize English equity and justice.

to lift the veil of Isis. To pierce to the heart of a great mystery. Proclus mentions a statue of Isis, which bore the inscription, "I am that which is, has been, and shall be. My veil no one has lifted. The fruit I bore was the Sun."

Islam. The religion of MUHAMMAD, whose adherents are called Muslims, Moslems, Musulmans, Mohammedans. The word means *resignation* or *submission to the will of God.* MUSLIMS believe every child is born in Islam and would continue in the true faith if not led astray.

Islam emphasizes five duties: (1) bearing witness that there is but one God and one prophet, Muhammad; (2) reciting daily prayers; (3) giving appointed and legal alms; (4) observing the RAMADAN, a month's fast; (5) making a pilgrimage to Mecca at least once in a lifetime. See HADJI; KORAN.

Island of the Seven Cities. A kind of mythical Utopia. There seven bishops, who quitted Spain during the dominion of the Moors, founded seven cities. The legend says that many have visited the island, but no one has ever left it.

Islands of the Blessed. A mythical abode of dead heroes, called by the Greeks Happy Islands, and by the Romans Fortunate Islands. They are imaginary islands somewhere in the West, where the favorites of the gods are conveyed at death, and dwell in everlasting joy.

Isla y Rojo, José Francisco de (1703–1781). Spanish Jesuit and satirist. His best-known work is the *Historia del famoso predicador fray Gerundio de Campazas, alias Zotes* (1758), a satire aimed at bombastic and pedantic religious oratory. It was banned in Spain by the Inquisition, and the second part did not appear until after the expulsion of the Jesuits from Spain in 1767. Isla also wrote *Triunfo del amor y de la lealtad, o Día grande de Navarra* (1746), a satirical treatment of a celebration in Pamplona upon the accession of Ferdinand VI.

Isle of Dogs, The (1597). A lost play by Thomas NASHE and Ben JONSON. It was so scornfully satiric that it resulted in the imprisonment of Jonson and in the temporary closing of the theatres.

Isle Sonante, L' (*Fr.,* "Ringing Island"). The title of the first edition (1562) of 16 chapters of what is now known as Book V of Rabelais' GARGANTUA AND PANTAGRUEL. Ringing Island, which is the first of several islands visited by Pantagruel and his friends, is inhabited by variously colored birds named cardinjays, priestjays, etc., and one popejay, "unique in his species." Birds of passage who had migrated to the island from Nobreadland and Alltoomany, they pass their time in sumptuous living, warbling to the ringing of bells. The episode of these lucky folk who enjoy paradise "both in this world and the next" is a transparent satire on the luxurious living of the Roman Catholic clergy, who thus lured into their ranks many social outcasts and poverty-stricken people.

Ismene. In Greek legend, daughter of Oedipus and Jocasta. Antigone was buried alive by the order of King Creon, for burying her brother Polynices, slain in combat by his brother Eteocles. Although she had actually been too timid to do so, Ismene declared that she had aided her sister, and requested to be allowed to share the same punishment. The episode occurs in Sophocles' ANTIGONE.

Ismeno. In the GERUSALEMME LIBERATA of Tasso, an enchanter who advises and aids the infidel forces against the Crusaders attacking Jerusalem. At one point, he brings the Arab chieftain Solimano to the battle by transporting him in a cloud. Later he enchants a forest near the Christian camp so that the Crusaders cannot build any more war machines. This spell is broken by Rinaldo.

Isocrates (Isokrates) (436–338 B.C.). An Attic orator, a pupil of SOCRATES. He founded a school and taught some of the greatest future statesmen, orators, and philosophers. When Philip of Macedon conquered Greece, he committed suicide. Of his orations, 21 have been preserved.

Isolde. See ISEULT.

Isolt. See ISEULT.

Israel (*Heb.,* "contender with God"). In the Old Testament, it is the name given to Jacob after he wrestled with the angel of the Lord (Gen. 32:28). Thus, it is also the name given to the Jewish nation descended from him, frequently referred to as the *Children of Israel.*

Israel Potter: or, Fifty Years of Exile (1855). A novel by Herman MELVILLE. The book is based on Henry Trumbull's biography, *Life and Remarkable Adventures of Israel Potter* (1824). In search of freedom and adventure, Israel becomes involved in the battle of Bunker Hill. He meets three Americans: Benjamin Franklin, who robs him while masquerading as a friend; John Paul Jones, who genuinely befriends him; and Ethan Allen, who possesses America's most admirable characteristics. Israel's personality is a mixture of the virtues and faults of all three men. An archetypal American, he is taken prisoner by the English, exiled for 50 years, and returns home to die. Melville suggests, at the end of this satirical novel, that the best hope for America is in her pioneering West.

Israfil, Israfel, or Uriel. The Muslim angel of music, possessed of the most melodious voice of all God's creatures. It is he who, on Judgment Day, is to sound the last trump of resurrection. Along with Gabriel and Michael, he was one of the three angels, according to the Koran, who warned Abraham of Sodom's destruction.

Israfel is the title of one of Edgar Allan Poe's poems (1831), and also of Hervey Allen's biography of Poe.

Issa. See KOBAYASHI ISSA.

Istar. See ISHTAR.

Isthmian games. Games consisting of chariot races, running, wrestling, boxing, and other sports. They were held by the ancient Greeks in the Isthmus of Corinth every alternate spring, the first and third of each Olympiad. They were instituted, according to the myth, in honor of MELICERTES.

Isumbras, Sir. See Sir ISENBRAS.

italic. A style of type. *Italic type* or *italics* (the type in which the letters, instead of being erect, as in roman, slope upward from left to right, *thus*) was first used by Aldo Manuzio in printing the Aldine classics. It was called by him cursive, a running hand (from Lat. *curro*, I run). Vergil was the first author printed in this type (1501).

It Can't Happen Here (1935). A novel by Sinclair LEWIS. It presents a fancied fascist dictatorship in the U.S., set up by Berzelius Windrip, a New England demagogue who is elected to the presidency. Doremus Jessup, a Vermont editor, fights Windrip, is arrested, escapes, and joins an underground movement in Canada headed by Walt Trowbridge, Windrip's opponent in the election.

Ithuriel. In Milton's PARADISE LOST, an angel who, with Zephon, is commissioned by Gabriel to search for Satan after the latter has effected his entrance into Paradise. He is armed with a spear, the slightest touch of which exposes deceit.

It Is Never Too Late to Mend (1853). A novel by Charles READE. This fictional study of the discovery of gold in Australia and the British convict system is notable for the character of Isaac Levi, one of the first serious attempts to portray the Jew favorably in fiction.

Iturbide, Agustín de (1783–1824). Mexican soldier and emperor. After fighting against Hidalgo and Morelos in the Spanish army, Iturbide joined the rebel forces and contributed to the final victory over Spain in 1821. Exploiting the confusion that followed the separation from Spain, Iturbide, the self-styled father

of Mexican independence, seized power and had himself proclaimed emperor in 1822. During his brief reign as Agustin I, he was harassed by financial difficulties, by disgruntled generals, and by republican critics. He was deposed in 1823, and when he attempted to return to power the following year, he was captured and shot.

Iudushka. Nickname of Porfiri Golovlyov in Mikhail Saltykov's novel THE GOLOVLYOV FAMILY. His nickname means "Little Judas" and he is referred to as a bloodsucker. He lives up to his reputation as he takes over the family estates from his despotic mother and weakling brothers. He is regarded as a supreme portrayal of unctuous heartlessness.

Iulus. See ASCANIUS.

Ivan IV or Ivan the Terrible (1530–1584). Czar of Russia (1533–1584). Ivan engaged in a power struggle throughout his reign with the nobility (the boyars). During this time he consolidated the Muscovite state, the core of the future Russian empire, and gained an undying reputation for ferocious cruelty toward his enemies—a predilection which alternated with bouts of sensuality and piety. His squabbles with the boyars induced him to set up his own private state within the Muscovite state. Ivan's realm, called the *Oprichnina*, had its own courts, administration, and army. The rest of the country, called the *Zemshchina*, was ostensibly ruled by a prince appointed by Ivan, although the puppet ruler's power was slight.

Ivan's stormy career has provided the basis for many literary and dramatic works by Russian authors, as well as a two-part film by Sergei Eisenstein. Ivan's own literary remains consist of several letters in an acrimonious correspondence with Prince Andrei Mikhailovich Kurbski, who fled to Lithuania when the Czar began his reign of terror in Russia.

Ivanhoe (1819). A novel by Sir Walter SCOTT. The action occurs in the period following the Norman Conquest. The titular hero is Wilfred, knight of Ivanhoe, the son of Cedric the Saxon, in love with his father's ward Rowena. Cedric, however, wishes her to marry Athelstane, who is descended from the Saxon royal line and may restore the Saxon supremacy. The real heroine is REBECCA the Jewess, daughter of the wealthy Isaac of York, and a person of much more character and charm than the mild Rowena. Yet Ivanhoe finally rejects her in favor of Rowena. Richard the Lion-heart in the guise of the Black Knight and Robin Hood as LOCKSLEY play prominent roles, and the novel is further emblazoned with a colorful entourage of chivalric knights and fair ladies. The frenzied variety of the action, with the pageantry of a tournament and a great flame-engulfed castle, makes this the most enthralling of Scott's works. See Brian de BOIS-GUILBERT; Reginald FRONT DE BOEUF; and ULRICA.

Ivanov, Vsevolod Vyacheslavovich (1895–   ). Russian novelist and short-story writer. Ivanov ran away from home while in his teens and worked at a variety of jobs, including that of a circus clown and as a fakir and dervish. His first story was printed in a Siberian newspaper and attracted the attention of Maksim Gorki, who helped and encouraged the young writer. After the civil war, in which he fought first for the Whites and then for the Reds, Ivanov went to Petersburg and joined the SERAPION BROTHERS. His novels, *Colored Winds* (*Tzvetnye* *vetra;* 1922) and *Blue Sands* (*Golubye peski;* 1923), and his stories, such as *Partisans* (*Partizany;* 1921) and *Armored Train No. 14–69* (*Bronepoyezd No. 14–69;* 1922), are exotic in both theme and treatment, written in the ornate prose style popular in the 1920's. The inherent primitivism that Ivanov depicts as a constant factor in human behavior eventually displeased Soviet critics, who felt he should deal more with life's social aspects. Ivanov then toned down the highly colored prose of his earlier work and made his stories more conventional, with some loss of vigor and excitement. His later work includes an autobiographical novel, *The Adventures of a Fakir* (*Pokhozhdeniya fakira;* 1935), and a war novel *The Taking of Berlin* (*Vzyatiye Berlina;* 1945).

Ivanov, Vyacheslav Ivanovich (1866–1949). Russian poet. A classical scholar, Ivanov was the leader of the St. Petersburg branch of SYMBOLISTS from 1905 to 1911, when he moved to Moscow. His earlier poetry was a compound of classical references and archaic Slavic diction, with an admixture of Nietzschean philosophy. His later *Roman Sonnets* (*Rimskiye sonety*), written just before World War II, dispense with ornateness and archaism, achieving powerful effects in simple, direct lines. Ivanov's study of Dostoevski (1932) examines the novelist's work as creations of myth. Ivanov emigrated in 1924 and settled in Italy. He died in Rome, after becoming a Roman Catholic convert.

Ives, Charles [Edward] (1874–1954). American composer and businessman. The income from his insurance firm, Ives & Myrick, supported his musical experiments. In his works, which include symphonies, and choral and chamber music, he anticipated modern techniques of later composers. His *Sonata No. 2* (subtitled *Concord, Mass., 1840–1860*) has four movements, labeled: *Emerson, Hawthorne, The Alcotts, Thoreau.* The inspiration of these transcendentalists he explains in *Essays Before a Sonata* (1920). Ives' work has only recently received public attention.

Ives, James Merritt. See CURRIER AND IVES.

ivory gate. See DREAMS, GATES OF.

Ivy Day in the Committee Room. A short story in James Joyce's DUBLINERS (1914). It is an account of a conversation between a group of party political workers on the anniversary of the birth of Charles Stewart Parnell. The disunity, corruption, and pettiness of these small politicians is contrasted with the idealism of Parnell, whom these characters hypocritically idolize.

Ixion. In Greek mythology, a Lapith king. He tried to seduce Hera, but Zeus shaped a cloud in her likeness and he lay with it. Zeus bound him to a fiery wheel that perpetually rolls through the sky. The phantom, later called Nephele, bore Centaurus, ancestor of the centaurs.

Iyangar, Venkatesa (1891–   ). Kannada novelist, short-story writer and essayist, known affectionately in India as "Masti." Eleven volumes of his stories have been collected under the title *Sanna Kathegalu:* they show charm, humor, wit, compassion, and great narrative fluency.

Iyengar, K. R. Srinivasa (1908–   ). Indian critic writing in English; head of the department of English in Andhra University. His major work has been the assessment and publicizing of Indian creative writing in English. His main study is *Indian Writing in English* (1962).

J

Jabberwocky. A well-known mock-heroic ballad by Lewis Carroll, found in THROUGH THE LOOKING-GLASS. It contains a number of words coined by the author himself, including PORTMANTEAU WORDS such as slithy, a compound of lithe and slimy, mimsy, a compound of flimsy and miserable, etc. The Jabberwock is a species of dragon.

J'accuse (I accuse). The title of Emile ZOLA's famous open letter addressed to President Faure of France (first appearing in the newspaper *Aurore,* January 13, 1898), in denunciation of the Dreyfus affair. Zola used the phrase *"j'accuse"* several times in the letter, addressing himself to the injustices perpetrated by the war department. After a year of exile in England, Zola returned to France, a hero for the part he had played in this national crisis. See Alfred DREYFUS.

Jack and Jill. A well-known nursery rhyme. It is said to be a relic of a Norse myth, accounting for the dark patches in the moon. The two children are supposed to have been kidnaped by the moon while drawing water, and they are still to be seen with the bucket hanging from a pole resting on their shoulders.

Jack and the Beanstalk. A nursery tale. It is found among a wide variety of races from Icelanders to Zulus. Jack is a very poor lad, sent by his mother to sell a cow, which he parts with to a butcher for a few beans. His mother, in her rage, throws the beans away, but one of them grows during the night as high as the heavens. Jack climbs the stalk, and, by the direction of a fairy, comes to a giant's castle, where he begs food and rest. This he does thrice, and in his three visits steals the giant's red hen, which lays golden eggs, his money bags, and his harp. As he runs off with the last treasure, the harp cries out, "Master! master!" which wakes the giant, who runs after Jack. But the nimble lad cuts the beanstalk with an axe, and the giant is killed in his fall. As we know it, this story is of Teutonic origin. According to a frequently advanced theory, the "beanstalk" is the ash, Yggdrasil, of the *Eddas,* the giant is All-Father, whose three treasures are the wind, the rain, and the red hen which lays golden eggs (the sun). Jack typifies Man, who avails himself of these treasures and becomes rich.

Jack Ketch. See John KETCH.

Jacks, Lawrence Pearsall (1860–1955). English philosopher and Unitarian minister. He wrote books about Smokeover, an imaginary industrial city, and such works as *The Revolt Against Mechanism* (1934).

Jackson, Andrew (1767–1845). 7th president of the U.S. (1829–1837), sometimes known as "Old Hickory." Jackson fought in the American Revolution at the age of 13, was imprisoned by the British, and later became a backwoods lawyer in what is now Tennessee. In 1791 he married Mrs. Rachel Robards in the erroneous belief that she had obtained a divorce from her husband. Although they were remarried immediately after the divorce was granted in 1793, Jackson's enemies used the scandal as a political weapon until Mrs. Jackson's death in 1828. From 1798 to 1804 he was a judge of the Tennessee supreme court. Commissioned a major general in the U.S. army during the War of 1812, Jackson defeated the British at New Orleans (1815), an exploit that won him a national reputation. In 1818, as leader of an expedition to quell Indian depredations near the Georgia border, he entered Spanish-held East Florida and executed two British subjects. Although there were diplomatic repercussions, Jackson was not punished.

He was narrowly defeated for the presidency by John Quincy ADAMS in 1824 but was elected in 1828 after a campaign that portrayed Jackson as a symbol of the common man. During his first term he introduced the "spoils system" on a large scale and relied heavily on a KITCHEN CABINET of unofficial advisers. At a Jefferson's Day dinner in 1830, he chagrined supporters of states' rights by proposing a toast to "Our Union: It must be preserved," to which Vice President John CALHOUN replied, "The Union, next to our liberty, most dear." Jackson broke definitively with Calhoun the following year, partly as a result of a quarrel over the social status of Margaret EATON, wife of the secretary of war. (See NULLIFICATION.) Jackson's opposition to the 2d Bank of the U.S., which he attacked as an organ of monopoly and privilege, was the main issue of the 1832 campaign. After his re-election, Jackson had federal funds withdrawn from the bank and deposited in state institutions that were known as pet banks. This policy contributed to the growing financial disorder which culminated in the Panic of 1837. By that time Jackson's successor, Martin Van Buren, had been inaugurated, and the ex-president had retired to The Hermitage, his estate near Nashville. Perhaps the most significant aspect of Jackson's administration was his expansion of presidential power.

Jackson, Charles [Reginald] (1903–1968). American novelist and short-story writer. Jackson is best known for THE LOST WEEKEND, his first novel, a vivid report on the life of an alcoholic. His subsequent novels showed a continued preoccupation with pathological states of mind: *The Fall of Valor* (1946) has a homosexual theme, and *The Outer Edges* (1948) tells of the murder of two children by a sexual degenerate. *The Sunnier Side* (1950) and

Earthly Creatures (1953) are collections of short stories.

Jackson, Helen [Maria Fiske] Hunt (1830–1885). American poet, novelist, and essayist. She is best known for her novel RAMONA. Her sympathetic attitude toward the Indians in the novel had earlier manifested itself in the tract, *A Century of Dishonor* (1881). *Mercy Philbrick's Choice* (1876) is a novel supposedly dealing with the life of Emily Dickinson, who was a friend of the author.

Jackson, Holbrook (1874–1948). English literary scholar and editor. He is best known for his study of *The Eighteen Nineties* (1913).

Jackson, Shirley (1919–1965). American novelist and short-story writer. Her most famous tale, THE LOTTERY deals with a ritualized lottery in a small American town. It is not until the final lines of the story that death by stoning is revealed as the prize of the lottery. In a similar way, many of her stories and all her novels deal with the fantastic and the terrifying. *Hangsaman* (1951) shows a sensitive girl's flight into fantasy while attending a progressive girls' school. By way of contrast, *Life Among the Savages* (1953) and *Raising Demons* (1957) are autobiographical books describing with much humor the life of a middle-class intellectual family in a small New England town. Miss Jackson's other novels include *The Bird's Nest* (1954), *The Sundial* (1958), *The Haunting of Hill House* (1959), and *We Have Always Lived in the Castle* (1962).

Jackson, Thomas Jonathan. Known as "Stonewall" Jackson (1824–1863). American general. Considered one of the ablest Confederate generals in the Civil War, Jackson played an important role in both of the battles at BULL RUN and conducted a brilliant campaign in the Shenandoah Valley (1862), defeating the Union forces at Front Royal and Winchester. He died a few days after being accidentally wounded by his own men at CHANCELLORSVILLE. The words he supposedly said as he lay dying, "Let us cross the river and rest in the shade of trees," have inspired several poems and suggested the title of Ernest Hemingway's *Across the River and into the Trees* (1950). John Greenleaf Whittier paid tribute to Jackson after his death in BARBARA FRIETCHIE, based on an apocryphal incident.

Jack the Ripper. Popular name of an unknown London criminal to whom were attributed a number of gruesome murders (1888–1889).

Jacob. A biblical patriarch of the book of Genesis, whose 12 sons were the founders of the 12 tribes of ISRAEL. As a young man, he purchased the birthright of his brother ESAU for a mess of pottage and, by impersonating him, secured from his blind father ISAAC the blessing intended for Esau (see REBEKAH). To win Rachel's hand, he served her father Laban for seven years, but was then given her less attractive sister Leah instead; whereupon he served another seven years, which "seemed to him but a short while so great was the love he bore her." Jacob is famed for the shrewdness with which he accumulated wealth while in Laban's service (Gen. 24:34). For his later life, see BENJAMIN; JOSEPH.

Jacob's ladder. The ladder seen by Jacob in a vision (Gen. 28:12). *Jacob* is a slang name for a ladder; and steep and high flights of steps going up cliffs are often so called.

Jacob, Max (1876–1944). French poet, prose writer, painter. A friend of Guillaume Apollinaire and his circle, he was writing poetry concerned with "nocturnal nightmares" and "day hallucinations" before the official beginning of Surrealism. Most famous are his early poems in prose, *Le Cornet à Dés* (1917), and verse, *Le Laboratoire Central* (1921). Other works include *La Défense de Tartuffe* (1919), reflecting his conversion to Catholicism; *Les Pénitents en maillot rose* (1925); and *Derniers Poèmes* (1945).

Jacobean. Pertaining to the reign of James I of England (James VI of Scotland), 1603–1625. With the accession of James I, a national spirit that had begun to make itself felt as early as 1600 (see ELIZABETHAN) became more pronounced. The dour and pedantic Scot who acceded to the throne had none of the symbolic value of his predecessor, "Good Queen Bess." The nation grew increasingly factious, particularly on the religious question. In 1605 the GUNPOWDER PLOT, an attempt by a group of Roman Catholics to blow up Parliament, increased the animosity. On the intellectual plane the new discoveries in science and astronomy made it increasingly clear that the beautifully ordered universe of PTOLEMY, the large world of which man was the microcosm, was a pleasant fiction that would have to be traded in for the more realistic but less comforting world of COPERNICUS. Skepticism and doubt, together with an acute self-consciousness, became the dominant note, which SHAKESPEARE—who strode both Elizabethan and Jacobean ages like a Colossus—sounded in HAMLET (1601) and in MEASURE FOR MEASURE (1604–1605).

In prose the new mood was reflected in the reaction against the rhetorical, elaborate Ciceronianism of the Elizabethans. The new prose style, modeled after SENECA and TACITUS, was a more concise and flexible instrument, better suited to the new prose form, the essay. The essay, which had been developed by Montaigne, was imported and perfected by Francis BACON, whose aphoristic style established the dominant tone of that form. But the prevailing mood was better represented by Robert Burton's massive ANATOMY OF MELANCHOLY, a detailed treatment of the affliction that characterized the age. Independently of these currents the Jacobean age also witnessed one of the greatest achievements of English prose: the King James or Authorized Version of the BIBLE.

The poetry of the Jacobean age can be characterized in terms of the two poets who dominated it, Ben JONSON and John DONNE. The poetry of Jonson and his followers was generally derived from classical models and attempted to bring to English poetry the classical virtues of restraint, form, lucidity, and decorum. The cavalier poets later in the century looked to Jonson's poetry as their chief English model. From John Donne, however, derives the more important strain of metaphysical poetry. In metaphysical poetry the Jacobean reaction against the Elizabethan qualities of generous, rich profusion and abounding optimism is most clearly focused. In drama, "Jacobean melancholy" invaded both comedy and tragedy. In the comic area it produced vivid, scathing satire of human rapacity in such plays as Ben Jonson's VOLPONE and THE ALCHEMIST and in John MARSTON's THE MALCONTENT. In tragedy it resulted in some of the most memorable studies of evil in the history of

drama. Webster's THE WHITE DEVIL and THE DUCH-
ESS OF MALFI, Tourneur's THE REVENGER'S TRAGEDY,
Ford's 'TIS PITY SHE'S A WHORE, Middleton and
Rowley's *The Changeling* focus with an almost savage intensity on human, specifically sexual, corruption. Jacobean dramatists, heavily patronized by the
pleasure-loving court, were called upon to create elaborate masques in the splendid settings of Inigo JONES
as well as the courtly pastoral drama associated with
BEAUMONT AND FLETCHER. Finally, it was in the
Jacobean age that Shakespeare's greatest work was
produced. The Jacobean element in Shakespeare is
reflected in his refusal after 1600 to return to the
charming simplicity of the early comedies or to the
patriotic fervor of the histories. His mature work,
whether the tragedies or the later "romances," never
loses sight of the existence of evil as an operative
force in life.

Jacobi, Friedrich Heinrich (1743–1819). German novelist and popular philosopher who stressed
intuition and faith as opposed to rationalism. His
thought is related to that of Hamann and Herder,
and in his early career is close to the STURM UND
DRANG movement. The concept of NIHILISM is his
invention, but not his creed. His best-known novel
is *Aus Eduard Allwills Papieren* (*From the Papers of
Edward Allwill,* last version 1792).

Jacobins. (1) Name given the Dominican friars
in France because in Paris they first established themselves (1219) in the Rue St. Jacques.

(2) A political club, originally called the *Club
Breton,* formed by liberal members of the National
ASSEMBLY at Versailles (1789). On their removal to
Paris, they met in the hall of an ex-convent of the
Jacobins (hence their name). Although only mod-
erately democratic in the beginning, they became in-
creasingly radical and were a prime force in the
Revolution. Many of their more moderate members
broke off and formed their own clubs, notably the
FEUILLANTS. Among the best-known Jacobins are
MIRABEAU, ROBESPIERRE, DANTON, and MARAT. The
term "Jacobin" has come to denote a violent radical.

Jacobites. The partisans of JAMES II and, after
William III superseded him, the partisans of James's
heirs. They maintained the indefeasible right of the
house of Stuart to the throne and engaged in two
fruitless rebellions: first to enthrone James's son ("the
Old PRETENDER"), and later, his grandson (Bonnie
Prince Charlie, or "the Young Pretender"). The
Jacobites remained a powerful and disturbing political
influence for generations. See the FIFTEEN; the FORTY-
FIVE; WARMING-PANS.

Jacobowsky and the Colonel (*Jacobowsky und
der Oberst,* 1944). A satirical comedy by Franz
WERFEL in which an anti-Semitic Polish colonel is
led from behind the Nazi lines by a clever Jew.

Jacobs, William Wymark (1863–1943). English
story writer. His comic tales about sailors and rustics
were collected in *Snug Harbor* (1931). *The Monkey's
Paw* is a powerful horror story.

Jacobsen, Jens Peter (1847–1885). Danish poet
and novelist. Jacobsen began his career as a student
of botany and zoology; he introduced the scientific
theories of Darwin to Denmark. His body of creative
work is small and was all produced after he retired
to his native Thisted as a tubercular patient in 1873.
Naturalistic in his subject matter, Jacobsen writes in

a careful, precise style. The novel *Fru Marie Grubbe*
(1876) is a psychological study; *Niels Lynne* (1880)
portrays an atheist in the modern world. His stories,
noted for their skillful use of language, were published as *Mogens og andre Noveller* (*Mogens and
Other Stories,* 1882).

Jacob's Room (1922). A novel by Virginia
WOOLF, her first original and distinguished work.
The life story, character, and friends of Jacob Flanders are presented in a series of separate scenes and
moments. There are numerous little descriptions of
scenes and people that do not enter into his life at
all—such as an old woman selling matches and an
irrelevant conversation in another room—but help to
provide a complete, rounded world. The story of this
sensitive, promising young man carries him from his
childhood, through college at Cambridge, love affairs
in London, and travels in Greece, to his death in the
war. At the end, instead of describing his death, Virginia Woolf describes his empty room.

Jacopo della Quercia (1367–1438). Italian sculptor. One of the first of the great Renaissance sculptors,
Jacopo is noted for his luxuriant style, revealed in
the reliefs surrounding the doors of the Church of
S. Petronio at Bologna, and for the expressive power
of his other efforts in low relief. He influenced such
painters as MASACCIO and such fellow sculptors as
Michelangelo.

Jacopone da Todi (c. 1230–1306). Italian poet.
After 10 years of penance following his wife's death
in 1268, he became a Franciscan monk. His hymns
reveal a fervent mysticism, and he is possibly the
author of the *Stabat Mater Dolorosa.*

Jacquard, Joseph Marie (1752–1834). French
inventor. Jacquard produced a loom (1801) that
revolutionized the technique of inwoven designs. He
was later awarded a pension and elected to the Legion
of Honor (1819).

Jacquerie, La (1358). An unsuccessful insurrection of the French peasants of Ile-de-France, provoked by their oppression under the noble class while
King Jean II was in captivity in England. Acts of
great violence and cruelty were committed first by
the peasantry, who had sworn to kill every nobleman in France, and then by Charles the Bad of
Navarre and his nobles in their suppression of the
revolt and their reprisals. The name *Jacquerie* came
from the 14th-century use of *Jacques* as a generic
name for the peasant, connoting the humiliation of
serfdom.

Jacques, Pauvre. See PAUVRE JACQUES.

Jacques le fataliste (1796). A novel by Denis
DIDEROT. It was possibly Laurence Sterne's remark,
"Digressions, incontestably, are the sunshine; they are
the life, the soul of reading," that inspired Diderot to
write this, his last important work and longest novel.
The story, intentionally disorderly in structure, is a
burlesque recitation of Jacques' love affairs, as told
to his master, but this framework in itself is of practically no importance since it is interrupted constantly
by digressions and stories within stories; in which
the characters comment on their own tales, and even
the reader is constantly brought into the narrative.
Some of the interpolated stories are well known, for
example, the tale of Mme. de la Pommeraye who exacts vengeance from her faithless lover, or the tale
of the immoral Father Hudson, in which evil tri-

umphs. In this complex work, Diderot is concerned with the problems of the novel as a literary medium to depict reality, with the philosophic problem of determinism versus fatalism, and with defining a mature attitude toward life.

Jade Emperor. The chief god of the triad of popular Taoism.

Jael. See SISERA.

Jagannath. See JUGGERNAUT.

Jaggers, Mr. In Charles Dickens' GREAT EXPECTATIONS, the lawyer who is Pip's legal guardian and Miss Havisham's man of business.

Jahannam or **Jehennam.** The name of the Muslim Hell, or the first of its seven divisions. The word is the same as the Hebrew GEHENNA.

Jalna. See MAZO DE LA ROCHE.

Jaloux, Edmond (1878–1949). French novelist and critic. His novels are delicately realistic accounts of the inner life of restless souls, such as *Le Reste est silence* (1909), *L'Incertaine* (1918), and *La Chute d'Icare* (1936).

James I (1566–1625). Stuart king of England (1603–1625). The son of Mary Queen of Scots and Lord Darnley, he ruled effectively in Scotland as James VI for 20 years before the death of Elizabeth when he succeeded to the throne of England. There his awkwardness, pedantry, and Scottish accent were against him; his insistence on divine right and attempts to keep peace with Spain created a popular resentment which helped bring on the English Civil War. James was called "the English Solomon" and "the Wisest Fool in Christendom" on account of his impractical learning and literary ambitions. His most famous work was *Daemonologie* (1599), a treatise denouncing witches, but it was his *Essays of a Prentice in the Divine Art of Poesy* (1584), a critical treatise, and *Poetical Exercises at Vacant Hours* (1591) which led English poets to hope that he might become their patron; however, he is known to have assisted only Ben Jonson. He also wrote a well-known *Counterblaste to Tobacco* (1604), refuting the alleged virtues of the plant.

James II (1633–1701). Stuart king of England (1685–1688). The son of Charles I, he became a Roman Catholic, and succeeded to the throne after the death of his brother Charles II. Convinced that James planned to rule as absolute monarch and to restore Catholicism to England, seven representatives of the property-owning classes offered the throne to William of Orange, the king's Protestant son-in-law. After William had landed at Torbay in Devon (1688), James, finding himself without military and popular support, fled to France, where he was cordially received by Louis XIV. In an attempt to recover his throne, he landed in Ireland (1689), but was decisively defeated at the battle of the Boyne (1690). See GLORIOUS REVOLUTION.

James, Henry [Jr.] (1843–1916). American novelist, short-story writer, and man of letters. A major figure in the history of the novel, James is celebrated as a master craftsman who brought his great art and impeccable technique to bear in the development of abiding moral themes: the relationship between innocence and experience, especially as exemplified in the confrontation of American and European civilizations; the dilemma of the artist in an alien society; the achievement of self-knowledge through psychological and moral perception. With an approach to the art of fiction that resembled the research of the careful historian, James admitted into his stories and novels only that which could be represented as the perception or experience of his characters. With this approach to the problem of "point of view" in the novel, James achieved reality and unity, and it is perhaps in this respect that he had the strongest effect on subsequent writers.

James came from a distinguished family: his grandfather was one of the first millionaires in America; his father, the Swedenborgian Henry James, Sr., was a writer and lecturer in the fields of philosophy and theology; his brother was the psychologist William JAMES. Thus, the novelist grew up in an atmosphere that encouraged his becoming what he thought all novelists should be: "one on whom nothing is lost."

James entered Harvard Law School in 1862, but withdrew at the end of a year. Always a scribbler, he wanted to write seriously, and in 1864 his first story, *A Tragedy of Error*, appeared in the *North American Review;* he soon caught the attention of William Dean Howells who, as editor of the *Atlantic Monthly,* helped and encouraged James; in 1871 James's first novel, *Watch and Ward,* was published serially in the *Atlantic.* Between 1864 and 1871 he wrote a number of stories and astute reviews for both the *Atlantic* and the *Nation.* It was during this period, too, that he made his first independent trip to Europe. (He had spent much of his youth in Europe, as had his three brothers and sister, traveling there with his family and attending various schools.) The trip marked the beginning of his fascination with the theme of the American in Europe. During his second European trip (1872–1874) he wrote his best story to date: *A Madonna of the Future,* the story of an artist who never manages to paint the perfect madonna.

In 1875, after much thought, James decided to make his home abroad, settling first in Paris—where he knew Maupassant, Flaubert, and Turgenev—and finally in England (1876) where he spent the rest of his life. The 1870's, in England, saw the first real blossoming of James's talent. THE PASSIONATE PILGRIM AND OTHER STORIES appeared in 1875, followed in rapid succession by RODERICK HUDSON, THE AMERICAN, THE EUROPEANS, DAISY MILLER, and *Confidence* (1879). The major theme running throughout this work—the international confrontation of European and American civilizations—is posed clearly and unambiguously at this early stage: Christopher Newman in *The American* is basically innocent and naïve as he comes into contact with sophisticated and evil De Bellegardes. In his later work, James was to see his theme in a more complex light: the innocently unaware may themselves be the cause of evil in others.

In 1879, James published *Hawthorne,* a book in which James pays tribute to Hawthorne as a writer who accomplished much despite the cultural aridity of his surroundings. WASHINGTON SQUARE, set in the New York of James's childhood, was published a year later. The climax of this early period is THE PORTRAIT OF A LADY, considered by many to be not only James's finest but one of the finest novels in English. The 1880's also saw the publication of THE BOSTONIANS, THE PRINCESS CASAMASSIMA, and THE ASPERN PAPERS. The publication of THE TRAGIC MUSE, for many, marks the beginning of the more complex prose style generally associated with James. An interesting study of an actress, it preludes James's excursion into play-writing during the 1890's. The plays were all more or less unsuccessful, and few would claim much for them, but the effect of them on his fiction was marked. His stories and novels of the late 90's show a radical concern with experiment and with the adaptation of dramatic technique to fiction; this was the beginning of James's later style of involved sentences in which every thought and image is qualified, and the sentence is itself presented as a work of art. WHAT MAISIE KNEW, THE TURN OF THE SCREW, THE AWKWARD AGE, and THE SACRED FOUNT are all products of these experiments.

With the turn of the century, James entered into his last and perhaps his greatest period, publishing in rapid succession three long and complex novels: THE WINGS OF THE DOVE, THE AMBASSADORS, THE GOLDEN BOWL. Difficult as many have found them, the novels mark the pinnacle of James's art. This period also saw the publication of such famous short stories as *The Beast in the Jungle* (1903), a story of a man who waits for a special fate only to find that his fate was to be the man "to whom nothing was to have happened"; *The Birthplace* (1903), the story of a couple who become caretakers at a Shakespeare-like birthplace; and *The Jolly Corner* (1908), a complicated tale of a man who meets his alter ego as a ghost.

In 1904, James came to the U.S. and toured the country, producing on his return to England THE AMERICAN SCENE. The major effort of these years, however, went into the task of writing the critical prefaces and making, where needed, the revisions for the reissue of his works in the New York edition (1907-1909), a venture that ultimately ran to 26 volumes. The prefaces, important comments on his work and craft, were later republished as *The Art of the Novel* (1934), edited by R. P. Blackmur. After his brother William's death in 1910, James turned to another major undertaking, the writing of three autobiographical volumes: *A Small Boy and Others* (1913), *Notes of a Son and Brother* (1914), and the unfinished *The Middle Years* (1917). Two novels were left incomplete at his death in 1916: *The Sense of the Past* and *The Ivory Tower*, both published in 1917. James became a British subject in 1915 as a measure of support for the British cause in World War I. See SPOILS OF POYNTON, THE.

James, Jesse [Woodson] (1847-1882). American bandit. After riding with Quantrill's guerrillas during the Civil War, Jesse and his brother Frank committed daring railroad and bank robberies in the Middle West during the 1870's, becoming popular heroes. When a large reward was offered for their capture, Robert Ford, a member of the James gang, earned it by shooting Jesse in the back. His murder was narrated in an anonymous ballad, *Jesse James*.

James, The General Epistle of. A New Testament book. It is a letter to the entire Christian Church. The date and authorship of this letter are not known. Traditionally it has been ascribed to James, the first bishop of Jerusalem and the brother of Jesus; this would date the work before A.D. 62 when James was martyred. Others feel that the epistle was written about the year 90 by an unknown church

father. The writer reminds his readers of their moral obligations as Christians and calls for not only a faith in Christ but for Christian action in life as well.

James, William (1842-1910). American philosopher, physiologist, psychologist, and teacher. The son of Henry James, Sr., and the brother of Henry James, he began to teach at Harvard in 1872. A gifted writer, he produced works on theology, psychology, ethics, and metaphysics, coining such phrases as "the bitch goddess success." He was distinctly American in the concepts he advanced, and his approach to metaphysics was frankly commonsensical. He objected to the pure and highly "logical" but unreal systems of Idealist metaphysicians. Emphasizing the role of the nature of the knower in the character and validity of knowledge, he insisted that any view of the world is a compromise between the objectively given and the personally desired. He gave a series of lectures on PRAGMATISM at the Lowell Institute and later at Columbia University that was published as *Pragmatism* (1907) and *The Meaning of Truth* (1909). Turning away from abstractions, verbal solutions, fixed principles, and pretended absolutes, he looked for concreteness and facts, action and power. He argued that "the ultimate test for us of what a truth means is the conduct it dictates or inspires." The same attitude characterizes *The Varieties of Religious Experience* (1902), which contends that any article of religious faith is "true" when it provides emotional satisfaction. *The Principles of Psychology* (1890, 1892) shows James as a keen observer of sense data; one chapter, devoted to "The Stream of Thought," advances the concept of the STREAM OF CONSCIOUSNESS, later an important and revolutionary fictional technique. In other books, James discusses *The Will to Believe* (1897), *Human Immortality* (1898), *The Sentiment of Rationality* (1905), and *A Pluralistic Universe* (1919). See Charles Sanders PEIRCE.

Jameson, [Margaret] Storm (1897-   ). English novelist who often sets her stories in Yorkshire. *The Lovely Ship*, *The Voyage Home*, and *A Richer Dust* (1927-1931) comprise a trilogy about a ship-building family. Her other books include *The Hidden River* (1955), *A Cup of Tea for Mr. Thorgill* (1957), and *The Road from the Monument* (1962).

Jameson Raid (1895-1896). A raid on Johannesburg, South Africa. It was led by the Englishman Sir Leander Starr Jameson (1853-1917). It was an attempt to overthrow the Boer government during the troubles between the Boers and English in the gold mines. Jameson was captured and handed over to the British for trial, but was released shortly and later became prime minister of Cape Colony (1904-1908). See BOER WAR.

James the Greater, St. One of the 12 apostles of Jesus and the patron saint of Spain. He was the brother of John and a son of Zebedee. Legend states that, after his missionary journey to Spain and his subsequent death in Palestine, his body was placed in a boat with sails set, and that next day it reached the Spanish coast; at Padron, near Compostela, they used to show a huge stone as the veritable boat. According to another legend, it was the relics of St. James that were miraculously conveyed to Spain in a ship of marble from Jerusalem. A knight saw the ship sailing into port, his horse took fright, and plunged with its rider into the sea. The knight saved himself by "boarding the marble vessel," but his clothes were found to be entirely covered with scallop shells. The saint's body was discovered in 840 by divine revelation to Bishop Theodomirus, and a church was built at Compostela as a shrine for the relics. St. James is commemorated on July 25, and is represented in art sometimes with the sword by which he was beheaded and sometimes attired as a pilgrim, with his cloak covered with shells. He is also known as Santiago, a variation of St. James (Span., *San Diego*).

James the Less, St. One of the 12 apostles of Jesus. His attribute as a saint is a fuller's club, in allusion to the instrument by which he was put to death after having been thrown from the summit of the temple at Jerusalem in A.D. 62.

Jamestown. The first permanent English settlement in the New World, founded (1607) on the site of the abandoned Spanish settlement of San Miguel, and named for King James I. It was the capital of Virginia until 1698. The first settlers suffered great hardships, especially during the starving years of 1609–1610. John Smith was an original settler, but left in 1609. Jamestown was burned down during Bacon's Rebellion (1676). Before its restoration in modern times, the only surviving relics were the tower of the church and a number of tombs.

Jammes, Francis (1868–1938). French poet and novelist. His pastoral elegies describe his native region of the Pyrenées with sensuous and sentimental simplicity. The poems of *De l'angélus de l'aube à l'angélus du soir* (1897) were written during the time of his friendship with André GIDE, as were *Le Triomphe de la vie* (1902) and the novel *Le Roman du lièvre* (1903). Then he drew closer to Paul Claudel and was converted to Catholicism in 1905, after which his poems were more religiously inspired, such as *Clairières dans le ciel* (1906) and *Les Géorgiques chrétiennes* (3 vols., 1911–1912). Among his novels are *M. le curé d'Ozeron* (1918); *Le Poète rustique* (1920), modeled on himself; and *Cloches pour deux mariages* (1924).

Janaka. In Hindu legend, the foster father of Sita. He was the king of Mithila and discovered Sita

Jamestown: contemporary woodcut
of Capt. Smith's capture.

when he was ploughing the land; he is praised in the *Ramayana* for his extraordinary performances of charity and penance.

Jane Eyre (1847). A novel by Charlotte BRONTË. In both heroine and hero the author introduced types new to English fiction. Jane Eyre is a shy, intense little orphan, never for a moment, neither in her unhappy school days nor her subsequent career as a governess, displaying those qualities of superficial beauty and charm that had marked the conventional heroine. Jane's lover, Edward Rochester, to whose ward she is governess, is a strange, violent man, bereft of conventional courtesy, a law unto himself. Rochester's moodiness derives from the fact that he is married to an insane wife, whose existence, long kept secret, is revealed on the very day of his projected marriage to Jane. Years afterward the lovers are reunited.

Jane Seymour (1509?–1537). Third wife of HENRY VIII of England, mother of Edward VI. A lady in waiting to Catherine of Aragon and then to Anne Boleyn, Jane caught the fancy of the king in 1535. The following year Anne Boleyn was executed, and less than two weeks after her death Henry and Jane were privately married. She gave birth to Henry's first son in 1537, an event that was met with great public rejoicing, but she died 12 days later.

Jane Shore. See Jane SHORE.

Janice Meredith (1899). An historical novel by Paul Leicester FORD. It takes place during the American Revolution, and is the story of a Tory's patriotic daughter, who falls in love with a bond-servant named Charles Fownes. He is later revealed to be John Brereton, a colonel in the Continental army.

Janissaries or **Janizaries** (Turk., *yenitscheri*, new corps). A celebrated militia of the Ottoman empire, raised by Orchan in 1326, originally, and for some centuries, compulsorily recruited from the Christian subjects of the Sultan. It was blessed by Hadji Bektash, a saint, who cut off a sleeve of his fur mantle and gave it to the captain. The captain put the sleeve on his head, and from this circumstance arose the fur cap worn by these foot guards. In 1826, having become too formidable a threat to the state, they were abolished after a massacre in which many thousands of the Janissaries perished.

Jannings, Emil (1887–1950). Swiss-born actor of German-American parentage. He began his stage career with Max Reinhardt at the Deutsches Theater in Berlin, and made his screen debut in 1916 in Lubitsch films. From 1926 to 1929 he enjoyed enormous success in Hollywood, and in 1932 he returned to the stage. He is especially remembered for his portrayals in the German films *The Last Laugh* and *The Blue Angel*, with Marlene Deitrich.

Jansen, Cornelius. See JANSENISM.

Jansenism. The doctrines of the sect of Roman Catholics known as Jansenists, derived from the teachings of Cornelius Jansen (1585–1638), professor of exegesis at Louvain and later the bishop of Ypres. An opponent of the Jesuits, Jansen advocated reforms based, he claimed, upon the teachings of Augustine. Posthumously published in *Augustin* (1640), his tenets included irresistible grace, original sin, and "the utter helplessness of natural man to turn to God." The Jansenists' declaration of man's personal relationship with God resembled Calvinist doctrine and influenced the thinking of both Racine and Pascal. Louis XIV opposed the movement, whose influence was felt at court, in society, and in French letters (see Port-Royal), and the Jansenists were finally put down by Pope Clement XI in his bull *Unigenitus* (1713).

Januarius, St. (Ital., San **Gennaro**; ?272–?305). Patron saint of Naples. A bishop of Benevento, martyred during the Diocletian persecution, he is commemorated on September 19. His head and two vials of his blood are preserved in the cathedral at Naples, where the congealed blood is said to bubble and liquefy three times a year: on the Saturday before the first Sunday in May, on September 19, and on December 16. It is also said that this occurs whenever the head is brought near to the vials.

January and May. See Merchant's Tale.

Janus. One of the most ancient of Roman deities. Originally the god of light who opened the sky at daybreak and closed it at sunset, in time he came to preside over all beginnings and endings, all entrances and exits. He is often represented as having two faces, one in front and one behind, one to see into the future and one to see into the past. Doors (*ianuae*) were under his protection. The first month after the winter solstice, January, was sacred to him, and since 153 B.C. the first day of Janus' month has marked the beginning of the year. His principal temple was near the Roman forum. The doors of this temple were kept open in time of war and locked in time of peace. From the time of the earliest kings to the time of Augustus, these doors were closed only four times, twice during the latter's reign.

Japanese literature. The first literary productions date to the Nara period (710–794), which was marked by the wholesale importation of Chinese cultural elements. Native Japanese poetry is represented by the Man'yoshū, a collection of pre-Nara and Nara poems, many of which reflect indigenous Japanese concepts. In this period the first histories, based on the Chinese model, were composed and much emphasis was laid on the study of Buddhist scriptures. The Heian period (794–1185) saw a great literary flowering, marked by the novels and diaries of women writers. Although Chinese literature, particularly poetry, continued to exert considerable influence, new, purely Japanese tendencies came to the fore. The Tale of Genji by Murasaki Shikibu, a celebrated court lady, is regarded as the greatest single piece of Japanese literature; it has continued to influence the writers of Japan even to the present century. Diaries, some of them amusingly irreverent accounts of court life (Pillow-book of Sei Shonagon), feature the writings of this age. The succeeding Kamakura period (1185–1333) was a time of warfare and natural disaster. Its literature is colored by a pessimistic resignation, partly Buddhist inspired, to the uncertain and transitory nature of life during this era (Account of My Hut). Tales of military valor, originally the transmitted stories of ballad singers, were written down and became a permanent part of the literature (Tales of The Heike). Military unrest and natural calamities continued during the Muromachi period (1333–1600), although the country was unified for the first time. It was in this age that no drama evolved, under the sponsorship of the great warlords. The Tokugawa period (1600–1868),

which saw Japan at peace after centuries of almost constant warfare, was an age of many new literary departures. The Tokugawa family, imposing a rigid feudal hierarchy based on Neo-Confucian thought and ethics, set a firm and inflexible code of behavior for its subjects. Studies of the Chinese classics were encouraged and Buddhism, although the official religion, was severely regulated. Nevertheless, the merchant class, which was formally placed at the lowest of social levels, was responsible for a great new literary flowering. The merchants, because of inherent weaknesses in the feudal system, gained great wealth and power, which was reflected in the writings of the time. A new society developed, known as the floating world (*ukiyo*), which centered around the entertainment districts, the gay quarters, and the theaters. With it came this new literature: the stories of Ihara Saikaku, detailing the life of shopkeepers, courtesans, and humble people, and the puppet plays (joruri) and kabuki of Chikamatsu Monzaemon, which attained great popularity and are still performed. In art the *ukiyoe* wood-block prints portray graphically the life depicted in the literature. Poetry saw the rise of haiku under the direction of Matsuo Bashō, reflecting a more sensitive approach to life and nature. With the arrival of the Americans and Europeans in the mid-19th century the Tokugawa regime began to collapse, and in 1868 the Imperial Court was returned to prominence with the Meiji Restoration. A great wave of Western influences swept Japan: imitation of the Occident influenced all phases of life; the literary scene was no exception. Vast numbers of Western works were translated and imitated, various European literary and artistic movements had their vogues. Nevertheless works representative of the Japanese tradition continued to appear, especially in the pre-World War II period, when nationalistic sentiments encouraged such a trend. In the postwar period American influence has been strong and much Western material in all fields has appeared in Japanese. Throughout the 20th century there have been many novelists of exceptional talent and originality; a number of their works have appeared in English translation. Japan is a country of great literary productivity which accounts for its being the second greatest (after Russia) publisher of books in the world.

Japhet or **Japheth.** A name for Iapetus, introduced by Milton in Paradise Lost. He was also one of the sons of Noah and, according to legend, the father of Histion from whom descended the French, Italian, German, and British peoples.

Jaquenetta. A blowsy peasant wench who is wooed in histrionic style by Don Adriano de Armado in Shakespeare's Love's Labour's Lost.

Jaques. In Shakespeare's As You Like It, a lord, attendant on the banished duke in the forest of Arden. A philosophical idler, cynical, melancholy, and contemplative, he has little to do with the plot, but his musings furnish some of Shakespeare's most frequently quoted lines, notably from the speech on "the Seven Ages of Man":

All the world's a stage,
And all the men and women merely players:
They have their exits and their entrances;
And one man in his time plays many parts,
His acts being seven ages.

Jaques-Dalcroze, Emile (1865–1950). Swiss composer and inventor of eurhythmics. Eurhythmics coordinates bodily movement with music systematically to develop the physical experience of music, especially rhythm. This system has influenced modern dance. Jaques-Dalcroze founded the Institut Jaques-Dalcroze in Geneva, wrote folklike compositions and several expository and pedagogical works, among them *Rhythm, Music and Education* (1922).

Jardin des Plantes. Familiar name for what was originally the *Jardin du Roi* (1635), and is now the *Muséum d'Histoire Naturelle* (1794) in Paris. At first the site served as the royal garden for medicinal herbs; today the *Jardin des Plantes,* equipped with classrooms, laboratories, and museums, is a center of experimental scientific study.

Jarley, Mrs. In Charles Dickens' OLD CURIOSITY SHOP, a kindhearted woman, mistress of a traveling wax-work exhibition. She is kind to Little Nell and employs her as a decoy duck to "Jarley's unrivalled collection."

Jarndyce, Mr. See BLEAK HOUSE.

Jarnés [Millán], Benjamín (1888–1949). Spanish novelist. The elaborate style of his work, which often strays to the borders of poetry, is apparent in his best-known novels: *Mosén Pedro* (1924); *Vida de San Alejo* (*Saint Alexis,* 1928), an interesting biography; and *Castelar, hombre del Sinaí* (1935).

Jarrell, Randall (1914–1965). American poet, novelist, and critic. Jarrell served in the Air Force during the Second World War, and a considerable portion of his poetry deals with the war. Among his collections of verse are *Blood for a Stranger* (1942), *Little Friend, Little Friend* (1945), *Losses* (1948), *The Seven-League Crutches* (1951), and *Selected Poems* (1955). Some of his critical essays have been collected in *Poetry and the Age* (1953) and *A Sad Heart at the Supermarket* (1962). *Pictures from an Institution* (1954) is a novel satirizing life at a women's college.

Jarry, Alfred [-Henry] (1873–1907). French dramatist and novelist. Jarry is most famous for his epic burlesque UBU ROI (1896) and its sequels, and for the novel *Le Surmâle* (1902). Both works are considered major precursors of surrealism. Although the coarseness of his language was deliberately shocking, Jarry's humor was often metaphysical in nature. He would, for example, give a logical demonstration in lucid style of an absurd proposition.

Jason (Iason). In Greek mythology, the son (christened Diomedes) of Aeson. He led the ARGONAUTS to recover the GOLDEN FLEECE. Saved by his mother from Aeson's brother Pelias, who had seized the throne of Iolcus, he was reared by CHIRON. When he returned to claim the throne, he was sent to capture the Fleece. Thanks to the aid of Medea, he succeeded, killed Pelias, and became king of Ephyre (Corinth). Later, when he divorced Medea to marry Glauce, she killed her two children by Jason and escaped to Athens. Jason lost favor with the gods and wandered as an outcast until his old age, when the prow of his old vessel, the Argo, fell on him and killed him.

Jaspers, Karl (1883–1969). German philosopher. In 1913 he became an unsalaried lecturer on psychology at Heidelberg; he was made a full professor of philosophy in 1921. The Nazi regime secured his dis-

missal in 1937, but he was reinstated in 1945. After 1949 he lectured at the University of Basel. Jaspers is one of the founders of existentialism. From the beginning his interest in psychiatry provided the particulars for his search for a "perennial philosophy." His concern in this direction distinguishes him from his fellow-existentialists. He is less iconoclastic than other modern philosophers, such as Sartre. Although his system is rigorously logical, it acknowledges a transcendental power with which man seeks to communicate. Among his works are *Psychology of World Conceptions* (*Psychologie der Weltanschauungen;* 1919), *Man in the Modern Age* (1933), *On Truth* (*Von der Wahrheit;* 1947), *The Question of German Guilt* (1947), *The Perennial Scope of Philosophy* (1949), and *Tragedy Is Not Enough* (1953).

Jatayu. In Hindu legend, the eagle-king of birds. In the *Ramayana* he dies trying to save Sita from the clutches of Ravana. He is a symbol of unswerving loyalty and self-sacrifice.

Jaurès, Jean Léon (1859–1914). French socialist leader. Jaurès defended Captain Dreyfus in his newspaper *La Petite République.* With Briand, he founded (1904) and edited the daily *L'Humanité.* Jaurès was elected several times to membership in the Chamber of Deputies; in that capacity he expounded his socialist convictions eloquently. *Histoire socialiste collective* (1879–1900), a history of France from the Socialist perspective, was written under his direction. In 1914, at the outbreak of World War I, Jaurès was assassinated by a French chauvinist.

Java Head (1919). A novel by Joseph HERGESHEIMER. In his examination of the American past, Hergesheimer turned to the China trade that helped make New England rich. Gerrit Ammidon, the son of a famous Salem shipowner and retired captain, whose home is called Java Head, brings back from the Orient a Chinese wife, Taou Yuen, of aristocratic family. But she is received with kindness only by the wife of her husband's brother, and in addition arouses passion in a dissolute neighbor. Lured into a room she commits suicide by taking opium in order to escape him. In the end, the bereaved husband marries a girl he had once been fond of and sails back to the Orient.

Javert. In Victor Hugo's LES MISÉRABLES, the relentless pursuer of Jean Valjean. An officer of the police, Javert is the personification of the law's inexorability. He pursues the ex-convict Jean Valjean relentlessly, but finally commits suicide rather than arrest his prey.

Jay, John (1745–1829). American diplomat, jurist, and public official. After serving in the Continental Congress and as joint commissioner in making peace with Great Britain, he was secretary of foreign affairs under the Confederation. Upon the adoption of the Constitution, which he defended as one of the authors of THE FEDERALIST papers, he became chief justice (1789–1795) of the Supreme Court. In 1794 he was made special envoy to Great Britain to settle differences that had arisen over British failure to comply with the Treaty of 1783. The resulting treaty, known in the U.S. as Jay's Treaty, provided for British evacuation of the Northwest Territory and set up machinery for settling other grievances, though it was silent about British violations of American neutral rights during the Anglo-French war. As Jay had foreseen, the treaty was extremely unpopular; he was denounced in the press and burned in effigy.

jazz. Syncopated music of American Negro and possibly African origin that, in the 20th century, grew out of the dance and folk music of the American Negro and out of elements derived from Protestant hymns and march tunes. Among the predecessors of jazz are work songs, SPIRITUALS, ragtime, and blues (which has continued to be the main vocal form of jazz). Different jazz styles are identified with the successive decades of this century: hot jazz, or Dixieland, in the twenties; swing in the thirties; bebop in the forties; cool and progressive jazz in the fifties.

The extraordinary vitality of jazz, particularly in its rhythms, has extended its popularity throughout the world. It has influenced literature and other arts both implicitly and explicitly, for jazz also often connotes certain attitudes on the part of its listeners and performers; e.g., a freedom of behavior and feeling of exclusiveness that have interested writers since the twenties. Among the earliest of these writers were F. Scott Fitzgerald, John Dos Passos, and James T. Farrell. A resurgence of interest in the people associated with jazz has accompanied the rise of beat writing.

Some poets, both beat and otherwise, have imitated the rhythms of jazz, especially BLUES. Among them are Langston Hughes, Vachel Lindsay, Gregory Corso, Allen Ginsberg, and Gary Snyder. See George GERSHWIN; Aaron COPLAND.

Jazz Age. A term used to designate the period of the 1920's in the U.S. At that time the apparent emotional abandon of jazz seemed best to express the spirit of determined unconventionality, gaiety, and dissipation of the American boom era that followed World War I. Such dances as the "Black Bottom" and "Charleston" went hand in hand with "speakeasies," "petting parties," and the bobbed hair, short skirts, and new freedom of behavior of the "flapper." F. Scott FITZGERALD was one of the first to use this term by titling one of his works *Tales from the Jazz Age* (1922). Other writers of this period include John Dos Passos and James T. Farrell.

J.B. (1958). A verse drama by Archibald MacLeish. Based on the biblical story of Job, it is noted for its circus-tent setting and play-within-a-play structure. In contrast with Job, *J.B.* shows modern man in a universe whose laws he cannot understand; while the Voice from the Whirlwind offers an answer which is irrelevant to the human problem of how to live, the play simply affirms man's capacity to "endure and Love."

Jean Barois (1913). A long novel, written almost entirely in dialogue, by Roger MARTIN DU GARD. Its hero decides that conscience compels him to leave the church, and though he finds few answers to problems of morality and conscience in agnosticism, he remains a free-thinker until his old age, when he returns to the church, more through fear of death than out of conviction. The novel deals in part with the Dreyfus affair and with its shattering effect upon French intellectual life.

Jean Christophe (1904–1912, 10 vols.). A novel series by Romain ROLLAND. The hero, Jean Christophe Kraft, is a German-born musician who travels through France and Germany, observing and criticizing contemporary civilization. A satire on modern society, the massive work is also a sensitive analysis of the artist's isolated position in his world. Rolland, speaking through his musician hero, proposes that the purpose of art is to express moral truth and thus to combat the disintegration of values.

Jean de Meun[g]. Pen name of **Jean Clopinel** (c. 1250–c. 1305). French poet and scholar. His continuation of the ROMANCE OF THE ROSE satirizes most existing institutions of his day and makes Nature the standard for all moral and social judgments in a series of lucidly reasoned arguments.

Jean des Entommeures, Frère. See FRIAR JOHN.

Jean Jacques. The given name of Jean Jacques ROUSSEAU, by which he is often called.

Jeanne d'Arc. See JOAN OF ARC.

Jeanneret, Charles Edouard. See LE CORBUSIER.

Jean Paul. See Jean Paul Friedrich RICHTER.

Jean Santeuil (1952). An unfinished novel, written 1895–1899, by Marcel PROUST. It is largely an adapted version of his own life until 1895. Many of the characters and incidents are prototypes of those in his major work, *Remembrance of Things Past* (1913–1927), though none of the names are the same.

Jedermann. See EVERYMAN.

Jeeves. The perfect English valet. He appears in many stories by P. G. WODEHOUSE.

Jeffers, Robinson (1887–1962). American poet. He is known for his concern with the introversion of modern culture; his belief in extreme individualism, tending toward a Nietzschean adulation of the hero; his attraction to strong, primitive types; and his quasi-mystical preoccupation with sexual abnormality. The son of a minister, educated in the classics from early childhood, Jeffers based many of his narrative poems on biblical and classical sources. After two romantic volumes, *Flagons and Apples* (1912) and *Californians* (1916), he wrote TAMAR, AND OTHER POEMS. This volume, which caused the recognition of his unusual dramatic power, included among its contents THE TOWER BEYOND TRAGEDY. The title poem of ROAN STALLION, TAMAR, AND OTHER POEMS, his next collection, was based on a Monterey incident in which a man was killed by his own horse. Jeffers used the incident to contrast the primitive sexuality of the stallion with the degenerate lusts of man.

The Women at Point Sur (1927) deals with a minister who tries to found a new religion but is driven mad by his conflicting desires. The title poem of CAWDOR, AND OTHER POEMS is based on Greek mythology; DEAR JUDAS, AND OTHER POEMS is biblical. *Descent to the Dead* (1931) contains *At the Fall of an Age,* a dramatic poem dealing with the execution of Helen by Polyxo 20 years after the fall of Troy. THURSO'S LANDING reveals, perhaps more than any other of Jeffers' poems, his abhorrence of modern civilization. His many other volumes include *Give Your Heart to the Hawks and Other Poems* (1933), reiterating his idea that man must go beyond humanity if he is to survive; *Solstice and Other Poems* (1935), containing an early use of the Medea story, to which Jeffers returned in *Medea* (1946); *Such Counsels You Gave to Me and Other Poems* (1937), *Selected Poetry* (1938); *Be Angry at the Sun* (1941); *The Double Axe* (1948); and *Hungerfield, and Other Poems* (1954).

Jefferson, Thomas (1743–1826). Third president of the U.S. (1801–1809). A graduate of the College of William and Mary, Jefferson was admitted to the bar in 1767 and sat in the Virginia House of Burgesses from 1769 to 1775. As a delegate to the Continental Congress (1775–1776), he drafted the DECLARATION OF INDEPENDENCE. While he was a member of the Virginia House of Delegates (1776–1779), he supported the abolition of primogeniture and entail, the establishment of religious freedom, and the separation of church and state. After serving as wartime governor of Virginia and as a member of congress, he succeeded Franklin as minister to France, where he published his *Notes on Virginia* (1784–1785), still considered a valuable source of information about the natural history of Virginia as well as about 18th-century political and social life. He was named secretary of state under Washington, but resigned in 1793 as a result of long-standing political and personal differences with Alexander Hamilton and his supporters. Jefferson's championship of states' rights and agrarian interests distinguished him and his followers from the Hamiltonians and resulted in the emergence of the Democratic-Republican Party, of which Jefferson was the leader. He was the presidential candidate of the new party in 1796, but ran second to John ADAMS, the Federalist nominee, and, in accordance with the practice then followed, became vice president. In 1798, Jefferson and James Madison prepared the Virginia and Kentucky Resolutions in reply to the Federalists' ALIEN AND SEDITION ACTS.

In the election of 1800, Jefferson tied with Aaron Burr in electoral votes and was chosen president by the House of Representatives with the support of Hamilton, who considered Jefferson the lesser of two evils. Important events of his administration were the Tripolitan War, the LOUISIANA PURCHASE, and the short-lived Embargo Act, designed to preserve American neutrality rights.

After 40 years of public service, Jefferson retired permanently to his home at MONTICELLO in 1809, devoting much of his time to the creation of a university for Virginia. He was reconciled with his old political opponent, John Adams, and the two men, from 1811 to their deaths, carried on a voluminous correspondence, which is one of the most interesting in American letters. Perhaps the most versatile of the founding fathers, he is remembered for his faith in the capacity of the people to govern themselves through representative institutions. On his tombstone at Monticello is the inscription he ordered: "Author of the Declaration of American Independence, of the Statute of Virginia for religious freedom, and Father of the University of Virginia." His other writings include *A Summary View of the Rights of British America* (1774), *A Manual of Parliamentary Practice* (1801), and *Life of Captain [Meriwether] Lewis* (1817).

Jeffreys, George. 1st Baron **Jeffreys of Wem** (1648–1689). Welsh-born English jurist. As chief justice and lord chancellor of England, he supported the efforts of James II to rule as an absolute monarch. His conduct at the trials known as the BLOODY ASSIZES, over which he presided, made his name a byword for injustice and brutality. When James was overthrown, Jeffreys was imprisoned and died in the Tower of London.

Jeffries, Richard (1848–1887). English writer and novelist. He wrote *Gamekeeper* (1877) and *Red Deer* (1884), two collections of sketches, and the novels *Wood Magic* (1881) and *Bevis* (1882). These books are distinguished by their close and poetic observation of nature, particularly animal life.

Jehovah. In the Bible, the Christian version of the word used for the name of God, the Almighty, the Supreme Being in the Hebrew Scriptures. It is a transliteration of the four Hebrew letters *Y, H, W, H*, which form the incommunicable name of God. These four letters are called the tetragram. Since the Jews consider the name of God too sacred to be pronounced, the tetragram is read aloud as Adonai or Elohim, when encountered in the Scripture. The original form and pronunciation of the tetragram has been lost over the centuries; there is evidence that it may have been Yahwe or Yave, but certainly not Jehovah.

Jehu. In the Old Testament, the son of Nimshi, who overthrew the Ahab dynasty and took over the throne. He put to death King Joram, son of Ahab, the evil queen mother, Jezebel, and all the prophets of Baal. A *jehu* is a humorous appellation for a coachman, in reference to the swift chariot which Jehu drove (II Kings 9:20).

Jekyll, Dr. See STRANGE CASE OF DR. JEKYLL AND MR. HYDE, THE.

Jellyby, Mrs. In Charles Dickens' BLEAK HOUSE, an enthusiastic, unthinking philanthropist who forgets that charity should begin at home. She would do anything for the poor fan-makers and flower girls of distant Borrioboola-Gha, but shamefully neglects her own children and would send away a poor beggar dying of starvation on her doorstep.

Jenkins, Winifred. In Tobias Smollett's novel HUMPHREY CLINKER, Miss Tabitha Bramble's illiterate maid. An earlier Mrs. MALAPROP, she exhausts the possibilities of humor in English misspelling.

Jenkins' Ear, War of. The popular name of a war between England and Spain (1739–1741) declared by Sir Robert Walpole when the English mariner Robert Jenkins declared that a Spanish captain, upon boarding his vessel, had cut off his ear. The conflict was absorbed in the War of the Austrian Succession.

Jenkinson, Ephraim. A sharp old swindler in Oliver Goldsmith's novel THE VICAR OF WAKEFIELD. He sells the vicar's son Moses a pair of green spectacles for the money with which Moses was supposed to have purchased a harness horse. His eventual reformation saves the Primrose family from ruin.

Jenner, Edward (1749–1823). English physician and discoverer of vaccination. His best known work is *An Inquiry into the Causes and Effects of the Variolae Vaccinae* (1798). He first performed public vaccination on his own son in 1796, but it was not until 1853 that the practice was made compulsory in England.

Jennie Gerhardt (1911). A novel by Theodore DREISER. Jennie's harsh German father forces her to leave home when he discovers that she is pregnant; an Ohio senator had promised to marry her but died before he could carry out his intention. She becomes the mistress of the scion of a wealthy family, Lester Kane, who is finally forced by his family to give her up. He marries in his own class, becomes ill, and is nursed by Jennie. When he dies she steals in to his funeral, afraid to speak to his family. Jennie's daughter dies, and she is left to face life alone, but with the characteristic acceptance she has shown all along.

Jennifer Lorn (1923). A novel by Elinor WYLIE. Her first novel, it deals with 18th-century England and India at the time of Warren Hastings. It is a satiric study of a pompous aristocrat, seen through the eyes of his wife. The title is a pun: Jenny forlorn.

Jenseits von Gut und Böse. See BEYOND GOOD AND EVIL.

Jensen, Johannes Vilhelm (1873–1950). Danish novelist, poet, and essayist. Jensen attained literary prominence with the publication of *Himmerlandsfolk* (*Himmerland Tales*, 1898), stories of his native Jutland. *Kongens Fald* (*The Fall of the King*, 3 vols., 1900–1901), his first successful novel, paints a vivid and appreciative although sometimes critical portrait of Denmark and her people. Philosophically committed to Darwinism, Jensen published *Den Lange Rejse* (*The Long Journey*, 6 vols., 1908–1922), an evolutionary study of the Cimbrians, i.e., the Teutonic race, which moves from the baboon stage of the preglacial age to the time of Christopher Columbus. In his novels and even in his lyric verse, Jensen expressed his Darwinist convictions. From 1906 to 1940 eight volumes of *Myter* (*Myths*) appeared, containing poetic and subtle stories and essays. He was awarded the Nobel prize for literature in 1944.

Jensen, Thit Marie Kirstine (1876–1957). Danish novelist, sister of Johannes Jensen. Her early novels, among them *Martyrium* (1905), *Hemskoen* (1911), *Gerd* (1918), *Den erotiske Hamsta* (1919), and *Af Blod er du kommet* (1928), portray peasant life and express vigorous feminist convictions. Later she turned from present reform to Denmark's past, producing such fine historical novels as *Valdemar Atterdag* (2 vols., 1940), *Drotten* (2 vols., 1943), and *Rigets Arving* (2 vols., 1946).

Jephthah's daughter. The only daughter of Jephthah, judge of Israel. She went to greet him on his return home from victory over the Ammonites, unaware that he had vowed to offer up to Jehovah the first thing that met him. Her story is told in *Judges*.

Jeremiah. An Old Testament book. The prophet Jeremiah, who gave his name to the book, lived in Jerusalem during the time of the fall of this city to the Babylonians. With the destruction of the city and the temple, the emphasis in Jeremiah turns from the nation to the individual. The root of the prophet's religion is in his own heart, rather than a temple building. Matthew reports that Jesus was thought to be the returned Jeremiah.

Jeremy (1919). A semiautobiographical novel by Hugh WALPOLE about the daily life of a small boy. *Jeremy and Hamlet* (1923) and *Jeremy at Crale* (1927) are sequels.

Jericho. One of the oldest inhabited sites in Palestine, perhaps the oldest in the world. Mesolithic flints associated with fortifications are traceable to the ninth millennium B.C., a "proto-Neolithic" culture predates the eighth. Jericho was the first city conquered by the Israelites under Joshua after they crossed the Jordan into their Promised Land.

Jeroboam. In the Old Testament, the son of Nebat who "made Israel to sin" (I Kings 15:34).

Under his leadership, 10 tribes revolted against REHOBOAM, the son of Solomon, and set up a separate northern state with Jeroboam as king. Because of the idol worship he initiated, his name has become a byword for wickedness. A very large wine bottle or flagon is called a *jeroboam,* in allusion to his power and strength.

Jerome, St. (full Latin name, **Sophronius Eusebius Hieronymus;** c. 340–420). One of the fathers of the Western Church and translator of the Latin version of the Bible known as the VULGATE. He is generally represented as an aged man in a cardinal's dress, writing or studying, with a lion seated beside him. Legend has it that while St. Jerome was lecturing one day, a lion entered the schoolroom and lifted up one of its paws. All the disciples fled, but Jerome, seeing that the paw was injured, drew a thorn from it and dressed the wound. The lion, out of gratitude, showed a wish to stay with its benefactor.

Jerome, Jerome K[lapka] (1859–1927). English novelist and playwright, best known as a humorist. His works include *Three Men in a Boat* (1889), a novel, and *The Passing of the Third Floor Back* (1908), a modern morality play set in a boarding house.

Jerusalem. A city in Palestine. It is a holy city for Christians, Jews, and Muslims. A Canaanite city long before the arrival of the Israelites, Jerusalem was captured by David (c. 1,000 B.C.) who made it his capital city. David's son Solomon built his famous temple in Jerusalem, but after his death the city began to decline in importance. Under Solomon's son, Rehoboam, the city was sacked by the Egyptians (920 B.C.). A weak city, it remained fairly secure for two centuries until the Assyrians began to invade Judah in the middle of the eighth century. Most of the kingdom was lost in ransom, but the city itself was spared until 586 B.C., when it fell to the Babylonians, who destroyed it almost completely.

More than a century later (c. 420) Jerusalem was rebuilt under Nehemiah. The city was captured again by Alexander the Great in 332 B.C. After a period of domination by the Seleucid kings of Antioch, the revolt of the MACCABEES restored rule of the city to the Jews.

Jerusalem became a Roman city in 46 B.C. under Herod who rebuilt it on a grand scale. Revolts in A.D. 66–70 and 132–135 saw the city leveled again. Under Byzantine control for five centuries, it fell to the Muslims in 638.

Modern Jerusalem is a city divided between the Jews and Arabs who fought bitterly for it when the state of Israel was created in 1948.

Jerusalem. A long, mystical poem (1804) by William BLAKE in which he presents his theory that the world of imagination is a world of eternity after death.

Jerusalem (1901–1902). A collection of stories by Selma LAGERLÖF, dealing with an old peasant family, the Ingmars of Ingmarson, and their devotion to the family farm in Sweden. The title refers to a pilgrimage to Jerusalem, for which the land is finally sold at auction by one member of the family. Another Ingmar, however, renounces his fiancée and marries a rich woman in order to save the farm.

Jerusalén Conquistada (1609). A historical epic by Lope de VEGA. Although the theme is the unsuccessful attempt of Richard the Lion-Hearted to capture Jerusalem from the Saracens, it contains much legendary and nonhistorical material, such as the participation of Alfonso VIII of Spain in this crusade.

Jerusalem Delivered. See GERUSALEMME LIBERATA.

Jesse. In the Old Testament, the father of David. A *Jesse tree* is a genealogical tree, usually represented as a vine or as a large brass candlestick with many branches, tracing the lineage of the house of David from Jesse to Jesus, it having been prophesied that the Messiah would be a "rod out of the stem of Jesse." (Isa. 11:1.) Jesse is himself sometimes represented in a recumbent position with the vine rising out of his loins. A stained-glass window showing Jesse and the tree tracing the ancestry from him to Jesus is called a *Jesse window.*

Jesse, F[ryniwyd] Tennyson (18?-1958). English novelist, dramatist, journalist, and criminologist. Her best novel was *The Lacquer Lady* (1929). She described a number of cases for the *Notable British Trials* series.

Jessel, Miss. See TURN OF THE SCREW, THE.

Jessica. The rebellious daughter of Shylock in Shakespeare's MERCHANT OF VENICE. "Wise, fair, and true," she elopes with Lorenzo, but is practical enough to take with her a portion of her father's treasure.

jester. See FOOL.

Jesuit Martyrs of North America. Eight French missionaries whom the Indians martyred in the 17th century in New York and Canada: the priests Isaac Jogues, Jean de Brébeuf, Noël Chabanel, Anthony Daniel, Charles Garnier, Gabriel Lalemant, and the laymen René Goupil and John Lalande. All eight were canonized by Pope Pius XI in 1930 and celebrated in an epic poem, *Brébeuf and his Brethren,* by the Canadian poet Edwin John Pratt (1883-   ).

Jesuits. A name applied to members of the Society or Company of Jesus, founded in 1534 by St. Ignatius of LOYOLA. From the first six disciples made by Ignatius, four of whom were Spaniards, the order had grown to over 1000 at the time of his death in 1556. Jesuits were particularly active in three fields: education, missionary endeavor in non-Catholic lands, and the development of deeper spiritual life.

The order was founded to combat the Reformation and to propagate the Roman Catholic faith among the heathen, but through its discipline, organization, and methods of secrecy it soon acquired such political power that it came into conflict with both the civil and religious authorities. It was driven from England in 1579, from France in 1594, from Venice in 1607, from Spain in 1767, from Naples in 1768; in 1773 it was suppressed by Pope Clement XIV, but was revived in 1814.

Owing to the casuistical principles maintained by many of the leaders of the older organization and attributed to the order as a whole, the name *Jesuit* acquired a very opprobrious signification both in Protestant and Roman Catholic countries. A *Jesuit* or *Jesuitical person* came to connote a deceiver or prevaricator.

Jesus or **Jesus Christ** (Heb. "the Messiah"), or **Christ Jesus.** Known also as **Jesus of Nazareth.** Born between 4 and 6 B.C. and crucified about A.D. 28.

One of the world's major religious figures, he is regarded by his followers as the Messiah predicted by the Old Testament prophets (Isa. 9: 2-6). The events of his life are recorded in the four Gospels of the New Testament. His genealogy is traced through David to Abraham.

Miraculous events occurred at his birth, but little is known of his youth and young manhood. He was born and lived in a time of distress and oppression. After his baptism by John the Baptist, he gathered 12 disciples (see APOSTLES) and began to teach his message of God's redeeming love for all mankind, the necessity of repentance, and the duty of the individual to God and to other men. Through his doctrine of salvation for mankind and his extraordinary healing powers, he had a large following among the common people. He became suspect with the authorities, both Roman and Jewish, because of his popularity and his attacks on the hypocrisy of the privileged. He foretold the advent of a new Kingdom of God, which the priests regarded as blasphemy and the Romans as sedition.

After his ministry in Galilee, he went to Jerusalem for the observation of Passover. There, after the Last Supper, JUDAS ISCARIOT, one of the disciples, betrayed him to the authorities. He was arrested by the Roman soldiery, tried, and crucified. His followers believe that after three days he rose from the dead and later ascended to heaven to assume his rightful place with God.

The Christian Church was founded by the followers of Jesus, after his death. He is viewed as the word of God made flesh (John 1:14), the divine Incarnation that became fully human to redeem mankind. Through a series of Church councils, the nature of Jesus' exact relation to the Godhead was defined in the concept of the TRINITY, the three-person union of Father, Son, and Holy Spirit.

Jeune Alcidiane, La. See Marin le Roy GOMBERVILLE.

Jeune fille Violaine, La. See TIDINGS BROUGHT TO MARY, THE.

Jeune Parque, La (The Youngest of the Fates, 1917). A long poem by Paul VALÉRY. Written in a free-flowing version of classical rhymed Alexandrine couplets, it takes the form of a dramatic monologue. The young speaker is a maiden; she is simultaneously fearful of and fascinated by the desire awakening within her, for the violation of her self that will mark the beginning of her participation in the life process and her responsibility for new life.

Jevons, William Stanley (1835-1882). English economist and logician. He was a pioneer in the application of statistics to economics. Among his numerous books are *Pure Logic* (1864), *Theory of Political Economy* (1878), and *The State in Relation to Labour* (1882).

Jewett, Sarah Orne (1849-1909). American novelist and short-story writer. Her familiarity with her native Maine countryside enabled her to become one of the most successful of the local-color writers. Miss Jewett's pictures of New England life were described as "poetic realism" by Edward Garnett. *Deephaven* (1877), a collection of sketches of life in rural Maine, was her first successful book. Her masterpiece, THE COUNTRY OF THE POINTED FIRS, a series of episodes taking place in a Maine seaport town, is considered a minor classic.

Jew, the Wandering. See WANDERING JEW, THE.

Jew of Malta, The (probably performed in 1589; quarto of 1633, first extant edition). A romantic tragedy by Christopher MARLOWE. *The Jew of Malta* is essentially a dramatic portrait of one man, Barabas. At first the Jewish merchant, counting his "infinite riches in a little room," shares the longing for some extraordinary power and the ability to express his desire in stirring poetry that characterize other Marlovian heroes. He is a man of some dignity, unjustly persecuted by hypocritical Christians. But during the course of the play he degenerates from a human being who commands sympathy into a caricature of the grasping, greedy Jew dominated by his desire for gold. Barabas murders his daughter and an entire nunnery with poisoned porridge, performs other atrocities, and dies in an absurdly grotesque manner by falling into a bubbling caldron.

Jezebel. In the Old Testament, the wife of AHAB, who married him before he became king of Israel. After establishing the Phoenician worship of Baal at her husband's court, she was put to death at the order of JEHU.

A painted jezebel refers to a flaunting woman of bold spirit but loose morals (see II Kings 19:30). John Masefield's poetic drama *King's Daughter* (1923) is based on the story of Jezebel and Jehu.

Jibanananda Das (1899–1954). Bengali poet. He was born in East Pakistan. Considered to be the finest exponent of "pure poetry" in India, he taught English literature in a college in Calcutta. Of his published volumes, the finest is *Banalata Sen,* translated into English in 1962.

Jiménez, Juan Ramón (1881–1958). Spanish poet. His work, which has had the greatest impact upon contemporary Spanish poetry, brought Jiménez the Nobel Prize for literature in 1956. Educated at Seville, the poet resided in Madrid for some years before the civil war sent him into exile. His earlier volumes are lyrical, full of delicate metaphors, and stress folk motifs; these include *Ninfeas* (1900), *Baladas de primavera* (1910), and the more traditional, spiritual work, *Sonetos espirituales* (1917). The last-mentioned year also marks the publication of *Diario de un poeta recién casado* (1917), the poet's first venture into the field of "pure poetry." It is characterized, as is his later work, by a striving for simplicity, free verse, intense concentration, and condensation of form. Perhaps his best-known work is the prose poem *Platero y yo* (1917), which relates the wanderings of the poet and his poetical donkey through Andalusia. Jiménez's poetry may be surveyed in the anthology of his own selection, *Tercera antología poética* (1942).

Jimson, Gulley. The passionate, comic artist hero of Joyce Cary's novel THE HORSE'S MOUTH.

Jingle, Alfred. In Charles Dickens' PICKWICK PAPERS, a strolling actor who imposes for a time on the members of the Pickwick Club. He is discovered to be a scoundrel and an imposter.

jingo. A word from the meaningless jargon of the 17th century conjurers. Probably it was substituted for God, in the same way as are *gosh, golly,* and the like. In Motteux' translation of Rabelais (1694), where the original reads *par Dieu* (Bk. iv. lvi), the English rendering is "By jingo." There is a possibility that the word is Basque *Jinko* or *Jainko,* God, and was introduced by sailors.

The later meaning of the word, a blustering so-called patriot who is itching to go to war on the slightest provocation, or a chauvinist, is taken from a music-hall song by G. W. Hunt, which was popular in 1878 when the country was supposed to be on the verge of intervening in the Russo-Turkish War on behalf of the Turks:

We don't want to fight; but, by Jingo, if we do,
We've got the ships, we've got the men, and got the money too.

The Russophobes became known as the *Jingoes,* and such policy has been labeled *Jingoism* ever since.

jinn or **genii** (singular, *jinnee*). Demons of Muslim legend thought to have been created from fire 2000 years before Adam was made of clay. Fable holds that they were governed by a race of kings named Suleyman, one of whom built the pyramids. Living chiefly in Mount KAF, they assume the forms of serpents, dogs, cats, monsters, or even human beings and become invisible at will. Evil jinn are hideously ugly, while the good are exquisitely beautiful. See AFREET; EBLIS; GIAN BEN GIAN.

Jinnistan. The Arabian fairyland.

Jo. In Charles Dickens' BLEAK HOUSE, a poor little outcast living in one of London's decaying tenements. The child wanders about from place to place until he finally dies of want and neglect. He is one of Dickens' most poignant characters.

Joad, C[yril] E[dwin] M[itchinson] (1891–1953). English philosopher. Many of his books are of a popularizing nature; among them are *Essays in Common Sense Philosophy* (1919), *Great Philosophies of the World* (1931), and *Guide to Modern Thought* (1933).

Joad family. The central characters in John Steinbeck's novel THE GRAPES OF WRATH. Escaping from the dust bowl of Oklahoma during the depths of the depression, they migrate to California as fruit pickers.

Joan, Pope. A mythical female pope, fabled in the Middle Ages to have succeeded Leo IV (855). The vulgar tale is that Joan conceived a violent passion for the monk Folda and in order to get admission to him assumed the monastic habit. Being clever and popular, she was elected pope, but was discovered through giving birth to a child during the enthronement.

Joan La Pucelle. Shakespeare's name for JOAN OF ARC, whom he depicts in HENRY VI: PART I as "a vile fiend and shameless courtezan."

Joanna or **Joan the Mad.** Also known as **Juana la Loca** (1497–1555). Spanish queen. The daughter of Ferdinand and Isabella, she married (1496) Philip the Fair of Flanders, whose infidelities probably aggravated her mental disorder. By him she bore the future Charles V. Although she inherited the crown of Castile upon the death of Isabella in 1504, the death of Philip (1506) increased her derangement, and Ferdinand sent her to live in seclusion in Tordesillas, while he became regent of Castile. At the time it was widely rumored that she was sane and was merely the victim of her family's machinations.

Joan of Arc. *Fr.* **Jeanne d'Arc** or **Darc.** Later known as the **Maid of Orleans,** *Fr.* **La Pucelle** (1412–1431). French heroine. A deeply religious peasant girl of the village of Domrémy, she began at 13 to have visions in which she identified the voices of St. Michael, St. Catherine, and St. Margaret. Henry VI of England had been crowned king of France in 1422, and when the English began their siege of Orleans in 1428, Joan become convinced that the saints had chosen her to repulse the English and conduct the French Dauphin to be crowned at the Reims cathedral. She finally convinced the Dauphin of her mission and, in male attire, led the French troops to victory at Orleans and elsewhere (May and June, 1429) and stood beside Charles VII at his coronation in July. But then she was not given sufficient troops, and her military campaign began to fail; she was taken prisoner in May, 1430, by the Burgundians, who sold her to their English allies six months later.

They did not want the English to execute her, however, until they could defame her in the eyes of the French peasants and troops, who regarded her as a saint. So she was turned over to the French ecclesiastical courts, the weak Charles not daring to interfere, and was tried on 12 charges of sorcery, wantonness in cutting her hair and wearing men's clothes, and blasphemous pride in regarding herself as responsible directly to God rather than to the Church. Worn out by the examination and condemned to the stake, she finally signed a recantation of her alleged sins; her sentence was commuted to life imprisonment. But in the next few days she resumed male attire and repudiated her recantation, so she was handed over to a secular English court and burned at the stake (May 30, 1431). After confused legal proceedings to shift the blame for her death, Joan was officially declared innocent in 1456; she was canonized as a saint in 1920.

The official records of her trial give the best account of the historical Joan. In literature she is treated variously as a witch, as in Shakespeare's *Henry VI,* reflecting contemporary English sentiment; with skepticism toward the mystic aura surrounding her belief in her voices, as in Voltaire's *La Pucelle* (1738, pub. 1755); or with complete acceptance of the supernatural element, making her a romantic heroine, as in Schiller's tragedy *Die Jungfrau von Orleans* (1801). Famous accounts of her life include the one in Michelet's *History of France* (1833–1867), Mark Twain's *Personal Recollections of Joan of Arc* (1896), and Anatole France's *Life of Joan of Arc* (1908). More recent plays about her include G. B. Shaw's *Saint Joan* (1923) and Jean Anouilh's *L'Alouette* (1953; translated by Christopher Fry as *The Lark,* 1955).

Job. An Old Testament book. The greatest poetic drama in the Old Testament, it is one of the most philosophically involved books in the Bible. The unknown, undated author deals with the problem of undeserved suffering and God's justice in the framework of an antique folk legend. Job and his friends discuss the question of whether suffering is always the punishment for sin and conversely whether sin is always punished.

The Lord, confident of Job's faith, permitted Satan to test him; thereupon, his wealth vanished, his children died and he was smitten with boils. Yet, despite his wife's advice to "curse God and die," he remained steadfast, and his faith was rewarded. (See ELIHU.)

In the Koran, Job's wife is said to have been either Rahmeh, daughter of Ephraim, son of Joseph, or Makhir, daughter of Manasses; and the tradition is recorded that Job, at the command of God, struck the earth with his foot from the dunghill where he lay, and instantly there welled up a spring of water with which his wife washed his sores and they were miraculously healed.

Job's comforter. One who intends to sympathize with you in your grief, but says that you brought it on yourself, thus in reality adding weight to your sorrow.

Job's post. A bringer of bad news.

Jocasta (Iokaste). See OEDIPUS.

Jocelyn (1836). A narrative poem by Alphonse LAMARTINE. The hero is a priest. As a lad he finds refuge from war in an Alpine cave, where he lives with another boy, who turns out to be a girl named Laurence. Although he loves her, he remains true to his priestly vows and leaves her for a life of self-denying devotion.

Jochumsson, Matthías (1835–1920). Icelandic poet and playwright. Although he founded modern drama in Iceland, he is most famous as a fine lyric poet. Elegaic, religious, and nature poems appear in the collections *Ljóðmoeli* (1884) and *Grettisljóð* (1897).

Jōdo Buddhism. See AMIDISM.

Joel. An Old Testament book named for its author. A very approximate date of 350 B.C. has been assigned to the writing. The central event is a devastating plague of locusts, described in terms of an apocalyptic vision. The return of God's love is foretold and with it the wealth of the land.

Joe Miller's Jests. A book of jokes compiled by John Mottley in 1739. He named it for Joseph Miller (1684–1738), a popular comedian of the day who could neither read nor write. The term Joe Miller has become synonymous with a stale joke.

John (1167–1216). King of England (1199–1216). The youngest son of Henry II and ELEANOR OF AQUITAINE, he was nicknamed "Lackland," because he had not shared in the division of Henry's territory; he was probably Henry's favorite son, however, and his subsequent rebellion against his father broke the old king's heart. John succeeded to the throne upon the death of his childless brother Richard I, successfully thwarting the claim of his nephew Arthur of Brittany. As a result of John's famous quarrel with Pope Innocent III over the selection of Stephen LANGTON as archbishop of Canterbury, England was laid under an interdict and the king was declared deposed; in 1213, however, John submitted to the pope, going so far as to make England a fief of the papacy. The following year John invaded France in an attempt to regain the provinces of Normandy, Anjou, and Touraine, which he had previously lost, but he was decisively defeated by Philip II of France at the battle of Bouvines. Meanwhile, John's arbitrary practices had aroused the ire of the English nobles, who compelled him to sign the MAGNA CARTA in 1215. He is the subject of KING JOHN, a play by Shakespeare, and is a character in Scott's *Ivanhoe* (1819).

John, St., also **St. John the Evangelist** or **the Divine.** One of the twelve, frequently called "the

Joe Miller's *JESTS:*

OR, THE

WITS

VADE-MECUM.

BEING

A Collection of the moſt Brilliant JESTS; the Politeſt REPARTEES; the moſt Elegant BONS MOTS, and moſt pleaſant ſhort Stories in the *Engliſh* Language.

Firſt carefully collected in the Company, and many of them tranſcribed from the Mouth of the Facetious GENTLEMAN, whoſe Name they bear; and now ſet forth and publiſhed by his lamentable Friend and former Companion, *Elijah Jenkins,* Eſq;

Moſt Humbly INSCRIBED

To thoſe CHOICE-SPIRITS *of the* AGE,

Captain BODENS, Mr. ALEXANDER POPE, Mr. Profeſſor LACY, Mr. Orator HENLEY, and JOB BAKER, the Kettle-Drummer.

LONDON:

Printed and Sold by T. READ, in *Dogwell-Court, White-Fryars, Fleet-Street.* MDCCXXXIX.

(Price One Shilling.)

Title page of *Joe Miller's Jests* (1739).

beloved disciple," since he is referred to as "that disciple whom Jesus loved" in the narrative of the Gospel of St. John. He was one of the sons of Zebedee and brother of St. James the Great. His day is December 27, and he is usually represented bearing a chalice from which a serpent issues, in allusion to his driving the poison from a cup presented him to drink. Tradition says that he took the Virgin Mary to Ephesus after the Crucifixion, but there is no evidence to support this. Most scholars now agree that while John was an influential leader of the early church, he was not the author of the fourth Gospel, the *Epistles of John,* or *The Revelation of St. John.* All of these works date after A.D. 80; Papias, a second century Christian writer, reports that John was killed in Palestine before A.D. 70.

John, Don. In Shakespeare's MUCH ADO ABOUT NOTHING, the jealous and vindictive bastard brother of Don Pedro, prince of Arragon. His plot against Claudio and Hero nearly succeeds, but he is finally undone and punished.

John, The Epistles of. Three short books of the New Testament. They are letters addressed to all Christians. The first two warn against the false teachings that had been filtering into the Church, with a special condemnation of Gnostic ideas. The third shows concern for an ambitious, arrogant young church official with whom the writer intends to deal personally. All three are held to be the work of one man, an elder of the church in Ephesus, named John (not to be confused with the apostle). Stylistic similarities plus an agreement in outlook indicate that this man was also the author of the fourth Gospel.

John, The Gospel According to St. The 4th book of the New Testament. The most spiritual of the accounts of Jesus' life, its emphasis is more on interpreting the meaning of his life and death than in recording the events. See JOHN, THE EPISTLES OF.

John Brown's Body (1928). A epic poem by Stephen Vincent BENÉT. A narrative of the Civil War, it opens with a prelude on the introduction of slavery, which is followed by a description of John Brown and his raid on Harpers Ferry. The poem, which considers both sides of the conflict with sympathy, includes sketches of famous participants, battles, the hardships of those on the home front, etc.

John Bull. The English nation personified, or the typical Englishman. Represented as a bluff, kind-hearted, bull-headed farmer, the character originated in John ARBUTHNOT's political satire *The History of John Bull,* which was first published in 1712 as *Law is a Bottomless Pit.* In Arbuthnot's work "John Bull" is the Englishman, the Frenchman is termed "Lewis BABOON," and the Dutchman "Nicholas FROG." See Lord STRUTT. In the early years of the 19th century there was a scurrilous journal of this name, and in 1906 the name was adopted for a British weekly edited by Horatio Bottomley.

John Bull's Other Island (1904). A play by George Bernard SHAW. It was written at the request of William Butler Yeats for the Irish Literary Theatre, the group that later became the Abbey Theatre, Dublin. As might be expected the play deals with the conflict between the Irish and the English over home rule. The preface, written after the play, is strictly political, but the drama is subtle, having neither hero nor villain. The Irishman, Larry Doyle, is sensitive, imaginative, and more mature than his English friend Tom Broadbent. Broadbent's life is more straightforward, simpler than Doyle's; he is practical, adaptable, less bothered by thinking or feeling.

The conflict between the two men is in their characteristics, not their personalities. By the end of the play Tom has assumed all of Larry's ties with his birthplace in Ireland: his girl, his Parliamentary candidacy, even control of his property. This happens, not through conniving—Tom is too honest—but through Larry's reticence and Tom's blunt ambition.

John Dory. A popular ballad of the 14th century, often referred to in later literature. John Dory was a French pirate who was taken prisoner by the English.

John Gabriel Borkman (1896). A play by Henrik IBSEN. The story of a man who sacrificed love for ambition, *John Gabriel Borkman* expresses Ibsen's belief that the only unforgivable sin is "to murder the love-life in a human soul." As a young man, Borkman dreamed of power and broke his engagement to Ella Rentheim because Hinkel, the man whose help he needed to succeed, wanted to marry her. Borkman then married Ella's sister, but Ella persistently refused Hinkel's proposals. Finally Hinkel exposed Borkman's misappropriation of the bank's money, and Borkman was sent to jail. The action of the play concerns the meeting, after many years, of Ella and Borkman, and the attempts of Ella, Borkman, and Mrs. Borkman to influence young Erhart Borkman to choose his duty to his relatives, rather than his right to live for his own happiness.

John Gilpin (1782). A humorous ballad by William Cowper; its full title is *The Diverting History of John Gilpin, Showing How He Went further than He Intended and Came Safe Home Again.* Gilpin's wife says to him, "Though we have been married twenty years, we have taken no holiday"; and at her advice the well-to-do linen draper agrees to make a family party, and dine at the Bell, at Edmondton. Mrs. Gilpin, her sister, and four children go in the chaise, and Gilpin promises to follow on horseback. The horse begins to trot, and then to gallop, and John, a bad rider, flies through Edmondton, and never stops till he reaches Ware. Here he heads his horse back towards Edmondton, but is unable to stop until he reaches his original starting place in London. The model for John Gilpin was a Mr. Beyer, of Paternoster Row, who died in 1791.

John Halifax, Gentleman (1856). A novel by Dinah Maria Mulock Craik. It is a moralistic tale concerning an orphan who by perseverance and fortitude establishes himself in life and marries the heroine, Ursula March.

John Hancock. See John Hancock.

John Henry (1931). A novel by Roark Bradford. See John Henry.

John Marr and Other Sailors (1888). A collection of 25 poems by Herman Melville. Marr and other sailors invoke the spirits of their long-dead shipmates. The poems are chiefly nostalgic in mood.

Johnny Appleseed. See Johnny Appleseed.

John of Gaunt. Duke of Lancaster (1340–1399). English noble. The fourth son of Edward III and the father of Henry Bolingbroke (later Henry IV), he was the founder of the house of Lancaster and, during his lifetime, one of the most powerful figures in England. In Shakespeare's Richard II, he is an English nationalist who, upon his death-bed, utters one of literature's most moving expressions of patriotism:

> This royal throne of kings, this scepter'd isle,
> This earth of majesty, this seat of Mars,
> This other Eden, demi-paradise,
> This fortress built by Nature for herself
> Against infection and the hand of war,
> This happy breed of men, this little world,
> This precious stone set in the silver sea,
> Which serves it in the office of a wall,
> Or as a moat defensive to a house,
> Against the envy of less happier lands;
> This blessed plot, this earth, this realm,
>   this England . . .

John of the Cross, St. Also known as San Juan de la Cruz. Religious name of **Juan de Yepes y Alvarez** (1542–1591). Spanish mystic and poet. Known as the "ecstatic Doctor," he became a Carmelite in 1563 and took an active part in Saint Teresa's

efforts to reform the order. He was canonized in 1726.

In his verse he blended his religious ardor and his gift for rich poetic imagery to produce what has been called "the supreme expression of Spanish mysticism." His best-known poems include *Noche oscura del alma, Llama de amor viva,* and the *canciones* of *La subida al Monte Carmelo.*

John o'Groat's House. Popularly considered the most northerly point in Great Britain. Originally, a building is said to have occupied this site, which is on the coast of Caithness, in Northern Scotland, near Duncansby Head; it had an eight-sided room with a door in each side and an octagonal table within. The story is that it was built by John o'Groat (or Jan Groot) who came from Holland with his two brothers in the reign of James IV of Scotland. They purchased lands, and in time the o'Groats increased, so that there came to be eight families of that name. They met regularly once a year in the house built by the founder, but on one occasion a question of precedency arose, and John o'Groat promised them the next time they came he would contrive to satisfy them all. Accordingly he built his eight-sided room, and the building became so noted that ever after the place has borne the name, *John o'Groat's House.*

Johns, Orrick (1887–1946). American poet and editor. Johns was a radical in politics and in poetry; *Second Avenue,* which won the *Lyric Year* poetry prize (1912), had a deliberate social concern. His poetry was collected in *Asphalt* (1917), *Black Branches* (1920), and *Wild Plum* (1926). He also wrote *Time of Our Lives: The Story of My Father and Myself* (1937).

Johnson, Andrew (1808–1875). 17th president of the U.S. (1865–1869). A self-educated ex-tailor, Johnson served as governor of Tennessee and as a member of the House of Representatives. Elected to the U.S. Senate in 1856, he was the only senator from any of the 11 seceded states who remained loyal to the Union when the Civil War broke out. He was Abraham Lincoln's running mate in 1864 and succeeded to the presidency after Lincoln's assassination. When Johnson attempted to carry out Lincoln's conciliatory policies toward the defeated South, he clashed with radical Republicans who demanded a harsher Reconstruction program under Congressional supervision. In 1868 he dismissed Secretary of War Edwin Stanton in defiance of the Tenure of Office Act (1867), which forbade the removal, without Senate approval, of officials whose appointments had been confirmed by the Senate. As a result, Johnson was impeached by the House of Representatives, but in the Senate trial was acquitted by a single vote, a two-thirds majority being needed for conviction.

Johnson, Esther (1681–1728). Lifelong friend of Jonathan Swift, immortalized by him as "Stella" in Journal to Stella. Their friendship began in 1689 in the home of Swift's patron, Sir William Temple (she may have been Temple's natural daughter), when Swift became her tutor, and they remained close friends until her death. There is unconvincing evidence that they were secretly married in 1716.

Johnson, James Weldon (1871–1938). American poet and lawyer. The first Negro admitted to the Florida bar since Reconstruction days, Johnson was a vigorous spokesman for his race. He edited *The*

Book of Negro Poetry (1922) and several collections of spirituals. He is also known for *God's Trombones* (1927), a collection of seven sermons in free verse. Among his other books are *The Autobiography of an Ex-Colored Man,* a novel (1912); *Fifty Years and Other Poems* (1917); *Black Manhattan* (1930); *Along This Way* (1933), his autobiography; and *Selected Poems* (1936).

Johnson, Lionel [Pigot] (1867–1902). English poet and critic. Johnson was a classicist, disciple of Walter Pater, and member of the RHYMERS' CLUB. He wrote *Poems* (1895) and *Post Liminium* (1911), a book of essays.

Johnson, Lyndon B[aines] (1908–1973). 36th president of the U.S. (1963–1969). After graduating from Southwest State Teachers College in San Marcos, Texas, in 1930, Johnson taught in the Houston public schools before going to Washington as secretary to a member of Congress. There he attracted the attention of President Roosevelt, who named him Texas state director of the National Youth Administration in 1935; Johnson was himself elected to the House in 1937 and served until 1948 when he won a seat in the U.S. Senate, defeating his rival by only 84 votes. As leader of the Democratic majority in the Senate from 1955 to 1961, Johnson became known as a superb legislative strategist who often won Democratic support for the policies of a Republican administration. After an unsuccessful bid for the Democratic presidential nomination in 1960, Johnson accepted the vice-presidential nomination on the ticket headed by John F. Kennedy and succeeded to the presidency after Kennedy's assassination in 1963.

Johnson, Pamela Hansford (1912–   ). English novelist and literary critic, wife of C. P. SNOW. Among her books are *This Bed Thy Center* (1935), *Six Proust Reconstructions* (1958), *The Humbler Creation* (1960), and *An Error of Judgement* (1962).

Johnson, Robert Underwood (1853–1937). American poet, editor, and public official. Johnson was editor of *Century Magazine* (1909–1913) and helped to establish the Hall of Fame at New York University; he was its director from 1919 to 1937. He helped to secure better copyright protection for authors, and served as ambassador to Italy (1920–1921). A volume of *Poems* was published in 1902, and enlarged in later editions; Johnson's memoirs are called *Remembered Yesterdays* (1923).

Johnson, Samuel (1696–1772). American philosopher, theologian, and teacher. The first native disciple of the 18th-century movement of rationalism, he is considered one of the most important thinkers of early America. His works include *An Introduction to the Study of Philosophy* (1731), *A System of Morality* (1746), and *Elementa Philosophica* (1752), which was printed by Benjamin Franklin. Johnson also served as the first president (1753–1763) of King's College (now Columbia University).

Johnson, Samuel. Known as **Dr. Johnson** (1709–1784). English lexicographer, essayist, poet, and moralist, the major literary figure in the second half of the 18th century; he was referred to as the GREAT CHAM OF LITERATURE. After being a schoolmaster and a bookseller for six years in Lichfield, the town of his birth, he left for London in 1737, with his tragedy *Irene* under his arm, and remained there permanently.

He was employed by Edward Cave, the founder of THE GENTLEMAN'S MAGAZINE, and contributed regularly essays, poems, Latin verses, and reports on Parliamentary debates to that publication. In 1738 he published his poem *London* which was compared favorably with the maturer works of Pope; in 1749, *Irene* was produced and indifferently received, and in the same year appeared *The Vanity of Human Wishes,* a poem marked with the pessimism that pervaded his life.

Meanwhile, he was earning renown as a prose moralist, notably with his periodical essays THE RAMBLER and THE IDLER, and later with his philosophical romance RASSELAS, which, though not distinguished for its action, is a cogent presentation of Johnson's moral views and his abiding theme: the vanity of human wishes and the impossibility of human happiness in an imperfect world. His literary style, often referred to as "Johnsonese," is severely balanced, Latinate, and pithy.

The monumental DICTIONARY OF THE ENGLISH LANGUAGE (1755) secured his reputation as a scholar and, though faulty, it was highly useful. His edition of Shakespeare (1765), historical and interpretative in approach, greatly stimulated Shakespearean scholarship. His *Preface to Shakespeare* is sometimes considered one of his finest pieces of prose. In defending Shakespeare for not following the "rules," he makes a good case for imaginative truth while attacking the classical unities: "The objection arising from the impossibility of passing the first hour at Alexandria, and the next at Rome, supposes, that when the play opens, the spectator really imagines himself at Alexandria, and believes that his walk to the theatre has been a voyage to Egypt, and that he lives in the days of Anthony and Cleopatra. Surely he that imagines this may imagine more."

His last years were spent in the society of other great men. Of this facet of Johnson's career—that of conversationalist—we have BOSWELL's LIFE OF SAMUEL JOHNSON, LL.D., to inform us. In person slovenly, in manner abrupt and even rude, driven by fears of insanity and damnation, suffering from hypochondria, he yet emerges from Boswell's *Life* as a man of essential kindness, generosity, and sociability. He had married (1735) a woman 20 years his senior to whom he was devoted; her death (1752) may have caused him to seek more and more the society of men with whom he could indulge his fondness for conversation. In 1764 the LITERARY CLUB was founded, and here Johnson found an outlet for conversation; he cultivated the art consciously and even admitted that he sometimes talked for the sake of victory.

In 1773, at the age of 64, he was prodded into taking a walking tour of the Hebrides with Boswell. His account of it, *A Journey to the Western Isles of Scotland* (1775), is overshadowed by Boswell's *The Journal of a Tour of the Hebrides with Samuel Johnson, LL.D.* which is the more lively for having Johnson as its subject. His last published work, in 10 volumes, is the biographical and critical LIVES OF THE POETS. See Hester Lynch THRALE.

Johnson Over Jordan (1939). A play about time by J. B. PRIESTLEY. Johnson, an aviator in an accident, re-experiences events from his past life.

Johnston, Mary (1870–1936). American historical novelist. She is known as the author of some of the best of the historical romances that were so popular at the beginning of the 20th century. Her second novel, To Have and to Hold, which is still read, was her most successful. It was followed by *Audrey* (1909). Most of her books are set in Virginia, *The Long Roll* (1911) and *Cease Firing* (1912) describing the Civil War from the Confederate point of view. Miss Johnston later became interested in mysticism, feminism, and socialism, and these found their way into such books as *Silver Cross* (1922).

John the Baptist, St. Patron saint of missionaries. He is so regarded because he was sent "to prepare the way of the Lord." He baptized Jesus in the river Jordan. John the Baptist was a fearless denouncer of the sins of his contemporaries who was thrown into prison and later beheaded because he opposed Herod's act of making away with his brother to secure his brother's wife Herodias. For the use of this story in drama and opera, see Salome.

Joinville, Jean de (1224–1317). French chronicler. As royal seneschal he accompanied Louis XI on his first crusade (1248–1252); his *Histoire de saint Louis* (1305–1309) is a colorful first-person narrative of the events of the crusade and of his friendship with the king.

Jolas, Eugene (1894–1952). American editor and founder of the experimental magazine transition. Born in Union City, N.J., Jolas spent his childhood in Lorraine. While still a youth, he returned to the U.S., worked on various newspapers, and became passionately interested in the contemporary avant-garde. He then went to Paris, where in 1927 he founded his famous magazine. A brilliant editor, trilingual from childhood, Jolas gave encouragement to numerous important writers in the 20's and 30's. His anthology *Transition Workshop* (1949) contains representative selections of the work he published and encouraged.

Jolliet or **Joliet, Louis** (1645–1700). Canadian-born French explorer. Though intended for the priesthood, Jolliet became a merchant and is remembered for his trips through the Mississippi Valley and the regions of the Gulf of St. Lawrence and Hudson Bay. See Jacques Marquette.

Jolly Beggars, The (1785, pub. 1799). A poem by Robert Burns written in the form of a cantata with recitative. It presents a series of songs by a group of beggars who tell variously of their sorrows, their wretchedness, their cynicism and disillusionments, and their scorn for the church and the nobility. The setting of the poem is "Poosie Nansie's" disreputable inn at Mauchline. (See also The Holy Fair.) It is considered by many critics to be Burns's most accomplished work.

Jolly Roger. See black flag.

Jolyon. A character in John Galsworthy's The Forsyte Saga. Young Jolyon is the most sensitive member of the Forsyte family. He marries Soames Forsyte's former wife, Irene.

Jonah. In the Old Testament, the prophet said to have been swallowed by a mammoth fish, and the Old Testament book bearing his name. Instructed by Jehovah to preach in the great but wicked city of Nineveh, he willfully took ship in another direction. When a storm arose, the sailors, after casting lots, threw Jonah into the sea to appease the Deity. He was swallowed by a whale in whose belly he lived for three days until "the great fish" deposited him on dry land. He then went to Nineveh where he was the cause of widespread repentance.

Jonathan. See David.

Jonathan Wild, the Great. *The Life of Mr. Jonathan Wild* (1743). A novel by Henry Fielding. Jonathan Wild was a famous highwayman and receiver of stolen goods (1682–1725), but his life has little relation to this ironic satire on tyranny and political innocence. Wild is meant to be an ironic representation of Sir Robert Walpole.

Jones, David (1895–). Anglo-Welsh water-color painter and writer. He has written In Parenthesis, *The Anathemata* (1954), a long fragmented fusion of prose and poetry about the history of Britain, and *Epoch and Artist; Selected Writings* (1959).

Jones, Sir **Henry Arthur** (1851–1929). English playwright. Influenced by Ibsen, his plays deal with social relationships and social problems. Among his works are *Breaking a Butterfly* (1885), *Saints and Sinners* (1891), Michael and his Lost Angel, and *Mrs. Dane's Defense* (1900).

Jones, Inigo (1573–1652). English architect. He is also well known for his designs of sets, costumes, and stage machinery for court masques written by Jonson, Heywood, and Davenant. These designs were of unprecedented elaborateness and ingenuity and had considerable influence upon later theater design. The elegance and grace of his architectural work, which was based on classical Renaissance elements, earned him the title of "the English Palladio." Among the buildings still in existence are the Banqueting Hall at Whitehall and the Queen's House at Greenwich.

Jones, James (1921–). American novelist. Born in Robinson, Ill., Jones joined the U.S. army, which provided the material for his massive and forceful first novel, From Here to Eternity, that established his reputation. The book, which won a National Book Award, aroused a critical storm, many

Inigo Jones's design for Whitehall Palace (London).

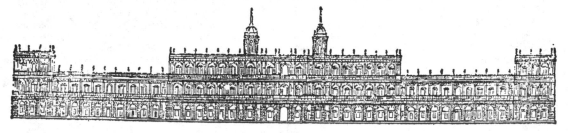

deploring the lurid language and shocking incidents, others admiring its vitality and force. His second novel, *Some Came Running* (1957), is concerned with the vagaries, mostly sexual, of small-town life. *The Pistol* (1959), a novella, and *The Thin Red Line* (1962), a full-length novel, are both concerned with the military.

Jones, John Paul (1747–1792). Scottish-born American naval officer, famed for his exploits in the Revolution. In a naval engagement off the coast of England (1779), Jones captured the British warship *Serapis,* although his own vessel, the BONHOMME RICHARD, was sunk. In response to a British demand for surrender during the battle, Jones is said to have replied: "I have not yet begun to fight!" He is the model for the hero of Cooper's novel *The Pilot* (1823) and a prominent character in Winston Churchill's *Richard Carvel* (1899).

Jones, Robert Edmond (1887–1954). American stage designer. Known for the sets he did for some of the most notable theatrical productions of the first half of the 20th century, he frequently worked with experimental troupes, among them the Washington Square Players, the Provincetown Players, the Greenwich Village Theater, and the Theatre Guild. He also was the author of *The Dramatic Imagination* (1941).

Jones, Lady Roderick. See Enid BAGNOLD.

jongleurs. Medieval entertainers, including acrobats, jugglers, and exhibitors of animals as well as musicians and reciters of poetry. They entertained at the courts of the nobility, and also in public places, especially near the shrines and churches along the routes of pilgrimages. It was the jongleurs who sang the CHANSONS DE GESTE, FABLIAUX, and other romances and lyrics written by the TROUVÈRES, although sometimes a jongleur was also a trouvère: that is, he would be both poet and singer-musician. Jongleurs permanently employed by a court were called *ménestrels,* or minstrels, and the security they enjoyed allowed them to devote more time to literary composition, so that by the 14th century there was considerably more specialization of function between composers and performers.

Jonson, Ben (1573–1637). English dramatist and poet. His father having died a month before his birth, Jonson was raised as the stepson of a bricklayer, and briefly entered this trade after leaving school. Though considered the most learned of the Elizabethan dramatists, his formal education seems to have been limited to his years at the Westminster School, where he was sent at the expense of its master, William Camden. He spent a short time as a soldier in the Netherlands, returned to England and, some time not later than 1592, married. During the next six years he probably existed as an actor and dramatic hack-writer, reworking old plays. His first original play, EVERY MAN IN HIS HUMOUR, was performed in 1598, with Shakespeare as a member of the cast. A comedy that already gives evidence of Jonson's brilliant gift for caricature and comic realism, it presents a group of assorted characters, each dominated—almost possessed—by one overriding characteristic, or HUMOR. Later in 1598 Jonson killed a man in a duel, and was imprisoned and charged with manslaughter. While in prison he was converted to Catholicism, to which he adhered for 12 years. He

narrowly escaped execution, but was released by benefit of clergy, forfeiting his property and receiving a brand on his left thumb. This incident, however, seemed to have few untoward effects on him, and the following year a sequel to his first play, called *Every Man Out of His Humour,* was produced at the Globe Theater. Less coherent in plot, and containing more blatant caricatures, it assailed the morals and foibles of the age, and contained (in response to John MARSTON's satiric portrait of him in HISTRIOMASTIX) veiled attacks on some of his fellow playwrights. *Cynthia's Revels,* which followed in 1600, was a flinging down of the gauntlet in the now-raging WAR OF THE THEATERS between Jonson, Marston, and Thomas DEKKER. Marston and Dekker retaliated with plays satirizing Jonson, and Jonson came back into the fray with *The Poetaster* (1601). Dekker answered with *Satiromastix, or The Untrussing of the Humorous Poet* in 1602, but Jonson did not take up the stage aspects of the war again. He turned to tragedy, writing the play *Richard Crookbacke* and SEJANUS HIS FALL, the latter performed at the Globe in 1603. A classical tragedy dealing with the attempt of the upstart Sejanus to overthrow the Emperor Tiberius, it lacks the verve and color of his comedies and the depth of characterization and psychological insight requisite for tragedy. Jonson only essayed one more tragedy, *Catiline* (1611), also based on classical models.

After the accession of James I in 1603 Jonson turned most of his energies to writing MASQUES for the new court, working for a time with the architect Inigo JONES on sets and stage effects. He developed the antimasque, a satiric or grotesque interlude juxtaposed against the imaginative and usually lighthearted content of the rest of the work. His quarrel with his fellow playwrights was evidently patched up, for in 1604 he collaborated with Dekker on *The King's Entertainment* and with Marston and George Chapman on *Eastward Ho* in 1605. When Marston and Chapman were imprisoned because James I found some parts of the play unflattering to the Scots, Jonson voluntarily joined them.

Though his masques far outnumber his plays during the Jacobean period, the five comedies he then wrote are the crowning pieces of his dramatic career: VOLPONE, OR THE FOX (performed 1605 or 1606, printed 1607); EPICENE, OR THE SILENT WOMAN (performed 1609; printed 1610); THE ALCHEMIST (1610); BARTHOLOMEW FAIR (1614); and *The Devil is an Ass* (1616). Colorful, crowded canvases filled with all manner of contemporary English types, these comedies satirize hypocrisy and greed, exploiters and gulls, rogues and fools; and as Jonson points out in the title of the last piece, the devil himself is a mere piker compared to humankind and its capacity for mischief.

In 1616 Jonson published the first folio edition of his collected works. Two years later he went on an extended holiday to Scotland, where he visited with the Scotch poet William Drummond. From this visit came Drummond's recollections of their *Conversations at Hawthornden,* a source of many of Jonson's opinions and an implicit portrait of the man as seen through the eyes of his friend.

The plays of Jonson's last period never reached the heights he had achieved before, though he re-

mained until the end of his life the greatest figure
of the English stage, the acknowledged leader of the
gatherings of men of letters at the MERMAID TAVERN.
His last plays include *The Staple of News* (1625);
The Magnetic Lady (1632); and *Tale of a Tub*
(1633). The lovely pastoral drama *The Sad Shepherd*
(printed 1641), was left uncompleted at the time
of his death.

A classicist who took the Roman writers for his
models, a humanist who would engraft classical control and purity on English forms, and a moralist
to whom the drama was a means of instruction and
of criticism, Jonson both reflects the temper of his
age and anticipates the more rock-ribbed classicism
of the Augustan period. His poetry, notable for its
balance, its control, its unadorned simplicity that
is not without lyricism, prefigured the later lyrics
of the 17th-century Cavalier poets, the "sons of Ben."
Among his *Epigrams,* published in the first folio of
1616, are the two well-known poems mourning the
deaths of his first daughter and his seven-year-old
son; *The Forrest,* also in the first folio, contains the
famous *To Celia,* beginning "Drink to me, only,
with thine eyes." The second folio, published in
1640, contains *Underwoods,* a collection of miscellaneous poems.

Jormungard. See MIDGARD SERPENT.

Jorrocks. A famous amateur sportsman, a Cock-
ney grocer passionately interested in the hunt, created
by Robert Smith SURTEES. He appeared in *Jorrocks'
Jaunts and Jollities, the Hunting, Shooting, Racing,
Driving, Sailing, Eating, Eccentric and Extravagant
Exploits of that Renowned Sporting Citizen, Mr.
John Jorrocks of St. Botolph Land and Great Coram
Street* (1838), and other books.

jōruri. Japanese puppet theater. Developed during the Tokugawa period (1600–1868), its most important plays were written by CHIKAMATSU MONZAE-
MON. The dolls are operated by puppet masters
visible to the audience. The roles and narrative explanation of the story are rendered by a reciter
(*gidayu*). Many of the same plays are used also in
the *kabuki* theater.

Josaphat. See BARLAAM.

José, Don. A Spanish officer in Bizet's opera
CARMEN, in love with Carmen.

Joseph. An Old Testament hero of the book
of Genesis. The younger son and favorite of his
father Jacob, he was hated by his 10 older brothers
who sold him as a slave to a caravan going to Egypt.
There, with his master Potiphar, he rose to a position of responsibility, but was maligned and imprisoned upon his refusal to respond to the advances
of POTIPHAR'S WIFE (Gen. 39). In time, he was set
free and, as a result of his interpretations of the
king's dreams, made prime minister. Pharaoh's
dreams of seven lean cattle swallowing up seven
fat cattle and seven lean ears of corn devouring seven
full ears were said to betoken the coming of famine,
and Joseph was therefore installed as food administrator. During the famine, his brothers came to
Egypt to buy corn and after a dramatic series of
events (see BENJAMIN), Joseph revealed his identity
and brought about their migration to Egypt. See
JOSEPH AND HIS BROTHERS.

Joseph, St. Husband of the Virgin Mary. He is
the patron saint of carpenters, because he was of that

craft. In art, Joseph is represented as an aged man
with a budding staff in his hand. His day is March
19.

Joseph II (1741–1790). Holy Roman Emperor
(1765–1790). The son of Maria Theresa, he was
called the revolutionary emperor because of his rigorous policy of social and economic reform within the
Austrian dominions, which he ruled after her death
in 1780.

Joseph and His Brothers (**Joseph und seine
Brüder;** 1933–1943). A tetralogy of novels by
Thomas MANN, based on the biblical story of JOSEPH:
Die Geschichten Jaakobs (*The Stories of Jacob,* 1933),
Der junge Joseph (*Young Joseph,* 1934), *Joseph in
Ägypten* (*Joseph in Egypt,* 1936), and *Joseph der
Ernährer* (*Joseph the Provider,* 1943). In these four
thick volumes, Mann has expanded the original story
tremendously, but most of the added episodes and digressions contribute not so much to the tale itself as
to the characters' depth and symbolic significance.
In its over-all attitude, the *Joseph* tetralogy is neither
ambiguous like *The Magic Mountain* nor tragic
like *Doktor Faustus,* but unqualifiedly redemptive.
Joseph's return from the pit into which he is cast
by his brothers is symbolically connected with
Christ's Resurrection, among other things, and indicates the redemption of man from death, whose
realm is dominant in most of Mann's earlier writing.

Joseph Andrews (1742). Hero and shortened
title of *The History of the Adventures of Joseph
Andrews and of his friend, Mr. Abraham Adams,
written in Imitation of the Manner of Cervantes,*
a novel by Henry FIELDING. Joseph Andrews, a prudent, brawny, pleasant young man, is intended to be
the brother of Samuel Richardson's heroine PAMELA.
His widowed employer, Lady BOOBY, dismisses him
from his position as footman for refusing her advances, and he flees London to rejoin his own true
love, Fanny Goodwill. On hearing the news of his
disgrace, Fanny rushes to meet him. Both are set
upon by thieves, but are providentially rescued by
Parson ADAMS, and the three return to their parish,
where Joseph and Fanny, after comic-opera reversals
and discoveries, are married in triumph. The time
of the novel is coincident with *Pamela,* which it
parodies and transcends. See Mrs. SLIPSLOP; Parson
Oliver TRULLIBER.

Joseph of Arimathea. The rich Jew, probably
a member of the Sanhedrin, who believed in Jesus
but was afraid to confess it, and after the Crucifixion
begged the body of Jesus and deposited it in his own
tomb (Matt. 27:57–60). Legend relates that he was
imprisoned for years, during which time he was
kept alive miraculously by the Holy GRAIL, and that
on his release by Vespasian, about A.D. 63, he brought
to Britain the Grail and the spear with which Longinus wounded Jesus, and there founded the abbey
of GLASTONBURY, beginning the conversion of Britain.

The origin of these legends is to be found in a
group of apocryphal writings of which the *Evange-
lium Nicodemi* is the chief one. These were worked
upon at Glastonbury between the 8th and 11th
centuries, and were further embellished by Robert de
Boron in the 13th century; the latter version was
used by Malory in his *Morte d'Arthur* (c. 1469).

George Moore introduces Joseph of Arimathea into
his novel *The Brook Kerith* (1915).

Josephson, Matthew (1899–   ). American editor and biographer. Along with many other young writers, Josephson became an expatriate during the 1920's. He helped to found and edit a number of little magazines, including *Secession, Broom,* and *transition;* he later served as assistant editor of the *New Republic.* Among his numerous biographies and books on business and politics are *Zola and His Time* (1928), *Jean-Jacques Rousseau* (1932), *The Robber Barons* (1934), *The President Makers* (1940), and *Life Among the Surrealists* (1962).

Josephus, Flavius. Original name, **Joseph ben Matthias** (A.D. 37–?95). Jewish historian and general. Imbued with deep admiration for Rome and its institutions, he managed in his later years to live in the sunshine of the favor of the emperors Vespasian and Titus. This was after the defeat of his people in their revolt (A.D. 66) against the Romans in Jerusalem, in which he had taken an active part. Among his writings are *History of the Jewish War* (7 books in Aramaic and Greek) and *Antiquities of the Jews* (in 20 books).

Joshi, Gaurishankar Govardhandas. Pen name **Dhumketu** (1892–   ). Indian novelist and dramatist in Gujerati, one of the Indian languages. He wrote more than 50 books in a wide range of styles, among them the famous *Jivan-rang* (*Life's Colors*), an autobiography.

Joshua. In the Old Testament, the successor of Moses and the name given to the 6th book of the Old Testament. Forty years before leading the Israelites into the Promised Land, he had been one of the 12 spies who reported favorably on Canaan; he was thus one of the two Israelites whom Jehovah permitted to enter it. He was a valiant fighter who gradually conquered the land. One of his most striking exploits was his commanding the sun to stand still (Josh. 10:12–13). See CALEB.

Josiah Allen's Wife. The pen name of Marietta HOLLEY.

Josquin. Full name **Josquin des Prés** (c. 1440–1521). The most celebrated French composer of his day. Josquin began and ended his life in Burgundy (now Belgium), but spent much of his life in Italy, in the service of the Sforza family, and of Popes Innocent VIII and Alexander VI. He wrote secular *chansons* in French, but his most important works are his masses, and above all, his motets. Their style humanized the mechanical compositional practices of the 15th century, and paved the way for the great flowering of polyphony in the 16th century.

Josse. A jeweler in Molière's comedy L'AMOUR MÉDECIN. Lucinde, the young daughter of Sganarelle, pines away, and the anxious father asks his neighbors what they would advise him to do. Josse replies that he would buy the young lady a beautiful piece of jewelry. Sganarelle's answer is, "You are a jeweler, Monsieur Josse (*Vous êtes orfèvre, Monsieur Josse*), and are not disinterested in your advice!"

Jötun[n]heim or **Utgard** (Old Norse, "outer ward"). In Norse mythology, one of the Nine Worlds, the home of the giants, situated at the northernmost edge of the universe. One of the roots of the ash tree Yggdrasill extends into it.

Jotuni, Maria (1880–   ). Finnish novelist, short-story writer, and playwright. She is best known for her plays, which blend humor with psychological insight and are cleverly constructed. *Klaus Lovhikon Herra* (*Klaus, the Master of Lovhikko,* 1941) received a Finnish drama award; other plays include *Miehen Kylkiluu* (1914), *Kultainen vasikka* (1918), and *Kurdin prinssi* (1932).

Jouhandeau, Marcel (1888–   ). Pen name: **Marcel Provence.** French fiction writer, essayist, dramatist. Among the novels that give a bitterly introspective and cynical account of his own married life are *Monsieur Godeau intime* (1926), *Monsieur Godeau marié* (1933), and *Chroniques maritales* (1938). Cruel portraits of his town are painted in *Les Térébinte* (1926), and *Chaminadour* (3 vols., 1934–1941). His short stories include *Astaroth* (1929), *L'Amateur d'imprudence* (1932), and *Elise* (1933).

Jourdain, Monsieur. The title character of Molière's LE BOURGEOIS GENTILHOMME. He is the prototype of the bourgeois who, elevated by sudden wealth to the upper ranks, makes himself ridiculous by his attempts to imitate a gentleman's manners and accomplishments. Much of the fun of the play derives from the awkward figure M. Jourdain cuts as the pupil of dancing and fencing masters and professors of philosophy. One of his remarks is especially noted: he expresses his astonishment that he has been talking prose all his life and that he never knew it till his professor told him.

Journal of a Voyage to Lisbon, The (1755). A prose account of a voyage to Portugal made by Henry FIELDING to recover his health; it is Fielding's last published work.

Journal of the Plague Year, A (1722). A famous account of the epidemic of bubonic plague in England during the summer and fall of 1665 by Daniel DEFOE. It purports to be an eyewitness report by a resident of London named "H. F.," and is remarkable in its convincingness as such, considering the fact that Defoe was only five years old when the plague ravaged London. Some of the details, such as the bell-man ringing his bell and calling, "Bring out your dead," seem more authentic than the original accounts reported in such works as the *Diary of Samuel Pepys.*

Journal to Stella. A private diary kept by Jonathan SWIFT from 1710 to 1713 in the form of letters addressed to "Stella," Swift's name for his friend Esther JOHNSON. *Stella* being the Latin word for *star,* the name was fancifully arrived at from equating this with the Greek word for star, *aster,* and Esther. The journal reveals the author's hopes, anxieties, social life, political intrigues. Baby talk sprinkles the correspondence. See PPT; PRESTO.

Journey's End (1929). A play by Robert Cedric SHERRIFF. It is set in the British trenches of World War I. The three main characters are Stanhope, the once idealistic school-hero of 18-year-old Raleigh who has just come to the front and Osborne, a former teacher. In the course of the play both Osborne and the boy are killed. Stanhope is still alive, but he drinks constantly to calm his shattered nerves and to hide his constant fear.

Journey's End played successfully in England and America.

Journey to the End of the Night (*Voyage au bout de la nuit;* 1932). A novel by Louis Ferdinand CÉLINE, about the driftings of the cynic Ferdinand in World War I and afterward. The work caused a scandal by the coarseness of its language and the violence of its despairing pessimism.

Jouve, Pierre Jean (1887–   ). French poet, novelist, and critic. At first closely associated with the ABBAYE GROUP, influenced by UNANIMISM and Romain Rolland, Jouve wrote stories of the war and poems of pacifist protest against it. His early poetry was collected in *Heures* (1919, 1920) and *Tragiques* (1923). In 1924 he turned to Catholicism and to Freudian psychoanalysis. The resultant energetic mingling of religious and sexual imagery produced his best work: the poems of *Les Noces* (1928); *Le Paradis perdu* (1929); *Sueur de Sang* (1933); *Kyrié* (1938); and the novels *Paulina 1880* (1925); *Le Monde désert* (1926); *Histoires sanglantes* (1931); and *La Scène capitale* (1935).

Jouvet, Louis (1885–1951). French actor, director, and producer. Jouvet worked with Jacques COPEAU in the *Théâtre du Vieux-Colombier* before becoming the director of the *Comédie des Champs-Elysées* in 1924, and establishing his own company at the *Théâtre de l'Athénée* in 1934. In the drama he sought to achieve a blend of the intellect and the fancy, through the skillful use of light to focus upon the inner drama, combined with stylized staging and acting. Plays by Jules Romains, Marcel Archard, and Jean Giraudoux were produced at his theater, as well as imaginative interpretations of Molière.

Jove. Another name for JUPITER.

Jovellanos, Gaspar Melchor de (1744–1811). Spanish statesman, economist, and man of letters. Appointed a magistrate in Seville (1767) and in Madrid (1778), he was banished to his native Asturias in 1790 because of his progressive views. He returned from exile to serve briefly as minister of justice, only to fall from favor again. From 1801 to 1808 he was a prisoner in Majorca. Refusing to collaborate with the Bonapartists, he was a prominent member of the Central Junta and helped convene the *Cortes* of Cadiz.

His finest work is the well-known *Informe sobre la ley agraria* (1794), ostensibly a report on a projected code of agrarian law, but in reality an enlightened program for extensive economic reform. In *Defensa de la Junta Central* (1810), he outlined his moderate political ideas.

Jovellanos also wrote verse in the classical tradition. His best poems are probably his didactic and philosophical satires, notably *A Arnesto, sátira contra la mula educación de la nobleza* and *El estado de España, bajo el gobierno de Godoy*. His play *El delincuente honrado* (1794) introduced lachrymose comedy in the manner of Diderot to Spain. His other works include *Elogio de las bellas artes* (1782), an evaluation of medieval Spanish art, and *Pelayo* (1792), a tragedy.

Jovial Crew, A, or The Merry Beggars (1641). A comedy by Richard BROME. The fears of the wealthy and kindly Squire Oldrents are realized when his two daughters, Rachel and Meriel, along with their sweethearts and Oldrent's trusted steward, Springlove, run off to join a band of roving beggars. However, the girls are soon discomforted and return with the steward, who proves to be the squire's illegitimate son.

Joyce, James (1882–1941). Irish novelist, short story writer, and poet. He is regarded as one of the greatest literary talents of the 20th century, and is known for his revolutionary innovations in the art of the novel. Joyce's technical innovations include an extensive use of the interior monologue (see STREAM OF CONSCIOUSNESS) and other experimental narrative techniques; the use, in FINNEGANS WAKE, of a unique language of invented words, puns, and complex allusions; and the use of a complex network of symbolic parallels drawn from mythology, history, and literature. Joyce is also famous for his detailed rendering of Dublin life, his objective presentation of organic functions, his extraordinary psychological penetration, his robust humor, and his sensitivity to auditory impressions (he had a lifelong passion for vocal music). Before other writers had imitated his techniques and critics had explained his methods, his books were denounced as obscure, unintelligible, nonsensical, and obscene.

Joyce was raised in the kind of environment that might be least expected to produce a revolutionary genius. Son of an ordinary, chronically insolvent civil servant and a conventionally pious mother, and eldest of a family of 10 children, Joyce's youth was marked by poverty and the struggle to maintain solid middle-class respectability. He was educated at a succession of excellent Jesuit schools, where he received a thorough training in Catholic and scholastic doctrines and in several languages. Joyce's rebellion against his family background, against Catholicism, and against Irish nationalism (see THE DAY OF THE RABBLEMENT), are described in his largely autobiographical novel, A PORTRAIT OF THE ARTIST AS A YOUNG MAN. "I will not serve that in which I no longer believe," says the hero, Stephen Dedalus, "whether it call itself my home, my fatherland, or my church: and I will try to express myself in some mode of life or art as freely as I can, using for my defence the only arms I allow myself to use—silence, exile, and cunning." In 1902 the 20-year-old Joyce left Dublin to spend the rest of his life in exile in Paris, Trieste, Rome, and Zurich, with only an occasional brief visit to Ireland. But the world he had rejected remained basic to all his writing. From the short stories in DUBLINERS to *Finnegans Wake,* his subject matter is the city of Dublin, its streets, topography, history, and residents, and, to a somewhat lesser extent, biographical details of his own childhood and youth. The Catholicism he had rebelled against remained so ingrained in him that its doctrines and methods of thought, its symbolism and scholasticism, strongly color all his writings.

Always an admirer of Ibsen, Joyce's earliest publication was an essay on *Ibsen's New Drama* in the *Fortnightly Review* of 1900. He also wrote two collections of poems, CHAMBER MUSIC and *Pomes Penyeach* (1927), and a play, EXILES.

Joyce had a difficult life. In 1904 he ran away to Trieste with Nora Barnacle, an almost entirely uneducated Dublin chambermaid, whom he met on June 16 of that year (the same day on which the action of ULYSSES takes place). On account of his antireligious principles they were not married until many years later. With their two children they wandered about Europe, while Joyce earned an inadequate living teaching languages and doing clerical work; he earned almost nothing from his writings until his last years. His poor eyesight deteriorated until he was almost blind; like Milton, he had to depend in his work on memory and the secretarial help of friends. His books were banned by censors, pirated by publishers, and misunderstood by the public. His much-loved daughter became insane and had to be confined in an institution.

A perfectionist who sought to fill his mature work with a network of complex internal echoes and allusions, Joyce toiled long hours at his writing and repeatedly revised and polished his work. *Ulysses* required seven years to complete (1914–1921), and *Finnegans Wake,* which was known until its publication as *Work in Progress,* took 17 years (1922–1939).

Joyeuse. The name given to Charlemagne's sword in medieval romances.

Joyous Gard (Fr., *La Joyeuse Garde*). In Malory's *Morte d'Arthur* (c. 1469), the castle of Sir Launcelot. It was given to him by King Arthur for defending Queen Guinevere's honor against Sir Mador. It is supposed to have been at or near Berwick-on-Tweed, but the Arthurian topography is very indefinite.

Juana Inés de la Cruz, Sor. Religious name of **Juana Inés de Asbaje y Ramírez** (1651–1695). Mexican poet and dramatist. Sor Juana's love for knowledge, the quality that governed her entire life, first became evident at the age of three when she coaxed her sister's tutor into teaching her how to read. Her intelligence and learning attracted wide attention, and at 14 she became lady-in-waiting to the viceroy's wife. When a panel of 40 scholars and theologians questioned her to determine whether her wisdom came from God, she emerged from the ordeal, as the viceroy reported, like a galleon harried by shallops. Her zeal for study led her to contemplate becoming a nun, though some have maintained, on the basis of the love poetry that she was writing at the time, that a blighted romance was another cause. After a short and unsuccessful stay in a Carmelite convent at the age of 16, she took her final vows in the Order of St. Jerome in 1669. In the convent, Sor Juana continued her studies despite the opposition of some prelates.

Sor Juana's literary production was merely one facet of her intellectual activity. She has described her surprise on learning that not everyone wrote poetry; her own verse, while revealing great technical virtuosity and some gongoristic traits, is on the whole as unaffected and spontaneous as the scientific deductions she made while watching an egg fry or the spinning of a top. Among her most famous poems are the *redondillas,* or quatrains, in which she "rationally describes the irrational effects of love" and those in which she censures men for being critical of qualities in women that they themselves have caused. *Primer sueño,* a long poem modelled on Góngora's *Soledades* (1627), is an analysis of sleep, describing how man's soul is dazzled at night by its vision of the universe and tries unsuccessfully to comprehend its laws. For church holidays she wrote numerous *villancicos,* or carols, and *autos sacramentales,* or one-act religious plays, the most notable of which are *El divino Narciso* (1692) and *El cetro de José* (1692). Her plays include the comedies *Los empeños de una casa,* written between 1680 and 1686, and *Amor es más laberinto,* written in 1688

with Juan de Guevara. Of her extant prose pieces, the best known is the *Respuesta a Sor Filotea* (1691), a rebuttal to clerical criticism, in which she discusses her devotion to learning and her difficulties in overcoming the hardships inflicted on her sex.

Juan de la Cruz, San. See JOHN OF THE CROSS, St.

Juan Manuel, Infante Don (1282–?1349). Spanish statesman and writer. A nephew of Alfonso X, Juan Manuel was an important political figure as well as an outstanding prose writer. His masterpiece is *El Conde Lucanor* or *Libro de Patronio;* completed about 1335, it is a collection of 50 "exemplary tales," some of oriental origin, which illustrate the counsels of Patronio to his pupil, Count Lucanor. His other extant works include *Libro de los estados,* which contains an adaptation of the story of Barlaam and Josaphat, and *Libro del caballero y del escudero,* a treatise on chivalry and encyclopedia of medieval knowledge.

Juárez, Benito (1806–1872). Mexican statesman. A full-blooded Zapotec Indian, Juárez became the leader of *La Reforma,* a liberal, anticlerical movement for political, economic, and social reform. Named president in 1857, he fought the French-supported regime of MAXIMILIAN, whom he defeated in 1867, and ruled Mexico until his death. Though *La Reforma* was at best a qualified success, Juárez occupies a place in Mexican hagiography similar to that held by Lincoln in the U.S.

Juarez und Maximilian (1924). A play by Franz WERFEL. It is about the rising of Mexican patriots to throw off the rule of the Austrian emperor MAXIMILIAN. Werfel concentrates more on the luckless emperor than on the Mexicans, and the play ends with his execution and funeral.

Jubal. In the Old Testament, the son of Lamech and Adah. As "father of all such as handle the harp and organ" (Gen. 4:21), he is said to have invented wind and stringed instruments. George Eliot has a narrative poem of this title (1874).

jubilee. In Jewish history, the year of jubilee was every fiftieth year, which was held sacred in commemoration of the deliverance from Egypt. In this year the fields were allowed to lie fallow, land that had passed out of the possession of those to whom it had originally belonged was restored to them, and all who had been obliged to let themselves out for hire were released from bondage. The year of jubilee was proclaimed with trumpets of ram's horn, and takes its name from Hebrew *yobel,* "a ram's horn."

Judah. In the Old Testament, the 4th son of Jacob; also, the name of the most powerful of the 12 tribes of Israel. After the death of Solomon, king of Israel, 10 tribes seceded under JEROBOAM, and the remaining kingdom, with its capital at Jerusalem, was known thereafter as Judah.

Judas Iscariot. The disciple who betrayed Jesus. Judas' specific act of betrayal was to cause the arrest of Jesus by the Roman soldiery by identifying him with a kiss in the Garden of Gethsemane. He was paid for this act 30 pieces of silver. Matthew (27:3–10) records that Judas returned the money to the Jewish priests and then hanged himself (see ACELDAMA). The version in Acts (1:16–20) has Judas dying by "falling headlong" after which "he burst asunder . . . and all his bowels gushed out."

Judas is known as one of the blackest villains in history. Dante in the INFERNO places Judas in the mouth of Satan. There are numerous allusions to his crime in figures of speech: a Judas kiss, 30 pieces of silver, and the name itself all signify treachery and deception.

There have also been many attempts to explain the motives of Judas. Early Christians felt that Judas acted as he did for the silver; however, the amount he was paid was not any great fortune, 30 pieces being about the price of one slave. Modern theorists feel that Judas was dissatisfied with Jesus' actions and wanted to force him into a situation where he would have to assert his divine powers and establish a glorious new order on earth. If this was the case it is obvious that Judas had no understanding of Jesus' message or ministry.

Judas Maccabaeus. The Hebrew patriot who gained decisive victories against the Syrians. In 165 B.C., he entered Jerusalem and reconsecrated the Temple; Hanukkah, the Jewish feast of dedication, commemorates this event. See MACCABEES.

Jude, St. One of the 12 disciples, also known as Thaddeus. He is represented in art with a club or staff, and a carpenter's square, in allusion to his trade. His day is October 28. According to tradition, he was shot to death by arrows in Armenia.

Jude, The General Epistle of. A New Testament book. It is a general letter denouncing heretical teaching. The identity of the author is not known definitely. One of Jesus' half brothers was called Jude; some scholars feel that he was also the apostle Jude.

Jude the Obscure (1895). Thomas HARDY's tragic last novel. This story dramatizes the conflict between carnal and spiritual life, tracing Jude Fawley's life from his boyhood aspirations of intellectual achievement to his miserable, early death. His passions entangle him in marriage with Arabella, an insensitive, animalistic woman who gives birth to a son, but then deserts them both. Jude then falls in love with his cousin, Sue Bridehead, an intelligent, sensitive, high-strung girl. She marries the decaying schoolteacher, Phillotson, but, finding him physically repellent, she flees to Jude. They both obtain divorces, but Sue, guilt-ridden over her desertion of her husband, cannot bring herself to take the step of marrying Jude, so they live together and have children, scorned by society. "Because there were too many," the children are killed by Arabella's son, a grotesque boy also named Jude, who subsequently hangs himself. Broken by this tragedy, Sue goes back to Phillotson and Jude returns to Arabella. Soon thereafter Jude dies.

Judges. A book of the Old Testament. An historical account of the tribes of Israel between the times of Joshua and Samuel (c. 1225–1020 B.C.). The Israelites had just invaded Canaan; the book tells of their attempts to subdue the former inhabitants and settle the land. Parts of the book are contemporaneous with the events; the rest are later additions. Judges had its present form by 500 B.C.

Judgment Day. See STUDS LONIGAN.

Judgment of Paris, The. A mythological beauty contest of goddesses. It led to the TROJAN WAR. Angry at not having been invited to the famous wedding of Thetis, Eris, the goddess of discord, threw into the gathering a golden apple bearing the inscription "For

the fairest." It was claimed by Hera, Athene, and Aphrodite. They took it to Paris, a son of Priam, who was then a shepherd on the slopes of Mount Ida. As the handsomest man in the world, he was regarded as an authority. Hera promised him greatness, Athene warlike prowess, and Aphrodite the love of the world's most beautiful woman in return for his vote. He awarded the apple to Aphrodite, and won for his pains the disastrous love of Helen. This famous subject was a favorite with artists both in classical times and the Renaissance.

Judgment of Solomon. See SOLOMON, JUDGMENT OF.

Judith. A legendary Jewish heroine of Bethulia whose story is told in the Apocryphal book bearing her name. To deliver her native city from the onslaught of Holofernes, general of the Assyrian king Nebuchadnezzar, she entered his camp and slew him in his drunken sleep. When she showed the head of Holofernes to her countrymen, they rushed on the invading army and put it to complete rout.

In his tragedy *Judith* (1841), Friedrich HEBBEL deepens the story's psychological complexity by having Judith become intimate with Holofernes before murdering him. Jean GIRAUDOUX adapted the story for his play *Judith* (1931).

judo. See JUJITSU.

Judson, E[dward] Z[ane] C[arroll]. Pen name, **Ned Buntline** (1823–1886). American adventurer and dime novelist. Judson's career was more incredible than any of the 400 dime novels he is said to have written. He was an inveterate duelist, led the Astor Place riots against the English actor Macready, was an organizer of the nativistic Know-Nothing Party, and during the Civil War was dismissed from the Union army for drunkenness.

In the meantime, he was a prolific writer of dime novels, a genre that he is credited with originating. Some he published in a magazine he founded, *Ned Buntline's Own;* later he worked for the publishing firm of Beadle & Adams. On a trip to the West he met William F. Cody and wrote a play, *The Scouts of the Plains* (1872) for him; it was Judson who named the famous scout Buffalo Bill. Judson also wrote hymns and lectured on temperance.

He undoubtedly had an astonishing knack with words and once wrote a novel of more than 600 pages in 62 hours. His dime novels have become collector's items. A few characteristic titles are *Magdalena, The Beautiful Mexican Maid* (1847), *The Black Avenger* (1847), and *Stella Delorme, or, The Comanche's Dream* (1860).

Juggernaut or **Jagannath.** A Hindu deity, literally "Lord of the World." His temple is at Puri, in Orissa, eastern India. Juggernaut is regarded as the remover of sin, and his image is on view three days in the year. The first day is the *Snanayatra,* or the Pilgrimage of the Bath, when the image is washed. Ten days later the image is taken in its chariot to a nearby temple. It was formerly erroneously supposed that on this day, known as the *Rathayatra* or the Journey by Chariot, fanatical devotees threw themselves beneath the wheels of the enormous, decorated chariot, in the hope that they would attain *moksha* or liberation from the cycle of birth and rebirth. Hence, the phrase *the car of Juggernaut* is used of customs, institutions, and traditions beneath which people are ruthlessly and unnecessarily crushed.

jujitsu. Literally "soft art." A Japanese system of self-defense without weapons. It is based entirely on the principle that the opponent's own (superior) strength can be used to defeat him. A *jujitsu* expert is able to nullify his attacker, not by meeting strength with strength, but by using specialized applications of momentum, balance, and leverage to disable or paralyze. *Judo* is a refined, modern version of *jujitsu*. Both are practiced as sports in Japan.

Jukes, The, a Study in Crime, Pauperism, Disease and Heredity (1877). A report of the New York Prison Association by Richard Louis Dugdale (1841–1883). The subjects are the descendants of several sisters who lived in New York toward the end of the 18th century. The study is a sociological companion to fictional studies of the decline and fall of families.

Julia. In Shakespeare's Two GENTLEMEN OF VERONA, the faithful love of Proteus. She follows him to Milan, disguised as a page, forgives him his inconstancy, and finally wins him back.

Julia de Roubigné (1777). A sentimental and theatrical novel by Henry MACKENZIE modeled upon Jean Jacques Rousseau's NOUVELLE HÉLOÏSE. Although she loves Savillon, Julia is forced to marry the count de Montauban. Misunderstanding and groundless jealousy bring tragedy to them all.

Julian, surnamed **the Apostate.** Full Latin name, **Flavius Claudius Julianus** (A.D. 331–363). Roman emperor, nephew of Constantine the Great. Although educated in monastic schools, Julian renounced Christianity when he became emperor (361). He attempted to drive out Christianity and to reinstate a polytheism based on Neoplatonic philosophy. He was, however, killed fighting in Persia before he could carry through his plans.

Julian calendar. See Julius CAESAR.

Julian emperors. A collective name for the Roman emperors Augustus, Tiberius, Caligula, Claudius, and Nero, as members by birth or adoption of the family of Julius Caesar. As a member of the Julia gens, or clan, Julius Caesar traced his ancestry back to Iulus, son of Aeneas; Vergil chose Aeneas as the hero of his great, nationalistic epic, the *Aeneid*, for this reason.

Caesar, a family name of the Julia gens, was assumed as a surname by Augustus as Julius Caesar's adopted son, and from him was handed down to all the Julian emperors either by adoption or by female descent. Though the Caesar family became extinct with the death of Nero, subsequent emperors retained the name Caesar as part of their title. The name survived to the 20th century in the forms of Czar and Kaiser.

Julie ou la Nouvelle Héloïse. See NOUVELLE HÉLOÏSE, JULIE OU LA.

Juliet. The passionate young heroine of Shakespeare's ROMEO AND JULIET. The love of this wildly romantic girl for Romeo, the son of her father's bitterest enemy, brings about her own death and that of her lover. Strong in spirit, she refuses to marry the husband that her family chooses and secretly weds Romeo. Her speeches contain some of Shakespeare's most beautiful and famous poetry:

> O Romeo, Romeo! wherefore art thou Romeo?
> Deny thy father, and refuse thy name;
> Or, if thou wilt not, be but sworn my love,
> And I'll no longer be a Capulet. . . .
>   O! be some other name:
> What's in a name? that which we call a rose
> By any other name would smell as sweet.

(2) In Shakespeare's MEASURE FOR MEASURE, the gentle, loyal betrothed of Claudio. Her pregnancy is the cause of Claudio's imprisonment for immorality.

Julius II, Pope. See DELLA ROVERE.

Julius Caesar (c. 1599). A tragedy by William SHAKESPEARE. It deals with the conspiracy against Julius CAESAR, his assassination, and the defeat of the conspirators by Marc ANTONY and Octavius CAESAR.

The crafty and ambitious CASSIUS, envious of Caesar's political and military triumphs, forms a conspiracy against him. Although BRUTUS, a man of great integrity, loves Caesar, he is persuaded to join the conspiracy by Cassius, who argues that Caesar's power is a threat to Rome's freedom. Ignoring the entreaties of his wife, CALPURNIA, who has dreamed of his death, Caesar goes to the Senate on the Ides of March and is assassinated by the conspirators. When Antony discovers Caesar's body, he feigns friendliness towards the conspirators and asks only that he be allowed to speak at Caesar's funeral. His oration so inflames the people that the assassins are driven out of Rome. Antony, joined by Lepidus and Octavius, engages the conspirators in battle at Philippi. Cassius' rash suicide weakens the army and turns the tide of battle. Brutus is routed and falls on his own sword rather than be taken captive.

Shakespeare's source for the play was Sir Thomas North's translation (1579) of Plutarch's *Lives*.

July Revolution (1830). An uprising (July 27–29) of the people of France against the reactionary Bourbon dynasty. The newspapers, protesting the abolition of freedom of the press, fanned the fires of the insurrection. After some fighting in barricaded streets King Charles X abdicated. The Bourbon-Orléans line then succeeded to the throne in the person of Louis PHILIPPE, "the citizen-king."

Jung, Carl Gustav (1875–1961). Swiss psychologist and author. Jung received his M.D. degree from the University of Basel in 1900. He then attended lectures by the pioneer French psychologist Pierre Janet at the Salpêtrière at Paris and worked with Eugen Bleuler, head of the Zurich school of the new depth-psychology. In 1909 he and Sigmund FREUD, the head of the Vienna School, traveled to Clark University in Worcester, Mass., to lecture and receive honorary degrees. He broke with Freud four years later, not because he differed with the master in fundamentals but because Freud could not agree with some of the applications which Jung was beginning to see for psychology. In 1912, Jung had published *Wandlungen und Symbole der Libido* (*Psychology of the Unconscious,* Engl. trans., 1916; revised for the *Collected Works* as Vol. 5, *Symbols of Transformation*), in which he presented several concepts alien to Freudian psychology. For Jung, the term "libido" itself signified a wider area than for Freud. Perhaps the most significant and important departure from orthodox Freudianism was Jung's theory of the collective unconscious advanced in this work. According to this concept, mankind shares a common and inborn unconscious life, not limited to the experience of any one individual, which is expressed in dreams, fantasies, and mythologies in the form of archetypal images and symbols. Among other of Jung's many contributions to psychology are his formulation of introvert and extrovert types (found in *Psychological Types,* 1923), his development of analytical psychology, his use of the association method, and his extensive work on symbology. An 18-volume edition of Jung's collected works is now in preparation by the Bollingen Foundation.

Jung Deutschland (Young Germany). A German literary movement of about 1830–1848. Its name was coined by Ludolf WIENBARG. He and the other important authors in the movement, LAUBE, GUTZKOW, and MUNDT, did not actually constitute a group until their names were linked in a Prussian edict (1835) prohibiting their writings. Their principal desire was to break away from the idealism that had characterized most previous German literature in the 19th century, for they felt that every literary work should take a stand on the real political and social problems of the day. Specifically, they advocated freedom of thought—which was by no means a fact under the oppressive Prussian and Austrian regimes of the time—emancipation of women, and frequently, free love. See Heinrich HEINE; BIEDERMEIER.

Jünger, Ernst (1895–   ). German novelist and essayist. His works show the influence of existentialism, especially the philosophy of Martin Heidegger. His best-known novel is *Auf den Marmorklippen (On the Marble Cliffs,* 1939).

Jungfrau von Orleans, Die. See MAID OF ORLEANS, THE.

Jungle, The (1906). A novel by Upton SINCLAIR. Seldom has a book been the subject of more widespread discussion than this appallingly grim account of life in the Chicago stockyards. It depicts with vivid and brutal realism the experiences of a Slavic immigrant, Jurgis Rudkus, and his wife, Ona. Jurgis becomes debased and then, in accordance with Sinclair's own creed, turns to socialism as a way out.

Jungle Books, The (1894–1895). A series of animal stories for children in two volumes by Rudyard KIPLING. The central figure is the human MOWGLI, brought up by Mother Wolf and instructed in the lore of the jungle.

Junius Letters. A series of anonymous letters, the authorship of which has never been finally settled, which appeared in Woodfall's *Public Advertiser* in London from January, 1769 to January, 1772. Junius was apparently an ardent Whig partisan of the Grenville faction and a bitter opponent of the administrations of the duke of Grafton and Lord North. His daring address to the king brought a libel suit against his printer, but a London jury refused to convict him. The author himself said, "I am the sole depositary of my secret, and it shall die with me." The letters were probably written by Sir Philip Francis (1740–1818), but many other authors have been suggested.

Junker. A member of the landed aristocracy of Germany, particularly east of the Elbe. The Junkers gained ascendency in Prussia during the early 18th century, when they represented a political philosophy of competent, military oligarchy, but with the de-velopment of the German national state in the 19th century, the Junkers became political and social reactionaries. It was not until after World War II that their large estates were redistributed.

Juno. In Roman mythology, the wife of JUPITER and queen of the gods. Like her Greek counterpart, HERA, she was the special protectress of marriage and of women. In Vergil's *Aeneid,* she is represented as the bitter foe of the exiled Trojans.

The Junonian bird was the peacock, dedicated to the goddess-queen.

Juno and the Paycock (1924). A comitragedy by Sean O'CASEY. Again the background of the Irish Civil War of 1922, the action concerns the attempt of Juno Boyle to overcome the triple menace of war, poverty, and drunkenness which result in the destruction of her family. Juno's heroic posture, which is defined in terms of her unillusioned, long-suffering grasp of reality, is contrasted to that of her husband, the "Paycock," a vain, posturing—but extremely funny—weakling who hides from reality behind a bottle and a flow of fine language. The initial production, which starred Sara Allgood as Juno and Barry Fitzgerald as the husband, represented one of the finest triumphs of the ABBEY THEATRE.

junta (Sp.). In Spain, a council or legislative assembly other than the Cortes, which may be summoned either for the whole country, for one of its separate parts, or for some special object only. The most famous is that called together by Napoleon in 1808.

Junto. In English history, a faction of Whigs who exerted great influence during the reigns of William III and Queen Anne. The name was first applied to the advisors of Charles I. The word is a corruption of *junta.*

Jupiter or **Juppiter** (from early Lat., *Diespiter,* "Father of the sky"). The ancient Italian sky-god and the supreme deity of Roman mythology, also known as Jove and corresponding roughly to the Greek ZEUS. He was the special protector of Rome and, as Jupiter Capitolinus—his temple being on the Capitoline hill—presided over the Roman games. He knew and could influence the course of history and made known the future to man by means of signs in the heavens, by the flight of birds, and, most awesomely, by the stroke of his lightning bolt.

Jurgen (1919). A novel by James Branch CABELL. This book, which became a *cause célèbre* and gave the author popular fame, forms part of an elaborate series of novels laid in the imaginary realm called Poictesme. Jurgen, a middle-aged pawnbroker, is married to a nagging wife who suddenly disappears. Jurgen goes in search of her, but actually he is in quest of his own lost youth. By magical dispensation, he finds himself 21 again and sets out on a series of strange adventures, including visits to Heaven and Hell, in which he meets a lost sweetheart and encounters a host of mythical persons. At the end he returns home, finds his wife there, and is glad to be a middle-aged, henpecked husband again.

Jusserand, Jean Jules (1855–1932). French writer, diplomat, and student of English literature and history. He was minister at Washington, D.C. (1902–1925), and the only non-American ever to head the American Historical Society. In 1917 he received the Pulitzer prize in History for his *With Americans of Past and Present Days.*

Justice (1910). A drama of social protest by John GALSWORTHY. A young lawyer's clerk, William Falder, forges a check in order to secure funds to free the woman he loves from her husband's cruelty. He serves a three-year prison sentence; on his release, his struggle to live down his past ends in tragedy. The play's title is ironic. Although Falder is treated justly according to the law, he is in fact treated very inhumanely by his employers, the court, the prison officials, and, on his release, by almost everybody. A basically good man, he is destroyed by society and "justice." Galsworthy's play was influential in the reform of English prison administration.

Justine (1791). A novel by the Marquis de SADE, celebrating a sexually persecuted heroine.

Justine. See ALEXANDRIA QUARTET, THE.

Justinian I. Called **Justinian the Great.** Full Latin name, **Flavius Anicius Justinianus** (483–565). Emperor of the BYZANTINE EMPIRE (527–565) during its most brilliant period. He married THEODORA (525). In 531 he bought a peace treaty with the Persians. In the West his generals Belisarius and Narses destroyed the Vandal kingdom in Africa and defeated the Ostrogoths in Italy, retaking Rome in 536.

Justinian's reign is highlighted by the amount of building that took place in the Empire (Sant' Apollinare in Classe and San Vitale, both in Ravenna, and Santa Sophia in Constantinople) and the code of laws he had published, the *Corpus Juris Civilis,* now called the Justinian Code. This codification is the foundation of the Roman law still used in many European countries.

Just So Stories (1902). Children's animal stories written and illustrated by Rudyard KIPLING, giving amusing and fanciful answers to such questions as why the leopard has spots or the elephant a trunk.

Jutland, Battle of. One of the greatest naval battles in history. It was fought in 1916 off Jutland peninsula between the German and British fleets. It won for England the undisputed control of the North Sea. Curiously it was the British fleet that sustained the heavier casualties.

Juvenal. Full Latin name, **Decimus Junius Juvenalis** (A.D 60?–?140). Satirist of Roman vices under the empire. Of his life little is known, although most early accounts agree that he spent some time in military service and ended his life in exile for having criticized a popular stage performer who was a special favorite of the emperor Domitian. He is the author of 16 satires, divided traditionally into 5 books. In these biting attacks on public manners and morals. Juvenal shows himself to have been a sharp observer of his fellow men. "Whatever men do," he announces in his first satire, "their devotion, their fear, their rage, their pleasure, their joys, their conversations—all these will make up the potpourri of my little work"; and he fulfills his pledge with the bitter gusto of an inspired cynic. Unlike Horace, the other great satirist of Roman letters, Juvenal seldom places himself among the foolish, the corrupt, and the frustrated; and while Horace's satires are conversational in tone and meter, Juvenal's are tight, rhetorical, and finely polished. He excels in sketching memorable vignettes and small portraits etched in vitriol. His satires abound in witty observations and terse proverbs, among which is the motto *mens sana in corpore sano,* "a sound mind in a sound body."

K

K., Joseph. The hero of Kafka's THE TRIAL. His initial, like that of K. in THE CASTLE, is the same as Kafka's. This is an example of the way Kafka often introduces elements of himself into his works behind the mask of a character. See Gregor SAMSA.

ka. In Egyptian mythology, a double that survived after a man's death if a statue of him were made into which it might enter and certain other rites were performed. Such a statue, placed usually near the mummy in the tomb, came to be called a *ka*.

Kaaba (Arabic *kabah,* a square house). The holiest shrine of the Muslims. Located at Mecca, in the center of the Great Mosque, it is said to have been built first by Adam, who received pardon there 200 years after his expulsion from Paradise, and rebuilt by Ishmael and Abraham after the Flood. In the northeast corner is the famous black stone. See HAJAR-AL-ASWAD.

Kabale und Liebe (Love and Intrigue, 1784). A bourgeois tragedy by Friedrich SCHILLER. The theme is the love across social barriers of Luise Miller, a musician's daughter, and Ferdinand von Walther, an aristocrat. Ferdinand's father opposes their love, and following the advice of a jealous schemer at court, unwittingly causes the lovers' death.

Kabir, Humayan (1906–   ). Indian man of letters. Born in Bengal, he was educated at Calcutta and Oxford universities. From 1958 to 1962 he was minister of scientific research and cultural affairs in the Indian government. He wrote *Men and Rivers* (1942), a novel, and edited *Green and Gold* (1960), an anthology of Bengali writing.

kabuki. Japanese theater. Developed together with *jōruri* during the Tokugawa period (1600–1868), it catered to the tastes of the newly arisen merchant class. Kabuki plays are either historical dramas or domestic works, performed by male actors only. The greatest Kabuki playwright was CHIKAMATSU MONZAEMON, who wrote originally for *jōruri* and whose plays were later rewritten for *kabuki* presentation. *Kabuki* is still performed extensively today.

Kaddish (*Aram.,* "holy"). In Judaism, the prayer recited to hallow the name of God. Since medieval times, it has been repeated by mourners as a declaration of their faith. It is used in the synagogue to close a section of the service.

Kadr, Al. The night on which the Koran was sent down to Muhammad. Al Kadr is supposed to be the seventh of the last ten nights of RAMADAN, or the night between the 23d and 24th days of the month.

Kaf, Mount. In Muslim myth, the huge mountain that served as the chief dwelling place of the JINN. According to legend, the earth was sunk in its middle. Its foundation is the emerald SAKHRAT, the reflection of which gave the azure hue to the sky.

from Kaf to Kaf. From one extremity of the earth to the other. The sun was supposed to rise from one of its eminences and to set on the opposite.

Kaffir (*Arab.,* "infidel"). A term of contempt for non-Muslims, chiefly in Africa. Hence the name came to be applied in the Western languages to either all or some of the Bantu races in Southern Africa, including the Zulus of Natal.

Kafka, Franz (1883–1924). Bohemian writer of Jewish descent. He is known especially for the unique visionary character of his novels, stories, parables, and sketches, all written in German. His thought is related to that of Søren Kierkegaard, and his writings center on the problematic existence of modern man.

Japanese print of a kabuki actor.

In them, a world of absurdity and paradox, of aimlessness and futility, and sometimes of faint hope, is revealed just beneath the surface of the everyday world. Specific problems Kafka explores, mainly through symbolism and allegory, include the utter incomprehensibility of God and the psychological ambivalence of family relationships, especially between father and son. His own strained family life, as well as his intense personal concern with religious problems, undoubtedly contributed much of the material for his work. But despite the atmosphere of human misery and futility that pervades most of his writing, Kafka did not entirely lack comic detachment, and he often shows a fine sense of humor. His style is remarkably precise and lucid, despite the grotesque unreality of the occurrences that it is used to describe, and his stories, in their combination of clarity and unreality, have often been compared to dreams. Less than one quarter of Kafka's entire production consists of finished works, the most famous of which are the stories, *The Judgment* (*Das Urteil;* 1913), THE METAMORPHOSIS, and *In the Penal Colony* (*In der Strafkolonie;* 1919). When he died of tuberculosis, all his unfinished writings, including the three novels, THE TRIAL, THE CASTLE, and AMERIKA, were left in manuscript form with his friend Max BROD with orders that they be burned, but Brod preserved and edited them.

Kahn, Gustave (1859–1936). French poet. A member of the school of SYMBOLISTS, Kahn, with Jules Laforgue, is considered to be the originator of vers libre. Kahn discarded the set line length and introduced such devices as assonance and internal rhyme for rhythmic purposes. His volumes of poetry include *Les palais nomades* (1881), *Chansons d'amant* (1891), *La Pluie et le beau temps* (1895), and *Le Livre d'images* (1897).

Kaikeyi. In the RAMAYANA, the daughter of Kekaya and one of the three chief queens of DASHARATHA, king of Ayodhya.

kailyard (*Scot.,* "kale" or "cabbage patch"). The name of a group of Scottish writers of the 1890's who wrote partly in dialect on humble, homespun topics. They took their name from the line, "There is a bonnie briar bush in our kailyard," which was the motto of the poem *Beside the Bonnie Briar Bush,* written by John Watson (1850–1907) under the pen name Ian Maclaren. Other members of the school beside Maclaren included James M. Barrie and Samuel R. Crockett.

Kaiser, Georg (1878–1945). German playwright. Belonging to the movement of EXPRESSIONISM, his plays turn, not on personal interaction among individualized characters, but rather on conflicts of ideas as exemplified in contrasting human types; often, in fact, his dramatis personae are nameless. His early writing (pre-1914), consisting mainly of satirical comedies in the tradition of such authors as Sternheim and Wedekind, is of no significance, but, with the coming of World War I, he was finally able to give effective expression to a deep longing for human redemption. In FROM MORN TILL MIDNIGHT, he depicts the complete emptiness of modern life, but in *Der Brand im Opernhaus* (*The Fire in the Opera-House,* 1918) he sees a possible solution for the individual in love. He preaches the salvation of peaceful society through individual sacrifice in *Die Bürger*

von Calais (*The Burghers of Calais,* 1914), but he also envisions the possibility of an increasingly deindividualized society leading to ultimate cataclysm in his GAS trilogy. His later works, which follow the same general thematic lines, include *Nebeneinander* (*Side by Side,* 1923), an interesting formal experiment involving three parallel plots; *Lederköpfe* (*Leather Hoods,* 1928), an anti-militaristic piece; *Mississippi* (1930), a religious play in which love is the spark of hope; and *Das Floss der Medusa* (*The Raft of the Medusa,* 1943), a children's tragedy.

Kalb, Johann. Known as **Baron de Kalb** (1721–1780). German army officer. While serving as a major general in the American Revolutionary army, he was mortally wounded at the battle of Camden, S.C.

Kalevala. Finnish national epic. It was compiled from popular songs and oral tradition by the Finnish philologist Elias Lonnrott (1802–1884), who published his first edition of 12,000 verses in 1835, and a second edition, nearly twice as long, in 1849. There is an account of the origin of the world, followed by the adventures of the three sons of Kaleva: the hero WAINAMOINEN, ILMARINEN, and the gallant Lemminkainen. The plot takes them to Pohjola, a dismally cold land to the north, both to fight for the return of the lost SAMPO and to find a bride for Wainamoinen. It was written in unrhymed, alliterative, trochaic verse; and a German translation in the same meter suggested to H. W. Longfellow both the form and the epic style for his *Hiawatha* (1855).

Kali. Hindu goddess. From her Calcutta receives its name, *Kali-ghat,* the steps of Kali, i.e., those by which her worshipers descend from the bank to the river Ganges. As wife of Shiva, she symbolizes the essence of destruction and bloodthirstiness, and the THUGS sacrificed their victims to her. Her naked idol is black and besmeared with blood; she has red eyes, four arms with blood-stained hands, matted hair, huge fanglike teeth, and a protruding tongue that drips with blood. She wears a necklace of skulls, ear rings of corpses, and is girdled with serpents. She is described as "terrible and beautiful, terribly beautiful" by a contemporary Indian poet. She plays a major role in Thomas Mann's "legend of India," *The Transposed Heads* (1940), where she is also Durga and Parvati, her two benign aspects. See SAKTISM.

Kalidasa (3rd century?). Sanskrit dramatist, sometimes referred to as the "Shakespeare of India." He wrote three plays, SHAKUNTALA, *Vikrama and Urvasi, Malaviki and Agnimitra;* two narrative poems, RAGHUVANSHA and *Kumara-sambhava;* and three long lyrics, *Meghaduta* (*The Cloud Messenger*), *Ritusamhara* (*The Cycle of Seasons*), and *Sringaratilaka.*

Kalilah and Dimnah. See BIDPAI, FABLES OF.

Kallas, Aino Julia Maria (**Krohn**) (1878–1956). Finnish-Estonian novelist. Finnish born, she married an Estonian scientist and wrote in the native language of her new land. Few of her novels have appeared in English; among those translated are *The White Ship* (1924), *Eros the Slayer* (1927), and *The Wolf's Bride* (1930).

Kalyb. The legendary "Lady of the Woods." She is said to have kidnapped St. George from his nurse, brought him up as her own child, and endowed him

K

with gifts. St. George enclosed her in a rock, where she was torn to pieces by spirits.

Kama. Also known as **Kamadeva** or **Kandarpa.** In Hindu mythology, the god of love. His wife is Rati (voluptuousness), his friend the season *vasanta* (spring); he rides on a sparrow, and holds in his hand a bow of flowers and five arrows which stand for the five senses. He was shriveled into cinders by the eye of Shiva, because Kama stirred passion in Shiva who was practicing penance; later Kama was reborn as Pradyumna.

Kamakura. Japanese historical period (1185–1333) following the Heian. The military clans in Eastern Japan gained the ascendency, destroying the power of the imperial court in Kyoto. New forms of Buddhism, notably Amidism and Zen, arose; a literature developed, centering on military chronicles that reflected the uncertainties of a period of incessant warfare and natural disasters. Kamakura is a small city south of Tokyo, where the military government, or shogunate, had its headquarters. A colossal bronze statue of the seated Buddha, known as the *Daibutsu,* is in Kamakura.

Kama-sutra (Sans. *kama,* love; *sutra,* science). A detailed account of the art and technique of Indian erotics by the sage Vatsyayana (first century?).

Kamboja. In ancient Indian history, the territory to the east of Kashmir and beyond the Himalayas.

Kamenev, Lev Borisovich (1883–1936). Russian Communist leader. With Stalin and Zinoviev, he formed the triumvirate ruling Russia after Lenin's death. By 1929, Stalin had taken the upper hand, and in 1936 he purged both his colleagues.

Kami. A god or divinity in SHINTO, the native religion of Japan. The title is also given to *daimyōs* or governors, and is about equal to "lord."

Kamsa. In Hindu mythology, the uncle of KRISHNA. He is Krishna's unremitting enemy.

Kandarpa. See KAMA.

Kandinsky, Wassily (1866–1944). Russian painter. He was a cofounder, with Franz Marc, of the BLAUE REITER, and a pioneer in abstract expressionist painting. In 1910 he rejected representational art and he evolved a style of turbulent, vividly colored abstractions. After 1920 his style gradually became orderly and strict. The works of this later period are limited to brightly colored dots, bundles of straight or broken lines, rectangles, and circular forms, but these shapes are handled with great freedom and inventiveness. From 1922 to 1933, Kandinsky taught at the BAUHAUS, where he did important work in his basic course on the theory of form and published *Punkt und Linie zu Fläche (Point and Line to Plane,* 1926).

Kane, Harnett [Thomas] (1910–   ). American writer. He is best known for *Louisiana Hayride: American Rehearsal for Dictatorship* (1941), the story of the Huey Long administration. In addition to other nonfiction, he has written several popular biographical novels, including *Bride of Fortune* (1948), about the wife of Jefferson Davis; *The Lady of Arlington* (1953), a story based on the life of Mrs. Robert E. Lee; and *The Gallant Mrs. Stonewall* (1957).

Kangaroo (1923). A novel by D. H. LAWRENCE. Set in Australia, it is notable for its vivid account of that country, largely drawn from Lawrence's own experience. The central characters of Richard Lovat Somers and Harriet Somers are closely based on Lawrence and his wife Frieda LAWRENCE. The novel is largely concerned with their difficult marriage relationship, in which the husband keeps trying unsuccessfully to assert his will over his wife. Kangaroo is the nickname of an invented character, Benjamin Cooley, the leader of a political party whose platform is a combination of fascism and Lawrence's own doctrine of "blood-consciousness."

K'ang-hsi. The Chinese era 1662–1722. K'ang-hsi was a period of great literary and scholastic activity.

Kannon. See KUAN-YIN.

Kansas-Nebraska Act (1854). In U.S. history, an act of Congress that provided for the territorial organization of Kansas and Nebraska. The principle of popular sovereignty, which permitted the admission of new states into the Union with or without slavery according to the decision of local governments, was incorporated in the bill, thereby rescinding the MISSOURI COMPROMISE. Because of the popular sovereignty provision, "bleeding Kansas" became a battleground for proslavery and antislavery forces. See John BROWN; Stephen A. DOUGLAS.

Kant, Immanuel (1724–1804). German philosopher. Kant's attempt to define precisely the domain of rational understanding is a landmark in Western thought. On the one hand, he opposed Hume's skepticism, the idea that pure reason is of no real use in understanding the world, and on the other, he challenged enlightenment faith in the unlimited scope of reason. The basic formulation of what is called his critical philosophy is contained in the CRITIQUE OF PURE REASON, the CRITIQUE OF PRACTICAL REASON, and the CRITIQUE OF JUDGMENT. His ideas were used by Schiller as the basis for aesthetic theories and marked the beginning of German idealistic philosophy, which was developed by Fichte, Schelling, and Hegel. The quiet regularity of Kant's everyday life in Königsberg, where he was a university professor (1770–1804), became proverbial. According to an anecdote of Heinrich Heine, the residents of the town set their watches by Kant's daily walks.

Kantemir, Antiokh Dmitryevich (1709–1744). Russian poet. Kantemir helped to form the classic tradition in Russian literature. He is known chiefly for his satires, written in imitation of those of Horace and Boileau. Although he made Russians aware of European classical culture, Kantemir's own work had little direct influence. His prosody, based on the number of syllables in each line of verse, was supplanted by the accentual verse introduced by Mikhail Lomonosov.

Kantor, MacKinlay (1904–   ). American novelist. He is known for his popular historical novels, especially those dealing with the Civil War. *Andersonville* (1955), which won a Pulitzer Prize, is a lengthy and grimly realistic story of the infamous Confederate prison. *Long Remember* (1934) and *Arouse and Beware* (1936) also have Civil War backgrounds, the former centering on the battle of Gettysburg. *The Voice of Bugle Ann* (1935), the story of a hound, became very popular. Kantor also wrote the scenario for the movie *The Best Years of Our Lives* (1947), and many earlier novels. *Spirit Lake* (1961) is an account of the massacre of 30 settlers near Spirit Lake, Iowa, in 1857.

Kanva. In Kalidasa's play, SHAKUNTALA, the foster father of Shakuntala.

Kapital, Das. See CAPITAL.

Kapp Putsch. A revolt in Berlin (1920) staged by army officers seeking to replace the Weimar Republic with an authoritarian state. The *putsch* collapsed when the unions shut off all public utilities.

Karamazinov. In Feodor Dostoevski's THE POSSESSED, a satirical portrait of Ivan TURGENEV, whose aesthetic posing and love of Western culture Dostoevski detested.

Karamazov, Feodor Pavlovich. In Feodor Dostoevski's BROTHERS KARAMAZOV, the father of the Karamazovs. He is a lustful, buffoonish character who thoroughly enjoys his sensual life and the sense of his degradation and only occasionally reveals a contempt for himself because of his unwholesome nature. The shock and disapproval of others only inspires him to further antics. Some of his sensual zest is contained in each of his sons in varying degrees, but none can match him for sheer animalism. He is the model of rampant irrationalism whose favorite mode of expression is the *non sequitur*.

Dmitri Fyodorovich Karamazov. Also known as *Mitya*. The eldest of the Karamazov brothers. Dmitri has inherited more of his father's lustiness than his brothers, but is saved from the old man's depravity by his own innately noble nature. Accused of his father's murder, he refuses to defend himself adequately, because by so doing he would injure the reputation of his ex-fiancée, KATERINA IVANOVNA. The most full-blooded of the characters in the novel, Dmitri is also one of Dostoevski's most successful character creations.

Ivan Fyodorovich Karamazov. Also known as *Vanya*. The intellectual member of the Karamazov family. Ivan is used by Dostoevski to represent the dead end to which he believed rationalism led. Tortured by the injustice and suffering in the world, Ivan "returns the ticket" to God, rejecting salvation from a Being who has allowed such a world to exist. Ivan both pities man's weakness and despises him for being so weak. Both of these attitudes are revealed in his "Legend of the GRAND INQUISITOR," a parable he recites to Alyosha during their most prolonged discussion. Ivan's guilt for wishing for his father's death rends him, culminating in his hallucinatory conversations with a shabby, imaginary Devil who espouses many of Ivan's own ideas in a debased form, much as the bastard Smerdyakov does.

Alexei Fyodorovich Karamazov. Also known as *Alyosha*. The youngest son of Feodor Pavlovich. Alyosha is a novice at the monastery who intends to become a monk, but his mentor, the elder Zosima, orders him to go into the world and serve God there. Although he is a religious mystic, Alyosha is much less removed from normal human concerns than Dostoevski's other famous mystic, Prince Myshkin of THE IDIOT. Despite his evident purity of heart, Alyosha admits to having a streak of the Karamazov sensuality in him. In the novel, he acts as the constant, sorrowful, and patient observer of his tormented father and brothers.

Smerdyakov. The illegitimate son of Feodor Pavlovich, who raped the boy's half-wit mother and later took the bastard into his house as a servant. Smerdyakov is a composite of cheap foppishness and second-

rate intellect. He adopts Ivan's nihilistic ideas wholesale, perverts them in his own less fertile brain, and under their influence eventually commits the murder for which Dmitri is blamed.

Karamzin, Nikolai Mikhailovich (1766–1826). Russian writer and historian. He introduced the romanticism of Jean Jacques Rousseau and the romanticism of the early 19th-century English writers into Russian literature. His best-known works are *Letters of a Russian Traveller* (*Pisma russkogo puteshestvennika;* 1790–1791), based on his journey through Europe; *Poor Liza* (*Bednaya Liza;* 1792), a sentimental love story; and the multi-volume *History of the Russian State* (*Istoriya gosudarstva rossiskogo;* 1818–1824). Besides his introduction of new sensibilities and themes into Russian literature, Karamzin is important for his linguistic reforms. He attempted to make literary Russian less heavy in style by introducing French syntax and terms into the language.

Karatayev, Platon. The wise peasant in Count Leo Tolstoi's novel WAR AND PEACE. His message of the goodness of the natural, simple life affects the spiritual development of Pierre Bezukhov, one of the book's main characters.

Karenina, Anna. See ANNA KARENINA.

Karlfeldt, Erik Axel (1864–1931). Swedish poet. Karlfeldt's work is characterized by its purposely archaic style and its basis in folklore and custom, in such collections as *Fridolins visor* (1898), *Fridolins lustgård* (1901), and *Hösthorn* (1927). In 1918 he refused the Nobel prize for literature, arguing that his work was unknown outside of Sweden. The prize was awarded to him posthumously in 1931.

karma (*Sans.,* "action, fate"). In Buddhism and Hinduism, the name given the results of action, especially the cumulative results of a person's deeds in one stage of his existence as controlling his destiny in the next. Among Theosophists the word has a rather wider meaning, viz., the unbroken sequence of cause and effect; each effect being, in its turn, the cause of a subsequent effect.

Karoon or **Karun.** The Arabic form of *Korah* of the Old Testament, who, according to the commentators of the Koran, was the most wealthy and beautiful of the Israelites. It is said that he built a large palace overlaid with gold, with doors of solid gold. He was the Croesus of the Muslims and guarded his wealth in a labyrinth.

Kartaphilos. See CARTAPHILUS.

Karttikeya. Also known as **Skanda** and **Kumara.** The Hindu god of war. He is said to have been born without a mother and to have been adopted by the Pleiads or Krittikas, for which reason he is sometimes called "the son of Krittikas." He rides on a peacock, with a bow in one hand and an arrow in the other.

Kaswa, al. Muhammad's favorite camel. It fell on its knees in adoration when the prophet delivered the last clause of the Koran to the assembled multitude at Mecca. This is one of the dumb creatures admitted into the Muslim paradise.

Katayev, Valentin Petrovich (1897–   ). Russian novelist, short story writer, and playwright. His first important novel was *The Embezzlers* (*Rastratchiki;* 1927), a comic picaresque about two officials who make off with a large sum of money and go through hilarious adventures before being caught.

Another popular comic work of the same period is Katayev's play SQUARING THE CIRCLE (*Kvadratura kruga;* 1928).

In 1932, Katayev published TIME, FORWARD!, one of the better novels depicting the Five-Year Plan in Russia. His next novel, *Lone White Sail* (*Beleyet parus odinoki;* 1936), is set in Odessa, Katayev's birthplace, during the period of the 1905 revolution. The story, obviously autobiographical, deals with the adventures of two young boys in the exotic seaport. The same two boys, grown into manhood, appear in Katayev's novel about wartime partisans in Odessa; *For the Power of the Soviets* (*Za vlast Sovetov;* 1949).

Katerina Ivanovna. In Feodor Dostoevski's THE BROTHERS KARAMAZOV, the former fianceé of Dmitri Karamazov. One of Dostoevski's "infernal woman" characters, Katerina refuses to abandon Dmitri, because of her gratitude to him for helping save her father from disgrace. So tenacious is she that she is described as being in love only with her own virtue. Ivan, the second brother, is in love with her, but their relationship is mainly a harrowing series of sadistic and masochistic scenes. Finally incensed at Dmitri's rejection of her, Katerina is instrumental in bringing about his conviction for his father's murder.

Katharina. The fiery and ungovernable daughter of the bewildered Baptista in Shakespeare's TAMING OF THE SHREW. "Renowned in Padua for her scolding tongue," Katharina is wooed and won in wild and highhanded fashion by the equally high-spirited Petruchio.

Katharine Walton. See PARTISAN, THE.

Kathasaritsagara (*Sans.,* "great ocean of stories"). A collection of stories in Sanskrit consisting of 22,000 verses in 124 chapters. They were written by the Kashmiri poet Somadeva of the 11th century. According to some the work is a recast of the "larger ocean," the *Brihat-kathasaritsagara* of the fifth century.

Käthchen von Heilbronn, Das (pub. 1810). A play by Heinrich von KLEIST. It is Kleist's most romantic work, a kind of dramatized fairy tale. Käthchen, apparently a young commoner, is drawn to the count von Strahl by a mysterious, irresistible love and refuses to leave his side. Her perfect devotion survives through a number of knightly and supernatural adventures, and it is finally discovered that she is the emperor's daughter. She and the count marry in the end.

Katmir or Kratim. In the Koran, the dog of the SEVEN SLEEPERS. It spoke with a human voice, and said to the young men who wanted to drive it out of the cave, "I love those who love God. Go to sleep, masters, and I will keep guard." The dog kept guard over them for 309 years, and neither slept nor ate. At death it was taken up into paradise.

He wouldn't give a bone to Katmir, or *he wouldn't throw a bone to the dog of the seven sleepers* is a traditional Arabic reproach, applied to a very niggardly man.

Katsushika Hokusai (1760–1849). Japanese painter and wood-block artist. His highly individual work had considerable influence on Western painting.

Kaufman, George S[imon] (1889–1961). American playwright. The author of numerous popular

From Katsushika Hokusai's *War Between the Han and Ch'u.*

plays and musical comedies, Kaufman worked with a number of well-known writers. His long series of collaborations with Marc CONNELLY included DULCY; *To the Ladies* (1922), a comedy on home life; BEGGAR ON HORSEBACK; and *Merton of the Movies* (1922), a satire on Hollywood. With Moss HART, Kaufman wrote *Once in a Lifetime* (1930), another satire of Hollywood; YOU CAN'T TAKE IT WITH YOU; *I'd Rather Be Right* (1937), a satire on the New Deal; *The American Way* (1939), a paean to democracy; THE MAN WHO CAME TO DINNER; *George Washington Slept Here* (1940), a satire on the city dweller's urge to buy and renovate a house in the country; and other plays.

Kaufman worked with Edna FERBER on several plays: *Minick* (1924), based on one of Miss Ferber's short stories; *The Royal Family* (1927), dealing with a theatrical family resembling the Barrymores; *Dinner at Eight* (1932), an exposé of high society; *The Land Is Bright* (1941); and *Bravo!* (1948). With Morrie Ryskind he wrote the book for the Ira and George GERSHWIN musical OF THEE I SING. With Howard Dietz he collaborated on *The Band Wagon* (1931), with Ring Lardner on *June Moon* (1929), with Alexander Woollcott on *The Dark Tower* (1933), with Nunnally Johnson on *Park Avenue* (1946), and with Leueen MacGrath, his second wife, on *The Small Hours* (1951).

Kautsky, Karl (1854–1938). German Marxist. He denounced the revisionist socialism of Eduard Bernstein and Jean Jaurès, as well as the revolutionary socialism of the Russian Bolsheviks.

Kavanagh (1849). A romance by Henry Wadsworth Longfellow. Mr. Churchill, the local schoolmaster, is unable to see the drama going on around him, while he attempts to be an author. Two girls fall in love with Fairmeadow's new minister, Kavanagh. Alice Archer, a poor girl, must nurse her invalid mother. Cecilia Vaughn, rich and beautiful, wins the minister, who is blind to Alice's love. The two leave Fairmeadow, and Alice wastes away and dies. On the couple's return, Kavanagh and Churchill discuss literature, and the latter must confess that his romance is still unwritten. The book delighted many discerning readers; it is an amusing and romantic vision of a small New England town, in which passions are either satirized or sentimentalized.

Kavanagh, Patrick (1905-1967). Irish poet. He wrote the long poem *The Great Hunger* (1942), about poor Irish farming people and their hunger both for land and life, and the collection *Come Dance with Kitty Stobling* (1960).

Kaverin, Venyamin. Pen name of **Venyamin Aleksandrovich Zilberg** (1902-). Russian novelist and short-story writer. Kaverin was a member of the Serapion Brothers, in which he joined Lev Luntz in advocating more attention to Western literary methods. His special favorite was Edgar Allan Poe. His early stories, published in the collection *Craftsmen and Apprentices* (*Mastera i podmasterya;* 1923), show an attention to plot that sets them apart from the typical works of the time with their diffuse construction and ornate prose. Kaverin's best early novel is *The Artist Unknown* (*Khudozhnik neizvesten;* 1931), the story of a young artist's problems in finding a place for himself in the new society after the revolution. Another novel with a similar theme, although less complex in its structure, is his *The Fulfillment of Desires* (*Ispolneniye zhelanii;* 1934–1935), translated into English as *The Larger View.* Kaverin's next novel, *Two Captains* (*Dva kapitana;* 1939), was an adventure story of Arctic exploration with some detective elements thrown in.

In 1949, Kaverin published the first part of a novel entitled *The Open Book* (*Otkrytaya kniga*), the story of a young girl who becomes a prominent bacteriologist. This fragment was not well received. In 1956, during the relaxed period following Stalin's death, Kaverin issued another part of the novel, a section entitled *Searches and Hopes* (*Poiski i nadezhdy*), which proved to be an outspoken criticism of Soviet scientific bureaucracy and the chauvinistic concern for Russian primacy in all fields, in this particular case, penicillin research. Kaverin was critized for the story and, along with other writers he defended his views before the Moscow Union of Writers.

Kawabata Yasunari (1899–1972). Japanese novelist and literary critic. Two of his novels have appeared in English, translated by Edward Seidensticker: *Yukiguni* (*Snow Country,* 1935, 1947); *Sembazuru* (*Thousand Cranes,* 1955). In 1968 he was awarded the Nobel prize in literature.

Kay, Sir. In Arthurian legend, King Arthur's seneschal (steward). In the Welsh tale, *Kulhwch and Olwen* (c. 1100), Sir Kay is a great hero—a wound from his sword, no physician might heal. In later tales, such as *Lancelot* (c. 1180) by Chrétien de Tryes and *Le Morte d'Arthur* (c. 1469) of Malory, he becomes the rude and boastful knight whose sharp tongue is always stirring up trouble and who is inept in combat; yet Arthur always defers to him. In *Le Morte d'Arthur,* he is the son of Sir Ector, King Arthur's foster father.

Kaye-Smith, Sheila (1887-1956). English regional novelist. Set in Sussex, her best novels are *Sussex Gorse* (1916) and *Joanna Godden* (1921). Other works include *Mrs. Gailey* (1951) and *Quartet in Heaven* (1952).

Kazantzakis, Níkos (1883-1957). A Greek poet and novelist. Born in Crete, Kazantzakis took a law degree at Athens, then traveled widely for several years. From 1919 to 1947 he held, off and on, a variety of governmental posts. In his first novel, *Toda Raba,* written in 1929, he declared, "I am a mariner of Odysseus with heart of fire but with mind ruthless and clear." This essential ambivalence, the conflict between Dionysus and Apollo, between flesh and spirit, was the fundamental subject of his life and his writings. Zorba, the hero of Zorba the Greek, the novel that established Kazantzakis' reputation in America, was beset by the same conflict; it is central also to his next great novel, The Greek Passion. The author's preoccupation with the dual nature of man found its ultimate expression in his monumental poem, The Odyssey: A Modern Sequel.

Kazantzakis was influenced by philosophies as remote from one another as those of Dante, Lenin, and Buddha. His principal mentors, however, were Nietzsche, whose works he avidly read, and Bergson, under whom he studied in his youth. Like his hero Odysseus, Kazantzakis valued freedom above all other blessings. Yet, he believed that the ultimate good is not freedom, which, in any case, can never be achieved, but the passionate, often tragic *search* for freedom. Though greatly admired by such figures as Albert Schweitzer and Thomas Mann, and repeatedly nominated for the Nobel prize, Kazantzakis' writings became known in America only toward the end of his life.

Kazin, Alfred (1915-). American literary critic. His works of criticism include *On Native Grounds* (1942), *The Inmost Leaf* (1955), and *Contemporaries* (1962). Of his own native grounds in Brooklyn, Kazin wrote an appealing book of memories and reflections, *A Walker in the City* (1951).

Keable, Robert (1887-1927). English novelist and clergyman. *Simon Called Peter* (1921), his portrait of a disillusioned clergyman, was a best seller and perhaps autobiographical in nature.

Kean, Edmund (1787-1833). English actor. He was unrivaled in his day as a tragedian; his greatest successes were Shakespearean roles, notably Othello, Richard III, and Lear. His excessive drinking ruined his career and his health.

Keats, John (1795-1821). English poet. The oldest of four children, Keats was born in London. His father, a livery-stable keeper, died when Keats was eight and his mother six years later. The following year, when he was 15, he was withdrawn from school by his guardian and apprenticed to an apothecary-surgeon. In 1815 he entered a London hospital as a medical student, and though he received his certificate to practice he soon gave up medicine in order to devote himself entirely to poetry. In the autumn of 1816 he gained the acquaintance of the influential editor of the *Examiner,* Leigh Hunt, who published his sonnet *On First Looking into Chapman's Homer* (1816) and through whom he later met Shelley and Wordsworth. The following year saw the publication of his first collection, *The Poems of John Keats*. He then began work on *Endymion* (1818), a long allegory of imagination in search of ideal beauty; the story is based on the Greek myth of the shepherd ENDYMION on Mount Latmos who was loved by Selene, the goddess of the moon. Though Keats may have attached enough hopes to the poem to be troubled by the attacks of unfriendly critics, he was maturing rapidly both as a poet and as a critic of his own work and soon spoke of *Endymion* as "mawkish" and "slipshod." There is little truth in the popular belief, stimulated by Shelley's preface to his elegy ADONAIS, that Keats wasted away and died as a result of the "savage criticism" of *Endymion*, which "produced the most violent effect on his susceptible mind . . . [ending] in the rupture of a blood-vessel in the lungs."

In 1818 Keats had to cut short a walking tour because of a severe sore throat, possibly the first sign of his illness. He then nursed his brother Tom, suffering from tuberculosis, until Tom's death in the beginning of December. He had met Fanny Brawne in September, and he became engaged to her at Christmastime. Between the autumn of 1818 and the summer of 1819, Keats composed his finest poetry. He worked on *Hyperion,* a Miltonic blank-verse epic of the Greek myth of Creation, but left it after a little more than two books had been completed. The story was to deal with the Titan Hyperion, god of the sun, and his overthrow by Apollo, representative of the new generation of gods headed by Zeus.

In January, 1819, he began THE EVE OF ST. AGNES; the story, which he probably got from Boccaccio, is based on the medieval belief that on St. Agnes' Eve a girl who follows certain rituals will see her future husband in her dreams. He wrote LA BELLE DAME SANS MERCI, a haunting and mysterious ballad, and began to compose his great odes—*Ode on Melancholy,* ODE ON A GRECIAN URN, *Ode to Psyche,* ODE TO A NIGHTINGALE—adapting elements of the rhyme-scheme of both Petrarchan and Shakespearean sonnets. Notable for their sensuous imagery and sustained feeling, these odes are among the finest in English.

By summer he was at work on *Lamia,* an allegorical poem based on a story, found in Burton's *Anatomy of Melancholy,* of a youth who met a phantasm in the shape of a lovely woman and went to live with her. At their wedding, the woman was revealed to be a serpent (a lamia), and all her possessions mere illusions which, with her, vanished "in an instant." He began a revision of *Hyperion,* called *The Fall of Hyperion,* and *The Eve of St. Mark,* both of which were left incomplete. By the fall of 1819 his tuberculosis had progressed until he could do little but revise and prepare his poems for publication. This third and final collection, *Lamia, Isabella, The Eve of St. Agnes and Other Poems,* appeared in July of 1820. In February of that year he had suffered his first hemorrhage. Bothered by financial problems, frustrated and unhappy in his unconsummated relationship with Fanny Brawne, he became progressively worse until a doctor warned that another English winter would kill him. In August he refused an invitation from Shelley, whom he knew slightly, to spend the winter at the Shelleys' villa in Italy. He borrowed money and sailed for Italy in September, accompanied by the young painter Joseph Severn, and died in Rome the following February.

Probably the most talented of the English romantic poets, Keats wrote a surprisingly large body of poetry before his early death. Practically all the finished poems of the 1818–1819 group are the work of a mature poet, and a few of them, such as the magnificent *To Autumn,* are among the finest examples of English lyric poetry. His letters are of particular interest not only for their biographical value but for their poetic and philosophic insights. See ISABELLA, OR THE POT OF BASIL.

Keb. See GEB.

Keble, John (1792–1866). Anglican clergyman and poet. Keble's Oxford sermon on *National Apostasy* was considered by Cardinal Newman to be the start of the OXFORD MOVEMENT. He was professor of poetry at Oxford (1831–1841) and author of a popular collection of religious verse, *The Christian Year* (1827), as well as several volumes of sermons and essays.

Keeldar, Shirley. See SHIRLEY.

Kelland, Clarence Budington (1881–1964). American newspaperman and novelist. A reporter early in his career, he later became editor of *The American Boy* and wrote books for juveniles. His fame rests on the title character of his 1921 novel, *Scattergood Baines.* A shrewd, fat Yankee promoter, Baines appeared in a succession of humorous novels and short stories, including *Scattergood Pulls the Strings* (1941). Among Kelland's other books are *Dynasty* (1929), *Archibald the Great* (1943), *No Escape* (1952), and *Monitor Affair* (1960).

Keller, Gottfried (1819–1890). Swiss novelist and poet, writing in German. He is known especially for his ability to combine bourgeois good sense and humor with powerful symbolism and subtle psychological perception. After failing to realize his youthful ambition of becoming a painter, he turned to poetry in 1842. He was involved in the Swiss civil disputes of the time, and a number of his early poems are in the manner of such liberal political poets as Herwegh and Freiligrath. During 1848–1855, he traveled and studied in Germany, completing his first major narrative work, the novel GREEN HENRY, (*Der grüne Heinrich;* first version, 1854; second, 1879–80) which was shortly followed by a collection of stories, *Die* LEUTE VON SELDWYLA. Most of his later years were spent comfortably in Zürich where, during 1861–1876, he was a government official. Outstanding among his later works are the *Sieben Legenden* (*Seven Legends,* 1872), treating the early period of the Christian era. In them, he weaves a delicately ironic web of both Christian and pagan elements, by which he implies his own preference for a secularized view of religion, an idea that reflects the strong influence of Feuerbach.

Keller, Helen [Adams] (1880–1968). American memoirist, essayist, and counselor on international relations for the American Foundation of the Blind. Disease deprived her of sight and hearing at the age of 19 months; cut off from human communication, the child finally learned the relationship between words and things from her devoted teacher, Anne

Sullivan Macy (1866–1936). When she was 10 years old, her "Teacher" helped her learn to speak. Miss Keller graduated from Radcliffe College *cum laude* in 1904. Mrs. Macy remained her companion until her death. Helen Keller received several honorary degrees from universities all over the world. She wrote *The Story of My Life* in 1902 (reissued, 1947); among her other books are *Optimism* (1903), *The World I Live In* (1908), *Out of the Dark* (1913), *The Open Door* (1957), and *Helen Keller's Teacher: Anne Sullivan Macy* (1955). Several books have been written about Helen Keller; in 1954, a movie called *The Unconquered* was based on her life story. *The Miracle Worker* (1959), a Broadway play and later a movie, dramatized Anne Sullivan Macy's first success in communicating with Helen as a child.

Kelly, George [Edward] (1887–   ). American playwright. He first achieved fame with *The Show-Off* (1924), a satire on American success stories. CRAIG'S WIFE won a Pulitzer Prize. Later plays included *Behold the Bridegroom* (1927) and *The Fatal Weakness* (1946).

Kelmscott Press. A cooperative publishing and printing enterprise established by William MORRIS on his English country estate in 1891. It was noted for the beauty of paper, binding, and typography in the books it published. The *Kelmscott Chaucer* is considered the masterpiece among these. See CHAUCER.

kelpie or kelpy. In Scottish folklore, a spirit of the waters in the form of a horse. It was supposed to take delight in the drowning of travelers, but also occasionally to help millers by keeping the mill wheel going at night.

Kemble, Charles (1775–1854). English actor. His noted family of actors included his brother John Philip Kemble (1757–1823) and Sarah SIDDONS. Charles was manager of Covent Garden from 1822. His daughter **Frances Anne or Fanny Kemble** (1809–1893) was a popular leading lady who resided alternately in England and the U.S. She wrote several autobiographical books, a play, *The Star of Seville* (1837), and a collection of notes on Shakespeare.

Kemp, Harry [Hibbard] (1883–1960). American writer, poet, and vagabond. *Tramping on Life* (1922) and *More Miles* (1927) are fictional accounts of his vagabond days. His poetry includes *Chanteys and Ballads* (1920) and *The Thresher's Wife* (1914), a narrative poem. *Judas* (1910) is a four-act play.

Kemp, William (fl. c. 1600). English comedian and dancer. He acted in the plays of William Shakespeare and Ben Jonson. He was an important member of Shakespeare's company until 1600, and later traveled widely on the continent. Kemp's *Nine Daies Wonder* is an autobiographical account of his famous morris-dance from London to Norwich.

Kempis, Thomas à. See THOMAS À KEMPIS.

Kempner, Alfred. See Alfred KERR.

Kemp Owyne. A medieval Scottish or English ballad. It deals with the transformation of Isabel into a "loathly lady" by her stepmother's magic and with her deliverance by the fortitude and courage of the knight Kemp Owyne. Kemp is the Scottish word for champion.

Kenelm, St. An English saint, son of Kenwulf, king of Wessex in the early 9th century. He was only seven years old when, by his sister's order, he

Kemps nine daies vvonder.
Performed in a daunce from
London to Norwich.

Containing the pleasure, paines and kinde entertainment
of *William Kemp* betweene *London* and that Citty
in his late Morrice.

Wherein is somewhat set downe worth note; to reprooue
the slaunders spred of him: many things merry,
nothing hurtfull.

Written by himselfe to satisfie his friends.

LONDON

Printed by *E. A.* for *Nicholas Ling*, and are to be
solde at his shop at the west doore of Saint
Paules Church 1600.

Title page of Kemp's *Nine Daies Wonder* (1600).

was murdered at Clente-in-Cowbage, Gloucestershire. The murder, says Roger of Wendover, was miraculously reported at Rome by a white dove, which alighted on the altar of St. Peter's, bearing in its beak a scroll with these words:

> In Clent cow pasture, under a thorn
> Of head bereft, lies Kenelm king-born.

Kenilworth (1821). A novel by Sir Walter SCOTT, famous for its portrayal of Queen Elizabeth and her court. The other principal characters are Robert Dudley, the earl of Leicester, who entertains ambitions of becoming king-consort, and his beautiful, unhappy wife, Amy Robsart. She suffers neglect, insult, and finally death at his hands. Kenilworth is a magnificent castle near Stratford, now ruined.

Kennan, George (1845–1924). American journalist. The Century Company commissioned him to visit Russia and Siberia, a trip that involved a 5,000-mile trek by dogsled; he was also sent to the front in the Spanish-American and Russo-Japanese wars. From these experiences Kennan published *Siberia and the Exile System* (2 v., 1891), *Campaigning in Cuba* (1899), and several other volumes.

Kennedy, John Fitzgerald (1917–1963). 35th president of the U.S. (1961–1963). The son of Joseph P. Kennedy, Boston financier and former ambassador to England, and the grandson of a popular mayor of Boston, Kennedy was born into an atmosphere of wealth and prominence. After attending the London School of Economics (1935–1936), he entered Harvard University, from which he graduated with honors in 1940. During World War II, Kennedy served as the commander of a PT boat in the South Pacific and was decorated by the navy for the courage and leadership he displayed after his boat was rammed by a Japanese destroyer during a night action in the Solomons.

Kennedy's political career began in 1946 when he was elected to Congress as a representative from Massachusetts. He was re-elected in 1948 and 1950, and in 1952 defeated Henry Cabot Lodge for a seat in the Senate. As a senator, Kennedy quickly became a leader of the moderate liberal wing of the Democratic Party and won prominence as a member of the Senate Foreign Relations Committee and the Select Senate Committee on Improper Labor-Management activities. In 1956 he was a leading contender for the Democratic vice-presidential nomination, and in 1960, after impressive victories in a number of state presidential primaries, he became the Democratic nominee for president, winning the election by a narrow margin over Vice-President Richard Nixon. He was the first Roman Catholic and the youngest man ever to be elected to the presidency.

During his brief administration, Kennedy launched the Peace Corps to aid underdeveloped areas, demanded the withdrawal of Soviet weapons from Cuba, and encouraged the Negro drive for full civil rights. On Nov. 22, 1963, Kennedy was shot to death as he rode in a motorcade in Dallas, Texas. His accused assassin, Lee Harvey Oswald, was himself killed on November 24 by Jack Ruby, a Dallas night club operator, in full view of the nation's television audience.

Kennedy was the author of *Why England Slept* (1940), an analysis of the causes of England's failure to rearm before World War II; *Profiles in Courage* (1956), a Pulitzer Prize-winning collection of essays dealing with congressional leaders who, in historically critical moments, placed conscience over political expediency; and *The Strategy of Peace* (1960), which presented a statement of Kennedy's aims in international affairs.

Kennedy, Margaret (1896–1967). English novelist. Author of the best-selling THE CONSTANT NYMPH, she also wrote the novels *Return I Dare Not* (1931), *Troy Chimneys* (1953), and *The Forgotten Smile* (1961).

Kennicott, Carol. See MAIN STREET.

kenning. In Anglo-Saxon poetry, a figure of speech using a descriptive circumlocution in place of the common noun. Examples are "whale-road" or "gannet's bath" for "sea," and "ash-wood" for "spear." *Beowulf* contains a number of excellent examples of kennings.

Kensington Gardens (1722). A mock-heroic descriptive poem by Thomas TICKELL in which Kensington Gardens, then only a few years completed, is peopled with fairies. The gardens are the royal domain of Oberon, and the hero is Albion, son of "Albion's royal blood," who was stolen thence by the fairy Milkah. He later falls in love with Kenna, daughter of Oberon, and after many adventures and a war caused by Oberon's opposition, they are married. Kensington Gardens is a royal park in London, and site of the Great Exhibition of 1851.

Kent, earl of. In Shakespeare's KING LEAR, the honest courtier banished by Lear for interceding on behalf of Cordelia. Under the assumed name of Caius, Kent continues to serve Lear.

Kentigern, St. (c. 510–601). The patron saint of Glasgow, born of royal parents. He is said to have founded the cathedral at Glasgow, where he died. He is represented with his episcopal cross in one hand, and in the other a salmon and a ring, in allusion to the well known legend:

Queen Langoureth had been false to her husband, King Roderich, and had given her lover a ring. The king, aware of the fact, stole upon the knight in sleep, abstracted the ring, threw it into the Clyde, and then asked the queen for it. The queen, in alarm, applied to St. Kentigern, who after praying, went to the Clyde, caught a salmon with the ring in its mouth, handed it to the queen, and was thus the means of restoring peace to the royal couple, and of reforming the repentant queen.

The Glasgow arms include the salmon with the ring in its mouth, and also an oak tree, a bell hanging on one of the branches, and a bird at the top of the tree:

The tree that never grew,
The bird that never flew,
The fish that never swam.
The bell that never rang.

The oak and bell are in allusion to the story that St. Kentigern hung a bell upon an oak to summon the wild natives to worship.

St. Kentigern is also known as St. Mungo, for *Mungho* (i.e., dearest) was the name by which St. Servan, his first preceptor, called him. His day is January 13.

Kenton, Simon (1755–1836). American soldier and Indian fighter, famous in frontier legends. At one time a scout for Daniel Boone, he fought in the American Revolution and in the War of 1812. See Simon GIRTY.

Kentucky Cardinal, A (1894). A novel by James Lane ALLEN. The hero, Adam Moss, is a nature lover who reluctantly cages a Kentucky cardinal at the capricious demand of his jealous betrothed, Georgianna. To their great remorse, the bird dies, but the two are reconciled. *Aftermath* (1896) is a sequel.

Kentucky Tragedy, the. A murder and suicide which took place in 1825. Anna Cook, a Kentucky girl who had been seduced by Col. Solomon P. Sharp, married an attorney, Jeroboam O. Beauchamp, in 1825. She made her husband take an oath to kill her seducer. Beauchamp stabbed Sharp to death the same year in Frankfort, Ky. He was tried, denied his guilt, but was convicted. The evening before his execution, Anna joined him, and both took laudanum. His wife died, but Beauchamp lived to be hung the next day.

The dramatic possibilities of the crime inspired many works. Beauchamp wrote his own *Confession* (1826). Thomas Holley Chivers treated the theme in his verse drama *Conrad and Eudora* (1834); Poe used it in POLITIAN. Charlotte Mary Barnes wrote a tragedy called *Octavia Bragaldi* (1837); Mary E. MacMichael wrote *The Kentucky Tragedy* (1838); Charles Fenno Hoffman treated the same story in his romance *Greyslaer* (1849). The popular Southern novelist William Gilmore Simms wrote *Beauchampe* in 1842. In recent years, two well-known works have been based on the story: Robert Penn Warren's WORLD ENOUGH AND TIME and Joseph Shearing's *To Bed at Noon* (1951).

Kenyon Review, The. A quarterly founded by members of the Kenyon College faculty in 1939. John Crowe RANSOM was the first editor. The magazine stressed close structural criticism and reviews of important new trends in the arts. The advisory board initially included Allen TATE, Mark VAN DOREN, Robert Penn WARREN, and other writers of reputation. In 1951, Ransom edited the anthology *The Kenyon Critics: Studies in Modern Literature from the "Kenyon Review."*

Kepler, Johannes (1571–1630). German astronomer. He helped to establish the validity of the Copernican system by his empirical formulation of the laws of planetary motion. Using the precise data of Tycho BRAHE, he discovered that all planets move in elliptical orbits with the center of the sun as one of the foci, that the speed of a planet is related to its orbital position, and that the speeds of the different planets have a mathematical relationship to one another.

Kerenski, Aleksandr Feodorovich (1881–1970). Russian revolutionary leader. He became the head of the provincial government in 1917 after Czar Nicholas II's abdication. He was overthrown by the Bolsheviks in October, 1917, because of his moderate policies, and fled to Paris.

Kern, Jerome [David] (1885–1945). American composer of musical comedies. The best was undoubtedly SHOW BOAT. Some of his songs, such as *Ol' Man River* and *Smoke Gets in Your Eyes,* are still favorites.

Kerner, Justinus (1786–1862). German poet, writing for the most part in folk-song style. Though a medical doctor, he was especially interested in occult phenomena, and his famous *Die Seherin von Prevorst* (*The Prophetess of Prevorst,* 1829) is the record of his experiences with a visionary, somnambulist peasant woman whom he treated with mesmerism. The poets of Swabian romanticism, including Schwab, Uhland, and Lenau, were frequent guests at his house.

Kerouac, Jack (1922–1969). American novelist and poet. Recognized as one of the leading representatives of the BEAT MOVEMENT, Kerouac wrote in a "spontaneous prose" that parallels the long, loose line employed by many of the beat poets. Like the poets he has been sharply criticized for lack of organization and for extolling the amorality of his characters, who seem concerned only with self-gratification. His best-known novels include *On the Road* (1957), *The Subterraneans* (1958), *The Dharma Bums* (1960), and *Big Sur* (1962).

Kerr, Alfred. Pen name of **Alfred Kempner** (1867–1948). German critic. His critical writings, especially on drama, were influential. His works were collected in 1917 under the title *Die Welt im Drama* (*The World in Drama*).

Kerr, Orpheus C. The pen name of Robert Henry Newell, author of the ORPHEUS C. KERR PAPERS.

Kessel, Joseph (1898–   ). Argentinian-born French novelist of Russian parentage. Kessel is best known for *Le Lion* (1958), a novel set in a wild animal reserve in Kenya. His other books include *La Steppe rouge* (1922), short stories of the Russian revolution, and adventure tales of war and aviation, such as *L'Equipage* (1923); *Crossroads* (*Fortune carrée;* 1932); and *Army of Shadows* (*L'Armée des ombres;* 1944).

Kessel, Maurice. See Maurice DRUON.

Kesten, Hermann (1900–   ). German novelist. He is known for his attacks on Nazism in such works as *Die Zwillinge von Nürnberg* (*The Twins of Nürnberg,* 1946).

Ketch, John. Known as **Jack Ketch** (d. 1686). English hangman and executioner, notorious for his barbarity. His name appeared in a ballad as early as 1678, and by 1702 it was associated with the executioner in Punch and Judy puppet-plays, which had recently been introduced from Italy.

Kevin, St. An Irish saint of the 6th century. Legend relates that, like St. Senanus, he retired to an island where he vowed no woman should ever land. Kathleen tracked him to his retirement, but the saint hurled her from a rock, and her ghost never left the place while he lived. A rock at Glendalough (Wicklow) is shown as the bed of St. Kevin. Moore has a poem on this tradition (*Irish Melodies,* iv).

Key, Ellen (1849–1926). Swedish feminist and author. While she was a prominent figure in Sweden, her works, proposing radical social views, gained her fame outside her own country. Her pacifist and feminist sympathies, as well as her broad humanitarian concerns, find expression in *Barnets århundrade* (*The Century of the Child,* 1900), *Kvinnorörelsen* (*The Woman Movement,* 1909), and *Kriget, freden och framtiden* (*War, Peace, and the Future,* 1914).

Key, Francis Scott (1779–1843). American lawyer and author of THE STAR-SPANGLED BANNER.

Keyes, Frances Parkinson (1885–1970). American novelist. Mrs. Keyes has written dozens of books since her first novel, *The Old Gray Homestead* (1919). Her best-known novel, *Dinner at Antoine's* (1948), is a murder mystery set in modern New Orleans a few weeks before Mardi Gras. *The Chess Players* (1961) is a fictional version of the life of the 19th-century American chess master Paul Morphy.

Keyes, Sidney (1922–1943). English poet. He was killed in World War II just as he was beginning to show his originality and talent. *Collected Poems* appeared in 1946.

Keyne, St. A Celtic saint, daughter of Brychan, king of Brecknock in the 5th century. Concerning her well, near Liskeard, Cornwall, it is said that if a bridegroom drinks therefrom before his bride, he will be master of his house, but if the bride gets the first draught, she will rule. Southey has a ballad, *The Well of St. Keyne* (1798), on this tradition. The man leaves his wife at the porch and runs to the well to get the first draught, but when he returns, his wife tells him his labor has been in vain, for she has "taken a bottle to church."

Keynes, John Maynard. 1st baron of **Tilton** (1883–1946). English economist. Originator of the so-called New Economics, Keynes lectured in economics at Cambridge from 1908 until his death, became an editor of the *Economic Journal* in 1912, and wrote such works as *The Economic Consequences* *of Peace* (1919), denouncing as unrealistic the reparations of the treaty of Versailles; *A Tract on Monetary Reform* (1923); *The End of Laissez-Faire* (1926); *A Treatise on Money* (1930); *The General Theory of Employment, Interest, and Money* (1936), his most influential and best-known work; and *How to Pay for the War* (1940). Keynes served on the staff of the Treasury from 1915 to 1919 and was its principal representative at the Paris Peace Conference of 1919. During the 30's he advised wide government expenditure as a counter measure to deflation and depression. Though his suggestions were less followed in Great Britain, they became the foundation of President Roosevelt's recovery program in the U.S. At the close of World War II, Keynes was influential in the planning for the World Bank and for the stabilization of international currency. Though his doctrine of deficit spending has been widely opposed, he was undoubtedly the most brilliant British economist of his time, and his influence is still apparent in British and U.S. government economic planning.

Keyserling, Count Hermann Alexander (1880–1946). Estonian social philosopher and mystic of German stock. Deprived of his estates by the Russian Revolution, he founded at Darmstadt the *Schule der Weisheit* (School of Wisdom). His thought was conditioned by contact with many cultures and the direct result of his far-flung travels, which earned him the well-deserved epithet of "the wandering philosopher." His final ideal was a synthesis of the Western notion of doing with the oriental notion of being. His books include *Reisetagebuch eines Philosophen* (1919) or *Travel Diary of a Philosopher* (1925) and THE BOOK OF MARRIAGE.

Kezia. A little girl, the heroine of Katherine MANSFIELD's stories about her childhood in New Zealand.

Khadijah. Muhammad's first wife and, according to the Koran, one of the four perfect women. The other three are Fatima, the prophet's daughter, Mary, daughter of Imran, and Asia, wife of the Pharaoh drowned in the Red Sea.

khedive. The title, from 1867 to 1914, of the ruler of Egypt, as viceroy of the sultan of Turkey. The word is Turkish, derived from Persian, and means a prince or viceroy.

Khepera. An Egyptian solar deity represented by the beetle.

Khlebnikov, Velemir Vladimirovich (1885–1922). Russian poet. One of the originators of FUTURISM in Russia, Khlebnikov was an inventive poet whose searchings for new poetic techniques helped revivify Russian poetry. His fellow futurist Vladimir Mayakovski described him as "the Columbus of new poetic continents now settled and cultivated by us." Khlebnikov, who had a love for old Slavic culture, replaced his original first name, Viktor, with the more archaic name Velemir.

Khnemu. An Egyptian ram-headed deity, worshiped especially in the region of the 5 cataracts of the Nile.

Khodasevich, Vladislav Felitzyanovich (1886–1939). Russian poet. He began publishing verse in 1908, but most of his best work appeared after the revolution. He emigrated in 1922 and became one of the best Russian *émigré* poets. His best-known collec-

tion of poetry is *The Heavy Lyre* (*Tyazhiolaya lira;* 1921).

Khrushchev, Nikita Sergeyevich (1894–1971). Russian leader of the government and Communist Party of the Soviet Union (1953–1964). A factory worker, Khrushchev joined the Communist Party in 1918 and began a rapid rise through the ranks. In 1939 he was elected to the Soviet Union's ruling body, the Politburo (renamed the Presidium in 1952). He was named in 1949 as a secretary of the Communist Party Central Committee. After Stalin's death he became first secretary of the Party, sharing power with Georgi Malenkov, who was chairman of the Council of Ministers (the head of the government). Malenkov resigned in 1955, and Nikolai Bulganin became head of state, to be replaced by Khrushchev in 1958. He was deposed and disgraced in 1964.

Khrushchev's speech at the 20th Congress of the Communist Party in 1956 created a sensation by its violent attacks on the memory of the past dictator Stalin. The de-Stalinization campaign instituted by Khrushchev created a freer atmosphere that was quickly reflected in Soviet literature. In spite of this new atmosphere, named "the thaw" from the title of a novel by Ilya Ehrenburg, Khrushchev has kept a watchful eye on the work of Soviet writers and has several times personally admonished them to maintain the correct spirit of loyalty to the Party and state. This has been an insistent demand, even though the degree of freedom of Soviet writers has increased measurably since the Stalin era.

Ki. In Sumerian mythology, the primeval earth goddess. Born of Nammu, the sea, she bore the air-god Enlil by her brother-consort An, with whom she was originally joined as one. Enlil separated them, An becoming the upper sky. In religion she was supplanted by such younger counterparts as NINTU.

Kiblah or **Keblah.** The point of adoration toward which Muslims turn when they worship; i.e., the direction of the KAABA at Mecca. In mosques, the direction is shown by the *mihrab,* or hole in the interior wall.

Kid, The (1947). A poem by Conrad AIKEN. It deals with the legendary William Blackstone who is said to have greeted Boston's first settlers on what is now Boston Common. His later wanderings and other American heroes are also described.

Kidd, William. Known as **Captain Kidd** (1645?–1701). Scottish-born English pirate. Kidd was originally an affluent ship owner and sea captain who saw service against French privateers during King William's War and was later engaged by the British government to suppress piracy in the Indian Ocean. By 1799 a combination of circumstances, including a mutinous crew, had induced Kidd to turn to piracy; he captured several vessels and was declared a pirate by British authorities. Informed that he would be pardoned, he landed at Boston and was promptly arrested. He was sent to England, tried, and hanged at Execution Dock in London.

After his death, Kidd became a legendary figure in both England and the U.S. He became the hero of many ballads, his ghost was seen on several occasions, and numerous attempts were made to unearth a fabulous treasure which he supposedly buried in various points ranging from Oak Island, Nova Scotia to Gardiner's Island, N.Y. Cooper referred to Kidd in several works, notably *The Water Witch* (1830), a novel. The influence of the Kidd legend is also evident in Poe's short story *The Gold Bug* (1843), and Stevenson's novel *Treasure Island* (1883).

Kidnapped (1886). A historical novel by Robert Louis STEVENSON. It deals with the adventures of David Balfour, the young hero, and Alan BRECK, a Jacobite who is considered one of Stevenson's most interesting and best-drawn characters. A sequel, *Catriona*, was published in 1893.

Kielland, Alexander Lange (1849–1907). Norwegian novelist, short-story writer, and playwright. Although his own background was wealthy and aristocratic, Kielland's writing was spurred by a strong sense of social protest. In *Arbeidsfolk* (1881) he criticizes the bureaucracy, and in *Sankt Hans Fest* (1887) he denounces the clergy. *Garman og Worse* (1880) and *Skipper Worse* (1882) are tempered by childhood memory and display a clear beauty of style.

Kieran, John [Francis] (1892–   ). American newspaperman. An excellent sports columnist and authority on Shakespeare and bird life, he is best known for his prodigious memory which he displayed on the radio quiz show "Information Please." Kieran has written several books on his specialties, the most recent being *Natural History of New York City* (1959).

Kierkegaard, Søren Aabye (1813–1855). Danish philosopher. The early years of his life were dark and cheerless, his home a lonely, gloomy place. Kierkegaard published his first philosophical works under pseudonyms. In contrast to Hegel's objective philosophy, he proposed, in such works as *Stadier paa Livets Vej* (*Stages on Life's Way*, 1845) and *Gjentagelsen* (*Repetition*, 1843), a system based on faith, knowledge, thought, and reality. In *Enten Eller* (*Either-Or*, 1843), he discusses the razor-edge decision made by man's free will, which determines his personal relation to God. In 1846, events in his private life led him to experience a deeper commitment to Christianity and to attack with new vigor orthodox, organized religion. For Kierkegaard the relation with God must be a lonely, agonizing experience of a man's inner solitude. During his lifetime he was not recognized in Denmark as a genius; a rebel against secure bourgeois morality, he was mocked and reviled for his unorthodox views and for the strange, ungainly figure he cut on the cheerful streets of Copenhagen. The 20th-century revival of Kierkegaard was initiated by the German philosophers Heidegger and Jaspers, and furthered by members of the French existentialist movement, notably Sartre and Camus.

Kikuchi Kan (1888–1948). Japanese popular writer of prodigious output. Author of numerous short stories, novels, plays, and magazine serials. See *Madman on the Roof* (1923) translated by Y. T. Isasaki and G. Hughes.

Killers, The (1927). A short story by Ernest HEMINGWAY. One of Hemingway's most famous works, this story has as its protagonist Nick Adams, the same figure who appears in many of the stories of IN OUR TIME. Two city gunmen enter a small-town lunchroom to inquire about Ole Andreson, an ex-prizefighter, whom they announce they are going to kill for having double-crossed them. Nick, a customer in the lunchroom, goes to warn Andreson in his rooming-house, but Andreson, knowing that there is no final escape for him, refuses to help himself. The story does not really deal with urban gangsters; its focus is on Nick and the effect on him of the acceptance of violence.

Killigrew, Thomas (1612–1683). English dramatist and theater manager. A favorite of Charles II, he wrote several plays, including the licentious tragicomedy *The Parson's Wedding* (1640). He is also remembered as the founder of the first Theatre Royal (1663) in Drury Lane.

Kilmansegg, Miss. The heroine of Thomas HOOD's satirical poem *Miss Kilmansegg and her Precious Leg* (1828). She is an heiress of great expectations who has an artificial leg of solid gold.

Kilmer, [Alfred] Joyce (1886–1918). American poet. He is remembered chiefly for his poem *Trees,* which was published first in *Poetry* in August, 1913, won its author national fame, and became the title poem of *Trees and Other Poems* (1914). Kilmer had earlier published a collection, *Summer of Love* (1911), and published another one later, *Main Street and Other Poems* (1917). He was killed in France during World War I. His wife, Aline Kilmer (1888–1941), was also a poet and published several collections, including *Candles That Burn* (1919) and *The Poor King's Daughter and Other Poems* (1925).

Kim (1901). A novel of Indian life by Rudyard KIPLING. The hero, an Irish boy named Kimball O'Hara, is an orphan shifting for himself in Lahore. He attaches himself to a holy man, an old lama from Tibet who is on a quest for the mystic River of the Arrows, and together the pair roam about India. By accident Kim is recognized by his father's Irish regiment and much against his wishes is sent to school. During the long vacations he still tramps with his beloved lama. His intimate knowledge of India makes him a valuable asset to the English Secret Service, in which he wins renown while still a boy. The book abounds in brilliant descriptions of Indian scenes.

King, Clarence (1842–1901). American geologist and author. King presented to Congress a plan for the survey of the Cordilleran ranges from eastern Colorado to the California boundary. He was placed in charge of the approved project, and, leading a corps of geologists, was the first to explore and describe the Yosemite Valley, an area of about 100 miles in width. The monumental *Report of the Geological Exploration of the Fortieth Parallel* (1870–1878), one of the finest of government publications, included the results of the survey. King, a gifted writer, also published a volume called *Mountaineering in the Sierra Nevada* (1872; rev. ed., 1902); appearing first in *The Atlantic Monthly*, the book includes scientific description as well as vivid narrative. In 1871, King met Henry Adams, with whom he traveled and whose work he greatly influenced. Once considered by many an ideal American, King suffered financial loss during the business depression in 1893. During 1894, he suffered a nervous breakdown and remained in Bloomingdale Asylum for several months. He died of tuberculosis, alone and uncared for, in an Arizona tavern.

King, Edward. See LYCIDAS.

King, Henry (1592–1669). English poet and churchman, bishop of Chichester. An intimate friend of Donne and possibly his first editor, he was also close to Ben Jonson and Izaak Walton. King wrote two volumes of verse: *Psalmes of David Turned into Meter* (1651) and *Poems, Elegies, Paradoxes and Sonnets* (1657).

King Arthur and the Emperor Lucius. See MORTE D'ARTHUR, LE.

King Cole. See COLE, KING.

King Horn. See HORN, KING.

Kingis Quair (1424, pub. 1783). A long poem by James I of Scotland. Written while the king was a prisoner in England, it laments his fortune and celebrates a beautiful woman, Lady Jane Beaufort, whom he married. *Quair* is an older form of *quire*, "booklet." In modern times, Maurice Hewlett has written a novel called *The Queen's Quair* and James Leslie a trilogy called *A Scots Quair*.

King James Bible. See BIBLE, ENGLISH VERSIONS.

King John, The Life and Death of (c. 1595). A historical play by William SHAKESPEARE. The action concerns the efforts of the weak and despicable King JOHN to fend off the royal claims of Arthur, duke of Brittany, who is supported by the king of France. In spite of the able support of Philip FAULCONBRIDGE, John alienates the English nobility and runs disastrously afoul of the pope. In the end he is poisoned, and his son, Henry III, becomes king. An earlier play, *The Troublesome Reign of King John* (pub. 1591), was once attributed to Shakespeare.

Kinglake, Alexander William (1809–1891). English historian. He described a tour of the Near East in *Eothen, or Traces of Travel Brought Home from the East* (1844), considered a classic English travel book. His *Invasion of the Crimea* (1863–1887) is a detailed account of the Crimean War.

King Lear (c. 1605). A tragedy by William SHAKESPEARE. Seeking peace in his old age, the weary Lear, king of Britain, resolves to divide his kingdom among his three daughters GONERIL, REGAN, and CORDELIA, but first he requires that they make declarations of their love for him. The first two, crafty and insincere, profess their love in the most grandiloquent terms and are each rewarded, in turn, by the bestowal of a third of the kingdom. Cordelia, the youngest and favorite, then disappoints Lear by stating that she loves him according to her bond "nor more, nor less." Rage blinds him to the deeper, truer love of Cordelia, and he divides the portion designed for her between her sisters. Thus undowered, she is taken by the king of FRANCE for his wife. Lear now begins to suffer for his foolish vanity. It quickly becomes clear, as he spends a month first with one and then the other, that Goneril and Regan are grasping hypocrites and that they are bent on humiliating Lear. Goneril refuses to put up his entire retinue and demands that he reduce it to 25; Regan puts Lear's servant, the faithful earl of KENT, in the stocks. In a famous scene, Lear goes out upon the heath in a raging storm and raves with the agony of madness. Cordelia, learning from Kent of her father's condition, brings an army from France to Britain's shores. Goneril and Regan unite against this threat. Cordelia sends attendants out after her father, and they are happily reunited in a tent in the French camp. In the battle that follows, Cordelia's army is defeated and they are taken prisoner. Goneril poisons Regan for love of EDMUND, the evil bastard son of GLOUCESTER; then stabs herself.

By an order countermanded too late, Cordelia is hanged in prison and Lear, broken-hearted, dies soon after. A subplot, paralleling the main plot, involves Gloucester, who allows the jealous Edmund to turn him against his real son, EDGAR, who loves him. See duke of ALBANY; duke of CORNWALL; OSWALD; Lear's FOOL; LEIR, KING.

King Lent. An anglicism for Carêmeprenant, the ruler of Tapinois, or Sneaks, Island in Rabelais' GARGANTUA AND PANTAGRUEL. His body and limbs resemble inanimate objects, so that his feet suggest guitars and his skin is like a gabardine jacket. He personifies the Lenten customs of fasting and penitence which Rabelais thought unnatural.

Kingmaker. Epithet for Richard Neville, earl of Warwick (1420–1471). He was so called because, when he sided with Henry VI, Henry was the king, but when he sided with Edward IV, Henry was deposed and Edward crowned king. He was killed at the battle of Barnet.

King of Misrule. See LORD OF MISRULE.

King of the Wood. Lat., *Rex Nemorensis.* The priest of Diana who must pluck the golden bough (as Aeneas did before his descent into the underworld) and then slay his predecessor in a duel before entering on his office at Aricia on the shores of a lake (now Lago di Nemi) in the Alban Mountains, where the goddess had a sacred grove. A discussion of this myth is the opening passage in, and explains the title of, Sir James G. Frazer's THE GOLDEN BOUGH.

King Philip (died 1676). Name given by English settlers to Metacomet, the son of Massasoit and chief of the Wampanoag tribe. During King Philip's War (1675–76), the most important Indian uprising in New England, Wampanoag, Narragansett, and Nipmuck warriors made sudden raids on frontier settlements; many towns were destroyed and captives taken, including the famous Mrs. Mary ROWLANDSON. Although the Indians were initially successful, the movement collapsed after Philip's death. See also Benjamin TOMPSON.

Kings, The First Book and **The Second Book of.** Two books of the Old Testament. Together these books—originally one—relate the history of Israel from the last years of David to the Babylonian Exile. They record the glories of Solomon's reign (c. 960 B.C.) and the decline of the Southern Kingdom, which followed, ending with the destruction of the temple in Jerusalem in 586 B.C.

king's evil. Scrofula. It was so called from a notion that prevailed from the reign of Edward the Confessor to that of Queen Anne that it could be cured by the royal touch. The Jacobites considered that the power did not descend to William III and Anne because the divine hereditary right was not fully possessed by them, but an office for such healing remained in the Prayer Book till 1719. Prince Charles Edward, when he claimed to be prince of Wales, touched a female child for the disease in 1745; but the last person touched in England was Dr. Johnson, in 1712, when only 30 months old, by Queen Anne.

The French kings laid claim to the same divine power from the time of Clovis (A.D. 481). On Easter Sunday, 1686, Louis XIV touched 1,600 persons, using these words: *le Roi te touche, Dieu te guérisse.*

Kingsley, Rev. Charles (1819–1875). English clergyman, novelist, and poet. Kingsley was much involved in the social reform movements of his time, having been strongly influenced by Carlyle. His earliest novels, ALTON LOCKE and *Yeast* (1851), deal with CHRISTIAN SOCIALISM, a movement with which he was associated. His best-known books are the historical romances HYPATIA, WESTWARD HO!, and HEREWARD THE WAKE, and his fairy tale THE WATER BABIES. A review of his in *Macmillan's Magazine* led to the famous church controversy with Cardinal Newman, which moved the latter to publish his *Apologia Pro Vita Sua*. See MUSCULAR CHRISTIANITY.

Kingsley, Henry (1830–1876). English novelist and journalist, brother of Charles KINGSLEY. His best-known works are the romantic novels *Geoffrey Hamlyn* (1859) and *Ravenshoe* (1862). He wrote several other novels, of which *The Hillyars and the Burtons* (1865) and *Mademoiselle Mathilde* (1868) are worthy of note, and a number of short stories, essays, and children's books.

Kingsley, Sidney (1906–   ). American actor and playwright. He is the author of the Pulitzer Prize-winning drama MEN IN WHITE and of the popular DEAD END. Later plays include *The Patriots* (1942), written with his wife, Madge Evans Kingsley, and *Darkness at Noon* (1951), an adaptation from the book by Arthur Koestler.

King, the Greatest Alcalde, The. See MEJOR ALCALDE EL REY, EL.

Kingu. A Bablyonian demigod. He was a general and consort of Tiamat, in the WAR OF THE GODS. After her defeat, Marduk killed him and fashioned man out of his blood and bones.

King William's War (1689–1697). A war waged by Great Britain and its American colonies against France and its Indian allies. It was the American phase of the war between the Grand Alliance and Louis XIV and was concluded by the Peace of Ryswick.

Kinsmen, The. See SCOUT, THE.

Kipling, Rudyard (1865–1936). English novelist, poet, and short story writer. Born in India of English parents, he was taken to England at the age of six and spent six unhappy years there, later described in *Baa Baa, Black Sheep*. In 1878 he entered the United Services College in North Devon, and his experiences there later served as the basis for STALKY AND Co. Kipling returned to India at the age of 17 where his father had secured him a post at the *Civil and Military Gazette* of Lahore; the collection of verses *Departmental Ditties* (1886) and the collection of stories PLAIN TALES FROM THE HILLS were originally written for the *Gazette*. The stories that he produced as editor, during his last two years in India, of the Allahabad *Pioneer* were collected into *The Phantom Rickshaw* (1889).

Kipling returned to England via Japan and America, writing letters during the trip that were to form *From Sea to Sea* (1899). Once in London, he enjoyed spectacular success: all his Indian volumes were republished, and he followed up quickly with LIFE's HANDICAP, THE LIGHT THAT FAILED, and BARRACK-ROOM BALLADS, the collection of poems that included GUNGA DIN, FUZZY WUZZY, *Danny Deever*, and MANDALAY. He wrote *The Naulahka* (1892) in collaboration with Charles Wolcott Balestier, whose sister Caroline he married in the same year. They settled in Vermont, and during the next five years

Kipling published *Many Inventions* (1893), THE JUNGLE BOOK (1894), *The Second Jungle Book* (1895), *The Seven Seas* (1896), and *Captains Courageous* (1897). After bitterly quarreling with his brother-in-law Beatty, Kipling returned to England. Except for a brief visit to New York in 1899, when his daughter died of pneumonia and he almost died of the same disease, Kipling never returned to the U.S., and spoke of it with bitterness despite the fact that, with the exception of Mark Twain, no other author had been so popular there as Kipling. In the years between 1897 and 1914, he published *The Day's Work* (1898), *Stalky and Co.* (1899), KIM, JUST SO STORIES, the only book that Kipling himself illustrated, *The Five Nations* (1903), *Traffics and Discoveries* (1904), *Puck of Pook's Hill* (1906), *Actions and Reactions* (1909), *Rewards and Fairies* (1909), *A Diversity of Creatures* (1917), *The Irish Guards in the Great War* (1923), a memorial to his only son John, fallen in battle, *Debits and Credits* (1926), *Limits and Renewals* (1932), and *Something of Myself* (1937), an autobiography left unfinished at his death.

Kipling was one of the first English poets to exploit the Cockney dialect. While his life-long glorification of imperialism has antagonized some critics and caused them to miss his more poetic side, it has had no effect on his popularity. See RECESSIONAL; SOLDIERS THREE; WEE WILLIE WINKIE; MAN WHO WOULD BE KING, THE.

Kipps (1905). A novel by H. G. WELLS. Arthur Kipps is a draper's apprentice who suddenly acquires wealth and makes comic efforts to fit into his new social world. Eventually he marries a housemaid and settles down to a happy, simple life.

Kirby, William. See GOLDEN DOG, THE.

Kirchhoff, Gustav Robert (1824–1887). German physicist. With Robert Bunsen, he developed the method of spectrum analysis and explained the FRAUNHOFER LINES.

Kirilov, Alexei Nilich. In Feodor Dostoevski's THE POSSESSED, a fanatically rebellious atheist who resolves to commit suicide, asserting man's freedom from his terrible fate—death. The idea has been implanted in the half-mad Kirilov by STAVROGIN. The revolutionary Pyotr VERKHOVENSKI tries to persuade Kirilov to leave a suicide note confessing to the murder of SHATOV, who has been killed by Verkhovenski's group.

Kirkland, Caroline [Matilda Stansbury]. Pen name, **Mrs. Mary Clavers** (1801–1864). American writer. Mrs. Kirkland, who traveled to the West with her missionary husband expressed her disillusionment with the crudeness of pioneer life in three books of semifictional narrative: *A New Home—Who'll Follow* (1839), *Forest Life* (1842), and *Western Clearings* (1845).

Kirkland, Joseph (1830–1894). American novelist. The son of Caroline KIRKLAND, he was one of the earliest exponents of realism. Kirkland was known for his frank and powerful studies of life in the Middle West. His best novel, *Zury, The Meanest Man in Spring County* (1887), was taken from his own grim youthful experience.

Kirkrapine. See FAERIE QUEENE, THE.

Kirkup, James (1923–   ). English poet, novelist, and playwright. Among his collections of poetry are *The Cosmic Shape* (1947), *A Spring Journey* (1954), and *The Prodigal Son* (1959). *The Love of Others* (1962) is a novel, and *Upon This Rock* (1955) is a play.

Kirov, Sergei Mironovich (1886–1934). Russian revolutionary leader. One of Stalin's chief aides and a member of the praesidium (1930–1934), Kirov was the Communist Party's secretary for the Leningrad area whose assassination in 1934 set off the purges of 1936–1937.

Kirsanov, Pavel Petrovich. In Ivan Turgenev's novel FATHERS AND CHILDREN, the chief antagonist of the nihilist BAZAROV. Pavel Petrovich, who defends the aristocratic way of life against the iconoclastic young radical, is called by Bazarov "an archaic phenomenon" and an "idiot."

Kirshon, Vladimir Mikhailovich (1902–1938). Russian dramatist. His plays, which champion the Soviet world against all forms of intervention and counterrevolution, include *Konstantin Terekhin* (*Rust*, 1927) and *Khleb* (*Bread*, 1930).

Kishar. See ANSHAR.

kismet (from Turk., *qismat*, portion, lot). Fate; the fulfilment of destiny.

Kissbreech, Lord. An anglicism for Seigneur de Baisecul, the plaintiff in the great lawsuit against Lord SUCKFIST in Rabelais' GARGANTUA AND PANTAGRUEL.

Kiss Me Kate (1948). A musical comedy with libretto by Bella and Samuel SPEWACK and music by Cole PORTER. Based on Shakespeare's *The Taming of the Shrew*, it contains some of Porter's best-known songs and is often considered his best musical.

Kit-cat Club. A club formed in the beginning of the 18th century by the leading Whigs of the day, whose meetings were held in the house of Christopher Catt, a pastrycook. Catt's mutton pies, which were eaten at the club, were also called *kit-cats*, and probably gave the club its name. The publisher Jacob Tonson was secretary, and the members included Richard Steele, Joseph Addison, William Congreve, Samuel Garth, John Vanbrugh, Robert Walpole, and William Pulteney. Their portraits by Sir Godfrey Kneller were reduced to three-quarter length in order to accommodate them to the size of the clubroom wainscot. Hence, a three-quarter portrait is still called a *kit-cat*.

kitchen cabinet. A name applied to President Andrew Jackson's informal advisers (1829–1833). The name was used in a derogatory manner by Jackson's political opponents, with particular reference to Francis P. Blair and Amos Kendall, both of whom were connected with the pro-Jackson newspaper *The Globe*.

Kitely. In Ben Jonson's EVERY MAN IN HIS HUMOUR, a rich elderly merchant. He is convinced that his young wife has made him a cuckold. His "horns i' the mind are worse than o' the head." Ironically, his wife is equally suspicious of his activities.

Kithara. See GREEK MUSIC.

Kittredge, George Lyman (1860–1941). American teacher and scholar. Kittredge, who taught at Harvard University from 1888 to 1936, was known as a great Shakespearean authority. Among his important works were *The Language of Chaucer's "Troilus"* (1894), *English and Scottish Popular Ballads* (1904), with H. C. Sargent; *Chaucer and His*

Poetry (1915); *Sir Thomas Malory* (1925); *Witchcraft in Old and New England* (1929); and an edition of *The Complete Works of Shakespeare* (1936).

Kivi, Aleksis. Pen name of **A. Stenvall** (1834–1872). Finnish novelist, playwright, and poet. Regarded as his country's greatest 19th-century writer, Kivi found inspiration for his best work in the country life of Finland. In *Kullervo* (1864) he dramatized an episode from the *Kalevala*, while in the comedy *Nummisuutarit* (*Shoemakers of the Heath*, 1864) and in the novel *Seitsemän Veljestä* (*Seven Brothers*, 1870) he depicted Finnish peasant life with a realism and humor that have never been matched by any other writer. He is also noted for his numerous collections of lyric verse.

Kjartan. In the LAXDALE SAGA, a young Icelander in love with the strong-willed heroine Gudrun. When he returns home from the Danish court and learns Gudrun has married his cousin Bolli, he takes a wife of his own, Hrefna. During the ensuing feud between the two couples, Kjartan continues to love Gudrun and defend her even when she is in the wrong.

Klaboterman. The kobold of the phantom ship, CARMILHAN.

Klabund. Pen name of **Alfred Henschke** (1890–1928). German poet, playwright, and novelist. He was a versatile writer with expressionistic leanings and wide cultural interests. His novels include *Pjotr* (*Peter the Great*, 1923), *Borgia* (1928) and *Rasputin* (1929).

Klaus or **Claus, Peter.** German legendary hero, the prototype of RIP VAN WINKLE. Klaus is a goatherd of Sittendorf who is led into a deep dell, where he finds 12 knights silently playing skittles. He drinks of their wine and is overpowered with sleep. When he awakens, he is amazed at the height of the grass; and upon discovering how strange his village seems, he realizes he has been asleep for 20 years.

Klee, Paul (1879–1940). Swiss painter. Generally considered one of the great masters of modern painting, Klee spent much of his life in Germany; he joined the BLAUE REITER group in 1912 and taught at the BAUHAUS from 1920 to 1929. Interested in the abstract meaning of pictorial representation, he was a highly original metaphysical painter, who by his playful line and subtle use of color created an art of great whimsy and spontaneity.

Kleist, Ewald von (1715–1759). German poet and grand-uncle of Heinrich von Kleist. He is most famous for his long philosophical lyric *Der Frühling* (*The Spring*, 1749) and for his heroic *Ode an die preussische Armee* (*Ode to the Prussian Army*, 1757).

Kleist, Heinrich von (1777–1811). German dramatist and novella writer, considered by many the greatest of all German authors in both genres. As a young man, he was induced by his family to undertake a career in the Prussian army, but in 1799 he resigned his commission and began an intensive study of mathematics and philosophy in hopes of perfecting his mind and gaining intellectual control over his destiny. In 1801, however, after reading Kant, his faith in the perfectability of knowledge was shattered, and for the first time he turned decisively to a career in writing. During 1801–1802 he worked on two plays, *Robert Guiskard* and *Die Familie Schroffenstein* (*The Schroffenstein Family*, pub. 1803), a tragedy of errors influenced by Shakespeare's *Romeo and*

Juliet. Though he never carried the latter beyond a fragmentary stage, he felt that it would be his *magnum opus,* and parts of it were highly praised by Wieland; but in 1803, in a fit of despair, he destroyed the manuscript, and the fragment of it that he published in 1808 consisted only of some 500 lines restored from memory. The year 1803, however, also saw the completion of his great comedy THE BROKEN JUG. He then spent three years as a government official in Königsberg. But in 1807 he went to Dresden where, with his friend Adam Müller (1779–1829), he founded the periodical *Phöbus* (1808) in which his greatest novella, MICHAEL KOHLHAAS, appeared. By 1809 he had also completed several more plays: an adaptation of Molière's *Amphitryon,* DAS KÄTHCHEN VON HEILBRONN, and PENTHESILEA.

Around 1808, along with the growing anti-Napoleonic movement in Germany, Kleist's interests became more patriotic. In 1810, again with Müller, he began editing the *Berliner Abendblätter* (*Berlin Evening News*) in which he took a firm stand against Napoleon; and in the same year he completed his last play, the strongly patriotic PRINZ FRIEDRICH VON HOMBURG. But in 1811, after his newspaper had been closed by the government, after all hope had faded of a successful German uprising against Napoleon in the near future, and in despair about his lack of literary recognition, he took his own life.

In form, Kleist's dramas show the clear influence of Schiller's classicism; but Kleist's characters, unlike Schiller's, have no clearly defined structure of moral principles and personal standards upon which to base their actions. They tend more to vacillate unpredictably among various attitudes, to show more the nervousness and insecurity of the modern individual. Some theoretical background to Kleist's dramatic style may be found in his essay *Über das Marionettentheater* (*On the Puppet-Theater,* 1810), in which he suggested that man's self-consciousness hinders his freedom of action, that man cannot act purely and simply in accordance with conscious ideas or standards.

Kline, Franz (1910–1962). American painter. A creator of abstract paintings, he built tension and movement by means of deliberate, wide brush strokes in his large black and white canvases.

Klinger, Friedrich Maximilian (1752–1831). German dramatist of the STURM UND DRANG, which took its name from the title of his play of 1776. His works are noted for boldness of expression and freedom of form. Goethe helped him through Giessen university.

Klingsor or Klingshor. An evil magician in medieval German legend. His small role in Wolfram von Eschenbach's *Parzival* (13th century) is greatly expanded in Wagner's opera PARSIFAL. He also appears in the stories of the WARTBURG singing contest.

Klondike. A region in the Yukon Territory of Canada, famous for its gold mines. See Robert William SERVICE.

Klopstock, Friedrich Gottlieb (1724–1803). German poet in the movement of irrationalism. In his preference for classical forms, especially the elegy and ode, and his virtually total rejection of rhyme, he was consciously attempting to develop for the German language a classical perfection of its own that would place it on a par with Greek and Latin. His major work is a religious epic in hexameters, *Der Messias* (*The Messiah,* 1773; final version, 1800), which shows the influence of Milton and pietism. He was deeply patriotic and hoped to be remembered as a prophet of his country's future greatness. This side of him appears in much of his lyric and in his dramatic trilogy (1769–1787) celebrating Hermann, the Germanic hero who defeated the Romans in the first century. His most famous prose work, *Die Deutsche Gelehrtenrepublik* (*The German Republic of Letters,* 1774) proposes the outlines of a utopian state in Germany, and parallels the poet's more practical efforts toward the founding of a German Academy. See ARMINIUS; BODMER; GOTTINGER HAIN.

Klotho. See the FATES.

Knaben Wunderhorn, Des (*The Boy's Wunderhorn;* vol. 1, 1805; vol. 2, 1808; vol. 3, 1818). A collection of folk songs edited by Clemens BRENTANO and Achim von ARNIM, named for the first song in it. As opposed to Herder's earlier cosmopolitan collection of *Volkslieder* (*Folk Songs,* 1778–1779), the *Wunderhorn* contains only German songs and was intended to draw attention specifically to the German folk spirit. It is not, however, a scholarly work, for Brentano and Arnim frequently made their own changes in the material they collected.

Knecht, Josef. The hero of Hesse's MAGISTER LUDI. Though he rises to the position of master in the hierarchy of the glass-bead game, the fact that his name in German means servant is a central indication of the book's pervasive irony. Even as he dominates the game, he is dominated by it.

Kneller, Sir Godfrey (1649?–1723). German-born English portrait painter. Highly successful, he served English kings from Charles II to George I.

Knickerbocker, Diedrich. A character invented by Washington IRVING.

Knickerbocker's History of New York. See HISTORY OF NEW YORK FROM THE BEGINNING OF THE WORLD TO THE END OF THE DUTCH DYNASTY, A; Washington IRVING.

Knight, Eric (1897–1943). Anglo-American writer. Knight's best-known tales are laid in Yorkshire, particularly *The Flying Yorkshireman* (1937), in which he created the character of Sam Small. His other works include the popular juvenile *Lassie Come Home* (1940), the novel *This Above All* (1941), and the short-story collection *Sam Small Flies Again* (1942).

Knight, G[eorge] Wilson (1897–   ). English literary critic. His studies of Shakespeare's plays were controversial and influential; in them he treats the plays as poems expressing cosmic ideas through patterns of imagery. Among his books are *The Wheel of Fire* (1930), *The Shakespearean Tempest* (1932), *The Mutual Flame* (1955), and *The Golden Labyrinth* (1962).

Knight, Sarah Kemble. Known as **Madam Knight** (1666–1727). American schoolteacher. She is known for the diary in which she recorded observations and impressions of a journey made on horseback from Boston to New York in the winter of 1704–1705. Published in 1825, her *Journal* is a firsthand source of information on the transportation, housing, manners, and speech of early 18th-century New England.

Knightly, Mr. See EMMA.

Knight of the Burning Pestle, The (c. 1607). A comedy by Francis Beaumont. (See BEAUMONT AND FLETCHER.) A performance of a play called *The London Merchant* is interrupted by a grocer who insists upon interspersing it with scenes from his own concoction, *The Knight of the Burning Pestle*, with his apprentice Ralph in the leading role. In the hilarious potpourri that follows, hackneyed sentimental scenes from bourgeois romance are laced with scenes from the grocer's effort, a parody of chivalric romance with Ralph cast as a kind of Don Quixote. The whole thing is continuously interrupted with comments by the grocer and his wife.

Knight of the Garter. See GARTER, ORDER OF THE.

Knights, The (Hippeis). A comedy by Aristophanes. Because of its political topicality, this play is less interesting to modern audiences than some others by Aristophanes. It is remarkable, however, for the freedom with which the playwright is able to attack the powerful Athenian demagogue CLEON and for the fact that it was awarded a first prize.

Knight's Gambit (1939). A book of interrelated stories by William FAULKNER. Dealing with the various inhabitants of YOKNAPATAWPHA COUNTY, *Knight's Gambit* is a collection of detective stories in which Gavin STEVENS, the county attorney, ferrets out the real culprits and saves the innocent. The book is ingenious and skillfully narrated; perhaps the best story is *Monk,* which deals with an idiot who is imprisoned for a murder he did not commit and who finally is incited to kill the warden who has befriended him.

Knights of Labor. A pioneer U.S. labor organization. Founded as a secret league in Philadelphia in 1869, it aimed at the regulation of wages, of the degree of skill to be exacted from workmen, and of the length of a day's work, as well as attempting to control strikes. The league decided when a strike was to take place and when the workmen of the union might resume work.

Knights of Malta. First called "Knights of St. John of Jerusalem," otherwise "Knights of Rhodes," the most celebrated religious military order of the Middle Ages.

Knight's Tale, The. One of the CANTERBURY TALES of Geoffrey CHAUCER, a chivalric romance adapted from Boccaccio's TESEIDA. Theseus of Athens defeats Creon at Thebes, and the royal Theban cousins Palamon and Arcite are imprisoned in a tower. They see Emily, sister of Theseus' wife Hippolyta, walking in a garden; both fall in love with her. Arcite is released and banished from the territory, but he returns and works disguised as a court servant. Palamon escapes from prison, also determined to win Emily; the cousins meet by accident and determine to fight the next day in knightly regalia for the right to love her. Theseus interrupts the battle and orders that in a year the combatants will each bring 100 knights to a tourney. Emily prays to Diana that both warriors will forget their quarrel and desert her, but her prayer is rejected. Palamon prays to Venus that he may win his beloved, while Arcite prays to Mars that he may triumph in the battle. Accordingly, Saturn arranges that Arcite be victorious in the joust, but be thrown by his horse as he rides toward Emily. Dying, he yields Emily to Palamon, and after a suitable time the two are happily married.

Knoblock, Edward (1874–1945). British playwright, scenarist, and novelist. His works include *Kismet* (1911), *Milestones* (with Arnold Bennett; 1921), and *Grand Hotel* (from the novel by Vicki Baum).

Knowles, James Sheridan (1784–1862). Irishborn English playwright and actor. He wrote both verse tragedies, such as *Caius Gracchus* (1815) and *Virginius* (1820), and comedies, such as *The Hunchback* (1832) and *The Love-Chase* (1837).

Know-Nothing party. In U.S. history, a popular name for the American party, which reached its greatest influence in 1854–1855. Its program called for the exclusion of Catholics and foreigners from public office and for other nativist measures. It was originally a secret society whose members answered questions with "I don't know." The party split over the slavery issue and faded after the election of 1856.

Knox, John (1505–1572). Scottish reformer and founder of Presbyterianism. He was twice at Geneva in personal contact with Calvin (1554, 1556–1558). He published six tracts dealing with religion in Scotland; the best known are his *Blasts of the Trumpet Against the Monstrous Regiment of Women* (1st and 2nd, 1558). They were not meant for Queen Elizabeth but offended her deeply. Knox preached throughout Scotland against Mary Queen of Scots, whom he simply called "Jezebel," and against Catholicism in general.

Knut. See CANUTE.

kōan (Ch. *Kung-an*). In ZEN Buddhism, the problem or case to be meditated upon. Frequently paradoxical, and usually concerned with the sayings and actions of Chinese CH'AN (Zen) masters, it is one of the methods used for training in Japanese Rinzai Zen. A *kōan* is always studied under the guidance of a Zen master. There are some 1,700 *kōans*.

Kobayashi Issa (1763–1827). Japanese *haiku* poet. He is noted for the humorous and simple treatment of his subjects. He was a prolific writer of both poetry and prose.

Kober, Arthur (1900–   ). Polish-born American writer and playwright. Kober is noted for his dialect stories set in the Bronx or Hollywood. These appeared in the *New Yorker* and were later reissued in several books, the best known being *Having Wonderful Time* (1937), the story of a group of vacationers in the Berkshires who try to improve themselves culturally. It became a play (1937) and was later made into a successful musical called *Wish You Were Here* (1952).

kobold. In German folklore a mischievous house spirit, similar to Robin Goodfellow or the Scottish Brownie. It is also a gnome who works in the mines and forests.

Koch, Martin (1882–1940). Swedish journalist and author. A pioneer in the Swedish proletarian novel, Koch describes the strike of 1909 and the struggles of laborers in his naturalistic novel *Arbetare* (*Workers,* 1912). His concern with social problems appeared again in *Guds vackra värld* (*God's Lovely World,* 2 vols., 1916), a treatment of crime.

Koch, Robert (1843–1910). German physician, one of the pioneers of modern bacteriology. He discovered the anthrax and tuberculosis bacilli and did research on cholera, malaria, and other diseases. He was awarded the Nobel Prize for medicine in 1905.

Koel or **Kokila.** An Indian bird often mentioned in imaginative writing. The poignance of the koel's song is supposed to convey the sad sweetness of frustrated or alienated love. In Sanskrit it is called the *parabhrita,* "brought up by another," because the female koel leaves her eggs in the nest of a crow, where they are hatched.

Koestler, Arthur (1905–   ). Hungarian novelist and essayist. Bilingual from childhood, Koestler became a German-language journalist and a writer of popular articles on science. In 1926 he left Europe for Palestine, and remained in the Near East for some time. His life from his childhood until the end of this period is described in the first volume of his autobiography, *Arrow in the Blue* (1952). In 1931 he became a member of the Communist Party. While covering the Spanish Civil War for an English newspaper, he was captured by the Fascists early in 1937 and spent three months in prison under sentence of death before being released through British intervention. His war and prison experiences he recorded in *Spanish Testament* (1938) and in the shorter *Dialogue with Death* (1942). *The Invisible Writing* (1954), the second volume of his autobiography, deals with the seven-year period of his membership in the Communist Party. At the beginning of the Second World War he was arrested in France as a refugee and sent to the detention camp at Le Vernet, about which he wrote in *Scum of the Earth* (1941). He was released in 1940, and after the end of the war became a British subject.

Among his nonfiction works are *The Yogi and the Commissar* (1945), essays; *Promise and Fulfillment* (1949), a report of the fighting between the Jews and the Arabs after the partition of Palestine; *Insight and Outlook* (1949); *The Trail of the Dinosaur* (1955); *Reflections on Hanging* (1957), which helped end capital punishment, except in special cases, in England; and *The Lotus and the Robot* (1961), an examination of Eastern and Western thought. He is perhaps best known for his novel *Darkness at Noon* (1941), based on the Moscow trials during the 1930's. His other novels include *The Gladiators* (1939), based on Spartacus and the slave revolt; *Arrival and Departure* (1943); *Thieves in the Night* (1946), a story of Jewish settlers of Palestine in the 1930's; and *The Age of Longing* (1951).

Kohlhaas, Michael. See MICHAEL KOHLHAAS.

Kokoschka, Oskar (1886–   ). Austrian painter and playwright. Known as an exponent of EXPRESSIONISM, he is primarily significant as a painter. His plays, however, with their tendency to depict extreme human agony in almost abstract terms and with their use of an ecstatic and compressed diction, contributed considerably to the development of expressionist dramatic style. The best known are *Mörder, Hoffnung der Frauen* (*Murderer, Hope of Women,* 1907), *Hiob* (*Job,* 1917), and *Orpheus and Eurydice* (1918).

Kolchak, Aleksandr Vasilyevich (1874–1920). Russian admiral. The leader of the anti-Bolshevik forces in the Far East during the civil war in Russia, he advanced far into western Russia before having to retreat. He was captured and executed by the Bolsheviks.

Komsomol. The youth organization of the Soviet Communist Party.

Königsmarke, The Long Finne: A Story of the New World (1823). A novel by James Kirke PAULDING. An amusing satire, the book tells of the trials of a Finnish immigrant in the Delaware colony of New Sweden.

Koo, V[i] K[yuin] Wellington (1887–   ). Chinese statesman. He represented his country on the Council of the League of Nations (1932–1934); was ambassador to France (1936–1941); ambassador to England (1941–1946); ambassador to the U.S. (1946–1956). "Wellington" became part of his name through sound association with the original Wei-chün.

Kopit, Arthur (1937–   ). American playwright. His plays, often distinguished by their dark humor, by their mixing of realistic and antirealistic elements, and by the longest titles in theatrical history—except, perhaps, for those of the Restoration—have caused certain critics to classify him among the playwrights of the absurd. His works include *On the Runway of Life You Never Know What's Coming off Next* (1958); *Oh Dad, Poor Dad, Mama's Hung You in the Closet and I'm Feeling So Sad* (1960); *The Day the Whores Came out to Play Tennis* (1963); and *Mhil'daiim* (1963).

Korah. An Old Testament Levite, his name signifying "ice." He led a rebellion against Moses and Aaron for which he was swallowed by the earth (Num. 16; 26:9–11). His descendants, the Korahites, were temple musicians.

Koran. The ISLAM Bible, the sacred book of the Muslims. In Arabic, the word means reading, from *quran;* the variant form, *Alcoran,* has a prefixed article. Written in the purest Arabic, it is considered the Word of God, the uncreated and eternal truth revealed to Muhammad by the angel Gabriel. The tradition that the text should be transmitted orally had to be broken under the third Caliph, Othman, when the best Koran reciters had fallen in battle. There are 114 *Suras* or chapters in the Koran, unnumbered but individually named. Historically, the subject matter is of Jewish, and to a lesser extent, of Christian origin.

Kore. See PERSEPHONE.

Korneichuk, Alexander Evdokimovich (1905–1972). Russian dramatist. Noted for their use of Ukrainian themes and their strong nationalistic and militaristic devotion to the Soviet regime, his plays include *On the Ukrainian Steppes* (1941), a sequel, *Guerillas on the Ukrainian Steppes* (1942), *The Front* (1942), *The Sinking of the Squadron* (1934), *Truth* (1937) and *Mr. Perkins' Mission to the Land of the Bolsheviks* (1944). He has won three Stalin Prizes.

Körner, Theodor (1791–1813). German patriotic poet who died in the wars of liberation against Napoleon (1813–1815). His best-known collection is *Leier und Schwert* (*Lyre and Sword,* 1814).

Kornilov, Lavr Georgyevich (1870–1918). Russian general. The commander of the troops in Petrograd after the revolution (1917), he attempted to overthrow the Kerenski regime, and afterwards fought against the Bolsheviks in the civil war until his death.

Korobochka. A dull-witted woman landowner in Nikolai Gogol's DEAD SOULS. Her fear that Chichikov, the swindler-protagonist of the novel, may be cheating her in their strange business deal is instrumental in exposing Chichikov.

Korolenko, Vladimir Galaktionovich (1853–1921). Russian writer and political radical. He was instrumental in helping the young Maksim Gorki get his start in literature. Korolenko, who was exiled to Siberia for six years by the Czarist government, was also opposed to the Bolshevik regime, an attitude he forcefully expressed in letters to Anatol Lunacharski, the future commissar of education. Korolenko's best works are *Makar's Dream* (*Son makara;* 1885), a short story depicting the death of a Siberian native; *Tongueless* (*Bez yazyka;* 1895), a humorous story of three non-English speaking peasants in America; and *The History of My Contemporary* (*Istoriya moego sovremennika;* 1910–1922), an autobiographical work.

korrigans. Nine fays of Breton folklore. They can predict future events, assume any shape they like, move as quickly as thought from place to place, and cure diseases or wounds. They are not more than two feet high, have long flowing hair, which they are fond of combing, dress only in a white veil, and are excellent singers. Their favorite haunt is beside some fountain. They flee at the sound of a bell or benediction, and their breath is most deadly.

Korzybski, Alfred [Habdank] [Count] (1879–1950). Polish-born American semanticist. Korzybski came to the U.S. in about 1915. He founded what he called "general semantics," an approach to semantics that rejects the Aristotelian language structure, with its *is* of identity, as tending to confuse words with the things for which they stand, to see propositions as either "right" or "wrong," and to limit severely the levels of abstraction. Among his writings is *Science and Sanity: An Introduction to Non-Aristotelian Systems and General Semantics* (1933). With other general semanticists, he often expressed his views in *ETC., A Review of General Semantics.*

Koshar-wa-Khasis. Divine artisan of the Canaanite pantheon. In THE POEMS OF BAAL and THE POEM OF AQHAT, he fashions weapons and palaces for the gods. In this respect he is clearly parallel with the Greek HEPHAESTUS. His Phoenician counterpart seems to be Chusor.

Koskenniemi, Veikko Antero. Pen name of V. A. Forsnäs (1885–1962). Finnish poet. A university professor and scholar, he is known for his skill as a lyric poet. Careful artistry and subdued melancholy characterize the poems of *Runoja* (1906) and *Sydän ja Kuolema* (1919) and the ballads of *Kurkiaura* (1930).

Kotzebue, August von (1761–1819). German dramatist. His *Sämtliche dramatische Werke* (*Complete Dramatic Works,* 1827 ff.) fill 44 volumes, but though he was popular in his time, none of his plays is today considered any more than oversentimentalized melodrama. He was ridiculed by the poets of German romanticism, and his reactionary political writings led to his murder by a university student.

Koussevitzky, Sergey Alexandrovitch (1874–1951). Russian-born conductor. He began his career as a performer on the double-bass, first conducted publicly in Berlin (1908), and came to the U.S. to conduct the Boston Symphony Orchestra (1924–1949).

He directed the Berkshire Music Festival at Tanglewood and championed modern music.

Krafft-Ebing, Baron Richard von (1840–1902). German neurologist. His *Psychopathia Sexualis* (1886) is a famous collection of psychiatric case histories.

Kramm, Joseph (1908–). American playwright. He is best known for *The Shrike* (1952), a play about a man who tries to commit suicide to escape an overpossessive wife. It won a Pulitzer Prize.

Krapp's Last Tape (1958). A one-act play by Samuel BECKETT. Its one character, Krapp, an old man, plays back tapes of monologues he recorded when young and ridicules the passions and ambitions of his youth and middle years, which have come to nothing. In the light of his broken-down old age, hope and optimism seem absurd, and we are made aware of the futility and meaninglessness of life.

Kreisler, Fritz (1875–1962). Austrian-born violin virtuoso and composer. His colorful career includes an amusing hoax by which he convinced the public that many of his own works were written by Baroque or Classical composers. He wrote some memoirs: *Four Weeks in the Trenches: The War Story of a Violinist* (1915) about his experiences in the Austrian army.

Kremlin. A walled section of Moscow, containing cathedrals and palaces dating back to the 15th century. There are 20 towers of various sizes and architectural styles. The largest building, the Great Kremlin Palace, is now used for sessions of the Supreme Soviet, the Soviet Union's governing body. Until Peter the Great moved the capital to St. Petersburg in 1712, the Kremlin was the residence of the Czars. After the revolution it became the seat of government and a symbol of Soviet power.

Kretzer, Max (1854–1941). German novelist. He is known only for his early works, which show affinities with the movement of naturalism, especially *Die Betrogenen* (*The Betrayed Ones,* 1882), *Die Verkommenen* (*The Fallen Ones,* 1883), and *Meister Timpe* (*Master Timpe,* 1888). All these novels stress the needs of the proletariat and reflect Kretzer's socialist sympathies.

Kriemhild. Heroine of the NIBELUNGENLIED, known as **Gudrun** in the VÖLSUNGA SAGA and **Gutrune** in Wagner's RING DES NIBELUNGEN.

Krishna (*Sansk.,* "the black one"). One of the greatest of the Hindu deities. The god of fire, lightning, storms, the heavens, and the sun, he is usually regarded as the eighth *avatar* of VISHNU. One legend relates that Kamsa, the demon-king of Mathura, committed great ravages so that Brahma prayed to Vishnu to relieve the world of this distress. Vishnu plucked off two hairs, one white, the other black, and promised they would revenge the wrongs of the demon-king. The black hair became Krishna.

Another legend says that Krishna was the son of Vasudeva and Devaki. When he was born among the Yadava tribe at Mathura, between Delhi and Agra, his uncle King Kamsa, who had been warned by a prophecy that this nephew would slay him, sought to kill Krishna, who was, however, smuggled away. He was brought up by shepherds, and later he killed his uncle and became king of the Yadavas. He is often represented playing on his divine flute and attracting the *gopis* or cowherdesses to dance the *rasa-lila* around him in the moonlight. To Arjuna on the battlefield (see BHAGAVADGITA), he becomes a provider of divine consolation and inspiration. See MAHABHARATA.

Kriss Kringle. The Pennsylvania Dutch Santa Claus. On Christmas Eve, arrayed in a fur cap and strange apparel, he goes to the bedroom of each good child, where he leaves a present in the stocking that is hung up in expectation of his visit. The word is a dialectal variant of High German *Christkindle*, "the little Christ child," and has undergone such radical changes because it is no longer associated with either of its component parts.

Kristin Lavransdatter (1920–1922). A trilogy of historical novels by Sigrid UNDSET. Re-creating a woman's life in the devout Catholic Norway of the 13th and 14th centuries, this great romance appeared in successive volumes: *The Bridal Wreath* (*Kransen;* 1920), *The Mistress of Husaby* (*Husfrue;* 1921), and *The Cross* (*Korset;* 1922).

Kröger, Tonio. See TONIO KRÖGER.

Kronos. See CRONOS.

Krook. In Charles Dickens' BLEAK HOUSE, proprietor of a rag-and-bone warehouse where everything seems to be bought and nothing sold. He is a grasping drunkard who eventually dies of spontaneous combustion.

Kropotkin, Prince Piotr Alekseyevich (1842–1921). Russian social philosopher and geographer. A leading theorist of anarchism, Kropotkin took part during the 1870's in the revolutionary movement against the Czarist government. To escape arrest, he emigrated to Europe and settled in England (1876). He returned to Russia in 1917, but was no friendlier to the Bolsheviks than he had been to the Czars. His most famous book, *Zapiski revolyutzionera* (*Memoirs of a Revolutionist,* 1899), describes the social ferment during the reign of Alexander II.

Krull, Felix. See CONFESSIONS OF FELIX KRULL; CONFIDENCE MAN.

Krupp. A German family in control of the corporation that built and managed the greatest ordnance works in modern Germany. The firm was founded in 1811 by Friedrich Krupp (1787–1826) as a steel mill, and expanded rapidly under Alfred Krupp (1812–1887). Bertha (1886–1957), after whom the World War I cannon Big Bertha was named, wed Gustav von Bohlen und Halbach (1870–1950); he was made the firm's head and took the Krupp name. His son Alfried (1907–1967), the last sole owner, agreed in 1967 to the sale of stock in the company.

Krutch, Joseph Wood (1893–1970). American critic, essayist, and teacher. Krutch was a drama critic for *The Nation* for many years, as well as an English professor at Columbia University and elsewhere. His critical works include *Edgar Allan Poe: A Study of Genius* (1926), one of the first psychoanalytical interpretations of literature; *Five Masters, a Study in the Mutations of the Novel* (1929); and *The American Drama Since 1918* (1939; revised in 1957). His essays are collected in *The Modern Temper* (1929), *The Measure of Man* (1954), and *Human Nature and the Human Condition* (1959), in which he discussed the need for humanistic values in a mechanized so-

ciety. *The Desert Year* (1952) and *The Best of Two Worlds* (1953) deal with natural history.

Krylov, Ivan Andreyevich (1769–1844). Russian fabulist. In his early career both dramatist and journalist, Krylov published his collections of fables from 1809 on. They have become classics in Russian literature and were translated into English by the British historian Sir Bernard Pares in 1927.

Kshatriya. See CASTE.

Kuan-yin (Sans. *Avalokitesvara;* Jap. *Kannon*). Chinese Buddhist deity, the BODHISATTVA of Mercy. She is much represented in painting and sculpture and the object of popular veneration.

Kubera or **Kuvera.** In Hindu mythology, the god of wealth. He was the half-brother of Ravana, the demon-king of Ceylon.

Kublai Khan (1216–1294). Mongol emperor of China after 1259 and grandson of Genghis Khan. He established his court at what is now Peking (1264) and founded the Yuan dynasty, which ended in 1368. His kingdom, finally extending as far as Russia, flourished under his patronage of commerce and culture. His reign was vividly described by Marco POLO, and the splendor of his court inspired S. T. Coleridge's poem KUBLA KHAN.

Kubla Khan (1797). An unfinished poem by Samuel Taylor COLERIDGE. According to Coleridge, the poem was composed in an opium-induced sleep; when he awoke he immediately began to set it down, but was interrupted by a visitor, and when he returned to his task, he found that the rest of the poem had vanished from his memory. A precursor, to some extent, of both symbolism and surrealism, the poem is considered one of his best. See XANADU.

Kūkai (774–835). Japanese priest, founder of Shingon Buddhism. The most literate scholar of his time, he was influential in the introduction of Chinese learning to Japan. His command of the Chinese language and the diversity of his writings marks him as one of the major literary figures of the early Heian period (794–1185). He is known posthumously as Kōbō Daishi.

Ku Klux Klan. A name given to two American secret societies. The original Ku Klux Klan was formed about 1866, in Pulaski, Tenn.; an organization for ex-Confederates, it was dedicated to Southern white political supremacy. It developed into a secret society whose purpose was frightening Negroes into submission. In April, 1867, the Grand Wizard or Cyclops of the Pulaski group, Nathan Bedford Forrest, called a convention of delegates to Nashville. At

Poster of the Klan dealing with carpetbaggers (1869).

this convention the Klan declared its principles, which were to protect the weak and aid the enforcement of the Constitution. Two years later, Forrest disbanded the group when it proved to be an instrument of violence. In 1870 and 1871, Congress passed the Ku Klux Klan acts, to deal with offenders.

In 1915, a new Ku Klux Klan was organized on a nationwide basis in Georgia. Its avowed aims were to maintain "pure Americanism" and white supremacy; it attacked Negroes, Catholics, Jews, as well as such ideas as birth control, Darwinism, pacifism, and the repeal of prohibition. In the early 20's, the Klan was reputed to have a membership of 5 million throughout the U.S. After its terroristic activities were exposed in newspapers after 1923, it began to splinter and decline; it still exists, but in a limited form.

Many novelists have written about the Klan, both favorably and unfavorably. In Thomas Nelson Page's RED ROCK, the hero is a Klan leader. A clergyman, Thomas Dixon, Jr., made the Klan the subject of several novels, including the sensational *Clansman* (1905); this novel, the basis of the motion picture *The Birth of a Nation* (1915), is credited with reviving interest in the society. Two anti-Klan novels are Howard Fast's *Freedom Road* (1944) and Ward Greene's *King Cobra* (1940).

The name of the society is taken from the Greek word *kuklos,* meaning band or circle; it is often referred to with the abbreviation K. K. K.

kulak. A wealthy Russian peasant. The name, derived from the word for "fist," was used derogatorily by Soviet authorities who exterminated the class in the 1920's to make way for the collectivization of agriculture.

Kulhwch and Olwen (c. 1100). One of the tales in the Welsh MABINOGION. This prose narrative is especially important, being perhaps the earliest, full-fledged Arthurian romance. Kulhwch, the hero, gains the help of Arthur and his followers in accomplishing the hard tasks set by the giant Ysbaddaden, whose beautiful daughter Olwen he seeks to win.

Kulturkampf (*Ger.,* cultural battle). The struggle between Bismarck and the Roman Catholic church in the 1870's. Considering the church a threat to national unity, Bismarck imposed laws restricting Catholic worship and education, expelled the Jesuits, and forced many bishops into exile.

Kumara. See KARTTIKEYA.

Kumarbi. In Hurrian mythology, the supreme god. Kumarbi is probably best known for his role in the Hittite myth of the Stone Monster. After nine years as vizier of the sky god ANU, Kumarbi revolted. He won the ensuing battle by emasculating Anu with his teeth, but was soon alarmed to discover that Anu's two children were growing inside him. After a good deal of trial and error, Kumarbi managed to give birth to them. The second of these children promptly overthrew Kumarbi and replaced his true father, Anu, on the throne. On the advice of the lord of the sea, Kumarbi now impregnated a mountain. which, in due course, labored mightily and brought forth a baby made of stone. The delighted Kumarbi named the infant Ullikummi and arranged to have it placed on the right shoulder of Upelluri, the giant who held up earth and heaven, standing in the midst of the ocean. The stone child grew most remarkably,

and soon his immense size threatened to topple heaven itself. Neither the might of the gods nor the wiles of ISHTAR could prevail against it. Finally, EA, the god of wisdom, severed his legs at the ankles with a magic knife, and the stone monster fell into the sea. Thus ended Kumarbi's revolt.

Kunitz, Stanley J[assipon] (1905–). American poet and editor. Though his work is not widely known, Kunitz is regarded as one of the better American metaphysical poets. His first volume of poetry was *Intellectual Things* (1930); *Passport to the War* appeared in 1944. His *Selected Poems, 1928–1958* (1958) was awarded a Pulitzer Prize. With Howard Haycraft he has edited a number of biographical dictionaries of authors, including *British Authors of the Nineteenth Century* (1936), *American Authors: 1600–1900* (1938), *Twentieth Century Authors* (1942), and *British Authors before 1800* (1952).

Künstlerroman (*Ger.,* artist novel). A type of novel popular in GERMAN ROMANTICISM. It is basically a BILDUNGSROMAN (novel of education) in which the hero finally becomes an artist or poet, and thus the form reflects a characteristic romantic interest in the growth of the artist as a person. The most important examples are Tieck's *Franz Sternbalds Wanderungen* (*Franz Sternbald's Wanderings,* 1798) and Novalis' *Heinrich von Ofterdingen* (1802). In later literature, Joyce's *A Portrait of the Artist as a Young Man* (1916) is such an artist novel.

Kuomintang. The three parts of this Chinese term mean *nation, people,* and *party.* The Kuomintang is the nationalist, republican party that was organized chiefly by Dr. Sun Yat-sen and gained control of most of China in 1926–1927. After years of civil war, the communists finally gained control of the mainland (1949) and the Kuomintang, under Chiang Kai-shek, was forced to Taiwan, which it now governs.

Kuprin, Aleksandr Ivanovich (1870–1938). Russian novelist and short-story writer. Kuprin left Russia during the civil war, but returned two years before his death. His work covers a wide range of subjects. Best known are the short novel *Poyedinok* (*The Duel,* 1905), a story of army life in a provincial garrison; *Yama* (*The Pit,* 1915), an account of a Russian brothel; *V tzirke* (*The Circus Wrestlers,* 1905); *Shtabs-kapitan Rybnikov* (*Captain Rybnikov,* 1906), a spy story; and *Granatovyi braslet* (*The Bracelet of Garnets,* 1911), a sentimental love story.

Kur. The Sumerian underworld and the dragonlike lord thereof. He carried off ERESHKIGAL and fought with Enki, who pursued him. He was destroyed in two other myths by NINURTA and INANNA, respectively. Obviously related to many other dragons slain by heroes of Semitic mythology, he also seems to have had some of the characteristics of the Greek Hades.

Kurma. See VISHNU.

Kürnberger, Ferdinand (1821–1879). German novelist. He is most famous for his *Der Amerika-Müde* (*Tired of America,* 1855), which treats the life of Nikolaus Lenau.

Kurosawa Akira (1910–). Japanese film director. A large number of his films have been successfully shown in the West. *Rashōmon* won first prize at the Venice Film Festival (1951).

Kurtz. See HEART OF DARKNESS.

Kuru. In Hindu mythology, a legendary monarch. From him are descended the Kauravas and Pandavas, whose contests form the subject of the epic, the *Mahabharata*. He was a prince of the lunar race, reigning over the country around Delhi.

Kurusu Saburo (1888–1954). Japanese diplomat. He was special envoy to the U.S. (Nov.–Dec., 1941) during negotiations cut short by the attack on Pearl Harbor.

Kuvera. See KUBERA.

Kyd, Thomas (1557?–1594). English dramatist. A scrivener by profession, Kyd became the author of the most popular drama of his day with his Senecan revenge-play THE SPANISH TRAGEDY (produced between 1584 and 1589). He may have written a lost play on Hamlet, and is thought to have worked on parts of Shakespeare's *Titus Andronicus* and *Henry VI. Arden of Feversham* is sometimes attributed to him, as is the anonymously published *Soliman and Perseda* (written c. 1588). In 1593 he was sharing a room with Christopher Marlowe, and was arrested with him for atheism and heresy. Possibly suffering from his imprisonment and disgrace, he died the following year.

Kyoto. Old capital of Japan (794–1868), formerly known as Heian. It was the site of the imperial court until moved to Tokyo in the Meiji period (1868–1912). Famous as a cultural and sight-seeing center, it has numerous Shinto shrines, Buddhist temples, objects of art, and places of scenic beauty.

Kyrie eleison (Gr., "Lord have mercy"). Originally an invocation to the Greek sungod. This petition is the first fixed chant in most Western Eucharistic liturgies, and is also used in the liturgies of the Eastern churches.

L

Laban. In the Old Testament, the uncle of JA-COB and father of Leah and Rachel. Jacob served him for 14 years in order to marry Rachel.

labarum. The standard borne before the Roman emperors. It consisted of a gilded spear with an eagle on the top. From a cross-staff hung a splendid purple streamer, with a gold fringe, adorned with precious stones. CONSTANTINE THE GREAT added Christian symbols to the Roman military symbols at the time of his vision and subsequent conversion to Christianity.

Labé, Louise (1524?–1566?). French poet. Celebrated for her talent and beauty, she was one of the best-known of the school of French poets centered at Lyons. In the elegies and sonnets included in her *Oeuvres* (1555), she expressed in a direct, intense style the torments of a passionate nature which had been profoundly marked by an unhappy love. The wife of a wealthy rope-maker, she was sometimes called *la belle cordière.*

Labe, Queen. The Circe of the Arabians, who, by her enchantments, transformed men into horses and other brute beasts. She is introduced into the *Arabian Nights* when Beder, a prince of Persia, marries her, defeats her plots against him, and turns her into a mare. Restored to her proper shape by her mother, she turns Beder into an owl, but the prince ultimately regains his own form.

Labiche, Eugène [Marin] (1815–1888). French playwright. Responding to the Second Empire's demand for farcical comedy, Labiche wrote a long series of popular plays including *Un Chapeau de paille d'Italie* (1851) and *La Poudre aux yeux* (1862). The delightful *Le Voyage de M. Perrichon* (1860)—perhaps his best-known comedy—was written in collaboration with Edouard Martin.

labors of Hercules. See HERACLES.

La Bruyère, Jean de (1645–1696). French writer and moralist of the neoclassical period. La Bruyère's sympathies lay with the ancients in their literary battle with the moderns, and, in addition to being conservative, his outlook was deeply misanthropic. His most famous work, *Caractères de Théophraste traduits du grec, avec les caractères ou les Moeurs de ce siècle* (*Characters of Theophrastus Translated from the Greek, with Characters or the Manners of This Century,* 1688), is a piece of social satire in the manner of Theophrastus, combining maxims with character portraits of French social types and individuals of the day.

Labyrinth (Labyrinthos). The palace of Minos in Knossos, the Minoan capital of Crete, said to have been devised by Daedalus. According to the legend, it was a mazelike building in the center of which the MINOTAUR was imprisoned. The word has come to be applied to any structure with many confusing passages. The origin of the word is not known, but it may be connected with *labrys,* the double ax constantly used in the religious symbolism of ancient Crete.

Labyrinthine Ways, The. See POWER AND THE GLORY, THE.

La Calprenède, Gauthier de Costes de (1610–1663). French dramatist and novelist. He is best known for his enormous historical romances: *Cassandre* (10 vols., 1642–1645), *Cléopâtre* (12 vols., 1648) and *Pharamond, ou l'histoire de France* (12 vols., 1661–1663). La Calprenède's novels abound in complex plots, detailed descriptions, literary portraits, and Oriental settings.

Lacedaemon (Lakedaimon). An ancient name of Laconia, and of SPARTA, its chief city. (See LACONIC.)

La Chaise, Père François d'Aix de (1624–1709). French Jesuit confessor to Louis XIV. His favorite retreat near Paris later became the site of the cemetery popularly known as the *cimetière du Père-Lachaise.*

Lachaise, Gaston (1882–1935). French-born American sculptor. He is known for his long series of ample, vigorous female figures.

La Chaussée, Pierre Claude Nivelle de (1692–1754). French dramatist, inventor and champion of the COMÉDIE LARMOYANTE (*Fr.,* "sentimental comedy"). His most famous play is *Le Préjugé à la mode* (1735), in which the fashionable attitude of making light of a wife's love is criticized. Many of his other plays, among which are *Mélanide* (1741) and *L'Ecole des mères* (1744), are somewhat moralizing. He was elected to the ACADÉMIE FRANÇAISE in 1736.

Lachesis. See the FATES.

Laclos, Pierre [Ambroise François] Choderlos de (1741–1803). French artillery officer and author of the epistolary novel LES LIAISONS DANGEREUSES. The novel depicts the immorality of his times, particularly corrupt and cynical seducers of innocence. He was a member of the JACOBIN club, became a general, and played an important military role in the French Revolution.

Laconic, Laconian. Pertaining to Laconia or its main city, SPARTA. Hence laconic, sparing of words, as the Spartans were reputed to be.

Lacretelle, Jacques de (1888–   ). French novelist. His books are usually psychological analyses of lonely characters, such as *Silbermann* (1922), about a young Jewish student, and *Les Hauts Ponts* (4 vols., 1932–1935), about a woman's passion for her family estate. Other novels include *Marie Bonifas* (1925) and *A Man's Life* (*Amour Nuptial;* 1929).

Ladislaw, Will. In George Eliot's MIDDLEMARCH, the gay young artist whom Dorothea Brooke marries after the death of her first husband, the desiccated Mr. Casaubon.

Lady Chatterley's Lover (1928). A novel by D. H. LAWRENCE, presenting the author's mystical theories of sex in the story of Constance, or Connie, the wife of an English aristocrat who runs away with her gamekeeper. Her husband, Sir Clifford, is a physical and emotional cripple. The gamekeeper, MELLORS, is a forthright, individualistic man, uncontaminated by industrial society. Because of the frank language and detailed descriptions of love-making, the book was banned in England and the U.S. as obscene. After historic court cases the ban was lifted in the U.S. in 1959 and in England in 1960.

Lady Day. See ANNUNCIATION, THE DAY OF THE.

Lady Geraldine's Courtship (1844). A poem by Elizabeth Barrett BROWNING. The lady falls in love with a peasant-poet, whom she marries. The poem contained a tribute to the poetry of Robert Browning, which prompted a warm letter from him and their subsequent meeting, romance, and marriage.

Lady Into Fox (1922). A novel by David GARNETT. It is a delicate, solemn fantasy about a man whose wife suddenly turns into a fox—and their consequent marital problems.

Lady Macbeth. See MACBETH.

Lady of Pleasure, The (1635). A comedy by James SHIRLEY. The good Sir Thomas Bornwell becomes increasingly alarmed at the growing extravagances of his wife, Aretina. Pretending to become converted to her spendthrift ways, he turns to gambling and begins paying attention to the beautiful widow, Celestina, Lady Bellamour. Eventually, as he had hoped, Aretina becomes alarmed and returns to modesty and thrift.

Lady of the Aroostook, The (1879). A novel by William Dean HOWELLS. Lydia Blood sails for Europe on the *Aroostook;* a delicate young schoolteacher, she is traveling for her health. The only woman passenger, she attracts the attention of Staniford, who gradually recognizes the nobility of character beneath her village rusticity. Lydia's Venetian relatives are interested only in knowing whether Staniford is socially suitable for her. Although Lydia is free of European social restraints, she reveals her upbringing in her shock at Sunday opera and Venetian immorality.

Lady of the Fountain, The. A medieval Welsh tale from the MABINOGION in which are found King Arthur and his court. This tale has a remarkable parallel in the story YVAIN by Chrétien de Troyes.

Lady of the Lake. In Arthurian legend, an obscure, supernatural figure endowed with magical powers. In Malory's *Morte d'Arthur* (c. 1469), she lives in a castle in the midst of a magical lake, which prevents access to her. She steals LAUNCELOT in his infancy and plunges with him into her home in the lake; hence, Launcelot comes to be called *Lancelot du Lac* (Launcelot of the Lake). When he has grown to manhood, she presents him to King Arthur. It is from the Lady of the Lake that Arthur receives the magical sword EXCALIBUR; he takes it from the mysterious arm extending above the surface of the lake.

She is also known as Nimuë or Vivien, the mistress of MERLIN, whom she ultimately imprisons forever in a tower. The Lady of the Lake appears in later works, notably in Tennyson's *Idylls of the King* (1859–1885) and James Branch Cabell's *Jurgen* (1919).

Lady of the Lake, The (1810). A long narrative poem by Sir Walter SCOTT. It tells of Ellen Douglas, who lives with her father near Loch Katrine, and of the varied fortunes of her suitors in troubled times of border warfare. One of her suitors is the king of Scotland, but she finally chooses the bold Malcolm Graeme.

Lady of the Lamp. See Florence NIGHTINGALE.

Lady or the Tiger?, The (1882). A short story by Frank R. STOCKTON. Stockton originally called the story *The King's Arena* and read it at a party given by a friend. Its reception there was so good that he elaborated it and sent it to the *Century Magazine.* It was the most famous story the magazine ever published; its plot is simple but unique. In a barbaric land a handsome youth is audacious enough to fall in love with the king's daughter and she with him. His offense is discovered, and he is condemned. In a great arena he must walk up to two doors and open one of them; behind one door is a beautiful maiden who would be given to him in marriage; behind the other is a ravenous tiger. The princess learns the secret of the doors and signals the young man to open the door on the right. Who comes out, asked Stockton, the lady or the tiger? Stockton wrote another story supposed to solve the puzzle, *The Discourager of Hesitancy* (1887), but it also cleverly left the query unanswered.

Lady's Not for Burning, The (1949). A play in verse by Christopher FRY.

Lady Windermere's Fan (1892). A comedy of manners by Oscar WILDE. Annoyed at her husband's persistent interest in Mrs. Erlynne, a woman of little reputation, Lady Windermere decides to leave him and run away with Lord Darlington. Mrs. Erlynne, actually Lady Windermere's mother who deserted her husband and daughter years ago for a lover who then left her, finds the note and rushes to Lord Darlington's apartments. Here, without revealing her identity, she persuades Lady Windermere not to take this rash step and succeeds in rushing her off in a carriage just as Lord Darlington appears with Lord Windermere. Lord Windermere immediately notices his wife's fan; Mrs. Erlynne comes forth and generously assumes guilt, saying that she mistook it for her own, thus saving her daughter's reputation at the expense of her own. She succeeds, however, in convincing Lord Augustus Lawton that it was in his interests that she came to Lord Darlington's rooms, and the two marry.

Laelaps. In classical mythology, a powerful dog. It was given by Artemis to Procris who gave it to Cephalus. While pursuing a wild boar it was metamorphosed into a stone. The name, which was originally that of one of Actaeon's fifty dogs, means "the hurricane."

Laelius. See DE AMICITIA.

Laertes. In Shakespeare's HAMLET, the son of Polonius and brother of Ophelia. A well-meaning but impetuous young man, he contrasts with the introspective and indecisive Hamlet, whose death he causes.

Laestrygonians (Laistrygones). A fabulous race of cannibal giants who lived in Sicily. Odysseus sent two of his men to request that he might land, but the king of the place ate one for dinner and the other fled. The Laestrygonians assembled on the coast and threw stones against Odysseus and his crew; they fled with all speed, but many men were lost.

La Farge, Christopher (1897–1956). American poet and novelist. Originally an architect by profession, La Farge published a long narrative poem, *Hoxsie Sells His Acres* (1934), dealing with childhood recollections and followed it in 1939 with *Each to the Other,* a novel in verse about a happy marriage. Among his other works are *Poems and Portraits* (1940); *The Wilsons* (1941), a collection of interrelated short stories; *Mesa Verde* (1945), a play in verse; and *The Sudden Guest* (1946), a novel about the 1938 and 1944 New England hurricanes. La Farge was a grandson of the artist John La Farge, a nephew of Father John La Farge, and a brother of Oliver La Farge.

La Farge, John (1880–1963). American Jesuit leader and writer. He became well known for his dedicated and highly successful work in rural American missions, which led to the founding of the National Catholic Rural Life Conference. Beginning in 1928, he was for many years the director of the Catholic Laymen's Union. From 1942 to 1948 he was first executive editor, then editor-in-chief of the Jesuit weekly *America,* and he continued as an editor for many years thereafter. Known for his contributions to the causes of minority groups, Father La Farge was the author of several books on the Jesuits and on racial problems. His highly praised autobiography, *The Manner Is Ordinary,* appeared in 1953, and he completed *Reflections on Growing Old* just a month before his death. He was an uncle of Oliver and Christopher La Farge.

La Farge, Oliver [Hazard Perry] (1901–1963). American anthropologist and writer. He is best known for his works dealing with the American Indian, especially his notable first novel, LAUGHING BOY. A member of several anthropological expeditions to Arizona, Mexico, and Guatemala, La Farge was particularly interested in the Navaho and throughout his life was an eloquent spokesman and champion for the American Indian. *Tribes and Temples* (1945) is a book on archeology. *Sparks Fly Upward* (1931) and *All the Young Men* (1935) were collections of short stories. *The Eagle in the Egg* (1949) is a novel based upon his experiences as an officer in the army's Air Transport Command. *Raw Material* (1945) is his autobiography. La Farge and his brother, Christopher, were grandsons of the artist John La Farge, and nephews of Father John La Farge.

Lafayette, Marquis de. Marie Joseph Paul Yves Roch Gilbert du Motier (1757–1834). French statesman and general, known as "the Hero of the Worlds." He served (1777–1781) the American cause during the Revolutionary War as a major general in Washington's army. On furlough in France from 1778 to 1780, he did much to cement Franco-American relations. Active in French politics, he advocated moderation during the French Revolution. He was forced to flee to Austrian lines in 1792 after failing in his

attempted *coup d'état* against the revolutionary government in Paris, and returned to Paris in 1799. He did not engage in politics during the Napoleonic era, but after the Bourbon Restoration (1815–1830) he was one of the leaders of the liberal opposition. It was he who persuaded the leaders of the 1830 revolution to accept Louis Philippe as their monarch, saying the famous words: "Take him, he will make the best of republics." At Lafayette's suggestion, Louis Philippe appeared on the balcony of the Hôtel de Ville, wrapped in the TRICOLOR. Lafayette lived to regret his decision, becoming quite disappointed in the July Monarchy.

La Fayette, Comtesse de. Born **Marie Madeleine Pioche de La Vergne** (1634–1693). French novelist. Although Comtesse de La Fayette borrowed the format of her early work *Zayde* from de Scudéry, her novels *La Princesse de Montpensier* (1662) and LA PRINCESSE DE CLÈVES (1678) are unmarred by the sentimentality and extravagance that characterize the works of her predecessor. With these simply and soberly written romances, melancholy in mood, Comtesse de La Fayette originated the French novel of character.

Lafcadio's Adventures (Les Caves du Vatican; 1914). A satirical farce by André GIDE. Also known in translation as *The Vatican Swindle,* the book caricatures various types in society by means of the three brothers-in-law and their many relations who comprise its major characters. The plot concerns the confusion resulting from a swindler's scheme to extort money by falsely reporting that the pope has been kidnapped and organizing a conspiracy to liberate him. The interest of the book, however, focuses on the apparently unmotivated murder of one of the brothers by Lafcadio, a bastard relative.

Lafeu. In Shakespeare's ALL'S WELL THAT ENDS WELL, an old French lord sent to conduct Bertram to the royal court on the king of France's invitation.

Lafitte or **Laffitte, Jean** (1780?–?1826). French pirate and smuggler. Lafitte seems to have reached the neighborhood of New Orleans around 1809 as the head of a band of smugglers and privateers. During the War of 1812 he offered his services to Andrew Jackson and took part in the battle of New Orleans. Later he returned to his freebooting in Texas.

The subject of many legends, he was the hero of *Lafitte, The Pirate of the Gulf* (1836), a best-selling romance by Joseph Holt Ingraham. He also appears in Hervey Allen's *Anthony Adverse* (1933). Lord Byron, in a note to *The Corsair* (1815), suggested some likenesses between his hero and Lafitte.

La Follette, Robert M[arion] (1855–1925). American statesman. An opponent of Republican Party regulars in his native Wisconsin, La Follette was elected district attorney of Dane County in 1880 and served in Congress from 1885 to 1891. In 1900 he won the GOP gubernatorial nomination by acclamation and after his election, instituted an extensive reform program that included opposition to political bosses, establishment of the direct primary, and regulation of the railroads. In the U.S. Senate (1906–1925), he continued his battle against the "interests." As leader of the newly formed Progressive Party, he sought the 1912 presidential nomination but lost it to Theodore Roosevelt. He opposed President Wilson's foreign policy and argued against U.S. entry into the League of Nations. In 1924 he won nearly five million votes as the presidential candidate of the Progressives.

His son, Robert M. La Follette, Jr. (1895–1953), was appointed to the elder La Follette's Senate seat in 1925 and served until 1946 when he was defeated by Joseph R. McCarthy.

La Fontaine, Jean de (1621–1695). French author. A prolific writer of comedies, lyrics, elegies, ballads, and licentious tales, La Fontaine is remembered primarily for his FABLES CHOISIES, MISES EN VERS and his CONTES ET NOUVELLES EN VERS. Despite disputes with the French Academy, police condemnation of his *Contes,* and royal disfavor, La Fontaine was little distracted from his work and remained in the eyes of the world a vagabond, dreamer, and lover of pleasure, drifting happily from one patron to another throughout his highly productive literary career.

Laforet, Carmen (1921–   ). Spanish novelist. Her first work, *Nada* (1945), won great acclaim in Spain. This is a simple tale centering about the experiences of a young girl who settles in Barcelona after completing her education. Her more recent works include *La isla y los demonios* (1952), set in the Canary Islands, and *La mujer nueva* (1955), which relates the fall and spiritual regeneration of an adulterous woman.

Laforgue, Jules (1860–1887). French poet. Laforgue, with Gustave Kahn, is considered to have invented vers libre, as free verse is known in the 20th-century. Associated with the SYMBOLISTS, his volumes of poetry include *Les Complaintes* (1885), *L'Imitation de Notre-Dame la lune* (1886), and *Le Concile féerique* (1886). *Moralités Légendaires* (1887) is a collection, published posthumously, of satires upon old tales. Laforgue exerted considerable influence upon the form, rhythm, attitude, and subject matter of T. S. Eliot's early poetry.

Lagado. In Jonathan Swift's GULLIVER'S TRAVELS, the capital of Balnibarbi, the continent neighboring LAPUTA. Lagado is celebrated for its Academy of Projectors, where scholars spend their time in such useless projects as extracting sunbeams from cucumbers and converting ice into gunpowder.

Lagerkvist, Pär (1891–   ). Swedish novelist, playwright, and poet. Lagerkvist is a moralist without a system of belief; profoundly humanistic, he probes the human mind and heart with agonized honesty. During the troubled decade of the 1930's, he spoke out against tyranny, Nazism, and totalitarianism. He published *Bödeln* (*The Hangman;* 1933) to show the evil of violence. His best-known novels are *Dvärgen* (*The Dwarf;* 1945), BARABBAS, and *The Sibyl* (1956). He was awarded the Nobel Prize for literature in 1951.

Lagerlöf, Selma (1858–1940). Swedish novelist and short-story writer. Uncomfortable with the literary realism current in her day, Selma Lagerlöf returned to the past for her stories and wrote in a romantic, imaginative manner. Her best known works are the novels GÖSTA BERLINGS SAGA and JERUSALEM. *Nils Holgerssons underbara resa genom Sverige* (*The Wonderful Adventures of Nils;* 1906–1907) and *Further Adventures of Nils* (1911), are fanciful accounts of a young boy's adventures as he travels over Sweden on the back of a wild goose. In 1909, Selma Lagerlöf received the Nobel prize for literature.

Lagrange, Joseph Louis (1736–1813). French-Italian mathematician. He received great acclaim during his lifetime, and was highly honored by Frederick the Great, Louis XVI, and Napoleon.

La Guardia, Fiorello H. Known as **the Little Flower** (1882–1947). American political leader. From 1901 to 1906 LaGuardia worked for the U.S. consular service in Europe and from 1907 to 1910 was an interpreter on Ellis Island in New York harbor. Elected to Congress in 1916, he resigned to become an air force officer during World War I, then returned to the House, where he served from 1923 to 1933. In 1933 he was elected mayor of New York on an anti-Tammany reform ticket. During his three terms as mayor, La Guardia conducted an energetic, incorruptible administration; sponsored an ambitious public-works program; and secured the adoption of a new city charter. In 1941–1942 he headed the U.S. Office of Civilian Defense and in 1946 was director of the UN Rehabilitation and Reconstruction Administration.

Lahamu. See LAHMU.

Lahar. The Sumerian god of cattle.

Lahmu and Lahamu. A Babylonian god and goddess. Born of the union of fresh water (Apsu) and salt water (Tiamat), they in turn were the parents of Anshar, a sky-god, and Kishar, an earth-goddess.

La Hogue, Battle of. The successful naval operations of the English and Dutch fleets against the French off the coast of Normandy (May 19 to 23, 1692). La Hogue itself is a harbor which served as the base of Louis XIV's attempted invasion of England.

lai. (1) A verse form in medieval French verse, composed of three-line units rhymed *aab.*

(2) also **lay.** A short narrative poem using the material of the medieval romances or the *fabliaux,* of the type written by MARIE DE FRANCE. These *lais* are not to be confused with the *Lais* (or *legs,* meaning legacies) written by François VILLON.

Laing, Alexander [Kinnan] (1903–   ). American poet and teacher. He is author of several volumes of verse, including *Fool's Errand* (1928) and *The Flowering Thorn* (1933), and of a discourse on poetry, *Wine and Physic* (1934). A teacher at Dartmouth, he has written an epic of the clipper-ship era, *The Sea Witch* (1933), and a prose work dealing with the same subject matter, *Clippership Men* (1945). Laing has also edited horror stories. With R. A. Lattimore, he published *American Sail, a Pictorial History* (1961).

Laïs. Name of two celebrated Greek HETAERAE or courtesans. The earlier was the most beautiful woman of Corinth, who lived at the time of the Peloponnesian War. The beauty of Laïs the Second so excited the jealousy of the Thessalonian women that they pricked her to death with their bodkins. She was the contemporary and rival of Phryne and sat to Apelles as a model. Demosthenes claims that she sold her favors for 10,000 Attic drachmae.

laissez-faire (*Fr.,* "let do," that is, "let people and things alone"). The principal tenet of laissez-faire is that problems should be allowed to work themselves out without planning or regulation. It is, specifically, the principle of noninterference by government in commercial affairs. The phrase comes from the motto of the PHYSIOCRATS, a school of French economists of the mid-18th century: *Laissez faire, laissez passer* (let do, let pass). The physiocrats wished to have all customs duties abolished and demanded free circulation for their goods, thus anticipating the later free traders. Jean Claude Marie Vincent de Gournay (1712–1759) is generally credited with being the author of the motto. Adam SMITH was the principal exponent of laissez-faire theories in England, from where they later spread to the United States. As embodied in the writings of Smith, the principle has become one of the bulwarks of capitalist economics.

Laius (Laios). See OEDIPUS.

Lake poets, also called **Lake school.** A name applied to a group of poets in the 19th century, including Wordsworth, Coleridge, and Southey, making reference to their residences in the Lake District of England (Westmoreland, Cumberland, Lancashire). The name was first used as an epithet of derision by the *Edinburgh Review,* but has long since lost its disparaging connotations.

Lakmé (1883). A romantic opera by the French composer Léo DELIBES. The libretto by Gondinet and Gille is based on Loti's novel *The Marriage of Loti* (1880), and is Oriental in character. It contains the famous "Bell Song."

Laksmi or Lakshmi. One of the consorts of the Hindu god Vishnu, and mother of Kama, the god of young love. She is goddess of beauty, wealth, and pleasure, and the *Ramayana* describes her as springing, like Venus, from the foam of the sea.

Lal, P. (1929–). Indian poet writing in English. He has published *The Art of the Essay* (1952); *The Parrot's Death and Other Poems* (1960); *Love's the First* (1962), poems; and adaptations of six *Great Sanskrit Plays* (1963).

Lall, Anand (1911–). Indian novelist writing in English. He was consul-general of India in New York, 1951–1954. He wrote *The House at Adampur* (1956), a study of the decaying Indian *zamindari* class, and *Seasons of Jupiter* (1960).

Lallans. A Scottish dialect used by some modern Scottish poets. It is a synthetic language, made up of the dialects of the Scottish lowlands and elements from the Scottish literary language of the past. See SCOTTISH RENAISSANCE.

Lalla Rookh (1817). A series of four Oriental tales in verse held together by a story in prose, by Thomas MOORE. The narrative tells of Lalla Rookh, daughter of the emperor of Delhi who, on a journey to meet her betrothed, is entertained by the young Persian poet Feramorz; he relates four tales of romance and she falls in love with him. Ultimately she discovers that he is her betrothed.

The four tales he entertained her with are:

(1) *The Veiled Prophet of Khorassan* in which the chief figure is the prophet Hakem ben Haschem who wears a silver gauze veil "to dim the lustre of his face" or rather to hide its extreme ugliness.

(2) *Paradise and the Peri,* about a Peri who is told she will be readmitted to heaven if she brings the gift most dear to the Almighty. After a number of unavailing offerings she brings a guilty old man, who weeps repentantly. The Peri offers the Repentant Tear and the gates of Heaven fly open.

(3) *The Fire Worshippers,* about Hafed, the fire worshiper, who, when betrayed to the Muslims,

throws himself in the sacred fire and is burned to death.

(4) *The Light of the Harem,* about Nourmahal, who regains the love of her husband, the Mogul Emperor Jehangir, by means of a magic spell.

lama. A Buddhist monk or priest in Tibet. Prior to 1959, when he was forced to flee from the Chinese, the Dalai Lama had been both the temporal and spiritual leader of the Tibetans. Ruling from the Potala, a huge palace-lamasery in Lhasa, the Dalai Lama is considered a reincarnation of Avalokitesvara, the ancestor of the Tibetan race.

Lamarck, Chevalier de. Jean Baptiste Pierre Antoine de Monet (1744–1829). French naturalist. Lamarck advocated views on organic evolution which are sometimes mistakenly interpreted as representing Darwinism in a preparatory stage. In his *Philosophie zoologique* (1809), he held that an organism reacts to a new or changing environment by fitting developments; he did not hold, as did Darwin, that a new or changing environment permits the survival of the accidentally fittest. Lamarck also introduced new principles in the classification of animals and originated the term *vertebrate* and *invertebrate*. See Charles Robert DARWIN.

Lamartine, Alphonse Marie Louis de (1790–1869). French poet, writer, and statesman. Lamartine's work is marked by a preoccupation with nature, religion, and love, all subjectively presented (see ROMANTICISM). He is regarded as the first truly romantic poet in French literature. Among his published volumes are *Les Premières méditations* (1820), *Les Nouvelles méditations* (1823), and *Les Harmonies poétiques et religieuses* (1830). His narrative poems include *Jocelyn* (1836), dealing with a priest's love, and *La Chute d'un ange* (1838). A liberal in his beliefs, Lamartine tended toward radical republicanism in politics. Serving as a deputy for several years, he distinguished himself as an orator. A leader in the Revolution of 1848, he became the virtual chief of the provisional government, but fell from power upon the coup d'état of Napoleon III (1852).

lamasery. A Buddhist monastery (or convent) of Tibet or Mongolia, presided over by a LAMA, who corresponds to a Christian abbot.

Lamassu. In Babylonian religion, one of a race of semidivine beings. The Lamassus were visualized as colossal bulls or lions with human heads. Statues of them flanked the entrances of palaces and public buildings.

lamb. In Christian art and imagery, Jesus is often symbolically represented as a lamb, in allusion to John 1:29, "Behold the Lamb of God, which taketh away the sins of the world." The reference is to his sacrificial act for the redemption of the sins of all men.

Lamb, Lady Caroline (1785–1828). English novelist, the wife of William Lamb (later 2d Viscount Melbourne, prime minister to Queen Victoria). She is better known for her nine-months' intrigue with Lord Byron than for any of her novels. She was neurotic and demanding, and Byron soon tired of her. She took revenge in an anonymous novel, *Glenarvon* (1816), which contains a caricature of the poet. After Byron's death she gave way to conduct of such impropriety that Melbourne was forced to separate from her.

Lamb, Charles. Pen name **Elia** (1775–1834). English essayist of the romantic period, a schoolmate of Coleridge and friend of other figures of English romanticism. He attempted work in the fields of drama and poetry, but was most successful in the personal essay. His writings in this form are known for their humor, whimsy, and faint overtones of pathos. He was also a perceptive critic with a special sympathy for the work of Elizabethan and early 17th-century writers: a sympathy that is reflected in his own vivacious, idiosyncratic style.

His essays are contained in the two series entitled *Essays of Elia,* which appeared in *The London Magazine* from 1820 to 1823 and from 1824 to 1825, being collected and published in 1823 and 1833, respectively. Outstanding single essays are: A Dissertation on Roast Pig; *A Chapter on Ears; Mrs. Battle's Opinions on Whist;* Dream Children; and *The Superannuated Man.* Other works of Lamb are *The Tale of Rosamund Gray and Old Blind Margaret* (1798), a prose narrative; *John Woodvil* (1802), a dramatic tragedy; *Tales from Shakespeare* (1807), adaptations for children written in collaboration with his sister, Mary Lamb; *The Adventures of Ulysses* (1808), another book for children; *Specimens of English Dramatic*

Caricature of Charles Lamb.

Scratched on Copper from Life in 1825 by his friend Brook Pulham.

Poets Contemporary with Shakespeare (1808); *Album Verses* (1830), poetry.

Though he was much loved for his personal sweetness and good humor, Lamb's life was marked by frustration and sorrow. Because of a stammer, he was unable to qualify for a university position and went to work as an accountant for the East India Company, where he stayed until 1825. There was a strain of insanity in the family, and Mary Lamb had several attacks of madness, during one of which she killed her mother. Lamb, who himself suffered from alcoholism and stayed for a while in a sanatorium, took care of her.

Lamb, Harold [Albert] (1892–1962). American writer. Lamb is known for his vivid and popular historical studies and biographies: *Genghis Khan* (1927), *Tamerlane* (1928), *The Crusades* (2 vols., 1930, 1931), *The March of Muscovy: Ivan the Terrible* (1948), *Constantinople: Birth of an Empire* (1957), and many others. As these titles indicate, Lamb was primarily interested in Asia and the Near East.

Lamber, Juliette. See Juliette Adam.

Lambert, Marquise Anne-Thérèse de (1647–1733). French writer. Famed for her salon, which was reputed to exercise influence in the appointment of members to the French Academy and where aristocracy and men of letters freely mixed, the marquise de Lambert expressed her high moral principles in two instructive works: *Avis d'une mère à son fils* (*A Mother's Advice to her Son;* 1726) and *Avis à sa fille* (*Advice to her Daughter;* 1728).

Lamentations of Jeremiah, The. An Old Testament book. It is ascribed to the prophet Jeremiah, but is probably the work of various authors. It is comprised of five poems, the first four of which are alphabetical acrostics. The book's theme is that suffering is the result of sin.

Lamerok, Sir. In Arthurian legend, one of the knights of the Round Table. In Malory's *Le Morte d'Arthur* (c. 1469), he is the son of King Pellinore. He becomes the lover of Queen Margawse and her son Sir Gawain kills him.

La Mettrie, Julien Offroy de (1709–1751). French physician and philosopher, the most notorious materialist of his day. His most famous work, *L'Homme machine* (1747), shows how thought depends on matter, not on God or the soul, and that though man is a machine, he is too complicated ever to be completely understood.

lamia. A female phantom. Her name was used by the Greeks and Romans as a bugbear to children. She was a Libyan queen beloved by Zeus, but robbed of her offspring by the jealous Hera. In consequence she vowed vengeance against all children, whom she delighted to entice and devour.

Witches in Middle Ages were called lamioe, and Keats's poem *Lamia* (1820), which relates how a bride when recognized returns to her original serpent form, represents one of the many superstitions connected with the race. Keats's story came (through Burton) from Philostratus' *De Vita Apollonii,* Bk. iv. In Burton's rendering, the sage Apollonius, on the wedding night

found her out to be a serpent, a lamia. . . . When she saw herself descried, she wept, and desired Apollonius to be silent, but he would not be moved, and thereupon she, plate, house, and all that was in it, vanished in an instant; many thousands took notice of this fact, for it was done in the midst of Greece. *Anatomy of Melancholy,* Pt. iii. sect. ii, memb. i, subsect. i

Lammas. Elements of the word are "loaf" and "mass." Formerly a harvest festival, *Lammas Day* falls on August 1.

Lamming, George (1927–   ). West Indian writer. *In the Castle of My Skin* (1953) is an evocation of village life in his childhood home of Barbados.

Lamont, Corliss (1902–   ). American writer and teacher. The son of a millionaire banker, Thomas W. Lamont, he taught courses in philosophy and Russian civilization at Cornell, Columbia, and Harvard. Politically a leftist, Lamont has expressed his views in a book called *You Might Like Socialism* (1939), and in several pamphlets, including *The Myth of Soviet Aggression* (1953), *Challenge to McCarthy* (1954), and *The Congressional Inquisition* (1954). Among his other books are *Issues of Immortality* (1932), *Russia Day by Day* (1933), *The Independent Mind* (1951), and *The Illusion of Immortality* (1935; rev. 1950, 1959).

Lampedusa, Giuseppe di. See LEOPARD, THE.

Lamplighter, The (1854). A novel by Maria Susanna Cummins (1827–1866), originally published anonymously. The author's first book, it was an immediate success; sentimental and materialistic, it was typical of the best-selling women's novels of the time. Gerty, the heroine, is brought up in squalid surroundings, from which she is rescued by a kindly old lamplighter, Trueman Flint. She finds a playmate named Willie, and is taken into the home of Emily Graham, a rich blind girl, when Flint dies. There Gerty learns that her father is really Emily's brother, who ran away from home when he accidentally blinded his sister. Finally, she marries Willie, who has become wealthy and successful. The fantastic sales of *The Lamplighter* puzzled Nathaniel Hawthorne, who complained that the America of his time was "wholly given over to a d—d mob of scribbling women."

lampoon (F. *lampon,* from the refrain *lampons,* let's drink, in 17th-century French satirical drinking songs). A malicious, often scurrilous satirical piece, in prose or poetry, attacking an individual's character or appearance. The lampoon flourished in 17th- and 18th-century England. It fell into disuse as a result of a revulsion of public feeling, as well as of modern libel laws. The term is still in use, however, both as noun and verb, for any piece of pointed mockery of an individual or institution. A generalized use is seen in the name of the Harvard University humor magazine, *The Harvard Lampoon.*

Lancastrian. A member or supporter of the English royal house of Lancaster during the Wars of the Roses.

Lancelot, Sir. See LAUNCELOT.

Landino, Cristoforo (1469–1527). Florentine teacher and critic. Connected with the circle of Lorenzo de' Medici, he gave lectures on poetry and rhetoric and wrote the commentary for a 1481 edition of Dante that included some designs by Botticelli. His most famous critical work is the *Disputationes Camaldulenses,* which consists of discussions

on literary subjects supposedly held at the monastery of Camaldoli in 1468.

Landino, Francesco (1325–1397). Italian composer, poet, and organist. The most important composer of 14th-century Italy, Landino was renowned for singing to his own organ accompaniment, musical settings of his own poems. He won a laurel crown at a tournament in Venice in 1364; Petrarch was on the jury.

Land of Nod. See NOD, LAND OF.

Land of Promise. See PROMISED LAND.

Landon, Letitia Elizabeth (1802–1838). English poet and novelist. Her sentimental poems, usually signed L.E.L., were a popular feature of annuals during the third and fourth decades of the century. She also wrote several novels, including *Esther Churchill* (1837).

Landor, Walter Savage (1775–1864). English poet, literary critic, and prose writer. Landor is best remembered for his interest in the classics and for the severity and intellectual coldness of his lyrics, many of which were written in direct imitation of Greek and Latin models. Among his works are *Gebir* (1797), an Oriental tale in blank verse; *Count Julian* (1812), a tragedy; *Imaginary Conversations* (1824–1853), a series of discussions between historical figures on a variety of subjects; *Citations and Examination of William Shakespeare* (1834), literary criticism; *Pericles and Aspasia* (1836), imaginary letters; *Poemata et Inscriptiones* (1847), Latin verse; *The Hellenics* (1847), poems on Greek subjects; *Last Fruit Off an Old Tree* (1853); *Antony and Octavius* (1856), dramatic dialogues; *Heroic Idyls* (1863). *Rose Aylmer* is his best known lyric.

In his youth, Landor was influenced by the revolutionary atmosphere of the time and was forced to leave Oxford because of his opinions. In 1808 he went off with a regiment he had raised to fight Napoleon in Spain. He tried to institute humanitarian reform on his estate in Wales but failed, and for a number of years lived in Italy. His poetry was never popular in his own time.

land o' the leal. The land of the faithful or blessed. It is a Scotticism for a hypothetical land of happiness, loyalty, and virtue; hence, the equivalent of heaven.

Landseer, Sir Edwin Henry (1802–1873). A famous English animal painter. He drew Sir Walter Scott's dogs with the poet in their midst. His paintings owe their popularity largely to the etchings made of them by his brother Thomas Landseer (1795–1880).

Land's End. The most westerly point in England. Called Bolerium in ancient geography, Land's End is on the southwest coast of Cornwall, and consists of granite cliffs, 60 to 100 feet high.

Lang, Andrew (1844–1912). Scottish scholar and man of letters. In a controversy with Max Müller he held that literary mythology is the outgrowth of anonymous folklore. He wrote several books of graceful verse, collaborated with Samuel Henry Butcher on a well-known prose translation of the *Odyssey* (1879), and edited numerous volumes of fairy tales.

Lang, Fritz (1890–   ). German motion-picture director and producer. Among his notable films are *Destiny* (1921), *Dr. Mabuse* (1922), and *M* (1931).

Langbehn, Julius (1851–1907). German popular philosopher, opposed to materialism and rationalism. His *Rembrandt als Erzieher* (*Rembrandt as Educator,* 1890), published anonymously, was a best-seller.

Langer, Susanne K. (1895–   ). American philosopher and teacher. Mrs. Langer's interest in the symbol-making function of the mind led her into aesthetics and to her book *Philosophy in a New Key: A Study in the Symbolism of Reason, Rite, and Art* (1942). It was influenced by the work of the German philosopher Ernest Cassirer, whose *Language and Myth* she translated in 1946. *Feeling and Form; A Theory of Art* appeared in 1953; 10 of Mrs. Langer's lectures on philosophy and aesthetics were printed in *Problems of Art* (1957).

Langland or **Langley, William.** See under PIERS PLOWMAN.

Langner, Lawrence (1890–1962). Welsh-born American playwright and producer. Langner came to the U.S. in 1914 and shortly thereafter organized the Washington Square Players; the group performed several of his early plays, including *Another Way Out* (1916), a popular one-act drama. Out of the Washington Square Players grew the Theatre Guild, of which Langner was the founder and, after 1919, the director. He also founded the American Shakespeare Festival Theatre and Academy of Stratford, Conn. In addition to adapting foreign plays for the American stage, Langner collaborated with his wife, Armina Marshall, on several successful plays. *Pursuit of Happiness* (1934) deals with a Hessian soldier involved in the old American custom of bundling. The Langners also conducted their own summer theater in Westport, N.Y., until 1959. Langner's *G.B.S. and the Lunatic* (1963) describes the business relationship between the Theatre Guild and George Bernard Shaw.

Langton, Stephen (c. 1150–1228). English prelate, statesman, and scholar, Archbishop of Canterbury (after 1207). King John refused to recognize his appointment until 1213, and Langton became the leader of the barons in their struggle against John, representing them with his signature on the MAGNA CARTA.

Langtry, Lily. Born **Emily Charlotte Le Breton** (1852–1929). English actress, known as the "Jersey Lily," famous for her great beauty. She went on the stage in 1881 in the role of Kate Hardcastle in Goldsmith's *She Stoops to Conquer.*

langue d'oc and **langue d'oïl.** The two groups of medieval Romance dialects that emerged from Vulgar Latin in Gaul, named after the word for "yes" in each group. The *langue d'oc* was spoken in the region of southern France and northern Italy known as Provence. The *langue d'oïl* was spoken in France north of a line running approximately from the mouth of the Gironde River east to the Alps; it was the ancestor of standard modern French (in which *oïl* became *oui*).

Lanier, Sidney (1842–1881). American poet. After graduating from Oglethorpe University in his native Georgia in 1860, Lanier enlisted in the Confederate army and, in 1864, was captured and imprisoned for four months at Point Lookout, Md. He emerged from the war afflicted with the tuberculosis that remained with him for the rest of his short life. Prevented by economic necessity from devoting

himself to literature, Lanier worked at odd jobs after the war. In 1873 he settled in Baltimore, becoming first flutist with the Peabody Symphony Orchestra.

Considered one of the most accomplished poets of the American South in the latter half of the 19th century, he tried to achieve in his work the auditory effect of music and experimented with varying metrical patterns and unusual imagery. Much of his poetry shows an affinity with that of the Pre-Raphaelites and Swinburne. His best-known poems include *The Symphony* (1875), a denunciation of industrialism designed to illustrate the close relationship between poetry and music; THE MARSHES OF GLYNN; and *The Song of the Chattahoochee* (1883), notable for its successful combination of alliteration, onomatopoeia, and melody. Lanier also wrote *Tiger Lilies* (1867), a novel based on his Civil War experiences, and three works of criticism, *The Science of English Verse* (1880), *The English Novel* (1883), and *Shakespeare and His Forerunners* (1902).

Lanigan, George Thomas (1845–1886). Canadian-born American journalist and humorous poet. He sometimes published under the pseudonym of G. Washington Aesop. Lanigan worked on the New York *World* from 1874 to 1883 and published two volumes, *Canadian Ballads* (1864) and *Fables* (1878). He is chiefly remembered for his poem *Threnody for the Ahkoond of Swat* (1878), which was inspired by an item in the London *Times.* One of Lanigan's best sayings was that he dreamed of the day "when the singular verb shall lie down with the plural noun, and a little conjunction shall lead them."

Lantern Land. The land of literary charlatans, pedantic graduates in arts, doctors, professors, prelates, and so on. They were ridiculed as "Lanterns" by Rabelais (with a side allusion to the divines assembled in conference at the Council of Trent) in his *Gargantua and Pantagruel.*

Laocoön (Laokoön). In Greek mythology, a Trojan priest who, having offended the gods, was strangled by sea serpents. In Vergil's *Aeneid,* he draws down the anger of Athena by warning the Trojans not to accept the Trojan horse and by hurling his javelin into the hollow flank of the wooden statue dedicated to her. She sends two huge sea snakes to the shore where Laocoön, assisted by his two sons, is sacrificing to Poseidon. The monsters choke the three to death.

The famous group of sculpture representing these three in their death agony, now in the Vatican, was discovered in 1506, on the Esquiline Hill in Rome. It is a single block of marble, and is attributed to Agesandrus, Athenodorus, and Polydorus of the school of Rhodes in the second century B.C. The discovery lent tremendous impetus to the renascence of interest in the classical period and had great impact on the art world.

In a famous treatise on the limits of poetry and the plastic arts (1766), Lessing uses this group as the peg on which to hang his dissertation, called *Laocoön.*

Laocoön, or On the Limits of Painting and Poetry (Laokoon, oder Über die Grenzen der Malerei und Poesie; 1766). An essay by Gotthold Ephraim LESSING. It seeks to dispute the idea that art criticism and literary criticism may be based on the same principles. The fundamental point is that a painting exists in space and all its parts are perceived simultaneously, whereas a work of literature exists in time and its parts are perceived one after another. On this basis, Lessing develops an extensive theory of the respective domains of painting and poetry, in which he challenges some of Winckelmann's ideas. Lessing uses the statue "Laocoön" as one of his central examples.

Laodamia. In classic myth, the wife of PROTESILAUS, who was slain before Troy.

Laodicean. One indifferent to religion, caring little or nothing about the matter. The reference is to Revelation 3:14–18 where the Christians of the city of Laodicea are "lukewarm."

Laomedon. In classic myth, a king of Troy, the father of Priam. He is remembered chiefly for his ingratitude in refusing to give the rewards he had promised to Apollo for pasturing his flocks on Mount Ida, to Poseidon for building the walls of Troy, and to Heracles for rescuing his daughter Hesione from the sea-monster sent by Poseidon. Heracles slew him and all his sons but Priam in revenge.

Lao Tzu. Legendary Chinese sage, supposedly contemporary with Confucius (6th century B.C.) and regarded as the founder of TAOISM. Lao Tzu is also the name of the basic text of the Taoist religion; it is more commonly known as the TAO TE CHING.

Lapiths (Lapithai). A Thessalian tribe. They were neighbors of the CENTAURS, with whom they had a famous battle. The Lapiths invited the Centaurs to the wedding of their king Pirithous to Hippodamia. Under the influence of wine, the Centaurs tried to carry off the Lapith women, including even the bride, but were roundly defeated. During the battle, an invulnerable Lapith leader named Caeneus was driven into the ground by the Centaurs, since he could not be killed. This Caeneus had been a girl until, upon being violated by Poseidon and granted a boon, she chose to become a man and invulnerable. The battle of Centaurs and Lapiths was a favorite subject for Greek artists. It appeared on the PARTHENON, the Theseum at Athens, and the temple of Apollo at Basso, as well as on numberless vases.

Laplace, Marquis Pierre Simon de (1749–1827). French astronomer and mathematician. Laplace made discoveries in celestial mechanics and set forth a nebular hypothesis of cosmogony (*Exposition du système du monde;* 1796) which is essentially similar to that advanced by Immanuel Kant.

Laputa. The flying island which Gulliver visits in Jonathan Swift's GULLIVER'S TRAVELS. It is largely inhabited by abstract philosophers. In this third voyage, technical knowledge is extensively satirized. Laputans, in their preoccupation with the theoretical and with innovation in technical methods, are ill equipped for living in society. Swift regarded Laputan ingenuity as misplaced. See LAGADO; GLUBDUBDRIB.

Lara. See CORSAIR, THE.

Lara, Cantar de los siete infantes de. A lost Spanish epic, or *cantar de gesta,* parts of which are preserved in the *Crónica general* of Alfonso X and in the *Crónica de 1344.* Menéndez Pidal used these fragments as the basis for his reconstruction, *La leyenda de los infantes de Lara* (1896).

The legend deals with the seven sons of Gonzalo Gustios, lord of Salas, or Lara. Gonzalo González, youngest of the brothers, incurs the enmity of his aunt, Doña Lambra, by killing her cousin, Alvar Sánchez, at a tournament celebrating her marriage to Ruy Velázquez. As a result, a bloody vendetta ensues. Spurred by his wife, Ruy Velázquez asks Almanzor, military governor of Córdoba, to kill Gonzalo Gustios, but the magnanimous Moor merely holds him captive. Meanwhile, as a result of Velázquez' machinations, the sons and their old tutor, Nuño Salido, are killed while fighting against the Moors. They are later avenged by their half-brother, Mudarra, the offspring of their father's union with a Moorish slave.

This legend has formed the basis of many later works, notably Juan de la Cueva's *Tragedia de los siete infantes de Lara,* Lope de Vega's *El bastardo Mudarra,* and the romantic epic *El moro expósito* (1834) by Angel Saavedra, duque de Rivas.

La Ramée, Pierre. Known as **Petrus Ramus** (1515–1572). French philosopher, grammarian, and mathematician. He is known for his opposition to Aristotelian logic, which he attacked in his *Dialectique* (1555). He was a victim of the MASSACRE OF ST. BARTHOLOMEW.

Larbaud, Valery (1881–1957). French poet, fiction writer, critic. His *Poèmes par un riche amateur* (1908) and especially the *Journal d'A. O. Barnabooth* (1913) are lyrical reflections upon his many travels and express his yearning for some unattainable absolute. He was a close friend of James Joyce, and helped to launch *Ulysses* in 1922.

Lardner, Ring[gold Wilmer] (1885–1933). American humorist and short-story writer. He is known for his bitterly humorous and satirical stories and sketches of 20th-century American life, told in the language of baseball players, boxers, songwriters, stockbrokers, stenographers, chorus girls, etc. Lardner's first important work was YOU KNOW ME AL, letters of a baseball player which first appeared in the *Saturday Evening Post.* Previously, he had published a collection of verse, *Bib Ballads* (1915), and a long series of books followed, including HOW TO WRITE SHORT STORIES; *The Love Nest and Other Stories* (1926), a collection that includes the famous story *Haircut; The Story of a Wonder Man* (1927), a satirical autobiography; and *June Moon* (1929), a play written with George S. Kaufman, satirizing the song writers of Tin Pan Alley.

lares. Household gods of the ancient Romans, usually referred to in the singular (lar), there being one lar to a household. The lares were protective, and were usually deified ancestors or heroes. The *lar familiaris* was the spirit of the founder of the house who, never leaving, accompanied his descendants in all their changes. See PENATES.

Lark, The (L'Alouette; 1953). A play by Jean ANOUILH about JOAN OF ARC. It was translated into English by Christopher Fry.

Larkin, Philip [Arthur] (1922–   ). English poet and novelist. He has been a leader in the English antiromantic movement of the 1950's. *The Less Deceived* (1955) is a collection of witty poems. *Jill* (1946) and *A Girl in Winter* (1947) are novels.

La Rochefoucauld, Duc François de (1613–1680). French writer. In his *Mémoires* (1662), La Rochefoucauld records his political activities, describing his efforts to destroy the power of Cardinal Richelieu over the royal family and his participation in the battle of the FRONDE. After 1652 he abandoned politics for a sheltered intellectual life. The *Maximes* (*Maxims*, 1665) are concise and biting observations upon society and human nature, illustrating his conviction that self-interest is the spring of human conduct and that men delude themselves in pretending to virtue or disinterested behavior.

Larra [y Sánchez de Castro], Mariano José de. Known as *Fígaro* (1809–1837). Spanish journalist, literary critic, and author. The penetrating intelligence of this thoroughly romantic spirit brought him fame through his articles concerning Spanish regional life. These appeared in the 14 issues of the biting and satiric magazine *El pobrecito hablador* (1832–1833), which Larra edited and wrote himself. His reputation established, he went on to become one of the leading journalists of the period. His novel *El doncel de don Enrique el Doliente* (1834) and the drama *Macías* (1834) deal with the tragic loves of a minstrel who figures in Spanish literature as one of the authors who contributed to the *Cancionero de Baena*, an anonymous collection of medieval Spanish lyrics.

Larsen, Wolf. See SEA WOLF, THE.

Lars Porsena. See Lars PORSENA.

larvae. A name among the ancient Romans for malignant spirits and ghosts. The larva, or ghost, of the emperor Caligula was often seen (according to Suetonius) in his palace.

La Salle, Sieur de. Robert Cavelier (1643–1687). French explorer in North America. La Salle descended the Mississippi River to the Gulf of Mexico (1682), claiming the entire valley for France. He named the region Louisiana after the French king Louis XIV.

Lasca, Il. See Anton Francesco GRAZZINI.

Lascaris, Constantine (1434–1501). Greek scholar and teacher in Italy during the Renaissance. After teaching at Milan and Naples, he settled at Messina, where his school drew such northerners as Bembo for Greek studies. His Greek grammar was very popular in Italy and throughout Europe at the time.

Lascaris, John (1445–1535). Greek scholar in Italy during the Renaissance. He lectured at Florence and published there the first edition of the Planudean Anthology, part of the *Greek Anthology* as the entire collection was later called.

Las Casas, Bartolomé de (1474–1566). Spanish-born Dominican missionary and historian. He came to Santo Domingo in 1502 and was the first priest ordained in the New World (1510). In 1514, Las Casas suddenly became aware of the injustice with which the Indians were being treated in America, and subsequently devoted himself entirely to promoting their welfare, usually with the support of the crown, but against the bitter opposition of the Spanish settlers. *Brevísima relación de la destrucción de las Indias* (1552), his vivid, but probably exaggerated, account of Indian sufferings, was instrumental in fostering the long-lived "black legend," which denigrated the colonial policies of Spain in America. His major work, *Historia general de las Indias* (1875), is an important source for the early period of colonization in Latin America.

Laski, Harold J[oseph] (1893–1950). English political scientist. A convinced Marxist but not a Communist, he was an authority on American politics, history, and law.

Laski, Marghanita (1915–   ). English novelist and critic. She is the author of *Little Boy Lost* (1949), about an orphan, and *The Victorian Chaise Longue* (1954), a tale of the supernatural. Among her other works are *The Offshore Island* (1959), a play, and *Ecstasy: A Study of Some Secular and Religious Experiences* (1961).

Lassalle, Ferdinand (1825–1864). German socialist. His program of state socialism, or cooperation between worker and government, was criticized by Marx. His life is the source of George Meredith's novel *The Tragic Comedians* (1880).

Lassus, Orlandus de. Also **Orlando di Lasso.** Original name **Roland Delattre** (1530–1594). Flemish composer and choirmaster. Though, with Palestrina, he represents the apogee of 16th century polyphonic composition for voices, he also understood and composed for the instruments of his day. He left over 1,250 compositions at his death, including Italian canzoni, French chansons, secular madrigals, sacred motets, psalm-settings and masses.

Last Days of Pompeii, The (1834). A historical novel by Edward BULWER-LYTTON. The young Greek lovers, Glaucus and Ione, are thwarted in their intentions by Ione's rancorous guardian. The eruption of Vesuvius fortuitously allows them to escape to happiness.

Last Leaf, The (1907). A short story by O. HENRY. None of O. Henry's tales is more characteristic of his technique and sentiment than this account of a girl who lies, desperately ill of pneumonia, in a Greenwich Village apartment and makes up her mind to die as soon as the last leaf of five drops off the vine outside her window. One leaf hangs on, and she recovers—but there is a typical O. Henry twist to the ending.

Last of the Barons, The (1843). A historical novel by Edward BULWER-LYTTON dealing with the Wars of the Roses. The hero is Richard Neville, earl of Warwick, known as the Kingmaker. The novel traces his downfall. Sybil Warner and her father Adam Warner are important characters.

Last of the Just, The. See André SCHWARZ-BART.

Last of the Mohicans, The (1826). A novel by James Fenimore COOPER, the second of THE LEATHER-STOCKING TALES. The plot revolves around the efforts of Alice and Cora Munro to join their father, the British commander at Fort William Henry, near Lake Champlain. Their course is blocked by Magua, the leader of a group of Hurons, who are leagued with the French against the British in the war. The schemes of Magua, an evil Indian, are frustrated by Uncas, the last of the Mohicans, his father, Chingachgook and their friend Hawkeye (see Natty BUMPPO). The rhythm of the book is set by a series of thrilling attacks, captures, flights, and rescues. At the climax, Cora is killed by Magua and Uncas dies trying to save her.

Last Puritan, The (1936). A novel by George SANTAYANA. Subtitled *A Memoir in the Form of a Novel,* the book is a study of Oliver Alden, descendant of an old and wealthy New England family, who comprises in himself the Puritan characteristics of austerity, single-mindedness, gravity, and conscientious, scrupulous devotion to purpose. He is out of place in the civilization of the 20th century; as a friend of his in the novel says, "In Oliver Puritanism worked itself out to its logical end. He convinced himself, on Puritan grounds, that it was wrong to be a Puritan. . . . He thought it his clear duty to give Puritanism up, but couldn't." Oliver is presented in the prologue of the novel supposedly as a former student of the author at Harvard University and one of the young men killed during World War I. (Santayana later stated that he was partly based on W. Cameron Forbes.) In style, subject matter, and approach, *The Last Puritan* recalls the novels of Henry James.

Last Rose of Summer, 'Tis the. The title and first line of a song, generally known from the second act of the opera *Martha* (1847) by Flotow. It was written (1813) by Thomas Moore to the tune of an old air.

Last Supper. The last meal shared by Jesus and his 12 apostles. They celebrated the PASSOVER, then Jesus gave his followers bread and wine, thus instituting the sacrament of the Eucharist, also known as the Lord's Supper, and Holy Communion. The original occasion has been the subject of many works of art, the most famous of which is a fresco by Leonardo da Vinci in the refectory of Santa Maria delle Grazie, Milan. It shows the consternation of the disciples when Jesus told them that he would be betrayed that night.

Last Time I Saw Paris, The (1942). A book of reminiscences by Elliot PAUL. After the Germans took Paris in World War II, Paul set down in carefully interwoven episodes this nostalgic remembrance of Paris. The title was taken from a popular song of the 1940's. In *Springtime in Paris* (1950), Paul told of revisiting Paris.

Late George Apley, The (1937). A novel by John P. MARQUAND. Subtitled *A Novel in the form of a Memoir*, the story is told by Horatio Willing, a staid and polished annotator, who manages to satirize himself as he recounts the life of the recently deceased George Apley, a conventional, tradition-bound, but somewhat pathetic Bostonian. A highly successful book, it was awarded a Pulitzer Prize and later dramatized (1946) by its author and George S. Kaufman.

Lateran. See SAINT JOHN LATERAN.

Lathrop, George Parsons (1851–1898). American poet, biographer, and editor. Lathrop founded the American Copyright League in 1883, was editor of the Boston *Sunday Courier*, and associate editor of the *Atlantic Monthly*. In 1871, he married Rose Hawthorne LATHROP, and five years later wrote a *Study of Nathaniel Hawthorne* (1876), her father. He also published several collections of verse, among them *Rose and Roof-Tree* (1875) and *Dreams and Days* (1892).

Lathrop, Rose Hawthorne [Mother Mary Alphonsa] (1851–1926). American poet, memoirist, humanitarian. The second daughter of Nathaniel Hawthorne, she married George Parsons LATHROP in 1871. The marriage was unhappy, and Lathrop became a heavy drinker. In 1891, both husband and wife were converted to Roman Catholicism; working together, they established the Catholic Summer School of America and wrote a history of the Order

of the Sisters of Visitation, published as *A Story of Courage* (1894). In 1895, the Lathrops separated permanently. Mrs. Lathrop began to work in a hospital, and after her husband's death was received into the Dominican order as Mary Alphonsa. In 1901, she bought a home in Westchester County, N.Y., which she named Rosary Hill Home, and devoted the rest of her life to the care of incurable cases of cancer. In 1897 she published her *Memories of Hawthorne*.

Latimer, Hugh (1485?–1555). English bishop and Protestant martyr. Latimer was made bishop of Worcester in 1535, but resigned because he felt unable to accept the Act of the Six Articles of 1539. On the accession of Mary he was committed to the Tower, and was burned at the stake for heresy in 1555.

Latini, Brunetto (c. 1220–c. 1294). Italian philosopher and scholar, Dante's teacher. He wrote a didactic poem, the *Tesoretto*, in rhymed couplets of seven-syllable verse. His major work, the prose *Livre du Trésor* (c. 1265), was written in French and soon translated into Italian as *Tesoro* by Bono Giamboni; it is an encyclopedic "treasure book" of medieval scholastic knowledge.

Latin Quarter (*Fr.* **le Quartier Latin**). The University quarter of Paris on the left bank of the Seine. For centuries it has been a center for artists, writers, students, intellectuals, and Bohemians of all varieties and from many lands.

Latinus. The legendary king of the Latini, the ancient inhabitants of Latium. According to Vergil's AENEID, Latinus had been advised by an oracle to give his daughter, LAVINIA, in marriage to a stranger. Accordingly, he offers her to Aeneas, but Turnus, king of Rutuli, declares that she is betrothed to him. The contest between Aeneas and Turnus is settled by single combat, in which Aeneas is victorious.

Latitudinarians. Members of the liberal faction of the Church of England in the time of Charles II. They opposed the doctrinal rigidity of both the High Church and the Puritans. The term came to be applied to those persons who attach little importance to dogma and what are called orthodox doctrines.

Latmos, Mount. The mountain where ENDYMION pastured his flocks when Selene, goddess of the moon, fell in love with him.

La Tour du Pin, Patrice de (1911–   ). French poet. After the youthful lyrics of *La Quête de Joie* (1933), he collected the succeeding volumes into *Une Somme de Poésie* (1946), a long and allusive work interspersed with prose speculations which give it a mythological and philosophical unity. The development of the adolescent concerned only with himself into an adult involved with the fraternity of men provides subject and pattern for the work. *Le Second Jeu* (1959) stresses again that the man is born only through the death of the child, and leads La Tour du Pin to the third stage, the Christian confrontation with the mystery of God.

Latzko, Andreas (1876–   ). A Hungarian writer. His best-known book, *Men in War* (1917), is a war novel of pacifist tendencies.

Laube, Heinrich (1806–1884). German novelist and dramatist. His most famous work is the novel *Das junge Europa* (*Young Europe*, 1838 ff.), which attempts to define a unifying connection between the

JUNG DEUTSCHLAND (*Young Germany*) movement of which he was a representative and the other liberal young movements in Europe at the time, such as La Jeune France and Giovane Italia.

Laud, William (1573–1645). English prelate. The son of a clothier, he rose to the rank of archbishop of Canterbury (1633) and became one of the foremost supporters of Charles I, representing absolutism in both Church and State. His attempts to impose High Church conformity in Scotland and England aroused the bitter opposition of the Puritans. Impeached for treason by the Long Parliament (1640), he was condemned and beheaded.

lauda. Religious songs popular in Italy during the medieval and early Renaissance periods. These used the BALLATA form and were composed for lay confraternities. The outstanding early master of *lauda* was Jacopone da Todi (1230–1306). As the form developed in his hands and in those of his successors, it became increasingly dramatic, with dialogue, action, and setting assuming dominance. As such, it became the Italian equivalent of the mystery play, called the SACRA RAPPRESENTAZIONE (sacred representation). Though plays of this type dwindled in popularity in the later Renaissance, they left their influence on the secular and neoclassical drama, which replaced them in popularity. During the Renaissance, some *lauda* were still written, but not for large religious organizations; usually they were conceived as texts for musical setting, to be performed by individual artists or as part of religious services.

Laughing Boy (1929). A novel by Oliver LA FARGE. Centering around the ill-fated love of Laughing Boy for Slim Girl, it is noted for its sensitive and accurate depiction of Navaho culture and psychology. La Farge's first novel, it was awarded a Pulitzer Prize.

Laughing Philosopher, The. See DEMOCRITUS.

Launce. In Shakespeare's Two GENTLEMEN OF VERONA, the clownish servant of Proteus. Launce is especially famous for his remarks to his dog Crab, "the sourest-natured dog that lives."

Launcelot, Sir. In ARTHURIAN LEGEND, the most famous of the knights of the Round Table. In the

Launcelot at a tournament. From a
French romance (1513).

early Welsh legends of King Arthur, he does not appear, but almost seems a French innovation since we first find him figuring importantly in the 12th-century *Lancelot, or the Knight of the Cart* by Chrétien de Troyes. He comes to full growth, however, in Malory's *Morte d'Arthur* (c. 1469), as do so many of the other Arthurian characters.

In most versions he is the son of King Ban of Benwick, and his full title is Sir Launcelot du Lac (see LADY OF THE LAKE). In almost all versions in which he appears, he is the champion and lover of Queen GUINEVERE and the favorite of King Arthur. In Malory's version, he begets Sir GALAHAD by ELAINE, when he is deceived into believing that she is Guinevere, and he is then driven to madness for a long period by the jealousy of Guinevere. Most of his exploits are in the name of the queen, one way or another, and sometimes they take the form of rescuing her, as, for example, from being burnt at the stake. He is finally exiled by King Arthur who afterwards comes to war with him at Benwick. In a combat with Sir GAWAIN, Launcelot mortally wounds that knight; then, going back to England, he finds King Arthur dead, the Round Table dissolved, and Queen Guinevere become a nun. He himself becomes a monk and dies not long after Guinevere. Launcelot is a major figure in Tennyson's *Idylls of the King* (1859–1885) and in the narrative poem *Lancelot* by Edwin Arlington Robinson. See JOYOUS GARD.

Launcelot Greaves, The Adventures of Sir (1760). A rambling, satiric novel by Tobias SMOLLETT. It is an attempt to adapt DON QUIXOTE to the 18th century by creating a benevolent reformer so disinterested as to seem mad. The hero, Sir Launcelot Greaves, is a well-bred and noble-minded young English squire of the George II period, half-crazed by love. He sets out, attended by Captain CROWE, to detect fraud and to right the wrongs of the world. After sundry adventures which give the author opportunity for satiric treatment of English life, he is welcomed back by his faithful love Aurelia Darnel. The novel was among the first serialized in English.

Laura. The beloved of PETRARCH and the subject of his collection of lyrics called *Rime* (verses) or *Canzoniere* (song book). The poet says he first saw her in the church of St. Claire at Avignon on April 6, 1327, fell in love, and was inspired to write poetry. Her death, on the same date 21 years later, resulted in a profound spiritual crisis with which the poet struggled for the remainder of his life. Who Laura actually was is still a controversial matter. It was formerly thought that she was a certain Laure de Noves of Avignon, born in 1308, wedded to Hugues de Sede and the mother of 11 children, who died in the great plague of 1348. Modern scholars reject this identification in favor of the idea that Laura is a poetic fiction, a symbol of the poet's aspirations as well as a focal point of his psychological conflicts. In the poems, Petrarch frequently puns on the name because of its resemblance to the Italian words for *air* and *laurel* (hence, inspiration and fame). The name has been used by poets ever since, in love poems addressed to a similar idealized lady. Robert Tofte entitled his 1597 collection of love lyrics *Laura;* Lord Byron used the name for the Venetian lady who marries *Beppo* in the poem of the same name; and Schiller wrote a series of poems to Laura.

laureate. See Poets Laureate.

Laurence, Friar. The wise and kindly Franciscan friar in Shakespeare's Romeo and Juliet who marries the young lovers. He hopes that the alliance will end the feud between the Montagues and Capulets.

Laurent, Jacques. Pen names: **Jacques Laurent-Cely, Cécil Saint-Laurent, Albéric Varenne** (1919–). French novelist and historian. The risqué popular novels he has published as Saint-Laurent, such as *Caroline chérie* (1947) and *Clotilde* (1957), are better known than his more serious *Les Corps tranquilles* (1948) and *Le Petit Canard* (1954).

Laurie, Annie (1682–1764). The subject of a Scottish song (c. 1700). A daughter of Sir Robert Laurie of Maxwellton, Dumfriesshire, she married Alexander Ferguson. The song was written by the man she rejected, William Douglas. It was revised and set to music by Lady John Scott (1855).

Lauriers sont coupés, Les (We'll to the Woods No More, 1888). A novel by Edouard Dujardin. It is considered the first example in fiction of an intended interior monologue (see stream of consciousness). Daniel Prince, a young Frenchman, is in love with an actress, Léah d'Arsay, and pretends to himself to be satisfied with a merely "Platonic" relationship, although he actually wishes to make her his mistress. She allows him to believe that she is about to grant him her favors, but after she has secured a sum of money from him she skillfully puts him off. He therefore resolves never to see her again. The story is told through the thoughts and impressions of the hero as he walks in the street, meets friends, sits in a restaurant, rides in a carriage, and visits Léah. James Joyce is said to have read this book about 1901 and to have been partly influenced by it while writing *Ulysses*. Dujardin himself claimed to have been influenced in his technique by Richard Wagner's device of the musical *Leitmotiv*, by the dramatic monologue of Robert Browning, and by the psychological monologue of Dostoevski.

Lautréamont, Le Comte de. Pen name of Isidore Lucien Ducasse (1846–1870). French poet. Born in Montevideo, Uruguay, Lautréamont came to Paris in 1867. In 1868 he published his first work, *Les Chants de Maldoror*. His poetry, marked by despair, violence, and savagery, possesses the quality of a surrealist nightmare.

Lautrec. See Henri de Toulouse-Lautrec.

Laval, Pierre (1883–1945). French politician. A member of the Chamber of Deputies (from 1914) and premier (1931–1936), Laval is remembered for his policy of collaboration with the Germans during the Occupation. He was ousted as vice-premier of the Vichy government by Pétain (Dec., 1940) but reinstated through German pressure as administrative chief of state. At the end of the war, Laval was tried by a French court for high treason and executed by a firing squad.

Lavater, Johann Kaspar (1741–1801). Swiss divine and poet. In his *Physiognomische Fragmente zur Beförderung der Menschenkenntnis und Menschenliebe* (*Physiognomical Fragments for the Promotion of Knowledge and Love of Man*, 1775 ff.), on which Goethe collaborated, he founded the study of "physiognomy." See phrenology.

Lavengro: The Scholar, Gypsy, Priest (1851).

A novel by George Borrow. Mingling autobiography with fiction, the author relates the wanderings of a young man who is interested in philology and becomes intimate with a family of gypsies. His adventures are resumed in the sequel, *The Romany Rye* (1857). The name Lavengro, which means philologist in the language of the gypsies, was applied to Borrow in his youth.

Lavinia. (1) In Vergil's Aeneid, the daughter of Latinus. She is betrothed to Turnus, king of the Rutuli. When Aeneas lands in Italy, Latinus makes an alliance with the Trojan hero and promises to give him Lavinia as his wife. After Aeneas defeats the angry Turnus, he marries Lavinia and becomes by her the ancestor of Romulus, the mythical founder of Rome. The ancient city of Lavinium near Rome was said to have been built by Aeneas and named after her.

(2) In Shakespeare's Titus Andronicus, the daughter of Titus. Described as "gracious Lavinia, Rome's rich ornament," she is abducted and married to her betrothed, Bassanius, to prevent her forced marriage to his brother Saturninus. Later the evil sons of the vengeful Tamora slay Bassanius, rape Lavinia, and cut off her tongue and hands.

Lavoisier, Antoine Laurent (1743–1794). French chemist. Lavoisier, who discovered oxygen and the composition of air (at the same time as Priestley), is one of the founders of modern chemistry. He is best known for his theory of the indestructibility of matter. His reforms in chemical nomenclature are the basis of the system still in use. In 1794, he was guillotined by the Revolutionists.

Lavransdatter, Kristin. See Kristin Lavransdatter.

Law, John. See Mississippi Bubble.

Law, William (1686–1761). English devotional writer who was influenced in later life by the philosophy of the German mystic Jakob Böhme. He is the author of the *Serious Call to a Devout and Holy Life* (1729), which strongly influenced the Evangelical revival in England, and is especially remembered for his attack on Bernard Mandeville's *Fable of the Bees* (1723). In 1740, Law became the spiritual advisor to Edward Gibbon's aunt, as well as to John and Charles Wesley.

Lawless, Emily (1845–1913). Irish novelist and poet. Her best-known works are the novels *Hurrish* (1886) and *Grania* (1892). *With the Wild Geese* (1902), a volume of poems, is also noteworthy.

Lawrence, St. The patron saint of curriers. He was broiled to death on a gridiron. He was deacon to Sextus I and was charged with the care of the poor, the orphans, and the widows. In the persecution of Valerian (258), being summoned to deliver up the treasures of the church, he produced the poor under his charge and said to the praetor, "These are the church's treasures." He is generally represented as holding a gridiron, and is commemorated on August 10.

The phrase *lazy as Lawrence* is said to take its origin from the story that when being roasted over a slow fire he asked to be turned, "for," said he, "that side is quite done." This expression of Christian fortitude was interpreted by his torturers as evidence of the height of laziness, the martyr being too indolent even to wriggle.

Lawrence, D[avid] H[erbert] (1885–1930). English novelist, short-story writer, poet, and essayist. He is known for his frequently misunderstood but basically idealistic ideas about sexual relations, and for his interest in primitive religions and nature mysticism. Lawrence regarded sex, the primitive subconscious, and nature as cures for what he considered modern man's maladjustment to industrial society. His philosophy, life history, and prejudices are inextricably involved in his writings; many of his views are expressed in WOMEN IN LOVE and LADY CHATTERLEY'S LOVER. SONS AND LOVERS is a partly autobiographical novel which deals with the author's boyhood and adolescence as the son of a coal miner. Lawrence struggled to become a teacher, then an established member of London's literary society, but he never ceased to rebel against Anglo-Saxon puritanism, social conventions, and mediocrity. He was attracted to the Nietzschean idea of the superman, and expressed his idea of the hero in his novels KANGAROO and THE PLUMED SERPENT.

Lawrence's work, of great volume and variety, is uneven in literary value. At its best it is marked by intensity of feeling, psychological insight, vivid evocation of events, places, and particularly nature. A controversial figure, he is regarded by some critics as the greatest of modern English novelists; most concede that he is a major writer in spite of his overfondness for preaching, his obscurantism, and his ranting attacks on the people and institutions he regarded as his enemies. Lawrence's other novels are *The White Peacock* (1911), *The Trespasser* (1912), THE RAINBOW, *The Lost Girl* (1920), *Aaron's Rod* (1922), and *The Boy in the Bush* (1924), in collaboration with M. L. Skinner. Among his short novels are *St. Mawr* (1925), THE MAN WHO DIED, and *The Virgin and the Gipsy* (1930). Lawrence's short stories, which do not have the faults of his novels, are widely admired. Among them are THE PRUSSIAN OFFICER, THE CAPTAIN'S DOLL, *Sun*, *The Fox*, THE WOMAN WHO RODE AWAY, *The Man Who Loved Islands*, THE ROCKING-HORSE WINNER, and THINGS. His early fiction tends to be fairly conventional and realistic while his later work is more immersed in the subconscious and rich in symbolism. Some of his later short stories, however, are taut and naturalistic.

Lawrence's first published works were poems (see MIRIAM). He began by writing in the school of imagism. His best-known poems are in free verse, about the individual, inner nature of animals and plants: *Fish*, *Snake*, *Mountain Lion*, and *Bavarian Gentians* are among them. *Birds, Beasts and Flowers* (1923) is a well-known collection. *Look! We Have Come Through* (1917) is a collection of poems about his relationship with his wife, Frieda von Richthofen LAWRENCE. *Pansies* (1929) is a collection of didactic, satiric, and iconoclastic poems, which was seized as immoral by the English authorities on its first publication.

Lawrence's fine, vivid collections of travel sketches are *Twilight in Italy* (1916), *Sea and Sardinia* (1921), *Mornings in Mexico* (1927), and *Etruscan Places* (1927). His most influential book of criticism is *Studies in Classical American Literature* (1923), which contains brilliant, eccentric insights into American writers from Benjamin Franklin to Walt Whitman. *Psychoanalysis and the Unconscious* (1921) and *Fantasia of the Unconscious* (1922) are statements of his philosophy. He wrote a great many colloquial, iconoclastic essays, including *Pornography and Obscenity* (1930), *Reflections on the Death of a Porcupine* (1934), and *Democracy* (1936). He also wrote *Movements in European History* (1921), under the pen name of Lawrence H. Davidson, and a few unsuccessful plays. His interesting *Letters* were edited by Aldous Huxley (1932).

Even after Lawrence established himself in London literary circles—he was a close friend of Aldous Huxley (see POINT COUNTER POINT), and of Katherine Mansfield and J. Middleton Murry—he still had many troubles. He suffered from tuberculosis, saw his books banned as obscene, and was persecuted during World War I for his supposed pro-German sympathies. Disgusted by England, he left it to travel with his wife, but he was continually disappointed in his quest for a homeland and congenial associates. At one time or another, Lawrence lived in Italy, Germany, Ceylon, Australia, New Zealand, Tahiti, the French Riviera, Mexico, and the southwestern part of the United States. In Taos, New Mex., an artists' colony, he once dreamed of setting up an ideal social community. (See Mabel Dodge LUHAN.) At the end of his life he was extravagantly admired by several women who called him "Lorenzo," regarded themselves as his disciples, and engaged in jealous quarrels over his attentions. After Lawrence's death a number of people who had known him published books and memoirs about him, both unfriendly and adulatory, often attacking each other. Among these remembrances were those of J. Middleton Murry, Catherine CARSWELL, Mabel Dodge Luhan, Dorothy BRETT, Richard ALDINGTON, E. T. (see MIRIAM), and his wife.

Lawrence, Frieda von Richthofen (1879–1956). Aristocratic German wife of D. H. LAWRENCE. She was married to Professor Ernest Weekley, an English philologist, and had three children when she met Lawrence and eloped with him in 1912. Lawrence described their stormy, happy marriage in his writings, especially in the collection of poems *Look! We Have Come Through* and in the novels WOMEN IN LOVE and KANGAROO. She wrote *Not I, But the Wind . . .* (1934), a memoir of her husband. Her brother, Manfred von Richthofen, was a celebrated German aviator during World War I.

Lawrence, James (1781–1813). American naval officer. During the War of 1812 he commanded the *Chesapeake* in an engagement (June 1, 1813) with the British frigate *Shannon* near Boston harbor. Mortally wounded, Lawrence is said to have shouted, "Don't give up the ship!" The British captured the *Chesapeake*, but Lawrence's last words became a popular slogan in the U.S. navy.

Lawrence, Josephine (1897?–   ). American newspaperwoman and novelist. She writes of the common problems faced by average people in such books as *Head of the Family* (1932), *If I Have Four Apples* (1935), *No Stone Unturned* (1941), *The Web of Time* (1953), *All Our Tomorrows* (1959), and *Hearts Do Not Break* (1960).

Lawrence, T[homas] E[dward]. Known as **Lawrence of Arabia** (1888–1935). English soldier, archaeologist, and author. He is famous for his activities in arousing and directing a successful rebellion of the Arabs against the Turks during World War I, for his account of his exploits in *Seven Pillars of Wisdom* (1926), and for his enigmatic personality. During the war he became an almost legendary figure in the Middle East; after the war, he received a number of honors and was offered, but refused, the Victoria Cross and a knighthood. He retired from public life to write the *Seven Pillars of Wisdom*, an abridgement of it called *The Revolt in the Desert* (1927), and a prose translation of Homer's *Odyssey* (1932). Meanwhile he sought still more obscurity by joining the Air Force as a private under the name of Shaw. His journal from this period was published as *The Mint* (1955). There has been much interest in, and controversy about, Lawrence's psychological motivations. B. H. Liddell-Hart, Robert Graves, and Richard ALDINGTON are among those who have written about him.

Lawrence, Sir Thomas (1769–1830). English portrait painter. A child prodigy, he succeeded Sir Joshua REYNOLDS as principal painter to the king in 1792. He was the graceful and romantic portraitist of the most brilliant society of England, and after his reputation spread to the continent, he painted the European princes and the heroes of the Napoleonic wars.

Lawrence of Arabia. See T. E. LAWRENCE.

Lawson, John Howard (1895–   ). American playwright. He is known for his experiments in expressionism in the 1920's and his later plays expressing proletarian sympathies. *Processional* (1925), set in a West Virginian town during a coal strike, is perhaps the best known of his plays influenced by the expressionist movement. *Loud Speaker* (1927), on American politics, *The International* (1928), dealing with a worldwide revolution of the proletariat, and *Marching Song* (1937), dealing with a sit-down strike, are all examples of his proletarian plays. Among his books is *Film in the Bottle of Ideas* (1953).

Laxdale Saga. An Icelandic saga of the early Middle Ages, dealing chiefly with the wilful, selfish, and much-married Gudrun who falls in love with Kjartan. While Kjartan is at the court of King Olaf, his cousin Bolli tells Gudrun that Kjartan has become friendly with Olaf's sister Ingebjorg. Vindictively, Gudrun marries Bolli; when Kjartan returns to Iceland and hears of the marriage, he marries Hrefna, also vindictively. He gives to Hrefna an ornate coif, which Ingebjorg had originally sent with him as a gift for Gudrun, and this causes Gudrun to precipitate a feud between the two families by having the coif stolen. There follows a series of raids and battles in which Kjartan is eventually killed through the machinations of the woman who really loved him and whom he loved.

Laxness, Halldór [Kiljan] (1902–   ). Icelandic poet, novelist, and playwright. One of the great figures in modern Icelandic literature, Laxness, who was awarded the Nobel Prize for literature in 1955, passed through several spiritual stages during the course of his literary career. A world traveler, he discovered expressionism in Germany, surrealism in France, and was converted to Catholicism in Luxembourg. The novels *Undir Helgahnúk* (*Under the Holy Mountain,* 1924) and *Vefarinn mikli frá Kasmír* (*The Great Weaver from Kashmir,* 1927) portray the spiritual turmoil of Laxness and the discontent

that led him to the church. He turned to Communism during a visit to the U.S.; when he returned to Iceland in 1930, he published *Alpýðubókin* (*The Book of the People*), a collection of essays expressing his new Communist views. Laxness' finest work, however, appears in the three novels set in an Icelandic fishing village: *Salka Valka* (1936), *Sjálfstoett fólk* (*Independent People,* 2 vols., 1934–1935), and *Ljós heimsins* (*The Light of the World,* 4 vols., 1937–1940). These novels are a rich blend of social criticism, vivid lyricism, and a turbulent, highly exciting prose style. The simple village girl, the sturdy farmer, and the victimized poet who contains an inextinguishable spark of life emerge as symbols from the grand canvas of the work. His *Paradise Reclaimed* was published in 1962.

lay. See LAI.

Layamon. See BRUT, THE.

Lay of the Last Minstrel (1805). A narrative poem by Sir Walter SCOTT. Lady Margaret of Branksome Hall, "the flower of Teviot," is beloved by Baron Henry of Cranstown, but a deadly feud exists between the two families. The poem celebrates the martial prowess and amorous success of the baron.

Lays of Ancient Rome (1842). A series of ballads by Thomas Babington MACAULAY. The chief ballads are *Horatius* (see HORATIUS COCLES), THE BATTLE OF THE LAKE REGILLUS, and *Virginia*.

Layton, Irving (1912–   ). Romanian-born Canadian poet. Layton's family settled in Montreal in 1913. He studied agriculture, served in the Royal Canadian Air Force, and was an editor of *Preview*, an experimental literary magazine published in the 1940's. He is known for his poems of rebellious protest against the social inequalities he saw both in the countryside and the city; often he purposely shocked readers with harsh, "unpoetic" images. His works include *Here and Now* (1945), *In the Midst of My Fever* (1954), *The Bull Calf and Other Poems* (1956), and *The Swinging Flesh* (1961).

Lazarillo de Tormes, La vida de (1554). A PICARESQUE novel by an anonymous author, sometimes identified with Diego HURTADO DE MENDOZA. Divided into seven chapters or *tratados,* it is the autobiography of the wily Lázaro, who describes his experiences with the various masters whom he served: the blind man, the miserly priest, the proud but hungry squire, the mendicant friar, the seller of indulgences. He ends his career as town-crier of Toledo. Written with vigorous realism and irony, *Lazarillo* was enormously popular and inspired several sequels. It is considered the greatest Spanish work in this genre.

Lazarus. (1) In the New Testament, a character in one of Christ's parables who begged daily at the gate of the rich man Dives (Luke 16:19).

(2) Another better-known Lazarus of the New Testament is the brother of Mary and Martha of Bethany, whom Jesus raised from the dead after four days (John 11:12).

Lazarus, Emma (1849–1887). American poet and translator. She translated Heine's poems and published a novel, *Alide: An Episode in Goethe's Life* (1874). This early work, flowery and romantic, would not have won her a reputation. In 1882, however, her indignation was kindled by the Russian pogroms; she set out to defend and glorify the Jewish people. *Songs of a Semite* (1882) includes her best poem, *Dance to Death*. Her sonnet *The New Colossus* (1883) is inscribed on the pedestal of the Statue of LIBERTY. *By the Waters of Babylon* (1887) showed the influence of Whitman.

Lazarus Laughed (1927). A drama by Eugene O'NEILL. It deals with Lazarus after his resurrection by Jesus. The man to whom new life has been given goes about preaching a new religion of love and eternal life, symbolized by laughter. He eventually goes to Rome and causes a sensation there, finally being stabbed by Caligula in the great amphitheater of the city but affirming until the last his belief in the triumph of life. Seven masked choruses, symbolizing varying periods of life, are used in this play.

le, la, l'. For titles beginning with these words, see following words.

Leacock, Stephen (1869–1944). Canadian humorist and political scientist. His satirically humorous short stories and essays were very popular; among them are *Nonsense Novels* (1911), *Moonbeams from the Larger Lunacy* (1915), and *The Garden of Folly* (1924). He also wrote standard works on political science, and studies of Mark Twain (1932) and Charles Dickens (1933).

League of Nations. A league to promote international cooperation and peace, formed after World War I. Its headquarters were at Geneva, Switzerland. Its members were the signatories of the treaty of VERSAILLES on behalf of the Allies, with certain other states, including Germany and the U.S.S.R. Although it was created largely through the exertions of President Woodrow WILSON, the U.S. Senate refused to ratify the treaty of Versailles, and thus the U.S. was never a member of the league.

During the 1920's the league was able to settle a few minor disputes between nations, and its contributions in the fields of refugee rehabilitation, public health, and international labor problems were considerable, but it had no power to enforce its policies in cases of war waged by important nations. It failed especially to be effective at the invasion of Ethiopia by Italy (1935), of Manchuria by Japan (1931), and also during the Civil War in Spain (1936–1939). Several members, including Italy, Japan, and Germany, resigned from the league in the late 1930's. It was formally dissolved on April 18, 1946, its material and moral heritage being taken over by the UNITED NATIONS.

Leah. In the Old Testament, the daughter of Laban and sister of Rachel. She became one of the wives of JACOB.

Léandre. (1) In Molière's *Les Fourberies de Scapin* (*Rogueries of Scapin*, 1671), the son of Géronte. During the absence of his father, he falls in love with Zerbinette, whom he supposes to be a young gypsy but who is in reality the stolen daughter of Argante, his father's friend. SCAPIN raises the money to ransom the girl from the gypsies and Léandre marries her.

(2) In Molière's LE MÉDECIN MALGRÉ LUI, the lover of Lucinde.

leaning tower. The campanile of the cathedral of Pisa, Italy. About 180 feet in height, it began to lean during its construction in the 12th century, and this condition has worsened until it is now about 17 feet out of plumb.

Lear, Edward (1812–1888). English painter and writer. He is known for his LIMERICKS and nonsense verse, marked by absurd humor, whimsy, and fantasy. These are inimitable in their kind, and perennial classics of English humorous verse. *The Owl and the Pussycat* (1871) is his best-known set of verses. His books include *A Book of Nonsense* (1846), *Nonsense Songs, Stories, Botany, and Alphabets* (1871), *More Nonsense Songs* (1872), and *Laughable Lyrics* (1877). Lear was also the author of interesting illustrated travel books, such as a *Journal of a Landscape Painter in Greece and Albania* (1852) and so prominent a painter of landscape and animals that he once gave drawing lessons to Queen Victoria.

Learchus (Learchos). See INO.

Leatherstocking Tales, The. A series of five novels by James Fenimore COOPER. The novels appeared in the following sequence: THE PIONEERS (1823), THE LAST OF THE MOHICANS (1826), THE PRAIRIE (1827), THE PATHFINDER (1840), and THE DEERSLAYER (1841). The series follows the career of Natty BUMPPO from his youth (*Deerslayer*) to his death (*The Prairie*). An abridgement of the five novels was made by Allan Nevins in a single volume called *The Leatherstocking Saga* (1954).

Leaves of Grass. A collection of poems by Walt WHITMAN. First published in 1855, it was revised and augmented every few years until the poet's death in 1892. The first edition, unsigned, contained only 12 untitled poems. The first and longest was later called SONG OF MYSELF. In 1855 the poems were preceded by a preface declaring Whitman's poetic credo. "The United States themselves," he said, "are essentially the greatest poem." The country's genius is the common people; the poet must be "commensurate" with the people and "incarnate" the spirit and geography of the States. Echoing *Walden* (1854), Whitman praises simplicity. A great poem, he says, is for "all degrees and complexions and all departments and sects." The poem's form was to be organic; it must grow out of the demands of its subject.

The book, radical in form and content, takes its title from the themes of fertility, universality, and cyclical life. Critics have noted the influence of Shakespeare and the Hebraic poetry of the Bible.

As he revised and added to the original edition, Whitman arranged the poems in a significant autobiographical order. In the final poems, the poet, though dead, survives in his work. In 1881, the permanent order of the volume was established; all later work was assigned to an annex. The final or "death-bed" edition was issued in 1892.

Leavis, F[rank] R[aymond] (1895–   ). English literary critic. One of the CAMBRIDGE CRITICS, he edited the influential magazine *Scrutiny* (1932–1953). Making it his business to maintain standards in English literature and criticism, Leavis wrote controversial essays attacking what he considered mediocre and dilettante work. Above all, he required literature to have moral value and to be concerned with the health of society. He found the qualities he admired in the novelists George Eliot and D. H. Lawrence, and praised them extravagantly. Leavis' criticism was very influential in England. His chief works are *New Bearings in English Poetry* (1932), *Revaluations* (1936), *The Great Tradition: George Eliot, James, and Conrad* (1948), *The Common Pursuit* (1952), and *D. H. Lawrence, Novelist* (1955). Much of the material in these books first appeared in *Scrutiny*, which served as a vehicle for the ideas of Leavis and of other Cambridge critics who shared some of his principles.

Le Beau. In Shakespeare's As You Like It, a garrulous French courtier, "his mouth full of news," attending on Duke Frederick.

lebensraum. See Karl HAUSHOFER.

Lebyadkin, Marya Timofeyevna. In Feodor Dostoevski's novel THE POSSESSED, the crippled half-wit STAVROGIN has married for obscure and perverse reasons that are not clarified. She is portrayed in the tradition of the Russian "holy fool" and, along with SHATOV, is the vehicle for the expression of many of Dostoevski's own religious ideas.

Lebyadkin, Captain. The comical and unscrupulous brother of Marya Timofeyevna, Stavrogin's half-wit wife. He calls himself a retired army captain, although doubt is cast on the truth of this by the narrator. Lebyadkin, who callously mistreats his sister, continually tries to extort money from Stavrogin for her support. He is murdered along with Marya at the end of the novel.

Le Charlier, Jean. See Jean GERSON.

Leconte de Lisle, Charles Marie René (1818–1894). French poet, leader of the PARNASSIANS. A dislike for the excessive subjectivity and exaggerated emotionalism of the romantic writers caused him to write poetry that was objective in content and austere in style. Leconte de Lisle gave voice to dark pessimism, and his hatred for the ugly industrial civilization in which he lived led him to seek his subjects in the past or in strange, distant places. His works include *Poèmes antiques* (1852), *Poèmes barbares* (1862), *Histoire populaire du Christianisme* (1871), *Poèmes tragiques* (1884), and *Derniers Poèmes* (1895). His drama *L'Apollonide* (1888) and the verse tragedy *Les Erinnyes* (1889) are also well known.

Lecoq, Monsieur. A brilliant French detective created by Emile GABORIAU. Monsieur Lecoq appears in several novels: *Monsieur Lecoq* (1869), *L'Affaire Lerouge* (1866) and *Le Dossier no. 113* (1867). He is one of the first of the famous detectives of literature and a precursor of Sherlock Holmes.

Le Corbusier. Real name, **Charles Edouard Jeanneret** (1887–   ). Swiss-born French architect and painter. He is known for his contributions to functionalism. Among these are the corner window, the glass façade, the use of ferroconcrete in buildings, and the elevated traffic ramp. Le Corbusier is an innovator in city planning. His suggested plans for Algiers and St. Dié are no less influential than his planning, undertaken in 1951, of the new town of Chandigarh for the Indian government. He is the author of *Towards a New Architecture* (1923). Among his best-known works are the Radiant City of Marseilles (1946–1952) and the chapel at Ronchamp (1955). As a painter, Le Corbusier demands of art a total submission to its architectural setting. About 1918, with Amédée Ozenfant, he developed purism with the idea of preventing cubism from becoming a mere decorative ornament. He adopted the machine as an object of absolute perfection and rejected every accidental detail in his rigorous compositions. Yet at no time did Le Corbusier condemn lyricism, but rather sought rules, both in painting

and architecture, proper to the creation of a setting that would satisfy the very nature of man as he conceives it, with its need for light, order, and joy.

Lecouvreur, Adrienne (1692–1730). French actress. The greatest tragedienne of her day on the French stage, Lecouvreur substituted unaffected delivery for the then current bombastic, declamatory style of tragic acting. The church's refusal to grant her burial in consecrated soil provoked an anticlerical scandal and aroused Voltaire to compose an elegy on her death. Lecouvreur is the subject of a play by Scribe and Legouvé and of an opera by Cilèa, both based on the unfounded tradition that she was poisoned by a rival in love.

Lectern, The. See LUTRIN, LE.

Leda. In Greek mythology, the wife of Tyndareus. She was the mother by Zeus (who is fabled to have come to her in the shape of a swan) of two eggs, from one of which came Castor and Clytemnestra, and from the other Polydeuces and Helen. There are, however, many versions of their birth. The subject of Leda and the Swan has been a favorite with artists; Paul Veronese, Correggio, and Michelangelo have all left paintings of it.

Ledoux, Louis V[ernon] (1880–1948). American poet and critic. Head of the firm of Ledoux & Co., chemists and assayers, Ledoux wrote such volumes of verse as *Songs from the Silent Land* (1905), *The Soul's Progress and Other Poems* (1906), and *The Shadow of Aetna* (1914). Following one of his main interests, he wrote *The Art of Japan* (1927) and *Japanese Prints of the Primitive Period* (1942).

Ledwidge, Francis (1891–1917). Irish nature poet. He wrote *Songs of the Field* (1914) and *Songs of Peace* (1916). He was killed in World War I.

Lee, Ann (1736–1784). English mystic and founder of the American Shaker society in Watervliet, N.Y. (1776). She claimed the power of discerning spirits and working miracles. She was known to her followers as "Ann the Word" or "Mother Ann" since they were convinced that she was the manifestation of the female counterpart of Christ.

Lee, Henry. Known as **Light-Horse Harry Lee** (1756–1818). American soldier and statesman. The father of Robert E. Lee, he was a brilliant cavalry commander in the Revolutionary War and received his nickname because of his quick movements in the field. His eulogy of Washington (1799) contains the famous words: "First in war, first in peace, and first in the hearts of his countrymen."

Lee, Laurie (1914–   ). English poet. The author of simple lyrics, mostly about nature, he has written *The Bloom of Candles* (1947) and *A Rose for Winter* (1955). *Cider with Rosie* (1959) is an autobiography.

Lee, Lorelei. The heroine of Anita Loos's novel GENTLEMEN PREFER BLONDES. Not very bright but an enterprising young lady, she is a remarkably successful "gold-digger."

Lee, Manfred B. See Ellery QUEEN.

Lee, Nathaniel (c. 1653–1692). English dramatist. His bloody and extravagant tragedies, extremely popular in his time, include *The Rival Queens, or The Death of Alexander the Great* (1677); *Mithridates, King of Pontus* (1678); and *Caesar Borgia* (1680). He also collaborated with Dryden.

Lee, Robert E[dward] (1807–1870). American soldier. The son of Henry Lee, he was graduated from West Point in 1829, fought in the Mexican War, and commanded the marine detachment that quelled John Brown's abortive insurrection in 1859. Although Lee favored preservation of the Union, loyalty to his native Virginia, where his family had long been prominent, led him to refuse field command of the U.S. army in 1861 and to accept command of the state's forces. Named commander of the Army of Northern Virginia in 1862, he thwarted McClellan's Peninsula Campaign against Richmond in the Seven Days' Battles (1862), suffered a technical defeat at ANTIETAM, and won engagements at Fredericksburg and CHANCELLORSVILLE. His defeat at GETTYSBURG began the attrition of Confederate strength that compelled him to surrender to Grant at Appomattox Courthouse on April 9, 1865. After the war, Lee became president of Washington College in Virginia, which was later renamed Washington and Lee University in his honor. An excellent strategist and leader of men, Lee is admired in both North and South for his courage and chivalry.

Lee, Vernon. Pen name of **Violet Paget** (1856–1935). English novelist, essayist, and writer on aesthetics, politics, and Italian art and life. *Euphorion* (1884) is a study of Renaissance art.

Leech, Margaret (1893–   ). American writer. Her works in the field of American history and biography are known for their careful research and readable style. For *Reveille in Washington* (1941), an account of life in the capital during the Civil War, she received a Pulitzer Prize. Her other books include *Anthony Comstock, Roundsman of the Lord,* written with Heywood Broun (1927), and *In the Days of McKinley* (1959), another Pulitzer Prize winner.

Leech-gatherer, The. See RESOLUTION AND INDEPENDENCE.

Le Fanu, Joseph Sheridan (1814–1873). Irish novelist, journalist, and balladeer. He is known for his mystery novel *Uncle Silas* (1864), and his tales of the supernatural, the best of which is *The House by the Churchyard* (1863). His work compares favorably with that of Poe and Wilkie Collins. He was a distant relative of the 18th-century playwright Sheridan.

Lefèvre d'Etaples, Jacques. See Jacques Lefèvre d'ETAPLES.

left, right, center. Names applied to political positions. In the amphitheater where the French National Assembly of 1789 convened, the nobles still commanded sufficient respect to be given places of honor to the *right* of the president. The radicals moved naturally as far away from them to the *left* as they could. The moderates found themselves squeezed in between in the *center*. Hence the political connotations of these terms. Carlyle, in *The French Revolution* (1847), was one of the first to speak in English of "the extreme Left." Such derivatives as *leftist, leftism,* and the like, did not come into general use until after the Russian Revolution (c. 1920).

Legalist School. Chinese political philosophy of the 4th and 3d centuries B.C. Largely based on the teachings of the HAN FEI TZU, it called for harsh and expedient means for gaining political and military control. Its teachings were adopted during the Ch'in Dynasty.

Le Gallienne, Eva (1899–   ). English-born American actress, director, and producer. The daughter of the English writer Richard Le Gallienne, she founded (1926), directed, and acted in the Civic Repertory Theater in New York, and was cofounder of the American Repertory Theatre (1946). She is noted for her continuing interest in repertory theater in the U.S. In addition, she has translated many of Ibsen's plays and has written an autobiography *At 33* (1934), continued in *With a Quiet Heart* (1953).

Legenda Aurea. See GOLDEN LEGEND.

Legend of Good Women, The (c. 1386). Unfinished poem by Geoffrey CHAUCER, of over 2700 lines in decasyllabic couplets. In the prologue, which contains the best poetry, the poet describes his delight at wandering through the meadows on a May morning, especially celebrating the daisy. He falls asleep and dreams that the god of Love, attended by Queen Alceste, appears and berates him for having translated the *Romance of the Rose* and written *Troilus and Criseyde,* thereby discouraging men from the service of COURTLY LOVE. Alceste intercedes, pointing out Chaucer's exaltation of love in other works, and suggests that he be allowed to redeem himself by writing a collection of 20 lives of women who have served Love truly and well. There follow nine short narratives, modeled on stories by Vergil and Ovid, about women who suffered or died because they were faithful in love and (except for the first two stories) because men were treacherous: Cleopatra; Thisbe; Dido; Hypsipyle and Medea, both betrayed by Jason; Lucrece; Ariadne; Philomela; Phyllis, betrayed by Demophon; Hypermnestra.

Legend of Montrose, The (1819). A novel by Sir Walter SCOTT, dealing with the struggle between the Royalists and the Parliamentarians in the time of Charles I. Interwoven with this are the amorous quandaries of the heroine, Annot Lyle.

Legend of Sleepy Hollow, The (1819). A tale by Washington IRVING, collected in his SKETCH BOOK OF GEOFFREY CRAYON, GENT. The story takes place at Sleepy Hollow, now Tarrytown, N.Y. ICHABOD CRANE, the local schoolmaster, courts Katrina Van Tassel. The affair is interrupted when Crane's rival, Brom Bones, masquerades as a headless horseman, and scares the schoolmaster out of town.

Legends of the Alhambra, The (1832; enlarged, 1852). A group of tales and sketches on Spanish subjects by Washington IRVING. The book grew out of Irving's sojourn in Spain as a member of the U.S. Embassy, in 1826. The legends deal with the clashes between Spaniard and Moor. Irving, an admirer of Moorish civilization, invests the tales with glamour and mystery.

Léger, Aléxis St.-Léger. See St.-John PERSE.

Léger, Fernand (1881–1955). French artist whose paintings, murals, tapestries, mosaics and stained glass windows exercised a profound influence upon his time. In 1917 he began to construct his compositions from mechanical elements such as radiators, railway wheels, or cogs; human figures were themselves treated as machines. Léger's art gradually became more human, achieving a liveliness, and gaiety, while retaining its monumental quality. His construction workers, mechanics, divers, or picnickers were constructed in bright flat colors increasingly dissociated from his strong and direct drawing but full of movement and power.

Legion of Honor (Légion d'honneur). A French order of distinction and reward instituted by Napoleon Bonaparte in 1802 for either military or civil merit. The order has continued to exist in France during the 19th and 20th centuries.

Legree, Simon. The overseer in Harriet Beecher Stowe's UNCLE TOM'S CABIN. He flogs Uncle Tom, causing his death, when the latter refuses to reveal the hiding places of two runaway women slaves. His name has become a synonym for a brutal taskmaster.

Lehár, Franz (1870–1948). Hungarian composer of operettas. He wrote THE MERRY WIDOW; *The Count of Luxemburg* (1909); and others.

Lehmann, John (1907–   ). English editor, brother of Rosamond Lehmann. He edited the influential left-wing magazine *New Writing* and its successor from 1936 to 1950 (publishing the work of Auden and other left-wing poets), and edited *The London Magazine* from 1954. His autobiographies are *The Whispering Gallery* (1955) and *I Am My Brother* (1960).

Lehmann, Lotte (1888–   ). German-born concert and operatic soprano. She is especially famed for her interpretation of German lieder. She wrote a novel, *Orplied mein Land* (1937; translated, *Eternal Flight,* 1938), and two autobiographies: *Anfang und Aufstieg* (1937; translated, *Midway in My Song,* 1938) and *My Many Lives* (1948).

Lehmann, Rosamond (1903–   ). English novelist. She is the daughter of L. C. Lehmann, long on the staff of *Punch,* and sister of John Lehmann and of Beatrix Lehmann, an actress. *Dusty Answer* (1927) is about the emotions of a young girl growing up, especially during her years at college. *Invitation to the Waltz* (1932) describes the experiences of a girl at her first elegant party. *The Ballad and the Source* (1945) is an experimental novel in which the most violent events that afflict three generations of a tragically doomed family are narrated by a 14-year-old girl in the order in which she hears about them. She also wrote *A Note in Music* (1930), and *The Echoing Grove* (1953). A writer of grace and sensibility, her work may be compared with that of Virginia Woolf and Elizabeth Bowen.

Leibniz or **Leibnitz, Gottfried Wilhelm** (1646–1716). German philosopher. A major figure in the German enlightenment, he believed in a pre-established harmony, created by God, of matter and spirit. His statement that "this is the best of all possible worlds" was ridiculed by Voltaire in CANDIDE for its supposedly irresponsible optimism; actually, however, Leibniz meant his statement in a metaphysical sense and did not intend it to be directly applied to everyday life. In his *Monadologie* (1714), Leibniz maintains that the divine order of the universe is reflected in each of its parts, the smallest unit being the monad. The happiness of man is in striving for harmony with God, the original creator of harmony. Leibniz formulated the calculus in 1676, independently of Newton.

Leicester, earl of. See Robert DUDLEY, earl of Leicester.

Leiden des jungen Werthers, Die. See SORROWS OF YOUNG WERTHER, THE.

Leif Ericson. See Leif ERICSON.

Leigh, Augusta. See Anne Isabella MILBANKE.

Leino, Eino. Pen name of **Armas Eino Leopold Lönnbohm** (1879–1926). Finnish poet, playwright, and novelist. Considered the outstanding lyric poet of modern Finland, Leino published many collections of highly subjective verse. In such works as *Ajan Aalloilta* (*The Waves of Time,* 1899) and *Helkavirsia* (*Helga Hymns,* 1903), he gave expression to the feelings of his people and to his own intense emotional life.

Leipzig, battle of. Also called the **battle of the nations** (October 16–18, 1813). A famous battle where the French under Napoleon Bonaparte were badly defeated by the allied forces of Prussia, Austria, Sweden, and Russia.

Leir, King. A central figure in a tale in the HISTORY OF THE KINGS OF BRITAIN by Geoffrey of Monmouth. His story is much the same as that found in Shakespeare's great tragedy KING LEAR: Leir divides his kingdom among his three daughters; he rejects Cordelia, and is subsequently rejected by Goneril and Regan. In this tale, however, the king goes to France to enlist the aid of Cordelia, reconquers Britain, and, when he dies, is buried under the river Soar. For his tragedy, Shakespeare seems to have made use of the version of Leir's story found in Holinshed's *Chronicles.*

leitmotiv or **leitmotif** (*Ger.,* "leading motive"). In the Wagnerian music drama, a theme consistently reappearing with the reappearance of a given character, problem, emotion, or thought. The term has also been applied to a corresponding device in literature. Thomas Mann has used the leitmotiv technique in conscious emulation of Wagner. For instance, in *The Magic Mountain,* each appearance of Settembrini is accompanied by the same brief description of his clothes.

Leland, Charles Godfrey. See Hans BREITMANN.

Lélia (1833). A novel by George SAND. The highly romantic tale describes the tragically misdirected feelings of love that motivate the various characters. These include Lélia, the lovely heroine; her sister Pulchérie, a prostitute; Sténio, an idealistic young poet; and Magnus, a priest who becomes insane.

Lely, Sir Peter. Originally **Pieter Van der Faes** (1618–1680). Dutch-born English portrait painter. He migrated to England in 1641, where his studio became a school that introduced Dutch technique to the artistically isolated English.

Lemaître, [François Elie] Jules (1853–1914). French writer and critic. Lemaître served as drama critic for the *Journal des Débats* and was noted for his lively impressionistic articles, refreshing for the spontaneity of their reactions. His essays and reviews were published in the 7-volume series *Contemporains* (1855–1899), the 8th volume appearing posthumously in 1918, and in his 10-volume *Impressions de Théâtre* (1888–1898) whose 11th volume also appeared posthumously (1920).

Lemnos. The island where Hephaestus fell when Zeus flung him out of heaven. One myth connected with Lemnos tells how the women of the island, in revenge for their ill-treatment, murdered all the men. The Argonauts found the place an "Adamless Eden." They were received with great favor by the women; as a result of their few months' stay the island was repopulated, and the queen, Hypsipyle, became the mother of twins by Jason.

Lemon, Mark (1809–1870). English playwright, editor. Author of some 60 plays, numerous novels, essays, and children's books, Lemon is remembered as one of the founders and first editor (1841–1870), of *Punch*, the English magazine of humor and satire, whose tone and popularity he did much to establish.

Le Morte d'Arthur. See MORTE D'ARTHUR, LE.

Lemoyne, Jean Baptiste. See Sieur de BIEN-VILLE.

Lemprière, John (1765–1824). English classical scholar who compiled the reference work *Bibliotheca Classica, or Classical Dictionary* (1788), dealing with classical history and mythology.

lemures. The name given by the Romans to the spirits of the dead, especially specters which wandered about at nighttime to terrify men.

Lemuria. The name given to a lost land that supposedly connected Madagascar with India and Sumatra in prehistoric times.

Lenau, Nikolaus. Name at birth: **Edler von Strehlenau Niembsch** (1802–1850). Hungarian-born Austrian poet. His lyrics are marked by a striking exactness of imagery and an occasionally morbid personal intensity that reflects the instability of his temperament. He wrote two religious epics pleading for tolerance, *Savonarola* (1837) and *Die Albigenser* (*The Albigensians*, 1842), and an epic-dramatic *Faust* (1836). In 1832 he came to the U.S., hoping to begin a new, idyllic existence, but returned disappointed to Germany in 1833, and in 1844 he went mad. See Ferdinand KÜRNBERGER.

Lenclos, Anne. Known as **Ninon de Lenclos** (1620–1705). French lady of fashion. Famous for her wit and beauty, she conducted a dazzling salon and numbered among her lovers the most distinguished men of the day. In the novel *Clélie*, her friend Madeleine de Scudéry drew a portrait of her under the name Clarisse.

Lenin, Nikolai. Pseudonym of **Vladimir Ilyich Ulyanov** (1870–1924). Russian Communist leader. Lenin, who led the BOLSHEVIKS to power in 1917, was born in Simbirsk (now called Ulyanovsk in his honor), the son of a provincial schoolmaster. His elder brother Alexander was executed in 1887 for an attempt on the life of Czar ALEXANDER III. Lenin, who studied at the universities of Kazan and St. Petersburg where he became a profound student of Marxism, entered revolutionary activity in the 1890's. Much of his time was spent in Siberian exile or abroad. In 1903 he became a leader of the Bolshevik faction of the Social Democratic Party, having been largely responsible for the schism that split the party, the other faction being known as the Mensheviks. Lenin's drive and astuteness as a practical revolutionary led the Bolsheviks to power in the *coup d'état* of October (November by the Western calendar) of 1917. He became the head of the Soviet state and retained the post until his death. Like his colleague Trotsky, Lenin had a background of bourgeois culture and apparently was little interested in the manipulation of cultural life of the kind that took place in the Soviet Union under Stalin. His giant mausoleum in Red Square, Moscow, is a national shrine to the Russians.

Lennox. In Shakespeare's MACBETH, a Scottish noble. He informs Macbeth of Macduff's flight to England.

Lenore (1774). A ballad in folk style by Gottfried August BÜRGER, in which a soldier appears after death to his sweetheart and carries her with him on horseback to the graveyard where a macabre marriage is celebrated by departed spirits.

Lenormand, Henri René (1882–1951). French dramatist. His plays, influenced by Freudian theory, show the psychological conflicts of men at the mercy of the forces of nature. *Time is a Dream* (*Le Temps est un songe;* 1919), *Failures* (*Les Ratés;* 1920), *The Dream Doctor* (*Le Mangeur de rêves;* 1922) and *Man and His Phantoms* (*L'Homme et ses fantômes;* 1924) are among his better known works.

Lenz, Jakob Michael Reinhold (1751–1792). German dramatist of the STURM UND DRANG, admirer of Goethe. His plays, which are distinguished by a revolutionary realism and looseness of form, include *Der neue Menoza* (*The New Menoza*, 1774) and *Die Soldaten* (*The Soldiers,* 1776).

Leo X, Pope. See MEDICI.

Leo XIII. Original name: **Gioacchino Pecci** (1810–1903). Pope (1878–1903), and Italian poet. His encyclical *Rerum Novarum* (1891), urging reform in favor of the working classes, is significant for its liberal approach. He wrote poetry in Italian and Latin and in 1832 was admitted to the ARCADIAN ACADEMY, whose bicentenary (1890) he later celebrated in a long poem praising Metastasio, Parini, and Alfieri. Also noted is his ode written on New Year's Eve, 1900, in which he calls for spiritual renewal and the avoidance of war in the coming century.

Leodegraunce, King. See ROUND TABLE.

León [y Román], Ricardo (1877–1943). Spanish novelist. His works of popular fiction include *Casta de hidalgos* (*A Son of the Hidalgos,* 1908), a descriptive narrative, and *El amor de los amores* (*The Wisdom of Sorrow*, 1910), a study in mysticism.

Leonard, William Ellery (1876–1944). American poet and educator. He is best known for the sonnet sequence, *Two Lives* (1925), which forms an autobiographical account of Leonard and his first wife. He also published several volumes of verse, including *A Man Against Time* (1945), *The Vaunt of Man and Other Poems* (1912), and *The Lynching Bee and Other Poems* (1920). *The Locomotive God* (1927) is his autobiography. A student of Lucretius, Leonard translated his poems (1916), wrote a study of his life and poetry (1942), and helped edit the Latin text.

Leonardo da Vinci (1452–1519). Italian painter, sculptor, architect, engineer, scientist, poet, and musician. A universal genius and one of the greatest intellects in the history of mankind, Leonardo was born at Vinci, near Florence, and became in 1466 an apprentice to VERROCCHIO. The latter's *Baptism of Christ* contains an angel and landscape features probably executed by his pupil, who was already his superior. In 1482, he went to Milan where he worked for Lodovico Sforza as an engineer as well as a designer of costumes and scenery for court entertainments. He also made sketches for churches, painted the murals and ceiling pictures of the Sforza castle, and worked on problems of irrigation and central

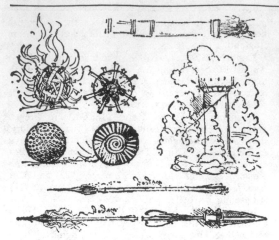

Leonardo da Vinci: sketches for war machines.

heating. In 1502, he served for a time as military engineer to Caesar Borgia. An offer from the French king, Francis I, took him to France in 1516, where he stayed until his death. Misfortune and Leonardo's own habit of endlessly experimenting with pigments have left few of his paintings to posterity. The best known are *The Adoration of the Magi* in the Uffizi; *The Madonna in the Grotto* (c. 1495) and *Mona Lisa* (also called LA GIOCONDA, 1503), both in the Louvre; and the LAST SUPPER (1495–?1498) in the Milan church of S. Maria delle Grazie. *The Battle of Anghiari*, done in 1505 at Florence in competition with Michelangelo, survives only in drafts. His style in painting is characterized by the use of *sfumato,* or blurring of outlines. the mysterious effects of chiaroscuro, the clarity of composition, and the over-all tone of serenity. In sculpture, only sketches remain of the destroyed equestrian statue of Francesco Sforza and of the unfinished one of the *condottiere* Trivulzio. He left no architectural works, but his sketches for buildings and even whole cities were influential for his contemporaries. As engineer and scientist, Leonardo was led by his avid curiosity to speculate about and experiment with various mechanical devices, including guns and cannon, flying machines, parachutes, hydraulic works, submarines, and spiral staircases. In his notebooks, there are some 5,000 pages of sketches and comments that reveal his concern with anatomy, botany, and mathematics, including mechanical perspective drawings, studies of people and animals, caricatures, plant studies and landscapes. He left also a treatise on painting, *Trattato della pittura* (1489–1518), which has been extracted from the notebooks. Here he espoused again his favorite motif: fidelity to nature, which must be observed directly, not through abstractions or Aristotle or Galen. It was this attention to things themselves which produced the paradox of Leonardo's life, for he accomplished hardly a fraction of his schemes, so overwhelmed was he by the need to investigate and know everything. But even his most tentative ideas and experiments were years ahead of his time and simply beyond the capacities of his contemporaries.

Leonato. In Shakespeare's MUCH ADO ABOUT NOTHING, the governor of Messina, father of Hero and uncle of Beatrice. He joins with Don Pedro in bringing Beatrice and Benedick together and later forgives Claudio for having doubted Hero's virtue.

Leoncavallo, Ruggiero (1858–1919). Italian operatic composer and librettist. He is best known for *I Pagliacci* (1892).

Leone. In the ORLANDO FURIOSO of Ariosto, a Greek prince, and prospective husband of Bradamante. His rival, Ruggiero, wins Bradamante by defeating her in a duel, but he is wearing Leone's armor! Finally, Leone gives up to Ruggiero his right to wed Bradamante.

Leonidas. A Spartan king and hero (fl. early 5th century B.C.). He resisted the Persians at Thermopylae with only three hundred Spartans and was slain with all his forces at the pass.

Leonov, Leonid Maksimovich (1899–   ). Russian novelist, dramatist, and short-story writer. Leonov fought with the Red Army during the civil war. He published some short stories during the early 1920's, but first attracted attention in 1924 with a long story, *The End of a Petty Man* (*Konetz melkogo cheloveka*). The story, dealing with the acceptance of the revolution by a member of the old generation, foreshadowed a theme Leonov and others were to take up often in later works. Leonov's first novel, *The Badgers* (*Barsuki*; 1925), dealt with the conflict between the city and countryside during the civil war. The conflict is personified in two brothers, one of whom leaves the village for the city and eventually comes back at the head of an armed force sent to quell a revolt led by his brother. Leonov's second novel, considered by some critics as his best work, is THE THIEF, which is set in the period of the New Economic Policy in Russia.

Leonov's other novels are *Soviet River* (*Sot;* 1930), *Skutarevski* (1932), *Road to the Ocean* (*Doroga na okean;* 1935), and *Russian Forest* (*Russki les;* 1953). His best-known plays include *The Orchards of Polovchansk* (*Polovchanskiye sady;* 1936), *Nashestviye* (*Invasion;* 1942), and *Lyonushka* (1943). One of his best wartime works was the short novel *The Taking of Velikoshumsk* (*Vzyatiye velikoshumska,* 1944), describing a Red Army offensive in the Ukraine.

Leonov is noted as one of the foremost stylists of Soviet prose. His rich and exuberant language and his predilection for complex intrigues in his stories have caused critics to cite him as a follower of Dostoevski, although this influence is only plainly evident in his novel *The Thief.*

Leontes. In Shakespeare's WINTER'S TALE, the king of Sicilia, husband of Hermione and father of Perdita. Consumed with blind, unreasoning jealousy, he accuses his wife of adultery and tries to poison his friend Polixenes. When he finally realizes his folly, he is stricken with remorse.

Leopard, The (*Il Gattopardo,* 1956). An historical novel by Giuseppe Tomasi, prince of Lampedusa (1896–1957), Sicilian novelist. It describes the impact of Garibaldi's invasion of Sicily and the subsequent unification of Italy on a proud, aristocratic Sicilian family devoted to the Bourbon kings. The novel is celebrated for its refined, poetic style.

Leopardi, Count **Giacomo** (1798–1837). Italian poet. A self-taught prodigy, afflicted by physical deformity and spinal disease, he distinguished himself at an early age with the lyrical beauty and intense melancholy of his poetry. All his writings express belief in a cosmic nature that is unalterably hostile to man and the chief obstacle to human happiness. This pessimism provides the connective motif in the various collections of his verse: *Canzoni* (1824), *Versi* (1826), and *Canti* (1836). It is treated philosophically in the brief dialogue-essays *Le Operette Morali* (1824) and the miscellany of aphorisms *Pensieri* (1834–1837).

Leopardi described himself as an ardent patriot and a confirmed classicist, but he revealed romantic tendencies in asserting that imagination rather than reason is the true source of poetic inspiration.

Lepanto, battle of (Oct. 7, 1571). A naval engagement in the gulf of Corinth, fought between the forces of the Ottoman Empire and those of a Holy League comprising Spain, Venice, and the papacy. Under the leadership of Don John of Austria, the Christians overwhelmingly defeated the Turks, ending their naval domination of the Mediterranean. Cervantes took part in the battle and was wounded in the left hand.

Lepidus, Marcus Aemilius (d. 13 b.c.). A member, with Octavius and Mark Antony, of the Second Triumvirate (43–33 b.c.). He was forced by Octavius into retirement.

Leporello. In Mozart's opera Don Giovanni, the valet of Don Giovanni.

leprechaun. An elflike creature in Irish folklore, often associated with shoemaking and the guarding of hidden treasure. He is usually characterized by small stature, supernatural qualities, and a puckish sense of humor. Modern treatment of the leprechaun may be found in James Stephens' fantasy *The Crock of Gold* (1912) and in William Butler Yeats's *Fairy and Folk Tales* (1888).

Lermontov, Mikhail Yurievich (1814–1841). Russian poet and novelist. In his work and his life he was the outstanding example of the influence of Byronic romanticism on Russian literature. His reputation as a poet in the 19th century was exceeded only by Pushkin's. Many of Lermontov's works are set in the Caucasus, where he was exiled for a poem denouncing court circles after Pushkin's death. He returned to St. Petersburg later, was exiled again for dueling, and was killed in a duel in the Caucasus. A few months before, he had described a death similar to his own in a short poem *Son* (*A Dream*). His most famous poems are *Angel, Demon, Mtsyri* (*The Novice*), and *Zaveshchaniye* (*The Testament*). Lermontov's only completed novel, A Hero of Our Time, was important in the development of the Russian novel, marking a transition from the earlier form of a cycle of stories to the traditional novel form of the later 19th century. It consists of five stories, centering around the romantic hero Pechorin, which are presented out of their chronological sequence for purposes of suspense and retardation of the narrative, just as later novelists were to do. Lermontov's psychological analysis of the hero and realistic treatment of the secondary characters, also, anticipate the work of the great 19th-century Russian realists.

Lernean hydra. See Hydra.

Lesage or **Le Sage, Alain René** (1668–1747). French novelist and dramatist. His early works are translations of Spanish authors, such as Rojas, Lope de Vega, Calderón, and others; these works caused no comment. His first original work, *Crispin, rival de son maître* (1707), a comedy, made him a repu-

tation. It was soon followed by the novel *Le Diable boiteux* (1709), an imitation and enlargement of Luis Vélez de Guevara's *El Diablo cojuelo* (1641). Asmodeus, as this novel is sometimes called in English translation, is an unrelated series of satirical tableaux, more descriptive than moralistic, of life in 18th-century France. His next play *Turcaret, ou le Financier* (1708) is a bitter satire on money and financiers, and caused a great scandal. After this comedy, Lesage wrote some 100 farces or comedies of manners, often interspersed with popular airs, for the Théâtre de la Foire. His masterpiece, *Histoire de Gil Blas de Santillane* (definitive ed. 1747), is considered by some critics to be the first novel of manners. Lesage wrote three other picaresque novels, *Don Guzman d'Alfarache* (1732), *Estevanille Gonzalès* (1734), and Le Bachelier de Salamanque (1736), and some inferior minor works of fiction. Celebrated for his animated style, and for his vivid and dramatic presentation of human foibles and absurdities, he had a marked influence on Fielding, Smollett, and Sterne, the English novelists.

Lesbian. Pertaining to Lesbos, one of the islands of the Greek Archipelago. It pertains also to Sappho, the famous poetess of Lesbos, and to the practices of female homosexuality (Lesbianism) attributed to her.

Lesbino. In the Gerusalemme Liberata of Tasso, the youthful page of Solimano, the leader of the Arab forces pitted against the Crusaders. The lad is killed by the knight Argillano, whom the bereaved Solimano then kills in revenge.

Lescaut, Manon. See Manon Lescaut.

Leskov, Nikolai Semionovich (1831–1895). Russian novelist and short-story writer. Leskov, whose parents died when he was 17, supported himself as a civil servant, estate manager, and journalist in various provincial towns, until at the age of 30, he became a journalist in St. Petersburg. His first large literary work, the novel *Nekuda* (*No Way Out*, 1864), won little critical acclaim. The radical critics held sway over literature at the time and Leskov had displeased the radicals with some of his journalistic articles. His next novel, *Na Nozhakh* (*At Daggers Drawn*, 1870–1871), depicted young radicals in a manner that enraged the radical camp still more. Leskov was disinclined to placate the critics, even though their influence was able to delay his recognition as a major writer. He eventually attained this recognition with the general reading public for the humor and raciness of his stories and for his remarkable prose, which is full of puns, colloquial expressions, folk etymologies, and neologisms. Many of his most popular stories are set in the milieu of the clergy and Old Believers, which Leskov had had ample time to observe during his early years in the provinces. Leskov was one of the early masters of the narrative technique termed *skaz* by Russian critics: the re-creation in prose of indigenous oral narration, by reproducing the speech mannerisms, cadence, and vocabulary of a fictional narrator. Leskov often placed the *skaz* narration in the framework of the story by having the recorder of the story meet a character who relates the tale in his own words.

Leskov's most popular works include the novel *Soboryane* (*Cathedral Folk*, 1872), and the tales *Zapechatlionni angel* (*The Sealed Angel*, 1873), *Ocharovanni strannik* (*The Enchanted Wanderer,*

1874), *Melochi arkhiyereiskoi zhizni* (*Details of Episcopal Life*, 1880), and *Skaz o tul'skom kosom levshe i o stal'noi blokhe* (*The Left-handed Smith of Tula and the Steel Flea*, 1882).

Les Misérables. See MISÉRABLES, LES.

Lespinasse, Julie Jeanne Eléonore de (1732–1776). French letter-writer. She was the companion and protégée, from 1754 to 1763, of the blind Mme du DEFFAND. Together, they conducted for a time a sparkling literary salon; later, her own salon became a center for the *Encyclopédistes* (see ENCYCLOPÉDIE). She was a friend of d'Alembert, the marquis de Mora, and the comte de Guibert. To this latter are addressed her passionate love letters, *Lettres de Mlle de Lespinasse*, with their constant theme, *Je ne fais qu'aimer, je ne sais qu'aimer* (Fr., "I do nothing but love, I can do nothing but love"). The letters were published by Guibert's widow in 1809.

Lesseps, Vicomte Ferdinand Marie de (1805–1894). French diplomat and engineer. The original conceiver of the Suez Canal, de Lesseps received a concession from Said Pasha, viceroy of Egypt in 1854. He completed the canal in 10 years (1859–1869). De Lesseps was also, unfortunately, president of a French company that began work on cutting through the isthmus of Panama (1881–1888). The scheme collapsed and de Lesseps was condemned for misappropriation of funds, although his sentence was never carried out.

Lessing, Doris [May] (1919–   ). English novelist, short-story writer, and essayist, born and for many years resident in Southern Rhodesia. Her intense commitment to socialism and to other causes is reflected in her work. She began a series of novels about *Martha Quest* in 1952. *The Grass is Singing* (1950) and *This Was the Old Chief's Country* (1951) are set in Africa. *In Pursuit of the English* (1960) is a sociological essay. *The Golden Notebook* (1962) is an ambitious experimental novel about a modern "liberated" woman.

Lessing, Gotthold Ephraim (1729–1781). German dramatist, aesthetician, and critic, a strong advocate of religious tolerance. His thought has roots in the enlightenment but is not cramped by a too strict rationalism. Perhaps more than any other, he was responsible for the emergence of German drama as a significant contribution to world theater; in his critical work *Hamburgische Dramaturgie* (*Hamburg Dramaturgy*, 1767–1768), he attacked the formalism of neo-classicism and called for a drama in which the form springs from the dramatist's vision of life. Among his more general works on aesthetics are the *Briefe, die neueste Literatur betreffend* (*Letters, Concerning the Most Recent Literature*, a periodical with Christoph Nicolai, 1759–1765), which includes a Faust fragment and a classic attack on Johann Gottsched; LAOCOÖN, OR ON THE LIMITS OF PAINTING AND POETRY; and *Wie die Alten den Tod gebildet* (*How the Ancients Represented Death*, 1769). Late in his life, he wrote a number of tracts on theological subjects, the best known of which is *Erziehung des Menschengeschlechts* (*Education of the Human Race*, 1780). His most famous dramas are *Miss Sara Sampson* (1755), MINNA VON BARNHELM, EMILIA GALOTTI, and NATHAN THE WISE.

Les Six. A group of French composers: Darius MILHAUD, Arthur HONEGGER, Francis POULENC, Georges Auric (1899–   ), Louis Durey (1888–   ), and Germaine Tailleferre (1892–   ). A music critic coined this soubriquet in comparing these composers with "THE FIVE" Russians. Although they joined Erik SATIE, their mentor, and Jean COCTEAU, their spokesman, in decrying the pretentiousness of Romanticism and admiring the directness of popular music, they seldom met, and developed different musical styles. They collaborated without Durey on Cocteau's ballet *Les Mariés de la Tour Eiffel* (1921).

L'Estrange, Sir Roger (1616–1704). English journalist, political pamphleteer, and translator. In 1663 he became surveyor of printing presses and licenser of the press and established *The Public Intelligencer* and *The News*, both of which ceased publication in 1666. He later edited the *Observator*, in which he attacked the Whigs. His best-known translation is *The Fables of Aesop* (1692).

Lethe (Gr. *letho, latheo, lanthano,* to cause persons not to know). In Greek mythology, one of the rivers of Hades. The souls of all the dead are obliged to taste its water, that they may forget everything said and done when alive. See STYX.

Leto. In Greek mythology, a daughter of the Titans Coeus and Phoebe and mother by Zeus of Apollo and Artemis.

Leto, Pomponio (1428–1498). Italian scholar. He was prominent during the Renaissance as the leader of a group of Humanists and men of letters who formed one of the first modern academies at Rome.

Letter, The. See CASUARINA TREE, THE.

Letters from an American Farmer (1782). A group of essays by CRÈVECŒUR, under the pseudonym of J. Hector St. John. They deal with farm life on the American frontier in the 18th century, sometimes idealizing it in the tradition of Jean Jacques Rousseau, yet depicting realistically the hard unpleasant facts of the social life and customs in the American colonies. Crèvecœur sees America as a refuge for the persecuted and oppressed peoples of the world.

Letters of Unknown Men. See EPISTOLAE OBSCURORUM VIRORUM.

Letters on the Study of History (1752). A political and philosophical treatise by Henry ST. JOHN, Viscount Bolingbroke, setting forth the concept that "history is philosophy teaching by examples." St. John proclaims a new Tory position which, in effect, is no different from the Whig doctrines of the Revolution of 1688.

Lettres de Mon Moulin (Letters from My Windmill, 1866). A collection of short stories by Alphonse DAUDET depicting country life in Provence with skill and sympathy.

Lettres provinciales. See Blaise PASCAL.

Leucadia's Rock. A promontory, the south extremity of the island Leucas or Leucadia in the Ionian Sea. According to legend, SAPPHO leapt from this rock when she found her love for Phaon unrequited. At the annual festival of Apollo, a criminal was hurled from Leucadia's Rock into the sea; but birds of various sorts were attached to him in order to break his fall, and if he was not killed, he was set free.

Leucippus (Leukippos; fl. 450 B.C.). A Greek philosopher. His atomist theory held that all matter is composed of an irreducible and unchanging set of atoms. Always in motion, the atoms circulate in a void, and link to form an unlimited number of worlds. See DEMOCRITUS.

Leucothea (Leukothea). See INO.

Leute von Seldwyla, Die (The People of Seldwyla; vol. 1, 1856; vol. 2, 1874). A collection of humorous novellas by Gottfried KELLER, all set in the fictional Swiss town of Seldwyla. The two best-known ones are *Kleider machen Leute* (*Clothes Make the Man*), about a man who is taken for a Polish nobleman and, with an eye to his personal advantage, continues the pose, and *Spiegel, das Kätzchen* (lit., Spiegel, the Little Cat, trans. as *The Fat of the Cat*), about a down-and-out cat who sells his cat-fat to a magician without fully realizing that in order to relinquish his fat, he must be killed.

Leutnant Gustl (1901). A short novel by Arthur SCHNITZLER. An early experiment in the technique of stream-of-consciousness, this story probes deeply into the mind of a young officer whose traditionally based values are put to a severe test by the prospect of a duel.

Levana (from Lat., *levare*, "to raise up"). In Roman mythology the goddess who watched over newborn infants. It was in her name that the father accepted the infant as his legitimate offspring; he did this by the ritual of lifting the child from the ground and raising it aloft. In *Suspiria de Profundis* (1845), Thomas De Quincey writes of an opium dream in which he beheld the goddess.

Levelers or **Levellers.** In English history, a group of ultrarepublicans during the Civil War, who wanted to give all men the right to vote and to end class distinctions. John LILBURNE was one of the leaders of the sect, which was active from 1647 to 1649, when it was suppressed by Cromwell's troops.

In Irish history, an illegal association of 18th-century agrarian agitators, also called WHITEBOYS.

Lever, Charles James (1806–1872). Irish novelist. His early novels, reminiscent of student and military life, are his best, and include THE CONFESSIONS OF HARRY LORRIQUER, *Charles O'Malley* (1841), and *Tom Burke of Ours* (1843). These books are highly anecdotal, notable for their swift and witty narrative and comic secondary characters. In his day, Lever was an extremely popular writer.

Leverkühn, Adrian. The hero of Thomas Mann's novel DOKTOR FAUSTUS. He is a contemporary composer, and in several places Mann has used actual music of Arnold Schoenberg to describe the fictional works of his protagonist. In order to achieve a breakthrough into the most sublime realms of art, Leverkühn, like the legendary FAUST, makes a pact with the powers of evil. Like Faust, he himself is utterly destroyed by the forces he has set in motion, but the magnificence of his music remains as a monument. The name *Leverkühn* suggests "one who lives boldly."

Leverrier, Urbain Jean Joseph (1811–1877). French astronomer. Leverrier determined mathematically, on the basis of previously observed irregularities in the motion of the planet Uranus, the existence and exact position of another planet. Galle, a German astronomer, discovered the planet (1846) and named it Neptune. The same discovery was made independently by the English astronomer J. C. Adams.

Leverson, Ada (1865–1936). English novelist. She is well known for her literary friendships; she befriended Oscar Wilde during his trial. Her urbane, witty novels are in the manner of Wilde; *The Limit* (1911) is a typical work.

Levertov, Denise (1923–   ). English-born American poet. Of Welsh and Jewish parentage, Miss Levertov married an American and came with him to the U.S. in 1948. Recognized as one of the most accomplished of the younger poets, she shows the influence of William Carlos Williams and Wallace Stevens and writes poetry that is lyrical, graceful, and of colloquial simplicity. Her collections include *Overland to the Islands* (1958), *With Eyes at the Back of Our Heads* (1959), and *The Jacob's Ladder* (1961).

Levi (1). In the Old Testament, one of the sons of the patriarch Jacob. The tribe of his descendants are known as Levites, the priestly tribe of the Israelites (Deut. 21:5).

(2) In the New Testament, a name for Matthew.

Levi, Carlo (1902–   ). Italian writer. He is especially noted for his book CHRIST STOPPED AT EBOLI. Other books include *Le Parole Sono Pietre* (1955), a study of Sicily, and *Il Futuro Ha Un Cuore Antico* (1956), a study of Soviet Russia. His novel *The Watch* (*L'Orologio;* 1950) is set in the turbulent period following World War II. *La Doppia Notte dei Tigli* (tr. 1962 as *The Linden Trees*) records his impressions of a visit to Germany, a nation split both by artificial borders and its sense of guilt for the past while enjoying prosperity.

leviathan. A word from the Hebrew, meaning literally "that which gathers itself together in folds," and given in the Bible to a mythical sea serpent (Job 41:1; Isa. 27:1; Ps. 104:26). The name is also applied to the whale and the crocodile, and by extension it has come to mean something vast and formidable of its kind.

Leviathan, or the Matter, Form, and Power of a Commonwealth, Ecclesiastical and Civil (1651). A treatise on the origin and ends of government by Thomas HOBBES. This work, a defense of secular monarchy, written while the Puritan Commonwealth ruled England, contains Hobbes's famous theory of the sovereign state.

Hobbes, following the trend of his time, tended to regard politics as a branch of physical science, a kind of social physics. Comparing the motion of physical bodies to human behavior, he argued that just as physical things, when left to themselves, pursued their own direction, so individuals, when uncontrolled, naturally followed their own direction, their private self-interest. Thus, in his view, the first principle of human behavior was egoism, or self-interest, and it was this egoism that was the root of all social conflict. He believed that social peace could only be achieved within a stable government which had an absolute authority over its subjects and its institutions. Since the attainment of all desirable social ends was hindered by the "war of all against all," it was necessary that men agree among themselves, upon the basis of a social contract, to accept a common and absolute power that would protect them from themselves and from each other, keep the peace, and allow thereby a moderate satisfaction of human desires.

Levin, Konstantin. See ANNA KARENINA.

Levin, Meyer (1905–   ). American journalist and writer of fiction. He is known for his studies of American Jewish life, especially in the city of Chicago. His first novel *Reporter* (1929) was based on his own experiences as a Chicago newspaperman. *The Golden Mountain* (1932) contains stories of the Chassidim, a remarkable sect of medieval Jewish mystics. *The Old Bunch* (1937) is a novel about 11 boys and 8 girls of Jewish parentage, all graduating from the same Chicago high school in 1921. More recent books are *My Father's House* (1947); *Compulsion* (1956), a fictional study of the Leopold-Loeb case; *Eva* (1959), the story of a Jewish girl in flight from the Nazis during World War II, and *The Fanatic* (1964).

Levine, Jack (1915–   ). American painter. He is known for his satirical portraits and mordant social commentaries.

Leviticus. A book of the Old Testament. It was written about 475 B.C. and records the religious and ceremonial law of the Jews in the period after the rebuilding of the temple in 516 B.C. In an effort to give the book greater authority, the author ascribes it to Moses. It is the basic compendium of Jewish law.

Levy, Benn [Wolfe] (1900–   ). English playwright. His works include *Mrs. Moonlight* (1928), *Art and Mrs. Bottle, Springtime for Henry* (1931), and *Topaze* (from the French of Marcel Pagnol).

Lewes, George Henry (1817–1878). English scientific writer and critic. Lewes is better known for his connection with the novelist George ELIOT than for his own work; the two lived together as man and wife from 1854 (Lewes being separated from his first wife), and he discovered and fostered her talent. He was the first editor of the *Fortnightly Review* (1865–1866). His plays and novels were never successful; his works on marine biology, physiology, and psychology (fields in which he did original scientific work) are dated; but his *Biographical History of Philosophy* (1845–1846), *Life of Goethe* (1855), and *Actors and the Art of Acting* (1875) retain some interest.

Lewis, Alun (1915–1944). Welsh poet, killed in World War II. *Ha! Ha! Amongst the Trumpets* (1945) is a posthumous collection of verse.

Lewis, Cecil Day. See Cecil DAY-LEWIS.

Lewis, C[live] S[taples] (1898–1963). English novelist, literary critic, and writer of essays on Christian theological and moral problems. Lewis wrote science fiction in the form of interplanetary fantasies which are really Christian allegories of good and evil: *Out of the Silent Planet* (1938), *Perelandra* (1943), and *That Hideous Strength* (1945). *The Problem of Pain* (1940) and THE SCREWTAPE LETTERS (1942) were widely read works of Christian apologetics. Among his important books of literary criticism are *The Allegory of Love* (1936), a study of the medieval courtly tradition; *Preface to Paradise Lost* (1942); and *An Experiment in Criticism* (1961).

Lewis, D[ominic] B[evan] Wyndham (1894–1969). Welsh-born English humorist, essayist, and biographer. Lewis is perhaps best known as a whimsical, chatty essayist in the manner of Chesterton. His humorous works include *A London Farrago* (1922), *At the Green Goose* (1923), *At the Sign of the Blue Moon* (1924), and *On Straw and Other Conceits* (1927). He also edited with Charles Lee an anthology of bad verse, *The Stuffed Owl* (1930), and conducted a humor column for the London *News Chronicle* under the name Timothy Shy, which he used as co-author with Ronald Searle of *The Terror of St. Trinian's* (1954).

In addition, Lewis has written several scholarly and colorful biographies, including *François Villon* (1928), *King Spider* (1930), *Emperor of the West* (1932; U.S. title, *Charles of Europe*), *Ronsard* (1944), *The Hooded Hawk* (1946; republished as *James Boswell*, 1952), *Doctor Rabelais* (1957), and *Molière: The Comic Mask* (1959). Despite the similarity in names, he is not related to novelist and painter Wyndham Lewis.

Lewis, Matthew Gregory (1775–1818). English novelist and dramatist, author of the famous GOTHIC NOVEL *Ambrosio, or* THE MONK, for which he was known as "Monk Lewis." A lover of poetry, Lewis collaborated with Sir Walter Scott and Robert Southey in a collection of verse, *Tales of Wonder* (1801). Lewis' contributions included some of the earliest translations of the German romantics Goethe and Herder. He was a successful dramatist and a liberal who did his best to alleviate the condition of the slaves on his Jamaica plantation, where he died. See ALONZO THE BRAVE.

Lewis, [Harry] Sinclair (1885–1951). American novelist. Born in Sauk Centre, Minn., Lewis was an awkward, lonely boy, something of a dreamer. After his graduation from Yale in 1908, he spent several years in newspaper and editorial work. His first novel, *Hike and the Aeroplane* (1912), was a story for boys. He achieved moderate success with his early novels, and two of them—*Our Mr. Wrenn: The Romantic Adventures of a Gentle Man* (1914) and *The Job: An American Novel* (1917)—contain hints of the satire and realism that were to be characteristic of his best work.

According to Mark Schorer, Lewis' biographer, the appearance of MAIN STREET in 1920 was "the most sensational event in 20th-century American publishing history." Although there were some howls of outrage, in general both the critics and the public were delighted with Lewis' devastating portrayal of the smugness and provincialism of the American small town, as typified by Gopher Prairie, the novel's mythical locale. Lewis next directed his barbs at the American businessman in BABBITT, in many ways an extension of *Main Street.* In ARROWSMITH, often considered his best work, he attacked the venality and pettiness that impede the search for scientific truth. Although Lewis was awarded a Pulitzer Prize for *Arrowsmith*, he promptly refused to accept it, because the terms of the award state that it is to be given, not for literary merit, but for the best presentation of "the wholesome atmosphere of American Life." Other successes of this period were ELMER GANTRY and DODSWORTH.

Lewis was awarded the Nobel Prize in 1930, the first American to win such an honor. But his work declined in the 1930's, and he tended to make peace with the attitudes he had earlier satirized. *Ann Vickers* (1933) traces the career of a neurotic woman who starts as a social worker and ends as the mistress of a politician. *The Prodigal Parents* (1938) presents rebellious children in an unsympathetic light. Perhaps the most vigorous of Lewis' work in the 30's was

It Can't Happen Here, a warning about the possibility of fascism in the U.S. Among his later novels are *Cass Timberlane* (1945), the story of an older man's love for his young and unsuitable wife; *Kingsblood Royal* (1947), about racial prejudice; and *The God-Seeker* (1949), about a missionary in Minnesota in the 1840's.

There is much disguised biography in Lewis' work, and many suggestions of Lewis himself in his characters. A romancer as well as a realist and satirist, he loved the Babbitts and Main Streets of America even as he deplored them.

Lewis, [Percy] Wyndham (1882–1957). English novelist, essayist, and vorticist painter. A vitriolic satirist, Wyndham Lewis wrote the notable satiric novels Tarr, The Apes of God, and the trilogy The Human Age. His largest output consisted of essays written to express his near-fascist political views and his literary opinions. Trained as an artist, Lewis first attracted attention, before World War I, as the leader of the school of painting known as vorticism. In association with Ezra Pound, he edited the little magazine Blast (1914–1915). With Pound, T. S. Eliot, and James Joyce, he sympathized with a French-inspired movement to reject "romanticism" and return to "classicism." The four were sometimes called "the men of 1914." *Blasting and Bombardiering* (1937) is an autobiography about Lewis' experiences in action in the second half of the war. Lewis' sympathy with fascism came to a peak in the years between the wars; at the outbreak of World War II he emigrated to Canada, describing his experience, in fictional form, in *Self-Condemned* (1954). *Rotting Hill* (1951) is a novel purporting to demonstrate the decay of England under postwar socialism. In 1949 Lewis began to go blind.

Among Lewis' other works are poems (1933); *The Wild Body* (1927), a collection of short stories; the novels *Snooty Baronet* (1932), *The Revenge for Love* (1937), and *The Red Priest* (1956); and the autobiography *Rude Assignment* (1950). Some of his political and literary tracts are *The Art of Being Ruled* (1926), Time and Western Man, *The Lion and the Fox: the role of hero in the plays of Shakespeare* (1927), *Hitler* (1931), *Men Without Art* (1934), and *The Demon of Progress in the Arts* (1954).

In his heyday in the 1920's Wyndham Lewis was thought as original and exciting as James Joyce. Since then he has been neglected.

Lewis and Clark Expedition (1804–1806). An expedition across the U.S. to the Pacific Ocean led by Meriwether Lewis (1774–1809) and William Clark (1770–1838). Starting out from St. Louis in the spring of 1804, the party of 23 soldiers, three interpreters, and one slave ascended the Missouri River, spent the winter among the Mandan Indians of North Dakota, and descended the Columbia River to the Pacific late in 1805. The expedition showed that an overland route to the Pacific was feasible and provided scientific data about the previously unexplored region. *The Original Journals of the Lewis and Clark Expedition* were edited by R. G. Thwaites in 1904–1905. See Sacajawea.

Lewisohn, Ludwig (1883–1955). German-born American editor, teacher, critic, and writer. Lewisohn, who came to America as a boy, became an authority on German literature and translated works of Hauptmann, Rilke, and others. Some of his critical works are *The Modern Drama* (1915), *The Spirit of Modern German Literature* (1916), *The Story of American Literature* (1937), and *Goethe* (2 vols., 1949). He treated the problems of Jews in *The American Jew* (1950) and other volumes. This subject also found its way into his fiction; among his novels are *The Island Within* (1928), *The Last Days of Shylock* (1931), *Anniversary* (1948), and *In a Summer Season* (1955). He also published memoirs in *Up Stream* (1922) and *Mid-Channel: An American Chronicle* (1929).

Lexington. A town in Massachusetts, site of the first engagement of the American Revolution (April 19, 1775). General Gage sent 700 men to destroy the American supply depot at Concord, 21 miles from Boston. At Lexington, 5 miles from Concord, the troops ran into 70 armed minutemen, forewarned by Paul Revere, who forced them to withdraw. Moving on to Concord, the British were turned back at the Concord bridge and shot at from behind walls and trees. They retreated to Boston under fire of gathering swarms of minutemen. Estimates of the casualties vary.

Ley, Robert (1890–1945). German Nazi, noted for his extreme anti-Semitism. As head of the Labor Front (1933–1945), he mobilized German war industry and supervised the slave labor camps. He committed suicide after his capture by the Allies.

Lhasa. The capital of Tibet and sacred city of Tibetan Buddhists. Its chief buildings are monasteries, some of which are 1,200 years old, and the Potala, palace of the Dalai Lama. Prior to Chinese occupation, Lhasa was the goal of religious pilgrims from all over the Himalayan plateau. Not open to Westerners until the British forced entry in 1904, Lhasa is still known as the Forbidden City. In 1959 the Dalai Lama fled to India to escape the Chinese who had assumed control of Tibet in 1951.

L'Hermite, François. Known as **Tristan l'Hermite** (1602–1655). French author and playwright. The popularity of his tragedy *La Mariane* (1636) rivaled that of *Le Cid*, and *La Mort de Sénèque* (*The Death of Seneca*, 1644) is the finest French tragedy on a classical theme outside of Corneille's and Racine's. The comedy *Le Parasite* (1654) introduced to the French stage the stock parasitic figure of Latin comedy, and the autobiographical novel *Le Page Disgracié* (*The Disgraced Page*, 1642–1643) recounts episodes from the author's erratic youth.

L'Hospital or **L'Hôpital, Michel de** (1505–1573). Chancellor of France (1560–1568) and the most celebrated French orator of his century. His speeches urging religious tolerance and justice during the religious wars are notable for their simplicity and honesty. The complete *Œuvres* of L'Hospital were published in 1824–1825.

Liaisons dangereuses, Les (1782). An epistolary novel by Pierre Choderlos de Laclos. The novel deals with the corruption of innocence and virtue by Valmont, a libertine, and his equally vicious and immoral mistress, Mme de Merteuil, for their own amusement. It is essentially a study of the fascination and power of evil, and one is struck by the absence of frivolity and sentimentality in this work;

the battle of the sexes is depicted with utter seriousness and humorlessness. The style is Racinian in its brilliance, lucidity, and precision, diabolical in its impassivity.

Liar, The. See MENTEUR, LE.

Libation-Bearers, The. See House of ATREUS.

Libellus Merlini. See MERLIN.

Liber. An Italian god of wine, later identified with the Greek DIONYSUS, known in Rome as BACCHUS. He and his feminine counterpart, Libera, were honored at the festival of the *Liberalia* on March 17.

liberal arts. In the Middle Ages, the seven branches of learning: grammar, logic, rhetoric, arithmetic, geometry, music, and astronomy. In modern times, the liberal arts include the languages, sciences, philosophy, history, and related subjects. The term is a translation of Latin *artes liberales,* so called because their pursuit was the privilege of the freemen who were called *liberi.* See QUADRIVIUM.

Libertins (Libertines). A sect of French freethinkers and skeptics of the 17th and 18th centuries, precursors of VOLTAIRE and the encyclopedists. Advocates of total freedom of thought and conscience, the *Libertins* questioned the doctrines and morality of all received religion and were continually accused of atheism and immorality. The greatest religious thinkers of the day, including Bossuet and Pascal, denounced their views, and ultimately the *Libertins'* own poor conduct discredited their name.

Liberty, Statue of. A colossal statue, *Liberty Enlightening the World,* which stands on Liberty (formerly Bedloe's) Island, at the entrance to New York harbor. Dedicated in 1886, it was a gift of the French people, and commemorates the alliance between the two nations during the American Revolution. Of bronze, it stands 152 feet high on a pedestal almost 150 feet high, and represents a woman, draped, holding a lighted torch in her upraised hand. It is the work of Frédéric Auguste Bartholdi (1834–1904). On its base is carved a sonnet, *The New Colossus,* by Emma Lazarus, which ends with the lines:

> Give me your tired, your poor,
> Your huddled masses yearning to breathe free,
> The wretched refuse of your teeming shore,
> Send these, the homeless, tempest-tost, to me
> I lift my lamp beside the golden door!

Liberty Bell. The bell in Independence Hall, Philadelphia, which was rung when the Continental Congress adopted the Declaration of Independence. First cast in London (1752) with the inscription, "Proclaim Liberty throughout all the Land unto all the Inhabitants Thereof," it was recast in Philadelphia (1753) with the same legend, and cracked in 1835 when it was tolled for the death of John Marshall.

liberty cap. A symbol of freedom. When a slave was manumitted by the Romans, a small Phrygian cap, usually of red felt, called *pilëus,* was placed on his head; he was termed *libertinus* (a freedman), and his name was registered in the city tribes. When Saturninus, in 100 B.C., possessed himself of the Roman Capitol, he hoisted a similar cap on the top of his spear, to indicate that all slaves who joined his standard should be free; Marius employed the same symbol against Sulla; and, when Caesar was murdered, the conspirators marched forth in a body with a cap elevated on a spear, in token of liberty. In the French Revolution, the cap of liberty (BONNET ROUGE) was adopted by the revolutionists as an emblem of their freedom from royal authority.

Libethra. The place in Greece where the nightingales sing most sweetly. It is there that the Muses buried the fragments of ORPHEUS' body.

Library, The. See APOLLODORUS.

Library of Alexandria. See ALEXANDRIAN LIBRARY.

Libro de buen amor, El. See Juan RUIZ.

Libya. The name given by the Greeks to Africa in general. The Romans used the word sometimes as synonymous with Africa, sometimes for that section on the Mediterranean which included Carthage.

Libya was also a goddess whom the Greeks identified as a daughter of the Egyptian king Epaphos and mother of Belus and Agenor.

Licenciado Vidriera, El. One of the tales in Cervantes' NOVELAS EJEMPLARES. It is really a collection of aphorisms, uttered by a demented law student who believes that he is made of glass but who, like Don Quixote, displays amazing insight and perspicacity.

Lichas. In Greek mythology, the friend of HERACLES who brought him Deianira's fatal tunic. He was thrown into the sea by Heracles.

Li-chi. See BOOK OF RITES.

lictor. In ancient Rome, an officer attending a magistrate. A dictator, for example, had 20 lictors, a consul 12, a praetor 6, and so on. The lictor bore the FASCES as the insignia of his office. He cleared the way, enforced respect for his superior, and arrested offenders and executed condemned criminals.

Liddell, Alice. See Henry George LIDDELL.

Liddell, Henry George (1811–1898). English classical scholar and dean of Christ Church (1855–1891). He is the author, with Robert Scott, of the standard *Greek Lexicon* (1843; last revised 1925). He also wrote a *History of Ancient Rome* (1855). His daughter Alice Liddell was the original Alice, the child for whom Lewis Carroll wrote his famous *Alice's Adventures in Wonderland* and *Through the Looking-Glass.*

Lidia. In the ORLANDO FURIOSO of Ariosto, a princess of Lidia whose spirit is encountered by Astolfo in his journey through Hell. There among those sinners who are being punished for treating their lovers cruelly in life, she tells Astolfo her story, revealing her cruelty to her suitor Alceste.

Lido. A reef and sandbank outside the lagoon of Venice, famous as a fashionable bathing resort on the Adriatic.

Lie, Jonas [Lauritz Idemil] (1833–1909). Norwegian novelist, playwright, and poet. Financial difficulties caused Lie, always fascinated by literature, to begin his professional literary career. In 1870 he published *Den Fremsynte;* both this first novel and later volumes of stories, *Trold* (1891–1892), mingle realistic with fantastic elements. His studies of family life in the middle classes—among them *Lodsen og hans Hustru* (1874), *Familjen paa Gilje* (1883), and *Kommandørens Døtre* (1886)—are his finest work.

Lie, Trygve (1896–1968). Norwegian statesman and secretary-general of the United Nations (1946–1953). Formerly Norwegian minister for foreign affairs (1940; 1941–1945), Lie served in the cabinet as minister of justice (1935–1939) and minister of commerce (1939–1940).

Liebelei. See LIGHT O' LOVE.

Liebknecht, Karl (1871–1919). Socialist leader in the German Reichstag, son of Wilhelm LIEB-KNECHT. As a member of the SPARTACIST PARTY, he opposed the war policies of the government and supported the Russian Bolsheviks. The proletarian revolt that he organized with Rosa Luxemburg in 1919 was suppressed by the provisional government, and he was shot.

Liebknecht, Wilhelm (1826–1900). German socialist and associate of August Bebel. He helped to found the German Social Democratic Party in 1869.

Lied von Bernadette, Das. See SONG OF BERNA-DETTE, THE.

Lien Chi Altangi. Narrator and central figure of Oliver Goldsmith's epistolary novel THE CITIZEN OF THE WORLD, a Chinese who, for all his philosophy, cannot help being surprised by the follies of Goldsmith's England. He also prophesies the successful revolution of the American colonies and the rise of Russia.

Lif. See VALI.

Life and Death of Mr. Badman, The (1680). An allegorical dialogue by John BUNYAN, in which Mr. Wiseman tells of the vicious life and habits and the eventual death of Mr. Badman, using his story to point out the folly of wickedness.

Life Is a Dream. See VIDA ES SUEÑO, LA.

Life of Galileo, The (Leben des Galilei; 1938–1939). A play by Bertolt BRECHT. Written in the style of the EPIC THEATER, it concerns Galileo's conflict with the church. Brecht deliberately makes Galileo a very unheroic figure, always ready to compromise his principles when pressure is put on him. The play is not so obviously tendentious as most of Brecht's later works, but there are several anachronisms in which Marxist doctrine is propounded.

Life of Samuel Johnson, LL.D., The (1791). A biography by James BOSWELL, generally considered the greatest in the English language. Boswell met Dr. Samuel JOHNSON in 1763 in London and visited him periodically from that time, spending a great deal of time with him in the three years before Johnson's death. Boswell's method is of particular note: occasionally he made notes on the spot during Johnson's conversation; more often, however, from the habit of a lifetime, he made notes in his copious journals nightly on the events and conversation of the day, and for this, he had a prodigious memory to serve him. He questioned Johnson himself, prodding him into talk, and questioned Johnson's friends; after Johnson died, he was in constant quest of letters and anecdotes. He was greatly aided in his task by Edmund MALONE, who went over the last draft of the manuscript. Boswell's aim and achievement was completeness; no detail was too small for him, and on this very point Dr. Johnson remarked to him: "There is nothing, Sir, too little for so little a creature as man." Boswell's achievement is twofold: first he was able, from his scrupulously accurate memory, to record faithfully the brilliance and wit of Dr. Johnson's conversation; second, he had the artistry to transform a painstaking, almost scholarly profusion of detail into a perceptive, lifelike portrait. The result is a

Illustration for *The Life and Death of Mr. Badman* (1680).

study in depth of a complex and fascinating man who was the prime moving force in the literary world of his time. Although Boswell's *Life* is indisputably the finest of the many biographies of Johnson, Sir John Hawkins's *Life* (1787) is a better source for young Johnson, and Hester Lynch THRALE saw more of Johnson's intimate, domestic side.

Life on the Mississippi (1883). An autobiographical account by Mark TWAIN. The book describes the apprenticeship of a river pilot, and the excitement of life on the river. The second half of the book was added seven years after the first part was published; it records Twain's revisit to the river in 1882.

Life's Handicap, Being Stories of Mine Own People (1891). A volume of short stories of India, including THE MAN WHO WAS, by Rudyard KIPLING.

Life with Father (1935). A collection of sketches by Clarence DAY. In them the author recalls with delightful humor the not-always-easy life with his eccentric and domineering father. In spite of the elder Day's tyrannizing, however, his very feminine wife nearly always managed to get her way. The book was dramatized in 1939 by Howard LINDSAY and

Russel CROUSE and achieved the longest unbroken run of any American play. The second book of sketches, *Life with Mother* (1936), was dramatized by the same playwrights but had only a moderately successful run.

Life with Mother. See LIFE WITH FATHER.

Lifthrasir. See VALI.

Ligea (Ligeia). In classical myth, one of the three SIRENS.

Ligeia (1838). A tale by Edgar Allan POE. Ligeia, the narrator's mysterious dark-haired wife, dies after a lingering illness. He later remarries, though he does not love his fair Rowena. In the lavishly furnished English abbey to which they move, Rowena dies. The narrator, affected by opium, sees signs of life return to the corpse. Finally she rises; the Lady Rowena has been transformed into Ligeia.

Light-Horse Harry Lee. See Henry LEE.

Light in August (1932). A novel by William FAULKNER. The book reiterates the author's concern with a society that classifies men according to race, creed, and origin. Joe CHRISTMAS, the central character and victim, appears to be white but is really part Negro; he has an affair with Joanna Burden, a spinster whom the townsfolk of Jefferson regard with suspicion because of her New England background. Joe eventually kills her and sets fire to her house; he is captured, castrated, and killed by the outraged townspeople, to whom his victim has become a symbol of the innocent white woman attacked and killed by a Negro. Other important characters are Lena GROVE, who comes to Jefferson far advanced in pregnancy, expecting to find the lover who has deserted her, and Gail Hightower, the minister who ignores his wife and loses his church because of his fanatic devotion to the past.

Lightnin' (1918). A play by Winchell SMITH and Frank BACON. Its 1,291 performances set a record for its day. Bacon himself played the leading role of Lightnin' Bill Jones, owner of a hotel which lies half in Nevada and half in California. An amusing liar, Lightnin' has numerous troubles, but manages entertainingly to solve them all.

Light o' Love (Liebelei; 1894). A play by Arthur SCHNITZLER. It is a more serious treatment of the erotic themes that Schnitzler had stated earlier in *Anatol* (1891). The naïve young heroine Christine commits suicide when she learns that her lover has died dueling over another woman.

Light that Failed, The (1890). A novel by Rudyard KIPLING. Through his experience as an illustrator in the Sudan, the hero, Dick Heldar, wins both professional success and a firm friend in the war correspondent Torpenhow. He is in love with his foster sister Maisie, now also an artist, but Maisie is shallow and selfish and does not appreciate his devotion. Dick gradually goes blind from a sword cut received in the Sudan, working courageously against time on his painting, *Melancholia*. Although Maisie is summoned by Torpenhow, she heartlessly leaves Dick to his fate, and he carries out his plan of dying at the front. In a later edition a happy ending is provided.

Li Hung-chang (1823–1901). Chinese statesman; long the major force in foreign policy, after the emperor. Visited Europe and U.S. (1898). Commis-

sioned to restore peace after the BOXER uprising (1900). Often referred to as "the Bismarck of Asia."

Lilburne, John (1614?–1657). English political agitator and Puritan pamphleteer, noted for his rancorous temper. He was imprisoned several times for printing unlicensed books and for verbal attacks on persons of authority. See LEVELERS.

Liliencron, Detlev von (1844–1909). German poet. All his youth was spent as an officer in the Prussian army, in which he served through three wars, and his army experiences form the background for his first and most important volume of poems, *Adjutantenritte (An Adjutant's Rides,* 1884). In this book, he emphasizes a subjective but realistic treatment of the individual experience, as opposed to the emphasis on formal polish and generalized experience in such authors as Heyse and Geibel. These characteristics made his writing important in the budding movements of NATURALISM and IMPRESSIONISM.

Liliom (1909). A play by Ferenc MOLNÁR. It was produced in New York in 1921. The hero is a disreputable but fascinating side-show barker. One act shows him before the judges of the other world; another, on earth again with a single chance to redeem himself. The play was made into the musical play *Carousel* (1944), by Richard Rodgers and Oscar Hammerstein.

Lilith. In Talmudic tradition, a demon, probably of Babylonian origin, said to haunt wildernesses in stormy weather and be especially dangerous to children and pregnant women. She is referred to as "the screech-owl" (Isa. 34:14), and as "the night monster" in the Revised Version. Hebrew legend holds that she was created simultaneously with Adam and was his first wife, but, refusing to be considered his inferior, she left him and was expelled from Eden to a region of the air. In Arabic mythology, she married the Devil and became the mother of evil spirits. Superstitious Jews put four coins in the chambers occupied by their wives inscribed with the names of Adam and Eve and the words, "Avaunt thee, Lilith!" Goethe introduced her in his *Faust* (1790–1833), and Dante Gabriel Rossetti in his *Eden Bower* (1870) made the serpent the instrument of Lilith's vengeance against Adam.

Lillibulero or Lilliburlero. A political song, popular during the English revolution of 1688 and still the most savagely thunderous of British marching songs. The music is by Henry Purcell. The text by Thomas Wharton (c. 1686) satirizes James II and the Catholics, using the refrain "Lillibulero bullen a la" which is said to have been used as a watchword by the Irish Catholics in their massacre of the Protestants (1641). The song was included by Bishop Percy in his *Reliques.*

Lilliput. The country of Gulliver's first voyage in GULLIVER'S TRAVELS by Jonathan Swift. The Lilliputians are about 1/12 human size, and Gulliver is a giant among them. At first he falls in with their views, takes an interest in their disputes, helps them, and accepts their honors to him as real praise; he is soon disillusioned when the little creatures grudge him food and propose binding him lest he fend for himself. Their smallness is not merely a matter of stature; the pettiness of their lives is used by Swift to mirror the pettiness of human beings. See BIG-

ENDIANS; BLEFESCU; LOW HEELS AND HIGH HEELS;
QUINBUS FLESTRIN.

Lillo, George (1693–1739). English dramatist.
He is remembered chiefly for the sentimental bourgeois tragedy THE LONDON MERCHANT.

Lilly, William (1602–1681). English astrologer.
He issued a series of prophetic pamphlets and almanacs from 1644 to 1680 and wrote *Christian Astrology* (1647). As Sidrophel he is satirized in Samuel
Butler's *Hudibras* (1663–1678).

lily. A flower of innumerable varieties. There
is a tradition that the lily sprang from the repentant
tears of Eve as she went forth from Paradise. In
Christian art, the lily is an emblem of chastity, innocence, and purity. In pictures of the Annunciation,
Gabriel is sometimes represented as carrying a lily
branch, while a vase containing a lily stands before
the Virgin, who is kneeling in prayer. St. Joseph
holds a lily branch in his hand, indicating that his
wife Mary was a virgin.

lily of France. The *fleur-de-lis* (*Fr.*, "flower of
the lily"; the iris). It is an emblem of France. The
device of Clovis was three black toads, but the
story goes that an aged hermit of Joye-en-valle saw a
miraculous light stream one night into his cell, and
an angel appeared to him holding an azure shield of
wonderful beauty, emblazoned with three gold lilies
that shone like stars, which the hermit was commanded to give to Queen Clotilde. She gave it to
her royal husband, whose arms were everywhere
victorious, and the device was thereupon adopted as
the emblem of France. Tasso, in his *Jerusalem Delivered,* terms the French *gigli d'oro* (golden lilies).
It is said the people were commonly called *Liliarts,*
and the kingdom *Lilium* in the time of Philippe le
Bel, Charles VIII, and Louis XII.

limbo (Lat., **limbus,** "border, edge"). The abode
of souls that through no fault of their own are
debarred from heaven. It is particularly identified
with the souls of righteous men that lived before the
coming of Christ and with the souls of unbaptized
infants. Believed to be located near the region of hell,
it is the setting for the first stage of the journey in
Dante's *Commedia.* The word has come to refer
more generally to the condition of being lost or confined to a state of neglect or oblivion.

limbus of the moon. A legendary land. On the
moon was treasured everything wasted on earth;
misspent time and wealth, broken vows, unanswered
prayers, fruitless tears, abortive attempts, unfulfilled
desires and intentions. In Ariosto's *Orlando Furioso,*
Astolpho found on his visit to the moon that bribes
were hung on gold and silver hooks; princes' favors
were kept in bellows; wasted talent was kept in
vases, each marked with the proper name. Pope
describes the place in *The Rape of the Lock* (canto
v). Pope tells us that when the Lock disappeared:

> Some thought it mounted to the lunar sphere,
> Since all things lost on earth are treasured there,
> There heroes' wits are kept in pond'rous vases,
> And beaux' in snuff-boxes and tweezer-cases.
> There broken vows and death-bed alms are found
> And lovers' hearts with ends of ribbon bound,
> The courtier's promises, and sick man's prayers.
> The smiles of harlots, and the tears of heirs
> Cages for gnats, and chains to yoke a flea,
> Dried butterflies, and tomes of casuistry.

Hence the phrase, *the limbus of the moon.*

Limehouse. Violent and vitriolic abuse of one's
political opponents; so called out of compliment to
an oratorical display by Mr. Lloyd George at Limehouse, London, on July 30, 1909, when he poured
forth scorn and abuse on dukes, landlords, financial
magnates, etc., many of whom, in the course of later
events, became his best friends. It is also the name
of London's Chinatown.

limerick. A humorous, usually epigrammatic
piece of verse in five lines of mixed iambic and
anapestic meter, lines 1, 2, and 5 in trimeter and
3 and 4 in dimeter, rhyming a-a-b-b-a. The form,
the origins of which are uncertain, was popularized
by Edward LEAR in his *Book of Nonsense* (1846).
Following Lear's practice, the first line of most limericks ends in a place name, usually the place of
origin or residence of the protagonist of the verse.
The last line, in most of Lear's limericks, repeated the
place name instead of furnishing another rhyme
upon it, but most modern limericks end with a rhyme
word instead of a repetition. The subject of the typical limerick is likely to be somewhat ribald and puns
and plays on words are often included. The limerick has a wide oral circulation and, being a truly
popular form of verse, is often of anonymous authorship. The following is an example:

> There once was a man from Nantucket
> Who kept all his cash in a bucket;
>   But his daughter named Nan
>   Ran away with a man,
> And as for the bucket, Nantucket.

Linacre, Thomas (1460?–1524). English physician and classical scholar, one of the earliest representatives of British humanism. He was physician to
Henry VIII and one of the founders of the College
of Physicians in London (1518). Among his students
were Sir Thomas More and Erasmus. He was the
author of *Rudimenta Grammatica* (1523), a Latin
grammar; a Latin translation of Galen; and various
medical works.

Lincoln, Abraham (1809–1865). 16th president
of the U.S. (1861–1865). Born in a log cabin in
Hardin (now Larue) County, Ky., Lincoln lost his
mother, Nancy Hanks Lincoln, in 1818, while the
family was living in Indiana. In 1831 he settled in
New Salem, Ill., where he studied law and worked as
a store-keeper, postmaster, and surveyor; in 1836
he was admitted to the bar. From 1834 to 1841 he
served in the state legislature as a Whig and supporter of Henry Clay. While Lincoln was living in
New Salem, he met Ann Rutledge (1816–1835), to
whom he became engaged and who died in 1835;
their romance has inspired many legends for which
there is little concrete evidence. The truth about
Lincoln's relationship to Mary Todd, whom he married in 1842, has also been distorted, largely as a
result of the writings of William HERNDON, Lincoln's
law partner, who disliked Mrs. Lincoln intensely.

After serving one term (1847–1849) in Congress,
where he voiced his opposition to the Mexican War,
Lincoln returned to his flourishing law practice in
Illinois. Stirred to renewed political activity by the
sectional agitation of 1854, Lincoln soon aligned himself with the newly formed Republican Party and ran
for the U.S. Senate against Stephen A. DOUGLAS in
1858; although Lincoln lost the election, his famous

debates with Douglas won him national prominence. In 1860 he won the Republican presidential nomination over such rivals as William SEWARD largely because of his conservative record on the slavery question, but the Southern states seceded from the Union soon after his election. His first Inaugural address was conciliatory: he emphasized the indissolubility of the Union, but promised not to interfere with slavery where it already existed. During the Civil War, which began with the Confederate attack on Fort SUMTER, Lincoln did not hesitate to use his extensive powers as commander-in-chief, and although Northern Democrats and members of his own party often assailed his war policies, he handled his opponents with aplomb. In the election of 1864 he easily defeated George B. McCLELLAN, who had often tried his patience in the early days of the war. In his second Inaugural address, he asked the nation "to finish the work we are in . . . with malice toward none, with charity toward all." Just after Lee's surrender, Lincoln was shot by John Wilkes BOOTH and died the following day.

Now transformed into a major American folk hero, Lincoln has been the subject of numerous literary works. Among the best-known poems about him are Walt Whitman's O CAPTAIN! MY CAPTAIN! and WHEN LILACS LAST IN THE DOORYARD BLOOM'D. He is a character in many novels and stories, notably Henry Ward Beecher's Norwood (1867), Edward Eggleston's The Graysons (1888), and Winston Churchill's THE CRISIS. His early life is the subject of Robert E. Sherwood's play ABE LINCOLN IN ILLINOIS. Edgar Lee Masters wrote a hostile biography, Lincoln the Man (1931), while another poet, Carl Sandburg, offered a vivid portrayal in the six volumes of ABRAHAM LINCOLN. See Mary Todd LINCOLN; GETTYSBURG ADDRESS; EMANCIPATION PROCLAMATION.

Lincoln, Mary Todd (1818–1882). Wife of Abraham LINCOLN. Descended of a distinguished Kentucky family, Mary Todd was courted by Lincoln when she moved to Springfield, Ill., in 1839 to live with her sister, Mrs. Ninian W. Edwards, who was the daughter-in-law of the state governor. There is no contemporary evidence for the story that the wedding was scheduled for Jan. 1, 1841, and that the groom failed to appear; some emotional crisis in Lincoln's life, however, probably did lead him to delay the marriage, which took place in 1842. Despite the testimony of William HERNDON, Lincoln's law partner, the Lincolns' married life was probably happy, though some difficulties arose after his election to the presidency, when Mrs. Lincoln was accused of extravagance and disloyalty to the Union cause. Her mind weakened by her husband's assassination and by the loss of three of her four sons, she was adjudged insane in 1875 but declared competent the following year.

Lind, Johanna Maria. Known as Jenny Lind or Madame Jenny Lind-Goldschmidt (1820–1887). Swedish coloratura soprano, called "the Swedish Nightingale." She made her début as Agatha in Der Freischütz (1838). She was introduced to the U.S. by P. T. Barnum (1850–1852). She married (1852) Otto Goldschmidt, a German-born composer and pianist, and toured the continent. A resident of England during her last years, she was professor of singing at the Royal College of Music (1883–1886).

Lindbergh, Anne Morrow (1906–   ). American writer. The wife of Charles A. LINDBERGH, she has described their flights together in North to the Orient (1935) and Listen! The Wind (1938). Her controversial essay, The Wave of the Future (1940), was influenced by her husband's isolationism and was regarded by some as an apologia for fascism. She also wrote Gift from the Sea (1955), essays especially addressed to women; The Unicorn and Other Poems (1956); and Dearly Beloved (1962).

Lindbergh, Charles A[ugustus] (1902–   ). American aviator. Lindbergh is best known for his solo flight across the Atlantic on May 20–21, 1927, the first in history. With Fitzhugh Green he wrote an account of the flight called We (1927); the title refers to Lindbergh and his plane, The Spirit of St. Louis. In 1929 he married Anne Morrow, the daughter of the U.S. ambassador to Mexico, Dwight Morrow. The tragic kidnaping and death of their infant son, Charles, Jr., in March, 1932, resulted in the passing of "Lindbergh laws" which make interstate kidnaping a federal offense. The Lindberghs moved to Europe in 1935, where he worked with Alexis Carrel on the mechanical heart. In the years immediately preceding World War II, Lindbergh was an advocate of American neutrality. He wrote Of Flight and Life (1948) and an autobiography, The Spirit of St. Louis (1953), which was awarded a Pulitzer Prize. See Anne Morrow LINDBERGH.

Lindsay, Howard (1889–1968). American actor, director, producer, and playwright. In collaboration with Russel CROUSE, he dramatized LIFE WITH FATHER, in which he and his wife played the leading roles for five years. Also with Crouse, he wrote State of the Union (1945), which won a Pulitzer Prize, and produced Arsenic and Old Lace (1941). Lindsay also worked with Damon Runyon on A Slight Case of Murder (1935); with Irving Berlin on Call Me Madam (1950); and with Richard Rodgers and Oscar Hammerstein on The Sound of Music (1959).

Lindsay, Jack (1900–   ). Australian poet, novelist, and classical scholar. His Marxist, mass-declamation poems were popular in England in the leftist 1930's. Most of his novels are historical, about ancient Greece and Rome, such as Caesar is Dead (1935). His other works are polemical writings on Russia and Marxism, literary criticism, translations from Greek and Latin, and the history Byzantium into Europe (1952). He was the son of Norman Lindsay.

Lindsay, [Alfred William] Norman (1879–   ). Australian artist and novelist. Lindsay, the son of a physician, turned to art at an early age, and worked later for a Melbourne paper. His pen drawings hang in English galleries. A novel, Red Heap (1913), was censored in Australia but well received in America under the title Every Woman's Son. His talent for satire and plot are discernible in The Cautious Amorist (1934) and Age of Consent (1938). He has been described by critics as a "true humorist," while his writing has the "gauntness of Australia." Other works include A Curate in Bohemia (1913), The Magic Pudding (1919), Pam in the Parlor (1934), Halfway to Anyway (1947), and Dust or Polish (1950).

Lindsay, [Nicholas] Vachel (1879–1931). American poet. Known for the dramatic and auditory effects of his poetry, he read from the lecture platform with theatrical gestures and intonation in an effort to make a love of poetry public property. His own work dealt in the main with American subjects and heroes, patriotism, and a mystic faith in the earth and nature. The crusading spirit was strong in Lindsay, and for a time he lectured for the Anti-Saloon League in the winter; in the summer (1912) he walked from Illinois to New Mexico, exchanging for meals the poems collected in *Rhymes to Be Traded for Bread* (1912). In the following year he published one of his best-known poems, GENERAL WILLIAM BOOTH ENTERS INTO HEAVEN. THE CONGO and THE SANTE FE TRAIL were published in 1914. Among others of his more famous single poems are *A Gospel of Beauty* (1908), *A Net to Snare the Moonlight* (1913), *The Eagle That Is Forgotten* (1913), *Abraham Lincoln Walks at Midnight* (1914), *The Chinese Nightingale* (1917), *The Ghost of the Buffaloes* (1917), and IN PRAISE OF JOHNNY APPLE-SEED. *The Golden Book of Springfield* (1920) is a prose work giving a Utopian picture of his native city. His other books include *Adventures While Preaching the Gospel of Beauty* (1914), *The Art of the Moving Picture* (1915), *The Golden Whales of California and Other Rhymes in the American Language* (1920), *The Candle in the Cabin* (1926), *Every Soul Is a Circus* (1929). His *Selected Poems* (1931) were edited by Hazelton Spencer.

As his poetic powers failed, Lindsay became weary and disillusioned. In 1931 he committed suicide by drinking poison.

Lingard, Captain. As a young man, the hero of Joseph Conrad's THE RESCUE; in later life, in AN OUTCAST OF THE ISLANDS and ALMAYER'S FOLLY, a powerful white trader who takes Almayer and Willems for protégés.

linguistic philosophy. See LOGICAL POSITIVISM.

Linklater, Eric (1899–   ). Scottish novelist. He writes witty novels of travel, fantasy, and satire. He is best known for *Juan in America* (1931). Among his other books are *Roll of Honour* (1961) and *Husband of Delilah* (1962).

Linnaeus, Carolus. The latinized name of the great Swedish botanist Carl von Linné (1707–1778). In his *Systema Naturae* (1735), he outlined what was largely adopted as the *Linnaean classification* or *system* of plants. It is also known as the *sexual system*. It differs from Jussieu's system (1789), by which it was superseded, in that it made no attempt to show the relationship of species and genera. Hence the name *artificial system* as opposed to Jussieu's *natural system*. Linnaeus' *Species Plantarum* (1753) is considered the foundation of modern botanical nomenclature.

Linné, Carl von. See Carolus LINNAEUS.

Lins do Rego, José (1901–1957). Brazilian novelist. In the sensitive, realistic novels of his "sugar-cane cycle" (*Ciclo da Cana-de-Açúcar*), Lins do Rego depicted the decline of the patriarchal society that revolved around the sugar plantations of northeastern Brazil. The works usually included in the cycle are *Menino de Engenho* (1932), *Doidinho* (1933), *Banguê* (1934), *O Moleque Ricardo* (1935), and *Usina* (1936). In *Pedra Bonita* (1938) and other novels, he portrayed aspects of rural life in the arid portions of this same region.

Lin Yu-t'ang (in English usually **Yutang**) (1895–   ). Chinese teacher, translator, editor, and writer. Lin attended Harvard Graduate School, after which he returned to China to teach. He founded and wrote for several English and Chinese periodicals and edited textbooks. He is chancellor of Nanyang University, Singpore, and head of the Arts and Letters Division of UNESCO. Lin has written several books interpreting China and her people; among these are *My Country and My People* (1935), *A History of the Press and Public Opinion in China* (1936), *The Wisdom of Confucius* (1938), and *The Chinese Way of Life* (1959). He has written and translated short stories, among them *Famous Chinese Short Stories* (1952) and *Widow, Nun and Courtesan* (1951). Among his other books are *A Leaf in the Storm* (1941); *Between Tears and Laughter* (1943); and an anthology, *The Wisdom of China and India* (1942). His most recent works are *The Importance of Understanding* (1960) and *The Red Peony* (1962).

lion. The "king of beasts." This animal figures perhaps more than any other in legend, symbolism, and heraldry. In religious art, the lion is an emblem of the Resurrection. According to tradition, the lion's whelp is born dead, and remains so for three days, when the father breathes on it and it receives life. Another tradition is that the lion is the only animal of the cat tribe born with its eyes open, and it is said that it sleeps with its eyes open.

St. Mark the Evangelist is symbolized by a lion because he begins his gospel with the scenes of St. John the Baptist and Christ in the wilderness. The device of Venice is the winged Lion of St. Mark. St. Jerome befriended lions. (See ANDROCLES, HERACLES, and UNA for legends of lions.)

Ever since 1164, when it was adopted as a device by Philip I, duke of Flanders, the lion has figured largely, and in an amazing variety of positions, as a heraldic emblem.

Lion Gate. The gate leading from the ancient Greek city of Mycenae in Argolis to the acropolis. It is about 10 feet high and wide, has monolithic jambs and a huge lintel. Above the lintel is a great slab with a relief of two affronted rampant lions which account for the name. It was built in the Mycenaean era (1400–1100 B.C.).

Lipchitz, Jacques (1891–   ). Russian-born French sculptor. Established in New York since 1941, he has composed powerful figures, notably of bulls, in which the play of light on rough surfaces and on large masses contributes to a great feeling of movement; he has also done monumental semihuman standing columns of interpenetrating circular forms and shafts.

Li Po or **Li Tai Po** or **Li Tai Peh** (c. 701–c. 762). Chinese poet, considered one of the greatest. Fond of wine, fencing, and adventure, he traveled widely, then retired to the mountains as one of the Six Idlers of the Bamboo Streams. Admired by the emperor for his learning and his poetry, he was brought to the royal court, but palace intrigue and his part in the rebellion of An Lu-shan (775–776), forced him to leave and resume his wanderings. Imperial orders, however, allowed him to obtain free wine, and he formed another group of companions called the Eight Immortals of the Wine Cup. According to legend he drowned one night trying to embrace the reflection of the moon near his boat. His poems are passionate lyrics about wine and love, rich in delicate, imaginative imagery of natural beauty. See Arthur Waley, *The Poetry and Career of Li Po* (1950).

Lippi, Fra Lippo or **Filippo** (1406–1469). Italian painter. A Florentine monk of the Carmelite order, he painted religious easel paintings and frescoes in a style stressing charm, imaginative detail, and sinuous outline. He was influenced primarily by Masaccio, Fra Angelico, and Donatello, and in turn was the teacher of Botticelli. Among his best-known works are *The Madonna with Saints* and the *Virgin and Child with Saints and Angels*. His restlessness as a monk, which caused him to leave his monastery, inspired Browning's famous poem FRA LIPPO LIPPI.

His son **Filippino** (1475–1504), who studied with his father's pupil Botticelli, also became famous as a painter of religious scenes. His masterpieces include the *Madonna Appearing to Saint Bernard,* the *Madonna and Child with Angels,* the *Allegory of Music,* and the frescoes of the Strozzi Chapel in the Florentine church of S. Maria Novella. He also finished the frescoes left incomplete by Masaccio in the Brancacci Chapel of the Carmine.

Lippmann, Walter (1889–   ). American journalist. After aiding in the preparations for the peace conference after World War I and holding important editorial positions on the *New Republic* and New York *World,* Lippmann became famous for the thoughtful and reasoned political comments of his influential newspaper column, which he began to write in 1931 for the New York *Herald Tribune.* He has lucidly set forth his social philosophy in several influential volumes, including *Public Opinion* (1922), *A Preface to Morals* (1929), *The Good Society* (1937), and *The Public Philosophy* (1955).

Lippold, Richard (1915–   ). American sculptor. He is known for constructions of metal plates and wires, such as the hanging *Orpheus and Apollo* in the New York Lincoln Center Philharmonic Hall.

Lismahago, Captain. In Tobias Smollett's novel HUMPHREY CLINKER, an eccentric, superannuated veteran officer of the Indian wars who marries Miss Tabitha BRAMBLE. He is a forbidding Scotsman, singular in dress and in manners, conceited, disputatious, and rude. Though most tenacious in argument, he can yield to Miss Tabitha, whom he wishes to conciliate.

Lissauer, Ernst. See HYMN OF HATE.

Liszt, Franz (1811–1886). Hungarian composer and virtuoso pianist. A child prodigy, he first performed in public at the age of nine. He studied in Vienna under Czerny and Salieri, in Paris under Reicha. He lived at Geneva (1835–1839) with the Comtesse d'Agoult, by whom he had three children, one of whom was Cosima, who later married Richard Wagner. Liszt was court Kapellmeister at Weimar from 1848 to 1859. In 1865 he entered the Franciscan order at Rome (1865) and was thenceforth known as the Abbé Liszt. He died at Bayreuth (1886) in the midst of a Wagner festival. He was outstanding as a piano teacher as well as a performer.

Much of his music, especially from the last 20 years of his life, is marked by daring innovations in form and harmonic relations, which have fascinated and influenced composers ever since, even though he had no true disciples or imitators. His works include the *Faust Symphony* (1853–1861), the *Dante Symphony* (1856); twelve symphonic poems, including *Les Préludes* (after Lamartine), two piano concertos; much piano music, notably the *Années de Pèlerinage* and the 20 Hungarian Rhapsodies (1851–1886); two oratorios, several masses, and other church music; songs, and organ pieces.

Literary Club, The. A group founded by Sir Joshua REYNOLDS and Samuel JOHNSON in 1764 under the simpler title of "The Club." They met weekly for conversation at The Turk's Head Tavern in Gerrard Street, Soho, until 1783, when the tavern was converted to a private dwelling. They continued at various meeting-places until the end of the century. The members included Edmund Burke, Thomas Percy, James Boswell, Edward Gibbon, David Garrick, Oliver Goldsmith, and Adam Smith, among other famous 18th-century figures.

Litigants, The. See PLAIDEURS, LES.

Little, Henry. The inventor-hero of Charles Reade's PUT YOURSELF IN HIS PLACE.

Little, Thomas. Pseudonym under which Thomas MOORE's *Poetical Works* of 1801 were published. Moore is called by this name in Byron's *English Bards and Scotch Reviewers.*

Little Clay Cart, The or **The Toy Cart** (Sans., *Mrichchhakatika*). A Sanskrit comedy ascribed to King Shudraka and variously assigned to the 3rd to 10th centuries. The hero is Charudatta, an impoverished Brahmin merchant, the heroine the lovely courtesan Vasantasena. The villain of the play, Sansthanaka, the king's brother-in-law, smothers Vasantasena in a remote garden and accuses Charudatta of the crime, but Vasantasena recovers and appears just in time to save her lover from execution. An important subplot is concerned with a successful conspiracy to overthrow the reigning monarch. Goethe paraphrased the drama in his poem *Der Gott und die Bayadere,* and it was made the basis of a popular ballet *Le Dieu et la bayadère* which was staged throughout Europe about the year 1830. The drama itself was produced in New York by the Neighborhood Playhouse players in 1924–1925.

Little Corporal. An epithet applied to Napoleon Bonaparte after the battle of Lodi in 1796. Bonaparte stood barely five feet two inches in height.

Little Dorrit (1855–1857). A novel by Charles DICKENS. William Dorrit, with his three children Edward, Fanny, and Amy (who is Little Dorrit), lives in prison where he is confined for debt. Little Dorrit was born in the prison, spends most of her life there, and ultimately, chooses to be married there. The three children try to make a living outside the prison and bring back their earnings each night. Little Dorrit does her part by sewing for Mrs. Clennam. Suddenly, her father comes into a fortune and the whole family becomes as pretentious and despicable as they were formerly objects of compassion. Only Little Dorrit remains unchanged with her father's changing fortune, retaining her sweet and generous disposition. She grows to love Arthur Clennam, middle-aged son of Mrs. Clennam, who has recently returned from India; he helps to free her father from prison. In Arthur's struggle with the civil service's CIRCUMLOCUTION OFFICE, Dickens levels an attack on bureaucracy. Arthur is sent to prison for debt and Little Dorrit labors to help him. Their love ends happily, and they are married in Marshalsea prison. This novel is one of Dickens' strongest attacks on bureaucratic inefficiency and the practice of imprisonment for debt.

Among the many memorable characters in the book are the soft-hearted Meagles family; the BARNACLES; and Mr. and Mrs. PLORNISH. See MARSHALSEA.

Little Em'ly. See PEGGOTTY.

Little-Endians. See BIG-ENDIANS.

Little Entente. See ENTENTE.

Little Eva. A character in Harriet Beecher Stowe's UNCLE TOM'S CABIN.

Little Foxes, The (1939.) A play by Lillian HELLMAN. In telling the story of the Hubbard family, it depicts unfavorably the rise of industrialism in the South and condemns the new breed of Southerners as rapacious and ruthless—like "the little foxes who spoil the vines" of the biblical verse. *Another Part of the Forest* (1946) deals with an earlier stage in the Hubbards' career.

Little Gidding. The home of an Anglican lay religious community in England in the 17th century. It was composed of the family and friends of Nicholas FERRAR, who was intimate with the poets George Herbert and Richard Crashaw. It is the setting for the novel *John Inglesant,* by J. H. Shorthouse, and for T. S. Eliot's poem *Little Gidding* (see FOUR QUARTETS). The community was dispersed by the Parliamentarians in 1647, during the Civil War.

Little John. A chief follower of ROBIN HOOD in the English Robin Hood ballad cycle. He was a big stalwart fellow, first named John Little (or John Nailor), who encountered Robin Hood and gave him a sound thrashing, after which he was rechristened, Robin standing as godfather. He appears in Scott's novel *The Talisman* (1825).

Little Lord Fauntleroy. A story for children by Frances Hodgson BURNETT (1886), illustrated by Reginald Birch. The seven-year-old hero, Cedric Errol, is the son of a disinherited English father and an American mother. His title of Lord Fauntleroy he would normally inherit from his grandfather, an English earl, who has, however, never forgiven the boy's father for marrying an American. On the death of the father the boy is summoned to England, leaving his mother, whom he calls "Dearest," in the poverty-stricken quarters where they have been living in New York. He so completely wins the hearts of his English relatives that they are soon persuaded to extend to "Dearest" a cordial welcome. Little Lord Fauntleroy is a striking figure, dressed in black velvet with lace collar and yellow curls, and his name passed into common usage as referring either to a certain type of children's clothes or to a beautiful but pampered and effeminate small boy.

little magazines. A name applied to small, noncommercial, usually short-lived periodicals whose aim is to promote avant-garde writing. These magazines, frequently the only means of expression available to young, unknown experimental writers, have provided a meeting-ground for writers and thereby sometimes formed the nucleus of new literary movements. They were a major factor in the literary revolution of 1910–1920.

The little magazine form goes back to the mid-19th century with the Transcendentalist magazine THE DIAL (1840–1844), *The Philistine* (1895–1915), and *The Mirror* (1893–1920) in America, and *The Germ* (1850) and *The Yellow Book* (1894–1897) in England. Between 1910 and 1920 little magazines began to appear in abundance: *The Blue Review* (England, 1911), POETRY (1912), *Blast* (England, 1914), THE LITTLE REVIEW (1914), *Bruno's Weekly* (1915), THE SEVEN ARTS (1916), *The Dial* (1917). During the 1920's a number of magazines were published by American expatriates in London and Paris: *The Criterion* (London, 1922), TRANSITION (Paris, 1927), *Exile* (Paris and Chicago, 1927), *Broom* (Rome, then London, then New York, 1921–1924), *Secession* (Vienna, Berlin, New York, 1922–1924). The most important American little magazines during this period were *The Double Dealer* (1921), *The Fugitive* (1922), and *The Chicago Literary Times* (1923).

The late 20's and 30's saw a shift in emphasis away from the more purely literary little magazines toward two new forms: the politico-literary journal, such as the *New Masses* (1926), which was dominant during the 30's, and the quarterly review, such as the *Prairie Schooner* (1927), which became important in the late 30's and have continued to be widely influential critical and usually academic journals. New magazines in the 30's and 40's included *The Harkness Hoot* (1930), *Story* (1931), THE PARTISAN REVIEW (1934), *New Directions in Prose and Poetry* (1936), THE KENYON REVIEW (1939), *Furioso* (1939), *Accent* (1940), *Chimera* (1942), *Quarterly Review of Literature* (1943), *Hudson Review* (1948), and *Cronos* (1947). In reaction against the quarterlies, which were no longer avant-garde and were critical more than creative, a new group of little magazines appeared during the 50's, many of them with titles borrowed from now-defunct magazines of the twenties: *The Dial, The Seven Arts, Transatlantic Review, Contact.* Practically all the major writers of the 20th century had their early work published in little magazines: Sherwood Anderson, Van Wyck Brooks, Hart Crane, E. E. Cummings, John Dos Passos, Theodore Dreiser, T. S. Eliot, William Faulkner, Robert Frost, Ernest Hemingway, James Joyce, D. H. Lawrence, Marianne Moore, Eugene O'Neill, Katherine Anne Porter, Ezra Pound, Gertrude Stein, Dylan Thomas, William Carlos Williams, Edmund Wilson, and others. Critical studies of the little magazines include F. J. Hoffman's *The Little Magazine* (1946).

Little Minister, The (1891). A novel by J. M. BARRIE. The hero, Gavin Dishart, is a young preacher in the Scottish village of Thrums. He struggles in vain against his love for the irresistible gypsy, Babbie, and marries her on impulse. The parish is scandalized. The two are separated, but after many vicissitudes, the Little Minister regains both his prestige and his bride.

Little Nell. See OLD CURIOSITY SHOP, THE.

Little Orphant Annie (1885). A poem in Hoosier dialect by James Whitcomb RILEY. Orphant Annie tells hair-raising tales about the goblins, and is finally carried off by them. A comic strip by Harold Gray is called *Little Orphan Annie.*

Littlepage Manuscripts, The (1845–1846). A series of three novels by James Fenimore COOPER: SATANSTOE, *The Chainbearer,* and THE REDSKINS. Presumably related by several generations of Littlepage men, the novels deal with the antirent controversy and its historical background. In this now forgotten issue, the tenants of the New York patroons, suffering hardships, refused to pay rent. Cooper defended the landlords' rights, insisting that the tenants had enjoyed years of advantages in the bargain. Cooper saw, in this controversy, a crisis in American democracy; if contracts could be broken by mob rule, democracy would turn to anarchy.

The three novels become progressively weaker, as Cooper's political principles outweigh those of his art. The trilogy marks the end of his most creative period.

Little Red Riding-Hood. A nursery tale. It comes to us from *Le Petit Chaperon Rouge* (1697) of Charles PERRAULT (in his CONTES DE MA MÈRE L'OYE), though with slight alterations the story is common to France, Germany, and Sweden and probably originated in Italy. A little girl bringing a present to her grandmother is devoured by a wolf who has disguised himself in the old lady's ruffled nightcap. The brothers GRIMM added a happy ending to the tale: a huntsman slits open the wolf and restores the child and her grandmother to life.

Little Review, The (1914–1929). An American literary periodical. It was published, first in Chicago, later in New York and Paris, under the editorship of Margaret Anderson, and championed all the 20th-century experimental movements, publishing the work of outstanding English, American, and European writers of the period. When James Joyce's *Ulysses* appeared in installments (1918–1921), four issues were confiscated and burned by the Post Office.

Little Shepherd of Kingdom Come, The (1903). A novel by John Fox, Jr. The highly sentimental story deals with Chad Buford, a shepherd of doubtful parentage who, before going to fight in the Civil War, comes to live for a while at the Cumberland Mountain settlement which is used in the book's title. The novel was dramatized by Eugene Walter in 1916.

Little Tragedies (Malen'kiye tragedi; 1830). Four short dramatic works in blank verse by Aleksandr PUSHKIN. The short dramas, which Pushkin referred to as "essays of dramatic investigation," are studies of character in four varied situations. *The Stone Guest* (*Kamyenni gost'*) is a re-telling of the Don Juan legend. *Mozart and Salieri* (*Motzart i Sal'yeri*) depicts Salieri's jealousy of Mozart's artistic genius and his legendary poisoning of Mozart. *The Covetous Knight* (*Skupoi rytzar'*) is a study of the effects of avarice. *The Feast during the Plague* (*Pir vo vremya chumy*), translated from the English drama *City of the Plague* by John Wilson, shows the evil effects on human behavior of imminent death. All four of the small dramas are regarded as being among Pushkin's most powerful poetic work.

Little Women, or Meg, Jo, Beth, and Amy (1868, 1869). A widely read story for young people by Louisa May ALCOTT. The heroine is Jo March, the tomboyish and literary member of the family, who retires to the attic when "genius burns." Meg, her older, pretty sister, marries a young tutor, John Brooke, and reappears in the sequel, *Little Men* (1871), with her twins, Daisy and Demi. Gentle, music-loving Beth dies young. The fashionable and artistic Amy finally marries Laurie, a high-spirited boy who had long been Jo's boon companion, but who failed to persuade her to marry him. Jo herself becomes the wife of a kindly old German professor, Mr. Bhaer; in *Little Men*, she and the professor turn their home into a school for boys. *Jo's Boys* (1886) is a second sequel.

Litvinov. The hero of Ivan Turgenev's novel SMOKE, who allows his former lover, Irina, to disrupt his love affair with Tanya.

Lives of the Poets, The (1779–1781). A collection of biographical and critical essays on 52 English poets from Cowley to Johnson's contemporaries by Samuel JOHNSON. It is noted for its approach; Johnson was interested in establishing a causal relationship between the artist's life and his art:

To judge rightly of an author we must transport ourselves to his time, and examine what were the wants of his contemporaries, and what were his means of supplying them.—*Life of Dryden*

His criticism was vigorous and articulate. He considered Dryden, Pope, Swift, and Addison the most important authors of the Restoration and Queen Anne periods. Some of his critical opinion has been discredited with the perspective of time; the romantics deplored his failure to appreciate the odes of Thomas Gray and Milton's work, and his attack on metaphysical poetry, in the *Life of Cowley*, is not compatible with the modern view. However, Johnson's *Lives* remains an achievement beyond the "correctness" of its critical evaluations.

Livingstone, David (1813–1873). Scottish-born English missionary and explorer in Africa. After working in a cotton mill from the age of 10, he went to college in 1837, received a medical degree in 1840, and left England for South Africa as a medical missionary. He discovered Lake Ngami (1849), Zambesi River (1851), the Victoria Falls of the Zambesi (1855), and Lake Nyasa (1859). On his return to England (1864) he published *Narrative of an Expedition to the Zanzibar and Its Tributaries* (1865). Appointed British consul in central Africa, he went back with the express purpose of wiping out slave trade and determining the watershed of the Nyasa-Tanganyika region. Exhausted and near death, he spent some months in Ujiji; in 1871 an expedition was sent out under Sir Henry M. Stanley (1841–1904) to find Livingstone and their famous encounter began with Stanley's anticlimactic, "Dr. Livingstone, I presume?" Livingstone died in a village on the south shore. His body was taken to England and buried in Westminster Abbey. His journals for the years 1866 to 1873 were published as *Last Journals of David Livingstone in Central Africa* (1873). Livingstone's example was followed by many missionaries and his influence was considerable in reducing slave trade.

Livius Andronicus (fl. 3d century B.C.). Founder of Roman epic poetry and drama. He was a Greek slave who, after being freed by his master Livius, whose name he adopted, introduced both comedies and tragedies in Latin on Greek models for performance in Rome. He also made a Latin translation of Homer's *Odyssey* which was used for centuries in Roman schools. His importance is due to the fact that he gave the Romans their first contact with Greek literature in translation.

Livre de mon ami, Le. See Anatole FRANCE.

Livy. Full Latin name, **Titus Livius** (59 B.C.–A.D. 17). Roman historian. His *Ab Urbe Condita Libri,* the history of Rome from the founding of the city, was written in 142 books of which only about 36 have been preserved. We have, however, summaries of all but two of the missing books; these outlines, written by an unknown scholar of the fourth century, give an indication of the vast scope of the work which extended from the mythological beginnings of Rome down to A.D. 9. Though Livy's research must have been voluminous, it was unscholarly; his information is often inaccurate, and his facts are sometimes self-contradictory. But scientific history was not his primary objective. He wished to hold up to his countrymen the great panorama of their past, to recall to them the glories of their ancestors, and to urge them to abandon the decadent ways they had. In this sense his aim was similar to that of Vergil in his *Aeneid.* Livy's style is one of polished rhetorical brilliance; the speeches which he puts in the mouths of historical personages are masterful, both as oratory and as character analysis.

A native of Patavium (Padua), Livy began his great work about 26 B.C., but did not publish his first 21 books until A.D. 14. Excerpts were, however, in circulation much earlier, for Asinius Pollio, who died in A.D. 4, had occasion to criticize Livy's "patavinitas." This was apparently a reference to his provincial, Paduan manner of expression, evidence of which scholars have not been able to detect in Livy's prose.

Liza of Lambeth (1897). The first novel of W. Somerset MAUGHAM. It depicts the life and loves of Liza, a girl of the London slums. Written in the tradition of naturalism, it is filled with minute descriptions of poverty, violence, and physical and psychological illness. The novel was considered shocking when it was first published.

Llareggub or Llaregyb. See UNDER MILK WOOD.

Llewellyn, Richard. Pen name of **Richard David Vivian Llewellyn Lloyd** (1907–   ), Welsh novelist. Llewellyn wrote the very popular Welsh novel How GREEN WAS MY VALLEY. His other books include *None But the Lonely Heart* (1943), *A Few Flowers for Shiner* (1950), *The Flame of Hercules* (1957), *Chez Pavan* (1959), and *Up, Into the Singing Mountain* (1961).

Lloyd George, David (1863–1945). British statesman of Welsh descent. Succeeded Asquith as prime minister (1916–1922) and directed British policies during World War I and in the negotiation of peace terms. Instituted negotiations resulting in the establishment of the Irish Free State. Author of *War Memoirs* (6 vols., 1933–1936) and *The Truth About the Peace Treaty* (2 vols., 1938). Created Earl Lloyd-George of Dufor (1945). See LIMEHOUSE.

Lloyd's of London. An association of underwriters, merchants, shipowners, and brokers. The company deals principally with ocean-borne commerce, marine insurance, and the publication of shipping intelligence, but it has a worldwide reputation of being willing to insure almost anyone against almost anything. The company is so called because the society was founded in 1688, at a coffee house kept in Lombard Street by one Edward Lloyd. In 1774, the offices, or *Lloyd's Rooms,* were moved to the Royal Exchange, where they still are.

Lloyd's books. Two enormous ledgerlike volumes, placed on desks at the entrance (right and left) of Lloyd's Rooms. They give the principal arrivals, and all losses by wrecks, fire, or other accidents at sea.

Lloyd's List. A periodical, in which the shipping news received at Lloyd's Rooms is published. It has been issued regularly since 1726, and as a daily since 1800.

Lloyd's Register. A register of ships, English and foreign, published yearly.

Lludd and Llefelys. See MABINOGION, THE.

local color. In reference to literature, the concrete details of natural scenery, architecture, language, local custom and tradition, used by authors to lend a sense of authenticity to their work. Local color writing flourished in the U.S. during the post-bellum 19th century. Native manners and dialect were frequently exploited for humorous effect. Among the outstanding local colorists of the Far West were Bret Harte and Joaquin Miller; New England scenes and characters were delicately recorded by Sarah Orne Jewett and Rose Terry Cooke. In the Middle West, Edward Eggleston and John Hay employed local color, while Hamlin Garland and Edgar Lee Masters, under the influence of the new realism, presented their devastating studies of local life. The South was nostalgically or accurately portrayed by George Washington Cable, Lafcadio Hearn, Charles Egbert Craddock, Joel Chandler Harris, Thomas Nelson Page, and Grace Elizabeth King.

Local color writing in the United States may be traced back as far as James Fenimore Cooper's SATANSTOE, Washington Irving's Knickerbocker's HISTORY OF NEW YORK, Charles Brockden Brown's WIELAND, and Nathaniel Hawthorne's THE SCARLET LETTER. Among the 20th-century American writers whose work local detail enriches are William Faulkner, Ellen Glasgow, J. P. Marquand, O. Henry, Edith Wharton, James T. Farrell, John Steinbeck, and Sherwood Anderson.

In Great Britain, writers who employ local color to a significant degree include J. M. Synge, Sean O'Casey, Thomas Hardy, Arnold Bennett, A. E. Housman, and Winifred Holtby. In the novels and stories of James Joyce, the atmosphere of Dublin is vividly evoked. In France, Guy de Maupassant reveals the details of life in Normandy; Alphonse Daudet, Frédéric Mistral, and Jean Giono have written of Provence.

Locarno Pact or Treaty. A series of five treaties between Germany and Belgium, France, Great Britain, Italy, Poland, and Czechoslovakia (October 1925). They were negotiated at Locarno in Switzerland with the purpose of guaranteeing peace and the existing territorial boundaries.

Lochiel. The title of the head of the clan Cameron. The hero of Thomas CAMPBELL's poem *Lochiel's Warning* (1802) is Donald Cameron, known as the Gentle Lochiel. He was one of the Young PRETENDER's stanchest adherents, and escaped to France with him after Culloden (1746). He took service in the French army, but died two years later.

Lochinvar. A young Highlander, hero of a ballad in Scott's MARMION. Being in love with a lady already committed to an unenviable marriage, he persuades her to dance one last dance, during which he swings her into his saddle, and makes off with her before the bridegroom and his servants can recover from their astonishment.

Locke, David Ross. See Petroleum Vesuvius NASBY.

Locke, John (1632–1704). English philosopher. Educated at Christ Church, Oxford, Locke was a lecturer in Greek, rhetoric, and philosophy at that university and apparently practiced medicine, though he never received a medical degree. He became confidential secretary to the earl of SHAFTESBURY, who was one of the proprietors of Carolina, and wrote a well-known constitution for the colony in 1669. Suspected of complicity in Shaftesbury's plots against the government, Locke was forced to leave England and lived in the Netherlands from 1684 to 1689. After the accession of William and Mary, he was appointed commissioner of appeals.

Locke's most famous work is AN ESSAY CONCERNING HUMAN UNDERSTANDING, an inquiry into the nature of knowledge. His *Two Treatises on Government* (1690), written in defense of the Glorious Revolution, exerted enormous influence on British and American political thought. The Declaration of Independence, in particular, echoes his contention that government rests on popular consent and that rebellion is permissible when government subverts the ends—the protection of life, liberty, and property—for which it is established. Locke also wrote *Some Thoughts Concerning Education* (1693), *The Reasonableness of Christianity* (1695), and four *Letters on Toleration* (1689–1692, 1765).

Locke, William J[ohn] (1863–1930). English popular novelist, author of the best-selling novel THE BELOVED VAGABOND. He also wrote *The Morals of Marcus Ordeyne* (1905), *The Glory of Clementina Wing* (1911), and *The Great Pandolfo* (1925).

Locker-Lampson, Frederick. Before 1885, **Frederick Locker** (1821–1895). English poet. He was noted for his light verse and elegant *vers de société*. He was the author of *London Lyrics* (1857), and editor of *Lyra Elegantiarum* (1867), an anthology of light verse. Lampson was the maiden name of his second wife.

Lockhart, John Gibson (1794–1854). Scottish editor and writer. He published the sketches of Edinburgh life *Peter's Letters to his Kinsfolk* (1819), under the pseudonym Peter Morris, and translated *Ancient Spanish Ballads* (1823). At the age of 23 he wrote for *Blackwood's Magazine* a series of four articles, signed "Z," dealing with the supposed COCKNEY SCHOOL of poetry and excoriating Leigh Hunt and John Keats. Though the ruffianly tone of these articles is abusive and though to later generations many of Lockhart's adverse judgments seem as vicious as they are obtuse, especially in their confusion of enmity with criticism, Lockhart enjoys a high reputation in English letters, his life of his father-in-law Sir Walter Scott (7 vols., 1837–1838) ranking second only to Boswell's *Johnson* among the great biographies in the language. Lockhart also published a biography of Robert Burns (1828).

Lockit. See BEGGAR'S OPERA, THE; THREEPENNY OPERA, THE.

Locksley. In Scott's IVANHOE, a name assumed by Robin Hood, who appears as an archer at the tournament. It is said to have been the name of the village where the outlaw was born.

Locksley Hall (1842). A poem by Alfred TENNYSON. The hero takes a last look at Locksley Hall, the remote seaside mansion where he spent his youth. Here he fell in love with his cousin Amy, who, yielding to social and parental pressure, married a rich "clown." Though disgusted by the weakness of women and the mercenary corruption of the age—he even considers exiling himself to some tropic island—his youthful belief in progress and in the high destiny of Europe reasserts itself. In 1886 Tennyson published *Locksley Hall Sixty Years After*, a sequel.

Lockyer, Sir Joseph Norman (1836–1920). British astronomer. He initiated (1866) the spectroscopic observation of sunspots. He investigated the chemistry of the sun, and, in 1868, determined the presence in its atmosphere of an unknown element to which the name helium was given (from Greek *helios*, "the sun")—a name that it has kept although helium was later discovered to exist also in the earth's atmosphere.

Loco-Focos. The radical urban wing of the Democratic party in New York in the mid-1830's. They favored the abolition of monopolies and advocated "hard" (as opposed to paper) money. They derived their name from a Tammany Hall meeting in 1835 at which the Democratic regulars nominated a ticket, ignoring the protests of the radicals, and turned out the lights in order to evict them. The radicals then obtained candles, which they lit with the new self-igniting matches called loco-focos, and proceeded to select their own candidates.

Locrine. In Geoffrey of Monmouth's HISTORY OF THE KINGS OF BRITAIN, king of England and son of BRUTE. His love for Estrildis, daughter of a German king, causes his jealous wife Gwendolen to raise arms against him. Locrine is slain, and Gwendolen, assuming power, drowns Estrildis and her daughter SABRINA. According to Geoffrey, England (Loegria) received its name from him.

Locusta. One who murders those she professes to nurse or take care of. The original Locusta was a professional poisoner living in Rome about A.D. 54. She poisoned the emperor Claudius at Agrippina's bidding and was hired by Nero to poison Britannicus. She was put to death under the emperor Galba.

Lodge, Thomas (1558?–1625). English poet, playwright, and prose writer. The son of the Lord Mayor of London, Lodge was educated at Oxford and became one of the group in London known as the UNIVERSITY WITS. Considered by some to be the best of the imitators of LYLY and the Euphuistic style (see EUPHUISM), Lodge wrote several prose romances, the first of which was *The Delectable History of Forbonius and Pisceria* (1584). During a voyage to the Canary Islands he wrote *Rosalynde, Euphues' Golden Legacie* (printed 1590), his most famous work. Based to some extent on the medieval tale of Gamelyn, it provided Shakespeare with the plot for As YOU LIKE IT. Lodge's poetry includes *Scillaes Metamorphosis, Enterlaced with the Unfortunate Love of Glaucus* (1589; reissued as *Glaucus and Scilla*). As the first example of a classical story given romantic treatment in verse, it may have influenced Shakespeare's VENUS AND ADONIS. *Phillis,* a sonnet sequence, was published with the narrative poem *The Complaint of Elstred* in 1593. *A Fig for Momus* (1595), based on the satires of Horace, is one of the earliest English verse satires.

THE

Lamentable Tragedie of

Locrine, the eldeſt ſonne of King *Brutus*, diſcour-
ſing the warres of the *Britaines*, and *Hunnes*,
with their diſcomfiture:

The Britaines *victorie with their Accidents, and the
death of* Albanact. *No leſſe pleaſant then
profitable.*

Newly ſet foorth, oуerſeene and corrected,
By *VV. S.*

LONDON
Printed by Thomas Creede.
1 5 9 5.

Title page of *Locrine*. Possibly by George Peele,
it was mistakenly included in the Shakespeare
Third Folio.

Only two of Lodge's plays have survived: *A Looking
Glass for London and England*, written with Robert
GREENE in about 1590, published in 1594; and *The
Wounds of Civil War*, produced c. 1587, published
1594. Some critics believe Lodge may have had a
hand in Part II of Shakespeare's HENRY VI and in
KING JOHN. In the latter part of his life Lodge became a physician, and his writings after that time
are confined to more serious and edifying subjects,
such as a *Treatise on the Plague* (1603) and a translation of Seneca.

Lodi, League of (1454). A 25-year nonaggression pact signed by the major states of Italy. Negotiated by the Venetians, it is regarded as the first
triumph of modern diplomacy.

Lodovico. In Shakespeare's OTHELLO, kinsman
to Brabantio, father of Desdemona.

Lofting, Hugh (1886–1947). English-born American writer, author and illustrator of children's books.
Lofting created the amiable and fantastic Dr. Dolittle,
the title character of several popular and imaginative
works such as *The Story of Dr. Dolittle* (1920), *The
Voyages of Dr. Dolittle* (1922), and *Dr. Dolittle's
Garden* (1927).

Loftus, Cissie. Stage name of **Marie Cecilia
McCarthy** (1876–1943). Scottish actress. She starred
on the stage and in early motion pictures. She was
famous for her sparkling impersonations of other
stage and screen stars.

Log, King. A king who rules in peace and quietness, but never makes his power felt. It is an allusion
to the fable of the frogs who asked for a king. Jupiter
first threw them down a log of wood, but they
grumbled at so spiritless a king. He then sent them
a stork, which devoured them eagerly.

logical positivism. A leading school of 20th-cen-
tury philosophy. Logical positivists believe man's
thoughts, ideas, and concepts are dependent on his
command of language, so they approach truth and
logic through a study of language. The school had
its origin in Vienna but it is now centered at Oxford
in England. It was much influenced by the writings
of Ludwig WITTGENSTEIN. Logical positivism is also
known as linguistic philosophy and its exponents are
often called the Oxford philosophers. A. J. AYER is
a leading English member of the school. Linguistic
philosophy has profoundly influenced literary criticism in England. See CAMBRIDGE CRITICS.

Logistilla. In the ORLANDO FURIOSO of Ariosto,
the sister of the witch Alcina. Herself a symbol of
reason and virtue, she teaches Ruggiero to ride the
Hippogriff and gives Astolfo a book that enables him
to break enchantments, and a horn whose sound has a
shattering impact on all who hear it.

Lohengrin. A son of Percival or Parsifal in German legend, the Knight of the Swan. He appears at
the close of Wolfram von Eschenbach's *Parzival* (c.
1210), and in other German romances, where he is
the deliverer of Elsa, a princess of Brabant, who has
been dispossessed by Telramund and Ortrud. He
arrives at Antwerp in a skiff drawn by a swan,
champions Elsa, and becomes her husband on the sole
condition that she shall not ask his name or lineage.
She is prevailed upon to do so on the marriage night,
and he, by his vows to the Grail, is obliged to disclose
his identity, but at the same time disappear. The swan
returns for him, and he goes, but not before re-
transforming the swan into Elsa's brother Gottfried,
who, by the wiles of the sorceress Ortrud, had been
obliged to assume that form. Richard Wagner has an
opera based on the subject, composed (words and
music) in 1847.

Lohenstein, Daniel Caspar von (1635–1683).
German dramatist, poet, and novelist of the late
baroque period. Like the poems of Hofmann von
Hofmannswaldau, his plays are rich and sensual in
language and imagery. Unlike Gryphius, who often
gives his heroes a martyr's death, Lohenstein's tragedies frequently end in suicide—showing less of an
attempt to remain within Christian teachings. His
most famous tragedies are *Cleopatra* (1661), *Ibrahim
Sultan* (1673), and *Sophonisbe* (1680). His historical
novel *Arminius* (1689) reveals many parallels with
the actual political situation of the time and embodies
the author's own views.

Loki. In Scandinavian mythology, the Satanic
Aesir god of strife and evil who fathered the 3 monsters with the giantess Angerboda: the Midgard serpent, Fenris, and Hel. As enemy of the good gods,
he artfully contrived the death of BALDER. He was
finally bound to a rock by 10 chains and tortured by

drops of venom from a serpent overhead. One legend holds that he will remain captive until the Twilight of the Gods, when he will break his bonds. Another story says that he was freed at RAGNAROK when he and Heimdall slew each other.

Lokman. A fabulous personage, the supposed author of a collection of Arabic fables. The name is based on Luqman, the title of the 31st Sura of the Koran, in which it is stated, "We gave to Luqman wisdom." Like Aesop, he is said to have been a slave, noted for his ugliness.

Lollards. A name given, sometimes disparagingly, to members of the 14th-century English movement in England associated with John Wyclif and his demands for ecclesiastical reform. The Lollards held that the Church in England had become so encrusted with false doctrine as to be virtually useless and that the only true way of life was one based on the Bible. They particularly objected to the wealth and power of the clergy and advocated that the Church practice the poverty exemplified by Christ in the Gospels. The Lollards' rise into prominence during the latter half of the 14th century can best be understood in the historical context of the times: while the great mass of the people were plagued by warfare, pestilence, and poverty, the English clergy by skillful abuse of ecclesiastical prerogatives had amassed enormous power, wealth, and property. The Lollards reached the height of their strength in the decade following Wyclif's death: in 1395, it was said that one out of every two Englishman was a Lollard. Under the house of Lancaster in the 15th century, they were more and more sternly repressed and, waning in numbers, responded to their loss of strength by ever-increasing fanaticism. In part their decline was due to a loss of leadership; in the 16th century, to all practical intents and purposes, the Lollards had ceased to exist. Though it cannot be claimed that the Lollards sparked the English Reformation, the movement bore important fruit: the placing of the clergy under lay jurisdiction, the curbing of clerical abuses (especially in the form of the reduction in ecclesiastic holdings and possessions), and the insistence that the Bible through translation into the vernacular be made available to the reason of common men and women are all due, directly or indirectly, to the legacy left by the Lollards.

Lomax, John Avery (1872–1948). American folklorist and collector of folk songs. These he published in numerous books. His work has been continued by his son **Alan Lomax** (1915–   ), who has collected thousands of American and European folk songs by means of phonograph recordings, many of which are in the Library of Congress; some are also available on commercial recordings.

Lombard. A banker or money-lender. They are so called because the first English bankers were from Lombardy, and set up in Lombard Street (London), in the Middle Ages. The name Lombard is a contraction of Longobards. Among the richest of these Longobard merchants was the celebrated Medici family, from whose armorial bearings the pawnbrokers' insignia of three golden balls may have been derived (see St. NICHOLAS). The Lombard bankers exercised a monopoly in pawnbroking until the reign of Elizabeth I.

Lombard, Peter (c. 1100–c. 1164). Italian scholastic theologian. He studied Aristotelian philosophy under Pierre ABÉLARD, then himself became a teacher at Paris. He is often called Master of the Sentences (Lat., "Magister Sententiarum") because of his compilation of the *Sententiarum Libri Quatuor* (*Four Books of Sentences*). These volumes contain quotations from the authorities on doctrinal questions, with objections and replies also from "the sayings of the fathers." The fourth volume, concerning the nature of the sacraments, was especially important at the time; the whole work became a theological textbook and inspired innumerable commentaries.

Lomonosov, Mikhail Vasilyevich (1711–1765). Russian scholar and poet. He is considered the founder of modern literary Russian and the first to introduce what became standard Russian prosody. The son of a fisherman, Lomonosov became one of the most versatile and brilliant Russians of his time. He made valuable contributions in chemistry, mathematics, grammar, and rhetoric. He formed modern literary Russian by establishing a working relationship between the Old Church Slavonic language and the Russian vernacular, producing a literary language that rivals any other for richness and flexibility. Realizing that the old-style syllabic versification, based on the number of syllables in a line, was not fitted for Russian, Lomonosov introduced a system based on accents—alternating stressed and unstressed syllables. This system became the standard one used by the great classic Russian poets. Not until the early 20th century were new methods of versification introduced into Russian by Aleksandr Blok.

London, Jack. Real name, **John Griffith London** (1876–1916). American writer. Born in San Francisco, an illegitimate child, London was for a time the highest-paid and best-known writer in America. Brought up in dire poverty, he had already been at the age of 20, a hobo, a sailor, and a Klondike adventurer. Largely self-educated, he was influenced by the ideas of Darwin, Marx, and Nietzsche, and his work is marked by sympathy with the poor; prophecies of world revolution and a future socialist state; emphasis upon the primitive, the powerful, the cruel; and a predilection for the violent, usually embodied in an animal or a superman.

Going to the Klondike in 1897, London began writing stories of his Alaskan experiences for various magazines. These were collected in *The Son of the Wolf* (1900). His first novel, *A Daughter of the Snows* (1902), stresses his belief in Anglo-Saxon superiority, seen often in his later books. In 1903 came his most popular and enduring book, THE CALL OF THE WILD, the story of the dog Buck; WHITE FANG was a sequel. THE SEA-WOLF, again based on his own experiences, is an attempt to portray the Nietzschean superman. *The Game* (1905) is a novelette about a prizefighter, engaged to be married, who dies in his last fight. *Before Adam* (1906) describes the experiences of mankind in the far distant past; THE IRON HEEL turns to the future. MARTIN EDEN is a partly autobiographical novel in which the hero commits suicide, just as London was ultimately to do. *John Barleycorn* (1913), a tract against drinking, is also autobiographical. THE VALLEY OF THE MOON shows London's faith in socialism. *The Star Rover* (1915) describes trances experienced by a man in prison.

Best Short Stories of Jack London (1945) and *Tales*

of Adventure (1956) are selections of his stories. Leonard D. Abbott made a collection of London's *Essays of Revolt* (1926), and Philip S. Foner has edited *Jack London: American Rebel* (1947), a collection of his socialist writings.

London Merchant, The (1731). A bourgeois tragedy by George LILLO. It depicts the seduction of George Barnwell by the villainous Sarah Millwood and his subsequent crimes and degradation. The play, which was highly popular in its time, is chiefly remembered as an extreme example of sentimentality and bathos.

Loneliness of the Long Distance Runner, The (1959). A long short story by Alan SILLITOE. A boy who is sent to reform school for robbing a bakery narrates his own story. The corrupt society that has made him a delinquent is incidentally analyzed. The boy scores a triumph over the warden of the reformatory and the Establishment in general by deliberately losing in a long-distance race against another school.

Long, Gabrielle Margaret Vere (1886–1952). Prolific English novelist who wrote under 6 or 10 pen names. As Marjorie Bowen she wrote historical romances, such as *The Viper of Milan* (1906). As Joseph Shearing she wrote historical novels usually based on actual criminal cases, such as *Lucile Cléry: A Woman of Intrigue* (1932).

Long, Huey [Pierce] (1893–1935). American politician. Perhaps the most notorious as well as the most successful of American demagogues, Long began his career as a traveling salesman and later studied at Tulane University, completing the three-year law course in seven months. Having served as railroad commissioner of Louisiana, he was elected governor in 1928 and consolidated his power by placing his followers in strategic positions. After the failure of an attempt to remove him from office (1929), he was elected to the U.S. Senate in 1930 and, retaining the governorship until 1932, made himself master of the state; he provided Louisiana with good schools and highways during his term as governor, built a new state capitol at Baton Rouge, and helped the state university. In 1934 he announced a Share-Our-Wealth program to provide financial security for every American. After declaring himself a candidate for the presidency, he was assassinated on the steps of the state capitol by Dr. Carl A. Weiss, who was killed by Long's bodyguards.

Long's career inspired several novels, including Hamilton Basso's *Sun in Capricorn* (1942) and John Dos Passos' *Number One* (1943). Although Robert Penn Warren has denied that the character of Willie Stark in his ALL THE KING'S MEN should be identified with Long, the similarity is striking.

Longaville. In Shakespeare's LOVE'S LABOUR'S LOST, one of the three young lords who join Ferdinand, king of Navarre, in an oath of celibacy and study. He becomes enamored of Maria.

Long Day's Journey into Night (1956). A play by Eugene O'NEILL. An autobiographical drama, it was apparently written before July 22, 1941, when O'Neill presented the manuscript to Carlotta, his third wife. It deals with the Tyrone family: the father, mother, and two sons. The only other character is Cathleen, a servant girl. The father is a celebrated actor; the older son is a drunkard and ne'er-do-well.

A harrowing domestic tragedy, the play offers a clear insight into the character of O'Neill himself.

Longest Journey, The (1907). A novel by E. M. FORSTER. Its main character is Rickie Elliot, a student at Cambridge University. Lame, an orphan, and weak-willed, he neglects his good friend, Stewart Ansell, to marry Agnes Pembroke. Agnes, a shallow girl, with her brother influences Rickie to cheat his half brother, Stephen Wonham. Rickie finally redeems himself when he loses his life in saving Stephen's. The novel is notable for its picture of the intellectual and social life of Cambridge students.

Longfellow, Henry Wadsworth (1807–1882). American poet, translator, romancer, and college professor. Longfellow is two poets: one, the popular schoolroom image of the wise but harmless old man who wrote A PSALM OF LIFE, THE CHILDREN'S HOUR, and THE VILLAGE BLACKSMITH; and the other, the serious but limited poet who wrote MEZZO CAMMIN and was the subject of a recent study by the critic Newton Arvin.

Descended from old New England families, Longfellow went to Bowdoin College in Maine and then to Europe to study languages. On his return, he became professor of languages at Bowdoin and married Mary Potter. Dissatisfied with life in Maine, he turned to reminiscences. The result was his first book, the Irvingesque series of travel sketches *Outre-Mer: A Pilgrimage Beyond the Sea* (1835). After another trip to Europe, he accepted the chair of modern languages at Harvard, succeeding George Ticknor. His wife had died in Rotterdam on the European trip.

At home, Longfellow wrote HYPERION, a romance in which he modeled his heroine on Frances Appleton, whom he had met in Europe. In the same year, he published his first volume of poems, VOICES OF THE NIGHT, and three years later, his second, *Ballads and Other Poems* (1842). In 1843, after another trip to Europe, he married Frances Appleton. Her father gave the pair, as a wedding present, the beautiful Cambridge mansion, Craigie House. Longfellow lived in the house for the rest of his life, and it is now dedicated to his memory.

Increasingly interested in narrative forms, he produced a series that helped to establish a native mythology: EVANGELINE, THE GOLDEN LEGEND, HIAWATHA, THE COURTSHIP OF MILES STANDISH, and TALES OF A WAYSIDE INN. To these he added a long prose romance of curious charm, KAVANAGH.

In 1861, at the height of his fame, Mrs. Longfellow died. The poet's shock and sorrow prevented his working for several years. He finally finished his translation of *The Divine Comedy* (1865–1867) and his religious poem, *Christus* (1872). In his last years he added to his volumes, expanding earlier editions, and writing a number of sonnets.

His poetry and values have been subject to great reversals in critical opinion. Never profound or powerfully original, he did have a sound lyric sense and an effective understanding of European culture. His work, however, is rooted in literature, rather than life; there is always a feeling of aloofness in his lines. Longfellow's immense popularity did a great deal to develop audiences for poetry in America. See ARSENAL AT SPRINGFIELD, THE; BUILDING OF THE SHIP, THE; MY LOST YOUTH; WRECK OF THE HESPERUS, THE.

Longinus. See ON THE SUBLIME.

Longinus, or **Longius.** The traditional name of the Roman soldier who stabbed Jesus with a spear at the crucifixion.

Longinus, Cassius (c. 220–273). Greek rhetorician and philosopher. A Neo-Platonist and the teacher of PORPHYRY, he is not to be confused with the unknown author of the treatise, ON THE SUBLIME. Longinus taught at Athens, and counseled Queen ZENOBIA at Palmyra. He was executed by Aurelian for his loyalty to the queen.

Long Parliament. In English history, the Parliament that assembled in November, 1640, after the dissolution of the Short Parliament. The Long Parliament impeached the earl of STRAFFORD, passed the GRAND REMONSTRANCE and, after the final rupture with CHARLES I in 1642, conducted the CIVIL WAR against the king's forces. In 1648, the members who were willing to come to terms with Charles were ousted during PRIDE'S PURGE. The remaining members constituted the RUMP PARLIAMENT, which was forcibly dissolved by Oliver Cromwell in 1653 but was twice recalled in 1659. Early in 1660, after the Rump assembled and was joined by the members expelled in 1648, the Long Parliament declared itself dissolved.

Longstreet, Augustus Baldwin (1790–1870). American lawyer, clergyman, editor, writer, and college president. Longstreet, in addition to many activities, founded and edited the *States Rights Sentinel* in Atlanta in 1834, and wrote a classic of regional humor, GEORGIA SCENES. Later he wrote a series of short stories and a novel, *Master William Mitten* (1864).

Longus (4th or 5th century A.D.). Greek writer, supposed author of DAPHNIS AND CHLOË.

Long Valley, The (1938). A collection of 13 stories by John STEINBECK. They deal with the life of people in the Salinas Valley in California, especially in relation to the migrants who have come into the valley. Best known of the tales is *The Red Pony,* separately printed in 1945.

Lonigan, Studs. See STUDS LONIGAN.

Lonsdale, Frederick (1881–1954). British playwright. He is best known for his sophisticated comedies such as *The Last of Mrs. Cheyney* (1925).

Look Back in Anger (1957). A play in 3 acts by John OSBORNE, one of England's Angry Young Men. Tied down by his working-class origins, Jimmy Porter turns his resentment against English class values on his upper-class wife, Alison. Although he has brought her down to his own level of poverty, it gradually becomes apparent that only by breaking her spirit can he revenge himself for the injustices he has suffered, but Alison remains impassive in the face of his insults and cruelty. When a childhood friend, Helena, learns that Alison is pregnant, she persuades her to leave Jimmy. Helena then becomes his mistress and scapegoat, but because she is incapable of real suffering he can take no pleasure in her. When Alison comes back in complete despair after having lost her baby, Jimmy is able to show her his love, and they are finally united in their mutual degradation and pain.

Look Homeward, Angel: A Story of the Buried Life (1929). A novel by Thomas WOLFE. It describes the childhood and youth of Eugene GANT in the town of Altamont, state of Catawba (said to be Asheville, N.C.), as he grows up, becomes aware of the relations among his family, meets the eccentric people of the town, goes to college, discovers literature and ideas, has his first love affairs, and at last sets out alone on a mystic and romantic pilgrimage. OF TIME AND THE RIVER is a sequel.

Looking Backward: 2000–1887 (1888). A utopian novel by Edward BELLAMY. The author describes a collectivist Boston society in the year 2000. Its hero transported into the future, the book advocates the peaceful evolution of society until it reaches the point of state socialism. The book was extremely popular; numerous other writers adopted Bellamy's plot and characters to qualify or attack his theme, and the book led to the forming of a Nationalist Party to advocate his principles.

Loos, Anita (1893–   ). American humorous writer. Her famous light satire GENTLEMEN PREFER BLONDES inspired a play (1925), a sequel, *But Gentlemen Marry Brunettes* (1928), a musical comedy (1949), a movie (1953), and the title of her autobiography, *This Brunette Prefers Work* (1956). Miss Loos is also the author of the play *Happy Birthday* (1946) and numerous film scenarios.

Lope de Vega. See Lope Félix de VEGA CARPIO.

López de Ayala [y Herrera], Adelardo (1828–1879). Spanish statesman and dramatist. He is best known abroad as an exponent of the moral tendency that infused 19th-century Spanish drama, in spite of the fact that he attained the rank of prime minister of the Spanish government. His plays include *El tanto por ciento* (1861), dealing with wealth and honor in love, and *Consuelo* (1870). His delicate and lyrical sonnets have also added to his reputation.

López de Ayala, Pero or **Pedro.** Also known as **the Chancellor** or **el Canciller Ayala** (1332–1407). Spanish statesman, poet, and historian. His chronicles of the reigns of Peter the Cruel, Henry II, John I, and Henry III are distinguished by their dramatic style and psychological penetration. As a poet he is best known for *Rimado del Palacio,* a miscellaneous compilation containing religious verse as well as realistic satire on contemporary society. He also wrote a treatise on falconry and translations of the works of Boethius, St. Isidore, and Boccaccio.

López de Mendoza, Iñigo. See marqués de SANTILLANA.

López Velarde, Ramón (1888–1921). Mexican poet. A disciple of Leopoldo Lugones, López Velarde wrote about love, religion, and his homeland in a style characterized by the use of eccentric, unexpected words and images. The poems in *La sangre devota* (1916) and *Zozobra* (1919) deal with the spiritual and carnal aspects of love, showing the poet's final disenchantment and dismay at his failure to satisfy either his physical appetites or the demands of his soul. *La suave patria,* his best-known poem, which appears in *El son del corazón* (1932), is an ironic but tender tribute to his native province.

López y Fuentes, Gregorio (1895–   ). Mexican novelist. His best-known novel is *El indio* (1935), in which he reveals the injustices inflicted upon Mexico's Indians in the early decades of the 20th century and realistically describes tribal customs and institutions.

Lorca, Federico García. See Federico GARCÍA LORCA.

Lord Jim (1900). A novel by Joseph CONRAD. It is about a man's lifelong efforts to atone for an act of instinctive cowardice. The young Jim is one of the officers of the *Patna* who frantically take to the boats when their ship appears to be sinking—leaving their passengers, eight hundred Muslim pilgrims, to apparently certain death. But the ship survives and is towed to port, and Jim becomes a wandering outcast. Eventually he wins a measure of satisfaction and self-respect from a busy, useful life among the natives of Patusan, who put complete confidence in *Tuan* Jim (Lord Jim). His life comes to its second crisis when a group of white men whom he has befriended betray his trust by murdering Dain Waris, his best friend, the son of the old chief Doramin. In spite of the pleas of the native girl he loves, Jim immediately gives himself up to native justice and is killed by Doramin. He wins back his lost honor and triumphs in death. The story is told obliquely, through Marlow's account of his own experiences and stories and letters from his friends.

Lord of Burleigh, The (1842). A ballad by Alfred, Lord TENNYSON. In the guise of a village painter the noble-born hero courts and wins a simple country maiden; but, when he takes her home to his castle, she feels out of place and pines away and dies.

Lord of Misrule. Sometimes **King,** or **Abbot of Misrule.** An official appointed to oversee the horseplay of Christmas festivities during the 15th and 16th centuries. In Scotland he was called the Abbot of Unreason; in France, *L'abbé de Liesse* (jollity). At Oxford and Cambridge one of the Masters of Arts superintended both the Christmas and Candlemas sports, for which he was allowed a fee of 40s. A similar "lord" was appointed by the lord mayor of London, the sheriffs and the chief nobility. These mock dignitaries often had other officers under them, and were furnished with hobby-horses, dragons, and musicians. Polydore Vergil says the Feast of Misrule was derived from the Saturnalia, the disorderly Roman festival held in December.

Lord of the Flies (1955). A novel by William GOLDING about a group of boys stranded on a paradisal island after a plane crash. In spite of the efforts of a few leaders to form an organized society, the group reverts to primitive religious rites and ritual murder. Children's adventure stories and anthropology are powerfully combined with Eden and original sin.

Lord Ormont and His Aminta (1894). A novel by George MEREDITH. It is based on the career of the earl of Peterborough, who rendered distinguished service at Valencia but in later life nourished resentment against the government, which had recalled him for high-handedness in 1707. He married Anastasia Robinson, the singer, but made no public acknowledgment of the marriage for many years. In the novel the names are changed, and the heroine, Aminta, remedies her equivocal position by eloping with Matthew Weyburn and opening a school in the Alps.

Lord Ullin's Daughter (1809). A ballad by Thomas CAMPBELL. Lord Ullin's daughter elopes with the Chief of Ulva's Isle, and is pursued by her father with a party of retainers. The lovers reach a ferry, and promise to give the boatman "a silver pound" to row them across the Lochgyle. The waters are very rough, and the father reaches the shore just in time to see the boat capsize, and his daughter drowned.

Lorelei or **Lurlei.** The name of a rock cliff that juts into the Rhine near Bingen and is known as a danger to shipping. Clemens Brentano, in his ballad "Lore Lay" (included in the novel *Godwi*, 1800–1801), was the first to associate the rock with a woman of the same name; and the poem is so convincingly folklike in style that Brentano's invention came to be regarded as a genuine folk legend. But Brentano's Lore Lay is only a woman, and it was not until Heinrich HEINE's famous poem *Die Lorelei* (1827) that the now-popular idea of a siren sitting atop the rock and luring ships to their destruction by her singing was actually created.

Lorenzetti, Ambrogio (1265?–1348) and **Pietro** (fl. 1306–1348). Italian painters of the early Sienese school. Ambrogio is noted for his allegorical fresco *The Effects of Good Government* and for his paintings of religious subjects. His brother Pietro is noted for his *Deposition* fresco and for the *Madonna and Child with Saints* in the church of St. Francis at Assisi.

Lorenzo. In Shakespeare's MERCHANT OF VENICE, the impractical but honest young man with whom Jessica, the daughter of Shylock, elopes.

Lorenzo. The name by which D. H. LAWRENCE was known to his admirers and disciples.

Loretto, the house of. Santa Casa, the reputed house of the Virgin Mary at Nazareth. It was miraculously translated to Fiume in Dalmatia in 1291, thence to Recanati in 1294, and finally to a plot of land belonging to a certain Lady Lauretta, near Ancona, Italy, around which the town of Loretto sprang up. The chapel contains bas-reliefs showing incidents in the life of the Virgin, and a rough image traditionally held to have been carved by St. Luke. See Richard CRASHAW.

Lorimer, George Horace (1867–1937). American editor (1899–1936) of the *Saturday Evening Post.* Lorimer also wrote two "inspirational" books, advocating rugged individualism: *Letters from a Self-Made Merchant to His Son* (1902) and *Old Gorgon Graham* (1904).

Lorna Doone, a Romance of Exmoor (1869). A historical novel by R. D. BLACKMORE set in 17th-century Devonshire at the time of the rebellion of the duke of MONMOUTH. The young hero, John Ridd, falls into the hands of the Doones, an outlaw clan. He is saved by Lorna Doone, a mere child, and when he comes of age, he sets out to find her again. Because the Doones killed his father he hates them, but protects Lorna against them, and finally, learning that she is the kidnaped daughter of a Scottish nobleman, marries her.

Lorrain, Claude. Originally, **Claude Gellée** or **Gelée** (1600–1682). French landscape painter. At the age of 27, Claude Lorrain established himself permanently in Rome, where he studied the surrounding countryside and the varying aspects it assumed with the passage of the day. Acknowledged a master during his lifetime, he permanently influenced the art of landscape painting. His calm and poetic, idyllic scenes are known for their golden light.

Los de abajo (The Underdogs, 1916). A novel by Mariano AZUELA. Ignored for years after its first appearance in a Spanish-language El Paso newspaper, *Los de abajo* is now generally regarded as the best of the many novels inspired by the Mexican Revolution. Written in a spare, colloquial style, the novel consists of a series of sharply etched vignettes that recount the career of Demetrio Macías, the leader of a band of ignorant, often bestial, peasants. Through Macías, Azuela brilliantly re-creates the blind, apparently futile struggle of the nameless masses who took up arms for a cause they did not understand and, swept along by the turbulence of the revolution, continued fighting because they did not know how to stop.

Lost Chord, The (1858). A once popular poem by Adelaide Anne Procter (1825–1864), daughter of Bryan Waller PROCTER. She wrote it under the pseudonym of Mary Berwick; it begins "Seated one day at the organ . . ." and was set to music by Sir Arthur Sullivan.

Lost Colony of Roanoke. See ROANOKE ISLAND.

lost generation. A term used to refer to the generation of men and women who came to maturity during World War I (1914–1918); specifically it refers to their experiences in the war itself, to the social dislocations following it, and to their rootlessness and disillusionment. Gertrude Stein is said to have coined the term in a conversation with Ernest Hemingway, whose early novels are considered to typify the attitudes and behavior of the lost generation. *The Lost Generation* (1931) by Malcolm Cowley dealt with the subject.

Lost Lady, A (1923). A novel by Willa CATHER. The "lost lady" of the title is Marian Forrester, the charming young wife of a rugged pioneer and railroad-builder. She is seen, with a naïveté that becomes the most delicate irony and revelation, through the eyes of Niel Herbert, an adoring young boy. Her husband's death leaves Marian in financial difficulties, and she becomes the mistress of Ivy Peters, an aggressive businessman of the new generation. After Peters marries and moves into the Forrester mansion with his wife, she disappears and is heard of again only by rumor as the wife of a wealthy Englishman in South America.

Lost Weekend, The (1944). A novel by Charles JACKSON. It is a realistic study of an alcoholic who first resists, then succumbs to his passion for liquor. On a five-day "lost weekend" much of his life flashes before him. The title has become a catchword for a drunken fling of major proportions.

Lot. In the Old Testament, the son of Haran and nephew of Abraham, who accompanied his uncle to Canaan and divided the land with him. Lot was one of the inhabitants of the wicked city of SODOM and escaped by the intervention of an angel, just before the city was destroyed by fire and brimstone, but Lot's wife was turned into a pillar of salt for ignoring the warning not to look back at the city (Gen. 19:26).

Lot, King. In Arthurian romance, king of Orkney and one of the kings subdued by Arthur. In Malory's *Morte d'Arthur* (c. 1469), he is the husband of MARGAWSE and father of the knights Gawain, Aggravaine, Gaheris, and Gareth.

Lothair. A novel by Benjamin DISRAELI (1870). The hero, Lothair, is a young English nobleman who, upon coming of age, inherits a great fortune. The plot centers about the struggle of the Anglican Church, the Church of Rome, and the revolutionary societies of Italy to secure his money and support. One of the most interesting characters of the book is the witty Lord St. Aldegonde. A primary cause for the popularity of the book was the interest taken by the English public in identifying the persons of prominence who appeared in it as characters only slightly disguised.

Loti, Pierre. Pen name of **Louis Marie Julien Viaud** (1850–1923). French novelist. His career as a naval officer sent him to distant places, providing him with the exotic backgrounds for many of his novels, which were sentimental in theme and luxurious in setting. *Aziyadé* (1879) is set in Constantinople, *Le Mariage de Loti* (1880) in Tahiti, and *Madame Chrysanthème* (1888) in Japan. In his sensuous and impressionistic style, Loti gave voice to a persistent melancholy. Although his travel romances first brought him fame, it was the publication of his three novels of Breton life—*Mon Frère Yves* (1883), PÊCHEUR D'ISLANDE, and *Matelot* (1893)—that won him enduring acclaim.

Lotis. See LOTUS.

Lotte in Weimar. See BELOVED RETURNS, THE.

Lottery, The (1949). A short story by Shirley JACKSON. This quietly told tale describes an annual lottery held since time immemorial in a small American town. Only in the final lines of the story does it become apparent that the winner is to be stoned by the other townspeople.

Lotto, Lorenzo (1480–1556). Italian painter. A leading figure of the Venetian Renaissance, he painted religious themes and secular portraits in his native Loreto, in Venice, and in other northern cities. His best-known works—*Portrait of Andrea Odoni, Virgin and Child with Saints and Angels, The Maiden's Dream*—reveal a style recognizable by the alabaster texture given to flesh by the manipulation of light and shade. *The Maiden's Dream*, an enigmatic allegory, best reveals his characteristic tone—sad, almost sinister.

lotus. A name of many plants. To the Egyptians, it was various species of water-lily, to the Hindus and Chinese the Nelumbo (a water-bean, *Nymphaeaceae speciosum*), their sacred lotus, and to the Greeks *Zizyphus Lotus,* a North African shrub of the natural order *Rhamneae,* the fruit of which was used for food.

According to Muhammad a lotus tree stands in the seventh heaven, on the right hand of the throne of God, and the Egyptians pictured God sitting on a lotus above the watery mud.

The lotus is a symbolic flower in Indian religion and literature. Brahma sits on a lotus and is himself born out of the lotus in Vishnu's navel. The Buddha is always depicted seated on a lotus; the Tibetan prayer chant is *Om mani padme hum* (I salute the jewel in the lotus). Growing in stagnant village ponds, the flower stands for the emergence into light from the darkness and sensuality of the phenomenal world; the leaves, unaffected by water, symbolize the *atman* (self) unpolluted by the attractions of the *gunas* (senses); and the daytime opening and nighttime closing of the flower suggest the timeless day and night of Brahma in the context of Hindu metaphysical belief.

The classic myth is that Lotis, a daughter of Poseidon, fleeing from Priapus was changed into a tree, which was called Lotus after her. Another story goes that Dryope of Oechalia was one day carrying her infant son, when she plucked a lotus flower for his amusement, and was instantaneously transformed into a lotus.

Lotus-eaters or **Lotophagi.** In Homeric legend, a people who ate the lotus-tree. The effect of this was to make them forget their friends and homes, and to lose all desire of returning to their native country, their only wish being to live in idleness in Lotus-land (ODYSSEY, ix).

Hence, a lotus-eater is one living in ease and luxury. Tennyson wrote one of his best-known poems on this subject.

Lotus Sūtra. (Sans. *Saddharma-pundarīka*; Ch. *Fahua ching*; Jap. *Hokke kyō*). Buddhist *sūtra* of great popularity in China and Japan. The *T'ient'ai* (Jap. *Tendai*) and *Nichiren* sects base their teachings on this work.

Loubet, Emile (1838–1929). French statesman and president of France (1899–1906). Loubet, with other liberals, sought revision of the Dreyfus case.

Louis XIV. Called **Louis the Great, le Roi Soleil** (the Sun King), and **le Grand Monarque** (1638–1715). King of France (1643–1715). The greatest autocratic monarch that France has ever known, he left his country bankrupt through his wars, conquests, and extravagances. His reign was marked by his lavish patronage of art, literature, and women, and coincided with the greatest flowering of French civilization to date. Louis secretly married Mme de MAINTENON, the last of his many mistresses, after the death of his first wife, Marie Thérèse of Spain.

Louis XVI (1754–1793). King of France. He married MARIE ANTOINETTE in 1770, and in 1774, on the death of his grandfather Louis XV, he began his reign; he was deprived of his powers by the Legislative ASSEMBLY in 1792 and was beheaded in 1793. See BAKER; VÉTO, M. ET MME.

Louis XVII. See DAUPHIN.

Louis, Pierre. See Pierre LOUŸS.

Louise. See Gustave CHARPENTIER.

Louise, the Glee-maiden. A prominent character in Scott's FAIR MAID OF PERTH. Enamored of Prince James of Scotland, she flings herself from a precipice at his death.

Louisiana Purchase (1803). The acquisition of Louisiana from France during the consulship of Napoleon by the U.S. for approximately $15 million. Alarmed by the threat implicit in Spain's retrocession of Louisiana to France in 1800, President Jefferson appointed James Monroe to purchase New Orleans and West Florida from the French. Napoleon, however, had abandoned his projects for a French empire in the New World and offered to sell the whole of Louisiana instead. The purchase of Louisiana, a vaguely defined tract of some 828,000 square miles lying between the Mississippi River and the Rocky Mountains, more than doubled the area of the U.S.

Louis Philippe (1773–1850). King of France (1830–1848). A son of Philippe Egalité, he was the first elected king of France. At the insistence of Thiers and Lafayette, Louis Philippe was elected constitutional monarch after the deposition of Charles X (see JULY REVOLUTION). A partisan of the Revolution in his youth, and democratic in the first years of his reign, he became, more and more, a typical Bourbon and absolutist. He himself abdicated the throne after the revolution of February, 1848, and died in exile at Claremont, England.

Lounsbury, Thomas Raynesford (1838–1915). American scholar and educator. A professor of English literature at Yale, he wrote a *History of the English Language* (1879), *Life of James Fenimore Cooper* (1882), and edited Chaucer's minor poems and the works of Charles Dudley Warner. A student of Early and Middle English, he was one of the original members of the American Academy of Arts and Letters, and a fellow of the American Academy of Arts and Sciences.

Loup Garou. See WERWOLF.

Lourdes. See BERNADETTE OF LOURDES.

Louÿs, Pierre. Pen name of **Pierre Louis** (1870–1925). French poet and novelist. A close friend of André Gide and Paul Valéry, he still remained primarily a disciple of the Parnassian school of José-Maria de Hérédia, whose daughter he married in 1899. *Astarte* (1891) is a collection of Hellenistic poetry; *Aphrodite* (1896) is a novel of Alexandrian manners. Although much of his fiction, such as the short story *Les Aventures du roi Pausole* (1901), was intended to shock conventional morality, Louÿs was essentially a worshiper of form and beauty, and a moralist. His other works include *La femme et le pantin* (1898), *Le Crépuscule des Nymphes* (1925), *Psyché* (1927), and *Poésies* (1927).

Love and Intrigue. See KABALE UND LIEBE.

Love and Mr. Lewisham (1900). A semi-autobiographical novel by H. G. WELLS. Mr. Lewisham is a rather comical young English science teacher and, later, college student. He reluctantly gives up his schemes for an ambitious scientific, literary, and political career when he falls in love and marries ordinary, domestic Ethel. The teaching and college background are like Wells's own; after an unsuccessful first marriage he always feared domestic confinement.

Loved One, The (1948). A novel by Evelyn WAUGH. It is a very funny, biting satire on American life, especially Hollywood mortuary practices, and on the more universal themes of love and death. The hero finally cremates the heroine in a dogs' cemetery.

love feast. A meal or banquet in token of brotherly love and friendship. It is often used as a synonym for the agape, or common meal, shared by early Christians, which originally always preceded the Lord's Supper.

Love for Love (1695). A comedy by William CONGREVE. The extravagant Valentine agrees to relinquish his inheritance to his sea-faring brother Ben if his father, Sir Sampson Legend, will pay his debts. Valentine's attempts to regain his inheritance are unsuccessful until the resourcefulness of his devoted Angelica extricates him from his predicament. Among the well-known lesser characters are Prue, Angelica's rustic cousin, and Jeremy, Valentine's enterprising servant.

Lovelace, Richard (1618–1658). English poet. One of the CAVALIER POETS, Lovelace was known for his grace, his handsome appearance, and his aristocratic gallantry. A passionate Royalist, he was imprisoned twice by Parliament during the Civil War and ruined himself supporting Charles I. He died in a London slum in great poverty.

Lovelace's poetry is very uneven: a large proportion of it is lifeless, extravagant, and labored, but he wrote a few lyrics whose nobility and grace equal anything of the period. Such are To ALTHEA FROM PRISON; *To Lucasta, Going Beyond the Seas* (1649); and To LUCASTA, GOING TO THE WARS.

Lovelace, Robert. The principal male character in Samuel Richardson's novel CLARISSA HARLOWE. He is a polished libertine who is kind and considerate to all who acknowledge his power, but ruthless (to himself and to Clarissa) in his search for proven affection. He is killed in a duel by Colonel Morden, Clarissa's cousin.

Love Me Little, Love Me Long (1859). A novel by Charles READE. It is concerned with the successful wooing of Lucy Fountain, the heroine, by David Dodd, a seaman completely at home on shipboard but extremely ill at ease on land. In a sequel, *Hard Cash* (1863), David's struggles to bring home a large sum of money result in his losing his mind, and as "Silly Billy Thompson" he escapes from a burning lunatic asylum to a frigate and lives through a series of exciting adventures before fate restores to him his reason, his wife, his exuberant daughter Julia, and his bank account of "hard cash." This novel was written as an exposure of conditions in the private lunatic asylums of England and as such aroused much discussion.

Lover, Samuel (1797–1868). Irish novelist, painter, and song writer. A successful portrait artist, Lover later turned to writing on Irish themes. His novel *Rory O'More* (1839) was avidly received, as was HANDY ANDY, an entertaining story of a singularly inept Irishman. His sympathetic portrayal of the Irish peasantry and his popular songs and ballads helped to herald the dawning of Irish Nationalism.

Lover's Complaint, A. An anonymous poem. It was attributed to William SHAKESPEARE on the basis of its inclusion in the first edition of the *Sonnets of Shakespeare* in 1609. The poem, which is somewhat wooden and stilted in its manner, is not generally regarded as a legitimate item in the Shakespearean canon.

Love's Labour's Lost (c. 1594). A comedy by William SHAKESPEARE. FERDINAND, king of Navarre, and his friends, Berowne or BIRON, Longaville, and Dumain, take an oath to eschew the company of women and devote themselves to study for three years. The charming princess of France arrives with her three vivacious ladies, Rosaline, Maria, and Katherine, on a diplomatic mission and, because of Ferdinand's vow, is housed in a pavilion outside the city gates. Despite their oath, the four gentlemen fall in love with the four ladies: Ferdinand with the princess, Biron with Rosaline, Longaville with Maria, and Dumain with Katherine. Discovering each other's perfidy, the gentlemen acknowledge love's power and decide to pursue the ladies, who gently mock them for their conceits. Learning that the king

Title page of *Love's Labour's Lost*. It is the first title page to bear Shakespeare's name (1598).

of France has died, the ladies are obliged to leave, but they assign various penances to the four suitors and promise to return to them in a year.

The play cannot be attributed to any early source, and the plot, which is based on current court life, is presumed to be of Shakespeare's invention. See HOLOFERNES.

Loves of the Angels (1822). The stories of the love of three angels for mortal women, in verse, by Thomas MOORE. The stories are founded on Eastern and rabbinical tales.

Love Song of J. Alfred Prufrock, The (1915). A poem by T. S. ELIOT. Said to have been written when Eliot was still an undergraduate at Harvard, it was first published in *Poetry* magazine after he had settled in England. Through the person of the poem's narrator, J. Alfred Prufrock, Eliot explores a kind of death in life and suggests the spiritual decay of his society. Prufrock, a middle-aged man of anonymous respectability, differs from those around him only in his greater degree of self-awareness and suffering. Conscious of the sterility of his world, he longs to make some significant gesture, but lacking the necessary will and passion, puts the matter off in introspection. The poem ends on a note of hopelessness. Completely paralyzed by social habit and a sense of his own futility, Prufrock will never escape and is finally identified with his surroundings.

Love, the Doctor. See AMOUR MÉDECIN, L'.

Loving (1945). A novel by Henry GREEN. Set in an Irish castle during World War II, it is a picture of the lives of the owners and their many servants. On this level, the book is a light, witty social comedy. Each of the characters loves some person or idea, and the different kinds of love are revealed by an ironical juxtaposition of scenes. The central characters are Raunce, the butler, and Edith, a maid, both of whom grow mature as their love develops. This love is emphasized by various recurrent symbols, like an imaginary cave of fairy gold. The gold is later replaced by a valuable ring whose loss and recovery is a focal point of the plot and a touchstone for the attitudes of the various characters.

Lowell, Amy [Lawrence] (1874–1925). American poet, critic, and biographer. A member of an old and distinguished New England family, Amy Lowell became a serious student of poetic forms. She is known for her association with and leadership in the imagist movement, in accordance with which she wrote numerous poems in free verse and "polyphonic prose." Her first book was *A Dome of Many-Coloured Glass* (1912). A year after its publication she met Ezra Pound and others in the imagist movement in England and subsequently became the leader of the movement in this country. Although Pound complained that she converted IMAGISM into "Amygism" she did much to sponsor imagist poets and edited a number of imagist anthologies. Celebrated as a personality as well as an artist, she was eccentric in behavior, keeping a large troupe of dogs, smoking large black cigars, and using language of extreme frankness. One of her best single poems is *Lilacs* (1925); several others are familar to readers of anthologies, notably *Patterns*. Among her books of poetry are SWORD-BLADES AND POPPY SEED, *Men, Women, and Ghosts* (1916), *Can Grande's Castle* (1918), and *What's O'Clock* (1925). Among her critical works are *Six French Poets* (1915), A CRITICAL FABLE, and a two-volume biography of Keats (1925). Her *Complete Poetical Works* (1955) were edited by Louis Untermeyer.

Lowell, James Russell (1819–1891). American poet, editor, critic, and diplomat. Although he was born into a distinguished Brahmin New England family, Lowell favored democratic ideas, attacked slavery, and was an early admirer of Lincoln. Trained for the law, he turned instead to journalism; he contributed to *The Dial,* and founded a short-lived magazine, *The Pioneer.*

In 1844, Lowell married Maria White, poet and firm abolitionist. Four years later, he published THE BIGLOW PAPERS, First Series, which brought him to the notice of the literary world. The dialogue between Hosea Biglow, the Yankee farmer, and his friends was especially important for its use of authentic New England dialect. The interest in language was to remain with Lowell throughout his career. In the same year, his long poem, THE VISION OF SIR LAUNFAL, was published; long a favorite among schoolchildren, it is far from his most significant work. Lowell's satirical, often accurate, always amusing A FABLE FOR CRITICS was also published during this important literary year.

His reputation established, Lowell became a leader of what is now called the popular, conservative school of American letters. After travel abroad, he succeeded Longfellow to the chair of modern languages at Harvard, and in 1857 was appointed as the first editor of *The Atlantic Monthly.* In 1861, he became co-editor with Charles Eliot Norton of the *North American Review.*

Lowell's active public life included the positions of minister to Spain and to England; in both countries he was an able spokesman for democracy. See COMMEMORATION ODE.

Lowell, Robert [Traill Spence], Jr. (1917–   ). American poet. One of the Lowell family of Boston, he is considered a leading poet of his generation. Many of his poems are set in New England, and several of them deal with his ancestors. His conversion to Catholicism in 1940 is reflected in many of the poems in his first collection, *Land of Unlikeness* (1944). A number of poems in this privately printed book were included in *Lord Weary's Castle* (1946), for which he was awarded the Pulitzer Prize. His poetry is complex and intense, occasionally ironic, and is marked by a strong sense of rhythm. *The Mills of the Kavanaughs,* of which the title poem is a dramatic narrative set in Maine, appeared in 1951. *Life Studies* (1959) is an autobiographical piece in prose and verse; *The Old Glory* (1964), a verse drama.

Lower Depths, The (*Na dne;* 1902). A drama by Maksim GORKI. The best known of Gorki's works, it is set among the derelicts of a sleazy flophouse. The theme of the play is the problem of whether to live without illusions and on one's own strength or to shield oneself from the pain of life by accepting a romanticized view of things. These choices are supported by the thief Satin and the wandering pilgrim Luka. A highly similar theme was used by U.S. playwright Eugene O'Neill in his drama, *The Iceman Cometh.*

Lowes, John Livingston (1867–1945). American teacher and scholar. Lowes taught at several universities before he joined the Harvard faculty (1918–1939). Among his works are *Convention and Revolt in Poetry* (1919), an account of action and reaction in the history of poetry; *The Road to Xanadu* (1927), an examination of the sources of Coleridge's *Kubla Khan* and *The Ancient Mariner;* two books on Chaucer; and two collections of essays, *Of Reading Books and Other Essays* (1930) and *Essays in Appreciation* (1936).

Low Heels and High Heels. Two great political factions in the LILLIPUT of Jonathan Swift's GULLIVER'S TRAVELS who are also called the Tramecksan and Slamecksan. The High Heels are the Tories, and the Low Heels are the Radicals. The king is a Tramecksan, the heir-apparent a Slamecksan.

Lowndes, Mrs. Belloc. Pen name of **Marie Adelaide Lowndes,** born Belloc (1868–1947). English novelist. The sister of Hilaire Belloc, she wrote historical and mystery novels, including *The Lodger* (1913), a murder story based on the crimes of Jack the Ripper.

Lowry, Malcolm (1909–1957). English novelist and traveler. He wrote *Ultramarine* (1933), a sea story in experimental, impressionistic style; UNDER THE VOLCANO, a psychological, symbolical novel about Europeans living in Mexico; *Hear Us O Lord* *from Heaven Thy Dwelling Place* (1961), a collection of novellas and short stories; and *Selected Poems* (1962).

Loyola, St. Ignatius of (1491–1556). The founder of the Society of Jesus (the order of JESUITS). He is depicted in art with the sacred monogram I.H.S. on his breast, or as contemplating it, surrounded by glory in the skies, in allusion to his claim that he had a miraculous knowledge of the mystery of the Trinity vouchsafed to him. He was a son of the Spanish ducal house of Loyola, and after being severely wounded at the siege of Pampeluna (Pamplona) (1521) he left the army and dedicated himself to the service of the Virgin. His Order of the Society of Jesus, which he projected in 1534, was confirmed by Paul III in 1540. His *Spiritual Exercises* (*Exercitia;* 1548), a manual of devotions and prayer, is considered a remarkable treatise on applied psychology as an inducement to mystic vision.

Lubbock, Percy (1879–). English literary critic. He is best known for his book *The Craft of Fiction* (1921).

Lucan. Full Latin name, **Marcus Annaeus Lucanus** (A.D. 39–65). Roman poet and prose writer. He wrote the *Pharsalia*, an epic in 10 books on the civil war between Caesar and Pompey. No other work of his is extant. He was, like Brutus and Cassius before him, an aristocrat and a rebel; like them, he regretted the lost republic and hated the regime of the Caesars. He joined PISO's CONSPIRACY against Nero, was denounced and, like Seneca, was ordered to commit suicide. He was only 25 when he took his own life.

Lucan enjoyed a great vogue during the Middle Ages, but of late has been more criticized than praised for his exaggerated treatment of the war between Caesar and Pompey.

Lucas, E[dward] V[errall] (1868–1938). English novelist, poet, essayist, and man of letters. He wrote numerous essays in the manner of Charles Lamb, on whose work he became an authority. Among his collected essays is *Adventures and Misgivings* (1938). He was also a prolific writer of novels, such as *Over Bemerton's* (1908) and *The Barker's Clock* (1931); travel books, such as *A Wanderer in London* (1906) and *French Leaves* (1931); biographies, such as *The Life of Charles Lamb* (1905); poetry; and art criticism.

Lucas, F[rank] L[aurence] (1894–1967). English writer and literary critic. He was the author of such works as *Decline and Fall of the Romantic Ideal* (1936) and *The Greatest Problem and Other Essays* (1960).

Luce, Clare Boothe (1903–). American playwright and widow of the late Henry LUCE. Although she has written a novel, *Stuffed Shirts* (1931), under the name of Clare Boothe Brokaw, her literary reputation rests on her plays. Among them are *The Women* (1937), an antifeminine play set on Park Ave.; *Kiss the Boys Good-bye* (1938), a satire set in Hollywood; and *Margin for Error* (1939), an anti-Nazi mystery melodrama. She also wrote *Europe in the Spring* (1940), observations on her travel abroad at the time of Germany's invasion of France and the Low Countries.

Mrs. Luce became more and more interested in politics and served two terms in Congress (1943–

1947). She later became U.S. ambassador to Italy (1953–1956).

Luce, Henry R[obinson] (1898–1967). American editor and publisher. With Briton Hadden, Luce founded TIME, the weekly news magazine, in 1923. *Fortune,* a monthly for businessmen, followed in 1930, and *Life,* the weekly picture magazine, appeared in 1936. Luce also published *Sports Illustrated, Architectural Forum,* and (until 1964) *House and Home.* He was married to author and diplomat Clare Boothe LUCE.

Lucentio. In Shakespeare's TAMING OF THE SHREW, a young man who comes to Padua to "deck his fortune with his virtuous deeds." He is immediately smitten with Bianca and resorts to a number of tricks in order to win her hand.

Lucia di Lammermoor (1835). An opera by Gaetano DONIZETTI. It is based on Sir Walter Scott's *Bride of Lammermoor.* In the opera Lucy Ashton is Lucia, Arthur Bucklaw is Arturo, and Edgar of Ravenswood is Edgardo. Bucklaw does not recover from the wound given him by his bride, as he does in the novel, and Edgardo, instead of being swallowed up in the quicksands, kills himself. The opera contains a celebrated "Mad Scene" for Lucia, and a popular "Sextet."

Lucian. The chief character in THE GOLDEN ASS of Apuleius. His behavior when changed into an ass, which he remains throughout most of the book, satirizes the follies and vices of the age.

Lucian (Loukianos, c. 120–200). A Greek satirist. He was the most brilliant wit of Greek letters under the Roman empire. A free-thinker, he was often referred to in his own time as the blasphemer and later compared with Swift and Voltaire. He wrote rhetorical, critical, and biographical works, romances, dialogues, poems, and other works. His *Voracious History,* a mock narrative of travel, is the archetype of such books as Swift's *Gulliver's Travels.* His *Dialogues of the Dead* have been called brilliant satires of the living. He is regarded as the inventor of the satirical dialogue. His novel, *Lucius, or The Ass* may have been based on a work by Lucius of Patrae that also served as a model for Apuleius' *The Golden Ass.*

Luciana. The meek and gentle sister of the shrewish Adriana in Shakespeare's COMEDY OF ERRORS. She is wooed by Antipholus of Syracuse.

Lucifer. The morning star. The Hebrew name for it was figuratively applied by Isaiah to Nebuchadnezzar, the proud but ruined king of Babylon; "Take up this proverb against the King of Babylon, and say . . . How art thou fallen, from heaven, O Lucifer, son of the morning!" (Isa. 14:4,12). It was later claimed that SATAN, before he was driven from heaven for his pride, was called Lucifer. In Marlowe's *Doctor Faustus* and Dante's *Inferno* Lucifer is the ruler of hell. In Milton's *Paradise Lost,* Lucifer is called Satan after his fall.

Lucifer, Lawrence. The narrator in Lawrence Durrell's novel THE BLACK BOOK.

Lucifera, Queen. See FAERIE QUEENE, THE.

Lucile (1860). A narrative poem by Owen MEREDITH. The heroine is beloved by two bitter rivals, an English lord and a French duke. She loves the former, but misunderstandings keep them apart. Many years later the lord's son and the duke's niece fall in love, are separated by the old rivalry, but are reunited through the efforts of Lucile, who has become a nursing nun.

Lucilius. In Shakespeare's JULIUS CAESAR, a friend of Cassius and Brutus. Captured by the enemy at Philippi, he pretends to be Brutus, but Antony, recognizing him, asks that he be treated with kindness for he would like to count such a man among his friends.

Lucina. In Roman mythology, a goddess of childbirth. She was sometimes identified with JUNO.

Lucinde. (1) The heroine of Molière's comedy L'AMOUR MÉDECIN. She is the daughter of Sganarelle. As she has lost her spirit and appetite, her father sends for four physicians, who all differ as to the nature of the malady and the remedy to be applied. Lisette, her waiting woman, sends in the meantime for Clitandre, the lover of Lucinde, who comes disguised as a doctor. He tells Sganarelle that the disease of the young lady must be reached through the imagination and prescribes a mock marriage. As his assistant is in reality a notary, the marriage turns out to be a real one, and Lucinde, who has been pining because her father disapproved of her beloved, is cured.

(2) The heroine of Molière's LE MÉDECIN MALGRÉ LUI. Géronte, her father, wants her to marry Horace, but as she is in love with Léandre she pretends to have lost the power of articulate speech, to avoid a marriage which she abhors. Sganarelle, the woodcutter, is introduced as a doctor specialising in dumb cases, and soon he sees the state of affairs. He takes with him Léandre as an apothecary; the young lady receives a perfect cure, an elopement.

Lucius Apuleius. See APULEIUS, LUCIUS.

Luck of Roaring Camp, The (1868). A short story by Bret HARTE. This is a sentimental tale of gold-rush miners and their false toughness. Dying, Cherokee Sal, a prostitute who frequents the mining camps, gives birth to a child the miners adopt and name Thomas Luck. The following year the camp is destroyed in a flood, and one of the miners, Kentuck, dies holding the infant in his arms. The story established Harte's fame after its first printing in his magazine, *The Overland Monthly.*

Lucky Jim (1954). A best-selling novel by Kingsley AMIS. The title is ironic, since the story is about the comic misfortunes of Jim Dixon, a young, lower-middle-class instructor at an English university. The book satirizes the academic "racket" and cultural pretensions. See ANGRY YOUNG MEN.

Lucrece. See LUCRETIA.

Lucretia. In Roman legend, the daughter of Spurius Lucretius, prefect of Rome, and wife of Tarquinius Collatinus. She was dishonored by Sextus, the son of the king Tarquinius Superbus. Having avowed her dishonor in the presence of her father, her husband, and their friends Junius BRUTUS and Valerius, she stabbed herself. The outcome was an insurrection which changed the magistracy of kings to that of CONSULS. The story of Lucretia has been dramatized in French by Antoine Vincent Arnault in his tragedy *Lucrèce* (1792) and by François Ponsard in 1843; in Italian by Alfieri in *Brutus;* in English by Thomas Heywood in *The Rape of Lucrece* (1630), by Nathaniel Lee in *Lucius Junius Brutus* (17th century), and by John H. Payne in *Brutus or The Fall*

of Tarquin (1820). Shakespeare selected the same subject for his poem *The Rape of Lucrece* (1594).

Lucretius. Full Latin name, **Titus Lucretius Carus** (98?–55 B.C.). Roman poet. He was the author of the unfinished *De Rerum Natura* (*On the Nature of Things*), a didactic poem in six books, setting forth in outline a complete science of the universe based on the philosophies of DEMOCRITUS and EPICURUS. The purpose of the work was to prove, by investigating the nature of the world in which man lives, that all things—including man—operate according to their own laws and are not in any way influenced by supernatural powers. Lucretius hoped thereby to free himself and all men from the yoke of religious superstition and the fear of death. The poem is arranged as follows:

Book I. All things are made up of eternal atoms which move through infinite space.

Book II. The entire world of material substances is produced through the joining together of these atoms.

Book III. The mind and the spirit are also an arrangement of atoms, in this case exceedingly more subtle. At death the individual soul is dispersed as its imperishable atoms fly apart.

Book IV. Sensation, perception, and thought are all produced by the images which are emitted by external surfaces.

Book V. The world, as we know it, was created by a fortuitous concourse of atoms.

Book VI. All natural phenomena can be explained according to this atomic theory.

De Rerum Natura is the only large-scale poem written in dactylic hexameter which has come down to us from the period of the Roman republic and is, with the possible exception of Vergil's *Aeneid,* the most ambitious poem written in Latin. Its scientific and philosophical argumentation often rises to magnificent heights of emotional power, intensified by an eloquent simplicity of diction and by the great passion of the poet's conviction. Lucretius was prevented by his suicide from completing the final draft of the poem; Cicero was said to have prepared the manuscript for publication.

Tennyson's dramatic monologue *Lucretius* repeats the legend that the poet committed suicide in a fit of insanity induced by a love potion given him by his wife.

Lucullus (110–57 B.C.). A wealthy Roman noted for his banquets and self-indulgence. On one occasion, when a superb supper had been prepared, being asked who were to be his guests, he replied, "Lucullus will sup tonight with Lucullus."

Lucy, St. Patron saint for those afflicted in the eyes. She is supposed to have lived in Syracuse and to have suffered martyrdom there about 303. One legend relates that a nobleman wanted to marry her for the beauty of her eyes, so she tore them out and gave them to him, saying, "Now let me live to God." Hence she is represented in art carrying a palm branch and a platter with two eyes on it. Her day is December 13.

Lud. One of the kings in the HISTORY OF THE KINGS OF BRITAIN by Geoffrey of Monmouth. According to Geoffrey, London (Kaerlud) received its name from Lud. He was buried near what is still known as *Ludgate.*

Lud's Town. London, so called from King Lud.

Ludendorff, Erich (1865–1937). Quartermaster-General in the German High Command (1916–1918). He was more powerful than either Hindenburg or Kaiser Wilhelm II during the last years of World War I. Acknowledging German defeat, he ordered the formation of a constitutional government to negotiate with the Allies. Later, he supported HITLER, then deserted him. See BEER-HALL PUTSCH.

Ludwig, Otto (1813–1865). German novelist and playwright who popularized the term poetic realism as a description of the realistic trend in German literature of his time. His own works, realistic in style, include the novel *Zwischen Himmel und Erde* (*Between Heaven and Earth*, 1856), about the tragic conflict of two brothers in love with the same woman; *Der Erbförster* (*The Forester*, 1850), a domestic tragedy; and *Die Makkabäer* (1854), a play in verse about the revolt of the Maccabees.

Luftwaffe (Ger., "air weapon"). The air force of Nazi Germany, organized by Hermann GOERING.

Lug. In the Gaelic mythological cycle, a hero of the people called the TUATHA DÉ DANANN. Later, he becomes an important god for the Sons of Mil, who are said to be the first Celts in Ireland. See BALOR.

Lugnasad. August 1, one of the 4 great feast days of the ancient Celtic year. See SAMAIN; BELTINE; IMBOLC.

Lugné-Poë, Aurélien-François (1869–1940). Actor and producer. An actor at the *Théâtre d'Art* of Paul FORT, he later became director of the theater (1893) and called it *Théâtre de l'oeuvre*. Lugné-Poë encouraged new dramatic talent: Crommelynck, Sarment, Salacrou, and Marcel Achard were first played in his theater. The avant-garde *Théâtre de l'oeuvre*, begun as a symbolist theater, sought to return poetry and an atmosphere of mystery to the French stage.

Lugones, Leopoldo (1874–1938). Argentine poet. The outstanding exponent of MODERNISM in Argentina, Lugones was a close friend of Rubén Darío, whom he resembled in verbal virtuosity and ingenuity. In his first books of poetry—*Las montañas de oro* (1897), *Los crepúsculos del jardín* (1905), and *Lunario sentimental* (1909)—he revealed a penchant for startling but beautiful imagery and rhythmical experimentation. His return to poetic orthodoxy was signaled by his *Odas seculares* (1910), written to commemorate the centenary of Argentine independence. In this and later works, including *Romancero* (1924) and *Poemas solariegos* (1928), he expressed his ardent love of country in a style that became progressively less personal and more realistic. His prose writings include *La guerra gaucha* (1905), poetic accounts of episodes in Argentina's war for independence, and *Las fuerzas extrañas* (1906), fantastic short stories.

Luhan, Mabel Dodge (1879–1962). American patroness of the arts and memoirist. Famous for her salons in Italy and New York in the early 20th century, she cultivated close associations with Max Eastman, D. H. Lawrence, John Reed, Gertrude Stein, and Carl Van Vechten. She told of their lives and hers in a four-volume autobiography, *Intimate Memories* (1933–1937). She had three husbands before she married a Pueblo Indian and settled down in Taos, N.M., where she was a vital force behind the art colony there. She also wrote *Lorenzo in Taos* (1932) about her relationship with Lawrence.

Lu Hsun (1881–1936) Pseudonym of **Chou Shu-jen.** Chinese short-story writer, essayist, and educator. A leader in the movement to overthrow the Ch'ing government and an ardent reformer, he is idolized by the communists. Many of his stories have been translated into English by Chi-chen Wang, in *Ah Q and others* (1941).

Luke, St. Patron saint of painters and physicians, author of the *Gospel of St. Luke* and the *Acts of the Apostles* in the New Testament. Tradition says he painted a portrait of the Virgin Mary; *Col.* iv. 14 states that he was a physician.

Luke, The Gospel According to St. The 3rd book of the New Testament. One of the SYNOPTIC GOSPELS, it was the third account of the life of Jesus to be written, the author using Mark and Matthew as sources, as well as other documents now lost. It has high literary merit and a strong humanitarian appeal. The author is almost certainly the Greek physician who was a traveling companion of Paul and the author of The Acts of the Apostles.

Lully, Jean Baptiste or **Giovanni Battista Lulli** (1632–1687). Florentine-born French composer. Known as the originator of French opera, he was appointed court superintendent of music by Louis XIV in 1653, and received his French naturalization patent in 1661. Out of the music that he composed for court entertainments, notably the ballets of Benserade and the *comédie-ballets* of Molière, he developed French opera with its characteristic accompanied recitatives, dramatic scoring, and balletic interludes. In 1672, Lully founded the Académie Royale de Musique, which later became the Paris Opéra, and for which he composed 20 or more operas and ballets to librettos by QUINAULT. Reflecting the fashion of the day in their choice of classical subjects (*Alceste*, 1674; *Proserpine*, 1680), these works held the stage for almost a century.

Lunsford, Sir Thomas (c. 1610–c. 1653). English jailer and long-time governor of the Tower of London. He was noted for his vindictive temper. Samuel Butler mentions him in *Hudibras*.

Lunt, Alfred (1893–   ). American actor. With his wife, Lynn FONTANNE, he has appeared on stage in *The Guardsman, Elizabeth the Queen, The Taming of the Shrew, Idiot's Delight, Amphitryon 38, The Sea Gull,* and *The Visit of the Old Lady.*

Luntz, Lev Natanovich (1901–1924). Russian playwright and critic. An active member of the SERAPION BROTHERS, Luntz was especially insistent on Russian writers looking to the West for their methods, particularly for ways of handling plot. He advised Russian writers to pay attention to such authors as Conan Doyle and Rider Haggard. Besides his work publicizing the viewpoint of the Serapion Brothers, Luntz also wrote four plays: *The Outlaw* (*Vne zakon;* 1921), *The Apes are Coming* (*Obezyany idut;* 1921), *Bertrand de Born* (1922), and *The City of Truth* (*Gorod pravdy;* 1923–1924).

Lun-yü. See ANALECTS.

Lupercalia. In ancient Rome, an annual festival, held on February 15, probably in honor of FAUNUS, worshipped under the name of Lupercal. The worshippers gathered at a grotto on the Palatine where Romulus and Remus were supposed to have been suckled by the wolf (lupus). It was a festival of expiation and purification, and goats and a dog were sacrificed. Youths smeared with sacrificial blood ran round the Palatine carrying thongs of goat's hide (*februa*); women struck by them were supposedly made fertile. The ceremony survived into Christian times; it was suppressed A.D. 494.

Lurcanio. The brother of Ariodante in a tale from the ORLANDO FURIOSO of Ariosto. He charges Ginevra, the heroine, with having caused the suicide of his brother, in despair over her alleged unfaithfulness. As a result, she is doomed until rescued by Rinaldo and the returned Ariodante, who had survived.

Luria (1846). A poetic drama, written in Elizabethan style, by Robert BROWNING. The titular hero, a noble Moor, leads the army of Florence to victory against the Pisans, but the Florentines distrust him and summon him to trial. Overwhelmed by their ingratitude, he ends his life with poison. The poem is based on a historical character of the 15th century.

Lurlei. See LORELEI.

Lusíadas, Os (The Lusiads, 1572). An epic poem by Luis de CAMÕES. It relates the illustrious actions of the Lusians, or Portuguese, of all ages, but deals principally with the exploits of Vasco da GAMA and his comrades in their "discovery of India." Gama sailed three times to India. It is the first of these voyages (1497) which is the theme of the epic, but its wealth of episode, the constant introduction of mythological "machinery," and the intervention of Bacchus, Venus, and other deities make it far more than the mere chronicle of a voyage. Bacchus is the guardian power of the Muslims, and Venus, or Divine Love, of the Lusians. The fleet first sails to Mozambique, then to Quiloa, then to Melinda in Africa, where the adventurers are hospitably received and provided with a pilot to conduct them to India. In the Indian Ocean, Bacchus tries to destroy the fleet, but the "silver star of Divine Love" calms the sea, and Gama arrives in India safely.

Interwoven in the poem are episodes based on notable events in Portuguese history, such as the death of Inés Castro and the victory of Aljubarrota.

Lusitania. (1) The ancient name for Portugal (2) A British transatlantic liner torpedoed without warning by a German submarine off the coast of Ireland on May 7, 1915. She sank in 18 minutes with a loss of 1198 lives, including 124 Americans. Indignation over this act contributed to U.S. entry into World War I.

Lustra (1916). A collection of poems by Ezra POUND. The title, from the Latin, refers to the offerings made by Roman censors "for the sins of the whole people." Pound also issued a collection called *Lustra of Ezra Pound* (1917), an extension of the earlier volume, containing *Near Perigord*.

Lutetia (from Lat. *lutum,* mud). The ancient name of Paris, which, in Roman times, was merely a collection of mud hovels. Caesar called it *Lutetia Parisiorum* (the mud town of the Parisii), from which comes the present name Paris.

Luther, Martin (1483–1546). German religious reformer. He was an Augustinian monk and the professor of biblical exegesis at Wittenberg where, in 1517, he posted his critique of the Roman Catholic Church's practices, the NINETY-FIVE THESES which are usually regarded as the original document of the REFORMATION. From then on, he was the center of a

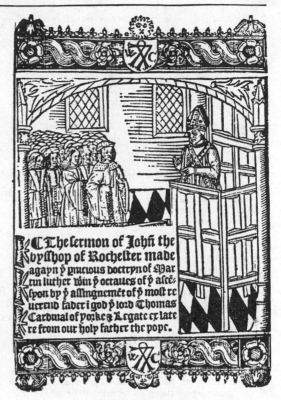

Title page of St. John Fisher's sermon against Luther (preached 1521). Fisher was later beheaded by Henry VIII.

violent religious upheaval in Germany where—among the humanists, for example—there had already been a great deal of feeling against Rome. The most important of Luther's later contributions to the controversy were his pamphlets *An den Christlichen Adel deutscher Nation* (*Address to the Christian Nobility of the German Nation,* 1520) and *Von der Freiheit eines Christenmenschen* (*On Christian Liberty,* 1520). His principal contention was that man is justified by faith alone, and not by works. On the basis of this idea of a personal faith, he favored the abolition of many church rituals and challenged the supreme authority of the pope. He was excommunicated in 1521 and then appeared before the Diet of Worms, where he took a firm stand upon his views and was put under the ban of the Holy Roman Empire. The elector of Saxony, however, undertook to protect him; and in a safe retreat, Luther began his translation of the Bible into German (New Testament, 1522; Old Testament, 1534). His other works include the *Sendbrief von Dolmetschen* (*Letter on Translation,* 1530), defending his rendering of the Bible, and 40 *Kirchenlieder* (*Church-Songs,* 1524), among which is the famous hymn *Ein feste Burg ist unser Gott* (*A mighty fortress is our God*). His *Tischreden* (*Table-Talk*) is a valuable source of detail about his personality and beliefs. See Philipp MELANCHTHON; Ulrich von HUTTEN; Thomas MURNER.

Lutrin, Le (The Lectern, cantos 1-4, 1674; cantos 5-6, 1683). A mock-heroic poem by Nicolas BOILEAU.

It satirizes a dispute between the treasurer and the choirmaster of the Sainte-Chapelle over the positioning of a choir lectern. The treasurer triumphs, but the poem ends with a reconciliation. Boileau not only lampoons clerical pomposity and pettiness with merciless irony, but manages, by contriving a battle in a bookshop, to comment satirically upon the literary feud between the ancients and the moderns. (See QUERELLE DES ANCIENS ET DES MODERNES.)

Luxemburg, Rosa (1870–1919). German socialist. She was killed with Karl LIEBKNECHT by the provisional government, because of her leading position in the SPARTACIST PARTY revolt of 1919.

Luzán Claramunt de Suelves y Gurrea, Ignacio de (1702–1754). Spanish scholar and critic. A bilingual academician, he is known for his championship of the neoclassic cause in Spanish literature. His ideas are contained in the treatise *Poética, o reglas de la poesía en general y de sus principales especies* (1737), which advocated a didactic poetry and adherence to the three unities in the drama. He also gained fame as a result of his Latin compendium of Descartes' ideas.

Lycaon (Lykaon). In classical mythology, a king of Arcadia. Desirous of testing the divine knowledge of Zeus, he served human flesh on his table, for which the god changed him into a wolf. His daughter, Callisto, was changed into the constellation Bear, whence this is sometimes called *Lycaonis Arctos.*

Lyceum (Lykeion). A grove and gymnasium on the banks of the Ilissus, in Attica. ARISTOTLE taught philosophy there as he paced the walks. The name is sometimes used to stand for Aristotle's philosophic school.

Lycidas (1637). An elegiac poem by John MILTON, commemorating the death of Edward King (1612–1637), a Cambridge schoolmate who was drowned in the Irish Sea. The title is taken from the name of a shepherd in Vergil's third *Bucolic.* One of the most famous English elegies, *Lycidas* is not only concerned with King's untimely death, but attempts to deal with a world in which the good die young and false priests and poets prevail. Milton's solution is partly that of the Christian—ultimately God's justice will win out on earth; meanwhile virtue is rewarded in heaven—and partly that of the dedicated humanist poet—true genius is interconnected and immortal and enjoys a special relationship to, and survival in, the powers and beauties of the natural world. *Lycidas* has the strength and majesty of Milton's mature poetry and is consciously a poem of self-renewal and dedication to great work ahead.

Lycurgus (Lykourgos). A legendary legislator of Sparta. He is referred to by Herodotus and Xenophon, but nothing certain is known about him. His reforms are dated, as a result of archaeological evidence, at 600 B.C. Lycurgus is credited with transforming the Spartans from an art- and luxury-loving people into the stern and disciplined state-directed citizens of the sixth century.

Lycus (Lykos). See AMPHION.

Lydgate, Dr. See MIDDLEMARCH.

Lydgate, John (c. 1360–c. 1451). English poet and priest. Lydgate studied in both English and European universities, and was ordained as a priest in 1397. He was a close friend of the son of CHAUCER,

and knew the elder poet, whose influence is obvious in much of Lydgate's work. An amazingly versatile and prolific writer, he is one of the few poets of merit in the 150-year period between the death of Chaucer and the beginnings of the Elizabethan period. However, though his work was esteemed only less than that of Chaucer during the 16th century, his prolixity and medieval attitudes make him little read today. Among his numerous works are two allegorical poems, the *Complaint of the Black Night* and the *Temple of Glass;* the *Troy Book* (1412–20), based on the *Historia Troiana* of Guido delle Colonne; *The Story of Thebes* (1420–22); *The Pilgrimage of Man* (c. 1424), a translation of a work by Guillaume de Deguileville; and the FALLS OF PRINCES (1430–38), based on a French prose version of Boccaccio's *De Casibus Virorum Illustrum.*

Lydian mode. See GREEK MUSIC.

Lyly, John (1554?–1606). English prose writer, poet, and dramatist. Lyly gained a reputation as a wit at Oxford, and took M.A. degrees both at Oxford and Cambridge. He went to London, where he became one of the UNIVERSITY WITS, and tried to gain a place at court. Though associated with the court for a number of years, he never gained the position of

Title page of Lyly's *Campaspe* (1584).

Campaspe,

Played beefore the Queenes Maieſtie on newyeares day at night, by her Maieſties Childre, and the Children of Paules.

(∵)

¶ Imprinted at London for Thomas Cadman. 1584.

Master of Revels for which he had hoped. He came under the patronage of Edward Vere, earl of Oxford, and wrote the first part of his most famous work, *Euphues, the Anatomy of Wit* (1579), for which he was immediately acclaimed. The following year he published the second part of this work, called *Euphues and his England*. The balanced, elegant, and highly artificial style of these pieces was very possibly Lyly's own invention. It was widely imitated for many years, notably by Robert GREENE and Thomas LODGE, and has come to be known as Euphuistic (see EUPHUISM; EUPHUES).

Lyly succeeded in becoming the vice-master of the acting company of the Children of St. Paul's, for whom he wrote plays to be presented at court. Of the eight plays he wrote for the Children the best known are *Alexander and Campaspe* (1584; reissued as *Campaspe,* 1591); *Endimion* (1591); and *Midas* (1592). He took his plots from Greek and Roman classic literature and transformed them into charming, ornate allegories of court flirtations and intrigues and the political affairs of the time, and refined and intellectualized comedy from its former and cruder state. All but one of his plays (*The Woman of the Moon,* 1597) were written in Euphuistic prose.

Lyly was involved on the side of the bishops in the Martin MARPRELATE CONTROVERSY, although only one pamphlet thought to be his has survived. Called *Pappe with an Hatchet* (1589), it was answered by Gabriel HARVEY in *Advertisement for Papp-Hatchet and Martin Marprelate,* which was appended to his *Pierce's Supererogation.*

Lynceus (Lynkeus). One of the ARGONAUTS and brother of Idas. He was so sharp-sighted that he could see through the earth, and distinguished objects nine miles off. He and his brother were killed in a fight with their fellow Argonauts, Castor and Polydeuces.

Lynch, Benito (1885?-1951). Argentine novelist. Lynch is best known for his depiction of the Argentine gaucho and for the homely fidelity with which he described rural life in Argentina. (See GAUCHO LITERATURE.) His books include *Los caranchos de La Florida* (1916), which relates the conflict between the domineering master of La Florida ranch and his impetuous son; *El inglés de los güesos* (1924), a love story of an English scientist and a gaucho girl; and *El romance de un gaucho* (1930), which is written entirely in gaucho idiom.

Lynd, Robert (1879-1949). Anglo-Irish essayist and journalist. He wrote essays in the manner of Charles Lamb; among his collections are *Books and Authors* (1922) and *In Defence of Pink* (1939). His wife, Sylvia **Lynd** (1888-1952), was a poet and novelist.

Lyonnesse. A legendary land in medieval romance. It was located near Land's End, off the coast of England; at present, it is submerged "full forty fathoms under water." King Arthur came from this mythical country, and the battle of Lyonnesse was the final conflict between Arthur and Sir Mordred.

Lyons, Eugene (1898-   ). Russian-born American journalist. At one time warmly sympathetic to Soviet Russia, Lyons became disillusioned and vigorously attacked the regime in articles and books, including *The Red Decade* (1941). He was editor of *American Mercury* (1939-1944) before becoming a senior editor for *Reader's Digest.*

lyre. See GREEK MUSIC.

Lyrical Ballads (1798). A volume of poems by Samuel Taylor COLERIDGE and William WORDSWORTH; a second edition was published in 1800, and a third in 1802. It was the first important publication of the poetry of the romantic period in English literature, and is considered one of the landmarks of literature. Wordsworth's contributions were his poems of country scenes and people, written in plain language and style, and his *Tintern Abbey.* Coleridge's principal contribution was *The Rime of the Ancient Mariner.* The second edition of *Lyrical Ballads* contains a preface by Wordsworth explaining his theory that poetry should be drawn from the everyday life and speech of men; this preface came to be considered the manifesto of English ROMANTICISM.

Lysander. In Shakespeare's MIDSUMMER NIGHT'S DREAM, a young Athenian in love with Hermia. He escapes with her into the woods in order to prevent her marriage to Demetrius.

Lysander (Lysandros, died 395 B.C.). Spartan naval and military commander. He defeated the Athenians at Aegospotami in 405 B.C., thus ending the PELOPONNESIAN WAR.

Lysistrata (c. 415 B.C.). The title and heroine of a comedy by ARISTOPHANES. It deals with an effective women's peace organization. In the 21st year of the Peloponnesian War, Lysistrata persuades the wives of Athens and Sparta to shut themselves up away from their husbands until peace shall be concluded. She has the satisfaction of dictating the terms.

Lyttelton, George. Baron **Lyttelton** (1709-1773). English author and statesman who was in the forefront of the opposition to Sir Robert Walpole. His works include *Letters from a Persian in England* (1735), an imitation of Montesquieu's *Lettres Persanes;* and *Dialogues of the Dead* (1760).

Lytton, Edward George Earle Lytton Bulwer-. See Edward George Earle Lytton BULWER-LYTTON.

Lytton, Edward Robert Lytton Bulwer-. See Owen MEREDITH.

M

Maartens, Maarten. Pen name of **Joost Marius William van der Poorten-Schwartz** (1858–1915). A Dutch author. He wrote almost exclusively in English. Although he wrote novels and stories chiefly of his native Holland, he was more admired elsewhere. His writings had an almost austere moral tone, although he was not an admirer of any organized religion.

Maat. Egyptian goddess of truth, justice, law, and the daughter of Ra and wife of Thoth. On Osiris' scales of justice, she placed her symbol, an ostrich plume, opposite the scale holding a human heart.

Mab or **Queen Mab** (perhaps from the *Welsh* "mab," a baby). In 15th-century English and Welsh legend, the queen of the fairies, an honor later given to Titania. She is described in Shakespeare's *Romeo and Juliet* as the "fairies' midwife"—i.e., she is employed by the fairies as midwife to deliver man's brain of dreams. Excellent descriptions of Mab are given by Shakespeare (*Romeo and Juliet*, Act I, scene 4), by Ben Jonson, by Herrick, and by Drayton in NYMPHIDIA (1627).

Mabinogion, The. A collection of medieval Welsh tales first translated into English (1838–1849) by Lady Charlotte GUEST. The tales, 11 in all, were preserved in two Welsh sources: *The White Book of Rhydderch* (written about 1300–1325), and *The Red Book of Hergest* (1375–1425). Though the tales were, for the most part, not committed to writing until the 14th century, internal evidence indicates that they originated far earlier. KULHWCH AND OLWEN, for example, is at least early 11th century, and reflects in language and custom an even more ancient time.

These 11 prose tales fall into three divisions. The first, called "The Four Branches of The Mabinogi," includes *Pwyll, Branwen, Manawydan,* and *Math.* The second, called "Independent Native Tales," includes *The Dream of Macsen Wledig, Lludd and Llefelys, The Dream of Rhonabwy,* and *Kulhwch and Olwen,* the last being the earliest Arthurian tale in Welsh. The third grouping consists of three comparatively late Arthurian romances: THE LADY OF THE FOUNTAIN; *Peredur, Son of Efrawg,* an early PERCIVAL story; and GERAINT SON OF ERBIN.

Most of the stories are concerned with Celtic mythological subjects and filled with folk themes. Archaisms in custom and language reflect an ancient time when such tales were not written down, but were memorized and transmitted orally from generation to generation.

The title word, *Mabinogion,* is a modern term appended to the collection by Lady Charlotte Guest. See ARTHURIAN LEGEND.

Macaire, Richard de. The name of the murderer of Aubrey de Montdidier, in the old French legend. Dragon, the Dog of MONTARGIS, who belonged to de Montdidier, showed such an aversion to Macaire that suspicion was aroused. Macaire and Dragon were pitted in single combat, and the man was killed, after confessing his guilt.

McAllister, [Samuel] Ward (1827–1895). American lawyer and social arbiter. He introduced the term "the Four Hundred" to describe the cream of American society; the figure refers to the number of people who could be accommodated in the ballroom of Mrs. William Astor.

macaroni (It., *maccheróne*). A coxcomb. The word is derived from the Macaroni Club, instituted in London about 1760 by a set of flashy men who had traveled in Italy, and introduced at Almack's subscription table the new-fashioned Italian food, *macaroni.* The macaronis were the most exquisite fops that ever disgraced the name of man; vicious, insolent, fond of gambling, drinking, and dueling, they were (c. 1773) the curse of Vauxhall Gardens.

There is a tradition that an American regiment raised in Maryland during the War of Independence was called The Macaronis from its showy uniform. This may explain the allusion in the American song, *Yankee Doodle.*

macaronic verse. Verses having foreign words ludicrously distorted and jumbled. It seems to have been originated by Odaxius of Padua (born about 1450), but was popularized by his pupil, Teofilo FOLENGO (Merlinus Coccaius), a Mantuan monk of noble family, who published a book entitled *Liber Macaronicorum,* a poetical rhapsody made up of words of different languages, and treating of "pleasant matters" (1520).

Macaronic Latin is a name for Dog Latin, modern words with Latin endings, or a mixture of Latin and some modern language. Presumably the word macaronic comes from the Italian food, which was originally a mixture of coarse meal, eggs, and cheese.

MacArthur, Charles (1895–1956). American newspaperman and playwright. He wrote *Lulu Belle* (1926) with Edward Sheldon, about a Negro Carmen; *Salvation* (1928) with Sidney Howard, about a lady evangelist; *The Front Page* (1928) with Ben Hecht, a play about newspaper life; *Twentieth Century* (1932) also with Hecht, a satire on Hollywood; and other plays. In 1929 he began writing and producing movies in Hollywood. He was married to Helen Hayes, the actress.

MacArthur, Douglas (1880–1964). American general. A graduate of West Point, MacArthur had a distinguished military career, with notable service in the Philippines, before being named commander

of the U.S. forces in the Far East in 1941. After the
Japanese attack on the Philippines, he was forced to
abandon Manila and retreat to Bataan Peninsula. In
1942 he was evacuated to Australia and named commander-in-chief of the Allied forces in the southwest
Pacific. In 1945, MacArthur, now a five-star general,
was given command of all U.S. army forces in the
Pacific; he accepted the formal Japanese surrender
on the U.S.S. *Missouri* and directed the Allied occupation of Japan. Named commander of the UN troops
in Korea in 1950, he was removed by President
Truman in 1951 because of his public statements
urging that stronger military action be taken against
Communist China. He returned to a hero's welcome
in the U.S. and made a memorable address to a joint
session of Congress (April 19, 1951), in which he
said, "Old soldiers never die; they just fade away."

Macaulay, Dame **Rose** (1889–1958). English
novelist. Her early novels were notable for their
wit, urbanity, and mild satire. The best known were
POTTERISM, *Told by an Idiot* (1923), *Crewe Train*
(1926), and *Staying with Relations* (1930). *They
Were Defeated* (1932, U.S. title *The Shadow Flies*)
is an excellent historical novel about Robert Herrick
and 17th-century intellectual life. Her post-World
War II novels are marked by irony and tenderness;
The World My Wilderness (1950) is about a wild
young girl in conflict with civilization, and *The
Towers of Trebizond* (1956) describes a religious and
historical pilgrimage in the Middle East.

Macaulay, Thomas Babington (1800–1859).
English statesman, poet, historian, essayist, and biographer. He is best known for his *History of England
from the Accession of James the Second* (1848, 1855,
1861), a work extremely popular in his day, marked
by a colorful style and vivid presentation. His LAYS
OF ANCIENT ROME, narrative poems dealing with Roman heroes, were also popular. In addition he wrote a
number of well-known historical and biographical
essays under the guise of book reviews for the
Edinburgh Review and a series of biographies of
literary figures for the *Encyclopædia Britannica*.
Macaulay was a staunch Whig and an advocate of
moderate reforms. He served in the House of Commons, was a member of the Supreme Council of
India, and Secretary of War. In 1857 he was made
Baron Macaulay of Rothley. Macaulay's prose style,
much admired in its day, is somewhat pontifical and
monotonous; similar qualities vitiate his poems. Much
of his prose writing, however, in spite of stylistic
faults, instances of insensitivity, prejudice, and exaggeration, remains interesting in itself and as an
expression of Victorian tastes and standards. His
essays are collected in *Critical and Historical Essays*
(1843).

Macbeth (c. 1606). A tragedy by William
SHAKESPEARE. Shakespeare's shortest play, *Macbeth*
has been described as a study in fear. It is thought
that the play may have been written as a tribute to
James I because of its emphasis on the supernatural, a
subject in which he was interested, and its flattering
portrayal of the origins of the Stuart line, to which
he belonged.

Two victorious generals, Macbeth and BANQUO, are
accosted on a deserted heath by three mysterious
witches, who prophetically hail Macbeth as thane
of Glamis, thane of Cawdor, and future king of

Scotland and then tell Banquo that his sons will sit
upon the throne. Macbeth is already thane of
Glamis, and when he learns that the title of the
traitorous thane of Cawdor is to be bestowed upon
him, his ambition to be king is kindled. When his
wife, Lady Macbeth, hears of the prophecy, she urges
Macbeth to kill King DUNCAN and caustically reproaches him for his scruples. Macbeth reluctantly
acquiesces, murders Duncan, and is proclaimed king.
Fearing the second part of the witches' prophecy,
Macbeth engages two assassins to murder Banquo
and his son FLEANCE, but Fleance escapes them. When
Macbeth learns that the Scottish thane MACDUFF has
joined Duncan's son MALCOLM, who is raising an
army in England to proceed against him, he orders
the death of Lady Macduff and her children. Lady
Macbeth, driven mad by her conscience, finally commits suicide, and Macbeth is slain by Macduff, who
has returned to Scotland with the English forces.
Malcolm is then proclaimed king.

The direct source of the play is Holinshed's *Chronicles* (1577). It records the career of a real Macbeth
(died c. 1058), who killed Duncan of Scotland in
1040, seized the throne, and was overthrown by Malcolm, Duncan's son, 17 years later.

The sleep-walking scene in Act V, in which Lady
Macbeth, tormented by the memory of her victims,
tries to wash imaginary bloodstains from her hands,
is one of the most famous in Shakespeare.

Maccabees. The family of Jewish heroes, descended from Mattathias the Hasmonaean and his
five sons: John, Simon, Judas, Eleazar, and Jonathan.
They delivered the race from the persecutions of the
Syrian king Antiochus Epiphanes (175–164 B.C.) and
established a line of priest-kings, which lasted until
Herod's reign in 37 B.C. Their exploits are told in
I and II Maccabees, the last two books of the Apocrypha. See JUDAS MACCABAEUS.

McCaig, Norman (1910–   ). Scottish poet.
He is the author of sensuous, speculative verse mainly
on Scottish themes. *Riding Lights* (1955) is a collection of poems.

MacCarthy, Sir Desmond (1878–1952). English
literary and dramatic critic and journalist. He is the
author of *Portraits* (1931), *Drama* (1940), and other
books.

McCarthy, Joseph R[aymond] (1908–1957).
American politician. McCarthy was elected to the
U.S. Senate from Wisconsin in 1946. As chairman of
the Senate Permanent Investigating Subcommittee, he
conducted an investigation of communism in the
government that aroused great controversy because
of McCarthy's sensationalistic and irresponsible methods. After a series of hearings (1953–1954) on alleged
subversion in the U.S. army, McCarthy was formally
condemned by the Senate.

McCarthy, Mary (1912–   ). American novelist, short-story writer, and critic. Her scathing satires
of American literary life acquire a particular effectiveness from being thinly disguised *romans à clef* and
from being couched in a prose style which has a
classic fluidity and precision. Born in Seattle, Wash.,
Miss McCarthy and her brother, actor Kevin Mc-
Carthy, lost both of their parents in the influenza
epidemic of 1918. As a result, she spent her childhood being passed around among relatives of vastly
different backgrounds, an experience she recounts

with chillingly detailed accuracy in *Memories of a Catholic Girlhood* (1957). After graduating from Vassar in 1933, she was engaged as a book reviewer for *The Nation* and *The New Republic,* which provided the experience for a group of loosely connected short stories published as *The Company She Keeps* (1942). In 1937 she became the drama reviewer for the *Partisan Review* and quickly established herself as the severest, as well as the wittiest, critic of the New York stage. Her theater pieces have been collected under the title *Sights and Spectacles, 1937–1956* (1956). Members of the *Partisan Review* group figure prominently in two of her other novels, *The Oasis* (1949) and *A Charmed Life* (1955). She also drew upon her experience as a college teacher for her satirical *The Groves of Academe* (1952). Her latest novel *The Group* (1963) brought her to the attention of a larger audience, which tended to solidify her position as America's foremost female author. A former wife of Edmund Wilson, she is the author of a collection of short stories, *Cast a Cold Eye* (1950), as well as *Venice Observed* (1956) and *The Stones of Florence* (1959), pictorial studies of the two cities, and *On the Contrary* (1961), a collection of articles on contemporary subjects.

McCaslin. A family in Go Down, Moses and other works by William Faulkner. Among the first families to settle in Yoknapatawpha County, the McCaslins evidence—more directly than any other Faulkner characters—the guilt of slaveholding, which continues to influence their lives after the Civil War. The founder of the family is [Lucius Quintus] Carothers McCaslin, father of Uncle Buck and Uncle Buddy (both white) and of Tomasina ("Tomey"), who is born a black slave. Incest is added to miscegenation when Carothers seduces Tomasina. Isaac ("Ike") McCaslin is the son of Uncle Buck and the last male McCaslin to bear the name. He is the principal character in the short-story *The Bear.* Unable to accept the family guilt, he refuses to inherit the family property which passes to Carothers McCaslin ("Cass") Edmonds, the great-grandson of the first McCaslin. Uncle Buck, who also appears in THE UNVANQUISHED, and Uncle Buddy do not believe in slavery and invent a system whereby their slaves can earn their freedom. Lucas Beauchamp, who also appears in INTRUDER IN THE DUST, is a part-Negro grandson of the first McCaslin; his friend and rival is his part-Negro cousin Isaac ("Zack") Edmonds, who temporarily steals Lucas' wife.

McCauley, Mary. Known as **Molly Pitcher** (1754–1832). American Revolutionary heroine. She earned the name of Molly Pitcher when she carried water to thirsty American soldiers during the battle of Monmouth (June 28, 1778). After her husband fell, she manned his cannon through the rest of the battle.

McClellan, George B[rinton] (1826–1885). American general. A West Point graduate who had become a railroad executive, McClellan was named commander of the Union forces in 1861. Although he had great organizing ability, his reluctance to take offensive action against the enemy exasperated President Lincoln, and he was relieved of one command after another until his retirement in 1863. In 1864 he was the unsuccessful Democratic candidate for president against Lincoln. There is still consid-

erable controversy about McClellan; many historians have charged him with ineptitude and even with disloyalty, while others, notably J. G. Randall, have contended that he was the great Union general of the war. See ANTIETAM.

McClure, S[amuel] S[idney] (1857–1949). Irish-born American editor. Having arrived in the U.S. in 1866, McClure studied at Knox College and later worked for the *Century Magazine.* In 1884 he created a revolution in publishing by starting the first newspaper syndicate, the purpose of which was to reprint in serial form material that had already been published.

In 1893 McClure founded *McClure's Magazine,* which became the most influential periodical in the country, particularly because of its muckraking articles. (See MUCKRAKERS.) In 1906, at its peak, McClure's partner, John S. Phillips, along with Ida M. Tarbell, Ray Stannard Baker, and Lincoln Steffens resigned because of differences with McClure. They founded the *American Magazine,* which continued the policies of *McClure's* and became equally influential. In 1914 McClure suspended his own magazine and later revived it briefly. It became part of the *New Smart Set* in 1929 and expired in 1933. McClure spent his last years in retirement. *My Autobiography* (1914) was ghost-written by Willa Cather.

McClure appears twice in fiction. R. L. Stevenson, whom he helped to win an audience, presented him as Jim Pinkerton in *The Wrecker* (1892). Less friendly is the characterization of him as Fulkerson, an aggressive Westerner, in W. D. Howell's *A Hazard of New Fortunes* (1890). A biography, *Success Story: The Life and Times of S. S. McClure,* by Peter Lyon, appeared in 1963.

MacCool, Finn. See FIONN MAC CUMHAIL.

McCormack, John (1884–1945). Irish-born American lyric tenor. He sang opera roles and German lieder with immense refinement of style. In later years, he was famous for his concert programs of Irish songs.

McCormick, Anne O'Hare (1882–1954). American journalist. As foreign correspondent and columnist for the New York *Times,* she was the first woman to receive a Pulitzer Prize in journalism (1937). An eloquent and prescient writer, she predicted the rise of Mussolini well ahead of her colleagues. *The World at Home* (1956) is a selection of her writings.

McCrae, John (1872–1918). Canadian physician and poet. He wrote *In Flanders Fields,* an inspirational poem popular during World War I.

McCullers, Carson [Smith] (1917–1967). American novelist and short-story writer. Recognized as one of the talented literary artists of her generation, Carson McCullers was born in Georgia and studied music in New York. Her first novel was *The Heart Is a Lonely Hunter* (1940), a parable on fascism told as the story of a deaf-mute in a small Southern town. *Reflections in a Golden Eye* (1941) is a tale of violence at a peacetime army post in the South. With A MEMBER OF THE WEDDING, her reputation, already established in literary circles, became widespread. *The Ballad of the Sad Café* (1951) contains the title novelette, dramatized by Edward Albee in 1963, and a selection of short stories. It was followed by *The Square Root of Wonderful,* a play (1958), and *Clock Without Hands,* a novel (1961).

McCutcheon, George Barr (1866–1928). American newspaperman and novelist. Best known for his romance GRAUSTARK and two sequels, McCutcheon also wrote the very popular *Brewster's Millions* (1902), a farcical account of the results of unexpectedly inheriting a fortune.

McDiarmid, Hugh. Pen name of **Christopher Murray Grieve** (1892–   ). Scottish poet, critic, and translator. He is a leading figure in the SCOTTISH RENAISSANCE. His poems are written in LALLANS, a synthetic Lowland Scots dialect. He is an ardent Marxist and Scottish Nationalist, and much of his poetry is concerned with social and political themes; many of his poems are satires. He writes of the conditions of the poor in his country, the state of society in his time, and the hope of a future under socialism. His published volumes of poetry include *Sangschaw* (1925), *Pennywheep* (1926), *First* and *Second Hymn to Lenin* (1931, 1932), and *A Kist of Whistles* (1946). For a collection of his poetry published in 1961 McDiarmid drew upon his 12 published volumes of poetry as well as previously uncollected poems. *Lucky Poet* (1934) is an autobiography. His critical works include *Contemporary Scottish Studies* (1924) and *At the Sign of the Thistle* (1934). He collaborated on *Scottish Scene* (1934) with Lewis Grassic Gibbon.

MacDonagh, Donagh (1912–1968). Irish poet and dramatist. The son of Thomas MacDonagh, he wrote the ballad-comedies *Happy as Larry* (1946) and *God's Gentry* (1951).

MacDonagh, Thomas (1878–1916). Irish poet and patriot. He was executed after the Irish Easter Week rebellion. His *Poetical Works* was published in 1916.

Macdonald, Flora (1722–1790). Scottish Jacobite heroine who aided Prince Charles Edward Stuart in his escape after the battle of CULLODEN. She resided in the United States (1774–1779), where her husband Allan Macdonald was a brigadier general in the British Army during the American Revolution. See PRETENDER.

MacDonald, George (1824–1905). A Scottish novelist and poet best known for the juvenile fantasy *At the Back of the North Wind* (1871).

MacDonald, [James] Ramsay (1866–1937). British statesman. In 1924, he organized the first Labour ministry in the history of Britain.

MacDowell, Edward Alexander (1861–1908). American composer of symphonic poems, piano sonatas, and orchestral suites. His widow founded in his memory the MacDowell Colony for musicians, artists, and writers at Peterborough, N.H., where talented persons may work undisturbed the year round, in picturesque surroundings. His most popular work is *Woodland Sketches* (1896).

Macduff. In Shakespeare's MACBETH, the thane of Fife and a former friend of Macbeth. Horrified at the crimes which Macbeth has committed and deeply loyal to his country, he joins Malcolm in England and returns with him to Scotland to unseat Macbeth. Macduff, who was "from his mother's womb untimely ripp'd," slays Macbeth, thus fulfilling the witches' prophecy that no man born of woman could harm him.

Lady Macduff. The wife of Macduff. She and her children are murdered at Macbeth's order when it is discovered that her husband has joined Malcolm's forces.

McFee, William [Morley Punshon] (1881–   ). English-born American novelist and essayist. McFee ran away to sea in 1906, and many of his books have a sea setting. His first book, *Letters from an Ocean Tramp* (1908), was followed by *Casuals of the Sea* (1916), which deals with an impoverished family in a London suburb. *Command* (1922), one of his best novels, laid in Salonika, is the story of a mediocre man's rise to heroism. He also wrote *The Harbourmaster* (1932), about a sea-loving man who stays on land; *Sailors of Fortune* (1929), short stories; and *Harbours of Memory* (1921), essays. Many of his stories are told by Chief Engineer Spenlove, whom McFee acknowledges as his "garrulous, ironic, goateed *alter ego.*"

M'Fingal. A verse satire by John TRUMBULL. The first canto was published shortly after Lexington and Concord in 1775; in 1782 Trumbull lengthened and reissued the poem, which was immensely popular. Modeled on Samuel Butler's *Hudibras* (1663–1678), it ridicules extremism on both sides of the Revolution, especially the bombastic oratory of the Scotch-American Tory, M'Fingal, who is tarred and feathered, repents, and prophesies final victory for the colonists.

MacFlecknoe (1682). A satirical poem by John DRYDEN. It is directed against Thomas SHADWELL, who was to succeed Dryden as poet laureate in 1689. The title of the poem comes from the name of Richard Flecknoe (c. 1600–c. 1678), an Irish priest noted for his bad verse. Dryden depicts Shadwell as Flecknoe's successor in the monarchy of nonsense. Pope used the poem as a model for his *Dunciad* (1728–1743).

McGee, Thomas D'Arcy (1825–1868). Irish-born Canadian editor, public official, poet, and political agitator. McGee was at first a violent advocate of the Irish Confederation; after being arrested, he escaped to the U.S., where he gradually lost his revolutionary zeal. He finally settled in Montreal, where he founded the *New Era,* was elected to the Legislative Assembly, became president of the Council, and was active in the movement for a Canadian Federation. When that was established he was chosen a member of the Dominion parliament and the minister of agriculture and emigration. He was assassinated by a political enemy. He wrote *Irish Writers of the 17th Century* (1846) and a collection of *Poems* (1869).

McGinley, Phyllis [Mrs. Charles Hayden] (1905–   ). American writer of light verse and books for children. A humorous writer and clever versifier, Miss McGinley was awarded a Pulitzer Prize for *Times Three: Selected Verse from Three Decades* (1960). Her numerous collections of verse include *On the Contrary* (1934), *Pocketful of Wry* (1940), *A Short Walk from the Station* (1951), *Love Letters of Phyllis McGinley* (1954), and *Merry Christmas, Happy New Year* (1958). She has also written several books for children, among them *The Horse Who Lived Upstairs* (1944) and *Sugar and Spice* (1960). *The Province of the Heart* (1959) is a collection of her essays.

McGuffey, William Holmes (1800–1873). American educator and textbook compiler. College teacher and president, McGuffey was known to thousands of Americans as the author of their first schoolbook. The series began in 1836 with the *First* and *Second Readers.* The *Primer, Third,* and *Fourth Readers* appeared in 1837, the *Speller* in 1838, the *Rhetorical Guide* in 1841, the *Fifth* and *Sixth Readers* in 1844 and 1857. He collaborated with his younger brother, Alexander Hamilton McGuffey, on the "Eclectic Series." The books have sold 122 million copies, with new editions issued as recently as 1920. McGuffey was a political conservative who supported the Hamiltonians rather than the Jeffersonians; his Readers reflect his point of view.

Machado de Assis, Joachim María (1839–1908). Brazilian novelist and poet. Widely regarded as Brazil's greatest novelist, Machado de Assis was the son of a Negro house painter and a humble Portuguese woman. He first earned his livelihood as a typesetter and as a journalist, but in his mid-20's he began to be recognized for his creative writing. In 1869 he married a Portuguese woman of distinguished family and, although afflicted by epilepsy, led a conventional private life until his death. In 1897 he founded and became first president of the Brazilian Academy of Letters.

In its musicality and detachment, his verse reflects the influence of the French Parnassians. Two of his best-known poems are the ironical sonnet *Círculo Vicioso* and the perceptive *Mosca Azul,* which appear in *Occidentaes* (1900). Other collections include *Chrysalidas* (1864) and *Phalenas* (1870).

The serenity that characterizes the poetry of Machado de Assis is also present in his novels; they have been compared to those of Henry James in their psychological probing, and to those of Laurence Sterne in their philosophical humor and whimsical digressions. In such works as *Memórias Posthumas de Braz Cubas* (*Epitaph for a Small Winner,* 1881), *Quincas Borba* (1891), and DOM CASMURRO, his masterpiece, Machado de Assis emerges as a skeptic who observes humanity with few illusions but great understanding.

Machado [y Ruiz], Antonio (1875–1939). Spanish poet. His use of landscape and his desire for simplicity and sincerity link this leader of Spanish poetry to the GENERACIÓN DEL 98. His first volume, *Soledades* (1903), concentrates upon the background of Seville, which it renders in somber tones. Better known, and more characteristic of his verse, is the volume *Campos de Castilla* (1912). This work contains such poems as *El dios ibérico* and *Las encinas.* His is a serious poetry of message, clothed in form, with the accent on spiritual meditation. With his brother, Manuel MACHADO, he is the coauthor of several successful dramas.

Machado [y Ruiz], Manuel (1874–1947). Spanish poet and dramatist. The brother of Antonio MACHADO, he is a more colorful and sensuous poet, particularly in his use of native Andalusian folk motifs. His early volumes, which have been well received, include *Alma* (1902) and *Museo* (1910). In the drama, he collaborated with his brother to write the well-known *La Lola se va a los puertos* (1930) and *La duquesa de Benamejí* (1932), which reveal the French influence upon his work.

Machaon. A son of ASCLEPIUS. One of the Greek heroes in the TROJAN WAR, he was skilled in medicine and cured the wounds of many of his fellow-soldiers.

Machau[l]t, Guillaume de (1300?–1377). French poet and composer. He was in the service of the king of Bohemia until 1346, of the royal house of France thereafter, and simultaneously holder of several ecclesiastical positions. He was the chief of a school of lyric poets including Eustache Deschamps and Jean Froissart, establishing the rigid forms for the *ballade, chant royal, rondel,* and *lai.* By introducing material from his personal life into his lyrics, he marked the transition from the impersonal conventions of troubadour poetry to the introspection of François Villon.

His long narrative poems include the *Jugement du roy de Navarre* (c. 1349); *Le livre du voir-dit,* supposedly the true story of the love he inspires in a young girl, though old himself, because of his poetry; *La Prise d'Alexandrie* (c. 1370). Chaucer borrowed from the *Livre de la fontaine amoureuse* for his BOOK OF THE DUCHESSE, and was probably significantly influenced by Guillaume's work in general.

Macheath, Captain. See BEGGAR'S OPERA, THE; THREEPENNY OPERA, THE.

Machen, Arthur (1863–1947). Welsh novelist, essayist, and journalist. Preoccupied with black magic and the horrors of the supernatural, he wrote short novels on these subjects, such as *The Great God Pan* (1894). *The Hill of Dreams* (1907) is about the aura of a terrifying past which surrounds an old Roman fort. His other books include *Strange Roads* (1923), *Notes and Queries* (1926), and *Dreads and Drolls* (1926).

Machiavelli, Niccolò (1469–1527). Florentine statesman and political philosopher. He is famous for his *Il Principe* (THE PRINCE) and other political, historical, and literary writings. His early experience as an envoy for the Florentine republic filled him with first-hand knowledge of Italian political squabbles and intrigues and of powerful figures like Caesar Borgia, and shaped his thought; the need to report these affairs precisely and economically shaped his style. At the same time he read widely and deeply in ancient historical writers. In 1512, the return of the Medici to Florence left him without position, but the enforced exile gave him the time to compose *The Prince* and his other masterpiece, the *Discorsi* (*Discourses*), between 1513–1517. Other writings that followed include a book on the art of war, a discourse on the government of Florence, a life of the condottiero Castruccio Castracani, and a history of Florence. His literary efforts include the *Clizia* and LA MANDRAGOLA (*The Mandrake*), the latter comedy one of the best produced during the Italian Renaissance; a Novella entitled BELFAGOR; and a dialogue on the Italian tongue. *Il Principe,* dedicated to a younger member of the Medici clan, and in part motivated by a desire to show how useful its author could be as a political advisor, ranges from philosophical discussion of the nature and origins of principalities to realistic and practical comments on the relations between a prince and his subjects. The ruthlessness of Borgia towards his enemies is praised, but senseless cruelty condemned; Italian politics are viewed with cynicism, but there is also an idealistic and stirring call to unity. Much emphasis is placed upon the military, especially the need for citizens rather than mercenaries to do the fighting necessary to protect any state. In the more leisurely *Discorsi* on Livy, where the method is to compare ancient and modern events and draw from the comparison aphorisms of universal validity, Machiavelli makes clear his true republican sentiments. The ideal government is a republic in which the various social and political groups are given a say. The *Mandragola,* his most famous literary work, tells a typical novella story in the dramatic manner of Roman comedy. Its young lovers triumph over an old fool through the assistance of a fiendish parasite and a nodding confessor. The cynicism of the play reinforced the reputation Machiavelli soon gained for being a teacher of treachery, intrigue, and immorality. His criticism of contemporary Christianity earned him the censure of the Church and spurred the popular portrait of him as a diabolical anti-Christ. In Elizabethan England, where his influence reached Spenser, Raleigh, and Bacon, his name became a popular synonym, especially in the drama, for diabolical cunning. In later years, the term *Machiavellian* came to connote cynical politics; *The Prince* became a handbook for tyrants and dictators. Modern opinion has reversed this trend, so that he is now regarded as a pioneer of political science; his republicanism and patriotism are stressed; and though the originality and value of his thought are now questioned, there is unanimous praise for his style and his literary genius. In modern times, Somerset Maugham's *Then and Now* (1946), which is based on the *Mandragola,* shows the literary influence. Similarly, there is H. G. Wells's novel *The New Machiavelli.*

Machine Infernale, La. See INFERNAL MACHINE, THE.

Mackail, J[ohn] W[illiam] (1859–1945). English classical scholar and educator; author of books on classical and English poetry. Among his books are *Latin Literature* (1895) and *Lectures on Poetry* (1911).

McKay, Claude (1890–1948). Jamaican-born American poet and novelist. His *Home to Harlem* (1928), the story of a Negro soldier returning home after World War I, was the first best seller written by a Negro. Of his other novels, *Banjo* (1929), a story of Marseilles, is perhaps the best. His verse was published in the collections *Songs of Jamaica* (1911), *Constab Ballads* (1912), *Spring in New Hampshire and Other Poems* (1920), and *Harlem Shadows* (1922).

MacKaye, Percy [Wallace] (1875–1956). American poet and dramatist. He is known for his interest in the community theater and his use of older literature as the point of departure for his plays. *The Canterbury Pilgrims* (1903), a successful blank-verse play, was produced by E. H. Sothern and Julia Marlowe as were the dramas *Jeanne d'Arc* (1906) and *Sappho and Phaon* (1907). Other plays include THE SCARECROW; CALIBAN BY THE YELLOW SANDS; *Rip Van Winkle* (1920), a libretto for Reginald De Koven's opera; *This Fine-Pretty World* (1923), a comedy of folkways; and *The Mystery of Hamlet, King of Denmark—Or What We Will* (1949), a tetralogy of verse plays dealing with the major characters of Shakespeare's play up to the time the play begins.

McKenna, Stephen (1888–1956). English novelist. Most of his novels are about the social and political inner circle of London. His best-known work is *Sonia* (1917).

McKenney, Ruth (1911-1972). American journalist and humorist. Although she is best known for the amusing *My Sister Eileen* (1938), she wrote a serious account of economic and social conditions in Akron, Ohio, from 1932 to 1936 in *Industrial Valley* (1939). Her other works include *The Loud Red Patrick* (1947), sketches about her grandfather; *Love Story* (1950), an account of her marriage and motherhood; and *Mirage* (1956), a novel about Napoleon. See Nathanael WEST.

Mackenzie, Sir Compton (1883-1972). English novelist and writer of essays, memoirs, and other nonfiction. SINISTER STREET is one of his best-known novels. In later life he wrote farcical comic novels, such as *Whisky Galore* (1947) and *Thin Ice* (1956). As a young man Mackenzie was converted to Catholicism, Scottish nationalism, and to islands (he lived on Capri, two Channel islands, and Barra in the Outer Hebrides). His early writings were often iconoclastic, but he later became an English institution, and was knighted in 1952. Among his works are the novels *Carnival* (1912) and *The Four Winds of Love* (1937-1940), *Gallipoli Memories* (1929), *Literature in My Time* (1933), *Catholicism and Scotland* (1936), *Aegean Memories* (1940), *On Moral Courage* (1962), and *My Life and Times: Octave One* (1963).

Mackenzie, Henry (1745–1831). Scottish novelist who is variously known as "The Man of Feeling" (after the title of his famous novel) and "The Addison of the North." His early works include the ballad imitations *Duncan* (1764) and *Kenneth* (1765), which reflect his interest in the revival of medieval art forms, but he soon turned to sentimental fiction and produced THE MAN OF FEELING. His other novels are THE MAN OF THE WORLD and JULIA DE ROUBIGNÉ. His periodicals in essay form, the *Mirror* (1779-1780) and the *Lounger* (1785-1787) contain notable critiques of the poetry of Robert Burns and of contemporary German literature. Sir Walter Scott was considerably influenced by Mackenzie's writings.

McKerrow, R[onald] B[runlees] (1872–1940). English pioneer bibliographer. His *Introduction to Bibliography for Literary Students* (1927) is a standard work.

McKinley, William (1843–1901). 25th president of the U.S. (1897–1901). A veteran of the Civil War, McKinley was elected to Congress in 1876, and became known as a champion of high tariffs. After two terms as governor of Ohio, he was the Republican presidential nominee in 1896, defeating William Jennings Bryan. The SPANISH-AMERICAN WAR occurred during his first term. Running on a platform that promised voters a "full dinner pail," he again defeated Bryan in 1900, but was assassinated by an anarchist, Leon Czolgosz, in Buffalo, N.Y.

Mackintosh, Elizabeth. Pen names, **Gordon Daviot; Josephine Tey** (1896–1952). Scottish novelist and playwright. She wrote plays, notably the successful historical drama *Richard of Bordeaux* (1933). Under the name Josephine Tey she wrote mystery novels, including *The Franchise Affair* (1951).

Macklin, Charles (c. 1700-1797). English dramatist and actor. He is remembered for his two fine comedies *Love a la Mode* (1759) and *The Man of the World* (1781). He was also one of the best actors of his time. See SHYLOCK.

MacLeish, Archibald (1892-   ). American poet. After an early volume of poetry, *Tower of Ivory* (1917), he became an expatriate in Paris and remained there until 1928. During this period he was greatly influenced by Ezra Pound, T. S. Eliot, and the French symbolists. He published two volumes of short lyrics, *The Happy Marriage* (1924) and *Streets in the Moon* (1926), both of which show his experiments in form and metrics. Two long poems also belong to the Paris period: THE POT OF EARTH and THE HAMLET OF A. MACLEISH. In *Nobodaddy* (1926), a verse play based on the story of Adam, Eve, Cain, and Abel, MacLeish turned to "the dramatic situation which the condition of self-consciousness in an indifferent universe" presents.

In 1932, MacLeish published CONQUISTADOR, which was awarded a Pulitzer Prize. Throughout the 30's, he continued to publish volumes of verse, but he attracted more attention with his verse plays, each having a timely political message generalized into a universal problem of human nature: PANIC, taking its point of departure from the depression years; *The Fall of the City* (1937), written during Hitler's rise to power, showing the people of an unnamed city accepting through blind fear a conqueror whose power is only imagined. The latter, like *Air Raid* (1938), was written as a radio script.

During World War II, MacLeish became more and more involved in the world's problems. He was appointed Librarian of Congress in 1939; he then held successively the post of director of the Office of Facts and Figures (1941-1942), assistant director of the Office of War Information (1942-1943), and assistant secretary of state (1944-1945). His poetry of this period was public and patriotic. He also wrote numerous essays dealing with social and political questions.

MacLeish won his second Pulitzer Prize with *Collected Poems 1917-1952* (1952), a third with his verse drama *J.B.* (q.v.). Among other important works of the 1950's are *Hypocrite Auteur* (1952), a poem calling on poets to invent new metaphors for their age; *The Trojan Horse* (1952), a radio play and satire on the Communist scare; and *Songs for Eve* (1954), a recasting of Eve as the heroine of intellectual and spiritual curiosity. Recent books by MacLeish include *Freedom Is the Right to Choose: An Inquiry into the Battle for the American Future* (1951) and *Poetry and Experience* (1961).

MacLennan, Hugh (1907-   ). Canadian novelist. He is the author of *Barometer Rising* (1941), *Two Solitudes* (1945), *Each Man's Son* (1951), *The Watch That Ends The Night* (1959), and *Scotchman's Return* (1960).

MacMahon, Comte Marie Edmé Patrice Maurice de (1808-1893). Marshal of France and 2nd president of the Third Republic (1873-1879). MacMahon was successful as a commander in three wars, but was defeated in the fourth by the Prussians at the battle of Sedan.

McMaster, John Bach (1852-1932). American historian. He is best known for his eight-volume *History of the People of the United States* (1883-1913), in which he stressed the social and economic aspects of the country's past rather than the military.

MacMorris, Captain. In Shakespeare's HENRY V, a captain in the army during the French campaign. Like his fellow captains, the Scottish Jamy and the Welsh Fluellen, he is typical of the stout British soldiers who overcame a much larger French force at Agincourt.

MacNeice, Louis (1907-1963). Irish-born English poet. He was associated with W. H. Auden and other left-wing poets during the 1930's, but was not as closely committed to Marxist doctrines as they were. His poetry is characterized by its colloquial, sometimes humorous tone and its use of contemporary ideas and images. His volumes of poems include *Blind Fireworks* (1929), *Collected Poems* (1949), *Autumn Sequel* (1954), *Eighty-Five Poems* (1961), and *Solstices* (1961). MacNeice was a classical scholar and a lecturer in Greek and Latin; he wrote a verse translation of *The Agamemnon of Aeschylus* (1936) and also one of Goethe's *Faust* (1951). *Out of the Picture* (1937) is a verse drama in the Auden manner. He collaborated with Auden on *Letters From Iceland* (1937). From 1941 he wrote a number of works for the British Broadcasting Corporation; *The Dark Tower and Other Radio Scripts* appeared in 1947.

McNeile, Herman Cyril. Pen name, **Sapper** (1888-1937). English writer of crime and adventure fiction. He created the hero BULLDOG DRUMMOND, a modern Robin Hood.

Macpherson, James (1736-1796). Scottish poet, writer, literary forger. In 1760 he published *Fragments of Ancient Poetry Collected in the Highlands of Scotland, and Translated from the Gallic or Erse Language.* Shortly thereafter he published first FINGAL, AN ANCIENT EPIC, and then TEMORA, AN EPIC POEM, purportedly translations from the Gaelic of the 3d-century bardic hero OSSIAN. The Ossianic poems —in actuality, a literary hoax—aroused a great deal of interest, the author collecting funds from a number of well-known literary figures, such as John Home and Hugh Blair, to make a tour through the Highlands in search of epic material. The London critics, especially Samuel Johnson, soon became suspicious, however, and Macpherson failed to make further Ossianic "discoveries." After his death, investigation revealed that Macpherson had liberally edited traditional Gaelic poems and added passages of his own. These pseudo-Gaelic poems are written in poetic prose marked by rhapsodic descriptions of nature and an atmosphere of vague mystery and melancholy. Although critics do not now consider them to be of much literary value, they had an important influence on the development of romanticism in France and Germany.

Macpherson's later writing was historical and political, including *Introduction to the History of Great Britain* (1771), *History of Great Britain from the Restoration to the Accession of the House of Hanover* (1775), and *Original Papers, Containing the Secret History of Great Britain* (1775). All three showed a bias against Britain and the ruling house of the time. For a while, the author was in the U.S. as secretary to the governor of Florida; in the last years of his life, he held a number of comfortable political sinecures at home.

Macready, William Charles (1793–1873). English tragedian, noted for his portrayals of Macbeth, Cassius, Lear, Henry IV, and Iago, among others. By 1837 he was in the first rank of his profession. He made several trips to the U.S.; during the last of these the Astor Place Riot occurred (May 10, 1849), taking the lives of 22 persons and injuring 36 others outside the Astor Place Opera House in New York City. The riot involved partisans of Macready and Edwin Forrest, an American actor, and was occasioned by a resurgence of anti-British feeling.

McTeague (1899). A novel by Frank NORRIS. Forbidden to practice dentistry when Marcus Schouler informs the authorities that he lacks both license and diploma, McTeague grows brutish and surly, while his wife, Trina, who had won $5,000 in a lottery, becomes a miser. He eventually murders Trina, steals her money, and is pursued into Death Valley by Schouler. McTeague kills Schouler, but the latter manages to handcuff their wrists. Tied to the corpse, McTeague is doomed to die of thirst in the desert.

MacWhirr, Captain. A heroic sea captain in Joseph Conrad's novel TYPHOON.

Madame Bovary (1856). A novel by Gustave FLAUBERT. With flawless style, Flaubert creates the life and fate of the Norman bourgeoise Emma Bovary. Unhappy in her marriage to a good-hearted but stupid village doctor, Emma finds her pathetic dreams of romantic love unfulfilled. A sentimental, discontented, and hopelessly limited person, she commits adultery, piles up enormous debts, and finally takes her own life in desperation. The novel's subject, the life of a very ordinary woman, and its technique, the amassing of precise detail, make *Madame Bovary* one of the crowning works in the development of the novel.

Mad Anthony Wayne. See Anthony WAYNE.

Madariaga [y Rojo], Salvador de (1886–). Spanish poet and academician. A multilingual author, exile from Spain, and Oxford professor, Madariaga is bent on the opening up of Spanish culture to foreign audiences. His wide range of interests is apparent in his varied styles and subjects. His works include the novels *La jirafa sagrada* (*The Sacred Giraffe*, 1925) and *The Heart of Jade* (*El corazón de piedra verde;* 1944); the poetic volumes *Romances de ciego* (1922), and *Rosa de cieno y ceniza* (1941); the essays *Shelley and Calderón and other essays on English and Spanish poetry* (1920) and *Don Quixote: An Introductory Essay in Psychology* (1934); the biographies *Hernán Cortés* (1941) and *Bolívar* (1951); and a historical interpretation, *España* (*Spain*, 1942), his best-known work.

mad as a hatter. A popular simile. The probable origin of this phrase is "Mad as an *adder*" (AS, *naeddre;* AS, *atter,* "poison"), but evidence is wanting. It was popularized by Lewis Carroll (*Alice's Adventures in Wonderland,* 1865), but was well known earlier and was used by Thackeray in *Pendennis* (1849).

Madeleine, M. In Victor Hugo's novel LES MISÉRABLES the assumed name under which Jean Valjean gains wealth and becomes mayor of a French town.

Madeleva, Sister Mary [Mary Evaline Wolff] (1887–1964). American poet, teacher, and essayist. She is the author of *Knights Errant and Other Poems* (1923), *Gates and Other Poems* (1938), and *Christmas Eve and Other Poems* (1938). Among her prose works are two books on Chaucer (1925, 1951) and *The Pearl—A Study in Spiritual Dryness* (1925).

Madelon. One of the 2 ridiculous snobs in Molière's comedy LES PRÉCIEUSES RIDICULES.

Madero, Francisco I[ndalecio] (1873–1913). Mexican revolutionary leader and statesman. Hailed as Mexico's deliverer after the ouster of dictator Porfirio Díaz, Madero was elected president in 1911. Although honest and well-intentioned, Madero failed to sense the need for social and economic reform and was unable to cope with the conflicting demands of revolutionaries and conservatives. In 1913 he was overthrown by his commanding general, Victoriano Huerta, and shot.

Madge, Charles Henry (1912–). English poet and professor of social science. His volumes of precise, intellectual poetry include *The Father Found* (1941).

Madgulkar, Vyankatesh (1927–). Indian novelist. Born in the village of Madgul in Bombay State, Madgulkar won literary prominence in India with a collection of village sketches, published in 1949. His novel *The Village Had No Walls* (1960) is a shrewd, accurate presentation of life in a Marathi village.

Mad Hatter. See HATTER.

Madison, Dolly [Payne Todd] (1768–1849). Wife of James Madison, whom she married in 1794. Mrs. Madison was unofficial first lady during the administration of Jefferson, a widower, and her fame as a charming, tactful hostess grew after her husband assumed the presidency. When the British burned Washington in 1814, she rescued many official papers and a portrait of George Washington from the White House. After Madison's death, she again became a social leader in Washington though her last years were marred by financial difficulties.

Madison, James (1751–1836). Fourth president of the U.S. (1809–1817). After serving in the Continental Congress during the American Revolution, Madison was elected to the Virginia House of Delegates where he helped secure passage of Thomas Jefferson's bill for religious freedom. As a member of the Constitutional Convention (1787), he played a dominant role in the framing of the Constitution, which he later defended in the FEDERALIST papers. He continued his close association with Jefferson, with whom he prepared the Virginia and Kentucky Resolutions condemning the ALIEN AND SEDITION ACTS and under whom he served as secretary of state. After Madison's election to the presidency, continued friction with Great Britain over U.S. neutral rights led to the War of 1812, which found the U.S. unprepared and disunited. Its opponents, especially in New England and New York, dubbed it "Mr. Madison's war." In the last years of his administration, Madison advocated tariff protection and a strong army.

Madness of Heracles, The. See HERACLES.

Mad Poet. Epithet of Nathaniel Lee (c. 1653–1692). He was confined for four years in Bedlam, and wrote some of his best poetry there.

Madras House, The (1910). A play by Harley GRANVILLE-BARKER. The Madras House is a great business concern. The characters are the various members of the family that control it and the employees to whom it provides a means of livelihood. Philip Madras and his wife, Jessica, the central figures, represent the new generation.

madrigal. An Italian verse form of uncertain origin and etymology, the earliest known being those of Petrarch. It is made up of a single stanza in which long and short lines appear without regularity. After Petrarch's time, it became a vernacular equivalent for the classical epigram, with its amatory subject matter treated wittily or humorously. In the 16th century the composing and singing of single and groups of madrigals became the rage, as such composers as Gesualdo, Luca Marenzio, and Claudio Monteverdi turned their talents to the form. The fashion reached England by the turn of the century with William Byrd and Thomas Morley.

Madwoman of Chaillot, The (La Folle de Chaillot; 1945). A play by Jean GIRAUDOUX. A delightfully eccentric old woman manages to exploit and defeat the exploiters and financiers of Paris.

Maecenas, Gaius Cilnius (d. 8 B.C.). Roman statesman and patron of letters. As a friend and adviser of the young Octavius Caesar, he was instrumental in arranging the Peace of Brundisium (41 B.C.), which temporarily reconciled Octavius with Mark Antony. He was not a fawning creature of the emperor, for on one occasion he publicly reproved Octavius by warning him against becoming a common butcher (*carnifex*) of his own people. It was Maecenas who organized the cultural resources of the principate by subsidizing the work of young artists, among whom were VERGIL and HORACE. His munificence as a patron has made his name proverbial.

maenads. In Greek mythology, the female attendants of DIONYSUS. The word means mad or frenzied women, also called Bacchae. See BACCHANTS.

Maerlant, Jacob van (c. 1235–c. 1300). Flemish poet who stimulated the cultivation of a Flemish literature distinct from the French. About 1264 he adapted a number of romances from the French, such as Benoît de Sainte-Maure's history of Troy and some of the Grail legends. Then he began metrical translations and adaptations of didactic works on government, ethics, and natural history, and of the Bible and histories by Josephus. His most important work, although he died before completing it, is the *Mirror of History* (begun 1284), a history of the world based on the *Speculum majus* of Vincent of Beauvais (d. 1264).

Maeterlinck, Maurice (1862–1949). Belgian poet, dramatist, and essayist. His literary career began with the publication of two volumes of poetry: *Douze chansons* (1896), and *Serres chaudes* (1889), both mysterious and dreamy in subject matter and mood. Maeterlinck's fame, however, rests on his symbolic dramas, played chiefly at the *Théâtre de l'oeuvre* of LUGNÉ-POË. *La Princesse Maleine* (1889), his first success, was followed by *L'Intruse* and *Les Aveugles* (1890), *L'Intérieur* (1894), and PELLÉAS ET MELISANDE (1892). Antinaturalistic in its subject, Maeterlinck's drama portrayed the inner conflict of the individual, not the external struggle between man and his world. Antinaturalistic in method as well, it abandoned a realistic portrait of life as seen for a symbolic expression of the inner life. The romantic melancholy of his early plays was succeeded by a faith in the spiritual life of all living things. The plays *Aglavaine et Selysette* (1896), *Monna Vanna* (1902), and *L'Oiseau bleu* (1909) were more hopeful in mood, founded on that belief in the spirit expressed in the essays of *La Sagesse et la destinée* (1898) and *Le Temple enseveli* (1902). The mystery of human life and death that preoccupied Maeterlinck led him to write studies of flowers and animals who share in this mysterious existence: *La Vie des abeilles* (1901), *L'Intelligence des fleurs* (1907), and *La Vie des termites* (1927). In 1911 Maeterlinck was awarded the Nobel prize for literature.

Maeztu y Whitney, Ramiro de (1875–1936). Spanish man of letters. Originally a member of the GENERACIÓN DEL 98, he later abandoned their social program, turning to ardent support of traditional Roman Catholicism in Spain. This is best expressed in his most famous work, the essay *Defensa de la hispanidad* (1934). His other works include *Hacia otra España* (1899), *La crisis del humanismo* (1919), and *Don Quijote, Don Juan y La Celestina* (1926).

Magda (Die Heimat, lit., *Home;* 1893). A melodramatic play by Hermann SUDERMANN, which presents the conflict between the mores of the bourgeois homestead and the bohemian life of urban artists.

Magellan, Ferdinand. Port. **Fernando de Magalhães** (1480?–1521). Portuguese navigator. After serving the king of Portugal in India and the Moluccas, or Spice Islands, Magellan fell into royal disfavor and offered his services to Charles V of Spain, from whom he won permission to sail to the Orient by a westward route. Leaving Spain in September, 1519, with five ships, he sailed down the eastern coast of South America, exploring the estuary of the La Plata river. After wintering at Port St. Julian, where Magellan quelled a mutiny among his men, the expedition entered what is now known as the Strait of Magellan and sailed northwestward, reaching the Ladrones (now Mariana) Islands on March 6, 1521. A month later Magellan discovered the Philippines. He made an alliance with a native chief and was killed on the island of Mactan while fighting on his behalf. His ships continued the voyage, but only one managed to return to Europe (1522), completing the first circumnavigation of the globe.

Maggie: A Girl of the Streets (privately printed, 1893; published, 1896). A novel by Stephen CRANE. The first realistic American novel, *Maggie* is the story of a girl of the New York slums, doomed by family and environmental forces to a life that she is unable to escape. The tone of the novel is set in its opening scene of boys fighting in the streets. In this Darwinian jungle even the toughest have difficulty in surviving. Maggie Johnson is the daughter of a brutal father and a drunken mother. She goes to work in a collar factory, falls in love with Pete, a bartender who is a friend of her brother Jimmie, and is seduced by him. Her mother disowns her; she becomes a prostitute, and in despair she finally kills herself. Her final degeneration becomes almost an allegory.

The novel, like THE RED BADGE OF COURAGE, is episodic in structure, relying on irony for its dramatic effect. Crane revised the original edition before the book was republished in 1896, eliminating some of the more melodramatic sections.

Magi (Lat., *pl.* of *magus*). Literally "wise men"; specifically, the Three Wise Men of the East bringing gifts to the infant Saviour. Tradition calls them Melchior, GASPAR, and Balthazar, three kings of the East. The first offered *gold,* the emblem of royalty; the second, *frankincense,* in token of divinity; and the third, *myrrh,* as a symbol of death.

Medieval legend calls them the Three Kings of Cologne, and the Cathedral there claims their relics. They are commemorated on January 2, 3, and 4, and particularly at the Feast of the Epiphany.

Among the ancient Medes and Persians the Magi were members of a priestly caste credited with great occult powers. After Zoroaster's death, they adopted the Zoroastrian religion and spread its influence to Egypt and Asia Minor. In Camões' *Lusiad,* the term denotes the Indian Brahmins.

magic carpet. See CARPET, MAGIC.

Magic Flute, The (Die Zauberflöte; 1791). An opera by Wolfgang Amadeus MOZART, with libretto by Emmanuel Schikaneder. It is written in the form of a *Singspiel,* or German ballad opera, with spoken dialogue instead of recitative. The Queen of the Night gives a magic flute to the prince, Tamino, who offers to rescue her daughter Pamina from the palace of the high priest Sarastro. Tamino finds Pamina, and also discovers that Sarastro is not evil, but a magnanimous priest of Isis and Osiris. The priest permits Tamino to undergo the ordeal of the search for truth, but he is not to speak. In his trials he meets Pamina, who is mystified by his silence and nearly kills herself. The lovers finally arrive at the temple of success, and Sarastro blesses them. Mozart and his librettist were both Masons, at a time when Masonry was outlawed in Austria, and they saw in this opera a way to advertise some of the Masonic ideals.

Magic Mountain, The (Der Zauberberg; 1924). A novel by Thomas MANN. Written in the tradition of the BILDUNGSROMAN, it is concerned with young Hans CASTORP and his personal development at Haus Berghof, a tuberculosis sanatorium in the Swiss Alps. In the book's symbolism, the sanatorium with its international clientele is a scale model of Europe on the eve of World War I; the pervasive atmosphere of sickness and death symbolizes a general European decadence, and the sanatorium's isolation indicates an unhealthy separation between artistic or intellectual life (the mountain) and the vital and active life below. Hans first comes there to visit his cousin Joachim Ziemssen, intending to stay only three weeks; but the place mysteriously attracts him, the discovery of a minute pulmonary defect induces him to remain, and he stays there for seven years. During this period, the other characters act upon him essentially as two forces; on the one hand, there are those like SETTEMBRINI, PEEPERKORN and Dr. Behrens, the vigorous, outgoing head physician, that attract him to the side of reason and vital, nondecadent activity; on the other, such figures as Clavdia CHAUCHAT, Leo NAPHTA and Dr. Krokowski, the assistant physician interested in psychoanalysis, hypnotism, and spiritism, draw him toward the mysterious and decadent, occult and aesthetic aspects of life. Hans's development reaches a climax when he gets lost in the snow and has an internal vision in which he first sees a classical temple surrounded by a society of beautiful and enlightened men, but then finds that inside the temple two old hags are tearing apart and devouring a child. The import is that even the highest attainments of reason (symbolized by the temple) must contain an element of deadly pagan decadence and that the two contradictory human tendencies toward enlightened, constructive activity and toward superstitious, destructive decadence are inseparable. But Hans's confrontation with this truth occurs on an intellectual plane and does not lead him to make any active personal commitment. At the end of the book, he has left the mountain and is a German soldier in World War I, but the reader feels that he is still basically an uncommitted and unfulfilled young man.

Mágico prodigioso, El (**The Wonder-Working Magician**). A drama by Pedro CALDERÓN DE LA BARCA, considered the best of his religious plays. It is the story, reminiscent of the Faust legend, of the pagan philosopher Cipriano who makes a pact with the devil to gain the love of Justina, a Christian who has previously rejected him. The devil tempts her in vain, and Cipriano, admiring her virtue, also becomes a Christian. The two then suffer martyrdom at the hands of the Roman governor of Antioch.

Maginn, William (1793–1842). Irish writer. He is known for his satires and parodies in *Blackwood's* magazine. He was editor of *Fraser's Magazine* (1830–1837).

Magister Ludi (*Lat.,* "master of the game"). The title of the English translation of *Das Glasperlenspiel* (*Ger.,* "the glass-bead game," 1943), a novel by Hermann HESSE. The story is set in a fictitious future in which culture is dominated by the glass-bead game. The game, which in its highest form is practiced only by a chosen few, is fundamentally a combination of music and mathematics but includes elements from virtually all human disciplines; it provides a center about which the artistic and intellectual world may orient itself, avoiding what the narrator considers the fragmentation and dilettantism of the 20th century. Still, Hesse makes clear by constant irony that he himself does not regard this culture as an ideal utopia, that it is rather to be seen as the imagined realization of a number of potentialities, some valuable and some dangerous, inherent in our own civilization. The story itself concerns the life of Josef KNECHT, of his rise to the lofty position of *magister ludi* and of his ultimate fall, the tragedy of a life dedicated entirely to the world of the spirit.

Magna Carta or **Charta** (1215). The "Great Charter" of England. It permanently guaranteed the principle that the king's power must be limited by law. Embittered by King JOHN's misgovernment, his levying of heavy taxes to support his foreign wars, and his personal injustice and cruelty toward potential rivals among the nobility, the barons advised by Stephen LANGTON compelled John at Runnymede to sign a document clarifying their feudal relationship. Most of the provisions sought redress for grievances; the two later glorified as the basis of modern government and bills of personal rights were the clauses establishing the principle that the king could not levy taxes without the consent of a "counsel of the realm," and that he could not imprison a free man or deprive him of his property except by the judgment of his peers or the law of the land. Pope Innocent III suspended Langton for siding against the king and annulled the Charter, which incited a civil war; but when John and the Pope died in 1216, Langton compelled a re-issue of the Charter in Henry III's name, and a confirmation of it when the young king came of age.

Magnalia Christi Americana (1702). A history of the church in New England by Cotton MATHER. Designed to extol "God's beautiful work," especially "the great achievements of Christ in America," the book stresses the virtues of New England's religious life, the dangers of backsliding, and the need for reform. Although Mather's display of erudition is sometimes pretentious, the book gives a good picture of life in colonial New England.

magnetic mountain. A mountain of medieval legend, which drew out all the nails of any ship that approached within its influence. It is referred to in *Mandeville's Travels* (c. 1371) and in many stories, such as the tale of the Third Calender and one of the voyages of SINBAD THE SAILOR in the *Arabian Nights*. It is also the title of a book of poems by Cecil Day-Lewis (1933).

Magnificat. The song of praise of the Virgin Mary, her response when she was greeted by her cousin Elizabeth in the house of Zacharias (Luke 1:46–55). It begins "My soul doth magnify the Lord" (*Magnificat anima mea Dominum"*). As a part of the vesper service of the Roman Catholic Church it has been in use since the beginning of the sixth century, and in the Anglican service for over 800 years.

It has been set to music numerous times, a famous version being Johann Sebastian Bach's *Magnificat in D* (1723), a superb cantatalike work for orchestra, chorus, and soloists.

Magnificent Ambersons, The (1918). A novel by Booth TARKINGTON. The middle volume of a trilogy called *Growth* (1927), it tells the story of George Amberson Minafer, a pampered young snob, whose family has for two generations been a source of pride and awe to the inhabitants of their Midwestern town. He does a good deal to ruin the life of his mother and other people but finally adopts a more wholesome attitude toward life. The book is also a study of the decay of one American aristocracy and the rise of another.

Magnificent Lovers, The. See AMANTS MAGNIFIQUES, LES.

Magog. See GOG.

Magwitch, Abel. In Charles Dickens' GREAT EXPECTATIONS, Pip's convict benefactor and father of Estella. He is a terrifying, simple man with a long memory for good and ill turns. When he returns illegally to England to see what kind of a gentleman his "dear boy" Pip has become, old enemies inform on him and, after an abortive flight, he dies.

Mahabharata. One of the 2 great epic poems of ancient India, the other being the *Ramayana,* about 8 times as long as the *Iliad* and *Odyssey* together. It is a great compendium, constantly added to; by A.D. 350 it had acquired something of its present form. Some parts are traditional and very ancient, others have been added as late as A.D. 600.

Its main story is the long struggle between the five Pandavas, or sons of Pandu, and the Kauravas, a name applied, from their ancestor Kuru, to the family of Dhritarashtra, Pandu's brother, who refuses to give up the throne of his nephews, the rightful heirs. Of the five Pandavas, the most heroic are Yudhishthira, the eldest, who finally gains the kingdom, and Arjuna, who wins the hand of the lovely Draupadi in open contest and brings her home as the wife of all five brothers. The legend is that his mother, not knowing what he was bringing, asked him to share whatever he possessed equally with all his brothers. Friendly to the Pandavas and very prominent throughout a large part of the epic is Krishna, an *avatar* of Vishnu, and adviser to Arjuna in his pacifist dilemma on the battlefield (see BHAGAVAD-GITA). After the death of Krishna, Yudhishthira tires of his throne, and the five Pandavas, accompanied by their wife and dog, start out to seek admission to the heaven of Indra on Mount Meru. Only Yudhishthira and the dog succeed in completing the journey; when the dog is refused admittance, Yudhishthira refuses to enter. The dog turns out to be Dharma, the god of justice, and all the Pandavas are admitted into heaven. The epic also contains the famous Savitri episode, the tale of NALA and Damayanti, and is in fact an encyclopaedia of Hindu life, legend, and thought. "What is not in the *Mahabharata,*" says the *Mahabharata,* "is not to be found anywhere else in the world." See GANESH.

Mahabhasha (Sans., *maha,* great; *bhasha,* language). A 1st century B.C. dissertation on Sanskrit grammar by Patanjali. He is considered an authority.

Mahadeva. See SHIVA.

Mahagonny. See RISE AND FALL OF THE TOWN MAHAGONNY.

Mahan, Alfred Thayer (1840–1914). American naval officer and historian. A lecturer in naval history and tactics at the Newport War College, Mahan is known mainly for *The Influence of Sea Power upon History, 1660–1783* (1890), in which he showed the overriding importance of naval power. His ideas influenced naval policy in the U.S., Great Britain, and Germany.

Mahāyāna. See BUDDHISM.

Mahdi (Arabic, *the divinely directed one*). The expected Messiah of the Muslims who is to lead to victory the hosts of Islam. A title often assumed by leaders of insurrection, it is applied especially to Muhammad Ahmed (1843–1885) who led the uprising of 1883 and who is said to be sleeping in a cavern until the time he will return to life to overthrow Dejal (Antichrist). The Shiahs or SHIITES believe that the Mahdi has lived and that the twelfth Imam, who disappeared about 873, will someday come out of hiding to rule the Muslim world.

Mahendra. See INDRA.

Mahler, Gustav (1860–1911). Austrian composer and conductor, born in Bohemia. He directed the Imperial Opera in Vienna from 1897 to 1907, and conducted at the Metropolitan Opera House in New York in 1907. He was conductor of the New York Philharmonic Orchestra in the season of 1909–1910. He wrote ten symphonies, the last unfinished. The second or *Resurrection Symphony* (1894) has a choral finale, using as its text an ode by Klopstock; the eighth or *Symphony of a Thousand* (1907) is entirely choral, in two vast movements. The first sets the medieval hymn "Veni Creator Spiritus"; the second, the final scene of Goethe's *Faust. Das Lied von der Erde* (*The Song of the Earth;* 1908) is a setting for solo voices and orchestra of a cycle of poems by the Chinese Li-Po. Mahler's widow, Alma Mahler, then the widow of Franz Werfel, wrote a biography, *Gustav Mahler, Memories and Letters,* in 1946.

Mahomet. See MUHAMMAD.

Mahony, Francis Sylvester. Pen name **Father Prout** (1804–1866). Irish humorist. He is best known for his *Prout Papers* (1834–1836), ostensibly the autobiographical remains of a rural Irish priest. Mahony was himself a priest, but passed most of his life as a traveler and man of letters.

Mahoun or **Mahound.** Names of contempt for Muhammad as a Muslim and a Moor, particularly in romances of the Crusades. The name is sometimes used as a synonym for the devil.

Maia. In Greek mythology, originally a mountain nymph in Arcadia who became the mother of HERMES.

Maid Marian. In the English ROBIN HOOD ballad cycle, the sweetheart of Robin Hood. In one version, she loved Robin Hood when he was the earl of Huntington. When he was outlawed for debt, she followed him into the forest dressed as a page and lived among his men as a virgin huntress until the marriage rites could be performed. This is a late version, arising in Tudor times. Originally she was the May queen in the early English May-day dances.

Maid of Orleans, The (**Die Jungfrau von Orleans;** 1801). A romantic tragedy by Friedrich SCHILLER, based on the life of Joan of Arc. Schiller emphasizes Joan's determined idealism and her refusal to be diverted from her transcendent goal by earthly temptations. He varies the usual story in that Joan dies in battle and not at the stake.

Maids, The (**Les Bonnes;** 1948). A play by Jean GENET. Two sisters, Claire and Solange, have betrayed their mistress's lover to the police, and to complete their treachery they poison her tea while she prepares to follow him to the penal colony. But Madame, learning that her lover has been freed, departs and leaves her tea undrunk. In order that her sister may join the elite of the criminal and the saint, Claire takes Madame's place as victim and forces Solange to poison her. The place illustrates two preoccupations central to Genet's work: human identity is seen exclusively as a shifting succession of masks, roles, and states, and moral values are systematically inverted, evil being assigned the hierarchical place more traditionally reserved for good.

Maid's Tragedy, The (c. 1611). A tragedy by BEAUMONT AND FLETCHER. By order of the king, Amintor is forced to renounce his beloved Aspatia and marry Evadne, sister of his closest friend, Melantius, who has just returned a hero from the wars. But, on her wedding night, Evadne reveals that she is the king's mistress, a fact that Amintor later confides to Melantius. Enraged, Melantius plots against the king. He makes his sister repent and promise to kill the king, while he foments a successful revolution. Meanwhile, Aspatia, disguised as her brother, has been fatally wounded in a duel with Amintor. Evadne, after killing the king, kills herself when Amintor refuses to forgive her. Then

The Maids Tragedie.

AS IT HATH BEENE
diuers times Acted at the *Black-Friers* by
the Kings Maiesties Seruants.

Newly perused, augmented; and inlarged, This second Impression

London,
Printed for *Francis Constable,* and are
to be sold at the White Lion in
Pauls Church-yard. 1622.

Title page of Beaumont and Fletcher's
Maid's Tragedy.

Amintor discovers that the "man" he has slain is Aspatia and takes his own life. Melantius tries to follow his example, but is restrained by the new king who promises to abide by the lessons of these bloody events.

Mailer, Norman (1923–   ). American novelist. Born in Long Branch, N.J., and educated at Harvard, Mailer spent two years in the Pacific Theater with the army during World War II. He is best known for THE NAKED AND THE DEAD, generally considered the best novel by an American about World War II. His next book was *Barbary Shore* (1951), a half-symbolic, half-realistic novel dealing with radical political ideologies. It was followed by *The Deer Park* (1955), a sensational novel of similar style about Hollywood. That book's leading character, Sergius O'Shaugnessy, also appears in *Advertisements for Myself on the Way Out,* part of a projected novel presented in the autobiographical collection, *Advertisements for Myself* (1959). Mailer also wrote *Death for the Ladies, and Other Disasters* (1962), a collection of poems, and *The Presidential Papers* (1963), an indictment of American politics.

Mains sales, Les. See DIRTY HANDS.

Main Street (1920). A novel by Sinclair LEWIS. The book that first established Lewis' reputation as an important writer, it is both a satire and an affectionate portrait of Gopher Prairie, a typical American town, which was undoubtedly suggested by Sauk Centre, Minn., where Lewis was born. The heroine, Carol Kennicott, chafes at the dullness and sterility of her existence as the wife of the local doctor and tries unsuccessfully to make the townspeople conscious of culture and refinement. For a time she leaves to lead her own life, but eventually returns to make a kind of peace with "Main Street." The book aroused considerable controversy; Meredith Nicholson attacked it in *Let Main Street Alone!* (1921), and Carolyn Wells burlesqued it in *Ptomaine Street, The Tale of Warble Petticoat* (1921).

Maintenon, Marquise de. Françoise d'Aubigné (1635–1719). Mistress and 2nd wife of Louis XIV. After the death of her husband, the crippled poet SCARRON, Mme de Maintenon became governess to the children of Louis XIV and Mme de Montespan. In 1674, she became the royal mistress and in 1684 the wife of the king. A Protestant by birth, she is thought to have exercised some religious influence over Louis.

Main-Travelled Roads (1891). A collection of short stories and sketches by Hamlin GARLAND. These tales, set in the Dakotas and Iowa, are local-color stories realistically told in a manner which owes much to William Dean Howells. Most of the stories depict the grim lives of farmers who are at the mercy not only of the elements but of rapacious landlords as well. *Under the Lion's Paw*, a much-anthologized piece, is one of the most characteristic.

Mair, Charles (1838–1927). Canadian poet. In his poetry Mair revealed a strong attachment to the soil and to the American pioneers; he is credited with having strongly influenced western immigration. His most famous work, *Tecumseh* (1886), describes the western movement of the white man. He also wrote *Dreamland and Other Poems* (1868) and *The Last Bison* (1891).

Mairet, Jean (1604–1686). French playwright. Author of numerous tragedies and tragicomedies, Mairet is considered to have introduced the classical unities into French drama with his pastoral tragicomedy *Silvanire* (1630), later formulating a theory of the unities in the preface to the published version of the play. *Sophonisbe* (1634), based on the legend of SOPHONISBA, is generally reckoned the first true tragedy in French, for it conforms not only to the rules but to the style of classical tragedy, especially in strict simplicity of theme and rigorous exclusion of the comic. A protégé of Richelieu, Mairet was for a time one of the cardinal's *cinq auteurs*.

Maironi, Piero. The hero of *Piccolo Mondo Moderno* (1901) and *Il Santo* (1906), two novels by Antonio FOGAZZARO. The story of Piero's father, Franco Maironi, which is told in *Piccolo Mondo Antico* (1896), the first novel of this series, prepares the way for an understanding of Piero's inner struggles. In *Piccolo Mondo Moderno*, Piero has an insane wife, Elisa, and is passionately in love with Jeanne Dessalle, a married woman who is estranged from her worthless husband. Elisa recovers her sanity just before she dies. At the end of the novel, Piero renounces his property and all thought of Jeanne. In *Il Santo*, Jeanne finds him as Benedetto, a lay brother in a Benedictine monastery. The news that her husband has died has little effect on him; he has become the spokesman of a new Christianity which will accept and make use of the findings of modern science. His ideas arouse tremendous opposition from within the Catholic Church, but Jeanne, whose love can find

no other outlet, manages to ward off much of this opposition through her powerful friends. He sends for her on his death bed. A fourth novel, *Lelia* (1911), deals mainly with the love affair of the titular heroine and Massimo Alberti, a young doctor and disciple of Benedetto, "the saint."

Major Barbara (1905). A play by George Bernard SHAW. Barbara Undershaft is a major in the Salvation Army; her father is the millionaire owner of an armament company. When Undershaft and a whisky distiller donate money to the Army, Barbara cannot stand the hypocrisy of accepting this "tainted money," and she resigns. While never fully agreeing with her father, Barbara comes to accept his theory that poverty, not sin, breeds crime. The poor are not blessed, says Undershaft, they are cursed. This was advanced social theory in 1905 when complacent Edwardian England accepted the poor as a necessary evil.

All money is tainted, says Shaw; the problem then is to remove the taint and have a fairer distribution. Even with its moral and economic message, *Major Barbara* has a wealth of comic and arresting characters in the play.

Major Prophets. See PROPHET.

Making of Americans, The (1925). A "novel" by Gertrude STEIN. Written in 1906–1908, with no dialogue and no action, it presents the history of three generations of the author's own family, and by extension, the history of everyone else in the past, present, and future. Composed in a simpler style than much of the author's later work, it is marked by frequent verbal repetition to suggest repetition in time.

Malachi. An Old Testament prophetic book. Written about 460 B.C., it connects the economic hardships of the period with the moral laxness of the people. There are special denunciations of the priesthood.

Malade imaginaire, Le (The Imaginary Invalid, 1673). A COMÉDIE-BALLET by MOLIÈRE and his last play. The hypochondriac ARGAN allows himself to be victimized by the doctors PURGON and DIAFOIRUS and, in order to have a doctor in the family, tries to force his daughter to marry Diafoirus' son. His second wife, however, who in reality does not love him but his wealth, schemes to send the daughter off to a convent. To test his wife's love, Argan pretends death, and thus discovers his wife's greed and his daughter's loyalty. A final ballet with interpolated Latin doggerel parodies the admission of a doctor to the Paris faculty.

Malagigi or **Malagise (Fr. Maugis).** In the Carolingian legends a great magician and paladin of Charlemagne. In the *Morgante Maggiore* of Pulci and in the Orlando poems of Boiardo and Ariosto he frequently aids the paladins with his magic (see ORLANDO FURIOSO). He is the brother of Bradamante, the warrior maiden.

Malamud, Bernard (1914–   ). American novelist and short-story writer. Malamud was born and raised in Brooklyn, the setting for much of his work. His first novel, *The Natural* (1952), is an allegorical story about a baseball player. *The Assistant* (1957) deals with a poor New York Jewish shopkeeper and his assistant. *The Magic Barrel* (1958), a collection of short stories, won the National Book award. *A*

New Life (1961) deals with a New Yorker who goes to teach in a college in the Pacific Northwest. *Idiots First* (1963) is a collection of short stories.

Malaparte, Curzio. Pen name of **Curzio Malaparte Suckert** (1898-1957). Italian writer. Malaparte, who cast his lot alternately with fascism and democracy, strongly reflects D'Annunzio's influence. *Kaputt* (1944) is an account of his experiences with Hitler's armies during the Russian campaign. *The Skin* (*La Pelle;* 1949) describes his career as Italian liaison officer with the U.S. Fifth Army. A collection of short stories, *Racconti Italiani,* was published in 1959.

Malaprop, Mrs. (from Fr. *mal à propos,* "out of place"). A character in Sheridan's comedy THE RIVALS, noted for her blunders in the use of words. "As headstrong as an *allegory* on the banks of the Nile," is one of her gross misapplications. She has given us the word *malapropism* to denote such mistakes.

Malaquais, Jean (1908-   ). Polish-born French novelist. *Les Javanais* (*The Men from Java,* 1939, also translated as *Men from Nowhere*) is the violent story of a community of outcasts starving for a mining company. *Le Gaffeur* (*The Joker,* 1953) is a nightmarish fantasy. Other works include *Journal de guerre* (*Jean Malaquais' War Diary,* 1943), and *World Without Visa* (*Planète sans Visa;* 1947).

Malatesta (It., "evil head"). The name of an Italian family which dominated the city and environs of Rimini during the Renaissance. Its symbol was an elephant. Of the several CONDOTTIERI it produced, the most infamous was Sigismondo Pandolfo Malatesta (1417-1468), who combined a love of learning and patronage of the arts with a taste for cruelty and tyranny that earned him universal hatred. It was an earlier Malatesta, Giovanni, who murdered the lovers Paolo and Francesca, an event recalled by Dante in the famous episode of the *Inferno*.

Malavoglia, I (The House by the Medlar Tree or **The Malavoglias,** 1881). A novel by Giovanni VERGA. It is celebrated for its sympathetic and perceptive portrayal of a Sicilian fisherfolk family (the Malavoglias) and its vivid depiction of the provincial town (Aci-Trezza) where they live. The Malavoglias are a family seemingly doomed by an ineluctable fate. When their vessel sinks, drowning Padron 'Ntoni's son, his grandson 'Ntoni joins the navy to support the family. The upshot of his first acquaintance with the world outside Trezza is his rebellion against family traditions. He refuses to continue the fishing trade, eventually refusing to work altogether. As a result, the family's meager fortune rapidly declines. 'Ntoni's mother and younger brother die, his proud grandfather Padron 'Ntoni dies in a pauper hospital, and 'Ntoni is forced by circumstances to leave Trezza without hope or destination.

Malbecco. See FAERIE QUEENE, THE.

Malbrouk or **Marlbrough.** Very old song. The French song, *Malbrouk s'en va-t-en guerre* (Marlborough is off to the wars), is said to date from 1709, when the duke of Marlborough was winning his battles in Flanders. It did not become popular till it was applied to Charles Churchill, third duke of Marlborough, at the time of his failure against

Cherbourg (1758). It was further popularized in becoming a favorite of Marie Antoinette about 1780, and being introduced by Beaumarchais into *Le Mariage de Figaro* (1785). The tune is thought to be much older. According to a tradition recorded by Chateaubriand, the air came from the Arabs, and the tale is a legend of Mambron, a crusader.

Malcolm. In Shakespeare's MACBETH, the elder son of the murdered king, Duncan of Scotland. Aware of Macbeth's treachery, Malcolm flees to England, raises an army, and returns to dethrone Macbeth. After Macbeth's death, he becomes king of Scotland.

Malcontent, The (1604). A drama by John MARSTON. Altofronto, the deposed duke of Genoa, assumes the guise of a cynical, jesting malcontent named Malvole. Aurelia, wife of the usurping Duke Pietro, is seduced by her husband's chief minister, Mendoza, who also connives with Malvole against Pietro. But Malvole informs Pietro, sends him into hiding, and then proclaims his death. Mendoza assumes the throne, banishes Aurelia, plots to kill the outspoken Malvole, and aims to marry Maria, Altofronto's (Malvole's) wife. Malvole then reveals himself to Pietro, has him renounce the ducal throne, and gains his support. At a ball, the masked plotters surround Mendoza and depose him.

Maldon, Battle of (late 10th century). Old English poem, a fragment of 325 lines in ALLITERATIVE VERSE. In the heroic style it describes the unsuccessful stand (991) of the English under Byrhtnoth against a Viking invasion.

Malebranche, Nicolas (1638-1715). French philosopher, scientist, and theologian. He is known as one of the best prose writers of his century. In his principal work, *La Recherche de la Vérité* (*The Search for Truth,* 1674-1675), Malebranche took issue with the metaphysics of DESCARTES, though admiring his physics and method. Denying the interaction of spirit and matter, Malebranche declared that God arranges an exact correspondence between our notions of material objects and the motions of the objects themselves, for He is the sole source and cause of both. This ingenious solution to the Cartesian dualism antagonised the Jansenists and Bossuet, among others, because of its pantheistic overtones, and embroiled Malebranche in endless controversy; the doctrine also won him many disciples, including Leibniz. Malebranche's later writings, mostly on religious and moral subjects, include *Conversations Chrétiennes* (*Christian Conversations,* 1676), *Méditations Chrétiennes* (*Christian Meditations,* 1683), and *Entretiens sur la métaphysique et la religion* (*Conversations on Metaphysics and Religion,* 1688).

Malecasta, Queen. See FAERIE QUEENE, THE.

Maleger. See FAERIE QUEENE, THE.

Malengin. See FAERIE QUEENE, THE.

Malentendu, Le. See MISUNDERSTANDING, THE.

Malesherbes, Chrétien Guillaume de Lamoignon de (1721-1794). French statesman. His liberal policy made the publication of the ENCYCLOPÉDIE possible. He defended Louis XVI at his trial before the National Convention in 1792, during the French Revolution. He himself was arrested as a royalist and guillotined.

Malevitch, Casimir (1878-1935). Russian painter. In 1913 he derived from CUBISM the rigid geometrical abstractions called Suprematism, in which all painting is reduced to the use of the square, the triangle, the circle, and the cross. *White Square on White Background* (1919) illustrates the subtlety that this simplification can attain in its extreme manifestation.

Malherbe, François de (1555–1628). French writer. Official court poet, Malherbe became the virtual literary dictator of France during the early 17th century. Of neoclassic tendencies, he advocated a poetry of order, rationality, and simplicity; opposing all colorful eccentricity in verse, he condemned the affectation, emotionalism, and decorative qualities of the late-baroque poets. Better known for his influence than for his own writings, Malherbe wrote the poem *Consolation de Monsieur du Périer sur la mort de sa fille* (*Consolation of Monsieur du Périer upon the Death of His Daughter,* 1598) and a sycophantic *Ode* (1600) to Marie de Médicis.

Malibrán, María Felicitá. Born **García** (1808–1836). Spanish contralto, taught by her father, Manuel García. A romantic figure, she burned out her life by overwork, sacrificing herself to her singing.

Malign Fiesta. See HUMAN AGE, THE.

Mallarmé, Stéphane (1842–1898). French poet. Mallarmé is known as one of the leaders of the SYMBOLISTS and the formulator of their aesthetic theories. His own work shows the influence of Baudelaire, Poe, Verlaine, and the Pre-Raphaelites. Marked by elliptical phrases, Mallarmé's poetry employs condensed figures and unorthodox syntax. Each poem is built about a central symbol, idea, or metaphor, and consists of subordinate images that illustrate and help to develop the idea. Often obscure, his work never fails to be evocative and exciting. *L'Après-midi d'un faune* (*The Afternoon of a Faun,* 1876) which inspired Debussy to write his well-known *Prélude;* LE CYGNE; HÉRODIADE; and *Le Tombeau d'Edgar Poe* are outstanding examples of Mallarmé's method.

Mallet, David (1705?–1765). Scottish poet and scholar who collaborated with James THOMSON in the masque *Alfred* (1740). His best-known work is the ballad *William and Margaret* (1724), which later collected in Thomas Percy's RELIQUES. Mallet's chief work of scholarship is his edition (1754) of the works of Henry St. John, Viscount Bolingbroke.

Mallet-Joris, Françoise [formerly **Françoise Mallet**] (1930–). Belgian-born French novelist. While still in her teens she wrote THE ILLUSIONISTS (1950), which, like its sequel *The Red Room* (1953), shows the defensive cruelty and cynicism of those who would love. *The House of Lies* (*Les Mensonges;* 1956) and *Café Céleste* (*L'Empire céleste;* 1958) use a Flemish realism of detail to expose tragedies of self-delusion. Other works include the elaborately constructed THE FAVORITE (1961), and *Cordelia* (1954), a collection of short stories.

Malleus Maleficarum (**Hammer of Witches,** 1484). One of the most famous books of witchcraft and black magic, published in Cologne, by Henry Kramer and James Sprenger.

Mallison, Charles or Chick. A character in several works by William FAULKNER. The nephew of Gavin STEVENS, Chick grows from childhood to young manhood in four of Faulkner's novels. As a child he narrates part of *The Town;* as a 16-year-old boy he is instrumental in proving Lucas Beauchamp innocent of murder in INTRUDER IN THE DUST; and as a young man he narrates part of *The Mansion* and is an interested observer in KNIGHT'S GAMBIT.

Mallock, William Hurrell (1849–1923). English novelist. He is best known for his elaborate *roman à clef* THE NEW REPUBLIC.

Malone, Edmund (1741–1812). Irish literary critic and Shakespearean scholar. He left Ireland for London to devote himself to literature and became a part of the literary and political scene, counting among his friends Dr. Johnson, Sir Joshua Reynolds, Bishop Percy, Edmund Burke, and Horace Walpole. He was the first literary critic to establish a chronology of Shakespeare's plays in his *Attempt to ascertain the order in which the plays of Shakespeare were written* (1778), this work supplementing Johnson's edition of Shakespeare (1765). His own edition of Shakespeare was published in 1790. He also published an edition of Reynolds' works (1797) and an edition of Dryden (1800). A shrewd literary detective, he was one of the first to doubt the authenticity of Thomas Chatterton's Rowley poems and the purported Shakespearean works of William Ireland. He was probably the ablest research scholar of his day and provided invaluable aid to Boswell in his final draft of Johnson's biography.

Malone Dies (**Malone Meurt;** 1951). A novel by Samuel BECKETT. As Malone, a bum, lies dying, alone in bed in a strange room, he remembers his past life. By the end we realize that Malone was actually a murderer and that in his pathetic, senile, lonely state he is an image for the condition of all men. Beckett uses the stream-of-consciousness technique throughout. The novel is linked to MOLLOY and THE UNNAMABLE.

Malory, Sir Thomas (c. 1408–1471). English writer. He is the author of LE MORTE D'ARTHUR, the finest medieval prose collection of Arthurian romance. It was completed (c. 1469) while he was in prison and printed in 1485. Very little is known about Malory's life except for his rendering of the Arthurian romances. He was a member of Parliament (1445) and, in 1451, was imprisoned for various offenses and remained in jail until his death.

Malraux, André (1901–). French novelist and critic. Malraux went to Indo-China as an archeologist and became active in revolutionary politics there, in China, and later in Spain. The theme of social revolution dominates the novels *The Conquerors* (1928), set in Canton, China, during the 1925 insurrection; MAN'S FATE (1933); and *Man's Hope* (*L'Espoir;* 1937), which takes place during the Spanish civil war. Such revolutions are used as the symbol of oppressed man's struggle for dignity through revolt against his fate. By braving death for the life of their revolutionary doctrines, the leading characters transcend the individual self and accept a fate that binds them to all men. *Days of Wrath* (*Le Temps du mépris;* 1935) describes an underground Communist leader in Hitler's Germany; *The Walnut Trees of Altenburg* (*Les Noyers de l'Altenburg,* 1943) is a novel of ideas about human potential, its setting the two world wars.

In *The Psychology of Art* (3 vols., 1947–1950; adapted as *The Voices of Silence,* 1951) Malraux describes art as another way in which mankind as a whole transcends individual man's mortal destiny and is ennobled. He analyzes the history of art as the search for an absolute, which is man's religious aspiration. His other works include the novel *The Royal Way* (1930) and the essays *La Tentation de l'Occident* (1926) and *La Métamorphose des Dieux* (1957).

Under the French Fifth Republic, headed by Charles de Gaulle, André Malraux occupies the position of Minister of State in charge of Cultural Affairs.

Maltese Falcon, The (1930). A detective novel by Dashiell HAMMETT. It was one of the first novels of the "hard-boiled" school, and it marked the first appearance of Hammett's famous "private eye," Sam SPADE. Dealing with the theft of a jewel-encrusted falcon descended from the Knights Templars, the story was as romantic in content as it was realistic and tough in manner.

Malthus, Thomas Robert (1766-1834). English political economist. In 1798, the year that he became a curate of the Church of England, Malthus published *An Essay on the Principle of Population as it affects the Future Improvement of Society, with Remarks on the Speculation of Mr. Godwin, M. Condorcet, and other Writers*, in which he set forth the Malthusian doctrine that population increases in a geometric ratio while the means of subsistence increases in an arithmetic ratio, and that crime, disease, war, and vice are necessary checks on population. In the 1803 revision of his work, Malthus suggested moral restraint as a fifth check. Malthus' works also include *An Inquiry into the Nature and Progress of Rent* (1815) and *Principles of Political Economy* (1820).

Malthusian doctrine. See Thomas Robert MALTHUS.

Maltz, Albert (1908–   ). American writer of plays, fiction, and scenarios. While studying at Yale with George Pierce Baker and George Sklar, Maltz wrote *Merry-Go-Round* (1932), a play about political corruption in New York City, which was closed by censors and then reopened after vigorous public protests. With Sklar, Maltz also wrote *Peace on Earth* (1933), a pacifist play. His other works include a book of short stories, *The Way Things Are* (1938); the novels *The Cross and the Arrow* (1944) and *The Journey of Simon McKeever* (1949); and several film scenarios, including *The Pride of the Marines* (1945).

Malvolio. In Shakespeare's TWELFTH NIGHT, the steward of Olivia. He is a smug, pompous fool who secretly aspires to his mistress' love. Annoyed by his conceit and priggishness, Sir Toby Belch, Sir Andrew Aguecheek, and Maria concoct a scheme to turn Olivia against him. Maria forges a letter in the handwriting of Olivia, leading Malvolio to believe that his mistress returns his love. He falls into the trap, and when Olivia shows astonishment at his absurd conduct, he keeps quoting parts of the letter until he is shut up in a dark room as a lunatic.

Mambrino. A legendary pagan king introduced by Ariosto into his ORLANDO FURIOSO. He wears a helmet of pure gold, which makes him invulnerable, but is taken by Rinaldo. In the *Don Quixote* of Cervantes, the hero insists that a barber's basin is actually the precious helmet of Mambrino.

Mamelukes (Arab. *mamluc,* a slave). The slaves from the Caucasus in Egypt. Formed into a standing army, in 1254 they raised one of their body to the supreme power. They reigned over Egypt until 1517, when they were overthrown by the Turkish sultan, Selim I. The country, though nominally under a Turkish viceroy, was subsequently governed by twenty-four Mameluke beys. In 1811 the Pasha of Egypt, Muhammad Ali, by a wholesale massacre annihilated the Mamelukes.

mammon. An Aramic word used in the New Testament to personify riches and worldliness; the god of this world, or of avarice, cupidity. In the Bible, the word occurs in Matt. 6:24 and Luke 16:13: "Ye cannot serve God and mammon." Both Spenser with his cave of Mammon (*Faerie Queene,* 1590) and Milton, by identifying him with Vulcan (*Paradise Lost,* 1667) make Mammon the epitome of the evils of wealth and miserliness.

the Mammon of unrighteousness. Money (Luke 16:9).

Mammon, Sir Epicure. A wealthy lecher in Jonson's comedy THE ALCHEMIST.

Man Against the Sky, The (1916). The title poem of a book of verse by Edwin Arlington ROBINSON. In this long elegaic work, man is symbolized as a lonely figure seen against the sky at sunset, the sunset itself representing death, World War I, and the universe described by modern science. Robinson examines five creeds that explain life and death, rejects them, and finally asserts a simple stoicism as a way of life.

Man and Superman (1905). A play by George Bernard SHAW, subtitled "A Comedy and a Philosophy." The comedy is the eternal pursuit of the male by the female; the philosophy is Shaw's brand of religion, creative evolution. These two elements are coordinated in the brilliant, discursive Don Juan in Hell scene in Act III.

John Tanner, rational, morally passionate, and defiant of tradition, is plotted for, chased after, and caught by Ann Whitefield who, like most Shavian women, is instinctive, hypocritical, charming, and triumphant.

While in flight from Ann, Tanner dreams the scene of Don Juan in Hell. In a long, witty dialogue—the kind that Shaw excelled in—Don Juan (Tanner), Doña Ana (Ann), the Statue from Mozart's opera *Don Giovanni,* and the Devil, discuss the questions so far evoked by the action of the play. Don Juan describes the moral passion or "Life Force" that drives the universe forward. He explains to the sneering Devil that it is the idea of God depending on man to get his will done that gives human life meaning. The superman of the title is the person who is able to detect and follow the will of the universe while suppressing his own. Don Juan is a superman; Tanner is not.

Man and Superman is usually performed without the Don Juan scene; however, the work has its essential unity in this episode. *Don Juan in Hell* has been acted separately and also been given many dramatic readings.

Manassas. See BULL RUN.

Manchu. See CH'ING.

Mancini. The family name of the five nieces of Cardinal MAZARIN who were brought from Rome by their uncle and played a conspicuous part in French society. Although Louis XIV fell passionately in love with Marie (1639–1715), she was married to the prince of Colonna. Hortense (c. 1646–1699) was the most beautiful of the sisters; she abandoned her husband, who had taken the name of Mazarin, and settled in England, where she was a favorite at the court of Charles II. Marie Anne (1649–1714), who became duchess of the duke of Bouillon, was an intellectual leader and the patroness of La Fontaine and other writers. The other sisters were Laure (1636–1657) and Olympe (1640–1708), who married, respectively, the duke of Mercoeur and the count of Soissons.

Manciple's Tale, The. One of the CANTERBURY TALES of Geoffrey CHAUCER. In the *Prologue* the Host and the Manciple tease the Cook for being drunk. Finally the Manciple shares his own wine with the Cook, and begins his story, based on Ovid's version of a popular folk tale. The archer Phebus has a white crow that can sing as sweetly as a nightingale and speak human language. One day the crow reports to Phebus that his beloved wife has entertained a lover in his absence. Phebus kills her with an arrow, but afterward breaks his bow in remorse and grief. Then he turns bitterly on the crow for having disturbed, unasked, his unsuspicious bliss; he plucks the bird's feathers, turns him black, takes away his power of speech, changes his sweet song to a raucous croak, and flings him to the Devil—thus accounting for the present appearance of all crows and serving as a warning to all tattle-tales.

Mandalay (1892). A popular poem by Rudyard Kipling, first published in BARRACK-ROOM BALLADS. It was later set to music and became a standard amateur-night baritone air, with the famous refrain:

Oh, the road to Mandalay, where the flyin'-fishes play,
An' the dawn comes up like thunder outer China 'cross the Bay!

Mandarins, The (1954). A novel by Simone de BEAUVOIR. It portrays leading existentialists during and after World War II. It includes a fictionalized version of the argument between Jean Paul Sartre and Albert Camus over the subjugation of philosophical ideals to the need to act.

Mandelshtam, Osip Yemilyevich (1891–?1940). Russian poet. Belonging to the early Soviet period, Mandelshtam's poetry is a model of the classically concise and finished work striven for in ACMEISM. His output was small, mostly contained in the collections *Stone* (*Kamyen'*; 1913) and *Tristia* (1922). His obvious lack of enthusiasm for the Soviet regime ended in his arrest during the purges of the 1930's. He is believed to have died in a concentration camp.

Mandeville, The Travels of Sir John (c. 1371). Famous book of travels. It purports to be a guidebook for pilgrims to Palestine, but goes on to describe the marvels that the author claims to have seen in Africa and the Orient: some real, such as the Pyramids, some highly fictitious, such as the people with no heads but eyes in their shoulders. According to the work itself, Sir John Mandeville (or Maundeville) was born at St. Albans, left England in 1322, roamed widely, and finally came under a new name to live at Liège in 1343, writing his *Travels* about 1357. He has been variously identified with French writers of

THE
Voyages & Travels
OF
Sir John Mandevile, Knight.

Wherein is set down the Way to the *Holy Land*, and to *Hierusalem :* As also to the Lands of the Great *Caan*, and of *Prestor John :* to *Inde*, and divers other Countries : Together with many and strange Marvels therein.

LONDON,
Printed for *R. Scott, T. Basset, J. Wright, and R. Chiswel,* 1677.

Title page of *The Travels of Sir John Mandeville* (1677).

Liège such as Jean de Bourgoigne à la Barbe (d. 1372) and Jean d'Outremeuse. Actually, the work was probably originally compiled (1366–1371) in French, from early 14th-century travel books, and soon translated into Latin and English.

Mandragola, La (The Mandrake). A comedy of the Renaissance written by Niccolò MACHIAVELLI in 1504. The plot involves the attempt of a young Florentine, Callimaco, to win Lucrezia, wife of Nicia, an old fool. The servant Ligurio joins with the mother and the confessor (Fra Timoteo) of the young wife to help Callimaco succeed. The title of the play refers to the fact that, at one point in the play, Nicia is persuaded by Callimaco, posing as a doctor, that his wife must be given mandrake to combat her supposed sterility.

mandrake. An herb found in southern Europe and northern Africa. Its globose yellow berries were once believed to have aphrodisiac powers. The root of the mandrake often divides in two and presents a rude appearance of a man. In ancient times human figures were cut out of the root and wonderful virtues ascribed to them, such as the production of fecundity in women (Gen. 30:14–16). It was said that mandrakes could not be uprooted without producing fatal effects upon the uprooter, and so a cord would be fixed to the root and tied around a dog's neck, and the dog, being chased, would draw out the mandrake and, theoretically, die. Moreover, it was believed that

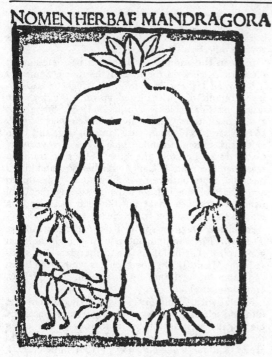

NOMEN HERBAF MANDRAGORA

The mandrake. From a 15th-century herbal.

a small dose of mandrake made a person vain of his beauty, while a large one made him an idiot, and also that when the mandrake was uprooted it uttered a scream, in explanation of which Thomas Newton, in his *Herball to the Bible,* wrote, "It is supposed to be a creature having life, engendered under the earth of the seed of some dead person put to death for murder." Mandrakes were sometimes called "love apples," from the old notion that they excited amorous inclinations; hence Venus is called Mandragoritis, and the Emperor Julian, in his epistles, tells Calixenes that he drank mandrake juice nightly as a love potion. The narcotic and stupefying properties of the herb were well known to the ancients, and it was commonly said of a very indolent and sleepy man that he had eaten mandrake.

Mandricardo. In the Orlando epics of Boiardo and Ariosto, a ferocious warrior, king of Tartary, and son of Agricane (Agrican). He comes to France to avenge his father, slain by Orlando, and fights alongside Agramante (Agramant) in the battle against Charlemagne. He is killed by RUGGIERO.

Manet, Edouard (1832–1883). French painter. Generally regarded as the originator of IMPRESSIONISM, as early as 1863 he had executed two of his greatest and most controversial works: *Lunch on the Grass* and *Olympia.* Noted for his versatility and creative originality, he was equally adept whether painting portraits, still lifes, landscapes, or scenes from contemporary life.

Manette, Dr. Alexander. A character in Charles Dickens' A TALE OF TWO CITIES. His spirit has been broken by 18 years of unjust imprisonment in the Bastille. After his release he recovers somewhat, but severe anxiety produces relapses in the form of partial amnesia and a longing for his old prison occupation of cobbling. He is something of a hero in the eyes of the revolutionists because of his imprisonment in the Bastille, and when the Defarges learn that his daughter will marry Darnay, nephew of the hated St. Evrémonde, they are greatly disturbed.

Lucie Manette. The heroine of the novel, daughter of Dr. Manette, a gentle girl dedicated to her father.

Manetti, Gianozzo (1396–1459). Florentine Humanist. He wrote in 1452 a treatise *On the Dignity and Excellence of Man* (*De dignitate et excellentia hominis*), which anticipates the similar work of Pico della Mirandola in asserting the Renaissance theme of individual worth and glory.

Man For All Seasons, A (1961). A play by Robert Bolt (1924–   ). It is based on the life of Sir Thomas MORE and his controversy with Henry VIII.

Manfred. Prince of Otranto and the central figure in Horace Walpole's *Castle of Otranto.*

Manfred (1817). A dramatic poem by Lord BYRON. The hero, Count Manfred, sells himself to the prince of Darkness and lives wholly without human sympathies in splendid solitude among the Alps.

Man Friday. A faithful, versatile, and willing attendant, from the young savage in Defoe's ROBINSON CRUSOE. Found by Crusoe on a Friday, he was kept as his servant and companion on the desert island.

Manhattan Transfer (1925). A novel by John Dos PASSOS. The book presents a picture of life in New York City during the 1920's through passages of impressionistic description and the simultaneous stories of several people from varying levels of society. The title, taken from the railroad station where people changed trains to get to and from the metropolis, is in itself suggestive of the shifting variegated life of the city. Although the novel has no central hero, Jimmy Herf, a journalist divorced by his actress wife, is perhaps the character of greatest interest. Only slightly less important are Bud Korpenning, a young man who fails in the city and commits suicide; Joe Harland, a Wall Street gambler, who loses his fortune and becomes a beggar; and Ellen Thatcher Ogelthorpe, Herf's former wife, who is a successful actress but loses the man she loves and is unable to find happiness. The final effect of this panoramic impression of a swarming metropolis is one of frustration and defeat.

Mani, Manes, or Manichaeus. The founder of Manichaeism, born in Persia, probably about 216. He was prominent at the court of Sapor I (240–272) but crucified by the Magians in 277. See MANI-CHAEANS.

Manichaeans or Manichees. Followers of the Oriental dualistic religion of Manichaeism, founded 242 by MANI. Their principal doctrine concerns the conflict between Light, or goodness, and Darkness, identified with chaos or evil. The system was drawn from the ancient Babylonian and Persian nature worship and influenced Christianity as late as the 13th century. For many centuries, Babylon, and then Samarkand, were the centers of Manichaeism.

manifest destiny. A 19th-century slogan that expressed the conviction of many Americans that the U.S. was destined to rule the entire North American continent. The earliest known appearance of the phrase was in an editorial (1845) in *The United States Magazine and Democratic Review* by John L. O'Sullivan, who wrote that foreign powers opposed the annexation of Texas in order to hinder "the fulfilment of our manifest destiny to overspread the continent allotted by Providence for the free development of our yearly multiplying millions."

Manilius, Marcus or **Gaius.** Roman poet of the early 1st century. He is reputedly the author of the learned astrological poem *Astronomica* in five books.

Manilov. In Nikolai Gogol's Dead Souls, a character wholly given over to idle dreaming. The term *Manilovism* has since been used to describe indulgence in such vague reverie.

Man in Black. A character in Oliver Goldsmith's novel The Citizen of the World who professes to be parsimonious, but is profusely generous, and who finds the truest way of finding esteem is to give nothing away. He is disappointed in ambition as well as in love.

Man in the Iron Mask. A mysterious French prisoner. He was held for over 40 years by Louis XIV at Pignerol and other prisons, ultimately dying in the Bastille (November 19, 1703) with his identity still undisclosed. His name was given as "Marchiali" when he was buried. Subsequently, many conjectures as to the real identity of Marchiali were advanced. One possibility was General du Bulonde, who in 1691 raised the siege of Cuneo against the order of Catinat. In 1891, Captain Bazeriès published in *Le Temps* translations of some cipher dispatches, apparently showing that this was the solution; but if it was, it could only be part of it, and Bulonde would have had to have taken the place of some earlier masked prisoner, for *l'homme au masque de fer* was at Pignerol in 1666 and was transferred to the island of St. Marguerite 20 years later, that is, well before the siege of Cuneo.

Other persons who have been suggested are a twin brother of Louis XIV—or, perhaps, an illegitimate elder half brother whose father is given as either Cardinal Mazarin or the duke of Buckingham—and Louis, duc de Vermandois, the natural son of Louis XIV by De la Vallière, who was imprisoned for life because he gave the dauphin a box on the ears.

Among the less likely names that have been put forward are the duke of Monmouth; Avedick, an Armenian Patriarch; Fouquet, the disgraced French minister of finance; the duc de Beaufort, who disappeared at the siege of Candia in 1669; and Mattioli's secretary, Jean de Gonzague.

Since the private papers of Louis XIV and the correspondence of his minister Louvois and Barbezieux were made available to Franz Funck-Brentano, it has become apparent that the man in the iron mask was Count Girolamo Mattioli, minister to the duke of Mantua, a theory now widely accepted. In 1678 he acted treacherously toward Louis in refusing to give up the fortress of Casale—the key to Italy—after signing a treaty promising to do so, and in consequence was lured onto French soil, captured, and imprisoned at Pignerol.

It was in 1790 that the Abbé Soulavie put forth the theory that the mysterious personage was a twin brother of Louis XIV. This supposition was accepted in tragedies on the subject by Zschokke in German and Fournier in French. In Dumas' romance *The Iron Mask*—sometimes published separately, but originally a part of his *Vicomte de Bragelonne*—a conspiracy to substitute the Man in the Iron Mask for his royal brother is all but successful.

man in the moon. A man seen by some among the dark patches on the face of the moon. Some say it is a man leaning on a fork, on which he is carrying a bundle of sticks picked up on a Sunday. The origin of this fable is Num. 15:32–36. Some add a dog also; thus Quince in *A Midsummer Night's Dream* says, "This man with lantern, dog, and bush of thorns, presenteth moonshine"; *The Testament of Cresid* says "he stole the bush." Another tradition says that the man is Cain, with his dog and thorn bush, the thorn bush being emblematical of the thorns and briars of the fall, and the dog being the "foul fiend." Some poets make out the man to be Endymion, taken to the moon by Selene.

manitou. A great spirit of the American Indians. The word is Algonquin, and is used of both the great good spirit (Gitche-Manito) and the great evil spirit (Matche-Manito). The good spirit is symbolized by an egg, and the evil one by a serpent. (Longfellow, *Hiawatha*, xiv.)

Mankowitz, Wolf (1924–   ). English novelist, film and television writer, and authority on porcelain. He usually writes realistic, humorous stories about the working life of London. His best-known works are *A Kid for Two Farthings* (1953; filmed 1955), about a small slum boy who thinks his goat is a unicorn, and *Expresso Bongo* (1958–59; filmed 1960), about London's tin-pan alley.

Manley, Mary de la Rivière (1672–1724). English playwright and political pamphleteer. She is chiefly remembered as the author of *Secret Memoirs and Manners of Several Persons of Quality of Both Sexes from the New Atalantis* (1709, usually known as *The New Atalantis*), and its continuation, *Memoirs of Europe* (1710), both scandalous, licentious chronicles of contemporary politics and society; for these two works she was arrested, and subsequently released. She was active as a political writer during the Tory regime of 1710–1714 and was well known to Jonathan Swift, whom she succeeded as editor of the periodical *Examiner* (1711). She was also the author of many plays and a romanticized autobiography, *Rivella* (1714).

Mann, Heinrich (1871–1950). German novelist, elder brother of Thomas Mann. Around the time of World War I, his political and social attitudes were a great deal more militantly liberal than his brother's, and this led to a serious dispute between them. His interest in topical matters is also reflected in his novels, the most famous of which is *Professor Unrat oder Das Ende eines Tyrannen* (*Professor Filth, or A Tyrant's End*, 1905), a diatribe against inhumanity in the schools. Fritz Lang's famous motion picture *The Blue Angel* (1929) is based on this novel.

Mann, Horace (1796–1859). American lawyer, educator, and legislator. After a childhood of hardship, Mann became a lawyer and practiced in Massachusetts, where he served as state representative (1827–1833) and state senator (1833–1837). In 1837, after trying to educate the public on the proper treatment of the insane, he turned from politics to education. As secretary of the state board of education, he labored to improve the public schools, increase teacher salaries, and set up teacher-training schools.

An enemy of religious bigotry, he fought against sectarian control of schools. In 1848, he was elected to the House of Representatives, where he held firm antislavery views. He was defeated as Free Soil candidate for governor of Massachusetts and was appointed president of Antioch College. Although he struggled for four years to maintain the ideal of a liberal education for all, the college was sold for debt in 1859. In addition to 12 *Annual Reports,* Mann published *Lectures on Education* (1845).

Mann, Thomas (1875–1955). German novelist and essayist. Awarded the Nobel Prize for literature in 1929, he is known for his many narrative psychological studies of the artistic temperament, for his extensive and penetrating explorations into Greek, Hebrew, Germanic, and Eastern mythology, and for the enlightened literary and social criticism found in both his imaginative and his discussive works. As a boy, Mann early became aware of the existence of two worlds between which his own life was divided: the solid, bourgeois, commercial world of his family, and the more mysterious, spiritual world of his own artistic inclinations. This awareness, in turn, developed into a dualistic pattern of thought which, in many variations and refinements, followed him throughout his career. The terms "spirit" and "life" (*Geist* and *Leben*) are used to define this dualism: the realm of art, of imagination and the mind, of the decadent artistic personality, on the one hand; and that of everyday reality, of the relatively wholesome bourgeois temperament, on the other. The early influence of Schopenhauer, Wagner, Nietzsche, and the German romantic poets strengthened the belief that ordinary life and activity were not adequate for the artist's inner needs. In his first novel BUDDENBROOKS, Mann treats this problem on a large scale, but his personal feelings are seen more clearly in the story TONIO KRÖGER which, though it affirms art, is filled with a nostalgic longing for the solidity of bourgeois life. Mann wanted very much to affirm both spirit and life, and he achieved at least a fictional synthesis between them in his next novel, *Königliche Hoheit* (*Royal Highness,* 1909), the story of a decadent young prince who eventually comes to grips with reality in his marriage to a rich but untitled American girl. Soon afterwards, however, Mann again began treating the tragic potentialities of artistic decadence, especially in the great novella DEATH IN VENICE; it was in this work, also, that his explorations of the vague borderline area between the psychological and the occult, and of the continuing relevance in modern reality of ancient, mythical forces and configurations, began to assume the form that became definitive for his later writing.

Concerned, as he was, with problems of a primarily spiritual nature, Mann remained aloof from the political controversies centering about World War I, though urged by his brother Heinrich MANN to make a liberal commitment. The essays in his *Betrachtungen eines Unpolitischen* (*Reflections of a Non-Political Man,* 1918) reflect his attitude at this time, as does his novel THE MAGIC MOUNTAIN, in which political themes are treated as little more than a symbol for Europe's spiritual and intellectual condition. But the rise of Fascism and Nazism soon obliged him to take a more interested and liberal stand politically, which may be seen both in essays, such as the anti-Nazi *Appel an die Vernunft* (*Appeal to Reason,* 1930), and in stories, such as MARIO AND THE MAGICIAN. In 1933, Hitler's government forced Mann into exile; in 1939 he came to the U.S., and in 1944 became an American citizen. During these years, he was active in many liberal pursuits, of which wartime broadcasts to the German people were only one. His post-World War II novel DOKTOR FAUSTUS reflects a deep and intense concern for the political fate of his native Germany. After the war he made frequent trips to Europe; he died in Switzerland.

Mann's other important works include *Leiden und Grösse der Meister* (*The Sufferings and Greatness of the Masters,* 1935), literary essays; THE BELOVED RETURNS, a novel; *Die vertauschten Köpfe* (*The Transposed Heads,* 1940), a short novel based on an Indian legend; JOSEPH AND HIS BROTHERS, a tetralogy of novels; and CONFESSIONS OF FELIX KRULL: CONFIDENCE MAN, a novel.

manna. The food miraculously supplied to the Children of Israel during their 40 years of wandering in the Sinai Peninsula. What they took for God's gift is now believed to have been the sweet secretions of various insects that feed on desert trees.

Mannerheim, Baron **Carl Gustaf Emil von** (1867–1951). Finnish army commander and political leader. Mannerheim served as supreme commander and regent in Finland after the declaration of independence from Russia (1918–1919). He commanded the Finnish army in 1939–1940, and again in 1941–1944. Appointed field marshal in 1933 and marshal of Finland in 1942, he served as president of Finland from 1944 to 1946.

Mannering, Mary. Stage name of **Florence Friend** (1876–1953). English actress. She appeared in England and America under the management of Daniel Frohman. She was married to the American actor James K. Hackett. She had starring roles in *Janice Meredith, The Truants, A Man's World,* and *The Garden of Allah.*

mannerism. In general, an exaggerated adherence to a particular manner or style. More particularly, the term refers to a style originating in Italy and current in 16th-century European art and architecture. In mannerism, which was a reaction to the canons of the High Renaissance, imbalance and conflict became central; exaggeration and effects of illusion were important as methods of expression; and, in painting, spatial distortion and elongation of the human figure were used to emphasize the effect of struggle. Elements of mannerism are evident in the work of Caravaggio and El Greco, among others. By the end of the century, mannerism had been superseded by the baroque, a style that it directly foreshadowed.

Mannin, Ethel (1900–   ). English novelist and essayist. She has written on politics (she was successively socialist, then anarchist), pacifism, and child care. Her novel *Venetian Blinds* (1933) is a study of working-class life. Other books include *Brief Voices* (1959), an autobiography; *A Lance for the Arabs* (1962), a travel book; and *Curfew at Dawn* (1962).

Manninen, Otto (1872–1950). Finnish poet and translator. In his two collections of verse *Säkeitä*

(*Stanzas,* 2 vols., 1905–1910) and *Virran Tyven* (*The Calm of the Stream,* 1925), Manninen exhibits a fineness of mind, a subtlety of emotion, and a beautiful perfection of form. As a professor and scholar, he is known for his translations from French, German, and Greek: among them Homer, Goethe, and Molière.

Manningoe, Nancy. A character in William Faulkner's short story *That Evening Sun Go Down* and in his Requiem for a Nun. Although it is mentioned in *The Sound and the Fury* that Nancy is murdered by her husband after the end of *That Evening Sun,* she is resurrected by Faulkner to play an important part in *Requiem for a Nun,* in which she is Temple Drake's confidante and nursemaid to the latter's children. Because Nancy's past is as sordid as her own, Nancy is the one person whom Temple can trust. Unlike Temple, however, Nancy is able to face the question of guilt and responsibility honestly.

Mannyng, Robert or **Robert of Brunne** (c. 1264–c. 1340). English poet and chronicler, member of a Gilbertine monastery after 1288. His works popularize religious and historical material in an early Middle English dialect of great importance in linguistic history. His best-known work is Handlyng Synne; the first part of his chronicle *The Story of England* (c. 1338) is an adaptation in octosyllabic couplets of Wace's history, the second part a translation in rhyming alexandrines from a history written in French rhyme by the English chronicler Peter of Langtoft (d. 1307?), continuing English history through the death of Edward I.

Man of Feeling, The (1771). A novel by Henry Mackenzie, also used as an epithet for the author. The "man of feeling" is named Harley, a sensitive, bashful, kind-hearted, and sentimental hero. The novel follows the style of Laurence Sterne in its structure of episodic adventures, keyed to moods and sentiments, and in its imitation of the dreamlike fantasy of *Tristram Shandy.*

Man of Law's Tale, The. One of the Canterbury Tales of Geoffrey Chaucer, based on an episode in Nicholas Trivet's *Anglo-Norman Chronicle* (c. 1335) and John Gower's version of it in his *Confessio Amantis* (1390). It is written in rhyme royal and told in the manner of a medieval legend, Constance (or Cunstance) representing an extreme degree of resignation or uncomplaining fortitude. The Sultan of Syria becomes a Christian in order to wed Constance, daughter of the Emperor of Rome. His mother, however, successfully schemes to set Constance adrift in a rudderless boat. She is washed ashore in Northumberland, where a rejected suitor frames a murder charge against her. A miracle proves her innocence to King Alla (or Ella), who then makes her his queen. In his absence she bears his son, Maurice; but the king's mother, anxious to rid the land of Christianity, has Constance set adrift once more with the child. They are rescued by a Roman senator and live with his family until Alla, who had killed his mother as soon as he learned what had happened, discovers them by chance. The reunited family then return to live happily in Northumberland.

Man of Mode, The, or, Sir Fopling Flutter (1676). A comedy by Sir George Etherege. It deals with the attempt of Dorimant to shed one mistress for another and his final match with yet another lady, the wealthy Harriet Woodvil, his equal in intellect and sophistication. Meanwhile, Dorimant's friend Bellair wins the hand of his beloved Emilia, despite the rivalry of his own father. The most remarkable character in the play is Sir Fopling Flutter, the personification of dandyism. Part of the play's success was due to the fact that the characters were based on real people; Beau Hewitt, a notorious fop, was the model for Sir Fopling Flutter, while Dorimant and Bellair are thought to be patterned on Lord Rochester and Etherege, respectively.

Man of Property, The. See Forsyte Saga, The.

Man of Sin (II Thess. 2:3). The Roman Catholics say the Man of Sin is Antichrist. The Puritans applied the term to the pope; the Fifth-Monarchy men to Cromwell; many modern theologians apply it to that "wicked one" (identical with the "last horn" of Dan. 7) who is immediately to precede the second advent.

Man of the World, The (1773). A sentimental novel by Henry Mackenzie written as a companion piece to The Man of Feeling. The chief protagonist is a villain named Sindall, who is a crude descendant of the literary villains of Samuel Richardson.

Manon Lescaut (1731). A novel by Abbé Prévost, the full title of which is *L'Histoire du Chevalier des Grieux et de Manon Lescaut.* It is the story of a brilliant and talented young man who, as a student of philosophy with the brightest of futures, meets Manon Lescaut, a fascinating lower-class woman. She inspires in him a love for which he almost ruins his life in his efforts to satisfy her whims and expensive tastes; for her sake, and in spite of the fact that she is rarely faithful to him, he steals, lies, borrows money, is imprisoned, exiles himself with her, and gravely wounds the son of the governor of Louisiana in a duel. She dies of exhaustion in his arms in the desert where they have fled to escape the consequences of the duel. The novel inspired numerous other works, notably two operas: *Manon* (1884) by Massenet and *Manon Lescaut* (1893) by Puccini.

Manrique, Jorge (1440?–1479). Spanish poet and soldier. His fame rests on a single poem, *Coplas por la muerte de su padre,* an elegy written shortly after the death of his father, grand master of the military order of Santiago, in 1476. In simple, almost colloquial language, the grieving son describes his father's virtues, then submerges his personal sorrow to reflect on the impermanence of all earthly endeavor. Longfellow's translation of the poem is well known.

Man's Fate (La Condition humaine; 1933; also translated as **Storm over Shanghai**). A novel by André Malraux very freely based on the Shanghai insurrection of 1927. The Communist Reds take over the city in a shaky alliance with Chiang Kai-shek's Blues, who then turn against them and retake the city. Although the work moves swiftly, it is a probing psychological study of the men involved in the uprising.

Mansfield, Katherine. Real name, **Kathleen Mansfield Murry** (wife of John Middleton Murry), born **Beauchamp** (1888–1923). New Zealand–born short-story writer. Her short stories, influenced by the work of Anton Chekhov, are notable for their poetic delicacy, psychological penetration, and sensitive understanding of children and women. Katherine

Mansfield usually follows the SLICE OF LIFE technique, describing a few typical hours in her characters' lives. Her stories are centered around some small but significant event that captures the meaning of the whole story or clarifies the character of the hero or heroine. Among her best-known stories are BLISS, A DILL PICKLE, THE GARDEN PARTY, and a number of stories, beginning with *Prelude* in 1918, which evoke her New Zealand childhood.

Her first collection of stories was *In a German Pension* (1911); *Bliss* (1920) established her reputation. Subsequent collections were published under the titles *The Garden Party* (1922) and *The Dove's Nest* (1923). After her death Murry edited and published some additional stories, her poetry, a collection of her criticism, and her journals and letters.

Katherine Mansfield had an unfortunate early life before she met Murry in 1912, including a stillborn illegitimate child and a divorce. Her later life was clouded by her brother's death in World War I. Ill health forced her to travel much in France and Germany, and eventually she died of tuberculosis. She was associated with Murry in editing and writing stories and criticism for a number of little magazines and for the *Athenaeum*. She was a friend of D. H. Lawrence, Aldous Huxley, and Virginia Woolf, and is said to be represented by the characters of Gudrun in Lawrence's *Women in Love* and Beatrice Gilray in Huxley's *Point Counter Point*.

Mansfield, Richard (1854–1907). English actor, born in Berlin. He appeared on the English stage (1877–1882) and in America (from 1882). He is famous for the title role in Rostand's *Cyrano de Bergerac* and the dual roles in Stevenson's *Dr. Jekyll and Mr. Hyde*.

Mansfield Park (1814). A novel by Jane AUSTEN. Fanny Price is adopted into the family of her rich uncle, Sir Thomas Bertram. Brought up with the four Bertram children, she is condescendingly treated as a poor relation by "Aunt NORRIS." Of her cousins, only Edmund, a young clergyman, appreciates her fine qualities, and she falls in love with him. He, unfortunately, is irresistibly drawn to the shallow, worldly Mary Crawford. In the meantime, Mary's attractive, unscrupulous brother Henry flirts violently with Maria Bertram, Edmund's sister, who is already engaged. Realizing his intentions are not serious, the disappointed Maria goes through with her marriage as planned. Henry turns his attentions to Fanny, falls in love with her, and proposes marriage. She refuses him. Henry then induces Maria to leave her husband and elopes with her. Mary Crawford takes this scandal very lightly, opening Edmund's eyes to her true nature. He turns to Fanny for comfort, falls in love with her, and marries her.

Mansion, The. See HAMLET, THE.

Mantalini, Madame. See NICHOLAS NICKLEBY.

Mantegna, Andrea (1431–1506). Italian painter and engraver. The great master of the early Renaissance, he worked principally in Padua and in Mantua. His study of classical sculpture and architecture, which he illustrated with archeological accuracy, led to the evolution of a style that is austerely controlled and of a metallic intensity. Despite their ascetic flavor and sculptural quality, his works have brilliance of color and a feeling of movement and space. Their hitherto unknown realism and dramatic power, reinforced by the assimilation of Florentine discoveries of perspective and foreshortening, made Mantegna's works a magnet for other artists. His unusual line engravings influenced Raphael, Holbein, and Dürer. His frescoes of the Gonzaga family in the Sala degli Sposi at Mantua, the earliest example of illusionist decoration of walls and ceilings, anticipated Correggio, Tiepolo, and the baroque penchant for trompe l'œil. The Venetian school founded by the Bellini family owed its early inspiration to his work, for he was the brother-in-law of Giovanni and Gentile Bellini. One of the tragedies of World War II was the partial destruction of Mantegna's series of paintings of *The Martyrdom of St. James* (Padua, Eremitani Chapel).

Man That Corrupted Hadleyburg, The (1900). A story by Mark TWAIN. A stranger leaves a sack of money in a bank in Hadleyburg, with a note instructing the cashier to give the sack to the person who makes a certain remark; secret letters then come to 19 prominent townsmen, telling them the supposed remark. All prepare to claim the treasure, which turns out to be a sack of lead; all are exposed, and the hypocrisy of the American small town is laid bare.

mantle of fidelity. A legendary garment. It appears in the old ballad *The Boy and the Mantle* in Percy's *Reliques* as a mantle "which would become no wife that was not leal." Queen Guinevere tries it, but it changes from green to red, and red to black, and seems rent into shreds. Sir Kay's lady tries it, but she fares no better; others follow, but only Sir Cradock's wife can wear it. The theme is a very common one in old story; Spenser used it in the incident of Florimel's girdle.

Mantuan, The. Medieval epithet for VERGIL.

Mantuanus (The Mantuan), Battista Spagnoli (1448–1516). Mantuan Humanist and Carmelite monk, widely known in Renaissance Europe for his Latin works. Of great importance are his 10 *Eclogues*, derived from Vergil and Petrarch, which were used as texts in the classrooms of Europe. His style and treatment of the eclogue genre influenced such writers as Erasmus and Spenser, especially the latter's *Shepheardes Calender* (1579). Shakespeare probably studied the *Eclogues* in grammar school; in *Love's Labour's Lost* Holofernes quotes a few words from the first eclogue and exclaims, "Old Mantuan, . . . who understandeth thee not, loves thee not."

Manu. In Hindu mythology, one of a class of progenitors of mankind. The seventh Manu, from whom stem all men now living, is comparable to Noah in that he survived the deluge in an ark.

Manu's Lawbook. A codification of Hindu laws and customs, written around the fifth century B.C.

Manuel, Dom. In the novels of James Branch CABELL, a swineherd who rises to be count of Poictesme, a mythical medieval realm. After his death he is known as "the Redeemer." To JURGEN, the titular hero of Cabell's most famous novel, are ascribed the many legends that are told of Manuel. Manuel's descendants in a complex genealogy appear in many of the other novels, all of which reveal Cabell's ironic view of mankind as striving, like Manuel, for the unattainable.

Man Who Came to Dinner, The (1939). A play by Moss HART and George S. KAUFMAN. A friendly burlesque on Alexander WOOLLCOTT, it deals with Sheridan Whiteside, a guest in the home of a

Middle Western family. He is immobilized as the result of an accident, meddles in family affairs, and insults virtually everyone in town. His health regained, he prepares to leave—only to break his leg again.

Man Who Died, The (1929). A short novel by D. H. Lawrence, first published under the title *The Escaped Cock*. It is a retelling of the story of Christ's resurrection. Lawrence, however, does not have Christ go to heaven, but has him mate with the priestess of Isis and declare that spiritual love and emphasis on death and heaven are a denial of life. The story is an ecstatic, symbolic presentation of Lawrence's personal religion.

Man Who Died Twice, The (1924). A blank-verse narrative by Edwin Arlington Robinson. It is the story of a composer who, in a fit of self-reproach, destroys the manuscripts of two symphonies and prepares to die. He recovers to write a third symphony and he attains salvation by joining some street evangelists.

Man Who Laughs, The (L'Homme qui Rit; 1869). A historical romance by Victor Hugo. The novel's hero, Gwynplaine, was deliberately disfigured during childhood by cuts made upward from the sides of his mouth to his ears. Inwardly kind and gentle, his outward appearance is that of a monster with a horrible grin. The willful and perverse duchess Josiana is attracted by his deformity. Only the pure love of a blind girl, Dea, rescues Gwynplaine from such a perverted liaison. When Dea dies, her protector commits suicide.

Man Who Was, The (1891). One of Rudyard Kipling's best-known short stories, published in *Life's Handicap* and later dramatized. The man, a mere "limp heap of rags," is living testimony to the cruelty of the Russians who have kept him prisoner long after the Crimean War. Though amnesic, he recognizes his name in the regimental records, but lives only a few days.

Man Who Was Thursday, The (1908). A novel by G. K. Chesterton. It is a fantastic, witty allegory concerning anarchists, spies, and detectives. The theme, expressive of Chesterton's Catholicism, is the primacy and sanctity of order.

Man Who Would Be King, The (1889). A short story by Rudyard Kipling, originally published in his volume *The Phantom Rickshaw*. By dint of his natural shrewdness the white trader Daniel Dravot sets himself up as god and king in Kafristan, dividing the kingdom with his servant, Peachey Carnehan. A woman discovers that he is human and betrays him. After suffering terrible torture, Peachey escapes to tell the tale, but Dravot is killed.

Man Without a Country, The (1863). A story by Edward Everett Hale. Philip Nolan, a U.S. Navy officer, is involved in Aaron Burr's treason. In a moment of anger he expresses the wish never to hear the name of his country again. His desire is carried out as a sentence; for 55 years, Nolan is transferred from vessel to vessel, never landing and never hearing of his country through people, books, or newspapers.

Man with the Golden Arm, The (1949). A novel by Nelson Algren. Set in the slums of Chicago, the novel, which won a National Book Award in 1950, tells the story of Frankie Machine (Francis

Majcinek) who is said to have a "golden arm" because of his sure touch with pool cues, dice, his drumsticks, and his heroin needle. Unable to free himself from his slum environment, Frankie is finally driven to suicide.

Man with the Hoe, The (1899). A poem by Edwin Markham. Inspired by Millet's celebrated painting of that title, it is a spirited protest against the wrongs of labor.

Man'yōshū (Collection of Myriad Leaves). The first Japanese poetry anthology (mid 8th century), containing some 4,500 poems written mostly during the seventh and eighth centuries. The poems reflect largely indigenous thought and beliefs and are one of the few literary sources for knowledge of Japan prior to the importation of the Chinese thought and culture of the T'ang Dynasty (618–906).

Manzoni, Alessandro (1785–1873). Italian novelist, poet, and dramatist. The leader of the Italian romantic school, he is especially known for his great historical novel I Promessi Sposi. Manzoni was a patriot, a liberal, and a Catholic whose poetic and religious sensibility found expression in his fiction; in his *Osservazioni Sulla Morale Cattolica* (1819), an essay on the power of Christian ethics to transmute human life; and in his five hymn-poems entitled *Inni Sacri* (*Sacred Hymns*, 1822). His two tragedies *Il Conte di Carmagnola* (1820) and *Adelchi* (1821) are noteworthy for their moral, religious, and patriotic themes and for the author's intentional disregard of the traditionally accepted Aristotelian unities.

In his historical fiction Manzoni strove to synthesize historical fact and poetic imagination. His ultimate aim was to show the operation of divine providence in the everyday, seemingly insignificant actions of men. *I Promessi Sposi* became a model for subsequent Italian novels—for example, the work of D'Azeglio, Grossi, and Niccolini—and the refined modern Florentine that Manzoni used as a literary language established a precedent for modern Italian prose. Verdi honored his memory in his *Manzoni Requiem* (1874).

Mao Tse-tung (1893–   ). Chairman of Central Committee of Chinese Communist Party. One of the early party leaders, he took part in the "Long March" (1934–1935), headed the Chinese Communist Party (1935), fought the Nationalists and the Japanese. He proclaimed the People's Republic (1949) and negotiated a 30-year treaty with Russia (1950). Author of many books, his *Selected Works* have appeared in several volumes (1954–   ). His essay *On Guerrilla Warfare* has been translated into English (1961) and is considered a definitive work on this subject.

Map or Mapes, Walter (c. 1140–c. 1209). Welshborn English courtier and satirist, later archdeacon of Oxford (1197–1209), a favorite at the court of Henry II. He was long considered the author of a lost prose version of the Launcelot story on which later accounts of the Arthurian legends were partly based, but the only work he is definitely known to have written is *De Nugis Curialium* (*Courtiers' Trifles*, 1180–1193), a collection of witty anecdotes, court gossip, and satirical denunciations. He was also reputed to be the author of large quantities of Goliardic verse; he certainly wrote light verse of this type, but not nearly as much as has been attributed to him.

Maradick. A character who recurs in various novels by Hugh WALPOLE. He first appears as the hero of *Maradick at Forty* (1910), and in subsequent novels as a mysterious figure in London clubs. He is connected with the village of "Treliss" in Cornwall.

Marañón [y Posadillo], Gregorio (1888–1960). Spanish writer, physician, and professor of medicine. A versatile intellectual, Marañón was interested chiefly in the field of endocrinology. However, this did not prevent him from acquiring a reputation as a literary and historical scholar. He is best known for his detailed treatment of specific figures, as in *Las ideas biológicas del padre Feijóo* (1934), *Tiberio; historia de un resentimiento* (TIBERIUS: A STUDY IN RESENTMENT; 1939), and the earlier and well-known *Ensayo biológico sobre Enrique IV de Castilla y su tier..po* (1930).

Marat, Jean Paul (1743–1793). Swiss-born French politician and physician. At the beginning of the FRENCH REVOLUTION he published the paper *L'Ami du Peuple* (1789), in which he advocated a republican form of government. With DANTON and ROBESPIERRE, he overthrew the GIRONDISTS. He was assassinated in his bath by Charlotte CORDAY on July 13, 1793.

Marathon. A plain in Attica, northeast of Athens. Here the Greeks won a victory over the Persians (490 B.C.) that ended Darius' Greek ambitions. According to tradition, the news of the victory was brought back to Athens by a runner, PHEIDIPPIDES, whose feat is commemorated in the modern marathon races, usually fixed at 26 miles, 385 yards.

Marble Faun, The (1860). A novel by Nathaniel HAWTHORNE. Donatello, an Italian count, resembles the Faun of Praxiteles in appearance as well as in his natural spirits. An innocent admirer of Miriam, the darkly beautiful, mysterious art student, he is driven to kill her strange pursuer, Antonio. The act catapults him into reality; sinning, he moves from innocence to experience. The murder scene is witnessed by Hilda, a pure, pale artist. Guilty through her inadvertent participation in the crime, Hilda must confess the secret to a Catholic priest; later she and the sculptor Kenyon reveal their love. Donatello, matured by his crime, becomes a moral being and turns himself over to the authorities. In telling his story, Hawthorne treats the theme of the fortunate fall. Setting the novel in Rome, the author employs the landscape of that center of art and faith to add to the richness of the work.

Marbury vs. Madison (1803). The first case in which the U.S. Supreme Court declared that an act of Congress was contrary to the Constitution and was therefore invalid. The decision was delivered by Chief Justice John Marshall for "the unanimous Court." The precedent established in this case greatly increased the power of the court.

Marc, Franz (1880–1916). German artist. A founder of the BLAUE REITER group, he is known for his expressionist paintings of animals.

Marceau, Félicien (1913–   ). Real name **Louis Carett.** Belgian novelist, essayist, and playwright. Balzacian in technique, such novels as *Chair et cuir* (1951), *Bergère légère* (1953; translated as *The China Shepherdess*), and *Les Elans*

du Coeur (1955) reveal Marceau as a shrewd observer of the social scene. The style of the novels is without a trace of romanticism, lucid to the point of coldness. As author, Marceau plays the role of detached observer. His satire, often cruelly derisive, brutally rips the mask from the social comedy which he perceives. In his plays, *L'Oeuf* (1956), *La Bonne Soupe* (1958) and *L'Etouffe-Chrétien* (1960), a deep pessimism lies beneath the keen wit. Farcical antics and comic buffoonery, as in Samuel Beckett's *En Attendant Godot*, express a nihilistic vision of absurdity and despair. But Marceau believes more optimistically than the dramatists of the ABSURD, that with his will and intelligence man can combat absurdity.

Marcel, Gabriel (1889?–   ). French philosopher, dramatist, and critic. He introduced the writing of Sören Kierkegaard to France about 1925, and, a convert to Catholicism, became the leading French exponent of Christian EXISTENTIALISM, as presented in his *Metaphysical Journal* (1927), *Being and Having* (*Etre et avoir;* 1935), *Homo Viator: Introduction to a Metaphysic of Hope* (1944), *The Philosophy of Existence* (1949), *The Mystery of Being* (*Le Mystère de l'être;* 1951). The importance of intuition and faith is also the theme of his plays, such as *La Grâce* (1921), *A Man of God* (*Un Homme de Dieu;* 1925), and *The Beacon* (*Le Fanal;* 1936). In 1969 he won the Goncourt prize for his novel *Creezy.*

Marcellus and **Bernardo.** In Shakespeare's HAMLET, 2 officers on night watch at Elsinore. They are the first to see the ghost of Hamlet's father.

March, Fredric (1897–   ). American actor. Since 1927 he has been married to the actress Florence Eldridge (1901–   ). He has appeared, often with his wife, in such notable plays as *The Skin of Our Teeth, A Bell for Adano, Long Day's Journey into Night,* and also in motion pictures.

March, Joseph Moncure (1899–   ). American newspaper critic and poet. He is known for the two narrative poems *The Wild Party* (1928) and *The Set-Up* (1928). Both are hard-boiled stories, written in staccato rhythms and highly colloquial diction.

March, William. Pen name of **William Edward March Campbell** (1893–1954). American novelist and short-story writer. March's best-known novel is probably *The Bad Seed* (1954), the story of Rhoda Penmark, a charming but homicidal eight-year-old; it was dramatized by Maxwell Anderson in 1955. *October Island* (1952) deals with a missionary's wife who is transformed into a modern goddess by the natives on a South Sea island. He also wrote *Company K* (1933) and two collections of short stories, *Some Like Them Short* (1939) and *Trial Balance* (1945).

Marche, Olivier de la. See RHÉTORIQUEURS, LES GRANDS.

Märchen (*Ger., little tale*). A favorite narrative form in GERMAN ROMANTICISM. The term includes, but has a wider range than the English fairy tale. On one hand, it can refer to the simple *Volksmärchen* (folk tale), such as those collected by the brothers Grimm, or to tales written in imitation of the folk style. On the other, it can refer to the deeply philosophical, allegorical form of the *Kunstmärchen* (art tale), the definitive example of which is Goethe's *Das Märchen* (1798). NOVALIS and Brentano also used this form. Basically, a *Märchen* is short and moves in a fantastic realm rather than in the real world. It usually has a happy ending, but not necessarily, as is seen in some written by Tieck. See E. T. A. HOFF-MANN.

March Hare. A character in Lewis Carroll's ALICE'S ADVENTURES IN WONDERLAND. At a mad tea party he offers Alice wine when there is none, and when reprimanded for putting butter in the Hatter's watch, he replies, "It was the *best* butter." The fact that hares are unusually shy and wild during March, their rutting season, gave rise to the popular expression "Mad as a March hare." Carroll's March Hare is a burlesque of the expression.

Marchioness, the. The half-starved girl-of-all-work in Charles Dickens' OLD CURIOSITY SHOP. As she has no name of her own, Dick SWIVELLER calls her the Marchioness when he plays cards with her because it seems "more real and pleasant" to play with a Marchioness than with a domestic slavey. When Dick Swiveller falls sick, the Marchioness nurses him and he afterward marries her.

Marco Millions (1928). A play by Eugene O'NEILL. The Marco of O'Neill's play is Marco Polo, who is used as a whipping boy to express the dramatist's scorn for mercenary souls. His Marco is interested only in making his million; he does not see that Kublai Khan's daughter is in love with him and he serves her only for the bonus he hopes to receive. At last, he marries a fat, commonplace Venetian.

Marcus Aurelius. Full Latin name, **Marcus Aurelius Antoninus** (121–180). Roman emperor (161–180) and Stoic philosopher. As emperor, he was beset by internal disturbances—famines and plagues—and by the external threat posed by the Germans in the north and the Parthians in the east. As year after year he witnessed the gradual crumbling of the Roman frontiers, he turned more and more to the study of Stoic philosophy. Between battles he wrote down the philosophical reflections which were later collected and published as *The Meditations of Marcus Aurelius.* This collection of precepts (written in Greek) is perhaps the most readable exposition of Stoic philosophizing that we possess.

Mardi and a Voyage Thither (1849). A novel by Herman MELVILLE. His first literary treatment of metaphysical, ethical, and political problems, the book is overwhelmed by complexity. Begun as a narrative of adventure, it concludes as an allegory of mind.

A symbolic quest for Absolute Truth is undertaken by five men: Taji, the young monomaniacal hero; Babbalanja, a philosopher; Yoomy, a poet; Mohi, a historian; and King Media, a man of common sense. On King Media's boat, they sail through the island archipelagoes of Mardi (the world), stopping at various countries, including Vivenza, the U.S. Taji, who most resembles Melville, kills an Island priest, Aleema, in order to rescue Yillah, a beautiful white woman of seeming prelapsarian innocence. Yillah disappears, and Taji's search for her becomes a search for truth and lost innocence. He, in turn, is sought by Hautia, the incarnation of sophisticated sexuality, who haunts him for the murder of Aleema. She becomes a symbol for guilt, and the need for repentance. Taji, pursued and pursuing, is last seen alone, sailing on desperate seas.

Mardi Gras (Fr., "fat Tuesday"). Last day of the pre-Lenten carnival in France, Shrove Tuesday. It is celebrated with all sorts of festivities. In Paris a fat ox used to be paraded through the principal streets, crowned with a fillet, and accompanied by mock priests and a band of tin instruments in imitation of a Roman sacrificial procession. In the U.S., New Orleans is famed for its Mardi Gras celebration. See also SHROVETIDE.

Marduk. A Babylonian warrior god. He was the son of Ea, the god of water and wisdom. When the other gods are all terrified by the invasion of Tiamat, the dragon of the sea, Marduk slays her. He makes heaven and earth of the two halves of her body and creates man of the bones and blood of Kingu, one of Tiamat's henchmen. Part of Marduk's supremacy in the pantheon of Assyria and Babylonia was due to the fact that he was the local BAAL of Babylon. See WAR OF THE GODS.

Marfisa (Marphisa). A warrior maiden in the Orlando poems of Boiardo and Ariosto. In the version of Boiardo, she is the sister of RUGGIERO, and like him an ally of the pagan forces. In Ariosto, she joins him as a convert to the Christian faith and becomes an ally of the paladins fighting for Charlemagne.

Marganorre. In an episode from the ORLANDO FURIOSO of Ariosto the father of two youths, Cilandro and Tanacro, both killed by the love of women. In revenge Marganorre punishes all the women who come by his castle. He is punished in turn by Ruggiero.

Margarete. See GRETCHEN.

Margaret of Anjou (1430–1482). French-born queen of England. The daughter of René I of Anjou, she married Henry VI in 1445 and gave birth to her only son, Edward, in 1453, the same year in which Henry suffered a temporary fit of insanity. The rivalry between her and Richard, duke of York, who had been heir presumptive until the birth of Edward, brought on the Wars of the Roses between the houses of Lancaster and York. In 1471 she was captured, and Edward was killed at Tewkesbury, Henry dying in the Tower of London soon afterwards. She was freed in 1475.

In HENRY VI: PARTS I, II, and III, Shakespeare chronicles her development into a savage and imperious woman whom Richard Plantagenet calls:

> She-wolf of France, but worse than wolves of France,
> Whose tongue more poisons than the adder's tooth!

She also appears in RICHARD III.

Margaret of Navarre. Also known as **Marguerite de Navarre, Marguerite de Valois,** and **Marguerite d'Angoulême** (1492–1549). French queen and author. The sister of Francis I of France, she married Henri d'Albret, king of Navarre, after the death of her first husband, and transformed his court into a refuge for humanists, among them Marot, Calvin, and Lefèvre d'Etaples. Instilled with Platonic and Petrarchan mysticism, she devoted her life to culture and sacrifice for those she loved. She expressed her religious fervor and intimate joys and sorrows in such works of poetry as *Miroir de l'âme pécheresse* (1531) and *Les Marguerites de la Marguerite des Princesses* (1547). In the HEPTAMERON she produced the first collection of French tales. Rabelais dedicated the third book of *Gargantua and Pantagruel* (1532–1564) to her soul. She is sometimes referred to as *marguerite des marguerites* (*Fr.*, "pearl of pearls"), the name by which Francis called her.

Margaret of Valois. Known as **Queen** or **Reine Margot** (1553–1615). French queen. The daughter of Henry II of France and Catherine de Médicis, she married Henry of Navarre (later Henry IV of France) in 1572. The childless marriage was dissolved in 1599. Known for her learning and loose living, she was the author of interesting letters and *Mémoires* (1628).

Margaret Ogilvy (1896). A biography of his mother by J. M. Barrie.

Margawse or **Morgause, Queen.** In Arthurian legend, the wife of King Lot and mother of the knights Gawain, Gareth, Gaheris, and Aggravaine. In Malory's *Morte d'Arthur* (c. 1469), she is also the mother, by King Arthur, of Sir Mordred. Margawse's son, Sir Gaheris, beheads her when he finds her with her lover, Sir Lamerok; Sir Gawain kills Lamerok. Margawse is Bellicent in Tennyson's *Idylls of the King* (1859–1872).

Marguérite. The heroine of Gounod's opera *Faust* and Boito's *Mefistofele*. She is based on the Gretchen in Goethe's *Faust*.

Margutte. A demigiant in the Morgante Maggiore of Pulci. A glutton and a vulgar scoundrel, Margutte remains an excellent and loyal companion to Morgante. He dies of laughter on seeing a monkey pulling on his (Margutte's) boots. One of the prime sources of Rabelais in his Gargantua and Pantagruel, Margutte was referred to by Leigh Hunt as the first and greatest unmitigated scoundrel in history.

Maria. Olivia's maid in Shakespeare's Twelfth Night. A lively, quick-witted shrew, she instigates the intrigues against Malvolio and eventually marries Sir Toby Belch, Olivia's uncle.

María (1867). A novel by Jorge Isaacs (1837–1895), Colombian poet and novelist. Perhaps the most widely read South American novel, *María* is a romantic idyll which describes the ill-starred love affair between the title character and her cousin Efraín. Although the plot is cloyingly sentimental by contemporary standards, the author's picture of life in Colombia's Cauca Valley, where the action takes place, retains its freshness and charm.

Maria Chapdelaine. See Louis Hémon.

Maria D'Aquino. The supposed natural daughter of King Robert of Naples, loved and celebrated by Giovanni Boccaccio as Fiammetta. It is now accepted that she and her affair with the author are entirely fictional.

Mariage de Figaro, Le, ou La folle journée. See Figaro.

Mariage forcé, Le. See Sganarelle (3).

Maria Magdalena (1844). A play by Friedrich Hebbel in the tradition of the bourgeois tragedy, which goes back ultimately to Diderot. It is the tragedy of a girl named Klara who is pregnant by her worthless fiancé and becomes involved in a web of conflicting motives and obligations—including love for another man and fear of social reproach—that leads to her suicide.

In the preface to this play, Hebbel outlines his theory, largely influenced by Hegel, that great drama is only produced at moments in world history when an old order and a new order are in conflict. He believed that in his own day the world spirit was undergoing a crisis of self-consciousness which would eventually lead to a firmer, less superstitious basis for human institutions, and *Maria Magdalena* is intended to depict this crisis. The last words of the play are spoken by Klara's father, who is a representative of unbending tradition, and are "I don't understand the world any more." The play's title refers to the fact that, in her tragedy, Klara is symbolically purged of evil as St. Mary Magdalene was.

Mariamne. The wife of Herod the Great. Friedrich Hebbel, in his tragedy *Herodes und Mariamne* (1850), makes Mariamne a prefiguration of the coming age of Christianity, thus reinterpreting the conflict between her and Herod as that between modern and pagan world orders.

Mariana. The rejected fiancée of Angelo in Shakespeare's Measure for Measure. She remains faithful to him and pleads with Duke Vincentio to spare his life.

Marianne. The heroine of Marivaux's novel *La Vie de Marianne*. She combines virtue and coquetry; her reactions to the complicated series of events comprising her life are minutely analysed by the author.

Maria Stuart. See Mary Stuart.

Maria Theresia or **Theresa** (1717–1780). Archduchess of Austria and queen of Hungary and Bohemia (1740–1780). The War of the Austrian Succession (1740–1748) and the Seven Years' War (1756–1763) were fought during her reign to defend the Hapsburg dominions, which she inherited. Among her many children were Marie Antoinette and Joseph II.

Marichi. In the Ramayana the half-brother of Ravana. Ravana orders him to assume the form of a golden deer to lure away Rama so that Ravana could abduct Rama's wife, Sita.

Marie Antoinette (1755–1793). Queen of France, wife of Louis XVI, whom she married when she was 15. As daughter of Maria Theresa of Austria, she sought Austria's aid against French Revolutionaries. In 1791 she counseled Louis XVI to attempt flight from France, an attempt which ended in their imprisonment. They were regarded as traitors and Marie Antoinette was guillotined on Oct. 16, 1793. Her personal charm, her naïve ignorance of practical life, her extravagance, and her frank and courageous honesty contributed to her unpopularity both at court and with the French masses, who contemptuously called her *l'Autrichienne* (*Fr.,* "the Austrian woman"). When she was told that a revolution was threatening because the people had no bread, she is said to have replied, "Let them eat cake." See Diamond; Madame Déficit; M. et Mme. Véto; baker. See illustration on page 636.

Marie de France (c. 1200). French medieval poetess, thought to have been the half sister of Henry II of England. Most of her life seems to have been spent at the English court and her writings had a considerable influence on English writers. She is famous for her Breton lais, verse-narrative romances full of Celtic atmosphere and often making use of Arthurian materials. Some 15 of these lais are known, among them that of Sir Launfal. She also wrote a collection of beast fables, based on Aesop, called *Ysopet* or *Isopet* (little Aesop). See Breton lai.

Marie de Médicis (1573–1642). Italian-born queen of France. The second wife of Henry IV, whom

Marie Antoinette en route to the guillotine.
Sketched by Jacques Louis David.

she married in 1600, she was regent for her son Louis XIII from 1610 to 1617. She was forced to leave France in 1630 by her archrival Richelieu.

Marignano, battle of (1515). The meeting at which the French king Francis I defeated Massimiliano Sforza, heir of the deposed Lodovico, duke of Milan, thus consolidating French control over Lombardy.

Marin, John (1872–1953). American painter. He was one of the New York artistic vanguard whose one-man shows were presented by Alfred STIEGLITZ at the beginning of the century. Marin used his major medium, watercolor, for his great subjects, New York's skyscrapers and the coast of Maine.

Marina. In Shakespeare's PERICLES, the daughter of Pericles. He leaves her in Tarsus in the care of his friends Cleon and Dionyza, who eventually attempt to assassinate her. She is abducted by pirates, sold into a brothel, but at last marries Lysimachus, governor of Mytilene, and is reunited with her family.

Marinell. See FAERIE QUEENE, THE.

Marinetti, Filippo Tommaso. See FUTURISM.

Marinism. A 17th-century literary style characterized by excessive ornateness and affectation. It was named after Giambattista Marino, the Italian poet famous for his artificial comparisons, pompous and overwrought descriptions, and conceits. See GONGORISM.

Marino or Marini, Giambattista (1569–1625). Italian poet. During a colorful lifetime spent mainly at Italian and French courts, he produced a collection of lyrics, *La Lira;* a group of iconographic poems, *La Galeria;* pastoral idylls, such as *La Sampogna;* and a sacred epic (1632) on the Massacre of the Innocents. His masterpiece is the *Adone* (1623), a long mythological poem centered around the love of Venus and Adonis. Its style—like that of his own earlier poems and that of the Marinists, his followers—features elaborate conceits, frequent plays on words, rhetorical devices, and a floridly sensuous tone. His extension of Petrarchan love motifs and his preference for themes from classical Roman mythology are also characteristic of Marinism. In the following centuries, a reaction against Marinism, seen as part of a larger decadence (*secentismo,* or 17th-centuryism), lowered his reputation to near oblivion. Recently, he has returned to literary discussion as a major example of the baroque style in poetry.

Marino Faliero (1820). A historical tragedy in verse by Lord BYRON. Faliero, the 49th doge of Venice, joins a conspiracy to overthrow the republic, but he is betrayed and subsequently beheaded upon the Giant's Staircase, where doges traditionally take the oath of fidelity. Though the historical Faliero joined the conspiracy in hope of becoming king, Byron explains Faliero's complicity as the result of his fury at the Council of Forty for meting out an insufficient sentence to Michel Steno, an indecent young noble who has scurrilously libeled the *dogaressa.*

Mario and the Magician (Mario und der Zauberer; 1930). A story by Thomas MANN. It is told from the point of view of a German family in an Italian resort town. Centering about the performance of a magician named Cipolla who brutally humiliates several members of his audience by hypnotic means, the story is at least partly intended as a warning against a masochistic fascination with the oppression of fascism, but it is nonetheless a convincing work of art. Cipolla is finally shot and killed by a very ordinary young waiter named Mario, whom he has mocked in an especially cruel way.

Marion, Francis (1732?–1795). American Revolutionary soldier. He was known as "the Swamp Fox" because of his skill in retreating—Indian-fashion —to swamps and forests after quick and effective raids on British forces. He participated in the battle of Eutaw Springs, S.C. (Sept. 8, 1781). William Cullen Bryant wrote a *Song of Marion's Men* (1831). See KATHERINE WALTON.

Maritain, Jacques (1882–   ). French Catholic philosopher and man of letters. Reared as a Protestant, Maritain was converted to Roman Catholicism in 1906; Charles Péguy and Léon Bloy were influential figures in his spiritual development. Bergson, his teacher, restored his sense of the Absolute but was severely criticized by Maritain in *La Philosophie bergsonienne* (1914). The philosophy of St. Thomas Aquinas, an ordered system able to reconcile faith and reason and to acknowledge the coexistence of freedom and the divine in man, alone could satisfy his needs. Systematically and energetically, he published critical studies of those philosophers whose thinking seemed to him faulty or inadequate. In *Antimoderne* (1922) and *Trois Réformateurs* (1925) he levels a sharp attack against Luther, Descartes, Rousseau, and Pascal for distorting modern thought. His own philosophy, neo-Thomism, is expounded in *Eléments de phi-*

losophie (1923–1930), *Distinguer pour unir, ou les Dégres de savoir* (1932), *Humanisme intégral* (1936), and *Confession de foi* (1941), first published in English as *I Believe* (1939). Maritain came to America after the fall of France in 1940 and taught at Columbia, Princeton, and the Institute of Medieval Studies in Toronto.

A brilliant although often dogmatically assertive thinker, Maritain has made significant contributions to the fields of aesthetics, ethics, and politics. *Art et Scolastique* (1920) is a lucid attempt to use scholastic philosophy as the basis of an aesthetic. His political works include *Scholasticism and Politics* (1940), *Le Crépuscule de la civilisation* (1941) and *The Rights of Man and Natural Law* (1943).

Marius, [Caius] (157–86 B.C.). Roman general, consul, and leader of republican Rome's popular party. Born of plebeian stock, Marius was a lifelong, fanatical foe of the privileged aristocracy. After a brilliant career as soldier and strategist, he won, in 107 B.C., the Roman consulate. Soon after he led a successful campaign against the African prince Jugurtha (107–105). It was here that his career first intercepted that of the aristocrat Lucius Cornelius SULLA, the man who was to become his mortal enemy. Through 15 years (105–90) Marius and Sulla vied for popular acclaim. In 90, after the Social War had been successfully concluded, Roman civil war broke out. For four bloody years thereafter, Rome was the pawn of these two ruthless generals. As one rival recovered, the other's supporters were purged. The reprisals did not end with the death of Marius (86), but continued until Sulla was absolute master of Rome (82).

Marius the Epicurean (1885). A philosophic romance by Walter PATER. The hero is a Roman noble of the time of Marcus Aurelius, and the book records his sensations and ideas rather than outward events. Though he makes no formal profession of Christianity, Marius is greatly drawn to it through his friend Cornelius and his own high principles and deeply religious nature. His death is of such a nature that the Christian Church looks upon him as a martyr.

Marivaux, Pierre Carlet de Chamblain de (1688–1763). French dramatist and novelist. He is most famous for those of his comedies which analyze the vicissitudes of the heart during courtship: timidity, jealousy, misunderstandings—in brief, the subtle psychological aspects of the game of love. Among this type of play are *Le Jeu de l'amour et du hasard* (1730), *Les Fausses confidences* (1737), and *L'Epreuve* (1740). Other plays by Marivaux are mythological, social, philosophical, or romanesque in theme, and his treatment of them is strikingly fanciful. His subtly nuanced, precious language is so peculiar to him that the term *marivaudage* has been coined to describe it. Marivaux's two unfinished novels *La Vie de* MARIANNE (1731–41), completed by Mme RICCOBONI, and *Le Paysan parvenu* (1735), combine penetrating analyses of characters' states of mind, and a vivacious, often realistic picture of all classes of Parisian society.

Marjorie Daw (1873). A short story by Thomas Bailey ALDRICH. Edward Delaney creates the character of a neighbor girl, Marjorie Daw, to amuse his languishing friend, John Fleming, in their correspondence. Delaney's description of Marjorie so intrigues Fleming that, when he recovers, he comes to claim her hand. The girl's abashed creator flees before his friend arrives. The story first appeared in *The Atlantic Monthly*.

Mark, St. The author of the *Gospel of St. Mark*, the second book of the New Testament. Little is known about his life. He is famed as the patron saint of Venice.

Mark, King. In the medieval legend of TRISTAN AND ISEULT, king of Cornwall, husband of Iseult, and uncle of Tristan. He has the misfortune to be in the generally unsympathetic position of cuckold, but, in most versions, the drama of the tale in which his wife and favorite nephew are lovers is intensified by the nobility and sensitivity of King Mark. In the version of Gottfried von Strassburg (c. 1210) particularly, the psychological conflict becomes the more acute through the character of the king whose understanding of the situation makes of him a tragic figure almost surpassing in importance the lovers themselves. In Malory's *Morte d'Arthur* (c. 1469), on the contrary, he is a base figure intent only on the death of Sir Tristram (Tristan). See TRISTRAM OF LYONESS.

Mark, The Gospel According to St. The 2nd book of the New Testament. One of the SYNOPTIC GOSPELS, it is generally held to be the earliest account of Jesus' life; scholars date it about A.D. 70. Tradition ascribes it to John Mark (Marcus), the traveling companion of Paul and friend of Peter. The narrative is simple and is obviously written for Christians who wanted a history of Jesus. Mark was a source for the later gospels of Luke and Matthew.

Markandaya, Kamala (1923–   ). Indian novelist writing in English. A journalist in Britain since 1947, Markandaya has published *Nectar in a Sieve* (1955), and *Some Inner Fury* (1959).

Markham, Edwin (1852–1940). American poet. He is best known for his protest against the exploitation of the poor in THE MAN WITH THE HOE. The popular success of the poem was due both to its message and to its sonorous and rhetorical style; its popularity allowed Markham to abandon teaching and to devote himself to writing and lecturing. His *Lincoln, the Man of the People*, published in *Lincoln, and Other Poems* (1901), has also been widely known and read. Markham published several other volumes of verse, including *The Ballad of the Gallows Bird* (1896), *Gates of Paradise and Other Poems* (1920), and *Collected Poems* (1940).

Markham, Gervase (1568?–1637). English writer on war, horsemanship, forestry, cookery, and hawking, and author of poems and plays. Markham is remembered especially for his versified account (1595) of Sir Richard GRENVILLE's heroic naval battle against the Spanish fleet (a theme also treated by Tennyson) and for *The English Arcadia* (1607).

Marko Kraljevic. Literally, Marko, son of the king, a Serbian national hero. Prominent also in Bulgarian and Romanian folk lore, he lived, according to popular tradition, 300 years, fighting all the time against foreign oppressors, especially the Turks. Historians give him about 60 years (1335?–1394).

Mark Rutherford, The Autobiography of (1881). A novel by William Hale WHITE. With its sequel *Mark Rutherford's Deliverance* (1885), it presents the story of an idealistic young minister tormented by intellectual skepticism, his break with the church, and the gradual working out of his ideals in a life of social service.

Marlborough, 1st duke of. John Churchill (1650–1722). English military leader. The son of the impoverished Sir Winston Churchill, he was assisted in advancing his fortunes by his sister Arabella, who was the mistress of the duke of York, later James II. At the outbreak of the War of the Spanish Succession (1702–1712), he was named commander of the English forces and defeated the French at the battles of Blenheim, Ramillies, Oudenarde, and Malplaquet. His wife Sarah, the famous duchess of Marlborough, was Queen Anne's closest friend for many years.

Marlow. The narrator of a number of tales and novels by Joseph CONRAD. He is a kind of detective of the conscience, who studies the moral dilemmas of other men in order to understand himself better. By using this character to narrate the stories (usually to his friends, at night, to the accompaniment of drinks and cigars), Conrad is able to develop the impersonal, oblique method of storytelling employed by Henry JAMES. Marlow describes and analyzes the various sources from which he has collected his information and comments on the significance of the events he narrates. Among the tales he tells are LORD JIM, YOUTH, HEART OF DARKNESS, and CHANCE.

Marlowe, Christopher (1564–1593). English dramatist and poet. Born at Canterbury, the son of a shoemaker, Marlowe attended Benet College (now Corpus Christi), where he took his B.A. in 1584, his M.A. in 1587. His life has become a legend, with its gay disdain for all convention, its irreverence, its reckless vitality. He was killed in a quarrel with a man named Ingram Frizer over the settlement of a tavern bill for supper and ale.

Considered the greatest figure in Elizabethan drama before Shakespeare, Marlowe raised the conventional, academic tragedy of his time, rigidly held within the limitations of the Senecan form, to a level of serious and emotionally gripping art. TAMBURLAINE, his first play, appeared in 1587. Blank verse, formerly stiff and wooden, sprang to life in his hands; the splendid utterances of the Scythian conqueror earned Marlowe's verse the praise of "mighty line." *The Tragical History of* DR. FAUSTUS, not entered on the *Stationer's Register* until 1601, was probably performed in 1588; THE JEW OF MALTA was probably produced in 1589. Each of these dramas is dominated by a single character whose force of personality alone gives unity to the play. Tamburlaine, Faustus, and Barabas are all gripped by a master passion, a Renaissance longing for infinite beauty or riches or power. In *Edward II,* entered on the *Stationers' Register* in 1593, Marlowe revealed a ripening and maturing of his dramatic and lyrical gifts. The play has less surface glitter and a graver, wiser understanding of human weakness and limitation. No longer dependent on the superhuman power of one main figure for its coherence, *Edward II* contains several finely drawn characters and is skillfully plotted. Its poetry, too, is less startling but far more subtle in its varied use of the blank verse line. Marlowe may also have written *Dido, Queen of Carthage* (c. 1593, with Thomas NASHE) and *The Massacre at Paris* (1593). Some scholars believe he may have had a hand in the

writing of some of Shakespeare's plays, among them *Titus Andronicus, Henry IV,* and *Richard III.*

Marlowe's lyric poetry is graceful, musical, and warmly sensuous. It includes a translation of Ovid's *Amores* (c. 1597); *Hero and Leander* (1598) based on the poem by Musaeus, left unfinished at Marlowe's death, and completed by George CHAPMAN; a translation of the first book of Lucan's *Pharsalia,* published in 1600; and the famous lyric *The Passionate Shepherd,* published in *England's Helicon* (1600).

Marlowe, Julia. Real name: **Sarah Frances Frost** (1866–1950). English-born American actress. She was particularly successful in Shakespearean roles, especially after her second marriage (1911) to E. H. SOTHERN. The most acclaimed of their joint appearances was in *Romeo and Juliet.*

Marmeladov. A drunken, Micawber-like character in Feodor Dostoevski's CRIME AND PUNISHMENT. His comicality is compounded with tragedy when he reveals to Raskolnikov that his daughter SONYA has been forced into prostitution to support the family. Marmeladov dies after being struck by a coach in the street.

Marmion, A Tale of Flodden Field (1808). A romantic narrative poem by Sir Walter SCOTT, set in the time of Henry VIII. Lord Marmion rejects his betrothed, Constance, and attempts unsuccessfully to secure the wealthy Lady Clare in marriage. Ultimately he is slain at the battle of Flodden Field (1513). See LOCHINVAR.

Mármol, José. See AMALIA.

Marmontel, Jean François (1723–1799). French critic, dramatist, and short-story writer. He contributed articles on literature to the ENCYCLOPÉDIE. His works include the tragedy *Denys le tyran* (1748); the novels *Bélisaire* (1766), a plea for religious tolerance, and *Les Incas, ou La Destruction de l'empire du Pérou* (1777), an indictment of slavery; and the *Contes moraux* (1761–1786). His *Mémoires d'un père* (1804), written for his children, offers a valuable picture of 18th-century French society. He became a member of the French ACADEMY in 1763.

Marnix, Philip van. Baron **Sint Aldegonde** (1538–1598). A Flemish writer and statesman, active in the liberation of the Netherlands and the propagation of Protestantism. His *De Byencorf der h. Roomscher Kercke (The Beehive of the Holy Church of Rome,* 1569) is a fierce and Rabelaisian attack on Catholicism. He is the putative author of the Dutch national song "Wilhelmus van Nassouwen."

Maro, Publius Vergilius. See VERGIL.

Marot, Clément (1496-1544). French poet, known for his light and graceful lyrics. His work marks the transition between medieval poetry, whose elaborate techniques were perpetuated by the RHÉTORIQUEURS, and the poetry of the Renaissance, which modeled itself after classical and Italian forms. He brought to the tortured poetic techniques of the Rhétoriqueurs a natural facility for playing with words and the sparkle of an engaging personality. He treated the modern forms, such as the Italian sonnet which he introduced into French literature, with the same freshness and vivacity. A critical spirit led him to question traditional Catholic doctrines and to undertake his famous translation from Latin of the Psalms (1541-1543). This religious independence caused him to be suspected of sympathizing with the Protestant reform movement and cost him imprisonment and periodic flights into exile in Navarre and Ferrara and in Calvin's Geneva (1542–1543). His buoyant verve, satirical wit, and elegant, tactful gaiety endeared him, alone of all the 16th-century poets, to the classic poets of the 17th century.

Marpessa. In Greek legend, daughter of Evenus, courted by both Idas and APOLLO. When Idas opposed his mortal strength to that of the god and carried her off, Zeus intervened to insure Marpessa the lover of her own choice. Fearing that Apollo would tire of her when she lost her youth, she decided in favor of Idas.

Marprelate controversy. The name given to the vituperative pamphlet war (1588–1590) between the Puritans and the Church of England. In 1588 appeared a number of pamphlets, printed by a secret press and purportedly written by one Martin Marprelate, attacking the Established Church and particularly the Episcopacy. Thinking that the best way to answer "Martin" would be in his own trenchant, witty style, the church authorities secretly hired writers—notably Robert GREENE and Thomas NASHE—to publish replies. In 1590 the Marprelate press was discovered and the printer, one Penry, executed. The real author may have been Job Throckmorton, who escaped execution. Seven of the Marprelate pamphlets are extant, and contain some of the best satirical writing of the time.

Marquand, John P[hillips] (1893–1960). American novelist. He is best known for his studies of upper-class New Englanders struggling to maintain their aristocratic, Puritan standards in the 20th century. These are contained in THE LATE GEORGE APLEY, WICKFORD POINT, and H. M. PULHAM, ESQ. Marquand also wrote a number of popular detective stories about the keen-witted Mr. MOTO. Marquand's shorter writings were collected in *Thirty Years* (1954). His later books include *B. F.'s Daughter* (1946), about a domineering tycoon and his domineering offspring; POINT OF NO RETURN; *Melville Goodwin, U.S.A.* (1951), the story of a typical American military officer; *Sincerely, Willis Wayde* (1955), a satirical business novel; *Women and Thomas Harrow* (1958), about the New York theater of the 1920's. The posthumously published *Timothy Dexter Revisited* (1960) returns to Newburyport, Mass., the setting of the earlier *Lord Timothy Dexter* (1925). See Timothy DEXTER.

Marquette, Jacques. Known as **Père Marquette** (1637–1675). French Jesuit missionary in North America. Marquette accompanied Jolliet down the Wisconsin and Mississippi rivers and across Lake Michigan. He described the journey in *Voyage et découverte de quelques pays et nations de l'Amérique Septentrionale (Journey and Discovery of Several Countries and Nations of Northern America,* 1681).

Marquina, Eduardo (1879–1946). Spanish poet and dramatist. Marquina was a leading exponent of modernism in Spanish poetry. His early works, *Odas* (1900) and *Vendimión* (1909), are somewhat romantic in tone and infused with a pantheistic flavor. Later the poet turned to social problems as in *Canciones del momento* (1910) and *Tierras de España* (1914). As a playwright he achieved success with his historical dramas, particularly with *Las hijas del Cid*

(1908), *Doña María la Brava* (1909), and his masterpiece, *En Flandes se ha puesto el sol* (1910), which deals with the campaigns in the Low Countries during the reign of Philip II.

Marquis, Don[ald Robert Perry] (1878–1937). American newspaperman and humorist. In his early career an assistant editor to Joel Chandler Harris, who encouraged his tendency toward fantasy, Marquis was known for his columns "The Sun Dial" in the New York *Sun* and "The Lantern" in the New York *Tribune.* His most memorable writings are his stories and verses about ARCHY AND MEHITABEL. Among other characters created by Marquis were Clem Hawley, the Old Soak, an uninhibited enemy of prohibition; Hermione and her Little Group of Serious Thinkers, all apostles of the platitudinous; the Cave Man and his battered lady love. These appeared in several books, including *Hermione* (1916), *The Old Soak* (1916), and *Love Sonnets of a Cave Man and Other Verses* (1928). *Noah an' Jonah an' Cap'n John Smith* (1921) is a poem depicting the celestial reminiscences of the three dead mariners. *The Dark Hours* (1924) is a play about the last days of Jesus. At his death, Marquis left an incomplete autobiographical novel, *Sons of the Puritans,* which was later published (1939).

Marriage of Figaro, The. See FIGARO.

Marriage of Heaven and Hell, The (1790). The chief prose work of William BLAKE, setting forth his doctrine of Contraries and emphasizing the negative side of his dualistic thinking. He writes: "Without Contraries is no progression. Attraction and repulsion, reason and energy, love and hate, are necessary to human existence." He denies matter as reality, eternal damnation, and the right of authority; specifically, he attacks the rationalism of 18th-century Protestantism for reducing moral complexities to oversimplified formulas.

Marriage of William Ashe, The (1905). A political novel by Mrs. Humphry WARD dealing with the married life of Ashe and his turbulent, unconventional wife, Kitty, and her lover, Geoffrey Cliffe. The story is said to be based on the characters of, and the relationships existing between Melbourne, Lady Caroline Lamb, and Byron.

Marric, J. J. See John CREASEY.

Marrow controversy. A prolonged struggle in Scotland between Puritanism and Presbyterianism. It arose when Edward Fisher's *Marrow of Modern Divinity* (1644), a book of ultra-evangelical tendency, was condemned by the General Assembly in 1718.

Marryat, Captain **Frederick** (1792–1848). English novelist. Marryat wrote his first novel, *Frank Mildmay, or the Naval Officer* (1829), in his late thirties after a distinguished career in the British Navy. With his expert knowledge of nautical life, his vigor and humor, he produced some outstanding early specimens of the novel of the sea. Such books as *Peter Simple* (1834), *Mr. Midshipman Easy* (1836), and *Masterman Ready* (1841; first in a series of books for children) excel in the depiction of character and incident, and still possess a considerable degree of vitality.

For many years Marryat's books were favorites of boys all over the English-speaking world. He is also well known for his *Diary in America* (1839), a generally negative view of the United States written during travels here.

Mars. An Italian god of fertility whose month, March, began the spring season of growth and fruitfulness and who later took on the aspects of the Greek god of war, ARES. In Rome the great park and parade ground, the Campus Martius, was dedicated to him; when war was declared, the general would come before his legions and, striking a shield against the ground, would intone the words *Mars vigilat* ("Mars, awake!"). In Roman poetry the word *Mars* is often used, through personification, as a synonym for war.

Camões introduces him in the Portuguese epic *The Lusiad* (1572) as typifying divine fortitude; as BACCHUS, the evil demon, is the guardian of the power of Islam, so Mars is the guardian of Christianity.

Marschallin, The. See ROSENKAVALIER, DER.

Marse Chan (1884). A story by Thomas Nelson PAGE. Written in dialect, the story is told by the servant of a likable Southerner, whom he calls Marse Chan. The hero and his beloved are separated by family pressures, but are reconciled just before he is killed on the battlefield. She mourns him for the rest of her life. *Marse Chan* is the most famous of Page's nostalgic stories of antebellum Southern life.

Marseillaise, La. The hymn of the French Revolution. Claude Joseph ROUGET DE LISLE, an artillery officer in garrison at Strasbourg, composed both the words and the music (April 24, 1792) with the title *Chant de guerre pour l'armée du Rhin.* On July 30, 1792, volunteers from Marseilles entered Paris singing the song, and the Parisians, enchanted with it, called it the *Chant des Marseillais* and later *La Marseillaise.* It has often been made use of by later composers, as for instance by Schumann in his music for Heine's poem *The Two Grenadiers* (1840), and by Tchaikovsky in his *Festival Overture, "1812"* (1880).

Marsh, Ngaio (1899–   ). New Zealand detective story writer and theatrical producer. "Ngaio" is the Maori word for "flowering tree," pronounced Ny-o. Among her works are *A Man Lay Dead* (1934), *Death in Ecstasy* (1937), *Night at the Vulcan* (1951), *False Scent* (1960), and *Hand in Glove* (1962).

Marshall, George C[atlett] (1880–1959). American general and statesman. A graduate of Virginia Military Institute (1901), Marshall served in the Philippines and with the American Expeditionary Forces during World War I. From 1919 to 1924 he was an aide to General Pershing. Named army chief of staff in 1939, he became the second non-West Pointer to hold this post and played a leading role in formulating Allied strategy during World War II. After going to China in 1945 as special ambassador in an unsuccessful attempt to mediate between Chiang Kai-shek and the Chinese Communists, Marshall was appointed secretary of state by President Truman. On June 5, 1947, in a commencement speech at Harvard, he outlined the principles of the European Recovery Program (known as the Marshall Plan) by which the U.S. contributed to the postwar rehabilitation of Europe. Marshall also served as secretary of defense from 1950 to 1951. In 1953 he was awarded the Nobel Peace Prize.

Marshall, John (1755–1835). American jurist. After serving as one of the commissioners in the X.Y.Z. Affair, Marshall was secretary of state for a short time. He was named chief justice of the Supreme Court in 1801. During his 34 years on the bench, he greatly increased the influence of the Supreme Court and interpreted the Constitution so as to strengthen the federal government at the expense of the states. See MARBURY VS. MADISON.

Marshalsea. A prison in Southwark, London, long used as a debtors' prison but abolished in 1842. It is described in LITTLE DORRIT by Charles Dickens, whose father had once been consigned to it. The spelling of the name is derived from "marshalcy."

Marshes of Glynn, The (1878). A poem by Sidney LANIER. Often considered his masterpiece, it was contributed to a volume of 175 poems by noted authors, none of whom signed his name. In this poem, notable for its skillful and varied use of anapestic measure, Lanier reached the height of his lifelong attempt to reconcile the techniques of music and poetry. Its lush imagery sensuously depicts the sea marshes of Glynn County, Ga., visited by Lanier in 1875.

Marsigli, Luigi (c. 1330–1394). Italian humanist. An Augustinian monk and disciple of Petrarch, he is considered one of the early Humanists by virtue of his influence on scholars who gathered about him in Florence in what was a prototype of the later academies of the Renaissance.

Marsile, Marsilius, Marsiglio. A king of the Saracens in medieval romances. See ROLAND, CHANSON DE.

Marston, John (c. 1575–1634). English satirist and dramatist. His plays are almost all concerned with depictions of unbalanced love and lust. In his best work, THE MALCONTENT and THE DUTCH COURTEZAN, his satiric power is couched in a dramatic structure which, if not extraordinary, is at least adequate. In other works, such as *The Insatiate Countess* (pub. 1613), dramatic structure all but disappears, and moral indignation degenerates to the level of hysteria. His other plays include *Histriomastix* (1599), *Antonio and Mellida* (1599), *Antonio's Revenge* (1600), *Jack Drum's Entertainment* (c. 1600), *What You Will* (1601), and *Sophonisba* (c. 1605–1606), a tragedy.

Ben Jonson attacked Marston in *The Poetaster* (1601), but they were reconciled and collaborated with George Chapman on *Eastward Ho* (1605), a comedy. Because the play contained passages offensive to the Scottish followers of James I, the three playwrights were briefly imprisoned.

Marston also wrote *The Metamorphosis of Pigmalions Image* (1598) and *The Scourge of Villanie* (1598), coarsely satirical poems.

Marston Moor. A plain in Yorkshire, England, scene of a battle (1644) during the CIVIL WAR. A combined Scottish and Parliamentary army led by Sir Thomas Fairfax and Oliver Cromwell defeated the Royalist forces under Prince Rupert of Bohemia, nephew of Charles I. As a result of the victory, Parliament won control of northern England.

Marsuppini, Carlo (1398–1453). Italian poet and man of letters. A member of the Medici circle and chancellor of Florence, he translated Homer and continued the Humanist tradition begun by the previous generation of Petrarch, Marsigli, and Salutati.

Marsyas. A Phrygian flute-player. He challenged Apollo to a contest of skill, and, being beaten by the god, was flayed alive for his presumption. From his blood arose the river so called.

Martano. A great braggart in the ORLANDO FURIOSO of Ariosto, he wins Origille (Origilla) from Grifone (Gryphon) but behaves in cowardly fashion during a tourney held at Damascus. While Grifone is asleep, Martano steals his armor and masquerading as Grifone goes to receive the victor's honors, due from king Norandino. He then flees with Origille until brought back by Grifone's brother, Aquilante (Aquilant). Eventually he is hanged.

Martel, Charles. See CHARLES MARTEL.

Martello tower. A circular masonry fort. The word is a misinterpretation of the original *Mortella*, from *Cape Mortella* in Corsica where a Martello tower repulsed an attack by the British fleet in 1794. In Joyce's *Ulysses,* Stephan Dedalus and his friend Buck Mulligan live in one in Dublin.

Martext, Sir Oliver. In Shakespeare's As YOU LIKE IT, a vicar whom Touchstone mocks.

Martha, St. The sister of Lazarus and Mary. When Jesus came to their house, Mary sat at his feet and listened, but Martha "was cumbered about much serving" and complained of her sister to Jesus. She is the patron saint of good housewives and is represented in art in homely costume, bearing at her girdle a bunch of keys and holding a ladle or pot of water in her hand.

Martí, José [Julian] (1853–1895). Cuban poet and essayist. Martí is famous, not only as the "apostle" of Cuban independence, but also as one of the most original and influential writers of Latin America. As a youth he was imprisoned and later deported from Cuba because of his opposition to Spanish rule; he remained an exile for most of his life. From 1881 to 1895 he resided in New York, earning a precarious livelihood as a newspaper correspondent, as Uruguayan consul, as a teacher and translator. At the same time he tirelessly collected funds, made speech after speech, and founded the Cuban Revolutionary Party in order to prepare a military expedition that would drive the Spaniards from the island. In 1895, Martí decided to return to Cuba to take advantage of renewed revolutionary sentiment there. His journal, *Diario de Cabo Haitiano a Dos Ríos* (1941), and letters to family and friends record his emotions as he and General Máximo Gómez reached Cuba with four companions and joined other insurgents. During a skirmish at Dos Ríos, Martí disobeyed Gómez' order to retreat and was killed by Spanish soldiers.

Martí, the poet, is often regarded as a forerunner of MODERNISM, though in reality his work belongs to no school. His verses, written in a fresh, uniquely personal style deal ardently, sometimes mystically, with familial and romantic love, freedom, and death. His best-known poems are in three collections: *Ismaelillo* (1882), addressed to his young son; *Versos libres,* written mainly in 1882 but not published until the 20th century; and *Versos sencillos* (1891). Many of his prose works, such as the essays *Nuestra América* (1891) and *Simón Bolívar* (1893), express his faith in the future greatness of Hispanic America. A perceptive critic of the U.S., Martí also wrote articles on

such topics as *Coney Island* (1881), *Emerson* (1882), *Jesse James* (1882), and *Walt Whitman* (1887).

Martial. Full Latin name, **Marcus Valerius Martialis** (A.D. 42?–?102). Latin epigrammatist born in Spain. He spent most of his life in Rome and, as a witty man of letters, was accepted in high imperial circles. His friends included the emperors Titus, Domitian, and Trajan as well as the litterateur Pliny the Younger. Martial's favorite form of writing was the epigram. His epigrams have come down to us in 15 books and present a graphic picture of life and manners in first-century Rome. Unlike his satiric contemporary Juvenal, Martial seems to have aimed more for elegant grotesquerie than for the exposure of moral evils.

Martianus Capella or **Marcian** (fl. 5th century). Latin author of North Africa. He is best known for his *De Nuptiis Philologiae et Mercurii* (*Concerning the Marriage of Mercury and Philology*), an allegorical work on the seven liberal arts, which is mentioned by Chaucer in the *House of Fame* and the *Merchant's Tale.*

Martin, St. The patron saint of innkeepers and drunkards. Usually he is shown in art as a young mounted soldier dividing his cloak with a beggar. He was born of heathen parents but was converted in Rome, and became bishop of Tours in 371, dying at Caudes forty years later. His day is November 11, the day of the Roman *Vinalia,* or Feast of Bacchus; hence his purely accidental patronage (as above), and hence also the phrase *Martin drunk.*

The usual illustration of St. Martin is in allusion to the legend that when he was a military tribune stationed at Amiens, he once, in midwinter, divided his cloak with a naked beggar, who craved alms of him before the city gates. At night, the story says, Christ Himself appeared to the soldier, arrayed in this very garment.

Martin, Violet. See E. O. SOMERVILLE.

Martin Chuzzlewit, The Life and Adventures of (1844). A novel by Charles DICKENS. Wealthy old Martin Chuzzlewit, Sr. is surrounded by a greedy, grasping, selfish family: Anthony Chuzzlewit, his brother; the villainous Jonas, Anthony's son; and Seth PECKSNIFF, a crafty hypocrite. Detecting incipient selfishness and greed in his grandson, young Martin, Chuzzlewit turns him from the house almost penniless; Martin is in love with Mary Graham, an orphan raised by the old Chuzzlewit. Thus turned away, Martin travels to the U.S. with his loyal friend Mark TAPLEY. Here he becomes an architect for the Eden Land Corporation, a fraudulent enterprise in which he loses everything. He contracts a fever and almost dies. He returns home to England cured of his selfishness by his difficult experiences in America, his grandfather accepts him, and he and Mary Graham are married. A subplot deals with Jonas Chuzzlewit, who tries to poison his old father, murders Montague Tigg because Tigg knows his secret, and marries Mercy Pecksniff, making her utterly miserable. He commits suicide to save his neck from the gallows.

In *Martin Chuzzlewit* Dickens slashes away at the ignorant provincialism of Americans (the section of the book which takes place in the U.S. was extremely offensive to the American public) and dissects the selfish, grasping nature of Englishmen of the Chuzzlewit variety. One of Dickens's most memorable characters, Sarah GAMP, appears in this novel.

Martin du Gard, Roger (1881–1958). French novelist and dramatist. An objective narrative and rational analysis of the intellectual and moral problems of the pre-World War I generation characterize both JEAN BAROIS and the eight-part series LES THIBAULTS. The novel *The Postman (Vielle France; 1933)* is a satiric study of small town life, as are the peasant farces for the stage *Le Testament du Père Luleu* (1914) and *La Gonflue* (1928). Martin du Gard's other works include the short novel *La Confidence africaine* (1931) and the drama *Un Taciturne* (1931). He received the Nobel Prize in 1937.

Martineau, Harriet (1802–1876). English author, a voluminous writer on religion, economics, and government. Deaf from early childhood, Miss Martineau was raised in a stern, resolutely pious, and intellectual atmosphere. Her earliest works, such as *Devotional Exercises for the Use of Young Persons* (1823), were of a religious character, but she became famous for a series of stories illustrating the economic theories of such contemporary thinkers as Malthus, Ricardo, and Mill. These tales, *Illustrations of Political Economy* (1832–1834); *Poor Laws and Paupers Illustrated* (1833); and *Illustrations of Taxation* (1843), combine sentimental fiction with dreary paraphrases of fact and theory. They were immensely popular in their time. Of continuing interest is her *Autobiography* (1877) and her unfavorable critiques of America, *Society in America* (1837) and *Retrospect of Western Travel* (1838). She also wrote children's stories, two novels, and a condensed translation of Comte's *Philosophie Positive* (1853). Her later work shows a reaction against religious principles. Her brother, James Martineau (1805–1900), was a Unitarian clergyman and author of philosophical works, very highly regarded in his day. His better-known books include *Types of Ethical Theory* (1885) and *The Study of Religion* (1888).

Martine-Bellême, Thérèse. See RED LILY, THE.

Martin Eden (1909). A novel by Jack LONDON. Partly autobiographical, it is the story of an unsuccessful writer who is rejected by his wealthy fiancée; only Russ Brissenden, a socialist poet, appreciates his work. When Eden becomes rich and famous, the very people who once rejected him try to court his favor. In disgust, he leaves for the South Seas, but commits suicide on the way.

Martínez de la Rosa, Francisco (1787–1862). Spanish statesman and dramatist. Although his political career carried him through the posts of emissary, ambassador, and prime minister, he is better known as a dramatist, particularly as one representative of the drift from the classic to the romantic; he is credited with the first widely acclaimed romantic drama, *La conjuración de Venecia* (1834), which is set in 14th-century Venice. He is also the author of *Abén Huyeya* (1836), a historical drama containing romantic elements which deals with the Christian campaign against the Moors in the Alpujarras.

Martínez de Toledo, Alfonso. Also known as the **archpriest** or **arcipreste of Talavera** (1398–?1470). Spanish prose writer. He is best known for *El Corbacho* or *Reprobación del amor mundano,* similar in some respects to Boccaccio's *Corbaccio*. A forerunner of the picaresque novel, the work is noted for its scathing denunciation of the foibles and vices of women.

Martínez Ruiz, José. Known as **Azorín** (1873–1967). Spanish essayist and novelist. His sensitive use of the Castilian landscape links Azorín to the GENERACIÓN DEL 98; in fact, he was the first to call the group by this name. Though he attempted nearly every literary genre, he excelled as an essayist. In *El alma castellana* (1900), he revealed the characteristics for which he is best known: an emphasis on the recurrence of time and a style characterized by short sentences and an accumulation of seemingly insignificant details. He also wrote two autobiographical novels, *La voluntad* (1902) and *Antonio Azorín* (1903), the latter furnishing him with his pseudonym, and *Una hora de España (An Hour of Spain, 1560–1590,* 1924).

Martínez Sierra, Gregorio (1881–1947). Spanish dramatist. Though he was the author of a volume of verse and several novels, Martínez Sierra's fame rests on his plays, particularly the widely translated *Canción de cuna (The Cradle Song,* 1911). A skillful depiction of convent life, the play centers about an abandoned child discovered upon the steps of a convent. The second half of the work finds the child come of age and ready to leave the convent for the world. The drama reveals Martínez Sierra to have been influenced by Benavente. Most of his work was written in collaboration with his wife, María Lejárraga, though her name did not always appear as co-author.

Martín Fierro (1872). A narrative poem by José Hernández (1834–1886), Argentine poet and journalist. The principal poetic work of the gaucho genre, it is a first-person account of the life of an Argentine gaucho who is drafted from his idyllic life on the pampas into the harsh discipline of the army. He rebels, becomes an outlaw, and joins the Indians. The second part, *La Vuelta* (1879), describes his return to a more humane and advanced society. Written in authentic gaucho dialect, the poem is a nostalgic tribute to a vanished way of life and has become the national epic of Argentina. See GAUCHO LITERATURE.

Martinus Scriblerus. See Martinus SCRIBLERUS.

Marvel, Ik. See Donald Grant MITCHELL.

Marvell, Andrew (1621–1678). English poet. Balance and detachment, strong features of Marvell's poetry, seem to characterize most of his life. During the English Civil War he was a tutor in the household of Lord General Thomas Fairfax and later became assistant to John Milton when the latter was Latin secretary of the Commonwealth; but he was also a good friend of Lovelace, who was a Royalist, and he never approved of the execution of Charles I. During the Commonwealth he was elected to Parliament and served ably in public offices until his death. He was instrumental in saving Milton from punishment after the Restoration.

One of the METAPHYSICAL POETS, Marvell is best known for his early, largely lyric, poetry, including THE GARDEN, TO HIS COY MISTRESS, *Bermudas,* THE DEFINITION OF LOVE, AN HORATIAN ODE UPON CROMWELL'S RETURN FROM IRELAND, and *A Dialogue Between the Soul and Body.* Typically, most of these poems represent a tacit, unresolved debate between two or more opposing values: contemplation vs.

activity, nature vs. civilization, power vs. justice, etc. In his later days he wrote satirical poetry directed against Stuart policies, such as *The Last Instructions to a Painter,* a verse satire on the Dutch War. His work is distinguished by lyric grace, striking conceits and images, and a rare intellectual balance and subtlety. Most of his poems were not published until 1681 and the satires not until 1689, after the Glorious Revolution.

In the 18th century, Marvell was known as a satirist, Swift praising this aspect of his work. The Romantics, Wordsworth and Lamb especially, appreciated his lyric poems, but it was the 20th century which saw a great revival of interest in him, in part through T. S. Eliot's influence as a critic.

marvellous boy, the. Thomas CHATTERTON, in an allusion to him by Wordsworth in *Resolution and Independence:*

> I thought of Chatterton, the marvellous boy,
> The sleepless soul, that perished in his pride.

Marx, Karl (1818–1883). German socialist who, with Friedrich ENGELS, formulated the principles of dialectic materialism, or economic determinism. Marx used Hegel's concept of the dialectic to explain history as a series of antitheses and syntheses; but whereas the Hegelian dialectic describes the conflict of ideas leading to the development of reason and freedom, the Marxian dialectic operates in terms of economic forces. Marx maintained that economic structure is the basis of history, and determines all the social, political, and intellectual aspects of life. The evils of capitalist society cannot be abolished by reform, therefore, but only by destruction of the whole capitalist economy and establishment of a new classless society (See THE COMMUNIST MANIFESTO). Because of his revolutionary activities, Marx spent most of his life outside Germany, and his major work, CAPITAL, was written in London, where he also organized the First INTERNATIONAL, an association of European socialists, in 1864. His ideas had great influence on Nikolai Lenin and the development of Russian communism.

Marxism. The economic, political, and social doctrines of Karl MARX, Friedrich ENGELS, and their disciples and successors; the practice of these doctrines, specifically in countries with Communist systems of government. Marxism accepts as virtually axiomatic dialectical materialism, the labor theory of value, and the economic determination of all human actions and institutions; it is characterized by a belief in the class struggle as the fundamental force in history and holds that the increasing concentration of industrial power in the capitalist class and consequent aggravation of misery among the workers must inevitably lead to the revolutionary seizure of power by the proletariat, the dictatorship of the proletariat, and, ultimately, the establishment of a classless society. Evolutionary Marxism holds that power will accrue to the proletariat by economic evolution and that therefore revolution is unnecessary.

Though few works of literary value can be called Marxist in any technical sense, many writers have in emotional tone and moral bias echoed certain Marxist ideas, generally in protest against economic misery and injustice rather than out of any formal allegiance to Marxism. Despite elements which resemble or derive from Marxist ideology, their writings may more accurately be classed as PROLETARIAN LITERATURE.

Mary I. Mary Tudor, often called **Bloody Mary** (1516–1558). Queen of England (1553–1558), daughter of HENRY VIII and Catherine of Aragon. Mary was declared illegitimate after her parents' marriage was dissolved, but was nevertheless proclaimed queen after the death of her half-brother, Edward VI, in 1553. She restored Catholicism in England, which had been Protestant for nearly twenty years. Despite strong popular opposition she married Prince Philip of Spain, a Catholic and a foreigner. In 1555 began the persecution and burning of Protestants under the reinstated heresy laws; nearly three hundred persons went to the stake in the last years of her reign. She is the subject of Victor Hugo's tragedy *Mary Tudor* (1833) and Tennyson's play *Queen Mary* (1876).

Mary, Queen of Scots. Mary Stuart (1542–1587). Daughter of James V of Scotland, mother of JAMES I OF ENGLAND and VI of Scotland, and titular queen of Scotland from six days after her birth until her abdication in favor of her son in 1567. Betrothed to the dauphin of France as a child and married to him in 1558, Mary did not actually reign in Scotland until after the death of her husband in 1560. In 1565 she married her cousin Henry, Lord Darnley, by whom she had a son, James. Darnley arranged the murder of David Rizzio, one of Mary's favorite councillors, and Darnley himself was murdered, possibly with Mary's complicity, shortly after (see CASKET LETTERS). The earl of Bothwell, who was probably responsible for Darnley's death, captured Mary, and after making a token resistance, she married him. The Scottish lords then rose up against Mary, and she was imprisoned and forced to abdicate. In 1568 she fled to England, where she was again put in prison. There were several Catholic plots to free Mary and put her on the English throne; from a Catholic point of view Queen ELIZABETH was both illegitimate and a heretic, and Mary the rightful claimant to the throne, both in terms of legitimate descent and faith. However, Mary was allowed to live in semiconfinement until the outbreak of the BABINGTON CONSPIRACY, after which she was brought to trial for conspiring against the life of the queen. She was condemned and executed in 1587.

Mary is a prominent character in Sir Walter Scott's *Abbot* (1820), which deals with her flight to England. She is the subject of Schiller's tragedy *Maria Stuart* (1800); Björnstjerne Björnson's drama *Maria Stuart* (1864); Swinburne's trilogy of verse dramas *Chastelard* (1865), *Bothwell* (1874), and *Mary Stuart* (1881); Maurice Hewlett's romance *The Queen's Quair* (1904); and John Drinkwater's *Mary Stuart* (1921).

Mary, the Virgin. The mother of Jesus. Jesus was her first child; Matthew (13:55) and Mark (6:3) mention other children by her husband Joseph. The day of neither her birth nor death is known. She may have been with Jesus on his travels; she was present at the Crucifixion where Jesus entrusted her to the care of John. Her last appearance is in the first chapter of Acts (Acts 1:13) shortly after the Resurrection. In the Roman Catholic Church she is an object of special veneration. She is an extremely popular subject in religious painting and sculpture where she is usually called "the Madonna."

Mary Barton (1848). A novel by Mrs. GASKELL. A work of great realism, it deals with the inhumanities suffered by the impoverished weavers of Manchester.

Maryland, My Maryland (1861). A poem by James Ryder RANDALL. First printed in the New Orleans *Delta* (April 26, 1861), it was reprinted all over the South; sung to the tune of the German Christmas song, *O Tannenbaum, O Tannenbaum,* it was adopted as a favorite battle song by Confederate soldiers. The title of Edmund Wilson's study of the literature of the American Civil War, *Patriotic Gore* (1962), is taken from Randall's poem.

Mary Magdalene. In the New Testament one of the followers of Jesus. She may have been the harlot whom Jesus rescued from her evil life (Mark 16:9). She is identified by the name of her home town, Magdala, which was famous for its immorality. Mary Magdalene was present at the Crucifixion and was one of the first to see the open tomb three days later.

Mary of France. Mary Tudor (1496–1533). Queen consort (1514–1515) of Louis XII of France, favorite sister of Henry VIII of England. Mary's love for Charles Brandon, and her marriage to him after the death of her royal husband, are the subject of Charles Major's novel *When Knighthood Was in Flower* (1898).

Mary Olivier (1919). A novel by May SINCLAIR. Using the psychology of Freud and the subjective technique of Joyce, she examines the mind and development of a girl brought up in a repressive Victorian household. Other members of the family become neurotic, but she finds an outlet in writing poetry and has a love affair.

Mary Stuart (Maria Stuart; 1800). A tragedy by Friedrich SCHILLER. It treats the conflict between Elizabeth I and Mary Queen of Scots, while the latter is in England awaiting execution for her crimes. In Schiller's version, though Elizabeth wants Mary out of the way, she is unable to make a final decision about commanding her death, and in the end, she contrives to make it seem as though a hasty official had been responsible for Mary's execution.

Masaccio. Real name, **Tommaso di Giovanni** (1401–1428). Florentine painter. He is often called "the true father of Renaissance painting" as his influence on his contemporaries was more immediate and fruitful than that of GIOTTO, of whom he was, however, the logical successor and modern embodiment. Masaccio stressed simplicity and evocative gesture rather than movement, and brought about a revolution in painting through his ability, learned from Brunelleschi, to construct convincing spatial relationships, and through his mastery in creating the illusion of heaviness and weight by means of light and shade. His frescoes in the Brancacci Chapel of the Church of the Carmine in Florence, though unfinished, served as a training school for Florentine painters of succeeding generations, even to the time of MICHELANGELO. Among the best known of the Brancacci frescoes, later completed by Filippino Lippi, are *St. Peter Enthroned, Adam and Eve,* and *The Tribute Money.* Another of his most famous works, in S. Maria Novella at Florence, is *The Holy Trinity,* *the Virgin and St. John the Evangelist, with Two Donors.*

Masaniello. Original name: **Tommaso Aniello** (1622?–1647). Italian fisherman who led the revolt in Naples in July, 1647. When his property was seized because his wife had smuggled flour, he led a popular uprising against the Spanish authorities. The viceroy was forced to flee, and Masaniello and his followers took over the government. Although the viceroy granted several concessions, Masaniello was assassinated, probably by his own followers. Auber's opera *La Muette de Portici* (1828), with a libretto by Eugène Scribe, is based on Masaniello's revolt.

Masaoka Shiki (1867–1902). Japanese poet. He was influential in reviving the *Haiku* and restoring it to the prestige it had enjoyed during the Tokugawa period (1600–1868).

Masaryk, Tomáš [Garrigue] (1850–1937). Czechoslovak statesman and philosopher regarded as the father of independent Czechoslovakia. His son **Jan [Garrigue] Masaryk** (1886–1948), also a liberal statesman, was murdered or committed suicide in Prague after the communist coup of 1948.

Mascagni, Pietro (1863–1945). Italian composer. He is famous for his one-act opera CAVALLERIA RUSTICANA (1890).

Masdeu, Juan Francisco de (1744–1817). Spanish Jesuit historian. Masdeu settled in Italy following the expulsion of the Jesuits from Spain (1767). He devoted the remainder of his career to his 20-volume *Historia crítica de España y de la cultura española* (1783–1805), a scholarly treatment of Spanish civilization.

Masefield, John (1878–1967). English poet, dramatist, and novelist; from 1930, Poet Laureate of England. He is best known for his sea poems, such as those collected in *Salt Water Poems and Ballads* (1902); his poems *Sea Fever* and *Cargoes* appear in many anthologies. As a boy he went to sea as a cadet officer. He then spent a number of years wandering around the world, doing odd jobs, including working as a bartender's assistant in New York. His novels, including *Lost Endeavour* (1910), *Sard Harker* (1924), and *The Bird of Dawning* (1933), are romantic adventure stories, packed with color and action.

Masefield made his reputation with a long narrative poem, THE EVERLASTING MERCY. Like many of Masefield's other early poems, it is notable for its realistic, robust background of country life and its sometimes harsh, unpoetic language. Masefield admired Chaucer; his narrative poem *Reynard the Fox* (1919), about a hunt, is particularly Chaucerian. Among his other long narrative poems are *The Widow in the Bye Street* (1912), about a devoted mother and a son who kills his rival in love, and *Dauber* (1913), the tragic story of an artist-sailor who is the butt of all his companions' jokes. He wrote a number of verse plays, of which THE TRAGEDY OF NAN is the best known. He also wrote journalism, literary criticism, and military and nautical history. His *Gallipoli* (1916) is a remarkable account of that World War I campaign, and *The Nine Days' Wonder* (1941) describes the evacuation of Dunkirk. Among his other books are *Shakespeare* (1911), *On the Hill* (1949), *So Long to Learn* (1952), and *The Bluebells* (1961).

Masham, Lady **Abigail** (d. 1734). Daughter of the London merchant Francis Hill, first cousin of the duchess of Marlborough, and a friend of Jonathan Swift. As a favorite of Queen Anne, superseding the duchess of Marlborough, she exercised much influence at court.

Masks and Faces. See PEG WOFFINGTON.

masochism. A sexual abnormality in which one takes pleasure in being abused or tortured. See Leopold von SACHER-MASOCH.

Mason, A[lfred] E[dward] W[oodley] (1865–1948). English novelist, author of romantic tales of adventure and detection, often set in exotic countries. *The Four Feathers* (1902) concerns the vindication of a man thought to be a coward. *At the Villa Rose* (1910), *The House of the Arrow* (1924), *No Other Tiger* (1927), and *Fire over England* (1936) are among his other works.

Mason, Perry. See Erle Stanley GARDNER.

Mason, William (1725–1797). English poet, playwright, and clergyman. His works include the dramatic poems *Elfrida* (1752) and *Caractacus* (1759); *The English Garden* (1772–1781), a poem; and *Memoirs of Gray* (1775), the result of his life-long friendship with the poet Thomas Gray. Gray immortalized Mason by giving him the nickname "Scroddles."

Mason and Dixon's line. Originally the boundary line separating Maryland and Pennsylvania, laid (1763–1767) by the English astronomers and surveyors Charles Mason and Jeremiah Dixon. It lies in 39° 43′ 26″ north latitude. At the time of the Civil War the name was used to designate the line separating the free states from the slave states.

Maspero, Sir **Gaston Camille Charles** (1846–1916). French Egyptologist. Noted chiefly for his remarkable discoveries at the temple of Karnak, Maspero also wrote a number of books on archeology.

masque (mask). A form of dramatic entertainment. The masque, like drama itself, probably finds its origins in primitive fertility rites. It appears in a number of societies in a variety of forms, although in almost all cases culminating in an impromptu dance or *komos* in which both spectators and performers engage. In the Middle Ages the masque took the form of an unexpected visit to a friend's house by a group of masked players and musicians who would provide a spontaneous entertainment.

In England the masque had a dual development, on the one hand resulting in thinly disguised fertility rites such as the St. George "Sword Dance" folk plays, and on the other in the elaborate court entertainments which make their first appearance in the early years of the 16th century during the reign of Henry VIII.

These court festivities were continued (with considerably less profligacy) under the reign of Elizabeth, but it is not until the reign of James I (1603–1625) and his pleasure-loving wife, Anne, that the masque in England develops the lavish, ornate, and elaborate spectacle for which it is known. The men who made the greatest contribution to the development of the masque were Inigo JONES and Ben JONSON. Jones, an architect trained in Italy and heavily influenced by Italian neoclassicism, was responsible for the magnificence of the spectacle. Jonson, who inherited a masque tradition, which was essentially one of pantomime and

Costumes for a masque by Inigo Jones

in which there were no dramatic values, emphasized dialogue and song, giving the airy nothings of the Elizabethan masque a substantial literary framework. He also introduced the anti-masque, a comic interlude which parodied the major plot. The collaboration of Jonson and Jones ushered in the golden age of the masque. Together they achieved a balance of lyrical grace and sumptuous splendor that has never been equalled in stage entertainments. Inevitably, however, they quarreled over the relative importance of their contributions, and with the dissolution of their partnership and, ultimately, the success of the Puritan Revolution, the masque disappeared from England.

Among Jonson's masques are *Hymenai* (1606); *The Masque of Beauty* (1608); *The Hue and Cry after Cupid* (1608); *The Masque of Queens* (1609); *Oberon, the Faery Prince* (1611). Other writers of masques were George Chapman, Beaumont and Fletcher, and Thomas Middleton. John Milton's COMUS, though titled a masque, is often considered to be more of a pastoral drama.

Massacre of St. Bartholomew. The slaughter of French Protestants begun on the eve of St. Bartholomew's Day, Aug. 24, 1572. Authorized by Charles IX at the instigation of his mother Catherine de Médicis, the persecutions continued for several weeks and spread from Paris to the provinces. It has been estimated that some 30,000 persons were killed, including Gaspard de Coligny and Pierre La Ramée.

Massacre of the Innocents. See INNOCENTS, MASSACRE OF THE.

Massenet, Jules Emile Frédéric (1842–1912). French composer of oratorios, operas, cantatas, and biblical dramas. He is best known for his operas *Manon* (1884), *Thaïs* (1894), and *Werther* (1892).

Masses, The. A left-wing magazine, founded in 1911 and especially noteworthy after Max EASTMAN became editor in December, 1912. Socialist and pacifist in viewpoint, it stressed literature, art, and the spoofing of the bourgeoisie. Eastman ran the magazine until its suppression by federal authorities in December, 1917. Contributing editors included Floyd

Dell, John Reed, Louis Untermeyer, and Art Young. It was succeeded in March, 1918, by the doctrinaire *The Liberator,* which Eastman edited for a while and which became associated with the Communist Party in 1922. The weekly *New Masses,* which appeared in 1926, was a successor to *The Liberator;* it became a monthly in 1948 under the name *Masses & Mainstream.* Samuel Sillen was editor, and Howard Fast, W. E. B. DuBois, and Paul Robeson were among the contributing editors.

Massey, Gerald (1828–1907). English poet, journalist. An unschooled millhand, Massey educated himself, becoming an advocate of Chartism and Christian Socialism. His career suggested to George Eliot the theme of FELIX HOLT. He is the author of *Poetical Works* (1857) and *My Lyrical Life* (1899), a memoir.

Massinger, Philip (1583–1640). English dramatist. After attending Oxford, Massinger went to London, where he won the friendship of such men as Tourneur, Dekker, and Fletcher, with all of whom he later collaborated. His best-known play is the satiric comedy A NEW WAY TO PAY OLD DEBTS, whose principal character, the acquisitive Sir Giles Overreach, was long a favorite role among actors. Among the plays usually ascribed to him alone are *The Duke of Milan* (1620), a tragedy; *The Maid of Honor* (c. 1621), a romantic drama based on a story told by Boccaccio; *The Great Duke of Comedy* (1627), a romantic comedy; and *The City Madam* (1632), a comedy. The religious emphasis of some of his works, notably *The Maid of Honor* and *The Virgin Martyr* (1622), on which he collaborated with Dekker, has fostered the belief that he was converted to Roman Catholicism. With Nathan Field he collaborated on the tragedy *The Fatal Dowry* (1619), and he may have shared in the writing of HENRY VIII and THE TWO NOBLE KINSMEN. The manuscripts of some of his lost plays were reputedly destroyed in the 18th century when a cook in the household of Bishop John Warburton used them to line pie dishes.

Master Builder, The (1892). A play by Henrik IBSEN. *The Master Builder* departs from the social subjects of the bulk of Ibsen's work and deals, both realistically and symbolically, with the spirit of the artist seeking to surpass its own limitations and the conflict between one's own needs and the needs of others. Master Builder Solness is afraid of being crushed by the younger generation of architects, as he himself has crushed the builders before him; yet he finds in the girl Hilda both the younger generation he fears and the strength of purpose he lacks. Through her urging, he attempts to do "the impossible": to climb, in spite of his vertigo, to the top of the high spire he has built on his new house, and then to build, with Hilda, "the loveliest thing in the world"—a castle in the air. He reaches the top of the spire, but falls and is killed.

Master Leonard. In medieval demonology, the grand master of the witches' Sabbaths. He had the shape of a goat with three horns and a black human face.

Master of the Sentences. See Peter LOMBARD.

Master Peter's Puppet Show. See RETABLO DE MAESE PEDRO, EL.

Masters, Edgar Lee (1868–1950). American poet and novelist. A lawyer by training, Masters is famous for his SPOON RIVER ANTHOLOGY, a series of "auto-epitaphs" giving a dramatic and realistic picture of village life in the Middle West. Masters had earlier published several collections of verse, beginning with *A Book of Verses* (1898). None of these books attracted much attention. *Spoon River,* in the tradition of E. W. Howe, Joseph Kirkland, Hamlin Garland, and other attackers of small-town life, immediately gained Masters a large following. His later collections of verse include *Songs and Satires* (1916), *Starved Rock* (1919, *Domesday Book* (1920), *Poems of the People* (1936), and *Illinois Poems* (1941).

Masters wrote several novels, including the trilogy *Mitch Miller* (1920), *Skeeters Kirby* (1923), and *Mirage* (1924). He wrote biographies of Vachel Lindsay (1935), Walt Whitman (1937), and Mark Twain (1938). *Lincoln, the Man* (1931), the only one of his later books to attract wide attention, was an attack on the Civil War president. *Across Spoon River* (1936) was an autobiography. Masters was buried in the cemetery of Petersburg, Ill., the village which, with Lewistown, Ill., he had used as the scene of his famous work.

Masters, John (1914–   ). India-born English novelist. A resident of the U.S., he is best known for his romantic novels on episodes in Indian history such as *Bhowani Junction* (1954). His books include *Fandango Rock* (1959), *The Venus of Konpara* (1960), and *The Road Past Mandalay* (1961).

Masters, The (1951). A novel by C. P. SNOW. Part of the STRANGERS AND BROTHERS series, it describes the negotiations and struggles for power at the election of a new president of a Cambridge college.

mastersingers. See MEISTERSINGERS.

Masuccio Salernitano. Pen name of Tomaso Guardati (c. 1415–c. 1480). Italian author of the *Novellino* (1476), a collection of 50 *novelle.* One of the stories is an early version of the Romeo and Juliet tale, from which Da Porto took his influential version.

Matadero, El (*Sp.,* "the slaughterhouse"; 1871). A story by Esteban ECHEVERRÍA. Written during the 1830's, *El matadero* is the unfinished draft of a novel denouncing the brutality of the dictatorship of Juan Manuel de Rosas. Its crude realism standing in sharp contrast to the romanticism that characterizes Echeverría's poetry, the story is set in a Buenos Aires slaughterhouse where henchmen of Rosas murder a member of the opposition who passes by.

Matali. In Hindu mythology, the charioteer of Indra.

Mather, Cotton (1663–1728). American clergyman, theologian, and writer. The grandson of Richard Mather and John Cotton, Mather was a child prodigy who entered Harvard at the age of 12 and became an erudite historian and folklorist, as well as a staunch Puritan and tireless writer on an encyclopedic range of subjects. Although he was inclined to believe in witchcraft and is often regarded as the epitome of Puritan fanaticism, he upheld the authority of reason and called Isaac Newton "our perpetual dictator." One of his many quarrels stemmed from his spirited defense of inoculation for smallpox, then a highly suspicious practice. Among his best-known works are *The Wonders of the Invisible World* (1693), a discussion of witches and the supernatural; MAGNALIA

CHRISTI AMERICANA; and *The Christian Philosopher* (1721), essays attempting to reconcile science with religion.

Mather, Increase (1639–1723). American clergyman and theologian. The son of Richard Mather and father of Cotton Mather, he was a well-known preacher, served as president of Harvard College (1685–1701), and played an important part in the Salem witchcraft trials, though he criticized the extremism of the trials in *Cases of Conscience Concerning Evil Spirits* (1693). Among his better-known works are *Life and Death of Richard Mather* (1670), *A Brief History of the War with the Indians* (1676), and AN ESSAY FOR THE RECORDING OF ILLUSTRIOUS PROVIDENCES. Like his son, he was influenced by the growing scientific spirit of his time and upheld inoculation for smallpox.

Mather, Richard (1596–1669). English-born American clergyman. Mather came to Dorchester, Mass., in 1635 and became an important leader in the establishment of the Congregational Church in America. He is probably best known as one of the compilers of the BAY PSALM BOOK. Increase Mather was his son.

Mathew, Father **Theobald** (1790–1856), called The Apostle of Temperance. He was an Irish priest at Cork whose successful temperance campaigns made him influential throughout Ireland and in America, where he was partly responsible for the Temperance Movement.

Mathieu, Noël. See Pierre EMMANUEL.

Title page of a sermon by Increase Mather.
The first book printed in Boston (1675).

Matisse, Henri (1869–1954). French painter and sculptor. He sought to combine line and color so that each, while retaining its individual quality, would enhance the other. His style evolved from the contrast of patterns shown in 1920's in his favorite theme of the *Odalisque,* through daringly simplified interiors with plants and women, and culminates during his last years in bold figures cut from paper.

Matsuo Bashō (1664–1694). Japanese HAIKU poet. He is generally acknowledged as the developer and greatest master of this form. His writings are said to have been deeply influenced by ZEN Buddhism.

Matsuoka Yosuke (1880–1946). Japanese foreign minister (1940–1941). From the age of 13, he was American-educated, working his way through school and college. He pursued a diplomatic career in Japan from 1904. He was head of Japanese delegation at League of Nations' sessions (1932–1933) when his country was condemned for the "Manchurian incident." As prime minister he concluded the Tripartite Pact with Germany and Italy (1940) and Neutrality Pact with Russia. After Germany's attack on Russia, Matsuoka was replaced in a reorganized Japanese cabinet. He died while on trial accused as a war criminal.

Matsya. See VISHNU.

Matta Echaurren, Roberto (1912–   ). Chilean abstract artist associated with SURREALISM. His paintings, lighted by iridescent yellows and deep reds, are full of movement and mystery.

Matthew, St. Also called **Levi.** One of the 12 disciples of Jesus. He was a publican or collector of tolls paid for goods and passengers coming to Capernaum by the Sea of Galilee. He is the author of the *Gospel of St. Matthew,* the first book of the New Testament. According to tradition, Matthew was slain by the sword in Parthia.

Matthew, Master. In Ben Jonson's EVERY MAN IN HIS HUMOUR, a melancholy "poet." His literary efforts are plagiarisms of earlier (and better) authors.

Matthew, The Gospel According to St. The 1st book of the New Testament. One of the SYNOPTIC GOSPELS, it is the most comprehensive and authoritative life of Jesus. There is internal evidence that this gospel was written for Jewish readers: Old Testament prophecies are explained in terms of Jesus, whose ancestry is traced back through David to Abraham. The date of its composition is usually put after A.D. 75; its actual authorship is uncertain. Since it was written in Greek and does not seem to be an eyewitness account, it is unlikely that, as traditionally ascribed, its author was actually Matthew the Apostle.

Matthews, [James] Brander (1852–1929). American teacher, critic, and author. Professor of English at Columbia, Matthews specialized in drama. Among his books are *The Theaters of Paris* (1880), *The Development of the Drama* (1903), *The Principles of Playmaking* (1919), and *Shakespeare as a Playwright* (1913). Matthews stimulated the study of American literature, and clarified the technique of the short story. His best novel, *A Confident Tomorrow* (1899), is set in New York City.

Matthiessen, F[rancis] O[tto] (1902–1950). American teacher and critic. Matthiessen taught at Yale and Harvard, and, in 1947, went to Salzburg as an exchange professor. He published a diary of his months in Salzburg and Czechoslovakia in *From the Heart of Europe* (1948). Before his suicide in 1950 he had contributed a significant body of criticism. His well-known works include *The Achievement of T. S. Eliot: An Essay on the Nature of Poetry* (1935), *American Renaissance: Art and Expression in the Age of Emerson and Whitman* (1941), *Henry James: The Major Phase* (1944), and *The James Family: Including Selections from the Writings of Henry James, Senior, William, Henry, and Alice James* (1947). In 1949, Matthiessen began work on the posthumously published *Theodore Dreiser* (1951); he also wrote the introduction to and edited *The Oxford Book of American Verse* (1950). In October, 1950, a memorial issue of the *Monthly Review* was dedicated to Matthiessen; the material, a selection from his books along with essays and statements by students and friends, was reissued as *F. O. Matthiessen 1902–1950: A Collective Portrait* (1950), edited by Paul Sweezy and Leo Huberman. In 1952, *The Responsibilities of the Critic: Essays and Reviews,* selected by John Rackliffe, was published.

Maturin, Charles Robert (1787–1824). Irish novelist, one of the leading writers of the GOTHIC NOVEL. His most famous work is MELMOTH THE WANDERER, a story of the sale of a soul to the devil in exchange for prolonged life. In this book, Maturin achieves power and psychological validity, but generally his work is marred by excesses of horror and mystification. His other books include *The Fatal Revenge* (1807), *The Wild Irish Boy* (1808), *The Milesian Chief* (1811), *Women, or Pour et Contre* (1818), and *The Albigenses* (1824). He also wrote a successful play, *Bertram* (1816).

Maud (1855). A poem by Alfred TENNYSON. An extended dramatic monologue in a number of poetic forms, it describes the growth of love in an embittered, rather morose young man for Maud, the daughter of the man who has ruined him. Ultimately, the hero kills Maud's brother in a duel; her death and his tragic exile follow.

Maude, Aylmer (1858–1938). English writer and translator. He is best known for his translations of Leo Tolstoi's novels.

Maude, Cyril (1862–1951). English actor and manager. He founded The Playhouse (London, 1907). He was married to Winifred Emery (1862–1924), an actress and the descendant of a long line of actors.

Maud Muller (1854). A narrative poem by John Greenleaf WHITTIER. It records a chance meeting between the wealthy judge, and Maud, a rustic beauty. She laid aside her rake, and gave him a drink from the spring. Each married someone of more suitable station in life, but was tormented by regretful illusions:

For of all sad words of tongue or pen,
The saddest are these: "It might have been."

Maugham, Robin. Pen name of Lord **Robert Cecil Romer Maugham** (1916–   ). English novelist, nephew of Somerset Maugham. Among his novels, which usually deal with psychological peculiarities, are *The Servant* (1948), *The Man with Two Shadows* (1958), and *The Slaves of Timbuktu* (1961).

Maugham, W[illiam] Somerset (1874–1965). English novelist, short-story writer, and playwright.

Although he uses plots and material of intended popular appeal, Maugham's work is distinguished by his skillful craftsmanship, and by his satire, cynicism, and ironical detachment. His novels include LIZA OF LAMBETH, his first novel, inspired by his experiences as an interne in London's Lambeth slums; *Mrs. Craddock* (1902); *The Magician* (1908), a novel based on the character of Aleister CROWLEY; OF HUMAN BONDAGE, a partially autobiographical novel and generally considered to be his finest; THE MOON AND SIXPENCE; *The Painted Veil* (1925); *Ashenden: or, The British Agent* (1928), based on the author's experience as a World War I secret agent; CAKES AND ALE; *The Narrow Corner* (1932); *Theatre* (1937); THE RAZOR'S EDGE; *Then and Now* (1946); and *Catalina* (1948).

A great traveler, Maugham set many of his stories in the tropics. These works were studies of mixed marriages, class differences, and the effects of the stress of the climate on white people. Among the best known of his short stories are MISS THOMPSON and THE CASUARINA TREE. Now admired for his technique as a short-story writer, Maugham was originally known as a playwright. Among his best remembered witty, cynical, and frankly commercial plays are *The Circle* (1921), *Our Betters* (1923), and *The Constant Wife* (1926). *The Summing Up* (1938), *A Writer's Notebook* (1949), and *The Vagrant Mood* (1952) are autobiography and literary chat. *The Art of Fiction* (1955) is a collection of introductions to 10 great novels which he cut down to what he considered a proper length. Maugham was awarded the Order of Merit after his 80th birthday.

Maugis. See MALAGIGI.

Maule, Matthew. The old wizard in Hawthorne's THE HOUSE OF THE SEVEN GABLES.

Mauley, Sir Edward. The real name of the "BLACK DWARF" in Scott's novel of that title. Because of sensitiveness over his physical deformity and cynical disillusionment at having been robbed of his bride by his best friend, he lives alone and acquires the reputation of being in league with the Devil. Gradually, however, he wins many friends through his wisely directed kindness to all who seek his help, and at last he comes out of his retirement and assumes his own name and station.

Maundy Thursday. The Thursday before Easter. It commemorates the Last Supper, at which Christ instituted the EUCHARIST. After supper, Christ washed his disciples' feet, and gave them a new commandment (Lat. *mandatum*), that they love one another. For this reason, some churches still hold foot-washing ceremonies on this day.

Maupassant, Guy de (1850–1893). French short-story writer and novelist. A member of the naturalist school, Maupassant chose the subjects for his stories and novels chiefly from Norman peasant life, the Franco-Prussian War, the behavior of the bourgeoisie, and the fashionable life of Paris. A pupil of Gustave Flaubert, he brought the same careful attention to the writer's craft as did his master. Stories such as the famous *En Famille, Le Rendezvous, The Necklace, and The Umbrella* are built around simple episodes from the humble life of every day. In tone, the tales are marked by objectivity, detachment, and a fine use of irony. Maupassant's style is direct and simple, with attention to realistic detail. His vision of human existence is somber, for he sees clearly the toil, suffering, and the bitterly ironic happenings that twist human lives. Among his novels are *Une Vie* (1883), about the frustrating existence of a Norman wife; *Bel-Ami* (1885), which depicts an unscrupulous journalist; and PIERRE ET JEAN.

Mauriac, Claude (1914–). French literary critic and novelist of the NEW WAVE, son of François Mauriac. His critical works led up to *The New Literature* (*La Littérature contemporaine*, 1958), a discussion of the new novelists who turn their back on tradition in order to risk discovery. He then began to write experimental novels that record the simultaneous dialogue and thoughts of a number of people: *Toutes les femmes sont fatales* (1957), *Dinner Party* (*Le Dîner en ville*; 1959), and *The Marquise Went Out at Five* (*La Marquise sortit à cinq heures*; 1961).

Mauriac, François (1885–1970). French novelist, essayist, and dramatist. His native Bordeaux is the setting for most of his short novels, which present psychological analyses of middle-class characters tormented by the absence of the grace of God. A Catholic intensely concerned with the problem of sin and redemption, Mauriac presents the attempts—and inevitable failures—of those who seek satisfaction in money, property, and especially in human love. In his novels sensual desire is always sinful and eventually destructive, marriages are hateful duels between the partners. Family relationships become enslaving bonds, and even love breeds tragedy through its fiercely possessive jealousy and its attempt to manipulate another life. Yet those individuals whose passionate quests for self-fulfillment lead them deepest into sin are usually those whose capacity for self-knowledge eventually makes them most capable of spiritual fulfillment. Those who pride themselves on their virtue remain most guilty of emotional coldness and spiritual sterility. Thus the women in *Genitrix* (1923) and *A Woman of the Pharisees* (*La Pharisienne;* 1941) harm everyone around them with their "good" intentions. A father and son find that their romantic yearnings lead only to *The Desert of Love* (1925); the family circle becomes a *Vipers' Tangle* (*Le Noeud de Vipères;* 1932). Mauriac is best at describing the anguish of suffering, rather than suggesting possible solutions for man's quest. His most successfully drawn characters, as in *A Kiss for the Leper* (*Le Baiser au Lépreux;* 1922) and THÉRÈSE DESQUEYROUX (1927) cannot achieve either earthly happiness or the salvation of divine love.

His *Life of Jesus* (1936) and *The Son of Man* (1958) present aspects of Christ as human sufferer. The development of his own philosophy is revealed through his reactions to literature and life in *God and Mammon* (1929), his *Journal* (5 vols., 1936–1953), and *The Stumbling Block* (*La Pierre d'achoppement*, 1948).

Mauriac's other novels include *Young Man in Chains* (*L'Enfant chargé de chaines;* 1913); *Flesh and Blood* (*La Chair et le sang*, 1920), *Questions of Precedence* (*Préséances*, 1921), *The Enemy* (*Le Mal;* 1924), *Lines of Life* (*Destins;* 1928), *The Frontenac Mystery* (1933), *The Dark Angels* (*Les Anges Noirs;* 1936), and *The Weakling* (*Le Sagouin;* 1951). His plays include *Asmodée* (1937), *Les Mal Aimés*

(1945), *Passage du malin* (1947), and *Le Feu sur la terre* (1951). His collections of poetry are *Les Mains jointes* (1909), *Orages* (1925), and *Le Sang d'Atys* (1940). Mauriac was awarded the Nobel Prize in 1952.

Maurice, [John] Frederick Denison (1805–1872). English theologian and reformer, founder of CHRISTIAN SOCIALISM. Maurice was one of the most influential of Victorian thinkers, involved in many progressive movements. A founder of Queen's College for Women and a teacher at the Working Men's College, he was also active in the Cooperative movement and was a liberalizing force in the Anglican Church, in which he was a priest. He was a friend of Charles Kingsley and John Ruskin, and wrote numerous books of sermons and works on divinity and social thought, including *Theological Essays* (1859) and *Social Morality* (1869).

Maurois, André. Pen name of **Emile Herzog** (1885–1967). French biographer, novelist, and essayist. He is best known for his vivid biographies of Shelley (*Ariel*, 1923), Disraeli (1927), Byron (*Don Juan*, 1930), Proust (1949), Georges Sand (*Lélia*, 1952), Victor Hugo (*Olympio*, 1955) and three generations of Alexandre Dumas (*The Titans*, 1957). *The Miracle of England* (1937) and *The Miracle of France* (1948) are popular histories. In *The Silence of Colonel Bramble* (1918) and *Les Discours du docteur O'Grady* (1922) he presents humorous portraits of his British comrades when he served as a liaison officer in World War I. His novels include *Bernard Quesnay* (1926), *Atmosphere of Love* (*Climats*, 1928), *The Family Circle* (1932), and *September Roses* (1956; also translated as *The Temptress*). He wrote a history of the U.S. in the 20th century, *From the New Freedom to the New Frontier* (1963).

Maurras, Charles [Marie Photius] (1868–1952). French political journalist and literary critic. An editor of *L'Action Française*, he made it the nucleus of a Catholic royalist movement at the turn of the century, but was disavowed by the Pope and the claimant to the throne in the 1920's. *L'Avenir de l'intelligence* (1905) outlines his concepts of order and traditionalism; his *Dictionnaire politique et critique* (1932–1934) supports classicism in art and literature.

mausoleum. A tomb of great size. It is so called after Mausolus, king of Caria in the 4th century B.C., whose wife Artemisia built for him a majestic sepulchral monument at Halicarnassus in Asia Minor. Parts of this sepulcher, which was one of the SEVEN WONDERS OF THE ANCIENT WORLD, are now in the British Museum.

The most important mausoleums are that of Augustus; that of Hadrian, the castle of St. Angelo at Rome; that of Henry II of France, erected by Catherine de Médicis; that of St. Peter the Martyr, built by G. Balduccio in the 14th century in the church of St. Eustatius; and that erected to the memory of Louis XVI.

Mauthe dog. A ghostly black spaniel that for many years haunted Peel Castle in the Isle of Man. It used to enter the guardroom as soon as candles were lighted, and leave it at daybreak. While this specter was present the soldiers forbore all oaths and profane talk. On one occasion a drunken trooper entered the guard-room alone out of bravado, but lost his speech and died in three days. Scott refers to the dog in *Lay of the Last Minstrel* (1805) and *Peveril of the Peak* (1823).

Mauve Decade, The (1926). A book by Thomas BEER surveying the American literary and social scene of the 1890's. The color yellow had already been described as typical of the period in England, and Beer, trying similarly to capture the essence of the decade in America, chose mauve as the significant tone: "pink turning to purple."

Mavor, Osborne Henry. See James BRIDIE.

Max. See Sir Max BEERBOHM.

Max, Prince. Nickname of Prince **Maximilian of Baden** (1867–1929). Last chancellor of the German Empire (1918) at the end of World War I. He influenced the abdication of Kaiser WILHELM II and the establishment of the Weimar Republic.

Maxime. The treacherous conspirator in Pierre Corneille's CINNA. He betrays Cinna to the emperor Augustus, out of love for the beautiful AMÉLIE.

Maximes. See François de LA ROCHEFOUCAULD.

Maximilian. Full name, **Ferdinand Maximilian Joseph** (1832–1867). Archduke of Austria. The younger brother of Francis Joseph I, he was made emperor of Mexico (1864–1867) by Napoleon III, who hoped to establish a French satellite in the Western Hemisphere. The opposition of Mexican liberals, U.S. protests, and political troubles in France led Napoleon to abandon Maximilian; after the withdrawal of the French forces, Maximilian was captured and shot by the Mexican leader Benito JUÁREZ. See CARLOTA.

Maximilian, prince of Baden. See MAX, Prince.

Max Müller, Friedrich (1823–1900). German-born British philologist best known for his *Sacred Books of the East* (49 vols., 1879–1894). He was a major influence, not only in linguistic studies, but on comparative religion and mythology.

Max und Moritz. See Wilhelm BUSCH.

Maxwell, William [Keepers] (1908–   ). American novelist and short-story writer. Maxwell is noted for his sensitive evocation of the recent American past, particularly the Midwest of the decades before and after World War I. His novels include *They Came Like Swallows* (1937), *The Folded Leaf* (1945), *Time Will Darken It* (1948), and *The Chateau* (1961).

Maxwell, William Babbington (1866–1938). English novelist and son of the popular Victorian novelist Mary Elizabeth BRADDON. Maxwell's second book, *The Ragged Messenger* (1904), was a best seller, and was dramatized and filmed three times. *The Guarded Flame* (1906) consolidated his success. He lived to produce close to 40 books, including an autobiography, *Time Gathered* (1937).

May, Phil (1864–1903). English caricaturist. He is noted for his studies of London characters, such as the coster-girl, the street waif, etc. In 1896 he became a member of the staff of *Punch*.

maya. A term in Hindu Vedantic philosophy. Maya refers to the cosmic illusion on account of which the One appears to be the Many and the Absolute appears as the relative. *Maya* is also associated with the ignorance that prevents man's realization of his identity with Brahman; on the esthetic plane, *maya* governs the realm of *rasa*, or the essence of esthetic relish. Some associate *maya* with *sakti*, the creative and adhesive energy in the phenomenal world.

Maya. A group of American Indians who inhabited parts of what are now Mexico, Guatemala, and Honduras. The "Old Empire" of the Mayas, which flourished between the fourth and ninth centuries, saw the rise of independent city states, such as Copan, Palenque, and Tikal, centered in southern Yucatan. For reasons that are still not clear, these were abandoned, and a "New Empire" later developed in northern Yucatan, which was dominated by the three cities of Chichen Itzá, Mayapan, and Uxmal. The greatest achievements of the Mayas were in the fields of astronomy, mathematics, and the calendar; their system of hieroglyphic writing was more advanced than that of any other American Indians. The Spaniards tried to subjugate the Mayas throughout the 15th century, but the conquest was not complete until the fall of Tayasal, the last Maya stronghold, in 1697. The investigations made by John Lloyd Stephens (1805–1852), American diplomat and archaeologist, which he described in *Incidents of Travel in Central America, Chiapas, and Yucatan* (1841) did much to arouse interest in Maya civilization.

Mayakovski, Vladimir Vladimirovich (1893–1930). Russian poet. Mayakovski, the outstanding poetic talent of the early Soviet period, was born in Georgia, the son of a forester. The family moved to Moscow in 1906, after the death of his father. Mayakovski joined the Social Democratic Party in 1908, and for the next two years spent a good bit of time in prison for his political activities. In 1910 he began to study painting, but soon afterwards was convinced by friends that his true talent was poetic. In 1912, Mayakovski signed the manifesto, *A Slap in the Face of Public Taste,* issued by the futurists. The aim of FUTURISM that seemingly most attracted him was its rejection of tradition in art. The group's concern with formal experimentation in literature engaged his interest. As he was later to show, however, he was not so willing to neglect the content of his poetry as were some of the other futurist poets. Mayakovski's first published work was a small book of four poems entitled *I* (*Ya;* 1913). This early work, with its startling imagery and powerful rhythms, created a stir, and Mayakovski was marked as one of the more original young poets. He confirmed this estimate with his next work, *A Cloud in Trousers* (*Oblako v shtanakh;* 1914–1915), a long poem which carried the depoetization of the language of poetry to an extreme limit. The characteristic features of Mayakovski's work were all present in this work: the declamatory nature of the lines, obviously fitted for being shouted from a platform; the hyperbolic imagery, forceful rhythm, and often coarse language. Mayakovski had virtually accomplished single-handed the revolt against the smooth, mellifluous poetry written by the symbolist poets. He went another step beyond the innovations in modern Russian verse introduced by Aleksandr Blok. While Blok had based his verse on a line that took into account the number of stresses (ignoring the number of unstressed syllables), Mayakovski abandoned metrical structure altogether, relying on rhythmic factors for his poem's organizing principle. His chief means of poetic organization were the rhymes, often unusual and striking, which linked his irregular lines.

Mayakovski triumphally greeted the revolution with such works as *Ode to the Revolution* (*Oda revolyutzi;* 1918), *Left March* (*Levyi marsh;* 1918), and the long poem *150,000,000* (1920). He also produced one of the first successful plays of the Soviet era, *Mystery-Bouffe* (*Misteriya buff;* 1918), a political satire in verse predicting the downfall of capitalism.

Throwing himself into the work of establishing the revolution, Mayakovski put his poetic talents at the service of the Russian telegraph agency, composing slogans and painting posters. He also composed many propaganda verses and read them before crowds of workers throughout the country. In 1923 he helped form LEF (Left Front), an organization of futurists who hoped to make their brand of art the standard one in the new Soviet society. Mayakovski edited the organization's journal, also entitled *LEF*, until 1925. The struggle between the radical approach of the LEF artists and the more conservative elements advocating realism in art finally ended in the closing of the journal. Mayakovski went on an extended tour of Western Europe, Latin America, and the U.S. During his three-month stay in the U.S., he wrote an appreciative poem about the Brooklyn Bridge (1925). On his return to Russia in 1927 he attempted to revive the magazine *LEF* under the title *The New LEF* (*Novyi LEF*). This venture lasted for just one year. A new conservative organization, RAPP (Association of Proletarian Writers) was gaining control of Soviet literature. Mayakovski's awareness that the bureaucratism he had fought was triumphing is reflected in two satirical plays: *The Bedbug* (*Klop;* 1928) and *The Bathhouse* (*Banya;* 1929).

Mayakovski continued his traveling and public readings. His troubles with literary opponents were compounded with unhappy romantic experiences. The burden became too much to bear, and in April, 1930, Mayakovski shot himself. Just five years earlier, he had harshly criticized the suicide of the poet Sergei Esenin.

Among Mayakovski's best-known longer poems are *Vladimir Ilyich Lenin* (1924), a eulogy to the Soviet leader; *All Right!* (*Khorosho!;* 1927); and *With Full Voice* (*Vo ves golos;* 1929–1930), an unfinished poem. Other well-known poems include *The Backbone Flute* (*Fleita—pozvonochnik;* 1915), *I Love* (*Lyublyu;* 1922), *Back Home* (*Domoi;* 1925), *Conversation with a Tax Collector about Poetry* (*Razgovor c fininspektorom o poetom;* 1926), and *Letter from Paris to Comrade Kostrov on the Nature of Love* (*Pismo tovarishchu kostrovu iz parizha o sushchnosti lyubvi;* 1928).

May Day. The 1st day of May. Vergil says that the Roman youths used to go into the fields and spend the *calends* (1st) of May in dancing and singing in honor of Flora, goddess of fruits and flowers. The English consecrated May Day to Robin Hood and the Maid Marian, because the famous outlaw died on that day. Villagers used to set up and dance around a Maypole, crown a May queen, and spend the day in archery, morris dancing, and other amusements. See EVIL MAY DAY.

Mayer, Julius Robert (1814–1878). German physicist. He formulated the theory of the conservation of energy, which asserts that energy, although convertible from one form to another, is never created or destroyed. Similar work was done by the German physicist Hermann Helmholtz (1821–1894) and the English scientist James Prescott Joule (1818–1889).

Mayerling. A village in Austria, the site of the royal hunting lodge where the bodies of Archduke Rudolf, crown prince of Austria, and his mistress, Baroness Marie Vetsera, were found on Jan. 30, 1889. Although the official report stated that they had committed suicide, it is generally believed that Rudolf, partly because of despair over his father's command to end the affair, shot the baroness and then killed himself.

Mayflower. The ship on which 102 Pilgrims sailed from Southampton, England, to Massachusetts in 1620. See John CARVER and MOURT'S RELATION.

Upon their arrival in America after the 63-day voyage, the Pilgrims drew up the *Mayflower Compact*, an agreement binding them together in a "civil body politic" for the government of the colony. It remained the fundamental charter of the Plymouth Colony until its absorption by the Massachusetts Bay Colony in 1691.

Maynard, Theodore (1890–1956). English-born American poet, biographer, and essayist. A Catholic convert, he wrote mainly on religious subjects. His *Collected Poems* was published in 1946.

Mayor of Casterbridge, The (1886). A novel by Thomas HARDY. Michael Henchard, an unemployed farmhand, becomes very drunk at a fair and sells his wife and baby for five guineas to a sailor named Newson. The next day, remorse-stricken, he takes an oath not to drink for twenty years and begins a fruitless search for his family. Eighteen years later, when the reformed and prosperous Henchard has become mayor of Casterbridge, his wife, Susan, and Elizabeth-Jane, now eighteen, reappear. Newson had been reported dead at sea and Susan has returned to be reunited with Henchard. After Susan dies, Henchard learns that his daughter died in infancy, and that Elizabeth-Jane is actually Newson's daughter, a fact which he conceals from her. A domineering, lonely man, he clings to her as his fortunes decline because of his differences with his astute Scottish assistant, Donald Farfrae. Then the memory of Henchard's sale of his wife is publicly revived, and he reverts to his drinking habits. Newson, not dead after all, returns to claim Elizabeth-Jane, who soon marries Farfrae, now the new mayor of Casterbridge. Henchard, deserted, wanders off and dies in dejection.

Mayor of Zalamea, The. See ALCALDE DE ZALAMEA, EL.

May Queen, The (1842). A ballad by Alfred, Lord TENNYSON. It tells of the pride, the heartlessness, and the remorseful death of Alice, the village beauty. It contains the often parodied line:

For I'm to be queen o' the May, mother, I'm to be queen o' the May.

Mazarin, Jules (1602–1661). French cardinal and statesman of Italian birth. Succeeding Richelieu as prime minister in 1642, Mazarin was retained by the queen regent, Anne of Austria, after the death of Louis XIII. A wealthy collector of books, Mazarin bequeathed his library to France; his collection of theological and historical writings forms the core of the Bibliothèque Mazarine in Paris. See BIBLE, SPECIALLY NAMED EDITIONS.

Mazeppa, Ivan (1644-1709). A famous Cossack hetman, hero of Byron's poem *Mazeppa* (1819) and of Pushkin's drama *Pultowa*. He was born of a noble Polish family in Podolia and became a page in the court of John Casimir, king of Poland. He intrigued with Theresia, the young wife of a Podolian count, who had the young page lashed naked to a wild horse, which was then turned loose. In the Ukraine, Mazeppa was released and cared for by Cossacks and in time became hetman and prince of the Ukraine under Peter the Great of Russia. Byron makes Mazeppa tell his tale to Charles XII of Sweden after the battle of Pultowa, in which he had deserted to Charles and fought against Russia.

Mazikeen or **Shedeem.** A species of demons in Jewish mythology resembling the Arabian *Jinn* and said to be the agents of magic and enchantment.

swells out like the Mazikeen ass. The allusion is to a Jewish tradition that a servant, whose duty it was to rouse the neighborhood to midnight prayer, one night mounted a stray ass and neglected his duty. As he rode along the ass grew bigger and bigger, until at last it towered as high as the tallest edifice where it deposited the servant. The next morning he was found there.

Mazzini, Giuseppe (1805-1872). Italian patriot. An active member of the CARBONARI, he founded (c. 1831), the secret revolutionary society YOUNG ITALY whose purpose was to liberate and unify Italy under a republican form of government. Later he fomented uprisings in Mantua, Milan, and Genoa. Although he gave every assistance to the expeditions of Garibaldi, he refused to support the monarchy established under Victor Emmanuel II of Sardinia, remaining a staunch republican to the end of his life.

Mc. For names beginning with *Mc-,* see under MAC-.

Mead, Margaret (1901-   ). American anthropologist and psychologist. Her first work, *Coming of Age in Samoa* (1928), was a study of adolescent girls in a noncompetitive, permissive culture. She later made a number of other expeditions to study the customs of primitive peoples, marriage, and general sexual behavior, particularly relating to rites of adolescence. She has lectured on psychology and written frequently for both scholarly journals and popular magazines. Among her many books are *Growing Up in New Guinea* (1930), *An Inquiry into the Question of Cultural Stability in Polynesia* (1930), *Sex and Temperament in Three Primitive Societies* (1935), *Male and Female* (1949), *Soviet Attitudes Toward Authority: An Interdisciplinary Approach to Problems of Soviet Character* (1951), *New Lives for Old* (1956), and *An Anthropologist at Work* (1959).

Meal-Tub Plot (1679). A pretended conspiracy against Protestants. Fabricated by Thomas Dangerfield (d. 1685), it was so called because he said that the papers relating to it were concealed in a meal-tub in the house of Mrs. Cellier, a Roman Catholic. She was tried for high treason and acquitted, while Dangerfield was convicted of libel, whipped, and pilloried.

Mean, The (Chung-yung). One of the Chinese FOUR BOOKS. Originally one chapter from the BOOK OF RITES, it became important during the Sung Dynasty (960-1279), when it became required reading for aspirants to Chinese officialdom. It discusses basic moral concepts.

Meander (Maiandros). The modern Menderes River in Asia Minor. It dried up when Phaëton drove the sun chariot. Its proverbial windings are comparable to those of the labyrinth of Minos.

Measure for Measure (c. 1604). A comedy by William SHAKESPEARE. After deputizing ANGELO to enforce Vienna's long-ignored laws, Duke VINCENTIO purports to leave the city but actually remains to observe the proceedings, disguised as Friar Lodowick. Angelo revives an old statute against fornication and sentences CLAUDIO to death for seducing JULIET, his betrothed. When Claudio's sister, ISABELLA, a religious novice, pleads for his life, her beauty stirs Angelo's repressed passions; he promises her Claudio's freedom if she will yield herself to him, a suggestion which she angrily spurns. Claudio at first approves of her behavior but, overwhelmed by the thought of death, weakens and begs her compliance. Overhearing their conversation, Vincentio, still in monk's garb, proposes that Isabella pretend to accede to Angelo's request. In her place, however, he will send MARIANA, who was formerly betrothed to Angelo but who has been spurned since the loss of her dowry. The plan is successful and, although Angelo breaks his promise by demanding Claudio's life, Friar Lodowick manages to save him. Revealing his true identity, Vincentio castigates Angelo for his severity and orders him to marry Mariana, while he himself sues for the hand of Isabella.

The main source of the play is George Whetstone's *Promos and Cassandra* (before 1578), which is based upon a story in Giraldo Cinthio's *Hecatommithi* (1565).

Mecca. In Arabia, the birthplace of Muhammad and the holiest of Muslim cities. It is to Mecca that all pious Muslims make the *hadj* or pilgrimage at least once during their lifetime.

Mecisteus (Mekisteus). See SEVEN AGAINST THEBES.

Meck, Nadezhda Filaretovna von (1831-1894). TCHAIKOVSKY's patroness, widow of a Russian railroad contractor. She helped Tchaikovsky by getting him commissions for his work and (1877) by making him a substantial annual allowance. They never met, but corresponded continuously, she being known as his "beloved friend."

Medal, The (1682). A satirical poem by John DRYDEN. Like Dryden's ABSALOM AND ACHITOPHEL, it was aimed at the earl of Shaftesbury, who had recently been exonerated from a charge of high treason. His Whig followers had a medal cast to commemorate the event.

Médard, St. Bishop of Noyon and Tournai in the 6th century. He founded the festival of the rose at Salency, which was continued even in the 20th century, the most virtuous girl in the parish receiving a crown of roses and a purse of money. This custom is the basis for De Maupassant's story *Le Rosier de Madame Husson* on which, in turn, Benjamin Britten based his opera *Albert Herring* (1947). Legend says that a sudden shower once fell which wetted everyone to the skin except St. Médard, who remained perfectly dry, for an eagle had spread its wings over him. Ever after he was termed *maître de la pluie* (master of the rain). It is said of him, as of St. Swithin, that if it rains on his holy day, it will rain for 40 days thereafter.

Medb. In early Irish literature, she is queen of Cruachain, wife of Ailill, and dire enemy of the hero Cú Chulainn. It is she who instigates the great conflict of the CATTLE-RAID OF COOLEY, and ultimately she brings about the death of Cú Chulainn.

Medea (Medeia). In Greek mythology, a sorceress and priestess of Hecate, daughter of the Colchian king Aeetes, and wife of Jason, later of Aegeus. Falling in love with Jason, she helped him to steal the GOLDEN FLEECE and to murder her half-brother Apsyrtus to delay their pursuers. (See ARGONAUTS.) Purified of murder by her aunt Circe and married to Jason among the Phaeacians, she returned with him to Iolcus. There she persuaded the three daughters of Jason's enemy PELIAS that she could rejuvenate him if they would cut him in pieces. Alcestis refused, but her sisters did so, and when Pelias was dead, Jason's Argonauts captured the city and placed Pelias' son Acastus on the throne.

Medea laid claim to the throne of Ephyre (Corinth), where Aeetes had once reigned, for Jason. Although he owed most of his successes to her, Jason later repudiated her in order to marry Glauce, daughter of Creon. Medea murdered her two children by Jason and escaped in a chariot drawn by winged serpents to Athens, where she married AEGEUS. After trying to poison his son Theseus, she was banished and ultimately returned to Colchis.

Medea was sympathetically portrayed by APOLLONIUS OF RHODES in his epic *Argonautica* and by EURIPIDES in his drama *Medea*, which told of her revenge on Jason, but neither forgot that she was both witch and barbarian. Robinson JEFFERS based his poetic drama *Medea* on the story of the Euripides play. The story has also been the subject of operas by M. A. CHARPENTIER (1693) and CHERUBINI (1797), both entitled *Medée*.

Médecin malgré lui, Le (The Doctor in Spite of Himself, 1666). A comedy by MOLIÈRE. Forbidden by her father GÉRONTE to marry the penniless Léandre, LUCINDE feigns dumbness. Géronte searches in vain for a skilled doctor to cure her. The woodcutter SGANARELLE, forced by his wife to masquerade as a specialist, earns an enormous fee from Géronte merely by reciting nonsensical medical jargon; he accepts a bribe from Léandre, takes the young man on as his ostensible apothecary, and restores Lucinde's speech so successfully that Géronte begs Sganarelle to make her dumb again. Sganarelle replies that he cannot do that, but he can make Géronte deaf. Lucinde elopes with Léandre, but Géronte is mollified upon learning that Léandre has inherited a fortune from his uncle. The character Sganarelle is one of Molière's supreme comic creations.

Médée (Medea, 1635). The first tragedy of Pierre CORNEILLE. Modeled on Euripides and Seneca, it relates Medea's bloody vengeance upon the faithless Jason. While superior to earlier French tragedies, the play does not attain the simplicity and restraint of Corneille's later works.

Medici. The famous Florentine family that rose to prominence during the Italian Renaissance on the wings of economic power and widespread cultural activities. Though the name suggests "doctor" or "medicine," the family accumulated its wealth in banking and trading, bourgeois origins that did not prevent its members from eventually joining the highest nobility of Europe.

Cosimo de' Medici (1389–1464), called *Pater Patriae* (Father of his Country) and the first of the family to exert cultural influence by his patronage of artists and writers and his encouragement of learning.

Lorenzo de' Medici (1449–1492), called *Il Magnifico* (The Magnificent), the grandson of Cosimo and the most famous of all the Medici. He was a patron of Ficino and Poliziano, Pico della Mirandola, Verrocchio, Della Robbia, Botticelli, Leonardo da Vinci, the young Michelangelo, and a host of other famous Renaissance artists. He himself wrote Petrarchan and other kinds of verse, sacred drama, and literary criticism. An astute politician, he kept his city-state secure and Italy united through the expert use of diplomacy. His death brought on the regime of Savonarola in Florence and the French invasions of the Italian peninsula. Historians have seen him as the embodiment of much of the Renaissance spirit.

Giovanni de' Medici (1475–1521), son of Lorenzo who reigned as Pope Leo X (1513–1521).

Giuliano de' Medici (1478–1516), youngest son of Lorenzo, duke of Nemours, and a minor poet popular in the literary salons of his day. Castiglione made him an interlocutor in the *Cortegiano*.

Giulio de' Medici (1478–1534), nephew of Lorenzo who reigned as Pope Clement VII (1523–1534). During his pontificate the sack of Rome by imperial forces took place (1527). Cellini, who worked for him, described the scene memorably in his *Autobiography*.

Giovanni de' Medici (1498–1526), called *Giovanni delle Bande Nere,* descendant of the younger branch of the Medici, a famous military commander. The black armor of his feared troops gave him and them the name *Bande Nere* (Black Bands). He was also known as "the Invincible," and praised by Aretino, who was with him when he died of a wound received in battle. Though he was only 28 at the time of his death, he has been called the greatest soldier produced by Italy during the 16th century.

Two female members of the family became queens of France: CATHERINE DE MÉDICIS, wife of Henry II, and MARIE DE MÉDICIS, who married Henry IV in 1600.

Médico de su honra, El (The Physician of his Own Honor). A drama by Pedro CALDERÓN DE LA BARCA, the most extreme of his honor tragedies. Doña Mencia, in love with Prince Enrique, is forced to marry Don Gutierre. However, the prince continues to pay her attention, although she tries to dissuade him. Don Gutierre, erroneously believing that his honor has been besmirched, has a surgeon bleed his wife to death. Since Don Gutierre has operated within the limits of the code of honor, the king condones his act.

Medina. A city in Arabia, the second holy city of the Muslims. It was called Yathrib before Muhammad fled there from Mecca, but afterward Medinat-al-nabi (the city of the prophet), from which its present name is derived. See HEGIRA; FAERIE QUEENE, THE.

Medium, The (1946). A two-act opera by Gian Carlo MENOTTI about a female charlatan, a medium who is haunted by her own hoax.

Medmenham Abbey. A ruined Cistercian abbey near Marlow on the Thames. It became the meeting place for the Hell-fire Club, founded by Sir Francis Dashwood in 1745 with John Wilkes and Bubb Dodington among its members. Its convivialities became orgies and its ritual was a mockery of all religion.

Medoro. In the ORLANDO FURIOSO of Ariosto, a Moorish youth of great beauty but humble origins; he is page to Agramante and is wounded in the battle for Paris between the pagan and Christian forces. ANGELICA cares for him and soon the two fall in love, thus precipitating the jealousy and madness of Orlando. The two lovers flee to Cathay, where Medoro takes the throne.

Medusa (Medousa). The chief of the Gorgons of Greek myth. It is said she dallied with Poseidon in Athene's temple and the goddess, outraged, changed Medusa's hair into serpents and made her face so terrible that it turned the beholder to stone. PERSEUS, with a sword given to him by the god Hermes, was able to cut off her head by looking only at her reflection in Athene's shield. From the dead Gorgon's blood sprang PEGASUS, the winged horse, and Chrysaor, her children by Poseidon. Perseus used Medusa's head to rescue ANDROMEDA, and later gave it to Athene in gratitude for her protection. Athene wears it on her shield and on her breastplate.

Medwin, Thomas (1788–1869). English biographer and cousin of Shelley. In 1821 he was with Shelley and Byron in Italy. His *Memoir of Shelley* (1833) was later expanded into *The Life of Shelley* (2 vols., 1847).

Meiji. Japanese period (1868–1912). It marks the emergence of Japan as a modern state. Under the banner of the restoration of the imperial family, various clans joined to bring an end to the Tokugawa shōgunate. This period saw an intense Westernization and modernization with the introduction of Occidental scientific knowledge, culture, and literature. A constitution was established, parliamentary government instituted, and Japan changed from an isolated feudal nation to a world power. Military victories were gained over China (1894) and Russia (1905) and Korea was annexed in 1910. Translations from Western literary, scientific, and philosophical works were made on a wholesale scale and much of Japanese literary production was influenced by the Occidental example. The emperor during the period was Mutsuhito (1852–1912). Meiji is the name designated for his reign.

Meilhac, Henri. See Ludovic HALÉVY.

Meinhold, Wilhelm (1797–1851). German author, famous especially for his skill in historical realism. His tale *Maria Schweidler, die Bernsteinhexe* (*Marie Schweidler, the Amber Witch*, 1843) was taken, at its publication, for an authentic chronicle from the 17th century.

Mein Kampf (My Struggle, 1924). An autobiographical work by Adlof HITLER, in which he revealed his program for political action in Germany. It was dictated to Rudolf Hess during their imprisonment after the BEER-HALL PUTSCH.

Meister, Wilhelm. See WILHELM MEISTER.

Meistersingers (*Ger.*, **mastersingers**). Members of German guilds of poets and singers, who attempted to preserve, in the 14th through 16th centuries, the medieval art form of the MINNESINGERS. The Meistersingers, of whom the most famous were Hans SACHS and Hans Folz, usually formed organizations similar to the craft guilds of the day: the title of "master" was given only to those who had proven their creative and vocal talent, and singing contests were often held among the masters. In general, however, the *Meistergesang* ("master-singing") is regarded as a degeneration of the Minnesang, retaining the external form but relinquishing the immediacy and artistic power of the original.

Meistersinger von Nurnberg, Die (1868). A comic opera by Richard WAGNER. The hand of the fair young Eva Pogner, daughter of the town goldsmith, is promised as the prize for a Nuremberg singing contest. The chief rivals are Beckmesser the town clerk, and a young knight, Walther von Stolzing, who is loved by Eva and has dreamed a beautiful song. He is hampered, however, by his ignorance of all the petty artificial rules of the songfest. Walther's cause is championed by Hans SACHS, the cobbler, and with his aid Beckmesser is put to confusion. Walther sings his *Preislied* and scores a triumph. Beckmesser is patterned on Edward Hanslick, a distinguished music critic who had annoyed Wagner by refusing to be impressed with his skill as a poet. Sachs is a fictional portrait of the historical poet.

Meitner, Lise (1878–1968). Austrian physicist. In collaboration with Otto HAHN she did highly important work in nuclear fission.

Mejor alcalde el rey, El (The King, the Greatest Alcalde). A historical drama by Lope de VEGA. It is based on an anecdote about King Alfonso VII (1126–1157). In this work, Lope contrasts royal justice with feudal tyranny.

Sancho, a poor peasant, is in love with Nuño's daughter Elvira. Don Tello, a feudal lord of the region, consents to the marriage but, on seeing Elvira, determines to possess her himself and carries her off to his castle. When Don Tello ignores Sancho's protests, the injured youth goes to the king and begs him to send a strong *alcalde,* or judge, to see that justice is done. The king himself, disguised as an

Medusa. From a Greek vase painting (fifth century B.C.).

alcalde, orders Don Tello to release Elvira. When Don Tello refuses, the king, revealing his identity, orders the arrogant noble to be executed. First, however, he is forced to marry Elvira so that she may inherit his property as his widow and share it with Sancho.

Melampus (Melampous). In Greek mythology, a seer. He understood the language of birds and beasts. This accomplishment saved his life when he overheard some woodboring worms remarking that the roof over his head was about to fall. He was the first mortal to practice the art of healing. He also appears to have been the first psychiatrist to recognize a castration complex. Phylacus of Phylace, king of Phylace, had imprisoned Melampus for trying to steal Phylacus' famous cattle as a wedding gift for Melampus' brother Bias. Learning of Melampus' special gifts after the episode of the roof, he promised Melampus both freedom and the cattle if Melampus would cure Phylacus' son Iphiclus of impotence. Eavesdropping on a pair of vultures, Melampus learned that Iphiclus had been terribly frightened as a child on seeing his father approaching him with a gelding knife, bloodstained from some rams. Melampus fed Iphiclus a potion made of the rust of the knife and he was cured.

Melanchthon, Philipp (1497–1560). German religious reformer, friend and follower of Luther, and nephew of Johann Reuchlin. (*Melanchthon* is a Hellenized form of his actual German surname *Schwarzerd,* which was interpreted as "black earth.") A noted humanist scholar, Melanchthon began as a professor of Greek, and because of his pedagogical endeavors, was known as "praeceptor Germaniae" ("the teacher of Germany"). His most important religious works are the *Loci Communes Rerum Theologicarum* (*Common Topics in Theology,* 1524), the first extensive formulation of Protestant doctrine, and the *Augsburg Confession* (1531) which he helped to draft. His desire to reconcile Roman Catholicism and Protestantism led to difficulties in his relationship with Luther.

Melba, Nellie (the stage name of **Helen Porter Armstrong,** born **Mitchell;** 1861–1931). Australian coloratura soprano. She made her début as Gilda in *Rigoletto,* was soon admired everywhere, and became the prima donna of the Royal Opera at Covent Garden, London. She was made Dame of the British Empire in 1918. She inspired two operas: *Hélène* (1904) by Saint-Saëns, and *Elaine* (1892) by Bemberg, as well as the delicacies peach melba and melba toast. *Melodies and Memories* (1925) is her autobiography.

Melchior. See MAGI.

Meleager (Meleagros). A hero of Greek legend, son of Oeneus of Calydon and Althaea. He was distinguished for throwing the javelin, for slaying the CALYDONIAN BOAR, and as one of the ARGONAUTS. It was declared by the Fates that he would die as soon as a piece of wood then on the fire was burnt up, whereupon his mother snatched the log from the fire and extinguished it. After Meleager had slain his maternal uncles, who had tried to prevent him from giving the boar's head to Atalanta for drawing first blood, his mother threw the brand on the fire again, and Meleager died.

Melibee. One of the CANTERBURY TALES of Geoffrey CHAUCER. It is told by Chaucer after the Host interrupts his narration of the rhyme of Sir THOPAS. It is a long prose didactic work, closely translated from a French adaptation of the Latin *Liber Consolationis et Consilii* by Albertanus of Brescia (c. 1193–c. 1270). Melibee (or Melibeus) returns from the fields to find that three of his enemies have beaten his wife Prudence and killed his daughter Sophie. Grieving, he rages about vengeance, but Prudence begins to reason with him, husband and wife both making extensive use of proverbs and quotations from scholastic authorities. Finally Prudence persuades him and his repentant enemies to come together in peace, and Melibee forgives them, hoping that God will likewise forgive human trespasses.

Melicertes (Melikertes). In Greek mythology, the son of Athamas and INO. Ino leaped with him into the sea. Possibly a Greek form of the Phoenician Melkarth, he became the sea-god Palaemon.

Mélisande. (1) The heroine of Maeterlinck's play PELLÉAS ET MÉLISANDE. She is a beautiful creature of mysterious origins.

(2) Another name for the water-sprite MELUSINA.

Melisenda, Melisendra. In medieval Spanish romance, the daughter of Charlemagne and the wife of Don Gayferos (Gwyferos). She is captured by the Moors and imprisoned for seven years before her husband rescues her. In the second part of Cervantes' *Don Quixote* the story is played as a puppet show. This scene from the novel was made into a one-act opera, EL RETABLO DE MAESE PEDRO, by Manuel de Falla.

Melissa. A prophetess in the ORLANDO FURIOSO of Ariosto, who lives in Merlin's cave. Bradamante, the warrior maiden, asks her to use an enchanted ring and rescue her beloved Ruggiero, who is in the power of the lovely witch Alcina. Assuming the form of Atlantes, she rescues Ruggiero and Astolfo, then disenchants all the forms metamorphosed in the island. Later, posing as Rodomonte, she persuades Agramante to break the league which was to settle the contest by single combat, thus precipitating a general battle.

Melkarth. The BAAL of Tyre. His name ("lord of the city") may appear in Greek mythology as MELICERTES, and is thought by some to bear a relation to Heracles.

Mell, Max (1882–   ). Austrian dramatist. His early plays on religious themes, all strongly influenced by Hofmannsthal's *Jedermann* (*Everyman,* 1911), include *Das Apostelspiel* (*The Apostle Play,* 1922), *Das Schutzengelspiel* (*The Play of the Guardian Angel,* 1923) and *Das Nachfolge-Christi-Spiel* (*The Play of the Imitation of Christ,* 1927). Later, he attempted to recreate the grandeur of classical tragedy in his SEVEN AGAINST THEBES (*Sieben gegen Theben,* 1932), but he soon turned toward more nationalistic ideas in *Das Spiel von den deutschen Ahnen* (*The Play of the German Ancestors,* 1935) and in *Der Nibelungen Not* (*The Distress of the Nibelungs,* 1944) which draws from the medieval *Nibelungenlied.* Among his recent works is a historical *Jeanne d'Arc* (*Joan of Arc,* 1957).

Mellichampe. See PARTISAN, THE.

Mellors. In D. H. Lawrence's novel LADY CHATTERLEY'S LOVER, the gamekeeper lover of the aristocratic heroine. He is an ideal Lawrence hero, forthright, sexually potent, and close to nature. Lawrence himself was of working-class origin and his wife, Frieda, of an aristocratic family.

Melmoth, Sebastian. A name adopted by Oscar WILDE after his exile to France following his release from prison in England. Melmoth is from Maturin's novel MELMOTH THE WANDERER; Sebastian is after St. SEBASTIAN, whose martyrdom was suggested by the arrows on Wilde's prison garb.

Melmoth the Wanderer (1820). A horrific GOTHIC NOVEL by Charles MATURIN. The hero, Melmoth, sells his soul to the devil in exchange for prolonged life. The pact can be canceled if Melmoth finds anyone willing to accept the same terms, but no one, not even those in the worst of circumstances, is willing to make the bargain.

Melozzo da Forlì (1438–1494). Italian painter. He was a follower of Piero della Francesca, though much more emotional than his austere master. He is best known for his paintings of music-making angels and of *Pope Sixtus and his Court*, a Vatican mural.

Melpomene. In Greek mythology, the MUSE of tragedy.

Melusina or **Mélisande.** A fairy in medieval French romance who is turned into a water sprite, fish-shaped from the waist down. She resumes human form when she marries Count Raymond of Poitiers, but he must promise never to see her on Saturdays, for then her mermaid appearance returns. He builds her the castle of Lusignan and others, but one Saturday secretly observes her in her bath. Melusina is now forced to leave and wander as a spirit forever. Jean d'Arras recorded the story in 1387.

Melvil, Count Renaldo de. See FERDINAND COUNT FATHOM.

Melville, Herman (1819–1891). American novelist, short-story writer, and poet. Member of a once prominent New York family, Melville was raised in an atmosphere of financial instability and genteel pretense. After the death of his father in 1832, he tried several jobs to help the family, among them clerking in a bank, school teaching, and going to sea.

His first voyage to Liverpool became the background for his fourth novel, REDBURN, the story of a young boy's initiation into manhood. Next he sailed for the South Seas, where he deserted his ship, the *Acushnet,* and took refuge among the cannibalistic Typees. Escaping from this beguiling imprisonment, he became involved in a mutiny, worked in Hawaii, and finally sailed home with the navy in 1844. He had never considered writing as a career, but, at the behest of friends, published his travel memoirs. TYPEE: A PEEP AT POLYNESIAN LIFE was a literary success, and the new author continued his adventures in a second book, OMOO.

Melville, who had been sporadically educated, now began reading widely to broaden his knowledge of the world's literature. Marrying Elizabeth Shaw in 1847, he moved to New York. His next book, MARDI AND A VOYAGE THITHER, begins as an adventure story but ends in philosophical allegory. Melville, intoxicated by metaphysics, was no longer content with the comparatively simple aims of his earlier books. In *Mardi,* Melville makes his first real use of a questing hero and a consciously symbolic level of meaning. Discouraged by the book's failure, the young author, now a father, dashed off *Redburn.* Apparently a return to autobiographical adventure, *Redburn* was a financial success. The following year, Melville wrote WHITE JACKET; OR, LIFE IN A MAN-OF-WAR, based on his life in the navy. Unable wholly to ignore symbolic significance, he does introduce a deeper meaning in both books, especially in *White-Jacket.*

Traveling to England, Melville arranged for the English publication of his books. In 1851 he completed his masterpiece, MOBY-DICK: OR, THE WHALE. An epic of a literal and metaphysical quest, it belongs to no genre. Although characters appear and disappear without explanation, and point of view changes, the book succeeds. Melville's contemporaries did not appreciate it, however, and mentally exhausted, he began PIERRE; OR, THE AMBIGUITIES. A pessimistic, deeply personal book, Pierre mirrors its author's psychological state.

Melville supported his family, during the 1850's, by farming and writing stories for magazines. Among these tales are BARTLEBY THE SCRIVENER, and BENITO CERENO. He also wrote a serialized novel, ISRAEL POTTER: OR, FIFTY YEARS OF EXILE, an ironic view of the state of American democracy. His last prose, until his final years, was the cynical and satirical novel THE CONFIDENCE-MAN, HIS MASQUERADE.

Melville then traveled to England, where he saw his friend Nathaniel HAWTHORNE for the last time. Troubled and exhausted, he visited the Holy Land, returning to New York in 1857. After an unsuccessful attempt at lecturing, he became a customs inspector in New York, a job he held for 20 years.

Unnoticed by the literary public, he turned to writing poetry. Among his poetic works are BATTLE-PIECES AND ASPECTS OF THE WAR, CLAREL: A POEM AND PILGRIMAGE IN THE HOLY LAND, JOHN MARR AND OTHER SAILORS, and TIMOLEON. Published posthumously were two books: a volume of poetry called *Weeds and Wildings* (1924) and the novella BILLY BUDD, FORETOPMAN.

Like other American artists in the latter half of the 19th century, Melville was a member of the literary underground. He had a small coterie, but was remembered, if at all, as the man who had lived with cannibals. It was not until the 1920's that he began to be recognized as one of the greatest of American writers. See PIAZZA TALES, THE.

Member of the Wedding, The (1946). A novel by Carson McCULLERS. A perceptive study, it tells the story of a motherless girl, 13-year-old Frankie, who wants to accompany her brother and his wife on their honeymoon. The wedding is seen through her eyes; as a chorus to her remarks and thoughts, one hears her six-year-old cousin and the Negro cook. The author's highly successful dramatic version of the novel was produced in New York in 1950.

Memling, Hans (c. 1430–1495). Flemish painter. He is known for the sweetness of his melancholy Madonnas, as well as for his sensitive handling of portraits and landscape backgrounds.

Memmi, Albert (1920–   ). Tunisian-born French novelist. Memmi wrote of the poignant failure of the meeting of different cultures and religions in *The Pillar of Salt* (*La Statue de Sel,* 1953) and *Strangers* (*Agar;* 1955).

Memnon. An Oriental or Ethiopian prince. In the TROJAN WAR, he went to the assistance of his uncle Priam and was slain by Achilles. His mother

Eos (the Dawn) was inconsolable for his death, and wept for him every morning.

The Greeks called the statue of Amenophis III, in Thebes, that of Memnon. When first struck by the rays of the rising sun, it is said to have produced a sound like the snapping asunder of a cord. Poetically, when Eos kissed her son at daybreak, the hero acknowledged the salutation with a musical murmur. *Memnon* is the title of a novel by Voltaire, the object of which is to show the folly of aspiring to too much wisdom.

Mémoires d'Outre-Tombe (Memories from beyond the Tomb, 1848–1850). A volume of personal reminiscences by François René de CHATEAU-BRIAND. Written during the period 1811–1841, the work was first published in *La Presse.*

Memoirs of a Midget (1921). A novel by Walter DE LA MARE. It is a fantastic romance, in which the world is seen from the midget's-eye-view of the heroine.

Memoirs of Barry Lyndon, Esq., Written by Himself, The (1844). A novel by William Makepeace THACKERAY. The Irish narrator, Redmond Barry, is an utter scoundrel and manages to involve himself in a steady succession of affairs, which he writes of as though he were invariably in the right, "the victim of many cruel persecutions, conspiracies and slanders." He courts and wins the widowed Countess Lyndon, spends her money and keeps her in his power, but finally goes from bad to worse and dies in the Fleet prison.

Mena, Juan de (1411–1456). Spanish poet and scholar. Educated in Italy, Mena served as Latin secretary to King John II of Castile. His best-known work is *El laberinto de Fortuna* or *Las trescientas,* an allegory suggested by Dante's *Paradiso,* in which the poet is transported to the palace of Fortune, where he is offered a vision of the past, present, and future. Mena is also remembered for having introduced many neologisms of Latin origin into the Spanish language.

Menaka. In Hindu legend, the heavenly nymph, seducer of Visvamitra. Her daughter is Shakuntala. The gods sent her to distract Visvamitra from his penance.

Menander (Menandros; 342–292 B.C.). An Athenian comic playwright, perhaps the best-known writer of New Comedy. His work was practically unknown until 1905, when considerable sections of three plays were discovered on a papyrus in Egypt. In 1957 the only extant complete play of Menander was discovered in Egypt, *Dyskolos (The Bad-tempered Man).* Although he employed the type characters and standard plot devices of New Comedy, Menander was a sophisticated and witty playwright. Many of the better-known plays of Plautus and Terence were adapted from his works.

Men and Women. See Robert BROWNING.

Mencius, The. One of the Chinese FOUR BOOKS. It concerns the teachings of the Confucian philosopher Mencius (372–289 B.C.), compiled by his disciples after his death. After the Sung dynasty (960–1279) it became one of the basic texts in the Chinese educational system. Mencius, living in a time of constant warfare, advanced a doctrine which maintained that the original nature of man was good and that through virtue and benevolence on his part the ruler could inspire similar sentiments in his subjects. See James Legge, The *Works of Mencius* (1895). The Chinese spelling of Mencius is Mêng-tzŭ. See CONFUCIANISM.

Mencken, H[enry] L[ouis] (1880–1956). American newspaperman, editor, and writer. Mencken began his career on the Baltimore *Herald;* he joined the *Sun* papers in 1906. In 1908 he became literary editor of the *Smart Set;* with George Jean NATHAN he edited the magazine from 1914 to 1923. In 1924, he and Nathan founded THE AMERICAN MERCURY, which became known for its "debunking" articles and its section entitled "Americana." Mencken excelled at framing insults and elicited violent retorts from those he labeled the "booboisie." He attacked Puritanism, conservatism, religion, and countless other subjects. In 1918, he was diverted from his usual occupations by his developing interest in American English; in a detailed and well-organized volume called THE AMERICAN LANGUAGE, he opened up a new field of study. In 1933, Mencken withdrew from *The American Mercury;* he continued his vitriolic attacks, however, against Hoover, Wilson, and Roosevelt and his New Deal. Critics credit Mencken with skill at satire, and admire the vigor and trenchancy of his attacks on the shams of his day; but they also call attention to his intolerance, frequent crudity, and misinformation.

Mencken's views are best promulgated in these collections of his essays: *A Book of Burlesques* (1916), *Damn: a Book of Calumny* (1917), and *Prejudices* (6 vols., 1919–1927). He also wrote many other books, among them *Ventures into Verse* (1903), poems; *George Bernard Shaw, His Plays* (1905); *Philosophy of Friedrich Nietzsche* (1908); *The Artist* (1912) and *Heliogabalus* (1920), plays; and *Menckeniana: A Schimpflexicon* (1927), compiled from unfavorable press notices about Mencken. His autobiography was published in three volumes: *Happy Days* (1940), *Newspaper Days* (1941), and *Heathen Days* (1943). Mencken appears as the character E. K. Hornbeck in the play *Inherit the Wind* (1955), by Jerome Lawrence and Robert E. Lee.

Mendel, Gregor [Johann] (1822–1884). Austrian botanist and Augustinian monk. Through his breeding experiments with peas in the monastery garden, he formulated the laws of heredity bearing his name and laid the foundation for modern genetics.

Mendelssohn[-Bartholdy], [Jakob Ludwig] Felix (1809–1847). German composer-conductor and pianist. He was a grandson of Moses Mendelssohn. He became instrumental in reintroducing the works of Bach, performing in 1829 that composer's *Passion According to St. Matthew* for the first time since Bach's death. He became conductor at the Gewandhaus, Leipzig, in 1835. He composed symphonies (among them the *Reformation* in 1830, the *Italian* in 1833, and the *Scotch* in 1842); overtures (*A Midsummer Night's Dream* in 1826, *The Hebrides* in 1830–1832, *Ruy Blas* in 1839, and others); piano concertos in G minor (1831) and D minor (1837); a famous violin concerto in E minor (1844); choral works, especially the oratorios *St. Paul* (1834–1836) and *Elijah* (1846–1847); complete music for Shakespeare's *A Midsummer Night's Dream* (1843); and many smaller works. His earliest mature work shows superb craftsmanship and a great melodic gift, but the many works he later wrote show little development in technique or deepening of expression.

Mendelssohn, Moses (1729–1786). Popular German Jewish philosopher who, with his friend Lessing, was a staunch defender of religious tolerance. His major work is *Phädon* (1767), the title taken from Plato's *Phaedo,* which supports belief in the immortality of the soul. Dorothea Veit was his daughter. Felix Mendelssohn, the composer, was his grandson.

Mendès, Catulle (1841–1909). French poet and man of letters. Mendès founded the *Revue fantaisiste* (1859), a poetry review which first published several of the Parnassian poets. In his *Légende du Parnasse contemporain* (1884) he describes the beginnings of the new poetic movement. See PARNASSIANS.

Mendicant Orders. Orders of the Franciscans (Grey Friars), Augustines (Black Friars), Carmelites (White Friars), and Dominicans (Preaching Friars). So called from the wandering mode of life in the early years of the orders, before permanent homes were allowed.

Mending Wall (1914). A poem by Robert FROST. The dramatic situation of the poem is simple: once a year Frost and a neighbor mend the wall which separates their property. Frost, however, contends that the wall is unnecessary, while the neighbor simply repeats the saying of his father, "Good fences makes good neighbors."

Menelaus (Menelaos). In Greek mythology, a son of ATREUS, brother of Agamemnon, and husband of Helen. His wife's abduction by Paris was the ostensible cause of the Trojan war. Menelaus was king of Lacedaemon or Sparta. He appears prominently not only in the *Iliad* but in three plays by Euripides, *The Trojan Woman, Helen,* and *Andromache.*

Menen, Aubrey (1912–   ). English novelist and essayist, of East Indian and Irish parentage. Much of his work, such as the autobiography and essay *Dead Man in the Silver Market* (1953), is directed against nationalism and group prejudice. *The Prevalence of Witches* (1948) is a satiric novel about the difference between tribal and British civil law in a remote Indian province. He has also written comedies of Italian life, such as *The Duke of Gallodoro* (1952).

Menéndez Pidal, Ramón (1869–   ). Spanish literary historian. He is considered the chief romance-language philologist and medieval authority in Spain, and his scholarship has inspired a generation of literary historians and critics. He is also a linguistics specialist of major repute. His works include *La leyenda de los infantes de Lara* (1896); his critical text in 3 volumes, *Cantar de mio Cid* (1908–1912); *La España del Cid (The Cid and his Spain,* 1930); and *Los orígenes del español* (1926). Menéndez Pidal founded the *Revista de filológia española* (1914), a journal; he also established the Madrid Center of Historical Studies (1907).

Menenius Agrippa. In Shakespeare's CORIOLANUS, an aged counsellor and friend to Coriolanus. "One that hath always loved the people," he represents the judicious attitude of the Roman nobility, aware of their own superiority and yet aware that the people must be flattered to maintain peace.

Mêng Tzǔ. See MENCIUS, THE.

Men in White (1933). A play by Sidney KINGS-LEY. It reveals the internal workings of a hospital when a surgeon is faced with a conflict between love and professional duty. The play won a Pulitzer Prize in 1934.

Menken, Adah Isaacs (1835–1868). American actress and poet. Her stage career began in New Orleans in 1857, while her poems were appearing in the *Cincinnati Israelite* and the New York *Sunday Mercury.* A frequent subject of scandal, she charmed many writers, including Joaquin Miller, Bret Harte, Mark Twain, Dickens, Reade, Swinburne, Rossetti, Dumas père, and Gautier. Her flamboyantly romantic autobiographical verse was published in a volume called *Infelicia* (1868).

Mennonite. A member of an evangelical Protestant sect. Originating in Switzerland during the 16th century, they took their name from Menno Simons (1492–1559), a Dutch religious reformer who belonged to the less fanatical wing of the Anabaptists from which they sprang. Personal regeneration by adult baptism, a refusal to bear arms and take oaths, and rejection of worldly concerns, as exemplified in a uniform plainness of dress, are among their characteristic tenets. The sect still exists in Holland and Germany although most of its membership is now to be found in Canada and the U.S., the Amish Church being one of its major branches.

Menoeceus (Menoikeus). In Greek mythology, a son of Creon. When, in the war with the SEVEN AGAINST THEBES, Tiresias predicted that Thebes would be saved only if one of its heroes voluntarily sacrifices himself for the city, Menoeceus promptly flung himself from the walls.

Men of Good Will. See Jules ROMAINS.

Menotti, Gian Carlo (1911–   ). Italian-born American composer and librettist. His best-known operas include *The Telephone* (1947), THE MEDIUM, THE CONSUL, AMAHL AND THE NIGHT VISITORS, and *Maria Golovin* (1958).

Menshevik. See BOLSHEVIK.

Menteur, Le (The Liar, 1643). A comedy by Pierre CORNEILLE. It concerns the misadventures of the inveterate but sympathetic liar, Dorante, who ultimately confuses the name of the lady he is courting with that of another and so embroils himself in lies that his only recourse is to transfer his affections to the other lady.

Mentor. An old man, mentioned in the ODYSSEY. In his care Odysseus left his son Telemachus on embarking for the Trojan War. He appears prominently at the beginning of the *Odyssey;* his name has become synonymous with a wise and faithful counselor.

Men Without Women (1927). A collection of 14 short stories by Ernest HEMINGWAY. The finest examples of Hemingway's mastery of description, dialogue, and atmosphere are to be found in this volume. The story most often anthologized is THE KILLERS, a narrative remarkable for its aura of impending doom and dramatic restraint. *The Undefeated* and *Fifty Grand* deal with one of Hemingway's favorite subjects—the courage of an aging man. *Hills Like White Elephants* and *A Simple Inquiry,* both consisting of dialogue and a few vividly drawn descriptions, appear to be simple, almost trivial sketches, but have a sinister and dramatic undertone.

Mephistopheles. Also **Mephistophiles, Mephistophilis, Mefistofele, Mephostophilus.** Name of the demonic tempter in all the literary versions of the FAUST legend, although his characteristics vary among them. The derivation is disputed, possibly Greek for not loving the light and thus the lord of the darkness, possibly Hebrew for destroyer and liar. Mephistopheles inherits his varying form and personality from both the Christian system of demonology, in which he is one of the seven chief devils, and from the pagan Germanic tradition of the kobold, or mischievous familiar spirit. Thus he is never identified with the Devil who is the fallen angel Lucifer, although he resembles him in part; he is more the pure fiend of pagan superstition in the earlier stories, and by Goethe's time the fiendish sneerer at all values has an air of urbane sophistication.

In Goethe's *Faust,* Mephistopheles is the tempting spirit of hell who uses his supernatural powers in Faust's service, after receiving a contract to the effect that Faust will sacrifice his soul to him at death. Mephistopheles characterizes himself as "der Geist, der stets verneint" ("the spirit who always negates"), that is, the spirit of absolute destruction, whose wish is that the entire world return to nothingness. Faust, on the other hand, never desires destruction for its own sake, but is always in some sense idealistic, despite the constant immorality of the means he employs for his ends. The pact between Faust and Mephistopheles, unlike that in other versions of the story, sets no time limit. Faust is to continue living with Mephisto as his servant until the time when he is so completely satisfied that he begs the present moment not to pass away.

He appears in Gounod's opera *Faust,* and Boito's opera *Mefistofele.* He is mentioned by Shakespeare (*Merry Wives,* i.I) and Fletcher as *Mephostophilus,* and appears prominently in Marlowe's *Dr. Faustus* as *Mephostopilis.*

Mercator, Gerhardus. Latin for **Gerhard Krämer** (1512–1594). A Flemish geographer. He is especially remembered for the system of projection, first used in his map of 1568 and now known as Mercator's projection, in which the meridians are drawn as parallel lines so that only comparatively small areas can be made to appear in correct relative dimensions.

Mercer, Cecil William. See Dornford YATES.

Merchant of Venice, The (c. 1595). A comedy by William SHAKESPEARE. In order to finance BASSANIO's voyage from Venice to Belmont to win the hand of PORTIA, Antonio, a Venetian merchant, borrows money from the Jew SHYLOCK and signs a bond stipulating that if the money is not repaid within three months Shylock may cut a pound of flesh from Antonio's body. In Belmont, Bassanio is about to wed Portia when he learns that the ships from which Antonio would have obtained the money to pay Shylock have been lost and that Shylock is demanding his pound of flesh. After a hasty wedding, Bassanio returns to Venice to attend his friend's trial. Without telling her husband, Portia obtains legal advice and, accompanied by her maid NERISSA, appears at the trial disguised as a lawyer. She wins the case by insisting that Shylock may take neither more nor less than the exact pound of flesh specified in the bond and that, if in the process a single drop of blood is shed, Shylock must pay for the infraction with his life. Because he had sought the life of a Venetian citizen, Shylock also loses half his property

to Antonio, but the merchant returns it to him on the condition that it be bequeathed to Shylock's daughter JESSICA, who has recently eloped with LORENZO, a friend of Bassanio. The play ends happily as Portia reveals her identity to her astonished husband and Antonio's ships are recovered.

The sources of the plot are a play called *The Jew,* first mentioned in 1579, Fiorentino's *Il Pecorone* (1558), and the *Gesta Romanorum* (c. 1472).

Merchant's Tale, The. One of the CANTERBURY TALES of Geoffrey CHAUCER. The Merchant bewails his own unhappy marriage, then begins his tale with the arguments for wedded bliss which persuade the aged knight January to marry young May despite anxious warnings from his friends. At the marriage feast his squire Damyan falls sick of a passion for her, and she cures him by writing that she will respond. January becomes blind and possessively jealous, but May steals an impression of the key to January's private garden, and Damyan precedes the couple there one day and climbs into a pear tree. Meanwhile, in a marital argument between the rulers of Fairyland, Pluto says he will restore January's eyesight to see May betray him, and Proserpina vows to help her fool him anyway. May asks January to help her into the pear tree to taste the fruit. Soon January can see his wife happily sporting with Damyan, and roars with rage. May replies that his new sight must be distorted as yet, and complains that she had learned she might cure his sight by struggling with a man in a tree, but now is getting no thanks for her successful undertaking. January is convinced, and in the *Epilogue* the Host exclaims bitterly over the slyness of women.

Mercier, Louis (1870–1935). French poet of the Forez region. Mercier describes his native countryside in *Voix de la terre et du temps* (1903), *Le Poème de la maison* (1906), and *Les Pierres Sacrées* (1920). His novels *Hélène Sorbiers* (1912) and *Les Demoiselles Valéry* (1923) exalt peasant life.

Mercilla, Queen. See FAERIE QUEENE, THE.

Mercury. The Roman equivalent of the Greek HERMES, son of Maia and Jupiter to whom he acted as messenger. He is probably of totally Greek origin, brought to Rome by Greek traders. He was the god of science and commerce, the patron of travelers and, also, of rogues, vagabonds, and thieves. Hence, the name of the god is used to denote both a messenger and a thief. Mercury is represented as a young man with winged hat and winged sandals (*talaria*), bearing the caduceus and sometimes a purse.

Mercury fig (Lat., *Ficus ad Mercurium*). The first fig gathered off a fig tree was by the Romans devoted to Mercury. The proverbial saying was applied generally to all first fruits or first works.

Mercutio. In Shakespeare's ROMEO AND JULIET, an elegant and high-spirited young nobleman, kinsman of Prince Escalus and Romeo's friend. When Romeo refuses to quarrel with Tybalt, Mercutio, who does not know that Romeo's animosity towards the Capulets has diminished since his secret marriage to Juliet, draws his sword in exasperation and is slain by Tybalt.

Mercutio is one of the most highly coveted of Shakespearean roles, actors often preferring Mercutio's mocking wit to the blander and less biting lyricism of Romeo. His famous Queen Mab speech, in which he describes the nocturnal activities of the mischievous fairy queen who delivers men of their dreams, is a masterpiece of spontaneous fancy:

O! then, I see, Queen Mab hath been with you.
She is the fairies' midwife, and she comes
In shape no bigger than an agate-stone
On the fore-finger of an alderman . . .

Mère Coquette, la. See Philippe QUINAULT.

Meredith, George (1828–1909). English novelist, poet and critic. Born into a family of naval outfitters, Meredith spent two years in a Moravian school in Germany and there developed cosmopolitanism of outlook and encountered the excesses of German romanticism. Twice married, he supported himself until 1894 as a newspaper writer and reader for a publisher. His poetry includes *Poems* (1851), MODERN LOVE, a marital tragedy based on his own unhappy first marriage; *Poems and Lyrics of the Joy of Earth* (1883), a celebration of evolutionary naturalism and his finest collection of verse; *Ballads and Poems of Tragic Life* (1887); *A Reading of Earth* (1888); *A Reading of Life* (1901); and *Last Poems* (1910). His fiction includes *The Shaving of Shagpat* (1855), an Oriental fantasy in extravagant style; *Farina* (1857), a lampooning of German romanticism; THE ORDEAL OF RICHARD FEVEREL, the partly autobiographical tragedy of an educational theory mistakenly applied; EVAN HARRINGTON; *Sandra Belloni* (1864), a burlesque of sentimentalism; RHODA FLEMING, a rural melodrama; *Vittoria* (1866), his only historical novel; *The Adventures of Harry Richmond*, a picaresque romance (1870); *Beauchamp's Career* (1874), a political novel mixed with romantic intrigues; *The Tale of Chloe* (1879), a tragedy; THE EGOIST, a biting study of selfishness; *The Tragic Comedians* (1880), a fictionalized biography of the Jewish socialist leader Ferdinand Lassalle; *Diana of The Crossways* (1885); *One of Our Conquerors* (1891); LORD ORMONT AND HIS AMINTA; *The Amazing Marriage* (1895); and an unfinished novel, *Celt and Saxon* (1910). The influence of Meredith's father-in-law Thomas Love Peacock is evident in the writer's hatred of egotism and sentimentality, in his affirmation of the intellectual equality of women with men, and above all in his belief in the beneficial power of laughter—a belief expounded in the critical work *The Idea of Comedy and the Uses of the Comic Spirit* (1877), in which he put forth the thesis that comedy corrected the excesses of sentimentality, selfishness, and vanity. Though Meredith's later novels are marred by an opacity of dialogue, narration, and style, and though many of the ideas that placed him politically and socially ahead of his time now seem dated, the evolutionary philosophy of his poetry and prose, the happy acceptance of life as a process of becoming, has lost little of its power. In 1905, Meredith was awarded the Order of Merit.

Meredith, Owen. Pen name of **Edward Robert Lytton Bulwer-Lytton,** 1st earl of **Lytton** (1831–1891). English poet and diplomat. The son of Edward George BULWER-LYTTON, the novelist, Meredith was once termed "third among living poets" and won the qualified praise of the Brownings and George Meredith. His works include *The Wanderer* (1857), LUCILE, and *King Poppy* (1892).

Meres, Francis (1565–1647). English critic. His *Palladis Tamia, Wits Treasury,* published in 1598, contains the most complete and extensive contemporary references to Shakespeare now extant. His work is invaluable to scholars engaged in establishing the chronology of Shakespeare's plays.

Merezhkovski, Dmitri Sergeyevich (1865–1941). Russian historical novelist, poet, and critic. Merezhkovski, who published his first collection of verse in 1888, was one of the Russian symbolists. With his wife, Zinaida HIPPIUS, he opened a salon in St. Petersburg, holding meetings of the Religious and Philosophical Society founded by him. This group, whose purpose was to spread mystical philosophical ideas, for a time attracted the poets Aleksandr Blok and Andrei Bely. Merezhkovski's own ideas of the dualism of flesh and spirit in human history were expressed in his trilogy of historical novels, entitled *Christ and Antichrist.* The separate volumes were *Death of the Gods* (*Smert' bogov;* 1895), also known as *Julian the Apostate; The Gods Reborn* (*Voskreseniye bogi;* 1902), also known as *Leonardo da Vinci;* and *Peter and Alexis* (*Piotr i Aleksei;* 1905). Merezhkovski also used antithetic contrast in his critical study *Tolstoi and Dostoevski* (1901–1902). He and his wife emigrated to France in 1919.

Mérimée, Prosper (1803–1870). French novelist and man of letters. The fondness for literary hoaxes, which was one of Mérimée's characteristics, showed itself at the outset of his literary career with the publication of *Théâtre de Clara Gazul* (1825). These six plays presented to the public as translations from the work of a Spanish actress were actually Mérimée's own work. Mérimée is known as a writer of vivid and skillful historical novels. Although fiery passions are portrayed, in exotic settings, Mérimée uses irony to control his tone. His works include *La Chronique du Temps de Charles IX* (1829), *Colomba* (1841), *Carmen* (1852), and *La Double Méprise* (1833). A student of archaeology, Mérimée served as Inspector General of historical monuments in France. During the Second Empire, he held the position of senator. His novel CARMEN was made by Georges Bizet into one of the finest and most durable of all operas.

Merivale, Philip (1886–1946). English actor and writer. He was a member of F. R. Benson's Shakespearean Company (1906). He visited the U.S. in *Scarlet Pimpernel* (1910). Merivale played in many modern and Shakespearean roles. He is the author of *The Wind Over the Water, Knut at Roeskilde,* and *The Peace of Ferrara.*

Merlin. The marvelous magician who plays an important role in ARTHURIAN LEGEND. His origins seem distinctly Celtic, and especially in early Welsh writings he figures prominently. Perhaps the first known full-fledged treatment of him is to be found in the *Libellus Merlini* (*Little Book of Merlin;* c. 1135), a Latin tract written by Geoffrey of Monmouth which was later incorporated into his *History of the Kings of Britain* (1137). In this work, Merlin has all the flavor of an ancient Celtic druid, removing, for example, the great stones of Stonehenge from Ireland to Amesbury by his magic. Most important to the legends of Arthur, however, it was Merlin in Geoffrey of Monmouth's work who arranged for UTHER PENDRAGON to go to IGRAINE in the likeness of her husband, for it was from that meeting that Arthur was born. Merlin the magician was elaborated on by Wace in *Roman de Brut* (1155), and achieved full growth in Malory's *Morte d'Arthur* (c. 1469), where he is the force behind Arthur's achievement of the throne and otherwise instructs Arthur, insuring his continuing invincibility and future greatness as king. Then the great seer and magician proceeds to fall in love with the LADY OF THE LAKE, the sorceress who, soon tiring of him, imprisons him for eternity in an enchanted tower.

Merlin also appears in Spenser's *Faerie Queene* (1590–1596), Tennyson's *Idylls of the King* (1859–1885), T. H. White's *The Once and Future King* (1958), and C. S. Lewis's *That Hideous Strength* (1945). See ROUND TABLE.

Merlin (1874). A poem by Ralph Waldo EMERSON. Analyzing the methods of the poet, Emerson advises waiting for inspiration, rather than mechanically devising a form. Whitman, rather than Poe, would have been admired by the author of "Merlin."

mermaid. A fabulous marine creature, half woman and half fish. She is allied to the Siren of classical mythology. Popular stories of the mermaid probably arose from sailors' accounts of the manatee (dugong), a cetacean whose head has a rude approach to the human outline, and the mother of which while suckling her young holds it to her breast with one flipper, as a woman holds her infant in her arm. If disturbed, she suddenly dives under water and tosses up her fishlike tail.

In Elizabethan plays the term is often used for a courtesan. Cf. Massinger's *Old Law,* iv, 1, Shakespeare's *Comedy of Errors,* iii, 2.

Mermaid Madonna, The (Panageia e Gorgona, E; 1949). A novel by Stratis MYRIVILIS. The story is a curious but effective combination of folk lore and realism. A sea nymph grows up in a modern fishing village in Mytilene (the author's native Lesbos) but, like Undine, cannot be happy in the bonds of an ordinary mortal marriage. The book is remarkable for its blending of the stuff of myth with a living and detailed picture of the day-by-day existence of Greek fishermen.

Mermaid Tavern. A famous English tavern of the early 17th century. In Bread Street, Cheapside, it was a meeting place for the wits, literary men, and men-about-town. Among those who met there were Ben Jonson, Sir Walter Raleigh, Francis Beaumont, John Fletcher, John Selden, and possibly Shakespeare. In his *Lines to Ben Jonson* Beaumont wrote:

> What things have we seen
> Done at the Mermaid! Heard words that have been
> So nimble, and so full of subtile flame,
> As if that every one from whence they came
> Had meant to put his whole wit in a jest.

Merodach. See MARDUK.

Merope. (1) One of the PLEIADES. Merope is dimmer than the rest, because, according to Greek legend, she married Sisyphus, a mortal. She was the mother of Glaucus.

(2) In classic myth, the daughter of Oenopion, king of Chios. Her too-eager lover ORION was blinded for his treatment of her.

(3) The mother of Aepytus by Cresphontes, king of Messenia. Her royal husband was murdered by Polyphontes, who possessed himself of both throne and widow, but years later Aepytus returned under pretext of claiming a reward for having murdered Cresphonte's son and avenged his father's death. This legend is the subject of a drama by Euripides, now lost, and dramas in Italian by Maffei (1731) and Alfiero, in French by Voltaire, and in English by Matthew Arnold.

(4) The wife of Polybus, king of Corinth, who adopted OEDIPUS. In some versions of the legend Polybus is called Periboea.

Merovingians. The first dynasty of Frankish kings (reigned 428–751). CLOVIS I was the most important, establishing the capital at Paris; after 638 the nominal kings lost all real power to the officials called mayors of the palace, a position held by the CAROLINGIANS until they assumed the crown.

Merrilies, Meg. A brilliant and exotic character, the half-crazy queen of the gypsies who appears in Scott's GUY MANNERING. She is the nurse of the young heir before he is kidnaped, and recognizes him when he returns as Brown. She is also the subject of a poem by Keats.

Merrill, Stuart [Fitzrandolph] (1863–1915). American-born French poet. An early American expatriate and a lifelong socialist, he lived most of his life in France and wrote his works in French. The only book of his to appear in English was *Pastels in Prose* (1890), a collection of translations from 19th-century French symbolist writers. His own poetry was part of the symbolist movement and appeared in *Les Gammes* (1887) and *Les Fastes* (1892). Merrill's most important work is *Une Voix dans la Foule* (1909), expressing deep pity for the suffering of man.

merry. Originally, "pleasing, delightful"; hence, "giving pleasure; mirthful, joyous."

The old phrase *Merrie England* (*Merry London,* etc.) merely signified that these places were pleasant and delightful, not necessarily bubbling over with merriment; and so with *the merry month of May.*

Merry Andrew. A buffoon, jester, or attendant on a quack doctor at fairs. The name is said by the English antiquary Hearne—with no evidence—to derive from Andrew Borde (d. 1549), physician to Henry VIII, who to his vast learning added great eccentricity. Matthew Prior wrote a poem on *Merry Andrew.* Andrew is a common name in old plays for a manservant, as Abigail is for a waiting woman.

Merry Mount. See Thomas MORTON.

Merry Widow, The. Operetta in 3 acts by Franz LEHÁR. It was produced (1905) as *Die Lustige Witwe.* The leading characters are Princess Sonia and Prince Danilo.

Merry Wives of Windsor, The (c. 1598). A comedy by William SHAKESPEARE. Sir John FALSTAFF, knowing that Mrs. Ford and Mrs. Page control the purse strings in their respective households, decides to seduce them, but the two ladies learn of his scheme and resolve to make a fool of him. When he is informed of Falstaff's designs by the disgruntled NYM and PISTOL, Mr. Ford, who doubts his wife's fidelity, disguises himself as a Mr. Brook and, pretending to be another aspirant for Mrs. Ford's favors, engages Falstaff to intercede for him. After the unsuspecting Falstaff has undergone several misadventures—including a ducking in the Thames—in his pursuit of Mrs. Ford and Mrs. Page, the ladies and Mr. Ford, who by now knows of his wife's plan and is convinced of her virtue, reveal themselves to the old lecher and pardon him. A subplot deals with the romantic affairs of Mrs. Page's daughter Anne, who is courted by SLENDER, Dr. CAIUS, and FENTON, whom she loves and with whom she eventually elopes.

No single source for the play, which makes use of several traditional comic devices, has been identified.

Meru, Mount. The Olympus of Hinduism; a fabulous mountain in the center of the world, 80,000 leagues high, the abode of Vishnu, and a perfect paradise.

Méséglise Way. See REMEMBRANCE OF THINGS PAST.

Meshach. See SHADRACH, MESHACH, AND ABED-NEGO.

Mesmer, Franz Anton. See MESMERISM.

mesmerism. A method of medical treatment by hypnosis developed by the Austrian physician Franz Anton Mesmer (1734–1815), who called it "animal magnetism." He cured hysterical patients by what are now known to be hypnotic methods, but attributed his success to a magnetic power, pervading the whole universe, which was concentrated in his own person. In 1778, he went to Paris where he established his famous clinic.

Messager, Charles. See Charles VILDRAC.

Message to Garcia, A (1899). An essay by Elbert HUBBARD. Hubbard based his tale on a newspaper story about a certain Lt. Andrew Summers Rowan (1857–1943), who had been given a mission by the war department to make his way to the Cuban insurgents in revolt against Spain, and learn something of their numbers and the possibility of cooperation with the U.S. Rowan accomplished his task against great odds, and finally reported the results of his interview with General Calixto García Iñiguez to the U.S. government. Hubbard retold the story, using it as a pretext for a sermon. The story sold out at once, and millions of reprints were issued during World War I; the reason for its popularity was Hubbard's moral: no matter what odds you face in the performance of your duty, you must carry out the assigned task, you must carry *your* message to Garcia.

Messalina, Valeria (d. A.D. 48). Notorious Roman empress. The third wife of the emperor CLAUDIUS of Rome, she was executed by order of her husband. Her name has become a byword for lasciviousness and incontinency. Catherine II of Russia (1729–1796) has sometimes been called "the modern Messalina."

Messer Gaster (*Gr.*, "stomach"). In Rabelais' GARGANTUA AND PANTAGRUEL, the prosperous master of arts who lives with Dame Pénie (*Lat.*, "poverty"). He symbolizes Rabelais' view that progress and civilization are spearheaded by the energetic poor who want more, not by the sluggish rich, whose wants are satisfied. Though Messer Gaster is monstrously greedy and his cult of gluttony is repulsive, it is precisely his vital need for bread that has led to the invention of all the arts.

Messer Marco Polo (1921). A novel by Donn BYRNE. Purporting to be the real story of Marco Polo, it is told by Malachi Campbell, an Ulsterman. Polo is described as falling in love with the daughter of Kubla Khan. When her magicians save him from

death in the desert, he stays, marries her, and returns to Venice only in old age after her death.

Messiah, The (1742). The most popular oratorio in the English language, music by George Frideric HANDEL, libretto compiled from the Bible by the Rev. Charles Jennens. First performed in Dublin, it treats the life of Christ in a spiritual and theological manner, rather than in a narrative.

mester de clerecía. A Spanish poetic style of the Middle Ages. In contrast to the popular MESTER DE JUGLARÍA, it produced verse characterized by the erudition and refinement that were then the exclusive property of the clergy. Its aims were didactic and moral. Themes were drawn from religion, legend, and history, and the meter known as CUADERNA VÍA was invariably used. Among the earliest exponents of this trend were the 13th-century poet Gonzalo de BERCEO and the unknown author of the LIBRO DE APOLONIO.

mester de juglaría. A Spanish literary style of the Middle Ages. The term was used as early as the 12th century to describe the popular, anonymous epics recited by minstrels, or *juglares*. See MESTER DE CLERECÍA.

Metamorphoses. A series of tales in Latin verse by the Roman poet OVID. Dealing with mythological, legendary, and historical figures, they are written in

Title page of Arthur Golding's translation of Ovid's *Metamorphoses* (1567).

The. xv. Bookes of P. Ouidius Naſo, entytuled Metamorphoſis, tranſlated oute of Latin into Engliſh meeter, by Arthur Golding Gentleman, A worke very pleaſaunt and delectable.

With ſkill, heede, and iudgement, this worke muſt be read, For elſe to the Reader it ſtandes in ſmall ſtead.

1567

Imprynted at London, by Willyam Seres.

hexameters, in 15 books, beginning with the creation of the world and ending with the deification of Caesar and the reign of Augustus. *Metamorphoses* is also the title of a satire by Apuleius more commonly known as THE GOLDEN ASS.

Metamorphosis, The (Die Verwandlung; 1915). A story by Franz KAFKA. Often regarded as Kafka's most perfect finished work, *The Metamorphosis* begins as its hero, Gregor SAMSA, awakens one morning to find himself changed into a huge insect; the story proceeds to develop the effects of this change upon Gregor's business and family life, and ends with his death. It has been read as everything from a religious allegory to a psychoanalytic case history; but its really attractive qualities are its clarity of depiction and attention to significant detail, which give its completely fantastic occurrences an aura of indisputable truth, so that no allegorical interpretation is necessary to demonstrate its greatness.

metaphor. In figurative language, an implied comparison identifying the two things compared with each other. As distinguished from simile, in which the comparison is stated, metaphor pretends that the two things compared are identical; the comparison is understood. Thus, in "the waves were soldiers moving," the poet (Wallace Stevens) does not expect to be taken literally; he is comparing the waves, his first term, with moving soldiers, his second term. Through metaphor, as through other figures of speech (SIMILE, METONYMY, PERSONIFICATION, and SYNECDOCHE, for example), the poet seeks to concretize his meaning, thereby making his poem more vivid and immediately appealing to the senses.

An extension of the metaphorical process may lead to the development of a symbol; in a symbol, the comparison is no longer even implied, the second term stands for the first, and the first is no longer present. This is easily grasped when we think of universal symbols, such as the flag for a nation or the cross for Christianity. ALLEGORY is also an extended metaphor.

metaphysical poets or school. A term generally applied to several English poets of the early 17th century. Their poetry is marked by highly complex and greatly compressed meanings; by complex and long-sustained CONCEITS; by a frequent avoidance of smooth and regular meter in order to achieve dramatic or conversational effects; by unusual syntax and an unconventional type of imagery chosen from philosophy, religion, and theology, and the arts, crafts, sciences, and ordinary daily life of the period in which the poets lived.

The most famous of the metaphysical poets are John DONNE, George HERBERT, Richard CRASHAW, Francis QUARLES, Andrew MARVELL, Henry VAUGHAN, Thomas TRAHERNE, Abraham COWLEY, and John CLEVELAND. Donne is the founder of the school and is considered its greatest member; Herbert, Crashaw, and Marvell follow in importance; Cowley and Cleveland are regarded as the most culpable in the use of farfetched conceits.

These poets, among whom there is wide variation in individual style, represented a reaction against the tradition of the Elizabethan sonnet sequence of the late 16th century, the products of which had become feeble and overconventionalized as the vogue died out, and a return in some ways to the cruder, more homely type of imagery in poetry of the middle of the

16th century, as well as to the scholasticism of the Middle Ages. The awakening interest in science in the early 17th century is also considered to have had an influence on metaphysical poetry. Its complex conceits, most popularly associated with the school, were paralleled and excelled in "fantastic" character in the baroque Spanish and Italian schools, and its use of imagery from the trades, professions, arts, and crafts was foreshadowed by practice in Italian and French poetry of the 16th century and by a critical recommendation in the DÉFENSE ET ILLUSTRATION DE LA LANGUE FRANÇAISE of Joachim du Bellay.

The poets in this loosely associated school were first called "metaphysical" by Samuel Johnson in his study of Cowley in his *Lives of the English Poets* (1779–1781), in which he condemns them for their excessive use of "learning" in their poetry. The term had been implied, however, in the early condemnations of the poets by Drummond of Hawthornden and Dryden. In the 20th century, interest in the metaphysical poets was revived, and their work was highly praised by such English and American critics as H. J. C. Grierson, T. S. Eliot, I. A. Richards, William Empson, Allen Tate, John Crowe Ransom, and Cleanth Brooks. Eliot, Richards, and Brooks use metaphysical poetry, especially that of Donne, as examples in their studies of poetic theory.

A number of 20th-century poets came under the influence of the metaphysicals and revealed this influence varyingly in their own work; according to critics, these include T. S. Eliot, Louise Bogan, Horace Gregory, Elinor Wylie, Ruth Pitter, Richard Eberhart, John Crowe Ransom, Allen Tate, Hart Crane, Wallace Stevens, and R. P. Blackmur. Gerard Manley Hopkins is regarded as a 19th-century poet whose work greatly shows metaphysical influence, and the poetry of Emerson, Jones Very, and Emily Dickinson has also been called metaphysical.

Metastasio, Pietro. Original name, **Pietro Trapassi** (1698–1782). Italian poet and dramatist. Associated with the ARCADIAN ACADEMY, he became court poet at Vienna (1730), serving the Emperor Charles VI and later the Empress Maria Theresa. Although his work served as a basis for many oratorios, cantatas, and operas, the most famous being Mozart's *La Clemenza di Tito* (1791), he is also known for his own lyrical dramas, such as *Demetrio, Demofoonte, Olimpiade,* and *Attilio Regolo,* which were produced from 1730 to 1740. Generally, his themes were taken from classical history, mythology, and the Bible. He was noted for the melodious quality of his style and for proverblike comparisons.

metempsychosis (Gr., from *meta,* beyond, and *empsychoun,* to animate). Transmigration of souls. The doctrine, originating in India and Egypt, that the human soul after death enters into another body, human or animal.

meter. In English verse, the measurement used in determining the rhythm of a line insofar as established by the regular or almost regular recurrence of accented syllables. (Other, less important factors that determine the rhythm of a line include the length of syllables, sense, and rhyme.) Meter is based on units called feet, each foot being a set relationship between one accented syllable and one or two unaccented syllables. The four types of feet in English verse are IAMB, TROCHEE, ANAPEST, and DAC-

TYL; occasional variations, such as SPONDEE, occur. Verse lines are named according to the type of foot they contain and the number of feet in the line. A line made up of five iambs, for example, is called iambic PENTAMETER.

Classical meters, upon which subsequent European versification is based, depended not upon alternations of accent as in English verse but on quantity or length of syllables. For the purposes of meter, one long syllable counted as two short syllables. Obviously, however, quantity plays a part in the nuances of rhythm in English meter. "Ten" and "strange," though they both be accented in a line, do not have the same value, and the poet is as aware of such quantitative distinctions as he is of alternation of accent. See SCANSION.

Method acting. See STANISLAVSKI SYSTEM.

Methodism. The doctrines of a Protestant denomination, originally of an evangelical nature, which grew from a loose religious association formed at Oxford University in 1729 by a group which included John and Charles WESLEY, and George Whitefield. The name began as a term of derision applied by the Oxford students to the members of the association because they displayed a methodical regularity in their meetings for Scriptural study and spiritual edification, and in their fasts and prayers. John Wesley's sermons are still the doctrinal standard of the Methodist communion. In the course of time, the movement became even more widely evangelical and broke away from the Church of England.

Methuselah. In the Bible, the son of Enoch. He is the oldest man mentioned in the Bible where it states that he died at the age of 969 years (Gen. 5:27).

Gelett Burgess entitled one of his humorous volumes *Maxims of Methuselah* (1907). George Bernard Shaw wrote *Back to Methuselah* (1921), a play.

metonymy. In rhetoric, a figure of speech using substitution of the name of an object for that of something related, usually a larger concept. Examples are "scepter" substituted for "sovereignty," "the ring" for "boxing," and so on.

Metternich, Prince **Clemens von** (1773–1859). Chancellor of Austria (1809–1848). His reactionary policies dominated European diplomacy from the Congress of Vienna (1814–1815) until the revolutions of 1848. He worked to maintain the security of Austrian power through a continental balance of power and suppression of nationalistic and liberal forces. During the insurrection of 1848 in Vienna he fled to England.

Meursault. See STRANGER, THE.

Mew, Charlotte (1869–1928). English poet. Her small output includes some Georgian verse and some individual, somber poems. Collections of her poems are *The Farmer's Bride* (1915) and *The Rambling Sailor* (1929).

Mexican War (1846–1848). A war between the U.S. and Mexico, caused mainly by Mexican resentment against the annexation of Texas (1845) and by boundary disputes arising out of the annexation. During the war, California was conquered, and U.S. forces under General Winfield Scott captured Mexico City. By the terms of the treaty of Guadalupe-Hidalgo, Mexico gave up its claims to southern Texas and ceded to the U.S. all of Mexico north of the Rio Grande and the Gila River—about a million square miles of land. In return, the U.S. agreed to pay $15 million and to assume the claims of U.S. citizens against Mexico. Many Whigs opposed the war, claiming that it was motivated solely by the desire for territorial expansion. The war was an important training ground for many Civil War generals, including Grant, Sherman, and Lee.

Meyer, Conrad Ferdinand (1825–1898). Swiss poet and novella-writer. Among German-language poets, he was a pioneer in the use of symbolist techniques; that is, he often did not directly express his feelings and thoughts, but tended to let them be tacitly implied in an objective description (see DINGGEDICHT). He is also famous for his historical ballads, and many of his novellas are based on historical material from the Italian Renaissance: for example, *Plautus im Nonnenkloster* (*Plautus in the Convent*, 1882) and *Die Hochzeit des Mönchs* (*The Monk's Wedding*, 1884). Like his poems, they are objective and realistic on the surface, but deeply metaphysical in essence.

Meyerbeer, Giacomo. Pen name of **Jakob Liebmann Beer** (1791–1864). A composer of German birth, but of the French school. Immensely popular in their day, his grand, somewhat grandiloquent operas have lost favor, partly for want of singers who can muster the grand style. Chief among them are *Robert le Diable, Les Huguenots, Le Prophète,* and *L'Africaine.*

Meyerhold, Vsevolod Emilievich (1874–1940). Russian director and actor. Known for his stylized, highly theatrical productions, Meyerhold began his career as an actor with the Moscow Art Theatre. He later became manager of the Revolutionary Theatre, in Moscow, where in his staging of political propaganda plays he introduced such innovations as dispensing with the theatrical curtain, the use of the bare stage, and purely symbolic scenery.

Meynell, Alice [Thompson] (1847–1922). English poet and essayist. A convert to the Roman Catholic religion, she carried her religious beliefs into her writings. Volumes of her poetry include *Preludes* (1875), *Poems* (1893), *Later Poems* (1901), *Father of Women* (1918), and *Last Poems* (1923). Among her books of essays are *The Rhythm of Life* (1893), *The Color of Life* (1896), *The Children* (1896), *The Spirit of Peace* (1898), *Ceres Runaway* (1910), and *The Second Person Singular* (1921). She and her husband Wilfrid Meynell befriended the poet Francis THOMPSON when he was living in London in poverty and loneliness. Her daughter Viola Meynell, author of novels and short stories, wrote *Alice Meynell, a Memoir* (1929).

Mezentius. A legendary king of Caere in Etruria. Noted for his cruelty and impiety, he put his subjects to death by binding them to dead men and then leaving them to starve. According to Vergil's AENEID, he was driven from his throne by his subjects and fled to Turnus, king of the Rutuli. When Aeneas arrives, he fights with Mezentius and slays both him and his son Lausus.

Mezzo Cammin (1842). A sonnet by Henry Wadsworth LONGFELLOW. The poet laments that his ambition to build a "tower of song" has been defeated by sorrow. The title, from Dante, refers to the fact that Longfellow was in the "middle way" of his life, 35 years old. The sorrow to which he refers is evidently the death of his first wife, Mary Potter.

M'Fingal. See under *Mac*.

Micah. The 6th Minor Prophet of the Old Testament, whose prophecy is recorded in the book bearing his name. He predicted the fall of Israel and Judah, but saw hope of redemption in the Messiah.

Micawber, Mr. Wilkins. A well-known character in Charles Dickens' DAVID COPPERFIELD. He is a great projector of bubble schemes sure to lead to fortune, but always ending in grief. In spite of his indigence, he never despairs; he feels certain that something will "turn up." Having failed in every adventure in England, he emigrates to Australia where he becomes a magistrate. Micawber is said to be drawn from Dickens' father.

Michael (1800). A narrative poem by William WORDSWORTH. It tells the story of an honest, hardworking herdsman whose virtues are ill rewarded by the failures of both his nephew and son.

Michael, St. The great prince of all the angels and leader of the celestial armies.

> And there was war in heaven: Michael and his angels fought against the dragon; and the dragon fought and his angels, and prevailed not.—*Rev*. xii, 7, 8

> Go, Michael, of celestial armies prince,
> And thou, in military prowess next,
> Gabriel; lead forth to battle these my sons
> Invincible; lead forth my armed Saints
> By thousands and by millions ranged for fight.
>   Milton, *Paradise Lost*

His day (St. Michael and All Angels) is September 29 (see MICHAELMAS DAY), and in the Roman Catholic Church he is also commemorated on May 8, in honor of his apparition in 492 to a herdsman of Monte Gargano. In the Middle Ages he was looked on as the presiding spirit of the planet Mercury, and bringer to man of the gift of prudence.

In art St. Michael is depicted as a beautiful young man with severe countenance, winged, and clad in either white garments or armor, bearing a lance and shield, with which he combats a dragon. In the final judgment he is represented with scales, in which he weighs the souls of the risen dead.

Michael and his Lost Angel (1896). A play by Henry Arthur JONES. It portrays the struggle of the stern and upright young minister, Rev. Michael Faversham, to resist his love for Mrs. Lesdon, a wilful, lovable, irresistible woman who comes suddenly into his life and will not be put out. He sins and forces himself to make public confession, but finds he cannot forget her.

Michael Angelo. See MICHELANGELO.

Michaelis, Karin (1872–1950). Full name **Katharina Marie Bech Michaelis.** Danish novelist and short-story writer. She lived in the United States for many years and spent time in both Austria and Germany. *Den farlige Alder* (*The Dangerous Age*, 1910), the best known of her many novels, is a perceptive psychological study of a woman.

Michael Kohlhaas (1808). A novella by Heinrich von KLEIST. It is set in the 16th century and Kleist calls its hero "one of the most upright and, at the same time, most terrifying men of his time." Kohlhaas, a common horse-trader, is tricked into leaving two of his best horses at the nearby castle of a dissolute young nobleman, and when he returns, he finds that they have been ruined by being used in the fields. After failing to obtain restitution from the government, he takes the law into his own hands, gathers a band of men, razes the nobleman's castle, and burns several cities in his quest for justice. The book then develops into a constantly wider field, embracing the religious struggles and international politics of the time, and the occult operations of fate. Finally, Kohlhaas obtains twofold justice in that his horses are returned in perfect condition and he is executed for his crimes. The story is not based on historical fact.

Michaelmas Day. September 29, the Festival of St. Michael and All Angels. In England it is one of the "quarter-days" when rents are due and the day when magistrates are elected. It also gives its name to the full term of the English universities.

Michaux, Henri (1899–   ). Belgian poet. His visits in Asia and South America produced *Qui je fus* (1927), *Ecuador* (1929), and *Un Barbare en Asie* (1932). The hero of *Plume* (1930), who symbolizes modern man in his futile revolt against a hostile world reappears in some of the prose poems of *Epreuves, Exorcismes* (1945). This volume describes the German Occupation, but also discovers the mystic joy and peace of creation that exorcises the anguish of life's absurdity. *Espace du dedans* (1944) is a selection of his poetry.

Michelangelo [Buonarotti] (1475–1564). Italian sculptor, architect, painter, and poet of the Renaissance. One of the greatest and most influential artists of all time, he was born in Florentine territory and began his apprenticeship in the studio of the painter GHIRLANDAIO at Florence. Later he studied antique sculpture under Bertoldo in the Medici academy, where he produced his first carving, the relief entitled *The Rape of Dejanira*. In the Florence of the time he also absorbed the influence of Giotto, Dante, Savonarola, and the Neoplatonist circle of FICINO. His study of anatomy during this period was important for his later treatment of the human form. His first trip to Rome in 1496 produced the *Bacchus* statue, and in 1498, the famous *Pietà* of the Vatican. Having returned to Florence, he finished in 1504 the colossal statue of *David* and the famous cartoon for the *Battle of Cascina,* in competition with Leonardo da Vinci. The painting was never finished, and only partial studies and copies remain, but CELLINI and VASARI assert that it was considered a marvel of the age. In 1504, Michelangelo also completed his *Holy Family,* one of his best-known paintings. Called to Rome again by Pope Julius II, for the purpose of executing the pope's tomb, he grew impatient with papal procrastination and left in a huff, refusing urgent pleas to remain. After a reconciliation with Pope Julius, he executed a huge bronze statue of him for the cathedral of Bologna (1507), but it was melted down shortly thereafter. In 1508, the pope diverted him from the tomb project to paint the ceiling of the Sistine Chapel, which was finally unveiled in 1512. This masterpiece consists of scenes from Genesis—the Creation to Noah—frescoed the length of the vault. Around these scenes he painted architectural motifs (molding, ribs, pilasters), and where they intersected he inserted the Old Testament prophets, the sibyls, and, in the spandrels, the Atlases

—figures bursting with power and vitality despite the mellow hues consistently employed. During the next three decades the artist worked sporadically on the Julian tomb, which was finally abandoned. Its surviving elements include the colossal *Moses* now in S. Pietro in Vincoli, and the unfinished figures of captives and slaves.

Back in Florence again, Michelangelo carved the Medici tombs for Lorenzo and Giuliano de' Medici in the new sacristy of S. Lorenzo, with the celebrated reclining figures of *Day, Night, Dawn,* and *Dusk,* as they are called (1520–1524). He also erected the Laurentian Library (1523–1534) in this period. During the remaining decades of his life, spent mainly in Rome, he painted the celebrated *Last Judgment* on the end wall of the Sistine Chapel (1542), erected the Palazzo Farnese (1547), laid out the current plan of the Capitoline Hill, and erected the dome of St. Peter's, begun in 1547. Among his surviving literary works are letters and some 200 poems, mainly sonnets, addressed to Vittoria COLONNA and the young boy Tommaso Cavalieri, for whom he felt a platonic affection. First published in bowdlerized form by his grandnephew in 1623, they were finally given to the world in their original state in 1863. The poems have been translated by Wordsworth, Southey, Symonds, Emerson, Longfellow, Norton, and Santayana. They reveal Michelangelo's preoccupation with his art, his struggle to reconcile a Platonic sense of the beauty of the human form and of all material things as a revelation of the soul within, and the Christian sense of sin he remembered in the sermons of Savonarola and the poetry of Dante. During the last week of his life he worked on the so-called Rondanini *Pietà,* which, like several others done at this time, reveals the depth of his spiritual struggle. In addition to acknowledging with the past the greatness of individual works, modern opinion credits Michelangelo with having written the best lyrics of the Italian *cinquecento,* with being the inspiration of the stylistic movements known as MANNERISM and BAROQUE and responsible for the direction taken by art for the next two centuries after his death.

Michelet, Jules (1798–1874). French historian. Michelet is noted for the vividness and penetration of his accounts of French history. He consistently expressed sympathy for the proletariat and the ideals of 1789, and consistently opposed the Church, the crown, and the bourgeoisie. His great work is *Histoire de France* (1833–1867).

Michelet came from a background of poverty and secured his education through his own efforts. He lost his position as professor in the Collège de France because of his attacks on the Jesuits. Later, when Napoleon III assumed power and destroyed Michelet's hopes for liberty, he was dismissed from his employment in the national archives.

Micromégas (1752). A philosophic tale by VOLTAIRE, which discusses the relativity of dimensions and the insignificance of mankind in the universe. It is written in imitation of Cyrano de Bergerac's *Histoire comique* and of Jonathan Swift's *Gulliver's Travels.* Micromégas, a 120,000-foot-tall inhabitant of the star Sirius, and his friend from Saturn, a "dwarf" 6,000 feet tall, visit the earth. Micromégas has about 1,000 senses, and the Saturnian about 72, which, he complains, aren't enough. They happen to observe a shipload of scientists through a microscope they fashion from a diamond. The earthlings proudly describe humanity's scientific accomplishments and religious history. The giants are impressed with the scientific knowledge of humans, but are horrified by the stupidity of religious wars and dogmas. Before leaving the earth, Micromégas bequeaths to the scientists a book containing the correct answers to philosophic questions. When the men open it later, they find only blank pages. In his description of the Saturnian giant, Voltaire satirizes the French philosopher and scientist Bernard de Fontenelle. The work is a satire on the philosophic systems of Descartes, Leibniz, and Nicolas de Malebranche.

Midas. A legendary king of Phrygia. He requested of the gods that everything he touched might be turned to gold. His request was granted, but as his food became gold the moment he touched it, he prayed the gods to take this favor back. He was then ordered to bathe in the Pactolus, and the river ever after rolled over golden sands.

Another story about Midas tells that, when appointed to judge a musical contest between Apollo and Pan, he gave judgment in favor of the satyr; whereupon Apollo in contempt gave the king a pair of ass's ears. Midas hid them under his Phrygian cap, but his barber discovered them, and, not daring to mention the matter, dug a hole and relieved his mind by whispering in it, "Midas has ass's ears," then covering it up again. The rushes were ever after murmuring the secret to the winds.

Middle Ages. The period of European history extending roughly from 476 (the fall of the Roman Empire) to 1453 (the capture of Constantinople by the Turks), although the dates vary with each nation. During this period FEUDALISM was the characteristic form of social and economic organization. In the 8th century the CAROLINGIANS established a connection between the Roman Catholic Church and the power of the kings and emperors as highest feudal lords. It was an uneasy alliance, however, resulting in a continuous struggle between the Church and the kings for supreme temporal authority.

The early part of the period (until about the 12th century) is occasionally referred to as the DARK AGES because of the supposed extinction of culture and learning. It is true that classical Greek and Roman manuscripts existed only in ecclesiastical libraries and were largely though certainly not totally ignored; the revival of general interest in classical learning and literature led to the RENAISSANCE. The Church dominated such education and scholarship as there was: compendiums of knowledge were written in the monasteries, and the great universities began as colleges of theology and divinity. But by the 12th century a fair amount of new literature was being written, largely under the patronage of the royal and ecclesiastical courts, based both upon the oral folklore traditions and upon scholastic learning.

Middlemarch: A Study of Provincial Life (1871–1872). A novel by George ELIOT, with a double plot interest. The heroine, Dorothea BROOKE, longs to devote herself to some great cause and for a time expects to find it in her marriage to Rev. Mr. Casaubon, an aging scholar. Mr. Casaubon lives only eighteen months after their marriage, a sufficient period to disillusion her completely. He leaves her his estate with the ill-intentioned proviso that she will forfeit it if she marries his young cousin Will LADI-SLAW, whom she had seen frequently in Rome. Endeavoring to find happiness without Ladislaw, whom she has come to care for deeply, Dorothea throws herself into the struggle for medical reforms advocated by the young Dr. Lydgate. Finally, however, she decides to give up her property and marry Ladislaw. The second plot deals with the efforts and failure of Dr. Lydgate to live up to his early ideals. Handicapped by financial difficulties brought about by his marriage to the selfish and ambitious Rosamond Vincy, and by the opposition of his medical associates, he drifts into cultivating a wealthy practice at the expense of his medical standards. There is a subplot dealing with the love affair of Rosamond's brother Fred Vincy and Mary Garth, the daughter of Caleb Garth, the builder.

Middleton, Thomas (1580–1627). English dramatist. One of the most popular playwrights of his period, Middleton possessed considerable comic and satiric talents but seldom gave way to caricature. His observation was keen and balanced, so that his characterizations remain, on the whole, remarkably credible. His masterpieces are, perhaps, THE CHANGELING, written with Thomas Rowley and one of the most powerful tragedies of the period, and A TRICK TO CATCH THE OLD ONE, one of the best comedies of manners. Among the finest of his other plays are THE ROARING GIRL, written with Thomas Dekker, *A Mad World, My Masters* (c. 1606), *Women, Beware Women* (c. 1623), *A Chaste Maid in Cheapside* (c. 1612), *No Wit, No Help Like a Woman's* (1613?), *Michaelmass Term* (c. 1606), *A Game at Chess* (1624), and *The Family of Love* (c. 1606), as well as a number written in collaboration with William Rowley: *A Fair Quarrel* (1616); *The Old Law* (1599?); an undated masque entitled *The World Lost at Tennis; The Mayor of Queenborough* (c. 1618); and *The Spanish Gipsy* (1623), in which John Ford was also a collaborator.

Midgard. The region of earth in Scandinavian mythology, meaning, literally, the yard in the middle. The abode of the first man and woman, Ask and Ember, it was made from the body of YMIR and was joined to Asgard by the rainbow bridge, Bifrost.

Midgard serpent (also known as *Jormungard,* the earth's monster, and *Midgardsorm,* the serpent of Midgard). In Scandinavian mythology, the venomous serpent, fathered by Loki, the spirit of evil, and the brother of Hel and Fenris. He lay at the root of the celestial ash until Odin cast him into the ocean, where he grew so large that in time he encompassed the earth and was forever biting his own tail. Thor finally killed him with his hammer, but his flood of venom drowned the god.

Midrash. The rabbinical investigation into, and interpretation of, the Old Testament writings. It began when the temple at Jerusalem was destroyed, and was committed to writing in a large number of commentaries between the 2nd and 11th centuries. Three ancient Midrashim contain both the HALACHAH, which deals with the legal sections of the Bible and the HAGGADAH, treating the nonlegal.

midsummer day. June 24, the Feast of the Nativity of St. John the Baptist. Its eve (June 23) is called midsummer night. It occurs near the time of the Summer solstice, which was associated with solar ceremonies long before the Christian era. The bonfires still lighted in parts of Europe on the eve are relics of these customs.

Midsummer Night's Dream, A (c. 1594). A comedy by William SHAKESPEARE. Plans are on foot for the wedding of THESEUS, duke of Athens, and the Amazon queen HIPPOLYTA, whom he has defeated in battle. EGEUS, an Athenian, has promised his daughter HERMIA to Demetrius, and although she is in love with Lysander, the duke orders her to obey her father. The two lovers escape to the forest, followed by DEMETRIUS and by HELENA, who is in love with Demetrius. Here they are found by OBERON, king of the fairies, his queen TITANIA, with whom he is extremely disgruntled, and the merry PUCK. Puck has a magic love-juice that will make the one whose eyelids are anointed fall in love with the first object he sees upon awaking. As Puck uses the potion somewhat indiscriminately a strange comedy ensues, but eventually Demetrius abandons Hermia to Lysander

Title page of Shakespeare's *A Midsummer Night's Dream* (1600).

FOLGER SHAKESPEARE LIBRARY

A
Midfommer nights
dreame.

As it hath beene fundry times publickely acted, by the Right honourable, the Lord Chamberlaine his feruants.

Written by William Shakefpeare.

¶ Imprinted at London, for *Thomas Fifher,* and are to be foulde at his fhoppe, at the Signe of the White Hart, in *Fleeteftreete.* **1600.**

and devotes himself to Helena. At the duke's marriage feast, which celebrates three weddings in place of one, BOTTOM the weaver and his blundering group of players present as an interlude the play of PYRAMUS and Thisbe.

There is no single source for the play. The story of Theseus and Hippolyta is found in Chaucer's *Knight's Tale* as well as in Plutarch's *Lives*. The "tragical comedy" of Pyramus and Thisbe is a burlesque of the tale in Ovid's *Metamorphoses*.

Mies van der Rohe, Ludwig (1886–1969). German architect. Last director of the BAUHAUS, he came to the U.S. in 1938. His design of the new campus of the Illinois Institute of Technology exerted a great influence on contemporary architecture. A master of the rectilinear and of elegant mass relations, he has brought the glass wall, with its metal grid, to a refinement exemplified by the famous Seagram Building in New York City (1958).

Mignon. In Goethe's *Wilhelm Meisters Lehrjahre* (see WILHELM MEISTER), a young girl whom Wilhelm finds in a troupe of side-show performers and buys from her brutal guardian. She is Italian in origin and filled with a constant yearning to return to her sunny native land. Her complete devotion to her savior Wilhelm is too deep and mystical to be considered a simple manifestation of love between the sexes; and in fact, everything about her is permeated with a sense of mystery. She wilts, finally, in her uncongenial northern surroundings, and dies. Her story, considerably altered, formed the basis for the once-popular opera *Mignon* (1866) by Ambroise Thomas.

Mikado or the town of Titipu, The. A GILBERT AND SULLIVAN comic opera. Nanki-Poo, the son of the Mikado, traveling in disguise, falls in love with Yum-Yum, the lovely ward of Ko-Ko, the Lord High Executioner. Ko-Ko, who never beheads anyone, is now informed by Pooh-Bah, Lord High Everything Else, that he will lose his office unless there is an execution within a month. Nanki-Poo agrees to be the victim if he may marry Yum-Yum. When the Mikado is told that his son, Nanki-Poo, has been executed, his wrath is fearful, but luckily Ko-Ko's report of the execution was false, so all is well.

Milbanke, Anne Isabella. Called **Annabella** (1792–1860). English heiress and wife of Lord BYRON. A beautiful and rigorously moral woman, she was unsuited to a man of Byron's temperament. The two were married in 1815 and separated a year later, after the birth of their daughter Augusta Ada. It was rumored at the time that the separation was caused by Lady Byron's discovery of an incestuous relationship between the poet and his half sister Augusta Leigh; it is more certain, however, that Byron was tired of his strait-laced wife and would have encouraged any belief that assured a separation.

Miles. See TURN OF THE SCREW, THE.

Miles Gloriosus (Lat., "boastful soldier"). A comedy by PLAUTUS. The hero is Captain Pyrgopolynices, a character who is the prototype of a long line of military braggarts in European and English drama.

Milesian Fables. A Greek collection of witty but obscene short stories, written, or more likely compiled by Aristides of Miletus (2d century B.C.). They were translated into Latin as the *Milesiae Fabulae* by Sisenna about the time of the civil wars of Marius and Sulla, and were greedily read by the

luxurious Sybarites, but are no longer extant. Similar stories, however, are still sometimes called Milesian Tales.

Milesians. Properly, the inhabitants of Miletus. The name has also, however, been given to the ancient Irish, because of a legend that two sons of Milesius, a fabulous king of Spain, conquered the country and repeopled it after exterminating the Firbolgs that lived there at the time.

Milesian School. A school of Greek philosphers originating in Miletus. It was of the period preceding Plato. The Milesians tried to find a unifying principle for the universe in a basic world-stuff which maintained its integrity throughout all physical change. Water, air, and the infinite were suggested. The members of the school were THALES, ANAXIMANDER, and ANAXIMENES.

Milhaud, Darius (1892–   ). French composer, member of LES SIX. In his many works he has explored the possibilities of jazz style, as in the ballet *La Création du monde* (*The Creation of the World*, 1923); Latin American music, as in *Saudades do Brasil* (a piano suite, 1921); and polytonality. His operas include *La Brebis égarée* (1910; *The Lost Sheep*, based on a novel by Francis Jammes), *Christophe Colomb* (1930; to a book by Paul Claudel), and others based on Greek legends and plays, such as *Médée* (1939).

Mill, John Stuart (1806–1873). English philosopher and economist. A precocious child, he was put through a rigorous education by his grim and exacting father, James Mill (1773–1836), a utilitarian philosopher. In 1823 he entered India House as his father's assistant, became assistant examiner in 1828, was in charge of relations with native states (1836–1856), and chief of office in 1856, retiring with a pension when the East India Company dissolved in 1858.

Mill formed the Utilitarian Society (1823–1826) for reading and discussing essays at the home of Jeremy Bentham. He was chief contributor to the *Westminster Review* and was recognized as a leading utilitarian before the age of 20. His first literary undertaking of note was the editing of Bentham's *Rationale of Judicial Evidence* (1825). After a severe mental crisis (1826–1827), at the root of which was probably the strict training by his father, he departed somewhat from the utilitarianism of Bentham and his father by humanizing it and introducing a note of idealism. His first successful work was *System of Logic* (1843). Mill's best-known works are a series of treatises, including *On Liberty* (1859), *Thoughts on Parliamentary Reform* (1859), *Representative Government* (1861), *Utilitarianism* (1863), and *Examination of Sir William Hamilton's Philosophy*, (1865), a defense of association philosophy. Mill was a member of Parliament (1865–1868), voted with the Radical party, and advocated women's suffrage. His later works include *The Subjection of Women* (1869), *The Irish Land Question* (1870), and *Autobiography* (1873). He lived the last years of his life at Avignon in France. See UTILITARIANISM.

Millais, Sir John Everett (1829–1896). English painter. With Holman Hunt and Daniel Gabriel Rossetti, he originated the PRE-RAPHAELITE BROTHERHOOD (1848). He illustrated the works of Trollope and of Tennyson, and painted portraits of Gladstone, Disraeli, Wilkie Collins, Carlyle, John Bright, Irving,

Tennyson, and other distinguished men of his day. After 1870, his work deviated from Pre-Raphaelite style and subject matter.

Millamant. See WAY OF THE WORLD, THE.

Millay, Edna St. Vincent (1892–1950). American poet. One of the best-known poets of her time, she is noted for her verse of the 1920's, celebrating life, love, and moral freedom with lyrical gaiety and freshness. After her graduation from Vassar and the appearance of her first volume, *Renascence and Other Poems* (1917), she went to live in Greenwich Village, and for a time acted with the Provincetown Players, who produced some of the plays she had written at college. With her second book of poetry, A FEW FIGS FROM THISTLES, she began to reach the reading public. In 1923 she won a Pulitzer Prize for THE HARP-WEAVER AND OTHER POEMS. Influenced by Shakespeare, Keats, and Gerard Manley Hopkins, she retained conventional forms and was especially noted for her sonnets. Among her later books of poetry are *The Buck in the Snow and Other Poems* (1928), *Fatal Interview* (1931), CONVERSATION AT MIDNIGHT, *Huntsman, What Quarry?* (1939), and *Make Bright the Arrow* (1940). Her *Collected Poems* were published in 1956. Her other works include *Three Plays* (1926); *Aria da Capo* (1920), also a play; *The King's Henchman* (1927), an opera with music by Deems Taylor. She also wrote satirical sketches, such as *Distressing Dialogues* (1924), under the pen name of Nancy Boyd.

After her marriage in 1923 to Eugen Boissevain, Miss Millay lived in the Berkshires, leaving their farm only for occasional travel or public readings. As time went on, she wrote less and less, her later poetry being concerned with political and social themes. See RENASCENCE.

Mille, Pierre (1864–1941). French short story writer and journalist. An authority on colonial life, he is best known as the humorous creator of Barnavaux (*Sur la vaste terre*, 1906) of the French Foreign Legion. This hero reappears in *Under the Tricolor* (1908) and *Louise and Barnavaux* (1912). *The Monarch* (1914), and *Partonneau* (1924), which deals with colonial administration, are among his other works.

Miller, Alice Duer (1874–1942). American poet, playwright, and novelist. Her light, entertaining novels *The Charm School* (1919) and *Come Out of the Kitchen* (1916) were successfully dramatized. *Gowns by Roberta* (1933) formed the basis of the musical comedy *Roberta*. *The White Cliffs of Dover* (1940), the fervid and sentimental verse eulogy she wrote about England during the dark days of World War II, became a great popular success. Her *Selected Poems* (1949) were collected by her son after her death.

Miller, Arthur (1915–). American playwright and novelist. Miller began writing plays at the University of Michigan. Returning to New York, he published a novel, *Focus* (1945), an ironical study of race prejudice. *All My Sons* (1947), his first successful play, dealt with the emotional aftermath of World War II. The Pulitzer Prize-winning DEATH OF A SALESMAN established Miller as one of the leading playwrights of his generation. The play exemplified Miller's contention that tragedy is possible in the modern theater and that its proper hero is the common man. THE CRUCIBLE confirmed his already secure reputation. Miller won a second Pulitzer Prize and the New York Drama Critics' Circle Award for *A View from the Bridge* (1955). His *Collected Plays* appeared in 1958. The scenario for his film, *The Misfits* (1961), which evolved from a short story published in *Esquire* (1957), was issued in book form in 1961. *After the Fall* (1964), an autobiographical drama which was the first production of the Lincoln Center Repertory Theater in New York City, caused considerable controversy, partly because of the characterization of Maggie, supposedly modeled on Miller's second wife, the actress Marilyn Monroe.

Miller, Henry (1891–). American writer. After holding various jobs—including a position as employment manager for the Western Union Telegraph Co.—Miller became an expatriate, living in France for a nine-year period beginning in 1930. During these years he published the books usually considered his best: the controversial TROPIC OF CANCER; *Black Spring* (1936), stories and sketches including *The 14th Ward; Tropic of Capricorn* (1938), an autobiographical work about the hilarious years with Western Union; *Max and the White Phagocytes* (1938), a collection of stories, many of which were reprinted in the later *The Cosmological Eye* (1939).

Miller was in Greece when World War II began. One product of the Greek trip was *The Colossus of Maroussi* (1941), a highly praised travel book which saw the genius of Greece, not in her ruins, but in the spirit of her living people. On his return to America, Miller made a nationwide tour; his critical reaction to the country was contained in *The Air-Conditioned Nightmare* (1945) and its continuation, *Remember to Remember* (1947). In 1949, Miller published *Sexus*, the first of a long autobiographical double trilogy called *The Rosy Crucifixion*, which includes *Plexus* (1953) and *Nexus* (1960). *The Books in My Life* (1952) lists hundreds of obscure volumes by which Miller was profoundly affected. He has written several pieces on literary censorship, among them an eloquent letter to the Supreme Court of Norway after it banned *Sexus*; it was reprinted with other material from the trial in *Henry Miller—Between Heaven and Hell: A Symposium* (1961). Miller's extensive correspondence with Lawrence Durrell was published in 1962.

Miller, Joaquin. Pen name of **Cincinnatus Hiner** (or **Heine**) **Miller** (1837–1913). American poet. As a boy, Miller traveled west from Indiana with his impoverished family; they settled in Oregon, and, at the age of 17, Miller ran away to the California gold fields. He led an adventuresome life, mixing schoolteaching, editing, living with Indians, and establishing a pony express route between Washington and Idaho. He wrote two volumes of poetry during this period, but received no attention. Arriving in London in the early 1870's, he posed as a Westerner, wearing cowboy boots and sombrero. It is said that he smoked three cigars at once, and bit the ankles of English debutantes, thus confirming the image that the English had of American Westerners. *Songs of the Sierras* (1871), earlier published in England, was well received there. In 1873, Miller wrote a prose autobiography, *Life Among the Modocs*. Returning to California, he continued to behave in an eccentric manner. Several other volumes of poetry were published, including *Specimens* (1868), *Songs of the Sunlands* (1873), *The Danites in the Sierras* (1881), and *Complete Poetical Works* (1893). Miller's most famous poems are *Columbus* and *Kit Carson's Ride;* learned by thousands of school children, they are extravagant celebrations of the vigor of the West.

Miller, Merle (1919–). American novelist. An editor of *Yank* in World War II and later an editor of *Harper's Magazine,* Miller won critical praise for his novel *That Winter* (1948), the story of three veterans after the war. *Island 49* (1945) was an earlier war novel. He dealt with freedom of expression in the novel *The Sure Thing* (1949) and the nonfiction *The Judges and the Judged* (1952). His later works include *Reunion* (1954) and *A Gay and Melancholy Sound* (1961).

Miller, Perry [Gilbert Eddy] (1905–1963). American historian. A member of the faculty of Harvard University from 1931 until his death, Miller is best known for his two-volume analysis of *The New England Mind,* a work notable for its erudition, profundity, and wit. In the first volume, *The Seventeenth Century* (1939), he examined the origins and implications of the religious, political, and social thought of the Puritans; the sequel, *From Colony to Province* (1953), covers the period from 1657 to 1731, with emphasis on the figure of Cotton Mather. Miller also edited *Images, or, Shadows of Divine Things* (1948), a compilation of itemized manuscript notes by Jonathan Edwards. His other works include *Orthodoxy in Massachusetts* (1933); *The Raven and the Whale* (1956), a literary study of Poe and Melville; and *Errand into the Wilderness* (1956), a collection of essays.

Miller's Tale, The. One of the CANTERBURY TALES of Geoffrey CHAUCER, based on a French *fabliau.* The Host asks the Monk to follow the Knight with a tale, but the drunken Miller insists on telling a ribald story. Alison, young wife of the old carpenter John, scorns the attentions paid her by Absolon, a foppish parish clerk, but would gladly return those of Nicholas, a young scholar boarding in their house. Nicholas convinces John that a second Flood is coming, and persuades him to suspend three tubs in the attic, so that they can float away in safety. John falls asleep in his tub, and Nicholas and Alison steal down from theirs to the bedroom. Absolon begs outside for a kiss, and Alison offers her rump at the dark window. Furiously insulted, Absolon borrows a hot brand from the smithy and returns, pretending to beg a second kiss in exchange for a gold ring. For a joke, Nicholas sticks his rump out this time, and is thoroughly scorched. His cries for water awaken John, who thinks the Flood has come and cuts loose his tub; he crashes through to the ground and is thereafter considered a fool by the townsfolk.

Milles, Carl (1875–1955). Swedish sculptor. A pupil of Rodin, Milles achieves the powerful quality of his sculpture through the clarity and simplicity of his clean, strong lines. Some of his finest work, sculptured allegorical figures, may be seen at Rockefeller Center in New York City. In Stockholm and Göteborg there are fountains created by Milles. Fre-quently made of bronze, his fountains use light and water skillfully as part of the entire design.

Millet, Jean François (1814–1875). French painter. One of the leaders of the BARBIZON SCHOOL, he extended his landscapes to include scenes of peasants, whose earthy bodies express Christian resignation and the dignity of work. Among his best-known works are *The Angelus* and *The Man with the Hoe,* which inspired Edwin Markham's poem of that title.

Millin, Sarah Gertrude (1889–1968). South African novelist. She is the author of *God's Stepchildren* (1924), a tragic story of Cape colored people; *The People of Africa* (1951), a history; *Two Bucks Without Hair* (1957); and *The Wizard Bird* (1962).

Millis, Walter (1899–1968). American journalist and military historian. A former reporter for the New York *Herald Tribune,* Millis is the author of books about the Spanish-American War and World Wars I and II. His latest book is *Arms and Men: A Study of American Military History* (1956).

Mill on the Floss, The (1860). A novel by George ELIOT. The principal characters are Maggie Tulliver and her brother Tom, who grow up together at Dorlcote Mill, united by a strong bond in spite of their opposite temperaments. Maggie is loved by Philip Wakem, the deformed son of the lawyer responsible for the ruin of Maggie's father, but Tom's opposition makes the relationship impossible. Later, she falls in love with Stephen Guest, the handsome and passionate fiancé of her cousin Lucy Deane. They go off together on impulse, and although Maggie repents before it is too late, her return is misconstrued and her life is made desperately unhappy. Only death unites her with Tom; the two are drowned together in a great flood of the Floss.

Milne, A[lan] A[lexander] (1882–1956). English dramatist, novelist, and humorous journalistic writer, now best remembered for his children's books. First written for his son, CHRISTOPHER ROBIN, *Winnie-the-Pooh* (1926) and *The House at Pooh Corner* (1928) have a toy bear, POOH, as their hero. *When We Were Very Young* (1924) and *Now We Are Six* (1927) are collections of verse for children. Milne was also a successful dramatist of the 1920's. His whimsical, rather sentimental plays include THE TRUTH ABOUT BLAYDS, the comedy *Mr. Pim Passes By* (1920), and the fantasy *The Dover Road* (1923). *The Red House Mystery* (1922) is a detective story.

Milo. An athlete of Crotona. It is said that he carried a four-year-old heifer through the stadium at Olympia, and ate the whole of it afterward. When an old man, he attempted to tear an oak tree in two, but the parts closed upon his hands, and he was devoured by wolves while held fast by the tree.

Milosz, Oscar Venceslas [or Vladislas] de Lubicz (1877–1939). Lithuanian-born French poet, dramatist, diplomat. His early poetry shows the influence of symbolism and his interest in the occult: *Le Poème des décadences* (1899) and *Les Sept Solitudes* (1904). Later poetry and the plays *Miguel Mañara* (1912) and *Mephiboseth* (1914) continue to explore spiritual problems and the mystery of the universe. His metaphysics are explained in *Ars magna* (1924) and *Les Arcanes* (1926).

Miltiades (540?–489? B.C.). A tyrant of the Thracian Chersonese. As a general of the Athenian forces, he defeated the Persians at MARATHON. He later died in prison for having tricked the Athenians into giving him a large force of ships in order to settle a private grudge.

Milton (1804). A symbolic poem by William BLAKE in which the poet John Milton returns from heaven and corrects the misinterpretations given to his works on earth. Eventually he enters the spirit of Blake himself and preaches redemption and forgiveness.

Milton, John (1608–1674). English poet and prose writer, one of the best-known and most respected figures in English literature.

Milton's father, a London notary who was raised a Catholic but became a convert to the Church of England, gave his talented son the best of educations. After private tutoring, the boy entered St. Paul's School and Cambridge, then was supported through five years of independent study, and finally sent on a two-year tour of Europe to perfect his learning. During this period Milton wrote some of his most brilliant poetry, including L'ALLEGRO and IL PENSEROSO, the masque COMUS, and the splendid elegy LYCIDAS, as well as other poems in English and Latin. He returned to England before the outbreak of the Civil War, for a while conducting a sort of private school in which two of his pupils were his nephews, the writers Edward and John PHILLIPS, and supporting the Puritan cause in various tracts and pamphlets. In 1649, his reputation as a learned controversialist won him the position of Latin secretary to Cromwell, in which office he handled correspondence with foreign nations and was apologist for the Commonwealth to the world at large. In 1657, Andrew Marvell became his assistant—by 1652 his grueling work had cost Milton his eyesight. After the Restoration he was arrested and fined, but escaped imprisonment or death, probably (in part) through Marvell's intervention. Aged, blind, his public career over, his hopes for a godly and republican England dashed, Milton turned to a cherished plan of composing a great national epic and in 1667 published his masterpiece, PARADISE LOST, following it in 1671 with its sequel, *Paradise Regained,* and the fine dramatic poem SAMSON AGONISTES.

Milton was a noble and difficult man. Though he was a Puritan, morally austere and conscientious, some of his religious beliefs were unconventional to the point of heresy, and a number of his works, such as the AREOPAGITICA and the DOCTRINE AND DISCIPLINE OF DIVORCE, came into conflict with the orthodox or official Puritan stand. He was also a humanist, convinced of the high possibilities of human nature, a lover of music, literature, and the various amenities of civilized life. Milton's character was a paradoxical mixture that combined passion, sensuality, pride, and ambition with high idealism, self-discipline, self-sacrifice, and fortitude. He was least admirable in some of his personal relationships, specifically with Mary Powell, the first of his three wives, and with his three daughters to whom he showed little understanding or consideration; and in some of his controversial writings he also revealed arrogance and coarseness.

Milton's writing reflects his rich and divided nature. Perhaps the most characteristic theme of his work is "temptation"—a theme running from

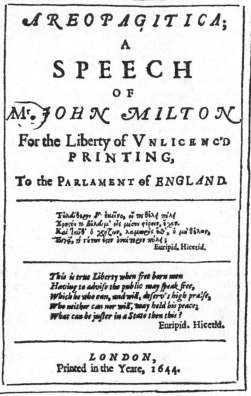

NEW YORK PUBLIC LIBRARY

Title page of Milton's *Areopagitica* (1644).

L'Allegro and Il Penseroso down to Samson Agonistes, the temptations being sensual enjoyment, pride, and passivity, all of which must be met by the resolute, God-instructed-and-supported will. His style ranges from the fresh luxuriance of such works as Comus to the force and masculinity of his great sonnets to the sonority and lofty eloquence of Paradise Lost. His prose is complex, highly rhetorical, with passages of great power.

In addition to those mentioned above, the following works of Milton are of importance: *On the Morning of Christ's Nativity* (1629); such sonnets as *When I Consider How My Light Is Spent* (*On His Blindness*), *On the Late Massacre in Piedmont, Methought I Saw My Late Espoused Saint* (all written between 1652 and 1658); and such prose writings as *Of Education* (1644), *Eikonoklastes* (1649), and *Defensio pro Publico Anglicano* (1651). See EIKON BASILIKÉ; Thomas ELLWOOD.

Mimir. The Scandinavian god of wisdom, a water demon. He was one of the most celebrated of the giants. The Vanir, with whom he was left as a hostage, cut off his head. Odin embalmed it by his magic art, pronounced over it mystic runes, and ever after consulted it on critical occasions. Mimir dwelt under the roof of Yggdrasill, where was Mimir's Well (*Mimisbrunnr*), in which all wisdom lay concealed, and from which Mimir drank with the horn Giallar. Odin gave one of his eyes to be permitted to drink of its waters, and thereby became the wisest of the gods.

Minerva. The Roman goddess of wisdom and patroness of the arts and trades, fabled to have sprung, with a tremendous battle cry, fully armed from the head of Jupiter. Remarkably similar to the Greek ATHENE, she became identified with her. She was one of the three chief deities, the others being Jupiter and Juno. She is represented as grave and majestic, clad in a helmet, with drapery over a coat of mail, bearing the aegis on her breast.

Minerva Press. A printing establishment in Leadenhall Street, London, famous in the late 18th century for its trashy, ultrasentimental novels, which were characterized by complicated plots and the labyrinths of difficulties into which the hero and heroine got involved before they could be married.

Ming. Chinese dynasty (1368–1644). A native Chinese house that replaced the Mongols of the Yüan dynasty. This era was famous for naval expeditions to Arabia and Africa and the enormous amount of printed works on all subjects which appeared. Blue and white Ming porcelain is highly esteemed.

Minister's Black Veil, The (1836). A tale by Nathaniel HAWTHORNE. Parson Hooper covers his face with a black veil, as a symbol of secret sorrow and sin. "What mortal," he asks, "might not do the same?" The emblem, separating him from friends and from happiness, is not removed even at his death.

Minister's Wooing, The (1859). A novel by Harriet Beecher STOWE. In 18th-century Newport, Mary Scudder is wooed by the orthodox minister, Samuel Hopkins. Truly in love with her cousin, James Marvyn, she will not marry him, for he has not been "saved." When James is reported dead in a shipwreck, Mary accepts the minister. She is prepared to marry him, when James returns, having found both salvation and a fortune. Hopkins releases Mary, and the book ends happily.

Miniver Cheevy (1907). A poem by Edwin Arlington ROBINSON. An ironic character sketch, it tells of Miniver and his longing for the Middle Ages, his scorn of money, although he "is sore annoyed without it," and his general feeling of having been born out of his time.

Minna von Barnhelm (1767). A comedy by Gotthold Ephraim LESSING. Major von Tellheim, because of a question of honor and military justice, refuses to marry Minna, whom he has long loved. To overcome his hesitation, Minna pretends to be poverty stricken and in dire need, whereupon Tellheim rushes to her aid. In the end, Tellheim gets both Minna and satisfaction for his honor.

Minnehaha. A Sioux word meaning waterfall, or laughing water. In Longfellow's HIAWATHA, Minnehaha is the Sioux maiden who becomes Hiawatha's bride.

Minnesingers. The lyric poets of the German courts in the 12th and 13th centuries. The **Minnesang** is by definition a song of love, although the Minnesingers also sang of religion and politics. Their poetry was greatly influenced by that of the Provençal TROUBADOURS and the tradition of COURTLY LOVE; they were succeeded by the MEISTERSINGERS. The most famous Minnesingers, usually men of the lower nobility, include Heinrich von Veldeke and

Friedrich von Hausen (12th century), then GOTTFRIED VON STRASSBURG, WALTHER VON DER VOGELWEIDE, and WOLFRAM VON ESCHENBACH. See also WARTBURG.

Minor Prophets. See PROPHET.

Minos. In Greek mythology, the king and lawgiver of Crete. At his death he became a judge in the underworld. The beginning of his reign was somewhat disturbed by the episode of the MINOTAUR, the last by the treachery of his daughter Ariadne in helping THESEUS to kill the beast and release the Greek captives. In spite of this, another daughter, Phaedra, married Theseus, who had abandoned Ariadne. Theseus lived to regret it.

Minos may well have been the name given to a dynasty of priest-kings of Crete, whose magnificent palace at Knossos has been extensively excavated and restored. He gave his name to the Minoan period, about 2500 to 1400 B.C., during which Crete was a predominant power in the Eastern Mediterranean area.

Minotaur, The. In Greek mythology, a monster with a bull's head on a human body. Poseidon sent a bull from the sea as a sign to prove MINOS' right to become king of Crete, but Minos failed to sacrifice it to him. In revenge, the god caused Minos' wife Pasiphae to conceive a passion for the bull. Aided in satisfying it by DAEDALUS, she bore the Minotaur, whose name was Asterius. It was shut up by Minos in the LABYRINTH. Every ninth year it was fed with fourteen youths and maidens, a tribute exacted from Athens, until Theseus killed it with Ariadne's aid.

In Minoan Crete, a sacred bull was regarded as the animal form of the priest-king Minos, consort of the high priestess of the Mother-goddess, Pasiphae. A version of the Minotaur story based on the discoveries of modern archaeology and anthropology is told in *The King Must Die,* a popular novel by Mary RENAULT.

Minstrel, The; or The Progress of Genius (1771). The chief poem of James BEATTIE, dealing with the growth of a young poet's mind. Edwin, under the instruction of a hermit, passes through the various dreams of youth to a survey of moral duties, and is told at length of man's cultural progress. Beattie himself, describing the poem, wrote: "It is a moral and descriptive poem, written in the stanza of Spenser, but not much in his style. The hint of the subject was taken from Percy's 'Essays on the English Minstrels.'"

Minturno, Antonio (c. 1500–1574). Italian literary critic and bishop of Ugento. His works, the *De Poeta* (1559) and *Arte poetica* (1563), shaped the thought and practice of Tasso, Ronsard, and Sidney, especially the latter's *Apologie for Poetrie* (1595).

Minuit, Peter (1580–1638). Dutch governor of New Netherland (1626–1631). He purchased Manhattan Island (1626) from the Indians for trinkets valued at 60 guilders (about $24).

Minutemen. The armed citizens or militiamen who, just prior to and during the American Revolution, agreed to be ready to fight at a minute's notice. The term is also used specifically for the militia organized in Massachusetts. The Minuteman, a statue by Daniel Chester French, stands at Concord, Mass.

Mirabeau, Comte de. Honoré Gabriel Victor Riqueti (1749–1791). French orator and revolutionary leader. In spite of his early notoriety as a pleasure-seeker, his unusual gift for oratory won him a firm and respected place in public life. One of the most important figures in the first two years of the Revolution, he advocated a limited, or constitutional, monarchy after the English model. Although his popularity died down gradually, his oratorical prowess enabled him to continue to sway the National Assembly. His death was the result of a dissolute life.

Mirabell. See WAY OF THE WORLD, THE.

Miraben. (*Sans.*, sister Mira). Name of the Rajput princess who gave up all worldly possessions to follow Krishna, the Hindu god. It became the Hindu name of Miss Madeleine Slade, daughter of the British admiral Sir Edmond Slade, when she left England in 1925 to join Gandhi. She remained in India and established a center, Gopal Ashram, to help the peasants, along the lines of Gandhi's teachings.

miracle plays or **miracles** (13th-16th centuries). Medieval dramas presenting miracles of the Virgin Mary or the saints. There are about 40 extant French miracles from the 14th century, all in octosyllabic couplets with a short prose sermon. Many of the English miracle plays were adapted from the French; there is more variation of metrical form, however. In English drama the miracle plays also include what are now usually called the MYSTERY PLAYS, and the terms are generally interchangeable. See MORALITY PLAYS; INTERLUDE.

Mira de Amescua, Antonio (1574?-1644). Spanish dramatist and priest. After serving the count of Lemos in Naples, he became archdeacon of his native Guadix in 1631. He is best known for *El esclavo del demonio,* a drama about a hermit who makes a pact with the devil but is ultimately saved through divine intervention. His other plays include *La rueda de la fortuna* and numerous *autos sacramentales.*

Miranda. The innocent daughter of Prospero in Shakespeare's THE TEMPEST. Raised without human companions, she is overcome with awe at the first men she sees:

> O, wonder!
> How many goodly creatures are there here!
> How beauteous mankind is! Oh, brave new world,
> That has such people in't!

She marries Ferdinand, son of Alonso, who is her counterpart in innocence and purity.

Miriam. (1) A Hebrew prophetess of the Old Testament, the elder sister of Moses and Aaron, who led the celebrative music and dances of the Hebrew women after Moses brought the Israelites across the Red Sea (Exod. 15:20).

(2) A mysterious, beautiful, and passionate art student in Rome in Hawthorne's *Marble Faun* (1860).

(3) A poem by John Greenleaf Whittier (1870) about a Christian maiden and her Muslim lord.

(4) In D. H. Lawrence's novel SONS AND LOVERS, the shy, intense farm girl who is the first love of Paul Morel. She also occurs in Lawrence's early poems. The character is based on the girl in Lawrence's own life who first encouraged his writing and submitted some of his early poems to Ford Madox Ford, then editor of *The English Review.* Ford published several, and handed the manuscript of Lawrence's first novel, *The White Peacock,* to Edward

Garnett, who saw to its publication. "Miriam" wrote *D. H. Lawrence, a Personal Record* (1936) under the initials E. T.

Miró [Ferrer], Gabriel (1879-1930). Spanish novelist. A delicate writer, he is best known for his treatment of religious themes, as in *Las Figuras de la pasión del Señor* (1916), *Nuestro padre San Daniel* (*Our Father, Saint Daniel,* 1921), and *El obispo leproso* (1925).

Miró, Joan (1893-   ). Spanish abstract painter. His works, notably *Harlequin's Festival* and *Composition* (1936) are full of fantasy and humor.

Mirour de l'omme. See SPECULUM MEDITANTIS.

Mirror for Magistrates, The. A work, in verse, on the fall of great men in English history, modeled after Boccaccio's *De Casibus Virorum Illustrium* and Lydgate's *Falls of Princes.* The first edition (1559) contained nineteen tragedies written by various authors; each tragedy is purportedly narrated in the first person by the ghost of its subject. The second edition added eight more tragic histories, including Thomas Churchyard's *Shore's Wife* (see Jane SHORE) and Thomas Sackville's *Induction* and *Complaint* of the duke of Buckingham. The best piece in the collection, the *Induction,* is one of the most important examples of early Elizabethan verse, and is considered to be inaugural of a new age.

The Mirror for Magistrates was avowedly of moral rather than purely literary purpose, intended to warn contemporary rulers to study tragic stories and thereby learn to avoid tragedy. It is interesting primarily

Title page of *A Mirror for Magistrates* (1st ed., 1559).

as a reflection of the new Renaissance conception of man in which not only fickle Fortune but moral flaws in a great man's character are responsible for his tragic end. The *Mirror* was very popular, and appeared in numerous editions and expansions from 1559 to 1610.

Misalliance (1910). A play by George Bernard SHAW. Almost a fantasy, *Misalliance* is one of Shaw's most loquacious plays. Its central theme is the variety of relationships between parents and their children. Hypatia Tarleton wants to get married, as she explains to her mother, not for love, but to have something happen. Her family and the family of her suitor are all present. Nothing happens, but the conversation goes on apace. The arrival on stage, via a plane crash, of a Polish lady acrobat and her handsome pilot finally moves the plot to a conclusion of sorts when Hypatia says, "Papa: buy the brute for me," meaning the pilot.

In the last scene, Mr. Tarleton says, "I suppose there's nothing more to be said." "Thank goodness," answers Hypatia. Most audiences have agreed.

Misanthrope, Le (The Misanthropist, 1666). A comedy by MOLIÈRE. The play centers on ALCESTE, who has vowed to speak and act with complete honesty and no longer to adhere to the conventions of a hypocritical society. Pursued by the pretended prude Arsinoé, unable to accept the affection of the gentle and sincere Eliante, Alceste is in love with the sharp-tongued, vain coquette Célimène, epitome of all that he despises. After losing a lawsuit in which justice was on his side, Alceste resolves to abandon society and asks Célimène to accompany him. She refuses to give up her gay life, and he departs alone, gloomy and disillusioned.

Miscellany, Poetic. See TOTTEL'S MISCELLANY.

Misérables, Les (The Miserable Ones, 1862). A novel by Victor Hugo. The central figure of the tale is the convict Jean Valjean. One of society's victims, Valjean, originally an honest peasant, stole a single loaf of bread to feed his sister's starving family and was sentenced to five years in prison at hard labor. He was caught trying to escape, and given a 19-year term on the galleys. On his release he has become a hardened criminal until he is befriended by a bishop and enabled to begin life anew. He becomes M. Madeleine, a successful industrialist and mayor of a northern French town, but, because of an impulsive, bitterly regretted former crime, he is discovered and compelled to return to prison by the implacable, ever-searching detective Javert. Escaping once again, Valjean befriends an unhappy woman of the streets, Fantine, and rescues her daughter Cosette from the abusive family with whom she has been living. The canvas of *Les Misérables* is an enormous representation of innumerable episodes and characters. Among the most famous chapters are the account of the battle of Waterloo and Valjean's flight through the Paris sewers.

Miserere. The 51st psalm (50th in the Latin numbering). It is so called because its opening words are *Miserere mei Deus* (Have mercy upon me, O God).

Mishima Yukio. Pen name of Hiraoka Kimitake (1925–1970). Japanese novelist and composer of modern *Kabuki* and *No* drama. A prolific and inventive writer, many of his works have been trans-lated into English: *Kamen no Kokuhaku (Confessions of a Mask,* 1949) and *Shiosai (Sound of Waves,* 1954), translated by Merideth Wetherby; *Five Modern No Plays* (1950–1955), translated by Donald Keene; *Kinkakuji (The Temple of the Golden Pavilion,* 1956), translated by Ivan Morris.

Mishnah (*Heb.,* "repetition"). The collection of moral precepts, traditions, and law forming the basis of the TALMUD. Compiled by Rabbi Judah I (c. 135–220), the Mishnah is divided into six parts: (1) agriculture; (2) Sabbaths, fasts, and festivals; (3) marriage and divorce; (4) civil and penal laws; (5) sacrifices; (6) holy persons and things. See GEMARA.

Misrule, Abbot or **Lord of.** See LORD OF MISRULE.

Mississippi Bubble. The SOUTH SEA BUBBLE of France (1717–1720), projected by John Law (1671–1729), a Scot. Law proposed that in return for his exclusive control of trade in Louisiana, on the banks of the Mississippi, he would assume the national debt of France. It was a notorious fiasco.

Miss Julie (1888). A long one-act play by August STRINDBERG. Described by the author as a naturalistic tragedy, the play has twin centers of conflict in the love-hate relationship of men and women and the social relationship of the upper and lower classes. Miss Julie is the daughter of a count. She has been brought up by her mother to hate men, and when, to express her contempt for them, she forced her fiancé to jump over a horsewhip at her command, the man broke the engagement. As the plays opens, Miss Julie joins in a servants' party and flirts with Jean, a footman. She seduces him and, unable to live with the conflicts this act creates in her, commits suicide.

Miss Lonelyhearts (1933). A novel by Nathanael WEST. The story of a man who writes an "advice to the lovelorn" column, the theme of the book is the loneliness of the individual in modern society. The hero tries to live the role of omniscient counselor he has assumed for the paper, but his attempts to reach out to suffering humanity are twisted by circumstances, and he is finally murdered by a man he has tried to help.

Miss Lulu Bett (1920). A short novel by Zona GALE. The heroine, a plain but not unattractive woman of 34, is disdained by her married sister's family and exploited by them as a household drudge. When her sister's brother-in-law, Ninian, arrives, Lulu Bett's salvation begins, and she shows courage, initiative, and wisdom. The author's dramatization (1921) of the novel was awarded a Pulitzer Prize.

Missouri Compromise (1820). In U.S. history, an act of Congress by which Maine was admitted into the Union as a free state, Missouri as a slave state, and slavery was barred from the territory acquired in the Louisiana Purchase north of the line 36° 30'. This act, which kept the number of free and slave states equal, was the first of numerous attempts to settle differences between the North and South. It was repealed in 1854 with the passage of the Kansas-Nebraska Act.

Miss Ravenel's Conversion from Secession to Loyalty (1867). A novel by John William DE FOREST. Dr. Ravenel, a New Orleans doctor, is forced to leave Louisiana when he refuses to support the Confederate cause; he and his daughter, Lillie, who remains loyal to the South, move to New Boston (obviously New Haven, where De Forest lived). There the Southern girl is wooed by two army officers; her marriage to the unfaithful and unstable Carter ends with his death in battle, and she finally recognizes her devotion to Colbourne. The book satirizes puritanical New England, and includes realistic battle scenes anticipating those in Stephen Crane's *Red Badge of Courage* (1895).

Miss Thompson (1921). A short story by W. Somerset MAUGHAM. The Reverend Alfred Davidson, a repressed missionary on a South Sea island during the rainy season, attempts to convert Sadie Thompson, a carefree young tart, to religion. His efforts are successful, but when he seduces her, she reverts to her former ways. Guilty and despairing, he commits suicide.

The story was dramatized as *Rain* in 1922 by John B. Colton and Clemence Randolph. Actress Jeanne Eagels scored her greatest success in the role of Sadie.

Mister. For titles beginning with *Mister*, see also under Mr.

Mister Johnson (1939). A novel by Joyce CARY. Set in Nigeria, it is the story of an African clerk called Johnson who is so imaginative that he believes in his own stories, and so is a rogue and a liar as well as a poet. He finally commits a murder and is executed.

Mister Roberts (1946). A novel by Thomas HEGGEN. It is about a popular lieutenant (j.g.) on a U.S. Navy cargo ship in World War II. The novel depicts the boredom of the men on the ship, their dislike of the captain, and their fondness for Mr. Roberts. The novel was adapted for the stage (1948) by Joshua Logan and later filmed.

Mistral, Frédéric (1830–1914). French poet, famous as a member of Le FÉLIBRIGE, an association of Provençal poets. With Roumanille, he gave new life to the language and literature of Provence. In the tongue of his native region, Mistral wrote the pastoral *Mirèio* (1859), the narrative *Lou Pouème dou Rose* (1897), and the lyrics of *Lis Isclo d'or* (1875).

Mistral, Gabriela. Pen name of **Lucila Godoy Alcayaga** (1889–1957). Chilean poet. The daughter of a rural schoolmaster who often composed songs and poems for village fiestas, Gabriela also became a teacher. Her first verses were inspired by an unhappy romance with a man who committed suicide, and in 1914 she won a poetry contest in Santiago with her *Sonetos de la muerte*, which were later included in her first collection, *Desolación* (1922). All her work is a variation on the single theme of love. Initially, she expressed her own tragic and frustrated passion; her outlook grew, however, until it encompassed all creation, particularly children and the humble and persecuted everywhere. The change is reflected in the title of her collection of songs and rounds for children, *Ternura* (1924), or "tenderness." Later she donated the proceeds of *Tala* (1938) for the relief of Basque children orphaned in the Spanish Civil War. Acclaimed as an educator as well as a poet, she received the Nobel Prize for literature in 1945.

Misunderstanding, The (Le Malentendu; 1944). A play by Albert CAMUS. Known also under the translated title *Cross Purposes*, it exposes different ways in which men and women fail to face themselves and communicate with each other in their common plight before the unresponsiveness of the universe.

Mitchell, Donald Grant. Pen name: **Ik Marvel** (1822–1908). American writer and farmer, Mitchell wrote largely for newspapers and magazines, and later wrote of his travels. His first popular book was REVERIES OF A BACHELOR, followed by a sequel, *Dream Life* (1851). He also became the first editor of "The Easy Chair" for *Harper's Magazine*. In 1852, after more time abroad, he settled at his family farm in Connecticut. The love of rural pleasures dominates his writings, among which are *Fudge Doings* (1855), *Doctor Johns* (1866), and *Rural Studies* (1867).

Mitchell, James Leslie. Pen name: **Lewis Grassic Gibbon** (1901–1935). Scottish novelist, archaeologist, and historian. Under his pen name he wrote the trilogy of novels *A Scots Quair* (1932–1934), which is regarded as a major work of Scottish literature. (*Quair* is an older form of *quire*, booklet.) The trilogy consists of *Sunset Song, Cloud Howe,* and *Grey Granite*. Mitchell collaborated with Hugh MacDiarmid on *Scottish Scene* (1934). Under his own name he published a number of popular romances, books on explorers and exploration, and *The Conquest of the Maya* (1934), a standard history of Mayan civilization. See SCOTTISH RENAISSANCE.

Mitchell, Margaret (1900–1949). American novelist. Mrs. Mitchell wrote only one book—the best-selling Civil War novel, GONE WITH THE WIND. She wrote it during a long period of hospitalization.

Mitchell, S[ilas] Weir (1829–1914). American physician and writer of historical novels. Noted as a writer of historical romances and psychological studies, he specialized in neurology as a doctor, thus combining his talent for historical narrative with his professional insight into human psychology. *Hugh Wynne: Free Quaker* (1897) is, perhaps, his best book, but he produced several other novels of value, including *Roland Blake* (1886), a story of a possessive woman set in the Civil War; *The Adventures of François* (1899); and *The Red City* (1907), a novel laid in Revolutionary Philadelphia.

Mitchison, Naomi [Margaret] (1897–   ). English writer of novels, short stories, plays, and poetry. She is also a classical scholar and political and educational reformer. Among her historical novels of ancient Greece and Rome are *The Corn King and the Spring Queen* (1931) and *The Conquered* (1923). Other books include *The Rib of the Green Umbrella* (1960), *The Young Alfred the Great* (1962), and *Memoirs of a Space Woman* (1962).

Mitford, Mary Russell (1787–1855). English novelist and dramatist. Her magazine sketches of country life, collected as *Our Village* (5 vols., 1824–1832), are notable for their continuing freshness, sympathetic humor, and naturalism. Of her plays, *Foscari* (1826) and *Rienzi* (1828) were the most successful. She also wrote a novel, *Atherton* (1854); several volumes of reminiscence, *Recollections of a Literary Life* (1852); and a number of collections of poetry and children's stories.

Mitford, Nancy (1904–   ). English author. Her witty and ironic satirical novels include *Pursuit of Love* (1945), *Love in a Cold Climate* (1949), *The Blessing* (1951), and *Don't Tell Alfred* (1961).

She edited *Noblesse Oblige: an enquiry into the identifiable characteristics of the English aristocracy* (1956) and popularized the terms U (upper class) and Non-U.

Mithras or **Mithra.** A Persian god. Probably ancient, his cult was little known west of Assyria until the first century B.C. As Rome extended its rule into Asia, the cult became very popular, especially with Asian traders and mercenaries in the Roman army. It soon came into favor with the Roman emperors, and was the principal rival of Christianity until the time of Constantine. It did not wholly disappear in the Near East until the domination of Islam.

In spite of the wide popularity of Mithraism, there is no record of the actual myth attributed to the god. This is probably due to the fact that it was a mystery religion whose secrets were as well kept by its initiates as those of the Eleusinian mysteries. The very little that is known of Mithras himself has been deduced from the many extant icons. Most of these represent the young god sacrificing the sacred bull, often in the presence of the sun-god. The strong rivalry of Mithraism with Christianity resulted in part from the striking resemblance of a number of their rituals. Both involve shepherds, a flood escaped in an ark, and a communion service. These factors point to the remarkable uniformity of mythological themes throughout the Near East.

Mithridate (Mithridates, 1673). A tragedy by Jean RACINE. Drawn loosely from Roman history, it centers around Mithridate, the aged enemy of Rome, who is betrothed to the young Greek girl Monime. When he is reported dead in battle, his son Pharnaces attempts to force Monime into marriage. Monime begs Xiphares, Mithridate's second son, to protect her. When Mithridate returns alive to learn of Pharnaces' act, he orders his son to marry the princess of Parthia. Pharnaces refuses, is arrested, and reveals that Xiphares also loves Monime. Mithridate discovers that Monime returns Xiphares' love, and, when Pharnaces leads a Roman attack against him, he orders Monime to poison herself and, believing defeat imminent, stabs himself. Xiphares routs his treacherous half brother and the Romans, and, before dying, Mithridate bestows his blessing and his betrothed on his loyal son.

Mithridates. King of Pontus (120–63 B.C.). To guard against being poisoned by his enemies, he so accustomed his system to poisons of various sorts that when, on being conquered by the Romans, he wished to end his life by this means it was impossible for him to do so. For this reason, an antidote against poison is called a mithridate.

Mitra, Premendra (1904–   ). Bengali poet and novelist. He is also known for his children's stories and as a magazine editor. He received the Rabindra Prize for *Sagar Theke Phera,* poems, and the Padma Sri, a high government honor, in 1961.

M'liss (1863–64). A novella by Bret HARTE. It is the story of a neglected child among the rough characters in a mining camp, during the days of the gold rush.

Mnemosyne. Goddess of memory and mother by Zeus of the nine MUSES of Greek mythology. She was the daughter of Heaven and Earth (Uranus and Ge). A mere personification of memory, she was not worshiped.

Moby Dick, or The White Whale (1851). A novel by Herman MELVILLE. A story of whaling as well as being a profound symbolic study of good and evil, the book was almost forgotten at the time of its author's death.

Moby Dick, the great white whale, is pursued by the monomaniacal Captain Ahab, whose ivory leg is testimony to their last encounter. The crew of Ahab's ship, the *Pequod,* is composed of a mixture of races and religions, including the God-fearing mate Starbuck; three primitive harpooners, Queequeg, Daggoo, and Tashtego; the Negro cabin boy, Pip; and the fire-worshiping Parsee.

The whale, perhaps representing knowledge of reality, is hunted by Ahab at the cost of his own dehumanization and the sacrifice of his crew. It seems to be a sacrilegious quest, and only Ishmael, who does not share the greed and pride of most of the others, is saved. He is borne up out of the vortex of the sinking ship on the coffin prepared by his friend Queequeg. Sustained by a belief in love and human solidarity, he alone remained to tell the tale. Ahab, determined to pierce the "pasteboard masks" of this world to glimpse reality, is tied to the whale by his harpoon line, and continues his pursuit even in death.

Mock Turtle. A character in Lewis Carroll's ALICE'S ADVENTURES IN WONDERLAND. The Mock Turtle, who is always weeping, shows Alice how to dance the Lobster Quadrille. His conversation consists largely of puns and ingenious plays on words, and he himself is "the thing mock turtle soup is made from." The original illustrator of the book, John TENNIEL, accordingly gave the Mock Turtle the head, tail, and hooves of a calf.

Modern Chivalry. A once widely popular satirical novel by Hugh Henry BRACKENRIDGE, published in parts between 1792 and 1805 and reissued with final additions in 1815. It is a sort of American *Don Quixote* in which the hero, Captain Farrago, and his man Teague O'Regan leave Pennsylvania to travel about and "observe human nature," meanwhile drawing an unflattering picture of manners in the early republic. The novel satirizes primarily the rule of political upstarts, of whom the scalawag Teague is chief. In Part II, when Farrago becomes governor of a backwoods community, the settlers are persuaded to give the vote to beasts as well as men and to make use of a monkey clerk and a hound lawyer. "The great moral of this book," Brackenridge concludes, "is the evil of men seeking office for which they are not qualified."

Modern Instance, A (1882). A novel by William Dean HOWELLS. Bartley Hubbard, a shrewd young journalist, marries the passionate Marcia Gaylord, against the wishes of her father. The story begins in Equity, Maine, but Bartley and his wife soon leave for Boston. Working as a free-lance writer, the self-indulgent Bartley progressively disintegrates morally; Marcia's fierce possessiveness adds to the strain of their relationship. Deserting his wife and child, Bartley is not heard from in two years. When he tries to procure a divorce in an Indiana court, his attempt is frustrated by Marcia's enraged father; Squire Gaylord gains the decree in his daughter's favor, dying in the law court. Bartley, later shot in a brawl, dies in a Western town; Marcia and her child return to the East, where Ben Halleck, who has always loved her, debates the morality of marrying a divorced woman.

The book was considered daring on its publication for its open handling of the problem of divorce.

modernismo or modernism. A literary movement that arose in Spanish America in the late 19th century and was subsequently transmitted to Spain. In their quest for pure poetry, the modernists displayed a dazzling verbal virtuosity and technical perfection that revolutionized Spanish literature.

According to some critics, the publication of José Martí's *Ismaelillo* (1882) marks the beginning of the movement. Others assert that, while Martí exerted enormous influence on Spanish-American writing and thought, his poetry is so individual that he cannot be considered even a precursor of modernism. There is no disagreement, however, as to the dominant role of Rubén Darío, whose work defined and stimulated modernism in America and in Spain. The publication of his *Azul* (1888) is sometimes said to signify the birth of modernism, and *Prosas profanas* (1896) is held to show modernism at its zenith. Other early modernist poets (often considered precursors of the movement) were Manuel Gutiérrez Nájera, José Asunción Silva, and Julián Casal (1863–1893), the Cuban. Modernists of the later, or post-1896, phase include Leopoldo Lugones, José Enrique Rodó, Julio Herrera y Reissig, José Santos Chocano, Amado Nervo, and Rufino Blanco Fombona.

In rebellion against romanticism, from which, however, they were not always able to free themselves, the modernists drew their initial inspiration and technique from European, particularly French, sources. From French Parnassians and symbolists, such as Gautier, Coppée, and Verlaine, came their pessimism and melancholy, their belief in "art for art's sake," their zeal for technical excellence and musicality, their love of exotic imagery and a vocabulary in which swans (one of Darío's favorite symbols), peacocks, gems, and palaces abound. Another distinctive characteristic of the modernists was their unceasing experimentation with old and new verse forms. In their desire to escape from the sordidness of reality, the early modernists usually shunned political and native themes. Their successors, however, inspired no doubt by the impassioned verses that Darío hurled at Theodore Roosevelt and his ode to Argentina, turned increasingly to American subjects, as exemplified by Chocano's *Alma América* (1906). In prose writing, particularly the essay, modernism fostered a new simplicity and elegance, the finest examples of which are to be found in the works of Rodó.

Modern Love (1862). A sequence of 50 poems by George Meredith. Containing 16 lines each, they present the various thoughts and emotions of a married couple who perceive that their love for each other is dying, the husband occasionally speaking in the first person. The sequence is considered to have been based on Meredith's own difficulties in his unfortunate first marriage with Mary Ellen Nicolls.

Modern Painters (5 vols., 1843–1860). A critical treatise on painting by John Ruskin. The purpose of the first volume, which concentrated almost exclusively on landscape painting, was to prove the superiority of contemporary artists, especially Turner, over the old masters. Its brilliant style and original ideas established his reputation as an art critic. The four succeeding volumes cover a far wider area and expound Ruskin's views on the principles of true art in general.

Modest Proposal, A (1729). The shortened title of *A Modest Proposal for Preventing the Children of the Poor People in Ireland from being a Burden to their Parents or Country; and for making them beneficial to their Publick,* a pamphlet by Jonathan Swift. The pamphlet, which is a masterpiece of bitterness and irony, turns the tables on a favorite theory of contemporary Whig economists: that people are the real wealth of a nation. The terrible suffering in Ireland is revealed in the mocking suggestion that the poor should devote themselves to rearing children to be killed and sold for eating. Swift gives recipes and six advantages of his proposal.

Mogg Megone (1835). A long narrative poem by John Greenleaf Whittier. Intended as a framework for a series of New England sketches, the story is melodramatic, a tale of seduction and murder. Mogg Megone, an Indian sachem, is killed by a white girl named Ruth Bonython. The poem includes an indictment of war.

Mogul Empire. The Muslim-Tartar Empire in India. It began in 1526 with Baber, great-grandson of Timur, or Tamerlane, and split up after the death of Aurangzeb in 1707, the power passing to the British and the Mahrattas. The emperor was known as the *Great* or *Grand Mogul;* besides those mentioned, Akbar, Jahangir, and Shah Jehan are the most noteworthy.

Mohammed. See Muhammad.

Mohism. See Mo Tzu.

Moïra (1950). A novel by Julien Green. The hero Joseph Day, obsessed by puritanism, can see physical love only as sinful. His revulsion, linked to a compulsive interest, causes him to commit a crime and to destroy his life.

Moley, Raymond (1886–   ). American journalist and educator. Appointed assistant secretary of state (1933) by President Franklin D. Roosevelt and a member of the so-called brain trust, Moley described the inner workings of the administration in *After Seven Years* (1939). From 1928 to 1954 he was professor of public law at Columbia University and in 1937 became a contributing editor of *Newsweek*.

Molière. Pen name of **Jean Baptiste Poquelin** (1622–1673). French comic dramatist. Born in Paris, son of an upholsterer who served the royal household of Louis XIV, Molière received his education under the Jesuits at the Collège de Clermont. In 1643 he became an actor and cofounder of the *Illustre Théâtre,* for which he wrote his first plays, notable among them L'Etourdi, and *Le Dépit Amoureux* (*The Amorous Vexation,* 1659). Initially unsuccessful in Paris, the company toured the provinces from 1645 to 1658, returning to the capital when the king granted it a theater in the Louvre, the Théâtre du Petit-Bourbon. The playwright's first success in Paris was also his first comedy of manners, Les Précieuses Ridicules, a one-act prose satire on the affectation and absurd pretension displayed by members of such refined salons as the Hôtel de Rambouillet. Enormously popular, the play was followed by Sganarelle, a one-act comedy in verse. The company moved to the Palais Royal the following year. *Dom*

Garcie de Navarre (1661), its first production in its new home, was a failure. In the same year Molière completed *L'Ecole des Maris* (*The School for Husbands;* see SGANARELLE (2)) and the first of his many COMÉDIE-BALLETS, LES FÂCHEUX. Presented to the king during a sumptuous entertainment at his country mansion, *Les Fâcheux* met with a delighted reception, won Molière a pension, and marked the beginning of the playwright's years as a royal favorite. A marriage to Armande Béjart, in 1662, proved unhappy and probably provided the embittering experience that led to the writing of one of Molière's masterpieces, LE MISANTHROPE. L'ECOLE DES FEMMES revealed a psychological penetration unprecedented in the comic theater of the period, but the author's unsparing power of ridicule attracted the attention of disgruntled clergymen, courtiers, physicians, and rival dramatists—all victims of Molière's merciless wit— and Boileau and the king himself were forced to defend Molière against attacks. The *Critique de l'Ecole des Femmes* (*Criticism of The School for Wives*) and the *Impromptu de Versailles* (both 1663) constituted Molière's own reply to his critics and enemies, followed in 1664 by *Le Mariage Forcé* (*The Forced Marriage;* see SGANARELLE (3)) and *La Princesse d'Élide.* A three-act version of LE TARTUFFE produced the same year aroused clerical opposition and the play was forbidden until 1667 when, presented as *L'Imposteur* (*The Impostor*), it received a second interdiction. The ban was finally lifted in 1669, and *Le Tartuffe* enjoyed its deserved popularity and established itself as one of Molière's greatest comic achievements. Because of continuing attacks, DOM JUAN OU LE FESTIN DE PIERRE had to be taken out of the repertory, and with L'AMOUR MÉDECIN, LE MÉDECIN MALGRÉ LUI, and *Mélicerte, Pastorale Comique,* and *Le Sicilien* (all written in the winter of 1666–1667) the company passed through a period of financial hardship. AMPHITRYON was a success, and the company enjoyed a degree of good fortune for five years with L'AVARE, *George Dandin* (1668), *Monsieur de Pourceaugnac* (1669), LE BOURGEOIS GENTILHOMME, LES AMANTS MAGNIFIQUES, *Psyché* (1671), on which Molière collaborated, *Les Fourberies de* SCAPIN (*The Rogueries of Scapin,* 1671), *La Comtesse d'Escarbagnas* (1671), and LES FEMMES SAVANTES. After taking the part of Argan in the fourth performance of his last comedy LE MALADE IMAGINAIRE, Molière collapsed from a sudden and severe hemorrhage and died the same day. At the insistence of the clergy he was denied holy burial.

Sometimes called the father of modern French comedy, Molière rejected the Italianate farces and comedies of intrigue dear to his predecessors, for his was a theater relying on sound observation of the foibles and complexities of human nature and on an incomparable skill in humorous presentation. Actor and director, as well as author, Molière could boast a total command of his art; few playwrights can equal his understanding of dramatic construction and effect his sparkling verse or comic strength. His virtuosity ranged from the most buffoonish farce, full of gaiety and absurdity, to the highest comedy, where the subtlety of his observation rivals many tragedians'. Molière's masterpieces are those plays in which, attacking hypocrisy and vice, he created characters that have become immortal types. His gallery of peasants,

noblemen, servants, and bourgeois offers not only an astonishingly wide view of 17th-century French society but also a telling moral: the wise man is he who observes moderation and remains within the bounds that good sense imposes on nature. Though many of the episodes and plots of his plays are borrowed, though—unlike Shakespeare—he dealt mainly in types rather than in individuals, and despite his occasionally arbitrary denouements and the faults of style inevitable in hasty writing, Molière's work triumphs over its weaknesses; a laughing yet compelling advocate of all that is natural and reasonable in man and an enemy of all that is false and pretentious, Molière remains to this day without rival in the comic exposition of human character.

Molinet, Jean. See RHÉTORIOUEURS, LES GRANDS.

Molinos, Miguel. See QUIETISM.

Moll Flanders (1722). The heroine and shortened title of *The Fortunes and Misfortunes of the Famous Moll Flanders, &c. who was Born at Newgate, and during a Life of continued Variety for Threescore Years, besides her Childhood, was Twelve Year a Whore, five time a Wife (whereof once to her own Brother), Twelve Year a Thief, Eight Year a Transported Felon in Virginia, at last grew rich, liv'd Honest, and died a Penitent. Written from her own Memorandums,* a PICARESQUE novel by Daniel DEFOE written in the form of an autobiographical memoir. The extraordinary title-page gives one aspect of the novel—the providential escape of Moll from a continued course of wickedness—but it gives little idea of Defoe's sympathetic realism; it is one of the earliest social novels in English.

Molloch, May, or **The Maid of the Hairy Arms.** An elf of folklore. She mingles in ordinary sports, and will even direct the master of the house how to play dominoes or draughts. Like the White Lady of Avenel, May Molloch is a sort of Banshee.

Molloy (1951). A novel by Samuel BECKETT. The first part is the story of a disintegrating old cripple's odyssey to reach his mother before he dies. The second part is an account of a search for him by the bullying petty official Moran and his young son; they are acting on the instructions of a Kafkaesque higher authority. None of them reaches his goal. The novel is a bitter, comic rendering of man's despairing condition and his quest for better things. It is linked to MALONE DIES and THE UNNAMABLE.

Molly Maguires. The members of an Irish secret society, organized in 1843. Stout, active young Irishmen dressed up in women's clothes, blackened their faces, and otherwise disguised themselves to surprise those employed to enforce the payment of rents. Their victims were ducked in bogholes, and many were beaten unmercifully.

From about 1854 to 1877, the members of a similar secret society in the mining districts of Pennsylvania were known by this name. They figure in Sir Arthur Conan Doyle's *The Valley of Fear* (1915), a long Sherlock Holmes story.

Molly Mog (1699–1766). An innkeeper's daughter who became the most celebrated beauty and toast of London in the first half of the 18th century. John Gay wrote a ballad to Molly entitled *Fair Maid of the Inn.*

Molly Pitcher. See Mary McCAULEY.

Molnár, Ferenc (1878–1952). Hungarian playwright. A native of Budapest, he was a war correspondent on the Austro-Hungarian front (1914–1918). His plays, many of which have been successfully produced in the U.S., are usually comedies, civilized in outlook, ingenious in theme and plot. They include *The Devil* (1907), LILIOM, *The Guardsman* (1910), *The Swan* (1920), *The Play's the Thing* (1925), *The Good Fairy* (1930), and *No Greater Glory* (1934). He is also the author of several novels, of which *The Paul Street Boys* (1907) is the best known.

Moloch or **Molech.** A title, "the king," for a Canaanite baal. He was propitiated with the sacrifice of first-born children, who were killed and burned in the "high places." The Hebrew prophets inveighed against his widespread worship among the Israelites, some aspects of which seem to have been frequently applied to the worship of Yahweh.

Moltke, Count Helmuth Karl Bernhard von (1800–1891). Chief of staff of Prussia (1861–1891) and the German Empire (1871–1891). He helped Bismarck to reorganize the army and directed the military campaign of the Franco-Prussian War (1870).

Moltke, Helmuth von (1848–1916). Chief of the German General Staff (1906–1914). Because of his hesitant attack and subsequent retreat in the battle of the Marne (1914), he was replaced by Falkenhayn. Nephew of Count von MOLTKE.

moly. A mythical herb. It was given, according to Homer's ODYSSEY, by Hermes to Odysseus as an antidote against the sorceries of Circe, who had turned his crew into swine.

Molza, Francesco Maria (1489–1544). Italian poet. Modenese by birth, he spent most of his literary life at Rome, which inspired his best-known work, *La ninfa Tiberina* (*The Nymph of the Tiber*), a pastoral poem in octaves.

Mommsen, Theodor (1817–1903). German historian. His best-known work is his unfinished *Roman History* (*Römische Geschichte;* 1854–1856); it is particularly notable for its admiring portrayal of Julius Caesar, whom Mommsen described as "the complete and perfect man," and for its aura of contemporaneity. He won the Nobel Prize for literature in 1902.

Mommur. The capital of the empire of Oberon, king of the fairies. It is here that he is said to have held his court.

Momus (**Momos**). The sleepy god of the Greeks, son of Nyx (Night). He was always railing and carping. Being asked to pass judgment on the relative merits of Poseidon, Hephaestus, and Athene, Momus railed at them all. He said the horns of a bull ought to have been placed in the shoulders, where they would have been of much greater force; as for man, he said Zeus ought to have made him with a window in his breast, whereby his real thoughts might be revealed.

Monaco, Lorenzo (c. 1370–c. 1425). Italian painter. Sienese by birth but Florentine by training, he was the master of Fra Angelico and Fra Lippo Lippi, both like himself members of the clergy. The style of the easel pictures he painted is characterized by exquisite color, graceful line, and tender feeling. As a Dominican friar he naturally painted religious subjects exclusively, his best known being *The Meet-*

ing at the Golden Gate in the Church of the Holy Trinity at Florence.

monad. See Gottfried Wilhelm LEIBNIZ.

Mona Lisa. See GIOCONDA, LA.

Monastery, The (1820). A novel by Sir Walter SCOTT set in the reign of Queen Elizabeth, in which the supernatural White Lady of the Avenels appears.

Mondrian, Piet[er Cornelis] (1872–1945). Dutch painter, a leader of the STIJL school. Influenced by cubism, he continued to investigate abstraction, limiting his compositions until he reduced them to a play of horizontal and vertical lines on a light background, with only a few areas of solid, primary color.

Monet, Claude (1840–1926). French painter. As Monet is one of the founders and leading representatives of IMPRESSIONISM, it is fitting that his view of Le Havre entitled *Impression, Sunrise,* which was rejected for the Salon of 1863, should have given its name to the movement. Today Monet is regarded as one of the greatest of all landscape painters; his luminous landscapes in which water adds a frequent note, as in his treatment of Venice and of the sea, are noted for their use of light, Monet's great interest and forte. In 1891, he painted haystacks in a series of studies observing the effects of light at different times of the day and under varying conditions. He continued this experimentation in his paintings of Rouen Cathedral; in these works form is transmuted by dazzling light or mist into a new poetic harmony. His no less beautiful, later paintings of *Water Lilies,* which concentrate upon the reflection of light and color as perceived through water, may be viewed from a purely abstract point of view.

Monikins, The (1835). A social satire by James Fenimore COOPER. The monikins of the title are monkeys whose homes are in the polar regions. They persuade Noah Poke, a Connecticut sea captain, and Sir John Goldencalf to accompany them on a visit to their countries. Three monikin lands are visited, which obviously represent the U.S., France, and England; they are all treated in a bitterly sarcastic way. A lengthy book, *The Monikins* has never found an audience.

Monime. The young Greek girl beloved by the aged Mithridate, in Jean Racine's tragedy MITHRIDATE.

Monk, The (1795). Best-known, shortened title of *Ambrosio, or the Monk,* a GOTHIC novel by Matthew Gregory LEWIS. Ambrosio, abbot of the Capuchins at Madrid, is renowned for his holy life. Matilda, a young noblewoman, is so smitten by his eloquence that she enters the abbey, disguised as a monk. Her passion, however, soon discloses itself; Ambrosio succumbs, and goes from crime to crime, until he is discovered and condemned to death by the Inquisition. Supposedly following the example of Matilda (who is actually a demon in disguise), he now bargains with Lucifer for release. The Devil, as usual, barely performs his part by "releasing" Ambrosio in a desert waste. Ambrosio enrages him by a gesture of repentance, and the Devil dashes him to pieces against the rocks.

Monker and **Nakir.** Two black angels in Muslim mythology who interrogate the dead after burial, inquiring the name of their Lord and prophet. Their voices are like thunder, their aspects hideous. If the scrutiny is satisfactory, the soul is gently drawn from the lips of the body; otherwise, the body is beaten by flaming iron clubs and the soul is wrenched forth by racking torments.

Monkey. See Hsi Yü Chi.

Monk Lewis. See Matthew Gregory Lewis.

Monk's Tale, The. One of the Canterbury Tales of Geoffrey Chaucer. In the *Prologue* the Host complains that his wife is not more like Prudence in the tale of *Melibee;* then he asks a merry tale of the Monk, jokingly lamenting that such a virile-looking man is forbidden procreation. The Monk says he can tell a hundred tragedies "of the falls of illustrious men." He tells 17 tragedies in eight-line stanzas, written about 1374 (before the *Canterbury Tales* were begun), except for the account of Bernabo of Milan, murdered by his nephew in 1385, and possibly the accounts of Ugolino, Pedro of Spain, and Pedro of Cyprus. Besides these "modern instances" of the reverses of Fortune, there are examples taken from the Bible, mythology, and history: Lucifer, Adam, Samson, Heracles, Nebuchadnezzar, Belshazzar, Zenobia of Palmyra, Nero, Holofernes, Antiochus of Syria, Alexander the Great, Julius Caesar, Croesus of Lydia. In the *Prologue* to the Nun's Priest's Tale the Knight interrupts the Monk, complaining of the "heavyness" of so much woe, and wishing to hear about a rise to prosperity for a change.

Monluc, Blaise de (1502?–1577). French memorialist and marshal of France. His *Commentaires* (1592), which Henry IV called the "soldier's Bible," are written in a crude, spontaneous style. They reveal him as a man of action, cold-blooded and ruthless, and provide a valuable eye-witness report of a turbulent period.

Monmouth, duke of. James Scott (1649–1685). Claimant to the throne of England. Known also by the names of James Fitzroy, James Crofts, and "the Protestant Duke," he was the natural son of Charles II, who named him duke of Monmouth in 1663. His religion, his clemency to the Scottish Covenanters, whom he defeated at Bothwell Bridge, as well as a persistent rumor that his mother had been secretly married to Charles led some Protestants to urge that he be named heir to the throne in place of James II, the king's brother, whose Roman Catholic sympathies were well known. After the death of Charles, he led the unsuccessful uprising against James which is known as Monmouth's Rebellion, but he was defeated at Sedgemoor and beheaded. He is the Absalom of Dryden's Absalom and Achitophel. See Bloody Assizes.

Monmouth's Rebellion. See Duke of Monmouth.

Monocle de Mon Oncle, Le (1923). A poem in 12 sections by Wallace Stevens. A dramatic monologue, the poem has been interpreted both as a commentary on the inspiration of youth and the sadness of age and as a celebration of "the faith of forty," an affirmation of the imagination of middle age as opposed to the invalid fancy of youth.

Monodante. In the Boiardo poem, Orlando Innamorato, an old king of India, father of Ziliante, Brandimarte, and Orrigille. Orlando rescues his son Ziliante from the witch Morgana and restores him to his father.

monometer. In prosody, a line of verse containing one metrical foot. This may be in any meter, usually identified together with the name of the meter, as iambic monometer, trochaic monometer, etc.

monosyllabic foot. In English prosody, a foot in accent meter composed of a pause and an accented syllable, or an accented syllable followed by a pause. An example is

o LONG/ (pause) LONG/ will the LA/dies STAND

from the ancient Scottish ballad *Sir Patrick Spens.*

Monro, Harold (1879–1932). English poet and critic. Associated with the Georgians, he is best remembered for founding and running the Poetry Bookshop, and for his work as an editor. He generously encouraged younger poets.

Monroe, Harriet (1860–1936). American editor and poet. Born in Chicago, she was chiefly known for founding and editing Poetry: A Magazine of Verse. This magazine, which is still published, became immensely influential among American poets. With Alice Corbin Henderson, Miss Monroe edited the anthology *The New Poetry* (1917). Her own poetry was collected in *Valeria and Other Poems* (1892), *You and I* (1914), and *Chosen Poems* (1935). The *Passing Show* (1903) consists of five verse plays.

Monroe Doctrine. A statement of U.S. foreign policy first presented to Congress by President James Monroe (1758–1831) in 1823. The presidential message resulted from a suggestion by George Canning, foreign secretary of Great Britain, that his country and the U.S. issue a joint declaration warning the quadruple Alliance not to attempt the restoration of Spanish rule in the newly independent republics of South America. At the urging of Secretary of State John Quincy Adams, who did not want the U.S. "to come in as a cockboat in the wake of the British man-of-war," Monroe and the Cabinet decided on a unilateral statement. Scholars still disagree as to Adams' precise role in the wording of the doctrine though he is often regarded as its chief architect. Monroe's statement declared in part that the U.S. would not permit Europe to extend its political system to the Western Hemisphere and that it would not interfere with existing European colonies in America or in the internal affairs of Europe.

Monsarrat, Nicholas (1910–   ). English novelist, author of *The Cruel Sea* (1951), a best-selling novel about naval combat in World War II. He also wrote *The Story of Esther Costello* (1953), *The Tribe That Lost Its Head* (1956), and *Smith and Jones* (1963).

Monsieur Beaucaire (1900). A novelette by Booth Tarkington. A French duke in the days of Louis XV, seeking adventure, goes to England as a barber in order to find just the right bride. He falls in love with the beautiful Lady Mary Carlisle, but eventually returns to France to marry his cousin.

Monsieur Ouine (1946). A novel by Georges Bernanos. A bitter, unhappy study of the anguish of modern man, *Monsieur Ouine* has as its hero a man who comes to loathe his own flesh and to feel tormented scorn for all mankind.

Monsieur Teste (1947). A fictional sketch by Paul Valéry. *An Evening with Mr. Teste (Une Soirée avec Monsieur Teste;* 1896) was the first sketch of a character who represents pure consciousness or mind (*teste* derives both from the old form of the French *tête,* meaning "head," and from the Latin *testis,* meaning "witness"). *A Letter from Mme Emilie Teste* (*Lettre d'Emilie Teste;* 1924) added the character of his wife who, representing soul and sensibility, attempts to describe the way their marriage works. Valéry later added other letters, dialogues, sketches, and diary excerpts to present Teste from other angles.

Monstre Gai. See HUMAN AGE, THE.

Montagu, Mrs. **Elizabeth** (1720–1800). English author and BLUESTOCKING, known as "the queen of the blues." She was the author of a sensational defense of Shakespeare against Voltaire in her *Essay on the Writings and Genius of Shakespeare* (1769).

Montagu, Lady **Mary Wortley** (1689–1762). English BLUESTOCKING, best known for her lively and amusing letters published in *Turkish Letters* (1763), and *Letters and Works* (1837). Her other works include *Town Eclogues* (1716) and *Court Poems by a Lady of Quality* (1716). She introduced small-pox inoculation into England on her return from Constantinople, where her husband had been am-bassador. She was the cousin and early patroness of Henry Fielding, and a close friend of Alexander Pope until their bitter quarrel of 1727–1728. Pope, in his MORAL ESSAYS, satirized her notorious slovenli-ness in the character of "Sappho."

Montague. See CAPULET AND MONTAGUE.

Montague, C[harles] E[dward] (1867–1928). English essayist, novelist, short-story writer, and journalist. His most important work reflects his com-bat experience in World War I. Montague attacks militarism and romantic patriotism in *Disenchant-ment* (1922), a mixture of essay and autobiography, and in the novels *Rough Justice* (1926) and *Right Off the Map* (1927). *A Writer's Notes on his Trade* (1930) is a collection of essays on prose style. C. E. Montague was noted as chief editorial writer and theater critic of the *Manchester Guardian.*

Montaigne, Michel [Eyquem] de (1533–1592). French moralist and creator of the personal essay. His father, kindled by the enthusiasms of the Renais-sance, hired a tutor who spoke only Latin to Mon-taigne until he was six and had him awakened every morning by music. He became a counselor in the Bordeaux *Parlement,* where he met Etienne de la Boétie, a young judge who encouraged his interest in philosophy and whose death affected him deeply. In 1571 he retired to his château in Dordogne and devoted himself to reading and writing until 1580, when he published the first two books of his ESSAYS. After a trip through Switzerland, Germany, and Italy, partly in search of treatment for gall stones, he served two terms as mayor of Bordeaux. As a re-sult of an outbreak of the plague, he and his family spent six months wandering through the countryside, an experience which he described in the third book of *Essays.*

Montale, Eugenio (1896–   ). Italian poet. His verse expresses a deeply pessimistic view of man and nature and is strongly reminiscent of the work of Leopardi. *Ossi di Seppia* (1925), *Le Occasioni* (1949), and *La Bufera e Altro* (1957) are songbooks of collected poems, Among his other works are a "notebook" of translations, *Quaderno di Traduzioni*

(1948), and a prose composition, *La Farfalla di Dinard* (1960). See HERMETICISM.

Montalembert, Comte **de. Charles Forbes** (1810–1870). French journalist and politician. With Lamennais, he founded the journal *L'Avenir* (1830) in which he upheld the interests of the Roman Catholic Church and the clergy. In the days of the Second Empire, Montalembert published his *Des Intérêts Catholiques au XIX⁰ Siècle* (1852) and *L'Eglise Libre dans l'Etat Libre* (1863), both works strongly supporting Roman Catholicism.

Montalvo, Juan (1832–1889). Ecuadorian essay-ist. A bitter foe of tyranny, Montalvo attacked Ecua-dorian dictator Gabriel García Moreno in the pages of his journal *El Cosmopolita.* When he heard of García Moreno's assassination, he declared, "My pen has killed him!" His savage polemical essays, the *Catilinarias* (1880), were directed against a new dictatorship and contributed to his being banished from Ecuador. His best known work, *Siete tratados* (1882), consists of seven treatises on moral and literary subjects, including a famous comparison be-tween Washington and Bolívar. He also wrote *Capítulos que se le olvidaron a Cervantes* (1895), a successful imitation of Cervantes. Montalvo is not considered a profound or original thinker and is esteemed today largely because of the fecundity and vigor of his style.

Montano. In Shakespeare's OTHELLO, an official in the government of Cyprus. He is wounded by Cassio in a drunken brawl.

Montargis, Dog of. A dog named Dragon in French legend. He belonged to Aubrey de Mondidier, who was murdered by the villain Richard de MACAIRE in 1371 near the castle of Montargis. Dragon's be-havior drew suspicion on Macaire, and the king ordered a trial by combat between man and dog. Dragon defeated Macaire, who confessed. Guilbert de Pixérécourt (1773–1844) dramatized the tale as *Le Chien de Montargis* (1814).

Montauran, Marquis de. The hero of Balzac's novel LES CHOUANS, leader of royalist peasant insur-rectionists at the time of the French Revolution.

Montchrétien, Antoine de (c. 1575–1621). French playwright and economist. Monchrétien's tragedies—*Sophonisbe* (1596), *La Reine d'Ecosse* (*The Queen of Scotland*), *Les Lacènes, David, Aman* (all published in 1601), and *Hector* (1604), written in his youth—were derived from biblical, classical, and historical sources and retained the device of the chorus as a means of achieving extended lyric inter-ludes. In 1615 the versatile Montchrétien wrote the *Traité de l'économie politique* (*Treatise on Political Economy*), a work which is credited with giving the new science its name and which, though of pro-tectionist tendency but free-trade aspirations, had enormous influence upon the policies of Richelieu and Colbert.

Monte Cristo, Count of. See COUNT OF MONTE CRISTO.

Montefeltro, Federico da. Duke of Urbino (1422–1482). Italian nobleman. Captain general of the Church, he was famous for his political wisdom and his patronage of learning and the arts. The palace he built in his city state became one of the great courts of the Renaissance, a magnet for the illustrious and the talented men of his day. During the reign of his son Guidobaldo, the continuing splendor of the court was captured by Castiglione, who made it the physical and spiritual setting of THE COURTIER.

Montefeltro, Guidobaldo da (1472–1508). Italian nobleman. Son of Federico and duke of Urbino, he married Elisabetta Gonzaga, who maintained his splendid court while he was ill. He is affectionately recalled by Castiglione in THE COURTIER, which is set in 1507 at the ducal court.

Montesinos. One of Charlemagne's PALADINS in medieval romance. Receiving an affront at the French court, he retired to La Mancha in Spain and lived in a cave. Cervantes' Don Quixote visits this cave, where he falls into a trance and has visions of Montesinos and other heroes.

Montespan, Marquise de. Born, **Françoise Athénaïs de Rochechouart** (1641–1707). Mistress of Louis XIV of France and mother of 8 of his children. She performed notable service to French letters as a patroness of Racine and Boileau. She and her husband, the marquis de Montespan, appear as characters in Bulwer-Lytton's drama *The Duchess de la Vallière* (1836) and in Sir Arthur Conan Doyle's romance *The Refugees* (1893).

Montesquieu, Baron de La Brède et de. Charles Louis de Secondat (1689–1755). French lawyer, philosopher, and man of letters. He is noted for his *Lettres persanes* (1721), a series of 160 fictional letters exchanged—for the most part—between two Persians, satirizing Parisian institutions, individuals, gambling, religious intolerance, and royal power. Montesquieu's *Considérations sur la grandeur et la décadance des Romains* (1734) demonstrates how a democracy, once having lost these public virtues that constitute the very essence of its existence, perishes through tyranny. His most famous work, *De l'Esprit des lois* (1748), analyzes the relation between human and natural law. See THE SPIRIT OF LAWS.

Montessori, Maria (1870–1952). Italian physician and educator. The first woman in Italy to receive a medical degree, after working with defective and feeble-minded children, she opened in 1907 in the slums of Rome the first of her *case dei bambini* ("children's houses"). Based on the premise that children can educate themselves, the Montessori method endeavors to develop the child's initiative by emphasizing individual liberty and the training of the senses and muscles through special exercises and games.

Monteverdi, Claudio (1567–1643). Italian composer, the dominant figure in the history of early Baroque music. His most important works are the operas *Orfeo* (Mantua, 1607), *Il ritorno d'Ulisse in patria* (Venice, 1641), and *L'incoronazione di Poppea* (Venice, 1642); eight books of madrigals, which, from the fifth book of 1605, have parts for instruments as well as voices; his church music, especially the *Vespers* of 1610, and the works written from 1613 on, at St. Mark's, Venice. His works are noted for their dramatic expressivity, adventurous harmonies, and careful orchestration.

Montezuma or **Moctezuma II** (1480?–1520). Aztec emperor (.1503–1520). Having tried unsuccessfully to dissuade Cortés and the Spaniards from proceeding to the Aztec capital at Tenochtitlán, Montezuma was kidnapped and held as a hostage soon after their arrival. He continued to rule as chieftain and apparently won the affection of his captors. During an Indian uprising, he was struck on the forehead by a shower of stones, as he was addressing his subjects, and died 'a few days later. He is the principal character in an opera, *Montezuma* (1964) by Roger Sessions, with a libretto by Giuseppe Borgese.

Montfleury, Antoine Jacob (1640–1685). French actor and playwright. He is remembered as the bitter enemy and rival of Molière, rather than for his comedies which include *L'Ecole des Jaloux* (*The School for the Jealous*, 1664) and *La Fille Capitaine* (*The Girl Captain,* 1672).

Montgolfier, Joseph Michel (1740–1810) and his brother **Jacques Etienne Montgolfier** (1745–1799). French inventors. Their balloon, filled with heated air, made the first passenger ascent at Annonay on June 5, 1783.

Montgomery, L[ucy] M[aud] (1874–1942). Canadian novelist. A school teacher and the wife of a Presbyterian minister, L. M. Montgomery became by accident a popular writer of juveniles. Asked to prepare a short serial for a Sunday School paper, she drew on her memories of her girlhood on Prince Edward Island to produce *Anne of Green Gables* (1908), which became a world-wide success. She also wrote *Anne of Avonlea* (1909) and many other books for girls.

Montherlant, Henry de (1896–1972). French dramatist, novelist, and essayist. His major theme, the haughtily superior male who both asserts and scorns his power, appears in early novels like *The Bullfighters* (*Les Bestiaires;* 1926). *The Bachelors* (*Les Célibataires;* 1934; also translated as *Lament for the Death of an Upper Class* and *Perish in Their Pride*) ironically describes the decadent aristocracy in the austerely elegant and cruelly trenchant style for which Montherlant is noted. In later works he goes on to portray the true aristocrat: the capable, courageous, virile man of rigorous integrity, doomed to intellectual and spiritual solitude if he would avoid the modern sin of mediocrity. Montherlant usually portrays women as selfish and inadequate creatures who use love as a tool to destroy men and to undermine their sense of moral absolutes.

The novel series *Les Jeunes Filles* includes *Young Girls* (*Les Jeunes Filles;* 1936), *Pity for Women* (*Pitié pour les femmes;* 1936), *The Demon of Good* (*Le Demon du Bien;* 1937), and *The Lepers* (*Les Lépreuses;* 1939), the last two also translated together as *Costals and the Hippogriff*. His plays, set amid the wars, famines, and domestic turmoil of Renaissance Italy and Spain, seek a universality applicable to contemporary Europe. They include *Queen After Death* (*La Reine Morte;* 1942), *No Man's Son* (*Fils de personne;* 1943), *Malatesta* (1946), *The Master of Santiago* (1947), *Tomorrow the Dawn* (*Demain il fera jour;* 1949), *Port-Royal* (1954), and *Don Juan* (1958).

Among his other novels are *Le Songe* (1922), set in World War I, and *La Petite Infante de Castille* (1929); *Desert Love* (*L'Histoire d'amour de la rose de sable;* 1954) is selections from an earlier unpublished work based on his stay in Africa.

Month in the Country, A (*Mesiats v derevne;* 1850). A play by Ivan TURGENEV. Natalia, the bored wife of a provincial landowner, falls in love with her son's tutor, as does her ward, Vera. The rivalry remains unresolved, the tutor being sent away while Natalia lapses once again into ennui. In style and content, the play anticipates the dramas of Chekhov.

Monticello. The home of Thomas JEFFERSON, situated on his estate three miles east of Charlottesville, Va. Jefferson himself designed the house and supervised its construction, which was begun in 1770.

Montmartre. A Parisian district. It is distinguished for its night life and for its literary and artistic associations. It overlooks the city from the north. Its name is thought to be derived from Mons Martyrum where the patron saint of France, St. Denis, and two companions were beheaded.

Montpensier, Duchesse de. Anne Marie Louise d'Orléans (1627–1693). French princess, known in her life and remembered as *"La Grande Demoiselle."* Daughter of Gaston d'Orléans, the brother of Louis XIII, the duchesse de Montpensier was frustrated in her hope of marrying Louis XIV when she sided against the royalists during the second FRONDE; she then spent a period in disgrace before returning to the court and asking permisison to marry the French courtier and soldier, the future duc de Lauzun. The king objected to the match; Lauzun was imprisoned, and she was not able to obtain his release for 10 years, and then only by ceding a huge portion of her estates to the king's bastards. She finally married Lauzun, was unhappy, and devoted herself to religious affairs and to the writing of her lively *Mémoires,* which were published after her death in 1729. Her romance *La Relation de l'Ile Imaginaire (Account of the Imaginary Isle)* and *La Princesse de Paphlagonie* were published under the name of her secretary, Jean SEGRAIS.

Mont-Saint-Michel and Chartres (privately printed, 1904; published, 1913). An historical and philosophical study by Henry ADAMS. The volume is subtitled *A Study in 13th-Century Unity,* and complements the later EDUCATION OF HENRY ADAMS. Adams sees the century 1150–1250 as "the point in history when man held the highest idea of himself as a unit in a unified universe." At that point, philosophy, thelogy, and the arts were all informed by faith. The book begins by discussing the Norman style and spirit of the 12th-century cathedral at Mont-Saint-Michel. From this precursor, Adams moves to the culminating moment in the 13th century, when the Virgin of Chartres was a viable symbolic link between reason and intuition, science and religion. By 1250, according to Adams, St. Thomas' scholasticism, with its emphasis on reason, had begun to destroy coherence.

Moodie, Susanna [Strickland] (1803–1885). English-born Canadian novelist. After her marriage to J. W. D. Moodie, an army officer, Mrs. Moodie sailed with him and her sister, Catherine Parr TRAILL, to Canada in 1832. She described the hardships experienced by pioneers like herself in the Canadian wilderness in *Roughing It in the Bush, or Life in Canada* (1852). Mrs. Moodie also wrote several poems and novels, including *Mark Hurdlestone* (1853) and *Geoffrey Moncton* (1856).

Moody, Dwight Lyman (1837–1899). American evangelist. In 1860 Moody retired from business to devote himself to missionary endeavors, preaching to large numbers in both the U.S. and Great Britain. On his third trip to the British Isles (1873–1875), which fostered a large-scale religious revival there, he was accompanied by organist and singer Ira David Sankey (1840–1908), who collected the famous *Gospel Hymns,* popularly referred to as "Moody and Sankey hymns." Moody founded the Northfield Seminary for girls (1879), Mount Hermon School for boys (1881), and the Chicago Bible Institute (1889).

Moody, William Vaughn (1869–1910). American poet, dramatist, and educator. Moody's reputation has rested on a few often anthologized lyrics, such as *Gloucester Moors* and *An Ode in Time of Hesitation.* But from 1900 until the time of his death, his greatest effort was devoted to the drama. *The Masque of Judgment* (1900), *The Fire Bringer* (1904), and the incomplete *The Death of Eve* (1912) form a trilogy of verse dramas. THE GREAT DIVIDE is his best-known play. *The Faith Healer* (1909) was his final drama before his untimely death. See Trumbull STICKNEY.

Moon and Sixpence, The (1919). A novel by W. Somerset MAUGHAM. Based closely on the life of Paul Gauguin, it tells of Charles Strickland, a conventional London stockbroker, who in middle life suddenly decides to desert his wife, family, and business in order to become a painter. He goes to paint in Tahiti, where he takes a native mistress. Eventually Strickland dies of leprosy.

Moon-Calf (1920). A novel by Floyd DELL. Based in part on Dell's own experiences, *Moon-Calf* is the story of Felix Fay, a lad of "the lower classes" in a little Illinois community. Deep in daydreams as a result of his reading, he has an unfortunate love affair, and abandoning his childhood sweetheart, goes to Chicago in the hope of finding a more satisfactory existence. In the sequel, *The Briary-Bush* (1921), after having thoroughly explored literary life in the city, Felix returns to marry the girl he left behind.

Moonstone, The (1868). A novel by Wilkie COLLINS. It concerns the disappearance of the Moonstone, an enormous diamond that once adorned a Hindu idol and came into the possession of an English officer. The heroine, Miss Verinder, believes her lover, Franklin Blake, to be the thief; other suspects are Blake's rival and three mysterious Brahmins. The mystery is solved by Sergeant Cuff, possibly the first detective in English fiction.

Moore, Brian (1921–   ). Irish novelist. Moore was educated in Ireland and later emigrated to Canada and to the U.S. His prize-winning first novel, *The Lonely Passion of Judith Hearne* (1956), deals with a middle-aged spinster in a Belfast boardinghouse. Later works include *The Feast of Lupercal* (1957), *The Luck of Ginger Coffey* (1960), and *An Answer from Limbo* (1962).

Moore, Clement Clarke. See A VISIT FROM ST. NICHOLAS.

Moore, Douglas [Stuart] (1893–1969). American composer. Moore prefers American themes, and the lyric stage has inspired his best works. Among his operas are THE DEVIL AND DANIEL WEBSTER (1938), based on the short story by Stephen Vincent Benét; *The Ballad of Baby Doe* (1955; libretto by

John Latouche); and The Wings of the Dove (1961), based on the novel by Henry James.

Moore, G[eorge] E[dward] (1873–1958). English philosopher. A resident at Cambridge University and editor of the periodical *Mind* from 1921 to 1947, he wrote *Principia Ethica* (1903) and *Philosophical Studies* (1922).

Moore, George (1852–1933). Irish novelist, playwright, poet, and critic. Moore was a cofounder of the Literary Theater at Dublin, from which the Abbey Theatre developed, and author of the plays *The Strike at Arlington* (1893) and *The Bending of the Bough* (1900). His fiction, revealing traces of the influence of Balzac, Flaubert, and Zola, includes *Confessions of a Young Man* (1888), and Esther Waters. *Memoirs of My Dead Life* (1906) and the trilogy *Hail and Farewell* (1911–1914) are autobiographic in content, while *Héloise and Abélard* (1921) and *Aphrodite in Aulis* (1931) are beautifully styled romances, the first historical, the second legendary. In his criticism, Moore was an influential defender of the impressionist school of painting and of the naturalist school of literature. His books of poetry include *Flowers of Passion* (1878) and *Pagan Poems* (1881). See Brook Kerith, The; Irish Renaissance.

Moore, Henry [Spencer] (1898–). English sculptor. Poised between realism and abstraction, he has formed a style which retains the inherent qualities of the sculptured material, whether bronze, stone, or wood. His style is typified by the hollowing-out of the human form in an effort to make space as meaningful as mass.

Moore, Marianne [Craig] (1887–1972). American poet. Born in St. Louis, Mo., she was educated at Bryn Mawr College and was the acting editor of *The Dial* from 1925 to 1929. Her poetry is of the type called objectivist, presenting in each poem an object, scene, person, or bit of information precisely expressed and meticulously delineated. Her work is distinguished by wit, irony, intellectual appeal, compact, individual metrical patterns in syllabic verse. She was particularly fond of animals, and much of her imagery springs from the animal world.

Miss Moore's first book, *Poems* (1921), was published without her knowledge by two friends, Hilda Doolittle (H.D.) and Robert McAlmon. Her later works include *Observations* (1924); *Selected Poems* (1935); *The Pangolin and Other Verse* (1936); *What Are Years?* (1941); *Nevertheless* (1946); *Collected Poems* (1951), awarded the Bollingen and Pulitzer prizes; *The Fables of La Fontaine* (1954), translations; *Predilections* (1955), essays; *Like a Bulwark* (1956); and *O To Be a Dragon* (1959).

Moore, Merrill (1903–1957). American psychiatrist and poet. A member of the Southern Fugitives, he was a specialist in the sonnet form, known for his large quantities of verse. His books include *The Noise That Time Makes* (1929), *Six Sides to a Man* (1935), *Poems from The Fugitive* (1936), *M: One Thousand Autobiographical Sonnets* (1938), *Clinical Sonnets* (1949), and *More Clinical Sonnets* (1952).

Moore, Mrs. In E. M. Forster's novel A Passage to India, an intuitive, half-mystical elderly woman with an Oriental understanding of Indian people and religions.

Moore, Thomas (1779–1852). Irish poet of the romantic period. He is known for his graceful lyrics and Irish folk songs, set to traditional tunes, which he published in *Irish Melodies* (1807–1835). Some of the famous songs of this collection are *The Harp That Once Through Tara's Halls, The Minstrel Boy,* and *Believe Me, If All Those Endearing Young Charms.* Lalla Rookh and Loves of the Angels, narrative poems with an Oriental setting, were also very popular. Additional writings by Moore include *Poetical Works* (1801), published under the pseudonym of Thomas Little; *The Two-Penny Post Bag* (1813), satires; *The Epicurean* (1827), a novel; pieces dealing with the adventures of the Fudge Family; a *History of Ireland* (1846); and several biographies, including one of Byron (1830), a close friend of Moore. Moore came to be regarded as the national poet of Ireland, and he was, next to Byron, the most popular writer of verse in the English romantic period. Subsequently, however, his work has been deprecated for its shallowness and sentimentality.

Moore, Thomas Sturge (1870–1944). English poet, critic, and translator. He was associated with the aesthetes of the 1890's, but was more severely classical and more experimental than they were; he translated the poetry of the French symbolists. He was also associated with the Georgians. His *Selected Poems* appeared in 1934.

Moorehead, Alan [McCrae] (1910–). Australian writer. From 1930 to 1946, Moorehead was a journalist in Australia and England. Later he wrote such books as *Gallipoli* (1956), about the ill-fated Gallipoli campaign of World War I; *The Russian Revolution* (1958); *No Room in the Ark* (1959), a report on animal life in Africa; *The White Nile* (1960); *The Blue Nile* (1962); and *Cooper's Creek* (1964), about the Burke and Wills expedition in 19th-century Australia.

Mopsus (Mopsos). A seer of Greek mythology and one of the Argonauts. He interpreted many omens and the words of the Argo's talking prow. On the homeward journey he was killed by a snake in Libya.

Moraes, Dom (1938–). Indian poet writing in English. Educated at Jesus College, Oxford, he won the Hawthornden Prize for poetry in 1957 with *A Beginning,* after which appeared *Poems* (1960), and a book of travel in India, *Gone Away* (1959).

Moral Essays. Four didactic poems in the form of letters, by Alexander Pope which include: *Of the Use of Riches* (1731), *Of the Knowledge and Characters of Men* (1733), another *Of the Use of Riches* (1733), and *Of the Characters of Women* (1735). See Lady Mary Wortley Montagu.

morality plays or **moralities** or **(Fr.) moralités** (15th–16th centuries). Allegorical dramas of the late Middle Ages. Although presented as popular pageants the way the mystery plays were, they are different in that the characters are always abstract personifications (Mercy, Truth, Everyman, King, Church) rather than figures of Biblical history or individually characterized personalities; the mystery vividly portrays an event in religious history, whereas the morality is the dramatic presentation of a sermon. Most famous of the English morality plays is Everyman; others include *The Pride of Life* (c.

1400), *The Castle of Perseverance* (c. 1405?), *Wisdom* (c. 1460). The French *moralités* were often indistinguishable from farces, and by the end of the 15th century the English morality plays also included many scenes of broad comedy burlesquing the everyday life of the time or turning to political satire. Thus in the 16th century the morality play developed into the INTERLUDE.

Moral Rearmament. See OXFORD GROUP MOVEMENT.

Morand, Paul (1888–). French novelist, diplomat, playwright. Morand is best known for the stories in *Ouvert la Nuit* (1922) and *Fermé la Nuit* (1923), and for his novels *Green Shoots* (*Tendres Stocks;* 1921) and *Europe at Love* (*L'Europe galante;* 1925). All these works depict the atmosphere of the 1920's. Afterward he turned to studies of racial and social groups, such as *Black Magic* (1928) and *Living Buddha* (1927), and of cities, such as *New York* (1936).

Morante, Elsa (1912–). Italian poet and novelist, former wife of Alberto Moravia. Her most successful novel is *Arthur's Island* (*L'Isola di Arturo;* 1957).

Moratín, Leandro Fernández de (1760–1828). Spanish dramatist. The son of poet and dramatist Nicolás Fernández de Moratín, he was apprenticed to a jeweler as a youth, but he later turned to diplomacy and traveled extensively throughout Europe. His career was ruined as a result of his collaboration with the Napoleonic invaders of Spain. After the fall of Joseph Bonaparte, he fled to France, where he remained in permanent exile, living in constant fear of imaginary assassins.

Moratín's literary reputation rests on his five plays, which are notable for their successful blending of French classicism and the traditional drama of Spain. His masterpiece, *El sí de las niñas* (1806), is a charming comedy directed against parental tyranny. Only slightly inferior are *La comedia nueva* or *El café* (1792), a satire on contemporary dramatists, and *La mojigata* (1804), an acute analysis of hypocrisy. He also wrote a prose satire on bad writers, *La derrota de los pedantes* (1789), and translated Shakespeare's *Hamlet* and several works by Molière.

Moravia, Alberto. Pen name of **Alberto Pincherle** (1907–). Italian novelist and short-story writer. His numerous works are noted for their realism and emphasis on sexuality as a means of character analysis. Moravia's protagonists, who belong, for the most part, to the middle and lower classes, are incapable of positive reactions to the reality life thrusts upon them. Moravia's first and perhaps most typical novel is *The Time of Indifference* (*Gli Indifferenti;* 1929). Among his later, more significant works are *Mistaken Ambitions* (*Le Ambizioni Sbagliate;* 1935), *The Fancy Dress Party* (*Le Mascherate;* 1941), *Agostino* (1945), *The Woman of Rome* (*La Romana;* 1947), *La Disubbedienza* (1948), *Conjugal Love* (*L'Amore Coniugale;* 1949), *The Conformist* (*Il Conformista;* 1951), *A Ghost at Noon* (*Il Disprezzo;* 1954), *Two Women* (*La Ciociara;* 1957), and *The Empty Canvas* (*La Noia;* 1960). Moravia is a recognized leader of the neorealist school of writing that emerged after World War II.

Moravian Brethren (Ger., *Mährische Brudergemeinde*). A pietistic sect based on the evangelical 15th-century movement led by the Bohemian reformer, John Hus. After much persecution it was restored in 1722 by Count ZINZENDORF in a Silesian town called Herrnhut (hence the original German name of the group, *Herrnhutter*). The immediate purpose was to use Herrnhut as a sanctuary for religious refugees from Moravia and Bohemia. Many of the Moravian Brethren emigrated to the U.S. after 1735. A permanent settlement arose in Pennsylvania.

Morax, René (1873–). Swiss playwright. Known for *Le Roi David* (1921), with music by Arthur Honegger, Morax also wrote *Guillaume Tell* (1914); and *Charles le Téméraire* (1944).

Mordant, Sir. See FAERIE QUEENE, THE.

Mordecai. In the Old Testament, the uncle of ESTHER. Through his wise counsel to his niece when she became queen, he helped save the Jewish people from the plots of Haman.

Mordred, Sir. In Arthurian legend, one of the knights of the Round Table, traditionally the treacherous one. In Malory's *Morte d'Arthur* (c. 1469), he is the bastard son of King ARTHUR and Queen MARGAWSE, and half brother of her other sons. When King Arthur goes to France on a military expedition, Sir Mordred usurps the throne and attempts to marry GUINEVERE (his stepmother). Upon receiving the news, Arthur hastens back to England to fight Mordred, and in the ensuing battle, each gives to the other his death blow.

The name is spelled *Modred* in Tennyson's *Idylls of the King* (1859–1885), where a much altered version of the story is given. Here, Modred does not try to seduce Guinevere but rather to expose her liaison with Launcelot. With 12 other knights he forces his way into the queen's chamber when Launcelot is there.

In the Welsh *Mabinogion,* Mordred appears as Medrawd. Like Arthur, Mordred may have originated in an actual, historical figure. See ANNALES CAMBRIAE.

More, Hannah (1745–1833). English writer, reformer, and philanthropist. Her writings include *Percy* (1777) and *The Fatal Falsehood* (1779), tragedies; *Village Politics* and *Repository Tracts* (1792), religious tracts on reforming the poor; and *Coelebs in Search of a Wife* (1809), a novel.

More, Henry (1614–1687). English philosophical writer and poet. A saintly man and a loyal Royalist, he was one of the leaders of the CAMBRIDGE PLATONISTS. Among his chief works are *An Anti-dote against Atheism* (1653), *Divine Dialogues* (1668), and *A Brief Discourse of the Real Presence* (1681).

More, Paul Elmer (1864–1937). American critic. While at Harvard, More met his fellow-student Irving Babbitt and, under his influence, renounced his interest in romanticism and espoused Babbitt's interest in neo-humanism, classicism, and restraint. However, he never entirely lost his love for Oriental literature and mysticism and was himself something of a contemplative. Between 1901 and 1914 he was an active journalist, writing many of the essays collected in his *Shelburne Essays* (11 vols., 1904–1921) and establishing his principles in the doctrine of the NEW HUMANISM. In the *Demon of the Absolute* (1928) he warned against absolutist creeds, urged philosophical dualism, advocated standards of taste based on tradition, argued against romanticism and sentimental humanitarianism, and particularly condemned the naturalistic writers. Among his later works are *The Greek Tradition* (5 vols., 1921–1931), the *New Shelburne Essays* (3 vols., 1928–1936), and *Pages from an Oxford Diary* (1937), an autobiography.

More, Sir Thomas (1478–1535). English statesman, lawyer, humanist, saint, poet, and author, and a friend of Erasmus, Colet, and other leading scholars of the time. A leading figure of English humanism, More was one of the most versatile and talented men of his age. His writings include a biography of Pico della Mirandola (1510); *The History of Richard III* (written c. 1513, posthumously published, 1543), which was based on an earlier account by Cardinal Morton. Utopia (1516), his most famous work, was written in Latin. A loyal defender of Roman Catholicism, he engaged in vigorous controversies with the Protestant heretics of the time, especially William Tyndale, against whom he wrote *A Dialogue Concerning Heresies* (1528).

More held important positions in the government of his time, being a Member of Parliament, an envoy on several missions abroad, a court official, and ultimately Lord Chancellor, succeeding Cardinal Wolsey in 1529. Though he had been a long-time friend and favorite of Henry VIII, More was a staunch Catholic and could not accept Henry's position announced in 1531 that the English king, and not the Italian Pope, was the head of the Church in England. More resigned from the Chancellorship in 1532. He wrote a justification of his position in *An Apology of Sir Thomas More* (1533). Two years later, Parliament passed a bill requiring that all subjects take an oath acknowledging the supremacy of Henry over all other foreign kings, including the Pope. More refused, was imprisoned, and finally executed a year later. He was beatified in 1886 and canonized by Pope Pius XI in 1935.

He is the subject of a memorable biography, *The Life of Sir Thomas More* (1557?, reprinted 1935), by his son-in-law William Roper, and of a modern play *A Man for All Seasons* (1961) by Robert Bolt.

Moréas, Jean (1856–1910). Pen name of **Jannis Papadiamantopoulos.** French poet. Born in Athens, Moréas was closely associated with the symbolists and published such volumes of poetry as *Les Syrtes* (1884) and *Les Cantilènes* (1886). His later work, however, was deliberately classical in both form and content. The lyrics that appear in *Les Stances* (1899–1901, and posthumously in 1920) are fine examples of his restrained, quiet classicism.

Moreau, Frédéric. The central character in Gustave Flaubert's novel L'Education Sentimentale.

Morel, Charles. A violinist in Marcel Proust's Remembrance of Things Past. The son of the servant of the narrator's great-uncle Adolphe, he becomes the homosexual lover of the Baron de Charlus and then of Robert de Saint-Loup, as well as a procurer of women for Albertine.

Morel, Paul. See Sons and Lovers.

Moreland, Catherine. See Northanger Abbey.

Morelos, José María (1765–1815). Mexican priest and revolutionary leader. An able organizer and administrator, Morelos became one of Hidalgo's chief aides and took command of the revolutionary forces after the latter's death. In 1813 he convened a congress at Chilpancingo which declared Mexico's independence and drafted the country's first constitution. Morelos was later captured and shot by the Spaniards.

Moretti, Marino (1885–   ). Italian novelist, poet, and short-story writer. He began his prolific career as a writer in 1905, when he associated himself with the circle of poets nicknamed the Crepuscolari. He turned from poetry to prose soon after and has since written some 40-odd volumes of novels and short stories. Most of his works have a markedly provincial setting (Cesenatico and the surrounding region along the shores of the Adriatic). His fiction suggests De Amicis in the note of sentimentality struck by the themes he developes. Pascoli appears to have influenced his simple and unassuming style. Moretti's short-story collections include *Pesci Fuor d'Acqua* (1914), *Conoscere il Mondo* (1919), and *Personaggi Secondari* (1920). His most successful novels are *La Voce di Dio* (1920) and *La Vedova Fioravanti* (1941). Among his many other novels are *Il Sole del Sabato* (1916), *Guenda* (1918), *Né Bella Né Brutta* (1921), *I Due Fanciulli* (1922), *I Puri di Cuore* (1923), and *Mia Madre* (1923).

Morgan, Charles (1894–1958). English novelist. His novels, which are sensitive but difficult and mannered, are not generally popular. Morgan is, however, a winner of the Femina Prize, the Hawthornden Prize, and the James Tait Black Memorial Award, and his work is highly regarded in France and other European countries. Morgan served as an officer in the navy, and his first novel, *The Gunroom* (1919), had to be withdrawn because of its unfavorable picture of navy life. Most of his novels deal with problems of morals and aesthetics in a faintly mystical tone; among them are *Sparkenbroke* (1936), *The Voyage* (1940), *The Empty Room* (1941), *The Judge's Story* (1947), and *The River Line* (1949). He was for many years drama critic of the London *Times*. The philosopher George Moore appointed him his literary executor. He married Hilda Vaughan, the novelist.

Morgan, Sir Henry (1635?–1688). Welsh buccaneer. During hostilities between England and Spain, he captured Portobelo, Panama, and ravaged the coasts of Cuba and Maracaibo. Named commander-in-chief of the entire naval force of Jamaica, he captured Panama City after a bitterly fought battle (1671). He was later appointed lieutenant-general of Jamaica. Morgan has appeared in numerous literary works, among them *Cup of Gold* (1940), a novel by John Steinbeck.

Morgan, John Pierpont (1837–1913). American financier. The Morgans, one of the leading banking families in the U.S., financed numerous important business enterprises, and helped to support many public institutions, particularly the Metropolitan Museum of Art. J. Pierpont Morgan became a notable art and book collector, and his great library in New York City, separately housed in a beautiful building, contains valuable manuscripts and rare books. His son, **J. Pierpont Morgan, Jr.** (1861–1943), turned this library over to public use in 1924.

Morgana. An enchantress, identified with the Lady of the Lake in Orlando Furioso, and also with Morgan Le Fay, the fairy sister of King Arthur. In the Orlando poem of Ariosto she dwells at the bottom of a lake where she keeps her treasure. In

Boiardo's version of the Orlando story she is simply Lady-Fortune, but then takes on the attributes of a witch.

Morgana, Fata. See FATA.

Morgan le Fay. One of the most mysterious figures in Arthurian legend, and one who appears in most versions but in different guises. Almost always she is a sorceress or in other ways has supernatural powers. Sometimes she is the sister of ARTHUR, sometimes his half sister, and almost always she is his enemy, or the enemy of Guinevere. In Malory's *Morte d'Arthur* (c. 1469), she is forever plotting against Arthur, and once she succeeds in stealing from him the sword Excalibur, giving it to her lover in order that he might kill Arthur. In SIR GAWAIN AND THE GREEN KNIGHT, she is an unobtrusive old woman who remains in the background, for the most part, and is only revealed in the end to be "Morgan the goddess," who plotted the action of the tale. Oddly, however, with all her animosity toward Arthur, it is she, in some versions, who takes him to Avalon to be healed of his wounds after the great final battle. Also it is to be noted that, in Malory's *Morte d'Arthur,* she is the only one of Arthur's enemies who is not ultimately vanquished by him. She also appears in ORLANDO FURIOSO, ORLANDO INNAMORATO; and OGIER THE DANE.

Morgante Maggiore, Il. The comic masterpiece of the Florentine Renaissance poet Luigi PULCI, it is a burlesque version of the Carolingian material inspired by the style and technique of the CANTASTORIE. Completed in twenty-three cantos and published in 1470, it appeared in an edition of 1483 with five added cantos, hence the title "The Greater Morgante." *Morgante* is the name of the giant who figures prominently in the plot. In 1822, Lord Byron's translation of the first canto of the poem appeared in his *The Liberal,* edited jointly with Leigh Hunt. The tale relates the adventures of Orlando, who leaves the Paris court of Charlemagne in anger at the instigations of Gano of Maganza (Ganelon). At the monastery of Chiaramonte he defeats two giants but spares the third, Morgante, who becomes his shield-bearer and companion. The giant aids Orlando and the other paladins in their various adventures in pagan lands. They are also assisted by the magician Malagigi and the fiend Astarotte, who is a theologian and philosopher. When temporarily separated from Orlando, Morgante meets the demigiant Margutte, a charming fellow, but an immense glutton who is proud of his ability as a thief and liar. He joins Morgante in several feats of appetite, treachery, and thievery until he dies in a fit of laughter at the sight of a monkey wearing his (Margutte's) boots. Soon after, his loyal friend, Morgante, also dies, of a crab bite, and is buried by the grief-stricken Orlando. The final cantos of the poem retell the famous battle of Roncisvalle (Roncesvalles), the death of Orlando, the punishment of Gano, and the further adventures of Rinaldo. The final octaves praise the inspirer of the poem, Lucrezia Tornabuoni, mother of Lorenzo de' Medici, and ask God's mercy for its author.

Morgenstern, Christian (1871–1914). German poet, known for the grotesque poems in his collection *Palmström* (1910). His significance as a serious poet was long overshadowed by the immense popularity of his humorous *Galgenlieder* (*Gallows Songs,* 1905), but he is now receiving more critical attention.

Morgiana. In the *Arabian Nights,* the clever female slave of Ali Baba who appears in the story ALI BABA AND THE FORTY THIEVES. She discovers that the robbers have been brought to her master's house concealed in jars of oil, and kills them by pouring boiling oil into the jars. Then, recognizing the captain of the thieves dining with Ali Baba, she stabs him during the dagger dance and marries the nephew of her grateful master.

Morglay. The sword of Sir BEVIS OF HAMTON; also, a generic name for a sword.

Morier, James [Justinian] (1780–1849). English diplomat and novelist. He is known for *The Adventures of* HAJJI BABA OF ISPAHAN and *The Adventures of Hajji Baba of Ispahan in England* (1828), in which he satirizes Western civilization in the tradition of Montesquieu's *Lettres Persanes.* The books reflect Morier's intimate knowledge of Near-Eastern chararacter, gained during his service as English ambassador to Persia.

Mörike, Eduard (1804–1875). German poet, generally considered the greatest in the 19th century after Goethe. Gottfried Keller later characterized him as "this son of Horace and a fine Swabian lady," by which he meant that Mörike's poetry combines classical balance and monumentality (Horatian qualities), sophisticated charm and wit (the lady), and deep feeling for his Swabian homeland. Like the poets of Swabian romanticism, Mörike sometimes wrote folklike lyrics, but he was also capable of a powerful classical style not unlike that of Klopstock and Hölderlin. His thought is generally close to that of the conservative BIEDERMEIER movement, with an affirmation of most bourgeois values. On the surface, his life was quiet and modest. He was educated in theology and served, at various times, as a Protestant pastor and a girls' school literature teacher. He was, however, never free of internal torment, the result of unhappy youthful loves, an unhappy marriage in 1851, religious doubts, and dissatisfaction with the clergy as a profession. This double character of his life is reflected in his verse which, beneath its careful consciousness of form and economy, often expresses an abysmal melancholy. He especially favors the theme of transience: the transience of love, as in *An eine Aolsharfe* (*To an Aeolean Harp,* written 1837) and *Ein Stündlein wohl vor Tag* (*A Little Before Dawn,* written 1857), or of life in general, as in *Denk' es, o Seele* (*Remember, O My Soul,* written 1852). He was also highly skilled in description, and his *Auf eine Lampe* (*On a Lamp,* written 1846) is considered an early example of the DINGGEDICHT. His prose works include a highly sentimental novel *Maler Nolten* (*Painter Nolten,* 1832) which in form is quite daring, embodying voluminous lyric and even dramatic insertions, and the masterful novella MOZART AUF DER REISE NACH PRAG.

Mori Ōgai (1862–1922). Japanese physician and litterateur. After spending four years in Germany, he became a surgeon in the Imperial Army, rising to the rank of surgeon-general. An indefatigable translator and writer of original works, he was one of the major contributors to the introduction of Western literature and ideas to Japan during the

Meiji period. See *Wild Geese* (1959) translated by Kingo Ochiai and Sanford Goldstein.

Morison, Samuel Eliot (1887–   ). American historian. A prolific writer whose work is outstanding both for its scholarship and its felicity of style, Morison taught at Harvard University from 1915 to 1955; he wrote several books about the university, including *Harvard College in the Seventeenth Century* (2 vols., 1936). His other works on early New England include *Builders of the Bay Colony* (1930) and *The Puritan Pronaos* (1936), reissued as *The Intellectual Life of Colonial New England* (1956), in which he stressed Puritan interest in literature and learning.

Morison's findings as commodore of the Harvard Columbus Expedition (1939–1940) furnished him with material for his masterly biography of Columbus, *Admiral of the Ocean Sea* (2 vols., 1942), which won a Pulitzer Prize; a one-volume edition appeared as *Christopher Columbus, Mariner* (1955). An officer in the U.S. Naval Reserve (1942–1951), Morison was official navy historian during World War II and wrote a *History of United States Naval Operations in World War II* (15 vols., 1947–1962), upon which he based his subsequent *Two-Ocean War* (1963). He is also the author of *Strategy and Compromise* (1958) and *John Paul Jones: A Sailor's Biography* (1959), another Pulitzer Prize winner.

Morituri te salutamus (Lat., "We [who are] about to die salute you"). A phrase with which, according to tradition, Roman gladiators greeted the emperor before they began their contests.

Morley, Christopher [Darlington] (1890–1957). American novelist, journalist, and essayist. After returning from England, where he was a Rhodes scholar, Morley worked on several magazines and served as contributing editor of the *Saturday Review of Literature* from 1924 to 1941. A dabbler in many literary genres, he wrote poetry, plays, essays, and novels. His best-known novels are *Parnassus on Wheels* (1917); its sequel, *The Haunted Bookshop* (1919); *Where the Blue Begins* (1922); *The Trojan Horse* (1937); and *Kitty Foyle* (1939). *The Old Mandarin* (1922) is a collection of free-verse "translations" of the sayings of a supposititious Chinese mandarin. *John Mistletoe* (1931) is Morley's autobiography.

Morley, Henry (1822–1894). English man of letters. Professor of literature at University College, London, he edited several collections of English classics. His magnum opus is *English Writers* (1864–1894), a 10-volume history of English literature down to the death of Shakespeare.

Morlocks. In a story by H. G. Wells, a race of underground monster-men. See TIME MACHINE, THE.

Morose. A character in Jonson's comedy EPICENE, OR THE SILENT WOMAN. He is a miserly old man who wants a wife, but also wants silence in his house.

Morpheus. Ovid's name for the son of Sleep and the god of dreams; so called from the Greek word *morphe* (form), because he gives these airy nothings their form and fashion. Hence the name of the narcotic: morphine or morphia.

Morrigan. In Gaelic literature, a battle goddess appearing chiefly in the mythological cycle. She is one of the TUATHA DÉ DANANN, and is later worshiped as a goddess by the Sons of Mil.

Morris, Gouverneur (1752–1816). American statesman and diplomat. A member of the Continental Congress, he was a delegate to the Constitutional Convention and American minister to France (1792–1794). His diary, a valuable sourcebook for the period, was edited by his great-granddaughter, Beatrix Cary Davenport, as *A Diary of the French Revolution, 1789–1793* (1939).

Morris, Sir Lewis (1833–1907). Welsh lawyer and writer of English verse. He was one of the founders of the University of Wales (1893). Author of *The Epic of Hades* (1876–1877), *The Ode of Life* (1880), and *Songs of Britain* (1887), among other volumes, his poetry was ridiculed by the *Saturday Review* and severely criticized by the *Athenaeum*.

Morris, Peter. See John Gibson LOCKHART.

Morris, William (1834–1896). English artist, designer, poet, and socialist. An admirer of John Ruskin's writings and of Gothic architecture, Morris trained as an architect but eventually studied painting with Dante Gabriel Rossetti. Unable to find suitable furniture or draperies for his house, he set up the manufacturing and decorating firm eventually known as Morris & Co., and did much to raise British standards of taste in furniture and ceramics as well as to revive interest in stained glass and textiles. Morris' poetic writings include *The Defence of Guenevere, and Other Poems* (1858), reflecting his interest in the Middle Ages; *The Life and Death of Jason* (1867), on a classical theme; and *The Earthly Paradise* (1868–1871), on an ingeniously combined classical and medieval theme. As a result of two trips to Iceland, Morris translated the Norse sagas and wrote his masterpiece, *Sigurd the Volsung* (1876), a narrative poem evoking the heroic legendary North An enemy of evil social conditions, which he believed fostered physical ugliness, Morris joined the socialist Democratic Federation in 1883 and helped form the Socialist League in 1885. His political convictions led to the writing of numerous socialist works in prose and verse, including *Socialism, Its Growth and Outcome* (1893). Among Morris' other works are translations of the *Odyssey* (1875) and the *Aeneid* (1887), the morality play *Love is Enough* (1873), *The Water of the Wondrous Isles* (1897), and *The Story of the Sundering Flood* (1898). See KELMSCOTT PRESS.

Morris, Wright (1910–   ). American novelist. Morris is best known for *The Home Place* (1948), a novel about a man who brings his family back to a Nebraska farm. In this book and *The Inhabitants* (1946), photographs taken by Morris complement the text. His other works include *Field of Vision* (1956), *Love Among the Cannibals* (1957), *Territory Ahead* (1958), *Ceremony in Lone Tree* (1960), and *Cause for Wonder* (1963).

Mortal Antipathy, A (1885). A novel by Oliver Wendell HOLMES. As a child, Maurice Kirkwood was accidentally dropped from the arms of his cousin, Laura, into a thorn bush. Thereafter, he faints away whenever he enters the presence of an attractive woman. Years later he is cured when the girl he subsequently marries rescues him from a fire. The book is the least successful of Holmes's three "medicated" novels.

Mort dans l'âme, La. See ROADS TO FREEDOM, THE.

Mort de Pompée, La (The Death of Pompey, 1642). A tragedy by Pierre CORNEILLE. It depicts Ptolemy's assassination of Pompey, the frustration of his plot aganist Caesar, and the coronation of Cleopatra. The bravery with which Pompey's widow Cordelia faces Caesar and the charm with which Cleopatra masters him are vividly presented.

Mort de Sénèque, La. See François L'HERMITE.

Morte Arthur, The Alliterative. See ARTHURIAN LEGEND.

Morte d'Arthur, Le (c. 1469). An English prose rendition of the legends of King ARTHUR by Sir Thomas MALORY. It was first printed in the year 1485 by William CAXTON who assembled the whole and presented it as one continuous narrative, entitling it *Le Morte d'Arthur*. The evidence of the Winchester Manuscript (recently found) indicates, however, that Malory really wrote this famous work as eight separate romances, and a modern edition presents the material in that manner under the title *The Works of Sir Thomas Malory*.

In these eight romances, ARTHURIAN LEGEND assumed ultimate and splendid shape. Malory's primary purpose in writing this material seems to have been, simply, the telling of a good story, and few will argue that he did not succeed. Even in his own era, the *Morte d'Arthur* enjoyed great popularity in many countries, and the influence it has had on subsequent generations cannot be overemphasized.

Written while Malory was in jail, the eight tales seem to have been taken from many English and French sources. One of them, called *The Tale of*

A page from Malory's *Le Morte d'Arthur* (1529).

King Arthur, retells the traditional story of Arthur's conception, birth, and coronation, and in this tale are to be found Queen IGRAINE, UTHER PENDRAGON, Sir ECTOR, Sir KAY, and MERLIN, the great magician. The other seven tales are *King Arthur and the Emperor Lucius, Sir Launcelot du Lake, Sir Gareth, The Book of Sir* TRISTRAM OF LYONESS, *The Tale of the Sangreal, The Book of Sir Launcelot and Queen Guinevere,* and *Le Morte d'Arthur.* Malory used, as some titles suggest, materials not originally part of the Arthurian tradition; however, the Tristan and Iseult legend and the quest for the Holy Grail are admirably intermingled with Arthurian materials.

Malory's tone in the *Morte d'Arthur* is primarily nostalgic: he is looking back to the days when knighthood was in flower and chivalry the great convention. Times past are brought to life again, in his pages, full of the color of curious quests, and the excitement of tournaments in which the knight rode to combat wearing a token of his chosen lady.

Malory's influence on later writers was very important: *Le Morte d'Arthur* was a source book for Spenser's *The Faerie Queene,* for example, and also for Tennyson's *Idylls of the King,* written in so much more recent times, as well as many other writers less well recognized.

Morton, David (1886–1957). American poet and teacher. A professor of English at Amherst, Morton published several volumes of verse and was especially noted for his sonnets. Among his books are *Ships in Harbour* (1921), *Harvest* (1924), *All in One Breath* (1939), *Poems 1920–1945* (1945), *Like a Man in Love* (1953).

Morton, John (c. 1420–1500). Cardinal, Archbishop of Canterbury, English statesman. Though he had been Bishop of Ely under Edward IV, Morton found no favor with Richard III, who had him arrested. He escaped to the continent, where he worked for the cause of the Earl of Richmond. Richmond became Henry VII, and during his reign Morton was made Archbishop of Canterbury (1486), Lord Chancellor (1487), and was appointed Cardinal by the Pope in 1493. He wrote in Latin a history of Richard III, which Sir Thomas MORE, at one time a member of Morton's household, translated into English. More's own *Richard III* is based largely on Morton's account.

Morton, Sarah Wentworth (1759–1846). American poet. Known as "the American Sappho," she wrote with "sensibility," and her contemporaries admired the "warbling eloquence" of her verses. She collected them in *Ouabi, or The Virtues of Nature* (1790), *Beacon Hill* (1797), and *The Virtues of Society* (1799). She was mistakenly thought to be the author of THE POWER OF SYMPATHY, now attributed to William Hill Brown.

Morton, Thomas (1590?–1647). English-born American adventurer. Settling in Mount Wollaston (now Quincy), Mass., he established a colony which he named Ma-re Mount. The maypole revels of the colony's Anglican settlers and their trade with the Indians, to whom they sold weapons, aroused the ire of the Puritans, and a force under Miles Standish was dispatched to oust Morton. He was arrested and shipped to England but later returned. Abroad he published *New English Canaan* (1637), a caustic description of New England, dubbing Miles Standish

"Captain Shrimp." His escapades are the subject of Hawthorne's allegorical short story *The Maypole of Merry Mount* (1836).

Mosby, John Singleton (1833–1916). American scout and ranger in the Confederate army. He commanded an unofficial group of bold adventurers who lived on booty; he was asked to form a regular company, but preferred leading rangers, although the number of volunteers varied from day to day. His efficient operations made him greatly feared, but he was never captured by the Federals. When Lee surrendered, Mosby disbanded his group and began to practice law in Warrenton, Va. A friend and admirer of General Grant, he was consul at Hong Kong (1878–1885), and an assistant attorney for the department of justice (1904–1910). He is the author of *Mosby's War Reminiscences, and Stuart's Cavalry Campaigns* (1887) and *Stuart's Cavalry in the Gettysburg Campaign* (1908).

Mosca (Lat. "fly"). In Ben Jonson's VOLPONE, the shrewd and rascally servant of Volpone. He believes that "almost all the wise world is little else, in nature, but parasites and sub-parasites."

Moschus (Moschos, 2d century B.C.). A bucolic Greek poet born in Syracuse. Only a few of his pastorals survive.

Moscow Art Theatre. A Russian theatrical organization founded by Konstantin STANISLAVSKI and Vladimir Nemirovich-Danchenko in 1898. A repertory group, it became world-famous for its naturalistic, highly artistic productions. Closely identified with Anton CHEKHOV, whose major plays it first staged, and later with Maksim Gorki, the Moscow Art Theatre exercised an enormous influence on the course of 20th-century theater.

Moses. In the Old Testament (Exod. 1; Deut. 34), the Hebrew lawgiver who led the Israelites out of Egypt through the wilderness and to the Promised Land. Because Pharaoh had decreed that all Hebrew boy babies should be killed, Moses' mother put him in a basket and left him in the bulrushes, where he was found and adopted by Pharaoh's daughter. Later, he identified himself with his own people and, because he killed an abusive Egyptian taskmaster, was forced to flee the country. He returned, called down on Pharaoh's recalcitrant head the TEN PLAGUES and led the Children of Israel out of Egypt, passing through the Red Sea on dry land. For 40 years he led his discontented, rebellious followers through the wilderness and was mediator for them with Jehovah, with whom he spoke on Mount Sinai when receiving the TEN COMMANDMENTS. Moses is spoken of in the Bible as the meekest of all men (Num. 12:3); but on one occasion he impulsively and vaingloriously struck a rock to bring water out of it, and for this sin he was punished by being forbidden to enter the Promised Land. He was, however, given a glimpse of it from Mount PISGAH, where he died. George Eliot wrote a poem *The Death of Moses*.

Moses, Anna Mary [Robertson]. Known as **Grandma Moses** (1860–1961). American primitive painter. She started late in life to reproduce rural scenes of her childhood in New England.

Moslem. See MUSLIM.

Mosses From an Old Manse (1846). A collection of 25 tales and sketches by Nathaniel HAW-THORNE. One of the finest collections of stories in American literature, the book contains YOUNG GOODMAN BROWN, THE BIRTHMARK, RAPPACCINI'S DAUGHTER, and THE CELESTIAL RAILROAD. The opening sketch describes the Concord parsonage in which Hawthorne wrote the tales.

Mot. A Canaanite god of the underworld and of aridity. In THE POEM OF BAAL, Mot challenges Baal's supremacy over the earth, and, luring him to the underworld, destroys him. Baal's body is recovered by his sister Anat and the sun goddess Shapash and he eventually revives. He conquers Mot, who henceforth, when he appears on earth at all, is forced to confine himself to the desert places.

Moth. (1) A quick-witted servant to Don Adriano de Armado in Shakespeare's LOVE'S LABOUR'S LOST. Glib and impertinent, he never tires of mocking his master.

(2) A fairy in Shakespeare's MIDSUMMER NIGHT'S DREAM. See PEASE-BLOSSOM.

Mother (Mat', 1907). A novel by Maksim GORKI. It depicts the regeneration of a frightened old woman when she throws herself into the revolutionary movement in Russia. The woman, Pelageya Nilovna, gradually realizes that the cause that her son Pavel Vlasov serves is important and necessary. As she becomes more involved in the movement herself, her timidity disappears, and she emerges a live, fearless human being. The novel, which is less an artistic work than a Marxist propaganda tract, is cited by Soviet critics as a model of SOCIALIST REALISM.

Mother Courage and Her Children (Mutter Courage und ihre Kinder; 1939). A play by Bertolt BRECHT. Written in the style of the EPIC THEATER, it describes the wanderings of Mother Courage, a woman who makes her living by following the army and selling trifles to the soldiers. Despite many admirable qualities, Mother Courage pays dearly for her economic dependence upon militarism. One by one, her three children are perverted by or caught in the trap of war. Each eventually dies a violent death, and Mother Courage is left alone.

Mother Goose. See CONTES DE MA MÈRE L'OYE.

Mother Hubberds Tale (1591). A poem by Edmund SPENSER. An animal fable supposedly related by Mother Hubberd, the *Tale* deals with the adventures of a Fox and an Ape. It is thought to be an early satire directed against some members of Elizabeth's court.

mothers, the (die Mütter). Mysterious figures in Part II of Goethe's FAUST. Faust has promised to make Helen of Troy appear to the imperial court in a magical vision. To help him fulfill his promise, Mephistopheles sends him to the mysterious realm of the mothers, who may be described as the guardians of all possible *forms* that existence may assume, but without the corresponding *substance*. Faust returns with a magical cauldron, by means of which he produces the vision. Goethe himself said that he had no specific reason for using the word *mothers*, but that it simply occurred to him.

Motherwell, William (1797–1835). Scottish poet, journalist, and antiquary. He is known for several collections of ballads and as author of *Poems, Narrative and Lyrical* (1832). The best of his poems are naïve and tender Scottish lyrics.

Motley, John Lothrop (1814–1877). American historian and diplomat. After graduating from Harvard at 18 and studying at Göttingen, Motley wrote *Morton's Hope: or, The Memoirs of a Young Provincial* (1839), a semiautobiographical novel. His best-known historical work is the three-volume *Rise of the Dutch Republic* (1856), in which he emphasized the conflict between William of Orange, who represented Protestantism and freedom, and Philip II of Spain, symbol of Catholicism and absolutism. Motley was minister to Austria (1861–1867) and to Great Britain (1869–1870).

Motley, Willard (1912–1965). American novelist. His first book, *Knock on Any Door* (1947), the story of the progressive criminal hardening of a boy in the Chicago slums, was acclaimed as a remarkably powerful and challenging novel. *We Fished All Night* (1951) and *Let No Man Write My Epitaph* (1958) also deal with poverty and crime.

Moto, Mr. A clever, fictional, Japanese sleuth who appears in stories by John P. MARQUAND. They were collected in *Thank You, Mr. Moto* (1936) and other volumes. Mr. Moto also appears in *Stopover Tokyo* (1957).

Mott, Frank Luther (1886–1964). American professor of journalism. A former head of the school of journalism at the State University of Iowa and at the University of Missouri, Mott won the Pulitzer Prize in 1939 for a three-volume *History of American Magazines* (1930–1938). A fourth volume appeared in 1957. He is also the author of *American Journalism 1690–1940* (1941) and *Golden Multitudes: The Story of Best Sellers in the United States* (1947).

Mottram, Ralph Hale (1883–1971). English novelist. He wrote the successful novel *The Spanish Farm* (1924). Mottram's matter and manner are similar to those of John Galsworthy, who first encouraged him to write. His other books include *Musetta* (1960), *Time's Increase* (1961), and *To Hell, with Crabb Robinson* (1962).

Mo Tzu (470–391 B.C.?). Chinese philosopher. He advocated universal love, pure utilitarianism, and free will. His doctrines were highly critical of Confucianism and were of considerable importance in the late Chou period, although by Han times his school no longer existed. See Y. P. Mei, *The Ethical and Political Works of Motse*. His philosophy is known also as Mohism.

Mouches, Les. See FLIES, THE.

Mountain, the (Fr., *la Montagne*). The extreme democratic party in the French Revolution. The members, many of whom were Jacobites, were known as *les Montagnards* because they seated themselves on the highest benches of the hall in which the National Convention met. Their leaders were Danton, Robespierre, Marat, St. André, Legendre, Camille Desmoulins, Carnot, St. Just, and Collot d'Herbois. Extreme radicals in France in later times were often called *Montagnards*.

Mountolive. See ALEXANDRIA QUARTET, THE.

Mount Vernon. The home and burial place of George WASHINGTON, situated on the Potomac River near Alexandria, Va. Originally known as the Hunting Creek plantation, the estate was renamed by Lawrence Washington, George's half brother, in honor of Admiral Vernon of the British navy, under whom Lawrence served in an unsuccessful attack on Cartagena in 1740. The main part of the house was built by Lawrence, who died in 1752, and additions were made by George, who rented the estate until he inherited it upon the death of Lawrence's widow in 1761. The estate became a public monument in 1860.

Mourning Becomes Electra (1931). A trilogy of plays by Eugene O'NEILL. Based on the *Oresteia* of Aeschylus, they are set in a stark New England, in which the Puritan conscience can function as the American equivalent of the Furies. Agamemnon is represented by Ezra Mannon, a general returning from the Civil War. His wife, Christine, corresponds to Clytemnestra; his daughter (Electra) is Lavinia, his son (Orestes), Orin. Christine, assisted by her lover, Adam Brant, poisons her husband. Lavinia, also in love with Brant, persuades Orin to revenge their father's death. Brant is murdered, Christine commits suicide, and Orin and Lavinia travel to the South Seas in an unsuccessful attempt to forget. On their return Orin, too, kills himself and Lavinia retires to the Mannon house. The play's central theme is the conflict between Puritanism and romantic passion.

Mourt's Relation (1622). The earliest narrative of the Plymouth Pilgrims. Known as *Mourt's Relation* from the name of the author of its preface, it consists mainly of letters from various colonists to their friends and families in England. Also included is a journal kept by William BRADFORD during the voyage of the *Mayflower* and the early settlement of Plymouth.

Mowgli. A native baby brought up by Mother Wolf with her cubs, in Kipling's JUNGLE BOOKS. After a boyhood spent with the animals of the jungle, he finally becomes a man among men.

Mozart, Wolfgang Amadeus (1756–1791). Austrian composer. A child prodigy, he performed on the clavier, violin, and organ for an enthusiastic European nobility. He became a prolific composer, producing more than 600 works, including 49 symphonies, as well as masses, operas, and much chamber music. His genius appears in a perfection of form and graceful melody. The *Requiem* was finished posthumously by Franz Xaver Süssmayr. Mozart's operas are unequalled; the best known are *Le Nozze di Figaro* (1786; see FIGARO), DON GIOVANNI, *Così fan tutte* (1790), and THE MAGIC FLUTE.

Mozart and Salieri. See LITTLE TRAGEDIES.

Mozart auf der Reise nach Prag (**Mozart on his Trip to Prague**, 1856). A novella by Eduard MÖRIKE. It is set in 1787 as Mozart and his wife are on their way from Vienna to Prague for the premiere of *Don Giovanni*. There is little plot and the author concentrates primarily on depiction of mood, combining a feeling of essential joy in Mozart's creative energy with a sense of melancholy premonition about Mozart's impending death.

Mr. For titles beginning with *Mister,* see also under *Mister*.

Mr. Bennett and Mrs. Brown (1924). An essay by Virginia WOOLF. She attacks the naturalistic novelists Arnold Bennett, John Galsworthy, and H. G. Wells, asserting that their books are not truly realistic because they disregard the moment-by-moment workings of the human mind.

Mr. Britling Sees It Through (1916). A novel by H. G. WELLS. It analyzes the effects of the first two years of World War I on the emotional and intellectual life of Mr. Britling, an English writer who loses a son and a German friend on different sides in the war. He is finally able to build an optimistic philosophy for the future.

Mr. Isaacs: A Tale of Modern India (1882). A novel by F. Marion CRAWFORD. It deals with a Persian diamond merchant named Abdul-Hafiz-ben Isak whose kindly but contemptuous treatment of his three wives is disturbed by the beautiful and noble Englishwoman, Miss Westonhaugh. He is saved from his dilemma only by her death, but he emerges spiritually enriched.

Mr. Norris Changes Trains (1935, U.S. title *The Last of Mr. Norris*). A novel by Christopher ISHERWOOD. Set in Berlin during Hitler's rise to power, it is the story of the narrator's innocent friendship with odd, corrupt Mr. Norris. While pretending to be a sincere Communist, Mr. Norris is actually selling information to fascists and foreigners. Mr. Norris's masochistic sexual aberrations add to the impression that he is a symbol of the whole corrupt, disintegrating society.

Mr. Perrin and Mr. Traill (1911). A novel by Hugh WALPOLE. Set in an English boys' boarding school, it is an account of the inbred, tense lives of the teachers, especially of the elderly Mr. Perrin. When young Mr. Traill arrives, is successful and popular with the boys, and becomes engaged to the girl with whom Mr. Perrin is in love, the older man develops an obsession and tries to murder his young rival.

Mr. Polly, The History of (1910). A novel by H. G. WELLS. Mr. Polly is a timid, middle-aged tradesman who escapes from his domineering wife and dreary small-town existence by setting his house on fire—intending, but comically failing, to commit suicide. Supposed dead, he wanders around the countryside, living a life of freedom and whimsical adventure. Eventually he serves the fat landlady of the Potwell Inn with comic chivalry, and establishes a new life with her.

Mrs. Dalloway (1925). A novel by Virginia WOOLF. It describes the events of a day in the life of Clarissa Dalloway, an English society woman. Peter Walsh, whom she loves but has rejected because she is afraid his possessive love would infringe on her own personality, arrives as a visitor from India. In the evening she holds a party. Through interior monologues and the STREAM OF CONSCIOUSNESS method, characters and past lives of herself, her family, and her friends are revealed. A complementary character is SEPTIMUS WARREN SMITH, who has retreated entirely into a private world, and gone mad; he finally commits suicide. Mrs. Dalloway and Septimus never meet, but their lives are connected by external events (such as an airplane overhead or a bus passing both), and by the fact that they both think the same kinds of thoughts.

Mrs. Miniver (1939). A collection of sketches by Jan STRUTHER. Mrs. Miniver is a middle-class Englishwoman whose everyday life at the beginning of World War II is described. The book was made into a very popular movie.

Mrs. Warren's Profession (1898). A play by George Bernard SHAW. Mrs. Warren's profession is prostitution, a secret she has kept from her 22-year-old daughter Vivie. When Mrs. Warren does explain to Vivie how she has been able to raise her in comfort and refinement, the daughter is, at first, sympathetic to her mother's candor and liberality. However, when Vivie learns that her mother not only was a madam but still is, she icily rejects her. Disillusioned, but unsentimental, Vivie is ready to start her own life.

Because of its subject matter, *Mrs. Warren's Profession* caused a storm of protest from the public and was closed when it was first produced in New York by Arnold DALY. It was not produced in England until 1925.

Mrs. Wiggs of the Cabbage Patch (1901). A novel by Alice Hegan RICE. The "Cabbage Patch" of this extremely popular book is a group of shanties along the railroad track in a Kentucky town. Here Mrs. Wiggs, a plucky, resourceful widow, lives with her five children, including her daughters Asia, Australia, and Europena. A love story is interwoven, and a wealthy young man and his former fiancée are reconciled in the process. *Lovey Mary* (1903) was a sequel.

Mr. Weston's Good Wine (1927). A novel by T. F. POWYS. In this fantasy Mr. Weston is a kind of God-figure who has two kinds of wine and two lessons to teach: the acceptance of love and of death.

Much Ado About Nothing (c. 1598). A comedy by William SHAKESPEARE. There are two main plots. One concerns the love affair of BEATRICE and BENEDICK, who become betrothed as a result of the clever schemes of their friends, each one being told that the other is pining away in unrequited passion. The other plot deals with a conspiracy against CLAUDIO, who is engaged to Beatrice's gentle cousin HERO. Don JOHN, who hates Claudio, stages a pretended assignation between Borachio, one of his followers, and Margaret, Hero's maid, who is garbed as her mistress. Claudio, who witnesses the scene and suspects Hero's virtue, rejects his bride at the altar, but through the good offices of kindly Friar Francis, the matter is finally cleared up. Many sources have been suggested for the plot, since similar tales have been told by Bandello, Ariosto, and Spenser. See DOGBERRY; LEONATO; Don PEDRO.

muckrakers. In U.S. history, a group of reformers whose writings drew public attention to corruption in politics and business and to other social ills. The term was first used, in a deprecatory sense, by Theodore Roosevelt, who likened them to the character in *Pilgrim's Progress* who is so busy raking mud that he cannot perceive the celestial crown held above him.

Muckraking reached its height in the first decade of the 20th century. The spearhead of the movement was *McClure's Magazine* with other mass-circulation periodicals, such as *Collier's* and *Cosmopolitan,* following its lead. Among the outstanding examples of muckraking literature are books based on articles that first appeared in these magazines: Ida M. Tarbell's *History of the Standard Oil Company* (1904), Lincoln Steffens' *Shame of the Cities* (1904), and Samuel Hopkins Adams' *The Great American Fraud* (1906). Other famous exposures include David Graham Phillips' *The Treason of the Senate* (1906), Burton J. Hendricks' *Story of Life Insurance* (1907), and Ray Stannard Baker's *The Railroads on Trial* (*McClure's,* 1906). Many novelists also turned to muckraking, notably Upton Sinclair, who assailed the meat-packing industry in The Jungle.

Mudarra. See Lara, Cantar de los siete infantes de.

Mudra-Rakshasa. A 7th-century Sanskrit play, *The Signet Ring of Rakshasa,* by Vishakadatta. It is concerned with the machinations of Chanakya, the minister of Chandragupta Maurya, emperor of India in the third century b.c., in attempting to subdue Rakshasa, the recalcitrant minister of the Nandas, dynastic rulers of a neighboring kingdom. There are no female characters in the play, since it deals with political intrigue, a subject not considered edifying for feminine tastes.

Mufti. An Arabic word meaning an official administrator of Muslim law. When the office of Grand Mufti of Constantinople was abolished in 1924, the place was filled by the Grand Mufti of Jerusalem.

In English, the term is used to denote *civil* costume, as distinguished from military or official.

Muhammad, Mahomet, Mohammed (Mecca, 570–Medina, 632). From the Arabic, "the praised one"; the founder of Islam, the Muslim religion. He adopted this name about the time of the Hegira to apply to himself the Old Testament Messianic prophecies (Haggai 2:7). His original name is given both as Kotham and Halabi.

When Muhammad introduced his system to the Arabs, they asked for miraculous proofs. He then ordered Mount Safa to come to him, thanked God when it did not move for "it would have fallen on us to our destruction," and went to the mountain to pray. This is the origin of the phrase, *if the mountain will not come to Muhammad, Muhammad must go to the mountain,* often used of one who bows before the inevitable.

Voltaire was the author of a drama, *Mahomet* (1738); James Miller wrote an English version called *Mahomet the Imposter* (1740).

Muir, Edwin (1887–1959). Scottish poet, translator, and literary critic. He published his *First Poems* in 1925, but he did not attain general recognition as an important 20th-century poet until his *Collected Poems* appeared in 1952. His work is characterized by its simple and direct style and its concern with dream imagery and archetypal myth and fable. Like other modern poets, he is indebted to the poetry of the 17th-century metaphysical poets and to the psychology of Jung and Freud, and he deals with contemporary intellectual, emotional, and social problems. During the 1930's he and his wife, Willa Muir, published translations of the works of Franz Kafka, introducing him to the English reading public. His autobiography, *The Story and the Fable* (1940; revised and expanded as *Autobiography* in 1954), with its evocations of childhood and its use of dream and fable, is an interesting book in its own right and a useful background to his poems. Muir was brought up on a poor Scottish farm and obliged to earn his living as a clerk in Glasgow at the age of 14. Deeply conscious of his Scottish heritage, he wrote *Scottish Journey* (1935) and other topographical and political books. His books of literary criticism include

Latitudes (1924), a collection of the essays he contributed to *The Freeman* under the editorship of Van Wyck Brooks; *The Structure of the Novel* (1928); and *The Estate of Poetry* (1962). His works of fiction include *The Marionette* (1927) and *Poor Tom* (1932).

Muir, John (1838–1914). Scottish-born American naturalist and writer. Muir, who migrated with his father to a Wisconsin farm, described his early experiences in *The Story of My Boyhood and Youth* (1913). Between 1863, when he left the University of Wisconsin, and 1868, when he settled for six years in the Yosemite Valley, Muir traveled thousands of miles afoot through Wisconsin, Illinois, Indiana, and Canada; he also made a journey from Indiana to Mexico, the journal of which he published as *A Thousand Mile Walk to the Gulf* (1916).

Muir had the naturalist's keen eye, a poetic appreciation of nature, and a gift for style. A lover of animals, he repeatedly expressed his wonder and admiration for the intelligence of beasts. *Stickeen* (1909) is a loving tribute to the loyalty and resourcefulness of his little half-wild dog.

Much of Muir's life was devoted to saving the natural beauties of the West from destruction by commercial exploitation, and his letters report his constant, heart-breaking struggle to prevent man from ruining the beauties of nature. His other works include *The Mountains of California* (1894), *Our National Parks* (1901), and *The Yosemite* (1912).

Mukhopadhyay, Prabhat Kumar (1868–1938). Bengali novelist and short-story writer, considered the finest prose writer in the language after Tagore. Among his better known collections of stories are *Navakatha (New Tales)* and *Deshi o Bilati (Local and Foreign).*

Mulciber. See Vulcan.

Müller, Friedrich Max. See Friedrich Max Müller.

Müller, Wilhelm (1794–1827). German poet in the movement of romanticism. His best-known work is the lyric cycle *Die schöne Müllerin* (*The Lovely Miller-Girl,* 1821) which was made famous by Franz Schubert's musical settings.

Mullins, Priscilla. See Courtship of Miles Standish, The.

Mulock, Dinah Maria. See Dinah Maria Mulock Craik.

Mumford, Lewis (1895–   ). American writer, philosopher, historian, and teacher. Mumford's diverse books all explore the relation of modern man to both his natural and his self-created environment. A study of the works of Patrick Geddes, Scottish biologist and sociologist, stimulated his interest in city and regional planning, and in 1924 Mumford helped to found the Regional Planning Association of America. In his books *The Brown Decades* (1931), *The Culture of Cities* (1938), *City Development* (1945), and *The City in History* (1961) he shows how the city expresses man's civilization but also influences its development. *The Culture of Cities* is part of Mumford's four-volume study called *The Renewal of Life,* which also includes *Technics and Civilization* (1934), *The Condition of Man* (1944), and *The Conduct of Life* (1951). In these books Mumford described the emergence of the modern scientific world and stressed man's obligation to use his now nearly infinite resources to help create a better life.

Mumford's *Sticks and Stones* (1924) was one of the first histories of American architecture. He collected his articles on architecture in a volume called *From the Ground Up* (1956). Two other important works are *The Golden Day* (1926), a pioneer study of 19th-century American literature, and *Herman Melville* (1929). Mumford also published *Green Memories* (1947), a biography of his son, Geddes, who was killed at 19 in World War II.

Mummu. In Babylonian mythology, the dwarfish counselor of Apsu. He supported him in the WAR OF THE GODS, and was conquered with him.

Munch, Edvard (1863–1944). Norwegian painter. A precursor of the German expressionist movement, Munch was influenced by the postimpressionists, particularly Van Gogh and Gauguin. He painted landscapes and portraits that were more an expression of a tormented inner state than the representation of external reality. Among his well-known works are *Summer Night, The Scream, Death in the Room, The Sick Child, Ashes,* and *Portrait of A. Strindberg.*

Munday [or **Monday**], **Anthony** (c. 1553–1633). English dramatist, actor, and pamphleteer. Munday's varied activities, which included acting as a spy on English Catholics in Rome and Paris, resulted in his being named as the official pageant writer for the City of London, a post coveted by Ben Jonson, during the reign of James I. The great majority of his dramatic works were written in collaboration with other writers and include SIR THOMAS MORE (1595), *The Downfall of Robin Hood* (1598), *The Death of Robin Hood* (1598), and *Fedele and Fortunio* (1585).

Mundt, Theodor (1808–1861). German novelist, historian, and liberal journalist. His most famous work is *Moderne Lebenswirren (The Confusion of Modern Life,* 1834), a novel which, like other products of the JUNG DEUTSCHLAND ("Young Germany") movement, attempts to attack directly specific social problems of the time.

Munera. See FAERIE QUEENE, THE.

Munich Crisis. A European diplomatic crisis of September 1938. War was threatened by the demand of Adolf Hitler for the incorporation into Germany of a group of Sudeten Germans living in a region that had been given to Czechoslovakia as part of its national territory by the Treaty of Versailles at the close of World War I. In an effort to prevent war, Neville Chamberlain, prime minister of Great Britain, conferred with Hitler at Berchtesgaden and later made a peace treaty at Munich, Germany, which permitted the annexation of the Sudeten region to Germany in return for a pledge by Hitler that the independence of the remainder of Czechoslovakia would be respected. Chamberlain believed that "peace in our time" had been achieved, but Hitler's pledge was not kept. The Munich agreement indirectly strengthened Hitler for his later aggression against Poland (September 1939), which brought about World War II.

Munin. See HUGIN AND MUNIN.

Munro, Hector Hugh. See SAKI.

Münster Anabaptists. The thousands of fanatical ANABAPTISTS, led by a tailor, who seized Münster, Germany in 1534 and occupied it for a year.

Lutherans and Catholics, opposed to social revolution, drove them out.

Mur, Le. See WALL, THE.

Murasaki Shikibu (978?–1015?). Japanese court lady. She wrote a great novel, THE TALE OF GENJI, and an important diary, *Murasaki Shikibu nikki.*

Murat, Joachim (1771–1815). French general. Murat aided NAPOLEON BONAPARTE in the coup d'état of 1799. He married Napoleon's sister Caroline and was created marshal of France and prince of the imperial house in 1804. Made king of Naples in 1809, he took the title of Joachim I and became known as "the Dandy King." Murat joined Napoleon on his return from Elba, but was later captured and executed.

Murder in the Cathedral (1935). A drama in verse by T. S. ELIOT. It deals with the assassination of St. Thomas à Becket, the archbishop of Canterbury who opposed King Henry II's attempt to limit the privileges of the clergy. In the play, Thomas is tempted by offers of worldly happiness, power, and influence, but rejects them in order to obey what he regards as the laws of God; he is martyred. The language of the play is mostly ritualistic and liturgical, spoken in a chorus by the women of Canterbury and in monologues and formal exchanges by the other characters. The interlude is a sermon by Becket to his invisible congregation. The villains, four tempters in Part one and four knights and murderers in Part two, are comic figures, expressing modern attitudes in colloquial language. The first work Eliot completed in his attempt to revive poetic drama on the English stage, *Murder in the Cathedral* is generally regarded as his best play.

Murders in the Rue Morgue, The (1841). A story by Edgar Allan POE. A mother and daughter are brutally murdered in a crime that baffles the police. Poe's amateur detective, C. Auguste DUPIN, solves the mystery.

Murdoch, Iris (1919–   ). English novelist and Oxford University lecturer in philosophy from 1948 to 1962. Her novels are noted for their wit, intricacy, and sensitivity of style, as well as for their psychological penetration and philosophical implications. Their structure is elaborate and unrealistic, often concerning a group of characters who become involved with each other through a complex network of love affairs. Man's need for love and for freedom is explored as part of his greater need to affirm his own reality. See UNDER THE NET, THE BELL, AN UNOFFICIAL ROSE. Among Iris Murdoch's other works are the novels *The Flight from the Enchanter* (1956), *The Sandcastle* (1957), *A Severed Head* (1961), *The Unicorn* (1963), and a study of the philosophy of Jean-Paul Sartre (1953). She is married to John Bayley, the literary critic.

Murdstone, Edward. See DAVID COPPERFIELD.

Murfree, Mary Noailles. Pen name **Charles Egbert Craddock** (1850–1922). American author of local-color stories and novels set in the Tennessee mountains. She was one of the first to present the Southern mountaineer realistically in her collection of dialect stories, *In the Tennessee Mountains* (1884). *The Prophet of the Great Smokey Mountains* (1885) is a novel, dealing with the Cayce family and a local preacher who sacrifices his life to save a "revenooer." *In the Clouds* (1887) also deals with the Great

Smokies. In addition to her local-color books, Miss Murfree wrote a series of Southern historical novels.

Murger, Henri (1822–1861). French writer. Murger is best known for *Scènes de la Vie de Bohème* (pub. 1848 serially; 1851 in book form), which formed the basis for Puccini's opera *La Bohème*. In it, Murger paints a picture of the world he knew well, that of the colorful but uncertain existence of the artist in Paris.

Murillo, Bartolomé Esteban (1617–1682). Spanish painter. He is best known for sentimental religious paintings, such as his *Immaculate Conceptions,* characterized by soft outlines and warm colors.

Murner, Thomas (1475–1537). German priest and satirical writer. He was a humanistically educated Franciscan and the most spirited opponent of Luther in Germany. His anti-Lutheranism is most clearly expressed in his biting prose work *Von dem grossen Lutherischen Narren* (*Of the Great Lutheran Fool,* 1522); also among his works is a satirical poem *Narrenbeschwörung* (*Exorcism of Fools,* 1512) which was influenced by Sebastian Brant's *Das Narrenschiff* (*Ship of Fools*).

Muromachi. Japanese historical period (1333–1600) marked by the rise of military leaders from the lower ranks of society, culminating in the unification of Japan under Toyotomi Hideyoshi. It saw the development of a highly ornate and sumptuous art. *Nō* drama developed during this period.

Murphy, Arthur (1727–1805). English playwright, journalist, and actor. His major farces include *The Way to Keep Him* (1760), *Three Weeks after Marriage* (1776), and *Know Your Own Mind* (1777), in which Murphy presents women as comic "types" in human nature. His important tragedies are *Orphan of China* (1759), showing the influence of Voltaire, *The Grecian Daughter* (1772), and *Alzuma* (1773), a neoclassical play dealing with Peru. See Euphrasia.

Murray, [George] Gilbert [Aimé] (1866–1957). Australian-born English classical scholar, poet, and translator. He is known for his many, very poetic translations from all the great Greek dramatists. He also wrote such works as *The Rise of the Greek Epic* (1907), *Four Stages of Greek Religion* (1912), and *Greek Studies* (1946). A great public figure, he held several important positions, was chairman of the League of Nations Union, and wrote on public affairs.

Murray, Lindley (1745–1826). Scottish-American grammarian, called the "Father of English Grammar." He is best known for his *Grammar of the English Language* (1795).

Murry, John Middleton (1889–1957). English essayist, journalist, and literary critic. The husband of Katherine Mansfield, he was the friend of many leading English and European figures in art and literature. (See Aldous Huxley's Point Counter Point and D. H. Lawrence's Women in Love.) His criticism is mystical and romantic, and emphasizes the biography and psychology of the author. Among his studies are *Fyodor Dostoyevsky* (1916); *Countries of the Mind* (1922, 1931); *To the Unknown God* (1924); *Keats and Shakespeare* (1925); *Son of Woman* (1931), a psychoanalytic study of D. H. Lawrence; and *Jonathan Swift* (1954). He also wrote poetry and fiction and books on sociology and politics.

He edited *The Journal of Katherine Mansfield* (1954) and wrote about her life and work; *Between Two Worlds* (1924) is his revealing autobiography published just after her death. He edited the *Athenaeum* (1919–1921), the *Adelphi* (1923–1930), and a number of little magazines.

muscular Christianity. Healthy or strong-minded Christianity, which braces a man to fight the battle of life bravely and manfully. The term was applied to the teachings of Charles Kingsley—somewhat to his annoyance, for he was less concerned with personal fortitude than a program of vigorous social action by the Church at large.

Muses. In Greek mythology, the nine daughters of Zeus and Mnemosyne; originally goddesses of memory only, but later identified with individual arts and sciences. The paintings of Herculaneum show all nine with their respective attributes:

(1) Calliope, Muse of epic poetry. Her symbols are a tablet and stylus, sometimes a scroll.

(2) Clio, Muse of history. Her symbol is a scroll, or an open chest of books.

(3) Erato, Muse of love poetry. Her symbol is a lyre.

(4) Euterpe, Muse of lyric poetry. Her symbol is a flute.

(5) Melpomene, Muse of tragedy. Her symbols are a tragic mask, the club of Heracles, or a sword. She wears the cothurnus, and her head is wreathed with vine leaves.

(6) Polyhymnia, Muse of sacred poetry. She sits pensive, but has no attribute, because deity is not to be represented by any visible symbol.

(7) Terpsichore, Muse of choral song and dance. She is usually represented by a lyre.

(8) Thalia, Muse of comedy. Her symbols are a comic mask, a shepherd's crook, and a wreath of ivy.

(9) Urania, Muse of astronomy. Her symbol is a staff pointing to a globe.

music (harmony) of the spheres. A theory of Pythagoras. He, having ascertained that the pitch of notes depends on the rapidity of vibrations, and also that the planets move at different rates of motion, concluded that the planets must make sounds in their motion according to their different rates; and that, as all things in nature are harmoniously made, the different sounds must harmonize. In this originated the old theory of the harmony of the spheres. Kepler has a treatise on the subject. See spheres.

Musics Duel (1646). A free translation by Richard Crashaw of a Latin poem by the Jesuit Famianus Strada. Describing a musical contest between a nightingale and a lutist, the poem is a tour de force of verbal music, ingeniously imitating the sweetness and variety of song.

Musil, Robert (1880–1942). Austrian novelist. He is best known for the extraordinary depth of psychological and cultural analysis built into his enormous unfinished novel *Der Mann ohne Eigenschaften* (*The Man Without Characteristics*). Of this work, which has had considerable influence upon German prose down to the present, Musil completed two volumes: *Reise an den Rand des Möglichen* (*Trip to the Limit of Possibility,* 1930) and *Ins tausendjährige Reich* (*Into the Millennium,* 1932); a fragmentary third was published posthumously in 1943. Among his other works, the best known is *Die*

Verwirrungen des Zöglings Törless (*The Confusions of Young Törless*, 1906), a short novel.

Muslim or **Moslem.** A follower of Muhammad. The word comes from the present participle of the Arabic *aslama,* to be safe or at rest, from which ISLAM is also derived.

Musset, Alfred de (1810–1857). French poet, novelist, and dramatist. Musset's early poetry partakes both of Byronic wit and Byronic passion (see RO-MANTICISM); it probes introspectively into the ecstasies and despairs of love. His celebrated love affair with George Sand ended diastrously in 1835 and this brought a darker coloring to his subsequent life and work. His poetic works include *Contes d'Espagne et d'Italie* (1830), *Premières poésies* (1829–1835); and *Poésies nouvelles* (1836–1852), which includes the series of lyrics for which he is best known, *Les Nuits.*

Musset's plays—comedies of manners called *comédies-proverbes,* as many of the titles were taken from proverbs popular at the time—also include fanciful comedies in the style of Shakespeare. Among his plays are *On ne Badine pas avec l'Amour* (1834), *Barberine* (1835), *Un Caprice* (1837), and *Il Faut qu'une porte soit ouverte ou fermée* (1845). *La Confession d'un enfant du siècle* (1836) is an autobiographical novel.

Mussolini, Benito (1883–1945). Italian dictator. Originally a socialist agitator, he later advanced a program of economic controls and national expansion that appealed to many Italians in the troubled years after World War I. In 1922 he led his followers in the famous march on Rome that resulted in his appointment as prime minister; he then proceeded to mold the Italian government to the ideals of FASCISM, stifling all opposition. Embarking on an aggressive foreign policy, he conquered Ethiopia (1935–1936), withdrew from the League of Nations, and entered World War II on the side of Germany. After the Allied invasion of Italy, he was deposed and imprisoned, but was rescued by the Germans, who installed him as head of a puppet state in northern Italy. Forced to flee, he was recognized by partisans and shot, together with his mistress Clara Petacci.

Mussorgski, Modest Petrovich (1837–1881). Russian composer. He is best remembered for his opera BORIS GODUNOV (1874), based on the play by Aleksandr Pushkin. The work is famous for its choral passages and it is sometimes said that the chorus is the protagonist rather than Boris. His other works include *Night on Bald Mountain* and *Pictures at an Exhibition* (orchestrated by Maurice Ravel, originally for piano). Mussorgski was a close friend of Nikolai Rimsky-Korsakov who revised much of Mussorgski's music after his death.

Mussulman. Another name for MUSLIM.

Mustardseed. See PEASE-BLOSSOM.

Mut. In Egyptian mythology, the mother goddess of Thebes. She is the wife of Amen and is sometimes called Amaune.

Mutability Cantos (1609). Two cantos and two stanzas by Edmund SPENSER, dealing with Mutability. They are thought to be a part of the unfinished seventh book of THE FAERIE QUEENE.

Mutiny on the Bounty (1932). A historical novel by Charles NORDHOFF and James Norman HALL. This vivid narrative is based on the famous mutiny which members of the crew of the *Bounty,* a British

war vessel, carried out in 1789 against their cruel commander, Captain William BLIGH. The authors kept the actual historical characters and background, using as narrator an elderly man, Captain Roger Byam, who had been a midshipman on the *Bounty.* The story tells how the mate of the ship, Fletcher Christian, and a number of the crew rebel and set Captain Bligh adrift in an open boat with the loyal members of the crew. The book was followed by two others, forming a trilogy: *Men Against the Sea* (1934), which tells of Bligh and his men in the open boat, and *Pitcairn's Island* (1934), which describes the mutineers' life on a tiny Pacific island for 20 years.

The original idea of writing a book on the mutiny occurred to Hall as far back as 1916, when he was browsing in a Paris bookstore. Eventually he wrote the English, Nordhoff the Polynesian, chapters, but the work as a whole was in the truest sense a collaboration, each man contributing heavily to the work of the other.

Mutsuhito. See MEIJI.

Mütter, Die. See MOTHERS, THE.

Mutter Courage und ihre Kinder. See MOTHER COURAGE AND HER CHILDREN.

MVD. See CHEKA.

My Ántonia (1918). A novel by Willa CATHER. It deals with the life of Bohemian immigrant and native American settlers in the frontier farmlands of Nebraska. The heroine, Ántonia Shimerda, is forced to work as a servant on the farms of her neighbors after her father kills himself in despair at his failure to become a successful farmer. She elopes with a railway conductor, but returns home, and eventually becomes the patient and strong wife of a Bohemian farmer, Anton Cuzak, the mother of a large family, and a typical woman of the pioneer West. *My Ántonia* is notable particularly for its lucid and moving depiction of the prairie and the lives of those who live close beside it.

Myers, Frederic William Henry (1843–1901). English poet and essayist. Myers' poetry resembles Swinburne's in its emphasis on verbal color and music. His volumes include *Poems* (1870), *Saint Paul* (1869), and *The Renewal of Youth* (1882). He was a founder of the Society for Psychical Research (1882).

Myers, L[eopold] H[amilton] (1881–1944). English novelist. He wrote *The Near and the Far* (1943), a series of novels consisting of the three novels collected in *The Root and the Flower* (1929–1935) and *The Pool of Vishnu* (1940). They are set in the ancient India of the emperor Akbar, and combine modern psychology and philosophy with Eastern religious ideas.

My Last Duchess (1842). A poem in the form of a dramatic monologue by Robert BROWNING. The speaker is the Renaissance duke of Ferrara who, while negotiating a marriage with the daughter of a count, indicates to the count's agent a portrait of his former wife, his "last Duchess." As he speaks of her, there is the intimation that, because she did not properly appreciate the honor bestowed upon her by his marrying her, he arranged for her murder.

My Life (Moya zhizn'; 1896). A long story by Anton CHEKHOV, subtitled *The Story of a Provincial.* The hero of the tale, Poleznev, rejects his position as a member of the intelligentsia and follows Tolstoian teachings by supporting himself as a laborer. The story has been cited as Chekhov's criticism of Tolstoi's preachments, but the trial at most seems to be an examination of their doctrinal effects.

My Lost Youth (1855). A poem by Henry Wadsworth LONGFELLOW. Based on the author's boyhood in Portland, Maine, its continual refrain is:

A boy's will is the wind's will,
And the thoughts of youth are long, long thoughts.

Robert Frost's *A Boy's Will* derives its title from this poem.

My Old Kentucky Home. A song by Stephen FOSTER. Supposed to have been inspired by a home he visited in Bardstown, Ky.

Myrivilis, Stratis (1892–1969). Greek author and journalist. Born on the island of Lesbos, Myrivilis studied philosophy at the University of Athens. A war hero during the succession of wars that involved his native country between 1912 and 1922, he was again active during World War II, this time in the Greek underground, and since then has been an opponent of Communism. Although well known in Europe for his novels, short stories, and poems, and to some degree for his journalism, he became known to readers of English only after the translation of his best-known novel, THE MERMAID MADONNA.

Myrmidons. In classic mythology, a people of Thessaly. They followed ACHILLES to the siege of Troy, and were distinguished for their savage brutality, rude behavior, and thirst for rapine. They were originally ants, turned into human beings by Zeus to populate the island of Oenone.

Myrrha. In Byron's historic drama *Sardanapalus* (1819), an Ionian slave. She was the beloved concubine of Sardanapalus, the Assyrian king. She rouses him from his indolence to resist Arbaces the Mede, who aspires to his throne; when the king finds his cause hopeless, she induces him to mount a funeral pyre, which he fires with her own hand, and, springing into the flames, she perishes with him.

Myrrha or **Smyrna.** The mother of ADONIS, in Greek legend. She is fabled to have had an unnatural love for her own father, and to have been changed into a myrtle tree.

Myrtilus (Myrtilos). See PELOPS.

Myshkin, Prince. See IDIOT, THE.

Mysteries of Paris, The (Les Mystères de Paris; 1842–43). A romance by Eugène SUE. The kaleidoscopic life of Paris, painted in a lively and dramatic manner, serves as the subject of this novel.

Mysteries of Udolpho, The (1794). A GOTHIC NOVEL by Mrs. Ann RADCLIFFE. The heroine, Emily de St. Aubert, has been brought up by a loving father in sunny Provence. On her father's death, she is left in the hands of her foolish aunt Madame Cheron, who imprudently marries Montoni, an adventurer. The scene moves to Montoni's melancholy Gothic castle in the Apennines, from which he pillages the countryside. Emily's existence is enlivened by her aunt's death from Montoni's persecutions, by the attentions of Montoni himself, and by the discovery that there is a mystery surrounding her birth. Eventually, she escapes and returns to Provence, where she solves the mystery and marries her lover, the chevalier de Valencourt, from whom she had been estranged by her aunt's folly.

Mysterious Mother, The (1768). A blank-verse Gothic tragedy by Horace WALPOLE, which deals with the theme of incest.

Mysterious Stranger, The (written 1898; pub. 1916). A story by Mark TWAIN. A boy in Eseldorf (Jackass Village), Austria, in the year 1590, is sitting with his two friends when Satan makes their acquaintance. Disguised as a well-dressed and pleasing stranger named Philip Traum, Satan convinces the boy of the falseness of morals, the kindness in killing a cripple, and the nonexistence of heaven. Destroying the boy's ideals, he vanishes. The book expresses Clemens' most pessimistic view of "the damned human race."

Mystery of Edwin Drood, The. See EDWIN DROOD, THE MYSTERY OF.

mystery plays or **mysteries** or (*Fr.*) **mystères** (13th-16th centuries). Medieval dramas based on the Old and New Testaments and the Apocrypha. In English the term is usually used interchangeably with MIRACLE PLAYS, and thus can also include plays based on the lives of the saints. The mystery plays grew out of dramatically expanded presentations of the events of Christ's life in church liturgy. As these liturgical dramas were lengthened, and enlivened with touches of realism and popular humor besides, they were moved to the porch or courtyard of the church; as the players were drawn more and more from the laity, the presentations moved to the public square or market place, although still given on the occasion of some religious holiday.

Most towns in England had at least a few presenta-

A page of manuscript from the York mystery plays.

THE BRITISH MUSEUM

tions by their own craft guilds or parish clerks, or by visiting players; and about a dozen of the large towns developed large cycles of mystery plays after 1311, when the Corpus Christi day festival was confirmed, and the plays were given annually as commercial pageants under civic control. Each cycle presented a series of episodes beginning with the Fall of Satan and continuing through Biblical history, with particular development of the details of Christ's life and resurrection. Each play was performed by the members of an appropriate craft or trade guild: for instance, the story of Noah by the shipwrights, the Last Supper by the bakers, etc. They used stage sets on wheels, so that the performance could be easily repeated in as many as a dozen different sections of a town during the day.

The plays are generally metrical, although of various verse forms. Their interpolation of wholly secular comic by-play into the religious material was the beginning of modern drama. There is the characterization of individuals, earthy and realistic humor, and a great deal of fairly coarse buffoonery. Aside from the individual plays unconnected with the cycles, there are four major collections: the 48 *York Plays* (early 14th century); the 32 TOWNELEY MYSTERIES (middle 14th-early 15th century, also called *Wakefield Mysteries*); the 25 *Chester Plays* (14th century), which are less dramatic and humorous, and resemble more closely the serious French *mystères;* and the 42 so-called *Coventry Plays* (15th century), which were probably actually performed by a traveling company. The plays by the unknown WAKEFIELD MASTER are considered the best.

The French *mystères,* usually Christmas or Easter pageants, were presented after 1371 by *confréries,* or fraternities of players. In 1402 the *Confrérie de la Passion* was given the royal commission for the pres-entation of the Easter Passion play, and it soon monopolized religious drama. However, it often joined forces with other groups who presented popular farces; comic scenes were thus introduced into the *mystères,* which continued to be given into the 16th century. Compare MORALITY PLAYS.

Mystery, meaning something beyond human comprehension, is (through French) from the Lat. *mysterium* and Gr. *mustes,* from *muein,* to close the eyes or lips. It is from this sense that the plays were called *mysteries,* though, as they were frequently presented by members of some single guild, or *mystery* in the sense (from *ministerium*) of a trade, handicraft, or guild, even here the words were confused and opening made for many puns.

Myth of Sisyphus, The (Le Mythe de Sisyphe; 1942). An essay by Albert CAMUS. It is the first outline of his theory of the ABSURD: conscious man confronting an unintelligible universe. Man yearns to know, and absolute knowledge is impossible; thus the lucid man must live in the absence of hope. Yet rejecting both despair and suicide, Camus urges that life and creation are possible within the narrow limits of what man does know. He makes the mythical Sisyphus his hero of the absurd: to him, at least, belong his rock, his awareness of his fate, and his futile struggle towards the heights, which is enough to fill a man's heart and thus make him happy.

mythological cycle. In GAELIC LITERATURE, a series of Old Irish sagas that survive in medieval manuscripts, but date from much earlier. Here the exploits of the heroes of the TUATHA DÉ DANANN, the later gods of the Celts, are related. Among the major tales in the mythological cycle are *The Wooing of Etain,* THE BATTLE OF MOYTURA, and *The Nurture of the Houses of the Two Milk-Vessels.*

myxolydian mode. See GREEK MUSIC.

N

Naaman. In the Old Testament, a Syrian commander and warrior in the service of the king of Damascus. When he was stricken with leprosy, he sought and was cured by the Hebrew prophet Elisha, of whose power he had heard through a captive Israelite maid. While still serving his master, an enemy of the Israelites, he brought back to Damascus some earth from Samaria so that he might worship the God of Israel on Israel's soil. See RIMMON.

Nabokov, Vladimir (1899–   ). Russian-born novelist and poet. Born of a noble Russian family, Nabokov was educated in England, lived in Europe, and came to America in 1940. His style is unusually fine, lucid, and controlled. *Lolita* (1958), a droll and satirical novel of Professor Humbert Humbert's passion for a 12-year-old "nymphet," created something of a sensation; the theme of an older man's fascination for a young girl appears in several others of his books, including *Laughter in the Dark* (1938) and in one of the stories in *Nabokov's Dozen* (1958; reprinted as *Spring in Fialta*). Among his other books are *The Real Life of Sebastian Knight* (1941), *Bend Sinister* (1947), *Pnin* (1957), *Invitation to a Beheading* (1959), and *Pale Fire* (1962). *The Gift* (1963) is a translation of a novel he wrote in Russian during the 30's. His *Poems* appeared in 1959.

Naboth's vineyard. See AHAB.

Nabuco, Joaquim (1849–1910). Brazilian statesman and writer. The son of a wealthy landowner, Nabuco was a leader in the struggle against slavery, which he combatted by political activity and in writings such as *O Abolicionismo* (1883). After the overthrow of the Brazilian monarchy, Nabuco retired from public life temporarily but later served as ambassador to the U.S. (1905–1910). Cosmopolitan in outlook, he spent many years in France and England and was an enthusiastic supporter of the Pan-American movement. His finest literary work is probably his autobiography, *Minha Formação* (1900), in which he gives a vivid portrait of slaveholding society in 19th-century Brazil.

Nadja (1928). A poetic novel by André BRETON. It is based on his own love affair with a woman of psychic tendencies.

Nag, Kalidas (1892–   ). Bengali historian and teacher. A professor of Indian history at Calcutta University from 1923 to 1955, he wrote *The Discovery of Asia* (1961) and *Greater India* (1963).

Nahum. Old Testament prophet. He foretold the fall of Nineveh in the book bearing his name. He saw this fall as God's vengeance on Assyria and a hope for Israel. The book was probably written between 663 B.C. and the fall of Nineveh in 612 B.C.

naiads. In Greek mythology, water nymphs.

Naidu, Sarojini (1879–1949). Indian poet writing in English. She organized flood relief work in India (1908), was the first Indian woman president of the Indian National Congress (1925), and lectured in India and the U.S. (1928–1929). Sometimes called "the nightingale of India," she exemplifies in her light, delicate, sentimental verse the romantic phase of Indian poetry in English; author of *The Golden Threshold* (1905), *The Bird of Time* (1912), and *The Broken Wing* (1915–1916).

Naipaul, V[idiadhar] S[urajprasad] (1932–   ). Trinidad-born Indian novelist and critic, who resides in London and writes in English. He writes comic novels of Caribbean life, such as *The Mystic Masseur* (1957).

Naïve and Sentimental Poetry, On (Über naive und sentimentalische Dichtung; 1795–1796). An essay by Friedrich SCHILLER. In it, he develops at length the distinction between the "naïve" poet, who seeks to depict objectively the balanced whole of life, and the "sentimental" poet, who is concerned more with depicting the ideals for which men should strive. Clearly enough, he was thinking of Goethe as the naïve poet and himself as the sentimental poet. Parallel to this distinction, he describes two types of character: the realist, who acts in accordance with an objective view of reality, and the idealist, who bases his actions upon a subjective ideal. The importance of this essay in Schiller's dramatic development can be seen in the fact that, whereas all his earlier heroes had been idealists, the heroes of his next two plays, *Wallenstein* (1798–1799) and *Mary Stuart* (1800), were realists.

Naked and the Dead, The (1948). A novel by Norman MAILER. It tells the stories of the members of an American infantry platoon invading a Japanese-held island in the Pacific during World War II. It is generally regarded as the finest novel to be written about the war.

Nala. In Hindu legend a king of Nishadha and husband of Damayanti, whose story is one of the best-known in the *Mahabharata*. Damayanti, through enchantment, falls in love with Nala without ever having seen him. The gods, however, want her for themselves and employ the unsuspecting Nala as their emissary and advocate; she declares that none but Nala shall possess her, whereupon the gods appear in Nala's shape and Damayanti is obliged to make her choice, which she does, correctly. Nala is showered with magic gifts by the gods and the wedding is celebrated. Nala later loses everything by gambling and becomes a wanderer, while Damayanti returns to her father's court. The lovers are reunited after many trials and adventures in which magic plays a large part.

Namby Pamby. See Ambrose PHILIPS.

Namo, duke of Bavaria. One of Charlemagne's PALADINS in medieval romances.

Nana (1880). A novel in the ROUGON-MACQUART series by Emile ZOLA. Nana, the heroine of this novel, is the daughter of Gervaise, central character in L'ASSOMMOIR. A product of the squalid atmosphere depicted in that novel, she becomes a prostitute and leads a similarly dissipated existence. One of Zola's themes in this series of novels is the transmission of traits through heredity; another is the significant influence of the environment in shaping human beings.

Nancy. In Charles Dickens' OLIVER TWIST, a poor misguided girl who loves the villain Bill SIKES. In spite of her surroundings she still has some good feelings and tries to help Oliver and prevent a burglary planned by Fagin. Sikes, in a fit of passion, strikes her with the butt end of a pistol and kills her.

Nanna. The Sumerian moon-god. The son of Enlil and Ninlil, he married Ningal, who bore him Utu, the sun-god. He was the chief deity of Ur in the Sumerian period.

Nanna. In Scandinavian mythology, the wife of BALDER who, when the blind god Hoder slew her husband, threw herself upon his funeral pyre and was burned to death.

Nansen, Fridtjof (1861–1930). Norwegian explorer and statesman. He is famous for his expeditions in his exploring vessel *Fram,* in which he searched for the North Pole and explored the north Atlantic ocean (1893–1896). In 1918 he was chosen chairman of the Norwegian Association for the League of Nations; in 1927 he represented Norway on the League of Nations Disarmament Committee. Nansen received the Nobel Peace Prize (1922) for his attempts to repatriate prisoners and his efforts to alleviate the Russian famine. In 1930 a refugee office in Geneva was opened by the League of Nations in his name. He was the author of *Eskimo Life* (1891), *In Night and Ice* (1897), *Through Siberia* (1914), and *Russia and Peace* (1923).

Nantes, Edict of. A decree (1598) issued by Henry IV of France establishing qualified religious toleration for French Protestants. They were granted liberty of conscience and the right to worship publicly in certain localities as well as some political and juridical rights. The edict marked the end of France's religious wars. Louis XIV's revocation of the Edict of Nantes in 1685 ended toleration and was followed by a mass migration of Protestants to the Netherlands, England, and America.

Naomi. In the Bible, the mother-in-law of RUTH whose story is told in the Old Testament book of that name.

Naphta, Leo. In Thomas Mann's novel THE MAGIC MOUNTAIN, a tubercular Latin teacher in the Davos school near Haus Berghof. He is an Austrian Jew who has been converted and become a Jesuit; and his attitudes, like his background, are a welter of violent contradictions. At various times he seems to represent both spiritualism and materialism, both socialism and reaction. In his long debates with SETTEMBRINI, he upholds mysticism and faith against reason and empiricism, absolutism and authority against enlightenment and liberalism. His self-contradictory nature is epitomized when he meets Settembrini for a duel, and, rather than firing at the latter, kills himself.

Napier, John, Laird of Merchiston (1550–1617). Scottish mathematician. Napier is famous as the inventor of logarithms, which he explained in *Mirifici Logarithmorum Canonis Descriptio* (1614).

Napoleon Bonaparte. Napoleon I. Original name, **Napoleone Buonaparte** (1769–1821). Emperor of France (1804–1815). Napoleon, born in Corsica and educated at French military schools, began his astoundingly successful military career as a very young man. Involved in the Revolution, he was imprisoned but managed to avoid the bloodletting of Robespierre's Reign of Terror. While serving the Directory, his victory in northern Italy during the campaign against Austria raised him to the position of national hero. His following campaign, in Egypt, was thwarted by the English victory of Nelson and the loss of the French fleet in the battle of the Nile. Returning to Paris at the time of a collapse in the government, Napoleon launched the coup d'état of 18 *Brumaire* (November 9, 1799) that set him firmly upon the path of destiny.

Now first consul, he was elected consul for life in 1802. Napoleon's coronation as emperor of France took place on Dec. 2, 1804. The empire had been carved out of a series of military and political victories but the Napoleonic dreams of glory and grandeur included the founding of a dynasty. In 1796, the Little Corporal had married Joséphine Beauharnais, but Napoleon divorced his wife, the first empress, when he was forced to abandon hope that she would provide him with an heir, marrying Marie Louise, archduchess of Austria (1810). As emperor, Napoleon enacted various important internal reforms in the economy and the legal system; but it was the victories of the empire under the Old Guard, consisting of Marshal Ney, Davout, Murat, and others, that made Napoleon a living legend and maintained his reign. The history of Europe during these years is the history of Napoleon's conquests, a chronicle of the gradual spread of his power throughout continental Europe.

Napoleon had captured the age, both in fact and in spirit, but there remained limits to even his sovereignty. After Nelson's second crushing defeat of the French fleet at Trafalgar, Napoleon was obliged to abandon any plans for the invasion of England. Furthermore, the English under Wellington, had landed an army on the Iberian peninsula, aiding the Spanish and the Portuguese who were seeking to restore the Bourbon line and remove the economic weight of Napoleon's continental system, the blockade of England. Napoleon, thus, turned eastward, beginning the disastrous campaign on the Russian front that was to prove his undoing. At Borodino, he defeated the Russians under Kutuzov but paid a high price for his victory. Reaching Moscow, he found the city abandoned and in flames; the long retreat westward from Russia cost the Napoleonic Corps more than two-thirds of its men. Napoleon himself had returned to France to organize a new army. This force was defeated at the battle of Leipzig, which resulted in the fall of Paris to the coalition allies, organized by Pitt and Metternich and led by Wellington (1814). Forced to abdicate, Napoleon was banished to the island of Elba; 10 months later, he escaped and returned to France in a final effort to regain power. But history's tide was no longer his to command, and after the brief triumphant glory of the Hundred Days, he was crushed at the BATTLE OF WATERLOO (June 18, 1815). His last years were spent in exile on the island of St. Helena.

A figure of great interest, not only to historians but to other writers as well, an enormous amount of literature has been written about Napoleon, including such works as Arthur Conan Doyle's *Uncle Bernac,* Sardou's *Madame Sans Gêne,* and George Bernard Shaw's *Man of Destiny.*

Napoleon II. Napoleon François Charles Joseph Bonaparte. Duke of **Reichstadt** (1811–1832). Son of Napoleon I and Marie Louise. At his birth he was given the title of the king of Rome. Also known as *l'Aiglon* (Fr., "the Eaglet"), he was named by his father as his successor upon his abdication (1814), but he never ruled. From 1814 until his death, he lived at the court of Vienna, under the control of Metternich. Edmond Rostand made Napoleon II the hero of his drama *L'Aiglon* (1900).

Napoleon III. [Charles] Louis Napoleon [Bonaparte] (1808–1873). Emperor of France (1852–1871). The 3rd son of Louis Bonaparte, king of Holland, and Hortense Beauharnais, Louis Napoleon was born in Paris but spent the early years of his career in exile (1815–1830). Returning to France, he favored the Revolution of 1848. Elected to the National Assembly, he became president of the Republic in 1848. Louis Napoleon soon began to pursue his absolutist policies; suppressing the Republicans he became dictator by coup d'état (1851). In 1852, he proclaimed himself Napoleon III. This period in French history is known as the Second Empire. Eugénie Marie de Montijo de Guzmán became the bride of the emperor on January 29, 1853. Napoleon's plans for a Roman Catholic, French empire in Mexico resulted in the disastrous Maximilian Affair (1863–1867). This was followed by the Franco-Prussian war (1870–1871). During the war Napoleon III was captured at Sedan and held prisoner for the duration. In 1871 he was deposed by the National Assembly. Retiring to England with his wife and family, he spent the remainder of his life there.

Napoleon of Notting Hill, The (1904). A novel by G. K. CHESTERTON. It is a fantasy of the future, when London is an orderly, conformist, dull city. The people elect a king who restores medieval pageantry and the autonomy of the separate sections of London. Because the provost of the Notting Hill section objects to having a new highway built, he engages the rest of the London boroughs in ingenious, medieval-style battle. "Napoleon" and the king are both killed.

Nara. The first Japanese historical period (710–794). It is notable for the flowering of Buddhist art and learning and the introduction of Chinese culture. The earliest recorded histories, *Kojiki* (712) and *Nihongi* (720), and the anthology of ancient poetry, the *Man'yoshu,* are products of this age. Nara was the first capital of Japan.

Naraka. The hell of Hindu mythology. It has 28 divisions, in some of which the victims are pecked by ravens and owls; in others they are doomed to swallow boiling hot cakes, or walk over burning sands. Each division has its name: *Rurava* (fearful) is for liars and false witnesses; *Rodha* (obstruction) for those who plunder a town, kill a cow, or strangle a man; *Sukara* (swine) for drunkards and stealers of gold, and so on. Naraka, in Hindu conception, is not an eternal hell, only a temporary one.

Narasinha. See VISHNU.

Narayan, R. K. (1906–). Indian novelist who writes, in English, sensitive and humorous novels and short stories about Indian life. Usually set in the make-believe town of Malgudi, his works include *Swami and Friends* (1935), *Waiting for the Mahatma* (1955), *Printer of Malgudi* (1957), and *Man-Eater of Malgudi* (1961).

Narcisse Parle (Narcissus Speaks). The title of 2 poems by Paul VALÉRY. First a sonnet (1890), then a longer monologue (1891), the idea was entirely rewritten to become *Fragments du Narcisse* (1922) and finally appeared as the libretto *Cantate du Narcisse* (1938). Narcissus, in love with his own reflection in the water, symbolizes the self seeking its own perfect image. The image, however, is shattered into fleeing ripples when Narcissus tries to kiss it.

Narcissus (Narkissos). In Greek mythology, a beautiful youth. He was beloved by the nymph ECHO. When he repulsed her, caring for no woman's love, she caused him to fall in love with his own reflection in a pool. He pined away for longing for this image and was changed into the flower that bears his name. The psychological term narcissism, a neurotic obsession with one's own person, is derived from this story.

Narrative of A. Gordon Pym, The (1838). A novelette by Edgar Allan POE. A New England boy stows away on a whaler, surviving mutiny, savagery, cannibalism, and wild pursuit. At the end of the story, the hero drifts toward the South Pole in a canoe; before him, out of the mist, rises a great white figure. There is some confusion in detail, because Poe, serializing the story, often did not pick up the loose ends. Based on the factual travels of J. N. Reynolds, whose book Poe had reviewed, the tale deals with situations later to intrigue Melville.

Narrenschiff, Das. See SHIP OF FOOLS, THE.

Nasby, Petroleum V[esuvius]. Pen name of **David Ross Locke** (1833–1888). American journalist and humorist. In 1861, while he was coeditor of the *Jeffersonian* in Findlay, Ohio, Locke met the town loafer and drunkard attempting to obtain signatures to a petition advocating the exile of all Negroes from town. The few Negro families in Findlay were respectable, industrious citizens, and the irony of the occurrence both amused and angered Locke. A few days later a letter appeared in the *Jeffersonian* signed Petroleum V. Nasby, an alleged Copperhead. The letter was an ironic, bitter attack on those whose views paralleled the town drunkard's.

After becoming editor, later owner, of the Toledo *Blade* in 1865, Locke continued to publish his Nasby letters for 16 years. Funny as he seemed to the readers of his day, Nasby was a serious, satirical creation. This drunken, bigoted, cowardly advocate of white supremacy and states' rights by espousing the Southern cause made it look ridiculous. Several collections of Nasby letters appeared, beginning with *The Nasby Papers* (1864).

Naseby (1645). A battle during the English CIVIL WAR in which Parliament's New Model Army under Sir Thomas Fairfax and Oliver Cromwell defeated the Royalist forces. The victory gave control of the English midlands to Parliament and broke the royal power.

Nash, Ogden (1902–1971). American writer of light verse. He is known for his sophisticated whimsy and satire, his adept use of the pun and distorted rhyme, and the inimitable cleverness of his free-verse style. Much of his writing has appeared in the *New Yorker,* and he has done much to establish that magazine's characteristic tone of statement. Nash's many collections of verse include *Free Wheeling* (1931), *Hard Lines* (1931), *Happy Days* (1935), *The Bad Parent's Garden of Verse* (1936), *I'm a Stranger Here Myself* (1938), *Versus* (1949), *The Christmas That Almost Wasn't* (1957), *Boy Is a Boy* (1960), and *Everyone But Thee and Me* (1962). He also wrote the lyrics for the musical comedies *One Touch of Venus* (1943), with S. J. Perelman, and *Two's Company* (1952).

Nashe or **Nash, Thomas** (1567–1601). English satirist and dramatist. A graduate of Cambridge and one of the UNIVERSITY WITS, Nashe was a brilliant and original writer and an outstanding personality of his time. His first published piece is the preface to the *Menaphon* of Robert GREENE (1589), in which he attacked pompous contemporary writers; he continued his assessment of contemporary literature in *An Anatomie of Absurdities* (1589). The Martin MARPRELATE CONTROVERSY gave him a further opportunity to exercise his lively wit; under the pseudonym of "Pasquil" he replied to the Marprelate pamphlets in *A Countercuff Given to Martin Junior* (1589); *The Return of the Renowned Cavaliero Pasquil of England* (1589); and *The First Part of Pasquil's Apology* (1590). *Pierce Penniless, His Supplication to the Devil* (1592) is a satire on contemporary society. Nashe entered a bitter controversy with Richard and Gabriel HARVEY, whom he attacked in *Strange News of the Intercepting of Certain Letters* (1593, also known as *Four Letters Confuted*); apparently repenting, he apologized to Gabriel Harvey in the preface to *Christ's Tears over Jerusalem* (1593). Before this pamphlet appeared, however, Harvey had printed a tract denouncing Nashe, and the next edition of *Christ's Tears* had a new and scathing preface. In 1596 he published a still more violent attack on Harvey in *Have with You to Saffron-Walden*. The feud was brought to an end by ecclesiastical order in 1599.

Also among Nashe's writings is THE UNFORTUNATE TRAVELLER, OR THE LIFE OF JACK WILTON (1594). A prose romance of adventure, it is a precursor of the English novel, and is notable for its detailed, journalistic style. Some critics consider it to be one of the finest examples of prose fiction of the period.

Only one of Nashe's plays has survived, a satirical masque called *Summer's Last Will and Testament* (1593). He may have collaborated with Christopher Marlowe on *Dido, Queen of Carthage* (c. 1593), and prepared the unfinished play for the stage after Marlowe's death. He worked with Ben Jonson on *The Isle of Dogs* (1597, not extant), a comedy which

Title page of Nashe's *Pierce Penniless* (1592).

resulted in Jonson's imprisonment for a time for having attacked the state.

Naso, Publius Ovidius. See OVID.

Nasr-ed-Din. In Turkish legend, a famous jester, sometimes called the Turkish Tyll Eulenspiegel and, like Eulenspiegel, the hero of many pranks that have been collected in a jest book and attributed to him. He is said to have died about 1410.

Nasser. The Arabian merchant whose fables were the delight of the Arabs. D'Herbelot tells us that when Muhammad read them the Old Testament stories they cried out with one voice that Nasser's tales were the best; upon which the Prophet gave his malediction on Nasser and all who read them.

Nast, Thomas (1840–1902). German-born American political cartoonist and illustrator. Nast's first political cartoon appeared soon after he joined the staff of *Harper's* in 1862. With his gift for devastating caricature, he chastised Andrew Johnson and supported Grant in two presidential campaigns. The greatest battle of his career, however, was his attack against the Tweed Ring, which had the finances of New York City completely in its control.

Nast, always conservative and usually Republican, came out strongly against race prejudice, while he attacked the income tax, inflation, and the reduction of the armed forces. He is credited with having been the first to use the donkey as a symbol for the Democratic Party, the elephant for the Republicans, and the tiger—the emblem of Tweed's old Americus Fire Company—for Tammany Hall.

After leaving *Harper's* in 1886, Nast tried unsuccessfully to establish a weekly of his own. He died of yellow fever while serving as consul at Guayaquil, Ecuador.

Natchez, Les (1826). A romance by François René de CHATEAUBRIAND. Written between 1797 and 1800, *Les Natchez* is based partly on the writer's own experiences in America. René, the hero tortured by romantic melancholy, flees to an Indian tribe and marries an Indian girl. The book closes as their romance ends in bloody violence.

Nath, Phanishwar. Pen name Renu (1925-   ). Indian writer in Hindi. Born in a village in Bihar in central India, he participated in the Quit India movement (1942) directed by Gandhi against the British. His first novel, *Maila Anchal* (1954), started a new realistic trend in Hindi fiction; another novel, *Parti Parikatha,* appeared in 1957, his short stories in 1959.

Nathan, George Jean (1882-1958). American drama critic and editor. Nathan devoted most of his energies to the interpretation of the theater; he was noted for his wit, cynicism, sophistication, and erudition. Nathan and H. L. MENCKEN, two scornful commentators, worked together on the *Smart Set,* and later on THE AMERICAN MERCURY. Nathan, who wrote play reviews for *The New Yorker* and other periodicals, established a magazine of his own, *The American Spectator*. With Mencken he wrote *Europe after 8:15* (1914) and *The American Credo* (1920). Among his other books are *Mr. George Jean Nathan Presents* (1917), *The Autobiography of an Attitude* (1925), *The World of George Jean Nathan* (1952), and *The Theater in the Fifties* (1953).

Nathan, Robert (1894-   ). American novelist. Known for his whimsical, sentimental, or satirical fantasy, Nathan has written more than 25 novels and novelettes, nearly all of them popular successes. His books include *Jonah* (1925), a new version of the biblical story; *One More Spring* (1933), presenting a touchingly happy solution to the economic depression; *Portrait of Jennie* (1940), concerned with a painter and a little girl from another world; and *They Went On Together* (1941), dealing with war refugees. Among his latest novels are *The Color of Evening* (1960), *The Wilderness Stone* (1961), and *A Star in the Wind* (1962).

Nathaniel, Sir. A verbose curate in Shakespeare's LOVE'S LABOUR'S LOST. Like HOLOFERNES, he embodies Elizabethan pedantry.

Nathaniel Lee. See MAD POET.

Nathan the Wise (Nathan der Weise; 1779). A drama by Gotthold Ephraim LESSING. It is set in Jerusalem during the Crusades. The title character is a Jewish trader who has come to look upon all religions as forms of one great truth. A Christian knight falls in love with Nathan's adopted daughter Recha, and the development of this situation involves the Sultan Saladin, a Muslim, so that all three faiths are brought into close contact. In the end, it is discovered that the knight and Recha are actually brother and sister, and that both are the children of Saladin's brother. The blood relationship among these three characters symbolizes the essential unity of the three religions.

National Institute of Arts and Letters. See AMERICAN ACADEMY OF ARTS AND LETTERS.

National Socialist German Workers' Party. See NAZI.

National Velvet (1935). A novel by Enid BAGNOLD. The heroine of the book, a young girl called Velvet, is jockey of the winning horse in the English Grand National horse race.

nation of shopkeepers. This phrase, applied to Englishmen by Napoleon in contempt, comes from Adam Smith's *Wealth of Nations,* a book well known to the emperor. Smith wrote:

> To found a great empire for the sole purpose of raising up a people of customers, may at first sight appear a project fit only for a nation of shopkeepers.

Native Son (1940). A novel by Richard WRIGHT. It is the story of a Negro youth, Bigger Thomas, the product of a Chicago slum, whom society victimizes because of his race. He commits two murders, is defended in court by a Communist lawyer, and is condemned to death. Wright's first novel, it stresses the sensational but it is also highly forceful, moving, and skillful. It is based partly on Wright's own experiences and partly on the case of Robert Nixon, a Chicago Negro, who was electrocuted in 1938 for murder.

Natsume Sōseki (1867-1916). Japanese novelist. A leading literary figure of the Meiji period, his humorous novel *Waga hai wa neko de aru* (*I Am a Cat,* 1905) has seen several English translations.

naturalism. A movement in fiction begun in France in the latter half of the 19th century. Revolting against the subjectivism and imaginative escapism which seemed to characterize the Romantic school, the naturalist writers were influenced by the biological theories of Darwin and the social determinism of Taine. The new movement sought to depict human society and the lives of the men and women who compose it as objectively and truthfully as the subject matter of science is studied and presented. Stendhal, Balzac, and Flaubert were forerunners of the movement; the GONCOURT brothers, MAUPASSANT, DAUDET, and above all ZOLA formulated the principles and engaged in the practices of naturalism. In technique their work was marked by an objective, detached method of narration, meticulous accuracy of detail, and scholarly care in the documentation of historical background. Its subjects were drawn from the lower strata of society and no detail of their sordid, unhappy lives was spared. Emphasis was placed on the social environment of the characters and on the totally subordinate relation of the individual human being to it. In the naturalistic novel, there is a pervading sense of the control exerted over the actions and destinies of the characters by impersonal social, economic, and biological forces. Human free will is shown as weak and almost completely ineffectual. Despite similarity of method, however, there was a difference in the aims of the naturalist writers. The Goncourt brothers engaged in a cold analysis of social misery, while Flaubert justified his minutely descriptive method on aesthetic grounds. Zola employed both his technique and his subject matter in the service of his passionate zeal for social reform.

In England, the novels of George GISSING, Thomas

HARDY, and Samuel BUTLER show affinities with naturalist writings; Somerset Maugham's *Liza of Lambeth* is in the tradition of Zola.

Naturalism in America, which appeared just before the turn of the 20th century, was to some extent an outgrowth of realism and was largely influenced by the spread of the theories of evolution, historical determinism, and mechanistic philosophy. The earliest naturalistic novel was Stephen Crane's MAGGIE: A GIRL OF THE STREETS, but Crane did not continue to work in this vein. Frank NORRIS and Jack LONDON, whose early naturalistic novels were the first to follow Crane's, became perhaps more famous as exponents of naturalism than as artists in their own right. Theodore DREISER is also considered a naturalist, as is the later writer James T. FARRELL. The proletarian literature of the 30's was in some ways an outgrowth of naturalism, though the similarities between the two are largely due to their common emphasis on the lower class.

Naturalism in German literature was a short-lived but important movement of about 1882–1891. The most important documents from its early phase are the *Kritische Waffengänge* (*Critical Passages-at-Arms*, 1882–1884) by the brothers HART, a critical periodical; *Moderne Dichtercharaktere* (*Modern Figures in Poetry*, 1884), an anthology of verse edited by Hermann CONRADI; and *Revolution der Literatur* (*Revolution of Literature*, 1886), a collection of essays by Karl Bleibtreu. In all these works, however, what the authors wanted was not *realism* and *objectivity* in style as much as simple *naturalness*, in opposition to what they saw as the classicistic posturing of such authors as Heyse and Geibel. They wanted genuine, heartfelt sentiment and expression in literature—which they found in LILIENCRON's poetry, for example—and preferred genuine romantics to affected realists. In addition, they felt that German authors should concentrate on timely German subject matter; it was for this reason that they liked such writers as Anzengruber and Wildenbruch, while entirely rejecting the exotic "professorial novels" of Dahn and Ebers.

It was not until the later phase of the movement, with the early plays of Gerhart Hauptmann and the works on which Holz and Schlaf collaborated, that German naturalism tended toward an emphasis on exact and detailed realism. The basic elements of the dramatic technique of late naturalism may be summarized as follows: (1) emphasis on simple family situations rather than on heroism or historic events; (2) the complete avoidance of didacticism or artificiality in dialogue, and the use of dialect where appropriate; (3) the avoidance of monologues and asides; and (4) the avoidance, as much as possible, of obvious plot contrivance. Holz, in his *Die Kunst, ihr Wesen und ihre Gesetze* (*Art, Its Essence and Its Laws*, 1891), gives a theoretical justification for such realistic techniques.

Naturalism in Germany was quickly superseded, and even in the works of such men as Sudermann, Halbe and Kretzer there are strong nonnaturalistic tendencies. But the naturalistic emphasis on genuineness of expression and respect for the unique individual experience as such strongly influenced impressionism and expressionism.

natural school. A Russian literary movement, particularly strong in the 1840's, which originated with the critic Vissarion BELINSKI. The school held that literature's task was to give a truthful representation of reality with the aim of criticizing society by depicting its true nature.

Nature (1836). An essay by Ralph Waldo EMERSON. It is the best expression of the Transcendentalist philosophy. Emerson sees Nature as Commodity in its practical functions, as Beauty in the delight it arouses, and as Discipline in the education it gives the Reason and Understanding. The essay treats man's relationship with nature, and its values. Behind every natural fact, the Transcendentalist finds a spiritual truth.

Natya-shastra. A Sanskrit treatise on dramatics, elaborating the theory of RASA, by BHARATA (first century).

Nausea (*La Nausée*, 1938). A novel by Jean-Paul SARTRE. It is also known in English translation under the title *The Diary of Antoine Roquentin*. The historian Roquentin records the process of his "nausea," a violent feeling of disgust inspired by the overwhelming fact that things and people cannot help existing, and yet there is "absolutely no reason for existing." Rejecting concepts of a cosmic purpose or of human progress as illusions, he is horrified by the absurdity of human life and the ugliness of its pretenses. Anny, his former mistress who returns to him, confesses similarly that she no longer experiences "perfect moments," which she used to feel when the opportunity offered by a "privileged situation" had been harmoniously completed. When she leaves him again, Roquentin discovers that, because there is no more reason to live, he is free despite the deathlike loneliness of this freedom. He concludes that the only possible escape from the oppressiveness of the accident of existence is through the act of creation, and contemplates writing a book so beautiful that he can accept himself.

Nausicaa (**Nausikaa**). In Homer's ODYSSEY, daughter of Alcinous, king of the Phaeacians. She conducts Odysseus to the court of her father when he is shipwrecked on the coast. Homer's portrait of this young lady is refreshingly human and believable.

Navagiero, Andrea (1483–1529). Venetian Humanist. Navagiero edited classical texts for the Aldine press, was the official historian of Venice, and served as librarian of St. Mark's. While in Spain on an embassy to Charles V, he persuaded the poet Boscán to write Petrarchan verse in Spanish, thus inaugurating Petrarchism in Spain. His Latin poems, entitled *Lusus* (*Light Pieces*) were imitated by Thomas Lodge.

Navas de Tolosa, Las. A plain in southern Spain, the site of a battle (1212) between the forces of the Muslim states of the Iberian peninsula and those of the kingdoms of Castile, Leon, Aragon, Portugal, and Navarre. Despite their superior numbers, the Muslims were completely defeated in what was the greatest Christian victory of the Reconquest.

Naxos. The largest island of the Cyclades group in the Aegean Sea. It is celebrated for its wine and appears in legend as DIONYSUS' favorite island. It was here that Theseus deserted ARIADNE, whom Dionysus found, consoled, and married. The island figures prominently in the account of Acetes, the Tyrrhenian mariner, who alone among his fellows did not conspire to abduct Dionysus to Egypt and subsequently became a Bacchanal on Naxos.

Nazareth. The village in lower Galilee, Palestine (now north Israel) where Jesus lived as a boy and young man, and learned the trade of carpentry.

Nazarite. A word from the Hebrew *nazar,* "to separate." It refers to one separated or dedicated by a vow to the Lord; Nazarites in the Old Testament refrained from intoxicating drink and allowed their hair to grow (Num. 6:1–21).

Nazi (shortening of the word *nazional*). A member of the National Socialist German Workers' Party. Hitler, who helped found the party in 1920, outlawed all others in 1933. Nazism, which was anticommunist, anti-Semitic, anticapitalist, and antiintellectual, had a strong emotional appeal for the discontented German people. See FASCISM; Karl HAUSHOFER.

Nebo, Mount. See PISGAH.

Nebuchadnezzar. The greatest king of Assyria. His reign lasted forty-three years (604–561 B.C.). He restored his country to its former prosperity and importance, practically rebuilt Babylon, restored the temple of Bel (Baal), erected a new palace, embanked the Euphrates and probably built the celebrated Hanging Gardens. In the Old Testament narrative he besieges Jerusalem, is victorious and carries the Jews away captive into Babylon. His name became the center of many legends, and the story related in Daniel (4:29–33) that he was one day walking in the palace of the kingdom of Babylon and said, "Is not this great Babylon that I have built . . . by the might of my power, and for the honor of my majesty?" and "the same hour . . . he was driven from men, and did eat grass as oxen, and his body was wet with the dew of heaven, till his hairs were grown like eagles' feathers, and his nails like birds' claws," is probably an allusion to the suspension of his interest in public affairs, which lasted, as his inscription records, for four years. Nebuchadnezzar was the king who, according to the account in Daniel, put the three Hebrews, Shadrach, Meshach, and Abednego into the fiery furnace for refusing to bow down to a golden image.

Necessary Angel, The (1951). A collection of essays on poetry by Wallace STEVENS. The major theme of the essays is the relation of the imagination—"the necessary angel"—to reality, and the way it invests reality with meaning.

Necessity of Atheism, The. See Percy Bysshe SHELLEY.

Nechayev, Sergei Genadyevich (1847–1882). Russian revolutionary. Noted for his unscrupulous and audacious escapades, Nechayev provided the basis for the characterization of Pyotr Verkhovenski in Dostoevski's novel *The Possessed*. It was Nechayev's manner of operation, however, rather than his actual achievements, that made him a legend in Russian revolutionary history. He allowed nothing to stand in the way of his revolutionary schemes. Friend and enemy alike were used as instruments to further his plans. The organizations and large numbers of followers that Nechayev claimed to head were largely products of his imagination. For a short time he managed to win the favor of the eminent revolutionary Mikhail Bakunin, but his unprincipled behavior eventually alienated the anarchist leader.

Nechayev's most famous exploit was the murder in 1869 of a student named Ivanov, a member of a small revolutionary group headed by Nechayev. For his part in planning the crime, which was arranged to elicit strict obedience from the other members of the group, Nechayev was arrested in 1872 and imprisoned in the fortress of Peter and Paul in St. Petersburg. He died there at the age of 35. A crime similar to the Ivanov murder was planned and carried out by Verkhovenski in *The Possessed*.

Necker, Jacques (1732–1804). Swiss-born French banker and statesman. He succeeded Turgot as minister of finance in 1776. His *Account Rendered*, which dispelled any illusions about the economic equilibrium of the monarchy, brought about his dismissal in 1781. He resumed office in 1788–1789, and again in 1789–1790. He was the husband of Suzanne NECKER and father of Mme de STAËL.

Necker, Suzanne. Born Curchod (1739–1794). Wife of the French financier and statesman Jacques NECKER, mother of Madame de STAËL. She was famous earlier and at the time of the French Revolution as hostess to political and literary leaders. She wrote on literary and moral subjects, including *Réflexions sur le divorce* (1749).

nectar. The drink of the gods of classical mythology. Like their food, AMBROSIA, it conferred immortality.

Nehemiah. In the Old Testament, a Hebrew whom Artaxerxes, the Persian king, sent to help rebuild Jerusalem (c. 420 B.C.) after the Babylonian captivity. Also, a book of the Old Testament called by his name.

Nehru, Jawaharlal (1889–1964). English-educated Hindu political leader. He joined Gandhi's movement and later became second only to Gandhi in influence throughout India. He was four times president of the Indian National Congress. In 1947 he became the first prime minister of India. He wrote *The Unity of India* (1941).

Neihardt, John G[neisenau] (1881–   ). American short-story writer and poet. Neihardt is best known for *The Lonesome Trail* (1907), a collection of short stories of pioneering heroes and Indians, and for his epic cycle of the West, the five book-length narrative poems, *The Song of Hugh Glass* (1915), *The Song of Three Friends* (1919), *The Song of the Indian Wars* (1925), *The Song of the Messiah* (1935), and *The Song of Jed Smith* (1941). The poet laureate of Nebraska, Neihardt also published several novels; a volume of lyric poetry, *A Bundle of Myrrh* (1907); and a play, *Two Mothers* (1921).

Nekhlyudov, Prince. See RESURRECTION.

Nekrasov, Nikolai Alekseyevich (1821–1878). Russian poet and editor. He was a prominent figure in the radical wing of literature during the middle years of the 19th century. Nekrasov's first collection of poems appeared in 1840, but they received no special attention. His first literary success was as an editor. In 1846 he edited and published the popular *Peterburgski sbornik* (*Petersburg Anthology*), which contained Dostoevski's first novel, *Poor Folk*. From 1847 to 1866, Nekrasov edited *Sovremennik* (*The Contemporary*), in which appeared the early works of Tolstoi, Goncharov, and Turgenev. *Sovremennik* was suppressed for political reasons, and, in 1868,

Nekrasov became editor of *Otechestvennye Zapiski* (*Fatherland Notes*), which he made as popular and influential as *Sovremennik* had been.

Nekrasov's poetry typifies the concern with social, rather than literary, values which was characteristic of the literature of his period, especially among liberal and radical writers. His verse tends more to popular than to literary usages of language and often contains elements based on or taken from folklore. His best-known poems are *Korobeiniki* (*The Pedlars*, 1861), *Moroz-Krasnyi Nos* (*Frost the Red-nosed*, 1863), and *Komu na Rusi zhit' khorosho* (*Who Lives Well in Russia*, 1863–1877).

Nekrasov, Viktor Platonovich (1911–). Russian novelist and short-story writer. Nekrasov fought at Stalingrad during World War II; in 1946 published *In the Trenches of Stalingrad* (*V okopakh Stalingrada*), a novel based on his experiences there. His later work includes a novel entitled *Home Town* (*V rodnom gorode;* 1954), set in Kiev after World War II. He has also written a series of travel sketches, *On Both Sides of the Ocean* (*Po obye storony okeana;* 1962), whose favorable comments on life in the U.S. have drawn Khrushchev's personal condemnation.

Nelson, Horatio. Viscount **Nelson** (1758–1805). English naval hero who, although he was victorious at the battle of Trafalgar (1805), was fatally wounded. His liaison with Emma, Lady HAMILTON was the subject of numerous books and plays, notably *Lady Hamilton* by Alexandre Dumas and *Divine Lady* by Mrs. L. Adams Beck. See NILE, BATTLE OF THE.

nembutsu. See AMIDISM.

Nemean. Pertaining to Nemea, the ancient name of a valley in Argolis, Greece, about ten miles southwest of Corinth.

The Nemean games were among the four great national festivals of Greece, celebrated at Nemea every alternate year, the second and fourth of each Olympiad. Legend states that they were instituted in memory of Opheltes (Archemorus), an infant who died from the bite of a serpent as the expedition of the SEVEN AGAINST THEBES was passing through the valley. The victor's reward was at first a crown of olive leaves, but subsequently a garland of ivy. Pindar has 11 odes in honor of victors.

In another myth, the Nemean lion kept the people of the valley in constant alarm. The first of the twelve labors of HERACLES was to slay it. He could make no impression on the beast with his club, so he caught it in his arms and squeezed it to death. Heracles ever after wore the skin as a mantle.

Nemerov, Howard (1920–). American poet, novelist, and short-story writer. Nemerov's first novel was *The Melodramatists* (1949), a satire. In a similar satirical vein was *Federigo, or, The Power of Love* (1954) and *The Homecoming Game* (1957). *A Commodity of Dreams*, a collection of short stories, appeared in 1959. His poetry, which has a considerable range of style and power, has been collected in *The Image and the Law* (1947), *Guide to the Ruins* (1950), *The Salt Garden* (1955), *Mirrors and Windows* (1958), and *New and Selected Poems* (1960).

Nemesis. The classical Greek personification of righteous anger. She exacts retribution from all who violate the natural order of things, either by break-

ing a moral law or through an excess of riches or happiness. Hesiod calls her the daughter of Night. Other legends say she is the daughter of Oceanus or of Dike (Justice). Her principal sanctuary was at Rhamnus in Attica where there was a statue of her, said to be carved by Phidias from marble the Persians had brought to Marathon as the material for their trophy, presumptuously counting on victory in advance.

Nemirovich-Danchenko, Vladimir Ivanovich (1859–1943). Russian director, dramatist and, with Konstantin Stanislavski, cofounder of the MOSCOW ART THEATRE. His works include *My Life in the Russian Theatre* (1937) and the play, *Kremlin Chimes* (1942).

Nemo, Captain. The hero of TWENTY THOUSAND LEAGUES UNDER THE SEA by Jules Verne.

Nemours, duc de. Gaston de Foix (1489–1512). French soldier, known as "the Thunderbolt of Italy." The nephew of Louis XII, he organized a brilliant campaign against the Spaniards in Italy and died after a great French victory at Ravenna.

Nennius (c. 800). An early medieval Welsh historian. He is important in connection with the origins of Arthurian literature. He specifically mentions an Arthur, crediting him with a part in 12 victories over invading Anglo-Saxons, and with killing 960 by himself. See ARTHURIAN LEGEND.

neoclassicism. The revival or adaptation of classical taste and style. In English literature, it is especially used to describe the spirit underlying much of the work of the late 17th and 18th centuries. Racine, Voltaire, Addison, Swift, and POPE are typically neoclassical in their approach to art. Their connection with the classical past is exemplified by their emphasis on traditionally classic values, such as sense of form, balance, discipline, dominance of reason, restraint, unity of design and aim, clarity, and proportion.

Neo-Confucianism. See CONFUCIANISM.

neo-humanism. See NEW HUMANISM.

neoimpressionism. A French artistic movement. Founded, about 1886, upon the recently formulated optical and color theories of such scientists as Edouard Root and Michel Eugène Chevreul, neoimpressionism sought to create a scientific method for the empirical division of tone used by the impressionists (see IMPRESSIONISM). The neoimpressionists carried the technique of division to its inherent extreme in their use of pointillism, which consisted of juxtaposing tiny dots of pure color upon a white canvas, thus allowing the eye alone to unite the strokes and create the impression of tone. Pointillism is best embodied in the work of Georges SEURAT. Paul Signac (1863–1935) was the leading spokesman of the movement.

Neoplatonism. Nineteenth-century term to describe the philosophy of PLOTINUS, developed during the 3rd century. The last great Greek philosophic synthesis, it was influenced by PLATO in its division between sensible and intelligible, and by ARISTOTLE in its equation of Being with intelligence. The basic impulse of Neoplatonism is man's return to God through reason. It asserts three levels of reality: that of non-Being, Nature, vegetative existence, sensible things; that of Being, Intellect (*Nous*), Plato's Ideas; and, finally, the level of Beyond Being, the One, the Good. It is with this last and for Neoplatonists most real level that union is to be achieved. The fundamental concept is unity. The philosophy is based on the assumption that there is Truth. One must awake from the sleep of this world into superconsciousness. This highest level of awareness is incommunicable by the intellect; it is an upward journey of the soul. These ideas were found highly congenial by the developing Christian philosophy. The relationship to St. Augustine has been indicated. There is evidence of the influence of Neoplatonism in the early German Idealism of Hegel and Bergson.

Neoptolemus or **Pyrrhus.** A son of Achilles. He was called Pyrrhus from his yellow hair, and Neoptolemus because he was a new soldier, or one who came late to the siege of Troy. According to Vergil, it was this youth who slew the aged Priam. He married Hermione, daughter of Helen and Menelaus. On his return home he was murdered by Orestes at Delphi. He is an important and sympathetic figure in Sophocles' PHILOCTETES. See ANDROMACHE.

Neo-realism. See the NEW WAVE.

NEP. See NEW ECONOMIC POLICY.

Nepenthe or **Nepenthes** (Gr. *ne*, not, *penthos*, grief). An Egyptian drug mentioned in the *Odyssey* (iv. 228). It was fabled to drive away care and make persons forget their woes. Polydamna, wife of Thonis, king of Egypt, gave it to Helen, daughter of Zeus and Leda. Poe mentions it in *The Raven:* "Quaff, oh quaff this kind Nepenthe and forget the lost Lenore."

Nephele. See IXION; the GOLDEN FLEECE.

Nephelococcygia. See CLOUD-CUCKOO-LAND.

Nephthys. An Egyptian goddess, sister and wife of Set. Both she and Set are associated with the ritual of the dead.

Nepomuk, St. **John of** (1340?-?1393). The patron saint of Bohemia. As confessor to the queen of King Wenceslaus IV he refused to reveal to the king what the queen had confessed, and the king caused him to be drowned in the river Moldau at Prague. Canonized in 1729.

Neptune (**Neptunus**). The Roman god of the sea. Originally a water god of little importance, he became an important deity through identification with the Greek POSEIDON, especially after Rome was a significant maritime power. The god was represented as an elderly man of stately bearing, bearded, carrying a trident, and sometimes riding a dolphin or a horse.

Nereids. The sea nymphs of Greek mythology. They were the fifty daughters of NEREUS and gray-eyed Doris. The best known are AMPHITRITE, THETIS, and GALATEA.

Nereus. In classic mythology, father of the water nymphs. Nereus was a very old prophetic god of great kindliness. His scalp, chin, and breast were covered with seaweed instead of hair.

Nergal. The Sumerian king of the underworld, son of ENLIL and NINLIL.

Néricault, Philippe. See Philippe DESTOUCHES.

Nerissa. In Shakespeare's MERCHANT OF VENICE, the clever waiting-woman and confidante of Portia. Possessing a fair share of her mistress' elegance and wit, Nerissa marries GRATIANO and accompanies Portia to Venice disguised as a law clerk.

Nero. Original name, **Lucius Domitius Ahenobarbus** (A.D. 37-68). Emperor of Rome (54-68).

When he was adopted by CLAUDIUS, he took the name Caius Claudius Nero. At first acclaimed by all as a liberal and sober leader, the young emperor lost little time in correcting this impression. To please his mistress POPPAEA, he had his wife Octavia murdered, and, when Poppaea was pregnant, he killed mother and child by kicking her to death. He amused himself with playing the harp and taking part in athletics in the Circus, and he was always able to coerce a large attendance at both performances. In the summer of 64 A.D., a great fire destroyed a sizable portion of the city. The story that the mad emperor lit the fire "to see how Troy looked when it was in flames" and that he occupied himself musically "while Rome burned" is now generally held to be a legend. He did, however, blame the Christians for the fire and persecuted them cruelly for several years.

After the fire, Nero rebuilt Rome, and erected for himself the DOMUS AUREA. In the meantime conspiracies had been forming. In one of them, PISO's CONSPIRACY, the poet Lucan and the philosopher SENECA were involved, and both men were ordered to commit suicide. This they did, and their stoic deaths further incensed the populace against the emperor. In 68, after Nero returned from a concert tour of Greece, the armies installed Galba as emperor, declared Nero an enemy of the state, and would have executed him had he not first taken his own life. He is a prominent character in Sienkiewicz' *Quo Vadis?* (1896). Stephen Phillips wrote a poetic drama entitled *Nero* (1906). See AGRIPPINA; BRITANNICUS.

Nerthus or **Hertha.** A German or Scandinavian goddess of fertility, or Mother Earth. The name is found in Tacitus. The goddess was worshiped on an island. She roughly corresponds to the classical Cybele, and is probably confused with the Scandinavian god Njorthr or NIORD, the protector of sailors and fishermen. *Nerthus* and *Njorthr* alike mean benefactor.

Neruda, Pablo. Pen name of **Neftalí Ricardo Reyes** (1904-). Chilean poet. After the appearance of *Veinte poemas de amor y una canción desesperada* (1924) had established Neruda as one of Chile's most promising poets, the Chilean government appointed him to various consular posts in Europe and Asia. In 1934 he was assigned to Madrid, where he mingled with Spanish writers such as Manuel Altolaguirre, with whom he founded (1935) a literary review called *Caballo Verde para la Poesía*. In the same year Neruda published a translation of William Blake's *The Visions of the Daughters of Albion* and *The Mental Traveller*. His outspoken sympathy for the Loyalist cause during the Spanish Civil War led to his recall in 1937, but he soon returned to Europe to aid in the settlement of republican refugees in America. From 1939 to 1943 he was Chilean consul in Mexico. Upon returning to Chile, Neruda became active in politics, was elected to the senate, and joined the Communist Party. When the party was declared illegal in Chile, Neruda was expelled from the senate. After spending several years in exile, he returned to Chile in 1953.

Neruda's earliest poetry—*La cancion de la fiesta* (1921), *Crepusculario* (1923), and *Veinte poemas*—is reminiscent of MODERNISM in form and tone. The poetry of the next stage in Neruda's career, especially *Residencia en la tierra*, I and II (1933; 1935), shows the poet trying to depict in each single stroke the full measure of his intuition and experience; written in a style that is usually described as surrealistic, these poems create an anguish-ridden world of chaos, desolation, and decay.

His political and social sensibilities stirred by the defeat of the Spanish Loyalists, Neruda began to see himself in relation to mankind. In such works as *Tercera residencia* (1947), *Canto general* (1950), *Odas elementales* (1954), and *Estravagario* (1958), Neruda—now a militant communist—became the people's poet and sought, above all, to communicate. Though there is considerable debate over the merits of Neruda's later work—a debate, moreover, that is often clouded by the intrusion of politics—he is widely regarded as the greatest Spanish-American poet since Darío.

Nervo, Amado (1879–1919). Mexican poet. As a young man, Nervo studied for the priesthood, an experience reflected in the mysticism that characterizes much of his work. When he was forced to leave the seminary for financial reasons, he turned to journalism and was the cofounder of the *Revista Moderna*, an influential modernist review. From 1905 to 1918 he held a diplomatic post in Madrid and at his death was Mexican minister to Argentina and Uruguay.

Nervo's early works, such as *Perlas negras* (1898), *Poemas* (1901), and *Jardines interiores* (1905), place him in the mainstream of MODERNISM. Subsequently, however, his poetry became more subjective and revealing, and such works as *Serenidad* (1914) and *Elevación* (1917) express the asceticism and tranquillity of the poet's later years.

Nessus (Nessos). In Greek mythology, the centaur responsible for the death of Heracles. Heracles had ordered him to carry his wife Deianira across a river; when the centaur attempted to carry her off, Heracles shot him. In revenge, Nessus gave Deianira his bloody tunic, telling her that it would preserve her husband's life. Later, when Heracles was unfaithful to her, she gave it to him as a present. The centaur's blood, together with the hydra's poison with which Heracles' arrow had been smeared, clung to his body, setting his flesh afire. The pain was so great that he immolated himself. Deianira hanged herself from remorse.

Nest of Gentlefolk, A (Dvoryanskoe gnezdo; 1859). A novel by Ivan TURGENEV. It tells the story of the tragic love affair between the hero Feodor Ivanovich Lavretzki and Liza Kalitina. Lavretzki is about to marry Liza when his first wife, whom he has believed dead, returns to him. Liza goes into a convent, and Lavretzki is left to his bleak duty. The novel, which poetically evokes the peaceful atmosphere of the provincial Russian feudal estate, had a great success on its publication.

Nestor. The oldest and wisest of the Greek generals who fought at Troy. The son of Neleus and king of Pylos, in the western Peloponnesus, he was accustomed to offering sage advice at considerable length on every occasion. Robert Graves has ironically pointed out that Nestor's counsel, though highly respected, generally turned out to have disastrous consequences. Heinrich SCHLIEMANN, the famous amateur archeologist, thought that he had discovered Nestor's cup, described in detail in the *Iliad*. Recent excavations on the site of Pylos prove that it was indeed a highly important center in Mycenaean times. Nestor appears in Shakespeare's *Troilus and Cressida*.

Nestorians. Followers of Nestorius (d. c. A.D. 451), patriarch of Constantinople. He maintained that Christ had two distinct natures, and that Mary was the mother of His human nature, which was the mere shell or husk of the divine. The sect spread in India and the Far East, and remains of the Nestorian Christians, such as their inscriptions, are still found in China, but the greater part of their churches were destroyed by Tamburlaine about 1400. Rumors of influential Christian centers in the East may have given rise to the legend of PRESTER JOHN.

Nestroy, Johann (1801–1862). Austrian playwright and actor. He is best known for his humorous satires, such as *Der böse Geist des Lumpacivagabundus oder Das liederliche Kleeblatt* (*The Evil Spirit of Lumpacivagabundus or The Dissolute Cloverleaf*, 1835). He also wrote parodies of such authors as Hebbel and Richard Wagner.

Nets to Catch the Wind (1921). A book of poems by Elinor WYLIE. The first collection of her poetry to bear her name, it contained some of her most characteristic verse. Many of the poems are in the metaphysical vein, the title being taken from the 17th-century poem *The Devil's Law Case* by John Webster. *Velvet Shoes* and *The Eagle and the Mole*, two of the author's best-known poems, were first printed in this volume.

Neveu de Rameau, Le (Rameau's Nephew, 1891). A satirical character sketch by Denis DIDEROT, written (1762) in the form of a dialogue between Diderot and Rameau, the nephew of the French composer Jean Philippe Rameau. Written in the most vivacious style, Diderot gives a character sketch of the nephew of the celebrated musician; he is a lazy, original, hare-brained, sensual, utterly frank social parasite, whose gifts for pantomime, conversation, monologue, and music serve Diderot well in his biting satire on contemporary society and the artists who either pleased or displeased him.

Neveux, Georges (1900–). Russian-born French dramatist and screenwriter. Much influenced by his surrealist friends, he produced highly poetic and symbolic plays which take place in a world of dream and fantasy. Chief among these works are *Juliette ou la Clef des songes* (1930) and *Le Voyage de Thésée* (1943).

Nevins, Allan (1890–1971). American historian and journalist. A graduate of the University of Illinois, Nevins was an editorial writer for the New York *Evening Post* (1913–1923) and for the *Nation* (1913–1918). In 1931 he was appointed professor of history at Columbia University, where he remained until 1958, when he became a senior research associate at the Huntington Library in San Marino, Calif.

Nevins won Pulitzer prizes for two of his earlier works: *Grover Cleveland* (1932) and *Hamilton Fish: The Inner History of the Grant Administration* (2 vols., 1936). He studied the U.S. from 1847 to 1861 in *The Ordeal of the Union* (2 vols., 1947) and *The Emergence of Lincoln* (2 vols., 1950), continuing the story in *The War for the Union* (2 vols., 1959), part of a projected four-volume work on the Civil War. With Frank E. Hill, he wrote *Ford* (1954–1963), a three-volume study of the great automotive pioneer and the company he founded; another work dealing with a prominent American businessman is *Study in Power: John D. Rockefeller* (2 vols., 1953). Other works by Nevins include *The Gateway to History* (1938) and *Herbert H. Lehman and His Era* (1963).

New Apocalypse. A romantic, surrealistic movement in English poetry. Led by G. F. Hendry, G. S. FRASER, and Henry TREECE in 1939, it was formed in reaction to the social poetry of W. H. Auden and others which was dominant in the 1930's. The movement was short lived. Only George BARKER and Dylan THOMAS wrote the kind of poetry its leaders advocated.

New Atlantis, The (1627). A Utopian fable by Francis BACON, published in an unfinished state after his death. It is an account of a voyage to the island of "Bensalem," and of the government and manners of its people. Of particular interest is the Bensalem institution for scientific study, "Solomon's House," which provided inspiration for the founding of the Royal Society.

Newbery, John (1713–1767). English publisher of newspapers and children's books. Newbery published the daily newspaper, *The Public Ledger* (1760–1761) which featured Oliver Goldsmith's "Chinese Letters" or *Citizen of the World* and contributions by Samuel Johnson. He also brought out the famous 20-volume collection of voyage narratives called *The World Displayed; or, a Curious Collection of Voyages and Travels* (1759–1761; 1774–1778; 1790). The "Newbery Medal," established by Frederic Melcher, is awarded annually (since 1921) for the best children's book written by an American.

Newbolt, Sir Henry (1862–1938). English poet. He wrote hearty, patriotic poems, such as *Drake's Drum* and *The Fighting Téméraire.* He also wrote on naval history, and was appointed official Naval Historian in 1923.

Newby, P[ercy] H[oward] (1918–   ). English novelist and short story writer. *The Retreat* (1953) is a study of madness, isolation, and love. Set in Egypt, like several of Newby's other works, *The Picnic at Sakkara* (1955) is an odd, ironic comic novel.

Newcomes, The (1855). A novel by William Makepeace THACKERAY. The plot is loose and complex, dealing with three generations of Newcomes. The lovable Colonel Thomas Newcome is a man of simple, unworldly tastes and the utmost honor. The colonel's son, Clive, an artist, is in love with his cousin Ethel Newcome, who, however, is urged by her brother to consider a more ambitious marriage. Clive, despairing of winning Ethel, marries Rosey Mackenzie, with whom he finds he is mismated. But Rosey dies in the course of time and Clive finally marries Ethel.

New Criticism. A movement in 20th-century American literary criticism. Although the term was first used by Joel SPINGARN in an address at Columbia University in 1910, it was not generally known until John Crowe RANSOM used it as the title of a book on critical methods in 1941. The New Critics are united in their emphasis on dealing with the text directly; they insist that the work of art be considered as an autonomous whole, rather than as an excuse for biographical, cultural, or social speculations. Beyond this point, the New Critics differ widely: Kenneth BURKE has emphasized literature as symbolic action; Yvor WINTERS has been concerned with the moral aspects of form and style; R. P. BLACKMUR has investigated the larger meanings of language; Cleanth BROOKS has dealt with the ambiguity of poetic statement.

The New Criticism derived in part from the writings of Ezra POUND and T. S. ELIOT. It tended to accept Eliot's definition of the English tradition in poetry, with its emphasis on the 17th century. With John Crowe Ransom at the center, the movement was also closely associated with the writers at Vanderbilt University who published the magazine *The Fugitive* (1922–1925).

Later, Yale University attracted several of the New Critics to its faculty. Although the movement has been rejected as too limited in many quarters, it has left its mark on contemporary criticism; careful scrutiny of the text has become an accepted approach, even for those embracing other critical methods.

New Deal. A name applied to the program of recovery and reform initiated by President Franklin D. ROOSEVELT in 1933. He first used the phrase in a speech to the Democratic convention on July 2, 1932, when he said, "I pledge you, I pledge myself, to a new deal for the American people."

The New Deal is generally divided into two phases. The first, lasting from 1933 to 1935, aimed at alleviating the economic hardships caused by the depression of 1929. During the Congressional session known as the "Hundred Days" (March 9 to June 16, 1933), legislation was enacted to regulate banks and currency (Emergency Banking Relief Act), to curtail unemployment (Civil Conservation Corps Reforestation Relief Act), and to raise farm prices (Agricultural Adjustment Act); the Tennessee Valley Authority was created to improve social and economic conditions in a seven-state area; and the National Industrial Recovery Act, which was declared unconstitutional in 1935, was passed to stimulate industry and lessen unemployment.

Roosevelt's message to Congress on Jan 4, 1935, in which he asked for social reform legislation, is regarded as the opening of the second phase of the New Deal (1935–1939). This period saw the creation of a Works Progress Administration (1935) to relieve unemployment and the enactment of the National Labor Relations Act (1935), which guaranteed unions the right to bargain collectively. Other legislation included a Social Security Act (1935), to provide unemployment compensation and old-age and survivors insurance, and the Fair Labor Standards Act (1938), establishing a minimum wage and a maximum work week.

Newdigate, Sir Roger (1719–1806). English antiquarian and founder of the Newdigate Prize at Oxford for English poetry.

New Economic Policy or **NEP.** A period of temporary return to capitalist trade and activity in the Soviet Union during the early 1920's. The policy was designed to help restore the country's war-damaged economy. The period was one of disillusionment on the part of many Communists and of rife opportunism and chicanery in economic life. The atmosphere of the time is well rendered in Leonid

Leonov's novel *The Thief,* and in the comic novels of Ilf and Petrov.

Newell, Robert Henry. See Orpheus C. Kerr Papers.

New England Nun, A, and Other Stories (1891). A collection of 20 stories by Mary E. Wilkins Freeman. Realistic and ironic, the stories represent Mrs. Freeman's best writing. The well-known opening story tells of a woman who experiences relief when her betrothed returns from seeking his fortune only in order to marry another woman.

New England Primer, The. A textbook used in early New England to teach children the alphabet and the rudiments of reading. The earliest extant edition is dated 1727, and millions of copies were sold as late as the 19th century. The author of the primer is unknown, but the pocket-sized book was similar to contemporary English volumes. Included in the 1749 edition were an alphabet with verses and illustrations, rules for behavior, several hymns, the prayer *Now I Lay Me Down to Sleep,* and pious stories of several martyrs. See illustration on page 2.

Newgate. A famous English prison. Newgate Gaol was originally merely a few cells over the gate; the first great prison was built in 1422, and the last in 1770–1783. For centuries it was the prison for London and for the County of Middlesex. It was demolished in 1902, and the Central Criminal Court (opened 1905) erected on its site.

New Grub Street (1891). A novel by George Gissing. It deals in grimly realistic fashion with the struggles and compromises of the modern literary world. The hero is Edwin Reardon, a novelist whose valiant attempts to maintain the standards of his art in the face of financial pressure are opposed by an unsympathetic wife. In sharp contrast to Reardon is his friend Jasper Milvain, a critic, whose cleverness and lack of moral or artistic integrity ultimately bring him great success.

New Harmony. A collectivist community founded in Indiana in 1825 on the former site of a Rappite religious settlement. New Harmony was sponsored by Robert Owen, who instituted communal ownership among the members. Dissension arose almost immediately, and the project was abandoned in 1828 at great financial loss to Owen.

new humanism or **neo-humanism.** A term applied to a movement in early 20th-century American literature and philosophy in which classical restraint and conservative values were upheld in an attempt to create standards for the judgment of literature and art to counter the "romantic excesses" of the 19th century. William C. Brownell is considered by some to have first formulated the principles that were adopted by the leaders of the movement, which was at its peak during the late 1920's and early 1930's. Irving Babbitt and Paul Elmer More were its most articulate advocates. Norman Foerster edited *Humanism and America* (1930), a collection of representative essays. After a vituperative battle with the literary radicals, led by H. L. Mencken, the humanist movement was eclipsed by the development of the New Criticism.

New Life, The. See Vita Nuova, La.

New Machiavelli, The (1911). A novel by H. G. Wells. Full of the author's ideas on politics and citizenship, it is almost a handbook of English political life on the eve of World War I. It is written in the form of the autobiography of Richard Remington, who has left England, his wife, and a brilliant political career to elope with Isabel Rivers to Italy.

Newman, Christopher. See American, The.

Newman, Ernest (1868–1959). English music critic. He championed the musicodramatic ideas of Christoph Willibald Gluck and Richard Wagner in *Gluck and the Opera* (1895), *Wagner as Man and Artist* (1914), and other books. He wrote some excellent biographies, such as *Hugo Wolf* (1907) and *The Life of Richard Wagner* (1933; 4 v.).

Newman, John Henry Cardinal (1801–1890). English churchman and author, famous as the leader of the Oxford Movement. He took an outstanding part in the theological controversies involved in the movement and in 1845, after resigning the position that he held as Protestant vicar of St. Mary's, was converted to the Roman Catholic Church. In 1846 he was ordained a priest and in 1879 was made a cardinal. Throughout his career he continued to engage in bitter controversies, especially with the Protestant clergyman and novelist Charles Kingsley and with the Catholic Cardinal Manning. His most famous work, Apologia pro vita sua, a history of his intellectual development and conversion to Catholicism, was written to refute charges made against him by Kingsley. Among his other works, those in prose being marked by a clear, quiet, and smoothly flowing style, are *Lyra Apostolica* (1834), a collection of religious lyrics published with hymns of other authors and including Newman's *Lead, Kindly Light; Loss and Gain* (1848), a partially autobiographical novel dealing with the Oxford Movement; A Dream of Gerontius, a mystic religious poem; *Grammar of Assent* (1870), analyzing religious belief; *The Idea of a University Defined* (1873), a collection of lectures that had an important influence on later theories of liberal arts education. See Tracts for the Times.

New Masses. See Masses, The.

New Men, The (1954). A novel by C. P. Snow. The new men are the scientists of the atomic age. The novel is concerned with their moral dilemmas during the development of the atomic bomb. It is part of the Strangers and Brothers series.

New Model Army. The name given to the Parliamentary army organized (1645) in the English Civil War after the passage of the Self-Denying Ordinance. It was commanded by Thomas Fairfax and later by Oliver Cromwell.

New Netherland. The name of New York while it was a Dutch colony (1624–1664). In the latter year it was seized by the English and renamed in honor of the duke of York.

New Republic, The (1877). A novel, satiric of contemporary English society and ideas by William Hurrell Mallock. In it many actual persons are disguised by other names, among them Ruskin, Jowett, Arnold, Pater, Huxley, and Tyndall. The action of the novel is a week-end discussion, at an English country house, of the prevalent ideas and interests of the day. The novel is notable for the penetration and wit of its characters' conversations.

Newsome, Chad. See Ambassadors, The.

New Testament. The 2d part of the Christian BIBLE. It tells of the embodiment of God's covenant with man in the coming of Jesus Christ. The 27 short books contain the four Gospels narrating the life of Jesus, the early history of the Church, letters by Church fathers to various congregations that have become cornerstones of Christian ethics and the apocalyptic Revelation of St. John.

Newton, Sir **Isaac** (1642–1727). English mathematician and natural philosopher. One of the greatest geniuses the world has known, he made three scientific discoveries of fundamental importance: first, the method of fluxions, which forms the basis of modern calculus; second, the law of the composition of light; and third, the law of universal gravitation, which he presented to the world in his major work PRINCIPIA. Among his other works are *Method of Fluxions* (1693), *Optics* (1704), and *Chronology of Ancient Kingdoms Amended* (1728). The story that Newton's hypothesis on gravity was inspired by the fall of an apple was first told by Voltaire, who claimed to have heard it from the scientist's niece.

New Wave, the (la Nouvelle Vague), including the **New Novel (Nouveau Roman)** and the **New Theater (Nouveau Théâtre).** A literary and cinematic movement originating in a cross-influence of novel and film in France of the late 1950's. Although the New Wave does not constitute a definite school and though it has no unified code, Alain ROBBE-GRILLET and Nathalie SARRAUTE are considered the leading theorists of a group of young writers, film scenarists, and directors who propose to continue the line of experiment marked by Proust, Kafka, Joyce, and Faulkner. The novels of such writers as Michel BUTOR, Marguerite DURAS, Claude MAURIAC, Robert PINGET, and Claude SIMON, and the films of such directors as Philippe de Broca, Claude Chabrol, Jean-Luc Godard, Louis Malle, Jean-Pierre Mocky, Alain RESNAIS, and François Truffaut constitute an attempt to evolve an art of appearances which, omitting all social and moral judgments and fixed values, concentrates on the rigorously exterior description of objects and events in order to reveal the character seeing or experiencing them; thus, events often take place not in chronological time, but in the time of human experience, memory, and fantasy. The leading dramatists of the New Theater, a related movement, are Jean GENET, Eugène IONESCO, and Samuel BECKETT.

As individual differences among the writers and directors popularly associated with the New Wave become more apparent, the term is seen to be less meaningful, and it has been repudiated by many of those to whom it was most commonly applied.

New Way to Pay Old Debts, A (c. 1625). A comedy by Philip MASSINGER. The avaricious Sir Giles Overreach, in order to obtain more money, has confiscated the property of his nephew Frank Wellborn, and is planning to have his daughter Margaret marry, against her wishes, the wealthy Lord Lovell. Margaret, however, loves Tom, the stepson of Lady Allworth, who offers to aid the lovers. She pretends to be in love with Frank who, on the basis of this splendid match, obtains money from his uncle. Margaret elopes with Tom, Lord Lovell marries Lady Allworth, and Sir Giles, from rage and despair, loses his mind.

A NEW WAY TO PAY

OLD DEBTS
A COMOEDIE

As it hath beene often acted at the Phœnix in Drury-Lane, by the Queenes Maiesties seruants.

The Author.

PHILIP MASSINGER.

LONDON,
Printed by *E. P.* for *Henry Seyle*, dwelling in *S. Pauls* Church-yard, at the signe of the Tygers head. Anno. M. DC. XXXIII.

Title page of *A New Way to Pay Old Debts* (1633).

New Yorker, The. An American weekly magazine founded in 1925 by Harold Ross. It specializes in short fiction, cartoons, verse, reviews, and sophisticated and literate commentary. Although avowedly "not for the old lady in Dubuque," it is widely read throughout the country. Among its features are "The Talk of the Town," consisting of comments and anecdotes, often written until recent years by E. B. WHITE; "Profiles," biographical sketches of unusual, interesting, or little known personalities; and examples of unconscious humor selected from current books and periodicals. Leading contributors have included James THURBER, Robert Benchley, Wolcott Gibbs, Ogden Nash, John O'Hara, Dorothy Parker, S. J. Perelman, J. D. Salinger, Rebecca West, and Edmund Wilson. Since the death of Ross in 1951, the magazine has been edited by William Shawn.

Nexø, Martin Andersen (1869–1954). Danish proletarian novelist and short-story writer. Born in the slums of Copenhagen, Nexø worked as a herd boy and a shoemaker's apprentice. He developed a warm sympathy for the poor and a faith in the innate goodness of man; his convictions led him to practical action, as a social democrat and later as a member of the Communist Party. *Pelle Erobreren* (*Pelle the Conqueror*, 1906–1910) was the first of his novel series dealing with the struggles of the working classes. Its subject is the Danish labor movement and its hero, Pelle, is a trade-union leader. In English the work was divided into four parts: *Boyhood, Apprenticeship, The Great Struggle,* and *Daybreak. Ditte Menneskebarn* (5 vols., 1917–1921) related the story of a poor, suffering servant girl. Among Nexø's other works are *Soldage* (1903), an account of travels in Andalusia, and *Under aaben Himmel* (*Under the Open Sky: My Early Years,* 1938), an autobiography.

Ney, Michel. Duc d'Elchingen. Prince de la Moskova (1769–1815). French marshal and Napoleonic military commander. Although made a peer by Louis XVIII, Ney supported Napoleon after his return from Elba and commanded the Old Guard at WATERLOO. After the Hundred Days, he was condemned and shot for treason (December 7, 1815).

Nezhdanov. The central character of Ivan Turgenev's novel VIRGIN SOIL. A student who is anxious to work in the revolutionary movement, Nezhdanov kills himself when he realizes he is not really a believer in the cause.

Nibelungenlied, The. A medieval German epic poem in four-line stanzas. It was probably written about 1190 or 1200, but the author and the exact original version are unknown. Although based on Scandinavian legends as told in the poetic EDDA and the VÖLSUNGA SAGA, it draws further on German legend and omits much of the supernatural material; Siegfried, for instance, is no longer a descendant of the Scandinavian god Odin, but the son of the king of the Netherlands and a typical hero of medieval romance.

Siegfried sets out for Worms to woo the famous beauty Kriemhild. Her three brothers, Burgundian kings, learn from their retainer Hagen that Siegfried is the hero who killed the Nibelung kings and took their name, their treasure of gold, and their cape of darkness, which makes the wearer invisible. Hagen also explains that Siegfried's skin is almost entirely invulnerable, for, except for a spot covered by a fallen leaf, it became horny when he bathed in the blood of a dragon he had slain.

Siegfried helps the three brothers fight the Saxons, then agrees to help one of them, Gunther, in courting Queen Brunhild of Iceland, on the condition of his own marriage to Kriemhild. Brunhild has vowed that she will marry the man who can best her at hurling a spear, throwing a stone, and jumping. Siegfried in his magic cape stands beside Gunther and invisibly accomplishes the difficult feats for him, so the double marriage is celebrated. But Brunhild is still suspicious about Gunther's strength, and on their wedding night she ties him in a knot and hangs him on the wall. He appeals to Siegfried, who, again invisible, wrestles her into pleased submissiveness and takes her girdle and ring, which he gives to Kriemhild. Then one day the two queens argue fiercely before the cathedral, and Kriemhild proves with the girdle and ring that Brunhild had been duped in accepting Gunther.

At this point Brunhild's role, so important in the *Völsunga Saga,* becomes vague, and that of the retainer Hagen becomes dominant. Presumably jealous for Gunther's sake of Siegfried's glory, Hagen tricks Kriemhild into revealing Siegfried's one vulnerable spot and arranges a great hunt, during which he murders Siegfried. He seizes the treasure hoard from Kriemhild (it had been her wedding gift from

Siegfried), and sinks it in the Rhine in collaboration with her brothers. The grieving widow broods on her wrongs, and when Etzel (Attila, king of the Huns) proposes marriage, she accepts on condition that he aid her plans for vengeance. After the wedding they invite her brothers for a visit, then attack them with the help of the heroes Hildebrand and Dietrich of Bern. When Hagen, the last living Burgundian, refuses to tell where the treasure is, Kriemhild kills him. At this point Hildebrand, horrified at the carnage caused by one woman, turns against her and kills her, leaving Etzel and Dietrich to lament the dead.

Wagner drew partly on this material for his opera DER RING DES NIBELUNGEN.

Nicander (Nikandros, fl. 2d century B.C.). A Greek poet and grammarian, born in Ionia. Both of his two surviving poems are on medical subjects.

Nicanor. The husband and victim of the evil queen Cleopatra in Pierre Corneille's tragedy RODOGUNE.

Niccoli, Nicolò (1364–1437). Florentine Humanist. He gathered and copied Greek and Latin manuscripts, during the REVIVAL OF LEARNING in the Renaissance.

Niccolini, Govanni Battista (1782–1861). Italian dramatist. His tragedies, which presented historical instances of Italy's long struggle against domestic despotism and foreign domination, served to highlight the resistance of Italian patriots to their Austrian, Spanish, and Papal rulers during the Risorgimento. Among his tragedies are *Nabucco* (1816), *Giovanni da Procida* (1830), and *Arnaldo da Brescia* (1838), his most famous work.

Nicene Creed. The creed formulated by the COUNCIL OF NICAEA (A.D. 325) on the basis of older wordings, specially designed to combat the heresy of Arianus. The controversial *filioque* clause in this creed, which was largely responsible for the Great Schism of 1054, was recognized by the Council of Toledo in 589.

Nichiren. Japanese Buddhist sect founded by Nichiren (1222–1282). It bases its teachings on the LOTUS SUTRA and claims that Japan is the true center of Buddhism and the Lotus Sutra is the ultimate teaching of the historical Buddha. Noted for the fanaticism of its priests and adherents, it gained great strength during the Kamakura period (1185–1333). A post-World War II phenomenon has been the growth of a splinter group, the Sōka Gakkai with more than five million members. It is an active force in Japanese politics and shows extreme right-wing and ultranationalistic tendencies.

Nicholas, St. One of the most popular saints in Christendom, especially in the East. He was the patron saint of Russia, of Aberdeen, of parish clerks, of scholars (who used to be called *clerks*), of pawnbrokers (because of the three gold balls that he gave to the daughters of a poor man to save them from earning their dowers in a disreputable way), and of little boys (because he once restored to life three little boys who had been cut up and pickled in a salting tub to serve for bacon). He is invoked by sailors (because he allayed a storm during a voyage to the Holy Land) and against fire. Finally, he is the original of SANTA CLAUS.

Little is known of his life, but he is said to have

been bishop of Myra (Lycia) in the early 4th century. One story relates that he was present at the Council of Nicaea (325) and there buffeted Arius on the jaw. His day is December 6, and he is represented in episcopal robes with three purses of gold balls, or three small boys, in allusion to one of the above legends.

Nicholas I (Nikolai Pavlovich; 1796–1855). Czar of Russia (1825–1855). His reign is noted for its extremely conservative, reactionary character, which was perhaps, in part, a direct result of the DECEMBRIST REVOLT that occurred upon his accession to the throne. Two other events that made Nicholas tighten his grip on the country even more were the Polish uprising of 1830–1831 and the 1848 revolutions in Europe. The Czar's determination to keep insurrection out of his country extended even to his personal censorship of the work of the great Russian poet Aleksandr Pushkin. The closing years of Nicholas' reign were marred by the debacle of the Crimean War (1854–1856), which clearly showed the corruption and inefficiency of the Czarist government.

Nicholas II (Nikolai Aleksandrovich; 1868–1918). Czar of Russia (1894–1917). Nicholas II's reign, filled with misfortunes and blunders, ended in the abolition of the monarchy and the revolution of 1917. The czar was not strong enough to deal with the social and political upheaval in his country, even if anything could have been done about it at such a late stage.

Even before the First World War, the influence at court of such sinister characters as the monk Rasputin had made even the supporters of the monarchy uneasy. The "Bloody Sunday" massacre in January, 1905, also contributed to the revolutionary mood of the people. On this occasion, a large procession of workers, on their way to the Winter Palace to place their petitions before the czar, were fired on by troops, and hundreds of workers were killed and wounded. A general strike was called throughout the country, and the government all but toppled. Only the granting of the Constitution of 1905 and the promise of liberal reforms stopped the 1905 revolutionary movement from succeeding. During this period, the government also had had the problem of the Russo-Japanese War (1904–1905), the destruction of the Russian fleet at Tsushima in May, 1905, stirring general discontent.

The next, and final, severe test of the regime started in 1914 with Russia's entry into World War I. Defeats on the battlefield and confusion and mismanagement at home finally brought about Nicholas' abdication in March, 1917. This was the first step in the Russian Revolution which culminated in October, 1917, with the seizure of power by the Bolsheviks. The czar and his family were put to death by the Bolsheviks in July, 1918.

Nicholas V, Pope. Tommaso Parentucelli (1398–1455). At the age of 49 he succeeded to the papacy and remained an outstanding patron of Humanism and the arts until his death. He founded the Vatican library and laid the architectural plans for Renaissance Rome.

Nicholas Breakspear. See ADRIAN IV.

Nicholas Nickleby (1838–1839). A novel by Charles DICKENS. When Nicholas' father dies leaving him penniless, his uncle Ralph Nickleby refuses to help him. Having his mother and his sister Kate to support, Nicholas sets about to make a living. He first serves as usher to Mr. Wackford SQUEERS, schoolmaster at Dotheboys Hall; the brutality of Squeers and his wife, especially toward a poor, half-witted boy named Smike, causes Nicholas to leave in disgust. Smike runs away from school to follow Nicholas, remaining his follower until he dies. Next Nicholas joins the theatrical company of Mr. Crummles, and finally he secures a good post in a counting house owned by the benevolent CHEERYBLE BROTHERS. In the meantime, Kate NICKLEBY has been working for Madame Mantalini, a milliner. Ralph Nickleby tries to lure her from her innocence by encouraging his friend Sir Mulberry Hawk to make unseemly advances toward her. He is foiled in this, and in his plan to force Madeline Bray to marry his friend Gride, by Nicholas, who interferes and saves his sister from Mulberry Hawk and who himself falls in love with Madeline Bray. Ralph tries to retaliate by injuring Nicholas through Smike, who finally dies. Ralph's final blow, the discovery that Smike was his son, causes him to commit suicide. Nicholas marries Madeline and Kate marries the Cheerybles' nephew Frank.

This novel attacks schools and schoolmasters in much the same way that OLIVER TWIST attacks the workhouses. Dickens' ruthless exposure, through Dotheboys Hall, of actual conditions in many schools in England, where the pupils were half starved and taught nothing, led to the closing or reformation of many such institutions. See Newman NOGGS; INFANT PHENOMENON.

Nichols, Anne. See ABIE'S IRISH ROSE.

Nichols, Robert (1893–1944). English poet and dramatist, associated with the GEORGIANS. *Ardours and Endurances* (1917) is a collection of war poems.

Nickleby, Kate. In Charles Dickens' NICHOLAS NICKLEBY, sister of Nicholas. She is beautiful, pure-minded, and loving. She works hard to assist in the expenses of housekeeping and shuns the attempts of her uncle Ralph and others to lead her astray.

Mrs. Nickleby. Widowed mother of Nicholas and Kate. She is a weak, vain woman who imagines an idiot neighbor is in love with her because he tosses cabbages and other articles over the garden wall.

Nickneven. A gigantic, malignant hag of Scottish superstition. William Dunbar has well described this spirit in his *Flyting of Dunbar and Kennedy.*

Nick of the Woods, or the Jibbenainosay (1837). A novel by Robert Montgomery BIRD. "Bloody Nathan," scorned by the pioneers as a timid Quaker who abhors all violence, is later revealed to be the feared killer of Indians, "Nick of the Woods." Bird describes the causes and symptoms of Nathan's split personality with remarkable psychological insight; he presents the Indians as brutish savages, in protest against James Fenimore Cooper's idealization. His background as a dramatist serves Bird well; he maintains suspense despite the complexity of plot.

Nicodemus. In the New Testament, a Pharisee who came to visit Jesus by night (John 3:2). After the crucifixion, he brought myrrh and aloes and helped Joseph of Arimathaea with the burial of Jesus.

Nicolai, Christoph Friedrich (1733–1811). German enlightenment philosopher. He was a friend of Lessing, with whom he edited the *Letters, Concerning the Most Recent Literature* (*Briefe, die neueste Literatur betreffend;* 1759–1765). He was, however, more narrowly rationalistic than Lessing and less amenable to progressive ideas, as is seen in his *Feyner kleiner Almanach* (*Fancy Little Almanac,* 1771 ff.), in which he satirically attacked Herder.

Nicole, Pierre (1625–1695). French theologian. An ardent Jansenist and a solitary resident at Port-Royal, Nicole defended JANSENISM against its enemies in a series of letters much in the manner of the *Lettres Provinciales* of Pascal: *Les Imaginaires, ou lettres sur l'hérésie imaginaire* (*The Imaginary Ones, or Letters on the Imaginary Heresy,* 1664) attempted to prove that the supposed Jansenist heresy, if it existed at all, was at best a tiny matter, while *Les Visionnaires, ou seconde partie des Lettres sur l'hérésie imaginaire* (*The Visionary Ones, or Second Part of the Letters on the Imaginary Heresy,* 1667) rebutted the attack of DESMARETS DE SAINT-SORLIN on Jansenist doctrine. Nicole aided Antoine ARNAULD in drafting *La Perpétuité de la Foi de l'Eglise Catholique touchant l'Eucharistie* (*The Perpetuity of the Faith of the Catholic Church Concerning the Eucharist,* 1669–1676) and accompanied him into exile, but soon managed to placate the authorities and to return. Nicole's earlier *Essais de morale et instructions théologiques* (*Essays on Ethics and Theological Instructions,* 1671), less controversial than many of his writings, was widely admired.

Nicoll, Allardyce (1894–). English writer on the theater. He teaches in the Harkness School of the Drama at Yale University. He is the author of *A History of Restoration Drama* (1923).

Nicolson, Sir Harold (1886–1968). English biographer, historian, diplomat, and journalist. He was the husband of Victoria SACKVILLE-WEST. Among his books are *The Development of English Biography* (1928), *The Congress of Vienna* (1946), *Benjamin Constant* (1949), *The Evolution of Diplomatic Method* (1954), and *The Age of Reason* (1960).

Nicomachean Ethics. See ARISTOTLE.

Nicomède (1651). A tragedy by Pierre CORNEILLE. It relates the triumph of Nicomède, conqueror of Cappadocia, over the hostile machinations of his father, the king of Bithynia, of his stepmother Arsinoé, of the Roman ambassador Flaminius, and of his own half brother Attale. Nicomède parries all intrigue skillfully and magnanimously and, with the eventual help of Attale, frustrates a plot to imprison him in Rome. The play, by virtue of the characterization of the central stoical figure, is one of Corneille's most striking.

Niebuhr, Reinhold (1892–1971). American theologian. After serving as pastor in Wright City, Mo., and Detroit, Mich., where he took an active interest in labor problems, Niebuhr joined the faculty of the Union Theological Seminary. One of the most important and influential of American theologians, he persistently emphasizes the reality of sin and the tragic estate of man in his fallen condition, and decries the secular tendency to discount sin. He sees the problem of modern man as one in which power and technocracy have brought confusion and meaninglessness, and the task of Christianity as ministering to the

world as well as to the spirit. Among his books are *Moral Man and Immoral Society* (1932), *The Children of Light and the Children of Darkness* (1944), *Christian Realism and Political Problems* (1953), *The Self and the Drama of History* (1955), *Leaves from the Notebook of a Tamed Cynic* (1956), and *Beyond Tragedy: Essays on the Christian Interpretation of History* (1961).

Niemöller, Martin (1892–). German Protestant minister, opposed to Nazi control of the church. He was put in a concentration camp (1938) and released after the war.

Nietzsche, Friedrich (1844–1900). German philosopher, classical scholar, and poet. He is most famous for the theory of the ÜBERMENSCH (superman) which he developed in THUS SPAKE ZAPATHUSTRA. As early as his *Unzeitgemässe Betrachtungen* (*Untimely Observations,* 1873–1876), he had sharply criticized the systematic philosophy of the earlier 19th century, especially that of Hegel; and throughout his career, he continually sought to penetrate beyond all rational, systematic schemes to the irrational, human level beneath, as in his well-known BEYOND GOOD AND EVIL. His complete rejection of Christianity was based on the belief that Christianity leads man's thoughts away from this world and into the next, thus making him less capable of coping with earthly life; he felt that Christianity teaches men how to die but not how to live. In his early career, especially in THE BIRTH OF TRAGEDY, his views were influenced by Schopenhauer. His own lyrics strongly influenced the poetry of expressionism. Other well-known works are *Menschliches, Allzumenschliches* (*Human, All Too Human,* 1878), *Der Antichrist* (1888), and *Ecce Homo* (1888). In 1889 he went insane and remained so until he died. See Elisabeth FÖRSTER-NIETZSCHE.

Nievo, Ippolito (1831–1861). Italian novelist and poet. His most successful work is the lengthy novel *Le Confessioni di Un Italiano* (1858), republished as *Le Confessioni di Un Ottuagenario* (1867), which recounts events occurring in Italy during the 82 years covered in the fictitious narrator's reminiscences. Nievo himself, an ardent patriot, served as a member of Garibaldi's Red Shirts.

Niflheim. A legendary realm of Scandinavian mythology. In contrast to Valhalla, the abode of fallen warriors, Niflheim is said to have received all those who died of disease or old age. It existed from the beginning in the North, in endless cold and everlasting night; Hela ruled over it. In its center was the well Hvergelmir, from which flowed 12 rivers.

Nigger, The (1909). A play by Edward SHELDON. It is one of the earliest uses of the familiar theme of the white man who discovers that he has Negro blood. In this case the man is a state governor who is about to sign a bill that will harm the financial interests of a cousin. The latter threatens to reveal the secret, but the governor signs the bill anyway.

Nigger Heaven (1926). A novel by Carl VAN VECHTEN. One of the first novels about Negro life in Harlem, the book takes its title from the topmost gallery where Negroes were required to sit in theaters. Set in the jazz era, the novel is filled with melodramatic episodes, and ends with a murder of which the hero is falsely accused. It is, nevertheless, noteworthy as a true and understanding exploration of the Negro's suffering and aspirations, the more remarkable that it was written by a white man.

Nigger of the 'Narcissus,' The (1897). A novel by Joseph CONRAD. Less a narrative than a study of men's characters under stress, the story is centered on a Negro sailor, James Wait, who is dying of tuberculosis. The brooding presence of death brings out the best and the worst in the crew of the *Narcissus*. In this tense atmosphere Donkin, a mean-spirited agitator, almost manages to stir the crew to mutiny.

Night Flight (Vol de Nuit; 1931). A novel by Antoine de SAINT-EXUPÉRY about the air line director Rivière. Rivière must appear harsh and ruthless in order to raise his pilots above self-pity and to extract from them that supreme effort through which aviation will achieve victory over the night.

nightingale. For the classical legend, see PHIL-OMELA. There is a passage in T. S. Eliot's *The Waste Land* which confuses the nightingale with the night-jar:

> . . . yet there the nightingale
> Filled all the desert with inviolable voice
> And still she cried, and still the world pursues,
> "Jug Jug" to dirty ears.

This is unfair. No nightingale ever cried "Jug Jug." The goatsucker does and *nightjar* is another name for it, not *nightingale*.

Nightingale, Florence (1820–1910). English nurse and hospital reformer, known as the Lady with the Lamp. Early interested in nursing, she inspected schools and hospitals throughout England and in Europe, and spent several months (1849–1950) at a Roman Catholic hospital at Alexandria, Egypt. She trained (1850–1851) as a nurse at the Institute of Protestant Deaconesses at Kaiserwerth, studied further in Paris, and in 1853 returned to London to take charge of a woman's hospital. At the news of the suffering of the wounded in the Crimean War, she volunteered her services and, at the head of a group of 38 nurses, set up a hospital at Scutari in November, 1854, soon after the battle of Balaklava. Here she set up stringent observance of sanitation and by 1855 the death rate from cholera, typhus, and dysentery had fallen from about 50 per cent to about 2 per cent. She worked tirelessly and ceaselessly, making her nightly rounds with lamp in hand and performing administrative duties as well as nursing. After the war, with funds donated as a testimonial to her services she founded (1860) the Nightingale home at St. Thomas's Hospital for the training of nurses, and thereafter, for 30 years, helped to establish nursing homes in England. She was not able to participate actively in nursing since her own health had been ruined during her war service. In 1907, she became the first woman to receive the Order of Merit.

Nightmare Abbey (1818). A novel by Thomas Love PEACOCK. In this book, Peacock satirizes the leading figures and concepts of romanticism in England in his day. Among the characters, Mr. Flosky is considered to represent Coleridge, Scythrop Glowry, Shelley, and the extravagant Mr. Cypress is a caricature of Lord Byron.

Night Over Taos (1932). A regional drama by Maxwell ANDERSON. It deals with a clash between American frontiersmen and the Mexican patriarchate of Taos in 1847.

Night Thoughts on Life, Death and Immortality (1742–1746). A poem by Edward YOUNG, written in nine books in blank verse. Although its full title reads *The Complaint; or, Night-Thoughts on Life, Death and Immortality*, the poem is commonly referred to as simply *Night Thoughts*. It is the most specifically theological of the major works of the age. It contains the reflections of the poet late at night on "life, death and immortality," a long soliloquy urging an erring youth, Lorenzo, to turn to virtue, and a vision of the Judgment Day and eternity thereafter, with a description of the magnificence of the starry heavens. The poem contains many autobiographical allusions: Young refers to the successive deaths of his wife, his step-daughter, and her husband. The characteristic theme in the poem, aside from its sentimental and orthodox elements, is upward progress through endless gradations of being:

> Nature revolves, but man advances; both
> Eternal; that a circle, this a line.

It is one of the outstanding examples of the melancholy "GRAVEYARD SCHOOL" in eighteenth-century English literature.

Nihilism (from Lat., *nihil*, "nothing"). An ex-

Title page of Young's *Night Thoughts* (1st ed., 1742).

THE

COMPLAINT:

O R,

Night-Thoughts

O N

LIFE, DEATH, & IMMORTALITY.

Sunt lacrymæ rerum, & mentem mortalia tangunt. VIRG

L O N D O N:
Printed for R. DODSLEY, at TULLY's Head in *Pall-Mall.* 1742.

[Price, One Shilling]

treme form of 19th-century revolutionism, indignantly disclaimed by Karl Marx, which took form in Russia in the 1850's, and was specially active in the 1870's and later, under Bakunin. It aimed at anarchy and the complete overthrow of law, order, and all existing institutions, with the idea of re-forming the world *de novo*. The following was the code of the Nihilists: (1) annihilate the idea of a God, or there can be no freedom; (2) annihilate the idea of right, which is only might; (3) annihilate civilization, property, marriage, morality, and justice (4) let your own happiness be your only law. The name was given to them by the novelist Turgenev in his FATHERS AND CHILDREN. Dostoyevsky portrays Nihilism in *The Possessed* and *The Brothers Karamazov*.

Nikolayeva, Galina Yevgenyevna (1914–   ). Russian novelist. Her long novel *A Battle on the Way* (*Bitva v puti;* 1957) is one of the more interesting recent Soviet works. The novel has an unusually large part of it given over to nonpolitical and generally forbidden areas of exploration, such as an unhappy love affair and descriptions of the work of the secret police.

Nile, battle of the. A naval engagement fought in Abukir Bay, near Alexandria, Egypt (August 1, 1798). The British fleet under Horatio NELSON defeated the French fleet under Brueys. As a result of the victory, Napoleon's expedition to Egypt ended in failure, and Nelson earned for himself the epithet of "the hero of the Nile."

Nimier, Roger (1925–1962). French novelist, essayist, and journalist. He was noted for his refusal to take anything seriously. An insolent and nonchalant wit characterized his work, such as the novels *The Blue Hussar* (1950) and *Children of Circumstance* (*Les Enfants tristes;* 1951), and the essays in *Le Grand d'Espagne* (1950).

Nimmo, Chester. A politician, hero of a trilogy of novels by Joyce Cary. See PRISONER OF GRACE, A.

Nimrod. In the Old Testament, the son of Cush, famous for his exploits as "mighty hunter before the Lord" (Gen. 10:9). Thus, the name refers generally to any daring or outstanding hunter. Alexander Pope says of Nimrod that he was "a mighty hunter, and his prey was man" (*Windsor Forest,* 1713); so also does Milton interpret the phrase (*Paradise Lost,* 1667).

Nims, John Frederick (1913–   ). American poet and teacher. Nims works in both "modernist" and traditionalist forms, though the harshness of many of his scenes makes even his most formal poems seem ragged and strained. Among his works are *The Iron Pastoral* (1947) and *Knowledge of the Evening: Poems 1950–1960* (1960). He edited *The Poems of St. John of the Cross* (1959).

Ninazu. A Sumerian god of the underworld, son of ENLIL and NINLIL.

nine. A mystical number. From the earliest times the number nine has been regarded as a mystical number of peculiar significance. Deucalion's ark, made by the advice of Prometheus, was tossed about for nine days before it stranded on the top of Mount Parnassus. There were nine MUSES, frequently referred to as merely "the Nine." There were nine Gallicenae or virgin priestesses of the ancient Gallic oracle; and Lars Porsena swore by the nine gods, who were Juno, Minerva, and Tinia (the three chief), Vulcan, Mars, Saturn, Hercules, Summanus, and Vedius;

while the nine of the Sabines were Hercules, Romulus, Esculapius, Bacchus, Aeneas, Vesta, Santa, Fortuna, and Fides.

There were nine rivers of Hell, or, according to some accounts, the Styx encompassed the infernal regions in nine circles. Milton makes the gates of Hell "thrice three-fold; three folds are brass, three iron, three of adamantine rock." They have nine folds, nine plates, and nine linings.

In the early Ptolemaic system of astronomy, there were nine spheres; hence Milton, in his *Arcades,* speaks of the "celestial syrens' harmony that sit upon the nine enfolded spheres." They are those of the Moon, Mercury, Venus, the Sun, Mars, Jupiter, Saturn, and the Firmament, or that of the fixed stars, and the Crystalline Sphere. In Scandinavian mythology there were nine earths, HEL being the goddess of the ninth; there were nine worlds in NIFLHEIM, and ODIN's ring dropped eight other rings (nine rings of mystical import) every ninth night.

In folk tale, nine appears many times. The ABRACADABRA was worn nine days, and then flung into a river; in order to see the fairies one is directed to put "nine grains of wheat on a four-leaved clover"; nine knots are made on black wool as a charm for a sprained ankle; if a servant finds nine green peas in a peasecod, she lays it on the lintel of the kitchen door, and the first man that enters in is to be her cavalier; to see nine magpies is most unlucky; a cat has nine lives; and the nine of diamonds is known as the Curse of Scotland.

There are nine orders of ANGELS; in heraldry, there are nine marks of cadency and nine different crowns recognized; and among ecclesiastical architects there are nine crosses.

Nine Days' Wonder. Something that causes sensational astonishment for a few days, then is forgotten. Like so many other concepts that grew up in the Middle Ages, such occurrences are predicted with numerological exactitude: three days are spent in amazement, three in discussion, and in three more interest subsides completely. In Elizabethan times, an event widely advertised as a nine days' wonder was William Kemp's morris dance from London to Norwich, undertaken on a bet. Kemp was a famous comedian and dancer of jigs, who was an important member of Shakespeare's company at the Globe Theatre.

1984 (1949). A satirical novel by George ORWELL. Set in the society of the future, toward which Orwell believed both extreme right- and left-wing totalitarianism were heading, it is the story of a man and a girl who rebel. In this terrifying society there is no place for truth, for historical records are destroyed and propaganda replaces information. Thought and love are punished, while privacy is impossible. Placards everywhere say: "Big Brother is watching you." Big Brother represents Stalin, and the satire is chiefly directed against Russia.

1919 (1932). A novel by John Dos PASSOS, the 2nd of his trilogy U.S.A. (q.v.). It takes the characters introduced in THE 42ND PARALLEL, with a few additions, through World War I and presents a kaleidoscopic picture of the war years.

Like the other novels of the trilogy, *1919* uses the "newsreel" and "camera eye" techniques; it also contains brief biographical sketches of such public figures as Theodore Roosevelt, J. P. Morgan, Woodrow Wilson, and the Unknown Soldier.

Ninety-five Theses. The original document of the Reformation, nailed on the door of the castle church at Wittenberg by Martin LUTHER on Oct. 31, 1517. Essentially, it was an indictment of the venality of the Roman Catholic Church and, especially, of the common practice of selling indulgences in connection with the sacrament of penance. Luther contended that, after confession, absolution was dependent only upon the sinner's faith and divine grace, not upon the priest. At this point, Luther was not an advocate of actual separation from the church of Rome.

Ninety-three (Quatre-vingt-treize; 1879). A historical novel by Victor HUGO. Set in the France of 1793, the novel involves in its action Marat, Danton, and Robespierre. The principal roles in this highly melodramatic work are played by the marquis de Lantenac, his nephew Gauvain, and a former priest with republican sympathies named Cimourdan.

Nine Worthies of London. A kind of chronicle-history in mixed verse and prose of 9 prominent citizens of London. It was published in 1592 by Richard Johnson, author also of *The Seven Champions of Christendom*. His Worthies are:

Sir William Walworth, who stabbed Wat Tyler, the rebel, and was twice Lord Mayor (1374, 1380).

Sir Henry Pritchard, who (in 1356) feasted Edward III (with 5,000 followers); Edward the Black Prince; John, king of Austria; the king of Cyprus; and David, king of Scotland.

Sir William Sevenoke, who fought with the dauphin of France and built twenty almshouses and a free school (1418).

Sir Thomas White, merchant tailor, who, in 1553, kept the citizens loyal to Queen Mary during Wyatt's rebellion.

Sir John Bonham, who was entrusted with a valuable cargo for the Danish market, and made commander of the army raised to stop the progress of the great Solyman.

Christopher Croker, who became famous at the siege of Bordeaux, and companion of the Black Prince when he helped Don Pedro to the throne of Castile.

Sir John Hawkwood, who was one of the Black Prince's knights, and immortalized in Italian history as Giovanni Acuti Cavaliero.

Sir Hugh Caverley, who was famous for ridding Poland of a monstrous bear.

Sir Henry Maleverer, generally called Henry of Cornhill, who lived in the reign of Henry IV. He was a crusader, and became the guardian of "Jacob's well."

The names of Sir Richard Whittington and Sir Thomas Gresham are "conspicuous by their absence."

Ninhursag. See NINTU.

Ninlil. A Sumerian goddess of air, the wife of ENLIL. Following the sage advice of her old mother Nundarshegunu, Ninlil so delighted Enlil, the storm-god, that he came to her in three different forms. The resulting offspring were Nergal, the king of the underworld, Ninazu, another underworld deity, and a third deity who remains unknown.

Ninmah. See NINTU.

Ninon de Lenclos. See Anne LENCLOS.

Ninshubur. The herald of INANNA in Sumerian mythology.

Ninsun. A Babylonian goddess, the mother of GILGAMESH.

Nintu. Also called **Ninhursag** and **Ninmah.** A Sumerian mother goddess. Possibly a later form of the ancient earth-goddess KI, she created human beings, molding six varieties of them from clay. To the water god ENKI, she bore Ninsar, who in turn bore him Ninkur, upon whom Enki fathered Uttu, the goddess of plants. When Enki ate the plants, he was cursed by Nintu, but he eventually persuaded her to remove the curse, in return for various gifts.

Ninurta or **Ningirsu.** Sumerian and Babylonian god of war, the south wind, and artificial irrigation. He was the hero of a fragmentary epic poem that tells of his successful war on the dragon KUR. Following the advice of his talking weapon Sharur, Ninurta, a son of Enlil, moves against Kur, a monster often associated with the underworld. At first defeated, Ninurta returns to the battle and destroys Kur completely. His death, however, adversely affects the normal behavior of the waters upon which the land depends for irrigation. Ninurta therefore guides the flood waters into the Tigris, and the fertility of the fields returns. Of the stones that were flung in his battle with Kur, Ninurta blesses those that had been on his side and curses the others. In many respects, this myth is the forerunner of innumerable others in which a hero slays a dragon. See WAR OF THE GODS; POEM OF BAAL, THE.

Ninus. Son of Belus, husband of the legendary SEMIRAMIS, and the reputed builder of Nineveh. In the Pyramus and Thisbe travesty in Shakespeare's *Midsummer Night's Dream* (c. 1595), the lovers meet at his tomb.

Niobe. Mythical queen of Thebes, daughter of TANTALUS and wife of AMPHION. She boasted that she had borne many children, whereas LETO had borne only two. Leto complained of the insult to her children, Apollo and Artemis, and they avenged her by killing all Niobe's children and, in some versions, her husband as well. Grief-stricken, Niobe returned to her homeland, Lydia. There, at her own request, Zeus turned her to stone on Mount Sipylus, and she may be seen there to this day constantly weeping.

Niord or **Njorthr.** The Scandinavian god of the sea, the protector of seafaring men. He ruled the winds, calmed the seas, and warded off fire. He was one of the Aesir, and father, by his wife Skadhi, of Frey and Freya. His home was Noatun, the place of ships. The name means benefactor.

Nippur. An important city of ancient Sumeria. It was the cult center of the god Enlil.

nirvana (*Sans.,* blowing out, extinction). In Buddhist teaching, a complete annihilation of the 3 main ego-drives for money, fame, and immortality. It also signifies enlightenment and the deliverance of the self from transmigration, because annihilation of the ego-drives destroys past KARMA and does not create new *karma*.

Nisard, Désiré (1806–1888). French literary critic. Violently opposed to romanticism, Nisard is noted for his rigid respect for 17th-century NEOCLASSICISM. His *Histoire de la littérature française* (1844–1861) is his best known work.

Nisus and Euryalus. In Vergil's AENEID, young Trojans who accompany Aeneas from Troy and win great distinction in the war against Turnus. In Book IX of the *Aeneid,* they enter the enemy camp in the dead of night but are detected by the Rutulians. Euryalus is slain and Nisus dies trying to save him.

Nivoix, Paul. See Marcel PAGNOL.

Njal. See BURNT NJAL.

Njorthr. See NERTHUS; NIORD.

NKVD. See CHEKA.

Nō. Japanese theater. The plays deal largely with well-known historical themes, often with Buddhistic overtones, and are frequently of much literary merit. The acting is highly stylized; masks, elaborate costumes, music, and a chorus are integral parts of the performance. Developed in court and noble society during the Muromachi period (1333–1600), its greatest exponent was SEAMI MOTOKIYO. Nō is influenced greatly by Zen Buddhism.

Noah. A righteous man in the Old Testament whom God chose to spare from the Flood that covered the face of the earth. During the 40 days and nights of the deluge, Noah lived in the ark, which he had built and where, with his own family, he had taken the animals, two by two, following God's command. The ark finally came to rest on Mount Ararat, and Noah with his three sons Shem, Ham, and Japheth, their families, and the various birds and animals came out safely to repopulate the world. According to the biblical narrative, the first rainbow then appeared as God's promise the world would not be so destroyed again. (Gen. 6–9). See FLOOD MYTHS.

According to legend, Noah's wife was unwilling to go into the ark; the quarrel between the patriarch and his wife forms a prominent feature of *Noah's Flood,* in the Chester and Townley mystery plays. In the Koran, Noah's wife, known as Waila, tries to persuade the people that her husband is mad.

Noailles, Comtesse **Anna de** [born Princesse **de Brincovan**] (1876–1933). French poet. She published nine volumes of lyric and romantic poetry and an autobiography, *Le Livre de ma vie* (1932).

Nobel, Alfred Bernhard (1833–1896). Swedish engineer and industrialist. Nobel amassed a great fortune from his discoveries of synthetics and explosives (especially dynamite) and their manufacture, and from his interests in Baku oil fields. He was also an unsuccessful writer of novels and plays. He left over $9 million to establish the Nobel Prizes.

Nobel Prizes. Annual monetary awards of variable amounts (about $100,000 in 1972) made to persons who have benefited mankind through their contributions in the fields of physics, chemistry, medicine, literature, and work for peace. They are paid out of a fund established for that purpose by the will of Alfred Nobel. The awards are presented in Stockholm and in Oslo (peace prize) on the anniversary of Nobel's death (Dec. 10) each year, but they are occasionally reserved in one or more categories.

The literary awards are selected by the Swedish Academy of Literature. The recipients have been: 1901, René François Armand Sully Prudhomme (Fr.); 1902, Theodor Mommsen (Ger.); 1903, Björnstjerne Björnson (Nor.); 1904, Frédéric Mistral (Fr.) and José Echegaray y Eizaguirre (Sp.); 1905, Henryk Sienkiewicz (Pol.); 1906, Giosuè Carducci (It.); 1907, Rudyard Kipling (Eng.); 1908, Rudolf Eucken (Ger.); 1909, Selma Lagerlöf (Swed.); 1910, Paul von Heyse (Ger.); 1911, Maurice Maeterlinck (Belg.); 1912, Gerhart Hauptmann (Ger.); 1913, Rabindranath Tagore (Ind.); 1914, none; 1915, Romain Rolland (Fr.); 1916, Verner von Heidenstam (Swed.); 1917, Karl A. Gjellerup (Dan.) and Hendrik Pontoppidan (Dan.); 1918, none; 1919, Carl Spitteler (Swiss); 1920, Knut Hamsun (Nor.); 1921, Anatole France (Fr.); 1922, Jacinto Benavente y Martínez (Sp.); 1923, William Butler Yeats (Ir.); 1924, Wladislaw S. Reymont (Pol.); 1925, George Bernard Shaw (Br.); 1926, Grazia Deledda (It.); 1927, Henri Bergson (Fr.); 1928, Sigrid Undset (Nor.); 1929, Thomas Mann (Ger.); 1930, Sinclair Lewis (Am.); 1931, Erik Axel Karlfeldt (Swed.); 1932, John Galsworthy (Eng.); 1933, Ivan Bunin (Fr., Russ. b.); 1934, Luigi Pirandello (It.); 1935, none; 1936, Eugene O'Neill (Am.); 1937, Roger Martin Du Gard (Fr.); 1938, Pearl S. Buck (Am.); 1939, Frans Eemil Sillanpää (Finn.); 1940 to 1943, none; 1944, Johannes V. Jensen (Dan.); 1945, Gabriela Mistral (Chilean); 1946, Hermann Hesse (Ger.); 1947, André Gide (Fr.); 1948, Thomas Stearns Eliot (Eng.); 1949, William Faulkner (Am.); 1950, Bertrand Russell (Eng.); 1951, Pär Lagerkvist (Swed.); 1952, François Mauriac (Fr.); 1953, Sir Winston Churchill (Eng.); 1954, Ernest Hemingway (Am.); 1955, Halldór Laxness (Ice.); 1956 Juan Ramón Jiménez (P.R.); 1957, Albert Camus (Fr.); 1958, Boris Pasternak (Russ., declined); 1959, Salvatore Quasimodo (It.); 1960, Alexis Léger (St. John Perse) (Fr.); 1961, Ivo Andric (Yugo.); 1962, John Steinbeck (Am.); 1963, Giorgos Seferis (Seferiades) (Gr.); 1964, Jean-Paul Sartre (Fr.); 1965, Mikhail Sholokhov (Russ.); 1966, S. Y. Agnon (Pol.–Isr.) and Nelly Sachs (Ger.–Swed.); 1967, Miguel Angel Asturias (Guat.); 1968, Yasunari Kawabata (Jap.); 1969, Samuel Beckett (Ir.–Fr.); 1970, Aleksandr Solzhenitsyn (Russ.); 1971, Pablo Neruda (Chile); 1972, Heinrich Böll (Ger.).

noble savage. The concept of a superior primitive man, uncorrupted by civilization. The first known use of the phrase occurs in Dryden's *Conquest of Granada* (1672). According to the Roman historian Diodorus Siculus, a contemporary of Julius Caesar, just such untainted savages are described in the works of the early Greek authors Jambulus and Euhemerus. In modern times, from the 15th century, this ideal man was often described in exaggerated terms in the travel accounts written by explorers, missionaries, and emigrants from Europe. The Italian historian of the 15th century, Pietro Martire Anghièra, who knew Columbus, Vespucci, Magellan, and other explorers, praises the virtuous conduct of the savages of the Antilles; the pastor Jean de Léry, who accompanied the French admiral and explorer Nicholas Durand de Villega[i]gnon to Brazil, undertakes to defend the savage Brazilians; Father Lejeune, a Jesuit missionary, in his *Relation* of 1634, defends the Canadian savages; Father Du Tertre, a Dominican, exalts the virtuous simplicity of West-Indian savages in his *Relation* of 1654. The noble savage's supposedly simpler, purer, less inhibited emotional responses and his religious life, uncomplicated by numerous conflicting dogmas or by persecution, served as subject matter for invidious comparisons between occidental civilization and the more perfect savage cultures. Frequently the noble savage also supposedly lived under just and reasonable laws which, when compared to European authoritarian governments, were made to seem infinitely more desirable. Literally hundreds of travel books describing such utopias were extremely popular from the 16th to 19th centuries and gave impetus to emigration from Europe to the new world. Rousseau, though aware that a return to the primitive state was impractical, nevertheless used the myth of the noble savage to give substance to the anathemas he hurled against civilization. Voltaire's INGÉNU serves as an example of the convention of the noble savage. Chateaubriand's novels dealing with the American Indian, RENÉ, ATALA, and LES NATCHEZ, portray the romantic, sentimentalized aspects of this myth; its influence is also to be found in the Indian novels of James Fenimore Cooper. See PRIMITIVISM.

Noctes Ambrosianae (1822–1835). A series of papers on literary and topical subjects, in the form of dialogues, contributed to *Blackwood's Magazine*. They were written principally by John WILSON under the pseudonym Christopher North. The title is taken from AMBROSE'S, a public house where Wilson and his friends met; Wilson recorded their talks with wit and vivacity. Although he often used imaginary characters, he impersonates James Hogg and William Maginn with great humor.

Nod, Land of. A land referred to in the Bible. It is said that "Cain went . . . and dwelt in the Land of Nod" (Gen. 4: 16). It was there that he found a wife. The phrase may mean merely "the land of wandering" rather than a definite locality.

Nodier, Charles (1780–1844). French poet, novelist, and short-story writer. During the early years of the romantic period, Nodier produced such tales as *Smarra ou les Démons de la nuit* (1821), and *Trilby ou le Lutin d'Argail* (1822). These contain the elements of fantasy, horror, and melancholy that characterize the Gothic novel. Nodier's own novels include *Le Peintre de Salzbourg, journal des émotions d'un cœur souffrant* (1803) and *Jean Sbogar* (1818). *Essais d'un jeune barde,* a collection of poetry, was published in 1804.

No Exit (Huis Clos; 1944). A play by Jean-Paul SARTRE. It is also known in English under the title *In Camera.* The scene of the play is a drawing room into which a man and two women who have died are escorted. Unable to leave, they discover that "hell is other people." At the end, when the door is finally opened, they find they are inseparable and cannot leave.

Noggs, Newman. In Charles Dickens' NICHOLAS NICKLEBY, Ralph Nickleby's clerk. He is a tall man of middle age with goggle eyes set in a cadaverous face and one miserable suit of clothes. This kindhearted dilapidated fellow "kept his hunter and hounds once," but ran through his fortune. He discovers a plot of Ralph, which he confides to the Cheeryble brothers; they frustrate it and then provide for Newman.

Nogueira Pessôa, Fernando António. See Fernando António Nogueira PESSÔA.

Nolan, Philip. The fictional chief figure in THE MAN WITHOUT A COUNTRY by Edward Everett Hale. There was a real Philip Nolan, a horse-trader, who was a historical personage killed on the Mexican border (1801). Hale explains in *The Real Philip*

Nolan (1901) that only his novel *Philip Nolan's Friends* (1876) was based on the historical Nolan.

nom de guerre. A French phrase originally and literally meaning "war name," now merely meaning a pseudonym or assumed name. It was customary at one time for everyone who entered the French army to assume a name; this was especially the case in the times of chivalry, when knights were known by the device on their shields.

nominalism. One of two rival doctrines in the disputes of the medieval schoolmen (see SCHOLASTICISM). It held that all abstractions, or universals, such as the general concept of a circle, of truth, of beauty, and the like, are mere names, rather than realities in themselves, and that only a particular and individual object or event has reality. It logically resulted in what was considered a heretical attitude toward the concept of the Trinity. See REALISM; Pierre ABÉLARD.

Nomura Kichisaburo (1877–   ). Japanese ambassador to the U.S. (1940–1941). He conducted the negotiations interrupted by the Japanese attack on Pearl Harbor.

nonconformists or **dissenters.** In England, members of Protestant bodies who do not conform to the doctrines of the Church of England. The term was used particularly to refer to the 2,000 clergyman who left the church in 1662 rather than submit to the Act of Uniformity, which demanded "unfeigned assent to all and everything contained in the Book of Common Prayer."

nones. In the ancient Roman calendar, the 9th (Lat., *nonus*) day before the IDES. In the Roman Catholic Church, Nones is the office for the ninth hour after sunrise, or 3:00 P.M.

Non Sum Qualis Eram Bonae sub regno Cynarae. See CYNARA.

Non-U. A term, meaning "not upper class," popularized in England by Nancy MITFORD. The term was invented by Professor Alan Ross in 1954 for a philological study which provides a set of rules for categorizing Englishmen as U or Non-U according to their speech habits.

Noon Wine (1937). A short novel by Katherine Anne PORTER. It was reprinted in the collection of three novels entitled *Pale Horse, Pale Rider* (1939). In Miss Porter's deceptively simple style, it tells the story of Mr. Thompson, an ineffectual farmer who kills a disagreeable stranger who he imagines is attacking his eccentric but valuable · hired man. Though acquitted of murder, Thompson commits suicide.

Norandino. A king of Damascus in the ORLANDO FURIOSO of Ariosto. He proclaims a tournament, which attracts the knight Grifone and the braggart Martano. The latter takes credit for Grifone's deeds by appearing in his armor to claim the victory. When Grifone persuades Norandino of Martano's treachery, the king has him hanged. See also ORIGILLE and AQUILANTE.

Nordhoff, Charles Bernard (1887–1947). American writer. He is best known for the trilogy narrating the story of the ship *Bounty,* on which he collaborated with James Norman HALL: MUTINY ON THE BOUNTY, *Men Against the Sea* (1933), and *Pitcairn's Island* (1934). Nordhoff drove an ambulance in France in 1916 and later joined the Lafayette

Escadrille. In 1920 he went with Hall to Tahiti, where they remained for many years. *The Fledgling* (1919) is an account in diary form of his flying experiences during the war. Both *The Pearl Lagoon*, adventures in the South Seas, and *Picaro*, a novel about two brothers in Guadaloupe whose destinies were bound up with airplanes, appeared in 1924. *The Derelict* (1925), another novel of adventure in the South Seas, was the last book Nordhoff wrote alone.

Norma. An opera by Vincenzo BELLINI (1831) with a libretto by Romani. The heroine, Norma, is a Druid priestess, secretly married to a Roman proconsul. When she discovers that he is planning to seduce a sister priestess, she gives herself up to vengeance but at the last minute shares the tragic fate she has brought upon him.

Norman Conquest, The. See WILLIAM THE CONQUEROR; Battle of HASTINGS.

Normans or **Norsemen.** See VIKINGS.

Norns. In Scandinavian mythology, the three demigoddesses who presided over the fates of both men and gods. The three were known as URDUR, VERTHANDI, and SKULD, or Past, Present, and Future. Originally there was only one Norn, Urdur, but later the two others were added. They appeared at the cradle upon the birth of a child, and dwelt at the root of the sacred ash, Yggdrasill, sprinkling it from the fountain Norna to preserve it from decay. See FATES.

Norris, Aunt or **Mrs.** A character in Jane Austen's novel MANSFIELD PARK. She is a satirical portrait of the typical busybody.

Norris, [Benjamin] Frank[lin] (1870–1902). American novelist. Known for his naturalistic depictions of life in the U.S., Norris was born in Chicago. In his youth, he studied art in Paris and wrote medieval romances, such as *Yvernelle: A Tale of Feudal France* (1892), but at the University of California he read Zola and began work on McTEAGUE. He later reported the Boer War, joined the staff of the San Francisco *Wave*, and went to Cuba to cover the Spanish-American War.

His first published novel was *Moran of the Lady Letty* (1898), a tale of adventure in which a captain's daughter takes command of the ship and is rescued by a shanghaied sailor. *McTeague,* one of the first naturalistic novels in America, appeared the following year. After two more romances, *Blix* (1899) and *A Man's Woman* (1900), Norris began a trilogy on the growth, sale, and consumption of wheat. Of the three volumes planned, only THE OCTOPUS, Norris' most ambitious work, and THE PIT were written. *Vandover and the Brute* (1914), a naturalistic story of the degeneration of a man suffering from lycanthropy, was written in 1894–1895.

Norris explained his literary credo in an essay *The Responsibilities of a Novelist* (1903), in which he declared that the novelist must always be able to say, "I never truckled; I never took off the hat to Fashion and held it out for pennies. By God, I told them the truth."

Norris, Kathleen [Thompson] (1880–   ). American short-story writer and novelist. *Mother* (1911), the story of a schoolteacher and her mother, was a best-seller. *Certain People of Importance* (1922) is considered her best novel. She also wrote a

play, *Victoria* (1933), and a collection of short stories, *Bakers' Dozen* (1938).

North, Christopher. See John WILSON.

Northanger Abbey (1818). A novel by Jane AUSTEN. Visiting Bath with her friend Mrs. Allen, an older but flighty, irresponsible woman, Catherine Morland falls in love with Henry Tilney, a young clergyman. Believing her to be wealthy, Henry's father invites Catherine to Northanger Abbey, the Tilney home. Greatly influenced by her reading of Mrs. RADCLIFFE's novel *Mysteries of Udolpho,* Catherine sees Northanger Abbey as a house of nightmarish mysteries and is terrified by her own imagination. Her visions of medieval horror prove groundless, of course. However, she is soon ordered out of the house by Henry's dictatorial father when he discovers that she is not wealthy. Henry follows her and persuades her to marry him. The novel gives Jane Austen an opportunity to satirize the Radcliffe school of romantic mystery and treat a favorite theme of feminine self-delusion.

northeast passage. A way from the Atlantic to the Pacific and on to India from Europe eastward round the north extremity of Asia. Its discovery was often attempted even in the 16th century.

After the discovery of America, there was much talk of a northwest passage through to the East by way of the Atlantic, and explorers were constantly sailing up the bays and rivers of the American coast in hopes of finding such a passage. This search accounts for Henry Hudson's exploration of the Hudson River and Hudson Bay.

North Star (Polaris). See GREAT BEAR.

northwest passage. See NORTHEAST PASSAGE.

Northwest Passage (1937). A historical novel by Kenneth ROBERTS. It describes Major Robert Rogers' expedition in 1759 to destroy the Indian town of St. Francis and his search for an overland route to the Northwest. Roberts used Rogers' own *Concise Account of North America* (1765) and unearthed lost documents for the facts of his story.

Northwest Territory. An American territory northwest of the Ohio River, comprising practically all the land owned as unsettled territory by the 13 colonies at the time of the Declaration of Independence. It was ceded to the federal government by the various states laying claim to it, and from it were formed the states of Ohio, Indiana, Illinois, Michigan, and Wisconsin.

Norton, Caroline Elizabeth Sarah. Born **Sheridan** (1808–1877). English writer, granddaughter of Richard Brinsley SHERIDAN. She was famous for her wit, beauty, and marital troubles, the last of which occasioned her letter, addressed to the queen, in criticism of the divorce laws; she was influential in bringing about the change in attitude toward married women of the time. A strong vein of social protest and autobiography runs through her verse, such as *A Voice from the Factories* (1836), and her prose, such as *The Wife and Woman's Reward* (1835). She is said to be the original of George Meredith's heroine in *Diana of the Crossways* (1885).

Norton, Charles Eliot (1827–1908). American teacher and man of letters. Professor of the history of fine art at Harvard, Norton was a frequent contributor to periodicals. In 1865 he helped to found and edit *The Nation*. Norton was active as translator, editor, biographer, and bibliographer. His friendships with famous men and women of his time make his *Letters* (1913) valuable documents.

Norton, Thomas (1532–1584). English lawyer and poet. A staunch anti-Catholic, he translated Calvin's INSTITUTES (1559). With Thomas SACKVILLE, he was author of the first English tragedy in blank verse, GORBODUC, OR FERREX AND PORREX (performed 1561; published 1565). Norton wrote the first three acts of the play, Sackville the last two.

Norumbega. Early map-makers' name for a region and its chief city vaguely situated on the east coast of North America. On the map of Hieronimus da Verrazano (1592) it reads Aranbega, and coincides more or less with Nova Scotia. It was sought in vain in the region of the Penobscot River by Champlain in 1604. Whittier wrote a poem *Norembega* dealing with the search for this fabulous city. The word Norumbega is possibly of Indian origin.

Norway, Nevil Shute. See Nevil SHUTE.

Nostradamus. Real name **Michel de Nostre-Dame** (1503–1566). French astrologer and physician. His famous *Centuries* (1555), a book of prophecies, caused much controversy and was condemned by the papacy in 1781.

Nostromo (1904). A novel by Joseph CONRAD. Set in the South American republic of "Costaguana," it is an exciting, complicated story about capitalist exploitation and revolution on the national scene, and personal morality and corruption in individuals. Charles Gould's silver mine helps to maintain the country's stability and its reactionary government, but absorption in the mine warps his character and makes him neglect his gentle wife, Doña Emilia. When the revolution comes, Gould puts a consignment of silver in the charge of Nostromo, the magnificent, "incorruptible" *capataz de cargadores* (foreman and leader of the dock hands). Chance and vanity make Nostromo decide to bury the silver and to pretend that the boat in which he was shipping it sank. Trying to protect his silver he is later killed by his fiancée's father. Silver is the pivot of the whole story. It is the cause of the foreign capitalist intervention and exploitation that in turn causes the revolution. It corrupts and destroys some men, and reveals the strengths, weaknesses, and ruling passions of others. Dr. Monygham is a proud man who never forgives himself for once breaking under torture. Martin Decoud, a journalist, is a cynic and sensualist who kills himself rather than endure enforced isolation. Giorgio Viola is a noble, idealistic and dedicated old republican. His daughter Linda continues to love Nostromo through all his unfaithfulness. Conrad's narration is complex and oblique, not following a normal time-sequence. He starts half-way through the events of the revolution and proceeds by way of flashbacks and glimpses into the future.

Notables. In French history, an assembly of nobles, or notable men, appointed and convoked by the king to form a special deliberative council. The first significant assembly of Notables occurred in 1554, although they are mentioned earlier in French history. They were convened again in 1626 by Richelieu, and not again until 1787 (160 years later), when Louis XVI called them together in an attempt to relieve the nation of some of its pecuniary embarrass-

ments. The last time they convened was November 6, 1788.

Not by Bread Alone (Ne khlebom yedinym; 1956). A novel by Vladimir DUDINTZEV. Noted for its criticism of the Soviet bureaucratic establishment, the story concerns the efforts of a young Soviet inventor, Lopatkin, to get his invention accepted by the authorities. He is blocked by an unscrupulous factory director, Drozdov, a careerist who has no interest in anything but his own cozy spot in the hierarchy. Through intrigue, Lopatkin is arrested and sent to a labor camp. When he is released, he finds Drozdov still in power. The authorities are at last ready to accept his invention, but Lopatkin is no longer interested in personally participating in an order that allows Drozdovs to go on prospering. He is left facing a continual struggle against such a system.

Notebooks of Malte Laurids Brigge, The (Die Aufzeichnungen des Malte Laurids Brigge; 1910). A novel by Rainer Maria RILKE. The hero, a young Danish poet, has come to Paris, and the novel is written as though it were no more than a collection of his notebook entries, in which observations on immediate experience, reminiscences of youth, and speculations about life and art are seemingly indiscriminately mixed. The book's over-all structure, which emerges only gradually, is a symbolic repetition of the story of the Prodigal Son.

Notes from Underground (Zapiski iz podpol'ya; 1864). A long story by Feodor DOSTOEVSKI. Touching on many of the philosophical problems dealt with in his novels, the story is divided into two parts. The first part is a monologue in which the narrator philosophizes, poses and then laughs at his posing, and defends himself in advance against criticism of his ideas; the second is a recounting of adventures from the narrator's life which illustrate some of the ideas propounded in the first part of the story. On one level, the work is a complex psychological portrait of the narrator, the underground man. On another level, it is a polemic against the positivist philosophy of the radical thinkers in Russia, who believed in the rationality of man and the possibility of social betterment through material progress. The narrator not only disagrees intellectually with the radicals; he himself embodies the irrationality which he insists is the essence of man. The story, one of Dostoevski's most powerful and original works, is usually considered the starting point of Dostoevski's literary maturity.

Notes Toward a Supreme Fiction (1942). A long poem by Wallace STEVENS. It marked his tendency to shift away from the rich metaphor and imagery of his earlier poetry toward a more abstract poetic statement about the nature of poetry. It is divided into three sections labeled "It Must be Abstract," "It Must Change," and "It Must Give Pleasure."

No Time for Comedy (1939). A play by S. N. BEHRMAN. It is concerned with a playwright who has the urge to deal with the serious problems and tragedies of his time, but has the talent only for light comedy.

Notre Dame de Paris. See HUNCHBACK OF NOTRE DAME.

Nouman, Sidi. Hero of *The History of Sidi Nouman*, one of the tales in the ARABIAN NIGHTS. He is an Arab who marries Amine, a very beautiful woman, who eats her rice with a bodkin. Sidi, wishing to know how his wife can support life and health without more food than she takes in his presence, watches her narrowly, and discovers that she is a ghoul, who goes by stealth every night and feasts on the freshly buried dead. When Sidi makes this discovery, Amine changes him into a dog. After he is restored to his normal shape, he changes Amine into a mare, which every day he rides almost to death.

Nourritures terrestres, Les. See FRUITS OF THE EARTH, THE.

Nouvelle Héloïse, Julie ou la (1791). An immensely successful epistolary novel by Jean Jacques ROUSSEAU. It is the moralistic story of a wife, Julie d'Etanges, beset by her former lover, SAINT-PREUX. Her husband, M. de Wolmar, invites him to live with them; Saint-Preux leaves because of the impossible situation, but is recalled by the dying Julie. He promises to remain after her death to educate her children. It is a philosophic novel exalting virtue and the natural man, as opposed to hypocritical social morality.

Nouvelle Revue Française, La. A review of literature and the arts, founded in 1909 by André GIDE, Jacques COPEAU, and Jacques RIVIÈRE. Reflecting the independent spirit of its founders, the magazine sought to discover and to encourage new authors. Its interest in the new, however, was combined with a belief in permanent aesthetic values transcending any contemporary trend. During the years before and after the First World War, the *Nouvelle Revue Française* exercised considerable influence in the French literary world. Its members began a publishing house, the *maison d'éditions de la nrf*, which has since been taken over by Gaston Gallimard.

Nouvelle Vague, la. See NEW WAVE, THE.

Novalis. Pen name of **Friedrich Leopold Freiherr von Hardenberg** (1772–1801). German poet and novelist, the leading poet of early GERMAN ROMANTICISM. From the pietism of his parents, the mysticism of Jakob Böhme, and the ideals of his fellow romantics, he developed a unique personal faith in the mystical unity of all things. He believed that man had once lived in complete union with nature and had been able to communicate directly with the world of animals, plants, and objects. This union, however, had been lost, and man's goal must be to regain it. His ideas about history were similar. In his essay, *Die Christenheit oder Europa* (*Christianity, or Europe*, written 1799), he urges that Europe strive toward the establishment of a new universal church, and thus regain the spiritual unity of the Catholic Middle Ages, which had been lost in the Reformation. His young fiancée, whom he adored, died in 1797, and many of his subsequent works, including the prose-poems *Hymnen an die Nacht* (*Hymns to the Night*, 1800), express a mystical yearning for death. His unfinished novel, HEINRICH VON OFTERDINGEN, a highly allegorical BILDUNGSROMAN some sections of which are in the form of MÄRCHEN, treats the growth of a young poet in an idealized medieval Europe. It was also in this novel that the symbol of the BLUE FLOWER, which was later taken to represent all romanticism, first appeared. Some of Novalis' religious poems have been included in Protestant hymnbooks. His friends F. Schlegel and Tieck edited his works after he died.

Novelas ejemplares (Exemplary Novels, 1613). A collection of 12 tales by Miguel de CERVANTES SAAVEDRA. To Cervantes and his contemporaries, the word *novela* meant a short story in the Italian manner rather than a novel. He added the word *ejemplares*, however, to indicate that he had avoided the licentiousness of his Italian models. Although the stories vary in style and content, the best are those which give free rein to the author's personal experience and practical philosophy, such as RINCONETE Y CORTADILLO and EL COLOQUIO DE LOS PERROS. The other stories are *La gitanilla*, *El amante liberal*, *La española inglesa*, EL LICENCIADO VIDRIERA, *La fuerza de sangre*, *El celoso extremeño*, *La ilustre fregona*, *Las dos doncellas*, *La señora Cornelia*, and *El casamiento engañoso*. Sometimes included in the collection is the ribald *Tía fingida*, first published in 1814; its authenticity, however, is doubtful.

novelette. A long short story. Of 15,000 words or somewhat more, it is less considerable in length than the NOVELLA.

novella. The Italian word for the short prose narrative, popular during the medieval and Renaissance periods. As the etymology suggests, the tales were originally news, or "What is new?" and concerned mainly the events of town and city life that were worth repeating—from a clever remark made by a local wit to a joke played on the town idiot by clever ruffians, from stories of clever seductions to tales of grim revenge taken by a husband on his betrayers. As these tales gathered into collections, they were joined by other tales of a more literary type: legends and anecdotes from ancient and modern history, oriental folk tales, courtly and romantic episodes. The earliest known collection, *Le cento novelle antiche* (*The Hundred Ancient Tales*), also known as the *Novellino*, was of anonymous authorship; its tales are short and simple. But as the form developed in the hands of artists such as Franco Sacchetti, Boccaccio, Matteo Bandello, and Basile the style, structure, length, and psychological subtlety of the stories made them popular with learned audiences throughout Europe. Their chief literary influence was on playwrights such as Shakespeare, who used them for his plots. His *Romeo and Juliet*, for example, began as a *novella* by Da Porto.

In the modern period, the term is used in English to designate a serious fictional form that is somewhere between the novel and the short story in length. Also sometimes called the nouvelle, the novella probably contains from 30,000 to 40,000 words, as compared to a full novel of a minimum of 60,000 words, and often of twice that and more. See NOVELETTE.

Novello, Ivor. Originally **Ivor Novello Davies** (1893–1951). English actor, composer, and film star. He wrote the song *Keep the Home Fires Burning*. The author of a number of musical revues, he also wrote for the legitimate theater. His plays include *The Truth Game* (1928) and *Symphony in Two Flats* (1929).

Novello, Vincent (1781–1861). English organist. He composed and edited sacred music, and introduced to England unknown works of Haydn, Mozart, and

Palestrina. He was the founder of the music publishing firm, Novello & Co., the first firm to print cheap music.

Novikov, Nikolai Ivanovich (1744–1818). Russian satirical journalist. During the reign of CATHERINE THE GREAT, he published *The Drone* (*Truten*'; 1769–1770), *The Painter* (*Zhivopisetz;* 1772–1773), and *The Purse* (*Kosheliok;* 1774), all of which were leading periodicals of the day, as well as a number of books. His jibes at Russian society, and, what was worse, at the government, displeased the empress, and in 1791 he was imprisoned. After his release in 1796 by Czar Paul, he lived on his own estate for the rest of his life.

Novum Organum (*Lat.*, "new instrument"; 1620). A philosophical treatise written in Latin by Francis BACON. The second part of his projected INSTAURATIO MAGNA, it presents Bacon's statement of his inductive method of interpreting nature and organizing knowledge, by which the results of experience are studied, and a general conclusion regarding them is reached. This method was the opposite of the procedure of reasoning deductively from a given postulate by means of the syllogism which was the universal practice among the Scholastic philosophers of his day.

The *Novum Organum* also contains an exposition of Bacon's concept of the four "Idols," or false images of the mind, which he saw hindering the attainment of true knowledge: (1) Idols of the Tribe, errors originating in human nature itself; (2) Idols of the Cave, errors originating in the peculiar psychology of each individual; (3) Idols of the Market-Place, errors and confusions of language originating in social and practical intercourse among men; (4) Idols of the Theater, errors originating in formal systems of philosophy, each of which presents a world of its own, like a stage play.

Noyes, Alfred (1880–1958). English poet, critic, and essayist. He is chiefly known for his narrative verse and ballads dealing with English history. His epic poem, *Drake* (1906–1908), appeared in *Blackwood's Magazine* in serial form and was awaited just as eagerly as a serial novel. His *Collected Poems* appeared in 1947. His best-known single poem is *The Highwayman.*

Noyes, John Humphrey (1811–1886). American religious leader. A believer in perfectionism and the second coming of Christ, he declared himself sinless in 1834, and was thereupon requested to withdraw from Yale; his license to preach was revoked, and Noyes wandered among groups of perfectionists in the country. He returned to his home in Putney, Vt. and formed a community known as the Bible Communists (1836). This group adopted communism, and published its religious views. Noyes soon asserted a belief in polygamy; complex marriage was practiced in Putney, Vt. in 1846. Noyes was forced to flee to New York where he and his followers established the prosperous ONEIDA COMMUNITY. During the following years, Noyes published several volumes, including *Bible Communism* (1848), *Male Continence* (1848), and *Scientific Propagation* (1873), as well as a *History of American Socialisms* (1870). His organizational skill made the Oneida Community the longest-lasting and most successful of American utopian experiments. In 1879, Noyes was forced by public disapproval to flee to Canada.

Nozdryov. A hard-drinking, loudmouth bully in Nikolai Gogol's DEAD SOULS. Nozdryov cheats at cards with Chichikov, the hero, then threatens to have the latter beaten for pointing out the fact. Nozdryov's coarseness makes him the only character who is totally immune to Chichikov's subtle wiles.

Nubbles, Kit. In Charles Dickens' OLD CURIOSITY SHOP, a shambling, awkward, red-faced lad employed for a time to wait on Little Nell and do all sorts of odd jobs at the Old Curiosity Shop. When Little Nell and her grandfather lose the shop to Quilp and disappear one night, Kit, their only faithful friend, sets out to find them. He catches up with them only after Little Nell has died. Later, he is falsely accused of theft and saved from transportation by the Marchioness.

Nuclea (1952). Drama by Henri PICHETTE presenting poetic visions first of war, "The Infernals," then of love, "The Human Heaven."

nullification, doctrine of. In U.S. history, a theory, held largely in the South and particularly in South Carolina, that the federal union is primarily a league of states and that a state may declare an act of Congress invalid if it exceeds constitutional restrictions on federal power. The doctrine was most effectively set forth by John C. CALHOUN. In 1832 South Carolina passed an ordinance nullifying the tariff acts of 1828 and 1832, but President Jackson's determination to enforce federal authority and the passage of a compromise tariff ended the controversy.

Numa Pompilius. The legendary 2nd king of Rome (715–672 B.C.). The nymph EGERIA favored him with secret interviews and taught the lessons of wisdom and law that he embodied in the institutions of his nation.

Numa Roumestan (1881). A political novel by Alphonse DAUDET. It relates the rise to power of the titular hero, a Provençal of sufficient wit, ambition and impudence to win notable success in the field of politics. He is said to have been drawn from Léon Gambetta.

number of the beast. 666; a mystical number of unknown meaning but referring to a certain man mentioned by St. John. It is also known as the *Apocalyptic number.*

Numbers. A book of the Old Testament. It records Israel's trip through the wilderness from Mt. Sinai to Moab, on the border of the Promised Land. The book contains much Mosaic law; Moses is portrayed as a prophet to whom God speaks directly. The date of its composition is not known; it was once thought to be contemporaneous with the events, but it is now dated 400 to 800 years later.

Núñez Cabeza de Vaca, Alvar. See Alvar Núñez CABEZA DE VACA.

Núñez de Balboa, Vasco. See Vasco Núñez de BALBOA.

Nuns Fret Not at Their Convent's Narrow Room (1807). A sonnet by William WORDSWORTH. It celebrates the pleasure of the poet in maintaining discipline of the sonnet form.

Nun's Priest's Tale, The. One of the CANTERBURY TALES of Geoffrey CHAUCER. The Host agrees with the Knight that the MONK's TALE is gloomy, and turns to one of the priests accompanying the Prioress to demand something merry. The Priest makes a mock-heroic epic of one of the episodes in the fables of REYNARD THE FOX. The cock Chauntecleer (or Chanticleer) is described as belonging to a widow and ruling seven hens, his favorite being Pertelote. One dawn he wakes in fright, having dreamed a fox was after him. Pertelote calls him a coward and cynically suggests indigestion as the cause. He lectures her severely on the importance of dreams, citing numerous examples from scholarly authorities of people who dreamed accurately of coming disasters.

Nevertheless, he lets Pertelote distract him, but the fox Don Russell indeed awaits him. The fox flatters him that he only wants to hear if the cock has as fine a voice as his father. Chauntecleer closes his eyes to crow, and is seized. Hearing the shrieks of Pertelote and the other wives, the widow sets many men and animals to chase the raider. Chauntecleer tricks Don Russell into opening his mouth to taunt his pursuers, and flies into a tree, resisting all the fox's further enticements.

Nuremberg Trials (1945–1946). The trials of 22 major Nazi leaders, conducted in Nuremberg by an inter-Allied tribunal after World War II. Hermann Goering, Rudolph Hess, Robert Ley, and Joachim von Ribbentrop were among the defendants tried for war crimes against humanity.

Nurse, Juliet's. The garrulous old confidante of Juliet in Shakespeare's ROMEO AND JULIET. She aids Juliet in her love affair with Romeo, badgering her all the while with good-natured raillery.

Nut-Brown Maid, The. An English ballad (given in Percy's *Reliques*), probably dating from the late 15th century. It tells how the "Not-browne Mayd" is wooed and won by a knight who pretends to be a banished man. After describing the hardships she would have to undergo if she married him, and finding her love true to the test, he reveals himself to be an earl's son, with large hereditary estates in Westmorland.

Nycteus. See AMPHION.

Nym. In Shakespeare's HENRY V, a rascally camp follower with the English forces. In THE MERRY WIVES OF WINDSOR, he appears as a crony of Sir John Falstaff.

Nymphidia (1627). A poem by Michael DRAYTON, dealing with romantic problems at the court of King Oberon and Queen Mab. The story is told to the poet by Nymphidia, an attendant of the queen. The description of the fairy court, people, and events —all diminutive in scale—is a remarkable feat.

Nyx. In classic mythology, the goddess of night. A very ancient personification of night, she was probably never worshiped as an anthropomorphic deity.

O

Oak, Gabriel. See FAR FROM THE MADDING CROWD.

Oates, Titus (1649–1705). English perjurer and fabricator of the Popish Plot. An ordained Anglican minister, he was expelled from his living, became a Roman Catholic, and was later expelled from two Jesuit colleges. In 1678, Oates and Israel Tonge, a London clergyman, concocted what became known as the Popish Plot, charging that the Roman Catholics planned to assassinate Charles II, place the duke of York (later James II) on the throne, and turn the country over to the Jesuits. The story was widely believed; Oates was granted a large pension by the government, and, as a result of the public uproar, some 35 innocent persons were executed. After the accession of James II, Oates was convicted of perjury, flogged, and imprisoned, but he was pardoned by William III in 1689, and his pension was restored. In 1698, he became a Baptist, but was soon expelled from the congregation for hypocrisy.

Oath of the Tennis Court. The oath taken by the French National ASSEMBLY in 1789. After it had been prevented by Louis XVI from using its normal meeting place, the Assembly convened at the tennis-court building on June 20, 1789, where it took the oath never to disband until France had been given a constitution. As this negated the power of the king, the event is often considered the beginning of the FRENCH REVOLUTION.

Obadiah. (1) A Minor Prophet of the Old Testament and the name of the book which records his prophecy, denouncing the Edomites and foretelling Israel's restoration.

(2) A slang term for a Quaker.

(3) A household servant in Sterne's novel *Tristram Shandy* (1759–1767). There is also an Obadiah in Fielding's novel *Tom Jones* (1749).

Oberman (1804). A novel by Etienne Pivert de SÉNANCOUR. Written in the form of letters, it greatly influenced the romantic movement of the 19th-century. The novel in part describes the author's wanderings in the forest of Fontainebleau and in Switzerland. Sénancour's restlessness, his disillusionment, and his torment of body and soul are, however, the real subject of his work. In its analytical, introspective concerns, *Oberman* foreshadows the development of modern fiction.

Oberon. In medieval legend, the king of the fairies. Probably an outgrowth of Alberich, the king of the elves, he appears in the medieval French romance HUON DE BORDEAUX as the son of Julius Caesar and Morgan Le Fay.

In Shakespeare's MIDSUMMER NIGHT'S DREAM, he is a strong-willed figure who resorts to a trick to obtain from Titania, his wife, the services of her changeling page. He dispatches Puck to anoint the sleeping queen with a love potion. In her drugged state, she makes love to Bottom and is so ashamed when she awakes that she agrees to Oberon's demand.

Obey, André (1892–). French dramatist best known for *Noah* (1931), *Lucretia* (1931), and his collaboration with Denys AMIEL on *The Wife With the Smile* (1921).

Obiter Dicta. Title of three books of essays by Augustine BIRRELL (1884; second series, 1887; *More Obiter Dicta*, 1924). An *obiter dictum* is an incidental and unbinding opinion given by a judge and hence any incidental comment.

objective correlative. A phrase coined by T. S. ELIOT in his essay *Hamlet* (1919). The term refers to the external equivalent of an inner emotional reality. Thus a scene, action, image, verse rhythm, or any other artistic device that expresses a subjective state may be regarded as its objective correlative.

objectivism. (1) In philosophy, a theory emphasizing external reality or the objective truth of man's knowledge; also, in ethics, stressing the objectivity of moral good.

(2) In literary history, a term used to describe a movement or theory of composition in which material objects are selected, and studied and presented for their own sakes rather than for any extraneous purposes, such as their suitability for symbolizing an emotion or intellectual concept of the author. The work of William Carlos Williams, who first used the term, is a good example of objectivism; Marianne Moore and Wallace Stevens have also been called objectivist poets. See IMAGISM; SYMBOLISM.

Oblomov (1859). A novel by Ivan GONCHAROV. The work is one of the outstanding classics of Russian realistic fiction of the 19th century. The hero, Ilya Ilyich Oblomov, a Russian landowner living in St. Petersburg, is the embodiment of physical and mental laziness. His chief activities are indulging in reveries while lying on his couch and occasionally quarreling with his gloomy, coarse servant Zakhar. Oblomov's robe and slippers, his almost constant apparel, become part of his character in the course of the book. Oblomov ignores his business affairs, although the estate on which he depends for his income and comfortable existence is being mismanaged and rapidly going to ruin. Contrasted to Oblomov is his friend Andrei Shtoltz, the model of the efficient man of business. All his efforts to rouse Oblomov to some kind of action end in failure. Not even the love offered by the young Olga Ilinskaya can move Oblomov to give up his way of life. Although he loves Olga, Oblomov chooses the peaceful, effortless existence he can have by marrying Agaf'ya Pshenitzyna, his land-lady. Olga marries Shtoltz, and Oblomov, coddled by Agaf'ya, sinks deeper into reverie and financial ruin until he dies.

Goncharov's novel holds a secure place in classic Russian literature on the basis of the characterization of its central character. Oblomov has come to symbolize all that is slothful in man's nature. The reasons cited by critics for his inactivity range from the social situation in Russia under serfdom to the superior sensibility of the hero. Since the well-known essay by the critic Nikolai DOBROLYUBOV, *Chto takoye oblomovshchina? (What is Oblomovshchina?* 1859), the main emphasis in Russian criticism has been on the social aspect of Oblomov's malady. The novel has also been regarded as a forerunner of later psychological discoveries because of the hero's anxieties, self-questioning, his reliving childhood in a dream, and the part these things are shown to play in his adult life.

Obregón, Alvaro (1880–1928). Mexican soldier and political leader. Carranza's ablest general in the struggle that followed the overthrow of Francisco Madero, Obregón became president in 1920. During his administration some economic and social reform was initiated, especially in education, but there was continuing conflict with the U.S. and the Roman Catholic Church. Reelected in 1928, Obregón was assassinated by a religious fanatic before he could take office.

O'Brien, Fitz-James (1828–1862). Irish-born American writer. He is noted for his remarkable short stories of the weird and uncanny, including *The Diamond Lens* (1858) and *What Was It* (1859). He wrote primarily for magazines and today he is considered among the forerunners of the modern science-fiction writer.

O Captain! My Captain! (1865). A poem by Walt WHITMAN. Commemorating the death of Abraham Lincoln, it is written in conventional rhyme and meter. The Captain, who has brought the ship of state to a safe port, has "fallen cold and dead."

O'Casey, Sean (1884–1964). Irish dramatist. Born and reared in a Dublin slum, O'Casey very early in life developed the two abiding concerns that were to characterize his life and work: a fierce uncontrolled vitality of language and a rigid, uncompromising social conscience. The artistic fusion of these elements has resulted in two of the most powerful plays written in the 20th century, JUNO AND THE PAYCOCK and *The Plough and the Stars.*

Hindered by bad eyesight, so that he was unable to read until the age of 12, O'Casey compensated for his late start by developing a voracious appetite for books. At the same time he became active in the revolutionary movement as an organizer of the transport strike of 1913 and a member of the Irish Citizens Army. He also joined the Gaelic League, learned the Irish language, and gained an entrée into the literary world.

The first of his plays to be produced was *The Shadow of a Gunman* (1923), a play presented by the Abbey Theatre, with which O'Casey was to be associated for the next six years. In 1924, the Abbey presented *Juno and the Paycock.* Regarded by many as O'Casey's masterpiece, *Juno* is a masterly blend of comedy and tragedy, set against the background of the Irish civil war. The production of *The Plough and the Stars* (1926) was greeted with rioting on the Dublin streets, as a result of the alleged anti-Irish sentiment of the play. In 1928 the Abbey Theatre rejected O'Casey's next play, *The Silver Tassie,* the rejection resulting in O'Casey's breaking his connection with the Abbey. *The Silver Tassie,* an expressionist drama dealing with World War I, was produced in London in 1929. *Within the Gates,* another play in the expressionist mode, appeared in 1933, revealing once again his strong sympathy with the lower classes. O'Casey's subsequent plays have been less successful, frequently hampered by the somewhat doctrinaire socialist message imposed upon them. Among these are *Purple Dust* (1940), *The Star Turns Red* (1940), and *Red Roses for Me* (1947).

In 1939, O'Casey published *I Knock at the Door,* the first book of his six-volume autobiography. It was followed by *Pictures in the Hallway* (1942), *Drums Under the Window* (1945), *Inishfallen Fare Thee Well* (1949), *Rose and Crown* (1952), and *Sunset and Evening Star* (1954). "Autobiography" is perhaps too precise a term for these highly lyrical, occasionally florid, always vivid accounts of his struggle to wrest some order and significance from the anarchic events of the first half of the 20th century. See IRISH RENAISSANCE.

Occam or **Ockham, William of** (c. 1285–1349). English scholastic philosopher and theologian, known as "Doctor Invincibilis" and "Venerabilis Inceptor." He joined the Franciscans, was a partisan of strict observance in their controversy over evangelical poverty, and became general of the order in 1342. In his *Dialogus* (c. 1343) he summarizes many of his previous writings, contesting the temporal power of the Pope and asserting that a king has independent authority in civil affairs.

Occam's philosophy was greatly influenced by his teacher Duns Scotus, although later they were rivals in scholastic disputes. He revived a modified Nominalism, maintaining the distinction between concrete realities and the abstraction of universals. Thus he claimed that purely intellectual abstractions are not valid knowledge and that reasoning must be based on experimental proof. In this view, the basis of the later position known as theological scepticism, the existence and attributes of God are not susceptible of proof by human reason, but can only be approached through intuition.

Occasion. See FAERIE QUEENE, THE.

Occleve or **Hoccleve, Thomas** (c. 1369–c. 1450). English poet, a copy clerk in the Privy Seal Office. He addressed to Prince Hal, later Henry V, his *De Regimine Principum (On the Governance of Princes,* c. 1411–1412), a treatise of 5463 lines in rhyme royal on the responsibilities of rulers, adapted from earlier similar works. Its long autobiographical preface (2,000 lines) includes a eulogy of Chaucer. Other autobiographical poems include *La Male Règle* (1406), about his unruly youth, and *Complaint* and *Dialogue to a Friend* (both c. 1421–1422), about his nervous breakdown. Of his other minor poems and translations, his *Mother of God,* a lyrical hymn to Mary, was formerly attributed to Chaucer.

Occupation, the. During World War II, especially, the occupation of France by German forces (1940–1945). See VICHY government.

Oceanus (Okeanos). In Greek myth, a river. It was believed to flow in a boundless circle around the earth. Homer names Oceanus as the origin of all things, including the gods. In Hesiod's *Theogony* he is a Titan, son of Uranus and Ge (Heaven and Earth). Oceanus and his wife Tethys bore 3,000 sons, the Rivers, and 3,000 daughters, the Water Nymphs (Oceanides). He appears in Aeschylus' Prometheus Bound.

Ochiltree, Edie. One of Sir Walter Scott's more engaging characters, a garrulous, kind-hearted, wandering beggar in The Antiquary.

Ochino, Bernardino (1487–1564). Italian Capuchin monk. Ochino became vicar-general of the Capuchin order (1538) but was attracted to the ideas of the Protestant reformers Juan de Valdés and Reginald Pole. He finally fled Italy and traveled about Europe, stopping in England from 1547 to 1553. His surviving works include *Prediche* and *Dialoghi*, sermons and dialogues in which he embodies his religious thought.

Ochs, Adolph Simon (1858–1935). American publisher and editor. In 1896, Ochs came to New York, after losing most of his money in the panic of 1893; he bought *The New York Times,* which had been nearly destroyed by the Hearst and Pulitzer competition. Realizing that his newspaper could not compete with the sensational dailies, he appealed to readers with the slogan: "All the news that's fit to print." Dignified and nonpartisan, offering additional features including book reviewing, foreign news coverage, and financial reporting, *The New York Times* rapidly increased its circulation, becoming one of the most influential newspapers in the country. Ochs also published the Philadelphia *Times* (1902–1912) and the Philadelphia *Public Ledger* (1902–1912). His interest in public welfare led him to found the Chattanooga Lookout Mountain Park and make possible the publication of the *Dictionary of American Biography.*

Ochs von Lerchenau, Baron. See Rosenkavalier, Der.

Ockham, William of. See William of Occam.

Ocnus, rope of. Profitless labor. Ocnus, in Roman fable, was always twisting a rope, but an ass ate it as fast as it was twisted.

O'Connell, Daniel (1775–1847). Irish nationalist, statesman, and orator. He was a prominent lawyer who became known as an opponent of the Act of Union (1801), the Church of Ireland, and the civil disabilities placed on Catholics because of their religion. He founded the Catholic Association, which, gaining quietly and impressively in strength and numbers, was suppressed in 1825. O'Connell was elected to Parliament (1828), but refused to take his seat until Wellington's hard-won Catholic Emancipation Act (1829) went through Parliament. He was elected (1841) lord mayor of Dublin. When the Tory Sir Robert Peel became prime minister, O'Connell resumed his agitations for an independent Ireland. He re-established the Catholic Association, Peel declared it illegal, and O'Connell was tried and convicted for conspiracy; the decision was reversed by the House of Lords. O'Connell's stay in prison, however, weakened his health and he died on his way to Italy to convalesce. A radical group within O'Connell's, Young Ireland, steadily gained adherents to the violent policy that O'Connell had consistently opposed.

O'Connor, Flannery (1925–1964). American novelist. Born in Georgia, Miss O'Connor takes Southern settings for the locale of her stories. *Wise Blood* (1952), her first novel, was praised for its originality and stark power. *The Violent Bear It Away* (1960) is a quasi-comic novel populated with compelling and grotesque characters. *A Good Man Is Hard to Find* (1955) is a collection of some of her short stories. She was considered among the most promising of the younger contemporary novelists.

O'Connor, Frank. Pen name of Michael O'Donovan (1903–1966). Irish short-story writer and author of poetic translations from Gaelic. He was encouraged by Æ and was for a time one of the directors of the Abbey Theatre. O'Connor's work is noted for its sense of humor, its realism, and its poetic sensitivity. *Guests of the Nation* (1931) is a collection of short stories about the Irish-English troubles. *Dutch Interior* (1940) is a collection of separate stories which together paint a discouraging picture of Irish life. Later stories, such as *The Holy Door* and *Uprooted,* are fine comedies. *An Only Child* (1960) is a memoir of the author's childhood and youth.

O'Crohan, Thomas (1856–1937). Irish author of *The Islandman* (1929), an autobiography in Gaelic of a peasant from the Blasket Isles. He states that his purpose in writing is "to set down the character of the people about me so that some record of us might live after us, for the like of us will never be again."

octameter. In prosody, a line of verse containing eight metrical feet, which may be in any meter, usually identified together with the name of the meter, as iambic octameter, trochaic octameter, etc. Octameter is the longest line designated by a special term; beyond octameter, it would be necessary to speak of the nine-foot line, ten-foot line, and so on. Such lengthy lines, however, are rare.

Octavia (d. 11 B.C.). Roman matron. The sister of Octavius Caesar, she married Mark Antony after the death of her first husband in 41 B.C. Antony divorced her in 32 when Cleopatra came into his life. One of her daughters by Antony became the mother of Caligula, and the other the grandmother of Nero.

She is a character in Shakespeare's Antony and Cleopatra, in which she is described as being "of a holy, cold, and still conversation." She also appears in Dryden's All for Love.

Octavius Caesar. See Augustus.

Octopus, The (1901). A novel by Frank Norris. The first of a projected trilogy on American wheat, the novel depicts the struggle for power between California wheat ranchers and the railroad, "the octopus" that encircles and strangles them. With its epic sweep, the novel includes two love affairs, one involving the mystical Vanamee, and comes to a climax with a pitched battle between farmers and railroad men. The Pit is its sequel.

Octoroon, The (1859). A play by Dion Boucicault. Based on an English novel, the play treats the subject of slavery. Zoë, a slave of mixed blood, must be sold by a man who loves her to another, whom they both hate. The first of many works treating the theme of mixed blood, the play was revived in New York during 1961.

ode. In prosody, a lyric poem of exalted emotion, devoted to the praise or celebration of its subject.

(1) The Pindaric Ode was first composed in ancient Greece by Pindar and other poets for choral recitation, and written in units of three stanzas each, called respectively the strophe, antistrophe, and epode. The chorus moved up one side of the orchestra chanting the strophe, down the other chanting the antistrophe, and came to a stop before the audience to chant the epode. The ode continued in this way to its end. Modern poets using this form do not, of course, write for such performance, but they still use its basic construction. Their first three stanzas usually have rhyme and are constructed with great freedom and variety; the pattern then repeats these three stanza forms as a unit throughout the poem.

(2) The Horatian or stanzaic ode is written in a succession of stanzas that follow the pattern of the first stanza, which may be in any form. Horace used this form, as did Keats in his *Ode to a Nightingale*.

(3) The irregular ode is a modern invention and has no regular pattern at all; it came about through misunderstanding (by the English poet William Collins) of the Pindaric form. William Wordsworth's *Ode: Intimations of Immortality* is perhaps the best-known example.

Ode: Intimations of Immortality from Recollections of Early Childhood (1807). A famous poem by William WORDSWORTH. It is based on the Platonic doctrine of "recollection," which asserts that the process of learning is actually only a recollection to the adult mind of knowledge gained in a pre-existent spiritual realm and lost to the individual at birth. Wordsworth's poem celebrates the child who, "trailing clouds of glory," still retains in infancy memories of his celestial abode. Although the mature man has forgotten this knowledge, we are told, he can regain it by heeding his intuition and remembering his own childhood.

Ode on a Grecian Urn (1819). A famous ode by John KEATS. It describes the perfection and timelessness of art, as contrasted to the living world of change, in the figures of the youth and his "unravished bride" whom he can never possess and never ceases desiring:

Forever wilt thou love, and she be fair!

Odessa Tales (1927). A collection of short stories by Isaak BABEL. Set in the Soviet writer's birthplace, the Black Sea city of Odessa, the stories are also known as *Jewish Tales* (*Yevreiskiye rasskazy*).

Ode to a Nightingale (1819). A poem by John KEATS. It expresses the emotions of the poet as he listens to the song of the nightingale: his visions of sensuous beauty and his melancholy as he feels his own mortality in contrast to the immortality of the bird's song:

Thou wast not born for death, immortal Bird!
No hungry generations tread thee down;
The voice I hear this passing night was heard
In ancient days by emperor and clown:
Perhaps the self-same song that found a path
Through the sad heart of Ruth, when, sick for home,
She stood in tears amid the alien corn;
The same that oft-times hath
Charm'd magic casements, opening on the foam
Of perilous seas, in faery lands forlorn.

Ode to the West Wind (1820). One of the best-known poems by Percy Bysshe SHELLEY. In it the poet addresses the wild, strong wind of autumn—as he was once, "tameless, and swift, and proud"—and implores that it may now inspirit him with its force.

Scatter, as from an unextinguished hearth
Ashes and sparks, my words among mankind!
Be through my lips to unawakened earth
The trumpet of a prophecy! O, Wind,
If Winter comes, can Spring be far behind?

Odets, Clifford (1906–1963). American playwright. Odets was acclaimed in the 1930's as an outstanding proletarian dramatist. His first two plays, which are often considered his best, are concerned with the class struggle: WAITING FOR LEFTY and AWAKE AND SING. He continued to use socialist themes in his succeeding plays. *Till the Day I Die* (1935) deals with the Communist underground movement in Nazi Germany. *Paradise Lost* (1935) depicts the decline of a middle-class family. *Golden Boy* (1937) portrays a young Italian-American who should have been a violinist but who chooses the easier way to fame through boxing. *Night Music* (1940) and *Clash by Night* (1941) are two later plays written before Odets turned to Hollywood. With *The Country Girl* (1950), later made into a movie, he managed to repeat his early success. The play marks the end of his preoccupation with political themes; it centers on the struggle of a young woman to remain faithful to her dissolute husband. *The Flowering Peach* (1954) was less successful.

Odets was at first an actor with the Theatre Guild; in 1931, he became one of the founders of the Group Theatre, which later produced his best-known plays.

Odette de Crécy. A cocotte in Marcel Proust's REMEMBRANCE OF THINGS PAST. At first "the lady in pink" introduced to the narrator by his great-uncle Adolphe, she becomes the mistress and then the wife of Charles SWANN, and by him the mother of Gilberte. After Swann's death she marries his rival, de Forcheville; then, a widow again, she becomes the mistress of the duc de Guermantes.

Odin. The Scandinavian name of the Anglo-Saxon god Woden. He was the supreme god of the later Scandinavian pantheon, having supplanted THOR.

Odin was god of wisdom, poetry, war, and agriculture, and on this latter account Wednesday (*Woden's day*) was considered to be specially favorable for sowing. He was god of the dead also, and presided over the banquets of those slain in battle. See VALHALLA. He became the *All-wise* by drinking from Mimir's fountain, but purchased the distinction at the cost of one eye, and is usually represented as a one-eyed man wearing a hat and carrying a staff. His remaining eye is the Sun.

The father of Odin was Bor. His brothers are Vili and Ve. His wife is Frigga. His sons are Thor and Balder. His mansion is Gladsheim. His court as war god is Valhalla. His two black ravens are Hugin (thought) and Munin (memory). His steed is Sleipnir. His ships are Skidbladnir and Naglfar. His spear is Gungnir, which never fails to hit the mark aimed at. His ring is called Draupnir, which every ninth night drops eight other rings of equal value. His throne is Hlidskjalf. His wolves are Geri and Freki. He will ultimately be swallowed up by the Fenris wolf at Ragnarok.

Odin, the promise of. The most binding of all oaths to a Norseman. In making it the hand was passed through a massive silver ring kept for the purpose, or through a sacrificial stone, like that called the Circle of Stennis.

Odoardo (Edward). An English baron in Tasso's epic, GERUSALEMME LIBERATA. He joins the Crusade with his warlike wife Gildippe. During the final struggle for the holy city he dies with his wife on the battlefield.

O'Donovan, Michael. See Frank O'CONNOR.

Odorico (Oderic). A false knight in Ariosto's epic ORLANDO FURIOSO. He is supposed to help Zerbino and Isabella escape together but instead falls in love with Isabella himself. But she is taken from him by a band of robbers who plan to sell her into slavery. Later, after her rescue, Zerbino punishes Odorico by forcing him to defend and keep the company of the old hag Gabrina, for a period of one year.

Odrovir or **Odhrevir.** The "poet's mead" of the Norse gods. It was made of Kvasir's blood mixed with honey, and all who partook of it became poets. Kvasir was the wisest of all men, and could answer any question put to him. He was fashioned out of the saliva spat into a jar by the Aesir and Vanir on their conclusion of peace, and was slain by the dwarfs Fjalar and Galar.

Odysseus. The hero of Homer's ODYSSEY and an important figure in many other classical myths. In the ILIAD and the *Odyssey,* he is shrewd and wily, but also generous and noble. In the works of later authors he becomes, for the most part, cruel and cunning. This is his character, for instance, in Sophocles' tragedy *Philoctetes.* He appears also in a humorous treatment of the episode of Polyphemus' cave in Euripides' satyr play *Cyclops.* He is one

of the great epic characters of literature. He was called ULYSSES by the Romans.

Odyssey. An epic poem by HOMER. It recounts the adventures of ODYSSEUS on his way home to Ithaca after the TROJAN WAR. Though written in heroic verse, it has been called the first novel because of its exciting narrative and the effective use of flashbacks to heighten the dramatic action. The poem opens on Ogygia, the far western island of the sea nymph Calypso. She has kept Odysseus imprisoned on her island for seven years, offering him immortality as an inducement to stay with her, but Odysseus insists on returning to his wife PENELOPE. The story now turns to Odysseus' son TELEMACHUS, back home in Ithaca. Penelope's suitors have been eating them out of house and home. Resolving, under the influence of Athene, to be a man, he sets out to find his father. He first consults NESTOR in Pylos, then Menelaus in Sparta, who tells Telemachus that he has learned of Odysseus' captivity in Ogygia.

Meanwhile, on Zeus' orders, Calypso has released Odysseus. Shipwrecked on the PHAEACIAN island of Scherie, he is befriended first by the young Nausicaa, then by her parents, King Alcinous and Queen Arete. At a banquet, he reveals his identity and tells the story of his wanderings. After leaving Troy and making a raid on the Ciconians, he landed in the country of the LOTUS-EATERS. There some of his men ate the lotus, which made them forget their homes, and they had to be carried away by force. Next time they landed on the island where the Cyclops lived; they were trapped by Polyphemus in his cave, and those not eaten escaped by a trick after blinding the Cyclops. It is this deed that won the enmity of Poseidon, the father of Polyphemus. Reaching the island of Aeolus, Odysseus was given the unfavorable winds in a leather bag, so that they were blown straight toward home. But Odysseus' men, thinking that the bag held treasure, opened it, and they were

Odysseus tied to the mast of his ship as he listens to the sirens' music. From a Greek vase painting (5th century B.C.).

blown back to Aeolus' island, where the god refused to help them again. The cannibal LAESTRYGONIANS destroyed all but one of Odysseus' ships. Odysseus and his crew reached Aeaea, where the enchantress CIRCE turned most of the men into swine. However, Hermes gave Odysseus a herb called moly which saved him, and he frightened Circe into changing his men back to their normal shapes. Next, Odysseus descended into HADES to learn from the ghost of TIRESIAS how he would reach home. Following Circe's advice, he was able to avoid SCYLLA and Charybdis, with a loss of only six men, and sailed past the SIRENS without danger by putting wax in his men's ears. Odysseus, however, had himself tied to the mast so that he could enjoy their song. The crew would probably have reached Ithaca in safety, had not the men stolen the cattle of Helios on the island of Thrinacia, for which crime the ship was destroyed by a thunderbolt, and only Odysseus was saved by being cast ashore on Ogygia.

When they hear this harrowing tale, the Phaeacians send Odysseus home to Ithaca on one of their ships, laden with rich presents. After he has landed, Poseidon avenges himself on the Phaeacians by turning the ship into stone. Disguised by Athene as a beggar, Odysseus stays in the hut of the faithful swineherd Eumaeus while he determines how to rid his house of suitors. At first he is recognized by his old dog Argus, somewhat later by his mother Anticleia. He is ridiculed by the suitors and by the beggar IRUS, whose jaw Odysseus breaks. With Telemachus' help, Odysseus hides the suitors' weapons, locks them in the great hall of the palace and shoots them down with his bow. His wife and aged father are finally reunited to him and he reestablishes himself as king of Ithaca, when Athene calms the resentment of the suitors' families.

The *Odyssey*, like the ILIAD, was attributed by the ancient Greeks to the poet Homer. Many modern scholars feel that this masterful dramatic structure and fairly consistent style are his work, for the most part at least. However, it is thought to be a somewhat later composition than the *Iliad*, although belonging to the same general period. Also, while the *Iliad* is a collection of mythical material that grew up about an event that actually seems to have occurred toward the end of the Mycenaean era, the *Odyssey* is largely a collection of folk tales, many of which are easily recognizable in the tales of other lands. These tales have been given continuity and coherence by attributing the adventures to a single hero, and, moreover, by reworking each incident so that it contributes to a consistent picture of that hero. The consistency of the author's concept of Odysseus as a fictional character can be appreciated by comparing him with Heracles, whose saga is also the result of a gradual accretion of unrelated tales, but whose adventures were never told in a unified work of literature.

The monumental and complex figure of Odysseus and the chief work in which his adventures were told have had a perennial fascination for later writers. The most remarkable work that has been inspired by the Odyssey was James Joyce's novel ULYSSES, in which a single day's events in the life of Leopold Bloom, a notably unheroic Jewish citizen of Dublin, are made to conform to the pattern of the *Odyssey*.

More recently, the Greek poet Nikos KAZANTZAKIS undertook to relate the further adventures of Odysseus in *The Odyssey: A Modern Sequel*.

Odyssey: A Modern Sequel, The (1938). An epic poem by Nikos KAZANTZAKIS. It was translated into English verse by Kimon Friar in 1958. The poem was begun in 1925 and reworked through seven versions, and was intended as the summation of the author's philosophical attitudes. It contains 24 books, and is richly flavored with the idioms and rhythms of Greek folk songs and legends, the earthy language of shepherds and fishermen. The poem's prologue and epilogue are invocations to the sun; fire and light supply the poem's dominant imagery. The journeys of Odysseus are presented as an agonized but ecstatic struggle toward freedom and purity of spirit.

The modern sequel is grafted to the Homeric epic at Book XXII, just after Odysseus has slain the suitors of Penelope. Although the mythological setting is retained for its hero's further adventures in Ithaca, Sparta, Crete, and down the length of Africa to his death at the South Pole, Kazantzakis has said that his Odyssey is "a new epical-dramatic attempt of the modern man to find deliverance by passing through all the stages of contemporary anxieties and by pursuing the most daring hopes."

Oedipe (Oedipus, 1659). A tragedy by Pierre CORNEILLE. Based on the *Oedipus Rex* of Sophocles, it is marred by the addition of Dirce, a character invented by the author, sister of Oedipus and beloved of Theseus, prince of Athens. The *Oedipe* (1718) of VOLTAIRE, his first tragedy, suffers from a similar irrelevancy, the introduction of Jocasta's former lover Philoctetes, who is briefly suspected of murdering Laius.

Oedipus (Oidipous). In Greek mythology, the son of Laius, of the Theban dynasty founded by Cadmus, and of Jocasta (or Epicasta). He is the tragic hero of many dramas, most notably of Sophocles' *Oedipus Rex* (*Oidipous Tyrannos*) and *Oedipus at Colonus* (*Oidipous epi Kolonoi*). His story is told also in the *Iliad* and in the many works dealing with his sons (see SEVEN AGAINST THEBES).

In the most familiar version of the myth, Laius, having learned from an oracle that he would be killed by his own son, thrust a spike through the infant's feet and had him exposed on Mt. Cithaeron. Rescued by a shepherd, he was raised by the childless king Polybus of Corinth and his wife Periboea (or Merope) as their own son. When he grew to manhood, Oedipus was warned by the Delphic oracle that he would kill his father and marry his mother. Avoiding Corinth in horror, he met Laius on the road and, not knowing him, killed him in an argument. He proceeded to Thebes, which was then being ravaged by the SPHINX. When Oedipus answered her riddle, the Sphinx killed herself and the regent Creon offered him the throne of Thebes and the hand of Laius' widow Jocasta, who was Creon's sister. Later, famine struck Thebes and the Delphic oracle advised Creon to cast from the city the slayer of Laius. The seer TIRESIAS and an old shepherd revealed Oedipus' identity, Jocasta committed suicide, and Oedipus blinded himself with her brooch.

Banished from the city and shunned by his sons,

Eteocles and Polynices, he cursed them and wandered, an outcast, for many years. At last, his faithful daughter Antigone led him to a grove at Colonus sacred to the Eumenides. Creon tried to force his return to Thebes so that his body, buried outside the gates, would magically protect the city in war. But Theseus, the king of nearby Athens, defended him and, dying, Oedipus promised that his tomb would guard Athens from harm.

The story of Oedipus was told also by Seneca in his tragedy *Oedipus* and by Jean Cocteau in his play *The Infernal Machine* and in his libretto for Stravinsky's opera *Oedipus Rex*. In the 13th-century *Golden Legend* of Jacobus de Voragine and other medieval works, the Laius-Jocasta-Oedipus myth was attached to the legend of Judas Iscariot. It is a theme common in folk lore.

Oedipus at Colonus (Oidipous epi Kolonoi). See OEDIPUS.

Oedipus complex. Attachment to a parent of the opposite sex. Sigmund Freud used this term to describe a supposedly universal emotional process in which young boys are sexually attracted to their mothers and resent their fathers as rivals. Given normal family relationships, the conflict is resolved in childhood; otherwise, it may result in many emotional problems in adult life. See OEDIPUS.

Oedipus Rex (Oidipous Tyrannos). See OEDIPUS.

Oehlenschlaeger, Adam Gottlob (1779–1850). Danish poet and playwright. The leader of the romantic movement in Denmark, Oehlenschlaeger enjoyed a period of intense creativity during his early years. *Guldhorne* (*The Gold Horns*, 1802) is a romantic poem that exalted the glory of his country's past. His poetic dramas, based on Scandinavian myth and legend, include *Sanct-Hansaften-Spil* (*The Play of St. John's Eve*, 1803) and *Aladdin* (1805). Among his northern tragedies are *Hakon Jarl* (*Earl Hakon*, 1848) and *Baldur hin Gode* (*Baldur the Good*, 1808). In 1829, Oehlenschlaegar was crowned poet laureate of the Scandinavian countries.

Oenomaus (Oinomaos). See PELOPS.

Oenone (Oinone). In classic myth a nymph of Mount Ida. She had the gift of prophecy, and told her husband PARIS that his voyage to Greece would involve him and his country (Troy) in ruin. According to the legend, Paris came back to her beseeching her to heal his severe wounds, but she refused, and changed her mind too late. When the dead body of old Priam's son was laid at her feet, she stabbed herself. This story forms the subject of Tennyson's *Oenone* and *The Death of Oenone*.

Oenone. In Jean Racine's tragedy PHÈDRE, the nurse of Phèdre. She persuades her mistress to declare her passion to Hippolyte, and she later convinces King Theseus that Hippolyte made advances to Phèdre. Thus, it is Oenone who brings about the ruin of Hippolyte and Phèdre. Realizing this, she kills herself.

Oenopion (Oinopion). In classic myth, father of Merope, to whom the giant ORION made advances. Oenopion, unwilling to give his daughter to him, put out the giant's eyes in a drunken fit.

O'Faolain, Sean (1900–   ). Irish novelist, short-story writer, biographer, playwright, and teacher. *A Nest of Simple Folk* (1933) describes the movement of some ordinary Irish people toward a decision to join in the rebellion. *Bird Alone* (1936) and *Come Back to Erin* (1940) are novels which, like most of his later work, attack Irish provincialism and the repressive censorship of Catholicism. He is the author of biographies of Eamon DE VALERA (1933) and the Irish patriot Daniel O'Connell (1938). *I Remember! I Remember* (1961) is a book of short stories. See IRISH RENAISSANCE.

Off Broadway. See BROADWAY.

Offenbach, Jacques (1819–1880). German-born composer of French operettas. Some of his more than 90 such works are *Orphée aux Enfers* (1858), *La Belle Hélène* (1864), and *La Vie Parisienne* (1866). His best and most serious work, TALES OF HOFFMANN, was not produced until the year after his death (1881).

Of Human Bondage (1915). A novel by W. Somerset MAUGHAM. Its hero is Philip Carey, a sensitive, talented, club-footed orphan who is brought up by an unsympathetic aunt and uncle. It is a study of his struggle for independence, his intellectual development, and his attempt to become an artist. Philip gets entangled and obsessed by his love affair with Mildred, a waitress. After years of struggle as a medical student he marries a nice girl, gives up his aspirations, and becomes a country doctor. The first part of the novel is partly autobiographical, and the book is regarded as Maugham's best work.

O'Flaherty, Liam (1897–   ). Irish novelist and short-story writer. Although he has spent much time wandering adventurously around the world, O'Flaherty always writes about the Irish life among the poor and in his native Aran Islands. THE INFORMER, a novel about the Irish revolution, is his best-known book. Much of his finest work appears in his short stories, many of them masterpieces of bare, lyrical realism: *Spring Sowing* (1926), *Two Lovely Beasts and Other Stories* (1948), and other collections. *Famine* (1937) is a historical novel. He wrote several "melodramas of the soul," novels compounded, like Graham Greene's, of the thriller and the psychoanalytic case history: *The Black Soul* (1925), *Mr. Gilhooley* (1926) and *The Assassin* (1928). Autobiographical and travel books are *Two Years* (1930) and *I Went to Russia* (1931). See IRISH RENAISSANCE.

Of Mice and Men (1937). A novelette by John STEINBECK. Dramatized for the theater in 1937, it deals with the friendship between two migrant workers in California: Lennie Small, a giant half-wit of tremendous strength, and George Milton, who acts as Lennie's protector. The two dream of owning a farm of their own one day, but Lennie accidently kills a girl who has tried to seduce him, and George is forced to shoot him to keep him from an angry lynch mob.

Of Thee I Sing (1931). A musical comedy with book by George S. KAUFMAN, Morrie Ryskind, and Ira Gershwin and music by George GERSHWIN. It satirizes American party politics, showing a presidential campaign conducted on a platform of Love. John P. Wintergreen, the party candidate, is to marry the winner of an Atlantic City beauty contest. It was the first musical to win a Pulitzer Prize.

Of Time and the River: A Legend of Man's Hunger in His Youth (1935). A novel by Thomas WOLFE. It is a sequel to LOOK HOMEWARD, ANGEL, in which Eugene Gant, the hero, spends two years as a graduate student at Harvard, returns home for the dramatic death of his father, and teaches literature in New York City at the "School for Utility Cultures" (New York University). Eventually he tours France, returning home financially and emotionally exhausted. When the manuscript of the novel was submitted to Maxwell Perkins of Scribner's, it was several thousand pages long. Perkins helped Wolfe to edit and divide the material into two sections, some of which was included in The Web and the Rock.

Og. According to rabbinical mythology, an antediluvian giant (Deut. 3:11) saved from the Flood by climbing on the roof of Noah's ark. Og's bedstead, made of iron, was above 15 feet long and nearly seven feet broad. Legend relates that Og picked up a mountain to hurl at the Israelites but got so entangled with his burden that Moses was easily able to kill him.

Ogden, C[harles] K[ay] (1889–1957). English scholar, inventor of Basic English. He wrote with I. A. Richards The Meaning of Meaning (1923), and The System of Basic English (1934).

Ogham or **Ogam.** The traditional alphabet of the ancient British and Irish people. It was used in writing on wood or stone and was supposedly invented by one Ogma. Ogham, and the language associated with it, was employed by the druids; it died in the fifth century with the coming of Christianity.

Ogier, François. See Tir et Sidon.

Ogier the Dane. A hero of medieval French romances, one of Charlemagne's paladins. He is probably based on the Frankish warrior Autgarius, who first opposed Charlemagne, then joined him. According to tradition, however, he is held as hostage for his father Geoffrey of Dannemarch (probably a region in the Ardennes, but later understood as Denmark). He gains Charlemagne's favor for his deeds in Italy, but kills the queens's nephew to retaliate for the death of his own son in a quarrel, and is pursued and imprisoned. Released to fight against the Saracens in Spain, he again wins favor and is eventually given the fiefs of Hainaut and Brabant.

According to another legend, Morgan le Fay has him brought to Avalon when he is 100 years old. She introduces him to King Arthur and rejuvenates him, sends him out to fight for France, but snatches him back before he can marry, to wait until he is next needed.

He is identified with the Danish national hero Holger Danske.

OGPU. See Cheka.

ogres. In nursery and fairy tales, giants of very malignant disposition. They live on human flesh. The word was first used (and probably invented) by Charles Perrault in his Contes (1697), and is thought to be made up from Orcus, a name of Pluto, the god of Hades.

o'Groat, John. See John o'Groat's House.

Ogygia. Calypso's island in the Odyssey. Odysseus has been kept captive on Ogygia by Calypso for seven years when the poem opens. The island is generally identified with Gozo, near Malta.

O'Hara, John [Henry] (1905–1970). American short-story writer and novelist. Noted for his uncanny ear and skillful rendering of dialogue, O'Hara, who was born in Pottsville, Pa., began his career as a newspaperman. His short stories and novels, many of them set in the fictitious town of Gibbsville, Pa., form a commentary on contemporary American manners and morals. Among his best-known short-story collections are The Doctor's Son and Other Stories (1935) and Pal Joey (1940), which was made into a successful musical with music and lyrics by Richard Rodgers and Lorenz Hart. As a novelist, O'Hara established his reputation with Appointment in Samarra (1934), his famous first novel, and Butterfield 8 (1935), which deals with the promiscuous Gloria Wandrous. His later books include A Rage to Live (1949), Ten North Frederick (1955), From the Terrace (1958), Sermons and Soda-Water (1961), The Cape Cod Lighter (1962), Elizabeth Appleton (1963), The Hat on the Bed (1963), and The Horse Knows the Way (1964).

O'Hara [Alsop], Mary (1885–). American writer. After writing scenarios in California, she moved to a ranch in Wyoming and wrote three novels about horses: My Friend Flicka (1941), Thunderhead (1943), and The Green Grass of Wyoming (1946). She discusses her own novel, The Son of Adam Wingate (1952), in Novel-in-the-Making (1954). She is also a composer of popular musical works, among which Wyoming Suite for Piano (1946) is the most ambitious.

O'Hara, Scarlett. The willful and colorful heroine of Margaret Mitchell's historical novel Gone with the Wind.

O'Higgins, Bernardo (1778–1842). Chilean general and statesman. The natural son of Irish-born Ambrose O'Higgins, who served as viceroy of Peru, he became commander of Chile's revolutionary forces in 1813. Defeated by the Spaniards at Rancagua, he fled to Argentina where he joined San Martín's army of liberation. After the army's heroic march across the Andes, San Martín and O'Higgins were victorious at the battles of Chacabuco and Maipu and declared the independence of Chile (1818). As supreme director of Chile, O'Higgins proved a vigorous, enlightened ruler, but clerical and conservative opposition to some of his reforms and his harsh treatment of political opponents led to his ouster in 1823. He spent the rest of his life in Lima, Peru. A province of Chile is named for him.

Ohm, Georg Simon (1787–1854). German physicist for whom the practical unit of electrical resistance is named.

Oh! Susanna. A song by Stephen Foster, from his Songs of the Sable Harmonists (1848). It was immensely popular in the California gold rush of 1849.

Oidipous epi Kolonoi. See Oedipus.

Oidipous Tyrannos. See Oedipus.

Oil! (1927). A novel by Upton Sinclair. Based on the Teapot Dome scandal of the Harding administration, it is the story of Bunny Ross, the son of a wealthy oil operator, who discovers that politicians are unscrupulous and that oil magnates are equally bad. In time he becomes a socialist.

O'Keeffe, Georgia (1887–). American painter. With fastidious craftsmanship, she has painted severe abstractions and symbolic juxtapositions of flowers and animal skulls. She was married to the photographer Alfred Stieglitz (1864–1946).

Okies. A term applied in the 1930's to dispossessed farmers from the Dust Bowl region. After the devastating dust storms of the 1930's, these men and their families, most of whom were from Oklahoma, were forced to leave their land and seek work elsewhere. Many of them became migrant workers in the fruit orchards of California. John Steinbeck's novel THE GRAPES OF WRATH is about an Okie family.

Oklahoma! (1943). A musical comedy based on *Green Grow the Lilacs* by Lynn RIGGS, with music by Richard RODGERS, libretto by Oscar HAMMERSTEIN and choreography by Agnes De Mille. With its many memorable songs, it set an all-time record of durability for musicals.

Old Bailey. A famous old prison in London, formerly a feudal castle.

Old Believers. In Russian history, dissenters opposed to the 17th-century liturgical reforms of Patriarch Nikon. The disagreement resulted in a split in the Russian Church during the 17th century. One of the leaders of the dissidents was the priest Avvakum, who described in his autobiography the sufferings he endured for his cause. In 1667 a church council excommunicated Avvakum and his followers, branding them with the name *Raskolniki* (schismatics) by which the sect continued to be known.

Oldbuck, Jonathan. In Scott's ANTIQUARY, the laird of Monkbarns, an old antiquary devoted to the study and accumulation of old coins and medals. Although he is sarcastic, irritable, and a woman hater, his character is tempered with kindness and humor.

Oldcastle, Sir John (1377?–1417). The model for Shakespeare's famous character Sir John FALSTAFF. A play called *Sir John Oldcastle*, now ascribed to Anthony Munday, was printed in 1600 as the work of Shakespeare. There are indications that in both parts of *Henry IV* the name Oldcastle was originally used but later changed to Falstaff.

Old Comedy. A style of Greek comedy; plays of ARISTOPHANES are the only surviving examples. Like tragedy, it evolved from the rituals in honor of DIONYSUS, and the two have in common the use of the chorus in PARODOS, EXODOS, and lyric interludes between episodes of dialogue. Comedy, however, apparently developed out of the parts of the Dionysiac festivals most directly concerned with fertility: ritual marriage and feast, bawdy jokes and songs. This ancient religious sanction accounts for both the obscenity and the freedom of political commentary in the plays. Other characteristics of Old Comedy are the *pnigos*, a kind of patter song sung by the chorus in one breath; the *agon* (contest), in which the two halves of the chorus argue violently over some contemporary question; and the *parabasis*, in which the chorus address directly to the audience an elaborate plea to reward the author with their approval. Old Comedy reached its end with the defeat of Athens in the Peloponnesian War, after which freedom of speech was greatly curtailed.

Old Creole Days (1879). A collection of short stories by George W. CABLE, dealing with 19th-century New Orleans. Noted for their local color and their use of dialect, the stories are a blend of realism and romance. *Madame Delphine,* included in later editions of the book, was a tale of miscegenation, as was *'Tite Poulette.* Other stories were *Ah Poquelin,* the story of a former slave trader; *Café des Exilés,* a tale with a smuggling plot; and *Belles Demoiselles,* a story about a proud father's loss.

Old Curiosity Shop, The (1840). A novel by Charles DICKENS. The heroine, Nell Trent, better known as Little Nell, lives with her grandfather, an old man who keeps a curiosity shop. In order to make some money for Little Nell, the grandfather borrows from the hunchback Daniel QUILP. An obsessive gambler, the grandfather loses all that he has and Quilp takes over the Old Curiosity Shop. Little Nell and her grandfather leave and roam about the countryside as beggars. They meet Thomas Codlin and his traveling puppet show and work for Mrs. JARLEY's Wax Works. Mr. Marton, a kindly schoolmaster, gives them a house near an old church, and Little Nell tends the graves. When Kit NUBBLES, their only friend, and the grandfather's brother finally locate them after a long search, Little Nell is dead; her grandfather dies shortly thereafter. Kit marries Barbara and tells the story of Little Nell to his children. The Old Curiosity Shop is torn down to make way for a new building. Many modern readers have found Dickens overly sentimental about Little Nell. Some well-known characters from the book include Sampson and Sarah BRASS; Dick SWIVELLER; the MARCHIONESS.

Oldenbourg, Zoë (1916–   ). Russian-born French historical novelist. *The World Is Not Enough* (*Argile;* 1946) and its sequel *The Cornerstone* (*Pierre Angulaire;* 1953), as well as *Destiny of Fire* (*Les Brûlés;* 1960), take place during the Crusades of the Middle Ages. *The Awakened* (*Réveillés de la vie;* 1956) and its sequel *The Chains of Love* (*Les Irréductibles;* 1958) concern émigrés in pre- and postwar Paris.

Old English Annals. See ANGLO-SAXON CHRONICLE.

Old Folks at Home, The (1851). A song by Stephen FOSTER. It is also called *Swanee River,* because it begins, "Way down upon the Swanee River ... "

Old Fortunatus (1599). An allegorical comedy by Thomas DEKKER. An old beggar offered wisdom, strength, health, beauty, long life, or riches by the goddess Fortune, chooses the latter. She gives him an inexhaustible purse which brings little but trouble to the foolish old man and his equally silly sons; they wander through the world, buffeted by Vice and Virtue, until they perish miserably and Fortune reclaims the purse. See illustration on page 734.

Old Glory. A popular name for the flag of the United States of America.

Old Ironsides. (1) Popular name for U.S.S. CONSTITUTION.

(2) A poem by Oliver Wendell HOLMES (1830). Written when Holmes read of the navy's plan to scrap the old frigate, the poem roused popular opinion, and the *Constitution* was saved.

Old Maid, The (1924). A novelette by Edith WHARTON. One of the four books included in the volume OLD NEW YORK, it tells the story of Tina, Charlotte Lovell's illegitimate daughter, who is brought up by Charlotte's cousin in ignorance of her true origin. The dramatization by Zoë Akins in 1935 won a Pulitzer Prize.

THE

Pleafant Comedie of

Old Fortunatus.

As it was plaied before the Queenes
Maieftie this Chriftmas , by the Right
Honourable the Earle of Notting-
ham, Lord high Admirall of England his Seruants.

LONDON

Printed by S. S. for William Afpley, dwelling in
Paules Church-yard at the figne of the
Tygers head. 1 6 0 0.

Title page of Dekker's *Old Fortunatus* (1600).

Old Man and the Sea, The (1952). A novelette
by Ernest HEMINGWAY. It movingly depicts an old
Cuban fisherman who has been 84 days without a
catch. Far from port on the 85th day he hooks a
gigantic marlin, and, against great odds in a battle
lasting two days, brings the fish alongside and har-
poons it. Soon sharks appear, and the old man breaks
his knife after he has killed only a few; during the
last night of the voyage home, the sharks devour all
but the head of the great fish. The story has been
interpreted as an allegory of man's inevitable defeat in the struggle with existence; in spite of defeat,
however, man can fight with dignity, courage, and
stoicism.

Old Man of the Mountains (Sheikh-al-Jebal).
Hassan-i-Sabbah, the founder of the ASSASSINS. He
died in 1124.

Old Man of the Sea. A strange and alarming
character in the story of SINDBAD THE SAILOR in the
Arabian Nights. A seemingly harmless if down-at-the-
heels old man, he climbs onto the shoulders of the
obliging Sindbad, and refuses to get off. He clings
there for many days and nights, much to the discomfort of Sindbad, but the sailor finally escapes by
making the old man drunk.

**Old Man's Comforts and How He Gained
Them, The** (1799). A poem by Robert SOUTHEY,
best known through the parody of it written by Lewis
Carroll in his *Father William* (1865).

Old Men at the Zoo, The (1961). A fable by
Angus WILSON. He uses the animals at the zoo and
their human administrators and keepers to satirize
various forms of government.

Old Mortality (1816). A novel by Sir Walter
SCOTT. It deals with the struggle between the Covenanters and the Cavaliers in 1679. Old Mortality, who
tells the story to the supposed author, Jedediah Cleish-
botham, is an eccentric itinerant whose whole life is
given over to cleaning the moss from old gravestones,
cutting new inscriptions, and erecting new stones for
fallen Covenanters.

Old Mortality (1939). A short novel by Katherine Anne PORTER. It appeared in the collection
PALE HORSE, PALE RIDER, which also included *Noon
Wine,* as well as the title story. The child Miranda
has heard for many years her family speaking with a
nostalgia that approaches reverence of her now dead
aunt, who had been known for her grace and beauty.
In adolescence, however, Miranda comes to realize
that her aunt was actually a totally self-centered
woman to whose whims several other people had been
sacrificed. Miranda, grown to young womanhood, is
also the heroine of *Pale Horse, Pale Rider.*

Old New York (4 vols., 1924). A series of four
novelettes by Edith WHARTON, each dealing with a
decade in the years 1840 to 1880. *False Dawn* is
about Lewis Raycie, who buys pictures so far in advance of his time that his father disinherits him.
THE OLD MAID is considered the best of the group.
The third volume, *The Spark,* deals with an elderly
man who comes under the influence of Walt Whitman. In *New Year's Day,* a wife sacrifices herself
to obtain money for a sick husband, only to be
scorned by society.

Old North Church. Popular name of Christ
Episcopal Church, Boston, Mass. It was dedicated in
1723. On April 18, 1775 lanterns were hung in the
belfry to signal Paul Revere of the coming of the
English forces. The church is still in use.

Old Possum. A name assumed by T. S. ELIOT.
It is used in his collection of comic and whimsical
verse *Old Possum's Book of Practical Cats* (1939).

Old Pretender. See PRETENDER.

Old South Church. An historic landmark, affectionately called "Old South," in Boston, Mass. Built
in 1729, it was often used before the Revolution for
mass meetings too large for Faneuil Hall, including
a protest meeting after the Boston Massacre and another which ended in the Boston Tea Party.

Oldstyle, Jonathan. A pen name used by Washington IRVING. He signed his satirical letters to the
New York *Morning Chronicle* (1802–1803) with this
pseudonym.

**Old Swimmin' Hole and 'Leven More Poems,
The** (1883). A book of poems by James Whitcomb
RILEY. It was his first volume written in Hoosier
(Indiana) dialect and was signed "Benj. F. Johnson."
One of Riley's most popular poems, *When the Frost
is on The Punkin,* is included.

Old Testament. The first part of the Christian
BIBLE, identical in content with the Hebrew scriptures. The theme of the Old Testament is God's
covenant with Israel. It contains the history of Israel,
its laws as given by God, its triumphs and failures
as a nation, its return to God's love, and its eternal
hope through righteousness. In the Hebrew canon

the Old Testament has three divisions: the Law, or Torah, comprising the first five books known as the PENTATEUCH; the eight books of the Prophets; and the Hagiographa, or Writings, which includes the poetical books Proverbs, Job, Ruth, Ecclesiastes, etc.

Oldtown Folks (1869). A novel by Harriet Beecher STOWE. Oldtown is actually South Natick, Mass.; the book takes place shortly after the Revolution. The most interesting characters are Horace Holyoke, a young man with spiritual visions, and Sam Lawson, the comic commentator.

Old Vic. Affectionate name for the Royal Victoria Hall in London. As a theater it first opened in 1818 as the Coburg. The name was changed in 1833. The specialties of the house were extravagant melodramas. In 1871 it became a music hall, later an opera house and movie theater.

With Sir George Dance's gift of £25,000 in 1914, the Old Vic was able to establish itself as the home theater for a Shakespearean company. By 1916 the entire works of Shakespeare had been performed on its stage.

It was badly damaged in World War II. A new theater houses the famous Shakespeare company, but the Old Vic is still used as a rehearsal hall.

old wives' tale. A term for a gossipy or unconvincing story, from Tyndale's translation of I Tim. 4:7. It is the title of a drama by George Peele (c. 1595).

Old Wives' Tale, The (1908). A novel by Arnold BENNETT. It is a naturalistic study of the environment and character development of two sisters, Constance and Sophia Baines, who are brought up together in their parents' store in Bursley, one of the Five Towns. Constance stays in Bursley, marries the good apprentice, Samuel Povey, and inherits the business. The more adventurous Sophia elopes to Paris with a young ne'er-do-well who deserts her. She finally establishes herself as the successful keeper of a *pension*, and lives peacefully through the siege of Paris and other contemporary events. In her old age she returns to Bursley to live—and die—with her widowed sister. The novel is remarkable for its sense of passing time and its detailed, sympathetic picture of ordinary women's lives.

Olger Danske. See HOLGER DANSKE.

Olimpia. In the ORLANDO FURIOSO of Lodovico Ariosto, the daughter of the count of Holland. Because she loved Bireno, duke of Selandia, she refused the hand of Arbante, son of King Cimosco of Frisia. To avoid the wedding, she has Arbante killed, but Bireno is captured by Cimosco. When Orlando rescues Bireno, the two are free to wed, except that Bireno has fallen in love with the daughter of Cimosco while in captivity. When Bireno deserts Olimpia, she is trapped by brigands and exposed to the Orc, a sea monster. After Orlando rescues her, she weds Oberto, king of Ireland.

Olindo. The lover of Sofronia in a famous episode of Tasso's GERUSALEMME LIBERATA. He offers to substitute for her at the stake but is condemned to die with her instead. Finally, they are both rescued by the warrior maiden Clorinda and marry.

Oliosha, Yuri Karlovich (1899–1960). Russian novelist and short-story writer. He is best known for his short novel ENVY, one of the outstanding works of prose fiction in Soviet literature. The novel was well received at first, but later Soviet critics condemned its preoccupation with private emotions and its implied satire on the Soviet scene. Oliosha insisted on his right to deal with the subjects he chose, and, after making a speech at the first meeting of the Union of Soviet Writers in 1934, he was rarely heard from again, though his reputation was rehabilitated in 1957 when a selection of his works was published. His collected stories originally appeared in a volume entitled *The Cherry Stone* (*Vishnyovaya kostochka;* 1930). He is also the author of an adventure novel, *Three Fat Men* (*Tri tolstyaka;* 1928), and a play, *A List of Blessings* (*Spisok blagodeyany;* 1931).

Oliphant, Laurence (1829–1888). English novelist. Oliphant wrote entertainingly of his worldwide adventures, and evidenced a talent for social satire in his novel *Piccadilly* (1866). He later became involved in spiritualism.

Oliphant, Margaret (1828–1897). Scottish novelist. She is chiefly known for her books dealing with provincial English society in the 19th century. Among her works are *Passages in the Life of Mrs. Margaret Maitland* (1849); *Chronicles of Carlingford* (1863–1876), including *Salem Chapel* (regarded as her best novel), *The Perpetual Curate, The Rector, Miss Marjoribanks,* and *Phoebe Junior; A Beleaguered City* (1880); and *Autobiography* (1899).

olive. In ancient Greece sacred to Pallas Athene. She was said to have made it her gift to the Athenians, thereby gaining their loyalty in preference to their previous patron Poseidon. It was a symbol of peace, and also an emblem of fecundity: Athenian brides wore or carried olive garlands as ours do a wreath of orange blossom. A crown of olive was the highest distinction of a citizen who deserved well of his country, and was the highest prize in the Olympic games.

The phrase "to hold out the olive branch," meaning to make overtures to peace, alludes, of course, to its ancient identification with peace. On some ancient Roman medals, the legendary King Numa is shown holding an olive twig, indicative of his peaceful reign.

Oliver. Orlando's envious older brother in Shakespeare's As You Like It. He forces his brother to flee to the Forest of Arden, but is reconciled with him when Orlando saves his life. He eventually weds Celia.

Oliver Twist (1837–1839). A novel by Charles DICKENS, depicting the world of poverty, crime, and the workhouse of 19th-century London. The novel was written against the background of the new Poor Law of 1834, which ended the supplemental dole to the poor and forced husbands, wives, and children into separate workhouses in the name of utilitarian efficiency.

Oliver, a foundling, is born in the workhouse where he commits the unspeakable crime of asking for more gruel. He is apprenticed by Mr. BUMBLE to the undertaker Mr. Sowerberry, but soon runs away only to fall into the hands of a gang of thieves headed by FAGIN. With the aid of Jack Dawkins (the ARTFUL DODGER), NANCY, Bill SIKES, and Charley BATES, Fagin tries to make Oliver into a thief. The wealthy Mr. Brownlow tries to rescue Oliver, but through the machinations of the evil Monks, who has a special interest in corrupting him, Oliver is kidnapped by Fagin's gang; he is forced to take part in a burglary during the course of which he is wounded. He is nursed by Mrs. Maylie and her foster child Rose (later revealed to be Oliver's aunt). Eventually the secret of Oliver's parentage is disclosed; Monks is his half brother and has tried to ruin Oliver in order to retain all their father's property. In the end, Monks, Fagin, and the gang are brought to justice. Mr. Brownlow adopts Oliver and educates him. In *Oliver Twist,* one of his most popular novels, Dickens illustrates that poverty breeds crime and that the road from the workhouse to Fagin's gang is a short and straight one.

Olives, Mount of. A ridge east of Jerusalem. Jesus used to go to the Mount of Olives to pray and meditate in the evening. It was here perhaps that he taught his disciples the Lord's Prayer. At the foot of its western slope is the garden of GETHSEMANE.

Olivia. The rich young countess wooed by Orsino in Shakespeare's TWELFTH NIGHT. Although she is in mourning for her dead brother and "hath abjured the company and sight of men," she falls in love with Orsino's page, who is Viola in boy's disguise. She finally weds Viola's twin brother, Sebastian.

Olivier. Also **Oliver, Oliviero, Ulivieri.** The close friend of Roland among the paladins of Charlemagne, gifted with the moderation and common sense that Roland lacks. His family is at war with Charlemagne, so that Roland and Olivier meet as dueling opponents. When their long and chivalrous battle is stopped by divine intervention, they become sworn friends, and Roland is engaged to Olivier's sister. The *Chanson de* ROLAND describes the death of all three.

As Oliviero he appears prominently in Pulci's *Morgante Maggiore* and Boiardo's *Orlando Innamorato.* In Ariosto's *Orlando Furioso* he joins Orlando (Roland) and Brandimarte in a great duel with the pagan leaders AGRAMANTE and GRADASSO at Lipadusa; he is seriously wounded, but survives.

Olivier, Sir **Laurence [Kerr]** (1907–   ). English actor of stage and screen. He made his debut on the English stage (1924) in *Byron* and in America (1929) in *Murder on the Second Floor.* He established his reputation in 1931 in *Private Lives* with Noel Coward and Gertrude Lawrence. He has had a long association with the Old Vic Company and is best known for his Shakespearean roles. He has produced and directed three movies in which he stars: *Henry V, Hamlet,* and *Richard III.*

Ollivant, Alfred (1874–1927). English novelist. His book *Bob, Son of Battle* (1898) is one of the world's most famous dog stories, to be compared with the animal stories of Anna Sewell (*Black Beauty*), Marshall Saunders (*Beautiful Joe*), and Albert Payson Terhune (*Lad*).

Ol' Man Adam an' His Chillun (1928). A book of stories about Negroes by Roark BRADFORD. It was from these stories that Marc Connelly wrote the famous play THE GREEN PASTURES.

Olmedo, José Joaquín. See VICTORIA DE JUNÍN, LA.

Olney. A country parish in England where William COWPER boarded with Mrs. Mary Unwin and received the religious ministrations of the Rev. John Newton, whom he assisted for a time in charitable activities in the parish. Newton, by forcing Cowper to incessant religious exercises, subjected the poet to a nervous strain which brought on an attack of insanity in 1773. During this period the *Olney Hymns* (1779) were written. The hymn, *Light Shining out of Darkness* contains the famous stanza:

> God moves in a mysterious way,
> His wonders to perform;
> He plants his footsteps in the sea,
> And rides upon the storm.

Olson, Elder (1909–   ). American poet and critic. Olson is a critic of the Neo-Aristotelian school associated with the University of Chicago. His own poetry, often of a humanist and religious bent, has been collected in *The Cock of Heaven* (1940), *Things of Sorrow* (1943), and *The Scarecrow Christ* (1945).

Olympic games. The greatest of the four sacred festivals of the ancient Greeks. It was held at Olympia every fourth year, in the month of July. The festival commenced with sacrifices and included all kinds of contests of sport, ending on the fifth day with processions, sacrifices, and banquets to the victors, who were garlanded with olive leaves. In 1895 an international committee met in Paris in the interests of establishing modern *Olympic games* to which various countries should send contestants. The first games of the new series were held at Athens in 1896, and after that date they occurred every four years with the exception of the duration of World Wars I and II.

Olympus (Olympos). The home of the gods of ancient Greece. There Zeus held his court; the mountain is about 9800 ft. high, on the confines of Macedonia and Thessaly.

Om. Among the Brahmans, the mystic equivalent for the name of the Deity. It was adopted by modern occultists to denote absolute goodness and truth or the spiritual essence.

Om mani padme hum (I salute the jewel in the lotus). The mystic formula of the Tibetans and northern Buddhists. It is used as a charm and for other religious purposes. They are the first words taught to a child and the last uttered on the deathbed of the pious. The lotus symbolizes universal being and the jewel the individuality of the speaker.

O'Malley, Grace. Gaelic name, **Graine Ni Maille** (fl. 1550–1600). Irish princess. A member of a famous family of sea-farers, she commanded a large fleet of war galleys that preyed on English ships and coastal villages. There are numerous legends about her career, and she may have inspired one of the episodes in James Joyce's *Finnegans Wake* (1939).

Omar Khayyám (d. 1123). Persian astronomer-poet. Born at Naishápúr, in Khorastan, Iran, as Abu-'l-fat'h 'Omar, son of Ibrahim the Tentmaker, Omar adopted as his poetic name the designation of his father's trade, Khayyám. He spent his whole life in his native town, where he studied under the celebrated teacher the Imam Mowaffak and was later granted a pension by the Vizier Nizam ul Mulk, a former schoolfellow, becoming known far and wide as a scholar and astronomer. He was one of a commission of eight appointed by Malik Shah to revise the calendar, and was the author of astronomical tables and a book on algebra, as well as the celebrated collection of quatrains, the RUBÁIYÁT OF OMAR KHAYYÁM.

Never popular in his own country, Omar's poetry had been preserved only in mutilated manuscripts, among which the one in the library of the Asiatic Society, Calcutta, is perhaps the most nearly complete;

it contains 516 *rubáiyát* (or *rubáis*). Edward FITZ-GERALD translated 101 of them from the original Persian into English. The *Rubáiyát* is a series of quatrains rhymed *a-a-b-a* (or sometimes *a-a-a-a* in the original), each one expressing a complete thought. Of Omar's thought, FitzGerald wrote: "Omar . . . pretending sensual pleasure as the serious purpose of Life, only diverted himself with speculative problems of Deity, Destiny, Matter and Spirit, Good and Evil, and other such questions."

omega. See ALPHA.

Omnibus Bill. A congressional bill dealing with a number of different subjects. A famous American Omnibus Bill was the Compromise of 1850.

Omoo: A Narrative of Adventures in the South Seas (1847). A novel by Herman MELVILLE. The book begins by recapitulating the ending of TYPEE, in which the hero escapes on the whaler *Julia*. The crew of the *Julia* mutinies, and is imprisoned on the island of Tahiti. Melville and his friend, Doctor Long Ghost, are released, and explore the island together. *Omoo* is superior in style to *Typee;* Bembo, Jermin, and the Doctor are vivid characters. The title of the book is a Polynesian word for a rover, one who wanders from island to island.

O'More, Rory. The name of 3 famous Irish rebel chiefs of the 16th and 17th centuries. The name appears frequently in Irish poetry.

Omphale. In Greek mythology, a queen of Lydia. Heracles was sold to her as a slave. For her he rid Lydia of robbers and other pests, and they had several children. The idea that they changed clothes, Omphale wearing the lion's skin and Heracles woman's dress, was spread only by later writers such as Ovid.

omphalos. See DELPHIC ORACLE.

On American Taxation. A famous speech by Edmund BURKE, delivered in the English Parliament on April 19, 1774, urging that the duty on tea imported into the American colonies be repealed. It was not successful.

On Conciliation with the American Colonies. A speech by Edmund BURKE, delivered in the English Parliament in March, 1775, in an effort to prevent disaffection between Great Britain and the colonies in America by granting them autonomy. Burke hoped for a system that might preserve both English superiority and colonial liberty. For his resolution in favor of conciliation, his speech won only 58 votes.

One Day in the Life of Ivan Denisovich (*Odin den' Ivana Denisovicha;* 1963). A short novel by Aleksandr Solzhenitzyn (1918–   ). It describes conditions in a Soviet prison camp during the Stalin era. This short book traces in excruciating detail the struggle of one prisoner to stay alive and to snatch what meager comforts he can find during a typical day in the camp.

The book was apparently a revelation to persons inside the Soviet Union as well as abroad. In terms of internal Soviet affairs, it was one more step in the de-Stalinization campaign begun by Khrushchev's speech at the 20th Communist Party Congress in 1956.

Solzhenitzyn, a former schoolteacher, had himself been an inmate of a prison camp.

Oneida Community. A perfectionist religious society established in New York State in 1847 by John Humphrey NOYES. An experiment in practical communism, the community developed an excellent school system, ran a 900-acre farm, and governed itself democratically. The original 40 settlers grew to some 300; they manufactured steel traps and silver-plated ware. Their system of polygamy and polyandry, developed for the purpose of scientific propagation, aroused public disapproval. The community was abandoned in 1879, but reorganized as a business corporation two years later.

O'Neill, Danny. The hero of a series of novels by James T. FARRELL: *A World I Never Made* (1936), *No Star Is Lost* (1938), *Father and Son* (1940), *My Days of Anger* (1943) and *The Face of Time* (1953). At the outset, Danny is brought up in a lower-middle-class Irish-Catholic background in Chicago, similar to that of the hero of STUDS LONIGAN. He goes to live with more well-to-do relatives, however, and is shown as a quiet little boy with a precocious knowledge of baseball. He grows up to be a sensitive young man, becoming a student at the University of Chicago and rebelling against the life accepted by Studs Lonigan. Danny, who is thought to be based on the author himself, also appears briefly in the Lonigan series.

O'Neill, Eugene [Gladstone] (1888–1953). American playwright. By common consent considered the greatest American dramatist, he is one of the most significant figures in the recent history of the theater. The winner of the Nobel Prize in 1936, O'Neill is famous for his technical experiments, being a pioneer in the use of myth on the modern stage. Influenced by German expressionism and the ideas of Freud and Nietzsche, his grim and moving psychological studies of men and women in the America of his time sometimes employ religious symbolism.

The son of James O'Neill and Ella Quinlan, both actors, O'Neill spent his early youth in restless wandering, working at odd jobs about the country and taking several voyages at sea, which provided him with much material for his plays. In 1912 he entered a tuberculosis sanitarium and there began reading plays and eventually writing them. Of this early work only *Thirst and Other One-Act Plays* (1914) was published; O'Neill spent a further apprenticeship at the Harvard Workshop directed by George Pierce Baker.

Crucial in his development was his association in 1916 in Provincetown, Mass., with George Cram Cook, Susan Glaspell, and the PROVINCETOWN PLAYERS. *Bound East for Cardiff,* a one-act play describing the last moments of a dying seaman, was produced by them in 1916. Other plays of the sea followed, including *The Long Voyage Home* (1917), concerning sailors in a London bar after a voyage; *Ile* (1917), the story of a captain who insists on continuing his hunt for whale oil at the expense of his wife's sanity and the threat of a mutiny; *The Moon of the Caribbees* (1918), telling of the crisis on the steamer *Glencairn* when women come aboard; and *Where the Cross Is Made* (1918), the tale of another obsessed captain. These were collected in *Bound East for Cardiff and Other Plays* (1916) and *The Moon of the Caribbees and Other Plays* (1919). In 1948 four of the plays were revived under the collective title *S.S. Glencairn.*

O'Neill's first full-length play was BEYOND THE HORIZON, the winner of a Pulitzer Prize. THE EMPEROR JONES indicated that O'Neill's naturalism was being modified by the expressionism of Strindberg. ANNA CHRISTIE, another play of the sea, won a second Pulitzer Prize for O'Neill; *Gold* (1921) was a full-length expansion of the earlier *Where the Cross Is Made*. THE HAIRY APE again combined expressionism and naturalism.

With DESIRE UNDER THE ELMS, O'Neill's interest in Freudian psychology was combined with his growing interest in the theories of Nietzsche. In ALL GOD'S CHILLUN GOT WINGS, a play about Negroes and whites, O'Neill helped to destroy the convention of caricaturing Negroes in literature. In these years he also wrote THE GREAT GOD BROWN and MARCO MILLIONS.

STRANGE INTERLUDE, another Pulitzer Prize winner, is a psychological study notable for the use of asides and soliloquy. MOURNING BECOMES ELECTRA, a trilogy based on Aeschylus, attempts to transform the Greek concept of fate into psychological and environmental determinism. *Ah, Wilderness* (1933), a nostalgic play about an adolescent boy, and *Days Without End* (1934) mark the end of O'Neill's early productivity. His name did not return to Broadway until 1946 when *The Iceman Cometh*, a treatment of social outcasts, was produced. *A Moon for the Misbegotten* (1957) and *A Touch of the Poet* (1958) were part of a larger cycle of plays O'Neill was working on at the time of his death. LONG DAY'S JOURNEY INTO NIGHT, produced in 1956 but written before 1941, is largely autobiographical, with moments equalling the best of the O'Neill of the early period. See LAZARUS LAUGHED.

One of Ours (1922). A novel by Willa CATHER. It tells the story of Claude Wheeler, a boy who grows up on a Western farm, goes to a Western university, enters the army, and is later killed in France. The book, which is based in part on the letters of a relative of Miss Cather's who died in World War I, was awarded a Pulitzer Prize.

One-upmanship (1952). A humorous book by Stephen POTTER which explains how to keep one-up on the Joneses.

Onions, Oliver (1873–1961). English novelist. He changed his name to George Oliver but continued to publish under his original name. He wrote novels of grim realism and ghost stories, including *Mushroom Town* (1914), *Ghosts in Daylight* (1924), and *Poor Man's Tapestry* (1946). Onions married the novelist Berta RUCK.

Onís [y Sánchez], Federico de (1885–   ). Spanish academician, philologist, and critic. Onís is a student of the famous Spanish scholar Menéndez Pidal. Having been a member of the faculty of several universities, he came to the U.S. where he joined the faculty of Columbia University (1916); here he remained as chairman of the department of Spanish during the period 1929–1954. His most famous work is the *Antología de la poesía española e hispanoamericana* (1934).

onomatopoeia. The formation of words imitating the sound of the object or action expressed, as in buzz, hiss, clack, bang, and twitter. In rhetoric, the figure of speech in which the writer deliberately reproduces in the sound of the words he selects the actual sound that he is describing or that is connected with his subject. Poe's *Bells*, the hissing passage in Milton's *Paradise Lost* where Satan's minions

turn into snakes, and the famous frogs' chorus in Aristophanes' satirical play *The Frogs* are all good examples of onomatopoeia.

On the Eve (Nakanunye; 1860). A novel by Ivan TURGENEV. The heroine, Elena STAKHOVA, is wooed by three men: the scholar Bersenev, the sculptor Shubin, and the civil servant Kurnatovski. Unmoved by all of them, she immediately falls in love at first sight with the Bulgarian revolutionary, INSAROV. Elena feels she has at last found her goal in life, to fight for social justice by Insarov's side. She leaves with him to continue the struggle for freedom in Bulgaria. Insarov dies on the way, but the inspired Elena goes on to carry on his work. Although he was attempting to show a young revolutionary acting in a positive manner, Turgenev was criticized by the radicals for portraying him as a Bulgarian and not as a Russian.

On the Sublime (Peri Hypsous). A Greek treatise of unknown author and date. It is attributed to Dionysius or Dionysius Longinus, and was probably written in the first half of the 1st century A.D. The treatise finds five sources of the sublime in literature: significant thoughts, intense emotion, powerful figures of speech, excellence in choice of language, and effective organization. The author states that a passion for novelty often converts the sublime into the ridiculous. The sublime has universal appeal. The author discusses the possibility of "noble error," saying that sublimity, not correctness, enables man to approach the gods. He cites Homer, Plato, and Demosthenes as examples. The treatise was first published by Robortello in 1554, and was translated by Boileau in 1674. It was widely admired, particularly by Dryden, Addison, Pope, Goldsmith, Reynolds, Hurd, Fielding, and Gibbon.

Open Boat, The (1898). A short story by Stephen CRANE. Often considered the greatest of his works in this form, it is based on a personal experience of the author. It deals with four men who have escaped in a small open boat from their sinking ship: the captain, the cook, an oiler, and a newspaper correspondent. They discuss the possibilities of being saved, sight land, and await help that does not come. After a whole night of drifting just off shore, they attempt to land the boat. In the process three of the men come ashore successfully, but the oiler dies, just as he is about to reach safety. Told in a style of great understatement and economy, the story carries far more significance, weight, and drama than the slight plot would seem to indicate.

open-door policy. The principle of giving equal opportunity and recognition to all foreign nations in matters of trade. See John HAY.

Ophelia. In Shakespeare's HAMLET, the young and innocent daughter of Polonius and sister of Laertes. Dutifully, she obeys Polonius' request that she spurn Hamlet's advances and later permits her father to spy on her and Hamlet. After the death of Polonius, she loses her mind. The scene in which her madness is poignantly revealed is one of the most famous in literature.

Opheltes. A character in Greek mythology. As the SEVEN AGAINST THEBES were on the way to their fatal war, they stopped at Nemea. HYPSIPYLE, a former queen of Lemnos, and now a slave to King

Lycurgus, was caring for Opheltes, the king's infant son. Left alone while she showed the soldiers a spring, the child was killed by a snake. The Seven killed the snake and instituted the Nemean Games in honor of the child. The seer Amphiaraus, one of the Seven, saw the event as an evil omen and renamed the child Archemorus (Beginner of Death or Doom). Opheltes is thought to have been a form of the familiar infant god of Cretan mythology.

Ophir. An ancient country or region—perhaps in southeastern Arabia—noted for its gold, as well as for its silver, ivory, and precious stones. According to Old Testament narrative, it was the source of the treasure of King Solomon (I Kings 10:11).

O Pioneers! (1913). A novel by Willa CATHER. Her second novel and the first to be set in Nebraska, it tells of how Alexandra Bergson, on the death of her father, takes over the care of her family and the management of the farm. The other Bergsons are weak or dull, but Alexandra, energetic and courageous, succeeds in building up a prosperous farm. Her hopes for the future of her young brother Emil are blasted when he is killed by a jealous husband, but eventually her loneliness comes to an end with her marriage to Carl Linstrum. Alexandra's deep devotion to the land dominates the novel.

Opitz, Martin (1597–1639). Early German critic and baroque poet. He is especially famous for his *Buch von der Deutschen Poeterey* Book on German Poetry, 1624), in which he set forth the poetic principles which were to be quite closely followed by subsequent baroque poets writing in German. Opitz, who was strongly influenced by Ronsard and the Pléiade in France, believed that poetry must be based on the models of classical antiquity, and he endeavored to show how the German language could be suited to these models. His own work includes many translations from Greek and Latin, and many poems in classical forms such as the elegy and ode.

Oppenheim, E[dward] Phillips (1866–1946). English novelist, popular and prolific writer of thrillers. He produced an average of more than three novels a year for over 50 years. Among his works are *The Long Arm of Mannister* (1910), *The Moving Finger* (1911), and *The Great Impersonation* (1920).

Oppenheim, James (1882–1932). American poet and writer of fiction. Oppenheim was early a social worker in New York, and the life of the city's slums furnished him with the material for his first book of short stories, *Dr. Rast* (1909). After two potboiling novels, he published *Songs for the New Age* (1914), the volume that marked his arrival as a serious writer. In 1916 he founded and edited the magazine SEVEN ARTS, with which Van Wyck Brooks and Waldo Frank were also connected. The poems of *Songs for the New Age* (1914), *The Solitary* (1919), *The Mystic Warrior* (1921), and *The Golden Bird* (1923) were strung together with connecting lines in *The Sea* (1923). During World War I, Oppenheim became interested in psychiatry, an interest reflected in *The Book of Self* (1917), a poetic treatment of psychiatry, and in *Your Hidden Powers* (1923) and *Behind Your Front* (1928).

Ops. In Roman myth, a goddess of plenty, identified with the Greek RHEA.

Optic, Oliver. The pen name of William Taylor ADAMS, a prolific writer for boys, author of the *Army and Navy* series, *Starry Flag* series, and others.

optimism. The doctrine that "whatever is, is right," that everything which happens is for the best. It was originally set forth by Leibniz from the postulate of the omnipotence of God, and is cleverly travestied by Voltaire in his *Candide, ou l'Optimisme,* where Dr. Pangloss continually harps on the maxim that "all is for the best in this best of all possible worlds."

oracle (Lat. *oraculum,* from *orare,* to speak, to pray). The answer of a god or an inspired priest to an inquiry respecting the future; the deity giving the response; or the place where the deity could be consulted. In ancient Greece there were many oracles, some of which were consulted by men of other nations. Perhaps the best known was the Delphic oracle, but the oracle of Zeus at Dodona, one of the most ancient, was very highly respected. The oracle of Trophonius, in Boeotia, was perhaps the most awesome. Other famous oracles were as widely separated as that of Heracles at Gades, in Spain; that of Zeus (or Amen), in Libya; and that of Ares, in Thrace.

One reason for the reputation for infallibility enjoyed by many oracles was that their answers were given in such ambiguous terms that they were sure to be right, no matter what happened. A famous example of this, told by Herodotus, was the sad experience of Croesus, who, on consulting the oracle about whether he should make war on Persia, was told that if he did, he would overthrow a great empire. He optimistically assumed that the empire was Persia—but it was his own empire of Lydia. Greek drama and myth is full of stories of oracles that turn out to be right, often after many years, and usually to the great sorrow of the recipient who has failed to accept the admonition.

Oracle of the Holy Bottle. A translation of *l'Oracle de la Dive Bouteille,* situated "near Cathay in Upper India," to which Pantagruel, Panurge, and Friar John journey in Rabelais' GARGANTUA AND PANTAGRUEL in an effort to learn whether Panurge should marry. They approach the temple through vineyards, descend through subterranean passages, and eventually pass through the gates of the temple itself, over which is the inscription "In wine, truth." There the Pontiff Bacbuc (*Heb.,* "bottle") leads Panurge unto a side chapel where the Holy Bottle is sitting in the middle of a fountain. Bacbuc casts something into the fountain, whereupon the water begins to bubble, and the Bottle makes a cracking sound like "Trinch!" (*Ger.,* "Drink!"). Bacbuc declares this to be a perfect answer and gives Panurge what appears to be a book but is in fact a flask full of wine so that he may interpret the oracle. The potion inspires Friar John and Panurge to recite doggerel. Bacbuc then sends the joyful party home, reminding the travelers that many secrets of nature are yet to be revealed by time and study.

Oracles, History of. See Bernard le Bovier de FONTENELLE.

Orage, Alfred Richard (1873–1934). English journalist and psychologist. Orage had been a lecturer on theosophy when a large, anonymous donation allowed him to buy the *New Age* and make it a

Socialist weekly. He attracted many distinguished contributors to the *New Age* such as G. B. Shaw, H. G. Wells, Hilaire Belloc, G. K. Chesterton, Arnold Bennett, Katherine Mansfield, and Richard Aldington. He gave up his weekly after the founding of the rival *New Statesman*. Orage was a remarkably clear expositor of a broad economic philosophy.

orange girls. In English theaters during the Restoration, the girls who sold refreshments to the spectators were called "orange girls." Nell Gwyn (1650–1687) began her career as an orange girl.

Orator Hunt. See Henry HUNT.

Orators, The (1932). A work by W. H. AUDEN in prose and some verse. It presents the author's early political and psychological ideas through symbolic satirical scenes from English middle-class life. Among the sections are *Address for a Prize-Day, Letter to a Wound,* and *Journal of an Airman.* The *Journal* is an account of the campaign against the enemy— disease and inertia in middle-class society and the individual consciousness.

Orc. In the ORLANDO FURIOSO of Lodovico Ariosto, a great sea monster that devours human beings. When Angelica is exposed to him on a rock, Ruggiero, riding the back of his winged steed, the Hippogriff, rescues her by dazzling the beast with the fatal glow of a burnished shield.

orchestra. In ancient Greek theaters, the large, circular dancing floor occupied by the chorus. Surrounded on three sides by tiers of seats, and on the fourth by a raised platform for the principal actors, it had an altar of Dionysus at its center. It was used by the chorus in their dances and songs, and also for processions and pageantry.

Orcus. A Latin name for HADES, the abode of the dead.

Orczy, Baroness **[Emmuska]** (1865–1947). Hungarian-born English novelist and playwright. She is the author of THE SCARLET PIMPERNEL and other stories of romance and detection.

ordeal (AS, *ordel,* related to *adoelan,* "to deal, allot, judge"). An ancient Anglo-Saxon and Teutonic practice of rendering justice in disputed questions of criminality by subjecting the accused person to a physical test, such as by battle, fire, water, or the like. This method of "trial" was based on the belief that God would defend the right, even by miracle if needful. All ordeals, except the ordeal by battle, were abolished in England by law in the early 13th century.

In *ordeal by battle,* the accused person was obliged to fight anyone who charged him with guilt. This ordeal was allowed only to persons of rank.

Ordeal by fire was also for persons of rank only. The accused had to hold in his hand a piece of red-hot iron, or to walk blindfolded and barefoot among nine red-hot ploughshares laid at unequal distances. If he escaped uninjured, he was accounted innocent, *aliter non.* This might be performed by a deputy.

Ordeal by hot water was for the common people. The accused was required to plunge his arm up to the elbow in boiling water, and was pronounced guilty if the skin was injured in the experiment.

Ordeal by cold water was also for the common people. The accused, being bound, was tossed into a river; if he *sank* he was acquitted, but if he *floated* he was accounted guilty. This ordeal remained in use

for the trial of witches to comparatively recent times.

In the *ordeal by the bier,* a person suspected of murder was required to touch the corpse; if he was guilty, the "blood of the dead body would start forth afresh."

In *ordeal by the cross,* plaintiff and defendant had to stand with their arms crossed over their breasts, and he who could endure the longest won the suit.

The *ordeal by the Eucharist* was for priests. It was supposed that the elements would choke him, if taken by a guilty man.

Ordeal of Richard Feverel, The (1859). A novel by George MEREDITH, with the subtitle *A History of Father and Son.* The plot concerns the tragic working out of Sir Austin Feverel's self-evolved system of education; in applying the precepts of this system to the upbringing and education of his son Richard, Sir Austin expects to create a perfect specimen of manhood. Richard is tutored at home by an uncle, Adrian Feverel, and is carefully protected from any untoward contact with the opposite sex. In spite of the system, however, Richard falls in love with Lucy Desborough, a girl beneath his station, and is forced to marry her. Sir Austin refuses to see Lucy and attempts to punish Richard by maneuvering to keep them apart, with the result that Richard succumbs to the attractions of a clever woman of low repute, while Lucy, in his absence, is approached by an aristocratic libertine. Bessie Berry, Richard's old nurse, a person much loved for her good judgment and large heart, finally succeeds in extricating Lucy from her difficulties. In the meantime, the repentant Richard lingers abroad, until his uncle Austin Wentworth, a man of tolerance and understanding, effects a reconciliation between Lucy and Sir Austin. Richard then returns, but when he hears of the libertine's insult to Lucy's honor, he challenges him to a duel, is badly wounded, and on recovery learns that Lucy has died of brain fever. Richard is mentally broken, and the failure of his father's system is complete.

order. In classical architecture, a column with its entablature viewed as a unit fully characteristic of a given style. It is customary to distinguish three orders of Greek architecture (Doric, Ionic, and Corinthian) and two Roman orders (Tuscan and Composite). The Parthenon on the Athenian acropolis, often considered antiquity's most perfect building, conforms to the Doric order with its simple capitals and massive columns.

Order of the Garter. See GARTER, ORDER OF THE.

O'Regan, Teague. See MODERN CHIVALRY.

O'Reilly, John Boyle (1844–1890). Irish-born American journalist, poet, and novelist. An ardent Fenian, O'Reilly was sentenced to penal servitude because of his revolutionary activities while in the British army and was deported to Australia. His powerful novel, *Moondyne* (1879), about convict life there was based on his own experiences. As a result he helped gain the freedom of all Irish military prisoners in Australia. The editor for many years of the Boston *Pilot,* he also published such books of poems as *Songs from Southern Seas* (1873). He was one of the first Americans to publish the poetry of Oscar Wilde.

O'Reilly, Persse. In James Joyce's novel FINNEGANS WAKE, the author, hero, or singer of *The Ballad of Persse O'Reilly.* Delivered in H. C. Earwicker's tavern, it is a gay, complex song having to do with

Earwicker's misdeed in the park. The name is derived from the French *perce-oreille*, meaning earwig; O'Reilly is therefore another incarnation of Earwicker himself. The ballad has often been anthologized.

Oresteia (458 B.C.). A trilogy of plays by AESCHYLUS, the only extant trilogy of Greek dramas. It includes *Agamemnon, The Libation-Bearers,* and the *Eumenides.* See the House of ATREUS.

Orestes. In Greek mythology, the son of Agamemnon and Clytemnestra. Aided or abetted by his sister Electra, he killed his mother and her lover Aegisthus to avenge his father, whom they had murdered. He appears in more Greek dramas than any other personage, notably in Aeschylus' *Oresteia,* Sophocles' ELECTRA, and Euripides' ELECTRA, *Iphigeneia in Tauris, Orestes,* and *Andromache.* See the House of ATREUS.

Orestes (408 B.C.). A drama by EURIPIDES. The main theme is the revelation of the character of Orestes and his friends, who are shown to be bungling criminals. The play opens on Orestes asleep, tormented by the Erinyes for the murder of his mother. He and Electra beseech Menelaus to help them escape their city's death penalty, but he refuses on the urging of Tyndareus, the father of Clytemnestra and Helen. Orestes and Pylades set out for the Argive Assembly, where Orestes makes a fool of himself and ensures his condemnation. Electra, Orestes, and Pylades decide to kill Helen and hold Hermione as hostage against Menelaus. The most unusual messenger scene in Greek tragedy follows, in which a Phrygian slave from Helen's retinue jumps onto the stage and blurts out in jumbled language what has happened within. At the conclusion, Orestes and Pylades have set the palace afire and are preparing to murder Hermione; Electra is about to set fire to the whole city; Menelaus is shouting helplessly from below, calling the townspeople to his aid. Then, Apollo appears from above and dictates the solution: Orestes is to marry Hermione; Electra and Pylades will be married; Menelaus must find himself a new wife, since Helen has been taken up into the sky as a beacon for sailors. The

Orestes killing Aegisthus. From a Greek vase painting.

artificial *deus ex machina* is convincing by its very absurdity; it is a fitting conclusion to a bitter play.

Orfeo and Heurodis. The tale of ORPHEUS and Eurydice, with the Gothic machinery of elves or fairies. It exists in a number of ballad versions. Sometimes Eurydice is also called Lady Isabel.

Organon, the. See ARISTOTLE.

Orgoglio. See FAERIE QUEENE, THE.

Orgon. In Molière's comedy TARTUFFE, the wealthy ex-officer who was victimized by the hypocrite Tartuffe. His credulity and faith in the scheming humbug can scarcely be shaken even by the evidence of his senses. Eventually, by a ruse, his wife reveals to him Tartuffe's true nature.

Oriane. See GUERMANTES.

Oriani, Alfredo (1852–1909). Italian poet, novelist, dramatist, and writer on history, politics, and social problems. His fiction is noted for its highly ornate and ponderous style suggestive of that of Victor Hugo, Eugène Sue, and other French serial novelists in vogue during the second half of the 19th century.

Oriani had a taste for unusual plot situations which act as catalysts for the pathological states of mind common to his characters. Among his better-known novels are *Gelosia* (1894), which describes an unsuccessful *ménage à trois; La Disfatta* (1896), in which a child's death destroys all vestiges of love and hope in his parents; *Vortice* (1899), which describes in detail a planned suicide; and *Olocausto* (1902), whose protagonist is forced into prostitution at the age of 16 and dies as a result of the loss of her childhood innocence.

An Hegelian idealist who subscribed to the mystique of national mission, Oriani often enunciated extremist views on nationalism and imperialism which made him a precursor of fascism.

Among his political writings are *Fino a Dogali* (1889), inspired by the Italian campaign in Africa; *Il Nemico* (1892); *La Rivolta Ideale* (1908); and *La Lotta Politica in Italia* (1892), a three-volume study of Italian political institutions from the Middle Ages to the 19th century.

Oriflamme (*Fr.,* "flame of gold"). The ancient banner of the kings of France. First used as a national banner in 1119, it was a crimson flag cut into three triangular pennants to represent tongues of fire. It was carried on a gilt staff and a silken tassle hung between each flame. Originally the banner of St. Denis, the sacred Oriflamme became royal property in 1082. It was carried at Agincourt in 1415. It was said that the sight of it blinded any infidel. In the 15th century the Oriflamme was succeeded by the blue standard powdered with fleur-de-lis, and the last heard of the original Oriflamme is a mention on the inventory of the Abbey of St. Denis dated 1534.

Origen (c. 185–c. 253). One of the Greek Fathers of the Church. The head of the catechetical school in Alexandria, in Caesarea. He wrote prolifically and collated the HEXAPLA.

Origille or **Orrigille (Origilla).** In the Orlando poems of Matteo Maria Boiardo and Lodovico Ariosto, the beloved of the knight Grifone. She deserts him for the braggart Martano. In the Boiardo poem, ORLANDO INNAMORATO, she is revealed to be the daughter of Monodante and sister of the warrior Brandimarte.

Original Sin. The sin of all at birth. In orthodox Christian theology, the belief that all men are born with the taint of sin resulting from the primal disobedience of ADAM AND EVE in eating the fruit of the forbidden tree. This sin is held to be removed by the Sacrament of BAPTISM.

Origin of Species. Full title *On the Origin of Species by Means of Natural Selection, or the Preservation of Favoured Races in the Struggle for Life* (1859). A work by Charles DARWIN. In it he develops his theory of evolution by natural selection. Darwin argues that every species develops or evolves from a previous one and that all life is a continuing pattern. His objects of study were the variations from generation to generation in domestic plants and animals. In the "struggle for existence," common to all life, an animal or plant that inherits an unfavorable variation is not likely to survive and produce offspring. The severe conditions in the environment tend to kill off individuals with unfavorable variations in favor of "the SURVIVAL OF THE FITTEST," that is, individuals with favorable variations. Darwin concludes that there exists a "natural selection" of favorable variations, which produces new varieties. While subsequent investigation has superseded some of Darwin's arguments, *Origin of Species* remains one of the most influential books ever published.

Orillo. A monstrous magician in Lodovico Ariosto's ORLANDO FURIOSO. He is capable of reintegrating his body when it is cut to pieces. Astolfo, learning from a book given him by the enchantress Logistilla that Orillo's life depends on literally one hair of his head, decapitates him and, with the headless body in pursuit, plucks out each hair until he finds it; the head then dies and the body falls lifeless from its horse.

Orinda the Matchless or **The Matchless Orinda.** See Katherine PHILIPS.

Orion. In Greek mythology, a famous hunter. In the many unreconciled variants of his story, he appears as an amiable if rather lustful giant. In one tale, he is blinded by Oenopion, king of Chios, to prevent his marriage to Oenopion's daughter; travels eastward toward the home of the sun, with a boy on his shoulders to guide him; and finally has his sight restored by the sun's rays. Two other legends, his pursuit of the Pleiades, and his death from a scorpion's sting as a result of trying to ravage Artemis, are astronomical myths that try to explain the relative positions of the constellations Orion, the Pleiades, and the Scorpion.

O'Riordan, Conal Holmes O'Connell. Pen name, **Norreys Connell** (1874–1948). Irish novelist and playwright. He succeeded John Millington Synge as director of the ABBEY THEATRE in 1909. Among his novels are *The Fool and His Heart* (1896) and *Adam of Dublin* (1920).

Oriskany. A village in Oneida County, N. Y., site of one of the bloodiest battles of the American Revolution (Aug. 6, 1777). About 800 American militiamen, under General Herkimer, on their way to the relief of Fort Stanwix, were ambushed by a detachment of Indians and British. Although the ensuing battle was a victory for the Americans, their forces were too weakened to proceed to Fort Stanwix.

Orithyia (Oreithyia). In classic mythology, a nymph. The north wind BOREAS loved her, and she bore him two sons, Zetes and Calais, who became famous as winged warriors in the company of the ARGONAUTS.

Orlando. (1) The courageous hero of Shakespeare's As You LIKE IT, who challenges Duke Frederick's wrestler to prove his mettle. In love with Rosalind, who leads him a merry chase through the Forest of Arden, he typifies the fashionable Elizabethan "lovesick swain," penning verses to Rosalind and hanging them on trees.

(2) The Italian name of Charlemagne's paladin ROLAND.

Orlando (1928). A fantastic novel by Virginia WOOLF. Orlando begins as a young Elizabethan nobleman and ends, 300 years later, as a contemporary young woman based on the author's friend, Victoria Sackville-West. The novel contains a great deal of literary history and brilliant, ironic insights into the social history of the ages through which Orlando lives. Orlando starts life as a male poet and ends as an equally intense and able woman poet in order to emphasize the author's belief that women are intellectually men's equals. The novel is thus a companion-piece to the feminist essay *A Room of One's Own*.

Orlando, Vittorio Emanuele (1860–1952). Italian statesman. Named prime minister in 1917, he was one of the Big Four at the Versailles Peace Conference in 1919. After clashing with Wilson over territorial concessions to Italy, he left the conference; although he later returned, the failure of the Versailles treaty to incorporate Italian demands resulted in his resignation. He withdrew from public life during the fascist regime.

Orlando Furioso (Roland Mad). A romantic epic by Lodovico ARIOSTO. It was written in 1516 with 40 cantos, and in a longer version of 46 cantos in 1532. Its plot continues where BOIARDO broke off his ORLANDO INNAMORATO; like the earlier poem, the subplots involving Charlemagne's paladins and various pagan knights are interwoven (*intrecciatura*). The magic and enchantments of the earlier poem are continued and expanded, but with an ironic tone that contrasts strongly with the seriousness of Boiardo yet avoids the burlesque of PULCI and other popular treatments of the material.

The poem begins with the escape of Angelica from the custody of Duke Namo of Baviera, to whom Charlemagne had entrusted her in hopes of avoiding conflict between Orlando (see ROLAND) and his cousin RINALDO, both desperately enamored of her. She flees to the island of Ebuda, where she is captured and exposed to a sea monster from which she is rescued by RUGGIERO. Orlando, who has dreamt of her plight, arrives at Ebuda to save OLIMPIA instead. Continuing his search for Angelica, he is detained in the enchanted castle of Atlante until his beloved rescues him. Angelica then disappears again and arrives at Paris, where a great battle has taken place; she meets the wounded Moorish youth Medoro, cares for him, and elopes with him to Cathay. Orlando goes mad with grief at this betrayal. ASTOLFO takes his winged horse to Ethiopia, then mounts the chariot of Elijah and, with Saint John as his guide, travels to the moon. There he recovers the lost wits of Orlando, who recovers upon sniffing the urn in which they lie. As the poem nears its end, the siege of Paris is broken and AGRAMANTE killed. Ruggiero, converted to Christianity, wins his BRADAMANTE after defeating the last pagan warrior RODOMONTE in a furious battle.

Thus, despite its title, the poem is really centered on Ruggiero, the progenitor with Bradamante of the Este family. Like Boiardo, the poet flatters his patrons of the Ferrara court in this imaginary genealogy. Similar emphasis is given to descriptions of such delightful creatures as Astolfo's hippogriff and such memorable places as the grotto of the witch Melissa and the island of oblivion ruled by the enchantress Alcina. Unlike his predecessors, Ariosto makes use of the opening octaves of each canto to set forth his personal views and critical comments.

The *Furioso* was the most influential of the early Orlando poems. In England its popularity during the Renaissance is attested by Robert Greene's play *The History of Orlando Furioso* (1594), Spenser's *Faerie Queene* (1590; 1596), and the translation done by Sir John Harington in 1591, presumably as a penance imposed by his godmother, Queen Elizabeth. Numerous artists have used the characters and incidents of Ariosto's poem for paintings and musical works, witness the *Alcina* of Handel.

Orlando Innamorato (Roland In Love). A romantic epic by Matteo Maria BOIARDO, who first blended the chivalric material of the Carolingian stories with the amorous motifs of the Arthurian cycle. Written in octaves, its first two books (of 29 and 31 cantos respectively) appeared in 1487; the third book was unfinished, breaking off at the ninth canto. The entire poem was rewritten by Berni in pure Tuscan, and ARIOSTO continued its plot in his ORLANDO FURIOSO.

At Paris, where thousands of knights have gathered for a tournament, the pagan princess Angelica suddenly appears. She has come from Cathay to sow discord in the ranks of the paladins and thus render them helpless before the Saracens, led by Agramante, emperor of Africa, and Gradasso, king of Sericana. One by one, Charlemagne's knights desert the court in pursuit of Angelica or each other. In the many subplots that follow, all interwoven (*intrecciatura*), the paladins Orlando (see ROLAND), RINALDO his cousin, Astolfo, and Brandimarte undergo various enchantments, combats with giants and pagan warriors, and timely rescues. The pagan warrior RUGGIERO, descended from the Trojans, is introduced as the forerunner of the Este family, who were Boiardo's patrons. When the poem breaks off, Ruggiero has not been reunited as yet with the warrior maiden Bradamante, sister of Rinaldo and the object of his love. The pagan forces still threaten Charlemagne at Paris.

Orléans, Anne Marie Louise d'. See Duchesse de MONTPENSIER.

Orleans, the Maid of. See JOAN OF ARC.

Ormondo. In Torquato Tasso's GERUSALEMME LIBERATA, a Saracen warrior who plans to kill Goffredo, the Christian general, by disguising himself and his men as crusaders. When he approaches the general in his disguise, Goffredo who has learned of the plot kills him immediately.

Ormulum (c. 1200). Middle English religious poem by an Augustinian monk named Orm (Orrm, Ormin). The extant manuscript of 20,000 unrhymed lines, alternately of eight and seven syllables, is a fragment comprising only one eighth of the projected work. The poem paraphrases Latin texts from the

THE BODLEIAN LIBRARY, OXFORD

A page from the *Ormulum* manuscript (13th century).

New Testament used in the Mass, following each with a homily explaining its meaning. Tediously repetitive, the work has little literary value, but its verse form and language are historically important as one of the first examples of English poetry after the Norman conquest, as is Orm's use of a phonetic spelling as a guide to pronunciation.

Ormuzd. The principal deity of the ancient Zoroastrians and modern Parsees. He is the angel of light and good, and creator of all things, according to the Magian system. He is called *Ahura Mazda,* the good god, and is said to be in perpetual conflict with AHRIMAN, over whom he will ultimately triumph. The Latin form is *Oromasdes.* See ZOROASTER.

Oromasdes. See ORMUZD.

Orosius, Paulus (5th century). Spanish historian and theologian. He became a disciple of St. Augustine of Hippo, who encouraged him to write the Latin *Adversus Paganos Historiarum,* a general history of the world refuting the pagan assertion that Christianity was responsible for the decline of the Roman Empire. Now ignored, it was once very popular; King ALFRED translated it, making a number of additions, particularly about Germanic history.

Orozco, José Clemente (1883–1949). Mexican painter. He is known for his murals, deeply nationalistic in character, which depict the social and political conflicts of his country.

Orphan Angel, The (1926). A novel by Elinor WYLIE. It tells the hypothetical story of what might have happened to Shelley in America if he had been rescued from drowning by an American ship. A highly imaginative story, it emphasizes Mrs. Wylie's preoccupation with the romantic poet.

Orpheus. In Greek mythology, a fabulous musician. A son of the muse Calliope and Apollo or Oeagrus, he was born in Thrace and was a devotee of Dionysus. He married Eurydice, a dryad, but she was killed by a snake while fleeing the advances of ARISTAEUS. Orpheus descended into HADES to find her. His playing of the lyre so delighted even Hades himself that Orpheus was permitted to take Eurydice back with him, provided that he did not look at her until they arrived in the upper world. When they were nearly there, however, he no longer heard her behind him, and looked back. Eurydice returned to Hades.

Inconsolable, Orpheus would have nothing to do with other women. The Thracian women, outraged by this behavior, tore him to pieces in a bacchanalian revel—and Orpheus thus suffered the same fate as his god Dionysus. The fragments of his body were collected by the Muses and buried at the feet of Mt. Olympus, but his head, which had been thrown into the river Hebrus, was carried into the sea and came ashore on the island of Lesbos. There it became a famous oracle.

The story of Orpheus and Eurydice has been a favorite subject for dramatists and composers. The first extant opera, by Jacopo Peri, was based on it, as were many others, including those by Monteverdi and Haydn; the most famous is Gluck's *Orpheus and Eurydice (Orfeo;* 1762). Of the many dramatic versions of the story one of the most unusual is *Orfée,* a motion picture by Jean Cocteau.

Orpheus C. Kerr Papers (1862–1871). A series of humorous letters by Robert Henry Newell (1836–1901), American journalist. Printed in daily newspapers during the Civil War, the letters were finally published in five volumes. Newell invented his pen name as a pun on the swarm of wartime office seekers in Washington. Using the devices of misspelling, overstatement, and anticlimax, he related war incidents and imaginary situations, and included sentimental verse. One genuinely funny letter gives the results of an imaginary contest for the writing of a new national anthem; entries supposedly submitted by Emerson, Holmes, Aldrich, Whittier, Longfellow, and others display Newell's wit and skill as a parodist.

Orphic Sayings (1840–1844). A series of philosophic epigrams by Bronson ALCOTT. They dealt with temptation, conscience, enthusiasm, hope, speech, and nature; with each issue of *The Dial* in which they appeared, the sayings became increasingly mystical and less intelligible.

orphism (6th century B.C.). A Greek mystic cult popular at that time. Its mysteries were supposedly taught to men by ORPHEUS. They centered about the myth of Zagreus, son of Zeus and Persephone, who was torn to pieces by the TITANS at Hera's orders. For this crime, Zeus destroyed the Titans and swallowed the heart of Zagreus, who was reborn of SEMELE in the person of Dionysus. The orphic rites apparently included the tearing and eating of animals representing Zagreus, whose myth was probably Thracian or Phrygian in origin. The notion, peculiar to the orphics, that human beings contained elements of both divinity and evil was explained by the fact that men were created from the ashes of the Titans, who, evil themselves, had nevertheless swallowed the divine Zagreus. Although orphism differed from both orthodox myth and popular cult, it influenced PLATO, PINDAR, and the PYTHAGOREANS.

Orsini, Felice (1819–1858). Italian revolutionist. He is remembered chiefly for his attempted assassination (Jan. 14, 1858) of Napoleon III. He was executed at Paris.

Orsino. The sentimental duke of Illyria in Shakespeare's TWELFTH NIGHT. He is in love with Olivia, but finally marries Viola. His famous words open the play:

> If music be the food of love, play on . . .

Orson. In the French romance VALENTINE AND ORSON, the brother who grows up "the wild man of the forest" until overcome by his twin. He eventually rescues Fezon from the Green Knight and marries her.

Ors y Rovira, Eugenio D'. Known as **Xenius** (1882–1955). Spanish author and art critic. A student of philosophy and law, he wrote *La bien Plantada* (1920), a novel, and *Guillermo Tell* (1926), a play—both successful. However, it is in the field of art criticism that his true merit lies, particularly in such works as *Poussin y El Greco* (1922), *Tres horas en el Museo del Prado* (1923), *Cézanne* (1924), *La vie de Goya* (1929), and *Pablo Picasso* (1930).

Ortega y Gasset, José (1883–1955). Spanish philosopher. One of the leading philosophers of the 20th century, he received his early education at the hands of the Jesuits, went on to the University of Madrid, and after receiving his doctorate, traveled to Germany in order to continue his studies. It was at this time that he came under the influence of the philosophy of Kant, apparent in much of his work. His studies completed, he returned to Spain, accepting the chair in metaphysics at the University of Madrid. It was from this position that he exerted his influence upon Spanish philosophy and 20th-century ideas. In 1936 he was exiled by the Civil War, but returned to Spain in 1945. His first book was the absorbing *Meditaciones del Quijote* (1914). This was followed by his essays which appeared in eight volumes spread out over the period 1916–1934 and titled *El Espectador. España invertebrada* (1921) is a critical review of decadence in Spanish literature and an attempt to locate the roots of Spain's decadence. Best known abroad are *El tema de nuestro tiempo (The Modern Theme,* 1923), *La deshumanización del arte e ideas sobre la novela (The dehumanization of art and notes on the novel,* 1925), and *La rebelión de las masas (The Revolt of the Masses,* 1930). This last work is a subtle analysis of the decaying effects of mob control upon government and the arts.

Ortnit or **Otnit.** Earlier **Hartnit.** German legendary hero, as in the HELDENBUCH. He wins his bride by fighting giants, but is later slain by a dragon. His brother Wolfdietrich (earlier Hardheri) then kills the dragon and marries Ortnit's widow.

Orville, Lord. See EVELINA, OR THE HISTORY OF A YOUNG LADY'S ENTRANCE INTO THE WORLD.

Orwell, George. Pen name of **Eric Blair** (1903–1950). English novelist, essayist, and critic. He was an independent-minded socialist, and his first works were largely studies of working-class life and culture. Educated at Eton, Orwell was typical of the gentleman-radical. His years with the Imperial Police in Burma provided material for the novel *Burmese Days* (1934), an attack on British imperialism, and for essays such as the title essay in the collection *Shoot-*

ing an Elephant (1950). His years as a vagabond doing odd jobs for a living are described in *Down and Out in Paris and London* (1933). *The Road to Wigan Pier* (1937) is a discussion of social problems; *Keep the Aspidistra Flying* (1936) and *Coming Up for Air* (1939) are comic novels about ordinary working people. Orwell is notable for the simplicity of his style and his journalistic or documentary approach to fiction. This method was followed by a number of leftist writers of the 1930's.

Homage to Catalonia (1938) expresses Orwell's disillusionment during the Spanish Civil War, in which he fought on the Republican side. It describes the internal dissension between the Republican and Communist allies, and Communist deceit and intellectual dishonesty. Orwell's last, best-known novels are ANIMAL FARM and *1984* (q.v.), biting satires on communism.

Osaka. A city in western Japan, formerly known as Naniwa. It was Japan's cultural center during the Tokugawa period (1600–1868). Known also as a commercial center, it was eclipsed by Tokyo during the Meiji period (1868–1912).

Osborn, Henry Fairfield (1857–1935). American paleontologist and archaeologist. He was curator of vertebrate paleontology of the American Museum of Natural History from 1891. His works include *The Age of Mammals* (1910); *Men of the Old Stone Age* (1915); *Origin and Evolution of Life* (1917); *Evolution and Religion in Education* (1926).

Osborne, John (1929–   ). English playwright. His first play, LOOK BACK IN ANGER, lent its name to the group of modern English writers now known as the "angry young men." Osborne and his contemporaries have attacked the static English social system, with particular denunciation of the Establishment. They have felt a vacuum in English culture and by Osborne's admission have looked to the U.S. to fill this void.

His plays include *The Entertainer* (1957), written for Laurence Olivier, the story of a cheap, sordid music hall entertainer; *Epitaph for George Dillon* (with Anthony Creighton; 1958) about a truculent, perhaps intelligent young man who becomes involved with a family of stupid people, later marrying the daughter; and *Luther* (1961), an historical drama about the German monk's split with the Catholic Church.

Osborne, Thomas (d. 1767). English bookseller and printer who, together with Samuel Rivington, published Richardson's novel *Pamela*. Alexander Pope satirized him in the *Dunciad* and Samuel Johnson beat him for his impertinence.

Osborne, Thomas Mott (1859–1926). American prison reformer. He was warden of Sing Sing Prison from 1914 to 1916 and founded the Mutual Welfare League under which prisoners of Sing Sing exercised self-government. He was the author of *Within Prison Walls* (1914).

Osbourne, Lloyd (1868–1947). English writer. The stepson of Robert Louis STEVENSON, he collaborated with Stevenson on *The Wrong Box* (1889) and other books.

O'Shea, Kitty. See Charles Stewart PARNELL.

Osiris. The supreme god and king of eternity of ancient Egypt, whose name means many-eyed. He was thought to be judge of the dead, ruler of the kingdom of the Other World, creator, god of the Nile, and constant foe of his twin brother and son Set, the principle of evil. He was slain by Set who cut his body into 15 pieces, but was buried by his wife Isis and revenged by Horus and Thoth. Because he was resurrected to an eternal reign in heaven, he symbolized hope for life beyond the grave and fostered the process of mummification. He was usually depicted as a mummy wearing the crown of upper Egypt, but sometimes also as an ox. He was the father of Anubis.

Osmond, Gilbert. See PORTRAIT OF A LADY, THE.

Osric. In Shakespeare's HAMLET, a court fop, contemptible for his affectations. He serves as umpire in the duel between Hamlet and Laertes.

Ossa. See PELION.

Ossian. The legendary Gaelic warrior, son of FIONN MACCUMHAIL, who became a bard in his old age and is supposed to have lived about the end of the third century. It is to him that James MACPHERSON ascribed the authorship of a group of poems published from 1760 to 1763; Macpherson claimed that he had translated them from manuscripts collected in the Scottish Highlands, and a great controversy as to their authenticity was aroused. The Ossianic poems, compared at the time to the works of Homer, could move the poet Thomas Gray to write, "Imagination dwelt many hundred years ago in all her pomp on the cold and barren mountains of Scotland." It was soon generally agreed, however, that Macpherson, although compiling from ancient sources, was the principal author of the poems as published. See FINGAL, AN ANCIENT EPIC; TEMORA, AN EPIC POEM.

Ostend Manifesto. A declaration made in 1854 by the ministers of the U.S. in England, France, and Spain, "that Cuba must belong to the United States." It occasioned great discussion.

Ostia (from Lat. *ostium*, river mouth). The ancient Roman port at the mouth of the Tiber through which most goods shipped to and from Rome had to pass. Archaeologists have unearthed the remains of Roman *insulae*—three- and four-story buildings—which are the precursors of our modern apartment houses. The site now lies inland because of the heavy deposits of material left by the Tiber.

ostracism (from Gr. *ostrakon*, an earthen vessel). Exclusion from society or common privileges. The word arose from the ancient Greek custom of banishing one whose power was a danger to the state, the voting for which was done by the people recording their votes on tiles or potsherds. See ARISTIDES.

Ostrovski, Aleksandr Nikolayevich (1823–1886). Russian dramatist. Ostrovski's plays laid the foundation for realistic Russian drama. He produced almost 50 in all, both comedies and tragedies, many of them set among the conservative merchant class of Moscow. His first published play was *The Bankrupt* (*Bankrot;* 1847, produced in 1850 as *Svoi lyudi—sochtiomsya*). His best-known works include *Poverty Is No Crime* (*Bednost' ne porok;* 1854), THE DIARY OF A SCOUNDREL, *Easy Money* (*Beshenie dengi;* 1870), *The Forest* (*Les;* 1871), and his masterpiece, THE STORM. He also wrote a fairy tale in verse, *Snegurochka* (*The Snow Maiden;* 1873) which formed the basis for the opera by Rimski-Korsakov (1880).

Ostrovski, Nikolai Alekseyevich (1904–1936). Russian novelist. He wrote the popular novel *How* *the Steel Was Tempered* (*Kak zakalyalas' stal'*; 1932–1934), a success story of a young cripple, Pavel Korchagin, who overcomes his handicaps to become a writer and teacher. The story was based on Ostrovski's own life. Its Marxist moralizing has made it one of early Soviet literature's most praised productions.

O'Sullivan, Maurice (1904–1950). Irish author of *Twenty Years A-growing* (1933), an autobiography in Gaelic of an Irish peasant from the Blasket Islands.

Oswald. In Shakespeare's KING LEAR, the villainous servant of Goneril. He tries to kill Gloucester, but is prevented by Edgar who kills him.

Otage, L'. See HOSTAGE, THE.

Othello, The Moor of Venice (c. 1604). A tragedy by William SHAKESPEARE. Othello, a Moorish general in the service of Venice, appoints CASSIO as his chief lieutenant, unwittingly arousing the enmity of IAGO, his ensign, who thinks that he has better claim to the post. Partly to avenge himself for the slight and partly out of sheer malice, Iago devises a scheme to undo both Cassio and unsuspecting Othello, who regards Iago as a loyal, trustworthy friend. After causing the dismissal of Cassio by a trick, Iago hints to Othello that his bride Desdemona, the daughter of BRABANTIO, has had illicit relations with Cassio. Although Othello is reluctant to believe Iago's accusations, his worst fears are confirmed when, as a result of Iago's machinations, a handkerchief which he gave to Desdemona is found in Cassio's possession. Enraged, Othello strangles Desdemona. EMILIA, Iago's wife and Desdemona's faithful servant, discovers her husband's plot and denounces him. Othello now realizes his horrible mistake and, after asking that he be remembered as one who "lov'd not wisely but too well," commits suicide. Iago is condemned to torture for his crimes.

The source of the play is Cinthio's *Hecatommithi* (1565). Two operas called *Otello,* one by Rossini (1816) and another by Verdi (1887), have been based on Shakespeare's play.

Other Voices, Other Rooms (1948). A novel by Truman CAPOTE. The hero, 13-year-old Joel Knox, comes to his father's dilapidated mansion at Skully's Landing. There he comes in contact with the effeminate Randolph, with the Negro Jesus Fever and his daughter, and with his own invalid father. Beyond is the mysterious Cloud Hotel where Joel achieves self-awareness and a sense of the emptiness of Skully's Landing. Sometimes described as a story of initiation, the book has also been interpreted as symbolizing a search for the Holy Grail and a search for the father.

otium cum dignitate (*Lat.,* "leisure with dignity"). Retirement after a person has given up business and has saved enough to live on in comfort. The words were taken as a motto by Cicero.

Otranto, battle of (1480). During this engagement the Turks, led by Muhammad II, captured and massacred the inhabitants of the southern Italian city on the Adriatic, an audacious act that shocked the continent. But in the following year, allied Italian and European powers recaptured the city.

ottava rima. In prosody, a stanza of eight lines rhyming a-b-a-b-a-b-c-c. The form arose in Italy in the 14th century and was used by Boccaccio, Tasso, Ariosto, and many other Italian poets. In English it is usually written in iambic pentameters; it has been used, for example, by Keats in *Isabella*. In *Don Juan,*

Byron strikes the mock-heroic, almost burlesque note which has come to be associated with the form.

Ottone (Otho). In Torquato Tasso's GERUSALEMME LIBERATA, a brave knight among the crusaders. When the infidel warrior Argante challenges the Christians to single combat, Ottone is the first to accept; but he is killed ruthlessly, in utter disregard of the laws of chivalry, by the ferocious Argante.

Otus (Otos) and Ephialtes. In Greek mythology, giant twin sons of Aloeus (or Poseidon) and Iphimedia. Enormous at nine years old, they tried to pile Mount PELION on Mount Ossa in order to war with the gods on Olympus, but Zeus killed them. Before their death they had managed to imprison Ares in a bronze bowl, where he stayed for more than a year.

Otway, Thomas (1652–1685). English dramatist. He is best known for his heroic tragedy VENICE PRESERVED, one of the finest tragedies of the Restoration. With the exception of *The Orphan, or The Unhappy Marriage* (1680), a domestic tragedy, about twin brothers in love with the same woman, the rest of his plays are of little merit. See SCAPIN.

Ouïda. See Louise de la RAMÉE.

Our American Cousin (1858). A comedy by Tom TAYLOR. A work of no particular merit, this play will always be remembered as the one Abraham Lincoln was watching when he was assassinated by John Wilkes Booth (April 14, 1865).

Our Mutual Friend (1864). A novel by Charles DICKENS. The "mutual friend" is John Harmon, friend of Mr. BOFFIN and the Wilfers (see Reginald WILFER), who has been left a fortune on condition that he marry Bella Wilfer. Since he has never met Bella, has not been home for 14 years, and is reported to have been murdered, he returns under the assumed name of John Rokesmith and acts as secretary to Mr. Boffin, who is to have the Harmon money if the will's conditions are not fulfilled. John and Bella fall in love, marry, and live for a time on John's earnings. Finally, Boffin turns over the fortune and Rokesmith again becomes John Harmon.

Some recent critics consider this novel as one of Dickens' finest from the point of view of conscious artistry, although it lacks the spontaneity of his earlier works. Dust as a symbol of money saturates the atmosphere of the book. Dust, deceit, and death fill the novel, reflecting Dickens' increasing pessimism about the responsibility of upper middle-class society and life in general. Other characters in the book include Lizzie HEXAM; Mr. and Mrs. VENEERING; Silas WEGG; Eugene WRAYBURN; and Jenny WREN.

Our Old Home (1863). A book of sketches by Nathaniel HAWTHORNE. Written during his consulship in Liverpool (1853–1857), it is a delightful record of his literary pilgrimages to the homes of English writers. He amusingly describes his consular duties, including his uneasy presence at British civic banquets.

Oursler, [Charles] Fulton (1893–1952). American writer. He is best known for his popular religious books, *The Greatest Story Ever Told* (1947), as a series of radio broadcasts; 1949, in book form) and *The Greatest Book Ever Written* (1951). He also wrote motion-picture scenarios and plays, including *The Spider* (1927), with Lowell Brentano, which had a long run on Broadway. He was associated with

many magazines and became a senior editor of
Reader's Digest in 1944.

Our Town (1938). A play by Thornton WILDER.
The action takes place in a typical New England
town, Grover's Corners, New Hampshire. The Stage
Manager, a garrulous Yankee, sits at the side of the
bare stage talking intimately to the audience as the
play unfolds. He describes the characters and the setting. Act I is entitled "Daily Life"; the citizens engage in their customary pursuits, while Professor Willard and Editor Webb comment on them objectively.
In Act II, "Love and Marriage," Emily, daughter of
Editor Webb, and George, son of Dr. Gibbs, fall in
love and marry. In Act III, "Death," Emily dies in
childbirth, and is buried in the town cemetery. The
ancient dead in the cemetery speak of their peace, and
their perception of eternal harmony in the universe.
The play was awarded a Pulitzer Prize.

outcaste. See CASTE.

Outcast of the Islands, An (1896). A novel by
Joseph CONRAD. It concerns the earlier lives of some
of the characters in ALMAYER'S FOLLY. The outcast is
Willems, who falls in love with the native girl Aissa;
she is given him in return for his help in throttling
Almayer's trade. Finally Aissa shoots Willems. See
Captain LINGARD.

Outcasts of Poker Flat, The (1869). A short
story by Bret HARTE. A group of ne'er-do-wells—the
gambler John Oakhurst, two prostitutes, and a drunkard—are expelled from Poker Flat, a mining camp.
They are joined by an eloping young couple when a
blizzard traps them all. The outcasts sacrifice themselves, one after another, for the young woman, who
dies with them. Her lover returns too late with help.

Outis (*Gr.,* "nobody"). The alias of the wily
Odysseus in the cave of POLYPHEMUS. When the monster roars with pain after being blinded by Odysseus
and his crew, his brother giants ask from a distance
who is hurting him. "Outis," thunders out Polyphemus, and his companions go their way.

Outlook, The (1893–1935). An American
weekly. It superseded *The Christian Union* (1870–
1893) which had been edited first by Henry Ward
Beecher and then by Lyman ABBOTT. Theodore Roosevelt wrote reform articles for *The Outlook* when he
joined the staff in 1909. Hamilton Wright Mabie was
another noted staff member. In 1928 the magazine
absorbed *The Independent*. It became a monthly in
1932 as *The New Outlook*.

Out of Africa. See Isak DINESEN.

Out of the Cradle Endlessly Rocking (1859).
A poem by Walt WHITMAN. The poet, a child, walks
on the beach at moonlight and hears the mourning
song of a bird; no longer an innocent, he asks the
sea for the secret, and the waves whisper the "low
and delicious word death,/ And again death, death,
death, death."

Outre-Mer (1835). A series of travel sketches by
Henry Wadsworth LONGFELLOW.

Outsider, The (1956). A best-selling book of
philosophic and literary essays by Colin WILSON.
After describing various real individuals and fictional
persons who were social misfits, Wilson claims that
these "outsiders" are actually ideal heroes. Van Gogh,
Nijinsky, Lawrence of Arabia—all were existentialists
who sought God and some transcendent meaning in
human existence.

Outward Bound. See Sutton VANE.

Overbury, Sir Thomas (1581–1613). English
poet and prose writer, one of the early 17th-century
CHARACTER WRITERS. When his clever series of prose
sketches, *Characters,* was published in 1614, his didactic poem *A Wife* was included in the same volume.
Overbury was imprisoned in the Tower of London
and killed by slow poison at the instigation of Lady
Essex, whose marriage to his patron Robert Carr
(later the earl of Somerset) he had opposed.

Overcoat, The (**Shinel'**; 1842). A short story
by Nikolai GOGOL. Regarded as one of the major influences toward the development of realism in Russian literature, the story concerns a poor clerk in the
St. Petersburg civil service, Akaki Akakyevich Bash-
machkin. He is a miserable old man who is tormented by his callous fellow workers and who has
only one thing to console him: his love of copying
documents in his hovel at night. Copying is all he
feels capable of doing, and when other, slightly more
demanding work is offered him in the office, he
refuses it. Akaki's life begins to change a little, when
he goes to the tailor to have his threadbare coat repaired for the coming winter. The coat is too ragged
to be patched any more, and Akaki is persuaded to
let the tailor make him a new coat. He saves his
money carefully, buys the material and the imitation
fur for the collar, and has the coat made. The new
garment draws attention at the office, and Akaki is
even invited to a party. On the way home from the
party, delirious with wine and the happiness of his
new status, he is robbed of his precious coat. His
frantic appeals to the authorities are futile, and the
heartbroken Akaki dies. Following his death, mysterious thefts of coats, right off the backs of honest
citizens, begin in St. Petersburg. Even the official who
had irascibly refused Akaki his aid is robbed of his
coat. The story ends with a hesitant policeman approaching a man he believes to be the thief and being
threateningly turned on by the man. The policeman
timidly retreats, and the mysterious figure disappears
in the night.

Gogol's story was hailed as one of the first pieces
of literature to deal in a sympathetic way with the
poor and downtrodden ordinary people of 19th-cen-
tury Russia. Dostoevski has been quoted as saying
about himself and his fellow writers: "We all came
from beneath Gogol's Overcoat."

Overdone, Mistress. A bawd in Shakespeare's
MEASURE FOR MEASURE. Like the foolish Master Froth
and the lusty tapster Pompey, she embodies the rampant licentiousness that Angelo attempts to suppress
in Vienna.

Øverland, Arnulf (1889–   ). Norwegian poet.
Øverland's first verse collections—*Den ensomme fest*
(*The Lonely Feast,* 1911); and *De hundrede violiner*
(*The Hundred Violins,* 1912)—contained highly personal poems that were bitter and melancholy in tone.
This sober introspection was to be replaced, however,
by intense social concerns. Moved by suffering and injustice, he celebrated the brotherhood of socialism in
such collections as *Berget det blå* (*Blue Mountain,*
1927), *Hustavler* (*Laws of Living,* 1929), and *Jeg
besverger dig* (*I Conjure Thee,* 1934). Øverland
voiced anger and cried a warning against Nazism in
Den røde front (*The Red Front,* 1937). During the
German invasion of Norway, his poems were circu-

lated anonymously; in simple, strong language they asked the Norwegian people to endure with courage. These poems, later published as *Vi overlever alt* (*We Shall Live Through All*, 1945), cost the poet time in a German concentration camp. Since the war he has published *Tilbake til livet* (1946) and *Fiskeren og hans sjel* (1950).

Overland Monthly, The. An American magazine published in California from 1868 to 1875 and from 1883 to 1933. During its first two and a half years, it was edited by Bret HARTE, and pictured a huge California grizzly on its cover. Harte printed *The Luck of Roaring Camp, Plain Language from Truthful James,* and other stories in the magazine. The *Overland* also published other early California writers, among them Ina Coolbrith, Charles Warren Stoddard, and Edward Rowland Sill. Among the contributors to its later revival were George Sterling, Gertrude Atherton, Edwin Markham, and Jack London.

Overreach, Sir Giles. See NEW WAY TO PAY OLD DEBTS, A.

Over-Soul, The (1841). An essay by Ralph Waldo EMERSON. The writer expresses his concept of a primal Mind, a cosmic unity. This "soul of the whole," of which all men partake, is the keystone of Emerson's philosophic thought. The essay is included in his *First Series.*

Ovid. Full Latin name **Publius Ovidius Naso** (43 B.C.–?A.D. 17). Roman poet, the first major writer to grow up under the empire. Although his parents had destined him for a career in law and had sent him to Athens to complete his studies, he decided to become a poet. He returned to Rome and, in a short while, gained the reputation of being the most brilliant poet of his generation. His first series of poems were light, sophisticated love elegies, *Amores.* He followed this success with the *Heroides,* where he first displayed his unique gift for psychological insight by composing dramatic monologues in the form of love letters written between mythological lovers, such as Paris and Helen, Hero and Leander. His *Ars Amatoria* (*The Art of Love*) was an instant success and established him, at the age of 40, as the undisputed arbiter of elegance for an upper-class Roman society that could no longer take itself seriously and that was generally disillusioned by the failure of the old Roman ideals to maintain the republic.

Ovid's greatest work, the METAMORPHOSES, reflects in its very theme the disillusionment of his generation. In 15 books of legends, he wrote the history of the world from chaos to the apotheosis of Julius Caesar. This great historical epic is written, not in terms of the destiny of Rome, which was Vergil's concern, nor in terms of the gradual decline of Roman virtue, which Livy described in his history, but in terms of the instability of the forms of nature. A woman is transformed into a bird, stones become people, a girl becomes a laurel tree. The poems of metamorphosis are linked with transitions that are so smooth that the reader comes to accept each tale of sudden change, not as bizarre and fanciful, but as a comment on the unpredictable nature of things.

Ovid was himself doomed to suffer a severe "metamorphosis"—from the witty cosmopolitan, whom Rome had hailed as the fit successor to Vergil, to a tired, lonely old man living out the last ten years of his life among fur-skinned barbarians. For some unknown indiscretion he was, in A.D. 8, exiled by Augustus to Tomi, a bleak fishing village on the northwest coast of the Black Sea. From there he sent poetic supplications to the Emperor and to his own influential friends that this sentence of banishment might be rescinded. These poems, sometimes sublime, often merely pathetic, were published as two collections of poetry, the *Tristia* ("songs of sadness"), and the *Epistulae ex Ponto* ("Letters from the Black Sea"). Despite his petitions, Ovid never returned to the city he loved. The greatest Roman poet of his age, he died in 17 on the bleak rim of the empire.

In the Middle Ages the poetry of Ovid was one of the major sources of Western man's knowledge of his own antiquity. Again, Ovid became an arbiter of elegance—this time for the medieval courts of love. He was revered as the great preceptor of courtly love. Through the Renaissance up to modern times his poetry has been respected as a treasury of mythic themes, the suggestiveness and psychological content of which have inspired the imagination of writers from Dante to Ezra Pound.

Owain. The hero of a 12th-century legend, *The Descent of Owain,* written by Henry of Saltrey, an English Cistercian monk. Owain is an Irish knight of King Stephen's court who, by way of penance for a wicked life, enters and passes through St. Patricks's Purgatory.

Owen, Robert (1771–1858). Welsh-born English manufacturer, pioneer in British socialism. A self-made business man, he became manager and part owner of cotton mills in New Lanark, Scotland in 1800. Here, for 25 years, he engaged not only in his business, but in educational, philanthropic, and propagandistic activities as well; he improved social conditions in the little mill town, laid particular stress on education, was the first to establish an infant school, inaugurated programs of adult education, and founded his Institution for the Formation of Character. His aim was to reorganize society on the basis of small, cooperative communities of from 800 to 2,500 members, combining agriculture and industry and organizing production and consumption. In 1824 he went to the U.S. and founded (1825) the New Harmony Community in southern Indiana, which lasted only until 1827. Although his ideas were received enthusiastically in the U.S., the failure of his project cost him nearly all his fortune and interest in his theories waned. Back in England, several other projects failed, but, undaunted, he continued the propagation of his ideas until his death at the age of 87.

Owen, Wilfred (1893–1918). English poet. He is considered the best of the poets who wrote in and about World War I. Influenced by Siegfried Sassoon, whom he met in an army hospital, Owen wrote technically experimental poems expressing his hatred of war and savagely and ironically describing the cruelty and horror he saw about him at the battlefront. Among his best-known poems are DULCE ET DECORUM EST, *Anthem for Doomed Youth,* and *Strange Meeting.* His use of alliterative assonance instead of regular rhyme influenced younger poets, especially W. H. Auden. Owen, who was killed a week before the Armistice, published only four poems during his lifetime and was unknown as a poet until Siegfried

Sassoon published his *Poems* in 1920. Owen's well-known poetic manifesto includes the statement that "My subject is War, and the pity of War. The Poetry is in the pity."

Owl and the Nightingale, The (c. 1200). Early Middle English poem, of 1704 lines in octosyllabic couplets. It is a lively debate and exchange of personal abuse: the nightingale berates the owl for being ugly and singing only of misfortune, while the owl accuses her of enticing men to sin with her frivolous and amatory songs. The work is often interpreted allegorically as the conflict between gay pleasure-seeking and spiritual gravity, or between the new courtly love poetry and religious didactic literature.

Owlglass or Howleglas, Tyll. See EULEN-SPIEGEL.

Oxford, Edward de Vere, earl of (1550–1604). English courtier and poet, a favorite of Queen Elizabeth. He was regarded as typical of the group of courtly lyric poets, which included Sir Philip Sidney, Sir Fulke Greville, and Sir Walter Raleigh. He was known among his contemporaries as somewhat of a fop and considered to be the object of satire in Gabriel HARVEY's *Speculum Tuscanismi* (1583), dealing with Italianate young Englishmen. Oxford was a patron of writers and actors; John LYLY served as his secretary and dedicated *Euphues and His England* (1580) to him. His verse is found in a number of poetic miscellanies, especially *A Hundred Sundry Flowers* (1573), which he may have edited. He was one of the jury at the treason trial of Lord Essex, and served as Lord Great Chamberlain at the coronation of James I. He has been one of the candidates for the "real" authorship of Shakespeare's plays.

Oxford Group Movement. An American evangelist, Frank Nathan Buchman (1878–1961), organized the Oxford Group Movement at Oxford, England (1921), sometimes called, in brief, the Oxford Movement or Buchmanism. It has no connection with the original Oxford Movement, emphasizing moral awakening through fellowship, public confession, and purity. Since 1939, the movement has been known as Moral Rearmament.

Oxford Movement, the. A movement in the Church of England, originating at Oxford around 1833 under the leadership of E. B. PUSEY, John Henry NEWMAN, and John KEBLE, which sought to bring back into the service of the Church much of the ritual and ornaments that had been dispensed with at the time of the Reformation, to emphasize neglected sacraments, practices, and doctrines, such as Confession, monastic or conventual life, and Apostolic Succession. A number of its followers, as did Newman, ultimately became Roman Catholics. See TRACTS FOR THE TIMES.

Oxford philosophers. See LOGICAL POSITIVISM.

oxymoron. In rhetoric, an apparent contradiction in terms deliberately employed for effect. An example in the use of a qualifying adjective whose meaning is contrary to that of the noun it modifies, such as strenuous idleness, wise folly, etc.

Oz, the Land of. The setting for the *Wonderful Wizard of Oz* (1900) and other fantastic stories by L[yman] Frank BAUM. A mythical kingdom extremely popular with American children.

Ozymandias (1818). A famous sonnet by Percy Bysshe SHELLEY, first published by Leigh Hunt in his *Examiner*. It is an ironic commentary on the vanity and futility of a tyrant's power.

P

pacifism. The doctrine professed by those people who, on moral or religious grounds, refuse to participate in activities of organized violence, especially war. During World War I English and American pacifists, among whom a number of well-known writers, artists and other intellectuals were included, were harshly treated, being fined, imprisoned, and in general socially ostracized by their former friends. William Jennings Bryan, Woodrow Wilson (at the beginning of his presidential career), Bertrand Russell, and Randolph Bourne were pacifists at this time. In the twenty years following World War I pacifism grew to be a comparatively influential international movement, especially among youth, and was supported by numerous religious and political organizations, both conservative and radical. Its culmination occurred about the middle of the 1930s, in the annual anti-war "strikes" held at a number of American schools, colleges, and universities, in the Oxford Oath, originating at Oxford University in England, by which students swore not to fight in any war waged by their national governments under any circumstances, and in the passage of legislation by the U.S. Congress to insure American neutrality in time of war. President Franklin D. Roosevelt was for a while identified with a speech in which the words "I hate war" occurred. With the rearmament of Germany, however, under Adolf Hitler, the avowed military ambitions of Fascist Italy and Nazi Germany, and the outbreak of the Spanish Civil War (1936), pacifism began to lose its popularity. An important factor in this change was the new stand of the U.S.S.R. and the national Communist parties, which had formerly encouraged the pacifist movement but now condemned only an "imperialist war" and advocated the formation of a Popular Front against Fascism. With the beginning of World War II, pacifism had lost its former influence, although legislation whose passage had been secured in England and the U.S. during the period of the movement's power permitted pacifists who could prove a bona fide basis for their beliefs—usually an acceptable religious creed—to become "conscientious objectors" and live together in camps at their own expense, exempt from military service but not permitted their former freedom until the end of the war. The Quakers have been outstanding among traditional religious pacifists.

Pacolet. The dwarf in the romance of VALEN-TINE AND ORSON. He has a magic wooden horse on which he carries the twins and Clerimond from the dungeon of Ferragus to Pepin's court.

Pactolus. A small river of Lydia in Asia Minor, a tributary of the Hermus. The fact that it carried gold was explained by the story of Midas, whose ability, given him by Dionysus, to turn everything he touched into gold proved disastrous when it affected also his food, and was mercifully transferred by the god to the waters of the river. By the time of Augustus the Pactolus had ceased to produce gold.

Paderewski, Ignace [Jan] (1860–1941). Polish pianist, composer, and statesman. He was one of the greatest and most popular pianists of all time. He donated a large part of the proceeds from his concerts to the cause of Polish nationalism. In 1919 he was chosen premier of the new Polish Republic, returned to the concert stage in 1920, but rejoined the Polish government as president of parliament after it was exiled by the invasion of 1939. His best-known composition is a Minuet in G for piano. He is the subject of many biographies and panegyrics.

paean. From Paian, in Greek mythology the "healer of the gods"; the name was later applied specifically to the god APOLLO. In time it acquired the meaning of a song, hymn, or chant to Apollo, of a triumphant nature; hence a triumphal song in general.

paeon. In classical prosody, a metrical foot which included three short syllables and one long syllable. They are distinguished as (1) the first paeon, with the first syllable long and the succeeding three short, (2) the second paeon, with the second syllable long and the first, third and fourth short, and so on. In English prosody, the first paeon occasionally appears singly in accent meter in such words as "SHADOWI-ness," and "LINGeringly," in which an extra unaccented syllable seems crowded into the normal English limit of nonaccents.

Paganini, Nicolò (1782–1840). Italian violinist and composer. According to tradition, a supreme virtuoso in technical accomplishment, he was a performer and personality of extraordinary fascination. He wrote concertos and many other pieces for violin, notably the 24 *Caprices,* Op. 1, for solo violin. These works were transcribed for the piano in studies by Liszt and Schumann, and were the source of themes for piano variations by Brahms and Rachmaninoff. *Harold in Italy* by Berlioz was commissioned by Paganini.

Page, Mr. In Shakespeare's MERRY WIVES OF WINDSOR, a gentleman living at Windsor. When Sir John Falstaff makes love to Mrs. Page, Page himself assumes the name of Brook, to outwit the knight. Sir John tells the supposed Brook his whole "course of wooing," and how nicely he is bamboozling the husband.

Mrs. Page. Wife of Mr. Page, of Windsor. When

Sir John Falstaff makes love to her, she joins with Mrs. Ford to dupe him and punish him.

Anne Page. Daughter of the above, in love with Fenton. Slender calls her "the sweet Anne Page."

William Page. Anne's brother, a schoolboy.

Page, Stanton. See Henry B. FULLER.

Page, Thomas Nelson (1853–1922). American lawyer, novelist, essayist, historian, and diplomat. Page was deeply affected by the "Old Dominion" Virginia ideals of chivalry and family. Although he became a lawyer, he soon turned to literature and achieved his first success with the story MARSE CHAN; it was later included in a volume called *In Ole Virginia* (1887). Page's novel, RED ROCK, which treated Southern resistance to the policies of the Reconstruction, was a best seller. Dominated by a sentimental outlook, his work includes *Two Little Confederates* (1888), a children's story; *Gordon Keith* (1903) and *John Marvel, Assistant* (1909), two novels; *The Old South* (1892) and *Social Life in Old Virginia* (1897), collections of essays. Page was ambassador to Italy from 1913 to 1919.

Page disgracié. See François L'HERMITE.

Paget, Violet. See Vernon LEE.

Paghat. Sister of the hero in the Canaanite THE POEM OF AQHAT. She tracks down his killer and avenges her brother.

Pagliacci, I (The Players). An opera by Ruggiero LEONCAVALLO (1892). The characters are traveling players; Nedda, the wife of Canio, the showman; Tonio, a member of the company; and Silvio, a villager who has long been in love with Nedda.

Pagnol, Marcel (1895–   ). French playwright, screenwriter, and film critic. After *Les Marchands de gloire* (1924), written with Paul Nivoix (1893–1958), Pagnol became famous for the satire TOPAZE (1928). His witty trilogy of life in Marseilles (*Marius* [1929], *Fanny* [1931], and *César* [1936]) was produced in film form.

Pailleron, Edouard (1834–1899). French dramatist. Pailleron's fame rests on his play *Le Monde où l'on s'ennuie* (*The World Where One Grows Weary*, 1881), a clever, animated piece of satirical writing, which mocks the ridiculous affectation of would-be ladies.

Pain, Barry Eric Odell (1865–1928). English humorist. He was popular at the beginning of the century, especially for his comedy of manners *Eliza* (1900). He also wrote parodies and ghost stories.

Pain Dur, Le. See HOSTAGE, THE.

Paine, Albert Bigelow (1861–1937). American biographer, editor, novelist, and writer for children. His biography of Thomas Nast (1904) proved so successful that he was asked to write other biographies. It is in connection with Mark Twain that Paine is chiefly remembered; Twain liked the Nast biography so much that he accepted Paine's proposition that the latter become his secretary and official biographer. From this association emerged Twain's *Speeches* (1910), edited by Paine; Paine's *Mark Twain, A Biography* (1912); *Mark Twain's Letters* (1917); and *Mark Twain's Autobiography* (1924), edited by Paine. Paine also wrote *Moments with Mark Twain* (1920) and edited *The Family Mark Twain* (1935). Paine's attitude toward his subject is one of warm admiration rather than critical objectivity.

Paine, Thomas (1737–1809). English pamphleteer and political radical. The son of a Quaker corsetmaker, Paine came to America in 1774. Famous for his activities in behalf of the colonies during the American Revolution, as well as in France during the French Revolution, he consistently urged revolt and independence instead of reform and tried to promote world revolution. Among his works are *The Case of the Officers of Excise* (1772), a plea for higher wages to excisemen, of whom he had been one; COMMON SENSE; THE AMERICAN CRISIS, a series of pamphlets supporting the American Revolution; *Public Good* (1780), in which he urged that western lands become the property not of one colony but of the nation; *Dissertations on First-Principles of Government* (1795), an attack on monetary inflation in the American colonies; THE RIGHTS OF MAN; THE AGE OF REASON, for which he was denounced as an atheist.

Paine lived a turbulent career, beginning in a variety of humble occupations. He held several official positions in the colonies during the Revolution but made enemies and subsequently lost favor. In England he was tried for treason *in absentia* and outlawed because of some seditious passages in *The Rights of Man*. In France he was made an honorary citizen by the republican government (1792) and was a delegate to the Convention, until the more radical government of the Reign of Terror came into power and imprisoned him as an enemy Englishman. He died in the U.S. amid poverty and calumny, denounced as a radical, a drunkard, and an atheist, and was denied burial in consecrated ground. His remains were lost after being taken to England for reburial. In later years he came to be regarded as an American patriot and an important crusader for democratic rights.

Painted Veils (1920). A novel by James Gibbons HUNEKER. An experimental, satirical fantasy, it has for its background the art world of New York City, introducing many real people under their own names. Because the morals of the fictional characters are for the most part free and easy, the book, which was privately printed, was considered in its day highly daring.

Painter, William (1540?–1594). English prose writer. A clerk at the Tower of London and at one time a schoolmaster, Painter is best known for *The Palace of Pleasure* (1566–1567), a collection of 101 tales translated from classic and contemporary sources, especially Boccaccio's *Decameron* and Bandello's *Novelle*. Widely read, the book supplied plots to the leading Elizabethan poets and playwrights. Shakespeare's *All's Well That Ends Well, Timon of Athens, Coriolanus, Romeo and Juliet,* and *Lucrece* may all derive from Painter's collection.

Pair of Blue Eyes, A (1873). A novel by Thomas HARDY. Elfride Swancourt, the daughter of a rector, is loved by Stephen Smith; she starts to elope with him, but changes her mind and returns home. Later she loves and is loved by Henry Knight, but Mrs. Jethway, a spying neighbor, writes Knight of Elfride's former experience, and the lovers quarrel. Sometime later the two men, each intending to be reconciled with Elfride, meet on a train, but they arrive only in time for her funeral. She has married, but, loving Knight, has pined away and died.

Palace of Art, The (1830). An allegorical poem by Alfred, Lord TENNYSON. Its object is to show that love of art will not alone suffice to make men happy.

Palace of Pleasure, The. See William PAINTER.

paladins. Knights-errant, usually referring to the companions of Charlemagne in medieval romances. The twelve most illustrious were known as *The Twelve Peers* (*Fr. Les Douze Pairs*), but the lists of their names vary widely. The *Chanson de* ROLAND lists Roland (Orlando), OLIVIER, Ivon, Ivory, Otton, Berengier, Samson, Anseis, Gerin, Gerier, Engelier, and Gerard. However, there are other important knights referred to as paladins in the *Chanson,* in Pulci's MORGANTE MAGGIORE, in Boiardo's ORLANDO INNAMORATO, and in Ariosto's ORLANDO FURIOSO: ASTOLPHO, Florismart, FIERABRAS (Ferumbras), GANELON (Gan), MALAGIGI (Maugis), Namo (Nami), OGIER THE DANE, RINALDO (Renault), and Archbishop TURPIN. These and other knights are also the protagonists of lesser known CHANSONS DE GESTE.

Palaemon (Palaimon). See INO.

Palamedes. One of the heroes against Troy. In Greek legend he was the reputed inventor of lighthouses, scales and measures, the discus, dice, etc., and was said to have added four letters to the original alphabet of Cadmus. It was he who detected the madness assumed by Odysseus to avoid entering the TROJAN WAR by putting his infant son Telemachus in the way of the plow the supposed madman was driving. In revenge Odysseus achieved Palamedes' death.

Palamedes. In Arthurian romance, a Saracen knight. He is overcome in single combat by TRISTAN. Both love Iseult, the wife of King Mark, and after the lady has been given up by the Saracen, Tristan converts him to the Christian faith, and stands as his godfather at the font.

Tasso introduces a Palamedes of Lombardy in his *Gerusalemme Liberata.* He joins the Crusaders with his brothers, Achilles and Sforza, and is shot by Corinda with an arrow.

Palamon and Arcite. See KNIGHT'S TALE.

Palaprat, Jean. See PATHELIN, LA FARCE DE MAISTRE PIERRE.

Palazzo Vecchio. The town hall of Florence, Italy. The austere, castlelike structure was built in the 13th and 14th centuries.

pale horse. See FOUR HORSEMEN OF THE APOCALYPSE.

Pale Horse, Pale Rider (1939). A short novel by Katherine Anne PORTER. It tells the story of a short-lived love affair during the influenza epidemic of the First World War between a young Southern newspaperwoman and a soldier. Like most of Miss Porter's work, it is written in a limpid, somewhat spare style that suggests far more than it says. The novel gave its name to the collection of three short novels in which it appeared, the others being NOON WINE and OLD MORTALITY.

Palemon and Lavinia. A poetic version of Boaz and Ruth told by James Thomson in *Autumn* (1730), a section of his poem THE SEASONS. Palemon is also the name of the hero in Falconer's narrative poem *The Shipwreck* (1756).

Palemone. See TESEIDA.

Palestrina. Full name **Giovanni Pierluigi da Palestrina** (c. 1525–1594). Italian composer. His usual name comes from Palestrina, the city of his birth. The greatest Italian composer of the 16th century, he is best known for his more than 100 masses and numerous motets, which have long been considered a yardstick of judgment for polyphonic music used in the Roman Catholic Church.

Paley, William (1743–1805). English theologian and philosopher. His theory of UTILITARIANISM differs from that of Jeremy Bentham's in that it sanctions the supernatural. His most important treatises include *Principles of Morals and Political Philosophy* (1785), a Cambridge textbook; *Horae Paulinae* (1790); and the *View of the Evidences of Christianity* (1794).

Palgrave, Francis Turner (1824–1897). English poet and critic, best known for his anthology THE GOLDEN TREASURY. He also wrote Wordsworthian lyrics, ballads on events in English history, and hymns. Collections of his verse include *Visions of England* (1881) and *Amenophis* (1892).

palindrome (Gr. *palin dromo,* to run back again). A word or line the same backward and forward. Examples are *Madam, I'm Adam,* also *Roma tibi subito motibus ibit amor.* They have also been called Sotadics, from their reputed inventor, Sotades, a scurrilous Greek poet of the 3d century B.C.

Probably the longest palindrome in English is

> Dog as a devil deified
> Deified lived as a god;

and others well known are

> Lewd did I live, evil I did dwel,

and Napoleon's famous reputed saying,

> Able was I ere I saw Elba.

A celebrated Greek palindrome is ΝΙΨΟΝΑΝΟΜΗΜΑΤΑΜΗΜΟΝΑΝΟΨΙΝ. It means "wash my transgressions, not only my face."

palinode. A recantation. It is named for the poem by Stesichorus in which he recanted his former harsh words about HELEN of Troy. Chaucer's *Legend of Good Women* is a palinode.

Palinurus. In Vergil's AENEID, the steersman of Aeneas and the first Trojan to be killed in Italy. Overcome with sleep, he tumbles from the helm into the sea off the coast of Lucania, and, swimming to shore, is murdered by the natives.

Palinurus. The pen name of Cyril CONNOLLY. Connolly thinks Palinurus fell into the sea through a typically modern will to failure.

Palissot [de Montenoy], Charles (1730–1814). French satirical dramatist. Most of his comedies are *pièces à clef* (Fr., "key-plays"; see ROMAN À CLEF). *Les Originaux ou le Cercle* (1755) and *Les Philosophes* (1760) perfidiously satirize some of the Encyclopedists, such as Diderot, Rousseau, Helvétius, and Duclos. His *La Dunciade ou la Guerre des sots* (1764), imitated from Alexander Pope's *Dunciad,* and his *Petites lettres contre de grands philosophes* (1757) both pursue this same theme.

Palladio, Andrea (1508–1580). Italian architect. His study of Roman architecture led him to develop an original style of design incorporating classical elements. Among his famous buildings are the churches of *San Giorgio Maggiore* and *Il Redentore* at Venice; the *Villa Capra,* or *Rotonda,* at Vicenza (c. 1567), which was the first modern example of integrated landscape and building; and *Palazzo Chiericati* also at Vicenza (1550). He also wrote a treatise, *Four Books of Architecture* (*Quattro libri dell'architettura;* 1570), that raised great interest throughout Europe and was translated into English by Inigo JONES; its drawings served to disseminate his ideas and to make the Palladian style the basis of English Georgian architecture in the 18th century.

Palladis Tamia. See Francis MERES.

Palladium (Palladion). Wooden statue of Pallas ATHENE in the city of Troy. It was said to have fallen from heaven. It was believed that so long as this statue remained within the city, Troy would be safe, but if ever it were removed, the city would fall into the hands of the enemy. The statue was carried away by the Greeks, and the city burnt by them to the ground. Later, Argos, Sparta, and Athens all claimed to possess this statue.

Pallas. (1) An epithet of the Greek goddess ATHENE, and sometimes also of the Roman Minerva. There are two main explanations of its origins. Apollodorus relates that Athene accidentally killed her playmate Pallas, daughter of the river-god Triton, and that, in token of her grief, she placed her friend's name before her own. In another tale, Pallas was a giant and the father of Athene. When he attempted to violate his daughter, she flayed him and took his skin for her aegis, his wings for her shoulders, and his name to add to her own.

(2) In the THESEUS legend, the son of Pandion and the father of fifty sons, the Pallantids. He plotted to steal the throne of Athens from his brother Aegeus, Theseus' father, but he and all his sons were killed by Theseus.

Pallavicino, Gasparo (1486–1511). Lombard nobleman. He was a friend of Castiglione, who made him one of the interlocutors in THE COURTIER.

Pall Mall. A fine thoroughfare in the West End of London. It was named in the early 18th century because the game of Palle-malle (Ital. *palla,* ball, *maglia,* mallet) was played there.

Palma, Ricardo (1833–1919). Peruvian writer. As a young man, Palma combined political activity with literature, producing dramas and poems in the romantic style. Disillusioned by the turbulence of Peruvian politics, Palma decided to devote himself exclusively to literature and history. In 1872 he published the first collection of his delightfully ironic TRADICIONES PERUANAS, the work upon which his reputation as a writer is based. From 1883 to 1912 he was director of Peru's national library, acquiring thousands of volumes to replace those that had been destroyed during the so-called War of the Pacific (1879–1883). At his death he was generally regarded as Peru's foremost man of letters.

palmer. A Pilgrim to the Holy Land who carried a palm staff and spent his life visiting holy shrines and living on charity. At the dedication of palmers, prayers and psalms were said over them as they lay prostrate before the altar; they were sprinkled with holy water, and then received the consecrated palm branch, sign of their office.

Palmer, George Herbert (1842–1933). American philosopher and teacher. A professor at Harvard, he excelled as a critic and expositor of philosophy, though he was not an innovator. Among his philosophic works are *The Field of Ethics* (1901), *The Nature of Goodness* (1903), *The Problem of Freedom* (1911), and *Altruism: Its Nature and Variety* (1919). Palmer wrote a biography of his wife, *The Life of Alice Freeman Palmer* (1908); Mrs. Palmer was the president of Wellesley College (1882–1887). Palmer also wrote literary and critical books, and published a much-admired translation of the *Odyssey* (1884).

Palmerín. The hero of several 16th-century Spanish romances of chivalry that rivaled *Amadís of Gaul* in popularity. According to tradition, the first work in the series, *Palmerín de Oliva* (1511) was written by an anonymous lady of Augustobriga. However, it may have been written by Francisco Vázquez of Ciudad Rodrigo, to whom is also attributed the second part, *Primaleón* (1512). The final work of the series, *Palmerín de Inglaterra* (1547–1548), is considered the best and was one of the volumes spared from condemnation in *Don Quijote.* Although it is sometimes ascribed to Luis Hurtado, the author was probably Francisco de Moraes, a Portuguese. Robert Southey published an English translation, *Palmerin of England,* in 1807.

Palmerston, 3d Viscount. **Henry John Temple** (1784–1865). English statesman. He was prime minister from 1855 to 1858 and from 1859 to 1865. He opposed construction of the Suez Canal. He supported a policy of neutrality in the U.S. Civil War, but intervened successfully in a number of threatened and actual international conflicts in favor of the *status quo* or the restitution of liberal order.

Palmieri, Matteo (1406–1475). Florentine writer. He is the author of a dialogue, *Della vita civile* (*On the Civil Life*) on the training of the ideal citizen. His *Città di vita* (*City of Life*) is a long philosophical poem in terza rima, influenced by Dante.

Palmyra. The Biblical Tadmor, a city east of Syria. After the revolt of its queen Zenobia, it was destroyed by the Emperor Aurelian (273 A.D.).

Paltock, Robert (1697–1767). English lawyer and author, principally known for the extraordinary fantasy and romance, *The Life and Adventures of Peter Wilkins, a Cornish Man* (1751), which describes a country of flying women.

Paludan, Jacob (1896–). Danish novelist and essayist. A pessimistic critic of modern society, Paludan paints a dark, bitter portrait of Denmark at the beginning of World War I in his novel cycle *Jørgen Stein* (2 vols., 1932–1933). In the novel *Fugle omkring Fyret* (*Birds Around the Light,* 1925), he depicts a small, quiet fishing village of simple people whose values are corrupted when an artificial harbor is constructed.

Pamela, or Virtue Rewarded (1740–1742). An epistolary novel in two parts by Samuel RICHARDSON, generally considered to be the first modern English novel. In the first part Pamela is *Aggressive Chastity,* in the second, *Provocative Prudence.* A simple, unsophisticated, fifteen-year-old country girl, Pamela Andrews has a surprising tendency for self-analysis. She is the maidservant of a wealthy woman who dies and whose son, Mr. B., pursues her with base intentions. He kidnaps her and tries to seduce her, but is deterred by the tenacity of her resistance. She then convinces him to marry her and sets about to reform him. The story is told in a series of letters from Pamela to her parents, and reads like a private journal. See B., MR.

Pan (Gr., *all, everything*). An Arcadian god of pastures, forests, flocks, and herds of Greek mythology; also, the personification of deity displayed in creation and pervading all things. He is represented with the lower part of a goat, and the upper part of a man. He invented the musical pipe of seven reeds, which he named SYRINX.

Legend has it that at the time of the Crucifixion, just when the veil of the Temple was rent in twain, a cry swept across the ocean in the hearing of many, "Great Pan is dead," and that at the same time the responses of the oracles ceased forever. *The Dead Pan,* a poem by Elizabeth Barrett Browning (1844), is founded on this legend. Pan is also the subject of her poem *A Musical Instrument* and of Robert Browning's *Pan and Luna.*

Panacea (Gr., *all-healing*). In Greek myth, the daughter of Asklepios, god of medicine. She was merely a personification of the idea of a cure-all.

In the Middle Ages, the search for the panacea was one of the alchemists' self-imposed tasks. Fable tells of many panaceas, such as the Promethean unguent, which rendered the body invulnerable; Aladdin's ring; the balsam of FIERABRAS; and Prince Ahmed's apple.

Panathenaea (Panathenaia). An Athenian festival in honor of Pallas Athene. Under the Tyrant PISISTRATUS, it was given great importance and became the occasion for a contest of bards and other cultural events. It was probably for this festival that the many versions of the *Iliad* and the *Odyssey* were collated and standardized.

Panchatantra. A collection of fables in Sanskrit. The compilation is supposed to have been ordered in the fifth century by King Amarasakti of South India for the edification of his sons. There is an English translation (1955) by Arthur W. Ryder.

Pancrace. In Molière's *Mariage Forcé,* a doctor of the Aristotelian school, who involves himself in constant absurdity in his attempts to apply his cumbersome logical analysis to trivial matters. When his adversary cannot agree, he calls him *"un ignorant, un ignorantissime, ignorantifiant, et ignorantifié."* See SGANARELLE.

Pandarus (Pandaros). In Greek legend, a Lycian leader, one of the allies of Priam in the TROJAN WAR. In the classic story he is depicted as an admirable archer, slain by Diomedes and honored as a hero-god in his own country. In medieval romance he is represented as such a despicable fellow that the word *pander* is derived from his name. In Boccaccio's FILOSTRATO he is Criseida's young cousin. Chaucer, in his *Troilus and Criseyde* (see TROILUS), makes him Criseyde's uncle, a worldly-wise, but sympathetic character. Shakespeare, in his drama of *Troilus and Cressida,* represents him as procuring for Troilus the good graces of Cressida, and in *Much Ado About Nothing,* it is said that Troilus "was the first employer of panders."

pandemonium (Gr., "all the demons"). A wild, unrestrained uproar, a lawless, infernal tumult. The word was first used by Milton, in PARADISE LOST as the name of the principal city in Hell, "the high capital of Satan and his peers."

Pandora. In Greek mythology, the first woman.

PROMETHEUS had made an image and stolen fire from heaven to endow it with life. In revenge, Zeus commanded Hephaestus to make a woman, who was named Pandora (i.e., the All-gifted), because each of the gods gave her some power that was to bring about the ruin of man. Zeus gave her a vessel which she was to present to him who married her. Prometheus distrusted Zeus and his gifts, but Epimetheus, his brother, married the beautiful Pandora, and, against advice, accepted the gift of the god. As soon as he opened the jar all the evils that flesh is heir to flew forth, and have ever since continued to afflict the world. According to some accounts the last thing that flew out was Hope, but others say that Hope alone remained. Some versions blame Pandora's curiosity for the disaster.

Pandora's box came to mean a present that seems valuable, but is in reality a curse, like that of MIDAS, who found his very food became gold, and so uneatable.

Pan-Germanism. A movement to incorporate all German peoples in one political organization and to extend German influence generally. It reached a height before World War I, and was continued by Adolf Hitler.

Pangloss, Dr. (*Gr.,* "all tongue"). The pedantic old tutor to the hero in Voltaire's CANDIDE, OU L'OPTIMISME (1759). His distinguishing feature is his incurable and misleading optimism; he sees and endures all sorts of misfortune, but to the end he reiterates "All is for the best in this best of all possible worlds." He is said to have been based on the philosopher Leibniz, but it is more likely that Voltaire had in mind the German philosopher Christian von Wolff (or Wolf, 1679–1754), who popularized Leibniz's works, and whom Voltaire must have read.

Panic (1935). A verse play by Archibald MacLEISH. The play attempts to show how human panic converted the financial crashes of the 1930's into catastrophes as inevitable as natural disasters. MacLeish here rejected blank verse in favor of accentual meter.

Pan Michael. The third of a Polish historic trilogy by SIENKIEWICZ. See WITH FIRE AND SWORD.

Panormita, il. Antonio Beccadelli (1394–1471). Italian Humanist and scholar. He served as a secretary at the Naples court and was crowned with the laurel by the Emperor Sigismund in 1432. He was and still is noted for his authorship of a collection of epigrams, obscene in content, called *Hermaphroditus* (1425). The surname Panormita was derived from the Latin name of his native city, Panormus (Palermo).

Panova, Vera Fiodorovna (1905–1973). Russian novelist. Her first successful work was *Traveling Companions (Sputniki;* 1947), describing the lives of a group of people working on a hospital train during World War II. Its focus on the human elements of the situation and its high quality of craftsmanship, in characterization and language, are also to be found in some of Panova's later books, such as *Kruzhilikha* (1948), which is set in a factory whose name gives the novel its title, and *Seasons of the Year (Vremena goda;* 1953), about life in an industrial town.

Pantagruel. The principal character of Rabelais' great satire, GARGANTUA AND PANTAGRUEL. The name,

Title page of Françoys Rabelais' *Pantagruel* (1532).
Rabelais' name is anagrammed as Alcofrybas Nasier.

meaning "all-thirsty," had originally been given to a little sea devil in 15th-century mystery plays who threw salt into the mouths of drunks to stimulate their thirst.

Capitalizing on the popularity of a contemporary chapbook about a marvellous giant called Gargantua, Rabelais introduced Pantagruel, the son of GARGAN-TUA and BADEBEC, *in Les Horribles et espovantables faictz et prouesses du très renommé Pantagruel, Roy des Dipsodes, fils du grand géant Gargantua* (1532), which later came to be known as Book II. Born during a terrible drought, Pantagruel is covered with hair at birth, like a young bear, and is so strong that though he is chained to his cradle he breaks his bonds into 500 pieces with a single blow of his infant fist. The tale goes on to recount his fabulous childhood feats, his tour of the universities and his life with PANURGE in the Latin Quarter of Paris, and his conduct of the war against the Dipsodes in Utopia. Aside from the realistic description of student life and the famous letter in which Gargantua, extolling the recent revolution in learning, instructs his son to immerse himself in all the new studies, the book remains on the whole faithful to medieval tradition.

In Books III–V Pantagruel continues as the hero, but he becomes less and less the fabulous giant and more the personification of the Renaissance man in search of knowledge and the good life.

Pantagruelion. The name given by Rabelais to hemp, partly because Pantagruel was the first to use it as a hangman's rope, but especially because, like Pantagruel, "the inspiration and exemplar of all jovial perfection," hemp "contains the highest efficacy, energy, and competence and force."

Pantagruelism. According to Rabelais, "a certain gaiety of spirit produced by a contempt of the incidentals of fate." The term is now used to refer to coarse or boisterous humor that has a satirical or serious intent.

Pantaloon or **Pantaleone.** A stock character in old Italian comedy. A thin, emaciated old man who always appeared in slippers, he was the father of COLUMBINE. He later became a figure in English pantomime.

Panthea. In classical history the wife of Abradatus, king of Susa. He joined the Assyrians against Cyrus, and she was taken captive. Cyrus refused to visit her, that he might not be tempted by her beauty, and Abradatus, charmed by this restraint, joined his party. Shortly afterward, he was slain in battle, and Panthea put an end to her life, falling on the body of her husband. Zenophon's *Cyropoedia,* in which her history is related, is said to be "the first extant example of a prose love-story in European literature."

pantheism (from Gr. *pan,* all, and *theos,* god). The doctrine that God is everything and everything is God. This monistic theory was elaborated by SPINOZA, who, by his doctrine of the Infinite Substance, sought to overcome the opposition between mind and matter, body and soul. During the romantic period and later, Wordsworth, Shelley, Emerson, Tennyson, and others expressed various doctrines of pantheism in their writings.

Pantheon (from Gr. *pan.,* all, and *theos,* god). A temple dedicated to all the gods; specifically, that erected at Rome by Agrippa, son-in-law to Augustus. It is circular, nearly 150 feet in diameter, and of the same total height; since the early 7th century, as Santa Maria Rotunda, it has been used as a Christian church.

The Panthéon at Paris was originally the church of St. Geneviève, built by Louis XV and finished in 1790. The following year the Convention gave it its present name, and set it apart as the shrine of those Frenchmen whom their country wished to honor.

pantisocracy. A scheme for an ideal social community in America, planned by COLERIDGE and Robert SOUTHEY in 1794. The community was to be based on the theories of Rousseau and Godwin and was to be located on the banks of the Susquehanna River in Pennsylvania. The scheme never materialized because of the lack of financial backing.

Panurge (*Gr.,* "all-doer"). In Rabelais' GARGAN-TUA AND PANTAGRUEL, the high-spirited rogue who becomes Pantagruel's companion. In Book II, when Pantagruel first meets him in Paris, he is suffering from a chronic malady called "impecunitis," which he has 63 methods of curing, "the most honorable and ordinary of which was filching." He proves to be "a quarrelsome fellow, a sharper, a toper, a roisterer, and a profligate, if there ever was one in the city of Paris. In every other respect, he was the best fellow in the world." Later, in the war against the Dipsodes, he displays a remarkable talent for ruse and cunning.

It is his inability to decide whether or not to marry that forms the basis of the plot in Books III to V. Although he still displays dialectical genius in his defense of borrowers and debtors in Book III and cunning in dispatching the dishonest DINGDONG in Book IV, he is characterized chiefly by cowardice in these latter books. During the tempest in Book IV, for example, he is reduced to hysterical blubbering, which he later dismisses with the statement, "I fear nothing by danger." See also FURRY LAWCATS and THAUMASTE.

Panza, Sancho. The squire of DON QUIXOTE in Cervantes' novel. He is a short, pot-bellied rustic, full of common sense, but without a grain of "spirituality." He is famous for his proverbs. Panza, in Spanish, means *paunch*.

Panzini, Alfredo (1863–1939). Italian novelist, historian, essayist, and short-story writer. He was a literary disciple of Carducci, and his writings are significant for their carefully worked, classically intoned style.

For the most part, Panzini's fiction lacks a convincing treatment of character and a sustained interest in plot development. He excels instead in isolated lyrical vignettes, similar in form to Carduccian neoclassicism and similar in tone to the delicate moods of the Crepuscolari poets.

His novels include *Wanted: A Wife* (*Io Cerco Moglie;* 1920), *La Madonna di Mamà* (1915), *Santippe* (1914), *Il Mondo E' Rotondo* (1920), *Il Padrone Sono Me* (1922), *La Pulcella Senza Pulcellaggio* (1925), and *Viaggio Con La Giovane Ebrea* (1935). He also wrote two essay-novels, *La Lanterna di Diogene* (1910) and *Viaggo Sentimentale di Un Povero Letterato* (1919), and two short-story collections, *Piccole Storie del Mondo Grande* (1901) and *Fiabe della Virtù* (1911).

Paolo and Francesca. Guilty lovers whose history is one of the most famous episodes in Dante's *Inferno*. They are in the second circle, that of the carnal sinners, blown lightly about by stormy winds as they had been by their passions when alive. Married to an unattractive man for political reasons, Francesca da Rimini had fallen in love with Paolo Malatesta, her husband's handsome brother, while they were innocently reading together the story of Launcelot. (See GALEOTO.) Her husband discovered their guilt and put them both to death (c. 1289). Another version, as in Stephen Phillips' poetic drama *Paolo and Francesca* (c. 1900), is that Paolo was sent by his brother to escort the bride from her home in Ravenna, with the same results. The story of the unhappy pair is also the subject of *Francesca da Rimini* (1901), a verse tragedy by Gabriele D'ANNUNZIO, which has passages of great lyric beauty; D'Annunzio dedicated this work to Eleonora Duse, who played the title role in its first production. Other dramas on this theme have been written by Silvio Pellico, G. H. Boker, and F. M. Crawford. Leigh Hunt wrote a poem, *The Story of Rimini* (1816), about the unhappy lovers. They are also the subject of a tone poem (1877) by Tchaikovsky and an opera (1914) by Riccardo Zandonai.

papacy. See POPE.

Papefigues. See POPE-FIGS.

Papen, Franz von (1879–   ). German diplomat. He was Nazi ambassador to Austria (1934–1938) and Turkey (1939–1944). He was acquitted at the NUREMBERG TRIALS.

Paphian. Relating to Venus or rather to Paphos, a city of Cyprus, where Venus was worshipped; a Cyprian; a prostitute.

Paphnutius (Paphnuce). The chief character in THAÏS, a novel by Anatole France. He is a young monk who destroys himself in converting Thaïs, a famous courtesan.

Papimaniacs. An anglicism for Papimanes, in Rabelais' GARGANTUA AND PANTAGRUEL, the inhabitants of the isle of Papimany, who exist in the hope of laying eyes on their idol, the pope. Their leader is Bishop Stoutmoron (*Fr.,* "Homenaz"), and their holy book the papal decretals. The episode of the Papimaniacs is a thinly disguised satire on the Roman Catholic Church.

Papini, Giovanni (1881–1956). Italian writer and philosopher. One of the founders of the philosophical journal *Leonardo* (1903–1907), he was known as a bitter opponent and critic of Christianity. After World War I, he was converted to Roman Catholicism and transformed into an exponent of religious orthodoxy. His highly successful *Life of Christ* (*Storia di Cristo;* 1921) was published shortly afterwards. Other writings include *Un Uomo Finito* (*The Failure;* 1912), an autobiographical novel; *Sant' Agostino* (1929) and *Dante Vivo* (1933), biographies; and *Gog* (1931), a satire on modern society.

parabasis. See OLD COMEDY.

Paracelsus (1835). A narrative poem by Robert BROWNING. The hero is Bombastus Paracelsus (1493–1541), a famous Swiss physician who was said to have delved deep into alchemy and to have kept a small devil prisoner in the pommel of his sword. In the poem, Paracelsus, at 20, thinks knowledge the supreme good, and on the advice of two friends retires to a seat of learning. Eight years later, dissatisfied, he falls in with Aprile, an Italian poet, and resolves to seek the supreme good in love. Again he fails, and, when dying in a cell in the hospital of St. Sebastian, deserted by all but one friend, he declares the supreme good to be "To see good in evil, and a hope in ill-success."

Paraclete (Gr. *parakletos,* Helper, Advocate). The Holy Spirit as Comforter or Advocate. Abelard gave this name to the oratory of his hermitage at Nogent-sur-Seine.

Parade's End. A series of novels by Ford Madox FORD, consisting of *Some Do Not* (1924), *No More Parades* (1925), *A Man Could Stand Up* (1926), and *The Last Post* (1928), all published together as *Parade's End* in 1950. The series describes the adventures in love and war of Christopher Tietjens, an old-fashioned gentleman of the English governing class. Ford draws a brilliant picture of the social changes brought about by the First World War. Before the war, Tietjens is nobly faithful to his impossible wife. But trench warfare seems to him a symbol of the disintegration of his whole society. He has a mental breakdown, goes to live with a girl he loves, and gives up his position, wealth, and historic family ties.

paradise. The land of the blessed. The Greeks borrowed this word from the Persians; it originally denoted the enclosed and extensive parks and pleasure grounds of the Persian kings. The Septuagint translators adopted it for the garden of Eden, and New Testament writers applied it to heaven, the celestial abode of the blessed dead. Dante's *Paradiso*, the third part of his *Divine Comedy*, describes the poet's journey through the 10 spheres of paradise.

Paradise Lost (1667). An epic poem in 12 books by John MILTON. Often considered the greatest epic in any modern language, it tells the story

> Of Man's first disobedience and the fruit
> Of that forbidden tree whose mortal taste
> Brought death into the World, and all our woe,
> With loss of Eden.

SATAN rouses the panic-stricken host of fallen angels with tidings of a rumor current in Heaven of a new world about to be created. He calls a council to deliberate what should be done, and they agree to send him in search of this new world. Passing the gulf between Heaven and Hell, Satan disguised as an angel enters the orb of the Sun, and, having obtained the information he seeks, goes to Paradise in the form of a cormorant. Seating himself on the Tree of Life, he overhears Adam and Eve talking about the prohibition made by God, and at once resolves upon the nature of his attack. GABRIEL sends two angels to watch over Paradise, and Satan flees. Sent to warn Adam of his danger, RAPHAEL tells him the story of Satan's revolt and expulsion from Heaven, and why and how this world was made. After a time Satan returns to Paradise in the form of a mist, and, entering the serpent, induces Eve to eat of the forbidden fruit. Adam eats "that he may perish with the woman he loved." Satan returns to Hell to tell his triumph and Sin and Death come into the world. As Michael leads the guilty pair out of the garden, he shows them a vision of humanity's misery—but, as he explains, the Son of God has already offered himself as ransom for man, and, in Him, man shall ultimately be victorious over Satan.

In 1671, *Paradise Regained* (in four books), written by Milton on suggestion of his Quaker friend Thomas Ellwood, was published. The subject is Christ's triumphant resistance to Satan's temptation, regaining the Paradise lost by Adam and Eve. The New Testament narrative is followed and enlarged upon; Satan, for instance, appeals not only to hunger, ambition, and pride, but also to the love of humanistic learning and art. *Paradise Regained* has never been as popular as its predecessor. The earlier poem is distinguished by richness and sonority of style, heroic characterization, and action on a grand, cosmic scale, while the verse of the sequel is generally far more austere and simple, and its action is much more restricted. See ADRAMELECH, ARIOCH, ABDIEL, BEELZEBUB, ITHURIEL, JAPHET, LUCIFER, PANDEMONIUM, URIEL, UZZIEL, ZEPHON.

Paradise of Dainty Devices, The. An English poetical miscellany (see TOTTEL'S MISCELLANY) of the Elizabethan period. First published in 1576, by 1606 it had gone through at least 10 editions. Its contents, originally compiled by Richard Edwards, show a taste for pious and serious works.

Paradise Regained. See PARADISE LOST.

Paradiso (Paradise). Part III of the DIVINE COMEDY by DANTE. BEATRICE and Dante are transported to the sphere of fire, where Dante first hears the musical harmony of the heavenly spheres. They move through the eight concentric heavens of the Moon, Mercury, Venus, Sun, Mars, Jupiter, Saturn, and the Fixed Stars, meeting in each heaven those of the blessed spirits notable for its appropriate virtue. Dante asks and Beatrice answers many specific questions about the nature of good and evil, original sin, transubstantiation, and the like. The ninth heaven is the Primum Mobile, divided into the nine orders of the angels. And beyond it is the Empyrean, a river of radiant light in the center of which is God's court, pictured as a white rose whose tiers of petals hold angels and beatified souls, united in the glorification of God. Here, as throughout the nine heavens, every participant is equally content with his position in the regions of bliss, but the closer a spirit is to God, the greater the intensity both of his joy and of the celestial light he reflects. Beatrice, who had originally been the one to petition that Dante be granted this extraordinary tour, now resumes her place in the rose, and is replaced by St. Bernard, who bids Dante to contemplate the Virgin Mary and himself prays her to allow the visitor a glimpse of the Godhead. Dante has been so thoroughly purified that, although still a mortal, his own will is totally merged in the Love and Will of the Creator, and he is thus capable of gazing for a moment on the supremely radiant light of the Trinity in Unity.

paradox. A statement or proposition seemingly contrary to common sense, yet possibly true in fact and full of significance, at least in part because of its contradictory qualities. "Waging the peace" is a concept that is paradoxical in this sense. Sometimes a paradox is implied, sometimes explicit. The paradox as a rhetorical device is full of surprises and often produces a memorable passage. Oscar Wilde and Gilbert K. Chesterton were masters of the literary use of paradox. See IRONY.

Parashurama. See VISHNU.

Parcae. The Latin name for the FATES. The three were Nona, Decuma, and Morta. Parcae is from the Latin *pars,* "a lot"; the corresponding Moirai of the Greeks is from the Gr. *meros,* "a lot."

Pardo Bazán [de Quiroga], Emilia (1852–1921). Spanish novelist. The only child of the count of Pardo Bazán, she wrote numerous critical and scholarly works and was professor of modern romance literatures at the University of Madrid. Although she is known for having introduced French naturalism into Spain, her work also contains elements of traditional Spanish realism and romanticism. Her finest novels are *Los Pazos de Ulloa* (1886) and its sequel, *La madre naturaleza* (1887); these works, which describe the gradual degeneration of an aristocratic family, are notable for their evocation of the Galician countryside. Her other novels include *La tribuna* (1882), *El cisne de Vilamorta* (1885), and *La quimera* (1905), a partly autobiographical work illustrating the spiritualist orientation of her later years. Some of her best short stories of Galicia are collected in *Cuentos de Marineda* (1892).

Pardoner's Tale, The. One of the CANTERBURY TALES of Geoffrey CHAUCER. In the *Prologue* the Pardoner boastfully reveals both the fraudulent tricks he uses in selling supposedly holy relics, and his own vices, particularly his hypocrisy in preaching primarily against cupidity when his own motives are purely avaricious. Then he gives a sample sermon, railing against gluttonous excess, drunkenness, gambling, and swearing. He uses as an *exemplum* the story, of Oriental origin, about three young revelers who determine to slay Death because he has just killed one of their comrades with the plague. Asked where they can find Death, an old man directs them to a tree, where they find a great pile of gold. They draw lots and send the youngest back to town for food and wine. The remaining two plot to kill him, so as to split the gold only two ways, while he puts poison in the wine, so as to keep all the treasure himself. When he returns, they stab him, then drink the wine; thus all three indeed find Death. The Pardoner boldly follows his sermon with an attempt to sell his relics; he turns first to the Host, who repulses him rudely, so that the Knight has to intervene to prevent a quarrel.

Paré, Ambroise (1517–1590). A French surgeon, often called the father of modern surgery. He introduced the practice of ligature of arteries in place of cautery in amputations. He was court physician to Henry II, Francis II, Charles IX, and Henry III.

Pareto, Vilfredo (1848–1923). Italian economist and sociologist. In 1893, after a career as a mining engineer, he became professor of political economy at Lausanne University. A man of vast erudition, he applied methods of mathematical analysis to general economic theory. His best-known work is *Trattato di Sociologia Generale* (*The Mind and Society,* 1916). Pareto's contempt for democratic institutions being well known, Mussolini and his followers claimed him as the creator of fascist ideology.

pariah. A member of a very low caste of Hindus in South India, from a word meaning a drummer. It was these who beat the drums at certain festivals. Europeans often extended the term to those of no caste at all; hence it is applied to outcastes in general.

Paribanou. In the tale of "Prince Ahmed and Paribanou" in the *Arabian Nights,* a fairy who gives Prince AHMED a tent so small that a lady may carry it about as a toy, but which, when spread, will cover a whole army.

Paridell, Sir. See FAERIE QUEENE, THE.

Parini, Giuseppe (1729–1799). Italian poet. Highly didactic in tone and intention, his poems are critical of the corruption and injustices of 18th-century society, the moral being shown through subtly humorous satire. *Il Giorno* (*The Day,* 1763–1765, 1801) is a long poem in blank verse which ostensibly gives instruction in fashionable ways of spending time, but in reality pokes fun at the sterile life of the aristocracy. Like *Il Giorno,* Parini's *Odi* (1764–1795) call attention to the ills of society and the need for immediate reform.

Paris. (1) In Greek legend, the son of Priam, king of Troy, and Hecuba; and through his abduction of HELEN the cause of the siege of Troy. Before his birth Hecuba dreamed that she was to bring forth a firebrand, and, as this was interpreted to mean that the unborn child would bring destruction to his house, the infant Paris was exposed on Mount Ida. He was, however, brought up by a shepherd under the name of Alexander, and grew to perfection of beautiful manhood. When the golden APPLE OF DISCORD was thrown on the table of the gods, it was Paris who had to judge between the rival claims of Hera, Aphrodite, and Athene. (See JUDGMENT OF PARIS.) He awarded the apple and the title of "Fairest" to Aphrodite, who in return assisted him to

Illustration from the manuscript of the *Life of Offa* by Matthew Paris.

THE BRITISH MUSEUM

⁊ ꝯ complices emulos nꝛos: fidelit reꝯo Et procul dubio post morte meam que notꝑ.

carry off Helen, for whom he deserted his wife, OENONE. At Troy Paris earned the contempt of all by his cowardice, and he was fatally wounded with a poisoned arrow by Philoctetes at the taking of the city.

(2) In Shakespeare's ROMEO AND JULIET, a young nobleman to whom Juliet is betrothed against her will.

Paris, Matthew (c. 1200–1259). English historian, most famous of the chroniclers at the Benedictine monastery of St. Albans. He revised the chronicles of England kept by his predecessors John of Cella (covering the period through 1188) and Roger of Wendover (through 1235), and continued a lively record of events in England and Europe until 1259, the whole work being called the *Chronica Majora.* He abridged it (c. 1253) as the *Historia Minor,* also called *Historia Anglorum,* covering the period 1067–1253. He also compiled and probably contributed to series of lives of the abbots of St. Albans and lives of the saints.

Parisina (1816). A poem by Lord BYRON. It describes the illicit love of Parisina, the wife of Azo, the marquis of Ferrara, and Hugo, his natural son. The action is founded on fact, occurring in the life of Niccola III of Ferrara who had the lovers beheaded.

Parizade, Princess. The heroine of one of the tales of the *Arabian Nights,* the "Story of the Sisters who Envied their Younger Sister." She is most famed for her adventures while in search of the Talking Bird, the Singing Tree, and the Yellow or Gold-Colored Water. After she finds these treasures, her troubles are at an end.

Parker, Dorothy [Rothschild] (1893–1967). American writer of short stories, verse, and criticism. Noted for her caustic wit, as drama critic on *Vanity Fair* and later *The New Yorker* she often drew blood with such critical sallies as her remark in her review of an unsuccessful Broadway play that Katharine Hepburn's acting ran "the whole gamut of emotions from A to B." Her works in verse are equally sardonic, usually dry, elegant commentaries on such themes as departing or departed love. The collection *Enough Rope* (1926) contains the often-quoted *Resume,* on suicide, and *News Item,* about girls who wear glasses. Her short stories, which were collected in *After Such Pleasures* (1933) and in *Here Lies* (1939), are as imbued with a knowledge of human nature as they are deep in disenchantment; among the best known are *Big Blonde* and *A Telephone Call.* She also wrote a play, *Close Harmony* (1924), with Elmer Rice.

Parker, Sir Gilbert (1862–1932). Canadian novelist. He was the author of *The Seats of the Mighty* (1896), a best-selling novel about the fall of Quebec in 1759.

Parker, Louis Napoleon (1852–1944). English dramatist and composer. He is best known for his comedy *Pomander Walk* (1910), the historical play *Disraeli* (1911) which starred George Arliss, and the drama *Joseph and His Brethren* (1913). He translated many of the plays of Edmond Rostand.

Parker, Matthew (1504–1575). English prelate. Chaplain to Anne Boleyn (1535) and dean of Lincoln (1552), he was during Mary's reign deprived of preferments, but became the second Anglican arch-bishop of Canterbury under Queen Elizabeth (1559). He was extremely influential in Anglicanism. He published the revised *Bishops' Bible* (1572).

Parker, Theodore (1810–1860). American clergyman, writer and abolitionist. Parker was a Harvard graduate and a pastor of the Unitarian congregation at West Roxbury, Mass. He was an active member of the Transcendentalist Club and wrote often on its doctrines; the best statement of his unorthodox beliefs is contained in his sermon, *On the Transient and Permanent in Christianity* (1841). He rejected the church and scripture, relying on a personal intuition of God. He was constantly in trouble with the orthodox members of the church for his religious and later his social sentiments. He was an ardent abolitionist and supported many advanced social notions.

Parkman, Francis (1823–1893). American historian. Having contracted a severe case of what he called "Injuns on the brain" as a boy, Parkman made a trip to Wyoming in 1846 during which he lived with and studied the Sioux Indians, an experience he described in *The Oregon Trail* (1847). Upon his return to the East, Parkman suffered a physical and nervous breakdown and remained a semi-invalid for the rest of his life; afflicted with extremely weak eyesight, he constructed a wire frame that enabled him to write with his eyes closed. In 1851 he published *History of the Conspiracy of Pontiac,* the first volume of his series on the struggle between Great Britain and France for control of North America. To Parkman, the eventual success of the British represented the victory of progress over reaction. The other volumes of the series, which is distinguished by its documentation from original sources and by Parkman's virile style and narrative skill, are *Pioneers of France in the New World* (1865), *The Jesuits in North America* (1867), *LaSalle and the Discovery of the Great West* (1869), *The Old Regime in Canada* (1874), *Count Frontenac and New France under Louis XIV* (1877), *Montcalm and Wolfe* (1884), and *A Half-Century of Conflict* (1892). Parkman also wrote *Vassall Morton* (1856), a semiautobiographical novel.

Parley, Peter. See Samuel Griswold GOODRICH.

Parliamentary novels. A series of novels about political life by Anthony TROLLOPE, including PHINEAS FINN, *Phineas Redux* (1874), *The Prime Minister* (1876), and *The Duke's Children* (1880). The hero is Phineas Finn, a young Irishman, but Plantagenet Palliser, duke of Omnium, plays a prominent role.

Parliament of Fowls, The (probably c. 1382). A poem by Geoffrey CHAUCER, almost 700 lines in RHYME ROYAL. After reading Cicero's account of Scipio Africanus' appearance to the younger Scipio in a dream, the poet himself dreams that Scipio Africanus conducts him to a garden where he sees the Temple of Venus. Then he comes to a hillside where all the fowls have gathered at the bidding of Nature to choose their mates, for it is Saint Valentine's Day. Nature declares that the royal tercel eagle has first choice, and he chooses the lovely formel eagle. Two tercels of lower rank contest the claim, one declaring he has loved her longer, the other that he loves her most truly. The other fowls begin a lively dispute over the three claims, each bird according to its character, until Nature finally refers the choice to the formel eagle, who asks for a year to make up her mind. The other birds quickly choose their mates, sing a rondel, and fly away.

Parmenides of Elea (fl. 485 B.C.). A Greek philosopher, founder of the Eleatic School. Parmenides' philosophy is expressed in his long poem known as *On Nature,* of which only fragments survive. The goal of Parmenides' intellectual journey is light, the symbol of unity and knowledge. The philosopher was not concerned with the origin of the universe; he maintained that the world is an unchanging whole, that motion and change are only illusion, and that unity is truth. In these beliefs the Eleatic School opposed the MILESIAN SCHOOL.

Parmigianino, Il. Real name, **Francesco Mazzola** (1504-1540). Italian painter. In his native Parma and in Rome and Bologna, he painted religious subjects, scenes from mythology, and portraits. In his best-known works—*The Madonna of the Long Neck, The Visitation, The Dresden Madonna,* and *Portrait of Antea*—he displays the characteristics of the Mannerist style: a witty and perverse upsetting of High Renaissance idealism; rejection of contemporary achievements in creating rational space and realistic human forms; and an ambiguity of meaning which may reflect deep religious feelings. He is a link between the elongated, twisting figures of Michelangelo and those of El Greco.

Parnassians. French school of poetry (1860-1880). The Parnassians reacted against the excessive emotionalism and subjectivity of the romantic movement, advocating instead that poetry be calm, detached, and meticulously precise in technique. Their reaction against romanticism and their emphasis on precision and objectivity closely parallels the growth of realism and naturalism in drama and the novel. The Parnassians were first published in the *Revue fantaisiste* (1861). The school's leader was Charles Leconte de Lisle, whose poetry appeared in the *Parnasse Contemporain* (1866) along with the work of Gautier, Banville, Baudelaire, Sully Prudhomme, Verlaine, and Mallarmé.

Parnassus (Parnassos). A mountain in Phocis, Greece. It has two summits, one of which was consecrated to Apollo and the MUSES, the other to Dionysus. Owing to its connection with the Muses (though they were more often associated with Mt. Helicon), Parnassus came to be regarded as the seat of poetry and music. Delphi was located on the southern slope of Parnassus.

Parnell, Charles Stewart (1846-1891). Irish nationalist leader, a Member of Parliament. He ceaselessly agitated for Home Rule in Ireland, winning William Gladstone and the Liberal party over to his side and uniting a number of dissident elements in his own country, until his career was brought to an end by accusations concerning his private life made by his enemies. He was named corespondent in a divorce suit (1890) initiated by one Captain O'Shea against his wife Kitty. Parnell is known for the devoted partisans and violent enemies that his policies and his personality created among the Irish people. He is referred to frequently throughout the works of James Joyce, to whom he was a political hero. See PHOENIX PARK.

Parnell, Thomas (1679-1718). Irish poet and clergyman, a member of the SCRIBLERUS CLUB and a friend of Steele and Addison. He provided the preface, *Essay on the Life, Writings, and Learning of Homer,* to Pope's translation of the *Iliad* (1715-1720). His major works include the meditative poems *A Hymn to Contentment* (1714), *A Night Piece on Death* (1721), and the famous moral apologue *The Hermit* (1721). After Parnell's death, his poems were edited and published by Pope in 1721 with a dedicatory tribute to his poetic style.

parodos. In classical Greek drama, the first choral passage in a tragedy or comedy, recited or sung as the chorus enters the orchestra. It was named for the passageways between the sides of the raised stage and the ends of the tiers of the seats; through these two passageways the chorus entered, and later left in the EXODOS.

parody. In literature, a comic or satirical imitation of a piece of writing exaggerating its style and content in a sort of *reductio ad absurdum,* playing especially upon any weakness in structure or meaning of the original. *A Christmas Garland,* by Max Beerbohm, *Condensed Novels,* by Bret Harte, and *Father William,* by Lewis Carroll, are examples; the last named has become famous in its own right, and almost nobody remembers that it was written as a parody of a poem of the same name by Robert Southey.

Parolles. In Shakespeare's ALL'S WELL THAT ENDS WELL, a cowardly braggart and wastrel whose influence on Bertram is partially responsible for the latter's rejection of Helena. At one point in the play, he is led blindfolded among his friends and, in the belief that he has been captured by the enemy, vilifies them to their faces.

Parr, Catherine. See CATHERINE PARR.

Parrington, Vernon L[ouis] (1871-1929). American teacher, historian, biographer, and critic. In 1927 Parrington published the Pulitzer-Prize-winning volume, *The Colonial Mind.* This work became the opening section of his *Main Currents in American Thought* (1927-1930), left unfinished at his death. Parrington frankly admitted in the preface to his first volume: "The point of view from which I have endeavored to evaluate the materials is liberal rather than conservative, Jeffersonian rather than Federalistic." His analysis is, therefore, more satisfactory when he deals with authors who were exponents of liberalism: Roger Williams, Tom Paine, Emerson, Thoreau, Hamlin Garland, and Jefferson. His history has been attacked for its emphasis on social or economic themes but despite these criticisms, *Main Currents* has been highly regarded by students of American literature.

Parsees or **Parsis.** The modern Zoroastrians who reside mainly in the Bombay section of India. They are descendants of a group of Zoroastrians who fled to India from Persia during the Muslim persecutions of the seventh and eighth centuries. Their name means people of Persia, and is derived from the old Persian province of Parsa. Although influenced by the Hinduism of India, they still maintain the main tenets of the Zoroastrian religion. A sacred fire is kept burning in their churches as a symbol of the Divine light that burns in man's soul. See ZOROASTER.

Parsifal (1882). An opera by Richard WAGNER largely based on the PARZIVAL of Wolfram von Eschenbach. The evil KLINGSOR has enchanted the beautiful Kundry and uses her to lure the knights of the GRAIL into breaking their vows of chastity. In this way he has taken the sacred lance which wounded Christ from its guardian AMFORTAS, and has wounded him with it. But the innocent Parsifal resists Kundry's kiss, and when Klingsor hurls the spear at him, it comes safely to his hand. Parsifal has to wander through many adventures, for he had failed in his ignorance to understand the ceremony of the Grail when he had been permitted to observe it; but eventually he returns to become king of the Grail, freeing Kundry from her spell by baptizing her, and healing Amfortas with a touch of the sacred lance.

Parson's Tale, The. Last of the CANTERBURY TALES of Geoffrey CHAUCER. It is a long prose sermon, replete with pious quotations, on the way of Penitence by which the soul may progress toward God. Contrition is followed by Confession, which involves an awareness of the difference between venial and deadly sins. An exposition of the seven deadly sins is interpolated, with the various branches of each, and the virtues which serve as remedies against them. The discussion of the manner of Confession is then resumed, followed by an explanation of Satisfaction, or the undertaking of penances, which is the last stage of Penitence.

A short paragraph, known as Chaucer's *Retractions,* is attached to the end of this tale. Chaucer prays God's forgiveness for those of his works that are frivolous or sinful, including most of the *Canterbury Tales,* and hopes that his moral works—the translation of Boethius, the homilies, and the lives of saints—will serve as penance.

Partage de Midi. See BREAK OF NOON.

Parthenius (Parthenios, fl. 1st century B.C.). Greek grammarian and poet. The only work of his that has come down to us is *Love's Woes (Peri Erotikon Pathematon),* consisting of 36 love stories. Parthenius taught Vergil Greek. A learned slave, he is said to have been freed in old age.

Parthenon. The great temple on the Athenian Acropolis to Athene *Parthenos* (i.e., the Virgin). Many of its sculptured friezes and fragments of pediments are now in the British Museum among the Elgin Marbles. The Temple was begun by the architect Ictinus about 450 B.C., and the embellishment of it was mainly the work of PHIDIAS, whose colossal chryselephantine statue of Athene was its chief treasure.

Parthenopaeus (Parthenopaios). See SEVEN AGAINST THEBES.

Parthenope. One of the SIRENS of Greek mythology. When she and her sisters drowned themselves in chagrin at Odysseus' escape, her body was washed ashore at the present site of Naples, where the first settlement was named for her.

Partisan, The, a Tale of the Revolution (1835). A novel by William Gilmore SIMMS. The first novel in a trilogy dealing with the American Revolution in South Carolina, *The Partisan* centers on the events between the fall of Charleston and Horatio Gates's defeat at Camden, and on the actions of Major Singleton and Colonel Walton, patriots and aristocratic landholders. Its sequel, *Mellichampe, a Legend of the Santee* (1836), deals with the time between the defeat at Camden and the arrival of Nathaniel Greene, and with the rivalry between Ernest Mellichampe, a patriot, and Barsfield, a Tory, for the hand of Janet Berkeley. The military action in *Katharine Walton, Or, the Rebel of Dorchester* (1851), the third novel of the trilogy, is nearly the same as that in *Mellichampe;* the central characters are Colonel Walton, who appears in *The Partisan,* and his daughter Katharine, who marries Singleton, also the hero of the earlier book. The most famous character in the trilogy is Captain PORGY, sometimes considered the best comic character in American romantic fiction.

Partisan Review. An American literary magazine founded in 1934. At first wholly identified with the radical left wing in politics, it diverged after 1937 from orthodox Marxism and became more and more politically independent and concerned with intellectual, literary, and artistic questions. Edited by Philip Rahv, one of its founders, and William Phillips, its staff has included F. W. Dupee, Dwight Macdonald, and Mary McCarthy. Always concerned with avantgarde writing, the magazine printed parts of James T. Farrell's *Studs Lonigan* before it appeared in book form. Other contributors have included Lionel Trilling, Richard Chase, Robert Gorham Davis, Saul Bellow, T. S. Eliot, Wallace Stevens, and Edmund Wilson. Several collections of material from the magazine have been published: *The Partisan Reader —1934-1944* (1946), *The New Partisan Reader* (1953), *Stories in the Modern Manner* (1953), and *More Stories in the Modern Manner* (1954).

Partridge. In Henry Fielding's TOM JONES, the attendant of Tom Jones, faithful, shrewd, and of childlike simplicity. His excitement in the playhouse when he goes to see Garrick in *Hamlet* is described in a famous chapter. Partridge has been both barber and schoolmaster before attaching himself to Tom Jones.

Partridge, Bellamy (1878–1960). American writer. He is known especially for *Country Lawyer* (1939), a book based on the life of his father. *The Big Family* (1941) was the story of a lawyer's household of eight children. *January Thaw* (1945), which became a Broadway play, told of a city couple living in a renovated Connecticut farmhouse. Among Partridge's many other books are *The Old Oaken Bucket* (1949) and *The Roosevelt Family in America* (1936).

Parvati. See KALI.

Parzival (early 13th century). A verse epic by WOLFRAM VON ESCHENBACH, adapted from the *Perceval* of Chrétien de Troyes. Parzival is the guileless fool, totally innocent of sin and guilt. Leaving his wife Kondwiramur to visit his mother, he chances upon the castle of the Holy GRAIL, where its guardian AMFORTAS has been told that only a guileless fool's sympathy can heal his wound. But Parzival obeys the laws of courtly etiquette rather than those of religion and humanity, and fails to ask the cause of his host's suffering. He thus must leave the castle, and later that of King Arthur. He is determined now to win the Grail despite his disgrace, but cannot until a hermit helps him renew his humility and his pure faith in God. Then his achievements allow him to be received at the Round Table, and he asks the questions which will cure Amfortas, becomes king of the Grail, and is reunited with his wife.

For Wagner's use of this material see PARSIFAL, for the Arthurian version see PERCIVAL.

Pascal, Blaise (1623–1662). French philosopher, scientist, mathematician, and writer. At 12 years of age he discovered Euclid's axioms unaided; at 16 he wrote a treatise on conic sections, and at 18 he invented a calculating machine. He formulated the first laws of atmospheric pressure, equilibrium of liquids, and probability, and invented the hydraulic press. In 1654 a mystical experience caused his conversion to Jansenism, and a year later he retired to Port-Royal to end his days writing philosophical treatises. In the 18 *Lettres Provinciales* (1656–1657), he sided with the Jansenists in a dispute over grace, and his argument in these 18 letters, graceful and ironic in style, routed the Jesuit opposition, quoting them verbatim to their own disadvantage and greatly damaging the Jesuit cause. The PENSÉES, fragments of a projected apology for the Christian religion, appeared in their entirety (1844) only after Pascal's death.

Pascoli, Giovanni (1855–1912). Italian poet. The reputed inspirer of much modern Italian poetry, he is noted for the exactness of his descriptions, his novel rhythmic patterns, and his predilection for modest, simple, rural, and domestic themes. His poems appeared in the collections *Myricae* (*Tamarisks,* 1891); *Poemetti* (1897); *Canti di Castelvecchio* (1903); *Nuovi Poemetti* (1906), showing the influence of French symbolism; *Poemi Conviviali* (1904); *Odi e Inni* (1906); and *Poemi del Risorgimento* (1913).

Pasiphaë. In Greek legend, a daughter of the Sun and wife of Minos, king of Crete. She was the mother of Ariadne, and also (through intercourse with a white bull given by Poseidon to Minos) of the MINOTAUR.

Pasolini, Pier Paolo (1922–). Italian poet, novelist, and motion-picture director. His poetry and such novels as *I Ragazzi di Vita* (1955) and *Una Vita Violenta* (1959) are significant for their use of dialect as a literary medium. The working class and the slums of Rome figure prominently in both his novels and his films. Associated with the postwar group of leftist Italian intellectuals, Pasolini is an outspoken member of the Italian Communist Party.

Pasquier, Etienne (1529–1615). French humanist, poet, and historian. A friend of the poets of the *Pléiade,* he himself wrote a volume of love poems, the *Monophile* (1554). In his *Recherches de la France* (1560–1621), a history of France based on solid documentation, he made astute observations on French medieval and Renaissance poetry that revealed him as the first French literary historian and critic.

Pasquier Chronicles, The (La Chronique des Pasquier; 10 vols., 1933–1945). A novel series by Georges DUHAMEL about a bourgeois Parisian family in the early 1900's.

pasquinade. A lampoon or political squib, having ridicule for its object. See PASQUINO.

Pasquino. The popular Italian title applied to the torso of a classical statue discovered in the Roman ruins (1501) and located in today's Piazza di Pasquino. The figure, it is said, derives its name from an Italian tailor, before whose house it was unearthed. It soon attracted anonymous satirists who found it a convenient place to attach their scurrilous verses on current events; this libelous verse and imitations of it were called *pasquinades,* and the word is occa-

Pasquino dressed in mourning for
Cardinal Caraffa (1511).

sionally applied to present-day political squibs and satiric comments. On April 25, as an annual custom, the statue was dressed to represent a pagan deity or classical figure; this occasion might merit the anonymous contributions of more notable writers such as Aretino, but though collections of *pasquinades* were published, the vogue has long since passed away.

Passage to India, A (1924). An ironic, compassionate novel by E. M. FORSTER about the difficulties of friendship between the races in British-ruled India. Adela Quested's hallucination that the friendly young Indian, Dr. Aziz, has assaulted her in the Marabar Caves gives rise to hysterical racial feeling in the community. In this atmosphere even Mr. Fielding, the liberal English principal of a local college, finds his friendship with Dr. Aziz shattered by a misunderstanding. Adela, who has come to India to visit her fiancé, the City Magistrate Ronny Heaslop, is traveling with his mother, Mrs. Moore. Mrs. Moore is an intuitive, half-mystical woman, and she has an Oriental understanding of Indians and India. Like Adela, she has an unpleasant experience in the ancient Marabar Caves; the echo in the cave seems to tell her of the worthlessness of life, and she has a nervous breakdown. However, she remains an influence for good, persuading Adela to take back her accusation against Dr. Aziz. The Indians come to regard Mrs. Moore as a goddess and almost worship her. Ronny breaks off his engagement with Adela, who he feels has betrayed the English by putting the truth above racial prejudice.

The novel is notable for its strong mystical flavor and its treatment of Indian religions. Mrs. Moore passes from sympathy with poetic Islam, Dr. Aziz's religion, to Hinduism, the religion of destruction and creation which is practiced by the odd Professor Godbole.

Passeur, Stève (1899–   ). French dramatist. He is the author of such brutal plays as *L'Acheteuse* (1930), *Je Vivrai un grand amour* (1935), *Le Témoin* (1936), and *La Traîtresse* (1946).

Passing of the Third Floor Back, The. See Jerome K. JEROME.

Passionate Pilgrim, The (1599). A collection of lyric poems. It was published by William Jaggard, an English printer, with an announcement on the title page that they were "By W. Shakespeare." Only about four of the poems are now considered to be Shakespeare's; others are by Griffin, Barnfield, Marlowe, and lesser-known writers.

Passionate Pilgrim, The, and Other Stories (1875). A collection of short stories by Henry JAMES. The title story was one of a number of pieces stimulated by his trip abroad in 1869–1870. It tells of Clement Searle, who goes to England, long the object of his dreams, to claim a rich estate. The tale is ironic and tragic, but full of James's own passionate love of England.

Passion Play (Ger., *Passionspiel*). A dramatic presentation of the suffering, crucifixion, and resurrection of Christ, usually performed during Holy Week. Similar to the MIRACLE PLAY, such representations developed during the 13th to 16th centuries and are still common. The most famous is that given every 10 years (with a few omissions) by the village of Oberammergau in Bavaria. It was first performed there in 1633, when the villagers vowed to repeat it regularly in gratitude for escape from a plague epidemic.

Passover (*Heb.* Pesach). The most important Jewish feast. It commemorates the events recorded in the Old Testament (Exod. 12) when Jehovah killed the Egyptian first-born while sparing the Israelites. This was the last of the TEN PLAGUES and the one that forced Pharaoh to release the Jews from their bondage.

On the first evening of the Passover the family celebration of Seder takes place; symbolic foods are served, and the story of the Exodus is read by the head of the household.

Pasternak, Boris [Leonidovich] (1890–1960). Russian lyric poet and novelist. Pasternak, the son of a well-known portrait painter, was educated at the universities of Moscow and Marburg, majoring in philosophy. He published his first poetry in 1912. Two collections of his lyrics in 1922 and 1923, *My Sister Life* (*Sestra moya zhizn'*) and *Themes and Variations* (*Temy i variyatzi*) brought him recognition as one of the most important young poets of the early Soviet period. He was connected for a while with the literary group of futurists led by Vladimir Mayakovski, but soon went his own way. For Pasternak, this involved writing a difficult, personal poetry that displeased the Soviet censors, who were gaining more and more control of literature during the 1930's. After publishing two long poems, *1905* (1926) and *Lt. Schmidt* (*Leitenant Shmidt;* 1927), Pasternak turned to translations for almost a decade, rendering some excellent Russian versions of Shakespeare's tragedies, as well as works from the German, French, and Georgian. During these years Pasternak was also at work on a novel. The work was rejected for publication in Russia, but appeared in 1957 in an Italian translation and in English in 1958. This novel, DOCTOR ZHIVAGO created a sensation in the West, principally because of its obvious rejection of Marxism and its general disaffection from the Russian revolutionary experiment. In 1958, Pasternak was awarded the Nobel Prize for literature, but the furor stirred up in the Soviet Union forced him to reject the award. After living for years in peaceful and productive obscurity, he became the object of everyone's attention, hounded by newsmen from the West in search of sensational copy and by literary watchdogs in his own country who demanded his exile from Russia. His example of courage and fortitude in the face of both onslaughts and the deep humanism so forcefully expressed in his work made him the idol of the younger generation of Russian poets and writers. He died after a brief illness in 1960, and his funeral assumed the character of a protest demonstration against the regime that had sought to silence him.

Besides his novel, Pasternak's prose work includes an autobiographical sketch, *Safe Conduct* (*Okhrannaya gramota;* 1931), and several short stories, including the memorable *Aerial Ways* (*Vozdushnye puti;* 1933).

Pasteur, Louis (1822–1895). French chemist. Famous for his discoveries in applied bacteriology, Pasteur's most sensational work concerned the development of a curative treatment for hydrophobia. Popularly, his name is associated with the process called *pasteurization,* which he developed, that causes the destruction of pathogenic organisms in milk and other liquids.

Pastime of Pleasure, The. See Stephen HAWES.

Paston Letters (1422–1509). A series of letters and legal documents written by and to three generations of the Paston family in Norfolk, England. They are a valuable source of information about English history, as well as the business and social customs of the upper middle class of the time.

Pastor, Antonio. Known as **Tony Pastor** (1837–1908). American theater manager. From 1881 to 1908 he managed the Fourteenth Street Theatre, a variety house, also known as Tony Pastor's. He was a pioneer in the development of vaudeville. Among the performers who played in his theaters were Weber and Fields, Nat Goodwin, and Lillian Russell.

pastoral. A term now applied to almost any kind of work depicting a more or less idealized rural life. In a stricter sense, it is a kind of poetry dealing with shepherds and country folk, first written by the Greek poet THEOCRITUS.

As part of the general revival of classical literature, Italian poets of the Renaissance period cultivated the ancient pastoral types and stirred a renewed interest and activity in them throughout Europe. Latin eclogues were written by Dante, Petrarch, and Boccaccio, mostly in imitation of Vergil; Pontano, Spagnoli, and other humanists later continued to write in Latin, but the Italian eclogues of Rota, Boiardo, and Castiglione paved the way for a vernacular treatment of the form. The pastoral romance, pioneered by Boccaccio's *Ameto,* was later revived with great influence by Sannazzaro in his *Arcadia.* There was no classical precedent except the primarily mythological satyr play for a pastoral drama. But the interest in pastoral generally, and in the drama, led to the advent of the pastoral play. Poliziano's *Orfeo* of 1480 had pastoral elements, but the first wholly pastoral play was Beccari's *Sacrificio* (1554). Tasso's AMINTA (1573) and Guarini's IL PASTOR FIDO (1590) were the climax of the trend.

Of less importance but equally in the tradition were the many pastoral lyrics (short poems, especially sonnets, with pastoral settings, characters, or brief incidents) written by such poets as Bernardo Tasso, Tansillo, and Marino. The so-called pastoral idyll, a short narrative poem dealing with an erotic episode from mythology, always included pastoral elements (as in Lorenzo de' Medici's poem *Corinto*); but these are more correctly called mythological poems or Ovidian narratives, as in Boccaccio's *Ninfale Fiesolano* and Marino's *Sampogna.*

Although pastoral poetry, almost by definition, always represents country life in a good light, it may be fairly true to the facts of rural existence. However, according to the conventions of the genre, which were largely established by sophisticated urban poets, the country is the abode of innocence and health, eloquent and musical shepherds, proud and beautiful maidens. Such a vision has provided a convenient setting for motifs of romantic love, either because the innocence of the shepherd's world lent itself to a special kind of erotic titillation—as in Longus' *Daphnis and Chloe* where the lovers, after embracing, are too naïve to know what to do next—or because Arcadia could be so much kinder to ideals of romantic love than the real world—as in most pastoral poetry of the Elizabethan and Spenserian schools where the lady is perfectly beautiful, the lover infinitely devoted, the world always at Spring.

Another use to which the pastoral has been put stemmed from the early identification of the piping shepherd with the poet. A pastoral poem, such as *October* from Spenser's *The Shepherd's Calendar* (1579), could serve as a vehicle for discussion of the poet's craft and place in society. This identification also gave rise to the pastoral elegy, in which the poet, in the role of a shepherd, mourns the death of a gifted colleague. Milton's *Lycidas* (1637), Shelley's *Adonais* (1821), and Matthew Arnold's *Thyrsis* (1861) are notable examples of this form, reserved exclusively for dead poets.

A final, major function of pastoral has been the implicit or explicit criticism of the corruption, sterility, and falseness of life in city or court. This aspect is significant in the work of many classical authors, including Vergil in his *Bucolics* and *Georgics,* and is recurrent throughout English literature, gaining a new emphasis with the Romantic movement.

The pastoral was long ago adapted to prose in romances like Sidney's *Arcadia* (1590) and Mlle de Scudéry's *Cyrus* (1650), and its conventions have been burlesqued and disguised in all sorts of ways without changing their essential significance. For example, one of the several poems by William Carlos Williams called *Pastoral* is set on a city street, the only "sheep" are a flock of city sparrows, the only "shepherd" an old man gathering dog-lime in a gutter,

and his tread
is more majestic than
that of the Episcopal minister
approaching the pulpit
of a Sunday.

In other words, the humble, simple man (the shepherd) still puts the proud, complicated man to shame.

Pastoral Symphony, The (La Symphonie Pastorale, 1919). A tale by André GIDE. A Swiss pastor adopts and educates the blind orphan Gertrude, but tries to keep her from falling in love with his son Jacques, ostensibly from Christian scruples. On the eve of an operation which may restore the girl's sight, frightened that she may love him less than Jacques when she can see, the pastor yields to the desire which he has suppressed under self-deceptive hypocrisy and seduces the girl. Her sight restored, Gertrude understands for the first time the truth about the people around her and the suffering which she has indirectly caused the pastor's wife and children. She commits suicide. Written in the form of the pastor's diary, the tale is remarkable for its restrained and oblique irony and for the sharpness of the author's observations on the hypocrisy which masquerades as Christian pity and duty.

Pastorella. See FAERIE QUEENE, THE.

Pastor Fido, Il (The Faithful Shepherd). A Renaissance pastoral play by Giambattista GUARINI, begun in 1580 and finally published in 1590. Its author called it a tragi-comedy, a new genre that combined a tragic plot with a happy ending, thus precipitating a major literary debate at the time. The plot stems from the lingering anger of Diana wth the people of Arcadia because of a past incident involving the infidelity to Aminta of the nymph Lucrina. To placate the goddess, the oracle says, two people of divine descent must wed and a faithful shepherd must be found whose pity will atone for the past cruelty of Lucrina. The two Arcadians of divine descent are Silvio and Amarilli, but the former prefers hunting to women, and the latter is loved by and loves the shepherd Mirtillo. Amarilli's rival, Corisca, arranges to have her condemned for breaking her vows to Silvio, in hopes of winning her himself. Finally, the revelation of Mirtillo's divine descent enables him to marry Amarilli; and his willingness to die for her, also, satisfies the goddess' other demand. At the same time, Silvio consents to marry Dolinda, who has made him fall in love at last, and Corisca is pardoned.

Past Recaptured, The. See REMEMBRANCE OF THINGS PAST.

Patchen, Kenneth (1911–1972). American poet and novelist. He is noted for often surrealistic poems, which combine humor and fantasy; sometimes sentimental, they are always distinguished by striking imagery. Often concerned with the injustices and tragedies of 20th-century American life, Patchen has frequently illustrated his poems with his own abstract paintings. His books of poetry include *Before the Brave* (1936), *Dark Kingdom* (1942), *Panels for the Walls of Heaven* (1947), *Selected Poems* (1947), *Red Wine and Yellow Hair* (1949), and *Because It Is* (1960). His prose includes *The Journal of Albion Moonlight* (1941) and *Memoirs of a Shy Pornographer* (1949).

Patelin. See PATHELIN, LA FARCE DE MAISTRE PIERRE.

Pater, Walter [Horatio] (1839–1894). English essayist and critic. A leader in the 19th-century revival of interest in Renaissance art and humanism, he was a formulator of the doctrine that art and aesthetics are in themselves one of the ends of life. His works, noted for their stylistic purity and precision, include *Studies in the History of the Renaissance* (1873); the philosophic novel MARIUS THE EPICUREAN, generally considered his masterpiece; *Plato and Platonism* (1893); the partly autobiographical *The Child in the House* (1894); *Greek Studies* (1895); and the five posthumously published chapters of *Gaston de Latour* (1896), a novel left unfinished at his death. See ART FOR ART'S SAKE; RHYMER'S CLUB.

paternoster (*Lat.*, "Our Father"). The Lord's Prayer; from the first two words in the Latin version. Every tenth bead of a rosary is so called, because at that bead the Lord's Prayer is repeated; the name is also given to a certain kind of fishing tackle, in which hooks and weights to sink them are fixed alternately on the line, somewhat in rosary fashion.

a paternoster-while. Quite a short time; the time it takes to say a paternoster.

Paterson (Books I-V; 1946, 1948, 1950, 1951, 1958). A long poem by William Carlos WILLIAMS. Set in Paterson, N.J., the poem is a statement on contemporary civilization. Williams uses one dominant metaphor throughout: the city is the human mind beside the river of time; the language of contemporary events (the waterfall) gives the only kind of meaning possible in the flux of time. The poem is composed of lyrics, narrative episodes, prose interludes, bits of letters, etc., to comprise an ecstatic statement on human life.

Pathelin, La Farce de maistre Pierre (c. 1470). An anonymous medieval French FARCE famous for the artfully cheating lawyer Pathelin (or Patelin). Having himself cheated the woolen-draper Joceaume, he comes to court to defend the shepherd Aignelet, charged with stealing Joceaume's sheep. Joceaume gets so confused in making his complaints that the judge keeps demanding, "revenons à ces moutons" (let us come back to these sheep), a line later quoted by Rabelais and since become a proverbial plea to get back to the subject. The play was adapted as *L'Avocat Pathelin* (1706) by Jean Palaprat (1650–1721) and L'Abbé David Augustin de Brueys (1640–1723).

pathetic fallacy. A phrase invented by John RUSKIN to designate the illusion that external objects seem actuated by human feelings, particularly when one is under great emotional strain. Thus when a poet is tormented by grief, he is apt to ascribe to inanimate nature either sympathy or heartless cruelty. Tennyson's *In Memoriam*, Shelley's *Adonais*, and other elegies are especially noteworthy for eloquent effects gained by the use of the pathetic fallacy.

Pathfinder, The, or The Inland Sea (1840). A novel by James Fenimore COOPER, in the LEATHERSTOCKING series. The story takes place in the Lake Ontario region in 1760, during the French and Indian Wars. Pathfinder, or Natty BUMPPO, relinquishes his claim to Mabel Dunham's hand, when he discovers that she loves Jasper Western. Jasper, suspected of being a traitor, is finally vindicated. The best episode in the book involves Dew-of-June, Cooper's most successful Indian heroine, and the siege of the blockhouse.

Paths of Glory. See Humphrey COBB.

Patience or Bunthorne's Bride (1881). A comic opera by GILBERT AND SULLIVAN. The hero, Bunthorne (a caricature of Oscar Wilde) is pursued by a whole troop of lovesick ladies.

Patience Worth. A mysterious spirit who according to her own account, which was dictated on the ouija board in 1913 to Mrs. John H. Curran of St. Louis, lived in 1649 "across the sea." She is the reputed author of two or three works of fiction, especially one, published under the title *Patience Worth*, which received wide publicity.

Patmore, Coventry [Kersey Dighton] (1823–1896). English poet. As a young man, he was an associate of the Pre-Raphaelites and contributed to *The Germ*. His best-known works are *Angel in the House*, a long poetic celebration of married love, containing *The Betrothal* (1854), *The Espousals* (1856), *Faithful Forever* (1860), and *The Victories of Love* (1862); *The Unknown Eros* (1877); and several fine sonnets. After the death of his first wife in 1864, he was converted to Roman Catholicism. *Rod, Root, and Flower* (1895) is a volume of prose meditations, chiefly on religious subjects.

Patmos. The Greek island of the Sporades in the Aegean Sea (now called *Patmo* or *Patino*). On this island an unknown exile, a prisoner of Rome, wrote *the Revelation of St. John the Divine.* The name is used figuratively for a place of banishment or solitude.

Paton, Alan (1903–   ). South African novelist and humanitarian worker. One of the founders of the Liberal Association of South Africa, he wrote CRY, THE BELOVED COUNTRY and *Too Late the Phalarope* (1953), novels about problems of race relations.

patrician. Properly speaking, one of the *patres* (fathers) or senators of Rome, and their descendants. As they held for many years all the honors of the state, the word came to signify the magnates or nobility of a nation, the aristocrats.

Patrician, The (1911). A novel by John GALSWORTHY. The patrician is Eustace Caradoc, son of an aristocratic family and conservative member of Parliament. He comes under the influence of Mr. Courtier, leader of the liberal opposition, who believes in giving the people more democratic freedoms. Caradoc also has an affair with a woman who is separated from her husband. Eventually his family persuades him to return to his former views.

Patrick, St. (c. 373–464). The apostle and patron saint of Ireland. He was born at what is now Dumbarton; his father was Calpurnius, a deacon and Roman official. As a boy he was captured in a Pictish raid and sold as a slave in Ireland. He escaped to Gaul about 395, where he studied under St. Martin at Tours before returning to Britain. There he had a supernatural call to preach to the heathen of Ireland, so he was consecrated and in 432 landed at Wicklow. He at first met with strong opposition, but, going north, he converted first the chiefs and people of Ulster, and later those of the rest of Ireland. He founded many churches, including the cathedral and monastery of Armagh, where he held two synods. He is said to have died at Armagh and to have been buried either at Down or Saul. One tradition gives

Glastonbury as the place of his death and burial; Downpatrick Cathedral claims his grave.

St. Patrick left his name to numerous places in Great Britain and Ireland, and many legends exist of his miraculous powers: healing the blind, raising the dead. Perhaps the best known tradition is that he cleared Ireland of its vermin. In commemoration of this, St. Patrick is usually represented banishing the serpents. He is shown with a shamrock leaf, in allusion to the tradition that when explaining the Trinity to the heathen priests on the hill of Tara he used this as a symbol.

Patrick, John (1905–   ). American playwright. He won a Pulitzer Prize for his adaptation of Vern Schneider's novel, *The Teahouse of the August Moon* (1953). Patrick has written several other plays, including *The Hasty Heart* (1945), the story of a convalescent soldier based on the author's experiences as an ambulance driver in World War II. He has also written scenarios for many films.

Patrick's Purgatory, St. A cave in a small island in Lough Derg (a lake near Pettigoe in Donegal). In the middle Ages it was a favorite resort of pilgrims who believed that it was the entrance to an earthly Purgatory. The legend is that Christ Himself revealed it to St. Patrick and told him that whoever would spend a day and a night therein would witness the torments of Hell and the joys of Heaven. Henry of Saltrey tells how Sir Owain visited it, and Fortunatus, of the old legend, was also supposed to be one of the adventurers. It was blocked up by order of the Pope on St. Patrick's Day, 1497, but the interest in it long remained, and the Spanish dramatist Calderón wrote a play on the subject, *El Purgatorio de San Patricio.* See MARIE DE FRANCE.

Patroclus (Patroklos). In Homer's ILIAD, a loyal friend of Achilles. Achilles, angry at Agamemnon, refused to fight with the Greeks but, seeing them hard pressed, Patroclus begged to be allowed to join them, and Achilles finally gave him his own armor. Leading the Myrmidons into the battle, Patroclus was slain by Hector. Grief and fury over Patroclus' death caused Achilles to re-enter the fighting.

patroons. The name given to a class of large landholders in New Netherland, those who within a four-year period had established a settlement of fifty persons. The patroons held their feudal privileges until the Anti-Rent War of the 1840's.

Pattee, Fred Lewis (1863–1950). American literary historian and teacher. He viewed American literature as popular expression rather than as the production of an elite. Among his works are *A History of American Literature* (1896), *The Development of the American Short Story* (1923), *The New American Literature* (1930), and *The Feminine Fifties* (1940). *Penn State Yankee: The Autobiography of Fred Lewis Pattee* (1953) was published posthumously.

Paul, St. The great apostle and missionary of Christianity, author of the principal *Epistles* of the New Testament. As Saul of Tarsus he was originally one of the most bitter persecutors of the early Christians, but he was converted by a vision on the road to Damascus. His missionary travels, described in the *Acts of the Apostles,* took him "in journeyings often, in peril of rivers, in peril of robbers . . . in perils in the sea, in perils among false brethren." He was

finally beheaded at Rome. He is patron saint of preachers and tentmakers (see *Acts* 18:3). Originally called Saul, his name, according to tradition, was changed in honor of Sergius Paulus, whom he converted (*Acts* 13:6–12).

His symbols are a sword and open book, the former the instrument of his martyrdom, and the latter indicative of the new law propagated by him as the apostle of the Gentiles. He is represented of short stature, with bald head and gray, bushy beard; legend relates that when he was beheaded at Rome (A.D. 66), after having converted one of Nero's favorite concubines, milk instead of blood flowed from his veins. He is commemorated on June 30.

Paul, Elliot [Harold] (1891–1958). American writer and journalist. For a number of years an expatriate in France and Spain, he was one of the founders and editors of the avant-garde periodical TRANSITION. His early novels, *Indelible* (1922), *Impromptu* (1923), and *Imperturbe* (1924), were hailed by a small circle of admirers. Perhaps his best book, *The Life and Death of a Spanish Town* (1937), is based on personal observation and tells the story of a Spanish town destroyed by Franco during the civil war. The nostalgic THE LAST TIME I SAW PARIS was his most popular work. In 1939, Paul published a burlesque detective novel, *The Mysterious Mickey Finn,* and its success seems to have led him to concentrate for a time on detective fiction. Among his crime novels were *Hugger-Mugger in the Louvre* (1940) and *Mayhem in B-Flat* (1940).

Paulding, James Kirke (1778–1860). American novelist, dramatist, and historian. Early in his life, Paulding became friendly with Washington Irving and his brother William; they formed the nucleus of a literary group whose most important production was SALMAGUNDI; OR THE WHIM-WHAMS AND OPINIONS OF LAUNCELOT LANGSTAFF, ESQ., AND OTHERS. Paulding's early writings were satirical and violently anti-British. They include a second series of *Salmagundi Papers* (1819–1820), THE DIVERTING HISTORY OF JOHN BULL AND BROTHER JONATHAN, and a sequel, *The History of Uncle Sam and His Boys* (1835). He also wrote a number of long poems and serious histories. Among his novels are KÖNIGS-MARKE, THE LONG FINNE, and THE DUTCHMAN'S FIRESIDE.

Paulding served as naval commissioner and secretary of the navy (1838–1841).

Paul et Virginie (1787). An idyllic, highly successful romance by BERNARDIN DE SAINT-PIERRE. Paul and Virginia, two fatherless children, are brought up on the Isle of France (now Mauritius) by their mothers in virtuous poverty and ignorance, far from corrupt civilization. They fall in love during their adolescence. When a long-forgotten aunt summons Virginia by letter to Paris, she is loath to leave Paul. She does go, however, remaining away from the island two years. Unable to adjust either to her aunt or to civilization, Virginia returns, but a storm sinks her ship, and she dies within sight of Paul, who himself dies of grief later. The nostalgic evocation of a lost paradise and the sumptuous descriptions of nature and landscapes have assured this work enduring success.

Paulina. In Shakespeare's WINTER'S TALE, the generous, strong-minded wife of ANTIGONUS and the loyal friend of Queen Hermione. At the end of the play, Antigonus having been eaten by a bear, she marries Camillo.

Paul Revere's Ride (1861). A narrative poem by Henry Wadsworth LONGFELLOW telling of the midnight ride of the Revolutionary patriot Paul Revere, to spread the news of an expected British raid.

Paul's Case. See YOUTH AND THE BRIGHT MEDUSA.

Paumanok. The Indian name for Long Island. It is used by Walt Whitman in *Leaves of Grass*.

Pausanias (2nd century A.D.). Greek traveler and geographer. His accounts of the monuments of ancient Greece before their destruction are of extreme value in research.

Paustovski, Konstantin Georgiyevich (1892–1968). Russian short story writer and journalist. After his war service, Paustovski worked in Odessa, where he became a friend of Isaak Babel. Paustovski was encouraged in his literary career by Maksim Gorki, for whom he worked on a journal from 1929 to 1937. He is the author of many nature stories, tales for children, and a three-volume autobiography. He has been consistently outspoken in his defense of liberalism in Soviet literary policy, and was one of the chief defenders in 1956 of Vladimir Dudintzev, who was under attack for his novel, *Not by Bread Alone*.

pauvre Jacques (Fr., "poor Jacques"). The absent sweetheart of a lovelorn maiden. Marie Antoinette sent to Switzerland for a lass to attend the dairy of her "Swiss village" in miniature, which she arranged in the Little Trianon (Paris). The lass was heard sighing for *pauvre Jacques*, and her longing made a capital sentimental amusement for the court idlers. The swain was sent for, and the marriage consummated.

Pavese, Cesare (1908–1950). Italian novelist and translator. In collaboration with Elio Vittorini, he translated and brought to the attention of the Italian public the works of many important modern American writers. His own novels and short stories show a mingling of realism, poetic feeling, and social sympathy. Among the more outstanding of his works are *La Spiaggia* (1942), *Feria d'Agosto* (1946), *Il Compagno* (1947), *La Bella Estate* (1949), *The Moon and the Bonfires* (*La Luna e I Falò;* 1950), *Il Mestiere de Vivere* (1952), *Notte di Festa* (1953), and *Fuoco Grande* (1959).

Pavia. A city in northwestern Italy. It was the site of a famous battle (1525) between the French under Francis I and an imperial army composed of Spanish, German, and Italian troops. The French were overwhelmingly defeated, and Francis himself was taken prisoner. He was freed after signing the short-lived treaty of Madrid (1526) with Charles V, by which France yielded Burgundy to Charles and renounced its suzerainty over Flanders and Artois.

Pavlova, Anna (1885–1931). A Russian ballerina of immense popularity. She was particularly famous for her ballet *The Dying Swan,* choreographed by Michel Fokine.

Payn, James (1830–1898). English novelist. He was a voluminous writer of popular novels, hardly read today, such as *Lost Sir Massingberd* (1864) and *A Woman's Vengeance* (1872). He contributed to *Household Words,* edited by his friend Charles Dickens, and was editor of the *Cornhill Magazine* from 1883 to 1896.

Payne, John (1842–1916). English poet and translator. Principally known for his version of the ARABIAN NIGHTS (nine vols., 1882–1884).

Payne, John Howard (1791–1852). American actor, playwright, and poet. At 15, Payne had already written a drama called *Julia, or, The Wanderer* (1806). Member of an impoverished family, he was sent to college on funds raised by his father's friends; in less than a year, Payne returned to the New York theater. He created a sensation in his acting roles, and traveled to England, where he wrote and acted in plays. On the verge of bankruptcy, he wrote *Brutus, or, The Fall of Tarquin* (1818); later, in debtors' prison, he wrote *Therese, Orphan of Geneva* (1821), making enough money to gain his freedom. Payne's greatest triumph was his *Clari, The Maid of Milan* (1823). This play included the song *Home, Sweet Home,* with music by Sir Henry Bishop. It became highly popular, but Payne, having sold the play outright, was not able to collect royalties. He continued to write, but could never avoid poverty. In England, he courted Mary Shelley, widow of the poet, but his suit was unsuccessful. In America, theatrical benefit performances raised almost $10,000 for him. Daniel Webster and other friends obtained the post of consul in Tunis for Payne; he held this job off and on until his death. A member of the Knickerbocker School, Payne collaborated with his friend, Washington Irving, on a comedy called *Charles II* (pub. 1917).

P.C. The Roman *Patres conscripti.* See CONSCRIPT FATHERS.

Peace, The (Eirene, 421 B.C.). A comedy by ARISTOPHANES. Trygaeus, a farmer, flies up to heaven on a huge dung beetle to find out from Zeus what has happened to the goddess Peace, who has been so long away from Greece. He finds that War has hidden her in a pit under a heap of stones. Farmers and workingmen from every part of Greece help Trygaeus to rescue the goddess. The play ends with a great feast, demonstrating the joys of peace. It was written when Athens and Sparta had been long at war.

Peachum. See BEGGAR'S OPERA, THE; THREEPENNY OPERA, THE.

Peacock, Thomas Love (1785–1866). English novelist and poet. Satirical and critical in subject and often extravagant in style, his novels include HEADLONG HALL, *Melincourt* (1817), NIGHTMARE ABBEY, CROTCHET CASTLE, and GRYLL GRANGE. Peacock caricatured contemporary figures by the device of bringing a group of thinly disguised eccentrics together and letting their conversation, often ridiculous, fill the book.

Peacock Throne. A throne built (1628 to 1635) at Delhi, India, for the Indian ruler, Shah Jehan. He also built the Taj Mahal. Each of its twelve pillars was decorated with two peacocks glittering with gems. A century later (1739), Nadir Shah took it to Persia.

Peake, Mervyn (1911–1968). English poet, novelist, and painter. He is the author of *Titus Groane* (1946) and its sequel *Gormenghast* (1951), both grotesque, fantastic novels.

Peale, Charles Wilson (1741-1827). American portrait and genre painter. He was instrumental in the founding of the Pennsylvania Academy of Fine Arts. Two of his sons also achieved distinction: Raphaelle Peale (1774–1825), a painter of still life and still-life deceptions, and Rembrandt Peale (1778–1860), a portrait artist.

Pearl. The illegitimate child of Arthur Dimmesdale and Hester Prynne in Hawthorne's THE SCARLET LETTER.

Pearl, The (late 14th century). A poem by the so-called PEARL POET. It combines the alliterative technique of Old English poetry with a complex metrical structure. There are 101 stanzas of 12 octosyllabic lines, arranged in groups of five stanzas with interlocking rhymes and refrains. The poet loses a beautiful white pearl, probably a symbol both of his two-year-old daughter and of theological purity or grace. Falling asleep at the scene of his loss, he dreams he has entered a shining world where he recognizes his loved one in the matured and pearl-decked maiden who speaks to him from across a river. She assuages his grief, describing her joyful state as one of the mystical brides of Christ. Finally the poet is permitted a glimpse of her abode, the New Jerusalem, and describes it in a vivid adaptation of the Scriptural Apocalypse. He tries to cross the river, but instead awakens to find himself filled with a new spiritual strength.

Pearl, The (1947). A novelette by John STEINBECK. Kino, an Indian pearl-fisher in the Gulf of California, and his wife, Juana, have a baby who is bitten by a scorpion. Kino finds a large pearl to pay the doctor, but it brings only tragedy.

Pearl of Orr's Island, The (1862). A novel by Harriet Beecher STOWE. Mara Lincoln, the "pearl" of the title, is brought up in the Maine village of Orr's Island by her grandparents. They later adopt Moses, a Spanish boy with whom Mara falls in love. After many complications, she dies, and he marries her friend Sally.

Pearl Poet, The (late 14th century). Supposed author of a manuscript containing four alliterative poems in a West Midland dialect of Middle English: THE PEARL, *Purity* (or *Cleanness*), *Patience,* and SIR GAWAIN AND THE GREEN KNIGHT, although it is not certain that *Sir Gawain* was actually composed by the same author as the first three. *Purity* and *Patience* are didactic poems drawing heavily on Biblical stories; there are indications that the Pearl Poet was also familiar with the French and Italian literature of the time.

Pearse, Padraic (1879–1916). Irish poet and patriot. During the Easter Week rebellion (1916) he was commander-in-chief of the Irish republican forces and president of the provisional government; he was shot by a British firing squad. His *Collected Works* appeared in 1918. The poets Thomas MacDonagh and Joseph Plunkett were among those who died with him.

Peary, Robert Edwin (1856–1920). American naval officer and arctic explorer. Peary reached the North Pole on April 6, 1909. The claim of Dr. Frederick Cook that he had reached the Pole on April 21, 1908, was later discredited, though the controversy has never been entirely stilled. Peary's wife, Josephine Diebitsch Peary, who accompanied him on earlier ex-

peditions, wrote *The Snow Baby* (1901), an account of her daughter, who was born farther north than any other white child.

Peasant Bard. An epithet applied to Robert Burns (1759–1796).

Peasants (Muzhiki; 1897). A long story by Anton CHEKHOV. Its somber picture of peasant life in Russia stirred up a heated debate, generally divided according to political convictions, about the accuracy of Chekhov's portrayal.

Peasants' Revolt, The. See TYLER'S REBELLION.

Pease-Blossom. In Shakespeare's MIDSUMMER NIGHT'S DREAM, one of four fairies of Titania who serve as personal attendants to Bottom. The others are Cobweb, Moth, and Mustardseed.

Peau de chagrin, La (The Wild Ass's Skin, 1830). A novel, part of LA COMÉDIE HUMAINE, by Honoré de BALZAC. The hero, Raphael, receives a piece of magic skin that will insure the gratification of his every desire. The skin, however, and the life of its owner, grow smaller with each wish. After a brief hedonistic fling, Raphael seeks frantically for some way to stretch the skin. His attempts fail, and while yet a young man he dies.

Pêcheur d'Islande (An Iceland Fisherman, 1866). A novel by Pierre LOTI. Each year the fishermen who live on the coast of Brittany make a voyage to the waters off the shores of Iceland for the long fishing season. Loti describes the loneliness of this existence and the bitter struggle between the men and the sea from which they draw their livelihood. The element of romantic adventure which characterizes Loti's popular, earlier work is not absent, however, for the hero becomes involved in the war between France and China, and dies in Singapore before reaching home.

Pechorin. See HERO OF OUR TIME, A.

Peck, George Wilbur (1840–1916). American newspaperman and humorist. His widely read, highly popular stories about Peck's Bad Boy first appeared in the Milwaukee *Sun,* which Peck owned and edited (1878–1890). They were subsequently collected in such volumes as *Peck's Bad Boy and His Pa* (1883). Though the stories are no longer read, their title phrase remains as a popular byword.

Peck, Harry Thurston (1856–1914). American classical scholar, teacher, editor, and writer. Peck, a professor of Latin at Columbia University, edited *The Bookman,* a literary journal, from 1895 to 1902. The author of many books ranging from biography to poetry, he edited *Harper's Dictionary of Classical Literature and Antiquities* (1897), and the *New International Encyclopedia* (1892, 1900–1903). Peck committed suicide as the result of personal scandal.

Pecksniff. In Charles Dickens' MARTIN CHUZZLEWIT, a canting hypocrite who is eventually exposed and denounced by Chuzzlewit, Sr., for trying to force Mary Graham to marry him. His two daughters are Charity and Mercy. The first is a thin shrew eventually jilted by a young man who really loves her sister. Mercy is pretty and true-hearted, and is made miserable in her marriage to Jonas Chuzzlewit.

Pecorone, Il. See Ser Giovanni FIORENTINO.

Peder Victorious. See GIANTS IN THE EARTH.

Pedro II. Known as **Dom Pedro** (1825–1891). Emperor of Brazil (1831–1889). The son of Pedro I, who abdicated in 1831, Pedro ruled with moderation and justice despite his extensive powers. He brought the country peace and stability, though the early part of his reign was marked by civil war and difficulties with foreign nations. A man of considerable intellectual attainments, Pedro encouraged education and scholarship in Brazil. In his travels to Europe and the U.S., he avoided official circles and sought out writers and scientists such as Pasteur, Victor Hugo, Longfellow, and Whittier. Gradually, however, the monarchy lost the support of its principal allies; the army and the clergy were dissatisfied, and the abolition of slavery in 1888 alienated the powerful landowning class. In 1889, Pedro was forced to abdicate and was exiled to France, where he died.

Pedro, Don. The genial prince of Arragon in Shakespeare's MUCH ADO ABOUT NOTHING. He helps Claudio woo Hero and conspires with Leonato to bring together the warring Beatrice and Benedick.

Peel, Sir Robert (1788–1850). English statesman. He was prime minister from 1834 to 1835 and again in 1841. He reorganized the Bank of England, initiated reforms in Ireland, supported free trade and the emancipation of the Jews. As chief secretary for Ireland (1812–1818), he instituted the Irish constabulary, from which came the nickname "peelers," a term later extended to designate London police as well. See BOBBY.

Peele, George (1558?–1597?). English playwright and poet. The holder of an M.A. degree from Oxford, a UNIVERSITY WIT notorious for his dissipated life, Peele wrote numerous works including plays, pageants, lyrics for use in his plays, and verse celebrating various occasions of honor in the lives of noble patrons. The influence of John LYLY can be seen in his plays, notably *The Arraignment of Paris* (performed c. 1581, printed anonymously 1584), *The Old Wives' Tale* (1595), and *The Love of King David and Fair Bethsabe* (written c. 1588, performed 1599). *The Merrie Conceited Jests of George Peele* (printed 1607) is supposedly an account of his reckless life, but the incidents reported are largely exaggerated or entirely apocryphal. Among his poems are *Polyhymnia* (1590) and *The Praise of Chastity* (printed in *The Phoenix Nest*, 1593).

peeler. See Sir Robert PEEL.

Peeperkorn, Pieter. In Thomas Mann's novel THE MAGIC MOUNTAIN, a rich Dutch coffee planter who comes to Haus Berghof with Clavdia CHAUCHAT. He is the novel's single representative of a robust and active, rather than lax and decadent, life of the senses. He has a huge appetite and speaks in broken, incoherent sentences, which suggest that his basic energy defies all discipline. Under his influence, Hans CASTORP begins to think of leaving the sanatorium and leading a normal life. But Peeperkorn does not last long; deeply aware that he is past his physical prime, he soon commits suicide by poison.

Peeping Tom of Coventry. See GODIVA, LADY.

Peer Gynt (1867). A verse drama by Henrik IBSEN. A satiric fantasy, the play takes as its hero the legendary Peer Gynt of Norse folklore. The boastful, capricious, irresponsible Peer goes through life thinking quite well of himself, though there is no more reality to his personality than there is to an onion when one has peeled all the layers away. Peer has many amazing adventures in many lands, alternately ships missionaries and idols to China, makes and loses money, saves his own life in a shipwreck by letting another drown, and finally comes up before the Button Molder, who tries to melt him in his ladle. Peer is horrified at the idea of losing his precious identity, though he has no true self. However, he is saved by Solveig, who has always loved him, and in whose mind he has existed as a real personality.

Peers, The Twelve. See PALADINS.

Pegasus (Pegasos). In classic myth, the winged horse of the Muses. He was born of the sea foam and the blood of the slaughtered MEDUSA. He was caught by BELLEROPHON, who mounted him and destroyed the Chimaera. But when Bellerophon attempted to ascend to heaven, he was thrown from the horse, and Pegasus mounted alone to the skies to become the constellation of the same name. According to a highly embroidered version by Ovid, when the Muses contended with the daughters of Pieros, Mount Helicon rose heavenward with delight; but Pegasus gave it a kick, stopped its ascent, and brought out of the mountain the soul-inspiring waters of the fountain HIPPOCRENE.

Peggotty, Clara. In Dickens' DAVID COPPERFIELD, the faithful nurse of David, who, with the other members of her family, is a great aid and comfort to him in his early childhood.

Dan'el Peggotty. Clara's brother. Dan'el is a Yarmouth fisherman, living with his nephew Ham Peggotty and his brother-in-law's child Little Em'ly, in an odd, ship-like house where David loves to visit as a child. He is a bachelor and Mrs. Gummidge keeps house for him.

Em'ly Peggotty. Daughter of Dan'el's brother-in-law, better known as Little Em'ly. She is engaged to Ham, but being fascinated by David's old schoolmate STEERFORTH, is seduced by him and runs off with him. She is later reclaimed and emigrates to Australia with Dan'el and Mrs. Gummidge.

Ham Peggotty. Dan'el's nephew. Ham loves Little Em'ly, but loses her to Steerforth. A simple, honest, warm-hearted fisherman, he is drowned attempting to rescue Steerforth from the sea.

Péguy, Charles [Pierre] (1873–1914). French poet, essayist. Of peasant stock, he became an ardent polemicist for the causes of Catholicism, nationalism, and socialism. In *Marcel* (1898) he projected the idea of the perfect socialist state based on the harmonious union of Christianity and France. He founded the bimonthly review *Cahiers de la quinzaine* (1900–1914), which introduced a number of important new authors in addition to publishing Péguy's polemics on contemporary affairs, such as his defense of Dreyfus. He absorbed in his native Orleans the story of Joan of Arc, who became for him the symbol of the unity of the two mystiques, Catholicism and France, which he exalted in his poems *Jeanne d'Arc* (1897) and *Le Mystère de la charité de Jeanne d'Arc* (1909). Other poems include *Le Porche du mystère de la deuxième vertu* (1911), *The Mystery of the Holy Innocents* (1912), and *Eve* (1913). English collections of his work are *Basic Verities: Prose and Poetry* (1943), *Men and Saints* (1944), and *God Speaks: Religious Poetry* (1945).

Peg Woffington (1853). A novel by Charles READE, first brought out as a drama entitled *Masks and Faces* (1852). Its heroine is the famous Irish actress Margaret Woffington (1714?–1760). In both play and novel, proof of her art is given in two extraordinary impersonations: she first imitates a famous tragic actress of the day so skillfully that she deceives an entire dramatic company, and she later substitutes her own face for the face of her portrait, which has been painted by James Triplet and is being inspected by a group of critics. The plot centers on the relations of Peg and Ernest Vane, a married man who falls in love with her during a sojourn in town. When she learns that he is already married and has no serious intentions, she determines on revenge but, won over by the naïveté and charm of Mrs. Vane, renounces her purpose.

Peirce, Charles Sanders (1839–1914). American logician, scientist, and philosopher. His early work in astronomy, gravity, and geodetics was original and competent, but did not attract much notice. Peirce studied under Louis Agassiz, lectured on the philosophy of science at Harvard, and published a number of papers on logic. In an article written for *Popular Science Monthly*, and called *How to Make Our Ideas Clear* (1878), he published the first full statement of PRAGMATISM. William JAMES, to whom pragmatism owes its fame as a movement, first used the term in 1898, crediting Peirce as the originator. Peirce's pragmatism, however, differs from James's; it is more like the idealism of Josiah ROYCE, and includes a belief in universals and an Absolute, which James and his followers rejected. The majority of Peirce's papers on logic, metaphysics, mathematics, religion, psychology, and many other subjects, were published posthumously. Charles Hartshorne and Paul Weiss edited the *Collected Papers of Charles Sanders Peirce* (6 v., 1931–1935). Never given much recognition, outside of a small professional group, during his lifetime, Peirce has since come to be regarded as one of the most brilliant men of his time, and an outstanding American philosopher.

Peleus. In Greek mythology, a son of Aeacus, king of Aegina. With his brother Telamon, he killed their half-brother Phocus to prevent his inheriting the kingdom. Banished, he became ruler of a part of Phthia, but accidentally killed his co-ruler Eurytion as they hunted the CALYDONIAN BOAR. Fleeing to Iolcus, he rejected the advances of Acastus' wife Cretheis and she accused him of trying to violate her, but Chiron helped him escape Acastus' treacherous revenge. Hera arranged for him to marry THETIS and she bore him Achilles. As she was placing the child in the fire to immortalize him, Peleus cried out in horror and she deserted both in anger. Later Peleus sailed with the ARGONAUTS. He outlived his son and his grandson Neoptolemus. As an old man he appears in Euripides' tragedy ANDROMACHE, defending the heroine from persecution.

Pelias. In Greek mythology, a son of Poseidon. He seized the throne of Iolcus from his half-brother Aeson. When Aeson's son Jason claimed the throne, Pelias sent him with the ARGONAUTS to recover the GOLDEN FLEECE. Jason returned with MEDEA, who tricked Pelias' daughters into killing Pelias.

pelican. In Christian art, a symbol of charity. It is also an emblem of Jesus Christ, by "whose blood we are healed." St. Jerome gives the story of the pelican restoring its young ones destroyed by serpents, and his salvation by the blood of Christ. The old popular fallacy that pelicans fed their young with their blood arose from the fact that when the parent bird is about to feed its brood, it macerates small fish in the large bag against its breast, transfers the macerated food to the mouths of the young.

The medieval Bestiary explains that the pelican is very fond of its brood, but when the young ones begin to grow they rebel against the male bird and provoke his anger, so that he kills them; the mother returns to the nest in three days, sits on the dead birds, pours her blood over them and revives them, and they feed upon the blood.

the Pelican State. Louisiana, which has a pelican in its device.

Pelion and Ossa. Mountains in Thessaly. In Greek mythology, the giant sons of Aloeus or Poseidon, Otus and Ephialtes, planned to pile Ossa on Mount Olympus, and Pelion on Ossa in order to carry on their somewhat obscure quarrel with the gods. Zeus, however, struck them down while they were still in their downy-cheeked youth. This story is told by Homer; later writers often confused them with the GIANTS and the TITANS, who also warred on heaven. "Heaping Pelion upon Ossa" has come to mean adding difficulty to difficulty.

Pelléas et Mélisande (1892). A drama by Maurice MAETERLINCK. Mélisande is found wandering wretchedly about in the forest by Golaud, a grandson of King Arkel, who marries her and takes her to court, although she will disclose nothing about herself. Her sadness and charm win her first the sympathy and then the love of Pelléas, Golaud's brother. While talking with Pelléas she loses her wedding ring, and at that same moment Golaud meets with an accident, but she nurses him back to health. Golaud's little son Yniold, the child of a former marriage, unwittingly confirms his father's growing suspicions. Finally Pelléas and Mélisande decide to part and meet for a last interview, but the jealous Golaud kills Pelléas, and after the birth of her child, Mélisande dies. Claude Debussy made this play into a fine opera in 1902.

Pelles, King. In Malory's *Morte d'Arthur* (c. 1469), the father of ELAINE, grandfather of Sir Galahad and related to Joseph of Arimathea.

Pellico, Silvio (1789–1854). Italian writer and patriot. The editor of IL CONCILIATORE, he was arrested as a suspected member of the CARBONARI in 1820, and was shuttled between prisons in Milan and Venice and the notorious Spielberg dungeon (Moravia) until his release in 1830. He narrated his prison experiences in *Le Mie Prigioni* (1832) wherein he tells how adversity confirmed his previously wavering Christian faith. A spirit of Christian forgiveness pervades the book so that Cesare Balbo observed that it was more damaging to Austria than the loss of a battle. He also wrote poetry, several verse tragedies, and made a translation of Byron's *Manfred.*

Pellinore, King. In Malory's *Morte d'Arthur* (c. 1469), the hunter of the Questing Beast. He is the father of Lamerok, Percival, Agglovale, Dornar, and Torre, all knights of the Round Table. Sir Gawain kills him in revenge for the death of his own father, King Lot.

Peloponnesian Wars (431–404 B.C.). A struggle between Athens, a democratic sea power, and Sparta, an oligarchical, conservative state. THUCYDIDES, who fought in the war, considered the cause to be Athens' rise to greatness; later historians have thought that the conflict arose out of commercial rivalries involving Corinth. The Spartans won an important victory at the battle of Mantinea (418 B.C.). The defection of ALCIBIADES during the ill-favored expedition to Sicily (415 B.C.) gave Sparta increased strength. When the Athenian fleet was destroyed at Aegospotami (405 B.C.), Sparta succeeded in reducing Athens to a second-rate power. Most of our information about the war comes from Thucydides' history; the later years are related in XENOPHON's *Hellenica*. Aristophanes lampooned warmongers and demagogues repeatedly in his comedies. Euripides' THE TROJAN WOMEN was in part a protest against atrocities committed in the war.

Pelops. In Greek mythology, a son of TANTALUS. The Peloponnese was named after him. As an infant he was served at a banquet given by his father for the gods. Failing to notice, Demeter ate a part of his shoulder, but the other gods were horrified. They condemned Tantalus to torture in Hades, and revived Pelops by boiling him; Demeter gave him a new shoulder of ivory. Making the beautiful child his favorite, Poseidon took him to Olympus.

As a young man, Pelops sued for the hand of Hippodamia, the daughter of Oenomaus, king of Pisa. Her suitors were required to flee with her in their chariots while Oenomaus pursued them, armed. Many had been killed thus, but Pelops persuaded Oenomaus' charioteer Myrtilus to place linchpins of wax in the chariot. Oenomaus was killed, but, when Myrtilus demanded the payment agreed on, a night with Hippodamia, Pelops killed him also, and was cursed by him.

Pelops subjugated much of the northern Peloponnese. Unable to subdue Stymphalus, king of Arcadia, he invited him to a banquet, where he treacherously killed him. The crime caused a famine throughout Greece, which was ended only by the prayers of Aeacus. Hippodamia bore many children to Pelops, including Atreus and Thyestes (see the House of ATREUS) and Pittheus. Through jealousy she caused the death of his son by the nymph Astyoche, Chrysippus, whom Laius carried off to Thebes. The sanctuary of Pelops at Olympia was one of its most sacred spots.

Pemán, José María (1898–   ). Spanish poet and dramatist. His verse, strongly Roman Catholic in its orientation, appears in the collections *El barrio de Santa Cruz* (1931) and *Elegía a la tradición española* (1931). His dramas have been more successful, particularly *El divino impaciente* (*A Saint in a Hurry*, 1935), *La Santa Virreina* (1939), and *Edipo* (1954), considered his finest work.

penates. In ancient Rome, guardian deities of the household and of the state, usually referred to in the plural. They were like personifications of the natural powers, and whereas the LARES protected and warded off danger, it was the duty of the penates to bring wealth and plenty.

Pendennis, The History of (1848–1850). A novel by William Makepeace THACKERAY. The hero, Arthur Pendennis, known as Pen for short, is spoiled by his mother and by Laura BELL, a distant relative of his own age with whom he grows up. He goes through the university, enters London society, writes a successful novel, becomes editor of the *Pall Mall Gazette*, and is involved in love affairs of varying character with the actress Miss Fotheringay (stage name of Emily Costigan), with Fanny Bolten, a London porter's daughter, and with Blanche Amory, daughter of Lady Clavering. He finally marries Laura, who has always loved him, and whom he has grown to love. Pen's uncle, Major Arthur Pendennis, and his friend George Warrington play prominent roles.

Pendragon. An ancient British title, denoting chief leader or king. It was conferred on a chief when he was invested with the supreme power in times of danger, and is particularly identified with Uther Pendragon, father of King Arthur. The word is derived from the Welsh *pen*, "head" and *dragon* (the reference being to the war chief's dragon standard). It corresponds to the Roman *dux bellorum*.

Geoffrey of Monmouth recorded a legend describing the origin of the title. Aurelius, the British king, was poisoned by Ambron during the invasion of Pascentius. As a consequence, "there appeared a star at Winchester of wonderful magnitude and brightness, darting forth a ray, at the end of which was a globe of fire in form of a dragon, out of whose mouth issued forth two rays, one of which extended to Gaul and the other to Ireland." Uther ordered two golden dragons to be made, one of which he presented to Winchester, and the other he carried with him as his royal standard, whence he received the title Pendragon.

Penelope. The wife of ODYSSEUS and mother of Telemachus in the ODYSSEY. While Odysseus was away from Ithaca during the Trojan War and on his subsequent wanderings, Penelope was besieged by suitors. She put them off by various devices, the cleverest being to say that she would decide on which she would marry when she had finished weaving a shroud for her father-in-law. At night she raveled out what she had woven by day. The suitors eventually discovered the ruse, but Odysseus fortunately returned to slay them all and rescue Penelope from her dilemma.

Peneus. A river in Thessaly. Also the name of the god of the river who was the father of Daphne.

Penguin Island (*L'Ile des pingouins*; 1908). A novel by Anatole FRANCE. It deals with French history in a satiric manner. The old Breton monk Saint Maël lands on an island and in his semiblindness fails to perceive that the inhabitants whom he baptizes are penguins and not men. They are, however, changed to men by God, and the island is carefully towed back to shore by the monk. A highly ironic and imaginative account of the development of civilization comprises the remainder of the novel.

Penitentes. A religious order in New Mexico. It puts on an annual Passion Play in the course of which the practice of self-flagellation is indulged in. The Penitentes are Roman Catholics, though the practice is condemned by the Church. See FLAGELLANTS.

Penitential Psalms. Seven psalms expressive of contrition. In the Christian tradition they have been recited together as a devotion. They are Psalms 7, 32, 38, 51, 102, 130, and 143. All except the first are one number lower in the Latin numbering.

Penn, William (1644–1718). English Quaker, founder of Pennsylvania. In 1681, Penn obtained a grant of land from James II where Quakers might live without fear of religious persecution. In the new colony, which was named Pennsylvania in honor of Penn's father, he established a liberal government, permitted religious freedom, and maintained friendly relations with the Indians. A prolific writer, Penn is best known for *Some Fruits of Solitude* (1693), a collection of religious and moral maxims.

Pennant, Thomas (1726–1798). English antiquary, traveler, and noted naturalist. He is the author of *British Zoology* (1766) and the *History of Quadrupeds* (1781). He appears as a correspondent of the author in Gilbert White's *Natural History of Selborne* (1789).

Penrod (1914). A novel by Booth TARKINGTON. This account of the humorous adventures and escapades of Penrod Schofield, a typical 12-year-old boy in a Midwestern community, has been widely read and highly popular; it was followed by *Penrod and Sam* (1916) and *Penrod Jashber* (1931). All three were collected in the omnibus volume *Penrod: His Complete Story* (1931).

Pensées (Thoughts, 1844). A collection of reflections on religion by Blaise PASCAL, found in fragmentary form after his death. The first edition (1670) abridged the *Pensées* in order to soften their strongly Jansenist tone, but the edition of 1844 is faithful to the original manuscript. It is Pascal's view that man —less than God yet more than the animals—is a helpless creature suspended between the great unknowns of past and future, birth and death. A frail reed in a vast universe, he is yet a thinking reed: *"L'homme n'est qu'un roseau, le plus faible de la nature, mais c'est un roseau pensant."* The Christian telling of man's fall from grace and the possibility of redemption must be true, because only thus can the contradictions in man's nature be explained. Faith cannot be gained by reason alone, for logic must be aided by God's grace, which speaks to the heart: *"Le coeur a ses raisons que la raison ne connaît pas."* (The heart has its reasons, which reason does not know.) A testament of religious faith, the fragmentary *Pensées* offer perceptive insights into the human condition, revealing Pascal's power of lucid reasoning and the depth of his Christian belief.

Pensées sur la comète. See Pierre BAYLE.

Penseroso, Il (1632). A poem by John MILTON. It celebrates the "pleasures" of melancholy, contemplation, solitude, and study. The thematic opposite of its companion piece L'ALLEGRO, it shares the latter's qualities of style: rich verbal music and an extraordinary range and opulence of fancy.

pentameter. In prosody, a line of verse containing five metrical feet in any METER, usually identified together with the name of the meter, such as iambic pentameter, trochaic pentameter, etc. The iambic pentameter is the English heroic line; it is also the standard line in English blank verse, the heroic couplet, the sonnet, and other forms.

Pentateuch (from Gr. *penta,* "five," and *teuchos,* "a tool, a book"). The first 5 books of the Old Testament, also called the *Law of Moses:* Genesis, Exodus, Leviticus, Numbers, and Deuteronomy. The Pentateuch relates the history of the Jews from the Creation to the death of Moses. See ELOHISTIC AND JEHOVISTIC SCRIPTURES.

the Samaritan Pentateuch. The Hebrew text as pre-

THE BRITISH MUSEUM

Anglo-Saxon paraphrase of the Pentateuch (996).

served by the Samaritans; it is said to date from 400 B.C.

Pentecost (Gr. *pentecoste,* "fiftieth"). A Jewish festival on the fiftieth day after the second day of Passover, which commemorates the giving of the Tablets of the Law to Moses. It was adopted as a Christian festival, also called WHITSUNDAY, to commemorate the descent of the Holy Ghost on the Apostles on the day of Pentecost (*Acts* 2).

Pentelic. Pertaining to Mount Pentelicus near Athens, Greece. The white marble used for the Parthenon came from the quarries of Mount Pentelicus. Hence, Pentelic came to connote the whiteness of marble.

Penthesilea (Penthesileia). In classic myth, a queen of the AMAZONS. She was slain by ACHILLES when she came to the aid of the Trojans after the death of Hector. Her beauty and courage won for her a sincere lament from her slayer.

Penthesilea (pub. 1808). A tragedy by Heinrich von KLEIST, in which both Penthesilea and Achilles die. It was on the basis of this play that Goethe made his notoriously unfair judgment of Kleist as a "hypochondriac northerner," by which he meant that, in his opinion, Kleist concentrated too strongly on the violently passionate, tragic potentiality of human nature and overlooked possibilities for wholesome balance.

Pentheus. A king of Thebes, and grandson of Cadmus. His tragic fate is told in Euripides' play *The Bacchants.*

People of Seldwyla, The. See LEUTE VON SELDWYLA, DIE.

People, Yes, The (1936). A poem by Carl SANDBURG. It is composed in alternating passages of prose and free verse, narrative and homily, copybook English and slang. It celebrates the vigor of the American people and expresses hope for their progress, in spite of social injustice and economic inequality.

Pepys, Samuel (1633–1703). English politician, best known for his *Diary*. The son of a tailor, Pepys had as a patron Sir Edward Montagu, the earl of Sandwich, and was in a position to meet the outstanding personalities of his day. He was secretary of the admiralty from 1673 to 1688 and, also, served in Parliament and as president of the Royal Society. After the accession of William III, he lost all his offices and was briefly imprisoned for his Stuart sympathies.

Written in shorthand between 1660 and 1669 and not deciphered until 1825, when it was published in part, the *Diary* was never intended for the public eye. It not only presents a vivid picture of an age, but is a uniquely uninhibited and spontaneous revelation of its author's life and character.

Perceforest, King. A legendary king of Britain. Perceforest is the hero of an old romance first printed in Paris in 1528. According to the narrative, he was crowned king of Britain by the shipwrecked Alexander the Great. He was called *Perceforest* because he dared to pierce, almost alone, an enchanted forest, where women and children were most cruelly treated.

Percival, Perceval, or **Percivale.** In Arthurian legend, one of the most famous knights of the Round Table, figuring especially in the quest for the GRAIL. His first appearance in literature is in the French poem *Perceval, ou le conte du Graal*, written c. 1175, by Chrétien de Troyes. *Peredur, Son of Efrawg*, a medieval Welsh tale of Arthurian romance included in the *Mabinogion*, is a parallel of Chrétien's *Perceval*. From the time of Chrétien on, he appears in almost all the Arthurian romances; he is Sir Percival in Malory's *Morte d'Arthur* (c. 1469) and the PARZIFAL or PARSIFAL of the German versions.

In general, his story begins with his boyhood in the forest and his complete ignorance of the ways of knights and warriors and of courtly manners. He then goes to King Arthur's court where he commits one gaucherie after another; he is trained as a knight, however, and goes on to become one of the best knights of the Round Table. His quest for the Grail is the main incident of the story and ends with his being awarded a sight of it. Late versions of his story usually present him as a virgin knight. Malory's *Morte d'Arthur* was Tennyson's source for his version in *Idylls of the King* (1859–1885).

Percival. In Virginia Woolf's novel THE WAVES, a character who does not appear but who acts as a unifying force, since the six leading characters all admire him deeply. He is killed by a fall from a horse in India, and his death serves as a symbol of all death. A completely unified character, he is symbol of all that his friends aspire to be; their final meeting at Hampton Court atones for an occasion when Bernard failed to meet Percival there.

Percy, Sir Henry. Known as **Hotspur** (1364–1403). English soldier, eldest son of Henry Percy, 1st earl of Northumberland. He joined Owen Glendower's rebellion against Henry IV and was killed at the battle of Shrewsbury. Called Hotspur because of his fiery and uncontrollable temper, he contrasts with the cool-headed Prince Hal in Shakespeare's HENRY IV: PART I.

Percy, Bishop Thomas (1729–1811). English antiquarian, scholar, and poet. He is best known for his RELIQUES OF ANCIENT ENGLISH POETRY, the most important work in the 18th-century ballad revival. His achievement was more that of a popularizer than an editor; a capricious selection, *Reliques* includes old ballads, political songs from the 17th century, and ballads by Percy's contemporaries, as well as by himself. Nevertheless, his collection reawakened a taste for English balladry and influenced the poetry of the romantics.

Percy's Reliques. See RELIQUES OF ANCIENT ENGLISH POETRY.

Perdita. The virtuous and beautiful daughter of Hermione and Leontes, king of Sicilia, in Shakespeare's WINTER'S TALE. As an infant she is abandoned by her father's orders and is raised by a shepherd as his daughter. Despite her supposedly humble birth, the nobility of her nature is apparent, and Polixenes says of her:

> This is the prettiest low-born lass that ever
> Ran on the green-sord: nothing she does or seems
> But smacks of something greater than herself;
> Too noble for this place.

Mary Robinson, who played the role of Perdita at Drury Lane in 1779 and became the mistress of the prince of Wales, later George IV, adopted the name as a pseudonym.

Perdix. See TALUS (2).

Pereda, José María de (1833–1906). Spanish novelist. An outstanding realist of conservative political and social views, Pereda wrote almost exclusively about his native Santander. His best-known works are *Sotileza* (1885), which has been called the finest Spanish novel about the sea, and *Peñas arriba* (1895), dealing with peasant life in the highlands, or *montaña*, of Santander. He also wrote *El buey suelto* (1878), an attack on bachelorhood; *Don Gonzalo González de la Gonzalera* (1879); *El sabor de la tierruca* (1882); and two collections of of short stories, *Escenas montañesas* (1864) and its continuation, *Tipos y paisajes* (1871).

Peredur, Son of Efrawg. See PERCIVAL.

Père Goriot, Le (Father Goriot, 1834). A novel, part of LA COMÉDIE HUMAINE, by Honoré de BALZAC. Père Goriot's consuming passion is his devotion to his two ungrateful daughters, Mme de Nucigen and Mme de Restaud. He deprives himself of everything for them, including his self-respect. Married to wealthy men, the two sisters are ashamed of their father's bourgeois manners, but they expect him to extricate them from financial difficulties. After sacrificing his last silver plate, Goriot dies of apoplexy. In a characteristic gesture, the daughters send empty carriages to the funeral. See Eugène de RASTIGNAC.

Peregrine Pickle, The Adventures of (1751). A PICARESQUE novel by Tobias SMOLLETT. The hero, an imaginative young man with a flair for practical jokes whose rascality often shades into villainy, grows up under the tutelage of his aunt, Grizzle Pickle, and her madcap husband, the one-eyed veteran, Commodore Hawser TRUNNION. After an ignoble attempt to seduce his friend's sister, Amanda, he dissipates the fortune inherited from Trunnion on false friends and extravagances, and is reduced to poverty, jail, and misanthropy. Upon his father's death, however, he is left a second fortune, and he marries Amanda. See

Tom PIPES; Lieutenant Jack HATCHWAY; Cadwallader CRABTREE.

Père humilié, Le. See HOSTAGE, THE.

Perelman, S[idney] J[oseph] (1904–   ). American humorist. Perelman published his first book, *Dawn Ginsbergh's Revenge,* in 1929; with that publication his fame was secured, and he moved to Hollywood to do gag- and script-writing. Most of Perelman's work is first published in magazines such as *The New Yorker* before it appears in book form. Although he has satirized almost every aspect of contemporary society, some of his most effective barbs have been directed against the entertainment and advertising industries. Among his books are *Strictly from Hunger* (1937), *Westward Ha! or, Around the World in 80 Clichés* (1948), *The Swiss Family Perelman* (1950), *The Road to Miltown, or, Under the Spreading Atrophy* (1957), and *The Rising Gorge* (1961). His best-known play, *One Touch of Venus* (1943), was written in collaboration with Ogden Nash. A collection, *The Most of S. J. Perelman,* was published in 1958.

Pérez de Ayala, Ramón (1881–1962). Spanish poet, critic, and novelist. He is known for his charming combination of intellectuality and warmth. This is apparent in his poetry, which includes the volumes *El sendero innumerable* (1916) and *El sendero andante* (1924). The best example of his criticism is the two-volume work *Las máscaras* (1917), which focuses upon contemporary Spanish drama. Pérez de Ayala, however, is best known as a distinguished novelist. His novels, which are pointed at the human condition and often reach a symbolic level, include *Tinieblas en las cumbres* (1907), *A. M. D. G.* (1910), which deals with life in a Jesuit boarding school, and *Tres novelas poemáticas: Prometeo, Luz de domingo, La caída de los Limones* (*Prometheus, Sunday Sunlight, and The Fall of the House of Limon,* 1916).

Pérez Galdós, Benito (1843–1920). Spanish novelist and dramatist. A native of the Canary Islands, Pérez Galdós devoted himself to writing after the publication of his first novel, *La fontana de oro,* in 1870. Often compared to Balzac, he was an enlightened progressive who sought to reproduce in his work every facet of human existence.

In the 46 novels of his *Episodios nacionales* (1873–1912), he traced Spanish history from the battle of Trafalgar to the restoration of the monarchy in 1875; thoroughly documented, they reveal the author's ability to evoke the spirit of a bygone age. Simultaneously, Pérez Galdós was writing several thesis novels which reflect his liberal, mildly anticlerical views. Among these are *Doña Perfecta* (1876), showing the tragic effects of religious bigotry; *Gloria* (1877), about a Roman Catholic girl who is unable to marry the Jew she loves; and *La familia de León Roch* (1879), which describes a marriage ruined because of the religious differences between husband and wife. Some of Pérez Galdós' finest works are in the series called *Novelas españolas contemporáneas,* which includes *Fortunata y Jacinta* (4 vols., 1886–1887), a masterly study of the bourgeoisie of Madrid; *Angel Guerra* (3 vols., 1891), an analysis of modern mysticism; and *Misericordia* (1897), about the underworld of Madrid.

With *Realidad* (1892), *El abuelo* (1897), and *Casandra* (1905), Pérez Galdós created a new genre, the dialogued novel, in which the author's intrusions are totally suppressed and the characters portray themselves only by their words and deeds. Later he adapted these works for the stage. His other dramas include *La loca de la casa* (1893) and *Electra* (1901).

perfectibilism. The doctrine of man's individual and social perfectibility. In Thomas Love Peacock's novel HEADLONG HALL there is a Mr. Foster who is represented as "perfectibilian."

Pergolesi, Giovanni Battista (1710–1736). Italian composer. His short life and sudden death from consumption shortly after his first success made many legends grow up about him, and led to the practice of ascribing to him works of other composers. For instance, nearly all the "works of Pergolesi" which Stravinsky used as the basis of his ballet *Pulcinella* are spurious. Pergolesi's best works are an *opera buffa, La Serva Padrona* (*The Maid as Mistress,* 1733) and the *Stabat Mater* for women's voices and orchestra (1736).

Peribáñez y el comendador de Ocaña (c. 1614). A drama by Lope de VEGA. It takes place during the reign of Enrique III (1309–1406). The *comendador,* or governor, of Ocaña is attracted to Casilda, bride of the peasant Peribáñez, but she spurns his advances. After making Peribáñez captain of a peasant company and sending him away, the *comendador* tries to take Casilda by force but is surprised in the act by Peribáñez, who has returned unexpectedly. Peribáñez kills the *comendador,* then recounts the whole affair to the king, who pardons him.

Periboea. See OEDIPUS.

Pericles (Perikles, c. 500–429 B.C.). An Athenian statesman. Pericles dominated Athens from about 460 B.C. to his death. Influenced by the philosopher Anaxagoras, he lost the superstitious beliefs held by many of his countrymen. His political ideal was a democratic Athens, leader of the Greek world. To this end he attempted to bring about a Greek union, but, when resisted by Sparta, he converted the Delian Confederacy into an Athenian empire. He pursued an imperialistic policy, while instituting democratic reform in Athens. A striking innovation was the payment of the *archons* and members of the Assembly. As a result of this reform, the qualification of wealth for the holding of public office could be dropped. Further, the *Areopagus,* or council of former *archons,* which had had the power of supervising the administration and judging crime, was relieved of these powers. Its censorial powers over the private lives of citizens were also abolished, and the wealthy and conservative institution was limited to duties without political significance.

In 430 B.C. Pericles was charged with misuse of public funds; it was thought that he used the treasury of the Delian League for the beautification of Athens. However, he was re-elected as general the following year, and died in 429 B.C., a victim of the plague.

Athens owes the Parthenon, Propylaea, the long wall to Piraeus, and many temples to Pericles' program of civic embellishment. He was also widely known for his eloquence, which is reported by Thucydides. The historian records Pericles' *Funeral Oration,* supposedly delivered by the general in honor of the Athenians who died in the Battle of Samos (440 B.C.). The speech exhorts the Athenians to have courage. Pericles also led the Athenians in battle at the opening of the Peloponnesian War.

He took as mistress the *hetaera,* or courtesan, AsPASIA (fl. 440 B.C.), who was famous for her beauty and intelligence. Her home became the center of the literary and philosophical life of Athens. It is said that she aided Pericles in matters of public policy, and helped to compose his speeches. She was condemned to death for impiety, but the eloquence of Pericles saved her life. Their son was later legitimatized and made a citizen by the Athenians.

The period 460–429 B.C. is often referred to as The Periclean Age, or the Golden Age of Athens.

Pericles, Prince of Tyre (c. 1608). A drama by William SHAKESPEARE and another author, presumably George Wilkins. The plot is believed to be derived from Lawrence Twine's *Pattern of Painful Adventures* (1576) and John GOWER's *Confessio Amantis* (1390). Gower himself is a character in the play, appearing as the Chorus.

At Antioch, Pericles arouses the enmity of King Antiochus by guessing that the king has an incestuous love for his daughter. Pursued by the wrath of Antiochus, he is forced to leave Tyre and go on a journey. At Pentapolis, where he has been shipwrecked, he wins a tournament for the hand of King Simonides' daughter THAISA, whom he marries. Hearing of Antiochus' death, Pericles sets sail for Tyre with his wife, who gives birth to a daughter during a storm at sea but falls into such a deep state of unconsciousness that she is presumed dead. Her body is placed in a chest which is thrown overboard and is later washed ashore at Ephesus. Thaisa is revived by Cerimon, an Ephesian lord, and, believing her husband to be dead, becomes a votaress in the temple of Diana. Meanwhile, Pericles leaves his infant daughter MARINA in Tarsus to be reared by Cleon and his wife Dionyza. Sixteen years later, the jealous Dionyza tries to kill Marina, but the girl is saved by pirates who place her in a brothel in Mytilene. Lysimachus, governor of the city, is so struck by her beauty and virtue that he purchases her freedom. Pericles, who has been told that Marina is dead, finds her in Mytilene and blesses her union with Lysimachus. Guided by the goddess Diana, who has appeared to him in a vision, Pericles then goes to Ephesus where he is finally reunited with Thaisa.

Perilous Castle. The border castle of the Scottish James DOUGLAS. It was so called in the reign of Edward I because, during border warfare, Douglas destroyed several English garrisons stationed there and vowed to be revenged on anyone who dared to take possession of it. It is the location of Sir Walter Scott's novel CASTLE DANGEROUS.

Peripatetic School. The school of philosophy founded by ARISTOTLE. It was so named because Aristotle used to walk about as he taught his disciples. The covered walk of the LYCEUM was called the *Peripatos.* THEOPHRASTUS and Strato led the school after Aristotle's death, and gradually turned it wholly to scientific research. After 1 B.C., the Peripatetics produced expositions of Aristotle's work. Finally the school turned to Neoplatonism.

Periquillo sarniento, El (*Sp.,* "the mangy little parrot"; 1816). A picaresque novel by José Joaquín FERNÁNDEZ DE LIZARDI. Modeled on Alemán's *Guzmán de Alfarache* and Lesage's *Gil Blas,* the book relates the adventures of Periquillo, an engaging rogue, in a pungent, colloquial style; the result is a realistic picture of Mexican society on the eve of independence. Interspersed throughout the narrative are didactic essays in which Fernández denounced the sloth of the middle class, the abuses of the clergy, the defects of the educational system, and other evils.

Perissa. See FAERIE QUEENE, THE.

Perkin Warbeck (c. 1633). A tragedy by John FORD, based on the rise and fall of the Yorkist pretender to the English throne. Perkin appeared during the reign of Henry VII and claimed to be Richard, son of Edward IV, whom Richard III was alleged to have murdered in the Tower. For a while, he enjoyed the backing of James IV of Scotland and enlisted considerable popular support in England. But his allies eventually deserted him, and he was captured by Henry and executed. In the play he maintains his claim to the very end. The real Perkin Warbeck (c. 1474–1499) was a Walloon of humble origin who became the tool of anti-Tudor forces; he confessed his true identity before he died.

Perpétuité de la foi de l'église catholique touchant l'Eucharistie, La. See Antoine ARNAULD.

Perrault, Charles (1628–1703). French writer and critic. Perrault took a leading role in the controversy between the ancients and the moderns. In the poem *Le Siècle de Louis le Grand* (*The Century of Louis the Great,* 1687) he asserted the superiority of the age of Louis XIV over that of the Roman emperor Augustus, and his *Parallèles des Anciens et des Modernes* (*Parallels between the Ancients and the Moderns,* 1688–1697) is a series of dialogues surveying the arts and pointing out the progress made by writers of Perrault's own day over those of the past. Perrault also collected and published a book of fairy tales, LES CONTES DE MA MÈRE L'OYE.

Perry, Bliss (1860–1954). American educator and literary critic. At the turn of the century he was an editor of the *Atlantic Monthly* but left the magazine for Harvard, where he became one of the nation's most beloved teachers. His most important critical books are *Walt Whitman: His Life and Works* (1906) and *Emerson Today* (1931). *And Gladly Teach* (1935) is his autobiography.

Perry, Matthew Calbraith (1794–1858). American naval officer. Chosen by President Fillmore to negotiate a treaty with Japan, which at that time refused to have contact with the West, Perry arrived in Yedo Bay with his naval squadron in 1853 and succeeded in delivering a letter from Fillmore to the emperor. The following year he returned and concluded a treaty of peace, amity, and commerce, bringing about the entrance of Japan into world affairs.

Perry, Oliver Hazard (1785–1819). American naval officer. After serving in the Tripolitan War, Perry was given command of the U.S. naval forces on Lake Erie during the War of 1812. On Sept. 10, 1813 he decisively defeated the British fleet on Lake Erie and announced the victory to Gen. W. H. Harrison in a famous message, "We have met the enemy and they are ours." Perry, who was the older brother of Matthew Calbraith Perry, died of yellow fever after concluding a diplomatic mission to Venezuela.

Perse, St. John. Pen name of Aléxis St. Léger Léger (1887–   ). French poet and diplomat. His childhood on a family-owned island near Guadaloupe is reflected by the recurrence of sea imagery in his poems; his travels as ambassador to the Far East (1916–1921) and his studies in early pagan philosophy and in geology perhaps account somewhat for his works' exotic flavor, their colorful settings, such as the unspecified Asiatic lands in ANABASE and the imaginary oriental kingdom by the sea in *Seamarks (Amers; 1957)*. The poems are written in lines of irregular length, ranging from a single word to a short paragraph, with a fluid, resonant rhythm like that of an incantation.

Indeed, Perse's work as a whole has a hymnlike tone of mystery and passion, although devoted not to God but to the vast scope of human experience and the triumphal joy of man's exploration and conquest of the universe and of himself.

The poet as creator is a dominant theme, as in *Exil* (1942), in which he is prince of lands which are void until he gives them existence in a poem. Panoramas of mankind's history and natural landscapes blend through a rich vocabulary and occasionally unusual syntax in a symphonic progression of images; the thematic unity of each piece is symbolized by one dominant image, as in *Rains (Pluies; 1943), Snows (Neiges; 1944), Winds (Vents; 1946), Chronique* (1960). Early poems include *Eloges* (1911; revised 1925, 1948) and *Amitié du Prince* (1924). Among others, T. S. Eliot and Archibald MacLeish have translated his poems into English, Rainer Maria Rilke into German.

The other half of Perse's "double life" is Aléxis Léger, who entered the French Foreign Service in 1914 and became a specialist in Far Eastern affairs. In 1940, he went into exile and lived in the U.S., working for the Library of Congress, until his return to France in 1959. Perse was awarded the Nobel Prize for Literature in 1960.

Persephone. Also known as **Kore.** In Greek mythology, both queen of the underworld and goddess of the reviving crops. In the latter capacity, she is identified as the daughter of DEMETER, abducted by Hades. However, Hades himself was Plouton, a god of the wealth of the fertile earth which springs up from beneath the ground, so Persephone's two worlds are essentially the same. With her mother, she plays an important role in the ELEUSINIAN MYSTERIES. Her Roman counterpart was called Proserpina.

Perseus. A hero of Ancient Greece. He was worshiped as divine at Athens. Epics relate that he was the son of Zeus by Danaë, daughter of King Acrisius of Argos. The Delphic oracle had predicted that Danaë would bear a son who would kill his grandfather, so Acrisius cast Danaë and Perseus adrift in a chest. Zeus caused the waves to carry them to the isle of Seriphus, where Dictys, a fisherman and the brother of King Polydectes, rescued them. When Perseus was a young man, Polydectes desired Danaë and, wanting to get rid of her son, tricked him into promising the head of the Gorgon Medusa as a gift, a hopeless task. But Perseus, aided by the gods, killed Medusa and secured the head, which turned all who looked on it to stone. He rescued ANDROMEDA with its help and, returning with her to Seriphus, turned Polydectes and his friends to stone. Later, while taking part in the games at Larissa, he accidentally killed his grandfather Acrisius with a discus, thus bringing the early prophecy to pass. Perseus and Andromeda founded the family of the Perseids, from whom Hercules descended.

Pershing, John J[oseph] (1860–1948). American general. A graduate of West Point, Pershing served in Cuba during the Spanish-American War. In 1913 he suppressed an insurrection in the Philippines and in 1916 commanded the border campaign against the Mexican bandit and revolutionary Francisco Villa. That year he became a major general. In 1917 he was placed in command of the American Expeditionary Forces in France. When the great offensive of July, 1918, began, the American army under Pershing opened the way for the collapse of the German forces. He served as army chief of staff from 1921 until his retirement in 1924. In 1931 he published *My Experiences in the World War* (2 vols.), a work for which he received a Pulitzer Prize in history.

Persians, The (Persai, 472 B.C.). A tragedy by AESCHYLUS. In this play, Aeschylus relates the humiliating return of Xerxes to his capital of Susa after his defeat in the Persian wars. A principal figure in the play is Xerxes' mother Atossa. It is remarkable for the compassion that Aeschylus, who himself had fought the Persians, shows for his former enemies in their defeat, which he attributes to the pride and arrogance of Xerxes. *The Persians* is the only extant Greek tragedy that dealt with figures of recent history, instead of ancient myth.

Persian Wars, the (500–c. 449 B.C.). Wars between Persia and Greece. The Persian king Darius, enraged at the defiance of Athens and Eretria, which had delayed his conquest of the Ionian cities of Asia Minor, moved against the two cities in revenge. Hippias, the exiled son of Pisistratus, traitorously led 30,000 Persians to the plain of Marathon, terrain supposedly favorable to the Persian cavalry. There 11,000 Greeks under Miltiades, fighting in close array, won a glorious victory (490 B.C.). This battle ended the first Persian War, and Darius, busy putting down a revolt in Egypt, did not live to return to Greece. After his death in 485 B.C., his successor Xerxes spent three years preparing for the second Persian War. Athens was then under the leadership of Themistocles, and the Greek states had joined in a defensive confederation. At the invasion of Xerxes, the Spartan Leonidas and an army of 6,000 Greeks defended the narrow pass of Thermopylae (480 B.C.). Betrayed by the traitor Ephialtes, Leonidas detached most of his army, and with 300 Spartans and 700 Thespians, held back the Persians until all were slain. Simonides wrote a famous epitaph for the valorous Greeks. Upon hearing the news of the defeat at Thermopylae, the Greek fleet retired to Salamis. There they encountered the Persians, and routed them. See THEMISTOCLES. After the defeat of Salamis, Xerxes left his army under the leadership of Mardonius. In 479 B.C., the Greeks won a complete victory in the battle of Plataea. Further battles were fought during the next thirty years, but the Greeks had assumed the aggressive position. Some mark the end of the Persian Wars at 479 B.C.; others consider the final date to be 449 B.C., when the Peace of Callias was established. Our knowledge of the Persian Wars comes from the history of HERODOTUS, which covers the course of the wars to 479 B.C.

Persius. Full Latin name, **Aulus Persius Flaccus** (A.D. 34–62). Roman satiric poet. He was a friend of Lucan and greatly influenced by Horace. He is the author of six satires which expound the tenets of Stoicism.

Personae (1909). A volume of poems by Ezra POUND. The title, literally translated from the Latin, means "masks of the actor," recalling Yeats's demand that the poet objectify his experience through an imagined personality, a mask. The second book of his poems published, it also reveals Pound's indebtedness to the monologues of Browning's *Men and Women.* Pound also used *Personae* as the title for later collections of verse.

personification. A figure of speech attributing human characteristics or feelings to nonhuman organisms, inanimate objects, or abstract ideas. ALLEGORY frequently employs personifications; the Giant Despair in John Bunyan's *Pilgrim's Progress,* for example, is a personification; that is, the abstract concept of despair is represented as a person. But the use of personification is by no means confined to allegory. Keats, for example, personifies the Grecian urn in his *Ode to a Grecian Urn* as a "Sylvan historian," an "unravished bride of quietness" and a "foster-child of silence and slow time."

Persuasion (1818). A novel by Jane AUSTEN. The heroine, Anne Elliott, and her lover, Captain Wentworth, were engaged for eight years before the story begins, but Anne broke the engagement in deference to family and friends. Upon being thrown into her company again, Wentworth realizes that he is still drawn to Anne. When he is certain that she, too, still loves him, he renews his offer of marriage and the two lovers are united. Anne is gentle, sensitive, and charming; the author wrote of her, "She is almost too good for me."

Pertelote. See under NUN'S PRIEST'S TALE.

Pertwee, Roland (1886–1963). English playwright and novelist. His works for the theater include *Seein' Reason* (1913), *Hell's Loose* (1929), and *Heat Wave* (1929). He also wrote for magazines and acted in the companies of H. B. Irving and Charles Hawtrey.

Perugino, Il. Real name, **Pietro Vannucci** (c. 1445–1523). Italian painter from Perugia. He was the teacher of RAPHAEL, who employed the same refinement of style and sweetness of manner. Among his best-known works are *Apollo and Marsyas* and *Christ Handing the Keys to St. Peter* (1482), one of the wall frescoes of the Sistine Chapel.

Pervigilium Veneris (Lat., "vigil of Venus"). A famous short Latin poem by an anonymous writer of the 2nd or 3rd century. It celebrates the spring festival in honor of Venus, goddess of love and increase. T. S. Eliot uses a plaintive quotation from this poem toward the end of *The Waste Land: Quando fiam uti chelidon . . .* ("When shall I become as the swallow?").

Peshkov, Aleksei Maksimovich. See Maksim GORKI.

Pessôa, Fernando António Nogueira (1888–1935). Portuguese poet. Reared and educated in South Africa, he wrote three volumes of *English Poems* (1921). Later he became an influential figure in the Portuguese *modernista* movement, publishing his verse in such reviews as *Orféu* and *Presença.*

He wrote under his own name and three pseudonyms —Alberto Caeiro, Ricardo Reis, and Alvaro de Campos—each of which supposedly represented a distinct facet of his personality. His *Obras Completas* were published from 1942 to 1956.

Pestalozzi, Johann Heinrich (1746–1827). Swiss educational reformer. His work influenced the methods of education in elementary schools in Europe and America.

Peste, La. See PLAGUE, THE.

Pétain, Henri Philippe (1856–1951). French general, later politician. Marshal of France (1918), Pétain won fame as commander in chief of the French army under Marshal Foch in World War I. The elderly war hero, serving as *President du Conseil,* signed an armistice with Germany in 1940. During the Occupation (1940–1944), he served as head of the Vichy government, collaborating with the Germans. Pétain was tried by a French tribunal at the end of the war and convicted of high treason, but the death sentence was commuted to life imprisonment.

Peter, St. One of the 12 disciples of Jesus, noted for his impulsive nature. More incidents are related of him in the *Gospels* than of any other disciple. He was first called Simon, but Jesus changed his name and addressed to him the words on which the authority of the Papacy is based, "Thou art Peter, and upon this rock (Lat. *petra,* rock) I will build my church; and the gates of Hades shall not prevail against it; I will give unto thee the keys of the kingdom of Heaven; and whatsoever thou shalt bind on earth shall be bound in heaven; and whatsoever thou shalt loose on earth shall be loosed in Heaven."

At the time of Jesus' arrest, Peter denied three times that he knew him before the cock crew, as he had been warned that he would. After the crucifixion he became a principal and many of his missionary activities are related in the *Acts.* He figures in numerous popular tales as the keeper of the door to Heaven, to whom saints and sinners present themselves for admittance. Peter is the patron saint of fishermen, having been himself a fisherman. His day is June 29, and he is usually represented as an old man, bald, but with a flowing beard, dressed in a white mantle and blue tunic, and holding in his hand a book or scroll. His peculiar symbols are the keys and a sword. Tradition tells that he confuted Simon Magus, who was at Nero's court as a magician, and that in 66 he was crucified with his head downward at his own request, as he said he was not worthy to suffer the same death as Jesus.

Peter, The General Epistles of. Two books of the New Testament. The first epistle, probably a genuine Petrine letter, gives encouragement to the Christians who were then suffering persecution. It was written prior to A.D. 65. The second letter was not written by Peter; it dates from the middle of the second century. It denounces moral laxity in the Church.

Peter Bell (1819). A poetical tale by William WORDSWORTH. The potter Peter Bell is about to steal an ass, which he sees standing alone by the river, but, upon approaching it, he discovers that the ass is watching the body of its drowned owner. Bell returns the ass to the poor man's widow; on his way to her he has several experiences that cause him to change his outlook on life, hitherto one of insensitivity to human values and to beauty. The poem was written in 1798; Shelley burlesqued it as *Peter Bell the Third.*

Peter Ibbetson (1891). A novel by George DU MAURIER. It is the story of the strange, idealistic dream life of the incarcerated Peter Ibbetson, a deranged murderer. It was the basis of an opera by Deems Taylor.

Peterkin, Julia [Mood] (1880–1961). American novelist and short-story writer. She is noted for her books dealing, both realistically and sympathetically with the Gullah Negroes of South Carolina, her native state. Her best-known novel is SCARLET SISTER MARY. *Black April* (1927) is the story of the title character's domination over all the other Negroes on an isolated plantation. Her other books include *Green Thursday* (1924); *Bright Skin* (1932); *Roll, Jordan, Roll* (1933), a collection of photographs with text by Mrs. Peterkin; and *Plantation Christmas* (1934).

Peter Lombard. See Peter LOMBARD.

Peterloo Massacre. A riot at St. Peter's Field, Manchester, England, on Aug. 16, 1819. An assembly of 60,000 men, women, and children, mostly from the laboring classes, had gathered to hear Henry HUNT speak on parliamentary reform and the repeal of CORN LAWS. The military was sent out to break up the group, and charged on the crowd with drawn sabers, killing 11 and wounding over 400. The name Peterloo is ironic, referring to the fact that the same Tory government that claimed credit for Waterloo ordered the assault on the crowd at St. Peter's Field. Shelley wrote an indignant poem, *The Masque of Anarchy* (pub., 1832) on the incident.

Peter Pan (1904). A children's drama by J. M. BARRIE. The boy hero, Peter Pan, has run away to the Never-Never-Land to escape growing up; here he lives in the trees with the fairies. One day he shows the Darling children, Wendy, Michael, and John, how to fly and persuades them to come home with him. They have many adventures, particularly at the hands of Peter's enemy Captain Hook, leader of a band of pirates. The Indian princess, Tiger Lily, and Tinker Bell, the unseen fairy, protect the children. Finally the Darling children must go home, but Wendy promises to come again every spring. A long succession of actresses, notably Maude Adams, and including Pauline Chase, Cissie Loftus, Eva Le Gallienne, and Mary Martin, have played Peter.

Peter Porcupine. See William COBBETT.

Peter Quince at the Clavier (1923). A poem by Wallace STEVENS. It is built on a musical analogy; the poet, seated at the clavier, retells part of the biblical story of Susanna and the Elders in the Apocrypha. He draws the conclusion that "beauty is momentary in the mind . . . / But in the flesh it is immortal."

Peter Rugg, the Missing Man (1824). A story by William Austin (1778–1841), American lawyer, public official, and writer. It first appeared in the *New England Galaxy,* and has since been frequently anthologized. Peter Rugg, caught in a thunderstorm, swears that he will not stop and take shelter before he reaches Boston; he is condemned to roam about between Hartford and Boston forever. The tale bears resemblance to RIP VAN WINKLE and the story of the Wandering Jew. It is referred to in Nathaniel Hawthorne's *A Virtuoso's Collection* (1842), and

both Louise Guiney and Amy Lowell used it as a basis for ballads.

Peter Schlemihls wundersame Geschichte (Peter Schlemihl's Remarkable Story, 1814). A story by Adalbert von CHAMISSO. It tells, with both sympathy and humor, the adventures of a young man who gives up his shadow to a gray stranger in return for Fortunatus' purse. The careful balance between the fantastic subject and the matter-of-fact style in which it is treated is the story's chief merit. At the end, Peter renounces his ill-gotten wealth, luckily finds a pair of seven-league boots, and using this conveyance to make trips all over the world, devotes his life to scientific research. *Schlemihl* (lit., beloved of God) is a Yiddish word and refers commonly to a clumsy, unfortunate person for whom nothing ever seems to work out right.

Peter's pence. Before the Reformation, an annual tribute to the Pope of a penny. It was paid by every English householder who held land of a certain value. The term is now used to denote voluntary contributions by Roman Catholics to the Papal Treasury.

Peter the Great or **Peter I (Piotr Alekseyevich;** 1672–1725). Czar of Russia (1689–1725). More than any previous ruler, Peter Europeanized Russia, when necessary forcibly imposing Western ideas and customs on his subjects. He visited western Europe in 1697–1698, gathering information and hiring teachers and technicians to take back to Russia. Peter's energy was unlimited, and his interests covered a wide range. He founded the Russian navy, reorganized the army on Western lines, instituted obligatory service to the state by the gentry class, bound the administration of the church to that of the state, reformed the Russian alphabet, and gained Russian outlets on the Baltic Sea by driving out the Swedes. On the marshes at the mouth of the Neva River on the Baltic, he built Russia's "window on the West," St. Petersburg, making it the capital instead of Moscow. In 1721 the title of emperor was taken by Peter. The designation was also used by succeeding rulers.

Peter's reforms created Russian civilization and set its direction for the next 200 years. His introduction of Western ways to the Russian gentry classes laid the basis for the split between the upper classes and the peasantry that was to plague Russian society until the 1917 revolution. Besides the far-reaching effects of his action on Russian society, Peter's personality also had a strong impact. The chief response in literature to this impact is Pushkin's poem *The Bronze Horseman.* Another of Pushkin's poems, *Poltava,* deals with Peter's victory in 1709 over Charles XII of Sweden. The Czar is the subject of Aleksei Tolstoi's historical novel, *Piotr Pervyi (Peter the First).*

Peter the Hermit. Known as **Peter of Amiens** and **Pietro L'Eremita** (1050?–1115). French monk. He was one of the instigators of the First Crusade (1096–1099), which he preached widely and enthusiastically. He actually led one segment of the crusade to Asia Minor in 1096. He is introduced by Tasso in the epic GERUSALEMME LIBERATA, where he advises and exhorts the Christian forces against the infidel armies. It is he who first proposes Goffredo (Godfrey of Bouillon) as the supreme commander. Later, revealing the genealogy of Rinaldo of Este, he describes the founding of the house of Este, Tasso's patrons at Ferrara.

Petitioners and Abhorrers. Two political parties in the reign of Charles II, initially defined by their opposite attitudes on the issue of the right of English subjects to petition the king to assemble Parliament. The Petitioners, supporting the right to petition, were in favor of strong parliamentary government and opposed the succession of James II. They formed the nucleus of the Whig party. The Abhorrers, who disapproved of petitioning, maintained the royal prerogative of independent rule and favored James's succession. Their successors were the Tories and the Jacobites.

Petition of Right (1628). A declaration of Parliament reluctantly accepted by Charles I, providing that no forced loans or taxes were to be imposed without Parliament's consent. It also condemned arbitrary imprisonment and the billeting of troops in private houses. It is one of the chief documents of English constitutional government.

Petit Pierre, Le. See Anatole FRANCE.

Peto. In Shakespeare's HENRY IV: PART I and PART II, an associate of Sir John Falstaff.

Petrarch. Ital., **Francesco Petrarca** (1304–1374). Italian poet and scholar. A major force in the development of the Renaissance and European culture generally, he was born at Arezzo and spent much of his early life at Avignon and Carpentras, the former city being the seat of the papacy during the so-called Babylonian captivity. Although he studied law at Bologna, his primary interests were in Latin and Greek literature and in writing. As scholar and poet, he soon grew famous enough to be crowned at Rome on April 8, 1341, with the coveted laurel, in a ceremony that had not been seen since ancient times. The latter part of his life was spent in wandering restlessly from city to city in northern Italy, despite the welcome he received everywhere as an international celebrity. Like his friend Boccaccio, he was avidly interested in classical antiquity and fostered its revival. His learning, sound scholarship, and critical spirit made him a founder of Renaissance HUMANISM. Several factors set him apart from his medieval contemporaries and later earned him the designation of the first modern man: his love of nature, evidenced by the descriptions of Vaucluse in his writings and the then unusual feat of mountain climbing; his frank confession of and meditation on psychological conflicts; his preference for Plato over Aristotle; and, most of all, his human treatment of his love for LAURA, which transcended the conventions of courtly love. A prolific correspondent, he wrote many important letters. Among his Latin works are *De viris illustribus* (*On Illustrious Men*); the epic poem *Africa*, which has Scipio Africanus as its hero and the love of Masinissa and Sophonisba as its key romantic episode; the dialogue *Secretum*, which reveals in a debate with St. Augustine Petrarch's "secret" conflict—his love of Laura and the laurel (fame) opposed to his spiritual yearnings; an incomplete treatise on the cardinal virtues, *Rerum memorandarum libri*; *De vita solitaria* (*On the Solitary Life*); *De otio religioso* (*On the Virtue of the Religious Life*); *Bucolicum carmen*, 12 eclogues; *Invecta contra medicum* (*Invective Against Doctors*); *De Remediis utriusque fortunae* (*Remedies Against One and the Other Fortune*), his most popular Latin prose work, translated into English in 1579 by

Thomas Twyne; an *Itinerarium,* or guide book, to the Holy Land; *De sui ipsius et multorum ignorantia* (*On His Own Ignorance and That of Others*), against the Aristotelians.

Equally influential, especially during the Renaissance, were his Italian poems, collected in a *canzoniere*, or songbook. Usually called *Rime* or *Rime sparse* (*Scattered Lyrics*), they include sonnets, canzoni, sestine, ballate and madrigals, divided by later editors into two parts: *In vita* and *In morte di Madonna Laura* (*During the Life* and *After the Death of My Lady Laura*). Modern scholars no longer believe that Laura was a real woman, but it is admitted that she is more realistically presented than the conventional lady of the Provençal troubadours and the literature of courtly love, that she is less ethereal than the *donna angelicata* (angelic lady) of his immediate Italian predecessors, the *stil-novisti* (followers of Dante's "sweet new style"), and especially Beatrice. Some of the poems are addressed to friends; others deal with contemporary personages and affairs; still others are religious; but the dominant theme is Laura, whose beauty and actions enamour the poet and cause him both joy and despair, for she is unattainable, and the poet would be a lesser man and a lesser poet were his desire to be fulfilled. This conflict is recorded in detailed psychological terms, albeit formalized by figurative language and the other devices of literary style. Upon her death, the poet finds that his grief is as difficult to live with as was his former despair, but the mood and the tone become more spiritual and a consolatory note appears. These poems were the source of European Petrarchism, which everywhere dominated lyric poetry for centuries after. Petrarch's other vernacular work, the *Trionfi,* is in terza rima and partly inspired by Dante. It describes allegorical processions or "triumphs" of Love, Chastity, Death, Fame, Time, and Eternity, including historical and literary persons among whom Laura appears again. The poet was still revising the work when he died in 1374.

His immense influence in England began with Chaucer, who used for his *Clerk's Tale* Petrarch's translation into Latin of the *Griselda* story in the *Decameron,* as well as a poem from the *Rime* for the *cantus Troili* in *Troilus and Criseyde.* Later, English Petrarchism started its long journey in the poems of Wyatt and Surrey, and from there continued to exert its power through the 19th century. During the English Renaissance, when every lyricist was touched by the *Rime,* there was also great interest in the *Trionfi,* as the translation of Henry Parker, Lord Morley, in 1550 reveals. Shelley's poem, *The Triumph of Life,* indicates its later impact. Among the Latin works, the *De Remediis* proved especially popular with English readers and authors.

Petrie, Sir **Flinders** (1853–1942). A world renowned English Egyptologist. His excavations in Egypt and Palestine led to many discoveries in archeology and anthropology. He was the author of numerous books on ancient civilizations.

Petrified Forest, The (1935). A play by Robert E. SHERWOOD. Set in the Arizona desert, the drama deals with Alan Squier, an unsuccessful New England author who is hitchhiking to California. Arriving at a gasoline station and cheap lunchroom, he persuades a gangster to kill him, first revising his insurance policy. He makes the daughter of the lunchroom proprietor his beneficiary, so that she can escape from her sordid environment.

Petronius, Gaius (d. A.D. 66). *Arbiter Elegantiae* (judge of elegance), as Tacitus calls him, at the court of Nero. He is probably the author of the *Satyricon*, a fragmentary manuscript in prose and verse which is considered one of the first examples of the novel form and gives a vivid, sardonic, and extremely realistic picture of the luxuries, vices, and social manners of the imperial age of ancient Rome. Almost the only historical evidence of Petronius' existence is to be found in the 16th book of the *Annals* of Tacitus, where it is reported that he committed suicide to escape being put to death by Nero. He figures importantly in *Quo Vadis* (1896) by Sienkiewicz. See TRIMALCHIO.

Petruchio. In Shakespeare's TAMING OF THE SHREW, a highhanded gentleman of Verona who undertakes to tame the haughty Katharina, the title character. He marries her and reduces her to lamblike submission with his wit, spirit, and vigor.

Petry, Ann (1911–). American novelist and short-story writer. She is known for her first novel, *The Street* (1946), set in New York's Harlem. *Country Place* (1947) and *The Narrows* (1953) have Connecticut as their background. She is also the author of several juvenile books.

Petty, Sir William (1623–1687). English political economist and statistician. His *Treatises of Taxes and Contributions* (1662, 1667, 1685) contain the first statement of the economic doctrine that price depends upon the labor invested in production.

Peveril of the Peak (1822). The longest of Sir Walter SCOTT's novels. Julian Peveril, a Cavalier, is in love with Alice Bridgenorth, a Roundhead's daughter, and the action is interwoven with the "Popish Plot" of 1678. The 108 characters include a gallery of memorable historical figures.

Peyrefitte, Roger (1907–). French novelist. *Special Friendships* (*Les Amitiés particulières;* 1944) concerns the secret and tragic friendship of two boarding-school adolescents. *Diplomatic Diversions* (*Les Ambassades;* 1951) and *Diplomatic Conclusions* (*La Fin des Ambassades;* 1953) are witty and worldly accounts of Athens in 1937–1938, where Peyrefitte was in diplomatic service. The satiric *Keys of St. Peter* (1955) and *Knights of Malta* (1957) involve ironic clerical intrigues. Other works include *The Exile of Capri* (1959) and the essay *South from Naples* (*Du Vésuve à l'Etna;* 1952).

Pfaff's Cellar. A famous tavern at 653 Broadway, near Bleecker Street, New York City. A meeting place for Bohemians of the 1850's, Walt Whitman, Henry Clapp, Ada Clare, Fitz-James O'Brien, Bayard Taylor, George Arnold, Adah Menken, and William Winter were frequent visitors. The group was scattered by the Civil War, but the Bohemians had written so much in praise of Pfaff's that it flourished as a tourist attraction for many years.

Phaeacians (Phaiakes). In Greek mythology, a seafaring people. They befriended Odysseus and the ARGONAUTS. In the Odyssey, their island is named Scherie; in the *Argonautica* it is called Drepane. They were ruled by the kindly king Alcinous, who respects the counsel of his even more sympathetic wife Arete. Their daughter Nausicaa encounters Odysseus on the beach, and, after entertaining him royally, her parents send him back to Ithaca in one of their ships, which Poseidon turns to stone in revenge. They also defend the Argonauts from a pursuing Colchian ship after Arete has arranged for a hasty marriage between Jason and Medea.

Phaedo (Phaidon). A dialogue by PLATO. In it, Phaedo, a disciple of SOCRATES, describes the last hour of his teacher's life. Socrates and his friends discuss the possibility of the immortality of the soul. The doctrine of ideas and the theory of reminiscence are the most important arguments.

Phaedra (Phaidra). In Greek mythology, a daughter of Minos and Pasiphaë and wife of THESEUS. Theseus had previously abandoned her sister Ariadne. She fell in love with her stepson Hippolytus. When he scorned her, she committed suicide, but left a message for Theseus claiming that Hippolytus had tried to violate her. This story is the subject of Euripides' tragedy HIPPOLYTUS, Racine's masterpiece *Phèdre*, and many other works, including Mary Renault's historical novel *The Bull from the Sea*. It is obviously based on the same widespread folk tale as that of Joseph and Potiphar's wife. BELLEROPHON was another Greek hero to suffer from the same revenge on the part of a woman whose advances he had scorned.

Phaedria. See FAERIE QUEENE, THE.

Phaedrus (Phaidros). A dialogue by PLATO. In it Socrates and his friend Phaedrus discuss the difference between conventional rhetoric, which attempts to persuade regardless of truth, and true rhetoric, based on dialectic. As illustration, the subject of love is discussed in both styles. The dialogue includes the famous simile in which the soul is compared to a charioteer (the rational element) driving a black steed (the irrational appetites) and a white steed (the spirited element).

Phaëthon (*Gr.*, the shining one). In classical myth, the son of HELIOS or Phoebus, the Sun. He undertook to drive his father's chariot, but was upset and thereby caused Libya to be parched into barren sands, and all Africa to be injured, the inhabitants blackened, and vegetation nearly destroyed. He would have set the world on fire had not Zeus transfixed him with a thunderbolt.

Phaon. See FAERIE QUEENE, THE.

Pharisees (Heb. *perûshim*, from *perash*, "to separate"). In the Bible, those ascetic separatists who attempted to regulate their lives according to the Old Testament ideal of the oral Law given by God to Moses. Because the Pharisees were highly self-righteous, refusing to hold intercourse with other men, the term "Pharisee" has become derogatory. Jesus attacked their hypocrisy: "Woe unto you, scribes and Pharisees, hypocrites!" (Luke 11:44).

Pharnace. In Jean Racine's tragedy MITHRIDATE, the disloyal son of the titular hero. He conspires to take his father's betrothed for his own bride and attempts, eventually, to betray his father to Rome.

Pharos. One of the SEVEN WONDERS OF THE ANCIENT WORLD. It was a lighthouse built by Ptolemy Philadelphus on the island of Pharos, off Alexandria, Egypt. It was 450 feet high, and, according to Josephus could be seen at the distance of 42 miles. Part of it was blown down in 793; the rest was destroyed by an earthquake in the 14th century. The name has become synonymous with lighthouse.

Pharsalia. See LUCAN.

Pharsalus, battle of (48 B.C.). The decisive battle between CAESAR and POMPEY. When Caesar crossed the RUBICON, Pompey and other members of the Senatorial Party fled to Thessaly where Caesar pursued them and defeated them near the town of Pharsalus.

Phebe. In Shakespeare's As You LIKE IT, a young shepherdess who falls in love with the disguised Rosalind. When she realizes her mistake, she marries Silvius, the shepherd.

Phedon. See FAERIE QUEENE, THE.

Phèdre (1677). A tragedy by Jean RACINE. It is based upon Euripides' *Hippolytus*, but with the emphasis shifted from Hippolytus to PHAEDRA. During the absence of her husband, King Theseus, Phèdre conceals her passion for her stepson HIPPOLYTE, but receiving false word of Theseus' death, she is urged by her nurse OENONE to declare her love. Horrified, Hippolyte repulses her and upon Theseus' return asks permission to leave the court. Oenone convinces the king that Hippolyte made advances to her mistress, and Theseus calls upon Neptune, his protector, to destroy his son. Hippolyte refuses to accuse the queen directly, but inflames her jealousy by declaring his love for Aricie, a captive princess (the character is Racine's invention). In despair, Phèdre commits suicide, but the disclosure of her guilt comes too late for Neptune has already destroyed Hippolyte.

Pheidippides. (1) A Greek runner. He was famed for his exploits at the time of the battle of MARATHON. Browning makes him the hero of a poem in his *Dramatic Idylls*.

(2) See CLOUDS, THE.

phenomenology. In philosophy and metaphysics, the description and classification of *phenomena*, or acts of perception, as the only objects of knowledge possessing ultimate reality. In the 20th century the phrase is particularly identified with the work of Edmund HUSSERL, who sought to establish a foundation for all the sciences by describing the formal structure of phenomena.

Pherecydes of Leros (Pherekydes). See APOLLODORUS.

Phidias. Greek sculptor of the 5th century B.C. He supervised the rebuilding of the Acropolis instituted by Pericles. The Parthenon and most of the other great monuments of Athens date from this period. His Olympian Zeus at Elis and his Athene Parthenos (438), both colossal chryselephantine statues, are known from descriptions and more or less doubtful copies. Fragments of his frieze for the Parthenon have survived; they are among the greatest existing works of sculpture. Phidias died in prison under a charge of sacrilege, brought by the enemies of Pericles, for having represented Pericles and himself on the shield of Athene.

Philadelphia Story, The (1939). A comedy by Philip BARRY. Tracy Lord, a young heiress, finds her old Philadelphia family traditions too restrictive, especially after an escapade with a reporter on the eve of her second marriage. When everything becomes mixed up on the morning of the wedding, C. K. Dexter Haven, Tracy's first husband, takes the place of the pompous bridegroom and remarries Tracy.

Philaster, or Love Lies A-Bleeding (1609). A tragi-comedy by BEAUMONT AND FLETCHER. Philaster, heir to the throne of Sicily, is forced to live at the court of the usurping king of Calabria and Sicily. Arethusa, the king's daughter, who loves Philaster, is about to be married to the lecherous Pharamond, prince of Spain. However, Pharamond's lecheries become known and the engagement is broken off. Pharamond avenges himself by accusing Arethusa of having an affair with Bellario, Philaster's page now in her service. The distracted Philaster first offers his life to Arethusa and Bellario and then tries to kill them. He is arrested and entrusted to the custody of Arethusa, who saves his life by marrying him. Arethusa's honor is finally cleared when it is revealed that Bellario is really a young girl who entered Philaster's service because of her infatuation for him. Meanwhile, an uprising forces the king to restore Philaster's titles and lands.

Philemon. See FAERIE QUEENE, THE.

Philemon, The Epistle of Paul to. A New Testament book. A short personal letter from Paul to the master of a runaway slave who carried the letter on his return trip. Paul asks Philemon to forgive Onesimus, the slave. It is the only personal letter to an individual in the New Testament; it shows the new Christian social order which harmoniously included reformed slaves, rabbis, and pagans.

Philemon and Baucis. In Greek and Roman mythology, poor cottagers of Phrygia, husband and wife. In Ovid's account in *Metamorphoses*, they entertained Jupiter so hospitably that he promised to grant them whatever request they made. They asked that both might die together, and it was so. Philemon became an oak, Baucis a linden tree, and their branches intertwined at the top.

In the second part of Goethe's *Faust*, Philemon and Baucis are an old couple who refuse to sell their home at any price. Because theirs is a part of the land that he is redeeming from the sea, Faust, with the aid of Mephistopheles, dispossesses them, and they die of the shock.

Philip II (382–336 B.C.). King of Macedon (359–336 B.C.). Philip assumed charge of the Macedonian government as regent for his nephew Amyntas, whom he later set aside. The first few years of his reign were marked by his successful dispersal of rivals for the throne. Philip reorganized the Macedonian army on the basis of the phalanx. He extended Macedonian territory to include the gold mines of Mt. Pangaeus. Attempting to push into Greece, he eased Athens out of her possessions on the Thermaic Gulf. He married Olympias, who gave birth to Alexander in 356 B.C.

On the capture of Olynthus, Athens sent envoys to Philip to negotiate the peace of Philocrates, which was disapproved by Demosthenes. Philip soon broke the treaty and overran Thrace. The combined forces of Thebes and Athens were defeated, but Philip, who admired the Athenians, was lenient in his treatment of prisoners. About to move against Persia, he was assassinated by an agent of Olympias, who was jealous of his new consort. It is said that Alexander knew of the plot. Philip's reign marked the end of the city-state in Greece, paving the way for a Greek nation. Philip's aim, frustrated by his death, was to bring Greek culture to Macedon.

Philip II (1527–1598). King of Spain. The son of Charles V and Isabella of Portugal, Philip succeeded to the throne in 1556 upon his father's abdication. His first wife was Mary of Portugal, who died giving birth to the ill-starred Don CARLOS; in 1554 he married Mary Tudor of England and upon her death (1558) was an unsuccessful suitor for the hand of Elizabeth I. He arrived in Spain in 1559, never again to leave the Iberian Peninsula.

The most powerful monarch in Christendom, Philip ruled not only Spain, but the Netherlands, Franche Comté, Sicily, Sardinia, Naples, and Milan, as well as the Spanish possessions in America. In 1580, upon the extinction of the Aviz dynasty, he also acquired the crown of Portugal. This vast empire he ruled virtually alone, making all decisions, whether trivial or important, himself.

Often pictured, especially by northern European writers, as a tyrannical religious bigot, Philip was determined to strengthen royal power in Spain and to unify the peninsula, a policy which led him to suppress religious heterodoxy there and to curtail the traditional "liberties" of Aragon. The outbreak of a serious Protestant revolt in the Netherlands in the 1560's led him to aim at the subjugation of England, a design that was thwarted by the astute diplomacy of Elizabeth and the defeat of the Spanish ARMADA in 1588. He also intervened actively in the religious and dynastic struggles of France, but his efforts to control that country were checked by the accession of HENRY IV, though the latter's conversion to Catholicism represented a partial victory for Philip. He also warred with the powerful Ottoman Empire, winning a signal victory at LEPANTO in 1571. The burden of paying for this ambitious foreign policy rested almost entirely on Spain, especially Castile, which continuously skirted financial disaster despite the influx of American treasure and suffered a serious economic decline.

A bibliophile and a patron of art, Philip amassed a fine collection of rare books and paintings at the ESCORIAL, where he died and lies buried.

Philippi. A town in Macedonia, the scene of the defeat of the forces of BRUTUS and CASSIUS by those of Octavius (later Augustus) and Mark Antony in 42 B.C.

Philippians, The Epistle of Paul the Apostle to the. A New Testament book. It is a letter of thanks and encouragement written by Paul to the church at Philippi. Paul was in prison and had received presents from the Philippians; he writes to thank them and to encourage them in the face of persecution. The letter is filled with joy and a sense of triumph, and it indicates the strength of Paul's faith.

Philips, Ambrose (1675?–1749). English poet and friend of Addison and Steele. Pope's spiteful attacks on him began when a writer for *The Guardian* praised Philips' *Pastorals* and ignored Pope's *Pastorals*, both works having appeared in the same volume of Jacob Tonson's *Miscellany* (1709). Pope referred to him as "Namby Pamby," a nickname originally conferred on Philips by Henry Carey, because he thought it fitted his "eminence in infantile style." Philips is best known for his play *The Distrest Mother* (1712), an adaptation of Racine's *Andromaque*.

Philips, John (1676–1709). English poet. He is chiefly known for *The Splendid Shilling* (1705), a learned "Miltonic" burlesque contrasting the pleasures of a rich man with the sorrows of a penniless poet.

Philips, Katherine (1631–1664). English poet, known as "the Matchless Orinda." The leader of a literary salon in Cardigan, Wales, she adopted the name Orinda in her correspondence with Sir Charles Cotterell, who styled himself Poliarchus. Her translation of Corneille's *Mort de Pompée* was successfully produced in 1663, and was included in a collection of her *Poems* (1667).

Philip Sparrow (c. 1500). A long, quick-running, rambling, tenderly humorous elegy for a pet bird by John Skelton, employing fragments from the office for the dead. The poem was probably suggested by Catullus' dirge for a dead sparrow. Philip is the traditional name for sparrows, derived from the sound of the bird's chirp.

Philip the Apostle. One of the original 12 disciples. While he was active during the ministry of Jesus, Philip is not mentioned after the Resurrection. He is traditionally supposed to have preached in Hierapolis. During the Middle Ages, Philip the Apostle was confused with Philip the evangelist. The latter was one of the seven deacons ordained by the apostles as recorded in Acts.

Philistines. In the Old Testament, the inveterate enemies of the Israelites, fought against by Samson, David, and other Jewish heroes. In modern usage, the term refers to ignorant, ill-behaved persons lacking in culture or artistic appreciation and only concerned with materialistic values. Matthew Arnold first used the word in this sense by adapting it from the German *Philister*, the term applied by the university students to the townspeople, or "outsiders." This usage is said to have arisen at Jena, because after a "town and gown" row in 1689, which resulted in a number of deaths, the university preacher took for his text "The Philistines be upon thee" (Judg. 16).

James Branch Cabell introduced the country of *Philistia* into his satiric romances, notably *Jurgen* (1919).

Phillips, David Graham. Pen name, **John Graham** (1867–1911). American journalist and novelist. He is known for his muckraking articles, especially the series entitled *The Treason of the Senate*, which appeared in *Cosmopolitan* in 1906. Phillips wrote numerous novels exposing political corruption and social problems, such as *The Great God Success* (1901), *The Cost* (1904), *The Deluge* (1905), and *The Conflict* (1911). Several of the novels, as well as his only play, *The Worth of a Woman* (1908), deal with his era's changing attitudes toward the feminine sex. His most important novel was *Susan Lenox: Her Fall and Rise* (1917), a realistic, well-documented account of a country girl who becomes a prostitute and later a successful actress. Phillips was murdered by a madman who thought that he had been maligned and slandered by the author's *The Fashionable Adventures of Joshua Craig* (1909).

Phillips, Edward (1630–?1696) and **Phillips, John** (1631–1706). English writers. Both were nephews of John MILTON and were educated by him. The former was tutor to the son of John Evelyn, wrote a valuable memoir on Milton and a number of books, including a popular philological dictionary, *New World of Words* (1658). John Phillips acted as secretary to Milton and published a reply in Latin to an anonymous attack on him. He is best known for his diatribe against Puritanism; *A Satyr Against Hypocrites* (1655).

Phillips, Wendell (1811–1884). American abolitionist and reformer. Phillips dismayed the exalted Boston circles in which he moved by becoming an ardent antislavery agitator in the mid-1830's. A long-time ally of William Lloyd Garrison, Phillips was particularly noted as a superb speaker whose informal, direct delivery contrasted with the bombast then in vogue. After the Civil War, he devoted himself to economic reform, denouncing "the present system of finance, which robs labor and gorges capital. . . ."

Phillpotts, Eden (1862–1960). Prolific English novelist. His novels of Devon rural life, written in the Thomas Hardy tradition, include *Down Dartmoor Way* (1895), *Children of the Mist* (1898), and *The Good Red Earth* (1901). Among his other works are *The Changeling* (1943) and *Through a Glass Darkly* (1951).

Philoctetes (Philoktetes). Greek hero in the TROJAN WAR. On the way to Troy he was bitten by a serpent. The wound proved so noxious and Philoctetes' pain so great that his companions abandoned him on the island of Lemnos. He remained there for ten years, nursing his wound and his hatred of the Greeks. Ultimately, however, his former companions learned from the captured Trojan seer Helenus that Troy could fall only before the arrows of Heracles. These had descended to Philoctetes from his father Poeas, who had received them for the service of lighting Heracles' funeral pyre. Odysseus and NEOPTOLEMUS (or Diomedes) sailed to Lemnos. According to Sophocles' tragedy *Philoctetes*, they would have tricked him into going with them or taken him by force except for the compassion of Neoptolemus. In the end, Heracles appeared and commanded Philoctetes to go. He was cured by Machaon, the son of Asclepios. Philoctetes then killed Paris with one of the arrows and Troy soon fell.

Philomela. In Greek legend, daughter of Pandion, king of Attica. According to one version of the story, TEREUS, king of Thrace, brought Philomela to visit his wife, Procne, who was her sister. He dishonored her, and cut out her tongue that she might not reveal his conduct. Tereus told his wife that Philomela was dead, but Philomela made her story known by weaving it into a peplus, which she sent to Procne. In another version Tereus married Philomela, telling her that Procne was dead, and it was Procne whose tongue was cut out and who wove the telltale story. In each case the end is the same. Procne, in revenge, cut up her own son Itys, or Itylus, and served the flesh to Tereus. The gods changed all three into birds; Tereus became the hoopoe, his wife the swallow, and Philomela the nightingale (in Latin versions), which is still called Philomel (lover of song) by the poets. Matthew Arnold's *Philomela*, Coleridge's *Nightingale*, and Swinburne's *Itylus* are among the best-known poems based on the tale.

Philomena. See FILUMENA.

philosophers' stone. The hypothetical substance which, according to the medieval alchemists, would convert all baser metals into gold. Its discovery was the prime object of all the alchemists, and to the wide and unremitting search that went on for it we are indebted for the birth of the science of chemistry, as well as for many inventions. According to one legend, Noah was commanded to hang up the true and genuine philosophers' stone in the ark, to give light to every living creature therein. Another relates that Deucalion had it in a bag over his shoulder, but threw it away and lost it.

philosophes. A group of 18th century French thinkers, scientists, and men of letters. They held that human reason ought to be the supreme guide in human affairs and therefore opposed those institutions and creeds which they found irrational, constraining, or superstitious. Though the *philosophes* differed widely in their separate views, they were united in their skeptical attitude toward religious and political authority and helped induce a climate of popular disrespect for government and church which contributed directly to the French Revolution. Despite censorship difficulties, the *philosophes* were able to publish their great work, the *Encyclopédie* (1751–1766), a systematic classification of all human knowledge marked by its rigorous rationality, its utter contempt for superstition and its blunt skepticism toward religion. In addition to Diderot, who was chief director of the *Encyclopédie*, the most important *philosophes* were d'Alembert, Buffon, Condillac, Condorcet, Helvétius, d'Holbach, Marmontel, Morellet, Raynal, Rousseau, Turgot, and Voltaire, many of whom were at one time or another imprisoned or otherwise persecuted for expressing their views too freely.

Philosophy of Composition, The (1846). A critical essay by Edgar Allan POE. The poet explains the methodical manner in which he composed THE RAVEN. Choosing the death of a beautiful woman as the most poetic of all subjects, he rationally dissects the melodic effects of his work. Poe believed that a poem must be brief, and its proper tone, melancholy.

Philostrate. In Shakespeare's MIDSUMMER NIGHT'S DREAM, the master of the revels who arranges the wedding festivities of Theseus and Hippolyta.

Philostratus (Philostratos, fl. c. 210). Greek author, also known as the Athenian. To him, the third of his family to bear the name, are attributed two important works: *Lives of the Sophists* and the fictional biography of APOLLONIUS OF TYANA. The latter work was the subject of religious controversy between Christians and pagans.

Philoxenos of Leucadia. An ancient Greek epicure. Of him it is told that he wished he had the neck of a crane, that he might enjoy the taste of his food the longer (Aristotle, *Ethics,* 111, 10).

Phineas Finn (1869). The first of the so-called Parliamentary novels by Anthony TROLLOPE. Phineas, a poor young Irishman, is elected to Parliament and comes to London, leaving Mary Flood-Jones, his sweetheart, behind. In London he becomes enamored of several ladies, quarrels with the leading members of his party, resigns, and returns home to Mary.

Phineus. In classic myth, a blind soothsayer. He was tormented by the harpies. Whenever a meal was set before him, the harpies came and carried it off.

The ARGONAUTS delivered him from these pests in return for his information respecting the route they were to take in order to obtain the GOLDEN FLEECE. He also appears in the *Argonautica* of Apollonius of Rhodes.

Phips or **Phipps, Sir William** (1651–1695). American colonial governor of Massachusetts. His administration, during which the Salem witchcraft trials occurred, was attacked as neglectful, and he was called to England by the king. Cotton Mather wrote a laudatory biography of Phips (1697).

Phiz. Pen name of **Hablot Knight Browne** (1815–1882). English illustrator and caricaturist. Famed for his illustrations of the works of Charles Dickens, he first made his reputation when, in 1836, Robert Seymour died and he succeeded him as illustrator of *Pickwick Papers*. He subsequently illustrated the works of Charles Lever and Harrison Ainsworth; he was also noted for his contributions to *Punch*.

Phlegethon (Gr. *phlego,* to burn). In classic myth, a river of liquid fire in HADES. It flowed into the river ACHERON. For the other rivers, see STYX.

phlogiston. An imaginary substance used by 17th- and early 18th-century chemists to explain what is now called oxidation. The Germans Georg Ernest Stahl (1660–1734) and Johann Joachim Becher (1635–1682) were among its advocates. The belief that burning substances gave off phlogiston was not challenged until Lavoisier, using precise scales, discovered that burning substances combined with oxygen from the air.

Phobos. Literally, panic fear. It is personified by the ancient Greeks as one of the sons of Ares, god of War, the other being Deimos (terror). The twin satellites of the planet Mars, Phobos and Deimos, were discovered in 1877.

Phocas. In Pierre Corneille's tragedy HÉRACLIUS, the murderer of the Emperor of the East and the usurper of his throne.

Phocus (Phokos). In Greek mythology, a son by Psamathe of AEACUS, king of Phthia. Killed by his jealous half-brothers Telamon and Peleus, he was the eponymous ancestor of the Phocians.

Phoebus (from Greek *phoibos,* bright). An epithet of APOLLO, particularly in his quality as the god of light. The name often stands for the sun personified.

Phoenician Women, The (Phoinissai; 410 B.C.). A drama by EURIPIDES. In this, the longest extant Greek play, Euripides treated the events of the war of the SEVEN AGAINST THEBES, and more. Oedipus lives imprisoned in the palace; Creon's son Menoeceus kills himself when Tiresias predicts that his death will save the city; Jocasta kills herself on failing to separate the brothers; Creon declares that Antigone shall marry his son Haemon, but she defies him and goes into exile with Oedipus. Parts of this story also were told in Aeschylus' SEVEN AGAINST THEBES, SENECA's *Phoenissae,* and STATIUS' epic *Thebais.* Parts of it are found in Sophocles' ANTIGONE and Euripides' THE SUPPLIANT WOMEN. See EPIGONI.

Phoenissae (Phoinissai). See SEVEN AGAINST THEBES.

phoenix. A mythical Arabian bird, the only one of its kind. At the end of a certain number of years, it was said to make a nest of spices, sing a melodious dirge, flap its wings to set fire to the pile, consume itself in the ashes, but come forth with new life to repeat the former one.

It is to this bird that Shakespeare refers in *Cymbeline* (c. 1610) and in his poem, *The Phoenix and the Turtle.*

The phoenix was adopted as a sign over chemists' shops because of its association with alchemists. It was also regarded as a symbol of immortality.

phoenix period or *cycle.* The period between the transformations of the phoenix, generally supposed to be 500 years but sometimes estimated as high as 1500 years.

Phoenix and the Turtle, The (1601). A poem by William SHAKESPEARE. It was published with a group of poems in a volume called *Loves Martyr: Or Rosalin's Complaint* by Robert Chester. An obscure, enigmatic, but strikingly effective work. it has provoked a great deal of critical speculation as to its merit and its meaning.

Phoenix Nest, The (1593). A poetic miscellany edited by "R. S. of the Inner Temple, gentleman." One of the finest of Elizabethan collections, it contains poems by Lodge, Breton, Raleigh, and others.

Phoenix Park. An amusement area in Dublin where on May 6, 1882 the then newly-appointed lord secretary of Ireland, Lord Frederick Cavendish, and the under-secretary, Thomas H. Burke, were murdered by members of the revolutionary Fenian movement. In retaliation the English government instituted severe repressions and attempted to implicate the Irish parliamentary leader, Charles Stewart Parnell. In James Joyce's novel *Ulysses,* the Phoenix Park murders are discussed in the scene which takes place in the newspaper office.

phooka, pooka, or **púca.** A many-shaped hobgoblin of Irish folklore, whom some see as akin to Shakespeare's Puck. Samain (the first of November) is of special importance to him, and it was said that he used to appear on this day out of a certain hill as a great and terrible horse, able to speak in a human voice and answer the questions of passers-by.

phrenology. The study of relationships between the formation of the skull and specific character traits. It was founded by GALL. Lavater began a study of the correlation between facial characteristics and character traits. He called his science "physiognomy."

Phrixus (Phrixas). See GOLDEN FLEECE, THE.

Phrygian cap. See BONNET ROUGE; LIBERTY CAP.

Phrygian mode. See GREEK MUSIC.

Phryne (4th century B.C.). A famous Athenian courtesan. She acquired so much wealth by her beauty that she offered to rebuild the walls of Thebes if she might put on them this inscription: "Alexander destroyed them, but Phryne the hetaera rebuilt them.' She is said to have been the model for Praxiteles' Cnidian Venus, and also for Apelles' picture of Venus rising from the sea.

Phrynicus (Phrynichos, 6th century B.C.). An Athenian playwright. Only fragments of his many plays remain, but he was highly regarded by his contemporaries and for generations thereafter. It is said that one of his plays proved so distressingly moving to the Athenians that he was fined. According to tradition, he was the first playwright to introduce female characters in his plays, though the parts were played by men.

Phylacus (Phylakos). See MELAMPUS.

Physician of His Own Honor, The. See MÉDICO DE SU HONRA, EL.

Physician's Tale, The. One of the CANTERBURY TALES of Geoffrey CHAUCER. After a digression on the raising of young girls, the Physician tells the story of the judge Apius and VIRGINIA, purportedly from Livy, but resembling more the version in the 13th-century *Romance of the Rose*. According to the Physician, Virginia's father tells her at home that she must die by his hand or else be shamed by the lecherous Apius. She weeps, but voluntarily accepts her death. Apius condemns her father to be hanged, but the people revolt, and the judge commits suicide in prison.

physiocrats. Name given to a French school of economic theorists of the latter part of the 18th century. François QUESNAY is considered to be the founder and leader of physiocracy, though many of his ideas are to be found in the writings of earlier French economists, such as Jean Claude Vincent, sieur de Gournay; Sébastien Vauban; and Pierre de Boisguilbert. Among other economists who subsequently elaborated on Quesnay's thought are the marquis de Mirabeau, Mercier de la Rivière, Anne TURGOT, and Pierre Samuel DU PONT DE NEMOURS. The term "physiocrat" combines two Greek words meaning *nature* and *rule*, and implies the economic view that only natural resources constitute national wealth, that only agriculture and mining are really productive, and that industry and commerce, though not to be neglected, add nothing to national wealth. Agricultural methods, according to this doctrine, should be scientifically improved, since only abundant production coupled with fair prices can create prosperity. Absolute freedom of trade, and an economic policy of *laissez faire* (free competition) will establish a natural economy, from which all other benefits will flow. A single tax is to be levied at the very source of wealth, i.e., on the land, and any tax on manufacturers and traders would be futile, since they would pass their tax burden onto the farmer. Though physiocracy died partly because of its failures, and possibly because of ridicule on the part of contemporaries, it did influence the classical school of economists, notably Adam Smith. The founder of the single-tax movement in America, Henry George, was directly influenced by the physiocrats.

Physiologus (Physiologos, 2d century). An anonymous Greek collection of allegories concerning animals and other things in nature. In the fifth century, Latin translations of the *Physiologus* became popular throughout Europe. They constitute the foundation of the bestiaries of the later Middle Ages.

Pia, Emilia (d. 1528). Italian lady. The widowed heiress of the noble Carpi family, she lived at Urbino as the companion of its duchess Elisabetta Gonzaga. She has the nominal leadership of the discussions that form THE COURTIER of Castiglione.

Piazza Tales, The (1856). A collection of six long short stories by Herman MELVILLE. His finest stories, they were all published individually in magazines. In *The Bell Tower*, the artist Bannadonna attempts to rival the power of God, but is destroyed by his own creation. Similar in theme, *The Light-ning-Rod Man* is refused a sale: his unwilling customer believes that man, who cannot control God, should not fear Him. *The Encantadas, or The Enchanted Isles* is a collection of ten descriptive sketches based on Melville's 1841 voyage to the Galápagos Islands. Introducing the volume is a section called *The Piazza*. *The Piazza Tales* conclude with two excellent short stories, BENITO CERENO and BARTLEBY THE SCRIVENER.

picaresque. An adjective from the Spanish *pícaro* (rogue) used to describe a genre of literature in which the life and adventures of a rogue are chronicled. Although the picaresque takes many forms—for example, memoirs, plays, ballads—its best expression is found in the novel.

The picaresque novel is typically a realistic depiction of the criminal element in society; it is usually an autobiographical account of a peripatetic rogue of "loose" morals. The retelling of his adventures in the service of a series of masters, and of his various ways of outwitting them, affords the author an opportunity to make humorous, satiric sketches of types in various levels of society. Moralizing, in greater and lesser degrees of serious intent, is also characteristic. Stylistically, the picaresque novel usually displays plainness of language and faithfulness to petty detail; the tone is often cynical. The structure is that of a series of loosely connected episodes; there being no plot, these could end at any time or go on endlessly, since neither character nor incident is treated developmentally. The hero, or picaroon, who may be thought of as an anti-hero need not be a man; it may be a woman or an animal.

Picaresque elements are found in the *Satyricon* of Petronius, in *The Golden Ass* of Apuleius, in the mediaeval *fabliaux* and animal epics, and in the work of François Villon. It was not established as a genre, however, until the publication of the anonymous *La vida de* LAZARILLO DE TORMES (1554), which was one of the most widely read books of the century. The next picaresque novel was GUZMÁN DE ALFARACHE (1599–1605) by Mateo Alemán. Cervantes took up the manner with the stories *El Coloquio de los perros* and *Rinconete y Cortadillo* in his NOVELAS EJEMPLARES, and elements of the picaresque are to be found in DON QUIXOTE. *Historia de la vida del Buscón* (1626) by Francisco de Quevedo is a further example of the genre.

The picaresque novel in Spain declined after the mid-17th century; the last of the Spanish series is usually given as *Periquillo el de las gallineras* (1668). Early in the 18th century the picaroon appeared in France, notably in Lesage's GIL BLAS which was highly popular. Initially the genre was so firmly established as Spanish that the French writers gave their novels Spanish settings and their characters Spanish names, but inevitably the form underwent many modifications. By the time the English picked it up, in the 18th century, the picaroon's criminality was often mere prankishness; he was crafty and lived by his wits, and although hard-hearted, he was often lovable and essentially good. Outstanding examples of the English picaresque novel of the 18th century are Defoe's MOLL FLANDERS and the novels of Smollett, notably *The Adventures of* RODERICK RANDOM and *The Adventures of* PEREGRINE PICKLE; the middle section of Fielding's TOM JONES may also be considered picaresque. Some latter-day novels—for example, Mark Twain's *Huckleberry Finn* and Saul Bellow's *The Adventures of Augie March*—are sometimes loosely described as picaresque.

Picasso, Pablo [Ruiz y] (1881–   ). Spanish painter and sculptor. Picasso, who with Georges Braque founded CUBISM, is probably the most influential and certainly the most famous artist of the 20th century. Born in Málaga, the son of a Basque drawing teacher, he learned the rudiments of his art from his father, and then studied in Barcelona and Madrid. In 1901 he held his first exhibition in Paris, having visited there for the first time a year previously, and in 1904 he settled permanently in the French capital. During the next decade, Paris was to witness the greatest art revolution in its history; the impressionists had already been accepted, if not approved of, and the search for a truly modern form of 20th-century art was in the hands of the postimpressionists.

Picasso's early work gives no hint of the break that he was shortly to make with tradition. Strictly representational in content, it is generally divided into a so-called blue period (1901–1904) and rose period (1904–1906)—the terms being derived from the basic tonality of color used at each time—and in both periods it reflects the influence of such French artists as Manet, Degas, and Toulouse-Lautrec and of the great Spanish masters. Then, in 1907, Picasso produced *Les Demoiselles d'Avignon,* his famous and influential canvas, which inspired by primitive African sculpture directly foreshadowed cubism, and from that moment on he was in the forefront of modern art.

A figure of protean diversity, Picasso has participated in most of the artistic styles and movements of the 20th century. Gradually moving away from cubism, after 1917 he began to explore the possibilities of neoclassicism. He returned to a modified form of cubism; then, in the middle 1920's, his work gradually became surrealistic in style and content. In recent years he has seemed concerned with creating works of pure fantasy. Picasso has also constantly sought to extend the range of the artist's resources; in 1912, while experimenting with cubism, he evolved the new medium of collage. Extraordinarily prolific, he has done distinguished work in sculpture and in nearly every form of the graphic arts, as well as in such allied fields as ceramics, mosaics, and stage designing. Among his most famous paintings are *Guernica, The Three Musicians,* and *The Guitarist.*

Piccadilly. A well-known London thoroughfare. It is named for Pickadilly Hall, a house that stood near the corner of Sackville Street in the early 17th century.

Piccini or **Piccinni, Niccolò** (1728–1800). Italian opera composer. He is remembered principally for a feud (1774–1780) between his followers (Piccinists), and the admirers of C. W. Gluck (GLUCKISTS).

Piccolomini, Die. See WALLENSTEIN.

Piccolomini, Enea Silvio de. See PIUS II.

Pichette, Henri (1924–   ). French poet and dramatist. The avant-garde drama NUCLEA (1952) presents his nightmare vision of hate and war, and his demanding dream of love and peace. His poetry includes *A-poèmes* (1947), *Dents de lait, dents de loup* (1959), and *Odes à chacun* (1961).

Pickle, Peregrine. See PEREGRINE PICKLE.

Pickwick, Samuel. In Charles Dickens' PICKWICK PAPERS, the founder of the Pickwick Club. An unsophisticated, innocent man, he is caught up in a breach of promise suit brought against him by Mrs. BARDELL. When he refuses to pay damages, he is put into Fleet Prison, accompanied by Sam WELLER. When released he dissolves the club and retires to a house outside London with Sam Weller and Weller's bride, who acts as housekeeper.

Pickwick Papers (1836–1837). A novel by Charles DICKENS, first published serially under the pseudonym Boz. Originally intended as mere prose sketches to accompany the illustrations of the popular caricaturist Seymour, *The Posthumous Papers of the Pickwick Club* (the series' formal title) were an almost immediate success, and made Dickens famous. The book is made up of letters and manuscripts about the club's activities. The chief character is Samuel PICKWICK, founder of the club, a most naïve and benevolent elderly gentleman. As chairman of the Pickwick Club, he travels about with his fellow club members and acts as their guardian and advisor.

in a Pickwickian sense. Said of words or epithets usually of a derogatory or insulting kind, that, in the circumstances in which they are employed, are not to be taken as having quite the same force or implication as they normally would have. The allusion is to the scene in chapter I where Mr. Pickwick accuses Mr. Blotton of acting in a "vile and calumnious manner," whereupon Mr. Blotton retorts by calling Mr. Pickwick a humbug. It finally is made to appear that both use the offensive words only in a Pickwickian sense and that each has, in fact, the highest regard and esteem for the other. The book is one of Dickens' most quoted and it contains many of his well-known characters, or caricatures, including Mrs. BARDELL; Serjeant BUZFUZ; Messrs. DODSON AND FOGG; Mr. and Mrs. Leo HUNTER; Alfred JINGLE; Augustus SNODGRASS; Tracy TUPMAN; Mr. WARDLE; Samuel WELLER; and Nathaniel WINKLE.

Pico della Mirandola, Count Giovanni (1463–1494). Italian humanist, philosopher, and author. In 1484, he came to Florence and joined the so-called Florentine Academy, actually a literary gathering sponsored by the Medici family. Pico knew Latin, Greek, Hebrew, and Arabic, and was one of the first Christian scholars of the Cabala. Unlike his friend Ficino, he was interested in the more esoteric writing of the philosophical tradition. It was his idea that all knowledge could be reconciled and systematized. In 1486, at the age of 24, he published a series of 900 conclusions or theses, ranging from logic to the Cabala, and offered to take on all challengers of his ideas. After the church found 13 of them heretical, he fled to France for a time but returned to continue his studies. His best known work in modern times is the Latin oration *De dignitate hominis* (*On the Dignity of Man*), which was prefaced to his 900 theses as the opening salvo in the expected debate. It has been regarded as a typical RENAISSANCE expression of the renewed faith in the power and stature of the human creature. In England, he was especially influential on Colet and Sir Thomas More, the latter having translated some of his work and written a life of him.

Picrochole (*Gr.* "who has a bitter bile"). In Rabelais' GARGANTUA AND PANTAGRUEL, the despot of Lerne, who declares war on the kingdom of Grandgousier, Gargantua's father. When the power-mad tyrant, using a quarrel between his bakers and Grandgousier's shepherds as a pretext for attack, begins ravaging the countryside, Grandgousier is obliged to send for Gargantua, who leaves his studies in Paris to defend his homeland. Gargantua and Friar John win the war, Picrochole and his counselors flee, and peace is restored. The war is waged in the vicinity of Chinon, where Rabelais was born, and the narrative faithfully portrays its people and their customs. In describing the war, Rabelais expressed his own humanist ideal of reasoned and benevolent government as opposed to unbridled tyranny.

Picture of Dorian Gray, The (1891). A fantastic, moral novel by Oscar WILDE. The plot concerns a beautiful youth, Dorian Gray, who has his portrait painted by Basil Hallward. Hallward also introduces Dorian to Lord Henry Wotton, who initiates the youth in a life of vice. The painting, it turns out, has supernatural powers, and while Dorian remains young and beautiful throughout his deterioration, the portrait changes, reflecting his real state of degeneracy. Finally Dorian kills Hallward and then stabs the painting; he is then found dead with a knife through his heart, his face the very picture of corruption while the portrait, restored to what it was, hangs over him portraying a young, innocent, handsome man.

Picus. In Roman mythology, a soothsayer and augur; husband of Canens. In his prophetic art he made use of a woodpecker (*picus*), a prophetic bird sacred to Mars. Circe fell in love with him, and, as he did not respond to her advances, changed him into a woodpecker, whereby he still retained his prophetic power. These tales appear to have built up about a figure that was originally no more than the sacred woodpecker itself.

Pied Piper of Hamelin. A magician in German folk lore. According to legend, the town of Hamelin was plagued with rats in 1284. A mysterious stranger in particolored clothes appeared and offered to rid the town of the destructive vermin for a specified sum of money. The leaders of the town agreed to the contract, and the stranger began to play his pipe. The rats came swarming from the buildings and followed him to the river Weser, where they drowned. But then the town leaders refused to make the agreed payment, so the Pied Piper returned, once more playing his pipe. Only this time it was all the children of the town whom he enchanted and lured away to vanish behind a door in the Koppenberg hill.

Robert Browning told the story in his poem *The Pied Piper of Hamelin* (1842); Josephine Preston Peabody used it in her verse play *The Piper* (1909).

Pierce, Lorne (1890–1961). Canadian editor and writer. As editor-in-chief of the Ryerson Press, Pierce encouraged young Canadian writers and founded several awards for literature. His works include *Marjorie Pickthall, A Book of Remembrance* (1925), *Master Builders* (1937), and *Grace Coombs: Artist* (1949).

Pierian spring. Inspiration, from Pieria where the MUSES were born.

Pierre et Jean (1888). A short novel by Guy de MAUPASSANT. This psychological study of two brothers shares in the concentrated force of Maupassant's short stories.

Pierre Nozière. See Anatole FRANCE.

Pierre, or The Ambiguities (1852). A novel by Herman MELVILLE. Pierre Glendinning, a young writer, leaves his ancestral home and rejects his mother and his fiancée, Lucy Tartan, in an effort to protect the interests of Isabel, a beautiful woman who has convinced him that she is his illegitimate sister. They move to New York, where Pierre's recognition of incestuous desires transforms him from an innocent to a stormy cynic. Disowned, forced to live in poverty, and struggling to write, he eventually commits suicide in prison. In pursuit of truth, he has caused the deaths of his mother, Isabel, and Lucy.

Pierrot (*Fr.,* "Little Peter"). A favorite character of the old Italian drama and of pantomime, a sort of clown lover. Pierrot is traditionally played by a tall, thin young man with his face and hair covered with white powder or flour. He wears a white gown with very long sleeves and a row of big buttons down the front. Pierrot is the lover of Pierrette, or sometimes of Columbine. From the simple figure of the early pantomime, poets and artists have gradually evolved another, more romantic Pierrot, an artist-lover of soaring imagination who grimly hides his real passions behind a comic mask. Among many others, the French Gaspard Deburau, Charles Baudelaire, Jules Laforgue, and Theophile Gautier, the English Ernest Dowson, and the Canadian Bliss Carman have written of this new Pierrot. Ernest Dowson's dramatic fantasy, *The Pierrot of the Minute,* is the best known of several short plays on the subject. An interesting collection of poems on Pierrot (as well as Pierrette, Columbine, Harlequin, and the other pantomime characters) is given in *Mon Ami Pierrot, Songs and Fantasie,* compiled by Kendall Banning.

Piers Plowman. Full title: **The Vision of William Concerning Piers Plowman** (c. 1362–c. 1387). Middle English poem usually attributed in whole or in part to a hypothetical William Langland or Langley (c. 1332–c. 1400). Actually, there are three different versions of the poem (c. 1362, 2579 lines; c. 1377, 7241 lines; c. 1387 or 1393?, 7353 lines), by at least two and perhaps even five different writers. Although contemporary with Chaucer's work, it is written in ALLITERATIVE VERSE like old English poetry and uses a deliberately rustic or archaic dialect.

It is an allegorical moral and social satire, written as a "vision" of the common medieval type. The poet falls asleep in the Malvern Hills and dreams that in a wilderness he comes upon the tower of Truth (God) set on a hill, with the dungeon of Wrong (the Devil) in the deep valley below, and a "fair field full of folk" (the world of living men) between them. He describes satirically all the different classes of people he sees there; then a lady named Holy Church rebukes him for sleeping and explains the meaning of all he sees. Further characters representing abstract personifications (Conscience, Liar, Reason, etc.) enter the action; Conscience finally persuades many of the people to turn away from the Seven Deadly Sins and go in search of St. Truth, but they need a guide. Piers (Peter), a simple Plowman, appears and says that because of his common sense and clean conscience he knows the way and will show them if

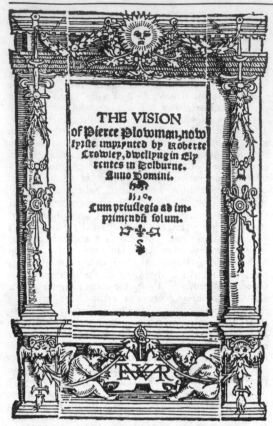

THE VISION of Pierce Plowman, now fyrste imprynted by Roberte Crowley, dwellyng in Elye rentes in Holburne. Anno Domini. 1550. Cum priuilegio ad imprimendum solum.

Title page of *Piers Plowman* (1st edition, 1550).

they help him plow his half-acre. Some of the company help, but some shirk; and Piers becomes identified with Christ, trying to get men to work toward their own spiritual salvation, as well as toward their own material relief from the current abuses of worldly power. In the last section of the poem, much less coherent, the dreamer goes on a rambling but unsuccessful summer-long quest, aided by Thought, Wit, and Study, in search of the men who are Do-Well, Do-Bet, and Do-Best.

pietism. The name given to a vague and widespread Protestant movement in 18th-century Germany, which stressed emotional piety and the pure Christian life, as opposed to rationalism and outward formalization in religion. The principal pietistic sect was the MORAVIAN BRETHREN.

Pietro d'Abano. See Pietro d'ABANO.

Pieyre de Mandiargues, André (1909–). French poet. His prose poems, such as *Soleil de Loups* (1951), *Le Lis de Mer* (1956), and *Feu de braise* (1959), often resemble short stories.

pig in a poke. A blind bargain. The French phrase is *acheter chat en poche* ("to buy a cat in a pocket"). The reference is to a common trick in days gone by of trying to palm off on a greenhorn a cat for a suckling pig. If he opened the sack he "let the cat out of the bag," and the trick was disclosed.

Pigwiggen. A fairy knight in Drayton's NYMPHIDIA, in love with Queen Mab. He combats the jealous Oberon with great fury.

Pilate, Pontius. A Roman procurator (governor) of Judaea in the first half of the 1st century, before whom Jesus was tried. Failing to persuade the mob of Christ's innocence, he yielded, washing his hands before them and condemning Jesus with the words, "Take ye him, and crucify him: for I find no fault in him" (John 19:6). Tradition has it that Pontius Pilate's later life was so full of misfortune that, during Caligula's time, he committed suicide in Rome. His body was cast into the Tiber, but it is said that because evil spirits disturbed the water, it had to be retrieved and taken to Vienna; there, it was thrown into the Rhone, eventually coming to rest in the recesses of a lake on Mount Pilatus opposite Lucerne. Another legend states that the suicide occurred so that he might escape the sentence of death passed on him by Tiberius because of his having ordered the crucifixion of Christ; and yet another, that both he and his wife became penitent, embraced Christianity, and died peaceably in the Faith.

Tradition gives the name Claudia Procula, or Procla, to Pilate's wife, and by some she has been identified with the Claudia of II Tim. 4:21.

Pilate's voice. A loud, ranting voice. In the old Mystery plays, all tyrants were made to speak in a rough, ranting manner.

Anatole France wrote a short story about Pilate's later life called *The Procurator of Judaea* (1892).

Pilgrimage. A series of 9 novels by Dorothy RICHARDSON. Using the STREAM-OF-CONSCIOUSNESS technique, she portrays the mind and follows the emotional development of her heroine, Miriam Henderson. The novels in the series are: *Pointed Roofs* (1915), *Backwater* (1916), *Honeycomb* (1917), *The Tunnel* (1919), *Interim* (1919), *Deadlock* (1921), *Revolving Lights* (1923), *The Trap* (1925), *Oberland* (1927), *Dawn's Left Hand* (1931), *Clear Horizon* (1935), and *Dimple Hill* (1938).

Pilgrims. The name given to the English Puritans who sailed to America on the MAYFLOWER, and by extension to any early Puritan settlers of New England. The *Mayflower* Pilgrims, unlike the other Puritans of Massachusetts, were Separatists, in that they sought complete independence from the Established Church of England. Originally from Scrooby, England, they first emigrated to the Netherlands (c. 1606), where they could worship freely. More than half of this group sailed to America on the *Mayflower*.

Pilgrim's Progress from This World to That Which Is to Come, The (Part I, 1678; Part II, 1684). A prose allegory by John BUNYAN. The author purports to have a dream in which he sees Christian, who is weeping and wondering what to do to avoid the destruction of himself, his family, and his town that is prophesied in the Bible. Evangelist comes, warns Christian to flee, and tells him to journey to the Wicket-gate beneath the shining light in the distance. Closing his ears to the entreaties of his family and neighbors to remain, Christian flees the City of Destruction and sets out for the Celestial City beyond the Wicket-gate. He wanders into the Slough of Despond, from which he cannot get out because of the weight of the burden of sin on his back, until at last he is rescued by Help. He meets Mr. Worldly-Wiseman, who urges him to give up his dangerous journey, have his weighty burden removed by Mr. Legality, and settle down in the comfortable village of Morality nearby; Christian is ready to follow Mr. Worldly-Wiseman's counsel, but is rescued by Evangelist, who warns him against being led astray again. At the Wicket-gate, Christian is let in by Mr. Good-will and shown the straight and narrow way that leads to the Celestial City. He comes to the Cross, and his burden of sin falls from his back and rolls into the Holy Sepulchre nearby. Soon he comes upon three men, fettered and asleep, called Simple, Sloth, and Presumption; they give no heed to his warnings to wake and seek the Celestial City. Then he comes upon Hypocrisy and Formalist, climbing over the Wall to get on the narrow way; Christian warns them that they may be counted as thieves and trespassers because they have not come through the Wicket-gate. They go on together until they come to the Hill Difficulty; Christian takes the narrow road over the steep hill, while his two companions take the easier paths, called Danger and Destruction, around it. At the top of the Hill he meets Timorous and Mistrust, who turn back because they fear greater difficulties ahead. He rests at the House Beautiful, where he talks with the damsels Discretion, Prudence, Piety, and Charity. They show him the Delectable Mountains ahead, and send him on his way armed against attackers. He goes down into the Valley of Humiliation, where he meets the fiend Apollyon; they fight for more than half a day before Christian, himself wounded, vanquishes the enemy. He then must pass through the Valley of the Shadow of Death, which is full of Hobgoblins, Satyrs, and Dragons of the Pit. He meets a pilgrim named Faithful, and they describe their journeys to one another. Evangelist appears and predicts the troubles they will encounter in the town of Vanity, where a year-round fair sells all the empty things of the world. At Vanity Fair the two pilgrims cause a great hubbub by their refusal to buy anything and are arrested. Faithful is tried and sentenced to be burned at the stake, after which a heavenly Chariot carries him off into the clouds. Christian escapes and is joined by Hopeful, who had been converted by the example of Faithful. They come to the plain of Ease and beyond it the Hill of Lucre, where they are tempted to dally with a free silver mine. Soon they come to a pleasant river, which runs alongside the narrow way for a while, but before long the path goes away from the River and becomes rough, and Christian leads Hopeful into a more pleasant path nearby. Night falls and they become lost, and in the morning they are near the Doubting Castle, where they are caught by the Giant Despair. He locks them in a dungeon and beats them, until finally Christian remembers that he has a key called Promise which will unlock the door. They go back to the narrow way, which soon leads them to the Delectable Mountains, where they talk with the shepherds called Knowledge, Experience, Watchful, and Sincere. Going on, they enter the Enchanted Ground, on which they have been warned not to sleep, and they converse to stay off drowsiness. At length, they come to the country of Beulah, which is within sight of the Celestial City. Two angels tell them that to get to the City they must cross the River of Death; in the water Christian is afraid, but is encouraged by Hopeful. On the other side they are met by angels who lead them to the gate of heaven.

The Pilgrim's Progress, with its vivid characterization, direct and colorful style, and beauty of language, has been one of the most widely read books in the English language. Because of its immense popularity Bunyan was encouraged to write a second part which, unfortunately, has not the power of the original book. Part II deals with the pilgrimage to the Celestial City of Christian's wife, Christiana; accompanying her are their children, Mercy, a neighbor, and Mr. Great-heart, who is given them for a guide.

Pillars of Hercules. Two opposite promontories at the entrance of the Mediterranean, one in Spain and the other in Africa. The tale is that they were bound together till Hercules tore them asunder in order to get to Gades (Cadiz). The ancients called them Calpe and Abyla; we call them Gibraltar and Mount Hacho.

I will follow you even to the pillars of Hercules. To the end of the world. The ancients supposed that these rocks marked the utmost limits of the habitable globe.

Pillow-book of Sei Shōnagon, The (Sei Shōnagon nikki). Japanese diary (c. 1002). Its authoress, Sei Shōnagon, was a lady-in-waiting in the Heian court. Witty and brilliantly written, the work occupies a unique position in Japanese literature. Translated by Arthur WALEY.

Pilnyak, Boris. Pen name of **Boris Andreyevich Vogau** (1894–?1937). Russian novelist. One of the outstanding practitioners of the rich, ornamental prose style popular with Soviet writers in the 1920's, he was a victim of the purges in the 1930's. His first novel, *Golyi God (Naked Year;* 1922), is an account of the revolution. *Krasnoye derevo (Mahogany;* 1929) depicted the period of the New Economic Policy (NEP) in 1921–1928, when a return to a limited form of capitalism was allowed in the Soviet Union. Pilnyak was reprimanded when *Krasnoye derevo* was published abroad before being approved by the Soviet authorities. He revised the work and included part of it in a longer novel, *Volga vpadayet v kaspiiskoye morye (The Volga Flows to the Caspian Sea;* 1931), which dealt with the first Five Year Plan. Pilnyak was arrested in 1937 and sent to a labor camp. His subsequent fate is unknown.

Pilot, The (1823). A novel by James Fenimore COOPER. The first of Cooper's sea stories, the novel was written to prove that he could do better than Scott. The central character is Mr. Gray, modeled on John Paul Jones. The most fully drawn character in the book, however, is Long Tom Coffin, a nautical version of Natty BUMPPO. The book, valued for its exciting portrayal of life and combat at sea, has maintained its popularity.

Pilpay, Fables of. See BIDPAI, FABLES OF.

Piltdown man. An alleged extinct manlike primate. It was reconstructed from the remains of two skulls found early in the 20th century at Piltdown, near Lewes, in Sussex, England. It was exposed as a hoax in 1953. The skull was proved modern, and the jawbone an ape's.

Pinabello. In the ORLANDO FURIOSO of Lodovico Ariosto, a treacherous nephew of Gano of Maganza. He hurls the warrior maiden Bradamante from a cliff, but she survives and later kills him.

Pinafore, H.M.S., or The Lass that Loved a Sailor (1878). A comic opera by GILBERT AND SULLIVAN. The plot hinges on the fact that Josephine, the daughter of the Captain of *H.M.S. Pinafore*, refuses the advances of the all-important Sir Joseph Porter because she loves a "common sailor" named Ralph Rackstraw. Finally Little Buttercup, the bumboat woman, confesses to having exchanged the two babies, Ralph Rackstraw and the Captain, as nurse long years before.

Pinch. In Shakespeare's COMEDY OF ERRORS, a schoolmaster and conjurer who tries to exorcise the supposedly insane Antipholus of Ephesus.

Pincherle, Alberto. See Alberto MORAVIA.

Pincher Martin (1956; in the U.S., *The Two Deaths of Christopher Martin*). A novel by William GOLDING about a shipwrecked man and his struggle to keep alive on a bare rock. He remembers his selfish past life with the "eat or be eaten" principles, and in his dying delirium imagines he is eaten himself (perhaps, ironically, by God). In a surprise ending Golding shows that his hero actually died in the wreck, so that the rock has been either a dream or a kind of purgatory. The name Pincher is from the slang "pinch," to steal.

Pinckney, Charles Cotesworth (1746–1825). American statesman. He was a member of the Constitutional Convention and was one of the three Americans involved in the X Y Z AFFAIR. When the French agents attempted to obtain bribes from him, he replied: "No! No! Not a sixpence!" Because of this reply, the slogan "Millions for defence, but not one cent for tribute" has been erroneously ascribed to him. In 1804 and 1808 he was the unsuccessful Federalist candidate for the presidency.

Pindar (Pindaros) (522 or 518–432 or 438 B.C.). Greek poet also known as the Dircaean Swan. He was born near Thebes, and his works, about one fourth of which survive, are mainly EPINICIA composed on commission to celebrate famous victors at the Olympian, Pythian, Nemean, or Isthmian games. They were mainly intended to be sung by a chorus at some later celebration in honor of the victor, rather than immediately. Pindar was immensely admired both in his own day and in centuries to come.

His works combine gravity of manner with strikingly bold images. The onrushing beat of his verse has been compared to that of Kipling. Pindar was aristocratic in his sympathies and conservative in both politics and religion. He refused, for example, to credit the famous story of TANTALUS feeding his son Pelops to the gods, for he could not believe that the gods would be cannibals. Since Pindar's Epinicia are generally concerned with mythical subjects, reserving praise of the mortal victor for the end of the ode, his works are a fine source of legend. According to tradition, he was criticised by Corinna, a popular poet, for having failed to use myth in his first poem. In his next he used it so extravagantly that she warned him to "sow with the hand, not with the sack."

Pindar, Peter. See John WOLCOT.

Pindarus. In Shakespeare's JULIUS CAESAR, a slave of Cassius, who had taken him prisoner in Parthia. He discharges Cassius' last command to kill him and flees from the battlefield.

Pinero, Sir Arthur Wing (1855–1934). English dramatist, actor, and essayist. He is chiefly remembered for his dramas dealing with social problems. He acted (1874–1881, 1885) both modern and Shakespearean roles. His plays include *The Magistrate* (1885), *The Schoolmistress* (1886), *Sweet Lavender* (1888), *The Profligate* (1889), THE SECOND MRS. TANQUERAY, *The Notorious Mrs. Ebbsmith* (1896), TRELAWNY OF THE WELLS, *The Gay Lord Quex* (1899), *Iris* (1903), *The Thunderbolt* (1908), and *Mid-Channel* (1909). As a critic he wrote *Browning as a Dramatist* (1912) and *Robert Louis Stevenson as a Dramatist* (1914).

Pinfold, Gilbert. A middle-aged writer, hero of the partly autobiographical novel *The Ordeal of Gilbert Pinfold* (1957) by Evelyn WAUGH.

Pinget, Robert (1920–   ). French novelist and dramatist of the NEW WAVE. Pinget creates his absurd situations and farcical characters with reckless gaiety. His heroes, who resemble the tragicomic clowns of Samuel Beckett, are put through quick paces and given a colorful poetic jargon to speak. Among his works are *Entre Fantoine et Agapa* (1950), *Mahu ou le Matériau* (1952), *Baga* (1956), *Graal Flibuste* (1957), and *Le Fiston* (1959).

pin money. A lady's allowance of money for her own personal expenditure. At one time pins were a great expense to a woman, and in 14th- and 15th-century wills there are often special bequests for the express purpose of buying pins.

Pinocchio, The Adventures of (Le Avventure di Pinocchio; 1883). A children's story written by Collodi, the pen name of Carlo Lorenzini (1826–1890), a native of Florence, Italy. The hero of the tale is Pinocchio, a puppet come-to-life, whose many escapades serve to teach him (and his young readers) to distinguish right from wrong. Unique is the puppet's nose which grows larger when he tells a lie and returns to normal size when he tells the truth. Walt Disney produced a full-length animated cartoon of the story (1940).

Pinter, Harold (1930–   ). English playwright. He is one of a number of young playwrights in England and America who have begun their careers writing for television. Pinter's plays are characterized by repetitive dialogue with an emphasis on the *non sequiturs* of conversation. His works include *The Birthday Party* (1958), *A Slight Ache* (television 1959), *The Dwarf* (television 1960), *The Room* (1960), THE DUMBWAITER, *The Caretaker* (1960), and THE COLLECTION.

Pinturicchio or **Pintoricchio, Il.** Real name, Bernardino di Betto (c. 1454–1513). Italian painter from Perugia. Known as "the Little Painter" because of his small stature, he excelled in large-scale decoration. His narrative scenes are characterized by a superb arrangement of figures and a mastery of space composition and landscape. These qualities, found also in Perugino and other Umbrian painters, influenced the art of Raphael. Pinturicchio's best-known works include the series of scenes from the life of PIUS II in the library of the Siena cathedral; the decoration of the Borgia apartments of the Vatican; and the wall fresco of the Sistine Chapel, *The Circumcision of the Sons of Moses*.

Pioneers, The, or the Source of the Susquehanna (1823). A novel by James Fenimore COOPER. The character of Natty BUMPPO here makes his first appearance in print as an older man, who has witnessed the coming of civilization to the wilderness. The story takes place in upper New York State, in the village of Templeton, founded by Judge Temple. The central conflict in the book concerns the opposition between the laws of nature, upheld by Natty, and the laws of civilization. Symbolic of this opposition are two incidents; in the first, Natty kills a deer for food, in Indian fashion. The white settlement seeks to punish him for failing to respect the seasonal hunting laws it has established. On the other hand, there is the wholesale slaughter of pigeons by the civilized inhabitants of Templeton, with no purpose but sport. A second moral question involves the true ownership of Judge Temple's lands. The marriage of Elizabeth Temple and Edward Effingham, heir of the true owner, resolves the difficulty. Natty, like Huck Finn, heads for the far West to escape confining civilization. See LEATHERSTOCKING TALES, THE.

Piovene, Guido (1907–   ). Italian essayist, historian, and novelist. He is well known for his penetrating analysis of Italian and American cultural relations, *De America* (1953). An accomplished stylist, he produced his best novel in *Letters of a Novice* (*Lettere di Una Novizia;* 1941).

Piozzi, Mrs. See Hester Lynch THRALE.

Pip. See GREAT EXPECTATIONS.

Piper of Hamelin. See PIED PIPER OF HAMELIN.

Pipes, Tom. In Tobias Smollett's novel PEREGRINE PICKLE, a taciturn, battered, retired boatswain's mate. Living with Commodore TRUNNION, he speaks chiefly in whistles.

Pippa Passes (1841). A poetic drama by Robert BROWNING. Pippa is a poor child who works all year, except for one holiday on New Year's Day, in the silk mills at Asolo in Italy. The drama hinges on her chance appearance "at critical moments in the spiritual life-history of the leading characters in the play." Pippa passes, singing some song, and her voice and words alter the destinies of the men and women who overhear her. Her own life is altered by her final song. Her famous first song, which ends,

> God's in His heaven—
> All's right with the world!

while often quoted as revealing naïve optimism on Browning's part, is actually mainly an expression of Pippa's innocent and trusting character.

Pirandello, Luigi (1867–1936). Italian dramatist and novelist. He is known for his symbolical and psychological dramas and satires, which aroused much controversy because of their alleged obscurity during the 1920's. SIX CHARACTERS IN SEARCH OF AN AUTHOR is his most celebrated play. Others are *The Living Mask* (*Enrico IV;* 1922), *So It Is, If It Seems So* (*Cosi E' Se Vi Pare;* 1918), *As You Desire Me* (*Come Tu Mi Vuoi;* 1931), *Tonight We Improvise* (*Questa Sera Si Recita a Soggetto;* 1932), and *Tutto Per Bene* (1937). His nontheatrical works include *Il Fu Mattia Pascal* (*The Late Mattia Pascal;* 1904), *The Outcast* (*L'Esclusa;* 1893), and *One, None, and a Hundred Thousand* (*Uno, Nessuno, e Centomila;* 1926), and the vast repertoire of short stories entitled *Novelle Per Un Anno* (1922–1936).

In both his dramas and his fiction Pirandello explored the many faces of reality. His characters are invariably confronted with the "problems" of several "truths" or "realities," depending upon the individual's way of interpreting what seems to him to be real and true. The relentless pessimism that pervades his work was best articulated by a character in the short story *La Veglia* (*The Deathwatch*): "I'm not suffering on my account, or on your account. I'm suffering because life is what it is."

Pirandello spent most of his early career as a professor of literature in an Italian girls' school. After his success as a writer for the stage, he founded his own theater in Rome and took his own acting company on tours with his plays throughout Europe. He was awarded the Nobel Prize for literature in 1934.

Pirates of Penzance, The (1879). A comic opera by GILBERT AND SULLIVAN. It concerns the capers of a band of pirates, a bevy of girls, and a Major General.

Pirenne, Henri (1862–1935). Belgian historian. Pirenne's most famous work is his *Historie de Belgique* (1900–1932), a seven-volume study. He is noted for the new emphasis he placed on economic, social, and religious factors in determining the course of history.

Pirithous (Perithoos). King of the LAPITHS in Thessaly, and friend of Theseus. He was the husband of Hippodamia, at whose wedding feast the Centaurs offered violence to the bride, thus causing a great battle.

Piron, Alexis (1689–1773). French poet, epigrammatist, satirist, and dramatist. His best-known comedy in verse is *La Métromanie* (1738), a satire on poets and poetasters. His vicious tongue and redoubtable gift for repartee made even the great Voltaire flinch.

Pisan Cantos, The (1948). Ten sections of the CANTOS of Ezra Pound. Written while the poet was imprisoned in a U.S. army stockade in Italy as a result of his radio broadcasts for the Italian Fascists, *The Pisan Cantos* reflect this experience. Pound turns back to the essential things, to nature, to regain his lost emotional and spiritual balance. He frequently refers to his fellow prisoners, army guards, and the physical surroundings at Pisa. One of the most intense literary controversies of the 20th century was initiated when Pound, accused of treason, was awarded the BOLLINGEN PRIZE in 1948.

Pisanello, Il. Real name **Antonio Pisano** (c. 1395–1455). Italian painter and sculptor. He is noted for his easel paintings and his cast medallions, done in a style that embodies the transition between Gothic and Renaissance. The best known of the medallions are those of the Visconti and Gonzaga families; his paintings include the famous *Vision of St. Eustace* and *St. George and the Princess of Trebizond*, which reveal his skill in rendering animals with incomparable realism.

Pisanio. In Shakespeare's CYMBELINE, the kindly servant of Posthumus Leonatus. Ordered to murder his master's wife Imogen, he allows her to escape and sends a bloody napkin to Posthumus as proof of the murder.

Pisano, Andrea (c. 1305–1349). Italian sculptor. He is noted for the reliefs he carved with Giotto on the campanile, or bell tower, of the Florence cathedral, and for the first of the famous series of three bronze doors in the baptistery of the same city. The other two doors were done by Ghiberti.

Pisano, Nicolò (c. 1220–c. 1278) and his son **Giovanni** (c. 1250–1320). Italian sculptors from Pisa. Working individually, the Pisani contributed many statues and reliefs to the leading churches of Pisa, Siena, and Pistoia. The style of Giovanni, though more Gothic and less inclined to imitate the antique than that of his father, attracted and influenced the youthful Michelangelo.

Pisarev, Dmitri Ivanovich (1840–1868). Russian radical journalist. Although born a member of the gentry class, Pisarev became a leading spokesman for the young nihilists of the 1860's. Most of the articles that established Pisarev's reputation were written while he was in prison, from 1862 to 1866, for publishing illegal pamphlets. Pisarev's ideas on literature and art were even more extreme than those of the radical critics Chernyshevski and Dobrolyubov. While these two men saw art as a worthy pursuit when it served a social purpose, Pisarev tended to deny any value at all to art. He attacked Pushkin's work as a waste of time and once claimed that a pair of boots was more important than a play by Shakespeare. Elements of the nihilist ideology remained in radical thinking, but the force of the movement began to lessen after Pisarev's accidental death by drowning in 1868.

Pisemski, Alexei Feofilaktovich (1820–1881). Russian novelist, dramatist, and short-story writer. The son of an impoverished nobleman, Pisemski spent his early life in the provinces. There he acquired the intimate knowledge of provincial life and of peasant character that became a prominent feature of his literary works. His interest in literature began early, and he was already writing stories before he finished secondary school. After graduation from Moscow University, he entered government service and remained a civil servant for most of his life. Pisemski's first published work was the short novel *Tyufyak* (*The Muff*, 1850), a somberly realistic study of a family tragedy. The combination of an objective narrative manner and a pessimistic attitude toward his subjects and toward life marked most of Pisemski's writings. His best-known works are *Ocherki iz krest'yanskogo byta* (*Sketches from Peasant Life*, 1856), a collection of short stories; the novel A Thousand Souls; and the drama A Hard Lot.

Pisgah. In the Bible, the mountain in Moab, northeast of the Dead Sea, from which Moses, unable to enter Canaan, was allowed to view the Promised Land (Deut. 34:1). Mount Nebo was one of its summits.

Browning uses *Pisgah-Sights* (1876) as the title of a poem about a man viewing his whole life while in the throes of death.

Pisistratus (**Peisistratos**, 612?–527 b.c.). The greatest of the tyrants of Athens. Although he respected and, for the most part, retained the constitution of his predecessor Solon, he made himself tyrant in 560 b.c. and, except for brief periods of exile, held that position for the rest of his life. His reign was characterized by stability, prosperity, and cultural advancement. He either instituted or significantly altered the festival called the Greater Panathenaea, at which he introduced contests of bards. Tradition says that he arranged for the editing of the works of Homer, which had many variant forms. Dramatic contests were added to the festival of Dionysia, and it may have been at this time that Thespis' plays were performed.

Piso's conspiracy (a.d. 65). A plot against the life of the tyrannical emperor Nero instigated by C. Calpurnius Piso. When the plot was discovered, Piso committed suicide. Many distinguished persons involved in the conspiracy, including Lucan and Seneca, were ordered to commit suicide and took their own lives.

Pissarro, Camille (1830–1903). French impressionist painter. Intended by his family for a career in business, Pissarro finally convinced his father of his absorbing interest in painting and went to Paris to study in 1855. He exhibited at the *Salon des Refusés* (1863) and remained loyal to the unpopular impressionist movement despite great personal hardship. His home at Louveciennes and all his paintings were destroyed by the Germans in 1871, while he was in London. Recognition did not come to Pissarro until he was nearly 60 years old. His early admiration for the delicate, dappled landscapes of Corot is reflected in his own work—*Le Verger* (the orchard) and *Le Bûcheron* (the woodcutter), for example. Never extreme or daring in technique, fine, small strokes and subtle tonal shading characterize his landscapes.

Pistol. A cowardly braggart, in the tradition of the *capitano* of the *commedia dell'arte*, whose bombastic words are filled with quotations from old plays. He appears in Shakespeare's Henry IV: Part II and The Merry Wives of Windsor as Sir John Falstaff's ensign. He is promoted to lieutenant in Henry V. His wife is Mistress Nell Quickly.

Pit, The (1903). A novel by Frank Norris. The second part of the unfinished trilogy *Epic of the Wheat*, of which The Octopus was the first, this posthumously published novel is composed of three elements: the adventures of Curtis Jadwin, who attempts to corner the Chicago wheat market in "the pit" of the stock exchange; the love story of Jadwin's wife Laura; and the story of the wheat itself, the life force which Norris intended as the great central theme of the trilogy.

Pit and the Pendulum, The (1842). A story by Edgar Allan Poe. The narrator, a victim of the Spanish Inquisition, is condemned to death by torture. He narrowly escapes death by falling into the pit, as he moves around his dark cell. Bound to a board, a pendulum swings a knife across his body. He escapes by enticing the prison rats to gnaw through his ropes. Then the walls of his cell become molten; as they close in around him, he is forced to the edge of the pit. Fainting, about to fall, he is rescued by the successful opposing army.

Pitcairn Island. A Polynesian island. It was colonized by refugee mutineers from the H.M.S. *Bounty* (see Mutiny on the Bounty), who were the ancestors of its present natives. It was named after the British midshipman Robert Pitcairn (1747?–1770?) who first sighted the island (July 2, 1767) from H.M.S. *Swallow*.

Pitcher, Molly. See Mary McCauley.

Pitoëff, Georges (1886–1939). Russian-born French actor, director, and producer. In 1919 Pitoëff came to Paris with his *Compagnie Pitoëff* and produced Henri Lenormand's play *Le Temps est un songe*. In 1934 he and his actress wife established their company at the theater *Les Mathurins*. A stark simplicity in stage settings and subtle lighting effects placed the emphasis on the inner struggles of the characters. Pitoëff produced plays by modern Russian and French dramatists, with the works of Shaw, O'Neill, and Pirandello.

Pitt, William. 1st earl of Chatham. Called **the Elder Pitt** (1708–1778). English statesman and orator; "the Great Commoner." He entered Parliament in 1735 as a Whig and was made paymaster-general under the duke of Newcastle. When Newcastle resigned (1756), George II asked Pitt to form a new government, but Pitt was unsuccessful. When Newcastle returned (1757) and Pitt was made secretary of state, success was achieved; Newcastle kept Parliament in line and Pitt vigorously pursued the Seven Years' War. Pitt resigned in 1761, returned as head of government in 1766, but resigned (1768) because of ill health. Pitt recognized the foolishness of George III's policies toward the American colonies, and while he did not wish to grant them their independence, tried to use his influence on their behalf.

Pitt, William. Called **the Younger Pitt** (1759–1806). English statesman, second son of William Pitt, 1st earl of Chatham, and considered by many to have been the greatest of England's prime ministers. He entered Parliament in 1780; by 1782 he was chancellor of the exchequer, and leader of the House of Commons. In 1783 he became prime minister and remained in office until 1801, one of the longest ministries in English history. During this period he effected major reforms in financing the public debt, in customs duties, and in the administration of India, which he took out of the hands of the East India Company. He resigned in 1801, resumed office in 1804, and retired in 1806, just two weeks before his death.

Pitter, Ruth (1897–   ). English poet. She is the author of delicate lyrics on nature, love, and religious themes. Her books include *A Mad Lady's Garland* (1934) and *Urania* (1951).

Pitti Palace. A palace in Florence, Italy, completed in the 16th century by Cosimo de' Medici. It is now one of the world's outstanding art galleries.

Pius II. Real name, **Enea Silvio de Piccolomini.** Known as **Aeneas Silvius** (1405–1464). Pope (1458–1464), Sienese scholar and man of letters. He first came to prominence, at the Council of Basel, which sent him on a mission to England and the Scottish court of James I. Later he took up secretarial duties at the court of Emperor Frederick III, where he produced several literary works, the most popular being his long novella, *Historia de duobus amantibus* (*The History of Two Lovers*). It was translated from the original Latin into Italian, French, German, and English. In 1458, he was elected to the papacy as Pius II; in referring to his former support of councils as superior to the popes in authority, he made the famous remark, "Hold to Pius, spit out Aeneas!" His series of *Commentaries* (*Commentarii*) on his life and times are among the best and most valuable writings of the early Renaissance. The painter Pinturicchio recorded his visage and activities in several frescoes on the walls of the library of the cathedral of Siena.

pixie or **pixy.** A mischievous sprite or fairy. Pixies are especially prevalent in the folklore of Cornwall and Devon, where some hold them to be the spirits of infants who have died before baptism. The pixy monarch has his court like Oberon, and sends his subjects on their several tasks. The word is probably Celtic in origin, but its actual history is unknown.

Pizarro, Francisco (1470?–1541). Spanish conqueror of Peru. The illegitimate son of a Spanish army officer, Pizarro was a swineherd before he left for America, where he settled in Panama. In 1522 he formed a pact for the conquest of Peru with Diego de Almagro and Fernando de Luque, a priest. After two unsuccessful expeditions, Pizarro won the support of Charles V, who named him governor and captain-general of Peru while Almagro was relegated to a secondary position. In 1531 Pizarro left for Peru, leaving Almagro in Panama to recruit additional men. Reaching the city of Cajamarca, Pizarro and his men seized ATAHUALPA, the Inca emperor, and slew a large number of Indians. Although Atahualpa complied with Pizarro's demand that he produce a huge ransom, he was later executed. By 1535, when Pizarro founded Lima, the Inca empire had been vanquished; however, he now had to contend with Almagro, who claimed the city of El Cuzco for himself. Almagro was defeated and killed at the battle of Las Salinas (1538), but partisans of his assassinated Pizarro in Lima three years later.

Placebo (Lat., "I shall please," or "be acceptable"). The Vespers of the Dead, so called because this is the first word of the first antiphon of the service: *Placebo Domino in regione vivorum* ("I shall please the Lord in the land of the living"; *Ps.* cxvi, 9). In the Middle Ages, those who wished to get something out of the relatives of the deceased made a point of attending the service, so that the phrase "to sing *Placebo*" came to mean "to play the flatterer or sycophant." Chaucer, who in the Merchant's Tale gives this as a name to a parasite, has:

Flatereres been the develes chapelleyns that singen
evere *Placebo.—Parson's Tale*

place in the sun. A favorable position affording room for development, a share in what one believes one has a natural right to have. The phrase was popularized by Wilhelm II of Germany during the crisis of 1911. In his speech at Hamburg (Aug. 27), he spoke of the German nation taking steps that would make "sure that no one can dispute with us the place in the sun that is our due."

The phrase had been used by Pascal some 200 years earlier.

Plague, The (La Peste; 1947). A novel by Albert CAMUS. The Algerian port of Oran is overwhelmed by an epidemic of bubonic plague, although modern medicine does its best to quarantine the city and isolate the stricken and the dead within. The emergency forces many to make character-revealing decisions; yet death plays no favorites, and life continues much the same after the calamity. The doctor Bernard Rieux represents those who, despite everything, simply do what they can for the cause of human life and hope for the possibility of occasional human joy.

Plaideurs, Les (**The Litigants**, 1668). A comedy by Jean RACINE. The magistrate Dandin, driven mad by his mania for judging, is kept locked up by his son and hears cases from the attic and cellar windows, among them, those arising from neighborhood and household quarrels. The farcical highlight of the play is the trial of Dandin's own dog for eating a chicken. After an elaborate prosecution and defense, Dandin condemns the dog to death, but he commutes the sentence out of compassion for the pups. The play abounds in burlesques of the legal corruption and pomposity of Racine's day.

Plain Language From Truthful James (1870). A humorous poem by Bret HARTE. Humorist Bill Nye and the mining camp character, "Truthful" James, attempt to get the better of a Chinese named Ah Sin in the card game, Euchre. Ah Sin is too good for them until they discover he has 24 Jacks up his sleeve. The poem has often been reprinted under the title *The Heathen Chinee*, and was unsuccessfully dramatized as *Ah Sin* by Harte and Mark TWAIN in 1877.

Plain Tales from the Hills (1888). A volume of short stories of life in India by Rudyard KIPLING, first published in Calcutta. It contains the first story about the famous trio of Ortheris, Learoyd, and Mulvaney.

Planché, James Robinson (1796–1880). English dramatist and writer on heraldry and costumes. He is best remembered for his *History of British Costumes* (1834). He wrote, translated, and adapted over 150 burlesques, extravaganzas, and pantomines.

Planck, Max [Karl Ernst Ludwig] (1858–1947). German physicist whose introduction of the quantum theory greatly influenced modern physics. He received the Nobel Prize in 1918.

planets. The heavenly bodies that revolve around the sun in approximately circular orbits. They are so called because, to the ancients, they appeared to wander (Gr., *planasthai,* through Lat. and OFr, "to wander") among the stars, instead of having fixed places.

Only five of the planets were known to the ancients (the earth, of course, not being reckoned): Mercury, Venus, Mars, Jupiter, and Saturn; to these were added the sun and the moon, making seven in all. Among the astrologers and alchemists, the Sun (Apollo) represented gold, the Moon (Diana) represented silver, Mercury represented quicksilver, Venus represented copper, Mars represented iron, Jupiter represented tin, and Saturn represented lead. According to astrology, some planet, at the birth of every individual, presides over his destiny. Some of the planets, such as Jupiter, are lucky; others, such as Saturn, are unlucky.

Plantagenet (from O.Fr. *planta genista* ("sprig of broom"). The surname, originally a nickname, of the Angevin line of English kings (1154–1399). As a family cognizance, it was first assumed by Geoffrey, count of Anjou (d. 1151), during a pilgrimage to the Holy Land, as a symbol of humility. By his wife Matilda, daughter of Henry I of England, he was father of Henry II, the first of the house of Plantagenet to occupy the throne.

Plataea, Battle of. See PERSIAN WARS.

Platen, August Graf von (1796–1835). German poet. His verse, though classicistic and highly form-conscious, often expresses a deep pessimism. His collected *Gedichte* (*Poems*, 1828, expanded 1834) include many sonnets and poems in Oriental forms. Heinrich Heine, in his *Die Bäder von Lucca* (*The*

Baths of Lucca, 1830), uses Platen's homosexuality as the basis for a witty but vicious attack on him.

Platina [Bartolommeo Sacchi] (1421–1481). Italian scholar, humanist, and academician. He is noted for his *Vitae pontificum* (*Lives of the Popes*).

Plato (Platon. c. 427–c. 348 B.C.). A Greek philosopher and prose writer. Born at Athens of a noble family, Plato aspired to political activity. Dismayed at the inequities of the Athenian tyranny, and later at the execution of his teacher Socrates under the democracy, he turned toward philosophy in search of an alternative to the unstable and unjust public life of the time. He also sought unity behind the changing impressions of the visible universe.

After Socrates' death, Plato went to Megara and possibly visited Egypt and Cyrene. During this decade the dialogues that emphasize the personality of Socrates are supposed to have been written. At the age of 40, Plato visited Sicily and Italy, and twice returned there later in life, hoping vainly to influence Dionysius II, tyrant of Syracuse, to establish a Platonic government. On his return to Athens Plato founded the Academy, at which discussion and research were stimulated in mathematical and astronomical fields, in practical legislation, in the art of definition, and in natural history.

All Plato's writing, except for the *Apology* and the *Letters,* are in the dialogue form. Of the 35 dialogues, 29 are considered genuine. In the earliest dialogues, Socrates is the principal figure. This group includes the *Charmides, Crito, Euthyphro, Hippias Minor, Ion, Laches,* and *Lysis.* The *Apology* records Socrates' defense at his trial. These dialogues are philosophically inconclusive, but are considered best to represent the historical Socrates. In a second group, Socrates is the spokesman for Plato's views or Plato's interpretation of Socrates. These include *Alcibiades, Cratylus, Ethydemus, Gorgias, Menexenus, Meno, Parmenides, Phaedo, Phaedrus, Protagoras, Republic, Symposium,* and *Theaetetus.* A third group of dialogues, written in Plato's later years, include *Critias, Philebus, Politicus, Sophist, Timaeus,* and *Laws.* The last was unpublished at Plato's death.

The dialogue, as Plato used it, is a literary form, not merely a vehicle for the expression of a philosophical system. Plato's philosophy emerges, not in a systematic or didactic way, but through the use of dramatic setting and myth. Therefore summary or paraphrase easily distorts Plato's thinking.

The core of his philosophy is the doctrine of ideas. Form and idea are used interchangeably to designate that which remains the same through all the manifestations of a material thing or a virtue. An idea for Plato, contrary to its common English usage, is something outside the mind. He posited a realm of truth or being in which the ideas reside, as distinct from the world of opinion, or Doxa. Through the soul, the mediator between the ideas and appearances, we may obtain knowledge.

Tradition has it that Plato was originally named Aristocles, and only later called Plato (broad) because of his wide forehead, his robust physique, the quality of his writing, or a variety of other explanations.

Platonic love. A popular term for spiritual comradeship or love between persons of opposite sexes; the friendship, usually of man and woman, without sexual implications. The phrase is founded on a mis-interpretation of a passage toward the end of the *Symposium* in which Plato is extolling not the non-sexual love of a man for a woman, but the loving interest that Socrates took in young men—which was pure, and therefore noteworthy in ancient Greece of that period.

Plautus, Titus Maccius (254?–184 B.C.). The greatest comic playwright of Rome. Son of a peasant family, he worked as a stagehand in a traveling the-atrical troupe. This job afforded him nothing but experience, and when the group disbanded, he was left penniless. He was obliged to return to Rome and work in a flour mill; here he found the time to com-pose his first verse comedies. He subsequently wrote and produced about 130 plays, of which 21 are still extant in more or less complete form. In them he Romanized many of the plots and characters of New Greek Comedy (see MENANDER). Through his plays he introduced to the non-Greek world charac-ters which have since become part of traditional western European comedy, among them the braggart soldier (in his MILES GLORIOSUS) and the sly servant (in his *Pseudolus*). In his treatment of stock comic plots he displayed a mastery of language and meter, and a seemingly inexhaustible supply of wit—some-times subtle, often humorously coarse. (See TRANIO.)

Plautus' play the *Menaechmi* was the source for Shakespeare's *Comedy of Errors;* and his comedy about the old miser and his pot of gold, the *Aulu-laria*, supplied the model for Molière's *L'Avare*.

Playboy of the Western World, The (1907). A play by John Millington SYNGE. Christie Mahon, a timid peasant boy, flees home, convinced that he has killed his father. His act is treated by the people to whom he flees as a piece of heroic audacity and the lionization results in the transformation of his per-sonality. The plot, however, is the mere backdrop for the most fertile and vigorous dialogue written for the stage since Shakespeare. The play, which contained some imagined insults to "Irish womanhood," met with a storm of protest, culminating in the "Playboy riots" that took place in Dublin in 1908 and later when it was produced in New York and Philadelphia.

Playfair, Sir Nigel (1874–1934). English actor and manager. He produced John Drinkwater's *Abraham Lincoln* (1919) and *The Beggar's Opera* by John Gay (1920).

plebiscite. In Roman history, a law enacted by the *comitia*, or assembly of tribes. In modern politi-cal terminology, it is the direct vote of the whole body of citizens of a nation on a question phrased in definite terms.

Pléiade, la. A group, first known as the Brigade, of young 16th-century French poets. Led by Pierre de RONSARD, they boldly asserted themselves with the publication of Joachim DU BELLAY's DÉFENSE ET ILLUSTRATION DE LA LANGUE FRANÇAISE. Condemning the poetry of the RHÉTORIQUEURS and of Clément MAROT, they sought to revitalize French literature through study and imitation of Greek and Roman writers. Later on they modified some of their prin-ciples, avoiding too servile an imitation of classical models, and by 1555 they were truly representative of French Renaissance poetry. The members of the Pléiade were Ronsard, Du Bellay, Jean Antoine de BAÏF, Etienne Jodelle, Pontus de Tyard, Rémy Bel-leau, and Jean Dorat, their former teacher who had first revealed to the poets the treasures of classical literature.

Pleiades. The most prominent cluster of stars in the constellation Taurus. Especially, it includes the seven larger ones out of the great number that compose the cluster; so called by the Greeks, possibly from Gr. *plein*, "to sail" because they considered navi-gation safe at the return of the Pleiades, and never attempted it after those stars disappeared.

In Greek myth, the *Pleiades* were the seven daughters of Atlas and Pleione. They were trans-formed into stars, one of which is invisible and known as the lost Pleiad. Some say this star is Electra mourning over the destruction of the city and royal race of Troy. Others say it is Merope, ashamed to show herself because she married a mortal, Sisyphus.

Pletho, George Gemistus (1355–1452). Greek scholar. He came to Italy for the council held at Florence and Ferrara (1438–1439) to unify the Greek and Roman churches, and stayed to teach Platonism and NEOPLATONISM. Through the Florentine intellec-tual center stimulated by Cosimo de' Medici, he in-fluenced the Revival of Learning and Italian Renais-sance Humanism.

Pliny the Elder. Full Latin name, **Caius Plinius Secundus** (A.D. 23–79). Latin author. He is known for his *Historia Naturalis* (*Natural History*), which was regarded as a scientific source book during the Middle Ages. His zeal for scientific research led him to Pompeii, in A.D. 79, where he studied the erup-tions of Mt. Vesuvius; here he died when the city was destroyed.

Pliny the Younger. Full Latin name, **Caius Plinius Caecilius Secundus** (A.D. 62–113). The nephew and adopted son of PLINY THE ELDER, he rose to a high and respected rank in imperial society. His friends included Quintilian, Martial, Suetonius, Tacitus, and the emperor Trajan. His collected let-ters give a vivid account of the social, literary, and political life of his times.

Plomer, William (1903–   ). South African novelist, short-story writer, poet, and traveler. Among his volumes of short stories are *I Speak of Africa* (1928) and *Four Countries* (1949). His novels *Turbott Wolfe* (1926) and *Sado* (1931) explore con-flicts between different cultures. *Museum Pieces* (1952) is a satire on English society.

Plornish, Thomas. In Charles Dickens' LITTLE DORRIT, a plasterer whose trade renders him eternally lime-whitened. His young wife is somewhat slat-ternly and has been prematurely dragged by care and poverty into wrinkles.

Plotinus (Plotinos; c. 204–c. 270). A Greek philosopher of Neoplatonism. After studying in Alexandria with AMMONIUS SACCAS, he settled in Rome. He persuaded his friend the Emperor Gal-lienus to build a city for philosophers, to be gov-erned according to the laws of Plato. Plotinus' own philosophy had no political significance; he lived in a time of political chaos and mystery religions. Porphyry, his biographer and student, relates that he refused to eat meat, and that he attained the state or mystical union with God four times while Por-phyry knew him. The treatises, arranged into En-neads or groups of nine, were written during the last 17 years of Plotinus' life. He broke his vow of silence with regard to Ammonius' doctrines only because other students were reporting them mistakenly. Plotinus is reported by Porphyry as ashamed of his bodily existence, and reticent about revealing biographical information.

Plowman, Piers. See PIERS PLOWMAN.

Plumed Serpent, The (1926). A novel by D. H. LAWRENCE. It is a powerful, vivid evocation of Mexico and its ancient Aztec religion. Kate Leslie, an Irish visitor to Mexico, goes to a bullfight and is horrified by the vulgar cruelty of modern Mexico. But then she meets Don Ramón, a scholar and political leader, and General Cipriano, a military leader, and becomes involved in their resurrection of the ancient Mexican religion. For Lawrence, this religion is characterized by "blood consciousness," emotional and symbolic depth, and sex awareness. It is marked by dominance of the male over the female and the political leader over the masses, a Nietzschean type of superman. Don Ramón, the sexual, political, and religious hero of the book, is regarded as the reincarnated Quetzalcoatl, the Plumed Serpent that the Aztecs used to worship. He rises to lead the people, drawing them away from "outworn" Christianity toward the Aztec religion. Eventually the cult spreads over the whole of Mexico and Kate, too, comes under its spell. She marries General Cipriano, who is regarded as Huitzilopochtli, god of war, and in spite of the rebelliousness of her European character, she passively submits to his male domination. The views Lawrence expresses in it are typical of his later period.

Plunkett, Joseph Mary (1887–1916). Irish poet and patriot. He was executed for his part in the Easter Week rebellion of 1916. His *Poems* appeared in 1916.

Pluralité des mondes, Entretiens sur la. See Bernard le Bovier de FONTENELLE.

Plutarch (Ploutarchos) (A.D. c. 46–c. 120). A Greek biographer. Except for some meager details—that he was born at Chaeronea, that he visited Rome and Athens, and possibly Alexandria, but spent most of his life in Chaeronea as a priest of the Delphic Apollo—nothing is known of his life. His biographical and philosophical writings show that he was one of the most erudite men of his age. His surviving works are confined to the *Moralia*, a book of essays on many subjects, and the famous *Parallel Lives*, arranged mainly in pairs in which a Greek and a Roman are contrasted. His subjects, who included Demosthenes and Cicero, were statesmen or generals. In the process of writing about them, he described many important historical events with immense skill, if sometimes doubtful accuracy. His accounts are the livelier for the fact that he invents dialogue and describes the emotions of the personages involved. Shakespeare's *Julius Caesar, Coriolanus,* and *Antony and Cleopatra* are all based on Plutarch in the famous translation based by Thomas North in 1579. The *Moralia* is concerned with an amazing range of subjects including the education of children, advice on marriage, the oracles, the face in the moon, and the reasoning of animals.

Pluto. See HADES.

Plutus (Ploutos). In Greek mythology, the god of riches—originally the fertility of the earth. Hence the phrase rich as Plutus, and the term *plutocrat,* one who exercises influence or possesses power through

his wealth. The legend is that he was blinded by Zeus so that his gifts should be equally distributed and not go only to those who merited them. *Plutus* was the name of ARISTOPHANES' last extant play.

Plymouth Rock. The ledge in the harbor of Plymouth, Mass., where the *Mayflower* Pilgrims landed (Dec. 21, 1620). They had previously landed at Provincetown, Mass., on Cape Cod.

Plyushkin. An incredibly miserly landowner in Nikolai Gogol's DEAD SOULS. After completing his business transactions with him, the hero Chichikov is almost subjected to the hospitality of the house: a year-old Easter cake that Plyushkin has been saving for a special occasion.

pnigos. See OLD COMEDY.

Pnyx. Athenian hill, approximately one quarter of a mile west of the ACROPOLIS. The assembly held its meetings there in a large amphitheater with a capacity of 20,000 citizens. The hill was used for this purpose from the time of Cleisthenes (fl. 507 B.C.) until the end of the fourth century.

Pobedonostzev, Konstantin Petrovich (1827–1907). Russian jurist and government administrator. A firm believer in the principle of absolutism, he was a bulwark of political reaction under Czars ALEXANDER III and Nicholas II. As Procurator of the Holy Synod, the highest lay office of the Orthodox Church, Pobedonostzev had immense influence, which he consistently used to uphold the old regime and to combat liberal tendencies in Russia.

Pocahontas (c. 1595–1617). Daughter of Powhatan, an Indian chief of Virginia. Her real name was Matoaka, Pocahontas being a pet name meaning "playful." She is said to have rescued Captain John Smith when her father was about to kill him, although the authenticity of the event is still disputed. She later married John Rolfe (1585–1622), a Jamestown settler, bringing the colonists peace with the Indians for eight years. In 1616, baptized under the name of Rebecca, she was brought to England, presented at court as a princess, and became an object of curiosity and of frequent allusion in contemporary literature.

Pocahontas appears in numerous literary works, notably J. N. Barker's drama, *The Indian Princess* (1808), and John Davis's *The First Settlers of Virginia* (1805) and J. E. Cooke's *My Lady Pokahontas* (1885), both novels.

Po Chü-i or **Po Lo-t'ien** (772–846). Chinese poet of the T'ang Dynasty. His work is marked by a satiric vein, and possesses great narrative power and a keen sense of observation. See Arthur Waley, *The Life and Times of Po Chü-i* (1949).

Poe, Edgar Allan (1809–1849). American poet, critic, and short-story writer. Poe's stormy personal life, further confused by an unscrupulous literary executor, postponed honest evaluation of his place in American literature.

The child of theatrical parents, Poe was orphaned early in life. He was taken into the home of John Allan, who did not adopt him, but became his godfather. From 1815 to 1820 the Allans lived in England, where Poe studied at a classical academy. During the next decade Poe and John Allan quarreled more and more frequently. When Mrs. Allan died, and her widower remarried, the two severed relations. Up to 1831, when he came to New York, Poe had entered and left several schools, including West Point, and had enlisted in the Army. He had already published TAMERLANE AND OTHER POEMS, and AL AARAAF.

In 1831, he published his *Poems;* content and preface show the influence of the English romantic poets. He won a story contest with *MS. Found in a Bottle,* and began to write the poetic drama POLITIAN. His newly established reputation gained him the position of editor of the *Southern Literary Messenger* in Richmond. He contributed such stories as BERENICE and *Hans Pfaal,* and began the serialization of THE NARRATIVE OF A. GORDON PYM in 1837. Leaving the *Messenger,* he went to Philadelphia to work on *Burton's Gentleman's Magazine.*

In 1836, Poe married his 13-year-old cousin, Virginia Clemm. She died eleven years later, and he addressed the famous ANNABEL LEE to her. Issuing TALES OF THE GROTESQUE AND ARABESQUE, he then began writing his tales of ratiocination.

Poe came to New York in 1845, and worked on the *Evening Mirror,* in which his poem THE RAVEN was published. The poem established Poe's national reputation. He became co-editor, and then proprietor of his own paper, *The Broadway Journal,* which collapsed in 1846.

Virginia Clemm died of tuberculosis in 1847. Poe, cared for by Mrs. Clemm and his female admirers, continued to write several important pieces, among them THE PHILOSOPHY OF COMPOSITION, ULALUME, and EUREKA. A series of drinking bouts left him exhausted. In October of 1849, he was found seriously ill by a friend, and he died several days later, at the age of 40.

Although Poe felt that he was primarily a poet, his tales of horror and ratiocination have become increasingly popular. He is respected for his books of criticism, as well as for the day-to-day newspaper reviews he turned out.

Poe exercised the greatest influence on the French poet, Charles Baudelaire, who wrote several articles about him, and translated his work. Through Baudelaire, his influence extended to Mallarmé, Valéry, Rimbaud, and others of the symbolist school. See Thomas Holley CHIVERS; CITY IN THE SEA, THE; LIGEIA; WILLIAM WILSON; MURDERS IN THE RUE MORGUE, THE; PIT AND THE PENDULUM, THE; GOLD BUG, THE; TELL-TALE HEART, THE; PURLOINED LETTER, THE; POETIC PRINCIPLE, THE.

Poem of Aqhat, The. A Canaanite epic poem. It was discovered during the excavation of the ancient city of UGARIT (now Ras Shamra) in the early 1930's. It was written in an early Semitic script in cuneiform characters on clay tablets dating from about the 14th century B.C. Though less clearly associated with religious ritual than THE POEM OF BAAL, found in Ugarit at the same time, it nevertheless contains many of the basic elements commonly found in seasonal rites. It is also an astronomical myth similar to that of ORION, in which the physical juxtaposition of certain constellations apparently resulted in their association in legend.

At the beginning of the poem, an old chieftain named Danel (or Daniel) observes an elaborate rite beseeching Baal to grant him a son. Baal intercedes with the chief deity EL on his behalf and El consents. Danel celebrates his good fortune, and in due time

Aqhat is born to his wife Danatiya. Sometime thereafter the divine artisan Koshar-wa-Khasis is entertained by Danel as the god is returning from his Egyptian forge with a load of new bows for the gods. In return, Koshar presents his host with one of the bows as a present for Aqhat.

Unfortunately, this bow had (as well as can be judged from the fragmentary remains of the poem) been intended for the goddess Anat, a warlike Canaanite counterpart of the Greek Artemis. She offers Aqhat (now a youth) wealth and immortality in return for the bow, but he spurns them. With threats she wins El's permission to take vengeance on Aqhat. Seductively, she lures the youth to the city of the moon god, and there her henchman Yatpan kills him. She then weeps for Aqhat and promises to revive him. The clumsy Yatpan drops and breaks the divine bow, so Anat's efforts have been in vain. Moreover, the murder has brought famine on the land, which lasts for seven years.

Danel learns of Aqhat's death. Shooting down the eagles that hover about, he finds his son's remains and buries them with proper ceremony, at the same time cursing the unknown murderer. After seven years of mourning, Aqhat's sister Paghat sets out to avenge him. Hiding clothes and weapons of a soldier under her dress, she seeks out the professional assassin Yatpan, who, under the influence of drink, reveals himself as the murderer of Aqhat.

Although the rest of the poem is lost, it is generally agreed, on the basis of numerous parallel myths of the death and resurrection of a young god, that Aqhat too was eventually revived.

Poem of Baal, The. A Canaanite epic poem of undetermined antiquity. Lengthy fragments of this poem were discovered at the site of ancient UGARIT (now Ras Shamra) in Syria in the early 1930s. The clay tablets on which it appears date from about the 14th century B.C., but the poem itself was probably several centuries older. It was written in cuneiform characters in a Semitic dialect that was deciphered within a few years after its discovery. The poem relates the myth that grew out of certain important Canaanite religious rituals. These myths include a combat between fertile and infertile seasons of the year, and the death and revival of a young god: elements common to most parts of the eastern Mediterranean area.

The epic begins with a fragmentary section that apparently describes rivalry for dominion over the earth between Yam, the dragon god of the sea and all inland waters, and Ashtar, the young god of artificial irrigation. Ignoring the warning of the sun goddess Shapash, Ashtar demands of the Bull God El (the supreme deity) that Yam be deposed in Ashtar's favor, but El confirms Yam's supremacy, on the grounds that Ashtar is inadequate to this exalted position. Soon, however, El's son Baal, the rain god and spirit of fertility, challenges the power of Yam. Emissaries from Yam to the divine assembly frighten the other gods, but Baal boasts that he will destroy Yam. Although El has to pacify Yam's messengers, Baal causes the divine smith, Koshar-wa-Khasis, to make him two thunderbolts for weapons. In a protracted battle, Baal subdues Yam.

Baal now complains that, although he rules the earth, he has no palace there. After driving Yam back into the sea, the war-goddess Anat, Baal's ally, accompanies him to the abode of the mother of the gods, Asherat, El's consort, in order to present his plea. On their approach, Asherat is at first alarmed, but becomes friendly when she sees the rich gifts that they have brought, and promises Baal that his dominion will continue. After feasting her guests, Asherat presents Baal's case to El, who agrees that he may have his palace. Koshar-wa-Khasis plans the palace, but cannot persuade Baal to allow him to put windows in it, for Baal feels that Yam will steal away his young brides. When he has finally disposed of Yam, however, Baal consents to the windows. When he opens them, the windows of Heaven will open likewise and rain will fall on the earth, fertilizing it. Baal feasts the gods and makes a royal progress about his kingdom, the earth.

In his pride, Baal now challenges a more formidable enemy than Yam: Mot, the god of death and the underworld, and of aridity, which meant death to vegetation. He sends his messengers Gupan and Ugar (Vine and Field) to Mot's abode beyond the northern mountains to demand that he confine himself henceforward to the underworld and the deserts of the earth. Mot, however, invites Baal to banquet with him in the underworld. Though terrified at the prospect, Baal feels that he cannot refuse. By way of precaution, he smears himself with red ochre to warn off demons and gains strength (and a son) by copulating eighty-eight times with a heifer. He then descends into the underworld and is reported as dead.

El mourns for Baal in sackcloth and ashes, and even with self-mutilation. Anat does likewise, but afterwards she determines to seek him in the underworld. With the aid of Shapash (who, as the sun, visits there every night), she recovers Baal's body. His burial is accompanied with numerous animal sacrifices. Ashtar now sits on Baal's throne, but his feet do not reach the footstool and he realizes that he is not adequate to take Baal's place. Anat roams through the earth in search of Baal, and demands that Mot release him, but he repeatedly refuses. After some months she slays Mot in a fury.

El dreams that Baal is alive and rejoices in his imminent return. On his orders, Anat sends Shapash to find Baal. Resurrected, Baal subdues his enemies, including the revived Mot, who at last surrenders. Anat takes savage vengeance on Mot's allies, but is finally persuaded by Baal, who again reigns supreme, that peace must be restored to earth and heaven.

Apart from its intrinsic interest, *The Poem of Baal* is of great importance for the light it sheds on primitive myth and ritual, and on certain hitherto obscure passages in the Old Testament. Considerable parts of the books of Joel and Zephaniah seem to have been deliberate satires on Canaanite myth in ritual, which the Hebrews regarded as heathen. In other cases, they ascribed to Yahweh feats that are here attributed to Baal, such as the conquering of the dragon of the sea by the storm-god: "Awake, awake, put on strength, O arm of the Lord; awake, as in the ancient days, in the generations of old. Art thou not it that hath cut Rahab, and wounded the dragon? Art thou not it which hath dried the sea, the waters of the great deep?" (Isaiah 51:9–10). There are shades of Greek myth too: the dominion over earth, sea, and underworld among Baal, Yam, and Mot, are identical

with the division among Zeus, Poseidon, and Hades; Anat's mourning for the dead fertility god Baal is similar even in phraseology to the accounts of the mourning of Aphrodite for Adonis, or Demeter for Persephone. The unexplained hostility of El, Asherat, and many other gods toward Baal in the poem recalls the relegation of the older gods to positions of lesser importance when Cronos was conquered by Zeus, and the resulting wars with Giants and Titans, offspring of Ge, who, like Asherat, was the mother of the gods.

Poetaster, The (1601). A satirical comedy by Ben JONSON. In it he attacked Thomas Dekker and John Marston during the WAR OF THE THEATERS.

Poetical Miscellanies. See TOTTEL'S MISCELLANY.

poetic diction. The choice of words in poetry. Diction has always been of particular importance in poetry, since only a combination of the right words can make a poem memorable. Poetic diction should be distinguished from "poetic" diction, which has come to have a pejorative significance: the use of the archaisms and poetic clichés favored by poetasters.

Poetic Principle, The (1850). An essay by Edgar Allan POE. The poet criticizes the didactic elements in poetry; beauty is the poem's proper province. The essay, published posthumously, includes 11 poems, English and American, as examples of fine poetry.

Poetics, The (Peri Poietikes, 335–322 B.C.). A treatise by ARISTOTLE. It was composed over a period of time. All the arts, says the philosopher, have their origin in imitation or *mimesis*. Poetry springs from this instinct for imitation and from the instinct for harmony and rhythm. Aristotle makes the famous observation that poetry is more philosophical than history, since it expresses universals rather than particulars.

The objects of imitation in poetry are men in action. If they are presented as better than they are in actual life, the genre is tragedy; if worse, it is comedy. Epic poetry and tragedy have the same characteristics, except that epic admits only the narrative meter. Further, epic has no limits of time, while tragedy confines itself to a single revolution of the sun. Tragedy excites the emotions of pity and fear, effecting a release, or *catharsis*. Elements of the tragic plot are reversal of situation and recognition. The hero's fortunes fall from good to bad as a result of his tragic flaw, or *hamartia*. Aristotle disapproves of the use of the DEUS EX MACHINA, saying that the unraveling of the plot must arise out of the action of the plot itself.

This exhaustive treatise, the first devoted wholly to literary criticism, has influenced all literatures, most notably the 17th-century French classical drama. Aristotle's definitions have become a part of our critical language.

poet laureate. In England, an official court poet appointed by the sovereign. His duty was, in Jonson's time, to compose odes in honor of the sovereign's birthday and in celebration of state occasions of importance, in return for £200 a year and a butt of sack.

The first poet laureate officially recognized as such was Ben Jonson, for he was the first appointed to carry out the duties, but the first to bear the actual title was Sir William Davenant. In earlier times there had been an occasional *Versificator Regis,* and Chaucer, Skelton, Spenser, and Samuel Daniel were each called poet laureate, though not appointed to that office. The complete list of laureates:

Ben Jonson	1619–1637
Sir William Davenant	1638–1668
John Dryden	1668–1688
Thomas Shadwell	1689–1692
Nahum Tate	1692–1715
Nicholas Rowe	1715–1718
Laurence Eusden	1718–1730
Colley Cibber	1730–1757
William Whitehead	1757–1785
Thomas Warton	1785–1790
Henry James Pye	1790–1813
Robert Southey	1813–1843
William Wordsworth	1843–1850
Alfred Tennyson	1850–1892
Alfred Austin	1896–1913
Robert Bridges	1913–1930
John Masefield	1930–1967
Cecil Day-Lewis	1968–1972
Sir John Betjeman	1972–

The term arose from the ancient custom in universities of presenting a laurel wreath to graduates in rhetoric and poetry. There were once doctors laureate, bachelors laureate, etc.; in France today authors of distinction continue to be "crowned" by the Academy.

Poetry: A Magazine of Verse. An American magazine founded in 1912 and devoted to the publication of poetry. Under the editorship of Harriet Monroe, it was one of the first little magazines and a part of "the Chicago Renaissance," early in the century. It published, and often introduced, the work of such leading American and English poets as Vachel Lindsay, Carl Sandburg, Ezra Pound, T. S. Eliot, and Hart Crane. Many important spokesmen for the new movement in American literature have served as associate, foreign, and contributing editors—e.g., Ezra Pound, Yvor Winters, and Wallace Fowlie. Other editors of the magazine, which is still in existence, have included Morton Zabel, Peter De Vries, Hayden Carruth, and Karl Shapiro. See IMAGISM.

Poetry and Truth. See DICHTUNG UND WAHRHEIT.

Poet's Corner. The southern end of the south transept of Westminster Abbey. It is said to have been first so called by Oliver Goldsmith because it contained the tomb of Chaucer. Addison had previously (*Spectator*, No. 26, 1711) alluded to it as "the poetical Quarter." Besides Chaucer's tomb, it contains that of Spenser, and either the tombs of or monuments to Drayton, Ben Jonson, Shakespeare (a statue), Milton (a bust), Samuel Butler, Davenant, Cowley, Prior, Gay, Addison, Thomson, Goldsmith, Dryden, Dr. Johnson, Sheridan, Burns, Southey, Coleridge, Campbell, Macaulay, Longfellow, Dickens, Thackeray, Tennyson, and Browning.

Pogány, Willy (1882–1955). Hungarian-born American artist, illustrator, mural painter, and stage and costume designer.

Pogodin, Nikolai. Pen name of **Nikolai Feodorovich Stukalov** (1900–1962). Russian playwright. His early plays, such as *Tempo* (*Temp*; 1930) and *Poem about an Axe* (*Poema o topore*; 1930), deal with the problems encountered during the first Five-Year Plan. One of his most successful plays was *Aristocrats* (*Aristokraty*; 1934), about the rehabili-

tation of a band of outcasts and undesirables at a labor camp in northern Russia. Two plays portraying Lenin were *Man with a Gun* (*Chelovek s ruzhiom*; 1937) and *The Kremlin Chimes* (*Kremliovskiye kuranty*; 1941). A recent interesting play by Pogodin was *Petrarch's Sonnet* (*Sonet Petrarki*), published during the period of the thaw after Stalin's death. The play treats the question of love in Soviet society and broadly hints that there are areas, such as those of the emotional life of a person, that the Party would do well to keep away from.

Poictesme. An imaginary country of medieval Europe which is the scene of many of the romances of James Branch Cabell, notably JURGEN, *Figures of Earth,* and *Domnei*. In THE CREAM OF THE JEST, the scene is laid partly in a Virginia town and partly in Poictesme.

Poincaré, Raymond (1860–1934). French statesman and writer. Appointed premier in 1912, Poincaré served as president of the Republic from 1913 to 1920 leading France through the war years. Reappointed premier during the reparations crisis, he held office from 1922 to 1924, and from 1926 to 1929. Poincaré was elected to the French academy in 1909; his chief work is *Au Service de la France: Neuf années de souvenirs* (1926).

Poins. In Shakespeare's HENRY IV: PART I and PART II, a companion of Prince Hal and Falstaff at the Boar's Head Tavern.

Point Counter Point (1928). A novel by Aldous Huxley. It presents a satiric picture of London intellectuals and members of English upper-class society during the 1920's. Frequent allusions to literature, painting, music, and contemporary British politics occur throughout the book, and much scientific information is embodied in its background. The story is long and involved, with many characters; it concerns a series of broken marriages and love affairs, and a political assassination. The construction is elaborate, supposedly based on Bach's *Suite No. 2 in B Minor*. It is also a novel within a novel. Philip Quarles, a leading character in the novel, is himself planning a novel, which echoes or "counterpoints" the events going on around him. Quarles is a critical portrait of Huxley himself. The only sympathetic characters in the novel are Mark Rampion and his wife Mary, idealized portraits of D. H. Lawrence and his wife Frieda. The diabolical, sexually depraved Spandrell is said to be based on Baudelaire, and Everard Webley, whom he assassinates, on Sir Oswald Mosley, leader of the British fascist movement. Denis Burlap and Beatrice Gilray are said to represent J. Middleton Murry and Katherine Mansfield.

pointillism. See NEOIMPRESSIONISM.

Point of No Return (1949). A novel by John P. Marquand. Its theme is the ambition of a businessman, Charley Gray, to win promotion in the bank in which he is employed. While he waits anxiously for the announcement of the promotion, he revisits his home town, Clyde, Maine, where he relives his past.

Poirier, Louis. See Julien GRACQ.

Polaris (North Star). See GREAT BEAR.

Pole, Reginald (1500–1558). English Roman Catholic prelate. A friend of Sir Thomas More, he opposed the divorce of Henry VIII. He was archbishop of Canterbury (from 1556) during the reign of Queen Mary, and largely responsible for the persecutions of Protestants.

Polexandre. See Marin le Roy GOMBERVILLE.

Polinesso. In the ORLANDO FURIOSO of Lodovico Ariosto, the evil instigator of discord between Ginevra and Ariodante. Polinesso, who had hoped to win Ginevra himself, persuades Ariodante that his beloved is unfaithful, and is killed by Rinaldo when his plot is exposed.

Politian. See Angelo POLIZIANO.

Politian: A Tragedy (1835–1836). An unfinished poetic drama in blank verse, by Edgar Allan POE. The story, based on the actual murder case known as the KENTUCKY TRAGEDY, takes place in Italy. A lover, not yet the husband of the injured heroine, takes revenge.

Politick Would-Be, Lady. An English noblewoman traveling in Venice with her husband, in Jonson's comedy VOLPONE, OR THE FOX. In order to silence her maddening garrulity, Volpone tells her that her husband is dallying with Celia, the innocent wife of Corvino. Later, on the basis of no evidence, she testifies against Celia in court.

Politick Would-Be, Lord. An English nobleman residing in Venice in Jonson's comedy VOLPONE, OR THE FOX. The principal figure in a subplot that is often omitted from modern performances of the play, he is a caricature of a pompous Englishman living abroad.

Polixenes. The king of Bohemia and the father of Florizel in Shakespeare's WINTER'S TALE. Polixenes shows dignity and mercy in the face of Leontes' psychotic jealousy.

Poliziano, Angelo. Also known as **Politian.** Real name, **Angelo Ambrogini** (1454–1494). Italian poet and humanist. Called Poliziano after his birthplace, Montepulciano, he was a professor of Latin and Greek at the University of Florence, a tutor in the Medici household, and a member of the Florentine academy established by the Medici for the study of Greek philosophy. He also translated Latin and wrote verse in Latin and Italian. His best-known works are his *Stanze per la Giostra (Stanzas for the Joust)* and his short lyrics based on popular songs.

Polk, James K[nox] (1795–1849). 11th president of the U.S. (1845–1849). After serving in Congress (1825–1839) and as governor of Tennessee (1839–1841), Polk became the first "dark horse" presidential nominee and defeated Henry Clay, the Whig candidate, in 1844. Despite Polk's campaign slogan of "54° 40' or Fight," the troublesome Oregon controversy with Great Britain was settled through compromise during his administration, and the Mexican War added over one million square miles of territory to the U.S. As he had promised in 1844, Polk declined to run for a second term.

Pollaiuolo or **Pollajuolo, Antonio del** (1432–1498). Italian painter, sculptor and goldsmith. He is noted for his landscapes and his treatment of the human form to which he imparted vivid movement. Such artists as Dürer, Signorelli, and Verrocchio studied and were influenced by him. His best-known paintings are *Portrait of a Man, Labors of Hercules, David, The Martyrdom of St. Sebastian,* and *Tobias and the Angel.* His sculpture includes the *Hercules* and the tomb of Sixtus IV. His brother and collaborator **Piero** (1441–1496) is best remembered for his *Portrait of a Lady.*

Pollente. See FAERIE QUEENE, THE.

Pollice verso. See THUMBS DOWN.

Pollio, Gaius Asinius (75 B.C.–A.D. 4). Roman poet, orator, and statesman. After an early career in politics and in the army (48–38 B.C.), he retired from public life to devote himself to the advancement of learning. As a patron of literature he is remembered for three accomplishments: He saved VERGIL from being evicted from his ancestral farm in the land redistribution of 41 B.C. and introduced him to Maecenas; he set up the first public library in Rome; and he introduced the practice of public recitation by writers of their works in progress.

Pollock, Channing (1880–1946). American playwright and critic. Pollock wrote drama reviews for various newspapers and magazines including *Smart Set,* published novels, essays, and several popular songs, including *My Man* for Fannie Brice, and was the author of more than 30 plays. He dramatized (1904) *The Pit* by Frank Norris and wrote such popular plays as *The Sign on the Door* (1919) and *The Fool* (1922). *The Adventures of a Happy Man* (1939; enlarged 1946) and *Harvest of My Years* (1943) are autobiographical.

Pollock, Jackson (1912–1956). American abstract painter. After 1940 he developed the controversial "drip" technique of spattering paint on the canvas, generally using subdued colors—black, brown, and white—and covering the canvas with an over-all design of rhythmic curves and textured surface.

Pollux. See CASTOR AND POLYDEUCES.

Polly. A ballad-opera by John GAY (published 1729), a sequel to THE BEGGAR'S OPERA. It was not performed till 1777, and then only in an adaptation by Colman the elder, because of government resentment at Gay's satire.

Pollyanna (1913). A novel by Eleanor H[odgman] Porter (1868–1920), an American. The child heroine of the story is an expert at her favorite "Glad Game" of always looking at the bright side in her numerous trials. The word *Pollyanna* has become a synonym for the fatuous, irrepressible optimist who always makes the best of things for himself and other people. Mrs. Porter herself wrote *Pollyanna Grows Up* (1915), but several other sequels by other writers followed.

Polo, Marco (c. 1254–1324). Venetian traveler and adventurer. About 1263, Nicolo and Maffeo Polo (the father and uncle of Marco) visited the court of Kublai Khan, the first Europeans to do so. They returned to Venice in 1269 and, with Marco, left for the East again in 1271. After arriving at the mouth of the Persian Gulf, they abandoned their plan of traveling by sea and turned north, traversing Persia and Turkmen until they reached the Oxus river. They crossed the plain of Pamir and traveled on through the Gobi Desert until they reached Tangut, in the extreme northwest of China. Early in 1275 the three Polos were cordially received at Shangtu by the great Khan, who became especially fond of Marco. The young Polo studied the various native languages, and in 1277 he became a second-class commissioner in the Mongol bureaucracy. Traveling throughout the empire on missions for the

Khan, he journeyed from Tibet to Burma and as far as the southern states of India.

So popular at court were the Polos that Kublai Khan would not tolerate their leaving his empire. However, in 1292 they escorted a Mongol princess to Persia. The journey by sea took two years. The Polos went on through Constantinople to Venice, arriving unrecognized late in 1295.

While engaged in a sea battle with the city of Genoa in 1298, Marco Polo was captured and spent nearly a year in prison, during which time he dictated his *Book of Marco Polo* to Rustichello of Pisa.

Polonius. In Shakespeare's HAMLET, a garrulous courtier, typical of the pompous, sententious old man. He is the father of Ophelia and Laertes and lord chamberlain to the king of Denmark. His advice to his son, however, is justly famous. The speech contains this admonition:

> This above all: to thine own self be true,
> And it must follow, as the night the day,
> Thou canst not then be false to any man.

Polybius (Polybios, 202?–125 B.C.). A Greek historian of the Roman world. Taken as a hostage by the Romans in the Third Macedonian War, Polybius, a Greek statesman of prominence, became a tutor to the young Publius Scipio Aemilianus and his brothers. Though later free to return home, he accompanied Scipio to Carthage in the Third Punic War and was present when the city fell. He later saw the fall of Corinth. He wrote a reliable history of Rome from 262 B.C. to 120 B.C. in 40 books, of which only five are extant. Undistinguished as literature, this work is a sound source book for Roman history of this period.

Polycleitus (Polykleitos, 5th c. B.C.). The name of two Greek sculptors often confused. The former lived in Sicyon, the latter in Argos. The most famous statue of the elder of the two was the Doryphorus (Spear-Bearer). Polycleitus deduced a canon of the proportions of the human body and was immensely admired in his own day and long thereafter. The Argive Polycleitus was also highly successful, but his works are less well known.

Polycrates (Polykrates, 6th century B.C.). A tyrant of Samos. He was known and feared for his unfailing success in all his ventures. He won a number of wars with other Greek islands and even withstood an attack from the combined forces of Sparta and Corinth. For a time he was allied with Amasis, the king of Egypt, but Amasis grew so uneasy at his success that (according to the legend) he superstitiously demanded that Polycrates deliberately throw away one of his most valued possessions. Polycrates obligingly threw his favorite ring into the sea, and in a few days received it back again in the belly of a fish. Amasis broke off their alliance. A patron of the arts, Polycrates is particularly known for his friendship with Anacreon. His luck finally broke when, lured to the mainland by the envious Oroetes, satrap of Sardis, he was ignominiously crucified.

Polydamas. A Grecian athlete of immense size and strength. He was an Olympic victor in 408 B.C. According to the legends that grew up about him, he killed a fierce lion without weapons, stopped a chariot in full career, lifted a mad bull, and died at last in attempting to stop a falling rock.

Polydeuces. See CASTOR AND POLYDEUCES.

Polydorus (Polydoros). In classic myth, the youngest son of Priam and Hecuba. According to Homer (ILIAD, xx. 470), he was killed by Achilles, but other legends state that he was committed to the care of Polymestor, king of Thrace, who treacherously slew him. His ghost appears in Euripides' tragedy HECUBA, which tells of her revenge on Polymestor.

Polyeucte (1641). A tragedy by Pierre CORNEILLE. Derived from the *Vitae Sanctorum* of the 16th-century monk Surius, the play is set in Armenia in the early Christian era. Polyeucte, a newly baptized Christian, reviles the pagans and is imprisoned. Desiring martyrdom, he surrenders his wife Pauline to her first lover Severus, but she refuses to comply if her husband dies. Severus bravely attempts to save Polyeucte, but Pauline's father Felix, the Roman governor of the province, orders the execution of his son-in-law. Polyeucte's martyrdom subsequently provokes the conversions to Christianity of both Pauline and the repentant Felix.

Polyhymnia. The MUSE of lyric poetry, and inventor of the lyre.

Polyidus (Polyidos). A soothsayer. He advised Bellerophon to procure the horse PEGASUS for his conflict with the Chimaera. For his other adventures, see GLAUCUS.

Polynices (Polyneikes). In Greek legend, a son of Oedipus and Jocasta. See SEVEN AGAINST THEBES.

Polyolbion or **Poly-Olbion (1612–1622).** A long poem by Michael DRAYTON. Begun in 1598, it con-

Title page of Drayton's *Poly-Olbion* (1612).

sists of a "description of all the tracts, rivers, mountains, forests, and other parts of this renowned isle of Great Britain, with intermixture of the most remarkable stories, antiquities, wonders, rarities, pleasures, and commodities of the same."

Polyphemus (Polyphemos). The best known of the Cyclops of Greek mythology. A cyclops had a single eye in the middle of his forehead. Odysseus landing in Sicily with his crew during their wanderings described in Homer's ODYSSEY, comes to Polyphemus' cave. The monster imprisons them by pushing a stone against the entrance and dines on six of them. They manage to blind him and escape holding on to the undersides of Polyphemus' sheep. However, Polyphemus prays to his father Poseidon, and the god's enmity is the main cause of Odysseus' long wanderings. This story is humorously told in Euripides' satyr play *Cyclops.*

According to Ovid, this same Polyphemus was in love with the nymph Galatea, who, however, preferred the handsome ACIS. Polyphemus crushed him under a rock, from which thereafter flowed the river Acis, near Mount Aetna.

polyphonic prose. A type of free verse resembling prose in its thought sequence and published as a prose passage. Its use is outstanding in the poetry of Amy LOWELL.

Polyxena. In classic myth, a daughter of Priam and Hecuba. The early poets say little about her, but according to later legends she is the heroine of a tragic love affair with Achilles the Greek hero. See TROJAN WOMEN, THE.

Pomes Penyeach (1927). A collection of lyric poems by James JOYCE.

Pomona. In Roman mythology, the goddess of fruit trees. She was wooed and won by VERTUMNUS, god of the seasons.

Pompadour, Marquise de. **Jeanne Antoinette Poisson** (1721–1764). Mistress of Louis XV. She was established at Versailles (1745) and given the estate of Pompadour. She had great influence over the king, especially in internal affairs. Opposed to RICHELIEU's foreign policy, she was instrumental in bringing on the Seven Years' War, which ended in disaster for France. She protected writers of the ENCYCLOPÉDIE and spent enormous sums to pay artists to decorate her residences.

Pompey the Great. Full Latin name, **Gnaeus Pompeius Magnus** (106–48 B.C.). Roman general and statesman. He organized the First TRIUMVIRATE with Julius Caesar and Crassus in 60 B.C. He became a champion of the Senatorial Party. When Caesar crossed the RUBICON, Pompey and his followers fled to Northern Greece; Caesar pressed them, and they were decisively defeated at Pharsalus (48). Pompey then fled to Egypt where Ptolemy had him murdered. The earliest English tragedy based on the story of Pompey is *Pompey the Great, his faire Cornelia's Tragedy,* a translation into blank verse by Thomas Kyd from the French of Garnier.

Pomponazzi, Pietro (1462–1525). Italian philosopher. Influenced by the naturalistic school of Padua, where he studied and taught, Pomponazzi's major work, *De immortalitate animae,* published at Bologna in 1516, stirred controversy because it argued against the soul's immortality as an unreasonable tenet. In justifying his skepticism he distinguished

between objective truth and truth according to religion, a defense that echoed widely in the writings of Renaissance thinkers.

Ponce de León, Juan (c. 1460–1521). Spanish explorer. Ponce de León may have sailed to America on the second voyage of Christopher Columbus. In 1508 he conquered the island of Puerto Rico and subsequently became its governor. Seeking a legendary fountain of youth, supposedly located in a land called Bimini, he sighted the North American mainland on Easter Sunday, 1513, and upon landing called the region Florida, probably for *Pascua florida* ("flowery Easter"). After exploring much of the Florida coast, he returned to Puerto Rico. During a second expedition to Florida, he was wounded in a skirmish with the Indians and was taken to Cuba, where he died.

Pond, James B[urton] (1838–1903). American lecture manager. His clients included Henry Ward Beecher, Mark Twain, Sir Arthur Conan Doyle, Matthew Arnold, and many other well-known literary personages. He wrote his amusing reminiscences in *Eccentricities of Genius: Memories of Famous Men and Women of the Platform and Stage* (1900).

Ponderevo, Edward. The hero of H. G. Wells's novel TONO-BUNGAY. He invented and made a fortune from quack medicine.

Ponge, Francis (1899–   ). French poet. His prose poems, such as those in *Le Parti pris des Choses* (1942) and *Proèmes* (1948), depict the world with cold precision in a philosophic attempt to approach the essence of objective reality.

Ponocrates (*Gr.,* "strong"). In Rabelais' GARGANTUA AND PANTAGRUEL, the tutor who accompanies Gargantua when he goes to Paris to complete his education. After observing how Gargantua's former teachers had taught him nothing but lazy and sloppy manners and useless memorization from the breviary, Ponocrates institutes a new program of studies emphasizing first-hand observation in all fields of learning, physical exercise, and cleanliness.

Pons, Sylvain. See COUSIN PONS, LE.

Pons Asinorum (Lat., "the asses' bridge"). The fifth proposition, Bk. I, of Euclid. The first difficult theorem, which dunces rarely get over without stumbling.

Pontano, Giovanni. Also known as **Jovianus Pontanus** (1426?–1503). Italian humanist and poet. Born in Umbria, he moved to Naples in 1447 to begin his career as author and public figure. He was a founder and leading light of the Neapolitan academy, and many of its members appear as interlocutors in his dialogues. Among his Latin prose and verse, the group of poems entitled *De amore coniugali* (*On Married Life*) is outstanding. His eclogues, sensual lyrics, and didactic poems were widely admired and imitated, notably in England by George Chapman. He is considered an outstanding humanist and the author of some of the most natural Latin writing of the Renaissance.

Ponte Vecchio. An ancient bridge over the Arno in Florence, Italy. A covered gallery at the top connected the Pitti Palace with the Uffizi Gallery. Small shops have clustered like barnacles on the side of the bridge since the 14th century.

Pontiac (1720?–1769). American Ottawa chief. He participated in, and perhaps organized, the unsuccessful Indian uprising against the British known as Pontiac's War or Conspiracy (1763–1764). He is the subject of one of the first American dramas, *Ponteach, or the Savages of America* (1766), by Robert Rogers.

Pontiac's War or **Conspiracy.** See PONTIAC.

Pontifex, Ernest. See WAY OF ALL FLESH, THE.

Pontoppidan, Henrik (1857–1943). Danish novelist. Pontoppidan is most famous for his three series: *Det forjoettede Land* (3 vols., 1891–1895); *Lykke-Per* (8 vols., 1898–1904); and *Dødes Rige* (5 vols., 1912–1916). In his books he paints a somber, pessimistic portrait of Denmark and the Danish people. With Karl Gjellerup he received the Nobel Prize for literature in 1917.

Pontormo, Jacopo Carucci da (1494–1556). Italian painter. One of the leading mannerists and a disciple of Michelangelo and Dürer, he is known for a series of frescoes on the Passion of Christ (1522–1524) at Valdema, near Florence. His individual paintings include *Joseph in Egypt, The Resurrection, The Visitation,* and the portrait of a *Lady with a Lapdog.* He best exemplifies the neurotic and discordant strain in MANNERISM in his anticlassical treatment of figures, color, and space. See PARMIGIANINO; Rosso.

pony express. A privately owned American postal service of the 19th century. Riders carried mail between St. Joseph, Mo. and Sacramento, Calif. in 10 days, braving weather, isolation, and hostile Indians. At its height the service employed 125 riders, 400 station men and assistants, and 420 horses. Every 10 or 20 miles, the riders would change horses. At first the charge for delivery of each letter was five dollars; later, charges were reduced, although they never paid the costs of operation. Among the most famous of the riders were Buffalo Bill (William F. CODY) and Wild Bill HICKOK.

Pooh. The toy-bear hero of the near classical children's stories by A. A. MILNE. Pooh is one of an imaginative cast of characters, which includes Eeyore the Donkey, Tigger the Tiger, Piglet, and Roo, a small kangaroo. A Latin translation of *Winnie-the-Pooh,* published in 1962, was a best seller. *The Pooh Perplex* (1963), by Frederick C. Crews, lampoons various fashionable critical approaches by parodying them in the form of commentaries on *Winnie-the-Pooh.*

pooka. See PHOOKA.

Poole, Ernest (1880–1950). American journalist and novelist. Poole lived in a settlement house in the slums of New York City and wrote articles for magazines exposing the horrible conditions of the workers. In 1905 he traveled to Russia to report on the abortive revolution there. His first novel, THE HARBOR, was immediately popular. HIS FAMILY won a Pulitzer Prize. In 1917, Poole returned to Russia; from this trip came his accounts of Russian life, *The Village* (1918) and *The Dark People* (1918), and a volume of Russian tales and sketches, *The Little Dark Man* (1925).

Poole, William Frederick (1821–1894). American librarian. In 1848 Poole published a useful and famous work, *Poole's Index to Periodical Literature.* A forerunner of the *Readers' Guide to Periodical Literature,* it was enlarged in later editions and continued after his death.

Poor Clares. Nuns of the Order founded by St. Clare of Assisi (1194–1253). It is the equivalent for women of the Friars Minor (Franciscans).

Poor Folk (**Bednye lyudi;** 1846). A short novel by Feodor DOSTOEVSKI. The author's first published fictional work, written in the form of an epistolary novel, it tells of the hopeless love of Makar Alekseyevich DEVUSHKIN, a poor, timid clerk, for Varvara Alekseyevna Dobroselova, a poor young girl who lives in the building across the way from him. Despite Devushkin's frantic efforts to save Varvara, interspersed with the clerk's despairing bouts of drunkenness, Varvara is married to a wealthy landowner who carries her away. The work is remarkable for the vivid characterization, especially of Devushkin, solely by means of his letters to Varvara and her answers to him.

Poor Richard's Almanack. Composite name given to the almanacs issued from 1732 to 1757 by Benjamin FRANKLIN. From 1732 to 1747 their title was *Poor Richard;* the later numbers were called *Poor Richard Improved.* To *Poor Richard* are attributed most of Franklin's famous adages:

> Make haste slowly.
>
> God helps them that help themselves.
>
> Early to bed and early to rise,
> Makes a man healthy, wealthy, and wise.

See Richard SAUNDERS.

Poor Robin. A series of almanacs published in England from 1662 to 1828. The poet Robert Herrick is said to have assisted with the first numbers.

Poor White (1920). A novel by Sherwood ANDERSON. It describes the changes occurring in a Midwestern town when industrialism replaces the old agrarian, craft-centered society. The town itself is the protagonist of the early part of the book, and Anderson successfully depicts its shabbiness, isolation, and sterility. Hugh McVey, the central character, is an introverted inventor who does not become aware until it is too late that his own genius contributes to the corruption of his environment.

pope. The title of the spiritual ruler of the world's Roman Catholics. His other titles include bishop of Rome, Vicar of Christ, Supreme Pontiff of the Universal Church, Patriarch of the West, primate of Italy, archbishop and metropolitan of the Roman Province, and sovereign of the State of Vatican City.

The title "pope" came into use in the fourth century; until that time the usual title was bishop of Rome. According to tradition, St. Peter came from Antioch to Rome c. A.D. 41 and was martyred there c. 67. The papal see has since remained at Rome, except that in 1309 King Philip of France persuaded Clement V (who had been elected by a college of cardinals dominated by the French) to move to Avignon; the "Babylonian captivity" of the popes, as the era is called, lasted until 1377.

For centuries, the popes were powerful temporal rulers. The Papal States, which grew out of a nucleus of land grants in the fourth century and eventually spread over vast areas of Italy, were finally absorbed in 1870 by Victor Emmanuel II. The Lateran Treaty of 1929, however, granted the popes full sovereignty over Vatican City, an enclave in the heart of Rome.

According to the theory of Petrine succession, the popes are the rulers of all Christendom, by virtue of their succession to the see of St. Peter, the vicar (vicegerent) of Christ. This claim has always been rejected by the Protestant churches, and was the principal reason for the disunion (schism) of the Church of Rome and the churches of the Eastern (Orthodox) rite, which became definite in 1054 when Pope Leo IX condemned the patriarch of Constantinople.

Popes are elected at an assembly of the college of cardinals, known as the conclave. Balloting ends when one name has received two thirds plus one of the votes cast. In theory any Catholic, even a layman, is eligible for election; in practice the cardinals have always selected one of their own number, and he has most often been an Italian. The last non-Italian pope was Adrian VI of Utrecht, elected in 1522; the sole English pope was Adrian IV (Nicholas Breakspear) elected in 1154.

A list of the popes follows, to which is appended a list of antipopes and doubtful popes.

Popes:

St. Peter	41?– ?67
St. Linus	67– ?79
St. Anacletus (Cletus)	79– ?90
St. Clement I	90– ?99
St. Evaristus	99–?107
St. Alexander I	107–?116
St. Sixtus I	116–?125
St. Telesphorus	125–?136
St. Hyginus	136–?140
St. Pius I	140–?154
St. Anicetus	154–?165
St. Soterus	165– 174
St. Eleutherius	174– 189
St. Victor I	189– 198
St. Zephyrinus	198– 217
St. Callistus I	217– 222
St. Urban I	222– 230
St. Pontian	230– 235
St. Anterus	235– 236
St. Fabian	236– 250
St. Cornelius	251– 253
St. Lucius I	253– 254
St. Stephen I	254– 257
St. Sixtus II	257– 258
St. Dionysius	259– 268
St. Felix I	269– 274
St. Eutychian	275– 283
St. Caius	283– 296
St. Marcellinus	296– 304
St. Marcellus I	308– 309
St. Eusebius	309
St. Melchiades	310?– 314
St. Sylvester I	314– 335
St. Mark	336
St. Julius I	337– 352
St. Liberius	352– 366
St. Damasus I	366– 384
St. Siricius	384– 398
St. Anastasius I	398– 401
St. Innocent I	402– 417
St. Zosimus	417– 418
St. Boniface I	418– 422
St. Celestine I	422– 432
St. Sixtus III	432– 440
St. Leo I (the Great)	440– 461
St. Hilary	461– 468
St. Simplicius	468– 483
St. Felix III (or II)	483– 492

St. Gelasius I	492– 496
Anastasius II	496– 498
St. Symmachus	498– 514
St. Hormisdas	514– 523
St. John I	523– 526
St. Felix IV (or III)	526– 530
Boniface II	530– 532
John II	533– 535
St. Agapetus	535– 536
St. Silverius	536–?538
Vigilius	538– 555
Pelagius I	556– 561
John III	561– 574
Benedict I	575– 579
Pelagius II	579– 590
St. Gregory I (the Great)	590– 604
Sabinianus	604– 606
Boniface III	607
St. Boniface IV	608– 615
St. Deusdedit or Adeodatus I	615– 618
Boniface V	619– 625
Honorius I	625– 638
Severinus	640
John IV	640– 642
Theodore I	642– 649
St. Martin I	649– 655
St. Eugene I	655– 657
St. Vitalian	657– 672
Adeodatus II	672– 676
Donus I	676– 678
St. Agatho	678– 681
St. Leo II	682– 683
St. Benedict II	684– 685
John V	685– 686
Conon	686– 687
St. Sergius I	687– 701
John VI	701– 705
John VII	705– 707
Sisinnius	708
Constantine	708– 715
St. Gregory II	715– 731
St. Gregory III	731– 741
St. Zachary	741– 752
Stephen II (disputed)	752
Stephen III	752– 757
St. Paul I	757– 767
Stephen IV	768– 772
St. Adrian I	772– 795
St. Leo III	795– 816
Stephen V	816– 817
St. Paschal I	817– 824
Eugene II	824– 827
Valentine	827
Gregory IV	827– 844
Sergius II	844– 847
St. Leo IV	847– 855
Benedict III	855– 858
St. Nicholas I	858– 867
Adrian II	867– 872
John VIII	872– 882
Marinus I	882– 884
St. Adrian III	884– 885
Stephen VI	885– 891
Formosus	891– 896
Boniface VI	896
Stephen VII	896– 897
Romanus	897
Theodore II	?897
John IX	898– 900
Benedict IV	900– 903
Leo V	903
Sergius III	904– 911
Anastasius III	911– 913
Landus	913– 914
John X	914– 928

Leo VI	928– 929		Urban V	1362–1370
Stephen VIII	929– 931		Gregory XI	1370–1378
John XI	931– 936		Urban VI	1378–1389
Leo VII	936– 939		Boniface IX	1389–1404
Stephen IX	939– 942		Innocent VII	1404–1406
Marinus II	942– 946		Gregory XII	1406–1415
Agapetus II	946– 955		Martin V	1417–1431
John XII	955– 964		Eugene IV	1431–1447
Leo VIII	963– 965		Nicholas V	1447–1455
Benedict V	964		Callistus III	1455–1458
John XIII	965– 972		Pius II	1458–1464
Benedict VI	973– 974		Paul II	1464–1471
Benedict VII	974– 983		Sixtus IV	1471–1484
John XIV	983– 984		Innocent VIII	1484–1492
John XV	985– 996		Alexander VI	1492–1503
Gregory V	996– 999		Pius III	1503
Sylvester II	999–1003		Julius II	1503–1513
John XVII	1003		Leo X	1513–1521
John XVIII	1004–1009		Adrian VI	1522–1523
Sergius IV	1009–1012		Clement VII	1523–1534
Benedict VIII	1012–1024		Paul III	1534–1549
John XIX	1024–1032		Julius III	1550–1555
Benedict IX	1032–1045		Marcellus II	1555
Gregory VI	1045–1046		Paul IV	1555–1559
Clement II	1046–1047		Pius IV	1559–1565
Damasus II	1048		St. Pius V	1566–1572
St. Leo IX	1049–1054		Gregory XIII	1572–1585
Victor II	1055–1057		Sixtus V	1585–1590
Stephen X	1057–1058		Urban VII	1590
Benedict X	1058–1059		Gregory XIV	1590–1591
Nicholas II	1059–1061		Innocent IX	1591
Alexander II	1061–1073		Clement VIII	1592–1605
St. Gregory VII	1073–1085		Leo XI	1605
Victor III	1086–1087		Paul V	1605–1621
Urban II	1088–1099		Gregory XV	1621–1623
Paschal II	1099–1118		Urban VIII	1623–1644
Gelasius II	1118–1119		Innocent X	1644–1655
Callistus II	1119–1124		Alexander VII	1655–1667
Honorius II	1124–1130		Clement IX	1667–1669
Innocent II	1130–1143		Clement X	1670–1676
Celestine II	1143–1144		Innocent XI	1676–1689
Lucius II	1144–1145		Alexander VIII	1689–1691
Eugene III	1145–1153		Innocent XII	1691–1700
Anastasius IV	1153–1154		Clement XI	1700–1721
Adrian IV	1154–1159		Innocent XIII	1721–1724
Alexander III	1159–1181		Benedict XIII	1724–1730
Lucius III	1181–1185		Clement XII	1730–1740
Urban III	1185–1187		Benedict XIV	1740–1758
Gregory VIII	1187		Clement XIII	1758–1769
Clement III	1187–1191		Clement XIV	1769–1774
Celestine III	1191–1198		Pius VI	1775–1799
Innocent III	1198–1216		Pius VII	1800–1823
Honorius III	1216–1227		Leo XII	1823–1829
Gregory IX	1227–1241		Pius VIII	1829–1830
Celestine IV	1241		Gregory XVI	1831–1846
Innocent IV	1243–1254		Pius IX	1846–1878
Alexander IV	1254–1261		Leo XIII	1878–1903
Urban IV	1261–1264		St. Pius X	1903–1914
Clement IV	1265–1268		Benedict XV	1914–1922
Gregory X	1271–1276		Pius XI	1922–1939
Innocent V	1276		Pius XII	1939–1958
Adrian V	1276		John XXIII	1958–1963
John XXI	1276–1277		Paul VI	1963–
Nicholas III	1277–1280			
Martin IV	1281–1285			
Honorius IV	1285–1287			
Nicholas IV	1288–1292			
St. Celestine V	1294			
Boniface VIII	1294–1303			
Benedict XI	1303–1304			
Clement V	1305–1314			
John XXII	1316–1334			
Benedict XII	1334–1342			
Clement VI	1342–1352			
Innocent VI	1352–1362			

The term "antipope" is applied to a claimant to the papal throne whose election was not in accordance with the Church's canon law. Some pretenders were promoted by European rulers as political pawns; others were elected by a rival faction of cardinals. The most famous antipope was Clement VII; he was named in 1378 after the death of Gregory XI, who had just moved the papal see back to Rome from Avignon. A conclave at Rome elected Urban VI as Gregory's successor; Clement was named a few months later by the French cardinals. The resultant dispute, known as the Great Schism of the West, divided the Church. It was resolved in 1417 when the Council of Constance elected Martin V.

Antipopes and doubtful popes:

Novatian	251 –	?258
Felix II	355 –	358
Eulalius	418 –	419
Laurentius	498 –	505
Stephen II		752
Constantine II	767 –	768
Anastasius		855
Boniface VII		974
John XVI	997 –	998
Sylvester III		1045
Benedict IX	1047 –	1048
Honorius II	1061 –	1064
Clement III	1080, 1084 –	1100
Sylvester IV	1105 –	1111
Gregory VIII	1118 –	1121
Celestine II		1124
Anacletus II	1130 –	1138
Victor IV		1138
Victor IV	1159 –	1164
Paschal III	1164 –	1168
Callistus III	1168 –	1178
Innocent III	1179 –	1180
Nicholas V	1328 –	1330
Clement VII	1378 –	1394
Benedict XIII	1394 –	1423
John XXIII	1410 –	1415
Clement VIII	1424?–	1429
Benedict XIV		?1424
Felix V	1439 –	1449

Pope, Alexander (1688–1744). English poet and satirist, literary dictator of his age and regarded as the epitome of English neoclassicism. He was born a Roman Catholic at a time when England was violently anti-Catholic, and was educated largely at home; a severe illness in boyhood caused permanent damage to his health and disfigurement of his body. Pope's metrical skill was apparent very early in his *Pastorals* (1709; see Ambrose PHILIPS) which he said he wrote when he was 16. Known for its skillful use of the heroic or closed couplet, his poetry is characterized by technical finish, invective, and wit; it is satiric, epigrammatic, and didactic. Pope's best-known works include ESSAY ON CRITICISM, which made him famous at the age of 23; THE RAPE OF THE LOCK; *Messiah;* a Vergilian paraphrase of the Book of Isaiah, first published in *The Spectator* in 1712; *Windsor Forest* (1713), in praise of the Tory peace of Utrecht; *An Elegy to the Memory of an Unfortunate Lady* and *Epistle from Eloisa to Abelard* (1717), two passionate though rhetorical poems; translations of the *Iliad* (1715–1720) and the *Odyssey* (1725–1726); an edition of Shakespeare (1725); THE DUNCIAD; MORAL ESSAYS; AN ESSAY ON MAN; EPISTLE TO DR. ARBUTHNOT. The first complete edition of Pope's works was that published by William WARBURTON in 1751. In his *Essay on the Writings and Genius of Pope* (1756), Joseph Warton argued that Pope's claim to poetic greatness was limited by his cultivation of didacticism and wit, rather than sublimity and pathos, but that "in the species of Poetry wherein Pope excelled, he is superior to all mankind." Pope was wont to attack his contemporaries, often spitefully, as, for example, his attack on Joseph Addison in *Epistle to Dr. Arbuth-*

Title page of Pope's *Essay on Man*, designed by Pope.

not; because of this he was called the Wicked Wasp of Twickenham, from the name of the villa in which he lived. He was a Tory in politics, a friend of John Gay and Jonathan Swift, and a member of the SCRIBLERUS CLUB.

Pope-Figs. An anglicism for the Papefigues in Rabelais' GARGANTUA AND PANTAGRUEL. Once called Gaillardets (*Fr.,* "Goodfellows"), they had been reduced to ruin by the PAPIMANIACS after they had "made the fig at," or ridiculed, a portrait of the pope.

Popeye. A character in William Faulkner's SANCTUARY. An embodiment of pure evil, Popeye is a reptilian and perverted gangster and murderer who rapes Temple DRAKE and kills the half-wit Tommy. Popeye is finally hanged in Alabama for a murder he did not commit, having been busy, at the time of the supposed crime, murdering a man in Memphis. As repulsive as this degenerate representative of urban culture is, he, too, is in part the victim of his environment.

Popish Plot. See Titus OATES.

Poppaea. The mistress and later the wife of the Roman emperor NERO. She is a character in Seneca's Latin tragedy *Octavia,* appears in Sienkiewicz' historical novel *Quo Vadis* (1896), and is the heroine of Monteverdi's opera *L'Incoronazione di Poppea* (1642).

Popular Front. A term of the later years of the 1930's, during the Spanish Civil War (1936–1939) and again after the beginning of World War II (1939–1945). It signified an alliance between the capitalist democracies (especially the U.S. and Great Britain) and the U.S.S.R. against Nazi Germany, Fascist Italy, and, later, Japan. The Popular Front became a reality only after the German invasion of the U.S.S.R. in June 1941. The term is also applied to coalitions of certain progressive parties in Spain and France (after 1936), as those that supported the French cabinets of Léon Blum, Camille Chautemps, and Edouard Daladier, and opposed the Spanish insurgents in the early phases of the Civil war.

Populisme. A French literary movement. It advocated a literature written for and about the common working man. Essentially a revolt against mannered, aristocratic literature, *Populisme* defined its aims in two manifestos, of August 1929 and January 1930. Naturalistic in their minutely descriptive method and in their humble subject matter, the chief writers of the school were Eugène DABIT, Léon Lemonnier (1892–   ), André Thérive (1891–   ), and Louis Guilloux (1899–   ). The novels that best embodied the goals of *Populisme* were Dabit's *Hôtel du Nord* (1929), *Femme sans péché* (1931) by Lemonnier, *Sans Ame* (1928) and *Le Charbon ardent* (1929) by Thérive, and Guilloux's *Le Pain des Rêves*. An annual *Prix populiste* is still awarded.

Populist or People's Party. In U.S. history, a political party established in 1892 in Omaha, Neb., by farmers and laborers, primarily from the West, who were dissatisfied with Eastern financial and commercial policies. The Populists nominated James B. Weaver of Iowa as their presidential candidate and adopted a platform calling for the free and unlimited coinage of silver and gold at the ratio of 16 to one; government ownership of transportation and communications facilities; direct election of U.S. senators; and a graduated income tax. Their aim was "to restore the government of the Republic to the hands of the 'plain people,' with which class it originated." Weaver received over 1,000,000 votes in the election of 1892. In 1896 the Populists endorsed the candidacy of William Jennings Bryan, the Democratic nominee.

Porch, the. Another name for the Stoic school of Greek philosophy. See STOICISM.

Porgy (1925). A novel by DuBose HEYWARD. Set in Charleston, S.C., it deals with Negroes along Catfish Row. Central to the story is Porgy, a crippled beggar who becomes involved in a murder. Other characters include Bess, Sportin' Life, Crown, and Serena. With his wife, Dorothy, Heyward adapted the novel as a play (1927). The play in turn became the basis of George GERSHWIN's *Porgy and Bess* (1935), a folk opera which has become an American classic.

Porgy, Captain. A comic character created by William Gilmore SIMMS. He appears in Simms' trilogy about the American Revolution—THE PARTISAN, *Mellichampe* (1836), and *Katharine Walton* (1851)—and in *The Forayers* (1855) and WOODCRAFT. Porgy combines a Falstaffian paunch and love for food and drink with the more typical Southern virtues of bravery, gallantry, and generosity. He is bawdy, humorous, inventive, and a tireless practical joker. Many critics felt Simms was at his best when

describing the exploits of Porgy, although others, notably Poe, found Porgy "an unsufferable bore."

Porphyry (Porphyrios; Tyrian, Malchus; 233–c. 301). Greek Neoplatonist, the student and biographer of PLOTINUS. Porphyry is the source for all our information about his teacher. He arranged Plotinus' treatises into six groups of nine treatises (*Enneads*), and seems to have faithfully respected the text. He also wrote a life of Pythagoras and an introduction to Aristotle's *Organon*.

Porsena, Lars. In the 6th century B.C., king of Clusium in Etruria. He led an expedition against Rome, but was stopped from entering the city by the bravery of HORATIUS COCLES. After laying siege to Rome, he finally made peace on condition that the Romans give up some captured land and supply hostages.

This is the Roman legend. Scholars feel that it is an attempt to cover up a greater tragedy inflicted on Rome by the Etruscans as they, the Etruscans, moved southward before the invading Celts, passing through Rome as they fled.

Porte étroite, La. See STRAIT IS THE GATE.

Porteous Riot. A riot at Edinburgh in September, 1736. Captain Porteous was commander of the town guard and, at the execution of a smuggler named Wilson, ordered the guard to fire on the mob, which had become disorderly. Six persons were killed, and eleven wounded. Porteous was condemned to death, but reprieved, whereupon the mob burst into the jail where he was confined, and, dragging him to the Grassmarket (the usual place of execution), hanged him by torchlight on a barber's pole. As a result, Robert Walpole attempted to punish the Edinburgh populace too severely and was vehemently opposed. Sir Walter Scott introduces the riot in his *Heart of Midlothian*.

Porter, Cole (1893–1964). American composer of popular songs. His lyrics are often unusually witty. His best-known songs include *Night and Day* and *Begin the Beguine*. *Kiss Me Kate* (1948) is probably his most famous musical comedy.

Porter, Eleanor H. See POLLYANNA.

Porter, Gene[va] Stratton (1863–1924). American novelist. She is noted for the enormous popularity of her sentimental romances, set in the great Limberlost Swamp of Indiana, notably *Freckles* (1904) and *A Girl of the Limberlost* (1909). *Laddie* (1913) is a fictional version of the author's childhood in the Limberlost country. *Keeper of the Bees* (1925) was published posthumously.

Porter, Jane (1776–1850). English novelist. She is known for her popular romances *Thaddeus of Warsaw* (1803) and a very early historical novel, *The Scottish Chiefs* (1810), which was a forerunner to the romantic novels of her childhood friend, Sir Walter Scott.

Porter, Katherine Anne (1894–   ). American short-story writer and novelist. Miss Porter's stories are rich in psychological insight and symbolic import. Two well-known collections of her short stories are FLOWERING JUDAS and *The Leaning Tower* (1944). PALE HORSE, PALE RIDER is a collection of three short novels. SHIP OF FOOLS, a novel Miss Porter had worked on for 20 years, was hailed as a major achievement by many reviewers. Her essays on life and art were collected in *The Days Before*

(1952). Other books by Miss Porter are *Hacienda* (1934), a collection of short stories, and NOON WINE and OLD MORTALITY, short novels.

Porter, William Sydney. See O. HENRY.

Porthos. One of the famous trio in Dumas' THE THREE MUSKETEERS, and a prominent character in its sequels TWENTY YEARS AFTER and THE VISCOUNT OF BRAGELONNE. In physical stature the good-hearted Porthos is a giant, but in mental stature he is somewhat less grand.

Portia. (1) The clever and wise young heroine of Shakespeare's MERCHANT OF VENICE. Disguised as Balthazar, a young lawyer, she defends Antonio against Shylock's demand for a pound of his flesh. At first she tries to soften Shylock by pleading for mercy:

> The quality of mercy is not strain'd,
> It droppeth as the gentle rain from heaven
> Upon the place beneath: it is twice bless'd;
> It blesseth him that gives and him that takes.

Although this appeal fails to move Shylock, she manages to outwit him and win the case for Antonio. See BASSANIO.

(2) In Shakespeare's JULIUS CAESAR, the courageous and noble wife of Brutus and daughter of Cato. When Brutus is forced to flee from Rome after Caesar's assassination, she commits suicide by swallowing hot coals.

portmanteau word. A completely new word combining parts of two or more words. The word thus created expresses a combination of the meanings of its parts, as in the now common word *brunch*, created by combining the "br" of *breakfast* with the "unch" of *lunch*. Lewis Carroll introduced portmanteau words in *Through the Looking-Glass;* he says *slithy* means *lithe* and *slimy, mimsy* is *flimsy* and *miserable*, etc. Carroll called these portmanteau words because in them two meanings were "packed up" in one bag, as it were. Modern writers have made liberal use of such words, notably James Joyce in his *Finnegans Wake*.

Portolá, Gaspar de (1723?–?1784). Spanish governor of the Californias who marched 1,000 miles (1769) from Lower to Upper California, where he founded San Diego and Monterey. Father Junípero Serra was one of the diarists of the expedition.

Porto-Riche, Georges de (1849–1930). French dramatist, born of Italian-Jewish parentage. Porto-Riche won fame with his masterpiece *Amoureuse* (1891), a cynical comedy marked by great psychological insight. His later plays, *Le Passé* (1897), *Le Vieil Homme* (1911), and *Le Marchand d'estampes* (1917), never matched his initial success.

Portrait of a Lady (1917). A poem by T. S. ELIOT. It is about the lack of communication between a woman and a man who are trapped by the conventions of a dying social order. Both are conscious of their isolation, yet are equally unable to escape it. The lady of the poem is driven by her loneliness to reach out to the man, but realizes that she has nothing left to give. Her life, she knows, is an empty shell determined by empty forms and devitalized social rituals. He, evading her demands, seeks solace in humdrum habits and conventions.

Portrait of a Lady, The (1881). A novel by Henry JAMES. The motives that lead Isabel ARCHER,

a romantic New England girl who inherits an English fortune, to refuse other suitors and marry Gilbert Osmond are skillfully analyzed, and her subsequent disillusionment is traced in devastating detail. Osmond is a dilettante, an impoverished gentleman living in retirement in Italy with his daughter, Pansy, because his exquisite tastes and sensibilities make him scornful of the crudities of the modern struggle for existence. After Isabel's marriage she discovers that she has only served the purposes of her quasi-friend, Madame Merle, who, as Osmond's mistress and the mother of Pansy, brought the two together for the sake of Isabel's fortune. Osmond's fine sensibilities are likewise seen to be but the expression of an intensely egocentric, unpleasant nature. The novel has been generally considered one of James's finest works.

Portrait of a Man with Red Hair (1925). A novel by Hugh WALPOLE. It is a horror story and romance about two men, a girl, and a red haired, sadistic madman.

Portrait of the Artist as a Young Man, A (1916). A largely autobiographical novel by James JOYCE. It portrays the childhood, school days, adolescence, and early manhood of Stephen DEDALUS, later one of the leading characters in ULYSSES. Stephen's growing self-awareness as an artist forces him to reject the whole narrow world in which he has been brought up, including family ties, nationalism, and the Catholic religion. The novel ends when, having decided to become a writer, he is about to leave Dublin for Paris. Rather than following a clear narrative progression, the book revolves around experiences that are crucial to Stephen's development as an artist; at the end of each chapter Stephen makes some assertion of identity. Through his use of the stream-of-consciousness technique, Joyce reveals the actual materials of his hero's world, the components of his thought processes. *Stephen Hero,* the first version of the book, was written in about 1904 and published posthumously. It is longer and more conventional in form.

Port-Royal. A French Cistercian convent near Versailles, which in the 17th century became the center of JANSENISM. Its teachings greatly influenced both religion and literature, and Jesuit rivals induced Pope Innocent X to condemn certain Jansenist doctrines. In 1660, Louis XIV suppressed the community. Springing again into prominence, Port-Royal was razed in 1710, and permanently condemned three years later in the papal bull *Unigenitus* of Clement XI.

Porus. The Indian king in Jean Racine's tragedy ALEXANDRE LE GRAND.

Posada, José Guadalupe (1852–1913). Mexican graphic artist, folk illustrator, and political cartoonist. A fierce supporter of the downtrodden, he depicted horrors and tragedies in bold black and white, and did a series of popular satirical woodcuts of skeletons acting out daily activities.

Poseidon. The chief sea god of the ancient Greeks. According to the usual story, he was the son of Cronos and brother of Zeus, Hades, and other gods. When dominion over the universe was divided among these three gods, Poseidon was given the sea. He was also a god of horses, and may even have had a horse shape originally, and of earthquakes. He was married to Amphitrite. Inclined to be ill-tempered, it was Poseidon whose anger at Odysseus for blinding his son Polyphemus so long prevented that hero's return to Ithaca, in the ODYSSEY. It was enmity against Priam's father LAOMEDON, who had refused to pay Poseidon and Apollo for building the walls of Troy, that made the god side with the Greeks in the TROJAN WAR. In a contest with Athene for the patronship of Athens, Poseidon lost when the goddess' gift of the olive tree was judged a more valuable boon than Poseidon's horse.

Positivism. A philosophical movement of the 19th century. It was developed under the influence of the new discoveries in the science of the period, particularly outstanding in the thought of Auguste COMTE, regarded as its founder. Its chief principles call for: a study of the various sciences and an arrangement of them in a "scale of subordination," with those of greater complexity placed near the top of an ascending series; the assignment of sociology, with its study of past history and contemporary society and its attempts to solve persistent social problems, to a position at the summit of hierarchy; and a belief in the progress of mankind toward a superior state of civilization by means of the science of sociology itself. In the later years of his career, Comte, turning toward mysticism, attempted to convert sociology into a literal Religion of Humanity, with a set creed, rituals, and ceremonies for private and public use, the worship of great men and women of the past, saints' days, etc. As a church, Positivism lasted in France down through the 20th century, although this development of his philosophy alienated a number of early admirers from the side of Comte. J. S. Mill and G. H. Lewes were among the leading disciples of early Positivism in England. George Eliot's poem *The Choir Invisible* expresses its aspiration. Herbert Croly, first editor of the *New Republic,* was the first American child to be christened in the faith.

Possessed, The, or The Devils or The Demons (Besy; 1871–1872). A novel by Feodor DOSTOEVSKI. It has two plot lines, one depicting the revolutionary movement in Russia and the other tracing the strange career of Nikolai STAVROGIN, the enigmatic central character of the novel. Stavrogin is a brilliant, attractive, but emotionally sterile young nobleman, afflicted with a genuine spiritual nihilism as contrasted to the affected nihilism of the revolutionaries portrayed in the book. Stavrogin indulges in crime and debauchery, infects SHATOV and KIRILOV with ideas in which he himself does not believe, and accepts the love of Lizaveta Nikolayevna TUSHINA without being able to return it. On a whim he marries the cripple Marya Timofeyevna LEBYADKIN. The leader of the small revolutionary group, Pyotr VERKHOVENSKI, whose character was modeled on that of Sergei NECHAYEV, tries to persuade Stavrogin to join the conspiracy, knowing what an attraction Stavrogin would be as a figurehead. Verkhovenski manages the murder of Shatov, who has belonged to the revolutionary group and is attempting to break with it. This incident was based on one of Nechayev's notorious exploits. See SHIGALYOV.

The ending of the novel is bloody, with Marya Timofeyevna Lebyadkin and her brother being murdered and their home burned, ostensibly by the terrorists, Lizaveta a victim of mob vengeance, and both Kirilov and Stavrogin committing suicide.

Dostoevski intended the novel to show how lack of organic ties with the Russian people and adherence to Western political ideas wreak havoc with the Russian upper classes, represented by Stavrogin and the hapless revolutionaries. This aim was in part realized, that is, with Stavrogin but not with the revolutionary group who are a caricature, not a portrayal, of the reality in Russia at the time. Dostoevski's own hope for the salvation of his country is expressed by Shatov. The aristocracy must return to the Orthodox faith, which the people have never abandoned, and must lead the people in attaining the high destiny assigned to Russia: saving the world by revealing to it the "new word" of universal love and brotherhood contained in Orthodoxy.

Although he satirized the nihilists, Dostoevski also feared their effect and took them seriously. The epigraph to the novel from which the title comes refers to the demons cast out by Christ into the Gadarene swine. The nihilists in this case are regarded as the swine into which the demons haunting Russian society are cast.

A revolutionary of an older generation, Stepan Trofimovich Verkhovenski, Pyotr's father, is dealt with in a more genial manner than the nihilists. Stepan, who lives on the charity of Stavrogin's mother, Varvara Petrovna, typifies the milder radical of the 1840's, the time in which Dostoevski himself was a young Utopian socialist. Stepan is made ridiculous by his perpetual assertions that he is about to be arrested as a dangerous radical, although it is certain that no one fears him. The implication is plain, however, that such harmless drawing-room socialists as Stepan have figuratively, if not literally, fathered the more dangerous generation of nihilists.

One other satirical portrait in the book, that of the writer KARMAZINOV, is an instance of Dostoevski paying off an old personal foe, the novelist Ivan TURGENEV, on whom the characterization was obviously based. Karmazinov is depicted as a slavish worshiper of Western culture, a foppish egoist and poseur. His ostentatious farewell to literature, "Merci," read at a local literary evening, is reminiscent of similar proclamations occasionally issued by Turgenev.

Post, Emily [Price] (1873–1960). American writer on etiquette. Born to wealth and social position, she is best known for *Etiquette* (1922), which established her as an arbiter of polite American manners.

Post, Melville Davisson (1871–1930). American detective-story writer. A lawyer by profession, he is best known for his literate detective stories about Uncle Abner, a shrewd Virginia squire who protects the innocent and rights the wrongs of his community. The best of them were published as *Uncle Abner, Master of Mysteries* (1918).

Posthumus Leonatus. In Shakespeare's CYMBELINE, a "poor but worthy gentleman" who is secretly married to Cymbeline's daughter Imogen. His name comes from the fact that he was born just after his mother died in childbirth.

postimpressionism. A term coined by Roger FRY to denote a movement in modern art. It does not refer to a school, but to artists who sought independent self-expression and a pictorial reality distinct from the impressionist concentration on light effects. Among the most important postimpressionist painters are Cézanne, Gauguin, van Gogh, and Matisse.

Postl, Karl. See Charles SEALSFIELD.

Postumus. The friend of the poet HORACE, to whom, in Ode 14 of Book 2, he addresses the famous words: *Eheu! fugaces, Postume, Postume, labuntur anni* ("Alas! Postumus, Postumus, the flying years glide by").

Potash and Perlmutter (1910). The first collection of tales by Montague GLASS. Dealing with two partners in the cloak-and-suit business, and written in vernacular, the tales were immensely popular and were followed by *Abe and Mawruss* (1911), *Potash and Perlmutter Settle Things* (1919), and other volumes. Several of them were successfully dramatized.

pot-boiler. A literary or critical term meaning an inferior piece of work (e.g., a story or a painting) done merely for the sake of money: in other words, to keep the pot boiling, that is, to eat.

Potemkin, Grigori Aleksandrovich (1739–1791). A Russian field marshal and favorite of Empress Catherine of Russia, influential in her councils.

Potiphar Papers (1853). A series of satires of New York society by George William Curtis (1824–1892). The *Papers* relate the adventures of the newly rich Mr. and Mrs. Potiphar. They were dramatized as *Our Best People* in 1854. The most popular character was Mrs. Potiphar's friend and adviser, the Reverend Cream Cheese. Curtis, a Rhode Island-born essayist and editor, also wrote *Prue and I* (1856), a collection of essays on the theme that wealth is not a requisite of happiness.

Potiphar's wife. In the Old Testament and the Koran, the wife of Joseph's master in Egypt. JOSEPH fled from her advances, leaving his robe behind him, whereupon she accused him of evil and had him cast into prison (Gen. 34). Some Arabian commentators have called her Rahil, others ZULEIKA. The theme of this story is familiar in the myth and folk-lore of many lands, notably in the myth of PHAEDRA.

Potocka. Countess **Anna.** Born **Anna Tyczkiewicz** (1776–1867). A Polish writer. Her *Memoirs* are valuable as historic source material. They cover the period from 1794 to 1820 and give an account of Napoleon's stay in Warsaw (1806–1807).

Pot of Earth, The (1925). A long poem by Archibald MacLeish. It is based on the description of an ancient fertility rite in Sir James Frazer's *The Golden Bough*. Several themes are woven into the story, including that of the sexual maturation, marriage, and death in childbirth of a contemporary girl.

Potter, Beatrix (1866–1943). English writer and illustrator of inimitable stories for children. Her subjects were the rabbits, ducks, squirrels, hedgehogs, and cats that she observed in and near her home in the Lake District. As a young woman, she was kept by her father as a virtual recluse. After her marriage to William Heelis, she lived at Sawrey. Her painted backgrounds are said to have had the emotional feeling of a Constable. Her books include *The Tale of Peter Rabbit* (privately printed in 1900, published in 1902); *The Tale of Benjamin Bunny* (1904); *The Tale of Tom Kitten* (1907); *The Roly-Poly Pudding* (1908); *Jemima Puddleduck* (1910). She is the subject of a biography, *The Tale of Beatrix Potter,* by Margaret Lane (1946).

Potter, Stephen (1900–1969). English humorist. He is the author of *Theory and Practice of* GAMESMANSHIP (1947), *Some Notes on Lifemanship* (1950), and ONE-UPMANSHIP.

Potterism (1920). A novel by Rose MACAULAY. The work satirizes vulgarity, commercialism, and cheap journalism; hence the word has become a synonym for humbug and hypocrisy.

Poulenc, Francis (1899–1963). A French composer, one of LES SIX, known especially for his songs, choral works, and operas. The songs include settings of texts by Apollinaire and Ronsard; operas are based on plays by Apollinaire (*Les Mamelles de Tirésias;* 1947), Cocteau (*La Voix Humaine;* 1959), and Bernanos (*Les dialogues des Carmélites;* 1957); choral works include a *Mass in G* (1937) for double chorus; *Stabat Mater* (1951) for soprano solo, chorus, and orchestra; and a striking *Gloria* (1959) for the same forces.

poulter's measure. In prosody, a meter consisting of alternate ALEXANDRINES and FOURTEENERS, that is 12-syllable and 14-syllable lines. The name was given to this meter by George Gascoigne in the 16th century because it was said that poulterers—then called poulters—used sometimes to give 12 to the dozen, sometimes 14. It was a common measure in Elizabethan times.

Pound, Ezra [Loomis] (1885–1972). American poet, editor, and critic. One of the most influential literary figures in modern literature, he was born in Hailey, Idaho, of New England stock. After graduate work at the University of Pennsylvania, Pound went to live in Europe: first in Italy, then in England and France, and finally in Italy again. His first book, a small collection of poems entitled *A Lume Spento* (1908), was published in Venice. In England he was the guiding spirit and chief promoter of IMAGISM, a poetic movement that stressed the direct treatment of the object without unnecessary rhetoric, the free phrase rather than the forced metric, and utter clarity of image and metaphor. During his years in England, Pound edited the first anthology of imagist poetry (1914), founded and edited the vorticist magazine, *Blast,* served as foreign editor of POETRY and as London editor (1917–1919) of the LITTLE REVIEW. The most influential man of letters of his generation, his importance in the development of modern poetry can scarcely be overstated. He sought publishers for the early works of T. S. Eliot, Wyndham Lewis, James Joyce, William Carlos Williams, and many others. His own poetry during this period was published in *Exultations* (1909), PERSONAE, *Provença* (1910), *Canzoni* (1911), *Riposte* (1912), and LUSTRA.

Abhorring war and increasingly dissatisfied with the world around him, Pound eventually left England altogether, settling first in France and then in Italy. In the meantime, he had become interested in Chinese poetry, publishing in *Cathay* (1915) his adaptations of Ernest Fenollosa's translations of the poems of Li Po. He also made a study of Japanese classical drama, publishing *Noh, Or Accomplishment* in 1916. In 1919 appeared *Homage to Sextus Propertius,* a broad adaptation of Propertius and a very influential work. HUGH SELWYN MAUBERLEY marked Pound's farewell to England and to a period in his own life, expressing his hatred of war, dissatisfaction with the commercialism he felt prevalent in the arts, and growing concern with economic questions. These concerns are also felt in the CANTOS, Pound's epic work which he began in 1917—publishing the first sections in *Cantos I–XVI* (1925)—and continued to write and publish thereafter throughout the years.

Pound's concern with economic problems grew stronger throughout the 1920's and 1930's. Stemming from social credit theories, his views eventually propelled him into an acceptance of Mussolini and fascism. During World War II he started to broadcast fascist propaganda to the U.S. from Rome, an act which led to his arrest in May, 1945, by American forces, his confinement at Pisa (see THE PISAN CANTOS), and his trial in the U.S. Judged insane, Pound was committed to St. Elizabeth's Hospital in Washington, D.C. He remained there from 1946 to 1958, when he was finally released; charges against him were dropped, and he was allowed to return to Italy.

Pound's essays and works of criticism are almost as important as his poetic output. A voluminous contributor to magazines, he has published numerous prose volumes since *The Spirit of Romance* (1910; rev. 1953). Although literary and cultural questions are raised throughout these publications, from the early 20's on he has spent a growing amount of energy on purely polemical works on economic questions. Pound's prose works include *Pavannes and Divisions* (1918), *Instigations* (1920), *Indiscretions* (1923), *Antheil and the Treatise on Harmony* (1924), *How to Read* (1931), *ABC of Reading* (1934), *Polite Essays* (1937), *Guide to Kulchur* (1938; rev. 1951), and *The Literary Essays of Ezra Pound*, with an introduction by T. S. Eliot (1954).

Although Pound's erudition has often been attacked—from the layman's viewpoint that it is obscure and from the scholar's that it is not without occasional flaws—there is no question but that he has been instrumental in promoting a renewed general interest in the poetry of those periods with which he has been especially concerned, including those of medieval Provence and Anglo-Saxon England.

As has already been noted, Pound's importance is in his total effect as literary critic, essayist, promoter, editor, and adviser, as well as creator, practicing craftsman, and originator.

Poussin, Nicolas (1594–1665). French painter. The great master of the classical school, he worked chiefly at the studio he established in Rome. In his rational, clearly composed paintings of mythological, historical, and religious scenes, he imitated the measured gestures of antique sculpture and the clean draftsmanship and effortless order of Raphael. His work, which exerted an enormous influence on the course of art, embodies the ideal of the classical school, but his principles were later turned into sterile academism by his imitators.

Powell, Anthony [Dymoke] (1905–   ). English novelist. His books are comedies of manners and mild social satires directed against the chic world of fashion, the arts, and the upper, moneyed classes. His chief work is a long sequence of novels, a history of our own times, called A DANCE TO THE MUSIC OF TIME. Other novels by Anthony Powell are *Venusberg* (1932), a satire on totalitarian government; *Afternoon Men* (1931), *Agents and Patients* (1936); and *What's Become of Waring?* (1939).

Powell, Dawn (1897–1965). American novelist. Some of her witty novels are laid in small towns in the West; others deftly satirize the literary and entertainment world of Manhattan. They include *Whither* (1925), *The Bride's House* (1929), *The Tenth Moon* (1932), *The Locusts Have No King* (1948), *Cage for Lovers* (1957), and *Golden Spur* (1962).

Power and the Glory, The (1940). A novel by Graham GREENE, first published in the U.S. as *The Labyrinthine Ways*. Its hero, a drunken, lecherous priest in Mexico, withstands political persecution and dies a Christlike death.

Power of Darkness, The (Vlast' t'my; 1886). A tragedy by Count Leo TOLSTOI. The play's epigraph "when one claw is caught, the whole bird is doomed," refers to Nikita, a young peasant, who perpetrates a series of crimes. He seduces a young girl, Marina; poisons Peter, a wealthy peasant, and marries Peter's wife Anisya. He then seduces Anisya's stepdaughter, Akulina, and, when Akulina gives birth to his child, he kills the baby and buries it in the cellar. His conscience finally impels him to make a public confession of his crimes.

One of the outstanding peasant dramas in Russian literature, the play demonstrates that, despite Tolstoi's love for the peasants, he was not blind to their faults. The only character free from the crime and vice so vividly presented is Akim, Nikita's father; he is described as "God-fearing."

Power of Sympathy, The (1789). A novel generally regarded as the first to be written in the U.S. Long attributed to Sarah Wentworth MORTON because a subplot resembles an incident in her sister's life, it was probably written by William Hill BROWN. In a series of letters it tells how Harrington, the hero, is prevented from marrying the charming but socially inferior Harriot Fawcett by the discovery that she is his half sister. The shock of the discovery kills Harriot and Harrington commits suicide. Brown's purpose was to illustrate "the dangerous Consequences of Seduction" and "the Advantages of Female Education."

Powys, J[ohn] C[owper] (1872–1963). English novelist, essayist, and poet. He was the elder brother of Theodore Francis Powys and Llewelyn Powys, both writers; all three brothers felt a mystical love for nature. John Cowper was a friend and disciple of Thomas Hardy; in the novel WOLF SOLVENT the romantic hero retreats from the city to find happiness in the Dorset countryside. He was the author of more than 40 volumes, including *The Religion of a Sceptic* (1925); *A Glastonbury Romance* (1932); *Autobiography* (1934); *Enjoyment of Literature* (1938); *Owen Glendower* (1940), a historical romance; *The Inmates* (1952), a love story set in an insane asylum; and *All or Nothing* (1960).

Powys, Llewelyn (1884–1939). English essayist. He wrote sketches based on his experiences in East Africa (*Ebony and Ivory*, 1923), in Swiss tuberculosis sanatoria (*Skin for Skin*, 1925), and in Israel, the U.S., and Dorset. *Earth Memories* (1934) and *Dorset Essays* (1935) are among his best collections. See John Cowper POWYS.

Powys, T[heodore] F[rancis] (1875–1953). English novelist and short-story writer, the most original and best remembered of the three Powys brothers (see John Cowper Powys). Powys, who spent his whole life in the same Dorset village, wrote of village life with realism, grim humor, and a sense of life's tragedy, oddness, and mystery. Among his novels are *The Left Leg* (1923), *Mr. Tasker's Gods* (1925), MR. WESTON's GOOD WINE, *Unclay* (1931), and *The Two Thieves* (1932). *God's Eyes A-Twinkle* (1947) is a collection of short stories.

Ppt. In Jonathan Swift's JOURNAL TO STELLA, a cryptic abbreviation and pet name for Stella. It recurs throughout James Joyce's *Finnegans Wake*, where H. C. Earwicker uses it as a pet name for his daughter Isobel. See PRESTO.

Prado. The national museum of painting and sculpture in Madrid, Spain. It is next to the famous fashionable promenade of the same name. The word means "meadow."

Pradon, Nicolas (1632–1698). French playwright. His *Phèdre et Hippolyte* (*Phaedra and Hippolytus*, 1677), written and produced as part of an intrigue against the *Phèdre of* RACINE, influenced the latter to abandon the theater.

Praed, Winthrop Mackworth (1802–1839). English poet and parliamentarian. As the schoolboy editor of the *Etonian* (1820), in which some of his best poems appeared, Praed early achieved a minor literary reputation. He was elected to Commons in 1830, enlarging on his Cambridge reputation for brilliant oratory. Much of his verse is political; it is witty, but too topical to retain much interest. His best work is his graceful, amusing *vers de société,* published in numerous periodicals and collected in his *Poems* (1864).

praetor. In ancient Rome, one of 8 magistrates whose duty was to administer justice. They correspond roughly to modern Supreme Court justices. After his year in office, the praetor often went as propraetor to govern a province. See CURSUS HONORUM.

Praetorian Guard. In Roman history, the imperial bodyguard. It was organized by Augustus on the basis of the older praetorian cohorts, the bodyguards of the praetors. The Praetorian Guard grew more and more powerful, and many emperors were hardly more than its puppets. It survived to the time of Constantine the Great.

Praga, Emilio (1839–1875). Italian poet, painter, and short-story writer. A member of the SCAPIGLIATURA circle of young writers, Praga recounted personal experiences and depicted scenes with the eye of an impressionist painter in both his prose and verse. His poetry was published in collections whose titles indicate its coloristic quality: *Easel* (*Tavalozza;* 1862), *Pale Shades* (*Penombre;* 1864), *Transparencies* (*Trasparenze;* 1875), and *Fiabe e Leggende* (1867). His most successful prose work, *Le Memorie del Presbitero, Scene di Provincia* (1877), narrates the author's eventful stay in a priest's home in a remote Alpine village. The diary-novel was left unfinished at the time of Praga's death.

pragmatism (from *Gr.* pragma, "deed"). The philosophical doctrine that the only test of the truth of human cognitions or philosophical principles is their practical results. It does not admit "absolute" truth, as all truths change their trueness as their practical utility increases or decreases. The word was introduced in this connection about 1875 by the American logician C. S. PEIRCE, and was popularized by William JAMES, whose *Pragmatism: A New Name for Some Old Ways of Thinking,* lectures delivered at the Lowell Institute and Columbia University (1906–1907), was published in 1907.

Prairie, The (1827). A novel by James Fenimore COOPER, in the LEATHERSTOCKING TALES series. The story centers around the death of the aged Natty BUMPPO. Cooper contrasts the noble, disinterested Natty with the squatter Ishmael Bush and his family. Lawless and self-seeking, the squatters portend ill for the future of democracy. Cooper's prairie descriptions, which include an effective buffalo stampede and prairie fire, are derived from the *Journals* of Lewis and Clark.

Prasildo. A Babylonian knight in the ORLANDO INNAMORATO of Matteo Maria Boiardo. He fights beside his friend Iroldo at the siege of ALBRACCA. Earlier, he has fallen in love with Tisbina, Iroldo's wife. To divert him from suicide, she promises her love if he can fulfill certain impossible tasks. When he actually accomplishes them, Tisbina and Iroldo decide to take poison as the only honorable solution. Prasildo resolves to do the same, but the poison turns out to be harmless. Now Iroldo nobly decides to give up Tisbina and leave. Later, Prasildo flies to rescue his friend and risks his own life to save him.

Prater. A famous Viennese park. It is located on an island formed by the Danube and the Danube Canal. It was opened to the public in 1766 by Emperor Joseph II. The name (like Prado, derived from Lat. *pradum,* meadow) is often used for the amusement park, which is actually but a small part of the Prater.

Pratolini, Vasco (1913–   ). Italian novelist. His novels, which reflect the socialist ideology of his political convictions, characteristically describe the working-class quarters of his native Florence. Among his best-known works are *The Naked Streets* (*Il Quartiere;* 1945), *Cronaca Familiare* (1947), *A Tale of Poor Lovers* (*Cronache di Poveri Amanti;* 1947), *A Hero of Our Time* (*Un Eroe del Nostro Tempo;* 1949), and *Le Ragazze di San Frediano* (1961). He also wrote a trilogy called *Una Storia Italiana,* composed of the novels *Metello* (1955), *Lo Scialo* (*The Shawl,* 1960), and *La Costanza della Ragione* (1963).

Pratt, E[dwin] J[ohn] (1883–1964). Canadian poet. A native of Newfoundland, Pratt is best known for his heroic narratives. The most famous of these, *Brébeuf and His Brethren* (1940), deals with the Jesuit martyrs of North America. His other epics include *The Witches' Brew* (1925), *The Roosevelt and the Antinoë* (1930), and *Towards the Last Spike* (1952). They are concerned, respectively, with alcoholic prohibition, a rescue at sea, and the construction of Canada's first transcontinental railway.

prayer wheel. A device used by the Tibetan Buddhists as an aid to or substitute for prayer. The use of the prayer wheel is said to be founded on a misinterpretation of the Buddha's instructions to his followers that they should "turn the wheel of the law"—that is, preach Buddhism incessantly. A prayer wheel consists of a pasteboard cylinder inscribed with or containing the mystic formula *om mani padme* *hum* and other prayers. Each revolution represents one repetition of the prayers.

Preacher, the. The author of the Old Testament book ECCLESIASTES, once reputed to be Solomon.

Précieuses Ridicules, Les (The Ridiculous Snobs, 1659**).** A 1-act prose comedy by MOLIÈRE. The first of Molière's satires on a foible of contemporary society, it narrates how Madelon and Cathos, daughters of a provincial bourgeois and ardent admirers of the affectations of Parisian society, reject their suitors as insufficiently ornate in speech and dress; they will have no proposals without the garnish and flamboyance described in the novels of Madeleine de SCUDÉRY. The suitors avenge themselves by sending their valets to call on the ladies disguised as a marquis and a viscomte. The ladies are ravished by the extravagant behavior of their visitors, whom they take for men of the highest fashion, but when the trickery is revealed they are suitably mortified.

Precious Bane (1925). A novel by Mary WEBB. Set in the English county of Shropshire, it is a story of harsh farming life, and fierce, morose country people. Prudence Sarn, the narrator, finds a husband who appreciates her in spite of her hare lip. The novel became extremely popular when Stanley Baldwin, then prime minister, wrote an introduction to it in 1928. See also COLD COMFORT FARM. The title is from Milton's *Paradise Lost:*

> Let none admire
> That riches grow in Hell; that soil may best
> Deserve the precious bane.

Prelude, The (1850). A long autobiographical poem by William WORDSWORTH. It shows the growth of a poet's mind by tracing his own life from childhood on. Completed in 1805, it underwent many revisions before it was published. Wordsworth originally dedicated the poem to his friend Samuel Taylor Coleridge.

Pre-Raphaelite Brotherhood. A group of artists and poets formed in London in 1848 originally consisting of Holman HUNT, John Everett MILLAIS, and Dante Gabriel ROSSETTI. The discovery, in reproductions, of early Italian painting led them to adopt the title of Pre-Raphaelites and thus to stress their rejection of academism, which they traced to Raphael and the High Renaissance. The Brotherhood's publication, *The Germ,* was started in 1850 under the editorship of William Michael Rossetti, but only four numbers were published. Its object was "to enforce and encourage an entire adherence to the simplicity of nature," a principle applied to the writing of poetry as well as painting.

The artists in the brotherhood painted scenes of the childhood of Christ and the Virgin and represented contemporary scenes with a moral message; as a whole, the group had a strongly religious and moralizing cast. Accepted when they first exhibited in 1849, they were bitterly attacked the following year, notably by Charles Dickens, and thereafter became the target of raging criticism. They gained the powerful support of John Ruskin, who seriously advocated their principles. The group broke up in 1854, but enjoyed a brief revival through the young William Morris and Edward Burne-Jones in 1856 at Oxford. See FLESHLY SCHOOL OF POETRY.

Presbyterian. Pertaining to one of the Churches of Calvinistic origin. In it, as in the early Christian Church, the presbyters or elders are the medium through which the members govern the church.

Prescott, William Hickling (1796–1859). American historian. Prescott lost the use of his left eye in his junior year at Harvard when it was struck with a hard crust of bread thrown by a playful classmate. Shortly after his graduation, his right eye was seriously impaired. Wealthy enough to pay assistants and aided by a device called a noctograph, he was able to devote his life to historical research and composition. Prescott's high standards of scholarship and his ability to write dramatic, exciting narrative are most evident in the *History of the Conquest of Mexico* (1843) and *History of the Conquest of Peru* (1847), the works for which he is best known. He also wrote *History of the Reign of Ferdinand and Isabella* (1838) and *History of the Reign of Philip the Second* (1855–1858).

President of the U.S. The chief executive of the U.S. According to the Constitution, he must be a native-born American and must be at least 35 years of age. The original document did not impose restrictions on the number of four-year terms a president might serve, but no president had served more than two until Franklin Delano Roosevelt violated the tradition in 1940 by running for and winning a third term; as a result of the ratification (1947) of the 22nd amendment, the president is now limited to two terms. A list of the presidents follows:

George Washington	1789–1797
John Adams	1797–1801
Thomas Jefferson	1801–1809
James Madison	1809–1817
James Monroe	1817–1825
John Quincy Adams	1825–1829
Andrew Jackson	1829–1837
Martin Van Buren	1837–1841
William Henry Harrison	1841
John Tyler	1841–1845
James K. Polk	1845–1849
Zachary Taylor	1849–1850
Millard Fillmore	1850–1853
Franklin Pierce	1853–1857
James Buchanan	1857–1861
Abraham Lincoln	1861–1865
Andrew Johnson	1865–1869
Ulysses S. Grant	1869–1877
Rutherford B. Hayes	1877–1881
James A. Garfield	1881
Chester A. Arthur	1881–1885
Grover Cleveland	1885–1889
Benjamin Harrison	1889–1893
Grover Cleveland	1893–1897
William McKinley	1897–1901
Theodore Roosevelt	1901–1909
William Howard Taft	1909–1913
Woodrow Wilson	1913–1921
Warren G. Harding	1921–1923
Calvin Coolidge	1923–1929
Herbert C. Hoover	1929–1933
Franklin D. Roosevelt	1933–1945
Harry S. Truman	1945–1953
Dwight D. Eisenhower	1953–1961
John F. Kennedy	1961–1963
Lyndon B. Johnson	1963–1969
Richard M. Nixon	1969–

Prester John (John the Presbyter). A legendary Christian king and priest, supposed in medieval times to have reigned in the 12th century over a wonderful country somewhere in the heart of Asia. He appears in Ariosto's *Orlando Furioso* (1516), having furnished materials for a host of medieval legends including that of the Holy Grail.

According to Sir John Mandeville, he was a lineal descendant of Ogier the Dane, who penetrated into the north of India with 15 of his barons, among whom he divided the land. John was made sovereign of Teneduc and was called Prester because he converted the natives. Another tradition says he had 70 kings for his vassals, and was seen by his subjects only three times a year. So firm was the belief in his existence that Pope Alexander III (d. 1181), sent him letters by a special messenger. The messenger never returned. It is possible that the legend of Prester John rose from travelers' reports of colonies of NESTORIAN Christians encountered in Asia.

Presto. The name frequently applied by Jonathan Swift to himself in his JOURNAL TO STELLA.

Preston, Thomas (1537–1598). English dramatist and author of the florid tragicomedy *Cambises, King of Persia* (pub. 1569).

pretender. *The Old Pretender.* James Francis Edward Stuart (1688–1766), only son of JAMES II. He played one of the principal roles in the JACOBITE cause. He appears as a character in Thackeray's *Henry Esmond.* See FIFTEEN, THE; WARMING PANS.

The Young Pretender. Charles Edward Louis Philip Casimir Stuart (1720–1788), son of "the Old Pretender" and grandson of James II, sometimes called "the Chevalier" or "Bonnie Prince Charlie." As a result of his unsuccessful attempt to seize the Hanoverian throne (see the FORTY-FIVE), the hereditary jurisdiction of the Highland chiefs was taken away. He appears as a character in Scott's *Waverly,* and again in *Red Gauntlet,* disguised as Father Buonaventura.

Prévert, Jacques (1900–   ). French poet and screenwriter. Sometimes the lyricism of Prévert is turned to a mockingly satiric purpose; sometimes it is tender, wistful, evocative of gentle melancholy. In the poems of *Paroles* (1946) and *Spectacle* (1951) he ridicules the conformity and conventions of his world, while he praises the simple joys of love, of color and smell and sound. Prévert wrote scenarios for the films of Marcel CARNÉ, among them *Les Enfants du Paradis* and *Les Portes de la Nuit.*

Prévost d'Exiles, Antoine François, known as **Abbé Prévost** (1697–1763). French novelist and journalist. Prévost vacillated in his youth between a career in the army and one in the church, but, after entering the Benedictine order, his taste for a worldly life won. He feared ecclesiastical reprisals and fled to Holland (1729) and to England (1733), but returned to France in 1734. In order to earn money he wrote the seven-volume work *Mémoires et aventures d'un homme de qualité* (1728), the last volume of which contains his most famous story *L'Histoire du Chevalier des Grieux et de* MANON LESCAUT (1731). From 1733 to 1740, he published a periodical journal *Le Pour et le contre.* His other works include the romantic novels *Histoire de M. Cleveland* (1732–39) and *Le Doyen de Killerine* (1735). Through his translations of several of Richardson's novels, Prévost helped to introduce English literature into France.

Priam (Priamos). In Greek legend, king of Troy when that city was sacked by the Greeks, husband of Hecuba, and father of fifty children. Among the children were HECTOR, Helenus, PARIS, DEIPHOBUS, POLYXENA, TROILUS, CASSANDRA, and POLYDORUS. When Hector was slain, the old king went to the tent of Achilles and made a successful plea for the body of his dead son. After the gates of Troy were thrown open by the Greeks concealed in the wooden horse, Pyrrhus, the son of Achilles, slew the aged Priam. See TROJAN WAR.

Priamond. See FAERIE QUEENE, THE.

Priapus (Priapos). In Greek mythology, the ithyphallic god of reproductive power and fertility (hence of gardens) and protector of shepherds, fishermen, and farmers. In later times he was regarded as the chief deity of lasciviousness and obscenity.

Price, Fanny. See MANSFIELD PARK.

Prichard, Katherine [Susannah] (1884–   ). Australian novelist. Although born in Fiji, she was brought to Tasmania at the age of 3, and in time became the most distinctively Australian of writers. She taught in outback schools of Victoria and New South Wales, and spent six years in London, where the condition of the working class deeply stirred her sympathies. Because of these observations she became an apostle of what one critic called "extreme democracy." Her book *Wild Oats of Han* (1928) is largely autobiographical. During a literary period of 36 years, she published nine novels, two volumes of short stories and several plays. Her books include *The Pioneers* (1915), which won the 1,000-pound prize in an all-British novel competition; *Black Opal* (1921), a study of social relationships of the opal-mining community; *Working Bullocks* (1926), considered her best novel; *Coomaardo* (1929), a story of the relations between whites and the unspoilt blacks at an isolated northwest station; *Haxby's Circus* (1930); and *Intimate Strangers* (1937).

Prick of Conscience, The (early 14th century). A Middle English religious poem, of 9624 lines in rhymed couplets. Long attributed to Richard ROLLE OF HAMPOLE, it was the most popular poem in 14th-century England, describing the wretched nature of man and his inevitable sentence to the tortures of Hell or the joys of Heaven.

Pride, Thomas. See PRIDE'S PURGE.

Pride and Prejudice (1813). A novel by Jane AUSTEN. The story concerns the middle-class household of the Bennets. The empty-headed and garrulous Mrs. Bennet has but one aim in life: to find a good match for each of her five daughters. Mr. Bennet, a mild and indolent man given to witty cynicisms, refuses to take this vulgar project seriously; he ridicules his wife instead of giving her support in her schemes. One of the daughters, Elizabeth, becomes prejudiced against her future suitor, Darcy, because of his arrogance and his uncalled-for interference with his friend Bingley's courtship of her sister Jane. In interfering with Jane and Bingley, Darcy is influenced by Mrs. Bennet's undisguised husband-hunt and her impropriety in general; he mistakenly believes that Jane is only seeking an advantageous match and that her feelings are not sincere. In spite of his disapproval of the Bennet family, Darcy cannot keep himself from falling in love with Elizabeth and he proposes to her. The tone of the proposal (it is evident that his love for Elizabeth is a blow to his pride) and her own prejudice cause Elizabeth coldly to reject him. His subsequent support of a renewal of Bingley's suit with Jane and his sensitive assistance throughout the foolish elopement of young Lydia Bennet with an officer, Wickham, show Darcy's ability to recognize and correct his own false pride, and Elizabeth's prejudice dissolves. The two are reconciled and the book ends with their marriage and the marriage of Bingley and Jane. The novel contains two of Jane Austen's best-known minor characters, Mr. COLLINS and Lady Catherine de BOURGH.

Pride's Purge (1648). The forcible expulsion from the LONG PARLIAMENT of over 100 members who were inclined to compromise with the Royalist party. Acting under orders from the Parliamentary army, two regiments of soldiers led by Thomas Pride (d. 1658) entered the House of Commons and ousted the offending members. The remainder, about 60 in number, became known as the RUMP PARLIAMENT.

Priest, Judge. A well-known character appearing in a number of stories by Irvin S. COBB. A wise Kentucky judge, Priest acts as a local Solomon in getting people out of trouble and solving their problems with deep insight into human nature. *Old Judge Priest* (1915), the first of these books, was followed by *Down Yonder with Judge Priest and Irvin S. Cobb* (1932). *J. Poindexter, Colored* (1922) is a novel about the judge's servant Jeff. *Judge Priest Turns Detective* was published in 1937.

Priestley, J[ohn] B[oynton] (1894–   ). English novelist, playwright, and essayist. Priestley is best known as the author of the novel THE GOOD COMPANIONS. He is a fervent believer in the goodness of life, people, England, and humor, and many of his most successful works are happy comedies, full of Dickensian characters. Among his novels are *Benighted* (1927, U.S. title *The Old Dark House*), *Farthing Hall* (1929, with Hugh Walpole), ANGEL PAVEMENT, *Faraway* (1932), *Wonder Hero* (1933), *The Doomsday Men* (1938), *Let the People Sing* (1940), *Bright Day* (1946), and *Festival at Farbridge* (1951, U.S. title *Festival*).

Priestley's plays fall into two groups. Some are middle-class domestic comedies with some mild social commentary: DANGEROUS CORNER, *Laburnum Grove* (1933), *Eden End* (1933), and *An Inspector Calls* (1946). Others, influenced by the time theories of John William DUNNE, are experimental dramas concerned with problems of time: *I Have Been Here Before* (1937), TIME AND THE CONWAYS, and JOHNSON OVER JORDAN. *They Came to a City* (1943) is a fable about a utopia and the reactions of various persons to it.

Other works by Priestley are books of criticism, including *The English Comic Characters* (1925) and *Literature and Western Man* (1960). His social and political books include *English Journey* (1934), an account of some mining and industrial areas during the depression, and *The Arts Under Socialism* (1947). Among his volumes of autobiography and essays are *Midnight on the Desert* (1937), an evocation of a winter in Arizona; and *Journey Down a Rainbow* (1955), reports on life in Texas, with contrasting depictions of New Mexico Indian culture by his third wife, Jacquetta HAWKES.

Priestley, Joseph (1733–1804). English clergyman, chemist, and philosopher who pursued fruitful investigations into the nature of electrical discharges and discovered what is now called oxygen (1774). His theory of government, as set forth in his *Essay on the First Principles of Government* (1768), stipulates that the happiness of the majority is the great standard of all good government. He also published several works on religion, notably *History of the Corruption of Christianity* (1782) which was burned (1785) by order of the authorities. He spent the last decade of his life in the U.S. after his home in Birmingham, England, had been burned by a mob infuriated because of his sympathies with the French Revolution.

Primaleón. See PALMERÍN.

Primas. See GOLIARDIC VERSE.

Primaticcio, Francesco (1504–1570). Italian painter from Bologna. A follower of the mannerists PONTORMO and Rosso, he took his skill in large-scale decoration to France, where he founded the so-called School of Fontainebleau with Rosso and Nicolò del'Abbate (1509–1571). This importation of Italian Renaissance style influenced French artists who studied the decoration, in fresco and stucco, of the great Fontainebleau château.

primitivism. Term applied to a persistent tendency in European literature, art, and thought since the 18th century, stimulated by the acquisition of foreign colonies of low cultural development and by new discoveries in scholarship and the social sciences, to attribute superior virtue to primitive, non-European civilizations. J. J. ROUSSEAU was the first notable primitivist, with his doctrine of the natural man, and the widespread 18th-century veneration of the NOBLE SAVAGE had an important influence on the romantic movement. See ROMANTICISM. The American Indian was a favorite early exemplar of the Noble Savage. Later, primitivism expanded to include among the objects of its enthusiasm the violent, the crude, undeveloped, ignorant, naïve, nonintellectual or subintelligent of any kind, such as peasants, children, and idiots.

The following are literary figures of the 18th, 19th, and 20th centuries whose work embodies primitivism in one or another of its aspects: Macpherson (pseudo-Ossianic poems); Blake (innocence, childhood); Wordsworth (peasants, children, idiot boys); Chateaubriand and James Fenimore Cooper (the American Indian); Richard Wagner (pre-Christian religion and myth); Feodor Dostoevski (children, idiots); Tolstoi (peasants); Rimbaud (sadism, violence, the occult); Huysmans and the Decadents (sadism, violence, the cult of sensation); Pierre Loti (South Sea Islands); D. H. Lawrence (the mystical role of sex, the cult of sensation, primitive religion and ritual); Sherwood Anderson and Carl Van Vechten (the American Negro); and Ernest Hemingway (violence, cult of sensation). Primitivists in painting include Millet and van Gogh (peasants), and Henri Rousseau, a naïve, self-taught painter, was a favorite among primitivist art groups in the early part of the 20th century.

Primrose, Dr. Charles. The hero of Oliver Goldsmith's novel THE VICAR OF WAKEFIELD. He is a guileless, charitable, and unworldly clergyman.

Mrs. Deborah Primrose. The vicar's wife, full of motherly vanity, desirous to appear genteel, and ambitious for her two daughters.

George Primrose. The Oxford-bred son of the vicar. He becomes Captain Primrose and marries Arabella WILMOT, an heiress.

Olivia Primrose. The eldest daughter of the vicar. Pretty, enthusiastic, eager for adventure, she elopes with the unprincipled Squire THORNHILL who then abandons her after what seems to be a false marriage.

Sophia Primrose. The second daughter of Dr. Primrose. She is twice rescued by Sir William THORNHILL: once, when she is thrown from her horse into a deep stream; and, once, when she is abducted by his nephew's design.

primum mobile (*Lat.,* the first moving thing). In the Ptolemaic system of astronomy, the ninth (later the tenth) sphere. It was supposed to revolve around the earth from east to west in 24 hours, carrying with it all the other SPHERES.

Prince, F[rank] T[empleton] (1912–   ). English poet and literary scholar. His best-known collection of poems is *Soldiers Bathing* (1954).

Prince, The (Il Principe). A controversial political treatise by Niccolò MACHIAVELLI. Written during an enforced exile and dedicated to the Medici, it was completed by 1517 in 26 chapters. The opening chapters discuss the various types of principalities and in particular the difficulties of maintaining power in a newly acquired state. Examples of how rulers of the past and present handled new conquests suggest that one must often be ruthlessly despotic as well as cunningly magnanimous to keep corrupt human nature in obedience. Caesar Borgia is offered as a model prince; through the exercise of *virtù* (personal dynamism) and the adoption of force and fraud, he was able to maintain territories originally obtained through the influence of his father, Pope Alexander VI. His eventual failure is attributed to malign fortune, which influences the affairs of men even though it would be better to act on the assumption that it does not.

The importance of the soldiery and the use of citizen soldiers instead of militia and auxiliaries are defended in the middle chapters. Then the author takes up the character of the ruler, asserting that, although it is desirable to have a reputation for virtue, it is foolish to act in such a way that public applause comes before retention of power. Cruelty is sometimes mercy in disguise; it is much safer to be feared than loved. It is laudable to keep faith, but if necessary one must combine the cunning of the fox and the violence of the lion. A prudent prince avoids flatterers and sycophants.

In his final chapter, Machiavelli exhorts the princes of Italy to unite and expel the barbarians who are occupying its land.

Prince and the Pauper, The (1881). A novel by Mark TWAIN. Edward VI of England and a little pauper change places a few days before Henry VIII's death. The prince wanders in rags, while Tom Canty suffers the horrors of princedom. At the last moment, the mistake is rectified. The book, dedicated to Twain's two daughters, is a favorite among children.

Prince of Parthia, The (pub. 1765). A tragedy in blank verse by Thomas GODFREY. The first play written by an American, it was produced at the Southwark Theatre in Philadelphia on April 24, 1767. The plot deals with a villainous Parthian prince who murders his father and deprives his elder brother of the throne.

princeps (Lat., "first citizen"). The title assumed by Augustus Caesar upon establishing his new government in Rome in 27 B.C. Instead of adopting a more pretentious title, he chose princeps which was in good republican tradition, thus concealing his absolute authority behind a façade of republicanism. The term *principate,* derived from this, is applied to the form of government prevailing between 27 B.C. and A.D. 284.

Prince's Progress, The (1866). An allegorical poem by Christina ROSSETTI about a procrastinating Prince Charming who reaches his princess-bride to find she has died of despair while waiting for him.

Princess, The (1847). A long narrative poem by Alfred TENNYSON, especially noted for the songs introduced. Its general subject is the new woman, and its heroine, Ida, becomes the founder of a university to which only women are admitted. The Gilbert and Sullivan comic opera, *Princess Ida* (1884), is a "respectful operatic perversion" of *The Princess.*

Princess Casamassima, The (1886). A novel by Henry JAMES. The Princess Casamassima is the former Christina Light, who appears in RODERICK HUDSON; now, unhappily married, she decides to make a first-hand study of poverty and radicalism in London. The hero of the book is Hyacinth Robinson, the illegitimate son of an English nobleman and a Frenchwoman; though brought up in the London slums and a member of a radical underground movement, he makes his way into upper-class society, meets the princess, and is selected by the revolutionaries to commit an assassination.

Princesse de Clèves, La (1678). A novel by the comtesse de LA FAYETTE. It deals with the struggle of the princess of Clèves to remain loyal to her husband though drawn to the duc de Nemours. She eventually confesses her feelings to the prince, who dies in bitterness and despair. Focusing upon the characters' states of mind, the book is a precursor of the psychological novel and, as such, is of considerable importance in French literary history.

Princip, Gavrilo (1893?–1918). A Serbian student. He assassinated the Austrian Archduke Francis Ferdinand at Sarajevo (June 28, 1914), precipitating the first World War.

principate. See PRINCEPS.

Principia (1687). A work by Sir Isaac NEWTON. Its full title is *Philosophiae Naturalis Principia Mathematica* (*Lat.,* "the mathematical principles of natural philosophy"). The book is divided into three parts: "The Motion of Bodies," "The Motion of Bodies in Resisting Media," and "The System of the World." Because of its presentation of the law of gravitation and of Newton's rules for reasoning from physical events, its appearance signified the beginning of a new era in scientific investigation.

printer's devil. A printer's boy. Formerly a boy was employed to remove each newly printed sheet from a cylinder of the press. A 17th-century writer explained, "They do commonly so black and bedaub themselves that the workmen do jocosely call them devils." The black slave employed by Aldo Manuzio, a Venetian printer, was thought to be an imp, and Manuzio found it necessary in 1490 to issue a proclamation which read:

I, Aldo Manuzio, printer to the Doge, have this day made public exposure of the printer's devil. All who think he is not flesh and blood may come and pinch him.

Prinz Friedrich von Homburg (1821). A play by Heinrich von KLEIST. Prince Friedrich, cavalry general under the elector of Brandenburg in a war against the Swedes, dreams on the night before a crucial battle that he will be crowned with glory and will win the hand of the elector's niece Natalie. In the battle itself, however, he is confused and excited by the apparent nearness of his greatest desires; he attacks before the order is given, and though his charge carries the day, he is condemned to death for insubordination. He breaks down and begs for pardon, but when the decision about his fate is put in his own hands, he realizes the justice of the sentence and resigns himself to death. It is then that he is pardoned and, in a nearly exact repetition of the first dream scene, his dreams come true.

Prior, Matthew (1664–1721). English poet and diplomat, known chiefly for his epigrams, satires, and "society" verse. While still at Cambridge, Prior wrote with his friend Charles Montagu a clever attack on John Dryden, *The Hind and the Panther Transversed, or The Story of the Country-Mouse and the City-Mouse* (1687). His major works include *Alma: Or, the Progress of the Soul,* a long philosophical poem on worldly vanity in the form of a dialogue between Prior and his friend Richard Shelton; *Henry and Emma,* a paraphrase of the sixteenth-century NUT-BROWN MAID; SOLOMON ON THE VANITY OF THE WORLD; *Down-Hall* (1723), a ballad concerning a journey through Essex; *Carmen Saeculare* (1700), an "occasional" piece on William III; *The Secretary* (1696), a long poem recalling his experiences in diplomacy; and several prose works. Prior took part in several important European treaty negotiations of his time, including the Treaty of Ryswick (1697) and the Peace of Utrecht (1713), known as "Matt's peace."

Prioress's Tale, The. One of the CANTERBURY TALES of Geoffrey CHAUCER, a legendary miracle of the Virgin told in RHYME ROYAL. After an invocation to the Virgin Mary, the Prioress piously tells the story of a seven-year-old schoolboy who learns a hymn in honor of Mary and sings it on his way through the Jewish ghetto to school. Satan inspires the Jews to cut his throat and cast him in a pit; but Christ and Mary take pity on his anxious mother, and the child miraculously begins to sing again, so that his body is found and the murderers are hanged. The boy explains that Mary has laid a grain upon his tongue and commanded him to sing until it is removed, when she will take him to her. The abbot removes the grain, and the martyr gives up the ghost and is buried. The Prioress concludes with an allusion to the slaying of HUGH OF LINCOLN.

Priscian (fl. A.D. 500). A Latin grammarian at Constantinople. He is the author of *Institutiones Grammaticae,* which was so highly regarded as authoritative in the Middle Ages that the Latin phrase *diminuere Prisciani caput* ("to break Priscian's head") came into use when speaking of a violation of the rules of grammar.

Prisoner of Chillon, The (1816). A poem by Lord BYRON. It is freely based on the imprisonment of François de BONNIVARD, a 16th-century Genevan prelate and politician, in the dungeon of Chillon on the edge of Lake Leman. In the poem, he and his two brothers, victims of religious persecution, are chained in a lightless cell. The brothers die, are buried in the floor of the cell; years later the survivor is released—it hardly matters to him:

> My very chains and I grew friends,
> So much a long communion tends
> To make us what we are:—even I
> Regain'd my freedom with a sigh.

Prisoner of Grace, A (1952). The first novel in a trilogy by Joyce CARY. The story of Chester Nimmo, dynamic liberal politician, is told by his wife Nina, who is completely under his spell. *Except the Lord* (1953) is Nimmo's own story of his early struggles and ideals. *Not Honour More* (1955) is an account of Nimmo by Nina's second husband, Jim Latter, who thinks that his predecessor has really been a ruthless, time-serving hypocrite.

Prisoner of Zenda, The (1894). A popular romance by Anthony Hope HAWKINS. For three months the English hero, Rudolf Rassendyl, impersonates the king of RURITANIA, who is being held captive in the castle of Zenda. Rudolf finally secures the king's release, surrendering the crown and the hand of his beloved Princess Flavia to the rightful ruler. Though not the first novel of its kind, *The Prisoner of Zenda* began a trend of best-seller romances of high political adventure, a trend that lasted for 10 years.

Prisonnière, La. See REMEMBRANCE OF THINGS PAST.

Pritchett, V[ictor] S[awdon] (1900–   ). English novelist, short-story writer, and literary critic. His early stories, such as *Marching Spain* (1928), were set in Spain, while his later works are often Dickensian comedies about working-class types. Among his books are *Mr. Beluncle* (1951), a satire of suburban life, and *When My Girl Comes Home* (1961), a collection of short stories. Pritchett is literary editor of the *New Statesman and Nation.*

Private Life of the Master Race (Furcht und Elend des Dritten Reiches; 1938). A loose collection of realistic dramatic scenes by Bertolt BRECHT. It is an open attack on Nazism, the literal translation of its German title being "Fear and Misery of the Third Reich."

Private Papers of Henry Ryecroft, The (1903). A novel by George GISSING. The first part of the book is a brief biography of Ryecroft, whose diary Gissing is ostensibly publishing. The diary itself is divided into four sections: Spring, Summer, Autumn, and Winter, which contain reflections or *pensées* on the human condition.

Privy Council. The council chosen by the English sovereign originally to administer public affairs. By the 20th century it was never summoned as a whole except to proclaim the successor to the Crown on the death of the sovereign. The business of the Privy Council is now performed by committees (of which the Cabinet is technically one), such as the Judicial Committee of the Privy Council, and the great departments of State, such as the Board of Trade, Local Government Board, and Board of Education. All these are, in theory, merely committees of the Privy Council.

Prix Goncourt. The most sought-after and highly respected French literary prize. Established in 1903 under the terms of the will of Edmond Goncourt, it is given annually to the best volume of imaginative work in prose published during the year. In cases of a tie, novels are to be given preference over collections of short stories or sketches. The awarding of the prize is decided by the Académie Goncourt, an institution founded in 1896 in compliance with Goncourt's specifications. Consisting of 10 members, whose annual salary of 60 francs has never varied, the academy attempts to recognize and reward originality of talent and new and daring efforts in thought and form. The Goncourt prize is only 50 new francs, but it assures, on the average, a sale of 150,000 copies and royalties of 200,000 new francs to author and publisher alike. The record sale for a Goncourt winner was set by Robert Merle's *Week-end à Zuydcoote*, which printed 235,000 copies. Though the Prix Goncourt has established the reputation of numerous young writers, from Henri Barbusse (1914) to André Malraux (1933), it has not prevented that of other recipients from falling into oblivion even during their lives. The recipients of the Goncourt prize since its inception are:

1903 John Antoine Nau, *La force ennemie*
1904 Léon Frapié, *La maternelle*
1905 Claude Farrère, *Les civilisés*
1906 Jérôme and Jean Tharaud, *Dingley, l'illustre écrivain*
1907 Emile Moselly, *Terres lorraines*
1908 Francis de Miomandre, *Ecrit sur de l'eau*
1909 Marius-Ary Leblond, *En France*
1910 Louis Pergaud, *De Goupil à Margot*
1911 Alphonse de Chateaubriant, *Monsieur des Lourdines*
1912 André Savignon, *Filles de la pluie*
1913 Marc Elder, *Le Peuple de la mer*
1914 Adrien Bertrand, *L'Appel du sol*
1915 René Benjamin, *Gaspard*
1916 Henri Barbusse, *Le Feu*
1917 Henri Malherbe, *La flamme au poing*
1918 Georges Duhamel, *Civilisation*
1919 Marcel Proust, *A l'ombre des jeunes filles en fleurs*
1920 Ernest Pérochon, *Nène*
1921 René Maran, *Batouala*
1922 Henri Béraud, *Le Vitriol de lune; Le martyre de l'obese*
1923 Lucien Fabre, *Rabevel*
1924 Thierry Sandre, *Le chèvrefeuille*
1925 Maurice Genevoix, *Raboliot*
1926 Henri Deberly, *Le supplice de Phèdre*
1927 Maurice Bedel, *Jérôme, 60° latitude nord*
1928 Maurice Constantin-Weyer, *Un homme se penche sur son passé*
1929 Marcel Arland, *L'ordre*
1930 Henri Fauconnier, *Malaisie*
1931 Jean Fayard, *Mal d'amour*
1932 Guy Mazeline, *Les loups*
1933 André Malraux, *La condition humaine*
1934 Roger Vercel, *Capitaine Conan*
1935 Joseph Peyré, *Sang et lumières*
1936 Maxence Van der Meersch, *L'empreinte du Dieu*
1937 Charles Plisnier, *Faux passeports*
1938 Henri Troyat, *L'araigne*
1939 Philippe Hériat, *Les enfants gâtés*
1940 Francis Ambrière, *Les grandes vacances* (awarded 1946)
1941 Henri Pourrat, *Vent de Mars*
1942 Marc Bernard, *Pareils à des enfants*
1943 Marius Grout, *Passage de l'homme*
1944 Elsa Triolet, *Le premier accroc coûte deux cents francs*

1945 Jean-Louis Bory, *Mon village à l'heure allemande*
1946 Jean-Jacques Gautier, *Histoire d'un fait divers*
1947 Jean-Louis Curtis, *Les forêts de la nuit*
1948 Maurice Druon, *Les grandes familles*
1949 Robert Merle, *Week-end à Zuydcoote*
1950 Paul Colin, *Les jeux sauvages*
1951 Julien Gracq, *Le rivage des Syrtes*
1952 Béatrice Beck, *Léon Morin, prêtre*
1953 Pierre Gascar, *Le temps des morts*
1954 Simone de Beauvoir, *Les Mandarins*
1955 Roger Ikor, *Les eaux mêlées*
1956 Romain Gary, *Les racines du ciel*
1957 Roger Vailland, *La loi*
1958 Francis Walder, *Saint-Germain ou la négociation*
1959 André Schwarz-Bart, *Le dernier des justes*
1960 Award rescinded.
1961 Jean Cau, *La pitié de Dieu*
1962 Anna Langfus, *Les bagages de sable*
1963 Armand Lanoux, *Quand la mer se retire*
1964 Georges Conchon, *L'état sauvage*
1965 Jacques Borel, *L'adoration*

Proclus (Proklos; c. 410–485). A Greek Neoplatonic philosopher. Also known as the Successor because of his position as head of the Platonic Academy, Proclus presented the fullest systematization and extension of the Neoplatonic position. The last important pagan Greek philosopher, Proclus' life was related by his student Marinus. Forty-four years after Proclus died, the Emperor Justinian closed the schools of philosophy.

Procne. See PHILOMELA.

Procopius. A Byzantine historian who was private secretary (A.D. 527) to Belisarius, general of JUSTINIAN I, and accompanied him on his campaigns in the Persian, Vandal, and Gothic wars.

Procris. See CEPHALUS.

Procrustes (Prokroustes). In Greek legend, a robber of Attica. He placed all who fell into his hands upon an iron bed. If they were longer than the bed he cut off the redundant part; if shorter, he stretched them till they fitted it. He was slain by Theseus. He is also called Damastes.

Procter, Bryan Waller. Pen name: **Barry Cornwall** (1787–1874). English poet, author, better known for his friendship with many 19th-century authors than for his own work. He was close to such figures as Lamb, Leigh Hunt, Hazlitt, Scott, and later, Browning, Dickens, Thackeray, and Swinburne. A few lyrics of his *Poetical Works* (1822) survive, as does his biography, *Charles Lamb* (1866). His daughter Adelaide Anne Procter (1825–1864) is remembered for her poem THE LOST CHORD.

prodigal son. A repentant sinner from the parable of the prodigal son who "wasted his substance with riotous living" in a far country, but returned to his father's house and was forgiven (Luke 15:11–32). It has become a familiar motif in literature, as evidenced, for example, in Prince Hal's repentant behavior in Shakespeare's *Henry IV,* Part II (1598). It is the title of an oratorio by Arthur Sullivan (1869).

Professor, The (1938). A novel by REX WARNER. It is a political allegory about an idealistic, impractical president who is used as a tool by the extreme right and left in his government and is finally destroyed.

Professor Bernhardi (1912). A play by Arthur SCHNITZLER. In order to prevent a young girl from learning prematurely of her impending death, a Jewish medical professor prevents a priest from going to see her. The play is concerned with the religious and political consequences of this action, and develops into a critique of many trends in the society of the time, including anti-Semitism.

Professorenroman (Ger.). Literally, "professor's novel." In German literary history a very convenient term applied to novels which are crammed full of reliably correct historical detail but which remain absolutely devoid of literary inspiration.

Professor's House, The (1925). A novel by Willa CATHER. The central character is Godfrey St. Peter, a middle-aged professor who is victimized by his wife's ambition and his daughter's desire for a higher social position. The Southwest, in which Miss Cather had become increasingly interested, contributes numerous incidents and motifs, and her characters find the cliff dwellers' homes beautiful and deeply significant.

Progress and Poverty (1879). A treatise on economics by Henry GEORGE. The author tries to analyze why there is an increase in poverty with the increasing prosperity of a nation and attributes the cause to private ownership of land and the rising rate of rent in proportion to the rising value of the land. George's proposed solution is his famous single tax, by which only the return from rented land is made subject to taxation.

Progressive Party. In U.S. history, the name of three political parties. (1) The Progressive Party of 1912, also known as the Bull Moose Party, consisted of Republicans who had withdrawn from their party when it nominated W. H. Taft and not Theodore ROOSEVELT for president. In the ensuing election, Woodrow Wilson, the Democratic candidate, became president, but Roosevelt, with 88 electoral votes, ran ahead of Taft.

(2) The Progressive Party of 1924 represented dissident agrarian and labor groups. It nominated Robert LAFOLLETTE for president on a platform of radical character. He received over five million votes in the election.

(3) The Progressive Party of 1948 consisted mainly of Democrats opposed to the election of Harry S. Truman. It nominated Henry A. Wallace for the presidency on a platform of friendship for Russia and of numerous radical doctrines. Wallace polled over a million votes.

Prokofiev, Sergey Sergeyevitch (1891–1953). Russian composer and pianist. His best-known works include the *Classical Symphony* (1917), the opera *Love for Three Oranges* (1921; based on a comedy by Carlo Gozzi), and a fairy tale for narrator and orchestra *Peter and the Wolf* (1936). His later works are mostly unsuccessful attempts to comply with the Soviet ideal of "socialist realism."

Prokosch, Frederic (1908–   ). American poet and novelist. His poetry is marked by rich, sensuous imagery and an atmosphere of decay; his novels at first inclined toward the poetic, later becoming more sharply realistic. *The Assassins* (1936), *The Carnival* (1938), *Death at Sea* (1940), and *Chosen Poems* (1947) are books of his verse. His novels include *The Asiatics* (1935), *The Seven Who Fled* (1937), *The Idols of the Cave* (1946), and *Nine Days to Mulkalla* (1953). *A Tale for Midnight* (1955) is a study of the Cenci.

proletarian literature. A type of literature, at the height of its influence during the 1930's, especially in the U.S., which had as its aim a sympathetic portrayal of the lives and sufferings of the proletariat. Some of the leading writers of proletarian literature were Communists or Communist sympathizers, but to a large degree their work was a sincere response to an era of economic depression and to obvious social injustices.

In subject-matter and sympathetic approach to its characters, proletarian literature had its forerunners among the humanitarian novelists of the 19th century, such as Mrs. Gaskell, Dickens, George Eliot, Charles Kingsley, Victor Hugo, Harriet Beecher Stowe, Rebecca H. Davis, and Jack London, and such humanitarian poets as Thomas Hood, Elizabeth Barrett Browning, and Edward Markham. In its social perspective, it was preceded by the naturalists (Flaubert, the Goncourts, Zola) and by their American disciples, Stephen Crane and Frank Norris; by the Muckrakers; and by such "problem" novelists as W. D. Howells, Robert Herrick, and D. G. Phillips. Its technique is derived from that of the naturalists and the unaffiliated realists, such as Joseph Kirkland, E. W. Howe, and Hamlin Garland. The spirit of bitter or idealistic rebellion that animates its most characteristic examples had a precedent among the English and American romantics—Robert Burns, the early Wordsworth, Shelley, Emerson, Thoreau, and Walt Whitman. Whitman's exaltation of the "common man" was continued particularly by American proletarian poets.

Proletarian writers in the fields of fiction and theater include the following: Maxim Gorki, the early Gerhart Hauptmann, Liam O'Flaherty, Nexö, John Dos Passos, James T. Farrell, Barbusse, Erskine Caldwell, John Steinbeck, André Malraux, Clifford Odets, John Howard Lawson, Irwin Shaw, Marc Blitzstein, Albert Halper, Meyer Levin, Albert Maltz, Grace Lumpkin, Meridel Le Sueur, Henry Roth, Richard Wright, Waldo Frank, and Leane Zugsmith. Among proletarian poets are Carl Sandburg, Bertolt Brecht, Hugh MacDiarmid, Stephen Spender, Kenneth Fearing, Alfred Hayes, Muriel Rukeyser, Horace Gregory. Characteristic proletarian novels are *Man's Fate, In Dubious Battle,* and *Grapes of Wrath. Waiting for Lefty* and *Let Freedom Ring* are effective proletarian plays.

With the growth of the international ambitions of Nazi Germany and Fascist Italy, anti-Nazi and anti-Fascist works by such writers as Ralph Bates and Ignazio Silone came to be included in the category of proletarian. Leading organs of proletarian literature were the magazines *New Masses, The Anvil,* and *Partisan Review,* the last-named in its early period of publication only. A school of proletarian criticism also developed which sought to advance the notion that literature should concern itself with social and economic injustice and participate actively in the "class struggle," impelling its readers to "action" rather than causing them pleasure or turning them toward contemplation. It vigorously condemned theories of art for art's sake. Many of the above-mentioned writers abandoned their preoccupation with proletarian themes after the Second World War.

Unfortunately, few examples of proletarian literature reached a high level of art. Perhaps the most memorable were Silone's *Fontamara* and Steinbeck's *Grapes of Wrath*.

Promessi Sposi, I (The Betrothed, 1827). A romantic historical novel by Alessandro MANZONI, often considered the greatest Italian novel of modern times. The story tells of the attempts of Renzo and Lucia, two peasants in 17th-century Lombardy, to marry despite the bullying threats of a local grandee, Don Rodrigo. The lovers are assisted in their plight by their saintly confessor, Fra Cristoforo, and by Cardinal Borromeo who personifies Manzoni's ideal of the moral perfection of Catholic doctrine and practice. Their situation is worsened by the cowardice of their parish priest Don Abbondio, who typifies what the author considers a common type of human failing. The Nun of Monza figures as the willful sinner whose maliciousness harms the lovers and confirms her own moral turpitude. The "Unnamed" Signore (*L'Innominato*) represents the repentant sinner whose conversion protects Renzo and Lucia from Don Rodrigo and facilitates their marriage and the book's happy outcome.

The author's stated purpose in the novel is to show the workings of divine providence in history, specifically, in the day-to-day events in the life of a common man; hence the obvious moralizing of the text and the moral lessons implicit in the personalities of the characters. Among the many remarkable scenes in the book is that describing the plague in Milan.

Prometheus (Gr. "forethought"). In Greek mythology, a son of Iapetus and Themis, Asia, or Clymene. He stole fire from heaven. A champion of men against the gods, he tricked Zeus into choosing fat and bone as the god's portion of sacrifices, leaving the flesh for men. Angrily Zeus withheld fire from men, but Prometheus stole it in a fennel stock. As a punishment, Prometheus was nailed to a mountain, where an eagle tore out his liver by day and it grew again by night. Eventually HERACLES rescued him, or he was saved by Zeus himself. Man, meanwhile, had been afflicted by Zeus with innumerable ills through PANDORA. According to some stories, Prometheus was the creator of man, molding him of mud. It is likely that he was a pre-Hellenic fire-god who was replaced by Hephaestus. In Aeschylus' PROMETHEUS BOUND, he is a heroic figure, as he was in Shelley's narrative poem *Prometheus Unbound*.

Prometheus Bound (Prometheus Desmotes). A tragedy of unknown date by AESCHYLUS. Prometheus, who has stolen fire from heaven for man, is punished by Zeus by being fastened to a Scythian mountain by HEPHAESTUS. He tells a chorus of sympathetic ocean nymphs how he had once helped Zeus in his war with the Titans. The old god Oceanus enters, riding a strange, winged animal, and advises Prometheus to defy Zeus no longer. Io, now a heifer, enters and tells of her sorrow. Prometheus foretells a happy outcome after her further wanderings. He then says that Zeus himself will be destroyed by a son yet to be born to him, but only Prometheus knows who will be its mother. When Io is gone, HERMES tries to force Prometheus to reveal his secret, but he refuses unless he is released. With lightning and an earthquake, Zeus plunges Prometheus into Tartarus.

In this monumental play, Aeschylus deals with the theme of men's relation to the gods. *Prometheus*

Bound was the first play of a trilogy. The other two, *Prometheus Unbound* (*P. Lyomenos*) and *Prometheus, the Fire-Bearer* (*P. Pyrphoros*), are lost, but a fragment of the second shows that Prometheus remained in Tartarus for 30,000 years.

Prometheus Unbound (1820). A lyrical drama by Percy Bysshe SHELLEY, inspired by the Greek myth of PROMETHEUS. In Shelley's work, the chained and tormented Prometheus is a symbol of humanity; Jupiter, the usurper, represents the tyranny of kings and civil institutions; Demogorgon, the son of Jupiter and Thetis, is the Primal Power of the world and the spirit of Necessity or Destiny; Asia, Prometheus's wife, is ideal Love or Nature. Demogorgon drives Jupiter from his throne, Prometheus is released by Hercules (Strength) and reunited with Asia, and a golden age, where love and beauty reign, begins.

Promised Land. CANAAN or Palestine, so called because God promised Abraham, Isaac, and Jacob that their offspring should possess it (Gen. 12:7, 26:3, 28:13).

The expression has frequently been used in connection with the promise of the Balfour Declaration that the Jews should have a homeland in Palestine.

Promised Land, The (1912). An autobiography by Mary Antin (1881–1945), Russian-born American writer. It describes her life in Polotzk as the child of Russian Jews, her emigration to America at the age of 13, and her school days in Boston, where she found friends and opportunity.

Propertius, Sextus (49–15 B.C.). Roman poet and master of elegiac verse. His three books of poetry deal with his experiences in love as well as etiological myths and Roman history. The 20th-century American poet Ezra Pound made several modern imitations of him in *Homage to Sextus Propertius*.

Prophecy of Famine, The, a Scots Pastoral (1763). A satiric poem by Charles CHURCHILL chiefly attacking the taking over of important administrative offices in England by the Scots. It begins with a condemnation of the artificialities of English pastoral poetry and it parodies, in the dialogue between the Pessimist, Sawney, and the Optimist, Jockey, the first scene of *The Gentle Shepherd* by Allan Ramsay.

Prophet, the. In the Koran, the special title of MUHAMMAD. According to the Muslims, there have been 200,000 prophets, or interpreters of God's will, but only six of them, Adam, Noah, Abraham, Moses, Jesus, and Muhammad, have brought new laws.

Kahlil Gibran wrote a book called *The Prophet* (1923), which presents his mystical faith in the form of a prose poem.

The Great or Major Prophets. In the Old Testament, Isaiah, Jeremiah, Ezekiel, and Daniel; so called because their writings are more extensive than the writings of the other twelve.

The Minor or Lesser Prophets. Hosea, Joel, Amos, Obadiah, Micah, Jonah, Nahum, Habakkuk, Zephaniah, Haggai, Zechariah, and the author of Malachi.

Prophetess, the. A title of Ayeshah, the second and beloved wife of Muhammad. Like *Sultana,* it is used as a title of honor.

Proserpina or **Proserpine.** The Roman counterpart of the Greek goddess PERSEPHONE.

prosody. The broad study or science of how language is handled in the composition of poetry.

The term encompasses VERSIFICATION (meter, rhyme, traditional forms); Anglo-Saxon poetics; syllable-count methods and forms; FREE VERSE; distortion and dissonance applied to traditional methods; SPRUNG RHYTHM; and any specific stylistic rules or requirements of special poetic movements, as, for example, those of the imagists (see IMAGISM).

Prospero. The rightful duke of Milan who reigns over an enchanted island in Shakespeare's THE TEMPEST. Almost superhuman in his attributes, he is wise, firm, and philosophical, meting out justice to friend and enemy. His magical skills symbolize the power that man may attain by the use of his mind, though he is often impeded by the baser aspects of his nature. His is one of the most famous of Shakespeare's speeches:

> Our revels now are ended. These our actors,
> As I foretold you, were all spirits and
> Are melted into air, into thin air:
> And, like the baseless fabric of this vision,
> The cloud-capp'd towers, the gorgeous palaces,
> The solemn temples, the great globe itself,
> Yea, all which it inherit, shall dissolve,
> And like this insubstantial pageant faded,
> Leave not a rack behind. We are such stuff
> As dreams are made on; and our little life
> Is rounded with a sleep.

Prospero is often said to embody the philosophy at which the dramatist arrived toward the end of his life.

Prospice (1864). A poem by Robert BROWNING. Written soon after his wife's death, it expresses an optimistic and courageous attitude towards death. The title, taken from Latin, states the theme: "Look forward!"

Protagoras of Abdera (c. 490–420 B.C.). A Greek SOPHIST. His best-known statement, one of the two fragments of his works that have been preserved, is: "Of all things the measure is man, of the things that are that they are, and of the things that are not that they are not." Plato and Aristotle both regarded the comment as giving to appearances the status of truth. Protagoras also said that there is no way of knowing about the gods. He held that there are two accounts of everything and was able to teach the art of making the weaker account equally convincing.

Protekult. Proletarian Cultural and Educational Organizations, formed in Russia in 1917. Its purpose was to foster a literature created by proletarians for their own class. The contributions of the group to Soviet culture were negligible, however, and it was abolished in 1923.

Protesilaus (**Protesilaos**). The first Greek to die in the Trojan War. At the siege of Troy an oracle prophesied that the first Greek to step on land would be killed. Protesilaus took the honor upon himself and was promptly slain. His faithful wife Laodameia, who had kept a wax statue of him always beside her, now prayed that he should return for a brief while. His ghost appeared to animate the statue for three hours, but she willingly returned with him to Hades at the end of that time. According to another story, she killed herself when her father took away the statue.

Proteus. (1) In Greek legend, Poseidon's herdsman, an old man and a prophet. He was famous for his power of assuming different shapes at will. When caught, however, he was helpful to many Greek heroes by his foreknowledge. Proteus lived in a vast cave, and his custom was to tell over his herds of sea-calves at noon, and then go to sleep. There was no way of catching him but by stealing upon him at this time and binding him; otherwise he would elude anyone by a rapid change in shape. In Euripides' HELEN he is referred to as a former king of Egypt.

(2) In Shakespeare's Two GENTLEMEN OF VERONA, the inconstant friend of Valentine. Although he betrays Valentine and Julia, to whom he had vowed eternal love, he is forgiven by both of them and repents of his unfaithfulness. See FAERIE QUEENE, THE.

Prothalamion (1596). Lyric poem by Edmund SPENSER. It was written to celebrate the double wedding of Lady Elizabeth and Lady Katherine Somerset, daughters of the earl of Worcester.

Proudhon, Pierre Joseph (1809–1865). French socialist and anarchist. His most famous work *What Is Property* (*Qu'est-ce que la propriété?*; 1840) denounces private property as an institution which perpetrates inequality and injustice. A fiery reformer, Proudhon fled France in 1858 when his *La Justice dans la Révolution et dans l'Eglise* (1858), a work violently critical of church and state, was angrily received.

Proudie, Bishop and **Mrs.** Two of the best-known characters in Anthony Trollope's Chronicles of BARSETSHIRE. Mrs. Proudie is a formidable woman who propels her husband through life with unrelenting vigor. See BARCHESTER TOWERS.

Proust, Marcel (1871–1922). French novelist. Son of an eminent Catholic doctor and his Jewish wife, Proust grew up in their permanent home in Paris near the Champs-Elysées. His memories of visits to relatives in Auteuil and in Illiers were the material for the imaginary village of COMBRAY, the setting for the early part of his long and most important novel, REMEMBRANCE OF THINGS PAST. He suffered his first attack of asthma when he was nine; thereafter, his summer visits were to shore resorts on the English Channel, which he combined into the BALBEC of the novel.

In 1889 he joined the army for a year as a sub-officer. The following year, to satisfy his father's insistence that he should have a regular career, he entered the Sorbonne as a student of both law and political science. His real interest was philosophy, however; he was much influenced by the lectures of Paul Desjardins and of Henri Bergson, whose theories about time as subjectively lived contributed to Proust's.

At the Lycée Condorcet, where he had studied philosophy under Marie Alphonse Darlu, his schoolfellows and he had produced in 1887–1888 a number of ephemeral handwritten little magazines. Now, in 1892, the same group founded the printed review *Le Banquet,* which lasted for eight issues. Proust was one of the most prolific contributors of sketches and short stories, but his artificial although graceful style did not impress even his colleagues, except as revealing his apparently snobbish fascination with titled society. And indeed, the young Proust was steadily and deliberately making his way, despite his bourgeois origins, into higher and higher circles of the Faubourg St. Germain, the social elite of Paris. Similarly, although Anatole France wrote an introduction for *Pleasures and Days* (*Les Plaisirs et les jours;* 1896), a collection of sketches, stories, and poems in a variety of imitative styles, the book was received as the elegant but slight work of a literary dilettante.

In 1895, Proust began working on a long novel, which was published posthumously as JEAN SANTEUIL, finally abandoning it about 1899. These were also the years of the Dreyfus Case, during which Proust with Anatole France and other intellectuals actively protested the miscarriage of justice and demanded a retrial.

The aesthetic theories of John Ruskin attracted Proust who, in 1899, began a serious study of his works, translating *The Bible of Amiens* (*La Bible d'Amiens;* 1904) and *Sesame and Lilies* (*Sésame et les lys;* 1906) with notes and prefaces. Ruskin's descriptions of architecture also inspired Proust to make a number of trips to see the important buildings of France, Holland, and Venice.

After his father died in 1903 and his mother in 1905, Proust began to relinquish almost all his social ties, although he continued to travel a bit and to write for newspapers and reviews. In 1907 he moved to the apartment on Boulevard Haussmann famous for the cork-lined bedroom from which, in later years, he almost never stirred, partly to prevent serious asthmatic or nervous attacks, partly to avoid being distracted from his writing. By 1908 he had conceived and begun writing his life work, *Remembrance of Things Past*. The narrator of the novel is very like Proust in character and background. A neurotic, hypersensitive, asthmatic young man, who is even called in one place "Marcel," he courts fashionable society and romantic experiences, records his observations in great detail, introspectively analyzes his responses to them, and finally discovers his vocation in the writing of this novel. In shaping the narrator's personality, Proust omitted his own Jewish background, homosexuality, and hypochondria. All these attributes, transposed to other characters, are extensively analyzed, however, and the narrator's generalized conclusions about love, snobbery, art, literature, etc., are assumed to be Proust's own.

The only significant interruption to direct work on his masterpiece, was the writing (1908–1910) of *Contre Sainte-Beuve* (1954). Proust began this as a critical study, but it soon digressed into an analysis of his own processes of memory, thought, and emotion, and thus like *Jean Santeuil* was an exploratory preparation for his masterpiece. The first draft of *Remembrance of Things Past* was completed by 1912, and the first volume in print by 1913, but World War I delayed further publication, giving Proust time for "revisions" that expanded the work to nearly twice its original length: Proust died before the last three books were published.

Prout, Father. See Francis MAHONY.

Prouty, Olive Higgins. See STELLA DALLAS.

Provence, Marcel. See Marcel JOUHANDEAU.

Proverbs. The 20th book of the Old Testament, appearing directly after the Psalms. It contains, as the title indicates a collection of maxims and pithy statements, a considerable section of which were formerly ascribed to Solomon.

Provincetown Players. A group of actors, producers, and playwrights. It is known for its encouragement of native writers and its part in promoting a resurgence in the American theater after World War I. The group started as an acting company in Provincetown, Mass., under the direction of George Cram COOK. It produced plays by Cook and by his wife, Susan GLASPELL, and also by other dramatists, notably Eugene O'NEILL. The Players was organized in 1915; after moving to New York, the group continued to work until 1929. O'Neill was its most important discovery, but it eventually produced almost 100 plays by some of the most famous playwrights of the period.

Prozess, Der. See TRIAL, THE.

Prufrock, J. Alfred. See LOVE SONG OF J. ALFRED PRUFROCK, THE.

Prussian Officer, The (1914). A short story by D. H. LAWRENCE. It is about a sadistic Prussian army officer and his victim, a young orderly, who is finally driven to kill his tormentor.

Prynne, Hester. The heroine of Hawthorne's THE SCARLET LETTER.

Prynne, William (1600–1669). English Puritan lawyer, pamphleteer, and statesman, known for his attacks on popular amusements. His *Histriomastix* (1633), a long diatribe against actors and stage plays, contained indirect criticism of the royal family. As a result, he was expelled from his profession by the Star Chamber, sentenced to life imprisonment, and placed in the pillory, where he lost both his ears. He was released from prison in 1640 by the Long Parliament.

Psalm of Life, A (1839). A poem by Henry Wadsworth LONGFELLOW. Widely anthologized, though didactic and sentimental, the poem contains the well-known line: "Life is real! Life is earnest!"

Psalms. The 19th book of the Old Testament, containing 150 hymns, or songs to God. Many of them are ascribed to David, who was called "the sweet psalmist of Israel" (II Sam. 23:1).

Psellus, Michael Constantine. Called **Psellus the Younger** (11th century). Byzantine philosopher and statesman. He revived the study of Plato, was powerful at court from about 1042 to 1078, becoming prime minister under his pupil Michael VII, and wrote voluminously on history and politics, music, mathematics, science, etc.

Pseudodoxia Epidemica. See VULGAR ERRORS.

Psycarpax (Gr., "granary thief"). In the Greek BATTLE OF THE FROGS AND MICE, the son of Troxartas, the king of the Mice. The Frog-king offers to carry the young prince over a lake, but scarcely has he reached midway, when a water-hydra appears and King Frog, to save himself, dives under water. The mouse, being thus left on the surface, is drowned, and this catastrophe brings about the battle of the Frogs and Mice.

Psyche (Gr. breath; hence, life or soul). The heroine of the myth of CUPID (Eros) and Psyche, an episode in the GOLDEN ASS of Apuleius, second century A.D. She was a beautiful maiden beloved by Cupid, who visited her every night, but left her at sunrise. Cupid bade her never to seek to know who he was, but one night curiosity overcame her prudence; she lit the lamp to look at him, a drop of hot oil fell on his shoulder, and he awoke and fled. The abandoned Psyche wandered far and wide in search of her lover. She became the slave of Venus, who imposed on her heartless tasks and treated her most cruelly. But ultimately she was united to Cupid and became immortal. The kernel of the story, the theme of the lover who must not be named, is a common theme in folk lore.

psychoanalysis. A 20th-century method of psychiatric treatment attributing the greater part of human activity to motives of the unconscious mind. It endeavors, partly through analysis of the symbolic value of dreams, to bring "suppressed desires" into the sphere of consciousness and to strip them of their power or set them free to work in more normal channels. The prime mover in the field of psychoanalysis was Dr. Sigmund FREUD, who identified the libido—that is, the energy or driving force in living creatures—with the sex instinct. Freud's disciple and later rival Carl Jung rejected such a restriction. Further deviations from Freud's system were developed by Alfred Adler, Karen Horney, Harry Stack Sullivan, and others.

Psychoanalysis and particularly the theories of Freud and Jung have had enormous influence on literature. Prominent among the innumerable writers who have been affected by them are James Joyce, Eugene O'Neill, Thomas Mann, and T. S. Eliot. STREAM OF CONSCIOUSNESS techniques of narration, though in use earlier, were given added intensity and precision by writers who had studied Freud. Psychoanalytic theories have also been widely used in literary criticism.

Ptah. In Egyptian religion, the chief god of Memphis worshiped as the creative force of the world and molder of men. He was identified with the Greek Hephaestus and the Roman Vulcan.

Ptolemy. Full Latin name, **Claudius Ptolemaeus** (2nd century). Alexandrian astronomer and geographer. In his *Almagest* he described a new system of astronomy that was accepted until the 16th century. The Ptolemaic system, as it is called, stipulates that the sun, the planets, and the stars revolve around the earth. The movements of the heavenly bodies were plotted by a complicated arrangement of epicycles (small circles with their centers on the circumference of a larger one). Whenever a planet or star was observed moving out of its prescribed path, it was assumed that it had entered a new series of epicycles. By continually adding epicycles, the Ptolemaic system was made to work; however, it had become insanely complex with dozens of epicycles for a single planet when COPERNICUS advanced his uncomplicated theory of heliocentricity in 1530.

Public Advertiser, The. A London newspaper (1758–1793), edited by Henry Sampson Woodfall, in which the JUNIUS LETTERS appeared.

Public Occurrences, Boston. See BOSTON PUBLIC OCCURRENCES.

Pucci, Antonio (1310–1388). Florentine poet. The author of humorous sonnets, he is well-known for his public recitation of his works. He especially excelled in the tailed sonnet and in the use of terza rima. The latter is used in his *Noie* (*Annoyances*), a poem of a hundred tercets, each describing briefly something that galls the poet; it is related to the Provençal *enueg*.

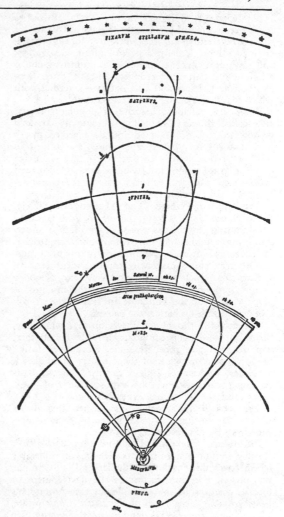

The Ptolemaic universe. From a work by Kepler.

Puccini, Giacomo (1858–1924). Italian composer of opera. Born into a musical family, Puccini was sent to the local conservatory of music; he was organist at a nearby church at 17 and, with a stipend from the queen, was able to attend the Milan Conservatory where he studied under Amilcare Ponchielli. Verdi regarded Puccini as the most talented Italian composer of his time, and, in the first quarter of this century, Puccini's popularity rivaled that of Verdi. Among Puccini's operas are MANON LESCAUT (1893); *La Bohème* (1896); *La Tosca* (1900), which brought him recognition as Verdi's successor; *Madama Butterfly* (1904)—at its première, Puccini's worst failure, only to become within the year one of his best-loved works; *The Girl of the Golden West* (1907); *Il Trittico* (1918), a trilogy of one-act operas including *Il tabarro, Suor Angelica,* and *Gianni Schicchi;* and TURANDOT, first performed in 1926.

Pucelle, La. Short for *La Pucelle d'Orléans* (the virgin of Orléans, i.e., JOAN OF ARC), *La Pucelle* is the title of an epic poem by Jean CHAPELAIN (cantos

1-12, 1656; 12 additional cantos, 1882) and of a mock-heroic poem by VOLTAIRE. Chapelain treats his subject reverently, but the work is critically considered a failure; Voltaire's poem, adroit, derogatory, and scathingly obscene, uses Joan as an instrument to assail superstition and credulity, and has often been attacked as tasteless and defamatory—a verdict with which many of Voltaire's admirers concur.

Puck. A mischievous sprite of popular folklore, also called Robin Goodfellow. Originally an evil demon, he was transformed and popularized in his present form by Shakespeare, who depicts him in A MIDSUMMER NIGHT'S DREAM as a merry wanderer of the night, "rough, knurly-limbed, faun-faced, and shock-pated, a very Shetlander among the gossamer-winged" fairies around him.

Pudd'nhead Wilson, The Tragedy of (1894). A novel by Mark TWAIN. David Wilson is called "Pudd'nhead" by the townspeople, who fail to understand his combination of wisdom and eccentricity. He redeems himself by simultaneously solving a murder mystery and a case of transposed identities.

Two children, a white boy and a mulatto, are born on the same day. Roxy, mother of the mulatto, is given charge of the children; in fear that her son will be sold, she exchanges the babies.

The mulatto, though he grows up as a white boy, turns out to be a scoundrel. He sells his mother, and murders and robs his uncle. He accuses Luigi, one of a pair of twins, of the murder; Pudd'nhead, a lawyer, undertakes Luigi's defense. On the basis of fingerprint evidence, he exposes the real murderer, and the white boy takes his rightful place.

The book implicitly condemns a society that allows slavery. It concludes with a series of witty aphorisms from Pudd'nhead's calendar.

Pudovkin, Vsevolod Ilarionovich (1893–1953). Russian motion-picture director. He was an innovator in film technique. Along with Sergei Eisenstein, he was one of the chief factors in the development of motion pictures in the early Soviet era. Among his films are *The Mechanism of the Brain, Chess Fever, Storm over Asia* (1929), and *General Suvorov.* He wrote two books, *Film Technique* (1933) and *Film Acting* (1935), in which he explored the possibilities of the motion pictures as an art form.

Pugachev, Emelyan Ivanovich (1743–1775). Russian Cossack soldier who led an uprising against CATHERINE THE GREAT. In 1773, posing as Catherine's late husband, Peter III, Pugachev formed an army of Cossacks, peasants, and escaped convicts. The band swept through southern Russia, capturing a number of important towns and cities along the Volga River. In 1774 the government forces finally broke the revolt and captured Pugachev. He was executed in Moscow in 1775. The poet Pushkin used the revolt as the basis for his novel, *The Captain's Daughter* (*Kapitanskaya dochka*).

Pugin, Augustus Welby Northmore (1812–1852). English architect and designer. Instrumental in reviving the Gothic style in England, he was responsible for the architectural decoration of the House of Parliament in London.

Pulchérie. In Pierre Corneille's tragedy HÉRACLIUS, the daughter of the murdered Emperor of the East. She is almost forced by the usurper Phocas to marry Héraclius, her own brother.

Pulci, Luigi (1432–1484). Florentine poet. A member of the circle around Lorenzo de' Medici, he served both the Medici family and the CONDOTTIERE Roberto Sanseverino while writing his comic masterpiece, the MORGANTE MAGGIORE. It is a mainly burlesque treatment of the epic material involving Charlemagne, Roland and the other paladins; it takes its title from one of the characters, the giant Morgante, and is called *maggiore* (greater) because a later edition (1483) had 5 more cantos added to the original 23. It influenced Folengo and Rabelais; in modern times, Byron translated the first canto superbly, and George Borrow used it in his *Lavengro* and *Romany Rye.*

Pulitzer, Joseph (1847–1911). Hungarian-born American journalist. Pulitzer began his career in 1868 as a reporter for the German daily *Westliche Post* in St. Louis and soon became its part-owner. He was also a lawyer active in politics, first as a Liberal Republican and later as a Democrat. In 1878 he bought the *St. Louis Dispatch,* which was soon merged with the *Evening Post* to become the *Post-Dispatch.* He bought the New York *World* in 1883, founded the *Evening World* in 1887, and made both of them prosperous enterprises. Their prestige and circulation declined after a sordid war with the dailies of William Randolph Hearst in the late 1890's. Pulitzer had retired from active control in 1890 because of ill health, but his directives eventually restored the papers to respectability. See PULITZER PRIZES.

Pulitzer Prizes. Annual awards in journalism and letters made by the trustees of Columbia University. They were endowed by the will of Joseph PULITZER, who also left money to found the University's School of Journalism. The nominees are screened by juries appointed in each category, and recommended to the trustees by the Advisory Board on the Pulitzer Prizes.

There are eight journalism awards: to a newspaper, for public service, and for "distinguished examples" of editorial writing, cartooning, news photography, and national, international, local spot news, and local investigative reporting. In letters, the awards are for distinguished works by American authors in the fields of fiction, U.S. history and biography, drama, poetry, and (since 1962) for a work not eligible in any other existing category. There is also a prize for a larger musical work, and four fellowships. Literary works awarded the Pulitzer Prize:

Fiction: 1918, Ernest Poole, *His Family;* 1919, Booth Tarkington, *The Magnificent Ambersons;* 1920, none; 1921, Edith Wharton, *The Age of Innocence;* 1922, Booth Tarkington, *Alice Adams;* 1923, Willa Cather, *One of Ours;* 1924, Margaret Wilson, *The Able McLaughlins;* 1925, Edna Ferber, *So Big;* 1926, Sinclair Lewis (author declined), *Arrowsmith;* 1927, Louis Bromfield, *Early Autumn;* 1928, Thornton Wilder, *Bridge of San Luis Rey;* 1929, Julia M. Peterkin, *Scarlet Sister Mary;* 1930, Oliver La Farge, *Laughing Boy;* 1931, Margaret Ayer Barnes, *Years of Grace;* 1932, Pearl S. Buck, *The Good Earth;* 1933, T. S. Stribling, *The Store;* 1934, Caroline Miller, *Lamb in His Bosom;* 1935, Josephine W. Johnson, *Now in November;* 1936, Harold L. Davis, *Honey in the Horn;* 1937, Margaret Mitchell, *Gone*

With the Wind; 1938, John P. Marquand, *The Late George Apley;* 1939, Marjorie Kinnan Rawlings, *The Yearling;* 1940, John Steinbeck, *The Grapes of Wrath;* 1941, none; 1942, Ellen Glasgow, *In This Our Life;* 1943, Upton Sinclair, *Dragon's Teeth;* 1944, Martin Flavin, *Journey in the Dark;* 1945, John Hersey, *A Bell for Adano;* 1946, none; 1947, Robert Penn Warren, *All the King's Men;* 1948, James A. Michener, *Tales of the South Pacific;* 1949, James Gould Cozzens, *Guard of Honor;* 1950, A. B. Guthrie, Jr., *The Way West;* 1951, Conrad Richter, *The Town;* 1952, Herman Wouk, *The Caine Mutiny;* 1953, Ernest Hemingway, *The Old Man and the Sea;* 1954, none; 1955, William Faulkner, *A Fable;* 1956, MacKinlay Kantor, *Andersonville;* 1957, none; 1958, James Agee, *A Death in the Family;* 1959, Robert Lewis Taylor, *The Travels of Jaimie McPheeters;* 1960, Allen Drury, *Advise and Consent;* 1961, Harper Lee, *To Kill a Mockingbird;* 1962, Edwin O'Connor, *The Edge of Sadness;* 1963, William Faulkner (posthumous), *The Reivers;* 1964, none; 1965, Shirley Ann Grau, *The Keepers of the House.*

Drama: 1918, Jesse Lynch Williams, *Why Marry?;* 1919, none; 1920, Eugene O'Neill, *Beyond the Horizon;* 1921, Zona Gale, *Miss Lulu Bett;* 1922, Eugene O'Neill, *Anna Christie;* 1923, Owen Davis, *Icebound;* 1924, Hatcher Hughes, *Hell-Bent for Heaven;* 1925, Sidney Howard, *They Knew What They Wanted;* 1926, George Kelly, *Craig's Wife;* 1927, Paul Green, *In Abraham's Bosom;* 1928, Eugene O'Neill, *Strange Interlude;* 1929, Elmer Rice, *Street Scene;* 1930, Marc Connelly, *The Green Pastures;* 1931, Susan Glaspell, *Alison's House;* 1932, George S. Kaufman, Morrie Ryskind, and Ira Gershwin, *Of Thee I Sing;* 1933, Maxwell Anderson, *Both Your Houses;* 1934, Sidney Kingsley, *Men in White;* 1935, Zoë Akins, *The Old Maid;* 1936, Robert E. Sherwood, *Idiot's Delight;* 1937, George S. Kaufman and Moss Hart, *You Can't Take It With You;* 1938, Thornton Wilder, *Our Town;* 1939, Robert E. Sherwood, *Abe Lincoln in Illinois;* 1940, William Saroyan, *The Time of Your Life;* 1941, Robert E. Sherwood, *There Shall Be No Night;* 1942, none; 1943, Thornton Wilder, *The Skin of Our Teeth;* 1944, none; 1945, Mary Chase, *Harvey;* 1946, Russel Crouse and Howard Lindsay, *State of the Union;* 1947, none; 1948, Tennessee Williams, *A Streetcar Named Desire;* 1949, Arthur Miller, *Death of a Salesman;* 1950, Richard Rodgers, Oscar Hammerstein II, and Joshua Logan, *South Pacific;* 1951, none; 1952, Joseph Kramm, *The Shrike;* 1953, William Inge, *Picnic;* 1954, John Patrick, *Teahouse of the August Moon;* 1955, Tennessee Williams, *Cat on a Hot Tin Roof;* 1956, Frances Goodrich and Albert Hackett, *The Diary of Anne Frank;* 1957, Eugene O'Neill, *Long Day's Journey Into Night;* 1958, Ketti Frings, *Look Homeward, Angel;* 1959, Archibald MacLeish, *J. B.;* 1960, George Abbott, Jerome Weidman, Sheldon Harnick, and Jerry Bock, *Fiorello!;* 1961, Tad Mosel, *All the Way Home;* 1962, Frank Loesser and Abe Burrows, *How to Succeed in Business Without Really Trying;* 1963, none; 1964, none; 1965, Frank Gilroy, *The Subject Was Roses.*

Poetry: 1922, Edwin Arlington Robinson, *Collected Poems;* 1923, Edna St. Vincent Millay, *The Ballad of the Harp-Weaver, A Few Figs from Thistles,* and other poems; 1924, Robert Frost, *New Hampshire: A Poem with Notes and Grace Notes;* 1925, Edwin

Arlington Robinson, *The Man Who Died Twice;* 1926, Amy Lowell, *What's O'Clock;* 1927, Leonora Speyer, *Fiddler's Farewell;* 1928, Edwin Arlington Robinson, *Tristram;* 1929, Stephen Vincent Benét, *John Brown's Body;* 1930, Conrad Aiken, *Selected Poems;* 1931, Robert Frost, *Collected Poems;* 1932, George Dillon, *The Flowering Stone;* 1933, Archibald MacLeish, *Conquistador;* 1934, Robert Hillyer, *Collected Verse;* 1935, Audrey Wurdemann, *Bright Ambush;* 1936, Robert P. Tristram Coffin, *Strange Holiness;* 1937, Robert Frost, *A Further Range;* 1938, Marya Zaturenska, *Cold Morning Sky;* 1939, John Gould Fletcher, *Selected Poems;* 1940, Mark Van Doren, *Collected Poems;* 1941, Leonard Bacon, *Sunderland Capture;* 1942, William Rose Benét, *The Dust Which Is God;* 1943, Robert Frost, *A Witness Tree;* 1944, Stephen Vincent Benét, *Western Star;* 1945, Karl Shapiro, *V-Letter and Other Poems;* 1946, none; 1947, Robert Lowell, *Lord Weary's Castle;* 1948, W. H. Auden, *The Age of Anxiety;* 1949, Peter Viereck, *Terror and Decorum;* 1950, Gwendolyn Brooks, *Annie Allen;* 1951, Carl Sandburg, *Complete Poems;* 1952, Marianne Moore, *Collected Poems;* 1953, Archibald MacLeish, *Collected Poems 1917–1952;* 1954, Theodore Roethke, *The Waking;* 1955, Wallace Stevens, *Collected Poems;* 1956, Elizabeth Bishop, *Poems, North and South;* 1957, Richard Wilbur, *Things of This World;* 1958, Robert Penn Warren, *Promises: Poems 1954–1956;* 1959, Stanley Kunitz, *Selected Poems, 1928–1958;* 1960, W. D. Snodgrass, *Heart's Needle;* 1961, Phyllis McGinley, *Times Three: Selected Verse from Three Decades;* 1962, Alan Dugan, *Poems;* 1963, William Carlos Williams (posthumous), *Pictures from Brueghel;* 1964, Louis Simpson, *At the End of the Open Road;* 1965, John Berryman, *77 Dream Songs.*

History: 1917, J. J. Jusserand, *With Americans of Past and Present Days;* 1918, James Ford Rhodes, *History of the Civil War;* 1919, none; 1920, Justin H. Smith, *The War with Mexico;* 1921, William Sowden Sims, with Burton J. Hendrick, *The Victory at Sea;* 1922, James Truslow Adams, *The Founding of New England;* 1923, Charles Warren, *The Supreme Court in United States History;* 1924, Charles Howard McIlwain, *The American Revolution: A Constitutional Interpretation;* 1925, Frederick L. Paxton, *A History of the American Frontier;* 1926, Edward Channing, *History of the U.S.;* 1927, Samuel Flagg Bemis, *Pinckney's Treaty;* 1928, Vernon Louis Parrington, *Main Currents in American Thought;* 1929, Fred A. Shannon, *The Organization and Administration of the Union Army, 1861–65;* 1930, Claude H. Van Tyne, *The War of Independence;* 1931, Bernadotte E. Schmitt, *The Coming of the War: 1914;* 1932, Gen. John J. Pershing, *My Experiences in the World War;* 1933, Frederick J. Turner, *The Significance of Sections in American History;* 1934, Herbert Agar, *The People's Choice;* 1935, Charles McLean Andrews, *The Colonial Period of American History;* 1936, Andrew C. McLaughlin, *A Constitutional History of the United States;* 1937, Van Wyck Brooks, *The Flowering of New England;* 1938, Paul Herman Buck, *The Road to Reunion 1865–1900;* 1939, Frank Luther Mott, *A History of American Magazines;* 1940, Carl Sandburg, *Abraham Lincoln: The War Years;* 1941, Marcus Lee Hansen, *The Atlantic Migration 1607–1860;* 1942, Margaret

Leech, *Reveille in Washington;* 1943, Esther Forbes, *Paul Revere and the World He Lived In;* 1944, Merle Curti, *The Growth of American Thought;* 1945, Stephen Bonsal, *Unfinished Business;* 1946, Arthur M. Schlesinger, Jr., *The Age of Jackson;* 1947, Dr. James Phinney Baxter 3d, *Scientists Against Time;* 1948, Bernard De Voto, *Across the Wide Missouri;* 1949, Roy F. Nichols, *The Disruption of American Democracy;* 1950, O. W. Larkin, *Art and Life in America;* 1951, R. Carlyle Buley, *The Old Northwest, Pioneer Period 1815–1840;* 1952, Oscar Handlin, *The Uprooted;* 1953, George Dangerfield, *The Era of Good Feelings;* 1954, Bruce Catton, *A Stillness at Appomattox;* 1955, Paul Horgan, *Great River: The Rio Grande in North American History;* 1956, Richard Hofstadter, *The Age of Reform;* 1957, George F. Kennan, *Russia Leaves the War;* 1958, Bray Hammond, *Banks and Politics in America— From the Revolution to the Civil War;* 1959, Leonard D. White and Jean Schneider, *The Republican Era: 1869–1901;* 1960, Margaret Leech, *In The Days of McKinley;* 1961, Herbert Feis, *Between War and Peace: The Potsdam Conference;* 1962, Lawrence H. Gipson, *The Triumphant Empire, Thunder-Clouds Gather in the West;* 1963, Constance Green, *Washington, Village and Capital;* 1964, Sumner Chilton Powell, *Puritan Village: The Formation of a New England Town;* 1965, Irwin Unger, *The Greenback Era.*

Biography: 1917, Laura E. Richards and Maude Howe Elliott, assisted by Florence Howe Hall, *Julia Ward Howe;* 1918, William Cabell Bruce, *Benjamin Franklin, Self-Revealed;* 1919, Henry Adams, *The Education of Henry Adams;* 1920, Albert J. Beveridge, *The Life of John Marshall;* 1921, Edward Bok, *The Americanization of Edward Bok;* 1922, Hamlin Garland, *A Daughter of the Middle Border;* 1923, Burton J. Hendrick, *The Life and Letters of Walter H. Page;* 1924, Michael Pupin, *From Immigrant to Inventor;* 1925, M. A. DeWolfe Howe, *Barrett Wendell and His Letters;* 1926, Harvey Cushing, *Life of Sir William Osler;* 1927, Emory Holloway, *Whitman, An Interpretation in Narrative;* 1928, Charles Edward Russell, *The American Orchestra and Theodore Thomas;* 1929, Burton J. Hendrick, *The Training of an American: The Earlier Life and Letters of Walter H. Page;* 1930, Marquis James, *The Raven* (Sam Houston); 1931, Henry James, *Charles W. Eliot;* 1932, Henry F. Pringle, *Theodore Roosevelt;* 1933, Allan Nevins, *Grover Cleveland;* 1934, Tyler Dennett, *John Hay;* 1935, Douglas Southall Freeman, *R. E. Lee;* 1936, Ralph Barton Perry, *The Thought and Character of William James;* 1937, Allan Nevins, *Hamilton Fish: The Inner History of the Grant Administration;* 1938, divided between Odell Shepard, *Pedlar's Progress,* and Marquis James, *Andrew Jackson;* 1939, Carl Van Doren, *Benjamin Franklin;* 1940, Ray Stannard Baker, *Woodrow Wilson, Life and Letters;* 1941, Ola Elizabeth Winslow, *Jonathan Edwards;* 1942, Forrest Wilson, *Crusader in Crinoline;* 1943, Samuel Eliot Morison, *Admiral of the Ocean Sea;* 1944, Carleton Mabee, *The American Leonardo: The Life of Samuel F. B. Morse;* 1945, Russel Blaine Nye, *George Bancroft: Brahmin Rebel;* 1946, Linnie Marsh Wolfe, *Son of the Wilderness;* 1947, William Allen White, *The Autobiography of William Allen White;* 1948, Margaret Clapp, *For-*

gotten First Citizen: John Bigelow; 1949, Robert E. Sherwood, *Roosevelt and Hopkins;* 1950, Samuel Flagg Bemis, *John Quincy Adams and the Foundations of American Foreign Policy;* 1951, Margaret Louise Coit, *John C. Calhoun: American Portrait;* 1952, Merlo J. Pusey, *Charles Evans Hughes;* 1953, David J. Mays, *Edmund Pendleton 1721–1803;* 1954, Charles A. Lindbergh, *The Spirit of St. Louis;* 1955, William S. White, *The Taft Story;* 1956, Talbot F. Hamlin, *Benjamin Henry Latrobe;* 1957, John F. Kennedy, *Profiles in Courage;* 1958, Douglas Southall Freeman (posthumous), *George Washington,* vols. I-VI, John Alexander Carroll and Mary Wells Ashworth, vol. VII; 1959, Arthur Walworth, *Woodrow Wilson, American Prophet;* 1960, Samuel Eliot Morison, *John Paul Jones;* 1961, David Donald, *Charles Sumner and the Coming of the Civil War;* 1962, none; 1963, Leon Edel, *Henry James: The Conquest of London and the Middle Years;* 1964, Walter Jackson Bate, *John Keats;* 1965, Ernest Samuels, *Henry Adams.*

General non-fiction: 1962, Theodore H. White, *The Making of the President, 1960;* 1963, Barbara Tuchman, *The Guns of August;* 1964, Richard Hofstadter, *Anti-Intellectualism in American Life.*

Pumblechook, Uncle. In Charles Dickens' GREAT EXPECTATIONS, Joe Gargery's uncle. He is patronizing to Pip until Pip comes into his fortune; then Pumblechook is extremely servile.

pun. A word-play in which two meanings appear in one word or in two words of identical sound. Used as a rather low form of wit, often in playful humor, a pun sometimes has deeply serious implications.

Ask for me tomorrow and you shall find me a grave man.
Shakespeare, *Romeo and Juliet*

Punch and Judy. The hero and heroine—and the title—of countless English puppet shows. In the traditional story, Punch, in a fit of rage, kills his infant child and bludgeons Judy, his wife, to death; although he is imprisoned, he manages to escape. Later he encounters and outwits several other characters, including the Devil. The irascible, humpbacked, hook-nosed Punch is thought to be derived from Pulcinella, the slow-witted servant of the *commedia dell'arte,* who was also a great favorite in Italian puppet shows. By about 1650, this character was appearing in puppet shows in France; transformed into the witty Polichinelle reaching England at the time of the Restoration, he became known as Punchinello or Punch. In their present form, Punch and his wife Judy, who was originally called Joan, date from about 1800.

Punchinello. See PUNCH AND JUDY.

Punic faith (Lat., *Punica fides*). Treachery, violation of faith, the faith of the Carthaginians. The Latin word *Punicus,* earlier *Poenicus,* meaning Phoenician, was applied to the Carthaginians, who were of Phoenician descent. The Carthaginians were accused by the Romans of breaking faith with them, a most extraordinary instance of the pot calling the kettle black; for whatever infidelity they were guilty of, it could scarcely equal that of their accusers.

Punic Wars. The three wars fought between Rome and Carthage in the third and second centuries B.C. The First Punic War (264–241 B.C.) was waged by Rome to prevent Carthaginian supremacy in Sicily. The second (218–202 B.C.) was fought over the Carthaginian advances in Spain, and it was during this war that HANNIBAL crossed the Alps with his army and ravaged Italy for nearly 15 years. At its conclusion Carthage was stripped of all its territories except its own city, and Rome was left mistress of the Mediterranean. The Third Punic War (149–146 B.C.) ended in the complete destruction of Carthage. See CATO THE ELDER.

puppet plays, Japanese. See JŌRURI.

Puranas (*Sans.* old material). A class of Sanskrit works, written around 500 B.C., serving as the secondary scriptures of Hinduism and containing the history and legends of the pantheon.

Purcell, Henry (1659–1695). The outstanding English Baroque composer. Purcell's early work consisted largely of church music. During the last few years of his life he turned his attention almost exclusively to music for the stage, and wrote one true opera *Dido and Aeneas* (1689?, libretto by Nahum TATE), and several so-called "English Operas," which are full-length musicodramatic works with spoken dialogue and elaborate scenic effects, similar to MASQUES. These works include: *King Arthur* (1691, libretto by Dryden); *The Fairy Queen* (1692, adapted from Shakespeare's *Midsummer Night's Dream*); *The Tempest* (1695?, adapted from Shakespeare by Shadwell); and *The Indian Queen* (1695, libretto by Dryden and Sir Thomas Howard). Purcell also composed incidental music, ranging from one song to long scenes, for 43 plays, including works by Aphra Behn (*Abdelazer*, 1695), Dryden (*Amphitryon*, 1690; *Aureng-Zebe*, 1692; *Love Triumphant*, 1694; *The Spanish Friar*, 1694–1695; four others), Congreve (*The Double Dealer*, 1693; *The Old Bachelor*, 1693), and works by 14 other playwrights.

Purchas, Samuel (1575?–1626). English author and clergyman, known for his editions of Elizabethan travel literature. His outstanding works are *Purchas His Pilgrimage, or Relations of the World and the Religions Observed in All Ages* (1613); *Purchas His Pilgrim: Microcosmus, or the Histories of Man* (1619); and *Hakluytus Posthumus, or Purchas His Pilgrims, Containing a History of the World in Sea Voyages and Land Travel by Englishmen and Others* (1625). The last-named work was compiled in part from material left by Richard Hakluyt. Coleridge is said to have used the narratives assembled by Purchas in his famous poems *The Rime of the Ancient Mariner* (1798) and *Kubla Khan* (1816).

Purdy, James (1923–   ). American novelist and short-story writer. Purdy's *Don't Call Me by My Rightful Name,* a collection of short stories, and *63: Dream Palace,* a novella, were privately published in 1956. Purdy was recognized as a writer of considerable talent, and in 1957 a commercial publisher combined the two privately printed books and issued them under the title *Color of Darkness.* Purdy employed the satiric and macabre fantasy he used in many of his short stories in his first novel, *Malcolm* (1959), a weird, picaresque tale that was highly praised by critics. *The Nephew* (1960) is a novel set in a region like the rural Ohio in which Purdy grew up; it deals with a retired schoolteacher who attempts

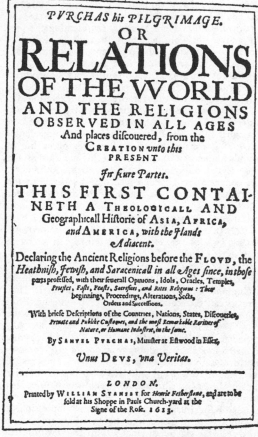

Title page of *Purchas His Pilgrimage* (1613).

to write a memorial booklet for her beloved nephew, who she fears has been killed.

Pure Land Buddhism. See AMIDISM.

Purgatorio (Purgatory). Part II of the DIVINE COMEDY by DANTE. Vergil conducts Dante up the mountain of Purgatory, or purification. At the foot in Ante-Purgatory are the negligent who for some reason delayed repentance for their sins and must wait as long as they delayed before beginning their ascent. A terrace makes an ascending spiral up the mountain, and repentant spirits toil forward on it, bowed beneath burdens appropriate to the sins of which they must be purged, and learning the corresponding virtues. The higher on the mountain the spirit is climbing, the less grievous the sin of which he is being cleansed, and the easier his progress, until at last he will be ready to join the blessed in Paradise. Dante must join in the labors of this ascent—although his progress is much more rapid than others—and he meets successively those doing penance for pride, envy, wrath, sloth, avarice, gluttony, and lust. Vergil explains that an instinct to love and desire is natural in man, and properly leads the soul to God. The first three sins are perversions of that instinct; sloth is the failure to pursue it; and the last three sins, although exercising the instinct, deflect it toward worldly objects and thus, at least temporarily away from God.

Having guided Dante as far as human intellect can go, Vergil leaves him at the entrance to the Earthly Paradise. Here Matilda, representing the perfect active life, conducts him through an Edenlike garden to BEATRICE, who represents the perfect contemplative life, or divine grace and revelation. After a series of allegorical appearances and adventures, representing the crises of the Roman Catholic Church, Beatrice prepares Dante for the ascent to Paradise.

Purgatory (1939). A short verse play by William Butler YEATS. For Yeats, purgatory is the condition of a spirit so obsessed by remorse or some other emotion that it constantly relives the crisis of its life in its old home. An old man and his son watch the ghost of the old man's mother in such a purgatory. The conversation between father and son reveals the family history and melodrama; at the end, the father kills his son in order to give his mother peace and put an end to the family's polluted blood.

Purgon. A quack doctor in Molière's comedy LE MALADE IMAGINAIRE. His favorite remedy, as his name suggests, is a purge.

purism. See LE CORBUSIER.

Puritans. Originally, seceders from the Church of England in the time of Queen Elizabeth I. They were so called because as radical, or Calvinistic, Protestants, who acknowledged only the authority of the "pure Word of God" as expressed in the Bible, they wished to "purify" the church of its Catholic heritage of doctrines, rites, and organization. Early persecution drove them to emigrate in large numbers to Europe and New England; later they played a major role in the social and religious conflicts of the 17th century. In both England and America the rigid morals of the Puritans and their stern suppression of various forms of recreation and art have made the word *puritanical* synonymous with narrow-mindedness.

Purloined Letter, The (1845). A story by Edgar Allan POE. A woman of royal rank is blackmailed by a cabinet minister on the basis of a compromising letter. The police, failing in the search, turn to the amateur, C. Auguste DUPIN, who is able to locate the purloined letter.

Purple Cow, The. A famous quatrain by Gelett BURGESS that first appeared in the *Lark* (1895).

> I never saw a PURPLE COW,
> I never HOPE to see one;
> But I can tell you, anyhow,
> I'd rather SEE than BE one.

Some years later, for obvious reasons, he recorded his sentiments with,

> Ah. Yes! I Wrote the PURPLE COW—
> I'm Sorry, now, I Wrote it!
> But I can Tell you Anyhow,
> I'll KILL you if you QUOTE it!

purple patches. Highly colored or ornate passages in a literary work that is, generally speaking, otherwise undistinguished. The allusion is to Horace's *De Arte Poetica:*

> Inceptis gravibus plerumque et magna professis,
> Purpureus, late qui splendeat, unus et alter
> Adsuitur pannus.

(Often to weighty enterprises and such as profess great objects, one or two purple patches are sewed on to make a fine display in the distance.)

Pursuit of Diarmuid and Gráinne, The. An early Irish tale from the FENIAN CYCLE. It is a variant of the Deirdre story and an early parallel to the Tristan and Iseult legend. Diarmuid, nephew of FIONN MAC CUMHAIL, runs off with Fionn's second wife Gráinne. The major part of the story concerns the life of the lovers in the wilderness, fleeing from Fionn and his forces, and finally being caught by Fionn.

Puru. In Hindu legend, the founder of the lunar dynasty.

Pururavas and Urvasi. A Hindu myth similar to those of Cupid and Psyche or Apollo and Daphne. King Pururavas fell in love with Urvasi, the heavenly nymph born as a result of the churning of the waters by the gods searching for the lost nectar of immortality, and she consented to become his wife on certain conditions. When these conditions were violated, she disappeared, and Pururavas, inconsolable, wandered everywhere to find her. Ultimately he succeeded, and they were indissolubly united. The best-known version of the story is found in Kalidasa's third century Sanskrit play, *Vikrama and Urvasi.*

Pusey, E[dward] B[ouverie] (1800–1882). Anglican theologian, associated with John Keble and John Henry Newman in the OXFORD MOVEMENT. Perhaps the staunchest controversialist and most learned theologian in the movement, Pusey became its virtual leader after Newman's conversion to Roman Catholicism, effecting many changes in the churches of England, such as the establishment of Anglican nunneries and the revival of private confession. His works consist mainly of controversies or doctrinal writings. See TRACTS FOR THE TIMES.

Pushkin, Aleksandr Sergeyevich (1799–1837). Russian poet, dramatist, novelist, and short-story writer. Russia's greatest poet, whose standing in his own country is equivalent to Shakespeare's in England or Goethe's in Germany, Pushkin almost singlehandedly created a classical literary heritage for Russian writers, producing the first good examples of work in almost every major genre.

Pushkin was a descendant on his father's side of an ancient noble family. On his mother's side he was a great-great-grandson of an Abyssinian Negro, Gannibal, who served under Peter the Great. Pushkin's poetry attracted attention even before he graduated from the Lyceum in 1817. He obtained a sinecure in the foreign ministry in St. Petersburg, led a fast-paced social life, and wrote *Ruslan i Lyudmila* (*Ruslan and Ludmilla,* 1820), a long poem based on folklore motifs. The work established him as one of the outstanding younger poets. Because of some politically indiscreet verses, Pushkin was transferred in 1820 to southern Russia. He traveled in the Caucasus, served in Bessarabia and Odessa, and continued his poetic works, which at this period show the influence of Byron in theme and treatment: *Kavkazski Plennik* (*The Captive of the Caucasus,* 1822), *Bakhchisaraiski Fontan* (*The Fountain of Bakhchisaray,* 1824), and *Tzygany* (*The Gypsies,* 1827). He also began his greatest work, EUGENE ONEGIN, a novel in verse.

Pushkin's trouble with the authorities continued. In 1824 he was expelled from government service and banished to his family estate. While there he wrote his famous historical tragedy, BORIS GODUNOV. Pushkin was on the family estate when the Decembrist revolt of 1825 took place. Several of his friends were involved in the affair, but he apparently had no connection with it. In 1826, Pushkin was given permission by Czar Nicholas I to return to St. Petersburg, where he resumed the active social life interrupted six years before. In 1829 he met 16-year-old Natalya Goncharova, whom he married two years later. In the autumn of 1830, while stranded by a plague quarantine on his country estate at Boldino, Pushkin wrote *Tales of* BELKIN, began the LITTLE TRAGEDIES, a cycle of four tragedies in verse, and completed his masterpiece, *Eugene Onegin*. After his marriage, he had little peace for such intense creative activity. His wife's frivolous social life was a constant source of irritation, and a growing family necessitated added income. In 1836 he founded the literary journal *Sovremennik (The Contemporary)*. Jealousy over his wife's attachment to a guards officer, Baron Georges D'Anthes, led to a duel, in January, 1837, in which Pushkin was fatally wounded.

Besides the poems mentioned, Pushkin produced a large body of lyric verse, as well as numerous long poems, including *Graf Nulin (Count Nulin, 1825), Domik v Kolomne (The Little House in Kolomna, 1830), Poltava (1828),* and THE BRONZE HORSEMAN. His prose work includes, besides the Belkin tales, *Dubrovski (1832–1833),* THE QUEEN OF SPADES, and *Kapitanskaya dochka (The Captain's Daughter, 1836),* an account of the PUGACHEV rebellion of the 1770's.

Much of Pushkin's work had an immense influence on later Russian literature. He was the master for all the poets who came after him in both lyric and narrative poetry. His character Ivan Belkin, the narrator of the Belkin tales and of the prose fragment *Istoriya sela Goryukhina (History of the Village of Goryukhino, 1830),* is one of the initial models of a realistic depiction of character in Russian literature. Eugene Onegin is one of the original SUPERFLUOUS MEN of Russian literature, the ancestor of Lermontov's Pechorin and of many of Turgenev's heroes. Tatyana, the heroine of *Onegin,* has been regarded as the ideal of Russian womanhood, and many later writers, again notably Turgenev, have modeled their heroines after her.

Pushkin's early poetic style was influenced by the classical styles of such 18th-century French writers as Voltaire, Evariste Parny, and André Chenier. The smoothness and balance of Pushkin's diction in his early works were learned from these authors and from his own compatriots who imitated them: ZHUKOVSKI and Konstantin Nikolayevich Batyushkov (1787–1855). *The Prisoner of the Caucasus* and *The Fountain of Bakhchisarai* are perhaps the best examples of Pushkin's early manner. In a letter of 1823, Pushkin wrote, "I don't like grafting European graces and French subtleties onto our old language. Roughness and simplicity suit it better." Pushkin's poetic style from this time on reflects these thoughts. His language becomes more concise than before, and it loses its mellifluent qualities, reaching the limits of simplicity in such late works as *Poltava (1828–1829)* and *The Bronze Horseman.* The shift in poetic style was accompanied by a change in Pushkin's relationship to his work: from that of a narrator who is sometimes subjectively involved in the work to that of an objective creator who is always outside the work. This objectivity is particularly evident in Pushkin's prose works. In these works, the language is extremely simple and straightforward, and instances can be found in the prose where Pushkin changed the ordinary Russian word order to make the language even more simple than it would be normally. Although many of his prose pieces—such as the Belkin tales, *The Queen of Spades,* and *The Captain's Daughter*—have been very influential in Russian literature because of their themes and characterizations, Pushkin's prose language was too experimental a medium to be more than a starting point for later writers.

Puss in Boots. A famous tale with many sources. It is best known from Charles PERRAULT's tale *Le Chat Botté* (1697). The cat is marvelously accomplished, and by ready wit or ingenious tricks secures a fortune and royal wife for his master, a penniless young miller, who passes under the name of the marquis de Carabas. In the Italian tale, Puss is called "Constantine's cat." Ludwig TIECK's play *Der gestiefelte Kater* (pub. 1797) also treats this theme.

Putain respectueuse, La. See RESPECTFUL PROSTITUTE, THE.

Putnam, George Palmer (1814–1872). American publisher. Putnam educated himself while working as an errand boy in a New York book store; in 1833, he began to work for the publishing firm of Wiley and Long; in 1840, the name was changed to Wiley and Putnam. He then opened an agency in London for the sale of American books, and wrote a volume called *American Facts* (1845) to instruct the British. In 1853, Putnam began the publication of *Putnam's Monthly Magazine,* one of the best of the mid-century American periodicals; he did not pirate English works unprotected by copyright, but encouraged and paid for the original work of American authors. A lifelong friend and admirer of Washington Irving, he published "Recollections of Irving" in *The Atlantic Monthly* (November, 1860). In 1866, Putnam established the publishing firm of G. P. Putnam, later changing it to G. P. Putnam & Sons (1871). Active in the fight for an international copyright law, he sponsored the cause of a native American literature.

Putnam, Israel (1718–1790). American army officer. He was commander-in-chief of the Revolutionary forces during the battle of Long Island (1776), though there is uncertainty over the extent of his responsibility for the disastrous American defeat.

Putnam, [Howard] Phelps (1894–1948). American poet. Putnam published two volumes of verse, *Trinc* (1927) and *The Five Seasons* (1930). At his death he left a long incomplete philosophical poem, *The Earthly Comedy.*

Putsch (Ger., "uprising"). A small armed revolt, such as the KAPP PUTSCH or BEER-HALL PUTSCH.

Puttenham, George (d. 1590). English author. He is known for *The Arte of English Poesie* (1589), a thoroughgoing analysis of the types and techniques of Tudor and Elizabethan poetry. Much esteemed in its day, the treatise is still regarded as a sourcebook of poetic theory of the English Renaissance. The work is sometimes attributed to George's brother, Richard Puttenham (1520?–1601?).

Put Yourself in His Place (1870). A novel by Charles READE. The hero, Henry Little, a laborer and inventor, struggles against the jealous antagonisms of the British trade unions, and his efforts to effect a reconciliation between them form the body of the narrative. The title is derived from the favorite saying of the philanthropist Dr. Amboyne, one of the book's important characters.

Pye, Henry James (1745–1813). English poet laureate (1790) who wrote occasional and ineffectual patriotic verse. His epic *Alfred* (1801) is considered his best work.

Pygmalion. A sculptor and king of Cyprus in Greek legend, who, though he hated women, fell in love with his own ivory statue of Aphrodite. At his earnest prayer the goddess gave life to the statue and he married his own creation.

The story is told in Ovid's *Metamorphoses,* and appeared in English in John Marston's *Metamorphosis of Pygmalion's Image* (1598). William Morris retold it in *The Earthly Paradise* (1868). In W. S. Gilbert's comedy, *Pygmalion and Galatea* (1871), the sculptor is a married man and his wife Cynisca is jealous of the animated statue Galatea, which, after considerable trouble returns to its original state. George Bernard Shaw's play PYGMALION takes its name from this legendary figure.

Pygmalion (1913). A play by George Bernard SHAW. Based on the classical legend, Shaw's work is about human relations and the delicate modern social order. The Pygmalion of the play is Professor Henry Higgins, a teacher of phonetics. He takes on Eliza Doolittle, a Cockney flower girl, as his student. She is transformed from a guttersnipe into an elegant woman, but then, like the statue of the legend, having come to life, she falls in love with Higgins. His is the responsibility for having made her a lady; she cannot return to her former life, but Shaw makes it clear that she does not marry the professor. *Pygmalion* was made into a successful musical comedy, *My Fair Lady* (1956).

pygmies (from Gr. *pygme,* the length of the arm from elbow to knuckles). The name used by Homer and other classical writers for a supposed race of dwarfs. They were said to dwell somewhere in Ethiopia. Fable has it that every spring the cranes made war on these creatures and devoured them. The pygmies required axes to cut down cornstalks. When HERACLES went to the country, they climbed up his goblet by ladders to drink from it, and while he was asleep two whole armies of them fell upon his right hand, and two upon his left. They were rolled up by Heracles in his lion's skin. Jonathan Swift used this legend in his *Gulliver's Travels.*

The term is now applied to certain dwarfish races of Central Africa, unknown until late in the 19th century, and of Malaysia.

Pylades. The son of Strophius and loyal friend of Orestes. He appears in several Greek dramas about Orestes, often as a mute character, but plays a noble role in Euripides' *Iphigenia in Tauris.* He married Electra. His friendship for Orestes, like that of Damon and Pythias, is proverbial. See IPHIGENIA and the House of ATREUS.

Pyle, Ernie (1900–1945). American war correspondent. Pyle's dispatches from the front during World War II were admired by soldiers and civilians alike for their honesty and warmth. He was killed by Japanese gunfire on a small island off the coast of Okinawa. Some of his columns were collected in *Here Is Your War* (1943) and *Brave Men* (1944).

Pym, John (1584–1643). English Parliamentary statesman and orator. As leader of the anti-Royalist extremists in the Long Parliament, he prosecuted the case against the earl of STRAFFORD and sponsored the GRAND REMONSTRANCE. His intransigence contributed to the outbreak of the Civil War.

Pyncheon. The name of the Salem family who built and lived in THE HOUSE OF THE SEVEN GABLES in Hawthorne's novel of that name.

Pynson, Richard (d. 1530). English printer. With Wynkyn de WORDE, he succeeded William CAXTON as king's printer. He introduced Roman type into England, and printed Alexander Barclay's *Ship of Fools* (1509) and an edition of Chaucer (1526).

Pyramus. A Babylonian youth in classical story (Ovid's *Metamorphoses*), the lover of Thisbe. Thisbe was to meet him at the white mulberry-tree near the tomb of Ninus, but she was scared by a lion and fled, leaving her veil, which the lion smeared with blood. Pyramus, thinking she had been killed committed suicide. When Thisbe returned she found her lover dead and stabbed herself. The legend says that their blood stained the white fruit of the mulberry-tree to its present color.

The "tedious brief scene" and "very tragical mirth" presented by the rustic tradesmen in Shakespeare's MIDSUMMER NIGHT'S DREAM is a travesty of this legend.

Pyrocles. See FAERIE QUEENE, THE.

Pyrrha. The wife of Deucalion in Greek legend. They were the sole survivors of the deluge sent by Zeus to destroy the whole human race, and repopulated the world by casting stones behind them. (See DEUCALION'S FLOOD.)

Pyrrhonism. A school of Greek philosophy named after Pyrrho (c. 365–275 B.C.). Pyrrho believed that virtue is the only good, and all other things are indifferent. Realizing the eternal nature of good helped him to achieve a tranquil state called *ataraxy.* In the field of action, Pyrrho relied upon convention and custom; only in the sphere of truth did he refuse to rely on human cognition. The attitude of Pyrrho was later refined, and referred to as SKEPTICISM.

Pyramus and Thisbe. From a book of romances (1494).

Pythagoras (6th century B.C.). A Greek philosopher and mathematician. Almost nothing is known of his life, except that he was born on the island of Samos; it is probable that he studied with Pherecydes and he may have visited Egypt. Reliable information even on his teachings is scant, but he is known to have been interested in mathematics, especially in relation to weights and measures, and musical theory. He is best known for his doctrine of the transmigration of souls and the harmony of the spheres, although the proof of the so-called Pythagorean theorem (the 47th proposition of Euclid, Book One) is also attributed to him. He founded a semi-monastic school of philosophy in Crotona, Italy, where he apparently practiced divination, among other arts. He was regarded by his contemporaries with mingled awe and suspicion, and many wild tales grew up of his supernatural powers. The meeting place of Pythagoras' secret society was set afire and the sect suppressed almost everywhere. Whether Pythagoras himself died at this time or later is uncertain. Among the tales told of him are that he had a golden thigh, that he recalled previous existences, including one as Euphorbus, who fought at Troy, and that he was an incarnation of the Hyperborean Apollo.

Pythagoreans. Followers of PYTHAGORAS. They lived almost monastic lives, observing many ascetical practices. In later times their doctrines became associated with ORPHISM.

Pythia. The title of the priestess of the famous DELPHIC ORACLE.

Pythian games. One of the four great national Greek festivals. These games were celebrated every four years at Delphi in honor of Apollo. The games were supposed to have been instituted by Apollo in commemoration of his slaying of the serpent Python. Prizes were also given for music, poetry, sculpture, and painting. See DELPHIC ORACLE.

Python. The monster serpent hatched from the mud of DEUCALION's FLOOD. It was slain near Delphi by Apollo. It was the ancient guardian of the shrine of the DELPHIC ORACLE and probably an oracular serpent.

Q

Q. See Sir Arthur QUILLER-COUCH.

quadrivium (Lat. *quadri,* four, and *via,* way). The collective name of the Schoolmen of the Middle Ages for the four liberal arts, arithmetic, music, geometry, and astronomy. The quadrivium was the fourfold way to knowledge. The threefold way to eloquence, the trivium (Lat. *tres,* three, and *via*), consisted of grammar, rhetoric, and logic. Together the quadrivium and trivium comprised the seven LIBERAL ARTS.

Quadruple Alliance. An international alliance for offensive or defensive purposes.

(1) In 1718, England, France, the Holy Roman Emperor, and the Netherlands formed such an alliance when Philip V of Spain sought to rescind the peace settlements reached after the War of the Spanish Succession.

(2) The best-known Quadruple Alliance was formed in 1814 by Great Britain, Austria, Prussia, and Russia to strengthen the coalition against Napoleon I; after Napoleon's final defeat, the alliance was renewed in order to insure the execution of the Treaty of Paris of 1815.

(3) In 1834, Great Britain, France, Spain, and Portugal formed an alliance in order to strengthen the constitutional government of Spain and the throne of Isabella II against the Carlists.

quaestor. In ancient Rome, one of 20 treasury officials. See CURSUS HONORUM.

Quai d'Orsay. The French Foreign Office, named from its location in Paris.

Quakers. A familiar name for members of the Society of Friends, an evangelical Christian religious sect founded by George Fox. They have no definite creed and no regular ministry, but are guided by their doctrine of INNER LIGHT. Their tenets include pacifism, a refusal to take oaths, and originally a characteristic simplicity in dress and speech (i.e., use of the archaic "Thee" and "Thou"). "Justice Bennett, of Derby," says Fox, "was the first to call us Quakers, because I bade him quake and tremble at the word of the Lord."

Quality Street (1901). A drama by J. M. BARRIE. When she sees that her lover, Valentine Brown, finds her disappointingly like a mousy spinster on his return from a long absence, Phoebe Throssel transforms herself into the younger, gayer girl that she was, calling herself Livvy, niece of Phoebe, and thus reconquers her love.

Quarles, Francis (1592–1644). English poet of the METAPHYSICAL SCHOOL. His religious poetry, similar to that of George Herbert, is marked by an elliptical, colloquial, or hortatory style and by striking imagery chosen from the everyday pursuits and interests of his time. He is best known for *Emblems* (1635), a book of poems accompanied by appropriate pictures, which won enormous popularity in its day. His other works include *A Feast for Worms* (1620), *Argalus und Parthenia* (1629), *History of Samson* (1631), *Divine Fancies* (1632), and *Hieroglyphics* (1638). See EMBLEM BOOKS.

Quasimodo. The deformed bell ringer of Notre Dame in Victor Hugo's novel, THE HUNCHBACK OF NOTRE DAME.

Quasímodo, Salvatore (1901–1968). Italian poet. He was awarded the Nobel Prize for literature in 1959. His work falls into two periods: a pre-World War II "hermetic" period characterized by a recondite style and metaphysical content (see HERMETICISM) and a postwar "engagé" period concerned with the interpretation of contemporary history, social conditions, and the aspirations of the common man. His verse of the first period includes the collections *Waters and Land* (*Acque e Terre;* 1929), *Sunken Oboe* (*Oboe Sommerso;* 1932), *Aerato and Apollyon* (*Erato e Apollion;* 1936), and *Poesie* (1938). Postwar works include *Ed E' Subito Sera* (1954), *Day After Day* (*Giorno Dopo Giorno;* 1947), *Il Falso e Vero Verde* (1956), and the songbook *Tutte Le Poesie* (1960). He has also translated Greek lyrics and various works of Molière, Shakespeare, and E. E. Cummings into Italian.

quatrain. In prosody, a stanza containing four lines in any meter, especially the ballad stanza, the *In Memoriam* stanza, which rhymes a-b-b-a, and the *Rubáiyát* stanza, which rhymes a-a-b-a.

quattrocento (It., "the four hundreds"). The Italian way of designating the 15th century. The term thus refers to the early RENAISSANCE, the age of HUMANISM, and the period of the REVIVAL OF ANTIQUITY, and in art history, to the century and the style of such artists as Masaccio, Botticelli, Fra Angelico, Ghiberti, Brunelleschi, and Donatello.

Queen, Ellery. Pen name of Frederic Dannay (1905–   ) and Manfred B. Lee (1905–1971). American detective-story writers and editors. The two are cousins whose fictional sleuth Ellery Queen has exercised his ratiocinative powers in numerous successful novels and stories since he made his first appearance in *The Roman Hat Mystery* (1929). Under the pseudonym Barnaby Ross, they also occasionally write about detective Drury Lane. Among their books are *Drury Lane's Last Case* (1933), *The Four of Hearts* (1938), and *The Origin of Evil* (1951). In 1941, they began to edit *Ellery Queen's Mystery Magazine,* making it the finest and best-known periodical in the field.

Queen Mab. See Percy Bysshe SHELLEY.

Queen of Hearts. A character in Lewis Carroll's ALICE'S ADVENTURES IN WONDERLAND. Every time she is crossed or defeated during her mad croquet match, the queen shouts "Off with his head!" at the offender. When Alice points out that the trial of the Knave of Hearts, alleged to have stolen some tarts, is being absurdly conducted, the queen replies irrefutably, "Off with her head!"

Queen of Spades, The (*Pikovaya dama*; 1833). A short story by Aleksandr PUSHKIN. Although it belongs to the Gothic tradition of horror the tale is unusual for the calm, matter-of-fact manner in which the breakdown of the gambler Germann is related. Pushkin's prose style in this story is at its barest and most simple. Tchaikovsky based an opera on the story.

Queffélec, Henri (1910–). French novelist. Concerned with crises of conscience and religious faith, he usually sets his novels in his native Brittany, often among the fishermen, as in *Island Priest* (*Un recteur de l'île de Sein*; 1944, filmed as *God Needs Men*) and *The Kingdom Under the Sea* (*Un Royaume sous la mer*; 1957). His other works include *Saint Anthony of the Desert* (1950) and *Frontier of the Unknown* (*Combat contre l'invisible*; 1958, also translated as *The Men of Damezan*).

Queiroz, José Maria Eça de. See José Maria EÇA DE QUEIROZ.

Quem quaeritis (Whom seek ye?) **trope.** A text in the medieval Easter liturgy. It was in the form of a dialog between the women and the angel at the empty tomb of the risen Christ. At about the beginning of the 11th century it began to be acted out during the service of Matins. The brief scene was gradually expanded, with priests, nuns, and choirboys taking the parts. From this simple beginning grew the medieval drama. See MYSTERY PLAYS.

Queneau, Raymond (1903–). French novelist, poet, and critic. Queneau is best known for the acid wit of such novels as *Skin of Dreams* (*Loin de Rueil*; 1944), and *Zazie* (1959). He has also published poetry, including *Chêne et chien* (1937), *Petite Cosmogonie portative* (1950), and *Si tu t'imagines* (1952).

Quennell, Peter [Courtney] (1905–). English poet, literary critic, and biographer. He is an authority on Byron and Ruskin. Among his books are *Baudelaire and the Symbolists* (1929), *Caroline of England* (1939), and *The Sign of the Fish* (1960). His parents, Charles Henry Quennell (1872–1935) and Marjorie Quennell (1884–) published a noteworthy series of popular educational books, including *A History of Everyday Things in England* (1918–1934; 4 vols.).

Quental, Antero Tarquínio de (1842–1891). Portuguese poet. Born in the Azores, he studied at the university of Coimbra, where he became a leader of the "Coimbra generation" of students who sought to revivify Portuguese literature. His famous pamphlet *Do bom senso e bom gosto* (1866) sparked the *questão Coimbra*, a bitter literary dispute in which the younger generation rebelled against the sterile romanticism, divorced from contemporary reality, that was exemplified by the works of the blind poet António Castilho. Influenced by Hegel and Proudhon, Quental was a socialist for a time but failed to find a creed that would satisfy his spiritual and moral aspirations. Having retired from public life in 1874, he returned in 1891 to his native island, where he took his own life in a public park.

As a poet Quental is best known for his sonnets, which constitute a spiritual autobiography of his tortured existence. About 150 of these are collected in *Sonetos Completos* (1886). He also wrote *Raios de Extinta Luz* (1859–1863) and *Primaveras Românticas* (1871), poems representative of his early romantic phase, and *Odas Modernas* (1865), in which he gave expression to his revolutionary views.

Quentin Durward (1823). A romantic novel by Sir Walter SCOTT set in 15th-century France. Durward, a gallant young member of Louis XI's Scottish Guards, seeks the hand of Isabella, countess of Croye. His suit prospers when he saves the king's life in a boar hunt.

Querelle des anciens et des modernes (Quarrel of the Ancients and the Moderns). A French literary battle of the late 17th century between the ancients (classicists), who believed that literature should adhere to models and even to themes of antiquity, and the modernists, who did not wish literature to be thus restricted. The first leading spokesman for the modernists, DESMARETS, was promptly condemned by BOILEAU. The ensuing dispute engaged the entire world of French letters and ended at the turn of the century with Boileau's partial capitulation.

Quesnay, François (1694–1774). Physician to Louis XV of France. As an economist, he contributed articles to the ENCYCLOPÉDIE, which, along with his *Tableau économique* (1758), were the basis for the theory adopted by the PHYSIOCRATS. His thought influenced, among others, Adam Smith.

Quesnel, Pasquier (1634–1719). French theologian. Quesnel was the chief spokesman after the death of Arnauld for the Jansenists in their dispute with the Jesuits. His enormously popular *Réflexions morales sur le Nouveau Testament* (*Moral Reflections on the New Testament*, 1671) was condemned in the papal bull *Unigenitus* (1713).

Quetzalcoatl. The nature god of various Indian tribes in Mexico prior to the Spanish conquest. His symbol was the *quetzal* or royal bird, known abroad as the emblem of Guatemala.

Quevedo [y Villegas], **Francisco Gómez de** (1580–1645). Spanish satirist, moralist, and poet. Born in Madrid of a good family, Quevedo studied at Alcalá. After a hasty flight from Spain to escape the consequences of a duel in which he had slain a noble (1611), Quevedo entered the service of the duke of Osuna in Italy. When Osuna fell from favor, Quevedo was exiled to his estate in La Mancha. In 1639 he was accused of having slipped into the king's napkin a satiric poem against the royal favorite, the count-duke of Olivares, and was imprisoned in the monastery of San Marcos in Leon. He was released in 1643, his health shattered.

A prolific writer who essayed nearly every genre, Quevedo is remembered mainly for his vitriolic satires, in which he mercilessly exposed the follies and vices of mankind. The best known are the picaresque novel EL BUSCÓN and the SUEÑOS, a series of burlesque descriptions of Hell. His other prose works include *Política de Dios* (1626), a treatise on Christian rule; *Marco Bruto* (1644), a commentary on Plutarch's life of Brutus; a life of St. Paul (1644); and translations from Seneca, Epictetus, and St. François de Sales.

In poetry as in prose Quevedo excelled as a satirist. Over 800 of his poems have been preserved, but the best of these are the picaresque ballads and light verses that enable him to display his wit and familiarity with low life. An excellent stylist, he used CONCEPTISM to good effect, though it sometimes marred his most ambitious works.

Quickly, Mistress Nell. In Shakespeare's HENRY IV: PART I and PART II and HENRY V, the excitable and stupid hostess of the Boar's Head Tavern in Eastcheap, frequented by Prince Hal, Sir John Falstaff and their disreputable crew. In THE MERRY WIVES OF WINDSOR, she becomes servant of all work to Doctor Caius and devotes her boundless energy to securing a husband for Anne Page. Her husband is Pistol.

Quiet Don, The (Tikhii Don; 4 vols., 1928–1940). A novel by Mikhail SHOLOKHOV. Regarded as the outstanding work of early Soviet literature, this four-volume work is an epic of the revolution's intrusion into the Don Cossack region of Russia and of the struggle between the old and new ways of life, both on the battlefields and within men's hearts. The hero of the work, a young Cossack named Gregor Melekhov, unlike the positive hero demanded by the Soviet literary doctrine of SOCIALIST REALISM, vacillates between the two choices. He is at first convinced that the Bolsheviks are right, then gives up this view and fights with the Whites in the Civil War, intending to help the Cossacks maintain their independence after the fighting is over. At the end of the novel, Melekhov is tending to favor the Bolsheviks again, but he is still not firmly convinced which side is best. His hesitation is set against the fanatical conviction of such Communists as Ivan Bunchuk, who is killed by Cossacks siding with the Whites. Even such characters as Bunchuk, however, are treated by Sholokhov as multidimensional human beings, rather than as the undeviating automatons that Soviet literary theorists would have preferred. There is reason to believe that Soviet authorities expected Sholokhov to convert Melekhov into a believing Communist at the end of his novel. By the time the fourth volume was published, they realized that the work was too popular to condemn severely and that they had to accept the novel as a Soviet literary classic, as it deserved to be for its artistic merits.

The first half of *The Quiet Don* was published in English as *And Quiet Flows the Don* (1934) and the second half as *The Don Flows Home to the Sea* (1941).

Quietism. A form of religious mysticism based on the doctrine that the essence of religion consists in the withdrawal of the soul from external objects and in fixing it upon the contemplation of God. Specifically, the term is applied to the creed professed by the Spanish mystic Miguel Molinos (1640–1696), who taught the direct relationship between the soul and God. His followers were called Molinists or Quietists.

Quijote de la Mancha, Don. See DON QUIXOTE.

Quiller-Couch, Sir Arthur [Thomas]. Pen name, **Q.** (1863–1944). English man of letters. Especially known as editor of The *Oxford Book of English Verse* (first published in 1900) and several other anthologies in that series, he was, from 1912 until his death, professor of English literature at Cambridge. He completed Robert Louis Stevenson's *St. Ives* (1893), and was the author of many novels, short stories, and romances, the most noted being *The Golden Spur* (1889) which, like most of the others, has for its background his native Cornwall. In addition, he wrote *Poems and Ballads* (1896) and published several volumes of literary criticism.

Quilp, Daniel. In Charles Dickens' OLD CURIOSITY SHOP, a hideous dwarf, cunning and malicious, who collects rents, advances money to seamen, and keeps a sort of wharf containing rusty anchors, huge iron rings, and piles of rotten wood; he calls himself a ship-breaker. He is on the point of being arrested for felony when he is drowned.

Quinault, Philippe (1635–1688). French playwright. Ill-starred love provides the subject for his tragedies: *La Mort de Cyrus* (*The Death of Cyrus*, 1656), *Amalasonte* (1657), and ASTRATE, ROI DE TYR. His most successful comedy, *La Mère Coquette* (*The Flirtatious Mother*, 1665), depicts the triumph of two young people's love over the amorous intrigues of their elders. Quinault supplied librettos for many of the ballets and operas of LULLY, and it is for his contributions to the French lyric theater that he is best remembered. His operas include *Alceste* (1674) and *Armide* (1686).

Quinbus Flestrin. A name given Gulliver in the first book of GULLIVER's TRAVELS by Jonathan Swift which means "man mountain" in the language of LILLIPUT. Swift's contemporaries occasionally refer to him by this name, and John Gay wrote an ode in honor of Quinbus Flestrin.

Quince, Peter. See BOTTOM.

Quint, Peter. See TURN OF THE SCREW, THE.

Quintana, Manuel José (1772–1857). Spanish poet and statesman. Two ideals—patriotism and liberalism—guided Quintana's public life and literary work. He denounced the Napoleonic invaders of Spain and took an active part in the Central Junta, only to be imprisoned by the reactionary Ferdinand VII. During the liberal period of 1820–1823 he served as director of public instruction.

His best-known poems are his patriotic odes, notably *A España, después de la revolución de marzo* and *Al armamento de las provincias españolas contra los franceses* (both 1808), in which nationalist fervor is wedded to classical form. He also wrote a majestic *Oda a la invención de la imprenta* (1800). His other works include two tragedies, *El duque de Viseo* (1801) and *Pelayo* (1805); *Vidas de los españoles célebres* (1807–1833), a series of nine biographies; and 10 letters to Lord Holland, written in 1823–1824, on contemporary Spanish politics.

Quintilian. Full Latin name, **Marcus Fabius Quintilianus** c. A.D. 35–c. 99). Spanish-born rhetorician and teacher of oratory in Rome (from A.D. 68). His most important work was his *De Institutione Oratoria* (*On the Training of an Orator*), which he published in 96 after a long and successful career of oratory and teaching. Like Cicero in his *De Oratore*, Quintilian proposes to give an educational schedule for the training of the ideal orator. Throughout, he emphasizes the importance of personal integrity and honest conviction in the art of public persuasion. The book is a valuable source for us today for it describes, in minute detail, the educational advantages available to the well-to-do Roman youth of the first century, and includes, as good and bad examples, selections from the works of Latin authors whose writings would otherwise have been entirely lost.

Quirinus. See ROMULUS.

Quiroga, Horacio (1878–1937). Uruguayan short-story writer. Quiroga wrote poetry and novels, including *Historia de un amor turbio* (1908), but he was most successful in the short-story form. Although he never lost his initial tendencies toward MODERNISM, his prose became clearer and his narrative technique more realistic. His best-known stories are set in the jungles of Misiones territory in Argentina where he spent many years. In some, such as those collected in *Cuentos de la selva* (1918) and *Anaconda* (1921), the protagonists are animals. The stories are characterized by haunting, imaginative depictions of the forces of nature, which seem to dwarf the fears and passions of his characters. Other collections include *Cuentos de amor, de locura y de muerte* (1917) and *La gallina degollada y otros cuentos* (1925).

Quisling, Vidkun (1887–1945). Norwegian polit-ical figure. He actively collaborated in the German conquest of Norway (1940) and became head of the State Council under the Nazis. After the German defeat he was tried and executed. His name has become a synonym for *traitor*.

Quixote, Don. See DON QUIXOTE.

Qumram manuscripts. See DEAD SEA SCROLLS.

Quoirez, Françoise. See Françoise SAGAN.

Quo Vadis? (1896). A historical novel by H. SIENKIEWICZ. It deals with the Rome of Nero and the early Christian martyrs. The Roman noble, Petronius, a worthy representative of the dying paganism, is perhaps the most interesting figure, and the struggle between Christianity and paganism supplies the central plot, but the canvas is large. A succession of characters and episodes and, above all, the richly colorful, decadent life of ancient Rome give the novel its chief interest. The beautiful Christian Lygia is the object of unwelcome attentions from Vinicius, one of the Emperor's guards, and when she refuses to yield to his importunities, she is denounced and thrown to the wild beasts of the arena. She escapes and eventually marries Vinicius, whom Peter and Paul have converted to Christianity. *Quo Vadis?* has been translated into nearly every language.

R

Ra. In ancient Egyptian religion, one of the most frequent names given to the sun god, the supposed ancestor of all the Pharaohs. He was worshiped as the creator and protector of men and the vanquisher of evil; it was said that men and women were made from his tears. He is usually represented with the head of a falcon and crowned with the solar disk and uraeus, the symbol of power over life and death. See AMEN; APOPHIS.

Raabe, Wilhelm (1831–1910). German realistic novelist. He is known for the pessimistic irony and cultural criticism found in the three novels that established his fame: *Der Hungerpastor* (*The Hunger-Pastor*, 1864), *Abu Telfan* (1868), and *Der Schüdderump* (1870). His style, however, often shows a benign, forgiving humor about his characters. In his later works, for example *Stopfkuchen* (1891), he began to experiment more with the form of the novel, and often created complicated time-structures.

Rab and his Friends (1859). A dog story by Dr. John BROWN. Rab is described as "old, gray, brindled, as big as a little Highland bull," extraordinarily faithful and affectionate.

Rabbi Ben Ezra (1855). A famous poem on old age by Robert BROWNING. First published in the collection *Dramatis Personae* (1864), it opens with the well-known lines:

> Grow old along with me!
> The best is yet to be,
> The last of life, for which the first was made.

The supposed speaker, Rabbi Ben Ezra (c. 1090–1168), was one of the most distinguished Jewish literati of the Middle Ages.

Rabble in Arms (1933). A historical novel by Kenneth ROBERTS. It continues the history of the Revolution which Roberts began in ARUNDEL. *Rabble in Arms* describes the defeat of Burgoyne's invasion by Benedict Arnold. Both stories undertake to humanize the Revolution by exploring the factual basis that underlies its myths.

Rabelais, François (1494?–1553). French scholar, humanist, physician, and author of the robust and outspoken GARGANTUA AND PANTAGRUEL. Having first entered the Franciscan and then the Benedictine orders, he left the confining environment of the monastery to study, practice, and teach medicine in Montpellier and Lyons. Twice he accompanied Jean du Bellay, bishop of Paris and later cardinal, to Rome, where he made archeological and botanical studies. From 1550 to 1553, Rabelais, who is sometimes known as "the curate of Meudon," held the parishes of Saint-Martin-de-Meudon and of Saint-Christophe-du-Jambet in the diocese of Mans, though he probably did not reside there. Throughout his life he published various works on medicine and translations in addition to his literary masterpiece. *Gargantua and Pantagruel* is filled with allusions to Rabelais' personal life, as well as to the contemporary French scene, humanistic studies which interested him, and observations he had made on his visits to Italy.

Rabelaisian. Coarsely and boisterously satirical in the Gallic comic tradition; grotesque, extravagant, and licentious in language; reminiscent of the literary style of Rabelais.

Rabicane or **Rabicano.** Argalia's horse in the Orlando poems of Matteo Maria Boiardo and Lodovico Ariosto (see ORLANDO FURIOSO). Argalia, the brother of Angelica, the princess of Cathay who enamors the paladins of Charlemagne, is killed by Ferragù.

Rabinowitz, Solomon J. See Sholem ALEICHEM.

Rachel. In the Old Testament, the daughter of Laban, wife of JACOB, and mother of Joseph and Benjamin. Jacob had been promised her hand in marriage if he worked seven years for her father. At the end of that time, he was tricked into marrying her sister Leah and was forced to serve another seven years for Rachel (Gen. 29–33). The phrase "Rachel weeping for her children and would not be comforted, because they are not" occurs in the New Testament in allusion to Herod's Massacre of the Innocents after the birth of Christ (Matt. 2:18).

Rachel or **Mademoiselle Rachel.** The stage name of Elisabeth Félix (1820–1858), a celebrated 19th-century actress of the Comédie Française.

Rachel. An actress in Marcel Proust's REMEMBRANCE OF THINGS PAST. At first offered to the narrator as a prostitute, she becomes the demanding mistress of Robert de SAINT-LOUP. At that time she is scorned by society, but later she is launched as a great actress by the duchesse de Guermantes.

Rachmaninoff, Sergey Vassilievitch (1873–1943). Russian-born composer and pianist. His music, often rhapsodic and impassioned, is very popular on the concert stage, especially his *Prelude in C-sharp minor* (1892) and the piano concertos. Although an expatriate after 1917, he was greatly admired in the Soviet Union.

Racine, Jean (1639–1699). French playwright. Born at La Ferté-Milon, near Soissons, the son of a petty official, Racine was orphaned at an early age and left in the care of a Jansenist grandmother who sent him in 1655 to the schools of Port-Royal. There he acquired a thorough education in doctrine, as well as in classical literature, and the combination of the Jansenist concept of original sin with the Greek concept of Fate was to exert considerable influence upon his later work. In 1658, Racine went to the Collège d'Hancourt, part of the university of Paris, where he discovered and delighted in the profane world of actors and the theater. He became a protégé of Chapelain and, after writing an ode on the marriage of Louis XIV—*La Nymphe de la Seine* (*The Nymph of the Seine*, 1660)—he managed to obtain a small pension. Fearful for the state of his soul and hoping to persuade him to enter the church, his family sent him to Uzès to live with a clergyman uncle, but Racine returned to Paris in 1662 to publish further odes and to cultivate the friendship of such men as Boileau, Molière, and La Fontaine. Molière produced Racine's first two tragedies: *La Thébaïde* (*The Thebaid*, performed 1664) and ALEXANDRE LE GRAND. Though not his finest work, these plays established Racine's reputation. ANDROMAQUE achieved as great a success as Corneille's *Le Cid*, and after the comedy LES PLAIDEURS, a satire on the judiciary and one of his few treatments of a contemporary subject, Racine challenged Corneille with BRITANNICUS, a historico-political tragedy very much in the older playwright's genre, and BÉRÉNICE, based on the same subject as Corneille's *Tite et Bérénice* and appearing at virtually the same time. The public held Racine the victor in the contest, and the young playwright, now at the height of his powers and of his career, went on to produce his greatest plays: BAJAZET, MITHRIDATE, IPHIGÉNIE EN AULIDE, and PHÈDRE (1677). Racine was elected to the French Academy in 1673. In 1677, the year of his marriage, he retired from the theater, discouraged by the elaborate intrigue conducted by his enemies against *Phèdre*, tempted by an appointment to the post of historiographer to Louis XIV, and reconciled with the Jansenists of Port-Royal. Racine devoted himself fully to his new duties, and aside from two biblical plays, ESTHER (1689) and ATHALIE (1691), commissioned by Madame de Maintenon for the schoolgirls of St. Cyr, he never again wrote for the theater. The works of his last years include four *Cantiques Spirituels* (*Spiritual Hymns*) and the *Abrégé de l'Histoire de Port-Royal*, published after his death.

Racine's tragedies resemble those of Corneille in their rigid adherence to a single theme shorn of all irrelevancies, in their loyalty to the classical unities, and in their careful exposition of character and depiction of powerful spiritual conflicts. He was no mere imitator, however, but rather the inheritor and modifier of a tradition. Though Racine's Hellenism is apparent in his frequent culling of themes from Greek originals, his main thematic preoccupations are passion and women. His depiction of the emotions and especially of the subverting, destructive power of love was severely criticized during his lifetime as being unnecessarily realistic. Compared to Corneille's, Racine's characters are ordinary beings, subject to superhuman passions but also to human doubts and fears; far from possessing the extraordinary determination of, for example, Corneille's Cid, they are subject to the fluctuations of feeble and uncertain wills, and in this respect reveal the influence of Racine's Jansenist upbringing. His most memorable characters are the fierce and tender women of his great tragedies; in these creatures, Racine accomplished the humanization of classical French drama.

Many might agree with La Bruyère, but few would regard his remark as condemnation, when he said that Corneille showed men "as they ought to be" and Racine "as they are." More would perhaps echo Brunetière, who praised Racine as the first to write "the literature of the passions of the heart."

Radcliffe, Mrs. Ann. Born **Ann Ward** (1764–1823). English novelist, known for her tales of terror in the convention of the GOTHIC NOVEL. Her books include *The Romance of the Forest* (1791); THE MYSTERIES OF UDOLPHO, her most popular novel; *A Sicilian Romance* (1790); *An Italian Romance* (1791); and *The Italian, or the Confessional of the Black Penitents* (1797), whose best-drawn character, the implacable, villainous monk Schedoni, is one of the prototypes of the Byronic hero.

Radhakrishnan, Sarvepalli (1888–   ). Indian educator and statesman. Radhakrishnan was professor of philosophy at Presidency College, Madras (1916–1917), and at Calcutta University (1921–1931, 1939–1941). He later served as ambassador to Russia and as vice president of India. In 1962 he became president of the country. He wrote *The Hindu View of Life and Indian Philosophy* (1923–1927) and edited and translated *The Bhagavad-Gita* (1948).

Radiguet, Raymond (1903–1923). French novelist and poet. At once lyrical and cynical in his accounts of the adolescent's emotional initiation, Radiguet showed his skill in such novels as *The Devil in the Flesh* (*Le Diable au corps;* 1923) and *Count d'Orgel* (*Le Bal du Comte d'Orgel;* 1924).

Radigund. See FAERIE QUEENE, THE.

Radio City. Popular designation of Rockefeller Center, a group of buildings in New York City. Built between 1931 and 1940, they were specially designed to house the city's leading commercial enterprises. The term is derived from the R. C. A. (Radio Corporation of America) Building, which is the center of the group and contains the studios of the National Broadcasting Company. Included in the group are a sunken plaza, landscaped gardens, outdoor sculpture, shops, restaurants, and a theater.

Radishchev, Aleksandr Nikolayevich (1749–1802). Russian writer. Radishchev's politically liberal book, *A Journey from Petersburg to Moscow* (*Puteshestviye iz Peterburga v Moskvu;* 1790), created a sensation during the reign of Catherine the Great. Radishchev had been educated at the University of Leipzig, where he picked up the liberal ideas prevalent in Europe at the time. He returned to Russia and became a customs official. His book, describing an imaginary trip between the two Russian cities, was an outspoken indictment of serfdom and the government. The Empress, already upset by the French Revolution, was enraged at the exposures and ordered Radishchev sentenced to death, but this was commuted to exile in Siberia. He was released on the accession of Paul I in 1801. Broken in physical and mental health, he committed suicide the following year. Radishchev was also the author of some technically fine poetry, including an *Ode to Liberty* (1781–1783) which forcefully expressed the liberal sentiments of his book.

Radványi, Netty. See Anna SEGHERS.

Raeburn, Sir Henry (1756–1823). Scottish portrait painter. Largely self-taught, he established himself in Edinburgh where he became known as the

Scottish Reynolds. He painted the fashionable and famous in straightforward portraits strengthened by insistent contrasts of light and shade.

Raffles. The hero of a series of novels by E. W. HORNUNG. He is a debonair, witty, and cricket-loving gentleman thief.

Raggedy Man, The (1890). A poem by James Whitcomb RILEY. Written in the Hoosier dialect of a little boy, it tells of his admiration for the farm's hired man. The Raggedy Man is also the beau of Lizabuth Ann, in Riley's *Our Hired Girl*.

Raghuvansha (*Sans.,* the race of Raghu). A narrative poem in Sanskrit. It is ascribed to KALIDASA. It deals with the story of RAMA, the hero of the RAMAYANA.

Ragnarok. In Scandinavian mythology, the Twilight of the Gods, or day of doom. It will result in the destruction of the universe: the heavens will disappear, the earth will be swallowed up by the sea, and fire will consume the elements. There will be a final battle between the gods of evil, Loki, Hel, Fenris and the Midgard serpent, and the good gods, Odin and his companions, during which all will be slaughtered. After Ragnarok there will be a regeneration of all things; a new world will arise repopulated by Lif and Lifthrasir. Ragnarok is translated into German as *Götterdämmerung,* which is the title of the fourth work in Wagner's RING DES NIBELUNGEN. See BIFROST; VALI.

Rahab. In the Old Testament, the woman of Jericho who protected the two Israelite spies sent by Joshua and managed their escape (Josh. 2). When the city was later to be destroyed, Joshua commanded that "only Rahab the harlot shall live, she and all that are with her in the house" (Josh. 6:18). She lived among the Israelites for a long time afterward.

Rahu. The demon who, according to Hindu legend, causes eclipses. He drank some of the nectar of immortality one day, but was discovered by the Sun and Moon, who informed against him, and Vishnu cut off his head. But he had already taken some of the nectar into his mouth, as a result of which the head was immortal; ever afterward he hunted the Sun and Moon, causing eclipses when he occasionally caught them.

Rai, Nawab. See Prem CHAND.

Raimondo di Tolosa. See RAYMOND IV.

Raimund, Ferdinand (1790–1836). Austrian playwright, associated with the highly successful People's Theater of Vienna. Many of his plays, such as *Der Alpenkönig und der Menschenfeind* (*The Alp-King and the Misanthrope,* 1828), were popular primarily because of their light-hearted humor and songs; but some, such as *Der Verschwender* (*The Squanderer,* 1834), lay more stress on serious moral teachings.

Rain. See MISS THOMPSON.

Rainbow, The (1915). A novel by D. H. LAWRENCE. It is about the emotional life and loves of three generations of the Brangwen family, farmers and craftsmen of Nottinghamshire, Lawrence's childhood home. Tom Brangwen, a farm youth, marries Lydia Lensky, a Polish widow of a political exile. Anna, Lydia's daughter by her first marriage, grows up as Tom's own child and marries her cousin, Will Brangwen, a strong-willed, morose man with a passion for wood carving. Most of the novel is about

Ursula, daughter of Anna and Will. A sensitive, high-spirited rebel, she escapes from her confining environment, as Lawrence himself did, by going to college and becoming a teacher. Her emotional life consists of a love affair with Anton Skrebensky, a Polish exile and officer in the British army, and an intense attraction to Winifred Inger, an older teacher. Winifred, an athletic, intellectual woman, and a feminist, marries Ursula's uncle; Ursula rejects Skrebensky. Ursula's story is continued in WOMEN IN LOVE, a sequel. When *The Rainbow* was published it was denounced as obscene, and a whole edition was destroyed by court order.

Raine, Kathleen (1908–   ). English poet. She writes romantic, religious poetry, in the manner of William Blake. Her *Collected Poems* appeared in 1956.

Rais, Gilles de. See Gilles de RETZ.

Raisuli, Ahmed ibn-Muhammad (1875?–1925). A brigand of Morocco. He created international incidents by kidnaping the London *Times* correspondent Walter Harris (1904); Perdicaris, an American (1904); and Sir Harry MacLean (1907). The sultan of Morocco met his ransom demands to avoid war with the powers involved. An American slogan of the time ran "Perdicaris alive or Raisuli dead!"

Rajagopalachari, Chakravarti (1879–1972). Indian statesman, writer, and translator. "Rajaji's" Tamil writings are popular in south India, and his English retellings of the *Ramayana* and the *Mahabharata* (1957) bring out the didactic element in the epics. His translation of *The Ayodhya Canto of the Ramayana, as told by Kamban,* appeared in 1961. Rajaji became India's governor general, succeeding Earl Mountbatten, in 1948; he retired in 1950. He founded the Swatantra (Freedom) Party in 1960.

Rake's Progress, The. A series of engravings by William HOGARTH. Depicting the career of a wealthy, foolish young gentleman that carries him through the pleasure-houses of London to the madhouse of Bedlam, the engravings served as the basis of the libretto that W. H. AUDEN and Chester Kallman wrote for Igor Stravinsky's opera *The Rake's Progress* (1951).

rakshas. The evil spirits of Hindu legend, guardians of the treasures of Kubera, the god of riches. They haunt cemeteries and devour human beings, and can assume any shape at will; their strength increases as the day declines. Some are hideously ugly, but others, especially the female spirits, allure by their beauty.

Raleigh or **Ralegh, Sir Walter** (1552?–1618). English explorer, courtier, poet, and prose writer. One of the favorites of Queen Elizabeth between 1581 and 1592, Raleigh helped his friend Edmund SPENSER arrange for the publication of the first three books of *The Faerie Queene;* also during this period he sent several expeditions to North America, though the Queen would not allow him to make the voyages himself. He fell from Elizabeth's favor in 1592, according to legend, because of his seduction of one of her maids of honor. He took advantage of being in the Queen's bad graces by making in 1595 an expeditionary voyage to South America, which he described in the colorful (and fanciful) *Discovery of Guiana.* He was reinstated at court during the last years of Elizabeth's reign, but at the accession of James I he was imprisoned on a flimsy charge of treason. He narrowly escaped execution, and was detained in the Tower (though in reasonable comfort) for the next thirteen years. In 1616 he was released on his promise to James I to discover gold in South America, providing that he neither intruded on Spanish possessions or pirated Spanish ships. Unfortunately, Raleigh attacked a Spanish settlement, and on his return to England was condemned and executed.

A true courtier poet, Raleigh did not publish his poetry but had it circulated in manuscript. As a result, only a few of his poems have come down to the present day. *Cynthia*, a long poem in honor of the Queen, was highly praised by Spenser, but only a fragment has survived. Among his best-known poems are *The Nymph's Reply to the Shepherd*, an answer to Christopher Marlowe's *Passionate Shepherd; The Lie; The Passionate Man's Pilgrimage;* and the sonnet beginning "Methought I saw the grave where Laura lay," prefixed to Spenser's *Faerie Queene*. In addition to a prose *History of the World* (of which only one volume was completed), Raleigh wrote a narrative of the sea-battle between the *Revenge* and a Spanish warship in which his cousin, Sir Richard Grenville, was killed; Tennyson's ballad *The Revenge* is largely based on Raleigh's account. The legend of the courteous Sir Walter spreading his cloak over a puddle that the Queen might cross dry-shod is mentioned by Sir Walter Scott in *Kenilworth*.

Raleigh, Sir Walter Alexander (1861–1922). English scholar and essayist. He was regarded by his contemporaries as a major authority on English literature. Among his works are *The English Novel* (1894) and *Shakespeare* (1907).

Ralph, James (1695?–1762). American writer. He accompanied Benjamin Franklin to London in 1724 and established himself there with the Thomsonian blank-verse poems *The Tempest* and *Night* (1727). His ballad opera *The Fashionable Lady* was, in 1730, the first play by an American to be produced on a London stage. Franklin refers to him in his *Autobiography*.

Ralph Roister Doister (performed c. 1553; published 1566). The earliest English comedy, written by Nicholas UDALL. Based on Latin models, it has five acts and is written in rhymed doggerel. The titular hero is a swaggering, blustering fellow who, urged on by Mathew Merygreeke, tries unsuccessfully to win Dame Christian Custance, a rich widow.

Rama. The seventh incarnation of VISHNU. Rama performed many wonderful exploits, such as killing giants, demons, and other monsters. He won Sita as his wife because he was able to bend the bow of Shiva in the court of Sita's father. He is the hero of the great Hindu epic, the RAMAYANA. A clever retelling of the Rama story, in the nature of a spoof, is *The Ramayana* (1954) by Aubrey Menen.

Ramachandra. See VISHNU.

Ramadan or Ramazan. The ninth month of the Muslim year, considered to be the Muslim Holy Month. From sunrise to sundown during this period, a strict fast is observed by all pious Muslims; only the sick, infirm, or pregnant are temporarily excused. See BAIRAM; KADR, AL.

Raman, Sir Chandrasekhara Venkata (1888–1970). Indian scientist. He discovered the light wave phenomenon known as the Raman Effect in 1928, was knighted in 1929, and received the Nobel Prize

for Physics in 1930. He was awarded the Franklin Medal of America in 1951 and the Bharat Ratna, the highest government honor in India, in 1954.

Ramayana (Sans., "Relating to Rama"). The history of RAMA, the great epic poem of ancient India, ranking with the *Mahabharata*. It is ascribed to the poet VALMIKI, and, as now known, consists of 24,000 stanzas in seven books. Parts of the *Ramayana* date from 500 B.C. The young hero, Rama, an incarnation (*avatar*) of the deity Vishnu, wins his bride, SITA, by bending the great bow that had belonged to the god Rudra. When about to be named heir-apparent of Ayodhya, Rama is exiled for 14 years through the jealousy of Kaikeyi, one of his father's wives, who desires the throne for her son, Bharata. Sita is carried off by RAVANA, the demon-king of Ceylon. A great part of the narrative is concerned with Rama's efforts to win her back. He secures the assistance of Vibhishana, Ravana's own brother and of HANUMAN, the great monkey-god, whose monkeys construct a bridge to Ceylon. After this alliance rescues Sita, Rama is welcomed back as the monarch of Ayodhya. But both Rama and the people fear that Sita has been defiled by her sojourn with the demon-king, and although she successfully undergoes an ordeal by fire, Rama sends her away. She wanders into the forest, finds shelter in the hut of Valmiki, and there gives birth to Rama's two sons, whom she brings up to be brave and noble youths. Eventually she is found by Rama and received back as his wife.

Rambler, The (1750–1752). A series of semiweekly essays written by Samuel JOHNSON, dealing with mores and literature. They were thought, at first, too difficult for a public trained on Addison's SPECTATOR. Some even found them dull, as did Lady Mary Wortley Montagu, who remarked that the *Rambler* "follows the *Spectator* with the same pace that a pack horse would a hunter."

Rambouillet, Hôtel de. The house in Paris where the marquise de Rambouillet founded the salon (c. 1615) out of which grew the *Académie française*. The members included Mme de Sévigné, Descartes, Richelieu, Bossuet, and La Rochefoucauld. Disgusted with the immoral and puerile tone of the times, they sought to restore delicacy and refinement to life and literature. Gradually they developed a language of their own, calling common things by uncommon names. The women became known as *Les précieuses* and the men as *esprits doux*. Although the coterie performed a good and lasting service, the growth of preciosity, pedantry, and affectation led to its disruption. Molière hastened its fall with two telling satires: *Les Précieuses Ridicules* (1659) and *Les Femmes Savantes* (1672).

Rameau, Jean Philippe (1683–1764). The most important French composer of the 18th century, whose works include the operas *Castor et Pollux* (1737) and *Dardanus* (1739); the opera-ballets *Les Indes galantes* (1735) and *Les Fêtes d'Hébé* (1739); two books of harpsichord pieces (1706 and 1741). He is also an important writer on musical theory; his *Traité de l'Harmonie réduite à ses Principes naturels* (1722) laid the foundation for modern harmonic theory.

Rameau's Nephew. See NEVEU DE RAMEAU, LE.

Ramée, Marie Louise de la. Pen name **Ouida** (1838–1908). English novelist, widely known for her flamboyant romances of fashionable life, such as *Under Two Flags* (1867), *Tricotrin* (1869), and *Moths* (1880). She also wrote animal stories and children's books, including *A Dog of Flanders* (1872) and *Bimbi* (1882). Her pseudonym was a childish version of Louise.

Ramillies. A village in Belgium, scene of one of the Duke of Marlborough's famous victories over the French during the War of the Spanish Succession (1706). The battle gave its name to various articles and modes of dress, such as the Ramillies wig.

Raminagrobis (*Lat.,* "the pondering tom-cat"). In Rabelais' GARGANTUA AND PANTAGRUEL, the dying poet whom Panurge consults when he cannot decide whether or not to marry. In reply he writes an equivocal verse advising both courses.

Also, one of the names given to the cat in La Fontaine's *Fables* (1678–1679) who arbitrates the quarrel between the weasel and the rabbit by eating them both.

Ram of the Zodiac. This is the famous Chrysomallon. Its GOLDEN FLEECE was the prize sought by Jason and the ARGONAUTS.

Ramona (1884). A historical romance by Helen Hunt JACKSON. The heroine, Ramona, of mixed Scottish and Indian blood, elopes with the noble Indian, Alessandro. The proud young man comes to a tragic end as the result of harassment by whites. The book helped to create a marked change in the attitude of white men toward the Indian.

Ramos, Graciliano (1892–1953). Brazilian novelist. Sometimes considered the finest Brazilian novelist since Machado de Assis, Ramos wrote about the northeastern state of Alagoas, where he was a merchant and public official. His first novel, *Caetés* (1933), was written in the mid-1920's and was published after the vivid style and sardonic tone of one of his official reports had won him national attention. Later, his radical political views brought him persecution and imprisonment. He spent his last years as a proofreader for a newspaper in Rio de Janeiro.

Ramos' novels are characterized by acute, though dispassionate, insight into the human mind and awareness of the inequities of social and economic conditions in northeast Brazil. *São Bernardo* (1934) is a first-person account of an unfeeling parvenu in the cane-growing littoral of Alagoas. In *Angústia* (*Anguish,* 1936), he utilized a stream-of-consciousness technique to weave the story of a man who is led to destruction through thwarted sexual desire. Set on the arid *sertão,* or backcountry, of Alagoas, *Vidas Sêcas* (1938) is an episodic work about a cowherd whose lot is difficult but who is uncontaminated by the corruption of the littoral.

Ramsay, Allan (1686–1758). Scottish poet and wigmaker who became a bookseller and edited old Scottish poems. He put together many collections of Scottish poetry, among them being *The Ever Green* (1724) and *The Tea-Table Miscellany* (1724–1727). His original works include *Patie and Roger* (1720) and *Jenny and Meggy* (1723), humorous pastorals, and *The Gentle Shepherd* (1725), a pastoral drama. Ramsay was also the first to have a circulating library in Scotland. His eldest son, Allan RAMSAY was a prominent portrait painter in Edinburgh.

Ramsay, Allan (1713–1784). Scottish portrait painter, eldest son of the poet Allan RAMSAY. A refined colorist and unaffected portraitist, he was named court painter to George III in 1767.

Ramsay, Mr. and Mrs. The central characters in Virginia Woolf's novel To THE LIGHTHOUSE. Mrs. Ramsay is a personification of creative womanhood; Mr. Ramsay is a typical intellectual male.

Ramsay, Sir William (1852–1916). British chemist. He was the first to advance proof that the emanation of radium produces helium during its atomic disintegration. He was awarded the Nobel Prize for chemistry in 1904.

Ramus, Petrus. Lat., for **Pierre La Ramée** (1515–1572). French philosopher and mathematician. A professor of philosophy in the Collège de France (1543), his anti-Aristotelian doctrine of logic, known as *Ramism,* became current in the English universities, principally at Cambridge. He was a victim of the massacre of St. Bartholomew.

Ramuz, C[harles] F[erdinand] (1878–1947). Swiss novelist. Ramuz stylized the peasant speech and life of his native region, analyzing the primitive emotions and spiritual climate of its people. He is best known for *The Reign of the Evil One* (*Le Règne de l'esprit malin;* 1922), *The End of All Men* (*Présence de la mort;* 1922, also translated as *The Triumph of Death*), and *When the Mountain Fell* (*Derborence;* 1936).

Ran or **Rana.** In Norse mythology, goddess of the sea, wife of Aegir, and mother of nine daughters of the waves. Her name signifies robbery, and it was she who caught seafarers in her net and drew them down to her dwelling beneath the water.

Rand, Ayn (?–   ). Russian-born American novelist. Her novels, *Anthem* (1936), THE FOUNTAINHEAD, *Atlas Shrugged* (1957), and *We the Living* (1959), are polemical and melodramatic vehicles for her ideas. In her so-called objectivist philosophy, she defends capitalism and attacks government controls because they may frustrate the self-interested, supermanlike individual whom she has pictured in her novels and expatiated on further in *For the New Intellectual: The Philosophy of Ayn Rand* (1961). She is also the author of a mystery play *The Night of January 16th* (1935).

Randall, James Ryder (1839–1908). American journalist, teacher, and poet. At the outbreak of the Civil War, Randall, inspired by Baltimore anti-Union sentiment, wrote his famous poem, MARYLAND, MY MARYLAND. A volume of *Poems* was published posthumously (1910).

Randolph, John. Known as **John Randolph of Roanoke** (1773–1833). American statesman and orator. A brilliant nonconformist whose eccentricity often bordered on insanity, Randolph was descended from a prominent Virginia family. He was elected to the first of his many terms in Congress in 1799 and became chairman of the House Ways and Means Committee at the age of 28. Although he initially supported the policies of Jefferson, he broke with the administration over its measures to acquire Florida, dubbing the president "St. Thomas of Cantingbury." In succeeding administrations he opposed the War of 1812 and the chartering of the second U.S. Bank; during the Missouri controversy, he emerged as a sectional leader. His attacks on the alliance of John

Quincy Adams and Henry Clay led the latter to challenge him to a duel (1826), in which neither was hurt. Randolph was appointed minister to Russia in 1830 but resigned shortly because of poor health. He was buried facing the West so that, it is said, he might keep his eye on Henry Clay.

Randolph, Thomas (1605–1635). English poet and dramatist. A brilliant scholar at Cambridge and a friend of Ben Jonson, Randolph wrote plays deeply influenced by classical drama. His *Hey for Honesty* (pub. 1651) is an adaptation of Aristophanes' *Plutus;* and his other plays, such as *Aristippus* (1630), *The Jealous Lovers* (1632), and *The Muses' Looking-Glass* (1638), reflect his academic background. He is best known for a few poems of a witty and intimate tone, such as *An Ode to Master Anthony Stafford* and *A Congratulatory to Mr. Ben Jonson* from his *Poems* (1638).

Random, Roderick. See RODERICK RANDOM.

Ranjit Singh (1780–1839). Indian maharaja. With the help of the British, he established a Sikh kingdom in the Punjab. He is known as the "Lion of the Punjab."

Ranke, Leopold von (1795–1886). German historian. Outstanding for his scientific approach to history, he relied entirely on contemporary, firsthand sources, which he subjected to the most rigorous analysis. His best-known work is his *History of the Popes (Die römischen Päpste;* 1834–1839).

Ransom, John Crowe (1888–   ). American poet and critic. Ransom attended and later taught at Vanderbilt University, where he was a member of the group known as the Fugitives; a staunch believer in Southern agrarianism, he also contributed to the symposium *I'll Take My Stand* (1930). (See AGRARIANS.) In 1937 he went to teach at Kenyon College where he became the founder and editor of the KENYON REVIEW. As a critic, he gave currency to the term NEW CRITICISM in a book by that title (1941). His literary essays appear in *God Without Thunder* (1930), *The World's Body* (1938), and *Poems and Essays* (1955).

Ransom's poetry, broadly showing the influence of the metaphysical poets, is marked by irony, criticism of the 20th-century industrial world, and nostalgia for the past, especially the aristocratic society of the South before the Civil War. His books of poetry include *Poems About God* (1919), *Chills and Fever* (1924), *Grace After Meat* (1924), *Two Gentlemen in Bonds* (1927), and *Selected Poems* (1945).

Ransome, Arthur (1884–1967). English writer, best known for his realistic books written for and about children. *Swallows and Amazons* (1931) describes a vacation spent sailing small boats.

Rao, Raja (1909–   ). Indian novelist writing in English. He studied at the University of Montpellier and at the Sorbonne and has published stories in French. He wrote *Kanthapura* (1938), *Cow of the Barricades* (1947), *The Serpent and the Rope* (1960).

Rape of Lucrece, The (1594). A long poem by William SHAKESPEARE, dealing with LUCRETIA.

Rape of the Lock, The (1714). A mock-heroic poem, often considered the best in the English language, by Alexander POPE. The first sketch of two cantos was published in 1712; the final version was in five cantos. The poem was based on a real incident: Lord Petre, in a thoughtless moment of frolic gal-

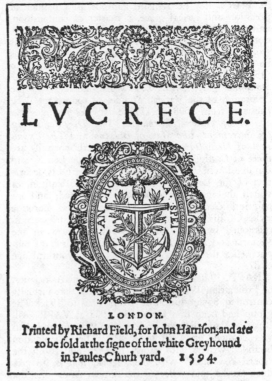

Title page of Shakespeare's *Rape of Lucrece* (1594).

lantry, cut off a lock of Arabella Fermor's hair, and this liberty gave rise to a feud between the two families. In his treatment of the incident, Pope employed an elaborate and elevated style from the classical epic: the description of a card-game as a battle, the final combat between beaux and belles, and the journey to the Cave of Spleen. The heroine, called BELINDA, indignantly demands back the ringlet, but after a fruitless charge it is affirmed that it has been transported to heaven, and henceforth shall "midst the stars inscribe Belinda's name."

Raphael. One of the principal angels of Jewish angelology. According to the apocryphal book of Tobit, he traveled with Tobias, instructing him how to marry Sara and drive away the wicked spirit, Asmodeus. In his *Paradise Lost* (1667) Milton calls him "the sociable spirit" and "affable archangel," and it is he who is sent by God to advise Adam of his danger. Raphael is usually distinguished in art by a pilgrim's staff, or is shown carrying a fish; this alludes to the fish he helped Tobias catch which miraculously cured Tobit's blindness.

Raphael. Real name, **Raffaelo Sanzio** or **Santi** (1483–1520). Italian painter. With Leonardo and Michelangelo forming the greatest trio of artists ever produced by a single age, Raphael was born in Urbino, and settled in Rome where he worked mainly at the Vatican. A versatile artist, he painted frescoes illustrating historical and mythological scenes, and executed many portraits, altar pieces, and delicate small paintings. As an architect, he designed the *Villa Madama* and the *Palazzo Cafarelli* in Rome, and was for a time in charge of the construction of

St. Peter's. But he remains famous as a painter of precision and lyrical grace, a master of composition, and the leading exponent of the Renaissance conception of human nobility. The most popular of his works are undoubtedly the many gentle Madonnas he painted, especially the *Madonna del Cardellino* (1506), the *Belle Jardinière* (1507), and the *Sistine Madonna* (1518). His best work, however, is the decoration of the Vatican *Stanze,* or rooms, for Pope Julius II from 1508 on. These frescoes include *The School of Athens, Parnassus, The Disputation on the Sacrament, The Mass of Bolsena,* and *The Expulsion of Heliodorus.* Among his superb portraits are those of Castiglione, Pope Julius II, Pope Leo X, and Bindo Altoviti. Of future importance were his decoration of the *Loggie* of BRAMANTE at the Vatican, in which the grotesque style was introduced; and his painting *Galatea,* which anticipated the Baroque style. Of his series of cartoons for tapestries, commissioned by Pope Leo X, seven are now in the Victoria and Albert Museum, London. His huge output belies the fact of his death at the youthful age of 37.

RAPP. The initials of the Russian Association of Proletarian Writers, an organization that virtually controlled Soviet literature from 1929 to 1932. The group had been first formed in 1925 as VAPP (All-Russian Association of Proletarian Writers) and then was changed in 1928 to RAPP. The organization hounded writers with orders to heed and fulfill the "social command" with their work, that is, to produce works that reflected the times. After the first FIVE-YEAR PLAN was over, RAPP had its power taken away when the Union of Soviet Writers was formed.

Rappaccini's Daughter (1844). A story by Nathaniel HAWTHORNE. Rappaccini, a doctor and devoted man of science, nourishes his beautiful daughter, Beatrice, on poisons, so that she, invulnerable, may aid him in his experiments with dangerous plants. Physically deadly, but pure in spirit, Beatrice drinks the antidote given her by a faithless suitor, knowing it will kill her. She reproaches her father for subordinating heart to head, depriving her of human existence. This theme is frequent in Hawthorne's work.

Rasa. (1) In Hindu legend, a mythical river in the sky.

(2) A theory of dramatic purpose and effect as propounded by Bharata.

(3) The central principle of Hindu esthetics. In the *Aitareya Upanishad* the sentence *Raso vai sah* (*The well-carved is the well-loved* in the sense that *Perfection alone is delectable*) suggests the ineffable nature of *rasa.* The *rasa-lila* is the dance of the divinely inspired *gopis* who, in honor of Krishna with whom they desire union, perform to his fluting in the moonlight.

Raskolnikov. See CRIME AND PUNISHMENT.

Rasmussen, Knud Johan Victor (1879–1933). Danish Arctic explorer. He made ethnological expeditions to North Greenland and developed the theory that Eskimos and North American Indians descended from the same Asian migratory tribes. Rasmussen was the author of *The People of the Polar North* (1908), *Myths and Legends from Greenland* (*Myter og Sagn fra Grønland;* 1921–1925), and *Across Arctic America* (1927).

Rasputin, Grigori Efimovich (1871–1916). Russian monk in the household of Czar Nicholas II. Despite his notoriously bad reputation, Rasputin wielded power at the court through his influence over the Czarina. He was assassinated by a group of Russian nobles on Dec. 30, 1916.

Rasselas, Prince of Abyssinia, History of (1759). A philosophical romance by Samuel JOHNSON, hastily written within a month of his mother's death to meet her funeral expenses. Rasselas is the youngest son of an Oriental despot who confines his children in the Happy Valley, a paradise. Rasselas, longing for the novelty of the world outside, escapes with his sister, Nekayah, and his mentor, IMLAC. They go to Cairo where Rasselas is warned by one example after another that romantic reverie, romantic love, the flights of the imagination, the daring speculations of philosophy, the great discoveries of science, all harm man by giving him an unrealistic estimate of what life has to offer and by encouraging false hopes. Ranging through all that nature and society have to offer, they find nothing that promises the happiness they expected, and they return to the Happy Valley.

The attack in *Rasselas* is directed against the optimism of the 18th century or, more generally, against all simple formulas that profess to lead man to happiness, against all glib generalizations about the goodness of nature and the satisfactions of solitude, learning, or social life. *Rasselas* has often been compared with Voltaire's *Candide;* the two works were published only a few weeks apart.

Ras Shamra. See UGARIT.

Rastignac, Eugène de. One of Balzac's best-known characters, appearing in several of the novels of *La Comédie Humaine,* notably LE PÈRE GORIOT and LA COUSINE BETTE. Introduced as a struggling young law student who has come to Paris to make his fortune, Rastignac quickly acquires practicality. He determines to conquer society by giving up his ideals and taking advantage of circumstances. By installing himself as the lover of Mme de Nucingen, the daughter of his fellow-boarder Père Goriot, he manages to better his fortunes. Later, he marries Augusta de Nucingen, the daughter of his former mistress, and becomes a prominent statesman, peer, and millionaire. Rastignac finally epitomizes ruthless, cynical ambition.

Ratan, Jai (1923–   ). Indian author writing in English. He was born in the Punjab, and now lives in Calcutta. He is the translator (with P. Lal) of Prem Chand's *Godan,* founder member of Writers Workshop (Calcutta), and author of a volume of short stories, *The Angry Goddess* (1962).

Rathenau, Walter (1867–1922). German industrialist and statesman. During World War I, he was in charge of mobilizing German production, and in 1922 became foreign minister of the Weimar Republic. He was assassinated by an anti-Semitic organization.

rationalism. Term applied to a trend in philosophic thinking toward emphasis on the reason and intellect, rather than the emotions and imagination. Aristotle and St. Thomas Aquinas are considered rationalists, and the 18th century was dominated by rationalist philosophy.

Ratliff, V. K. A character in William Faulkner's trilogy of novels beginning with THE HAMLET. A sewing-machine salesman who knows practically everyone in Yoknapatawpha County, Ratliff is a shrewd and humane observer, who narrates a good deal of the action. Elsewhere in the Yoknapatawpha saga, he is known as V. K. Suratt.

Rats, The (Die Ratten; 1911). A drama by Gerhart HAUPTMANN. A woman buys a child to satisfy her maternal instincts, pretends to her husband that it is her own and, when threatened by the child's real mother, has the woman killed. Eventually, when the child is taken from her, she kills herself. While this is going on, an actor of "the old school" continually laments the disappearance of tragedy from the modern world.

Rattigan, Terence Mervyn (1911–   ). English playwright. His works have been produced in England and America. His plays include *O Mistress Mine* (1945), *The Winslow Boy* (1947), THE BROWNING VERSION, *The Deep Blue Sea* (1952), SEPARATE TABLES, and *Ross* (an historical play about Lawrence of Arabia; 1960).

Räuber, Die. See ROBBERS, THE.

Ravana. The king of Lanka (Ceylon) and the 10-faced demon of Hindu legend. He was fastened between heaven and earth for 10,000 years by Shiva's leg, because he audaciously attempted to move the hill of heaven to Lanka. In the epic the RAMAYANA, he abducted Rama's wife, Sita.

Ravel, Maurice [Joseph] (1875–1937). French impressionist composer. Some of his best-known works are the song cycle *Shéhérazade* (1903; text by Tristan Klingsor), the operas *L'Heure Espagnole* (*The Spanish Hour*, 1910; libretto by Franc-Nohain) and *L'Enfant et les Sortilèges* (*The Child and the Enchantments*, 1925; libretto by Colette), and the ballets *Daphnis et Chloé* (1912) and *Boléro* (1928).

raven. A bird of ill omen. It is fabled to forebode death and bring infection and bad luck generally. The former notion arises from their following an army under the expectation of finding dead bodies to raven on; the latter notion is a mere offshoot of the former, since it was noted that pestilence kills as fast as the sword. In Christian art, the raven is an emblem of God's Providence, in allusion to the ravens that fed Elijah.

The fatal raven, consecrated to Odin, the Danish war god, was the emblem on the Danish standard, *Landeyda* (the desolation of the country), and was said to have been woven and embroidered in one noontide by the daughters of Regner Lodbrok, son of Sigurd, that dauntless warrior who chanted his death song (the *Krakamal*) while being stung to death in a horrible pit filled with deadly serpents. If the Danish arms were destined to defeat, the raven hung his wings; if victory was to attend them, he stood erect and soaring as if inviting the warriors to follow.

Raven, The (1845). A poem by Edgar Allan POE. Lost in melancholy memories of his dead love, the poet is startled by a tapping at his chamber door. A raven enters, and perching on the bust of Pallas Athene, answers the tormented questions of the bereaved lover with the mysterious, unchanging "Nevermore." Nevermore will he be reunited with his lost love. Poe's most famous poem, *The Raven* is the subject of his essay THE PHILOSOPHY OF COMPOSITION.

Ravenswood, Edgar. See BRIDE OF LAMMERMOOR, THE.

Rawlings, Marjorie Kinnan (1896–1953), American novelist. Best known for THE YEARLING, she moved to Cross Creek, Fla., in 1928 and began to use Floridian folklore and folkways in her work. Her first novel, *South Moon Under* (1933) is the story of a hunter who prefers the wilds to the urban communities that encroach upon his domain. She described the region where she lived in *Cross Creek* (1942).

Raw Youth, The (Podrostok; 1875). A novel by Feodor DOSTOEVSKI. In this book the author examines directly the reasons for what he sees as the "chemical decomposition" of Russian society in the late 19th century. The central character is Arkadi Makarovich DOLGORUKI, a young man in his early 20's, who is trying to find something solid to cling to in the disorder and chaos of the times. He settles on the idea of becoming a Rothschild, as he terms it: of amassing vast wealth, not for the sake of the money's monetary value, but for the sense of power it will give him.

Arkadi is the illegitimate son of the nobleman VERSILOV, who has been living with Arkadi's mother for some years. His nominal father, Makar Dolgoruki, has become a religious pilgrim. The youthful Arkadi goes to St. Petersburg to see Versilov, full of mixed love and hatred for his father. The nobleman—a brilliant, twisted product of the acceptance of Western ideas—charms the boy. Their closeness is short-lived, however, when Arkadi learns that his father is his rival for Katerina Nikolayevna Akhmakova. After a siege of brain fever, the anguished Arkadi begins to find peace, when the pilgrim Makar Dolgoruki arrives for a visit. The old man preaches love for all of God's creation and the need for all men to strive for seemliness in their relations with themselves and one another. Arkadi abandons his idea of becoming a Rothschild for the goal of attaining seemliness.

Ray, Man (1890–   ). American artist and photographer. Associated with the short-lived New York DADA movement (1917) and with SURREALISM in Paris, he is the creator of photographic montages. He has also made several abstract films.

Raymond IV. Called **Raymond de Saint-Giles** (d. 1105). Count of Toulouse (1088–1105). As a historical personage, he led a major force in the First Crusade (1096). In Torquato Tasso's GERUSALEMME LIBERATA he appears as **Raimondo di Tolosa,** one of the leading veterans among the Crusaders, especially noted for his Nestor-like wisdom. At one point in the story Tancredi (Tancred) breaks off his duel with Argante to seek Clorinda his beloved. Raimondo takes Tancredi's place, despite his age, but an angel appears to protect him from the furious blows of the infidel champion. Later it is he who kills King Aladino of Jerusalem and plants the Christian standard on the tower of David. He also appears in Sir Walter Scott's novel *Count Robert of Paris*.

Raymond, René. See James Hadley CHASE.

Razor's Edge, The (1944). A novel by W. Somerset MAUGHAM. The hero is a worldly young man who is converted to Hinduism and leaves his inheritance for the holy life.

Razumov. The central character in Joseph Conrad's novel UNDER WESTERN EYES. He is a Russian, a student, and an unsuccessful spy.

Read, Sir **Herbert [Edward]** (1893–1968). English poet and literary and art critic. He is best known for his books explaining movements in modern art (he published *A Concise History of Modern Painting* in 1959), and for his championship of art in education, industry, and society generally. His early poetry was imagistic and his later poetry more metaphysical; his volumes of *Collected Poems* appeared in 1946 and 1953. Read's literary criticism has been influential in spreading his enthusiasm for romanticism and "organic form," as in *Form and Modern Poetry* (1932). He was a supporter of both surrealism and communism, but turned from Marxism to anarchism on deciding that the Marxist system represented an imposed, not organic, political form. He is the author of *Poetry and Anarchism* (1938) and other books on literature in society. His literary criticism is also characterized by its psychoanalytic bent, notably in his study of *Wordsworth* (1930). He has also written *The Green Child* (1935), a novel, and *Annals of Innocence and Experience* (1940), an autobiography. Among his important later studies are *The Philosophy of Modern Art* (1952) and *The True Voice of Feeling* (1953).

Read, Opie [Percival] (1852–1939). American humorist and novelist. Read founded and edited the popular humorous magazine, *The Arkansas Traveler* (1882–1916). *The Jucklins* (1895) was one of the most popular of American novels. Read wrote more than 50 books, including *The Kentucky Colonel* (1890) and *Judge Elbridge* (1899).

Reade, Charles (1814–1884). English novelist. He is best known for his medieval romance CLOISTER AND THE HEARTH. In his other novels, he often deals with social problems and exposes social abuses. These include PEG WOFFINGTON; CHRISTIE JOHNSTONE; IT IS NEVER TOO LATE TO MEND; LOVE ME LITTLE, LOVE ME LONG; *Hard Cash* (1863); *Foul Play* (1869); PUT YOURSELF IN HIS PLACE; *The Wandering Heir* (1872); and *A Woman Hater* (1874). His plays include *Masks and Faces* (1852), *The Courtier of Lyons* (1854), and *Drink,* based on Zola's *L'Assommoir*.

Reading Gaol, The Ballad of. See BALLAD OF READING GAOL, THE.

realism. In philosophy, one of two rival doctrines in the disputes of the medieval Schoolmen (see SCHOLASTICISM). Derived from the theories of Plato, it held that only universal concepts, such as roundness, beauty, and the like, have reality, since they exist before any particular circle or beautiful object. See NOMINALISM; Pierre ABÉLARD.

The term *realism* is also used to describe literature that attempts to depict life in an entirely objective manner, without idealization or glamor, and without didactic or moral ends. Realism may be said to have begun with such early English novelists as Defoe, Fielding, and Smollett, and to have become a definite literary trend in the 19th century. In America, realism became an important movement in the 1880's, with William Dean Howells as its leading theorizer and Henry James as one of its main practitioners. It contributed to the growth of NATURALISM, with which it is sometimes identified, at the turn of the century. At present it is such a pervasive element in literature that it scarcely retains any distinct import.

Rebecca. In Scott's IVANHOE, the real heroine, daughter of Isaac the Jew. She loves Ivanhoe, who has shown great kindness to her and her father. When Ivanhoe marries Rowena, both Rebecca and her father leave England for the Continent.

Rebecca and Rowena (1850). A burlesque continuation of Scott's IVANHOE by William Makepeace THACKERAY. Ivanhoe is now a henpecked husband and Rowena makes him promise never to marry a Jewess, but after Rowena's death Rebecca becomes a Christian and she and Ivanhoe finally marry.

Rebecca of Sunnybrook Farm (1903). A story for girls by Kate Douglas WIGGIN. The 10-year-old heroine, Rebecca Randall, leaves her widowed mother and brothers and sisters to go to live with her two old-maid aunts, Miranda and Jane. Aunt Miranda, particularly, is a great trial, but Rebecca finds a friend in Emma Jane Perkins and a hero and admirer in Adam Ladd, whom she calls Mr. Aladdin. The book ends with her graduation from Wareham Academy in Maine. There was a sequel, *New Chronicles of Rebecca,* in 1907.

Rebekah. In the Old Testament, the wife of ISAAC and mother of JACOB and Esau. The meeting at the well between Rebekah and Abraham's servant, sent to seek a wife for Isaac, is one of the celebrated pastoral love stories (Gen. 24). It was Rebekah who helped her favorite son Jacob secure the birthright that should have been Esau's (Gen. 27:6).

Rebel, The (L'Homme Révolté; 1951). A long philosophical essay by Albert CAMUS. It expands the theory of the absurd first treated in THE MYTH OF SISYPHUS and explores the possible responses man can make in attitude and in action, rejecting equally suicidal despair and all promises of complete personal or social salvation. Camus distinguishes between philosophical rebellion, proper to the man of the absurd, and historical or political revolution, which promises salvation but consists merely of murder and a new tyranny.

Récamier, Mme **Jeanne Françoise Julie Adélaïde.** Born **Bernard** (1777–1849). French leader of society. The wife of a Paris banker and close friend of Mme de Staël, she was known for her wit and beauty. Mme Récamier's salons were filled with the most important people of her time, both in the arts and in politics. In later years, Chateaubriand became the indisputed center of this group and the object of Mme Récamier's devotion.

Recessional (1897). A famous poem by Rudyard KIPLING. It was written to celebrate the 60th anniversary of the reign of Queen Victoria. The title refers to the hymn that is sung at the close of a church service, while the choir is leaving the chancel and proceeding to the robing room. The poem includes a warning to the British people not to become over-confident, but to remember their obligations during their hour of greatest glory.

Recherche de l'absolu, La (1834). A novel, part of LA COMÉDIE HUMAINE, by Honoré de BALZAC. The main character, Balthazar Claes-Molina, spends a huge fortune and neglects his family in his monomaniacal quest for the "absolute," a philosopher's stone that will yield unending wealth.

Recherche de la Verité, La. See Nicolas MALE-BRANCHE.

Recherche du temps perdu, A la. See RE-MEMBRANCE OF THINGS PAST.

Red and the Black, The (Le Rouge et le Noir; 1830). A novel by STENDHAL. The author's most celebrated work, it is equally acclaimed for its psychological study of its protagonist—the provincial young romantic Julien SOREL—and as a satiric analysis of French social order under the Bourbon restoration. Its intensely dramatic plot is purposively romantic in nature, while Stendhal's careful portraiture of Sorel's inner states is the work of a master realist, foreshadowing new developments in the form of the novel.

Red Badge of Courage, The: An Episode of the American Civil War (1895). A novel by Stephen CRANE. More the story of the battle that rages inside the hero, Henry FLEMING, than of that between Confederate and Union soldiers, the novel is, as its author said, a psychological study of fear. Young Fleming has romantic notions of the hero he will be when he enters his first battle, but his illusions are soon destroyed and he turns and runs. Ironically, he receives his "red badge" when a fellow soldier strikes his head with the butt of a gun. He sees his friend Jim Conklin die and tries to find security in a secluded spot in the forest. After attempting to stop the advancing troops he thinks are doomed, Fleming returns to his comrades. During the battle on the next day, he gives up his illusions, merges with the great body of soldiers, and becomes, temporarily at least, a hero.

Crane's realism is remarkable, especially in view of the fact that he had not seen a battle at the time he wrote the book. His insight into the feelings and fears of soldiers provided a new experience to a public unaccustomed to reading about the seamier aspects of war. *The Red Badge of Courage* established Crane's reputation and remains his most popular book.

Red Book of Hergest. A Welsh manuscript of the 14th century. Its contents, highly interesting to the scholar, are used in the MABINOGION.

Redburn (1849). A novel by Herman MELVILLE. Young Redburn, on his first voyage as a sailor, discovers the thinly veiled selfishness behind the actions of most people. He sees death and despair in the slums of Liverpool, as he emerges from innocence into experience. The hero of Melville's only comic novel, Redburn is willing to take the world on its own terms.

Red Cavalry (Konarmiya; 1926). A collection of short stories by Isaak BABEL. It is based on the Soviet author's experiences with Budenny's cavalry regiment during the civil war in Russia.

Red Cross Knight, The. Central character of Book I of Spenser's FAERIE QUEENE. He is identified with St. George, the patron saint of England, and is a symbol of holiness.

Redgauntlet (1824). A novel by Sir Walter SCOTT, told in a series of letters. Sir Edward Redgauntlet is a Jacobite conspirator who aids the bid of the Young Pretender, Charles Edward, for the throne. The whole enterprise proves a fiasco, and Redgauntlet escapes abroad to become a prior. Two notable characters are Peter Peebles, a strange, unbalanced lawyer, and Wandering Willie, a blind fiddler.

Red Gloves. See DIRTY HANDS.

Red Jacket. Indian name **Sagoyewatha** (1758?–1830). American Indian chief of the Senecas. He received his name from the bright red jacket he wore, a gift of the British. At first hostile to the whites, especially Christian missionaries, he later became friendly but did not wish Indian lands ceded to the U.S.

Red Lily, The (Le Lys Rouge; 1894). A novel by Anatole FRANCE. When she meets and falls in love with the sculptor Dechartre, Thérèse Martin-Bellême is already the wife of one man and the mistress of another. Her story is one of passion and frustrated love.

Redon, Odilon (1840–1916). French painter and lithographer. He is known for his beautiful and delicate flower studies and for the deep blacks of his drawings and lithographs. Often depicting fantastic creatures and bizarre visions never quite completely divorced from reality, he was in close contact with Mallarmé and other symbolist writers who recognized affinities with his mystical, poetic work.

Red Rock (1898). A novel by Thomas Nelson PAGE. Page pictures the effect of war and Reconstruction on two old Southern families. The beginnings of the Ku Klux Klan are described, and its motives and actions justified. Red Rock is the old Gray estate, which the hero, Jacquelin Gray, is forced to see in the possession of another man after the Civil War. He gradually wins back the plantation and the love of his old playmate, Blair Cary.

Redskins, The, or Indian and Injin (1846). A novel by James Fenimore COOPER, the third of the LITTLEPAGE MANUSCRIPTS.

reductio ad absurdum. A proof of inference arising from the demonstration that every other hypothesis involves an absurdity. In common parlance, the phrase has come to signify the opposite; an argument that brings out the absurdity of a contention made.

Reed, Henry (1914–   ). English poet and writer for radio. His satirical poems about wartime bureaucracy appeared in *A Map of Verona* (1946).

Reed, John (1887–1920). American journalist and poet. Although he came from a wealthy Oregon family, Reed developed a serious interest in social problems, became friendly with Lincoln Steffens, and joined the staff of *The Masses*. His experiences as a correspondent during the Mexican Revolution furnished the material for his first book, *Insurgent Mexico* (1914). He covered the Eastern Front during World War I, then went to Russia, where he became an active supporter of the Bolsheviks. His eloquent eye-witness account of the Russian Revolution, *Ten Days That Shook the World* (1919), is considered his best work. After helping to found the Communist Party in America, Reed returned to Russia and remained there until his death.

Reed, Walter (1851–1902). American army surgeon. He headed a commission with James Carroll, Jesse Lazear, and Aristides Agramonte to investigate yellow fever in Cuba (1900). Their experiments with volunteers proved earlier contentions that the disease was transmitted by mosquitoes and defined the dangerous type. Sidney Howard's play *Yellow Jack* (1934) depicts their work.

Reese, Lizette Woodworth (1856-1935). American poet. For many years a high school teacher in Baltimore, she published several volumes of verse, from *A Branch of May* (1887) and *A Handful of Lavender* (1891) to *Pastures and Other Poems* (1933) and *The Old House in the Country* (1936). Her sonnet *Tears* became extremely popular.

Reeve's Tale, The. One of the CANTERBURY TALES of Geoffrey CHAUCER, based on a French *fabliau*. Oswald the Reeve takes the MILLER'S TALE as a personal insult, for he is also a carpenter, and retaliates in kind with his tale. The young scholars John and Alan resolve to watch carefully and stop the miller Simkin's gross cheating of their college. But Simkin lets loose their horse, so that they give chase, and proceeds to steal more grain than ever. When they return late, he scornfully offers them a bed for the night in the same room with his family. But in the dark Alan steals over to the lovely daughter's bed, and John, by moving the infant's cradle, tricks the wife into his own bed. The daughter tells Alan where the stolen grain is hidden, and he goes to wake John and boast of his exploits, but is also misled by the cradle and wakes Simkin instead. In the confused fight that follows, the wife knocks out Simkin by mistake, and the scholars escape with all their grain and a little more.

referendum. The submission to the people in general of any act of legislature. In the U.S. about half the states can exercise the referendum as to state matters. In municipal affairs about 300 cities use this principle of action.

Reflections on the French Revolution (1790). A treatise by Edmund BURKE, written in the form of a letter to a Frenchman. It attacks the leaders and principles of the French Revolution for their violence and excesses, and urges reform, rather than rebellion, as a means of correcting social and political abuses. This work was, in turn, attacked by Thomas PAINE. Burke had interpreted the Glorious Revolution (1688) and the American Revolution as just assertions of rights guaranteed by the British Constitution; he opposed the French Revolution because, he thought, it broke the framework of tradition altogether.

Reformation. The great 16th century movement against the authority of the Roman Catholic Church that brought about the establishment of Protestantism. The chief religious leaders of the Reformation were Martin LUTHER, John CALVIN, Ulrich ZWINGLI, and John KNOX. Although the movement originated as a protest against religious abuses, it had profound political implications as well. See THIRTY YEARS WAR.

Reform Bill. In English history, a bill that enlarges the number of voters in elections for the House of Commons, reducing inequalities in representation. The first of these, the Reform Bill of 1832, disfranchised boroughs of very few inhabitants (called rotten boroughs), giving increased representation to large towns and extending the number of holders of the county and borough franchise. The Reform Bill of 1867 went further in the same direction, and the Franchise Bill (1884) extended suffrage to nearly all men. In 1918 suffrage was given to all men over 21 and to women over 30; in 1928, all persons over 21 were eligible to vote. The background of George Eliot's *Middlemarch* is the Reform Bill of 1832.

Regan. In Shakespeare's KING LEAR, the 2nd daughter of Lear. Like her older sister, Goneril, she refuses to house her father's large entourage and later aids her husband, Cornwall, in plucking out Gloucester's eyes when he shelters Lear. After her husband's death, she plans to marry Edmund, but is poisoned by the jealous Goneril.

Regent Street. A street in London containing many fine shops; it was originally (1813) designed to connect Carlton House, then the residence of the Regent, with Regent's Park.

Regillus, Lake. A lake near Rome. It was the scene of a battle in which the Romans defeated the Latins (498 B.C.).

Régnard, Jean François (1655-1709). French comic dramatist. He was once captured by pirates and sold as a slave in Constantinople. He traveled extensively, settling finally in Paris where he wrote his autobiographical *Voyages* (1731). His fortune permitted him to live and entertain lavishly. Among his more celebrated comedies in verse are *Le Joueur* (*The Gambler,* 1696), *Les Folies amoureuses* (*Amorous Follies,* 1704), *Les Ménechmes* (1705), and his masterpiece, *Le Légataire universel* (1708). Régnard's plays are simply gay, witty, and sparkling, with no attempt at being profound; indeed, human sympathy is conspicuously absent. Régnard was long regarded as the closest successor to Molière.

Régnier, Henri de (1864-1936). French poet and novelist. As a member of the SYMBOLISTS and a disciple of Mallarmé, Régnier wrote verse, such as that published in *Tel qu'en songe* (1892) and *Les Jeux rustiques et divins* (1897), which was musical and skillful in its use of vers libre. In his later work—such volumes as *Les Medailles d'argile* (1900) and *La Sandale Ailée* (1906)—he returned to classical forms and sought themes for his poetry in antiquity. Régnier's best-known novel is *La Double Maitresse* (1900).

Rehoboam. A Hebrew king in the Old Testament, the son and successor of Solomon. During his leadership, the northern tribes revolted and, retaining the name Israel, formed a new kingdom under Jeroboam. His remark, "My father . . . chastised you with whips, but I will chastise you with scorpions" (I Kings 12:14), cost him the allegiance of the greater part of his kingdom; only the tribe of Judah and part of the tribe of Benjamin remained loyal.

Reid, Forrest (1875-1947). Irish novelist, biographer, and critic. Particularly sensitive to the thought and spirit of children, he wrote about them in the novels *Spring Song* (1916), *Pirates of the Spring* (1919), and *Young Tom* (1944). Reid also wrote a biography of Walter de la Mare (1929).

Reid, [Thomas] Mayne (1818-1883). Anglo-Irish novelist. He wrote spirited stories of the American frontier, such as *The Rifle Rangers* (1850), *The Scalp Hunters* (1851), *The Quadroon* (1856), and *Afloat in the Forest* (1865).

Reigen. See RONDE, LA.

Reign of Terror. A term applied to the period of anarchy, bloodshed, and confiscation in the FRENCH REVOLUTION. It may be considered to have begun on Jan. 21, 1793, with the execution of Louis XVI, or after May 31, 1793, when the GIRONDISTS fell; it extended to the overthrow of ROBESPIERRE and his accomplices on July 27, 1794. During this period thousands of persons were put to death. The name is also applied to similar cataclysms in the histories of other nations, such as the Red Terror of the Russian Revolution (March–Sept., 1917).

Reik, Theodor (1888–1969). Austrian-born psychoanalyst and writer. A pupil of Freud, Reik came to the U.S. in 1938 and ultimately departed from orthodox Freudianism. In *The Psychology of Sex Relations* (1945) he rejected the Freudian concept that neuroses have sexual roots. *Listening with the Third Ear* (1948) discusses the process of psychoanalysis. *Fragment of a Great Confession* (1949) is his autobiography. Other books include *The Secret Self* (1952), *The Haunting Melody* (1953), *The Search Within* (1956), *Of Love and Lust* (1957), *The Compulsion to Confess* (1959), *The Creation of Woman* (1960), and *The Need to Be Loved* (1963).

Reineke Fuchs (1794). An epic poem in hexameters by Johann Wolfgang von GOETHE, which retells the story of REYNARD THE FOX. Goethe lays stress upon the fact that the amoral man, even though his crimes may be harmful to others, is still useful to society because of his superior resourcefulness, and necessary to society as a balance to the gradual stultification of unchallenged morality.

Reinhardt, Max. Originally **Max Goldmann** (1873–1943). Austrian stage director and producer specializing in mass effects; he is best known for *Sumurun* (New York, 1912), *The Miracle* (London, 1911), and *Oedipus Rex.* He toured the U.S. in 1923, producing his pageant-play, *The Miracle.* Regularly every year at Salzburg he produced the mystery play *Everyman.* Upon Hitler's coming to power, Reinhardt left the continent, worked in England and America, became a film director in Hollywood, and, in 1937, put on Werfel's *Eternal Road* in New York City.

Rejected Addresses. See James and Horace SMITH.

Relations des Jésuites (Accounts of the Jesuits, 1632–1672). The reports of the French Jesuit missionaries to Canada, distributed in Paris under the title *Relations de ce qui est passé en nouvelle France (Accounts of What Has Happened in New France).* They remain to this day an invaluable source of information on early Canadian history.

Religio Laici (1682). A poem by John DRYDEN in defense of the Anglican religion. It preceded his famous defense of Catholicism, *The Hind and the Panther,* by only three years. The work is a witty and cogent argument for the middle way of Anglicanism.

Religio Medici (*Lat.,* "a doctor's religion"; 1643). The best-known work of Sir Thomas BROWNE, who called it "a private Exercise directed to myself." Published only after a pirated edition had appeared, it represents Browne's attempt to arrive at a warm and vital faith, one without cant or a spirit of exclusiveness, acceptable to a scientist. It is one of the great achievements in the ornate style of English prose.

Reliques of Ancient English Poetry (1765). A collection of ballads, sonnets, historical songs, and romances published by Thomas PERCY; more properly, it is one of the earliest histories of literature. It contains metrical romances and traditional ballads from

RELIQUES

OF

ANCIENT ENGLISH POETRY:

CONSISTING OF

Old Heroic BALLADS, SONGS, and other PIECES of our earlier POETS,

(Chiefly of the LYRIC kind.)

Together with some few of later Date.

VOLUME THE FIRST.

DURAT OPUS VATUM

LONDON:

Printed for J. DODSLEY in Pall-Mall.

M DCC LXV.

Title page of Percy's *Reliques* (1st edition, 1765).

the 15th and 18th centuries, all arranged in chronological order. In it appeared for the first time such famous ballads as *Sir Patrick Spens* and *Edward, Edward.*

Remarque, Erich Maria (1898–1970). German journalist and novelist. Like most of his generation, he was deeply affected by World War I, which is the subject of his most successful novel ALL QUIET ON THE WESTERN FRONT (*Im Westen nichts Neues;* 1929). Other novels are *Der Weg zurück (The Road Back,* 1931), *Arc de Triomphe* (1947), *Spark of Life* (1951), *A Time to Love and a Time to Die* (1954), *The Black Obelisk* (1957), and *Heaven Has No Favorites* (1961). He left Germany in 1932 because of Nazism, came to the U.S. in 1937, and has been a citizen since 1947.

Rembrandt [Harmenszoon van Rijn] (1606–1669). Dutch painter and etcher. Born in Leyden, he settled in Amsterdam in 1631 and quickly established himself as the finest portrait painter of the city. His wife died in 1642, leaving him a considerable fortune, but his popularity declined as his art became increasingly divergent from popular taste, and he sank into financial difficulties. A declaration of bankruptcy, in 1656, was followed by the sale of his property, including his art collection. His faithful companion, Hendrikje Stoffels, and his son Titus provided for him a position in their art-dealing firm, but both died before him.

The range of Rembrandt's art is unusually extensive. He painted numerous portraits, both of individuals and of groups, and he is as well known for the lively *Night Watch* or *Sortie of the Banning Cock Company* (1642) as for the splendid self-portraits in which he recorded the gradual alteration of his features with searching integrity and nobility. Here, as in his religious paintings and studies of the nude, he transfixed reality through harmony of color, light, and shadow. In many of his paintings a concentrated light falls on the central figure while the rest of the picture remains enveloped in dark but transparent shadows that continue to define details. Cool at first, this lighting gradually grew softer, the technique freer and simpler, until it became the mellowing color typified by the golden brown of his mature years.

Mention must also be made of his extraordinary etchings. The grandeur of his conception of the Crucifixion and of other scenes from the life of Christ is enhanced by the intense realism with which the poor of the city are represented, gathered around the holy figure. Also greatly prized are his pen-and-wash drawings, brief notations of great vigor and expressiveness, that further reveal this master as a great landscapist.

Remember the Maine. A slogan used in the SPANISH AMERICAN WAR after the destruction of the U.S. battleship *Maine* in Havana harbor.

Remembrance of Things Past (A la recherche du temps perdu; 16 vols., 1913–1927). A long novel in 7 parts by Marcel PROUST. Except for *The*

Past Recaptured, which is translated by Stephen Hudson, the English translation (1922–1931) is the work of C. K. Scott-Moncrieff. Proust's own French title indicates this great work's subject and theme; the narrator is "in search of lost time," and he finds in involuntary memories stimulated by some object or circumstance the true meaning of past experience. He could not appreciate this meaning at the time of the experience itself; and conscious attempts at recollection only serve to change his view of the experience, according to the perspective of the new self he has meanwhile become. But certain "privileged moments" of memory, evoked by unconscious associations, mean simultaneous existence in the past and present; they thus permit a glimpse of the essence common to both, a transcendental reality independent of time.

Otherwise, time invariably produces a kaleidoscopically changing series of patterns in people and their emotions, as well as in society and its fashions. The novel exposes the illusory nature of the narrator's early ideals, especially those regarding the permanence of love and the absoluteness of any hierarchy of values. Love, at first inspired by unattainability, becomes boring after consummation, unless continually stimulated by jealousy. Even the inhabitants of the fashionable and exclusive Faubourg St. Germain greatly disappoint the bourgeois narrator, once he has climbed carefully from salon to salon to view their supposedly gallant splendor and cultivated wit. In structure, the novel first introduces as opposite paths the Méséglise Way, which leads past Swann's bourgeois estate, and the Guermantes Way, leading toward a royally titled estate—both at first impossible for the narrator to enter. But he gradually discovers

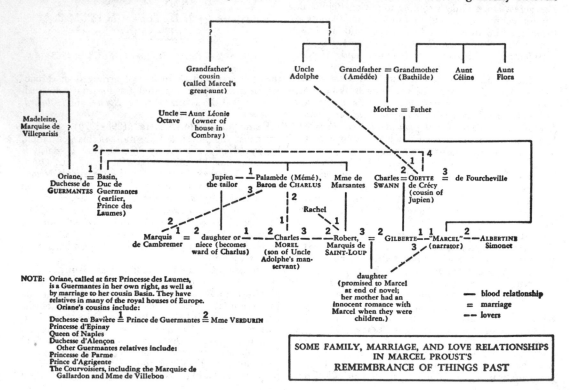

NOTE: Oriane, called at first Princesse des Laumes, is a Guermantes in her own right, as well as by marriage to her cousin Basin. They have relatives in many of the royal houses of Europe.
    Oriane's cousins include:
Duchesse en Bavière ≗ Prince de Guermantes ≗ Mme VERDURIN
Princesse d'Epinay
Queen of Naples
Duchesse d'Alençon
    Other Guermantes relatives include:
Princesse de Parme
Prince d'Agrigente
The Courvoisiers, including the Marquise de Gallardon and Mme de Villebon

— blood relationship
= marriage
-- lovers

SOME FAMILY, MARRIAGE, AND LOVE RELATIONSHIPS IN MARCEL PROUST'S
REMEMBRANCE OF THINGS PAST

the personal relationships that increasingly connect these families and the ways of life they represent. Eventually, even the superficial appearances of difference degenerate and take new shapes, until Swann's daughter—by a cocotte whom the Guermantes had formerly refused to meet—has married a Guermantes and offers her daughter by this marriage to the narrator as a mistress.

The analysis of love includes male and female homosexual relationships, showing their essential similarity to heterosexual ones. The analysis of snobbery exposes pathetic self-delusion as much as deliberate hypocrisy. In regard to artists and their work, as to everything else, anticipated pleasure always exceeds the actual pleasure at first meeting; but, after assimilation of the work of the actress Berma, the writer Bergotte, the composer Vinteuil, and the painter Elstir, the narrator does conclude that art can occasionally—as can dreams, but never life—express the associations that make perceptible the world of essential reality, which lies outside of lived Time.

Swann's Way (*Du côté de chez Swann*). After the *Overture* introduces most of the themes of the entire novel, the narrator recalls his childhood at home in Paris and with his relatives at COMBRAY, including his idealized love for SWANN's daughter, GILBERTE. He then recounts the story of Swann's love for ODETTE many years before, which is intertwined with the beginning of the rise of the VERDURINS.

Within a Budding Grove (*A l'ombre des jeunes filles en fleurs*). In Paris the narrator's love for Gilberte slowly ends. Two years later, when he is at BALBEC, he falls in love with a little band of frolicsome girls and particularly with ALBERTINE.

The Guermantes Way (*Le Côté de Guermantes*). The narrator, whose family have been tenants in the large GUERMANTES home in Paris, conducts his laborious ascent to the summit of high society, finally attending the duchesse de Guermantes' reception. He also describes SAINT-LOUP's passion for RACHEL, and the death of his own beloved grandmother.

Cities of the Plain (*Sodome et Gomorrhe*). The narrator discovers Baron CHARLUS' homosexuality and the changing nature of socially fashionable opinions—regarding the Dreyfus Case, for instance. After a reception given by the princesse de Guermantes, he returns to Balbec, where Charlus is launching MOREL at the Verdurins' *soirées*. He is about to break with Albertine when suspicions of her lesbian tastes arouse his horror and jealousy, and revive his love.

The Captive (*La Prisonnière*). Albertine is living in the narrator's Paris home, where he attempts to keep complete watch on her activities. The Verdurins provoke a scandalous rupture between Morel and Charlus. Albertine suddenly flees, just as the narrator is ready to dismiss her.

The Sweet Cheat Gone (*Albertine disparue*). The narrator seeks the return of Albertine, but after her death he observes the gradual encroachment of oblivion on grief until, on a trip to Venice, he finds his pain completely cured. Gilberte has become the social-climbing Mlle. de Forcheville; she marries Saint-Loup, who is now Morel's lover.

The Past Recaptured (*Le Temps retrouvé*). World War I accelerates the kaleidoscopic changes in society. The narrator attends a reception of the new princesse de Guermantes, actually the former Mme. Verdurin,

and finds most of his acquaintances almost unrecognizable. He has enjoyed three "privileged moments" of memory, and in contemplating them discovers that his vocation is to be the shaping of his experiences into a literary work of art.

Remington, Frederic [Cackrider] (1861–1909). American painter and illustrator. He is best known for his scenes of the American West and for his tense, animated drawings and sculptures of horses.

Remizov, Aleksei Mikhailovich (1877–1957). Russian novelist. Remizov, whose ornate prose style influenced such Soviet writers as Boris Pilnyak, Isaak Babel, and Yevgeni Zamyatin, left Russia in 1921 and lived in Paris for the remainder of his life. His works include *The Pond* (*Prud;* 1907), *The Fifth Pestilence* (*Pyataya chuma;* 1912), and *Flaming Russia* (*Plamennaya rossiya;* 1921).

Remus. See ROMULUS.

Renaissance, the. From the French word for *rebirth*. First used by 19th-century historians, it is a label for the period dating approximately from the mid-14th century to the end of the 16th century. During the period itself, the idea of a revival or rebirth of culture after the barbarism of the Dark Ages and the medieval period was a favorite notion of the Humanists; but they did not use the word itself. It was used at the time by such art historians as Vasari, whose reference was exclusively to the fine arts. With Michelet and Burckhardt, the term and the concept of the Renaissance came into general use. Since their day, controversy has centered on denigration of the Middle Ages, on the chronological limits of the period, on its applicability to science and philosophy of the time, on its causes, and even on its value as a term for widely differing phenomena in Europe, especially outside Italy. There is essential agreement, however, on the main ingredients of the era. These include the REVIVAL OF ANTIQUITY, the REVIVAL OF LEARNING, the activity of the Humanists, the increased secularization of social life, the burst of creativity in the fine arts, the cultivation of the arts, the growth of individualism in private as well as public life, the expansion of scientific and philosophical horizons, the creation of new social, political, and economic institutions, and the arrival of a new view of man and his world. In the literary sphere, the men of letters and the works of the period, from Petrarch to Shakespeare, represent an impressive roster unmatched before or since. There is a continuity of themes and forms as the wave of inspiration passed from Italy to France and Spain, then to England, where the novelle of Boccaccio and the sonnets of Petrarch were being read and imitated two centuries after their composition. See FRENCH RENAISSANCE; HUMANISM.

Renan, Ernest (1823–1892). French critic, writer, and scholar. Raised in poverty, Renan was a student preparing for the priesthood when he lost his faith in orthodox religion due to the influence of German philosophy and Semitic philology. Renan later became a relativist. From a tolerant, skeptical point of view, he realized that no one system of religious, scientific, or historical knowledge could claim absolute truth. A professor of Hebrew at the Collège de France, Renan's major influence was felt in the field of religion. In 1863 he published *La Vie de Jésus* (*The Life of Jesus*), the first work in a series called *Histoire des Origines du Christianisme* (*History of the Origins of Christianity*, 1866–1881). This study offered a new perspective on religious history, approaching the subject matter not merely in a factual, historical manner but as biography and psychology. Renan also published *Histoire du Peuple d'Israël* (*History of the People of Israel*, 1887–95), *Histoire générale des Langues Semitiques* (*General History of the Semitic Languages*, 1855), and *Dialogues Philosophiques* (1876). Anatole France, Paul Bourget, and Maurice Barrès were influenced by his work.

Renascence (1912). A poem by Edna St. Vincent MILLAY. It was first published in Mitchell Kennerley's *The Lyric Year*, an anthology of prize-winning poems which was part of the resurgence of poetry in the early 20th century. In the poem, the author describes a semimystical experience in which she experiences sin and suffering, desires death, but is then given a rebirth of innocence and knowledge of God.

Renault, Mary. Pen name of **Mary Challans** (1905–). British novelist. Miss Renault has produced novels on contemporary subjects, often drawing on her experiences as a hospital and war nurse, as well as on ancient and mythological subjects. Her works include *Purposes of Love* (1939); *Kind Are Her Answers* (1940); *The Friendly Young Ladies* (1944); *Return to Night* (1946); *North Face* (1948); *The Charioteer* (1953), a well-received and compassionate examination of homosexuality; *The Last of the Wine* (1956), set during the wars between Athens and Sparta; *The King Must Die* (1958); and *The Bull from the Sea* (1962), both recreations of the legend of Theseus.

Renault or **Renaud of Montauban** or **Reynold of Montalban.** One of Charlemagne's PALADINS, better known by his Italian name RINALDO.

René. A romance by François René de CHATEAUBRIAND, published first in *Le Génie du Christianisme* (1802), and as a separate volume in 1805. Set in America, the story's hero is a violently unhappy, morbidly introspective youth whose posture is typically romantic.

René, Le bon roi (1408–1480). Duc d'Anjou, comte de Provence, son of the French King Louis II. His daughter, Margaret of Anjou, married the English King Henry VI. Devoted to knight-errantry and hunting, and a patron of musicians and poets, René was more generous than his income warranted. He appears in Sir Walter Scott's ANNE OF GEIERSTEIN, and as Reignier in Shakespeare's *Henry VI*.

Reni, Guido (1575–1642). Italian painter. A product of the Bologna school of Eclecticism founded by the CARRACCI, he was the most famous painter of his day. A skillful designer, his ability may be seen in such works as the *Apollo and Marsyas,* the *Aurora* (1613), and the popular *Massacre of the Innocents* (1611), a key work of the COUNTER-REFORMATION style. His series of episodes from the life of Samson, especially the noteworthy *Triumph of Samson* (c. 1611), may be seen today in the Vatican.

Renn, Ludwig. Pen name of **Arnold Vieth von Golssenau** (1889–). German novelist. He is best known for his works on war, including: *Krieg* (*War*, 1928) and *Vor grossen Wandlungen* (translated as *Death Without Battle*, 1936).

Renoir, [Pierre] Auguste (1841–1919). French painter. One of the great masters of modern French painting, Renoir was born in Limoges. A leading impressionist, he painted pure luminous landscapes, nudes, still lifes, and many groups and portraits, e.g., *Madame Charpentier and her daughters* in the Metropolitan Museum of Art, New York. After a brief period in the 1880's during which he enclosed his forms in a precise line, he resumed his earlier style, painting women and nudes with even greater freedom and vigor, and never abandoning his sensuous, visual delight in life and the world around him.

Renoir, Jean (1894–). French motion-picture director. Among the most notable of his many films are *Grand Illusion* (1937), *The Rules of the Game* (1939), and *The River* (1950). The son of Auguste Renoir, he is also the author of *Renoir, My Father* (1962), a vivid and affectionate reminiscence of the famous impressionist painter.

Repington, Charles à Court (1858–1925). British soldier and military correspondent. His gossipy *The First World War* (1920) and *After the War* (1922) made free use of private conversations and letters, causing much scandal.

Repplier, Agnes (1855–1950). American writer. She is known for the grace, wit, and learning of her personal essays. Among her many collections are *Books and Men* (1888), *Essays in Miniature* (1892), and *Compromises* (1904). *In Pursuit of Laughter* (1936) was in effect a history of humor. She also wrote biographies of Roman Catholic subjects.

Representative Men (1850). A series of biographical sketches by Ralph Waldo EMERSON. The men discussed are Shakespeare, the Poet; Plato, the Philosopher; Goethe, the Writer; Swedenborg, the Mystic; Napoleon, the Man of the World; and Montaigne, the Skeptic. The essays are preceded by an introduction dealing with the "uses of great men." The book is modeled on Carlyle's *On Heroes, Hero Worship and the Heroic in History*. The two volumes reveal the difference in their author's feelings about democracy. Unlike Carlyle, Emerson believed that great men are representative of their time, rather than apart from it.

Reprieve, The. See ROADS TO FREEDOM, THE.

Republic, The. A dialogue by PLATO. In it Socrates' interlocutors are Cephalus, Polemarchus, Thrasymachus, and Plato's brothers, Glaucon and Adeimantus. The dialogue begins with an attempt at the definition of justice. Socrates remarks that before justice can be found in the individual, it must be sought in the state. Describing the ideal state, Plato's Socrates divides the citizens into three classes: the guardians, the soldiers, and the workers or producers. Democracy and tyranny are both rejected. Temperance and restraint must characterize all three classes. Political justice would confine each to his proper function.

Requiem for a Nun (1951). A novel by William FAULKNER. Written in three prose sections, which provide the background, and three acts which present the drama in the courthouse and the jail, the novel centers on Temple DRAKE, one of the main characters of SANCTUARY. In the interval of the eight years separating the events of the two books, Temple has married Gowan Stevens and borne two children; she is being blackmailed by Pete, brother of her lover in

Sanctuary, and is planning to run away with him when Nancy MANNINGOE, her Negro servant, kills Temple's youngest child. Her attempts to gain a pardon from the governor for Nancy finally bring out Temple's own involvement in and responsibility for the crime.

Rescue, The (1920). A novel by Joseph CONRAD. Its hero, Captain LINGARD, is faced with a moral choice: he has to choose between the rajah he has promised to serve and the woman he loves.

Resnais, Alain (1922–). French film director associated with writers of the NEW WAVE. He uses the techniques of this school in films such as *Hiroshima mon amour* (1959), scenario by Marguerite Duras, and *Last Year at Marienbad* (1961), scenario by Alain Robbe-Grillet.

Resolution and Independence (1807). A poem by William WORDSWORTH. Sentimentally portraying the sad lot of an old and crippled leech-gatherer whom the poet encounters on one of his country walks, it was originally entitled *The Leech-gatherer*. It was parodied by Edward Lear in *Incidents in the Life of My Uncle Arly* and by Lewis Carroll in *The White Knight's Ballad*.

Respectful Prostitute, The (La Putain respectueuse; 1946). A play by Jean-Paul SARTRE. It is set in the American South. Lizzie does not want to lie to help build a case against an innocent Negro. But the senator's son Fred needs a scapegoat for his cousin Thomas, who killed another Negro, and Lizzie is finally so thoroughly confused about relative rights and wrongs that she agrees.

Respighi, Ottorino (1879–1936). Italian impressionist composer, violinist, pianist, and conductor. His best-known works are the two tone poems: *Fontane di Roma* (*Fountains of Rome,* 1917) and *Pini di Roma* (*Pines of Rome,* 1924).

Restif or **Rétif de la Bretonne, Nicolas Edmé** (1734–1806). French novelist and dramatist, often labelled as the "Rousseau of the Gutter," or the "Voltaire of Chambermaids." He wrote some 250 volumes, many of which describe peasant life and lower-class women. To gather material for his works he was wont to prowl around Paris at night. In 1775 he published *Le Paysan perverti ou les dangers de la ville,* a four-volume novel about the corrupting influences of Paris on a young peasant. From 1780 to 1785 he published his 42-volume work on the lives of contemporary women, *Les Contemporaines ou Aventures des plus jolies femmes de l'âge présent.* His intimate knowledge of women is reflected in his self-appraisal: "Without women, I was a nonentity, without vigor, without energy, in a word, without a soul." *La Vie de mon père* (1779, 2 vols.) is perhaps his masterpiece. He also wrote a series of works under the general title of *Les Idées singulières* (1769–89), in which he advocated reforms in education, prostitution, the theater, and spelling. In his novels Restif presents a faithful picture of the last 30 years of the French monarchy, but some readers find his style coarse and the subject matter melodramatic and sometimes obscene.

Restoration. In English history, the period after the fall of the Commonwealth, when the Stuart dynasty returned to England in the person of Charles II, who became king in 1660. In its reaction to Puritan austerity and its imitation of French manners, the period gained a reputation for licentiousness and frivolity. It is marked in the field of English letters by characteristic developments in the drama (Dryden, Congreve, Wycherly, Farquhar), particularly in the prose comedy of manners; by the flourishing of song and verse satire (Dryden, Rochester); and by the productions of numerous diarists (Pepys, Evelyn). These forms, though they confirm the worldliness and dissoluteness of the Restoration, are only a partial expression of the age, which also saw remarkable accomplishments in prose composition, science, philosophy, and religion.

Resurrection (Voskreseniye; 1899). A novel by Count Leo TOLSTOI. The story deals with the spiritual regeneration of a young nobleman, Prince Nekhlyudov. In his earlier years, he seduced a young girl, Katyusha Maslova. She became a prostitute and later became involved with a man whom she is accused of poisoning. Nekhlyudov, serving on the jury, recognizes her and decides that he is morally guilty for her predicament. He decides to marry her, and when she is convicted he follows her to Siberia to accomplish his aim. Maslova is repelled by his reforming zeal. She marries another prisoner, but is finally convinced of Nekhlyudov's sincerity and accepts his friendship.

The novel, which is the weakest of Tolstoi's three large works, was very popular at the time of its publication. Tolstoi used the money received from it to help the Russian religious sect of Dukhobors to emigrate to Canada.

resurrection man, also called **body snatcher.** A purloiner or snatcher of newly buried bodies. Such bodies were sold to surgeons for dissection. The first instance on record of robbing a grave was in 1777, when the body of Mrs. Jane Salisbury was "resurrected" from the burial ground near Gray's Inn Lane. The term "resurrection men" was first applied in 1829 to two men who stole bodies for dissection and even murdered for this purpose. Jerry CRUNCHER in Dickens' *A Tale of Two Cities* is a resurrection man.

Retablo de Maese Pedro, El (Master Peter's Puppet Show, 1923). A one-act opera by Manuel de FALLA. It is based on a scene in Cervantes' *Don Quixote* in which the melancholy knight watches a puppet show in an inn-yard. He becomes so engrossed in the romantic tale of Charlemagne's daughter MELISENDA and her knight Don Gayferos that he beheads the villainous Moorish puppets and launches into an apostrophe to the institution of chivalry, while the puppeteer and his boy rescue their depleted company.

Retrieved Reformation, A (1909). A short story by O. HENRY. It relates the ironic fate of Jimmy Valentine, a burglar who decides to reform but is foiled when he shows his skill in opening a safe during an emergency. Jimmy is said to have been modeled on Jimmy Connors, O. Henry's fellow prisoner in the Ohio state penitentiary. Paul Armstrong based his successful play *Alias Jimmy Valentine* (1909) on the story.

Return, The (1910). A novel by Walter DE LA MARE, about a man possessed by a dead man's spirit. It is characterized by mysteriousness, grisly humor, and some satire of society.

Return of the Druses (1841). A verse tragedy by Robert BROWNING. The Druses, a semi-Islamic sect

of Syria, are attacked by Osman and take refuge in
one of the Sporades, placing themselves under the
protection of the knights of Rhodes. The knights
betray them, slaying all the sheiks except Djabal, who
is saved by Maäni. Djabal conceives the plan of revenging his people and leading them back to Syria,
and to this end he proclaims himself Hakim, the
incarnate god returned to earth, and thus becomes
leader of the exiled Druses. The Druses bargain with
Venice to betray the island in exchange for a convoy
for their own return. Aneal, a young Druse woman,
stabs the prefect of the island, but dies of bitter disappointment when she discovers that Djabal is a mere
impostor. His fraud exposed, Djabal stabs himself,
and Loys, a Breton count, leades the exiles back to
Lebanon.

Return of the Native, The (1878). A novel by
Thomas HARDY. Clym Yeobright, tired of city life,
returns from Paris to open a school on Egdon Heath,
and in spite of the opposition of his mother, marries
Eustacia Vye, a passionate, pleasure-loving girl who
hopes to persuade him to return to Paris. She has
been in love with reckless Damon Wildeve, who, to
spite her, married Clym's cousin, Thomasin. Clym's
eyesight fails and he becomes, for the time being, a
furze cutter. With the idea of becoming reconciled
to her son, Mrs. Yeobright walks over the heath to
his cottage, but Eustacia, entertaining Wildeve, does
not answer the door until Clym's mother leaves in
despair. Overcome with fatigue, she sinks down and
is found by Clym, unconscious and dying of an adder
bite. Clym learns enough to blame Eustacia, who subsequently drowns herself at a midnight rendezvous
with Wildeve, who also drowns attempting to rescue
her. Thomasin later marries Diggory Venn, the red-
dleman, and Clym becomes an itinerant preacher.

Retz or **Rais, Gilles [de Laval] de** (1404?–
1440). A Marshal of France who fought with Joan
of Arc against the English. A generous patron of the
arts, he turned to alchemy and sorcery to recoup his
fortune, and was said to have kidnaped and murdered children. He was tried and executed for heresy
and murder. It used to be thought that his history
was the origin of the story of BLUEBEARD.

Reuchlin, Johann (1455–1522). German jurist
and humanist, famous for his Greek and Hebrew
studies. His *De Verbo Mirifico* (*The Miraculous
Word,* 1494), a defense of Jewish literature and philosophy, brought him into conflict with the Dominicans and the apostate Jew Pfefferkorn, who advocated
the destruction of Jewish books. Other humanists, in
the EPISTOLAE OBSCURORUM VIRORUM, supported
Reuchlin in the dispute.

Reunion in Vienna (1931). A play by Robert E.
SHERWOOD. An exiled Hapsburg archduke returning
to Vienna arranges a rendezvous with his former
mistress, who has married a psychiatrist in his absence. The doctor is too involved in psychoanalytic
theories to be outraged at his cuckoldom: he believes
the affair will cure his wife of an obsession.

Reuter, Baron Paul Julius von. Original name
Israel Beer Josaphat (1816–1899). German-born
English capitalist. He established in Aachen (1849)
a telegraphic and pigeon post bureau for the collection and transmission of news. This was the beginning of Reuter's News Agency, which established its
headquarters in London in 1851.

Revelation of Saint John the Divine, The.
The only purely apocalyptic book in the New Testament. The unknown author, a prisoner of Rome on
the island of Patmos, saw a vision of the end of the
world and the final triumph of Jesus. The book is
highly symbolic and employs mystic numbers. See
ANTICHRIST.

Revenge, The (1878). A ballad by Alfred, Lord
TENNYSON. It recounts the fight of the ship *Revenge*
under Sir Richard Grenville against a fleet of 53
Spanish ships.

Revenger's Tragedy, The (1607). A Senecan
tragedy by Cyril TOURNEUR. It tells of the revenge
taken by Vendice upon a duke who had poisoned
Vendice's mistress when she refused his advances.
The play describes in almost grotesque detail the
incredible degeneracy of the duke and his court.

revenons à nos moutons (Fr.). Literally, "let us
come back to our sheep," a phrase used to express,
"Let us return to our subject." It is taken from the
14th-century French comedy *La Farce de Maître
Pathelin,* or *L'Avocat Pathelin* (line 1282), in which
a woolen-draper charges a shepherd with ill-treating
his sheep. In telling his story he keeps running away
from his subject, and to throw discredit on the defendant's attorney (Pathelin), accuses him of stealing
a piece of cloth. The judge must pull him up every
moment with, *"Mais mon ami, revenons à nos
moutons."* The phrase is frequently quoted by
Rabelais.

Reverdy, Pierre (1889–1960). French poet. A
friend of Apollinaire and those who were to form the
surrealist movement, he employs a technique that
makes use of fantastic, illogical, disturbing images.
His early work (1915–1922) is collected in *Plupart
du Temps* (1945), his later work in *Main-d'oeuvre*
(1949). Reverdy's poetic theories are explained in
Le Gant de crin (1926).

Revere, Paul (1735–1818). American patriot and
craftsman. A successful silversmith by trade, Revere
is best remembered for his midnight ride from Boston
to LEXINGTON on April 18–19, 1775, to warn the
colonists that British soldiers were on the march.
Revere's exploit is described in Longfellow's popular,
though inaccurate, ballad *The Midnight Ride of
Paul Revere* (1863).

**Reverie at the Boar's Head Tavern in East-
cheap, A** (1760). A dream-tale written by Oliver
GOLDSMITH in which the dreamer is transplanted back
in time and recounts the history of the Boar's Head
Tavern.

**Reveries of a Bachelor, or, A Book of the
Heart** (1850). A book by Ik Marvel (Donald Grant
MITCHELL). The four mildly sentimental reveries re-
veal a bachelor's thoughts on love and marriage.

Revival of Antiquity. One of the key aspects of
the RENAISSANCE and a leading activity of the advocates of HUMANISM in Italy during the 14th and 15th
centuries. It refers specifically to the search for lost
manuscripts, the recovery of statues, medallions, coins,
and other artifacts of classical civilization, a renewed
interest in the available remnants of Greek and Roman art, especially its sculpture and architecture, its
philosophy, and its literature. Finally, the term refers
to the putting into practice of classical precepts and
ideals in education, in political and social life, and in
the creation of works of art and literature.

Revival of Learning. Sometimes identified with the RENAISSANCE and HUMANISM. More accurately, the term refers to the quickening pace of activity in philology, scholarship, criticism, and education that occurred in Italy from the mid-14th through the 16th century, and in other European countries shortly thereafter. Modern theory attributes the revival to the economic and political conditions of the Italian city-states and petty kingdoms, where a craving for culture was a characteristic of the individual as well as the society.

Revolt of the Angels, The (La Révolte des anges; 1914). A satirical novel by Anatole FRANCE. A group of angels, weary of life in heaven, seek to amuse themselves in modern Paris. They finally defect to the ranks of Satan.

Revolutionary calendar. The calendar of the first French republic. Dated from Sept. 22, 1792, it divided the year into 12 months of 30 days each, with 5 (6, every leap year) additional days of celebration. The old system was restored by Napoleon on Dec. 31, 1805. See BRUMAIRE; THERMIDOR.

Rexroth, Kenneth (1905–   ). American poet. Rexroth has published many collections of his poetry, among them *The Phoenix and the Tortoise* (1944), *The Art of Worldly Wisdom* (1949), *Signature of All Things* (1950), and *In Defense of Earth* (1956). A self-educated linguist, he has made excellent translations of Oriental poetry and collected them in *One Hundred Poems from the Japanese* (1955) and *One Hundred Poems from the Chinese* (1956). *Bird in the Bush* (1959) and *Assays* (1962) are collections of essays. His ballet *Original Sin* was performed in 1961 by the San Francisco Ballet.

Reyes, Alfonso (1889–1959). Mexican essayist and poet. One of the young Mexican intellectuals who formed the circle known as the *Ateneo de la Juventud*, Reyes left his homeland soon after receiving his law degree in 1913. He lived in Spain until 1924 and subsequently served as Mexican minister or ambassador to France, Argentina, and Brazil. He returned permanently to Mexico in 1939.

Often considered the finest prose stylist of Spanish America since Rodó, Reyes was also an authority on the literature of Spain's golden age. He eschewed pedantry, however, and his work is remarkable for its subtlety, grace, and insight. His best-known book is probably *Visión de Anahuac, 1519* (1917), a depiction of Aztec civilization just before the Spanish Conquest. His collections of essays include *Capítulos de literatura española* (1939; 1945), *Pasado immediato y otros ensayos* (1941), *Ultima Tule* (1942), and *Tentativas y orientaciones* (1944). He also wrote *El deslinde* (1944), an introduction to literary theory; *Letras de la Nueva España* (1948), on the culture of colonial Mexico; and *La X en la frente* (1952), an interpretation of Mexico. *Ifigenia cruel* (1924) is a dramatic poem based on the classical legend.

Reyles, Carlos (1868–1938). Uruguayan novelist. Independently wealthy, Reyles was able to devote his life to writing and other intellectual pursuits. His early novels are naturalistic and emphasize psychological analysis. Among these works are *Beba* (1894), about the evil effects of consanguinity on both men and animals; *La raza de Caín* (1900), a study in abnormal psychology; and *El terruño* (1916), which reflects the author's familiarity with ranch life. His

best-known work is probably *El embrujo de Sevilla* (*Castanets*, 1922), a sensuous, lyrical novel, in which the Andalusian city itself is the dominant figure. He also wrote *El gaucho florido* (1932), another realistic portrayal of rural life.

Reymont, Wladyslaw Stanislaw (1868–1925). A Polish novelist, chiefly known for his four-volume masterpiece, *The Peasants*, for which he received the Nobel prize for literature (1924).

Reynaldo. In Shakespeare's HAMLET, a servant to Polonius. Polonius asks him to report on the conduct of his son Laertes, who is a student in Paris.

Reynard the Fox. A medieval beast-fable in French, Flemish, and German literature. It satirizes contemporary life by endowing animals with human personality traits, the major plot concerning the struggle for power between the cunning fox Reynard and the physically powerful wolf Isengrim (or Ysengrin): sly wit usually wins. Other characters for Reynard to outwit include King Noble the lion, Sir Bruin the bear, Tibert the cat, and Chanticleer the cock.

The ever-changing cycles of episodes derived from the countless animal fables circulating in Europe, Aesop's and others, as in MARIE DE FRANCE's *Ysopet*. (See ECBASIS CAPTIVI.) From the 12th to the 14th century the tales were circulated in numerous forms, with constant additions and changes. The Latin clerical satire *Ysengrimus* (1148) was a direct ancestor of the French *Roman de Renart*, which had been begun by 1180, when it was adapted by the German Heinrich der Glichezare as *Reinhart Fuchs*. Other related French works include *Renart le Nouvel*, by Jacquemart Gelée (13th century), and *Renart le Contrefet* (early 14th century). The expanded French *Roman* of 1210 was the basis of the Flemish *Van den vos Reinarde* (1250–1270). This was revised about 1380 with further borrowings from kindred collections, and a later Dutch version was probably the basis for William Caxton's English translation *Reynart the foxe* (1481). A Low German version called *Reinke de Vos* appeared in 1498, and others followed. By now the folk tale quality and often the humor were being subordinated to each author's specific didactic purpose; a gloss would accompany the text, explaining the political significance of the characters and events, interpreting the power struggle, for instance, as that between the Church, the Barons, and the King. Goethe published a modern German version, REINEKE FUCHS (1794), as did Jacob Grimm in 1834.

Before Caxton's translation, portions of the tale had been known in England as *Vox and the Wolf* (13th century), and Chaucer used part of the French material in his NUN'S PRIEST'S TALE.

Reynolds, Jeremiah N. (1799?–1858). American writer. The propagandizer of an extraordinary theory about the construction of the world's polar regions, he is credited with influencing the writings of Herman Melville and Edgar Allan Poe. Reynolds' story of *Mocha Dick* (1839), a fierce white whale, is said to have been the source of Melville's MOBY DICK. Poe introduced Reynolds' polar theories in his *Unparalleled Adventures of One Hans Pfaal* (1835) and championed them in other stories.

Reynolds, Sir Joshua (1723–1792). English portrait painter, working in the tradition of Titian and

Van Dyck. A very successful artist, he was a founding member of the Royal Academy and became its first president (1768). His famous 15 presidential *Discourses* were concerned with the education of the painter. He is admired for his paintings of women and children, and his portraits of men possess an admirable vigor. He was a friend and portrayer of Samuel Johnson, Edmund Burke, Oliver Goldsmith, David Garrick, and Richard Sheridan, and it was at his suggestion that the LITERARY CLUB was founded in 1764.

Rhadamanthys. In Greek mythology, son of Zeus and Europa and brother of Minos. He reigned in the Cyclades with such impartiality that at death he was made one of the judges of the infernal regions, with Minos and Aeacus.

Rhea. In Greek mythology, the wife and sister of CRONOS, and mother of Zeus and other Olympians. One of the TITANS, born of Ge (earth) and Uranus (sky), Rhea married her brother Titan Cronos and gave birth to Hestia, Demeter, Hera, and Poseidon. Cronos, having learned from his mother that one of his sons would dethrone him, swallowed them as soon as they were born. In order to avoid this fate for Zeus, Rhea bore him secretly and gave him to Ge, who arranged for his bringing up in Crete. Rhea, meanwhile, gave Cronos a stone wrapped in swaddling clothes, which he swallowed in place of Zeus.

Though a somewhat shadowy figure herself, Rhea was widely worshiped under other names, or identified with local earth-mother goddesses with similar functions. Her most famous counterpart is the Asian goddess CYBELE.

Rheingold, Das (The Rhine Gold). An opera by Richard Wagner. It is a long one-act prologue to the RING DES NIBELUNGEN.

Rhétoriqueurs, les Grands. A school of French poets which originated in the duchy of Burgundy toward the end of the 15th century and extended as a medieval anachronism well into the Renaissance of the 16th century. Its representatives were the last to compose on the medieval themes of courtly love and chivalry, but medieval poetic lyricism having died out with the passing of knighthood, the apparatus of allegory and mythology served now only to cloak banal moralising by such poets as Olivier de la Marche (c. 1422–1502) or Georges Chastellain (c. 1405/15–1475). This degeneration in content was accompanied by increasing complexity of technique. The *Art de rhétorique vulgaire* (1493) by Jean Molinet (1435–1507) and the *Grand et vray art de pleine rhétorique* (1521) by Pierre Fabry described the infinite variations in rhythm and rhyme scheme then in fashion. These handbooks gave a definite and complete formulation of the aims of the Rhétoriqueurs as found in the now long-forgotten Jean Meschinot, Guillaume Crétin, and their colleagues. Yet sterile as their preoccupation with technique proved to be, the Rhétoriqueurs were the first group of poets, before the PLÉIADE, to consider poetry as an exacting art worthy of respect in its own right.

Rhinoceros, The (1959). A play by Eugène IONESCO. The central character is a man caught by the fear of remaining a human being when his fellow citizens are achieving animalistic conformity by turning into rhinoceroses.

Rhoda Fleming (1865). A novel by George MEREDITH. The plot concerns the tireless efforts of the titular heroine, aided by her lover Robert Armstrong, to set right the affairs of her sister, Dahlia, who has been seduced by Edward Blancove, an irresponsible young nobleman. Rhoda obstinately believes in her innocence through a long series of revealing episodes, and, when she learns the truth, as obstinately forces her sister to marry a worthless man under the conviction that her only hope lies in becoming a married woman.

Rhodes, Cecil John (1853–1902). British financier. He amalgamated the diamond mines around Kimberley in South Africa under a corporation called the De Beers Consolidated Mines (1888). As prime minister of Cape Colony (1890–1896) he sought to establish a federal South African dominion under Great Britain. He instigated the JAMESON RAID (1895) in pursuit of his imperialistic aims. Its failure compelled him to resign as premier, but in spite of this he is remembered in South Africa as a great figure. He founded the Rhodes scholarships, which have enabled young men from all over the British Empire, from the U.S., and from Germany to study at Oxford University.

rhyme. In English prosody, the repetition of identical or similar accented sound or sounds. Full or perfect rhyme occurs when differing consonant sounds are followed by identical, accented vowel sounds, and any sounds that may come after are also identical. Foe, toe; meet, fleet; buffer, rougher are perfect rhymes.

Rhyme is classified according to the number of syllables contained in the rhyme as follows: masculine rhyme, in which the final syllables are accented and after differing initial consonants the sounds are identical (lark, stark; support, resort); feminine rhyme, in which accented, rhyming syllables are followed by identical, unaccented syllables (revival, arrival; flutter, butter); and triple rhyme, a kind of feminine rhyme in which accented, rhyming syllables are followed by two identical syllables (machinery, scenery; tenderly, slenderly).

Rhyme is also distinguished according to its position in the poem as follows: end rhyme, in which the rhyme occurs at the ends of lines; internal rhyme, in which at least one rhyme occurs within the line (as in Wilde's "Each narrow *cell* in which we *dwell*"); initial rhyme, in which the rhyme occurs as the first word or syllable of the line; cross rhyme, in which the rhyme occurs at the end of one line and in the middle of the next; and random rhyme, in which the rhymes seem to occur accidentally in any combination of the foregoing, often mixed with unrhymed lines.

Near rhyme or slant rhyme is the repetition of similar sounds instead of identical sounds or the coupling of accented-unaccented sounds that would be perfect rhymes if they were both accented. Because they involve degrees of identity of sound combinations, ALLITERATION, ASSONANCE, and CONSONANCE are considered to be near rhymes.

Historically, rhyme is a late-comer to poetry, having first come into use in the Western world around A.D. 200 in the Church Latin of North Africa; rhyme was unknown in classical prosody. It first became popular in medieval Latin poetry. The word rhyme comes from Provençal *rim* and was originally spelled rime, and still often is. The usual English spelling, rhyme, comes from a false identification with the Greek *rhythmos,* rhythm.

rhyme royal. In prosody, a stanza form containing seven lines of heroic (i.e. iambic pentameter) verse rhymed a-b-a-b-b-c-c. It is also known as the Troilus stanza because Geoffrey Chaucer popularized it in his poem *Troilus and Criseyde;* Chaucer also used it in his *Ballad of Good Counsel* and part of the *Canterbury Tales.* Written in later periods by Shakespeare and others, it supposedly received its name after James I of Scotland, who was both king and poet.

Rhymers' Club, The. A club in London. It was founded by William Butler Yeats and his friends in 1891. Pre-Raphaelite in character, its aims were to promote pure poetry and the aesthetic cult of Walter PATER. Its chief members were Yeats, Ernest Dowson, Lionel JOHNSON, and Arthur SYMONS.

rhyming slang. A kind of slang popular in Great Britain in the early 20th century, in which the word intended was replaced by one that rhymed with it, as "Charley Prescott" for waistcoat, or "plates of meat" for feet. When the rhyme was a compound word, the rhyming part was almost invariably dropped, leaving one who did not know the idiom somewhat in the dark. Thus Chivy (Chevy) Chase rhymes with "face"; by dropping the "chase," chivy remains, and becomes the accepted slang word. Similarly, daisies become boots, thus: daisy-roots will rhyme with boots; drop the rhyme and daisy remains. By the same process, sky is slang for pocket, the compound word which gave birth to it being sky-rocket." "Christmas," a railway guard, as "ask the Christmas," is, of course, from "Christmas-card"; and "raspberry," heart, is "raspberry-tart."

Rialto (From *rivo alto*). A famous commercial district in Venice, Italy. Shakespeare mentions it in *The Merchant of Venice.* It is also the name of a marble bridge in Venice built (c. 1590) across the Grand Canal.

Ribaut or **Ribault, Jean** (c. 1520–1565). French Huguenot navigator and colonist. With the support of Admiral Coligny, he tried unsuccessfully to establish a colony for French Protestants near Port Royal, S.C., having first laid claim to the territory of Florida for France in 1562. In 1565, he arrived at Fort Caroline, a new colony on the St. John's River in Florida, but he and most of the settlers were killed by Spaniards.

Ribbentrop, Joachim von (1893–1946). Diplomat in NAZI Germany. Ambassador to Great Britain (1936–1938) and foreign minister during World War II, he was sentenced to death at the NUREMBERG TRIALS.

Ricardo, David (1772–1823). English economist. It was reading Adam Smith's *Wealth of Nations* that caused Ricardo to devote himself to the study of political economy. *Principles of Political Economy and Taxation* (1817) is the most systematic exposition of his theory of rent, property, and wages, as well as the quantity theory of money. He wrote several earlier important economic studies, of which particularly the pamphlet *The High Price of Bullion* (1810) caused great discussion at the time of its publication.

Ricciardetto. In the MORGANTE MAGGIORE of Luigi Pulci and the ORLANDO FURIOSO of Lodovico Ariosto, a Christian knight and twin brother of the warrior maiden Bradamante. Out of love for Bradamonte, the pagan knight Ruggiero saves his life.

Riccoboni, Marie Jeanne (1713–1792). French comedienne, novelist. She wrote numerous sentimental romances, such as *Lettres de mistress Fanny Butler* (1756), *Lettres de milady Juliette Caterby* (1759), and a continuation of MARIVAUX's *La Vie de Marianne* (1751).

rice. The basic cereal food of warm climates. The custom of throwing rice after a bride comes from India, rice being, with the Hindus, an emblem of fecundity. The bridegroom throws three handfuls over the bride, and the bride does the same over the groom. Among Americans, the rice is thrown by neighbors and friends.

Rice, Alice Hegan (1870–1942). American novelist. The author of more than a dozen novels, she is remembered mainly for her immensely popular MRS. WIGGS OF THE CABBAGE PATCH and its sequel *Lovey Mary* (1903).

Rice, Elmer (1892–1967). American playwright. He is known for his use of experimental technique, his realism, and his portrayal of the problems of his time, especially social injustice. Trained as a lawyer, Rice gave his first play, *On Trial* (1914), a legal setting, as he did his later *Counselor-at-Law* (1931). He is better known, however, for the expressionistic THE ADDING MACHINE and for the realistic STREET SCENE. *The Left Bank* (1931) deals with American expatriates. The depression and the Nazi and Soviet menace provided subjects for *We, the People* (1933), *Judgment Day* (1934), *Between Two Worlds* (1934), *Two on an Island* (1940), and *Flight to the West* (1940). *Dream Girl* (1945) and the operatic version of *Street Scene,* for which Kurt Weill supplied the music (1947), were notably successful with the public. Rice, also a novelist, wrote *A Voyage to Purilia* (1930), *Imperial City* (1937), *The Show Must Go On* (1949), and other fiction.

Rice Christians. Converts to Christianity for worldly benefits, such as a supply of rice to East Indians. The term implies a profession of Christianity caused not by faith, but for profit.

Rich, John (1682?–1761). English actor, called "the father of Harlequins," and noted as a pantomime player. He was manager of the Lincoln's Inn Fields (1713–1732), the theater at which John Gay's THE BEGGAR'S OPERA was produced with such resounding success that it was said to have made "Rich gay and Gay rich."

Rich, Penelope, born **Devereux** (1562?–1607). Beloved of Sir Philip Sidney, the "Stella" of his sonnet sequence *Astrophel and Stella* (1591).

Rich, Richard (fl. 1609–1610). English adventurer. His *Newes from Virginia* (1610), a well-known ballad based upon his shipwreck in the Bermudas and his adventures in the Virginia colony, is said to have suggested to Shakespeare certain scenes in *The Tempest.*

Richard I, called **Coeur de Lion** or the **Lion-Hearted,** also **Richard Yea and Nay** (1157–1199). King of England (after 1189), son of Henry II and ELEANOR OF AQUITAINE. He spent only six months of his ten-year reign in England, but the troubadours and later writers glorified his courage, romanticizing his exploits as leader of the Third Crusade (1190–

Woodcut from the romance *Richard
Coeur de Lion* (1528).

1192), his captivity in Austria (1192–1194) while his brother John was plotting to supplant him, and his wars against Philip II to protect his French possessions. He is the hero of the anonymous metrical romance *Richard Coeur de Lion* (c. 1300) and Maurice Hewlett's *Richard Yea and Nay* (1900), which celebrate his adventures in Palestine, and is prominent in Sir Walter Scott's historical novels *The Betrothed*, THE TALISMAN, and IVANHOE.

Richard II (1367–1400). King of England (1377–1399). The son of Edward the Black Prince, he succeeded his grandfather Edward III while still a child. During his minority, the country was governed by his uncles, John of Gaunt, duke of Lancaster, and Thomas of Woodstock, duke of Gloucester. He is remembered for the bravery and presence of mind he displayed when he faced an angry mob during the Peasants' Revolt of 1381. Overthrown by Henry Bolingbroke, John of Gaunt's son and later HENRY IV, Richard was probably murdered at Henry's castle of Pontefract. In Shakespeare's RICHARD II, he is depicted as an engaging man but an ineffective ruler.

Richard III (1452–1485). King of England (1483–1485). The third son of Richard, duke of York, and brother of Edward IV, he took an active part in the Wars of the Roses. Upon Edward's death in 1483, he seized his nephews, the young Edward V and his brother Richard, and had himself declared protector. Later he assumed the crown, announcing that the two princes had died in the Tower of London. Richard was defeated and killed at the battle of Bosworth

Field by Henry Tudor, earl of Richmond (later Henry VII).

One of the most controversial figures in English history, Richard was often denigrated, especially in works of the Tudor era, such as Thomas More's *History of Richard III*, which was a source of Shakespeare's RICHARD III. Horace Walpole sought to vindicate him in *Historic Doubts on the Life and Death of Richard III* (1768). He now tends to be regarded, not as a blood-thirsty monster, but as a capable ruler who often behaved ruthlessly in a ruthless age.

Richard II, The Tragedy of (c. 1595). A historical tragedy by William SHAKESPEARE. The action begins with a conflict between Henry Bolingbroke and Thomas Mowbray, which King Richard resolves by banishing both. Upon the death of Bolingbroke's father, JOHN OF GAUNT, Richard confiscates Henry's inheritance to finance the Irish war. While Richard is in Ireland, Bolingbroke boldly invades England, and upon Richard's return, imprisons him. After Bolingbroke's coronation as HENRY IV, Richard is murdered by Sir Pierce of Exton, acting on a hint from the new king. Professing horror at the deed, Henry plans a pilgrimage to the Holy Land to do penance. The play is based upon the account in Holinshed's *Chronicles* (1577).

Richard III, The Tragedy of King (c. 1594). A historical tragedy by William SHAKESPEARE. A scheming Richard, duke of Gloucester and younger brother of Edward IV of the house of York, resolves to inherit the crown of the ailing king and systematically plans the extermination of all who hinder his succession. He causes the death of his brother George, duke of CLARENCE, and marries the Lady Anne, daughter-in-law of Henry VI. When Edward dies, Richard imprisons the two young sons of the late king in the Tower of London and, with the help of the duke of BUCKINGHAM, seizes power. In order to strengthen his position, he orders the murder of the princes and, after disposing of his wife, sues for the hand of Elizabeth, daughter of Edward IV. Meanwhile, the earl of Richmond, the representative of the rival house of Lancaster, has invaded England. At Bosworth Field, Richard's forces are defeated by Richmond; his horse having been killed, Richard fights desperately on foot, shouting "A horse! a horse! my kingdom for a horse." He is slain by Richmond, who is recognized as Henry VII and announces his intention of marrying Elizabeth, thus ending 30 years of conflict between the houses of York and Lancaster.

Shakespeare depicts Richard as a crafty villain whose soul is as deformed as his body, though the blackness of the portrait is relieved somewhat by Richard's courage, his wit, and his freedom from self-delusion. Written while Elizabeth, the granddaughter of Henry VII, ruled England, the play was enormously popular in its day and is largely responsible for the ill-repute in which Richard has long been held. It is Colley Cibber's alteration (1700) of the play that contains the line "Off with his head! so much for Buckingham!" which is often searched for in vain in the Shakespearean version.

Richard Carvel (1899). A historical novel by Winston CHURCHILL. One of the most popular novels ever written about the American Revolution, *Richard*

Carvel is an account, narrated by the hero, of his adventures aboard a slaver from which he is rescued by John Paul Jones. The book describes sea warfare, a London interlude, and a successful love affair.

Richard Coeur de Lion. See RICHARD I.

Richards, I[vor] A[rmstrong] (1893–). English literary critic, aesthetician, and poet. He is notable as one of the pioneers in the analytical method of criticism of the CAMBRIDGE CRITICS and the NEW CRITICISM. He published his influential *Principles of Literary Criticism* in 1924. Richards based his ideas on his studies in semantics, such as those presented in *The Meaning of Meaning* (1923), with C. K. Ogden as co-author. In his book *Science and Poetry* (1925) he argued that scientific discourse deals with truth, but that poetry makes pseudo-statements and should not be read for the facts it may convey but should be analyzed for its implications and connotations. In pursuit of the language of science and fact, Richards became interested in BASIC ENGLISH. He wrote *Basic English and its Uses* (1943) and a Basic English translation of *The Republic of Plato* (1942). He applied the study of semantics and of the exact meaning of words to literary criticism at the same time as the LOGICAL POSITIVISTS were applying it to philosophy. One of Richards' other important aesthetic theories is that poetry is valuable in a scientific society because its complexity and depth can help to give psychological balance to its readers. His other works include *Practical Criticism* (1929) and *How to Read a Page* (1942), demonstrations of his method of analytical criticism, and *Coleridge on Imagination* (1934). Among his collections of poetry is *The Screens and other Poems* (1960).

Richardson, Dorothy (1873–1957). English novelist. She was a pioneer and outstanding exemplar of the STREAM-OF-CONSCIOUSNESS school. Her novels are grouped together under the general title of PILGRIMAGE. Expressing above all the feminine sensibility, Dorothy Richardson's novels describe the thoughts, sense impressions, memories, and feelings that the heroine experiences.

Richardson, Henry Handel. Pen name of Henrietta Richardson; original name Ethel Florence Lindesay Richardson; married name Robertson (1870–1946). Australian novelist. Born in Melbourne and trained as a pianist, she devoted herself to her first love, writing, after her marriage. Her first books, beginning with *Maurice Guest* (1908), were influenced by her readings in French and Russian literature, particularly Flaubert, Tolstoi, and Dostoevski. With her third novel, *Australia Felix* (1917) her style became both more noticeably English and more surely her own. This was the first of a trilogy of novels with the general title *The Fortunes of Richard Mahony*, finished in 1930, which were regarded by many critics as an outstanding achievement.

Richardson, Henry Hobson (1838–1886). American architect. Trained in Paris, Richardson inspired the Romanesque revival in the U.S. at the end of the 19th century. His vigorous use of masonry is perhaps best exemplified by Boston's Trinity Church (1877).

Richardson, Samuel (1689–1761). English novelist. He is known for his expansion of the novel, for his interest in the psychological aspects of character, and for his highly emotional tone. He was one of the most successful printers of his day, having risen from an apprenticeship as a boy. In 1739, while working on a manual of letter-writing that two booksellers had asked him to prepare, Richardson took time off to write PAMELA, OR VIRTUE REWARDED. Pamela is generally considered to be the first modern English novel. CLARISSA HARLOWE and SIR CHARLES GRANDISON are his two other major novels; all three are epistolary in form.

Richard the Lion-Hearted. See RICHARD I.

Richelieu, duc de. Armand Jean du Plessis. Known as **Cardinal Richelieu** (1585–1642). French statesman and prelate. As chief minister under Louis XIII, he was largely responsible for the downfall of Protestantism and for the entrenchment of monarchic autocracy in France. An undistinguished writer himself (as is seen in *Testament Politique*), he was a patron of the literary arts, founding the Académie française (1635) and employing five authors (see CINQ AUTEURS), among them Corneille, to write plays under his direction. Richelieu appears as a character in de Vigny's *Cinq Mars* (*The Fifth of March*, 1826), in Bulwer-Lytton's historical drama *Richelieu, or the Conspiracy* (1838), and in Dumas' *Les Trois Mousquetaires* (*The Three Musketeers*, 1844). See DUPES, DAY OF.

Richter, Conrad Michael (1890–1968). American novelist and short-story writer. Richter's first novel, *The Sea of Grass* (1937), is the story of a cattle baron of the old Southwest and his hopeless battle against progress. His most ambitious work is a trilogy depicting a pioneer family over the years: *The Trees* (1940), *The Fields* (1946), and *The Town* (1950), which won a Pulitzer Prize. He is also the author of *The Light in the Forest* (1952), about a Pennsylvania boy brought up by Indians, and *The Water of Kronos* (1960), a symbolic fantasy.

Richter, Jean Paul Friedrich (1763–1825). Pen name, **Jean Paul.** Popular German novelist and aesthetician. Both the ironic humor of his style and the sometimes excessive sentimentality of his stories show the influence of Laurence Sterne. Also like Sterne, he often tinkered with the novel's structure by placing the author's preface in the middle, inserting long digressions, or weaving complex time-structures with multiple flashbacks. With his *Vorschule der Ästhetik* (*Introduction to Aesthetics,* 1804) he became one of the first theorists of the novel. He rejected both Weimar classicism and romanticism; the former because he felt it to be too cold, the latter because of its one-sided emotional idealism and failure to take the whole man into account. In turn, he was himself coolly received by both groups. His best-known novels are *Leben des vergnügten Schulmeisterlein Maria Wuz* (*Life of the Complacent Little Schoolmaster Maria Wuz,* 1790), *Siebenkäs* (1796–1797), *Titan* (1800–1803), and *Flegeljahre* (*Years of Indiscretion,* 1804–1805).

Richtofen, Frieda von. See Frieda von Richtofen LAWRENCE.

Ridd, John. See LORNA DOONE.

Riddle of the Sphinx, the. See the SPHINX.

Ridge, Lola (1883–1941). American poet, born in Ireland and raised in Australia. Her poetic technique owed much to imagism but also showed the influence of Walt Whitman. Her most famous poem was *The Ghetto;* published in the *New Republic* in

1918 and the title poem of her first collection that same year, it gave a pitiless picture of the New York slums. *Sun-Up* (1920) contained memories of Australia; *Red Flag* (1927) was a sonnet sequence; *Firehead* (1929) was an account of the Crucifixion inspired by the Sacco-Vanzetti case. She also published *Dance of Fire* (1935).

Ridler, Anne, born **Bradby** (1912-   ). English poet. She writes poems on domestic and religious subjects, and religious poetic dramas. Among her works are *The Shadow Factory, a Nativity Play* (1946) and *The Golden Bird and other Poems* (1951).

Ridley, Nicholas (1500?-1555). English bishop and Protestant martyr. Once chaplain to Henry VIII, Ridley helped Thomas CRANMER in the preparation of the two Prayer Books of Edward VI. He signed Edward's request that the crown be given to Lady Jane GREY and denounced Mary and Elizabeth as illegitimate. When Lady Jane was imprisoned he asked Mary's pardon for his denunciation of her, but he was arrested. With Hugh Latimer, he was burned at the stake for heresy.

Ridruejo, Dionisio (1912-   ). Spanish poet. A poet of simple but wide-ranging expression, he wrote *Plural* (1935), *En la soledad del tiempo* (1944), and the poems collected under the title *En once años,* which brought him the *Premio Nacional de Literatura* in 1950.

Rienzi, Cola di. Real name **Niccolo Gabrini** (1313-1354). Italian patriot, often called "the last of the Romans," who, for a time, restored the old Roman system of government, but failed and went to his death. He is the hero of Bulwer-Lytton's historical romance *Rienzi, the Last of the Tribunes* (1835) and Wagner's opera *Rienzi* founded on the novel (1841).

Riggs, Lynn (1899-1954). American playwright. His plays deal with life in Oklahoma and Texas, making special use of folk themes of that region. Among them are *Borned in Texas,* a romantic comedy written in Paris on a Guggenheim fellowship and produced on the stage as *Roadside* (1930); *Green Grow the Lilacs* (1931), a folk drama that formed the basis for Rodgers' and Hammerstein's OKLAHOMA!; *The Cherokee Night* (1936), a tragedy dealing with the decline of the Cherokee Indians in Oklahoma. He is also the author of *The Iron Dish* (1930), a volume of poetry.

Right, Declaration of (1689). An instrument submitted to William and Mary and accepted by them, setting forth the fundamental principles of the English constitution and limiting royal power. According to its provisions, the Crown cannot levy taxes without the consent of Parliament, nor keep a standing army in times of peace. In addition, Roman Catholics are barred from the throne. The document was confirmed by Parliament as the Bill of Rights.

Rights of Man, The (1791-1792). A political work by Thomas PAINE, defending the French Revolution against attacks made on it by Edmund Burke. In it Paine argues that civil government exists only through a contract with a majority of the people for the safe-guarding of the individual, and that if man's "natural rights" are interfered with by the government, revolution is permissible. As a result of this tract, Paine was forced to flee to France and was tried in England *in absentia* as a traitor.

Rigoletto. An opera by Giuseppe VERDI (1851) based on Victor HUGO's drama *Le Roi S'amuse* (*The King Amuses Himself*). The opera scene is laid in 16th-century Mantua instead of the court of Francis I of France, and the principal character becomes Rigoletto instead of Triboulet.

Rig Veda. See VEDAS.

Riis, Jacob [Augustus] (1849-1914). Danish-born American journalist and reformer. Arriving in America at the age of 21, Riis worked at odd jobs and learned at first hand of the squalor of New York slums. Later he became a police reporter for the N.Y. *Tribune,* and waged a single-handed battle against the terrible conditions in the New York City tenements. Finally his book, *How the Other Half Lives* (1890) attracted the attention of Theodore Roosevelt; the result was an improved water supply, child labor laws, playgrounds, the closing of police lodging-houses, and the elimination of the worst slum, the notorious Mulberry Bend. *The Making of an American* (1901) is Riis' own account of his life and crusades; it is his most famous book. Other works include *The Children of the Poor* (1892), *The Battle with the Slum* (1902), *Children of the Tenements* (1903), and *Is There a Santa Claus?* (1904).

Riley, James Whitcomb (1849-1916). American poet, lecturer, and newspaperman. Riley's real education was acquired not in school, but as a journalist in his native Indiana. He had an ear for the local Hoosier speech and published a series of poems in dialect in the Indianapolis *Journal.* The poems were collected as THE OLD SWIMMIN' HOLE AND 'LEVEN MORE POEMS in 1883, and made him not only famous, but the richest American writer of his time. He increased his income by lecturing and writing humorous sketches. He is remembered for his dialect poems, among them LITTLE ORPHANT ANNIE, THE RAGGEDY MAN, and *When The Frost is on the Punkin,* which have been called "comforting, familiar platitudes restated in verse."

Rilke, Rainer Maria (1875-1926). German poet. He is considered the most significant figure in 20th-century German lyric poetry. His early works, culminating in *Das Stundenbuch* (*The Book of Hours,* 1905), a collection of poems written in the person of a monk, show a strong tendency to seek escape from the real world in a highly subjective realm of half-religious, half-aesthetic anguish and ecstasy. His elevation of art to a personal religion, at this stage, reflects the strong influence of both German and French romanticism. But Rilke felt a very strong need to break away from his youthful subjectivity, and did so in his *Neue Gedichte* (*New Poems,* 1907), a collection which contains the most perfect examples of a relatively new type of poem called in German the DINGGEDICHT (thing-poem). His friendship with the sculptor Auguste Rodin, to whom he dedicated *Der neuen Gedichte anderer Teil* (*The Second Part of the New Poems,* 1908), significantly influenced the meticulous accuracy of observation reflected in his poems of this period. In his last and most famous works, including the DUINO ELEGIES and THE SONNETS TO ORPHEUS, Rilke developed a highly individualized style in which the minutest shades of meaning, not only in every word but even in prefixes, suffixes, and individual sounds, are carefully considered and made to contribute to the structure of the poem. Rilke's novel, THE NOTE-BOOKS OF MALTE LAURIDS BRIGGE, abounds in the same kind of radically daring but impressively accurate imagery that characterizes his poetry, and was, in its time, a bold experiment in narrative technique.

Rimbaud, Arthur (1854–1891). French poet. Rimbaud, a member of the SYMBOLISTS, became a forerunner of the surrealist school. His poetry is characterized by dramatic and imaginative vision, particularly in the realm of hallucination. Subtle and infinitely suggestive, his work uses words for tone-color, as in his famous *Sonnet des Voyelles,* and is partially written in free verse. Stylistically the poetry is marked by a distortion of common meaning and syntax, and by the grouping of images about a single central metaphor. His best known works are *Les Illuminations* (1886), *Le Bâteau Ivre* (*The Drunken Boat,* 1871) and *Une Saison en Enfer* (*A Season in Hell*). A striking and enigmatic personality, Rimbaud was raised in a poor and strictly religious home by his mother. He was an industrious, quiet, and irreproachably mannered student in a provincial school until the age of 15. Then suddenly, in savage rebellion, he ran away to Paris. He studied occult writings, Plato, the cabbala, and Buddhist scriptures, in order to make himself a seer. Believing the role of poetry to be one of mystic revelation, he deliberately debauched himself in order to reach a transcendent world through sin and suffering. For two years, he was closely associated with Paul Verlaine and had a powerful influence—morally corruptive but aesthetically fruitful—on the older poet. All of Rimbaud's known poetry was written prior to the age of 20, and he apparently spent the remainder of his short life as a trader in Africa. A poetic prodigy, Rimbaud is of vital import to 20th-century poetry.

Rime of the Ancient Mariner, The (1798). A poem by Samuel Taylor COLERIDGE. It deals with the supernatural punishment and penance of a seaman who heartlessly shot an albatross, a bird of good omen, in the Antarctic regions. The story is told by the Mariner himself—part of his penance is its periodic repetition—to the reluctant, fascinated listener, a man who was on his way to a wedding.

Rimmon or Ramman. A Babylonian storm-god. It was he who was worshiped by NAAMAN before his conversion to the worship of Yahweh. In *Paradise Lost,* Milton identifies Rimmon as one of the fallen angels.

Rimsky-Korsakov, Nicolai Andreyevich (1844–1908). Russian composer, a member of the nationalist "FIVE." He was a professor of composition (1871) at the St. Petersburg Conservatory. He wrote a treatise on orchestration, and his memoirs. In 1902 he met Stravinsky, who became his pupil. He is best known for his symphonic suites *Antar* and *Scheherazade,* and the *Russian Easter* overture. His operas based on Russian legends, include LE COQ D'OR.

Rinaldo or Ranaldo. One of the great heroes of medieval romance (also called Renault of Montauban, Regnault, Reynold, etc.), a paladin of Charlemagne and cousin of Orlando. One of the four sons of Aymon, he rides the famous horse Baiardo, or Bayardo. Though brave and ingenious, he is often given to violent and unscrupulous behavior. His rapacious instincts often lead him to act like a common plunderer.

He appears in Luigi Pulci's MORGANTE MAGGIORE, in Matteo Maria Boiardo's ORLANDO INNAMORATO, and in Lodovico Ariosto's ORLANDO FURIOSO. In Ariosto, he is the son of the fourth marquis of Este, lord of Mount Auban or Albano, eldest son of Amon or Aymon, nephew of Charlemagne, and brother to Bradamante. Like his cousin Orlando he falls in love with the fair Angelica, who detests him. The subsequent haggling of the two cousins over Angelica weakens the Christian camp against the pagan forces. In the GERUSALEMME LIBERATA (*Jerusalem Delivered*) of Torquato Tasso, he appears as Rinaldo d'Este, son of Bertoldo and Sophia, nephew of Guelfo. Craving fame rather than gold or power, he joins the First Crusade as an adventurer, though only 15. After slaying Gernando, his rival for a position of command, he is summoned to public trial by Goffredo, the leader of the Crusaders. In anger he deserts the Christian camp, as Achilles left the Greek army, to sulk over his treatment. He then falls into the power of the enchantress Armida, who detains him in her castle until Goffredo sends for him. Returned to the wars, he leads the Crusaders in a final assault on the city, which results in its capture.

Rinconete y Cortadillo. One of the tales in Cervantes' NOVELAS EJEMPLARES. Containing many elements of the PICARESQUE, it deals with two youths who travel to Seville, where they receive thorough training in crime and roguery at the thieves' school of Monipodio.

Rinehart, Mary Roberts (1876–1958). American detective-story writer. *The Circular Staircase* (1908) and *The Man in Lower Ten* (1909) established her reputation as a writer of detective stories that combined humor with ingenuity; the former novel was successfully dramatized by the author and Avery Hopwood as *The Bat* (1920). She also wrote numerous stories about a dauntless spinster called Tish and her two middle-aged cronies, Aggie and Lizzie; included in the series are *The Amazing Adventures of Letitia Carberry* (1911) and *Tish* (1916). One critic has called Mrs. Rinehart's autobiography, *My Story* (1931; rev., 1948), her finest book.

Ring and the Book, The (1868–1869). A long poem in 12 books by Robert BROWNING. Based on an Italian murder case of 1698, the story is presented in dramatic monologues spoken by 12 characters, each of whom approaches it from a different point of view. Guido Franceschini, a Florentine nobleman of shattered fortune, marries Pompilia Comparini, whom he believes to be an heiress. Pietro and Violante Comparini, learning that Guido is not wealthy as they believed, sue for the return of Pompilia's dowry, claiming that she is not really their daughter. Guido treats her so brutally that Pompilia, who is about to have a child, flees to Rome under the protection of Caponsacchi, a young priest. They are caught by her husband, and Caponsacchi, charged with adultery, is banished for three years; Pompilia is sent to a nunnery. Two weeks after her child is born, Pompilia and her supposed parents are murdered by Guido. He is arrested and admits his crime, and, though he claims that Pompilia's alleged adultery justified him, he is condemned and executed.

The "Book" of the title is an ancient record of the case which Browning found in Florence. The "Ring" refers to an Etruscan ring that had belonged to Mrs. Browning. In order to shape it an alloy had been added to the gold; when the ring was finished the alloy was burned off with an acid, and the pure gold remained. Thus, the facts of the case in the old manuscript were the gold that could be given form only when mixed with a "baser metal," the poet's imagination and interpretative fancy.

Ring des Nibelungen, Der. A prologue and three music-dramas or operas by Richard WAGNER. They are based on Scandinavian legends and were first performed together at Bayreuth in 1876. Although Wagner's principal source was not the NIBE-LUNGENLIED but the VOLSUNGA SAGA, the *Nibelungen-lied,* the *Elder* and *Younger Eddas,* and the *Eckelied* were also drawn upon for material. The interest centers about the magic ring made from the Rhine gold and the curse it brought to all who owned it.

The four operas may be briefly summarized as follows:

(1) *Das Rheingold* (*The Rhinegold,* 1869). In the bottom of the Rhine is a hoard of gold guarded by the Rhine Maidens. Alberich, the dwarf, forswears love to gain this hoard, which confers boundless power upon its possessor. From it he makes a magic ring. Meantime Wotan, chief of the gods, has given Freya, the goddess of youth and love, to the giants Fasolt and FAFNER as payment for their labor in building for him the castle Valhalla. Without Freya, everything grows old, even the gods. To get her back, Wotan and Loki steal the ring and the hoard from Alberich and trade them for the goddess. Alberich has put a curse on the ring; and accordingly, almost immediately the giant Fafner kills his brother Fasolt. As the opera ends, the gods go over the rainbow bridge to Valhalla.

(2) *Die Walküre* (*The Valkyrie,* 1870). Wotan is the father of two children, Siegmund and Sieglinde, who grow up on earth in ignorance of each other but who, by the desire of Wotan, are to mate in the interest of the coveted ring. Sieglinde has married Hunding, but when Siegmund comes, she goes with him into the forest. Wotan's wife, the goddess of marriage, insists that Siegmund be punished, and Wotan finally yields and entrusts the Valkyrie Brunhilde with the task. In spite of her orders, Brunhilde tries to protect Siegmund, but Hunding, finally aided by the angry Wotan, kills him. She succeeds, however, in escaping with Sieglinde, who is about to give birth to the hero Siegfried. Wotan punishes Brunhilde by making her a mortal woman asleep on a mountain peak surrounded by magic fire through which only a hero may pass.

(3) *Siegfried* (1876). Siegfried, since the death of his mother Sieglinde, has been brought up to the trade of the smithy by Mime, the dwarf, whom he hates. He remakes his father's sword and slays a dragon who is really the giant Fafner. A drop of the dragon's blood on his tongue makes him understand the language of the birds. Acting on the information they give him, he kills the treacherous Mime, secures the magic ring, and finds Brunhilde and marries her.

(4) *Götterdämmerung* (*The Twilight of the Gods,* 1876). Siegfried leaves the magic ring with Brun-hilde and goes to seek adventure. At the court of Gunther and his sister Gutrune, their half-brother Hagen, son of the dwarf Alberich, gives Siegfried a magic potion that causes him to forget Brunhilde and become a suitor for the hand of Gutrune. He even agrees to secure Brunhilde for Gunther and does so. Unable to understand his fickleness, Brunhilde denounces him and enters into schemes for revenge with the wily Hagen. At a hunting feast, just as Siegfried is remembering his past and calling for Brunhilde, he is killed by a thrust in the back from Hagen. The hero's body is burned on a funeral pyre; Brunhilde sacrifices herself in the flames; the Rhine overflows its banks; Gunther and Hagen perish in the struggle for the ring, which now returns to the Rhine Maidens, and Valhalla, with all the gods, is destroyed by fire.

Ringing Island. See ISLE SONANTE.

ring of Polycrates. See POLYCRATES.

Rinuccini, Ottavio (1562–1621). Florentine poet. Rinuccini's plays were used as librettos by the composers of the first operas. He was a member of the famous *Camerata dei Bardi,* a Florentine association of poets and musicians bent on reviving Greek tragedy in its original form, mistakenly believed by them to consist of a completely sung text. Along with Peri, Caccini, and V. Galilei, he produced texts suited to the new style of recitative (*recitar cantando*), which superseded the polyphonic style of the earlier Renaissance. In 1594, his *Dafne,* called a *favola per musica* (a fable to be set to music) was performed with the music of Peri in the new monodic or recitative style. Though only the text survives, the *Dafne* is considered the first opera by historians. (The word opera itself, however, and its synonym in Italian, *melodramma,* came into use after 1650.) In 1600, Rinuccini wrote the text for the *Euridice,* with music by Peri, for the marriage of Henry IV of France and Maria de' Medici. In 1607, he helped to launch the career of Monteverdi by supplying the text for his successful opera *Arianna,* performed at Mantua's ducal court. By 1637, operas were being performed publicly in the theaters of Venice.

Ripheus. A Trojan, highly praised for his justice and nobility of character in Vergil's *Aeneid.* He is one of the two pagans admitted to heaven by Dante in his *Paradiso.* See TRAJAN.

Ripley, George (1802–1880). American editor, reformer, and literary critic. After graduating from Harvard University, Ripley taught mathematics there while attending the Divinity School. He became a Unitarian minister in Boston, and studied German theology as he edited the *Christian Register.* In 1838 Ripley began to edit *Specimens of Foreign Standard Literature* (14 v., 1838–1852), translations of the philosophers whose work forms the basis of the American transcendentalist movement. On April 1, 1841, Ripley and 20 other members of the Transcendental Club moved to West Roxbury, Mass., where he became president of the community at BROOK FARM. After the disastrous fire of 1846, Ripley moved to Flatbush, L.I.; a contributor to the New York *Tribune,* he soon was recognized as an important influence in American letters. A founder of *Harper's New Monthly Magazine,* he also edited the *New American Cyclopedia* (16 v., 1858–1863, later revised).

Rip Van Winkle (1819). A tale by Washington IRVING, collected in his SKETCH BOOK OF GEOFFREY CRAYON, GENT. Certainly the most popular piece Irving ever wrote, the story is based on a folk tale. Henpecked Rip and his dog Wolf wander into the Catskill mountains before the Revolutionary War. There they meet a dwarf, whom Rip helps to carry a keg. They join a group of dwarfs playing ninepins. When Rip drinks from the keg, he falls asleep and wakes 20 years later, an old man. Returning to his town, he discovers his termagant wife dead, his daughter married, and the portrait of King George replaced by one of George Washington. Irving uses the folk tale to present the contrast between the new and old societies.

The story was adapted many times for the stage and opera house. The most famous adaptation was done by Dion Boucicault for the actor Joseph Jefferson, who played Rip for almost 40 years (1865–1904).

Rise and Fall of the Town Mahagonny (Aufstieg und Fall der Stadt Mahagonny; 1929). A play by Bertolt BRECHT with music by Kurt WEILL in a style similar to that of their *The Threepenny Opera.* Set in the U.S., it is strongly Marxist in thought, and is intended as an object lesson about bourgeois decadence. The town of Mahagonny, founded and populated entirely by pleasure seekers, is in Brecht's eyes a logical development of capitalistic society; it eventually collapses because of inherent economic and human contradictions. It is an example of what Brecht called EPIC THEATER.

Rise of David Levinsky, The (1917). A novel by Abraham CAHAN. Levinsky is a Russian Jew who emigrates to America and becomes, finally, the chief figure in the New York cloak-and-suit trade. Sometimes ruthless and unscrupulous, he becomes a rich man, but he does not attain happiness, and ends with neither family nor a real home. The novel is recognized as the first important novel dealing with immigrant life.

Rise of Silas Lapham, The (1885). A novel by William Dean HOWELLS. Silas, a self-reliant businessman who has become wealthy, moves to Boston. Building a pretentious home on Beacon Hill, he disgraces himself by drinking too much at a dinner party given by the social elite. Originally careless of the morality of his money-getting methods, Silas begins to recognize ethical standards. Although he is financially ruined by the end of the book, his "rise" reflects this change in attitude. Persis, his helplessly provincial wife, has been unable to guide her daughters' social careers; Penelope Lapham finally marries Tom Corey, member of a Brahmin family, and the two escape to Mexico. The novel is generally considered Howells' best.

Risorgimento (*Ital.,* "revival; resurrection"). The political movement, starting about 1831, whose objective was the liberation and unification of Italy. Its three great leaders were MAZZINI, GARIBALDI, and CAVOUR. *Risorgimento* was the name of a newspaper founded (1847) by Count Cavour.

rispetto (pl. rispetti). See STRAMBOTTO.

Ristori, Adelaide (1821–1906). Italian actress. One of the leading tragediennes of the European stage, she played principally in Paris, where the relative merits of her interpretations and those of Rachel at the Comédie Française were a subject of bitter controversy. In addition to her appearances in Italian and classical French drama, she was widely acclaimed for her portrayal of Lady Macbeth and of Maria Stuart in an Italian version of Schiller's tragedy.

Ritchie, Anne Isabella. Born Thackeray (1837–1919). Novelist, eldest daughter of William Makepeace THACKERAY. Although a novelist in her own right, her biographies of famous Victorians are her best work. These include *Lord Tennyson and His Friends* (1893) and *Chapters from Some Memoirs* (1894).

Ritson, Joseph (1752–1803). English antiquary and critic. He quarreled savagely with Thomas Percy over the editing of the RELIQUES OF ANCIENT ENGLISH POETRY, and with George Steevens over Steevens' edition of Shakespeare. He also attacked Thomas Warton's *History of English Poetry.* Ritson's collections of popular songs (*Select Collection of English Songs,* 1783–1793) are distinguished by faithful reproduction of the text and the inclusion of the ballad music—as in most modern collections. He is best known for his comprehensive collection of ballads and poems on *Robin Hood* (1795); the *Ancient English Metrical Romances* (1802), attacking the authenticity of romances in Percy's *Reliques;* and for the *Bibliographia Poetica* (1802), a catalogue of English poetry from the 12th to the 16th centuries. Ritson became insane shortly before his death.

Rittenhouse, Jessie B[elle] (1869–1948). American poet and anthologist. She is known for her anthologies of American verse, especially *The Younger American Poets* (1904). A founder of the Poetry Society of America, she published several books, including *The Door of Dreams* (1918), *The Lifted Cup* (1921), and *The Moving Tide: New and Selected Lyrics* (1939).

Rivals, The (1775). A comedy by Richard Brinsley SHERIDAN. Though less well known in name, this play is considered by some to be better than THE SCHOOL FOR SCANDAL. The plot is complicated: Sir Anthony Absolute wishes his son Captain Absolute to marry Lydia Languish. He does not know that Captain Absolute is already wooing her in the guise of the impecunious Ensign Beverly, a guise taken on to please Lydia's romantic dream of an elopement rather than marriage with a well-to-do baronet's son. Lydia's aunt Mrs. MALAPROP, disapproving of the penniless Beverly, threatens to take away half of Lydia's fortune if she marries him. She wishes Lydia to marry Captain Absolute. The plot is further complicated by the fact that Captain Absolute's friend Bob Acres is also in love with Lydia and challenges Beverly to a duel (not knowing that Beverly is really Absolute). Things get straightened out in the end, however, and Lydia, after scolding Captain Absolute for ruining her hopes of a romantic elopement, happily agrees to marry him.

Rivas, duque de. Angel Saavedra y Ramírez de Baguedano (1791–1865). Spanish poet and dramatist. As a youth Rivas was seriously wounded while fighting against the French during the Napoleonic invasion of Spain. Exiled in 1823 by Ferdinand VII because of his liberal tendencies, he lived in London, Paris, and Malta, where he met John Hookham Frere, who exerted a decisive influence on his literary career by introducing him to English romanticism. After his return to Spain in 1834, he inherited the title and held a number of important political positions.

Though Rivas' early writings were in the classical manner, he later became the champion of Spanish romanticism. The change was signaled by the lyric *El faro de Malta* (1828?) and by *El moro expósito* (1834), a long narrative poem in the style of Sir Walter Scott, dealing with the legend of the seven *infantes* of Lara. His prose-and-verse drama, DON ALVARO O LA FUERZA DEL SINO, first presented in 1835, had an impact on the Spanish theater comparable to that of Hugo's *Hernani* in France five years earlier. He also wrote *Romances históricos* (1841), a series of ballads on important events in Spanish history, such as the downfall of Alvaro de Luna and the victory of Pavia.

Rivera, Diego [Maria] (1886–1957). Mexican painter. His influence led to the formation of a purely national school of painting. He is best known for vast historical murals undertaken with the support of succeeding administrations. His fresco in Rockefeller Center in New York was removed because it was felt to be too radical in its political allusions. It was repainted in Mexico City. Currently in the hotel El Prado, it is covered by a heavy curtain to protect it from being defaced by Catholic or anticommunist demonstrators, and is only shown on special occasions.

Rivera, José Eustasio. See VORÁGINE, LA.

Rivera y Orbaneja, Miguel Primo de (1870–1930). Spanish political leader. By a military *coup d'état* he proclaimed a directorate of army and naval officers in Spain (Sept. 12, 1923) and made himself dictator. He later restored the original government and made himself premier. He resigned shortly before his death.

Rivière, Jacques (1886–1925). French critic and editor. One of the founders of the influential literary magazine the *Nouvelle Revue Française,* Rivière directed it from 1919 to 1925. His conversion to Catholicism is reflected in much of his literary criticism, such as *A la trace de Dieu* (1925), and in his correspondence with Paul Claudel (pub. 1926) and with Alain Fournier (4 vol., 1926–1927).

Rizal, José (1861–1896). Philippine novelist and national hero. He was sent into exile by the Spanish government because of his novel *Noli Me Tangere* (*The Lost Eden,* 1886), in which he criticized both the Spanish regime and the clergy. In 1896, on his return to the Philippines, he was charged with fomenting revolution and executed. Before his death he wrote a remarkable poem, *Mi último adiós.*

Rizzio, David (1533?–1566). An Italian musician in the service of Mary Queen of Scots. He became her private foreign secretary, arranged her marriage with Darnley, and finally attained such influence that he was attacked and killed in Queen Mary's apartment at Holyrood Palace in Edinburgh by Darnley, Morton, and Lindsay. Swinburne treats this event in *Mary Stuart: A Tragedy* (1881).

Road Not Taken, The (1915). A poem by Robert FROST. One of Frost's best-known poems, it describes how the narrator coming to a fork in the road is undecided on which way to go. Both roads seem very much alike. He takes the one less traveled —and "that has made all the difference."

Roads to Freedom, The (Les Chemins de la liberté). A trilogy of novels by Jean Paul SARTRE. *The Age of Reason* (*L'Age de raison;* 1945), set in 1938, presents Mathieu, a professor of philosophy trying to maintain his ethical freedom. *The Reprieve* (*Le Sursis;* 1945) is a panorama of the eight days preceding the Munich Pact in September, 1938. *Troubled Sleep* (*La Mort dans l'âme;* 1949; also translated as *Iron in the Soul*), shows varied reactions to the fall of France in 1940.

Road to Rome, The (1927). A play by Robert E. SHERWOOD. Influenced by George Bernard Shaw's *Caesar and Cleopatra* (1899), it is a plea against war presented in a comedy. The first of Sherwood's plays, it describes how Hannibal is prevented from capturing Rome by the allurements of Amytis, the wife of a pompous senator, Fabius Maximus.

Roanoke Island. An island off the coast of North Carolina, site of an ill-fated English colony (1584–1591), sponsored by Sir Walter Raleigh. Although previous attempts at settlement had failed, a group of new colonists arrived in 1587. The ships that sailed back to England for supplies did not return until 1591 and found no trace of the settlers, except for the word "Croatoan," the name of a friendly tribe of Indians, carved on the bark of a tree. The fate of the colony has never been discovered. Paul Green's historical pageant, *The Lost Colony* (1937), is presented annually on the island. See Virginia DARE.

Roan Stallion, Tamar, and Other Poems (1925). A collection of poems by Robinson JEFFERS. The title poem deals with the almost religious love of a woman named California for a magnificent red stallion, in which she sees godlike power and beauty. She permits the horse to trample her brutal husband to death, but then shoots the beast "out of some obscure human fidelity."

Roaring Girl, The (c. 1610). A comedy by Thomas MIDDLETON and Thomas DEKKER. The marriage of Mary Fitzallard and Sebastian Wengrave is opposed by the latter's arrogant and avaricious father, Sir Alexander. In order to force his father's compliance, Sebastian pretends to pay court to "the roaring girl," Moll Cutpurse. A woman who combines a knowledge of London's lowlife with a sort of manly virtue, Moll agrees to help Sebastian and act as go-between with Mary. Sir Alexander sends his spidery servant, Trapdoor, to gain Moll's confidence and bring about her downfall. However, Moll eludes the trap and succeeds, by pretending momentarily to be Sebastian's bride, in bringing about the wedding of the happy pair while gulling Sir Alexander into the bargain.

Robbe-Grillet, Alain (1922–   ). French novelist, critic, and farm engineer. Robbe-Grillet first described the *nouveau roman* or new novel in 1956, becoming the leading exponent of the NEW WAVE in literature. His own novels experiment with the presentation of space and time. The changing appearance of what the protagonist sees, noted with geometrical precision, conveys the human significance. In *The Voyeur* (1955) we watch a rape and murder by a traveling salesman, and in *Jealousy* (1957) we observe the powerful obsession of a banana plantation owner about his wife and his neighbor. Other works include *Les Gommes* (*The Erasers,* 1953), *In the*

The Roaring Girle.
OR
Moll Cut-Purse.

As it hath lately beene Acted on the Fortune-stage by the Prince his Players.

Written by *T. Middleton* and *T. Dekker.*

My case is alter'd, I must worke for my liuing.

Printed at *London* for *Thomas Archer,* and are to be sold at his shop in Popes head-pallace, neere the Royall Exchange. 1611.

Title page of Dekker and Middleton's *Roaring Girl.*

Labyrinth (1959), and the scenario for *Last Year at Marienbad* (1961).

Robbers, The (Die Räuber; 1782). A play by Friedrich SCHILLER. Karl Moor, the hero, is cheated out of his inheritance by his brother, and feeling himself cast out of human society, he forms a band of robbers. Some of the men who gather around him are mere opportunists, but others are genuine victims of social injustice. Thus, Schiller depicts the robber band in a morally ambiguous light, giving a possible justification for it as a protest against social evil. But in the end, Karl recognizes that antisocial action is not justifiable, and gives himself up to the authorities.

Robbia, Luca della (1400–1482). Florentine sculptor. He invented and developed glazed terra cotta as an inexpensive substitute for marble; in addition to being weather-resistant, the terra cotta had the advantage of vivid color. His nephew **Andrea** (1435–1525) used the new material for the *putti* (little angels) that appear in the spandrels of the arches of Brunelleschi's Ospedale degl' Innocenti in Florence. But Luca's masterpiece is his first work, the marble reliefs depicting boy musicians and child dancers in the *cantoria* of the Florence cathedral (1438).

Robert Elsmere (1888). A novel by Mrs. Humphry WARD dealing with 19th-century religious problems. The hero is a clergyman whose intellectual convictions force him to leave the church. His wife Catherine loves him but cannot share his changing faith. Following the lead of French and German religious critics, the book advocates that Christianity should abjure its supernatural origins and concentrate on social questions.

Robert of Brunne. See Robert MANNYNG.

Robert of Gloucester (late 13th century). English chronicler. A long metrical *Chronicle of English History* from earliest times (c. 1300) bears his name, but someone else probably wrote the earlier sections (to 1135). Most of the work is compiled from other chroniclers, but the last section (1256–1270) includes fresh contemporary reminiscences. The work is primarily of linguistic importance, showing the beginning of the transition from Old to Middle English.

Roberts, Sir Charles G[eorge] D[ouglas] (1860–1943). Canadian novelist and poet. He was among the first to write about the Canadian scene, and has been called the father of Canadian letters. Among his collections of poetry are *The Iceberg and Other Poems* (1934) and *Selected Poems* (1936). His books include *The Heart of the Ancient Wood* (1900), *In the Morning of Time* (1923), *They Who Walk in the Wild* (1924), and *Eyes of the Wilderness* (1933).

Roberts, Elizabeth Madox (1886–1941). American novelist. A regional writer, she is noted for her treatment of the pioneers and "poor whites" of Kentucky and the Virginias. Although her talent and insight were highly poetic and she wrote several books of verse, including *Under the Tree* (1922) and *Song in the Meadow* (1940), she is known primarily for her distinguished works of prose. *My Heart and My Flesh* (1927) is the story of a Southern girl and her attempt to find happiness through three different love affairs. *The Great Meadow* (1930) is a novel dealing with the settlement of Kentucky.

Roberts, Kenneth [Lewis] (1885–1957). American historical novelist. He is best known for his excellent novels of the colonial and Revolutionary periods, especially ARUNDEL, RABBLE IN ARMS, and NORTHWEST PASSAGE. Roberts based his novels on facts unearthed after careful research; the journals of men accompanying Benedict Arnold, which Roberts used for *Arundel,* were edited by him in *March to Quebec* (1939). *Oliver Wiswell* (1940) is a study of an American Tory at the time of the Revolution.

Robertson, E. Arnot. Pen name of Eileen Arbuthnot Robertson (1903–61). English novelist. Among her popular and witty novels are *Four Frightened People* (1931) and *The Signpost* (1944).

Robertson, Ethel F. Lindesay Richardson. See Henry Handel RICHARDSON.

Robertson, Morgan [Andrew] (1861–1915). American short-story writer. He never received recognition during his lifetime and was debt-ridden most of the time. Today Robertson is considered one of America's finest writers of sea stories. One of his best tales is *The Derelict Neptune* from *Spun Yarn* (1898), a collection of his short stories.

Robertson, William (1721–1793). Scottish historian and king's historiographer. His works include a *History of Scotland* (1759) and a *History of America* (1777); but he is best known for his *History of the Reign of Emperor Charles V* (1769), which drew the praise of both Edward Gibbon and Voltaire and was an important source for Schiller's *Don Carlos*.

Robert the Devil (*Fr. Robert le Diable*). Hero of medieval legend. Robert learns that the reason he has been using his strength exclusively for outrageous crimes is that his mother, hitherto childless, had prayed to the Devil for a son. He goes to a hermit to seek purification and undertakes the severe penances imposed, living as the mute court fool at the court of Rome and saving the city three times from the Saracens, but finally ending his days at the hermitage.

The legend became attached to the name of Robert, sixth duke of Normandy and father of William the Conqueror. The historical Robert was known for his cruelty, as well as his daring, and died (1035) on his return from a pilgrimage he made to Jerusalem as penance for his sins.

Versions of the composite story vary widely. It is the subject of a French metrical romance of 1496, a 15th-century English metrical romance, *Sir Gowther*, and a prose romance by Thomas Lodge (1591). In Meyerbeer's opera *Robert le Diable* (1831), libretto by Scribe and Delavigne, the setting is Italy. Bertram, the Devil in disguise, follows his son Robert around in hopes of making a contract for his soul. But Robert's foster-sister Alice helps him break the evil spell, and he marries Princess Isabella of Sicily.

Robert François Damiens (1715–1757), who attempted to assassinate Louis XV, was also called *Robert le Diable*.

Robeson, Paul (1898–   ). American Negro singer and actor. He has appeared in *The Emperor Jones* (1923), *Porgy and Bess, All God's Chillun Got Wings, Show Boat*, and *Othello*. An open Communist sympathizer, he lived abroad for many years, and returned to the U.S. in 1964.

Robespierre, Maximilien François Marie Isidore de (1758–1794). French Revolutionist. Undisputed master of the JACOBIN Club, he was called by the Parisians "the Incorruptible" for his uncompromising honesty and revolutionary fervor. In the year 1793–94, he dominated the COMMITTEE OF PUBLIC SAFETY which instituted the REIGN OF TERROR. While head of this committee, he and his two lieutenants, Louis de SAINT-JUST and Georges Couthon, gave every appearance of being masters of France. Robespierre was overthrown by the Convention on July 27, 1794. He and his fellow terrorists were sent to the guillotine without a trial, as they had sent so many others. During the 19th century the Robespierre legend enjoyed a revival among the lower classes as a champion of social revolution; others consider him to be an ambitious demagogue and dictator. See FRENCH REVOLUTION.

Robin. In Shakespeare's MERRY WIVES OF WINDSOR, the page of Sir John Falstaff.

Robin Adair. A song written by Lady Caroline Keppel, daughter of the second earl of Albemarle. She married Robert Adair, a young Irish surgeon, in 1758. The air was the old Irish tune of "Eileen Aroon," which her lover had sung to her.

Robin Hood. A legendary English outlaw and popular hero, best known through a cycle of ballads. It is said that he was born c. 1160 at Locksley, Not-

Title page of *A Mery Geste of Robyn Hoode* (1550).

tinghamshire; he is also said to have been the outlawed earl of Huntington, Robert Fitzooth, in disguise. He lived in the forest, either out of choice or because he was outlawed for debt. His chief haunt was Sherwood Forest in Nottinghamshire. Ancient ballads abound with anecdotes of his personal courage, his skill in archery, his generosity, and his great popularity. It is said that he robbed the rich to give to the poor, and that he protected women and children with chivalrous magnanimity. According to tradition, he was treacherously bled to death by the prioress of Kirkley; as an old man he had gone to her to be bled, and she let him die.

Robin Hood's companions in Sherwood Forest and Barnsdale, Yorkshire, were LITTLE JOHN, FRIAR TUCK, Will SCARLET, ALLAN-A-DALE, Will STUTLY, and MAID MARIAN. According to one tradition, Robin Hood and Little John were two heroes defeated with Simon de Montfort at the battle of Evesham. Robin Hood became a stock figure in the MAY DAY plays and festivities.

Robin Hood has long figured in English literature. He is first mentioned in a 1377 edition of *Piers Plowman*. The most important ballad series of which he is the hero is *A Lytell Geste of Robyn Hode* (1510), a near epic of 456 four-line stanzas.

Robin Redbreast. A common name for two different birds, one European, the other North American. The tradition is that when Jesus was on his way to Calvary, a robin picked a thorn out of his crown, and the blood that issued from the wound falling on the bird dyed its breast with red. Another fable, referred to in John Webster's *White Devil,* is that the robin covers dead bodies with leaves.

Robins, Elizabeth. Pen name, **C. E. Raimond** (1865?–1952). American actress and writer. She appeared in England in several of Ibsen's plays. Under her pen name she wrote *Below the Salt* (1896) and other fiction. Under her real name she turned to feminist writing. She dramatized her novel *The Convert* (1906) as *Votes for Women* (1906). Her *My Little Sister* (1913), dealing with the white-slave trade, was a sensational success.

Robinson, Edwin Arlington (1869–1935). American poet. He is known for his long narrative poems and objective psychological portraits of New England characters, usually written in blank verse, and for his creation of TILBURY TOWN, whose prototype was Gardiner, Me., where he spent his boyhood. Robinson privately printed 300 copies of *The Torrent and the River* (1896), his first book of poems, and, encouraged by the warmth of its critical reception, determined to make a career of writing. Published the following year with some changes, as *The Children of the Night,* the volume contained several of what were to become Robinson's best-known poems, among them *Luke Havergal, Richard Corey,* and *Two Men.* The poet moved to New York, and worked at various uncongenial occupations, hounded by poverty and depression. After the publication of CAPTAIN CRAIG, which included *The Book of Annandale,* Theodore Roosevelt, impressed by his work, secured a position in the New York City custom house for him. MINIVER CHEEVY first appeared as one of the poems in *The Town Down the River* (1910), and thereafter Robinson earned his living by writing, spending his summers at the MacDowell Colony in Peterboro, N.H. With the publication of THE MAN AGAINST THE SKY his reputation was firmly established. Although there are long narratives and dramatic monologues among them, the majority of the poems in these collections are short lyrics and character sketches.

Robinson's *Collected Poems* (1921), which was published the same year as his *Avon's Harvest,* won the first Pulitzer Prize to be awarded for poetry. He won the Pulitzer Prize again in 1925 for THE MAN WHO DIED TWICE and in 1928 for TRISTRAM. This long poem, which followed *Merlin* (1917) and *Lancelot* (1920), was the final volume of Robinson's Arthurian trilogy, and had a very considerable popular success.

His later books include CAVENDER'S HOUSE, *The Glory of the Nightingales* (1930), *Matthias at the Door* (1931), *Nicodemus* (1932), *Talifer* (1933), and *Amaranth* (1934)). His *Collected Poems* (1937) were published posthumously.

Despite the irony and pessimism of his work, Robinson is usually considered 19th century in tone. His poetry forms an important bridge from Whitman and Dickinson to the truly modern poets of the 20th century.

Robinson Crusoe (1719–1720). The hero and shortened title of *The Life and Strange Surprising Adventures of Robinson Crusoe, of York, Mariner,* a novel by Daniel DEFOE. Robinson Crusoe runs away to sea, is wrecked, and leads a solitary existence on an uninhabited island near the Orinoco river for 24 years. He meets the difficulties of a primitive existence with wonderful ingenuity and finds consolation in reading the Bible. At length he meets a human being, a young native whom he saves from death at the hands of cannibals. He calls him "MAN FRIDAY," because he met him on a Friday, and makes him his companion and servant. Crusoe and Friday share in a variety of adventures which include a fierce battle with cannibals, culminating in their recapturing a mutinous ship and returning to England. *Robinson Crusoe* is a manual of the qualities that have won the world from barbarism—courage, patience, ingenuity, and industry. Defoe founded this story on the adventures of Alexander SELKIRK. In a commentary, *Serious Reflections of Robinson Crusoe* (1720), Defoe claims that the novel is an allegory of his own life.

Roblès, Emmanuel (1914–   ). Algerian-born French novelist, dramatist, journalist. Known for his proletarian novel *Travail d'homme* (1942), Roblès also wrote *Les Hauteurs de la Ville* (1948), set in Algeria, and *Dawn on our Darkness* (*Cela s'appelle l'aurore,* 1952), which takes place in Sardinia. The drama *Montserrat* (1949) is set in Venezuela in 1812.

Robortelli, Francesco (1516–1567). Italian literary critic. He is famed for his pioneer edition (1548) of the *Poetics* of Aristotle. It included a Latin translation and commentary that were influential both in the history of Renaissance and later literary criticism.

Rob Roy. Nickname of **Robert Macgregor** (1671–1734). Scottish outlaw, comparable to England's Robin Hood. He was given the name Roy because of his red hair.

He is the title character of *Rob Roy* (1817), a novel by Sir Walter SCOTT, in which he rescues the hero, Francis Osbaldistone, from various difficulties. His exploits also enable Osbaldistone to marry Diana Vernon, the heroine.

roc. An enormous white bird in Arabian folklore. Said to be of such size and strength that it could carry elephants to its mountain nest where it devoured them, it appears in the *Arabian Nights,* most notably in the story of SINBAD THE SAILOR, where it transports Sinbad from the Valley of Diamonds.

Rochambeau, comte de. Jean Baptiste Donatien de Vimeur (1725–1807). French soldier. He joined, as commander of a French force, Washington's Continental Army in 1781; he helped besiege Cornwallis at Yorktown, and, with the French fleet, forced his capitulation in 1781. He was made marshal of France in 1791.

Rochefoucauld, duc de la. See Duc François de LA ROCHEFOUCAULD.

Rochester, Edward Fairfax. See JANE EYRE.

Rochester, 2nd earl of. John Wilmot (1647–1680). English courtier and poet. A favorite of Charles II, he was known in his day as "the Wicked Earl" for his profligate life, atheism, and obscene verse. Rochester, who died worn-out and repentant at the age of 32, was nevertheless a man with some amiable characteristics and a highly talented poet, author of a number of graceful lyrics and a few biting satires. His best-known poem is *A Satire Against*

Mankind (1675), a brilliant attack on *homo sapiens* and his pretensions to rationality.

Rocinante or **Rosinante**. In Cervantes' DON QUIXOTE, the steed of Don Quixote, "lean, lank, meagre, drooping, sharp-backed, and raw-boned." The name implies "that the horse had risen from a mean condition to the highest honor a steed could achieve, for it was once a cart-horse, and rose to become the charger of a knight-errant."

Rockefeller, John D[avison], Sr. (1839–1937). American industrialist and philanthropist. Rockefeller's Standard Oil Company, incorporated in 1870, soon controlled virtually all U.S. facilities for oil refining and transportation. In 1911 the Supreme Court ordered the dissolution of the Standard Oil Company of N.J., a holding company for the Rockefeller interests. At this time Rockefeller retired with a fortune estimated at one billion dollars and devoted the remainder of his life to worthy causes. His son John D. Rockefeller, Jr. (1874–1960) continued his father's business and philanthropic interests.

Rocking-Horse Winner, The (1933). A short story by D. H. LAWRENCE. It is about a small boy, the son of greedy parents, who rides himself to death on a demonic toy rocking-horse which prophesies the winners in the horse races.

Rockwell, Norman (1894–). American illustrator. He is chiefly known for his covers portraying folksy Americana for the *Saturday Evening Post*.

rococo. A later form of BAROQUE architectural style, originating in France in the first quarter of the 18th century. It was characterized by extreme freedom, playfulness, and grace achieved by a liberal use of flowing curves, irregular or broken rhythms, and elaborate ornament. The term is now applied to any flamboyant and excessively ornamental style.

Roderick or **Rodrigo**. A Spanish hero around whom many legends have collected. The thirty-fourth and last of the Visigothic kings, he came to the throne in 710 and was routed and probably slain, by the Moors under Tarik in 711.

One legend tells that he is befriended by a shepherd who is then rewarded with the royal chain and ring. Roderick passes the night in the cell of a hermit, who tells him that he must do penance by living for some days in a tomb full of snakes, toads, and lizards. After three days, the hermit goes to see him, and he is unhurt, "because the Lord kept his anger against him." The hermit goes home, spends the night praying, and goes again to the tomb. Rodrigo says, "They eat me now, they eat me now, I feel the adder's bite." His sins thus atoned for, he dies. According to other versions, he does not die but will come again in time of need. In one legend, he reappears at the Battle of Covadonga with the old rallying cry "Roderick the Goth! Roderick and victory!" and saves the day, but is seen no more.

Scott, in his *Vision of Don Roderick* (1811), portrays Roderick descending into an ancient vault near Toledo where he is shown a panoramic vision of Spanish history to the beginning of the 19th century. Walter Savage Landor made the Roderick legend the subject of his poetic drama, *Count Julian* (1812). Another famous Spanish hero named Roderigo is the Cid.

Roderick Hudson (1876). A novel by Henry JAMES. In this, the first of James's novels published in book form, the titular hero is a talented young American sculptor. Going to study in Rome under the aegis of a wealthy benefactor, he becomes gradually disillusioned about his art and utterly demoralized by his experience. Christina Light, with whom he falls disastrously in love, reappears as a character in THE PRINCESS CASAMASSIMA.

Roderick Random, The Adventures of (1748). A PICARESQUE novel by Tobias SMOLLETT modeled on Lesage's GIL BLAS. The titular hero, a young Scottish scapegrace in quest of fortune, narrates a succession of adventures. At one time he revels in prosperity, at another he is in utter destitution. Fleeing prosecution for having killed an officer in a duel, Roderick, accompanied by his comrade Hugh STRAP, runs off to sea and becomes a surgeon's mate. He subsequently meets and falls in love with Narcissa; her suitors, Sir Timothy Thicket and Lord Quiverwit, impede the progress of the romance. Thwarted in his plans, he flees to France and, supported by Strap's money, plans to marry Miss Melinda Goosestrap. Failing in these plans he goes to sea with his uncle Tom BOWLING and lands in South America where he meets the wealthy Don Rodrigo, who turns out to be his long-lost father. The triumphant exile returns, marries Narcissa, repurchases the family estate, and shows scorn for those relatives who had earlier scorned him.

Roderick, the Last of the Goths (1814). A narrative poem by Robert SOUTHEY. Roderick, the last king of the Visigoths, dishonors Florinda, daughter of Count Julian. In revenge, Count Julian, calling the Moors into Spain to help him, drives Roderick from his throne. Roderick assumes the robes of a monk and devotes his life to God in expiation. During a revolt against the Moors, Roderick, under the name of Father Macabee, persuades his cousin Pelayo to head the Christian forces. When Roderick has heard Florinda's confession (which partly absolves him) and makes peace with his mother and Count Julian, he reveals his identity, leaps into battle, and leads the Christian army to victory. He then disappears and Pelayo becomes the founder of the Spanish royal line. Generations later, a tomb bearing the name Roderick is discovered.

Roderigo. In Shakespeare's OTHELLO, a rejected suitor of Desdemona. Foolishly believing that Iago will help him win Desdemona, he becomes a dupe in Iago's plot against Othello.

Rodgers, Richard (1902–). American composer of musical comedies. With his lyricists, Lorenz Hart (1895–1943) and Oscar HAMMERSTEIN, he developed the musical into a more unified dramatic form than it had been previously. Among his most famous shows are *Pal Joey* (1940; with Hart), OKLAHOMA!, and *South Pacific* (1949).

Rodgers, W[illiam] R[obert] (1909–). Irish poet and clergyman. He is the author of verse in the manner of Gerard Manley Hopkins. He wrote *Awake, and other Poems* (1941).

Rodin, [François] Auguste [René] (1840–1917). French sculptor. One of the important influences in the development of 20th-century art, Rodin used his genius as a means of self-expression, to register emotion and to reveal character. His work, tortured and lyrical in turn, is strengthened by his rejection of any desire for surface finish: bronze retains the rough texture of clay; satin-smooth marble contrasts with roughly cut stone. Among his many famous works are *The Thinker, The Kiss, St. John the Baptist Preaching,* the monuments to Claude Lorrain and the one to Balzac, the portrait bust of Victor Hugo. There is a Rodin Museum in Paris and one in Philadelphia.

Rodman, Selden (1909–   ). American poet and critic. His best-known works include *Lawrence: The Last Crusade* (1937), a narrative poem concerning T. E. Lawrence; *The Airmen* (1941), a poem about the achievements of fliers throughout history; and *The Revolutionists* (1942), a play dealing with Toussaint L'Ouverture and Henri Christophe. As this last work indicates, Rodman has been greatly interested in Haiti. He has done much for Haitian art and written two books on the country: *Renaissance in Haiti* (1948) and *Haiti: The Black Republic* (1954). Among his other books are *The Amazing Year: A Diary in Verse* (1947), *Portrait of the Artist as an American* (1951), *The Eye of Man: Form and Content in Western Painting* (1955), and *Conversations with Artists* (1957). He has also edited a number of poetry anthologies.

Rodney, George Brydges. 1st baron **Rodney of Stoke-Rodney** (1719–1792). Governor of Newfoundland and noted English admiral who defeated the Spanish off Cape St. Vincent (1780) and the French under de Grasse off Dominica (1782).

Rodó, José Enrique (1871–1917). Uruguayan essayist. Rodó spent most of his uneventful life in Montevideo, where his home became a mecca for Latin-American intellectuals, especially after the publication of ARIEL, his most influential essay. *Los motivos de Proteo* (1909) is a series of related essays, undoubtedly influenced by Bergson, in which the dominant note is the unlimited possibility for the development of the human spirit. The essays on Montalvo and Bolívar in *El mirador de Próspero* (1913) are also well known. Regarded as the foremost prose writer of MODERNISM, Rodó wrote in a style remarkable for its marmoreal serenity and purity.

Rodogune (1644). A tragedy by Pierre CORNEILLE. The scheming queen Cleopatra, believing that her husband NICANOR, king of Syria, is dead, has married his brother Antiochus and banished his children. Nicanor, who has been a prisoner of the Parthians, avenges himself by announcing that he will return to Syria and marry Rodogune, princess of Parthia. Cleopatra arranges the ambush and murder of Nicanor and takes Rodogune prisoner. She recalls her two sons and announces that she will crown king whichever will kill Rodogune. The sons, Antiochus and Seleucus, both fall in love with Rodogune, who at first promises to marry whichever will kill Cleopatra but who eventually withdraws the condition and declares her love for Antiochus. Cleopatra pretends to favor their marriage, but murders Seleucus and poisons the wedding cup. In order to allay Antiochus' suspicions she is forced to drink from the cup herself, and she dies. This tragedy was Corneille's favorite of all his works.

Rodomonte. A Saracen hero in Carolingian legends, who appears as king of Sarza or Algiers in Matteo Maria Boiardo's ORLANDO INNAMORATO and Lodovico Ariosto's ORLANDO FURIOSO. Called the "Mars of Africa," he is the Saracen Achilles, commander of the armies sent against Charlemagne and the Christians by Agramante. His love is Doralice

(Doralis), princess of Granada, who runs off with Mandricardo, king of Tartary. At the wedding feast of Ruggiero and the warrior maiden Bradamante, Rodomonte appears in battle dress to denounce Ruggiero, a convert to Christianity, for betraying Agramante and the Saracen cause. In the combat that follows, Ruggiero slays him.

Rodríguez Alvarez, Alejandro. See Alejandro CASONA.

Roebling, John Augustus (1806–1869). German-born American civil engineer. He designed and manufactured the first wire rope in America. He also constructed several bridges, the most striking of which was the railroad suspension bridge at Niagara Falls (1851–1855). He was injured while making plans for a bridge over the East River between Manhattan and Brooklyn (the Brooklyn Bridge); his son, Washington Augustus ROEBLING, completed the job. John Roebling wrote many articles for periodicals and published *Long and Short Span Railway Bridges* (1869).

Roebling, Washington Augustus (1837–1926). American civil engineer. The son of John Augustus ROEBLING, he worked in his father's wire rope factory after receiving a degree in civil engineering; four days after the attack on Fort Sumter, he enlisted in the Union army, for which he built many important bridges. After the war he went to Europe to study caisson foundations of bridges, in order to assist his father on the Brooklyn Bridge project. When his father died as field work began, Washington Roebling succeeded him in the difficult work. In the spring of 1872, he was seriously injured at the bridge site; he directed the rest of the work, until its completion in 1883, from a house in Brooklyn. His health, permanently impaired by the bridge project, forced him to abandon professional engineering. He devoted the remainder of his life to collecting rare minerals; his collection is now housed in the Smithsonian Institution in Washington, D.C.

Roentgen, Wilhelm Konrad (1845–1923). German physicist who discovered X-rays (1895). He received the Nobel Prize for physics in 1901.

Roethke, Theodore (1908–1963). American poet. Roethke won a Pulitzer Prize for his *Collected Poems* (1954) and a Bollingen Prize for *Words for the Wind* (1958). One of the talented poets of his generation, he wrote in strict forms, employing witty and rational modes of thought, and he also used free forms, tending toward the surrealistic. Noted for their evocation of childhood and old age, Roethke's poems also abound in horticultural imagery. Other collections of his poetry are *Open House* (1941), *The Lost Son and Other Poems* (1948), *Praise to the End!* (1951), and *The Waking, Poems 1933–1953* (1953). *I Am! Says the Lamb* (1961) consists of light verse.

Rogero. See RUGGIERO.

Rogers, Henry Huddleston (1840–1909). American financier. Chief executive of the Standard Oil Company, Rogers was also a great admirer of Mark TWAIN. He advised the author on his tangled business affairs, and helped to bring about an agreement between Mark Twain and Harper & Brothers, by which this firm took complete charge of the works; the arrangement was greatly to the author's benefit. The correspondence between Mark Twain and Rogers, soon to be published, reveals hitherto unknown facts about the important decade of the 1890's in the life of a major author.

Rogers, Robert (1731–1795). American frontier captain and dramatist. His company of rangers became famous in 1756. As a loyalist, he was imprisoned at the start of the Revolution, but escaped and organized the Queen's Rangers. He fled to England (1780), where he received a pension from the government. Rogers wrote a drama about Pontiac's Conspiracy, *Ponteach* (1766), the first tragedy written on a native American subject. He is the central figure of Kenneth Roberts' novel NORTHWEST PASSAGE.

Rogers, Samuel (1763–1855). English poet and patron of men of letters. A friend of Wordsworth, Scott, and Byron, Rogers was noted for his biting, sarcastic wit in conversation. Much of Rogers' table talk is preserved in Alexander Dyce's *Recollections* (1856) and G. H. Powell's *Reminiscences* (1859). His carefully lifeless 18th-century-style poetry has not stood the test of time, though it was highly regarded in its day. His best-known poetic work is *The Pleasures of Memory* (1792).

Rogers, Will[iam Penn Adair] (1879–1935). American actor and humorist. He was widely popular in the U.S. for his vaudeville act of talking while swinging a lasso. He acted in many motion pictures, notably in *David Harum, Judge Priest,* and *Lightnin'.* He wrote a series of books with such titles as *The Cowboy Philosopher on Prohibition* (1919) and *The Illiterate Digest* (1924). From 1926 on he ran an extremely popular syndicated column on the news of the day, selections from which were published by Donald Day in *Sanity Is Where You Find It* (1955). An early enthusiast for aviation, he was killed in an airplane accident while flying in Alaska with the noted aviator Wiley Post.

Rogozhin. In Feodor Dostoevski's novel THE IDIOT, the sinister rich young man who has an insane passion for Natasha FILIPPOVNA. Violent as he is, Rogozhin is fascinated by the gentle Prince Myshkin. When he begins to see that Myshkin is a rival for Natasha's love, he attempts to kill the prince. Finally his jealousy drives him to murder Natasha.

Rogue Herries. See HERRIES CHRONICLE, THE.

rogue literature. A type of prose literature, popular in Elizabethan England, and regarded as a forerunner of the English novel. It dealt realistically and exuberantly with the lives and adventures of thieves, vagabonds, and tricksters of the London underworld and rural highways, often expanding from fact to fiction. Robert GREENE and Thomas NASHE were outstanding authors of rogue literature.

Rogueries of Scapin, The. See SCAPIN.

Röhm, Ernst (1887–1934). German Nazi. He was executed in a purge, probably because of a disagreement with Hitler over his leadership of the Storm Troops (S.A.).

Roi Soleil, le (The Sun King). A title adopted by LOUIS XIV when he took the sun as his emblem.

Rojas, Fernando de. See CELESTINA, LA.

Rojas Zorrilla, Francisco de (1607–1648). Spanish dramatist. A native of Toledo and a member of the order of Santiago, Rojas was strongly influenced by Calderón. His finest play, *Del rey abajo ninguno* or *García del Castañar,* deals with a peasant who mistakenly believes that the king has violated his honor; despite some gongoristic traits, the drama is

vigorous and direct. Rojas also wrote the amusing *Entre bobos anda el juego* and *Cada cual lo que le toca,* notable for its unconventional approach to feminine honor. His plots were borrowed by French dramatists such as Corneille, Lesage, and Scarron.

Rokesmith, John. See OUR MUTUAL FRIEND.

Roland or **Orlando.** The most famous of Charlemagne's paladins in medieval romances. His story grew up around the name of Hruotland of Brittany, historical leader of Charlemagne's rear guard in the defeat at RONCESVALLES. Tradition makes Roland the nephew of Charlemagne, his mother being the king's sister. He is the most perfect type of the devotedly loyal and courageous knight who sacrifices himself in service to his king. He is apt to be too trusting and unsuspicious in his dealings with others, too impetuous and determined in his decisions. These tendencies, however, are not treated as flaws, but as the necessary attributes of his pride and his admirably frank, straightforward nature. His close friend OLIVIER is thus his complement, being cooler and wiser in his advice.

Roland's story seems to have entered the tradition of French ballads by the 9th century and is said to have been sung by TAILLEFER in 1066. The *Chanson de Roland* (*Song of Roland*) is a French CHANSON DE GESTE probably written in the middle of the 11th century in Brittany. It has 4002 decasyllabic lines using assonance rather than rhyme, divided into lays or stanzas of unequal length. As the *Chanson* tells the story, Charlemagne has, in seven years of fighting, conquered all of Spain except Saragossa. The Saracen leader Marsile asks for a meeting to discuss a settlement in exchange for Charlemagne's departure from Spain. Roland warns of a trap, but the king accepts GANELON's advice to send a messenger to Marsile at Saragossa. Roland then successfully urges that Ganelon be the messenger. The angry Ganelon goes, but decides to accept Marsile's bribes and betray Roland. He has Roland appointed commander of the rear guard and informs Marsile of the planned route through the pass of Roncesvalles. Accordingly, Roland's 20,000 men are ambushed by 400,000 Saracens. Olivier begs Roland to sound his ivory horn and recall the main body of the army, but Roland refuses. The valorous deeds of the 12 PALADINS during this unequal contest occupy much of the poem. When only 60 men are still alive, Roland finally sounds his horn, at the third blast cracking it and bursting the veins of his own neck; but it is too late to save anyone. Roland and Olivier exchange farewells and are blessed by the Archbishop TURPIN; all are dead on the arrival of Charlemagne and his army, who then avenge the dead by defeating the Saracens. Aude, the sister of Olivier and the betrothed of Roland, dies upon learning of the disaster. Ganelon is found guilty and punished by quartering.

There are many episodes involving Roland that do not appear in the *Chanson,* but in other *chansons de geste*: fights with giants, various accounts of how he acquired his sword DURANDEL and his horn Olivant, and the like. Two important 12th-century Latin versions of the Roland story are the *Chronicle of Charlemagne,* erroneously attributed to the Archbishop TURPIN, and the anonymous poem *De Proditione Guenonis* ("Ganelon's betrayal").

Roland became known in Italian minstrelsy as

Orlando, and by the 15th and 16th centuries his loves and his adventures against the Saracens, along with those of the other paladins, had been thoroughly reshaped in Pulci's MORGANTE MAGGIORE, Boiardo's ORLANDO INNAMORATO, and Ariosto's ORLANDO FURIOSO.

Roland, Jeanne Manon Phlipon. Known as **Madame Roland** (1754–1793). Famous character in the French Revolution. Her house was the intellectual center of the GIRONDISTS. She was guillotined in 1793; according to tradition, her last words on the scaffold were, "Oh liberty! What crimes are committed in thy name!"

Rolfe, Frederick [William Serafino Austin Lewis Mary]. Pen name, **Baron Corvo** (1860–1913). English novelist and historian. He was a versatile, eccentric, learned and witty man and writer. Related to the group of DECADENTS of the 1890's, Rolfe claimed that he had received the title Baron Corvo as a gift. Converted to Catholicism, he tried unsuccessfully to become a priest. His novel *Hadrian the Seventh* (1904) is a kind of wish-fulfilment compensation for his failure, and a revenge on his enemies. *The Desire and Pursuit of the Whole* (published posthumously in 1934) is another novel full of personal attacks. *Stories Toto Told Me* (1898) are retellings of legends of Catholic saints. *Chronicles of the House of Borgia, In His Own Image* (1901) is an unusual historical work. See A. J. A. SYMONS.

Rolfe, John. See POCAHONTAS.

Rolland, Romain (1866–1944). French novelist, dramatist, essayist, and musicologist. Increasingly disturbed by the materialism of contemporary civilization, in 1889 Rolland began to write his long novel series JEAN CHRISTOPHE, a satirical criticism of the world he saw about him. A letter from Tolstoi and his friendship with Malwida von Meysenburg, who had known both Wagner and Nietzsche, greatly influenced his spiritual development. He evolved his own philosophy, a faith in humanity based on a pantheistic religion. An active participant in the Dreyfus case, Rolland collaborated with another Dreyfus sympathizer, Charles Péguy, on the semimonthly review *Cahiers de la quinzaine*. He advocated a new form of drama built on the traditions of French history, and wrote twenty plays himself on the theme of revolutionary heroism. *The Wolves* (*Les Loups;* 1898), *Danton* (1900), *The Fourteenth of July* (*Le Quatorze juillet;* 1902) and *Robespierre* (1938) are based on the French revolution. A professor of music at the Sorbonne from 1900 to 1912, Rolland published several works on music: *Histoire de l'opéra en Europe avant Lulli et Scarlatti* (1895), *Musiciens d'autrefois* and *Musiciens d'aujourd'hui* (1908). During World War I he wrote, from his place of retirement in Switzerland, *Above the Battle* (*Au-dessus de la Mêlée;* 1915), an influential essay of pacifist protest. *The Soul Enchanted* (*L'Ame enchantée;* 7 vols., 1922–1933) is a second novel series with a woman as its central character. In 1916 Rolland received the Nobel prize for literature.

Rolle of Hampole, Richard (c. 1290–1349). English hermit and mystic. He wrote about the soul's approach to the mystic state through Purgation of worldliness, Illumination through meditation and prayer, and finally joyful Contemplation of the presence of God: *Incendium Amoris* (*The Fire of Love*) and *Emendatio Vitae* (*The Mending of Life*) in Latin; paraphrases of the Psalms, with commentaries, and *The Form of Living* in English. He became spiritual adviser to several other recluses and had great influence in the 14th century with his emphasis on individual spiritual experience rather than the forms of religion. However, he was best known for the PRICK OF CONSCIENCE, which he probably did not write.

Rolling Stone, The. The name that O. HENRY gave to the magazine that he purchased and published from 1894 to 1895 in Austin, Tex. In 1913 his estate published a collection of stories, poems, and sketches called *Rolling Stones,* which included some pieces from the magazine.

Rollo Books. A once popular series of books for children by Jacob Abbott (1803–1879). The Lucy, Jonas, and Franconia books were by the same author. They told of simple adventures in a New England town and countryside and were packed with information and a fair amount of morals.

Rollo the Ganger or **Walker** (c. 860—c. 931). A leader of the VIKINGS. After conquering the area around Rouen in France, he received the territory by a treaty with Charles the Simple (c. 912), thus founding the Duchy of Normandy.

Rölvaag, Ole Edvart (1876–1931). Norwegian-born American novelist. He is known for his dramatic and realistic accounts of the life of Norwegian pioneers in the Dakotas, marked particularly by psychological studies of the characters. Rölvaag emigrated to America in 1896, attended, and later taught at, St. Olaf's College in Minnesota. *Letters from America* (1912) is an autobiographical novel cast in the form of letters written to relatives in Norway. Like all his novels, it was written in Norwegian and later translated into English. His best-known work is the trilogy that consists of GIANTS IN THE EARTH, *Peder Victorious* (1929), and *Their Father's God* (1931). *The Boat of Longing* (1933), inspired by the death of his youngest child, contrasts the scenery of Norway with the sordidness of the American city.

Romains, Jules. Pen name of **Louis Farigoule** (1885–1972). French novelist, dramatist, essayist, and poet. Romains was a leading exponent of UNANIMISM, in early poetry such as *La Vie unanime* (1908) and in novels such as *The Death of a Nobody* (1911) and *The Boys in the Back Room* (*Les Copains;* 1913). Raising the group to the status of divinity (*Manuel de déification;* 1910), he celebrated the soul of the city in the prose poems *Puissances de Paris* (1911) and the verse plays *L'Armée dans la ville* (1911) and *Cromedeyre-le-Vieil* (1920). In the 1920's he wrote a number of popular comedies, such as *Doctor Knock* (1923). The 27 novels of the cycle *Men of Good Will* (*Les Hommes de bonne volonté;* 1932–1947) present frescoes of modern French life between 1908 and 1933 in cities, armies, etc.

roman à clef. Literally, a novel with a key, or secret meaning. Such a work of fiction contains one or more characters and situations based upon actual persons and their lives. Often such novels skirt dangerously close to infringement of the libel laws. Contemporary novels that might be mentioned are *Point Counter Point,* by Aldous Huxley, and *The Mandarins,* by Simone de Beauvoir. See also LA CALPRENÈDE; SCUDÉRY.

romance. In medieval literature, a verse narrative (originally written in Old French or Provençal, which were "Romance" languages) recounting the marvelous adventures of a hero of chivalry. Such medieval romances fall into three main cycles: the Arthurian, based upon the life of King Arthur and his Knights of the Round Table; those retailing the life and deeds of Charlemagne and his most celebrated paladin, Roland; and those devoted to the exploits of Alexander the Great. Romances were written in English and German as well as in French; the vast majority of them were connected with one of these cycles, but German romances in particular drew upon Scandinavian and other sources as well.

In modern literature, i.e., from the latter part of the 18th century through the 19th, the term denotes a work of prose fiction in which the scenes and incidents are more or less removed from common life and are surrounded by a halo of mystery, an atmosphere of strangeness and adventure. The Gothic novels, such as Horace Walpole's *Castle of Otranto* (1764), are typical English romances.

In linguistics, the term is applied to languages developed from Latin, including Spanish, Portuguese, French, Italian, Romanian, and Provençal. English is made up of both Romance and Germanic elements, with a small Celtic element as well.

Romance (1913). A play by Edward SHELDON. One of the first plays to employ the flashback as a stage technique, it is the story of a young man who comes to tell his grandfather, a clergyman, of his intention to marry an actress. The grandfather unsuccessfully attempts to dissuade him by relating the great romance of his youth when he fell in love with an Italian opera singer.

Romance of the Rose (Roman de la Rose; 13th century). Medieval French poem in two parts. The first 4000 lines were written by Guillaume de Lorris about 1230 and form an allegory of the Art of Love modeled on Ovid's. The Lover is conducted by Idleness to a garden of roses where he meets such characters as Pleasure, Riches, and Sweet-Looks. He is attracted to one particular rosebud and tries to pluck it, but the god of love (Cupid) stops him with an arrow and explains to him the sufferings required by the code of COURTLY LOVE. Resolved to return to his Rose, the Lover is encouraged by Welcome but obstructed by Danger, Shame, and Slander. Reason urges him to abandon the attempt, but Pity and Venus finally help him attain a kiss. Thereupon Slander rouses Jealousy, who builds a wall around the Rose and imprisons Welcome, leaving the Lover to grieve.

The continuation of over 18,000 lines was written by JEAN DE MEUNG about 1275. Hypocrisy overcomes Slander; Nature allows the fire of Venus to drive away Danger, Shame, and Fear, and the Lover wins his Rose. The events of the story, however, are subordinate in this section to the long digressions in which the author flaunts the extent of his learning with a number of quotations. Here the main point is a series of satires from the bourgeois point of view: against the holders of political and economic power, against the friars, against popular superstitions, against women, and particularly against the artificial glorification of women in the aristocratic tradition of courtly love that had originally inspired Guillaume de Lorris' poem. Instead, Jean de Meung glorifies Nature, asserting that only the natural is good, whether in matters of love or of social institutions.

The *Romaunt of the Rose* attributed to CHAUCER is a translation, with additions, of the Guillaume de Lorris section and about one sixth of the Jean de Meung section. However, this is probably a 15th-century version of which only the first 1700 lines are actually Chaucer's.

Romancero gitano. See Federico GARCÍA LORCA.

Roman Comique. See Paul SCARRON.

Roman de Brut (1155). A verse chronicle in French by the Norman poet WACE. It is an adaptation of the Latin Chronicle HISTORY OF THE KINGS OF BRITAIN by Geoffrey of Monmouth. In this interpretation of ARTHURIAN LEGEND, the Round Table motif is introduced for the first time. See BRUT, THE.

Roman de la Rose. See ROMANCE OF THE ROSE.

Roman de Renart. See REYNARD THE FOX.

Roman de Troie. See BENOÎT DE SAINTE-MAURE.

Roman Empire, rulers of. The Empire was inaugurated 27 B.C., when Octavius received from the Senate the title "Augustus." He had been actual ruler since 31 B.C. when the Second TRIUMVIRATE was dissolved after the battle of Actium. The Republican constitution remained in force, but only formally; Augustus gradually assumed the titles of all the major offices. His reign is sometimes called the principate, from *princeps* (first citizen), the title he favored.

Augustus	27 B.C.–A.D. 14
Tiberius I	14– 37
Gaius (Caligula)	37– 41
Claudius I	41– 54
Nero	54– 68
Galba	68– 69
Otho; Vitellius	69
Vespasian	69– 79
Titus	79– 81
Domitian	81– 96
Nerva	96– 98
Trajan	98–117
Hadrian	117–138
Antoninus Pius	138–161
Marcus Aurelius; Lucius Verus (coemperors)	161–169
Marcus Aurelius	169–180
Commodus	180–192
Pertinax; Julianus I	193
Septimius Severus	193–211
Caracalla; Geta (joint emperors)	211–212
Caracalla	212–217
Macrinus	217–218
Elagabalus (Heliogabalus)	218–222
Alexander Severus	222–235
Maximinus I (the Thracian)	235–238
Gordianus I	238
Gordianus II	238
Pupienus; Balbinus; Gordianus III (joint emperors)	238
Gordianus III	238–244
Philip (the Arabian)	244–249
Decius	249–251
Gallus	251–253
Aemilianus	253
Valerian; Gallienus (joint emperors)	253–259
Gallienus	259–268
Claudius II (the Goth)	268–270
Quintillus	270
Aurelian	270–275
Tacitus	275–276

Florian	276
Probus	276–282
Carus	282–283
Carinus; Numerian (joint emperors)	283–284
Carinus; Diocletian (joint emperors)	284–285
Diocletian	285–286
Diocletian and Maximian	286–305
Galerius and Constantius I	305–306
Galerius, Maximinus II, Severus l	306–307
Galerius, Maximinus II, Constantine I (the Great), Licinius, Maxentius	307–311
Maximinus II, Constantine I, Licinius, Maxentius	311–312
Maximinus II, Constantine I, Licinius	312–314
Constantine I and Licinius	314–324
Constantine I (the Great)	324–337
Constantine II, Constans I, Constantius II	337–340
Constantius II and Constans I	340–350
Constantius II and Magnentius	350–353
Constantius II	353–361
Julian II (the Apostate)	361–363
Jovian	363–364

WEST (ROME) AND EAST (CONSTANTINOPLE)

Valentinian I (W); Valens (E)	364–367
Valentinian I and Gratian (W); Valens (E)	367–375
Gratian and Valentinian II (W); Valens (E)	375–378
Gratian and Valentinian II (W); Theodosius I (the Great) (E)	379–383
Maximus (usurper) and Valentinian II (W); Theodosius I (E)	383–388
Valentinian II (W); Theodosius I (E)	388–392
Eugenius (W); Theodosius I (E)	392–394
Theodosius I (E & W)	394–395
Honorius (W); Arcadius (E)	395–408
Honorius (W); Theodosius II (E)	408–423
Valentinian III (W); Theodosius II (E)	423–450
Valentinian III (W); Marcian (E)	450–455
Petronius Maximus (W); Avitus (W); Marcian (E)	455
Avitus (W); Marcian (E)	455–456
Majorian (W); Marcian (E); Leo I (E)	457
Majorian (W); Leo I (E)	457–461
Severus II (W); Leo I (E)	461–465
[interregnum W]; Leo I (E)	465–467
Anthemius (W); Leo I (E)	467–472
Olybrius (W); Leo I (E)	472–473
Glycerius (W); Leo I and Leo II (E)	473
Julius Nepos (W); Leo I and Leo II (E)	473–474
Julius Nepos (W); Zeno (E)	474–475
Romulus Augustulus (W); Zeno (E)	475–476

The empire in the West ended 476 when Romulus Augustulus was banished by the barbarian Odoacer. Zeno continued to rule in the East until 491. The Byzantine empire lasted until 1453, when Constantinople fell to the Turks. Charlemagne was crowned Emperor of the West in 800, the date usually accepted as the founding of the HOLY ROMAN EMPIRE.

roman-fleuve (*Fr.*, river-novel). A novel that deals with a set of characters over a long period of years, usually in a series of volumes. It came to be characteristic of French fiction during the first half of the 20th century. Outstanding examples are *Jean Christophe* by Romain Rolland; *Remembrance of Things Past* (*A la Recherche du temps perdu*) by Marcel Proust; *Les Thibaults* by Roger Martin du Gard; and *Men of Good Will* (*Les Hommes de bonne volonté*) by Jules Romains. Such English works as John Galsworthy's *Forsyte Saga* and C. P. Snow's *Strangers and Brothers* are also *romans-fleuves*.

Romano, Giulio. Real name, **Giulio Pippi** (1492–1546). Italian painter and architect. Although he is remembered primarily as the pupil and imitator of RAPHAEL, whom he assisted in many works, he produced on his own such paintings as the Moscow *Lady at Her Toilet* and such buildings as the *Palazzo del Té* at Mantua. While serving as artist-in-chief to Federigo Gonzaga, duke of Mantua, he also erected his own house in that city, a sturdy specimen of mannerist architecture. In his own day, he enjoyed fame of another kind because of a series of 16 lascivious engravings for which ARETINO supplied appropriate sonnets. For this work both artists were censured, and their joint effort suppressed.

Romanov or **Romanoff**. The last Russian royal house. The Romanovs were descended from Andrey Romanov (14th century). The first Romanov czar was Mikhail who was elected by a conference of nobles (*boyars*) in 1613. The direct male line ended with Peter II in 1730 and the direct female line in 1762 with Elizabeth. Peter III who succeeded Elizabeth was her nephew, his wife (Catherine the Great) was a German princess. The dynasty ended in July 1918 when Nicholas II, his wife and children were executed by the revolutionaries.

Roman Question. See VATICAN CITY.

Romans, The Epistle of Paul the Apostle to the. A book of the New Testament. It is a long letter written by Paul in A.D. 56 to the Christians in Rome. It is sometimes called the "Gospel of Saint Paul," being his most profound exposition of the nature of Christianity. In this letter is the core of Pauline thought: Christianity is a religion for the whole world, having its roots in the older prophetic religion of the Jews.

Romantic Comedians, The (1926). A novel by Ellen GLASGOW. Like the author's *They Stooped to Folly*, this novel is an ironical comedy of manners. The elderly Judge Honeywell, who belongs to the generation before World War I, marries 18-year-old Annabel Upchurch. The juxtaposition in age, manners, and values produces a rich comedy, told by Miss Glasgow with wit and compassion. Eventually Annabel runs away with Dabney Birdsong, leaving the judge looking longingly at the young nurse sent to take care of him.

romanticism. A term applied to the movement in European literature and the other arts that began toward the end of the 18th century. In emphasizing the imagination and emotions over reason and intellect, the movement was a reaction against NEOCLASSICISM.

The rise of romanticism was so gradual and it exhibited so many phases, some of them paradoxical, that a definition is nearly impossible. Broadly, romanticism might be said to involve the following characteristics: individualism; nature-worship; primitivism; an interest in medieval, Oriental, and vanished or alien cultures in general; philosophic idealism; a paradoxical tendency toward both free thought and religious mysticism; revolt against political authority and social convention; exaltation of physical passion; the cultivation of emotion and sensation for their own sakes; and a persistent attraction to the supernatural, the morbid, the melancholy, and the cruel.

The French writer Rousseau is considered the

father of romanticism, although its first manifestation as an organized movement appeared in Germany in the work of Schiller, Goethe, Novalis, Kleist, and Tieck, all early romantic leaders there, and especially in the idealist philosophies of Kant, Fichte, Schelling, and Hegel. Scattered English forerunners of romanticism in the later 18th century were Gray, Collins, Cowper, Burns, Chatterton, Blake, and the Gothic novel. The movement was given impetus with the publication of Percy's *Reliques* and Macpherson's *Ossian,* and was powerfully stimulated by the French Revolution. English romanticism flowered (1789–1832) in the work of Wordsworth, Coleridge, Shelley, Byron, Keats, Southey, Campbell, Moore, Leigh Hunt, Hood, Beddoes, Scott, Lamb, Hazlitt, De Quincey, and Landor.

In France, Mme de Staël and Chateaubriand were forerunners of romanticism after Rousseau, but there was no definite movement there until about 1820, lasting until about 1843. The chief influences in French romanticism were German and English and the outstanding literary representatives were Lamartine, Nodier, Béranger, Hugo, Musset, Vigny, Gautier, George Sand, Dumas *père,* Stendhal, Sainte-Beuve, and Mérimée. In the U.S., romanticism developed at a later date than in Europe, and was less well defined, exhibiting modifications from the peculiar nature of American culture of the time with a strong emphasis on humanitarianism and reform. Foreign influences were chiefly German idealism, Rousseauistic nature worship, the Gothic novel, and the historical romance and pseudo-popular ballad of Scott. Among American romantic writers were Charles Brockden Brown, Cooper, Irving, Simms, Bryant, Poe, Emerson, Thoreau, Very, Hawthorne, Melville, Longfellow, Whittier, Lowell, and Whitman. Transcendentalism (c. 1830–1861) is regarded as the clearest example of romanticism in the U.S.

Among the arts other than literature, romanticism is exemplified by Beethoven, Berlioz, Schubert, Mendelssohn, and Schumann in music, and by Delacroix, Ingres, Corot, and Millet in painting.

The romantic movement was arrested in its development in England after 1832, with only a brief revival under the pre-Raphaelite Brotherhood, and in the U.S. it was rapidly absorbed by native tendencies and other influences. In Germany, however, it persisted, continuing especially in the philosophies of Schopenhauer and Nietzsche, in the music dramas of Wagner, in the fiction of Mann, and in the poetry of Stefan George and Rilke. In France dominant romantic characteristics were developed by Baudelaire and through him passed to the Decadents, the Symbolists and, ultimately, the surrealists. See GERMAN ROMANTICISM.

Romany. A gypsy; or the gypsy language, the speech of the Roma or Zincali. The word is from Gypsy *rom,* a man, or husband. A *Romany rye,* one who enters into the gypsy spirit, learns their language, and lives with them as one of themselves. *Rye* is gypsy for gentleman.

romanzo (romance). Italian term for the genre of the romantic epic. In Italy this took the form of a long poem in OTTAVA RIMA dealing with the chivalric adventures and romantic loves of the knights of Charlemagne and of King Arthur. Sung on the streets by minstrels as well as written in the study

by learned poets, the *romanzi* reached their artistic peak in the work of BOIARDO and ARIOSTO, who wrote on the Orlando theme. TASSO's *Gerusalemme liberata* is an attempt at a stricter emulation of the classical epics of Homer and Vergil, but its variety of characters and incidents, its interweaving of plots, and its reliance on the marvelous and the magical make it the last of the Italian Renaissance *romanzi.* Mock *romanzi* that poked fun at the absurdities of the genre, especially the *Morgante Maggiore* of PULCI, also appeared during the period. In the same vein, the *Gargantua and Pantagruel* of Rabelais and the *Don Quixote* of Cervantes utilize the ingredients of the popular romantic epics in a satiric manner. In England, the chief influence of the *romanzo* can be seen in Spenser's *Faerie Queene.*

Romaunt of the Rose. See ROMANCE OF THE ROSE.

Rome. Known as the **Eternal City.** A city in central Italy, the capital of the Republic of Italy. In ancient times Rome was the capital and center of the Roman Empire. It then became, through Peter the first bishop of Rome, the home of the pope and the capital of early Christendom. Today the pope lives in the VATICAN CITY, which is wholly within the city's precincts, and Rome remains the center of the Roman Catholic religion.

Traditionally the city was founded by ROMULUS in 753 B.C. By 265 B.C. Rome controlled the entire Italian peninsula, having subjugated all the neighboring tribes. Victory in the three PUNIC WARS with Carthage (264–241, 218–202, 149–146 B.C.) gave Rome domination of the Mediterranean and made her most powerful state in the ancient world.

As a republic (753–31 B.C.), Rome had flourished. Under the dictatorship of Julius CAESAR and later under the emperors AUGUSTUS, TRAJAN, and HADRIAN, Rome became the capital of an empire that included virtually all the known world.

From the early days of the empire, various emperors had contemplated moving the capital from republican-minded Rome to an eastern city. In A.D. 330, CONSTANTINE THE GREAT moved the seat of empire to Byzantium on the Bosphorus, renaming it Constantinople. The Visigoths sacked Rome in 410. The city was repeatedly pillaged by barbarian tribes until JUSTINIAN I restored imperial power (536).

During this period the popes (as bishops of Rome) began to assume temporal power over the city. In 756 the Frankish king Pepin donated Rome to Pope Adrian I.

Medieval Rome was a dingy, mud-filled city with animals grazing in the Imperial Forum. The population shrank as low as 2,000 people. Even the papacy moved to France (1309–1377).

A new period of splendor began in the 15th century under the Renaissance popes. New churches and public buildings were erected, often using material from the ruinous buildings of Imperial Rome that littered the city. Rome was sacked again in 1527 by the soldiers of Charles V, but this only temporarily halted the rebuilding. The modern city is still dominated by the lavish baroque and rococo churches and palaces built in the 16th, 17th, and 18th centuries.

The popes lost sovereignty of the city in 1870, when Rome became the capital of the united nation of Italy. A symbolic temporal power was restored to the popes in 1929, with the creation of the Vatican City as an independent state.

Rome's outstanding feature as a city is the fact that its history as a center of political and religious importance is unparalleled in duration. This is visually evident in its abundance of historic architecture. Roman buildings from the classical age can be seen standing between a Renaissance church and a modern apartment house.

Rome, sack of. In 1527 the imperial armies of Charles V, inspired by the zeal of Protestant mercenaries from the northern countries, destroyed and pillaged the holy city. Pope Clement VII took refuge in the Castel Sant' Angelo and later fled the city.

Rome: when in Rome, do as Rome does. Conform to the manners and customs of those among whom you live. St. Monica and her son St. Augustine said to St. Ambrose: "At Rome they fast on Saturday, but not so at Milan; which practice ought to be observed?" To which St. Ambrose replied, "When I am at Milan, I do as they do at Milan; but when I go to Rome, I do as Rome does!"

Rome-Berlin Axis. In World War II, the alliance between Germany and Italy, created in 1936. Both countries later signed agreements with Japan.

Romeo and Juliet (c. 1596). A tragedy by William SHAKESPEARE. Romeo, the young heir of the Montagues, attends the great ball of the Capulets in disguise and falls in love with JULIET, the daughter of the house. (See CAPULET AND MONTAGUE.) Because of the deadly feud between the Montagues and Capulets, the lovers are married secretly in the cell of Friar LAURENCE. During a street brawl Romeo's friend MERCUTIO is killed by Juliet's cousin TYBALT. Enraged by his friend's death, Romeo kills Tybalt and is banished from Verona. In desperation Juliet, who is about to be married to Paris against her will, takes a sleeping potion given her by the friar to bring on a semblance of death. Romeo, hearing of her death before the friar's explanation reaches him, returns and drinks poison at Juliet's tomb. When she wakes up a few moments later to find him dead, she stabs herself. Realizing that their hatred has caused the tragedy, the two houses make a tardy, sorrowful peace.

Sentimental, romantic, and given to poetic expression of his love, Romeo is typical of the youthful Elizabethan swain. His best-known speech occurs in the famous balcony scene with Juliet:

But, soft! what light through yonder window breaks?
It is the east, and Juliet is the sun!
Arise, fair sun, and kill the envious moon,
Who is already sick and pale with grief,
That thou her maid are far more fair than she.

The first written version of the story of the ill-fated lovers appears in the *Novellino* (1476) of Masuccio Salernitano. The story was retold in Arthur Brooke's poetic *Tragical History of Romeus and Juliet* (1562) and in William Paynter's *Palace of Pleasure* (1567). Shakespeare most closely follows Brooke's version.

Gounod wrote an opera, *Roméo et Juliette* (1867), based on the Shakespearean plot, and Jean Anouilh has written a bitter and very realistic version of the story in his *Roméo and Jeanette*.

Romero, Pedro. A young bullfighter in Ernest

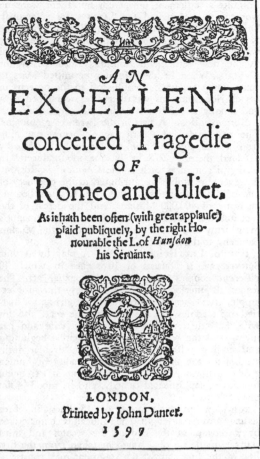

Title page of Shakespeare's *Romeo and Juliet* (1597).

Hemingway's novel *The Sun Also Rises*. Admired by the other characters for his style and courage, he has a short-lived affair with Lady Brett Ashley.

Rommel, Erwin (1891–1944). Commander of German forces in North Africa during World War II. He was involved in an attempt to assassinate Hitler in 1944.

Romola (1863). A historical novel by George ELIOT. After her marriage to the hedonistic Tito Melema, Romola, a young Florentine woman, comes under the influence of Savonarola; she finds peace through faith and dedication.

Romulus. Legendary and eponymous founder of Rome (753 B.C.) and its 1st king (753–716 B.C.). Descendants of AENEAS, Romulus and his twin, Remus, were sons of Mars and Rhea Silvia; Numitor, Rhea's father and king, was ousted by his brother Amulius who made Rhea a vestal virgin. Accordingly, when she gave birth, she was put to death and her two babies were thrown into the Tiber. They were washed ashore, suckled by a she-wolf, and found by a herdsman and his wife who brought them up. They were eventually recognized and overthrew Amulius, restoring Numitor as king. They then set about to found a city; they quarreled over the site for the city, and Romulus killed his brother in anger.

Romulus's settlement prospered, but there were no women, so he invited the SABINES for a festival. During the celebrations, the young Romans seized the Sabine women and drove off the men. The ensuing war was settled by making Sabines and Romans equal in the new settlement. Romulus ruled wisely for 37 years. When he died, Jupiter permitted Mars to come down and take Romulus off to the heavens in his chariot. Romulus was thereafter worshiped as a god among the Romans under the name Quirinus.

Roncesvalles. A pass in the Pyrenees mountains. The rear guard of Charlemagne's army, returning from a campaign in Spain, was ambushed and badly defeated there in 778 by Basque mountaineers. In medieval romances such as the *Chanson de* ROLAND, however, the ambush is attributed to the treachery of one of Charlemagne's knights, the Basques become an army of 400,000 Muslims, and the defeat of the rear guard is followed by the return of Charlemagne's main army and the retaliatory defeat of the Muslim Saracens, to the glory of Christendom.

Ronde, La (Reigen; 1900). A play by Arthur SCHNITZLER. It consists of 10 scenes in which 10 different couples prepare for the sexual act. The scenes all interlock with one another—thus, for example, after a scene between a young girl and a married man comes a scene between the man and his wife, and then a scene between the wife and her lover—and the whole play forms a circle beginning and ending with a prostitute. This circular form symbolizes the unending frenetic quality of human erotic behavior; but the play contains frequent touches of sophisticated comedy, and its mood is not one of despair.

rondeau. A lyric poem of 15 lines, in three stanzas of uneven length. The rondeau is characterized by a refrain, at the end of the second and third stanzas, made up of a fragment taken from the first line of the first stanza; the fragment may consist of a phrase, a clause, or as little as a single word. The rondeau form arose in France and its rules were enunciated in the 16th century. The rhyme scheme is: a-a-b-b-a, a-a-b-R, a-a-b-b-a-R, the R being the refrain. The following is an example:

> In after days when grasses high
> O'ertop the stone where I shall lie,
>   Though ill or well the world adjust
>   My slender claim to honoured dust,
> I shall not question or reply.
>
> I shall not see the morning sky;
> I shall not hear the night wind sigh;
>   I shall be mute, as all men must
>   In after days!
>
> But yet, now living, fain were I
> That some one then should testify,
>   Saying—*He held his pen in trust*
>   *To art, not serving shame or lust.*
> Will none?—Then let my memory die
>   In after days!
>   Austin Dobson, *In After Days*

See RONDEL; ROUNDEL; CHAUCERIAN ROUNDEL.

rondel. A verse form containing fourteen lines and two rhymes. The rondel arose in France in the 14th century, was written in English as early as the 15th century, and revived in the 19th. A two-line refrain is repeated in the rondel three times in its entirety. The rhyme scheme is A-B-b-a-a-b-A-B-a-b-b-a-A-B, or sometimes A-B-a-b-b-a-A-B-a-b-a-b-A-B. (A-B represents the refrain). There is also a rondel form of thirteen lines which omits either one of the last two refrain lines. The following example has thirteen lines:

> Love comes back to his vacant dwelling,—
>   The old, old love that we knew of yore!
> We see him stand by the open door,
> With his great eyes sad and his bosom swelling.
>
> He makes as though in our arms repelling,
>   He fain would lie as he lay before;—
> Love comes back to his vacant dwelling,
>   The old, old love that we knew of yore!
>
> Ah, who shall help us from over-spelling
>   That sweet, forgotten, forbidden lore!
> E'en as we doubt in our heart once more,
> With a rush of tears to our eyelids welling,
> Love comes back to his vacant dwelling.
>   Austin Dobson, *The Wanderer*

See RONDEAU, ROUNDEL, CHAUCERIAN ROUNDEL.

Ronsard, Pierre de (1524?–1585). French poet and leader of the PLÉIADE. He was destined by his father for a diplomatic career, but after spending four years as a page in the service of Francis I, he was struck by deafness and turned to humanistic studies and poetry. Inspired by the teaching of Jean Dorat at the Collège de Coqueret in Paris, Ronsard and his fellow-students Joachim Du Bellay and Jean Antoine de Baïf conceived a new program for French poetry, which Du Bellay elaborated in the DÉFENSE ET ILLUSTRATION DE LA LANGUE FRANÇAISE.

The succession of Ronsard's works testifies to his steady development and great versatility. Although his *Odes* (1550) were closely modeled after the work of Horace and Pindar, the *Amours de Cassandre* (1552), a collection of Petrarchan sonnets published with musical accompaniment, was characterized by the light, graceful style for which he is best known. The *Folâtries* (1553), *Mélanges* (1555), *Odes* (1555), and *Amours de Marie* (1555) are simple, sensual love poems which celebrate rustic pleasures and evoke the gentle atmosphere of Ronsard's native countryside. In the *Hymnes* (1555) he expressed his awe before the mysteries of the universe. With the outbreak of the religious wars, Ronsard the patriot produced the *Discours des Misères de ce Temps* (1562) and other political works that at first were conciliatory but became increasingly hostile to the Huguenots. He made an unsuccessful attempt at epic poetry with *La Franciade* (1572). His last and perhaps best collection of love poetry, *Sonnets pour Hélène* (1578), was written in the prevailing platonic style and betrayed the profound melancholy which dominated Ronsard as he saw death approaching.

Although widely acknowledged throughout Europe as the "Prince of poets," Ronsard, mindful of posterity's verdict, never ceased polishing and perfecting his work. After his death, his reputation suffered an eclipse until he was re-discovered by the 19th-century Romantics.

Room at the Top (1957). A best-selling novel by John BRAINE. It is the story of a young man's struggle to rise in his job and marry his boss's daughter—at the cost of his mistress's life.

Room of One's Own, A (1929). A feminist essay by Virginia WOOLF on the status of women and the difficulties of a woman artist. See ORLANDO.

Room with a View, A (1908). A novel by E. M. FORSTER. It is set mostly in Italy, a country which represents for the author the forces of true passion. The heroine, upper-middle-class Lucy Honeychurch, is visiting Italy with a friend. When she regrets that her hotel room has no view, lower-middle-class Mr. Emerson offers the friends his own room and that of his son. Among Lucy's experiences are a street murder at her feet, from which George Emerson rescues her, and getting lost at a picnic, at which George kisses her. On her return to England she becomes engaged to a shallow, conventional young man of her own class. But when she meets George again, she overcomes her own prejudice and her family's opposition and marries him.

Roosevelt, [Anna] Eleanor (1884–1962). American humanitarian and wife of President Franklin D. Roosevelt. She married Roosevelt, who was a distant cousin, in 1905, and, after his election to the presidency, became the most active first lady in American history; she engaged in social welfare work, took part in Democratic politics, served as assistant director of the Office of Civilian Defense (1941–1942), and conducted a newspaper column, *My Day*. After her husband's death, she was chairman of the Commission on Human Rights of the UN Economic and Social Council and represented the U.S. in the UN General Assembly from 1949 to 1952. In her last years, she was a leader in New York City reform politics. Her books include *This Is My Story* (1937), *My Days* (1938), *This I Remember* (1948), and *On My Own* (1958).

Roosevelt, Franklin Delano (1882–1945). 32nd president of the U.S. (1933–1945). Roosevelt was a fifth cousin of Theodore Roosevelt, who was also his wife's uncle. Educated at Groton and at Harvard University, he attended Columbia University Law School and married Eleanor ROOSEVELT in 1905. After his admission to the bar, he entered politics in 1910 as the leader of a group of insurgents against Tammany Hall in New York and won election to the state legislature. He supported Woodrow Wilson in 1912 and in 1913 was made an assistant secretary of the navy under Josephus Daniels. In 1920 he was nominated as the vice-presidential candidate on the Democratic ticket with James M. Cox and battled eloquently for the League of Nations. In August, 1921, he was stricken with poliomyelitis; he went to Warm Springs, Ga., to take the cure but, although his condition was somewhat improved, he remained a cripple for the rest of his life. He later established a foundation at Warm Springs to aid other victims of the disease.

After serving two terms as governor of New York, he ran for the presidency in 1932, defeating Herbert Hoover. Declaring in his first inaugural address that "the only thing we have to fear is fear itself," he dedicated his first administration to a NEW DEAL that would alleviate the economic distress caused by the depression of 1929. In 1936, he defeated Alfred Landon of Kansas to win reelection by a landslide, losing the electoral votes of only Maine and Vermont. Domestic matters occupied much of Roosevelt's second administration, during which he lost his fight

to enlarge the Supreme Court, but the worsening situation in Europe brought a new concern with foreign affairs as the president sought to sway public opinion in favor of international cooperation against aggressor nations, a policy that was bitterly attacked by isolationists.

Roosevelt defied a long-standing tradition in 1940 when he decided to run for a third term, defeating Wendell Willkie. Soon after his inauguration, he secured enactment of the Lend-Lease Act to aid Great Britain and met with Winston Churchill to frame the Atlantic Charter, a statement of Anglo-American aims for the future. When the U.S. entered World War II after the Japanese attack on Pearl Harbor on Dec. 7, 1941, which Roosevelt described as "a day which will live in infamy," he directed American mobilization and acted to ensure hemispheric solidarity; in 1944 he won an unprecedented fourth term by defeating Thomas E. Dewey. At the Casablanca conference (1943), Roosevelt and Churchill announced that the war would continue until the enemy surrendered unconditionally; at the Yalta meeting (1945) with Premier Stalin, several concessions were made to the Soviet Union in exchange for her entry into the war against Japan. Two months later Roosevelt was dead of a cerebral hemorrhage.

One of the most colorful and controversial presidents in American history, Roosevelt greatly expanded the scope of the federal government, particularly in the field of social and economic legislation. His enemies, however, accused him of dictatorial tendencies and denounced his encroachments on private enterprise. His extraordinary gift for communication was best shown in his press conferences, of which transcripts were always made, and in his famous radio "Fireside Chats."

Roosevelt's writings include *Looking Forward* (1933) and *On Our Way* (1934). Samuel I. Rosenman edited his *Papers and Addresses* from 1928 to 1945. Playwright Robert E. Sherwood, who was one of Roosevelt's speech writers, wrote about the president in *Roosevelt and Hopkins* (1948). FDR's early struggles against polio are described in Dore Schary's drama *Sunrise at Campobello* (1959).

Roosevelt, Theodore (1858–1919). 26th president of the U.S. (1901–1909). After his graduation from Harvard, Roosevelt turned to writing history, in which he was intensely interested all his life. His first book was *The Naval War of 1812* (1882). Then he entered politics and served from 1882 to 1884 as a Republican member of the New York legislature. When his first wife, Alice Lee, and his mother died within a few hours of each other, the grief-stricken Roosevelt went to the Dakota Territory where he ranched and won the approbation of the local residents. In 1886 he married Edith Carow.

Returning to politics, Roosevelt served as a member of the U.S. Civil Service Commission and as police commissioner of New York City, displaying in these posts the vigor and determination that were his hallmarks. At the same time he was writing his four-volume *Winning of the West* (1889–1896), an account of U.S. expansion after the Revolution.

He was assistant secretary of the navy in 1898 when the Spanish-American War broke out and he resigned to form the Rough Riders, a volunteer cavalry group that was to become famous for its charge up San

Juan Hill in Cuba. After Roosevelt had been elected governor of New York in 1898, Republican Party bosses who feared his independence and liberal views secured his nomination as William McKinley's running mate in 1900, only to see him become president upon McKinley's death in 1901. As chief executive, Roosevelt gained a reputation as a "trust-buster," particularly for his dissolution of the Northern Securities Co. (1902); he encouraged conservation of national resources and secured the passage of the Pure Food and Drug Act (1906) and the Hepburn Act (1906) to ensure stricter regulation of the railroads.

An advocate of a venturesome foreign policy, he effected the construction of the Panama Canal, won the Nobel Peace Prize for his successful intervention in the Russo-Japanese War (1905), and dispatched the U.S. Fleet on a round-the-world tour (1907–1909). His motto was "Speak softly and carry a big stick." After the inauguration of his "lieutenant," William Howard Taft, in 1909, Roosevelt traveled in Africa and Europe and returned to find a growing split between Republican conservatives and progressives. Breaking with Taft and unable to win the Republican nomination in 1912, he organized the "Bull Moose" Party, ran against both Taft and Woodrow Wilson, and took enough votes away from Taft to ensure Wilson's election.

In 1914 he led an expedition to South America and explored Brazil's River of Doubt, which was renamed Rio Teodoro in his honor. Later, he favored U.S. entry into World War I on the side of the Allies and was deeply disappointed when President Wilson prevented him from raising a volunteer division. His son Quentin was killed in action; in World War II his sons Kermit and Theodore died in active service.

Roosevelt's other writings include *The Strenuous Life: Essays and Addresses* (1900), *The New Nationalism* (1910), and *Theodore Roosevelt, An Autobiography* (1913). See Upton SINCLAIR.

Rootabaga Stories (1922). A book of children's stories by Carl SANDBURG. Written in a style nearer poetry than prose, it is rich in the language and cadence of folk song. It was followed by *Rootabaga Pigeons* (1923).

Roots of Heaven, The (Les Racines du ciel; 1956). A novel by Romain GARY about the idealist Morel's fight to save elephants—symbol of liberty—from extinction.

Rope of Ocnus. See OCNUS.

Rorschach test. An ink-blot test used in the diagnosis of psychopathologic conditions. It was developed by the Swiss psychiatrist Hermann Rorschach (1884–1922).

Rosalind. The courageous, witty, and charmingly sportive heroine of Shakespeare's AS YOU LIKE IT.

Rosaline. In Shakespeare's ROMEO AND JULIET, the niece of Capulet with whom Romeo is infatuated when the play opens. Although Romeo attends the ball of the Capulets in order to catch a glimpse of Rosaline, he dismisses her from his thoughts when he first sees Juliet. Rosaline is frequently mentioned in the first act of the play, but is not one of the characters.

Rosary, The (1909). A best-selling novel by Florence BARCLAY. The plain heroine, Jane, declines to marry a young artist who loves her, fearing that his passion for physical beauty will cause him to regret the marriage later. When he is blinded in an accident she goes to look after him as "Nurse Gray" and wins his love again.

Rosas, Juan Manuel de (1793–1877). Argentine dictator. Named governor of Buenos Aires province in 1829, Rosas controlled the entire country until 1852 when he was defeated at the battle of Caseros. This was a period of great intellectual ferment in Argentina, and many writers, usually from exile in Chile or Uruguay, produced literary works attacking the despotism and terror of the Rosas regime. Among these were Sarmiento's FACUNDO, Mármol's AMALIA, and Echevarría's EL MATADERO.

Roscellinus. See Pierre ABÉLARD; NOMINALISM.

Roscius. A first-rate actor; so called from Quintus Roscius (d. about 62 B.C.), the Roman actor, unrivaled in his grace of action, melody of voice, conception of character, and delivery.

rose. A flower of many symbolic connotations. Medieval legend asserts that the first roses appeared miraculously at Bethlehem as the result of the prayers of a "fayre Mayden" who had been falsely accused and was sentenced to death by burning. The burning brands changed to roses and she was saved.

The rose has been a emblem of England since the time of the Wars of the Roses, a contest that lasted 30 years, in which 80 princes of the blood, a large portion of the English nobility, and some 100,000 common soldiers were slain. It was a struggle for the crown between the houses of York (the white rose) and Lancaster (the red). When the parties were united in the person of Henry VII, the united rose was taken as his device.

Rose and the Ring, The (1854). A burlesque fairy tale by William Makepeace THACKERAY. The fun arises from the fact that the magic rose, which belongs to Prince Bulbo of Crim Tartary, and the magic ring worn by Prince Giglio of Paflagonia make their possessors seem both lovely and lovable. So long as she is allowed to wear either the rose or the ring, the Princess Angelica, Giglio's cousin, who has been wrongfully put in his place by her father, appears the most charming of individuals, but the moment she is deprived of them, she becomes the most ill-tempered and ugly. Rosalba, the deposed princess of Crim Tartary, shares with Giglio the favor of the all-powerful Fairy Blackstick, and although at their christenings she gave them each a little misfortune, she stands by them in their difficulties and brings their affairs to a happy ending.

Rose Bernd (1903). A tragedy by Gerhart HAUPTMANN. The titular heroine is unable to resist the advances of the men whose lust she awakens. Trapped by her sensuality, she gives birth to an illegitimate child, which she subsequently smothers. She is finally condemned by the society that has cynically used her.

Rose Garden at Worms, The. See ILSAN THE MONK.

Rosenberg, Alfred (1893–1946). German writer and leading Nazi. In his theoretical work, *The Myth of the Twentieth Century (Der Mythus des 20. Jahrhunderts;* 1930), he supported the anti-Semitic policies that he helped to administer. He was condemned to death at the NUREMBERG TRIALS. See ARYAN RACE.

Rosenberg, Isaac (1890–1918). English poet. He wrote passionate, original, muscular verse, chiefly about his experiences in the first World War; he was killed in action. His *Collected Works* appeared in 1937.

Rosencrantz and Guildenstern. In Shakespeare's HAMLET, 2 time-serving courtiers. They are willing to undertake any commission, however iniquitous, to please the king.

Rosenkavalier, Der (The Cavalier of the Rose, 1911). An opera composed by Richard STRAUSS to a libretto by Hugo von HOFMANNSTHAL. It is a bitter-sweet love story infused with much broad comedy, Viennese gaiety, and a certain nostalgia for the days of Vienna's flowering that were already slipping into the past at the time of composition. The principal characters are Baron Ochs, in love with the merchant's daughter Sophie Faninal; Princess von Werdenberg (known as the Marschallin); and her young admirer Octavian, who is also in love with Sophie. The rough and jovial country baron loses Sophie to his young rival, and the Marschallin reconciles herself to being too old for love.

Rose Tattoo, The (1951). A play by Tennessee WILLIAMS. Set in a Sicilian community on the Gulf Coast, the play deals with Serafina Delle Rose, a passionate and warm-hearted dressmaker, whose truckdriver husband has just been killed. Serafina, unwilling to believe rumors of her husband's infidelity, keeps his ashes in a marble urn in the house and remains a frustrated widow, until three years later she meets a younger truckdriver who, like her dead husband, has a rose tattoo on his chest. The play has a clownish humor usually lacking in Williams.

Rose Theatre. An Elizabethan playhouse. It was built in 1587 by Philip Henslowe and John Cholmley on the Bankside in Southwark. The Rose was occupied by the Lord Admiral's Men, featuring the famous tragedian Edward Alleyn, and in 1591–1592 by the Lord Strange's Men who later became Shakespeare's company, the Lord Chamberlain's Men.

Rosetta stone. A stone found in 1799 by M. Boussard, a French officer of engineers, in an excavation made at Fort St. Julien, near Rosetta, in the Nile delta. It has an inscription in three different languages: the hieroglyphic, the demotic, and the Greek. It was erected in 195 B.C., to honor Ptolemy Epiphanes, because he remitted the dues of the sacerdotal body. The great value of this stone is that it furnished the French Egyptologist Jean François CHAMPOLLION the key whereby he deciphered the Egyptian hieroglyphics.

Rosicrucians. A mystical society of religious reformers, who first appeared in Germany in the early 17th century and who were said to have a knowledge of magical secrets. Their symbol was a red rose upon a cross.

Rosmersholm (1866). A play by Henrik IBSEN. Johannes Rosmer has freed himself intellectually, but he is unable to cut his emotional ties to the life-destroying conventions embodied in Rosmersholm, his ancestral home. His invalid wife, Beata, has committed suicide to leave him free to marry the vital, strong-willed Rebecca West, but when Rosmer learns that Rebecca had subtly led Beata to believe that she must sacrifice herself, his faith in himself and his idealism die. He refuses to believe that Rebecca truly loves him unless she agrees to go the way of Beata; she consents willingly, and together she and Rosmer end their lives by leaping into the millrace.

Ross. In Shakespeare's MACBETH, a cousin of Macduff. He goes to England to inform Macduff of the murder of Lady Macduff and her children.

Ross, Harold [Wallace] (1892–1951). American editor. A dynamic, contradictory personality, Ross edited THE NEW YORKER from its founding in 1925 until his death. James Thurber, long associated with the magazine, wrote of him in *The Years with Ross* (1959).

Ross, Martin. See E. O. SOMERVILLE.

Rossellini, Roberto (1906–   ). Italian motion-picture director and producer. He began his film career by working on a number of documentaries for the Mussolini regime. In 1944, while the Germans were preparing to evacuate Rome, Rossellini began to work on his famous film, *Open City*. In it he sought to re-create as closely as possible the heroic action of the resistance movement among the people of Rome; it became a crucial film in the development of the Italian neorealist movement in cinema. Rossellini's next film, *Paisan* was also highly acclaimed. Among his subsequent films are *Germany Year Zero* (1947), *The Miracle* (1948), *No Greater Love* (1952), and *General della Rovere* (1960).

Rossetti, Christina Georgina (1830–1894). English poet of Italian parentage, sister of Dante Gabriel and William Michael Rossetti. She is known for her ballads and her mystic religious lyrics, marked by symbolism, vividness of detail, and intensity of feeling. Among her works are *Goblin Market, and Other Poems* (1862); THE PRINCE'S PROGRESS; *Sing-Song* (1872), a collection of verse for children; *Annus Domini* (1874); *A Pageant* (1881); *Time Flies* (1885), prose and verse; and *The Face of the Deep* (1892), an interpretation of the Apocalypse. *The Convent Threshold* (1862) is one of her best-known single works. Her first poems were published in *The Germ*, the Pre-Raphaelite publication, and she often modeled for painters in the PRE-RAPHAELITE BROTHERHOOD. After a serious illness in 1874 she was left an invalid and withdrew from the world, rarely receiving visitors or leaving her home.

Rossetti, Dante Gabriel. Full name, **Gabriel Charles Dante Rossetti** (1828–1882). English poet and painter of Italian parentage, brother of Christina and William Michael Rossetti. He was the driving force of the PRE-RAPHAELITE BROTHERHOOD. As a painter he had little formal training, revealed little technical ability, and is noted chiefly as a colorist. His best-known painting, *Ecce Ancilla Domini* (1850), is an emotive representation of the Annunciation.

His lyric poems are distinguished by richness and vividness of detail, mysticism and fantasy, and the frequent use of modified ballad form. His books of poetry include *The Early Italian Poets* (1861), translations of the lyrics of Dante, his contemporaries, and predecessors; *Poems* (1870), a collection that was at first buried in the coffin of Elizabeth SIDDALL, Rossetti's wife; and *Ballads and Sonnets* (1881). His best-known single works are THE BLESSED DAMOZEL, SISTER HELEN, *Troy Town,* and THE HOUSE OF LIFE. He also made a number of translations from the Italian, German, and French, the most outstanding of which is THE BALLAD OF DEAD LADIES of François Villon.

Rossetti, William Michael (1829–1919). Art critic and author, brother of Dante Gabriel and Christina Rossetti. He was one of the original members of the PRE-RAPHAELITE BROTHERHOOD, serving as editor of *The Germ*. He wrote a translation of Dante (1865) and a *Life of Keats* (1887); he also wrote memoirs of both his brother (1895) and his sister (1904).

Rossini, Giacchino Antonio (1782–1868). The dominant Italian operatic composer of the early 19th century. His more than 40 serious and comic operas were all written between 1810 and 1829, after which he wrote little but the *Stabat Mater* (1842) and the *Petite Messe solennelle* (1864). He settled in Paris in 1824, and there ended his days, famous as a wit and as a host. His most important operas are THE BARBER OF SEVILLE, *Otello* (1816), *La Cenerentola* (*Cinderella*, 1817), *Sémiramide* (1823), and *William Tell* (1829).

Rosso Fiorentino. Also known as **Il Rosso**. Real name, **Giovanni Battista de'Rossi** (1494–1540). Italian painter. A leading figure in the movement away from High Renaissance classicism towards mannerism, he is best known as a painter for his *Moses and the Daughters of Jethro* and *Deposition from the Cross*. He was also one of the leading decorators imported from Italy by Francis I to paint at Fontainebleau. The resulting "School of Fontainebleau" is regarded as a source of the later rococo style in France.

Rostand, Edmond (1868–1918). French poet and playwright. CYRANO DE BERGERAC (1897) is the most famous example of the poetic, romantic drama created by Rostand. A colorful and exciting portrait of the reign of Louis XIII, with an aspiring poet-lover for its hero, the play enjoyed tremendous popularity. The actress Sarah Bernhardt made famous the title roles of *La Princesse Lointaine* (1895), *La Samaritaine* (1897), and *L'Aiglon* (1900), the story of Napoleon's son. *Chantecler* (1910), an experimental play, has since won critical acclaim, but it was poorly received and put an end both to Rostand's meteoric rise to fame and to his dramatic career.

Rosten, Leo [Calvin]. Pen name, **Leonard Q. Ross** (1908–). Polish-born American humorist, political scientist, and teacher. He is best known for *The Education of H*y*m*a*n K*a*p*l*a*n* (1937), a series of amusing sketches based on his experiences as a teacher of English to adult immigrants. Under his own name he also wrote *Hollywood: The Movie Colony, the Movie Makers* (1941), an objective analysis of the motion-picture industry, and *Captain Newman, M.D.* (1961), a novel.

Rosten, Norman (1914–). American poet, radio writer, and playwright. Rosten has written vigorous poetry about contemporary life, which has been collected in *Return Again, Traveler* (1940) and *The Fourth Decade and Other Poems* (1943). *The Big Road* (1946) celebrates the building of the Alcan highway to Alaska. *This Proud Pilgrimage* (1938) and *First Stop to Heaven* (1941) were verse dramas. He has also written plays for the radio, including some on historical figures for *Cavalcade of America*. His later work includes *Songs for Patricia* (1951), *The Plane and the Shadow* (1953), and the

play *Mister Johnson* (1956) based on the novel by Joyce Cary.

Rostova, Natasha. The heroine of Count Leo Tolstoi's novel WAR AND PEACE. One of Tolstoi's greatest characterizations, Natasha matures in the course of the book from a charming but ingenuous girl into a woman of poise and devotion. Her tragic love affair with Prince Andrei Bolkonski takes much of the joy out of her life, but her eventual marriage to Pierre Bezukhov is a happy one.

Roswitha (also **Hrosvitha** or **Hrotsvitha**) (c. 935–c. 1002). German poet, dramatist, historian. A nun in a Benedictine convent in Saxony, she was among the first to adapt classical drama to a Christian purpose: she wrote six prose comedies revealing an effective sense of theater, modeled on the Latin comedies of Terence but devoted to the lives of saints, especially virgins. She also wrote eight narrative poems on religious subjects and a poetic chronicle in epic style celebrating the career of Otto I.

Rota, Bernardino (1509–1575). Italian poet. He is known for his Petrarchan sonnets, Italian eclogues, and Latin epigrams and elegies, all widely admired and influential in his day. These were published in the *Rime* (verses) of 1572.

Roth, Philip (1933–). American short-story writer. Many of Roth's short stories have been anthologized, and his *Goodbye, Columbus* (1959), a novella and several short stories, received a great deal of critical acclaim. Like most of his work, the novel *Letting Go* (1962) deals with contemporary Jewish life in America.

Rothko, Marc (1903–). Russian-born American painter. His canvases are reduced to two or three subtly harmonized, pulsating bands of color.

Rothschild. A family of internationally known German-Jewish financiers, whose banking house was established at Frankfort-am-Main near the end of the 18th century.

Rotrou, Jean de (1609–1650). French playwright. One of Richelieu's CINQ AUTEURS, Rotrou wrote his first play, *L'Hypocondriaque ou le mort amoureux* (*The Hypochondriac, or the Amorous Dead Man*, 1628), when he was 19, but produced his best work in his later life, including the comedies LES SOSIES and *La Soeur* (*The Sister*, 1648), the tragedies *Saint Genast* (1646) and *Venceslas* (1641), and the tragicomedy *Don Bernard de Cabrère* (1648). Often derived from Spanish and classical sources, Rotrou's plays marked an enormous stylistic advance over those of his predecessors and were the only dramatic works of their time considered to rival those of Corneille.

Rouault, Georges (1871–1958). French painter and printmaker. Apprenticed to a stained-glass maker, he retained in his work a vigorous black line that encircles bright spots of color. He has concentrated on the anguish of man's fate in figures of judges and clowns, and has poignantly pictured religious subjects.

Rouget de Lisle, Claude Joseph (1760–1836). A French army officer, composer of the words and music of LA MARSEILLAISE (1792), the French national anthem.

Roughead, William (1870–1952). A Scottish criminologist and authority on the "gentle art of murder." Lillian Hellman's play, *The Children's*

Hour (1934), is based upon an essay by Roughead concerning an old Edinburgh scandal. He was the editor of many volumes in the Notable British Trials series, and also wrote essays on crime collected in *Rascals Revived* (1940); *Reprobates Reviewed* (1941); and similar collections.

Roughing It (1872). A narrative by Mark TWAIN. The author describes the experiences he shared with his brother, Orion, when the two worked in a mining camp in Nevada in the early 1880's. Mark Twain traveled on to California and the Sandwich Islands; his book describes, in dramatic incidents, the people he met, from desperadoes to Brigham Young.

Rough Riders, the. Name given to the First Volunteer Cavalry serving in Cuba during the Spanish-American War, under Theodore Roosevelt and Leonard Wood. The Rough Riders distinguished themselves in their charge up San Juan Hill.

Rougon-Macquart, Les (1871–1893). A series of 20 novels by Emile ZOLA. Zola himself characterized the work as the natural and social history of a family under the Second Empire. This enormous work, exhaustive in its treatment of events, describes the world of the Rougon-Macquart family in minute detail. He depicts these human beings with brutal realism, sparing no detail of their sordid lives. The novels provided Zola with a laboratory in which he could experiment with his new naturalistic theories of fiction. A reformer at heart, Zola uses his naturalistic technique to dramatize the desperate need for social change. The thick volumes vary in their merit, but such works as L'ASSOMMOIR, LA DÉBÂCLE, NANA, LA TERRE, and GERMINAL are still widely read. See NATURALISM.

Roumanille, Joseph (1818–1891). French poet, leader of the FÉLIBRIGE.

roundel. An 11-line poem of particular structure. It is a variation of the French RONDEAU attributed to Swinburne, who popularized it in his *A Century of Roundels.* The first part of line one is repeated as a refrain in lines four and 11. The rhyme scheme goes a-b-a-R, b-a-b, a-b-a-R.

Roundheads. English Puritans of the reign of Charles I, and later, especially Cromwell's soldiers. They were so called because they wore their hair cut short, while that of the Royalists or Cavaliers was worn long, covering their shoulders.

Round Table. The table, in Arthurian legend, fabled to have been made by Merlin at Carduel for Arthur's father Uther Pendragon. Uther gives it to King Leodegraunce of Camiliard who in turn gives it to Arthur when Arthur marries Guinevere. To prevent any jealousy on the score of precedency, it was circular and seated 150 knights, with a place left in it for the GRAIL. The first reference to it is found in Wace's *Roman de Brut* (1155), but the fullest legendary details are from Malory's *Morte d'Arthur* (c. 1469).

Knights of the Round Table. According to Malory, there were 150 knights who had sieges (chairs) at the table. (See SIEGE PERILOUS.) Among the best known of the knights of the Round Table are Launcelot, Tristram, Lamerok, the three bravest; Torre, the first made; Galahad, the chaste; Gawain, the courteous; Gareth, the big-handed; Palamedes, the Saracen or unbaptized; Kay, the rude and boastful; Mark, the dastard; and Mordred, the traitor.

Rourke, Constance M[ayfield] (1885–1941). American writer. A specialist in U.S. folklore and humor, she wrote the first article on Paul Bunyan to appear in an American magazine (*New Republic,* 1918), but her best-known work is *American Humor: A Study of the National Character* (1931), which Lewis Mumford called "the most original piece of research that has appeared in American cultural history." She also wrote *Trumpets of Jubilee* (1927), *Davy Crockett* (1934), *Audubon* (1936), *Charles Sheeler, Artist in the American Tradition* (1938), and *The Roots of American Culture and Other Essays* (1942).

Rousillon, countess of. The mother of Bertram in Shakespeare's ALL'S WELL THAT ENDS WELL. She is deeply fond of her young ward Helena, whom Bertram is unwilling to marry because she is a commoner, and rebukes her son for his arrogance.

Rousseau, Henri (1844–1910). French primitive painter, known as *Le Douanier* (*Fr.,* the customhouse officer). A municipal toll employee, he retired in 1885 in order to paint and exhibited regularly thereafter. During these years he suffered from the ridicule and scorn of critics, although he gained the support of young writers and artists, particularly that of Guillaume Apollinaire. His is a simple world: he stiffly portrays his friends, sketches Paris and its surroundings, shares his enjoyment for the color of patriotic and military scenes, and also presents dreams of the jungle. These subjects are translated with a freshness and naïveté that reveal a rare sense for color and a unique sense of design.

Rousseau, Jean Jacques (1712–1778). Swiss-born French philosopher, author, political theorist, and composer. The son of a watchmaker, he set out on a life of wandering at the age of 16; he went to Turin where he was converted to Catholicism and served as footman to a wealthy family. He left Turin in 1731 and spent most of the next 10 years at Chambéry, Savoy, with Mme de WARENS, his benefactress. In 1741 he set out for Paris; became a secretary in the French embassy in Venice, but resigned, and returned to Paris where he became acquainted with the writers of the ENCYCLOPÉDIE, for which he wrote the article on musical notation. During this period he began his liaison with the half-literate servant-girl Thérèse Le Vasseur, by whom Rousseau said he had five children, all of whom he put in an orphan asylum. She later became his common-law wife, and accompanied him throughout his life. During his stay in Paris he wrote his ballet *Les Muses galantes* (*The Gallant Muses*), and light opera *Le Devin du village* (*The Village Soothsayer,* 1752). Rousseau became famous overnight by the publication of his first essay *Discours sur les sciences et les arts* (*Discourses on the Sciences and Arts,* 1750), in which he reacts against the 18th-century view that progress in the sciences and arts increases man's happiness; he argued that, on the contrary, they corrupt mankind. His second philosophical essay, *Discours sur l'origine et les fondements de l'inégalité parmi les hommes* (*Discourse on the Origin and Bases of Inequality among Men,* 1754) celebrates the "natural man" and indicts private property and the political state as causes of inequality and oppression. Rousseau returned to Geneva (1754), became a Protestant again, and returned to Paris. He lived at the Hermitage, a cottage built for him at Montmorency by Mme d'EPINAY. He fell in love with Comtesse d'Houdetot, Mme d'Epinay's sister-in-law, who was herself in love with another man. Rousseau's persecution complex began to show itself, for he quarreled with his friends and left the Hermitage to live nearby in the château of the duc de Luxembourg. Here he finished his immensely popular novel LA NOUVELLE HÉLOÏSE while still partially under the influence of his unrequited love affair. Here too Rousseau wrote his most famous and influential work THE SOCIAL CONTRACT and his EMILE. This latter work, because of its religious view, incurred the censure of the Sorbonne and the *Parlement*, and Rousseau was banished from France. He escaped to Switzerland, settling finally, at the invitation of David Hume, in England, where he started his CONFESSIONS, written from 1766 to 1770. Suspecting Hume, as he had suspected most of his friends, of a conspiracy against him, Rousseau quarreled with him and left England in 1767. Until 1770 he wandered with Thérèse and her mother from province to province, prey to intermittent delirium, finally returning to Paris where he lived in a state of poverty and near solitude. Here, protected from prying eyes by Thérèse, he wrote *Rêveries d'un promeneur solitaire* (*Daydreams of a Solitary Stroller*, 1776–1778), published in 1782, and a draft for a constitution for Poland, at the request of a Polish count. His only friend and contemporary disciple was BERNARDIN DE SAINT-PIERRE. He died at Ermenonville, near Paris; in 1794 his remains were transferred to the Panthéon in Paris.

Rousseau's closeness to nature, his sensitivity, individualism, rebellion against the established social and political order, his imagination and his glorification of the emotions make him the father of French ROMANTICISM. William Godwin and the leaders of the French Revolution of 1789 were among those influenced by his political ideas; Lamartine and de Musset were influenced by his style, as was Chateaubriand.

Roussin, André (1911–   ). French dramatist. His farcical comedies, such as *Bobosse* (1957), *Hélène* (1953), *La Petite Hutte* (1950), *Les oeufs de l'Autruche* (1950), and *Lorsque l'enfant paraît* (1952), generally revolve about the familiar romantic triangle. A skilled dramatic craftsman, Roussin enlivens his plays with light, witty dialogue.

Rover Boys. The heroes of a popular series of books for boys about life in preparatory school and college. The series included more than 30 titles, the first of which appeared in 1899. The books were written by Edward Stratemeyer under the pen name Arthur M. Winfield. Stratemeyer also created Tom SWIFT.

Rovetta, Girolamo (1851–1910). Italian novelist and dramatist. He is noted for his satirical treatment of the cultural and social values of the Italian bourgeoisie in the period following the Risorgimento. An uncompromising and pessimistic social critic, he was inspired by Balzac to write a "human comedy" pointing out the sordid economic and political interests that underlie the most praiseworthy ideals. His skill as a narrator is exceptional; his descriptions are precisely realistic; his language synthesizes dialect (usually Milanese) and colloquial modes of expression; his tone is at once satirical and cynical.

Rovetta's forte is his psychological analysis of character types. For example, Pompeo Barbarò, the protagonist of *Le Lagrime del Prossimo* (1887), is a pitiless moneylender and shrewd investor whose rapid rise to social and financial prominence is sparked by a remark he heard as a poor young man, that the real gentleman is one who knows how to steal. Among Rovetta's numerous plays might be cited *La Trilogia di Dorina* (1889), *I Disonesti* (1892), *La Realtà* (1895), *Romanticismo* (1903), and *Re Burlone* (1905).

Rowe, Nicholas (1674–1718). English poet and dramatist. He is best known for such tragedies as *Jane Shore* (1714), *The Fair Penitent* (1703), *Tamerlane* (1701), and *Lady Jane Grey* (1715). He also edited Shakespeare's plays, and was poet laureate (1715–1718).

Rowena. See IVANHOE.

Rowlandson, Mary (1635?–?1678). American pioneer and author of the first Indian-captivity narrative. The wife of a minister, she was taken captive with her six-year-old daughter in 1675 during King Philip's War, after an Indian attack on Lancaster, Mass. Her account of the event is *The Sovereignty and Goodness of God . . . Being a Narrative of the Captivity and Restauration of Mrs. Mary Rowlandson* (1682). One of the most popular American prose works of the 17th century, reprinted many times since, it gives a hair-raising picture of frontier perils.

Rowlandson, Thomas (1756–1827). English caricaturist. He is especially well known for his series of plates entitled *Tours of Dr. Syntax* (1812, 1820, 1821). He also illustrated books by Smollett, Goldsmith, Sterne, and others.

Rowley, Thomas. See Thomas CHATTERTON.

Rowley, William (c. 1585–c. 1637). English dramatist, best known for his collaboration with Thomas Middleton on THE CHANGELING. His own plays include *All's Lost by Lust* (1622) and *A Match at Midnight* (1633). He also collaborated with John Ford, Philip Massinger, John Fletcher, John Webster, and possibly, on a play now lost, with Shakespeare.

Rowson, Susannah Haswell (1762–1824). English-born American writer and actress. She came to Boston with her father, a British naval lieutenant, in 1767 but was forced to leave during the Revolution. CHARLOTTE TEMPLE, the only one of her novels which has been remembered, appeared in 1791 in England and three years later in the U.S. In 1793 she returned to America as an actress and, after leaving the stage, she ran a school for girls until her death.

Roxane. The wicked sultana in Jean Racine's tragedy BAJAZET. The heroine of Rostand's CYRANO DE BERGERAC is also named Roxane.

Roy, Gabrielle (1909–   ). Canadian novelist. Her first novel, *The Tin Flute* (*Bonheur d'occasion;* 1945), won France's Prix Femina in 1947. The story of a large French-Canadian family living in an impoverished quarter of Montreal, it was praised for its "vivid characterization, unflinching honesty, and dry-eyed compassion." Her later novels include *Where Nests the Water Hen* (*La petite poule d'eau;* 1950), *The Cashier* (*Alexandre Chenevert;* 1954), and *The Hidden Mountain* (1962). *Street of Riches* (*Rue Des-*

A Faire Quarrell.

With new Additions of M^r. *Chaughs* and *Trimtrams* Roaring, and the Bauds Song. *Neuer before Printed.*

As it was Acted before the King, by the Prince his Highnesse Seruants.

{ Written by *Thomas Midleton,* } Gent. and *William Rowley.*

Printed at London for *I. T.* and are to be sold at Christ Church Gate. 1617.

Title page of Middleton and Rowley's *A Fair Quarrel*.

chambault; 1955) is a collection of autobiographical sketches.

Roy, Jules (1907–). Algerian-born French novelist, dramatist, poet, and essayist. All his works are set in the wars he has observed as pilot and officer and analyze the nature of heroism. His novels are *Ciel et terre* (1943), *The Happy Valley* (*La Vallée heureuse;* 1946), *The Navigator* (1954), and *Unfaithful Wife* (*La Femme infidèle;* 1955). *Beau Sang* (1952), and *Le Fleuve rouge* (1957) are plays, while *Chants et prières pour des pilotes* (1943) is a collection of poetry.

Royal Society of London for Improving Natural Knowledge, The. An English scientific academy, founded in 1660 for the purpose of studying the whole field of knowledge and still in existence. Abraham Cowley and the chemist Robert Boyle had presented plans for such an organization, and among its members were included some of the leading literary, diplomatic, and scientific figures of the day. Samuel Pepys, who was admitted to the society in 1665 and later became its president, has a number of references to its meetings and its experiments in his famous diary. Isaac Newton was president from 1703 to 1727, and John Winthrop and Cotton and Increase Mather were leaders of a group of New England correspondents of the Royal Society. Thomas Sprat, bishop of Rochester, was historian of the organization, which sought, among other aims, to improve the English prose style of the time, making it simpler, clearer, and more suited to the needs of scientific ex-

position than the usual literary style then current. In this connection, an international language of symbols was proposed by Bishop Wilkins, considered to have been the Society's most important member.

The Royal Society was satirized in numerous contemporary works, including Shadwell's *Virtuosi* (1676), Swift's *Gulliver's Travels* (1726), and Samuel Butler's ELEPHANT IN THE MOON and *Satire on the Royal Society.*

Royce, Josiah (1855–1916). American philosopher, teacher, and essayist. After a series of teaching posts, Royce went to Harvard to replace William James, who was on leave; he remained there as a professor for the rest of his life. *The Religious Aspect of Philosophy* (1885) established Royce's famous theory of the Absolute. He held that if one admits the presence of evil in the world, it then necessarily follows that there is also an absolute principle of Truth, an all-knowing Mind or Universal Thought. James and Royce disagreed vigorously, and entered into a fruitful debate; James wrote that Royce's mind had nourished his, "as no other social influence ever has." Royce, the leader of the post-Kantian idealistic school in the U.S., also wrote *The Spirit of Modern Philosophy* (1892), *The Concept of God* (1897), *The Problem of Christianity* (1913), *Lectures on Modern Idealism* (1919), and other volumes. His *Fugitive Essays* (1920) deal with Shelley, George Eliot, and Browning. *The Feud of Oakfield Creek* (1887) was the philosopher's one attempt at fiction.

Rozanov, Vasili Vasilyevich (1856–1919). Russian writer, critic, and philosopher. He is best known for his views on the central place that sexuality holds in man's nature, forming the creative impulse on both the biological and the spiritual planes. His views were expressed in the collections of aphorisms entitled *Solitaria* (*Uyedinennoye;* 1912) and *Fallen Leaves* (*Padshiye listya;* 1913, 1915) in which he tries to convey not only his thought but his tone of voice through the prose. An avid admirer of Dostoevski, Rozanov published a penetrating study of the novelist, *The Legend of the Grand Inquisitor* (*Legenda velikogo inkvizitora;* 1894) in which he was the first to note the importance of Dostoevski's short work, *Notes from Underground.* Rozanov married Polina Suslova, the former mistress of Dostoevski.

Ruark, Robert [Chester] (1915–1965). American newspaper columnist and novelist. In his newspaper columns, Ruark revealed a gift for expressing aversion amusingly, often in a facetiously ungrammatical style. In *Grenadine Etching* (1947), he lampooned historical novels. He has also written two melodramatic and sensational novels, both of which are laid in Africa: *Something of Value* (1955) and *Uhuru* (1962). *Poor No More* (1959) is an embittered rags-to-riches saga set in the U.S. and Europe.

Rubáiyát of Omar Khayyám. A collection of quatrains by OMAR KHAYYÁM. Perhaps even better known in English than in the original Persian, 101 of the quatrains were translated by Edward FITZGERALD and published in 1859. The oldest-known manuscript of the original work is in the Bodleian Library, Oxford, and is dated at Shiraz, A.H. 865 (A.D. 1460). FitzGerald's translation, reputed to be extremely free but actually much closer to the original than has been supposed, is a masterpiece of English poetry in its own right. Omar's beautiful and world-weary concentration, in FitzGerald's rendering, upon sensual pleasure as the sole aim of living, helped establish the mood of the whole *fin de siècle* school of poetry in England.

Rubens, Peter Paul (1577–1640). Flemish painter. The greatest representative of baroque art in northern Europe, he was born and educated in Amsterdam. From 1600 to 1608, he was in the service of the duke of Mantua who sent him to Rome where he became strongly influenced by Italian printing. Thereafter, he returned to Antwerp where he entered the service of Albrecht and Isabella, who ruled the Netherlands as regents for Philip III of Spain. He was later entrusted with diplomatic missions that took him to Spain and England, and he undertook important commissions for the Spanish court. Exuberant religious paintings, classical fables, and allegories were produced at a stupendous rate in his workshop. These large-scale paintings are noted for their vitality, masterly execution, richness of color, and the vigorous, often rhythmic movement of their composition.

Rubicon. A small river separating ancient Italy from Cisalpine Gaul, the province allocated to Julius Caesar in the First TRIUMVIRATE. Fearing Caesar's growing power in Gaul, Pompey and the senate ordered Caesar to return to Rome without his army. When, in defiance of this order, Caesar crossed the Rubicon with his army (49 B.C.), he passed beyond the limits of his province, thereby becoming an invader of Italy and precipitating civil war. Hence, "to cross the Rubicon" is to take an irrevocable step.

Rucellai, Giovanni (1475–1525). Florentine courtier and dramatist. He is noted for his tragedies *Rosamunda* and *Oreste*. He also wrote *Le api* (*The Bees*), a celebrated version of the fourth book of Vergil's *Georgics*.

Ruck, Berta (1878–). English popular novelist, married to Oliver ONIONS. Among her works are *His Official Fiancée* (1914) and *Fantastic Holiday* (1953).

Rückert, Friedrich (1788–1866). German poet, known especially for his pioneering efforts in popularizing Oriental poetic forms and philosophical ideas in Germany. His works include *Geharnischte Sonette* (*Harnessed Sonnets*, 1814), a collection treating political themes of the day; a collection of *Kindertotenlieder* (*Songs on Children's Deaths*, 1872), set to music by Mahler; and *Die Weisheit des Brahmanen* (*The Wisdom of the Brahman*, 1836), collected translations from Oriental literature.

Ruddymane. See FAERIE QUEENE, THE.

Rudin (1856). A novel by Ivan TURGENEV. It traces the ineffectual career of the hero, Dmitri Nikolayevich Rudin. Typifying the philosophically inclined idealists Turgenev had encountered in his student days in Berlin, Rudin impresses almost everyone with his brilliant and high-minded talk. The hero does well when talking or dreaming, but decisive action is not in his line. The demands of a love offered him by Natalya Alekseyevna frighten him away. Rudin eventually does try to act and loses his life for it. During the 1848 revolt in Paris, he is shot while standing on top of a barricade, futilely waving a sword and trying to rally the retreating insurgents. Rudin has been characterized as one of SUPERFLUOUS MEN in Russian literature, a man unable to find a suitable cause to serve or proper outlet for his energies. Another view is that his nature would make him unable to act in any conditions.

Rudra (Sans., *rud,* to weep; *dra,* to run). The father of the tempest gods in the Hindu mythology of the *Vedas.* The legend says that as a boy he ran about weeping because he had no name, whereupon Brahma said, "Let your name be Rud-dra."

Rugby. A public school in England, founded in 1567. Its headmaster from 1828 to 1842 was Thomas Arnold, the father of Matthew Arnold. The book *Tom Brown's Schooldays* by Thomas Hughes concerns the school in the nineteenth century. A poem by Matthew Arnold is called *Rugby Chapel.* The game of Rugby football originated at this school.

Ruggiero or **Rogero.** A leading figure in Carolingian legends and in Matteo Maria Boiardo's ORLANDO INNAMORATO and Lodovico Ariosto's ORLANDO FURIOSO. He is the brother of Marfisa (Marphisa) and the ward of the magician Atlante (Atlantes). After the slaying of his mother, he was nursed by a lioness. From Atlante he receives an enchanted sword of such dazzling splendor that it numbs all who look upon it, but he casts it into a well because he regards it as unchivalrous. At first he fights with the pagan forces of Agramante, the African king, against Charlemagne and the Christian knights. Later, having met and fallen in love with the warrior maiden Bradamante (Bradamant), he becomes converted to Christianity and marries her. Ariosto's poem ends with their marriage feast and his election to the crown of Bulgaria. From their union comes the house of Este, the princely patrons of both poets at the court of Ferrara. See RODOMONTE.

In Torquato Tasso's GERUSALEMME LIBERATA (*Jerusalem Delivered*), Ruggiero is a Norman, son of Roberto Guiscardo. A member of the crusading army led by Goffredo (Godfrey) against the Saracens, he is killed by Tisaphernes in the final canto.

Ruggles of Red Gap. A humorous novel (1915) by Harry Leon WILSON, dealing with a British butler in a western pioneer town.

Ruisdael or **Ruysdael, Jacob van** (c. 1625–1682). Dutch landscape painter and etcher. His forest, shore, and mountain scenes reveal a sympathy and intimacy with nature. Calm and somewhat melancholy, they show his ability to interpret as well as represent nature.

Ruiz, Juan. Also known as the **archpriest or arcipreste of Hita** (c. 1283–?1350). Spanish poet. Little is known about the life of the archpriest, considered the greatest poet of medieval Spain, except what he himself relates in his realistic and humorous autobiography in verse, *El libro de buen amor,* which may have been composed while he was in prison. His purpose, the poet wrote, undoubtedly with tongue in cheek, was to warn readers of the pitfalls of *loco amor,* or foolish love. The contents of the work are varied; included are hymns to the Virgin and animal apologues as well as picaresque accounts of the author's love affairs and a description of a battle between Lord Flesh and Lady Lent in which the latter is vanquished. Among the outstanding characters is the old hag Trotaconventos, ancestress of LA CELESTINA.

Ruiz de Alarcón y Mendoza, Juan. See Juan Ruiz de ALARCÓN Y MENDOZA.

Rukeyser, Muriel (1913–   ). American poet. Her early work, especially *U.S. 1* (1938), dealing with the exploitation of working people along the U.S. highway of that name, is marked by proletarian sympathies. *Theory of Flight* (1935), published a year previously, shows her fondness for incorporating the world of 20th-century science and technology. Her later work is more concerned with the personal and the symbolic. Among her later collections are *A Turning Wind* (1939), *Beast in View* (1944), *The Green Wave* (1948), *Orpheus* (1949), *Chain Lightning* (1955), *Sun Stone* (1961), and *I Go Out* (1961). She has also written the biography *Willard Gibbs: American Genius* (1942) and paid tribute to Wendell Willkie in *One Life* (1957).

Rule Britannia. See Thomas Augustine ARNE.

Rumford, Count. See Benjamin THOMPSON.

Rumpelstiltskin or **Rumpelstilzchen.** A deformed dwarf in German folk tale. A king tells a miller's daughter he will marry her if she can really spin straw into gold. Helpless, she accepts the dwarf's offer to do it in exchange for her first child. Once queen, she grieves so bitterly when the child is born that the dwarf agrees to relent if in three days she can guess his name, which no one knows. On the third day he is so sure he will win the child that he is overheard muttering his name triumphantly to himself. When he hears his name from the queen, he destroys himself in his rage at losing.

Rump Parliament. In English history, a derisive nickname given to the fragment of the LONG PARLIAMENT that remained after PRIDE'S PURGE. Consisting of from 60 to 70 members, most of them INDEPENDENTS, the Rump voted for the execution of Charles I.

Rundstedt, Karl Rudolf Gerd von (1875–1953). German general. He commanded the army of occupation in France (1942–1944), and became commander-in-chief of the Western Front (1944–1945).

Runeberg, Johan Ludvig (1804–1877). Finnish poet. Though he wrote in the Swedish language, Runeberg was a leader of the Finnish nationalist literary movement of the 19th century. In addition to lyric poems and philological works, he wrote *The Elk Hunters* (1832), an epic of Finnish rural life; *King Fjalar* (1844), a Norse epic; and *Tales of Ensign Stål* (1848, 1860), a collection of prose and verse glorifying the Finnish soldiers of the 1808–1809 Russo-Finnish war. The *Tales* were instrumental in accelerating Finland's awareness of herself as a nation separate from Sweden and Russia, and they contain the poem *Vårt Land* (*Our Land*), which has become Finland's national anthem.

runes. Letters in various alphabets used by Teutonic peoples, especially in Scandinavia and the British Isles from the 2nd century to the 12th. The runic alphabets were adaptations of a Greek alphabet, simplified for facility in carving inscriptions on wood, stone, and metal. Each rune is the initial letter of its name (as the *m* letter is called *man*), and the name is also a common word (*man, horse, thorn, sun*); thus the runes were used as characters in ordinary spelling, but also as idea-symbols in composing magical incantations or charms.

Runnymede. An island (Charter Island) in the Thames in Surrey, where King John, on June 19, 1215, was forced to sign the Magna Carta. Cf. Kipling's poem, *The Reeds of Runnymede*. Some say the document was signed in the meadow on the south side of the Thames.

Runyon, [Alfred] Damon (1884–1946). American journalist and short-story writer. He is famous for his stories about such colorful Broadway characters as the Lemon Drop Kid and Harry the Horse. His style, so individual that it is called Runyonese, relies on Broadway slang, outrageous metaphors, and constant use of the present tense. Among his books are *Guys and Dolls* (1932) and *Blue Plate Special* (1934). He also wrote a play, *A Slight Case of Murder* (1935), with Howard Lindsay.

R.U.R. A play by Karel ČAPEK, produced in 1923. It deals with an imagined future state in which robots, enslaved to do work for men, revolt against their masters. The initials in the title stand for "Rossum's Universal Robots," the name of the commercial firm which manufactures the mechanical creatures.

Rural Rides. See William COBBETT.

Ruritania. An imaginary Central-European kingdom. It is the locale of THE PRISONER OF ZENDA and *Rupert of Hentzau* (1898) by Anthony Hope Hawkins.

Rush, Benjamin (1745–1813). American physician, member of the Continental Congress, and signer of the Declaration of Independence. Rush was a great admirer of Thomas Jefferson and like him had an informed and worthwhile opinion on almost every subject. As a medical man he was overly dogmatic in his insistence on bleeding as a form of therapy. However, his theory that the yellow fever epidemic of 1793 was caused partly by poor sanitation was advanced for the times and led him to be ostracized by the medical profession. His *Medical Inquiries and Observations Upon Diseases of the Mind* (1812) contains pioneer discoveries in psychoanalytic method and in the treatment of mental disorders.

Rush or **Rausch, Friar.** See FRIAR RUSH.

Ruskin, John (1819–1900). English writer and critic. The son of a wealthy merchant, Ruskin benefited from extensive travel and private drawing lessons during his youth. In the first volume of MODERN PAINTERS he included a spirited defense of the then much-misunderstood landscape painter John Turner, attracting attention with his clear style and his novel approach to art criticism. The four later volumes of this series, along with *The Seven Lamps of Architecture* (1849) and *The Stones of Venice* (3 vols., 1851–1853), a study of the development of Byzantine and Gothic architecture in Venice and of the city's moral, vital, and artistic decline, established Ruskin as a leading critic and stylist. Several of his lectures on art were published in *Lectures on Art* (1870), *Aratra Pentelici* (1871), *The Eagle's Nest* (1871), *Ariadne Florentina* (1873–1876), *Val d'Arno* (1874) and *Lectures on Landscape* (1898). He developed and expressed his philosophy of art in these and other works, including *St. Mark's Rest: The History of Venice* (1877–1884), *Morning in Florence* (1875–1877) and *The Bible of Amiens* (1880–1885). Believing that the "greatest picture" was the one that conveyed "to the mind of the spectator the greatest number of the greatest ideas" and classifying the greatest ideas in the categories of Power, Imitation, Truth, Beauty and Relation, Ruskin advocated a basically religious aesthetic, in which moral perception of beauty was superior to the merely sensuous and beauty itself revealed the attributes of God. His conviction that faith, morality, education, and good social conditions were prerequisites to the creation of good art led him to take up the cause of social and economic reform in such works as *The Political Economy of the Arts* (1857), UNTO THIS LAST, *Essays on Political Economy* (1862–1863), the widely read *Sesame and Lilies* (1865), and *Fors Clavigera: Letters to the Workmen and Laborers of Great Britain* (1885–1889). Ruskin's views deeply influenced the British socialist movement, just as his art history and criticism brought about the revival of interest in Gothic architecture. A scholar of enormously varied interests, he wrote works on botany, *Proserpina* (1875–1886); ornithology, *Love's Meinie* (1873–1878); and geology, *Deucalion* (1875–1883); and an unfinished autobiography, *Praeterita* (1885–1889). The term PATHETIC FALLACY was coined by Ruskin.

Russell, Bertrand. 3d Earl **Russell** (1872–1970). English philosopher, mathematician, and social reformer. His books on mathematics, philosophy, and logic include *Principia Mathematica*, with A. N. WHITEHEAD as co-author (1910–1913), which became a classic; *An Introduction to Mathematical Philosophy* (1919); *The Analysis of Mind* (1921); and *An Inquiry into Meaning and Truth* (1940). He wrote a number of essays on philosophic and scientific problems in a semipopularizing vein; among these are *The ABC of Relativity* (1925), *Religion and Science* (1935), and *A History of Western Philosophy* (1945). He has written numerous books expressing his unorthodox views on war, politics, sociology, and religion, and on such domestic matters as education, sexual relations, and divorce. Among these are *Mysticism and Logic* (1918), *The Practice and Theory of Bolshevism* (1920), *Marriage and Morals* (1929), *Education and the Social Order* (1932), *Freedom and Organization* (1934), *Let the People Think* (1941), *The Faith of a Rationalist* (1947), *Unpopular Essays* (1950), and *New Hopes for a Changing World* (1951). *Satan in the Suburbs* (1953) is a collection of fantastic short stories. Russell's writing is remarkable for its clarity and ease. In 1944 he was awarded the British Order of Merit, and in 1950 the Nobel Prize for Literature. In more recent works —*Common Sense and Nuclear Warfare* (1958), *Has Man a Future?* (1961), and *Unarmed Victory* (1963) —he concerns himself with the threat of nuclear war.

Intent on putting his beliefs into practice as well as publicizing them, Russell became involved in frequent difficulties with English and American authorities; toward the end of his life, internationally acclaimed as an important 20th-century thinker, he had become more notorious than ever. During World War I in England he was fined and imprisoned for his pacifist views. An experimental nursery school he ran with his wife from 1927 to 1932 was severely criticized. An appointment to teach at the City College of New York was withdrawn on the grounds that his teachings were immoral. When over 90 years old he founded the Committee of 100 in England, an influential militant group which campaigned, through civil disobedience, for nuclear disarmament and international morality. Russell was married four times.

Russell, George William. See A. E.

Russell, Lillian. Stage name of **Helen Louise Leonard** (1861–1922). American soprano. She first appeared in Tony PASTOR's Variety Theatre (1880) and sang for more than 35 years in burlesque and comic opera. Her beauty and figure (of the Gibson Girl type) made her a great popular favorite.

Russell, Mary Annette. See ELIZABETH.

Russell, Thomas. See Theobald Wolfe TONE.

Russell, William Clark (1844–1911). English novelist. After eight years in the British merchant service he became a journalist in London and wrote many stories of nautical adventure including *John Holdsworth, Chief Mate* (1875) and *The Wreck of the Grosvenor* (1877). He also wrote lives of Dampier (1889), Nelson (1890), and Collingwood (1891).

Russell, Sir William Howard (1820–1907). English journalist, one of the first and best known war correspondents, reporter for the London *Times* in the Crimean, American Civil, and Franco-German Wars. In the first he coined the phrase "the thin red line," applied to British Infantry at Balaclava. His *The War from the Landing at Gallipoli* (1855–1856), about the Crimean War, and *My Diary North and South* (1862), about the Civil War, are of particular interest.

Russian Primary Chronicle, The (Nachalnaya Letopis). Also known as **The Tale of Bygone Years (Povest' vremennykh let).** Historical annals of medieval Russia covering events from 852 to the early 12th century. The chronicle contains descriptions of historical occurrences, legends, and tales from folk tradition. Kiev was the center of the Russian nation when these annals were compiled, and their authorship was for years attributed to Nestor, a monk in a Kiev monastery. Nestor's authorship is now doubted by most scholars. Chronicles also survive from other Russian cities, such as Tver, Pskov, and Novgorod.

Russian Revolution. The events that began with the abdication of Czar NICHOLAS II in the spring of 1917 and ended with the seizure of power by the Bolsheviks in Nov., 1917. An earlier, unsuccessful attempt at revolution had taken place in 1905, when a series of strikes had obliged the czarist regime to promise full civil rights to the people and the establishment of Russia's first legislative body, the DUMA. After the storm had blown over, however, the government managed to avoid fulfilling most of its promises.

Early in 1917 military defeats by the Germans and internal chaos led to a series of strikes and mutinies among workers and soldiers, particularly in the capital of St. Petersburg. After the Czar abdicated in March, 1917, power was divided between a provisional government under Prince Lvov, set up by a committee of the Duma and the Soviet (council) of workers' deputies in St. Petersburg. Soviets also existed in Moscow and other cities. Lvov's government was replaced in July by a coalition government under Kerenski which was repeatedly attacked by the Bolsheviks. LENIN had returned to Russia from exile in April and immediately began agitation for the overthrow of the provisional government and the seizure of power by the Bolsheviks. In September the Bolsheviks won majorities in both the St. Petersburg and Moscow Soviets. Some Bolshevik leaders wanted to content themselves with this electoral gain, but Lenin's urging for a *coup d'état* prevailed. Shortly before the convening of a constituent assembly in November, the Bolsheviks seized power. The new regime, under Lenin, signed a peace treaty with Germany in March, 1918, and turned to defend itself against its enemies, known as the Whites, who had massed armed forces in the Volga region, the south, and in western Siberia. The civil war raged until late 1920, when the last remnants of the White army under General Wrangel were forced from the Crimea.

The outstanding literary work based directly on the revolution was Aleksandr Blok's long poem *The Twelve*. Many works have been devoted to the civil war, the most notable being those of Mikhail Sholokhov, Isaak Babel, Aleksandr Fadeyev, Boris Pilnyak, and Vsevolod Ivanov.

Ruth. The Moabite heroine of the Old Testament book that bears her name. After the death of her husband, she loyally refused to desert Naomi, his Hebrew mother: "Entreat me not to leave thee, or to return from following after thee; whither thou goest, I will go; and where thou lodgest, I will lodge; thy people shall be my people, and thy God my God" (Ruth 1:16). After accompanying her to Bethlehem, Ruth became a gleaner in the fields of the wealthy Boaz, whom she married.

Rutherford, Mark. See William Hale WHITE.

Rutledge, Ann. See Abraham LINCOLN.

Ruysbroeck, Jan van (1293–1381). A Flemish mystic, called the Ecstatic Doctor. He wrote mystical works in Flemish and Latin.

Ryder, Albert Pinkham (1847–1917). American painter. He lived as a recluse in New York City, working for years on end on glowing compositions in which he developed unerring patterns and rhythms. His subjects were drawn from the depths of his imagination and from the tales of William Shakespeare, Richard Wagner, and the Bible. His moonlit seas and night scenes range from calm to violence, but all reveal a sense of mystery and power. Ryder made his own pigments, often with bizarre ingredients, that have tended to darken and crack with time.

Rye House Plot (1683). In English history, an alleged conspiracy to assassinate Charles II and the duke of York (later James II) at Rye House in Hertfordshire. Lord William Russell and Algernon Sidney, partisans of the duke of Monmouth, were implicated and executed. It is now thought that both were entirely innocent of complicity.

Rymenhild. See King HORN.

Rymer, Thomas (1641–1713). English antiquary and critic. He attacked Beaumont and Fletcher in *The Tragedies of the Last Age* (1678), and criticized Shakespeare in *A Short View of Tragedy* (1692) for failing to observe the classical unities in *Othello* (1604), which he labelled a "bloody farce." He also wrote a tragedy, *Edgar, or the English Monarch* (1678), to show how it should be done.

Ryti, Rysto Heikki (1889–1956). President of Finland (1940–1946). Ryti was convicted on war-guilt charges and sentenced to 10 years of hard labor, but in 1949 he was pardoned on the grounds of poor health.

S

S.A. The abbreviated name of the *Sturmabteilung* (Storm Troops), the strong-arm bands organized by the Nazi Party in 1920. The S.A., which grew with the party, participated in parades and demonstrations and served as an instrument of terror. They were also called the Brownshirts. See S.S.

Saarinen, Eero (1910–1961). Finnish-born American architect. Though influenced by Mies van der Rohe, his creations—e.g., the Technical Center for General Motors, Warren, Mich. (1951–1956), Kresge Auditorium at the Massachusetts Institute of Technology, and the TWA Terminal at New York's Kennedy International Airport (1962)—are very much his own. His works are characteristically light and graceful and each is different from the others.

Saavedra y Ramírez de Baguedano, Angel. See duque de RIVAS.

Saba, Queen of. See SHEBA, QUEEN OF.

Saba, Umberto (1883–1957). Italian poet. His verse describes the homely personal episodes of his life as an Italian of Jewish ancestry from the narrow provincial society of Trieste. His poems have been collected in *Il Canzoniere* (5th ed., 1961).

Sabatini, Rafael (1875–1950). Italian-born English novelist. He wrote best-selling historical and adventure romances, among them *Scaramouche* (1921), about a strolling player during the French Revolution, and *Captain Blood* (1922), about a gentleman-pirate.

Sabbatical year. Originally, 1 year in 7 when the ancient Jews allowed all their land to lie fallow for 12 months. The practice was based on a law found in the books of Exodus, Leviticus, and Deuteronomy. The phrase is now used for a missionary's furlough or a year of vacation from a profession.

Sabine. In Pierre Corneille's tragedy HORACE, a nonhistorical character invented by the author. The sister of the slain Curiace, she entreats the emperor to allow her to be executed in place of Horace.

Sabines. An ancient Italian people, subjugated by the Romans about 290 B.C. The rape of the Sabine women, an important incident in the legendary history of Rome, was instigated by ROMULUS who needed wives for his men and solved the problem by telling them to help themselves to Sabine virgins after he had lured the male population away.

Sablé, Marquise **Magdeleine de** (c. 1599–1678). French patroness of letters. Her literary salon was second in importance only to the Hôtel de Rambouillet and influenced La Rochefoucauld in the writing of his maxims. The marquise's *Maximes et pensées diverses* (*Maxims and Various Thoughts*), largely her own work, was published in 1678.

Sabra. The legendary daughter of Ptolemy, king of Egypt. She was rescued by St. GEORGE from a dragon and ultimately married her deliverer. She was pure in mind, saintly in character, a perfect citizen, daughter, and wife. Her three sons, born at one birth, were named Guy, Alexander, and David. She died from the pricks of a thorny brushwood.

Sabrina. Latin name of the river Severn, named from the daughter of Estrildis and LOCRINE in Geoffrey of Monmouth's *History of the Kings of Britain*. Sabrina and her mother are drowned in the river Severn by Gwendolen. In John Milton's *Comus*, Sabrina is a nymph of the Severn.

Sacajawea (1787?–?1812). American Indian woman, probably of the Snake or Shoshone tribe. She served as guide and interpreter for the Lewis and Clark Expedition (1805), during which she bore a son to a Canadian trapper whom she had married by Indian rites.

Sacchetti, Franco (c. 1330–1400). Italian poet and prose writer. Born in Dalmatia of Florentine parents, he spent most of his life in Florence as a public official. His writings include sonnets, *canzoni, sestine* and *ballate,* as well as the then less familiar madrigals, *cacce,* and *frottole.* Many of these varied lyrics were intended for musical setting, since he composed himself and was associated with musicians writing in the *ars nova* style. His most famous poem is the pastoral *ballata* beginning "O vaghe montanine pasturelle" ("O lovely mountain shepherdesses"). In prose, his masterpiece is the *Libro delle trecentonovelle* (*Book of Three Hundred Tales*), a collection of novelle, of which some 200 pieces are extant. Unlike the *Decameron,* there is no structure or framing story to knit the tales together.

sacco benedetto (*Ital.*), **saco bendito** or **san benito** (Span., "the blessed sack or cloak"). The yellow linen robe with two crosses on it, and painted over with flames and devils, in which persons condemned by the Spanish Inquisition were arrayed when they went to the stake. (See AUTO-DA-FÉ.) In the case of those who expressed repentance for their errors, the flames were directed downward. Penitents who had been taken before the Inquisition had to wear this badge for a stated period. Those worn by Jews, sorcerers, and renegades bore a St. Andrew's cross in red on back and front.

Sacco-Vanzetti case (May–July, 1921). A celebrated murder trial in which two Italian anarchists, Nicola Sacco and Bartolomeo Vanzetti, were convicted of and condemned to death for the murder of a paymaster and a guard and the theft of over $15,000 at a shoe factory in South Braintree, Mass., on April 15, 1920. Both men denied any knowledge of the crime, and it was widely believed that they had been convicted largely because of their radical political views. The case aroused intense public interest, both in the U.S. and abroad, and defense committees succeeded in obtaining many stays of execution. In July, 1927, Governor Fuller of Massachusetts appointed a committee headed by President Lowell of Harvard to review the case; it upheld the original verdict, and Sacco and Vanzetti were executed the following month.

The case inspired numerous literary works, including Edna St. Vincent Millay's poem *Justice Denied in Massachusetts* (1927), Upton Sinclair's novel *Boston* (1928), and two plays by Maxwell Anderson, *Gods of the Lightning* (1928) and *Winterset* (1935). During their imprisonment the two accused men wrote hundreds of letters which possess considerable literary power. Vanzetti's final appeal has become a classic. A collection of the *Letters of Sacco and Vanzetti* appeared in 1928.

Sacher-Masoch, Leopold von (1836–1895). Austrian novelist whose name is the source of the word *masochism*. This abnormality is portrayed in many of his works, such as *Das Vermächtnis Kains (The Legacy of Cain,* 1870–1877) and *Falscher Hemelion (False Ermine,* 1873).

Sachs, Hans (1494–1576). German poet and dramatist, by trade a shoemaker, most skillful and famous of the MEISTERSINGERS. In addition to his more than 4,000 mastersongs, he wrote many poems on moral and religious subjects, the most famous being *Die Wittenbergisch Nachtigall (The Nightingale of Wittenberg,* 1523), an allegory in praise of Martin Luther, and an *Epitaphium* (1546) on Luther's death. His enormous dramatic production includes tragedies on classical, biblical, and medieval subjects, dialogues in defense of Protestantism, and many Shrovetide-plays, a genre which he carried to its highest perfection. He appears as a leading character in Richard Wagner's opera DIE MEISTERSINGER VON NÜRNBERG.

Sackville, Charles. 6th earl of **Dorset,** 1st earl of **Middlesex** (1638–1706). English poet and courtier. He was the friend and patron of poets, including Matthew Prior, Wycherly, Dryden, and others. His best-known poem, *To all you Ladies, now at Land* (1665), was written at sea during the Dutch War, the night before an engagement.

Sackville, Thomas. 1st earl of **Dorset** and Baron **Buckhurst**(1536–1608). English poet and statesman. Sackville is known for his authorship (with Thomas Norton) of *The Tragedy of* GORBODUC (1561), an important work in the history of English drama; and especially for his *Induction* to the 1563 edition of THE MIRROR FOR MAGISTRATES. The latter piece is the most famous part of the *Mirror,* and one of the most outstanding poems written in England between the death of Chaucer and the publication of Spenser's *Shepheardes Calender* (1579). The *Induction* is patterned after the classical Descent into Hades; in it the poet meets the personification of Sorrow, who leads him to Hell and shows him the ghosts of men ruined by their ambition. The *Induction* then introduces Sackville's *Complaint* of Henry, duke of Buckingham.

In later life, Sackville devoted himself to a public career, serving variously as a Member of Parliament,

ambassador, member of the Privy Council, Lord Treasurer, and Chancellor of Oxford University.

Sackville-West, Edward Charles (1901–1965). English novelist. A cousin of Victoria Sackville-West, he wrote light, witty novels, such as *Piano Quintet* (1925), and *The Sun in Capricorn* (1934). *Inclinations,* a book of critical essays, was published in 1949.

Sackville-West, V[ictoria] (1892–1962). English novelist, poet, and critic; associated with the BLOOMSBURY GROUP. Her best-remembered novels are *The Edwardians* (1930), a sensitive portrait of an era, and *All Passion Spent* (1931), an account of an unusual marriage relationship. *The Land* (1926) is a long poem about the year's cycle of an English farmer. She is particularly noted for her feeling for the English countryside and English history. A descendant of Thomas SACKVILLE, she was a member of an ancient family whose ancestral home was Knole Castle, originally a gift from Queen Elizabeth I to Thomas Sackville. ORLANDO, by Virginia Woolf, a close friend, was said to be a portrait of V. Sackville-West, her family's history, and Knole Castle, while she herself wrote *Knole and the Sackvilles* (1922), a family history. Her other books include *The Eagle and the Dove* (1943), a biographical study of St. Teresa of Avila and St. Thérèse of Lisieux; *The Garden* (1946), a book of poems; and *The Easter Party* (1953). She married Harold NICOLSON.

saco bendito. See SACCO BENEDETTO.

sacrament. Originally "a military oath" (Lat. *sacramentum*) taken by the Roman soldiers not to desert their standard, turn their back on the enemy, or abandon their general. The early Christians used the word to signify "a sacred mystery," hence its application to baptism, the Eucharist, and so on.

The sacraments interpreted by the Roman Catholic Church as having been commanded by Christ in the Gospels are Baptism and the Eucharist (Lord's Supper); the other five Sacraments of Christian tradition are Confirmation, Penance (Confession), Holy Orders, Matrimony, and Extreme Unction.

sacra rappresentazione (It., sacred representation). The Italian equivalent of the English and French mystery play, especially popular during the early Renaissance. Developed from the dramatic religious song called the LAUDA, these sacred dramas were elaborately performed by the young men and boys of religious organizations, with appropriate scenery and props. The subject was exclusively biblical and the favorite form the OTTAVA RIMA. Most of the authors are anonymous, but one, Belcari, is remembered as an outstanding composer of these plays. The form was used by Lorenzo de' Medici, in whose city of Florence they were especially cultivated by the learned as well as the folk. Poliziano's *Orfeo,* one of the earliest examples of the Renaissance revival of classical subjects in drama, actually owed its structure to the sacred play, rather than to Greek or Roman practice. Soon after, however, the strict classicism of the later Renaissance ended the influence and popularity of the sacred representation.

Sacred Fount, The (1901). A novelette by Henry JAMES. The title refers to the theory of the narrator that in an unequal marriage or liaison the older or weaker partner is refreshed and invigorated at the "sacred fount" of the younger or stronger personality, which in turn becomes depleted. At an English house party, the narrator attempts, by the use of his theory, to discover the relationships among his fellow guests.

Sacred Nine, the. The MUSES.

sacred thread. In Hindu custom, the *upavita*, worn by upper-caste members. It is a cotton thread of three strands, which a *guru* gives to a boy during the initiation ceremony, usually between 8 and 12 years.

Sacrifice, The (1633). A long poem by George HERBERT. It is a dramatic first-person account of the Crucifixion in which Jesus repeatedly stresses the paradoxes of His situation: His goodness to man, man's ingratitude; His actual power, His seeming weakness, etc.

Sacripante (**Sacripant**). In Matteo Maria Boiardo's ORLANDO INNAMORATO and Lodovico Ariosto's ORLANDO FURIOSO, the emperor of Circassia and one of the leading Saracen knights in the war between Charlemagne and the pagans. He is in love with Angelica, who allows him to be her champion for a time, but he does not win her.

Sade, Comte **Donatien Alphonse François de.** Known as **marquis de Sade** (1740–1814). French author. His works, because of their controversial subject matter, have been denied official publication by the French courts as recently as 1957. After completing his Jesuit education, Sade acquired various military ranks and took part in the Seven Years' War. Soon after his marriage at 23, much of the rest of his life was punctuated by violent scandals over his sexual conduct, netting him several prison sentences totaling some 30 years. After seven years of liberty from 1794 to 1801, he was again arrested for writing licentious books; he remained in prison to the end of his life. His works, many of which were written in prison, include *Justine ou les Malheurs de la vertu* (1791), *La Philosophie dans le boudoir* (1795), *Aline et Valcour* (1795), *Juliette* (1797), and *Les 120 Journées de Sodome* (1931–35)—in all, a dozen 2- to 10-volume novels, about 60 short stories, 20 plays, and many smaller works. Approximately one fourth of his manuscripts were burned by the police during the Consulate and the Empire. For years his works were considered to be the monstrous ravings of a delirious criminal mind, but recent criticism and psychiatric analysis of them have shown him to be a precursor of Nietzsche's superman, and a psychologist and analyst far ahead of his time, whose style, eloquence, language, and profundity of thought warrant his being given a permanent high place in French literature. See SADISM.

Sa'dī. Pen name of **Musharrif-uddīn** (born **Muslih-uddīn;** c. 1184–1291). Persian poet. As a young man he studied in Baghdad, returning to Persia about the time the ruler, Sa'd, was deposed by the Mongol invaders. It was in his honor that the poet took his pen name, Sa'dī. Depressed by conditions in Persia, Sa'dī became a wanderer, traveling in other countries for 30 years. While in exile his life varied from that of a renowned sheikh to that of a prisoner condemned to forced labor. In 1256 he returned to his birth place in Shiraz, Persia, where he lived, according to tradition, to the advanced age of 107.

Sa'dī is perhaps the most popular Persian poet of all time. His *Būstān* (*Fruit Garden*), GULISTAN (*Rose Garden*), and *Dīwān*, or collection of lyrics, are classics of Persian poetry. Sa'dī's polished style and the wit and poignancy of his sentiments have delighted readers everywhere.

sadism. A type of sexual perversion in which gratification is found by torturing the object of love. It is so called from comte (known as marquis) de SADE, the French writer whose works first brought such practices to public attention. The term has come to be popularly applied to any delight in causing suffering to others, sex not necessarily being involved. Sadism is usually associated with MASOCHISM.

Sadleir, Michael (1888–1957). English biographer and novelist. *Fanny by Gaslight* (1947) is his best-known novel. He wrote biographies of *Trollope* (1929) and others.

Sadoleto, Jacopo (1477–1552). Italian prelate and scholar. Bishop of Carpentras and later made a cardinal, he was noted for his Latin composition, including a treatise on education. In the Renaissance quarrel over languages, he championed the invincibility of Latin as the supreme tongue.

Safa. In Muslim myth, the hill in Arabia on which Adam and Eve came together after the 200 years during which they wandered, alone and homeless, over the earth.

Sagan, Françoise. Pen name of **Françoise Quoirez** (1935–   ). French novelist and dramatist who at 18 wrote BONJOUR TRISTESSE. Her later works also present, in a subdued, unemotional style, the innocent in search of experience, and their half-despairing, half-cynical disillusionment. Her novels are *A Certain Smile* (*Un Certain Sourire;* 1956), *Those Without Shadows* (*Dans un mois, dans un an;* 1957), *Aimez-vous Brahms?* (1959), and *The Wonderful Clouds* (*Les Merveilleux nuages;* 1962). *Château en Suède* (1960), and *Les violons, parfois* (1961) are both plays.

Sagittary. The name given in the medieval romances to the CENTAUR, a mystical monster, half horse and half man. Its eyes sparkled like fire and struck dead like lightning, and it was fabled to have been introduced into the Trojan armies. The Sagittary referred to in *Othello* was probably an inn, but may have been the Venetian Arsenal.

Saha, P. K. (1932–   ). Indian poet and novelist writing in English. Formerly editor of *Orient Review,* he has published a novel, *After the Sunlit Hour* (1956).

Sahitya Darpana. A Sanskrit treatise, *The Mirror of Literature*. Written by Visvanath Kaviraj, who lived in the court of King Narasingha, East India, in the 15th century, it explains the nature and forms of literary expression.

Saikaku. See IHARA SAIKAKU.

Saint. For all saints, see under their individual names.

Saint, the. In novels by Leslie CHARTERIS, the name by which the gentleman-burglar Simon Templar is known. He appears in *Enter the Saint* (1930), *The Saint Goes West* (1942), and several other works.

Saint-Amant, Marc Antoine de Gérard (1594–1661). French poet. An original member of the ACADÉMIE FRANÇAISE but subsequently condemned by Boileau, Saint-Amant was an uninhibited freethinker and wrote verse that was by turns outlandish, fanciful, and realistic. In addition to sonnets and lyrics, he produced burlesques and tavern songs, as well as an epic, *Moïse* (*Moses,* 1653).

St. Cloud. A suburb of Paris. It is notable for its palace, where many important events in French history took place. Built by Louis XIV (1658) on the site of an older castle, it was bought by Louis XVI for Marie Antoinette, and was later a favorite residence of Napoleon I and Napoleon III. Badly damaged during the Franco-Prussian War, it was afterward demolished.

Sainte-Beuve, Charles Augustin (1804–1869). French literary critic and man of letters. Sainte-Beuve's career as a critic can be divided into three periods. When he first began to practice journalism, writing for the *Globe* in Paris, he spoke out warmly and enthusiastically in favor of the romantic school. His passionate love affair with the wife of Victor Hugo, celebrated in the love lyrics of *Le Livre d'Amour* (1843), engendered a certain coldness between the poet and the young critic. His interest in ROMANTICISM considerably diminished, Sainte-Beuve was writing for the *Revue de Paris* and the *Revue des Deux Mondes* by 1831. During this second period, he developed his biographical and psychological approach, studying a literary work through the life and personality of its author. The third period saw Sainte-Beuve writing for the *Constitutionnel* and using a naturalistic method of criticism, placing emphasis upon historical background and social environment. Among his published works are *Portraits Contemporains* (1869–1871), *Portraits Littéraires* (1862–1864), *Chateaubriand et son Groupe Littéraire* (1861), and his collected weekly critical articles, *Causeries du Lundi* (1851–1862) and *Nouveaux Lundis* (1863–70). His criticism favors moderation, artistic unity, truth in the portrayal of life, and good taste. A strange individual, Sainte-Beuve was erratic in both his personal friendships and intellectual affiliations. He became caught up, at various times, in the swirling intellectual currents of his day: Saint-Simonism, liberal Roman Catholicism, Swiss Calvinism, scientific skepticism, and positivism.

Saint-Evremond, seigneur de. Charles de Marguetel de Saint-Denis (1613–1703). French wit and man of letters. Saint-Evremond attacked Mazarin's treaty with Spain in his *Lettre sur le Traité des Pyrénées* (*Letter on the Pyrenees Treaty,* 1656) and was forced in 1661 to flee to England. Well received by Charles II, he became a permanent member of the English court. In his critical essays, his poems, and his play *Comédie des Académistes* (*The Academists' Play,* 1643) Saint-Evremond displays a keen wit coupled with natural elegance.

Saint-Exupéry, Antoine de (1900–1944). French novelist, essayist, and aviator. In 1926 he began flying for a commercial airline across West Africa, later flew in South America, and was one of the pioneers in exploring flight over the desert, the Andes, and at night. Barely fictionalized, his experiences in the air became the material for the novels *Southern Mail* (*Courrier-Sud;* 1928), and NIGHT FLIGHT. Regretfully the pilots must abandon the terrestrial order of things, partially represented by women and their love, in order to discover the hidden treasures of experience represented by the stars. They give meaning to their lives by joining others who seriously accept the discipline of duty and the risk of death in a quest for a value greater than themselves.

Already the prose poet of the new world of the skies, Saint-Exupéry then rediscovered men's earth in WIND, SAND, AND STARS. *Flight to Arras* (*Pilote de guerre;* 1942), autobiographical account of a dangerous wartime mission, becomes an introspective analysis of the pilot's mind and the humanistic philosophy he has shaped for himself. Human relationships are the basis of his morality and the source of his joy in life; ties of love, however, should not mean looking at one another, but rather "looking together in the same direction."

Letter to a Hostage (1942) and the posthumous publication of his unfinished notebook of reflections as *The Wisdom of the Sands* (*Citadelle;* 1948) give further exposition of his moral philosophy. *The Little Prince* (*Le Petit Prince;* 1943) is a fairy tale whose mode of whimsy and fantasy cloaks a wise understanding of the significant values in human life.

Saint-Gaudens, Augustus (1848–1907). American sculptor. He is noted for his public monuments, symbolic figures, and portrait plaques in low relief. His *Reminiscences* were published in 1913.

Saint-Germain, Treaty of (1919). The peace treaty between Austria and the Allies after World War I. It confirmed the breakup of the Hapsburg monarchy.

St. Helena. An island in the South Atlantic, under English dominion, to which Napoleon Bonaparte was exiled following the battle of Waterloo. He died there in 1821.

Saint Joan (1923). A play by George Bernard SHAW. Produced three years after the canonization of St. JOAN OF ARC, Shaw's play shows her as an early nationalist and the prototype of the Protestant thinker who put her conscience before the judgment of the Church. She died because her new ideas were dangerous to both the Church and feudal society. In an epilogue Joan is surprised to learn of her sainthood; when she offers to return to earth she is again rejected, the usual fate of saints and geniuses according to Shaw.

St. John, Henry. Viscount **Bolingbroke** (1678–1751). English statesman, orator, and man of letters, who, during the reign of Queen Anne, was the leader of the Tory party in association with Robert Harley. He later propagandized his opposition to the government of Sir Robert Walpole in *The Craftsman* (1726), a periodical. His major works include the DISSERTATION UPON PARTIES (1835); the IDEA OF A PATRIOT KING (1749), an essay; and the LETTERS ON THE STUDY OF HISTORY, published posthumously in 1752. As a patron, Bolingbroke formed literary friendships with Swift, John Gay, John Arbuthnot, and Pope. An adherent of DEISM, he furnished Pope with many of the philosophical ideas used in the groundwork of the ESSAY ON MAN.

Saint John Lateran. A basilica, the cathedral church of the Pope as bishop of Rome. Adjoining is the Lateran Palace, scene of a number of Church councils known as Lateran councils. The name goes back to the Roman family Lateranus who owned a palace on the same site until the last owner was put to death by the Emperor Nero.

St. John Perse. See PERSE, ST. JOHN.

Saint-Just, Louis Antoine Léon de (1767–1794). French revolutionary leader and intimate of ROBESPIERRE. He was known as "the archangel of the Revolution" because of his incorruptibility and good looks. He was active in overthrowing the GIRONDISTS and instrumental in bringing on the REIGN OF TERROR. He was arrested and guillotined with Robespierre in 1794.

Saint-Laurent, Cecil. See Jacques LAURENT.

Saint-Loup, Marquis Robert de. A close friend of the narrator in Marcel Proust's REMEMBRANCE OF THINGS PAST. He is one of the GUERMANTES, and his relatives deplore his passion for the prostitute RACHEL. Eventually he marries GILBERTE, although he has become a homosexual, and is killed in World War I.

Saint Maël. The old Breton monk who preaches to the penguins in Anatole France's novel PENGUIN ISLAND.

St. Nicholas. A monthly magazine for children, edited (1873–1905) by Mary Mapes Dodge. Among its contributors were Louisa M. Alcott, Frank R. Stockton, Edward Eggleston, Mark Twain, Kipling, Palmer Cox, Howard Pyle, and others.

St. Paul's Cathedral. An Anglican cathedral in London. The original Gothic building was destroyed in the Great Fire of 1666. Christopher WREN designed the present St. Paul's, completed 1701. Its huge, smoke-blackened dome is a London landmark. Inside are tombs of Wellington, Nelson, and other notables including that of the architect.

St. Peter's Basilica. The largest church in Christendom. It can accommodate fifty thousand people, and in it most of the important papal functions are held. Donato Bramante laid out the plan in the form of a Greek cross. This was modified but Michelangelo used Bramante's ideas in bringing the plan to completion. The famous dome is Michelangelo's work. Bernini designed the colonnades of the *piazza* and the ornate baldacchino over the high altar.

Saint-Preux. The hero of Rousseau's novel LA NOUVELLE HÉLOÏSE. He is Julie's tutor and lover, and is drawn chiefly from Rousseau himself, who bore the same relation to comtesse d'Houdetot, Julie's prototype.

Saint-Saëns, [Charles] Camille (1835–1921). French composer of operas, symphonies, chamber music, and choral works. His works include the opera *Samson et Dalila* (1877), and the humorous suite *Le Carnaval des Animaux* (composed in 1886 as a musical joke; he did not permit its performance in public while he lived), and five well-known piano concertos.

Saint-Simon, comte de. Claude Henri de Rouvroy (1760–1825). French philosopher and social reformer. His social doctrines were developed by his disciples into a system called Saint-Simonianism. Within this system, all property is owned by the state, while the worker shares in it according to the amount and quality of his work. The basic principle of the state is that of association for the good of all. Surprisingly modern in their ideas, the Saint-Simonians not only advocated social equality, increased attention to education, and the abolition of hereditary rights, but also demanded disarmament.

Saint-Simon, duc de. Louis de Rouvroy (1675–1755). French courtier and writer. An aristocrat embittered by the frustration of his own political ambitions, Saint-Simon was sharply critical of bourgeois royal officialdom. His *Mémoires,* which present a vivid and candid picture of the life and the personalities of the fashionable court of Louis XIV, are colored by the tart disposition of their author, who admits that he cannot be impartial. Claimed by his creditors at his death and sequestered by the state the manuscript was not published until 1829, and an accurate edition did not appear until 1879. (See marquis de DANGEAU.)

Saison en Enfer, Une (A Season in Hell, 1873). A prose-poem by Arthur RIMBAUD. Called a psychological autobiography, the work, consisting of nine fragments, describes the poet's tortured spiritual experiences.

sake. Japanese rice wine.

Sakhrat. In Muslim legend, a sacred stone, one grain of which endows the possessor with miraculous powers. It is emerald in color and makes the sky blue by its reflection. See KAF, MOUNT.

Saki. Pen name of **Hector Hugh Munro** (1870–1916). Scottish writer of humorous, ironic, and macabre short stories. The young men Reginald and Clovis are heroes of a series of short stories in which they take gay revenge on the stupid and conventional adult world. Other stories are somber and macabre, such as *Sredni Vashtar, The Music on the Hill,* and *Esme. The Unbearable Bassington* (1912) is Saki's one novel. *Reginald* (1904), *The Chronicles of Clovis* (1912), *Beasts and Super Beasts* (1914), and *The Square Egg* (1924) are collections of stories. Saki was killed in action in World War I.

Saktism. A Hindu religious cult. Originating about the fifth century, it is based on the worship of a god's dynamic force personified in his female consort. The cult's worship of the fertile, productive energy of Nature (*sakti*) often degenerated into mere orgies. Kali, the consort of Shiva, was the chief object of veneration. See TANTRAS.

Sala, George Augustus Henry (1828–1895). English journalist. A prolific contributor to the Victorian popular press, he was a by-word, in his own day, for overblown and careless writing. He edited several magazines in the 1860's and produced sketches of London life, travel pieces, and war correspondence for Dickens' *Household Words, The Illustrated London News,* and the *Daily Telegraph. Things I Have Seen and People I Have Known* (1844) and *Life and Adventure* (1895) are memoirs.

Salacrou, Armand (1899–   ). French dramatist. Salacrou's works reveal a humanistic concern with man's sense of the ridiculous chaos of his life, and express sympathy for his anguished need to believe in God, in the face of death's inevitability. His plays include *Patchouli* (1930), *Atlas Hôtel* (1931), *L'Inconnue d'Arras* (1936), *La Terre est Ronde* (1938), *Les Nuits de la colère* (1946), *Dieu le savait* (1951), *Une femme trop honnête* (1956), and *Boulevard Durand* (1960).

Salamanca, The Bachelor of. See BACHELIER DE SALAMANQUE, LE.

Salamis. An island off the coast of Greece, not far from Athens. It is famous for the naval victory won by the Greeks over the Persians (480 B.C.) in the bay between it and Attica. See PERSIAN WARS; THEMISTOCLES.

Salammbô (1862). An historical novel by Gustave FLAUBERT. Set in ancient Carthage, the action of this book, a product of vivid and imaginative writing, is colorfully romantic. Before writing it, Flaubert made a voyage to Tunisia, thus carrying out his artistic theories of precise and accurate documentation literally.

Salanio and **Salerio**. In Shakespeare's MERCHANT OF VENICE, two merchants who are loyal friends of Antonio and who aid Lorenzo in his elopement.

Salarino. In Shakespeare's MERCHANT OF VENICE, a high-spirited merchant and a loyal friend to Antonio.

Salathiel. One of the names of the WANDERING JEW. The original Salathiel ben Sadi was a mysterious Jew of 16th-century Venice to whom the old legend became attached.

Salavin, Louis. Hero of a novel series (5 vols., 1920–1932) by Georges DUHAMEL about a man too sensitive and too afraid of life to be happy.

Salem witch-hunt (1692). A hysterical persecution of witches and wizards in Salem, Mass. It began when several young girls accused some old women of bewitching them. Hundreds of persons were accused; many were brought to trial at a special court set up by Governor William Phips; nineteen were hanged; and one, Giles Corey, pressed to death. The hysteria began to subside when several prominent persons, including Phips's wife, came under suspicion. The episode has frequently been described in literature: e.g., John Neal's *Rachel Dyer* (1828), a novel; Longfellow's *Giles Corey of the Salem Farms*, a dramatic poem in *The New England Tragedies* (1868); and Arthur Miller's *The Crucible* (1953), a play. See also Cotton MATHER; Increase MATHER; Samuel SEWALL.

Salerio. See SALANIO.

Salii. In ancient Rome, a college of 12 priests of Mars traditionally instituted by Numa Pompilius. The tale is that a shield fell from heaven, and the nymph Egeria predicted that wherever it was preserved the people would be the dominant people of the earth. To prevent its being surreptitiously taken away, Numa had 11 others made exactly like it, and appointed 12 priests as guardians. Every year these young patricians promenaded the city, singing and dancing, and they finished the day with a sumptuous banquet, with the result that *saliaris coena* became proverbial for a most sumptuous feast. The name *Salii* is derived from the word *salire*, "to leap or dance."

Salinas [Serrano], Pedro (1892–1951). Spanish scholar, critic, and poet. A well-known academician, he taught both at home and abroad, notably in the U.S. at Wellesley College and Johns Hopkins University. His critical studies, which include *Jorge Manrique o tradición y originalidad* (1947) and *La poesía de Rubén Darío* (1948), have been well received. His own poetry, however, is the source of his reputation; his works include the volumes *Fábula y signo* (1931), *Razón de amar* (1936), and *Todo más claro y otros poemas* (1949). Each of these is an individual investigation of the expression of love.

Salinger, J[erome] D[avid] (1919–). American novelist and short-story writer. Salinger won wide acclaim with his first novel THE CATCHER IN THE RYE, which captivated a whole generation of young people. His collection of stories, *Nine Stories* (1953), a majority of which originally appeared in *The New Yorker*, deals mainly with sensitive and troubled adolescents and children who are strongly contrasted with the empty world of their parents. In this collection, Salinger introduces the Glass family, notably in *A Perfect Day for Bananafish*, in which Seymour Glass, the oldest son, commits suicide. Members of the Glass family are also the subject of *Franny and Zooey* (1961) and *Raise High the Roofbeam, Carpenters and Seymour: An Introduction* (1963), long stories originally published in *The New Yorker*.

Salinger's style is clean and concise, and he is particularly noted for his faithful reproduction of colloquial speech. Perhaps no other writer of so few works has been the subject of so many scholarly analyses.

Sallust. Full Latin name, **Gaius Sallustius Crispus** (86–34 B.C.). Roman historian. His *Bellum Catilinae*, on the conspiracy of Catiline, and his *Bellum Jugurthinum*, on the war with Jugurtha, are extant. Sallust was the first artistic writer of Roman history. Like his Greek model Thucydides, he strove to give a vivid dramatic structure to a historical situation, and included brilliant speeches which, though they are fictitious, reveal the character of his historic personages with amazing force and subtlety. His style differs sharply from the rhetorical orchestration of Cicero; it is more like the style of the elder Cato—straightforward, condensed, and paradoxical.

Sally in our Alley (1729). A famous popular ballad in seventeen stanzas by Henry CAREY, composed before 1719 and first published in *Poems on Several Occasions* (1729):

> Of all the girls that are so smart
> There's none like pretty Sally;
> She is the darling of my heart,
> And she lives in our alley.

Salmagundi; or, The Whim-Whams and Opinions of Launcelot Langstaff, Esq. and Others (1807–1808). A humorous periodical published by Washington IRVING, his brother William, and James Kirk PAULDING. It was collected in book form in 1808 and is an American link between *The Spectator* and *Pickwick Papers*. Under fantastic pseudonyms, the writers discussed politics, theater, fashions, and manners in order to "instruct the young, reform the old, correct the town, and castigate the age." The papers were an immediate success; their bias was Federalist and conservative. Their wit makes them readable today. Paulding went on to do a second series, but it lacks the spontaneity and vitality of the first.

The word salmagundi first appeared in the 17th century; it refers to a spicy stewlike concoction, whose ingredients are as various as the contents of the book.

Salmon, André (1881–). French art critic, poet, novelist. Salmon did much to introduce such painters as Modigliani and Chagall to the public. His poems are often a kind of intuitive, almost surrealist reporting, such as *Prikaz* (1921), an epic of the Russian revolution, and *L'Age de l'humanité* (1922). *The Black Venus* (*La Négresse du Sacré-Coeur;*

1920), which paints a grotesque bohemia and underworld, is typical of his novels.

Salmoneus. In Greek mythology, a son of Aeolus. He was struck dead by Zeus for pretending to be a sky god. He made thunder by dragging bronze kettles and dried hides after his chariot and flung torches to represent lightning. These practices were actually primitive rainmaking ceremonies and were probably part of the priest-king's duties.

Salome. In the Bible, the daughter of Herodias and Herod Philip. When her mother divorced her husband and married his brother HEROD ANTIPAS, governor of Judaea, the prophet John the Baptist was imprisoned for denouncing the marriage. According to the New Testament narrative, Salome so pleased Herod by her dancing at his birthday feast that he promised her "whatsoever she would ask." She followed her mother's advice and demanded the head of John the Baptist on a platter (Matt. 14:6–11).

According to medieval legend, Herodias had been in love with John. Modern treatments of the story, such as Hermann Sudermann in his tragedy *The Fires of St. John* (1897), and Oscar Wilde in *Salomé* (1894), make Salome also infatuated with the prophet, and Herod infatuated with Salome. The opera *Salome* (1905) by Richard Strauss is based on Wilde's play. Flaubert has a short narrative called *Herodias, the Story of Salomé* (1877).

Saltus, Edgar [Evertson] (1855–1921). American novelist. Saltus is known for his emphasis on the exotic and erotic. *Mr. Incoul's Misadventure* (1887), his first "diabolical" novel of New York society, succeeded in shocking many with its sensational style.

Salomé: Aubrey Beardsley illustration for Wilde's play.

The Imperial Purple (1892) dealt with the scandals of the Roman emperors. It was followed by other books of its kind.

Saltykov, Mikhail Evgrafovich. Pen name, **N. Shchedrin** (1826–1889). Russian novelist and satirist. Saltykov attended the Lyceum at Tsarskoe Selo, where interest in literature was high. After his graduation in 1844, he joined the Petrashevski circle, a group of young intellectuals interested in the theories of the French utopian socialists. The novelist Feodor Dostoevski, also just beginning his career, was a member of the group.

The radical tone of one of Saltykov's early short novels, *Zaputannoye delo* (*A Complicated Affair*, 1848), attracted the attention of the Czarist censor and Saltykov was exiled to Vyatka in eastern Russia. His exile saved him from the severer treatment dealt to the Petrashevski circle in 1849, when the members were imprisoned, subjected to a mock execution, and sent to Siberia. Saltykov languished in Vyatka until 1856 when the amnesty following the death of Nicholas I released him. One result of his exile was *Gubernskiye ocherki* (*Provincial Sketches*, 1856), a collection of satirical pieces on provincial life, published under the pseudonym of N. Shchedrin.

From 1857–1862, Saltykov was again in the provinces, serving as vice-governor in Ryazan and Tver. Returning to St. Petersburg, he became the editor of the journal *Sovremennik* (*The Contemporary*) when its previous editor, Nikolai Chernyshevski, was exiled. In 1868, Saltykov took over the journal *Otechestvennye zapiski* (*Fatherland Notes*) in colaboration with the poet Nikolai Nekrasov. He continued to work on this journal until 1884. During this period he produced his best-known works. These include *Istoriya odnogo goroda* (*The History of a Town*, 1869–1870), a satirical history of an imaginary town; the novel THE GOLOVLYOV FAMILY, considered Saltykov's masterpiece; and *Skazki* (*Fables*, 1880–1885), in which Saltykov used the fable form for incisive comments on man and society.

Salus. In Roman myth, the goddess of health and good fortune. She became identified with the Greek Hygeia, the daughter of Aesculapius.

Salutati, Coluccio (1331–1406). Florentine scholar. A disciple of Petrarch, and one of the early Humanists, he was instrumental in bringing to Florence in 1397 the Byzantine scholar Chrysoloras, thus giving impetus to the revival of Greek studies at the university.

Salvation Army. A religious and charitable organization that grew out of the Christian Mission in London, established by the Methodist evangelist William BOOTH in 1865. From the beginning it devoted itself largely to work among the urban poor, criminals, alcoholics, and other neglected classes. The name Salvation Army, together with its semimilitary organization, was adopted in 1878 and goes back to a chance use of the phrase by Booth in reference to the work of his adherents. George Bernard Shaw has depicted the group in his *Major Barbara* (1905).

Salvation Nell (1908). A drama by Edward SHELDON. The heroine, Nell Sanders, is a scullery maid in a barroom. When she loses her job she goes to the Salvation Army where she meets Lieutenant Maggie O'Sullivan, who aids in Nell's reformation.

Salvini, Tommaso (1829–1916). Italian actor. A famous tragedian, he was noted for his interpretations of Shakespearean roles. He toured England and the U.S. with great success, winning special acclaim in the role of Othello.

Samael or **Sammael.** In rabbinical legend, the prince of demons who, in the guise of a serpent, was said to have tempted Eve. He was also known as the angel of death. See ADAM AND EVE.

Samain. November 1, the New Year's feast of the ancient Celtic year. Samain Eve, October 31, corresponds to the more modern HALLOWE'EN, and in Early Irish tales this was the time that the fairy mounds of Ireland opened, allowing supernatural beings to come out into the world. By the same token, Samain Eve was the time when the mysterious mounds became accessible to Irish heroes in search of glory and hidden treasure. With the coming of Christianity, Samain became ALL SAINTS' DAY.

Samaritan, Good. In the New Testament, a compassionate character who aids a man robbed and injured by thieves (Luke 10:30–34). The expression applies, in general, to any philanthropist who relieves the poor.

Sam Hill. A mythical individual of American origin, frequently referred to in such phrases as *fight like Sam Hill, swear like Sam Hill.* According to F. J. Wilstach, author of *A Dictionary of Similes,* the expression *what in Sam Hill* occurred at least as early as 1839 (in the Elmira, New York, *Republican*), and seems to have been well established in usage at that time. This date excludes a theory that Sam Hill was Sam Hall, the murderous chimney-sweep of an English song popular in 1848–1849. Mr. Wilstach is inclined to derive the fighting, swearing Sam Hill from the daemon Samael, and to see in references to him a satisfactory Puritan substitute for profanity. A simpler, not necessarily less probable explanation, treats the name as a playful euphemism for "hell."

Samient. See FAERIE QUEENE, THE.

Sammael. See SAMAEL.

Sammuramat. See SEMIRAMIS.

Sämpo. A precious object in the KALEVALA, usually described as a magic mill that grinds out meal, salt, and gold.

Sampson, Dominie. An extremely well-drawn character in Scott's GUY MANNERING. Tutor to the hero, Harry Bertram, he is described as "a poor, modest, humble scholar, who had won his way through the classics, but fallen to the leeward in the voyage of life." He is overfond of the exclamation "Prodigious!"

Samsa, Gregor. The hero of Kafka's THE META-MORPHOSIS. A traveling salesman, he awakens one morning to find himself changed into an insect. His name is a code form of the author's own, for by the substitution of *k* for *s* and *f* for *m, Samsa* becomes *Kafka.* See K.; Joseph K.

Samsāra. A Sanskrit word meaning the cycle of transmigration, birth, death, and rebirth.

Samson. In the Old Testament, the son of Manoah, famous for his prodigious strength and the many remarkable feats by which he routed his enemies, the Philistines. He became infatuated with Delilah, a Philistine woman, who discovered that the secret of his strength lay in his uncut hair; she betrayed him by cutting it off in his sleep so he was easily captured by the Philistines who blinded him and forced him to grind meal in the prison-house at Gaza. When, at the feast of the Philistine god Dagon, he was brought to the temple to be mocked by the people, he prayed to Jehovah for a return of his strength. He was enabled to pull down the two great pillars which supported the entire edifice, killing himself and all present (Judg. 13–16).

Milton made Samson the hero of his great poem *Samson Agonistes* (1671). The opera *Samson et Dalila* by Saint-Saëns (1877) also follows the Biblical story.

Samson's crown. An achievement of great renown, which costs the life of the doer.

Samson Agonistes (1671). A tragedy in blank verse by John MILTON. It deals with the captivity of the blinded Samson among the Philistines, his repudiation of the faithless Delilah, and his destruction of the Philistine temple. The agon, or struggle about which the play centers, is Samson's effort to renew his faith in God's support and his own mission. In structure the drama is closely modeled on Greek tragedy: there is a chorus; the action is confined to a single day; and the climactic event (the destruction of the temple) occurs off stage and is related by a witness.

Samuel. In the Bible, a judge and prophet, the religious and political reformer of early Israel, after whom are named two books of the Old Testament. At his birth, he was consecrated to temple service by his mother Hannah and, when still a child, heard Jehovah's voice in the night. He preserved the work of Moses in reuniting the people and established schools devoted to the cultivation of sacred poetry and song. After a long life as priest and leader, Samuel was forced to yield to the people's demand for a king and established Saul on the throne, though he prophesied loss of liberty. He also anointed David as future king.

samurai. (Jap., "guard"). Title of the feudal warriors of Japan.

Sánchez, Florencio (1875–1910). Uruguayan dramatist. Considered the outstanding dramatist of the Río de la Plata region, Sánchez turned to the theater after working as a journalist and participating in anarchist agitation. He wrote his first play, *M'hijo el dotor* (1903), in less than three weeks in order to earn enough money to marry his sweetheart, whose parents viewed his bleak prospects with disfavor. Dealing with the conflict between an old gaucho and his urbane, self-centered son, the play met with notable success. The struggle between the old order and new is also the theme of other plays by Sánchez, notably *La Gringa* (1904), which is concerned with racial animosity between native Argentines and Italian immigrants, and *Barranca abajo* (1905), a poignant elegy on the gaucho threatened by "progress." *Los muertos* (1905) deals with the urban middle classes. Sánchez' work has been likened to Ibsen's, because of its realism and emphasis on contemporary problems.

Sanctuary (1931). A novel by William FAULK-NER. Horace Benbow, an ineffectual intellectual, becomes involved in the violent events centering around Temple DRAKE, a young coed. Temple is raped by POPEYE, who murders a man trying to protect the girl. Carried off to a Memphis brothel by Popeye,

Temple later protects him and testifies against Lee Goodwin, who is accused of the murder. Benbow defends Goodwin at the trial and unsuccessfully tries to give shelter to his common-law wife. Temple's testimony ends all hope for Goodwin, who is lynched by the townspeople. Temple's story is continued in REQUIEM FOR A NUN.

sanctum sanctorum. See HOLY OF HOLIES.

Sanctus (Lat. "holy"). The oldest of the fixed chants in all historical Christian Eucharistic liturgies. The text, derived from the Book of Isaiah, begins "Holy, Holy, Holy, Lord God of Hosts." It is sung just before the Consecration.

Sand, George. Pen name of **Amandine Lucie Aurore Dupin,** Baronne **Dudevant** (1804–1876). French writer. George Sand is as famous for her love affairs with such prominent artistic figures as Alfred de Musset and Frédéric Chopin, as she is for her writings. In 1831 she left her husband, Baron Dudevant, and established herself in Paris. Her work is usually divided into three distinct periods, the first of which, intensely romantic, corresponds to her affair with Musset (see ELLE ET LUI). The novels of this period plead the right of free love for both men and women, and include such works as INDIANA, LÉLIA, and *Valentine* (1832). During the next decade George Sand became interested in various humanitarian reform movements and published such works as CONSUELO and *Le Meunier d'Angibault* (1845). Her last group of novels, studies of nature and of rustic manners, includes *La Mare au Diable* (1846), *La Petite Fadette* (1848), and *François le Champi* (1850).

Sandalphon. One of the three angels of rabbinical legend who receive the prayers of the faithful and weave them into crowns.

Sandburg, Carl (1878–1967). American poet. Known for his free verse, written under the influence of Walt Whitman and celebrating industrial and agricultural America, American geography and landscape, figures in American history, and the American common people, he frequently makes use of contemporary American slang and colloquialisms. Born in Galesburg, Ill., Sandburg left school at 13 and worked at a variety of odd jobs in his youth, traveled as a hobo to the West, served in the Spanish-American War, and worked his way through college. He was an advertising writer, a newspaper reporter, a correspondent in Sweden and Norway, and an editorial writer for the Chicago *Daily News*. Early in his career he evinced socialist sympathies, worked for the Social-Democratic Party in Wisconsin, and later was secretary to the first Socialist mayor of Milwaukee.

After an early pamphlet, *In Reckless Ecstasy* (1904), Sandburg began publishing his poems in Harriet Monroe's *Poetry*, becoming part of the Chicago Renaissance (See CHICAGO GROUP). With *Chicago Poems* (1916) and CORNHUSKERS, his reputation was established. These volumes were followed in the 20's by SMOKE AND STEEL, *Slabs of the Sunburnt West* (1922), *Selected Poems* (1926), and *Good Morning, America* (1928). Also in the 20's, Sandburg's energies were directed into three other areas. The most important of these was the beginning of his monumental study, ABRAHAM LINCOLN. His second area of interest was the collection of American folklore,

the ballads of THE AMERICAN SONGBAG. This was to be followed by *The New American Songbag* (1950). Finally, Sandburg began to publish books for children. The best known of these is ROOTABAGA STORIES, followed by *Rootabaga Pigeons* (1923), *The Rootabaga Country* (1929), and *Potato Face* (1930).

In the 1930's, Sandburg continued his celebration of America, especially with *Mary Lincoln, Wife and Widow* (1932); THE PEOPLE, YES; and the second part of his Lincoln biography, *Abraham Lincoln: The War Years* (1939). For the latter he received a Pulitzer Prize; he received a second Pulitzer Prize for his *Complete Poems* (1950). Among Sandburg's other prose works are *The Chicago Race Riots* (1919); *Steichen the Photographer* (1929), a biography of his brother-in-law; *Remembrance Rock* (1948), a novel; and *Always the Young Strangers* (1952), an autobiography of his youth.

Sandhurst. A parish in Berkshire, England. It is the seat of the Royal Military College, which corresponds to St.-Cyr in France and to West Point in the U.S.

Sandibar, Tales of. See SEVEN WISE MASTERS, THE.

Sandoz, Mari [Susette] (1901–1966). American biographer and historical writer. A native of Nebraska, Miss Sandoz is known especially for her biography of her pioneer father, *Old Jules* (1935), and for such nonfiction narratives as *Crazy Horse* (1942), *Cheyenne Autumn* (1953), *The Cattlemen* (1958), *Love Song to the Plains* (1961), and *These Were the Sioux* (1961). She also wrote several novels, including *Slogum House* (1937), *Capital City* (1939), and *Miss Morissa* (1955).

Sandys, George (1578–1644). English poet and translator, a traveler in the Orient, one-time resident of Virginia, and a courtier of Charles I. Sandys is best known for his translation (1626) of Ovid's *Metamorphoses*, but also wrote numerous Biblical paraphrases and translations.

Sangrado, Dr. An epithet applicable to an ignorant or quack doctor, from the doctor in the novel GIL BLAS DE SANTILLANE by Alain René LESAGE. Gil Blas, the hero, becomes his servant and pupil. Sangrado's knowledge of medicine is limited to prescribing bleeding and hot water. He is also known as the doctor of Valladolid.

Sangreal. See GRAIL.

Sangster, Charles (1822–1893). Canadian poet. Sangster is remembered as one of the first poets to make appreciative use of Canadian subjects. His works include *The St. Lawrence and the Saguenay and Other Poems* (1856) and *Hesperus and Other Poems* (1860).

Sanhedrin or **Sanhedrim.** The chief judicial council of the Jews from the 3rd century B.C. to A.D. 70. After the destruction of Jerusalem in 70, the Sanhedrin lost its temporal powers; it lasted until the fifth century as a purely religious body. Formerly it had acted as the supreme court in the interpretation of the complex Jewish law, having the power of life and death over the accused. It is not certain whether CAIAPHAS, when he judged Jesus, was acting as a member of the Sanhedrin or as an influential leader of the Jewish community.

Sankey, Ira D[avid]. See Dwight Lyman MOODY.

TO THE BEST OF MEN,
AND
MOST EXCELLENT OF PRINCES,
CHARLES,
BY THE GRACE OF GOD KING
OF GREAT-BRITAINE, FRANCE,
AND IRELAND:

LORD OF THE FOVRE SEAS;
OF VIRGINIA, THE VAST TER-
RITORIES ADIOYNING, AND
DISPERSED ISLANDS OF THE
VVESTERNE OCEAN:

THE ZEALOVS DEFENDOR OF
THE CHRISTIAN FAITH:

GEORGE SANDYS,
THE HVMBLEST OF HIS SERVANTS,
PRESENTS AND CONSECRATES
THESE HIS PARAPHRASES VPON
THE DIVINE POEMS,
TO RECEIVE THEIR LIFE AND ESTI-
MATION FROM HIS FAVOVR.

Dedication to Charles I from Sandys' *Paraphrases upon the Divine Poems* (1638).

San Martín, José de (1778–1850). Argentine general and revolutionary leader. After taking part in Argentina's struggle for independence from Spain, San Martín became governor of Cuyo province (1814–1817), where he organized an army to lead against Chile and Peru, the stronghold of Spanish power in South America. After an arduous trek across the Andes, San Martín and the Chilean patriot Bernardo O'Higgins defeated the Spaniards at Chacabuco and Maipu and declared the independence of Chile. Rejecting the political honors which the grateful Chileans offered him, San Martín turned to the liberation of Peru. Although he was able to declare Peru's independence in 1821, most of the territory included in the viceroyalty of Peru still remained in royalist hands, and San Martín, who was named dictator of Peru, resolved to seek the aid of Bolívar. After a famous meeting between the two liberators at Guayaquil (1822), San Martín, perhaps in the belief that his continued presence in Peru would delay the final victory, resigned his post and left the country, leaving a clear field for Bolívar. He spent his last years in Europe and died in France. His achievements were belatedly recognized by his countrymen, who had ignored or vilified him during his lifetime, and in 1880 his remains were brought to Argentina for final burial in Buenos Aires.

Sannazzaro, Jacopo (1456–1530). Neapolitan poet. Known also by his academic name of Actius Syncerus, he devoted most of his life to the service of the house of Aragon. His writings include Latin elegies, epigrams and piscatorial (or maritime) eclogues, the latter being the first attempts at the genre since Theocritus. His religious poem *De partu virginis* (*On the Virgin's Parturition*) was one of several Renaissance attempts at writing Vergilian epic on Christian subject matter and eventually influenced Milton. In Italian he wrote sonnets and *canzoni*, but his masterpiece is the *Arcadia* (1501–1504), a pastoral romance immensely popular and influential throughout Europe. Written between 1480 and 1485, it is divided into 12 prose chapters, each accompanied by 12 poems, and tells of the adventures of Sincero, who visits Arcadia to observe the pastoral life of its inhabitants. He returns to Naples in search of his beloved Fillide only to find her dead. The *Arcadia* was imitated by many European writers; in England, Spenser and Sidney are only two of his adapters, the latter using its title and some details for his own prose romance.

Sansfoy. See FAERIE QUEENE, THE.

Sansjoy. See FAERIE QUEENE, THE.

Sanskara. The 10 essential rites of Hindus of the first three castes. They take place at the conception of a child; at the quickening; at birth; at naming; when carrying the child out to see the moon; when giving him his first food to eat; at the ceremony of tonsure; during investiture with the sacred thread; at the close of his studies; at the ceremony of "marriage," when he is qualified to perform the sacrifices ordained.

Sansloy. See FAERIE QUEENE, THE.

Sansom, William (1912–   ). English novelist and short-story writer. He is the author of sinister Kafkaesque works such as the novel *The Body* (1949), an account of a paranoid delusion narrated by its victim, and the short stories collected in *Fireman Flower* (1944) and *Something Terrible, Something Lovely* (1954). Stories about restlessness and deception in love are collected in *The Face of Innocence* (1951) and *A Bed of Roses* (1954). *The Passionate North* (1950) and other collections of short stories vividly describe foreign backgrounds and are really travel books.

Sanson, Charles Henri (1740–?1795). Official executioner in Paris from 1788 to his death. He executed Louis XVI. His son and colleague, Henri, executed Marie Antoinette.

Sansonetto of Mecca. In Lodovico Ariosto's ORLANDO FURIOSO, a Saracen knight who had been baptized by Orlando and joined the Christian cause. He is Charlemagne's commander at Jerusalem.

Sans Souci (Fr., "carefree"). The palace built by FREDERICK II near Potsdam (1747).

Santa Anna or **Santa Ana, Antonio López de** (1795?–1876). Mexican general and political leader. Now generally regarded as a self-seeking opportunist who betrayed every cause he espoused, Santa Anna dominated Mexican politics for over 25 years. After serving as president (1834–1835), he led the Mexican assault at the Alamo. Taken prisoner at the battle of San Jacinto shortly afterwards, he was released when he promised to recognize the independence of Texas. He was provisional president and commander of the Mexican forces during the war with the U.S., but was deposed after the American victory. Again made president in 1853, he was exiled in 1855. In

1874 he was permitted to return to Mexico, where he died penniless and alone.

Santa Claus or **Santa Klaus.** The patron saint of children and bearer of gifts at Christmas. His name is a corruption of the Dutch form of St. Nicholas. His feast-day is December 6, and the vigil is still held in some places, but for the most part his name is now associated with Christmastide. The old custom used to be for someone, on December 5, to assume the costume of a bishop and distribute small gifts to good children.

Santa Fe Trail. The main overland route to the American Southwest and southern California in the years before the railroad. Originally traced by explorer William Becknell in 1821–1822, it began at Independence (originally at Franklin), Mo., proceeded along the prairie divide to the great bend of the Arkansas River, followed the river upward almost to the mountains, then turned south to Santa Fe. It is still the route of a transcontinental highway and of the Atchison, Topeka, and Santa Fe Railroad.

Josiah Gregg's *Commerce of the Prairies* (1844) is the classic account of the trail. Novels about the trail include Stanley Vestal's *'Dobe Walls* (1917) and Harvey Fergusson's trilogy, *Followers of the Sun* (1936).

Santa Fe Trail, The: A Humoresque (1914). A poem by Vachel LINDSAY. It contrasts industrial civilization at the beginning of the 20th century with the Rachel-Jane bird, which sings of love and eternal youth. It is notable for its radical sound effects.

Santa Sophia. The great metropolitan cathedral of the Greek Orthodox Church at Constantinople. It was built in the sixth century by Justinian, but since the capture of the city by the Turks (1453) has been used as a mosque. It was not dedicated to a saint named Sophia but to the Logos, the second Person of the Trinity, called *Hagia Sophia* or Sacred Wisdom.

Santayana, George (1863–1952). Spanish-born American philosopher, poet, novelist, and critic. He was known for his cosmopolitan viewpoint, his philosophic skepticism and materialism, his interest in the systems of Plato and Aristotle, and his fondness for the Greek and Roman classical ideals of beauty.

Santayana studied at Harvard University and later returned there to teach philosophy; among his students were Conrad Aiken, Robert Benchley, Felix Frankfurter, Walter Lippmann, and T. S. Eliot. In 1912 Santayana resigned from the university and went to live and travel in Europe, spending winters in Rome and summers in Paris. At the outset of World War II he moved to a Roman Catholic nursing home in Rome where he spent the rest of his life.

Santayana himself divided his work into two groups: the poetic, or personal, and the academic. The first group includes such works as *Lucifer: A Theological Tragedy* (1899), *Dialogues in Limbo* (1925), and THE LAST PURITAN. Santayana's memoirs, *Persons and Places*, were published in three volumes: *The Background of My Life* (1944), *The Middle Span* (1945), and *My Host the World* (1953).

In the academic group are *The Sense of Beauty* (1896), an outline of an aesthetic theory; *The Life of Reason, or, The Phases of Human Progress,* a five-volume work including *Introduction and Reason in*

Common Sense (1905), *Reason in Society* (1905), *Reason in Religion* (1905), *Reason in Art* (1905), and *Reason in Science* (1906), all based on a materialistic view of nature; *Skepticism and Animal Faith* (1923); and *Realms of Being,* including the four volumes *The Realm of Essence* (1927), *The Realm of Matter* (1930), *The Realm of Truth* (1937), and *The Realm of Spirit* (1940). In addition to many other works, Santayana dealt with the American scene in *Character and Opinion in the United States* (1921) and *The Genteel Tradition at Bay* (1931).

Santiago. See St. JAMES THE GREATER.

Santillana, marqués de. Iñigo López de Mendoza (1398–1456). Spanish poet. The nephew of the chancellor Ayala, Santillana was a great feudal lord who fought against the Moors and conspired against Alvaro de Luna, the powerful favorite of John II. Italian influences are evident in his two allegorical poems, *La comedieta de Ponza* and *Infierno de los enamorados,* and in his 42 sonnets, a form which he introduced to Spain. He is best known, however, for his charming *serranillas,* or mountain songs, such as the one about his encounter with the milk-maid of Finajosa. He also wrote *Proemio e Carta,* a letter on the nature of poetry addressed to the constable of Portugal, which is regarded as the first example of literary criticism in Spain.

Santos-Dumont, Alberto (1873–1932). A Brazilian pioneer aeronaut in France. His airship won a prize (1901) for making the first flight from St. Cloud around the Eiffel Tower and back. He also experimented with an airplane of a box-kite type (1906) and a monoplane (1909).

Sapper. See H. C. McNEILE.

Sapphic. A four-lined verse-form of classical lyric poetry. It is named after the Greek poetess Sappho, who employed it, the fourth line being an Adonic. There must be a caesura at the fifth foot of each of the first three lines, which run thus:

$$-\cup|--|-\|\cup\cup|-\cup|-\cup$$

The Adonic is

$$-\cup\cup|-\cup \ or --$$

All the night sleep came not upon my eyelids,
Shed not dew, nor shook nor unclose a feather,
Yet with lips shut close and with eyes of iron
　　Stood and beheld me.
　　　　　　　　　Algernon Charles Swinburne

Sapphira. A female liar. See ANANIAS.

Sappho (b. 612 B.C.). One of the most famous lyric poets of all time, a native of Lesbos. Except for a period of some years in Sicily, she lived in Lesbos all her life. Married and with a daughter, she was the leader of some kind of group of young girls who were devotees of music and poetry, and perhaps of Aphrodite. To some of these girls are addressed many of Sappho's poems. Classical writers called Sappho the tenth muse. Although her poems survive only in fragments, their lyrical intensity and economy prove that her reputation was not exaggerated. The legend that she flung herself into the sea on being rejected by the beautiful youth Phaon has been the subject of many works, from a section of Ovid's *Heroides* to plays by John Lyly (1584) and

Percy MacKaye (1907), both of which are named *Sappho and Phaon*.

Saracinesca (1887). A novel by F. Marion CRAWFORD. It is the first of four novels dealing with the fortunes of a great Italian family in Rome from 1865 to the 1890's. The novel was followed by *Sant' Ilario* (1889), *Don Orsino* (1892), and *Corleone* (1897).

Sarah or **Sarai**. In the Old Testament (Gen. 12–23), the wife of Abraham and mother of Isaac. After the birth of Isaac, which occurred in her old age in accordance with Jehovah's promise to make a great nation of Abraham, her name was changed from Sarai to Sarah. See HAGAR.

Sara Monday. The heroine of a trilogy by Joyce Cary. See HORSE'S MOUTH, THE.

Sarasvati. A sacred river in the Punjab in North India. It is personified by the ancient Hindus as the wife of Brahma and goddess of the fine arts. The river loses itself in the sands, but was fabled to become united with the Ganges and Jamuna.

Sardanapalus. The mythical last king of Assyria. His legend, as it grew up among the Greeks, combined the name of one historical ruler, Assurdanin-pal, with some of the exploits of another, ASSUR-BANI-PAL. An effete ruler, he nevertheless was said to have fought bravely against the rebellious Medes. When faced with inevitable defeat, he burned himself, his wife, and his treasures in the year 880 B.C.

Sardou, Victorien (1831–1908). French dramatist. The author of comedies and historical dramas that won him enormous popularity during his lifetime, Sardou excelled at clever plot construction. His light, shallow comedies of manners include *Les Pattes de mouche* (*A Scrap of Paper*, 1860), *Nos Intimes* (*Peril*, 1861), and *La Famille Benoîton* (1865). Sarah Bernhardt played the leading role in several of his historical dramas, including *Fédora* (1882), in which she triumphantly returned to the stage of Paris, and *La Tosca* (1887), on which Puccini based his opera of the same title.

Sarett, Lew (1888–1954). American poet. Sarett was a guide and forest ranger before he became a university teacher, and his poetry is often concerned with the American Indian and the creatures of the wild. Among his collections are *Many Many Moons* (1920), *The Box of God* (1922), *Slow Smoke* (1925), and *Collected Poems* (1941).

Sargasso Sea. A part of the North Atlantic Ocean. It derives its name from the great amount of seaweed (gulfweed or Sargassum) floating in it.

Sargent, John Singer (1856–1925). American painter. Born in Italy, he studied in Florence and Paris, and lived mostly in London. A fashionable and elegant portrait painter, he recorded surface observations with brilliant brushwork, if little insight. He was a distinguished watercolorist and also did murals for the Public Library and the Museum of Fine Arts in Boston.

Sarment, Jean (1897–). French dramatist. His plays, such as *Le Pêcheur d'ombres* (1921) and *Les Plus Beaux Yeux du monde* (1925), are peopled with poets and dreamers unable to face the reality of life.

Sarmiento, Domingo Faustino (1811–1888). Argentine statesman, educator, and writer. Completely self-educated, Sarmiento once wrote that he had tried to pattern himself on Benjamin Franklin. His political career began when he opposed the dictatorship of Juan Manuel de Rosas, whom he denounced in his greatest work, FACUNDO. He spent many years as an exile in Chile, where he wrote spelling books and primers, directed a secondary school, and founded the first normal school in South America. He returned to Argentina after Rosas had been overthrown and held several important political posts. In 1864 he was named Argentine minister to the U.S., a country he unabashedly admired. While he was returning to Argentina in 1868, he was informed that he had been elected president of the republic. During his six years in office, he reformed the country's educational system, encouraged large-scale immigration, and furthered advances in transportation and communications. He was, however, unable to diminish the personalism in Argentine politics, and when his term ended the country was divided by civil war.

A prolific writer whose complete works fill 52 volumes, Sarmiento was a romantic in style and literary outlook. In 1842 he engaged in a newspaper debate with Andrés Bello, the great grammarian and poet, in which he argued that linguists should describe, rather than prescribe, usage and that literature should emphasize content, rather than form. Other important works by Sarmiento are *Viajes* (1849), an account of a trip to Europe, Africa, and the U.S., and *Recuerdos de provincia* (1850), an engaging memoir of his childhood.

Saroyan, William (1908–). American short story writer, novelist, and playwright. He is known for his impressionistic stories and sketches, which exalt personal emotion and freedom and assert kindness and brotherly love as a human ideal. His short story *The Daring Young Man on the Flying Trapeze* (1934), a mingling of fantasy and realism, did much to establish his reputation. There followed such fiction as *Inhale and Exhale* (1936), *Three Times Three* (1936), *Peace, It's Wonderful* (1939), and the autobiographical *My Name Is Aram* (1940). *The Human Comedy* (1942) was a largely autobiographical novel about a little boy who delivers telegrams.

Saroyan's play *My Heart's in the Highlands* (1939) was a Broadway success and was followed by THE TIME OF YOUR LIFE, the winner of a Pulitzer Prize which the author refused, believing that commerce should not patronize art. This play was followed by *Love's Old Sweet Song* (1940) and *The Beautiful People* (1941). *Two by Saroyan* (which included *The Cave Dwellers*, 1958) was produced in 1961. Saroyan's later writing includes *The Adventures of Wesley Jackson* (1946), *The Bicycle Rider of Beverley Hills* (1952), *Papa, You're Crazy* (1957), and *Boys and Girls Together* (1963).

Sarpedon. (1) A brother of MINOS and Rhadamanthus and son of Europe. He was driven from Crete when Minos claimed the throne for himself alone.

(2) In the *Iliad* king of Lydia, son of Zeus and Laodameia. He fought with the Trojans in the Trojan War. Learning that he was fated to die at the hands of Patroclus, Zeus wept for him.

Sarpi, Fra Paolo (1552–1623). Venetian friar of the Servite order, theologian, scientist, and historian. An advocate of restraining church power in the temporal sphere, he defended the cause of the Venetian republic against the interdict of Pope Paul V in 1606. His masterpiece, the *History of the Council of Trent,* written between 1610 and 1618, was first published in London (1619) without its author's knowledge. Sarpi is credited with a memorable pun, made when he commented on a nearly successful attempt at assassination: "Agnosco stylum Romanae Curiae" ("I recognize the style [dagger] of the Roman Curia"). Popular with the English and with northern reformers in general, his works were translated into English; Milton, for example, mentions him favorably in the *Areopagitica.*

Sarraute, Nathalie (1902–). Russian-born French novelist. With *Tropismes* (1939), she began to experiment with presenting the fluctuations of human feelings and motivations by concentrating on the myriad minutiae of objects and impulses that fill human time as lived. In her preface to her *Portrait of a Man Unknown* (*Portrait d'un inconnu;* 1947), Jean-Paul Sartre called it an "antinovel." In the essays collected in *The Age of Suspicion* (*L'Ere du soupçon;* 1956), first published 1947-1955, Sarraute analyzed the techniques of what was to be called the NEW WAVE of fiction. Her later novels include *Martereau* (1953), *The Planetarium* (1959), and *Golden Fruits* (1962).

Sarto, Andrea del. Real name, **Andrea Vanucchi** (1486-1531). Florentine painter. He was known as *Andrea senza errore* (Andrea the faultless) because of his technically flawless fresco paintings, which he never retouched. Under the influence of RAPHAEL, he painted such notable works as the *Madonna delle Arpie* and *Portrait of an Architect.* His *Last Supper,* recalling that of LEONARDO, is also executed in the High Renaissance style, emphasizing balanced composition and noble gesture. His pupil was Pontormo, who reacted against his master's harmonious beauty and turned to mannerism. Andrea is the speaker in Robert Browning's famous dramatic monologue *Andrea del Sarto.*

Sartoris (1929). A novel by William FAULKNER. The book tells the story of the descendants of Colonel John SARTORIS, especially that of young Bayard who returns from World War I haunted by guilt feelings for the death of his brother, John. Driven by an urge for self-destruction, Bayard has a series of accidents. Because of his reckless driving, his grandfather, old Bayard Sartoris, rides with him in an attempt to force him to drive carefully, but young Bayard runs the car off the road and his grandfather dies of a heart attack. Young Bayard marries Narcissa Benbow, the sister of Horace Benbow who figures so prominently in *Sanctuary,* but his suicidal drive leads him to become a test pilot in Ohio, and he is killed. This is the first of Faulkner's novels to deal with YOKNAPATAWPHA COUNTY. The early history of the Sartoris family is described in THE UNVANQUISHED.

Sartoris, Colonel John. A leading character in William Faulkner's THE UNVANQUISHED and other novels and stories, and ancestor of the family treated in the novel SARTORIS. His many descendants and kinsfolk make up one of the important aristocratic families of Faulkner's imaginary world. He is believed to be reminiscent of Colonel William C. Falkner, the novelist's great-grandfather.

Sartor Resartus (*Lat.,* the tailor re-tailored, 1833-1834). A philosophical satire by Thomas CARLYLE. It purports to review a work on the philosophy of clothes by Diogenes Teufelsdröckh, an eccentric old professor of Things in General at Weissnichtwo (*Ger.,* know not where). Passages supposedly translated from the German and the editor's running comments weave a narrative of Teufelsdröckh's life, often considered of autobiographical interest. A restless, impressionable youth, he passes through one disillusioning experience after another. He attends the university, studies law, falls in love with the Rose Goddess, Blumine, who discards him for a more eligible suitor. After years of despair and wandering, he realizes that "here, in this poor, miserable, hampered, despicable Actual, wherein thou even now standest, here or nowhere is thy ideal. . . ."

Sartre, Jean-Paul (1905–). French philosopher, dramatist, novelist, and teacher. Born and educated in Paris, he began his career by teaching (1929), first in *lycées* (secondary schools) in the provinces and later in Paris. He also traveled widely before 1935, and, while in Germany (1933-1934), studied under the philosophers Edmund Husserl and Martin Heidegger, who greatly influenced his thinking. Before World War II he wrote several original psychological studies: *Imagination* (1936), *Emotions, Outline of a Theory* (*Esquisse d'une théorie des émotions;* 1939), and *The Psychology of Imagination* (*L'Imaginaire;* 1940). He became known, however, for a series of articles on contemporary literature which did much to popularize in France the works of American novelists such as Faulkner, Hemingway, Dos Passos, and Steinbeck. In 1938, Sartre published the novel NAUSEA and the next year the short stories in THE WALL, both books dramatizing the discovery of the meaninglessness of human life, which is the precondition for the philosophy of EXISTENTIALISM as Sartre later developed it.

He joined the French army in 1939 and was taken prisoner in Alsace in 1940. After nine months he escaped to Paris and resumed teaching. He took an active part in the underground Resistance movement, writing for clandestine publications such as *Combat.* The production of the play THE FLIES in 1943, despite the Nazi censorship of the Occupation, emphasized that the apparent pessimism of *Nausea* did not lead to nihilism for Sartre but to the active assumption of moral responsibility—the position Sartre described as being *engagé,* or actively engaged in the business of shaping one's life. The same year he published BEING AND NOTHINGNESS, the major exposition of his analysis of man's condition and potentialities.

The following year, No EXIT was produced, and, after the liberation of France, Sartre left his teaching position and organized (1946) the politico-literary review *Les Temps modernes.* He became internationally famous as the leader of a group of intellectuals, described in many of the works of his intimate friend Simone de BEAUVOIR. The Café de Flore where they gathered attracted tourists as well as disciples, and, for the rest of the decade, existentialism became a popular fashion as well as a serious and major influence on contemporary writers.

Albert CAMUS was one of the friends in Sartre's circle. Although his philosophical thinking started from similar assumptions, he was not an existentialist, and he disagreed publicly with Sartre on a number of issues, particularly that of ends and means. Sartre dramatized this issue in the controversial play DIRTY HANDS, which reflects his troubled sympathy with Communism. He defended this sympthay on occasion, on the grounds that one must be *engagé*, that even though there can be no perfect causes, one is obligated to support the least undesirable cause in order to act, in this case for the reform of existing social institutions. After the Soviet intervention in Hungary in 1956 he admitted total disillusionment.

Other important plays by Sartre include THE RESPECTFUL PROSTITUTE, *The Devil and the Good Lord* (*Le Diable et le bon Dieu;* 1951), *Kean* (1953), *Nekrassov* (1956), and *The Condemned of Altona* (*Les séquestrés d'Altona;* 1959), also translated as *Loser Wins. The Chips Are Down* (*Les Jeux sont faits;* 1947), later revised as a novel, and *In the Mesh* (*L'Engrenage;* 1948) are film scenarios.

Sartre's other works include the novel trilogy THE ROADS TO FREEDOM; the essays *Existentialism is a Humanism* (*L'Existentialisme est un humanisme*), first presented as lectures in 1945; *Baudelaire* (1947); *Literary and Philosophical Essays* (*Situations I;* 1947); *Saint Genet* (1952), an exploration of the philosophical and psychological aspects of Jean GENET's life; and *Search for a Method,* the prefatory essay to *Critique de la raison dialectique* (1960). He was awarded the Nobel prize in literature in 1964.

Sassoon, Siegfried (1886–1967). English poet, best known for his lyrics exposing the horrors of war. His volume *Counter-Attack and other Poems* (1918) contains angry, violent, and satirical poems about World War I trench warfare. He is also known for his fictional autobiography, called *The Memoirs of George Sherston* (3 vols., 1928–1936). The first volume, *Memoirs of a Fox-Hunting Man,* is a particularly vivid evocation of the life of the old English country gentry. *Siegfried's Journey* (1945) is a three-volume continuation of the autobiography.

During World War I Sassoon was wounded twice, received two medals for bravery, and attained the rank of captain, but he became a pacifist. He spent some time in the same hospital as Wilfred Owen and encouraged him in his writing.

Satan (*Heb.,* "adversary"). In Judaeo-Christian belief, the chief spirit of evil in the universe. He entered into Jewish religious thought during the Exile under the influence of the dualistic Persian theology of Zoroastrianism, and continued in Christian doctrine. It was Satan who, in opposition to God, tested Job and tempted Jesus in the wilderness. In early Christian writings he appeared as Christ's chief adversary. Many strange doctrines concerning Satan's continuing war with God were later considered heretical, but belief in the devil was an important factor in daily life throughout the Middle Ages and common up until modern times, though it no longer plays a widespread role in Christian theology.

The gods of one religion have often become the devils of an opposing religion. Following this principle, the Christian Devil acquired many characteristics of various "heathen" deities. In the early days of the Church, popular superstition added a whole company of demons to Satan's entourage. Later, many traits of Norse and Germanic gods and spirits enhanced his powers, notably the capacity to assume many forms, human and animal.

In PARADISE LOST, Milton follows the Talmudic tradition of Satan's expulsion from heaven for pride, and makes him monarch of hell. His chief lords are Beelzebub, Moloch, Chemos, Thammuz, Dagon, Rimmon, and Belial—all once powerful gods of the ancient Near East. His standard-bearer is Azazel. Milton's Satan is a daring, ambitious chieftain who believes that "'tis better to reign in hell than serve in heaven." In Dante's *Divine Comedy,* LUCIFER, rather than Satan, is the ruler of hell. See Phineas FLETCHER; SATANISM.

Satanic school. A name of a group of writers in the early part of the 19th century. They were said to show a scorn for all moral rules and the generally received dogmas of the Christian religion. The most eminent English writers of this school were Bulwer-Lytton, Byron, Moore, and Shelley. Of French writers, the leaders were Paul de Kock (1794–1871), George Sand, and Victor Hugo. The term was first used by Southey in the preface of his *Vision of Judgment* (1821).

Satanism. The worship of SATAN. A survival of heathen fertility cults, it gained impetus in about the twelfth century from the secret rebellion against the Church. The central ritual of the cult was the Black Mass, an insulting and sometimes grisly parody of the Christian mass. It was performed by an unfrocked priest, with the nude body of a reclining woman as the altar. The Host was sometimes stolen from a church; at other times it was the ashes and blood of murdered children. These practices, often connected with witchcraft, were supposed to have magical efficacy. They gave rise to the legend of the WITCHES' SABBATH, or WALPURGIS NIGHT.

Satanstoe (1845). A novel by James Fenimore COOPER. The first volume in the LITTLEPAGE MANUSCRIPTS, *Satanstoe* gives the historical background of the Anti-Rent dispute. Set in pre-Revolutionary New York, the book shows the trouble and expense incurred by patriotic landowners, in encouraging the settlement of outlying lands. The hero, Corny Littlepage, is the heir of an old Dutch family living at Satanstoe, a strip of land in Westchester County. Corny travels upstate to explore his father's lands, falls in love, and fights the French and Indians at Lake George.

Satie, Erik **[-Alfred-Leslie]** (1866–1925). French composer whose early rebellion against the ideals of romanticism earned him the adulation of LES SIX and others. He collaborated with Pablo Picasso and Jean Cocteau on the ballet *Parade* (1917).

Satin Slipper, The (**Le Soulier de Satin,** 4 vols.; 1928–1929). A poetic drama by Paul CLAUDEL, revised for the stage in 1943. The never-consummated passion of Don Rodrigue and Dona Prouheze (at first married to old Don Pélage) blazes across a baroque pageant of 16th-century Spain's domination of the seas, of Morocco, and of South America, until after the defeat of the Spanish Armada by the English. The love they cannot exchange is transmuted during their entire lives into the energy that explores a continent or holds an embattled fortress, and thus fulfills God's purpose. Because they accept the difficult challenge of bearing their separation loyally and nobly, their passion becomes the annealing flame that prepares them for spiritual joy; the symbol of this is the gay Dona Sept-Epées (Seven-Swords), who is actually Prouheze's daughter by her second husband, Don Camille, but spiritually the child of Rodrigue.

satori. Enlightenment in ZEN Buddhism. It is attained in Rinzai Zen as a product of successful intensive meditation and KŌAN practice; in Sōtō Zen by meditative sitting. An adept may have many *satoris* in the course of his Zen training.

Satsuma. One of the early powerful clans in Japan. *Satsuma ware* is a brand of china.

Saturday Night and Sunday Morning (1958). A novel by Alan SILLITOE. Arthur Seaton, the hero, is a young factory worker whose weekdays are devoted to a dull, evil-smelling job. His Saturday nights are devoted to drink, promiscuity and general rebellion, while on Sunday mornings he fishes peacefully in the country. Eventually he chooses the almost secure perpetual "Sunday morning" of marriage to a nice, ordinary girl.

Saturday Review. A weekly literary review founded in 1924 by Henry Seidel Canby, Christopher Morley, Amy Loveman, and William Rose BENÉT. Originally called *The Saturday Review of Literature,* it changed its name in 1952, because by then it covered social commentary, recordings, the drama, radio, television, and travel, as well as books. Among its other editors have been Bernard De Voto (1936–1938), George Stevens (1938–1940), and Norman COUSINS (since 1942).

Saturn. An Italian god of agriculture, later identified with the Greek CRONUS. He was the husband of Ops, goddess of plenty identified with the Greek RHEA. As a legendary king of Rome, Saturn was remembered for introducing agriculture, and his reign, considered a golden age, was commemorated by the SATURNALIA, a festival which lasted from the 17th to the 19th of December. During this period, presents were exchanged, and all people, even slaves, were freed from customary restraints. The temple of Saturn was located at the foot of the Capitoline hill.

Saturnalia. A time of unrestrained disorder and misrule. In ancient Rome, it was the festival of SATURN, and was celebrated from the 17th to the 19th of December. During its continuance no public business could be transacted; the law courts and schools were closed; no war could be started, and no malefactor punished. Under the empire, the festival was extended to seven days.

Satyrane, Sir. See FAERIE QUEENE, THE.

Satyricon. See PETRONIUS.

satyr play. A semiserious form of classical Greek drama. Presented at the end of a trilogy of tragedies by the same author, a satyr play apparently brought comic relief to the great festivals of drama. It treated serious mythological events in a grotesquely comic manner, but had the form of tragedy. The only surviving satyr plays are *Cyclops* by Euripides and a long fragment of Sophocles' *Ichneutai.* The first tells the famous story of POLYPHEMUS and Odysseus, the second the miraculous growth of the infant Hermes. As in all satyr plays, the chorus is made up of horse-tailed SATYRS. Because of its comic scenes with the drunken Heracles, Euripides' ALCESTIS resembles a satyr play.

satyrs. In Greek legend, a race of goat-men who dwelt in the woodlands. The most famous satyr was SILENUS. They were often shown as followers of DIONYSUS and spent much of their time in amorous pursuit of the nymphs.

Saul. (1) In the Old Testament (I Sam. 9–15), 1st king of Israel, anointed by Samuel when the people demanded a king. In his moods of despair, he was calmed by the harp playing of DAVID, but grew jealous of David's friendship with his son Jonathan and persecuted David. He and his son were slain on Mount Gilboa, while in battle against the Philistines.

(2) PAUL, the apostle, was known in Hebrew as Saul of Tarsus.

(3) Browning has a dramatic monologue, *Saul* (1845) whose speaker is David.

Saunders, Richard. Benjamin Franklin's pen name, under which he wrote the maxims in *Poor Richard's Almanack.*

Savage, Richard (1697–1743). English playwright and poet, who claimed to be the illegitimate son of the countess of Macclesfield and Richard Savage, fourth Earl Rivers. His friend Dr. Samuel Johnson wrote his biography in THE LIVES OF THE POETS, although the account there of his birth and ill treatment is now generally disbelieved. Some of his plays were acted in Drury Lane. In one of them, *Sir Thomas Overbury* (1723), he himself played the title role. Savage edited *Miscellaneous Poems and Translations* (1726), a well-known collection, and wrote *The Wanderer* (1729), a poem. He had an adventurous life, and died in debtor's prison.

Savoir, Alfred [born **Posznanski**] (1883–1934). Polish-born French dramatist. Savoir wrote a number of extravagantly farcical comedies, such as *The Tamer; or, English as It Is Eaten* (*Le Dompteur;* 1925) and *He* (*Lui;* 1929). *Banco* (1922) and *Baccara* (1927) are iconoclastic satires.

Savonarola, Fra Girolamo (1452–1498). The celebrated monk of Ferrara who came to Florence and preached reform. From the Dominican monastery of San Marco and the pulpit of the cathedral, his sermons and exhortations engulfed the city in a tidal wave of piety. After the ouster of the Medici family, he held political as well as spiritual power over the city; heeding his call to reform and purify, the people burned vanities, eschewed paganism, and practiced repentance. Finally, charges of disobedience, then heresy, brought his excommunication from the Church and his burning at the stake. His surviving sermons give some indication of why he was able to win adherents among the people and among such artists as Botticelli, Pico della Mirandola, Benvieni, Ficino, and the young Michelangelo. Savonarola is a leading character in George Eliot's *Romola,* and appears in Harriet Beecher Stowe's *Agnes of Sorrento* (1862).

Savoy, the. A precinct and parish of London between the Strand and the Thames. The famous Savoy Palace, the London residence of John of Gaunt, where Chaucer was married, once stood there. It was burned by the rebels under Wat Tyler, and rebuilt as a hospital. When Waterloo Bridge was built, the remains of the palace were all swept away. The Savoy Hotel and Theatre (1881) stand near the Strand, and the latter gave its name to the operas of Gilbert and Sullivan which were called the *Savoy Operas.* Members of the company that produced them were called Savoyards.

Savoyard, Vicar. A priest in Rousseau's educational romance EMILE, charged with Emile's religious instruction. His own liberal Christianism and sentimental deistic teachings are intended to make Emile follow his natural instincts and conscience in matters of religion, and to be wary of formal dogma.

Saxe, Comte **Hermann Maurice de.** Known as **marshal de Saxe** (1696–1750). Famous marshal of France who served under Marlborough and Prince Eugene, natural son of Augustus II of Saxony. He was victor at Fontenoy (1745) and was created marshal general (1747). His remarkable work on the art of war, *Mes Rêveries*, was published in 1757.

Saxo Grammaticus (c. 1150–c. 1220). Danish historian and poet. His *Gesta Danorum* or *Historia Danica* (c. 1185–1208) chronicles the history of Danish kings and heroes to 1185, interspersed with translations of earlier poetry. The account of Amleth (2d century B.C.) is the ultimate source for Shakespeare's HAMLET.

Sayers, Dorothy (1893–1957). English detective-story writer and author of books of Christian apologetics. Her sophisticated detective stories, with their urbane sleuth Lord Peter Wimsey, are popular among intellectuals: *Whose Body?* (1923), *Strong Poison* (1930), *The Nine Tailors* (1934), and many others. In later life she wrote plays, often religious, such as *The Man Born to Be King* (1942); books of amateur theology such as *Creed or Chaos* (1947); and translations of Dante (1949–1955).

Scaevola, Gaius Mucius. A legendary Roman youth who volunteered to assassinate Lars PORSENA when the latter besieged Rome (509 B.C.). Captured and asked for details of the plot, Scaevola refused to confess, and, in order to show that any attempt to force him to talk by torture would be vain, he thrust his right hand into the fire, holding it there until it was completely consumed. Lars Porsena thereupon released him and negotiated peace with Rome. He thereby earned the cognomen *Scaevola* (left-handed).

Scala, La. Opera house in Milan (1778), one of the largest and most important in the world.

scalds or **skalds.** Court poets and chroniclers of the ancient Scandinavians.

Scaligero, Giulio Cesare. Known as **Julius Caesar Scaliger** (1484–1558). Italian literary critic. He was born and spent his youth as soldier and student in northern Italy. In 1525, he moved to France as a physician and stayed there to become a leading advocate of the moralist approach to literature. His *Poetices* (1561), ostensibly a manual for writing Latin poetry, served to spread his critical ideas throughout Europe.

Scamander (Skamandros) or **Xanthos.** A river near the ancient city of Troy. It figures largely in the accounts of the TROJAN WAR.

scansion. In prosody, the term denoting the determination of the METER of a piece of poetry through the analysis, either written and detailed or done mentally in a general way, of the lines. The verb is "to scan," and any piece of writing or of speech can be scanned to determine its meter or its rhythm. Detailed scansion is accomplished by marking each syllable according to whether it is accented or not and analyzing the pattern of accents and nonaccents.

scapegoat. A sacrificial animal symbolically bearing the sins of a group. Part of the ancient ritual among the Hebrews for the DAY OF ATONEMENT laid down by Mosaic law (Lev. 16) was as follows: Two goats were brought to the altar of the tabernacle and the high priests cast lots, one for the Lord, the other for AZAZEL. The Lord's goat was sacrificed; the other was the *scapegoat*. After the high priest, by confession, had transferred his sins and the sins of the people to it, it was taken into the desert and allowed to escape.

The word has come to mean anyone who bears the blame for a group or another person.

Scapigliatura, La (Ital., "the disheveled ones"). An avant-garde literary circle that flourished in Milan c. 1860–1875. The name was coined by one of its founding members, Cletto Arrighi, pen name of Carlo Righetti (1830–1906), as an Italian equivalent of the "Bohème," the noted French circle of iconoclastic writers.

The Scapigliatura counted among its adherents Righetti; Arrigo BOITO; Giuseppe Rovani (1812–74), its chief exponent; Emilio PRAGA; and Iginio Ugo Tarchetti (1841–1869), "the Italian Edgar Allan Poe." These writers had a common objective in their declared war against the classical and Arcadian (see ARCADIAN ACADEMY) as well as against the moralistic traditions in Italian literature. They proposed Baudelaire and the budding school of French symbolists as models for Italian writers. Poe (known through Baudelaire's translations) was another model, as were Ernst Hoffmann and other German romantic writers of the bizarre and macabre.

The result of the Scapigliatura's antibourgeois, antitraditionalist stand was a fusion of interest in pathological characters, such as Tarchetti's *Fosca,* and a preference for realistic descriptions expressed in a direct, unaffected, and nonclassical language. VERGA, DE MARCHI, and CAPUANA were influenced by the Scapigliatura during their literary apprenticeships in Milan. The circle disbanded, having realized its *raison d'être,* when Capuana published his novel of psychological realism, *Giacinta* (1879), and Verga published his exemplar of realistic narrative, THE MALAVOGLIAS (1881).

Scapin. The central character in Molière's comedy *Les Fourberies de Scapin* (*The Rogueries of Scapin,* 1671). A clever and intrepid valet whose roguery provides the interest of the drama, he is the direct literary descendant of Scapino, the lively rascal who had long been one of the stock characters of the Italian stage. In Molière's comedy he is the valet of Léandre, son of Seignior Géronte. Léandre falls in love with Zerbinette, supposedly a gypsy, but in reality the daughter of Seignior Argante, stolen by gypsies in early childhood. Her brother Octave falls in love with Hyacinthe, whom he supposes to be Hyacinthe Pandolphe of Tarentum, but who turns out to be Hyacinthe Géronte, the sister of Léandre. The gypsies demand a large sum for the ransom of Zerbinette, and Octave requires sufficient money for his marriage with Hyacinthe. Scapin obtains both these sums from the respective fathers under false pretenses. At the end of the comedy he is brought into the wedding banquet on a litter, his head bound as though he were on the point of death. He begs forgiveness, which he readily obtains, and thereupon leaps up from the litter to join the banqueters.

Thomas Otway made an English version of this

play under the title *The Cheats of Scapin* (1677), in which Léandre is Anglicized into Leander, Géronte is called Gripe, and his friend Argante, the father of Zerbinette, becomes Thrifty, the father of Lucia.

Scaramuccia (*Fr.,* **Scaramouche**; *Eng.,* **Scaramouch**). A stock character of the Italian COMMEDIA DELL'ARTE. He is sometimes considered one of the *zanni,* or servants, though he may have more closely resembled the braggart soldier. The role was closely associated with Tiborio Fiorillo or Fiorilli (1608–1694), an Italian actor who often played in Paris.

Scarecrow, The (1908). A play by Percy MACKAYE. It is based on Hawthorne's *Feathertop,* the tale of a scarecrow brought to life. In the play the scarecrow becomes Lord Ravensbane, successfully woos Rachel Merton, and eventually chooses to die in order to save her from further grief. The play was made into the silent film *Puritan Passions* and was successfully revived on Broadway in 1953.

Scarlatti, Alessandro (1660–1725). Italian composer, the outstanding figure of the Late Baroque period in Italy. His many operas are an important milestone on the way to modern opera, and he also wrote over 600 cantatas for solo voices, as well as church music. His son **Domenico Scarlatti** (1685–1757), long resident in Spain, was a virtuoso harpsichordist and composer, famous for his sonatas for the harpsichord.

Scarlet, Will. One of the companions of ROBIN HOOD in the English Robin Hood ballad cycle. His name also occurs as Scadlock, Scarlock, and Scathlock. In one ballad he is the nephew of Robin Hood.

Scarlet Letter, The (1850). A novel by Nathaniel HAWTHORNE. Hester Prynne is condemned to wear the scarlet embroidered letter A on her breast, as punishment for her adultery. She resists all attempts of the 17th-century Boston clergy to make her reveal the name of her child's father. Her husband, an old physician who had remained in Europe, arrives in America to see her on the pillory. Assuming the name of Roger Chillingworth, he seeks revenge. Soon correctly suspecting the respected young minister, Arthur Dimmesdale, he constantly torments him without revealing the full extent of his knowledge. Pearl, the elfin child, is a constant trial to her mother; perverse, wild, an "outcast of the infantile world," she is the brilliant product of sin. Chillingworth succeeds in frustrating the escape of Hester, Arthur, and Pearl. In the final scene, the minister mounts the pillory with Hester and their child, revealing his guilt and the scarlet letter that remorse had etched on his breast. By this act he finally escapes Chillingworth's Satanic power, and dies in Hester's arms. The child, transfigured by the sorrowful scene, sheds tears for the first time. Kissing her father, she gives proof of her humanity.

The book treats Hawthorne's favorite themes. First, all men are guilty of secret sin. Secondly, greater than Dimmesdale's is Chillingworth's sin, for he has invaded the sanctity of another's soul.

Scarlet Pimpernel, The (1905). A novel by Baroness ORCZY. It is an adventure story of the French Revolution. The apparently foppish young Englishman, Sir Percy Blakeney, is found to be the daring Scarlet Pimpernel, rescuer of distressed aristocrats.

Scarlet Sister Mary (1928). A novel by Julia PETERKIN. The heroine of this realistic regional study is a Gullah Negro whose joyous spirit survives in spite of poverty, desertion, and nine children. Expelled from the church, she is readmitted after experiencing the death of her favorite son and seeing a vision of Christ's suffering. Written with insight and understanding, the book was awarded a Pulitzer Prize in 1929.

Scarlet Woman or **Scarlet Whore.** The woman seen by the author of the book of Revelations in his vision "arrayed in purple and scarlet color," sitting "upon a scarlet colored beast, full of names of blasphemy, having seven heads and ten horns," "drunken with the blood of the saints, and with the blood of the martyrs," upon whose forehead was written, "Mystery, Babylon the Great, the Mother of Harlots and Abominations of the Earth" (Rev. 17:1–6). The author was probably referring to Rome, which, at the time he was writing, was "drunken with the blood of the saints." Some Protestants have applied the words to the Church of Rome; and some Roman Catholics, to the Protestant churches generally.

Scarron, Paul (1610–1660). French novelist. His *Roman Comique* (*Comic Novel,* 1651), an account of a troupe of wandering comedians, is believed by scholars to be based upon the troupe of Molière. Scarron's realism and satire constituted a revolt against the artificial and excessively mannered writing of his time. Crippled by rheumatism at the age of 30, Scarron married Françoise d'Aubigné, who later became Mme de MAINTENON.

Scatterbrain, The. See ETOURDI, L'.

Scattergood Baines. See Clarence Budington KELLAND.

Scève, Maurice (1510?–1564?). French poet. The first of a group of French poets whose center was at Lyons, he wrote love poetry that reveals a profound spiritual uneasiness. His most famous collection of poems, the *Délie* (1544), betrays the Petrarchan influence—the conception of love progressing from the senses to pure idea. In fact, Scève was involved in the discovery of what was thought to be the tomb of Petrarch's Laura in Avignon (1543). His verse is marked by a subtle musicality which 19th-century SYMBOLISM was quick to appreciate. The symbolist poets brought Scève back into literary prominence after two centuries of neglect.

Schacht, Hjalmar (1877–1970). German financier. He was president of the Reichsbank for the Weimar Republic (1923–1930) and for the Nazis (1933–1939). Called the "financial wizard of the Third Reich," he was acquitted at the Nuremberg Trials.

Schahriah. In the *Arabian Nights,* the Sultan for whom the tales are told. When both his own wife and that of his brother prove unfaithful, Schahriah, imagining that no woman is virtuous, resolves to marry a new wife every night and have her strangled at daybreak. But SCHEHERAZADE, the Vizier's daughter, marries him in spite of his vow and contrives, an hour before daybreak, to begin a story to her sister, DINARZADE, in the Sultan's hearing, always breaking off before the story is finished. The Sultan grows interested in these tales and, after 1001 nights, revokes his decree, bestows his affection on

Scheherazade, and calls her the liberator of her sex.

Schauffler, Robert Haven (1879–). American poet and musical biographer. He is best known for the poem *Scum o' the Earth* (1912), a denunciation of race and religious prejudice. Other collections of his verse are *The White Comrade and Other Poems* (1920) and *The Magic Flame and Other Poems* (1923). He is also the author of *Music as a Social Force in America* (1927), *Beethoven—The Man Who Freed Music* (1929), and *The Unknown Brahms* (1933).

Scheffel, Joseph Viktor von (1826–1886). German popular novelist and poet, many of whose works are sentimentalizations of medieval themes. Examples are *Ekkehard* (1855), a novel, and *Frau Aventiure* (*Dame Adventure,* 1863), a collection of songs.

Scheffler, Johann. See Angelus Silesius.

Schéhadé, Georges (1910–). French dramatist and poet of Lebanese background. Schéhadé is known for the poetic, neo-surrealistic world of fairy tale and dream that characterizes his drama. The characters in such plays as *Monsieur Bob'le* (1951), *La Soirée des proverbes* (1954), *Histoire de Vasco* (1956), and *Les Violettes* (1960) seek desperately for innocence.

Scheherazade. The narrator of the tales of the *Arabian Nights* who tells her stories to her sister Dinarzade in the presence of her husband, the Sultan Schahriah, to keep him from strangling her at daybreak. The name is also the title of a famous orchestral suite by Rimsky-Korsakov, and a Fokine ballet, which is danced to its music.

Scheidemann, Philipp (1865–1939). German political leader. He declared Germany a republic after the abdication of Kaiser Wilhelm II (1918), and became its first prime minister (1918–1919).

Schelander, Jean de. See Tir et Sidon.

Schelling, Caroline, born **Michaelis** (1763–1809). Influential figure in German literary life during the period of romanticism. After the death of her first husband (1788), her erotic attachment to a French officer involved her in serious political trouble, from which she was rescued by August Wilhelm Schlegel, whom she then married in 1796. It is thought that she helped him with some of his essays on Shakespeare, and perhaps with his translations. Friedrich Schlegel was also deeply attached to her, and though he yielded to his brother, she clearly inspired many of his ideas on feminine emancipation. In 1803 she divorced A. W. Schlegel and was married, for the last time, to the young philosopher Schelling. Her letters later appeared in a collection entitled *Briefe aus der Frühromantik* (*Letters of Early Romanticism,* 1871) and offer many personal and literary insights into the romantic movement.

Schelling, Friedrich Wilhelm Joseph von (1775–1854). German philosopher and aesthetician of romanticism. His commitment to a pantheistic view of the universe is seen in his *Von der Weltseele* (*Of the World-Soul,* 1798) and *System des transcendentalen Idealismus* (*System of Transcendental Idealism,* 1800). He saw the universe as an organic, living whole that pervaded by a single spirit, and contended that "nature is visible spirit and spirit is invisible nature." He believed that the creative act of the artist is analogous to the act of world creation, since it comprehends both the material and spiritual aspects

of the world. Hegel and Hölderlin were both schoolmates and close friends of his, and all three shared the wish to see man and nature as parts of a single whole. See German romanticism.

Schickele, René (1883–1940). Alsatian novelist, poet, and playwright of French-German background, writing in German. He was noted especially for his advocation of a cultural unity between France and Germany. His best-known works are *Hans im Schnakenloch* (*Hans in the Mosquito-Hole,* 1915), a play, and *Das Erbe am Rhein* (*The Rhenish Heritage,* 1925–1931), a novel in three volumes.

Schiff, Sidney. See Stephen Hudson.

Schiller, [Johann Christoph] Friedrich von (1759–1805). German dramatist, poet, historian. From 1794 until his death, he was closely associated with Goethe, and the two authors, almost alone, led the movement known as Weimar classicism. The two men's tendencies, however were considerably different. Whereas Goethe's main strength was broad, epic development, always striving to comprehend the balanced wholeness of life, Schiller's talent lay in the treatment of fast-moving, dramatic action. He had more skill in creating and maintaining theatrical interest than Goethe did, and though his characters are often not as deep, they are usually more sharply defined than Goethe's.

Schiller's early prose plays are in the style of the Sturm und Drang, but tend to deal with more specific social problems than Goethe's early plays. The Robbers and Kabale und Liebe are examples. But after Don Carlos, the play in which this period culminated, Schiller began to have serious misgivings about the value of his writing and felt the need for a reappraisal of his aesthetic and philosophical principles. For the next decade he wrote no plays at all, and his most important writings were several treatises on aesthetics, all influenced by Kant, including: *Über Anmut und Würde* (*On Grace and Dignity,* 1793); *Briefe über die ästhetische Erziehung des Menschen* (*Letters on the Aesthetic Education of Man,* 1795), in which art is defined as the expression of a human play-drive, and its value seen in the cultivation of this drive; and On Naïve and Sentimental Poetry. These aesthetic writings provided the theoretical groundwork for his later dramatic style, which first appeared in Wallenstein. He had now given up much of his earlier unquestioning and tendentious idealism in favor of a more realistic, Goethean technique, which is also observable in Mary Stuart. But Schiller never entirely forsook his basic tendency toward idealism, and in fact took a strong turn back in that direction in his last plays, including The Maid of Orleans and Wilhelm Tell. These plays, however, are more polished and classical in form than his early *Sturm und Drang* works, and put more emphasis on general, moral ideas.

As a lyric poet, Schiller is more famous for his long didactic poems, including *Die Götter Griechenlands* (*The Gods of Greece,* 1788) and *Die Künstler* (*The Artists,* 1789). By profession Schiller was a historian and in 1791 was made a professor of history at the University of Jena. His most famous scholarly work is *Die Geschichte des Dreissigjährigen Krieges* (*History of the Thirty Years' War,* 1791).

Schism, the Great (1378–1417). The period when the Roman papacy was challenged by antipopes

who reigned at Avignon. THE COUNCIL OF CON-
STANCE (1414–1418), was responsible for its termination.

Schlaf, Johannes (1862–1941). German playwright and story-writer. He is known especially for
the works on which he collaborated with Arno HOLZ:
Papa Hamlet (1889), a collection of stories, and the
play *Die Familie Selicke* (*The Family Selicke*, 1890),
both of which are important in NATURALISM. Schlaf
showed his own talent, however, in the play *Meister
Oelze* (*Master Oelze*, 1892), which is a better work
than either of the collaborations.

Schlegel, August Wilhelm von (1767–1845); his
brother **Friedrich** (1772–1829). German romantic
poets and critics. August Wilhelm's poetry is of little
significance, but he was an extremely able critic and
scholar. His lectures at Berlin University, *Über schöne
Literatur und Kunst* (*On Literature and Art*, delivered 1801–1802), and those at Vienna, *Über dramatische Kunst und Literatur* (*On Dramatic Art and
Literature*, delivered 1807–1808), were instrumental
in formulating and publicizing the ideas of his fellow romantics. He also accompanied Madame de
Staël on her travels in Germany and many of her
ideas are borrowed from him. Among his other
works are translations of Calderón under the title
Spanisches Theater (1803), and translations of seventeen plays of Shakespeare (1797). His German *Shakespeare* was later continued by Tieck (1825) and is
still read today.

Friedrich Schlegel was a more original and creative
spirit than his brother, but often lacked the latter's
gift of stylistic clarity. He wrote hundreds of brilliant philosophical and critical aphorisms, which include many important statements about the romantic
movement. It was he who defined romantic poetry
as a "progressive universal poetry," and it was he
who first clearly defined the concept of romantic
IRONY. In his novel *Lucinde* (1799), he advocated
free love, but not on a purely sexual basis; he believed in full equality of the sexes and felt that a
man and a woman should not live together except
on terms of complete spiritual and sexual union. He
was a competent classical scholar and wrote a *Geschichte der alten und neuen Literatur* (*History of
Ancient and Modern Literature*, 1815). Among his
close friends were Novalis, Tieck, and Schleiermacher; like his brother, he was a lifelong admirer
of Goethe, but fell out with Schiller whom he attacked critically on occasion.

The two brothers together edited the romantic
periodical *Athenäum* (1798–1800). Central among the
ideas they held in common was a distinction between
classical (ancient) poetry as a "poetry of accomplishment," and romantic (modern) poetry as a "poetry
of yearning." Goethe makes a similar distinction in
Faust (see HELEN). The Schlegels are also credited
with a large part in the establishment of modern
literary critical techniques, in that they opposed the
18th-century ideal of the critic as a *judge* of art and
insisted that the critic must first of all *understand*
and *appreciate* the literary work on its own terms.
Both brothers, finally, were pioneers in the fields of
Romance philology and Sanskrit studies. See Caroline
SCHELLING; Dorothea VEIT; WEIMAR CLASSICISM; GER-
MAN ROMANTICISM.

Schlegel, Johann Elias (1718–1749). German
dramatist. Uncle of August Wilhelm and Friedrich
von Schlegel, he was an early admirer of Shakespeare
among the Germans and, though a student of Gottsched, his plays already show a tendency, which became very strong in Lessing, away from neo-classicism. Among his plays are *Hekuba* (1736) and
Orest (*Orestes*, 1739).

Schlegel, Margaret. The cultured, idealistic
heroine of E. M. Forster's novel HOWARDS END. Her
sister Helen is also an important character.

Schleicher, Kurt von (1882–1934). German
chancellor (1932–1933), succeeded by Hitler. He was
shot with his wife in a Nazi purge.

Schleiermacher, Friedrich Ernst Daniel (1768–
1834). German philosopher and Protestant theologian, important in the movement of ROMANTICISM.
In his *Reden über die Religion* (*Speeches on Religion*,
1799) and *Monologe* (*Monologues*, 1800), he developed the idea that every individual must establish an
entirely personal attitude toward religion. With his
friend Friedrich von Schlegel, he was a staunch advocate of equality between the sexes.

Schlemihl, Peter. See PETER SCHLEMIHLS WUN-
DERSAME GESCHICHTE.

Schlesinger, Arthur M[eier] (1888–1965). An
American historian. Schlesinger taught at Ohio State
and Iowa universities before joining the faculty of
Harvard University in 1924. His many important historical works include *The Colonial Merchants and the
American Revolution* (1918), *New Viewpoints in
American History* (1922), *The Rise of the City*
(1933), *Paths to the Present* (1949), and *Prelude to
Independence: The Newspaper War on Britain, 1764–
1776* (1958). *In Retrospect: The History of a Historian* (1963) is autobiographical.

Schlesinger, Arthur M[eier], Jr. (1917–   ).
American historian. The son and namesake of another
well-known historian, Schlesinger joined the faculty
of Harvard University in 1946. His best-known book
is probably *The Age of Jackson* (1945), for which
he was awarded a Pulitzer Prize; in it Schlesinger
maintained that the controlling beliefs and aims of
Jacksonianism came from the South and East, not
the West. He has also completed three parts of a
four-volume work on *The Age of Roosevelt: The
Crisis of the Old Order* (1957), *The Coming of the
New Deal* (1959), and *The Politics of Upheaval*
(1960). Schlesinger's other books include *Orestes A.
Brownson: A Pilgrim's Progress* (1939) and *The
Politics of Hope* (1960), essays written from the
liberal point of view. In 1961 Schlesinger was appointed special assistant to President Kennedy. In
1964, several months after Kennedy's assassination, he
resigned from his White House post to devote full
time to an account of the Kennedy administration.

Schliemann, Heinrich (1822–1890). A German
amateur archeologist famous for his excavations of
sites mentioned in Homer. He discovered the ruins
of a series of cities near the present Turkish village
of Hissarlik, though he guessed wrong as to which
of them was the Homeric Troy. He also did extensive
excavation at Mycenae. Though unscientific and even
careless in his approach, Schliemann made monumental discoveries, largely as a result of his belief,
then considered absurd, that the Homeric legends
were to a considerable degree historical fact.

Schloss, Das. See CASTLE, THE.

Schlumberger, Jean (1877–1968). French novelist and critic. Schlumberger is best known for the novel *Saint-Saturnin* (1931) and his essays in *Jalons* (1941) and *Nouveaux Jalons* (1943).

Schmidt, Kaspar. See MAX STIRNER.

Schmitz, Ettore. See Italo SVEVO.

Schnabel, Artur (1882–1951). Austrian pianist, teacher, and composer. Outstanding 20th-century interpreter of Beethoven's sonatas, of which he prepared a much-used edition. His compositions are in the atonal idiom of Schoenberg.

Schnitzler, Arthur (1862–1931). Austrian playwright and novelist. He is known for his stylistic experiments in both prose and drama and for his brilliance of psychological observation and depiction. Both of these qualities are found in his two best-known works, LEUTNANT GUSTL, a short novel, and LA RONDE, a play. His early play ANATOL is filled with characteristically Viennese wit and a vigorously amoral attitude toward erotic situations, which form the atmospheric background in many of his subsequent works. But though he continued to favor erotic themes, he became increasingly aware, in plays such as LIGHT o' LOVE and *Der grüne Kakadu* (*The Green Cockatoo,* 1899), of problems inherent in his early carefree attitude. Only once, in the play PROFESSOR BERNHARDI (1918), did he treat a completely nonsexual theme. Before turning to writing, Schnitzler had studied medicine and done research in psychiatry, which accounts in part for his ability to probe characters in depth.

Schoenberg, Arnold (1874–1951). Austrian-born composer and teacher. He is the inventor of the 12-tone or serial method of composition to provide a basis for unity and coherence in atonal music (see ATONALITY). His method and his music as well as his personal philosophy, which he expounded in many essays and several books such as *Style and Idea* (1950), have had a great impact on composers and musicians of many nations. Several of his students are major composers in their own right, among them Alban Berg, Anton von Webern, and Marc Blitzstein. When Thomas Mann described the 12-tone method in *Dr. Faustus,* Schoenberg demanded and received credit for his idea. The composer is also identified with the expressionism that affected various arts at the beginning of this century. His works include: *Verklärte Nacht* (1899; a tone poem based on *Zwei Menschen* by Richard Dehmel), *Pierrot Lunaire* (1912; 21 poems by Albert Giraud, in a German translation by O. E. Hartleben, for voice—in SPRECHSTIMME and instruments), *Suite for Piano* (1924, the first work based entirely on 12-tone techniques); *Ode to Napoleon* (1942, for speaker, strings, and piano; based on Lord Byron's poem).

Scholar-Gipsy, The (1853). A poem by Matthew ARNOLD. According to an old story current in Oxford, a student of that university, who years before wandered off to learn the gypsy traditions, still roams about. Arnold makes this lonely wanderer, whose life he regards as enviable in many ways, the hero of his poem.

Scholasticism (from *Lat.* schola, "school"). The philosophical system of the SCHOOLMEN of the Middle Ages. In schools first established under the Carolingians and usually attached to monasteries or cathedrals, the Schoolmen, as distinct from the practicing clergy, were involved in trying to synthesize a Christian system of logic and philosophy based on Aristotle and other ancient scholars. Their work was made even more difficult by the fact that very often the classical texts they had at their disposal were poor Latin translations from Arabic sources that were in turn dubious translations from the original Greek. Hampered by the Church's insistence that their results be reconcilable with Christian doctrine, the Schoolmen were often reduced to hair-splitting quibbles over methodology and terminology. Their most significant contribution to modern philosophy was their argument over the priority of essence or existence, which was the problem behind the opposition of NOMINALISM and REALISM. The climax of the first period (9th to 12th century) was reached in the work of Peter LOMBARD and Pierre ABÉLARD; the best of the second period was summarized by St. Thomas AQUINAS and John DUNS SCOTUS.

Schönherr, Karl (1867–1943). Austrian dramatist. He is best known for his peasant plays in the tradition of such writers as Raimund, Nestroy and Anzengruber. His two best works are *Erde* (*Earth,* 1908), about the unsuppressible vital energy of a mountain peasant, and *Glaube und Heimat* (*The Faith and the Homeland,* 1910), which also glorifies, in a historical setting, the strength and steadfastness of the common people. Schönherr was very attached to his native Tyrol and later, under the pressure of political and military events, brought out two frankly patriotic pieces: *Volk in Not* (*A People in Distress,* 1915) and *Der Judas von Tirol* (1928).

Schoolcraft, Henry Rowe (1793–1864). American ethnologist, explorer, geologist, and writer. After serving as geologist to the Lewis Cass expedition (1820) to Lake Superior, Schoolcraft was appointed Indian agent there. In 1832, he discovered the source of the Mississippi. Married to the daughter of a Chippewa chief, he gathered much of his Indian lore from his wife. As superintendent of Indian affairs for Michigan (1836–1841), he wrote his explorations and researches in a number of highly influential books. The first white man to translate Indian poetry, he was among the first seriously to study Indian legend and religion. Among Schoolcraft's books are *Travels in the Central Portions of the Mississippi Valley* (1825), *Algic Researches, Comprising Inquiries Respecting the Mental Characteristics of the North American Indians* (2 v., 1839), and *Personal Memoirs of a Residence of Thirty Years with the Indian Tribes* (1851). Schoolcraft's writings made a profound impression on Longfellow; repeating Schoolcraft's error, the poet confused the Iroquois Hiawatha with the Chippewa Manabozho, and set his famous verse narrative on the shores of Lake Superior, instead of in central New York.

School for Husbands, The. See SGANARELLE (2).

School for Scandal, The (1777). A comedy, one of the most popular in the English language, by Richard Brinsley SHERIDAN. Lady Sneerwell and a group of friends meet often at her house for the purpose of creating and spreading malicious gossip. Lady Teazle, attractive young wife of the much older Sir Peter, is a member of the circle. By making overtures to Lady Teazle, Joseph Surface, a hypocritical young man, tries to gain access to Maria, Sir Peter's ward. Although Maria is in love with Joseph's brother Charles, Sir Peter favors a match with Joseph. Joseph tells Lady Teazle that he is indifferent to Maria; after a quarrel with Sir Peter, Lady Teazle keeps an appointment at Joseph's rooms. Suddenly Sir Peter is announced, and Joseph hides Lady Teazle behind a screen. Sir Peter tells Joseph that he thinks his wife is in love with Charles and also speaks of the handsome settlement he intends to make on her. Overhearing this, Lady Teazle is full of remorse. Moments later Charles is shown in, and Sir Peter hides in a closet; he is thus able to hear Charles tell Joseph that his interest is entirely in Maria. Sir Peter comes out of hiding, and, while Joseph is called away, the screen topples, exposing a much chastened Lady Teazle. Meanwhile Sir Oliver Surface, wealthy uncle of Joseph and Charles, has returned from India with a plan to test the mettle of his nephews' characters. First, disguised as Mr. Premium, a usurer, he calls on Charles. Charles and his friends auction off the family portraits to Premium, but Charles refuses to sell the portrait of his Uncle Oliver. He sends some of the money to Stanley, an old relative who has asked him for assistance. Uncle Oliver, pretending to be Stanley, then calls on Joseph to ask for assistance and is refused; Joseph tells him that he can't help him because Uncle Oliver is so stingy. Joseph's duplicity is brought to light; Sir Peter and Lady Teazle are reconciled, and Maria and Charles are united.

School for Wives. See Ecole des Femmes, L'.

Schoolmaster, The. A celebrated treatise by Roger Ascham (1570), expressing the author's ideas on the education of the English youth of his time. It opposes foreign schooling, especially in Italy, favors the incorporation of athletics into the curriculum, and attacks English verse meter, while defending the use of English prose.

Schoolmen. The theologians of the Middle Ages. They lectured in the cloisters or cathedral schools founded by Charlemagne and his successors. They followed Aristotle and the Fathers of the Church (see Scholasticism), but attempted to reduce every subject to a system.

Schoolmistress, The. A poem by William Shenstone, written in Spenserian stanzas. It presents a burlesque picture of a village school of the author's time and of the elderly mistress who teaches and punishes her pupils.

School of Abuse, The. A Puritan treatise by Stephen Gosson (English, 1554–1634), written in 1579, attacking poets, actors, and playwrights on moral grounds. It was dedicated without authorization to Sir Philip Sidney, who answered it in his famous Apologie for Poetrie.

School of Silence. See Jean Jacques Bernard.

Schopenhauer, Arthur (1788–1860). German philosopher whose extreme pessimism is expressed in *The World as Will and Idea* (*Die Welt als Wille und Vorstellung;* 1819). He maintained that the desires and drives of men, as well as the forces of nature, are manifestations of a single will, specifically the will to live, which is the essence of the world. Since operation of the will means constant striving without satisfaction, life consists of suffer-

ing. Only by controlling the will through the intellect, by suppressing the desire to reproduce, can suffering be diminished.

Schorer, Mark (1908–   ). American novelist and critic. His fiction includes *A House Too Old* (1935) and *The Wars of Love* (1954), both novels, and *The State of Mind* (1946), a collection of short stories. He also wrote *William Blake: The Politics of Vision* (1946) and *Sinclair Lewis: An American Life* (1961).

Schreiner, Olive. Pen name **Ralph Iron** (1855–1920). South African novelist. Her best-known work is her semiautobiographical novel The Story of an African Farm. Although almost entirely uneducated, she was a fervent rationalist, feminist, and extreme liberal. Most of her later books were concerned with such problems as *The South African Question* (1899) and *Woman and Labor* (1911). Her other works include *Dreams* (1891), *Trooper Peter Halkett of Mashonaland* (1897), and The Story of an African Farm.

Schubert, Franz [Peter] (1797–1828). Austrian composer. Schubert was perhaps the finest composer of art songs the world has known; his catalogued works number nearly a thousand, of which nearly 600 are songs with piano. His favored poets were Goethe and Schiller, but he also set Shakespeare and Sir Walter Scott. He wrote much piano and chamber music, six masses, other church music, operas, and eight symphonies, of which No. 7, the "Great Symphony" in C major, and No. 8, "The Unfinished Symphony" in B minor, are the most remarkable.

Schulberg, Budd (1914–   ). American short-story writer and novelist. The son of a leading film producer, Schulberg first published a satirical study of a Hollywood mogul, What Makes Sammy Run? His next novel was *The Harder They Fall* (1947), the story of a prizefighter. The Disenchanted is a *roman à clef* based on F. Scott Fitzgerald's career. Schulberg's short stories were collected in *Faces in the Crowd* (1953), and he wrote the screenplay *On the Waterfront* (1954), published as a novel in 1955.

Schumann, Robert (1810–1856). German composer, pianist, and music critic, a representative and leader of the romantic school. Among his works are highly imaginative song cycles based on poems by Heine (*Dichterliebe*), Chamisso (*Frauenliebe und Leben*), and others, four symphonies, one piano concerto, and many sets of piano pieces with titles such as *Papillons* (*Butterflies*), *Carnaval*, *Kinderscenen* (*Scenes from Childhood*), and *Nachtstücke* (*Nightpieces*). He founded, in 1833, and edited the *Neue Zeitschrift für Musik* (*New Chronicle of Music*). His wife, **Clara Schumann,** born **Wieck** (1819–1896), was a fine pianist and a masterly interpreter of her husband's works. Schumann's last years were darkened by mental illness.

Schumann-Heink, Ernestine (1861–1936). German operatic contralto. She sang much in the U.S., and originated the role of Clytemnestra in Richard Strauss's opera *Elektra* (1909).

Schuschnigg, Kurt von (1897–   ). Chancellor of Austria (1934–1938), successor to Engelbert Dollfuss. When Germany invaded Austria, he was replaced by Seyss-Inquart and put in a concentration camp.

Schütz, Heinrich (1585–1672). Outstanding German composer of the 17th century. A pupil in Italy of Giovanni Gabrieli and Claudio Monteverdi, he introduced many of the new practices of Baroque music to Germany. He wrote the first German opera, *Dafne* (1627, music lost), but he is best known for his masterly setting of German Bible texts for use in services of the Lutheran Church.

Schutzstaffel. See S.S.

Schwab, Gustav (1792–1850). German poet, known for his ballads. His friends included Uhland and Kerner, and like theirs, his poetry shows traits of both romanticism and the Biedermeier style. His *Die schönsten Sagen des klassischen Altertums* (*The Most Beautiful Legends of Classical Antiquity*, 1838) was an attempt to popularize classical myths.

Schwartz, Delmore (1913–1966). American poet, short-story writer, and critic. Among Schwartz's collections of verse are *In Dreams Begin Responsibilities* (1938), *Genesis* (1943), *Vaudeville for a Princess* (1950), and *Summer Knowledge* (1959). He has translated Rimbaud's *A Season in Hell* (1939). *The World Is a Wedding* (1948) is a collection of his short stories, many of them dealing with the problems of Jewish life.

Schwarz-Bart, André (1928–   ). French novelist. His semihistorical *The Last of the Just* (*Les Derniers des Justes;* 1959) traces the martyrdom of the Jews through 36 generations of the Levy family, culminating with the death of Ernie in the Auschwitz German prison camp. *The Last of the Just* was awarded the Prix Goncourt in 1959.

Schwarzerd, Philipp. See MELANCHTHON.

Schweitzer, Albert (1875–1965). Alsatian philosopher, musician, theologian, and medical missionary. At 18 he began to study music in Paris with C. M. Widor, with whom he later edited the organ music of J. S. Bach. From the University of Strasbourg he received a Ph.D. in 1899, a Licentiate in Theology in 1900, and a doctorate in medicine in 1913. That same year he founded a medical mission at Lambaréné, Gabon (then French Equatorial Africa). Except for a few lecture and concert trips, he devoted his life to the mission.

His philosophy expounds what he called "reverence for life." It is an ethical system based on the mutual respect of all living things and calls for the fullest development of human resources.

Among his works are *Philosophy of Civilization* (1923), *The Quest of the Historical Jesus* (1906), *Out of My Life and Thoughts* (1932). He was awarded the 1952 Nobel Peace Prize.

science fiction. A genre of fantasy. It has its basis either in scientific fact or in a plausible kind of pseudo-science. The first significant science fiction writer was Jules VERNE, although Edgar Allan Poe had experimented with scientific fantasy in *The Unparalleled Adventure of Hans Pfall* and *The Narrative of Arthur Gordon Pym.*

The genre did not become widely popular until the 1940's and 1950's, when books and magazines devoted to it proliferated in the United States. A number of writers have made their reputation largely in this field, some of them having been scientists in their own right. Well known among these names are Isaac Asimov, Ray Bradbury, Robert A. Heinlein, and Theodore Sturgeon.

Scio. Another name for CHIOS.

Scipio Africanus, Publius Cornelius. Known as **Scipio the Elder** (237–183 B.C.). Roman general and politician. His successful invasion of Carthage in the Second PUNIC WAR caused the Carthaginians to recall HANNIBAL from Italy. Scipio decisively defeated Hannibal at Zama (202 B.C.).

Sciron (Skeiron). A robber of Greek legend. He was slain by THESEUS. He infested the parts about Megara, and forced travelers over the rocks into the sea, where they were devoured by a giant turtle. It was from these cliffs (known as the Scironian rocks) that INO cast herself into the Corinthian bay.

Scobellum. A very fruitful land mentioned in the SEVEN CHAMPIONS OF CHRISTENDOM. Its inhabitants were notorious for indulging in "a generality of vices." The gods punished them by transforming drunkards into swine, lechers into goats, scolds into magpies; i.e., into the animals that typify the vices.

Scobie. (1) In Graham Greene's novel THE HEART OF THE MATTER, the hero who is torn between love and religious duty.

(2) In Lawrence Durrell's novels THE ALEXANDRIA QUARTET, a comic old homosexual sailor.

Scogan's Jests. A popular jest book in the 16th century. It was said by Andrew Boorde (who published it) to be the work of John Scogan (sometimes called "Scoggin"), reputed to have been court fool to Edward IV. He is referred to anachronously, by Justice Shallow in 2 *Henry IV*, iii, 2.

Scopes trial (July, 1925). A court trial in Dayton, Tenn., in which John Scopes, a high school biology teacher, was found guilty of violating a state law that forbade teaching the theory of evolution. Clarence Darrow defended Scopes, and William Jennings Bryan directed the prosecution. Although Scopes was convicted, Bryan's was a Pyrrhic victory; taking the stand as an expert on the Bible, he was subjected to relentless cross-examination by Darrow, who ridiculed his simple fundamentalist creed; Bryan died five days after the trial. H. L. Mencken reported the "monkey" trial in some famous sardonic dispatches. The trial was the basis of the play *Inherit the Wind* (1955) by Jerome Lawrence and Robert E. Lee.

Scot or Scott, Michael (1175?–1234). Scottish-born medieval scholar. After studying at the universities of Oxford, Paris, and Toledo, he became attached to the court of Frederick II of Sicily; there he served as physician and astrologer and, with others, translated the works of Aristotle and Averroës into Latin. Famed for his occult learning, even in his own lifetime he was said to possess miraculous powers; and after his death this reputation spread, and he became known as a wizard and magician. He is mentioned by Dante in the *Inferno* and by Sir Walter Scott in *The Lay of the Last Minstrel.*

Scotia. Scotland; sometimes called Scotia Minor. According to the Venerable Bede, Scotland was called Caledonia until A.D. 258, when it was invaded by a tribe from Ireland and its name changed to Scotia.

Scotism or Scotists. See John DUNS SCOTUS.

Scotland Yard. The headquarters of the London Metropolitan Police. From this office all public orders to the force proceed. The original Scotland Yard was a short street near Trafalgar Square, so called from a palace on the spot, given by King Edgar (about 970) to Kenneth II of Scotland when he came to

London to pay homage and subsequently used by the Scottish kings when visiting England. New Scotland Yard, as it is officially called, is close by, on the Thames Embankment near Westminster Bridge.

Scots, Wha Hae (1794). A patriotic poem by Robert BURNS, celebrating the victory of Robert Bruce over the English King Edward II at the Battle of Bannockburn in 1314, and hailing liberty and independence for the Scottish nation. It is believed that Burns was strongly influenced in the writing of this poem by the French Revolution.

Scott, Dred. See DRED SCOTT DECISION.

Scott, Duncan Campbell (1862–1947). Canadian poet. He is best known for his poems about man's conflict with nature and about the Indians, to whom he devoted most of his professional life in the Canadian Civil Service. His *Complete Poems* appeared in 1926.

Scott, F[rancis] R[eginald] (1899–). Canadian poet. During the 1920's Scott was a member of the "Montreal school," a group of poets influenced by T. S. Eliot, and was instrumental in the publication of *New Provinces: Poems of Several Authors* (1936), which included some of his own experimental work, along with that of five other modernist poets. Later he was one of the editors of *Preview*, an experimental literary magazine. Scott's poetry is often witty and amusing, as when he pokes fun at Canadian poetic movements in *The Canadian Authors Meet;* elsewhere, however, he reveals a profound concern with social problems.

Scott, Geoffrey (1886–1928). English scholar. His study of *The Architecture of Humanism* (1914) was influential in reviving interest in the BAROQUE.

Scott, Michael (1789–1835). Scottish novelist. He wrote *Tom Cringle's Log*, a lively, colorful account of life in the West Indies in the early 19th century, and the slightly less effective *The Cruise of the Midge*. Both novels were published anonymously in 1836, after appearing in installments (from 1829) in *Blackwood's Magazine.*

Scott, Robert Falcon (1868–1912). An English antarctic explorer. He perished with his party on the return trip from the South Pole in 1912. The searching party found his records and diaries.

Scott, Sir Walter (1771–1832). Scottish novelist and poet of the romantic period. Deriving most of his material from Scottish history and legend, and influenced by medieval French romance, popular ballads, and the Gothic novel, he wrote narrative poetry at first; but when overshadowed in this field by Byron, he turned to the novel. His great achievement here lay in his exploitation of history as material for the novel, and with WAVERLEY he began the long series of works which proved him the master of the historical novel. In these romances he displays an arresting ability to recreate the atmosphere of an age in all its pageantry and detail. He was a skillful portrayer of character; his most brilliant figures are generally eccentric Scottish peasants, but his romantic lovers, usually aristocratic, tend to be somewhat uninteresting. His novels are written with an immense vigor, and achieved for him a vast public in England and on the Continent, where he strongly influenced Balzac and Tolstoy. Although by far the most popular novelist of his day, he has lost favor of late, partly because of the improbability of his plots, which he

admitted to turn on "marvellous and uncommon incidents," and partly because his romanticism now seems rather cloying.

His more notable poetic works include THE EVE OF SAINT JOHN; *Minstrelsy of the Scottish Border* (1802–1803), a collection of ancient Scottish ballads; THE LAY OF THE LAST MINSTREL; MARMION; and THE LADY OF THE LAKE. The best known of his novels are *Waverley,* GUY MANNERING, THE ANTIQUARY, OLD MORTALITY, THE BLACK DWARF, THE HEART OF MIDLOTHIAN, ROB ROY, THE BRIDE OF LAMMERMOOR, THE LEGEND OF MONTROSE, IVANHOE, THE MONASTERY, THE ABBOT, KENILWORTH, *The Pirate* (1822), THE FORTUNES OF NIGEL, PEVERIL OF THE PEAK, QUENTIN DURWARD, REDGAUNTLET, *The Betrothed* (1825), THE TALISMAN, WOODSTOCK, THE FAIR MAID OF PERTH, ANNE OF GEIERSTEIN, CASTLE DANGEROUS, and *Tales of a Grandfather* (1828–30).

Scott also wrote several dramatic works and a number of studies in biography and in the history, legends, and antiquities of Scotland. He contributed some articles to the *Encyclopædia Britannica* and also had a part in the foundation of the *Quarterly Review.*

As his fortune increased he built the baronial mansion of Abbotsford on the banks of the Tweed. In 1813 he refused the laureateship in favor of Southey. He was almost ruined when the publishing firm of Ballantyne, in which he was a partner, went into bankruptcy in 1826, and spent the rest of his life working to pay off the debts.

Scott was known to the readers of his day as The Wizard of the North. See WAVERLEY NOVELS.

Scott, William Bell (1811–1890). Scottish poet and painter, friend of Rossetti and Swinburne. Many of his best short lyrics and sonnets appear in the collection, *Poems* (1875). He was also the author of *Autobiographical Notes* (1892).

Scott, Winfield Townley (1910–1968). American poet. Scott worked for a number of years as a newspaperman and has taught at Bard College. In his poetry he often deals with New England characters and ideas, as in *Elegy for Robinson* (1936) and *Mr. Whittier and Other Poems* (1948). His poetry tends to be formally loose and is occasionally colloquial or autobiographical. Other collections are *Biography for Traman* (1937), *Wind the Clock* (1941), *The Sword on the Table* (1942), *To Marry Strangers* (1945), and *Collected Poems: 1937–1962* (1962). *The Dark Sister* (1958) is an epic of the Viking explorations in North America.

Scottish Chaucerians. A term applied to a group of Scottish poets in the late 15th and early 16th centuries who wrote in the tradition of Geoffrey CHAUCER. They are considered by critics to have written the best lyric poetry of their time. Gawain DOUGLAS, William DUNBAR, and Robert HENRYSON were the leaders of the Scottish Chaucerians.

Scottish Renaissance. A 20th-century revival of Scottish literature, chiefly poetry. It is characterized by its use of Scottish themes and usually written in the Scottish poetic dialect of LALLANS. The movement originated in the KAILYARD tradition of the 19th century. Its leading figure is the poet Hugh MACDIARMID; other poets associated with it are William Soutar, Robert Garioch, Douglas Young, and Sidney Goodsir Smith. James Leslie MITCHELL was a novelist of the Scottish Renaissance.

Scotus Erigena, Johannes (9th century). Christian theologian and philosopher, probably born in Ireland of Scottish parents. He came to the court of the Carolingian emperor Charles II before 847, directed the palace school, and greatly influenced later scholasticism. He wrote a treatise on predestination (c. 851) asserting the fundamental identity of philosophy and religion, and freedom of the will in both God and man; he was soon under attack for lack of orthodoxy. His translation, with commentary (c. 858), of the neo-Platonic treatise *On the Heavenly Hierarchy,* by Dionysius the Areopagite, was similarly controversial, although important in the development of medieval mysticism. His major work, the *Divisions of Nature (De Divisione Naturae,* c. 865–870), is also neo-Platonic, establishing God as the supreme intellect through whose will archetypal ideas are made manifest as created things; but it was attacked for pantheism because it made Nature the totality of all things and forces, whether creating or created, or both or neither.

Scotus, John Duns. See John DUNS SCOTUS.

Scourge of God. Epithet for Attila (406?–453), king of the Huns. He was so called by medieval writers because of the widespread havoc and destruction caused by his armies. The term was also applied to Genseric, king of the Vandals (d. 477), and to Tamerlane.

Scout, The (1854). A novel by William Gilmore SIMMS. Originally issued as *The Kinsmen* (1841), the novel is set against the background of the American Revolution and deals with the struggles of two half brothers in war and love.

Screwtape Letters, The (1942). A popular work on Christian moral and theological problems by C. S. LEWIS. It is in the form of a series of letters in which a devil, Screwtape, advises his nephew, Wormwood, on how to deal with his human "patients."

Scriabin[e], Alexander Nikolayevitch (1872–1915). Russian composer. His mysticism led to experiments with synesthesia and dissonance. His best-known works are *The Poem of Ecstasy* (1908) and *Prometheus (The Poem of Fire;* 1911).

Scribe, Augustin Eugène (1791–1861). French dramatist. Scribe, a prolific and popular playwright, wrote nearly 400 plays, many in collaboration with other writers. Gay, spirited comedies of manners, his dramas were constructed with skill but had little substance. Almost devoid of characterization, they depended on farcical plots. Among his most successful comic efforts were *Le Mariage de raison* (1826), *Le Mariage d'argent* (1828), *Le Camaraderie ou la courte échelle* (1837) and *Une Chaîne* (1841). He is known also for his many opera libretti.

Scriblerus, Martinus. A fictional character created by the SCRIBLERUS CLUB as a satire on pedantry and false taste. Martin, the son of Cornelius Scriblerus, has read everything but without discernment or taste. Supposedly, he is the author of Alexander Pope's *Peri Bathous, or the Art of Sinking in Poetry* (1727), a mock treatise on rhetoric satirizing the aesthetic theories of Longinus; of the *Origine of Sciences* (1732), ironically deriving modern learning from the ancient pygmies; and of *The Memoirs of the Extraordinary Life, Works, and Discoveries of Martinus Scriblerus,* a burlesque which was first printed in Pope's second volume of prose works (1741), but which was largely written by John Arbuthnot in 1714, in the heydey of the Scriblerus Club.

Scriblerus Club. An association formed in 1714 by John ARBUTHNOT, Alexander Pope, Jonathan Swift, John Gay, Thomas Parnell, and Robert Harley, earl of Oxford. The group met in Arbuthnot's apartments in St. James's Palace. Arbuthnot and Pope were the principal instigators of this project to combat pedantry and the abuses of learning. Although meetings ceased within the year, the spirit of Scriblerus lived on, kept alive by Pope's correspondence. Pope's DUNCIAD and the third book of Swift's GULLIVER'S TRAVELS are the most important works which sprang from this association. See Martinus SCRIBLERUS.

Scrooge, Ebenezer. See CHRISTMAS CAROL, A.

Scrutiny (1932–1953). An English literary review edited in Cambridge, England, by F. R. LEAVIS. It expressed the critical ideas of Leavis himself and of the CAMBRIDGE CRITICS.

Scudamore. See FAERIE QUEENE, THE.

Scudder, Horace Elisha (1838–1902). American editor and writer. Scudder described his happy and pious home in a book about his older brother, *Life and Letters of David Coit Scudder, a Missionary in Southern India* (1864). He graduated from Williams College and went to New York, where he taught private pupils and wrote two books for children, *Seven Little People and Their Friends* (1862) and *Dream Children* (1864). He joined Henry O. Houghton's publishing firm (later Houghton Mifflin), serving as literary editor. From 1890 to 1898, he was editor of *The Atlantic Monthly.* Scudder did more than any other individual to raise the standards of literature for children, through his own writings and through his editorial work. When the *Riverside Magazine for Young People* was started in 1867, he contributed stories and enlisted the aid of such distinguished writers as Hans Christian Andersen, Jacob Abbott, Frank R. Stockton, and Sarah Orne Jewett. As editor, he planned the "American Commonwealth Series" and the "Riverside Literature Series." He wrote the *Bodley Books* (1875–1887), popular juvenile books of travel; *Childhood in Literature and Art* (1894); and biographies of Noah Webster (1882), George Washington (1890), and James Russell Lowell (1901).

Scudéry, Madeleine de (1607–1701). French novelist. She was also known as Sapho, the name she gave herself in *Artamène, ou le Grand Cyrus* (10 vols.; 1649–1653). This novel and CLÉLIE, HISTOIRE ROMAINE intermix adventurous historical narrative with portraits of contemporary society, friends, and even the author herself in Persian, Greek, and Roman disguise, and abound in conversations expressing the author's opinion on a variety of practical subjects (see Anne LENCLOS). Scudéry is considered to have brought the sentimental romance to the height of its popularity with her enormous novels, which include *Ibrahim, ou l'Illustre Bassa,* the first *roman à clef* (1641) and *Almahide, ou l'Esclave Reine (Almahide, or the Slave as Queen,* 1660–1663). She and her brother, the dramatist Georges de Scudéry, were associated with the Hotel de Rambouillet, and her elaborate salons with their competitions in *précieux* gallantry were satirized in Molière's *Les Précieuses Ridicules.*

Scylla (**Skylla**). In Greek legend, a daughter of King Nisus of Megara. The daughter of Nisus promised to deliver Megara into the hands of her lover MINOS and, to effect this, cut off a golden hair on her father's head while he was asleep. Minos despised her for this treachery and Scylla threw herself from a rock into the sea. At death she was changed into a lark and Nisus into a hawk.

Scylla (**Skylla**) **and Charybdis.** In Greek mythology, two monsters. They endangered shipping through the narrow Straits of Messina between Italy and Sicily. Scylla, a female monster with twelve feet, six heads, each on a long neck and each armed with three rows of pointed teeth, barked like a dog as she sat on her rock on the Italian side of the straits. Homer called her a daughter of Crataeis, but later accounts make her a nymph who, because she was beloved by Glaucus, was changed by the jealous Circe into a monster. Across the straits, Charybdis supposedly lived under an immense fig tree; thrice every day he swallowed the waters of the sea and thrice threw them up again. In post-Homeric legends he is said to have stolen the oxen of Hercules, been killed by lightning, and changed into the whirlpool that bears his name.

The phrase "between Scylla and Charybdis" came to mean between two equal difficulties, between the devil and the deep sea. Horace says that an author trying to avoid Scylla drifts into Charybdis: i.e., in seeking to avoid one fault, he falls into another.

sea deities. In classical myth, besides the 50 Nereids, the Oceanides (daughters of OCEANUS), the Sirens, etc., a number of deities presiding over or connected with the sea. The chief of these are:

AMPHITRITE, wife of Poseidon, queen goddess of the sea.

GLAUCUS, a fisherman of Boeotia, afterward a marine deity.

INO, who threw herself from a rock into the sea, and was made a sea-goddess.

NEREUS and his wife DORIS. Their palace was at the bottom of the Mediterranean; his hair was seaweed.

OCEANUS and his wife TETHYS (daughter of Uranus and Ge). Oceanus was god of the ocean, which formed a boundary round the world.

PORTUMINUS, the protector of harbors.

POSEIDON, the chief sea god.

PROTEUS, who assumed every variety of shape.

THETIS, a daughter of Nereus and mother of Achilles.

TRITON, son of Poseidon.

Seafarer, The (8th century). Old English poem of about 100 lines in ALLITERATIVE VERSE. It speaks alternately of the joys and the sorrows of life at sea, then compares the pleasures of earth to those of heaven.

Sea Gull, The (**Chaika;** 1896). A play by Anton CHEKHOV. A four-act work, it established Chekhov as a major dramatist and was one of the first successful productions of the Moscow ART THEATRE. Two years earlier, the play had been presented in St. Petersburg with such poor results that Chekhov nearly abandoned writing for the stage. The plot deals with young Konstantin Gavrilovich Trepliov, his literary ambitions, and his love for Nina Mikhailovna Zarechnaya, a girl who aspires to become a great actress. Trepliov's hopes for literary greatness suffer a setback when a private performance of his play proves to be a failure, arousing mostly laughter from his audience. He fears that Nina has lost her love and respect for him, and is angered at her attentions to Trigorin, a well-known writer who has been a lover of Trepliov's mother, Irina Nikolayevna Arkadina. Trepliov in his despair kills a gull at the lake and places it at Nina's feet as a symbol of his ruined hopes. Nina leaves with Trigorin, after the stricken Trepliov has made an unsuccessful suicide attempt. Two years pass, during which Trepliov finally achieves his aim of becoming a capable writer. Nina returns, having been cast aside by Trigorin. In a semicoherent speech, she compares herself to the gull destroyed by a man's mere momentary whim. Nina leaves, and Trepliov, with his old griefs stirred once more, succeeds in his second suicide attempt.

Sealsfield, Charles. Pen name of **Karl Postl** (1793–1864). German author. His travel books, which were very popular, include the *Transatlantische Reiseskizzen* (*Transatlantic Travel-Sketches,* 1834), about his experiences (1823–1832) in the U.S. He also wrote a famous attack on Metternich in English, *Austria as It Is* (1828).

Seaman, Elizabeth Cochrane. Pen name, **Nelly Bly** (1867–1922). American journalist. As a muck-raker for the New York *World*, she had herself committed to the city's insane asylum on Blackwell's Island, and her account of the horrifying conditions there resulted in great improvements. Her most famous feat (1889) was her round-the-world trip in 72 days, 6 hours, 11 minutes, a record beating that of Jules Verne's hero in *Around the World in Eighty Days* (1873).

Seami Motokiyo (1363–1443). Japanese NŌ dramatist, author of numerous plays, many of which are still performed today. He was also a critic and the establisher of the aesthetic standards under which the plays are performed.

Search for Truth, The. See Nicolas MALEBRANCHE.

Seasons, The (1726–1730). A descriptive poem in blank verse by James THOMSON, in four parts—*Winter* (1726), *Summer* (1727), *Spring* (1728), *Autumn* (1730). The poem reflects the author's main convictions: his belief in progress, his fascination with the ideal of the Golden Age, his deistic views, and, above all, his sense of a universe ordered by divine harmony and reason. The poem contains the love episodes of Celadon and Amelia, Damon and Musidora, and PALEMON and LAVINIA.

Sea Wolf, The (1904). A novel by Jack LONDON. The ruthless power of Wolf Larsen, captain of the schooner *Ghost*, is challenged by Humphrey Van Weyden, a literary critic, and Maude Brewster, a poet, both of whom he has rescued. Later, when the three are wrecked on a deserted island, Maude and Van Weyden manage to escape to civilization, while Larsen dies, blind but still indomitable.

Sebastian. (1) The twin brother of Viola in Shakespeare's TWELFTH NIGHT. He is mistaken for Viola, who has assumed male disguise, and led off to the altar by the infatuated Olivia.

(2) The weak-willed but ambitious brother of Alonso, the king of Naples, in Shakespeare's THE TEMPEST. Prodded by the evil Antonio, he makes a

feeble attempt to assassinate his brother, but is stopped in time by Ariel.

Sebastian, St. Patron saint of archers. He was bound to a tree and shot at with arrows. Because the arrows stuck in his body as thickly as pins in a pincushion, he was also made patron saint of pinmakers. And as he was a centurion, he is patron saint of soldiers.

Sebastian, Dom (1554–1578). King of Portugal. Sebastian, who became king in 1557 upon the death of his grandfather, John III, dreamed of spreading Christianity to Asia and Africa and of winning new dominions for the crown of Portugal. Becoming involved in a civil war between rival claimants to the throne of Fez and Morocco, he was slain at the battle of Alcázarquivir. Because his body could not be identified with certainty, it was widely believed that he had merely been taken prisoner and that he would one day return to the throne. He was the subject of numerous literary works, notably Calderón's drama *El príncipe constante*, Dryden's tragicomedy *Don Sebastian* (1691), and Zorrilla's play *Traidor, inconfeso y mártir* (1849).

Second Empire. The reign of Emperor Napoleon III of France (1852–1870).

Second Mrs. Tanqueray, The (1893). A play by Arthur Wing PINERO, one of his most successful works. Paula, the titular heroine, is a woman "with a past" and in spite of Aubrey Tanqueray's hopes and efforts, is not very cordially accepted by his friends or by his 19-year-old daughter, Ellean. Ellean goes to Paris with a friend and there becomes engaged to Captain Ardale, a former lover of Paula. Paula tells Aubrey, who then forbids Ellean to see Ardale again. Ellean suspects Paula of ruining her love, and tells her that she always knew what kind of a woman she was. In the end Paula kills herself.

Second Nun's Tale, The. One of the CANTERBURY TALES of Geoffrey CHAUCER. Although written in 1373 before he thought of the plan for the *Tales*, it was included. It is an adaptation in RHYME ROYAL of the life of Saint CECILIA as told by medieval Latin sources. Cecilia, born of Roman nobility and raised a Christian, warns her bridegroom Valerian that an angel guards her at all times. Valerian goes to Saint Urban to be christened and finds on his return that he can see the angel, who gives Cecilia a crown of roses and him a crown of lilies, adjuring them to live a pure life. Cecilia also converts Valerian's brother Tiburtius, and they all perform many miracles. The pagan Almachius tries to make them sacrifice to Jupiter, but they refuse and are killed. Cecilia is the last; the executioner strikes her three times in the neck while she is in her bath, but she continues to preach and convert for three days. Saint Urban buries her body when she dies.

Second Sex, The. See Simone de BEAUVOIR.

Second Shepherd's Play, The (Secunda Pagina Pastorum). A medieval English miracle play, written at the end of the 14th century or the beginning of the 15th, and considered to have been from the hand of the WAKEFIELD MASTER. It deals with the Nativity in a vein of rollicking, farcical, almost burlesque realism, in terms of country life in Yorkshire at the time of the play's composition. It is the second in the Towneley cycle of plays to present the Adoration of the shepherds at Christ's Nativity, but

its success is due to the long, lively prefatory episode about the exposure of Mak the sheep-stealer, who pretends that a stolen sheep concealed in a cradle is his wife's new-born baby.

Secret Agent, The (1907). A novel by Joseph CONRAD. Set in a London back street, amid a group of anarchists, it is the story of Verloc, an agent-provocateur. He persuades his stupid, trusting brother-in-law Stevie to blow up the Greenwich Observatory. When Stevie blows himself up in the attempt, Verloc's wife, Winnie, who was devoted to her brother, kills Verloc. After a revolutionary steals her money while helping her to escape, she commits suicide.

Secrets de la Princesse de Cadignan, Les (1839). A novel by Honoré de BALZAC. The heroine is Diane de Cadignan, previously the duchess of Maufrigneuse. One of Balzac's most heartless and brilliant women, the princess is the mistress of many of the men who appear in the novels of LA COMÉDIE HUMAINE.

Secret Sharer, The (1912). A short story by Joseph CONRAD. A young captain takes on board, hides, and saves a murderer who is physically and psychologically his "double."

Section: Rock-Drill 85–95 de los Cantares (1956). A section following THE PISAN CANTOS in the longer CANTOS of Ezra POUND. After the purgatorial tone of the Pisan section, the *Cantos* move into a new phase, in which Pound begins to describe his paradise.

Sedaine, Michel Jean (1719–1797). French dramatist and librettist. He was the first to recognize the possibilities of combining a comic play with music, and is considered the founder of comic opera. His works include *Blaise le Savetier* (1759), written with the composer François André Danican known as Philidor; an opera *Aline, reine de Golconde* (1766), with music by Pierre Monsigny; *Richard Coeur de Lion* (1784), with music by André Grétry. His most famous play, *Le Philosophe sans le savoir* (1765), is the best example of the BOURGEOIS DRAMA. He was admitted to the French ACADEMY in 1768.

Sedan. A French city located on the Meuse river. Sedan is of great strategic importance and hence historical interest. The most famous battle of Sedan (September 1, 1870) resulted in the surrender to the Prussians of an army of 100,000 men under the direct command of Napoleon III. During World War I, Sedan was an important point in the German army's advance into France. In 1940, it was the gateway through which the German *Wehrmacht*, skirting the Maginot Line, poured westward.

Sedgemoor. A place in Somersetshire, England, scene of a battle (1685) between the Royalist army and the forces of the duke of Monmouth. Monmouth's troops were routed, and the duke himself was captured and later executed.

Sedgwick, Catharine Maria (1789–1867). American novelist. Called "the Maria Edgeworth of America," she wrote novels with authentic American settings that won her great popularity both in the U.S. and in Europe. Her best-known work was *Hope Leslie* (1827), a story of the Pequod War in 17th-century New England. She also wrote *Redwood* (1824), *Clarence* (1830), and *The Linwoods* (1835).

Sedley, Amelia. See VANITY FAIR.

Sedley, Sir **Charles** (1639?–1701). English dramatist and poet. Famous in his day for his profligacy and wit, Sedley was esteemed as a writer and patron of the arts by the earl of Rochester and by Dryden, who introduced him as Lisideius in his *Essay of Dramatic Poesy* (1668). Among his best-known works are *Bellamira* (1687), a comedy based on Terence's *The Eunuchs,* and the song *Phillis is my only joy.* His daughter Catherine (1657–1717), the clever, ugly countess of Dorchester, was mistress of James II.

Seeger, Alan (1888–1916). American poet. He enlisted in the French Foreign Legion at the outbreak of World War I and was killed in action. A thoroughgoing romantic, Seeger is best known for his famous poem *I Have a Rendezvous with Death,* which appeared in his *Collected Poems* (1916).

Seferis, Giorgos. Pen name of **Giorgos Seferiades** (1900–1971). Greek poet. Born in Smyrna, he and his family fled to Athens in 1914 to escape Turkish domination. He studied in Athens and Paris, and, after a period as a lawyer, he entered the foreign service. He first began to write poetry seriously early in his 30's in London, where he translated the poetry of T. S. Eliot into Greek. His own poems began to be known in English translations by Lawrence Durrell, Rex Warner, and others, and Henry Miller spoke of him enthusiastically in his *Colossus of Maroussi.* His fame culminated in 1963 when he was awarded the Nobel Prize for literature.

Seferis' verse is simple and spare in style, but imbued with a love of Greece and its past. In the words of the Swedish Academy, it symbolizes "all that is indestructible in the Hellenic acceptance of life."

Seghers, Anna. Pen name of **Netty Radványi,** born **Reiling** (1900–   ). German novelist with socialist convictions. She left Germany during World War II and, afterward, returned to East Berlin. Her most famous novel is *Der siebte Kreuz* (*The Seventh Cross,* 1939).

Segni, Bernardo (1504–1558). Italian historian and literary critic. He wrote an annotated Italian translation (1549) of Aristotle's *Poetics.*

Segrais, Jean Regnault de (1624–1701). French poet and man of letters. Author of a pastoral poem *Athis,* a novel *Bérénice,* and a collection of tales, *Les Divertissements de la Princesse Aurélianne,* he translated Vergil's *Aeneid* and *Georgics* into French verse. He allowed his name to be put to the first editions of two romances by his employer, the duchesse de MONTPENSIER, and of two novels, *Zayde* and *La Princesse de Clèves,* by his friend the comtesse de La Fayette.

Seian horse. Possession invariably bringing ill luck with it. The Latin proverb *Ille homo habet equum Seianum* refers to a tradition that Cneius Seius had an Argive horse, of the breed of Diomedes, of a bay color and surpassing beauty, but which was fatal to its possessor. Its next owner, Cornelius Dolabella, who bought it for 100,000 sesterces, was killed in Syria during the civil wars. Caius Cassius, who next took possession of it, perished after the battle of Philippi by the very sword that stabbed Caesar. Antony had the horse next, and after the battle of Actium slew the horse and then himself.

Sei Shōnagon. See PILLOW-BOOK OF SEI SHŌNAGON, THE.

Sejanus, His Fall (1603). A tragedy by Ben JONSON. It traces the life of Lucius Aelius Sejanus, favorite and chief minister of the Emperor Tiberius. He seduces Livia, the wife of Tiberius' son Drusus, whom he poisons; plots against Agrippina, the widow of the hero, Germanicus; and even aspires to the throne itself. However, because of his arrogance, he overreaches himself and is arrested and put to death (A.D. 31).

Selden, John (1584–1654). English jurist, scholar, and orientalist, known for his treatises, many of which were written in Latin and dealt with questions of law. Of humble birth, Selden was an outstanding lawyer and became especially known for his collection of Oriental manuscripts, which he willed to the Bodleian Library.

His scholarly publications include *De Diis Syriis* (1617), a study of Oriental religion, and *History of Tithes* (1618), which was suppressed because of the objections of the English clergy. Perhaps his best-known work is *Table Talk* (1689), a collection of his sayings compiled after his death by his secretary, Richard Milward.

Seldwyla. See LEUTE VON SELDWYLA, DIE.

Selene. The moon goddess of Greek mythology, daughter of Hyperion and Thea, and sister of Helios (the sun), corresponding to the Roman Luna. Selene had fifty daughters by ENDYMION, and several by Zeus, one of whom was called "The Dew." Selene is usually shown in a chariot drawn by two white horses. Late Greek mythographers identified her with ARTEMIS.

Title page of Selden's *Table Talk* (1689).

Table-Talk:
BEING THE
DISCOURSES
OF
John Selden Efq;
OR HIS
SENCE
Of Various
MATTERS
OF
WEIGHT and High CONSEQUENCE
Relating efpecially to
Religion and State.

Diftingue Tempora.

IONDON,
Printed for *E. Smith,* in the Year MDCLXXXIX.

Seleucidae. The dynasty of Seleucus Nicator (c. 358–280 B.C.), one of Alexander's generals. In 312 B.C. he conquered Babylon and succeeded to a part of Alexander's vast empire. The monarchy consisted of Syria, a part of Asia Minor, and all the eastern provinces. The line of the Seleucids reigned till about 64 B.C.

Seleucus. In Pierre Corneille's tragedy RODOGUNE, the stepson of the wicked queen Cleopatra, who murders him.

Self-Reliance (1841). An essay by Ralph Waldo EMERSON. The writer, in some of his best-known epigrammatic sentences, instructs his listener to discover his relationship with Nature and God, and then to trust his own judgment above that of all others. The essay is collected in Emerson's *Essays, First Series.*

Seljuks. A Perso-Turkish dynasty of 11 emperors over a large part of Asia. It lasted 138 years (1056–1194). It was founded by Togrul Beg, a descendant of Seljuk, chief of a small tribe that gained possession of Bokhara.

Selkirk, Alexander (1676–1721). A Scottish sailor whose narrative of his actual experience as a castaway suggested Daniel Defoe's ROBINSON CRUSOE. As the sailing-master of the privateer *Cinque Ports Galley,* Selkirk, at his own request, was left on the desolate island of Juan Fernández off the coast of Chile for four years and four months (1704–1709). His rescue and return to England by Captain Woodes Rogers caused the publication of many narratives of his history.

Selvaggio. The father of the Knight of Arts and Industry, and the hero of James Thomson's CASTLE OF INDOLENCE.

selve (It., "woods or forests"). During the Renaissance it was used in literature to describe improvisations or scattered thoughts provoked by varied subjects. This meaning came from the Latin *sylvae,* used by Statius to title a collection of occasional poems; for Cicero and the rhetoricians it meant a collection of materials from authors of note, useful in studying expression. Poliziano entitled his lectures *Sylvae* and Lorenzo de' Medici entitled one of his longer poems *Selve d'amore.*

Semele. In Greek mythology, the daughter of CADMUS and Harmonia and mother of Dionysus by Zeus. Six months pregnant by her unknown lover, she was persuaded by the jealous Hera to insist that he reveal himself. Zeus appeared as a thunderbolt and she died, but the unborn Dionysus was saved by Hermes. Semele was later rescued from Hades by her son under the name of Thyone. This raising of Semele, symbolizing the return of vegetation in the Spring, was widely celebrated. Semele seems to have been a Greek adaptation of Zemelo, a Phrygian earthgoddess.

Semiramis or **Sammuramat.** An Assyrian queen. All that is known of the historical queen, Sammuramat, is that she was the mother of the Assyrian king Ninus and a woman of immense importance through more than one reign. Perhaps Babylonian herself, she introduced a Babylonian god, Nebo, into the Assyrian pantheon. She fought effectively against both Medes and Chaldeans.

The legendary queen, Semiramis, on the other hand, is a figure known to various Greek writers, who believed her to be the daughter of the Syrian goddess Atargatis. Various legends claimed that she was fed as a child by doves (which fact later identified her with ISHTAR), married King Ninus, and after his death built Babylon and other great cities and monuments. At her death she became a dove. It was this fabulous creature, rather than the human queen, who was the heroine of Voltaire's tragedy *Sémiramis,* a drama by Calderón, and Rossini's opera *Semiramide.*

Semitic. Pertaining to the descendants of SHEM (Gen. 10) who are the Hebrews, Arabs, Assyrians, Aramaeans, and others. The word is now popularly used as a synonym for Jewish.

the Semitic languages. Ancient Assyrian and Chaldee, Aramaean, Syriac, Arabic, Hebrew, Samaritan, Ethiopic, and old Phoenician. The great characteristic of this family of languages is that the roots of words consist of three consonants.

Sen, Pradip (1928–   ). Indian poet writing in English. Strongly influenced by Catholic imagery and ideals, his poetry is characterized by tight technical discipline and deep feelings, especially in *And Then the Sun* (1960). He is a founder-member of Writers Workshop (Calcutta).

Sénancour, Etienne Pivert de (1770–1846). French man of letters. A forerunner of such romantics as Chateaubriand and a follower of Rousseau, Sénancour lived a melancholy, lonely existence. He escaped for a time to Switzerland where the majesty of nature seemed to satisfy the longings of his romantic spirit. Sénancour is most famous for his pessimistic novel in letter form, OBERMANN.

Senàpo (Senapus). In Lodovico Ariosto's ORLANDO FURIOSO and Torquato Tasso's GERUSALEMME LIBERATA, the king of Ethiopia. In Ariosto, he is tormented by Harpies until Astolfo arrives on the Hippogriff to chase them back to the gates of Hell. In the Tasso epic, he is the father of Clorinda, the warrior maid, whom he never knew because her mother had given the child away in fear of the suspicion its white complexion would arouse in him.

Sender, Ramón [José] (1902–   ). Spanish novelist. Sender resides in New Mexico, exiled from his native Spain because of his liberal views. His novels, strong and detailed, include *Imán (Earmarked for Hell,* 1929) dealing with the war in Morocco; *Siete domingos rojos (Seven Red Sundays,* 1932); *Contraataque (Counter Attack in Spain,* 1937), which describes the Spanish Civil War; and *Epitalamio del Prieto Trinidad (Dark Wedding,* 1942), considered his best work.

Seneca. Full Latin name, **Lucius Annaeus Seneca** (4 B.C.–A.D. 65). Roman philosopher and playwright. In A.D. 45 Seneca, a Spanish-born scholar, was chosen to become the tutor of the future emperor NERO. Seneca spent the major portion of his life studying and writing, and instructing his disciple Nero on the art of government and the virtues of a Stoic philosopher-king. When the young prince ascended the imperial throne in A.D. 54, Seneca remained his most trusted advisor and three years later, in 57, was honored by the conferral of a consulship. However, for reasons that are not entirely clear to historians, Seneca lost favor with the emperor and prudently withdrew from imperial politics and court society in 62. In 65 he was implicated in PISO's CONSPIRACY to assassinate Nero, and was commanded by his one-time pupil to kill himself. With Stoic composure, the philosopher had his veins opened and bled to death.

As a Roman philosopher, Seneca is second only to Cicero, and like Cicero was an adherent of the philosophy of Stoicism. He wrote, furthermore, the first and only Roman text book on physics, the *Quaestiones Naturales* (*Investigations in Natural Science*), which was an important source of knowledge (and misinformation) in the Middle Ages. His influence on Renaissance drama was considerable. Eight tragedies are ascribed to him; they are *Hercules, Troacles, Phoenissae, Medea, Phaedra, Agamemnon, Oedipus,* and *Thyestes.* Marked by violence and bloodshed, and characters of little individuality or differentiation, they had an important influence on the tragic drama of Italy, France, and, especially, of Elizabethan England.

Sénécal. A character in Gustave Flaubert's novel L'ÉDUCATION SENTIMENTALE. Sénécal, a political radical, is quick to change his allegiance when the Revolution of 1848 fails and Napoleon III assumes control of the government.

Sennacherib. In the Bible, an Assyrian king who captured and destroyed Babylon. His siege of Jerusalem in the days of Hezekiah is dramatically described: in the night, "the angel of the Lord went out, and smote in the camp of the Assyrians an hundred fourscore and five thousand" (II Kings 19:35). He was murdered by two of his sons while praying in a temple.

Byron has made the destruction of his army by disease the subject of a famous lyric, *The Destruction of Sennacherib* (1815).

Sennett, Mack. Original name, **Michael Sinnott** (1884–1960). American motion-picture producer and director. After acting for a time under the direction of D. W. Griffith, he became associated in 1912 with the Keystone Company. Here he began to produce his famous slapstick films, known as "Mack Sennett comedies." Among the actors who worked for him were Marie Dressler, Mabel Normand, Ben Turpin, Roscoe ("Fatty") Arbuckle, and Charlie Chaplin.

senryū. Japanese satiric verse. It follows the same syllabic system as HAIKU, but deals with subjects of a lighter vein.

Sense and Sensibility (1811). A novel by Jane AUSTEN in which two sisters, Elinor and Marianne Dashwood, represent "sense" and "sensibility" respectively. Each is deserted by the young man from whom she has been led to expect an offer of matrimony. Elinor bears her deep disappointment with dignity and restraint while Marianne violently expresses her grief. Elinor soon discovers why her lover, Edward Ferrars, has left her: he has been secretly engaged to Lucy Steele for four years, and, while he regrets the connection now, he feels honor bound to marry her. When his mother discovers his engagement to Lucy, a girl of inferior social standing, she disinherits him, settling her property on his younger brother, Robert. The sly Lucy, at this turn of events, shifts her interest to Robert. Thus released, Edward proposes to Elinor and is accepted. On the other hand, Marianne, with characteristic impetuosity, follows her lover John Willoughby to London where she only becomes more disillusioned with him. As she gradually recovers from her foolish love, she is able to

see, for the first time, the more quiet attractions of her old admirer, Colonel Brandon, and she finally marries him.

Sensitive Plant, The (1820). A poem by Percy Bysshe SHELLEY. The sensitive plant is a variety of mimosa; its outer leaves curl up when touched. The poem relates the mystic love of the plant for the "lady of the garden" and its death in the general ruin of the garden following the lady's demise.

Sentimental Journey, A (1768). An unfinished narrative by Laurence STERNE. Attacking sentimentalism in the guise of a tour through France and Italy, it is itself didactic in its sentimental emphasis on natural benevolence and philanthropy. Here Sterne moralizes so playfully as to present an almost delicate caricature of moralizing. It was long read seriously, even in such famous episodes as YORICK weeping over an ass chewing a thistle. Its first illustrator was William HOGARTH.

Sentimental Tommy (1896). A novel by J. M. BARRIE which, together with its sequel *Tommy and Grizel* (1900), relates the story of a young man overendowed with imagination who cannot resist playing the hero whenever his mood or the situation seem to call for it, often to the injury of his adoring Grizel. In spite of his spasmodic efforts, Tommy cannot succeed in being the faithful lover and husband she deserves. He meets an accidental death by hanging.

Separate Tables (1954). A play by Terence RATTIGAN. This work is actually two one-act plays set in the same English resort hotel. The minor characters remain the same in both acts; only the male and female leads change. The theme of both acts is the frustration and misunderstanding caused by the artificial social barriers errected between individuals. The loneliness and isolation of the guests in the hotel is symbolized by their separate tables in the dining room.

Sephardim. The group of Jews early settling in Spain and Portugal. See ASHKENAZIM.

sepoy. The Anglicized form of the Hindu and Persian *sipahi,* a soldier, denoting a native Indian soldier trained and disciplined in the British manner, especially one in the British Indian Army.

Sepoy Mutiny. A revolt of the Sepoy troops in British India during the transference of the administration of India from the East India Company to the British crown.

September Massacres. An indiscriminate slaughter, during the French Revolution, of Loyalists confined in the Abbaye and other prisons, lasting from Sept. 2 to 5, 1792. As many as 8,000 persons died.

Septimius Felton, or a Romance of Immortality (1871). An unfinished novel by Nathaniel HAWTHORNE. Discovered after his death, the manuscript was prepared and published by the author's wife. Set in both England and America, the story involves a hero of mixed Indian and English blood. He discovers the elixir of life, causes the death of his sweetheart, and finally disappears in England. The plot is further complicated by a long episode about a bloody footprint.

Septimus Warren Smith. A character in Virginia Woolf's novel MRS. DALLOWAY. Having retreated into a private world, he has gone mad; a conventional doctor's efforts to intrude and to cure him drive him to suicide.

Septuagint. The Greek version of the Old Testament and Apocrypha. It is so called because it was traditionally said to have been made by 72 Palestinian Jews in 72 days, during the third century B.C. at the command of Ptolemy Philadelphus. In abbreviated form, it is usually expressed as LXX, "The Seventy."

The first translators, working on the island of Pharos, translated only the Pentateuch. Greek translations of the other books were added by later writers. This version of the Bible was used in Mediterranean lands during the time of Christ and the early Church.

Serafimovich, Aleksandr. Pen name of **Aleksandr Serafimovich Popov** (1863–1949). Russian novelist. He wrote *The Iron Flood* (*Zheleznyi potok;* 1924), describing the civil war struggle between White and Red Cossacks in the Caucasus. The novel is a favorite of Soviet critics because of its Marxist emphases and interpretations.

Serafino de Ciminelli. Also known as **Serafino Aquilano** (1466–1500). Italian Renaissance poet. He is known as an inspired performer of supposedly improvised poems (*improvisatore*). A singer and a lutanist, he was widely traveled in important Renaissance circles. His *Rime* (1502) is composed of sonnets and other verses, particularly *strambotti*. This work was widely circulated and reaching England, was adapted and translated by Wyatt and Surrey. Ciminelli's verse favors exaggerated Petrarchism in the manner of Chariteo and Tebaldeo; his conceits invited the lyric reforms of Bembo.

Seraglio. The former palace of the Sultan of Turkey at Constantinople. Situated on the Golden Horn, it is enclosed by walls seven miles and a half in circuit. The chief entrance was *the Sublime Gate.* The chief of the large edifices was the *Harem,* or sacred spot, which contained numerous houses for the Sultan's wives and his concubines. The word is often used as a synonym for harem, as in Mozart's opera *The Abduction from the Seraglio.*

Serao, Matilde (1856–1927). Italian novelist. Her novels describe Neapolitan life in a realistic and sympathetic manner. *Il Paese di Cuccagna* (*The Land of Cockaigne,* 1891), her best-known work, humorously depicts the Neapolitan passion for the national lottery. Among her other novels are *Cuore Infermo* (1881), *Il Ventre di Napoli* (1884), *All'Erta, Sentinella!* (1889), *Terno Secco* (1889), *Addio, Amore* (1890), *Piccolo Romanzo* (1891), *Fantasia* (1892), and *Il Castigo* (1893).

seraphim. ANGELS. Seraphim belong to the highest order of angels, according to medieval angelology, especially distinguished by the ardency of their zeal and love. In the Bible, each seraph had six wings: "with twain he covered his face, and with twain he covered his feet, and with twain he did fly" (Isa. 6:2). Elizabeth Barrett Browning wrote a poem entitled *The Seraphim* (1838).

Serapion Brothers, the. An organization of writers formed in Russia during the 1920's. The group, which had no definite program, came together chiefly to advocate the right to nonconformity and freedom in literature. They especially were in reaction against the growing demands for literature to concern itself with political themes. Included in the group were Yevgeni Zamyatin, the oldest member and leading spirit, and younger writers such as Venyamin Kaverin, Konstantin Fedin, Mikhail Zoshchenko, Vsevolod Ivanov, and Nikolai Tikhonov. The name of the group was taken from a story called *The Serapion Brothers* by E. T. A. Hoffmann, in which one of the characters advocates unlimited freedom in literary work.

Serapis. An Egyptian deity, combining the attributes of Apis and Osiris. The temples of Serapis were called Serapea. The most famous Serapeum, at Memphis, was the burial place of the sacred bull Apis.

Sercambi, Giovanni (1348–1424). Italian writer. Born in Lucca, he is the otherwise unknown author of an untitled collection of *novelle,* first published in 1889. Based on the *Decameron* of Boccaccio, its basic plot involves the wanderings over Italy of a group of refugees from a 1374 plague. The author, a member of the company, tells the tales himself. The resemblance to Chaucer's *Canterbury Tales* is largely coincidental.

serendipity. A word coined by Horace WALPOLE to denote the faculty of making lucky and unexpected "finds" by accident. In a letter (January 28, 1754) he says that he formed it from the title of a fairy story, *The Three Princes of Serendip,* because the princes "were always making discoveries, by accidents and sagacity, of things they were not in quest of."

Serkin, Rudolf (1903–   ). Bohemian-born Austrian concert pianist, residing in the U.S. He is known for his interpretations of Mozart and Beethoven, and is director of a summer music school and festival at Marlboro, Vt.

Sermon on the Mount. In the New Testament, the sermon given by Christ to the multitudes and his disciples (Matt. 5–7) where he explains the essence of the true disciple and enunciates his teachings of love and righteousness. See BEATITUDES.

Serpentino. In Matteo Maria Boiardo's ORLANDO INNAMORATO and Lodovico Ariosto's ORLANDO FURIOSO, a brave knight and one of the best of the pagan warriors. He is defeated by the warrior maiden Bradamante. He is surnamed "de la Stella" because he is from the Spanish city of Estella.

Sertões, Os (Rebellion in the Backlands, 1902). A book, considered the chief classic of Brazilian literature, by Euclides da Cunha (1866–1909). The work, which has been called "the Bible of Brazilian nationality," defies classification. It is partly a geographical and sociological treatise that gives a brilliant description of the drought-ridden *sertão,* or hinterland, and its backward, poverty-stricken inhabitants. It is also a fast-paced narrative, full of pathos and suspense, that has sometimes been called a novel. The book recounts the heroic, though ill-fated, attempt of a religious zealot, "Antônio the Counsellor," and his followers to resist the authority of the central government in 1896–1897. In their settlement at Canudos, 300 miles northwest of Salvador, the rebels stubbornly held out against government troops until the last man was dead. Da Cunha was an engineer and journalist of Darwinian convictions who accompanied one of the military expeditions to Canudos as a newspaper correspondent. He turned the story of the rebels into a remarkable document, an indictment of Brazilian society for its neglect of the *sertão* as well as a stirring account of human misery and courage.

Service, Robert W[illiam] (1874–1958). English-born Canadian author. He led an adventurous, far-traveling life and wrote popular verse in the manner of Rudyard Kipling. His best-known ballad is *The Shooting of Dan McGrew*, and his most popular collection, *Songs of a Sourdough* (1907), later retitled *The Spell of the Yukon*.

Sesha. In Hindu mythology, the serpent who supports the world on his head.

Sesshū (1420–1506). Japanese painter. A Zen priest, he specialized in black and white landscape painting. Noted for his originality, simplicity, and sensitivity, his work greatly influenced later artists.

sestina. In prosody, a lyric poem of six stanzas of six lines each and an envoi or *tornada* of three lines. A specialized form of the Provençal *canso* and the Italian CANZONE, the sestina was developed sometime toward the end of the 13th century by the famed Provençal troubadour Arnaut Daniel. Admired and written by Dante and Petrarch in Italy, it was hardly used in France and England before the 19th century.

Instead of rhyme the sestina uses a pattern of repetition of the six words which terminate the six lines of the first stanza. (Not content with this, Swinburne invented a rhymed form of the sestina.) Such modern poets as Ezra Pound and W. H. Auden have written the sestina with notable success.

The arrangement of repetition is as follows:

Stanza I.	1–2–3–4–5–6
Stanza II.	6–1–5–2–4–3
Stanza III.	3–6–4–1–2–5
Stanza IV.	5–3–2–6–1–4
Stanza V.	4–5–1–3–6–2
Stanza VI.	2–4–6–5–3–1

The envoi contains inner repetition, as well as terminal repetition. Line one has word 2 in the middle, and 5 at the end. Line two has word 4 in the middle and 3 at the end, while line three has word 6 in the middle and 1 at the end.

Sestius or **Sextius, Publius.** Roman politician. He helped Cicero crush the conspiracy of CATILINE and was instrumental in bringing about the recall of Cicero from exile (57 B.C.).

Sestos. An ancient city on the European side of the Hellespont. Here Hero dwelt in the legend of HERO AND LEANDER.

Set. The Egyptian god of darkness, prototype of the Greek Typhon, the god of evil. He was the brother-son and deadly enemy of OSIRIS whom he slaughtered and cut into 14 pieces. Representations of Set portray him with a human body and the head of some unidentified mythological beast with pointed muzzle and high square ears.

Seton, Anya (1916–   ). American novelist. The daughter of the naturalist Ernest Thompson Seton, she is the author of *My Theodosia* (1941), a biographical novel about the daughter of Aaron Burr; *Dragonwyck* (1944), a "Hudson River Gothic" novel; and *Foxfire* (1950), about an Arizona mine. *Katherine* (1954) deals with 14th-century England. She also wrote *The Turquoise* (1946), *The Hearth and the Eagle* (1948), *The Mistletoe and Sword* (1955), and *Winthrop Woman* (1958).

Seton, Ernest Thompson (1860–1946). English-born American naturalist. His best-known book is *Wild Animals I Have Known* (1898), illustrated by himself.

Settembrini, Ludovico. In Thomas Mann's novel THE MAGIC MOUNTAIN, an Italian tubercular patient who befriends Hans CASTORP. He is concerned lest the young man succumb to the decadent atmosphere of Haus Berghof and frequently urges him to leave. He represents the classical European tradition of enlightened humanism and political liberalism.

Seurat, Georges (1859–1891). French painter. Seurat collaborated with Paul Signac in the foundation of NEOIMPRESSIONISM. His sensitive, controlled pointillism, with its emphasis on the repetition of simplified forms expressed in terms of light and shade, is best exemplified by *Sunday Afternoon on La Grande Jatte* (1886), in the Chicago Art Institute.

Seuss, Dr. See Theodor Seuss GEISEL.

Sevastopol Sketches (1855). Three stories by Count Leo TOLSTOI. They are based on his own experiences and observations at the siege of Sevastopol during the Crimean War. Tolstoi, who was an army officer at the time, was in the thick of the fighting at the most exposed point in the town's fortifications. The stories were a departure from the usual war descriptions. Tolstoi stripped away the tinsel and showed war, not as a heroic and glorious pastime, but as a dangerous, tedious, and bloody succession of horrors. In these stories, Tolstoi first used the stream-of-consciousness technique which he developed in his later work. In an article about the sketches, the Russian critic Nikolai Chernyshevski called the technique that of an "internal monologue," the first time this term was used in relation to the literary device.

The three stories are separately entitled *Sevastopol in the Month of December (Sevastopol v dekabre mesyatze)*, *Sevastopol in May (Sevastopol v maye)*, and *Sevastopol in August 1855 (Sevastopol v avguste 1855 goda)*. At the end of the second story are the famous lines: "The hero of my story, whom I love with all the strength of my soul, whom I have tried to reproduce in all his beauty and who always was, is, and will be beautiful, is truth."

seven. A mystic or sacred number. It is composed of four and three, which, among the Pythagoreans, were, and from time immemorial have been, accounted lucky numbers. Among the Babylonians, Egyptians, and other ancient peoples, there were seven sacred planets. The Hebrew verb *to swear* means literally to come under the influence of seven things; thus, seven ewe lambs figure in the oath between Abraham and Abimelech at Beersheba (Gen. 21:28), and Herodotus describes an Arabian oath in which seven stones are smeared with blood.

There are seven days in Creation, seven days in the week, seven graces, seven divisions in the Lord's Prayer, and seven ages in the life of man; climacteric years are seven and nine with their multiples by odd numbers; and the seventh son of a seventh son was held notable.

Among the Hebrews, every seventh year was sabbatical, and seven times seven years was the jubilee. The three great Jewish feasts lasted seven days; and between the first and second were seven weeks. Levitical purifications lasted seven days; Balaam would have seven altars, and sacrificed on them seven

The seven ages of man. Woodcut (1485).

bullocks and seven rams; Naaman was commanded to dip seven times in Jordan; Elijah sent his servant seven times to look out for rain; ten times seven Israelites went to Egypt, the exile lasted the same number of years, and there were ten times seven elders. Pharaoh in his dream saw seven kine and seven ears of corn; Jacob served seven years for each of his wives; seven priests with seven trumpets marched round Jericho once every day, but seven times on the seventh day. Samson's wedding feast lasted seven days; on the seventh he told his bride the riddle, he was bound with seven withes, and seven locks of his hair were cut off. Nebuchadnezzar was a beast for seven years.

In the Apocalypse, there are seven churches of Asia, seven candlesticks, seven stars, seven trumpets, seven spirits before the throne of God, seven horns, seven vials, seven plagues, a seven-headed monster, and the Lamb with seven eyes.

The old astrologers and alchemists recognized seven so-called planets. According to the Muslims, there are seven heavens.

Seven Against Thebes (Hepta epi Thebas, 467 B.C.). A tragedy by AESCHYLUS. It deals with the war between the sons of OEDIPUS for the throne of Thebes. It is the last play of a trilogy that included *Laius* and *Oedipus,* both now lost. The ending was changed by an unknown poet to conform to Sophocles' popular tragedy *Antigone* and the original ending is lost. Static in action, the play is martial in spirit; it may have been in part a tract urging Athens to fortify its acropolis. For the story, see THE SEVEN AGAINST THEBES.

Max MELL's *Sieben gegen Theben* (1932) is a German adaptation of the play.

Seven against Thebes, The. Seven mythical Argive champions. They waged war on Thebes. Cursed by OEDIPUS for consenting to his banishment, his sons, Eteocles and Polynices, agreed to occupy the Theban throne on alternate years, but Eteocles banished his brother. Polynices fled to Argos, where, with the help of ERIPHYLE, he won the support of King Adrastus, whose daughter he married. Their force was led by seven champions: Adrastus; his brother-in-law, the seer Amphiaraus, who foresaw that only Adrastus would survive the war; Adrastus' son-in-

law Tydeus, a hero from Calydon; Parthenopaeus, Hippomedon, Capaneus, and Polynices (though some accounts add the Argives Mecisteus and Eteoclus in place of the foreign leaders, Polynices and Tydeus).

Tydeus was sent ahead to demand Theban surrender; Eteocles refused and Tydeus was ambushed, but killed his fifty attackers and escaped. On the way to Thebes, the seven were dismayed by the death of the infant OPHELTES, which they regarded as an ill omen. Each of the champions stationed himself at one of the seven gates of Thebes; Eteocles assigned a general to defend each, reserving for himself the one menaced by Polynices. In the ensuing battle, the Argives were almost totally destroyed. Zeus struck Capaneus from a scaling-ladder for his impious boasting; Amphiaraus was swallowed by the earth; Athena would have saved the wounded Tydeus, but refused when she saw him eating the brains of an enemy; and the other Argive leaders died except for Adrastus, who was saved by his horse Arion. Polynices and Eteocles met in single combat and killed each other.

For more details of this bloody war, and its aftermath, see MENOECEUS, ANTIGONE, EVADNE, and EPIGONI. The story of the war was told by Aeschylus in his SEVEN AGAINST THEBES, by Euripides in his PHOENICIAN WOMEN and THE SUPPLIANT WOMEN, by SENECA in his *Phoenissae,* and by STATIUS in his epic poem *Thebais.*

Seven Arts, The (1916–1917). An American monthly periodical of literature and opinion founded by James OPPENHEIM. One of the best-known and shortest lived of the little magazines of the early 20th century, it ceased publication largely because its pacifist views made it a financial failure. Its aim was to provide a vehicle for the expression of ideas and forms to which the conservative journals of the day were closed. Van Wyck Brooks and Waldo Frank were among its editors.

Seven Champions of Christendom, The Famous History of the (1596). A medieval romance by Richard Johnson about the national patron saints of England, Scotland, Wales, Ireland, France, Spain, and Italy. Johnson relates that St. George of England was seven years imprisoned by the Almidor, the Black King of Morocco; St. Denys of France lived seven years in the form of a hart; St. James of Spain was seven years dumb through love for a fair Jewess; St. Anthony of Italy, with the other champions, was enchanted into a deep sleep in the black castle, and was released by St. George's three sons, who quenched the seven lamps by water from the enchanted fountain; St. Andrew of Scotland delivered six ladies who had lived seven years in the form of white swans; St. Patrick of Ireland was immured in a cell where he scratched his grave with his own nails; and St. David of Wales slept seven years in the enchanted garden of Ormandine, and was redeemed by St. George. See SCOBELLUM.

Seven Hills, the City of (Lat. *Urbs Septicollis*). Ancient Rome. The city was built on seven hills, which Servius Tullius surrounded with a line of fortifications. The hills are the Palatinus, the Capitolinus, the Quirinalis, the Caelius, the Aventinus, the Viminalis, and the Esquilinus.

seven last words of Christ. (1) "Father, forgive them; for they know not what they do."

(2) "Today shalt thou be with Me in paradise." (3) "Woman, behold thy son!" etc. (4) "My God, My God, why hast Thou forsaken Me?" (5) "I thirst." (6) "It is finished." (7) "Father, into Thy hands I commend My spirit."

seven names of God. Among the ancient Hebrews, the seven names for the Deity over which the scribes had to exercise particular care. They were El, Elohim, Adonai, YHWH (i.e., our *Jehovah*), Ehyeh-Asher-Ehyeh, Shadai, and Zebaot. In medieval times God was sometimes called simply *The Seven.*

Seven Pillars of Wisdom. See T. E. LAWRENCE.

Seven Sages of Rome, The. See THE SEVEN WISE MASTERS.

seven sciences. See LIBERAL ARTS.

seven seas. The Arctic and the Antarctic, North and South Pacific, North and South Atlantic, and the Indian oceans. Kipling called a volume of his poems *The Seven Seas* (1896).

Seven Sleepers. In Muslim and Christian legend, seven noble youths who fled in the Decian persecution of 250 to a cave in Mount Celion. After 309 years (or 230 years, according to some sources), they awoke, but soon died. Their bodies were taken to Marseilles in a large stone coffin, still shown in Victor's church. Their names are Constantine, Dionysius, John, Maximian, Malchus, Martinian, and Serapion. In the Muslim version the Sleepers had a dog named KATMIR who watched over them. This fable took its rise from a misunderstanding of the words in the Bible (I Cor. 15:18), "They fell asleep in Christ" (i.e., died). See TALISMAN.

Seventeen (1916). A novel by Booth TARKINGTON. Its hero is William Sylvanus Baxter, "Silly Billy," an adolescent in the throes of his first love affair. The object of his attention is Lola Pratt, whose chief occupation is lavishing baby talk on her pet dog Flopit and on her numerous admirers.

Seven Wise Masters, The. Also known as the **Tales of Sandibar** or **Sindibad** or **Syntipas.** A collection of Oriental tales (probably Indian, c. 100 B.C.) popularized in the Middle Ages through the French verse romance *The Seven Sages of Rome* (*Roman des Sept Sages,* early 14th century) and the prose variation *Dolopathos* (c. 1222-1225). A jealous stepmother tells her husband the king that his son is trying to seduce her, and the prince is condemned to death. For seven days the queen and the boy's seven wise teachers alternate in telling the king tales, the queen urging him that the prince is a dangerous rival, the sages demonstrating the untrustworthiness of women. Finally the prince, who has been silent for seven days, reveals the whole truth, and the queen is burned at the stake.

Seven Wonders of the Ancient World. A list of man-made wonders compiled by Hellenistic travelers. The first extant list was that made by Antipater of Sidon in the second century B.C.; a better known list by Philo of Byzantium was made somewhat later. The Seven Wonders included the pyramids of Egypt, the HANGING GARDENS OF BABYLON, the statue of Zeus at Olympia, carved by PHIDIAS, the temple of ARTEMIS AT EPHESUS, the tomb of king Mausolus (hence the term MAUSOLEUM) at Halicarnassus, the COLOSSUS at Rhodes, and any one of the following three: the PHAROS, the walls of Babylon, or the palace of Cyrus.

Seven Years War (1756-1763). The war against Frederick the Great of Prussia waged by France, Austria, and Russia. England aided Frederick with subsidies and Hanoverian troops. The war ended with the treaty of Hubertusburg by which Frederick retained all his dominions. The war carried with it the struggle between France and England overseas, which was settled in the Peace of Paris of 1763, leaving England predominant in India and America. See FRENCH AND INDIAN WAR.

Severn, Joseph (1793-1879). English painter. He is chiefly remembered as a friend of John Keats, whom he accompanied to Italy in 1820 and attended on his deathbed.

Sevier, John (1745-1815). American frontiersman, Indian fighter, and politician. During the Revolution he contributed to the American victory at King's Mountain on the border between the Carolinas (Oct. 7, 1780). He later served as the first governor of Tennessee. He is a character in Winston Churchill's novel *The Crossing* (1904).

Sévigné, marquise de. Born **Marie de Rabutin-Chantal** (1626-1696). French letter writer and lady of fashion. In letters to her daughter, Mme de Grignan and to a circle of intimate friends, Mme de Sévigné described the life of the court, city, and countryside, her domestic affairs, and her reading. These writings afford not only a picture of an age but a portrait of the woman herself—wise and witty, imaginative and affectionate.

Sewall, Samuel (1652-1730). English-born American statesman of early New England. He is known for his liberal views and for his *Diary* (1878-1882), written between 1674 and 1729, which gives a vivid picture of life and personalities in the Boston of his day and has been compared to the similar and more famous work of Samuel Pepys. Among his other writings are *The Revolution in New England Justified* (1691), which seeks to justify the deposition of the dictatorial English governor Andros; *The Selling of Joseph* (1700), one of the first antislavery tracts written in America; and *A Memorial Relating to the Kennebeck Indians* (1721), a brief appeal for charitable treatment of the Indians.

Sewall, who held a number of political offices in the Massachusetts colony, was one of the judges at the Salem witchcraft trials, but later repented publicly in church while his confession was read to the congregation.

Sewanee Review, The. A quarterly magazine founded in 1892 at the University of the South, Sewanee, Tenn. It has always been especially interested in Southern affairs, but in later years (under Allen Tate and his successors) the magazine has been chiefly noted as an organ of the NEW CRITICISM and of avant-garde writing in general.

Seward, Anna (1747-1809). English poet, known as "the swan of Lichfield." She bequeathed her poems to Sir Walter Scott, who published them with a memoir in 1810.

Seward, William Henry (1801-1872). American statesman. After serving as governor of New York, Seward was elected to the U.S. Senate in 1848. An opponent of slavery, he attacked the COMPROMISE OF 1850 and the Kansas-Nebraska Act, claiming that the struggle over slavery entailed irrepressible conflict between North and South. After an unsuccessful attempt to win the Republican presidential nomination in 1860, he became Lincoln's secretary of state and apparently thought that he could dominate the administration, but the president soon showed Seward his error. Considered one of the greatest American secretaries of state, he carried on a successful foreign policy during the Civil War and later secured the withdrawal of French troops from Mexico. On the night of Lincoln's assassination, Seward, who was recovering from injuries sustained in an accident, was wounded by an accomplice of John Wilkes Booth. Continuing as secretary of state under Johnson, he purchased Alaska from Russia for $7,200,000, a transaction once known as "Seward's Folly."

Sewell, Anna (1820–1878). English writer. She is best known for her highly popular BLACK BEAUTY, THE AUTOBIOGRAPHY OF A HORSE, which was translated into most European languages. She also wrote stories in prose and verse for children.

Sextus Empiricus (fl. 190). A Greek physician and Skeptical philosopher. In *Pyrrhonean Sketches* he defends the position of the Skeptics, as he does in his other work *Against the Dogmatists* and *Against the Schoolmasters* (*Adversus Mathematicos*). Although he adds nothing original, he gives useful information on the positions he attacks.

Seymour, Jane. See JANE SEYMOUR.

Seyss-Inquart, Artur von (1892–1946). Austrian Nazi. He succeeded Schuschnigg as chancellor (1938) and proclaimed union with Germany.

Sforza. Italian family that ruled in the second half of the 15th century at Milan. From their obscure origins as soldiers of fortune they established themselves as a princely house and one of the leading powers of Italy. Among those noted for their cultivation of the arts and their patronage of learning were Francesco Sforza (1401–1466) and his son Lodovico Sforza (1451–1508), both dukes of Milan. Lodovico, surnamed *il Moro* (the Moor) because of his swarthy complexion, is especially known for his employment of Leonardo da Vinci.

Sganarelle. In the comedies of Molière, a favorite name for the cowardly, domineering or unpleasant character:

(1) The titular character in *Sganarelle, ou Le Cocu imaginaire* (*The Imaginary Cuckold*, 1660). This farce hinges on the consequences of Sganarelle's finding and confiscating the miniature of a gentleman, which he thinks his wife has dropped. In reality, the miniature was dropped by Clélie, and the portrait is not that of Sganarelle's imaginary rival but of Lélie, her sweetheart.

(2) In *L'Ecole des maris* (*The School for Husbands*, 1661), Sganarelle and his brother Ariste are the guardians of the two young orphans, Isabelle and Léonore. The conceited and domineering Sganarelle expects to marry Isabelle, but forces her to lead such a dull, strict life that she dupes him and marries Valère instead.

(3) In *Le Mariage Forcé* (*The Forced Marriage*, 1664), Sganarelle is a rich man of 64 who promises marriage to Dorimène, a young girl in her teens. He decides at the last moment to withdraw from the alliance, but Dorimène's brother beats him ruthlessly until he consents to go to the altar.

(4) In L'AMOUR MÉDECIN, Sganarelle is the selfish father of Lucinde.

(5) In DOM JUAN, OU LE FESTIN DE PIERRE, Sganarelle is Don Juan's rather foolish, cowardly valet.

(6) In LE MÉDECIN MALGRÉ LUI, the last of the Sganarelle plays of which *Le Cocu imaginaire* is logically the sequel, Sganarelle is a woodcutter. Martine, his wife, wanting to get even for the blows he has dealt her, tells some inquirers who are looking for a doctor that he is a noted specialist but so eccentric that he will deny it until they beat him well. Sganarelle, beaten, is taken to the house of the apparently dumb Lucinde. The shrewd Sganarelle sees through her ruse and brings her lover Léandre to her in the guise of an apothecary.

Shackleton, Sir Ernest Henry (1874–1922). English antarctic explorer. He accompanied Robert F. SCOTT on his 1901 expedition, and later conducted several expeditions of his own. He described them in *The Heart of the Antarctic* (1909) and *South* (1919).

Shadow-Line, The (1917). A short novel by Joseph CONRAD. Its hero is a young captain who grows mature in the experience of taking his sailing ship through a difficult calm.

Shadows on the Rock (1931). A novel by Willa CATHER. In part a result of the author's interest in the Roman Catholic church, this work is an episodic narrative of life in Quebec during the last days of Frontenac. The story centers in the life of Cécile Auclair, a child recently emigrated from France.

Shadrach, Meshach, and Abednego. In the Old Testament, 3 Hebrews who, because of their refusal to worship a golden image, were cast by the command of Nebuchadnezzar into a fiery furnace. But although the furnace was made burning hot, the three men "came forth of the midst of the fire" unharmed, convincing Nebuchadnezzar of the power of their God (Dan. 3:22).

Shadwell, Thomas (c. 1642–1692). English dramatist and poet. He is best known as Dryden's original for the titular hero of MACFLECKNOE and for Og in *Absalom and Achitophel* (1682). These satirical portraits were inspired by Shadwell's *The Medal of John Bayes* (1682), a savage attack on Dryden as a member of the court party. Shadwell later became poet laureate when Dryden was deprived of the position upon the accession of William III. His best plays, distinguished equally by their coarseness and acute observation of manners of the day, are *Epsom Wells* (1672) and *The Squire of Alsatia* (1688).

Shaftesbury, 1st earl of. Anthony Ashley Cooper (1621–1683). English statesman. A Royalist during the Civil War, he was a member of the CABAL after the Restoration and was named lord chancellor in 1672. A fomenter of the Popish Plot and a supporter of the duke of Monmouth, he was satirized by Dryden, who made him the Achitophel in his ABSALOM AND ACHITOPHEL. See MEDAL, THE.

Shahn, Ben (1898–). Lithuanian-born American artist. At one time assistant to Diego Rivera, he has put his expressive talent to public use, doing commercial work and posters as well as drawings and paintings of social import.

Shah-nama (The Book of Kings). Persian epic poem by FIRDOUSI. The poet labored for 35 years on this work, finishing it in 1010. It consisted of 60,000 couplets, but not all have survived. A legendary treatment of Persian history, it immediately became the national epic. It chronicles the entire history of Persia from the creation of man to the Sasanian empire (A.D. 226–641). By writing this epic Firdousī preserved material that was on the verge of oblivion; he used now lost written sources and the dying oral traditions for his material. While *Shah-nama* has many heroes, its main theme is an expression of Persian pride and glory.

Shakers. A celibate sect of Second Adventists, founded in the 18th century in England by a secession from the Quakers and transplanted to the U.S. by Ann LEE. Their official name is "The United Society of Believers in Christ's Second Appearing" or "The Millennial Church"; their popular name was originally derisive and refers to the contortions they made during the religious dances of which their public form of worship chiefly consisted. Theologically, they hold that God is dual, comprising the eternal father and eternal mother, the parents of angels and of men.

Shakespeare, William (1564–1616). English poet and dramatist of the Elizabethan and early Jacobean period, the most widely known author in all English literature. Shakespeare was born at Stratford-on-Avon, the son of John Shakespeare, a man who attained some prominence in town affairs, and Mary Arden, a woman of good family. William was probably educated at the King Edward IV Grammar School in Stratford, where he learned Latin and a little Greek and read the Roman dramatists. At 18 he married Anne Hathaway, some seven or eight years his senior, who bore him a daughter Susanna, in 1583, and twins, Hamnet (who died in boyhood) and Judith, in 1585. There is no record of Shakespeare's activities between 1585 and 1592, when he is known to have been in London and is alluded to as an actor and playwright in a bitter passage in Robert Greene's *A Groatsworth of Wit*. There is some speculation that Shakespeare may have taught school during this period, but it seems more probable that in 1585, or shortly after, he went to London and began his apprenticeship as an actor.

The London theaters were closed from June, 1592, to April, 1594, because of the plague. How Shakespeare earned his living during this period is not precisely known, though he probably had some income from his patron, Henry Wriothesley, earl of Southampton, to whom he dedicated his first two published poems: VENUS AND ADONIS (1593) and THE RAPE OF LUCRECE (1594). *Venus and Adonis* is a long narrative poem based on Ovid and dealing with Adonis' rejection of the goddess of love, his death, and the consequent disappearance of beauty from the world; it was immensely popular, and went through six editions in nine years. Contemporary sources, however, indicate that the more conservative elements objected to what they considered the poem's glorification of sensuality, and it may have been in response to this that Shakespeare wrote *Lucrece,* which

Shakespeare's signature, one of six known.

praises chastity. The story of the rape of the Roman matron LUCRETIA by Tarquin, it is based on tales found in Ovid, Livy, and Chaucer's *Legend of Good Women,* and written in rhyme royal. Though a more polished and in some senses a better poem than *Venus and Adonis,* it suffers from excessive length and never found the popularity of the earlier poem.

In 1594, Shakespeare appears in contemporary records as a member of the Lord Chamberlain's company of actors. The most popular of the companies acting at Court, it lasted through the reign of Elizabeth and became the company of the King's Men under the patronage of James I. In 1599 a group of the leading actors of Chamberlain's Men—Shakespeare among them—formed a syndicate to build and operate a new playhouse; it was named the GLOBE, and became one of the most famous theaters of its time. Largely from his share of the income of the Globe (and of BLACKFRIARS, in which he also had an interest) Shakespeare became a moderately wealthy man. As early as 1597 he purchased New Place, a large house in Stratford.

By 1597, Shakespeare had written at least a dozen plays: comedies, patriotic histories, and one tragedy in the bloody-revenge style popular in the Elizabethan theater. The dates of these plays, and their order of composition, cannot be definitely established. The earliest plays include, among the histories, HENRY VI (Parts I, II, and III, 1590–1592), RICHARD III (1594), RICHARD II (1595), and KING JOHN (1596–1597); among the comedies, THE COMEDY OF ERRORS (1590–1592), TWO GENTLEMEN OF VERONA (c. 1592), LOVE'S LABOUR'S LOST (1593–1594), A MIDSUMMER NIGHT'S DREAM (1595–1596); and, among the tragedies, TITUS ANDRONICUS (1590–1592). The earliest plays, as might be expected, show the greatest influence of contemporary and classical models; the early comedies are conventional, artificial, filled with ingenious conceits, puns, and other elaborate wordplay, but they foreshadow his later great comedies in their careful structure. The *Henry VI* plays, though faulty in themselves, developed into an early triumph in *Richard II. Titus Andronicus,* Senecan in style and strongly influenced by Thomas Kyd's *The Spanish Tragedy,* is so unlike Shakespeare's mature tragedies that some critics dispute his authorship of it.

ROMEO AND JULIET (1596), Shakespeare's second tragedy, is a transitional work; like the early comedies, it tends to be artificial, but in its lyricism and its development of character it indicates the direction of Shakespeare's growth. His plays in the last years of the 16th century are primarily comedies and histories: the so-called joyous comedies, namely, THE MERCHANT OF VENICE (1596), THE MERRY WIVES OF WINDSOR (1597–1600), MUCH ADO ABOUT NOTHING (1598–1599), AS YOU LIKE IT (1599–1600), TWELFTH NIGHT (1599–1600); and the histories of HENRY IV (Parts I and II, 1597–1598) and HENRY V (1598–1599). It is in these plays that Shakespeare's great gift for character portrayal becomes evident as he brings to life SHYLOCK, FALSTAFF, JAQUES, and a host of memorable figures.

The great period of Shakespeare's tragedies is ushered in at the turn of the century with JULIUS CAESAR (1599–1600). In the intensely drawn character of Brutus from this play there is a foreshadowing of the heroes of the first two of the great tragedies:

HAMLET (1600–1601) and OTHELLO (1604). These profound explorations of the human spirit are developed with even larger range in KING LEAR (1605–1606), generally regarded as his greatest work, and with a sharper focus in MACBETH (1606) and ANTONY AND CLEOPATRA (1607–1608). TIMON OF ATHENS (1607–1608) and CORIOLANUS (1608–1609) are his final tragedies, and their enigmatic quality is shared by the other plays of this period: TROILUS AND CRESSIDA (1600–1602), a play variously described as a comedy or a tragedy and now generally regarded as a serious satire; ALL'S WELL THAT ENDS WELL (1602) and MEASURE FOR MEASURE (1604–1605), two of "the dark comedies."

The plays of Shakespeare's last period are sometimes described as comedies, but might be better termed romances or tragicomedies; clearly experimental, they are light-hearted and yet serious, romantically fanciful and yet symbolic. They include PERICLES (1608–1609), CYMBELINE (1609–1610), THE WINTER'S TALE (1610–1611), and THE TEMPEST (1611–1612).

HENRY VIII, a history play, is the final work attributed to Shakespeare; it is generally considered to be an inferior piece, and many scholars believe much of it to have been written by John Fletcher. Eighteen of Shakespeare's plays were published separately in quarto editions during his lifetime; a complete collection of his works did not appear until the publication of the FIRST FOLIO in 1623.

Shakespeare's achievements did not go unnoticed among his contemporaries. In 1598, Francis Meres cited "honey-tongued" Shakespeare for his plays and poems. With Shakespeare as their leading dramatist, the Chamberlain's Men rose to become the leading dramatic company in London, and, in 1603 were installed as members of the royal household, bearing the title of the King's Men.

Sometime after 1612, Shakespeare apparently retired from the stage and returned to Stratford. In January, 1616, he had his will drawn up; it included the famous bequest to his wife of his "second best bed." On April 25 of that year, he was buried at Stratford Church, and the monument over his tomb lists the day of his death as April 23, 1616.

Although Shakespeare was ranked among the foremost dramatists of his time by his contemporaries, evidence indicates that both he and his world looked to poetry, not playwriting, for enduring fame. In the years following the publication of *Venus and Adonis* and *Lucrece,* Shakespeare continued to write poems; his sonnets (see SONNETS OF SHAKESPEARE) were composed between 1593 and 1601, though not published until 1609. In 1599 there appeared a volume of 20 poems called THE PASSIONATE PILGRIM; Shakespeare's name was given on the title page, but only five of the poems (I, II, III, V, and XVII) are now believed to be his. A poem called THE PHOENIX AND THE TURTLE, attributed to Shakespeare, was published in Robert Chester's *Loves Martyr* (1601). A LOVER'S COMPLAINT, published at the end of the 1609 edition of the sonnets, is written in the same meter as *Lucrece* but seems to belong to a different period. Not all scholars agree that it is the work of Shakespeare.

During the 17th and early 18th centuries Shakespeare suffered at the hands of those—including Alexander Pope—who would "improve" him; his plays were frequently staged, but apparently he was not widely read. There was, however, a considerable upsurge of interest in his works, beginning in the middle of the 18th century and continuing with the enthusiastic criticism of Samuel Taylor Coleridge, Charles Lamb, and William Hazlitt. The 19th century also saw the growth of the theory that someone other than Shakespeare—usually Sir Francis Bacon —wrote his plays (see BACONIAN CONTROVERSY).

Shakespeare's sonnets. See SONNETS OF SHAKESPEARE.

Shakuntala. In Hindu mythology, the daughter of Visvamitra and Menaka. She is the heroine of KALIDASA's Sanskrit drama *Shakuntala.* She was abandoned on the banks of the river Malini and brought up by the hermit Kanva. While hunting one day King Dushyanta meets Shakuntala, falls in love with her, and persuades her to marry him. He gives her a ring before returning to his throne. Shakuntala gives birth to a son and sets out with him to find Dushyanta. She loses the ring while bathing and the king, enchanted by Durvasas' curse, does not recognize her. The ring is subsequently recovered by the king in the stomach of a fish he has caught. He then recognizes his wife and proclaims her his queen. Their son, Bharata, becomes the heir to the throne and later the founder of the race of the Bharatas.

The play, written in both poetry and prose, follows a highly traditionalized style. Like Attic Greek drama, the plot is taken from mythology and there is no effort to use suspense or to introduce elements into the story that are not already known to the sophisticated audience. Through his poetry and music the playwright seeks to evoke states of being and to elicit the emotions in his audience: love, mirth, energy (the heroic emotion), terror, disgust. Each scene is supposed to engender some emotional flavor, but not to run counter to the dominant emotion of the play, which in the case of *Shakuntala* is erotic.

Shākyamuni. See BUDDHA.

Shallow, Justice Robert. A weak-minded country justice in Shakespeare's HENRY IV: PART II, HENRY V and, more prominently, in THE MERRY WIVES OF WINDSOR. A braggart, he is fond of endlessly recounting his imaginary exploits. He is Slender's cousin.

shamanism. A primitive form of religion. Those who practice it believe that the world and all events are governed by good and evil spirits who can be propitiated or bought off only through the intervention of a witch doctor, or *Shaman.* The word is Slavonic; it comes from the Samoyeds and other Siberian peoples, but is now applied to American Indian and other primitive worship.

Shamash. The Babylonian sun-god. The son of Sin, the moon-god, and brother of Ishtar, he was a divine dispenser of justice. In this role it was he from whom HAMMURABI claimed to have received sanction for his code of laws. His wife was Aya, the Dawn. He is almost identical with the Sumerian god Utu.

Shandy, Tristram. See TRISTRAM SHANDY.

Shandy, Walter. In Laurence Sterne's novel TRISTRAM SHANDY, the father of the hero-historian. Walter's great aim is to rear his child to be a great man, but all his schemes are confounded by fate: the child is baptized Tristram not Trismegistus;

his nose is crushed by Dr. SLOP's forceps; a window-sash falls leaving Tristram circumcised or worse.

Shang or **Yin.** The first historical Chinese dynasty (c. 1523–1027 B.C.). Centering about the Yellow River with its capital at Anyang, it possessed a highly developed civilization. Exquisite Chinese bronzes and oracle bones, inscribed with an advanced form of writing, which date to this period, were unearthed in excavations in the late 1920's.

Shangri-La. In James HILTON's popular novel *Lost Horizon* (1933), a mythical land of eternal youth and safety from war, supposedly situated somewhere in the interior of Tibet. Shangri-La has come to mean any ideal refuge.

shanties (from Fr. *chanter* to sing). Songs sung by sailors at work, to ensure united action; also called *chanties*. They are in sets, each of which has a different cadence, adapted to the work at hand.

Shan Van Voght. An Irish patriotic song (1798). The title is a corruption of *Ant-sean bhean bhocht* (the poor old woman, i.e., Ireland).

Shapiro, Karl [Jay] (1913–   ). American poet, critic, and editor. Shapiro is best known for his poems of World War II, the best of which appeared in *V-Letter and Other Poems* (1944). Other collections include *Person, Place, and Thing* (1942), *The Place for Love* (1943), *Trial of a Poet and Other Poems* (1947), *Poems 1940–1953* (1953), and *Poems of a Jew* (1958). His critical works include *Essay on Rime* (1945), a philosophical discourse in verse, and *Beyond Criticism* (1953). *In Defense of Ignorance* (1960) is a collection of essays on modern poetry. He was editor of *Poetry* magazine from 1950 to 1956 and later was editor of *Prairie Schooner.*

Sharp, Becky or **Rebecca.** The central character in the novel VANITY FAIR by William Makepeace Thackeray. She is a cool, unprincipled, selfish girl, whose only object is to rise in the world from her obscure and poverty-stricken origins. "She was small and slight in person, pale, sandy-haired, and with green eyes, habitually cast down, but very large, odd, and attractive when they looked up."

Sharp, Margery (1905–   ). English novelist. Among her light, popular novels are *The Nutmeg Tree* (1937), *Cluny Brown* (1944), *Britannia Mews* (1946), *The Gypsy in the Parlor* (1953), and *The Turret* (1963).

Shatov, Ivan Pavlovich. In Feodor Dostoevski's THE POSSESSED, an earnest, awkward former student and friend of STAVROGIN whose father had been a servant in the household of Stavrogin's mother. He has become obsessed with the idea of the mission of Russia in saving the world with the unsullied Christianity preserved in Orthodoxy, a notion once casually dropped by Stavrogin. Shatov is a member of VERKHOVENSKI's revolutionary group. When he tries to quit, Verkhovenski has him murdered.

Darya Pavlovna Shatova. Ivan's sister, a ward in the household of Varvara Petrovna, Stavrogin's mother. The open-hearted Darya is in love with Stavrogin and immediately agrees to go away with him to begin a new life elsewhere. Before the plan is carried out, Stavrogin hangs himself.

Marya Ignatyevna Shatova. Ivan's wife, who returns to him on the evening of his murder and gives birth to a child, presumably fathered by Stavrogin.

Shatriya. See CASTE.

Shaun the Postman. In James Joyce's novel *Finnegans Wake,* the name by which Kevin, one of H. C. Earwicker's twin sons, is generally known. He represents the man of action. Shem is his opposite. See FINNEGANS WAKE.

Shaw, George Bernard (1856–1950). Irish dramatist, critic, and social reformer. Idealistic, prudish, afraid of intimacy, often shy, Shaw's public image was his own created caricature: "G.B.S." The beard, the mysticism, the eccentricities all belonged to G.B.S., whom Shaw used as the spokesman for his social, moral, and literary theories. Political and economic socialism, a new religion of creative evolution, anti-vivisection, vegetarianism, and spelling reform were a few of his causes. His plays and essays, never written solely to entertain, were the vehicles for Shaw's theories; G.B.S. was his press agent.

Shaw had written five unsuccessful socialist novels by 1884 when he met William Archer, who urged him to write modern, purposeful dramas as Ibsen had done. Through Archer, Shaw became music critic for a London newspaper. He was well known for his music reviews long before he became famous as a dramatist. He began to write for the stage in 1885. With most of his early plays either banned by the censor or refused production, Shaw sought a reading audience with his first published collection, *Plays Pleasant and Unpleasant* (1898), the pleasant plays being ARMS AND THE MAN, CANDIDA, *The Man of Destiny,* and *You Never Can Tell;* the unpleasant, *The Philanderer,* MRS. WARREN'S PROFESSION, and his first play, *Widowers' Houses.* It was for this volume that Shaw began the practice of writing the challenging, mocking, eloquent prefaces to his plays, the prefaces sometimes being longer than the plays themselves and covering a diversity of topics.

By 1900, some of Shaw's plays had been produced in the U.S. and in Germany, but not in England. His next collection of plays, *Three Plays for Puritans* (1900), contained THE DEVIL'S DISCIPLE, CAESAR AND CLEOPATRA, and CAPTAIN BRASSBOUND'S CONVERSION.

Before the outbreak of the First World War, and largely through the efforts of H. Granville-Barker, Shaw had been accepted in England; his position as a playwright was secure, and his fame worldwide.

Because of his attacks on British policy during the war and his continual irritation to reactionary elements in England, Shaw was widely unpopular for a time, but his international fame allowed him to speak his mind and write what he pleased.

Shaw wrote his best plays prior to, during, and shortly after the First World War. They include MAN AND SUPERMAN, JOHN BULL'S OTHER ISLAND (written at the request of William Butler Yeats for the Irish Literary Theater), MAJOR BARBARA, MISALLIANCE, *Fanny's First Play* (1912), ANDROCLES AND THE LION, PYGMALION, *Great Catherine* (1918), HEARTBREAK HOUSE, BACK TO METHUSELAH, and SAINT JOAN. He received the Nobel prize for literature in 1925.

A member of the FABIAN SOCIETY from its founding (1883), Shaw wrote many essays on socialism, politics, and economics and one longer work, *The Intelligent Woman's Guide to Socialism and Capitalism* (1928).

He wrote less as he grew older, but never stopped completely; he was at work on a comedy when he died at the age of 94. His last full-length play, *Buoyant Billions,* was produced in Zurich in 1948 "before a respectful if uncomprehending audience."

Always outspoken, with a barbed humor and wit, never satisfied with the conventional, Shaw conducted himself so that the adjective *Shavian* is descriptive of an iconoclastic way of life, rather than a literary form.

His fame and popularity rest on his plays, but John Mason Brown has observed, "This astonishing Mr. Shaw has been greater than anything even he has written."

Shaw, Henry Wheeler. See Josh BILLINGS.

Shaw, Irwin (1913–   ). American playwright, short-story writer, and novelist. He first wrote serials for radio, turning to the stage with his antiwar play BURY THE DEAD. *The Gentle People: A Brooklyn Fable* (1939) was a dramatic fantasy dealing with the threat of dictatorship. Shaw wrote other plays, but achieved even more success with two collections of short stories: *Sailor Off the Bremen* (1939) and *Welcome to the City* (1942). His first novel was THE YOUNG LIONS, a book set during World War II. His next novel, *The Troubled Air* (1950), dealt with the plight of the liberal caught between witch-hunting on the one hand, and Communist pressure on the other. Later works include *Lucy Crown* (1956) and *Two Weeks in Another Town* (1960). Shaw has also written a number of motion-picture scenarios.

Shays, Daniel. See SHAYS' REBELLION.

Shays' Rebellion (1786–1787). An uprising of western Massachusetts farmers against the foreclosure of mortgages on their property. The insurgents were led by Daniel Shays (1747–1825), a former captain in the Revolutionary Army, who was seeking to prevent their imprisonment for debt as a result of the very high land taxes levied after the Revolution. *The Duke of Stockbridge* (1879), a novel by Edward Bellamy, describes this episode.

Shchedrin, N. See Mikhail Evgrafovich SALTYKOV.

Shchepkin, Mikhail Semenovich (1788–1863). Russian actor. He is generally considered the finest of 19th-century Russia's actors. His realistic style paved the way for the drama of Ostrovski and Chekhov and the acting theories of Stanislavski.

She (1887). A romance by Rider HAGGARD. "She," or Ayesha, is an African sorceress whom death apparently cannot touch. The young English hero, Leo Vincey, sets out to avenge her murder of his ancestor, an ancient priest of Isis.

Shearing, Joseph. See G. M. V. LONG.

Sheba, queen of. The queen who visited King SOLOMON (I Kings 10), known to the Arabs as Balkis, queen of Saba. According to the Old Testament story, she came to Solomon "to prove him with hard questions," but on seeing him in all his glory and wisdom, had "no more spirit in her." One version of the story holds that she bore Solomon a son, Menelek, from whom the Abyssinians were descended.

Shedeem. See MAZIKEEN.

Sheean, [James] Vincent (1899–   ). American foreign correspondent and writer. He is best known for *Personal History* (1935), his interesting, best-selling autobiography. His other nonfiction works include *Not Peace but a Sword* (1939), a denuncia-

tion of fascism; *Lead Kindly Light* (1949), a tribute to Gandhi; *The Indigo Bunting, A Memoir of Edna St. Vincent Millay* (1951); *Nehru, The Years of Power* (1958); and *Dorothy and Red* (1963), an account of the marriage of Dorothy Thompson and Sinclair Lewis. He has also written a number of novels, including *Gog and Magog* (1930), *A Certain Rich Man* (1947), and *Lily* (1954).

Sheep Well, The. See FUENTEOVEJUNA.

Sheffield, John. 3rd earl of **Mulgrave,** 1st duke of **Buckingham and Normanby** (1648–1721). English political leader, poet, essayist, and dramatist, patron and friend of Dryden and Pope. He is remembered chiefly for his *Essay on Satire* (1680), which, published anonymously and attributed to Dryden, resulted in the latter's being attacked by some thugs engaged by the earl of Rochester.

Sheik, The (1921). A novel by the English popular novelist Edith Maude Hull. A preposterous story that made a semiscandalous sensation, it became the basis for a famous movie with Rudolph Valentino.

Sheldon, Charles M[onroe] (1857–1946). American clergyman. He is the author of the novel *In His Steps* (1896), one of the greatest all-time best sellers. Sheldon published other works of exhortation, but none achieved the fame of this book. From 1902 to 1925, he was editor of the *Christian Herald.*

Sheldon, Edward Brewster (1886–1946). American playwright. His best-known plays were melodramas based on the social problems current in the early 20th century. His first success was SALVATION NELL, written while he was still at Harvard. THE NIGGER created a furore because its hero is a white man with Negro blood, whose fiancée does not reject him. Later came THE BOSS, *The High Road* (1912), ROMANCE, and other successful plays. He also collaborated with Sidney Howard on *Bewitched* (1924), with Charles MacArthur on *Lulu Belle* (1926), and with Margaret Ayer Barnes on *Dishonored Lady* (1930).

Shellabarger, Samuel (1888–1954). American historical novelist and biographer. After teaching at Princeton (1914–1923), Shellabarger retired to write historical romances, such as *Captain from Castile* (1945), about the conquest of Mexico by Cortez; *Prince of Foxes* (1947), about Renaissance Italy; and *The King's Cavalier* (1950), about Renaissance France. He also wrote mysteries and light romances under the pen names John Esteven and Peter Loring. *The Chevalier Bayard* (1928) and *Lord Chesterfield* (1935; rev., 1951) are scholarly biographies.

Shelley, Mary Wollstonecraft. Born **Godwin** (1797–1851). English novelist, daughter of William GODWIN and Mary WOLLSTONECRAFT and second wife of Percy Bysshe SHELLEY. She wrote in the convention of the GOTHIC NOVEL. FRANKENSTEIN OR THE MODERN PROMETHEUS is her best-known work. Other romances are *Valperga* (1823), *The Last Man* (1826), *Lodore* (1835).

Shelley, Percy Bysshe (1792–1822). English poet. Although he was the son of a conservative country squire, Shelley was influenced early in life by the doctrines of the Enlightenment, ardently championing liberty and rebelling against the strictures of English politics and religion. While at Oxford he wrote and circulated a pamphlet called *The Necessity of Atheism,* and was sent down for "contumacy in refusing to answer certain questions" about it. In 1811, when he was 19, he eloped with 16-year-old Harriet WESTBROOK, and the pair spent the following two years traveling in England and Ireland, distributing pamphlets and speaking against political injustice. By 1814, however, an estrangement was growing between them, and they were separated. At about the same time he met William Godwin, whose *Political Justice* had strongly influenced the early direction of his thinking, and soon fell in love with Godwin's daughter Mary (see Mary SHELLEY). In the summer of 1814 he and Mary eloped to the Continent; though they did not believe in marriage because of its exclusiveness and limitations, they were married after Harriet committed suicide in 1816. Their household, however, was scarcely conventional, and after 1818 they lived exclusively in Italy, where Shelley did his best work.

Shelley's early poetry includes *Queen Mab*, written in 1812–1813, a long work inveighing against orthodox Christianity and secular tyranny, and *Alastor, or the Spirit of Solitude* (1816), an allegory of a youth seeking in vain for a being equal to his most perfect imaginings. His *Hymn to Intellectual Beauty*, conceived during a voyage on Lake Geneva with Byron in 1816, reflects Shelley's Platonism. He revised the early *Laon and Cythna*, an allegorical poem on the French Revolution, and renamed it *The Rise of Islam;* somewhat similar in ideological content to *Queen Mab*, it was the last long poem Shelley wrote before leaving for Italy in 1818. He was working on *The Cenci* (1819), a blank-verse drama on the unfortunate Beatrice CENCI, when news came of the PETERLOO MASSACRE at Manchester; inspired by outrage and pity, he wrote the *Mask of Anarchy*. He soon began working on PROMETHEUS UNBOUND, a lyric and symbolic drama for which he adapted elements from the Greek myth of Prometheus.

In 1819 the Shelleys moved to Pisa, where Shelley composed many of his shorter lyrics, among them THE CLOUD, *To a Skylark*, ODE TO THE WEST WIND, and THE SENSITIVE PLANT; with the earlier OZYMANDIAS (written 1817), these poems have become the most famous among Shelley's works, though their popularity has obscured his general recognition as a philosophical poet.

Among Shelley's last works are EPIPSYCHIDION, a passionate love poem addressed to Emilia VIVIANI; and ADONAIS, an elegy on the death of Keats modeled after the elegies of Bion and Moschus and frequently considered to be, of elegies in English, second only to Milton's *Lycidas*. In 1821, in response to Thomas Love Peacock's disparaging comments on the value of poetry in *The Four Ages of Poetry*, Shelley wrote his famous *Defence of Poetry*. Based somewhat on Sir Philip Sidney's essay, and drawing on ideas contained in the *Symposium* and *Ion* of Plato, the *Defence* is interesting primarily for the light it throws on Shelley's philosophical thought and his analysis of the value of the creative imagination.

In 1822 the Shelley household, which now included Jane and Edward Williams, moved to the Bay of Lerici, where Shelley wrote the poems addressed to Jane and sailed with Edward. He was at work on a long poem, *The Triumph of Life*, which was left incomplete when his boat was caught in a storm and he and Edward Williams were drowned. Their bodies were washed ashore at Viareggio where, in the presence of Lord Byron and Leigh Hunt, they were burned on the beach.

A thorough student of Greek, Shelley was a Platonist and a humanist, looking to the Athens of the time of Pericles as the ideal toward which present-day civilization should be directed. Though his enthusiasms had the spontaneity and impulsiveness of an adolescent, there can be little question of the sincerity of his beliefs or his dedication to his liberal ideals. Never an atheist, he rejected orthodox Christianity but always held to the idea of some "pervading spirit co-eternal with the universe," and rejected all conventions that he believed stifled love and human freedom. His poetry, typically abstract and allegorical, reflects his concern with the nature of transcendent reality.

Shem. In the Old Testament, the eldest of the three sons of NOAH, whose supposed descendants are called Semites (Shemites) from his name.

Shem the Penman. In James Joyce's novel *Finnegans Wake*, the name by which Jerry, one of H. C. Earwicker's twin sons, is generally known. He represents the artist. Shaun is his opposite. See FINNEGANS WAKE.

Shenstone, William (1714–1763). English poet, known for his pastoral verse, including songs, odes, ballads, and elegies. His major works include *The Judgment of Hercules* (1741), a poem; THE SCHOOLMISTRESS; and *Essays on Men and Manners*, prose *pensées* in the manner of La Rochefoucauld.

Sheol. See HADES.

Shepard, Benjamin Henry Jesse Francis (1848–1927). English-born American musician and essayist. Shepard became famous as a pianist during his 20's; when he began to write essays he took the pen name of Francis Grierson, so that his two talents would be judged independently. He lived abroad for many years, but in 1913 returned to the U.S. to devote himself to writing and lecturing. His first book, written in French and published in France, was *La Révolte Idéaliste* (1889); his other volumes include *Modern Mysticism and other Essays* (1899), *The Celtic Temperament and Other Essays* (1901), *The Valley of Shadows: Recollections, 1858–63* (1909), and *Abraham Lincoln, The Practical Mystic* (1921).

Shepard, Ernest H. (1879–   ). English illustrator and political cartoonist. Much of his work has appeared in *Punch*, but it is for his illustrations of A. A. Milne's Christopher Robin books and Kenneth Grahame's *Wind and the Willows* that he is most widely known.

Shepheardes Calender, The (1579). Twelve eclogues by Edmund SPENSER, one for each month of the year. The first and last eclogues are laments by the shepherd Colin Clout (a persona of Spenser) because the fair Rosalind does not return his love. The remaining ten are dialogues on love and other subjects among the shepherds.

Shepherd Kings. See HYKSOS.

Shepherd Lord. Epithet for Henry de Clifford, 10th baron of Westmoreland (d. 1523). He was sent by his mother to be brought up by a shepherd, in order to save him from the fury of the Yorkists. At the accession of Henry VII he was restored to all his rights and seigniories. His story is told by Wordsworth in *The Song for the Feast of Brougham Castle*.

Januarye.

The month of January from Spenser's *The Shepheardes Calender* (1597 edition).

Sheridan, Philip Henry (1831–1888). American Union general in the Civil War. His army was endangered at Cedar Creek while he was in conference with General Grant at Winchester; on that day, Oct. 19, 1864, he made a famous ride that turned imminent defeat into victory. His feat is celebrated in *Sheridan's Ride* (1865) by Thomas Buchanan Read. In 1883 Sheridan succeeded Sherman as commander of the U.S. army. His *Personal Memoirs* were published in 1888.

Sheridan, Richard Brinsley (1751–1816). Irish-born English dramatist, orator, and statesman. He wrote brilliantly polished, satirical comedies of manners that returned to the general vein of the Restoration period, although critics have pointed out that the moral tone of his works is not to be found in the drama of 17th-century England. He established himself as a versatile playwright within one year (1775) with the Covent Garden Theater productions of THE RIVALS, *St. Patrick's Day,* and *The Duenna,* a light opera. In 1776 he succeeded David Garrick as manager of the Drury Lane Theater. His other plays include THE SCHOOL FOR SCANDAL, *The Critic* (1779), and *Pizarro* (1799), a melodramatic tragedy.

Sherman, Frank Dempster (1860–1916). American writer of light verse. Among his collections are *Madrigals and Catches* (1887), *Lyrics for a Lute* (1890), and *Lyrics of Joy* (1904).

Sherman, William Tecumseh (1820–1891). American general. After succeeding Grant as commander of the Union forces in the West during the Civil War, Sherman captured Atlanta on Sept. 1, 1864 and began his famous March to the Sea, which cut the Confederacy in half. His men lived off the country, destroying enemy supplies, buildings, and

railroads, and so devastated the region that Sherman's name is still anathema in the South. After the war he performed important services in the West. When Republican leaders attempted to nominate him for the presidency in 1884, he replied, "I will not accept if nominated, and will not serve if elected." The remark that "war is hell," usually attributed to Sherman, probably stems from a speech (1880) in which he said, "There is many a boy here today who looks on war as all glory, but, boys, it is all hell."

Sherriff, Robert Cedric (1896–). English playwright and novelist. Among his plays are JOURNEY'S END, *Windfall* (1933), and *St. Helena* (with Jeanne de Casalis; 1934). His best-known novels are *The Fortnight in September* (1931) and *The Hopkins Manuscript* (1939). He has written motion picture scenarios.

Sherwood, Robert E[mmet] (1896–1955). American playwright and editor. Wounded in World War I, Sherwood early resolved to do all he could to stop future wars. This attitude appears in *Acropolis* (1933), which attacked Hitler, and IDIOT'S DELIGHT, a Pulitzer Prize-winning drama. Sherwood had earlier been drama critic of *Vanity Fair* (1919–1920), and associate editor and then editor of *Life* (1920–1928).

His first Broadway play was THE ROAD TO ROME, a comedy satirically attacking the concept of military glory. This was followed by *The Love Nest* (1927), *The Queen's Husband* (1928), *Waterloo Bridge* (1930), *This Is New York* (1931), REUNION IN VIENNA, THE PETRIFIED FOREST, ABE LINCOLN IN ILLINOIS, and THERE SHALL BE NO NIGHT.

Sherwood was extremely vocal in warning of the dangers of European totalitarianism. During World War II he was at various times special assistant to the secretaries of war and the navy, and director of the overseas operation of the Office of War Information. He helped write some of Franklin D. Roosevelt's speeches and later won his fourth Pulitzer Prize with *Roosevelt and Hopkins:An Intimate History* (1948). During this period, Sherwood did little writing for the stage, only *The Rugged Path* (1945) and a musical comedy, *Miss Liberty* (1949), with Irving Berlin. In the next years he wrote a number of movie scripts and plays for television.

She Stoops to Conquer, or, The Mistakes of a Night (1773). A comedy by Oliver GOLDSMITH. The story concerns young Marlow, a bashful young man who feels easy only with barmaids and serving girls. It is with reluctance that he sets forth to win the hand of Miss Hardcastle. Tricked into believing that the home of Mr. Hardcastle is a village inn, he treats her enraged father as if he were an impudent landlord. Miss Hardcastle takes advantage of the situation, posing first as the barmaid, then as a poor relative and thus conquers Marlow. The mistakes of the evening unravel with the arrival of Marlow's father who had arranged the match. Mr. Hardcastle forgives young Marlow and all ends happily. This comedy is noted for its rich characterizations and retains its deserved popularity.

Shestov, Lev. Pen name of **Lev Isaakovich Schwarzman** (1866–1938). Russian philosopher and critic. He is best known for his studies of Tolstoi, Dostoevski, and Nietzsche, and his doctrine of the primacy of irrationalism in human thought, expressed in his books *The Apotheosis of Groundlessness* (*Apofeoz bespochvennosti;* 1905), also known as *All Things Are Possible,* and *Athens and Jerusalem* (1938).

shibboleth. The password of a secret society; the secret by which those of a party know each other; also, a worn-out or discredited doctrine. The Ephraimites could not pronounce *sh,* so when they were fleeing from Jephthah and the Gileadites (*Judges* 12:1–16) they were caught at the ford on the Jordan because Jephthah caused all the fugitives to say the word shibboleth (which means "a stream in flood"), which all the Ephraimites pronounced as sibboleth.

Shigalyov. In Feodor Dostoevski's THE POSSESSED, a member of VERKHOVENSKI's revolutionary group. He is a burlesque portrait of a political theorist. Reporting on his plan for the new order after the revolution, the bewildered Shigalyov admits that in working out his ideas he began with unlimited freedom in the system and ended with unlimited despotism.

Shih-ching. See BOOK OF ODES.

Shiites or **Shiahs** (Arabic, *shiah,* a sect). Those Muslims who regard Ali as the first rightful Imam or Caliph (rejecting the three Sunni Caliphs), and do not consider the SUNNA, or oral law, of any authority, but look upon it as apocryphal. There are numerous Shiite sects, all of them regarded as heretical by the orthodox SUNNITES. Because of the Shiite doctrine of the MAHDI, a 12th Imam who is supposedly living in concealment through the centuries, but is expected to appear to rule Islam, the Shiites have had a political as well as a religious influence on the development of Islamism.

Shiloh, battle of (Apr. 6–7, 1862). A U.S. Civil War battle near Pittsburg Landing, Tenn. A Union army under Gen. Ulysses S. Grant was attacked and nearly defeated by the Confederates under Gen. A. S. Johnston. The arrival of reinforcements under Gen. Buell and Gen. Lew Wallace enabled the Union forces to drive the Confederates from the field, but they were too weakened for pursuit. Gen. Johnston was killed in the first day of fighting. The battle is sometimes called the battle of Pittsburg Landing.

Shimazaki Tōson (1872–1943). Japanese poet and novelist. His work shows strong Western influence. *Hakai* (*Broken Commandment,* 1906) concerns the *eta,* or outcast class, and was one of the earliest Japanese novels to deal with social problems.

Shin Buddhism. See AMIDISM.

Shingon or **Esoteric Buddhism.** A Japanese Buddhist sect. Introduced from China by Kukai, it gained wide popularity with Tendai Buddhism during the Heian period (784–1185). Shingon Buddhism centers its teaching on Vairocana, the Cosmic Buddha, and emphasized secret ritual, and learning, transmitted directly from master to disciple.

Shinto. The native religion of the Japanese. It emphasizes the worship of natural objects, ancient deities, and national heroes. From the Nara period (710–794) it coexisted with Buddhism and many of its gods were incorporated into the Buddhist pantheon. Although without a literature and fixed tenets, it has always held a firm place in Japanese religious life. The Meiji government accorded it state sponsorship (1868) and officially divorced it from Buddhist influences. The word *shinto* means literally "the way of the gods."

Shipman's Tale, The. One of the CANTERBURY TALES of Geoffrey CHAUCER, based on a popular *fabliau.* The monk John has claimed cousinship with a rich merchant in order to frequent his house and be near his wife. Just before the merchant departs on a business trip, the wife complains bitterly to John about her husband's miserliness and begs the loan of 100 francs to pay a debt for fine clothes. John then asks the departing merchant for a loan, takes the money to the wife, and spends the night with her. When the merchant returns, John thanks him for the loan and says he has already returned it to his wife. She, when questioned, claims she understood the money was meant as a gift because of the two men's friendship. The merchant decides the case is hopeless and accepts her offer to pay him back in their marriage bed.

Ship of Fools. Title of a number of allegorical satires lashing the weaknesses and vices of their times. The first popular one was Sebastian BRANT's *Das Narrenschiff* (1494), a poem in rhymed couplets assembling on a ship bound for Narragonia, the land of fools, representatives of every age, class, and quality among men. In exposing, among other things, abuses within the Church, it helped prepare the way for the Protestant Reformation. Written in an Alsatian dialect, it was almost immediately translated and adapted throughout Europe; in English the most famous versions were Alexander Barclay's *The Ship of Fools* (1509) and the anonymous *Cock Lovell's Bote* (c. 1510).

Ship of Fools (1962). A novel by Katherine Anne PORTER. It is an allegorical account of a voyage of the German ship *Vera* from Veracruz, Mexico, to Bremerhaven in 1931. The title of the book, taken from Sebastian Brant's 15th-century novel *Das Narrenschiff*, represents a "simple almost universal image of the ship of this world on its voyage to eternity."

Shipton, Mother. A fictitious English prophetess. She is first heard of in a tract of 1641, in which she is said to have lived in the reign of Henry VIII, and to have foretold the death of Cardinal Wolsey, Thomas Cromwell, Lord Percy, and others. In 1677, Richard Head the pamphleteering publisher, brought out a *Life and Death of Mother Shipton*, and in 1862 Charles Hindley brought out a new edition in which she was credited with having predicted steam engines, the telegraph, and other modern inventions, as well as the end of the world in 1881. Bret Harte named one of the characters in his story *The Outcasts of Poker Flat* (1869) Mother Shipton.

Shirer, William L[awrence] (1904–). American journalist. He vividly depicted the rise of Nazism in his CBS radio reports from Germany and in his *Berlin Diary* (1940). His massive history of *The Rise and Fall of the Third Reich* (1960) was a notable best seller.

Shirley (1849). A novel by Charlotte BRONTË. The story is set in Yorkshire at the end of the Napoleonic Wars. The depressed wool industry of the time, and the strife between workers and the hero, a mill owner named Robert Gerand Moore, figure in the plot. The heroine, Shirley Keeldar, was drawn from Charlotte's sister, Emily.

Shirley, James (1596–1666). English dramatist, often called "the last of the Elizabethans" because he was the last important dramatist writing when the theaters were closed by Parliament in 1642. He is best known for his comedies of manners, such as THE LADY OF PLEASURE, The *Witty Fair One* (1628), *Hyde Park* (1632) and *The Gamester* (1633), although he wrote at least two noteworthy tragedies: THE CARDINAL and *The Traitor* (1631). Other plays include *The Royal Master* (1638), *The Young Admiral* (1633), *The Doubtful Heir* (1640), *The Ball* (1632), and such masques as *The Triumph of Peace* (1634) and *Cupid and Death* (1653).

Shiva or Siva (Sans., *the blessed one*). The 3rd person of the Hindu trinity, or TRIMURTI, representing the destructive principle in life. Since in Hindu philosophy restoration is involved in destruction, Shiva is also the reproductive or renovating power. Shiva is a worker of miracles through meditation and penance, and hence is a favorite deity with the ascetics. He is a god of the fine arts, and of dancing. Shiva is also known as Hara, and Mehadeva, "the Great God." His consort is Kali.

Shoemaker's Holiday, The (1600). A comedy by Thomas DEKKER. Two young lovers, Rowland Lacey and Rose Otley, are determined to overcome the efforts of their parents to keep them apart. Rowland, who is supposed to be with the army in Europe, returns to London disguised as a Dutch cobbler, takes a job in the shop of the prosperous shoemaker Simon Eyre, and eventually reveals himself to Rose. After many complications, Rowland and Rose are married, and Simon, now Lord Mayor, declares a holiday.

shogun. The title of the actual ruler of Japan from the 12th century to the restoration of the emperor in 1868. The *shoguns* were hereditary military commanders-in-chief (the word means army leader), and took the place of the emperors, whom they kept in a state of perpetual confinement, but with some show of prestige.

Sholem or Shalom Aleichem. See Sholem ALEICHEM.

Sholokhov, Mikhail Aleksandrovich (1905–). Russian novelist. His famous novel THE QUIET DON is considered the major literary work written since the revolution. Born in the Don Cossack region of southern Russia, Sholokhov published his first volume of stories, *Don Tales* (*Donskiye rasskazy*) in 1925. The next year he began work on his major novel, *The Quiet Don,* a study of the conflicting loyalties set loose among the Don Cossacks by the revolution. The four-volume work was immensely popular, selling millions of copies in Russia and abroad. In 1936, Sholokhov was elected to the Supreme Soviet, the country's legislative body, and in 1939 he was awarded the Order of Lenin. He was the Nobel laureate in literature in 1965.

Between the publication of the third and fourth volumes of *The Quiet Don,* Sholokhov worked on a novel dealing with the collectivization of agriculture during the Five-Year Plan in Russia. This work, VIRGIN SOIL UPTURNED was less artistically successful than Sholokhov's masterpiece, but it gave a good picture of the misery caused by collectivization.

Sholokhov's place in Soviet literature, based mainly on his authorship of *The Quiet Don,* is a secure one. His novel is cited as a model to young writers, although recent trends have been away from his type of objective realism. In recent years, Sholokhov's role has been confined to that of a representative of the conservative wing of literature, chiding the younger writers for their modernist views and methods.

Shore, Jane (1445?–1527). Mistress of Edward IV. She left her husband, a London goldsmith, in 1470 to become the mistress of the king, and through her wit and beauty exerted great influence. After the death of Edward she continued to have political influence, thereby incurring the hatred of Richard III who accused her of practicing witchcraft. She was put to public penance and became a prisoner in London, remaining in poverty and disgrace until her death.

Thomas Churchyard, in 1563, and Nicholas Rowe, in 1714, wrote tragedies based upon her life, both entitled *Jane Shore.* She is also the heroine of a ballad included in Percy's *Reliques,* and appears in Shakespeare's *Richard III,* Thomas Heywood's *Edward IV,* and many other works of literature.

Shortest Way with the Dissenters, The. See Daniel DEFOE.

Short Happy Life of Francis Macomber, The (1938). A short story by Ernest HEMINGWAY. In this compact, taut, and dramatic story, the Macombers, an American couple, are on a safari in Africa with the Englishman Wilson as their guide. When confronted with a mad, wounded lion, Macomber proves himself a coward, is saved by Wilson, and earns his wife's utter contempt. On the next hunting expedition the following day, Macomber feels a gathering strength, and his wife, who has always found gratification in his weakness, is suddenly frightened by this new Macomber. His second chance comes with a wild buffalo. Cowardice vanishes, and, as he heroically tries to fell the onrushing beast, a bullet fired by his wife misses the buffalo and kills Macomber. The tale infuses Hemingway's favorite theme, cowardice as opposed to courage, with tragic overtones, and is one of the best of his shorter pieces.

Shorthouse, Joseph Henry (1834–1903). English novelist and Birmingham manufacturer, best known for his historical and religious novel *John Inglesant* (1881).

Short-Lived Administration. The English cabinet formed by William Pulteney on February 12, 1746. It lasted only two days.

Shostakovitch, Dmitri Dmitrievitch (1906–   ). Russian composer. His first symphony (1926) was very popular; later works were criticized in Russia for their "western decadence," especially the opera *Lady Macbeth of the District of Mtzensk* (1934; based on a story by Leskov). Official Soviet approval was restored with the performance of his famous *Symphony No. 5*. His *Symphony No. 7* (1942), depicting the German siege of Leningrad, was performed frequently by the allies during World War II.

Shōwa. See HIROHITO.

Show Boat (1926). A novel by Edna FERBER. In this popular book three theatrical generations appear: Captain Andy Hawks, who runs a showboat on the Mississippi and marries Parthy Ann, a prim New England schoolmarm; their daughter, Magnolia, who becomes an actress and runs off with the leading man Gaylord Ravenal; and their daughter Kim, who grows up to be a Broadway star. In 1927 the novel was made into one of the best known of all American musical shows, with music by Jerome Kern and libretto by Oscar Hammerstein, 2nd.

Shridharani, Krishnalal Jethalal (1911–1960). Indian writer who resided in the U.S. He described his dual life in *My India, My America* (1941) and *Warning to the West* (1942).

Shropshire Lad, A (1896). See A. E. HOUSMAN.

Shrovetide. A period of carnival and merrymaking ending with Shrove Tuesday, the last day before the beginning of the penitential season of Lent. The name of Shrove Tuesday derives from the fact that on this day people are "shriven," or absolved of their sins.

Shrovetide-play. See FASTNACHTSSPIEL.

Shu-ching. See BOOK OF DOCUMENTS.

Shui Hu Chuan. Chinese novel. A Robin Hood-type adventure, it describes the exploits of a 108-man robber band whose members had fled government oppression. Not attributable to one author, the story evolved over a period of centuries. Banned in the Ch'ing period (1644–1912). Translated by Pearl Buck, *All Men are Brothers* (1933).

Shuruppak. A very ancient Sumerian city. Of several ancient Near Eastern accounts of a deluge, the Biblical story is the only one in which the hero did not live in Shuruppak. See UTNAPISHTIM; ZIUSUDRA.

Shute, Nevil. Pen name of **Nevil Shute Norway** (1899–1960). English novelist. An aeronautical engineer and managing director of an airplane factory, Shute concocted his very popular novels out of plenty of technological detail and exciting plots. His early adventure stories include *An Old Captivity* (1940), *Pied Piper* (1941), and *No Highway* (1948).

Later novels were set in Australia: *A Town Like Alice* (1950, U.S. title *The Legacy*), *The Far Country* (1952), and *On the Beach* (1957), a piece of science fiction which predicts atomic destruction of the entire world. *Stephen Morris* (1961) consists of two novels found in manuscript after the author's death: *Stephen Morris* and *Pilotage*.

Shy, Timothy. A pen name of D. B. Wyndham LEWIS.

Shylock. The avaricious Jewish money-lender in Shakespeare's MERCHANT OF VENICE. When his daughter Jessica elopes, taking some of his money with her, he is more concerned with the loss of his ducats than the loss of his daughter. His hatred for the merchant Antonio is so great that he persists in obtaining a pound of flesh as forfeit for his bond until he is outwitted by Portia in the Venetian court.

One of the most controversial of Shakespearean roles, Shylock was played as a low-comedy character until Charles Macklin electrified London audiences in 1741 by making the despised usurer a tragic, dignified figure. His performance drew from Alexander Pope the comment, "This was the Jew that Shakespeare drew."

Although Shylock cannot be described as a likable or attractive character, he utters the moving speech:

Hath not a Jew eyes? hath not a Jew hands, organs, dimensions, senses, affections, passions? . . . If you prick us, do we not bleed? if you tickle us, do we not laugh? if you poison us, do we not die?

Sibelius, Jean (1865–1957). Finnish composer. A fervent nationalist, Sibelius wrote music—symphonies, songs, and choral works—that captures the spirit of Finnish mythology: remote, melancholy, and grand. The tone poem *Finlandia* (1899) is the most popular of his works.

sibyl. A prophetess of classical legend, who was supposed to prophesy under the inspiration of a particular deity. The name is now applied to any prophetess or woman fortuneteller. There were a number of sibyls, and they had their seats in widely separate parts of the world: Greece, Italy, Babylonia, Egypt, etc.

Plato mentions only one sibyl, the Erythraean, identified with Amalthaea, the Cumaean sibyl, who was consulted by Aeneas before his descent into Hades and who sold the SIBYLLINE BOOKS to Tarquin. Martianus Capella speaks of two, the Erythraean and the Phrygian; Aelian of four, the Erythraean, Samian, Egyptian, and Sardian. Varro tells us there were ten, the Cumaean, the Delphic, Egyptian, Erythraean, Hellespontine, Libyan, Persian, Phrygian, Samian, and Tiburtine.

The medieval monks adopted the sibyls, as they did so much of pagan myth; they made them 12 in number and gave to each a separate prophecy and distinct emblem.

Sibylline Books. A collection of oracles of mysterious origin, preserved in ancient Rome and consulted by the Senate in times of emergency or disaster. According to Livy, there were originally nine of these books; they were offered in sale by Amalthaea, the SIBYL of Cumae, to Tarquin; the offer was rejected, and she burned three of them. After 12 months, she offered the remaining six at the same price. Again being refused, she burned three more, and after a similar interval asked the same price for the three left. The sum demanded was then given, and Amalthaea never appeared again.

The three books were preserved in a stone chest underground in the temple of Jupiter Capitolinus, and committed to the charge of custodians chosen in the same manner as the high priests. The number of custodians was at first 2, then 10, and ultimately 15. Augustus had some 2,000 of the verses destroyed as spurious, and placed the rest in two gilt cases, under the base of the statue of Apollo, in the temple on the Palatine Hill, but the whole perished when the city was burnt in the reign of Nero.

A Greek collection in eight books of poetical utterances relating to Jesus Christ, compiled in the second century, is entitled *Oracula Sibylina* or the *Sibylline Books*.

sic (Lat., "thus"). A word sometimes inserted [sic] to indicate that the preceding word or phrase is reproduced exactly as in the original text, calling attention to the fact that it is wrong in some way.

Sic et Non (Yes and No). A compilation of theological arguments by Pierre ABÉLARD. It is notable as being an unprejudiced listing of all the arguments, pro and con, on the doctrinal questions of the Middle Ages with no attempt to draw conclusions.

Siddal, Elizabeth [Eleanor] (d. 1862). Wife of Dante Gabriel ROSSETTI who both before and after her marriage posed for his paintings and served as an inspiration for his poetry, notably *The Blessed Damozel*. A frail, lilylike beauty, she died just two years after her marriage. Rossetti, beside himself with grief, buried with her in her coffin the sole copy of a manuscript of poems dealing with their love and marriage; in 1869 the manuscript was recovered and published. *The House of Life* was contained in the collection.

Siddons, Sarah, born **Kemble** (1755–1831). English tragic actress, sister of John Philip and Charles KEMBLE. She appeared first at Drury Lane in the role of Portia. She became the leading Shakespearean actress of her time; her greatest role was Lady Macbeth.

Sidney, Algernon (1622–1683). English politician. During the Civil War he fought at Marston Moor and became a Parliamentary leader. He lived on the Continent after the Restoration until 1677. Known to be a supporter of the duke of Monmouth, he was accused of complicity in the RYE HOUSE PLOT and executed for treason.

Sidney, Sir Philip (1554–1586). English poet, scholar, soldier, and courtier, regarded by many as the perfect example of the Renaissance gentleman. Sidney came from a noble family, traveled extensively on the Continent, and was one of the most admired of Elizabeth's courtiers. With his uncle, the earl of Leicester, Sidney took part in a military expedition to the Low Countries, and was fatally wounded at Zutphen. According to the traditional story told by his friend and biographer Fulke Greville, the wounded Sidney gave his own water bottle to a dying foot soldier, saying "Thy necessity is greater than mine." His death was greatly mourned and celebrated in a number of elegiac poems, the best of which is Edmund SPENSER's *Astrophel*.

Only two of Sidney's poems were published during his lifetime, but his works were read and circulated among his friends. His essay entitled AN APOLOGIE

THE
COVNTESSE
OF PEMBROKES
ARCADIA,
WRITTEN BY SIR PHILIPPE SIDNEL

LONDON
Printed for William Ponfonbie.
Anno Domini, 1590.

Title page of Philip Sidney's *Arcadia* (1590).

FOR POETRIE (written c. 1580; published 1595) is perhaps the most eloquent and solid critical work of the Elizabethan period. *Arcadia* (written c. 1580, published 1590) is a pastoral romance in prose, interspersed with lyrics, which established that genre in England. ASTROPHEL AND STELLA (written 1580–1584, published 1591) created a vogue for the sonnet sequence in England. Sidney's poetry, though making much use of conventional Petrarchan elements, is distinguished by its metrical skill, its poignant, grave, and virile tone.

Siècle de Louis le Grand, Le. See Charles PERRAULT.

Siege of Corinth, The (1816). A poetical version by Lord BYRON of the siege that occurred in 1715. The lover of the daughter of the besieged Venetian governor betrays the citadel to the Turks, and then proceeds to blow up everybody, including himself.

Siege of Rhodes, The (1656). The first English opera. It was written by Sir William DAVENANT, with music in the prologue by Henry Lawes and "recitation music" by Dr. Charles Coleman and George Hudson.

Siege Perilous. Also called **The Perilous Seat.** In Arthurian legend, especially Malory's *Morte d'Arthur* (c. 1469), a vacant chair at the ROUND TABLE of King Arthur, reserved for the one predestined to achieve the quest of the Grail. It was the death of any other who sat in the chair. At the appointed time the name of GALAHAD is found on the Siege Perilous; he takes the chair and later goes on to win the quest of the Grail.

Siegfried. Hero of the first half of the NIBELUNG-ENLIED and the second half of Wagner's RING DES NIBELUNGEN. He is known as Sigurd in the VÖLSUNGA SAGA. Jean GIRAUDOUX gives a modern adaptation of Siegfried's story in his novel *Siegfried et le Limousin* (1922) and his play *Siegfried* (1928).

Siegfried Line. The western line of defense established by Germany in World War II, opposed to the Maginot Line in France.

Sienkiewicz, Henryk (1846–1916). Polish novelist. His WITH FIRE AND SWORD, *The Crusaders* (4 vols., 1900), and CHILDREN OF THE SOIL were well received in English translation, but he is best known for his historical novel of Nero's court, QUO VADIS? written in 1895. His portrait of the hero, Petronius Arbiter, is a memorable one. In 1905 he received the Nobel prize for literature.

Sieveking, Lance[lot de Giberne] (1896–   ). English writer and playwright. He is best known for his productions of radio and television plays on the BBC. He is the author of many radio plays; his works include *Dressing Gowns and Glue* (1919), *Stampede* (1924), and *Silence in Heaven* (1936). Among his books are *The Stuff of Radio* (1934), *Soul of a Heel* (1952), and *The Eye of the Beholder* (1957).

Signac, Paul. See NEOIMPRESSIONISM.

Sign of the Reine Pédauque, At the (La Rotisserie de la Reine Pédauque; 1893). A novel by Anatole FRANCE. The chief character is Jérôme COIGNARD.

Signorelli, Luca (1441–1523). Italian painter of the Umbrian school. A pupil of Piero della Francesca, he produced many easel and fresco paintings of religious and mythological subjects, but excelled primarily in rendering the nude. His great painting entitled *Pan*, formerly at Berlin, was the single most tragic loss in art during World War II. Although he assisted Botticelli in decorating the walls of the Sistine Chapel and painted in other rooms of the Vatican, the latter were painted over to allow their decoration by Raphael. His best surviving work is now the series of frescoes, *Heaven and Hell*, in the Orvieto cathedral.

Sigurd. See SIEGFRIED.

Sikes, Bill. In Charles Dickens' OLIVER TWIST, a brutal, violent house-breaker and thief. The only rudiment of a redeeming feature he possesses is a kind of affection for his dog. His murder of his mistress, Nancy, is a horrible but celebrated incident in the novel.

Sikh (Hindi, "one who is learning, a disciple"). Originally, a member of a monotheistic religious body which broke off from Hinduism in the Punjab in the 16th century. The Sikhs soon formed a military community, and in 1764 formally assumed independence. From 1849 to 1947 the Sikhs, as part of India, were ruled by the British. Reinforced with a code of the highest ascetic and moral ideals, the religion of the Sikhs, as propounded by the *gurus* (spiritual leaders), enjoins on every Sikh the strict observance of the "five K's": *kesha* (long hair), *kanga* (the hair comb), *kaccha* (the undergarment), *kada*

(the steel bangle), and *kirpan* (the dagger worn in self-defense). The orthodox Sikh neither smokes nor drinks. Sikhs are famous for their courage and fighting ability.

Silas Marner, or the Weaver of Raveloe (1861). A novel by George ELIOT. The author says that the book "is intended to set in a strong light the remedial influences of pure, natural, human relations." Silas is a lonely, embittered hand-loom weaver who long ago was accused of a theft of which his best friend was guilty, and so robbed of the girl he loved. He has no friends in Raveloe, the village to which he has come, and cares only to add a little more gold to the pile in his humble cottage. In close succession two strange events occur: he is robbed of his gold, and finds by chance a little yellow-haired baby girl whom no one claims. Gradually he is brought back into a more wholesome, normal life through his love for little Eppie. In the meantime, much of the story is concerned with the affairs of the two sons of Squire Cass, Dunstan and Godfrey. Dunstan, who is a wild reckless fellow, always in debt, disappears. Godfrey marries the girl of his choice, Nancy Lammeter. At last, after 16 years Silas' lost gold is found, together with the skeleton of Dunstan Cass. Godfrey now confesses that Eppie is the offspring of his earlier, secret marriage to a common woman who died the night Eppie was found; he asks Eppie to come and live with him and Nancy, but Eppie chooses to stay with Silas and eventually marries a village boy whom she has always known.

Si le grain ne meurt. See IF IT DIE. . . .

Silence. A country justice in Shakespeare's HENRY IV: PART II. When sober, he is dull and asinine; drunk, he is outrageously funny.

Silenus (Seilenos). In Greek mythology, an elderly follower of DIONYSUS. Originally there were many *sileni*, male spirits of the woods who became associated with the worship of Dionysus; later, Silenus was differentiated, and usually represented as a sly, cowardly, and often drunken old man. As such he appears in innumerable paintings of the Renaissance. He is a leading character in Euripides' satyr play *Cyclops*.

Silesius, Angelus. See ANGELUS SILESIUS.

Silhouette, Etienne de (1709–1767). French controller general of finances (1759). His rigid economies were ridiculed by certain members of the nobility who applied his name sarcastically to any mode or fashion that was plain or cheap; eventually it was used only in the restricted sense to apply to portraits in which the painter's expensive art is replaced by a profiled outline in plain black; hence, *silhouette*.

Sill, Edward Rowland (1841–1887). American writer of essays and verse. A professor of English at the University of California, he contributed essays to the *Atlantic Monthly* and wrote poems under the name of Andrew Hedbrooke. His best-known poems are *The Fool's Prayer* and *Opportunity*. Among his collections are *The Hermitage and Other Poems* (1868), *The Venus of Milo and Other Poems* (1883), and *Poems* (1887).

Sillanpää, Frans Eemil (1888–1964). Finnish novelist and short-story writer. His novels, which are sensitively written and reveal keen psychological insight, include *Hurskas Kurjuus* (*Meek Heritage*, 1919) and *Nuorena nukkunut* (*Fallen Asleep While Young,* 1931). In 1939, Sillanpää received the Nobel Prize for literature.

Sillitoe, Alan (1928–   ). English novelist. A factory worker who left school at 14, Sillitoe writes best about the lives of contemporary workers and their families in industrial towns. His heroes are young anarchists whose lives are constant struggles against conventional morality, employers, and the ESTABLISHMENT. His books include SATURDAY NIGHT AND SUNDAY MORNING; THE LONELINESS OF THE LONG DISTANCE RUNNER, a collection of short stories; *The General* (1960), an allegorical story about war and a general who captures the enemy's orchestra by mistake; *Key to the Door* (1962), about Brian Seaton, brother of the hero of his first novel; and *The Ragman's Daughter and Other Short Stories* (1964). See ANGRY YOUNG MEN.

Silone, Ignazio. Original name: **Secondo Tranquilli** (1900–   ). Italian novelist. Silone lived in his native Pescina, a small village in central Italy, until it was destroyed in 1915 by an earthquake that took the lives of his mother and several of his brothers. In 1922 he was editor of *Il Lavoratore,* a labor newspaper in Trieste, that was raided by the fascists. Although his brother was seized and was subsequently beaten to death in prison, Silone managed to elude capture, finding shelter among the Italian peasantry with whose life and cause his own work has so movingly and consistently identified itself. From 1930 to the fall of the fascist regime, he lived in Switzerland, where he wrote his two great novels: *Fontamara* (1934; revised, 1960) and BREAD AND WINE. They brought him international fame, though neither they nor his next novel, *The Seed Beneath the Snow* (*Il Seme sotto la Neve;* 1942), were published in Italy until after the war.

Once a fervent Marxist and member of the Communist Party, Silone described his disillusionment and break with the party (1930) in an essay in *The God that Failed* (1950), edited by Richard Crossman. At the same time he affirmed his faith in socialism as "an extension of the ethical impulse from the restricted individual and family sphere to the whole domain of human activity."

His other novels include *A Handful of Blackberries* (*Una Manciata di More;* 1952), *The Secret of Luca* (*Il Segreto di Luca;* 1956), and *The Fox and the Camellias* (*La Volpe e le Camelie;* 1961). He also wrote *Fascismus* (*Il Fascismo;* 1934), a history of fascism; *The School for Dictators* (*La Scuola dei Dittatori;* 1938), a satirical treatise on the training of dictators; and *Ed Egli Si Nascose* (*And He Hid Himself,* 1945), a play.

Silurist, the. See Henry VAUGHAN.

Silva, José Asunción (1865–1896). Colombian poet, considered a precursor of MODERNISM. A tragic figure of acute sensibility, Silva felt oppressed by the smug provincialism of his native Bogotá, against which he rebelled in bitter, though highly lyrical, verse. The death of a beloved sister is said to have inspired his best-known poem, *Nocturno III,* which displays the musicality and morbid melancholy, akin to Poe's, that distinguish his poetry. Another characteristic note is the nostalgic yearning for the past that is evident in the short poem *Vejeces.* He died by his own hand.

Silvanire. See Jean MAIRET.

Silver, Long John. See TREASURE ISLAND.

Silver Cord, The (1926). A play by Sidney HOWARD. It is one of the earliest psychological studies of a dominant mother to be presented on the stage. Mrs. Phelps has two sons, one of whom is unable to break away from her, while the other succeeds only through the help of his wife.

Silver-Fork school. A name given to a class of English novelists who gave undue importance to etiquette and the externals of social intercourse. The most distinguished are Lady Blessington (1789–1849), Theodore Hook (1716–1796), Bulwer-Lytton (1803–1873), Mrs. Trollope (1790–1863), and Disraeli (1804–1881).

Silvia. In Shakespeare's Two GENTLEMEN OF VERONA, the duke of Milan's virtuous and beautiful daughter, who is in love with Valentine. When Valentine's friend Proteus declares his love for her, she refuses him and chides him for his unfaithfulness to his friend. She runs away from her father's court to join Valentine when he is banished, and finally is allowed to marry him.

Silvius. A young shepherd, embodying Shakespeare's somewhat satirical view of pastoral love, in As YOU LIKE IT. He is in love with the shepherdess Phebe.

Simenon, Georges. Also **Georges Sim** (1903–   ). Belgian-born French novelist. Simenon is most famous for his detective stories, especially the series about Inspector Maigret, which includes *Les Fiançailles de M. Hire* (1933), *Le Coup de lune* (1933), and *La Maison du Canal* (1933). Later he wrote more ambitious psychological analyses of modern man, among them *La Neige était sale* (1948), *La Mort de Belle* (1952), *Lettre à mon juge* (1947), and *L'Ours en peluche* (1960).

Simeon Stylites. See STYLITES.

simile. In rhetoric, a figure of speech: a comparison between two things of a different kind or quality, usually introduced by "like" or "as." Simile is one of the two main figures of speech, the other being METAPHOR; in simile, the comparison made is explicit, whereas in metaphor it is implied. The object of both simile and metaphor is double: to achieve clarity and exactness of meaning; and to achieve vividness of presentation and style. An example of simile is:

> Now the chimney was all of the house that stood,
> Like a pistil after the petals go.
>
> > Robert Frost

Simms, William Gilmore (1806–1870). American novelist and poet. Born in Charleston, S.C., Simms had a varied career, marked by numerous misfortunes. Although he considered himself primarily a poet and published 18 volumes of verse up to 1860, his reputation rests on his historical novels. The first of these, *Guy Rivers* (1834), which deals with a fiendish Georgia bandit, was an outstanding success. Also included in the series known as "the Border Romances" are THE YEMASSEE and *The Cassique of Kiawah* (1859), in which Indians figure prominently, and two novels based on the KENTUCKY TRAGEDY: *Beauchampe* (1842) and its sequel, *Charlemont* (1846). The series called "the Revolutionary Romances" includes THE PARTISAN and its sequels,

Mellichampe (1836) and *Katharine Walton* (1851); *The Kinsmen* (1841), later revised as THE SCOUT; *The Sword and the Distaff* (1853), later issued as WOODCRAFT; and *The Forayers* (1855) and its sequel, *Eutaw* (1856).

In his romances Simms was a loyal follower of Sir Walter Scott and James Fenimore Cooper. His stories preserve a wealth of local tradition and vividly express many aspects of the American Revolution in South Carolina. An ardent defender of the Southern ideal of agrarian life, Simms was also steeped in Elizabethan literature, and one of his best characters, Captain PORGY, has been called "the American Falstaff."

A member of the CHARLESTON SCHOOL, Simms was surrounded by a coterie of young men in his later years, chief among them Paul Hamilton Hayne.

Simon. In the New Testament: (1) The original name of the disciple PETER (Matt. 10:2); (2) a Pharisee who entertained Jesus and criticized him for forgiving the sins of a woman of the streets who anointed his feet (Luke 7); (3) a sorcerer of Samaria, also called Simon Magus ("Simon the Magician"), rebuked by Peter because he attempted to buy the power of the Holy Spirit (Acts 8); this is the origin of the term *simony*, the buying of ecclesiastical power.

Simon, Claude (1913–). French novelist born in Madagascar, considered a member of the NEW WAVE of fiction. All his works are characterized by a fluid style of long, convoluted sentences. They give extremely detailed and precise descriptions of sensual impressions, yet often leave their essence or significance obscure. His most successful novels are *The Wind* (*Le Vent;* 1957) and *The Grass* (*L'Herbe;* 1958), both set in the rural south of France, and *The Flanders Road* (*La Route des Flandres;* 1960), in which three soldiers remember the fall of France in 1940.

Simonides (c. 506–467 B.C.). A Greek poet. Born at Ceos, he was the first Greek poet to make a living from his writing. He was highly admired by Classical writers. He is said either to have invented or perfected the epinicion, but is better known for his elegiac epigrams. Especially famous is his epitaph for those who died at Thermopylae. (See PERSIAN WARS.)

Simon Lee (1798). A poem by William WORDSWORTH, subtitled *The Old Huntsman with An Incident in which He Was Concerned.* The incident is that the poet helps Simon dig up the root of a tree, which causes him to relate the simple story of the old huntsman's life.

Simonov, Konstantin (1915–). Russian novelist, poet, dramatist, and short-story writer. Simonov attained popularity during the war with *Dni i nochi* (*Days and Nights,* 1945), a novel portraying the defense of Stalingrad, and a play, *Russkiye lyudi* (*Russian People,* 1942). Another war novel, *Zhivye i myortvye* (*The Living and the Dead,* 1962), deals with events in Russia in 1941 just after the Germans invaded the country. During the Stalinist era, Simonov managed to avoid dangerous or fatal entanglements with the government, in which other prominent Soviet authors so often became involved.

Simonson, Lee (1888–). American scenic designer. He early designed scenery for the Washing-

ton Square Players and later for the Theatre Guild, which he helped found. His sets for the Metropolitan Opera's production of *The Ring of the Nibelungen* (1948) were highly praised. Among his books are *The Stage Is Set* (1932) and *The Art of Scenic Design* (1950).

Simon the Canaanite or **Simon Zelotes** (the Zealot). One of the original 12 disciples. Almost nothing is known of this disciple except that at one time he had been a member of the Zealots, an ultranationalistic Jewish group.

Simple Cobler of Aggawam in America, The (1647). A tract by Nathaniel Ward, published under the pseudonym Theodore de la Guard. The book is a satirical denunciation of England and New England for being "tolerant," of England for the quarrel between Parliament and the Crown, and of the human race in general and women in particular for being silly. Ward's vitrolic, witty style has been compared to that of Elizabethan pamphlet writers such as Greene and Nash. Aggawam was an early name for Ipswich, Mass.

Simple Heart, A (*Un Coeur Simple;* 1877). A short story by Gustave FLAUBERT. Originally published in the volume *Trois Contes,* it portrays the life of Félicité, the servant of Mme Aubain—a small-town, bourgeois widow and mother of two children. Flaubert reveals himself as a true master of the genre in the careful strokes that picture the endless self-denial of Félicité's existence; only faith remains upon the canvas at the completion of the work.

simple life. An existence unhampered by the luxuries and artificialities of civilization. It implies a return to the life led close to nature as imagined by the pastoral poets. The phrase was taken as the title of a book by Charles Wagner (1901), a Lutheran preacher in Paris who was brought up in the pastoral surroundings of the Vosges, and was popularized by President Theodore Roosevelt. See PRIMITIVISM.

Simplicissimus. (1) The popular title of a novel (1668, expanded 1669) by Hans GRIMMELSHAUSEN. Its full title is *Der abenteuerliche Simplicissimus* (*The Adventurous Simplicissimus*). A picaresque story set during the Thirty Years War, it treats the development of its hero's originally simple soul toward resignation and wisdom. It is well known as a panorama of contemporary events, of the horrors and injustices of war, but its treatment of psychological development has caused some critics to give it a place in the growth of the *Bildungsroman* (novel of education or development).

(2) A satirical weekly, founded (1896) by Thomas T. Heine in Munich. Its last pre-Nazi editor was Franz Schoenberner whose *Confessions of a European Intellectual* (1946) was well received in America.

Simpson, Louis (1923–). American poet and novelist. Born in the British West Indies, Simpson came to the U.S. in 1940. With Donald Hall and Robert Pack, he edited *New Poets of England and America* (1957). Collections of his own poetry include *The Arrivistes* (1949), *Good News of Death and Other Poems* (1955), and *A Dream of Governors* (1959). His poems frequently deal with interpretation, usually ironic, of mythical subjects. He has written a novel, *Riverside Drive* (1962), and a critical study of James Hogg (1962).

simurgh. In Eastern legend, a huge bird who has seen the destruction of the world three times and has all the knowledge of the ages. He is perhaps identical with the ROC.

Sin. The Babylonian moon-god. An old man, he was the first of the astral deities and father by Ningal of Shamash (the sun-god), ISHTAR, and Nesku (the fire god). He rode in his moon boat through the sky at night. He is much like NANNA, the moon deity of Sumerian Ur.

sin. Failure to attain to the standard of behavior attributed to God's moral requirements. In Roman Catholic theology sins are distinguished as *venial* (those that do not forfeit the state of grace) and *mortal* (those that forfeit the state of grace and can be removed only by confession and absolution).

In Milton's *Paradise Lost* Sin is the Keeper of the Gates of Hell, together with Death. Described as half woman, half poisonous serpent, she sprang full grown from the head of Satan.

The Man of Sin (referred to in 2 Thess. 2:3) is generally held to signify the Antichrist. However, it was applied by the old Puritans to the Roman Pope, by the fifth monarchy men to Cromwell, and by many 19th-century theologians to "that wicked one" (identical with the "last horn" of Dan. 7) who was immediately to precede the second advent of Christ.

Sinbad or Sindbad the Sailor. A well-known story in the *Arabian Nights*. Sinbad is a Baghdad merchant who acquires great wealth by going on seven voyages. He describes these to a poor discontented porter, Hindbad, to show him that wealth can only be obtained by enterprise and personal exertion.

First Voyage. Being becalmed in the Indian Ocean, he and some others of the crew visit what they suppose to be an island, but which is really a huge whale asleep. They light a fire on the whale and the heat wakes the creature, which instantly dives under water. Sinbad is picked up by some merchants, and in due time returns home.

Second Voyage. Sinbad is left on a desert island where he discovers a ROC's egg fifty paces in circumference. He fastens himself to the claw of the bird and is deposited in the Valley of Diamonds. The next day, some merchants come to the top of the crags and throw into the valley huge joints of raw meat to which the diamonds stick; when the eagles pick up the meat, the merchants scare them from their nests and carry off the diamonds. Sinbad then fastens himself to a piece of meat, is carried by an eagle to its nest, and, rescued by the merchants, returns home laden with diamonds.

Third Voyage. This is the encounter with the Cyclops. See POLYPHEMUS.

Fourth Voyage. Sinbad marries a lady of rank in a strange island on which he is cast; when his wife dies, he is buried alive with the dead body according to the custom of the land. He makes his way out of the catacomb and returns to Baghdad, greatly enriched by valuables rifled from the dead bodies.

Fifth Voyage. The ship in which he sails is dashed to pieces by huge stones let down from the talons of two angry rocs. Sinbad swims to a desert island, where he throws stones at the monkeys who throw back coconuts in return. On this island, Sinbad encounters and kills the OLD MAN OF THE SEA.

Sixth Voyage. Sinbad visits the island of Serendip (Ceylon) and climbs to the top of the mountain where Adam was placed on his expulsion from Paradise.

Seventh Voyage. Sinbad is attacked by corsairs, sold into slavery, and employed in shooting at elephants from a tree. He discovers a tract of hill country completely covered with elephants' tusks, communicates his discovery to his master, obtains his liberty, and returns home.

Sinclair, May (1865–1946). English novelist. The best of her popular books were experimental in technique and based on the new Freudian psychology. A feminist, May Sinclair wrote her first novels about the lives of women and followed the point of view of George Bernard Shaw and H. G. Wells. *The Divine Fire* (1904), a study of a temperamental Cockney genius supposedly drawn from the poet Ernest Dowson made her famous. *Three Sisters* (1914) is a novel loosely based on the situation of the Brontë sisters, confined in a Victorian rectory. MARY OLIVIER is her best-known novel.

Sinclair, Upton [Beall] (1878–1968). American writer of novels and nonfiction. Sinclair, a remarkably prolific author, is known for his steady espousal of socialism and his concern with social and political problems. The first of his 80-odd books was the novel *Springtime and Harvest* (1901), later called *King Midas*. It was followed by *The Journal of Arthur Stirling* (1903), which was first regarded as factual rather than fictional. His best-known book, THE JUNGLE, created a sensation when published; it shocked President Theodore Roosevelt, who invited Sinclair to the White House, and was influential in the passage of the Pure Food and Drug Act (1906).

Sinclair used his earnings from *The Jungle* to found the cooperative Helicon Home Colony, near Englewood, N.J. The project, in which Sinclair Lewis participated briefly, was abandoned after a mysterious fire in 1907. In 1915, Sinclair moved to California. In 1934 he was the Democratic candidate for governor of the state, running on the famous EPIC (End Poverty in California) platform; after an acrimonious campaign, he was narrowly defeated.

Meanwhile, Sinclair continued to write steadily. Among his later novels are *The Metropolis* (1908), *Love's Pilgrimage* (1911), *King Coal* (1917), OIL, BOSTON, and *Affectionately Eve* (1961). His nonfiction works include *The Brass Check* (1919), a highly critical treatise on journalism, based on his own experiences; *American Outpost: A Book of Reminiscences* (1932); and *Upton Sinclair Presents William Fox* (1933). His *Autobiography* appeared in 1962.

With the rise of fascism and communism in Europe, Sinclair also became more interested in foreign affairs; he wrote a long series of popular novels, beginning with *World's End* (1940), which deal with Lanny Budd, scion of a wealthy family, who takes it upon himself to right the world's wrongs and becomes a prominent figure in international politics and intrigue.

Sindibad, Tales of. See SEVEN WISE MASTERS, THE.

Singer, Israel Joshua (1893–1944). A Polish-born novelist and playwright. He wrote in Yiddish. His best-known book is *The Brothers Ashkenazi*

(1936), a novel that has been translated into English, Danish, Swedish, and Dutch. He became a U.S. citizen in 1939.

Singh, Khushwant (1917–   ). Indian novelist writing in English. A lawyer by profession, he became a free-lance writer and has published three studies of Sikh culture, two short story collections, and two novels, *Mano Majra* (1956), an account of the partition days, and *I Shall Not Hear the Nightingale* (1959).

Sinis. In Greek mythology, a robber of the Isthmus of Corinth known as the Pine-Bender. He used to fasten his victims to two pine trees bent toward each other; they were rent asunder by the rebound. He was eventually captured by Theseus and put to death in this same way.

Sinister Street (1913–14). The best-known title in a series of novels by Compton MACKENZIE. An early archetype of the novel of growing up, it describes the childhood and youth of Michael and Stella Fane, illegitimate children of wealthy parents. The book was published in two volumes in England, and appeared in the U.S. as *Youth's Encounter* (1913) and *Sinister Street* (1914). *Plashers Mead* (1917), *Sylvia Scarlett* (1918), and *Sylvia and Michael* (1919) continue the story up to Michael's marriage.

Sinjohn, John. The pen name under which John GALSWORTHY published his early work.

Sinn Fein (Ourselves alone). The name given to the extreme home rule party in Ireland in the 20th century. It grew out of early nationalistic agitation but reached its greatest power with the Easter rebellion of 1916.

Sinon. The Greek who induced the Trojans to receive the wooden horse (Vergil: AENEID, ii, 102, etc.). Dante, in his INFERNO, places Sinon, with Potiphar's wife, Nimrod, and the rebellious giants, in the tenth pit of Malebolge.

Sio, Kewlian (1935–   ). Indian novelist and poet writing in English. Born of Chinese-Sikkimese parents, he lives and works in Calcutta; his writing reveals extreme sensitivity within a limited range. He has published a collection of stories, *A Small World* (1960).

Sion. Another name for Mount Hermon in the Anti-Lebanons. It is to be distinguished from ZION.

Sirat, Al (Arabic, "the path"). An imaginary bridge, in Muslim legend, said to span the distance between earth and paradise, yet be no wider than a spider's thread. Sinners fall into the abyss below.

Sir Charles Grandison (1753). An epistolary novel by Samuel RICHARDSON, which relates the love story of Sir Charles and Harriet Byron. The hero, a male counterpart of CLARISSA HARLOWE, is an ideal 18th-century gentleman who rescues Harriet from her abductor, Sir Hargrave Pollexfen. Sir Charles becomes enamored of Harriet, but is honor-bound to marry a beautiful Italian girl, CLEMENTINA DELLA PORRETTA, whom he has met on his travels abroad. Clementina rejects his proposal on the grounds of religion, leaving him free to marry Harriet. See Charlotte GRANDISON.

siren (Gr. *seiren,* entangler). A mythical monster, half woman and half bird. They were said by Greek poets (see ODYSSEY) to entice seamen by the sweetness of their song to such a degree that listeners forgot everything and died of hunger. Odysseus escaped their blandishments by filling his companions' ears with wax and lashing himself to the mast of his ship.

In Homeric mythology, there were but two sirens; later writers name three, PARTHENOPE, Ligea, and Leucosia, and the number was still further augmented by later writers. According to one tale, the Argonauts safely passed the sirens because Orpheus sang more ravishingly than they. Chagrined, they either flew away forever or committed suicide.

Sir Gawain and the Green Knight (c. 1370). A Middle English poem in ALLITERATIVE VERSE written by an unknown called the PEARL POET. The poem is one of four (all by the same writer) which appear in a single manuscript of the Cotton Collection.

Perhaps the greatest single ARTHURIAN LEGEND in English, this masterpiece of Middle English writing concerns the ordeal of the ideal knight, Sir GAWAIN. Two major motifs are utilized in the unfolding action: the so-called Beheading Game and the Temptation To Adultery.

Into the midst of New Year festivities at King Arthur's court bursts a green giant on horseback. He dares any of Arthur's knights to chop off his head on condition that in one year he be allowed to return the blow. Sir Gawain accepts the challenge, wields the axe successfully (the Green Knight calmly scoops up his head and leaves), and 12 months later sets out in search for the Green Chapel where he is to keep the bargain. After a long, bitter journey, he comes to a marvelous castle where he is entertained by Lord Bercilak, his beautiful wife, and an ugly old lady who quietly hovers in the background. Bercilak suggests to his guest an exchange-of-gifts game: every day he will bring to Sir Gawain what he gains hunting, and Sir Gawain will give him what he has won in the castle during the absence of the host. For two days, Sir Gawain is tempted to adultery by the beautiful wife of Bercilak; he resists, and each night, in accordance with their game, exchanges with Bercilak the kisses of the lady for animals from the hunt. On the third day, however, he accepts a supposedly magic sash of green silk from the lady, believing that it will save him from the Green Knight. That evening he fails to mention the sash during the exchange of gifts.

At the appointed time, he leaves the castle and goes for his tryst at the Green Chapel. Three times the Green Knight strikes at his neck. The first two strikes do not touch him because he twice resisted temptation, but the third blow nicks his neck slightly marking his failure with regard to the green sash.

The Green Knight turns out to be Bercilak, in the service of the ugly old lady who is really MORGAN LE FAY and who planned the entire affair.

Returning to King Arthur's court at Camelot, Sir Gawain swears always to wear the green sash around his waist as a reminder of moral lapse. His fellow knights, in tribute to Sir Gawain's courage, also place green sashes around their waists, to wear thereafter.

Siris: A Chain of Philosophical Reflections and Inquiries concerning the Virtues of Tar-Water (1744). A treatise by George BERKELEY, containing a recommendation and a list of the uses of tar water for medicinal purposes, as well as a somewhat mystical philosophy dealing with the utilization of tar water as a panacea.

Sir Launfal. A 12th-century BRETON LAI by MARIE DE FRANCE. In this narrative verse romance, Sir Launfal is one of the knights of King Arthur's court. He falls in love with a beautiful fairy who brings him great wealth and happiness, but pledges him to secrecy regarding the source. But the oath is violated when the envious Queen Guinevere goads him into admitting his love for someone else. Infuriated, Guinevere accuses him, as Potiphar's wife did Joseph, of having insulted her. Thereupon King Arthur swears that unless Sir Launfal can defend himself at trial, he will be either burned or hanged. Being told that he might save himself by producing his fairy mistress, Sir Launfal has to admit that by breaking his oath to her, he may never again expect her aid. Faced with a most miserable fate, he is, however, dramatically rescued by the beautiful fairy and carried off by her to Avalon.

There have been many adaptations of this romance, one of the best-known being a 14th-century English version bearing the same title. The material was also used centuries later in *The Vision of Sir Launfal* (1848) by James Russell Lowell.

Sir Patrick Spens. The title of a medieval Scottish sea ballad. It is a tragic tale of shipwreck based on the voyage of the titular Scottish hero. Though warned of a terrible storm, Sir Patrick Spens puts out to sea with his companions, and then:

> . . . O lang, lang may the ladies stand,
> Wi thair gold kems in their hair
> Waiting for thar ain deir lords,
> For they'll se thame na mair. . . .

Sir Thomas More. A chronicle play. Probably it was written by Anthony MUNDAY. It deals with three significant episodes in the life of Thomas More. One of these, an account of More's role in pacifying a rioting mob, was apparently rewritten by another playwright whom many reputable scholars believe to be Shakespeare. Since the play is extant in manuscript form, it is further argued that the relevant passages are in Shakespeare's handwriting.

Sir Thopas. See THOPAS.

Sisera. In the Old Testament, the Canaanite captain defeated by Barak and DEBORAH. Taking refuge in the tent of Jael, he was killed by her with a tent pin (Judg. 4–5).

Sisley, Alfred (1839–1899). French impressionist painter. Sisley rejected a career in business and, in 1862, went to study in the studio of Gleyre, where he met Monet and Renoir. His landscapes are usually set in the countryside near Paris, or near his birthplace of Moret, as in *Le Canal* and *La Barque pendant l'inondation*. The play of light over natural forms in his work is subtle and delicate. Muted blues, greens, and browns, his characteristic colors, contribute to a quiet, sometimes gently wistful, mood.

Sister Carrie (1900). A novel by Theodore DREISER. The author's first novel, it was officially published in 1900 but was not made publicly available until 1912 because of its outspoken frankness and supposed immorality. It is considered by many to be Dreiser's finest work. It tells the story of Carrie Meeber, an innocent country girl, who is exposed to the impersonal cruelty of Chicago in the 1890's.

From this life of bleak poverty and loneliness, she is rescued by a traveling salesman, Charles Drouet. Later, a wealthy married man, George Hurstwood, virtually absconds with funds in order to take her to New York. There Carrie goes on the stage, but as her star rises Hurstwood's sinks until finally, unknown to Carrie, he commits suicide, a destitute Bowery bum, while Carrie herself fails to find happiness, despite her success.

Sister Helen (1870). A poem by Dante Gabriel ROSSETTI about a young woman who destroys a false lover by melting a waxen image of him.

Sisters, The. The first story in James Joyce's DUBLINERS (1914). It is about a boy confronted with death for the first time. Through the conversation between his aunt and the two sisters of the dead man (a paralyzed old priest, his former teacher), the boy learns of the priest's insanity and finds a new, dubious light shed on the Catholic religion.

Sisyphus (Sisyphos). In Greek mythology, a son of Aeolus and the founder of EPHYRE. He is best known for his punishment for revealing Zeus's rape of Aegina to her father, the river Asopus: in Hades he rolls a huge stone up a hill, only to have it roll down again each time. When Autolycus stole his cattle, he avenged himself by stealing Autolycus' daughter Anticleia and thus became (according to some authorities) the true father of Odysseus, rather than Laertes, Anticleia's husband.

Sita (Sans., "furrow"). In Hindu mythology, the wife of RAMA. She was not born, but arose from a furrow when her father Janaka, king of Mithila, was ploughing. She is the heroine of the Hindu epic the RAMAYANA, which is largely concerned with her faithfulness under misfortune.

Sitting Bull (1834?–1890). American Sioux Indian chief. He was the leader of the Indian forces during the Sioux War of 1876–1877 and was present at the battle of the Little Big Horn during which a U.S. contingent under George A. CUSTER was wiped out. Forced to flee to Canada, he returned to the U.S. in 1881 and was settled on a reservation. He was killed by Indian police while trying to escape arrest.

Sitwell, Dame Edith (1887–1964). English poet and prose writer. She is known for the brilliant, experimental patterns of sound and imagery in her poems. From 1916 she edited *Wheels*, an annual anthology that printed gay, experimental, near-nonsense poems by herself, by her brothers, Osbert and Sacheverell, and by other writers. *Clowns' Houses* (1918) was her first successful volume of poetry. Her public reading of her long, difficult poem *Façade* in 1922 caused a sensation. *Gold Coast Customs* (1929) is a satirical poem. During World War II she began to write emotional, passionate, and religious poetry; *Still Falls the Rain*, which combines thoughts of the crucifixion with impressions of a London air raid, is one of her best poems. Other collections of poetry include *Gardeners and Astronomers* (1953) and *Music and Ceremonies* (1963). Her historical and critical works include *Alexander Pope* (1930), *Bath* (1932), *The English Eccentrics* (1933), and *A Poet's Notebook* (1943). *I Live Under a Black Sun* (1937) is a novel about Jonathan Swift. Born into a noble and ancient English family, Edith Sitwell, who was converted to Roman Catholicism in

1954, maintained a reputation for aristocratic eccentricity, habitually dressing in medieval costume. She was made dame of the British Empire in 1954. Her autobiography, *Taken Care of,* was published in 1965.

Sitwell, Sir Osbert (1892–1969). English poet and writer, brother of Edith and Sacheverell Sitwell. His most remarkable achievement is his five-volume autobiography, which is an interesting account of the Sitwell family background and a fine evocation of the aristocratic England of his own childhood and youth. The volumes are *Left Hand! Right Hand!* (1944), *The Scarlet Tree* (1945), *Great Morning* (1947), *Laughter in the Next Room* (1948), and *Noble Essences* (1950). *Tales My Father Taught Me* (1962) consists mainly of autobiographical anecdotes about the author's eccentric father. Sir Osbert's poetry, collected in *Argonaut and Juggernaut* (1919) and other volumes, is largely satirical, concerned with war and types of English character. He also has written fiction, plays, essays, and literary criticism.

Sitwell, Sacheverell (1897–). English poet and writer on art and travel; brother of Edith and Osbert Sitwell. Among his volumes of poetry are *The Hundred and One Harlequins* (1922), *Doctor Donne and Gargantua* (1930), and *Sacred and Profane Love* (1940). He has written on art, especially of the baroque period, on music, and on travel from the art-lover's point of view. *All Summer in a Day* (1926) is "an autobiographical fantasia"; *Golden Wall and Mirador* (1961) is a travel book about Peru.

Siva. See SHIVA.

Siward. In Shakespeare's MACBETH, the earl of Northumberland. He leads the English army that fights against Macbeth. His son, Young Siward, is slain in battle by Macbeth.

Six Characters in Search of an Author (Sei Personaggi in Cerca d'Autore; 1921). A play by Luigi PIRANDELLO. The action takes place on an unprepared stage, where a company of actors is being assembled for a rehearsal. Six persons appear, announce that they are the incomplete, unused creations of the author's imagination, and demand that they be permitted to perform the drama that was never written for them but is implied in their lives. The life stories of all six characters are then presented.

Six Nations. A confederation of North American Indians formed by the union of the Five Nations with the Tuscaroras in 1715.

1601 (1939). A sketch written about 1876, by Mark TWAIN. The piece is subtitled "Conversation as It Was by the Social Fireside in the Time of the Tudors." An amusing essay on manners, it was printed only privately for many years, because of its free use of Anglo-Saxon vocabulary.

Sixteen-string Jack. The almost affectionate nickname of a famous highwayman whose real name was John Rann and who is referred to in Boswell's *Life of Samuel Johnson*. He was renowned for his affectation of fine clothes and his nickname was an allusion to the many "strings" or ribbons he wore at his knees. He was hanged in 1774.

Sixtus IV, Pope. See DELLA ROVERE.

Skanda. See KARTTIKEYA.

skeleton at the feast. An Egyptian custom. Plutarch says that toward the close of Egyptian banquets a servant brought in a skeleton, and cried aloud to the guests, "Look on this! Eat, drink, and be merry; for tomorrow you die!" Herodotus says the skeleton was a wooden one, about 18 inches in length.

Skelton, John (c. 1460–1529). English poet. He is known for his satire, his humorous and realistic verse, and his short, "breathless" lines and irregular rhyme-scheme, called "Skeltonic meter." His surviving works include *A Garland of Laurel* (c. 1520), an allegorical poem dealing with the crowning of Skelton himself as a great poet; PHILIP SPARROW (c. 1500), a lyric mourning the death of a sparrow, the pet of a young girl; *Colin Clout* (c. 1519), a satire on the abuses of the Church; *The Bowge of Court*, a satire in allegory on life at the English court; *Magnificence, a Morality Play; The Tunning of Elinour Rumming*, a coarse and humorous work, giving a realistic picture of contemporary "low life"; *Why Come Ye Not to Court?* (c. 1523) and *Speak, Parrot,* satires on Cardinal Wolsey. Skelton received the title of Poet Laureate from both Oxford and Cambridge Universities and held an unofficial position as Laureate under Henry VIII. He was ordained a priest, but spent most of his time at court, where he made many enemies by his outspokenness. As a result of the hostility between him and Cardinal Wolsey, he was forced to seek refuge with the abbot of Westminster, with whom he stayed virtually as a prisoner until his death.

Skelton is considered a poet of the transition between England of the Middle Ages and the Elizabethan period, writing in the tradition of CHAUCER, GOWER, and LYDGATE, and the medieval Latin poets. Interest in his work was revived in the 20th century by Robert GRAVES, and Skeltonic meter is parodied in the early verse of W. H. AUDEN.

Title page of a collection of Skelton' works (c. 1560).

Skepticism. A movement in Greek philosophy. It was based on careful examination and deliberately suspended judgment. There were two main types of Skepticism, Pyrrhonism and Academic Skepticism. The last, beginning in the Platonic Academy c. 250 B.C., was founded by Arcesilaus. He believed that philosophic assent should always be withheld, because reasons could be adduced for any side of the question. The Skeptics confined knowledge to the impressions. They continued to influence Greek philosophy until the third century of the Christian era.

Sketch Book of Geoffrey Crayon, Gent., The (1819, 1820). A collection of tales and sketches by Washington IRVING. The book marked the beginning of the short story in America. At the time of publication, Irving's sketches of English landscape and customs were most popular, but the best loved and most permanently valuable tales in the collection are THE LEGEND OF SLEEPY HOLLOW and RIP VAN WINKLE.

Skimpole, Harold. In Charles Dickens' BLEAK HOUSE, an amateur artist, always sponging on his friends. It was said that the character was drawn from Leigh Hunt, who was much offended by it.

Skinner, Cornelia Otis (1901-   ). American actress and author. The daughter of Otis SKINNER, she made her first Broadway appearance with her father in *Blood and Sand* (1921), and thereafter wrote and acted in various plays and sketches. In 1937 she turned Margaret Ayer Barnes's novel *Edna His Wife* into a full-length play in which she played all the parts. She has also written a number of humorous books, perhaps the best known being the highly successful *Our Hearts Were Young and Gay* (1942), on which she collaborated with Emily Kimbrough.

Skinner, Otis (1858-1942). American actor. The father of Cornelia Otis SKINNER, he had a long and distinguished career on the stage. One of his most famous roles was that of the beggar in *Kismet*, a play that ran from 1911 to 1914. He also wrote several books about the theater, including *The Last Tragedian: Booth Tells His Own Story* (1939).

Skin of Our Teeth, The (1942). A play by Thornton WILDER. Unconventional in structure, it gives a panoramic picture of George Antrobus (man), his family, and their maid Sabina (the eternal temptress), who manage to survive the world upheavals from prehistoric times until the present. Wilder was awarded his third Pulitzer Prize for this play.

Skipper Ireson's Ride (1857). A ballad by John Greenleaf WHITTIER. This poem denounces Skipper Ireson, a Marblehead sea captain, for abandoning his crew. His ride is his tar-and-feathering by the village widows on his return. The poem's greatest interest lies in Whittier's attempt to imitate the sound of the Marblehead dialect.

Skuld. In Norse mythology, one of the three NORNS or Fates. She represents the future, her name being related to the word *shall*. Veiled, she was thought to face the future, scroll in hand.

Slavophiles. A 19th-century school of thought in Russia which stressed the uniqueness of Russian life and culture. The Slavophiles claimed that the Russian way of life, based on the faith of the Orthodox Church, was superior to that of the West, whose rationalism and weak religious faith doomed it to

decay. The leading Slavophile thinkers included Alexei Stepanovich Khomyakov (1804-1860), Ivan Vasilyevich Kireyevski (1806-1859), Yuri Fedorovich Samarin (1819-1876), and Konstantin and Ivan Aksakov, sons of the author Sergei Timofeyevich Aksakov. Although he was not an adherent of the group, some elements of Slavophile thought can be discerned in the writings of Feodor Dostoevski.

The Slavophiles were opposed by the so-called Westerners, who believed that Russia should adopt the social, political, and cultural ways of the West. Outstanding members of this group were Vissarion Belinski, Aleksandr Hertzen, and the novelist Ivan Turgenev.

Slawkenbergius, Hafen. An imaginary author, distinguished for the great length of his nose, in Laurence Sterne's novel TRISTRAM SHANDY. Slawkenbergius is referred to as a great authority on all lore connected with noses, and a curious tale, filled with sexual symbolism, is introduced from his hypothetical works about a man with an enormously long nose. Gogol based a short story called *The Nose* on Slawkenbergius' tale.

Sleeper, the. Widely used descriptive term. Epimenides, the Greek poet, is said to have fallen asleep in a cave when a boy, and not to have waked for 57 years, when he found himself possessed of all wisdom.

Medieval legends of those who have gone to sleep and been or are to be awakened after many years are very numerous. Such legends cluster around the names of King Arthur, Charlemagne, and Barbarossa. See the stories concerning ENDYMION, the SEVEN SLEEPERS, TANNHÄUSER, OGIER THE DANE, RIP VAN WINKLE, PETER KLAUS, and the Muslim MAHDI.

Sleeping Beauty, The. See BELLE AU BOIS DORMANT.

Sleipnir. Odin's gray horse. It had eight legs and could traverse either land or sea. The horse typifies the wind that blows over land and water from eight principal points.

Slender. In Shakespeare's MERRY WIVES OF WINDSOR, a country lout who aspires to the hand of "sweet Anne Page." His servant's name is Simple. Slender is a cousin of Justice Shallow.

Slessor, Kenneth (1901-   ). Australian poet and journalist. During the Second World War he was correspondent for Australia with the Second A.I.F. In 1944 he became the literary editor for the *Sydney Sun*. Edith Sitwell's anthology, *Wheels* (1916-1921), revealed to him the horizons of the new poetry, and started him writing verse that was to put him among the ranks of the foremost Australian poets. His work, highly individualistic, rich in imagery and unconventional rhythms, reveals a keen zest for life. His publications include *Thief of the Moon* (1924); *Earth Visitors* (1926), the visitors being pagan gods who come down to earth to court women; *Cuckoo Contrey* (1932); and *Five Bells* (1939), an elegy on the death of a dear friend.

slice of life. A phrase used to describe the work of naturalistic writers such as ZOLA who attempt to present a chunk of life complete, not modified by any selection or arrangement of material. The phrase is used for short stories that have no plot, climax, or structured form, but instead give an impression of the characters' daily life.

Slick, Sam. A Yankee of the Yankees, hero of Thomas HALIBURTON's *The Clockmaker or the Sayings and Doings of Samuel Slick of Slickville* (1837), first published as a series of letters in the *Nova Scotian*. Sam is a shrewd, ingenious New England clock peddler who does not scruple to take advantage of the slower-witted Nova Scotians among whom he peddles his wares. Sam Slick reappeared in a number of volumes and was finally sent abroad in *The Attaché, or Sam Slick in England* (1843–1844).

Slipslop, Mrs. A lecherous old maid and ancestress of Mrs. MALAPROP in Henry Fielding's JOSEPH ANDREWS.

Sloan, John (1871–1951). American painter. A member of "The Eight" or ASHCAN SCHOOL, he was a teacher and an organizer of the ARMORY SHOW and other early independent shows.

Sloane, Sir Hans (1660–1753). English physician and naturalist. He succeeded Sir Issac Newton as president of the Royal Society (1727–1741) and was president of the Royal College of Physicians (1719–1735). He also founded the Botanic Garden in 1721. He received by bequest the valuable library of the naturalist William Courten and, in turn, bequeathed it to England; it formed the basis of the collection in the British Museum. *Catalogue of Jamaica Plants* (1696), published in Latin, is Sloane's only noted work.

Slogger Williams. In Thomas Hughes' TOM BROWN'S SCHOOL DAYS, a bully whom Tom finally vanquishes.

Slop, Dr. A choleric, bigoted Catholic physician, in Laurence Sterne's novel TRISTRAM SHANDY. In attempting to demonstrate the use and virtues of a newly invented pair of obstetrical forceps, he crushes Tristram's nose (an event ominous for Tristram's father, who believes that all great men have large noses).

Sloper, Catherine. See WASHINGTON SQUARE.

Slough of Despond. See PILGRIM'S PROGRESS. Protestants have applied the words to the Church of Rome, and some Roman Catholics, to the Protestant churches generally.

Sly, Christopher. The principal character in the Induction to Shakespeare's TAMING OF THE SHREW. He is a keeper of bears and a tinker, the son of a peddler, and a drunken sot; he may have been an actual person from the village of Wincot, near Stratford-on-Avon. Sly is found dead drunk by a lord, who commands his servants to put Sly to bed, and on his waking to attend him like a lord and deceive him into thinking himself a great man. The play is performed for his entertainment.

A similar trick was played by the Caliph Haroun-al-Raschid on ABOU HASSAN in the "Sleeper Awakened" tale in *The Arabian Nights*; another is attributed to Philippe the Good, duke of Burgundy, in Burton's *Anatomy of Melancholy*.

Small Souls. The first of a series of novels by the Dutch author Louis COUPERUS (1863–1923). They deal with the Van Lowe family, a large and diverse group, many of them united by little except the custom of pleasing old Granny Lowe by spending Sunday evenings together at her home. The other novels of the series are *The Later Life*, *The Twilight of the Souls*, and *Dr. Adrian*. Constance Van Lowe causes a great scandal by her love affair, which ruins the career of the brilliant young diplomat Van Welcke, and the first books deal with the married life of this unhappy couple, who are held together only by their intense love for their small son Adrian. *The Twilight of the Souls* is the story of Gerritt Van Lowe, an apparently healthy, normal member of the family, with a pleasant, domestic wife and large brood of children, who, however, gradually goes to pieces under the influence of a morbid, neurotic fear. Among the other characters who appear throughout the novels are Ernest Van Lowe, a sensitive dilettante, who is as obviously morbid as his brother Gerritt was secretly so; Paul, the foppish idler (whom some critics consider a spokesman for the author's ideas) and the devoted old-maid sister and aunt, who gives herself unstintingly, yet nourishes a bitter resentment at being so made use of. *Dr. Adrian* tells of the career of Adrian Van Welcke, who becomes a physician with a strange power for healing.

Smart, Christopher (1722–1771). English poet and journalist, who frequently worked for the bookseller John NEWBERY. In 1756, a religious mania overtook him and he was confined to an asylum. During this period he wrote the incoherent poem *Jubilate Agno* (recently published as *Rejoice in the Lamb*), in which Smart declares, "For I am the Lord's News-Writer, the scribe-evangelist"; and his best-known work, *Song to David* (1763), a rhapsodic poem in praise of God. His religious concepts are close to those of William Blake.

Smectymnuus (1641). The title of a celebrated pamphlet attacking episcopacy. The title is composed of initial letters of the five writers: SM (Stephen Marshall), EC (Edmund Calamy), TY (Thomas Young), MN (Matthew Newcomen), UUS (William Spurstow). Milton published *An Apology for Smectymnus* (omitting a *u*) in 1642.

Smerdyakov. See KARAMAZOV.

Smetana, Bedřich (1824–1884). Bohemian composer whose opera *The Bartered Bride* (1866) is considered the national opera of Czechoslovakia. His best orchestral music is *Má vlast* (*My Country*), a set of six musical landscapes, of which *The Moldau* is best known.

Smike. See NICHOLAS NICKLEBY.

Smith, Adam (1723–1790). Scottish moral philosopher and political economist. He was educated at Glasgow and Oxford, and gave a series of lectures on English literature at Glasgow which were so popular that they had to be repeated the two following years. He was elected to the chair of logic at Glasgow in 1751 which he exchanged for the chair of moral philosophy the following year. With the publication of *Theory of Moral Sentiments* (1759), in which he expressed his ethical views, he won recognition as a contemporary writer of the first rank. His major work, THE WEALTH OF NATIONS was the first systematic formulation of classical English economics.

Smith, Alexander (1830–1867). Scottish poet, a member of the SPASMODIC SCHOOL. His best verse appears in *City Poems* (1857). He was also the author of *Dreamthorp* (1863), a book of essays, and numerous articles and critical pieces.

Smith, Alfred E[manuel] (1873–1944). American political leader. Born on New York's East Side, Smith joined Tammany Hall at an early age and held several city and state offices before being elected governor in 1919. He was an advocate of legislation to improve labor conditions and favored woman suffrage and the repeal of prohibition. After an unsuccessful bid for the Democratic presidential nomination in 1924, he ran for president in 1928 against Herbert Hoover and was defeated after an unusually vitriolic campaign; with his Roman Catholic faith, his opposition to prohibition, and his Tammany connections, he seemed to many, especially in the South and West, a symbol of the corrupt urban East. Later, Smith's views became more conservative, and he broke with his one-time ally, Franklin D. Roosevelt. In his last years, he was head of the corporation that managed New York's Empire State Building. Smith, who was dubbed "the Happy Warrior" by Roosevelt at the 1924 Democratic convention, was noted for the brown derby he habitually wore and for his colorful New York accent.

Smith, Betty [Wehner] (1904–1972). American novelist. Best known for her widely read first novel, A TREE GROWS IN BROOKLYN, she is also the author of more than 70 one-act plays and three other novels: *Tomorrow Will Be Better* (1948), *Maggie-Now* (1958), and *Joy in the Morning* (1963).

Smith, Dodie (1896–   ). English playwright. Among her works are *Autumn Crocus* (1930), *Touch Wood* (1933), and *Dear Octopus* (1938). Until 1936 she used the pen name C. L. Anthony. *I Capture the Castle*, a novel, appeared in 1948.

Smith, Ernest Bramah. Pen name, **Ernest Bramah** (1869–1942). English author of detective stories. He also wrote the suave, witty, and ironic Kai Lung books, about Chinese life and traditions: *The Wallet of Kai Lung* (1900), and *Kai Lung's Golden Hours* (1922).

Smith, George (1824–1901). English publisher. From 1846 he headed the publishing house of Smith, Elder & Co., which had been founded by his father George Smith (1789–1846). He published the early works of John Ruskin, *Jane Eyre* by Charlotte Brontë, *Henry Esmond* by Thackeray, the works of Robert Browning and Matthew Arnold, and the *Dictionary of National Biography*. Smith also founded the *Cornhill Magazine* of which Thackeray was an editor.

Smith, Goldwin (1823–1910). English historian. He was active in politics as an anti-imperialist and opponent of the Boer War; he was a regius professor at Oxford from 1858 to 1866.

Smith, H[arry] Allen (1907–   ). American newspaperman and humorist. One of the best of the Midwestern humorists, Smith is noted for such books as *Low Man on a Totem Pole* (1941), *Life in a Putty Knife Factory* (1943), and *The Complete Practical Joker* (1953). *People Named Smith* (1950) establishes the Smith clan as of great moment; *Rebel Yell* (1954) is a satire on some aspects of Southern life. *London Journal* (1952) is, in part, a parody of Boswell's famous diary. In 1961, Smith published *How to Write Without Knowing Nothing*.

Smith, James (1775–1839) and his brother **Horatio** or **Horace Smith** (1779–1849). English humorists. The Smiths are best known as joint authors of *Rejected Addresses* (1812), a classic of parody aimed at, among others, Wordsworth, Southey, Coleridge, Scott, and Byron. James subsequently produced three slight comedies, and Horace a number of more highly regarded novels and collections of humorous verse.

Smith, John (1616–1652). See CAMBRIDGE PLATONISTS.

Smith, John (1580–1631). English explorer and soldier of fortune. He came to Jamestown, Va., in 1607 and became president of the governing council of the colony. The legend of his rescue from death by Pocahontas is based on his own story, told in his *Generall Historie of Virginia, New-England, and the Summer Isles* (1624). He also made several expeditions to New England and helped to promote interest in the region. *A True Relation of . . . Virginia* (1608), another of Smith's works, is sometimes called the first American book.

Smith, Joseph (1805–1844). American religious leader and Mormon prophet. In 1820, Smith began to have supernatural visions, which appointed him prophet of a new religion; in 1827, according to his account, he got from the angel Moroni a book written in strange characters on golden plates. He translated the message as the *Book of Mormon* (1830), and on this book the Church of the Latter-Day Saints was founded the same year. Smith decided to move westward from Vermont with his followers; he went to Ohio (1831), Missouri (1838), and finally to Nauvoo, Ill. There on July 12, 1843, he proclaimed the doctrine of polygamy. Much opposition was aroused, especially in the columns of the Nauvoo *Expositor*. When Smith's followers destroyed the press of this paper, a warrant for his arrest was issued. He resisted, but was placed in jail at Carthage. An angry mob invaded the jail, and killed him. His son, **Joseph Smith, Jr.** (1832–1914) headed the Church of Jesus Christ of Latter Day Saints in Missouri and his nephew, **Joseph Fielding Smith** (1838–1918), later became a leader of the Utah Mormon Church.

Smith, Lillian (1897–1966). American novelist and social worker. Born in the South and for a time a music teacher in a mission school in China, Lillian Smith then became a social worker in the South and the publisher of a quarterly, *South Today*. She is best known for *Strange Fruit* (1944), her vividly written and widely read novel, dramatized in 1945 by the author and Esther Smith. The novel deals with the hopeless love of a white man and a Negro girl. Her nonfiction includes *Killers of the Dream* (1949; rev., 1961), *The Journey* (1954), *Now Is the Time* (1955), and *One Hour* (1959).

Smith, Samuel Francis (1808–1895). American clergyman born in Boston. He wrote *America* (*My Country, 'tis of Thee*), first published in 1832.

Smith, Seba (1792–1868). American teacher, editor, humorist, and poet. Born in Maine, where he attended school and contributed to various newspapers, Smith adopted the pseudonym of Major Jack Downing, contributing satirical letters to the Portland *Courier* (1830). Smith first attacked the local legislature and Maine customs, then went on to Washington and President Jackson. The Downing letters continued until the Civil War; several skits were produced about Jack Downing in New York theaters. As a semiliterate Yankee oracle, he was the predecessor of Artemus Ward, Hosea Biglow, and Sam Slick.

Smith, Thorne (1892–1934). American humorist. He is known for his ribald and impish books, especially *Topper* (1926), the story of a sober gentleman transformed into an adventurous romantic by two ghosts. *Topper Takes a Trip* (1932) is its sequel.

Smith, William (1727–1803). American educator and clergyman. In *A General Idea of the College of Mirania* (1753), he recommended for the colonies a practical type of higher education. The pamphlet attracted Benjamin Franklin, who invited Smith to become provost (1755–1779) of the College of Philadelphia, which became the University of Pennsylvania in 1791. An important cultural force in Philadelphia, Smith encouraged and published the poetry of Francis Hopkinson and Thomas Godfrey.

Smith, Winchell (1871–1933). American playwright. He collaborated with Byron Ongley on *Brewster's Millions* (1902), based on the novel by George Barr McCutcheon, and with Frank Bacon on Lightnin'.

Smoke (Dym; 1867). A novel by Ivan Turgenev. It combines the story of a love triangle with strictures on Russia's need to turn to the West for her civilization. The hero, Litvinov, in love with Tanya, is distracted by an old lover, Irina, who manages to break up the romance. The interjections of social comment, which harm the structure of the novel, are mostly made by Turgenev's mouthpiece in the book, Potugin.

Smoke and Steel (1920). A collection of poems by Carl Sandburg. The title poem is an attempt to find some kind of beauty in modern industrialism, with particular reference to the steel mills.

Smollett, Tobias [George] (1721–1771). Scottish-born English novelist and surgeon. After a vain attempt to sell a tragedy in London, he served as surgeon's mate on board the *Chichester,* took part in an ill-fated attack on the Spanish at Cartagena (1741), and lived for a few years on the island of Jamaica. On his return to England, he began writing his picaresque novels, including *The Adventures of* Roderick Random and *The Adventures of* Peregrine Pickle, both satiric works patterned on Lesage; *The Adventures of* Ferdinand Count Fathom, the memoirs of a Gothic villain; *The Expedition of* Humphrey Clinker, an epistolary novel; and *The Adventures of* Launcelot Greaves. He was fined and imprisoned for a libel that appeared in the *Critical Review,* which he edited from 1756 to 1763. He also published a *History of England* (1757–1758); *Travels Through France and Italy* (1766), a sardonic account of his travels; and *The Adventures of an Atom* (1769), a somewhat gross and virulent political allegory. During his last illness, he returned to Italy where he died.

Smollett is noted for his well-drawn eccentric characters, particularly those of a nautical type; these at times grotesque caricatures often draw interest away from the main plot to the incidental and to comic relief. Smollett expressed his conception of what a novel should be in his preface to *Ferdinand Count Fathom:*

A novel is a large diffused picture, comprehending the characters of life, disposed in different groups, and exhibited in various attitudes, for the purpose of an uniform plan, and general occurrence, to which every individual figure is subservient. But this plan cannot be executed with propriety, probability, or success, without a principal personage to attract the attention, unite the incidents, unwind the clue of the labyrinth, and at last close the scene, by virtue of his own importance.

Smuts, Jan Christian (1870–1950). A famous Boer leader in the Boer War. During World War I, he organized the South African forces. Prime minister of the Union of South Africa (1919–1924; 1939–1948), he was most influential in World War II.

Snodgrass, Augustus. In Charles Dickens' Pickwick Papers, an M.P.C. (Member of the Pickwick Club). He is a poetical young man who travels about with Mr. Pickwick. He marries Miss Wardle.

Snodgrass, W[illiam] D[eWitt] (1926–   ). American poet. Snodgrass' first volume of poetry, *The Heart's Needle* (1959), was awarded the Pulitzer Prize. The title refers to an Irish proverb that one daughter is a needle to the heart; in Snodgrass' poetry, always deeply personal, the reference is to his daughter by his divorced first wife. Considered one of the better contemporary young poets, Snodgrass combines sensitivity of perception with deep feeling; his forms tend to be traditional and regular, and though his poetry is polished and lyrical it contains a sometimes harsh humor that turns on puns. Many of his poems have appeared in magazines.

Snopes. A family in several novels and stories by William Faulkner, notably The Hamlet, *The Town,* and *The Mansion*. Residents of Yoknapatawpha County, the Snopeses typify the vicious and inhuman aspects of modern commercial civilization. The first Snopes to be mentioned is Ab, who is involved with a gang of horse thieves and killers in The Unvanquished; he reappears in the story Barn Burning and in *The Hamlet*. Ab's son, Flem, is a central character in the trilogy of which *The Hamlet* is the first volume. Flem works his way up from clerkship in a store to the presidency of a bank, is largely responsible for his wife's suicide, and drives her lover from town. Mink Snopes, who spends 40 years in prison for murdering Jack Houston, is a central character in *The Mansion* and is Flem's murderer. Eula Varner Snopes, Flem's wife, carries on an 18-year-long love affair with Manfred De Spain and later kills herself to keep her daughter, Linda, from scandal. Linda is a Snopes in name only; she is the illegitimate child of Eula and Hoake McCarron. Byron Snopes, who appears in *The Town* and Sartoris, writes anonymous letters to Narcissa Benbow and robs the Sartoris bank. Clarence, the son of I. O. Snopes, appears in Sanctuary and *The Mansion* and is an unscrupulous state senator. Other members of the family are I. O., a schoolteacher noted for his lengthy use of proverbs; Ike, the idiot ward of Flem who has a pathetic and tender attachment to Jack Houston's cow; Eck, an honest man and not a true Snopes; Montgomery Ward, who runs a "French post-card peep-show" before being run out of town; and Wallstreet Panic, who, like his father, Eck, is honest and not truly a Snopes.

Snorri Sturluson (1178–1241). Icelandic historian. His Heimskringla is a record of the kings of Norway from earliest times to 1177, as well as a collection of their sagas and poems. He expanded one of its sections into a separate *Olaf's Saga*. He also wrote *Prose Edda* (see Edda).

Snout, Tom. See Bottom.

Snow, Sir C[harles] P[ercy] (1905–   ). English novelist, scientist, and administrator. His novels, especially those in his Strangers and Brothers series, deal with problems of power and morality in contemporary managerial and scientific society. His analysis of THE TWO CULTURES claims that scientists are too much separated from the rest of educated English society, and too little appreciated and understood. In such novels as *The Search* (1935) and THE NEW MEN he gives a picture of scientists and their work and problems. C. P. Snow used his scientific training to move beyond a humble family background. His novel *Time of Hope* (1949) is partly autobiographical. During his years of scientific research in a Cambridge college he studied the workings of power in a small community, recording his findings in THE MASTERS and THE AFFAIR. During and after the war he did administrative work for the government and industry; he was knighted in 1957. He married the novelist Pamela Hansford JOHNSON.

Snow's novels were much admired during the 1950's, chiefly because of their documentary presentation of English society and social history. His statement that, in the future, novels must be less experimental and more closely related to man and his environment was influential and in keeping with the prevailing mood of the times.

Snow, Edgar [Parks] (1905–1972). American journalist. His *Red Star Over China* (1937), reporting the growing power of the Communists, won him national recognition. During World War II he was a war correspondent for the *Saturday Evening Post*. A six-month trip to Red China in 1960 resulted in the controversial *Other Side of the River* (1962).

Snow, [Charles] Wilbert (1884–   ). American poet. Snow is noted for his poems dealing with Maine. Among his collections are *Maine Coast* (1923), *The Inner Harbor* (1926), and *Down East* (1932). He was lieutenant governor of Connecticut in 1945–1946 and governor in 1946–1947. *Sonnets to Steve, and Other Poems* was published in 1957.

Snow-Bound, A Winter Idyll (1866). A long poem by John Greenleaf WHITTIER. An excursion into Whittier's boyhood, *Snow-Bound* evokes the memory of being snowed in on his father's Massachusetts farm. Sharply depicted details bring out the wondrous metamorphosis of the barnyard as the snow falls, and the cozy, homely indoor scene around the fire. Whittier nostalgically pays tribute to his family and their guests and adds a prayer for peace and brotherhood.

Snowe, Lucy. See VILLETTE.

Snow Image, The, and Other Twice-Told Tales (1851). A collection of 17 tales and sketches by Nathaniel HAWTHORNE. Among the best are ETHAN BRAND and *My Kinsman, Major Molineaux*.

Snow King. Epithet for Gustavus Adolphus of Sweden (1594–1632). He was so called by the Austrians because, said they, he "was kept together by the cold, but would melt and disappear as he approached a warmer soil."

Snows of Kilimanjaro, The (1938). A short story by Ernest HEMINGWAY. With a wealthy woman who has been keeping him, Harry, a writer, goes on a safari in Africa. There he hopes to "work the fat off his mind," so that he can set to work on all the things he has dreamed of writing. This dream is shattered when he develops gangrene in his leg. In the knowledge of death he reviews his life, and in a dream just before he dies he sees a legendary, gigantic, frozen leopard on the summit of Mt. Kilimanjaro.

Snug. See BOTTOM.

Snyder, Gary. See BEAT MOVEMENT.

Sobakevich. A bearlike character in Nikolai Gogol's DEAD SOULS. Everything about Sobakevich is huge and solid: his person, his furniture, and, especially, his appetite. At a banquet for the artful schemer Chichikov, Sobakevich creates a sensation by devouring a grandiose sturgeon that was to have served as the main course.

Sobrino. In Lodovico Ariosto's ORLANDO FURIOSO, a Saracen knight noted for his valor and wisdom. Called "the Sage," he is the Saracen NESTOR who advises the pagan king Agramante (Agramant) to entrust the outcome of the war with the Christians to a single combat, with the stipulation that the nation of the defeated warrior shall be tributary to that of the winner. When the Christian knight Rinaldo defeats the pagan champion RUGGIERO, Agramante breaks the agreement. Sobrino's displeasure causes him to accept soon after the Christian rite of baptism.

Social Contract, The (Le Contrat social; 1762). Chief work of Jean Jacques ROUSSEAU, a treatise on the origins and organization of government and the rights of citizens. Rousseau's thesis states that, since no man has any natural authority over another, the social contract, freely entered into, creates natural reciprocal obligations between citizens. The individual, as the basic political unit, surrenders his rights to the State, and is legally equal to all other members. The third book is a discussion of three forms of government: democratic, which Rousseau distrusts; aristocratic, which, if elective, is acceptable; and monarchic, which is preferable, if headed by an ideal ruler. Like Montesquieu, Rousseau states that practical, moral, and theoretical considerations should determine the best form of government for any people. That all minorities must submit to the general will or be banished is the conclusion of the fourth book. Though an individualistic work, it reveals Rousseau as a firm collectivist. Some critics assert that the injustices of collectivism and "democratic despotism" during the French Revolution and later in the 19th and 20th centuries were, in part, derived from this work.

socialism. A term used since the 1830's to describe any theory or social or political movement predicated upon communal or government ownership and control of production and distribution of goods. Socialism does not necessarily imply the abolition of private property, though it is characterized by public ownership of property directly affecting public interests. The societies advocated in Plato's *Republic* and Sir Thomas More's *Utopia* are socialist in nature, and the early Christian community has been held to have been socialist in that all property was communally owned. Socialist theories have been advanced by Robert OWEN in England and François Fourier (see FOURIERISM) in France, advocating the organization of society into cooperative communities. In 1847 Marx and Engels' COMMUNIST MANIFESTO laid down the principles of scientific socialism. The FABIAN SOCIETY in England, whose members included George Bernard Shaw and Beatrice and Sidney Webb, attempted to popularize the socialist cause. Guild socialism, an English movement of the early 20th-century, advocated government ownership of all industries, control and management being entrusted to a guild composed of all the manual and white-collar workers in each industry, who in turn were to be restricted by laws protecting consumers' interests. Socialism is generally regarded as distinct from Communism since, unlike the latter, it need not adhere to the tenets of MARXISM.

socialist realism. The officially supported artistic doctrine that has been more or less obligatory for Soviet writers and artists since 1932. The resolution of the Communist Party's Central Committee, which set up the Union of Soviet Writers, declared that "Socialist realism is the basic method of Soviet literature and literary criticism. It demands of the artist a truthful, historically concrete depiction of reality in its revolutionary development. Truthfulness and historical concreteness in the artistic depiction of reality must be combined with the task of reforming the ideas of the toilers and of educating them in the spirit of socialism." The writer Maksim Gorki was one of the early theoreticians of the doctrine, but Gorki's ideas about the relationship of literature to life contained elements of romanticism that later Soviet critics have tended to label "revolutionary romanticism," rather than realism. Shortly before his death, Gorki said: "I want literature to rise above reality and to look down on reality from above, because literature has a far greater purpose than merely to reflect reality. It is not enough to depict already existing things—we must also bear in mind the things we desire and the things which are possible of achievement." As the grip of Soviet control tightened on literature, the freedom of the artist to depict reality as he saw it or wished it to be was—officially, at least—subordinated to the demand for an art that showed the steady progress of Soviet society toward its socialist goal. The claim that society actually was progressing in that direction without setbacks was, of course, as much of a dream as Gorki's revolutionary romanticism, but this was not to be admitted by Soviet critics. Concomitant with the general depiction of a progressive society, there was also demanded the creation of positive heroes in Soviet literature. This was a sharp break with the literature of the 19th century, in which the protagonists were most often SUPERFLUOUS MEN, alienated from society and unable to find a useful purpose for their lives. The Soviet hero, on the contrary, was to be an active, healthy man, without hesitations and scruples about his role in society. He was to be a good Communist, a leader who knew exactly what to do to advance the cause of the building of socialism, and who was willing to sacrifice personal considerations to this task. This rigid formula laid down for Soviet writers to follow resulted in the deadness of so much of Soviet literature for three decades. Gorki's novel *Mother,* held up as an early example of socialist realism, fell more within the scope of Gorki's revolutionary romanticism. Another novel often cited as a model of socialist realism, Sholokhov's *The Quiet Don,* also fails to meet the test. His hero, Gregor Melekhov, resembles the 19th-century superfluous man more than he does a positive hero.

Since the doctrine was first propounded, Soviet writers have obviously had trouble adhering to the prescribed formula and producing readable literature. Occasionally one of the bolder Soviet authors openly questions the possibility of writing within such a narrow framework or questions the validity of such a doctrine at all. One of the recent critics of the theory, a pseudonymous writer who calls himself Abram Tertz, wrote in an essay on the subject: "What is socialist realism? What is the meaning of this strange and jarring phrase? Can there be a socialist, capitalist, Christian, or Mohammedan realism? Does this irrational concept have a natural existence? Perhaps it does not exist at all, perhaps it is only the nightmare of a terrified intellectual during the dark and magical night of Stalin's dictatorship? Perhaps a crude propaganda trick of Zhdanov or a senile fancy of Gorki? Is it fiction, myth, or propaganda?" Despite such sharp questioning by their own writers, Soviet authorities remain determined to retain the doctrine as a useful way to control literature in their country.

Society for Pure English (S. P. E.). An organization founded in 1913 by a committee of which Robert BRIDGES, Sir Walter RALEIGH, and Logan Pearsall Smith were members, with the object of directing popular taste and education in the development of the English language.

Society of Friends. See QUAKERS.

Society of Jesus. See JESUITS.

Socrates (Sokrates, c. 470–399 B.C.). A Greek teacher of wisdom. Socrates himself left no writings, and is known to us through the *Dialogues* of Plato, Aristotle's treatises, and Xenophon's discourses. His interest was in ethics. He is represented as believing that virtue is knowledge; all wickedness, he said, is due to ignorance. In his teaching, Socrates sought the universal definition of virtue through particulars. Aristotle credits him with developing inductive method. With self-knowledge the foundation for inquiry, Socrates would save men from leading "unexamined" lives. The Socratic method of teaching consisted in asking questions, and drawing out the answers from the student. Socrates himself pretended to be ignorant of the subject. The purpose of the method, which Plato called midwifery, was to show the student that the answers are contained in his own mind. Socrates always understated the truth, giving rise to the expression "Socratic irony." In 399 B.C. the Athenians tried Socrates on a charge of impiety and corruption of youth. He was sentenced to death, and drank hemlock, as described by Plato in the PHAEDO.

The only unfavorable view of Socrates occurs in Aristophanes' comedy THE CLOUDS, where he is caricatured as a representative of the Sophistic profession. The play, however, is professedly fictional, and is not accepted as history. See also XANTIPPE.

Sodom and Gomorrah. In the Old Testament, 2 cities of the Vale of Siddim destroyed by heaven with fire and brimstone because of their wickedness. Abraham persuaded Jehovah to spare Sodom if 10 righteous men could be found there, but this condition could not be fulfilled. Lot and his family were the only inhabitants who escaped the doomed city, but Lot's wife became a pillar of salt because she looked back.

Sodome et Gomorrhe. See REMEMBRANCE OF THINGS PAST.

Sofronia (Sophronia). A young Christian maiden, heroine of an episode in Torquato Tasso's GERUSALEMME LIBERATA. Aladino, king of Jerusalem, is advised by the enchanter Ismeno to remove the statue of the Virgin from a Christian church and place it in a mosque, to insure against the capture of the city. When the statue is stolen, Aladino orders the execution of the entire Christian community of Jerusalem. To avoid this fate, Sofronia offers herself as the culprit. Her lover Olindo then confesses the theft himself, in hopes of saving her. Aladino promptly sentences both to death, whereupon Clorinda, the Amazon warrior, appears to offer her services against the Christians in return for their lives. With Aladino's acceptance of the bargain, Sofronia and Olindo are free to wed.

Sohrab and Rustum. A narrative poem in blank verse by Matthew ARNOLD (1853), dealing with the legendary Persian hero Rustum and his son Sohrab. The two meet in single combat, in ignorance of their relationship, and Sohrab is slain.

Sōka Gakkai. See NICHIREN.

Soldati, Mario (1906–   ). Italian novelist. Noted for his terse, journalistic style, he is a prolific and versatile writer. He has written, among other works, *America Primo Amore* (1935); *Dinner with the Commendatore* (*A Cena col Commendatore;* 1952); *The Capri Letters* (*Le Lettere da Capri;* 1954); *The Confession* (*La Confessione;* 1955); *Il Vero Silvestri* (1957), based on the Pirandellian theme of truth and its many semblances; and *I Racconti* (1958), a collection of short stories.

Soldiers Three, and Other Stories (1880). A volume of short stories of life in India by Rudyard KIPLING. The soldiers three are the famous trio, Ortheris, Learoyd, and Mulvaney.

Soledades, Las. See LUIS de GÓNGORA Y ARGOTE.

Solemn League and Covenant. A league of the General Assembly of the Church of Scotland, the Westminster Assembly of English Divines, and the English Parliament in 1643, for the establishment of Presbyterianism and suppression of Roman Catholicism in both countries. Charles II swore to the Scots that he would abide by it, and therefore they crowned him in 1651 at Dunbar; but at the Restoration he not only rejected the Covenant, but had it burnt by the common hangman.

Solimano (**Solyman** or **the Soldan of Nicea**). King of the Turks and elected chieftain of all the Muslims in the wars against the Crusaders led by Goffredo in Torquato Tasso's GERUSALEMME LIBERATA. He is killed by Rinaldo of Este in revenge for the earlier slayings of Sveno and Argillano. His death brings to a victorious end the Christian assault on the Holy City.

Solinus. The kindly duke of Ephesus in Shakespeare's COMEDY OF ERRORS. Although he is moved to pity by Aegeon's story about the loss of his family, he is forced to arrest him because of the law which bars Syracusans from Ephesus. When Aegeon is discovered to be the father of Antipholus, who is under the duke's patronage, he pardons him.

Sologub, Feodor. Pen name of **Feodor Kuzmich Teternikov** (1863–1927). Russian novelist, poet, and short-story writer. Sologub was a schoolteacher until the success of his novel *Melkii Bes* (*The Petty Demon,* 1907) allowed him to devote himself entirely to writing. The hero of the novel, the evil and vindictive schoolteacher Peredonov, is one of the most striking and grotesquely unpleasant characters in Russian fiction. The novel expresses Sologub's sense of the evil reality of the world, stifling an ideal of good which is only sporadically glimpsed. Similar

ideas are found in his finely wrought poetry, in his stories, and in his other novels, *Tyazhelye sny* (*Bad Dreams,* 1896) and *Tvorimaya legenda* (*The Created Legend,* 1908–1912). His poetry places him with the Russian SYMBOLISTS. However morbid or perverse Sologub's ideas or stories, his literary ability is of high quality. His work has been generally ignored in the Soviet Union since his death.

Solomin. A character in Ivan Turgenev's novel, VIRGIN SOIL, who urges a gradual, evolutionary reform of the social system in Russia as opposed to the revolutionary methods of the young radicals.

Solomon. In the Old Testament, the wisest and most magnificent of the kings of Israel and the son of David and Bathsheba. When asked by Jehovah to be granted any wish, he wisely chose "an understanding heart" by which to judge the people (I Kings 3:9). He is perhaps most celebrated for his building of the famous temple which bore his name, and for his lavish entertainment of the queen of SHEBA. (See I Kings 2–11.) The glory of his reign gave rise to many legends in the Talmud and the Koran. See CARPET, MAGIC; OPHIR; SONG OF SOLOMON.

Solomon, Judgment of. A famous example of Solomon's wisdom. Two harlots came before the king bearing a live and a dead baby, and each claimed the live baby as her own. Solomon ordered that the live child be cut in half and shared between the two. One woman begged the king to give the living child to the other woman rather than kill it. Solomon at once knew that she was the true mother, and the people knew that "the wisdom of God was in him, to render justice." See CIRCLE OF CHALK, THE.

Solomon on the Vanity of the World (1718). A despondent verse soliloquy in three books by Matthew PRIOR in which he expresses the pessimistic notion that neither reason, pleasure, nor power overcome the vanity of human reason and effort, that "The Pleasures of Life do not compensate for the miseries." See ABRA.

Solomon's Temple. The central place of Jewish worship. It was erected by Solomon and his Tyrian workmen (probably on Phoenician models) on Mount Moriah, Jerusalem, about 1006 B.C. It was destroyed at the siege of Jerusalem by Nebuchadnezzar (586 B.C.), and some 70 years later the Temple of Zerubbabel was completed on its site. In 20 B.C. Herod the Great began the building of the last Temple—that of the New Testament—which was utterly destroyed during the siege of Jerusalem by Vespasian and Titus in A.D. 70. For many centuries the site has been covered by the splendid Muslim mosque, Haram esh Sherif.

Solon (c. 640–c. 558 B.C.). A Greek statesman and poet. He was elected *archon* (594–593 or 592–591 B.C.) in order to mediate between the oppressed poor and the rich few. He carried out extensive reforms to this end, but his true title to fame rests on his constitutional reforms. Although he retained a class system, he added the lowest class, the Thetes, and gave them a part in the Assembly and in the choice of magistrate. His radical measure was establishing courts of justice, Heliaea, administered by all the citizens. Even the magistrates, after they resigned their office, could be accused before the people.

Solon's reforms won him the title of founder of Athenian democracy. A man of moderation, a poet, legislator, traveler, and merchant, he embodied the best characteristics of the Greeks. He survived to see his reforms partially thrust aside under the tyranny of PISISTRATUS.

Soloviov, Vladimir Sergeyevich (1853–1900). Russian religious philosopher and poet. His mystic doctrine of Sophia (the eternal feminine, the divine wisdom) had a large influence on the symbolist poets Aleksandr Blok and Andrei Bely. Much of Soloviov's poetry reflects his mystical thought, although some of it is riotously witty nonsense verse. His major prose work is *Three Conversations* (*Tri razgovory;* 1899).

Solzhenitzyn, Aleksandr. See ONE DAY IN THE LIFE OF IVAN DENISOVICH.

Soma. An intoxicating drink. It was brewed by Hindu priests in ancient times, with accompanying mystic rites and incantations, from the juice of some Indian plant, and was drunk by the Brahmins as well as offered as libations to their gods. It was fabled to have been brought from heaven by a falcon, or by the daughters of the Sun, and it was itself personified as a god. Soma is one of the most important of the old Vedic deities, a sort of Hindu Bacchus. All the 114 hymns in the ninth book of the Rig Veda are invocations in his honor. In later mythology, Soma represented the moon, which was supposed to be gradually drunk up by the gods and then filled up again.

To drink the Soma. To become immortal, or as a god.

Somaize, sieur de. Antoine Beaudeau (1630–?). French man of letters. Author of the *Dictionnaire des Précieuses,* in which he defined the elaborate circumlocutions employed by the female habituées of the Hôtel de RAMBOUILLET (1660), Somaize took it upon himself to defend the Rambouillet circle against the barbs of Molière's *Les Précieuses Ridicules.*

Somerville, E[dith] O[enone] (1861–1949). Irish novelist who collaborated with Martin Ross, the pen name of her cousin Violet Martin, on many novels, including the humorous *Some Experiences of an Irish R. M.* (1899).

Somerville, William (1675–1742). English author known for his blank-verse poems *The Chase* (1735) and *Hobbinol, or the Rural Games* (1740), a burlesque epic dealing with his life in the countryside of Warwickshire.

Somnus. In Roman mythology, the god of Sleep, the son of Night (Nox) and the brother of Death (Mors).

Sonette an Orpheus, Die. See SONNETS TO ORPHEUS, THE.

Song of Bernadette, The (Das Lied von Bernadette; 1941). A novel by Franz WERFEL, concerning the life of Saint BERNADETTE OF LOURDES. Werfel, who was in France when the Germans invaded in 1940, is said to have taken refuge in the church of St. Bernadette and to have vowed to dedicate a book to the saint if he should escape. He did escape to the U.S. in 1940 and the novel appeared shortly afterward.

Song of Igor's Campaign, The. Also known as **The Tale of Igor's Campaign** and **The Igor Tale** (**Slovo o polku igorevye;** 1800). An anonymous late 12th-century heroic poem. Describing the ill-fated campaign of a Russian prince against the roaming Polovtzy tribes in 1185, it is regarded as one of the greatest literary masterpieces in Russian written before Pushkin's work. Rather than strictly an epic poem, the work is a mixture of epic, lyric, and sometimes oratorical styles. The only manuscript of the poem was discovered in the late 18th century. An edition of it was published in 1800, and the original manuscript was destroyed in the Moscow fire of 1812. Some scholars have expressed doubts about its genuineness, although a literary forger with such poetic talents could hardly have remained anonymous. The work is now generally accepted as authentic.

Song of Myself (1855). A poem by Walt WHITMAN. Nearly 2,000 lines long, it is probably his most important poem, containing his major themes. The poet celebrates himself; encompassing all, he gives everything significance. The poet-prophet sees the equality and the beauty of all things and all people; in his huge catalogues, he moves through space and time, the poet of wickedness as well as goodness. The grass, "a uniform hieroglyphic" transpiring from the graves of men and women, testifies to immortality and cyclical rebirth. Sounding his "barbaric yawp," Whitman departs, dissolving into the universe. If he is sought, he advises, "look for me under your bootsoles." His *Song,* containing the "origin of all poems," direct experience of life, is "good health" to its reader.

Song of Roland. See ROLAND.

Song of Solomon, The. One of the books of the Old Testament, "the song of songs." A love idyll, it was universally ascribed to Solomon until the 19th century; critics now consider it of later date. It is interpreted as an allegory of the union between Christ and his Church more frequently than as a type of Oriental love poem.

Song of the Lark, The (1915). A novel by Willa CATHER. The author said this was both her favorite novel and the one that satisfied her least. It tells the story of Thea Kronborg, a Colorado girl, the daughter of a Swedish clergyman, who has a talent for music. She goes to Chicago to study, has an unhappy love affair with Fred Ottenburg, a wealthy young man who cannot obtain a divorce to marry her, and eventually becomes a soprano at the Metropolitan Opera House in New York City, famous for her Wagnerian roles. Thea is to some extent drawn from the famous Wagnerian singer Olive Fremstad.

Song of the Open Road (1856). A poem by Walt WHITMAN. The road on which the poet travels, and on which he encounters and accepts all things, becomes symbolic of life. The universe itself is a road "for traveling souls."

Songs and Sonnets. See TOTTEL'S MISCELLANY.

Songs of Innocence (1789) and **Songs of Experience** (1794). Two series of poems, subtitled *Showing the Two Contrary States of the Human Soul,* by William BLAKE. The first group exults in the omnipresence of divine love and sympathy, even in face of sorrow; the second group, gloomy in tone, opposes the first and deals with the power of evil. Innocence and experience are two opposing states of the human soul; the poems of one group are set against the poems of the other. Thus we have *Infant Joy* against *Infant Sorrow, The Blossom* against *The Sick Rose, The Lamb* against THE TIGER, and *The Divine Image* against *The Human Abstract.* Often

A Poison Tree, one of Blake's *Songs of Experience.*

the same subject is treated in each group, as in *The Chimney Sweeper* and *A Little Boy Lost.* This dualistic thinking, so characteristic of Blake, is set forth in his most important prose work THE MARRIAGE OF HEAVEN AND HELL.

Song to David. See Christopher SMART.

sonnet. In prosody, a fourteen-line poem of a set rhyme scheme and movement. In English the sonnet is written in heroic verse, i.e., iambic pentameter. The earliest sonnet form was the Italian or Petrarchan sonnet, so called after Petrarch, its earliest major practitioner. Apparently the form developed after long experimentation from a kind of "little song" (*sonetto* in Italian and *sonet* in Provençal, from Latin *sonus,* sound). The 13th-century Italian poet Guittone of Arezzo established its rules. In structure it falls into the octave, or first eight lines, which state the proposition, and the sestet, or last six, which contain the resolution. A break between the octave and the sestet, and a minor thought-division between lines four and five and 11 and 12, are standard in the form. The rhyme scheme is a-b-b-a, a-b-b-a in the octave, and either c-d-e, c-d-e or c-d-c, d-c-d in the sestet. The Italian sonnet form was introduced in England early in the 16th century by Wyatt and Surrey, and sonnets and sonnet sequences, usually upon the subject of love, were soon a literary fashion.

However, English writers were not satisfied with the Italian form, and soon were experimenting with what became the English or Shakespearean sonnet, so called because Shakespeare was the greatest writer to use the form. As in the Italian sonnet, the rhyme scheme largely determines its movement. Rhymed a-b-a-b, c-d-c-d, e-f-e-f, g-g, it usually retains the Italianate break in thought between octave and sestet, but the epigrammatic force of the final couplet is so strong that it changes the whole character of the form; a major break comes between the 12th and 13th lines, and this sometimes becomes the main thought division of the poem.

Writers of sonnet sequences in the 16th century include Thomas Watson, Sir Philip Sidney, Samuel Daniel, Michael Drayton, Edmund Spenser, Henry Constable, Barnabe Barnes, Thomas Lodge, Giles Fletcher, and William Shakespeare. Milton, Wordsworth, Keats, Elizabeth Barrett Browning, and Christina Rossetti have written notable sonnets and sonnet sequences, in both the Italian and the Shakespearean forms. In the 20th century the sonnet has lost none of its popularity, having been written by Edwin Arlington Robinson, Edna St. Vincent Millay, Elinor Wylie, E. E. Cummings, W. H. Auden, and many others.

The two kinds of sonnet, first the Italian and then the Shakespearean, are illustrated in the following examples:

> Much have I travell'd in the realms of gold,
> And many goodly states and kingdoms seen;
> Round many western islands have I been
> Which bards in fealty to Apollo hold.
> Oft of one wide expanse had I been told
> That deep-brow'd Homer ruled as his demesne:
> Yet did I never breathe its pure serene
> Till I heard Chapman speak out loud and bold:
> Then felt I like some watcher of the skies
> When a new planet swims into his ken;
> Or like stout Cortez, when with eagle eyes
> He stared at the Pacific—and all his men
> Look'd at each other with a wild surmise—
> Silent, upon a peak in Darien.
>
> John Keats, *On First Looking
> into Chapman's Homer*

> Shall I compare thee to a summer's day?
> Thou art more lovely and more temperate:
> Rough winds do shake the darling buds of May,
> And summer's lease hath all too short a date:
>
> Sometime too hot the eye of heaven shines,
> And often is his gold complexion dimm'd:
> And every fair from fair sometime declines,
> By chance, or nature's changing course, untrimm'd.
>
> But thy eternal summer shall not fade
> Nor lose possession of that fair thou owest;
> Nor shall Death brag thou wanderest in his shade,
> When in eternal lines to time thou growest:
>
> So long as men can breathe, or eyes can see,
> So long lives this, and this gives life to thee.
>
> Shakespeare, *Sonnet XVIII*

sonnet sequence. A collection of SONNETS in which there is discernible, if only vaguely, some kind of development, whether it be narrative or psychological. In Petrarch's *Rime* (verses), the antecedent of most European and English sequences, the sonnets are mixed with madrigals and *canzoni,* but they are the chief vehicles of the story of the poet's love for

Laura in life and after her death. Outstanding English sequences include Sidney's *Astrophel and Stella,* Spenser's *Amoretti,* and Shakespeare's *Sonnets.*

Sonnets from the Portuguese (1850). A collection of sonnets by Elizabeth Barrett BROWNING, expressing the poet's love for her husband, Robert Browning, and presented to him as a gift. The basis for the title is probably the series of sonnets of the great 16th-century Portuguese poet Luiz de Camões (or Camoëns). The 43d sonnet in Mrs. Browning's series begins with the well-known line, "How do I love thee? Let me count the ways."

Sonnets of Shakespeare, The (printed 1609). A series of 154 sonnets by William SHAKESPEARE. Probably composed between 1593 and 1601, they are written in the form of three quatrains and a couplet that has come to be known as Shakespearean (see SONNET). Influenced by, and often reacting against, the popular sonnet cycles of the time, notably Sir Philip Sidney's *Astrophel and Stella,* Shakespeare's sonnets are among the finest examples of their kind. They fall into two groups, Sonnets 1–126 addressed to a beloved friend, a handsome and noble young man, and Sonnets 127–152 to a malign but fascinating "Dark Lady" whom the poet loves in spite of himself and in spite of her unworthiness. It is frequently suggested that the stolen mistress of Sonnets 40–42 is the Dark Lady; the poet's complaint in the second group indicates that she has been false to him with his friend. Several themes recur throughout the series, notably the inevitable decay brought by Time, and the immortalization of beauty and love in poetry. The final two poems (153–154), which do not seem to fit anywhere, are adaptations of a Greek epigram and were possibly early poetic exercises.

Critics disagree as to whether the *Sonnets* form a coherent and unified sequence, and whether they are simply fictional pieces written according to the Petrarchan conventions of the day or deep expressions of Shakespeare's intimate life. Perhaps the safest general conclusion is that the *Sonnets* fall into several related groups within the two main divisions, and that, because of their intensity of feeling, many if not most of them sprang out of the poet's personal experience. The dedication of the 1609 printing to a "Mr. W. H." has led many scholars to identify the beloved youth of the first group as Henry Wriothesley, earl of Southampton, to whom Shakespeare had dedicated *Venus and Adonis* and *The Rape of Lucrece.* Another theory is that William Herbert, earl of Pembroke, is the object of the dedication (as he was of the First Folio edition of Shakespeare's plays in 1623), although he was only in his teens during the period in which the poems were probably written.

Sonnets to Orpheus, The (Die Sonette an Orpheus; 1923). A cycle of sonnets by Rainer Maria RILKE. The sonnets are free and varied in form and center about the myth of Orpheus. One of the main ideas in the cycle is that in order to realize his true essence, man must make his nature fluid, must be capable of constant inner metamorphoses in order to exist on a par with the varied and changing world about him. Death is only one metamorphosis among many. Similar ideas may be found in the later poetry of Stefan George.

Son of the Middle Border, A (1917). An autobiographical narrative by Hamlin GARLAND. Garland tells of the westward migration of the Garland and McClintock families and of his own boyhood in the Middle West. Although he writes feelingly of the grandeur of the prairie, he also describes the bleakness and hardship of farm life that forced men like his father into what was by then a fruitless quest from frontier to frontier. The book was succeeded by *A Daughter of the Middle Border* (1921), *Trail-Makers of the Middle Border* (1926), *Memories of the Middle Border* (1926), and *Back-Trailers of the Middle Border* (1928).

Sons and Lovers (1913). A novel, autobiographical in character, by D. H. LAWRENCE. It deals with the family background, childhood, adolescence, and young manhood of Paul Morel, sensitive and talented son of an English coal miner in Nottinghamshire. His mother Gertrude, the educated daughter of puritanical middle-class parents, has married the miner in the heat of physical attraction. The marriage soon disintegrates; Walter Morel takes to drink and beats his wife and children, and Mrs. Morel pours all her possessive love upon her sons, especially Paul. The novel is concerned with Paul's painful introduction to the commercial world, his discovery of books and art, his growing discontent with his background of poverty and gloom, his developing talent for painting. It records his first love affairs with MIRIAM and with Clara Dawes. Because of the strong bond of love between him and his mother (a classical Oedipus complex), he is never able to give his affection wholly to either of the women, although both love him passionately. After his mother has died from cancer Paul decides to set out on an independent life of his own and rejects both Miriam and Clara.

The novel, which was attacked on its first publication because of its frankness in dealing with sexual matters, is in a more naturalistic vein than most of Lawrence's later work. Remarkable for its portrayal of English mining life, its vivid and moving characterizations, and its poetic descriptions of nature, it is considered one of Lawrence's best novels.

sons of Ben. English poets such as Thomas CAREW, Robert HERRICK, Richard LOVELACE, and John SUCKLING, who acknowledged Ben JONSON as their literary "father." Like him, they emulated the ease and polish of the Latin lyricists. The group is also called "the tribe of Ben" or (most commonly now) the CAVALIER POETS. It was their custom to meet with Jonson regularly at the Apollo Room of the Devil Tavern in London, membership in the "tribe" implying a certain convivial as well as poetic relationship.

Sons of Freedom. See DUKHOBORS.

Sons of Mil. In the mythological cycle of Gaelic literature, the 5th and last race to invade and inhabit Ireland. In effect, the Sons of Mil were the first Celts to come into Ireland and are presumably the ancestors of the present-day Irish. In order to win the island, they had first to engage in battle and defeat the TUATHA DÉ DANANN.

Sonya. The heroine of Feodor Dostoevski's CRIME AND PUNISHMENT, a saintly, gentle young girl who has been forced into a life of prostitution to support her father, the drunken Marmeladov, her stepmother, and their children.

Sophists. Greek philosophers of the 5th century B.C., masters of the arts of rhetoric and persuasion. They are considered the first professional teachers of Greece and the first to give practical help in politics. Since rhetorical training was the key to political power, these teachers emphasized the arts of persuasion. Originally, *sophist* was the Greek term for any skilled craftsman or artist; however, it was later applied to anyone who devoted himself to wisdom. Early Sophists such as GORGIAS and PROTAGORAS OF ABDERA were conservative: they affirmed things as they were and stood for the rule of law and order. The later Sophists, Hippias, ANTIPHON, Callicles, and Thrasymachus, were more radical; they opposed "nature" or man's individual instincts and desires to law or convention, and were the first to set forth the doctrine, later criticized by Plato, Thucydides, and Aristotle, that might makes right. Because the Sophists were in the service of the rich, a class inimical to democracy and held in contempt by Plato and Aristotle, the word Sophist was given a pejorative sense by these two men: they thought the object of the teachers was not genuine knowledge, and sophist in the general sense has come to mean anyone who makes the worse reason appear the better. The Sophists and their methods were caricatured in THE CLOUDS by Aristophanes, who erroneously placed Socrates among them.

Sophocles (Sophokles) (496–406 B.C.). Greek tragic dramatist. He was born at Kolonos, near Athens, and in his own day was probably the most generally admired of the three great Athenian dramatists. He was known not only for his poetic and dramatic gifts, but for his musical skill and his fine appearance; he was the *choragos* when the victory over Xerxes at SALAMIS was celebrated in Athens in 480 B.C. In addition to his work as a playwright, he also held military and political positions, and was a priest of Asclepius. He was only 27 when, with his first tragedy, he defeated AESCHYLUS in the playwright's contest. Evidence of his special position in the public esteem is the fact that ARISTOPHANES, who ridiculed Euripides and, to some extent, Aeschylus in *The Frogs,* spoke only with the greatest respect of Sophocles.

Although Sophocles wrote well over 100 plays, only 7 tragedies and a part of a SATYR PLAY remain. Best known of the plays are the three about OEDIPUS and his children—*Oedipus Tyrannos, Oedipus at Colonus,* and ANTIGONE—and the ELECTRA. He also wrote plays on AJAX, *The Women of Trachis* (see HERACLES), *Philoctetes,* and the *Ichneutai,* his fragmentary satyr play about the birth of Hermes. It was Sophocles who added a third speaking actor to the two used by Aeschylus, increased the size of the chorus, and abandoned the use of the trilogy in favor of single plays—his three plays on Oedipus were written over a period of 40 years.

Whereas both Aeschylus and Euripides, in different ways, may be said to have had a progressive attitude toward religion and social custom, Sophocles was more conservative. His chief interest was in the search for truth and self-understanding on the part of the individual in relation to the existing moral order, as in the case of Oedipus' relentless seeking after the murderer of Laius even though that knowledge brings with it his own destruction. His best dramas have never been excelled in their power and economy of expression.

A doubtful but highly popular tradition about Sophocles is that at the age of 90 he was hailed into court by his son Iophon as too senile to manage his own affairs. To prove the absurdity of this contention, Sophocles merely read a choral ode he had just written for the *Oedipus at Colonus.* As a matter of fact, Iophon himself became a tragic dramatist, as did Sophocles' grandson by his second son.

Sophonisba or **Sophoniba** (d. 204 B.C.). Daughter of Hasdrubal of Carthage, sister of Hannibal. Like her brother, she was reared to detest Rome. Originally affianced to Prince Masinissa of Numidia, she was married, for political reasons, to Syphax, Masinissa's rival. Masinissa defeated Syphax in battle and captured Sophonisba, but was compelled by Rome to give her up. Rather than fall into Roman hands, she willingly took the poison given to her by Masinissa. She is the subject of tragedies by Jean Mairet, Corneille, Voltaire, Trissino, Alfieri, and John Marston.

Sophronia. See TITUS AND GISIPPUS.

Sorbonne. The institution of theology, science, and literature in Paris founded by Robert de Sorbon, canon of Cambrai, in 1252. In 1808 the buildings, erected by Richelieu in the 17th century, were given to the University, and since 1821 it has been called the *Académie universitaire de Paris.*

Sordello (c. 1200–c. 1270). Italian TROUBADOUR who wrote in Provençal. He wrote a conventional didactic poem, *L'Ensenhamen d'onor,* and a bitter complaint against poor rulers, *Serventese* (1237), written on the death of his patron Blacatz. His fame, however, comes from his appearance in Dante's *Purgatorio* as a too zealous patriot, and in Robert Browning's psychological poem *Sordello* (1840).

Sordello (1840). A poem by Robert BROWNING. Against the background of restless southern Europe of the 13th century, it projects the conflicting thoughts of a poet about the best way of making his influence felt, whether by personal action or the power of song. Tennyson said that he had done his best with *Sordello,* but there were only two lines he understood—the first and the last—and they were both untrue:

> Who will, may hear Sordello's story told.

> Who would has heard Sordello's story told.

Sorel, Agnès [also called **Mlle de Beauté**] (1422–1450). Politically influential mistress (1444–1450) of the French king Charles VII.

Sorel, Georges (1847–1922). French advocate of social progress. In 1892 Sorel abandoned his career as a highway engineer to devote himself exclusively to the examination of social problems. A proponent of revolutionary syndicalism, he published his most famous work, *Réflexions sur la violence,* in 1908. Although Sorel turned to different agents to effect his purpose, his aim remained consistent: social progress through a spiritual revitalization of all sectors of society. The revitalization would occur, he believed, through spontaneous outbreaks of violence that would engender widespread enthusiasm and release human energy. Sorel's revolutionary doctrine did not depend upon an ideology; he emphasized not the source of the violence, whether proletariat or bourgeoisie, but its effect. At the turn of the century, he looked to the labor unions for revolutionary action, and later published *Matériaux pour une théorie du prolétariat* (1919). In an abrupt shift of sympathies, he collaborated with royalists and nationalists, and finally transferred his allegiance to Lenin and Mussolini. Among Sorel's works are *Le Procès de Socrate* (1889), an anti-intellectualist tract; *Introductions à l'économie moderne* (1903), a hopeful view of technology controlled and utilized to good purpose by man; and *Les Illusions de progrès* (1908).

Sorel, Julien. The protagonist of Stendhal's novel THE RED AND THE BLACK. Julien Sorel is a young man motivated by boundless ambition. Calculating and egotistical, he uses his love affairs to serve his drive for power. *Le Rouge* represents the red of the military while *Le Noir* is the black of the clergy, which for Julien, living in the aftermath of the Napoleonic dreams of glory, represents the one channel then open for advancement.

Sorrel, Hetty. See ADAM BEDE.

Sorrell and Son (1925). A popular novel by Warwick DEEPING. It is a sentimental account of an ex-officer's hard life as a hotel porter and the sacrifices he makes for his son. See IF WINTER COMES.

Sorrows of Young Werther, The (Die Leiden des jungen Werthers; 1774, final version 1787). A short novel by Johann Wolfgang von GOETHE, the first great popular success of his career. It is the story, in Goethe's words, of an artistically inclined young man "gifted with deep, pure sentiment and penetrating intelligence, who loses himself in fantastic dreams and undermines himself with speculative thought until finally, torn by hopeless passions, especially by infinite love, he shoots himself in the head." Werther's infinite love for an uncomplicated girl named Lotte who, however, marries a man with a much steadier, more bourgeois temperament than Werther's, at least partly reflects Goethe's own experiences. In its epistolary form the book was influenced by Richardson, and in its imagery and language by Macpherson's *Ossianic Poems*. See ZERRISSENHEIT. The book caused a wave of suicides among young German romantics.

Sosies, Les (1636). One of the most successful comedies of Jean de ROTROU. A retelling of the AMPHITRYON legend and a source of Molière's comedy on the same theme, the play takes its name from Sosie, Amphitryon's servant, who like his master is confronted with his own double—actually Mercury in disguise.

Sothern, E[dward] H[ugh] (1859–1933). American actor. The son of the famous English actor E. A. Sothern, he was closely associated on the stage with Julia MARLOWE, whom he married in 1911. They appeared together in a number of celebrated Shakespearean productions. Sothern won fame in such plays as *The Prisoner of Zenda, Henry Esmond*, and *If I Were King*. He also played Lord Dundreary in a revival of Tom Taylor's *Our American Cousin*.

Soubiran, André (1910–). French novelist. *The Doctors* (*Hommes en Blanc*, 1947) and *The Healing Oath* (1951) describe the sordid, then the redemptive qualities of hospital life and of sex for a young medical student. *Bedlam* (1955) describes an insane asylum.

Soulier de Satin, Le. See SATIN SLIPPER, THE.

soul of Pedro Garcias, the. Riches, from a story in the preface to Lesage's novel GIL BLAS DE SANTILLANE. Two students discover a tombstone with the inscription, "Here lies the soul of the licentiate Pedro Garcias." The more quick-witted student digs under the stone and finds 100 ducats. Lesage means that he hopes the reader of his novel will take heed of the moral lessons implied in it.

Soult, Nicolas Jean de Dieu. Duke of Dalmatia (1769–1851). Marshal of France under Napoleon Bonaparte (1804). Soult fought in many Napoleonic campaigns and aided Napoleon upon his return from Elba. He was recalled to France after living in exile and again made a marshal in 1820. From 1830 to 1834 and from 1840 to 1844 he served as minister of war.

Sound and the Fury, The (1929). A novel by William FAULKNER. Often considered Faulkner's best novel, the book is a radical experiment in form and technique. Three of the novel's four sections are the interior monologues of the three COMPSON brothers. With their hypochondriac mother and their vanished sister, Caddy, they are the sole surviving members of a decaying aristocratic family in Mississippi. The first section, seen through the eyes of the idiot Benjy, is literally "a tale told by an idiot, full of sound and fury." The second follows the thoughts of Quentin, a Harvard student whose world, built on a dying view of family honor and on his abnormally close ties to his sister Caddy, has been shattered by her seduction and hasty, loveless marriage.

The third section is a first-person narrative by greedy, petty-minded Jason, who has kept for himself the money Caddy has been sending for the support of her illegitimate daughter, Quentin. The final section is a third-person narrative focused on Dilsey, the Negro cook, whose patience and compassion are implicitly contrasted with the self-absorption and self-destructiveness of the Compsons.

Soupault, Philippe (1897–). French poet, novelist, and critic. At first closely associated with André BRETON in the DADA and SURREALIST movements, he left the group and began to write novels describing the social and moral degeneration of the 1920's, such as *Last Nights of Paris* (*Les Dernières Nuits de Paris*, 1928). *Age of Assassins* (*Le Temps des assassins*, 1945) is the story of his prison days. His critical works include books on Charlie Chaplin (*Charlot*, 1931), *James Joyce* (1944), *Lautréamont* (1946), and *Alfred de Musset* (1956).

Sousa, John Philip (1854–1932). American bandmaster and composer of marches. Among the best known of these are *Stars and Stripes Forever* (1897) and *El Capitan*, from his comic opera of that name (1896). He was known as the "March King."

South, Robert (1634?–1716). English churchman and writer. His *Sermons* (1692) are notable for their unusual liveliness, wit, and humor.

Southampton, 3rd earl of. Henry Wriothesley (1573–1624). English politician and soldier, patron of Shakespeare and other Elizabethan poets. Shakespeare's *Venus and Adonis* (1593) and *Rape of Lucrece* (1594) are dedicated to him. He was imprisoned for his part in Essex's rebellion (1601), but was released by James I. In 1605 he helped to equip an expedition to Virginia.

Southerne, Thomas (1660–1746). English dramatist. He was the author of such tragedies as *The Loyal Brother* (1682) and two plays based on novels by Mrs. Aphra Behn: *The Fatal Marriage* (1694) and *Oroonoko* (1695).

Southern Literary Messenger (1834–1864). American magazine founded at Richmond, Va. In December of 1835, Edgar Allan Poe assumed the editorship; his book reviews, stories, and critical essays gave the magazine a wide reputation. Poe raised its circulation from 500 to 3500, but the owner, T. W. White, gave him little compensation or appreciation. Poe was succeeded by Matthew F. Maury, a naval officer and oceanographer, whose articles, under the pseudonym of Harry Bluff, contributed to naval reorganization. George W. Bagby edited the magazine from 1860 to 1864. Revived in 1939 by the Dietz Press, it frequently reprinted Poe's original contributions.

Southern Review, The (1935–1942). An American literary quarterly. Founded at Louisiana State University, it was the third magazine in the South to bear such a title. Under the editorship of C. W. Pipkin, Cleanth Brooks, and Robert Penn Warren, it became one of the most distinguished of the little magazines of the 1930's, printing articles on literary criticism—often aligned with the New Criticism—philosophy, and politics, as well as stories and poems by outstanding 20th-century authors. Kenneth Burke, Katherine Anne Porter, John Crowe Ransom, and Allen Tate were among its regular contributors.

Southey, Robert (1774–1843). English romantic poet, one of the so-called Lake Poets. Though a leader in his day, he is considered by 20th-century critics to have been of mediocre talent. He wrote a great deal of verse, including the epic poems Thalaba The Destroyer; The Curse of Kehama; and Roderick, the Last of the Goths. He also wrote ballads, such as *The Battle of Blenheim;* didactic poems, such as The Old Man's Comforts; and much prose criticism and biography. If Southey's epics now seem tedious and diffuse, his ballads unmusical and moralizing, his prose is still esteemed. Such miscellanies as the *Common-Place Book* (1849–1851) and *The Doctor* (1834–1847) are erudite and valuable; while his short biographies of Nelson (1813), Cowper (1833), and Wesley (1830) are admired. In his youth, Southey joined with Coleridge in the scheme of pantisocracy and married Edith Fricker, whose sister married Coleridge. His early liberalism was superseded by a conservatism that was attacked in satire by Byron. Southey was Poet Laureate (1813–1843). In the last years of his life his mind gave way, and a brief bout of brain fever proved fatal.

South Sea Scheme or **Bubble.** A stock-jobbing scheme devised by Sir John Blunt, a lawyer, in 1710, and floated by the earl of Oxford in the following year. The object of the company was to buy up the national debt in return for the sole privilege of holding an extensive trade monopoly in the South Seas and in South America. Spain refused to give trading facilities, so the money was used in other speculative ventures and, by careful "rigging" of the market, £100 shares were run up to over 10 times that sum. The company at times rivaled in influence even the Bank of England (incorporated in 1694); but the highly inflated value of its stock caused, in 1720, England's first great stock-market panic in which thousands were ruined. Dr. John Arbuthnot wittily remarked that "the Government and South Sea Company have only locked up the money of the people upon conviction of their lunacy, as is usual in the case of lunatics, and intend to restore them as much as is fit for such people, as they see them return more and more to their senses."

Southwell, Robert (c. 1561–1595). English poet and author of religious writings. Southwell was ordained a Jesuit priest in Rome in 1584; two years later he was sent, at his own request, as a missionary to England, where his presence (after forty days) was legally treason. In 1592, after six years of secret service to English Catholics, he was arrested. He was imprisoned and repeatedly tortured for three years, and hanged in 1595. His religious tracts, such as *Mary Magdalen's Funeral Tears* (pub. 1609), were written before his imprisonment and probably fairly widely circulated in manuscript. Most of his poetry, which is concerned with the spiritual life, was composed while he was in prison. *Saint Peter's Complaint* was published anonymously in 1595, and followed shortly by *Maeoniae,* a supplementary volume. *A Fourfold Meditation of the Four Last Things* was published in 1606. *The Burning Babe,* which was highly praised by Ben Jonson, is Southwell's best-known poem.

South Wind (1917). A novel by Norman Douglas. It is set on the Capri-like island of Nepenthe, and is concerned with the group of exotic, odd, and learned characters who live there during a spring "season," blown on by the disturbing south wind. The flimsy thread of plot quietly embraces drunken orgies, intentional miscarriages of justice, forgery of art treasures, a religious revival, a volcanic eruption, fraud, blackmail, and murder. But the novel is less a story than a symposium—a series of long hedonistic and skeptical discussions of ethics, religion, art, food, and many other matters. These discussions are interspersed with Douglas's lightly satirical essays on the island's history and mythology. The island's free pagan values challenge the beliefs of a respectable visiting English bishop. He so modifies his ideas that by the end of the book he is condoning a murder.

Southworth, Emma Dorothy Eliza. Born Nevitte (1819–1899). American novelist, known as Mrs. E. D. E. N. Southworth. Mrs. Southworth married in 1841 and two years later was deserted by her husband; left with two children to support, she turned to teaching and novel-writing. The more than 60 melodramatic tales she wrote sold millions of copies. Her greatest triumph was *The Hidden Hand* (1859). Her *Works* (42 v.) were published in 1872.

Soviet literary policy. Soviet literature was freest during the years just after the revolution. Bolshevik leaders such as Lenin and Trotsky seemed willing to allow unfettered development of literature, barring any openly anti-Communist works. Not until 1928, when the literary organization RAPP (q.v.) gained dominance, was pressure put on writers. During the years of the first Five-Year Plan (1928–32), RAPP exhorted writers to heed the "social command" by producing the kind of literature RAPP said was needed at the time: depictions of contemporary social and economic problems. In 1932, RAPP was dissolved and the Union of Soviet Writers established. Apparently a step in the direction of greater freedom, the move actually made writers easier to watch and control by gathering them into a common organization. Further restraint was created by the proclamation of the doctrine of SOCIALIST REALISM which all writers were obliged to follow. Recalcitrant writers, who either did not heed the new standards or whose earlier work offended the authorities, were eliminated during the purges beginning in 1936. Among the outstanding authors who disappeared, presumably into prison camps, were Isaak Babel, Boris Pilnyak, and Osip Mandelshtam. Other writers, such as Yuri Oliosha, Anna Akhmatova, and Boris Pasternak, ceased to appear in print.

The war years saw a loosening of the iron grip on literature, although the Party showed it was still vigilant by castigating Mikhail Zoshchenko for his "personalistic" work, *Before Sunrise* (1943). Immediately after the war, the slight degree of freedom was quickly destroyed with the campaign against Western influences in Soviet culture led by Andrei ZHDANOV. The "anticosmopolitan" campaign began in 1946 with the expulsion of Zoshchenko and Akhmatova from the Writer's Union. From this time until Stalin's death (1953), literature was smothered by the close Party control. With Stalin gone, a gradual relaxation was felt in cultural life. Hints of this relaxation were contained in Ilya Ehrenburg's novel, *The Thaw* (1954), which gave its name to the new atmosphere. The thaw was given impetus by Nikita KHRUSHCHEV's anti-Stalin speech at the 20th Communist Party Congress in 1956. That year a number of works criticizing various aspects of Soviet life appeared, among the most publicized being Vladimir Dudintzev's novel *Not by Bread Alone*. A new tightening of controls came, however, after the Hungarian Revolution of late 1956.

In 1958 a new disciplinary problem presented itself to the government with the publication abroad of Pasternak's novel, *Dr. Zhivago*. The work, which had been refused for Soviet publication, was outspoken in its criticism of the Marxist attempts to order life to a set plan. Pasternak was expelled from the Writer's Union and threatened with expulsion from the country. He was obliged to reject the Nobel Prize offered him in 1959.

In recent years the Soviet leadership has tended to allow writers to work in a relatively relaxed atmosphere, clamping down only when works are too openly critical of the present Soviet society. Works exposing the evils of the Stalin regime, which is considered safely in the past, are allowed and even praised. The most sensational of such works has been Aleksandr Solzhenitzyn's short novel, *One Day in the Life of Ivan Denisovich*.

Sowerby, James (1757–1822). English artist and naturalist who illustrated botanical and conchological works. His great works are *English Botany* (1790–1814) and *English Fungi* (1797–1815).

Sowerby, Katherine Githa. English playwright and writer. Among her works are *Rutherford & Son* (1912), *Sheila* (1917), and *The Policeman's Whistle*

(1934). She collaborated with her sister Amy Millicent Sowerby on a number of children's books.

Spade, Sam. A private detective created by the novelist Dashiell HAMMETT. His first and most significant appearance was in THE MALTESE FALCON. Spade, a rough, tough, realistic man, was a far cry from the dilettantes who had been featured in most detective fiction up to his appearance.

Spanish-American War (1898). A war between the U.S. and Spain, stemming from a native revolt on the Spanish-held island of Cuba, in which Americans had long had a political and economic interest. The sensational reports of the "yellow press" about Spanish atrocities in Cuba aroused American resentment against Spain, as did the publication of a letter written by Dupuy de Lôme, Spanish minister to the U.S., in which he referred to President McKinley in derogatory terms. War hysteria reached its height when an explosion destroyed the U.S. battleship *Maine* in Havana harbor with the loss of 260 lives; although a naval court of inquiry could not discover who was to blame for the disaster, it was popularly attributed to Spanish agents. Although McKinley had previously followed a peaceful policy, he asked Congress to declare war on April 11, 1898. U.S. victories in the Philippines and Cuba led Spain to sue for peace in July. According to the terms of the treaty of Paris, Spain agreed to Cuban independence and ceded the Philippines to the U.S. for $20 million, as well as Puerto Rico and Guam. The conflict marked the emergence of the U.S. as a world power. See George DEWEY; Theodore ROOSEVELT.

Spanish Gypsy, The (1868). A poem by George ELIOT. It relates the tragic love story of Fedalma, a gypsy brought up as a noble Spanish girl, and Duke Silva, the commander of the Spanish fort. The couple are engaged, but, when Fedalma's father Zarca recognizes her and reveals her parentage, she believes it her duty to give up her lover and join her people. Silva, on the other hand, deserts his post and resolves to become a gypsy. During his absence the post falls, and Silva in desperation stabs Zarca. The lovers then part forever, Fedalma to lead the gypsies to Africa, Silva to seek pardon at Rome.

Spanish Main, the. Properly the northern coast of South America, going westward from the mouth of the Orinoco to the Isthmus of Panama, or a bit farther. It is the *main*-land bordering the Caribbean Sea, called by the Spanish conquerors *Tierra Firme*. The term is often applied, however, to the curving chain of islands forming the northern and eastern boundaries of the Caribbean Sea, beginning from Mosquito, near the isthmus, and including Jamaica, Hispaniola, the Leeward Islands, and the Windward Islands, to the coast of Venezuela in South America. It is carelessly used to refer to the Caribbean Sea. It often relates to the haunts of pirates who preyed on shipping to the Spanish colonies.

Spanish Tragedy, The (prod. between 1584 and 1589). A drama by Thomas KYD. A bloody tragedy of revenge in the popular Senecan style, *The Spanish Tragedy* deals with political intrigue between the Spanish and the Portuguese that explodes in the murder of Horatio, the son of the marshal of Spain Hieronimo. Horatio, in the arbor with his beloved Bel-Imperia, is slain by her brother and the prince of Portugal, who wants to marry her. Horatio's

The Spanish Tragedie:
OR,
Hieronimo is mad againe.

Containing the lamentable end of *Don Horatio*, and *Belimperia*; with the pittifull death of *Hieronimo*.

Newly corrected, amended, and enlarged with new Additions of the *Painters part*, and others, as it hath of late been diuers times acted.

LONDON,
Printed by W. White, for I. White and T. Langley, and are to be sold at their Shop ouer against the Sarazens head without New-gate. 1615.

Title page of Kyd's *The Spanish Tragedy*
(1613 edition).

body is left hanging in the arbor, where Hieronimo finds it and goes mad with grief. Finally Hieronimo conspires with Bel-Imperia to stage a play at a royal party at which the murderers are present. The villains are lured into taking parts in the play and are killed, and Hieronimo, to prevent himself from being tortured into naming his confederates, kills himself. In 1592 a prologue was added to the play, called *The First Part of Jeronimo* [sic], *or the Warres of Portugal*. This gives a somewhat different version of the story, and is thought by some critics to be the work of someone other than Kyd.

Spark, Muriel (1918–   ). Scottish novelist, poet, and critic. Her witty novels are strongly colored by her Catholicism. *Robinson* (1958) is about a wrecked plane and a hermit; *Memento Mori* (1959) is about old people plagued by mysterious phone calls, "a reminder of death." *The Ballad of Peckham Rye* (1960) deals with a London factory turned upside down by satanic Dougal Douglas, while *The Prime of Miss Jean Brodie* (1962) is concerned with a schoolteacher and her girl pupils.

Sparks, Jared (1789–1866). American historian and editor. As owner and editor of the *North American Review* (1824–1830), Sparks made it the most influential magazine in the U.S. Meanwhile, he had begun to compile his 12-volume edition of *The Writings of George Washington* (1834–1837); he also edited *The Works of Benjamin Franklin* (1836–1840) and two series of *The Library of American Biography* (1834–1838, 1844–1847), to which he contributed several sketches. Although his editorial methods were often faulty, Sparks rescued many important documents from oblivion and stimulated interest in American history. In 1839 he joined the Harvard faculty as the first professor of history in any American university. From 1849 to 1853 he was president of Harvard.

Sparta or **Lacedaemon (Lakedaimon).** The ancient capital of Laconia, in the southeast corner of the Peloponnesus. The victorious opponent of Athens in the PELOPONNESIAN WAR, Sparta was also opposed to that city in spirit. Aristocratic, conservative, and militaristic, the Spartans took pride in their courage, endurance, frugality, and discipline. Boys were taken from their mothers at the age of seven and lived in barracks until they were 30. No deformed Spartan children were allowed to live, and the newborn were washed in icy mountain streams. The Spartans were frugal even in speech, a fact that gave us the word laconic. Two famous figures of legend illustrate Spartan attitudes: the Spartan mother who, handing her son the shield he was to carry into battle, told him to come back either with it or on it; and the boy who, having hidden a stolen fox under his tunic, permitted it to gnaw his vitals rather than confess his theft. These characteristics were peculiar to the Dorian Sparta of Classical times. In the Mycenaean period, Sparta was known primarily as the capital of Menelaus' dominions, from which Helen was abducted by Paris.

Spartacist Party. A German revolutionary organization, led by Karl LIEBKNECHT and Rosa LUXEMBURG, which became powerful during World War I. It attempted to imitate the Russian Bolsheviks by organizing a proletarian uprising in 1919, but without success. It was named after the Roman slave Spartacus, who led a revolt in 73 B.C.

Spartacus (d. 71 B.C.). Roman slave and gladiator. He led an insurrection of slaves (73–71 B.C.), during which he routed several armies; he was finally defeated and killed by CRASSUS. Howard Fast's historical novel *Spartacus* (1951) is based on his life.

Sparti (Gr., "sown men"). Armed men. They grew from the dragon's teeth sown by Cadmus and by Jason (see ARGONAUTS). The dragon had guarded the sacred spring of Ares at Thebes. Both heroes defeated the Sparti by throwing a stone among them, which set them fighting each other to the death. Of the five surviving Sparti at Thebes who became Cadmus' followers, Echion married his daughter Agave and was the father of Pentheus, Chthonius was the father of Nycteus and Lycus, later kings of Thebes.

Spasmodic School. A name applied by William Edmonston AYTOUN to certain 19th-century poets, such as P. J. Bailey, Gerald Massey, Alexander Smith, and Sydney Dobell. Their work was characterized by forced conceits and unnatural style.

speakeasy. A tavern, restaurant, or cabaret that sold liquor illegally in the U.S. during the prohibition era. It was so called because in the 1920's admittance was surrounded by an air of secrecy and adventure, although police surveillance of speakeasies was actually quite lax.

Specimen Days and Collect (1882). A collection of notes and essays by Walt WHITMAN. The book begins with an account of the poet's youth, but concentrates on his Civil War experiences. Much of the material is adapted from notebooks Whitman kept during the period. Some reminiscences of his old age are included. The "Collect" is a group of literary essays.

Spectator, The (March, 1711–December, 1712). A famous series of essays by Joseph ADDISON and Richard STEELE. In these essays, purportedly edited by the members of the fictional Spectator Club, Mr. Spectator, a shy, observant gentleman who has settled in London, provides a picture of the social life of the times, while the individual concerns of the club's other members, Sir Roger de COVERLEY, Will Honeycomb, Andrew Freeport, and Captain Sentry, add narrative depth and interest.

Spectra and the Spectrist school. A literary hoax perpetrated by Witter BYNNER and Arthur Davison FICKE. Irked by the pretentiousness of the imagist and vorticist poets, they decided to found their own school of poetry and, using the names Emanuel Morgan and Anne Knish, published *Spectra: A Book of Poetic Experiments* (1916). The so-called school was taken seriously for nearly two years.

Speculum Meditantis, also known as **Speculum Hominis** or **Mirour de l'omme** (c. 1378?). Norman-French poem by John GOWER, of 30,000 lines in 12-line stanzas. A didactic work, it describes the contest for men's souls between the seven vices, with all their offspring by the Devil, and the seven virtues, with their offspring by Reason. In doing so, it gives a detailed "mirror of men" of all classes in contemporary life. It concludes that all men are corrupt and must turn to the Virgin Mary for mercy and aid.

Spedding, James (1808–1881). English author, editor of *Works, Life and Letters of Francis Bacon* (14 vols.; 1857–1874) and author of *Life and Times of Bacon* (1878), both of which have remained standard works. He was a close friend of Tennyson, Thackeray, and Edward FitzGerald.

Speed. In Shakespeare's Two GENTLEMEN OF VERONA, an inveterate punster and the clownish servant of Valentine. He is an "illiterate loiterer" whose dilatory ways belie his name.

Spence, Joseph (1699–1768). English biographer who wrote lives of such men as Stephen Duck, the so-called thresher poet, and Thomas Blacklock, a blind Scottish poet. Spence also collected examples of Alexander Pope's conversation; these were finally published as *Spence's Anecdotes* in 1820.

Spencer, Herbert (1820–1903). English philosopher and social scientist. He is known for his application of the scientific doctrines of evolution to philosophy and ethics, with a central principle, the "persistence of force," as the agent of all change, form, and organization in the knowable universe. In education, he scorned the study of the liberal arts and advocated that science be the chief subject of instruction.

Spencer's best-known works include *Principles of Psychology* (1855), and the 10-volume *System of Synthetic Philosophy,* the general title of the series that he announced in 1860 and to which he devoted the rest of his life. His *Autobiography* appeared in 1904.

Spence's Anecdotes. See Joseph SPENCE.

Spender, Stephen (1909–   ). English poet. A friend and follower of W. H. Auden, he was a leading member of the British group of Marxist poets of the 1930's. His poetry, especially in its later development, is more personal, lyrical, and romantic than that of his associates. It deals chiefly with his own emotional reactions as he contemplates unemployment, poverty, suffering, or injustice, or visualizes amelioration in a socialist state; many of his poems, especially his later ones, have an autobiographical basis; much of his work is characterized by imagery appropriate to an industrial and mechanical civilization. His *Collected Poems* appeared in 1954. Spender's autobiography, *World Within World* (1951), is valuable for its account of his friends W. H. Auden, Christopher Isherwood, Cecil Day-Lewis, and Louis MacNeice, and of his political beliefs and intellectual development. Spender also wrote *The Trial of a Judge* (1938), a poetic drama having the same theme as Rex Warner's novel THE PROFESSOR. His works of fiction include *The Burning Cactus* (1936) and his works of criticism include *The Destructive Element* (1935), *The Creative Element* (1953), and *The Making of a Poem* (1962). He coedited (with Cyril CONNOLLY) the magazine *Horizon* during World War II, and coedited the Anglo-American magazine *Encounter* from 1953.

Spengler, Oswald (1880–1936). German philosopher of history. His noted work *The Decline of the West* (*Der Untergang des Abendlandes;* 1918–1922) reflects the pessimistic atmosphere in Germany after World War I. Spengler maintained that history has a natural development in which every culture is a distinct organic form that grows, matures, and decays. He predicted a phase of "Caesarism" in the further development of Western culture, which, he believed, was in its last stage.

Spengler's attitude became very popular with the Nazi government, but he refused to enter into their persecution of the Jews. Being independently wealthy, he managed to exist in Germany, somewhat under a cloud, until the end of his life.

Spenlow, Dora. In Charles Dickens' DAVID COPPERFIELD, a warm-hearted, doll-like woman with no practical views of the duties of life or the value of money. She is the child-wife of David and loves to sit by him and hold his pens while he writes. After she dies David marries Agnes WICKFIELD. Dora is drawn from Dickens' wife.

Spens, Sir Patrick. See SIR PATRICK SPENS.

Spenser, Edmund (1552?–1599). One of the greatest English poets, and the first major English writer to arise after Chaucer. Born in London, Spenser was educated at the Merchant Taylors' School and Pembroke Hall, Cambridge. He was well acquainted with Plato and Aristotle, whose influences are clear in his works, with the Greek and Latin poets, and with the great Italian epics of Tasso and Ariosto. As early as 1569 he contributed some translations of Petrarch and the French poet Du Bellay to the *Theater for Worldlings,* an edifying volume of anti-Catholic propaganda. Also in his youth he wrote the hymns *In Honor of Love* and *In Honor of Beauty* (not published until 1596) which show his debt to Platonism. While at Cambridge he met Gabriel Harvey, a scholar and something of a pedant, but nevertheless a faithful and helpful friend, and the model for Hobbinol in THE SHEPHEARDES CALENDER. Harvey may have introduced Spenser to Sir Philip SIDNEY, the nephew of the earl of Leicester; in any event, in 1578 Spenser became a member of Leicester's household, and during this time formed with Sidney, Dyer, and others a literary club known as the Areopagus. Probably from the discussions of this club came the theories expressed in Sidney's *Apologie for Poetrie* and Spenser's *The English Poete*, a critical work which is not extant. In 1579, Spenser published his first important work, *The Shepheardes Calender*. Dedicated to Sidney, it contained 12 eclogues in the style of Vergil and Mantuan and is particularly notable for its use of various meters and its vocabulary, enriched both by foreign borrowings and a reviving of older English words.

By this time Spenser had probably begun to work on his great epic, THE FAERIE QUEENE. Most of the following years were spent in Ireland, where he first went in 1580 as secretary to Lord Grey of Wilton, who had been appointed lord deputy of Ireland. In about 1587, Spenser was given possession of Castle Kilcolman in County Cork, and it was here that he wrote *Astrophel*, an elegy on the death of Sidney. In 1589 he was visited by Sir Walter Raleigh, who urged him to go to London to arrange for the publication of the first three books of *The Faerie Queene*, and promised to present him to Queen Elizabeth. When Spenser returned to Ireland after an absence of nearly two years, he wrote his autobiographical pastoral COLIN CLOUTS COME HOME AGAINE (published, with *Astrophel*, in 1595), in which he allegorically describes his voyage with Raleigh, his admiration for Elizabeth, and includes an attack on the intrigues at court. During his visit to London, meanwhile, Spenser had been received with favor by Elizabeth, had seen the publication (1590) of the first three books of *The Faerie Queen*, and had been granted a royal pension of 50 pounds a year. 1591 saw the publication of his *Complaints*, which included revised versions of some of the poems that had appeared in the *Theater for Worldlings;* it also contained *The Teares of the Muses*, a complaint on the current status of poetry; *The Ruines of Time*, a lament on the deaths of Sidney and Leicester; and MOTHER HUBBERDS TALE, a satire in the form of an animal fable thought to be directed against Lord Burghley and the proposed marriage of Elizabeth to the French duc d'Alençon.

Spenser's courtship of Elizabeth Boyle probably occasioned most of the 88 sonnets in the *Amoretti*, and his marriage to her in 1594 inspired his magnificent EPITHALAMION (publ. with *Amoretti* in 1595). The PROTHALAMION, another marriage-poem, was written for the double wedding of the daughters of the earl of Worcester. In the same year appeared FOUR HYMNS TO LOVE AND BEAUTY, the first two the early poems to earthly love and beauty, the latter two on their celestial counterparts. During the winter of 1595–1596 he was again in London arranging for a reissuing of Books I–III of *The Faerie Queene* and the publication of the next three books. In 1598 he was recommended as sheriff of Cork; however, it was not long until the outbreak of Tyrone's rebellion, during which Castle Kilcolman was burned and Spenser forced to flee. He died shortly after in London,

apparently in bad straits but probably not "for lack of bread," as Ben Jonson reported. He left two cantos and two stanzas on mutability (publ. 1609), thought to have been intended for a future book of *The Faerie Queene. A View of the Present State of Ireland*, a prose defense of the repressive policy of Lord Grey of Wilton in Ireland, was not published until 1633.

A Protestant and a Platonist, Spenser was deeply concerned with the religio-historical problems of his age, and reflected in his work the Renaissance conception of poetry as the highest instrument of moral teaching. Deliberately archaic in style, he looked to Chaucer as the pure "well of English undefiled,' but he was no mere imitator of his master, and gave to English poetry both an enriched, romantic language, lines marked by their running sweetness of diction, and stanzas—called Spenserian—adapted from ottava rima but made particularly his own. Both the SPENSERIAN STANZA and the archaic language contribute to the mythic romance of *The Faerie Queene*, enveloping the scenes of chivalry and adventure with a singularly appropriate mistiness of style. An epic to compare with the great epics of the classical world and of Renaissance Italy, *The Faerie Queene* is simultaneously a nationalistic paean to the greatness of Elizabeth and her England, an imaginative romance, and a moral allegory of the soul of man on his quest for salvation.

Spenserian school. A group of English poets, including William BASSE, William BROWNE, Sir John DAVIES, and George WITHER, who flourished in the first part of the 17th century. In opposition to a growing fashion for more self-conscious, intellectual, and ingenious verse, they preserved the simpler lyric and pastoral tradition of the early Elizabethans, their chief model being Edmund SPENSER. Their typical form was the PASTORAL or pastoral dialogue (ECLOGUE), and their verse was characteristically musical, pictorial, and allegorical.

Spenserian stanza. Stanza devised by Edmund SPENSER for *The Faerie Queene*. Adapted from the Italian ottava rima, it is a stanza of eight decasyllable lines concluded by a ninth six-foot iambic line, or Alexandrine, and rhymes ababbcbcc:

> A Gentle Knight was pricking on the plaine,
> Ycladd in mightie armes and silver shield,
> Wherein old dints of deepe woundes did remaine,
> The cruell markes of many a bloody fielde;
> Yet armes till that time did he never wield:
> His angry steede did chide his foming bitt,
> As much disdayning to the curbe to yield:
> Full jolly knight he seemed and faire did sitt,
> As one for knightly guists and fierce encounters fitt.
>
>   (*The Faerie Queene*, I, i)

It has the advantage of tending to be less rapid and more sonorous than the Italian form, while still retaining a sense of motion suitable for a long poem dealing with heroic exploits. It was later used by Byron in his *Childe Harold*.

Speroni, Sperone (1500–1588). Paduan gentleman and author of many dialogues and discourses on varied subjects. Especially important was his *Dialogo sulle lingue (Dialogue on Language)* of 1540, which was used by such defenders of the vernacular as Du Bellay. He also wrote the influential and controversial tragedy *Canace* (1542).

Spewack, Bella (1899–   ) and **Samuel** (1899–1971). American playwrights and film scenarists. Mrs. Spewack, born in Hungary, has also written short stories; her husband, born in Russia, is the author of detective stories. They are best known for their plays, including *Clear All Wires* (1932); *Spring Song* (1934); *Boy Meets Girl* (1935), a well-known satire on Hollywood screen-writers; and for the two musical comedies *Leave It to Me* (1938) and KISS ME KATE, both with music by Cole Porter.

Speyer, Leonora (1872–1955). American poet. She won a Pulitzer Prize for her collection *Fiddler's Farewell* (1926). Among her other collections are *Canopic Jar* (1921) and *Naked Heel* (1931).

spheres. A particular concept in the Ptolemaic system of astronomy. The earth, as the center of the universe, was supposed to be surrounded by nine spheres of invisible space, the first seven carrying the "planets" as then known: (1) Diana or the Moon, (2) Mercury, (3) Venus, (4) Apollo or the Sun, (5) Mars, (6) Jupiter, and (7) Saturn. The eighth, the Starry Sphere, carried the fixed stars, and the ninth, the Crystalline Sphere, was added by Hipparchus in the 2d century B.C. to account for the precession of the equinoxes. Finally, in the Middle Ages, was added a solid barrier that enclosed the universe and shut it off from Nothingness and the Empyrean. These last two spheres carried neither star nor planet. See MUSIC OF THE SPHERES.

Sphinx. (1) A monster of Greek mythology with the face of a woman, the body of a lion, and the wings of a bird. The offspring of Echidna and Typhon or Orthus, she flew to Mount Phicium, near Thebes. There she propounded a riddle and devoured those young men who could not answer it. The most familiar version of this riddle, a common theme in folk lore, is as follows: What walks on four legs in the morning, on two at midday, on three in the evening? When OEDIPUS gave the correct answer (man, who crawls as an infant, walks upright as an adult, and uses a staff in old age) the Sphinx killed herself in chagrin.

(2) In Egypt, the Sphinx was represented as a wingless lion with the head and breast of a man, typifying the sun god, Ra. A colossal sphinx, near the Great Pyramid of Cheops, was ancient when the pyramid was built (c. 3000). Hewn out of the solid rock, it is 140 feet in length and its head 30 feet from crown to chin.

Emerson has a poem entitled *The Sphinx* (1841), as does Oscar Wilde.

Spielhagen, Friedrich (1829–1911). German author of many realistic, politically liberal novels about problems of his time, the most famous of which is *In Reih und Glied* (*Rank and File*, 1867). He also wrote a treatise entitled *Beiträge zur Theorie und Technik des Romans* (*Contributions to the Theory and Practice of the Novel*, 1883) which, though advocating realism, was opposed by the writers of naturalism.

Spillane, Mickey [Frank Morrison Spillane] (1918–   ). American detective-story writer. He is known for the blend of sex and sadism he lavishes on his blunt narrative; his chief character is Mike Hammer. *I, the Jury* (1947) is perhaps the best known of these works.

Spingarn, Joel E[lias] (1875–1939). American critic. A student of Benedetto Croce and influenced by the work of Santayana and Huneker in America, Spingarn helped shift critical emphasis away from such external considerations as history and biography and focus it solely on the work of art itself. He first outlined his views in an address called "The New Criticism." Delivered at Columbia University in 1910, it anticipated the NEW CRITICISM of the thirties and forties. In 1931 he compiled the most significant critical studies of three decades and published them as *Criticism in America: Its Function and Status*. Among his other writings are *A History of Literary Criticism in the Renaissance* (1899), *Creative Criticism* (1917; revised and expanded, 1931), and *Critical Essays of the 17th Century* (3 vols., 1908–1909).

Spinoza, Baruch (1632–1677). A famous Dutch philosopher of Portuguese-Jewish parents. He is regarded today as the most eminent expounder of the doctrine of pantheism. He kept aloof from academic obligations by making a living as a grinder of lenses.

Spirit of Laws, The (De l'Esprit des lois; 1748). A treatise on the principles and historical origins of law by Charles de MONTESQUIEU. Its theme may be understood in part by the whole title: "Concerning the spirit of laws, or the relationship which laws must have to the constitution of each government, to mores, religion, commerce, etc." Underlying man-made laws are natural, or universal, laws which may be broadly described thus: universal peace in all nature; the need for food; the need to reproduce in kind; and gregariousness. Once society is formed, it is necessary for human beings to formulate positive laws to govern that society. These positive laws are not deduced a priori but must take into account natural law, and, as the subtitle suggests, such considerations as the mores, climate, religion, commerce, population, and customs of each different society to which the laws apply. In seeking to establish positive laws perfectly just to all peoples, Montesquieu reveals himself to be a universal humanist for whom justice is the supreme political virtue. In this connection, it is interesting to note that he speaks out against slavery, aggressive war, cruel punishments, and religious intolerance. Of the three types of government which he analyzes, monarchic, republican, and despotic, Montesquieu shows a preference for a constitutional monarchy for France. He also admires the English constitution for its separation of powers. The last five books are a technical treatise on the Roman and Germanic origins of French law.

The somewhat incoherent plan of the work does not lessen its value as the first authoritative example of a comparative study of social institutions; it also, by implication, exposed grave abuses in the French monarchy and defects in contemporary civilization. For example, Montesquieu advocated separation of Church and State in legal matters and believed that civil law should not be used to condemn men for heresy or witchcraft. It is generally considered one of the most important polical treatises in existence; its influence on practically every constitution in the world (e.g., the American Constitution, and Catherine II's efforts to recodify Russian law) cannot be underestimated. Its literary style makes it eminently readable today.

spirituals. The religious folksongs of the American Negro slaves. While some spirituals are exuberant, the most characteristic express the slave's misery in bondage and his yearning for freedom, generally in Old Testament terms borrowed from the tales of the captivity of Israel, which the slave saw as analogous to his own. Spiritual melodies are often built on the pentatonic or other scales, closer to Greek or Hungarian modes than to the standard major and minor scales of Western music, and their free treatment of the third and seventh degrees occasionally results in the so-called blue note. While they are eminently susceptible to the simple tonic-subdominant-dominant harmonizations typical of the hymnbook, their rhythms retain the freedom, subtlety, and complexity common in African music. Not surprisingly, these traits were carried over into Negro secular song and dance music and became basic components of early jazz.

Spitteler, Carl. Pen name of **Felix Tandem** (1845-1924). Swiss poet and novelist, writing in German. He was heavily influenced by Nietzsche. His epic *Olympischer Frühling* (*Olympian Spring*, final version 1910) earned him the Nobel Prize in 1919. His prose works, the best known of which is *Conrad der Leutnant* (*Conrad the Lieutenant*, 1898), a short novel, show certain features of NATURALISM.

Spoils of Annwn, The. A 10th-century Welsh poem that briefly mentions King ARTHUR.

Spoils of Poynton, The (1897). A novel by Henry JAMES. The "spoils" of the title refer to a great art and furniture collection in a house at Poynton. When Owen Gereth, owner of the house, is unwilling to marry Fleda Vetch, his mother's choice, Mrs. Gereth removes the art treasures. After Owen's marriage to Mona Brigstock, he offers Fleda any object in the collection. She arrives at Poynton to find that the house has been destroyed in an accidental fire.

spondee. In English prosody, a foot of two accented syllables; in classical prosody, of two long syllables. The form in English is rare since most polysyllabic words contain a primary accent; when the spondee does occur, it is usually as two monosyllabic words, such as "ah, joy." In examining the subject, Poe found only three or four instances where spondee occurs in a single word; "football" was one instance. See METER.

Spooner, William Archibald (1844-1930). English dean and later warden of New College, Oxford. He acquired a (probably exaggerated) reputation for his "spoonerisms," witty or unwitting transpositions of sounds, technically known as metathesis: For example, "There is a roaring pain" for "There is a pouring rain." Spoonerisms form part of Joyce's technique in *Finnegans Wake*.

Spoon River Anthology (1915). A volume of verse epitaphs by Edgar Lee MASTERS. The men and women of Spoon River narrate their own biographies from the cemetery where they lie buried. Realistic and sometimes cynical, these free-verse monologues often contradict the pious and optimistic epitaphs written on the gravestones. The poems made their first appearance in *Reedy's Mirror* in 1914 and 1915, and William Marion Reedy himself was partly responsible for their inception: he gave Masters a copy of J. W. Mackail's *Select Epigrams from the Greek Anthology*, and the style of the Greek poems impressed Masters deeply. *New Spoon River* (1924) was a less successful sequel.

Sportsman's Sketches, A (*Zapiski okhotnika;* 1852). A collection of short stories by Ivan TURGENEV. Portraiting the life led on one of the typical great feudal estates in Russia, the *Sketches* with its perceptive descriptions by a fictional narrator of what he encountered on his rambles through the countryside brought Turgenev his first fame as an author. Because of the sympathetic attitude shown to the peasants and the often explicit condemnation of the landowners, the work has been interpreted as an attack on serfdom, which was abolished about 10 years after the book's publication.

Sporus. A favorite of the emperor Nero. The name was applied by Alexander Pope in his *Epistle to Dr. Arbuthnot* (1735) to Lord Hervey, and implied effeminacy.

S.P.Q.R. Senatus Populusque Romanus (Lat., "the Roman Senate and People"). Initials inscribed on the standards of ancient Rome.

Sprat, Thomas (1635-1713). English clergyman and writer. He is best known for his *History of the Royal Society of London* (1667), dealing with the Royal Society and philosophy in general and noted for the modernity of its style. Sprat was bishop of Rochester.

Sprechstimme (Ger., "speaking voice"). In music, the rhythmic declamation of a text at specified pitches but in a speaking voice. The effect is one of heightened, almost sung speech. The device was first used by Arnold SCHOENBERG in his song cycle *Pierrot Lunaire* (1912).

Sprigg, Christopher St. John. See Christopher CAUDWELL.

Spring, Howard (1889–). English popular novelist. He wrote *My Son, My Son!* (1938), *Fame is the Spur* (1940), supposedly based on the life of Ramsay MacDonald, *The Houses in Between* (1951), and *I Met a Lady* (1961).

Spring and Autumn Annals (Ch'un-ch'iu). One of the Chinese FIVE CLASSICS, it is a Chou Dynasty chronicle of the feudal state of Lu for the years 722-481 B.C. Traditionally said to have been compiled by Confucius.

sprung rhythm. A combination of ACCENT METER with certain stylistic devices. It is the term by which Gerard Manley HOPKINS designated his approach to rhythm in poetry. The word "sprung," he said, connoted for him something like "abrupt." Instead of the intense musicality of most poetry in accent meter, Hopkins sought the sense of halt, of impediments to smoothness. He used such stylistic devices as alliteration, a preponderance of Anglo-Saxon vocabulary, the deliberate use of archaic and provincial words and turns of phrase, and inversion of natural order, in order to suggest the power of Anglo-Saxon poetry, which he said had a great influence on him.

Spurgeon, Caroline (1869-1942). English literary scholar. Her study *Shakespeare's Imagery and What It Tells Us* (1935) has been influential.

Spy, The (1821). An historical novel by James Fenimore COOPER. Cooper's second novel, but his first success, the book is a mixture of fighting, espionage, and love. The central character is Harvey Birch, a Yankee peddler who risks his life as a double spy.

The action takes place in Westchester County, where both British and Americans have troops.

Square, Mr. [Thomas]. One of two tutors to Tom and Blifil in Henry Fielding's TOM JONES. Deistic in thought, Square spouts the "natural beauty of virtue." Actually, he is a great hypocrite. Both Square and THWACKUM satirize theological pedantry in education.

Squaring the Circle (Kvadratura kruga; 1928). A comedy by Valentin KATAYEV. The play's central characters are two mismatched couples who share a Moscow apartment. Eventually they change partners, thus uniting the two dedicated and the two frivolous ones.

Squeers, Mr. Wackford. In Charles Dickens' NICHOLAS NICKLEBY, the vulgar, conceited, ignorant schoolmaster of Dotheboys Hall. He steals the boys' money, clothes his son in their best suits, half starves them, and teaches them next to nothing. Ultimately, he is transported for purloining a deed.

Mrs. Squeers. Squeers' wife, a raw-boned, harsh, heartless virago, without one spark of womanly feeling for the boys in her charge.

Squire, Sir J[ohn] C[ollings] (1884–1958). English GEORGIAN poet and editor. He wrote fine parodies (*Collected Parodies,* 1921) and collaborated in writing a number of plays, including *Berkeley Square* (1928), with J. L. Balderston as co-author.

Squire's Tale, The. One of the CANTERBURY TALES of Geoffrey CHAUCER, an unfinished medieval romance. The first part tells of the birthday feast of the Tartar king Cambuscan (or Cambyuskan), to whom a mysterious knight brings four magical gifts —a brass horse, a mirror, a ring, and a sword—and explains their workings. In the second part Cambuscan's daughter Canacee goes out next morning wearing the ring, which enables the bearer to understand and speak with birds. She takes pity on a bitterly distressed falcon who tells her how her tercelet lover has deserted her for a kite. The section ends with a promise to describe the adventures of Cambuscan and his two sons, and the fights for Canacee's hand in marriage, but Chaucer never continued the tale. Spenser wrote a continuation in the fourth book of his *Faerie Queene.*

Squirrel-Cage, The (1912). A novel by Dorothy Canfield FISHER. Using the characters of a husband and wife, the book effectively contrasts the materialistic attitude of a social-minded and avaricious woman and the more altruistic attitude of the man she loves.

S.S. The abbreviated name of the Nazi *Schutzstaffel* (Elite Guard), organized in 1929 by Himmler. Members of the S.S., selected from the larger S.A., served as bodyguards for high officials and as supervisors of the concentration camps. They were also called Blackshirts. See S.A.

Ssu-ma Ch'ien (145?–90? B.C.) Chinese historian, author of the *Shih chi,* or *Records of the Historian,* the first major Chinese historical work. Son of a scholar, he served in the Imperial Court. He organized and edited ancient source materials, writing a masterpiece that set the pattern for all later DYNASTIC HISTORIES. He was castrated for having incurred the emperor's displeasure, but continued his work until its completion. See Burton Watson, *Ssu-ma Ch'ien: Grand Historian of China* (1958).

Stabat Mater (Lat. "The Mother was standing"). Opening words of a medieval Latin hymn which describes the suffering of the Virgin Mary at the foot of the Cross of Christ. It is ascribed to the 13th-century Franciscan Jacopone da Todi. It has been set to music by many major composers: Josquin des Prés, Palestrina, Pergolesi, Haydn, Schubert, Rossini, Verdi, and Dvořák, among others.

Stadler, Ernst (1883–1914). German poet. Influenced by Walt Whitman, Stadler himself contributed to the development of German EXPRESSIONISM. Collections of his poems are *Präludien* (*Preludes,* 1905) and *Der Aufbruch* (*The Departure,* 1914). He was killed in World War I.

Staël, Mme. de Born **Anne Louise Germaine Necker** (1766–1817). Swiss-French belle-lettrist. Her father, Jacques NECKER, was the French minister of finance; her husband, the Baron de Staël-Holstein, was Swedish ambassador to France. She is known for her celebrated salons, which were attended by leading literary and political figures, for her charm, talent for conversation, vigorous mind, and for her influence on ROMANTICISM in France. Among her works are *Lettres sur les écrits et caractère de Jean-Jacques Rousseau* (1788); *De l'Influence des passions* (1796); *Essai sur les fictions* (1795); *Considérations sur la Révolution française* (1818). DELPHINE and CORINNE are considered by some critics to be the first "modern" feminist, psychological, romantic novels; they anticipate the works of George Sand. In her *De la Littérature considérée dans ses rapports avec les institutions sociales* (1800), Mme de Staël attempted, among other things, to establish that literature develops qualitatively as social and political freedom increase. It was unanimously criticized because of its superficiality and simplistic literary prophecies. In *De l'Allemagne,* suppressed by Napoleon in 1811, but later published in London in 1813, she makes invidious comparisons between German and French culture and politics; in it she introduced German romanticism into France, thereby influencing greatly European thought and letters.

Mme de Staël was an outspoken critic of Napoleon, and was exiled from Paris several times. She traveled in Germany, Russia, England, Switzerland, and Sweden—hence her cosmopolitan attitude toward literature and politics. Her marriage was disappointing, and she had several love affairs. She inspired, in part, her Don-Juan-like lover, the Swiss novelist Benjamin CONSTANT DE REBECQUE, to write his ADOLPHE. Her influence has been found in the works of Lamartine, Victor Hugo, and Charles Nodier.

Stafford, Jean (1915–   ). American novelist and short-story writer. A serious writer and admirable stylist, she is particularly noted for evocative presentations of adolescence and childhood. Her first novel, *Boston Adventure* (1944), depicts Boston as perceived by a girl, the daughter of immigrants. It was followed by *The Mountain Lion* (1947), a study of a brother and sister in the years between childhood and adolescence. She has also published one other novel, *The Catherine Wheel* (1951), and a novelette, *A Winter's Tale* (1954). *Children Are Bored on Sunday* (1953) is a collection of her short stories.

Stagirite, the. See ARISTOTLE.

Stahl, Georg Ernest. See PHLOGISTON.

Stakhova, Elena. The heroine of Ivan Turgenev's novel ON THE EVE. Falling in love with the

Bulgarian revolutionary INSAROV, Elena leaves the comfort and safety of her home to follow him into the dangers of the battle for freedom in Bulgaria.

Stalin, Joseph. Real name, **Ioseph Visarionovich Dzhugashvili** (1879–1953). Russian political leader. Stalin, who succeeded Lenin as the ruler of Russia and thenceforth governed with an iron, dictatorial hand until his death, was born in Georgia. The son of a shoemaker, he attended a theological seminary in Tiflis for a short time. He joined the Social Democratic Party and actively entered the revolutionary movement in the late 1890's, often thereafter being imprisoned for his activities. In 1903 he sided with the Bolshevik faction, and in 1912 he went to St. Petersburg as a member of the Central Committee. He was imprisoned (1913–1917), but at the start of the revolution he was freed and became Lenin's lieutenant. After the revolution he served as commissar of nationalities until 1922 when he was made general secretary of the Communist Party's Central Committee. From this position he carefully built his power, and when Lenin died (1924) he was able to eliminate the opposition of Trotsky, KAMENEV, ZINOVYEV, and other rivals. By 1927, he was in uncontested command of the Party and the government. Instead of actively attempting to spread international revolution, Stalin concentrated on building Russia's strength, forming his national policy around the doctrine of "socialism in one country" as a base from which Communism could spread. He initiated the Five-Year Plan for industrial construction and the collectivization of agriculture. In the cultural field, he exercised a paternal watchfulness over writers and artists, exhorting them with such platitudes as "writers are engineers of the human soul." One of his most direct acts in the literary sphere was his declaration that the greatest Soviet poet was Vladimir Mayakovski—a pronouncement that was quickly heeded by Soviet critics. Stalin himself was the object of countless eulogistic writings, which fail to earn attention as literature.

Stalin purged the government and the army so thoroughly in the 1930's that he had complete control of Russia at the outbreak of World War II. In 1936, Russia had supported the Loyalists in the Spanish Revolution in opposition to Italy and Germany, the two fascist nations that helped Franco establish his government. Nevertheless, in 1939, Russia and Germany signed a nonaggression pact. When Hitler violated that treaty and invaded Russia in 1941, Stalin assumed command of the Russian armed forces. Russia suffered tremendous losses during the war, but on Germany's final defeat it was, under Stalin, one of the two great powers in the world, dominating the eastern hemisphere as no other modern nation had done. In his last years Stalin was loved, hated, and feared as no other living man.

After Stalin's death in 1953, a relaxation of controls was felt in Soviet literature. This period of relative freedom received the name of "the thaw," from the title of a novel by Ilya Ehrenburg. The writers were emboldened in their criticisms of past and current Soviet life by Nikita Khrushchev's anti-Stalin speech at the 20th Congress of the Communist Party in 1956. Previously forbidden themes were examined, such as the obstructionism of Soviet bureaucracy (in Vladimir Dudintzev's novel *Not by Bread Alone*) or the decay of the communist ideal (in the poetry of Yevgeni Yevtushenko). One of the most striking works dealing with the Stalinist regime itself was Aleksandr Solzhenitzyn's short novel, *One Day in the Life of Ivan Denisovich,* a depiction of life in a prison camp during Stalin's reign.

Stalky and Co. (1899). A collection of boys' stories by Rudyard KIPLING. They narrate the adventures of three schoolboys: Arthur Corkran, otherwise known as "Your Uncle Stalky," the Irish McTurk, and Beetle. Beetle is usually taken to be Kipling himself. McTurk is George Charles Beresford (d. 1938), and Stalky is Major General Lionel Charles Dunsterville (1866–1946).

Stallings, Laurence (1894–1968). American playwright and author. He is best known for WHAT PRICE GLORY?, a play on which he collaborated with Maxwell Anderson, and for *The First World War* (1933), a book of photographs and text presenting the horrors of World War I. *First Flight* (1925) and *The Buccaneer* (1925) are other plays written with Anderson. *Plumes* (1924) is a novel, largely autobiographical; *Deep River* (1926) is an operetta using New Orleans as a background, one of the first to make use of jazz; *Rainbow* (1928), written with Oscar Hammerstein 2nd, is another operetta set in the Far West. *The Doughboys: The Story of the AEF* appeared in 1963.

Stampa, Gaspara (c. 1523–1554). Italian Renaissance poet. Stampa spent most of her brief life in Venice. Here she recorded the emotional experiences of that life in a series of sonnets, madrigals, and elegies published as her *Rime* (1554). This work entitles her to a high place among the poets of the Renaissance period.

Stamp Act. A revenue act, known as Grenville's Stamp Act, passed by the English Parliament in 1765. It required that all legal documents, newspapers, almanacs, and commercial papers in the American colonies carry stamps showing that a tax had been paid on them. Led by Samuel Adams and James Otis, the colonists protested against the measure, and the Stamp Act Congress, the first intercolonial congress, petitioned the king to repeal the act. The request was granted in 1766.

Standard, Battle of the (1138). Battle fought near Northallerton. The English defeated the Scots under King David I, who was contesting King Stephen's right to the English throne on behalf of his niece Matilda.

Standish, Miles or **Myles** (1584?–1656). Military leader of the Pilgrims. He was largely responsible for the colonists' friendly relations with the Indians and led the party which arrested Thomas MORTON of Merrymount. He is the title character of Longfellow's THE COURTSHIP OF MILES STANDISH, for which, however, there is no historical foundation.

Stanhope, Lady Hester [Lucy] (1776–1839). English eccentric who established herself in the Levant and became legendary during her lifetime. From 1803 until his death in 1806, she was secretary and housekeeper for her uncle William Pitt. Four years later, leaving England forever, she made a pilgrimage to Jerusalem, and thereafter traveled widely in the Levant, camping among the Bedouin tribes, until she finally settled among the Druses on Mt. Lebanon. Adopting Eastern dress and practicing her own peculiar brand of religion, based partly on astrology, she gained such influence over the half-civilized tribes by her prophecies and pronouncements that they believed her divinely inspired—a view that came to be shared by certain English mystics and, eventually, by Lady Hester herself. Her life on Mt. Lebanon is described in *Eöthen, or Traces of Travel Brought Home from the East* (1844) by Alexander Kinglake.

Stanislavski, Konstantin. Stage name of **Konstantin Sergeyevich Alexeyev** (1865–1938). Russian actor and director. Cofounder (with Vladimir Nemirovich-Danchenko) and director (1898–1938) of the famous MOSCOW ART THEATRE, Stanislavski is also known for his theories of acting, which he set forth in such works as *An Actor Prepares* (1926), *Building a Character* (1950), and the autobiographical *My Life in Art* (1924). He rejected purely external theatrics in favor of a realistic style in which the actor seeks to identify with, or "live," his role, using his own psychological reactions. Sometimes called the STANISLAVSKI SYSTEM, his theories have been widely accepted by modern actors.

Stanislavski system. A method or discipline of acting developed by Konstantin STANISLAVSKI that seeks to give a performance complete realism. Realism in the theater was not originated by Stanislavski; however, it was in his MOSCOW ART THEATRE that a determined effort was made to achieve a deep realism through long, meticulous rehearsal periods and a precise formula for acting technique.

Stanislavski's productions were founded on three principles: (1) long, careful rehearsals; (2) complete rapport between actor and director, the latter to be a mirror for the actor's creativeness; (3) preparation of the actors themselves.

Norris Houghton in his book *Moscow Rehearsals* (1938) has enumerated the points in the actor's preparation that lie at the core of the Stanislavski system: (1) development and training of the actor's "instrument," i.e., his voice and body; (2) personal psychology, i.e., the actor must learn to isolate himself "in a circle" and not be distracted by the audience; (3) invention, i.e., the actor's re-creation of a situation in terms of his own impressions, associations, and memories; (4) complete immersion in the situation of the play; (5) "naïveté," i.e., the ability of the actor to have absolute belief in what he does and says; (6) contact with the other actors when they are in their roles; (7) memorization of common emotions in order to recall them at any time in any role; (8) rhythm—of the role and of the play; (9) mastery of the intrinsic personality or "kernel" of the character; (10) awareness of the point of the character, i.e., to be able to show in the performance what the character wants and why.

In America, the Stanislavski system has evolved into an acting technique known as "Method acting." The Actors' Studio in New York City, under the direction of Lee Strasberg, has trained many actors under principles based on Stanislavski's. Marlon Brando, a graduate of the Studio, gave a notable performance on Broadway as Stanley Kowalski in Tennessee Williams' *A Streetcar Named Desire* (1947). Brando's mannerisms and his appearance on stage in a torn undershirt caused some derogatory remarks, however, about the "grunt-and-groan method" and the "torn-shirt school."

Contemporary critics feel that a great many "Method" actors overlook the fact that Stanislavski emphasized external, as well as internal, training and did not give license to on-stage mumbling and hypernaturalistic twitchings and grimaces.

Stanley, Sir **Henry Morton** (1841–1904). Famous explorer, chiefly remembered for his expedition into Central Africa to find David Livingstone. The expedition was commissioned by James Gordon Bennett of the New York *Herald*. Stanley reached Livingstone in November 1871, greeting him with the now famous words, "Dr. Livingstone, I presume?" He published a number of books including *Through the Dark Continent* (2 vols.; 1878); *The Congo and the Founding of its Free State* (2 vols.; 1885); *In Darkest Africa* (2 vols.; 1890); etc.

Stanley, Thomas (1625–1678). English poet, translator, and miscellaneous writer. Stanley's love poems and his translations of the works of such poets as Petrarch, Lope de Vega, and Góngora are thought to have exceptional charm. His four-volume *History of Philosophy* (1655–1662) was for many years the standard work of its kind.

Stanton, Elizabeth Cady (1815–1902). American woman suffragist. The first woman's rights convention was held in Mrs. Stanton's home in Seneca Falls, N.Y., in 1848. With Lucretia Mott, she was one of the first agitators for woman suffrage. She was the first president of the National Woman Suffrage Association (1869–1890) and edited, with Susan B. Anthony, a militant magazine called *Revolution*. Also with Miss Anthony and Matilda Gage, she wrote *A History of Woman Suffrage* (6 v., 1881–1922). Elizabeth Cady Stanton's autobiography, *Eighty Years and More*, was published in 1898.

Stanton, Frank L[ebby] (1857–1927). American newspaperman and poet. He was noted for his daily column, *Just From Georgia*, in the Atlanta *Constitution*. Selections from the column were published by his daughter in 1927. He published several volumes of verse; his poem *Mighty Lak' a Rose* (1901) became famous as set to music by Ethelbert Nevin.

stanza. In prosody, a division of a poem containing one or more lines, separated by spacing from other like units; a group of lines standing together, apart from other such groups. Stanzas are defined according to the number of lines they contain as in the terms couplet; triplet or tercet; quatrain; quintet or cinquain; sestet, sextet, or sextain; septet; octave or octet. There are also numerous traditional stanza forms of a set length and rhyme scheme that have names, as: the ballad stanza, rhyme royal, ottava rima, the Spenserian stanza, terza rima, etc.

Stanzas may be of arbitrary length and plan, as in regular stanza forms, or they may be free and irregular, as in the irregular ode or most free verse forms. The thought may be continued from one stanza to another, or the stanza may be a closed thought unit. One stanza may and frequently does constitute a complete poem. On the other hand, many longer poems written in blank verse or heroic couplets are not divided into stanzas at all, but consist of an unbroken flow of lines divided, if at all, into larger parts such as numbered sections or cantos.

Stapledon, [William] Olaf (1886–1950). English novelist and philosopher. He wrote fantastic science fiction as a vehicle for his philosophical ideas. His novels include *Last and First Men* (1931) and *Star Maker* (1937).

Staple of News, The (1625). A comedy by Ben JONSON. The profligate young Pennyboy, Jr. becomes enamored of Lady Aurelia Clara Pecunia Do-All, the ward of his uncle, Richer Pennyboy. He woos her in extravagant fashion and ends in destitution— or seemingly so until it is revealed that his "ancient" companion is his wealthy father in disguise, and that he has been named heir to his uncle's wealth. Interwoven with the plot is Jonson's satire against the "Staple of News"—really Nathaniel Butter's *The Courant* or *Weekly News*, the first English newspaper—which printed all manner of misinformation to satisfy the appetites of its readers.

Star Chamber. A room in the Palace of Westminster. On its ceiling are gilt stars. Sittings of a very arbitrary and tyrannical court were held here under the early Stuarts. "Court of star chamber" or "star-chamber proceedings" are phrases still applied to any tyrannical tribunal.

Stark, Freya (1893–   ). English travel writer. Most of her adventurous traveling was done in the Middle East. She is the author of *The Valleys of the Assassins* (1934), *A Winter in Arabia* (1940), *East Is West* (1945), and *The Lycian Shore* (1956). Her work is notable for its shrewd observation and original thought.

Starrett, [Charles] Vincent [Emerson] (1886–   ). Canadian-born American writer and newspaperman. Starrett's books include such works as *Books Alive* (1940) and *Bookman's Holiday* (1942). An authority on Sherlock Holmes, he is the author of *The Private Life of Sherlock Holmes* (1933). He has also written poetry, short stories, detective novels, a bibliography of Stephen Crane's writings, humorous sketches, biographies, and novels.

Star-Spangled Banner, The. The national anthem of the United States. It was written by Francis Scott KEY in 1814 during the War of 1812. During the British bombardment of Fort McHenry, the gateway to the Baltimore defenses, Key was aboard a British man-of-war, detained on a mission to obtain the exchange of an American prisoner. The bombardment lasted throughout the night from September 13 to 14. A part of the poem was scribbled on the back of an envelope, when, after a long night of anxious waiting, "by dawn's early light," Key could see that the Stars and Stripes were still flying over the fort. It was sung to the tune of *To Anacreon in Heaven*, ascribed to the English composer John Stafford Smith (1750–1836). *The Star-Spangled Banner* became the national anthem by an act of Congress in 1931, though it had long held that position unofficially.

Starveling, Robin. See BOTTOM.

Stations of the Cross (Lat. *Via Crucis*, "the Way of the Cross"). A medieval devotion based on the events of Christ's Crucifixion. It originated in Jerusalem, where pilgrims followed the supposed path of Jesus, stopping at the places where specific events had taken place; prayers were said at each station, which number fourteen. Later, frescos, pictures, or sculptural representations were made of these events and placed in churches so that those who could not go to the Holy Land could make the devotion. The events:

1. Jesus is condemned to death.
2. He is made to bear His cross.
3. His first fall under the cross.
4. Jesus meets His sorrowing mother.
5. Simon of Cyrene helps to bear the cross.
6. Veronica wipes the face of Jesus.
7. Jesus falls the second time.
8. Jesus speaks to the daughters of Jerusalem.
9. Jesus falls the third time.
10. He is stripped of his garments.
11. He is nailed to the cross.
12. He gives up the Ghost.
13. He is taken down from the cross.
14. Jesus is laid in the sepulcher.

Statius, Publius Papinius (c. 45–96). Latin poet. He is the author of the *Thebais* (c. 91), an epic in twelve books dealing with Eteocles and Polynices, the quarrelling sons of Oedipus. He also wrote *Achilleis,* about the life of Achilles, and the five books of the *Silvae,* occasional poems. Statius appears as a character in Dante's *Purgatorio.*

Stavisky, Serge Alexandre (1886–1934). A remarkable Russian-born French swindler. He managed to sell 40 million francs' worth of worthless bonds to the French working people. The discovery of his huge fraud (December 1933) resulted in the downfall of two ministries. A trial that ended in January 1936 led to the conviction of nine persons. Stavisky's sudden death was probably suicide.

Stavrogin, Nikolai Vsevolodovich. The central character in Feodor Dostoevski's THE POSSESSED. A young nobleman tormented by a spiritual sterility, Stavrogin returns to his native provincial town, after several years of listless debauchery and crime in Moscow and abroad. He has capriciously married a crippled half-wit, Marya Timofeyevna Lebyadkin, and has become associated with the revolutionary plotter Pyotr VERKHOVENSKI, who wants Stavrogin as a figurehead for his movement. Unable to lose himself in either crime or political activity, or to find solace in religion, Stavrogin is also unable to respond to the love offered by Lizaveta Tushina. For a while he considers starting a new life with the adoring Darya Shatova, but he is unable to make the effort. He is haunted by the memory of a horrible crime which he finally confesses to the monk Tikhon. Some years before, he had violated a young girl and then allowed the frightened, tormented girl to hang herself. (The chapter containing this confession was not allowed to be published when the novel first appeared.) Finally, unable to live with his guilt, Stavrogin hangs himself.

Stealthy School of Criticism. A term coined by Dante Gabriel Rossetti in allusion to criticism published under a pseudonym. It was first used in a letter to the *Athenaeum,* December 16, 1871, with reference to a pseudonymous attack entitled THE FLESHLY SCHOOL OF POETRY published in the *Contemporary Review* of that year.

Stedman, Edmund Clarence (1833–1908). American poet, critic, anthologist, and businessman. Early in his journalistic career, Stedman turned to stock brokerage; he continued to write poetry and anthologize even after his change in vocation. His early verse was inspired by the Civil War and the abolitionist movement, but his best poem is *Pan in Wall Street* (1867).

Stedman's chief literary importance rests on his criticism and anthologies. He managed to persuade the reading public of the interest of the works of Poe and Swinburne, among others. His two large volumes of criticism, *Victorian Poets* (1875) and *Poets of America* (1885), were supplemented by two anthologies: *A Victorian Anthology* (1895) and *An American Anthology* (1900). The American volumes, significant for the estimation of Poe and Whitman, were early studies in American literature, a field hitherto barely explored. Stedman's work became very popular, and he was often referred to as the literary dean of his day.

Steel, Mrs. Flora Annie (1847–1929). English novelist. She is best known for *On the Face of the Waters* (1896), a well-documented relation of the Sepoy Mutiny in India. Among Mrs. Steel's other books, *From the Five Rivers* (1893) and *Tales from the Punjab* (1894) also provide good accounts of Indian custom and myth.

Steele, Richard (1672–1729). Irish-born English playwright and essayist, known for his writing in the periodicals THE TATLER and THE SPECTATOR in association with Joseph ADDISON. Steele took the initiative in the founding of these two journalistic

Title page of the collected edition of Addison and Steele's *The Spectator* (1747).

THE

SPECTATOR.

VOLUME *the* FIRST.

L O N D O N:

Printed for J. and R. TONSON and S. DRAPER.

MDCCXLVII.

enterprises, serving as the first editor of *The Tatler* under the name of Isaac BICKERSTAFF, and contributing the majority of the essays published in *The Tatler*. Other works by Steele include THE CHRISTIAN HERO, a pamphlet, and the plays *The Funeral* (1701), *The Lying Lover* (1703), *The Tender Husband* (1705), and *The Conscious Lovers* (1712). Steele was more journalistic than Addison: his subjects are lighter and less varied.

Steele, Wilbur Daniel (1886–1970). American short-story writer and novelist. Steele is best known for his stories and won the O. Henry Memorial Award four times with *For They Know Not What They Do* (1919), *Bubbles* (1926), *The Man Who Saw Through Heaven* (1927), and *Can't Cross Jordan* (1931). Among his novels are *Storm* (1914), *Undertow* (1930), *That Girl from Memphis* (1945), and *Their Town* (1952). He has also written several one-act plays, and with his second wife, Norma Mitchell, a full-length drama, *Post Road* (1935).

Steen, Marguerite (1894–   ). English popular novelist. She is the author of *Matador* (1934) and *The Sun Is My Undoing* (1941), a long historical novel about the slave trade.

Steendam, Jacob (1616–1672). Dutch merchant-poet, the first poet of colonial New York. After a trip to the Gold Coast for trade and adventure, he settled in New Amsterdam in 1649, buying property in Long Island and Manhattan. His chief works are the rhetorical *Klacht van Niew Nederlandt tot Haar Moeder* (*Complaint of New Netherlands to her Mother;* 1659), a versed allegorical history of the colony; and *'T Lof van Niew Nederlandt* (*The Praise of New Netherlands;* 1661), a 300-line idealized picture of colonial New York designed to encourage immigration.

Steerforth. In Charles Dickens' DAVID COPPERFIELD, David's hero at CREAKLE's school. Steerforth leads Em'ly PEGGOTTY astray; when he tires of her, he proposes that she marry his valet. Later he is shipwrecked off the coast of Yarmouth, and Ham Peggotty, who tries to rescue him, is drowned with him. Steerforth cuts a dazzling, attractive figure, but is arrogant, selfish, and heartless.

Steffens, [Joseph] Lincoln (1866–1936). American journalist. Born in San Francisco, Steffens had a somewhat restless and unrestrained youth. After studying in Europe, he became a journalist in New York City in 1892; he was managing editor of *McClure's Magazine* (1902–1906) and associate editor of the *American Magazine* and *Everybody's Magazine* (1906–1911).

Best known as one of the first MUCKRAKERS, Steffens exposed business and government corruption in articles that were collected in such works as *The Shame of the Cities* (1904), *The Struggle for Self-Government* (1906), and *The Upbuilders* (1909). He also wrote a candid and entertaining *Autobiography* (1931), in which he described his political views and his affiliation with liberal and radical causes.

Stegner, Wallace [Earle] (1909–   ). American novelist. With such novels as *The Potter's House* (1938), *On a Darkling Plain* (1940), and *Country Dance* (1948), Stegner became noted for his authentic depiction of American rural life. His short stories, concerned with much the same setting, have been collected in *Women on the Wall* (1950), *City of the*

Living (1956), and *A Shooting Star* (1961). *One Nation* (1945) is a study of minority groups in the U.S. *Mormon Country* (1942) and *Beyond the 100th Meridian* (1954) are both nonfiction, the latter a biography of the explorer and conservationist John Wesley Powell. *Wolf Willow* (1962) is a description of frontier life in Saskatchewan combining fact and fiction.

Steichen, Edward (1879–   ). American photographer. He commanded the photographic division of the air service during World War I. A pioneer in experimental photography, he has exhibited in art centers both here and abroad. Director since 1947 of the department of photography of the Museum of Modern Art in New York, he created its famous *Family of Man* exhibition (1955).

Stein, Charlotte von (1742–1827). The beloved of GOETHE, probably the most important woman in his life. She was married to an equerry who was much her intellectual inferior, and Goethe fulfilled her need for spiritual companionship. Goethe, in turn, when he came to Weimar in 1775, was in need of a sobering, stabilizing influence upon his character and it was this that she provided. Austere, highly intelligent, and older than the poet, she resisted his sensual tendencies and taught him the art of renunciation of personal desire. Though the intimate details of their love are not known, it is certain that even if she later did become his mistress, their relationship still remained primarily a spiritual one. Their love lasted unbroken from 1775 until Goethe's departure for Italy in 1786. In Italy, he experienced a sensual reawakening and when he returned, he and Charlotte had little left in common.

Her influence upon him, though, was lasting. The character of Iphigeneia in his *Iphigeneia in Tauris* (1787) is an adoring portrait of her, and the Princess in his *Torquato Tasso* (1790), though not a character as completely admirable, seems also to have been modeled after her. And finally, the theme of renunciation, which is extremely important in all Goethe's later works, is largely based on his experience with her.

Stein, Gertrude (1874–1946). American poet, novelist, and critic. For many years a leading American expatriate in Paris, she was the subject of wide literary controversy in the 1920's. Her unique and celebrated style, which was influenced by the psychological theories of William James and by modern French painting, is characterized by the use of words for their associations and sound, rather than for their literal meaning; an intricate system of repetition and variation on a single verbal theme; an avoidance of conventional punctuation and syntax; an emphasis on the presentation of impressions and a particular state of mind, rather than the telling of a story; and concreteness and extreme simplicity of diction, with preference for the common and monosyllabic vocabulary.

Miss Stein, who came of a wealthy family, studied psychology under William James at Radcliffe College and later studied medicine at Johns Hopkins University, specializing in brain anatomy. In 1903 she settled in Paris with Alice B. Toklas, her secretary, supposedly the author of THE AUTOBIOGRAPHY OF ALICE B. TOKLAS. She returned to America only once, in 1934, for a brief lecture tour. Becoming interested in

such artists as Picasso, Matisse, Braque, and Juan Gris, Miss Stein became both art critic and patron.

THREE LIVES was her first book. In part an example of primitivistic writing, it is regarded by many critics as her best. *Tender Buttons* (1914) is a poetic series of paragraphs about objects, often witty, often close to automatic writing. After *Geography and Plays* (1922), Miss Stein finally published THE MAKING OF AMERICANS, which was written some 20 years earlier. Of her many later works, the best known are FOUR SAINTS IN THREE ACTS, *In Savoy or "Yes" is for Yes for a Very Young Man* (1946) and *Four in America* (1947), essays on Washington, Grant, Wilbur Wright, and Henry James.

Miss Stein is noted for several famous lines, notably "A rose is a rose is a rose is a rose"; she is also the originator of the phrase, "the LOST GENERATION."

Steinbeck, John [Ernst] (1902–1968). American novelist and short-story writer. Awarded a Pulitzer Prize in 1940 and the Nobel Prize for literature in 1962, Steinbeck was born in Salinas, Calif. A writer of proletarian sympathies, he is noted for his realistic studies of life among the depressed economic classes of the U.S., especially the itinerant farm laborers of California.

Steinbeck's first book, *Cup of Gold: A Life of Sir Henry Morgan, Buccaneer, with Occasional References to History* (1929), reflected his long interest in the sea. He had specialized in marine biology at Stanford University and he later published two other books about sea life: *Sea of Cortez* with Edward F. Ricketts (1941) and *The Log of the Sea of Cortez* (1951), a reissue of the narrative part of the earlier volume with a biographical sketch of Ricketts.

Pastures of Heaven (1932), a collection of short stories about the inhabitants of the valley of that name, is the first example of Steinbeck's interest in the simple-minded, the "unfinished children of nature." *To a God Unknown* (1933) presents Steinbeck's strongest statement about man's relationship to the land. TORTILLA FLAT and IN DUBIOUS BATTLE established Steinbeck's reputation. OF MICE AND MEN, first conceived as a play, was dramatized the year of its publication. THE LONG VALLEY is a book of short stories.

THE GRAPES OF WRATH, Steinbeck's major novel, is, perhaps, the best example of the proletarian fiction of the 1930's. Realistic and naturalistic, it also expresses Steinbeck's mystical affirmation that all life is holy. *The Moon Is Down* (1942) deals with life in a German-occupied country of Europe during World War II. *Bombs Away: The Story of a Bomber Team* (1942) was the first of three nonfiction works, the other two being *Russian Journal* with photographs by Robert Capa (1948) and *Once There Was a War* (1958), excerpts from his own work as a war correspondent.

CANNERY ROW and its sequel *Sweet Thursday* (1954) deal with simple people living in a virtual state of nature. *The Wayward Bus* (1947) describes the sexual misadventures of a group stranded overnight in a California wayside station. THE PEARL is the story of a Mexican pearl-fisher. Steinbeck's most ambitious work since *Grapes of Wrath* is EAST OF EDEN, a long novel based partly on a biblical story. The novelette *The Short Reign of Pippin IV* (1957) is a light satire on modern French politics. Steinbeck's latest works are *Winter of Our Discontent* (1961) and *Travels with Charley* (1962), the account of his trip across the U.S. in the company of an elderly poodle.

Steinberg, Saul (1914–   ). Romanian artist, now a naturalized American citizen (1943). His witty drawings for the magazine *The New Yorker* have been collected in several volumes.

Steinway, Henry Engelhard (1797–1871). A German piano manufacturer, who began making one of the world's outstanding pianos in New York City in 1853. One of his sons, **William Steinway** (1853–1896) planned the first subway in New York.

Stella. Lady Penelope Devereux, the object of Sir Philip SIDNEY's affection celebrated in his sonnet series ASTROPHEL AND STELLA. She married Lord Rich.

Stella Dallas (1923). A novel by Olive Higgins Prouty (1882–   ), American novelist. It is a story of a New England woman who sacrifices herself for her daughter's happiness. This widely known work first appeared in serial form in a magazine, became a best seller as a book, was made into a play, a silent movie, a talking picture, and finally became a long-lasting radio soap opera.

Stendhal. Pen name of **Marie Henri Beyle** (1783–1842). French novelist and critic. Stendhal, one of France's greatest literary artists, played a major role in the development of the modern novel. His place lies somewhere between the romantic and realistic schools, for his plots and subjects are often violently melodramatic, yet his treatment of them is painstakingly realistic. Pointing the way toward the psychological novel, his probing, analytical studies of character deal with proud and egotistical natures involved in love and war. A great admirer of Napoleon Bonaparte and Lord Byron, Stendhal himself participated in several campaigns of the Napoleonic Wars, and his works are in part autobiographical. His most noted works are *Le Rouge et le Noir* (THE RED AND THE BLACK), *La Chartreuse de Parme* (THE CHARTERHOUSE OF PARMA), *Armance* (1827), and the unfinished *Lucien Leuwen* (1894). *Racine et Shakespeare* (1823) is a critical discussion of classicism and ROMANTICISM, and *De l'Amour* (1822) is a series of notes on the effects of love on a variety of temperaments.

stentor, the voice of a. A very loud voice. Stentor was a Greek herald in the Trojan War. According to Homer's *Iliad*, his voice was as loud as that of 50 men combined; hence stentorian, loud voiced.

Stephano. A drunken butler in Shakespeare's THE TEMPEST. Cast ashore with a wine cask during the tempest, he proceeds to involve the jester Trinculo and the monster Caliban in a drinking bout. The three concoct a harmless plot to oust Prospero; they steal his clothing, and are at last brought before him in an alcoholic stupor. They provide the low comedy in the play.

Stephansson, Stephan Gudmundsson (1853–1927). Icelandic-Canadian poet and novelist. In 1873 he left Iceland and came to Alberta, Canada, with his family. Directly influenced by the realist movement, Stephansson produced a novel series, *Bréf og ritgerðir* (4 vols., 1938–1948), which criticized existing social conditions. He also wrote many sensitive and beautiful nature poems; *Úti á víðavangi* (1894),

Andvökur (6 vols., 1909–1938), *Kolbeinslag* (1914), and *Vígslóði* (1920) are among his collections of verse.

Stephen. In Ben Jonson's EVERY MAN IN HIS HUMOUR, a country bumpkin. He is so stupid that "he shakes his head like a bottle to feel an there be any brain in it!"

Stephen, James Kenneth. Known as **J.K.S.** (1859–1892). English author of excellent light verse and parodies. His work is collected in the volumes *Lapsus Calami* (1891) and *Quo Musa Tendis?* (1896).

Stephen, Sir Leslie (1832–1904). English man of letters. Although Stephen took orders as a young man, he later became an agnostic, explaining his views in his *Essays on Free Thinking and Plain Speaking* (1873) and his *Agnostic's Apology* (1876). After having edited the *Cornhill Magazine* from 1871 to 1882, he became the first editor of the *Dictionary of National Biography* in the latter year. His books include *The History of English Thought in the Eighteenth Century* (1876), *The English Utilitarians* (1900), and *English Literature and Society in the Eighteenth Century* (1904). Stephen's first wife was Harriet Marian, the younger daughter of Thackeray. He was the father of Virginia WOOLF; another daughter, Vanessa, married the English art critic Clive Bell.

Stephens, James (1882–1950). Irish poet and fiction writer. He is best known for his whimsical tales and adaptations from Irish legend. *The Crock of Gold* (1912), a novel that combines humor, realism, and fantasy, is his best-known work. Among his other works of fiction are *The Charwoman's Daughter* (1912), *The Demi-Gods* (1914), *Irish Fairy Tales* (1920), *Deirdre* (1923), and *In the Land of Youth* (1924). As a poet, Stephens was a disciple of A. E., but he celebrated the Celtic twilight with more oddness and fantasy. His *Collected Poems* appeared in 1926. Stephens was associated with the IRISH RENAISSANCE.

Stephens, John Lloyd. See MAYA.

Steppenwolf, Der (The Wolf of the Steppes, 1927). A novel by Hermann HESSE. It is a treatment of the outsider, a very common theme in modern fiction. The hero, Harry Haller, exemplifies in modern terms the typical disintegration of German romantic characters (see ZERRISSENHEIT); he is torn between the frustrated artistic idealism of his inner life and the cold, inhuman nature of modern reality which, in his eyes, is characterized entirely by philistinism and technology. It is his inability to be a part of the world and the resulting loneliness and desolation of his existence that cause him to think of himself as a "Steppenwolf." The novel, which is rich in fantasy throughout, ends in what is called the magic theater, a kind of allegorical sideshow. Here, Haller learns that in order to relate successfully to humanity and reality without sacrificing his ideals, he must overcome his own social and sexual taboos, including his prejudice against technology.

Sterling, George (1869–1926). American poet and playwright. Sterling lived most of his life in Carmel and San Francisco and was a member of the Bohemian Club in the latter city. He had many Western admirers, but was known in the East largely through his poem *A Wine of Wizardry* (1907). He wrote numerous volumes of verse and several plays, such as *Rosamund* (1920) and *Truth* (1923). His many volumes of verse include *The Testimony of the Suns and Other Poems* (1903), *Beyond the Breakers and Other Poems* (1914), *Thirty-five Sonnets* (1917), and *Sonnets to Craig* (1928). Sterling also wrote *Robinson Jeffers: The Man and the Artist* (1926). He finally took his own life in a mood of depression.

Sterling, John (1806–1844). English essayist and poet. He formed a literary group (1838), the Sterling Club, including such members as Thomas Carlyle, Alfred Tennyson, and John Stuart Mill. His own work, including his best poem, *The Sexton's Daughter* (1837), is less well known than Carlyle's biography, *The Life of John Sterling* (1851).

Stern, G[ladys] B[ronwyn] (1890–   ). English novelist, short-story writer, and critic. She was of Jewish parentage and her best-known novels, those in the *Matriarch* series (1919–1935), are naturalistic chronicles of Jewish life. In 1947 she was converted to Catholicism. Among her volumes of autobiography are *Monogram* (1936) and *All in Good Time* (1954).

Sterne, Laurence (1713–1768). English novelist and clergyman. When, in 1759 at the age of 47, he published the first two volumes of TRISTRAM SHANDY, he emerged like a comet on the literary world from the complete obscurity of the small Yorkshire vicarship he had held since 1739. Though *Tristram* was denounced by Dr. Johnson, Richardson, Goldsmith, and others on both literary and moral grounds, Sterne was well received in London. Successive volumes of *Tristram* appeared until 1767, accompanied by volumes of *Sermons of Mr. Yorick* (1760–1769), as well as by A SENTIMENTAL JOURNEY. This tremendous output was accomplished in the face of the throes of consumption from which Sterne was to die—an autobiographical circumstance which he treats in volumes 7 and 8 of *Tristram*. Two views of his character have held sway. Sterne the accomplished scoundrel and Sterne the sentimental humorist. He was both by turns, although it is only fair to say that he did all in his power to propagandize the second. See ELIZA; BRAMINE'S JOURNAL, THE.

Sternhold and Hopkins. The popular name of an English metrical version of the Psalms of David. It was used in England and the American Colonies from the reign of Queen Elizabeth I until the end of the 17th century. It was mainly the work of Thomas Sternhold (d. 1549), and John Hopkins (d. 1570). The completed version appeared in 1562. The poetic style is poor; much of it is doggerel. It was ridiculed by Dryden in *Absalom and Achitophel*.

Stesichorus (Stesichoros; c. 640–555 B.C.). A Greek lyric poet. He was born in Sicily. The fragments that remain of his works justify the high reputation he bore in classical times, Longinus calling him "most like Homer." His unusual achievement was to write of heroic subjects with epic sweep, but in lyric verse. He was the first known poet to tell the story of Daphnis. For a famous legend about him, see HELEN.

Stevens, Gavin. A character in several works by William Faulkner. Educated at Harvard and Heidelberg, Stevens is a lawyer and later the county attorney in Jefferson, Miss.; he comments philosophically on events in YOKNAPATAWPHA COUNTY, although

Title page of Sternhold's *Certayne Psalmes* (1548).

he is rarely directly involved in them. He develops a hopeless love for Eula Varner Snopes in *The Town* and later for her daughter, Linda, in *The Mansion* (see THE HAMLET); he solves murders in KNIGHT'S GAMBIT and is a somewhat ineffectual but philosophic presence in INTRUDER IN THE DUST. Finally, to cure himself of his unrewarded love for Linda Snopes, he marries Melisandre Backus Harriss, a wealthy widow who appears in the title story of *Knight's Gambit*.

Stevens, John (1749–1838). American inventor, instrumental in the passage of the first American patent laws. His steamboat *Phoenix* (1808), built very shortly after Robert Fulton's *Clermont,* traveled from New York to Philadelphia and was the first sea-going steamboat in the world.

Stevens, Thaddeus (1792–1868). American statesman. As a member of Congress from Pennsylvania (1849–1853, 1859–1868), Stevens was an outspoken opponent of slavery and a leader of the radical Republicans who advocated a harsh policy toward the defeated South after the Civil War. He favored the impeachment of President Johnson but played a small role in the trial because of declining health.

Stevens, Wallace (1879–1955). American poet. He is known for his poetry influenced by the French symbolist movement, his recondite vocabulary, lavish imagery, metaphors of brilliant originality, and a rhetoric whose intricate stylizations were designed not only to please but to shock. In his later poetry Stevens turned away from his earlier preoccupation with the splendors of the West Indies, and wrote more of the harsher realities of New England, concerning himself with aesthetic problems. But until the end of his life his poetic style remained marked by a kind of intelligent dandyism, never soft or merely pretty, always hard as a diamond and regally controlled.

Part of the poetic renaissance shortly before World War I, Stevens' first works were published in *Poetry* in 1914. But it was not until 1923 that his first book of poems, *Harmonium,* was published. He wrote little throughout the 20's, adding only a few poems to the reissue of *Harmonium* in 1931. The 1930's, however, saw a fairly voluminous output; collections of the period are *Ideas of Order* (1935), *Owl's Clover* (1936), *The Man with the Blue Guitar and Other Poems* (1937). Later volumes are *Parts of a World* (1942), Notes Toward a Supreme Fiction, *Esthétique du Mal* (1945), *Transport to Summer* (1947), *Three Academic Pieces,* two poems and a prose address (1947), *The Auroras of Autumn* (1950), The Necessary Angel, *Collected Poems* (1954), and *Opus Posthumous* (1957).

A lawyer by profession, Stevens served for most of his life as an executive in an insurance company in Hartford, Conn., writing his poetry in his spare time and keeping the two spheres of interest so separate that some of his insurance colleagues never knew he was the established poet he had long since become. It has often been remarked that his life in business was contradictory to his main aesthetic creed; however, in his essays and in many of his poems, he emphasized the need of imaginatively transforming reality, of infusing an otherwise drab and meaningless existence with the meaning and beauty of poetry. See Peter Quince at the Clavier; Sunday Morning; Monocle de Mon Uncle, Le.

Stevenson, Adlai E[wing] (1900–1965). American statesman. The grandson and namesake of a former vice-president of the U.S., Stevenson graduated from Princeton, attended Harvard Law School and Northwestern University Law School, and was admitted to the bar in 1926. He interrupted his Chicago law practice to work for various government agencies, and during World War II was special assistant to the secretary of the navy (1941–1944) and headed a mission to Italy for the Foreign Economic Administration.

His long-time association with the United Nations began in 1945 when he was a member of the U.S. delegation to the UN conference in San Francisco. Later he served as senior adviser to the U.S. delegation to the UN and as alternate delegate. In 1947 he was elected governor of Illinois by a large plurality and instituted many extensive reforms. He was Democratic candidate for president in 1952 and in 1956, but was defeated both times by Dwight D. Eisenhower. He was appointed ambassador to the UN by President Kennedy in 1961.

Stevenson's addresses are remarkable for their insight, their fairness to opponents, their urbanity, and their incisive humor. Among Stevenson's books are *Call to Greatness* (1954), *What I Think* (1956), *Friends and Enemies* (1959), *Putting First Things*

First (1960), and *Looking Forward: Years of Crisis at the United Nations* (1964).

Stevenson, Burton [Egbert] (1872–1962). American writer and anthologist. His works include some 40 novels, mystery stories, books for children, and a play, *A King in Babylon* (1955). He is best known, however, for his anthologies: *The Home Book of Verse* (1912), *The Home Book of Verse for Young Folks* (1915), *The Home Book of Modern Verse* (1925), *The Home Book of Quotations* (1934), and *The Home Book of Bible Quotations* (1949).

Stevenson, Robert Louis [Balfour] (1850–1894). Scottish novelist, poet, essayist. A sickly child, Stevenson was tubercular all his life, in spite of which he lived adventurously, traveling widely. He studied civil engineering and prepared for the bar, but never took up the practice of law. A trip to Europe supplied the materials for *An Inland Voyage* (1878) and *Travels with a Donkey in the Cévennes* (1879). In France he met Mrs. Fanny Osbourne, followed her to the U.S. and married her, returning to Scotland in 1880. In rapid succession he published the collections of essays *Virginibus Puerisque* (1881) and *Familiar Studies of Men and Books* (1882); a collection of tales, *New Arabian Nights* (1882); *Silverado Squatters* (1883), his recollections of California; and the novel Treasure Island, one of his most popular books and the one which brought him fortune and renown. The following year, 1885, saw the publication of A Child's Garden of Verses, *The Body Snatcher,* and *Prince Otto,* and in 1886 came The Strange Case of Dr. Jekyll and Mr. Hyde and the historical romance Kidnapped, both of which have to this day retained their popularity with readers. In 1887, after a series of disappointing visits to European health spas, the Stevensons went to America; while at Saranac Lake, Stevenson wrote *The Master of Ballantrae* (1888). He and his wife moved on to the West Coast and set out for the South Seas; except for one trip to Sydney, Stevenson spent the last five years of his life on Samoa, living as a planter and chief of the natives. It was there that he wrote *The Wrecker,* in collaboration with his stepson Lloyd Osbourne (1892), *Island Nights Entertainments* (1893) and *Catriona* (1893), a sequel to *Kidnapped.* While dictating his Weir of Hermiston, Stevenson died suddenly of apoplexy. He was buried on his beloved island.

During his life Stevenson wrote half a dozen plays with various collaborators, among them his wife and stepson, none of them successful; his *Letters* were published in 1895, after his death. Though his novels are perhaps less successfully accomplished than his briefer tales and stories, his work is marked by his power of invention, his command of horror and the supernatural, and the psychological depth which he was able to bring to romance.

Stewart, J[ohn] I[nnes] M[ackintosh]. Pen name, **Michael Innes** (1906–   ). English novelist, scholar, and literary critic. Under his own name he is the author of *Character and Motive in Shakespeare* (1949) and the novel *Mark Lambert's Supper* (1954). Under his pen name he writes skillful detective stories, such as *Hamlet, Revenge!* (1937), *The Journeying Boy* (1949), and *The Man from the Sea* (1955).

Stickney, [Joseph] Trumbull (1874–1904). Swiss-born American poet and dramatist. After graduating from Harvard in 1895, Stickney studied at the Sorbonne and was the first American to receive that institution's *Doctorat des Lettres*. He went back to teach at Harvard and died of a brain tumor at the age of 30.

In his studies and in his general philosophy, Stickney was closely associated with William Vaughn MOODY, with whom he read much Greek literature. Moody wrote *The Fire-Bringer* (1904); Stickney preceded him with a work on the same theme, *Prometheus Pyrphoros* (1900), a group of somewhat pessimistic dramatic scenes, based directly on Greek sources, which sought to present Prometheus as a sort of hero of scientific progress. Stickney also prepared a collection of *Dramatic Verses* (1902). His *Poems* were collected in 1905.

Stieglitz, Alfred (1864–1946). American photographer. He sought to establish recognition of photography as an art, and was editor and publisher of *Camera Work* (1903–1917). After 1909 he began to show in his small Gallery 291 on Fifth Avenue, often for the first time, drawings by Rodin and Matisse, watercolors by Cézanne, works by Picasso, Toulouse-Lautrec, and young Americans such as John Marin and Georgia O'Keeffe, whom he married. He fought with high intelligence for the acceptance of modern art.

Stifter, Adalbert (1805–1868). Austrian novelist whose style reflects the tendency, found in much German literature of the time, away from romantic idealism and toward realism. His attachment to the common people and his sometimes excessive emphasis on the preservation of tradition align him, as well, with the conservative BIEDERMEIER movement. In the preface to his collection of narrative sketches, *Bunte Steine (Colored Stones*, 1853), he states that a boiling teakettle interests him as much as a volcano, that in even the most trivial phenomena, provided one knows how to look at them, the universal harmony of nature may be recognized. It is primarily this "gentle law" by which all things, small and great, are connected, that is depicted in Stifter's writing and that accounts for his extensive treatment of seemingly insignificant events and characters. His novel *Der Nachsommer (Indian Summer*, 1857) is one of the finest examples of the BILDUNGSROMAN.

Stijl, de [Style]. A Dutch 20th-century movement towards pure art. It received its name from an avant-garde periodical of that name, which was published between 1917 and 1928. Its founders were Piet MONDRIAN and the versatile writer and artist, Theo Van Doesburg (1883–1931). In its final form, *de Stijl* reduced artistic elements to the basic form of the rectangle and to the primary colors. It had a considerable influence on the Bauhaus, as well as on contemporary painting, typography, and commercial design.

Still, Clyfford (1904–   ). American painter. He formulated an abstract art of intense black areas cleft by vividly colored patches. He exerted a great influence in California, where he taught till 1950.

Still, James (1906–   ). American poet, novelist, and short-story writer. He is known for his writing dealing with the Kentucky mountains. *Hounds on the Mountain* (1937) is a volume of poetry;

River of Earth (1940), a novel; and *On Troublesome Creek* (1941), a collection of short stories.

Stilnovisti. A late 13th-century Tuscan school of Italian poets. They introduced what DANTE called a *dolce stil nuovo* ("sweet new style") in lyrical poetry. Reacting against the stylized conventions of the Provençal troubadours and the tradition of COURTLY LOVE, they achieved greater simplicity and sincerity in portraying the psychology of love and sorrow. Their poetry of love, however, is imbued with metaphysics and religion; the beloved lady becomes idealized as an "angelic woman," while love for her becomes an emotionally and spiritually ennobling experience that prepares a man for love of beauty and truth and God. This trend began with Guido GUINICELLI; its leading exponents were Guido CAVALCANTI and Dante.

Stirner, Max. Pen name of **Kaspar Schmidt** (1806–1856). German philosopher whose ideas foreshadowed existentialism. He advocated the supremacy of the individual ego, and launched an anarchistic attack on all the traditional social institutions that limit the development of the ego. His major work is *Der Einzige und sein Eigentum (The Individual and His Property*, 1845).

Stockton, Frank R. Real name, **Francis Richard Stockton** (1834–1902). American novelist, short-story writer, and editor. Although Stockton was widely admired by contemporaries for his humor, his ingenuity, and his narrative skill, his works are little read today, except for a few often anthologized stories, notably THE LADY OR THE TIGER? His novels include *Rudder Grange* (1879), about a newly married couple who take up residence in an abandoned house boat that ultimately gets adrift in Newark Bay, and *The Casting Away of Mrs. Lecks and Mrs. Aleshine* (1886), about two New England widows who are shipwrecked during an ocean voyage and find shelter on a desert island.

Stoddard, Richard Henry (1825–1903). American poet, book reviewer, editor, and public official. Stoddard held various jobs throughout his career in an effort to help his poverty-stricken family. In 1845, he began to publish his poetry, which he modeled on the work of the English Romantics and Victorians. Largely imitative and sentimental, his work includes *Footprints* (1849), *Poems* (1852), *The King's Bell* (1863), *The Book of the East and Other Poems* (1871), *The Lion's Cub with Other Verse* (1890), and *Recollections, Personal and Literary* (1903). Stoddard's best poem is *Abraham Lincoln: An Horatian Ode* (1865).

Stoic, The (1947). The last novel in a trilogy by Theodore DREISER. See TITAN, THE.

Stoicism. A school of Greek philosophy. It was founded by Zeno of Citium (c. 362–c. 264 B.C.) around 308 B.C. The Stoics were austere, advocating freedom from passions and desires. They equated the real with the material, and defined the active principle in the universe as Force or God. They sought to be in harmony with nature and the divine will, and their philosophy is characterized by a detachment from the outside world. The Stoicism later taught by EPICTETUS had more of a religious emphasis. Zeno's school was continued by Cleanthes and Chrysippus, and derived its name from the *Stoa Poikile*, a painted colonade or porch at Athens in which Zeno and his successors lectured. Stoicism was highly congenial to the Roman temperament, and has influenced Roman Law. See MARCUS AURELIUS.

Stoke Poges. A village in Buckinghamshire, England, where Thomas GRAY wrote some of his poems. He is buried there in St. Giles churchyard which is believed to be the scene of his ELEGY WRITTEN IN A COUNTRY CHURCHYARD.

Stoker, [Abraham] Bram (1847–1912). English writer. He is best known for *Dracula* (1897), a wild tale of vampires and werewolves. It has been made into several motion pictures and sequels. Stoker was also, for several years, business manager of the famous actor Sir Henry IRVING.

Stokowski, Leopold [Antoni Stanislaw Boleslawowicz] (1882–). English-born American conductor of the Philadelphia Symphony (1912–1941) and other orchestras. He wrote *Music for All of Us* (1943).

Stolberg, Christian, graf von (1748–1821) and his brother, **Friedrich Leopold,** graf von (1750–1819). German lyric poets and translators. Members of the GÖTTINGER HAIN group, they were influenced by Klopstock and the STURM UND DRANG. Friedrich, the more significant of the two, wrote a romance entitled *Die Insel* (*The Island*, 1788) and translated Macpherson's *Ossian* in 1806. The two together published a collection of *Vaterländische Gedichte* (*Patriotic Poems*, 1815). They both accompanied Goethe on his trip to Switzerland in 1775.

Stone, Irving (1903–). American writer. Stone has had a highly successful career as a writer of popular fictionalized biography. He created a sensation with his second book, *Lust for Life* (1934), recounting the life of Vincent van Gogh. He also edited some of van Gogh's writings in *Dear Theo: The Autobiography of Vincent van Gogh* (1937). He next wrote *Sailor on Horseback* (1938), about Jack London, and *Clarence Darrow for the Defense* (1941). His other best-selling books include *Immortal Wife* (1944), about Jessie Frémont; *Adversary in the House* (1947), about Eugene V. Debs; *The President's Lady* (1951), about Rachel Jackson; *Love Is Eternal* (1954), about Mrs. Lincoln; and *The Agony and the Ecstasy* (1961), about Michelangelo.

Stone, Lucy. Mrs. **Henry Brown Blackwell** (1818–1893). American woman suffragist; she insisted upon retaining her maiden name after marriage. Lucy Stone's first opponent in her battle for women's rights was her father, who refused her financial aid toward higher education. After several years of teaching, she was able to go to Oberlin College. After her graduation, she lectured against slavery and for woman suffrage. Although she had not intended to marry, she relented when Henry Blackwell promised to devote himself to her cause. With her husband, Lucy Stone edited the *Woman's Journal* (1872–1893). She helped to form the American Woman Suffrage Association in 1869.

Stone Guest, the. See DOM JUAN OU LE FESTIN DE PIERRE; LITTLE TRAGEDIES.

Stonehenge. The great prehistoric (Neolithic or early Bronze Age) monument on Salisbury Plain. It originally consisted of two concentric circles of upright stones, enclosing two rows of smaller stones, and a central block of blue marble, 18 feet by 4 feet, known as the Altar Stone. Many theories as to its original purpose and original builders have been propounded. It was probably used, if not built, by the Druids and from its plotting, which, it is certain, had an astronomical basis, it is thought to have been the temple of a sun god and to have been built about 1680 B.C.

The *-henge* of the name seems to refer to something hanging (A.S. *hengen*) in, or supported in, the air, viz., the huge transverse stones; but Geoffrey of Monmouth connects it with Hengist, and says that Stonehenge was erected by Merlin to perpetuate the treachery of Hengist in falling upon Vortigern and putting him and his 400 attendants to the sword. Aurelius Ambrosium asked Merlin to devise a memento of this event, whereupon the magician transplanted from Killaraus, in Ireland, the "Giant's Dance," stones which had been brought thither from Africa by a race of giants and all of which possessed magic properties.

Stony Point. A rocky promontory on the west bank of the Hudson, 35 miles north of New York City. American soldiers under General Wayne captured the British fort there in a surprise attack on the night of July 15, 1779. Although the position was abandoned three days later, the victory greatly bolstered American morale.

Stopping by Woods on a Snowy Evening (1923). A lyric poem by Robert FROST. The poet stops his horse to contemplate the beauty of the scene and then continues his journey:

> The woods are lovely, dark and deep.
> But I have promises to keep,
> And miles to go before I sleep . . .

It is one of Frost's most famous and most frequently discussed poems; he himself once said that he would like to have it printed on one page, followed by "forty pages of footnotes."

Stories of Jacob, The. See JOSEPH AND HIS BROTHERS.

Storm, The (Groza; 1860). A drama by Aleksandr OSTROVSKI. It depicts the tragedy of a young wife, Katerina, who tries unsuccessfully to break out of the stifling atmosphere of her life. No longer in love with her husband and weary of the dull merchant class milieu in which they live, Katerina seeks a change by having a love affair with Boris, a young man who is unable to provide her with the escape she seeks. Katerina confesses her infidelity, is hounded by her cruel mother-in-law, and finally commits suicide.

Storm, Theodor (1817–1888). German poet and novella-writer. He is an unparalleled master of the so-called frame-technique of narrative writing: that is, he often has a character in a story tell another story, so that the second is framed by the first. His novellas, most of which are permeated by a strong feeling for his North German homeland, include *Immensee* (1850), in which the romantic melancholy of Storm's early period may be seen; *Aquis Submersus* (Sunken in the Water, 1876) which, like *Immensee*, is a story of lost love, but is more realistic; and *Der Schimmelreiter* (The White-Horse Rider, 1888), a strongly realistic and deeply symbolic story about the man responsible for the dikes upon which his community's safety depends.

Storm and Stress. See STURM UND DRANG.

Storm Troops. See S.A.

Story of a Bad Boy, The (1870). A semi-autobiographical novel by Thomas Bailey ALDRICH. The hero, Tom Bailey, is not really bad; he is, as the author explains, "a real human boy." The book tells of Tom's youth in New Hampshire, and his early years in New Orleans with distant relatives. In Rivermouth, Tom gets into all kinds of mischief. This popular book was a forerunner of Mark Twain's *The Adventures of Tom Sawyer* (1876).

Story of an African Farm, The (1883). A novel by Olive SCHREINER, published under the pseudonym Ralph Iron. Most of the action takes place on a Boer farm in South Africa in the late 19th century. The principal characters are three childhood playmates: Waldo, son of the kindly, pious German overseer; Em, the good-hearted stepdaughter of Tant' Sannie, owner of the farm; and Lyndall, Em's talented orphan cousin. Lyndall grows into a woman of great beauty and power, but her life is unhappy. She separates Em from her lover, has a child by a man whom she refuses to marry, and soon afterward dies. Waldo, who has always loved her, outlives her only a short while.

Story Teller's Story, A (1924). An autobiographical narrative by Sherwood ANDERSON. Dealing with his life as a writer, it is a complement to *Tar: A Midwest Childhood* (1927), the fictional account of his early years.

Stout, Rex [Todhunter] (1886–   ). American detective-story writer. Stout is famous as the creator of Nero Wolfe, the adipose detective and orchid-fancier who solves all his cases at home and employs the likable Archie Goodwin to do his leg work. Wolfe first appeared in *Fer-de-Lance* (1934); he and Archie have solved many later cases, including *Some Buried Caesar* (1939), *Three Doors to Death* (1950), and *Before Midnight* (1955).

Stow, John (1525?–1605). English historian and antiquary. He published *The Woorkes of Geffrey Chaucer* (1561); *Summary of English Chronicles* (1565); and *A Survey of London* (1598, 1603), the most informative and reliable work on old London.

Stowe, Harriet Beecher (1811–1896). American novelist. Mrs. Stowe had two major interests: writing and religion. The daughter of a prominent Congregationalist clergyman, Lyman BEECHER, and the wife of another, Calvin Stowe, she was both attracted and repelled by orthodox doctrine. Although she finally became an Episcopalian, at several periods during her difficult life she turned to different kinds of spiritualism.

She was born in Connecticut, but her father moved the family to Cincinnati, where Harriet was married in 1836. She and her husband returned to New England, where she was visited, in 1848, by the vision that inspired UNCLE TOM'S CABIN. The book brought her immediate fame and fortune; the following year, she and her husband traveled abroad and were well received. During Mrs. Stowe's stay in England, she vigorously championed the cause of Lady Byron in a series of articles and books.

After the publication of articles and a sequel to *Uncle Tom's Cabin,* she based a number of books on her husband's childhood reminiscences of rural New England. These books, including THE PEARL OF ORR'S ISLAND, OLD-TOWN FOLKS, and *Poganuc*

People (1878), are among the first examples of local color writing in New England. The other important book by Mrs. Stowe is THE MINISTER'S WOOING, in which local color is mixed with a religious theme.

Strabo (c. 58 B.C.–c. A.D. 24). Greek geographer. Born in Pontus, he traveled widely through the Roman world and wrote a description of it in 17 books, *The Geography* (*Geographia*), nearly all of which are extant. His history of Rome in 47 books, beginning where Polybius' history ended, is lost.

Strachey, [Evelyn] John [St. Loe] (1901–   ). English writer on politics and minister in the Labour government (1946–1951). His best-known book is *The Coming Struggle for Power* (1932), a Marxist work predicting the doom of capitalism.

Strachey, [Giles] Lytton (1880–1932). English biographer and historian. A member of the BLOOMSBURY GROUP, he revolutionized the art of biography by writing humanized criticism, not panegyric, especially about the Victorians. His urbanity, irony, and witty malice are seen best in his most famous work, *Queen Victoria* (1921). He also wrote *Landmarks in French Literature* (1912), *Eminent Victorians* (1918), *Books and Characters* (1922), and *Elizabeth and Essex* (1928).

Stradivarius. See CREMONA.

Strafford, 1st earl of. Sir **Thomas Wentworth** (1593–1641). English statesman, favorite and chief adviser of Charles I. In 1640 he was named commander of the royal forces against a Scottish army that had invaded northern England. His failure to repel the Scots gave his enemies in Parliament, led by John Pym, an opportunity to accuse him of treason. He was condemned by a bill of attainder, which the king reluctantly signed, and executed. He is the central figure of Robert Browning's drama *Strafford* (1837).

Strait Is the Gate (La Porte étroite; 1909). A tale by André GIDE. Jerome woos his cousin Alissa, but, although she accepts and returns his spiritual love, she will not marry him, Alissa says that she prefers to please God by sacrificing her own worldly happiness to that of her sister, but she is fearful, too, of passion. When the sister no longer needs her sacrifice, Alissa fears that God does not think her capable of such holy selflessness and says she must continue to renounce her own happiness—and Jerome's for him—in order to prove her sincerity. She dies without even coming close to the mystic joy she sought.

strambotto. Italian folk lyric popular during the Middle Ages and the Renaissance with both rustic and aristocratic poets. Of uncertain etymology, the word may reflect an original link with folk dance. Its subject is love, treated either seriously or lightheartedly; its form consists of a stanza of eight 11-syllable lines rhyming *a b a b a b a b* or *a b a b a b c c* (as in *ottava rima*). The former scheme was preferred among the Sicilian poets of the 13th century, the latter by the Tuscan writers of the Renaissance, who also called the form a *rispetto*, perhaps because the poet pays his respects to the lady in these poems. In addition to single stanzas, there were also chains, or longer poems, made up of *strambotti* or *rispetti*. It differed from the *ottava rima* stanza mainly in content, the latter being regularly used for long narrative poems rather than single lyrics. But some *ris-*

petti also varied the rhyme scheme to *a b a b c c d d*. Among the better known writers who used the form were Poliziano and Lorenzo de' Medici.

Strange Case of Dr. Jekyll and Mr. Hyde, The (1886). A novel by Robert L. STEVENSON, the disturbing tale of the dual personality of Dr. Jekyll, a physician. A generous and philanthropic man, he is preoccupied with the problems of good and evil and with the possibility of separating them into distinct personalities. He develops a drug that transforms him into the demonic Mr. Hyde, in whose person he exhausts all the latent evil in his nature. He also creates an antidote that will restore him to his respectable existence as Dr. Jekyll. Gradually, however, the unmitigated evil of his darker self predominates until finally he performs an atrocious murder. His saner self determines to curtail these alternations of personality, but he discovers that he is losing control over his transformations, that he slips with increasing frequency into the world of evil. Finally, unable to procure one of the ingredients for the mixture of redemption, and on the verge of being discovered, he commits suicide.

The novel is of great psychological perception and strongly concerned with ethical problems.

Strange Interlude (1928). A play in nine acts, performed in two parts, by Eugene O'NEILL. The plot concerns the emotional and especially the sexual reactions of Nina Leeds, who subconsciously hates her father; she holds him responsible for preventing her from sleeping with her fiance before he was killed in France. She becomes a nurse and marries good-natured Sam Evans, but when she learns she is about to have a child she resorts to abortion, ostensibly because of a strain of insanity in his family. However, she has an affair with Dr. Darrell, becomes pregnant, and pretends their child is Evans'. When Evans dies, Nina marries a childhood admirer who reminds her of her father. The play caused a sensation by its use of a stream-of-consciousness technique. The characters speak in asides to reveal their true thoughts, in contrast to their conversation. The play was successfully revived in 1963.

Stranger, The (L'Etranger; 1942). A novel by Albert CAMUS. It reveals the ABSURD as the condition of man, who feels himself a stranger in his world. Meursault refuses to "play the game," by telling the conventional social white lies demanded of him or by believing in human love or religious faith. The unemotional style of his narrative lays naked his motives—or his absence of motive—for his lack of grief over his mother's death, his affair with Marie, his killing an Arab in the hot Algerian sun. Having rejected by honest self-analysis all interpretations which could explain or justify his existence, he nevertheless discovers, while in prison awaiting execution, a passion for the simple fact of life itself.

Strangers and Brothers. A series of novels by C. P. SNOW, started in 1940. The hero and narrator of the series is Lewis Eliot, a lawyer and government administrator. *Time of Hope* (1949) describes his childhood, education, and unhappy first marriage; *Homecomings* (1956) describes his successful later life and second marriage. THE MASTERS and THE AFFAIR are set in a Cambridge college. *Strangers and Brothers* (1940), *The Light and the Dark* (1947), THE NEW MEN, and *The Conscience of the Rich*

(1958) describe crises in the lives of his friends, in science and government. All the novels are about struggles for power and conflicts between private conscience and the public politics of power.

Strap, Hugh. In Tobias Smollett's novel RODERICK RANDOM, an ineffable Sancho Panza type whose fidelity and generosity are treated with disdain by Roderick.

Straparola, Giovan Francesco (c. 1480–1557). Italian writer. A native of Lombardy, he is the author of two books of *novelle, Le piacevoli notte* (*The Pleasureful Nights*, 1550–1553). Of the 75 *novelle,* some 20 are folk tales, marking the first appearance in European literature of a large group of such stories. Included among these folk tales are such favorites as *Beauty and the Beast, Puss in Boots,* and *The Singing Apple.*

Strasser, Gregor (1892–1934). German Nazi. His opposition to Hitler's policies led to his execution in a political purge. He was the brother of Otto Strasser.

Strasser, Otto (1897–   ). German political leader. The brother of Gregor Strasser, he was expelled from the Nazi Party in 1930 because of his socialist views. In 1933 he left Germany to conduct a program of opposition to Hitler.

Stratemeyer, Edward. See ROVER BOYS; TOM SWIFT.

Strato. In Shakespeare's JULIUS CAESAR, a faithful servant of Brutus. He holds the sword of Brutus as the latter runs upon it to kill himself.

Straus, Oskar (1870–1954). Austrian operetta composer, best known for *Der Tapfere Soldat* (1908; *The Chocolate Soldier,* based on *Arms and the Man,* by George Bernard Shaw).

Strauss, David Friedrich (1808–1874). German theologian. In *Leben Jesu* (*Life of Jesus,* 1835) he attributed a secular, mythical origin to the miraculous narrative of the gospels. See Ludwig FEUERBACH.

Strauss, Johann (1825–1899). Austrian composer and conductor, known as "The Waltz King." He succeeded to the conducting post of his father, Johann Strauss (1804–1849), also a well-known composer. Many of the younger Strauss's waltzes are still famous—among them the *Blue Danube, Artists' Life, Tales of the Vienna Woods.* His operetta *Die Fledermaus* (*The Bat;* 1874) is as much in the public favor as ever.

Strauss, Richard (1864–1949). German composer and conductor. He extended the musical ideas of Richard Wagner and Franz Liszt to their limits in tone poems, such as *Don Juan* (1889), *Till Eulenspiegels Lustige Streichen* (1895), and *Don Quixote* (1898), and in his three greatest operas, *Salome* (1905; based on Oscar Wilde's play), *Elektra* (1909; libretto by Hugo von Hofmannsthal), and DER ROSENKAVALIER (1911; libretto also by Hofmannsthal).

Stravinsky, Igor [Feodorovitch] (1882–1971). Russian-born composer. His creative output has spanned and deeply affected the entire development of modern music, from impressionism to neoclassicism and from tonality to polytonality and atonality. His first significant works, commissioned by Sergei DIAGHILEV's Russian Ballet, were *L'Oiseau de Feu* (1910; *The Firebird*), *Petrouchka* (1911), and *Le*

Sacre du Printemps (1913; *Rite of Spring*). The latter so startled its first audience that it provoked a riot. Later works seem restrained by comparison: *Histoire du Soldat* (1918; a pantomime, with narrator and instruments); *Oedipus Rex* (1927; an "opera-oratorio" using the Jean Cocteau version of Sophocles' play in a Latin translation in order to dissociate the text's sound from its meaning); *Symphony of Psalms* (1930); Symphony in C (1940); *The Rake's Progress,* an opera to a libretto by W. H. Auden and Chester Kallman; *Agon* (1957; ballet). Stravinsky has attempted to explain his musical aesthetic in his autobiography, *Chronicles of My Life* (1936), and *Poetics of Music* (1948), a group of lectures.

Strawberry Hill. The estate of Horace WALPOLE at Twickenham, Surrey, England. It was here that he established his private printing press (1757–1789) in the house he converted into "a little Gothic castle."

stream of consciousness. A narrative technique developed toward the end of the 19th century, often confused with interior monologue, and employed to evoke the psychic life of a character and depict subjective as well as objective reality. The term "stream of consciousness" was first used by William James in his *Principles of Psychology* (1890); the concept behind it—that ideas and consciousness in general are fluid and shifting, rather than fixed—contributed to a new approach to the novel. This approach was also given impetus by the new Freudian theories of the conscious and unconscious mind, and the Bergsonian concept of time as duration and of consciousness as an indivisible flux. As a literary term, "stream of consciousness" generally refers to the presentation of a character's thoughts, feelings, reactions, etc., on an approximated preverbal level and with little or no direct comment or explanation by the author. It is frequently difficult to distinguish absolutely between stream of consciousness and interior monologue, and the terms are sometimes used as if they were interchangeable. In general, the term "stream of consciousness" is used as the description of mental life at the borderline of conscious thought, and is characterized by the devices of association, reiteration of word- or symbol-motifs, apparent incoherence, and the reduction or elimination of normal syntax and punctuation to simulate the free flow of the character's mental processes. "Interior monologue" refers to a presentation of thoughts more consciously controlled and on a level closer to direct verbalization. The French writer Edouard Dujardin claims to have been the first to use the interior monologue in his *Les Lauriers sont coupés* (1887, trans. as *We'll to the Woods No More*). Another innovator was the English writer Dorothy Richardson, who recorded the psychic experience of one character in her 12-volume *Pilgrimage.* James Joyce brought the stream-of-consciousness approach to its highest form in *Ulysses* and *Finnegans Wake.* In America, William Faulkner's *The Sound and the Fury* is often given as a leading example of stream-of-consciousness writing, though only the first two sections of the book can be described as such; the third section, however, provides a good example of an interior monologue according to the differentiation made above. In England, Virginia Woolf adapted the stream-of-consciousness technique to slightly different uses in *To the Lighthouse, Mrs.*

Dalloway, and *The Waves.* It is no longer the "experimental" form it was once considered, and aspects of stream-of-consciousness techniques are evident in the work of most of the important writers to appear since the 1930's.

Streetcar Named Desire, A (1947). A play by Tennessee WILLIAMS. The winner of a Pulitzer Prize, it is set in the French Quarter of New Orleans where two streetcars named Desire and Cemetery run on a single track. It is the story of Blanche DuBois, a faded Southern belle, who comes to live with her sister, Stella, and the sister's husband Stanley. Annoyed at her pretensions to gentility and her flirtatious behavior, Stanley eventually warns a friend who had thought of marrying Blanche. With her hopes of marriage destroyed, Blanche confronts Stanley and provokes him into raping her. Finally, with her illusions still strong, she is taken away to a mental institution.

Street Scene (1929). A play by Elmer RICE. The play, using a naturalistic setting, presents life in a slum tenement and reaches its climax in a double murder. One of the first stage productions to include realistic sound effects throughout the performance, it was the winner of a Pulitzer Prize. Later it was given a musical score by Kurt Weill (1947).

Streicher, Julius (1885–1946). German Nazi journalist and political leader. He was editor of *Der Stürmer* (*The Stormer,* 1923–1945), a fanatical anti-Semitic periodical, and was sentenced to death at the Nuremberg Trials.

Strenia. The goddess who presided over the New Year festivities in ancient Rome. Tatius, the legendary Sabine king, entered Rome on New Year's Day, and received from some augurs palms cut from the sacred grove dedicated to Strenia. After his seizure of the city, he ordained that January 1 should be celebrated by gifts to be called *strenae,* consisting of figs, dates, and honey. The French word *étrenne,* "a New Year's gift," is derived from the name of this goddess.

Strephon. The shepherd in Sir Philip Sidney's *Arcadia* who makes love to the beautiful Urania. It is a stock name for a pastoral lover, while the name Chloe is frequently given to a Strephon's beloved.

Stresemann, Gustav (1878–1929). German foreign minister (1923–1929) who helped to negotiate the Locarno Pact (1925). He shared the Nobel peace prize with Aristide Briand in 1926.

Strether, Lambert. See AMBASSADORS, THE.

stricken deer. A term applied to William COWPER by himself and often used as an epitaph for the poet. It occurs in Book III of his poem THE TASK (1785). The reference is to Cowper's attacks of insanity and his morbid religious obsession of guilt. It is also the title of a biography of Cowper by Lord David Cecil.

Strickland, Agnes (1796–1874). English historian. She is known chiefly for her *Lives of the Queens of England* (12 vols., 1840–1848), written in collaboration with her sister Elizabeth Strickland (1794–1875), and for her *Lives of the Queens of Scotland and English Princesses* (8 vols., 1850–1859). She also edited *Letters of Mary Queen of Scots* (1843) and wrote several novels.

Strindberg, [Johan] August (1849–1912). Swedish playwright, novelist, and poet. The son of a serving woman and a bankrupted ex-gentleman, Strindberg knew poverty and misery from childhood. Later, he was variously employed as a journalist, a tutor, and an assistant at the Royal Library. His first significant play was *Master Olaf* (written in 1874 in prose, rewritten in verse in 1878, and first performed in the original version in 1881). It was followed by *Lucky Per's Travels* (1880), reminiscent of Ibsen's *Peer Gynt;* and *Sir Bengt's Wife* (1882), an answer to Ibsen's *A Doll's House* which Strindberg hated. In 1879, Strindberg first became the subject of literary excitement with his satirical novel *The Red Room,* which many critics consider the first example of modern Swedish realism. With the publication of the stories in *Married* (1884–1886) his fame became unpleasant notoriety, for these satirical, bitter narratives involved their author in a prosecution for blasphemy. He was acquitted, but the experience contributed to his feelings of persecution that culminated in his breakdown of 1896.

Strindberg embarked on the first of his unfortunate marriages in 1877. His relations with his wife, the former Siri Wrangel, probably formed the basis for the conflicts in the major plays of his realistic-naturalistic period: THE FATHER, *Comrades* (1888), and *The Creditors* (1890). These three works are centered on the duel between the sexes: the woman, ruthless and aggressive, asserts herself as the equal— if not the superior—of the man, usurps his masculine prerogatives of decision and leadership, and destroys him. Not until many years later, in the powerful DANCE OF DEATH, did Strindberg write of a husband who enslaves and torments his wife. In MISS JULIE, probably the best-known of the plays of this period, Strindberg depicts both sexual antagonism and class conflict in the figure of the aristocratic girl who seduces her father's footman.

In 1891 Strindberg's first marriage ended in a painful divorce. He married again in 1893, but this union lasted only a few years. He was beginning to show increased evidence of emotional disturbance, and his feelings of persecution were intensified by his difficulties in getting his plays produced; he had been forced to establish his own Experimental Theater in Copenhagen to have *Miss Julie* and *The Creditors* performed. He became interested in the physical sciences, but his experiments in chemistry were soon transformed into delvings into alchemy, occultism, and mysticism. In July of 1896 he suffered a psychological crisis which brought him to the edge of madness, an experience which he recorded in the autobiographical *Inferno* (1897) and *Legends* (1898), and expressed dramatically in the mystical and symbolic plays *To Damascus* (Parts I and II, 1898; Part III, 1904), *Advent* (1899), and *There are Crimes and Crimes* (1899). This period of crisis marks the beginning of what is perhaps the most interesting phase of his creative life; in order to give dramatic form to his new vision of life—a vision in which the inner world has as much, if not more, claim to reality than external experience—he wrote the haunting, surrealistic "dream-plays" that became the forerunners of modern expressionism. Gentler and less bitter than the plays of his realistic period, these dramas have a scope that ranges from the mystic surrealism of *A Dream Play* (1902) to the nearly naturalistic but tenderly mystical *Easter* (1901). As his emotional

health improved he turned again to Swedish history and wrote a series of dramas probably inspired by the historical plays of Shakespeare. Among them are *The Saga of the Volsungs, Gustavus Vasa* (a continuation of the story of the Vasa dynasty begun in *Master Olaf*), *Erik XIV,* and *Gustavus Adolphus.* In 1907 he and August Falck established the Intimate Theater in Stockholm, for which Strindberg wrote a series of four "Chamber Plays"; of these, only *The Spook Sonata* (1907) achieved marked success.

Strindberg's collected writings—plays, fairy tales, poems, short stories, prose sketches, essays, autobiographical writings, novels—fill 55 volumes. Particularly interesting are his autobiographical works, including *The Son of a Servant* (1886), *A Fool's Defense* (1893), and *Alone* (1903).

Strong, George Templeton (1820–1875). American lawyer, businessman, trustee of Columbia University, and memoirist. Strong, a prominent New Yorker, is famous for the *Diary* that he kept for 40 years, starting on Oct. 5, 1835. Filled with frank comment about the notable men and events of his time, it is an extremely valuable document; in 1952, Allan Nevins made a selection from the 5 million words, and published four volumes.

Strong, L[eonard] A[lfred] G[eorge] (1896– 1958). English novelist, short-story writer, poet, and critic. Some of his best stories are set on the fishing coasts of Ireland and display characters in elemental situations. His best novels are *The Garden* (1931) and *Sea Wall* (1933). *Travellers* (1945) is a collection of short stories; *Selected Poems* appeared in 1931.

strophe. From the Greek, literally a turn. Originally, that part of an ode which was sung by the Greek dramatic chorus as it moved in one direction, followed by an antistrophe when the chorus reversed the direction of its movement. Hence, in prosody, a stanza.

Struther, Jan. Pen name of Joyce Anstruther (1901–1953). English poet and novelist. Her best known book is MRS. MINIVER.

Strutt, Joseph (1749–1802). English antiquary and engraver. He is the author of *A Biographical Dictionary of Engravers* (1785–1786), *A Complete View of the Dress and Habits of the People of England* (1796–1799), and *The Sports and Pastimes of the People of England* (1801). An unfinished novel of Strutt's suggested the writing of *Waverley* to Sir Walter Scott.

Strutt, Lord. A verbal caricature of the king of Spain, originally Charles II (who died without issue), which can also be applied to his successor Philippe, duc d'Anson. Bearing the full name of Philip Lord Strutt, he appears in John Arbuthnot's political and allegorical satire *The History of* JOHN BULL.

Stryver, Bully. In Charles Dickens' A TALE OF TWO CITIES, a loud, aggressive lawyer, attorney for the defense in Darnay's trial at Old Bailey. The brilliant but dissipated Sydney CARTON is his clerk and writes all the cases that Stryver pleads in court.

Stuart, Prince Charles Edward. See PRETENDER.

Stuart, Gilbert [Charles] (1755–1828). American painter. After 17 years in England and Ireland, where he studied with Benjamin West and began a successful career, he returned to America in 1792. He gained fame for his portraits, among which is the well-known, unfinished "Athenaeum" head of George Washington in the Boston Museum of Fine Arts.

Stuart, James. See JAMES I OF ENGLAND AND VI OF SCOTLAND.

Stuart, James Francis Edward. See PRETENDER.

Stuart, Jesse [Hilton] (1907–). American poet, novelist, and short-story writer. He is known for his regional works dealing with the mountain region of Kentucky and its people. He won his early reputation with his short stories, collected first in *Head o' W-Hollow* (1936) and later in *Men of the Mountain* (1941) and other volumes. His first novel, *Trees of Heaven* (1940), describes a disagreement between two mountain men. *Taps for Private Tussie* (1943) presents an amusing and unfavorable account of Kentucky life. Other novels include *Hie to the Hunter* (1950) and *The Good Spirit of Laurel Ridge* (1953). Stuart has also published several volumes of verse, including *Man with a Bull-Tongue Plow* (1934), and *The Thread That Runs So True* (1949), an account of his experiences as a school teacher.

Stuart, Mary. See MARY, QUEEN OF SCOTS.

Stubbs or Stubbes, Philip (fl. c. 1583–1591). English Puritan who violently denounced the stage and other popular amusements in *The Anatomie of Abuses* (1583). Thomas NASHE answered with *The Anatomie of Absurdities* (1589).

Stubbs, William (1825–1901). English historian. He was appointed regius professor of modern history at Oxford in 1866, curator of the BODLEIAN LIBRARY in 1868, canon of Saint Paul's in 1879, and bishop of Chester in 1884. His major work is *The Constitutional History of England in its Origins and Development* (1874–1878).

Stuckenberg, Viggo (1863–1905). Danish poet. With his friends Claussen and Jørgensen, Stuckenberg initiated the neoromantic movement in Denmark. His poem *Den Vilde Jaeger* (*The Wild Huntsman*, 1894), mystical and medieval in its mood, marked a departure from the realistic school and its social concerns. Gentle melancholy, wistful tenderness, and a love for nature characterize his verse. Among Stuckenberg's collections of poetry are *Flyvende Sommer* (1898), *Aarsens Tid* (1905), and *Sidste Digte* (1906).

Studs Lonigan (1935). A trilogy by James T. FARRELL, consisting of *Young Lonigan, The Young Manhood of Studs Lonigan,* and *Judgment Day.* In relentlessly naturalistic style it presents the boyhood, adolescence, early manhood, and finally the death of William (Studs) Lonigan, the son of lower-middle-class Irish Catholic parents in Chicago. Although Studs as a boy displays sparks of vigor and ambition, the combined influences of his social and economic environment, his swaggering and vicious associates, and his narrow family, educational, and religious background serve to aggravate his weaknesses and lead him into a life of futile dissipation, which he recognizes as unsatisfactory, but from which he is unable to escape. The language of the streets, the monotony and crudity of the thought processes of Studs and his associates, and their numerous sordid sexual adventures are all frankly and faithfully reproduced, and there is extensive documentation in the depiction of the social background in the U.S. during the period between 1912 and the early 1930's.

Young Lonigan (1932) introduces Studs as a boy of 15 graduating from a Roman Catholic grammar school and starting out on the typical career of his class and time. He dreams of becoming a "great guy" and takes care to conform to the pattern of conduct set for him by his associates. Notable events are his initiation into the mysteries of sex (in which he is assisted by Iris, a promiscuous adolescent girl of the neighborhood) and his first sentimental attachment, of which Lucy Scanlan is the object.

In *The Young Manhood of Studs Lonigan* (1934), the career of Studs is carried through the period of the 1920's, during which he works as a house painter with his father and participates in the dissipations of the time. The culmination of the novel is a wild New Year's Eve party at which a girl named Irene is raped by Weary Reilley, one of Studs's companions.

Judgment Day (1935) records Studs's declining health, futile dissipation, love affair with Catherine Banahan, fruitless search for a job, and ultimate death from pneumonia. The climax of the novel is a dramatic death scene against the background of family lamentations and quarrels and of Roman Catholic prayers for the dead.

Sturluson, Snorri. See SNORRI STURLUSON.

Sturmabteilung. See S.A.

Sturm und Drang (storm and stress). A literary movement in late 18th-century Germany leading toward romanticism. The *Sturm und Drang,* which takes its name from the title of a play by Maximilian Klinger, was especially rich in drama and lyric poetry. Its other major figures were young Goethe, young Schiller, Reinhold Lenz, Heinrich Wagner, and Gottfried Bürger. In thought, the *Sturm und Drang* was strongly influenced by Edward Young, Rousseau, and Hamann. In its literary productions, emphasis was usually placed upon the energetic, daemonic, Promethean quality of the individual in opposition to the rationalistic ideal of the enlightenment and the formalism of French-influenced neoclassicism. The representatives of the *Sturm und Drang* admired Shakespeare and Ossian especially, and the effect of Herder's writings upon them can be seen in their frequent interest in folk material and the German past. They were not, however, so decidedly patriotic as the poets of the GÖTTINGER HAIN. Peripheral figures in the movement include Jacobi and Heinse.

Stutly, Will. In the English ROBIN HOOD ballad cycle, one of Robin Hood's followers. He was about to be hanged by the sheriff when Robin Hood and his men arrived and saved him at the very last minute.

Stuyvesant, Peter (1592–1672). Dutch director-general of New Netherland (1647–1664) until forced to surrender the colony to England. Fierce in appearance, a harsh ruler, he appears in Washington Irving's *A History of New York* (1809) as "Peter, the Headstrong." According to legend, his false leg was made of silver. His farm, *Bouwerij* (literally, "farm"), included the region of the Bowery in New York City.

stylites or **pillar saints** (Gr., *stylos,* pillar). A class of early and medieval ascetics, chiefly of Syria, who lived on top of pillars, from which they never descended. The most celebrated were Simeon Stylites, of Syria, and Daniel the Stylite of Constantinople. Simeon (d. 596) spent 68 years on different pillars, each loftier and narrower than the preceding, the last being 66 feet high. Daniel (d. 494) lived for 33 years on a pillar, and was not infrequently nearly blown from it by the storms from Thrace.

Tennyson wrote a poem, *St. Simeon Stylites* (1842). Paphnutius in Anatole France's *Thaïs* becomes a stylite for a time.

Stymphalus (Stymphalos). In Greek mythology, an Arcadian king. He was treacherously murdered by PELOPS. The crime caused a famine throughout Greece, which was finally ended by the prayers of the virtuous Aeacus.

Styron, William [Clark, Jr.] (1925–   ). American novelist. A Southerner, Styron shows the influence of Faulkner and Thomas Wolfe. His first novel, *Lie Down in Darkness* (1951), was highly praised. It concerns an alcoholic father and his daughter, a suicide in her early 20's. *Set This House on Fire* (1960), which takes place largely in Italy, was regarded by many critics as less powerful than the earlier book. Styron also wrote *The Long March* (1952), which appeared in *discovery*.

Styx. A river. According to classical mythology, it flowed seven times round the infernal regions. The five rivers of Hell are the Styx, ACHERON, COCYTUS, PHLEGETHON, and LETHE. Styx is also the deity of the river, a daughter of Oceanus and Tethys, and mother of Zelus (Zeal), Nike (Victory), Bia (Strength), and Kratos (Power).

Dante, in his *Divine Comedy*, places the rivers in different circles of the Inferno. Thus, he makes the Acheron divide the borderland from Limbo. The former realm is for the "praiseless and the blameless dead"; Limbo is for the unbaptized. He places the Stygian Lake of inky hue in the fifth circle, the realm of those who put no restraint on their anger. The fire-stream of Phlegethon he fixes to the eighth steep, the Hell of burning, where it snows flakes of fire, and where blasphemers are confined. He places the frozen river of Cocytus in the tenth pit of Malebolge, a region of thick-ribbed ice, the lowest depth of Hell, where Judas and Lucifer are imprisoned. Lethe, he says, is no river of Hell at all, but it is the one wish of all the infernals to get to it, that they may drink its water and forget their torments. It being, however, in Purgatory, they can never reach it.

Sublime Porte. The central office of the former Ottoman government in Constantinople; hence, the government or the Turkish empire itself. The term is French in origin, derived from the gate (*porte*) of the Sultan's palace where justice in ancient times was administered.

sub rosa (*Lat.*, "under the rose"). In strict confidence. The origin of the phrase is wrapped in obscurity, but the story is that Cupid gave a rose to Harpocrates, the god of silence, to bribe him not to betray the amours of Venus. Hence the flower became the emblem of silence. In 1526 it was placed over confessionals.

Subtle. A character in Ben Jonson's comedy THE ALCHEMIST (1610). An artful quack, Subtle is an "alchemist" who pretends to be on the eve of discovering the Philosopher's stone. Sir Epicure Mammon, a rich knight, is his principal dupe, but by no means his only one.

Suckert, Curzio Malaparte. See Curzio MALAPARTE.

Suckfist, Lord. An anglicism for Seigneur de Humevesne, defendant in the lawsuit instituted by Lord Kissbreech in Rabelais' GARGANTUA AND PANTAGRUEL. The trial having become hopelessly involved, the court calls in Pantagruel as judge. He insists that all the papers, which serve only to confuse the case, be burned and that the two parties present their arguments in person. Since the court still fails to understand the case, Pantagruel gives a garbled decision which has the unheard-of result of pleasing both parties.

Suckling, Sir John (1609–1642). English poet, courtier, and soldier. Suckling was known in his day for his wit, gaiety, extravagance, and love of gaming. He was implicated in the plot to rescue the earl of Strafford from the Tower of London in 1641 and died a fugitive in France, possibly a suicide, possibly the victim of a vengeful servant.

One of the CAVALIER POETS, Suckling was, however, influenced in some superficial effects by Donne. His poetry has the kind of ease, knowledgeability, and unaffected simplicity of diction that has traditionally formed, in England, the ideal of gentlemanly speech. In his poems he could play both the ardent lover and skeptic—although the latter pose gave more scope for the wit which distinguishes lyrics like the song "Why so pale and wan, fond lover?" from his play *Aglaura* (1637). Other works by Suckling include *Session of the Poets* (1637), a poem containing descriptions of Ben Jonson, Thomas Carew, and other contemporary writers, and *Brennoralt, or The Discontented Colonel* (1639), a play.

Suckow, Ruth (1892–1960). American novelist and short-story writer. Born in Iowa, she is known for her studies, generally realistic, of life in the Middle West. Her best-known work is *Country People* (1924), her first novel, which told the story of three generations of German-Americans. *The Bonney Family* (1928) and *New Hope* (1942) are both about ministers. Young women often occupied her attention, as in *The Odyssey of a Nice Girl* (1925) and *The Kramer Girls* (1930).

Sucre, Antonio José de (1795–1830). Venezuelan general and patriot. Considered one of the most high-minded of Hispanic America's revolutionary heroes, Sucre was the chief lieutenant and friend of Simón Bolívar. In 1822, Sucre's victory at Pichincha drove the Spaniards from Ecuador. In Peru he commanded the revolutionary army that defeated the Spaniards at Ayacucho, virtually ending the wars for independence. He fathered the creation of an independent Bolivia and reluctantly became its first president in 1826, only to resign in 1828. He was returning to his home in Quito after an unsuccessful attempt to keep Venezuela in Gran Colombia when he was mysteriously murdered near Pasto, Colombia.

Sudermann, Hermann (1857–1928). German playwright and novelist. In his plays, which include *Die Ehre* (*Honor,* 1888), *Sodoms Ende* (*Sodom's End,* 1890) and *Die Heimat* (lit. *Home,* trans. as MAGDA), he exercised a searching social criticism, which caused him to be associated by critics with the movement of NATURALISM. His dramatic technique, however, is far from naturalistic; his plots are contrived and he makes frequent use of monologues and asides. His novels include *Frau Sorge* (*Dame Care,* 1888), *Der Katzensteg* (*The Narrow Path,* 1889), and *Das hohe Lied* (*Song of Songs*, 1908), all of which, like his plays, deal with social questions.

Sudra. See CASTE.

Sue, Eugène. Real name **Marie Joseph Sue** (1804–1857). French novelist. A ship's doctor, he found the material for such sea stories as *Plik et Plok* (1831), and *La Vigie de Koatven* (1833) among his own adventures. Best known for his popular and sensational romances in the manner of Dumas père, Sue had a prolific and highly successful career. Among his works are THE MYSTERIES OF PARIS and *Le Juif Errant* (*The Wandering Jew*, 1844–1845).

Sueños, Los (1627). A series of prose satires by Francisco de QUEVEDO. Supposedly a description of the author's visits to Hell, they are notable for their incisive caricature of the men and institutions of contemporary society. Usually included in the series are *El sueño de las calaveras, El alguacil alguacilado, Las zahurdas de Plutón, El sueño del mundo por de dentro, La visita de los chistes, El discurso de todos los diablos,* and *La hora de todos.*

Suetonius. Full Latin name, **Gaius Suetonius Tranquillus** (A.D. 75?–?150). Roman biographer and historian. He was private secretary to the emperor Hadrian from about A.D. 119 to 121. The work for which he is principally remembered is *De Vita Caesarum* (*Lives of the Caesars*), a detailed account of the life and times of the first 12 emperors from Caesar to Domitian. Suetonius is also the author of a work on literary history, *De Viris Illustribus* (*Famous Men*). Of this work we possess only the biographies of Terence and Horace, and a fragment on the life of Lucan.

Title page of Suetonius' *Lives of the Caesars* (1542).

On les vend a Paris en la grand salle du palais, par Arnoul langelier tenant sa bouticque au deuxiesme pillier deuant la chappelle de messieurs les presidens.

Sufis. A Muslim sect of mystics, mentioned, for instance, by Omar Kháyyám. They are so named, from the Arabic word *suf* for wool, because they wore woolen garments to symbolize their renunciation of worldly comforts. Their ultimate goal is blissful union with the Supreme Being who may be reached by following the Law, the Way, and the Truth.

Suggs, Captain Simon. A rapscallion character created by the American humorist Johnson Jones Hooper (1815–1862). Hooper's reputation as a humorist is founded chiefly on his account of *Some Adventures of Captain Simon Suggs, Late of the Tallapoosa Volunteers* (1846). It was Suggs' guiding principle "to be shifty in a new country." The rowdy tales ridiculed many folkways of the South. Hooper wrote several other books, and became secretary of the Provisional Congress of the Southern States when the Civil War broke out. In his *Flush Times of Alabama and Mississippi* (1853), J. G. Baldwin, another Southern humorist, introduced a character named Simon Suggs, Jr., Esq., " a good trader and the mean boy of the school."

Sui. Chinese dynasty (590–618). Founded by Yang Chien (541–605), a vast canal system was established and the country reunited after a period of disunity following the Han, setting the stage for the T'ang Dynasty which followed.

Sukhovo-Kobylin, Aleksandr Vasilievich (1817–1903). Russian dramatist. He is known for his trilogy: *Krechinski's Wedding* (1855), *The Affair* (1869), and *The Death of Tarelkin* (1869).

Suleiman I. Known as the **Magnificent** (1496?–1566). A famous Turkish ruler. He encouraged the arts and sciences.

Sulla, Lucius Cornelius. Surnamed **Felix** (138–78 B.C.). Roman general, dictator, and reformer. He took part in various campaigns and was elected consul (88 B.C.). During the civil struggle between Sulla and MARIUS (88–82), Sulla led for the first time an army of Romans against Rome (88). In 81 he was appointed dictator. He reorganized the senate and the judiciary of Rome and was the first in Roman history to use the weapon of proscription.

Sullivan, Sir Arthur [Seymour] (1842–1900). English composer, best known for his collaboration with W. S. Gilbert on the GILBERT AND SULLIVAN OPERAS. He was also an accomplished organist and composer of sacred music and serious opera. His songs *The Lost Chord* and *Onward, Christian Soldiers* are widely known.

Sullivan, Frank [Francis John Sullivan] (1892–). American columnist and humorist. Long a columnist for the New York *World,* Sullivan is perhaps best known for his collection of clichés used in various professions, but he has used his light satiric wit in many fields. His later writings have often appeared in *The New Yorker.* His books include *The Life and Times of Martha Hepplethwaite* (1926), *Innocent Bystanding* (1928), *Sullivan at Bay* (1939), and *Moose in the Hoose* (1959).

Sullivan, Louis (1856–1924). American architect. A pioneer in the use of steel frames for high buildings, he practiced his craft principally in Chicago. Among his achievements are the stone

Auditorium building (1889) and the Carson, Pirie, and Scott store (1899–1904), both in Chicago. Sullivan's famous dictum, "Form follows function," influenced many architects, among them Frank Lloyd WRIGHT.

Sullivan, Mark (1874–1952). American journalist and historian. First winning recognition as a muckraker, he is best known for his lively six-volume history, *Our Times: The United States, 1900–1925* (1926–1936).

Sully, duc de. Maximilien de Béthune (1560–1641). French statesman. As finance minister under Henry IV, he reformed France's fiscal system by curtailing expenditures and correcting abuses. His *Mémoires des sages et royales oeconomies d'estat, domestiques, politiques, et militaires de Henry le Grand,* often referred to as the *Economies Royales* (*Royal Economies,* 1638) include a discussion of Henry's well-known though probably apocryphal plan to ensure permanent peace by means of a federation of European states. They are an invaluable historical source.

Sully, Thomas (1783–1872). English-born American painter. Sully established himself in Philadelphia. His fashionable portraits and less well-known historical scenes are noted for elegance and sensitivity to color.

Sully Prudhomme. Pen name of René **François Armand Prudhomme** (1839–1907). French poet. His early work—*Stances et Poèmes* (1865), *Les Solitudes* (1869), and *Les Vaines Tendresses* (1875)—is lyrical and expresses a delicate melancholy. Later volumes, however, such as *La Justice* (1878) and *Le Bonheur* (1888), stress impersonality and objectivity—favored techniques of the PARNASSIANS. In 1901, Sully Prudhomme received the Nobel Prize for literature.

Sumarokov, Aleksandr Petrovich (1718–1777). Russian dramatist and writer. The founder of classical drama in Russia and an important reformer of the poetic language, Sumarokov wrote in almost every classical genre. Among his 10 tragedies is an adaptation of *Hamlet.* In reaction to the "high" style of solemn odes based on the theory and practice of Mikhail LOMONOSOV, Sumarokov insisted on greater naturalness in poetic language. He was instrumental in introducing what became the modern love lyric into Russian poetry. He is best known for two classical plays, *Khorev* (1747) and *Zemir* (1751).

Sumer. An ancient nation of Mesopotamia. It is the oldest civilization known in the Near East, but its origins are still a mystery. Its language is neither Semitic nor Indo-European. It dominated most of Mesopotamia during the fourth millenium before Christ. Excavations at UR, NIPPUR, and other ancient cities have demonstrated that Sumer had a very rich culture. The Sumerian language continued as the hieratic language of Babylonia and Assyria for many centuries after the Sumerians themselves had disappeared and were forgotten. The very existence of Sumer was unknown until the relatively recent decipherment of ancient tablets bearing the cuneiform writing that was probably the invention of the Sumerians and the ancestor of Phoenician script. For much that has been learned of the Sumerian mythology, on which was based much of the mythology of Babylon and Assyria, see AN; ENKI; ENLIL; ERESHKIGAL; INANNA; KUR; NANNA; NINTU; ZIUSUDRA.

Summa Theologica. Full title, **Summa Totius Theologiae** (c. 1265–1274). Major philosophical treatise by St. Thomas AQUINAS. A "summary of all theology," it is still recognized as the doctrinal basis for all such teachings in the Roman Catholic Church. It applies the methodology of Aristotelian logic to problems of Christian doctrine, systematizing and quoting from the works of both classical and early Christian thinkers. Aquinas emphasizes the importance of logical argument in matters of reason, but the supremacy of revelation through scriptural and Church pronouncements in matters of faith. The work is in three sections: the first concerns the existence and nature of God and His universe; the second develops a moral philosophy, treating the virtues and vices from the practical viewpoint of society as well as from the theortical aspect; the third discusses the role of Christ and the sacraments in the salvation of the soul. Aquinas died before he could finish the third section, but his follower Reginald of Piperno completed it later according to Aquinas' design.

Summers, Montague (1880–1948). English Catholic priest and scholar. He is known for his eccentric belief in witchcraft and his popular books on the subject, including *The History of Witchcraft and Demonology* (1927); he was a friend of Aleister CROWLEY. He was also an authority on Restoration drama.

Summerson, Esther. See BLEAK HOUSE.

Summoner's Tale, The. One of the CANTERBURY TALES of Geoffrey CHAUCER. The Summoner, very angry at the FRIAR'S TALE, retorts that all friars are consigned to the most repulsive spot in Hell. He then tells a scatological tale of the come-uppance given a particularly greedy and hypocritical friar. Thomas, sick in bed, grows increasingly angry at the friar's use of pious argument to get gold from him, ostensibly for the convent where prayers are being said for the recovery of the invalid. The friar now exhorts him against his ire, telling numerous stories demonstrating how evil anger is. Thomas finally pretends to offer the friar a precious gift if he promises to divide it equally among his fellow friars, instructing him to reach under the covers behind his back because the gift is hidden with him in bed. The friar eagerly complies, and Thomas coarsely revenges himself. The friar rages to the lord of the village about the insult offered his order. The lord and his family, howeyer, simply ridicule him by holding a mock-scholarly discussion as to how the roar and odor of the offering can be equally divided, as stipulated, among the friar's colleagues.

Sumner, Charles (1811–1874). American statesman. After lecturing at Harvard Law School and spending several years in Europe, Sumner became active in Massachusetts politics and in various reform movements. In the U.S. Senate, where he served from 1851 until his death, he was an outspoken opponent of slavery. In 1856 he delivered a speech, later known as "The Crime Against Kansas," in which he denounced several proslavery senators, including Andrew Butler of South Carolina. A few days later, Butler's nephew, Rep. Preston Brooks, attacked Sumner in the Senate chamber, raining blows on him with his cane. As a result of his injuries, Sumner was not able to return to the Senate until 1859. During the Civil War he favored emancipation and later opposed the Reconstruction policy of President Johnson. In 1861 he was named chairman of the Senate Foreign Relations Committee, a post from which he was removed in 1872 after he made his "Naboth's Vineyard" speech against the proposed annexation of Santo Domingo.

Sumner, William Graham (1840–1910). American economist and social scientist. A professor of political and social science at Yale, Sumner was a champion of *laissez faire,* opposing labor unions and government regulation of business. His most enduring work is probably his pioneering sociological treatise *Folkways* (1907), in which he stressed custom as the basis of social institutions.

sumō. Japanese wrestling. Wrestlers undergo long apprenticeships, starting when young, and are trained to gain strength, agility, and weight. The sport enjoys tremendous popularity, particularly since the introduction of television.

Sumter, Fort. A fort in the harbor of Charleston, S.C., and the site of the first military engagement of the U.S. Civil War. After the secession of South Carolina in December 1860, Major Robert Anderson, U.S. commander in Charleston harbor, withdrew his men to Fort Sumter. The administration then had to decide whether to evacuate the fort or to send reinforcements. Delaying a final decision, President Lincoln dispatched provisions. When state authorities demanded that Anderson surrender, he offered to surrender when his supplies ran out. The South Carolinians, who knew that provisions would soon arrive, rejected Anderson's offer, and shore batteries under Pierre G. T. Beauregard opened fire on April 12, 1861. Historians still disagree as to Lincoln's role in the events preceding the attack, some arguing that he deliberately maneuvered South Carolina into firing the first shot of the Civil War.

sun. The source of light and heat, and consequently of life, to the whole world. Hence it is regarded as a deity and worshiped as such by all primitive peoples. It has a leading place in all mythologies. *Shamash* was the principal sun god of the Assyrians, *Merodach* of the Chaldees, *Ormuzd* of the Persians, *Ra* of the Egyptians, *Tezcatlipoca* of the Mexicans, and *Helios* (known to the Romans as *Sol*) of the Greeks. Helios drove his chariot daily across the heavens, rising from the sea at dawn and sinking into it in the west at sunset. The Scandinavian sun god *Sunna,* who was in constant dread of being devoured by the wolf Fenris (a symbol of eclipses), was similarly borne through the sky. In later times *Apollo* was also a sun god of the Greeks, but he was the personification not of the sun itself but of its all-pervading light and life-giving qualities.

Sun Also Rises, The (1926). A novel by Ernest HEMINGWAY. Considered by many critics to be his finest long work, it deals with "the lost generation" of Americans who had fought in France during World War I and then had expatriated themselves from the America of Calvin Coolidge. The story is told by Jake BARNES, rendered impotent from a war wound. Lady Brett ASHLEY, who is divorcing her husband, is in love with him. These two go to Spain with a group that includes Michael Campbell, whom

Brett plans to marry; Bill Gorton, a friend of Jake; a Greek nobleman; and Robert Cohn, an American-Jewish writer. Brett has an affair with Romero, a bullfighter whom the others respect for his grace and control in the face of danger; she eventually leaves him and returns to Michael. The fact that at the end nothing has really changed in life for any of the characters is exactly the point of the novel: for these disillusioned people, life can have no direction, no point toward which to develop.

Sunday Morning (1923). A poem by Wallace STEVENS. The narrator debates with a woman who feels "the need of some imperishable bliss." The lady must learn that "Death is the mother of beauty," that there is no transcendence, and that the earth is "all of paradise that we shall know."

Sung. Chinese dynasty (960–1279). Following the T'ang, this era saw the gradual disunion and partition of the empire. It was a period of great cultural ferment in which Ch'an established itself as the principal Buddhist sect and the Neo-Confucianism of Chu Hsi established Confucianism as the dominant political and ethical force.

Sunken Bell, The (Die versunkene Glocke; 1896). A verse-play by Gerhart HAUPTMANN. A bellmaker, Heinrich, loses his masterpiece when it falls into a lake. He himself, wandering around in the woods, meets and falls in love with the female elf Rautendelein, and decides to remain with her. His deserted wife Magda, however, throws herself into the lake and rings the bell to remind him of his guilt. Heinrich goes home, but finds Magda gone; he returns to the mountains, but finds Rautendelein married to the Frog King; and finally, he drinks the goblet of death.

Sunna (Arabic, "custom, divine law"). The sayings and example of Muhammad and his immediate followers insofar as they conform to the KORAN; hence, applied to the collections of legal and moral traditions attributed to the Prophet, supplementary to the Koran, as the Hebrew Mishna is to the Pentateuch.

Sunnites. The orthodox and conservative body of Muslims who consider the SUNNA as authentic as the Koran itself and acknowledge the first four caliphs as the rightful successors of Muhammad. They form the largest section of Muslims and are divided into four sects: *Hanafites, Hanbalites, Malikites,* and *Shafites.* See SHIITES.

Sun Yat-sen (1866–1925). Chinese statesman, called in China the "father of the Revolution." He founded the KUOMINTANG. He helped to bring about the revolution against the Manchus (1911), and was elected provisional president of the Chinese Republic. He retired in favor of Yuan Shih-kai, who became president of all China, but soon broke with Yuan over policy. Sun later headed a southern regime at Canton. Under the influence of the communist doctrines of Mikhail Borodin, he opposed General Tsao Kun (1924) and gained more influence in the north. He died of cancer. A large mausoleum was built in his honor at Nanking.

superfluous man. A term used to describe a specific type of protagonist in 19th-century Russian literature. Such a man is exemplified by Pushkin's Eugene Onegin, Lermontov's Pechorin, Goncharov's Oblomov, and Turgenev's Rudin. Characteristics of the type were an inability to act decisively in personal or social matters, and a lack of contact or involvement with the life of the society in which he lived. The condition was usually brought about by a combination of the character's private inadequacies or maladjustments and the deadening effect of a restrictive political and social regime. The radical critics of the 19th century proposed replacing the socially useless superfluous man with an exemplary positive hero. This task was finally accomplished by decrees after the Soviet regime was in power.

Superman. See ÜBERMENSCH.

Supervielle, Jules (1884–1960). Uruguay-born French poet, dramatist, fiction writer, who often describes the South American scene. His collections of poetry are: *Débarcadères* (1922), *Poèmes de la France malheureuse* (1941), and *The Shell and the Ear* (1951). *The Colonel's Children* (*Le Voleur d'enfants;* 1926), *Bolivar* (1936), and *Robinson* (1948) are plays. *The Survivor* (1928) and *Along the Road to Bethlehem* (1933) are both novels.

Suppliants, The. See SUPPLIANT WOMEN, THE.

Suppliant Women, The (Hiketides; c. 490 B.C.). The earliest surviving play by AESCHYLUS, and the first play of a trilogy. It concerns the flight of Danaus and his 50 daughters from Aegyptus, his brother, who has usurped the throne of Egypt. They plead for protection from the people of Argos, where their ancestress Io was born. King Pelasgus grants their request and defies the herald of Aegyptus, who arrives with his 50 sons to demand that the maidens marry them. The play is the first of a trilogy that told the myth of the murder on their wedding night of all but one of the young men by their Danaid brides. The other two plays are lost.

Suppliant Women, The (Hiketides; 421 B.C.). A drama by EURIPIDES recounting the successful plea of the mothers of the SEVEN AGAINST THEBES that Theseus, king of Athens, bury the bodies of their sons.

Supplices. See SUPPLIANT WOMEN, THE.

Suprematism. See Casimir MALEVITCH.

Sura. In Arabic, any one ethical revelation; thus each chapter of the Koran is a Sura.

surrealism. A literary, artistic, and philosophical movement, founded in 1924. Surrealism sought a reality above or within the surface reality, usually through efforts to suspend the discipline of conscious and logical reason, esthetics, or morality in order to allow the expression of subconscious thought and feeling.

Ever since symbolism there had been a growing interest in the irrational and in the technique of producing impressions through the startling juxtaposition of images. LAUTRÉAMONT, RIMBAUD, MALLARMÉ, and JARRY were considered the leading precursors of surrealism, and Guillaume APOLLINAIRE seems to have coined the name. World War I heightened the sense of protest against a purely scientific and materialistic world view, and strengthened the conviction that the intellect alone could not achieve complete understanding of life. After first voicing their despair through the DADA movement, the surrealist group announced themselves with André Breton's *Manifeste du surréalisme: Poisson soluble* (1924). Based on FREUD's theory of the unconscious, it claimed that through "automatic" writing and painting the subconscious

would dictate images and symbols in combinations which, however unexpected and incongruous to the conscious mind, which would actually reveal the true nature and content of the human soul. A second manifesto (1930) stressed the importance of investigation of dreams and psychic states.

Breton, with Louis ARAGON, René Crevel, Robert DESNOS, Paul ELUARD, Philippe SOUPAULT, and others, converted (1924) the Dada review *Littérature* to *La Révolution surréaliste*. In 1930 the title was changed to *Surréalisme au service de la révolution* (until 1933) in an attempt to claim that the movement was the representative of Communism in the arts. However, Communist leaders disavowed surrealism so that, forced to choose between them, Aragon officially left for Communism in 1932, Eluard in 1938.

In England Herbert READ tried to introduce "superrealism" as a manifestation of the principle of romanticism, but the original name survived; David Gascoyne and Hugh Sykes Davies were English surrealists. Giorgio di CHIRICO and Salvador DALI became the leading surrealist painters; others include Yves TANGUY and Max ERNST.

Few other writers and artists produced primarily surrealistic works, but many either were actively associated with the movement briefly or were greatly influenced by it: in painting, Paul Klee, Joan Miró, Pablo Picasso, and Pavel Tchelitchew; in literature, Jean Cocteau, St.-John Perse (France); Dylan Thomas (England); E. E. Cummings, Henry Miller, Anaïs Nin, William Carlos Williams (U.S.); and García Lorca (Spain).

Surrey, Henry Howard, earl of (1517?–1547). English poet and courtier attached to the court of Henry VIII. Surrey won various distinctions, particularly during the years (1540–1542) that his cousin, Catherine Howard, was married to the king. After her execution, however, his enmity with the Seymours finally led to his arrest on a trumped-up charge of treason. He was executed early in 1547. With Sir Thomas WYATT, Surrey helped introduce new Italian and French verse forms into English. His blank verse translations of Books II and IV of Vergil's *Aeneid* represent the first use of unrhymed iambic pentameter in English, and he is responsible for what is now known as the "Shakespearean" form of the sonnet. Forty of his poems were published in TOTTEL'S MISCELLANY (1557). His metrical smoothness and elegance led critics, until recent times, to regard him as superior to Wyatt, but many 20th-century critics favor Wyatt's poetry for its greater intensity of feeling.

Sursis, Le. See ROADS TO FREEDOM, THE.

Surtees, Robert Smith (1803–1864). English novelist and sports writer. He wrote the humorous fox-hunting sketches *Jorrocks' Jaunts and Jollities* (1838), which suggested the original plan of Dickens' *Pickwick Papers,* and other works of light fiction dealing mainly with the hunt. These include *Handley Cross* (1843), *Hillingdon Hall* (1845), and *Mr. Sponge's Sporting Tour* (1853). Although of minor literary value, his books preserve the spirit of the old English sporting life. See JORROCKS.

survival of the fittest. A concept of the Darwinian theory of evolution (see ORIGIN OF SPECIES). This principle maintains that the biological species best adapted to its environment will be the one to survive and perpetuate in its offspring. A popular misconception of this idea was that the species surviving was the one able to overcome its rivals in a literal, tooth-and-nail struggle. The phrase itself is said to have been coined by Herbert Spencer in a study on Darwinian natural selection.

Surya. In Hindu mythology, the god of the sun. In the older legends he presides over the gods of the sky, sharing the government of nature with Agni, lord of the gods of the earth, and Indra, lord of the gods of the air. The famous Sun Temple of Konarak, also known as the Black Pagoda, was constructed in the ninth century in eastern India to glorify Surya; its erotic friezes symbolize the multitudinous fertility of the sun, source of all energy.

Susanna and the Elders. A favorite subject among Renaissance and later artists. The *Story of Susanna,* one of the books of the Old Testament Apocrypha, tells how Susanna was accused of adultery by certain Jewish elders who had unsuccessfully attempted her chastity, how her innocence was proved by Daniel, and the Elders put to death.

Sutpen. A family in William Faulkner's ABSALOM, ABSALOM! Thomas Sutpen is the head of the family. Descended from poor whites, Sutpen acquires land in Mississippi from the Indians in 1833, and later marries Ellen Coldfield, daughter of a Jefferson merchant, in order to establish his respectability. Two children, Henry and Judith, are born of the marriage. Henry becomes a close friend of Charles Bon but kills him when he discovers that Bon, who wants to marry Judith, is their half brother and part Negro, the son of Thomas Sutpen and Eulalia Bon, who has Negro blood. After Bon's death, Judith brings up his son, Charles Etienne St.-Valery Bon.

Other characters connected with the Sutpen story are Rosa COLDFIELD, Ellen's sister, who is at one point engaged to Thomas Sutpen; Clytic (Clytemnestra) Sutpen, the daughter of Thomas and a Negro slave; Jim Bond, the idiot son of Charles E. St.-Valery and the last descendant of Thomas; and Wash Jones, who murders Thomas after the latter rejects the illegitimate child borne to him by Jones's granddaughter.

sutras. Ancient Hindu aphoristic manuals probably developed from 500 to 200 B.C. They give the rules of systems of philosophy, grammar, and other disciplines, and contain directions concerning religious ritual and ceremonial customs. They form a link between the Vedic and later Sanskrit literature and are so called from the Sanskrit *sutra* (thread), the aphorisms being, as it were, threaded together themselves and threading together other things.

In Buddhism *sutras* refer to the preachings of the historical Buddha. There are, however, hundreds of *sutras* composed after his death and many apocryphal ones composed in China. As the sayings of the Buddha they are venerated and are the most important sections of the TRIPITAKA.

Sutro, Alfred (1863–1933). British playwright and translator of Maeterlinck. His best play was *The Walls of Jericho* (1904).

suttee (Sans. *sati,* a virtuous wife). The Hindu custom of burning the widow on the funeral pyre of her deceased husband; also, the widow so put to death. In theory the practice was optional, but public opinion and the very severe form of ostracism

the defaulting widow had to endure left her practically no choice. The practice was declared illegal in British India in 1829.

Su Tung-p'o or **Su Shih** (1036–1101). Chinese poet of the Sung dynasty, noted also for his prose and painting. See Lin Yutang, *The Gay Genius* (1947).

Svengali. A Hungarian musician in George du Maurier's novel TRILBY. He controls Trilby's stage singing through his hypnotic power. Hence, a Svengali is one who can exercise a sinister, mesmeric influence over another.

Sveno. In Torquato Tasso's GERUSALEMME LIBERATA, the young Danish prince who is killed by Solimano, the Arab chieftain, before he can bring his forces to relieve the Crusaders assaulting Jerusalem. His sword and the avenging of his death are entrusted to Rinaldo of Este, his friend. The sole survivor of the massacre, Guelfo, tells the story to Goffredo and the other Crusaders.

Svevo, Italo. Pen name of **Ettore Schmitz** (1861–1928). Italian novelist. His best-known work is the psychological novel *La Coscienza di Zeno* (*The Confessions of Zeno,* 1923). Presented as a statement of self-analysis prepared by Zeno for a psychiatrist, it is an introspective study of the perpetual contradiction between his inner and outer desires. Svevo also wrote the novels *Una Vita* (*A Life,* 1892) and *Senilità* (1898). His technique has been compared to that of Joyce and Proust.

Svidrigailov. A sinister profligate in Feodor Dostoevski's CRIME AND PUNISHMENT. He admits to having violated young girls and to have caused the death of one of them. His final attempted seduction is of Raskolnikov's sister, Darya, whom he has followed to Petersburg after having tormented her when she was employed in his household. Svidrigailov shows no remorse for his acts, until one night, after saying he is going off to America, he shoots himself.

Swanhild. An old Norse legendary heroine, the daughter of Sigurd and Gudrun. She is falsely accused of adultery with the son of the king who is wooing her, and the king has his son hanged. She is sentenced to die by being trampled to death by wild horses, but is so beautiful that she must be blanketed before the horses will perform their task.

Swann, Charles. A neighbor and friend of the narrator's family in Marcel Proust's REMEMBRANCE OF THINGS PAST. Swann, who is partly Jewish, has an affair with ODETTE DE CRÉCY, whom he later marries, and is the father of GILBERTE. Himself a member of high society, he grieves that Odette is not similarly accepted.

Swann's Way. See REMEMBRANCE OF THINGS PAST.

swan song. The song fabled to be sung by swans at the point of death; hence, the last work of a poet, composer, or other creator. The fable that the swan sings beautifully just before it dies is very ancient, though baseless.

Swedenborg, Emanuel (1688–1772). Swedish theologian, scientist, and philosopher. During the first half of his career, he devoted himself to scientific research, and spent several years studying in Europe and in England. In 1716, Swedenborg published Sweden's first scientific journal, *Daedalus Hyper-*

boreus, and was appointed to the Royal Board of Mines. During his 25 years as an active member of this board, he published scientific books and articles in almost every field: mathematics, geology, anatomy, physiology, chemistry, and physics. The most important works of this period were *Opera Philosophica et Mineralia* (1734), *Oeconomia regni animalis* (1740), and *Regnum animale* (1744–1745). Between the years 1743 and 1745, Swedenborg experienced a spiritual crisis. Turning away from his former interests, he spent the last 25 years of his life in biblical study and the writing of religious philosophy. His most significant theological works are *Arcana Coelestia* (8 vols., 1749–1756), *Doctrina vitae pro Nova Hierosolyma* (*Divine Love and Wisdom,* 1763), and *Vera christiana religio* (*The True Christian Religion,* 1771). After his death his followers formed the New Church or New Jerusalem Church. Swedenborg's accounts of his mystical visions have influenced a number of writers, among them the English poet William Blake.

Swedish nightingale. A popular epithet for Jenny LIND, the Swedish singer.

Sweeney. A figure in several poems by T. S. ELIOT. He is symbolic of the sensual, brutal, and materialistic man of the 20th century. In *Sweeney Erect* and *Sweeney among the Nightingales,* rhyming, semicomic poems, he is set against the dignity and beauty of the classical past. *Sweeney Agonistes, Fragments of an Aristophanic Melodrama* (1932), is part of a play, striking in its use of music-hall rhythms and slang speech.

Sweet, Henry (1845–1912). An English philologist, regarded as the founder of modern phonetics.

Sweet Adeline. A well-known sentimental song. It was written in 1896 (publ. 1903) by Richard Gerard and Harry Armstrong. It was sung in colleges throughout the U.S., often in "barbershop quartets," especially by men in their cups.

Sweet Cheat Gone, The. See REMEMBRANCE OF THINGS PAST.

Swift, Jonathan (1667–1745). English satirist, poet, political writer, and clergyman. Born in Dublin of English parents, Swift received his education in Ireland. In 1689 he went to England and became secretary to Sir William TEMPLE, now retired at Moor Park from his distinguished political career. It was here that Swift met Esther JOHNSON; it was also here that he learned a great deal about politics and wrote his first important prose: THE TALE OF A TUB, a Rabelaisian and allegorical satire on the divisions in the Christian religion, and THE BATTLE OF THE BOOKS. Swift was the major political writer for the moderate Tories in their brief reign (1710–1714) under Robert Harley, producing the *Examiner* (1710), a newspaper in the Tory interest, and *The Conduct of the Allies* (1711), a masterly pamphlet of his party's plan for peace in the war of the Spanish Succession. His life during these years is reflected in his JOURNAL TO STELLA, a series of letters written for Esther Johnson. He was appointed dean of St. Patrick's Cathedral in Dublin (1713) by Queen Anne and remained in Ireland, except for brief excursions, for the rest of his life. He returned to politics again in 1724, this time as an Irish patriot in the person of "M. B. Drapier"; DRAPIER'S LETTERS were designed to incite the Irish against a new coinage, and a re-

ward of £300 was soon offered for discovering the author. It was well known that Swift was the author, but proof was needed and never obtained, for, by now, he was greatly loved in Dublin; his birthday thereafter was celebrated by Dubliners with the ringing of bells and bonfires. By this time, Swift had almost finished his masterpiece GULLIVER'S TRAVELS, which contained his bitterest denunciation of mankind. Of his many minor satires, the most celebrated are *An Argument Against Abolishing Christianity* (1708) and A MODEST PROPOSAL, both in prose; and *The Day of Judgment* (1731) and *Verses on the Death of Dr. Johnson* (1739). The 19th-century notion of a demonic, cynical Swift, an exaggeration used to explain the savage indignation of his satire, ignores his playfulness and love of fun, qualities evident throughout his work. Though he called himself a misanthrope, he always wrote for the betterment of mankind. He valued reason as a human attribute and became bitter at its abuse. A master impersonator, Swift often became the person in which he wrote: now he is "Isaac BICKERSTAFF," a clairvoyant astrologer; now the urbane "CADENUS," now the playful "PRESTO;" now "M. B. Drapier;" now "Lemuel Gulliver." The "true Swift" is still, and perhaps always will be, uncertain. See SCRIBLERUS CLUB.

Swift, Tom. A boy-inventor, hero of a long series of novels for boys. Tom's hair-raising adventures with all kinds of contrivances, some of which anticipated actual inventions, became widely popular and brought considerable wealth to his creator, Edward L. Stratemeyer (1862–1930), who also originated the ROVER BOYS series.

Swinburne, Algernon Charles (1837–1909). English poet and man of letters. He is known for his rebellion against Victorian social conventions and religion, his active sympathies with the movements and leaders of political revolution of his time, and the pagan spirit and musical effects of his poetry. He was an intense admirer of Shelley and Victor Hugo, and was influenced in his own work by Greek legend and Roman classic literature, medieval romance, and Elizabethan drama.

In his early career, Swinburne's behavior was eccentric, violent, and dissipated, calculated to shock the respectable people of his time. As alcoholism was rapidly undermining his health, he was taken into the home of Theodore WATTS-DUNTON in 1879 and stayed there for the rest of his life.

Swinburne's first published volume, *The Queen Mother. Rosamund. Two Plays* (1860) attracted no attention. With the publication of ATALANTA IN CALYDON, a drama in classical Greek form, he won fame. In the same year he published CHASTELARD, the first of three dramas on Mary Queen of Scots. This was followed closely by *Poems and Ballads: First Series* (1866), lyrics dealing chiefly with sensual love, which caused a scandal and was severely censured by some. *A Song of Italy* (1867) and *Songs before Sunrise* (1871) deal with the cause of Italian union and independence. The second drama of the Mary Queen of Scots trilogy was *Bothwell: A Tragedy* (1874) and *Poems and Ballads: Second Series* was published in 1878. *Mary Stuart,* the last of the trilogy, appeared in 1881, and *Tristram of Lyonesse,* an Arthurian poem in rhymed couplets, considered by some his finest work, in 1882. In *Marino Faliero* (1885) Swinburne reworks a theme previously treated by Byron. His last volumes of poems are *Astrophel* (1894), *A Tale of Balen* (1896), and *A Channel Passage* (1904). *The Duke of Gandia* (1908), a tragedy, is his last work. His prose works include *Essays and Studies* (1875), *Miscellanies* (1886), and astute critical writings on many modern writers including Blake, the Brontës, and Dickens. His later work is not considered to be as fine as the earlier. Among his best-known single poems are *Hymn to Artemis, Hymn to Proserpine, Hertha, Laus Veneris*, and *The Triumph of Time*. He wrote two novels dealing with the complexities of love, *Love's Cross Currents* (1905) and *Lesbia Brandon*, posthumously published (1952). See FLESHLY SCHOOL of POETRY.

Swinnerton, Frank (1884–   ). English novelist and critic; a prolific, professional, witty writer. He achieved fame with *Nocturne* (1917), a naturalistic novel about dull London people. Among his later novels are *The Cats and Rosemary* (1948), *Faithful Company* (1948), and *Death of a Highbrow* (1962).

Swiss Family Robinson, The, or Adventures in a Desert Island. A story for young people by J. R. Wyss (1813). It relates the adventures of a Swiss clergyman, his wife, and four sons, who are wrecked on a desert island.

Swithin or **Swithun, St.** (d. 862?). English ecclesiastic and bishop of Winchester. According to legend, he was buried, at his own wish, in the open air of the churchyard, so that the rain might fall from heaven upon his grave. After the new cathedral was built, the monks decided to honor him by removing his body into the church, but, as it rained day after day for 40 days thereafter, they finally assumed that the saint objected to their plan and abandoned it. Since then, tradition says that if it rains on St. Swithin's day (July 15), there will be rain for 40 days thereafter.

Swiveller, Mr. Dick. In Charles Dickens' OLD CURIOSITY SHOP, a dirty, smart young man, living in apartments near Drury Lane. His language is extremely flowery and interlarded with quotations. He is forever humming some dismal air. Mr. Swiveller is a clerk to Sampson BRASS; he is later turned away and falls sick of a fever through which he is nursed by the Marchioness, whom he marries.

Swope, Herbert Bayard (1882–1958). American newspaperman. He was awarded the first Pulitzer Prize in journalism for his dispatches to the New York *World* as a war correspondent with the German armies (1914–1916). He was executive director of the paper through its most brilliant era (1920–1929).

sword. A long-bladed weapon used for cutting or stabbing. The sword was the chief weapon of the romances. In the days of chivalry, a knight's horse and sword were his most treasured and carefully kept possessions, and his sword as well as his horse had its own name. The old romances, especially those of the Charlemagne and Arthurian cycles, are full of these names, among the more noteworthy of which are

Angurvadal (Stream of Anguish), Frithiof's sword.
Ar'ondight, the sword of Launcelot of the Lake.

Balmung, one of the swords of Siegfried, made by Wieland.
Colada, the Cid's sword.
Courtain (the Short Sword), one of the swords of Ogier the Dane; *Sauvagine* was the other, and each took Munifican three years to make.
Curtana, the blunted sword of Edward the Confessor.
Durandan, Durandal, or *Durandana* (the Inflexible), Orlando's sword.
Excalibur, the sword of King Arthur. (Lat., *ex cal*[ce] *liber*[are], "to liberate from the stone.")
Flamberge or *Floberge* (the Flame-Cutter), the name of one of Charlemagne's swords, and also that of Rinaldo and Maugis or Malagigi.
Glorius, Oliver's sword, which hacked to pieces the nine swords made by Ansias, Galas, and Munifican.
Gram (Grief), one of the swords of Siegfried.
Joyeuse (Joyous), one of Charlemagne's swords; it took Gallas three years to make.
Mimung, the sword that Wittich lent Siegfried.
Morglay (Big Glaive), Sir Bevis's sword.
Nagelring (Nail-Ring), Dietrich's sword.
Philippan, the sword of Antony, one of the triumvirs.

Sword Blades and Poppy Seed (1914). A collection of poems by Amy LOWELL. The second book of poetry that she published, it was especially important in its use of free verse and in containing the first English examples of polyphonic prose—rhythmical prose characterized by all the devices of verse except strict meter.

sword of Damocles. See DAMOCLES' SWORD.

Sybarite. An inhabitant of Sybaris, in South Italy, proverbial for its luxurious living and self-indulgence. The Sybarites piped their chief product, wine, down to the sea, so that they would not have to transport it. A tale is told by Seneca of a Sybarite who complained that he could not rest comfortably at night, and, being asked why, replied that he found a rose leaf doubled under him, and it hurt him. Sybaris was destroyed as a significant power in a war with nearby Crotona. Fable has it that the Sybarites taught their horses to dance to a pipe. When the Crotonians marched against Sybaris, they played on their pipes, whereupon all the Sybarite horses began to dance, disorder soon prevailed in the ranks, and the victory was quick and easy.

Sybil, or the Two Nations (1845). A novel by Benjamin DISRAELI. The two nations are the rich and the poor working class in England during the 1840's. The novel deals with the Chartist movement and the distressed condition of the laboring class during this period.

Sycorax. The evil witch who originally inhabited the island of Prospero in Shakespeare's THE TEMPEST. She imprisoned Ariel in a pine rift and left to posterity her son, the subhuman Caliban. When Prospero reaches the island, she is already dead.

sylphs. Elemental spirits of air. They are so named in the Middle Ages by Paracelsus and others, possibly from the Greek *silphe*, a kind of beetle, or a grub that turns into a butterfly. Any mortal who has preserved inviolate chastity may enjoy intimate familiarity with these gentle spirits, and deceased virgins were said to become sylphs, "and sport and flutter in the fields of air." Sylphs play an important part in Pope's *Rape of the Lock*.

Sylvander. In Robert BURNS's correspondence with Mrs. McLehose, the name taken by Burns, while Mrs. McLehose was called Clarinda. The correspondence was published in 1802, later withdrawn, and republished in 1845.

Sylvester, Joshua (1563–1618). English poet. He is best known for his translation of *La Semaine* by Guillaume du Bartas, which appeared in English as *Divine Weeks and Workes* (1605).

symbolists (Fr., *symbolistes*). A group of French poets who were active during the last 30 years of the 19th-century. Although the work of each writer was unique, and neither the aims nor the techniques of the movement were at all rigid, the poets did share certain basic convictions and used similar poetic methods. Symbolism in France began as a revolt against the cold impersonality of the realistic novel, and its minute descriptions of an objective, external reality. The rebel poets turned inward, in order to explore and express the shifting, subtle states of the human psyche. They believed that poetry should evoke and suggest, raising itself above the level of objective description only; hence, they sought poetic techniques that would make possible the re-creation of human consciousness. The symbol and the metaphor enabled them to suggest mysterious and inexpressible subjective emotion. Often the symbols were highly personal, and their use resulted in obscure, esoteric verse. At its finest, however, symbolist poetry achieved a richness of meaning, and created an awareness of the mystery at the heart of human existence.

As symbolism sought freedom from rigidity in the selection of subject matter, so it desired to free poetry from the restrictions of conventional versification. The art that seemed most to resemble poetry was, not that of the sculptured precision of plastic forms, but music; fluid melody and delicate lyricism characterized symbolist poetry. Poe, Baudelaire, and Wagner were admired by the symbolists; Rimbaud, Verlaine, and Mallarmé are generally considered the leaders of the school. Other members included Gustave Kahn, Henri de Régnier, Jules Laforgue, E. J. Corbière, Francis Vielé-Griffin, Jean Moréas, Maurice Maeterlinck, Marcel Schwob, Lautréamont, and Villiers de L'isle-Adam. Among the numerous symbolist reviews were *Vogue* (1886–1889), *Revue indépendante* (1886–1895), *Ermitage* (1890–1906), and *Revue Blanc* (1891–1903).

Symbolism, as a literary movement, was predominant in Russia from about 1896 to 1910. Its characteristics were an interest in mysticism and exotic lore, an intense concern with the aesthetic aspects of art, and an impressionistic poetic style. The main sources and influences on the group were the French symbolists, the Russian poets TYUTCHEV and FET, and the philosophical ideas of Vladimir SOLOVIOV. The earlier symbolists included Valeri Bryusov, Konstantin Balmont, Dmitri Merezhkovski, Feodor Sologub, and Zinaida Hippius. Best known among the younger generation were Vyacheslav Ivanov, Andrei Bely, and Aleksandr Blok, the greatest poet to emerge from the movement.

Symbolism did much to add new life to Russian poetry, which had fallen into decline during the last part of the 19th century because of the preponderance of great prose writers. The great amount of fine work produced by the symbolist poets earned the symbolist period—the most fruitful period since the time of Pushkin—the name of "the second golden age" (or "the silver age") of Russian poetry.

During the 20th century the use of symbolism became a major force in British literature. Symbolist poetry was introduced and popularized by Arthur SYMONS. George MOORE and the members of the RHYMERS' CLUB imitated it; W. B. YEATS was influenced by it in his early career and based his mature style on it; T. S. ELIOT adapted it in the development of his individual style and praised it in his criticism, influencing the critical tenets of the CAMBRIDGE CRITICS and the NEW CRITICS. But the most outstanding development of symbolism was in the art of the novel. The great 20th-century British novelists, James JOYCE especially, but also Joseph CONRAD, D. H. LAWRENCE, E. M. FORSTER, and Virginia WOOLF, wrote novels in which much of the meaning is conveyed through patterns of images and ideas and central suggestive symbols rather than through the traditional method of narrative and overt discourse.

Symonds, John Addington (1840–1893). English historian, scholar, and translator. He is best known for his *History of the Renaissance in Italy* (1875–1886), a study, often consisting of a series of impressionistic essays on separate subjects under the main heading, of the politics, culture, art, and literature of Italy in the 15th and 16th centuries. He also translated the *Autobiography of Benvenuto Cellini* (1888) and did other translations, notably of the Greek poets and the Italian Renaissance poets. In addition, he wrote verse and literary criticism.

Symons, A[lphonse] J[ames] A[lbert] (1900–1941). English biographer, bibliophile, and dandy. He is best known as author of *The Quest for Corvo* (1934), a life of Frederick ROLFE, Baron Corvo. His younger brother is Julian Symons, a writer.

Symons, Arthur (1865–1945). English critic and poet. His most important work was *The Symbolist Movement in Literature* (1899), which introduced English readers to the work of the French symbolist poets (see SYMBOLISM); it particularly influenced William Butler Yeats. Symons wrote poetry in the manner of the DECADENTS and displayed in himself the neurasthenic characteristics of that group. He described his irregular life and his spells of amnesia and madness in his *Confessions: A Study in Pathology* (1930).

Symphonie pastorale, La. See PASTORAL SYMPHONY, THE.

Symplegades. The "clashing rocks." They guarded the entrance to the Black Sea and crushed ships between them by moving quickly together. When the ARGONAUTS passed through them safely, by the advice of Phineus and the help of Hera, the rocks became fixed to the sea bottom and were harmless thereafter.

Symposium (Symposion; Banquet). A dialogue by PLATO. Each guest at the banquet speaks in honor of love, mainly between males. Phaedrus treats love mythically, Pausanias sophistically, Agathon poetically, and ARISTOPHANES comically. SOCRATES says that the priestess Diotima has taught him that love may take an intellectual form, creating the desire to produce things of beauty; poets and legislators experience this sort of love. The dialogue ends with the speech of ALCIBIADES, praising Socrates.

synecdoche. In rhetoric, the figure of speech giving the part instead of the whole for the sake of vividness of effect, as in "fifty head" for "fifty cattle," "nine bats" instead of "nine baseball players," etc.

synesthesia. A medical (or psychological) term describing the occurrence when, stimulating one sense organ another responds. It is as though nerve paths to the brain had become crossed like telephone wires. It is as though in eating one were to receive strong visual sensations of color rather than or along with sensations of taste. As a literary device, synesthesia has been used in certain types of poetry of the 19th and 20th centuries, especially that of the symbolists and their forerunners and disciples, to present imagery with extra vividness and to express intense and unusual experience. Poe, Rimbaud, and Hart Crane used synesthesia in their poetry, and Rimbaud's *Sonnet of the Vowels,* expressing the sounds of the common vowels in terms of colors, is an excellent example of the use of this device.

Synge, John Millington (1871–1909). Irish dramatist. Synge's tragically brief career established him as the foremost dramatist of the IRISH RENAISSANCE. He began his career by settling in France, where he spent his time translating the poetry of Mallarmé and other French symbolists. Here he met William Butler YEATS who persuaded him to return to the Irish countryside, where the peasants' speech still exhibited vigorous, exuberant, poetic qualities unmatched elsewhere in the world. Synge followed Yeats's advice with the result that he claimed his plays amounted to literal transcriptions of the language of western Ireland's peasants. His plays include *In the Shadow of the Glen* (1903); *Riders to the Sea* (1904), a one-act tragedy which achieves an almost Aeschylean starkness and grandeur; *The Well of the Saints* (1905); PLAYBOY OF THE WESTERN WORLD, generally regarded as his masterpiece; *The Tinker's Wedding* (1907); and the nearly completed *Deirdre of the Sorrows* (1910), one of the most distinguished recreations of Irish myth of the Celtic revival.

synoptic gospels. The first 3 books of the New Testament: the gospels according to Matthew, Mark, and Luke. They are so called from the Greek word *synoptikos* meaning a general view. These three accounts of Jesus' life have a similarity in matter, language, and order. Mark is thought to be the oldest; both Luke and Matthew use Mark as a source. A lost book containing the sayings of Jesus was also used by the authors of Matthew and Luke. This lost book, called *Q* from the German word *Quelle* (source), was one of the earliest Christian documents. Since it was probably only an anthology of Jesus' wisdom, Bible scholars have postulated that Mark was written to accompany *Q,* and supply biographical material.

The *synoptic problem* concerns the relation of these three gospels arising from their common features.

Syntipas, Tales of. See SEVEN WISE MASTERS, THE.

Syrinx. An Arcadian nymph of Greek legend. On being pursued by PAN she took refuge in the river Ladon, and prayed to be changed into a reed. The prayer was granted, and of the reed Pan made his pipes. Hence the name is given to the Pan pipe, or reed mouth organ, and also to the vocal organ of birds.

T

Tabernacles, Feast of. A Jewish festival. It lasts eight days, beginning on the 15th of Tishri (toward the end of September). It is kept in remembrance of the sojourn in the wilderness.

taboo. A custom among the South Sea Islanders that prohibits the use of certain persons, places, animals, things, or the utterance of certain names and words. It signifies that which is banned, interdicted or devoted in a religious sense. Thus, a temple is taboo and so is he who violates a temple. Not only so, but everyone and everything connected with what is taboo becomes taboo also. Captain Cook was taboo because some of his sailors took rails from a Hawaiian temple to supply themselves with fuel, and, being "devoted," he was slain.

With us, a person who is ostracized, or an action, custom, etc., that is altogether forbidden by society is said to be taboo or tabooed.

tabula rasa (*Lat.,* "a scraped tablet"). A clean slate—literally and figuratively—on which anything can be written. Thus we say that the mind of a person who has been badly taught must become a *tabula rasa* before he can learn anything properly.

Tacitus, Cornelius (A.D. 55?–?117). Roman historian. His most ambitious works were the *Historiae,* a history of his own times, from A.D. 69 to 96, and the *Annales,* a detailed account of events from the death of Augustus to the year 69. These two historical works were originally published in 30 books, only 11 of which have been preserved in complete form while 4 have survived in fragments. Tacitus is also famous for his *Germania,* a careful study of the manners and mores of the peoples of Germany. As a reporter and historian, he always sought to be scrupulously impartial, and, not content with a simple narration of events, he searched constantly for causes. His style, especially in his later work, is colored now and then with poetic diction, but is at the same time tightly organized, precise, and epigrammatic.

Tadzio. See DEATH IN VENICE.

Taft, Robert A[lphonso] (1889–1953). American statesman. The son of President William Howard Taft, he served as U.S. Senator from Ohio from 1939 until his death, becoming known as "Mr. Republican." In 1940, 1948, and 1952, he was an unsuccessful candidate for his party's presidential nomination. Taft's calm courage in the face of a painful death from cancer led to the writing of John and June Robbins' *Eight Weeks to Live* (1954). Taft was the author of *A Foreign Policy for Americans* (1951).

Taft, William Howard (1857–1930). 27th president of the U.S. (1909–1913). After graduating from Yale University and Cincinnati Law College, Taft held several posts in the Ohio and federal judiciary.

As the first civil governor of the Philippines (1901–1904), he introduced various reforms and established limited self-rule. He served as secretary of war (1904–1908) under Theodore Roosevelt and was the latter's choice to succeed him in the presidency. During his term in office, Taft continued his predecessor's policies and strongly enforced the antitrust laws, but he later broke with Republican progressives and with Roosevelt himself. In 1912 he ran unsuccessfully for a second term against Woodrow Wilson and Roosevelt, who had founded the Bull Moose Party after failing to receive the Republican nomination. In 1913 Taft became professor of constitutional law at Yale and served until 1921 when he was named chief justice of the Supreme Court.

Tages. In Etruscan mythology, a mysterious boy with the wisdom of an old man who was plowed up, or who sprang from, the ground at Tarquinii. He is said to have been the grandson of Jupiter and to have instructed the Etruscans in the arts of augury. The latter wrote down his teaching in 12 books, which were known as "the books of Tages," or "the Acherontian books."

Taggard, Genevieve (1894–1948). American poet. A writer and interpreter of poetry, she founded and edited *The Measure, a Journal of Verse* (1920–1926), and taught English at Mount Holyoke and Sarah Lawrence colleges. Among the numerous volumes of her collected verse are *For Eager Lovers* (1922), *Hawaiian Hilltop* (1923), *Not Mine to Finish* (1934), and *Slow Music* (1946). She also wrote *The Life and Mind of Emily Dickinson* (1930) and edited several anthologies.

Tagore, Rabindranath. Also written **Ravindranath Thakura** (1861–1941). Indian poet, novelist, story writer, and essayist in Bengali, awarded the Nobel prize for literature in 1913. He is known in his country for his lyrics and songs on nature, love, and childhood, and for his *Ravindrasangeet,* or poems set to music. In the West he is generally considered a poet of mysticism and religious feeling, and for three decades after the Nobel prize Tagore coteries and cults tended to misinterpret much of the fine poetry as Oriental mysticism. His early work strongly impressed Ezra Pound, who found in it a "new Greece," and W. B. Yeats, who did the introduction to *Gitanjali* (1912). Since then Tagore's influence in the West has steadily declined though in his homeland it is a massive literary phenomenon. He was also an educationist, founder of the "world university," Santiniketan, 100 miles from Calcutta. In his "dance dramas" (such as *Valmiki Prativa*) he employed opera for the purposes of the Bengali stage; in his last years he emerged as a symbolist painter of startling vividness and richness. He was knighted in 1915, but in 1919 resigned the honor in protest against the British repressive measures in Jallianwala Bagh in the Punjab. English translations of his work include: *The Crescent Moon* (1913), *One Hundred Poems of Kabir* (1914), *Chitra* (1916), a play; *The Gardener* (1917), *Lectures on Personality* (1917), *Red Oleanders* (1925), *Fireflies* (1928), *The Religion of Man* (1931), on his ideas of God; *Broken Ties, and Other Stories* (1925), *The Child* (1931), *The Golden Boat* (1932), *Collected Poems and Plays* (1936), *Farewell My Friend* (1940).

Ta-hsüeh. See GREAT LEARNING, THE.

Taillefer (d. 1066). Norman minstrel. According to WACE he rode with William the Conqueror's invading army, singing of the deeds of Charlemagne and Roland, and died at the battle of Hastings. It is uncertain whether he actually knew the *Chanson de Roland* or simply another version of the legend.

Taine, Hippolyte [Adolphe] (1828–1893). French philosopher, literary critic, and historian. Taine was influenced by Hegel, the positivism of COMTE, and the English Utilitarians. He is known for his emphasis on the role of scientific determinism in literature and history, particularly as exemplified in hereditary and environmental influences. One of Taine's most famous doctrines is that of the *faculté maîtresse,* or dominant trait, from which the critic hoped to deduce an author's career geometrically. His other significant theory is that of *race, milieu, et moment,* which linked Taine with the naturalistic school. Essentially this is the proposition that a literary or historical figure might be fully understood by considering the three forces that composed his biological inheritance: environment, the configuration of tradition, and the dominant trends at the time of his appearance. Among Taine's works are *La Philosophie de l'Art* (1865–1869), *Histoire de la Littérature Anglaise* (1864), *Nouveaux Essais* (1865), *Origines de la France contemporaine* (1875–1894) and *De l'intelligence* (1870).

T'ai-p'ing. Chinese rebellion (1850–1864).

Taishō. Japanese period (1912–1926). The name given to the reign of Emperor Yoshihito (1879–1926).

Taj Mahal. A mausoleum built by Shah Jahan for his favorite wife. Located outside Agra, India, it was begun in c. 1630 and completed in c. 1648. It is built of white marble and richly decorated with mosaics of semiprecious stones. With its reflecting pool and gardens it is considered one of the most beautiful buildings in the world.

Talavera, arcipreste of. See Alfonso MARTÍNEZ DE TOLEDO.

Tale of a Tub, The (1704). An allegorical satire by Jonathan SWIFT, written in 1696–1698. A ridicule of religious extremists, it is the tale of three brothers: Peter (the Roman Catholic Church), Jack (English dissenters or extreme Protestants), and Martin (the Lutheran or Anglican Church). The title comes from the nautical practice of throwing empty wooden tubs into the sea to divert whales who threaten a vessel. The tale is interspersed with ironic digressions, best known of which is the *Digression on Madness* revealing that the author himself, who impersonates a Grub Street hack writer, is an inmate of Bedlam. Along with *Tale of a Tub* were published two separate pieces, THE BATTLE OF THE BOOKS and *Discourse concerning the Mechanical Operation of the Spirit.* All

three are thematically related. The book gave Thomas Carlyle, in the next century, the idea for *Sartor Resartus.*

Tale of Genji, The (Genji monogatari). A Japanese novel of the Heian period by MURASAKI SHIKIBU. This vast chronicle of court life centers on the career of Prince Genji and the women with whom he was associated. Its style is highly ornate and the work is rich in poetry and elaborate word play. Reflecting pure Japanese traditions, it has had a tremendous influence on subsequent literature and art and is regarded unreservedly as the greatest single work in Japanese literature. It was translated by Arthur WALEY (1925–1933).

Tale of King Arthur, The. See MORTE D'ARTHUR, LE.

Tale of the Sangreal, The. See MORTE D'ARTHUR, LE.

Tale of Two Cities, A (1859). A novel by Charles DICKENS. The two cities are London and Paris; the background is the French Revolution, descriptions of which Dickens obtained from his friend Thomas Carlyle's *French Revolution.*

Dr. Alexander MANETTE, unjustly imprisoned for 18 years in the Bastille because of his knowledge of an attack on a peasant girl by the marquis de St. Evrémonde, is released from prison and waits in an attic above the wine shop of M. and Madame DEFARGE for his rescuers to take him back to England. Reunited with his daughter Lucie, they return to London safely. Years later they are called to Old Bailey to testify that they saw a young man named Charles DARNAY on the boat from France to England. A nephew of St. Evrémonde who has rebelled against his family and emigrated to England, Darnay is now falsely accused of treasonable activities. He is saved by the presence of Sydney CARTON, a dissolute young man, who bears a striking resemblance to Darnay; STRYVER, the defense counsel, points out the resemblance, stating that legal identification is impossible. Darnay and Carton become friends; both are frequent callers on the Manettes and both love Lucie. Darnay marries Lucie and they have a baby. Some time later, he hears from Paris that an old faithful servant has been unjustly imprisoned and hastens to his aid. In the revolution-torn city, Darnay, as a member of a hated aristocratic family, is imprisoned and sentenced to the guillotine. Sydney Carton now appears and intervenes; with bribery, and aided by his resemblance to Darnay, he drugs the latter, spirits him out of prison to safety, and takes his place on the guillotine. This he does out of his great love for Lucie and complete cynicism about himself. Darnay and Lucie are happily reunited in England. See Jerry CRUNCHER.

Tales from Shakespeare. See Charles LAMB.

Tales of a Traveller (1824). A collection of 32 tales and sketches by Washington IRVING. The book is divided into four parts; the first three concern, respectively, the tales of an English gentleman, the adventures of Buckthorne, a young writer, and the doings of some Italian brigands. The last section, *The Money Diggers,* is the best; set in Dutch New York, it gives Irving a chance to exploit folklore and sentiment in his most successful manner. The high point of the section, and of the book, is the story THE DEVIL AND TOM WALKER.

Tales of a Wayside Inn (1863). A collection of narrative poems by Henry Wadsworth LONGFELLOW. The work's structure is modeled on Chaucer's *Canterbury Tales* and Boccaccio's *Decameron*. Each of the tales is narrated by one in a group seated around the fireside of a New England tavern. Many of the stories reflect Longfellow's interest in the Middle Ages. Even when the event related is not ancient, as in the popular *Paul Revere's Ride,* it is presented as though it occurred long, long ago. Some of the more interesting tales include *Elizabeth, The Battle of Carmilhan, Emma and Eginhard,* and *The Saga of King Olaf.*

Tales of Hoffmann (1881). A fantastic opera by Jacques OFFENBACH (1881), based on three tales by the German author E. T. A. HOFFMANN. The successive acts deal with the love affairs and other adventures of the poet Hoffmann, which he recalls over the wine in a Nuremberg tavern.

Tales of My Landlord. The general title for several novels by Sir Walter SCOTT. The tales are supposedly told by the landlord of the Wallace Inn, a Scottish tavern. The novels are arranged thus: Series I, THE BLACK DWARF and OLD MORTALITY; Series II, THE HEART OF MIDLOTHIAN; Series III, THE BRIDE OF LAMMERMOOR and THE LEGEND OF MONTROSE; Series IV, *Count Robert of Paris* (1832) and CASTLE DANGEROUS.

Tales of the Grotesque and Arabesque (1840). A collection of short stories by Edgar Allan POE. His first book of tales, it includes THE FALL OF THE HOUSE OF USHER and BERENICE. In the preface, Poe explains that he based his tales, not on German Gothicism, but on the terror of the soul.

Tales of the Heike, The (**Heike monogatari**). Japanese military chronicle detailing the late 12th-century battles for control of Japan between the Taira (Heike) and Minamoto families. Stemming from oral traditions, the work achieved its present form in the mid-13th century.

Taliesin (fl. 550?). Early medieval Welsh bard. According to many sources, he produced a prodigious amount of fine poetry. He is mentioned in *Idylls of the King* (1859–1872) by Tennyson and is prominent in *The Misfortunes of Elphin* (1829) by Thomas Love Peacock. The architect Frank Lloyd Wright gave the name *Taliesin* to his residences in Wisconsin and Arizona.

talisman (Ar., *tilasman,* from late Gr., *telesma,* mystery). A charm, magical figure, or word, such as the ABRAXAS, which is cut on metal or stone under the influence of certain planets. It is supposed to be sympathetic to these influences, which it communicates to the wearer.

In Arabia, a talisman consisting of a piece of paper on which are written the names of the SEVEN SLEEPERS and their dog is used to protect a house from ghosts and demons. In order to free any place of vermin, a talisman consisting of the figure of the obnoxious animal is made in wax or consecrated metal, in a favorable planetary hour.

Talisman, The (1825). A historical novel by Sir Walter SCOTT, relating the adventures of Sir Kenneth, prince royal of Scotland, as a knight in disguise in the Holy Land under Richard Coeur de Lion. Richard and his noble enemy Saladin are leading characters. The talisman is an amulet of singular healing powers with which Saladin effects the cure of Richard's sickness.

Talleyrand-Périgord, Charles Maurice de (1754–1838). French statesman, commonly known as Talleyrand. He was minister of foreign affairs from 1797 to 1807, and was made grand chamberlain (1804) by Napoleon. He opposed Napoleon's Russian and Spanish policies, and after Napoleon's fall he helped restore the Bourbons. Louis XVIII made him minister of foreign affairs (1814) and grand chamberlain (1815). He represented France at the Congress of Vienna (1815) where his diplomatic tact succeeded in maintaining his country's territorial integrity. He resigned after Napoleon's defeat at Waterloo. In 1830 he became ambassador to Great Britain and helped form the Quadruple Alliance (1834). His *Mémoires* were published in 1891. See Mme de VERNON.

Talmud (*Heb.,* "instruction"). The body of Jewish civil and religious law, not contained in, but largely derived from the Pentateuch. The Talmud is divided into the MISHNAH and the GEMARA. The Mishnah gives a simple statement of a law or precept; the Gemara presents the discussion and debate on it.

When the Talmud is spoken of without any qualification, the reference is to the Babylonian Talmud, one of the two recensions of the Gemara. The other is the Palestinian Talmud, which is only one fourth the size of the Babylonian and is considered by Jews to have less authority.

Work on the Mishnah began in the time of the Maccabees. The 4,000 rules and postulations were codified and arranged by subject by Rabbi Judah I (c. 135–220). The schools in Palestine had codified their Gemara by the fourth century; the Babylonian scholars finished their Gemara in the sixth century.

Talus (Talos). (1) In Greek myth, the guardian of Crete; a giant of brass fashioned by Hephaestus for Minos. He kept strangers off the island by throwing huge rocks at approaching ships, or he would make himself red-hot and burn trespassers to death in his embrace. A single vein of blood ran from his head to his foot, where it was closed with a nail. Medea, coming to Crete with the ARGONAUTS, charmed the nail out by her magic, and Talos bled to death. In Spenser's FAERIE QUEENE (Bk. v) he is the "yron man" attendant upon Sir Artegal, and representing executive power—"Swift as a swallow, and as lion strong."

(2) An apprentice of DAEDALUS, also known as Perdix. Daedalus, according to a Greek myth, grew jealous of his skill as an artisan and threw him into the sea, but he was saved by being turned into a partridge (*perdix*). The invention that incited Daedalus' enmity is said to have been the saw.

Tamar, and Other Poems (1924). A collection of poems by Robinson JEFFERS. The little poem is loosely based on the biblical story of Tamar, the daughter of King David who was seduced by her brother. It deals with a modern Tamar living on the Monterey coast, who seduces her brother, a neighbor, and her father, communicates with the dead, and finally brings destruction to her entire family.

Tamayo, Rufino (1899–   ). Mexican semi-abstract, expressionist artist. He has done many murals, including one for the Bank of the Southwest in Houston, Texas.

Tambimuttu, Thurairajah (1916–). Ceylonese poet. He went to England in 1937 and launched *Poetry London,* and later *Poetry London-New York.* He was guest editor of *Poetry's* Indian number.

Tamburlaine. See TAMERLANE.

Tamburlaine the Great (in two parts; probably acted first in 1587, published in 1590). A romantic tragedy by Christopher MARLOWE, based on the history of TAMERLANE. A Scythian shepherd who becomes a fierce bandit and finally the victorious conqueror and king of Persia, the Tamburlaine of Part I is an embodiment of the Renaissance spirit: bold, defiant, eager to explore the possibilities of human life. Marlowe creates a hero who is free to act, unhampered by fate or external circumstance. At the end of Part I he is at the height of his glory; in Part II, however, his lust for power and his cruelty finally end in ruin. His character loses its magnetic ability to hold the play together, and before death conquers him, he himself disintegrates.

Tamerlane or **Tamburlaine.** Corruption of **Timur i Leng,** or Timur the Lame (1336–1405). Mongol conqueror, great-great-grandson of Genghis Khan. After establishing his capital at Samarkand, he conquered great parts of Russia, Persia, India, and central Asia, and died while preparing to invade China. TAMBURLAINE THE GREAT, a blank verse tragedy, was Christopher Marlowe's first play. In it Tamburlaine becomes a bloodthirsty, inhuman villain and the action consists of one atrocity after another. In Rowe's play *Tamerlane* (1702), the warrior appears as a calm, philosophic prince, out of compliment to William III. There is a poem called *Tamerlane* by Edgar Allan Poe.

Tamerlane and Other Poems (1827). A collection of poems by Edgar Allan POE. This group of youthful poems, published "by a Bostonian," was not successful. The poems reveal the influence of Byron and Shelley, and deal with Poe's favorite themes: pride, love, beauty, and death.

Taming of the Shrew, The (c. 1594). A comedy by William SHAKESPEARE. The "shrew" is KATHARINA, a maiden of such violent whims and tempers that it seems unlikely she will ever find a husband. Her father, BAPTISTA, refuses to allow her lovable younger sister BIANCA to marry any of her numerous suitors until Katharina is off his hands. Finally PETRUCHIO appears, marries Katharina in short order, and by his own abrupt highhandedness "tames" her to such good effect that he wins a bet with two other men on a test of their wives' obedience. Meanwhile, LUCENTIO, through the ruse of becoming Bianca's tutor while his servant Tranio assumes his name and clothing and presses his suit with her father, has succeeded in winning her hand. The entire play is enacted for the benefit of Christopher SLY, a drunken tinker who, in the opening "induction" scene, is taken to a nobleman's castle where he is fooled into thinking he is a nobleman himself.

The relationship of Shakespeare's play to an earlier anonymous play, *The Taming of a Shrew,* is disputed by scholars, but the plot elements of the two plays are similar. The opening episode concerning the induction of the drunken Sly is a common one in folk tales, as old as the *Arabian Nights.* The subplot involving Bianca and Lucentio is based on Ariosto's *I Suppositi,* translated by Gascoigne in 1566.

Tammany Hall. The headquarters (formerly on Union Square) of the controlling organization of the Democratic Party in New York City and State; hence, the party itself, and, as this has been the political target for so-called party abuses, the term "Tammany" is figuratively employed for municipal malpractice.

Tammany was the name of a 17th century Delaware chief, and the patriotic, anti-British leagues of pre-Revolutionary days adopted the name "St. Tammany" to ridicule the titles of loyalist organizations—Societies of St. George, St. Andrew, and so on. After the Revolution these leagues became anti-aristocratic clubs, but all soon died a natural death except "Tammany Society, No. 1," which was that of New York. This flourished, and was converted into a political machine by Aaron Burr in his conflict with Alexander Hamilton (c. 1798), and in 1800 played a prominent part in the election of Jefferson to the presidency.

Tammuz. A Near Eastern god of fertility. In some obscure manner, ISHTAR's love for him caused his death, and he descended into the underworld, leaving the earth barren. Ishtar mourned him, and eventually followed him into the underworld, from which, with the help of EA, she rescued him. With his father, Ningishzida, he became a gatekeeper at the palace of Anu, the god of heaven.

Tammuz was important, under one name or another, throughout the Near East. His earliest known form was the Sumerian shepherd-god, Dumuzi. He was most widely known in later times in the modified form of ADONIS.

Tamora. See TITUS ANDRONICUS.

Tam o'Shanter (1791). A narrative poem by Robert BURNS, based on the legend that no manner of spirit or sprite could cross the middle of a running stream. On his way home one night, a little drunk, Tam sees witches and warlocks dancing in the Kirk of Alloway. Delighted, he calls out to one "winsome wench" among the beldams, "Weel done, CUTTY SARK!" Immediately the lights go out, and the witches come down on Tam who rides for his life until he has reached the middle of the bridge over the DOON. Being past the middle of the stream, he is out of the witches' power, but his mare's tail is not, and Cutty Sark catches hold of this and pulls it off.

Tancred or **Tancredi.** Known as **Tancred of Altavilla** or **of Sicily** (d. 1112). Norman soldier and crusader. During the First Crusade (1096–1099), he took part in the siege of Jerusalem and the battle of Ascalon; he eventually became ruler of the principalities of Edessa and Antioch.

The character of Tancredi in Tasso's GERUSALEMME LIBERATA is based upon him. In the poem, he is second only to Rinaldo of Este in bravery and fighting ability among the crusaders encamped before Jerusalem. He is loved by two women, the Syrian maiden Erminia and the Persian warrior-maid CLORINDA, but it is the latter whom he loves. In a night attack, he unwittingly wounds Clorinda, who dies in his arms after receiving baptism from him and granting her forgiveness. His grief is tremendous, but he recovers in time, aided by a vision of her in heaven,

Tancred's vision of Clorinda.
From *Gerusalemme Liberata* (1590).

to defeat the infidel champion Argante and speed the capture of the holy city.

He was the subject of an opera, *Tancredi* (1813), by Rossini and a musical drama *Il Combattimento di Tancredi e Clorinda* (1624) by Monteverdi.

Tancred, The Revenge of. A tale from Giovanni Boccaccio's THE DECAMERON. Tancred sends to his daughter Ghismonda her murdered lover's heart in a gold goblet; she pours poison into it, drinks it, and dies.

Tancred, or the New Crusade (1847). A novel by Benjamin DISRAELI. Tancred is a young and highborn visionary who leaves the social circles of 19th-century London to travel in the East. In the Holy Land he experiences the great Asian mystery, which is to work regeneration for the West.

Tandem, Felix. See Carl SPITTELER.

Tandy, Napper. See Theobald Wolfe TONE.

Taney, Roger Brooke (1777–1864). American statesman. He was secretary of the treasury from 1833 to 1834. He became chief justice of the Supreme Court following John Marshall and is remembered for his association with the Dred Scott Decision in 1857.

T'ang. Chinese dynasty (618–906). The "Golden Age" of Chinese civilization, which saw vast expansion of the empire, great developments in Buddhism, particularly Ch'an, and a flowering of literature, science, and the arts. Such foreign religions as Zoroastrianism, Nestorian Christianity, and Manichaeanism were introduced, and Taoism flourished. Poetry reached heights unequaled in later centuries, Po Chü-i, Li Po, Tu Fu, and Wang Wei being products of this age. Prose literature gained stature, the compilation

of dictionaries and encyclopedias made great advances, and the prototypes of later drama and fiction can be traced to this period. Japan was greatly influenced by all phases of the culture of the T'ang Dynasty.

Tanglewood Tales (1853). A book for children by Nathaniel HAWTHORNE. The author retells six Greek myths, dealing with the same themes, revenge, the effects of time, strange transformations, that interest him in his major work. The book is a sequel to A WONDER-BOOK FOR BOYS AND GIRLS.

Tanguy, Yves (1900–1955). French SURREALIST painter. With the carefully controlled brushstroke, precision, and detail that is typical of the surrealist movement, Tanguy painted semi-abstract shapes against a background of distant horizons. By suggesting the infinity of space, his pictures create a mood of nostalgia and loneliness, which is offset by the whimsical, slightly comic quality of his forms. *Mama, Papa Is Wounded* (1927) is a characteristic work.

Taniguchi Buson (1716–1783). Japanese painter and *haiku* poet. He is generally ranked next to Matsuo Bashō as the greatest poet of the Tokugawa period (1600–1868).

Tanizaki Jun'ichirō (1886–   ). Japanese novelist. Dealing with both modern and ancient subjects, he has produced a large number of successful works. Best known are a modern version of the TALE OF GENJI and *Sasame yuki* (*Thin Snow*, 1942–48), translated as *The Makioka Sisters* by Edward Seidensticker. The latter details at length the everyday life of four sisters in Osaka in the late 1930's. Other works include: *Tade kuu mushi* (*Some Prefer Nettles*, 1928), translated by Seidensticker and *Kagi* (*The Key*, 1956), translated by Howard Hibbet.

tanka. The classic form of Japanese poetry, fixed centuries ago in a standard arrangement of five lines (with 5, 7, 5, 7, 7 syllables). It reduces, through the strict limits of its form, all poetic raw material to the concentrated essence of one static event, image, mood, etc. An example by Saigo Hoshi:

> Now indeed I know
> that when we said "remember,"
> and we swore it so,
> it was in "we will forget"
> that our thoughts most truly met.

See HAIKU.

Tannhäuser (13th century). A minor German minnesinger, or lyrical poet. He led a wandering life and went on a Crusade to the Holy Land. He was associated with the knight Tannhäuser of popular ballads, which relate how he discovers Venusberg (or Hörselberg), a magic land reached through a subterranean cave, and stays to enjoy its pleasures with the goddess Venus. At last he becomes conscious of having sinned, and journeys to the upper world to ask the Pope for absolution. The Pope replies that he should no more expect God's forgiveness than he could expect the papal scepter to bring forth green leaves. Tannhäuser departs in despair, but on the third day the papal staff bursts into blossom. Messengers are sent after him, but the knight has disappeared, having returned to Venusberg.

In WAGNER's adaptation for his opera *Tannhäuser* (1845) the hero returns from Venusberg to the court of the landgrave of Thuringia, where the landgrave's niece Elizabeth has been faithful to her love for him. His friend WOLFRAM VON ESCHENBACH persuades him to take part in the singing contest, for the winner is to marry Elizabeth. The last to sing, Tannhäuser bursts unwillingly into a song in praise of Venus, so wildly pagan that the other knights draw their swords to kill him. Elizabeth begs for his life, and he departs with a group of pilgrims to seek forgiveness at Rome. The Pope gives the legendary reply, and Tannhäuser returns weak and dejected. He is just in time to see the funeral of Elizabeth, who has died despairing that he would ever return. He falls sorrowfully dying on the bier just as more pilgrims arrive carrying the Pope's leaf-bearing staff.

Tansillo, Luigi (1510–1568). Italian poet. Born at Venosa, he traveled widely in the military service of the Spanish viceregal government centered at Naples. His experiences on land and sea are reflected in his didactic and humorous poems, one of which, the *Vendemmiatore* (*The Vintager*) was placed on the Index. In repentance, he wrote his *Lagrime di San Pietro* (*The Tears of Saint Peter*), one of the first poems in the counter-reformation style; it was used by Southwell in England and Malherbe in France. His sonnets, influenced by Petrarch and Chariteo, were also popular with lyricists of the late 16th century. See BRUNO.

Tantalus (Tantalos). In Greek mythology, a son of Zeus or Tmolus and progenitor of the house of ATREUS. He is best known for the punishment he suffers in Hades: suffering hunger and thirst, he stands in the midst of a lake, but when he bends to drink it dries up; a fruit-laden bough flies up when he reaches for it; and an overhanging stone threatens to crush him. The word *tantalize* recalls his tortures. The punishments were inflicted for various crimes. A favorite of Zeus, Tantalus betrayed his secrets and gave ambrosia to his friends. Offering a banquet to the gods on a Lydian Mount Sipylus, he served his dismembered son PELOPS. His theft of the golden dog that had watched over the infant Zeus caused Zeus to crush him under Sipylus. By Euryanassa, he was the father of Pelops, Niobe, and Broteas.

Tantras, the. Sanskrit religious writings, forming the holy scriptures of SAKTISM, a Hindu sect. The adherents worship the divine power in its female aspect (sakti). The *Tantras* consist of magical formulas, for the most part in the form of dialogues between Shiva and his wife Kali, and deal with the creation and ultimate destruction of the world, divine worship, the attainment of superhuman power, and final union with the Supreme Spirit (*purusha*). They are of comparatively recent date (sixth or seventh century). *Tantra* is Sanskrit for thread, or warp, and is used here as groundwork, order, or doctrine of religion.

Taoism. Chinese religious system based on the teachings of LAO TZU and CHUANG TZU. Developing almost contemporaneously with Confucianism, it called for a flight from conventional social obligations and envisions a transcendental world of the spirit. It opposed the pompous respectability of Confucianism's insistence on social order and duties, and provided a release from the burdens of the official philosophy. Emphasizing mystic, undefined worlds, Taoism gradually degenerated into a search for eternal life, and surrounded by a welter of superstition, eventually became a popular folk religion. Many of its teachings were absorbed by Confucianists and Chinese Buddhists. Early Buddhist texts were first translated from Sanskrit into Chinese using Taoist technical terms.

Tao te ching. Chinese Taoist text attributed to the sage LAO TZU. A brief work in 81 paragraphs, it combines both verse and prose passages of a mystic tone. Its meaning is highly obscure and thus subject to a great variety of interpretations. The work posits an Absolute or Tao, which is indescribable and precedes all things in the universe. It advocates a passive, unforced, yielding attitude that will permit one to remain in harmony with the Tao. The most reliable translations are: Arthur Waley, *The Way and its Power* (1935); J. J. L. Duyvendak, *Tao te ching, the Book of the Way and Its Virtue* (1954). See TAOISM.

Tapley, Mark. Martin's invariably cheerful servant and companion in Charles Dickens' MARTIN CHUZZLEWIT. Whatever the circumstances, he believes things will "come out jolly." He shares Martin's miseries in America, and on his return to England becomes landlord of the Blue Dragon inn.

tar or **Jack Tar.** A sailor. It is probably an abbreviation of tarpaulin, of which sailors' caps and overalls were made. Tarpaulins are tarred cloths, and are commonly used on board ship to keep articles from sea-spray.

Tara. A site in Meath, Ireland. There the kings, the clergy, the princes, and the bards used to assemble in a large hall to consult on matters of public importance. The name Tara's Psaltery or Psalter of Tara was given to the great national register or chronicles of Ireland, read to the assembled princes when they met in Tara's Hall in public conference.

Tarakee. A hero of Brahminical legend and miracle of ascetic devotion. He is fabled to have lived 1100 years, and spent each century in some astounding mortification.

tarantula. A large and hairy venomous spider (so-called from *Taranto,* a town in Apulia, Italy, where they abound). The bite of a tarantula was formerly supposed to be the cause of the dancing mania known as tarantism. This was an hysterical disease, common, epidemically, in southern Europe from the 15th to the 17th centuries. From this same insect the *tarantella* gets its name. This is a very quick Neapolitan dance (or its music) for one couple, and is said to have been based on the gyrations practiced by those whom the tarantula had poisoned.

Taras Bulba (1835). A short novel by Nikolai GOGOL. It is set during the 17th-century wars between the Poles and the Cossacks in the Ukraine. The old Cossack, Taras Bulba, and his two sons, Andri and Ostap, join the Cossacks in a campaign against the Poles. Andri falls in love with a Polish girl and deserts his comrades to be with her inside a besieged Polish fortress. Meeting Andri in a skirmish outside the fort, Taras kills his traitorous son. Meanwhile Ostap is captured and tortured to death by the Poles. Taras later suffers the same fate. The novel is rich not only in battle scenes but also in the language in which the Ukrainian countryside is described. The work ends with a famous description of the Dniester River with a wild duck, called in Russian a *gogol,* included in the scene.

The story has a biographical connection with Gogol. One of his Cossack ancestors, named Ostap Gogol, sided with the Poles during the 17th-century wars and once surrendered a fortress to them.

Tarassov, Lev. See Henri TROYAT.

Tar Baby (1880). One of the best-known stories of Joel Chandler HARRIS. It first appeared in book form in UNCLE REMUS, HIS SONGS AND HIS SAYINGS and later in *The Tar Baby Story and Other Rhymes by Uncle Remus* (1904). A tar doll set up by the roadside so irritates Brer Rabbit by its unresponsiveness that he strikes it until he is stuck tight.

Tarbell, Ida M[inerva] (1857–1944). American journalist, chiefly known for her exposés in *McClure's Magazine* (1894–1906). Her *History of the Standard Oil Company* (1904) is one of the best accounts of a monopoly.

Tarde, Gabriel (1843–1904). French sociologist and criminologist. His works include *Les Lois de l'imitation* (1890), *La Criminalité comparée* (1898), and *Etudes de psychologie sociale* (1898). Tarde viewed man as essentially dominated by the social environment, which supplies the goals of his motivations.

Tardieu, Jean (1902–   ). French poet and dramatist. His *Théâtre de Chambre* (1955) and *Poèmes à Jouer* (1960) are collections of one-act plays. Poetry collections include *Poèmes* (1944) and *Jours pétrifiés* (1948).

Tarkington, [Newton] Booth (1869–1946). American novelist and playwright. After studying at Princeton, where he founded the Triangle Club, Tarkington served in the Indiana House of Representatives in 1902–1903; his concern for politics is reflected in THE GENTLEMAN FROM INDIANA, his first novel, and *In the Arena* (1905). He also is noted for his stories of childhood and adolescence, particularly PENROD and SEVENTEEN. The title *Growth* (1927) was later given to his trilogy about urban life in the Midwest, which appeared as *The Turmoil* (1915), THE MAGNIFICENT AMBERSONS, for which he was awarded a Pulitzer Prize, and *The Midlander* (1923). He received another Pulitzer Prize for ALICE ADAMS. His other novels include MONSIEUR BEAUCAIRE, THE CONQUEST OF CANAAN, *The Plutocrat* (1926), *Mirthful Haven* (1931), *The Lorenzo Bunch* (1936), and *The Heritage of Hatcher Ide* (1941). He also wrote 25 plays, 11 of them with Harry Leon Wilson, notably *The Man from Home* (1907), which contrasts American innocence with European sophistication. *The World Does Move* (1928) is his autobiography, and *Your Amiable Uncle* (1949) consists of letters to his nephews.

Tarlton, Richard (d. 1588). English actor. A popular comedian, Tarlton became one of the Queen Elizabeth's Men in 1583. He was famous for his improvisations of doggerel verse, and may perhaps have been the prototype for Shakespeare's Yorick. Many collections of anecdotes supposedly originating with him were published, notably *Tarlton's Jests* in three parts (1592–1611).

tarot cards. A pack of fortunetelling cards. Their figures are said to be very ancient; they were used by the Egyptians, and may have originated in the rituals of fertility religions. T. S. Eliot (in *The Waste Land*), Charles Williams, Lawrence Durrell, and other modern writers refer to the cards.

Tarpa, Spurius Metius. A famous Roman critic of the AUGUSTAN AGE. He sat in the temple of Apollo with four colleagues to judge the merit of theatrical pieces before they were produced in public.

Richard Tarlton as a clown.

Tarpeian Rock. An ancient rock or peak (now no longer in existence) on the Capitoline hill, Rome. The name comes from Tarpeia, a vestal virgin and daughter of Spurius Tarpeius, governor of the citadel. According to legend, he agreed to open the gates to the Sabines if they would give his daughter "what they wore on their arms" (meaning their gold bracelets). The Sabines, thereupon, crushed her to death with their shields, and her body was hurled from the Tarpeian Rock. Subsequently, traitors were cast down from this rock, and so killed.

Tarquin. The family name of a legendary line of early Roman kings. Tarquinius Priscus, the fifth king of Rome, is dated 617–578 B.C. His son, Tarquinius Superbus, was the seventh (and last) king of Rome; it was his son, Tarquinius Sextus, who committed the rape of Lucrece, in revenge for which the Tarquins were expelled from Rome and a republic established. See LUCRETIA.

Tarr (1918). A novel by Wyndham LEWIS. It is a psychological drama about a group of Paris art students of various nationalities. The hero is Frederick Tarr, an Englishman, but the center of interest is Otto Kreisler, a German student through whom Lewis attacks German romanticism, nihilism, and militarism.

Tarsia, Galeazzo di (1520–1553). Italian Renaissance poet. He is best known for his lyrics, mainly sonnets of a Petrarchan nature; forged in bitter exile, they echo his national sentiment.

His *Canzoniere (Song Book)* was not published until 1617.

Tartarin. A famous comic character created by Alphonse DAUDET. He is the hero of *Aventures prodigieuses de Tartarin de Tarascon* (1872) and *Tartarin sur les Alpes* (1885). Tartarin, a native of Provence, is an amusing braggart who bubbles over with good humor and with hilarious, fantastic tales of his own escapades.

Tartarus (Tartaros). The infernal regions of classical mythology. Used as equivalent to HADES by later writers, by Homer it was placed as far beneath Hades as Hades is beneath the earth. It was here that Zeus confined the TITANS.

Tartini, Giuseppe (1692–1770). Italian violinist and composer of many concertos and sonatas. His *Devil's Trill* is a favorite showpiece.

Tartuffe, Le (Tartuffe, 1664). A witty comedy by MOLIÈRE. The religious hypocrite Tartuffe worms his way into the household of ORGON, a credulous fool who deeds all his property to the impostor and intends to marry his daughter to him. Orgon's wife Elmire tricks Tartuffe, who is unaware that Orgon is watching, into trying to seduce her; Orgon, finally understanding Tartuffe's true nature, orders him from the house. But Tartuffe, owning the house, evicts the family instead and arranges Orgon's arrest. The king intervenes at the last moment and Tartuffe is hauled off to jail. The word *tartufe* has come to mean religious hypocrite in the French language. The play itself was twice suppressed before permission to perform it freely was finally given.

Tarzan. A fabulous character created by Edgar Rice Burroughs (1875–1950). Although Burroughs wrote many other stories about the fantastic and unearthly, his main claim to fame is the Tarzan series. First appearing in *Tarzan of the Apes* (1914), this 20th-century folk hero is depicted as the son of an English nobleman, abandoned in Africa in his infancy. He is brought up by apes, learns to speak their language (and that of other animals as well), and goes through a long series of breathless adventures. Eventually Tarzan marries, has a son, and finally a grandson. Millions of copies of the Tarzan books have been sold, and they have been translated into 56 languages. Innumerable films have been made of his adventures, and he has long been a comic-strip favorite.

Task, The (1785). A long poem by William COWPER (1785), its purpose being, according to a statement by the author himself, "to discountenance the modern enthusiasm after a London life, and to recommend rural ease and solitude as friendly to the cause of piety and virtue." In its six books (*The Sofa, The Time-piece, The Garden,* etc.) it deals with a number of subjects in which the author was interested, such as nature, rural life, animals, simple, hard-working people, and social reform. Cowper's Christian orthodoxy, his insistence on the fallen state of man and on a God found necessarily in revelation and not merely in nature, make him bitterly hostile to Deism and limit his sympathy with scientific discovery to prove divine design. In its recollections of the inspiring and healing qualities of nature, and in its use of blank verse, it is considered a forerunner of some of the poetry of Wordsworth. The poem contains perhaps Cowper's most famous aphorism: "God made the country and man made the town."

Tasman, Abel J. (1602–1659). Dutch navigator. He went to the South Seas and discovered what he called Van Diemen's Land after the governor of the Dutch East Indies. It is the modern Tasmania.

Tasso, Bernardo (1493–1569). Italian diplomat and poet. He wrote Petrarchan lyrics and classical odes, as well as a romantic epic, *Amadigi* (1560), based on *Amadis of Gaul.* He was the father of Torquato Tasso.

Tasso, Torquato (1544–1595). Italian poet. He was born at Sorrento and educated by the Jesuits at Naples and by his father Bernardo Tasso, himself a distinguished man of letters. At Padua, he studied the law, then philosophy and eloquence under the influence of Speroni. Though only 18, he wrote a romantic epic, the *Rinaldo,* about the adventures of the hero, a cousin of Orlando (Roland) the paladin. In 1565, he went to Ferrara to serve the Este family and began work on his masterpiece, the GERUSALEMME LIBERATA (*Jerusalem Delivered*). During the decade he composed several discourses on the art of poetry and wrote the AMINTA, first performed at the Este court in 1573. A few years later, his physical and mental health began to disintegrate as his sensitive nature was racked by doubts about the critical and religious orthodoxy of his work and by suspicions of hostility towards him on the part of patrons and friends. In 1579 the duke of Ferrara placed him in an asylum, where he languished for seven years in misery, despite such visitors as Montaigne and many expressions of sympathy from the literary world. The fact that his writings in the asylum reveal an anguished rather than a deranged mind prompted later writers like Goethe to picture him as the victim of a romantic but forbidden attachment to the duke's sister Leonora (see TORQUATO TASSO). In 1586, upon his release, he found himself universally honored for his *Jerusalem,* which had appeared during his imprisonment. Despite further wanderings and continuing poor health, he completed in 1586 a tragedy, *Torrismondo,* and a creation poem, the *Mondo creato* (1607) as well as more critical treatises and many letters. In 1593, he completed a revised version of his masterpiece, called *Gerusalemme conquistata* (*Jerusalem Conquered*), to meet critical and ecclesiastical objections. But in Italy and elsewhere, the first version was and remains the celebrated work; the second version has lived only as a document of biographical value. In 1594, Pope Clement VIII planned to crown him with the laurel on the Capitol in Rome, but the poet died in April of 1595, before the ceremony could take place. From the time of Edward Fairfax's translation into English of the *Jerusalem Delivered* (1594 and 1600), Tasso strongly influenced English poets from Spenser to Byron.

Tassoni, Alessandro (1565–1635). Italian poet. He wrote a celebrated mock-heroic epic *La Secchia Rapita* (*The Rape of the Bucket,* 1624). It is made up of 12 cantos of octaves that narrate in epic style a struggle between the cities of Bologna and Modena over possession of a bucket.

Tate, [John Orley] Allen (1899–   ). American poet and critic. A graduate of Vanderbilt University, Tate was associated with the Fugitives and the Southern AGRARIANS. Like them he tended toward social and political conservatism, seriously stirred by the nonindustrial South. He contributed *Remarks on the Southern Religion* to the Fugitive symposium *I'll Take My Stand* (1930). Tate was Southern editor of *Hound and Horn* (1931–1934) and editor of the Sewanee Review (1944–1946).

His poetry is marked by a classical severity of form, with a tendency toward religious symbolism, satire, and intellectual complexity. His best-known poem is perhaps the much anthologized *Ode to the Confederate Dead.* His verse has appeared in *Mr. Pope and Other Poems* (1928), *Poems: 1928–1931* (1932), *The Mediterranean and Other Poems* (1936), and *Poems: 1922–1947* (1948). *The Fathers* (1928) is his one published novel.

Tate is as distinguished a critic as he is a poet. Instrumental in the New Criticism, he has published several collections of essays, including *Reactionary Essays on Poetry and Ideas* (1936), *Reason in Madness* (1941), *The Hovering Fly and Other Essays* (1945), and *The Forlorn Demon* (1953). He has also written biographies of Stonewall Jackson (1928) and Jefferson Davis (1929) and has edited several anthologies.

Tate, Sir Henry (1819–1899). English philanthropist. He built the Tate Gallery in London as a gallery for modern paintings (opened in 1897). Today it is the National Gallery of British Art.

Tate, Nahum (1652–1715). English playwright and poet. He is best known for his bowdlerized versions of works of more famous authors, particularly for his adaptation (1681) of Shakespeare's *King Lear* which gave the play a happy ending and remained the standard acting version until 1840. He collaborated with Dryden on the second part of Absalom and Achitophel and with Nicholas Brady on a *New Version of the Psalms* (1696), a widely used hymnal. His best independent work is *Panacea, a poem on Tea* (1700). Tate was poet laureate from 1692 to 1715.

Tatler, The. A series of periodical essays started by Richard Steele under the pseudonym of Isaac Bickerstaff (1709–1711). Joseph Addison and Jonathan Swift were also contributors. The essays are predominantly light satires and allegorical criticisms of contemporary mores which fall into five categories: entertainment, poetry, domestic and foreign news, and miscellaneous subjects. *The Tatler* was succeeded by The Spectator.

Tattersall, Richard (1724–1795). English horseman. Tattersall's horse-auction headquarters in London (1766) were known all over the world. The word *tattersall* is used in various languages as a synonym of horse market.

Tauchnitz, Christian Bernhard (1816–1895). German publisher, member of a family of printers and publishers. He is especially known for the "Tauchnitz Edition" (started in 1841) of a *Collection of British and American Authors.* The Tauchnitz volumes were English-language editions for sale on the Continent, not legally to be taken into American or British territory.

Taugenichts, Aus dem Leben eines. See Aus dem Leben eines Taugenichts.

Taunay, Viscount. Alfredo d'Escragnolle (1843–1899). Brazilian novelist and historian. Of French ancestry, Taunay fought in the Paraguayan war (1864–1870); *A Retirada da Laguna* (1871), which was originally written in French as *La Retraite de Laguna,* is an epic account of a famous retreat during the war. His fiction, which reflected the growing interest of Brazilian intellectuals in social problems, tends toward realism. *Inocência* (1872), his best-

known novel, is a tragic love story, notable for its depiction of the Brazilian hinterland.

Tawney, R[ichard] H[enry] (1880–1962). English historian. His *Religion and the Rise of Capitalism* (1926) is a classic study of the relationship between Protestantism and economic development in the 16th and 17th centuries.

Taylor, A[lan] J[ohn] P[ercival] (1906–   ). English historian. He has written especially about 19th- and 20th-century European history and the events leading up to the two World Wars. *The Course of German History* (1945), *Rumours of Wars* (1953), and *Origins of the Second World War* (1962) are among his books.

Taylor, Bayard (1825–1878). American man of letters. Apprenticed to a printer, Taylor left his work for a walking tour of Europe. He sent letters from Europe to several periodicals; they were collected in *Views Afoot; or, Europe Seen with Knapsack and Staff* (1846). The book, full of enthusiasm and good description, was an immense success. Taylor was then sent by the *Tribune* to report on the 1849 California gold rush. These experiences were published in another successful book, *Eldorado, or, Adventures in the Path of Empire* (1850). Taylor traveled widely as a journalist, even serving as historian on Commodore Perry's expedition to Japan. Throughout his career, however, Taylor thought of himself as a serious poet. In his *Home Pastorals* (1875) he dealt realistically with his own experience, but most of his verse is romantic, as in *Poems of the Orient* (1855). The best-known poem is the *Bedouin Song.* Taylor also wrote clever parodies and several novels; his translation of Goethe's *Faust* (1870–1871) won him academic recognition and the post of minister to Germany (1878).

Taylor, Edward (1642–1729). English-born American poet and clergyman. In 1668 he sailed to Massachusetts, entered Harvard College, and in 1671 became a minister in the frontier town of Westfield, Mass. An ultraconservative in theology, Taylor began to write pamphlets attacking the liberal ideas of Solomon Stoddard, the grandfather of Jonathan Edwards. In 1682, at the age of 40, he began to compose the *Preparatory Meditations,* 217 poems in six-line stanzas, written over a period of years. The poems, intended to "stir up" the affections before observing the Lord's Supper, celebrate in the metaphysical manner the glory, and also the difficulty, of man's relation to God. Around 1685, Taylor began his major long poem God's Determinations Touching His Elect.

Only two of Taylor's poems were published in his lifetime. A selection from his verse first appeared in 1939, but no complete edition of the *Meditations* was published until 1960. Still in manuscript are Taylor's sermons, and his *Metrical History of Christianity.* Most critics of American literature now consider Taylor the most important American poet before the 19th century.

Taylor, Jeremy (1613–1667). English clergyman and writer. His best-known work is the devotional book Holy Living and Dying. Taylor's prose is noted for its warmth and eloquence, its splendor of cadence and vividness of metaphor.

Taylor, John (1580–1653). English author, known as "the Water Poet" because he worked for a time as a waterman on the Thames River. He wrote a vast number of pamphlets and verses on a variety of subjects which were first collected in 1630. Among his best-known prose works is *The Penniless Pilgrimage* (1618), an amusing account of a journey from London to Edinburgh. Taylor was known for his eccentric exploits, one of which was sailing on the Thames in a boat made of brown paper.

Taylor, John (1808–1887). Leader in the Mormon Church. He took the side of Brigham Young and accompanied him to Utah. After Young's death in 1877, he became acting head of the church, accepted polygamy and was forced to hide from arrest by the government in 1884.

Taylor, Philip Meadows (1808–1876). English novelist and administrator in India. His best-known book, *Confessions of a Thug* (1839), deals with thuggism, the Indian terrorist cult of assassins of the early 19th century. His other novels provide an accurate and engaging picture of Indian life and history from the 17th to the 19th century. See THUG.

Taylor, Tom (1817–1880). English dramatist. Some of his better-known plays include the comedies *Masks and Faces* (1854, written with Charles Reade) and *Our American Cousin* (1858); the latter was a success in the U.S., and it was the play Lincoln was watching when he was assassinated at Ford's Theater in Washington by John Wilkes Booth. Taylor's serious melodrama *Ticket of Leave Man* (1863) is notable for its celebrated character Detective Hawkshaw.

Tchaikovsky, Peter Ilyich (1840–1893). Russian composer. His music, while having definite Russian characteristics, is not as fiercely nationalistic as that of his contemporaries, the St. Petersburg "FIVE." His music owes much to French and German models; the composer himself recognized his most serious weakness, a weak formal sense, when he said "I cannot complain of lack of inventive power, but I have always suffered from want of skill in the management of form." His strong points, warm and expansive melodies and moments of intense dramatic expression, have made many of his works popular with a wide audience. His best-known works are his three last symphonies (No. 4 in F minor, 1877; No. 5 in E minor, 1888; No. 6 in B minor, the *Pathétique,* his last work, 1893); the first piano concerto, in B flat minor (1875); the violin concerto (1878); symphonic poems, especially *Romeo and Juliet* (1869, 1880); and his three ballets: *Swan Lake* (1876), *Sleeping Beauty* (1889), and *Nutcracker* (1891–1892). The most popular of his 11 operas are *Eugene Onegin* and *The Queen of Spades,* both based on works by Pushkin. See Nadezhda von MECK.

tea ceremony. See CHA-NO-YU.

Teach, Edward. Known as **Blackbeard** (d. 1718). English pirate. Originally a privateer during the War of Spanish Succession, he cruised the Spanish Main and was killed in action. He is famous in pirate stories.

Teapot Dome. A tract of oil-bearing government land in Wyoming which figured in a major scandal of the Harding administration. A Senate investigating committee revealed that the Teapot Dome reserve and one at Elk Hills, Calif., had been transferred from the navy to Secretary of the Interior Albert B. Fall, who in turn had secretly leased the fields to private oil operators in 1922. It was also disclosed that the oilmen had lent Fall substantial sums of money. The leases were later canceled by the government, and Fall was convicted of bribery. The scandal inspired Upton Sinclair's novel *Oil!* (1927).

Tearsheet, Doll. A violent-tempered prostitute in Shakespeare's HENRY IV: PART II.

Teasdale, Sara (1884–1933). American poet. Known for the evocative intensity of her lyrics, she was for a time associated with the group that gathered around Harriet MONROE in Chicago. She received a special Pulitzer Prize for her *Love Songs* (1917). Other collections of her poetry include *Sonnets to Duse and Other Poems* (1907), *Helen of Troy and Other Poems* (1911), *Rivers to the Sea* (1915), *Flame and Shadow* (1920), *Dark of the Moon* (1926), and *Strange Victory* (1933). She also edited an anthology for young people, *Rainbow Gold* (1922). More and more withdrawn as the years went by, she committed suicide.

Tebaldi, Antonio. Also known by the Latinized name **il Tebaldeo** (1463–1537). Italian poet. Tebaldi is noted for his exaggerated Petrarchism, used in the manner of Serafino and Cariteo. His best-known work is the *Opere d'Amore (Amatory Verse,* 1534).

Tecumseh (1768?–1813). Shawnee chief, considered one of the greatest American Indian leaders. Determined to check the westward expansion of U.S. settlers, Tecumseh and his brother, the Prophet, formed a league of Northwest Indian tribes, which was supported by British officials in Canada. While Tecumseh was away, General William Henry Harrison defeated the Indians at the battle of Tippecanoe (1811) in what is now Indiana. During the War of 1812, Tecumseh, who had allied himself with the British, was killed at the battle of the Thames in Canada.

teddy boy. Post-World War II English teenager, usually of the juvenile delinquent type. So called from his group's fondness for pseudo-Edwardian costume.

Te Deum laudamus (*Lat.,* "We praise thee, O God"). Opening words of a Christian hymn of praise to the Trinity, attributed to Nicetas (c. 340), bishop of Remesiana in Dacia. It is traditionally sung at Matins or Morning Prayer services, and on occasions of great public thanksgiving, such as the end of a war. It has been set to music hundreds of times; notable settings are by Purcell, Handel, Haydn, Bruckner, Dvořák, and Verdi.

Tegnér, Esaias (1782–1846). Swedish poet, scholar, and bishop. After a university education at Lund, Tegnér was appointed a lecturer in aesthetics in 1803. By 1812 he was a professor with a chair of Greek; the leader of an intellectual circle, he remained at the university until 1826. Tegnér had been ordained in 1812, and he left the academic life to devote himself to his duties as bishop of Växjö. His finest poetry appeared in the collections of *Krigssång för skånska lantvärnet* (1808), *Sång till solen* (1813), *Hjälten* (1813), *Nattuardsbarnen* (1820; trans. by Henry Wadsworth Longfellow, *The Children of the Lord's Supper,* 1842), and *Frithiofs Saga* (1825). Although he is noted for the clarity of language and expression in his philosophical lyrics, Tegnér also wrote some fine love poetry.

Telamon. In Greek mythology, a son of Aeacus, king of Aegina. With his brother PELEUS, he killed their half-brother Phocus to prevent his inheriting the kingdom. Banished, Telamon became king of Salamis. He was one of the Argonauts and hunted the CALYDONIAN BOAR. He became the father of Great Ajax and Teucer.

Tel-el-Amarna. Ruins of an Egyptian city. It was built in the 14th century B.C. by the great liberal Egyptian ruler AKHENATON. About three hundred clay tablets, representing the diplomatic correspondence between the king of Egypt and the kings of Babylon and Assyria, written in cuneiform characters, were discovered there (1887). The ruins were further examined by Sir Flinders Petrie (1891–1892).

Telemachus (Telemachos). In classic legend, the only son of ODYSSEUS and Penelope. As a babe he was thrown in front of his father's plow as a test of that hero's pretended madness. When Odysseus had been absent from home nearly twenty years, Telemachus went to Pylos and Sparta to gain information about him. Nestor received him hospitably at Pylos, and sent him to Sparta, where Menelaus told him the prophecy of Proteus concerning Odysseus. Telemachus then returned home, where he found his father and assisted him in slaying the suitors. Telemachus was accompanied in his voyage by Athene, the goddess of wisdom, under the form of Mentor, one of his father's friends. He is the hero of *Les Aventures de Télémaque* (1699), a French prose epic by Fénelon. This once widely read story is based on the old legends but adds many incidents, notably Telemachus' love affair with the nymph Calypso, who had been so violently enamored of his father. See Stephen DEDALUS.

Télémaque (1699). A didactic romance by François de Salignac de la Mothe FÉNELON, written for his pupil, the duc de Bourgogne. Ostensibly relating the adventures of Telemachus, the son of Ulysses, the book bears no relation to the actual *Odyssey*: it is an imaginative narrative, a pretext for dissertations on politics, morals, education, and religion. Telemachus and his companion Mentor, in reality the goddess Minerva, are shipwrecked upon the island of Calypso. To save him from the nymph's temptations, Mentor throws Telemachus into the sea. A Phoenician ship carries the pair to the newly founded city of Salente, where Mentor is entrusted with the organization of the state. By this contrivance, Fénelon is able to expound his political and economic views, among them the necessity of good faith in international relations, the wisdom of treating conquered nations humanely, and the king's obligation to look after the welfare of his subjects. Not surprisingly, Fénelon's proposals for fair economic and legal systems offended Louis XIV, and the book brought its author into disfavor. It proved, nevertheless, the prototype of the religious and political tract disguised as a novel later employed by the philosophes.

Telephus (Telephos). In Greek legend, king of Mysia. He was wounded in single combat with ACHILLES and was told by an oracle that only that which had inflicted the wound could heal it. Disguised as a beggar he made his way to the hall of Agamemnon and succeeded in persuading Odysseus to scrape some rust from Achilles' famous Pelian spear and with it cure him of his wound. Aeschylus and Euripides wrote dramas on Telephus, but both are lost.

Telesio, Bernardino (1500–1588). Italian philosopher. One of the key figures in the Renaissance trend toward the modern scientific approach to nature, Telesio was influenced by the naturalistic school of Padua, where he studied and taught. His major work, *De rerum natura iuxta propria principia* (*The Phenomena of Nature According to Its Own Principles*, 1565–1586), outlined his approach.

Telford, Thomas (1757–1834). Scottish engineer. He built the Caledonian Canal, many bridges and roads in North Scotland, improved Scottish harbors, and constructed the Gotha Canal between the Baltic and North Seas. He was a friend of Thomas Campbell and Robert Southey.

Telipinu. Hittite god of fertility. The harsh, infertile winter was ascribed to his sleep, and seasonal rituals were performed to wake him and calm his anger at being awakened, thereby bringing back fertility to the earth. A myth explaining these rituals in terms of divine precedents was discovered on clay tablets in the ancient Hittite capital of Hattusas, now Boghazköy, Turkey. The earliest of the tablets are from the 15th century B.C., but the myth itself is far older.

At the beginning of the story, which may have been enacted annually as a ritual drama, Telipinu is so impatient to be off and find a quiet grove where he can sleep that he puts his boots on the wrong feet. When he is gone, the earth loses its verdure and gods as well as human beings live in misery. After the gods have searched in vain for Telipinu, a bee is sent to find him and sting him awake. It only succeeds in angering him until he nearly destroys the earth with floods. Man is called in to help and participates in a long series of magical rites led by the Kamrusepas, which succeed in luring Telipinu back from his retirement and eventually in appeasing his anger. Fertility returns to the earth and there is a great celebration.

Tell, Wilhelm or William. The legendary national hero of Switzerland. In the 14th-century Swiss uprising against Austrian rule, he was supposedly a popular leader. Because of his refusal to salute the cap of Gessler, the imperial governor, as a sign of allegiance to Austria, he was forced to attempt to shoot an apple from the head of his own son with his crossbow. He succeeded in doing so, but afterward dropped an arrow from his jacket. When Gessler asked him what the second arrow was for, Tell replied, "To shoot you, if I had killed my son." Gessler then ordered his imprisonment, but he was rescued by the peasantry and led his country to freedom from Austrian domination.

This legend is the subject of plays by Lemierre (1766), Schiller (1804), and Knowles (1840), and of Rossini's opera *William Tell* (1829).

Saxo Grammaticus tells a similar story about the Danish Toki who killed Harald, and many other variations of the legend are found in Scandinavian and English folklore.

Téllez, Fray Gabriel. See TIRSO DE MOLINA.

Telling the Bees (1858). A poem by John Greenleaf WHITTIER. The title is derived from the New England custom of telling the bees and draping their hives when a member of the family has died. A young man, coming to visit his beloved, sees that the hives are being covered. He assumes that her grandfather has died, but discovers that it is the girl herself.

Tell-Tale Heart, The (1843). A story by Edgar Allan POE. The murderer of an old man buries the dismembered body beneath the floor in his room. While the police are investigating, he begins to hear the heartbeats of his victim. He confesses in a frenzy. When the body is recovered, the murdered man's watch is found to be ticking.

Tellus (*Lat.,* "earth"). An ancient goddess of Rome, the symbol of fertility.

Temora, An Epic Poem (1763). One of the principal poems by James MACPHERSON and attributed by him to OSSIAN. Its title comes from the name given to the royal residence of the kings of Connaught. Cairbar has usurped the throne, having killed Cormac, a distant relative of Fingal (see FINGAL, AN ANCIENT EPIC), and Fingal has raised an army to dethrone the usurper. The poem begins with an invitation from Cairbar to Oscar, son of Ossian, to a banquet. Oscar accepts the invitation, but during the feast a quarrel is hatched in which Cairbar and Oscar are each killed by the other's spear. When Fingal arrives, a battle ensues in which Fillan, son of Fingal and the Achilles of the Caledonian army, and Cathmor, brother of Cairbar and the bravest of the Irish army, are both slain. Victory finally crowns the army of Fingal, and Ferad-Artho, the rightful heir, is restored to the throne of Connaught.

Tempe. A valley in Greece, between Mount Olympus and Mount Ossa. The word was employed by the Greek and Roman poets as a synonym for any valley noted for its cool shades, singing birds, and romantic scenery.

Tempest, Lady Betty. In Oliver Goldsmith's epistolary novel THE CITIZEN OF THE WORLD, a lady of beauty, fortune, and rank, whose head is turned by plays and romances. Having rejected many offers of marriage because her suitors do not come up to her ideal, she is gradually left in the cold until she becomes company only for aunts and cousins, a wallflower in ballrooms, and "a piece of fashionable lumber" in society generally.

Tempest, Marie. Stage name of Dame **Mary Susan Tempest** (1866–1942). English actress. She was best known in her early years for her roles in musical comedies, later changing to dramatic roles. She became a theatrical manager in 1911, and starred in her own productions. She was made a Dame of the British Empire in 1937.

Tempest, The (c. 1611). The last play of William SHAKESPEARE. PROSPERO, magician and philosopher, reigns over an enchanted island with his daughter MIRANDA. By use of magic, Prospero raises a tempest, causing a boat and its occupants to be washed ashore on the island. The boat contains the enemies who usurped Prospero's dukedom of Milan twelve years previously and cast him adrift on a bark with Miranda. The plot, planned by his brother ANTONIO and ALONSO, the king of Naples, miscarried through the kindliness of GONZALO, an old counsellor, who had fitted Prospero's bark with supplies, unbeknownst to his masters. FERDINAND, son of Alonso, is feared drowned by the others, but has landed alone on another part of the island, discovered Miranda, and fallen in love with her. Alonso, Antonio, and the others are led by the music of ARIEL, the invisible

sprite who serves Prospero, as they search for Ferdinand. At last they meet Prospero, who chastises them and orders them to right his wrongs. Alonso, rejoicing at finding Ferdinand alive, blesses the union of the young lovers and restores Prospero to his dukedom, whereupon Prospero renounces his magic and frees Ariel from his spell.

The play contains some of Shakespeare's famous lines and is among his most beautiful works. The existence of analogues to the play in Italian literature and elsewhere suggests the possibility of a source now lost. Prospero's speech renouncing magic was taken from a passage in Arthur Golding's translation (1565–1567) of Ovid's *Metamorphoses,* well known to Elizabethans. See CALIBAN; SEBASTIAN.

Templars or **Knights Templars.** An order of knighthood founded about 1118 to guard the passage of pilgrims to Jerusalem. Begun in poverty—the seal shows two knights riding on one horse—it was joined by many noblemen who brought great wealth to the order. Their independent conduct on the battlefield eventually became an embarrassment rather than an aid to the king of Jerusalem, and their wealth and political power a threat to the kings in Europe. Thus the order was savagely crushed by many rulers and officially suppressed by the Pope in 1312.

Temple. The site, in London, between Fleet Street and the Thames, formerly occupied by the buildings of the Knights TEMPLARS. The Temple Church, dating from 1185, was the last of these buildings to remain standing. Since 1346 the Temple has been in the possession of doctors and students of the law, who, since 1609, have formed the two Inns of Court known as the *Inner* and *Middle Temples.* The area was thoroughly wrecked by Nazi bombs in World War II.

Temple, Charlotte. See CHARLOTTE TEMPLE.

Temple, The (1633). A collection of 160 religious poems by George HERBERT. Deeply influential in its day, it inspired such works as Richard Crashaw's *Steps to the Temple* (1646).

Temple, Sir William (1628–1699). English diplomat, statesman, and author. At his estate at Moor Park in Surrey, Jonathan SWIFT worked as his secretary (1689 *et seq.*) helping him with his memoirs. It was here that Swift met Esther JOHNSON, a dependent of Temple's, when she was nine years old; he later immortalized her as "Stella."

Temple's best-known essay, *Of Ancient and Modern Learning,* started a controversy between Richard Bentley and Charles Boyle, the editor of a series of epistles which he and Sir William were satisfied had been written by the Sicilian tyrant Phalaris. Bentley showed them to be spurious. This wrangle brought forth Swift's famous THE BATTLE OF THE BOOKS.

Temps retrouvé, Le. See REMEMBRANCE OF THINGS PAST.

Tenant of Wildfell Hall, The (1848). A novel by Anne BRONTË. It concerns a marriage destroyed by a dissipated husband.

Tencin, Claudine Alexandrine Guérin de (1682–1749). French letter-writer, novelist, leader in Parisian intellectual circles, and mother of d'ALEMBERT (whom she callously left on a church doorstep). Her salons were the meeting place of many famous men, among whom were Marivaux, Montesquieu, and Bernard le Bovier de Fontenelle. The best of her three romances is the *Mémoires du comte de Com-minges* (1735). Though her conduct was considered scandalous and immoral, such men as the cardinal de Fleury, the grand-nephew of the cardinal de Richelieu, and Lord Chesterfield found it worthwhile to correspond with her because of her frank wit and vivacious style.

Ten Commandments. The Decalogue (*Gr.,* "ten words"), or the laws revealed at Mount Sinai to Moses on the 3rd month after the Israelites' deliverance from Egypt. The Ten Commandments forbid polytheism, idolatry, murder, adultery, theft, false testimony, and covetousness while commanding that God's name be revered, the Sabbath kept holy, and one's father and mother honored (Exod. 20:1-17). They were received by Moses on two tablets of stone.

Tendai. A Japanese Buddhist sect. It teaches an elaborate, comprehensive form of Buddhism. Introduced to Japan by Saichō (767–822), it is based on Chinese T'IEN-T'AI and emphasizes the teachings of the Lotus Sutra. Its headquarters were at Mt. Hiei, near Kyoto. The popularity of esoteric Shingon Buddhism obliged Tendai to incorporate Shingon's doctrines during the Heian period (794–1185). Mt. Hiei was long the center of Japanese learning and culture, and the leaders of almost all the new sects of Japanese Buddhism had their early training here.

Tender Is the Night (1934). A novel by F. Scott FITZGERALD. In the hedonistic setting of post-World War I Europe, a wealthy mental patient, Nicole, falls passionately in love with her young psychiatrist, Dick Diver. She finds her cure in marrying him, but as she achieves mental stability and emotional independence, he deteriorates. Finally Nicole leaves him for a man who will be her lover and not her caretaker, and Dick begins an irreversible decline into alcoholism and dissolution. Diver is perhaps a reflection of Fitzgerald himself, who had painful experiences with his mentally disturbed wife Zelda. Despite the book's many terrifying scenes, the warm tenderness of its writing lifts it into the realm of genuine tragedy. Fitzgerald kept reworking the book after its publication and initial failure with the public. After his death Malcolm Cowley made a new version (1951), in which the episodes were placed in chronological order and the flashback technique of the original version was abandoned.

Tennant, Kylie (1912–   ). Australian novelist. She was born in New South Wales, and educated at Brighton College and the University of Sydney. Her books appear to have grown out of her personal experiences. *Tiburnian* (1935), a prize-winning novel, is a realistic and grim story of the depression. *The Battlers* (1941) drew on the same locale and circumstances. Her writings always show a definite sense of place, and her descriptions are poetic. Her other books include *Foreaux* (1939), *Ride on Stranger* (1943), *Time Enough* (1943), and *Lost Haven* (1946).

Tenniel, Sir John (1820–1914). English illustrator and cartoonist on the staff of *Punch.* He is best known as the illustrator of *Alice's Adventures in Wonderland* and *Through the Looking Glass* by Lewis CARROLL. His illustrations have defined Carroll's characters in the public mind as sharply as the author's own descriptions. The cheery chubbiness of Tweedledum and Tweedledee, ...ne outsized head of the Duchess, the calf's head and feet of the Mock Turtle, and the Hatter's hat with its price tag "In this style 10/6" are all the products of the illustrator's fancy. Tenniel's pictures so perfectly capture the illogic and whimsy of the text that few editions of the books have been printed without them.

Ten Nights in a Bar-Room and What I Saw There (1854). A story by Timothy Shay Arthur (1809–1885), American editor and reformer. A melodramatic temperance tale, it was a favorite among American readers for more than 20 years; in 1858, Arthur's book was dramatized by William W. Pratt. As a play, it was more in demand than any other, with the exception of *Uncle Tom's Cabin.* An important influence in the passage of many temperance laws, its climax was little Mary's song at the saloon door, "Father, dear Father, come home with me now."

Tennyson, Alfred. 1st Baron **Tennyson,** commonly called **Alfred,** Lord Tennyson (1809–1892). English poet. Appointed Poet Laureate in 1850, he is considered highly representative of the Victorian age in England. In his early career, Tennyson was influenced by the English romantic poets, particularly John Keats. His poetry reflects the sensibility and the intellectual and moral values of his time and of the dominant Victorian social class, and is a characteristic

Tennyson's manuscript of *The Throstle.*

response of his time and class to the encroachments of science in the domain of religious faith. He was the favorite target for the attacks of English and American poets of the late 19th and early 20th centuries who, rebelling against Victorian standards, denounced him for sentimentality, insipidity, intellectual shallowness, and narrow patriotism. Later critics have praised him for his metrical skill and the distinguished imagery of some of his brief lyrics; his longer poems, however, are still regarded as suffering the aforementioned weaknesses.

Tennyson's works include the following: *Poems by Two Brothers* (1827), early verse with his brother Charles Tennyson TURNER; *Poems, Chiefly Lyrical* (1830); *Poems* (1832); *Poems* (1842); LOCKSLEY HALL; THE PRINCESS; IN MEMORIAM, often considered his greatest poem, though long; *Ode on the Death of the Duke of Wellington* (1852); MAUD; IDYLLS OF THE KING; ENOCH ARDEN; *Queen Mary* (1875), *Harold* (1876), and *Becket* (1884), historical tragedies in verse; *Tiresias, And Other Poems* (1885); *Locksley Hall Sixty Years After* (1886); *Demeter, And Other Poems* (1889); *The Death of Oenone* (1892).

Tennyson was immensely popular and successful throughout his later career; the one enduring shadow in his life, aside from those inspired by his sensitive and somewhat melancholy temperament, was caused by the death of his friend Arthur HALLAM. This early bereavement led not only to *In Memoriam,* but to a lifelong conflict between faith and doubt. See BREAK, BREAK, BREAK; CHARGE OF THE LIGHT BRIGADE, THE; CROSSING THE BAR; HIGHER PANTHEISM, THE; LORD OF BURLEIGH; MAY QUEEN; PALACE OF ART; REVENGE, THE.

Tenochtitlán. The capital of the Aztec empire and the site of modern Mexico City. Founded about 1325, the city was built on two marsh-bound islands in Lake Texcoco, which were connected to the mainland by a system of causeways; the islands were subsequently enlarged by means of floating gardens. It is said that Cortez wept when he saw the ruins of the city, completely destroyed in 1521 as a result of bitter fighting between Aztecs and Spaniards.

Ten Plagues. The plagues that facilitated the Jews' departure from Egypt (Exod. 7–12). All of these events are still common in this part of the world today. The final plague, the death of the Egyptian first-born, may have affected only the pharaoh's family. The first plague, the Nile turning to blood, was a flood of red silt from the Abyssinian headwaters.

Following closely on each other, these plagues seemed miraculous. In the Bible, they are attributed to the power of God acting through Moses and his brother Aaron. A recitation of the 10 plagues is part of the PASSOVER ritual.

Tenth Muse Lately Sprung Up in America, The (1650). The first volume of poems written in North America, by Anne BRADSTREET. Included in the collection are a *Dialogue between Old England and New* and the ambitious *Four Elements, Four Constitutions, Four Ages of Man, Four Seasons,* and *Four Monarchies,* the last an incomplete attempt at writing universal history. *Contemplations,* which appeared in 1678 in the second edition of *The Tenth Muse,* is generally considered her best work; it is a meditative and descriptive poem, probably influenced by Edmund Spenser and Giles Fletcher.

tercet. In prosody, a synonym for triplet or stanza of three lines. Specifically, a tercet is a three-line stanza used in the terza rima form and in the two three-line divisions of the sestet of the Italian sonnet.

Terence. Full Latin name, **Publius Terentius Afer** (185?–159 B.C.). Comic playwright of ancient Rome, second only to Plautus. Born in Carthage within a year of the death of Plautus, he was taken as a young man of 21 to Rome as the slave of the senator Terentius Lucanus. Impressed by the wit and learning of the young Carthaginian, his master set him free and helped him to continue his studies. His first play, the *Andria (Maid of Andros)* won him entry into what was called "the Scipionic Circle," the group of artists which was subsidized and encouraged by Scipio Africanus the Younger and his friend Laelius. His better-known works include the *Eunuchus,* the *Phormio,* and the *Adelphi.* He died at the age of 26.

Unlike his predecessor Plautus, Terence wrote thoughtful, psychologically refined comedies. He did not aim at strong wit or farcical effect but at sharp delineation of character and elegance of form. His faults stem, accordingly, from his virtues: he is sometimes dry and excessively refined, and often his plots display more skill than wit.

Teresa or **Theresa,** St., known as Santa **Teresa de Jesús** or St. **Teresa of Avila.** Real name: **Teresa de Cepeda y Ahumada** (1515–1582). Spanish nun and mystic. Born near Avila, she was devout even as a child and ran away from home at the age of seven to seek martyrdom among the Moors. In 1534 she became a Carmelite, later becoming mother superior of the order and the foundress of 17 new convents. The story of her intense spiritual life, with its moments of ecstasy and depression, and of her struggles to reform the order is told in her letters, over 400 of which have been preserved, and in the autobiographical *Libro de su vida* and *Libro de las fundaciones.* She was canonized in 1622.

Her finest mystical work is *Las moradas* or *El castillo interior* (1583), in which she guides the reader through the "abodes" of the human soul until he reaches the innermost chamber, the dwelling-place of God. She also wrote the *Camino de perfección* (1583), which discusses ways of achieving perfection in the religious life.

Though her meaning is occasionally obscure, her style is artless and vivid, offering an excellent example of colloquial Castilian of the 16th century.

Tereus. Mythical king of Thrace. He married Procne, daughter of King Pandion of Athens, but later seduced her sister Philomela, then cut out the latter's tongue so that Procne should not learn of his act. Philomela told the story in a piece of embroidery, and Procne avenged herself on Tereus by feeding him their son Itys at a banquet. Tereus tried to kill the two women, but was turned into a hoopoe, and they into a nightingale and a swallow. In the original Greek story, it is Procne who is the nightingale, but later Latin writers make Philomela the nightingale. Tereus appears in his form as a hoopoe in Aristophanes' THE BIRDS.

Termagant. The name given by the Crusaders, and by the authors of medieval romances, to a Saracen idol or deity. The Saracens were popularly supposed to worship the Termagant. He was introduced into the Morality plays as a most violent and turbulent person in long, flowing Eastern robes, a dress that led to his acceptance as a woman, whence the name came to be applied to a shrewish, violently abusive virago.

Hamlet speaks of "outdoing Termagant." In old drama the degree of rant was the measure of villainy. Termagant and Herod, being considered the beau-ideal of all that is bad, were represented as settling everything by club law, and bawling so as to "split the ears of the groundlings."

Terminus. The Roman god of bounds. A boundary stone with a bust of the god was called a *terminus.*

Terpander (c. 675 B.C.). Greek musician. He established at Sparta the first Greek school of music.

Terpine. See FAERIE QUEENE, THE.

Terpsichore. One of the 9 MUSES of ancient Greece, the Muse of dancing and the dramatic chorus, and later of lyric poetry. She is usually represented seated, holding a lyre. Hence the adjective *Terpsichorean,* pertaining to dancing.

Terre, La (The Soil, 1888). A novel by Emile ZOLA. One of the ROUGON-MACQUART series, the theme deals with greed for land. The characters, French peasants, are portrayed with merciless realism.

Terre des hommes. See WIND, SAND, AND STARS.

Terror. See REIGN OF TERROR.

Terry, Ellen [Alicia or Alice] (1847–1928). English actress. She was the mother of Edward Gordon Craig. She played Shakespearean roles with Henry Irving (1878–1902) and later toured the U.S., lecturing on Shakespearean subjects. G. B. Shaw admired her as an actress and as a personal friend. He wrote CAPTAIN BRASSBOUND'S CONVERSION for her. She was made a Dame Grand Cross, Order of the British Empire in 1925.

Terry, Phyllis Neilson- (1892–   ). English actress, the daughter of Ellen Terry's brother Fred. She played many Shakespearean roles in England, the U.S., and Canada.

Tertz, Abram. Pen name of an anonymous Russian writer. Supposedly a Soviet intellectual, Tertz has published a short novel, *The Trial Begins (Sud idiot;* 1960), and an essay on SOCIALIST REALISM. Both works reveal the author's dissaffection with Soviet society and especially with Soviet literary doctrine.

Teruel, Los amantes de. See Juan Eugenio HARTZENBUSCH.

terza rima. An Italian verse form in chain-rhymed TERCETS, the second line of each stanza rhyming with the first and third of the next. The poem or division of a poem in terza rima concludes either with an extra line added to the last stanza or with a separate couplet rhyming with the second line of the last stanza. The rhyme scheme is thus a-b-a, b-c-b, c-d-c, d-e-d-e or a-b-a, b-c-b, c-d-c, d-e-d, e-e. Terza rima may be written in any meter, but iambic pentameter is preferred in English. Dante's *Divine Comedy* was written in this form, which was introduced into England by Sir Thomas Wyatt in the 16th century and has been used by Shelley, Byron, and other English poets.

Teseida. The first Tuscan epic, written in octaves by Giovanni BOCCACCIO. Two friends, Arcita and Palemone of Thebes, vie for the love of Emilia,

sister to the queen of Athens, where they are prisoners. Theseus, king of Athens, orders a tournament to settle the quarrel; the wounded Arcita wins, but dies soon after betrothal to Emilia. As Arcita wished, Emilia then marries Palemone.

In addition to prefiguring the Orlando poems of Boiardo and Ariosto, the *Teseida* was used by Chaucer for *The Knight's Tale,* by Fletcher in *The Two Noble Kinsmen,* and by Dryden for his *Palamon and Arcite.*

Tess of the D'Urbervilles[, A Pure Woman] (1891). A novel by Thomas HARDY. Tess Durbeyfield, urged by her dissipated father and the necessities of a poverty-stricken household, takes service with the wealthy Mrs. D'Urberville. Here Alec, the son of the house, forces Tess into sexual relations with him, and she becomes pregnant. The child, however, dies in infancy, and Tess hires herself out as a dairy-maid on a farm. She falls in love with Angel Clare, a rector's son, and they marry. On their wedding night they indulge in mutual confessions. Though he expects to be forgiven for his own sinful past, Angel cannot forgive Tess for her past, in which she was victimized rather than sinful, and he deserts her. Some time later, Alec, now a preaching fanatic, entreats Tess to return to him. She does so in the belief that Angel will never relent, and in the face of growing poverty. When the repentant Angel returns, and finding Tess with Alec, prepares to leave once again, Tess stabs and kills Alec in desperation. She and Angel hide out for a time, but finally Tess is arrested and sentenced to death.

Testament of Beauty, The (1929). A long poem by Robert BRIDGES. In phonetic spelling and loose Alexandrines, it is an elaborate exposition of Bridges' Platonic philosophy.

Testi, Fulvio (1593–1646). Italian diplomat and poet. Noted for his writings against Spain and his imitations of Horace and Pindar, he began by following Marino, but turned to the influence of Chiabrera. His *Rime (Verses)* were first published in 1613.

Tête d'Or (1890, rev. 1894). A poetic drama by Paul CLAUDEL. Simon Agnel makes himself a warrior hero and tries to conquer the whole world.

Teternikov, Feodor Kuzmich. See Feodor SOLOGUB.

Tethys. In Greek mythology, a Titaness and a sea goddess, wife of OCEANUS; hence, the sea itself. Tethys was the daughter of Uranus and Ge and mother of the river gods.

tetragrammaton (*Gr.,* "four letters"). The Hebrew letters $Y, H, W, H,$ which spell the name of God. See JEHOVAH.

tetrameter. In prosody, a line of verse containing four metrical feet in any METER. Usually it is identified together with the name of the meter, as iambic tetrameter, trochaic tetrameter, etc.

Teucer (Teukros). In the ILIAD, the son of Telamon, and stepbrother of Telamonian Ajax. He went with the allied Greeks to the siege of Troy, and on his return was banished by his father for not avenging on Odysseus the death of his brother. He was the best archer among the Greeks.

Tey, Josephine. See Elizabeth MACKINTOSH.

Thackeray, William Makepeace (1811–1863). English novelist and satirist, best known for his satirical and moralistic studies of upper- and middle-class English life. Born in India of a wealthy merchant family, Thackeray moved to England at the age of six upon the death of his father. Leaving Trinity College, Cambridge, without a degree, he read law but abandoned the idea of the bar in order to explore journalism and art. Losing his inheritance in 1833, he spent three years in Paris studying unsuccessfully to be a painter. In 1836 he married Isabella Shawe and returned to England, resolved to try his luck as a writer. Thackeray gained a degree of recognition as a contributor of sketches to the *Times* and to *Frazer's Magazine* and as the author of such works as *The Yellowplush Correspondence* (1838), *A Shabby Genteel Story* (1840), *The Paris Sketch Book* (1840), THE FITZ BOODLE PAPERS, *The Irish Sketch Book* (1843), and *Notes of a Journey from Cornhill to Grand Cairo* (1846). His literary success, however, had been tragically offset in 1840 when his wife, having borne him three daughters, lost her sanity and never recovered it, though she survived Thackeray by 30 years.

From 1842 to 1851 Thackeray was on the staff of *Punch,* to which he contributed the satires later published as *The Book of Snobs* (1848). With the appearance of this work and of VANITY FAIR, he won a popular and critical reputation that he went on to consolidate with such novels as PENDENNIS; HENRY ESMOND and its sequel, THE VIRGINIANS; and THE NEWCOMES. His other works include the MEMOIRS OF BARRY LYNDON; several Christmas books, among them *Mrs. Perkins's Ball* (1846), REBECCA AND ROWENA, and THE ROSE AND THE RING; *The English Humourists of the Eighteenth Century* (1851) and *The Four Georges* (1855), lectures delivered in Great Britain and the U.S.; THE ADVENTURES OF PHILIP; and *The Roundabout Papers* (1863), essays written for the *Cornhill Magazine,* of which Thackeray was editor from 1860 to 1862. A novel, *Denis Duval* (1864), was left unfinished at his death. Shortly before he died, Thackeray was reconciled with Charles Dickens, with whom he had been feuding since 1858.

Thaïs (1890). A novel by Anatole FRANCE. Inspired by one of the tales in the *Golden Legend,* it is an ironic story of Paphnutius, a young Alexandrian debauché turned monk. Leading an ascetic life in the desert, he interprets his voluptuous dreams of the famous courtesan Thaïs as a call to convert her to Christianity. He succeeds in this aim, and she lives a short but saintly life as a hermit. Paphnutius, however, still dreams of her. In his attempt to hide from himself his lust for her, he mortifies his flesh relentlessly, and even spends some time as a STYLITE atop a high pillar. Finally he realizes his true feelings and tries to persuade her to flee the convent with him. As she dies, the abbess sends him away, horrified at the savagery that is finally revealed on his face.

Thaisa. The strong-willed and passionate daughter of Simonides, king of Pentapolis, in Shakespeare's PERICLES. She loves Pericles on sight and chooses him as her husband in spite of the misery to which he has been reduced by shipwreck.

Thalaba the Destroyer (1801). A poem by Robert SOUTHEY. It is decreed that Thalaba, a young Muslim, is to destroy Domdaniel, a submarine palace where a race of magicians meets. One of the magicians, Abdaldar, seeks to kill Thalaba, but dies in the attempt. Thalaba takes a magic ring from Abdaldar's finger; from the ring he learns that his father was

slain by one of the magicians. He learns that he will accomplish his revenge with faith and that the ring will protect him from the magicians. He succeeds in destroying Domdaniel and the sorcerers, but sacrifices his own life in so doing. He is ultimately united with his wife Oneiza in Paradise.

Thales (c. 624–c. 546 B.C.). A Greek philosopher of the MILESIAN SCHOOL. Regarded by some as the founder of Greek philosophy, he was considered one of the seven wise men of ancient Greece. He made several discoveries in geometry and astronomy, on one occasion accurately predicting an eclipse. Not satisfied with the answers provided by mythology, he searched for the primary substance in the universe, so that he could explain change as well as stability. He believed that water was this substance.

According to tradition, Thales replied to the charge of being an impractical philosopher by going into the olive-oil business, and becoming very wealthy.

Thalestris. A queen of the AMAZONS. She went with 300 women to meet Alexander the Great, under the hope of raising a race of Alexanders; hence, any bold heroic woman.

Thalia. One of the MUSES, generally regarded as the patroness of comedy. She was supposed by some, also, to preside over husbandry and planting, and is represented holding a comic mask and a shepherd's crook.

Thammuz or **Tammuz.** The Syrian and Phoenician name of ADONIS. His death occurs on the banks of the river Adonis, and in summer the waters become reddened with the hunter's blood. In the Bible, reference is made to the heathen "women weeping for Tammuz" (Ezek. 8:14).

Thamyris. A Thracian bard. He is mentioned by Homer (*Iliad,* ii.595). He challenged the Muses to a trial of skill, and, being overcome in the contest, was deprived by them of his sight and power of song.

Thanatopsis (1817). A poem by William Cullen BRYANT. Inspired by the English Graveyard School of poetry, Bryant's poem seeks comfort in Nature for death. The earth, tomb of mankind, will cover all who now laugh or chase their "favorite phantoms." The poet advises, then, that when our time comes to join the "innumerable caravan":

> ... approach thy grave,
> Like one who wraps the drapery of his couch
> About him, and lies down to pleasant dreams.

Thanatos. In Greek mythology, Death represented as a person. He appears in Euripides' ALCESTIS. Sleep (Hypnos) was his twin brother.

Thanet, Octave. See Alice FRENCH.

Thatcher, Becky. A young girl in Mark Twain's ADVENTURES OF TOM SAWYER. She is lost in the cave with Tom.

Thaumaste (*Gr.,* "admirable"). In Rabelais' GARGANTUA AND PANTAGRUEL, a great English scholar who goes to Paris attracted by the rumor of the great wisdom of Pantagruel. He proposes a disputation over philosophy, geomancy, the cabala, and other abstruse subjects to be carried on, not in words, but in gestures alone, "for these subjects are too profound for human words to explain them to my satisfaction." Panurge offers to dispute as his master's disciple, while Pantagruel arbitrates. The ensuing description of their pantomime is a masterly satire on the mechanical and empty arguments of the last of the scholastics. Finally, Thaumaste declares that he is fully satisfied, for "Panurge had told him even more than he had asked."

thaw, the. The name applied to the period of relative relaxation in Soviet life and culture following Stalin's death in 1953. The name was taken from the title of a novel by Ilya EHRENBURG, which was one of the first of a growing stream of works criticizing aspects of Soviet life. The unaccustomed freedom of writers to comment openly, if carefully, on their society reached its peak in 1956 with the publication of such works as Dudintzev's *Not by Bread Alone,* and Aleksandr Yashin's story *Levers.* Previously outlawed older writers such as Yuri Oliosha, Isaak Babel, and Anna Akhmatova were reprinted at this time. The growing concern of Soviet authorities at the criticism, spurred by the 1956 Hungarian revolution, brought a curtailment of the limited freedom the writers had been allowed.

Theaetetus (Theaitetos). A dialogue by PLATO on the nature of knowledge. Theaetetus, an Athenian mathematician, has been mortally wounded in the Corinthian War, and the news recalls to a friend a conversation Theaetetus and Socrates had once had. Varying definitions of knowledge are considered, but all are rejected. The subject is resumed in the dialogue called the *Sophist* which includes Socrates' comment that he is the midwife of men's thoughts.

Theagenes. See ETHIOPICA.

Theale, Milly. See WINGS OF THE DOVE, THE.

Theatre, The. An Elizabethan theater. The first English theater built expressly for performances, it was erected in Shoreditch by James BURBAGE in 1576. It was torn down when Burbage's sons erected the famous Globe Theatre.

Theatre Guild, The. A theatrical producing company. It developed from the Washington Square Players (1918) and built its own theater (1925), which cost a million dollars. It has specialized in giving the plays of George Bernard Shaw and Eugene O'Neill as well as reviving old plays and giving plays by newer American authors.

Théâtre de l'oeuvre. See Aurélien-François LUGNÉ-POË.

Théâtre Libre. See André ANTOINE.

Théâtre National Populaire. A theater created by the French government, under the direction of Jean Vilar. The aim of the new theater was to revitalize drama and to convey the life and excitement of the stage world to a wide audience. The plays, produced at the Palais de Chaillot in Paris, appeal to a range of interests: they are both French and foreign, classic and modern. Vilar is a director well suited to the attempt to establish a sense of communion between actors and audience. His staging is starkly simple; he imposes no footlights or elaborate props between the play and the playgoers.

Theban Eagle. An epithet applied to Pindar, born at Thebes (c. 520–435 B.C.). He was also called the *Theban Lyre.*

Thebes (Thebae). Called The Hundred-Gated, the chief town of the Thebaid, on the Nile in Upper Egypt, said to have extended over 23 miles of land. Homer says out of each gate the Thebans could send forth 200 war chariots.

It is here that the vocal statue of MEMNON stood, and here too are the tombs of the kings, the temple of Karnak, and large numbers of sculptures, sphinxes, etc. The village of Luxor now marks the spot.

Thebes (Thebai). Called the Seven-Gated, the chief city of Boeotia, according to legend named after the nymph Thebe (see AMPHION). Founded, according to legend, by Cadmus, it was the birthplace of Dionysus and the scene of the tragic events that began with the birth of Oedipus and continued through the wars of his sons (see SEVEN AGAINST THEBES) and grandsons, the Epigoni. It was still an important city in classical times.

Their Father's God. See GIANTS IN THE EARTH.

Their Wedding Journey (1871). A novel by William Dean HOWELLS. Treating the everyday scenes of American life with great fidelity, it follows the honeymooning couple Isabel and Basil March through New York City, Rochester, Niagara Falls, Quebec, and Montreal. Howells's first novel, it is largely autobiographical.

Thélème, abbey of (*Gr.,* "will, pleasure"). In Rabelais' GARGANTUA AND PANTAGRUEL, the abbey given by Gargantua to FRIAR JOHN for the aid he rendered in the war against PICROCHOLE. Built like a magnificent castle, it was the very reverse of a convent or monastery. Thélèmites were free to leave when they chose; they could marry, own wealth, and lived in perfect freedom. The only rule was "Do as thou wilt."

Themis. In Greek mythology, one of the TITANS, and goddess of Natural Law and Justice. She was regarded as an earth-goddess, and was one of the earliest patronesses of the DELPHIC ORACLE.

Themistocles (Themistokles; c. 528–c. 462 B.C.). An Athenian statesman and general. Thucydides spoke of him as a man of genius. He persuaded the Athenians to concentrate on the development of sea power, building up their fleet to 200 triremes. When the Persians led by Xerxes invaded Greece, Themistocles tried vainly to persuade the united Greeks to engage them by sea in the Bay of Salamis, where their more maneuverable vessels would have a tactical advantage. He then sent a message to the Persians that the Greeks were about to flee in disunity. The message had the intended effect, and the Persians at once surrounded the deliberating allies at Salamis. The battle (480 B.C.) was a great victory for the Greeks.

It was on Themistocles' advice that the Athenians rebuilt the walls of Athens and erected a walled way to her port at Piraeus. After the war, Themistocles became unpopular; he was vain and reportedly accessible to bribes. Ostracized, he moved to Argos, but was accused of treason. In time, he fled to the Persian court of Artaxerxes, where he was awarded the Asian kingdom of Magnesia. At his death, the Magnesians erected a statue of the "savior of Greece" in their market place.

Theobald, Lewis (1688–1744). English playwright and critic. In his *Shakespeare Restored* (1726), he attacked Pope's edition of Shakespeare, somewhat justifiably. Pope retaliated by making Theobald the king of Dullness in his first edition of *The Dunciad.*

Theocritus (Theokritos, early 3d century B.C.). A Greek poet. He was probably born in Syracuse. He is regarded as the inventor of the pastoral. Only about

30 of his works are extant; they include mainly the *Idyls*.

Theodora (508?–548). Empress of the Byzantine Empire, wife of JUSTINIAN I. She was an actress and noted for her beauty. She had great influence over Justinian and on the political and religious thinking at court.

Theodoric the Great (c. 454–c. 526). A king of the Ostrogoths who invaded Italy, then ruled it in peace after 493. He is the origin of the heroic Dietrich of Bern in Germanic legends such as the *Heldenbuch* and the *Nibelungenlied*, but there he is described as fleeing from Italy to the court of Etzel (Attila, king of the Huns).

Theognis (6th century B.C.). He expressed his distaste for the lower classes in elegiac verse. The collection attributed to him also contains the work of other poets.

Theon. A satirical poet of ancient Rome. He is noted for his mordant writings; hence, Theon's tooth means the bite of an ill-natured or carping critic.

Theophrastus (c. 370–285 B.C.). A Greek philosopher, successor to Aristotle. Originally named Tyrtamus, he was called Theophrastus or divine speaker by Aristotle, because of his eloquence. As the leader of the Peripatetic School, he continued the work of Aristotle in natural history and botany. The surviving fragments show little originality. His best known work is *Characters*, 30 satiric depictions of typical work weaknesses. See CHARACTER WRITERS.

Theory of the Leisure Class, The (1899). An economic treatise by Thorstein VEBLEN. Veblen held that the feudal subdivision of classes had continued into modern times, the lords employing themselves uselessly (as in hunting animals) while the lower classes labored at industrial pursuits to support the whole of society. The leisure class, Veblen said, justifies itself solely by practicing "conspicuous leisure and conspicuous consumption"; he defined waste as any activity not contributing to material productivity. H. L. Mencken later attacked Veblen in *Prejudices* (1919), calling the economist's theory of conspicuous waste "one per cent platitude and 99 per cent nonsense."

Theosophy (*Gr.*, theos, god; *sophia*, wisdom). A term applied in the 17th century to describe speculation that sought a deeper knowledge and control of nature than the current philosophical methods could achieve; this deeper knowledge of nature was to be obtained through a knowledge of God found in secret books and derived from a mystical interpretation of tradition. The term was specifically applied to the system of Jacob Boehme.

Later the term was adopted by the Theosophical Society founded (1875) in New York by Col. H. S. Olcott, Mme BLAVATSKY, and others. Their aims included the promotion of study of Eastern literature, religions, and sciences, and a study of the unfamiliar laws in nature and latent faculties in man.

Theotocopoulos, Kyriakos. See El GRECO.

Theresa of Avila, St. See TERESA DE JESÚS.

Thérèse Desqueyroux (1927). A novel by François MAURIAC. The title character, feeling herself stifled by the bourgeois proprieties of her marriage, attempts to poison her husband. She is acquitted at her trial, however, through her family's efforts to avoid scandal.

There Shall Be No Night (1940). A play by Robert E. SHERWOOD. Set in Finland, it deals with a brilliant neurologist who refuses to face the threat of war. When his native country is drawn into war with Russia and his only son is killed, he takes a stand. At his death, his American wife is left alone to defend their home. The play was awarded a Pulitzer Prize.

Thermidor (from Gr., *thermē*, "heat," and *doron*, "gift"). 11th month in the French REVOLUTIONARY CALENDAR, containing 30 days beginning July 19.

Thermidorians. The designation used for the milder French Revolutionists who took part in the *coup d'état* that overthrew ROBESPIERRE on Thermidor 9 of the second republican year (July 27, 1794), thus bringing to a close the Reign of Terror.

Thermopylae, Battle of. See PERSIAN WARS.

Thersander (Thersandros). In Greek mythology, a son of POLYNICES. By bribing ERIPHYLE, he won the support of her son Alcmaeon, who led the successful war of the Epigoni on Thebes to avenge their fathers. According to some stories, Thersander joined the expedition against Troy, but was killed in Mysia. In the AENEID, however, he is one of the Greek soldiers who hid in the TROJAN HORSE.

Thersites. In Homer's *Iliad* a deformed, scurrilous officer in the Greek army at the siege of Troy. He was always railing at the chiefs; hence, the name is applied to any dastardly, malevolent, impudent railer against the powers that be. Achilles felled him with his fist and killed him. In Shakespeare's TROILUS AND CRESSIDA he is "a slave whose gall coins slanders like a mint."

These Thirteen (1931). A collection of short stories by William FAULKNER. This volume contains one of the best known of all of Faulkner's stories, *A Rose for Emily*. It tells of an aristocratic, eccentric, and aging Southern spinster, Miss Emily Grierson, who has been courted by Homer Barron, a Yankee construction worker, who then disappears. When Miss Emily dies years later, having become a legend, the townspeople find the skeleton of Barron locked in an upstairs bedroom. The volume also contains two stories dealing with the Indians who inhabited the land before the white settlers arrived: *Red Leaves* and *A Justice*.

Theseus. The chief hero of Attica in ancient Greek legend; son of AEGEUS and the performer of innumerable exploits. He is sometimes also described as the son of Poseidon. He was brought up by his mother Aethra, but when he became strong enough to lift the stone under which his father's sword was hidden, he was sent to the court of Athens, where, in spite of the efforts of his father's wife MEDEA, he was recognized as heir to the throne. Among his deeds were the slaying of Procrustes, SCIRON, Sinis, the CROMMYONIAN sow; the capture of the Marathonian bull; the slaying of the Minotaur with the aid of ARIADNE, whom he subsequently deserted in Naxos; his war against the AMAZONS; his part in the expedition of the ARGONAUTS, and the hunt for the CALYDONIAN boar. He defends OEDIPUS in Sophocles' *Oedipus at Colonus*.

There are numerous versions of his war against the Amazons. He married the Amazonian queen who opposed him, known as either Antiope or Hippolyta (according to some accounts there were two sisters of these names) and took her home with him. After the death of this queen, he married PHAEDRA whose ill-fated infatuation with her stepson Hippolytus has formed the subject of many tragedies in which Theseus plays a part. In his old age he became unpopular with his people and was foully murdered by Lycomedes in Scyros, where he had taken refuge. He is the hero of two fine historical novels by Mary Renault, *The King Must Die* and *The Bull from the Sea.*

According to medieval legend, Theseus' title was duke of Athens and his duchess was Hippolyta. Under this title he plays a part in Chaucer's KNIGHT's TALE. In the *Knight's Tale,* he marries Hippolyta, and as he returns home with his bride and Emily, her sister, he is accosted by a crowd of female suppliants who complain of Creon, king of Thebes. The duke forthwith sets out for Thebes, slays Creon, and takes the city by assault. Many captives fall into his hands, among them the two knights Palamon and Arcite.

As the duke of Athens, Theseus appears in Shakespeare's MIDSUMMER NIGHT's DREAM. He is betrothed to Hippolyta, queen of the Amazons, and it is because of him that the action of the play takes place.

Thesmophoriazusai (411 B.C.). A comedy by ARISTOPHANES. The play is based on the notion that the women of Athens plan to kill Euripides for presenting them in so harsh a light in his plays—a crime of which, in real life, Euripides was not guilty. He tries to persuade the effeminate tragic poet Agathon to attend in women's dress the annual festival of Athenian women, the Thesmophoria, in order to plead Euripides' case. Agathon refuses, but lends his women's clothes to Euripides' father-in-law Mnesilochus. The Women Who Celebrate the Thesmophoria (the meaning of the title) resent Mnesilochus' arguments and, on penetrating his disguise, threaten to burn him. Euripides comes to the rescue and both men play several roles from Euripides' plays in hilarious attempts to outwit the women and a policeman. Finally Euripides is reconciled with the women.

Thespis (6th century B.C.). An Attic poet, regarded as the father of Greek tragedy. His chief contribution to drama, of which he may be considered the inventor, seems to have been that he gave lines of dialogue in dramatic narratives to specific members of the chorus, hitherto entirely performed by the whole chorus. Thus he would have performed a service similar to that of the unknown priests who first assigned the *Quem quaeritis?* line from the Easter gospel to individual voices, thereby giving birth to medieval drama.

Thessalonians, The First Epistle and **The Second Epistle of Paul the Apostle to the.** Two books of the New Testament. The first letter is possibly the oldest portion of the New Testament to be preserved in its original form. It was written c. A.D. 50 to the church at Thessalonica to answer questions about the expected second coming of Jesus. The second letter elaborates on the first.

Thetis. Greek sea-goddess, daughter of Nereus. She was loved by Zeus and Poseidon, but, when Themis or Prometheus disclosed that she was fated to bear a son greater than his father, Zeus quickly wedded her to the hero Peleus. Their wedding was a brilliant celebration attended by the gods, but marred by the incident of the APPLE OF DISCORD.

Thetis bore Achilles and proceeded to immortalize him by dipping him in the river Styx; only the heel by which she held him remained mortal. In another version, she held him in the fire, but when Peleus saw her and cried out, she dropped the child on the floor and left the house forever. When Achilles was grown to manhood, she warned him to return home from Troy in order to live a long life, but he preferred a short, glorious one. The tragic events recorded in the ILIAD resulted in part from her plea to Zeus to punish the Greeks for having offended her son. It was Thetis and Euronyme who caught Hephaestus when he was thrown out of heaven. She aided the ARGONAUTS to pass through the Clashing Rocks.

Thévenin, Denis. See Georges DUHAMEL.

They Knew What They Wanted (1924). A play by Sidney HOWARD. Tony Patucci, a California winegrower, misleads his mail-order bride-to-be, Amy, by sending her a picture of his handsome young hired man Joe. On their wedding day Tony breaks both his legs, and Amy, humiliated and confused, allows Joe to seduce her and becomes pregnant. Tony nearly kills the younger man, but finally allows Amy to stay. The play was awarded a Pulitzer Prize. It was later filmed, and still later became the basis of the musical *The Most Happy Fella* (1957) by Frank Loesser.

Thibault, Jacques Anatole François. See Anatole FRANCE.

Thibaults, Les (1922–1940). Novel series by Roger MARTIN DU GARD. In the tradition of the 19th-century naturalists, this work is marked by objectivity and by the amassing of precise detail. Two brothers, Jacques and Antoine Thibault, react as individuals to their bourgeois environment. Antoine leads a simple, dutiful existence while Jacques succumbs to his rebellious, adventurous temperament. The personal histories of the two main characters are set against a sweeping backdrop of world violence and chaos; both men die in the First World War.

Thief, Penitent. See DISMAS.

Thief, The (*Vor*; 1927). A novel by Leonid LEONOV. The book is set during the time of the New Economic Policy in Soviet Russia. The hero of the novel, Mitka Vekshin, has fought courageously during the civil war but emerges from the combat with inner conflicts about whether the killing was worthwhile. Disaffected with the humdrum life of building a society he is not sure he wants, he becomes a thief. The picture of the Moscow underworld, with its odd characters and the psychological probing of their personalities, reveals Dostoevski's influence on Leonov in this work. A further similarity is to be found in the novel's frenetically paced prose. The disillusionment with Soviet society implied in Leonov's description of life during the NEP period caused the novel to be severely criticized by Soviet reviewers. For years the work was not included in Leonov's collected works, and it is only after he recently revised it that it was reprinted at all.

Thiers, Louis Adolphe (1797–1877). French statesman and historical writer. A leader of the liberals (1863–1870) against Napoleon III (see JULY REVOLUTION), Thiers negotiated the peace treaty with Germany in 1871. He disposed of the Paris Commune, and was elected the first president (1871–1873) of the Third Republic. His most famous works are *Histoire de la Révolution française* (1823–1827) and *Histoire du consulat et de l'empire* (1845–1862).

Thiess, Frank (1890–   ). German novelist. His most famous work is *Abschied vom Paradies* (*Farewell to Paradise*, 1927).

thing-in-itself. See CRITIQUE OF PURE REASON; CRITIQUE OF JUDGMENT.

thing poem. See DINGGEDICHT.

Things. A short story by D. H. LAWRENCE, originally published in *The Lovely Lady* (1933). It is the cynical account of two American "idealists" who try to devote their lives to art, beauty, Buddhism, and European culture. They only succeed, however, in collecting material "things."

third estate. The third of the social classes, or "estates," according to political theory of medieval and feudal times. It comprised peasants, serfs, yeomen, and the early bourgeoisie; the nobles and clergy constituted the first two estates. In France the third estate was known as *tiers état* and was without representation until the Revolution of 1789, at which time it declared itself to be the National ASSEMBLY. The three estates together formed the *états-généraux* or States-General, which was something like the English Parliament.

Third Man, The (1950). A thriller by Graham GREENE. Concerned with love and intrigue in postwar Vienna, it was later made into a movie directed by Carol Reed.

Third Reich (Third Empire). The name given to Germany by Hitler during his dictatorship (1933–1945). In his terminology, the Holy Roman Empire was the First Reich and the German Empire of Bismarck the Second. The Third Reich, Hitler prophesied, would last a thousand years.

Thirkell, Angela (1890–1961). English novelist. She was the daughter of J. W. Mackail, granddaughter of Edward Burne-Jones, and cousin of Rudyard Kipling. She wrote light, popular novels about Anthony Trollope's BARSETSHIRE: *The Brandons* (1939), *Northbridge Rectory* (1942) and *Coronation Summer* (1953).

Thirteen Questions of Love. An episode in Giovanni Boccaccio's prose romance FILOCOLO. The hero, shipwrecked at Naples, is invited to join a party in a garden. One of the young ladies, FIAMMETTA, is chosen to preside over a discussion of love problems and to render a decision in each case. Since the statement of the problem involves the telling of stories, the whole scene is THE DECAMERON's frame story in embryo.

Thirty-Nine Articles, The. The articles of faith of the Church of England, the acceptance of which is obligatory on its clergy. They were originally issued in 1551 as 42, but in 1563 were modified and reduced to their present number. They received parliamentary authority in 1571.

Thirty-Nine Steps, The (1915). An adventure romance by John BUCHAN. Its hero and narrator, Richard HANNAY, uncovers a spy ring and forestalls an invasion of Britain. It was filmed by Alfred Hitchcock.

Thirty Tyrants, the. (1) The 30 magistrates appointed by Sparta over Athens at the termination of the PELOPONNESIAN WAR. This reign of terror, after one year's continuance was overthrown by THRASYBULUS (403 B.C.).

(2) In the Roman empire, those military usurpers who endeavored, in the reigns of Valerian and Gallienus (253–268), to make themselves independent princes, are also called the Thirty Tyrants. The number must be taken with great latitude, as only 19 are given, and their resemblance to those of Athens is extremely fanciful.

Thirty Years War (1618–1648). A war that devastated central Europe, especially Germany, and eventually involved most of the nations of Europe. It was originally a religious conflict between Protestants and Roman Catholics; northern Germany supported the former, and southern Germany, led by Austria, supported the latter. Later, political issues overshadowed religion as Sweden and France entered the struggle in an effort to crush the power of the Hapsburgs. The immediate cause of the war was a revolt (1618) of Bohemian Protestants whose religious rights had been violated by Austria. The Peace of Westphalia (1648) made territorial concessions to France and Sweden, recognized the independence of Switzerland and the Netherlands, and upheld the autonomy of the states of the German empire. It also confirmed the Peace of Augsburg (1555), which granted freedom of worship to the princes and free cities of Germany, and extended its provisions to include Calvinists.

Thisbe. See PYRAMUS.

This Side of Paradise (1920). A novel by F. Scott FITZGERALD. Amory Blaine, a handsome, wealthy, spoiled and snobbish young man from the Middle West, attends Princeton University and acquires a refined sense of the proper "social" values. Lacking all sense of purpose, he interests himself primarily in literary cults, vaguely "liberal" student activities, and a series of flirtations with some rather predatory young ladies that culminate in a genuine but ill-fated love for Rosaline Commase, who rejects him to marry a wealthier young man. During the war Amory serves as an officer in France, and upon his return home he embarks upon a career in advertising, world-weary, cynical, regretful, and not yet thirty years old. Virtually a record of the "LOST GENERATION" in its college days, the novel treats Fitzgerald's characteristic theme of true love blighted by money-lust and is remarkable for its honest and detailed descriptions of the early "Jazz Age." The book established Fitzgerald's reputation.

Thomas, St. One of the 12. He was the disciple of Jesus who doubted (John 21:25); hence the phrase, *a doubting Thomas*, applied to a skeptic. The story told of him in the Apocryphal *Acts of St. Thomas* is that he was deputed to go as a missionary to India, and, when he refused, Christ appeared and sold him as a slave to an Indian prince who was visiting Jerusalem. He was taken to India, where he baptized the prince and many others, and was finally martyred at Meliapore. His day is December 21.

Another legend has it that Gondoforus, king of the Indies, gave him a large sum of money to build a palace. St. Thomas spent it on the poor, "thus erecting a superb palace in heaven." On account of this he is the patron saint of masons and architects, and his symbol is a builder's square. Still another legend relates that he once saw a huge beam of timber floating on the sea near the coast, and the king unsuccessfully endeavoring, with men and elephants, to haul it ashore. St. Thomas desired leave to use it in building a church. When his request was granted he dragged it easily ashore with a piece of pack thread.

Thomas, Dylan [Marlais] (1914–1953). Welsh poet and prose writer. His poetry is remarkable for its lyrical power, its surrealism, its compact, vivid metaphors, its use of Christian and Freudian imagery, and its puns and intricate patterns of sound and meaning, influenced by the work of Gerard Manley Hopkins. It expresses Thomas' personal religion, celebrating the glory and wonder of procreation, growth, and death. He published his first volume of poetry, *Eighteen Poems*, in 1934; the leaders of the NEW APOCALYPSE movement in poetry imitated and advocated his visionary style. His *Collected Poems* appeared in 1953. Among Dylan Thomas' best-known individual poems are *And death shall have no dominion, Altarwise by Owl-light* (a sonnet sequence), *A Refusal to Mourn the Death, by Fire, of a Child in London, Do not go gentle into that good night, In My Craft and Sullen Art,* and *Fern Hill.*

Thomas' earliest prose works were surrealistic short stories; they were not published until 1955 when they appeared as *Adventures in the Skin Trade*. In the 1940's he worked on film and radio scenarios; he began to write more popular and humorous but still poetic prose, expressing his exuberant love of life. *Portrait of the Artist as a Young Dog* (1940) is a collection of stories about his childhood and youth; the title reflects Thomas' admiration for James Joyce. UNDER MILK WOOD (1954) is a radio play for voices. He also wrote *Quite Early One Morning* (1954) and *A Prospect of the Sea* (1955).

Through his radio work and his poetry readings in England and the U.S., Thomas achieved wide popular appeal. His reputation thrived on the storms of his private life, his tempestuous marriage with his wife Caitlin, and his alcoholism. His death in New York in 1953 was regarded as an international event, symbolic of the plight of the artist in modern society.

Thomas, Edith Matilda (1854–1925). American poet. A friend of Helen Hunt Jackson, she published several books of verse, including *A New Year's Masque and Other Poems* (1885), *Lyrics and Sonnets* (1887), and *The Flower from the Ashes* (1915).

Thomas, [Philip] Edward (1878–1917). English poet and critic. Associated with the GEORGIANS, he was for some years dismissed as just another old-fashioned nature poet, but he has recently been rediscovered as an original writer about life and the human consciousness. He was a friend of Robert Frost and the two poets' work is in many ways alike. He was killed in action during World War I. His *Collected Poems,* with a preface by Walter de la Mare, appeared in 1920; among his best-known single poems are *Old Man, Adlestrop,* and *The Glory*. His widow, Helen Thomas, wrote moving accounts of their relationship in *As It Was* (1926) and *World Without End* (1930).

Thomas, Norman [Mattoon] (1884–1968). American political leader and socialist. A graduate of Princeton University and an ordained Presbyterian minister, Thomas founded and edited *World Tomorrow* from 1918 to 1921. Eventually he resigned his ministerial duties to devote his entire time to writing

and speaking for social reform and pacifism. As a Socialist Party candidate he ran unsuccessfully for many offices, including the presidency (1928–1948). His books include *The Challenge of War* (1925), *Socialism of Our Time* (1929), *A Socialist's Faith* (1951), and *The Great Dissenters* (1961).

Thomas, Theodore (1835–1905). German-born American conductor. He founded in 1862 an orchestra bearing his name, which he conducted on many tours in America. He was the conductor of the New York Philharmonic from 1877 to 1891 and of the Chicago Symphony from 1891 to 1905.

Thomas à Becket. Also known as St. Thomas **Becket** or **Thomas of London** (1118?–1170). English prelate, archbishop of Canterbury (1162–1170). Against the lay interference of Henry II, he defended the rights of the Church without compromise. In 1164 he was forced to flee to France. Papal pressure brought about the king's reconciliation with him, but, after his return to England in 1170, he was murdered on December 29 in Canterbury Cathedral by four overzealous knights of Henry's court. Two years later he was canonized. His shrine was plundered by Henry VIII, and his name erased from the English church calendar. The lively company in Chaucer's *Canterbury Tales* are making a pilgrimage to St. Thomas à Becket's shrine. His martyrdom is the subject of T. S. Eliot's play *Murder in the Cathedral* and of Jean Anouilh's play *Becket*.

Thomas à Kempis. More properly, **Thomas Hammerken von Kempen** (c. 1380–1471). German monk and writer. He is generally regarded as the author of the IMITATION OF CHRIST. He entered the Augustinian monastery of Mt. St. Agnes in 1407, where he spent the rest of his life in meditation and writing.

Thomas Aquinas, St. See St. Thomas AQUINAS.

Thomism, Thomists. See St. Thomas AQUINAS.

Thompson, Benjamin, Count Rumford (1753–1814). American-born adventurer and scientist. A loyalist during the American Revolution, he entered the service of the elector of Bavaria and was created a count of the Holy Roman Empire. In England he made improvements in heating and cooking equipment for houses and helped organize the Royal Academy.

Thompson, Daniel Pierce. See GREEN MOUNTAIN BOYS, THE.

Thompson, Dorothy (1894–1961). American journalist. One of the most able newspaperwomen of her generation, she established her reputation as a foreign correspondent in Germany and Vienna during the 1920's. Later she wrote the widely syndicated column *On the Record*, in which she discussed foreign and domestic affairs. One of her books, *The New Russia* (1928), involved her in a controversy with Theodore Dreiser, whom she accused of plagiarizing from it. From 1928 to 1942 she was married to Sinclair Lewis; their marriage is the subject of *Dorothy and Red* (1963), an account by Vincent Sheean.

Thompson, Francis (1859–1907). English poet. He studied medicine in his early youth, but never received a degree. He was extremely unpractical and was unable to make a living for himself in London, failing at such diverse attempts as shoe-making, errand-running, and match-selling. He became addicted to opium, starved, and attempted suicide. During this period of misery, he wrote his earliest poems, some of which were accepted for publication by Wilfred Meynell in his magazine *Merry England*. Thereafter, Thomson lived with Wilfrid and Alice MEYNELL who nursed him and encouraged him in his writing.

His *Poems* (1893) contains his famous poem, THE HOUND OF HEAVEN; later publications include *Sister Songs* (1895), *New Poems* (1897), and the prose pieces *Health and Holiness* (1905), *Life of St. Ignatius Loyola* (1909), *Essays on Shelley* (1909), and *Life of John Baptist de la Galle* (1911). In color and imagery, Thompson's work shows the marked influence of Keats and Shelley, and in spirit and tone it is often akin to that of the metaphysical poets. A devout Roman Catholic, Thompson frequently presented ecstatic visions of heaven in his mystical poetry.

Thompson, Sadie. See MISS THOMPSON.

Thomson, James (1700–1748). Scottish-born English poet, known as a forerunner of romanticism in a period when neoclassicism held sway in literature, and except for Alexander Pope, the most celebrated poet of the first half of the 18th century. His best-known works are THE SEASONS and THE CASTLE OF INDOLENCE. Both poems are marked by their love of nature, fantasy, and sensuous imagery, all romantic qualities unique at the time of composition. Thomson was one of the first to write nature poetry in the manner of the later romantics. He also wrote *A Poem Sacred to the Memory of Sir Isaac Newton* (1727); *Sophonisba* (1731), a tragedy; *Liberty* (1735–1736), a long poem, which he considered his best work, setting forth the view that political liberty was attained in Greece, lost in the Middle Ages, and regained in Great .Britain; and the masque *Alfred* (1740), in which he collaborated with David Mallet, and which contains the famous *Rule, Britannia*.

Thomson, James (1834–1882). English poet, known for his savage melancholy, atheism, and political radicalism. Thomson had an extremely unhappy life. His alcoholic father was paralyzed when the poet was six; two years later his mother, who had suffered from acute religious melancholy, died. The virtually orphaned child was sent to an institution. For a time he was an army instructor in Ireland, there meeting the love of his life, a beautiful 16-year-old girl, Matilda Weller, who died before they could be married. Later he became a radical journalist and held a number of miscellaneous, precarious jobs. His death came as the result of chronic alcoholism. The despair engendered by his experience (and the philosophical pessimism of the late 19th century, as well) is best expressed in his THE CITY OF DREADFUL NIGHT, in which the poet pursues the enigma of fate through a magnificently realized, terrifying city of nightmare. Much of Thomson's work is in this vein, but some poems, such as his accounts of Cockney life in *Sunday at Hampstead* (1863) and *Sunday up the River* (1865) reveal a humorous, realistic side of his talent. His volumes of poetry include *The City of Dreadful Night* (1880); *Vane's Story and Other Poems* (1881); *Insomnia* (1881); and the posthumous *A Voice From the Nile* (1884). Many of his poems were published under the pseudonym Bysshe Vanolis or B.V., a compound of the names of Percy Bysshe Shelley and Novalis. He also wrote critical studies of Whitman, Heine, and numerous English writers, as well as notable translations of Leopardi.

Thomson, Virgil (1896–   ). American composer and muisc critic. An intimate friend of Gertrude Stein, he wrote two operas to her libretti: FOUR SAINTS IN THREE ACTS and *The Mother of Us All* (1947), the latter based on SUSAN B. ANTHONY's fight for women's rights. His witty and perceptive musical criticism is the basis of several books: *The State of Music* (1939), *The Musical Scene* (1945), *The Art of Judging Music* (1948), and others. He has also written some fine film music, including the score for Robert Flaherty's *Louisiana Story* (1948).

Thopas, Sir. One of the CANTERBURY TALES of Geoffrey CHAUCER, a stanzaic parody of minstrel romances, begun by Chaucer when the Host asks him for a tale. In greatly exaggerated detail Sir Thopas is described as an exemplary knight of Flanders who rides out, determined to love no one but an elf-queen. He meets the giant Olifaunt, escapes the stones thrown at him, and goes home to get his armor so he can give battle. At this point the Host interrupts, calling the rhyme "doggerel" and worse. Chaucer then offers to tell a "little thing in prose": see MELIBEE.

Thor. In Norse mythology, the Aesir god of thunder, second in importance to his father Odin. Perhaps the most widely worshiped of the gods, he was popular as the benevolent protector of man. His most precious possessions are his magic hammer, the thunderbolt Mjollnir, a belt of strength, and a pair of iron gloves. The giant who built the residence for the gods was paid by Thor with his mallet. When this hammer had fallen into the possession of the giant Thrym, Thor recovered it by dressing himself in Freya's clothes, pretending to be the fair goddess whom the giant wanted to be his bride in exchange for the hammer. Thor killed the Midgard serpent with his hammer but was drowned in his flood of venom. He was represented as a vigorous, red-haired youth, whose goat-drawn chariot created the thunder as it rolled by. From his name comes the word *Thursday*.

Thoreau, Henry David (1817–1862). American essayist, naturalist and poet. Born at Concord, Mass. and educated at Harvard, Thoreau began his career as a teacher. Through his older friend and neighbor, Ralph Waldo Emerson, he became a part of the Transcendentalist circle.

During Emerson's trip abroad in 1843, Thoreau took over the editorship of *The Dial*. Later that year he went to New York to tutor the children of Emerson's brother, William. He quickly returned to Concord, finding it a far more congenial place to live.

In 1845, Thoreau built a cabin at Walden Pond, on land owned by Emerson. He lived there for two years, two months, and two days; the experience was later described in his best-known work, WALDEN. During his stay at the pond, Thoreau was no hermit. He visited and entertained friends, worked his small plot of land, recorded observations of natural phenomena, and wrote the account of his trip with his brother, John. His first book, A WEEK ON THE CONCORD AND MERRIMACK RIVERS, was finally published in 1849.

During Thoreau's stay at Walden, he spent a night in jail, when he refused to pay his poll tax. He performed the gesture of civil disobedience to indicate his disapproval of the Mexican War. Later he explained his action in his essay on CIVIL DISOBEDIENCE.

Since his first book had sold so poorly, Thoreau was unable for five years to find a publisher for *Walden*. During this period he worked as a laborer and a surveyor and served in the family pencil business. He traveled to Maine, Canada, Cape Cod, and New York; these excursions were the basis of a series of posthumously published books and essays, including *A Yankee in Canada, The Maine Woods*, and *Cape Cod*.

Speaking publicly against the Fugitive Slave Law, he eloquently defended John Brown after Brown's capture in 1859. He died of tuberculosis in 1862 soon after his return from a trip to Minnesota. Politically the most conscious of the Transcendentalists, an acute observer of natural and social facts, Thoreau was an outstanding prose stylist. The *Journal* he kept from 1837 to the end of his life, the source of all his books, is an important literary document.

Thorndike, Dame Sybil (1882–). English actress and theatrical manager. She toured Egypt, Palestine, Australia, and New Zealand in the 1930's. She has starred in many moving pictures in England and the U.S. She was made a Dame of the British Empire in 1931.

Thornhill, Sir William. The uncle of Dr. Primrose's villainous landlord in Oliver Goldsmith's novel THE VICAR OF WAKEFIELD, who disguises himself as Mr. Burchell. Having exhausted a fortune by benevolence, he protects himself by acquiring a reputation for eccentric stinginess. After straightening out the affairs of the PRIMROSE family, he marries Sophia Primrose.

Squire Thornhill. Nephew of Sir William Thornhill, he is a libertine who abducts Olivia Primrose and casts the Vicar into jail. The unscrupulous squire is brought to terms by his uncle.

Thoth. In Egyptian religion, the god of wisdom, inventor of arts, sciences, and the system of hieroglyphics. He is represented with the head of an ibis on a human body. Sometimes he is shown holding in his hand the heart and tongue of Ra, the sun god, to symbolize his control of the intelligence of that great deity. The Greeks and Romans identified him with Hermes or Mercury. See IBIS.

Thou, Jacques Auguste de (1553–1617). French magistrate and historian. His *Histoire de mon temps*, published first in Latin (1604–1620) and finally in French translation (1734), is remarkable for its exactitude and its intelligent assessment of the period of the religious wars.

Thoughtless, Miss Betty. The heroine of a novel of that name by Mrs. Heywood (1697–1758). A virtuous, sensible, and amiable young lady, utterly regardless of the conventionalities of society, she is wholly ignorant of etiquette. She is consequently forever involved in petty scrapes most mortifying to her sensitive mind. Even her lover is alarmed at her *gaucherie*, and deliberates whether such a partner for life is desirable. Mrs. Heywood's novel is said to have suggested the more important *Evelina* of Fanny Burney.

Thoughts on the Comet. See Pierre BAYLE.

Thousand and One Nights. See ARABIAN NIGHTS.

Thousand Souls, A (Tysyacha dush; 1858). A novel by Alexei PISEMSKI. It traces the career of Kalinovich, an ambitious young man determined to make his way however he can. The title of the novel refers to the 1,000 serfs, or "souls," belonging to the woman Kalinovich marries to further his career.

Thrale, Hester Lynch, born **Salusbury** (1741–1821). English BLUESTOCKING. She met Samuel JOHNSON in 1764, and became perhaps his closest confidante until 1784, when, after the death of her first husband, he broke with her over her marriage to the Italian musician Gabriel Piozzi. After Johnson's death she published the *Anecdotes of Johnson* (1786) and *Letters to and from Johnson* (1788). Her diaries, published under the title *Thraliana* (1942), form a valuable source for Johnson's biography, as well as a delightful record of her volatile personality. Her letters to Queeny, her oldest daughter, are particularly notable.

Thrasea Paetus, Publius Clodius (d. A.D. 66). Roman senator and Stoic philosopher. He was a friend of Seneca and one of the keepers of the SIBYLLINE BOOKS.

Thrasybulus (Thrasyboulos). Athenian general. He aided ALCIBIADES in his victories over the Spartans (411–410 B.C.). He was exiled from Athens; upon his return he helped institute a more democratic form of government. In 389 B.C. he commanded the fleet against the Spartans and was killed in battle.

Threadneedle Street. The street in the City of London from Bishopsgate to the Bank of England. The Bank of England, which stands in this street, was nicknamed "the Old Lady of Threadneedle Street" in the late 18th century.

three. The perfect number of the philosopher Pythagoras. It is expressive of "beginning, middle, and end," wherefore he makes it a symbol of Deity. A Trinity is by no means confined to the Christian creed. The Hindu Trimurti consists of Brahma, the Creator, Vishnu, the Preserver, and Siva, the Destroyer. The world was supposed by the ancient Greeks to be under the rule of three gods: Zeus (heaven), Poseidon (sea), and Hades (underworld). The Fates are three, the Furies three, the Graces three, the Harpies three, the Sibylline books three times three (of which only three survived); the fountain from which Hylas drew water was presided over by three nymphs; the Muses were three times three; the pythoness sat on a three-legged stool, or tripod; and in Scandinavian mythology we hear of the Mysterious Three: Har the Mighty, the Like-Mighty, and the Third Person, who sat on three thrones above the rainbow.

Man is threefold (body, soul, and spirit); the world is threefold (earth, sea, and air); the enemies of man are threefold (the world, the flesh, and the devil); the Christian graces are threefold (Faith, Hope, and Charity); the kingdoms of nature are threefold (mineral, vegetable, and animal); the cardinal colors are three in number (red, yellow, and blue), and so on.

Three Lives (1909). A book of three stories by Gertrude STEIN. Written in a clear and masterly style, free from any of its author's later stylistic mannerisms, it consists of three character studies of women. *The Good Anna* deals with a kindly, but domineering German servingwoman; *Melanctha* is concerned with an uneducated but sensitive Negro girl; and *The Gentle Lena* is about a pathetically feeble-minded young German maid.

Three Men in a Boat. See Jerome K. JEROME.

Three Musketeers, The (Les Trois Mousque-taires; 1844). A famous historical romance by Alexandre DUMAS. With its sequels TWENTY YEARS AFTER and THE VISCOUNT OF BRAGELONNE, the novel covers the period of French history from 1625 to 1665. The central figure, D'Artagnan, is a real historical personage (Charles de Baatz d'Artagnan, 1623–1673), and much of the story's material is drawn from his memoirs. His three friends also have counterparts in history, even to their names. D'Artagnan, a gay young Gascon, arrives in Paris on a rawboned, yellow pony, with only three crowns in his pocket. Determined to become one of Louis XIII's guardsmen, he immediately involves himself in duels with Athos, Porthos, and Aramis, three of the most renowned fighters of the day. They welcome him into the fellowship of the Three Musketeers, and the narrow escapes and amazing exploits of these four friends form the subject matter of Dumas' exciting narrative.

Threepenny Opera, The (Die Dreigroschen-oper; 1928). A ballad opera by Bertolt BRECHT with music by Kurt WEILL, based on John Gay's THE BEGGARS' OPERA. Although Brecht follows the general outline of Gay's work, he concentrates more on depicting the social evils that drive individuals into crime. It is written in the style Brecht called EPIC THEATER.

Three Sisters, The (Tri sestry; 1901). A play by Anton CHEKHOV. Written in four acts, it is regarded by some critics as the best work in modern dramatic literature. The Prozorov sisters, Olga, Masha, and Irina, along with their brother Andrei, drag out a dull existence in a small provincial garrison town. Only the diversions afforded by the officers and the ever present dream of some day moving to Moscow keep the sisters going from one drab day to the next. Andrei, who has had dreams of becoming a professor, makes a bad marriage that thwarts his ambition and adds to his sisters' troubles. His wife, Natalya Ivanovna, becomes a domestic despot. Masha, who is married to the pedantic school-master Kulygin, tries to find happiness in a love affair with the officer Vershinin. The youngest sister, Irina, attempts to escape the drabness of her life by marrying Baron Tuzenbakh, another officer. The removal of the regiment from the town undoes Masha's plans, because Vershinin is married and cannot take her with him. Tuzenbakh is killed in a duel. The three sisters are left as they were at the beginning, deriving some faint pleasure from the cheerful sounds of the regiment band as it marches away, still clinging to their hopes for a better life.

Three Soldiers (1921). A novel by John Dos PASSOS. The book deals with three representative soldiers in the American army during World War I: Dan Fuselli, an Italian-American; Chrisfield, a farm-boy from Indiana; and John Andrews, a sensitive musician who longs to be a composer. Dos Passos was interested mainly in the story of Andrews, who joins the army hoping to find comfort by contributing to a righteous cause. Instead he encounters tyranny, aimlessness, red tape, and boredom. Eventually he deserts, and in the French countryside he begins to write music, only to be captured and taken away, leaving the sheets of his unfinished composition to be scattered and destroyed. That part of society represented by the military is the real villain of the book; it is possible to see in this early novel seeds of the later *U.S.A.* (q.v.).

three treasures (Sans., *triratna;* Ch., *san-pao;* Jap., *sambō*). In Buddhism, the Buddha, law (*dharma*) and the order (*sangha*).

three worlds. The concept of the universe in Hindu (Vedic) mythology. The *triloka* (Sans. *tri,* three and *loka,* world) or the universe was visualized as consisting of the earth, the middle space or atmosphere, and the ether or sky. By another interpretation it may also signify the world of men, of semi-divine creatures, and of gods. It sometimes refers to heaven, earth, and the territory of the demons. The three-forked river mentioned in Kalidasa's play *Shakuntala* refers to the descent of the holy river Ganges from heaven into the matted hair of Shiva who, in the midst of his severe practice of penance, received it on the earth.

Threnody (1847). An elegy on the death of his son by Ralph Waldo EMERSON. The poet's consolation is the belief that the dead person is "in Godhead found."

Through the Looking Glass (1872). A children's tale by Lewis CARROLL. A sequel to *Alice's Adventures in Wonderland,* the book tells of Alice's experiences when, curious about the world behind the mirror, she climbs over the mantel through the glass. In looking-glass country, everything is reversed, just as reflections are reversed in a mirror. Brooks and hedges divide the land into a checkerboard, and Alice finds herself a white pawn in the whimsical and fantastic game of chess that constitutes the bulk of the story. On her trip to the eighth square, where she at last becomes a queen, Alice meets talking flowers, looking-glass insects, a man in a white paper suit, such nursery-rhyme characters as Humpty Dumpty and the Lion and the Unicorn, and many others. When, after her coronation, Alice begins shaking the red queen, the red queen turns into Alice's cat, and Alice awakens from her dream. The ballad JABBERWOCKY is found in the tale.

Thrums. The scene of many of Sir James BARRIE's stories, notably *Window in Thrums* (1889) and THE LITTLE MINISTER. It represents Kirriemuir, Barrie's birthplace.

Thucydides (Thoukydides, c. 460–400 B.C.). An Athenian historian. He became a general and was sent to defend the Greek city of Amphipolis in Thrace (424 B.C.). Failing in his mission, he was exiled from Athens for 20 years. He was recalled in 403 B.C.; he is supposed to have been assassinated soon after. During his exile he wrote a history of the Peloponnesian War admirable for its objectivity in discussing contemporary events, its direct and descriptive style, and the author's grasp of cause and effect. It begins by tracing the history of the Hellenic race, and ends, unfinished, in 411 B.C., seven years before the wars ended. The best-known passages are those relating Pericles' *Funeral Oration,* the plague at Athens, and the Sicilian expedition. The painstaking reporting and acute political analysis vindicate Thucydides' claim that the work is a "possession for all time." See illustration on page 1006.

thug. Originally, a member of a religious body of northern India. KALI, the goddess of death in her aspect worshiped by this sect, could be propitiated only by human victims who had been strangled.

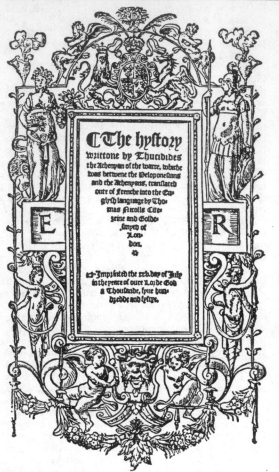

Title page of Thomas Niccol's translation of Thucydides' *History of the Peloponnesian Wars* (1550).

Hence, the thugs became a professional fraternity of stranglers who supported themselves by the plunder obtained from those they strangled. Their native name is *p'hansigars* ("stranglers"); that of *thug* ("cheat") was given them in 1810. Their methods were rigorously suppressed under British rule, and they were practically extinct by 1840. The word is now used in English for any ruffian.

Thule. The ancient name of an island or point of land 6 days' sail north of Britain. It was considered to be the extreme northern limit of the world. The name is first found in the account by Polybius (c. 150 B.C.) of the voyage made by Pytheas in the late fourth century B.C. Pliny says, "It is an island in the Northern Ocean discovered by Pytheas, after sailing six days from the Orcades." Others consider it to be Shetland, in which opinion they agree with the descriptions of Ptolemy and Tacitus. Still others assert that it was some part of the coast of Norway. The etymology of the name is unknown. Ultima Thule means the end of the world, the last extremity.

> Tibi serviat Ultima Thule.
> Vergil, *Georgics*, i, 30

thumbs down (Lat., *pollice verso*). A sign ordering death for a fallen gladiator. At the gladiatorial contests in ancient Rome, the winning gladiator turned to the spectators to ask whether he should kill his fallen enemy. If the spectators held out their arms with thumbs down, the victim must die; thumbs up meant that he was to be spared.

Thundertentronckh, Arminius von. A pseudonym under which Matthew ARNOLD wrote a number of satiric essays, chiefly for *The Pall Mall Gazette*. They were brought together in book form under the title *Friendship's Garland* (1871).

Thurber, James [Grover] (1894–1961). American essayist, short-story writer, and humorist. Thurber began his career as a journalist; in 1927, he met E. B. White, who introduced him to Harold Ross, the editor of a newly founded magazine, *The New Yorker*. During Thurber's years as a staff member he did much to establish the tone, style, and popularity of the magazine. Thurber turned his humor, his satire, and his irony on the follies of men and women, which he revealed in his lucid prose and inimitable drawings; nevertheless, he affirmed the power of love in a fantastic, often nightmarish world. His story *The Secret Life of Walter Mitty*, later made into a movie, describes the fantasies of a Caspar Milquetoast who imagines himself a hero. Among Thurber's other works are *Is Sex Necessary?* (1929), with E. B. White; *The Seal in the Bedroom and Other Predicaments* (1932); *The Middle-Aged Man on the Flying Trapeze* (1935); *Let Your Mind Alone* (1937); *The Male Animal* (1940), a play with Elliot Nugent; *Fables for Our Times* (1940); *The Thurber Carnival* (1945); *Alarms and Diversions* (1957); and *The Years with Ross* (1959), a memoir of Ross. *Lanterns and Lances* (1961) is a book of essays; *Credos and Curios* (1962) was published posthumously.

Thurio. In Shakespeare's TWO GENTLEMEN OF VERONA, Valentine's foolish, homely rival for the hand of Silvia. When the cowardly Thurio disavows his love for her in the face of danger, the duke of Milan, Silvia's father, consents to her marrying Valentine.

Thurso's Landing (1932). A narrative poem by Robinson JEFFERS. The poem deals with Helen Thurso's ambivalent attitudes toward her husband, whom she alternately loves and hates; toward her crippled brother-in-law, who loves her; and toward death itself, which simultaneously fascinates and repels her.

Thurston, E[rnest] Temple (1879–1933). English novelist and playwright. Among his sentimental novels are *The City of Beautiful Nonsense* (1909) and *Richard Furlong* (1913); among his plays, *The Wandering Jew* (1920) and *Charmeuse* (1930). He was at one time married to the novelist Katherine Cecil THURSTON.

Thurston, Katherine Cecil (1875–1911). English novelist. She was at one time the wife of E. Temple THURSTON. Her book *John Chilcote, M. P.* (1904; U.S. title, *The Masquerader*) was a best seller.

Thus Spake Zarathustra (Also sprach Zarathustra; 1883–1892). A philosophical narrative by Friedrich NIETZSCHE in which the ancient Persian philosopher Zarathustra (see ZOROASTER) is used as a mouthpiece for the author's views. In it, Nietzsche develops his doctrine of the ÜBERMENSCH, and the quasi-biblical style he uses underlines the prophetic character of his ideas.

Thwackum, Mr. [Roger]. One of two tutors to Tom and Blifil in Henry Fielding's TOM JONES. Thwackum is a high-church divine who believes in original sin, the natural depravity of man, and the necessity for seeking grace. Although he and SQUARE are contrasted to each other, they are both alike in their total lack of benevolence.

Thyestes. See the House of ATREUS.

Thyone. See SEMELE.

Thyrsis. A herdsman introduced in the *Idyls* of Theocritus, and in Vergil's seventh *Bucolic*. It has become a conventional name for any shepherd or rustic.

> Hard by, a cottage chimney smokes
> From betwixt two aged oaks,
> Where Corydon and Thyrsis, met,
> Are at their savoury dinner set.
> Milton, *L'Allegro* (1638)

See ARCADES AMBO.

thyrsus (thyrsos). A long pole with an ornamental head of a fir cone. It was carried by the votaries of DIONYSUS at the celebration of his rites. It has been suggested that the fir tree was an earlier source of intoxicating beverages than the vine.

Tiamat. In Babylonian mythology, the primeval sea seen as a dragon goddess. The wife of Apsu, the ancient god of the fresh waters, she was the mother of all the gods. In the famous creation myth of the WAR OF THE GODS, she fights against the younger gods, but is killed by Marduk, who, splitting her body, makes heaven of the upper half and earth of the lower.

Tibbs, Beau. A character in Oliver Goldsmith's THE CITIZEN OF THE WORLD. He is a poor, clever, dashing young man, who has the happy art of fancying he knows all the *haut monde*, and that all the *monde* knows him. He pretends that men of rank and fashion address him familiarly as "Ned."

Tiber. The river that flows through Rome to the Tyrrhenian Sea.

Tiberinus. In Roman myth, the god of the River Tiber.

Tiberius. Full Latin name, **Tiberius Claudius Nero** (42 B.C.–A.D. 37). Roman emperor (A.D. 14–37). The historians Tacitus and Suetonius labeled him a cruel tyrant, although modern scholars recognize his reign as one of sound administration and of benefit to the Empire. He was emperor when Jesus was crucified.

Tibullus, Albius (54?–18 B.C.). Roman elegiac poet. Only two books of his verse, both dealing with love and country life, have been preserved.

Tickell, Thomas (1685–1740). English poet who contributed to Steele and Addison's SPECTATOR. The fact that he published his intention to translate the *Iliad* caused a famous quarrel between Addison and Pope. Pope thought that Tickell's work was in reality instigated by Addison in opposition to Pope's own prior proposals to translate Homer. Tickell collected and edited the works of Addison (1721) to which he prefixed the famous lines *To the Earl of Warwick on the Death of Mr. Addison*. Among his best-known works are KENSINGTON GARDENS, a mock-heroic poem and COLIN AND LUCY, a ballad.

Ticknor, George (1791–1871). American historian and scholar. Ticknor studied Latin, Greek, Spanish, and French as a boy. After his graduation from Dartmouth he was admitted to the bar, but his scholarly interests drew him to the German university at Göttingen. There he admired German historical criticism, and returning to teach at Harvard, accepted the new Smith professorship of French, Spanish, and belles lettres. He reorganized his own department along the lines of Göttingen, and prepared a model *Syllabus of the Spanish Literature Course* (1823). Resigning from his teaching post in 1835, he wrote a three-volume *History of Spanish Literature* (1849, 1872). In 1864, he wrote a biography of his friend William Hickling Prescott. On his death, Ticknor left his collection of rare books on Spanish literature to the Boston Public Library.

Tidings Brought to Mary, The (L'Annonce faite à Marie; 1910). A poetic drama, revised 1948, by Paul CLAUDEL. An adaptation of Claudel's *La Jeune fille Violaine* (1892, rev. 1898), it symbolizes the struggle and the bond between spiritual devotion and the claims of human life and love. Pierre de Craon, architect of cathedrals, is set apart from life by his leprosy. Violaine Vercors kisses him in pity, and the affliction makes her a recluse, separated from earthly happiness and devoted to a religious vocation. Her fiancé, Jacques Hury, marries her sister Mara. But one Christmas Eve their infant dies, and Mara comes to Violaine, desperately demanding that Violaine hold the child and through her faith restore its life. Although Mara takes home a living baby, she notices that its eyes are now the color of Violaine's, and later murders her sister.

Tieck, Ludwig (1773–1853). German author. In his early career, he was a leading representative and popularizer of GERMAN ROMANTICISM, but later turned to realism. He contributed some sections to the pace-setting romantic work of his friend WACKENRODER, *Herzensergiessungen eines kunstliebenden Klosterbruders* (*Outpourings of the Heart of an Art-loving Lay Brother*, 1797); his play *Der gestiefelte Kater* (*Puss in Boots*, pub. 1797) is a classic example of romantic IRONY; his novel *Franz Sternbalds Wanderungen* (*Franz Sternbald's Wanderings*, 1798) is the definitive German KÜNSTLERROMAN; and he also wrote a number of MÄRCHEN (tales). The most significant work from his realistic period is the novella *Des Lebens Überfluss* (*Life's Overflow*, 1837). Among his friends were Novalis and the brothers Schlegel.

T'ien-T'ai (*Jap.*, TENDAI). Chinese Buddhist sect. Founded by Chih-k'ai (538–597), it was a highly syncretic intellectual school which based its teachings on the *Lotus Sūtra*. Most important from the sixth to eighth century, it was introduced to Japan in the Heian period (794–1185).

Tiepolo, Giovanni Battista (1696–1770). Venetian painter. He decorated churches and palaces in Venice, and palaces in Milan, Würzburg, and Madrid with religious and mythological scenes and imaginative depictions of events from ancient history. A rich colorist, he painted in a terse style of abbreviated contrasts of light and shade, with a rococo emphasis on movement, unusual perspective, and gaiety. German rococo was influenced by his work at Würzburg.

tiers état. See THIRD ESTATE.

Tietjens, Christopher. The hero of PARADE'S END by Ford Madox Ford. This series of novels is sometimes known as the Tietjens tetralogy.

Tietjens, Eunice [Strong] (1884–1944). American poet and novelist. For many years she was associated with Harriet Monroe on the staff of POETRY. Her own poetry was collected in such volumes as *Profiles from China* (1917) and *Leaves in Windy Weather* (1929). She also wrote several novels, including *Jake* (1921), and textbooks on Japan (1924) and China (1930). *The World at My Shoulder* (1938) is her autobiography.

Tiffany, Louis Comfort (1848–1933). American decorator and glassmaker. He was the son of the internationally established American jeweler Charles Lewis Tiffany (1812–1902). An interest in stained glass led him to develop a process for the manufacture of opalescent glass. He shaped this glass into decorative, intricately colored forms and vases which he called *favrile*.

Tiger, The. A poem by William Blake, included in his SONGS OF EXPERIENCE, celebrating the mystery and triumph of the creation of life. The well-known first stanza is as follows:

> Tiger! Tiger! burning bright
> In the forests of the night,
> What immortal hand or eye
> Could frame thy fearful symmetry?

Tiger at the Gates (La Guerre de Troie n'aura pas lieu; 1935). A play by Jean GIRADOUX. It was translated into English by Christopher Fry in 1955. The setting of the play is Troy just before the outbreak of the Trojan War. Peace-loving Hector keeps repeating ironically that "the Trojan War will not take place," eventually persuading Paris, Helen, and even the willing but dubious Ulysses to cooperate in avoiding battle. But the Trojan people have been inflamed for various reasons, and it is finally not the leaders' decision, but the inevitable consequence of a warmonger's lie, that precipitates the war.

Tighe, Mrs. Mary (1772–1810). Irish poet whose major poem *Psyche* (1805) was praised by John Keats.

Tikhonov, Nikolai Seminovich (1896–   ). Russian poet and short-story writer. His early verse—including his first collection *The Horde* (*Orda*; 1922)—revealed the influence of the Acmeist Nikolai Gumiliov in its concentration on adventurous themes and its precise, clear style. An early member of the SERAPION BROTHERS, Tikhonov later began the attempt to develop a narrative poetry for the recounting of revolutionary themes under the influence of Khlebnikov and Mayakovski. His work in the 1930's tended more toward realistic treatments, as is obvious in his collection. *The Shadow of a Friend* (*Ten druga;* 1935), and in the stories contained in *The Venturesome Man* (*Riskovannyi chelovek;* 1927).

Tilbury Town. An imaginary New England town created by Edwin Arlington ROBINSON. Used as the setting for many of Robinson's poems, it was derived in large part from his own home town of Gardiner, Me. Its inhabitants include Richard Cory, Miniver Cheevy, Flammonde, old Eben Flood, and other protagonists in the poems who are either privately or publicly outcast from the town.

Tilden, Samuel Jones (1814–1886). American statesman. He was governor of New York State from 1875 to 1876. As Democratic candidate for president of the U.S. (1876), he received more popular votes than the Republican candidate, Rutherford B. Hayes. An electoral commission was created to examine the contested returns in certain states. The committee reported in favor of Hayes, who was elected by one electoral vote. Tilden always believed that he had been wronged. The fortune that he bequeathed was used to establish a free public library in the city of New York.

Till or **Tyll Eulenspiegel, Ulenspiegel, Howleglas,** or **Owlglass.** See EULENSPIEGEL.

Tillich, Paul (1886–1965). German-born American philosopher and theologian. Forced to leave Germany because of the rise of Nazism, Tillich came to New York. He taught at the Union Theological Seminary from 1933 until 1955, when he became University Professor at Harvard. One of the leading contemporary American theologians, Tillich bases his theology on the estrangement of existence from its essence, of man from the divine, an estrangement symbolized by the Fall; the ultimate concern of man is to be reunited with the divine, with Being. Rather than emphasizing Jesus as either a historical personage or a social and ethical reformer, he sees Jesus as the Christ, the bearer of the New Being or creative power capable of overcoming the estrangement and reconciling existence with its essence. His major work is his *Systematic Theology*, in three volumes which appeared in the years 1951, 1959, and 1963. Among his other works are *The Courage to Be* (1952), *Love, Power and Justice* (1954), *The New Being* (1955), *Biblical Religion and the Search for Ultimate Reality* (1955), *Dynamics of Faith* (1957), and *Theology and Culture* (1959).

Tillotson, John (1630–1694). English writer and archbishop of Canterbury. His *Sermons* (1695–1704) and religious writings were very popular in their time and were admired by Dryden.

Tilly, count of. Johan Tserclaes (1559–1632). Flemish field marshal in the Thirty Years' War. He replaced Wallenstein in command of the Imperial forces (1630). In taking Magdeburg, his army committed great atrocities. He was defeated by Gustavus II in two engagements and mortally wounded in the second.

Tillyard, E[ustace] M[andeville] W[etenhall] (1889–1962). English literary scholar. He wrote important studies of Shakespeare and Milton and of the background of thought in their periods. Among his books are *The Elizabethan World Picture* (1944), *Shakespeare's History Plays* (1946), and *Studies in Milton* (1951).

Tilney, Henry. See NORTHANGER ABBEY.

Time. An American magazine founded in 1923 by Briton Hadden and Henry LUCE. Its official title is *Time, The Weekly News Magazine.* It is known for its diligent coverage of current events in a compressed, idiomatic, sometimes fantastic style that makes use of newly coined words, epithets, and unusual sentence structure.

Time and the Conways (1937). A play about time by J. B. PRIESTLEY. The Conway family experiences a future event in the present.

Time and Western Man (1927). A political and artistic manifesto by Wyndham LEWIS. He attacks Henri Bergson and the stream-of-consciousness technique in the novel. Lewis advocates fixity rather than flux, intelligence and the external rather than intuition and the internal, and classicism rather than romanticism.

Time, Forward! (Vremya, vperiod!; 1932). A novel by Valentin KATAYEV. Portraying the construction of the Magnitogorsk chemical works during Russia's First Five-Year Plan, it admirably conveys the rapid tempo of construction by its quickly shifting scenes, reminiscent of the cinematographic devices of John Dos Passos' early works.

Time Machine, The (1895). A science-fiction story by H. G. WELLS. The inventor of the time machine travels into the future and visits stages in the evolutionary degeneration of life. He sees the stage when the evil, apelike Morlocks (the descendants of our age's industrial workers) live underground and farm and eat the beautiful, aristocratic Eloi. He witnesses, too, the stage when giant crabs are the only surviving living things, and the sun and the earth are dying.

Time of Your Life, The (1939). A play by William SAROYAN. A blend of social consciousness and poetic symbolism, it is set in a waterfront saloon and takes as its themes the need to make the most of life, to be compassionate to the weak, and to oppose the enemies of life. A collection of lovable eccentrics represent the weak and Detective Blick of the Vice Squad personifies the forces of evil. The play was given the New York Drama Critics' Award and also the Pulitzer Prize for 1940, which Saroyan refused.

Times, The. A London newspaper (so named since 1788) founded by John WALTER as *The Daily Universal Register* in 1785.

Timias. See FAERIE QUEENE, THE.

Timocrate. See Thomas CORNEILLE.

Timoleon (1891). A volume of poetry by Herman MELVILLE, his last published work. Many of the poems were written early in the 1860's. Among the most interesting are *Art*, *The Garden of Metrodorus*, and *After the Pleasure Party*.

Timon of Athens (c. 1607). A tragedy by William SHAKESPEARE, perhaps written only in part by him. Timon, a generous host and patron of the arts, finds himself in financial difficulties and discovers, as the cynical APEMANTUS had predicted, that the so-called friends who had previously fawned on him now refuse to help him. Cursing mankind, Timon leaves Athens and settles in a cave where he finds a buried treasure of gold. There he meets ALCIBIADES, a general who has been banished by the Athenian senate when he pleaded for the life of a condemned soldier. Timon finances an expedition that Alcibiades is preparing against Athens and rewards his faithful servant FLAVIUS, exhorting him to show charity to no one. When word reaches Athens of Timon's gold, the senate sends a delegation to ask his aid against Alcibiades, but Timon rejects the request. Alcibiades, however, negotiates with the Athenians and is allowed to enter the city when he agrees to seek vengeance only from his and Timon's enemies. Just as the peaceful compromise is reached, it is learned that Timon has died in his cave, still inveighing against the human race.

The principal source of the play is Plutarch's *Life of Marcus Antonius,* translated into English (1579) by Sir Thomas North and retold also in Paynter's *Palace of Pleasure* (1567), though the story of Timon the Misanthrope was well known to Elizabethans.

Timotheus (446–357 B.C.). A renowned Greek musician and poet, referred to in *Alexander's Feast* by John Dryden.

Timothy. In the New Testament, one of the early Christians, a convert and associate of Paul.

Timothy, The Epistles of Paul the Apostle to. Two New Testament books. With **The Epistle of Paul to Titus,** they are called "the Pastoral Epistles" because of their theme of "care of the church." They are traditionally ascribed to Paul, but scholars feel that they were written by a disciple of Paul after his death in 65. Together they outline a course for church action and administration.

Timrod, Henry (1828–1867). American poet and journalist. A member of the CHARLESTON SCHOOL, he is known for his intensely emotional poems written in classical forms. During the Civil War, Timrod earned the title Laureate of the Confederacy. His *Collected Verse* was published in 1873. Timrod's best-known poems are *The Cotton Boll* and *Ethnogenesis.*

Tin Pan Alley. A popular and journalistic term for the section of New York City of the writers and publishers of popular songs. Later, it was applied by extension to the industry as a whole. Tin Pan Alley was at first located in the district around 14th Street, but later moved uptown to the Times Square area.

Tintern Abbey. A medieval abbey dating from the 13th century, located in Monmouthshire, England, on the river Wye. An ivy-covered ruin, it is well preserved except for the vaulting. Wordsworth wrote a poem, *Lines Composed a few miles above Tintern Abbey, on Revisiting the Banks of the Wye,* popularly though somewhat inappropriately known as *Tintern Abbey.*

Tintoretto. Real name, **Jacopo Robusti** (1518–1594). Venetian painter. Called *Il Furioso* because of the extreme rapidity with which he painted, he executed fine portraits and large decorative canvases, mainly in the Scuola di San Rocco and in the doge's palace of his native city. His vast imagination often took a mystical turn as he experimented with the mysterious effects of barely lighted interior and exterior scenes. A master of movement, he used perspective and foreshortening to give drama and excitement to his scenes from the New Testament. His leading works include the San Rocco frescoes—the largest collection of works by one painter in a single building to be found anywhere. The best known of these are *The Annunciation* and *The Agony in the Garden.* In the ducal palace are *Four Allegories of Venice* and *Bacchus and Ariadne.* In the Venetian Accademia are his paintings on the *Legend of the Body of St. Mark.* Having painted a *Crucifixion* from a revolutionary side view, he turned to the theme of the *Last Supper* and avoided frontality by setting the table in diagonal perspective. This latter, perhaps his single best-known work, is in the Church of San Giorgio Maggiore in Venice. Tintoretto's influence was immediately felt by Rubens and Rembrandt

Tiphys. In Greek legend, the name of the pilot of the *Argo*, the vessel of the ARGONAUTS.

Tippecanoe and Tyler too. The campaign slogan of the Whig party during the American presidential campaign of 1840. William Henry Harrison (1773–1841), the successful candidate for president, was nicknamed "Tippecanoe" from his victory over the Indians at Tippecanoe, Ind., in 1811. His running mate was John Tyler (1790–1862), who became president when Harrison died of pneumonia one month after his inauguration.

Tirant lo Blanch (Tirant the White, 1490). A Spanish romance of chivalry, dealing with the exploits of Tirant, a Breton prince. The first three parts were written by Johanot Martorell, and a fourth was added by Martí Johán de Galba. The work first appeared in Catalan, but it may have been originally written in Portuguese. It was praised by Cervantes in *Don Quixote*.

Tiresias (Teiresias). In Greek mythology, a Theban seer. His predictions played an important part in the lives of Oedipus and his descendants. Blinded in his youth at seeing Athene bathing, he received second sight as a consolation. He was transformed for a time into a woman as a result of seeing snakes coupling. As a result of this unusual experience, he was asked to settle an argument between Zeus and Hera as to whether men or women more deeply enjoyed the pleasures of love. He voted nine to one in favor of women. His blinding was recounted in *The Baths of Pallas*, a poem by CALLIMACHUS; in Euripides' *Bacchae* he is a convert to Dionysian rites. For his prophecies, see OEDIPUS, SEVEN AGAINST THEBES, and ANTIGONE. After prophesying the fall of Thebes before the EPIGONI, he died, his life having spanned seven generations. His bisexuality appears as a theme in T. S. Eliot's THE WASTE LAND and in Apollinaire's play *Les Mamelles de Tirésias* (1903).

Tir et Sidon (Tyre and Sidon, 1608). A tragedy in 2 parts by the French playwright Jean de Schelander (c. 1585–1635). Set in Phoenicia during the war between Tyre and Sidon, this long play centers on the ill-starred love of Belcar, prince of Sidon, and Méliane, princess of Tyre. Though originally culminating in four deaths, the play was rewritten 20 years later as a tragicomedy in the manner of Alexandre HARDY, a happy ending being substituted for the earlier catastrophe. The preface to the revised play, written by the cleric François Ogier, defends the mixing of comic and tragic elements on the stage as being closer to life than either the dramas of the ancients or those of their modern imitators.

Tirpitz, Alfred von (1849–1930). German admiral who organized the Imperial Navy that challenged British supremacy of the seas. As supreme commander of the fleet (1911–1916), he supported unrestricted submarine warfare during World War I.

Tirso de Molina. Pen name of Fray **Gabriel Téllez** (c. 1583–1648). Spanish dramatist. Born in Madrid, Tirso studied at Alcalá and became a Mercenarian friar in 1601. Thereafter he lived in Toledo, Santo Domingo, Salamanca, and Barcelona, rising to important positions in the order. In 1625 the Council of Castile recommended that he be enjoined from writing any more plays because of the scandal they were causing.

An avowed disciple of Lope de Vega, Tirso geared his plays to popular taste. He is said to have written more than 300 dramas, of which about 80 are extant. The finest of these is EL BURLADOR DE SEVILLA, in which the now universally known character of Don Juan was definitively delineated. His other plays include EL CONDENADO POR DESCONFIADO, considered the best religious drama of Spain; *La prudencia en la mujer,* a historical work dealing with the dowager queen Doña Maria, whose wisdom saves the throne for her son, Ferdinand IV; *Don Gil de las calzas verdes,* a cloak-and-sword play; and *Marta la piadosa,* about a female hypocrite. He also wrote two miscellaneous collections of verse, drama, and stories: *Los cigarrales de Toledo* (1624) and *Deleitar aprovechando* (1635).

Tisaferno (Tisaphernes). In the *Gerusalemme Liberata* of Tasso, one of the leading infidel warriors from India. Tisaferno is in love with Armida the witch, and has sworn to kill Rinaldo of Este, but he is killed by the latter in the final battle for the holy city.

Tisbina. See PRASILDO.

Tisiphone. One of the three ERINYES. Covered with a bloody robe, she sits day and night at hell-gate, armed with a whip. Tibullus says her head is coifed with serpents in lieu of hair.

'Tis Pity She's a Whore (c. 1627). A tragedy by John FORD about the fatal attraction of Giovanni for his beautiful sister, Annabella. She returns his affection and hesitates to choose between her suitors: Soranzo, Grimaldi, and Bergetto. The first of these has been having an affair with Hippolita, the wife of Richardetto, and has sworn to marry the lady should she become a widow. When word comes that Richardetto has been lost at sea, Soranzo rejects his pledge and continues to press his suit with Annabella. Meanwhile, Richardetto, disguised as a physician, has returned to watch his wife with her lover. When Annabella chooses Soranzo for her husband, Richardetto and the jealous Grimaldi join forces to kill him but murder the innocent Bergetto by mistake. At the wedding feast, Hippolita, double-crossed by Soranzo's servant Vasques, drinks a cup of poisoned wine she had intended for her erstwhile lover. Soon the reason for Annabella's marriage becomes apparent—she is pregnant by Giovanni. Soranzo plans to avenge himself by revealing the facts at a splendid banquet. To save her honor, Giovanni kills Annabella, proclaims her death at the banquet, stabs Soranzo, and is himself killed by Soranzo's followers.

Titan, The (1914). A novel by Theodore DREISER. It is the succeeding volume to THE FINANCIER and the second in the trilogy dealing with Frank Cowperwood. Having married Aileen Butler, his former mistress, and moved to Chicago, Cowperwood almost succeeds in his dream of establishing a monopoly of all public utilities. Dissatisfaction with Aileen leads him, however, to a series of affairs with other women; when the Chicago citizenry frustrate his financial schemes, he departs for Europe with Berenice Fleming, the lovely daughter of the madam of a Louisville brothel. Cowperwood, a powerful, irresistibly compelling man driven by his own need for power, beautiful women, and social prestige, at last experiences "the pathos of the discovery that even giants are but pigmies, and that an ultimate balance must be struck." In the final volume, *The Stoic* (1947), which was published posthumously, Dreiser concludes "the trilogy of desire" with an account of Cowperwood's life in England and his death after his return to the U.S.

Titania. The queen of the fairies and wife of OBERON in Shakespeare's MIDSUMMER NIGHT'S DREAM. Her name is mentioned by Ovid as an alternative for Diana, the moon goddess.

Titanic. The White Star liner that struck an iceberg in the Atlantic on April 14, 1912, during her maiden voyage and sank with the loss of over 1500 lives. A fabulous vessel whose 15 watertight bulkheads supposedly made her "unsinkable," the *Titanic* carried only enough lifeboats for 52% of the 2207 persons on board. Walter Lord's *A Night to Remember* (1955) is a minute-by-minute account of the disaster.

Titans (Titanes). In Greek mythology, offspring of Uranus and Ge. They appear to have been pre-Hellenic nature deities, consigned to near oblivion by the new pantheon headed by Zeus. Their names are CRONOS, OCEANUS, and IAPETUS, males, and RHEA, TETHYS, and THEMIS, females. Under the leadership of Cronos, they emasculated Uranus, who had hidden all but Cronos in the womb of earth. Rhea and Themis were both earth-goddesses, Oceanus and his wife Tethys were the progenitors of the sea gods—according to some accounts, all the gods. Besides the six above-mentioned Titans named in Hesiod's *Theogony*, there were Hyperion, a sun god; Koios (Coeus), Krios (Crius), Theia (Thia), Phoebe, and Mnemosyne. In many sources their descendants are also called Titans. It is generally believed that the protracted war that the Titans fought with Zeus, after he had overcome his father Cronos with the aid of his mother Rhea, reflects the prolonged conflict between the ancient Pelasgian inhabitants of Greece and their Hellenic conquerors.

Tite et Bérénice (1670). A tragedy by Pierre CORNEILLE. The emperor Titus is about to marry Domitia, who is actually in love with his brother Domitian, when the arrival of Bérénice, queen of Judea, reawakens his love for her. Realizing that her presence places Titus in jeopardy, Bérénice abandons hope of marrying him and departs. Titus in his turn surrenders Domitia to Domitian, who loves her. It is believed that the duchesse d'Orléans encouraged Racine and Corneille to write plays on this subject, each in ignorance that the other was doing the same. Corneille's intricacies of plot contrasted poorly with the simplicity of Racine's treatment, and Corneille's play was judged inferior. See BÉRÉNICE.

Tithonus. A beautiful Trojan of Greek legend, son of Laomedon, and beloved by Eos. At his prayer, the goddess granted him immortality, but as he had forgotten to ask for youth and vigor he grew old, and life became insupportable. He now prayed Eos to remove him from the world. This, however, she could not do, but she changed him into a grasshopper. Tennyson has a poem entitled *Tithonus*.

Titian. Real name, **Tiziano Vecelli** (c. 1477–1576). Italian painter. Titian was the greatest master of the Venetian school and one of the most influential artists in history. During a long and productive life, he gained a mastery of color that enabled him to achieve increased movement by disregarding symmetry of composition while restoring unity through chromatic balance. He also relied on color, rather than on the intensity of tone, to model forms and to describe lavish textures. Among his celebrated religious works are the Louvre *Entombment*, the Frari *Assumption* (1518), the *Pesaro Madonna*, and the moving *Pietà* of his final phase. His mythological works include the *Rape of Europa, Bacchus and Ariadne, Nymph and Shepherd*, and *Diana and Acteon*. Of his allegories, the best known are *Sacred and Profane Love* (c. 1510) and *The Three Ages* (1510). A superb portraitist, Titian did many versions of his patron, the Emperor Charles V, as well as the celebrated portrait of Pietro Aretino. He is now regarded as an important link between Renaissance and baroque painting, through his influence on such followers as Rubens, and in his appeal to the impressionists the remote antecedent of their style.

Titinius. In Shakespeare's JULIUS CAESAR, a friend of Brutus and Cassius. At Philippi he is sent by Cassius to determine the identity of some nearby troops. When Titinius is surrounded, Cassius erroneously concludes that the soldiers belong to the enemy army and, despairing of victory, orders Pindarus to kill him. Returning to find Cassius dead, Titinius takes his own life.

Titivil. See TUTIVILLUS.

Titurel. The first guardian of the Holy GRAIL according to medieval legend, and grandfather of AMFORTAS. WOLFRAM VON ESCHENBACH wrote a fragmentary verse epic *Titurel* (13th century), apparently intended as a prelude to his PARZIVAL, telling the early history of the Grail and the heroes designated to build a chapel for it.

Titus. Full Latin name, **Titus Flavius Sabinus Vespasianus** (A.D. 39–81). Roman Emperor (79–81). He completed the Colosseum and erected the triumphal arch known as the Arch of Titus. On this arch (still standing in modern Rome), the emperor had friezes carved to represent his conquest of the Jews (A.D. 70) and the looting and destruction of the Temple in Jerusalem.

Titus, The Epistle of Paul to. See TIMOTHY, THE EPISTLES OF PAUL THE APOSTLE TO.

Titus and Gisippus. A tale from Boccaccio's DECAMERON. It is the story of Titus, a Roman youth studying philosophy at Athens, who falls in love with Sophronia, the betrothed of his best friend, the Athenian Gisippus. The latter decides to give her up to Titus, who replaces him in the darkened nuptial chamber. Despite the clamor of outraged relatives, Sophronia accepts Titus as her husband and the two leave for Rome. Gisippus is left to face the combined anger of family and friends; this takes the form of rejection, which coupled with poor luck in his affairs, soon reduces him to abject poverty. He then goes to Rome in a wretched state, hoping to find Titus; but when he meets his friend, the latter fails to recognize him in his present state. Believing himself snubbed, he decides to end his life by accepting the guilt for a murder committed by another. As he is being tried by the triumvir Octavianus Caesar, Titus wanders into the court and soon realizes the identity of the defendant. Titus promptly tells Octavianus that he, not Gisippus, is guilty. This magnanimity stirs the true murderer to confess his crime, whereupon all three are freed. Finally, Gisippus marries Titus' sister, and the two couples live together in perfect joy and harmony thereafter.

Titus Andronicus (c. 1590). A tragedy by William SHAKESPEARE, based on Senecan models. The aging Titus Andronicus returns to Rome after a victorious war against the Goths, bringing as captives their queen Tamora and her three sons, one of whom is sacrificed by Titus to appease the souls of the slain members of his family. Declared emperor through Titus' intercession, Saturninus claims Titus' daughter LAVINIA as his wife. When Saturninus' brother Bassanius abducts Lavinia, Saturninus marries Tamora, who has sworn to avenge the death of her son. Through the intrigues of Tamora and her Moorish lover AARON, Tamora's sons kill Bassanius, rape Lavinia, and cut off her tongue and hands. Two of Titus' sons are accused of the murder and executed; another son, Lucius, is banished and proceeds against Rome with a Gothic army. Determined to exact vengeance for the crimes against his family, Titus kills Tamora's sons and serves their remains to her in a pie. After he has killed Lavinia to end her shame and has stabbed Tamora, Titus is slain by Saturninus, who is himself killed by Lucius. Lucius then tells the tale of his family's wrongs and is proclaimed emperor.

Neither the direct source of the play nor the extent of Shakespeare's share in the authorship has been clearly determined.

Tityus (Tityos). A giant of Greek mythology. His body covered nine acres of land. He tried to defile LETO, but Apollo cast him into Tartarus, where a vulture fed on his liver, which grew again as fast as it was devoured.

Tiu. See TYR.

Tivoli Gardens. A famous amusement park in Copenhagen, Denmark.

To Althea from Prison (1649). A poem by Richard LOVELACE. The poet maintains that true liberty, which comes from freedom of soul, cannot be threatened by chains or fetters. The last stanza contains the well-known lines:

> Stone walls do not a prison make,
> Nor iron bars a cage.

To a Waterfowl (1815). A poem by William Cullen BRYANT. The poem describes the flight of a bird, which renewed Bryant's belief in divine guidance.

Woodcut from *Titus Andronicus*.

FOLGER SHAKESPEARE LIBRARY

Tobacco Road (1932). A novel by Erskine CALDWELL. Jeeter Lester is an impoverished Georgia sharecropper who lives on Tobacco Road with his starving old mother, his sickly wife Ada, and his two children, 16-year-old Dude and Ellie May, who has a harelip. A third child, Pearl, has been married at the age of 12 to Lov Bensey, a railroad worker. When Jeeter's widowed preacher sister Bessie Rice induces Dude to marry her by buying him a new automobile, Dude accidentally wrecks the car and kills his grandmother. Pearl runs away from Lov Bensey; Ellie May happily goes to live with him; and Jeeter and Ada, left alone one night, perish when their shack burns down. The hapless Lesters, at once comical and shockingly degenerate, became widely familiar to the public through Jack Kirkland's dramatization (1933), which ran for 3,182 performances on Broadway.

Tobey, Mark (1890–   ). American artist. He is the originator of "white writing," a calligraphy of white lines inspired by Chinese writing, which he has also reduced to dense networks of thin angular white lines on a darker background.

Tobias. In the Apocrypha, the son of TOBIT. He left Nineveh to collect a loan for his father. Guided by the archangel Raphael, in disguise as Azarias, Tobias fell in love with and married his cousin Sara, seven of whose betrothed lovers had been carried off by the evil spirit ASMODEUS. With Raphael's aid, Tobias drove Asmodeus away.

Tobino, Mario (1910–   ). Italian novelist. His writings reflect his experiences as a practicing psychiatrist and his interest in the history of the anti-Fascist resistance movement during World War II. Among his more recent works are *The Women of Magliano* (*Le Libere Donne di Magliano;* 1953), inspired by his medical experience in hospital wards; *Il Deserto della Libia* (1952); the short story *La Brace dei Biassoli* (1956); and the novel *Il Clandestino* (1962), a lengthy chronicle of the resistance movement on the Tuscan coast. *Il Clandestino* has been critically acclaimed as an honest, fully documented account of the controversial partisan "war" against the Nazi-Fascist government of 1943–1945.

Tobit. The principal character of the Book of Tobit, a romance included in the Apocrypha. As a Jew in captivity at Nineveh, he buried the Hebrew dead, despite civil bans. Growing impoverished, miserable, and blind, he sent his son TOBIAS to collect a loan. When he returned, Tobias cured his father's blindness by applying to his eyes the gall of a fish, which had attacked him on the Tigris and which the archangel Raphael had helped him catch.

Tocqueville, Count **Alexis [Charles Henri Maurice Clérel] de** (1805–1859). French historian. De Tocqueville is known for his studies of the nature and operation of democracy. He sought to advance the rule of the people while simultaneously controlling undesirable tendencies. One of his best-known works, *Démocratie en Amérique* (*Democracy in America,* 1835–1839), is considered the first impartial and systematic study of American institutions. *L'Ancien Régime et la Revolution* (*The Old Regime and the Revolution,* 1856), a history of the French Revolution, was left unfinished at the time of his death. De Tocqueville held a number of official positions in the French government, at one time serving on a special mission to the U.S. He was later a deputy and then a minister under Louis Napoleon, a position from which he retired after the *coup d'état* of December 2, 1851.

Tod in Venedig, Der. See DEATH IN VENICE.

toga. The outer garment worn by Roman citizens when appearing in public. Hence, the Romans were known as the *gens togata,* or togaed people. The toga consisted of a single piece of undyed woolen cloth, cut almost in a semicircle and worn in a flowing fashion around the shoulders and body.

toga picta. The toga embroidered with golden stars that was worn by the emperor on special occasions and by a victorious general at his triumph.

toga praetexta. The toga with a purple border that was worn by children, by those engaged in sacred rites, magistrates, and others.

toga virilis. The plain, white toga worn by men (Lat., *virilis;* manly); it was assumed by boys when they reached 15 years of age.

To Have and Have Not (1937). A novel by Ernest HEMINGWAY. It deals with the effort of Harry Morgan, a native of Key West, to earn a living for himself and his family. He has operated a boat for rental to fishing parties, but during the depression of the 1930's he is forced to turn to the smuggling of Chinese immigrants and illegal liquor. While assisting a gang of bank robbers to escape, he is shot and mortally wounded. He dies gasping, "One man alone ain't got . . . no chance."

To Have and to Hold (1900). A historical novel by Mary JOHNSTON. One of the most popular historical novels published in the U.S., it is set in 17th-century Virginia. When Ralph Percy goes to Jamestown to choose a wife from a shipload of girls sent over from England, he little suspects the noble birth of the beautiful young woman who throws herself on his mercy. Jocelyn—fleeing the loathsome advances of Lord Carnal—at first despises Ralph, who becomes her husband. But, subsequently, adventures on land and sea reveal his courage, and love finally blossoms.

To His Angry God (1648). A poem by Robert HERRICK. After describing a period of spiritual affliction, the poet expresses confidence in its early termination.

To His Coy Mistress (1650). A poem by Andrew MARVELL, one of the great English love lyrics. The poet requests the lady's immediate favor; he would like to spend an aeon in compliment, as she deserves:

> But at my back I always hear
> Time's wingèd chariot hurrying near;
> And yonder all before us lie
> Deserts of vast eternity.

Toilers of the Sea (Les Travailleurs de la mer; 1866). A novel by Victor HUGO. Much of the tale's action centers about the steamboat *La Durande* and its trips between the isle of Guernsey and St. Malo. Tragically unrequited love, blissful young romance, and exciting adventure make this work another of Hugo's imaginative melodramas.

Tojo Hideki (1885–1945). Japanese minister of war (1940–1941), prime minister (1941–1944). He was executed for war guilt after an international trial.

Toki. See Wilhelm TELL.

Toklas, Alice B (1877–1967). See AUTOBIOGRAPHY OF ALICE B. TOKLAS, THE.

Tokugawa. Japanese period (1600–1868). Under the leadership of Tokugawa Ieyasu (1542–1616), the country was unified under a feudal government, the shōgunate, located in Edo (Tokyo), and the continued warfare of the previous centuries was replaced by a peace that lasted over 250 years. The imperial court was without power, foreigners were rigidly excluded and Christianity banned. A rigid feudal system, based on neo-Confucianism, assured a strict control of the nation by the Tokugawa family. A new bourgeois or merchant-oriented literature arose in Osaka, the commercial capital. The *kabuki* and *joruri* plays of Chikamatsu Monzaemon, the *haiku* of Matsuo Bashō, the stories of Ihara Saikaku and the *ukiyoe* wood-block prints were all products of this time. Economic decline, the rise of a merchant class, the arrival of Western nations, particularly the Americans under Admiral Perry, all contributed to the restoration of the imperial rule with the establishment of the Meiji government in 1868.

Tokyo. The world's largest city and capital of Japan. It was formerly known as Edo, when it was the capital of the shōgunate during the Tokugawa period (1600–1868).

Tolkien, J[ohn] R[onald] R[enel] (1892–   ). English author and scholar, professor of medieval English literature and philology. He wrote a series of books about the Hobbits, imaginary gnomelike creatures who have a world, language, and mythology of their own, and whose adventures involve struggles between good and evil. His trilogy *The Lord of the Rings* (1954–1956) consists of *The Fellowship of the Ring, The Two Towers,* and *The Return of the King.*

Toller, Ernst (1893–1939). German dramatist. He figured in the movement of EXPRESSIONISM, and was well known for his frequent and outspoken advocacy of a social revolution to follow World War I. He entered the German Army as a volunteer, but soon underwent a change of heart and, after his release in 1916, took part in pacifist movements for which he was imprisoned. His own development is reflected in that of the hero in his first play, *Die Wandlung (The Change,* 1919), who is prompted by the horrors of war to renounce his patriotism and commit himself to the cause of peace and a people's revolution. But Toller was no simple slave of socialist ideology; he was well aware that mass movements often injure the very social and moral ideals that they seek to promote, and his concern with this problem is seen in both the highly abstract *Masse Mensch (Man and the Masses,* 1920) and the historical *Die Maschinenstürmer (The Machine-Wreckers,* 1922). Toller was moving away from the simple ideal of revolution, and in another play, *Hinkemann* (1922), he all but left the realm of ideas to concentrate on the tragic human problems faced by a returning soldier. And finally, in his *Hoppla, wir leben! (Hurray, We're Living!,* 1927), a kind of political panorama, he expressed complete disillusionment with postwar Europe. Later, driven into exile by the Nazis, he committed suicide in New York.

Tolomei, Claudio (1492–1555). Sienese critic. In 1539 he published an important treatise on Tuscan poetry in which he argued for the use of classical meter, in preference to modern accentual meter. His ideas were influential among Renaissance authors who supported this losing cause.

Tolstoi, Aleksei Nikolayevich (1883–1945). Russian novelist, short-story writer, and dramatist. Born a count, Tolstoi was distantly related to Count Leo Tolstoi and to Ivan Turgenev on his mother's side of the family. He fought with the Whites during the civil war, emigrated in 1919, and returned to the Soviet Union in 1923, where his writings became extremely popular. His best-known works of fiction are *Khozhdeniye po mukam* (*Road to Calvary*, 1921, 1927, 1941), which is a trilogy describing the years before, during, and just after the revolution, and *Pietr Pervyi* (*Peter the First*, 1929–1945), a highly regarded historical novel. Tolstoi became one of the first Soviet science fiction writers with the publication of *Aelita* (1924), an account of a Russian landing on Mars.

Tolstoi or **Tolstoy**, Count **Leo** (**Lev Nikolayevich**; 1828–1910). Russian novelist and moral philosopher. Best known for his novels, he also wrote short-stories, plays, and essays. With Dostoevski, Tolstoi made the Russian realistic novel a literary genre that ranks in importance and influence with classical Greek tragedy and Elizabethan drama. Aside from his literary work, Tolstoi holds an important place in his own country's cultural history as an ethical philosopher, and religious reformer. He is especially known, both inside and outside of Russia, as an early champion of the non-violent protest and the source of much of that doctrine's moral force. He was an influential factor in the social restlessness that swept Russia before the 1917 revolution.

Tolstoi was born, one of four brothers, on the family estate of Yasnaya Polyana, south of Moscow. His father, Count Nikolai Ilyich Tolstoi, was a veteran of the 1812 Russian campaign against Napoleon. His mother died when Tolstoi was not quite two years old. In 1837 the family moved to Moscow so that the boys could receive a formal education, and that same year their father died, the care of the children passing to their aunts. The story of his happy childhood and the later years was described by Tolstoi in his autobiographical trilogy, CHILDHOOD, BOYHOOD, and YOUTH.

In 1844 Tolstoi enrolled in the University of Kazan, intending to study Oriental languages. His interest flagged, however, and he left the university in 1847 to settle on the Yasnaya Polyana estate. While at the university he had acquired the life-long habit of keeping a diary of his thoughts, plans, and accomplishments. This diary has been an invaluable source of information for his biographers. Entries for 1847 show that Tolstoi intended to follow a rigorous course of self-study while living on the estate; instead he turned his attention to running the estate and improving the condition of his peasants, but encountering the serfs' mistrust, he soon gave up this idea, also. The next few years were spent enjoying the pleasures of Moscow society. His diary shows that this enjoyment was often followed by periods of self-castigation and vows to improve himself.

In 1851, Tolstoi went to the Caucasus, joined the army, and took part in the Russian efforts to suppress the rebellious Caucasian mountain tribes. During the next year he completed and published the first volume of his trilogy, *Childhood,* which was published in the journal *Sovremennik* (*The Contemporary*). In 1854, he was transferred to Sevastopol where he took part in the defense of the city against the British and French during the Crimean War. During these years he completed several short works, including *The Raid* (*Nabeg;* 1853), *Boyhood,* and *The Woodfelling* (*Rubka lesa;* 1855). His greatest success, however, was his stories based on the defense of Sevastopol— *Sevastopol in the Month of December* (*Sevastopol v dekabre mesyatze;* April, 1855), *Sevastopol in May* (*Sevastopol v maye;* June, 1855), and *Sevastopol in August 1855* (*Sevastopol v avguste 1855 goda;* December, 1855). These stories, generally known as the SEVASTOPOL SKETCHES, made their author famous and opened St. Petersburg's literary circles to him. Tolstoi's aristocratic aloofness and youthful bravado alienated many of the literati, including the novelist Ivan Turgenev with whom Tolstoi was to have intermittent quarrels for years.

In 1857, Tolstoi made his first European trip. Western life made a bad impression on him. He recorded his reactions in a short piece entitled *Lucerne* (1857). After his return to Yasnaya Polyana, Tolstoi became interested in education for the children of his peasants. He opened a school for them on the estate in 1859, and took another trip abroad that year to study European educational methods.

In 1862, Tolstoi married Sofya Andreyevna Behrs. She was then 18 years old and he was 34. The following year he published one of his best early works, THE COSSACKS, on which he had been working for several years. He also began writing his great novel, WAR AND PEACE, with which he had been occasionally occupied since 1860. He had originally planned to set the time of the book in the 1850's and to make the hero one of the Decembrist rebels who had been exiled to Siberia in 1825. This plan gradually changed. Tolstoi moved the time of the main action to 1825, the year of the Decembrist revolt, and finally to the period before the 1812 invasion by Napoleon.

Tolstoi's next major work was ANNA KARENINA, his second greatest novel. While at work on this book, he was beset with those metaphysical torments which he described in A CONFESSION. Following his rejection of Orthodoxy and conversion to a religion of love based on a literal interpretation of the Sermon on the Mount, Tolstoi concentrated more on philosophical and religious writings than on pure literature. Even the works of fiction he produced are weighted with didactic messages. One outstanding work that successfully carries such an extraliterary burden is the story THE DEATH OF IVAN ILYICH. Tolstoi's belief in the simple life of poverty and toil had its counterpart in his new attitude toward art, which he expressed in his treatise on aesthetics, WHAT IS ART? The didactic moral element is also particularly noticeable in such works as *The Kreutzer Sonata* (*Kreitzerova sonata;* 1890), *Father Sergei* (*Otetz Sergei;* 1898), the novel RESURRECTION, and *The False Coupon* (*Fal'shivyi kupon;* 1904).

Tolstoi's main interest was in working out his religious and philosophical ideas. He wrote commentaries on the gospels and made translations of them and produced many tracts and pamphlets on religious subjects. His larger works on these subjects include

A Criticism of Dogmatic Theology (*Kritika dogmaticheskogo bogosloviya;* 1885), *What I Believe* (*V chiom moya vera;* 1883), and *What Then Must We Do?* (*Tak chto zhe nam delat'?;* 1886).

Tolstoi stressed the moral and ethical side of Christianity; he believed in the mystical doctrine of the inner light. He rejected the divinity of Jesus, regarding him only as the greatest of ethical teachers. He also rejected the ideas of an afterlife or a personal god. The main principles on which he based his teachings were love for all mankind and freedom from all forms of hatred and violence, including the appetites of greed, anger, and lust. From these principles sprang his doctrine of passive resistance to evil (with its corollaries of hatred of war and of the demands of the state, both of which are forms of violence). Tolstoi condemned capitalism, private property, and the division of labor. Civilization in general he regarded as bad, emphasizing the need to make life as simple and primitive as possible. He extolled the virtues of physical labor, of earning one's livelihood by the sweat of one's brow. Tolstoi himself undertook to make his own shoes and wore simple peasant blouses. While some of his followers tried to build social utopias on the basis of his ideas, Tolstoi himself was generally content to criticize the existing society in the light of his ideas. He was an effective and fearless critic. His criticisms of the government and of the church were answered by these two closely connected powers in 1901 in the form of Tolstoi's excommunication from the Russian Orthodox Church. Instead of harming his standing with the general public, the action seemed to make Tolstoi more popular. When the Czarist government executed numbers of people after the 1905 revolution, Tolstoi issued a scathing criticism of the policy in *I Cannot Be Silent* (*Ya ne mogu molchat';* 1908).

Besides his moral and religious writings, Tolstoi produced a number of moralizing tales for the people. Several of these are small masterpieces, despite their didacticism. They include *God Sees the Truth, But Waits* (*Bog pravdu vidit, da ne skoro skazhet;* 1872), *What Men Live By* (*Chem lyudi zhivy?* 1881), *Two Old Men* (*Dva starika;* 1885), and *Alyosha Gorshok* (1905). These stories were written in the simple, plain narrative manner that Tolstoi conceived as the best style for all good literature. Despite his self-restrictions regarding style, Tolstoi managed to produce several fine works of art in his later years. These include *Master and Man* (*Khozyain i rabotnik;* 1895) and the short novel HADZHI MURAD. He also wrote three major plays: THE POWER OF DARKNESS, *Fruits of Enlightenment* (*Plody prosveshcheniya;* 1890), and *The Living Corpse* (*Zhivoi trup;* 1900).

Tolstoi's ideas and way of life after his conversion put a strain on his family life. His views on the evil of private property and his desire to put all his literary work in the public domain especially irritated his wife, who knew that only the royalties from Tolstoi's books supported the large family. After years of estrangement from his wife and all of his children save his youngest daughter Alexandra, Tolstoi left Yasnaya Polyana in November, 1910, accompanied by Alexandra and his doctor. He was on his way to a monastery, but he was taken ill during the train journey and died at the small railway junction of Astapovo.

To Lucasta, Going to the Wars (1649). A poem by Richard LOVELACE. In it the poet asks his lady to forgive him for leaving her to go to war. The poem closes with the famous lines:

> I could not love thee, Dear, so much,
> Lov'd I not Honour more.

The Lucasta to whom Lovelace addressed this and other poems is said to have been his fiancée, Lucy Sacheverell.

Tom Brown's School Days (1857). A famous book for boys by Thomas HUGHES. It portrays life in an English public school. When Tom enters Rugby, he is a shy, homesick chap, but he is soon drawn into the life of the school and develops robust, manly qualities. A sequel, *Tom Brown at Oxford,* appeared in 1861.

Tom Jones[, a Foundling, The History of] (1749). A novel by Henry FIELDING, generally considered one of the masterpieces of English literature. Squire ALLWORTHY, who lives with his sister Bridget, returns home after a long absence to find an infant on his bed. Suspecting his servant Jenny Jones to be the mother, he names the baby Tom Jones, determines to rear him himself, and Jenny leaves town. Soon after, Bridget marries Captain Blifil, a fortune-hunter; they have a son, and Captain Blifil dies. Tom and young Blifil are raised together, taught by SQUARE and THWACKUM. Blifil, a malevolent boy, seizes every opportunity to misrepresent Tom and get him into trouble. Tom is a lusty, imprudent boy, but essentially benevolent. A rivalry over the attentions of Sophia Western, daughter of the neighboring Squire WESTERN, arises between them. Because of an affair with the gamekeeper's daughter, and because of Blifil's treachery, Tom is sent packing by Squire Allworthy. In the PICARESQUE section that follows, Tom meets with many adventures, some of them of a dissipated nature, on the road to London. Sophia, in the meantime, flees to London to escape the marriage which her father is trying to force with Blifil, who is only interested in her fortune. Soon the whole cast of characters is on the scene; Jenny Jones turns up to reveal that Squire Allworthy's sister Bridget, not she, is the mother of Tom. Blifil's cruelties to Tom over the years are exposed, Tom, promising to mend his ways, marries Sophia, and becomes the heir of Squire Allworthy. As a hero, Tom Jones is not overheroic; he is perhaps a model of generosity and manly spirit, but mixed with dissipation. Lord Byron called him "an accomplished blackguard."

Tomlinson, H[enry] M[ajor] (1873–1958). English writer. He is the author of reflective novels, essays, and travel books, all of which deal with ships and the sea. *The Sea and the Jungle* (1912), an account of a voyage to Brazil, is the best known of his books. *Gallions Reach* (1927) and *Morning Light* (1946) are among his novels; *The Turn of the Tide* (1945) is a fine collection of essays.

Tommy or **Tommy Atkins.** A British private soldier, as a Jack Tar is a British sailor. At one time all recruits were served out with manuals in which were to be entered the name, age, date of enlistment, length of service, wounds, medals, and so on of the holder. With each book was sent a specimen form showing how the one in the manual should be filled in, and the hypothetical name selected, instead of the lawyer's *John Doe* or *Richard Roe,* was *Thomas Atkins.* The nickname was popularized by Kipling.

> For it's Tommy this, and Tommy that, and
> "Tommy wait outside";
> But it's "Special train for Atkins" when the
> trooper's on the tide.
> *Tommy (Barrack-Room Ballads)*

Tommy and Grizel. See SENTIMENTAL TOMMY.
Tom o' Bedlam. A mendicant who asks charity on the plea of insanity. In the 16th and 17th centuries applications for admission to BEDLAM became so numerous that many inmates were dismissed half cured. These "ticket-of-leave" men wandered about chanting mad songs and dressed in fantastic costumes to elicit pity. Posing as these harmless innocents, a band of sturdy rogues appeared. Called "Abram men," they committed great depredations.
Tompson, Benjamin (1642–1714). Puritan poet and teacher, the first native-born American to publish a volume of poems in America. Born in Braintree (now Quincy), Mass., and brought up by foster parents, Tompson graduated from Harvard in 1662 and five years later became master of the Boston Latin School. In 1676 he published *New England's Crisis,* modeled on Francis Quarles's *History of Sampson* (1631). The title poem of the collection describes the towns of New England at the time of King Philip's War. It is especially notable for its use of pidgin English and Indian dialect, and for its concluding picture of a group of women building a fortress to protect Boston. Tompson was the first poet in colonial America to make extensive use of the contemporary scene.
Tom Sawyer, The Adventures of (1876). A novel by Mark TWAIN. Tom, a shrewd and adventurous boy, is at home in the respectable world of his Aunt Polly, as well as in the self-reliant, parentless world of Huck Finn. The two friends, out in the cemetery under a full moon, attempt to cure warts with a dead cat. They accidentally witness a murder, of which Muff Potter is later wrongly accused. Knowing that the true murderer is Injun Joe, the boys are helpless with fear; they decide to run away to Jackson's Island. After a few pleasant days of smoking and swearing, they realize that the townspeople believe them dead. Returning in time to hear their funeral eulogies, they become town heroes. At the trial of Muff Potter, Tom, unable to let an innocent person be condemned, reveals his knowledge. Injun Joe flees. Later Tom and his sweetheart, Becky Thatcher, get lost in the cave in which the murderer is hiding. They escape, and Tom and Huck return to find the treasure Joe has buried.

Clemens wrote three sequels to this popular book: *The Adventures of* HUCKLEBERRY FINN, *Tom Sawyer Abroad* (1894), and *Tom Sawyer, Detective* (1896).
Tom Thumb. The pygmy hero of an old nursery tale, popular in the 16th century. *The History of Tom Thumb* was published by R. Johnson in 1621 and a similar tale by Perrault (*Le Petit Poucet*), in 1697. The American midget Charles Sherwood Stratton (1838–1883) exhibited at side shows by P. T.

The History of *Tom Thumbe*, the *Little,* for his small stature surnamed, King ARTHVRS Dwarfe:

Whose Life and aduenturescontaine many strange and wonderfull accidents, publiined for *the delight of merry Time-spenders.*

Imprinted at London for *Tho: Longley.* 1621.

Title page of *The History of Tom Thumb* (1621).

BARNUM was popularly called "General Tom Thumb."
Tom Thumb the Great (1730). Best-known, shortened title of *The Tragedy of Tragedies; or, The Life and Death of Tom Thumb the Great,* a satirical burlesque by Henry FIELDING. Fielding's satire was directed at contemporary and Restoration drama, particularly heroic drama. Tom Thumb himself, in his diminutiveness, burlesques the grandness of the heroic hero. Fielding describes him as a little hero with a great soul.
Tom Titivil. The name of the devil in many of the medieval English morality plays.
Tone, [Theobald] Wolfe (1763–1798). Irish revolutionist who founded the United Irishmen with Thomas Russell and Napper Tandy of the UNITED IRISHMEN. (Napper Tandy is mentioned in the beginning of the famous Irish song *The Wearing of the Green.*) He set forth his policy of unity for Ireland in *A Review of the Conduct of Administration* (1790), *Hibernicus* (1790), and *An Argument on behalf of the Catholics of Ireland* (1791). Tone negotiated for a landing of the French in Ireland, but the fleet was scattered by a storm in 1796. The British captured him with a small French squadron off Lough Swilly in 1798 and were preparing to prosecute him for treason when Tone committed suicide.
tong (Chin., *t'ang,* hall). A Chinese secret society, especially in the U.S. Now either underground

or pacified, the tongs were once powerful in U.S. Chinatowns, and controlled an active traffic in drugs, vice, and gambling.

Tonio Kröger (1903). A story by Thomas MANN. It is about a young North German author who experiences very sharply the gulf between his artistic temperament and the wholesome, vital world of the bourgeois. But Tonio does not resign himself to isolation and decadence; at the end of the story, he realizes that his most sincere emotion is an undying love of the ordinary, of his northern countrymen's uncomplicated vitality, and that this love is the first source of all true value in his art.

Tono-Bungay (1909). A novel by H. G. WELLS. The narrator is George Ponderevo, son of the housekeeper on a large estate, who is apprenticed to his uncle, Edward Ponderevo, a small-town druggist. His fantastic uncle soon moves to London and makes a fortune from his quack medicine, "Tono-Bungay." George helps his uncle, ironically observes his rise in the world, and uses some of his money to set himself up as an airplane designer. George resembles H. G. Wells himself—the son of a housekeeper, apprenticed to a druggist, a socialist, and a man with a vision of progress through properly used science.

Tonson, Jacob (1656?–1736). English publisher. He held the copyright of *Paradise Lost* and published the works of Dryden and Addison and editions of Shakespeare and Beaumont and Fletcher. He also brought out a famous *Miscellany* (1684–1709), which Dryden edited and which included poetry by Pope, Swift, and others.

Tonti or **Tonty, Henry de** (c. 1650–1704). Italian explorer. He took part in several of La Salle's expeditions to the Mississippi Valley. The iron hand that he wore led the Indians to believe that he was endowed with magic powers.

Tooke, [John] Horne (1736–1812). English radical politician, known as "the philosopher of Wimbledon." His major works include two pamphlets, *The Petition of an Englishman* (1765), a defence of John Wilkes, *Two Pair of Portraits* (1790), a study of William Pitt and Charles Fox, and numerous philological tracts.

Topaze (1928). A play by Marcel PAGNOL satirizing corruption in city politics. It was filmed in 1933.

Tophet. A valley south of Jerusalem, at the extremity of GEHENNA or the Valley of Hinnom, where children were burnt alive in idolatrous rites as sacrifices to Moloch. There, the reformer-king Josiah threw dead bodies, ordure, and other unclean things, to prevent any further use of the place for religious purposes (II Kings 23:10); it was also the site of the destruction of Sennacherib's army (Isa. 30:31–33). A perpetual fire was kept burning in Tophet to consume the bodies, filth, etc., deposited there; hence, it was taken as symbolical of Hell. The name is Hebrew and may mean "a place to be spat upon," or may be connected with *toph,* a drum, in allusion to the drowning of the murdered children's cries by the beating of drums.

Torah. A Hebrew word, originally referring to the casting of a lot for sacred guidance, which gradually acquired the sense of oracle or divine revelation. In Jewish literature, it refers to God's total revelation; in a more particularized sense, it is the Pentateuch. It is also used to designate the scroll, always present in a synagogue, on which the Pentateuch is handwritten.

Torelli, Pompeo (1539–1608). Italian dramatist. In 1589 he wrote the *Merope,* the first version of this subject, which was treated later by Voltaire and Matthew Arnold.

Torquato Tasso (1790). A play by Johann Wolfgang von GOETHE, based on the life of the 16th-century Italian poet. Though classical in form, like his earlier *Iphigeneia in Tauris, Tasso* is not as optimistic about the ultimate solution of all human conflicts. Basically, it treats the incompatibility of the poet's inner nature with life in the external world: a theme not unlike that of THE SORROWS OF YOUNG WERTHER, except that there is no suicide. The play ends ambiguously, and it is not clear whether or how this disharmony is eventually resolved. See WEIMAR CLASSICISM; ZERRISSENHEIT.

Torquemada, Tomás de. See Spanish INQUISITION.

Torrès, Tereska (?–). French novelist. Her novels of passion have been translated from the French by her husband Meyer LEVIN. They include *Not Yet* (1958) and *Golden Cage* (1959).

Tortilla Flat (1935). A novel by John STEINBECK. It deals with the poor but carefree Danny and his friends Pillón, Pablo, Big Joe Portagee, Jesús María Corcoran, and the old Pirate, all of whom gather in Danny's house, which Steinbeck insists "was not unlike the Round Table." The novel contrasts the complexities of modern civilization with the simple life of these men.

Tor und der Tod, Der (Death and the Fool, 1899). A short lyric drama by Hugo von HOFMANNSTHAL. The central character, a nobleman named Claudio, is about to die, and the play concentrates on his inner development, which is revealed in encounters with the spirits of his dead mother, an old beloved, an old friend, and with death himself.

Tory. A word of Irish origin meaning "pursuer." First applied to Irish outlaws, it later became a nickname for those who opposed the exclusion of the duke of York (later James II, a Roman Catholic) from succession to the Crown. After 1689, the English Tories continued to incline toward the Stuarts, but after George III came to the throne, their policy became one of upholding the established church and state and of opposing liberalism. In this way it became the name of one of the two great English Parties. Today the Tory Party has given place in English politics to the Conservative. In the American colonies and during the Revolution, British loyalists were called Tories. A U.S. source of 1777 defines a Tory as "a thing whose head is in England, whose body is in America, and whose neck ought to be stretched."

Tosa Diary, The (Tosa nikki). Japanese diary attributed to Ki no Tsurayuki (d. 946). Humorous and elegant in style, it describes a trip from the Province of Tosa to Kyoto in 936. It was much imitated by later writers.

Tosca, La. A tragic opera by Giacomo PUCCINI (1900) based on the drama by Victorien SARDOU.

Toscanelli, Paolo (1397–1482). Italian astronomer, mathematician, and geographer, a friend of Nicholas of Cusa, whom he met at Padua, and an adviser to the architect Brunelleschi while he constructed the famous dome of the Florence cathedral. The bulk of his work is lost, despite his great reputation. His arguments for an Atlantic route to the East may have influenced the voyages of Columbus.

Toscanini, Arturo (1867–1957). Italian conductor, perhaps the greatest of this century. He was the principal conductor successively of La Scala, the Metropolitan Opera, the N.Y. Philharmonic, and the NBC Symphony Orchestra (organized especially for him in 1937). His repertory included many symphonic and operatic works, all of which he memorized. His interpretations of Verdi and Beethoven were especially admired.

totem. A North American Indian (Algonquin) word for some natural object, usually an animal, taken as the emblem of a person or clan on account of a supposed relationship. Totemism, which is common among primitive peoples, has a distinct value in preventing intermarriage among near relations, for if persons bearing the same totem (as, for instance, in the case of brothers and sisters) intermarry, the punishment is death. Another custom is that one is not allowed to kill or eat the animal borne as one's totem.

totem pole. The post standing before a dwelling on which grotesque and, frequently, brilliantly colored representations of the totem were carved and hung. It was often of great size, and sometimes so broad at the base that an archway was cut through it.

To the Lighthouse (1927). A novel by Virginia WOOLF. Using the techniques of STREAM OF CONSCIOUSNESS and SYMBOLISM, it has little plot, but a great deal of atmosphere, emotion, and poetry. The characters' moment-by-moment actions, sense impressions, and thoughts are described. The first section, called "The Window," describes a day during Mr. and Mrs. Ramsay's house party at their country home by the sea. Mr. Ramsay is a distinguished scholar and, in the eyes of Virginia Woolf, a typical male, whose mind works rationally, heroically, and rather icily. He is drawn from her father, Sir Leslie Stephen. Mrs. Ramsay is a warm, creative, intuitive woman, the center of the household. Among the various guests is Lily Briscoe, an artist. The Ramsays have arranged to take a boat out to the lighthouse the next morning, and their little son James is bitterly disappointed when a change in the weather makes it impossible. The second section, called "Time Passes," describes the seasons and the house, unused and decaying, in the years after Mrs. Ramsay's death. In the third section, "The Lighthouse," Mr. Ramsay and his friends are back at the house. He takes the postponed trip to the lighthouse with his now 16-year-old son, who is at last able to communicate silently with him and forgive him for being different from his mother. Lily Briscoe puts the last touches to the painting Mrs. Ramsay once inspired. The lighthouse, everyone's goal, symbolizes many things to many people. More like a prose poem than a conventional novel, the whole book is a statement about time and death and the permanence of art.

To the Virgins, To Make Much of Time (1648). A poem by Robert HERRICK whose theme is explicit in the title. It was set to a number of melodies, and the first lines gained proverbial familiarity:

> Gather ye rosebuds while ye may,
> Old time is still a-flying
> And this same flower that smiles to-day,
> Tomorrow will be dying.

Tottel's Miscellany (1557). Popular title for *Songs and Sonnets,* a "miscellany" or collection of poems by various authors, published by Richard Tottel in England. It contained 271 poems, chiefly lyrics, although epigrams, epitaphs, elegies, satires, pastorals, and narrative verse were included, as well as translations of Latin, Italian, and French poems. It introduced the use of *terza rima, ottava rima,* rondeau, the first English sonnets, and possibly the first original English blank verse. In the collection were 97 poems attributed to Sir Thomas WYATT, 40 to the earl of SURREY, 40 to Nicholas Grimald, and 94 to "Uncertain Authors." The majority of these poems had never before appeared in print, for courtier-poets, such as Wyatt and Surrey, circulated their verses among the court in manuscript. It was not considered fashionable for them to publish their own work (this rule did not hold in the case of translations of poems from foreign languages) and as a result contemporary poetry reached the general public only rarely, if at all.

The first publication of its kind, *Tottel's Miscellany* was extremely popular. It went through eight editions in thirty years, and was followed by a host of imitators which are known generally as the Elizabethan anthologies. They are of less importance than the original, which is considered to mark the beginning of modern English poetry.

Tottenham in Boots. A popular toast in Ireland in 1731. Mr. Tottenham cast the vote which threw out a government bill very obnoxious to the Irish, on the subject of the Irish Parliament. He had come from the country, and rushed into the House of Commons without changing his boots, just in time to give his vote, which prevented the bill from passing by a majority of one.

Touchstone. In Shakespeare's As YOU LIKE IT, a court jester who accompanies Rosalind to the Forest of Arden. He is a witty, cynical fellow who lists "the seven degrees of affront" in a famous speech: (1) the retort courteous, (2) the quip modest, (3) the reply churlish, (4) the reproof valiant, (5) the countercheck quarrelsome, (6) the lie circumstantial, and (7) the lie direct. His wit is realistic and biting, usually aimed at the foibles of mankind, and he openly insults his betrothed Audrey, who is too stupid to realize it.

Toulet, Paul Jean (1867–1920). French poet and novelist, best known for the epigrammatic and erotic verses in *Les Contrerimes* (1921).

Toulouse-Lautrec [Monfa], Henri [Marie Raymond] de (1864–1901). French painter. Descended from an old French family and physically misshapen, he became the supreme portrayer of Montmartre night life, with its dancers, actresses, singers, and women of the demimonde. He probed the emotional significance of his subjects, picturing them with an elegant, nervous line, expressively revealing. At first influenced by Edgar Degas and Japanese prints, he soon developed his own original style. His decorative posters and lithographs are also highly distinguished.

Tourgée, Albion W[inegar] (1838–1905). American novelist. Born in Ohio, Tourgée lived in several parts of the U.S. After practicing law, he served in the Federal army. In 1865, he moved to North Carolina and played an active part in the work of the Reconstruction. Ultimately forced by hostile pressure to return to the North, Tourgée wrote several novels, among them A Fool's Errand and Bricks Without Straw. These once widely read volumes describing the problems and inevitable failure of the Reconstruction made Southern themes current in American literature. During the last eight years of his life, Tourgée served as consul at Bordeaux, France.

Tourneur, Cyril (c. 1575–1626). English dramatist. He is the probable author of the bloody Senecan tragedy The Revenger's Tragedy and of the somewhat milder Atheist's Tragedy.

Tour on the Prairies, A (1835). A travel narrative by Washington Irving. The book is based on Irving's 1832 trip across territory now part of Oklahoma. Irving comments on the landscape, the Indians, and the life of the settlers. A less romantic picture is presented in the journal Irving kept, which has been recently published.

Toussaint. See All Saints' Day.

Toussaint L'Ouverture, Pierre. François Dominique (1743–1803). Haitian Negro soldier and liberator, a self-educated slave. In 1791 he led a successful revolt against white rule in San Domingo (Hispaniola [Haiti and the Dominican Republic] of today) and, through his administration, brought law and order to the island by 1801. When he asked Napoleon for approval of a constitutional form of government, Napoleon sent a French expedition against him under General Leclerc. Captured and taken back to France, he was imprisoned and died there 10 months later. He is the central figure of a historical novel, The Hour and the Man (1840), by Harriet Martineau. Black Majesty (1928) by John W. Vandercook is his biography, and he is a major character in the drama The Revolutionists by Selden Rodman. He is also the subject of poems by Wordsworth, Whittier, and Lamartine.

Tousseul, Jean. Pen name of Olivier Degée (1890–1944). Belgian novelist. He captured the spirit of his native peasant region in such novels as Jean Clarambaux (5 vols., 1927–1936).

Tovaritch. See Jacques Deval.

Tovey, Donald Francis (1875–1940). Musical essayist, composer, and pianist, best known for his scholarly exegeses of music in encyclopedias and books such as Musical Form and Matter (1934), Essays in Musical Analysis (6 v.; 1935–1939), and Beethoven (1945).

Tower, The (Der Turm; 1925). A verse-play by Hugo von Hofmannsthal. It is freely adapted from Calderón's Life Is a Dream, the most important of Hofmannsthal's additions to the orginal work being the character of Olivier, a demagogical dictator who assumes power after the old king's deposition and executes Prince Sigismund. Thus, Sigismund's final triumph, which is real in Calderón's work, becomes entirely symbolic in Hofmannsthal's.

Tower Beyond Tragedy, The (1924). A play in verse by Robinson Jeffers. This poetic drama is based on Agamemnon and The Libation Bearers, the first two plays of the Oresteia trilogy of Aeschylus, but Jeffers gives an enlarged role to Cassandra, the prophetess, and emphasizes the contrast between the incestuous desires of Electra and the desire of Orestes to break away from her and from all ties with humanity.

Tower Hill. An elevation near the Tower of London, the site of the execution of traitors. Among famous figures executed there were Sir Thomas More, the earl of Surrey, Strafford, and Archbishop Laud.

tower of Babel. See Babel.

Tower of London. A famous London prison for political prisoners. William the Conqueror and the monarchs who followed him built the various buildings included in the name Tower of London, which stand by the Thames. The Tower has been a prison for many distinguished persons including kings and queens. It is said that the last person sent to the Tower was Sir F. Burdett in 1810.

Town, The. See Hamlet, The.

town and gown. The two sections of a university town, composed of those who are not attached to the university and those who are. A town and gown row, therefore, is a collision, often leading to a fight, between the students and non-gownsmen.

Towneley Mysteries or Plays. One of the important cycles of English medieval mystery plays. They are also known as the Wakefield Mysteries because they were probably acted at the fairs of Widkirk, near Wakefield. They have a more popular, lively, and even jocular tone than the plays of the other cycles. See Wakefield Master, the.

Townsend, Morris. See Washington Square.

Townshend, Charles (1725–1767). English statesman and chancellor of the exchequer. In the "Townshend Acts" he introduced taxes on glass, paper, and tea in the American colonies. These taxes are considered prime causes of the American Revolution.

Toy Cart, The. See Little Clay Cart, The.

Toynbee, Arnold J[oseph] (1889–   ). English historian and student of international affairs. From 1920 to 1938 he wrote the yearly Survey of International Affairs. His greatest work is his 12-volume A Study of History (1934–1961), a condensed version of which became a best seller. Comparing the history of 21 different civilizations, he traces a cyclical pattern of growth, maturity, and decay in them all. He believes that societies thrive best in response to a challenge, and that a society's most important task is to create a religion; though our Western civilization is in its decay stage, he sees hope for the future formation of one spiritually oriented world society. Despite all his encyclopedic knowledge, Toynbee is more of a poet, mythologist, and metaphysician than an empirical historian.

Toynbee, Philip (1916–   ). English novelist. The son of Arnold Toynbee and grandson of Gilbert Murray, he writes experimental, subjective novels, including Tea with Mrs. Goodman (1947; U.S. title, Prothalamium) and The Garden to the Sea (1953).

Toyotomi Hideyoshi (1536–1598). First unifier of Japan. Arising from peasant stock, he served the famous warrior Oda Nobunaga (1534–1582), gaining and consolidating military control after the latter's death. He engaged in extensive campaigns against

Korea, which proved inconclusive. A patron of the arts, he is revered in folklore and legend as one of Japan's greatest military geniuses. His successors lost control of the nation to Tokugawa Ieyasu (1542–1616), founder of the Tokugawa shōgunate.

Tozzi, Federico (1883–1920). Italian novelist. His works are characterized by their descriptions of the author's unhappy adolescence in his native Siena (Tuscany). Tozzi's youthful protagonists are projections of himself at a time when he strove to find a sense of spiritual peace and intellectual understanding in a society dominated by irrational passions. His most outstanding novels are *Con Gli Occhi Chiusi* (1919), an idyllic tale about the innocent, selfless love of two sensitive adolescents; *Tre Croci* (1920), the title of which refers to the crosses that mark the graves of three brothers whose lack of moral fiber led them to three varieties of catastrophe; and *Il Podere* and *Ricordi di Un Impiegato*, both published posthumously in 1921.

Trachinian Women, The. See HERACLES.

Tracts for the Times (1833–1841). A series of 90 papers on theological and liturgical subjects. Published at Oxford, it is sometimes called the Oxford Tracts. They consist of extracts from · 17th-century High Church divines and church fathers, and contributions from John Henry NEWMAN, Richard Hurrell Froude (1803–1836), E. B. PUSEY, John KEBLE, and Isaac Williams. The tracts were launched with the object of arresting "the advance of Liberalism in religious thought," and reviving "the true conception of the relation of the Church of England to the Catholic Church at large." The series came to an end (at the request of the bishop of Oxford) with Newman's Tract No. 90 in which he stated that it is possible to interpret some aspects of the Thirty-Nine Articles of the Church in a manner not inconsistent with the Council of Trent. This tract was condemned by several bishops and heads of colleges, and a group of Tractarians, including Newman, entered the Roman Catholic Church. See OXFORD MOVEMENT.

Traddles, Tommie. In Charles Dickens' DAVID COPPERFIELD, a simple, honest young man who believes in everything and everybody. He is a classmate of David's at CREAKLE's school.

Tradiciones peruanas (1872–1906). The aggregate title of 10 volumes by Ricardo PALMA, consisting of *tradiciones,* or traditions, a literary form that Palma himself originated. Virtually defying classification, Palma's traditions are short sketches combining history, anecdote, and satire. Using a formula that called for a *soupçon* of truth, a great deal of invention, and painstaking attention to style, Palma covered virtually every aspect of the Peruvian past, though he was most at home describing the intrigues and amorous escapades of 18th-century Lima. Written in a pungent, ironical style reminiscent of that of the 17th-century Spaniard Francisco Quevedo, Palma's traditions have often been imitated but never equaled.

Tradition and the Individual Talent (1919). An essay by T. S. ELIOT. In this influential poetic manifesto the author asserts that a poet cannot write significant poetry in the 20th century unless he is steeped in the tradition and poetry of the past. The past will teach him to avoid romantic, autobiographical writing, and to concentrate on technique and impersonal, detached poetry.

Trafalgar, battle of (Oct., 1805). The greatest British naval victory, off Cape Trafalgar on the southwest coast of Spain, in the Napoleonic wars. Fifteen French and Spanish ships were either captured or destroyed by the British, who did not lose a single vessel. The brilliant victory was marred by the death in action of Horatio NELSON, the commander of the British fleet.

Trafalgar Square. One of the principal squares in London, named after Horatio Nelson's victory in the Battle of TRAFALGAR. It contains the Nelson monument and the site of Charing Cross; the National Gallery faces on it.

Tragedy of Nan, The (1908). A play in verse by John MASEFIELD. It is set in the early 19th century. Nan Hardwick's father was hanged for sheep-stealing; she now lives with her uncle and his tormenting wife. The aunt tells Dick Gurvil, whom Nan loves, about the death of Nan's father and he leaves her to marry the aunt's daughter. After this humiliation, Nan learns of her father's innocence. Unable to endure any more, she stabs Dick to death and goes to drown herself.

While the play is sordid and grimly realistic, it is written in a beautiful folk-poetry idiom.

Tragic Muse, The (1890). A novel by Henry JAMES. Nicholas Dormer, son of an eminent English statesman, gives up a brilliant career in Parliament, his godfather's promised fortune, and the hand of his beautiful and wealthy cousin, Julia Dallow, to become a portrait painter. He is inspired to do this by the example of his actress friend and "muse," Miriam Rooth.

Traherne, Thomas (1636–1674). English poet and clergyman. One of the later METAPHYSICAL POETS, Traherne is known for the emphasis placed in his poetry on what he regarded as the direct and untutored apprehension of truth on the part of children. His work is marked by simple diction and a vivid presentation of the common things of everyday life as the vehicles of mystical revelation. Traherne was not discovered as a poet until early in the 20th century; his manuscripts, which were recovered in 1895 from a London bookbarrow, were at first ascribed to Henry Vaughan. His best-known verse is included in *Poetical Works* (1903) and *Poems of Felicity* (1910). *Centuries of Meditations* (1908) is a collection of his prose sketches.

Traill, Catherine Parr [Strickland] (1802–1899). English-born Canadian writer and naturalist. Mrs. Traill came to Canada with her husband and her sister, Susanna MOODIE, in 1832 and settled near Rice Lake, Ontario. The two sisters wrote of the many trials and occasional rewards of frontier life with a frankness designed to disillusion the dupes of land agents. Mrs. Traill's *The Backwoods of Canada* (1836), a series of letters to her mother, is a good example of her candor and dry humor. Canada's natural beauties are described in *Rambles in the Canadian Forest* (1859) and other works.

Trail of the Lonesome Pine, The (1908). A novel by John Fox, Jr. The hero of this once enormously popular sentimental novel is John Hale, a young engineer who comes to the Kentucky mountain region in an attempt to industrialize the area.

He finds himself in the midst of a feud between the Tollivers and the Falins, falls deeply in love with the beautiful but illiterate June Tolliver, and, after sending her East to acquire an education, finally marries her. The novel was dramatized (1912) by Eugene Walter.

Train, Arthur [Cheney] (1875–1945). American novelist and writer of short stories. A graduate of Harvard Law School who had a highly successful legal career, Train is best known as the creator of the famous character Ephraim Tutt, the wise old lawyer who shrewdly uses his legal wits and skill to help persons in trouble. The Mr. Tutt stories originally appeared in the *Saturday Evening Post,* and were collected in more than a dozen books, notably the greatly admired *Mr. Tutt's Case Book* (1937), which became required reading in several law schools. Train also wrote *The Prisoner at the Bar* (1906), *My Day in Court* (1939), and *Tassels on Her Boots* (1940).

Trajan. Full Latin name, **Marcus Ulpius Trajanus** (A.D. 52?–117). Roman emperor (98–117). He was appointed by his predecessor Nerva in A.D. 97. It is said that Trajan, although unbaptized, was delivered from Hell in answer to the prayers of St. Gregory. He is one of the two pagans said to have been admitted to Heaven. See RIPHEUS.

Trakl, Georg (1887–1914). Austrian poet. Influenced by French SYMBOLISM, he had considerable influence on the development of German EXPRESSIONISM. A volume of *Gedichte* (*Poems,* 1913) was his only book to be published during his lifetime; but his works have since attracted much attention and many of his writings appeared in posthumous publications. He was a pharmacist in the German army and died in a military hospital, probably by his own hand.

Tranio. (1) A slave in PLAUTUS' comedy *Mostellaria.* He is a clever rogue who from that time on became a sort of stock character in Roman comedy.

(2) A faithful servant to Lucentio in Shakespeare's TAMING OF THE SHREW.

Transcendentalism. An American philosophic and literary movement centered in New England during the 19th century. A reaction against scientific rationalism, it relied upon intuition as the only way to comprehend reality in a world where every natural fact bodies forth a spiritual truth. Its chief spokesman, Ralph Waldo EMERSON, expressed the Transcendentalist belief that everything in man's world is a microcosm of the universe when he stated that "the world globes itself in a drop of dew." Emerson thus stressed the essential unity of all things, which are ordered by a Supreme Mind or Over-Soul. Man's soul is identical with the Over-Soul; it is this belief in the divinity of man that allowed Transcendentalists to disregard external authority and tradition, and to rely on direct experience. "Trust thyself," Emerson's motto, became the code of Henry David THOREAU, Bronson ALCOTT, Margaret FULLER, and other members of the Transcendental Club, an informal group organized in 1836 by the Rev. George RIPLEY.

An idealistic philosophy, Transcendentalism was shaped by the ideas of Plato and Plotinus. It took its name and many of its ideas from Kant's CRITIQUE OF PRACTICAL REASON (1788). The American writers were influenced by Continental thinkers, including Hegel, Schelling, Fichte, and Goethe. The doctrines of the German Transcendentalists were reflected in the works of Carlyle, Coleridge, and Wordsworth, to whom the Americans owe a great debt. Emanuel SWEDENBORG's mystical doctrines of contact with the spiritual world also profoundly influenced the New England writers.

Basic contemporary statements of Transcendental belief may be found in Emerson's essay *Nature* (1836) and in his lecture *The Transcendentalist* (1842).

transition (1927–1938). A monthly literary magazine founded in Paris with Elliot PAUL and Eugene JOLAS as editors. Its purpose was to encourage experimental writing. Works by Gertrude Stein, E. E. Cummings, Ernest Hemingway, and Hart Crane were among those published. From 1927 to 1930, sections of James Joyce's *Finnegans Wake,* then known as *Work in Progress,* appeared in the magazine.

Transome, Harold. See FELIX HOLT, THE RADICAL.

Trapassi, Pietro. See Pietro METASTASIO.

Trasimenus, Lake. Latin name of the modern Lago Trasimeno or Lago di Perugia in Etruria, Italy. It was the scene of a famous battle (217 B.C.) in the Second PUNIC WAR. The Carthaginians and Gauls under Hannibal almost completely destroyed a large Roman army under the consul Flaminius.

Traubel, Horace Logo (1858–1919). American editor and biographer. A friend of Walt Whitman during the poet's later years, Traubel was deeply influenced by Whitman. As a youth he had worked at various jobs; later he founded and edited two periodicals, *The Conservator* (1890–1919) and *The Artsman* (1903–1907). His political philosophy, a mixture of socialism and poetic mysticism, was expressed in these magazines and in Traubel's books: *Chants Communal* (1904), *Optimos* (1910), and *Collects* (1914). The titles reveal Whitman's influence, but Traubel's own work was unimpressive. As one of Whitman's three literary executors, he helped to publish several volumes by and about the poet. His own contribution was *With Walt Whitman in Camden* (3 v., 1906, 1908, 1914), part of a meticulously kept diary of daily conversations with Whitman. A fourth volume, edited by Sculley Bradley, appeared in 1953.

Traveller from Altruria, A (1894). A novel by William Dean HOWELLS. Aristides Homos has just returned from the utopian Altruria, where the socialistic regime is democratic and Christian. In a series of amusing conversations, Homos finds the American system inferior to the Altrurian.

Traveller, The (1765). A poem, subtitled *A Prospect of Society,* by Oliver GOLDSMITH. It undertakes to show that every state has a particular principle of compensation that equalizes the diverse lots of mankind. Goldsmith, however, in his survey of the cultural state of Europe, finds decay of the arts everywhere. Nine lines of the poem are said to have been added by Samuel Johnson.

Travels of Sir John Mandeville, The. See MANDEVILLE, THE TRAVELS OF SIR JOHN.

Travers, Pamela (1906–   ). An Australian author. Her books concerning the mythical nurse Mary Poppins are delightful stories for children.

Traversari, Ambrogio (1386–1439). Italian monk and Humanist who translated and edited the Greek

Fathers. At the reunion councils of the Eastern and Western churches, he wrote the final document in both Latin and Greek, which was published at Florence (1438–1439).

Traviata, La (**The Lost One**; 1853). An opera by Giuseppe VERDI, based on the drama *La* DAME AUX CAMÉLIAS by Alexandre Dumas *fils*, better known in America as *Camille*. In the opera, the heroine is Violetta Valery and the man she loves is Alfred Germont. The libretto is by F. M. Piavé.

Treason of the Intellectuals, The (**La Trahison des clercs**; 1927; also trans. **The Great Betrayal**). An essay by Julien BENDA that denounces the tendency of intellectuals to engage in politics as the defeatist surrender of intelligence to propagandistic ideology. Their engagement, Benda says, necessitates the abdication of their responsibility to consider abstract truth and justice.

Treasure Island (1883). A romance by Robert Louis STEVENSON. The story is told by Jim Hawkins, a young boy who learns of the whereabouts of a buried treasure from the papers of an old sailor staying at his mother's inn. He shows the treasure map to Dr. Livesey and Squire Trelawney, and the three determine to find it. They fit out a ship, the schooner *Hispaniola*, hire hands and set off for Treasure Island. Among the ship's crew are Long John Silver and some of his followers who are after the treasure for themselves. Jim Hawkins overhears their plans to mutiny, and with the rest of the crew is able to thwart them in the bloody battle that ensues. Finally they reach the island, and retrieve the treasure with the help of the marooned sailor Ben Gunn.

Treatise on the Astrolabe, A. See ASTROLABE.

Trebizond, George of (1395–1484). Greek scholar from Crete. One of the influential Greek immigrants to Italy during the Renaissance, he taught at Vicenza and Venice, then became a papal secretary. He is noted for his defense of Aristotle against the Platonists of the time.

trecento (It., "the three hundreds"). The Italian way of designating the 14th century, the age of Dante, Petrarch, and Boccaccio.

Treece, Henry (1912–1966). English poet. He was associated with the NEW APOCALYPSE movement in poetry. Among his collections of verse is *Invitation and Warning* (1942).

Tree Grows in Brooklyn, A (1943). A novel by Betty SMITH. This best-selling, warm-hearted book tells of the life of the sensitive child Francie Nolan, growing up in a city slum, and of Francie's parents, her lovable drunkard father and tender, determined mother.

Tregeagle. A fabulous giant of Dosmary Pool, Bodmin Downs, Cornwall. His allotted task is to bale out water with a limpet shell. When the wintry blast howls over the downs, the people say it is the giant roaring.

Treitschke, Heinrich von (1834–1896). German historian. A strong partisan of German unification under Prussia and an ardent nationalist, he is best known for his *German History in the Nineteenth Century* (*Deutsche Geschichte im XIX. Jahrhundert*; 1879–1894).

Trelawny, Edward John (1792–1881). English biographer and traveler. Trelawny's life included

episodes of naval service, privateering in the Indian Ocean, and action in the Greek rebellion of 1823. He was a close friend of Byron and Shelley and it was he who recovered Shelley's and Edward Williams' bodies after they had drowned. He is best known for his autobiographical *Adventures of a Younger Son* (1831) and *Recollections of the Last Days of Shelley and Byron* (1858).

Trelawny of the Wells (1898). A comedy by Arthur Wing PINERO. The actress heroine, Rose Trelawny, becomes engaged to a young aristocrat, but breaks her engagement to return to the stage. Nothing daunted, her lover follows and becomes an actor.

tremendismo. A technique employed by several 20th-century Spanish novelists. Its effect is based upon the accumulation of gory detail in a heavy and relentless manner. The most notable presentation of the technique is found in Camilo José CELA's novel, *La familia de Pascual Duarte*.

Trench, Richard Chenevix (1807–1886). The Anglican archbishop of Dublin (1863–1884) and a noted philologist and poet. He was active in the Philological Society, which supported his scheme for beginning the Oxford *New English Dictionary*. He was the author of *Poems from Eastern Sources* (1842), *The Study of Words* (1851), *English Past and Present* (1855), and *Alma and Other Poems* (1865).

Trent, Council of. A council of the Roman Catholic Church. It met intermittently from 1545 to 1563 in reaction to the Protestant Reformation (see COUNTER REFORMATION). Its discussions and its conclusions influenced art, including literature, in the period immediately following.

Trent, Nell. See OLD CURIOSITY SHOP, THE.

Trent's Last Case (1912). A classic detective novel by E. C. BENTLEY. Philip Trent, an English painter, poetry lover, and amateur detective, successively uncovers three different, plausible solutions to the murder of an American millionaire.

Trescott, Jimmie. A small boy, the principal character in Stephen Crane's WHILOMVILLE STORIES.

Trevelyan, Sir George Otto (1838–1928). English historian and statesman, nephew of Thomas Babington Macaulay. His chief work is the *Life and Letters of Lord Macaulay* (1876). He also wrote *The Early History of Charles James Fox* (1880) and *The American Revolution* (6 vols., 1899–1914). His son G. M. TREVELYAN, is also a historian.

Trevelyan, G[eorge] M[acaulay] (1876–1962). English historian. He is best known for his *History of England* (1926) and *English Social History* (1944). He was awarded the Order of Merit in 1930.

Trevisa, John de (1326–1412). English translator, vicar of Berkeley. In 1387 he completed an English version of Ranulf HIGDEN's Latin *Polychronicon*, with an essay justifying translation into the vernacular; his own English prose is vigorous and carefully style-conscious. He also translated (by 1398) the encyclopedia *De Proprietatibus Rerum*, by BARTHOLOMEW ANGLICUS, and a number of other Latin works, possibly including the Bible.

Trevor-Roper, H[ugh] R[edwald] (1914–   ). English historian. Among his books are a scholarly study of *The Last Days of Hitler* (1947), which was a popular success, and *Men and Events* (1958).

Trial, The (*Der Prozess*; 1925). An unfinished novel by Franz KAFKA. Insofar as it depicts the confrontation of an individual and a baffling bureaucracy, it is similar to Kafka's THE CASTLE. The hero of *The Trial,* a bank assessor named Joseph K., is accused, by a mysterious legal authority whose headquarters are in a rundown tenement, of an unnamed crime of which he knows nothing. The novel treats his many fruitless attempts to obtain justice from an authority with which he cannot even effectively communicate, and culminates in his utter frustration, his complete loss of human dignity, and his death like a dog. Like *The Castle,* this novel has been interpreted allegorically; but whereas *The Castle* is seen as a quest for divine grace, *The Trial* depicts a struggle for divine justice. On another level, Joseph K.'s relationship to his judges has been seen as symbolic of the psychological (and perhaps autobiographical) fact of inner guilt feelings based on no actual crime. A short section of *The Trial* was completed and published separately in 1919 under the title *Before the Law* (*Vor dem Gesetz*) in the collection *A Country Doctor* (*Ein Landarzt*). See K., JOSEPH.

Triamond. See FAERIE QUEENE, THE.

tribune. In ancient Rome, one of 10 magistrates whose duty was to represent the will of the plebeian populace. A tribune had the right to veto any decree of the Senate, any law of the comitia, and any public action of a magistrate. Their persons were considered sacred, and no one was allowed to hinder them in the performance of their official duties. See CURSUS HONORUM.

Trick to Catch the Old One, A (c. 1606). A comedy by Thomas MIDDLETON. A penniless rake, Theodorus Witgood, connives to get money from his avaricious uncle, Pecunius Lucre, by pretending to be engaged to the wealthy "Widow Medler," who is really a courtesan in disguise. Immediately, Widow Medler is the focus of all attention. Old Walkadine Hoard, Lucre's equally avaricious enemy, is first among those who wish to cut out Witgood and win the wealthy widow for themselves. Meanwhile, Witgood's creditors, anticipating prompt payment, lend him additional sums to finance his suit with the widow. On Witgood's advice, the widow assures her future by marrying old Hoard. To protect himself from his creditors, Witgood counters with a breach-of-promise suit which Hoard settles by paying Witgood's debts. At the wedding feast, the widow is unmasked but promises to make Hoard a good wife. At the same time, Witgood announces that he has married Mistress Joyce, Hoard's niece. All are reconciled in the joy of the celebration.

tricolor. A flag of three broad stripes of different colors, especially the national standard of France of blue, white, and red. The popular tale is that the insurgents in 1789 had adopted for their flag the two colors of Paris, red and blue, but that Lafayette persuaded them to add the Bourbon white to show that they bore no hostility to the king.

tricoteuses (*Fr.,* "knitters"). Parisian women who, during the French Revolution, used to attend the meetings of the Convention and other popular assemblies. While they went on with their *tricotage* (knitting), they encouraged the leaders in their blood-thirsty excesses. The royalists called them the "furies of the guillotine." Madame DEFARGE in Dickens's *A Tale of Two Cities* typifies such a woman.

Triffid. An animate, thinking vegetable hostile to man that nearly takes over the world in John WYNDHAM's science-fiction novel *The Day of the Triffids* (1951).

Trilby (1894). A novel by George DU MAURIER. Trilby O'Ferrall, a young artist's model in Paris, is beloved by three English art students. Her engagement to one of them, William Bagot, known as Little Billee, is broken off and she falls into the hands of a sinister Hungarian musician, SVENGALI. She becomes a great singer under his mesmeric influence, but loses her voice when he suddenly dies of heart failure. She sickens and dies soon after.

Trilling, Lionel (1905–). American critic, short-story writer, and novelist. Trilling's first published work was *Matthew Arnold* (1939); as in this book, he applied the methods of modern psychology and anthropology in his study of E. M. Forster (1943). *The Liberal Imagination* (1950) and *The Opposing Self* (1955) are two collections of literary essays. He has also written *The Middle of the Journey* (1947), a novel, and several short stories which have been frequently anthologized.

Trim, Corporal. In Laurence Sterne's novel TRISTRAM SHANDY, UNCLE TOBY's orderly. He is, like his master, a devotee of military ways, but, in sharp contrast to Uncle Toby, extremely eloquent.

Trimalchio. The vulgar and ostentatious multimillionaire of PETRONIUS' *Satyricon.* He is the subject of allusion on account of the colossal and extravagant banquet that he gave. He was the literary prototype of Jay Gatsby in F. Scott Fitzgerald's novel *The Great Gatsby* (1925), which was originally to be entitled *Trimalchio's Banquet.*

trimeter. In prosody, a line of verse containing three metrical feet in any METER. It is usually identified together with the name of the meter, as iambic trimeter, trochaic trimeter, etc.

Trimurti (Sans., *tri,* three; *murti,* forms). In Hindu metaphysics, the triune aspect of Brahman, the Supreme Spirit: BRAHMA the Creator, VISHNU the Preserver, SHIVA the Destroyer. The three, however, are one, since whatever is created must necessarily die after passing through a period of preservation.

Trinculo. In Shakespeare's THE TEMPEST, a "dull fool," the jester of Alonso. See STEPHANO.

Trinity, the. Also called the **Holy Trinity.** In Christianity, the name of God as he exists in his three persons or hypostases: the Father, the Son, and the Holy Spirit. They are coequal, coeternal, and indivisible. The Father is thought of especially as the Creator, the Son as the Redeemer, and the Holy Spirit as the Enlightener. The Trinitarian doctrine was evolved and enunciated in early Church councils; its various definitions have caused great controversies and schisms. Whether the Holy Spirit proceeds from the Father alone, or from the Father and the Son still divides the Eastern and Western Churches, the Eastern Church holding the former position (see FILOQUE CONTROVERSY).

The Latin word *trinitas* was first used c. 180 when the doctrine began to take form. The three-person nature of God is nowhere expressly stated in the Old Testament. In the New Testament, however, the doctrine of the Trinity is expressly and frequently taught, as, for example, in I John 5:7.

The essence of the Trinity is considered a mystery by the Church: a full understanding is not possible through human intelligence. The Trinity can be known only through divine revelation.

The concept of a three-person god is not unique to Christianity: such a relation exists in Hindu mythology (see TRIMURTI; THREE).

Triolet, Elsa. See Louis ARAGON.

Tripitaka. (*Pali,* "three baskets"). A three-part collection of sacred Buddhist writings: the *Vinaya-pitaka,* rules of discipline for Buddhist monks and nuns; the *Sutra-pitaka,* aphorisms and parables for laymen; the *Abhidhamma-pitaka,* an analytic study of consciousness and metaphysics.

Triple Alliance. (1) A treaty between England, Sweden, and Holland against Louis XIV in 1688. It ended in the treaty of Aix-la-Chapelle.

(2) A treaty between England, France, and Holland against Spain, 1717. In the following year it was joined by Austria, and became a Quadruple Alliance.

(3) A military alliance initiated between Germany and Austria-Hungary in 1879, which Italy joined in 1882. It lasted until the outbreak of World War I.

Triple Entente. See ENTENTE.

triplet. In prosody, a stanza containing three lines, also called TERCET.

Triptolemus (Triptolemos). A Greek hero and demigod. He was worshiped chiefly at Eleusis as the one who gave grain to man and the first instructor in agriculture. He was generally described as a son of Celeus and Metaneira. See DEMETER.

Trishanku. In Hindu mythology, a king of Ayodhya (the modern Oudh in central India) of the solar dynasty who asked Vashishtha to do special penance for him so that he might ascend to heaven with his body. The request horrified Vashishtha and Trishanku was condemned as a *chandala* (outcaste). In spite of the objections of the gods and Brahmins, the sage Vishvamitra agreed, but when Indra learned of this, he ordered Trishanku hurled through space. The fall was stopped by Vishvamitra's penance, but Trishanku continues to hang in mid-space as one of the stars. There is a meaningful reference to him in Kalidasa's *Shakuntala.*

Trissino, Giangiorgio (1478–1550). Italian poet and dramatist. Born in Vicenza, he wrote the first modern tragedy on Greek rather than Roman models, the *Sofonisba* (1515; see SOPHONISBA). Influenced by the *Poetics* of Aristotle, he wrote the play in the Greek style and pioneered experiments with Italian versions of Pindar and Horace. In 1547, he published a "correct" Homeric epic, *L'Italia Liberata dai Goti* (*Italy Liberated from the Goths*), which had taken 20 years to compose.

Tristan or **Tristram.** Hero of the great medieval cycle TRISTAN AND ISEULT, and sometimes a knight of the Round Table in the legends of King Arthur. He is generally depicted as a great lover, great warrior, great musician, champion dragon killer, skillful hunter, excellent seaman, a poet, and marvelous teller of tales (which is to say, some insist, that he was an expert liar). In addition, he is supremely handsome. But due to the accidental drinking of a magic potion, his life is governed by an undying love for ISEULT the Fair, even though she is married to his uncle, King MARK of Cornwall. See PALAMEDES; TRISTRAM OF LYONESS.

Tristan and Iseult. A great medieval cycle of tales revolving about the figures of TRISTAN and ISEULT. Evolving from Celtic sources with a theme irresistible to writers right up to the present day, this legend has been called one of the world's greatest love stories. The core motif is the Celtic tale of elopement of the king's nephew with the wife of the king (See DEIRDRE; THE PURSUIT OF DIARMUID AND GRAINNE). Tristan goes to Ireland to bring the beautiful princess, Iseult, to Cornwall where she is to become the bride of his uncle, King MARK. On the way, the pair drink a potion that causes them to become eternally in love with one another; this love gives rise to the drama of the cycle. The cycle incorporates many folk themes, such as the AMBIGUOUS OATH. No major, complete version of the cycle survives. Malory's MORTE D'ARTHUR incorporates the Tristan and Iseult legend into ARTHURIAN LEGEND.

The story of Tristan and Iseult has been used by Tennyson in his *Idylls of the King* (1859–1885), by Wagner in the music drama *Tristan und Isolde,* and by Edwin Arlington Robinson in *Tristram* (1927), to name a few. See Sir TRISTRAM OF LYONESS.

Tristan L'Hermite. See François L'HERMITE.

Tristram (1927). A narrative poem in blank verse by Edwin Arlington ROBINSON. The third of Robinson's Arthurian trilogy, preceded by *Merlin* (1917) and *Lancelot* (1920), the poem emphasizes and contrasts Tristram's love for Isolt, the wife of his old uncle, and his neglect of his own wife, Isolt of Brittany. The longed-for is unattainable, and the attainable, neglected.

Tristram of Lyoness, Sir. In *The Book of Sir Tristram of Lyoness* from Malory's MORTE D'ARTHUR, one of the most valiant knights of the Round Table. The story was drawn from the TRISTAN AND ISEULT tradition, a cycle originally separate from the legends of Arthur. Malory makes Tristram a knight of the Round Table and second only to Sir Launcelot. In this version, King MARK is a vengeful and ignoble enemy.

Tristram Shandy (1759–1767). Shortened title of *The Life and Opinions of Tristram Shandy, Gentleman,* a novel by Laurence STERNE in which Sterne declares that his one rule is to be spontaneous and untrammeled. The form is ostensibly a chaotic account by Tristram of his life from the time of his conception to the present and shows how much Sterne was influenced by John Locke's theory of the irrational nature of the association of ideas. The historian, however (except for a few brief flashes), never gets beyond the second or third year of his life. In between are sandwiched his "Opinions," long-winded and philosophical reflections on everything under the sun including his novel, and accounts of the lives of YORICK, his father Walter SHANDY, his mother, and his UNCLE TOBY. The form of the book is in fact the character of Tristram himself, doomed by improbably fantastic fatalities to write a hodge-podge instead of a history, to spend two years describing one, to describe events whose chain of causation is cosmic, whose significance is comically petty for all but the exasperated historian.

For Sterne, the actual content of consciousness,

what passes through the mind of the character at a given moment, "writing to the moment," and the accompanying reactions and gestures are of primary importance.

The novel is sprinkled with many typographical eccentricities such as a profusion of dots, dashes, asterisks, one-sentence chapters, blank pages and unfinished sentences. See Hafen SLAWKENBERGIUS.

Triton. In Greek mythology, a merman. Tritons are usually depicted as blowing on conch horns, and appear as minor figures in Greek legends.

Triumph of the Egg, The (1921). A collection of "impressions from American life" by Sherwood ANDERSON. The title story refers to a farmer whose failure in life is symbolized by his inability to perform a simple trick with an egg.

Triumvirate, First. In Roman history, an alliance formed (60 B.C.) by CAESAR, POMPEY, and CRASSUS to divide the power among them. Caesar received the consulship for the year 59 and a command in Cisalpine GAUL (extended to Transalpine Gaul) and Illyricum. Pompey received assignment of lands for his veterans and administration of the grain supply for himself. By a renewal of the Triumvirate in 56, Pompey received the consulship and command in Spain; Crassus obtained the consulship and command in the East, where he was killed in 53. The alliance between Pompey and Caesar was formally broken with the outbreak of civil war in 49. See RUBICON.

Triumvirate, Second. In Roman history, an alliance formed (43 B.C.) by Octavius (later AUGUSTUS), Mark ANTONY, and LEPIDUS. The triumvirs were to have consular power for three years, they appointed magistrates, and their decrees were valid as laws. The empire was divided among them: Octavius obtained Africa and the islands; Antony, Gaul; Lepidus, Spain and Narbonensis. The alliance was followed by the overthrow of the republicans under Cassius and Brutus at Philippi (42). Eventually, Lepidus, whose position in the alliance was minor, was banished and by the Treaty at Brundisium, Octavian received the West and Antony the East. Their union was broken in 31, and Antony was defeated at ACTIUM. This left Octavius sole ruler, and in gradual steps, he completed the transformation of Rome from a republic to an empire, as Augustus, its first emperor.

trivium. See QUADRIVIUM.

trochee. In English prosody, a metrical foot consisting of two syllables, the first accented and the second unaccented. The word "CAREFUL" is a trochee. The METER made up of such units is called trochaic meter, and the following lines are a good example:

> TELL me/NOT in/MOURNful/NUMbers
> LIFE is/BUT an/EMPty/DREAM
> FOR the/SOUL is/DEAD that/SLUMbers . . .
> Longfellow (*Psalm of Life*)

trochilus. A small Egyptian bird fabled by the ancients to enter with impunity the mouth of the crocodile and to pick its teeth, especially of the leech, which greatly tormented the crocodile. Allusions to it are common in 16th- and 17th-century literature.

troglodytes, les. The cave dwellers in Letters XI–XIV of MONTESQUIEU's *Lettres Persanes*. Their behavior illustrates satirically Montesquieu's belief that man must have a sense of justice if he is to organize and maintain society.

Troilus (Troilos). In classic myth, one of the sons of Priam. He was killed by Achilles in the TROJAN WAR. The loves of Troilus and Cressida, celebrated by Shakespeare and Chaucer, form no part of the old classic tale. Their story appeared for the first time in Dares Phrygius and Dictys Cretensis, then about the 12th century in BENOÎT DE STE.-MAURE, and in the 13th century in GUIDO DELLE COLONNE. Later it passed to Boccaccio, whose IL FILOSTRATO (1344)—where PANDARUS first appears in his role of pander—was the basis of Chaucer's TROILUS AND CRISEYDE. Shakespeare's drama by the same name, TROILUS AND CRESSIDA (c. 1609) follows the general outline of Chaucer's narrative. In the classic myth Cressida or Cressid, daughter of Calchas, a Grecian priest, is beloved by Troilus. They vow eternal fidelity to each other, and as pledges of their vow Troilus

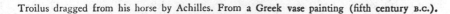

Troilus dragged from his horse by Achilles. From a Greek vase painting (fifth century B.C.).

gives the maiden a sleeve, and Cressid gives the Trojan prince a glove. Hardly has the vow been made when an exchange of prisoners is agreed to. Diomed gives up three Trojan princes, and is to receive Cressid in lieu thereof. Cressid vows to remain constant, and Troilus swears to rescue her. She is led off to the Grecian's tent, and soon gives all her affections to Diomed, even bidding him wear the sleeve that Troilus gave her in token of his love. Hence Cressida has become a byword for infidelity.

Troilus and Cressida (c. 1601). A tragedy by William SHAKESPEARE. During a truce between the Greeks and Trojans in the eighth year of the Trojan siege, Troilus, a Trojan prince, pursues his beloved Cressida (See CRISEYDE), though the girl pretends indifference. At last, through the offices of Pandarus, an assignation is arranged, and the two consummate their love, vowing eternal fealty. Meanwhile, Calchas, Cressida's father, who has gone over to the Greeks, accomplishes her exchange for a Trojan prisoner. She is brought to the Greek camp by Diomedes, who is taken with her beauty. After the Greeks and Trojans join in a friendly feast in Achilles' tent, Troilus discovers that Cressida is being unfaithful to him with Diomedes.

The subplot concerns the efforts of the Greeks to end the war and the insubordination of Achilles, who has been sulking moodily in his tent. Achilles finally bestirs himself when PATROCLUS, his closest friend, is killed by the great Hector, Troilus' eldest brother. After Achilles has slain the unarmed Hector, the Trojans sadly return to their city, led by Troilus, who castigates Pandarus for his lecherous offices.

The play's sources are Chaucer's TROILUS AND CRISEYDE and John Lydgate's *Siege of Troy* (c. 1420).

Troilus and Criseyde (c. 1385). A poem by Geoffrey CHAUCER, of 8239 lines in RHYME ROYAL. Although based on Boccaccio's IL FILOSTRATO, Chaucer's tale has considerably more individual characterization and humor. In the first book the Trojan prince TROILUS falls hopelessly in love with CRISEYDE, daughter of the Trojan prophet Calchas, who has fled to the Greeks; and PANDARUS offers to help him. He convinces Criseyde (Book II) that Troilus is dying of his love for her, encourages the pair to exchange letters, then arranges a meeting at a dinner given by Troilus' brother Deiphobus. Criseyde gives Troilus permission (Book III) only to serve her in the COURTLY LOVE tradition, but Pandarus soon manages to have them spend the night together in his own house. Calchas persuades the Greeks (Book IV) to demand his daughter in exchange for the return of Antenor to Troy, and the lovers bewail their separation; Criseyde promises, however, that she will contrive to return in ten days. Troilus sees her off (Book V), then immediately begins to grieve and worry. Criseyde, on the contrary, is seduced on the tenth day by the Greek Diomedes; though sincerely grieved at her infidelity to Troilus, she remains. Troilus dreams of the betrayal, hears it described by his sister Cassandra the prophetess, receives evasive answers from Criseyde when he writes, but is not convinced until he sees on a piece of Diomedes' armor the brooch he himself had given Criseyde. Then he rages into battle and fights frequently with Diomedes, but is finally killed by Achilles.

Troilus verse. Another name for RHYME ROYAL.

Troiolo. The hero of Giovanni Boccaccio's romance FILOSTRATO and the prototype of Chaucer's TROILUS.

Trojan Horse. A wooden horse in which, according to legend, the Greeks entered the city of Troy. Unable after 10 years to take the strong-walled city by force, the Greeks resorted to strategy. Under the supervision of the artisan Epeios, they built a huge, hollow wooden horse, secreted some of their best soldiers inside it, and left it before the gates of Troy. They then sailed away, leaving behind one of their number named Sinon. Pretending to hate the Greeks, who had supposedly ill-treated him, he told the Trojans that the horse was an offering to Athena; if brought inside the city, it would make Troy invulnerable. Laocoön, a priest of Apollo, warned them of a trick, but was immediately killed, with his sons, by a pair of sea-serpents. CASSANDRA's warnings also were, as usual, unheeded. The Trojans dragged the horse inside, making a breach in the wall. At night the hidden Greeks left the horse, unlocked the city's gates and after the other Greeks returned, Troy was quickly captured. The story was told by Homer in the ODYSSEY and by Vergil in the AENEID.

Trojan War, the. A war fought between Greek invaders and the defenders of Troy, probably near the beginning of the 12th century B.C. The archaeological discoveries of Heinrich SCHLIEMANN and others have shown that the classical tradition that began with Homer was based on an actual struggle for control of the important trade routes through and across the Hellespont, which were dominated by the city of Troy. About the events of this war and the return to their homes of the Greek generals there grew up a body of myth that was recounted in the ILIAD, the ODYSSEY, a number of lost epics, plays by the Athenian dramatists, and many other works down to the present day.

According to the more familiar versions of this complex myth, the cause of the war was the episode of the golden apple (see APPLE OF DISCORD), which resulted in the abduction by the Trojan prince Paris of Helen, the wife of Menelaus, king of Sparta. Earlier, most of the rulers of Greece had been suitors for Helen's hand and her father, Tyndareus, had made them swear to support the one chosen. Accordingly, they joined Menelaus and prepared to move against Troy under the leadership of Agamemnon, king of Mycenae. (See the House of ATREUS.)

After forcing Agamemnon to sacrifice his daughter IPHIGENEIA to insure fair weather, they sailed from Aulis. In the 10th year of the siege of Troy, Achilles withdrew from the fight in an argument with Agamemnon over possession of a female captive, but, grieved by the death of his friend Patroclus, he rejoined the fray and killed the Trojan leader Hector, son of Priam. By the use of the TROJAN HORSE, Greek leaders gained entrance to the walled city and Troy was overthrown and destroyed. Except for AENEAS and his clan, most of the Trojan men were killed and the women taken captive.

Among Greek dramas dealing with the war or its aftermath are Aeschylus' *Agamemnon*, Sophocles' *Philoctetes*, and four plays by Euripides, *Iphigeneia in*

Aulis, The Trojan Women, Helen, and *Andromache.* Homer and most later Greek authors wrote of the war in a heroic vein, but Euripides consistently, if mainly by implication, attacked it as the cause of senseless horror and suffering. The fall of Troy is also recounted at the beginning of Vergil's *Aeneid,* which claimed Aeneas as the founder of Rome.

The custom of claiming noble Trojan ancestry was widespread among European nations for a thousand years. As late as Elizabethan times Albion (England) was said to have been founded by Brutus, a descendant of Aeneas. In the Middle Ages, the legends of the Trojan War were best known through two Latin works attributed to Dictys Cretensis and Dares Phrygius, two supposed contemporaries of the war. On these two books BENOÎT DE SAINTE-MAURE based a long romance called the *Roman de Troie,* which became immensely popular and was the source in turn for many other medieval romances. See TIGER AT THE GATES.

Trojan Women, The (Troades; 415 B.C.). A tragedy by EURIPIDES. It relates the fate of the family of Priam at the fall of Troy. Priam and Hector are dead; their widows, Hecuba and Andromache, and the mad Cassandra are to be slaves. Troy is in flames; yet the Greek generals, fearful of the future, sacrifice Hector's sister Polyxena to the ghost of Achilles and fling his son Astyanax from the walls to end the royal line. In the midst of the horrors, Helen appears and, through sheer sexual attraction, easily sways her husband Menelaus from his intention to kill her. Her presence, vain and frivolous as ever, demonstrates the futility of the war that was fought for her sake.

In this play, which portrays the Greeks as cruel and cowardly, Euripides implicitly rebuked the Athenians for their recent brutal slaughter of the natives of Melos for remaining neutral in the war with Sparta. It is one of the most powerful indictments of war ever written.

Trollope, Anthony (1815–1882). English novelist. Although a post office official for many years, Trollope was a prolific writer, producing a large number of novels dealing with Victorian life. He declared that "a novel should give a picture of common life enlivened by humor and sweetened by pathos," which is a fair estimation of his own work. His best-known novels are those included in the two series, the so-called Chronicles of BARSETSHIRE and the Parliamentary novels. The latter, in which the British Parliament is the connecting thread, and which were overshadowed by Disraeli's popular novels of the same type, include PHINEAS FINN (1869), *Phineas Redux* (1874), *The Prime Minister* (1876), and *The Duke's Children* (1880). Among his other novels are *The Belton Estate* (1865), *The Claverings* (1867), THE EUSTACE DIAMONDS, *Ayala's Angel* (1881), and *Dr. Wortle's School* (1881). He also wrote a number of travel books, a study of W. M. Thackeray, and an *Autobiography* (1883). See BARCHESTER TOWERS.

Trollope, Frances, born **Milton** (1780–1863). English author of novels and travel books, mother of Anthony and Thomas Trollope. Her first book, the famous and derogatory *Domestic Manners of the Americans* (1832) was written after a three-year stay in the United States. Thereafter she wrote many travel books and novels, including *The Vicar of Wrexhill* (1837); THE WIDOW BARNABY; and *The Lottery of Marriage* (1846).

Trollope, Thomas Adolphus (1810–1892). English novelist and essayist, son of Frances, elder brother of Anthony Trollope. His books, which deal mainly with Italian life and history, include *A Decade of Italian Women* (1859); *Marietta* (1862); and *Beppo the Conscript* (1864).

trolls. In Teutonic mythology, the dwarfs who were said to live in underground caverns or beneath hills; they were represented as stumpy, misshapen and humpbacked, inclined to thievery, and fond of carrying off children and substituting their own. Because Thor used continually to fling his hammer after them, these hill people were especially averse to noise. The Troll King is a character in Ibsen's *Peer Gynt* (1867).

trope. (1) In rhetoric, a figure of speech employing a word or phrase out of its ordinary usage in order to give life to an idea; the most important types are METAPHOR, METONYMY, SYNECDOCHE, and IRONY.

(2) In music, (a) historically in liturgical music a final melodic or verse phrase added as decoration in Gregorian chant or the sung parts of the medieval Mass, and (b) a basic group of chords in the 12-tone scale, used by Josef Hauer.

Trophonius (Trophonios). An architect. He is celebrated in Greek legend as the builder of the temple of Apollo at Delphi. With his brother Agamedes, he also built a treasury for King Hyrieus in Boeotia, but so constructed it that they could easily steal from it. When Agamedes was trapped there, Trophonius cut off his head so that he might not be recognized. After his death he was deified and had an oracle in a cave near Lebadeia, Boeotia, which was so awe-inspiring that those who entered and consulted the oracle never smiled again. Hence a melancholy or habitually terrified man was said to have visited the cave of Trophonius.

Tropic of Cancer (1934). An autobiographical book by Henry MILLER. *Tropic of Cancer* was originally published in Paris, and was immediately banned by U.S. customs officials on the grounds of obscenity. When the first American edition (1961) appeared, it became a best seller. The book is a history of Miller's life in Paris during the early 1930's. Penniless and starving, he underwent a complete physical and spiritual degradation. The numerous philosophical ruminations that intrude on his story explain the poet's "heroic descent to the very bowels of the earth, the dark and fearsome sojourn in the belly of the whale." The poet's ascent from this abyss and his final emergence as "a bright, gory sun god cast up on an alien shore" are intended to inspire the reader with the same joy of life that Miller found after his sufferings.

Trotsky or **Trotski, Leon.** Real name, **Lev Davidovich Bronstein** (1879–1940). Russian Communist leader. First arrested for his revolutionary activities in 1898, he was sent to Siberia, but escaped under the alias of Leo Trotsky, the name he used for the rest of his life. After his escape he went to London where he worked with the exiled Lenin. Trotsky returned to Russia in 1905 to take part in the revolutionary attempt of that year. Once more arrested and sent to Siberia, he again escaped. He spent the next 12 years in exile in Europe and America.

When Czar Nicholas II abdicated in 1917, Trotsky again made his way home to Russia. After the Bolsheviks seized power, Lenin and Trotsky emerged as the two top men in the new government, the latter becoming the commissar for foreign affairs. Trotsky negotiated the treaty of Brest-Litovsk with Germany. In 1918 he was replaced as foreign minister and as commissar for war, a position he held until 1924, organized and directed the armies that repelled invasion on four fronts. Lenin, supported by Stalin, and Trotsky began to differ on ideological matters as early as 1919. When Lenin died in 1924, Stalin openly attacked Trotsky, and appointed him to less and less important positions. In 1927, Trotsky was exiled to Turkistan and, in 1929, banished from the U.S.S.R. He was assassinated in Mexico City (1940); his followers claimed that he was murdered on orders from Stalin, a claim later verified.

Trotsky viewed the Russian Communist Party as an instrument of international social revolution. He differed from Lenin and Stalin because he was not satisfied to concentrate on the consolidation of the Russian state and withdraw active support to the cause of immediately exporting the revolution beyond the Soviet Union's borders.

A brilliant intellect, Trotsky wrote many important books and pamphlets on the Communist revolution. His works include *The Defense of Terrorism* (1921), *Literature and Revolution* (1925), *My Life* (1930), and *The History of the Russian Revolution* (3 vols., 1932).

Trotwood, Miss Betsey. In Charles Dickens' DAVID COPPERFIELD, great-aunt of David. She lives with the likable lunatic, Mr. Dick. Miss Betsey's snappishness and briskness conceal great tenderness of heart. She takes in the runaway David, defends him against Mr. Murdstone, and becomes devoted to him.

troubadours. Poet-musicians of Provence in the 11th, 12th, and 13th centuries. They wrote short poems in the LANGUE D'OC following elaborate formal conventions, principally celebrating chivalry and the tradition of COURTLY LOVE. The leading troubadours, BERTRAN DE BORN and Bernard de Ventadour, were received at the court of ELEANOR OF AQUITAINE. Through her influence Provençal poetry was introduced at the courts of northern France, and its emphasis on romantic love began to enter the verse epics there (SEE TROUVÈRES). Other troubadour poets include Geoffrey Rudel, Peire Vidal, Guiraut de Bornelh, and Guilhem de Cabestan.

Troubled Sleep. See ROADS TO FREEDOM, THE.

trouvères. Medieval poets of northern France. They wrote in the LANGUE D'OÏL, principally narrative poems like the CHANSONS DE GESTE and shorter lyrics somewhat influenced by the Provençal poetry of the TROUBADOURS.

Trovatore, Il (The Troubadour, 1853). An opera by Giuseppe VERDI based on a Spanish drama by García Gutiérrez. It has one of the most complicated plots in all opera.

Troyat, Henri. Real name **Lev Tarassov** (1911–). Russian-born French novelist. *While the Earth Endures (Tant que la Terre Durera; 1947–*

1950) is a trilogy of historical novels that traces the effect of the 1917 revolution on an upper-class Russian family and describes their emigration to Paris. It includes *My Father's House, The Red and the White,* also translated as *Sackcloth and Ashes (Le Sac et la cendre),* and *Strangers on the earth (Etrangers sur la terre).* The cycle *The Seed and the Fruit (Les Semailles et les moissons;* 5 vols., 1953–1958), set in the early 20th century, concerns a middle-class French family, Amelie and Pierre and their daughter Elizabeth. A third series, *The Light of the Just (La Lumière des Justes;* 1959–   ) goes back to the time of Napoleon in Russia.

Truce of God. A Church attempt in 1041 to limit private war. The Church decreed that there should be no hostilities between Lent and Advent or from the Thursday to the next Monday at the time of great festivals. This *Truce of God* was confirmed by the Lateran Council in 1179, and was agreed to by England, France, Italy, and other countries; however, little attention was ever paid to it.

Truffaldino. In Matteo Maria Boiardo's ORLANDO INNAMORATO, a ferocious pagan king killed by Rinaldo. The latter had vowed Truffaldino's destruction for causing the death of the young maiden Albarosa.

Trulliber, Parson Oliver. A selfish, slothful, pig-raising high-church divine sharply contrasted with Parson ADAMS in JOSEPH ANDREWS by Henry Fielding.

Truman, Harry S. (1884–1972). 33rd president of the U.S. (1945–1953). Unable to obtain a college education, Truman managed his father's farm and clerked in a bank for a while. He served in the armed forces during World War I, then started an unsuccessful business venture as a haberdasher. Through the influence of Thomas J. Pendergast, the political boss of Kansas City and the surrounding region, he won a series of public offices: county judge, presiding judge of the court, U.S. Senator from Missouri. In the meantime, he had attended the Kansas City Law School for two years.

Having been elected vice-president as Franklin D. Roosevelt's running mate in 1944, Truman succeeded to the presidency when Roosevelt died on April 12, 1945. He made many momentous decisions toward the end of World War II, the most important of which was perhaps the use of the atomic bomb to end the war against Japan. He gave unwavering support to the United Nations and formulated the Truman Doctrine of aid to the free peoples of the world "resisting attempted subjugation by armed minorities or outside pressures." He generally followed his predecessor's policies in domestic matters.

In the 1948 election Truman surprised most experts by defeating Thomas E. Dewey. In what he regarded as his own presidency, he gave U.S. aid to the U.N. when North Korea, assisted by Russia and China, invaded South Korea in 1950. To him must be credited the Marshall Plan, designed to aid European rehabilitation and check communist expansion. Refusing to seek a third term, Truman returned to his home in Independence, Mo., where he prepared his memoirs, published as *Years of Decision* (1955) and *Years of Trial and Hope* (1956). He also wrote *Mr. Citizen* (1960).

Trumbull, John (1750–1831). American poet, a member of the HARTFORD WITS, known as the author of satires and bombastic patriotic poems in the neo-classic style. His works include *The Progress of Dulness* (1772–1773), a satire on contemporary methods of education; *An Elegy on the Times* (1774), a patriotic piece; M'FINGAL, an anti-British satire, issued in more than 30 editions in its time; essays in the style of *The Spectator;* several anonymous revolutionary essays; and a number of incidental poems. He also collaborated with Joel Barlow and other members of the Hartford Wits on THE ANARCHIAD.

Trumbull, in his time the most widely read poet of the Hartford school, came of an outstanding Connecticut family and was a child prodigy. He learned to read and write at the age of two, passed the Yale entrance examinations at seven, and entered the college at 13. During the period just before the Revolution, he studied law in the office of John Adams in Boston and took part in the political agitation of the times. Later he was a representative in the Connecticut legislature and a judge in the superior and supreme courts of that state.

Trumbull, Jonathan (1710–1785). Early American statesman. See BROTHER JONATHAN.

Trunnion, Commodore Hawser. The hero's choleric uncle in Tobias Smollett's novel PEREGRINE PICKLE. Trunnion is a one-eyed naval veteran who, though retired from the service because of injuries received in naval engagements, still keeps garrison in his own county house, which is defended with drawbridge and moat, and observes the routine of a battleship. He sleeps in a hammock, makes his servants sleep in hammocks, takes his turn on watch, and indulges his naval tastes in various other ways. Lieutenant Jack HATCHWAY is his companion. When he goes to be married, he rides on a hunter which he steers, like a ship, according to the compass.

Truth About Blayds, The (1921). A play by A. A. MILNE. A great writer confesses on his death-bed that every scrap of his distinguished work was stolen. After his death his family discreetly decides to suppress the whole affair.

Trygaeus (Trygaios). The hero of the Greek comedy THE PEACE (415 B.C.) by Aristophanes. This comedy was produced in the midst of the Peloponnesian war. The hero rides a dung beetle to Olympus in search of Peace, and finds that she has been thrown down a well. The gods are all away, so he rescues her and brings her back to Athens.

Tryphon. See FAERIE QUEENE, THE.

Tsurezure gusa. See ESSAYS IN IDLENESS.

Tuatha Dé Danann (*Gael.*, "the peoples of the goddess Dana or Danu"). In the Gaelic MYTHOLOGICAL CYCLE, one of the 5 original races to invade and inhabit prehistoric Ireland. They defeated the people before them, the Fir Bolg, and also were victorious on several occasions over the Fomorians, notably in the BATTLE OF MOYTURA. Ultimately, they themselves were conquered by the next invaders, the SONS OF MIL, last of the five races. After defeating the Tuatha Dé Danann, the Sons of Mil came to worship them as gods. Traditionally, they were given the lower half (underground) of Ireland and they dwell there, in the mounds, to this day. Among the heroes of the Tuatha Dé Danann who later were worshiped as gods by the Sons of Mil are Dadga, LUG, Mananaan Mac Lir, MORRIGAN, and Ogma. In modern folklore, the Tuatha Dé Danann are the Irish faeries and come out of the mounds on Samain Eve.

Tubal. In Shakespeare's MERCHANT OF VENICE, a wealthy Jew, the friend of Shylock.

Tubalcain. In the Old Testament, the 3rd son of Lamech and Zillah. He was the first smith, "an instructor of every artificer in brass and iron" (Gen. 4:22).

Tuck, Friar. See FRIAR TUCK.

Tuckerman, Frederick Goddard (1821–1873). American poet. Trained as a lawyer, Tuckerman spent most of his life as a recluse at Greenfield, Mass. In 1860, he published a slim volume of sonnets, which elicited high praise from Tennyson. After two further editions during the poet's lifetime, his work was neglected; in 1931, the poet Witter Bynner prepared an edition with a long and enthusiastic introduction. Since then, modern poets have admired Tuckerman's free use of the sonnet form in his melancholy verse.

Tudor, Henry. See HENRY VII.

Tudor, Mary. See MARY I; MARY OF FRANCE.

Tu Fu (712–770). Chinese poet of the T'ang Dynasty. He and LI PO are regarded as the greatest Chinese poets. A great stylist who endured much personal misfortune, his works reveal an unsurpassed depth and command of the poetic art of his time. Contrasting with the Taoistic flavor of Li Po's writings, Tu Fu was partial to Confucianism.

Tuileries. One of the oldest palaces in Paris. Its superb gardens were laid out by Louis XIV. The original palace, begun by Catherine de Médicis, is no longer in existence. The name means brickyard, from the previous use of the site it occupies.

Tulliver, Maggie and **Tom.** See MILL ON THE FLOSS, THE.

Tullus Hostilius. Legendary Roman king (673–641 B.C.). His period was distinguished by war between the HORATII and the Curiatii.

Tully. See CICERO.

Tun-huang. Oasis in Northwest China, present-day Kansu. It is the site of Buddhist caves where a walled-up library, hidden for a thousand years, was discovered by Sir Aurel Stein (1900). A vast cache of Buddhist texts, Chinese popular literature, and the like contributed much new knowledge to sinology. Here was found the world's first printed book, the *Diamond Sūtra* (868). Most of the material was brought to England by Stein and to Paris by Paul Pelliot.

Tupman, Tracy. In Charles Dickens' PICKWICK PAPERS, an M.P.C. (Member of the Pickwick Club), a sleek, fat young man, of very amorous disposition. He falls in love with every pretty girl he sees, and is consequently always getting into trouble.

Tupper, Martin Farquhar (1810–1889). English versifier whose facile, moralizing *Proverbial Philosophy* (four series, 1838–1867) went through some 50 editions and attained international vogue. A man who could write about anything (*e.g., Some Verse and Prose about National Rifle Clubs,* 1858), his name became synonymous with pretentious twaddle.

Turandot. Opera by Giacomo PUCCINI, first performed in 1926, two years after the composer's death. Act III was completed by Franco Alfano from the composer's sketches. The libretto is based on a play (1762) by Gozzi. Ferruccio Busoni also wrote an opera *Turandot* (1917) based on the same play.

Turberville, George (1540?–1610?). English poet and translator. He is best known for his translation of Ovid's *Heroides* (*The Heroical Epistles,* 1567), which contains some early experiments with blank verse. He also popularized, in translation, the Eclogues of Mantuan (*The Eclogs of the Poet B. Mantuan,* 1567). His original poems are collected in *Epitaphs, Epigrams, Songs, and Sonnets* (1567).

Turenne, vicomte de. Henri de la Tour d'Auvergne (1611–1675). French military leader. Turenne served in the Thirty Years' War and helped to bring about the Peace of Westphalia. He fought against the Fronde (1651) and recovered Paris for the king. In 1667 and 1672, he commanded armies under Louis XIV.

Turgenev, Ivan Sergeyevich (1818–1883). Russian novelist. Turgenev was born in Orol in south-central Russia and raised on the family estate at Spasskoye. His childhood was troubled by the continual bad feelings between his mother and father. His mother's feelings of resentment were often taken out on the children and servants.

In 1837 Turgenev graduated from the University of St. Petersburg, and the following year went to Germany to continue his studies at the University of Berlin, concentrating on classical languages, literature, and, especially, philosophy. Among his fellow Russian students at the university was Nikolai Stankevich (1813–1840), who had headed one of the famous philosophical circles of students at Moscow University in the early 1830's. Another fellow student of Turgenev's was the future anarchist leader Mikhail Bakunin. The intense interest in philosophical questions, the incessant talk, and the personality of Bakunin were all used to some extent in Turgenev's first novel, Rudin. In 1841, Turgenev returned to Russia, intending to make his career as a philosopher. The government abolished the teaching of philosophy, however, and the idle scholar spent his time going to the theater, carrying on a romance with Tatyana Bakunin, Mikhail's sister, and meeting the leaders of the intelligentsia. In 1843 he met the renowned Vissarion Belinski with whom he established a close friendship. Turgenev's despotic mother objected to his idleness, and in June he obtained a minor appointment in the civil service, which he held for almost two years.

During the winter of 1843, Turgenev made one of the most fateful meetings of his life, with Pauline Viardot-Garcia, a singer who was the wife of the French writer Louis Viardot. Turgenev fell in love with her almost at once, and the unrequited relationship continued for the rest of Turgenev's life. Pauline continued to live with her husband and to pursue her singing career, returning to Russia for concerts in each of the winters between 1843 and 1846. She did not return in 1846, however, and Turgenev went to France to see her. He lived on the Viardot estate and in Paris from 1847 to 1850. During this period he wrote the work that was to bring him his first literary success, A Sportsman's Sketches. He also wrote some of his best plays at this time, including A Month in the Country.

Since Turgenev's mother had died in 1850, he was at last financially independent and was freed from having to write all the time for living expenses. He became a member of the editorial board of *Sovremennik* (*The Contemporary*), which was headed at that time by the poet Nikolai Nekrasov. Turgenev left this literary milieu in 1856 to go abroad again; he returned to Russia in 1858, and during that summer he lived on his estate at Spasskoye, completing his second novel, A Nest of Gentlefolk (1869). In 1860 appeared his third novel On the Eve, and the autobiographical story, *Pervaya lyubov* (*First Love*). *On the Eve* did not appear in *Sovremennik,* as had most of Turgenev's previous work. The journal had virtually been taken over by the radical critics Nikolai Chernyshevski and Nikolai Dobrolyubov. Turgenev disagreed with their utilitarian view of literature, and they thought him too much of an aesthete. Another literary quarrel beset Turgenev in 1860. The novelist Ivan Goncharov, whose mental health was in decline, accused Turgenev of having plagiarized his novel *Obryv* (*The Precipice,* 1869) for parts of *On the Eve* and of having intercepted his letters to steal his ideas. Turgenev demanded that a panel of three literary men judge the case. This was done, and Turgenev was cleared. The novelist had more trouble to face, however, when his major novel, Fathers and Children, was published. The depiction of the central character, Bazarov, outraged both conservatives and radicals. The furor of criticism induced Turgenev to leave Russia, and thereafter he only returned for short visits to his native land. His next novel, Smoke, was, in part, a retaliation against the radicals and also against the conservative Slavophiles. Neither, Turgenev maintained, were on the right track. There was nothing in Russia nor the Russians worth working with. The salvation of the country could only come, Turgenev claimed, by turning to the civilization of the West. This novel, naturally, was not well received in Russia, which only further embittered Turgenev. The work also was the central point of a famous argument in Baden-Baden between Turgenev and Dostoevski. The two men had not been on good terms since the 1840's when both had been in the circle of young writers gathered around the critic Belinski. At that time Turgenev had reputedly enraged the sensitive Dostoevski with his barbed wit, and Dostoevski now supposedly paid back Turgenev by needling him about the poor reception of *Smoke.*

Turgenev's best work of his late years was the short novel *Veshnye Vody* (*Torrents of Spring,* 1872). His last attempt at a novel, Virgin Soil, was another effort to deal with the revolutionary movement in Russia, and again Turgenev met with hostile criticism. Ill with cancer of the spine, he made a few visits to Russia in his last years, on one of which he made peace with Tolstoi after a rift of almost 20 years' duration. In 1882 his *Stikhotvoreniya v proze* (*Poems in Prose*), his last notable work, was published. Turgenev died in 1883 on the estate at Bougival, France, which he shared with the Viardots. Pauline Viardot was at his bedside.

Turgenev was the first major Russian novelist of the late 19th century to become well known outside his own country. His reputation in the West diminished somewhat when the more powerful talents of Tolstoi and Dostoevski were revealed, but the esteem accorded Turgenev's artistic ability has remained high.

Turgot, Anne Robert Jacques. Baron **de l'Aulne** (1727–1781). French statesman, economist, and reformer, considered one of the founders of political economy. As comptroller general under Louis XVI, and disciple of the PHYSIOCRATS, he considered agriculture the sole source of wealth, and advocated greatly increased freedom (including freedom from taxation) for commerce and industry. He contributed articles to the ENCYCLOPÉDIE and influenced Adam Smith.

Turkey in the Straw. An American folk tune, probably of Irish or English origin, a favorite at square dances. The first published American version was a minstrel song, *Zip Coon* (1834).

Turm, Der. See TOWER, THE.

Turner, Charles Tennyson (1808–1879). English poet, older brother of Alfred TENNYSON. He wrote several volumes of poetry, mostly sonnets in a Wordsworthian style. These include *Sonnets and Fugitive Pieces* (1830), *Sonnets* (1864), and *Collected Sonnets* (1880). In 1830 he adopted the name Turner by the terms of his great-uncle's will.

Turner, Frederick Jackson (1861–1932). American historian. Turner is best known for his "frontier hypothesis," which he first presented at a meeting of the American Historical Association in 1893 in a paper called *The Significance of the Frontier in American History* (1894). Rejecting the traditional emphasis on the influence of the East and of Anglo-Saxon political institutions, Turner claimed that the form and spirit of American democracy were the direct product of the frontier with its free land, its stimulation of ingenuity and resourcefulness, and its dominant individualism. His thesis was immediately recognized as a historical idea of great importance and it opened up a new area for historical investigation; later historians, however, have challenged many of his interpretations.

Turner, who taught at the University of Wisconsin and at Harvard, also wrote *The Rise of the New West* (1906), *The United States, 1830–1850* (1935), and two collections of essays, *The Frontier in American History* (1920) and *The Significance of Sections in American History* (1932).

Turner, Joseph Mallord William (1775–1851). English painter. He began by painting vivid, romantic landscapes in the style of Claude Lorrain and Nicolas Poussin, but became increasingly concerned with the imaginative representation of light. He is famous for scenes of Venice in which forms lose their solidity and their outlines in the intense light of sky and water, and for storms at sea and effects of mist, smoke, and light. John RUSKIN extolled him in *Modern Painters* (1843).

Turner, W[alter] J[ames] R[edfern] (1889–1946). Australian-born English poet and writer of fiction and critical works, especially on music. He is the author of a few striking poems, notably the much-anthologized *Romance*.

Turn of the Screw, The (1898). A novelette by Henry JAMES. It is told from the viewpoint of the leading character, a governess in love with her employer, who goes to an isolated English estate to take charge of Miles and Flora, two attractive and precocious children. She gradually realizes that her young charges are under the evil influence of two ghosts, Peter Quint, the ex-steward, and Miss Jessel, their former governess. At the climax of the story, she enters into open conflict with the children, as a result of which Flora is alienated and Miles dies of fright. Some critics, notably Edmund Wilson, have interpreted the ghosts as products of the disordered mind of the governess, but most critics now agree that James intended them to have actual, objective existence, even though their exact nature remains ambiguous. The story was dramatized by William Archibald as *The Innocents* (1950) and was made into an opera by Benjamin Britten (1954).

Turnus. In Vergil's AENEID, the king of the Rutulians. His suit for Lavinia, daughter of Latinus, is favored by Amata, her mother. When Aeneas is promised the hand of Lavinia, Turnus, incited by the Fury Alecto, wages war on the Trojans. He is finally killed by Aeneas in single combat.

Turpin, Archbishop (d. 800?). French churchman, elected archbishop of Reims about 753. According to some legends, such as the *Chanson de* ROLAND, he was the religious leader among Charlemagne's paladins and died with Roland at Roncesvalles in 778. More frequently, he is erroneously considered the author of the *Historia de vita Caroli Magni et Rolandi* (usually called the *Chronicle of Charlemagne*), a Latin history of Charlemagne's exploits in Spain, actually written by monks in the 11th and 12th centuries.

Turpin, Richard. Known as **Dick Turpin** (1706–1739). English robber. The son of an alehouse keeper and partner of a highwayman, Tom King, whom he accidentally killed while firing at a constable, Turpin has been the subject of many ballads and legends. The incident of his famous ride from London to York in a single night on his steed, Black Bess, to establish an alibi first appeared in the novel *Rookwood* (1834), the fictionalized account of Turpin's life by Harrison Ainsworth. Turpin himself was finally hanged at York, having been convicted of horse stealing.

Tushina, Lizaveta Nikolayevna. In Feodor Dostoevski's THE POSSESSED, the young woman who gives herself to STAVROGIN, only to learn that he is incapable of returning love to anyone. She is murdered by a rampaging mob at the scene of the fire where the Lebyadkins were killed.

Tusser, Thomas (c. 1524–1580). English poet. He is known for his advice on domestic and farm problems presented in a form resembling later farmer's almanacs, but written in verse throughout. They were very popular in their day with the farmers and housewives of England. His works in this vein include *A Hundreth Good Points of Husbandry* (1557); *A Hundreth Good Points of Huswifery* (1570); and *Five Hundreth Good Points of Husbandry, United to as Many of Good Huswifery* (1573). Religious verse and moral maxims were included among information on crops, soil cultivation, weather, and the like.

Tutivillus. Later **Titivil**. A demon in medieval legend. He collects all the words mumbled or skipped over by priests in the performance of services, and bears them to hell to be recorded against the offender. Later the word is used for any tattletale fiend. See TOM TITIVIL.

Tutt, Ephraim. See Arthur TRAIN.

Tvardovsi, Aleksandr Trifonovich (1910–1971). Russian poet and editor. His first book of poems was *The Road to Socialism* (*Put k sotsializmu;* 1930). In 1936 he published *The Land of Muravia* (*Strana Muraviya*), a long narrative poem for which he received a Stalin prize. *Vasili Tiorkin,* another narrative poem about a jovial, courageous soldier, was published between 1941 and 1945 in installments. At the height of the post-Stalin thaw, Tvardovski published parts of a long poem, *Horizon Beyond Horizon* (*Dal' za dalyu;* 1956), which spoke out in favor of freedom in literary work. He was editor of *Novyi Mir,* the Soviet literary journal which often publishes the most nonconformist of Soviet writings.

Twain, Mark. Pen name of **Samuel Langhorne Clemens** (1835–1910). American humorist, newspaperman, lecturer, and writer. Born in Florida, Mo., Twain drew on his boyhood along the Mississippi River for characters and incidents in his best work. His formal schooling ended early, and he learned the printing trade. After writing for the Hannibal newspapers, he left for St. Louis, Philadelphia, and New York in 1853. Returning to the river in 1857, he became a Mississippi steamboat pilot until the Civil War ended river traffic. He wrote of this period in LIFE ON THE MISSISSIPPI; from river slang for two fathoms deep, he received his pen name.

Twain met Artemus Ward in mining camps in Nevada, learning from him the technique of lecturing successfully. Next he went to California as a roving correspondent, and worked for Bret Harte. His fame as humorist and storyteller was established with the publication of THE CELEBRATED JUMPING FROG OF CALAVERAS COUNTY. His lectures increased his reputation, but THE INNOCENTS ABROAD, product of a European trip, gave him a place in the world of letters and enough financial security to marry Olivia Langdon.

In the following year Twain wrote ROUGHING IT, TOM SAWYER, *A Tramp Abroad* (1880), THE PRINCE AND THE PAUPER, *Life on the Mississippi* (1883), HUCKLEBERRY FINN, and A CONNECTICUT YANKEE IN KING ARTHUR'S COURT. After a protracted European lecturing tour, during which one of his daughters died, he continued to write. Among the books published were THE TRAGEDY OF PUDD'NHEAD WILSON, THE MAN THAT CORRUPTED HADLEYBURG, and THE MYSTERIOUS STRANGER. In his last years Twain became a bitter satirist, famous for cynical epigrams. Some of his last essays, included in *Letters from the earth,* were first published in 1962. They reveal Twain as bitter and disillusioned in his last years.

A careful and conscious artist, Twain became a master of the technical devices of exaggeration, irreverence, and deadpan seriousness; sensitive to the sound of language, he introduced colloquial speech into American fiction. See *1601;* GILDED AGE, THE.

'Twas the Night Before Christmas. The popular title of A VISIT FROM ST. NICHOLAS.

Tweed, William Marcy (1823–1878). American politician, head of Tammany Hall. Known as "Boss" Tweed, he and the Tweed Ring of politicians swindled the treasury of New York City out of millions of dollars. Samuel J. Tilden was chairman of the Democratic State Committee that effected Tweed's downfall. Thomas NAST's remarkable cartoons in *Harper's Weekly* and the editorial views of *The New York Times* (1870) were significant influences on public opinion.

Tweedledum and Tweedledee. Names satirizing two quarreling and negligibly different schools of musicians. They were invented by John Byrom (1692–1763). Hence, used of people whose persons or opinions are "as like as two peas."

> Some say compared to Bononcini
> That Mynheer Handel's but a ninny;
> Others aver that he to Handel
> Is scarcely fit to hold a candle.
> Strange all this difference should be
> 'Twixt Tweedledum and Tweedledee.
>   J. Byrom

The duke of Marlborough and most of the nobility took the side of G. B. Bononcini (c. 1672–c. 1752), but the prince of Wales, with Pope and Arbuthnot, was for Handel. See GLUCKISTS.

Lewis Carroll introduced Tweedledum and Tweedledee into his *Through the Looking-Glass,* the sequel to *Alice in Wonderland,* where they sing the famous ditty of *The Walrus and the Carpenter.*

Twelfth Night. January 5, the eve of Twelfth Day, or the Feast of the EPIPHANY, twelve days after Christmas. It was formerly a time of great merrymaking, as the end of the secular celebration of Christmas.

Twelfth Night; or What You Will (c. 1600). A comedy by William SHAKESPEARE. The main plot hinges on the physical likeness between SEBASTIAN and his twin sister Viola, who are separated after a shipwreck off the coast of Illyria, each believing the other to be dead. Disguising herself as a boy and taking the name of Cesario, Viola becomes the page of ORSINO, the duke of Illyria, and falls in love with him. The duke, however, cherishes a hopeless passion for OLIVIA, who is in mourning for her dead brother and, aided by her pompous steward MALVOLIO, has forced her entire household to share her grief. When Cesario is sent by the duke to further his suit, Olivia is instantly smitten with the disguised Viola. Arriving in Illyria, Sebastian is mistaken for the page by Olivia, who sends for a priest and marries the astonished young man. The ensuing confusion is cleared up when Viola and Sebastian meet and recognize each other. Yielding Olivia to Sebastian, the duke decides to marry Viola, who has confessed her love for him.

The subplot concerns the machinations of MARIA, Sir Toby BELCH, and Sir Andrew AGUECHEEK against the pretentious Malvolio. Their efforts to remove him from Olivia's favor result in some of the finest low comedy in Shakespeare.

The play is based on an old Italian comedy *Gl'Ingannati* (1537) and later versions of it by Bandello, Belleforest, and Barnabe Rich.

Twelve, The (*Dvenadtzat';* 1918). A long poem by Aleksandr BLOK which is regarded as one of the best literary works produced by the Russian Revolution. The scene is the chaotic streets of St. Petersburg in the early days of the revolution, rendered by a striking mixture of poetry, bits of popular songs, and coarse colloquialisms. The 12 are a detachment of Red Guards patrolling the snowy streets. An ambiguous note was introduced by Blok when he inserted the figure of Jesus at the end of the poem. Blok's own explanation for this insertion did little to clarify the meaning of Jesus' presence in the work.

Twelve Chairs (Dvenadtzat stulyev; 1928). A humorous novel by ILF AND PETROV. It narrates the adventures of Ostap Bender, master crook, seeking to recover a cache of money hidden in one of a dozen identical chairs.

Twenty-six Men and a Girl (Dvadtzat' shest' i odna; 1899). A short story by Maksim GORKI. A group of wretched, slaving bakery-shop workers have their lives brightened each day by the visit of a pretty young girl who comes to buy buns. Their adoration for her turns to bitter rage when a swaggering boor bets them he can seduce the girl and succeeds.

Twenty Thousand Leagues Under the Sea (Vingt mille lieues sous les mers; 1870). A romance by Jules VERNE, remarkable for its prognostication of the invention of submarines. The central characters of the tale, in the process of exploring marine disturbances, are captured by the megalomaniacal Captain Nemo. An underseas tour in a strange craft and their ensuing escape conclude the work.

Twenty Years After (Vingt Ans après; 1845). A historical romance by Alexandre DUMAS, sequel to THE THREE MUSKETEERS. In this novel, the four friends find themselves on opposite sides of the uprising against Cardinal Mazarin known as the FRONDE. D'Artagnan and Porthos, still guardsmen, must support the regime. Athos, now a country gentleman, and Aramis, who has finally entered a monastery, join the intrigue. This second novel contains a generous share of excitement and adventure.

Twice-Told Tales, The (1837, 1842). A collection of tales and sketches by Nathaniel HAWTHORNE. The name of the volume is probably derived from the line in *King John:* "Life is a tedious as a twice-told tale." Among the most interesting pieces are *Howe's Masquerade, The Grey Champion, The Great Carbuncle,* and THE MINISTER'S BLACK VEIL.

Twicknam Garden (1633). A poem by John DONNE, dealing with the grief caused him by his mistress' perverse fidelity to her husband or lover. It is notable for its intensity of feeling and brilliance of conceit.

Twilight of the Gods. See RAGNAROK.

Two Cultures, The (1959). A controversial speech and pamphlet by C. P. SNOW. It claims that scientists are not sufficiently appreciated and that English society is divided into two cultures: the scientific, and the literary and humanistic. The literary and humanistic culture is of upper-middle-class origin, part of the ESTABLISHMENT, and conservative. The scientific culture is of lower-middle-class origin and of low status, but at the center of progress.

Two Deaths of Christopher Martin, The. See PINCHER MARTIN.

Two Gentlemen of Verona, The (c. 1592). A comedy by William SHAKESPEARE. The "two gentlemen" are Valentine and Proteus, close friends at first, but later rivals for the hand of Silvia, daughter of the duke of Milan, who wants her to marry THURIO. Proteus forgets his old love JULIA, plays his friend false, and brings about his banishment. SILVIA escapes to the forest to join Valentine, who has become an outlaw, and is pursued by Proteus and his page, who is really the doting Julia in disguise. Proteus finds Silvia and is about to make her submit to him when she is rescued by Valentine, who generously forgives his wayward friend. The duke then arrives on the scene and, impressed by Valentine's manly conduct, freely bestows his daughter upon him, while the repentant Proteus contents himself with marrying Julia.

The play is one of Shakespeare's lesser comedies. Its principal source is Jorge de Montemayor's *Diana* (1559), and its form is based on the early Italian comedies.

Two Noble Kinsmen, The (pub. 1634). A romantic drama by John FLETCHER, which was probably written in collaboration with SHAKESPEARE. The play takes place in Athens after the defeat of Thebes by Theseus. Two valiant Theban knights, Palamon and Arcite, spy Emilia, Theseus' sister-in-law, from their prison window. Each immediately falls in love with her. Later Arcite is released and Palamon escapes with the help of the jailer's daughter. They meet and duel in a forest where they are discovered by Theseus, who plans a great tournament. The winner will have the hand of Emilia; the loser will be executed. Palamon loses the tournament and is about to be beheaded when word comes that Arcite has been killed in a fall from his horse. With his last breath, Arcite relinquishes his right to Emilia's hand in Palamon's favor. The story of Palamon and Arcite was first told in Boccaccio's TESEIDA. See Philip MASSINGER.

Two on a Tower (1882). A novel by Thomas HARDY. It deals with the mutual love of the young astronomer Swithin St. Cleve and Lady Viviette Constantine. An early secret marriage between them is set aside by later developments, and, when St. Cleve finally returns from South Africa to the familiar observatory tower to propose marriage, Viviette falls dead in his arms.

Two Years Before the Mast (1840). A narrative by Richard Henry DANA, Jr. It is based on his own journal, written while he was a sailor. The book dwells on the brutality of the ship's captain, and the sailors' lack of redress. It did much to arouse public opinion, and led to legal action. In 1859, Dana added a final chapter describing a second trip to California. He continues the stories of several men he mentioned in the earlier part of the narrative. The book influenced both Melville and Conrad.

Tybalt. In Shakespeare's ROMEO AND JULIET, Lady Capulet's nephew and Juliet's cousin. Although the hot-tempered Tybalt recognizes Romeo at the Capulets' ball, old Capulet forbids him to harm a guest. Later he tries to pick a quarrel with Romeo, but the latter, Tybalt's kinsman since his secret marriage to Juliet, refuses to be baited. After Tybalt has slain Mercutio, however, the infuriated Romeo kills him.

Because Tybalt has the same name as the cat in the beast-epic *Reynard the Fox,* Mercutio addresses him as "rat-catcher" and "good king of cats."

Tyche. Literally Fortune. Originally the Greek goddess of chance, later in antiquity she was worshiped as the goddess of good fortune, who allots wealth and power to mortals. She is variously represented with a horn of plenty, a wheel, a rudder, or juggling a ball.

tycoon (from *Chin.*, "great sovereign"). A title taken by some of the Tokugawa *shōguns* of Japan. Today the term is used to refer to a magnate of industry in the U.S. and elsewhere.

Tydeus. In classic myth, one of the SEVEN AGAINST THEBES.

Tyler, John. See TIPPECANOE AND TYLER TOO.

Tyler, Moses Coit (1835–1900). American literary historian. After teaching English literature at the University of Michigan, Tyler was called to Cornell in 1881 to occupy the first chair of American history established in the U.S. One of the first scholars to examine American literature critically, he wrote *History of American Literature During the Colonial Time* (1878) and *Literary History of the American Revolution* (1897).

Tyler, Royall (1757–1826). American jurist, dramatist, and novelist. Although Tyler was a practicing lawyer who served as chief justice of the Vermont Supreme Court and as professor of jurisprudence at the University of Vermont, he is remembered as the virtual founder of American drama; his play THE CONTRAST was the first comedy to be written by a native American. Tyler also wrote *The Georgia Spec, or Land in the Moon* (1797), a comedy satirizing the YAZOO FRAUDS, and THE ALGERINE CAPTIVE, a novel.

Tyler's Rebellion. Also called the **Peasants' Revolt** (1381). Insurrection of the peasants of Kent and Essex. They demanded abolition of serfdom, the poll tax, and all restrictions on the freedom of labor and trade; under the leadership of Wat Tyler they sacked Canterbury, then several official buildings in London. The young Richard II met with Tyler and was having charters drawn up acceding to his demands; but Tyler insolently presented fresh demands the next day, and in the fighting that ensued Tyler was killed by William Walworth, Lord Mayor of London. In 1382 Parliament revoked the concessions that Richard had made. John Gower described the revolt in his VOX CLAMANTIS, Robert Southey in his dramatic poem *Wat Tyler* (1817).

Tyll or **Till Eulenspiegel, Ulenspiegel, Howleglas,** or **Owlglass.** See EULENSPIEGEL.

Tynan, Katharine (1861–1931). Irish poet and prose writer. Her work is based on her Roman Catholic and Celtic interests. Among her books of poetry are *Louise de la Vallière* (1885) and *Ballads and Lyrics* (1890). She also wrote several autobiographical volumes, including *Twenty-Five Years* (1913), *The Middle Years* (1917), and *Memories* (1924).

Tyndale, William (d. 1536). English Protestant preacher, known for his translation of the Bible into English. It was first printed at Cologne in 1525. He sent copies of his translation into England for distribution, but they were condemned by the bishops and burned. Tyndale also wrote pamphlets supporting the authority of the Bible and the king over the power of the Church and the Pope, and for awhile was favored by King Henry VIII, although he soon lost this favor when he disapproved of the king's divorce. He carried on a vigorous controversy with Sir Thomas MORE, and in 1536 was strangled and burned at the stake in Antwerp as a heretic. See BIBLE, ENGLISH VERSIONS.

Tyndareus (Tyndareos). Mythical king of Sparta, husband of Leda. Which of her children

First page of Tyndale's Gospel of St. Matthew (1525).

(Helen, Clytemnestra, Castor, Polydeuces) were also his is much disputed in mythology.

Typee[: A Peep at Polynesian Life] (1846). A novel by Herman MELVILLE. The hero and his friend Toby escape from their ship, and wander mistakenly into the valley of Typee, inhabited by cannibals. The Typees became their benevolent captors, refusing to allow them to leave. Toby escapes, while the hero, suffering from a leg wound, remains to be nursed by the lovely Fayaway. Tempted to enjoy a somnolent, vegetative existence, the moral American chooses to return to civilization. He regretfully leaves his island love, escaping on a cruising whaler.

Typhoeus. A giant of Greek mythology. He had a hundred heads, fearful eyes, and a most terrible voice. Zeus killed him with a thunderbolt, and he lies buried under Mount Aetna.

Typhon (Typhaon). A fire-breathing monster, the father of the Sphinx, the Chimaera, and other monsters. He is often identified with Typhoeus, a son of Tartarus and Ge, who begot the unfavorable winds or, according to other stories, is himself one of them. As one of the Hundred-handed Giants (Hekatoncheires), he warred against the gods and was banished by Zeus to Tartarus under Mount Aetna. Typhon is also the name used by the Greeks for the Egyptian Set, the god of evil, who killed his brother (or father) Osiris.

Typhoon (1903). A short novel by Joseph CONRAD. The stolid, seamanly Captain MacWhirr rides out a tempest and brings his crew and his cargo of Chinese passengers to safety.

Tyr or **Tiu.** The god of battle in Nordic legend,

second in importance to his brother Thor. He was one-handed since the day Fenris-wolf bit off the hand he once placed in its mouth as a pledge; thus, in battle, he could give victory only to one side. Also patron of athletic sports, he possessed a magic sword, which was said to insure victory.

tyrant (tyrannos). An absolute ruler. In ancient Greece the tyrant was merely the absolute ruler, the despot of a state, and at first the word had no implication of cruelty or what we call tyranny. Many of the Greek tyrants were excellent rulers, as were Pisistratus and Pericles, of Athens; Periander, of Corinth; Dionysius the Younger, Gelon, and his brother Hiero, of Syracuse; Phidion, of Argos; Polycrates, of Samos. The word *tyrannos* soon, however, obtained much the same meaning as it has with us.

tyrant's vein, a. A ranting, bullying manner. In the old Moralities the tyrants were made to rant, and the loudness of their rant matched the villainy of their dispositions.

Tyre and Sidon. See TIR ET SIDON.

Tyrian purple. A famous crimson or purple dye used by the Greeks and Romans. It was made in the city of Tyre and was very expensive. Hence it was worn by the nobility or the very wealthy.

Tyrtaeus (Tyrtaios). A lame schoolmaster and elegiac poet of Athens. He is said so to have inspired the Spartans by his songs that they defeated the Messenians (7th century B.C.). The name has hence been given to many martial poets who have urged on their countrymen to deeds of arms and victory.

Tyutchev, Feodor Ivanovich (1803–1873). Russian poet. After graduating from Moscow University in 1821, Tyutchev entered the diplomatic service and spent 20 years abroad, mostly in Germany. While there he became the friend of Heine and Schelling. He was one of the first Russian translators of Heine.

Tyutchev wrote and published in literary journals during his years of diplomatic service. It was not until the mid-1850's that his work was issued in a separate volume. From that time on, he was held in high esteem as a poet. His renown faded somewhat toward the end of the 19th century. It was revived through the influence of the symbolist poets, who considered Tyutchev one of their precursors. A distinctive feature of his work is his nature poetry, which often deals with the duality caused by the apparent order of the universe and the chaos that lies just beneath this seeming order. This idea is expressed clearly in one of his most famous lyrics, *Ne to chto mnite vy priroda* (*Nature is not what you think,* 1836). A duality of feeling is also evident in Tyutchev's love poems, where love is sometimes called "the key of life" and sometimes an "unequal struggle of two hearts." Many of his finest love lyrics were occasioned by Tyutchev's affair with Elena Aleksandrovna Deniseva, his children's governess. Among the more famous of Tyutchev's poems are *Silentium* (1833) and *Son na morye* (*Dream at Sea,* 1836).

Tzara, Tristan (1896–1963). Romanian-born French poet, best known for having founded the DADA movement in 1916. Tzara is the author of several dramatic or epic poems in a surrealistic style, such as *L'Homme approximatif* (1936).

Tzvetayeva, Marina Ivanovna (1892–1941). Russian poet. Much of Tzvetayeva's verse was published abroad, where she lived after 1922, having supported the Whites during the civil war. Some of her best poetry, which is typically written in powerful, staccato rhythms, is based on folk literature and legends. Tzvetayeva returned to the Soviet Union in 1939 and committed suicide two years later. Her poetry was admired by Boris Pasternak.

U

U. In England, "upper class." See Non-U.

Ubaldo of Sweden. In Torquato Tasso's Geru-salemme Liberata, a crusading knight sent along with Guelfo to bring back Rinaldo the Christian champion, who had left the camp in anger. He and Guelfo are assisted by the Hermit of Ascalon, who gives them a magic wand to ward off animals and a mirrorlike shield in which Rinaldo will see his disgrace. They travel to the distant Fortunate Isles, where the enchantress Armida keeps Rinaldo in bondage and free him. Ubaldo is believed to symbolize the power of reason over the senses in the allegorical scheme of the poem.

Übermensch (*Ger.,* superman). A term in Nietzsche's Thus Spake Zarathustra. The word, which had first occurred, only in passing, in Goethe's *Faust,* was used by Nietzsche to designate the goal of human existence. Despite the Nazi interpretation of his works, Nietzsche did not believe that the Germans were a race of supermen, nor did he believe that self-discipline and training, or racial purity, would ever develop such a race. The substance of his belief was simply that whereas every distinct human culture has its own unique goals, there exists a single universal human goal, the sum of all particular cultural goals, and this is the "Übermensch." He believed that man should completely commit himself to his earthly goals, that he should sacrifice his life for them, and that out of the self-destruction resulting from such sacrifice, the "Übermensch" would arise. It is not clear whether Nietzsche conceived of the "Übermensch" as an actual being or as an idea.

Ubu Roi (**King Ubu,** 1896). A play by Alfred Jarry which grew out of a farce written with a classmate at 15 to ridicule a pompous math teacher. A stylized burlesque, it satirizes the tendency of the successful bourgeois to abuse his authority and to become irresponsibly complacent. *Ubu enchaîné* (1900) less successfully parodies the tragic style.

Uccello, Paolo. Real name, **Paolo di Dono** (1397–1475). Florentine painter. In spite of his concentration on the elements of perspective and foreshortening—the contemporary discoveries of Alberti and Brunelleschi with which he was fascinated—his works, such as *St. George and the Dragon,* have the charming simplicity of a toylike world because of their decorative use of simplified forms and sharply outlined patterns of color. His best-known works are the three battle scenes he painted to commemorate the defeat of the Sienese by the Florentines at San Romano in 1432. They were commissioned by Lorenzo de' Medici for his palace, but the three com-ponent paintings have now been separated and are located in Florence, Paris, and London.

Udall or **Udal** or **Uvedale, Nicholas** (1504?–1556). English playwright, translator, and schoolmaster. Udall, Headmaster at Eton from 1534 to 1541, is chiefly remembered as the author of the first English comedy, Ralph Roister Doister. Somewhat similar to Plautus' *Miles Gloriosus,* it was probably first performed c. 1553, but not published until 1566. Udall also translated Terence, and wrote plays in Latin on theological subjects. He appears as a character in Ford Madox Ford's novel *The Fifth Queen.*

Uffizi Palace. A palace built by Vasari in the 16th century in Florence, Italy. It is now one of the world's most famous art museums. See Ponte Vecchio.

Ugarit. Ancient city on the sea-coast of Syria. For some centuries it was under the dominion of Egypt, but, after the battle of Kadesh, it came into the Hittite sphere. In both cases, however, Ugarit was an autonomous power. It is particularly important for the light its excavation has shed on the widespread Semitic culture of this period, which may have extended as far as Minoan Crete. Several important ancient documents have been discovered at Ugarit: The Poem of Baal, The Poem of Aqhat, and *The Poem of the Gracious Gods,* which have been useful to students of the Old Testament.

Ugly Duckling, The. A fairy tale by Hans Christian Andersen about a swan hatched among ducklings and mocked as an ungainly member of the brood, until finally it becomes apparent that he is a swan.

Ugolino. Count of Pisa (c. 1220–1289). Guelph leader whose history is one of the most famous episodes in Dante's *Inferno.* He is found frozen in the ice of the ninth circle, that of the traitors, gnawing on the head of the Ghibelline Archbishop Ruggiero, who first was Ugolino's ally in the betrayal of Pisa, then turned on him and imprisoned him with his four sons until they starved to death.

Uhland, Ludwig (1787–1862). German romantic poet. He is most famous for his ballads in folk style. He was a serious student of folklore, and his collection of *Alte hoch- und niederdeutsche Volkslieder* (*Old South and North German Folk-Songs,* 1844–1845) is an important scholarly work. His dramas, *Herzog Ernst von Schwaben* (*Duke Ernst of Swabia,* 1818) and *Ludwig der Bayer* (*Ludwig the Bavarian,* 1819), seek to further both the regional and national cultural awareness of Germany. Uhland himself was a politically active liberal. See Justinus Kerner; German romanticism.

ukiyoe (pictures of the floating world). Japanese color prints. Made from woodblocks, they were produced chiefly during the Tokugawa period (1600–1868). Subjects include *kabuki* actors, courtesans, landscapes, etc. They have been appreciated by Western art connoisseurs.

Ulalume (1847). A poem by Edgar Allan Poe. It was composed at the request of an elocutionist who wanted a poem for recitation. The narrator and his soul walk in a misty-mid-region on Hallowe'en. They are stopped, as they follow the planet Venus, by the door of the forgotten tomb of the narrator's beloved, the lost Ulalume.

ulema or **ulama** (*Arab.,* "learned"). In the Muslim countries, the learned classes, professionally trained to interpret the Koran and religious law. From the *ulema* are chosen the ministers of religion, doctors of law and administrators of justice. *Ulema* is the plural of *ulim,* a wise man.

Ullikummi. A stone monster of Hittite myth. He was the son of Kumarbi, a god in revolt against the sky-god Anu, who, following the advice of the lord of the sea, had impregnated a mountain.

Ullman, James Ramsey (1907–1971). American writer. Before he became a successful popular writer, Ullman wrote plays and then became a producer on Broadway. He was coproducer of *Men in White* (1930), which won a Pulitzer Prize, but after several later failures he went to South America where he followed the Amazon to the sea. The result was his book *The Other Side of the Mountain* (1938). The trip also provided the background for his later novel, *River of the Sun* (1951). *High Conquest* (1941) is a history of mountaineering; *The White Tower* (1945) is a novel about mountain climbing. Among his other books are the novels *Windom's Way* (1952), inspired by the story of Dr. Gordon Seagrave, and *The Day on Fire,* based on the life of Rimbaud.

Ulrica. In Scott's Ivanhoe, the weird sibyl at Torquilstone Castle, who dies in the conflagration there. In Verdi's opera *The Masked Ball,* she is the witch who predicts the peril that is to befall the two lovers.

Ulster. The northernmost province of Ireland. It was forfeited to the Crown in James I's reign in consequence of the rebellions of Tyrconnel and Tyrone, and colonized (1609–1612) by English and Scottish settlers, who were forbidden to sell land to any Irishman. Since then the Ulstermen have been intensely English and anti-Irish in sentiment and action and have refused on any terms to coalesce with the original inhabitants, who have ever been anti-British.

Ulster cycle. In Gaelic literature, a group of pagan sagas or romances that survive in medieval manuscripts but deal with much earlier periods. The sagas are peopled with the legendary heroes of Ulster among whom are King Conchobar, Medb and Ailill, Fergus, Cu Roi, Finnabair, Deirdre, Noisi, Emer, Bricriu Poison-tongue, Cathbad the Druid, Etain, Da Derga, Mac Datho, Conaire, Conall Cernach, and Cú Chulainn, the greatest hero of all. The most important tale from this cycle is Cattle-Raid of Cooley.

Ultima Thule. See Thule.

ultramontane party. The extreme papal party in the Roman Church. *Ultramontane* (beyond the mountains, *i.e.,* the Alps) meant Italy or the old Papal States. The term was first used by the French to distinguish those who looked upon the Pope as the fountain of all power in the Church from the Gallican school, which maintained the right of self-government by national churches.

Ulyanov, Vladimir Ilyich. See Lenin, Nikolai.

Ulysses. The Roman name of the Greek Odysseus, hero of Homer's *Odyssey* and a prominent character in the *Iliad.* He is called Ulysses in most English poetry, including the earlier translations of Homer. Tennyson wrote a poem *Ulysses* (1842), in which the hero in his old age speaks of his still active longing for adventure. In a modern reincarnation as Leopold Bloom, he is the hero of James Joyce's novel Ulysses.

Ulysses (1922). A novel by James Joyce. First published in Paris, and banned in the U.S. until 1933, it is now generally recognized to be the greatest 20th-century novel written in English. Its obscurity has made it the subject of much controversy. Virginia Woolf, William Butler Yeats, and Ezra Pound admitted to their confusion upon a first reading; T. S. Eliot, immediately recognizing its greatness, said the book would be a landmark because it destroys our civilization.

In *Ulysses,* Joyce has shifted from the personal, lyrical style of *A Portrait of the Artist as a Young Man* to the detached and impersonal style of the epic. Whereas his earlier book is affirmative in tone, *Ulysses* is a disillusioned study of estrangement, paralysis, and the disintegration of society.

The novel records the events of one average day, June 16, 1904, in the lives of its three leading characters: Leopold Bloom, his wife Molly, and Stephen Dedalus. The chronological pattern of these events provides the only narrative sequence in the book. Journeys about the city of Dublin are matched by inward journeys into the consciousness (see stream of consciousness), which Joyce expresses through journeys into the nature of language itself. On one level Joyce's style is as unrelentingly naturalistic as a movie reel, every detail, from a newspaper ad to a bodily function is recorded and dispassionately analyzed. But by means of these details, he captures the chain of stimulus and response—the material of experience—with a degree of accuracy and immediacy never before achieved in fiction. And by means of careful orchestration, these details become significant as symbols and raise the work above the level of simple naturalism.

It has been said that in order to fully understand *Ulysses* one must, at the very least, be familiar with the theology of the Roman Catholic Church, the history of heresy, Irish legend, European history, mythology, astronomy, Hebrew, Latin, Gaelic, and Gypsy slang. Joyce's method relates the time-world of Dublin to the timeless patterns of myth, history, and religion. The plan of the book parallels the *Odyssey.* Ulysses' 19 years of wandering is paralleled by the one-day pilgrimage of Bloom, an advertisement canvasser, and the commonplace occurrences of his day echo episodes in the *Odyssey.* Stephen is related to Telemachus, and Molly Bloom to Penelope, although through a complex network of literary and historical allusions, each character is associated with many other figures as well. The central theme, that of exile, is one that preoccupied Joyce. Both Stephen and Bloom are exiled from their home and family life, their country, and their religion. However Stephen is rejected because of his rejection of his dying mother—in a larger sense his rejection of Ireland—while Bloom is rejected by Ireland as a Jew. Bloom—in a sense a symbol for humanity—searches for fulfillment in social, political, and ethical terms, while Stephen—the artistic and uncompromising mind—searches for spiritual and emotional values. Whereas Ulysses on his odyssey gradually discovers the truth about himself and his relation to the gods, and finally returns to his homeland, Joyce's two exiles cannot find the key to their loneliness and frustration, and their potentialities for growth seem fated to be stunted by their environment. But the final section of the book belongs to Molly Bloom, an embodiment of the feminine, regenerative principle of the universe. Her famous soliloquy, in one uninterrupted long sentence, ends with the word yes—her affirmation of life and love.

Believing that man is rooted in matter, Joyce was the first novelist to give physical actualities the importance they have in life. In Ulysses he perfected the interior monologue. Throughout the book he parodies a variety of literary styles.

Una. The heroine of the 1st book of Spenser's Faerie Queene. She personifies Truth, her name being derived from the Latin unus, one. With the Red Cross Knight as her champion, she sets forth to relieve her royal parents who are being besieged by a dragon. She is soon parted from her knight, however, and she encounters a lion that becomes her attendant. She sleeps in the hut of Superstition, and on awakening meets Archimago (Hypocrisy) dressed as her knight. As they journey together, Sansloy overtakes her, exposes Archimago, kills the lion, and carries off Una to a wild forest. Fauns and satyrs rescue her and try to worship her; when she restrains them, they pay homage to her donkey. After she is delivered by Sir Satyrane, Archimago tells her that the Red Cross Knight is dead, but she subsequently learns that he is being held captive by the giant Orgoglio. She asks for help from King Arthur, who kills Orgoglio and rescues the knight whom Una takes to the house of Holiness, where he is carefully nursed back to health. Eventually, the Red Cross Knight kills the dragon, whose destruction was their original quest, and Una leads him to Eden where their marriage takes place. She is taken to represent Protestantism and Queen Elizabeth, as well as abstract truth; in this connection she is strongly contrasted with Duessa.

Unamuno [y Jugo], Miguel de (1864–1936). Spanish philosopher, poet, and novelist. The leading member of the Generación del 98, Unamuno is considered one of the major figures in the history of modern thought. The principal elements of his philosophy deal with tyranny and freedom and the problem of death versus life—here he advanced conclusions which anticipated modern existentialism, and the problem of 20th-century materialism. However, it is the second of these categories in which he most excelled. Unamuno explored the problems resulting from man's scientific awareness of the reality of death; this led him to the vision of the tragic nature of life—the agony of the spirit. In this he came quite close to the existential concept of the "absurd" or the "alone." His philosophical works include Del

sentimiento trágico de la vida en los hombres y en los pueblos (The Tragic Sense of Life in Men and in Peoples, 1913), his best-known work, and La Agonía del cristianismo (The Agony of Christianity, 1924). Among his novels, Paz en la guerra (1897), Niebla (Mist, A Tragi-Comic Novel, 1914), and Tres novelas ejemplares (Three Exemplary Novels, 1920) are the most highly praised. In the closing scene of Mist, the protagonist Augusto Pérez addresses the author himself, calling Unamuno a mere fiction, in a turn that is reminiscent of Pirandello. Unamuno was a prolific writer, and all his work in whatever form abounds with his philosophical ideas.

unanimism. A French school of thought in the early 20th century (c. 1907), based on the theory that the group is of prime importance and that the individual, especially the poet, can attain power and significance only by merging himself with a social aggregation of one kind or another, he himself being far less important than the collective whole. Georges Duhamel and Jules Romains were among the literary men associated with the school. Unanimism spread through the Abbaye Group. In 1908 Romains published a volume of poetry entitled La Vie unanime, and the unanimist influence is considered to be found in the collective emphasis of his Men of Good Will.

Uncle Remus, His Songs and His Sayings (1880). A famous book of folk tales by Joel Chandler Harris. They are told to a small white boy by whimsical, lovable Uncle Remus, an aging Negro servant, whose stories are based on traditional fables of his race. The tales, which include the story of Tar Baby, are ones that Harris himself heard as a boy and are fine examples of dialect and regional writing. Many of the characters are animals endowed with human qualities.

Uncle Sam. A commonly accepted personification of the U.S. government. It was originally a derogatory nickname for the federal government used by New Englanders opposed to its policies during the War of 1812. Uncle Sam may have been inspired by the nickname of a government inspector in Troy, N.Y., one Samuel Wilson, or it may represent an extension of the initials of the U.S. The Adventures of Uncle Sam (1816) by "Frederick Fidfaddy" seems to be the earliest use of the name in a book.

Uncle Toby. The lovable but almost totally inarticulate military uncle of the hero in Laurence Sterne's Tristram Shandy. His principal activity (he is incapacitated by a wound in his thigh) is to reconstruct all the military campaigns of Marlborough in miniature on a small bowling green. His speech is largely the whistling of tunes and a vain attempt to communicate his ideas through military palaver. See Widow Wadman; Corporal Trim.

Uncle Tom's Cabin, or, Life Among the Lowly (1852). A novel by Harriet Beecher Stowe. The book relates the trials, suffering, and human dignity of Uncle Tom, an old Negro slave. Cruelly treated by a Yankee overseer, Simon Legree, he dies as the result of a beating. Uncle Tom is devoted to Little Eva, the daughter of his white owner, Augustine St. Clare. Other important characters are the mulatto girl, Eliza; the impish Negro child, Topsy; Miss Ophelia St. Clare, a New England spinster; and

Marks, the slave catcher. The setting is Kentucky and Louisiana. The two most famous scenes are the death of Little Eva and the pursuit of Eliza and her baby over the Ohio River's ice floes. Eliza's husband, George, later joins her by using the UNDERGROUND RAILROAD.

The book, which Mrs. Stowe said was written by God, was a contribution to the abolitionist movement, but treats the situation in a balanced manner. There is admiration for the best of Southern gentility; the villain is a Vermonter. The book, extraordinarily popular, was followed by sequels and answers and counteranswers before 1860.

Uncle Tom's devotion to his white master led to the use of the pejorative term "Uncle Tomism," meaning undue subservience to white people on the part of Negroes.

Uncle Vanya (Dyadya Vanya; 1899). A play by Anton CHEKHOV, subtitled *Scenes from Country Life in Four Acts.* Uncle Vanya, Ivan Petrovich Voinitzki, for years has managed the estate of his brother-in-law, Aleksandr Vladimirovich Serebryakov, a retired professor. Vanya has given up his own dreams and ambitions to provide support for Serebryakov, whom he thinks is a great scholar. When he finally realizes that the old professor is somewhat of a fraud, Vanya feels cheated. His rancor against Serebryakov is increased by his love for the professor's young second wife, Yelena Andreyevna—a love that is not returned. He is thrown into fury and despair by Serebryakov's plan to sell the estate that Vanya has labored to make profitable. He unsuccessfully attempts to shoot the professor, then contemplates suicide. Serebryakov agrees not to sell the estate, and Vanya reconciled to his lot prepares to continue his drudgery.

Underdogs, The. See LOS DE ABAJO.

underground railroad. The organized secret system for transporting slaves to freedom before the Civil War. Negroes were frequently hidden on vessels bound from the South to New England, where they were helped further north, sometimes even to Canada. The program was supported by contributions from Northern abolitionists; many of its agents were Quakers.

Underhill, Evelyn (1875–1941). English mystical writer and poet. She is the author of the widely read study *Mysticism* (1911).

Under Milk Wood (1954). A radio play for voices by Dylan THOMAS. Written in poetic, inventive prose, it is full of humor, a joyful sense of the goodness of life and love, and a strong Welsh flavor. It is an impression of a spring day in the lives of the people of Llareggub, a Welsh village situated under Milk Wood. It has no plot, but a wealth of characters who dream aloud, converse with one another, and speak in choruses of alternating voices.

Under the Net (1954). A novel by Iris MURDOCH. It recounts the adventures of Jake Donaghue, who gets himself involved in film-making, horse racing, blackmailing, and dog-stealing, and finally becomes a hospital orderly. Unable to build for himself the kind of structured, successful life all his friends lead, he remains free—the goal of the existentialist. The "net" of the title refers to both the cage in which society tries to trap him and the falsifications it constructs through illogical words and theories.

Under the Volcano (1947). A novel by Malcolm LOWRY. Through the central character, Geoffrey Firmin, an ex-British consul and alcoholic living in Mexico, Lowry explores the gradual disintegration of a human being in despair. The book, which uses a variety of experimental techniques, is notable for its stylistic brilliance, as well as for the subtlety and depth of its characterizations.

Under Western Eyes (1911). A novel by Joseph CONRAD. It depicts the 19th-century Russian police state and extremist revolutionaries. Razumov betrays to the authorities his fellow-student Haldin, who has assassinated an official. Sent to Geneva as a government spy, Razumov falls in love with Haldin's sister Nathalie. He confesses the truth to the revolutionaries and is beaten, deafened, and run over by a tram car; finally he returns to Russia. The "Western eyes" are those of an Englishman who reads and comments on Razumov's journal.

Underwoods. The title of a collection of poems (1640) by Ben JONSON. Robert Louis STEVENSON adopted the title for a book of his own poems (1887).

Undine (1811). A tale by Friedrich von FOUQUÉ about the tragic love between the water-spirit Undine and a knight. Fouqué later made it into a libretto which was set to music by E. T. A. HOFFMANN, first performed in 1816. Jean GIRAUDOUX adapted the story of Undine in his play *Ondine* (1939).

Undset, Sigrid (1882–1949). Norwegian novelist. She is best known for her novels dealing with life in the Scandinavian countries during the Middle Ages. The daughter of a university professor, Sigrid Undset acquired her love of the medieval while helping her father with his research. She presents a vividly realistic picture of the past, combining with her scholarly knowledge a keen sense of psychological analysis and a powerful style. Among her historical works are KRISTIN LAVRANSDATTER; *The Master of Hestviken* (orig. title *Olav Audunnson,* 1925–1927), a tetralogy which includes *The Axe* (1928), *The Snake Pit* (1929), *In the Wilderness* (1929), and *The Son Avenger* (1930); and *Den Braendende Busk* (*The Burning Bush,* 1930). Undset's novels of the modern era concern themselves with social and psychological problems; her conversion to Roman Catholicism in 1924 is reflected in her fiction and in such studies as *Norske helgner* (*Saga of Saints,* 1934). Her personal life, too, was patterned on her medieval interests; she spent the later years of her life in a restored house dating from the year 1000, and dressed in the gown of a Norse matron of the Middle Ages. In 1928, Sigrid Undset was awarded the Nobel Prize for literature.

Unfortunate Traveller, The, or the Life of Jack Wilton (1594). A picaresque story by Thomas NASHE. A forerunner of the realistic novel of the style of Defoe, *The Unfortunate Traveller* deals with a page of King Henry VIII and his adventures in England and the Continent.

Ungaretti, Giuseppe (1888–1970). Italian prose writer and poet of the metaphysical "hermetic" school (see HERMETICISM). His poetry, characterized by a classically intoned style, treats themes of personal grief and sorrow. First introduced to the public in 1917 by Giovanni Papini, Ungaretti's verse is chiefly autobiographic in content. Collections of his poems include *L'Allegria* (1919), *Sentimento del Tempo*

(1933), *Poesie Disperse* (1945), *Il Dolore* (1946), *La Terra Promessa* (1950), and *Un Grido e Paesaggi* (1954). His works of prose consist of *Il Povero nella Città* (1949), *Il Taccuino del Vecchio* (1960), and *Il Deserto e Dopo* (1961).

unicorn (Lat., *unum cornu,* one horn). A fabulous animal. It is represented by medieval writers as having the legs of a buck, the tail of a lion, the head and body of a horse, and a single horn—white at the base, black in the middle, and red at the tip—jutting from the middle of its forehead; its body is white, head red, and eyes blue. The earliest author to describe it is Ctesias (400 B.C.). The medieval notions concerning it are summarized in the following extract:

The unicorn has but one horn in the middle of its forehead. It is the only animal that ventures to attack the elephant; and so sharp is the nail of its foot, that with one blow it can rip the belly of the beast. Hunters can catch the unicorn only by placing a young virgin in his haunts. No sooner does he see the damsel than he runs towards her, and lies down at her feet, and so suffers himself to be captured by the hunters. The unicorn represents Jesus Christ, who took on Him our nature in the virgin's womb, was betrayed to the Jews, and delivered into the hands of Pontius Pilate. Its one horn signifies the Gospel of Truth.—*Le Bestiaire Divin de Guillaume, Clerc de Normandie* (13th century)

The heraldic supporters in the old royal coat of arms of Scotland are two unicorns. When James VI of Scotland came to reign over England (1603), the unicorn supplanted the red dragon, representing Wales, as one of the supporters of the English shield, the other being the lion. The animosity that existed between the lion and the unicorn is allegorical for that which once existed between England and Scotland. A battle between the Lion and the Unicorn is an episode in *Through the Looking-Glass* (1872) by Lewis Carroll, and Spenser mentions it in his *Faerie Queene* (1590).

Union Rose. The combined emblematic rose of the houses of York and Lancaster. The petals are white and red: white representing York, and red representing Lancaster.

Unitarian. The name is derived from the belief that God is one single unit in person, as opposed to the doctrine of the TRINITY. The father of English Unitarianism was John Biddle (1615–1662).

United Irishmen. An Irish revolutionary organization founded in 1791 by Theobald Wolfe TONE, committed to the forcible overthrow of English rule in Ireland. Developed in the aftermath of the American and French revolutions, the society adopted an aggressive, belligerent character which paralleled these earlier rejections of tyranny. In its formative years the organization was identified as an essentially middle-class, Protestant faction, but its consistent support of Catholic enfranchisement enlisted many Catholics to its ranks. In 1794 the organization was outlawed and began to function as an underground movement. Increasing suppression resulted in an attempt on the part of the United Irishmen to engage in an alliance with Napoleon, with the purpose of driving the English from Ireland. Negotiations with the French resulted in a disorganized attempt to stage a rebellion in 1798. The rebellion, however, had been anticipated by the English, and,

by the time the French forces arrived to assist the rebels, the uprising had been put down. Wolfe Tone, who later committed suicide in prison, and the other Irish leaders were captured. The rebellion's chief effect lay in hastening the political union of England and Ireland, which occurred in 1800. The United Irishmen continued to function in small isolated groups after the rebellion, but never regained its former effectiveness.

United Nations. An international organization set up after World War II. The foundation for the UN was established during the war when the Allied powers, at various conferences, agreed upon the need for creating "a world family of democratic nations." Its initial meeting in San Francisco in 1945, with representatives of 51 nations present, resulted in the adoption of the UN charter. Within five years the UN had permanent headquarters in New York City, and by 1963 it had more than doubled its original membership, largely as a result of the admission of many newly independent African and Asian countries.

The principal bodies of the UN include the General Assembly, in which each nation has one vote; an 11-member Security Council, in which each of the five permanent members—the U.S., the U.S.S.R., the United Kingdom, France, and Nationalist China—has the veto power; a Secretariat, headed by the Secretary-General, which handles administrative and technical tasks; an Economic and Social Council with various regional commissions; and the International Court of Justice, the chief judicial organ of the UN. In addition, there are several subsidiary organizations, such as the World Health Organization, the Food and Agricultural Organization, and the International Bank for Reconstruction and Development (World Bank).

unities, the. The three dramatic unities: the rules governing the so-called classical drama. They are founded on Renaissance interpretations of passages in Aristotle's *Poetics,* and are hence sometimes styled the Aristotelean unities. Their principles are that in drama there should be (1) unity of action, (2) unity of time, and (3) unity of place. Aristotle lays stress on unity of action, meaning that an organic unity, or a logical connection between the successive incidents is necessary; but unity of time was deduced by Castelvetro, the 16th-century Italian scholar and critic, from the passage in the *Poetics* where Aristotle, in comparing epic poetry and tragedy, says that the former has no limits in time but the latter "endeavors, as far as possible, to confine itself to a single revolution of the sun, or but slightly to exceed this limit." The unity of time thus established, the unity of place followed almost perforce.

The theory of the three unities was formulated in Italy nearly a century before it was taken up in France, where it became, after much argument, the cornerstone of the literary drama. Its first modern offspring was *La Sophonisbe* (1629) by Mairet, though it was not till Corneille's triumph with *Le Cid* (1636) that the convention of the three unities can be said to have been finally adopted. The principle had little success in England, despite the later championship of Dryden (cf. his *Essay on Dramatic Poesy*), Addison (as exemplified in his *Cato*), and others. Ben Jonson's *The Alchemist* (1610) is perhaps the best example of the small class of English plays in which the unities of place and time have been purposely adhered to. In France, on the other hand, the three unities were much more strictly observed, and not until the momentous performance of Victor Hugo's *Hernani* did the old classical theories really give way to those of the modern romantic movement.

University Wits. A name for a group of young English writers of the later years of the 16th century. All had received their training at Oxford or Cambridge and came to London to embark on careers in literature. They were primarily pamphleteers and dramatists; many of them took part in the MARPRELATE CONTROVERSY and contributed to the growth of English satire. As dramatists they developed the Senecan revenge-tragedy, the use of bigger-than-life characters, such as Tamburlaine, the chronicle play, and the romantic comedy. Chief among them was Christopher MARLOWE; others were Robert GREENE, John LYLY, Thomas NASHE, Thomas LODGE, and George PEELE.

Unnamable, The (*L'Innommable*; 1953). A novel by Samuel BECKETT. It is an account, through the technique of stream of consciousness, of the empty existence of the most immobilized of Beckett's characters: he lives legless and armless in a large jar. The novel is linked to MOLLOY and MALONE DIES.

Unofficial Rose, An (1962). A novel by Iris MURDOCH. When an elderly gentleman becomes a widower and tries to return to his former mistress, his action precipitates a general round of "change partners" among his family and friends. His son Randall decides to leave his dull wife Ann, the unofficial or hedge rose of the title, for a more exotic woman. But the comedy and irony of the story are that no one decides anything through the exercise of free will, but is manipulated by circumstances and by other self-interested persons. Randall finds he has merely exchanged one servitude for another, and will probably return to Ann. This comic, philosophic novel qualifies the existentialist idea of freedom expressed in UNDER THE NET.

Unruh, Fritz von (1885–). German playwright and short story writer, a major figure in EXPRESSIONISM. Though an officer in World War I, he became known afterward for his passionate denunciations of war in such plays as *Ein Geschlecht* (*A Clan*, 1918) and *Platz* (*The Square*, 1920). He also attempted to further his democratic and humanistic ideals as a member of the Reichstag, but the rise of Nazism forced him to leave his homeland in 1932. His best-known narrative work is the story *Opfergang* (*The Way of Sacrifice*, written 1916, pub. 1919).

Unter den Linden. A famous avenue of linden trees in Berlin, now destroyed.

Untermeyer, Louis (1885–). American poet and anthologist. Untermeyer is widely known for such anthologies as *Modern American Poetry* (1919), *The Book of Living Verse* (1931), and *New Modern American and British Poetry* (1950). He has published several volumes of his own poetry, including *Burning Bush* (1928) and *Food and Drink* (1932). His superb parodies were reissued in *Collected Parodies* (1926). Among his other works are: *American Poetry Since 1900* (1923); *Moses*, a novel (1928); a

biography of Heine (1937); an autobiography, *From Another World* (1939); and a series of compact biographies, *Makers of the Modern World* (1955).

Unto This Last (1862). A collection of 4 essays by John RUSKIN. Dealing with employment and wages, the essays were originally published successively in 1860 in *Cornhill Magazine,* where they caused such disturbance that they were discontinued by the editor Thackeray. Although at the time Ruskin's ideas were thought to be chimerical, today practically every reform he advocated has been adopted.

Unvanquished, The (1938). A collection of interlocking stories by William FAULKNER. Set during the Civil War, it deals with the Sartoris family, whose modern history Faulkner recounted in SARTORIS. Composed of seven stories, which first appeared separately in magazines, the book centers primarily on the adventures of Bayard Sartoris and his Negro companion, Ringo. Colonel John SARTORIS and Miss Rosa, Bayard's grandmother, also figure prominently.

unwashed. In the phrase, the great unwashed. The first application of the term to the mob has been attributed to Edmund Burke and also to Brougham; perhaps to others, too. Carlyle has "Man has been set against man, Washed against Unwashed." (*French Revolution,* II. ii. 4).

Upanishads. The oldest speculative literature of the Hindus (10th century B.C.), a collection of treatises on the nature of man and the universe, forming part of the Vedic writings. They reveal great subtlety and sophistication, and combine abstract discussion with dialogue and illuminating metaphor. The word itself means "a sitting down (at another's feet)," in order to obtain spiritual truth. The basic Upanishadic contributions are: (1) the idea that the supreme Godhead, because it is completely attributeless, is incommunicable, but "realizable." (2) The individual, personal self (*atman*) is also the universal Self, but is unaware of this. (3) The phenomenal world of appearance exists on the relative plane of the lower truth and appears to be real without being so. (4) Yoga, or physical and spiritual discipline, is necessary for realizing the nature of and achieving the union between *atman* and Brahman.

Updike, John [Hoyer] (1932–). American novelist and poet. Considered one of the most promising of the younger contemporary novelists, Updike writes mainly of the lives of ordinary people in small-town Pennsylvania settings. His first book was a collection of poems, *The Carpentered Hen* (1958). *The Poorhouse Fair* (1959), a novel, was widely acclaimed, as was *Rabbit, Run* (1960). *The Centaur* (1963) was conceived as a kind of sequel to *Rabbit, Run* and deals with a central character who, in direct contrast to "Rabbit," is overburdened with a sense of responsibility and guilt. *The Same Door* (1959) and *Pigeon Feathers* (1962) are collections of short stories. *Telephone Poles and Other Poems* appeared in 1963.

Upelluri. In Hittite mythology, a giant who holds earth and heaven on his shoulders. Like the Greek ATLAS described by Homer, Upelluri carries earth as well as heaven, and stands in the middle of the ocean. Also like Atlas, he is not very intelligent and, consequently, is easily exploited. He was unaware that earth and sky were being piled on his shoulders, and did not notice when the gods separated them with a magic knife. Later, he is equally ignorant of the fact that the stone monster ULLI-KUMMI is standing on his right shoulder and growing to stupendous size.

Upham, Charles Wentworth (1802–1875). American clergyman, public official, historian, and biographer. After graduating from Harvard University, Upham became associate pastor of a Unitarian church. His sermon, *The Scripture Doctrine of Regeneration,* was printed in 1840. He also served in the Massachusetts legislature, was elected to Congress in 1853, and wrote a campaign biography of John C. Frémont. More important was his careful investigation of *Salem Witchcraft* (1867). He was married to Ann Susan Holmes, sister of Oliver Wendell Holmes. Nathaniel Hawthorne, who was removed from a post in the Salem Custom House as a result of Upham's political maneuvering, disliked the man intensely; he is supposed to have modeled the second Judge Pyncheon in *The House of the Seven Gables* on Upham.

Ur. Sumerian city dating from 4000 B.C. In its long history it rose and fell, was destroyed and rebuilt many times. The changing course of the Euphrates River finally robbed it forever of its greatness, leaving it stranded in the desert. Ur was the birth-place of ABRAHAM. The site has been extensively excavated by Sir Leonard Woolley. Among the finds was a small gold statuette of a goat caught in a thorn bush which is reminiscent of the ram sacrificed in place of ISAAC.

Urania. The MUSE of astronomy in Greek mythology, usually represented pointing at a celestial globe with a staff. Milton (*Paradise Lost* vii 1–20) makes her the spirit of the loftiest poetry, and calls her heavenly born (the name means the heavenly one) and sister of Wisdom.

Uranie. A sonnet by the French poet Vincent VOITURE. By many considered the finest sonnet of its day, it figured in the dispute between the *Uraniens* (partisans of Voiture) and the *Jobelins* (partisans of Isaac de BENSERADE).

Uranus (Ouranos). The ancient Greek personification of Heaven; son and husband of GE and father of the TITANS, the CYCLOPES and the Hundred-Handed. He hated his children and confined them in the depths of the earth, but his son Cronus, with the help of Ge, castrated him with a sickle and took his place.

Urbino. A town in the Marches of northern Italy. It became one of the celebrated city states of the Renaissance because of the cultural activities of the dukes of the Montefeltro family, especially Federico. Here Raphael and Bramante were born; painters like Uccello and Piero della Francesca worked in its palace; and Castiglione used its celebrated court as the setting for THE COURTIER.

Urdur, Urdhr, or **Urth.** The earliest and best known of the 3 NORNS of Scandinavian mythology. In the earliest conception, Urdur was the only Norn and her name was often identified with Death or **Hel.** When her two sisters, Skuld and Verthandi, were added, Urdur came to represent the past.

Urfaust (*Ger.,* "Original Faust"). The title generally given to an early, fragmentary version (c. 1775) of Part I of Goethe's FAUST. The manuscript is not Goethe's own but was copied by a young woman from his oral reading to a group of friends.

Urfé, Honoré d' (1568–1625). French writer. He is best known as the author of *L'Astrée* (1607–1627), a vast pastoral romance in prose which enjoyed great popularity and which influenced the development of the pastoral genre.

Uriah the Hittite. See BATHSHEBA.

Uriel. One of the 7 archangels of rabbinical angelology, sent to God to answer the questions of Esdras (II Esd. 4). In Milton's PARADISE LOST, he is "the Regent of the Sun," and "sharpest-sighted spirit of all in heaven." The name means "flame of God," or "angel of light." See ISRAFIL.

Uris, Leon (1924–   ). American novelist. Uris left school at 17 to join the Marines. *Battle Cry* (1953), his first novel, is a long account of the Marines in World War II. *The Angry Hills* (1955) deals with the Palestine Brigade that fought in Greece. *Exodus* (1958) is the story of the Jewish resettlement of Palestine and the creation of the state of Israel. *Mila 18* (1961) deals with the uprising of the Warsaw Ghetto during World War II.

Urizen. In William BLAKE's personal mythology, appearing in his mystical poetry and particularly in THE BOOK OF THEL and THE MARRIAGE OF HEAVEN AND HELL, the figure of Jehovah but, also a symbol of man in bondage. It represents the limiting mental power of reason, an analytical and destructive force which dominates man and against which man must struggle. Urizen is never destroyed, but is periodically regenerated by a union with Los (or the imagination) and Luvah (or passion).

Urquhart or **Urchard, Sir Thomas** (1611–1660). Scottish Royalist and author. He is chiefly known for his free but masterly translation (1653–1693) of the works of Rabelais, which was completed by P. A. Motteux in 1708. It is said that he died of a fit of laughter upon hearing that the throne had been restored to Charles II.

Ursa Major and **Ursa Minor.** See GREAT BEAR.

Urshanabi. A boatman in the Epic of GILGA-MESH. He rows the hero Gilgamesh across the sea of death to the island where lives the sage Utnapishtim.

Urth. See URDUR.

Urvasi. A Hindu heavenly nymph. In Rabindranath Tagore's Bengali poem *Urvasi* (1893), she is transformed from the chief dancing girl of Indra's heaven into a symbol of ideal beauty.

U.S.A. (1938). A trilogy by John Dos PASSOS, consisting of THE 42ND PARALLEL, *1919* (q.v.), and THE BIG MONEY. The novels give a panoramic picture of life in the U.S. in the period just before World War I, the period of the war and the armistice, and the boom era of the 1920's, ending with the first years of the depression. In addition to the life stories of countless characters, told in episodic fashion and narrative style, Dos Passos used three other devices—the "newsreel," the "camera eye," and impressionistic biographies of notable public figures—to create a broad, suggestive view of modern American life.

U.S.A. stresses sociological and economic determinism; greed, exploitation, opportunism, and dishonesty triumph, and the various characters find that they have no control over their lives. The only persons who emerge victorious are those who put aside all scruples and take advantage of the opportunities for material success. American radicals and radical movements also play an important role in the novels, with the more sincere radicals sometimes succeeding in preserving a measure of personal integrity.

Ushant: an Essay (1952). An autobiographical book by Conrad AIKEN. The title comes from the name of an island off the coast of Brittany. Told in the third person, the book mingles personal references with mention of literary associates in a kind of waking dream.

Ussher or **Usher, James** (1581–1656). Irish prelate and scholar. Named archbishop of Armagh and primate of Ireland in 1625, he wrote *Annales Veteris et Novi Testamenti* (1650–1654), a scheme of Biblical chronology. He had a remarkable library and left his books and manuscripts, among them the famous Book of Kells, to Trinity College, Dublin.

Utgard. See JÖTUNHEIM.

Utgard-Loki. In Norse mythology, the chief of the giants living in the infernal regions. Disguised as Skyrmir, he conducted Thor, Thialfi, and Loki to Jötunheim. There Fire, disguised as Logi, ate faster than Loki; Thought, disguised as Hugi, ran faster than Thialfi; Old Age, disguised as Elli, was stronger than Thor. When Utgard-Loki had told Thor about his tricks, he escaped the god's wrath by vanishing.

Uther Pendragon. The father of King ARTHUR, in Geoffrey of Monmouth's HISTORY OF THE KINGS OF BRITAIN (c. 1137), and other versions of the story of Arthur's birth and conception. With the help of Merlin, the magician, he visits IGRAINE in the guise of her husband, and, from that union, Arthur is subsequently born.

utilitarianism. The ethical doctrine that actions are right or good in proportion to their usefulness or as they tend to promote happiness; the doctrine that the end and criterion of public action is "the greatest happiness of the greatest number." John Stuart MILL coined the word *utilitarianism,* but Jeremy BENTHAM, the official founder of the utilitarian school, employed the word utility to signify that doctrine that makes "the happiness of man" the one and only measure of right and wrong.

Utnapishtim. The Babylonian Noah. An ancient sage, living with his wife on an island at the end of the earth, beyond the ocean of death, he tells the hero GILGAMESH the story of a great flood in which he played a role almost identical to that of Noah. With his wife, he was made immortal by the gods. He tells Gilgamesh the secret of a plant that restores youth—a herb that he himself has apparently never tasted, since he is described as very old. He is probably a Babylonian development of the Sumerian ZIUSUDRA.

Utopia (Gr., *ou,* not, *topos,* a place). Nowhere, the name given by Sir Thomas MORE to the imaginary island in his political romance of the same name, written in Latin (1516). Book I of *Utopia* is a dialogue, which presents a perceptive analysis of contemporary social, economic, penal, and moral ills in England; the second book is a narrative describing Utopia, a country run according to the ideals of the English humanists, where poverty, crime, injustice, and other ills do not exist. The classic English translation of *Utopia* is by Ralph Robinson (1551).

The name of this fictitious place, Utopia, has since been applied to all such ideal projections, including

Map of Utopia. From More's *Utopia* (1518).

even those which antedated More's, such as Plato's *Republic.* Others are Francis Bacon's *New Atlantis,* Samuel Butler's *Erewhon,* and several conceived by H. G. Wells, including his *A Modern Utopia* (1905).

In Rabelais' GARGANTUA AND PANTAGRUEL, Pantagruel goes to the kingdom of Utopia to defend its inhabitants, the Amaurotes (*Gr.,* "obscure ones"; the capital of More's Utopia was called city of the Amaurotes) against an invasion of the Dipsodes (*Gr.,* "thirsty ones"). Having followed the itinerary of the Spanish explorers around the Cape of Good Hope, Pantagruel passes several imaginary cities whose names mean "nothing" and "laughable" in Greek before arriving in Utopia. After the defeat of the enemy (see WERWOLF), Pantagruel becomes the leader of a group of Amaurotes who leave over-populated Utopia to settle in the country of the Dipsodes.

Utrillo, Maurice (1883–1955). French painter. Utrillo took his name from the Spanish journalist who adopted him, but he sometimes used his mother's name, Valadon, when signing his work. He began his artistic career in 1903 at a doctor's suggestion, as a possible cure for alcoholism and drug addiction. During the years 1910 to about 1920 he produced paintings at a frenzied rate of speed. The paintings are carefully controlled in technique, but the bleakness of the landscapes, the subdued, melancholy tones of the colors, and the tiny human figures dwarfed by towering buildings reflect the artist's own unhappy struggles. The city is pictured as a lonely, inhuman place roofed by a sullen gray sky. *Notre Dame de Paris, Le Square St. Pierre sous la neige,* and *Sacre Coeur de Montmartre* are among his well-known works. In later years Utrillo's paintings changed in mood and technique. The artist's inner state was reflected less in the work, which became more straightforwardly pictorial and replaced the shifting, subtle grays and whites with brighter, clearer colors.

Utu. The Sumerian sun-god, son of Nanna the moon-god. He is almost identical with the later Babylonian god SHAMASH.

Uz. In the Old Testament, the home of Job, a land east of Palestine (Job 1:1).

Uzziel. One of the principal angels of rabbinical angelology, the name meaning "strength of God." He was next in command to Gabriel and appears in Milton's PARADISE LOST.

V

Vache, Jacques. See André BRETON.

Vachell, Horace Annesley (1861–1955). English novelist. A prolific and popular writer, he is best remembered for his novel *The Hill* (1905), an idealization of boys' school life at Harrow.

vade mecum. A portable manual or handbook. The phrase is Latin and means "go with me."

Vafrino. In Torquato Tasso's GERUSALEMME LIBERATA, the shield-bearer of Tancredi (Tancred). At one point in the tale, he is sent as a spy to the Egyptian camp by Goffredo, Christian commander of the Crusaders. While there he learns, with the help of Erminia, that the infidels plan to send some of their warriors disguised as Crusaders into the battle in order to kill Goffredo. When the news is brought to Goffredo, the plan fails; the rout of the infidel forces produces a final victory.

Vailland, Roger (1907–1965). French novelist and dramatist. Vailland was an ironic iconoclast concerned with the rules according to which the "man of quality" must "play the game." *Playing for Keeps* (*Drôle de Jeu;* 1945) takes place during the Resistance; *The Law* (1957) is set in a southern Italian port. His other works include the novels *Turn of the Wheel* (*Les Mauvais Coups;* 1948) and *The Sovereigns* (*La Fête;* 1960), and the antireligious play *Héloïse et Abélard* (1947).

Vaishnava. Hindus worshiping VISHNU as supreme among the Hindu pantheon. Their sacred books are known as the *Vaishnava Puranas.* Much Hindu devotional literature is the work of Vaishnavite saints, chief among them being Chaitanya of Bengal.

Vaishya. See CASTE.

Vakhtangov, Eugene (1883–1922). Russian actor and director. His theatrical style deviated from the naturalism of the Moscow Art Theatre toward a more theatrical form including grotesque elements.

Valentine. (1) In Shakespeare's TWO GENTLEMEN OF VERONA, one of the titular heroes. He forgives his deceitful friend Proteus, who has caused him to be banished, and wins the hand of Silvia, whose father, the duke of Milan, at last recognizes his virtues.

(2) In Goethe's *Faust* and Gounod's opera of the same name, brother of Margaret.

(3) Heroine of Meyerbeer's opera *The Huguenots* (1836).

Valentine, Jimmy. The burglar hero of O. Henry's short story A RETRIEVED REFORMATION. He also appeared in a play based on this story by Paul Armstrong, *Alias Jimmy Valentine* (1909).

Valentine and Orson. An early French romance first printed in French in 1489, in English about 1550, and the subject of later plays and ballads. Valentine and Orson are the legendary twin sons of BELLISANT and Alexander of Constantinople. Abandoned in the woods in infancy, Orson is carried off and nursed by a bear, while Valentine is found and raised at Pepin's court. Later, Valentine tames Orson and makes a knight of him. A major episode involves PACOLET's rescue of the twins from the giant Ferragus. Valentine marries Clerimond, the giant's sister.

Valera, Eamon de. See DE VALERA.

Valera y Alcalá Galiano, Juan (1824–1905). Spanish novelist, critic, and diplomat. Valera's literary works reflect his urbanity and refinement, qualities that stemmed from his extensive reading and from his distinguished diplomatic career, during which he served as Spanish minister at Lisbon, Washington, and Brussels. His lucid and harmonious style is considered a model of 19th-century Castilian.

His first and best-known novel, *Pepita Jiménez* (1874), resulted from his mystical readings. Written partly in the form of letters, it is a psychological study of the inner struggles of a seminarist who falls in love with an attractive widow and eventually renounces the priesthood. He also wrote *El comendador Mendoza* (1877), *Doña Luz* (1879), and *Juanita la larga* (1895). Among his other works of fiction are the short stories *El pájaro verde* and *Parsondes* (both 1860) and the dialogue *Asclepigenia* (1878). Valera also exerted considerable influence as a critic, though his writings in this field are thought to be marred by excessive politeness.

Valerian. See SECOND NUN'S TALE.

Valéry, [Ambroise] Paul [Toussaint Jules] (1871–1945). French poet and critic. While studying for a law degree, Valéry met Pierre Louÿs and André Gide, and with them began attending (1891) Mallarmé's salons. The poem NARCISSE PARLE reflects the beginning of Valéry's concern with the interior drama of man's conflicting selves. He began an independent course of self-education in science, the arts, and history. *Introduction to the Method of Leonardo da Vinci* (1895) launched the theory that the processes of the creative mind are all analogous, whether the mind be turned toward science or toward any of the arts. It also distinguished between the limitations of real Being and the ideally pure Self, which contemplates reality and becomes conscious of the analogies uniting the essences of all things. In 1896 he wrote the first of the sketches collected as MONSIEUR TESTE, in which the central character represents pure mind or consciousness.

Valéry wrote very little more until 1912, when Gide, Louÿs, and Gaston Gallimard persuaded him to collect and revise the poetry he had written in the 1890's; in thus preparing his *Album de vers anciens* (1920), he again became interested in writing poetry. In 1913 he began LA JEUNE PARQUE, and after 1917 the poems in *Charmes* (1922), including LE CIMETIÈRE MARIN, *La Pythie, Ebauche d'un serpent,* and *Fragments du Narcisse.* All are dramatic monologues in fairly conventional poetic forms, worked and reworked by the poet in an attempt to reach his ideal of "crystal systems" of "pure poetry"; all symbolize some aspect of the tension between rational intellectual control and irrational possession by inspiration or passion, that is, between the freedom of detached contemplation and the surrender to involvement in life.

The dramatic monologue in Valéry's poetry became the dramatic dialogue in his prose. In *Dance and the Soul* (*L'Ame et la Danse;* 1921) Socrates represents the intellectual inquiry of total consciousness, whereas each of the other characters sees only in some limited way the Dancer who symbolizes life. In *Eupalinos, or the Architect* (1923), Socrates concludes that the act of creation is more important than knowing oneself, but regrets that in shaping one's actual life one has to exclude other potential lives. Valéry wrote the libretti for the melodramatic spectacles *Amphion* (1931) and *Semiramis* (1934), for which Arthur Honegger wrote the music, and a *Cantate du Narcisse* (1938). In 1940 he began writing fragments of two theatrical variations on the Faust legend; *Lust* and the ironical *Le Solitaire* were published posthumously as *Mon Faust* (1946).

After Valéry was elected to the French Academy in 1925, he became a public lecturer and administrator of cultural affairs at various times for the Academy, the League of Nations, and several universities. His numerous essays range from artistic and literary criticism to political comment.

Valhalla. The hall of the slain in Scandinavian mythology. The largest palace in Asgard, it has 450 gates so wide that 800 men can enter abreast. Here Odin feasts on mead and boar's meat with the heroes brought from mortal battles by the VALKYRIES. They go out every morning to fight with each other for sport, but their wounds are healed by the time they return for their banquet. See RING DES NIBELUNGEN.

Vali. (1) The guardian of justice in Scandinavian mythology, who was said to have grown to full stature in a day. The second son of Orin, he avenged the death of BALDER by using an arrow to kill his blind murderer, Hoder. Typifying new light after darkness, he was one of the few expected to survive the Twilight of the Gods, for justice was not to be banished from the earth.

(2) This was also an alternate name of the Scandinavian *Lifthrasir* (Desiring Life) who, with her mate, *Lif* (Life, also called *Vidar*), was to repeople the earth after RAGNAROK. Lif slew Fenris at Ragnarok to avenge Odin's death.

Valjean, Jean. See LES MISÉRABLES.

Valkyries, the. The maidens who are the choosers of the slain in Scandinavian mythology. They are the attendants of Odin in VALHALLA, usually 9 or 12 in number, sometimes divine, sometimes mortal princesses who become immortal. Brilliantly adorned, they ride into battle and select of those who are going to be killed the heroes who are worthy of dining with Odin. The Valkyries conduct them to Valhalla and become their cupbearers.

In earlier mythology they are associated with white clouds as maidens who can take the shape of swans. Brunhild is represented as a Valkyrie in the VÖLSUNGA SAGA and Wagner's RING DES NIBELUNGEN.

Valla, Lorenzo (1404–1457). Italian scholar. Born in Rome, he first taught in northern Italian universities, moved to Naples, where he was a secretary of King Alfonso, and then back to Rome as a papal secretary. His textual and historical criticism of ancient documents was one of the fruits of Italian Renaissance scholarship. Now remembered for his proof that the Donation of Constantine was based on a false document, he was equally noted then for his criticism of St. Jerome's version of the New Testament and for his *De linguae latinae elegantia,* which set standards for excellence in Latin. He influenced the thinking of later scholars like Erasmus.

Valle [Rossi], Adriano del (1895–   ). Spanish poet. Known for his beautiful sonnets, he wrote *Primavera portátil* (1934), *Los gozos del río* (1940), and *Arpa fiel* (1942).

Valle-Inclán, Ramón María del (1869–1936). Spanish writer. His most famous work is the four-volume *Sonatas* (1902–1905). This is an account of the adventures of the fictional marqués de Bradomín, in which each volume bears the name of a season in the year and symbolizes the state of love that corresponds to that particular season. Primarily a sensualist, Valle-Inclán was a romantic figure in his day. His other well-known works include the novels *Flor de Santidad* (1904) and *La Lámpara Maravillosa.*

Valley of Decision, The (1902). A novel by Edith WHARTON. Its central character is Duke Odo, who rules a late 18th-century Italian principality and wishes to give his people liberties which they are not ready to receive. By the time public opinion changes, the duke has returned to the conservative views of the class to which he was born, and is accordingly banished from his kingdom. Also woven into the plot is a love story involving Fulvia Vivaldi, daughter of a revolutionary theorist, who gives up the duke when he ascends the throne and is later killed by a bullet meant for him.

Valley of Humiliation. See PILGRIM'S PROGRESS.

Valley of the Moon, The (1913). A novel by Jack LONDON. In the fervor of his faith in socialism, London wrote this story of a strike in a California town, its consequences in the family life of Billy Roberts, a teamster and ex-prizefighter, and his final winning of happiness in the Valley of the Moon in Sonoma County.

Valley of the Shadow of Death. See PILGRIM'S PROGRESS.

Vallon, Annette. A young Frenchwoman with whom William WORDSWORTH had a brief affair while visiting France in 1792. A daughter, Caroline, was born, and Wordsworth corresponded with Annette for a while thereafter. It is believed that the poet returned to France to meet with the mother and child some time in 1802, shortly before his marriage to Mary Hutchinson. The affair was kept secret by the Wordsworth family and was discovered only in the 20th century.

Valmiki. The legendary author of the Hindu epic, the RAMAYANA. He was born a Brahmin, and is supposed to have lived by stealing until set right by Narada, the adviser of the gods. According to one story, he composed the *Ramayana* in a single inspired burst when he saw a hunter's arrow shoot down a mating bird; from *soka* (sorrow) flowed *sloka* (poetry).

Valmouth (1918). A novel by Ronald FIRBANK. Valmouth is Firbank's fantastic English village where Mrs. Yajñavalka provides Eastern massage and cultured conversation, society ladies practice religion and pursue men, and the homosexual hero comes home with a Negro bride. It was adapted into a successful musical comedy in 1958.

Valois. The name of the French royal house (1328–1589) that preceded the Bourbons.

Vamena or **Vamen.** See VISHNU.

vampire. A fabulous being. Supposed to be the ghost of a heretic, excommunicated person, or criminal, it returns to the world at night in the guise of a monstrous bat and sucks the blood of sleeping persons who, usually, become vampires themselves. Probably the most famous of modern vampires is Count Dracula, the hero of the novel *Dracula* by Bram Stoker. First filmed as *Nosferath the Vampire*, later as *Dracula*, this story was the first of a seemingly unending and progressively more dismal series of movies about vampires. The word is applied to one who preys upon his fellows: a "blood sucker." In the early 20th century, *vampire*, or *vamp*, meant a *femme fatale*, a beautiful but heartless woman who lures men to moral destruction.

Vanbrugh, Dame **Irene** (1872–1949). English actress. She married Dion Boucicault. On stage she was associated with Sir Herbert Beerbohm Tree, George Alexander, and others. She played many famous roles and toured extensively.

Vanbrugh, Sir **John** (1664–1726). English dramatist. His plays of the early 18th century mark the end of the Restoration and the beginning of the change from satirical wit to respectability in the English stage. They include *The Relapse* (1697), *The Provoked Wife* (1697), *The Confederacy* (1705), and *The Provoked Husband* (1728). Vanbrugh was also an architect and designed a number of buildings including Blenheim Palace and the Clarendon Building, Oxford.

Van Buren, Martin (1782–1862). Eighth president of the U.S. (1837–1841). The leader of a New York political faction known as the Albany Regency, Van Buren served in the U.S. Senate (1821–1828) and as secretary of state (1829–1831) under Andrew Jackson. Elected to the vice presidency in 1832 as Jackson's running mate, Van Buren defeated William Henry Harrison in the presidential election of 1836, but his popularity declined as a result of the economic distress engendered by the Panic of 1837. In the famous campaign of 1840, the Whigs appealed to the common man by presenting Harrison as a homespun frontier hero content with his log cabin and jug of hard cider while Van Buren was depicted as an aristocrat who dined off gold plate; Harrison won 234 electoral votes to Van Buren's 60. In 1844 the Democrats passed Van Buren over after he declared his opposition to the immediate annexation of Texas. Prominent among the New York BARNBURNERS, he ran unsuccessfully for the presidency as the FREE-SOIL

candidate in 1848, returning to the Democratic fold in 1852.

Vancouver, George (1758?–1798). English explorer. An associate of James COOK. He explored the Pacific coast of North America; the city of Vancouver in British Columbia was named in his honor. He wrote the *Voyage of Discovery to the North Pacific Ocean, and Round the World* (3 vols., 1798).

Vanderbilt, Cornelius (1794–1877). American financier, steamship and railroad executive. Vanderbilt operated steamship lines on the Hudson and Long Island Sound; he organized lines to California during the gold rush, and then to Europe. He made great sums of money by cutting rates until his competitors were forced out of business or into joining him; he also contributed toward the speed and comfort of travel. With his son, **William H. Vanderbilt** (1821–1885), he was largely responsible for the organization of the New York Central Railroad system. The Vanderbilts endowed Vanderbilt University and contributed to the New York College of Physicians and Surgeons and to the Metropolitan Museum of Art. **Cornelius Vanderbilt III** (1873–1942) was an inventor who patented devices for the improvement of locomotives and freight cars. His son, **Cornelius Vanderbilt Jr.** (1898–), a journalist, has published several books including *Experiences of a Washington Correspondent* (1924) and *The Living Past of America* (1955).

Van der Post, Laurens (1906–). South African writer and novelist. His striking travel books are *Venture to the Interior* (1951) and *The Lost World of the Kalahari* (1958), an account of a search for the vanishing Bushmen. Among his novels are *Flamingo Feather* (1955) and *The Heart of the Hunter* (1961).

Van Doren, Carl [Clinton] (1885–1950). American editor, critic, and writer. The brother of Mark Van Doren, he served on the Columbia University faculty from 1911 to 1930, and was headmaster of the Brearley School from 1916 to 1918. He acted as managing editor of the *Cambridge History of American Literature* (3 vols., 1917, 1918, 1921); literary editor of *The Nation* (1919–1922); editor for the *Literary Guild* and the *Living Library;* and a member of the committee on management of the *Dictionary of American Biography* (1926–1936). Van Doren helped to give the study of American literature a systematic place in university curricula; his biography of *Benjamin Franklin* (1938) won a Pulitzer Prize. Van Doren's special interest was American history of the late 18th century, his subject in *The Great Rehearsal* (1948). Other volumes include *The Life of Thomas Love Peacock* (1911), *The American Novel* (1921; rev., 1940), *Contemporary Novelists* (1922), *Sinclair Lewis* (1933), *What is American Literature?* (1935), *Jane Mecom, The Favorite Sister of Benjamin Franklin* (1950), and his autobiography, *Three Worlds* (1936).

Van Doren, Mark (1894–). American poet, critic, novelist, short-story writer, and editor. Mark Van Doren served as literary editor and film critic for *The Nation* during the 1920's; he also taught at Columbia University. A versatile man, he has written biographies and critical works, among them *Henry David Thoreau* (1916), *The Poetry of John Dryden* (1931) *Shakespeare* (1939), and *Nathaniel Haw-*

thorne (1949). His books of poetry include *Spring Thunder and Other Poems* (1924), *A Winter Diary and Other Poems* (1935), *The Mayfield Deer* (1941), *Spring Birth* (1953), and *Morning Worship and Other Poems* (1960). *Tilda* (1943) is a novel, and *Last Days of Lincoln* (1959) a play. Other works include *Nobody Say a Word, and Other Stories* (1953) and *Autobiography* (1958).

Van Druten, John [William] (1901–1957). English playwright; he later became an American citizen. His works include *Young Woodley* (1928); *Leave Her to Heaven* (1940); *The Voice of the Turtle* (1944); I REMEMBER MAMA; BELL, BOOK AND CANDLE; and *I Am a Camera* (a dramatization of Christopher Isherwood's *Berlin Stories;* 1952).

Van Dyck or **Vandyke**, Sir **Anthony** (1599–1641). Flemish painter. He studied briefly under Peter Paul Rubens and then came under the influence of Titian in Italy (1621–1626). He settled in England in 1632, becoming court painter to Charles I, whose likeness he transmitted to posterity in numerous portraits. He was knighted the same year and his name Anglicized to Vandyke. Although he painted some biblical and historical scenes, he is best known as a portrait painter, particularly of full-length courtly figures. The freedom of his drawing, the elegance and ease of his work, and the brilliance of his representation of rich fabrics exerted a tremendous influence on English art, as is evidenced in the work of the great portraitists of the 18th century.

Vane, Sir **Henry** (1613–1662). English governor of Massachusetts (1636–1637), who took the side of Anne Hutchinson when the Bay colony was divided upon her case. He returned to England and sat on the council of state although he did not take part in the execution of Charles I. A moderate Puritan and friend of Oliver Cromwell, Vane appears in Hawthorne's story *Howe's Masquerade* (1837).

Vane, Sutton (1888–1963). English playwright. His only major work is *Outward Bound* (pub. 1923) written when he was 26. It is an arresting work dealing with experiences beyond death. A small, diverse group of passengers on an otherwise deserted ship discover that they are dead and on the ship on its way to heaven and hell—"it's the same place." The work was a success in London and New York. It was revived in 1939 and has been filmed twice.

Van Eyck, Hubert and **Jan.** See Hubert van and Jan van EYCK.

Van Gogh, Vincent (1853–1890). Dutch painter. With Seurat, Cézanne, and Gauguin, Van Gogh is usually grouped as a postimpressionist. The emphasis laid by impressionism upon the recording of visual impressions seemed inadequate to him; he discovered his reality in the emotional responses of the individual self to the external world. A new definition of the reality that belonged upon the painter's canvas required a new technique. Although the impetus for Van Gogh's work—a love for all living things—never changed, he did undergo an evolution in artistic technique. His early paintings, such as the *Potato Eaters,* are sober, realistic portraits of life and landscape in his native Holland, painted in dark, grim colors with careful attention to detail. During the brief but productive period that he spent in Provence in the south of France (1888–1890), Van Gogh created canvases that recorded in violent, vi-

brant colors his emotional responses to nature and to human beings. Daring experiments with pigmentation and the use of bold, slashing brush strokes add to the vigor of the work. In the final paintings, such as *Cypress Road* or *Starry Night,* Van Gogh foreshadows the expressionist movement. The reality these paintings portray is an internal landscape; the images from the external world give concrete form to an inner state. In mood, too, the last paintings are different: lyricism is replaced by a dark brooding melancholy, and in such a work as *Cornfield with Black Crows* Van Gogh expresses a fearful vision of the world his suffering has led him to see. After spending some months in a mental institution, the painter took his own life in 1890 at the age of 37. His *Complete Letters* (3 vols., 1959), many of which are written to his loyal brother Theo, offer valuable insights into both the man and his work. Throughout his career Van Gogh produced numerous self-portraits; they offer a key not only to his artistic but also to his spiritual development, culminating in the ravaged faces and luridly bright colors of the portraits completed shortly before his death.

Vanini, Giulio Cesare Lucilio (1585–1619). Italian philosopher and physician. Vanini's interest in astrology, magic, and the occult, as well as in the more standard philosophy of Aristotle, made him an unwelcome visitor to both the Catholic and Protestant camps. He met a tragic end at Toulouse, where his suspected atheism and heresy caused him to be burned at the stake. His main works, the *Amphitheatrum* (1615) and *De admirandis . . . arcanis* (1617, *On the Admirable Secrets of Nature*), show him to have been in actuality an Averroist (see AVERROES) and pantheist.

Vanir. The Norse nature gods, once at war with the AESIR. After an exchange of hostages, the two races of gods made peace, and the Vanir were received in Asgard. Njord, the water god, was the chief; his son was Frey, his daughter Freya, and his wife Skadi. Noatun was their home.

Vanity Fair. In Bunyan's PILGRIM'S PROGRESS, a fair established by Beelzebub, Apollyon, and Legion in the town of Vanity and lasting all year round. Here are sold houses, lands, honors, preferments, titles, countries, kingdoms, and all sort of worldly pleasures.

Vanity Fair, a Novel without a Hero (1848). A novel by William Makepeace THACKERAY. The author said of the novel while he was writing it: "What I want to make is a set of people living without God in the world (only that is a cant phrase), greedy, pompous men, perfectly self-satisfied for the most part, and at ease about their superior virtue. Dobbin and poor Briggs are the only two people with real humility as yet. Amelia's is to come."

The two boarding-school friends, Amelia Sedley and Becky SHARP, are in marked contrast throughout the novel. Becky Sharp, clever, scheming, determined to get on in the world, first plays her cards to win Amelia's rich and stupid brother, Joseph Sedley. Failing that, she secretly marries Rawdon CRAWLEY, a younger son of Sir Pitt Crawley, at whose house Becky is governess. Rawdon, however, is disinherited, but the undaunted Becky manages to live at the height of fashion on a small income with the help of Lord Steyne. Rawdon finally becomes suspicious of his wife's relations with Steyne, and, when at last he discovers the truth, he departs to become the governor of Coventry Island, leaving his son by Becky to the care of his brother Pitt. This causes Becky to be completely ostracized, and she is forced to live by her wits on the Continent.

Meantime Amelia, loved by George Osborne and William Dobbin, has married the former, but he is killed in the battle of Waterloo. Because of her poverty, Amelia is forced to give her son, Georgy, into the care of his grandfather, Mr. Osborne, who will, however, have nothing to do with her. On Mr. Osborne's death, Georgy is left a fortune. Amelia and her brother, traveling on the continent, now meet Becky Sharp, and the latter gradually regains her old influence over Joseph Sedley. The faithful Dobbin, who has loved Amelia through thick and thin, is at last rewarded with her hand.

Van Loon, Hendrik Willem (1882–1944). Dutch-born American journalist and historian. A history teacher at several American universities, Van Loon wrote *The Fall of the Dutch Republic* (1913) and *The Rise of the Dutch Kingdom* (1915), both works of scholarship. He became assistant editor of the Baltimore *Sun* (1924) and was a distinguished radio commentator. He wrote children's books and edited several songbooks. He is best known, however, for his popularized surveys, enlivened with his own drawings: *Ancient Man* (1920), *The Story of Mankind* (1921), *The Story of the Bible* (1923), *Ships and How They Sailed the Seven Seas* (1935), *Van Loon's Lives* (1942), and many others.

Van Rensselaer, Kiliaen (1585?–1644). Dutch diamond merchant, who helped found the Dutch West India Co. (1621). Through an agent he bought from the Indians in America large tracts of land, which are at present the counties of Albany, Columbia, and Rensselaer, N.Y. His descendants in America constitute one of the oldest American families.

Van Tuyll, Isabella. See ZÉLIDE.

Van Twiller, Wouter or **Walter** (1580?–?1656). Dutch governor of New Netherland (1633–1637), succeeding Peter Minuit. He was a nephew of Kiliaen Van Rensselaer. He is satirized in Washington Irving's *History of New York* (1809) as "Walter the Doubter."

Van Vechten, Carl (1880–1964). American critic and novelist. He is known for his witty, satirical, and sophisticated novels of life among New Yorkers in the 1920's. *Peter Whiffle* (1922), his first novel, is an imaginary autobiography of a dilettante. *The Blind Bow-Boy* (1923) is a novel about homosexuality. *The Tattooed Countess* (1924) deals with fin-de-siècle Iowa. Van Vechten's best novel is NIGGER HEAVEN, a book about Harlem. He also wrote five books of music criticism, of which *Interpreters and Interpretations* (1917) is best known. His own *Sacred and Profane Memories* (1932) is a volume of autobiographical essays.

Vanzetti, Bartolomeo. See SACCO-VANZETTI CASE.

Varaha. See VISHNU.

Varchi, Benedetto (1503–1565). Florentine historian. He wrote a history of his native city and a treatise on language, the *Ercolano*. Posterity is indebted to him primarily because of his good sense in refusing the request of Cellini that he revise the style of the celebrated autobiography.

Varenne, Albéric. See Jacques LAURENT.

Varner, Eula. A rural Helen of Troy in William Faulkner's trilogy beginning with THE HAMLET. A mindlessly voluptuous woman married to the impotent Flem Snopes, she is beloved of nearly every man in the town of Jefferson and is the mistress of Manfred De Spain. Ultimately, however, she has the courage to commit suicide in order to save her daughter Linda from the shame of scandal over her mother.

Varro, Marcus Terentius (116–27 B.C.). Roman scholar, called by Quintilian "the most learned of the Romans." He arranged the library in Rome at the direction of Julius Caesar, and was appointed superintendent of another library by Augustus. He was the first Roman to attempt a thorough critical study of the Latin language. His *De Lingua Latina* was for many centuries the fundamental reference book for Latin grammarians. His treatise on agriculture, *De Agricultura*, was used by Vergil as a source of his four-book poem, the *Georgics*.

Varuna. In the early Hindu mythology of the Rig Veda, the lord of the universe; with Indra the greatest of the gods of the Vedic times (4000 B.C.). He is invoked as the night sky and his double, Mitra, as the day sky. In the later Vedic period his power is more and more confined to this one aspect of nature. In this post-Vedic period, however, he becomes the Hindu Neptune, represented as an old man riding a sea monster with a club in one hand and a rope in the other.

Vasari, Giorgio (1511–1574). Italian Renaissance painter, architect, and critic. Vasari is the author of the collection *Vite de' più eccellenti pittori, scultori e architettori* (*Lives of the Most Eminent Painters, Sculptors, and Architects*, 1550). The enlarged version of this work (1568) contained a total of 200 biographies. The longest of Vasari's lives is the selection devoted to Michelangelo, his favorite. Vasari's conception of a rebirth of the fine arts helped to shape the Renaissance itself.

Vasconcelos, José (1882–1959). Mexican educator, philosopher, and writer. Trained as a lawyer and a leading member of the intellectual group known as the *Ateneo de la Juventud*, Vasconcelos took an active part in the revolutionary movements that swept Mexico after 1910. As minister of education under President Alvaro Obregón, he initiated an outstanding program of mass education, especially in rural areas, that reflected his own passion for enlightenment. In 1929 he ran for the presidency, denouncing the corruption and militarism that infected Mexican politics; after winning only a small number of votes, he left the country, charging fraud. He was permitted to return in 1939.

During his years of exile, he wrote several works, notably *Etica* (1932) and *Estética* (1936), expounding his philosophical system, which was strongly influenced by Schopenhauer. At the same time he produced what may be his most enduring work—an impassioned, often bitter, autobiography consisting of five volumes: *Ulises criollo* (1935), *La tormenta* (1936), *El desastre* (1938), *El proconsulado* (1939), and *La flama* (1959). In these books, which reflect his increasingly conservative views and his conversion to Catholicism, he extolled Mexico's Hispanic tradition and fulminated against the U.S. Among his many other works are *Prometeo vencedor* (1920), a drama, and *La raza cósmica* (1925), in which he predicted the appearance of a new "cosmic race" of human beings in Latin America.

Vashti. In the Old Testament, the proud queen of King Ahasuerus before the days of Esther. Merry with wine, the king commanded his chamberlains to bring Vashti into the banquet hall to show the guests her beauty; when she refused to obey the insulting order, the angered king divorced her (Esther 1:10–19).

Vásquez de Coronado, Francisco. See Francisco Vásquez de CORONADO.

Vathek, an Arabian Tale (1786). A GOTHIC NOVEL by William BECKFORD. Vathek, the ninth caliph of the Abbasside dynasty is a haughty, effeminate monarch, induced by his sorceress mother, the Greek Carathis, and by his own curiosity and egotism to offer allegiance to Eblis, the Devil, in the hope of obtaining the throne of the pre-Adamite sultans. This he gains, only to find that it is a place of torture and that he is doomed to remain in it forever. In the final scene the hearts of the newly damned are set aflame with infernal fire.

This story of how the sadistic young caliph sold his soul to the devil is a notable contribution to the literature of horror that also includes *The Monk* by Matthew Lewis. Beckford's Orientalism is largely derived from the *Arabian Nights*.

Vatican City. A city-state enclave in Rome, Italy. It is the center of the Roman Catholic Church and is ruled by the pope. The Vatican City contains the basilica of St. Peter, the offices of the Papal See, and the Vatican Palace, the residence of the pope which also houses the famous papal libraries and museums.

This tiny state (108.7 acres) was established by the Lateran Treaty with Italy (1929). From late classical times the Roman Catholic Church had acquired vast amounts of land throughout Italy; the entire city of Rome was part of the papal states. In 1870, when Italy became a united nation under Victor Emmanuel II, the nation absorbed all the church lands and made Rome its capital city. The dispute over these confiscated lands became known as "the Roman Question." It was finally settled by Benito Mussolini and Pope Pius XI with the signing of the Lateran Treaty.

The Vatican City is a fully independent state. It has its own civil government under the direction of an appointed governor; it exchanges diplomats with other governments and has its own postal service.

Vatican Swindle, The. See LAFCADIO'S ADVENTURES.

Vatsyayan, S. H. (1913–). Indian poet and novelist in Hindu. Writing under the pen name *Agyeya* (Unknown), he has published over 25 volumes, including *Nadi ke Dvip* and *Shekhar*, an autobiographical novel.

vaudeville. A light entertainment consisting of a succession of acts, also called variety. The name comes from Vau-de-Vire (in Normandy, France) where the kind of song originally designated as "vaudeville" was common. In 1865, when Tony Pastor opened his Opera House in New York, he introduced this kind of entertainment, which was taken up later by the Keiths. A system of continuous vaudeville began in 1885, running two shows a day, from 11 a.m. to 11 p.m. Some famous vaudeville producers were Oscar Hammerstein, Alexander Pantages, and Marcus Loew. The Palace Theater in New York was formerly the principal home of vaudeville. Sarah Bernhardt and many lesser stars played in vaudeville.

Vaugelas, sieur de. Claude Favre (1585–1650). French grammarian. An original member of the ACADÉMIE FRANÇAISE, Vaugelas sought in *Remarques sur la langue française* (*Remarks on the French Language,* 1647) to formulate principles of correct French writing and speech based upon the example of the best writers and court speakers of his day. While he had no intention of fixing the French language in perpetuity, he had a lasting influence on the Académie's approach to linguistic reform.

Vaughan, Henry (1622–1695). Welsh-born English poet. Vaughan is often called "the Silurist" because he was born in South Wales, whose inhabitants were known as Silures in ancient times. One of the last of the METAPHYSICAL POETS, he wrote two volumes of secular verse, *Poems* (1646) and *Olor Iscanus* (1651), before turning to religious poetry. As he later explained, "The first that with any effective success attempted a diversion of this foul and overflowing stream (of secular verse) was the blessed man, Mr. George Herbert, whose holy life and verse gained many pious converts, of whom I am the least." His best-known work is *Silex Scintillans* (1650–1655), which includes *The Retreat, The World,* and *They Are All Gone into the World of Light.* His poetry is characterized by a mystical view of nature and is believed to have exerted considerable influence on Wordsworth.

Vaughan, Hilda (1892–). Welsh novelist. Married to the novelist Charles MORGAN, she is the author of *Her Father's House* (1930), *Pardon and Peace* (1943), and other novels of Welsh life.

Vaughan Williams, Ralph (1872–1958). English composer. His music displays an English character consciously derived from the English folk and classical tradition. This quality is evident in the operas *Hugh the Drover* (1911; libretto by H. Child) and *The Pilgrim's Progress* (1949; libretto by the composer), and many other works such as *A London Symphony* (1914; revised 1920).

Vauthier, Jean (1910–). French dramatist. His plays—*Le Capitaine Bada* (1952), *La Nouvelle mandragore* (1952), *Le Personnage combattant* (1955), and *Le rêveur* (1960)—use words almost like musical notes.

Vautrin. See Jacques COLLIN.

Vauvenargues, marquis de. Luc de Clapiers (1715–1747). French moralist and one-time army officer. Illness and battle wounds prevented him from realizing his ambitions in diplomacy and he was forced to live in poverty in Paris. An admirable man in every respect, he counted Marmontel and Voltaire among his few friends. In his *Introduction à la connaissance de l'esprit humain, suivie de réflexions et maximes* (1746), a rather summary personal discussion of ethics followed by some 600 maxims, he prefigures Rousseau in his belief in man's capacity for goodness, and in the human heart and passions. He has also left numerous smaller moralistic works, including some literary portraits.

Vaux, Thomas, 2nd baron **Vaux of Harrowden** (1510–1556). English poet and statesman, a prominent courtier of Henry VIII. He contributed lyrics to TOTTEL'S MISCELLANY and other collections.

Ve. The brother of Odin and Vili in Scandinavian mythology. He was one of the three deities who took part in the creation of the world, his role being to give the senses to the first man and woman, Ask and Ember. He, Odin, and Vili slew Ymir and drowned the whole race of the frost giants in his blood.

Veal, Mrs. The subject of *The True Relation of the Apparition of One Mrs. Veal* (1706), a convincing circumstantial report of a current ghost-story by Daniel DEFOE. Mrs. Veal, an imaginary person, is supposed to have returned from the dead on September 8, 1705, when she appeared to one Mrs. Bargrave of Canterbury. There were two accounts of the extraordinary affair prior to Defoe's; his continued to be popular throughout the century as an appendix to Drelincourt's *Consolations against the Fears of Death.*

Veblen, Thorstein [Bunde] (1857–1929). American economist and social philosopher, known for his trenchant criticism of 19th-century capitalism. Born in Wisconsin of Norwegian immigrant parents, Veblen studied at Carleton College, Johns Hopkins, and Yale (Ph.D., 1884) and taught at the Universities of Chicago and Missouri. His first published book, THE THEORY OF THE LEISURE CLASS, became an American classic in economics and sociology. He also wrote *The Theory of Business Enterprise* (1904), *The Instinct of Workmanship* (1914), and *The Vested Interests and the State of the Industrial Arts* (1919).

Vedas (*Sans.*, "knowledge"). The 4 sacred books of the Hindus: the *Rig Veda*, the *Yajur Veda*, the *Sama Veda*, and the *Atharva Veda*. They were composed around 2500 B.C. The first consists of prayers and hymns in verse, the second of prayers in prose, the third of prayers for chanting, and the fourth of formulas for consecration, imprecation, expiation, etc. See UPANISHADS.

Vega, Garcilaso de la. See GARCILASO DE LA VEGA.

Vega [Carpio], Lope [Félix] de (1562–1635). Spanish dramatist and poet, considered the greatest figure in Spanish literature after Cervantes. The world's most prolific playwright, he is also known as *El Fénix de los Ingenios* and *Monstruo de la Naturaleza* ("Prodigy of Nature"), the latter a name given to him by Cervantes. His reputation was such that the phrase "Es de Lope" became a synonym for perfection. According to his contemporary biographer Montalbán, he wrote about 1800 *comedias,* or plays, 400 AUTOS SACRAMENTALES, and many short sketches, interludes, and simple compositions accompanied by songs, which were woven into many of his plays. Four hundred twenty-six *comedias* and 42 *autos* have survived.

Virtually alone, Lope created the Spanish national drama, blending the most effective elements of earlier times. He elaborated some of his essential ideas in *El arte nuevo de hacer comedias* (*The New Art of Writing Plays,* 1609), a poetical essay in which he gave the rules for a new kind of play (*comedia nueva*) whose principal characteristics were violation of the unities, division of the play into three acts with the *dénouement* beginning about the middle of the last act, and the use of a variety of metrical forms in each play.

Lope's restless sensibility and ever-changing and contradictory personality made him understand the Spanish people, especially the masses, better than any other playwright. His works reflect his violent character and tumultuous existence, crowded with love affairs, elopements, abductions, and several marriages; his religious intolerance; and his profound love for his family. Even when he took holy orders (1614) after a religious crisis, he did not curtail his profane writing or his amorous proclivities.

Lope's plays, like those of Shakespeare, reveal him as a writer of artistic integrity as well as an ingenious craftsman who utilized dramatic themes and devices that would appeal to a mass audience. He knew that the people would applaud a play like *El niño inocente de la Guardia* because of its anti-Semitic theme, just as they would like *El remedio en la desdicha* and *Pedro Carbonero,* in which Moors are portrayed sympathetically, in accordance with popular sentiment.

Lope's characters are not given to reflection, unlike those of Calderón's more intellectual dramas. Instead, his personages are spontaneous, paradoxical, and unreasonable; accordingly, they are more engaging than Calderón's. It is difficult, in many of Lope's plays, to find a single central character. Sometimes there are two or three, a nobleman and common people, as in *El caballero de Olmedo;* sometimes the people themselves constitute the protagonist, as in FUENTEOVEJUNA.

Lope's most important and representative works are his historical plays based on national events, such as FUENTEOVEJUNA, PERIBÁÑEZ, and EL MEJOR ALCALDE, EL REY. In these three plays, the common people and the king are arrayed against a corrupt feudal nobility. Other well-known historical dramas are *El caballero de Olmedo, Porfía hasta morir, Las grandezas de Alejandro,* and *Roma abrasada.* He also wrote numerous heroic plays based on Spanish legends and chronicles, such as *El último godo,* dealing with Rodrigo, the last Visigothic king of Spain; *Las mocedades de Bernardo del Carpio; Las almenas de Toro,* about El Cid; and *El bastardo Mudarra,* about the legend of the seven *infantes* of LARA.

Among his COMEDIAS DE CAPA Y ESPADA, or cloak-and-sword plays, are *El acero de Madrid, Los melindres de Belisa, El perro del hortelano,* and *La moza del cántaro.*

His religious plays include *El vaso de elección, Barlaam y Josofat, El divino africano,* and *El serafín humano.* Among his *autos* are *El auto de los cantares, La siega, La locura por la honra,* and *El hijo pródigo.*

Although Lope is remembered chiefly for his plays, he also essayed other types of literature. LA DOROTEA, a long prose romance, is his best nondramatic work. His other prose works include *La Arcadia* (1598), a pastoral romance in which Lope appears as Belardo and the duke of Alba as Anfriso, and *El peregrino en su patria* (1604). His finest lyrics are collected in *Rimas sacras* (1614) and *Rimas humanas y divinas* (1634). He also wrote narrative poetry: the historical epics JERUSALÉN CONQUISTADA, *La Dragontea* (1598), which is directed against England and Sir Francis Drake, and *Corona trágica* (1627), about Mary Stuart; the romantic epic *La hermosura de Angélica* (1602), a sequel to Ariosto's *Orlando Furioso;* and the burlesque epic GATOMAQUIA. *Los pastores de Belén* (1612) is a prose-and-verse improvisation about the Holy Family. See GRACIOSO.

Veiller, Bayard (1869–1943). American playwright. He is noted for his mystery dramas. *Within the Law* (1912) deals with a young girl, railroaded to prison, who gets revenge on her accuser by a clever blackmail "within the law." He is also the author of two other popular plays: *The Thirteenth Chair* (1916), in which a medium catches a murderer, and *The Trial of Mary Dugan* (1927), which includes a meticulously arranged courtroom scene.

Veit, Dorothea (1763–1839). German novelist, daughter of Moses Mendelssohn. After divorcing her first husband, she became Friedrich Schlegel's mistress (1797) and married him in 1804. Their love is recorded in Schlegel's novel *Lucinde* (1799). In 1808 both she and Schlegel converted to Catholicism. She wrote a novel entitled *Florentin* (1801).

Velázquez, Diego Rodríguez de Silva y (1599–1660). Spanish painter. His early pictures represent common people with Caravaggiesque naturalism. In 1623, he became court painter to Philip IV, whom he continued to serve all his life, doing portraits and paintings among which *The Surrender of Breda* (1634) and *The Maids of Honor* (*Las Meninas*, 1656), both in the Prado, are among the most celebrated. Velázquez is renowned for his objectivity and for the dignity and reserve of his portraits. A sensitive observer of reality, he represented surface textures with a sketchy touch that is more suggestive than imitative, and revealed in his work a sure sense of color, creating both delicate and varied harmonies of tone.

Vélez de Guevara, Luis (1579–1644). Spanish dramatist and novelist. Born in Ecija, Vélez de Guevara was a page in the household of the archbishop of Seville and fought in Italy and Africa. Although he later won the favor of Philip IV, who appointed him usher of the king's chamber in 1625, he teetered continually on the brink of penury. His reputation for wit and merriment was such that Cervantes dubbed him *Quitapesares* ("Dispeller of cares").

He is said to have written some 400 plays, only 80 of which have survived, most of them dealing with historical subjects. The best known of these is *Más pesa el rey que la sangre,* dealing with Guzmán el Bueno, who placed loyalty to his king above love for his son. In *Reinar después de morir* he retold the legend of Inés de Castro, a Spanish *infanta* married to a Portuguese prince. She was murdered by conspirators and when the bereaved husband became king, he exhumed her body and crowned her in death.

The finest work by Vélez de Guevara is probably the satirical novel *El diablo cojuelo* (1641), which describes the adventures of Cleofás Leandro Pedro Zambullo, a student who releases a "limping devil" from a bottle in which he had been confined by a magician. To repay the kindness, the devil takes Cleofás on an aerial tour of Spain; he makes the roofs transparent, revealing the vices and follies of the citizens and offering a splendid framework for the author's witty commentary. The novel achieved great popularity in Europe as a result of Lesage's French imitation, *Le Diable Boiteux* (1707).

Vendages de suresne, les. See Pierre DU RYER.

vendetta. A blood feud of the kind originating in Sicily, Sardinia and especially in Corsica in the eighteenth century. "Feuding" among the mountaineers of Kentucky in the United States is a form of vendetta.

Veneering, Mr. and **Mrs.** A newly rich couple in Charles Dickens' OUR MUTUAL FRIEND. They live in a brand-new house with brand-new servants and shiny furniture, new just like that of their new friends. *The Veneerings* (1922) by Sir Harry Johnston is a novel in which these people are characters.

Venetian Glass Nephew, The (1925). A novel by Elinor WYLIE. This fantasy tells how Rosalba, a woman of flesh and blood, falls in love with and marries Virginio, who is made of glass. To harmonize herself and her husband she is willingly transmogrified by fire into porcelain.

Venice Preserved, or A Plot Discovered (1682). A tragedy in blank verse by Thomas OTWAY. Jaffeir, a Venetian gentleman now in reduced circumstances, has married Belvidera, daughter of the senator Priuli, who retaliates by disowning her. Jaffcir's friend Pierre persuades him to join a conspiracy to overthrow the Venetian government. After Renault, another of the conspirators, makes advances to Belvidera, Jaffeir reveals the plot to her and, at her urging, warns the senate. Although the senators promise to pardon Jaffeir and his fellow-conspirators, they are condemned to death. At the scaffold Jaffeir stabs Pierre to save him from an ignoble death and then kills himself. Belvidera, who has gone mad, also dies. Among the actresses well known for their interpretation of Belvidera were Elizabeth Barr, who created the role and with whom Otway was hopelessly in love, and Sarah Siddons.

It is believed that in the character of the foolish old senator Antonio, Otway was satirizing the earl of Shaftesbury.

Veni, Creator Spiritus (*Lat.,* "Come, Creator Spirit"). Medieval Latin hymn in honor of the Holy Ghost, author unknown. It was set by Mahler as the first movement of his *Symphony of a Thousand.*

veni, vidi, vici (*Lat.,* "I came, I saw, I conquered"). The words with which, according to Plutarch, Julius Caesar announced to his friend Amintius his victory at Zela (47 B.C.), in Asia Minor, over Pharnaces, son of Mithridates, who had rendered aid to Pompey. Suetonius, however, says that the words were displayed before his title after his victories in Pontus, and does not ascribe them to Caesar himself.

Venizelos, Eleutherios (1864–1936). A Greek statesman. He forced the abdication of King Constantine (1917) and brought Greece into World War I on the side of the Allies. He took part in the Peace Conference at Paris (1919), advocated a republic in Greece, was several times premier, and finally (1935), having opposed the government, was forced into exile. King George II, after his return to the throne (1935), granted him an amnesty.

Venus. In Roman mythology, the goddess of beauty and love. Originally of minor importance, she became, through identification with the Greek APHRODITE, one of the major characters in classical myth. She was the mother, by Anchises, of Aeneas.

In Camoëns' epic poem *The Lusiad* (1572), Uranian Venus is the impersonation of divine love and the presiding deity of the Lusians. The Isle of Venus is a paradise created for the Lusian heroes. Here Uranian Venus gives Vasco da Gama the empire of the sea.

In Wagner's opera *Tannhäuser* (1859), Venus is goddess of love and illicit delights, and entertains the hero in her magic grotto beneath the Venusberg.

Venus and Adonis (1593). A long poem by William SHAKESPEARE.

Venusberg. In German legend, a magic land of pleasure where Venus keeps her court. See TANN-HÄUSER. William Morris modernizes the setting in his poem *The Hill of Venus*, included in THE EARTHLY PARADISE.

verbatim et literatim (*Lat.*). Accurately rendered: word for word and letter for letter.

Vercel, Roger. Pen name of **Roger Auguste Crétin** (1894–1957). French novelist. He is best known for his psychological studies of the seafarers of Brittany and their families, such as *Captain Conan* (1934), *Northern Lights* (*L'Aurore boréale;* 1947), and *Ride Out the Storm* (*La Fosse aux vents;* 1949–1951).

Vercelli Book (Codex Vercellensis, 11th century? discovered 1822). A collection of manuscripts in Old English. It includes prose sermons and the poems *Andreas, Address of the Soul to the Body, Falseness of Men,* THE DREAM OF THE ROOD, and CYNEWULF's *The Fates of the Apostles* and *Elene.*

Vercors. Pen name of **Jean [Marcel] Bruller** (1902–). French novelist and essayist, founder of *Les Editions de Minuit* as a clandestine publishing house during the Resistance. The short novels *Put Out the Light* (*Le Silence de la mer;* 1942) and *Guiding Star* (*La Marche à l'étoile;* 1943) dramatically implied the need for intellectual resistance during the Occupation. His later works include satirical fables of modern man, such as *You Shall Know Them* (*Les Animaux dénaturés;* 1952) and *Sylva* (1961).

Verdad sospechosa, La (The Truth Suspected, c. 1619). A comedy by Juan Ruiz de ALARCÓN. The hero is Don García, a handsome young aristocrat who is an inveterate liar. Because of this flaw, he ends by losing the woman he loves. This play was the model for Corneille's *Menteur* (1643)

Verdi, Giuseppe (1813–1901). The most important Italian opera composer of the 19th century. All but a few of Verdi's works are operas. More a practical musician than a theorist, he at first completely accepted Italian operatic tradition, with its emphasis on vocal coloratura and beautiful melodies supported by conventional orchestral complements, and its reliance on the set forms of recitative and aria. Only as he matured did he develop his unique form of arioso as the basis of his style in his last two operas, *Otello* (*Othello*) and *Falstaff* (see THE MERRY WIVES OF WINDSOR).

Verdi was an ardent nationalist and was associated with the struggle for Italian independence. The death of the poet and patriot Manzoni led him to write his famous *Requiem Mass* in 1874. Among his operas are RIGOLETTO, IL TROVATORE, LA TRAVIATA, *Simon Boccanegra* (1857; revised 1881), *La Forza del Destino* (1862), *Don Carlo* (1867), AIDA, *Otello, Falstaff.*

Verdurins. The name of a *nouveau-riche* couple in Marcel Proust's REMEMBRANCE OF THINGS PAST. Insignificant themselves in the social hierarchy, the Verdurins affect scorn for the Guermantes and other aristocrats who ignore them. Fiercely possessive toward the little clan who attend their almost nightly *soirées,* they pride themselves on attracting and

launching literary, artistic, and musical celebrities. Gradually there is a narrowing of the social gulf between them and the elite, and Mme Verdurin eventually marries the prince de Guermantes.

Vere, Edward de, earl of Oxford. See OXFORD, EDWARD DE VERE, earl of.

Verga, Giovanni (1840–1922). Italian novelist and leader of the naturalistic school (called *verismo* in Italy). A regionalist writer, he is at his best when he describes the environment with which he was most familiar: the land and people of Sicily. As a young man, Verga left his native Catania and resided for a time in Florence and in Milan, where the action of his early novels takes place: *Una Peccatrice* (1866), *Storia de Una Capinera* (1871), *Eva* (1873), *Tigre Reale* (1873), and *Eros* (1875). His short story *Nedda* (1874) initiated his naturalistic depiction of Sicilian peasant life.

After Verga's return to Sicily (1879) appeared two collections of short stories: *Vita dei Campi* (1880) and *Novelle Rusticane* (1883), the latter containing the novella *Cavalleria Rusticana* which Pietro Mascagni reworked as an opera (1890).

The great novels of this period are I MALAVOGLIA and *Mastro Don Gesualdo* (1889). They were to be the first two novels of a projected five-novel cycle that was intended to depict man's struggle for material existence from the lowest, most primitive level of impoverished fisherfolk (*I Malavoglia*) to the highest pinnacle of wealth and power embodied in the "man of luxury" (the planned, but never realized, *L'Uomo di Lusso*). See SCAPIGLIATURA, LA; Federico DE ROBERTO.

Vergerio, Pietro Paolo (1370–1444). Italian Humanist educator. A student of Chrysoloras and Salutati, and secretary to Innocent VII, he impressed the emperor Sigismund at the Council of Constance and went to his court in Hungary, where he died. He was noted also for his educational theory, which was influential in the Renaissance.

Verges. See DOGBERRY.

Vergil. Full Latin name, **Publius Vergilius Maro** (70–19 B.C.). Roman poet. He was born in Andes, a small village near Mantua. After a preliminary education at Cremona, his father, a fairly prosperous farmer, sent him to Rome to study rhetoric and the physical sciences. The 17-year-old farm boy was, however, too shy and frail to stand up well in the competitive city. After several years, he gave up the ambition of becoming an advocate and, retiring to his father's farm, spent his time studying Greek philosophy and poetry.

Vergil was 25 in 44 B.C. when Julius Caesar was assassinated. All of the Roman world, even the small village of Andes in quiet, rustic Transpadane Gaul, was plunged into political chaos. Like all periods of political revolution in Roman Italy, the period from 44 to 40 was marked by large-scale confiscations and bloody reprisals—what the Romans termed proscriptions. In one of these mass confiscations (41), all the land in the neighborhood of Mantua and Cremona was confiscated, the owners were given notice to vacate, and their farms were resettled by veterans of Antony's army. Fortunately, however, through the influence of the gifted administrator and man of letters Asinius POLLIO, Vergil was not dispossessed. Instead, his poetry was taken by Pollio to MAECENAS, who was al-

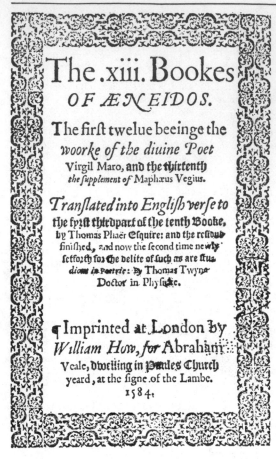

The .xiii. Bookes
OF ÆNEIDOS.

The firſt twelue beeinge the
woorke of the diuine Poet
Virgil Maro, and the thirtenth
the ſupplement of Maphæus Vegius.

Tranſlated into Engliſh verſe to
the fyrſt thirdpart of the tenth Booke,
by Thomas Phaër Eſquire: and the reſtous
finiſhed, and now the ſecond time newly
ſetfoɜth foɜ the delite of ſuch as are ſtu-
dious in Poetrie: By Thomas Twyne
Doctor in Phyſicke.

¶ Imprinted at London by
William How, foɜ Abraham
Veale, dwelling in Paules Church
yeard, at the ſigne of the Lambe.
1584.

Title page of Phaer's translation of Vergil's *Aeneid*.

ready what would be known today as the minister of culture. Maecenas was enthusiastic over these short pastoral compositions, then known generically as *eclogae* (see ECLOGUE), and urged the poet to organize them into publishable form. After several years of painstaking polishing, during which he added two or three more poems and fitted them into the arrangement of 10 idyls, he published the work under the title *Bucolica* (37). The BUCOLICS, apparently only artful variations on a theme by Theocritus, are, however, imbued with the spirit of postrepublican Rome, a spirit which looked back longingly to simpler times and forward with desperate hope to a new era of peace.

His fame now well established by the *Bucolics*, Vergil accepted the invitation of Maecenas to come and live on his estate in Naples and there begin work on a much more ambitious project, which Vergil had already outlined. The poet worked for seven years (37–30) on what was to be the great didactic poem of Rome: the *Georgica*, or "poems of farm life," also known as the GEORGICS. While Octavius Caesar was busy with the reconstruction of Rome's moral and political life, Vergil was occupied with the portrait of that archetypal builder and civilizer, the farmer. Like his *Bucolics*, Vergil's *Georgics* are superficially based on a Greek classic, Hesiod's *Works and Days*,

but, again like his first work, they are filled with an intense historical sense of the past and present and with the hope that Rome, under Octavius, would enter an era of peace.

After finishing the *Georgics*, Vergil immediately began work in the most exalted genre of classical literature, the epic. He gave consideration to several possible legends before he finally decided on the story of Aeneas, the Trojan prince whose descendants were supposed to have founded Rome and whom the Julian family claimed as their great ancestor. Again he made use of an ancient model, this time the *Iliad* and the *Odyssey* of Homer, and again created a work that was, in every sense, Roman. In this great 12-book myth, his countrymen were to see not only a symbolic summation of their history but a statement of their noblest aspirations for the future. The epic was never wholly completed. The poet died on Sept. 21, 19, after returning from a voyage to Athens. His unfinished AENEID was not destroyed, as he had wished, but was edited by his friends Varius and Tucca and, at last, published. Despite its minor imperfections—several obscure passages, a number of unfinished lines, and two or three inconsistencies in narrative—the *Aeneid* was at once accepted as the supreme epic of the Roman world.

Vergil was popular during the Middle Ages, partly because of his early acceptance by the early Christians as an inspired poet and partly because of the medieval habit of making magicians out of the poets and sages of antiquity. Dante, in his DIVINE COMEDY, has Vergil lead him through the infernal and purgatorial regions, considering him the wisest and most closely Christian of the ancient pagan poets.

Vergilio, Polidoro (c. 1470–1555). Italian diplomat and historian. He settled in England in 1502. A friend of Sir Thomas More and the other English Humanists, his *Anglica historia* (1534), a history, influenced native historians and through them Shakespeare's history plays.

Vergne, Marie Madeleine Pioche de la. See comtesse de LA FAYETTE.

Verhaeren, Emile (1855–1916). Belgian poet. The work of Verhaeren is always characterized by energy and unflagging vitality. Before World War I he entertained a faith in the possibility of universal brotherhood and in human progress. *Les Visages de la vie* (1899), *Les Forces Tumultueuses* (1902), *La Multiple Splendeur* (1906), and *Les Rhythmes souverains* (1910) all express this faith and are marked by exuberance and a joy in the life of sensation. *Les Flamandes* (1883) contains poems that describe Flemish life in lusty, vivid language; Verhaeren's interest in pictorial art is reflected in his poetry. The poems of *Les Villages illusoires* (1895) create symbols from the common people of his native region; they serve as concrete embodiments of his trust in man. A trilogy dedicated to his wife, *Les Heures Claires* (1896), *Les Heures d'après-midi* (1905), and *Les Heures de soir* (1911), is tender and quiet in mood. Gloom and despair were not, however, absent from Verhaeren's poetic repertoire. Another trilogy, *Les Soirs* (1888), *Les Débâcles* (1888) and *Les Flambeaux noirs* (1891), explores a bleak, unhappy state of soul. With *Les Flambeaux noirs*, Verhaeren began to experiment with *vers libre*, finding it more suited to the force of the feelings he sought to express. *Les Ailes Rouges de la Guerre* (1916) is a vigorous, bitter attack on the war, which brutally destroyed his hope in the future.

Verissimo, Erico (1905–   ). Brazilian novelist. Verissimo's novels are set in his native state of Rio Grande do Sul and in its capital city, Pôrto Alegre. Rich in characterization and extensive in scope, they show the influence of such writers as Aldous Huxley, John Dos Passos, and Ernest Hemingway. His best-known works include *Caminhos Cruzados* (*Crossroads,* 1935), which describes five days in the lives of the inhabitants of a suburban street in Pôrto Alegre; *Olhai os Lírios do Campo* (*Consider the Lilies of the Field,* 1938), about a wealthy doctor who reviews his past at the deathbed of a former mistress; and *O Resto É Silêncio* (*The Rest is Silence,* 1943), which studies the effect of a girl's suicide on seven people who witness her act. *O Tempo e o Vento* (*Time and the Wind*) is the title of a trilogy tracing the development of Rio Grande do Sul in the history of the Terra-Cambará family from the 18th through the 20th centuries; the first part of the third volume, *O Arquipélago,* appeared in 1961.

Verkhovenski, Pyotr Stepanovich. In Feodor Dostoevski's novel, THE POSSESSED, the leader of the revolutionary terrorist group. Pyotr, whose portrayal was partially based on the character of the infamous Sergei NECHAYEV, is depicted as cold and ruthless in his methods and strictly self-seeking in his goals. His aim is destruction for the pleasure of the thing, with no real interest in improving the lot of the oppressed people he claims to be helping. Personally he is shown to be an obnoxious boor. He is fascinated by the sinister STAVROGIN and quickly realizes the magnetism the man would exert as a figurehead of the revolutionary movement. He is unable, however, to persuade Stavrogin to lend himself to such a purpose. Verkhovenski's most diabolic act in the novel is the murder of SHATOV, who had been trying to resign from the revolutionary group. The incident was based on a real event from Nechayev's career.

Stepan Trofimovich Verkhovenski, the father of Pyotr Stepanovich, lives in retirement on the estate of Varvara Petrovna, Stavrogin's mother. Stepan is a representative of the mildly radical generation of the 1840's, who read Fourier and Saint-Simon, talked incessantly, and took no real action against the government. Stepan is, however, convinced that the authorities regard him as a dangerous radical and are constantly watching his every move. His harmlessness is contrasted to the menace represented by his nihilist son, Pyotr. The implication is that such men as Stepan, who wholeheartedly accepted Western ideas, prepared the ground for the growth of nihilism.

Stepan's distance from the ways of thought of the new generation is emphasized during a literary evening at which he passionately defends the value and autonomy of art against the ridicule of the young radicals whose views on such matters are strictly utilitarian.

Verlaine, Paul (1844–1896). French poet. Associated with the early SYMBOLISTS, Verlaine is noted for the grace, delicacy, and musical suggestiveness of his lyrics. Among his books are *Poèmes Saturniens* (1866), a volume in the style of the Parnassians; *Fêtes Galantes* (1869), written in a Watteaulike, 18th-century mood; *La Bonne Chanson* (1870), a celebration of the poet's joy at his coming marriage; and *Romances sans paroles* (1874). *Sagesse* (1881) contains poems of religious sentiment that reflect the poet's conversion to Roman Catholicism. Verlaine's personal life was disordered and tragic. He abandoned his young wife and in 1872 began his perverted, unhappy liaison with the young poet Rimbaud. This relationship, which ended in Brussels with a prison term for Verlaine and a bullet wound for Rimbaud, marked the beginning of a pitifully debauched existence that continued until the poet's death.

Verloc, Adolf. A spy and agent-provocateur in Joseph Conrad's novel THE SECRET AGENT. His wife Winnie is a central character.

Vermeer or **Van der Meer, Jan** (1632–1675). Dutch painter. Vermeer, who was born in Delft and lived there all his life, is the creator of some 35 highly prized known paintings. The work of a master colorist, these quiet interior scenes are characterized by an absence of sentimentality, by outstanding color harmonies—particularly of blues and yellows—and by an appreciation of light effects that led to the frequent inclusion of an open window as a source of light.

Verne, Jules (1828–1905). French writer. Verne's startling imaginative powers produced a number of semiscientific adventure stories that proved to be, not only universally popular with young people, but also almost unbelievably prophetic. He is best known for *A Voyage to the Center of the Earth* (*Voyage au centre de la terre;* 1864), *The Mysterious Island* (1870), TWENTY THOUSAND LEAGUES UNDER THE SEA, and AROUND THE WORLD IN EIGHTY DAYS.

Vernon, Mme de. The mother in Mme de Staël's DELPHINE. A cool-headed, intriguing egotist, she is considered to be a satirical, vengeful portrait of TALLEYRAND in feminine guise.

Veronese, Paolo. Real name, **Paolo Cagliari** (1528–1588). Venetian painter. Born in Verona, he excelled in large, brilliantly colored, and detailed paintings; these adorn the palaces and churches of his adopted city. Like Carpaccio, he favored the pageantry of a lively multitude of richly costumed figures in both his religious and allegorical works. His *Rape of Europa* and *Apotheosis of Venice,* the latter a spectacular essay in illusionist ceiling decoration, may be seen in the doge's palace. Two outstanding "festal" works are the *Marriage Feast at Cana* and *Feast at the House of Levi the Publican* (1573). The latter, originally entitled *Feast at the House of Simon,* was responsible for Paolo's arraignment before the Inquisition, which charged that he had violated official iconography in excluding the Magdalen and including dogs, German soldiers, buffoons, and dwarfs. Whereupon the painter simply changed the title to the present one, although he had made a moving plea for artistic freedom in handling such themes.

Veronica, St. A late medieval legend says that a maiden handed her handkerchief to Jesus on his way to Calvary. He wiped the sweat from his brow, returned the handkerchief to the owner, and went on. The handkerchief was found to bear a perfect likeness of the Saviour, and was called *Vera-Icon* (true likeness); the maiden became *St. Veronica,* and is commemorated on February 4. Milan Cathedral, St

Sylvester's at Rome, and St. Bartholomew's at Genoa all lay claim to the handkerchief.

Verrazano, Giovanni da (c. 1485–c. 1528). Florentine navigator who located the mouth of the Hudson River (1524) while seeking a northwest passage to Asia.

Verrocchio, Andrea del. Real name, **Andrea di Michele di Francesco de' Cione** (1436–1488). Florentine sculptor, painter, and goldsmith. Few of his works survive; but his *Baptism of Christ,* in which his young pupil LEONARDO DA VINCI participated, and other paintings reveal his skill in the subtle use of light—a lesson Leonardo remembered and perfected. His fame as a sculptor rests on the bronze *David* of 1476 and the celebrated equestrian statue of the *condottiere* COLLEONI at Venice (1479).

Versailles, treaty of (June 28, 1919). The treaty formally ending World War I, signed by the Allied powers and Germany in the Hall of Mirrors of the palace of Versailles. Similar treaties were accepted by Austria and Bulgaria on Sept. 12, 1919.

By the terms of the treaty, Germany was forced to accept responsibility for the damage caused to civilians by the war and was obliged to make financial reparations; her armed forces were also drastically reduced. She lost Alsace-Lorraine, the Saar Basin, Posen, parts of Schleswig and Silesia, and her overseas colonies. The covenant of the LEAGUE OF NATIONS was included as an integral part of the treaty.

Despite the efforts of President Woodrow WILSON, who headed the American delegation to the Paris peace conference that drafted the treaty, the U.S. Senate refused to ratify the document. Consequently, the U.S. did not join the League of Nations, which had been Wilson's great hope for the preservation of world peace.

versification. In prosody, the science of meter and rhyme in traditional verse composition, as contrasted with Anglo-Saxon prosody on the one hand and modern free verse on the other. See PROSODY.

Versilov. In Feodor Dostoevski's novel A RAW YOUTH, the natural father of the central character, Arkadi DOLGORUKI. Versilov is a representative of the "predatory type" of Russian 19th century man. Infected by Western ideas, without real religious faith, and cut off from a living contact with the Russian people, Versilov is shown as weak and artificial compared to Makar Ivanovich DOLGORUKI, the religious pilgrim.

versunkene Glocke, Die. See SUNKEN BELL, THE.

Verthandi. In Norse mythology, the second of the three sister NORNS or Fates. Active and straightforward, she personified the Present, her name being related to German *werden,* to grow, become.

Vertumnus or **Vortumnus.** In Roman mythology, the god of the changing seasons, who married POMONA. He courted her unsuccessfully in many guises until he finally appeared as an old woman and pleaded his own cause under cover of giving good advice.

Verwandlung, Die. See METAMORPHOSIS, THE.

Very, Jones (1813–1880). American poet. Licensed as a Unitarian minister, Very lived a retired life with his sisters in Salem, Mass., occasionally contributing to the Salem *Gazette* and the Christian *Register* and writing sonnets and lyrics celebrating religious visions and mysticism. At one time he was committed to

McLean Asylum in Somerville, Mass., but his friend Ralph Waldo Emerson insisted that he was "profoundly sane."

Very was associated with TRANSCENDENTALISM. His first book, *Essays and Poems* (1839), was edited and published by Emerson, and William Cullen Bryant and William Channing praised his sonnets highly. His work resembles that of Montaigne and the 17th-century metaphysical poets. Two posthumous collections are *Poems* (1883) and *Poems and Essays* (1886).

Vesalius, Andreas (1514–1564). Belgian anatomist. He was the first in modern times to dissect the human body. The Inquisition condemned him to death but his sentence was commuted to a pilgrimage to Jerusalem; on his return from there he was shipwrecked. His *De Humani Corporis Fabrica* is a treatise in seven books about the structure of the human body.

Vesey, Mrs. Elizabeth (1715?–1791). English poet and member of the BLUESTOCKING Club. She was nicknamed "the Sylph" by Mrs. Elizabeth MONTAGU.

Vespasian. Full Latin name, **Titus Flavius Sabinus Vespasianus** (A.D. 9–79). Roman emperor (69–79). The first of the Flavian emperors, he was chosen by his soldiers. He began the Colosseum. His name is immortalized by the *vespasiennes* (public toilets) in Paris.

Vespasiano da Bisticci (1421–1481). Italian scholar and book dealer. He is noted for his activities as a procurer and producer of beautiful manuscripts during the Italian Renaissance. He also wrote a collection of biographies, the *Vite d'uomini illustri del secolo XV*.

Vespucci, Amerigo (1451–1512). Florentine navigator. He visited the mouth of the Amazon in 1499 and explored the Brazilian coast in 1501. On the basis of these two voyages (and two others, probably fictional), described in his letters, and because he proclaimed his belief that the South American continent was not Asia but a new world, his name was given to the land. Actually, even if, as he claimed, he made a voyage in 1497 and reached the North American continent on June 16, others had preceded him there. The suggestion to name the new world after him was made by a German geographer and Humanist, Martin Waldseemüller (1470–1518), who had read and published the letters of Amerigo, which were later translated for the Hakluyt society (1894).

Vesta. The virgin goddess of the hearth of Roman mythology, corresponding to the Greek Hestia, one of the 12 great Olympians (see GODS OF CLASSICAL MYTHOLOGY). She was custodian of the sacred fire brought by Aeneas from Troy, which was never permitted to go out lest a national calamity should follow. See VESTALS.

Vestal, Stanley. See Walter S. CAMPBELL.

vestals. The six spotless virgins consecrated to VESTA. They tended the sacred fire brought by Aeneas from Troy and preserved by the state in a sanctuary in the forum at Rome. They were subjected to very severe discipline, and in the event of losing their virginity were buried alive. The vestal virgins also prepared from the first fruits of the May harvest the sacrificial meal for the LUPERCALIA, the Vestalia, and the Ides of September.

The word *vestal* has been figuratively applied to any woman of spotless chastity.

Vetalapanchavimsati (Sans., "twenty-five tales of a vampire"). Twenty-five Sanscrit tales by Somaveda taken from Book 12 of the KATHASARITSAGARA. They blend the bleak and the magical, the real and the fanciful, the grotesque and the lovely. Each ends with a question to which the wisest of men, king Trivikramasena, must give an answer. *The Transposed Heads,* by Thomas MANN, is a reconstruction of one of these.

Véto, M. et Mme. Name used for Louis XVI and MARIE ANTOINETTE during the French Revolution, because the king had been allowed a veto on the resolutions of the National Assembly. The name is used in the revolutionary song LA CARMAGNOLE.

Via crucis. See WAY OF THE CROSS; STATIONS OF THE CROSS.

Via Dolorosa. The way to the place of the Crucifixion. The way that Jesus followed from the Hall of Judgment to Golgotha, about a mile in length. See STATIONS OF THE CROSS.

Viana, Javier de. See GAUCHO LITERATURE.

Viaud, Louis Marie Julien. See Pierre LOTI.

Vicar of Christ. A title given to the Pope, symbolizing his claim to be the representative of Christ on earth.

Vicar of Wakefield, The (1766). A pastoral novel by Oliver GOLDSMITH. The story is told by Dr. Charles PRIMROSE, an unworldly, generous, and kindly vicar. With his wife, a woman with aspirations to gentility, his two daughters Olivia and Sophia, and his sons, George, Moses, and two smaller boys, he lives in quiet contentment until he loses his independent income. They move to humbler dwellings near the estate of Squire Thornhill, and there begin a series of misfortunes: Olivia is abducted and seduced by Squire Thornhill after a mock marriage ceremony; the vicar's house burns down and he is imprisoned for debt; Sophia is abducted by an unknown villain; and George, in attempting to avenge Olivia is imprisoned. The intervention of Sir William THORNHILL, the squire's uncle, straightens out the vicar's tangled affairs, which he himself has borne with remarkable fortitude; Sir William not only rescues Sophia, but marries her.

The book itself early became and has remained a classic, perhaps most of all because it reflects so truly the mellow wisdom and gentle irony of its author. See Ephraim JENKINSON; Miss Arabella WILMOT.

Vice, the. Also called **the Iniquity.** A character in medieval English mystery and morality plays. A buffoon who usually wore a cap with ass's ears, he was a boon companion of the devil.

Vice-Versa, or a Lesson to Fathers (1882). A fantastic novel by F. ANSTEY. It tells of the transformation of a father into his son and of the schoolboy son into his father.

Vichy government. French government during the German occupation of France (1940–1944) in World War II. See Henri-Philippe PÉTAIN.

Vico, Giambattista or Giovanni Battista (1668–1744). Italian philosopher and jurist. An opponent of Cartesian rationality, he anticipated Hegel's philosophy. Studies in the comparative history of law led him to formulate a concept of the relativity and evolution of human achievements which he applied to all the arts and sciences and to ideas in general. In *The New Science* (*La Scienza Nuova;* 1725–1730) he pro-

Olivia's abduction. From *The Vicar of Wakefield* (1766).

pounds a natural law of growth, decay, and regrowth through which all nations and civilizations must pass. The evolution of civilization is paralleled to the child's acquisition of knowledge through broadening experience; man, like the child, passes through the ascending stages of the senses, the imagination, and reason in his progression towards knowledge. In this scheme poetry properly belongs to the imaginative faculty midway between the physical senses and reason. Through Hegel, Vico influenced the aesthetic theories of De Sanctis and other literary critics of the romantic school.

Victoria. Full name **Alexandrina Victoria** (1819–1901). Queen of Great Britain and Ireland, empress of India. Her long reign (1837–1901) began on the death of William IV. In 1840 she married ALBERT, prince of Saxe-Coburg-Gotha, who died in 1861. Her name is used to describe the literature, and the characteristics, qualities, and attitudes of the period of her reign. See VICTORIAN.

Victoria, Tomás Luis de (c. 1548–1611). The most important Spanish Renaissance composer. Victoria was educated in Rome at the expense of King Philip II. He remained there nearly 30 years, then returned to Madrid in the service of the Empress

Maria, Philip's sister. A priest, Victoria's work was totally directed to the church, and his music is full of the ardor and exaltation of Spanish mysticism.

Victoria de Junín, La: Canto a Bolívar (1825). An ode by José Joaquín Olmedo (1780–1847), Ecuadorian poet and statesman. Dedicated to Simón Bolívar, the poem was inspired by the patriots' victories at Junín and Ayacucho, which virtually terminated the South American struggle for independence. In form and structure, the work reveals Olmedo's familiarity with the classics, and the opening lines closely imitate one of the odes of Horace. However, Olmedo's exuberance, imagination, and extravagant metaphors, which Bolívar himself satirized, make the poem one of the forerunners of the romantic movement in Latin America.

Victorian. Of or pertaining to the 64-year reign (1837–1901) of Queen Victoria of England, to the English people of the period, to their sentiments, beliefs, tastes, and accomplishments. In both literary and social history, Victoria's reign may be divided into two phases, each roughly 30 years long: the first period characterized by moderate and gradual political reforms, by the rapid growth of industry, by an enormous increase in population, by the rise to power of the industrial middle class, whose struggles with the working class and with the old aristocracy were to form the dominant theme of Victorian literature; and the second period characterized by a declining birth rate, by an increasingly jingoistic nationalism, by the looming specter of mass unemployment and economic crisis, by the tendency of the new science to undermine deeply held religious convictions, by the reflection in literature of a growing disillusionment with traditional moral values.

In the first half of Victoria's reign, England enjoyed unparalleled material prosperity and political stability. Prince Albert was sufficiently impressed by the achievements of his new country to urge that they be publicly compared with those of the other nations of the world. He became an active promoter of the "Great Exhibition of the Works and Industries of All Nations" held in London in 1851 under the glass arch of the Crystal Palace. Six million persons came from all parts of the kingdom and from nearly every corner of the world to view this great monument to Progress. After witnessing the opening ceremonies presided over by Queen Victoria, a reporter for *The Times* wrote:

Some saw in it the second and more glorious inauguration of their Sovereign; some a solemn dedication of art and its stores; some were most reminded of that day when all ages and climes shall be gathered round the throne of their Maker; . . . all contributed to an effect so grand and yet so natural, that it hardly seemed to be put together by design, or to be the work of human artificers.

Such was the complacent mood during the first half of Victoria's reign: a combination of pride in the stable constitutional government, of optimism generated by her increasing industrial prosperity, of an as yet unshaken confidence in the inherent rightness of the liberal and evangelical virtues of industriousness, self-reliance, temperance, piety, charity, and moral earnestness. William Makepeace Thackeray, though a self-proclaimed republican, composed odes to the Crystal Palace. Tennyson, after riding in the

first train to travel from Liverpool to Manchester, wrote "Let the great world spin for ever down the ringing grooves of change." Lord Macaulay began his *History of England* with the suggestion that "the general effect of this checkered narrative will be to excite thankfulness in all religious minds, and hope in the breasts of all patriots. For the history of our country during the last hundred and sixty years is eminently the history of physical, of moral, and of intellectual improvement." In the writings of lesser men, this characteristic pride, optimism, and confidence would often be transformed into a shoddy self-satisfaction, a naïve equating of success with right, and an arrogant belief in the inherent superiority of all things English—sentiments that later generations were to associate, rightly or wrongly, with the word *Victorian*.

The first half of Victoria's reign was a stable and prosperous period, but it was not stagnant. Well before Tennyson and Macaulay so eloquently celebrated the accomplishments of the age, others were diligently exposing its defects. In the 1830's Keble, Newman, and Pusey, as leaders of the OXFORD MOVEMENT, had sought to restore to the Anglican Church its original spiritual power and ritualistic beauty, to rid it of a bleak and literal evangelical "enthusiasm," to make it once again "more than a merely human institution." Throughout the 30's, 40's and 50's an increasing number of able writers turned their attention to current social evils that had been recently highlighted by Chartist agitation. The plight of the poor, the trials of the workingman, the evils of child labor, and the incessant conflict of the middle and working classes were examined in books such as Dickens' *Oliver Twist* and *Hard Times*, Mrs. Gaskell's *Mary Barton*, Kingsley's *Yeast* and *Alton Locke*, Carlyle's *Chartism* and *Past and Present*, Charlotte Brontë's *Shirley*, Meredith's *Evan Harrington*, Disraeli's *Sybil* and *Coningsby*.

In 1859, Charles Darwin's *Origin of Species* was published. Despite the caution with which he quietly presented his conclusions, they were immediately construed by those of orthodox views to be not only a challenge to the prevailing literal biblical interpretation but to be an affront to the best achievements of an age. Whether he had intended to do so or not, Darwin hastened the undermining of traditional Victorian values. Also published in 1859 was John Stuart Mill's brilliant essay *On Liberty*. Although he was once a Benthamite, Mill no longer believed that the good society could be based solely upon the crude doctrines of laissez-faire. He advocated a long series of reforms "to fit mankind by cultivation for a state of society combining the greatest personal freedom with that just distribution of the fruits of labour, which the present laws of property do not profess to aim at." And by questioning whether communal ownership or private property would best serve this end, he challenged no less effectively than Darwin the underlying Victorian assumptions.

Throughout the 60's, 70's, and 80's, the assaults upon mid-Victorian values increased in frequency and intensity. Matthew Arnold bitterly attacked the barbarians and Philistines in his *Essays in Criticism* and in *Culture and Anarchy*. John Ruskin extolled the beauties of nature and art and decried the ugliness of the industrial age in *Sesame and Lilies* and in

The Crown of Wild Olive. Thomas Huxley expounded, with somewhat less reticence than Darwin, the implications of evolution in *Man's Place in Nature* and in *The Physical Basis of Life.* Eventually Herbert Spencer became the only remaining political thinker to advocate the doctrine of laissez-faire, and in *Man versus the State* he justified his position by appealing, not to the old creed of self-reliance and industry, but to Darwin's theories of evolution.

By the last decade of the 19th century there was no respectable philosophical refuge in which one disposed to cling to his mid-Victorian intellectual heritage could take shelter. The old verities were being assaulted skillfully and with devastating effect from every possible angle by English authors, such as Butler, Conrad, Wilde, Wells, and Shaw, and by a growing number of foreign writers as well, including Zola, Maupassant, and Dostoevski. The average reader could either follow them in new and often disturbing directions or find relief from his humdrum existence by escaping to the South Seas with Robert Louis Stevenson and to the far-flung outposts of the empire with Rudyard Kipling.

Victory (1915). A novel by Joseph CONRAD. Axel Heyst lives the life of an exile in the South Seas. A man of integrity and generosity who distrusts the world, he helps those in trouble, including Lena, an unhappy girl he takes to his lonely island. Schomberg, the manager of the hotel where Lena worked, desires her and tells the fantastic, unscrupulous adventurer Jones, with his followers, that Heyst has treasure hidden on his island. The band of ruthless men invade the island sanctuary, and Lena is killed in an effort to save herself and her lover. It is the "victory" of their love and new-found purpose in life.

Vida, Girolamo or **Marco Girolamo** (c. 1485–1566). Italian poet. Cremona was his birthplace, but he spent most of his life at Rome in the service of his church, which made him bishop of Alba in 1532. He was famous for his Latin poetry, especially the *De Ludo Saccharum* (*The Game of Chess*) and the *Christius* or *Christiad,* an epic poem in the Vergilian manner on the life of Christ and the foundation of the Church. In 1527 he wrote *De arte poetica,* the first of many Renaissance treatises on the art of poetry. In England, Goldsmith translated the *Ludo,* Milton imitated the *Christias,* and Pope praised him in the *Essay on Criticism.*

Vida es sueño, La (**Life Is a Dream,** c. 1636). A play by Pedro CALDERÓN DE LA BARCA, considered one of the outstanding Spanish dramas of all time. This allegorical and philosophical play, through the symbolical character of the hero, Segismundo, explores the mysteries of human destiny, the illusory nature of mundane existence, and the conflict between predestination and free will.

Segismundo, a Polish prince, has been confined in a tower under the care of Clotaldo because astrologers had predicted that he would harm his father, King Basilio. After some years, the king decides to test the character of his son. Segismundo is drugged and brought to the palace where, since he is unaccustomed to human society, he behaves in a crude and violent fashion. Consequently, he is sent again to his confinement, convinced that the episode in the palace was a dream. Later the people revolt, liberate the prince, who is at first fearful that his new experience may not be real, and seize the kingdom. Segismundo is proclaimed king and, having learned that all life is a dream, decides that only virtue and nobility will give meaning to the dream.

Vidal, Gore (1925–   ). American novelist and playwright. Vidal's novels include *Williwaw* (1946), *The City and the Pillar* (1949), and *A Search for the King* (1950). *Visit to a Small Planet and Other Television Plays* was published in 1956; the title play, enlarged and rewritten, was successfully produced on Broadway in 1957. Vidal then wrote *The Best Man* (1960), a play about a presidential nominating convention; it, too, had a successful run on Broadway.

Vidar. See VALI.

Vidocq, François Eugène (1775–1857). French chief of detectives in Paris (1809–1827; 1832). Himself a clever criminal, his force consisted of ex-criminals who knew the ways of the underworld. On one occasion Vidocq organized a robbery himself and then investigated it as a police officer. M. LECOQ, a character created by Emile Gaboriau, is based on his character.

Vieira, Antônio (1608–1697). Portuguese-born Brazilian clergyman, orator, diplomat, and writer. Brought to Brazil at the age of six, Vieira soon identified himself with his new country although he later spent many years in Europe and became an important adviser to King John IV of Portugal. As a Jesuit preacher and missionary, he dedicated himself to the education and defense of the Indians; he also aroused the suspicions of the Inquisition because of his efforts on behalf of Portuguese Jews. His literary reputation rests largely on his letters and on his fiery, sometimes bombastic, sermons.

Vielé-Griffin, Francis. Original name, **Egbert Ludovicus Vielé** (1863–1937). French poet born in Virginia. Vielé-Griffin was educated and lived in Paris, where he became associated with the SYMBOLISTS. His poetical works include such collections as *Cueille d'avril* (1886), *Les Cygnes* (1887), *La clarté de vie* (1897), and *L'amour sacré* (1906).

Vienna, Congress of. The congress (1814–1815) by the powers of Europe after Napoleon's first abdication. It was called to settle the question of new boundaries. France kept the frontiers she had had in 1792; Prussia's territory was much increased; Poland was made into a new kingdom under the Czars.

Viereck, Peter [**Robert Edwin**] (1916–   ). American poet, teacher, and author. Born in New York City, Viereck has taught at Radcliffe, Smith, and Mount Holyoke colleges. He has written several works on political science, among them *Metapolitics: From the Romantics to Hitler* (1941), *Conservatism Revisited: The Revolt against Revolt* (1949), *Shame and Glory of the Intellectuals* (1953), *Dream and Responsibility: Tension between Poetry and Society* (1953), *Unadjusted Man: A New Hero for Americans* (1956), and *The Roots of the Nazi Mind* (1961). His novelette *Who Killed the Universe?* appeared in *New Directions* (1938). As a poet, Viereck is a classicist and a humanist; his poems, which are usually regular in meter and form, combine emotional lyricism and philosophic ideas in about equal parts. *Terror and Decorum* (1948), his first book of poems, won a Pulitzer Prize. Other collections include *Strike Through the Mask!* (1950), *The First Morning* (1952), *A Walk on Moss* (1956), and *The Persimmon Tree* (1956).

Vieth von Golssenau, Arnold. See Ludwig Renn.

Vigny, Comte Alfred Victor de (1797–1863). French poet, playwright, and novelist. One of the leaders of the romantic school, although not entirely typical of it in either his life or work, de Vigny wrote poetry marked by stoical despair and a bare, restrained classicism. Bleak and bitter, his work possesses a unique dignity. During the later years of his life, he retired almost entirely from public life, leading an isolated existence in what Sainte-Beuve called his *tour d'ivoire* (ivory tower). His volumes of poetry include *Poèmes* (1822), *Poèmes antiques et modernes* (1826), and *Les Destinées* (1864). *Chatterton* (1835) is highly esteemed by critics as an example of romantic drama, while *Cinq Mars* (1826) is an interesting pioneer attempt at a French historical novel. See ROMANTICISM.

Vikings. Danish and Norwegian sea pirates and adventurers of the 8th to 10th century (not to be confused with *sea-kings*, who were royal Norse chieftains). They were called *Norsemen* or *Normans* (north-men) by the Europeans whose coasts they plundered. They made important permanent settlements in England, France, and Iceland. Henrik Ibsen wrote a drama called *The Vikings* (1858).

Vilar, Jean (1912–1971). Director of the THÉÂTRE NATIONAL POPULAIRE.

Vildrac, Charles. Pen name of Charles Messager (1882–   ). French poet, dramatist, essayist, one of the ABBAYE GROUP. His plays present sympathetic psychological studies of workingmen, such as *The Steamer Tenacity* (*Le Paquebot Tenacity;* 1920), or of the lower middle class. Other works include the play *Michel Auclair* (1922) and the poems in *A Book of Love* (*Le livre d'amour;* c. 1910).

Vili. In Norse mythology, a mighty archer who, with his brothers Odin and Ve, slew the giant Ymir and created the world out of his body. When the first man and woman, Ask and Ember, were made, Vili gave them reason and motion.

Villa, Francisco or **Pancho.** Real name: **Doroteo Arango** (1877–1923). Mexican revolutionary leader. Originally a peon in the northern state of Chihuahua, Villa turned to cattle-rustling, becoming a hero to the local peasantry. With the outbreak of the Mexican Revolution, he joined in the struggle against Porfirio Díaz and Victoriano Huerta, and later vied with Venustiano CARRANZA for supreme power. A convention at Aguascalientes in 1914 failed to bring peace between the rival chieftains, and warfare continued until Villa's defeat by Alvaro Obregón, Carranza's lieutenant, at the battle of Celaya in 1915. Hoping to embarrass the Carranza government, Villa led a raid on Columbus, N.M., in 1916, killing several Americans. President Wilson responded by dispatching a punitive force under John J. Pershing into Mexico, and the two nations came close to war. Despite Carranza's efforts, Villa eluded capture and subsequently retired to a hacienda given to him after the successful revolt against Carranza in 1920. He was assassinated three years later, perhaps because of fear that he might oppose the presidential candidacy of Plutarco Elías Calles. Still a controversial figure in Mexico, Villa is regarded by some as a brigand, by others as a champion of the people. There is an excellent portrait of him in Martín Luis GUZMÁN's *Eagle and the Serpent* (1928).

Village, The (1783). A long poem by George CRABBE. It was written partly as a realistic response to the artificialities of the pastoral convention, particularly as exemplified in Oliver Goldsmith's THE DESERTED VILLAGE, which Crabbe considered a sentimentalized picture of rural life. *The Village* describes, in realistic terms, the hardships, evils, sordidness, and misery of the lives of country-dwellers of the day.

Village Blacksmith, The (1839). A poem by Henry Wadsworth LONGFELLOW. Melodic and very popular, it describes a New England smithy.

Villa-Lobos, Heitor (1887–1959). Foremost composer of Brazil. His style derives primarily from the folk and popular music of his country, which he collected and promoted in Brazilian schools and elsewhere. A popular series of works is his *Chôros*, Nos. 1–14; another is the *Bachianas Brasileiras*, Nos. 1–8.

villanelle. A lyric poem written in tercets and a closing quatrain, characterized by two refrain lines. These refrain lines are stated in the first stanza as lines one and three and return alternately in the succeeding stanzas as line three until the last stanza, where they are repeated in order as lines three and four. The rhyme scheme is: A^1-b-A^2, followed by a-b-A^1, a-b-A^2 as many times as desired, completed by a-b-A^1-A^2. The most frequent length is five tercets and a closing quatrain.

Originally a round-song of farm laborers, the name villanelle comes from Latin *villa*, or farm. Medieval French villanelles were irregular in form, but in the 16th century the form became fixed as it is known today. Such famous modern lyrics as *Do Not Go Gentle Into That Good Night*, by Dylan Thomas, are villanelles.

> O Singer of Persephone!
>   In the dim shadows desolate
> Dost thou remember Sicily?
>
> Still through the ivy flits the bee
>   Where Amaryllis lies in state,
> O Singer of Persephone!
>
> Simaetha calls on Hecate
>   And hears the wild dogs at the gate;
> Dost thou remember Sicily?
>
> Still by the light and laughing sea
>   Poor Polypheme bemoans his fate,
> O Singer of Persephone!
>
> And still in boyish rivalry
>   Young Daphnis challenges his note;
> Dost thou remember Sicily?
>
> Slim Lacon keeps a goat for thee;
>   For thee the jocund shepherds wait;
> O Singer of Persephone,
> Dost thou remember Sicily?
>
>   Oscar Wilde, *Theocritus*

Villard, Oswald Garrison (1872–1949). American editor. A champion of pacifism, free trade, minority rights, and a free and responsible press, he was editorial writer and owner of the New York *Evening Post* (1897–1918), manager and owner of *The Nation* (1918–1932), and a contributing editor of the magazine until 1940. His grandfather was William Lloyd Garrison.

Villari, Pascuale (1827–1917). Italian historian. His best-known works are *Storia di Girolamo Savanarola e de' Suoi Tempi* (1859–1861) and *Niccolò Machiavelli e i Suoi Tempi* (1877–1882).

Ville, La. See CITY, THE.

Villehardouin, Geoffroy de (c. 1150–c. 1213). French court advisor and historian. He took part in the Fourth Crusade, and his *Conquête de Constantinople,* considered one of the earliest important works in French prose, recounts the events from 1202 to the capture of Constantinople in 1207.

Villette (1853). A novel by Charlotte BRONTË. The English girl Lucy Snowe goes to the city of Villette in France to teach at a young girls' boarding school. There she meets the beautiful but egotistical Ginevra Fanshawe, a pupil who condescendingly becomes Lucy's friend and boasts of her admirers. One of these, Dr. John Bretton, turns out to be a childhood acquaintance of Lucy. He confesses to her that he hopes to marry Ginevra, and Lucy struggles to hide her love for him. One evening at a concert, Ginevra cruelly mimics his mother; disgusted, the doctor breaks with her. He, by chance, meets Polly, a friend of his and Lucy's from the past, and it becomes clear that the doctor and Polly love each other. In grief Lucy continues her work at the school, gradually feeling herself drawn to the professor Paul Emmanuel. Initially a bitter man, he mellows under her influence. Lucy is heartbroken when he announces that he must depart for the West Indies, but he later tells her privately that he has arranged for her to be headmistress of the school and that after his return in three years he plans to marry her. The city Villette is in reality Brussels, where Charlotte Brontë lived and studied during the years 1842–1844.

Villiers, George. See 1st duke and 2nd duke of BUCKINGHAM.

Villiers de L'Isle-Adam, Comte **Jean Marie Mathias Philippe Auguste de** (1838–1889). French writer of fiction and drama. Born into an aristocratic family in Brittany, he went as a young man to Paris, where he led the life of a Bohemian artist. In his dramas *Axël* (1890), *Elen* (1865), and *Morgane* (1866), Villiers de L'Isle-Adam displays flagrant romanticism. His tales, collected in *Contes cruels* (1883) and *Nouveaux Contes cruels* (1888), are written in a fantastic, macabre manner. His writing, often freighted with philosophical ideas, obscure and highly poetic, is generally considered as the immediate predecessor of the French SYMBOLIST movement.

Villon, François. Originally called **François de Montcorbier** or **François de Loges** (1431–?). French poet, considered the finest poet of the late Middle Ages. He adopted the last name of his patron, the chaplain of a university church who adopted him about 1438. A brilliant student, he received a Master of Arts degree from the Sorbonne before he was 21 (hence the title "Master Villon" occasionally used). However, he also excelled in the rowdier side of the student life of the time, cultivated disreputable society, and was involved in a number of brawls, in one of which he killed a priest (1455). Thereafter he was

repeatedly under arrest, sentenced to prison or to exile, or wandering to escape arrest for a series of brawls, robberies, and generally illegal escapades. His *Petit Testament* (1456) is a series of *Lais,* or "legacies," facetiously parodying the style of a legal testament; it explains that he is leaving Paris because of a broken heart (he was probably fleeing arrest) and bequeaths a number of worthless items to his friends and enemies.

But the *Grand Testament* (1461), the poem of 2,000 lines that made him famous, is melancholy and pathetic in some of its bequests, bitterly humorous in others. It includes a self-castigating review of his life as a beggar and thief, but also derides the vanity of all human life, whether or not overtly dissipated like his own. It is interspersed with *ballades* and *rondeaux,* including the *Ballade des Dames du temps jadis* (translated by Dante Gabriel ROSSETTI as *The Ballad of Dead Ladies*) and the *Ballade pour prier Nostre Dame,* addressed as a request to his mother to pray for him. In 1462 he was present at a street fight involving a death, and was sentenced to be hanged. This inspired him to write his own epitaph, the *Ballade des pendus,* or ballad of the hanged men, denouncing the justice of men and appealing for divine justice. His friends succeeded in having the sentence commuted in 1463 to ten years of banishment; Villon disappeared, and nothing further is known of him. His poems were first printed in 1489.

In the 19th century, Villon became popular as a Romantic rogue-hero, a colorful and sympathetic outlaw; episodes from his life (mostly legendary) appear frequently in literature, as in R. L. Stevenson's short story *Lodging for the Night.* D. G. Rossetti and A. C. SWINBURNE translated many of his ballads, and Bertolt Brecht adapted some of them for the lyrics of his *Threepenny Opera* (1928). J. H. Huntley made a largely fictitious Villon the hero of *If I Were King* (1901), adapted by Rudolf Friml for his operetta *The Vagabond King* (1925).

Vilmorin, Louise de (1902–). French novelist and poet. Vilmorin is known for her elegantly witty and perceptive fantasies and comedies of manners, such as the novels *Erica's Return* (1948), *Julietta* (1951), *Madame de . . .* (1951), and *Les Belles Amours* (1954).

Vincentio, Duke. The kindly, philosophical duke of Vienna in Shakespeare's MEASURE FOR MEASURE. Although he realizes that his forbearance has contributed to a decline in public morality, he is reluctant to initiate a program of reform himself and appoints Angelo to rule in his stead. He pretends to leave Vienna for Poland but, disguised as Friar Lodowick, remains in the city to observe Angelo's conduct in office.

Vinci, Leonardo da. See LEONARDO DA VINCI.

Vinland. See Leif ERICSON.

Vinteuil. A great composer of music in Marcel Proust's REMEMBRANCE OF THINGS PAST. He is an idealized composite of a number of 19th-century French composers. The "little phrase" from one of his sonatas, a recurrent motif in the novel, closely resembles one by Saint-Saëns. His daughter is revealed to be a lesbian and a sadist.

Viola. The heroine of Shakespeare's TWELFTH NIGHT and the twin sister of Sebastian. Disguising herself as a boy and taking the name of Cesario, she becomes page to Duke Orsino, with whom she falls in love. When her identity is revealed, Orsino weds her.

Viollet-le-Duc, Eugène Emmanuel (1814–1879). French architect and authority on Gothic art. A leader of the Gothic revival, he is responsible for the restoration of many of France's most historic cathedrals and medieval buildings. He is also famous for his great standard works, *Dictionnaire Raisonné de l'Architecture Française du XI° au XVI° Siècle* (10 vols., 1854–1869) and *Dictionnaire du Mobilier Français* (1855), which he himself illustrated.

Virgil. See VERGIL.

Virginia. A young Roman plebeian of great beauty, decoyed by APPIUS CLAUDIUS, one of the decemvirs, and claimed as his slave. According to tradition, her father L. Virginius, on hearing of it, hastened to the forum just as Virginia was about to be delivered up to Appius. He seized a butcher's knife and stabbed his daughter to the heart, crying "There is no way but this to keep thee free." He rushed from the forum and raised a revolt in which the decemvirs were overthrown and the old order of government was restored (449 B.C.). The story is told by Livy and has been retold by Petrarch, and by Chaucer in the *Doctor's Tale*.

Virginia (1913). A novel by Ellen GLASGOW. This story of a Southern woman is set in the years between 1884 and 1912. Virginia's marriage is unhappy; she is unable to adapt herself to a new environment, loses the respect of her husband and daughters, but manages to retain the love of her son. The book is, in essence, an analysis of social change and the new world facing women in the early 20th century.

Virginian, The (1902). A novel by Owen WISTER. Portraying cowboy life in Wyoming and in many ways the prototype of the modern Western, the story deals with the enmity between its unnamed hero and a local bad man called Trampas. When Trampas accuses the Virginian of cheating at poker and impugns his ancestry, the latter lays his pistol on the table and utters the immortal retort: "When you call me that, smile!" Trampas is eventually vanquished in a gun duel that constitutes the first "walkdown" in American literature, and the Virginian marries Molly Wood, a New England schoolteacher whom he has rescued from a marooned stagecoach.

Virginians, The (1857). A novel by William Makepeace THACKERAY. A sequel to HENRY ESMOND, it relates the story of George and Harry Warrington, the twin grandsons of Colonel Henry Esmond. The novel takes the two brothers, of differing tastes and temperaments, through boyhood in America, through various experiences in England, where they are favorites of their wicked old aunt, Baroness Bernstein (the Beatrix of *Henry Esmond*), and through the American Revolution, in which George fights on the British side and Harry on the side of his friend George Washington.

Virginius. See VIRGINIA.

Virgin Queen, the. ELIZABETH I of England.

Virgin Soil (Nov'; 1877). A novel by Ivan TURGENEV. It deals with the revolutionary movement in Russia. The student NEZHDANOV, who believes himself committed to the people's cause, carries off

Marianna, the daughter of a government official, who wants to "go to the people" with him and work for the peasants' freedom. Nezhdanov discovers that he is not really fitted to be a revolutionary leader and in despair kills himself. The stronger Marianna marries again, she and her husband SOLOMIN go off to work for a democratic Russia in a more gradual and realistic way.

Virgin Soil Upturned (Podnyataya tzelina; 2 vols.; 1932, 1960). A novel by Mikhail SHOLOKHOV. It depicts the turmoil caused by the collectivization of agriculture in the Don Cossack region of Russia.

Vischer, Friedrich Theodor (1807–1887). German critic and aesthetician, known for his attempts to provide a theoretical basis for literary realism. Among his works are *Kritische Gänge* (*Critical Paths*, 1844), a collection of essays, and a more systematic work, *Ästhetik* (*Aesthetics*, 1846).

Visconti. An Italian dynasty. Ruling Milan and its environs from the 12th through the mid-15th century, its members were noted for their patronage of such men of letters as Petrarch and for their political ferocity. Gian Galeazzo Visconti (1351–1402) became duke of Milan by treacherously ousting his uncle Bernabò (1323–1385), an event recalled by Chaucer in his *Canterbury Tales*. Their emblem, the viper, inspired Marjorie Bowen's *The Viper of Milan* (1906).

Viscount of Bragelonne, The (Le Vicomte de Bragelonne; 1848–1850). A historical romance by Alexandre DUMAS, the sequel to THE THREE MUSKETEERS and TWENTY YEARS AFTER. The reign of Louis XIV is the subject and setting for this third novel. The plot revolves about the schemings of ARAMIS, now bishop of Vannes, to attain power. *Louise de la Vallière* and *The Man in the Iron Mask*, originally part of *The Viscount of Bragelonne*, are now often published as separate works.

Vishnu. In Hindu metaphysics, the Supreme Spirit (Brahman), the Preserver in the TRIMURTI. He has had nine incarnations, or AVATARS: Matsya, a fish; Kurma, a tortoise; Varaha, a boar; Narasinha, a monster, half man and half lion; Vamena, a dwarf; Parashurama, a human (Rama with the axe); Ramachandra (the hero of the Ramayana); Krishna; and Buddha. There is one, Kalki, still to come in the form of a white horse with wings to destroy sin, the sinful, and all the enemies of the natural, stable order. Vishnu, also known as Hari, is usually represented as four-armed, carrying a club, a shell, a discus, and a lotus; a bow and sword are slung at his side. The Indian sect that worships him is known as the VAISHNAVA. Vishnu in his various forms and aspects is perhaps the most popular of the many Hindu deities. As the Preserver of the Trimurti he is at all times a kindly god in contrast to an intellectualized Brahma and a destructive Shiva.

Vision, A (1925). A book by William Butler YEATS, important for understanding some of the ideas in his poetry. He claimed that the spirits dictated much of it in automatic writing to his wife, the medium Georgie Hyde Lees. It states that history is cyclical and recurrent, proceeding for the individual as well as for mankind in a gyre, or corkscrew pattern. At death, men's souls transmigrate into other bodies and continue the pattern. It also states that all human personality types have their opposite, antithetical selves, or masks, and that the complete man should learn to assimilate the characteristics of his mask.

Vision of Columbus, The. See COLUMBIAD, THE.

Vision of Judgement, The (1822). A satirical poem by Lord BYRON. It satirizes an earlier poem by Robert Southey, *A Vision of Judgement* (1821), in the preface of which Byron was attacked for "lewdness and impiety." Byron ridicules Southey and treats with irreverent humor the subject of the earlier work: the entry of George III, recently dead, into heaven.

Vision of (or Concerning) Piers Plowman, The. See PIERS PLOWMAN.

Vision of Sir Launfal, The (1848). A narrative poem by James Russell LOWELL. Opening with the famous line, "What is so rare as a day in June?," the poem tells of Launfal's quest for the Grail. He fails until he shares his last crust with a beggar he had formerly scorned. His conversion complete, Launfal subsequently performs good works.

Visit, The. See VISIT OF THE OLD LADY, THE.

Visit from St. Nicholas, A (1823). A poem by Clement Clarke Moore (1779–1863). First published anonymously in the Troy, N.Y. *Sentinel*, the poem was widely appreciated. Moore reprinted it in *Poems* (1844). His retelling of the visit of the jolly old man, with his descent through the chimneys, became the standard version of the legend for his many readers. Moore was a scholar who taught Oriental and Greek literature at the General Theological Seminary in New York from 1823 to 1850.

Visit of the Old Lady, The (Der Besuch der alten Dame; 1956). A play by Friedrich DÜRRENMATT. An old billionairess returns to her destitute hometown and offers a huge sum of money for the life of the man who seduced and betrayed her when she was a girl. The citizens at first indignantly refuse to commit the murder, but eventually the temptation becomes too great and, at a full town meeting, they ritualistically execute the man. It was performed in New York as *The Visit*.

Vita Nuova, La (The New Life, c. 1293). A short work by DANTE, collecting his early sonnets and *canzoni* with prose commentaries. They are connected by an autobiographical prose narrative of the love for BEATRICE which inspired the poems. He only meets her twice, when he is 9 and 18, but adores her from afar. He feigns love for another woman to protect his true love, observes Beatrice's grief at the death of her father, foresees her own death, finds consolation after it happens with "a compassionate lady," but soon rededicates himself entirely to love of the memory of Beatrice. Finally a "new perception" of her in a vision makes clear the mystic significance of all these events, and he understands that he is not yet worthy to write about her ultimate meaning for him, but that he will—an intimation of her role to come in the DIVINE COMEDY. Both the poetry and the commentary, considering love for a woman as the first step in the soul's spiritual improvement toward a capacity for divine love, make the book a major work of the new poetic school of the STILNOVISTI. Dante Gabriel Rossetti wrote a popular English translation (1861).

Vitellius, Aulus (A.D. 15–69). Roman general. He was proclaimed emperor (January–December, 69) by his troops. Opposed by Vespasian, he was defeated and killed.

Vitrac, Roger (1901–1952). French dramatist. He continued in Alfred Jarry's style of bitterly satirical farce, as with *Loup-Garou* (1939).

Vitruvius. Full Latin name, **Marcus Vitruvius Pollio** (fl. c. 40 B.C.). Roman architect and military engineer. His celebrated *De Architectura Libri Decem* is the only classical work on architecture which has come down to us.

Vittorini, Elio (1908–). Italian novelist, critic, and translator who with Cesare Pavese pioneered in Italy the translation and study of modern American writers. A politically "engaged" writer, interested in the problems of contemporary society, he worked in the antifascist underground in World War II. His first full-length novel, *The Red Carnation* (*Il Garofano Rosso;* 1934; pub. 1948), describes the response of young students to fascism. *Erica* (1936) treats the theme of poverty in a world of cruelty and hypocrisy. *Conversazione in Sicilia* (*Conversation in Sicily,* 1941) marked a new phase in Vittorini's writing in its mythical theme, erudite style, and hidden symbolism. Allegory is prominent in *The Twilight of the Elephant* (*Il Sempione Strizza l'Occhio al Frejus;* 1948), which propounds the Marxist theme of the regeneration of the proletariat. Among his other "political" novels are *Uomini e No* (1945), which narrates his experiences in the underground, and *Le Donne di Messina* (1949).

Vittorino of Feltre (1373–1446). Italian Renaissance educator. He taught mainly at the court of Mantua. Like his equally famous contemporary, Guarino of Verona, he attained fame for educating young pupils, according to Greek ideals, in every aspect of physical, mental, and spiritual activity.

Vitus, St. A Sicilian youth. He was martyred with Modestus, his tutor, and Crescentia, his nurse, during the Diocletian persecution (303). In Germany it was believed in the 16th century that good health for a year could be secured by anyone who danced before a statue of St. Vitus on his feast day. This dancing developed almost into a mania, and came to be confused with chorea, which was subsequently known as St. *Vitus'* dance, the saint being invoked against it.

Vivaldi, Antonio (c. 1675–1741). Italian composer and violinist, known familiarly as *il prete rosso* (the red-haired priest). He wrote more than 400 concertos for various instruments and combinations of instruments, 38 operas, nearly all of which are lost, and church music, of which the *Gloria* (c. 1726) is well known.

Vivian Grey (1826). Benjamin DISRAELI's first novel, a political romance revolving around Vivian Grey, a charming, talented youth who persuades the stupid, vain marquis of Carabas to support an intrigue against his own government. After many convolutions, the plot fails, and Grey leaves England. Vivian has been regarded as a possible self-portrait of Disraeli.

Viviani, Emilia. The daughter of an Italian nobleman. Emilia was placed against her will in the convent of St. Anna, near Pisa. Percy Bysshe Shelley met her in 1820, was attracted by her beauty and sympathetic toward her plight, and took her as a flesh-

and-blood symbol of Ideal Beauty. He addressed his EPIPSYCHIDION to her in 1821.

Viviano. In Matteo Maria Boiardo's ORLANDO INNAMORATO and Lodovico Ariosto's ORLANDO FURIOSO, the brother of Malagigi, Aldigieri, and BRADAMANTE, as well as one of the outstanding Christian knights.

Vlaminck, Maurice de (1876–1958). French painter. With Matisse and Derain, Vlaminck led the FAUVE school of painting. Both his subjects and his technique are natural, simple, and almost primitive in the concentration upon elemental forces and basic color. The subjects he chooses from nature are violent, often brutal scenes of a raging sea, a bleak winter evening, or a hayfield with a burning orange sun making fire of the haystacks. His flower paintings, like his other work, use no modeling or detail but are vivid bursts of pure color. Vlaminck greatly admired Van Gogh and employed the technique of slashing raw bright pigment on his canvases to give a highly dramatic quality to his work. Among his most famous paintings are *Thatched Cottages, Storm*, and the dark, foreboding *Village Street*. Vlaminck saw both the fearful and the beautiful in the unthinking forces of nature; he captures with his painter's brush the energy and vitality he inevitably discovered.

Vogelweide, Walther von der. See WALTHER VON DER VOGELWEIDE.

Vogt, Nils Collett (1864–1937). Norwegian poet, playwright, and novelist. Vogt's intense spirit of rebellion joined with his fervent lyricism in his first collection of poetry, *Digte* (*Poems*, 1887). Abandoning the conservative beliefs he found in his home, the poet joined the radical movement of the 1880's in Norway. When these years of passionate commitment had drawn to a close, he began to express in his writings a tender nostalgia: *Fra gutt til mann* (*From Boy to Man*, 1932), a prose memoir, recreates the glorious time of his youth. Vogt felt a deep love for the stark beauty of his country; his poetry, always marked by courage and by a quiet strength, describes the dark firs and the bare mountains. Among his collections of lyric verse are *Fra vaar til høst* (*From Spring to Autumn*, 1894), *Det dyre brød* (*The Costly Bread*, 1900), *September brand* (*September Flame*, 1907), and *Hjemkomst* (*Homecoming*, 1917).

Voices of the Night (1839). A collection of poems by Henry Wadsworth LONGFELLOW. The book includes A PSALM OF LIFE and *Hymn to the Night*.

Voiture, Vincent (1598–1648). French poet. An original member of the French Academy, Voiture composed the sonnet URANIE, which was held to be so perfect that it involved him in a bitter dispute with a rival poet, Isaac de BENSERADE. Voiture's works were published posthumously.

Vol de Nuit. See NIGHT FLIGHT.

Volksbuch (Ger. "folk book"). A term popularized by Joseph GÖRRES, referring to the many cheap, easily understood books that were produced for the people in 15th and 16th-century Germany, roughly equivalent to the English chapbook. The most important folk books are those containing prose narratives, some of which, like EULENSPIEGEL and the FAUSTBUCH, assumed great importance in subsequent literary history.

Volksgeist (Ger. "folk spirit"). The national character or genius of a people, as distinguished from the entirely rational sense of humanity accepted during the enlightenment. This concept, which was formulated by HERDER, gained wide currency during the romantic era.

Volpone, or the Fox (1606). A comedy by Ben JONSON. Aided by his servant Mosca (the Fly), the avaricious Volpone (the Fox), a childless Venetian nobleman, devises a new method of adding to his hoard of gold. He pretends a lengthy illness in order to pique the expectations of his rascally associates, all of whom aspire to inherit his fortune: Voltore (the Vulture), a lawyer; Corbaccio (the Carrion Crow), a miserly old man; Corvino (the Raven), a knavish merchant. Mosca assures each, one by one, that he is in line for the fortune—thanks to Mosca's own efforts. Finally, Mosca whispers abroad that Volpone is near death. They rush to Volpone with rich gifts, in order to assure themselves of his favor. Corbaccio disinherits his own son in Volpone's favor; Corvino goes so far as to offer his wife to ensure his goodwill. After a series of complications, as logical as they are hilarious, Volpone, who is about to be outwitted by his own servant, reveals the whole plot in court, and all the participants are punished according to their crimes or their station in life. In 1928, Jules Romains and Stefan Zweig made a new version of the play which ends with Mosca inheriting all Volpone's money from the false will. Volpone, who will be executed if he turns out not to be dead, slinks away penniless. This version, more satisfactory for modern audiences, is the one commonly performed today. It was employed by George Antheil in his opera *Volpone* (1953). Jonson's play is generally recognized as one of the finest comedies of the Jacobean period.

Völsunga Saga. A Scandinavian prose cycle of legends, major source of the German epic poem THE NIEBELUNGENLIED and of Wagner's opera DER RING DES NIBELUNGEN, although names and plot details vary. The saga takes its name from Völsung, grandson of the god ODIN and father of Sigmund. The hero Sigurd (Siegfried) is Sigmund's son. He kills the dragon Fafnir, present guardian of a gold treasure and a magic ring, which carry the curse of their original owner from whom they were forcibly taken by the god LOKI. Sigurd then begins his travels, taking the treasure and the magic horse Grani, given him by Odin.

He awakens the sleeping Valkyrie maiden Brunhild, and they become betrothed; but he leaves her in search of adventure and becomes the friend of the three sons of a Rhine king, and their sister Gudrun (Kriemhild, Gutrune). He is given a magic potion which makes him forget Brunhild, and it is arranged that Sigurd will marry Gudrun if he helps her brother Gunnar (Gunther) win the hand of Brunhild, who has surrounded herself with a circle of fire that a prospective suitor must cross, since she assumes that none but Sigurd can do so. Sigurd rides through on his magic horse, but takes on Gunnar's appearance while winning Brunhild's promise of marriage. After he resumes his own shape, the double marriage is celebrated; but one day during a jealous argument Gudrun tells Brunhild about the deception. The enraged Brunhild has Sigurd killed, although still in love with him, then commits suicide. Gudrun eventually marries Atli (Attila, or Etzel, king of the Huns), who determines to get the treasure hoard, now in the hands of Gudrun's brothers. They sink the gold in the Rhine and die fighting in refusal to reveal where it is hidden. Gudrun avenges them by killing Atli and the sons she has borne him.

William MORRIS retold the saga in his *Sigurd the Völsung* (1876).

Voltaire. Pen name of **François Marie Arouet** (1694–1778). French satirist, philosopher, historian, dramatist, and poet. He is known for his enmity to organized religion and to fanaticism, intolerance, and superstition (which he attacked under the slogan, *Ecrasez l'infâme!* [Fr., "Crush the infamous thing!"]), for his biting wit and his prejudices, his generosity in helping the poor and oppressed, his personal vigor in spite of chronic ill health, his clever and swiftly moving philosophic tales, and his contributions to the objective study of history. His merciless satire and unorthodox ideas were a constant source of irritation to the political and religious authorities of his time.

One of the most famous and influential men in the history of thought, Voltaire had an extremely turbulent life. His early reputation was made as a dramatist and wit, the latter gift earning him a beating at the hands of the lackeys of the chevalier de Rohan, a nobleman whom he insulted. He was subsequently imprisoned for a few days (1725), and thereafter immediately exiled to England where he spent three years (1726–1729). There Voltaire met, and came under the influence of, Pope and Swift; he was much drawn to English political thought, and, in particular, to Newton and Locke, whose ideas he propagated in France. On his return to his native land, he enthusiastically introduced English literature, and particularly Shakespeare, to the French public. (In time, however, he was to regard Shakespeare's influence on the drama as deplorable.) After the publication of his *Lettres Philosophiques* (1734), Voltaire was again pursued by the government. He took refuge with Mme du CHÂTELET at Cirey, in Lorraine, where he remained, for the most part, from 1734 to 1749, writing historical works and dabbling in science. It was during this period, through the influence of Mme de Pompadour, that Voltaire was made royal historiographer (1743) of Louis XV, and a member of the French ACADEMY. After the death of Mme du Châtelet, Voltaire accepted FREDERICK II's invitation to visit him at his court in Berlin, where he stayed for three years until, in 1753, the two men became estranged. Their quarrels are celebrated: one of Voltaire's duties was to correct the monarch's attempts at French poetry. Angry at thus being treated as a subordinate, Voltaire on occasion referred to this chore as "washing the king's dirty linen." He fled from Prussia, not without first experiencing imprisonment: Frederick's revenge for the publication of Voltaire's *Diatribe du docteur Akakia*, a satire of Frederick's highly placed functionary Pierre Moreau de Maupertuis. Unwelcome elsewhere in Europe, Voltaire returned to Colmar, in eastern France; in 1775 he retired to a home in Geneva known as *Les Délices*. Here he continued publishing philosophic works and contributed articles to the ENCYCLOPÉDIE.

Because of the violent religious controversies he stirred up with reference to the article "Geneva" in the *Encyclopédie*, he thought it better to purchase an estate called FERNEY in 1758, where, safe from both the Swiss and the French governments, he could and did live comfortably for nearly all the rest of his life. Here he spent his time corresponding with the major figures of the time, receiving homage from innumerable visitors, managing his estate where he instituted social reforms, writing and producing plays, and publishing treatises (many anonymously) which violently denounced the cases of intolerance and injustice that came to his attention. Specifically, he aided many persons who were victims of injustice, notably the family of Jean Calas. It was from Ferney that Voltaire quarreled with Rousseau and inveighed against the Roman Catholic Church and Calvinism, winning fame all over Europe. When he returned once more to Paris just before his death, he was entertained sumptuously and honored as befitted a great man at the performance of his play *Irène* (1778). It proved too much for the 84-year-old man and he died shortly thereafter, on the 30th day of May. The Church denied him a Christian burial, but an abbot of his acquaintance brought his body to his own abbey in Champagne. In 1791, after the French Revolution, on which Voltaire had had such an important influence, his remains were transferred to the Panthéon in Paris.

Voltaire's major dramatic works, chiefly neoclassical in form (see NEOCLASSICISM), include OEDIPE (1718), *Brutus* (1730), ZAÏRE, *Alzire, ou les Américains* (1736), *Mahomet, ou le Fanatisme* (1742), *Mérope* (1743), *L'Orpheline de la Chine* (1755), and *Tancrède* (1760). Among his polemic and philosophic writings are the *Lettres philosophiques* (definitive edition 1737, known also as *Lettres sur les Anglais,* or *Lettres anglaises,* in the 1734 edition), in which he praises the religious practices of the Quakers, English politics, philosophy, science, and literature and, by implication, criticizes authoritarian France. The letters had been translated and published in England in 1733. In them Voltaire is impressed with England's progress in scientific thinking, and especially with the importance given to the experimental method in the works of Bacon, Locke, and Newton. The French *parlement* was quick to sense the heresy in these letters and ordered them burned in 1734. Other philosophic works are the *Traité de métaphysique* (1734), in which Voltaire insists that metaphysical matters are beyond human understanding; the *Discours en vers sur l'homme* (1738); the *Traité sur la tolérance* (1763), written as part of Voltaire's campaign to rehabilitate Jean Calas' memory; the *Dictionnaire philosophique portatif, ou la raison par alphabet* (1764); the *Sermon des cinquante* (before 1753), said to be one of the most violent pamphlets ever to have come from the pen of a major writer; *Le Philosophe ignorant* (1766); and *Les Questions de Zapata* (1767), which point out contradictions in Christian dogma. His philosophical poems include *Epître à Uranie* (known also as *Le Pour et le Contre,* 1722?), in which Voltaire shows that he conceives of God more abstractly than do revealed religions; *Le Mondain* (1736), which is both an apology for the epicurean way of life and an economic theory proclaiming the usefulness of luxury;

Poème sur le désastre de Lisbonne (1756), which treats the problem of evil in nature and the earthquake at Lisbon in 1755; and *Poème sur la loi naturelle* (1756), the aim of which is to establish the existence of a universal morality independent of any revealed religion. It is in the *Epître CIV à l'auteur du livre des trois imposteurs* (1769) that Voltaire wrote his oft-quoted observation on religion: "If God did not exist, it would be necessary to invent him." Of his historical works, the greatest are considered to be the *Histoire de Charles XII* (of Sweden) (1731); *Le Siècle de Louis XIV* (1751), in which Voltaire celebrates the progress of the arts, sciences, and letters of that epoch, giving wars a subordinate place; *Essai sur les mœurs et l'esprit des nations* (1756/69), which is regarded as the first history of civilization; *La Philosophie de l'histoire* (1765); and *Le Pyrrhonisme de l'histoire* (1770). His best known philosophical tales, which have become the most popular of his works, are ZADIG; *Bacbouc, ou le Monde comme il va* (1748); *Memnon, ou la Sagesse humaine* (1750); MICROMÉGAS; CANDIDE; *Jeannot et Colin* (1764); L'INGENU; *L'Homme aux 40 écus* (1767), a satire on French economic legislation; and *Le Taureau blanc* (1774), a satire on the Old Testament. Outstanding among his poems are LA HENRIADE; *Le Temple du goût* (1733), a satiric allegorical voyage in the realm of taste; and LA PUCELLE (1755, definitive edition 1762), an irreverent burlesque of Joan of Arc. Voltaire also wrote numerous light and witty verses on a variety of subjects. His more than 12,000 letters are still being edited in over 60 volumes by Theodore Besterman at the present date.

The name Voltaire is simply an anagram of Arouet l.j. (*le jeune*—Fr., "the younger," he having an elder brother), which Voltaire adopted in 1718.

Voltimand and **Cornelius.** In Shakespeare's HAMLET, 2 courtiers who are sent by Claudius to ask the king of Norway to prevent his nephew Fortinbras from attacking Denmark.

Voltore (the Vulture). An avaricious lawyer in Jonson's comedy VOLPONE, OR THE FOX.

Volumnia. In Shakespeare's CORIOLANUS, the "Junolike" mother of Coriolanus. In contrast to the gentle Virgilia, Coriolanus' wife, she is proud and fearless and has exerted great influence on her son's development. In Roman accounts of the story, the name Volumnia is given to the wife of Coriolanus, and his mother is called Veturia.

Volund. See WAYLAND.

Von. For names beginning with von, see also under name following.

Von Stroheim, Erich (1885–1957). German-American motion-picture director, actor, and writer. He arrived in the U.S. in 1909 and became a naturalized citizen in 1926. In 1919, he produced and directed the film *Blind Husbands,* in which he played the leading role and which he adapted from his novel *The Pinnacle.* Among the other films with which he is identified are *Greed* (1923) and *The Wedding March* (1927); his most notable role as an actor was in Jean Renoir's *Grand Illusion* (1937).

Vorágine, La (The Vortex, 1924). A novel by José Eustasio Rivera (1889–1928), Colombian poet and novelist. Considered the finest novel ever written about the *selva,* or tropical forest, of South America, *La Vorágine* describes the odyssey of the narrator, Arturo Cova, who enters the forest in search of a wayward mistress. It is the *selva,* however, that dominates the book; dark and menacing, teeming with life, it destroys the human beings who tamper with its mysteries. The book is also memorable for its picture of life among the wretched rubberworkers of the forest, who also succumb to its malignity.

Vortex, The (1923). A play by Noel COWARD. It is a serious work about a neurotic young man and his mother.

vorticism. A school of painting led by the English novelist Wyndham LEWIS. It was similar to FUTURISM.

Vortigern. One of the kings cited by Geoffrey of Monmouth in the HISTORY OF THE KINGS OF BRITAIN. He was ultimately betrayed by HENGIST AND HORSA, a fate foretold him by the wizard Merlin.

Voss, Johann Heinrich (1751–1826). German poet, member of the GÖTTINGEN HAIN group. His interest in bourgeois and peasant life is seen in his most famous work, the idyllic epic *Luise* (1795).

Vox Clamantis (c. 1382–1384). Latin poem by John GOWER, of 10,000 lines. The first third gives a vivid description of TYLER'S REBELLION of 1381, which serves as the occasion for the allegorical denunciation of the corruptness of men of all classes, particularly with regard to their political responsibilities.

Voynich, Ethel (1864–1960). English novelist. She is best remembered for *The Gadfly* (1897), a romance about the reunification of Italy.

Voysey Inheritance, The (1905). A play by Harley GRANVILLE-BARKER about financial ethics.

Voznesenski, Andrei (1934–   ). Russian poet. One of the leaders of the poetic renaissance in Soviet literature in the early 1960's, he studied architecture in Moscow, but gave up that career when his drawings were destroyed in a fire. His poetry attracted the attention of Boris Pasternak, and he became Pasternak's protégé. Voznesenski's collections of verse include *Parabola* (1960), *Mosaic* (*Mozaika;* 1960), and *The Triangular Pear* (*Treugolnaya grusha;* 1962).

Vronski, Count Aleksei. See ANNA KARENINA.

Vulcan. In Roman mythology, a son of Jupiter and Juno. Originally a destructive god of fire, he became identified with the Greek artisan-god HEPHAESTUS; thus he became the patron of smiths and other craftsmen. He was sometimes called *Mulciber,* the softener.

Vulgar Errors (1646). The popular title of a treatise by Sir Thomas BROWNE. The author, with an impressive display of recondite learning, confutes various errors and misconceptions in science, history, geography, etc. Its original title was *Pseudodoxia Epidemica, or Enquiries into Very Many Received Tenets and Commonly Presumed Truths.*

Vulgate. A Latin version of the Bible made by St. JEROME, under the commission of Pope Damasus (366–384). Jerome began his work in 382, using Greek and Hebrew sources. It is a liberally free, highly literate translation and is still the authorized Latin text of the Roman Catholic Church. Jerome's text was used in the first printed Bible, the Mazarin Bible (see BIBLE, SPECIALLY NAMED EDITIONS).

Vye, Eustacia. See RETURN OF THE NATIVE, THE.

W

Wace (c. 1100–c. 1175). Norman poet. He is especially important in Arthurian literature for his ROMAN DE BRUT. This graceful verse chronicle is an adaptation into French of the Latin *History of the Kings of Britain* (1137) written by Geoffrey of Monmouth, which exalts the deeds of King Arthur.

Wacht Am Rhein, Die (The Watch on the Rhine). A German national song, written in 1841 by Max Schneckenburger and set to music by Karl Wilhelm (1854). It provided the name for WATCH ON THE RHINE, a distinguished play by Lillian Hellman about the Nazis (1940).

Wackenroder, Wilhelm Heinrich (1773–1798). German author. His most important work, some parts of which were written by his friend Ludwig Tieck, is *Herzensergiessungen eines kunstliebenden Klosterbruders* (*Outpourings of the Heart of an Art-loving Lay Brother*, 1797). This revolutionary book deals for the most part with Renaissance painting, and because of its elevation of art to a religion, in opposition to the rationalistic art criticism of the 18th century, it may be considered the original work of GERMAN ROMANTICISM. Toward the end of the book, Wackenroder also treats music and prepares the way for the later romantic appraisal of music as the queen of the arts.

Waddell, Helen (1889–). English scholar, best known as a student of medieval literature. Among her well-known books on that period are *The Wandering Scholars* (1927); *Mediaeval Latin Lyrics* (1929), translations; and *Peter Abelard* (1933), a novel.

Wadman, Widow. In Laurence Sterne's novel TRISTRAM SHANDY, a comely widow who wishes to secure UNCLE TOBY for her second husband. Her wiles are disconcerted by Toby's total innocence, and her purpose perplexed because she, like the reader, is uncertain of the severity of the wound in Toby's thigh. Sterne introduces the Widow by a blank page on which the reader can write his own description.

Wagenknecht, Edward (1900–). American literary historian and anthologist. He is the author of such literary histories as *Cavalcade of the English Novel* (1943) and *Cavalcade of the American Novel* (1952). He has written accounts of Bernard Shaw (1929), Charles Dickens (1929), Mark Twain (1935), Hawthorne (1961), and Washington Irving (1962), the most important being *Longfellow: A Full-Length Portrait* (1955).

Wagner. In Goethe's FAUST, Faust's associate. Wagner is a hard-working, often pedantic scientist, and exemplifies precisely the meticulous, slow-moving character of scholarly life that Faust leaves behind by signing the pact with Mephistopheles.

Wagner, Heinrich Leopold (1747–1779). German poet and dramatist of the STURM UND DRANG. His plays include *Die Kindesmörderin* (*The Child-Murderess*, 1776), on a theme similar to that treated by Goethe in the figure of Gretchen, and *Prometheus, Deukalion und seine Rezensenten* (*Prometheus, Deukalian and his Reviewers*, 1775), a satire directed against Goethe's critics.

Wagner, Richard (1813–1883). German composer, conductor, and author. His operas (called by him "music dramas") form the major part of his output and, though his libretti for his operas often fail to reach the heights, the music generally overcomes their deficiencies. In his work, Wagner developed the concept of LEITMOTIV, an easily recognizable melodic gem associated with a character, situation, or emotion. As a reformer, he did away with the excessive *coloratura* and frequent artificiality of the prevailing operatic style, much as Gluck had done before him. The subject matter of most of his works is drawn from Nordic and Teutonic mythology or from history. His later works were conceived with a view toward performance at the *Festspielhaus* (Festival Playhouse), which he founded (1876) at Bayreuth.

His most extensive work is the cycle DER RING DES NIBELUNGEN. His other operas include TANNHÄUSER (1845), *Tristan und Isolde* (1865; see TRISTAN AND ISEULT), DIE MEISTERSINGER VON NÜRNBERG (1868), and the festival drama PARSIFAL (1882). In his lifetime, Wagner not only became famous for his work, but notorious for his extreme egotism, nationalism, and financial and emotional irresponsibility.

His wife, **Cosima Wagner** (1837–1930), a daughter of Franz LISZT, was instrumental in securing funds for the establishment of the Bayreuth *Festspielhaus*. Their son, **Siegfried Wagner** (1869–1930), was conductor of his father's works at Bayreuth from 1894 until his death. The composer's grandson, **Wieland Wagner** (1917–), is now the stage director at Bayreuth, and has proved a radical innovator in his simplified manner of staging Wagner's operas.

Wahabites. A Muslim sect whose object is to bring back the doctrines and observances of Islam to the literal precepts of the Koran. Their name is derived from their founder, Ibn Abdul Wahab (?–1787).

Wahlverwandtschaften, Die (The Elective Affinities, 1809). A novel by Johann Wolfgang von GOETHE, originally planned as a novella and intended for insertion into *Wilhelm Meisters Wanderjahre* (see WILHELM MEISTER). The title is a term from chemistry referring to the fact that when certain compounds are mixed, their component elements change partners, as it were. Likewise, in the novel, the marriage of two characters, Eduard and Charlotte, collapses when each of them finds a more suitable partner. Ottilie, Charlotte's young niece, arrives at their estate and Eduard falls immediately and passionately in love with her, while Charlotte's practical, sober nature is attracted to a captain who is also their house guest. Ottilie is the book's central character, and like Mignon in *Wilhelm Meister*, she is felt to be somehow in tune with mysterious natural forces in a way that others cannot understand. She is magnetically drawn to Eduard, as he is to her, but his passionate impatience is too much for her and she finally rejects him. Ottilie and Eduard both die in the end and are buried together.

Wailing Wall. A wall in Jerusalem where, according to tradition, the orthodox Jews gathered to lament the fall of the Jewish nation. At times the wall, which is near the site of the Temple of Solomon, now the Mosque of Omar, has been the scene of rioting between the Jews and the Muslims.

Wain, John (1925–). English novelist, poet, and critic. His best-known work is the picaresque comic novel *Hurry on Down* (1953; U.S. title, *Born in Captivity*). He also wrote the novels *Living in the Present* (1955), *The Contenders* (1958), *A Travelling Woman* (1959), and *Strike the Father Dead* (1962). *Nuncle and Other Stories* (1960) contains 10 short stories. *Weep Before God* (1961) is a collection of poetry. See Angry Young Men.

Wainämöinen. Known as the wise enchanter or singing musician, he is the hero of Finland's epic, Kalevala, and plays the role of the Finnish Orpheus.

Waiting for Godot (En Attendant Godot; 1952). A play by Samuel Beckett. It is a tragicomedy about two tramps, in which nothing happens except trivial events and conversations that suggest the meaninglessness of life. The two tramps Vladimir (Didi) and Estragon (Gogo) are continually aware of cold, hunger, and pain as they wait for Godot, who sends a boy to them each day to tell them he will come the next day. The tramps quarrel and contemplate suicide, separation, and departure, but they remain dependent on each other and never do anything. Their condition is reflected in the relationship between Pozzo and Lucky, the only passers-by, whom they at first mistake for Godot. Pozzo is a rich man who cruelly mistreats his servant, Lucky, driving him as if he were an animal. One of the most brilliant passages in the play is Lucky's monologue when he is forced to "think" for his master: it is a satirical and pitiful mixture of Christian, would-be profound and, banal, mechanical thought. Ironically, the pair are as dependent on one another as the two tramps are; on their second appearance Lucky, now dumb, is leading Pozzo, who has become blind. The play ends with the tramps still waiting for Godot to come; they wonder whether it is true that one of the thieves who was crucified with Christ was saved, and, if so, which one. Though the play is bleak and despairing, it is also richly humorous, asserting humanity's will to live in spite of everything.

Waiting for Lefty (1935). A play by Clifford Odets. Its subject is a taxi drivers' strike. Using an impressionistic flashback technique, Odets presents the situations of six people involved in the strike. At the climax the news that the popular committee-man Lefty has been murdered rouses the men to decisive action. *Waiting for Lefty* was one of the best known of the proletarian plays of the 1930's.

Wakefield Cycle. See Towneley Mysteries.

Wakefield Master, the (fl. 1400). Conjectural author of the leading works in the Towneley Cycle (see Towneley Mysteries) of English medieval miracle and mystery plays. He is thought to have been a man of humble birth, though well educated, and probably a secular priest, and is called the Wakefield Master because internal evidence in the plays suggests that they were performed by the local guilds of Wakefield, in southern Yorkshire. The plays attributed to him include *Noah, Herod, The Way of the Cross,* and the *First* and Second Shepherd's Play. Because of their humor, the unknown author has been called by some scholars the "first great comic dramatist in English literature."

Wakeman, Frederic (1909–), American novelist. After *Shore Leave* (1944), Wakeman wrote his best-known novel, *The Hucksters* (1946), a satirical attack on the advertising industry, based on the author's own experiences as an advertising copywriter. *Saxon Charm* (1947) depicts a Broadway producer as a scoundrel. Later novels include *The Wastrel* (1949) and *Deluxe Tour* (1956).

Walden, or, Life in the Woods (1854). A book by Henry David Thoreau. Convinced that "the mass of men lead lives of quiet desperation," Thoreau lived alone in a cabin at Walden Pond, Concord, from 1845 to 1847. His aim was to "front only the essential facts of life," to emancipate himself from slavery to material possessions. After giving these reasons for his experiment, Thoreau goes on to describe his observations and habits at Walden Pond, where he watched the seasons unfold. He does not encourage everyone to live in the woods, but rather urges that life be simplified so that its meaning may become clear.

Waldensians or **Waldenses.** Also called the **Vaudois.** Followers of Peter Waldo of Lyons, who began a reform movement in the Church about 1170. They threw off the authority of the Pope, bishops, and all clergy, appointed lay-preachers (women among them), rejected infant baptism and many other rites, and made themselves so obnoxious to the ecclesiastical powers that they met with considerable persecution. This they survived, and their descendants in doctrine still exist, principally in the Alpine valleys of Dauphiné, Provence, and Piedmont.

Waldseemüller or **Waltzemüller, Martin.** Called himself (in pseudo-Greek) **Hylacomylus** or **Ilacomilus** (1470?–?1518). A German cartographer. In his map of the world in 12 sheets, *Cosmographiae Introductio* (1507), he was the first to use the term America for the New World. See Amerigo Vespucci.

Waley, Arthur [David] (1889–1966). English scholar and translator of Oriental literature. His translations of Chinese and Japanese poetry, originally published in such volumes as *170 Chinese Poems* (1917) and *Japanese Poems* (1919), possess an intrinsic excellence in their own right and have also influenced many modern English and American poets (especially William Butler Yeats and Ezra Pound). He is also known for his equally distinguished translations in prose, including *The No Plays of Japan* (1921), Baroness Murasaki's novel The

TALE OF GENJI, THE PILLOW-BOOK OF SEI SHONAGON, and the Chinese Buddhist tale *Monkey* (1942), and as the author of a number of books of criticism on Chinese painting and literature.

Walker, James J[ohn] (1881–1946). American politician. Having served in the New York assembly and state senate, "Jimmy" Walker was elected mayor of New York City in 1925 and 1929. He was one of the most popular politicians in the state and became a symbol of the jazz era. As an avocation he wrote lyrics for popular songs, the most famous of which was *Will You Love Me in December as You Did in May?* (music by Ernest Ball, 1905). He allowed corruption to creep into the city government, was suspected of illegal transactions, and finally resigned in 1932. In 1940 he became an executive in the cloak and suit industry. Gene Fowler wrote an entertaining biography, *Beau James* (1949).

Walking Stewart. Nickname of **John Stewart** (d. 1822). English traveler, who traveled on foot through Hindustan, Persia, Nubia, Abyssinia, the Arabian Desert, Europe, and the U.S.

Walküre, Die (The Valkyrie). The second of the four operas of Wagner's RING DES NIBELUNGEN.

Wall, The (1950). A novel by John HERSEY. It recounts the harrowing story of the desperate but futile attempt of Warsaw Jews to defend the ghetto from extinction by the Germans. It was dramatized in 1961 by Millard Lampell.

Wall, The (Le Mur; 1939). A collection of short stories by Jean-Paul SARTRE. In the title story the central character awaits death in a Fascist prison during the Spanish civil war. Offered a reprieve if he tells where his leader is hiding, he decides to lie, not out of loyalty, for he has decided that the sacrifice of one man for another is meaningless, but simply to defy his captors. Soon released, he is surprised to learn that his companion had changed his hideout, and has been captured at the spot he had named.

Wallace, Alfred Russel (1823–1913). English naturalist and traveler. His independent formulation of a theory of evolution by natural selection is a most important contribution to science. His paper, *On the Tendency of Varieties to Depart Indefinitely from the Original Type,* was read before the Linnaean Society the same day as Darwin's paper (July 1, 1858). Among his other writings is a valuable description of a trip to the Amazon, *Travels on the Amazon and the Rio Negro* (1853).

Wallace, Edgar (1875–1932). English writer of popular fiction. Highly prolific, he wrote more than 150 thrillers, dealing with crime and detection, as well as many scenarios and plays. Among his books are *The Four Just Men* (1905) and *Sanders of the River* (1930).

Wallace, Lew[is] (1827–1905). American lawyer, novelist, and soldier. Wallace served in the Union army, in which he rose to the rank of major-general. During his political career, he was governor of New Mexico and Indiana, and minister to Turkey. Interested in Mexico, he published his first novel, THE FAIR GOD. With BEN-HUR: A TALE OF THE CHRIST, he achieved great popularity. Other books by Wallace include *The Life of Benjamin Harrison* (1888), *The Boyhood of Christ* (1888), and the popular *Prince of India* (1893).

Wallace, Sir William (1272?–1305). Scottish patriot, known as "the Hammer and Scourge of England." Wallace was a hero in the struggle against England for Scottish independence and was associated with Robert BRUCE. He led Scottish insurgents in a series of engagements against the English, but was ultimately betrayed to the English. He was tried at Westminster Hall, London, found guilty, and was hanged, drawn, and quartered.

Wallenstein. A trilogy of dramas by Friedrich SCHILLER, including *Wallensteins Lager* (*Wallenstein's Camp,* 1798), *Die Piccolomini* (*The Piccolomini,* 1799), and *Wallensteins Tod* (*Wallenstein's Death,* 1799), based on the fall of the German general Count Albrecht von Wallenstein (1583–1634). In Schiller's version, Wallenstein is tempted by the enormous strength he has built up as the principal general of Emperor Ferdinand II in the Thirty Years' War to entertain the idea of deserting the emperor and establishing his own political power. He never actually intends to commit treason, but the idea intrigues him, and he begins to correspond with the Swedish enemy. Jealous elements in the Viennese court discover this correspondence and use it to induce the emperor to outlaw Wallenstein. Wallenstein flees but is murdered by one of his generals.

Waller, Edmund (1606–1687). English poet. He was known for the smoothness and harmony of his verse, which was highly praised by Dryden. Two of his best-known poems are *On a Girdle* and *Go, Lovely Rose,* love lyrics from his *Poems* (1645). Although Waller was banished from England for participation in a Royalist plot during the Civil War, he later wrote a panegyric on Cromwell and a lament for his death. In the Restoration period he wrote verse praising Charles II.

Wall Street. A term for American business and moneyed interests, from the street of that name in New York City. There the financial operations of the country are centered.

Walpole, Horace. 4th earl of Orford (1717–1797). English author and historian. His *Memoirs,* covering the years 1746 to 1791, are among the most important and accurate sources of the period. Selections were published in 1822 and 1846. His *Anecdotes of Painting in England* (1762–1771) is the earliest attempt at a history of art in English; his estate at STRAWBERRY HILL in Twickenham, Surrey, in the process of rebuilding and remodeling (1754–1794) set a taste for refined Gothic architecture and gardening in England. He is best remembered for his encyclopedic *Correspondence*—noted, not only for the superb style of the letters, but also for the wide range of its matter—and for THE CASTLE OF OTRANTO, reputedly the earliest English GOTHIC NOVEL. His other major works include a *Catalogue of Engravers in England* (1763); *Historic Doubts on Richard III* (1768); and *A Letter from XoHo, a Chinese Philosopher at London to his Friend Lien Chi at Peking* (1757), an essay which influenced Oliver Goldsmith's *Citizen of the World.* Although he was the son of Sir Robert WALPOLE and served as a member of Parliament (1741–1767), Walpole himself took little interest in politics. His life was dedicated to literature and art, as a writer, a collector, and as the founder of Strawberry Hill Press which he opened in 1757. His great contribution was a minute history of himself, his friends, and his contemporaries. Leslie Stephen has said "The history of England throughout a very large segment of the eighteenth century is simply a synonym for the works of Horace Walpole." See MYSTERIOUS MOTHER, THE; SERENDIPITY.

Walpole, Sir Hugh [Seymour] (1884-1941). New Zealand-born English novelist. A prolific author, Walpole wrote short stories, criticism, miscellaneous essays, travel books, and plays, but he is best known for his many popular novels. They encompass a wide range of subjects and styles, perhaps the most distinguished being MR. PERRIN AND MR. TRAILL, a remarkable study of morbid psychology. His other novels include *The Wooden Horse* (1909); MARADICK *at Forty* (1910); *Fortitude* (1913), the story of a young man and his development as a writer; *The Dark Forest* (1916); *The Secret City* (1919); JEREMY; *The Cathedral* (1922), concerning the clergy's lives and politics in an English cathedral town; PORTRAIT OF A MAN WITH RED HAIR; and the tetralogy that form THE HERRIES CHRONICLE. His epistolary novel *Farthing Hall* (1929) was written with J. B. Priestley. The character of Kear in Somerset Maugham's CAKES AND ALE is said to have been a satirical portrait of Walpole.

Walpole, Sir Robert. 1st earl of Orford (1676-1745). English statesman. A leader of the Whig party in England, secretary of war (1708-1710), treasurer of the navy (1710-1711), he was twice prime minister and chancellor of the exchequer. He restored credit after the SOUTH SEA BUBBLE and abolished tariff duties on many articles. He stood for peace between France, England, and Spain. An expert in finance and especially commerce, he laid the basis for free trade in England. His ministry fell in 1742 because of his mismanagement of the war with Spain and also because of generally corrupt methods, particularly in rigged elections. He was the father of Horace WALPOLE.

Walpurgis Night or Walpurgisnacht. In German tradition, a WITCHES' SABBATH held on the Brocken, highest peak of the Harz Mountains, the night preceding May 1. The name comes from St. Walpurga (c. 710-c. 777), an English missionary nun who aided St. Boniface in Germany. Although she was actually believed to be a protectress against magic, her May 1 feast day became associated with the pagan traditions earlier assigned to that day. According to these, May 1 marked the official beginning of the agricultural season for men, so the witches held rendezvous with the devil the night before to celebrate the beginning of their own increase in activity. In Part I of his FAUST, Goethe uses the witches' festival as the background for a scene that shows at length the chaotic, magical realm in which MEPHISTOPHELES is at home. In Part II, as a parallel to this scene, there is a classical Walpurgis-night set in Greece, where Faust searches for Helen of Troy. In Thomas Mann's THE MAGIC MOUNTAIN, the chapter dealing with the Shrovetide festival is also entitled "Walpurgis-Night"; by using this title, Mann stresses the similarity of his chapter to both Goethe's scene and the popular legend.

Walsingham, Sir Francis (1530?-1590). English statesman. Walsingham was made secretary of state by Elizabeth in 1573 and, with Lord Burghley, he shared most of the administrative responsibilities of the government. Described as "exceeding wise and industrious," he persistently urged resistance to Spain in the Netherlands, and was alert to Catholic plots against Elizabeth in England. His spies discovered the BABINGTON CONSPIRACY before it could strike, and with its downfall came evidence of treason against MARY, QUEEN OF SCOTS. Walsingham urged Elizabeth to overcome her scruples and sign Mary's death warrant in order to put an end to the threat of Catholic uprisings to put Mary on the throne. He also learned in advance of the preparation of the Spanish Armada, and kept England posted as to its progress.

Waltari, Mika [Toimi] (1908-). Finnish novelist. Waltari is best known for *The Egyptian* (*Sinuhe, Egyptiläinen;* 1945), a long sensational novel about Sinuhe, a young physician. The hero lives among the Syrians, the Hittites, and the Babylonians; he succeeds in penetrating the labyrinth at Crete. The story and its film version were both popular in the U.S.

Walter [Schlesinger], Bruno (1876-1962). German-born conductor, pianist, and composer. He was an authority on the interpretation of works by Gustav Mahler, to whom he was assistant conductor in Hamburg and Vienna, and the Viennese Classicists, especially Mozart. Besides a few musical compositions he wrote a biography of Mahler (1936; translated into English and enlarged in 1958) and an autobiography, *Theme and Variations* (1946).

Walter, Eugene (1874-1941). American playwright. He is best known for such realistic melodramas as *Paid in Full* (1907) and *The Easiest Way* (1908). He also did dramatic adaptations of *The Trail of the Lonesome Pine* (1912) and *The Little Shepherd of Kingdom Come* (1916).

Walter, John (1739-1812). English journalist and publisher, who purchased the patents of an invention called "logotype" which permitted typesetting in units of words rather than of letters. His newspaper *The Daily Universal Register* (founded in 1785) became the London TIMES in 1788.

Walther von der Vogelweide (c. 1170-c. 1230). German minnesinger, most famous of the medieval lyric poets. He was attached to the Viennese court, but later became a wandering minstrel. He is noted for very often breaking with the conventions of traditional love poetry, and for making his poems a vehicle for his strong religious and political opinions, even at the risk of his patrons' disfavor. The German national song, *Deutschland, Deutschland über alles,* is an adaptation of one of his lyrics of patriotism and friendship. He appears as a contestant in the singing tourney in Wagner's opera TANNHÄUSER.

Walton, Izaak (1593-1683). English writer, best known for THE COMPLEAT ANGLER, a discourse on the quiet pleasures of fishing. Walton followed the trade of ironmonger, and in his youth became a close friend of John Donne and Ben Jonson. In his later years he spent much of his time at his beloved avocation, fishing, and in the company of various eminent clergymen, such as the bishop of Winchester, to whom his sweet and pious nature endeared him. Besides *The Compleat Angler,* Walton wrote biographies, usually called *Walton's Lives,* of such literary figures of his day as Donne (1640), Sir Henry

WOTTON (1651), Richard Hooker (1665), George Herbert (1670), and Bishop Robert Sanderson (1678). All his prose work is distinguished by great simplicity and grace of style, earnestness, and humor.

Walton, William [Turner] (1902–   ). English composer. He wrote *Façade,* the opera *Troilus and Cressida* (1954), the oratorio *Belshazzar's Feast* (1931) and many other works.

Wanderer, The (8th century?). Old English poem of over 100 lines in ALLITERATIVE VERSE. It is the poignant dramatic monologue of a warrior, now homeless and kinless, who laments the passing of his former glories and companions, singing an elegy of the times gone by.

Wandering Island. See FAERIE QUEENE, THE.

Wandering Jew, The. A legendary Jew condemned to wander the world until Christ's second coming. Although there are numerous variants of the story, the Jew is always said to have urged Christ to go faster in carrying the cross to Calvary, cruelly refusing him a moment's rest; and Christ's reply is that he goes, "but thou shalt tarry till I come." The Jew thereafter is periodically rejuvenated to the age of 30. His character changes, however; he is now extremely wise, and in his repentance he uses the time of his wandering to exhort other men to be mindful of their sins and avoid the wrath of God.

The story was very popular in medieval Europe, and there are numerous accounts of people having actually seen the Wandering Jew from the 13th to the 18th century. In Latin versions he is called Johannes Buttadeus (John the God-Smiter), with variant translations in the Romance languages, except Spanish and Portuguese, where his names mean John Hope-in-God. In German legend he is called Ahasuerus, and his wanderings often become symbolic of the wanderings of the Jewish people, doomed because of their rejection of Christ. In an early English version he is called CARTAPHILUS (*Kartaphilos*), and a later Italian one identifies him with the 16th-century Venetian Jew Salathiel ben Sadi. Some legends connect him with the WILD HUNTSMAN.

The figure of the Wandering Jew has appeared frequently in more recent literature, such as *Der ewige Jude* (1774), a fragmentary poetic epic by Goethe; *The Undying One* (1830), a Byronic poem by Caroline Norton; *Ahasuerus* (1833), a dramatic prose epic by Edgar Quinet (1803–1875) in which the Jew symbolizes humanity's progress through the ages; and the novels *Salathiel* (1829, retitled *Tarry Thou Till I Come*, 1900), by George Croly (1780–1860); *The Wandering Jew* (*Le Juif errant*; 1845), by Eugène Sue; *Prince of India* (1893), by Lew Wallace.

Wang Wei (707–761). Chinese poet of the T'ang Dynasty. Famed also as a painter and composer of brief prose pieces, he was greatly influenced by Buddhist thought.

Wang Yang-ming or **Wang Shou-jen** (1472–1529). Chinese Ming Dynasty philosopher, statesman and scholar. His school advocated a doctrine of intuitive knowledge through which self-perfection might be achieved. It opposed the elaborate investigation of the philosophy of past sages and of external things advocated by Chu Hsi's Neo-Confucianism.

Wang Yang-ming, although anti-Buddhist, was considerably influenced by CH'AN thought.

War and Peace (Voina i mir; 1864–1869). A novel by Count LEO TOLSTOI. Regarded as the author's masterwork, the story covers roughly the years between 1805 and 1820, centering around the invasion of Russia by Napoleon's army in 1812 and the Russian resistance to the invader. Over 500 characters, all completely and individually rendered, throng the pages of the novel. Every social level, from Napoleon himself to the peasant Platon KARATAYEV, is represented. Interwoven with the story of the war are narrations of the lives of several main characters, especially those of Natasha ROSTOVA, Prince Andrei BOLKONSKI, and Pierre BEZUKHOV. These people are shown as they progress from youthful uncertainties and searchings toward more mature understanding of life. Natasha exemplifies the instinctual approach to life that Tolstoi was later to preach as the way to true happiness. She is one of the most successfully created characters in the book and perhaps ranks as Tolstoi's greatest achievement in character creation. Everything from her girlish excitement at her first ball through her experiences of first love and her final role as wife and mother are depicted with perfect skill. The two main male characters, Prince Andrei Bolkonski and Pierre Bezukhov, represent contrasting approaches to life. Prince Andrei's struggles to find the meaning of life through his intellect end in the belated triumph of his calm acceptance of death as a natural and necessary end to life. Pierre, on the other hand, manages to find a sort of peace in living, chiefly with the aid of the simple wisdom preached to him by the peasant Karatayev. This wisdom, which was a large part of Tolstoi's later philosophy, was that life should be experienced emotionally and accepted naturally, rather than twisted into artificial forms by man's imperfect intellect. Prince Andrei and Pierre have one other thing in common, besides their searchings. Both are romantically connected with Natasha. Prince Andrei is engaged to her, then loses her to the rake Anatol Kuragin. He is reunited with her shortly before his death. After the war is over, Natasha becomes Pierre's wife.

While some writers have criticized the inclusion of the disparate themes of the historical, social, and personal in the novel, the book actually gains in its lifelike effect because of the mixture. The alternations of chapters describing the personal lives of the characters with those depicting battles and dealing with Tolstoi's philosophy of history are well-handled and carefully planned. The monumental size of *War and Peace,* its hundreds of characters, the variety of its action and scenes combine to make it an accurate portrait of the entire Russian nation. But far from being a static tableau, it has a vibrant animation and conveys the movement of people and history.

War Between the States. See AMERICAN CIVIL WAR.

Warburton, Eliot [Bartholomew Elliott George] (1810–1852). Irish writer and traveler. His best-known work, *The Crescent and the Cross* (1844) recalls his travels in Syria and Palestine. He also wrote historical novels such as *Memoirs of Prince Rupert and the Cavaliers* (1840) and *Darien* (1852).

Warburton, William (1698–1779). English theologian and bishop of Gloucester. He thought of himself as dominating Christian apologetics and literary scholarship of his own time. He was a friend of Alexander Pope and instrumental in persuading Pope to add a fourth book to his *Dunciad*. He was also Pope's literary executor (1744) and brought out the first complete edition of his work (1751). His edition of Shakespeare (1747) was severely criticized for want of literary judgment. He was defeated in a literary controversy by Robert Lowth (1765) who attacked his arrogance and lack of scholarship.

Ward, Artemus. Pen name of **Charles Farrar Browne** (1834–1867). American humorist, newspaperman, editor, and lecturer. After working for several New England newspapers, Browne moved to Ohio, where he contributed his first Artemus Ward letters to the Cleveland *Plain Dealer* in 1858. Ward, a shrewd and supposedly illiterate showman, wrote in Yankee dialect of adventures and misadventures with his traveling museum of wax figures (also a few "snaiks and other critturs"). The letters brought Browne a wide reputation, and he was made city editor of the *Plain Dealer*. After difficulties with the manager, he resigned in 1860; by that time, his character was so well known that he became merged with his creator. From Cleveland, Ward (better known than Browne) went to New York, where he wrote for *Vanity Fair*. Among the sketches he contributed was a fictitious interview with Lincoln that delighted the President. At this time, Ward published his first collection, *Artemus Ward, His Book* (1862), which sold 40,000 copies in a short time.

Ward's first lecture, *Babes in the Woods*, was a great success when it was delivered in 1861. A master of the dead-pan expression and the sudden pause, he amused his audience by the incongruity of his remarks. In the course of his travels, Ward met Mark Twain in Virginia City, Nev. In 1866 he departed for England, where he was made an editor of *Punch*, and later died of tuberculosis. He published only one more volume in his lifetime, *Artemus Ward, His Travels* (1865). Posthumously appeared *Artemus Ward in London* (1869), *Artemus Ward's Lectures* (1869), and *Artemus Ward: His Works Complete* (1875, 1890, 1910). Ward's most familiar techniques include cacography, or humorous misspellings, and what he himself called "ingrammaticisms." He loved puns and plays on words, burlesque and anticlimax, and pure absurdity. He exerted an important influence on Mark Twain and other American humorists.

Ward, Edward (1667–1731). English satirist and pub-keeper. His satirical travel pamphlets include *Trip to Jamaica* (1698), a vivid picture of a transatlantic crossing with an uncomplimentary account of the island of Jamaica, and *Trip to New England* (1699), containing a caustic commentary on the Boston blue laws. Ward is also the author of *The London Spy* (1698–1700), a monthly periodical describing "low-life," written in slang. It is a precursor of the *Tatler* and *Spectator* papers.

Ward, Mrs. **Humphry**. Born **Mary Augusta Arnold** (1851–1920). English novelist, granddaughter of Thomas Arnold. She wrote popular novels and was inclined toward philanthropy, social work, and religious polemics. Her more memorable works include ROBERT ELSMERE, *The History of David Grieve* (1892), *Marcella* (1894) and its sequel *Sir George Tressady* (1896), and THE MARRIAGE OF WILLIAM ASHE.

Ward, Nathaniel (1578?–1652). New England Puritan clergyman, born in England but forced to leave during the period of Puritan persecution. He is known for two works: THE BODY OF LIBERTIES, a code of laws for Massachusetts in the preparation of which Ward figured most prominently, and THE SIMPLE COBLER OF AGGAWAM IN AMERICA, written under the pseudonym Theodore de la Guard. Ward returned to England about 1647.

Ward, Wilfrid Philip (1856–1916). English Roman Catholic writer on religion and author of biographies of Cardinal Wiseman (1897) and Cardinal Newman (1912).

Wardle, Mr. In Charles Dickens' PICKWICK PAPERS, an amiable old country gentleman, who attends some of the meetings of The Pickwick Club, and feels a liking for Mr. Pickwick and his three friends.

Miss Isabella Wardle. Daughter of Mr. Wardle. She marries Augustus Snodgrass.

Miss Emily Wardle. Daughter of Mr. Wardle. She marries Mr. Trundle.

Ward No. 6 (Palata nomer shest'; 1892). A long story by Anton CHEKHOV. It depicts the gradual disintegration of Dr. Andrei Yefimich Ragin, the head of a mental hospital. Neglecting the miserable condition of the patients, he withdraws more and more into private study, thought, and alcohol. He finally reaches the point where he is unable to communicate with anyone except one of the inmates, Ivan Dmitrich Gromov, with whom he holds long talks on philosophical subjects. Ragin's unscrupulous assistant uses the doctor's eccentric behavior as a pretext for committing him to the hospital, where Ragin experiences the maltreatment he has allowed the patients to undergo for so many years. The realization of his part in the horror in which the patients live comes upon him just before his death.

Warens, Mme **Louise Eléonore de** (1700–1762). The first benefactress, mistress, and *chère maman* of Jean-Jacques ROUSSEAU, whom she took under her protection and installed as her companion at her farm *Les Charmettes* near Chambéry in the early years of his career (1729–1740).

Warfield, David (1866–1951). American actor. He is known for his starring roles in various productions by David Belasco. *The Auctioneer* (1901) was his first success, but he achieved even more fame in *The Return of Peter Grimm* (1911).

war hawks. In U.S. history, an epithet applied to Democratic Congressmen, mainly from the South and West, who demanded war with Great Britain after 1810. Among them were John C. CALHOUN, Henry CLAY, Langdon Cheves of South Carolina, and Felix Grundy of Tennessee. Southern war hawks hoped to obtain Florida from Spain, Great Britain's ally, while those from the Northwest wanted to end British influence in the area and acquire Canada in the process.

War Is Kind (1899). A volume of poems by Stephen CRANE. His second volume of verse, it contains epigrammatic parables similar to those in the earlier BLACK RIDERS but has a more pronounced vein of cynicism. The title poem, *Do not weep, maiden, for war is kind,* often considered one of Crane's best, is a good illustration of the dramatic irony that Crane used so successfully in both his poetry and prose.

warming-pans. Nickname of the JACOBITES. It was said that Mary of Modena, the wife of James II, never had a living child, but that on one occasion a child, introduced to her bedroom in a warming-pan, was substituted for her dead infant. This "warming-pan child" was the Old PRETENDER.

Warner, Charles Dudley (1829–1900). American essayist, editor, and novelist. Warner is remembered today chiefly for his collaboration with Mark Twain on THE GILDED AGE. In his own right, he edited the Hartford *Evening Post* (1861) and the *Courant* (1867); as editor of the American Men of Letters Series, he published biographies of Washington Irving and Captain John Smith. Warner's book of essays, *My Summer in a Garden* (1871), was praised as a worthy successor to Irving's sketches; his later volumes include *Backlog Studies* (1873), *Baddeck* (1874), and *Being a Boy* (1878). His trilogy of novels, *A Little Journey in the World* (1889), *The Golden House* (1895), and *That Fortune* (1899), satirized the era to which *The Gilded Age* had given a popular name. Warner also wrote travel books and literary criticism, and edited, with others, a multivolume *Library of the World's Best Literature*. Succeeding William Dean Howells in the "Editor's Study" of *Harper's* (1892), he was president of the American Social Science Association and the National Institute of Arts and Letters.

Warner, Rex (1905–   ). English novelist, poet, translator, and critic. THE PROFESSOR and THE AERODROME, his two best-known novels, are fantastic social and political allegories in the style of Franz Kafka. Among his other works are *Poems* (1937), the novels *The Wild Goose Chase* (1937) and *Why Was I Killed?* (1943), and the three biographical novels *The Young Caesar* (1958), *Imperial Caesar* (1960), and *Pericles the Athenian* (1963).

Warner, Sylvia Townsend (1893–   ). English novelist and short-story writer. Many of her novels are fantasies, filled with amiable witches and other quaint characters, *Lolly Willowes* (1926) being the best known of these. Her novel *The Corner That Held Them* (1948) is a reconstruction of medieval convent life. *A Spirit Rises* (1962) is a collection of short stories.

War of 1812. A war between Great Britain and the U.S., sometimes called the second American war for independence. The conflict was caused mainly by British violations of American neutral rights during the Napoleonic wars, though the desire of some Americans for territorial expansion, especially in Canada, was also a factor. (See WAR HAWKS.) Although the U.S. won several naval engagements, attempts to take Canada failed, and the British burned Washington in 1814. The treaty of Ghent (Dec. 24, 1814) restored peace but said nothing about the issues that had caused the war. Andrew Jackson's defeat of the British at New Orleans, the greatest U.S. land victory of the war, occurred two weeks after the signing of the peace treaty. See James MADISON; James LAWRENCE; Oliver Hazard PERRY;

CONSTITUTION; HARTFORD CONVENTION; and STAR SPANGLED BANNER, THE.

War of the Gods. A Babylonian epic poem. A myth of the creation of the world and the establishment of the divine hierarchy, it formed a part of the New Year festival, in which it may have been acted out. It is known as the *Enuma elish,* from its first words. The first gods were Apsu and his wife Tiamat, personifications respectively of the fresh and salt waters. From their union sprang two obscure gods of the deep, Lahmu and Lahamu, who, in turn, gave birth to Anshar and Kishar. They were the parents of ANU, the sky. Anu was the father of EA, the god of wisdom. After his birth a multitude of other gods came into being, but they were such a rowdy lot that Apsu, against Tiamat's advice, determined to destroy them all. Ea, however, drugged Apsu and his dwarfish counselor Mummu, killed Apsu, and imprisoned the dwarf. Tiamat promptly took the god Kingu for her consort.

Ea now married Damkina, who bore him Marduk, the storm-god. A mighty prince, he was given to such pranks as putting the winds on a leash. Many of the gods grew resentful, and asked the primal mother, Tiamat, to destroy him. She created a variety of hideous monsters and, placing Kingu at the head of her forces, prepared to make war on the principal gods, who supported Marduk. Ea and Anu were both quickly routed, but Anshar sent Marduk to fight Tiamat. Arming himself with bow and arrows, a bludgeon of thunder, and a flail of lightning, the young storm-god marched against the ancient goddess. After a terrible battle, he destroyed her and imprisoned her monsters in the depths of the earth. Splitting Tiamat's body into two pieces, he formed the firmament of one half, the foundations of the earth out of the other. He then determined the spheres of the chief gods: Anu was to rule the area above the firmament; Enlil, that between firmament and earth; Ea, the waters below the earth. In order to find someone to serve the gods, he finally created a puppet, man, out of the blood and bones of Kingu, who was killed for the purpose. In gratitude, the gods built the city of Babylon, which was crowned by a great shrine for Marduk.

This story, one of the oldest known creation myths, bears striking parallels to Greek myth, in which the primal father (URANUS) is destroyed by a descendant (CRONOS), and later the young storm-god (ZEUS) defeats various monsters spawned by the primal mother (GE) and imprisons them in the earth. Marduk's killing of Tiamat has its counterpart in Baal's killing of Yam, the dragon of the sea, in the Canaanite *Poem of Baal.*

War of the Theaters. A feud involving several Elizabethan playwrights. A personal quarrel between Ben Jonson on the one hand, and John Marston and Thomas Dekker on the other, was carried into the theaters when Jonson wrote *Cynthia's Revels* for the Children of the Revels at the Blackfriars Theatre. A little later he attacked Marston (who had apparently answered him with a play of unknown name produced by Paul's Boys) in the *Poetaster.* Thomas Dekker then attacked Jonson in *Satiromastix,* played by the Chamberlain's Men. The war of satire was popular with the public for two or three years, but quickly died out. It is referred to in *Hamlet* by the Player King.

War of the Worlds, The (1898). A science-fiction story by H. G. WELLS. It describes an invasion of England by Martians. A radio dramatization of it by Orson WELLES in 1938 caused widespread panic in the U.S.

Warren, Earl (1891–   ). American public official and jurist. After serving as district attorney of Alameda County in California and as state attorney-general, Warren was governor from 1943 to 1953. He was the Republican vice-presidential candidate in 1948 and was appointed chief justice of the U.S. Supreme Court in 1953. In the case of *Brown v. Topeka Board of Education* (1954), he presented a sociological argument that struck down the separate-but-equal doctrine which had been used to defend school segregation, maintaining that "separate educational facilities are inherently unequal."

Warren, Mercy [Otis] (1728–1814). American writer. A friend of the best-known public figures of her time, including John and Samuel Adams and Thomas Jefferson, she devoted her literary talents to the service of the American republic. Her works include *The Adulateur* (1773) and *The Group* (1775), two satirical dramas criticizing British rule in America; *Poems Dramatic and Miscellaneous* (1790); and a *History of the Rise, Progress, and Termination of the American Revolution* (1805).

Warren, Robert Penn (1905–   ). American poet and novelist. Warren was early identified with the Southern Fugitives and AGRARIANS and has been identified with the NEW CRITICISM in literature. He wrote *John Brown, The Making of a Martyr* (1929), an unsympathetic account of the emancipator, contributed to *I'll Take My Stand* (1930), and helped found and edit THE SOUTHERN REVIEW (1935–1942). Concerned with the regional interests of the South, Warren edited with Albert Erskine two anthologies: *A Southern Harvest* (1937) and *A New Southern Harvest* (1957).

Warren's early reputation was made with his poetry. Among his collections are *Thirty-Six Poems* (1935), *Eleven Poems on the Same Theme* (1942), *Selected Poems, 1923–1943* (1944), and *Brother to Dragons* (1953), a dramatic narrative in verse. While his poetry is noted for its vivid metaphor and brilliant descriptions, his novels have won him a far wider audience, beginning with *Night Rider* (1939), a story of the Kentucky Tobacco War. *At Heaven's Gate* (1943) was suggested by the career of Luke Lea, a corrupt Tennessee businessman and politician, but his two best-known novels are ALL THE KING'S MEN and WORLD ENOUGH AND TIME. *Circus in the Attic* (1948) is a collection of two novelettes and twelve short stories. Among his other fiction are *Band of Angels* (1955), a tale of miscegenation in the Civil War era; *The Cave* (1959), a philosophical novel; and *Wilderness* (1961), a historical novel of the Civil War period.

Warren is equally distinguished as a critic. With Cleanth Brooks he published *Understanding Poetry* (1938), one of the most popular of college textbooks. His essays have been widely published in literary journals, and his *Selected Essays* appeared in 1958.

Warrior Queen. See BOADICEA.

Wars of the Roses (1455–1485). A series of encounters between members of the house of York and the house of Lancaster for possession of the English throne. The Wars take their name from the roses, white for York and red for Lancaster, that were the emblems of the opposing factions. The parties were united after the Lancastrian Henry Tudor, earl of Richmond, defeated the Yorkist Richard III at the Battle of Bosworth (1485); Henry was proclaimed king (HENRY VII) and married Elizabeth of York, the eldest daughter of Edward IV.

Wartburg. A castle near Eisenach in Germany. Landgrave Hermann of Thuringia (d. 1217) welcomed wandering entertainers at his court there, and according to legend sponsored a *Sängerkrieg*, or minstrels' contest, in 1207 between WALTHER VON DER VOGELWEIDE, WOLFRAM VON ESCHENBACH, HEINRICH VON OFTERDINGEN, and other illustrious MINNESINGERS. This merged with another legend in which KLINGSOR, helped by the Devil, competes with Wolfram von Eschenbach, victoriously representing Christendom. These traditions, popularized in the poem *Der Wartburgkrieg* (*The Battle of Wartburg*, 13th century), were used by Wagner for the singing contest in his opera TANNHÄUSER.

Warton, Thomas (1728–1790). English literary historian, critic, and poet laureate (from 1785), son of Thomas Warton (c. 1688–1745), noted poet and teacher. His *History of English Poetry* (1774–1781) extends to the end of the Elizabethan age. It is the first history of English literature which still merits our attention. Like Richard Hurd, Warton regretted the loss of the medieval imaginative world:

We have parted with extravagancies that are above propriety, with incredibilities that are more acceptable than truth, and with fictions that are more valuable than reality.

This sentiment is reflected in his poetry as early as the *Pleasures of Melancholy* (1747).

Washington, Booker T[aliaferro] (1856–1915). American Negro educator. Born in Virginia of a Negro slave and a white man, he educated himself first at night school and then by working his way through Hampton Normal and Agricultural Institute (1872–1875). After some years of teaching, he returned to Hampton to teach Indian students. He established a night school for the needy, and was chosen to found Tuskegee Institute (1881). He organized the National Negro Business League in Boston (1901), before which he gave many important speeches. Washington wrote many books, the best known of which are *Up from Slavery* (1901) and *The Story of the Negro* (1909). In 1946, a bust and tablet in his honor were unveiled at the Hall of Fame in New York City.

Washington, George (1732–1799). First president of the U.S. (1789–1797), known as "the father of his country." Washington had little formal education, but early showed an aptitude for mathematics, and by the time he was 15 was a skilled surveyor. From 1753 to 1759 he was an officer in the French and Indian War. He was elected to the Virginia House of Burgesses in 1758 and successively reelected until the house was dissolved by the colonial governor in 1774. During the decade before the American Revolution, he became progressively more dissatisfied with British rule, particularly with the commercial regulations that required him and other Virginia planters to trade exclusively with Britain under conditions which he felt to be unfair to the colonists.

Washington was one of Virginia's delegates to the first and second Continental Congresses in 1774 and 1775, and was elected commander of the Continental Army in June, 1775. He was faced with the problem of directing an untrained and inexperienced army, composed primarily of militiamen whose terms of enlistment were short; his task was further complicated by a lack of supplies and the hesitancy on the part of Congress to establish the long-term enlistments necessary for a permanent army. In spite of his handicaps his leadership and success in the field were remarkable, and he won brilliant victories at Trenton and Princeton, N.J. (1776–1777) and at Yorktown (1781).

Having retired to his estate at MOUNT VERNON after the war, he returned to public life to preside at the Constitutional Convention in 1787. In 1789 he was unanimously elected president. During his administration he followed Hamilton's financial program, observed neutrality in the European wars, and crushed the WHISKY REBELLION, firmly establishing the authority of the new government. He declined a third term and prepared, with the help of several friends, his famous FAREWELL ADDRESS.

Numerous myths later grew up around the figure of Washington. The most famous of these was created by Mason Locke Weems whose biography of Washington (1800) contained the story that as a child Washington admitted having cut down a cherry tree because he could not tell a lie and was immediately forgiven by his astonished father. Another widely repeated story showed Washington throwing stones (some claimed silver dollars) across the Rappahannock River.

Some of the works of fiction in which Washington appears directly or indirectly are H. H. Brackenridge's *Modern Chivalry* (1792–1815), Charles Brockden Brown's *Ormond* (1799), Cooper's *The Spy* (1821), J. K. Paulding's *The Old Continental* (1846), S. Weir Mitchell's *Hugh Wynne, Free Quaker* (1897), Paul Leicester Ford's *Janice Meredith* (1899), Joseph Hergesheimer's *Balisand* (1924), and Kenneth Roberts' *Oliver Wiswell* (1940). Two 20th-century dramas dealing with Washington are Maxwell Anderson's *Valley Forge* (1934) and Sidney Kingsley's *The Patriots* (1942). See CONWAY CABAL; Henry LEE.

Washington Square (1881). A novel by Henry JAMES. As a boy, James had lived on Washington Square in New York City, at that time a fashionable residential district. The novel concerns Catherine Sloper, the shy daughter of wealthy, urbane, sardonic Dr. Austin Sloper. When young Morris Townsend, who is courting Catherine for her money, learns that her father will disinherit her if she marries him, he leaves her. Townsend renews his courtship after the doctor's death, but is rejected by Catherine, who lives on at Washington Square, an old maid. She has achieved her own kind of self-realization, freeing herself from the two men who had victimized her. The theme of the young, defenseless person trying to escape from the tyranny of an older, often

more knowledgeable adult, became a favorite theme for James.

Wasps, The (Sphekes, 422 B.C.). A comedy by ARISTOPHANES. *The Wasps* is an attack on Aristophanes' favorite butt, the Athenian demagogue Cleon, who had recently initiated the practice of paying citizens for jury duty. Philocleon (Cleon-lover), a foolish old man, suffers from an inordinate passion for jury duty. He resorts to all manner of ruses to escape from his house, where his sensible son Bdelocleon (Cleon-hater) is trying to keep him confined for his own good. Finally, the young man persuades his father to hold trials at home. In the first, a dog is tried for stealing cheese in a hilarious parody of legal proceedings. In spite of all his son's efforts, Philocleon remains unregenerate to the last.

Wassermann, August Paul von (1866–1925). German bacteriologist, known for his discovery in 1906 of a diagnostic test for syphilis.

Wassermann, Jakob (1873–1934). German novelist of international popularity. His writings, in their psychological realism, show the influence of Dostoevski. Among his novels are *Die Juden von Zirndorf* (*The Jews of Zirndorf*, 1897), *Caspar Hauser oder Die Trägheit des Herzens* (*Caspar Hauser, or Sluggishness of the Heart*, 1908) and *Der Fall Maurizius* (*The Case of Maurizius*, 1928). See Kaspar HAUSER.

Waste Land, The (1922). A long poem by T. S. ELIOT. Completely breaking from conventional modes of poetic expression in its condensed use of language, its wealth of literary and historical references, and its lack of narrative sequence, the poem occasioned a violent literary controversy on publication and has been the subject of an endless amount of critical explication ever since. In five sections it explores the different psychic stages of a soul in despair struggling for redemption. The waste land, throughout the poem a central image of spiritual drought, is contrasted with sources of regeneration relied upon in the past, such as fertility rituals and Christian and Eastern religious practices. The dominant imagery in the poem is drawn from Jessie L. Weston's *From Ritual to Romance*, a study of some of the themes of medieval romances and legends, such as the Grail story, which probably originated in ancient fertility religions. In medieval legend, the waste land and its ruler, the Fisher King, rendered sterile by a curse, were cured by a knight who underwent purifying ordeals. But doubt remains the burden of Eliot's poem, and there is no resolution at the end, when, in a decaying twilight world, the poet shores up his ruins with literary and religious fragments. Each one echoes a hope of rebirth, but they are in a medley of foreign languages, suggesting that they are nothing more than unassimilated memories.

The publication of *The Waste Land* was an important event in the development of modern English poetry. The technique of the poem was as radically new as that of *Ulysses*, and is in some ways similar. Both contrast the spiritual stagnation of the present with the myths of the past and use the city as a major symbol of paralysis; both are full of scenes, phrases, and references that have little meaning in themselves but echo and explain one another; and both depend upon the reader's knowledge of many works of literature, of various religions, and of history.

Following Ezra Pound's suggestion, Eliot reduced *The Waste Land* to about half its original length. The first version has disappeared.

Watch on the Rhine (1941). A play by Lillian HELLMAN. A German refugee in the U.S., whom Nazi agents want to intercept, is recognized by a hanger-on at the German embassy. The refugee kills the informer, and in so doing helps to awaken the American conscience to the danger of tyranny.

Water Babies, The, A Fairy Tale for a Land-Baby (1863). A fantasy by Charles KINGSLEY, concerning the adventures of little Tom the chimney-sweep who falls into a river and is transformed into a kind of miniature merman.

Waterhouse, Keith (1929–   ). English novelist. He is best known for his very funny and popular novel *Billy Liar* (1959). Billy is a likable Yorkshire youth whose congenital lying and fantasy-building involve him in endless trouble.

Waterloo, battle of (June 18, 1815). A decisive victory gained near Waterloo (a village south of Brussels) by the Allies over NAPOLEON BONAPARTE. The French numbered about 72,000; the combined forces of the British, the Dutch, and the Germans, under Arthur Wellesley, duke of WELLINGTON, numbered about 67,000; the Prussians, under Gebhard Leberecht von Blücher, made an additional 50,000. The Allies lost about 22,000 and the French about 37,000. Waterloo is the climax of the Hundred Days, which commenced with Napoleon's escape from Elba; his seizure of power ended, however, with the restoration of Louis XVIII on June 28, 1815.

The triumph of the "Iron Duke" over the "Man of Destiny" made Waterloo one of the most famous phrases of the period—second only to the name Bonaparte. Today it has come to mean failure and tragic, hope-shattering defeat. More than a battle, Waterloo marks the end of almost 20-years of European war, of the Napoleonic dreams of glory, of the spirit best captured in the novels of Stendhal—the 19th-century Waterloo had at last begun.

Watkins, Vernon (1906–   ). English poet. Born in Wales, he is known for his musical, mystical and visionary verse. Among his volumes of poetry are *The Ballad of the Mari Lwyd* (1941) and *Cypress and Acacia* (1959).

Watson, Thomas (1557?–1592). English poet, translator, and scholar. His best-known work is the *Passionate Century of Love* (1582), a hundred eighteen-line "sonnets" adopted from classical and contemporary Continental poets. He also wrote a Latin version of Tasso's *Aminta* (1585).

Watteau, Antoine (1684–1721). French painter. He is known for his charming pictures of small *fêtes champêtres,* or informal and fashionable gatherings in imaginary parks. His art is one of refinement and sensitivity; it is captivating because of the delicacy of its color harmonies and the poetry of its landscapes. His numerous drawings are spirited and accurate as well as elegant. His work was emulated by the rococo painters and decorators of the 18th century.

Watts, Isaac (1674–1748). English nonconformist theologian, hymn writer, author, and pastor. He is best known for his sacred poems, *Horae Lyricae*

(1706), *Psalms of David* (1719), and *Divine and Moral Songs for Children* (1720). He also wrote theological and philosophical works. He revolutionized the Protestant hymn and many of his hymns are still sung today. He is the author of the famous lines, "How doth the little busy bee," from one of his instructive poems for children.

Watts-Dunton, [Walter] Theodore (1832–1914). English critic and man of letters. SWINBURNE spent with him the later years of his life at Putney. He was well regarded as a critic in his day and left valuable memoirs, *Old Familiar Faces* (1916).

Wat Tyler. See TYLER'S REBELLION.

Waugh, Alec. Pen name of **Alexander Raban Waugh** (1898–   ). English writer. The brother of Evelyn Waugh, he gave a frank picture of life in an English boys' school in *The Loom of Youth* (1917). His later works include *Sunlit Caribbean* (1948), a travel book; *Island in the Sun* (1956), a novel; and *The Early Years of Alec Waugh* (1962), an autobiography.

Waugh, Evelyn (1903–1966). English novelist. His earliest and most famous novels are biting satires of the world of fashionable London society and the young intellectuals of the 1920's—the world also satirized in the early novels of Aldous Huxley. They are farcical comedies with undertones of violence, cruelty, and bitterness. Novels of this type are DE-CLINE AND FALL, *Vile Bodies* (1930), BLACK MISCHIEF, A HANDFUL OF DUST, *Scoop* (1938) which satirized newspapers and radio, and THE LOVED ONE. Waugh was converted to Roman Catholicism in 1930, and many of his later novels have as heroes Catholics of the gentlemanly type he formerly satirized. His satirical war novels are *Put Out More Flags* (1942) and the trilogy consisting of *Men at Arms* (1952), *Officers and Gentlemen* (1954), and *Unconditional Surrender* (1961; U.S. title, *The End of the Battle*), whose central character is Guy Crouchback. BRIDES-HEAD REVISITED, one of his best-known novels, has a strong Catholic background. *Helena* (1950) is a fictionalized biography of St. Helena, the mother of Constantine. Other books are *Tactical Exercise* (1957), a collection of short stories; *The Ordeal of Gilbert Pinfold* (1957), a self-portrait and an account of a hallucination; travel books with a rather aristocratic, imperialistic flavor; and critical works and biographies.

Waverley (1814). The first of Sir Walter SCOTT's historical novels, which established him as the foremost romantic novelist. The chief characters are Prince Charles Edward, the Young Pretender; the noble old baron of Bradwardine; and Captain Edward Waverley, the hero. Waverley is at first a captain in the royal army, but is cashiered for suspected Jacobite leanings. He then espouses the cause of the Pretender and joins his service. At the battle of Prestonpans he saves the life of the Englishman Colonel Talbot. When the Pretender's cause collapses, the colonel, out of gratitude, obtains a pardon for young Waverley, who then marries Rose Bradwardine and quietly settles down in the family seat at Waverley Honor.

Waverley Novels, the. A series of 32 novels and tales by Sir Walter SCOTT. The first novel of the series, *Waverley,* gave the series its name. The novels were published anonymously "by the author

of Waverley" who came to be known as the Great
Unknown. Originally, Scott published them anonymously because he feared that novel writing was beneath his dignity as a clerk of court; he discovered
that his anonymity increased sales and kept it up
until 1825, when his identity, by then generally
known, was disclosed.

Waves, The (1931). A novel by Virginia WOOLF.
Highly original, unconventional, and poetic, it describes the characters, lives, and relationships of six
persons living in England. The book is composed of
interior monologues (see STREAM OF CONSCIOUSNESS),
spoken by the six characters in rotation, and of interludes describing the ascent and descent of the sun,
the rise and fall of the waves, and the passing of the
seasons. These natural cycles symbolize the progress
of time, which carries the individual from birth to
death.

As children, the six live in the same house by the
seashore, and take lessons from the same governess.
Their early experiences influence their developing
personalities and remain valuable memories for the
rest of their lives. They have two reunions: one with
PERCIVAL in a restaurant, and one, in middle age, at
Hampton Court. The characters' life stories are revealed only incidentally, but their monologues throw
brilliant, subtle light on their various personalities.
The three men are various types of the artist: Bernard
is a life-loving storyteller; Neville is a meticulous
perfectionist; and Louis, an Australian with an inferiority complex, is vain, driving, and nourished by
tradition. The women, too, differ widely in character: Susan is domestic and maternal—she loves Bernard, but marries someone else; Jinnie is a flirtatious
society beauty and, like Neville, who loves only
Percival, does not marry. Rhoda, timid and mystical,
becomes the mistress of the other outsider, Louis,
and finally commits suicide. In a final monologue,
Bernard as an elderly man reviews the lives of himself and his friends, and feels himself flowing into
their consciousnesses like a wave into other waves.
He thinks that the six of them together make up
one complete person.

Wayland. A wonderful and invisible smith of
English legend. He is the English form of the
Scandinavian *Volund* or *Volunder*, a supernatural
smith and king of the elves. In *Frithiof's Saga* (13th
century), Volund forges the armor of Thorsten,
Frithiof's father, particularly a golden arm-ring
which descends to Frithiof as one of his most precious
possessions. According to the legend, King Nidud,
or Nidung, of Sweden cut the sinews of Volund's
feet and cast him into prison to avail himself of his
workmanship, but the smith made his escape in a
feather boat. Scott introduced Wayland or Wayland
Smith into his novel *Kenilworth* (1821). He is said
to have lived in a cromlech near Lambourn, Berkshire (since called *Wayland Smith's Cave*), and legend relates that, if a traveler tied up his horse there,
left sixpence for a fee, and retired from sight, he
would find the horse shod on his return. Kipling
has the tale of *Weland's Sword* in his *Puck of Pook's
Hill* (1906).

Wayne, Anthony. Known as "Mad Anthony"
Wayne (1745–1796). American general. He became
famous for his surprise attack on STONY POINT, N.Y.,
during the American Revolution. His decisive victory

over the Indians at the battle of Fallen Timbers
(Aug. 20, 1794) in northwestern Ohio secured the
Northwest frontier and served as evidence of the
stability of the new U.S. government.

Way of All Flesh, The (1903). A novel by
Samuel BUTLER, published posthumously. The hero,
Ernest, is the son of an English clergyman, Theobald
Pontifex. Few clergymen in fiction are as unsympathetic as this pious bully, nor is his docile, sanctimonious wife, Christina, any more lovable. The
story deals with one of Butler's favorite themes—
the relations between parents and children—and is
autobiographical in many details. It is, moreover, a
keenly satirical criticism of middle-class English family life. Ernest's school and university days are not
happy. He struggles with the problem of orthodoxy,
goes to live in the slums, is thrown into prison for
impulsive advances to a respectable girl, and marries
the extremely vulgar Ellen, who had been his
mother's maid. He is freed from this marriage by
the fact that Ellen was already married. Receiving
an inheritance from an aunt, he is able to devote his
life to literature, and finally wins some measure of
self-respect and genuine success.

Way of the Cross (Lat., *Via crucis*). A series
of pictures or images in a church (see STATIONS OF
THE CROSS) representing the successive stages of Jesus'
passion. The term also applies to the devotions said
at each of these representations.

Way of the World, The (1700). A comedy by
William CONGREVE. The plot revolves around the
efforts of the urbane and witty Mirabell to marry
Millamant despite the opposition of her aunt, Lady
Wishfort, to whom he has feigned passion in order
to disguise his suit for her niece. In the famous "bar-
gaining" scene, Mirabell and Millamant decide to
marry after negotiating an intricate agreement on
their various rights and responsibilities. The play is
now considered Congreve's greatest work; however,
the comparatively poor reception it received contributed to Congreve's decision to give up writing for
the stage.

We (*My*; 1924). A novel by Yevgeni ZAMYATIN.
Describing a regimented totalitarian society in the
26th century, it is an ancestor of such novels as Aldous Huxley's *Brave New World* and George Orwell's
1984. It was first published abroad in 1924. Publication in 1929 in a Russian version at Prague led to
Zamyatin's expulsion from the federation of writers
in Russia and his eventual departure from the country.

Wealth of Nations, The (1776). An influential
work on economics by Adam SMITH, the full title
of which is *Inquiry into the Nature and Causes of
the Wealth of Nations*. It is in this work that Smith
outlines a system of LAISSEZ-FAIRE economics based on
an absolutely free economy.

Wearing of the Green, The. An Irish patriotic
and revolutionary song, dating from 1798. Green was
the emblematic color adopted by Irish Nationalists.

Weaver, John V[an] A[lstyn] (1893–1938).
American newspaperman and writer. At the suggestion of H. L. Mencken, he wrote verse in slang.
His work includes *In American* (1921), *Finders*
(1923), and *More in American* (1926). *Love 'Em
and Leave 'Em* (1926), which he wrote with George
Abbott, was a successful play. *Trial Balance* (1931)

is his autobiography in verse. He also wrote three novels, including *Joy Girl* (1932), a satire of Hollywood life.

Weavers, The (Die Weber; 1892). A play by Gerhart HAUPTMANN, considered the finest work of German NATURALISM. Written entirely in dialect, it treats the economic plight of the Silesian weavers and centers about a weavers' revolt that had been put down some years before.

Web and the Rock, The (1939). A novel by Thomas WOLFE. Wolfe follows his autobiographical hero, George Webber (called Eugene Gant in LOOK HOMEWARD, ANGEL and OF TIME AND THE RIVER) to the "Enfabled Rock" of New York, where, in the midst of his youthful literary struggles, he meets the gifted scenic designer, Mrs. Esther Jack. During their love affair, he is at first entranced by and then disillusioned with the magic of the city that is so much a part of Esther's personality. At length George breaks from Esther's web of devotion and flees abroad to seek in an older culture the stability he could not find in the American city. YOU CAN'T GO HOME AGAIN is a sequel.

Webb, Mary (1881–1927). English novelist. She is best known as the author of PRECIOUS BANE and *The Golden Arrow* (1916). Her books, set on the Welsh borders, describe shy, untutored heroines in scenes of rustic violence and beauty. Her novels were brilliantly satirized by Stella Gibbons in COLD COMFORT FARM.

Weber, Die. See, WEAVERS, THE.

Weber, Karl Maria von (1786–1826). German composer best known for his romantic operas. *Der Freischütz* (1821) is based on the old legend of the hunter whose bullets, charmed by the devil, cannot miss; *Oberon* (London, 1826, sung in English) is based on the poem *Oberon* of Wieland. Weber employed the LEITMOTIF technique, which was later developed by Richard WAGNER.

Weber, Max (1864–1920). German sociologist and historian whose comprehensive view of society greatly influenced modern social science. His most controversial work is *The Protestant Ethic and the Spirit of Capitalism* (*Die protestantische Ethik und der Geist der Kapitalismus;* 1904–1905), an essay in which he related the rise of capitalist economy to the Protestant belief in the moral value of fulfilling one's worldly duties.

Weber, Max (1881–1961). Russian-born American painter, lecturer, and essayist on art.

Weber and Fields. A famous vaudeville team composed of Joseph Weber (1867–1942) and Lewis Fields (1867–1941). These comedians appeared together from the age of 10 on; they organized their own company, and later performed in movies and on the radio. Among their productions were *Whoop-Dee-Doo* and *Higgledy-Piggledy*.

Webster, Daniel (1782–1852). American statesman and orator. A native of New Hampshire, Webster was admitted to the bar in 1805. As a member of Congress (1813–1817), he attacked the War of 1812. He moved to Massachusetts in 1816 and, after two more terms in Congress, was elected to the U.S. Senate in 1827. A champion of nationalism as opposed to state sovereignty, he engaged in a famous debate (1830) with Senator Hayne of South Carolina in which he extolled "Liberty *and* Union, now and forever, one and inseparable!" After two futile attempts to win the Whig presidential nomination, he served as secretary of state (1841–1843), negotiating the Webster-Ashburton Treaty with Great Britain, which settled the dispute over the Maine boundary. In 1844 Webster was again elected to the Senate, where he favored the COMPROMISE OF 1850 in his Seventh of March speech, which began, "I wish to speak today, not as a Massachusetts man, nor as a Northerner, but as an American." His moderate stand cost him the support of abolitionists, and John Greenleaf Whittier denounced him in his poem *Ichabod* (1850). Whittier later condoned Webster's action in *The Lost Occasion* (1880). Webster is also a prominent character in Stephen Vincent Benét's THE DEVIL AND DANIEL WEBSTER.

Webster, Jean (1876–1916). American writer. The grandniece of Mark Twain, she is best known for *Daddy-Long-Legs* (1912), her sentimental, highly successful tale about an orphan, and its sequel, *Dear Enemy* (1915). She also wrote *When Patty Went to College* (1903) and *Just Patty* (1911), collections of stories for girls; the heroine is probably modeled on Adelaide Crapsey, whose verse Miss Webster edited.

Webster, John (1580?–?1625). English dramatist, noted for his passionate tragedies of revenge. His most famous plays are THE WHITE DEVIL and THE DUCHESS OF MALFI, both of which deal with

Title page of Webster's *The Duchess of Malfi* (1623).

actual events that occurred in Italy. He made additions to Marston's THE MALCONTENT and collaborated with Thomas Dekker on *Westward Ho* and *Northward Ho*, both of which were published in 1607. He also wrote *The Devil's Lawcase* (pub. 1623), a tragicomedy, and the tragedy *Appius and Virginia* (pub. 1654), to which Thomas Heywood probably contributed. He is perhaps the Elizabethan dramatist most frequently compared with Shakespeare because of the dynamism and poetic lyricism that characterize his best work.

Webster, Margaret (1905–1972). Anglo-American theatrical director and producer. The daughter of Ben Webster and Dame May Whitty, she made her debut as an actress with John Barrymore in *Hamlet* in London. She directed a notable series of Shakespearean plays starring Maurice Evans (1937–1939). In *Shakespeare Without Tears* (1942), she discussed the problems of producing Shakespeare's plays.

Webster, Noah (1758–1843). American lexicographer and author. A man of varied interests, Webster was a teacher, lecturer, journalist, lawyer, judge, scientist, gardener, and traveler. In politics, he was an ardent partisan of Federalism, advocating the adoption of the Constitution and a strong central government. While a resident in Amherst, Mass., he was president of the Amherst Academy (1820–1821) and helped to found Amherst College.

Webster believed that the American nation needed a language and literature of its own; he wrote a three-volume *Grammatical Institute of the English Language*. Parts II (1784) and III (1785) were a grammar and a reader, but Part I, commonly known as *Webster's Spelling Book* or the *Blue-Backed Speller* (1783), became a best seller in its own right. Used in all schools, it sold some 60 million copies in the course of the century and helped to make American orthography uniform.

Webster's great work, *An American Dictionary of the English Language* (1828), was revised in 1841. Upon Webster's death, George and Charles Merriam acquired the unsold copies and publishing rights to the work, bringing out in 1847 a revision edited by Webster's son-in-law, Chauncey A. Goodrich. This, the first Merriam-Webster unabridged dictionary, was followed by the *American Dictionary of the English Language* (1864), *Webster's International Dictionary* (1890), *Webster's New International Dictionary* (1909), *Webster's New International Dictionary, Second Edition* (1934), and *Webster's Third New International Dictionary* (1961). The broad scope of the 1961 edition excited critical controversy.

Wedekind, Frank (1864–1918). German playwright and actor. The scion of a wealthy family and destined for a respectable career in law, he left school to take a job advertising soup. While absorbing the divergent influences of the realist Hauptmann on the one hand, and of the symbolists Strindberg and Büchner on the other, he traveled as secretary to a circus. His first two plays, *The Young World* (*Die Junge Welt;* 1890) and *Spring's Awakening* (*Frühling's Erwachen;* 1891) dealt with the problems created by adolescent ignorance of sex. The latter caused a sensation that was repeated with the appearance of *Earth Spirit* (*Der Erdgeist;* 1899) and its sequel *Pandora's Box* (*Die Büchse der Pandora;*

1903), both of which treated sexual themes with revolutionary frankness that shocked many audiences. Wedekind and his actress wife played leading roles in many of these plays, which the author produced. Wedekind's plays were as important for their style as for their content; they are regarded as forerunners of German expressionism in the theater.

Wedgwood, C[icely] V[eronica] (1910–   ). English historian. She is known especially for her studies of the 17th century. Her works include *Oliver Cromwell* (1939), *The King's Peace, 1637–1641* (1955), *The King's War, 1641–1647* (1959), and *Poetry and Politics under the Stuarts* (1960).

Weekley, Ernest (1865–1954). English lexicographer. His books popularizing etymology include *The Romance of Words* (1912) and *Words and Names* (1932).

Week on the Concord and Merrimack Rivers, A (1849). A narrative by Henry David THOREAU. The book is the physical and spiritual history of a trip Henry and his brother John had made 10 years before.

Weems, Mason Locke (1759–1825). American clergyman, biographer, and bookseller. Known as "Parson" Weems, he was an itinerant evangelist and book agent. In 1800, he wrote a *History of the Life, Death, Virtues and Exploits of George Washington*. Vastly popular in its own day, the book was accepted as semifiction, and then took its place in American mythology. In its fifth edition (1806), the earliest known version of young Washington and the cherry tree is related. Aside from his other "biographies" of Franklin, Penn, and Marion, Weems wrote a number of moral tracts, among them *God's Revenge Against Murder* (1807) and *The Drunkard's Looking Glass* (1812).

Wee Willie Winkie, And Other Stories (1889). A book of short stories by Rudyard KIPLING. The story that gives the title to the book tells how six-year-old Percival William Williams, son of an officer of the British Indian Army, rescues the fiancee of his friend and hero, Lieutenant Brandis, and so "entered into his manhood." The name "Wee Willie Winkie" is an allusion to the familiar character of nursery rhyme who went about in his nightgown.

Wegg, Silas. In Charles Dickens' OUR MUTUAL FRIEND, a one-legged man who keeps a fruit stand. Mr. Boffin hires him to read aloud *The Decline and Fall of the Roman Empire*, a task somewhat beyond his powers. Wegg is a shrewd rascal and hopes to blackmail Boffin, but fails in the attempt.

Weidman, Jerome (1913–   ). American novelist. Weidman's first novel, *I Can Get It for You Wholesale* (1937) was so popular that he followed it with a sequel, *What's in It for Me?* (1938); both depict unscrupulous characters in the New York garment industry. His other novels include *Too Early to Tell* (1946), a satire on war propaganda, and *The Enemy Camp* (1958), dealing with anti-Semitism. *The Horse That Could Whistle "Dixie"* (1939) and *The Captain's Tiger* (1937) are short-story collections. His play *Fiorello!* (1959) won a Pulitzer Prize.

Weil, Simone (1909–1943). French philosophical writer. Jewish-born, she became interested in Catholicism and in Hellenic traditions of mystic spirituality.

Posthumous publication of her meditations include *Gravity and Grace* (*La Pesanteur et la grâce;* 1947), *The Need for Roots* (*L'Enracinement;* 1949), and *Waiting for God* (*Attente de Dieu;* 1950).

Weill, Kurt (1900–1950). German-born composer, known especially for his operas and musical comedies. Under the influence of the playwright Bertolt Brecht, he adopted a superficially popular style while retaining subtle techniques of modern art music. With Brecht he wrote his most famous work: *Die Dreigroschenoper* (1928; THE THREEPENNY OPERA, based on *The Beggar's Opera*). In the U.S. he worked with Maxwell Anderson on *Lost in the Stars* (1949; based on Alan Paton's *Cry the Beloved Country*) and *Knickerbocker Holiday* (1938; based on Washington Irving's *Father Knickerbocker*), and composed the "folk opera" *Down in the Valley* (1948) to a libretto by Arnold Sundgaard.

Weimar classicism (Ger., *Weimarer Klassik*). A literary movement in Germany, usually dated from GOETHE's return from Italy (1788) until SCHILLER's death (1805). During most of this period, Goethe was in Weimar itself and Schiller was in Jena, a small university town only a few miles away. From 1794 on, the two poets worked together closely, and in the main, it is their thinking and writing, their cooperative effort to establish and develop a new poetic humanism, that form the backbone of the movement. Wilhelm von HUMBOLDT, who was a friend of both poets, also contributed a good deal of critical thought to their endeavors; and though the brothers SCHLEGEL are usually thought of in connection with romanticism, they both influenced and were themselves influenced by the classical strivings of Goethe and Schiller.

The ideal of the Weimar classicists was one of harmony and balance, for which they took the ancient Greeks as their models, following WINCKELMANN. But neither Goethe nor Schiller believed in the rationalistic harmony of the enlightenment. Both sought, instead, an emotional and organic harmony based on the inward sympathy that unites all men, and on an unstrained, optimistic view of the relationship between man and the world. They thought that the ordinary man in his actions, as well as the artist in his works, should exercise restraint, but never at the expense of his essential humanity.

Goethe and Schiller cooperated on a collection of *Xenien* (1797; see XENION) in which, with a good deal of satire about other authors, they stated their own position within the literature of the time. Among Goethe's works, other central documents of Weimar classicism are *Iphigenia in Tauris* (1787), *Torquato Tasso* (1790), *Wilhelm Meisters Lehrjahre* (1795–1796), and *Hermann und Dorothea* (1797). Among Schiller's works, the essays on aesthetics are important for the movement, as are a number of lyric poems, including *Der Spaziergang* (*The Walk*, 1795), an imaginary excursion through the whole progress of human culture; *Würde der Frauen* (*Dignity of Women*, 1795), which attempts to define the eternal and unchanging spiritual relationship between man and woman; and *Das Lied von der Glocke* (*The Song of the Bell*, 1799), which takes the making of a town's church bell as the occasion for a eulogy on the communal spirit in human society.

Weimar Republic (1919–1933). The unofficial name for the German government, beginning with the formulation of its constitution in the city of Weimar and lasting until the dictatorship of Hitler. The republic was not very popular, largely because it had accepted the severe conditions of the Treaty of VERSAILLES (1919) after defeat in World War I.

Weir of Hermiston (1896). An unfinished novel by Robert Louis STEVENSON. Left unfinished at his death, this work promised to be Stevenson's masterpiece and contains some of his best writing. It is the story of Archie Weir, banished by his severe father, a judge, to live in solitude in the village of Hermiston. Here he meets Christina with whom he falls in love. The novel breaks off at this point; Stevenson intended to have Archie forced to commit a murder because of his love for Christina, tried and sentenced to death by his own father, and rescued by some relatives of Christina. Archie's father was to die of shock after his condemnation of his son.

Weissnichtwo. Nowhere. The word is German for "I know not where," and was coined by Carlyle in his SARTOR RESARTUS. It is the name of the place where Diogenes Teufelsdröckh holds his professorship of Things in General.

Welch, Denton (1915–1948). English novelist. He wrote two novels of adolescence noted for their sexual frankness: *Maiden Voyage* (1943) and *In Youth Is Pleasure* (1945). Though he was an invalid, he traveled a great deal; his interesting *Journals* (1952) were published posthumously.

Weld, Theodore Dwight (1803–1895). American abolitionist. At Utica Academy, N.Y., Weld fell under the influence of the revivalist, Charles Grandison Finney, and left school to become an itinerant preacher. By 1830 he was a confirmed abolitionist and helped to found Lane Seminary in Cincinnati, an abolitionist school whose president was Lyman Beecher. According to Harriet Beecher Stowe, Weld inspired her to write *Uncle Tom's Cabin*. In 1834, Weld was one of the founders of the American Anti-Slavery Society; he trained missionaries and wrote tracts for the group. Among these are *The Bible Against Slavery* (1837) and *American Slavery as It Is* (1839); G. H. Barnes and D. L. Dumond edited *The Correspondence of Theodore Weld* (1834).

Weller, Samuel. The center of comic interest in Charles Dickens' PICKWICK PAPERS, he is a bootblack at the White Hart and afterward servant to Mr. PICKWICK, to whom he becomes devotedly attached. When Pickwick is sent to the Fleet Prison, Sam Weller, rather than leave his master, gets his father to arrest him for debt. His colorful speech and his cunning on behalf of his master make him one of Dickens' most amusing characters. "Bless his old gaiters . . ." Sam Weller cries about Pickwick, "I never seen such a fine creetur in my days. Blessed if I don't think his heart must ha' been born 25 year arter his body, at least!"

Welles, Gideon (1802–1878). American journalist and politician. Welles was editor and part owner of the Hartford *Times* and a founder of the Hartford *Evening Press* (1856). Elected to the Connecticut legislature (1827–1835), he later served as secretary of the navy under Lincoln and Johnson (1861–1869). His introduction of ironclad battleships and his effective blockade of the Confederacy helped win the

Civil War. Welles's *Lincoln and Seward* (1874) was based on one of the many articles he wrote for *Galaxy* magazine. Autobiographical material is found in *The Diary of Gideon Welles* (3 v., 1911), edited by E. T. Welles, and in Welles's letters published in *The Magazine of History* (1924).

Welles, [George] Orson (1915–   ). American actor, radio and theatrical producer. Welles began his career in Dublin with the Gate Theater. In 1934 he directed the Woodstock Festival and later founded the Mercury Theater. He produced an all-Negro *Macbeth* and a provocative modern-dress *Julius Caesar*. His radio dramatization (1938) of H. G. Wells's *War of the Worlds*, done in the form of a newscast, caused a panic when people thought that the Martians had actually invaded the earth. In 1940, Welles wrote, directed, and starred in the motion picture *Citizen Kane;* he was later active in several movies and was especially noted for his controversial productions of *Macbeth* (1947) and *Othello* (1955). In recent years he has acted and produced chiefly in Europe.

Wellesley, Lady Dorothy (1889–1956). English poet. She was much admired by William Butler Yeats, who gave her more space in his *Oxford Book of Modern Verse* (1936) than he gave T. S. Eliot. Her poems of nature and elemental dream imagery appear in *Genesis* (1926) and other volumes; *Early Light: Collected Poems* was published in 1956.

Wellington, 1st duke of. Arthur Wellesley. Known as the **Iron Duke** (1769–1852). English general and statesman. He was chief in command, after the death of Sir John Moore (1761–1809), in the Peninsular War (1809), represented England at the Congress of Vienna (1814–1815), and defeated Napoleon at WATERLOO. A popular idol in England, he was prime minister from 1828 to 1830.

Wellman, Paul I[selin] (1898–1966). American writer. Wellman worked as a newspaperman in Kansas for 25 years, and it is with life in the West that almost all his books deal. He wrote several histories, including *Death on the Prairie* (1934) and *Death in the Desert* (1935), but he is best known for his highly popular novels. They include *Jubal Troop* (1939), *The Bowl of Brass* (1944), *The Walls of Jericho* (1947), *The Chain* (1949), *The Iron Mistress* (1951), *The Comancheros* (1952), and *The Female* (1953).

Wells, Carolyn (1869–1942). American anthologist, writer of humorous verse and detective stories. She is best known for her anthologies: *A Nonsense Anthology* (1902) and *A Parody Anthology* (1904). The sleuth in her detective stories is called Fleming Stone; they were published in the collection *Fleming Stone Omnibus* (1933). *The Patty Books* are a series of children's stories.

Wells, Charles Jeremiah. Pen name **H. L. Howard** (1799?–1879). English poet. A friend of Keats and Hazlitt, Wells abandoned poetry after the failure of two early works. One of these, the florid Marlowe-like verse drama *Joseph and His Brethren* (1823), was rediscovered in the 70's by Swinburne and Rossetti, highly praised, and republished (1876) shortly before the old man's death, enjoying a temporary vogue.

Wells, H[erbert] G[eorge] (1866–1946). English novelist and journalist. Wells is known for his science fiction, his satirical novels, and his popularized accounts of history and science. He is also known for his militant advocacy of socialism, feminism, evolutionism, rationalism, and the advancement of science. The first great writer of science fiction, H. G. Wells is author of THE TIME MACHINE, *The Island of Dr. Moreau* (1896), *The Invisible Man* (1897), THE WAR OF THE WORLDS, *The First Men in the Moon* (1901), *The Sea Lady* (1902), *The Food of the Gods* (1904), *In the Days of the Comet* (1906), and *The Country of the Blind* (1907). His best comic, satirical, and didactic novels are LOVE AND MR. LEWISHAM, KIPPS, ANN VERONICA, TONO-BUNGAY, *The History of Mr. Polly* (1910; see MR. POLLY), THE NEW MACHIAVELLI, *Marriage* (1912), *The Passionate Friends* (1913), *The Wife of Sir Isaac Harman* (1914), *The Research Magnificent* (1915), and MR. BRITLING SEES IT THROUGH. Most of these novels are concerned with improving men's living conditions and their attitudes toward life. His later novels are even more didactic and are now almost unread. Other later works were purely political, scientific, and sociological. Among these are his popular, near-classic survey, *Outline of History* (1920), and a compressed version of that work, *A Short History of the World* (1922). The *Outline* was the first work in a trilogy that continued with *The Science of Life*, written in collaboration with his son G. P. Wells and Julian Huxley (1929), and *The Work, Wealth, and Happiness of Mankind* (1932).

The son of a small tradesman and professional cricketer, Wells was apprenticed to a drygoodsman and a druggist before he made his way to the Royal College of Science, where he studied biology under Thomas Huxley. He became a teacher, and a Fabian. The novels *Love and Mr. Lewisham, Kipps*, and *Tono-Bungay* contain autobiographical elements. *The Book of Catherine Wells* (1928) is his appreciation of his second wife, a former student, written after her death. *Experiment in Autobiography* (1934) is an account of his life.

Wells's first sociological books were *Anticipations* (1901) and *Mankind in the Making* (1903), in which he criticized existing society. In *A Modern Utopia* (1905) he presented his remedies: internationalism, socialism, and the advancement and proper use of science. His *Men Like Gods* (1923) is a well-known tale depicting an ideal world. Like Shaw, Wells was attacked by the Catholic writers Hilaire Belloc and G. K. CHESTERTON for his progressive ideas; like his friend Arnold Bennett, he was attacked by Virginia Woolf for his old-fashioned naturalistic novels. In later life Wells became highly eccentric. His *The Open Conspiracy* (1928) proposed government by supermen and a new world religion based on physics; *The World of William Clissold* (1926) is a long didactic novel on the subject. Just before his death he reached a point of absolute despair for mankind in *Mind at the End of its Tether* (1946). Wells thought that man's scientific advances were totally outdistancing his intellectual and social development.

Deliberately aiming to achieve greatness as a prophet, journalist, and spokesman for progress, rather than as a novelist, Wells was considered to possess one of the most vigorous intellects of his period in England. We are still working toward many of the social and scientific goals he proposed.

Aerial warfare and the atomic bomb, which he "invented" in *The War in the Air* (1908) and *The World Set Free* (1914), have proved as apocalyptically destructive as he prophesied.

We'll to the Woods No More. See LAURIERS SONT COUPÉS, LES.

Welsh, Jane Baillie (1801–1866). Scottish-born wife of Thomas CARLYLE, whom she married in 1826. An exceptionally intelligent and charming woman, she is said to have suffered much from her husband's irritability, neglect, and ambition. A. J. Froude edited a collection of her *Letters* in 1883, and additional volumes have since been published. See CRAIGENPUTTOCK.

Welty, Eudora (1909–). American short-story writer and novelist. Born in Jackson, Miss., she is known for the perceptive artistry of her stories of small-town life in the Deep South. Her stories are collected in *A Curtain of Green* (1941), *The Wide Net* (1943), and *The Golden Apples* (1949). *Delta Wedding* (1946) is a sensitive novel about Southern family life. *The Ponder Heart* (1954) is a short novel dramatized successfully in 1956. She has an uncanny ear for colloquial speech, which she uses with richly comic effect, and her sense of the universal and mysterious gives her work an almost mythological dimension.

Wendell, Barrett (1855–1921). American teacher, scholar, and writer. Wendell was appointed to the Harvard faculty in 1880 and taught there until 1917. He gave the first course at Harvard in American literature; in later years he gave lectures on American literature and traditions at the Sorbonne. After publishing two novels, he wrote scholarly works (including *Cotton Mather, The Puritan Priest* (1891), *William Shakespeare* (1894), *The Temper of the 17th Century in English Literature* (1894)) textbooks, essays, and three short plays. He also wrote *The Traditions of European Literature* (1920). Wendell's principal work, however, was his *A Literary History of America* (1900). The volume extolled the contributions of New England, vented Wendell's prejudices against democracy, and wittily discoursed on American attitudes. A Boston Brahmin and an Anglophile, Wendell often indulged in a rhetorical flourish; he described Whitman's *Leaves of Grass* as "confused, inarticulate, and surging in a mad kind of rhythm which sounds as if hexameters were trying to bubble through sewage."

Wentworth, Captain. See PERSUASION.

Wentworth, Sir Thomas. See 1st earl of STRAFFORD.

werewolf. See WERWOLF.

Werfel, Franz (1890–1945). Austrian poet, novelist, and playwright. Among the best-known expressions of his religiously based yearning for a brotherhood of man are the novels: *Barbara oder Die Frömmigkeit* (translated as *The Pure in Heart*, 1929), *Die vierzig Tage des Musa Dagh* (*The Forty Days of Musa Dagh*, 1933) and THE SONG OF BERNADETTE. The same message, in an earlier, more expressionistic stage of development, is found in his collections of verse: *Der Weltfreund* (*Friend to the World*, 1911), *Wir Sind* (*We Are*, 1913) and *Einander* (*Each Other*, 1915). His earlier plays, such as *Der Spiegelmensch* (*The Mirror Man*, 1920), GOAT SONG, and JUAREZ UND MAXIMILIAN (1924) contain many

expressionist features and tend toward a tragic view of the conflict between good and evil; but he subsequently became more optimistic, as in *Der Weg der Verheissung* (*The Road of Destiny*, 1936), a triumphant dramatic unfolding of Jewish history, and JACOBOWSKY AND THE COLONEL (*Jakobowski und der Oberst*, 1944), a comedy. Werfel fled Germany and the Nazis in 1938, came to the U.S. in 1940, and died in California.

Werner, Zacharias (1768–1823). German dramatist. His plays, the most famous of which is *Der 24. Februar* (*The 24th of February*, 1810), pretend to probe deeply into the workings of fate, but are actually no more than unconvincing contrivances composed of improbable accidents. After divorcing his third wife, he became a Catholic priest (1814).

Werner, or The Inheritance. A verse drama by Lord BYRON, retold from *Kruitzner, or the German's Tale* in Harriet Lee's *Canterbury Tales*. Count Stralenheim has for years persecuted Werner, whose inheritance he has unjustly appropriated. In a moment of temptation, Werner steals a gold rouleau from the count; Werner's son Ulric, upon hearing him confess the theft, secretly murders the count. Werner secures his inheritance, but, learning that his son was the assassin, sends Ulric away with a curse.

Werther. See SORROWS OF YOUNG WERTHER, THE.

werwolf or **werewolf.** A legendary creature. A man-wolf (A.S. *wer*, man), i.e., a man who, according to medieval superstition, was turned—or could at will turn himself—into a wolf (the *loupgarou* of France). This creature had the appetite of a wolf, and roamed about at night devouring infants and sometimes exhuming corpses. Its skin was proof against shot or steel, unless the weapon had been blessed in a chapel dedicated to St. Hubert.

This superstition was once common to almost all Europe, and still lingers in certain remote areas. In the 15th century a council of theologians convoked by the Emperor Sigismund gravely decided that the werwolf was a reality.

Ovid tells the story of Lycaon, king of Arcadia, turned into a wolf because he tested the divinity of Jupiter by serving up to him a "hash of human flesh"; Herodotus describes the Neuri as having the power of assuming once a year the shape of wolves; Pliny relates that one of the family of Antaeus was chosen annually, by lot, to be transformed into a wolf, in which shape he continued for nine years; and St. Patrick, we are told, converted Vereticus, king of Wales, into a wolf.

Werwolf (Loup Garou). The giant captain of the Dipsodes, whom Pantagruel defeats in Rabelais' GARGANTUA AND PANTAGRUEL. The two engage in an epic duel to decide the victory, Werwolf armed with an enormous club, Pantagruel with a boat's mast which he uses as a spear. Pantagruel kills Werwolf and uses the dead giant's body like a scythe to mow down the enemy.

Wescott, Glenway (1901–). American novelist and poet. Wescott was born in Wisconsin and educated at the University of Chicago. His first book, *The Bitterns* (1920), was a volume of poems. *The Apple of the Eye* (1924), his first novel, was originally published serially in the *Dial*. His best-known book is the novel *The Grandmothers* (1927), a portrait of an American family. Although Wescott was for years an expatriate, he returned to the Middle West for material for *Good-bye, Wisconsin* (1928), a collection of short stories, and *The Babe's Bed* (1930). *Fear and Trembling* (1932) is a collection of essays. *The Pilgrim Hawk* (1940) and *Apartment in Athens* (1945) are novels with European settings.

Wesley, Charles (1707–1788). English Methodist clergyman and hymn writer, brother of John WESLEY. He composed some 6,500 hymns and left a *Journal*, published in 1849; he also accompanied his brother John on his missionary trip to Georgia.

Wesley, John (1703–1791). English evangelist and theologian, famous as the founder of METHODISM. In 1735, accompanied by his brother Charles WESLEY, he went to the U.S. as a missionary to the Indians and colonists in Georgia. Returning to England (1738) he established the first Methodist Church. In 1763 he drew up a legal deed stating that Methodist preachers should preach no other doctrine than that contained in his *Notes on the New Testament* and the first four volumes of his sermons. He was a powerful preacher, traveling all over England on horseback. He published his prose *Works* in 1771–1774. His *Journal* was published in 1909–1911.

West, Anthony (1914–   ). English novelist and critic. The son of Rebecca WEST and H. G. WELLS and now resident in the U.S., he is the author of *Heritage* (1955) and *The Trend Is Up* (1960). He is literary critic for *The New Yorker*.

West, Benjamin (1738–1820). American painter. A straightforward portraitist, his reputation was established by ambitious historical paintings which are criticized today for their dry exactitude of detail. He settled in England in 1763 and was appointed historical painter to George III in 1772; in 1792 he succeeded Sir Joshua Reynolds to the presidency of the Royal Academy. Among the numerous American artists who flocked to London to study with him were John Singleton Copley, Gilbert Stuart, and Samuel Morse.

West, Morris L[anglo] (1916–   ). Australian novelist. He is best known for his widely read novel, *The Devil's Advocate* (1959). He is also the author of *Gallows on the Sand* (1955), *Kundu* (1956), *Children of the Sun* (1957), *The Crooked Road* (1957), *Backlash* (1958), *Daughter of Silence* (1961), *Shoes of the Fisherman* (1963), and *Children of the Shadows* (1963).

West, Nathanael. Pen name of Nathan Wallenstein Weinstein (1904–1940). American novelist. An unusual and highly original talent, West is best known for two novels, MISS LONELYHEARTS and DAY OF THE LOCUST, that reveal his vision of the horror and emptiness of modern life. These and his two other short novels, *The Dream Life of Balso Snell* (1931) and *A Cool Million* (1934), constitute the entire contents of *The Complete Works of Nathanael West* (1959) with an introduction by Alan Ross. West and his wife, Eileen McKenney, the subject of Ruth McKenney's *My Sister Eileen* (1938), were killed in an automobile accident in California.

West, Dame Rebecca. Pen name of Mrs. **Cecily Maxwell Andrews,** born Fairfield (1892–   ). English novelist, critic, and essayist. Her best-known novels are *The Return of the Soldier* (1918), *The Judge* (1922), and *The Thinking Reed* (1936). *Black Lamb and Grey Falcon* (1942) is a study of Yugoslavia; *The Meaning of Treason* (1949) is a political and psychological study; and *The Court and the Castle* (1958) is literary criticism. As a young woman she was an ardent feminist and social reformer. Anthony WEST is her son by H. G. WELLS. She was awarded the D.B.E. in 1959.

Westbrook, Harriet (179?–1816). English schoolgirl who became the 1st wife of Percy Bysshe SHELLEY. A friend of Shelley's sisters, Harriet was unhappy at school and at home, and Shelley, possibly in an attempt to "rescue" her, eloped with her to Edinburgh in 1811. When they separated in 1814, she had borne him one child and was expecting another. She drowned herself in the Serpentine in 1816.

Westermarck, Edward Alexander (1862–1939). A Finnish philosopher. He wrote, among other books, *The Origin and Development of the Moral Ideas* (2 vols.; 1906–1908). *The History of Human Marriage* (1891) is his best-known work.

Western, Sophia. See TOM JONES.

Western, Squire. An irascible, hare-hunting Tory squire, father of the heroine of TOM JONES by Henry Fielding. He is singularly unlearned, very prejudiced and countrified, but fond of his daughter Sophia.

Western Reserve. A tract of land of 3,666,921 acres near Lake Erie which was "reserved" by Connecticut when the states ceded their western lands to the federal government after the Revolution. Connecticut gave up jurisdiction over the Western Reserve in 1800, but kept the title to the soil and sold it to individual purchasers.

Weston, Jessie L[aidley] (1850–1928). English writer and scholar. A specialist in the field of medieval legend and literature, she is best known for her book *From Ritual to Romance* (1920), her study of the origins and development of the legend of the Holy Grail, which provided the basis for T. S. Eliot's poem THE WASTE LAND.

West Point. The United States Military Academy at West Point, N.Y., on the Hudson River. Here most regular officers of the U.S. Army are trained.

West-Running Brook (1928). A book of poems by Robert FROST. His fifth volume of collected verse, it contains, besides the title poem, other well-known lyrics, such as ACQUAINTED WITH THE NIGHT, *The Bear,* and *The Egg and the Machine.* The title poem is a dialogue between husband and wife about a New England brook that perversely flows west instead of east.

Westward Ho! (1855). A romance of the Spanish Main by Charles KINGSLEY. The chivalric young Amyas Leigh contends relentlessly with the Spaniards in love and in war in actions that range from the jungles of Central America to the vales of Devonshire. The culmination comes when Amyas, now a captain, participates in the destruction of the Armada.

Wetzel, Friedrich Gottlieb. See BONAVENTURA.

We who are about to die. See MORITURI TE SALUTAMUS.

Wexley, John (1907–   ). American playwright. He is the author of *The Last Mile* (1930), which concerns the final days of a prisoner condemned to death. It is a strong plea for prison reform. *Steel* (1931) deals with the labor situation, and

They Shall Not Die (1934) is based on the Scottsboro trial.

Weyden, Rogier van der (c. 1400–1464). Flemish painter. Born in Tournai, he was originally called by the French form of his name, Roger de la Pasture. His clearly outlined figures are severe by comparison with the art of Jan van Eyck, but he revealed greater concern for the rhythmical movement and dramatic expression of his figures.

Whalley, Edward. See William GOFFE.

Wharton, Edith [Newbold Jones] (1862–1937). American novelist and short-story writer. A follower of Henry James, she is known for her studies of the tragedies and ironies of life, especially among the members of middle-class and aristocratic New York society in the 19th and early 20th centuries. Her work is marked by an interest in psychological characterization, a preoccupation with manners and morals, and an adherence to artistic form.

Born into one of New York's best families, she was at first criticized for her intellectual pursuits. Her first real success came with THE VALLEY OF DECISION, a novel of 18th-century Italy. In THE HOUSE OF MIRTH, she satirized the New York society that she knew so well. In 1907 she moved permanently to Europe, where she wrote *Madame de Treymes* and *The Fruit of the Tree* (both 1907), but she soon returned to America in her work, using the New England scene for what many consider her best and least typical work: ETHAN FROME.

After a minor novel, *The Reef* (1912), Mrs. Wharton wrote another book about the breakdown of traditional New York culture: THE CUSTOM OF THE COUNTRY. During World War I, she received the Cross of the Legion of Honor for her relief work in Paris. *The Marne* (1918) and *A Son at the Front* (1923) show the influence of her wartime experiences. *Summer* (1917) is a novel about the summer romance of a New England girl. In 1920 appeared THE AGE OF INNOCENCE, her highly successful novel of manners.

Of her later work, perhaps the best is OLD NEW YORK, a series of four novelettes that includes THE OLD MAID. *The Children* (1928) and its sequel *Hudson River Bracketed* (1929) deal with family problems. Of her several volumes of short stories, perhaps the best known is XINGU AND OTHER STORIES. *A Backward Glance* (1934), her autobiography, is well known for its picture of Henry James, her close friend and literary mentor.

What Every Woman Knows (1908). A play by J. M. BARRIE. The heroine, Maggie Wylie, is a plain but wise little woman with a humorous charm all her own. John Shand, a student who works as a railway porter in the summer, breaks into the house to investigate the library; Maggie's affectionate father and her brother, who regret that she has "no charm," offer the intruding student money with which to complete his education if he will ask Maggie to marry him five years later. In due course they are married, and with her encouragement and help, he enters Parliament. When he reveals a desire to elope with Lady Sybil Lazenby, Maggie manages to give him such a surfeit of that lady's company as to bring him back to her cured.

What Is Art? (Chto takoye iskusstvo?; 1897–1898). A treatise on aesthetics by Count Leo TOL-STOI. Tolstoi considered art an extension of morality and felt that it should be suffused with a morally uplifting spirit. To be good, in Tolstoi's terms, a work of art must also be simple enough to be understood by everyone, not only the well-educated. The feelings of the artist should be obvious in his work. In the Christian era these feelings should reflect a religious view of man's place in the world and his relation to God.

As examples of literature that transmit such feelings, Tolstoi lists Charles Dickens' *A Tale of Two Cities, A Christmas Carol,* and *The Chimes,* Victor Hugo's *Les Misérables,* Harriet Beecher Stowe's *Uncle Tom's Cabin,* and other works by Dostoevski, Schiller, and George Eliot.

As examples of "universal art" that convey "the simplest feelings of common life accessible to all men in the whole world," Tolstoi cites *Don Quixote,* the comedies of Molière, *David Copperfield, The Pickwick Papers,* and works by Gogol, Pushkin, and Maupassant.

Tolstoi's views on art and aesthetics became the framework for the doctrine of socialist realism in Soviet literature, where extraliterary standards are used to judge works of art.

What Maisie Knew (1897). A novel by Henry JAMES. Always interested in the "small expanding consciousness" of a child, James deals in this novel with 12-year-old Maisie Farange, whose divorced parents have subsequently remarried. Because custody of the child had been awarded to each of the parents for alternating periods of six months, Maisie presently learns that her stepfather and her stepmother are having adulterous affairs, just as earlier, she had been aware of her own parents' infidelities. Instead of corrupting her, this knowledge endows her with a precocious understanding of the adult world; ultimately, she decides to live with her old governess Mrs. Wix, instead of with either of her parents.

What Makes Sammy Run? (1941). A novel by Budd SCHULBERG. The hero, Sammy Glick, is a tough New York youth who works his way into a position of power in the motion-picture industry, where his harshness and crude manners are not out of place. A fast-paced novel, it is filled with much realistic detail of life in the movie colony.

What Price Glory? (1924). A play by Maxwell ANDERSON and Laurence STALLINGS. It is one of the first realistic American treatments of World War I. Centered on the rivalry of Captain Flagg and Sergeant Quirt for the favors of a French girl, the play caused a sensation by its frank presentation of the profanity and brutality of the professional soldiers and the wearying ugliness of war.

Wheatley, Phyllis or **Phillis** (1753?–1784). Negro poet, the first woman writer of her race in the U.S. In 1761 she was brought to America from Africa and purchased as a slave by John Wheatley, a Boston merchant. As a child she showed unusual intelligence and was given an education. Famous in her day, she was received in London aristocratic circles and her poetry was praised by George Washington. Later critics, however, have agreed with Thomas Jefferson that her *Poems on Various Subjects* (1773) "were below the dignity of criticism."

Wheelock, John Hall (1886–). American poet and editor. While still at Harvard, Wheelock published with his classmate Van Wyck Brooks *Verses of Two Undergraduates* (1905). In 1911 he published *The Human Fantasy*, his first book of verse, and began his association with the publishing house of Charles Scribner's Sons. His many later volumes of poetry include *The Beloved Adventure* (1912), *The Black Panther* (1922), *The Bright Doom* (1927), *Poems 1911–1936* (1936), *Poems Old and New* (1956), and *The Gardener and Other Poems* (1961). He was awarded the Bollingen Prize for his work in 1962. Wheelock has also written biography and has edited various books.

wheel of fortune. See FORTUNA.

When Johnny Comes Marching Home. A marching song of the Civil War. It was composed by the Union Army bandmaster, Patrick Sarsfield Gilmore (1829–1892). It has retained its popularity.

When Lilacs Last in the Dooryard Bloom'd (1867). A poem by Walt WHITMAN. With the return of lilacs in the spring, the poet mourns again the death of Abraham Lincoln. The thrush pours forth his carol of death, as the coffin slowly journeys through the land to its place of rest. A western star, sailing in the sky, "dropt in the night, and was gone." The song of death becomes victorious; the poet finally glorifies the "strong deliveress."

When We Dead Awaken (1900). A play by Henrik IBSEN. The play is a symbolic statement of a theme that can be found in almost all of Ibsen's dramas: that spiritual death is the price of denying love. The sculptor Rubek meets Irene, who had been the model for his masterpiece many years before, but whom he had not dared to love for fear that love would interfere with his art. She tells him that they both have been dead for many years. In an attempt to regain a life of the spirit they go up into the wild mountains; pressing on to the peak and the sunrise, they are swallowed up in a storm.

Where Angels Fear to Tread (1905). A novel by E. M. FORSTER. The first of Forster's novels, written when he was 26, it is set principally in Italy; its theme is the effect of that land's so different culture and atmosphere on insular, provincial British personalities. After Lilia Herriton, who as a widow of 33 has gone to Italy and married Gino Carelli, the carefree, irresponsible 21-year-old son of a dentist, dies in childbirth, her Herriton relatives decide that they must bring her infant son back to England to be properly brought up. Gino, however, refuses to relinquish his son; the sum of money that they offer as a bribe is of no avail; and when Harriet, Lilia's grimly conventional, self-righteous sister-in-law attempts to impose her will and abduct the baby, the child is accidentally killed. The title of the novel is taken from Alexander Pope's *Essay on Criticism:*

For fools rush in where angels fear to tread.

Whichcote, Benjamin. See CAMBRIDGE PLATONISTS.

Whig. An abbreviation of Whiggamore (*whig,* "to drive," and a *mare*). The name was first given to raiding parties in Western Scotland about 1648 and thence to Scottish Presbyterians. In 1679, it became a name for those opposed to James II's succession to the throne, and after that it was applied to one of the two chief political parties of England. In the latter part of the 19th century, the Whigs were replaced by the Liberal Party.

Whilomville Stories (1900). A collection of 13 stories by Stephen CRANE. Set in a town usually thought to be Port Jervis, N.Y., these tales are realistic and unsentimental sketches of childhood. Several are partly based on incidents from Crane's own youth. The title might be translated as "once-upon-a-time town," but the stories are less nostalgic than most stories about childhood. *Lynx-Hunting,* a comedy in which Jimmie Trescott shoots a cow, has as one of its characters Henry Fleming, the hero of THE RED BADGE OF COURAGE and the story *The Veteran.*

Whisky Rebellion or **Insurrection** (1794). An outbreak in western Pennsylvania, resulting from an attempt by the federal government to enforce an excise law passed in 1791, imposing duties on domestic distilled liquors. The rebellion was halted, proving the power of the new government to enforce its laws.

Whistler, James [Abbott] McNeill (1834–1903). American painter and etcher. Except for short periods of time, he lived abroad, especially in France, where he became a friend of the impressionists, and in England, where he became champion of the concept that divorces art from social, literary, or anecdotal significance. His refined, eclectic work is influenced by Japanese prints, from which he adapted the butterfly symbol that he used to sign his mature paintings. He used a restricted palette and simple patterns, relying for effect on delicate chromatic harmonies. The famous Louvre portrait of his mother is significantly entitled *Arrangement in Grey and Black*. Imperious and witty, he was the author of *The Gentle Art of Making Enemies* (1890).

white. A color symbolically denoting purity, simplicity, and candor; innocence, truth, and hope. The ancient Druids, and indeed the priests generally of antiquity, used to wear white vestments, as do the clergy of the Established Church of England when they officiate in any sacred service. The Magi also wore white robes. The head of Osiris, in ancient Egypt, was adorned with a white tiara; all his ornaments were white, and his priests were clad in white.

The priests of Jupiter and the Flamen Dialis of Rome were clothed in white, and wore white hats. The victims offered to Jupiter wore white. The Roman festivals were marked with white chalk, and at the death of a Caesar the national mourning was white; white horses were sacrificed to the sun; white oxen were selected for sacrifice by the Druids and white elephants are held sacred in Siam. The Persians affirm that the divinities are habited in white. In *Moby Dick,* Melville, in discussing the significance of the whale's unusual color, includes a long essay on white.

White, Antonia (1899–). English novelist. She is the author of sensitive novels such as *Beyond the Glass* (1954), which are usually about borderline psychological states.

White, E[lwyn] B[rooks] (1899–). American humorist and essayist. Beginning his career as a journalist, White sent several manuscripts to the recently founded *New Yorker* and was soon recruited for the staff, where he helped to start the witty "Talk of the Town" column. He conducted the

"One Man's Meat" department for *Harper's* from 1938 to 1943 and continued to contribute to *The New Yorker*. White published several volumes of poetry, including *The Lady Is Cold* (1929) and *The Fox of Peapack, and Other Poems* (1938). He collaborated with James THURBER on *Is Sex Necessary?* (1929); in 1941 White and his wife compiled *A Subtreasury of American Humor*.

Among White's other volumes are *The Wild Flag* (1946), *Here Is New York* (1949), *The Second Tree from the Corner* (1953), and two much-admired children's books: *Stuart Little* (1945) and *Charlotte's Web* (1952). In 1959 he edited a revision of *The Elements of Style* by William Strunk, Jr.

White, Edward Lucas (1866–1934). American novelist and short-story writer. A teacher of the classics in secondary schools in or near Baltimore, he is best known for *El Supremo* (1916), a novel about a 19th-century dictator in Paraguay. Also well known are two novels of Roman life, *The Unwilling Vestal* (1918) and *Andivius Hedulio* (1921).

White, Gilbert (1720–1793). English clergyman and naturalist, known for his *Natural History and Antiquities of Selborne* (1789), a classic scientific work in the field of ornithology.

White, Patrick (1912–   ). Australian novelist. Although born in London, White came from four generations of Australians. He spent his childhood in Sydney, in the outback where the eerie, dead landscape haunted his imagination and was later projected into much of his writing. The few years spent in the English public schools made him bitter about the system. For a while he worked in a New South Wales sheep station, where he did much reading and writing. His first novel, *Happy Valley* (1939), won a gold medal from the Australian Literature Society. The title is obviously ironical, since the book is a scathing analysis of a small Australian community. White's style, which reveals the influence of James Joyce and Gertrude Stein, exploits the stream-of-consciousness technique to its limits, but is at the same time unmistakably his own. His novels include *No More Reality* (1935), *The Aunt's Story* (1948), *The Tree of Man* (1956), a best seller; *Voss* (1957); and *Riders in the Chariot* (1961).

White, T[erence] H[anbury] (1906–1964). English writer of fantasies. *The Once and Future King* (1958) is a collection of his four Arthurian epics, beginning with *The Sword in the Stone* (1939). In 1961 the book was made into the musical *Camelot*. White also wrote *Mistress Masham's Repose* (1946), about a little girl and a community of Lilliputians.

White, Theodore H[arold] (1915–   ). American writer and journalist. White's nonfiction works include *Thunder Out of China* (1946), written with Annalee Jacoby; *Fire in the Ashes* (1953), an analysis of conditions in postwar Europe; and the Pulitzer Prize winner, *The Making of the President, 1960* (1961), a report on the presidential campaign and election. *The View from the Fortieth Floor* (1960) is a novel about the magazine world.

White, Walter [Francis] (1893–1955). American novelist and writer on race relations. White was for many years the executive secretary of the National Association for the Advancement of Colored People. His first novel, *Fire in the Flint* (1924), deals with lynching in a Southern town. *Flight* (1926) is a study of the middle-class Negro in Atlanta. *A Man Called White* (1948) is his autobiography; the title is a punning reference to the fact that the author, who was blond, fair-skinned, and blue-eyed, always identified himself with the Negroes.

White, William Allen (1868–1944). American newspaper editor. A liberal Republican, White was born and spent most of his life in Emporia, Kansas. In 1895, he became the owner and editor of the *Emporia Gazette,* which he developed into one of the best and most famous of small U.S. newspapers. He first won national attention with his editorial *What's the Matter with Kansas* (1896), which contributed to the election of William McKinley. His editorial tribute to his teen-aged daughter Mary, who died as the result of a riding accident, is also well known. White's other works include *A Certain Rich Man* (1909), a novel about the misdeeds and ultimate regeneration of a Kansas financier; *Puritan in Babylon* (1938), a biography of Calvin Coolidge; and *Autobiography* (1946), which won a Pulitzer Prize.

White, William Hale. Pen name **Mark Rutherford** (1831–1913). English novelist. He wrote *The Autobiography of* MARK RUTHERFORD, *Mark Rutherford's Deliverance* (1885), and other novels dealing with the spiritual struggle of a dissenter. White's work is known for its concern with morality and for its honesty and simplicity. He also translated Spinoza's *Ethics* (1883) and *Emendation of the Intellect* (1883) and wrote a number of journals and critical papers.

Whiteboys. Also called **Levelers.** A secret agrarian association organized in Ireland (c. 1760), so called because the members wore white shirts on their nightly expeditions. They threw down fences and leveled enclosures, and destroyed the property of harsh landlords, Protestant clergy, and tithe collectors.

White Company, The (1891). A historical romance by Sir Arthur Conan DOYLE. Its setting is the 14th century. The hero is Alleyne Edricson, one of the White Company of Saxon bowmen led by Sir Nigel Loring under the Black Prince. He wins both honor and the hand of Sir Nigel's daughter.

White Devil, The, or Victoria Corombona (pub. 1612). A tragedy by John WEBSTER. It is based on the story of Vittoria Accoramboni (c. 1557–1585), whose husband was murdered so that she might marry the duke of Bracciano. In the play, Vittoria's affair with Brachiano, as the duke is called, is encouraged by her diabolical brother, Flamineo. He and Brachiano dispose of Vittoria's husband Camillo and the duke's wife, Isabella. After being tried for murder and adultery, Vittoria is confined in a house for fallen women, but is rescued by Brachiano, with whom she elopes. To avenge Isabella's murder, her brother Francisco, duke of Florence, instigates a plot that results in the death of Brachiano, Vittoria, and Flamineo.

white elephant. A sacred animal of Siam in the days of the old kings of Ava. The holy white elephant bore the title of Lord, and had a minister of high rank to superintend his household. King of the White Elephant was the proudest title of the old kings of Ava and Siam. According to tradition, later kings of Siam used to make presents of white ele-

THE
WHITE DIVEL.

OR,

The Tragedy of *Paulo Giordano Vrsini*, Duke of *Brachiano*,

With

The Life and Death of Vittoria Corombona the famous Venetian Curtizan.

Acted by the Queenes Maiesties Seruants.

Written by IOHN WEBSTER.

Non inferiora secutus.

LONDON,
Printed by N.O. for *Thomas Archer*, and are to be sold
at his Shop in Popes head Pallace, neere the
Royall Exchange. 1612.

Title page of Webster's *The White Devil* (1612).

phants to courtiers whom they wished to ruin. This practice led to the use of the term white elephant to describe any expensive and unprofitable dignity or possession that is not worth the expense or responsibility of keeping it.

White Fang (1905). A novel by Jack LONDON. Written as a sequel to THE CALL OF THE WILD, *White Fang* tells of a wolf-dog who is gradually domesticated. White Fang is rescued from his brutal owner by Weedon Scott, a mining engineer, who tames the dog and takes him to his home in California, where the dog dies while defending his master's family against an escaped convict.

White Goddess, The (1947). An anthropological and mythological study by Robert GRAVES. He claims that the White Goddess, ancient female, fertility, and mother goddess, and goddess of the moon, became the Muse of poetry; and that poetry originated in the ritual worship of this goddess in primitive societies.

Whitehall. A street in London. On it are situated the chief government offices of the British Isles. By extension, the term refers to the governmental administration of the United Kingdom.

Whitehead, Alfred North (1861–1947). English philosopher and mathematician. His idealistic and mystical philosophy, which is aimed at a knowledge of God the Absolute, is based on his mathematical ideas. His best-known book, *Science and the Modern World* (1925), is a clear, layman's history of the development of science and an exposition of his own philosophy. Among Whitehead's other works are *Principia Mathematica* (1910–1913), with Bertrand RUSSELL as co-author, *The Aims of Education* (1929), and *Adventures of Ideas* (1933).

White Horse [of Uffington], the. Huge figure of a horse incised on a hill in Berkshire, England, by cutting away the turf covering the white chalk downs. It is 374 feet long, and was traditionally supposed to have been the emblem of the Saxons under Alfred the Great, cut into the hill to commemorate their victory over the invading Danes at Ashdown (871). It may actually have been cut by Belgic Gauls in the days of the Roman occupation. Thomas Hughes describes the periodic festival of cleaning the turf away from the figure in *The Scouring of the White Horse* (1859). In his poem *The Ballad of the White Horse* (1911) G. K. Chesterton makes the horse symbolic of Christianity under Alfred battling against Norse paganism.

White Jacket, or the World in a Man-of-War (1850). A novel by Herman MELVILLE. The voyage from Hawaii around Cape Horn to the Atlantic Coast is described in realistic detail. Melville reveals his distaste for the brutal and inhumane practices of the officers aboard a U.S. navy man-of-war. Some of the flogging scenes later convinced Congressmen to abolish that punishment. The white jacket for which the narrator is named, symbolic of his isolation and innocence, threatens to drown him when he falls from the mast. In this most dramatic episode, White Jacket succeeds in loosening the smothering folds of the jacket. Regaining his buoyancy, he rises while the hated garment sinks forever. A memorable character in the novel is Jack Chase, captain of the foretop; a natural leader and a sensitive and intelligent man, he reappears in many of Melville's works.

White Ladies. A species of *fée* in many countries. Their appearance generally forbodes death in the house. (See BANSHEE.) The belief is a relic of old Teutonic mythology, and the White Ladies represent Holda, or Berchta, the goddess who received the souls of maidens and young children.

German legend says that when the castle of Neuhaus, Bohemia, was being built, a White Lady appeared to the workmen and promised them a sweet soup and carp on the completion of the castle. In remembrance thereof, these dainties were long given to the poor of Bohemia on Maundy Thursday. She is also said to have been heard to speak on two occasions: once in December, 1628, when she said, "I wait for judgment!" and once at Neuhaus, when she said to the princes, "'Tis ten o'clock." The first recorded instance of this apparition was in the 16th century, and the name given to the lady is Bertha von Rosenberg. She last appeared, it is said, in 1879, just prior to the death of Prince Waldemar. She carries a bunch of keys at her side, and is always dressed in white.

In Normandy, the White Ladies lurk in ravines, fords, bridges, and other narrow passes, and ask the passenger to dance. If they receive a courteous answer, well; but if a refusal, they seize the churl and fling him into a ditch, where thorns and briers may serve to teach him gentleness of manners. The most famous of these ladies is *La Dame d'Aprigny,* who used to inhabit the site of the present Rue St. Quentin, at Bayeux, and *La Dame Abonde.*

white man's burden. Euphemism for the type of imperialism predominant in Europe, America, and especially Great Britain, at the end of the 19th century and the beginning of the 20th century. It was justified by many of its supporters as a moral duty devolving upon the "superior" white nations to guide and develop the "backward" peoples in their newly acquired colonies The term is from the title of a poem by Rudyard Kipling (1899) which is considered to be an excellent expression of the attitude of conservative British imperialists and of the author himself at the time of its composition.

white rabbit, the. A character in Lewis Carroll's ALICE'S ADVENTURES IN WONDERLAND. The white rabbit astonishes Alice when he rushes past her worriedly consulting his watch. Curious to know why he has a watch and where he is hurrying, Alice chases him and falls down a rabbit hole into Wonderland, where her adventures begin.

Whites and Blacks. See BIANCHI AND NERI.

White's Chocolate House. A popular meeting place in 18th-century London; it was opened by Francis White in 1697.

Whitman, Walt[er] (1819–1892). American poet, journalist, and essayist. Born near Huntington, Long Island, of mixed Dutch and English ancestry, Whitman early adopted the nickname, Walt, to distinguish himself from his father. After a few years of schooling, he learned the printing trade and worked in Brooklyn and Manhattan. For the next 15 years, he alternated between printing and writing jobs, with an interval as country schoolteacher. In 1842, he wrote his only novel, the temperance tract FRANKLIN EVANS. By 1846, he had become editor of the Brooklyn *Eagle,* a Democratic paper; in 1848 he lost his position because of his support of the Free Soil movement. After a trip to New Orleans on a short-lived journalistic venture, he founded his own paper, the *Freeman;* it folded in a year, because of conservative Democratic pressure.

Whitman held several odd jobs, working as carpenter and contractor, and published a few poems. None of these hinted that in 1855 he would publish a strikingly original book of poetry, LEAVES OF GRASS. The volume, with its 12 untitled poems, was not well received; it offended most delicate sensibilities with its ostensible vulgarity, but Emerson, a more perceptive critic, greeted Whitman "at the beginning of a great career." An expanded edition was published the following year.

In 1860, after a period of association with the bohemian group in New York, Whitman added two sections, CHILDREN OF ADAM and CALAMUS, to the third edition of his book. In 1862, when his brother George was wounded in the Civil War, Whitman went to Virginia to nurse him. He stayed on in Washington, volunteering to nurse in army hospitals. He published his war impressions in *Drum Taps* (1865), the sequel of which included the elegy for Lincoln, WHEN LILACS LAST IN THE DOORYARD BLOOM'D. Much of his wartime prose is included in SPECIMEN DAYS AND COLLECT.

When *Leaves of Grass* became more popular its author was dismissed from his government clerkship for having written an immoral book. His supporters rallied, and William D. O'Connor wrote a defense called *The Good Gray Poet* (1866). From this title came the unfortunate nickname, implying that Whitman was a benevolent but harmless old man. By 1868 his poems were becoming known in England, through the appreciation of William Rossetti. In 1870 a new edition was issued, containing the poem *Passage to India.* Shortly after, Whitman wrote DEMOCRATIC VISTAS.

After a paralytic stroke, he moved to Camden, N.J. He lectured in the East, visited Colorado and Canada, and published new editions. Purchasing a house on Mickle Street in Camden, he entertained writers and artists from all over the world. The house became the center of a band of disciples, who included Horace TRAUBEL, Dr. R. M. Bucke and Thomas Harned. At the time of Whitman's death in 1892, he had become a legend.

In his unorthodox form, the line is the rhythmical unit; meter is disregarded, but Whitman employs parallelism and tries to achieve a musical effect. His major themes include the sacredness of the self, the beauty of death, the equality of all people, the love of comrades, and the immortality of the soul. The popular poems that caused him to be admired as "the bard of democracy" have become secondary to CROSSING BROOKLYN FERRY, SONG OF MYSELF, OUT OF THE CRADLE ENDLESSLY ROCKING, and others, which identify him as a major poet. See SONG OF THE OPEN ROAD; O CAPTAIN! MY CAPTAIN!; John BURROUGHS.

Whitsunday. The Christian feast of PENTECOST. This old English name derives from the fact that those who were baptized at this time wore *white* garments. It and the two days following are the chief early summer holiday in England.

Whittier, John Greenleaf (1807–1892). American poet and editor. The poet's formal education was slight, but he read assiduously; before he was 20 he had published enough verse to bring him to the attention of editors and readers in the antislavery cause. A Quaker devoted to social causes and reform, Whittier worked zealously in behalf of a series of abolitionist newspapers and magazines. His first book, *Legends of New England in Prose and Verse,* was published in 1831; from then until the Civil War he wrote essays and articles as well as poems, almost all of which are concerned with abolition. See Daniel WEBSTER.

The Civil War inspired the familiar poem BARBARA FRIETCHIE, but the important change in his work came after the war. From 1865 until Whittier's death he wrote of religion, nature, and New England life; he became the most popular rural New England poet. He was the poet of the country folk whose vigorous speech is mirrored in his SNOW-BOUND.

In old age Whittier turned toward religious verse; many hymns still sung are excerpted from his long religious poems. His finest work was done in the rural poetic genre and includes *Snow-Bound,* TELLING THE BEES, SKIPPER IRESON'S RIDE, THE BAREFOOT BOY, MOGG MEGONE, and MAUD MULLER.

Whittington, Dick. Familiar name of **Richard Whittington,** lord mayor of London (1397–1398, 1406–1408, 1419–1420). According to popular legend, he was a poor orphan country lad who heard that London was "paved with gold" and went there to earn a living. When he was reduced to starvation, a kind merchant gave him employment in his family as the cook's helper, but the cook so ill-treated him that he ran away. While resting on the roadside, he heard the Bow bells, and they seemed to him to say "Turn again, Whittington, thrice lord mayor of London"; so he returned to his master. His master permitted him, with the other servants, to contribute to a ship bound for Morocco. Richard had nothing but a cat; this, however, he sent. It happened that the king of Morocco was troubled by mice, which Whittington's cat destroyed, and this so pleased his highness that he bought the mouser at a fabulous price. Dick commenced business with this money, soon rose to great wealth, married his master's daughter, was knighted, and thrice elected lord mayor of London. Except for Whittington's three elections as mayor, the legend bears little relationship to the recorded facts of his life.

whore of Babylon. An epithet for the Roman Catholic Church used by the early Puritans and some of their descendants. In the New Testament (Rev. 17–19) Babylon is the city of the ANTICHRIST.

Whyte-Melville, George John (1821–1878). English novelist. Whyte-Melville is best known for his lively episodic novels of hunting, such as *Market Harborough* (1861). He also wrote a number of historical romances, several volumes of poetry, and *Riding Recollections* (1878), a book on horsemanship. His work has considerable charm, and an air of straightforwardness and authenticity. Appropriately he met his death on the hunting field.

Wibberley, Leonard (1915–   ). Irish writer, resident in California. He has written humorous, fantastic political satires, including *The Mouse that Roared* (1955) and *The Mouse on the Moon* (1962).

Wickerwork Woman, The (Le Mannequin d'Osier; 1897). One of a series of novels by Anatole FRANCE. The tale involves the actions of its protagonist M. BERGERET.

Wickfield, Mr. In Charles Dickens' DAVID COPPERFIELD, a lawyer, father of Agnes. Uriah HEEP is his clerk.

Agnes Wickfield. Daughter of Mr. Wickfield. She is the most important woman in David's life and, in contrast to Dora Spenlow, a mature woman. After Dora dies, David marries Agnes.

Wickford Point (1939). A novel by John P. MARQUAND. It deals with a declining upper-class family that lives near Boston in tarnished splendor, supported by a trust fund and by obliging creditors. Arrogant and indolent, they rely completely on their vanished distinction.

Widdemer, Margaret (1890–   ). American writer. She first won fame with her poem *The Factories,* a denunciation of child labor; it was reprinted in *The Factories and Other Poems* (1915). She published several other collections of verse, the best of which was gathered in two volumes of *Collected Poems* (1928; 1957). She is also the author of numerous romantic and historical novels, two books for beginning writers, and a verse play: *The Singing Wood* (1926).

Widow Barnaby, The (1839). A novel by Frances TROLLOPE. The widow is a vulgar, pretentious husband-hunter, wholly without principle. She marries a degenerate clergyman in the sequel, *The Widow Married* (1840), and *The Barnabys in Amer-*

ica (1841) records unfavorable impressions of American travel.

Widsith (7th century?). Old English poem of over 140 lines in ALLITERATIVE VERSE. A wandering minstrel describes the kings he claims to have visited and from whom he received presents.

Wied, Gustav Johannes (1858–1914). Danish novelist, playwright, and short-story writer. One of Denmark's finest humorists, Wied produced work marked by sharp cynicism and bitter wit. His amused scorn for the absurdity of human existence mingles with a tender compassion. Wied's novels include *Sloegten* (1898), *Livsens Ondskab* (1899), and *Knagsted* (1902). *Menneskenes Børn* (2 vols., 1894) and *Circus Mundi* (1909) are collections of stories; *Det svage køn* (1900), *Dansemus* (1905), *Første Violin* (1898), and *Ranke Viljer* (1906; trans., $2 \times 2 = 5$, 1923) are among his plays.

Wieland, Christoph Martin (1733–1813). German poet and novelist, largely rococo in style. His satirical talent and political awareness are shown in the novel *Die Abderiten, eine sehr wahrscheinliche Geschichte* (*The Abderites, a Very Probable Story*, 1774), in which the characters and situations are meant to represent actual people and events. His *Geschichte des Agathon* (*Story of Agathon*, 1766; final version, 1798), on the other hand, is a more deeply psychological novel about the development of a youth in classical Greece, and is important as a predecessor to the *Bildungsroman* novel of education. Other important works include *Oberon* (1780), an epic; *Der deutsche Merkur* (*The German Mercury*, 1797–1803), a periodical edited by him which was a pioneering effort among German literary journals; and translations (1762–1766) of 11 plays of Shakespeare.

Wieland, or The Transformation (1798). A novel by Charles Brockden BROWN. Set in Pennsylvania, it deals with the sinister influence of a ventriloquist named Carwin upon the family of a German mystic, the Wielands. It is notable as the first American novel in the tradition of the Gothic romance.

Wienbarg, Ludolf (1802–1872). German publicist and aesthetician of the JUNG DEUTSCHLAND ("Young Germany") movement, whose main principles he outlined in his *Ästhetische Feldzüge* (*Aesthetic Campaigns,* 1834).

Wife of Bath's Tale, The. One of the CANTERBURY TALES of Geoffrey CHAUCER. It is famous for its long *Prologue* in which the Wife of Bath first argues against the virtues of virginity, and then uses an account of her life with five successive husbands to prove that the married state is happiest when the wife has the sovereignty. She boasts of all the tricks she used to keep her first four husbands in hand. The fifth, half her age, she married for love rather than money; when he made life difficult by reading antifeminist tales to put her in her place, she precipitated a fight and pretended he had nearly killed her, so that he repentantly offered to let her run everything—and thereafter they were tender to each other and never quarreled.

Her tale proves the same point. One of King Arthur's knights is condemned to death for ravishing a maid, but the ladies of the court intervene, and he is given a year to find out "what women most desire" and thus save his life. A foul witch offers to exchange the answer for his obedience to her next request. Accordingly, he pleases the court ladies with the answer that women most desire sovereignty over their husbands and their love, and the hag demands that he marry her. He takes her miserably to bed, and after a long lecture she offers him a choice: she can remain foul and guarantee loving fidelity, or she can become young and fair and probably make him a cuckold. He wisely says that she should make the choice, whereupon she is transformed into a beauty *and* promises fidelity as well.

Wiggin, Kate Douglas (1856–1923). A widely popular American writer of children's books and novels. She was best known for her *The Birds' Christmas Carol* (1887) and REBECCA OF SUNNYBROOK FARM.

Wigglesworth, Michael (1631–1705). English-born American poet and clergyman. For most of his life he served as Congregational minister and physician at Malden, Mass. In 1662 he published his most popular poem, THE DAY OF DOOM, based on a dream he had had nine days earlier. He also wrote *Meat Out of the Eater* (1669), a cycle of short theological poems almost as popular in its day as *The Day of Doom*, and lesser poems on religious subjects. Another long poem, *God's Controversy with New England*, was left in manuscript at his death and published in 1871. Considered by some critics Wigglesworth's best work, it is a bitter denunciation of backsliders in the Puritan colony.

Wight, Isle of. An island off the southern coast of England. Notable in literature as the residence of Alfred TENNYSON in the latter part of his life.

Wilbur, Richard (1921–). American poet. Wilbur has taught at Harvard and at Wesleyan universities. His poetry shows the influence of the metaphysical poets, particularly Andrew Marvell, and of Wallace Stevens. Usually rhymed and regular in meter, it is compact, textured, and partakes of both deep feeling and wit. His books include *The Beautiful Changes* (1947), *Ceremony and Other Poems* (1950), *Things of This World* (1956), *Poems* (1957), and *Advice to a Prophet, and Other Poems* (1961).

Wilcox, Mrs. Ruth. An intuitive, half-mystical elderly woman in E. M. Forster's novel HOWARDS END. The rest of her family are business people intent on property and material success.

Wild, Jonathan (1682–1725). A famous criminal, hanged at Tyburn for housebreaking. Tales of his six wives and of his gang of subordinates have become popular legend. Daniel Defoe made *Jonathan Wild* the subject of a romance (1725). Henry Fielding did the same in 1743, calling his novel *The Life of Mr. JONATHAN WILD THE GREAT*. In these romances he is a coward, traitor, hypocrite, and tyrant, unrelieved by human feeling and never betrayed into a kind or good action. The character is historic, but the adventures are in a measure fictitious.

Wild Duck, The (1884). A play by Henrik IBSEN. A satire on meddling, half-baked idealists, a poetic fantasy of illusions, and a realistic tragedy of human weakness, the play is unified by the symbolism of the wild duck and is one of Ibsen's most complex and compelling dramas. Hjalmar Ekdal is a weak, kindly, self-deluding man who believes himself to be on the verge of discovering a great invention; Gregers Werle, his old schoolfriend, is a crackpot idealist who is determined to free Hjalmar of his comforting—and necessary—illusions. Finally, through Werle's revelations, Hjalmar comes to believe that his beloved daughter, Hedvig, is not his own child. He rejects the girl, and Werle tries to persuade her that her adored father will come back to her if she sacrifices the thing she loves best—the wild duck. Hedvig, crushed by her father's rejection of her, kills herself.

Wilde, Oscar [Fingal O'Flahertie Wills] (1854–1900). Irish-born poet, dramatist, and novelist. During his undergraduate years at Oxford and as a disciple of Walter Pater, he became the leader of an aesthetic movement which advocated "ART FOR ART'S SAKE." He attracted a great deal of attention with his aestheticism, wearing long hair, dressing eccentrically, and carrying flowers in his hands while lecturing; the "art for art's sake" group was later satirized in Gilbert and Sullivan's *Patience*. Wilde was accused of homosexual practices, was tried and found guilty, and sentenced to imprisonment (1895–1897) with hard labor. On his release, physically, spiritually, and financially ruined, he went to Paris under the name of Sebastian MELMOTH. There he lived in bitterness and despair until his death.

Oscar Wilde caricatured by Max Beerbohm.

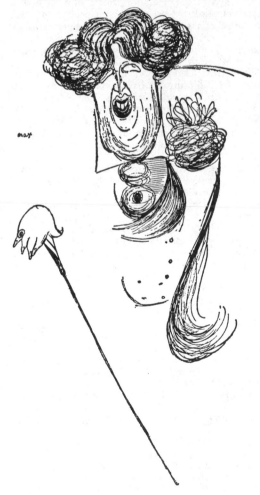

Wilde's works include *Poems* (1881); *The Happy Prince, and Other Tales* (1888), a collection of fairy tales and allegories; THE PICTURE OF DORIAN GRAY, a novel; *The House of Pomegranates* (1891), another collection of fairy tales; *Intentions* (1891), a collection of reviews and critical studies; LADY WINDERMERE'S FAN, a play; A WOMAN OF NO IMPORTANCE, a play; *Salomé* (1893), a play written originally in French and used as the basis for Richard Strauss' opera of the same title; *An Ideal Husband* (1895), a play; THE IMPORTANCE OF BEING EARNEST, a play, often considered his masterpiece; THE BALLAD OF READING GAOL; and *De Profundis* (1905). See DE PROFUNDIS; Lord Alfred DOUGLAS.

Wildenbruch, Ernst von (1845–1909). German playwright. His early works, such as *Die Karolinger (The Carolingians,* 1881) and *Väter und Söhne (Fathers and Sons,* 1882), are little more than overtheatrical attempts to imitate Schiller. Still, the vigor of his style and his frequent choice of specifically German themes appealed to some of the writers of naturalism; and he himself, in his later *Die Haubenlerche (The Crested Lark,* 1891), a "social drama," was influenced by naturalistic tendencies.

Wildenvey, Herman Theodore (1886–1959). Norwegian poet. With the publication of his first collection, *Nyinger* (1907), Wildenvey began a long career as popular lyric poet. His light, graceful, musical poems often depict young love. Among his volumes of verse are *Prismer* (1911), *Kjoertegn* (1916), *Ildorke stret* (1923), and *Fiken av tistler* (1925).

Wilder, Thornton [Niven] (1897–   ). American novelist and playwright, known for his sophisticated and ironic novels and for his successful plays, marked by touches of fantasy and experiments in theatrical technique. In 1926 he wrote *The Cabala,* an ironic novel of decadent Italian nobility; in the same year his first play, *The Trumpet Shall Sound,* was produced at a little theater. When his popular Pulitzer Prize-winning novel, THE BRIDGE OF SAN LUIS REY, was published a year later, Wilder's career was launched. From 1930 to 1936 he taught at the University of Chicago. *The Angel That Troubled the Waters* (1928) and *The Long Christmas Dinner* (1931) were collections of one-act plays; *Heaven's My Destination* (1934) was a comic novel. Wilder won his second and third Pulitzer prizes for the ever-popular play OUR TOWN, and for THE SKIN OF OUR TEETH. *The Merchant of Yonkers* (1938), a farcical play, was revived in 1955 as *The Matchmaker. The Ides of March* (1948) was a witty and learned epistolary novel about Julius Caesar. Wilder is presently working on a cycle of 14 plays, the first three having already been produced under the collective title *Plays for Bleecker Street.*

Wildeve, Damon. See RETURN OF THE NATIVE, THE.

Wild Goose Chase, The (1621). A comedy by John Fletcher. (See BEAUMONT AND FLETCHER.) It chronicles the attempts of the beautiful Oriana to win the love of the rakish Mirabel. She tries to provoke Mirabel's jealousy by having her disguised brother woo her and to awaken his pity by feigning madness. Finally, disguised as the daughter of a man whose life Mirabel once saved, she is able to trick him into a declaration of love. Meanwhile, Pinac and Belleur, Mirabel's companions, have, after many false steps, fallen for the charms of Rosalura and Lillia Bianca.

Wild Huntsman. A spectral hunter of medieval legend. With a pack of spectral dogs, he frequents certain forests and occasionally appears to mortals. One account has it that he was a Jew who would not suffer Jesus to drink out of a watering trough, but pointed to some water in a hoofprint as good enough for "such an enemy of Moses."

The Germans place him in the Black Forest; the French in the Forest of Fontainebleau, and confuse him with St. Hubert; and in England he has become Herne the Hunter, once a keeper in Windsor Forest, who "walks" in wintertime, about midnight, and blasts trees and cattle.

Wild Palms, The (1939). A novel by William FAULKNER. The book is composed of two narratives, alternating chapter by chapter. The title story deals with a young intern who falls in love with a married woman and flees with her to different parts of the country, trying to escape the civilization they fear will kill their love. The woman finally dies as the result of an abortion performed on her by her lover, who is imprisoned for life. The second story, later published separately as *The Old Man,* is also a study of society versus nature, of order juxtaposed with chaos. A convict is sent from prison to do rescue work during the great Mississippi flood of 1927. Finding a pregnant woman stranded by the rising water, he takes her into his boat and attempts to deliver himself and his charge back to the authorities—a task that, because of the violence of the flood, takes almost three months and is rewarded with an extended sentence.

Wilfer, Reginald. In Charles Dickens' OUR MUTUAL FRIEND, an impoverished clerk in VENEERING's drug-house, called "R. W." by his friends. In person Wilfer resembles an overgrown cherub; in manner he is shy and retiring.

Mrs. Wilfer. Wilfer's wife, a tall, angular, and majestic woman with a mighty idea of her own importance. "Viper!" "Ingrate!" and such epithets are household words with her.

Bella Wilfer. Daughter of Mr. and Mrs. Wilfer, affectionate spoiled beauty, "giddy from the want of some sustaining purpose, and capricious because she was always fluttering among little things." Bella ultimately marries John Harmon.

Lavinia Wilfer. Youngest sister of Bella, called "The Irrepressible," a tart, pert girl.

Wilhelm II (1859–1941). Emperor or kaiser of Germany and king of Prussia (1888–1918). After dismissing BISMARCK in 1890, he began a threatening foreign policy that aggravated the general instability of Europe. (See AGADIR CRISIS; ALGECIRAS CONFERENCE; Alfred von TIRPITZ). Although he was called the warlord during World War I, he eventually yielded his leadership of Germany to his generals, Ludendorff and Hindenburg. Upon the insistence of Prince MAX he abdicated and fled to Holland.

Wilhelm Meister. The central character of two novels by Johann Wolfgang von GOETHE, *Wilhelm Meisters Lehrjahre (Wilhelm Meister's Apprenticeship,* 1795–1796) and *Wilhelm Meisters Wanderjahre oder Die Entsagenden (Wilhelm Meister's Travels or The Renunciants,* 1829). The first, which is the original and classic example of the BILDUNGSROMAN, relates Wilhelm's progress from naïve, excitable youth to responsible manhood. He has dreams of becoming a great playwright and actor, but under the unobtrusive guidance of a mysterious Tower Society, whose existence he does not even suspect, he gradually comes to adopt a more modest and objective view of himself, and in the end, is accepted to membership in the society. The second novel is less of a connected narrative than the first and serves, like Part II of Faust, to allow Goethe to develop his ideas on a wide variety of subjects. In its course, Wilhelm finally discovers his true calling as a surgeon. See MIGNON.

Wilhelm Tell (1804). A play by Friedrich SCHILLER based on the legend of the famous Swiss hero, Wilhelm TELL. Schiller uses the play, and the figure of Tell, primarily as a vehicle for his own moral and political idealism.

Wilkes, John (1727–1797). English political reformer. A dissipated man of radical sympathies, he joined the fraternity called the Mad Monks of MEDMENHAM ABBEY, otherwise known as the Hellfire Club. In writing for *The North Briton*, a newspaper which he founded in 1762, he savagely attacked the government, and his paper was suppressed. Although he later was elected a member of Parliament, he was twice suspended for libel. He was a great favorite of the London mob, and was instrumental in securing certain rights for the people.

Wilkins, George (fl. 1607). English dramatist whose only extant play is *The Miseries of Enforced Marriage* (1607).

Wilkins, Sir George Hubert (1888–1958). Australian polar explorer and aviator. He took part in many Arctic expeditions between 1913 and 1922, and later led many of his own. Perhaps the most famous was the Wilkins-Ellsworth Nautilus Arctic Submarine Expedition, in 1931. He wrote about it in *Under the North Pole* (1931).

Wilkins, Mary E. See Mary Eleanor Wilkins FREEMAN.

Willard, Emma (1787–1870). American teacher and writer. In 1814, Miss Willard opened a female seminary in Vermont, where she taught many of the subjects usually barred from the curricula of schools for girls. In 1821, she moved to Troy, N.Y., where her famous school was first called the Troy Female Seminary, and then the Emma Willard School. She also founded the Willard Association for the Mutual Improvement of Female Teachers (1837). She wrote accounts of her travels, advanced a later accepted theory of blood circulation, and wrote verse. Her famous poem, called *Rocked in the Cradle of the Deep* (1830), was set to music by Joseph P. Knight.

Willard, Frances (1839–1898). American leader of the temperance movement, and teacher. Miss Willard was president of the Women's Christian Temperance Union (1879). She helped to organize the Prohibition Party and wrote *Glimpses of Fifty Years* (1889) and *Woman and Temperance* (1883).

William. In Shakespeare's As You LIKE IT, a rustic boor in love with Audrey.

William II. See WILHELM II.

William of Champeaux. See Pierre ABÉLARD.

William of Malmesbury (c. 1090?–c. 1143). English historian, librarian at the monastery of Malmesbury. He wrote a Latin history of England, the famous GESTA REGUM ANGLORUM, and continued it to 1142 in the sequel *Historia Novella* (*Modern History*); both books are important sources of information and lively anecdote, particularly on the period since the Norman conquest in 1066. He also wrote a *Gesta Pontificum Anglorum* (c. 1125), a history of the bishops and leading monasteries of England, as well as other works of ecclesiastical history and lives of the saints.

William of Newburgh (c. 1136–c. 1198). English historian. His Latin *Historia Rerum Anglicarum* (*History of English Affairs*), which covers the period from 1066 to 1198, is notable for its impartial insight into men and situations.

Williams, Charles (1886–1945). English novelist, poet, playwright, and critic. He wrote Christian thrillers such as *All Hallows Eve* (1945) which dealt with the conflict between good and evil in terms of sensational adventure, psychology, symbolism, black magic, and fantastic miracles. Peter Stanhope, the hero of *Descent Into Hell* (1937) is said to be a portrait of T. S. Eliot, whom Williams knew. He was also a friend of C. S. Lewis. Williams' best poetry is his strange, original, symbolic treatment of traditional Arthurian legends in *Taliessin Through Logres* (1938) and *Arthurian Torso* (1948), with C. S. Lewis as coauthor.

Williams, [George] Emlyn (1905–   ). Welsh stage and screen actor and playwright. His plays include *A Murder Has Been Arranged* (1930), *Night Must Fall* (1935), and *The Corn Is Green* (1938). Since the end of World War II, he has been most active as an actor. He has toured England and America giving dramatic readings of the works of Dickens and Dylan Thomas. *George* (1961) is an autobiography of his early years.

Williams, Oscar (1900–1964). American poet and anthologist. His own poetry, which is often concerned with the disorder of urban life, first appeared in two collections: *The Golden Darkness* and *In Gossamer Grey,* both published in 1921. After a long interval he published *The Man Coming Toward You* (1940), *That's All That Matters* (1945), and *Selected Poems* (1947). Williams has been an extremely successful anthologist, especially with his *Little Treasury* series. He has also edited other anthologies: *The War Poets* (1945) and *The Pocket Book of Modern Verse* (1954).

Williams, Roger (c. 1603–1683). English-born religious leader, founder of the Rhode Island colony. Immigrating to America in 1631, Williams settled in Massachusetts, but his unorthodox religious views and defense of the Indians resulted in his expulsion from the colony. With a few followers he founded a settlement at Providence, R.I. (1636), where he befriended the Indians and instituted a democratic form of government. He was also the first advocate of complete religious toleration in America.

Williams' writings include *A Key into the Language of America* (1643), a study of Indian languages; *Queries of Highest Consideration* (1644), a plea addressed to the English Parliament against the establishment of a national church; THE BLOUDY TENENT OF PERSECUTION, his most famous work; and *George Fox Digged Out of His Burrowes* (1676), an attack on the Quakers, uncharacteristic of his tolerant views.

Williams, Tennessee. Pen name of **Thomas Lanier Williams** (1914–   ). American playwright and writer of fiction. Best known for the primitive violence in his dramas—a quality he believes lurks beneath the surface of modern life—and for his realistic settings that, nevertheless make use of symbolic objects, Williams is often considered the most important American dramatist of the post-World War II era. His first play, *Battle of Angels* (1940), was unsuccessful; Williams later rewrote it as *Orpheus Descending* (1957). But with THE GLASS MENAGERIE, which won the New York Drama Critics' Circle Award, Williams established himself as an important dramatist. The theme of the lonely woman inhabiting a world of dreams was to remain one of Williams' favorites and was later given a violent turn in the Pulitzer Prize-winning A STREETCAR NAMED DESIRE. *Summer and Smoke* (1948) deals with a woman who, lost in dreams of her purity, is unable to respond to the man she loves and is driven into lonely spinsterhood. THE ROSE TATTOO is a humorous and sympathetic treatment of a Sicilian-American woman. More controversial was *Camino Real* (1953), an experimental play whose characters include Casanova, Don Juan, and Kilroy, the ubiquitous American G.I. CAT ON A HOT TIN ROOF, which won for Williams his second Pulitzer Prize, deals with the tensions and pretensions of a wealthy Southern family. *Suddenly, Last Summer* (1958), produced with *Something Unspoken* under the title *Garden District,* concerns a possessive mother and a homosexual son who use others for their own selfish purposes. The son is killed and devoured by a mob of starving children. Later plays include *Sweet Bird of Youth* (1959), *Period of Adjustment* (1960), *The Night of the Iguana* (1961), and *The Milk Train Doesn't Stop Here Any More* (1963).

Williams is also the author of *The Roman Spring of Mrs. Stone* (1950), a novel; *Hard Candy* (1954), a collection of short stories; and *Twenty-Seven Wagons Full of Cotton and Other One-Act Plays,* a collection of short plays later made into the movie *Baby Doll* (1956).

Williams, Ralph Vaughan. See Ralph VAUGHAN WILLIAMS.

Williams, William Carlos (1883–1963). American poet. He is known for his vivid, realistic, and precise recording in poetry of isolated, fleeting, and easily overlooked details of experience, chosen most often from a background of daily, commonplace living in the urban sections of the 20th-century U.S. Williams early knew Ezra Pound and Hilda Doolittle, and although he remained free from the mainstream of IMAGISM, the movement left its mark in his insistence that there are no poetic ideas except in things themselves.

The son of an English father and a Puerto Rican mother, Williams attended various schools, both in the U.S. and in Europe, and took medical training at the University of Pennsylvania, where he first knew Ezra Pound. For over 50 years he practiced medicine in Rutherford, N.J., publishing his first book of *Poems* in 1909. There followed numerous volumes of verse, later collections including *Journey to Love* (1955) and *Sappho* (1957). His poems were twice collected, in 1934 and 1938, and his collected early poems were issued in 1951. In 1946 the first book of

PATERSON appeared. Williams' most ambitious effort, the poem eventually included five books, the last published in 1958.

Primarily known as a poet, Williams also wrote numerous works of prose, both fiction and nonfiction. IN THE AMERICAN GRAIN is the most important of his work in the latter category. His fiction includes the novels *A Voyage to Pagany* (1928), *White Mule* (1937), and *In the Money: White Mule, Part II* (1940). *The Knife of the Times* (1932) and *Life Along the Passaic River* (1938) are collections of short stories. He also wrote several plays, including *A Dream of Love* (1948). *The Autobiography of William Carlos Williams* (1951) is a helpful and informative work. *Selected Essays* were published in 1954 and *The Selected Letters of William Carlos Williams,* in 1957. Williams won the Pulitzer Prize for poetry posthumously in 1963.

Williams-Ellis, Mrs. **Amabel** (1894–   ). English novelist, literary critic, and writer of sociological books. She is the sister of John Strachey and cousin of Lytton Strachey. Her best-known novel is *The Big Firm* (1938).

Williamson, Henry (1897–   ). English novelist and nature writer. He is best known for his animal stories, the most popular of which is *Tarka the Otter* (1927).

William Tell. See TELL, WILHELM.

William the Conqueror, known as **William the Norman** and the **Bastard of Normandy** (c. 1027–1087). King of England (after 1066). The natural son of Robert the Devil, duke of Normandy in France, William was a relative of Edward the Confessor, and married a descendant of Alfred the Great. Harold, earl of Wessex, had been forced by William (c. 1064) to swear to help him obtain the English succession. When Harold took the crown himself upon Edward's death, William invaded England and won the battle of HASTINGS (1066); as King William I he completed the "Norman Conquest," replacing the English nobility with Norman-French, and thus changing the social and eventually the cultural structure of England.

William Wilson (1839). A story by Edgar Allan Poe. An alter ego, the voice of conscience, begins to haunt William Wilson, while he is still at school. Never heeding his better self, William finally kills him. The story gave Robert Louis Stevenson the idea for *The Strange Case of Dr. Jekyll and Mr. Hyde* (1885).

Willis, Nathaniel Parker (1806–1867). American editor and writer. He served as foreign correspondent for the New York *Mirror* and published books of European tales. Willis advocated the use of an American language, inventing many new words; a member of the Knickerbocker School, he sought to foster a national literature. Willis' only popular piece today is the moralistic poem called *Unseen Spirits.* He wrote one novel, *Paul Vane, or, Parts of a Life Else Untold* (1857).

willow pattern. A favorite design for china, usually blue on white. It imitates, but does not copy, the Chinese style of porcelain decoration, introduced into England by Thomas Turner of Caughley about 1780, when the craze for things Chinese was at its height. It does not illustrate any Chinese story or legend, and is not Chinese in origin.

Will's Coffee-House. A famous coffeehouse of Queen Anne's time that stood at the corner of Bow Street and Russell Street, in Covent Garden, sometimes referred to as "Russell Street Coffee-House" and "The Wit's Coffee-House." It was the meeting place of the most prominent wits and literary men of the day. It was well known to Addison, who established his servant Button, in another coffeehouse, which eventually, as "Button's," became the headquarters of the Whig *literati*, as Will's had been of the Tory.

Willy, Colette. See COLETTE.

Wilmot, John. See 2nd earl of ROCHESTER.

Wilmot, Miss Arabella. A wealthy clergyman's daughter in Oliver Goldsmith's novel THE VICAR OF WAKEFIELD. Betrothed to Squire THORNHILL until his infamy becomes known, she is beloved by George PRIMROSE, the vicar's eldest son, whom she ultimately marries.

Wilson, Angus (1913–). English novelist and short-story writer. He maliciously satirizes almost all aspects of the lives of his large, Dickensian casts of characters. Most of his novels are about middle-aged or elderly people who have to recognize their past self-deceptions and readjust to society. Among his novels are HEMLOCK AND AFTER, ANGLO-SAXON ATTITUDES, THE MIDDLE AGE OF MRS. ELIOT, and THE OLD MEN AT THE ZOO. Some collections of short stories are *The Wrong Set* (1949), *Such Darling Dodos* (1950), and *A Bit Off the Map* (1957). *The Mulberry Bush* (1955) is a play. *The Wild Garden* (1964) is a non-fiction work in which Wilson attempts to explore the sources of his own creativity.

Wilson, Colin (1931–). English critic and novelist. He is the precocious author of the popular philosophical study THE OUTSIDER, and of *Religion and the Rebel* (1957). With Patricia Pitman, he compiled an *Encyclopedia of Murder* (1961). *Adrift in Soho* (1961) is a novel, and *The Strength to Dream* (1962) is a book of literary criticism.

Wilson, Edmund (1895–1972). American literary critic, novelist, poet, and editor. After his graduation from Princeton, where he was editor of a literary magazine, Wilson became a journalist. He performed editorial functions for the magazines *Vanity Fair* and the *New Republic,* and wrote book reviews and critical articles for the *New Yorker.* Wilson studied Hebrew and biblical manuscripts and in *Scrolls from the Dead Sea* (1955) revealed both his scholarship and reportorial skill. He edited an anthology of criticism by authors about authors called *The Shock of Recognition* (1943), and in *The Crack-Up* (1956) he put together uncollected pieces by F. Scott Fitzgerald, whom he had known at Princeton. *Memoirs of Hecate County* (1946), a collection of short stories, was banned after publication because of the candid treatment of sex in one story.

Among Wilson's volumes of literary criticism are *Axel's Castle* (1931), *The Wound and the Bow* (1941), and *Patriotic Gore: Studies in the Literature of the American Civil War* (1962). He also wrote *To the Finland Station* (1940), an account of socialist thought; *Travels in Two Democracies* (1936) and *Red, Black, Blond and Olive* (1956), two books reflecting his travel experiences in Russia; *Five Plays* (1954), a collection of his own work; *Poets, Farewell* (1929), a book of verse; and *I Thought of Daisy* (1929), a novel. In *The Cold War and the Income Tax* (1963), Wilson, who did not file tax returns from 1946 to 1955, related his difficulties with the Internal Revenue Service and his disenchantment with American civilization.

Wilson, Harry Leon (1867–1939). American novelist and playwright. He is best known for *Ruggles of Red Gap* (1915), a humorous novel about an English butler in a Western town, and *Merton of the Movies* (1922), about a small-town clerk who finally reaches Hollywood. *Merton* was dramatized in 1922 by Marc Connelly and George S. Kaufman. Wilson also collaborated with Booth TARKINGTON on *The Man from Home* (1907), a play.

Wilson, John. Pen name, **Christopher North** (1785–1854). Scottish writer. He is remembered for his contribution to *Blackwood's Magazine* of the greater part of the NOCTES AMBROSIANAE. He was among the first to recognize the genius of Wordsworth.

Wilson, John Dover (1881–1969). English Shakespearean scholar. He has written a number of critical studies and was chief editor of the New Cambridge edition of Shakespeare's plays (from 1921). His works include *Life in Shakespeare's England* (1911), *What Happens in Hamlet* (1935), and *Shakespeare's Happy Comedies* (1962).

Wilson, [Thomas] Woodrow (1856–1924). 28th president of the U.S. (1913–1921). Born in Staunton, Va., Wilson took his B.A. at Princeton University, studied law at the University of Virginia, and obtained a Ph.D. in history and political science at Johns Hopkins University, writing his doctoral dissertation on *Congressional Government* (1885). In 1890 he became professor of jurisprudence and political economics at Princeton and in 1902 was unanimously chosen president of the university. While there he did much to improve its academic standards and to democratize its social system.

Always keenly interested in politics, Wilson resigned from Princeton in 1910 to become the Democratic candidate for governor of New Jersey. Though he was supported by the state's conservative machine, he won election on a reform platform, and during his brief term he waged a successful fight against his former backers and enacted several liberal social and economic measures. At the Democratic national convention in 1912 Wilson was nominated after William Jennings Bryan threw his support to him, and he won the election as a result of the feud between Theodore Roosevelt and William Howard Taft that split the opposition.

Wilson was a moderate on political and economic questions, but his banking and tariff reforms were regarded as radical. As president, he gave new meaning to the "general welfare" clause of the Constitution, supplied vigorous executive leadership to Congress and to his party, and fought privilege. But he was unable to complete his projects for domestic reform because of the outbreak of the European war in 1914. Although Wilson tried to avoid U.S. participation in the conflict and won reelection in 1916 with the slogan "he kept us out of war," repeated German violations of American neutrality led him to ask Congress for a declaration of war in 1917, affirming that "the world must be made safe for democracy." (See LUSITANIA.) On Jan. 8, 1918, he announced a program of FOURTEEN POINTS as the basis for world peace.

After the cessation of hostilities, Wilson attended the Paris Peace Conference at the head of an American delegation conspicuous for the absence of senators and for the inclusion of only one Republican. Although he was the idol of the European masses, he was forced to make numerous concessions at the conference table in order to salvage his dream of a League of Nations that would ensure world peace. But the U.S. Senate refused to ratify the treaty of VERSAILLES, and Wilson, who refused to compromise with "the little group of wilful men" who were blocking the treaty, decided to take his case to the people. During a strenuous speaking tour, he suffered a stroke at Pueblo, Colo., and never fully recovered.

Wilson's writings include *The State* (1889), *Division and Reunion* (1893), *George Washington* (1897), *A History of the American People* (1902), and *Constitutional Government* (1908). His early essays and lectures were collected in *An Old Master and Other Political Essays* (1893) and *Mere Literature and Other Essays* (1896).

Winckelmann, Johann Joachim (1717–1768). German classical scholar, especially interested in painting and sculpture. He originated the concept of classical Greece as the home of "edle Einfalt und Stille Grösse" (noble simplicity and silent greatness), an ideal that influenced WEIMAR CLASSICISM. The final step in the destruction of Winckelmann's conception of Greece was taken by Friedrich Nietzsche in THE BIRTH OF TRAGEDY.

Wind in the Willows, The (1908). A classic fantasy for children by Kenneth GRAHAME. The characters are Mole, Water Rat, Mr. Toad, and other small animals, who live and talk like humans, but have charming individual animal characters. The book is a tender portrait of the English countryside.

windmills, to fight with. To face imaginary adversaries, combat chimeras. The allusion is to the adventure of DON QUIXOTE, who, when riding through the plains of Montiel, approaches 30 or 40 windmills, which he declares to Sancho Panza are "giants, two leagues in length or more." Striking his spurs into Rosinante, he drives at one of the "monsters dreadful as Typhoeus." His lance lodges in the sail, and the latter lifts both man and beast into the air. When the valiant knight and his steed fall they are both much injured, and Don Quixote declares that the enchanter Freston, "who carried off his library with all the books therein," had changed the giants into windmills.

Wind, Sand, and Stars (Terre des hommes; 1939). A series of tales and reflection by Antoine de SAINT-EXUPÉRY. Exupéry expresses a faith in the potential courage, nobility, and love of men, including the tiller of the earth as well as the explorer of unknown skies.

Windsor, duke of (1894–1972). Former king of Great Britain. The son of George V and Queen Mary, he ascended the throne as Edward VIII upon the death of his father in 1936. When it became known that the king planned to wed Mrs. Wallis Warfield Simpson, a twice-divorced American woman, he encountered the opposition of the Conservative ministry under Stanley Baldwin, who forced him to choose between her and the crown. He reported his decision in a memorable abdication speech, heard by a worldwide radio audience, in which he declared, "I have found it impossible to carry the heavy burden of responsibility and to discharge my duties as King as I would wish to do without the help and support of the woman I love." Edward, now known as the duke of Windsor, married Mrs. Simpson in 1937. From 1940 to 1945 he served as governor of the Bahama Islands. The duke recounted his life up to 1936 in *A King's Story* (1951).

Winesburg, Ohio (1919). A collection of 23 short stories by Sherwood ANDERSON. Most of the stories are connected by George Willard, a young reporter, who in undergoing the trials of adolescence is also in revolt against the barren narrowness of small-town life. Other characters have their own stories, often tales of sterility and thwarted happiness. The language of the book is simple and realistic, and many of the stories are told with a controlled lyric beauty.

Winfield, Arthur M. See ROVER BOYS.

Wings of the Dove, The (1902). A novel by Henry JAMES. Kate Croy is in love with the English journalist Merton Densher, but will not marry him until he is financially secure. When she discovers that her friend Milly Theale, an American heiress, has not long to live, she tells Densher to take an interest in Milly, who promptly falls in love with him. Before her death, Milly learns of Kate and Densher's true relationship, but she nevertheless leaves Densher her money. When the legacy in the form of a check arrives, Densher is anxious to refuse it. Kate, however, demands that he accept the money or promise that he is not in love with Milly's memory. When Densher can agree to neither of these, their romance is terminated. An opera based on the novel was produced in 1961 with libretto by Ethan Ayer and music by Douglas Moore.

Winifred, St. The patron saint of virgins. She was beheaded by Prince Caradoc for refusing to marry him. She was Welch by birth, and the legend says that her head falling on the ground originated the famous healing well of St. Winifred in Flintshire. Holywell, in Wales, is St. Winifred's Well, celebrated for its "miraculous" virtues.

Winkelried, Arnold von. Legendary hero of Switzerland. According to tradition he sacrificed himself at the battle of Sempach against the Austrians (1386) by rushing ahead of his companions and burying in his own body all the pikes of the enemy he could gather together. This created a gap in the Austrian front and enabled the Swiss to win a great victory.

Winkle, Nathaniel. In Charles Dickens' PICKWICK PAPERS, an M.P.C. (Member of the Pickwick Club). He is a young sportsman, considered by his companions to be a dead shot, a hunter, and skater, among other things. All these acquirements are, however, wholly imaginary. He marries Arabella Allen.

Winnie-the-Pooh. See POOH.

Winsor, Kathleen (1919–   ). American novelist. She is best known for *Forever Amber* (1944), a best-selling novel about a promiscuous Restoration beauty. She also wrote *Star Money* (1950), *The Lovers* (1952), and *America With Love* (1957).

Winter, John Keith (1906–   ). English novelist and dramatist. He is best known for his novel and play *The Rats of Norway* (1932). *The Shining Hour* (1934) was popular in the U.S.

Winters, [Arthur] Yvor (1900–1968). American poet and critic. Winters' criticism is considered part of the NEW CRITICISM in its close analysis of the literary work, but it differs in its insistence on moral evaluation: a poem must contain a rational statement about human experience. His books of criticism include *Primitivism and Decadence: A Study of American Experimental Poetry* (1937); *Maule's Curse: Seven Studies in the History of American Obscurantism* (1938); *The Anatomy of Nonsense* (1943); *In Defense of Reason* (1947), a collection of his first three books; *Edward Arlington Robinson* (1946); *The Function of Criticism: Problems and Exercises* (1957); and books on the poetry of Yeats (1960) and of J. V. Cunningham (1961).

In his poetry, Winters adheres to his critical theories on the necessity for balance between reason and emotion. His books of poetry include *The Immobile Wind* (1921), *The Magpie's Shadow* (1922), *The Bare Hills* (1927), *Before Disaster* (1934), *Poems* (1940), and *Collected Poems* (1952). He was awarded a Bollingen Prize in 1960.

Winterset (1935). A verse drama by Maxwell ANDERSON. Based on the SACCO-VANZETTI case, it deals with the son of an Italian radical whose father was executed for a murder he did not commit. In seeking to avenge himself on the actual murderer, the son, Mio, falls in love with Miriamne, the sister of one of the criminals. Through her love Mio is saved from the need for revenge, but both are killed by gangsters. Anderson had used the Sacco-Vanzetti theme unsuccessfully in an earlier play, *Gods of the Lightning* (1928, with Harold Hickerson).

Winter's Tale, The (c. 1611). A comedy by William SHAKESPEARE. POLIXENES, king of Bohemia, is invited to Sicilia by King LEONTES and unwittingly excites the jealousy of his friend because he prolongs his stay at the entreaty of Queen Hermione. Leontes orders CAMILLO to poison the royal guest, but instead of doing so, Camillo flees with him to Bohemia. Leontes now casts Hermione into prison, and orders that her infant daughter be abandoned on some deserted shore. Although the Delphic oracle asserts Hermione's innocence, Leontes remains unconvinced. After falling into a deep swoon, Hermione is reported dead. Leontes, now deeply repentant, goes into mourning. Sixteen years later, FLORIZEL, the son of Polixenes, falls in love with PERDITA, Leontes' lost daughter, who has been reared by a shepherd who found her near "the coast of Bohemia." When Polixenes forbids his son to marry a lowly shepherdess, the lovers, aided by Camillo, flee to Sicilia. There the identity of Perdita is revealed, and the lovers are married. Leontes and Polixenes, who has followed the fugitives, resume their friendship. Only the memory of the wronged Hermione mars the happiness of Leontes. He is then shown a perfect statue of Hermione which turns out to be the queen herself, who has been living in seclusion.

The play is based on Robert Greene's romance, *Pandosto: The Triumph of Time* (1588), and the character of the rogue AUTOLYCUS is derived from the second of Greene's "Conny-catching" pamphlets (1591–1592).

Winther, Rasmus Villads Christian Ferdinand (1796–1876). Danish poet. Two subjects dominated Winther's poetry: his love for woman's and nature's beauty. His finest piece of work is *Hortens Flugt* (*The Flight of the Stag*, 1855), an epic poem set in the Middle Ages, which describes his native Zealand. Among Winther's verse collections are *Sang og Sagn* (1839), *Lyriske Digte* (1848), *Brogede Blade* (1865) and *Efterladte Digte* (1879).

Winthrop, John (1588–1649). English-born leader of the Puritan exodus to America and governor of the Massachusetts Bay Colony 12 times. Orthodox and grave, he was a bitter opponent of Anne Hutchinson. Using the Bible as proof, he combatted the idea of democratic government and argued that there was "no such government in Israel." More than any other man he shaped the character of early New England. His *Journal*, partly published in 1790, appeared in full as *The History of New England from 1630 to 1649* (1825–1826). He is portrayed in Hawthorne's *The Scarlet Letter* (1850).

Winwar, Frances (1900–). Italian-born American biographer and novelist. Her family name was originally **Vinciguerra**, Winwar being the English translation. She is known for her highly colored, but usually accurate, biographies of famous people. Among these are *The Ardent Flame* (1927), about Francesca da Rimini; *Poor Splendid Wings* (1933), about the Pre-Raphaelites: *The Romantic Rebels* (1935), concerning Keats, Shelley, and Byron; *Oscar Wilde and the Yellow '90s* (1940); *The Life of the Heart* (1945), about George Sand; and *Immortal Lovers* (1950), about the Brownings. Among her novels are *The Sentimentalist* (1943) and *The Last Love of Camille* (1954).

Wishes to His Supposed Mistress (1646). A poem by Richard CRASHAW. Addressed to an ideal mistress, it presents a radiant picture of her physical beauty and gifts of spirit.

Wister, Owen (1860–1938). American novelist, short-story writer, and biographer. The grandson of the actress Fanny Kemble, Wister is best known for THE VIRGINIAN, a book whose hero became a prototype for later Westerns. He was a close friend and admirer of Theodore Roosevelt, to whom *The Virginian* is dedicated. *Philosophy Four* (1903) is a story of undergraduate life at Harvard. *Lady Baltimore* (1906) is a romantic novel laid in a Southern city. He also wrote *Lin McLean* (1897), six sketches and a poem about a Wyoming cowboy; a biography of *U. S. Grant* (1900); and *Roosevelt: The Story of a Friendship* (1930).

witch (A.S. *wiccian,* to practice sorcery). A sorceress. The typical witch is usually pictured as an old hag. There are many celebrated witches of history and legend, beginning perhaps with the *Witch of Endor* who, according to the Biblical narrative, called up the prophet Samuel from the dead to answer King Saul's questions concerning the fateful battle in which he would meet his death. The most famous witches in literature are the Three Weird Sisters whose prophecies concerning MACBETH started him on his ambitious and tragic course.

Pope Innocent VIII issued the celebrated bull *Summis Desiderantes* in 1484, directing inquisitors and others to put to death all practicers of witchcraft and other diabolical arts, and it has been computed that as many as nine million persons suffered

The witches in *Macbeth*. From
Holinshed's *Chronicles*.

of Yan III. *With Fire and Sword* has as its subject
the struggle between Russia and Poland. In the second novel, *The Deluge*, the subjects treated are the
settlement of the Teutonic Knights in Prussia, the
union of Lithuania and Poland with Russia brought
about by the marriage of a Lithuanian prince and Polish princess, and the conflict between Poland and Sweden in 1665. *Pan Michael*, the third novel of the series,
continues and concludes the history of Poland as a
separate nation of former centuries.

Within a Budding Grove (A l'ombre des jeunes
filles en fleurs). See REMEMBRANCE OF THINGS
PAST.

Within the Gates (1933). A drama by Sean
O'CASEY. The setting is a London park, where a
Bishop comes to learn more of the common people.
He meets, among others, two Park Chair Attendants,
an Atheist, a Policewoman, a Young Man in Plus-
Fours, two Nursemaids, a Guardsman, two Evangelists, a Young Whore, a Young Salvation Army Officer, and a group of Down-and-Outs. He hears of their
bitternesses, dreams, frustrations, and weaknesses;
and discovers that the Young Whore is his own
daughter. After she dies, affirming her faith in life,
the Bishop is overcome with shame at his past sin

death for witchcraft since that date. In the Massachusetts colony, witches in Salem were hanged or
pressed to death.

witches' Sabbath. The muster at nighttime of
witches and demons to concoct mischief. The witch
first anointed her feet and shoulders with the fat of
a murdered babe, then mounting a broomstick,
distaff, or rake, made her exit by the chimney, and
rode through the air to the place of rendezvous. The
assembled witches feasted together, and concluded
with a dance, in which they all turned their backs to
each other. Especially during medieval and Renaissance times, WALPURGIS NIGHT was believed to fall
on April 30. James Joyce's *Ulysses* and Thomas
Mann's *Magic Mountain* contain scenes based on the
tradition of the witches' Sabbath. Hawthorne's *Young
Goodman Brown* is a famous short story about a
New England witches' Sabbath.

Wither, George (1588–1667). English poet, one
of the SPENSERIAN SCHOOL of the early 17th century.
The verse publications upon which his reputation as
a poet is based include *The Shepherd's Pipe* (1614),
a collection of eclogues to which William Browne
and John Davies also contributed; *Shepherd's Hunting* (1615); *Fidelia* (1615); and *Fair Virtue* (1622).
He is also remembered for his *Collection of Emblems, Ancient and Modern* (1635), an EMBLEM
BOOK. Later Wither became a Puritan, writing numerous controversial pamphlets, hymns, and psalms of
rather inferior quality. He served in the Parliamentary army during the Civil War and on one occasion
was saved from hanging by the Royalists by the
plea of Sir John Denham that "whilst [Wither]
lived, he [Denham] should not be the worst poet in
England."

With Fire and Sword. The first of a trilogy of
historical novels (1890–1893) by SIENKIEWICZ dealing with the history of Poland from 1648 to the time

Title page of Wither's *Shepherd's Hunting* (1615).

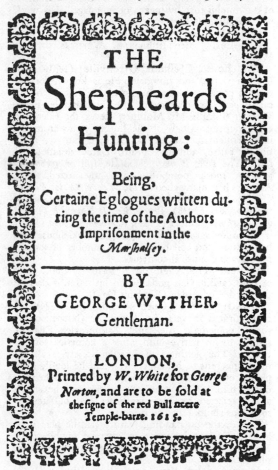

THE

Shepheards

Hunting:

Being,
Certaine Eglogues written du-
ring the time of the Authors
Imprisonment in the
Marshalsey.

BY
GEORGE WYTHER,
Gentleman.

LONDON,
Printed by *W. White* for *George
Norton,* and are to be sold at
the signe of the red Bull neere
Temple-barre. 1615.

and his former smugness. There are many references to social injustice, poverty, morality, and religion, and frequent songs and chants by single characters and a chorus.

Witla, Eugene. The hero of Theodore Dreiser's novel THE "GENIUS." The character is to a considerable extent autobiographical.

Witte, Count **Sergei Yulievich** (1849–1915). Russian statesman and administrator. Having started his career as a railway station agent, Witte rose to become, in turn, minister of communications and minister of finance. He was responsible for the rapid expansion of Russia's railway system, the building of the Trans-Siberian Railway, and the industrialization of Russia in the late 19th century. In 1905–1906, Witte served as the first constitutional prime minister in Russia.

Wittgenstein, Ludwig (1889–1951). An Austrian philosopher and professor at Cambridge University. In his highly regarded books *Tractatus Logico-Philosophicus* (1922) and *Philosophical Investigations* (1953), he proposed a critical method of linguistic analysis as the solution to most philosophic problems, which were the result, he argued, not of difficulty or inadequate knowledge, but of the systematic misuse of language by philosophers. "Philosophy," he said, "is a battle against the bewitchment of our intelligence by means of language." His work was a leading influence on LOGICAL POSITIVISM.

Wix, Mrs. See WHAT MAISIE KNEW.

wobblies. See INDUSTRIAL WORKERS OF THE WORLD.

Wodehouse, P[elham] G[renville] (1881–   ). English writer and humorist. He is known for numerous popular stories and novels about his whimsical upper-class characters: the Honourable Bertie Wooster, Psmith, Mr. Mulliner, Jeeves, the valet, and assorted peers. Much of the humor stems from the idle gentleman. The books contain fantasy, affectionate satire, and the absurd comic situations of farce. The style is very elaborate, full of verbal ingenuity, mock pomposity, and unexpected slang. Among his many books are *Leave It to Psmith* (1923), *The Inimitable Jeeves* (1924), *The Code of the Woosters* (1938), *Bertie Sees It Through* (1955), and *Author! Author!* (1962). *Performing Flea* (1953) is an autobiography and apologia. Wodehouse also has written and collaborated on a number of successful plays and musical comedies.

Woden. The Anglo-Saxon form of ODIN, chief of the Scandinavian gods. From his name is derived the word Wednesday (Woden's Day).

Woe from Wit (Gore ot uma; 1822–1824). A comic drama in verse by Aleksandr GRIBOYEDOV. A young nobleman, Aleksandr Andreyevich Chatzki, returns to his native land, after a homesick tour of Europe. The pettiness of Russian society is all the more apparent to his eager eyes, and he loudly complains of his disenchantment. His outspokenness causes him to be ostracized. In the end he stands alone, rejected by his sweetheart and buffeted by malicious rumors that he is insane.

One of the outstanding features of the play is its biting, pungent language in rhymed iambic verse. Many of the lines have become popular proverbial phrases.

Wolcot, John. Pen name: **Peter Pindar** (1738–

1819). English poet and physician, whose works include *Lyric Odes to the Royal Academicians* (1782) and *Epistle to the Emperor of China* (1817). His numerous satires incurred the wrath of William Gifford and James Boswell.

Wolf, Friedrich August (1759–1824). German philologist and Homeric scholar. His theory, that Homer's *Iliad* and *Odyssey* were the work of not one man but of several writers, was expounded in his *Prolegomena ad Homerum* (1795). His scholarly editions of Plato, Homer, Cicero and others are still sound.

Wolfdietrich. See ORTNIT.

Wolfe, Charles (1791–1823). Irish poet. The duties of a country curacy and an early death prevented Wolfe's leaving behind more than a single volume, the posthumous *Remains* (1825), but he has to his credit the most enduring of the Napoleonic war poems, *The Burial of Sir John Moore* (1816).

Wolfe, James (1727–1759). English general who defeated Montcalm in the battle of the Plains of Abraham at Quebec. Both Wolfe and Montcalm were fatally wounded. Wolfe is a prominent character in Thackeray's *The Virginians* and in Parkman's *Montcalm and Wolfe.*

Wolfe, Humbert (1885–1940). English poet. He is best known for his light satirical verse. *Lampoons* was published in 1925. His *Requiem* (1927) was widely read.

Wolfe, Thomas [Clayton] (1900–1938). American novelist. He was known for the intense individualism, extreme exuberance of spirit, frequently extravagant rhetoric, and mystical celebration of youth, sex, and America which characterize his usually autobiographical writings.

Wolfe was born in Asheville, N.C. At 15, he entered the University of North Carolina, where, with the encouragement of Frederick Koch, he wrote two plays which were produced by Koch's Carolina Playmakers: *The Return of Buck Gavin* (1924) and *The Third Night* (1938). At Harvard he studied playwriting under George Pierce Baker, writing *Welcome to Our City* (produced at Harvard, 1923) and working on *Mannerhouse* (1948), a play about the disintegration of a Southern family. Wolfe later taught at New York University and made several trips to Europe.

His first novel, LOOK HOMEWARD, ANGEL, was submitted to Maxwell Perkins of Charles Scribner's Sons as a huge, sprawling manuscript. Working with Perkins, Wolfe was able to bring the book to manageable size. After a short novel, *A Portrait of Bascom Hawke* (1932), Wolfe completed another massive manuscript, which, like his first novel, had as its hero the autobiographical Eugene GANT. After much editing the book was published as OF TIME AND THE RIVER. In 1935 Wolfe published a collection of short stories, *From Death to Morning,* and the following year published a lecture he had given on his own work, *The Story of a Novel.*

Wolfe's final work was done with the help of another editor, Edward C. Aswell of Harper & Brothers. In 1938 Wolfe suddenly died, leaving behind an eight-foot pile of manuscript which Aswell published as two novels and a book of short stories: THE WEB AND THE ROCK, YOU CAN'T GO HOME AGAIN, and *The Hills Beyond* (1941). Wolfe's

Letters to His Mother (1943) were edited by John Terry, and a further collection of *Letters* (1956) was made by Elizabeth Nowell.

Wolfert's Roost (1855). A collection of tales and sketches by Washington IRVING. Irving published the magazine pieces in an attempt to duplicate his earlier successes with similar volumes. Descriptions of Westchester County alternate with American fables and Spanish romances. The title of the book comes from the home Irving bought and remodeled as Sunnyside.

Wolfram von Eschenbach (c. 1170–c. 1220). German minnesinger, or lyric poet. He is known for three verse epics, PARZIVAL, *Willehalm,* and TITUREL, as well as a collection of love lyrics. His handling of chivalric themes often rebukes the usual traditions of knighthood and COURTLY LOVE, for instead of making women necessarily either sinful temptations or the objects of a grand but adulterous passion, he glorifies married love and a calmer kind of real affection.

Wolfram becomes a major character in Wagner's opera TANNHÄUSER; he is a close friend of Tannhäuser, although he is also secretly in love with Elizabeth. See WARTBURG.

Wolfskehl, Karl (1869–1948). German poet. He was a member of the circle about Stefan George, which often met at his house. Apart from his poetical writings, he published a volume of essays, *Bild und Gesetz (Image and Law,* 1930), and was co-editor with George of a collection entitled *Deutsche Dichtung (German Poetry,* 1901–1903).

Wolf Solent (1929). A novel by J. C. POWYS. Wolf Solent is a London teacher who returns to the Dorset village of his childhood (the Hardy country), seeking peace. The story is concerned with love, lust, mysticism, and the forces of nature.

Wollstonecraft, Mary (1759–1797). English author, best known for her *Vindication of the Rights of Woman* (1792), an argument for equality of women. In 1797 she married William GODWIN and died when their daughter Mary, later Mary Wollstonecraft SHELLEY, was born.

Wolsey, Thomas (c. 1475–1530). English Cardinal and Lord Chancellor. Wolsey became Privy Councillor to HENRY VIII in 1511, and was appointed Cardinal in 1515, the same year that he became Lord Chancellor. He had ambitions to become Pope, and cultivated a friendship with the Emperor Charles V to gain that end, but failed to be elected. When Henry wished to divorce Catherine of Aragon, Wolsey attempted to secure a divorce from the Pope—a course doomed to slow failure because Charles V, Catherine's nephew, effectively controlled the Papacy. Henry, displeased with Wolsey's conduct of the affair, deprived him of his offices (1529). A moving account of Wolsey's dismissal is given in Shakespeare's HENRY VIII, in which Wolsey's famous farewell is, however, generally thought to be the work of John Fletcher.

Woman in White, The (1860). A mystery novel by Wilkie COLLINS. The plot hinges on the resemblance of Laura Fairlie, an English heiress, to Anne Catherick, a mysterious woman in white, confined in a lunatic asylum. In order to secure Laura's money the unscrupulous Sir Percival Glyde thrusts her into the asylum in place of the dying Anne, but this villainy is finally exposed by her faithful lover,

Walter Hartright. A subsidiary villain is the subtle, sardonic Count Fosco.

Woman Killed with Kindness, A (1603). A tragedy by Thomas HEYWOOD. Mistress Anne, the sister of Sir Francis Acton, is married to John Frankford. Unwittingly, Frankford admits to his home the charming Master Wendoll, who succeeds in seducing Anne. Hearing rumors of this, Frankford surprises the two and banishes Anne forever from his sight, although he provides for her care and maintenance. Carrying the burden of her own guilt and her husband's "kindness," Anne pines and dies, having been reconciled with her husband on her deathbed.

Woman of No Importance, A (1893). A play by Oscar WILDE. The chief characters are Gerald Arbuthnot, his mother, and Lord Illingworth, a nobleman who has offered to make George his secretary. Mrs. Arbuthnot tries in vain to persuade George to refuse the offer. Only later, when George is about to attack Illingworth for kissing his fiancée Hester, does his mother confess that the nobleman is his father, who had seduced her as "a woman of no importance."

Woman Who Rode Away, The (1928). A short story by D. H. LAWRENCE, about a lonely and bored American woman in Mexico. Riding off alone into the mountains, she comes to a strange Indian tribe who imprison her and then sacrifice her to their god. The heroine is said to be based on his friend and patron Mabel Dodge LUHAN.

Women in Love (1920). A novel by D. H. LAWRENCE. Containing some of the clearest statements of Lawrence's own beliefs, it is a sequel to THE RAINBOW, and describes the later life of Ursula Brangwen and her sister Gudrun, a sculptor. Gudrun falls in love with Gerald Crich, a mining industrialist, but their relationship is marred by their possessive, destructive approach to love. In contrast, Ursula marries Rupert Birkin, a school inspector and spokesman for Lawrence, with whom she achieves an ideal sensual union. Birkin says that modern man exists in a living death because he allows his passionate, unconscious, true self to be imprisoned by his own intellect and by the pressures of industrial society. Man's salvation lies in his making a good, passionate marriage in which the lovers recognize each other's true separateness. He must complete his happiness by a different but similarly deep friendship with another man. Birkin offers this friendship to Gerald, who rejects it. When his affair with Gudrun ends, Gerald destroys himself in the mountains of the Tyrol, where they are all on vacation. The novel has a minimum of plot and action, but a great deal of philosophical discussion and description of the characters' emotional states and unconscious drives. Many of the ideas are expressed through symbolism. The characters and relationships in the novel are probably partially based on those of Lawrence and his wife Frieda Lawrence, John Middleton MURRY and his wife Katherine MANSFIELD. The friends shared a house in England in 1914–1915.

Wonder-Book for Girls and Boys, A (1852). A book for children by Nathaniel HAWTHORNE. The author retells, through a narrator, Eustace Bright, several Greek myths. TANGLEWOOD TALES was a sequel.

Wonder-horn, The Boy's. See KNABEN WUNDERHORN, DES.

Wonders of the Invisible World (1693). An account of the Salem witchcraft trials by Cotton MATHER. It purports to give evidence against the various victims of the trials and discusses witchcraft in general.

Wonders of the World. See SEVEN WONDERS OF THE ANCIENT WORLD.

Wonder-Working Magician, The. See MÁGICO PRODIGIOSO, EL.

Wood, Anthony or **Anthony à** (1632–1695). English antiquary. He wrote a Latin history of Oxford (1674) translated into English as *The History and Antiquity of the University of Oxford* (1792–1796). His *Athenae Oxonienses* (1691–1692) is a biographical dictionary listing famous Oxford graduates from the year 1500.

Wood, Charles Erskine Scott (1852–1944). American poet. His verse expresses his humanitarian and radical sympathies. In his early life, Wood served in the U.S. Army in the West, resigning because of the injustices against the Indians. He became a lawyer and, late in life, began writing. His best-known works are *The Poet in the Desert* (1915), a poetic dialogue on social injustice, and *Heavenly Discourse* (1927), a satire on war, injustice, and other social evils. He also wrote *Maia* (1918), *Circe* (1919), *Poems from the Ranges* (1929), and *Sonnets to Sappho* (1940).

Wood, Clement (1888–1950). American writer. He is the author of *Hunters of Heaven* (1929), a discourse on American poetry, and *The Complete Rhyming Dictionary and Poet's Craft Book* (1936). Deeply interested in social and racial injustice, Wood won considerable fame with his poem *De Glory Road*, the title poem of his 1936 collection. *The Greenwich Village Blues* (1926) is an earlier poetry collection.

Wood, Grant (1892–1942). American painter. He is known for his stark, often quietly ironical pictures of the Middle West, such as *American Gothic* or *Daughters of the Revolution.*

Wood, Mrs. Henry. Born **Ellen Price** (1814–1887). English novelist. Her enormously successful, frequently dramatized novel EAST LYNNE came to epitomize the ludicrous, tear-jerking melodrama of the later 19th century. No longer read now, she was a crude, sensational, prolific, and highly popular writer in her day.

Woodberry, George E[dward] (1855–1930). American critic, teacher, and poet. Still remembered for his teaching of comparative literature at Columbia University, Woodberry wrote poetry that is little known today. His critical studies, however, are still valuable, especially the biographies of Hawthorne (1902), Emerson (1907), and Poe (2 vols., 1909). He also edited with E. C. Stedman the 10-volume *Works of Edgar Allan Poe* (1894–1895). Among his other prose works are *Makers of Literature* (1900), *America in Literature* (1903), *The Appreciation of Literature* (1907), and *The Inspiration of Poetry* (1910). His books of poetry include *The North Shore Watch* (1890), *Wild Eden* (1899), *Ideal Passion* (1917), and *The Roamer, and Other Poems* (1920).

Woodcraft, or The Sword and the Distaff (1854). A novel by William Gilmore SIMMS. The book is set in the Charleston, S.C. area during 1782; the withdrawal of the British troops in December of that year is the chief historical event. Captain PORGY and his demobilized but loyal fellow soldiers return to his plantation to repair wartime devastation. Porgy rescues his slaves and those of the charming widow, Mrs. Eveleigh, from the scheming British officers and their dishonest American conspirators. He also pays the widow ardent but unsuccessful court. Because of Simms's favorable treatment of the lives of the slaves under their old masters, the book has been called his answer to *Uncle Tom's Cabin.*

Wooden Horse of Troy. See TROJAN HORSE.

wooden walls. Ships of wood. When Xerxes invaded Greece (480 B.C.), the Greeks sent to ask the Delphic oracle for advice and were told to seek safety in their wooden walls.

Woodham-Smith, Cecil (1896–   ). English biographer and historian. Her scholarly studies of figures in the Crimean War, *Florence Nightingale* (1950) and *The Reason Why* (1954), were popular successes. *The Great Hunger* (1962) is a study of the Irish potato famine of the 1840's.

Woodhouse, Emma. See EMMA.

Woodhull, Victoria Claflin (1838–1927). American reformer and lecturer. As a child, Victoria Woodhull gave spiritualistic performances, sold patent medicines, and told fortunes with her traveling family. Twice married, she moved to New York with her sister, Tennessee Celeste Claflin. The two sisters were befriended by Cornelius Vanderbilt, Sr., and founded *Woodhull and Claflin's Weekly* (1870–1876), a periodical devoted to social and political reform; they defended women's rights and free love. The first English translation of the *Communist Manifesto* (1872) and the story of the notorious Beecher-Tilton affair appeared in the *Weekly*. The Equal Rights party nominated Victoria Woodhull for President in 1872, with Frederick Douglass as her running mate. Moving to England, she married the scion of a wealthy banking family; her sister Tennessee married a baronet. With her daughter, Zulu Maud Woodhull, Victoria published a periodical entitled *Humanitarian* (1892–1901). Among the articles and pamphlets Victoria Woodhull wrote are *Origins, Tendencies and Principles of Government* (1871), *Stirpiculture* (1888), and *The Alchemy of Maternity* (1889). She and her sister are regarded as the models for Audacia Dangereyes in Harriet Beecher Stowe's novel *My Wife and I* (1871).

Woodstock (1826). A novel by Sir Walter SCOTT, dealing with the escapes of Charles II during the Commonwealth and his final triumphant entry into London. Shakespeare, Jonson, and Milton are among the minor characters.

Woodward, William E. (1874–1950). American writer. He is best known for his debunking biographies of George Washington (1926) and General Grant (1928). *Tom Paine: America's Godfather* (1945) is a more sympathetic biography. In addition to several novels, Woodward also wrote *A New American History* (1936) and *The Way Our People Lived* (1944).

Woolf, Leonard [Sidney] (1880–1969). English writer on politics and economics; husband of Virginia Woolf. As a young man he was in the Ceylon Civil Service and his earliest books were set in Ceylon; *The*

Village and the Jungle (1913) is a novel exposing some of the evils of colonialism. He was a member of the FABIAN SOCIETY. Among his other works are *Socialism and Co-operation* (1921); *Hunting the Highbrow* (1927); *The Hotel* (1939), a play; and *Principia Politica* (1953). In 1917 he and his wife founded the Hogarth Press.

Woolf, [Adeline] Virginia (1882–1941). English novelist, critic, and essayist. The daughter of Sir Leslie Stephen and wife of Leonard WOOLF, she was a member of the BLOOMSBURY GROUP. An exact contemporary of James Joyce, she is known, like him, as an experimenter and innovator in novel writing, especially in her use of the techniques of interior monologue and STREAM OF CONSCIOUSNESS. Her novels are noted for their poetic and symbolic quality. They are also known for their delicacy and sensitivity of style, their psychological penetration, their evocation of place and mood, and their background of historical and literary reference. Many of her novels are concerned with time, its passage, and the difference between external and inner time. Virginia Woolf was probably influenced by the ideas of Henri Bergson.

Her first two novels, *The Voyage Out* (1915) and *Night and Day* (1919), are fairly conventional and realistic. These were followed by JACOB'S ROOM, MRS. DALLOWAY, TO THE LIGHTHOUSE, ORLANDO, THE WAVES, THE YEARS, and BETWEEN THE ACTS. Her collections of short stories are *Monday or Tuesday* (1921) and *A Haunted House* (1944). She also wrote a great deal of literary criticism and many essays. Among her nonfictional works are *Mr. Bennett and Mrs. Brown* (1924); *The Common Reader* (1925, 1932), two series of literary essays; A ROOM OF ONE'S OWN; *Flush* (1933), on the spaniel pet of Elizabeth Barrett Browning; *Three Guineas* (1938), about women's emancipation (Virginia Woolf was an ardent feminist); *Roger Fry* (1940), a biography; *The Death of the Moth and Other Essays* (1942); and *A Writer's Diary* (1953).

In the home of her father, Sir Leslie Stephen, Virginia Woolf was reared in an atmosphere of literature and learning, receiving her education in her father's own extensive library and meeting many of the outstanding authors of the day. She was related to a number of the most distinguished scholarly families in England, such as the Darwins, the Symondses, and the Stracheys. The Bloomsbury group had its inception in the gatherings of former Cambridge University students and their friends which were held at the home of Virginia and her sister Vanessa (wife of Clive Bell). Virginia was married to Leonard Woolf in 1912. A few years later, with a single hand-press, they founded the Hogarth Press, which became a successful publishing house. It printed early works of Katherine Mansfield, E. M. Forster, T. S. Eliot, and Virginia Woolf's own first short stories, and it pioneered in introducing the works of Freud to English readers.

Virginia Woolf's books draw largely on her own life experience. Her childhood provides the background for her novel *To the Lighthouse,* and the sudden death of her favorite brother in 1906 is reflected in the deaths of Percival (in *The Waves*) and of Jacob (in *Jacob's Room*). Almost all her characters are members of her own leisured, intellectual,

upper-middle class. Many of her novels are set in London, where she lived for most of her life. In 1941, depressed by the war and afraid of the recurrence of a nervous breakdown, she committed suicide by drowning.

Woollcott, Alexander [Humphreys] (1887–1943). American journalist, drama critic, and writer. Woollcott was born in the Fourierist colony called the North American Phalanx. He became a journalist in New York and a leading member of the Round Table group, a number of well-known writers, musicians, and artists who gathered at the Algonquin Hotel. Woollcott carried on a radio program called "The Town Crier"; in this venture and in his magazine work for *The New Yorker* he established a reputation for sentimentality, egotism, and sharp insult. Later, Woollcott became a victim of others' wit. He was the acknowledged model for Sheridan Whiteside, an impossible egotist, in THE MAN WHO CAME TO DINNER by George S. Kaufman and Moss Hart. Woollcott, far from taking offense, played the role himself in a touring company. Among his books are *Shouts and Murmurs* (1922), *Enchanted Aisles* (1924), *The Story of Irving Berlin* (1925), and *Going to Pieces* (1928). He edited the anthologies *The Woollcott Reader* (1935) and *Woollcott's Second Reader* (1937).

Woolley, Sir [Charles] Leonard (1880–1960). English archaeologist. He made important excavations, especially in the Middle East. He wrote on the Sumerians and on Ur of the Chaldees; his book *Digging Up the Past* (1930) was a popular success.

Woolman, John (1720–1772). American Quaker leader and humanitarian. An itinerant preacher, he was among the first to protest Negro slavery. His simply written *Journal* (1774), a classic of its genre, was edited in 1871 by John Greenleaf Whittier, a fellow Quaker.

Woolson, Constance Fenimore (1840–1894). American novelist and short-story writer. Her greatuncle was James Fenimore Cooper. Born in New Hampshire, she traveled through America, lived in the South, and spent the rest of her life in England and Europe. A pioneer regionalist, Miss Woolson was impressed by the work of Bret Harte. Among her own writings are *Two Women* (1862), a long narrative poem; *Castle Nowhere* (1875), a collection of stories about French settlers in the Great Lakes region; *Rodman the Keeper* (1880), sketches about the South; *Anne* (1883), a novel about a Mackinac Island girl; *Horace Chase* (1894), a novel of the South; *The Front Yard* (1895) and *Dorothy* (1896), stories about Americans in Italy; and several other volumes. Praised by Henry James, most of her work first appeared in *The Atlantic Monthly, Harper's,* and *Century* magazines.

Worde, Wynkyn de. Real name Jan van Wynkyn (d. 1534?). English printer and stationer. He was born in Alsace and early in his career was an apprentice to William CAXTON. He published a number of well-known books of the time, including the fourth edition (1498) of Chaucer's *Canterbury Tales.*

Wordsworth, Dorothy (1771–1855). English writer and younger sister of William Wordsworth. Her *Journals* (1798, 1874, 1889, 1897, 1904, 1924), *Recollections of a Tour Made in Scotland* (1803), *Journal of a Mountain Ramble* (1805), and other similar works are records of her impressions and travels, many undertaken in the company of her brother, and are not only notable for their excellent style but also useful to Wordsworth students and biographers for the wealth of information on the poet which they contain. Dorothy wrote several short poems herself which were included in various editions of Wordsworth's poetic works. She spent the last 25 years of her life struggling against physical and mental illness.

Wordsworth, William (1770–1850). English poet. He is known for his worship of nature, his humanitarianism, his early sympathy with democratic liberalism, and his interest in the lives, the daily pursuits, and the common speech of common people. With his friend Samuel Taylor COLERIDGE, he was one of the early leaders of English ROMANTICISM. Wordsworth was particularly interested in instituting a reform in poetic diction which would employ, as he proposes in his famous preface to LYRICAL BALLADS, "a selection of language really used by men." His most ambitious works are THE EXCURSION, actually the first part of the uncompleted poem *The Recluse,* and THE PRELUDE, both long philosophical poems of autobiographical character. His earliest works, *An Evening Walk* and *Descriptive Sketches,* were published in 1793; the bulk of his best-known poetry is contained in *Lyrical Ballads* (1798), which he published jointly with Coleridge. Among his better-known shorter works are *Alice Fell;* MICHAEL; SIMON LEE; the *Lucy* poems; RESOLUTION AND INDEPENDENCE; *The Solitary Reaper;* PETER BELL; *The Idiot Boy; I Wandered Lonely as a Cloud; Elegiac Stanzas;* NUNS FRET NOT AT THEIR CONVENT'S NARROW ROOM; *The World is Too Much with Us; Lines Composed a Few Miles Above Tintern Abbey;* ODE: INTIMATIONS OF IMMORTALITY.

In his early youth Wordsworth was deeply influenced by the ideas of Jean Jacques Rousseau and William Godwin, and he enthusiastically supported the French Revolution. He visited France in 1792 and had a love affair with Annette VALLON, evidence of which was not uncovered until the 20th century. As he grew older, he lived peacefully in the Lake Country of northern England and became increasingly conservative in his political views and orthodox in his religion. In 1843 he was appointed poet laureate, succeeding Robert Southey. He is buried in the churchyard at Grasmere. See GOODY BLAKE AND HARRY FELL; DOVE COTTAGE; THE DAFFODILS.

Work in Progress. The title under which James Joyce's FINNEGANS WAKE was known until its publication. Sections were published before the whole work appeared in 1939.

Works and Days (Erga kai Hemerai). A long poem by HESIOD. This farmer's almanac of ancient Greece contains directions and advice concerning labor on the farm. It is a valuable guide to contemporary Greek life, and also gives what little is known of Hesiod's life.

Works of Sir Thomas Malory, The. See MORTE D'ARTHUR, LE.

World Court. The Permanent Court of International Justice. It was opened at The Hague (February 15, 1922) by the League of Nations. It had 15 judges who served for nine years. The court sat on all cases which states or members of the League brought before it and also on other matters provided for in international treaties and conventions. Before World War II, Germany, Italy, and Japan had handed in their resignations. The World Court came to an end in 1945 and was superseded by the International Court of Justice, provided for by the Charter of the United Nations.

World Enough and Time (1950). A novel by Robert Penn WARREN. It is based on the murder in Kentucky of Colonel Solomon P. Sharp by Jeroboam O. Beauchamp, whose trial was the sensation of 1826. (See KENTUCKY TRAGEDY.) The title is taken from Andrew Marvell's *To His Coy Mistress.*

World I Never Made, A (1936). A novel by James T. FARRELL. It is the first of a series of novels concerning Danny O'Neill.

Worldly-Wiseman, Mr. See PILGRIM'S PROGRESS.

World War I (1914–1918). The European war that began with Austria-Hungary's declaration of war on Serbia on July 28, 1914. The major belligerents were the Central Powers—Germany, Austria-Hungary, Turkey, and Bulgaria—and the Allies—Great Britain, France, Russia, Italy, and the U.S.

Although the immediate cause of the conflict was the assassination of Archduke FRANCIS FERDINAND of Austria by a Serbian nationalist on June 28, Europe had been on the verge of war for years as a result of the political, economic, and military rivalries of the great powers. Complicating the situation were such factors as the disintegration of the Turkish empire, the turbulence in the Balkans, and France's desire to avenge its defeat in the Franco-Prussian War of 1870–1871.

After Austria's declaration of war on Serbia, Russia ordered mobilization of her forces, and on Aug. 1 Germany declared war. Commencing hostilities against France, the Germans invaded Belgium in order to reach Paris from the northwest; the attack on Belgium, whose neutrality had been guaranteed by Germany, brought England into the war on August 4. In the east, the Germans smashed the Russian armies. Italy, an erstwhile ally of Germany and Austria, abandoned them and joined the Allies in 1915; Turkey came into the war on the German side, thus extending the area of conflict to the eastern Mediterranean.

In the U.S., President Woodrow WILSON sought to preserve American neutrality, but popular feeling gradually ran in favor of the Allies, particularly after the sinking of the LUSITANIA. When, after an interval of nonbelligerence toward America, Germany resumed unrestricted submarine warfare in Feb., 1917, the U.S. severed diplomatic relations with Berlin; in April war was declared. The entrance of American troops on the western front ended the stalemate. After a series of reverses the German armies retreated, the Berlin government fell, rebellion broke out in Germany, and an armistice was negotiated (Nov. 11, 1918).

The war killed millions, civilians as well as soldiers; it impoverished most of the world; it created a number of new nations when the German, Austrian, and Turkish empires were dismembered; and it hastened the RUSSIAN REVOLUTION of 1917. The treaty of VERSAILLES, moreover, carried within it the seeds of World War II.

The war inspired many literary works. Among the best novels dealing with the war are John Dos Passos' THREE SOLDIERS, Jaroslav Hašek's THE GOOD SOLDIER SCHWEIK, E. E. Cummings' THE ENORMOUS ROOM, Erich Maria Remarque's ALL QUIET ON THE WESTERN FRONT, and Ernest Hemingway's A FAREWELL TO ARMS. Poets who wrote about the war include Alan SEEGER, Wilfred OWEN, Siegfried SASSOON, John McCRAE, and Rupert BROOKE. Plays on this theme include WHAT PRICE GLORY by Maxwell Anderson and Laurence Stallings and JOURNEY'S END by Robert Cedric Sherriff. Poet Robert GRAVES described his war experiences in *Goodbye to All That* (1929), and T. E. LAWRENCE wrote about the Arab campaign against the Turks in his *Seven Pillars of Wisdom* (1926). See David LLOYD GEORGE; Georges CLEMENCEAU; Vittorio ORLANDO; WILHELM II; Paul von HINDENBURG; Eric LUDENDORFF; John J. PERSHING.

World War II (1939–1945). The global conflict that began officially with the German invasion of Poland on Sept 1, 1939. The major belligerents were the Axis powers—Germany, Italy, and Japan—and the Allies—Great Britain, France, the U.S.S.R., China, and the U.S.

The causes of World War II were intimately connected with those of WORLD WAR I and with the unfavorable conditions which remained after the treaty of VERSAILLES. Economic distress, together with the unpopularity and weakness of the WEIMAR REPUBLIC in Germany, led the way to the growth of FASCISM and the rise of Adolf HITLER. The LEAGUE OF NATIONS, the first world organization established to maintain peace and settle international disputes, was drastically weakened by the refusal of the U.S. to join. When the league did nothing but formally condemn Japan for its invasion of Manchuria in 1931–1932, many countries felt the need to protect themselves by building up armaments. In 1935 the league failed to prevent Italy's invasion of Ethiopia. Under Hitler, Germany began to rearm and sent troops into the Rhineland (1936) in violation of the Versailles treaty; she seized Austria in 1938, and in Aug. 1939, entered into a nonaggression pact with Russia.

After defeating Poland in 1939, the Germans invaded Norway and Denmark, the British were driven from the Continent, and France fell. On June 22, 1941, Germany attacked Russia.

On Dec. 7, 1941, the Japanese bombed Pearl Harbor in Hawaii and destroyed the greater part of the U.S. fleet there. The subsequent declarations of war by the U.S. included Germany and Italy, both of whom had made prior declarations of war on the U.S., as well as Japan. The latter country followed up her Pearl Harbor attack with others in the Pacific region, and the war became one that involved all the continents and all the oceans. The Japanese captured Wake, Guam, the Philippines, and other strategic islands before the Allied offensive, begun in the fall of 1942, began to dislodge them. However, it was not until President Harry S. Truman authorized the dropping of the first atomic bombs (on Hiroshima, Aug. 6, 1945; on Nagasaki, Aug. 9, 1945) that Japan was forced to surrender (Sept. 2, 1945).

After an Allied invasion of southern Italy, the Italian army and navy surrendered (Sept. 3, 1943), but German forces in Rome and to the north were not dislodged until the summer of 1944. On June 6, 1944, an immense invasion army of men and supplies, under the direct supervision of General Dwight D. EISENHOWER, had landed in France and forced the Germans to retreat across the Rhine. Germany surrendered unconditionally on May 7, 1945.

Among the best-known novels dealing with the war are Jan Struther's MRS. MINIVER, Thomas Heggen's MISTER ROBERTS, Norman Mailer's THE NAKED AND THE DEAD, Irwin Shaw's THE YOUNG LIONS, James Jones's FROM HERE TO ETERNITY, and Herman Wouk's THE CAINE MUTINY. Other novelists who have written about the war include John HERSEY, Pierre BOULLE, André SCHWARZ-BART, Erich Maria REMARQUE, Curzio MALAPARTE, and Konstantin SIMONOV. IDIOT'S DELIGHT and THERE SHALL BE NO NIGHT by Robert E. Sherwood and THE DEVIL'S GENERAL by Carl Zuckmayer are plays dealing with the war. *The Diary of* ANNE FRANK was by a Jewish girl in Nazi-occupied Holland. Winston CHURCHILL, prime minister of England from 1940 to 1945, wrote a six-volume history of the war called *The Second World War* (1948–1954). See Franklin D. ROOSEVELT; Joseph STALIN; Charles DE GAULLE; Benito MUSSOLINI; George C. MARSHALL; Douglas MACARTHUR; NUREMBERG TRIALS.

Worthies, the Nine. Nine heroes, three from the Bible, three from the classics, and three from romance. They were frequently bracketed together as in the burlesque Pageant of the Nine Worthies in Shakespeare's *Love's Labour's Lost*. They are: Joshua, David, and Judas Maccabaeus; Hector, Alexander, and Julius Caesar; Arthur, Charlemagne, and Godfrey of Bouillon.

Wotan. The old High German form of Odin, chief of the Scandinavian gods. This is the form used in the operas of Wagner's RING DES NIBELUNGEN, in which Wotan the Mighty plays a leading role.

Wotton, Sir Henry (1568–1639). English diplomat and poet. Wotton served as ambassador to Venice and later became provost of Eton College. He was an intimate friend of John Donne and a fishing companion of Izaak Walton, whose brief biography of Wotton was included in *Reliquiae Wottonianae* (1651), a posthumous edition of the latter's work. Wotton wrote poems of considerable charm, such as *On His Mistress, the Queen of Bohemia* (1624), and was the author of the statement that "an ambassador is an honest man sent to lie abroad for his country."

Wouk, Herman (1915–   ). American novelist. His most popular and famous work, THE CAINE MUTINY, was awarded a Pulitzer Prize. Wouk was born and educated in New York City. His first novel, *Aurora Dawn* (1947), was a fantasy lightly satirizing big business. It was followed by *The City Boy* (1948), the story of an 11-year-old boy and his experiences at a summer camp. *Marjorie Morningstar* (1955), Wouk's second best-selling novel, is the story of a middle-class Jewish girl who becomes enamored of the world of show business, but finally settles down to life as a suburban housewife. Another novel, *Youngblood Hawke* (1962), describes the life and career of an author partially modeled on Thomas Wolfe.

Would-be Gentleman, The. See BOURGEOIS GENTILHOMME, LE.

Woyzeck (pub. 1879, written 1836?). A fragmentary play by Georg BÜCHNER, about an imbecilic army private who murders his unfaithful common-law wife. It depicts, with powerful realism, the social and economic injustices that lead to both the wife's faithlessness and Woyzeck's murder of her; as such, it is a socialistic document. In style, it is extremely compact, a quick succession of short, meaningful scenes. For this reason, and because of its tendency to treat typical rather than individual phenomena, to depict human agony in the pure state, it has been regarded as a forerunner of expressionism. Alban Berg's 12-tone opera *Wozzeck* (1925) is based on the play.

Wozzeck. See WOYZECK.

Wrangel, Piotr Nikolayevich (1878–1928). Russian general. He fought against the Bolsheviks during the civil war. His forces, hard-pressed by the Red Army, evacuated the Crimea in 1920.

Wrayburn, Eugene. In Charles Dickens' OUR MUTUAL FRIEND, an indolent, moody, whimsical young man who loves Lizzie Hexam. After he is nearly killed by Bradley Headstone who also loves Lizzie, he reforms, and marries Lizzie, who saved his life.

Wreck of the Deutschland, The (1875). A poem by Gerard Manley HOPKINS. It celebrates the death of five nuns, drowned off the Welsh coast while sailing to the U.S. from religious persecution in Germany. In intricate stanzas, full of complex metaphor and allusion, the poet deals with the problem of suffering, his own and everyone's relationship with God, the decline of religion, and the nuns' happiness in dying in God's hands.

Wreck of the Hesperus, The (1841). A ballad by Henry Wadsworth LONGFELLOW. It was inspired by a newspaper account of an actual wreck at sea.

Wren, Sir Christopher (1632–1723). English architect. Following the great FIRE OF LONDON in 1666, he was entrusted with the reconstruction of innumerable churches and public buildings, notably St. Paul's Cathedral (1675–1710). His work is characterized by decorative interiors ornamented with designs and by graceful spires known for their inventive variety and for the technical resourcefulness of the construction. He is buried under the choir of St. Paul's; the tablet erected to mark the spot bears the Latin inscription: *Si monumentum requiris, circumspice* ("If thou seekest a monument, gaze around").

Wren, Jenny. A character in Charles Dickens' OUR MUTUAL FRIEND whose real name is Fanny Cleaver. She is a doll's dressmaker, a little, deformed girl, with a sharp, shrewd face and beautiful golden hair, who supports herself and her drunken father.

Wren, P[ercival] C[hristopher] (1885–1941). English novelist, soldier, and traveler. He is known for his adventure stories dealing with life in the French Foreign Legion. He wrote *The Wages of Virtue* (1916); *Beau Geste* (1924), a bestseller; and other novels.

Wright, Frank Lloyd (1869–1959). American architect. The creator of a strikingly individualistic, lyrical, and dramatic style, he is noted as one of the most important and influential architects of the modern era. His principles have been closely followed and studied by young architects around the world. Among the most famous works that show his use of the cantilever are the Imperial Hotel in Tokyo, Japan (1916–1922), built to withstand earthquakes; the Kaufmann House, Bear Run, Pa. (1936), boldly poised over a waterfall; and the Johnson Research Laboratory, Racine, Wis. (1949–1950), which is supported by a central cylinder. Wright's concern with relating building to site and with breaking down the enclosure of interior space by walls is illustrated by his headquarters at Taliesin West, near Phoenix, Ariz. (1938–1959), while the Guggenheim Museum in New York, with its spiral, wider at the top than bottom, shows his confident use of reinforced concrete. In spite of occasional paradoxes and contradictions, his many writings reveal a lively gift of narration and clarity of exposition. Ayn Rand's novel THE FOUNTAINHEAD is said to have been inspired by Wright and his famous predecessor and first employer, Louis SULLIVAN.

Wright, Richard [Nathaniel] (1908–1960). American novelist and short-story writer. Considered by many the most eloquent spokesman for the American Negro of his generation, he established his reputation with his powerful first novel, NATIVE SON. His other works include *Uncle Tom's Children* (1938), a collection of four novellas; *Black Boy* (1945), an autobiography of his youth; *The Outsider* (1953), a philosophical novel; *White Man, Listen!* (1957), on the evils of racial injustice; and *The Long Dream* (1958), a novel.

Wright, Wilbur (1867–1912) and **Orville** (1871–1948). American pioneers in aviation. They began experimenting with gliders at Kitty Hawk, N.C. Their first flight in an airplane with an engine was made at Kitty Hawk on Dec. 17, 1903. In 1908, France became the first country to recognize them, and, in 1909, the U.S. army adopted their plane. In the same year they founded the Wright Aeroplane Company.

Wriothesley, Henry. See 3rd earl of SOUTHAMPTON.

Wunderhorn, Des Knaben. See KNABEN WUNDERHORN, DES.

Wundt, Wilhelm Max (1832–1920). German physiologist and philosopher who established the first laboratory for experimental psychology (Leipzig, 1879). Similar work was done by Ivan Pavlov.

Wurdemann, Audrey [May] (1911–1960). American poet and novelist. She won a Pulitzer Prize with her second collection of verse, *Bright Ambush* (1934). She was the youngest poet ever to be so honored. Her other books of poetry include *The House of Silk* (1926), *The Seven Sins* (1935), and *The Testament of Love* (1938). With Joseph Auslander, her husband, she wrote two novels: *My Uncle Jan* (1948) and *The Islanders* (1951).

Wuthering Heights (1847). A novel by Emily BRONTË first published under the pen name Ellis Bell. Mr. Earnshaw, father of Catherine and Hindley, finds a waif on the streets of London and brings him home to raise with his own children. HEATHCLIFF, a strange, uncouth, passionate creature, is from the beginning, a disruptive influence in the Earnshaws' lonely, moorland home, Wuthering Heights. Catherine forms a passionate attachment to him while Hindley hates him, regarding him as a usurper and a rival in his father's affection. After Mr. Earnshaw's death, the household degenerates. In spite of her love for Heathcliff, Catherine lets fall a remark, overheard by him that it would degrade her to marry him; the furious Heathcliff steals off, disappearing for three years, and Catherine marries the well-to-do Edgar Linton. Years later, Heathcliff, mysteriously transformed into a wealthy and polished man, returns and is invited by Edgar, who has money troubles, to make his home at Wuthering Heights. Heathcliff accepts but deceitfully elopes with Edgar's sister, obviously to avenge himself on Catherine and her husband. Barred from the house, Heathcliff still manages a final meeting with Catherine before she dies in premature childbirth. Twelve years later, Heathcliff, now a widower, forces Catherine's daughter to marry his sickly son Linton, and upon the deaths of Edgar and of Linton he gains control of Wuthering Heights and of the young girl Cathy. When Heathcliff dies, the girl is at last free: she devotes herself to her young cousin Hareton, the uncouth and ignorant son of her uncle Hindley. The story, told by characters within the narrative and, to an extent, chronologically reshuffled, attains an almost mystical intensity. The adjective *wuthering,* in the title, is a Yorkshire word referring to turbulent weather.

Wyatt or **Wiat, Sir Thomas** (1503?–1542). English poet. Wyatt held a number of official positions under Henry VIII, including those of Member of the Privy Council, Ambassador to Spain, Member of Parliament, and Commander of the Fleet. During an official trip to Italy in 1527 he became acquainted with the work of the Italian love-poets. Later, his translations of PETRARCH introduced the sonnet into England. He was a friend of the earl of SURREY and had a strong influence on the writing of the younger man; together Wyatt and Surrey are credited with being the founders of the school of English lyric poetry which flourished during the remainder of the 16th and continued into the 17th century.

Wyatt's poetry is often characterized by extreme irregularity of rhythm, which 19th century scholars regarded as evidence of crude technique. In the 20th century, however, critics began to point out that this irregularity was often important in the total effect of the poems, comparing it with the dramatic rhythm in the work of John DONNE. Critics also have praised the vigor and authentic intensity of feeling in Wyatt's best poems, such as *They Flee from Me; My Lute, Awake;* and *In Eternum.* His work appeared in several anthologies, among them *The Court of Venus* (1542); *Seven Penitential Psalms* (1549); and TOTTEL'S MISCELLANY.

Wycherly, William (1640–1716). English comic dramatist of the Restoration, noted for the savagery of his satire, his cynical realism, and his coarse, mordant wit. Educated in France and at Oxford, Wycherly briefly contemplated a legal career. His first comedy, *Love in a Wood, or St. James' Park* (1671), won him the favor of the duchess of Clevelend, mistress of Charles II. This play was followed by *The Gentleman Dancing Master* (1672?) and his best works, THE COUNTRY WIFE and THE PLAIN DEALER. He incurred the king's displeasure by his secret marriage (c. 1680) to the widowed countess of Drogheda; after her death he became involved in lengthy litigation over her estate and spent seven years in a debtor's prison. Charles refused to help Wycherly out of his financial difficulties, but James II, who, it is said, had greatly admired *The Plain Dealer,* came to his rescue by paying his debts.

Wyclif, Wycliffe, or **Wiclif, John** (d. 1384). English theologian and reformer. Called "The Morning Star of the Reformation," Wyclif was one of the earliest antagonists of papal encroachments on secular power. He felt that all Christians should have access to the Bible in the vernacular and prepared the first complete English translation. It is thought that Wyclif himself translated the Four Gospels, and possibly the entire New Testament, while the Old Testament was done by his associates. The translation was completed c. 1388, but was not published until 1850. In addition to resisting the growth of the secular power of the papacy, Wyclif condemned monasticism, and attacked the foundations of medieval orthodoxy in his denial of the dogma of transubstantiation, from which the priesthood derived the basis of its power. He taught that all ecclesiastical and secular authority is derived from God and is forfeited when one is in a state of mortal sin. The followers of Wyclif were known as Wycliffites; however, the LOLLARDS, with whom they are often grouped, were not, strictly speaking, followers of Wyclif.

Wyeth, Andrew [Newell] (1917–   ). American painter. His tempera canvases realistically depict the people and scenes around his home in Chadds Ford, Pa.

Wylie, Elinor [Hoyt] (1885–1928). American poet and novelist. She is known for the precise and vivid imagery of her lyrics and the subtle analysis of emotion in her later love poems. Influenced by the Elizabethan and metaphysical poets, Elinor

Wyclif. From Bale's *Illustrium Majoris Britanniae Scriptorum* (1548).

Wylie derived the title of her first important book of poems, NETS TO CATCH THE WIND, from John Webster. She had published anonymously an earlier volume, *Incidental Numbers* (1912), and under her own name was to publish three more: *Black Armour* (1923), *Trivial Breath* (1928), and *Angels and Earthly Creatures* (1929). The last contains the well-known sonnet sequence *One Person. Collected Poems of Elinor Wylie* (1932) and *Last Poems of Elinor Wylie* (1943) were posthumously published.

Her novels, JENNIFER LORN, THE VENETIAN GLASS NEPHEW, THE ORPHAN ANGEL, and *Mr. Hodge and Mr. Hazard* (1928), all have a historical background for which she performed extensive research. *The Orphan Angel* centers on Shelley, her idol.

Wylie, Philip [Gordon] (1902–1971). American writer. A clever critic of American society, Wylie is best known for his attack on the "momism" of America in *Generation of Vipers* (1942). *Essay on Morals* (1947) is a strong criticism of organized religion, and *Opus 21* (1949) is an analysis of the sexual ills of American society. Wylie depicted the horrors of a future nuclear war in *Tomorrow* (1954) and in *Triumph* (1963).

Wyndham, John. Pen name of **John Beynon Harris** (1903–1969). English writer of science fiction. His fantastic *The Day of the* TRIFFIDS (1951) follows the fortunes of the survivors of a thermonuclear mistake.

Wynkyn de Worde. See WORDE, WYNKYN DE.

Wyoming Massacre (1778). The massacre in the Wyoming Valley of northeastern Pennsylvania by British loyalists and Iroquois of approximately 360 American settlers. *Gertrude of Wyoming* (1809), a narrative poem by the English poet Thomas Campbell, describes the event.

Wyss, Johan Rudolf (1781–1830). Swiss writer and philosopher. He is best known for *Der schweizerische Robinson* (1813; English translation 1820, THE SWISS FAMILY ROBINSON). He also is the author of the Swiss national anthem and collector of Swiss tales and folklore.

X

Xanadu. A province or region in China mentioned by Coleridge in his KUBLA KHAN as the site of the Khan's pleasure garden. *The Road to Xanadu* (1927) by the American John Livingston Lowes (1867–1945) is a unique study of the workings of the imagination, using Coleridge as an example.

Xanthus (Gr., Xanthos, reddish yellow). One of ACHILLES' two wonderful horses, Balios (piebald) being the other, and offspring of Zephyrus and the harpy Podarge. Being chided by his master for leaving Patroclus on the field of battle, Xanthus turned his head reproachfully and told Achilles that he also would soon be numbered with the dead, not from any fault of his horse, but by the decree of inexorable destiny (*Iliad,* xix). Xanthus is also the ancient name of the SCAMANDER River and of a city on its banks.

Xantippe or **Xanthippe.** The wife of the Greek philosopher Socrates. Her shrewish nature has made her name proverbial.

Xavier, St. Francis (1506–1552). Spanish Jesuit missionary, the "Apostle of the Indies." As a student in Paris he became a friend of Ignatius of Loyola and helped him establish the Society of Jesus (1534). He worked in Japan for several years and founded a mission in China. He was canonized, together with his master and friend, in 1622.

Xenion (*Gr.,* "stranger"). A two-line, usually satirical poem in the form of the classical epigram. Goethe's and Schiller's *Xenien* (1797; see WEIMAR CLASSICISM) are examples. "Xenien" is the German plural of the word.

Xenius. See Eugenio d'ORS Y ROVIRA.

Xenophon (c. 430–c. 355 B.C.). Athenian writer. In 401 B.C. Xenophon joined the force of mercenary Greeks recruited by Cyrus the Younger for the purpose of dethroning his older brother Artaxerxes. Cyrus was killed and Xenophon led the 10,000 Greeks through Persian territory to the Black Sea. His account of the expedition is known as the *Anabasis,* in which he portrays himself as the hero of the affair.

Xenophon, who had a great love for Sparta, fought with the Spartans against Athenians and Thebans in 394 B.C. The Athenians exiled him for this activity, and he subsequently lived in Sparta and Corinth. Among his other works, all of which seem to have survived in full, are the *Hellenica,* a continuation of Thucydides' history of Greece; the *Memorabilia of Socrates,* a popular philosophy; and the *Cyropedia,* a biography of Cyrus modified to suit Xenophon's didactic purpose. A famous part of the *Anabasis* is Xenophon's record of the Greeks crying "*Thalassa, thalassa,*" as they caught the first glimpse of their beloved sea.

Xerxes I (c. 519–465 B.C.). King of Persia, the son of Darius and Atossa. Concluding from a dream that the gods demanded war on the Greeks, he gathered a huge army and fleet. He constructed a bridge of boats over the Hellespont and reached Athens, but had to retreat after the battle of Salamis. He is an important figure in Aeschylus' tragedy THE PERSIANS. See PERSIAN WARS.

Xingu and Other Stories (1916). A collection of eight stories by Edith WHARTON. The title story satirizes the snobbish members of a women's luncheon club who discourse learnedly about Xingu—a Brazilian river—even though they know nothing about the subject. Also in the collection are *Coming Home, Autres Temps . . . ,* and *Bunner Sisters,* a novelette.

Xiphares. In Jean Racine's tragedy MITHRIDATE, the loyal son of Mithridate, who protects his father's betrothed and routs the Roman attack against him.

XYZ Affair (1797). A diplomatic incident that occurred when Charles PINCKNEY, John Marshall, and Elbridge Gerry were sent to Paris to negotiate a treaty of amity and commerce with France. The commissioners reported that three of Talleyrand's agents, designated in their correspondence as X, Y, and Z, had attempted to bribe them. The disclosure of the correspondence created a furor in both countries.

Y

Yahoo. In the fourth voyage of GULLIVER'S TRAVELS by Jonathan Swift, a race of filthy, loathsome brutes tamed by, and contrasted to, the virtuous and reasonable Houyhnhnms. Gulliver is discomfited by their resemblance to the human race. While the Houyhnhnms represent the highest attributes of mankind in their purest form, the beastly Yahoos represent Swift's conception of man living in a degenerate state of nature. See HOUYHNHNMLAND.

Yahweh. See JEHOVAH.

Yam or **Yamm.** The Canaanite god of the sea and inland waters. He is represented as a dragon. At the beginning of THE POEM OF BAAL, he has dominion over earth as well as sea, but after a protracted struggle, Baal, with the aid of his sister Anat, supplants him as lord of the earth. There are numerous references to this legend in the Old Testament, where Yam is referred to as Rahab or simply as the dragon, who was destroyed by Yahweh.

Yama. The god of the dead in Hindu mythology. The legend is that he was the first mortal to die, and was therefore made into a god. He is green in color, has four arms, is red-eyed, and rides a buffalo. The famous Savitri episode in the *Mahabharata* employs him as one of the major protagonists.

Yankee. Properly, a New Englander or one of New England stock. The term was extended to mean, first, an inhabitant of the North as apart from the South and, later, to comprise all citizens of the U.S. In the South, Northerners were often referred to as "Damyankees."

The word is generally taken to be a North American Indian corruption of *English* or of the French *Anglais*. There is also the story that in 1713 one Jonathan Hastings, a farmer of Cambridge, Mass., used the word as a puffing epithet, meaning "genuine," "what cannot be surpassed," as in a Yankee horse, Yankee cider, and so on. The students at Harvard, catching up the term, called Hastings "Yankee Jonathan." It soon spread, and became the jocose pet name of the New Englander.

Yankee Doodle. A quasi-national song of the U.S. Both the tune and several stanzas of *Yankee Doodle* were current early in the British colonies; the catchy tune seems to have inspired innumerable verses. The origin of the tune is disputed, and the words have traditionally been ascribed to Dr. Shuckburgh, a British army surgeon. The song seems to have been deliberately used by the British to provoke the American troops during the Revolution; the Americans, however, adopted the song as their own and created an image of the American in a rustic mold. The song was first printed in America in 1795.

Yarrow. A river in Scotland. Scott and Hogg have celebrated its legends, and Wordsworth wrote a poem called *Yarrow Revisited* (1835). *The Braes of Yarrow* is the title of an old Scottish ballad.

Yashin, Aleksandr. Pen name of **Aleksandr Yakovlevich Popov** (1913–   ). Russian poet and short-story writer. For *Aliona Fomina* (1949), his long poem glorifying work on the collective farm, Yashin received a Stalin prize. Most of his work deals with themes of peasant and village life. His short story, *Levers* (*Rychagi;* 1956), was one of the most discussed works of the recent thaw following Stalin's death. The story depicts the tyrannical behavior of Communist Party members toward subordinates on a collective farm.

Yates, Dornford. Pen name of **Cecil William Mercer** (1885–1960). English popular novelist. He wrote stories that blend adventure and light-hearted farce. The best known are those in the "Berry" series, starting with *Berry and Co.* (1921).

Yates, Edmund Hodgson (1831–1894). English novelist and editor. His differences with Thackeray ended in Yates's dismissal from the Garrick Club. This caused a long quarrel between Dickens and Thackeray which Thackeray, toward the end of his life, sought to patch up. As editor of the society weekly *The World,* Yates incurred the wrath of Lord Lonsdale and was imprisoned for libel in 1885. He wrote several novels including *For Better, For Worse* (1863) and *The Yellow Flag* (1872). In 1885 he published *Edmund Yates: his Recollections and his Experiences.*

Yatpan. The killer of the young hero in the Canaanite THE POEM OF AQHAT. He is hired by the goddess Anat to dispose of Aqhat and recover the divine bow which the youth refuses to give her. Yatpan, a most inefficient assassin, kills Aqhat, but promptly drops and breaks the bow, and, moreover, reveals his guilt to Aqhat's sister Paghat after drinking too much wine.

Yazoo Frauds (1795). A real estate speculation in which four land companies bribed the Georgia legislature in order to get large grants of land near the Yazoo River. The grants were later revoked. *The Georgia Spec; or Land in the Moon* (1797), a lost play by Royall Tyler, satirizes this episode.

Yearling, The (1938). A novel by Marjorie Kinnan RAWLINGS. Set in the scrub country of northern Florida, it recounts one year in the lives of a backwoods farmer, his wife, and his young son, Jody, who adopts an orphaned fawn and finds in the animal the love and companionship he craves. When the fawn begins to eat the family corn, Jody is ordered by his father to shoot him. The tragedy lifts

Jody out of his boyhood and into a more mature relationship with his parents. It was awarded a Pulitzer Prize.

Years, The (1937). A novel by Virginia WOOLF. More conventional than the author's other later books, and more popular when it was published, it is a chronicle of the Pargiter family from 1880 to "the present day." It is told in a series of nine separate but connected episodes which form a recurring cycle. It contains vivid evocations of London life.

Yeats, William Butler (1865–1939). Irish poet and dramatist. He is generally considered to be one of the greatest poets of the 20th century. The leader of the IRISH RENAISSANCE, he was largely responsible for founding the ABBEY THEATRE and encouraging its playwrights. The three major concerns of his life—art, Irish nationalism, and occult studies—are also central to his poetry and drama. His greatest work is in the poetry of his maturity and old age; it is characterized by its lyrical and dramatic qualities, its use of symbolism and the mythology of Irish folklore and the occult, its autobiographical and political themes, and its sensuous beauty, realism, precision, and economy.

He was the son of John Butler Yeats, a well-known Irish painter, and he himself studied painting for three years. Yeats's early poetry is characterized by a romantic affectation of melancholy and a preoccupation with "the Celtic twilight." *The Wanderings of Oisin* (1889), a long, mystical narrative poem based on Irish legend, and *The Lake Isle of Innisfree* (1893) date from this period.

In London, Yeats was a founding member of the Pre-Raphaelite RHYMER'S CLUB. On his return to Ireland in 1896 he became a leader of the Irish Renaissance. Believing that the Irish poet's task was to communicate with the Irish people, he wrote simple, direct poetry; *The Wind Among the Reeds* (1899) and *In the Seven Woods* (1903) are collections written during this period. Yeats met Maud GONNE when he was 23 and became indirectly involved in her political activities. He was in love with her during much of his life and used her as a central symbol in his poetry.

With Lady Gregory, George Moore, and others, Yeats founded in 1899 the theater society that was later to become the celebrated Abbey Theatre. He encouraged Lady Gregory and Synge to write plays for it, and he himself wrote many works for it, including THE COUNTESS CATHLEEN, *The Land of Heart's Desire* (1894), CATHLEEN NI HOULIHAN, and *Deirdre* (1907). Under the influence of Ezra Pound, whom Yeats met in 1912, he began to write ritualistic, symbolic dramas, with dance and music, in imitation of the Japanese NŌ plays. These plays, in prose and verse, often make symbolic use of Irish heroic legends, especially those about CÚ CHULAINN. Usually, like most of Yeats's work, they are concerned with peasants, aristocrats, beggars, wandering minstrels, and kings and queens; most of them are based on his mystical and occult ideas. THE HERNE'S EGG and PURGATORY are characteristic plays of this period.

Yeats had been interested in magic and occult philosophy since his Dublin days with A.E. (q.v.), and when he met Madame BLAVATSKY in London in 1887 he became a devoted student. He did not be-lieve in any orthodox religion, but since he felt that he needed some system of supernatural belief to give depth to his life and poetry, he half accepted the doctrines of THEOSOPHY, Hermetism (see HERMES TRISMEGISTUS), and spiritualism. In 1917 he married Georgie Hyde Lees, a spiritualist medium, and with the help of her trances and automatic writing composed A VISION, a prose work that combined a system of magic, a philosophy of history, and a philosophy of personality. Yeats's esoteric ideas provided a mythical background and a system of symbols for all his poetry, but especially for his later work.

In technique, Yeats's mature poetry was influenced by the work of John Donne, Walter Savage Landor, and Ezra Pound. It appeared in the volumes *The Green Helmet* (1910), *Responsibilities* (1914), *The Wild Swans at Coole* (1917), *Michael Robartes and the Dancer* (1920), *The Tower* (1928), and *The Winding Stair* (1929). Yeats prepared *The Collected Poems* (1933) himself, rewriting many of his early poems in accordance with his later stylistic ideas. Among the best-known individual poems are *Byzantium* and *Sailing to Byzantium; Easter 1916,* a commemoration of an incident during the Irish rebellion (see Padriac PEARSE); *A Prayer for My Daughter; Leda and the Swan; Among School Children; Lapis Lazuli; Long-Legged Fly;* and CRAZY JANE, a series of poems.

Yeats's prose works include *Fairy and Folk Tales of the Irish Peasantry* (1888); occult works, such as *The Celtic Twilight* (1893) and *The Secret Rose* (1897); collections of essays such as *Ideas of Good and Evil* (1903), *The Cutting of an Agate* (1912), and *Essays* (1937); and *Autobiographies* (1926). He edited the works of William Blake (1893).

At the end of his life Yeats was widely honored as one of the most important poets of the century. He was elected a senator of the Irish Free State in 1922 and was awarded the Nobel Prize for literature in 1923.

Yeats-Brown, Francis (1886–1944). English writer. He is best known for his autobiographical *Lives of a Bengal Lancer* (1930), which was partly based on his own service with the British Army in India. It expressed his love of adventure and interest in mysticism, especially in Yoga and Eastern religions.

yellow (AS, *geolo,* connected with Gr. *chloros,* green, and with *gall,* the yellowish fluid secreted by the bile). A color symbolically indicating jealousy, inconstancy, and treachery. In France the doors of traitors used to be daubed with yellow. In some countries the law ordained that Jews must be clothed in yellow, because they betrayed Christ; hence Judas, in medieval pictures, is arrayed in yellow. In Spain the vestments of the executioner were either red or yellow: the former to denote bloodshedding; the latter treason.

In heraldry and in ecclesiastical symbolism, yellow is frequently used in place of gold.

yellow peril. Danger from the yellow races. The term refers to a scare, originally raised in Germany in the late 1890's that the people of China and Japan would in a very few years have increased in population to such an extent that incursions upon the territories occupied by the white races, followed by massacres and every conceivable horror, would be inevitable.

Yemassee, The (1835). A historical novel by William Gilmore SIMMS. The book deals with the conflict between the South Carolina Yemassee Indians and the British in 1715. Occonestoga, the son of Sanutee, chief of the Yemassee, betrays his tribe, and is killed by his mother, Matiwan. Dying in the attack on Charleston, Sanutee is defeated by the novel's hero, a mysterious Captain Harrison. The captain, later revealed to be South Carolina's Governor Craven, marries Bess Matthews, a girl of the frontier. A central theme in this most popular of Simms's books is the helplessness of the Indians as they lose their lands to the advancing white civilization.

Yeomen of the Guard, The (1888). A comic opera by GILBERT AND SULLIVAN. The yeomen of the guard are the oldest military corps in England, having been instituted in 1485. They still wear 15th-century costumes, guard the Tower of London, and are familiarly known as "Beefeaters."

Yepes y Alvarez, Juan de. See St. JOHN OF THE CROSS.

Yevtushenko, Yevgeni (1933–). Russian poet. With Andrei Voznesenski, he stirred new interest in poetry in the Soviet Union during the early 1960's. Much of Yevtushenko's work expresses the impatience of the younger Soviet generation with the cant and smugness that had been growing throughout Stalin's reign. A return to the revolutionary fervor of the early Soviet period and a need to regain human values lost during Stalin's terror-laden rule are frequent demands of Yevtushenko's work. With such poems, he attracted crowds of thousands to his readings, often held in huge outdoor stadiums. His outspokenness has, however, caused him trouble with Soviet authorities. His poem *Babi Yar* (1962), was criticized for implying that the Soviet regime was guilty of anti-Semitism. The poem was a eulogy to the thousands of Jews killed at Babi Yar in the Ukraine during World War II. Shortly after the furor over this work died down, Yevtushenko again got into trouble by publishing his memoirs in France without obtaining Soviet permission. The criticisms of the Soviet system contained in the writings added to his difficulties.

Yggdrasill or **Ygdrasil** ("the horse of Yggr or Odin"). In Norse mythology, the great ash tree that supported the universe and sprang from the body of the giant Ymir. It had three roots, which extended to the realms of Asgard, Niflheim, and Totunnheim. Near it lay the well Urtharbrunn whose waters the Norns used to preserve the tree from decay. The squirrel Ratatosk ran up and down the trunk carrying strife. Four harts fed on Yggdrasill's foliage and an eagle and a hawk sat in its branches.

Yin. See SHANG.

Yin and Yang. A Chinese theory explaining the basic workings of the universe. Developed late in the Chou Dynasty (1027–256 B.C.), it was incorporated into Han period CONFUCIANISM. Yin is the female, passive, negative force; Yang, the male, active and positive. Together with the theory of the five elements (*wu hsing:* wood, metal, water, fire, and earth) elaborate formulas governing all human activity evolved. Each of the five elements had

powers and reactions, good and bad, in relation to the other elements, and each element was associated with specific heavenly bodies, periods of time, directions, colors, animals, numbers, bodily organs, and the like. Thus actions of human beings could be predetermined and regulated according to the interaction of the elements. Together with the teachings of the *Book of Changes,* these theories controlled human affairs and were consulted to determine marriage partners, propitious days, and related matters in both China and Japan. They are to a certain extent still current today.

Ymir. The primeval giant of Scandinavian mythology from whose body the world was said to be created. He was nourished by the four milky streams which flowed from the cow, Audhumla. One legend holds that while he slept, a man and woman grew out of his left arm and sons from his feet, thus generating the race of frost giants. A more popular account is that when Odin and his two brothers, Vili and Vi, slew Ymir and threw his carcass into an abyss, his blood formed the waters, his bones the mountains, his teeth the rocks, his skull the heavens, his brains the clouds, his hair the plants, and his eyebrow the wall of defense against the giants.

yoga (*Sans.,* "union, concentration, yoking"). Mental and spiritual exercises for the sake of self-illumination. Yoga puts special emphasis on meditation, but has an elaborate system of physical rules of procedure. The *Yoga-shastras* of Patanjali (first century B.C.) contain a wealth of detailed rules for the benefit of the aspiring yogi.

yogi. One who practices YOGA.

Yoknapatawpha County. An imaginary county in Mississippi which serves as a setting for many stories by William FAULKNER. Jefferson, the county seat, is modeled in part on Oxford, Miss. The novelist gave the county realistic detail, providing a map and population figures.

Yom Kippur. See DAY OF ATONEMENT.

Yonge, Charlotte Mary (1823–1901). English novelist of copious output. She was a disciple of John Keble, whose ideas she incorporated in her writings, and is faintly remembered for her historical novels such as *The Caged Lion* (1870) and for her bathetic romances of contemporary life, such as *The Heir of Redclyffe* (1853) and *Heartsease* (1854). Devout and charitable, sentimental and narrow, Miss Yonge herself stands as an epitome of Victorian propriety.

Yorick. In Shakespeare's HAMLET, the deceased jester of the murdered king of Denmark. His skull is apostrophized by Hamlet, who remembers him as "a fellow of infinite jest, of most excellent fancy." In Sterne's TRISTRAM SHANDY, Yorick is a humorous parson who claims descent from Shakespeare's Yorick.

Yorke, Henry. See Henry GREEN.

York Plays. See MYSTERY PLAYS.

Yorkshire Tragedy, The (c. 1606). An anonymous English tragedy in which a young woman marries a man who turns out to be a spendthrift and an ogre. He beats his wife, starves his children, and has little regard for the brother who is standing security for his numberless debts. When his brother is arrested, the husband goes mad, stabbing his wife and killing two of his children. Apprehended at last, he is filled with remorse as he is carried off to prison.

Yorktown. The capital of York County, Va., site of the surrender of Cornwallis (Oct. 19, 1781) which virtually ended the American Revolution.

Yoshida, Shigeru (1878–). Japanese politician. He was foreign minister (1945), leader of the Liberal Party, and prime minister (1946–1953, during which time he formed five cabinets).

You Can't Go Home Again (1940). A novel by Thomas WOLFE. In this sequel to THE WEB AND THE ROCK, George Webber, having returned from Europe, resumes his affair with Esther Jack and becomes a successful writer. He revisits his home town and is disillusioned by what he sees, an episode said to parallel Wolfe's own experience in Asheville, N.C.

You Can't Take It with You (1936). A comedy by Moss HART and George S. KAUFMAN. This Pulitzer Prize winner deals with the bizarre but supremely happy Vanderhof family in New York. They make fireworks in the cellar, write plays, and practice ballet, creating difficulties for the family's one conventional member, who wants to marry the scion of a wealthy but stuffy New York family.

You Know Me Al: A Busher's Letters (1916). A collection of short stories by Ring LARDNER. They are in the form of letters written by a half-literate baseball rookie, Jack Keefe. Perfectly capturing the vernacular speech, tone, and outlook of their protagonist, the stories are excellent examples of Lardner's characteristic mixture of humor and misanthropy.

Youma (1890). A novel by Lafcadio HEARN. One of Hearn's most distinguished works, it is based on the true story of a Negro girl's devotion to the daughter of her dead mistress during a slave insurrection in Martinique.

Young, Arthur (1741–1820). English agricultural theorist and author. His *Travels in France* (1792) describes conditions in France shortly before the Revolution.

Young, Brigham (1801–1877). American Mormon leader. Young was converted to Mormonism in 1832 and became head of a segment of the church in 1844, after the death of Joseph Smith, founder of the sect. A skillful organizer and administrator, he led the Mormon migration to Deseret, which was organized as the Utah Territory in 1850, and served as first territorial governor.

Young, Edward (1683–1765). English poet and playwright. He is best known today for NIGHT THOUGHTS ON LIFE, DEATH AND IMMORTALITY, written in defense of Christian orthodoxy against freethinkers and libertines, and CONJECTURES ON ORIGINAL COMPOSITION, IN A LETTER TO THE AUTHOR OF SIR CHARLES GRANDISON, his last and most brilliant prose essay. His other works include *Busiris* (1719) and *The Revenge* (1721), both dramatic tragedies; *The Universal Passion* (1725–1728), a series of satires; *The Brothers* (1753), another tragedy; and *Resignation* (1726), a long poem. In his youth, Young had hoped for a career as a lawyer, but was disappointed, spending most of his life as a country clergyman instead. He also carried on a long correspondence with Samuel Richardson, the closest literary friend of his later years.

Young, Francis Brett (1884–1954). English novelist and poet. He was a physician, and his novels deal largely with the medical profession. Among his popular novels are *Love Is Enough* (1927), *My Brother Jonathan* (1928), and *The City of Gold* (1939), set in South Africa. As a poet he belonged to the GEORGIAN group; *The Island* (1944) is a long poem about England.

Young Alcidiane. See Marin le Roy GOMBERVILLE.

Young England. A group of young aristocrats of the Conservative party (1833–1846) headed by DISRAELI and Lord John Manners. They wore white waistcoats, gave generously to the poor, and attempted to revive the courtly manners of the past. They are vividly portrayed in Disraeli's novels, notably CONINGSBY OR THE NEW GENERATION.

Youngest of the Fates, The. See JEUNE PARQUE, LA.

Young Goodman Brown (1835). A story by Nathaniel HAWTHORNE. Brown, a young Puritan, leaves Faith, his wife, for a night-time journey in the woods. Meeting an older man with a twisted staff, he learns that others have traveled the path before him. Sick at heart, he observes a witches' sabbath and discovers the presence of his own wife. The next morning Goodman Brown returns to Salem a changed man; stern, sad, and gloomy, he believes that all are blasphemers.

Younghusband, Sir Francis Edward (1863–1942). English Himalayan explorer. He led a military expedition to Lhasa that opened Tibet to Western trade (1904). Among his books is *India and Tibet* (1912).

Young Ireland. A militantly anti-English group developed in the 1840's by a dissident faction within the Catholic Association, an organization headed by the great Irish statesman Daniel O'CONNELL. The Catholic Association was opposed to the use of force in redressing its grievances with the English government, and the Young Ireland faction considered this position a fatal weakness. The severe economic privation (and human degradation) which was to reach such calamitous proportions as the result of the potato famine was already in progress in 1846 when the Young Ireland group, under the leadership of William Smith O'Brien (1803–1864) and Thomas Meagher (1823–1867), broke with the Catholic Association. By 1848 the plight was so great that violence was conceived of as the only alternative. The Young Ireland group planned an open rebellion, which however was more verbal than actual with the result that the rebels were arrested before any military action took place. Smith O'Brien and Meagher were sentenced to death and deported, and the Young Ireland group was scattered; many of its members later formed the FENIAN societies in Canada and the U.S.

Young Italy. An association of Italian republicans organized by Giuseppe Mazzini in 1831. Aimed at freeing Italy from Austrian domination and uniting it under republican government, it sought to attain these goals by direct agitation and insurrection.

Young Lions, The (1948). A novel by Irwin SHAW. The book, Shaw's first novel, begins on New Year's Eve, 1937 and weaves the stories of three men, who meet only in the climactic scene: Diestl, a Nazi ski instructor who epitomizes his nation's morality; Michael Whitmore, stage manager of a frivolous Broadway play, who drinks in the New Year, worrying about his wife's infidelity; and Noah Ackerman, a homeless Jew, first seen waiting for his father to die in a cheap California hotel. Ackerman, the book's most sympathetic character, marries a New Englander, with whom he enjoys a brief happiness; he fathers a son before, persecuted and exhausted, he is killed in a German wood. The book is one of the host of World War II novels that attempted to salvage meaning from the wreckage of war.

Young Lonigan. See STUDS LONIGAN.

Young Man, Adventures of a (1939). A novel by John Dos PASSOS. It tells the story of Glenn Spottswood, a young man of sensitivity and a strong sense of justice, who, interested in the labor movement, becomes closely involved with radicals and Communists. Disillusioned with American left-wing politics, Glenn goes to Spain as an ambulance driver in the civil war. His disillusionment continues there when the Communist leaders are suspicious of him because of his past. Arrested as a Trotskyite spy, he is finally killed carrying water to the firing-line.

The novel is the first of a trilogy about the Spottswood family. *Number One* (1943) is a study of a Southern politician strikingly like Huey Long, and *The Grand Design* (1949) is an unfavorable picture of the Roosevelt era. The trilogy was later published as *District of Columbia* (1952).

Young Manhood of Studs Lonigan, The. See STUDS LONIGAN.

Young Pretender. See PRETENDER.

Young Visiters, The (1919). The nine-year-old Daisy ASHFORD's story about Mr. Salteena, a butcher's son who rises to high society. The book is notable for its accurate but naïve observation of grown-ups, resulting in fine unconscious satire.

Yourcenar, Marguerite. Pen name of **Marguerite de Crayencour** (19?–   ). French novelist best known for *Mémoires d'Hadrien* (1951), a historical novel, and *Coup de grâce* (1939). The memoirs portray the emperor on the eve of his death and describe his reflections as he gazes out upon the city that seemed to him indestructible and that he now fears will fall. A world traveler, the author was able to use accurate historical and pictorial detail.

Youth (1902). A short story by Joseph CONRAD. Told by MARLOW, it is an account of his first dangerous voyage. His mature memory looks back on youthful emotion and illusion.

Youth and the Bright Medusa (1920). A collection of short stories by Willa CATHER. Dealing

with the theme of artistic sensibility and talent, the volume includes *Paul's Case,* an often anthologized short story of a psychotic boy.

Ys or Is. A legendary city off the coast of Brittany in France. Supposedly King Gradlon (5th century) held the only key to the floodgate in the dike that protected the city. His daughter, reveling with her lover, stole the key as a prank and flooded the city. Tradition says its cathedral can still occasionally be seen rising through the mists. In the opera *Le Roi d'Ys* (*The King of Ys,* 1888), by Edouard Lalo (1823–1892), it is a second princess, jealous of her sister's lover, who floods the city, then repents and sacrifices herself to the water to save the city.

Ysengrin or Ysengrimus. See REYNARD THE FOX.

Ysopet or Isopet. See MARIE DE FRANCE.

Yüan. A Chinese dynasty (1260–1368). It was established by the Mongols, who under Jenghis Khan (1162?–1277) had gradually consolidated power in Mongolia and Central Asia and eventually conquered the whole of China. This period was marked by a worldwide internationalization, with the distribution of Chinese products to the West and the introduction of much European knowledge to China. Marco Polo's visit was made during this dynasty. Literary advances were also made, particularly in the fields of drama and fiction.

Yvain, ou le chevalier au Lion. A 12th-century romance by CHRÉTIEN DE TROYES. It concerns the adventures of the knight Yvain. Following the directions of a giant, he arrives at a well, finds a golden basin near it, and splashes water from the basin on a stone dish. Immediately a great storm arises, and a mysterious knight comes forth to combat. Yvain emerges the victor from the struggle. He then comes to a castle and gains entrance with the assistance of a lady named Lunette, who shows him how to make himself invisible. While hidden in a room in the castle, he hears the widow of the slain knight weeping for her lost husband, and he falls in love with her. Lunette convinces the widow, Laudine, that since the magic well must be defended, it is most desirable that the man chosen as the new defender and husband be the one who vanquished the first knight. The argument is successful, and eventually Yvain marries Laudine. The remainder of the romance is concerned with his numerous other adventures, during which he rescues a lion from a serpent and thereby acquires the animal as a mascot.

Z

Zadig ou la Destinée (1748). A short novel by VOLTAIRE, first published in 1747 under the title of *Memnon, histoire orientale.* Zadig is a wealthy, honest, well-educated young Babylonian who learns how difficult it is to be happy in this world where almost everything goes wrong in spite of his efforts to do right. Every time he thinks he has achieved contentment, security, or love, something happens to rob him of them; yet he is able to go on by making use of the wisdom he has acquired so painfully from experience. In the end, the angel Jesrad reveals to him that there is no good without evil, or evil without good, and that all is trial or punishment, recompense or foresight. Zadig at last becomes a happy king and a sage. The inevitable Voltairian digs at religion, the clergy, and unjust sovereigns are apparent in this work.

method of Zadig. Drawing inferences from close observation. Zadig seemed to know so much about the king's horse, which had been lost, that he was accused of having stolen it. He said he had never seen it, but could describe it perfectly because "I saw the marks of horseshoes, all equal distances apart . . . [therefore] he gallops perfectly. The dust on the trees in this narrow road only seven feet wide brushed off a little right and left three and a half feet from the middle of the road . . . [therefore] he has a tail three and a half feet long. I saw beneath the trees, which made a cradle five feet high, some leaves newly fallen . . . [therefore] he was fifteen hands high . . ."

Zagreus. See ORPHISM.

Zaïre (Zara, 1732). A tragedy by VOLTAIRE. One of his best plays, it is said to have been inspired by Shakespeare's *Othello.* The sultan Orosmane has fallen in love with his captive Zaïre, a Christian girl who, as a child, had been carried off by the Turks and brought up in a seraglio in Jerusalem. She returns his love and a wedding is planned. Just before the marriage, Nérestan, Zaïre's childhood companion and fellow-captive, returns from France with the ransom for 10 knights. The ransom, however, has exhausted his fortune, and, unable to buy his own freedom, he surrenders himself. The good Orosmane refuses the ransom and frees everyone except Zaïre and another captive, the old Lusignan. Nérestan is visibly disappointed about Lusignan and secures Zaïre's promise to intervene in his behalf. Orosmane grants the old man his freedom, and when Lusignan is brought up from his dungeon, he meets for the first time Zaïre and Nérestan, whom he recognizes as his own lost son and daughter. He is horrified that Zaïre is a Muslim and, as a dying wish, asks her to be baptized. Zaïre postpones her wedding to accomplish this, arousing Orosmane's suspicions. He then intercepts a letter from Nérestan to Zaïre, which he mistakenly thinks is a love letter, and goes to the secret place where she is to be baptized. Seeing Nérestan, his suspicions are confirmed and he stabs Zaïre. When he learns the truth from Nérestan, he kills himself.

Zamoskvarechye. A section of Moscow, on the right bank of the Moscow River, inhabited mainly by merchants. Before the revolution it was famous as a center of old-fashioned Russian life, untouched by modern ways. Aleksandr OSTROVSKI used the section as the setting for many of his dramas. A good description of the life there is given by Apollon Grigoryev in *Moi literaturniye i nravstvenniye skitalchestva (My Literary and Moral Wanderings).*

Zamyatin, Yevgeni Ivanovich (1884–1937). Russian writer. Educated as a naval engineer, Zamyatin published his first tale *Provincial Things (Uyezdnoye)* in 1911. His other early tales include *At the Back of Beyond (Na kulichkakh;* 1914) and two satires on English life, which he had observed while in Britain on naval business: *The Islanders (Ostrovityane;* 1922) and *The Fisher of Men (Lovetz cheloveka;* 1922). After the revolution, Zamyatin helped organize the writers' group known as the SERAPION BROTHERS and became a leader and teacher of the circle's young writers. Zamyatin's major novel, WE, with its setting of a future totalitarian state, was a forerunner of Aldous Huxley's *Brave New World* and George Orwell's *1984.* Written in 1920, it could not be published in Russia, and when it was first published abroad in 1924, Zamyatin was castigated by the Soviet authorities, who denounced him as an "internal émigré" and expelled him from the federation of writers, shutting the pages of all journals and newspapers to him. He wrote a letter to Stalin, asking to be allowed to emigrate and the request was surprisingly granted, supposedly with the help of Maksim Gorki. Zamyatin moved to France in 1931 where he lived until his death.

Zamyatin's plays include *The Fires of St. Dominic (Ogni sv. dominika;* 1923), a satire of the Soviet secret police agency Cheka; *The Society of Honorary Bell Ringers (Obshchestvo pochotnykh zvonarei;* 1926); and *The Flea (Blokha;* 1925), a dramatization of a story by the 19th-century writer Nikolai Leskov.

Zamyatin described himself as a neorealist. He defined his method in the following way: "While neo-Realism uses a microscope to look at the world, Symbolism used a telescope, and pre-Revolutionary Realism, an ordinary looking glass." Zamyatin's almost surrealistic literary methods had a large influence on such younger Soviet writers as Vsevolod Ivanov and Yuri Olesha.

Zanoni (1842). A novel by Edward BULWER-LYTTON. The hero, Zanoni, manages by the aid of spirits to produce precious metals and to prolong his own life for many centuries, but he finally gives up his supernatural powers to marry an opera singer.

Zapata, Emiliano (1877?–1919). Mexican revolutionary leader. Zapata and the peasant army that he recruited in Morelos and other southern states participated in the revolutionary movement of 1910, devastating plantations and dividing the land among the peons. Although Carranza promised agrarian reform upon assuming power in 1915, Zapata was skeptical. Advising his followers to trust in nothing but their guns, he refused to come to terms with the government and skillfully eluded capture for years. After he was treacherously murdered by *currancistas*, he became a semilegendary figure.

Zara. See ZAÏRE.

Zarathustra. See THUS SPAKE ZARATHUSTRA; ZOROASTER.

Zaturenska, Marya (1902–   ). Russian-born American poet. She won a Pulitzer Prize for the collection *Cold Morning Sky* (1937). Other collections include *Threshold and Hearth* (1934), *The Listening Landscape* (1941), and *Terraces of Light* (1960). She has also written a life of Christina Rossetti (1949) and, with her husband, Horace Gregory, *A History of American Poetry, 1900–1940* (1946).

Zauberberg, Der. See MAGIC MOUNTAIN, THE.

Zauberflöte, Die. See MAGIC FLUTE, THE.

Zeami Motokiyo. See SEAMI MOTOKIYO.

Zechariah. An Old Testament book, the 11th of the Minor Prophets. It is in two parts. The first part dates from the restoration of the temple in Jerusalem (c. 530 B.C.), and is contemporaneous with HAGGAI, containing the same message. The second part, written after the death of Alexander the Great in 323 B.C., contains visions of Israel's future and Messianic prophecies.

Zeitblom, Serenus. The narrator of Thomas Mann's novel DOKTOR FAUSTUS. He is a childhood friend of the hero Adrian LEVERKÜHN. His very name, Serenus Zeitblom (literally, "serene time-flower"), suggests the complacency of the typical bourgeois and implies that he is simply the passive product of his age. He is, however, too intelligent to be caught up in the fever of Nazism. Thus, he is about halfway between Leverkühn's artistic genius, on the one hand, and his people's political madness, on the other, and is able to comment on both.

Zélide. Pen name of **Isabelle de Charrière**, born **Isabella van Tuyll** (1740–1805). Dutch-born Swiss author of breeding and beauty. One of her friends was James Boswell, who tried to marry her. She became a very close intellectual friend of Benjamin Constant.

Zemstvo. In Czarist Russia, a county council composed of local elected officials. The *Zemstva*, which were established by one of the reform laws of 1864, dealt with education, public health and welfare, roads, and food supply. They often had to operate under the handicap of restrictions imposed by the central government, which was suspicious of the democratic nature of the councils.

Zen Buddhism. A Buddhist sect. It was introduced from China to Japan during the late Heian (794–1185) and early Kamakura (1185–1333) periods by Japanese monks visiting the mainland and refugee Chinese priests. Known as CH'AN in Chinese, it emphasizes meditation and physical work as means to enlightenment, leaving scriptural study to advanced students. The two principal Japanese sects are Rinzai (Ch., *Lin-chi*) which was introduced by Eisai (1141–1215) and stems from the Ch'an of the Sung Dynasty (960–1279), and Sōtō (Ch., *Ts'ao-t'ung*), first brought to Japan by Dōgen (1200–1253). Rinzai gives particular stress to the study of KŌAN as a means to enlightenment; Sōtō, which contains many purely Japanese elements, concentrates on meditative sitting alone. Zen has had significant influence on various elements of Japanese culture: nō, the tea ceremony, martial arts, and literature. Zen was introduced to the West largely in the works of Daisetz Suzuki.

Zenger, John Peter (1697–1746). German-born American printer and journalist. He came to America in 1710 and established the *New York Weekly Journal* to oppose the policies of the provincial government. Brought to trial for seditious libel (1734–1735), he was defended by Andrew Hamilton and acquitted. The decision in this case helped to establish freedom of the press in America.

From the *Ten Ox-herding Pictures,*
a Chinese Zen text.

Zenobia (d. after 274). Queen of Palmyra, joint ruler with her husband Odenathus. On his death (267) she assumed complete control of the kingdom. Pretending to be closely allied to Rome, she stationed her armies all over the Near East, in Asia Minor, Syria, Mesopotamia, and Egypt. On the accession of Aurelian (270), she openly defied Rome and attempted to usurp the entire Eastern Empire. Her armies were defeated (271) and she was captured. Aurelian later pardoned her, but kept her exiled in Italy. Her name has come to signify a powerful, ambitious woman.

Zeno (Zenon) of Elea (fl. 460 b.c.). Greek philosopher, pupil and associate of PARMENIDES. Aristotle calls him the founder of dialectic. A clever logician, Zeno could draw his own conclusions from tenets his adversary admitted. He defended Parmenides' belief that motion and change are illusory in a series of brilliant paradoxes. In the best known of these, Achilles, the fastest runner, cannot catch the tortoise because he must first reach the point where the pursued started. In the meantime, the tortoise has advanced, however little, to a new position.

Zephaniah. An Old Testament prophetic book bearing the name of its author. It is apocalyptic and inspired the medieval *Dies Irae.* It was probably written before the reign of King Josiah (c. 640–609 b.c.), when many of Zephaniah's reforms were enacted.

Zephon. A guardian angel of Paradise in Milton's PARADISE LOST. With Ithuriel he is dispatched by Gabriel to find Satan after the latter's flight from Hell.

Zephyr (Zephyros). The west wind in classical mythology, son of Aeolus and Aurora, and husband of Iris. He was the rival of Apollo for the love of HYACINTH.

Zeppelin, Count Ferdinand von (1838–1917). German airship designer. He developed the dirigible balloon, named after him, which was used in World War I.

Zerbino. In Lodovico Ariosto's ORLANDO FURIOSO, a famous knight, son of the king of Scotland, brother of the fair GINEVRA, and friend to Orlando. His beloved, the Saracen princess Isabella, is kidnapped before their wedding; then Orlando rescues her and reunites them. But Zerbino is finally killed by Mandricardo and Isabella by Rodomonte, who builds a shrine to them.

Zerbrochene Krug, Der. See BROKEN JUG, THE.

Zerrissenheit (*Ger.,* "the state of being torn apart"). A German literary critical term, usually translated in English by "disintegration." It refers to the condition of a character, usually an artist, who is unable to reconcile the claims of his own subjective, ideal world with the necessities of the real, objective world. Examples are Goethe's characters Werther and Tasso, E. T. A. Hoffmann's Johannes Kreisler, and Harry Haller in Hesse's *Steppenwolf.*

Zetes. See ARGONAUTS.

Zethus (Zethos). See AMPHION.

Zeus. The supreme god of the ancient Greeks. He was the Greek version of an almost universally worshiped European god of atmospheric phenomena, especially thunder and lightning, of whom Jupiter is another example. As the god of kingship, he was king of the gods. His principal weapon was the thunderbolt; his famous fringed shield, the *aegis,* he

often shared with Athene. The most common of many stories of Zeus's origins was that he was a son of Cronos and Rhea. His mother bore him secretly, to save him from his voracious father, who had swallowed his brothers and sisters. He was brought up in a cave on Mount Dicte in Crete, where he was suckled by the goat AMALTHEIA, nursed by nymphs, and protected from discovery by the Curetes, sons of Rhea, who drowned his cries by dancing and clashing their shields.

Reaching manhood, Zeus overthrew his father, as his grandmother Ge had predicted. The universe was then divided between him and his brothers, whom Cronos had vomited up; Zeus received heaven, Poseidon the sea, Hades the underworld, with earth and their abode on Mount Olympus as their common property. Before the Olympian gods could establish their supremacy, however, they had to destroy the rebellious TITANS, the GIANTS, and the monster Typhon or TYPHOEUS, all of whom made war on heaven. Later, when the giants OTUS and Ephialtes warred with heaven, Zeus struck them down with his thunderbolts. Zeus also had to conquer a rebellion in his own family. His sister-wife Hera, his brother Poseidon, and his daugher Athene managed to bind him, but Thetis saved him by bringing the monster BRIAREUS to his assistance.

In various localities, Zeus was regarded as the consort of the reigning local goddess, often a pre-Hellenic earth-goddess. Later, the problem of his many wives was resolved by making him the remarkably unfaithful husband of Hera. Some of his many unions with other goddesses include that with Metis, who conceived Athene; with Themis, who bore him the Seasons and the Fates; with Eurynome, who bore him the Graces (Charites); with Demeter, who bore him Kore (Persephone); with Leto, who bore him Apollo and Artemis. His marriage to Hera, the powerful pre-Hellenic goddess of Argos, brought forth Hebe, Ares, and Eileithyia.

Zeus also had affairs with more or less mortal women, some of which led to famous offspring. Notable among these children were Dionysus, son of Cadmus' daughter Semele; Heracles, son of Alcmene; Perseus, son of Danae; Amphion and Zethus, sons of Antiope; Helen, Clytemnestra, and the Dioscuri (or some combination of them), children of Leda.

Zhdanov, Andrei Aleksandrovich (1888–1948). Russian politician and Soviet government official. Notorious for his policing of literature in the 1930's and 1940's, he replaced the assassinated Sergei Kirov as Communist Party secretary in Leningrad in 1934. Zhdanov led the campaign beginning in 1946 to oust "decadent" Western influences from Soviet literature. He delivered scathing speeches denouncing errant writers, particularly Mikhail Zoshchenko and Anna Akhmatova.

Zhukovski, Vasili Andreyevich (1783–1852). Russian poet and translator. His translations of such works as Schiller's *Maid of Orleans,* Byron's *Prisoner of Chillon,* and Gray's *Elegy* helped introduce Western romanticism into Russia. Zhukovski also produced a notable translation of Homer's *Odyssey* in 1849. His own poems were among the best written in Russian before Pushkin's work appeared. Besides his literary activity, Zhukovski was also a prominent figure in the Russian court. He was a tutor of the young Alexander II, who became Czar in 1855. His influence is reputed to have helped Pushkin in the younger poet's many scrapes with Czar Nicholas I's government.

Ziegfeld, Florenz (1867–1932). American showman. He introduced with his *Follies of 1907* a new type of stage entertainment, the revue, consisting of a medley of skits and light pieces with allusions to and re-enactments of the events of the past year, but the chief attractions of which were stage effects and pretty girls scantily clad. The *Follies* reached their height of popularity in the 1920's when they were imitated by other revues calling themselves *The Scandals, The Vanities,* etc.

Ziliante or **Gigliante.** In Boiardo's ORLANDO INNAMORATO and Ariosto's ORLANDO FURIOSO, the younger brother of Brandimarte and Orrigille and son of King Monodante of India. He is rescued by Orlando after falling into the power of the witch Morgana.

Zineura. The heroine of BERNABÒ OF GENOA, a tale from Boccaccio's THE DECAMERON. She is the prototype of Imogen in Shakespeare's *Cymbeline.*

Zinovyev, Grigori Yevseyevich. Real name, **Hirsch Apfelbaum** (1883–1936). Russian Communist leader. He shared power with Stalin and Kamenev after the death of Lenin. He and Kamenev were ousted from power by Stalin in the late 1920's, and in 1936 he was arrested and executed for alleged treason in the first of the notorious purge trials.

Zinzendorf, Count Nikolaus Ludwig von (1700–1760). German religious lyric poet and writer of hymns. He offered his estate to religious refugees from Moravia. A settlement of the MORAVIAN BRETHREN, known as Herrnhut, was established there in 1722.

Zion. One of the hills on which the city of JERUSALEM is built. On Zion was the fortified acropolis of the Jebusites which David's soldiers captured by stealth. The word *Zion* was later used to designate the whole city. Allegorically Zion refers to a house of God, Israel, or the Christian religion.

Zionism. The movement for colonizing the Jews in their old home, Palestine, the land of Zion. It led to the establishment of the modern nation of Israel.

Ziusudra. The Sumerian Noah. The single account discovered so far is fragmentary, but it appears to be very similar to the later version in the Babylonian epic of Gilgamesh, where the builder of the ark is named UTNAPISHTIM.

zodiac (Gr., *zodiakos,* pertaining to animals; from *zoon,* an animal). An imaginary belt or zone in the heavens. It extends about eight degrees each side of the ecliptic which the sun traverses every year. The zodiac was divided by the ancients into 12 equal parts, proceeding from west to east, each part of 30 degrees, and distinguished by a sign. These originally corresponded to the zodiacal constellations bearing the same names, but now, through the precession of the equinoxes, they coincide with the constellations bearing the names next in order.

Beginning with Aries, there are first six on the north side and six on the south side of the equator. Beginning with Capricornus, there are six *ascending* and six *descending* signs: i.e., six which ascend higher and higher toward the north, and six which descend lower and lower toward the south. The six northern signs are *Aries* (the ram), *Taurus* (the bull), *Gemini* (the twins), spring signs; and *Cancer* (the crab), *Leo* (the lion), *Virgo* (the virgin), summer signs. The six southern are *Libra* (the balance), *Scorpio* (the scorpion), *Sagittarius* (the archer), autumn signs; and *Capricornus* (the goat), Aquarius (the waterbearer), and *Pisces* (the fishes), winter signs.

Zoilus or **Zoïlos** (4th century B.C.). Greek rhetorician. A literary Thersites, shrewd, witty, and spiteful, he was nicknamed *Homeromastix* (Homer's Scourge), because he mercilessly assailed the epics of Homer, and called the companions of Odysseus in the island of Circe weeping porkers (*Choiridia klaionya*). He also flew at Plato, Isocrates, and other high game.

Zola, Emile (1840–1902). French writer and critic, leader of the naturalist school. Raised in the beautiful city of Aix-en-Provence, with his close friend Paul Cézanne, Zola came to Paris at the age of 18. He worked first as a clerk in a publishing house, and later became a journalist. In 1865 his first novel, *La Confession de Claude,* was published. With the publication of *La Fortune des Rougons* (1871), Zola began his 22-year, 20-volume experiment in the naturalistic novel entitled LES ROUGON-MACQUART. Scientific precision and scrupulous attention to detail mark his lengthy portrait of the Rougon-Macquart family. In 1880 he published *Le Roman Expérimental (The Experimental Novel)* in which he explained his naturalistic method and set forth his theories of fiction (see NATURALISM). For many years, Zola used his fiction in the service of his passion for social reform, but in his last novels—the two series *Les Trois Villes* (1894–1898) and *Quatre Evangiles* (1899–1903)—he speaks directly of his faith in a kind of Christian socialism, which would alleviate the misery and suffering he had long portrayed so faithfully. His zeal for reform and justice was translated into practical action when Zola penned his famous letter J'ACCUSE, in defense of Captain Dreyfus.

Zorba the Greek (Alexis Zorbas; 1946). A novel by Nikos KAZANTZAKIS. The hero, a still vigorous and passionate old Greek, personifies the Dionysian approach to life that fascinated his creator. He is contrasted with a pallid narrator, who, before meeting the overpowering Zorba, has preferred to contemplate life, rather than to live it. This novel established Kazantzakis' reputation in the English-speaking world.

Zoroaster or **Zarathustra.** The founder (about 1000 B.C.) of the Perso-Iranian national religion, Zoroastrianism, whose modern version is Parseeism. It was dominant in Western Asia from about 550 B.C. to A.D. 650, and is still held by many thousands in Persia and India. The theology is fundamentally dualistic in that the course of the universe is understood as a relentless struggle between Ormuzd (Ahura Mazda), the principle of light and goodness, and Ahriman (Angra Mainyu), the spirit of evil and darkness. Ormuzd will prevail, partly through the help of man whom he created to strengthen his forces. All souls will be purified by fire and a new heaven and earth will be established. Zoroaster, whose name is the Greek form of the Persian Zarathustra, established three commandments: good thoughts, good words, good deeds. See AVESTA; BACTRIAN SAGE; PARSEES.

Zorrilla y Moral, José (1817–1893). Spanish poet and dramatist. Born in Valladolid, Zorrilla became famous overnight in 1837 when he recited an elegy at the grave of poet Mariano de Larra, who had just committed suicide. He subsequently abandoned his wife, who was many years his senior, and lived in France and Mexico, where he enjoyed the patronage of the emperor Maximilian. After his wife's death in 1866 he returned to Spain. Though he was usually penniless, he received great popular acclaim and was honored with a golden crown in Granada in 1889.

One of Spain's outstanding romantic poets, Zorrilla was often facile and careless, but he possessed great dramatic and descriptive power which enabled him to recreate the atmosphere of a past age, as he showed in his many *leyendas,* or legends, of medieval Spain. His best-known verse includes the collection *Cantos del trovador* (1840–1841) and the unfinished *Granada* (1852), a richly ornamented account of the intrigues that preceded the city's fall.

Zorrilla's poetry has been largely overshadowed by the fame of his DON JUAN TENORIO, the most successful play of 19th-century Spain. Many of his other plays are based, like his poems, on episodes in Spanish history. Among these are *El zapatero y el rey* (1840–1841), *El puñal del Godo* (1842), and *Traidor, inconfeso y mártir* (1849).

Zoshchenko, Mikhail Mikhailovich (1895–1958). Russian satirist. He is famous for his short, pithy stories of the average Soviet citizen struggling to make his way in a world filled with red tape, regulations, and frustration. He studied law at the University of St. Petersburg, served in the army during the war, and in the Red Army in the civil war. He began his literary career when he joined the SERAPION BROTHERS in 1921. His first stories were published in the collection entitled *Stories Told by Nazar Ilyich Mr. Sinebryukhov* (*Rasskazy Nazara Ilyicha gospodina Sinebryukhova;* 1922). These and the several volumes of short stories published in later years show the influence of the ornamental styles of Leskov and Remizov and Zoshchenko's own mastery of *skaz*— the device of relating a story in the usually semi-literate language of a fictitious narrator, rather than the less vivid language of conventional narrative prose.

In 1943, Zoshchenko came under attack in the Soviet literary journals for his *Before Sunrise* (*Pered voskhodom solntza*), of which two parts were published that year. Although Zoshchenko referred to the work as a novel, it appears to be more a personal reminiscence, and this fact seemed the chief reason for the attacks. Three years later the Central Committee of the Communist Party issued a resolution criticizing various aspects of Soviet literature and singling out Zoshchenko and the poet Anna Akhmatova for special condemnation. Zoshchenko's wartime publication of his memoir was recalled and termed a "disgusting" work. Shortly afterward, in a speech the overseer of Soviet culture, Andrei Zhdanov, referred to Zoshchenko as a "vulgarian" in another bitter attack on the writer. After this onslaught, Zoshchenko virtually ceased publishing any new stories, except for a few second-rate efforts in 1947 and 1950.

Zosima. In Feodor Dostoevski's THE BROTHERS KARAMAZOV, the elder monk who preaches a message of love and forbearance which is considered to be the religious viewpoint of the author.

Zsigmondy, Richard (1865–1929). German chemist. With H. F. W. Siedentopf (1872–   ) he invented the ultramicroscope (1903) with which he investigated the nature of colloids. He won the Nobel Prize for chemistry in 1925.

Zuckmayer, Carl (1896–   ). German playwright. Though not so capable of profundity and poetry as Hofmannsthal, for example, and though not so much an innovator in dramatic form as the expressionists and Brecht, he has still won for himself an unchallenged place of honor in modern German drama. After a few abortive attempts at expressionism, he began to develop his main strength— the depiction of real and vital individuals—in *Der fröhliche Weinberg* (*The Merry Vineyard,* 1925) and *Schinderhannes* (1927), both of which treat country life in his own Rhenish homeland. Also in these plays, he began, in the form of satire, to voice his opposition to the tendency toward militarism and bureaucratic regimentation which was present in Germany at the time; and this satirical attitude then came into its own in his great comedy THE CAPTAIN OF KÖPENICK. But shortly after writing this play he was forced into exile by the rise of Nazism, and his next major success, written in the U.S., is an entirely serious protest against Hitler's government: THE DEVIL'S GENERAL. Among Zuckmayer's other significant plays are *Bellman* (1938), about an 18th-century Swedish minstrel; *Der Gesang im Feuerofen* (*Song in the Fiery Furnace,* 1950), about the resistance in occupied France; and *Das kalte Licht* (*The Cold Light,* 1956), a topical drama about a nuclear scientist turned traitor.

Zuleika. (1) In Arabic legend, the name traditionally ascribed to POTIPHAR'S WIFE whose advances were resisted by the virtuous Joseph (Gen. 39). Their story is told in the Persian *Yúsef and Zulaikha* by Nurreddin Jami (1414–1429); Zuleika is a common name in Persian poetry.

(2) The heroine of Byron's *Bride of Abydos* (1813).

Zuleika Dobson (1911). A fantastic, satirical novel by MAX BEERBOHM. Zuleika is a beautiful girl on a visit to Oxford University; every one of the undergraduates falls in love with her and drowns himself in despair.

Zweig, Arnold (1887–1968). German novelist. An advocate of socialism and Zionism, he is best known for the three novels of the Grischa cycle: *Der Streit um den Sergeanten Grischa* (*The Case of Sergeant Grischa,* 1927), *Junge Frau von 1914* (*Young Woman of 1914,* 1931) and *De Vrient kehrt heim* (*De Vrient Comes Home,* 1932). His other works include the novel *Versunkene Tage* (*Days Gone By,* 1938) and a discursive work, written in collaboration with Lion Feuchtwanger, on *Die Aufgabe des Judentums* (*The Task of Judaism,* 1933).

Zweig, Stefan (1881–1942). Austrian novelist, essayist and playwright. He is best known for the humanistic view of European culture he expressed in his numerous essays and biographies on major literary and historical figures, such as *Romain Rolland* (1920); *Drei Meister* (*Three Masters,* 1920) on Balzac, Dickens and Dostoevski; *Drei Dichter ihres Lebens* (*Three Poetic Self-Portraitists,* 1928) on Casanova, Stendhal and Tolstoi; *Erasmus von Rotter-*

dam (1934); *Maria Stuart* (1935) on Mary, Queen of Scots; and *Balzac* (1946). In his early career, he was influenced by the literary IMPRESSIONISM of such writers as his friend Hugo von Hofmannsthal, and developed a psychologically very subtle, sometimes mystical technique of character portrayal that served him well in both his biographical and his fictional works. Among the latter are the novel *Ungeduld des Herzens* (*Impatience of the Heart*, 1938), and numerous stories, including *Verwirrung der Gefühle* (*Confused Emotions*, 1926), *Sternstunden der Menschheit* (*Propitious Hours for Humanity*, 1928), and *Schachnovelle* (*Chess-Novella*, 1941). His best-known drama is the biblical *Jeremias* (1917), a pacifistic plea written during World War I. In 1938, Zweig left Austria, going first to England and then to Brazil where he committed suicide.

Zwingli, Ulrich or **Huldreich** (1484–1531). Swiss religious reformer. Ordained a priest in 1506, he delivered a series of sermons on the New Testament in Zurich in 1519 that launched the Protestant movement there. Although Zwingli, like other leaders of the Reformation, considered the Bible the sole source of authority and wanted to restore the purity of the early Church, he disagreed with Martin Luther's conception of the sacrament of the Eucharist; a conference at Marburg (1529) failed to settle their differences. Zwingli was killed in battle during the armed struggle between Zurich and the Catholic cantons of Switzerland.